PHILOSOPHY OF LAW

NINTH EDITION

PHILOSOPHY OF LAW

JOEL FEINBERG, LATE
University of Arizona

JULES COLEMAN
Yale Law School

CHRISTOPHER KUTZ
University of California, Berkeley

WADSWORTH
CENGAGE Learning™

Australia • Brazil • Japan • Korea • Mexico • Singapore • Spain • United Kingdom • United States

Philosophy of Law
Ninth Edition
Joel Feinberg, Jules Coleman, Christopher Kutz

Editor in Chief: *Lyn Uhl*
Publisher: *Clark Baxter*
Senior Sponsoring Editor: *Joann Kozyrev*
Development Editor: *Ian Lague*
Assistant Editor: *Joshua Duncan*
Editorial Assistant: *Marri Straton*
Market Development Manager: *Josh I. Adams*
Art Director: *Andrei Pasternak*
Manufacturing Planner: *Fola Orekoya*
Senior Rights Acquisition Specialist: *Amanda Groszko*
Production Service: *S4Carlisle Publishing Services*
Cover Designer: *Riezebos Holzbaur/ Tim Heraldo*
Cover Image: *©BAVARIA/Taxi/Getty*

For product information and technology assistance, contact us at **Cengage Learning Customer & Sales Support, 1-800-354-9706**

For permission to use material from this text or product, submit all requests online at **www.cengage.com/ permissions.**
Further permissions questions can be emailed to **permissionrequest@cengage.com.**

Library of Congress Control Number: 2012938894
Student Edition:
ISBN-13: 9781133942962
ISBN-10: 1133942962

Wadsworth
20 Channel Center Street
Boston, MA, 02210
USA

Cengage Learning is a leading provider of customized learning solutions with office locations around the globe, including Singapore, the United Kingdom, Australia, Mexico, Brazil and Japan. Locate your local office at **international.cengage.com/region**

Cengage Learning products are represented in Canada by Nelson Education, Ltd.

For your course and learning solutions, visit **www.cengage.com.**

Purchase any of our products at your local college store or at our preferred online store **www.cengagebrain.com.**

Instructors: Please visit **login.cengage.com** and log in to access instructor-specific resources.

Printed in the United States of America
1 2 3 4 5 6 7 16 15 14 13 12

For John Sexton, A true visionary
and an even better friend
J.C.

For my teachers, with gratitude;
for my students with hope.
C.K.

CONTENTS

THERE CURRENTLY IS a widespread and truly philosophical perplexity about law, occasioned by the events of the day and the legal proceedings to which they give rise. Increasing numbers of undergraduates have been attracted to courses in philosophy of law and social philosophy; law students, constantly challenged by the theoretical dimensions of law school subjects, are prompted more than ever to enroll in jurisprudence courses. These students are often disappointed by what seems to them an excessively abstract approach. Portentous terms such as law, morality, and justice are manipulated like counters in an uncertain game, and hoary figures from the past are marched by, each with a distinctive dogmatic pronouncement and a curious technical vocabulary. No wonder traditional jurisprudence often seems among the driest and most remote of academic subjects.

We have tried in this volume to relate the traditional themes of legal philosophy to the live concerns of modern society in a way that invigorates one and illuminates the other. The volume begins with essays by classic and contemporary figures on the essential nature of law and on the relation of law to morality or to other sources of principle outside the legal system. No attempt is made to give contending doctrines equal time or even to give them all a day in court. We have passed over much excellent material that might have been included, though this is sure to cause some displeasure in an area of jurisprudential concern that is so marked by doctrinal partisanship. Our endeavor is not to represent every important point of view, or to represent any in a truly comprehensive way, but instead to offer a series of selections that raise sharply the most important issues. Many of the philosophical issues debated in part 1 recur later in the book, where authors take up specific problems about liberty, justice, responsibility, and liability.

Although this ninth edition continues the tri-partite division of its ancestors, it is substantially different from the previous edition, with more than half of the selections changing. We made these changes partly in response to the advice of readers, who sought both the return of some old favorites, as well as increased coverage in a number of areas, especially the rule of law, critical theories of law, and law and economics. Of course, the addition of a new editor (Christopher Kutz) has prompted a different approach to the materials selected. We have this time included a substantial amount of material that appeared first in law journals—a decision occasioned by the quickly increasing philosophical sophistication of law school faculties. The conventions of law journal writing, however—particularly, the heavy use of citations—have forced us to frequently employ the editorial scissors, to keep selection lengths reasonable. Readers interested in pursuing the full discussions or seeing full citations are directed to the original law journal sources, most of which are available online.

Part 1 focuses on a range of issues organized around the traditional problems of jurisprudence and the rule of law. Our coverage of critical theories of law has entirely changed, to give more emphasis to the ways in which legal scholars have challenged some of philosophers' easy assumptions about law's neutrality and its capacity to serve very general, as opposed to sectarian, or class-, race-, or gender-bound interests. Our readings in international law also have changed, to give more depth to the concept of a law not bound to particular states.

Part 2 is organized around the central principles of political morality embodied in a liberal political order like our own. We have chosen a mix of classic and contemporary readings on constitutionalism, the criminalization of moral disapproval, and the basic liberties of a constitutional democracy. Our discussion of free speech reflects a shift in focus—from obscenity, in the previous edition, to blasphemy and religious offense—and includes discussions that arise in international contexts. (This highlights the peculiar traditions of the United States as just one example among a range of liberal approaches.) Our discussion of sexuality also has changed: although we have retained the legal cases concerning women's sexual autonomy, we have brought in new readings discussing the revolution represented by the fuller, but still sadly incomplete, incorporation of gays and lesbians into civic life. Our discussion of distributive equality and justice also is expanded.

Part 3 remains organized around philosophical issues that arise in the particular areas of the law. With our understanding that many teachers devote significant time to problems of criminal law and punishment, we have expanded our discussion of these topics, again with classic and new readings. Our discussion of private law now focuses more deeply on contract law as a paradigm.

We have endeavored to make changes reflecting the needs of the instructors who use this text, and to tailor our coverage to the public discussions that seem to us most energetic at the moment—showing how even classic pieces can cast new light on contemporary problems. We have tried, at the same time, to preserve the legacy of the late, great Joel Feinberg in our conception and execution of the book, and to keep as much of his distinctive authorial voice as we can.

We have benefited from the advice of many professors who have read or used some or all of the earlier editions of this book, especially the reviewers engaged in the development of the current edition: Nim Batchelor, Elon University; Brian Bix, University of Minnesota, Minneapolis; David Boersema, Pacific University; Kimberley Brownlee, University of Manchester; Maria Carl, Seattle University; Kenneth Ehrenberg, SUNY–Buffalo; Alexa Eodice, Iona College; Bruce Glymour, Kansas State; Thomas Halper, CUNY–Baruch College; Jacob Held, University of Central Arkansas; Carla Johnson, St. Cloud State University; Scott Lowe, Bloomsburg University; David MacAlister, Simon Fraser University; Rita Manning, San Jose State University; James McCartney, Villanova University; Vincente Medina, Seton Hall University; Ronald Novy, University of Central Arkansas; Anthony Reeves, SUNY–Binghamton; Katrina

Sifferd, Elmhurst College; Allan Silverman, Ohio State University; Donna Smith, Central Connecticut State University; Grant Sterling, Eastern Illinois University; Donald Turner, Hillsdale College; Lori Underwood, Christopher Newport University; and Lori Watson, University of San Diego. At Berkeley, Stephen Galoob has provided excellent research assistance. Finally, we have had an excellent editorial and production team at Cengage, and give particular thanks to our editor, Ian Lague, for his tireless and patient help.

Jules Coleman & Christopher Kutz

I would like to close this Preface with a personal note. Early adopters of this book will remember it as the "Feinberg–Gross" reader in the philosophy of law. No doubt much of its early and continued success is owed to their collaboration; especially perhaps to Joel Feinberg's impeccable reputation as a scholar, human being, and sympathetic reader of diverse texts. Several editions ago, Joel asked me to join the project and to take some responsibility for updating it and perhaps making its readings more relevant to students with interests beyond his area of expertise (criminal law). I happily undertook the charge but fear that there were times when my enthusiasm exceeded my ability to produce the right mix of materials.

As I had noted in the previous edition, and it remains as true today as it was then, the most difficult aspect of this project continues to be confronting the loss of Joel Feinberg, who in addition to being my teacher and mentor was my friend, colleague, and confidant. I know of no one who has represented the academic profession with more grace and integrity. Joel taught me not only how to be a philosopher, but how to treat people. I will be forever grateful for both of these lessons in life.

After Joel's passing, I undertook one revision of the reader on my own, and in doing so soon realized that I was not up to the solo task of carrying on the great tradition of this reader. Fortunately, I have been doubly blessed in the academy by having both great mentors and wonderful students. One of my mentors and dearest friends, John Sexton, has taught me two lessons that have made more and more of a difference to me as I work my way through life: the first is the possibility and value of seeking and finding redemption, and of the power of providing the chance for redemption to oneself, one's friends, and even one's "enemies." The second is that every loss or disadvantage provides an opportunity, and that the best way to deal with loss, pain, and hurt is to focus on the opportunity for positive change that it provides. In this case, the loss of Joel has provided me with the opportunity to bring someone else into the wonderful project that Joel and Hy began over a quarter century ago.

I don't know that there has been a professor of both law and philosophy who has had the good fortune that I have of being blessed by so many extraordinary students with such a broad range of scholarly interests. I have said on more than one occasion, however, that the real treat for me is that so many of these extraordinary students have proven themselves to be even better as persons than as scholars. Chris Kutz embodies all the virtues any teacher could ever hope for in a student, colleague, or friend. He is a broadly gauged, thoughtful, sympathetic, generous, and balanced intellectual who writes easily and beautifully. Perhaps more than any student I have had, he embodies the intellectual and personal attributes of Joel Feinberg himself; and so, bringing him into this project seemed only natural.

Though I frankly conceived of Chris as my junior partner at the outset (at least for this edition), within weeks our roles had been reversed, and I now feel as if I am hanging onto my position as an editor by a thread. This anthology is well on its way to being Chris's project, and that is as it should be. It is the only way that classic readers like this one can survive and flourish, and it is precisely as Joel Feinberg would have wanted it to be.

Jules Coleman

The Nature and Value of Law

THE QUESTION "What is law?" is often understood as a request to provide a definition of the word "law." This is a natural mistake, but a mistake nonetheless. The aim of the philosophy of law is to provide an account of the nature of law, rather than a definition of the term "law." Law is a complex social practice, and a philosophical theory of law is an account of that practice, not a definition or an account of the meaning of a word. Of course, the meaning of the term is bound up in interesting ways with the practice to which it refers, but an account of the content of the word is the province of the philosophy of language, not the philosophy of law. What kind of account of law is a philosophical theory of law? What kinds of questions does a philosophical account of law ask and answer, and what sort of illumination or understanding does it provide?

A theory of the law aspires to explain the distinctive nature of law. For some this amounts to a project of identifying law's essential nature: what is it about law that makes it the thing that it is? Water's essence—what makes it what it is—is its chemical composition, H_2O. A person's essence, arguably, lies in his or her DNA. So, does law have a comparable "essence" or nature? Most contemporary legal theorists resist the idea that law has an essential nature, and so they do not identify their project with discovering what that nature might be. Instead, they believe that law is characterized by distinctive features that help us to understand what it is and what is its place within our lives. Ronald Dworkin, for one, believes that the key concept in law is *coercion*. Law enforces its requirements through coercion, and if we hope to understand law, we need to see it through this concept. Unlike other forms of coercion, it is part of our concept of law that its use of coercion must be justified. To understand law is to see it through its claim to justify the use of coercion. Others, such as Joseph Raz, believe that the central concept of law is *authority*, and that in order to understand law one must view it through the lens of its claim to be exercising a legitimate authority. Perhaps the most important figure in contemporary legal philosophy, H. L. A. Hart, suggests that law's essence lies in its being a system of *rules*. For Hart, a philosophical account of law should explain central features of legal practice by exploring the relationship of law to other social practices with which it might be confused, such as morality and social convention.

Law seeks to regulate or govern human conduct. It does this largely through rules. Morality seeks to guide human conduct as well, also through rules. Law and morality, therefore, share the feature of guiding conduct through rules. Yet many legal norms are criticized on moral grounds, and many moral norms are not legally enforceable. Law and morality are related, but different. In what ways are they different and what is the relationship between them?

Here is one key difference: both law and morality impose obligations. With morality, the force of the obligation depends on the *content* of the obligation. For example, the force of an obligation not to kill is a function of the badness of killing; of an obligation not to lie of the badness of lying. But legal obligations are different—their force is independent of their content. A legal obligation to do X (or not to do Y) claims to have force just because it is imposed by law.

Some have thought that because the obligations laws impose are independent of their content, the capacity of law to guide behavior must depend on its capacity to sanction individuals who fail to comply with its demands. Sanctioning is an important feature of virtually all legal systems, and many famous philosophers of law, including Jeremy Bentham, have analyzed the nature of law in terms of sanctions. Bentham's contemporary John Austin is well known for his view that law is the order of a sovereign (properly so-called) backed by a sanction. Laws are commands backed by sanctions. However intuitive this position may be, it is clearly inadequate. After all, a pure sanctioning system, such as a system of threats issued by a local mafioso, makes no claim to *obligate*—to create duties for the individuals threatened. It merely gives them choices that cannot practically be refused. In contrast, law does create obligations, even when the threat of a sanction is unlikely (perhaps because there are not enough police). In fact, law necessarily creates obligations.

If we piece these initial considerations together, we can identify a very interesting puzzle that has occupied legal philosophy from the outset. One thing law, morality, and the mafiosi share is that they threaten to impose sanctions against those who fail to comply with their demands. One difference is that a mafioso doesn't claim that his directives impose moral obligations. Even if a particular mafioso boss did think of his demands as issuing in moral directives, we would have difficulty taking him seriously. After all, the mafioso boss epitomizes force and power, not moral authority. In contrast, both law and morality impose obligations and part of what justifies imposing sanctions on those who fail to comply with law or morality's demands is that they have failed to meet those obligations. In contrast, when the mafioso punishes someone who fails to comply with his threats, he cannot claim that he is merely exercising a power to penalize those who have failed to do what morality requires of them.

Law is not the mafiosi writ large; nor is it just another way of institutionalizing morality. It occupies its own place in the normative landscape and one of the central problems of legal philosophy is to characterize the place of law and the nature of the claims it makes against us. Morality and law differ from the mafiosi in that they impose and enforce genuine obligations, but they also differ from one another. Whereas the obligations morality imposes are based on the badness or wrongness of the actions it forbids, or the goodness of those it requires, the obligations the law imposes are based on the fact that the law imposes them. Of course, we can create new obligations for ourselves by promising; before we promise, say, to help a friend move, we may have no such obligation. But promising is something we do ourselves. The puzzle about law is how someone else—state officials—can obligate us just by *saying* that we have new legal duties. But so they claim when they pass a law.

To be sure, not everyone believes that law in fact obligates us morally to act as it demands. And everyone recognizes that even if law (or a legal official) claims to obligate us, it is sometimes mistaken. It sometimes fails in its efforts to impose moral requirements on us. Even if law doesn't always succeed in its aspiration to impose moral obligations, it nevertheless plays an important role in our lives. Law is one of the many ways in which we regulate our affairs with one another. We can do so through sanctioning systems as the mafioso does. We can do so through pricing systems as the market does. We can do so through informal norms, as closely knit communities do. Or we can do so by law. Why would reasonable people who aspire to act morally and to treat one another fairly and appropriately choose to govern many of their interactions through law? What is special about law? What, if anything, are its distinctive virtues?

Some theorists associate law with the virtue of justice, others with having our affairs regulated by principled consistency. Ronald Dworkin refers to the latter virtue as "integrity," and although integrity is different from justice, both are moral virtues or values. Others see the value of law in its ability to coordinate behavior among large and diverse groups of individuals spread out over large geographic areas. The law is like a traffic officer. It keeps us out of one another's way, and therefore enables each of us to pursue our projects, plans, and goals with minimal interference from others. Those who see law as a coordinating device view it instrumentally—not as embodying lofty moral ideals, but as providing us with the security necessary to exercise our autonomy safely and effectively.

Arguably, because law is so central to our lives, it deserves a measure of support from each of us. It deserves this support—what we may think of as "fidelity"—even if it does not impose moral obligations upon us to act as it requires. The idea of fidelity to law is an important one. Many political theorists have made a similar claim about democratic institutions. They argue that the value of having decisions made democratically calls for our supporting such institutions even when we disagree with the decisions they reach. Fidelity is a kind of support. To display fidelity to legal institutions is to defend them against attack and to support them through, among other things, one's tax dollars.

What is it about law—if anything—that leads to its deserving a measure of fidelity or support? Of course, the answer has something to do with what living under law provides: whether justice, integrity, or coordination of large-scale activities spread out over distance and time. But it also has something to do with the inherent characteristics of achieving these ends through law as opposed to some other means. Lon Fuller describes this as the internal morality of law—the canons of lawmaking that make law possible. These are the norms that create the values we associate with the rule of law. What are the norms that make law possible? Law cannot demand the impossible of us. It must make reasonably clear to us what it does demand. It can punish or sanction us only if it provides us with a reasonable opportunity to comply with its demands, and so on.

Once we introduce the notions of fidelity and obligation into our understanding of law and its characteristic, if not its essential, nature, we find ourselves drawn into thinking about the ways in which law and morality are unavoidably intertwined.

The mafioso boss can (and often does) demand the impossible. He does not constrain himself by concerns about giving his victims fair warning, nor does he worry about whether it would be wrong to impose punishment for rules that his victims are unaware of in advance. No doubt, one reason we do not believe that the mafioso boss's demands do not rise to the level of law is that there are no constraints he must follow when he issues orders.

It should be clear by now that many of the most important concerns in jurisprudence concern the relationship between law and morality. When we speak of law we use heavily moralized concepts. We speak of justice, rights, obligations, freedoms, and liberties. We often consult the law's requirements to help determine what actions we ought morally to undertake or which actions are morally permitted. Yet, as we noted above, many laws have been criticized for being immoral and many moral requirements are not legal requirements. How should we think about the relationship between law and morality? Many legal philosophers have thought that the place to begin is by asking whether there are any necessary connections between the two concepts. It is possible that even though law and morality are different, they are necessarily connected. On the other hand, if they are not necessarily connected, how are we to explain the importance law plays in determining what we have moral reason to do?

In the history of legal philosophy, two major schools of thought have emerged, based on the answers they provide to these questions. According to the first school, the *natural law* tradition, legal authority rests ultimately and necessarily on law's connection to morality revealed through reason. Some versions of natural law theory are said to require of each putative rule that it can be law only if it is consistent with or meets the demands of morality.

In other versions of natural law theory, morality is not a condition of something's being valid law so much as it is a condition for the legitimacy of a legal system as a whole. On this view, laws are the products of legal systems, provided that: (1) they are duly authorized by the procedures of a legal system, and (2) the rules of the legal system are by and large consistent with morality. Still other forms of natural law theory make a claim about the ultimate source of legal authority. They do not claim that each and every law must pass a moral test, nor do they assert that in order to be a legal system most laws would have to pass such a moral test. Instead they make a claim about the ultimate source of the authority to make law. On this view, law's authority must be conferred by morality.

The second major school of thought is known as *legal positivism*. Oftentimes, legal positivism is characterized in terms that suggest that it does little more than deny what natural law theory claims. If the natural lawyer claims that morality and law are necessarily connected, then legal positivism should be understood as the doctrine that there is no necessary connection between law and morality. If the natural lawyer claims that in order to be a law, a rule must satisfy the demands of morality, then legal positivism is the view that morality is not necessarily a condition of legality. If the natural lawyer claims that nothing can be a legal system unless the vast majority of its rules measure up to the demands of morality, then legal positivism is the view that there can be legal systems in which this is not the case.

Finally, if natural law theory claims that the authority of law is ultimately conferred by morality, then legal positivism claims that the authority of law rests on facts about persons, their behavior, and attitudes. Law has a social, not a moral basis. As we have seen, the nineteenth-century legal positivist John Austin suggested that the foundation of law is power and will. Law is the command of a sovereign, someone whose commands others habitually obey, but who does not habitually obey others. The source of the habit of obedience may be the power to threaten sanctions for noncompliance, and not the moral authority of the sovereign's commands. Austin's answer has been roundly criticized not just by natural lawyers, but by every important legal positivist who has followed him, most notably Hart.

Hart argues that law consists in the union of two distinct kinds of rules: what he calls primary and secondary rules. Where primary rules impose obligations, secondary rules can authorize individuals to create rules that impose obligations. Legislatures enact rules, such as penal codes, that make killing, assault, battery, and theft illegal. These are primary rules in Hart's sense. Other laws are secondary rules, such as the laws regulating how people can make enforceable agreements (contracts). Hart noticed, however, that since no one is commanded to make a contract, the laws of contract cannot be understood as commands of a sovereign. If law consists of both primary and secondary rules, we need something more than the idea of a command backed by obedience to account for law. Hart also noticed that legal systems contain a very important set of secondary rules: the rules that give legislatures the power to enact laws. All legal rules ultimately are grounded in what Hart calls a "rule of recognition," which is itself a secondary rule. The authority of all rules derives from this rule of recognition. This invites the question: what is the source of this rule's authority? The answer, according to Hart, is that the rule of recognition is authoritative among those whose behavior it guides because they regard it as binding on them. They take a certain normative attitude towards the rule of recognition. The authority of the law is thus grounded in facts about behavior and attitudes, not in morality.

In a sense, the central claim of positivists is that law has a social source—that law is the creation of a person or persons with the authority to create it. Similarly, natural lawyers are drawn to the view that for law to exist and function in the way it does, the authority to create law must have a moral foundation—though it is controversial what that foundation is. In contrast to both positivists and natural lawyers, Ronald Dworkin has suggested that the best way to uncover the nature of law is by investigating the *practices* of legal decision making. There are principles and norms that are imminent in the practice of legal interpretation. Judges cite sources in support of their decisions, and in doing so express the view that those sources are grounds for their decisions and thus part of the law. So every judge must have a view about what the grounds or sources of law are and what makes them so. According to Dworkin, the law is the best account of those principles that provide the grounds of law in a particular community.

Other legal theorists also are drawn to the practice of adjudication as the best lens through which one can come to understand the nature of law. Unlike Dworkin, however, these theorists are more prone to identify law with the decisions that judges reach, rather than the set of principles that make the best sense of the sources judges cite. It is the decision that has legal force, not the argument for that decision. On this view, the argument is a rationalization at worst, or merely a source of law at best, but not law. Law is what judges say it is. This view, which came into prominence at the beginning of the twentieth century in America with the work of the great judge Oliver Wendell Holmes, Jr. and the legal academics Jerome Frank and Karl Llewellyn, is called *legal realism*, and it continues to be enormously influential—indeed most American lawyers are probably best described as legal realists.

Whereas most realists hold a version of the view that the law is whatever judges say it is, and that legal texts are mere sources of law, the more persuasive view is that the law has a determinate content on most matters prior to a judge's resolution of a particular case. The judge is bound by the law, and reaches his or her decision in light of it. But that does not mean that the job of a judge is an uncreative one. Quite the contrary, it often falls to a judge to determine what the law is.

This brings us to matters of legal interpretation. How is someone—typically a judge—to determine what a law means or what the law requires? There are in fact two different but related issues involved in interpreting legal rules. Let us imagine a legal system in which we can identify all the binding legal sources—statutes, judicial opinions, executive orders, and the like—by virtue of their authoritative source. The first question to ask is, what do these statutes, orders, and precedents mean? A good example is the "cruel and unusual punishment" clause of the Eighth Amendment to the United States Constitution. What does the term "cruel" mean in this context? One view, sometimes referred to as *originalism,* holds that the term "cruel" today means exactly what the framers and adopters of the Constitution meant by it. That view does not by itself settle the matter, for we still need an account of the intentions of the framers. In other words, we might agree that "cruel" means today whatever those who voted for the Bill of Rights in 1791 meant by it—but how are we to figure out what they meant by the term? In using the word "cruel," we can agree that the Constitution's adopters meant to refer to some acts and not to others. But which ones? On one view, we can suppose that the framers meant to pick out those acts that they believed were cruel at that time or those that most of their contemporaries would have identified as cruel. Alternatively, the framers were men of the Enlightenment. They possessed a notion of progress, so we might suppose that they meant for the term to pick out actions that, at any given time in the country's history, would count as cruel according to the best theory of cruelty at that time, or actions that most individuals would, at that point, regard as cruel. Therefore, the first project of interpretation is to determine the semantic content or the meaning of the authoritative acts that constitute the community's law. This is no easy matter, as the previous example illustrates.

But there is more to interpretation than this. Imagine now that we have identified all the binding legal standards within our hypothetical community, and have determined what each individually means. We now have to figure out what the law of our community permits and requires of us, for the law is not just the long list of all the authoritative standards and their meanings. The force or content of the law is a result of how those authoritative texts are conjoined and combined with one another. It is a function of the practices of our community for connecting the standards and weighing them against one another, and of the principles that inform and regulate that practice. A judge presents a decision and opinion in a case. That opinion is an authoritative text. Another judge presents a decision and offers an opinion in a different case that explicitly contradicts the decision in the first case. What is the law on the matter as it comes before a judge in yet a third case? The answer to that question will depend in most jurisdictions on the relative levels of the courts. Was the judge in the second case sitting on a superior or inferior court to the judge in the first case? Were the two courts in distinct jurisdictions or the same jurisdiction? Which decision came before the other in relation to date? Now a legislature enacts a statute that supports the first judge and contradicts the second. What is the status of the law when a controversy arises before a third judge? Again, the answer will depend on whether our legal community is a democracy that defers to the legislature, whether the legislature has acted within the scope of its authority, and so on. These and other questions provide a lens through which we may look at the law from the perspective of those who apply it, and whose task it is to determine the law's content.

The more philosophical a judge or scholarly commentator is, the more likely he or she is to pause frequently to ask just what the rules are in the game of interpretation. What makes for an authoritative interpretation of a short and cryptic constitutional passage? Does the interpreter find all the clues inside the text itself? Or are there principles of justice outside the text to which he or she legitimately can refer in order to make better sense of the few clues provided by the text itself? Is evidence of the founding fathers' intentions ever relevant? Is it ever not relevant? Is anything apart from such evidence ever relevant?

When we consider jurisprudential questions, our natural instinct, as we have noted, is to explore the ways in which law is different from and yet connected to morality. Similarly, when we consider the nature of law, we tend to focus on the law of particular nation states. But this focus may be too narrow—especially in the modern world. Many of the most compelling and troubling problems of the day cross national borders; they involve conflicts between states (public international law) and conflicts between or among companies and organizations operating in many countries (private international law). No adequate jurisprudence can ignore questions about the status of international law. Moreover, the very feature of international law that makes it puzzling—the lack of a centralized enforcement system—makes it potentially illuminating for a general understanding of law.

Finally, it is worth asking what force so-called human rights have or should have. This is a question not only of what values our laws should reflect but also what our policies should be towards countries that flout human rights. It prompts us to ask what actions we might justifiably undertake to protect those whose rights are violated throughout the world.

The basic questions of jurisprudence may have an air of extreme abstractness about them. Yet answering them one way or another has the most practical and important implications for who we are and how we live.

CHAPTER ONE

The Rule of Law

1 Eight Ways to Fail to Make Law

LON L. FULLER

This chapter will begin with a fairly lengthy allegory. It concerns the unhappy reign of a monarch who bore the convenient, but not very imaginative and not even very regal-sounding name of Rex. . . .

Rex came to the throne filled with the zeal of a reformer. He considered that the greatest failure of his predecessors had been in the field of law. For generations the legal system had known nothing like a basic reform. Procedures of trial were cumbersome, the rules of law spoke in the archaic tongue of another age, justice was expensive, the judges were slovenly and sometimes corrupt. Rex was resolved to remedy all this and to make his name in history as a great lawgiver. It was his unhappy fate to fail in this ambition. Indeed, he failed spectacularly, since not only did he not succeed in introducing the needed reforms, but he never even succeeded in creating any law at all, good or bad.

His first official act was, however, dramatic and propitious. Since he needed a clean slate on which to write, he announced to his subjects the immediate repeal of all existing law, of whatever kind. He then set about drafting a new code. Unfortunately, trained as a lonely prince, his education had been very defective. In particular he found himself incapable of making even the simplest generalizations. Though not lacking in confidence when it came to deciding specific controversies, the effort to give articulate reasons for any conclusion strained his capacities to the breaking point.

Becoming aware of his limitations, Rex gave up the project of a code and announced to his subjects that henceforth he would act as a judge in any disputes that might arise among them. In this way under the stimulus of a variety of cases he hoped that his latent powers of generalization might develop and, proceeding case by case, he would gradually work out a system of rules that could be incorporated in a code. Unfortunately, the defects in his education were more deep-seated than he had supposed. The venture failed completely. After he had handed down literally hundreds of decisions, neither he nor his subjects could detect in those decisions any pattern whatsoever. Such tentative steps toward generalization as were to be found in his opinions only compounded the confusion, for they gave false leads

---

From Lon Fuller, *The Morality of Law*. Copyright 1964 by Yale University. Reprinted here by permission of the publisher, Yale University Press.

– 8 –

to his subjects and threw his own meager powers of judgment off balance in the decision of later cases.

After this fiasco Rex realized it was necessary to make a fresh start. His first move was to subscribe to a course of lessons in generalization. With his intellectual powers thus fortified, he resumed the project of a code and, after many hours of solitary labor, succeeded in preparing a fairly lengthy document. He was still not confident, however, that he had fully overcome his previous defects. Accordingly, he announced to his subjects that he had written out a code and would henceforth be governed by it in deciding cases, but that for an indefinite future the contents of the code would remain an official state secret, known only to him and his scrivener. To Rex's surprise this sensible plan was deeply resented by his subjects. They declared it was very unpleasant to have one's case decided by rules when there was no way of knowing what those rules were.

Stunned by this rejection Rex undertook an earnest inventory of his personal strengths and weaknesses. He decided that life had taught him one clear lesson, namely, that it is easier to decide things with the aid of hindsight than it is to attempt to foresee and control the future. Not only did hindsight make it easier to decide cases, but—and this was of supreme importance to Rex—it made it easier to give reasons. Deciding to capitalize on this insight, Rex hit on the following plan. At the beginning of each calendar year he would decide all the controversies that had arisen among his subjects during the preceding year. He would accompany his decisions with a full statement of reasons. Naturally, the reasons thus given would be understood as not controlling decisions in future years, for that would be to defeat the whole purpose of the new arrangement, which was to gain the advantages of hindsight. Rex confidently announced the new plan to his subjects, observing that he was going to publish the full text of his judgments with the rules applied by him, thus meeting the chief objection to the old plan. Rex's subjects received this announcement in silence, then quietly explained through their leaders that when they said they needed to know the rules, they meant they needed to know them *in*

advance so they could act on them. Rex muttered something to the effect that they might have made that point a little clearer, but said he would see what could be done.

Rex now realized that there was no escape from a published code declaring the rules to be applied in future disputes. Continuing his lessons in generalization, Rex worked diligently on a revised code, and finally announced that it would shortly be published. This announcement was received with universal gratification. The dismay of Rex's subjects was all the more intense, therefore, when his code became available and it was discovered that it was truly a masterpiece of obscurity. Legal experts who studied it declared that there was not a single sentence in it that could be understood either by an ordinary citizen or by a trained lawyer. Indignation became general and soon a picket appeared before the royal palace carrying a sign that read, "How can anybody follow a rule that nobody can understand?"

The code was quickly withdrawn. Recognizing for the first time that he needed assistance, Rex put a staff of experts to work on a revision. He instructed them to leave the substance untouched, but to clarify the expression throughout. The resulting code was a model of clarity, but as it was studied it became apparent that its new clarity had merely brought to light that it was honeycombed with contradictions. It was reliably reported that there was not a single provision in the code that was not nullified by another provision inconsistent with it. A picket again appeared before the royal residence carrying a sign that read, "This time the king made himself clear—in both directions."

Once again the code was withdrawn for revision. By now, however, Rex had lost his patience with his subjects and the negative attitude they seemed to adopt toward everything he tried to do for them. He decided to teach them a lesson and put an end to their carping. He instructed his experts to purge the code of contradictions, but at the same time to stiffen drastically every requirement contained in it, and to add a long list of new crimes. Thus, where before the citizen summoned to the throne was given ten days in which to report, in the revision the time was cut to ten seconds. It was made a crime, punishable by ten years' imprisonment, to cough, sneeze, hiccough, faint, or fall down in the presence of the king. It was made treason not to understand, believe in, and correctly profess the doctrine of evolutionary, democratic redemption.

When the new code was published a near revolution resulted. Leading citizens declared their intention to flout its provisions. Someone discovered in an ancient author a passage that seemed apt: "To command what cannot be done is not to make law; it is to unmake law, for a command that cannot be obeyed serves no end but confusion, fear and chaos." Soon this passage was being quoted in a hundred petitions to the king.

The code was again withdrawn and a staff of experts charged with the task of revision. Rex's instructions to the experts were that whenever they encountered a rule requiring an impossibility, it should be revised to make compliance possible. It turned out that to accomplish this result every provision in the code had to be substantially rewritten. The final result was, however, a triumph of draftsmanship. It was clear, consistent with itself, and demanded nothing of the subject that did not lie easily within his powers. It was printed and distributed free of charge on every street corner.

However, before the effective date for the new code had arrived, it was discovered that so much time had been spent in successive revisions of Rex's original draft that the substance of the code had been seriously overtaken by events. Ever since Rex assumed the throne there had been a suspension of ordinary legal processes and this had brought about important economic and institutional changes within the country. Accommodation to these altered conditions required many changes of substance in the law. Accordingly, as soon as the new code became legally effective, it was subjected to a daily stream of amendments. Again popular discontent mounted; an anonymous pamphlet appeared on the streets carrying scurrilous cartoons of the king and a leading article with the title: "A law that changes every day is worse than no law at all."

Within a short time this source of discontent began to cure itself as the pace of amendment gradually slackened. Before this had occurred to any noticeable degree, however, Rex announced an important decision. Reflecting on the misadventures of his reign, he concluded that much of the trouble lay in bad advice he had received from experts. He accordingly declared he was reassuming the judicial power in his own person. In this way he could directly control the application of the new code and insure his country against another crisis. He began to spend practically all of his time hearing and deciding cases arising under the new code.

As the king proceeded with this task, it seemed to bring to a belated blossoming his long-dormant powers of generalization. His opinions began, indeed, to reveal a confident and almost exuberant virtuosity as he deftly distinguished his own previous decisions, exposed the principles on which he acted, and laid down guidelines for the disposition of future controversies. For Rex's subjects a new day seemed about to dawn when they could finally conform their conduct to a coherent body of rules.

This hope was, however, soon shattered. As the bound volumes of Rex's judgments became available and were subjected to closer study, his subjects were appalled to discover that there existed no discernible relation between those judgments and the code they purported to apply. Insofar as it found expression in the actual disposition of controversies, the new code might just as well not have existed at all. Yet in virtually every one of his decisions Rex declared and redeclared the code to be the basic law of his kingdom. Leading citizens began to hold private meetings to discuss what measures, short of open revolt, could be taken to get the king away from the bench and back on the throne. While these discussions were going on Rex suddenly died, old before his time and deeply disillusioned with his subjects.

The first act of his successor, Rex II, was to announce that he was taking the powers of government away from the lawyers and placing them in the hands of psychiatrists and experts in public relations. This way, he explained, people could be made happy without rules.

THE CONSEQUENCES OF FAILURE

Rex's bungling career as legislator and judge illustrates that the attempt to create and maintain a system of legal rules may miscarry in at least eight ways; there are in this enterprise, if you will, eight distinct routes to disaster. The first and most obvious lies in a failure to achieve rules at all, so that every issue must be decided on an ad hoc basis. The other routes are: (2) a failure to publicize, or at least to make available to the affected party the rules he is expected to observe; (3) the abuse of retroactive legislation, which not only cannot itself guide action, but undercuts the integrity of rules prospective in effect, since it puts them under the threat of retrospective change; (4) a failure to make rules understandable; (5) the enactment of contradictory rules, or (6) the enactment of rules that require conduct beyond the powers of the affected party; (7) introducing such frequent changes in the rules that the subject cannot orient his action by them; and, finally, (8) a failure of congruence between the rules as announced and their actual administration.

A total failure in any one of these eight directions does not simply result in a bad system of law; it results in something that is not properly called a legal system at all, except perhaps in the Pickwickian sense in which a void contract can still be said to be one kind of contract. Certainly there can be no rational ground for asserting that a man can have a moral obligation to obey a legal rule that does not exist, or is kept secret from him, or that came into existence only after he had acted, or was unintelligible, or was contradicted by another rule of the same system, or commanded the impossible, or changed every minute. It may not be impossible for a man to obey a rule that is disregarded by those charged with its administration, but at some point obedience becomes futile—as futile, in fact, as casting a vote that will never be counted. As the sociologist Simmel has observed, there is a kind of reciprocity between government and the citizen with respect to the observance of rules.[1] Government says to the citizen, in effect, "These are the rules we expect you to follow. If you follow them, you have our assurance that they are the rules that will be applied to your conduct." When this bond of reciprocity is finally and completely ruptured by government, nothing is left on which to ground the citizen's duty to observe the rules.

The citizen's predicament becomes more difficult when, though there is no total failure in any direction, there is a general and drastic deterioration in legality, such as occurred in Germany under Hitler.[2] A situation begins to develop, for example, in which, though some laws are published, others, including the most important, are not. Though most laws are prospective in effect, so free a use is made of retrospective legislation that no law is immune to change ex post facto if it suits the convenience of those in power. For the trial of criminal cases concerned with loyalty to the regime, special military tribunals are established, and these tribunals disregard, whenever it suits their convenience, the rules that are supposed to control their decisions. Increasingly the principal object of government seems to be, not that of giving the citizen rules by which to shape his conduct, but to frighten him into impotence. As such a situation develops, the problem faced by the citizen is not so simple as that of a voter who knows with certainty that his ballot will not be counted. It is more like that of the voter who knows that the odds are against his ballot being counted at all, and that if it is counted, there is a good chance that it will be counted for the side against which he actually voted. A citizen in this predicament has to decide for himself whether to stay with the system and cast his ballot as a kind of symbolic act expressing the hope of a better day. So it was with the German citizen under Hitler faced with deciding whether he had an obligation to obey such portions of the laws as the Nazi terror had left intact.

In situations like these there can be no simple principle by which to test the citizen's obligation of fidelity to law, any more than there can be such a principle for testing his right to engage in a general revolution. One thing is, however, clear. A mere respect for constituted authority must not be confused with fidelity to law. Rex's subjects, for example, remained faithful to him as king throughout his long and inept reign. They were not faithful to his law, for he never made any.

NOTES

1. *The Sociology of Georg Simmel* (1950), trans. Wolff, § 4, "Interaction in the Idea of 'Law,'" pp. 186–89; see also Chapter 4, "Subordination under a

Principle," pp. 250–67. Simmel's discussion is worthy of study by those concerned with defining the conditions under which the ideal of "the rule of law" can be realized.

2. I have discussed some of the features of this deterioration in my article, "Positivism and Fidelity to Law," *Harvard Law Review*, 71, 630, 648–57 (1958). This article makes no attempt at a comprehensive survey of all the postwar judicial decisions in Germany concerned with events occurring during the Hitler regime. Some of the later decisions rested the nullity of judgments rendered by the courts under Hitler not on the ground that the statutes applied were void, but on the ground that the Nazi judges misinterpreted the statutes of their own government. See Pappe, "On the Validity of Judicial Decisions in the Nazi Era," *Modern Law Review*, 23, 260–74 (1960). Dr. Pappe makes more of this distinction than seems to me appropriate. After all, the meaning of a statute depends in part on accepted modes of interpretation. Can it be said that the postwar German courts gave full effect to Nazi laws when they interpreted them by their own standards instead of the quite different standards current during the Nazi regime? Moreover, with statutes of the kind involved, filled as they were with vague phrases and unrestricted delegations of power, it seems a little out of place to strain over questions of their proper interpretation.

2   The Rule of Law and the Importance of Procedure

JEREMY WALDRON

1. GETTING TO THE RULE OF LAW

The Rule of Law is one star in a constellation of ideals that dominate our political morality: the others are democracy, human rights, and economic freedom. We want societies to be democratic; we want them to respect human rights; we want them to organize their economies around free markets and private property to the extent that this can be done without seriously compromising social justice, and we want them to be governed in accordance with the Rule of Law. We want the Rule of Law for new societies—for newly emerging democracies, for example—and old societies alike; for national political communities and regional and international governance; and we want it to extend into all aspects of governments' dealings with those subject to them —not just in day-to-day criminal law, or commercial law or administrative law, but also in law administered at the margins, in antiterrorism law and in the exercise of power over those who are marginalized, those who can safely be dismissed as outsiders, and those we are tempted just to destroy as (in John Locke's words) "wild Savage Beasts, with whom men can have no Society or Security."[1] Getting to the Rule of Law does not just mean paying lip service to the ideal in the ordinary security of a prosperous modern democracy: it means extending the Rule of Law into societies that are not necessarily familiar with it; and in those societies that are familiar with it, it means extending the Rule of Law into these darker corners of governance as well.

When I pay attention to the calls that are made for the Rule of Law around the world, I am struck by the fact that the features that people call attention to are not necessarily the features that legal philosophers have emphasized in their academic conceptions.

Legal philosophers tend to emphasize formal elements of the Rule of Law, such as rule by general norms rather than particular decrees; rule by laws laid down in advance rather than by retrospective enactments; rule under a system of norms that has sufficient stability (is sufficiently resistant to change) so as to furnish for those subject to the norms a calculable basis for running their lives or their businesses; rules by norms that are made public, not hidden away in the closets of bureaucracy; rule by clear and determinate legal norms, norms whose meaning is not so obscure or contestable as to leave those who are subject to them at the mercy of official discretion. These are

---

[1] John Locke, *Two Treatises of Government* (Cambridge: Cambridge University Press, 1988), 274 (II: section 11).

formal aspects of the Rule of Law, because they concern the form of the norms that are applied to our conduct: generality, prospectivity, stability, publicity, clarity, and so on. But we don't just value them for formalistic reasons. In F.A. Hayek's theory of the Rule of Law, we value these features for the contribution they make to predictability which Hayek thinks is indispensable for liberty.[2] In Lon Fuller's theory, we value them also for the way they respect human dignity: "To judge [people's] actions by unpublished or retrospective laws … is to convey to [them] your indifference to [their] powers of self-determination."[3] (I shall say more about this in section 5.) In Fuller's theory, too, there is a hunch that if we respect dignity in these formal ways, we will find ourselves more inhibited against more substantive assaults on dignity and justice. That has proved very controversial, but it is further evidence of the point that the interests of those who adopt a formal conception of the Rule of Law are not just formalistic.

I have said that this formal conception is not what ordinary people have in the forefront of their minds when they clamor for the extension of the Rule of Law into settings or modes of governance where it has not been present before. Saying that is usually a prelude to a call for a more *substantive* vision of the Rule of Law. I am not as hostile as I once was to a substantive conception of this ideal.[4] I believe that there is a natural overlap between substantive and formal elements, not least because—as we have just seen—the formal elements are usually argued for on substantive grounds of dignity and liberty. I still believe that it is important not to let our enthusiasm for a substantive conception—whereby the Rule of

Law is treated as an ideal that calls directly for an end to human rights abuses or as an ideal that calls directly for free markets and respect for private property rights—obscure the independent importance that the formal elements I have mentioned would have even if these other considerations were not so directly at stake.[5] But it is probably a mistake to exaggerate the distinctiveness of our several political ideals or the clarity of the boundaries between them.

Still, it is not a substantive conception that I have in mind when I say that ordinary people are urging something other than the formal elements that I have mentioned when they clamor for the Rule of Law. Instead I have in mind elements of legal procedure and the institutions like courts that embody them. When people clamored recently in Pakistan for a restoration of the Rule of Law, their concern was for the independence of the judiciary and the attempt by an unelected administration to fire a whole slew of judges. When people clamor for the Rule of Law in China, they are demanding impartial tribunals that can adjudicate their claims.[6] And when advocates for the detainees in the American base at Guantanamo Bay clamor for the Rule of Law they are clamoring for hearings on their clients' comprehensive loss of liberty in which they or their clients would have an opportunity to put their case, confront and examine the evidence against them, such as it is, and make arguments for their freedom, in accordance with what we would say were normal legal procedures.[7]

[2]F.A. Hayek, *The Constitution of Liberty* (Chicago: University of Chicago Press, 1960), esp. Chs. 9–10.
[3]Lon Fuller, *The Morality of Law* (New Haven: Yale University Press, 1969), 162.
[4]See Jeremy Waldron, "The Rule of Law in Contemporary Liberal Theory," *Ratio Juris*, 2 (1989), 79. For a discussion of substantive Rule of Law ideas, see Paul Craig, "Formal and Substantive Conceptions of the Rule of Law: An Analytical Framework" [1997] *Public Law*, 467.
[5]See Jeremy Waldron, "Legislation and the Rule of Law," *Legisprudence* 1 (2007) 91, at 115.
[6]Editorial, "Gathering Storm," *The New York Times*, November 8, 2007: "The American Bar Association, its members horrified by events in Pakistan, has written to General Musharraf and condemned his profound breach of the rule of law." See also Letter, "Pakistan's Leaders Must Respect the Rule of Law," *The Times* (London), November14, 2007 (signed by chairs of Bar Associations in England, Scotland, Ireland, and Wales.)
[7]See, e.g., Editorial, "The Rule of Law in Guantánamo," *The New York Times*, October 11, 2008, and Laura Dickinson, "Using Legal Process To Fight Terrorism: Detentions, Military Commissions, International Tribunals, and the Rule of Law," *Southern Calif. L. Rev.* 75 (2002) 1407.

2. LAUNDRY LISTS

What sort of procedural principles do I have in mind? Theorists of the Rule of Law are fond of producing laundry lists of demands. The best known are the eight formal principles of Lon Fuller's "inner morality of law":[8]

1. generality;
2. publicity;
3. prospectivity;
4. intelligibility;
5. consistency;
6. practicability;
7. stability; and
8. congruence.

I think we need to match this list with a list of procedural characteristics which are equally indispensable. As a preliminary sketch,[9] we might say that no one should have any penalty, stigma or serious loss imposed upon them by government except as the upshot of procedures that involve:

A. a hearing by an impartial tribunal that is required to act on the basis of evidence and argument presented formally before it in relation to legal norms that govern the imposition of penalty, stigma, loss etc.;
B. a legally trained judicial officer, whose independence of other agencies of government is assured;
C. a right to representation by counsel and to the time and opportunity required to prepare a case;
D. a right to be present at all critical stages of the proceeding;
E. a right to confront witnesses against the detainee;
F. a right to an assurance that the evidence presented by the government has been gathered in a properly supervised way;

G. a right to present evidence in one's own behalf;
H. a right to make legal argument about the bearing of the evidence and about the bearing of the various legal norms relevant to the case;
I. a right to hear reasons from the tribunal when it reaches its decision, which are responsive to the evidence and arguments presented before it; and
J. some right of appeal to a higher tribunal of a similar character.

These requirements are often associated with terms such as "natural justice"[10] and as such they are important parts of the Rule of Law. I believe we radically sell short the idea of the Rule of Law if we understand it to comprise a list like Fuller's list (1)-(8) above without also including something like the procedural list (A)-(J) that I have just set out. We say the Rule of Law is violated when due attention is not paid to these procedural matters or when the institutions that are supposed to embody these procedures are undermined or interfered with. Equally I think we misrepresent the debate about whether the Rule of Law has also a substantive dimension if we do not contrast a possible list of substantive items—such as:

(α) respect for private property
(β) prohibitions on torture and brutality
(β) a presumption of liberty; and
(δ) democratic enfranchisement

—with *both* of the lists I have set out (the formal list and the procedural list) rather than with the formal list by itself.

3. FORM AND PROCEDURE IN THE WORK OF HAYEK, FULLER, AND DICEY

It is remarkable how little attention is paid to demands of this *procedural* kind—demands like (A) through (J)—in the literature in academic legal

[8]See also the lists in John Finnis, *Natural Law and Natural Rights* (Oxford: Clarendon Press, 1980), 270, John Rawls, *A Theory of Justice* (Oxford: Oxford University Press, 1971), 236–239, and Joseph Raz, "The Rule of Law and its Virtue," in his collection *The Authority of Law: Essays on Law and Morality* (Clarendon Press, 1979), at 214–219.
[9]I have adapted this list from A. Wallace Tashima, "The War on Terror and the Rule of Law," *Asian American Law Journal*, 15 (2008), 245, at 264.

[10]In the United Kingdom and elsewhere, the term "natural justice" is used to refer to the most elementary aspects of what Americans would call procedural due process. See, e.g., Paul Jackson, *Natural Justice* (London: Sweet & Maxwell, 1979).

and political philosophy devoted specifically to discussion of the Rule of Law.

The key chapter in F.A. Hayek's book, *The Constitution of Liberty*—the chapter entitled "Laws, Commands, and Order"—makes no mention whatever of courts or legal procedures: it is wholly concerned with the relation between formal characteristics like abstraction and generality and individual freedom.[11] Later chapters in that book do talk a little about courts, but hardly ever about their procedures.[12] The same is true of Hayek's later work on the Rule of Law, in his trilogy *Law, Legislation and Liberty*. Hayek talks a lot about the role of judges in Chapter 5 of the first volume of that work. But it is all about the role of judges in generating norms of the appropriate form, rather than about the procedures that characterize courtrooms.[13]

The case of Lon Fuller is even more instructive. Fuller calls his internal morality of law—comprising (1) generality, (2) publicity, (3) prospectivity, etc.—"procedural," but what he seems to mean is that it is not substantive. Fuller says this:

> As a convenient (though not wholly satisfactory) way of describing the distinction … we may speak of a procedural, as distinguished from a substantive natural law. What I have called the internal morality of law is in this sense a procedural version of natural law, though to avoid misunderstanding the word "procedural" should be assigned a special and expanded sense so that it would include, for example, a substantive accord between official action and enacted law. The term "procedural" is, however, broadly appropriate as indicating that we are concerned, not with the substantive aims of legal rules, but with the ways in which a system of rules for governing human conduct must be constructed and administered if it is to be efficacious and at the same time remain what it purports to be.[14]

In fact *substantive* can be contrasted either with *procedural* or with *formal*; the two contrasts are quite different and patently what Fuller has in mind is what we should call a formal/substantive contrast.[15] The features of his internal morality of law all relate to the form that legal norms take, not to either the procedure of their enactment or (more importantly) to the procedural mode of their administration. Among his nine desiderata, only one comes close to being procedural (in the sense I am distinguishing from formal), namely, the requirement of congruence between official action and law on the books—yet that is the one for which he says (in the passage quoted above) the word "procedural" should be assigned a special and expanded sense!

The point is that there is very little about due process or courtroom procedure in Fuller's account of law's internal morality in Chapters 2 and 3 of *The Morality of Law*.[16] Much the same is true of Fuller in his earlier response to H.L.A. Hart's Holmes Lecture.[17] There too Fuller focuses on what we should call formal characteristics of law—generality, publicity, consistency etc.—and his argument that they are prophylactics against injustice is based on an incompatibility between evil ends and law's forms.

> [C]oherence and goodness have more affinity than coherence and evil. Accepting this belief, I also believe that when men are compelled to explain and justify their decisions, the effect will generally be to pull those decisions toward goodness, by whatever standards of ultimate goodness there are. … [E]ven in the most perverted regimes there is a certain hesitancy about writing cruelties, intolerances, and inhumanities into law.[18]

---

[11]Hayek, *Constitution of Liberty*, pp. 148–161.
[12]See ibid., 218–19 for the suggestion that apart from the formal characteristics of the Rule of Law, its procedural aspects are unimportant: "[T]hey presuppose for their effectiveness the acceptance of the rule of law as here defined and … without it, all procedural safeguards would be valueless."
[13]F.A. Hayek, *Rules and Order*, Volume 1 of *Law, Legislation and Liberty* (Chicago: University of Chicago Press, 1973), 94–123.
[14]Fuller, *Morality of Law*, 96–7.

[15]Brian Tamanaha, *On the Rule of Law: History, Politics, Theory* (Cambridge University Press, 2004) gets this right by locating his discussion of Fuller in a chapter called "Formal Theories." That is then contrasted with a chapter called "Substantive Theories." Procedural theories don't rate a mention, but at least it is not assumed by Tamanaha that everything nonsubstantive is procedural.
[16]There is a reference to "due process" in Fuller, *Morality of Law*, 105–6, but that is in the technical sense of the term and it addresses whether ex post facto laws violate due process (in that sense).
[17]Lon Fuller, "Positivism and Fidelity to Law: A Reply to Hart," *Harvard Law Review*, 71(1959) 630.
[18]Ibid., 636–7.

The whole of his discussion along these lines, and the whole of his excoriation of Nazi "legality" has to do with legislative form not judicial procedure. That is the ground on which Fuller makes what we would call his "Rule of Law" argument.

I do not mean that Fuller was uninterested in procedure. Towards the end of Chapter 4 of *The Morality of Law*, there is some consideration about whether the internal morality of law applies to the processes by which allocative decisions are made by government agencies in a mixed economy. Fuller says we face problems of institutional design "unprecedented in scope and importance."

> It is inevitable that the legal profession will play a large role in solving these problems. The great danger is that we will unthinkingly carry over to new conditions traditional institutions and procedures that have already demonstrated their faults of design. As lawyers we have a natural inclination to "judicialize" every function of government. Adjudication is a process with which we are familiar and which enables us to show to advantage our special talents. Yet we must face the plain truth that adjudication is an ineffective instrument for economic management and for governmental participation in the allocation of economic resources.[19]

This seems to indicate an interest in procedural as well as formal aspects of the Rule of Law (and indeed a skepticism about their applicability across the board of all government functions).[20] But it is remarkable that the interest in the adjudicative process shown in this passage is not matched by anything in the earlier discussion in his book of the inner morality of law.

Fuller was in fact a great proceduralist, who made an immense contribution to our understanding of the judicial process.[21] Nicola Lacey has ventured the suggestion that Fuller would have been on much stronger ground in his argument with Hart had he focused on procedural and institutional as well as formal aspects of legality.[22] But he allowed Hart to set the agenda, with the crucial question "What is law and what is its relation to morality?" and did not force him to open that up, in any particular way to "What, in terms of institutional procedures, is a legal system, and what is the relation of all that to morality?"

Fortunately we are not bound to follow him in that. I think we can usefully pursue a procedural (and institutional) dimension of the Rule of Law as well as a formal dimension and distinguish both of them (separately as well as jointly) from a more substantive conception. There is certainly precedent for this elsewhere in the Rule of Law literature.

Albert Venn Dicey, for example, when he explained the Rule of Law as a distinguishing feature of the English Constitution, identified it in the first instance with the following feature:

> When we say that the supremacy or the rule of law is a characteristic of the English constitution, we ... mean, in the first place, that no man is punishable or can be lawfully made to suffer in body or goods except for a distinct breach of law *established in the ordinary legal manner before the ordinary Courts of the land*. In this sense the rule of law is contrasted with every system of government based on the exercise by persons in authority of wide, arbitrary, or discretionary powers of constraint.[23]

The passage I have emphasized is important. Without it, we tend to read the contrast between the rule of law and arbitrary government in terms of the application of a rule versus purely individualized application of punishment (without guidance by a rule). With it, however, the contrast between law and discretion has to do with institutions and procedures: a person must not be made to suffer except pursuant to a decision of a court arrived at in the ordinary manner observing ordinary legal process.

[19]Fuller, *Morality of Law*, 176.
[20]For the implications of this for Fuller's theory, see Jeremy Waldron, "The Appeal of Law: Efficacy, Freedom, or Fidelity," in *Law and Philosophy*, 13 (1994), 259, at 272–5.
[21]See Lon L. Fuller, "The Forms and Limits of Adjudication," *Harvard Law Review* 92 (1978), 353.
[22]See Nicola Lacey, "Out of the 'Witches' Cauldron?—Reinterpreting the Context and Reassessing the Significance of the Hart-Fuller Debate," in Peter Cane (ed.) *The Hart-Fuller Debate: 50 Years On* (Oxford: Hart Publishing, 2010), 1.
[23]A.V. Dicey, *Introduction to the Study of the Law of the Constitution*, Eighth edition of 1915 (Indianapolis: Liberty Classics, 1982), 110 (my emphasis).

When E.P. Thompson insisted (alarming his fellow Marxists) that the Rule of law was "an unqualified human good" and a "cultural achievement of universal significance,"[24] he did so by reference in large part to the importance of procedure:

> [N]ot only were the rulers (indeed, the ruling class as a whole) inhibited by their own rules of law against the exercise of direct unmediated force (arbitrary imprisonment, the employment of troops against the crowd, torture, and those other conveniences of power with which we are all conversant), but they also believed enough in these rules, and in their accompanying ideological rhetoric, to allow, in certain limited areas, the law itself to be a genuine forum within which certain kinds of class conflict were fought out. There were even occasions ... when the Government itself retired from the courts defeated.[25]

As I said earlier, in recent legal philosophy the phrase "the Rule of Law" is often used to conjure up a sort of laundry list of features that a healthy legal system should have. These are mostly variations of the eight formal desiderata of Lon Fuller's "internal morality,"[26] but occasionally procedural and institutional considerations creep in. Thus the fourth, fifth, and seventh items on Joseph Raz's list are the following: "(4) The independence of the judiciary must be guaranteed. ... (5) The principles of natural justice must be observed ... [o]pen and fair hearing, absence of bias, and the like ... (7) The courts should be easily accessible."[27] The justifications Raz gives often go to the issue of legal determinacy (e.g., "Since the court's judgment establishes conclusively what is the law in the case before it, the litigants can be guided by law only if the judges apply the law correctly"), but at least the procedural and institutional considerations rate a mention.

In many other discussions of the Rule of Law, however, the procedural dimension is simply ignored (or, worse, it is assumed thoughtlessly that the procedural dimension is taken care of by calling the formal dimension "procedural"). I do not mean that judges and courts are ignored. In the last *Nomos* volume devoted to this subject, there is extensive discussion of judicial authority and judicial discretion: some of it is about equitable decision by judges in hard cases (together with an intriguing account of the idea of practical wisdom as applied to the judiciary) and some of it is about the interpretive techniques that judges should use in difficult cases.[28] But if one didn't know better, one would infer from these discussions that problems were just brought to wise individuals called judges for their decision (with or without the help of sources of law) and the judges in question proceeded to deploy their interpretive strategies and practical wisdom to address those problems; there is no discussion in these papers of the highly proceduralized hearings in which problems are presented to a court, let alone the importance of the various procedural rights and powers possessed by individual litigants in relation to these hearings. Certainly there is no indication by any of the volume's contributors that the procedures themselves and the rights and powers associated with them are in and of themselves part of what we value under the heading of "the Rule of Law."

4. PROCEDURE AND THE CONCEPT OF LAW

Elsewhere I have remarked on an interesting parallel between the failure of some of our leading theorists of the Rule of Law to highlight procedural (as opposed to formal) considerations, and the failure of our leading legal philosophers to

---

[24]E.P. Thompson, *Whigs and Hunters: The Origin of the Black Act* (Harmondsworth: Penguin Books, 1977), 265–6.
[25]Ibid., 265.
[26]See for example, Finnis, *Natural Law and Natural Rights*, p. 270.
[27]Raz, "*The Rule of Law and its Virtue*," at 216–7.

[28]See the papers on equitable judgment and practical reason by Lawrence Solum, "*Equity and the Rule of Law*," in Ian Shapiro (ed.) *Nomos XXXVI: The Rule of Law*, (New York: New York University Press, 1994), 120; and Stephen Burton, "Particularism, Discretion, and the Rule of Law," ibid., 178. See also the papers on judges' interpretive strategies by Jack Knight and James Johnson, "Public Choice and the Rule of Law: Rational Choice Theories of Statutory Interpretation," ibid., 244; and William Eskridge and John Ferejohn, "Politics, Interpretation, and the Rule of Law," ibid., 265.

include procedural and institutional elements in their conception of law itself.[29]

For my part, I do not think we should regard something as a legal system absent the existence and operation of the sort of institutions we call courts. By courts, I mean institutions which apply norms and directives established in the name of the whole society to individual cases and which settle disputes about the application of those norms. And I mean institutions which do that through the medium of hearings, formal events which are tightly structured procedurally in order to enable an impartial to determine the rights and responsibilities of particular persons fairly and effectively after hearing evidence and argument from both sides.[30]

It is remarkable how little there is about courts in the conceptual accounts of law presented in modern positivist jurisprudence. The leading source is H.L.A. Hart's magisterial work, *The Concept of Law*. Hart conceives of law in terms of the union of primary rules of conduct and secondary rules that govern the way in which the primary rules are made, changed, applied and enforced. He certainly seems to regard *something like* courts as essential. When he introduces the concept of secondary rules, he talks of the emergence of "rules of adjudication" in the transition from a pre-legal to a legal society: "secondary rules empowering individuals to make authoritative determinations of the question of whether, on a particular occasion, a primary rule has been broken."[31] Notice, however, that this account defines the relevant institutions simply in terms of their output function—the making of "authoritative determinations ... of whether ... a primary rule has been broken." There is nothing on the distinctive process by which this function is performed.[32] A Star Chamber proceeding ex parte

without any sort of hearing would satisfy Hart's definition, so would the tribunals we call in the antipodes "kangaroo courts."

Much the same is true of Joseph Raz's view about the importance of what he calls primary norm-applying institutions in *Practical Reason and Norms*, and elsewhere.[33] Raz believes that norm-applying institutions are key to our understanding of legal systems (much more so than legislatures).[34] Now, there are all sorts of institutionalized ways in which norms may be applied, according to Raz, but "primary norm-applying organs" are of particular interest. Raz describes their operation as follows: "They are institutions with power to determine the normative situation of specified individuals, which are required to exercise these powers by applying existing norms, but whose decisions are binding even when wrong."[35] He tells us that "[c]ourts, tribunals and other judicial bodies are the most important example of primary organs."[36] In his abstract philosophical account, however, the operation of primary norm-applying institutions is understood solely in terms of output (and in terms of what is done with their output). Again there is nothing about mode of operation or procedure. Secret military commissions might meet to "determine the normative situation of specified individuals ... by applying existing norms," in the absence of the individuals in question and without affording any sort of hearing. The impression one gets from Raz's account is that a system of rule dominated by institutions like that would count as a legal system. Of course Raz would criticize such institutions, and as we have seen, he might use the ideal of the Rule of Law to do so.[37] But he seems to suggest that this is relevant to law only at an evaluative level, not at the conceptual level.

I think there is a considerable divergence here between what these philosophers say about the concept of law and how the term is ordinarily used. Most people, I think, would regard hearings

---

[29]See Jeremy Waldron, "The Concept and the Rule of Law," 43 *Georgia Law Review* (2008), 1–61.

[30]See Martin Shapiro, *Courts, A Comparative and Political Analysis* (Chicago: University of Chicago Press, 1981), 1–2; and Fuller, "The Forms and Limits of Adjudication," passim.

[31]H.L.A. Hart, *The Concept of Law*, Second Edition (Oxford: Clarendon Press, 1994), at 96.

[32]Hart acknowledges that of course secondary rules will have to define processes for these institutions (ibid., 97). But he seems to think that this can vary from society to society and that nothing in the concept of law constrains that definition.

[33]Joseph Raz, *Practical Reason and Norms*, New edition (Oxford: Oxford University Press, 1990), 134–7.

[34]Ibid., 132–3.

[35]Ibid., at 136.

[36]Idem.

[37]Raz, "The Rule of Law and its Virtue," at 217.

and impartial proceedings, and the safeguards that go with them, as an essential rather than a contingent feature of the institutional arrangements we call legal systems.[38] Their absence would for most people be a disqualifying factor, just like the absence of free and fair elections in what was alleged to be a democracy.

Moreover, a procedural conception of the Rule of Law helps bring our conceptual thinking about law to life. There is a distressing tendency among academic legal philosophers to see law simply as a set of normative propositions and to pursue their task of developing an understanding of the concept of law to consist simply in understanding what sort of normative propositions these are. But law comes to life *in institutions*. An understanding of legal systems that emphasizes argument in the courtroom as much as the existence and recognition of rules provides the basis for a much richer understand of the values and requirements that law and legality represent in modern political argument.

If it were up to me, I would bring the two concepts together—the concept of law and the concept of legality or the Rule of Law. I would suggest that the concept of law should be understood along Fullerian lines to embrace the fundamental elements of legality; but I would only argue this if the latter were understood to give pride of place to procedural and institutional elements. You may be relieved to hear that that is not the task of the present paper however; I have attempted this elsewhere and so have one or two others.[39] But it is not the received position. According to Joseph Raz and others you cannot understand what the Rule of Law is unless you already and independently understand what law is, and the characteristic evils law is likely to give rise to.[40] I mention this further conceptual debate in order to register the points that the absence of a proper emphasis on procedural aspects on either side—in the academic account of the concept of law and in the academic account of the Rule of Law—may have a common source and may have something to do with our inability to see the connection between the two ideas.

5. PROCEDURE AND THE UNDERLYING MORAL CONCERNS

When Fuller developed his formal principles of generality, prospectivity, clarity, stability, consistency—principles whose observance is bound up with the basics of legal craftsmanship[41]—legal positivists expressed bewilderment as to why Fuller called this set of principles a "morality."[42] He did so because he thought his eight principles had inherent moral significance. It was not only that he believed that observing them made it much more difficult to do substantive injustice; though this he did believe.[43] It was also because he thought observing the principles he identified was itself a way of respecting human dignity:

> To embark on the enterprise of subjecting human conduct to rules involves ... a commitment to the view that man is ... a responsible agent, capable of understanding and following rules.... Every departure from the principles of law's inner morality is an affront to man's dignity as a responsible agent. To judge his actions by unpublished or retrospective laws, or to order him to do an act that is impossible, is to convey ... your indifference to his powers of self-determination.[44]

I think what Fuller said about the connection between his formal principles and dignity can be said even more about the connection between procedure and dignity.

---

[38]See, for example, Jamil Anderlini, "Rewards and Risks of Chinese Legal Career," *Financial Times*, July 24, 2008, where a dissident Chinese lawyer, commenting on abuses of the "court" system in China, observes: "Actually, there is no real legal system in the western sense in China."
[39]See Waldron, "The Concept and the Rule of Law"; see also Nigel Simmonds, *Law as a Moral Idea* (Oxford: Oxford University Press, 2008).
[40]Raz, "The Rule of Law and its Virtue," 224.
[41]Fuller, *The Morality of Law*, esp. Ch. 2.
[42]See, e.g., H.L.A. Hart, "Book Review of Lon Fuller, *The Morality of Law*," *Harvard Law Review* 78 (1965), 1281 at 1284. For a characterization of Hart's bewilderment as disingenuous, see Jeremy Waldron, "Positivism and Legality: Hart's Equivocal Response to Fuller," *NYU Law Review*, 83 (2008) 1135, esp. 1154–6.
[43]Fuller, "Positivism and Fidelity to Law—A Reply to Professor Hart," at 636–7.
[44]Lon Fuller, *Morality of Law*, 162.

The essential idea of procedure is much more than merely functional: applying norms to individual cases. It is partly structural; it involves Martin Shapiro's idea of the triad structure:[45] a first party, a second opposing party, and above them a separate impartial officer with the authority to make a determination. Most importantly it is procedural: the operation of a court involves a way of proceeding which offers those who are immediately concerned in the dispute or in the application of the norm with an opportunity to make submissions and present evidence (such evidence being presented in an orderly fashion according to strict rules of relevance oriented to the norms whose application is in question). The mode of presentation may vary; but the existence of such an opportunity does not. Once presented, then the evidence is made available to be examined and confronted by the other party in open court. And each party has the opportunity to present arguments and submissions at the end of this process and answer those of the other party. In the course of all of this, both sides are treated respectfully, if formalistically, but above all listened to by a tribunal which (as Lon Fuller stressed in his work on "Forms and Limits of Adjudication") is bound in some manner to attend to the evidence presented and respond to the submissions that are made in the reasons it eventually gives for its decision.[46]

These are abstract characteristics, and of course (as I said) it would be a mistake to try to get too concrete given the variety of court-like institutions in the world. But they are not just arbitrary abstractions. They capture a deep and important sense associated foundationally with the idea of a legal system, that law is a mode of governing people that treats them with respect, as though they had a view or perspective of their own to present on the application of the norm to their conduct and situation. Applying a norm to a human individual is not like deciding what to do about a rabid animal or a dilapidated house. It involves paying attention to a point of view and respecting the personality of the entity one is dealing with. As such it embodies a crucial dignitarian idea—respecting the dignity of those to whom the norms are applied as *beings capable of explaining themselves.* None of this is present in the dominant positivist account; all of it I submit should be regarded as an essential aspect of our working conception of law.

6. APPREHENSIONS ABOUT LAWLESSNESS

Think of the concerns expressed about the plight of detainees in Guantanamo Bay from 2003 to the present. When jurists worried that the detention facility there was a "black hole" so far as legality was concerned,[47] it was precisely the lack of these procedural rights that they were concerned about. What the detainees demanded, in the name of the Rule of Law, was an opportunity to appear before a proper legal tribunal, to confront and answer the evidence against them (such as it was), and to be represented so that their own side of the story concerning their detention could be explained to a tribunal that (as I said) would be required to listen and respond to the arguments that were made. That was the gist of their habeas corpus demands. No doubt the integrity of these proceedings would depend in part on the formal characteristics of the legal norms (whether laws and customs of armed conflict or other antiterrorist laws) that were supposed to govern their detention, whose application in their case they could call in question at the hearings that they demanded; no doubt the formal features stressed by Fuller, Hayek and others would be important, because it is very difficult to make a case at a hearing if the laws governing detention are unacceptably vague, or indeterminate, or kept secret, etc. Even so, we still miss out on a whole important dimension of the Rule of Law ideal if we do not also focus on the procedural demands themselves

---

[45]Shapiro, *Courts*, at 1–2.
[46]Fuller, "The Forms and Limits of Adjudication", at 366–7.

[47]See, e.g., Johan Steyn, "*Guantanamo Bay: The Legal Black Hole*," Twenty-Seventh F.A. Mann Lecture, 25 November 2003; available at http://www.statewatch.org/news/2003/nov/guantanamo.pdf (last visited 9 May 2012).

which, as it were, give the formal side of the Rule of Law this purchase.[48]

These concerns are prominent not just in extreme cases like Guantanamo Bay. Among working lawyers, they have been at the forefront of concerns about the compatibility of the Rule of Law with the modern administrative state. When Dicey spoke of a "Decline in Reverence for the Rule of Law" in England at the beginning of the twentieth century, one of the things he had in mind was the transfer of authority to impose penalties or take away property or livelihood from courts to administrative entities, and the content of his concern was precisely that those entities would not act as courts acted, would not feel constrained by rules of procedure and other scruples of "natural justice" in the way that judges characteristically felt constrained.[49] True, even Dicey expressed this partly in terms of the existence of determinate rules:

> State officials must more and more undertake to manage a mass of public business…. But Courts are from the nature of things unsuited for the transaction of business. The primary duty of a judge is to act in accordance with the strict rules of law. He must shun, above all things, any injustice to individuals. The well-worn and often absurdly misapplied adage that "it is better that ten criminals should escape conviction than that one innocent man should without cause be found guilty of crime" does after all remind us that the first duty of a judge is not to punish crime but to punish it without doing injustice. A man of business, whether employed by a private firm or working in a public office, must make it his main object to see that the business in which he is concerned is efficiently carried out. He could not do this if tied down by the rules which rightly check the action of a judge.[50]

I guess one *could* parse this purely in terms of judges (as opposed to managers of public business) being bound by determinate rules—and then the whole thing could be brought in under Fuller's eighth principle of congruence.[51] But again, I think that would miss a whole dimension of the matter. It is not simply that one bunch of officials are bound to apply determinate rules while another bunch of officials are not; it is that the former operate in the context of highly proceduralized institutions in which procedural rights and duties of all sorts are oriented to allowing the application of determinate rules to be established fairly and minutely with ample opportunity for contestation. If we neglect this aspect of the Rule of Law, we make much of Dicey's concern about contemporary decline in regard for that ideal quite mysterious.

Something similar may be true of our concerns about the role of the Rule of Law in nation building. When theorists like Robert Barro argue that it is more important to secure the Rule of Law in a developing society than it is to secure the institutions of democracy, what they often have in mind is the elimination of corruption and the establishment of stable legal institutions.[52] We cannot understand these concerns unless we focus on the distinctive procedural features of legal institutions and their procedural integrity vis-à-vis the elimination of corruption, the securing of judicial independence, the guarantee of due process, and the separation of powers.

True, it has to be said also that sometimes when commentators call for the Rule of Law to be given priority over democracy in developing societies, what they mainly have in mind are quasi-substantive features like the protection of property, the proper enforcement of contracts, and the protection of outside investments, and

---

[48]It is also worth noting that the demand for a clear rule to apply to and regulate the detention is not only a demand for something which the potential detainees can use *ex ante* to guide their conduct: as though terrorists most wanted to know (and guide their action by) what they were forbidden to do! The demand for the formal aspects of the Rule of Law is often just a way of getting to the procedural aspects of the Rule of Law, which is what the detainees really care about.

[49]See Dicey's "Introduction" to the eighth edition of *Introduction to the Study of the Law of the Constitution*, at lv–lvii.

[50]Ibid., at lvii.

[51]Fuller, *The Morality of Law*, 39 and 81–91.

[52]Robert Barro, "Democracy and the Rule of Law," in B. Bueno de Mesquita and H. Root (eds.), *Governing for Prosperity* (New Haven: Yale University Press, 2000). See also R.D. Cooter, "The Rule of State Law versus the Rule-of-Law State: Economic Analysis of the Legal Foundations of Development," in E. Buscaglia, W. Ratliff, and R. Cooter (eds.), *The Law and Economics of Development* (Greenwich: JAI Press, 1997), 101.

the safeguarding of all this as against democratically enacted social-justice or environmental- or labor-rights legislation. Sometimes this is quite cynical.[53] I have argued vehemently elsewhere against this Washington-consensus-based abuse of the idea of the Rule of Law.[54]

7. LAW, ARGUMENTATION, AND PREDICTABILITY

When I set out my preliminary list of procedural characteristics of the Rule of Law at the beginning of this paper, I mentioned the requirement that those facing the imposition of penalty, stigma or serious loss at the hands of government must have the right to make legal argument about the bearing of the evidence and about the bearing of the various legal norms relevant to the case. I believe this is particularly important. But it also sets up an interesting tension between the procedural requirements of the Rule of Law and the formal requirements that relate to the determinacy of legal norms.

In the systems with which we are familiar, law presents itself as something one can make sense of. The norms that are administered in our legal system may seem like just one damned command after another, but lawyers and judges try to see the law as a whole; they attempt to discern some sort of coherence or system, integrating particular items into a structure that makes intellectual sense.[55] And ordinary people and their representatives take advantage of this aspiration to systematicity and integrity in framing their own legal arguments, by inviting the tribunal hearing their case to consider how the position they are putting forward fits generally into a coherent conception of the spirit of the law. These are not just arguments about what the law *ought to be*—made, as it were, in a sort of lobbying mode. They are

arguments of reason presenting competing arguments about what the law *is*. Inevitably, they are controversial: one party will say that such-and-such a proposition cannot be inferred from the law as it is; the other party will respond that it can be so inferred if only we credit the law with more coherence (or coherence among more of its elements) than people have tended to credit it with in the past. And so the determination of whether such a proposition has legal authority may often be a matter of contestation. Law in other words becomes a matter of argument.[56]

In this regard too, law has a dignitarian aspect: it conceives of the people who live under it as bearers of reason and intelligence. They are thinkers who can grasp and grapple with the rationale of the way they are governed and relate it in complex but intelligible ways to their own view of the relation between *their* actions and purposes and the actions and purposes of the state. Once again, I don't think we would accept that a society was governed by the Rule of Law if its judicial procedures did not afford parties the opportunity to make arguments of this kind in complex cases where the state was bearing down on them.

But this strand of the Rule of Law, this strand of dignitarian respect, has a price: it probably brings with it a diminution in law's certainty. On my view, the procedural side of the Rule of Law requires that public institutions should sponsor and facilitate reasoned argument in human affairs. But argument can be unsettling and the procedures that we cherish often have the effect of undermining the certainty and predictability that are emphasized in the formal side of the ideal.[57] By associating the rule of law with the legal process rather than with the form of the determinate norms that are supposed to emerge from that

---

[53]For examples, see the World Bank ideal of ROL as described by Frank Upham, "Mythmaking in the Rule of Law Orthodoxy," available at http://www.carnegieendowment.org/files/wp30.pdf (last visited 9 May 2012). See also the discussion in Waldron, "Legislation and the Rule of Law," at 118 ff.
[54]Waldron, "Legislation and the Rule of Law," passim.
[55]See also the discussion in Jeremy Waldron, "Transcendental Nonsense and System in the Law," *Columbia Law Review*, 100 (2000), 16, at 30–40.

[56]The legal philosopher who has done the most to develop this theme is of course Ronald Dworkin, particularly in *Law's Empire* (Cambridge, Mass.: Harvard University Press, 1986).
[57]See the discussion of the relation between civil disobedience and disputes about which laws are valid in Ronald Dworkin, *Taking Rights Seriously* (Cambridge, Mass.: Harvard University Press, 1977), 184–205. I have discussed this argumentative aspect of Dworkin's conception of the Rule of Law in Jeremy Waldron, "The Rule of Law as a Theater of Debate," Justine Burley (ed.), *Dworkin and his Critics* 319 (Oxford: Blackwell Publishing, 2004).

process, the procedural aspect of the Rule of Law seems to place a premium on values that are somewhat different from those emphasized in the formal picture.[58] The formal picture, particularly as it is put forward by thinkers like F.A. Hayek, emphasizes clarity, determinacy and predictability, as feature of governance that make private freedom possible.[59] The procedural idea sponsors a certain conception of freedom also: but it is more like positive freedom: active engagement in the administration of public affairs, the freedom to participate actively and argumentatively in the way that one is governed. And that positive freedom may stand in some tension with private freedom in Hayek's vision of liberty, which presupposes that law is determinate enough to allow people to know in advance where they stand and to have some advance security in their understanding of the demands that law is likely to impose upon them.

The tension may also be represented as a tension between various strands of dignity associated with the Rule of Law. Fuller, we saw, associated his formal criteria with a dignitarian conception of the legal subject as an agent capable of monitoring and freely governing his own conduct. In its action-guiding aspect, law respects people as agents; and the Rule of Law is sometimes represented as the conditions of such respect.[60] But how, it may be asked, can we maintain this mode of respect if law becomes contestable and uncertain as a result of argumentation? Insisting on an opportunity for argumentation respects dignity too but at the cost of diminishing the confidence that we can have in the dignity of law's self-application at the hands of ordinary individuals. On the other hand, it is worth remembering that law consists not only of determinate rules but also standards, and that law's confidence in

the possibility of self-application does not necessarily presuppose that it takes only the form of determinate rigid rules. Law's dignitarian faith in the practical reason of ordinary people may be an act of faith in their *thinking*—e.g., about what is reasonable and what is not—not just in their recognition of a rule and its mechanical application. And so also it may be an act of faith not just in their ability to apply general moral predicates (such as "reasonable") to their actions, but also to think about and interpret the bearing of a whole array of norms and precedents to their conduct—rather than just the mechanical application of a single norm.

So we cannot just brush the argumentative aspect of law's procedures aside, so far as the Rule of Law is concerned. I believe this tension in the Rule of Law ideal is largely unavoidable, and we should own up to the fact that the Rule of Law points as it were in both directions. I think we find symptoms of this tension in the ambivalence of the Rule-of-Law ideal so far as the role of judges in society is concerned and in a similar ambivalence about the role of litigation.[61]

There is no denying that theories that place great stress on legal certainty, predictability, and settlement, on the determinacy and intelligibility of the norms that are upheld in society, and on the relatively straightforward character of their administration by the state are among the most influential conceptions of the Rule of Law.[62] According to these conceptions, the most important thing that people need from the law that governs them is certainty and predictability in the conduct of their lives and businesses. There may be no getting away from legal constraint in the circumstances of modern life, but freedom is possible nevertheless if people know in advance how the law will operate and how they have to act if they are to avoid its application. Knowing in advance

---

[58]See Richard Fallon, "The Rule of Law as a Concept in Constitutional Discourse," 97 *Columbia Law Review* 1 (1997), at 6.

[59]See, for example, Hayek, *The Constitution of Liberty*, at 152–7.

[60]Raz, "The Rule of Law and its Virtue, at 214: "This is the basic intuition from which the doctrine of the rule of law derives: the law must be capable of guiding the behaviour of its subjects."

[61]See the discussion in Jeremy Waldron, "Is the Rule of Law an Essentially Contested Concept (in Florida)," *Law and Philosophy*, 21 (2002), 137.

[62]See also T. Carothers, "The Rule of Law Revival," 77 *Foreign Affairs* 95 (1998); and Jeffrey Kahn, "The Search for the Rule of Law in Russia," 37 *Georgetown Journal of International Law* 353, 359–361 (2006).

how the law will operate enables one to make plans and work around its requirements.[63] And knowing that one can count on the law's protecting certain personal property rights gives each citizen some certainty on what he can rely on in his dealings with other people and the state. Accordingly, they highlight the role of rules rather than standards, literal meanings rather than systemic inferences, direct applications rather than arguments, and *ex ante* clarity rather than labored interpretations.[64] The Rule of Law is violated, on this account, when the norms that are applied by officials do not correspond to the norms that have been made public to the citizens or when officials act on the basis of their own discretion rather than norms laid down in advance. If action of this sort becomes endemic, then not only are people's expectations disappointed, but increasingly they will find themselves unable to *form* expectations on which to rely, and the horizons of their planning and their economic activity will shrink accordingly. So it is natural to think that the Rule of Law must condemn the uncertainty that arises out of law's argumentative character.

But the contrary considerations embodied in the procedural side of the Rule of Law will not easily give way. As the late and lamented Neil MacCormick has pointed out, law is an argumentative discipline and no analytic theory of what law is and what distinguishes legal systems from other systems of governance can afford to ignore this aspect of our legal practice, and the distinctive role it plays in a legal system's treating ordinary citizens with respect as active centers of intelligence.[65] A fallacy of modern positivism, it seems to me, is its exclusive emphasis on the command-and-control aspect of law, or the norm-and-guidance aspect of law, without any reference

to the culture of argument that a legal system frames, sponsors and institutionalizes. The institutionalized recognition of a distinctive set of norms may be an important feature. But at least as important is what we do in law with the norms that we identify. We don't just obey them or apply the sanctions that they ordain; we argue over them adversarially, we use our sense of what is at stake in their application to license a continual process of argument back and forth, and we engage in elaborate interpretive exercises about what it means to apply them faithfully as a system to the cases that come before us.

When positivists in the tradition of H.L.A. Hart pay attention to this aspect of interpretation and argument they tend to treat it as an occasional and problematic sideline. The impression given is that in most cases the authoritative identification of legal norms using a rule of recognition is sufficient; once it is recognized, a legal norm can become a straightforward guide to official action. But, it is said, *occasionally* the language is unclear —because words have open texture or because our aims are indeterminate or because for some other reasons there is a hiccough in the interface between words and the facts that they apply to— and then unfortunately we have no choice but to argue the matter through.[66] And usually, the positivist will add, the upshot is that a court will just have to cut through the Gordian knot and make a new rule, which can be recognized and applied more readily without any attendant controversy.[67] But this account radically underestimates the point that argumentation (about what this or that provision means, or what the effect is of this array of precedents) is *business as usual* in law. We would be uneasy about counting a system that did not exhibit it and make routine provision for it as a legal system.

So: I don't think that a conception of law or a conception of the Rule of Law that sidelines the importance of argumentation can really do justice to the value we place on government treating

---

[63]See, especially, Hayek, *The Constitution of Liberty* 153 and 156–7.

[64]See also James R. Maxeiner, "Legal Indeterminacy Made in America: U.S. Legal Methods and the Rule of Law," *Valparaiso University Law Review*, 41 (2006), 517; and Antonin Scalia, "The Rule of Law as a Law of Rules," *University of Chicago Law Review*, 56 (1989), 1175.

[65]Neil MacCormick, *Rhetoric and the Rule of Law: A Theory of Legal Reasoning* (Oxford: Oxford University Press, 2005), at 14–15 and 26–8. I am greatly indebted to MacCormick's account.

[66]Hart, *The Concept of Law*, 124–36.

[67]Ibid., 135–6.

ordinary citizens with respect as active centers of intelligence. The demand for clarity and predictability is commonly made in the name of individual freedom—the freedom of the Hayekian individual in charge of his own destiny who needs to know where he stands so far as social order is concerned.[68] But with the best will in the word, and the most determinate seeming law, circumstances and interactions can be treacherous. From time to time, the free Hayekian individual will find himself charged with or accused of some violation. Or his business will be subject—as he thinks, unjustly or irregularly—to some detrimental rule. Some such cases may be clear; but others may be matters of dispute. An individual who values his freedom enough to demand the sort of calculability that the Hayekian image of freedom under law is supposed to cater to, is not someone who we can imagine always tamely accepting a charge or a determination that he has done something wrong. He will have a point of view, and he will seek an opportunity to bring that to bear when it is a question of applying a rule to his case. And when he brings his point of view to bear, we can imagine his plaintiff or his prosecutor responding with a point of view whose complexity and tendentiousness matches his own. And so it begins: legal argumentation and the facilities that law's procedures make for the formal airing of these arguments.[69] Courts, hearings and arguments—those aspects of law are not optional extras; they are integral parts of how law works; and they are indispensable to the package of law's respect for human agency. To say that we should value aspects of governance that promote the clarity and determinacy of rules for the sake of individual freedom, but not the opportunities for argumentation that a free and self-possessed individual is likely to demand, is to slice in half, to truncate, what the Rule of Law rests upon: respect for the freedom and dignity of each person as an active intelligence.

8. LEGAL PROCEDURES IN SOCIAL AND POLITICAL DECISION-MAKING

Alexis de Tocqueville famously remarked that "[s]carcely any political question arises in the United States that is not resolved, sooner or later, into a judicial question."[70] Does a proceduralist account of the Rule of Law, with its emphasis on due process and the sort of argumentation that one finds in courtrooms, endorse this characteristic? Is a society governed by the Rule of Law necessarily a society in which judicial procedures loom large in the settlement of social and political questions?

I think that is, for the most part, an unwarranted extrapolation. It is one thing to say that a person threatened by the government with penalty, stigma or serious loss must be offered an opportunity and a setting for argumentatively contesting that imposition. It is another thing to say that the courtroom setting, with its highly proceduralized modes of consideration, is an appropriate venue for settling general questions of common concern in a society. We may accept the procedural implications of the Rule of Law—along the lines of those set out in my list (A) through (J) in section 2—without denying that nevertheless in the end the legislature rather than the courtroom is the appropriate place for settling such matters. Certainly what happens in the courtroom, in argument about particular applications, may affect how the measures enacted in the legislature are subsequently understood. That, as I have said, may have an effect on predictability and we should not be in the business of trying to avoid that by minimizing the impact of judicial proceedings. Such an effect can and will accrue even in a society in which courts do not have the power to override legislation, and endorsing or accepting that effect by no means amounts to an endorsement of anything like judicial review of legislation.

I do not mean that the Rule of Law precludes judicial review of legislation. I believe that, as a

---

[68]See, e.g., Hayek, *The Constitution of Liberty*, at 148–61.
[69]There is a fine account of this in MacCormick, *Rhetoric and the Rule of Law*, at 12–31.

[70]Alexis de Tocqueville, *Democracy in America* (New York: Alfred Knopf, 1994), Vol. I, 280.

political ideal, it is neutral on the issue. In a society with a constitutional Bill of Rights and a practice of strong judicial review, the Rule of Law will require us to accept a much greater role for courts in public decision making than I have set out here. In such a society—I am thinking particularly of the United States—arguments made in courtrooms according to the procedural principles that I say are comprised in the Rule of Law will have a greater impact on the life of a society and a greater impact probably on social predictability than they have in a society with weak or no judicial review.[71] Also, the more robust the Bill of Rights, the more it will seem that the upshot of taking the Rule of Law seriously is substantive, not just procedural and formal. This I think is the gist of Dworkin's position on the Rule of Law in *A Matter of Principle*.[72]

Some people argue that the Rule of Law in a society is incomplete unless legislatures as much as executive agencies are bound to act in accordance with (higher) constraining laws. I do not accept that, though I understand the position. Some even say that the crucial distinction here is between the Rule of Law and rule *by law*, and they say that a system of legislative supremacy is an example of the latter but not the former. A position like this is sometimes associated with a general denigration of legislatures—as though in the end, the Rule of Law must amount to something other than the rule of men. The position is often associated with an almost mythic reverence for common law, not conceived necessarily as deliberately crafted by judges, but understood as welling up impersonally as a sort of resultant of the activity of courts. Hayek hints at some such nonsense when he writes in *The Constitution of Liberty* that most genuine rules of law:

> have never been deliberately invented but have grown through a gradual process of trial and error in which the experience of successive generations has helped to make them what they are. In most

instances, therefore, nobody knows or has ever known all the reasons and considerations that have led to a rule being given a particular form.[73]

In a similar way, the suggestion that legislatures need to be constrained by law rather than regarded as ultimate sources of law often involves a strange sort of constitutionalist mythology. It sees the framing of a constitution or a Bill of Rights as some sort of transcendent event—amounting to something other than the rule of men (by law): perhaps it is supposed to have been a spontaneous effulgence of unprecedented superhuman virtue hovering around the activity of giants like James Madison and the Federalists. But I see no reason to associate the Rule of Law with any such mythology, nor to embody in it any denial that law is human in origin and often the product of deliberate manufacture. Even if positivists (as I have argued) give an inadequate account of it, the Rule of Law is in the end the rule of positive law; it is a human ideal for human institutions, not a magic that somehow absolves us from human rule.

Having said that, let me add two final points, by way of qualification. First, even in systems of parliamentary supremacy, legislatures do act in ways that are constituted by rules, and procedural rules at that. (I mention this because sometimes when people allude to the procedural side of the Rule of Law, they have in mind the way laws are made rather than—as I have emphasized—the way they are administered.) They are—in their own way—highly proceduralized institutions and people rely on their articulated procedures as indicating the points of access at which citizens can hope to influence and participate in their proceedings. It is no accident that enemies of the Rule of Law, such as Carol Schmitt, sought comprehensively to disparage the rule-governed character of parliamentary democracy.[74]

Secondly, the Rule of Law applies not only within national polities but also increasingly

---

[71]For the contrast between strong and weak judicial review, see Jeremy Waldron, "The Core of the Case against Judicial Review," *Yale Law Journal*, 115 (2006), 1346.
[72]Ronald Dworkin, "Political Judges and the Rule of Law," in his collection *A Matter of Principle* (Cambridge, Mass.: Harvard University Press, 1985).

[73]Hayek, *Constitution of Liberty* 157. This line of thought is even more pronounced in Hayek's later work; see Hayek, *Rules and Order*, 72 ff.
[74]See e.g. Carl Schmitt, *The Crisis of Parliamentary Democracy* (Cambridge, Mass.: MIT Press, 1988).

between them. The Rule of Law as an international legal ideal remains undertheorized,[75] and I am afraid much of the work that has been done on it simply adopts uncritically the perspective of those who say, at the national level, that the ideal consists in determinacy, clarity, and predictability.[76] I believe there is much more to be said on this. I have tried to say some of it in some other writings,[77] and I will try to say more. For the moment this must suffice: to the extent that we take international law seriously, it will be the case that national legislatures like other national institutions will appropriately regard themselves as bound and constrained by law in what they do (whether they have a national Bill of Rights or not). The content of that constraint will be determined by the content of multilateral treaties (including human rights conventions), by customary international law, and by *ius cogens* provisions of various kinds. The character of the constraint will no doubt be determined, formally and procedurally (if not substantively), by the ideal of the Rule of Law, adapted to the international context. Accordingly it is a matter of some urgency—which more or less implies these days that legal philosophers are going to neglect it—to consider what that adaptation of this ideal to the international context involves.

3   Laws and Morals

H.L.A. HART

1. NATURAL LAW AND LEGAL POSITIVISM

THERE are many different types of relation between law and morals and there is nothing which can be profitably singled but for study as *the* relation between them. Instead it is important to distinguish some of the many different things which may be meant by the assertion or denial that law and morals are related. Sometimes what is asserted is a kind of connection which few if any have ever denied; but its indisputable existence may be wrongly accepted as a sign of some more doubtful connection, or even mistaken for it. Thus, it cannot seriously be disputed that the development of law, at all times and places, has in fact been profoundly influenced both by the conventional morality and ideals of particular social groups, and also by forms of enlightened moral criticism urged by individuals, whose moral horizon has transcended the morality currently accepted. But it is possible to take this truth illicitly, as a warrant for a different proposition: namely that a legal system *must* exhibit some specific conformity with morality or justice, or *must* rest on a widely diffused conviction that there is a moral obligation to obey it. Again, though this proposition may, in some sense, be true, it does not follow from it that the criteria of legal validity of particular laws used in a legal system must include, tacitly if not explicitly, a refernce to morality or justice.

It will be rightly observed that what makes sense of the thought that reason alone tells us that law "naturally" serves human interests is the tacit assumption that the proper end of human activity is survival, and this rests on the simple

[75]The papers that I have found most helpful include James Crawford, "International Law and the Rule of Law," *Adelaide Law Review*, 24 (2003), 3, and Mattias Kumm, "International Law in National Courts: The International Rule of Law and the Limits of the Internationalist Model," *Virginia Journal of International Law*, 44 (2003), 19.
[76]See Simon Chesterman, *The UN Security Council and the Rule of Law: The Role of the Security Council in Strengthening a Rules-Based International System* (Final Report and Recommendations from the Austrian Initiative) (Federal Ministry for European and International Affairs, 2004–2008, also published by the Institute for International Law and Justice, New York University School of Law). This report is available at http://papers.ssrn.com/sol3/papers.cfm?abstract_id=1279849 (last visited 9 May 2012).
[77]See Jeremy Waldron, "The Rule of International Law," *Harvard Journal of Law & Public Policy*, 30 (2006), 15; and "Are Sovereigns Entitled to the Benefit of the International Rule of Law?," New York University School of Law, Public Law & Legal Theory Research Paper Series, Working Paper no. 09-01 (2009), available at http://papers.ssrn.com/sol3/papers.cfm?abstract_id=1323383 (last visited 9 May 2012).

contingent fact that most men most of the time wish to continue in existence. The actions which we speak of as those which are naturally good to do are those which are required for survival; the notions of a human need, of harm, and of the *function* of bodily organs or changes rests on the same simple fact. Certainly if we stop here, we shall have only a very attenuated version of Natural Law: for the classical exponents of this outlook conceived of survival (*perseverare in esse suo*) as merely the lowest stratum in a much more complex and far more debatable concept of the human end or good for man. Aristotle included in it the disinterested cultivation of the human intellect, and Aquinas the knowledge of God, and both these represent values which may be and have been challenged. Yet other thinkers, Hobbes and Hume among them, have been willing to lower their sights: they have seen in the modest aim of survival the central indisputable element which gives empirical good sense to the terminology of Natural Law. "Human nature cannot by any means subsist without the association of individuals: and that association never could have place were no regard paid to the laws of equity and justice."[1]

This simple thought has in fact very much to do with the characteristics of both law and morals, and it can be disentangled from more disputable parts of the general teleological outlook in which the end or good for man appears as a specific way of life about which, in fact, men may profoundly disagree. Moreover, we can, in referring to survival, discard, as too metaphysical for modern minds, the notion that this is something antecedently fixed which men necessarily desire because it is their proper goal or end. Instead we may hold it to be a mere contingent fact which could be otherwise, that in general men do desire to live, and that we may mean nothing more by calling survival a human goal or end than that men do desire it. Yet even if we think of it in this common-sense way, survival has still a special status in relation to human conduct and in our thought about it, which parallels the prominence and the necessity ascribed to it in the orthodox formulations of Natural Law. For it is not merely that an overwhelming majority of men do wish to live, even at the cost of hideous misery, but that this is reflected in whole structures of our thought and language, in terms of which we describe the world and each other. We could not subtract the general wish to live and leave intact concepts like danger and safety, harm and benefit, need and function, disease and cure; for these are ways of simultaneously describing and appraising things by reference to the contribution they make to survival, which is accepted as an aim.

There are, however, simpler, less philosophical considerations than these which show acceptance of survival as an aim to be necessary, in a sense more directly relevant to the discussion of human law and morals. We are committed to it as something presupposed by the terms of the discussion; for our concern is with social arrangements for continued existence, not with those of a suicide club. We wish to know whether, among these social arrangements, there are some which may illuminatingly be ranked as natural laws discoverable by reason, and what their relation is to human law and morality. To raise this or any other question concerning *how* men should live together, we must assume that their aim, generally speaking, is to live. From this point the argument is a simple one. Reflection on some very obvious generalizations—indeed truisms—concerning human nature and the world in which men live show that as long as these hold good, there are certain rules of conduct which any social organization must contain if it is to be viable. Such rules do in fact constitute a common element in the law and conventional morality of all societies which have progressed to the point where these are distinguished as different forms of social control. With them are found, both in law and morals, much that is peculiar to a particular society and much that may seem arbitrary or a mere matter of choice. Such universally recognized principles of conduct which have a basis in elementary truths concerning human beings, their natural environment, and aims, may be considered the *minimum content* of Natural Law, in contrast with the more grandiose and more challengeable constructions

---

[1]Hume, *Treatise of Human Nature*, III. ii, "Of Justice and Injustice."

which have often been proffered under that name. In the next section we shall consider, in the form of five truisms, the salient characteristics of human nature upon which this modest but important minimum rests.

2. THE MINIMUM CONTENT OF NATURAL LAW

In considering the simple truisms which we set forth here, and their connection with law and morals, it is important to observe that in each case the facts mentioned afford a *reason* why, given survival as an aim, law and morals should include a specific content. The general form of the argument is simply that without such a content laws and morals could not forward the minimum purpose of survival which men have in associating with each other. In the absence of this content men, as they are, would have no reason for obeying voluntarily any rules; and without a minimum of cooperation given voluntarily by those who find that it is in their interest to submit to and maintain the rules, coercion of others who would not voluntarily conform would be impossible. It is important to stress the distinctively rational connection between natural facts and the content of legal and moral rules in this approach, because it is both possible and important to into quite different forms of connection between natural facts and legal or moral rules. Thus, the still-young sciences of psychology and sociology may discover or may even have discovered that, unless certain physical, psychological, or economic conditions are satisfied, e.g. unless young children are fed and nurtured in certain ways within the family, no system of laws or code of morals can be established, or that only those laws can function successfully which conform to a certain type. Connections of this sort between natural conditions and systems of rules are not mediated by *reasons*; for they do not relate the existence of certain rules to the conscious aims or purpose of those whose rules they are. Being fed in infancy in a certain way may well be shown to be a necessary condition or even a *cause* of a population developing or maintaining a moral or legal code, but it is not a *reason* for their doing so. Such causal connections do not

of course conflict with the connections which rest on purposes or conscious aims; they may indeed be considered more important or fundamental than the latter, since they may actually explain why human beings have those conscious aims or purposes which Natural Law takes as its starting points. Causal explanations of this type do not rest on truisms, nor are they mediated by conscious aims or purposes: they are for sociology or psychology like other sciences to establish by the methods of generalization and theory, resting on observation and, where possible, on experiment. Such connections therefore are of a different kind from those which relate the content of certain legal and moral rules to the facts stated in the following truisms.

(i) Human vulnerability. The common requirements of law and morality consist for the most part not of active services to be rendered but of forbearances, which are usually formulated in negative form as prohibitions. Of these the most important for social life are those that restrict the use of violence in killing or inflicting bodily harm. The basic character of such rules may be brought out in a question: If there were not these rules what point could there be for beings such as ourselves in having rules of *any* other kind? The force of this rhetorical question rests on the fact that men are both occasionally prone to, and normally vulnerable to, bodily attack. Yet though this is a truism it is not a necessary truth; for things might have been, and might one day be, otherwise. There are species of animals whose physical structure (including exoskeletons or a carapace) renders them virtually immune from attack by other members of their species, and animals who have no organs enabling them to attack. If men were to lose their vulnerability to each other there would vanish one obvious reason for the most characteristic provision of law and morals: *Thou shalt not kill.*

(ii) Approximate equality. Men differ from each other in physical strength, agility, and even more in intellectual capacity. None the less it is a fact of quite major importance for the understanding of different forms of law and morality that no

individual is so much more powerful than others that he is able, without co-operation, to dominate or subdue them for more than a short period. Even the strongest must sleep at times and, when asleep, lose temporarily his superiority. This fact of approximate equality, more than any other, makes obvious the necessity for a system of mutual forbearance and compromise which is the base of both legal and moral obligation. Social life with its rules requiring such forbearances is irksome at times; but it is at any rate less nasty, less brutish, and less short than unrestrained aggression for beings thus approximately equal. It is, of course, entirely consistent with this and an equal truism that when such a system of forbearance is established there will always be some who will wish to exploit it, by simultaneously living within its shelter and breaking its restrictions. This, indeed is, as we later show, one of the natural facts which makes the step from merely moral to organized, legal forms of control a necessary one. Again things might have been otherwise. Instead of being approximately equal there might have been some men immensely stronger than others and better able to dispense with rest, either because some were in these ways far above the present average, or because most were far below it. Such exceptional men might have much to gain by aggression and little to gain from mutual forbearance or compromise with others. But we need not have recourse to the fantasy of giants among pygmies to see the cardinal importance of the fact of approximate equality: for it is illustrated better by the facts of international life, where there are (or were) vast disparities in strength and vulnerability between the states. This inequality, as we shall later see, between the units of international law is one of the things that has imparted to it a character so different from municipal law and limited the extent to which it is capable of operating as an organized coercive system.

(iii) Limited altruism. Men are not devils dominated by a wish to exterminate each other, and the demonstration that, given only the modest aim of survival, the basic rules of law and morals are necessities, must not be identified with the false view that men are predominantly selfish and

have no disinterested interest in the survival and welfare of their fellows. But if men are not devils, neither are they angels; and the fact that they are a mean between these two extremes is something which makes a system of mutual forbearances both necessary and possible. With angels, never tempted to harm others, rules requiring forbearances would not be necessary. With devils prepared to destroy, reckless of the cost to themselves, they would be impossible. As things are, human altruism is limited in range and intermittent, and the tendencies to aggression are frequent enough to be fatal to social life if not controlled.

(iv) Limited resources. It is a merely contingent fact that human beings need food, clothes, and shelter; that these do not exist at hand in limitless abundance, but are scarce, have to be grown or won from nature, or have to be constructed by human toil. These facts alone make indispensable some minimal form of the institution of property (though not necessarily individual property), and the distinctive kind of rule which requires respect for it. The simplest forms of property are to be seen in rules excluding persons generally other than the "owner" from entry on, or the use of land, or from taking or using material things. If crops are to grow, land must be secure from indiscriminate entry, and food must, in the intervals between its growth or capture and consumption, be secure from being taken by others. At all times and places life itself depends on these minimal forbearances. Again, in this respect, things might have been otherwise than they are. The human organism might have been constructed like plants, capable of extracting food from air, or what it needs might have grown without cultivation in limitless abundance.

The rules which we have so far discussed are *static* rules, in the sense that the obligations they impose and the incidence of these obligations are not variable by individuals. But the division of labour, which all but the smallest groups must develop to obtain adequate supplies, brings with it the need for rules which are *dynamic* in the sense that they enable individuals to create obligations and to vary their incidence. Among these are rules enabling men to transfer, exchange, or sell their products; for these transactions involve the capacity to alter the incidence of those initial rights and obligations which define the simplest form of property. The same inescapable division of labour, and perennial need for cooperation, are also factors which make other forms of dynamic or obligation-creating rules necessary in social life. These secure the recognition of promises as a source of obligation. By this device individuals are enabled by words, spoken or written, to make themselves liable to blame or punishment for failure to act in certain stipulated ways. Where altruism is not unlimited, a standing procedure providing for such self-binding operations is required in order to create a minimum form of confidence in the future behaviour of others, and to ensure the predictability necessary for cooperation. This is most obviously needed where what is to be exchanged or jointly planned are mutual services, or wherever goods which are to be exchanged or sold are not simultaneously or immediately available.

(v) Limited understanding and strength of will. The facts that make rules respecting persons, property, and promises necessary in social life are simple and their mutual benefits are obvious. Most men are capable of seeing them and of sacrificing the immediate short-term interests which conformity to much rules demands. They may indeed obey from a variety of motives: some from prudential calculation that the sacrifices are worth the gains, some from a disinterested interest in the welfare of others, and some because they look upon the rules as worthy of respect in themselves and find their ideals in devotion to them. On the other hand, neither understanding of long-term interest, nor the strength or goodness of will, upon which the efficacy of these different motives towards obedience depends, are shared by all men alike. All are tempted at times to prefer their own immediate interests and, in the absence of a special organization for their detection and punishment, many would succumb to the temptation. No doubt the advantages of mutual forbearance are so palpable that the number and strength of those who would cooperate voluntarily in a coercive system will normally be greater than any likely combination of malefactors. Yet, except in

very small closely knit societies, submission to the system of restraints would be folly if there were no organization for the coercion of those who would then try to obtain the advantages of the system without submitting to its obligations. "Sanctions" are therefore required not as the normal motive for obedience, but as a *guarantee* that those who would voluntarily obey shall not be sacrificed to those who would not. To obey, without this, would be to risk going to the wall. Given this standing danger, what reason demands is *voluntary* cooperation in a *coercive* system.

It is to be observed that the same natural fact of approximate equality between men is of crucial importance in the efficacy of organized sanctions. If some men were vastly more powerful than others, and so not dependent on their forbearance, the strength of the malefactors might exceed that of the supporters of law and order. Given such inequalities, the use of sanctions could not be successful and would involve dangers at least as great as those which they were designed to suppress. In these circumstances instead of social life being based on a system of mutual forbearances, with force used only intermittently against a minority of malefactors, the only viable system would be one in which the weak submitted to the strong on the best terms they could make and lived under their "protection." This, because of the scarcity of resources, would lead to a number of conflicting power centres, each grouped round its "strong man": these might intermittently war with each other, though the natural sanction, never negligible, of the risk of defeat might ensure an uneasy peace. Rules of a sort might then be accepted for the regulation of issues over which the "powers" were unwilling to fight. Again we need not think in fanciful terms of pygmies and giants in order to understand the simple logistics of approximate equality and its importance for law. The international scene, where the units concerned have differed vastly in strength, affords illustration enough. For centuries the disparities between states have resulted in a system where organized sanctions have been impossible, and law has been confined to matters which did not affect "vital" issues. How far atomic weapons, when available to all, will redress the balance of unequal power, and bring forms of control more closely resembling municipal criminal law, remains to be seen.

The simple truisms we have discussed not only disclose the score of good sense in the doctrine of Natural Law. They are of vital importance for the understanding of law and morals, and they explain why the definition of the basic forms of these in purely formal terms, without reference to any specific content or social needs, has proved so inadequate. Perhaps the major benefit to jurisprudence from this outlook is the escape it affords from certain misleading dichotomies which often obscure the discussion of the characteristics of law. Thus, for example, the traditional question whether every legal system *must* provide for sanctions can be presented in a fresh and clearer light, when we command the view of things presented by this simple version of Natural Law. We shall no longer have to choose between two unsuitable alternatives which are often taken as exhaustive: on the one hand, that of saying that this is required by "the" meaning of the words "law" or "legal system," and on the other, that of saying that it is "just a fact" that most legal systems do provide for sanctions. Neither of these alternatives is satisfactory. There are no settled principles forbidding the use of the word "law" of systems where there are no centrally organized sanctions, and there is good reason (though no compulsion) for using the expression "international law" of a system which has none. On the other hand, we do need to distinguish the place that sanctions must have within a municipal system, if it is to serve the minimum purposes of beings constituted as men are. We can say, given the setting of natural facts and aims, which make sanctions both possible and necessary in a municipal system, that this is a *natural necessity*; and some such phrase is needed also to convey the status of the minimum forms of protection for persons, property, and promises which are similarly indispensable features of municipal law. It is in this form that we should reply to the positivist thesis that "law may have any content." For it is a truth of some importance that for the adequate description not only of law but of many other social institutions, a place must be reserved, besides definitions and ordinary statements of fact, for a third category of statements: those the truth of which is contingent on human beings and the world they live in retaining the salient characteristics which they have.

CHAPTER TWO

Natural Law Theory

4 An Introduction to the Principles of Morals and Legislation

JEREMY BENTHAM

CHAPTER I

OF THE PRINCIPLE OF UTILITY

Nature has placed mankind under the governance of two sovereign masters, *pain* and *pleasure*. It is for them alone to point out what we ought to do, as well as to determine what we shall do. On the one hand the standard of right and wrong, on the other the chain of causes and effects, are fastened to their throne. They govern us in all we do, in all we say, in all we think: every effort we can make to throw off our subjection, will serve but to demonstrate and confirm it. In words a man may pretend to abjure their empire: but in reality he will remain subject to it all the while. The *principle of utility*[1] cognises this subjection, and assumes it for the foundation of that system, the object of which is to rear the fabric of felicity by the hands of reason and of law. Systems which attempt to question it,

deal in sounds instead of sense, in caprice instead of reason, in darkness instead of light. But enough of metaphor and declamation: it is not by such means that moral science is to be improved.

II

The principle of utility is the foundation of the present work: it will be proper therefore at the outset to give an explicit and determinate account of what is meant by it. By the principle of utility is meant that principle which approves or disapproves of every action whatsoever, according to the tendency which it appears to have to augment or diminish the happiness of the party whose interest is in question: or, what is the same thing in other words, to promote or to oppose that happiness. I say of every action whatsoever; and therefore not only of every action of a private individual, but of every measure of government.

OF THE PRINCIPLE OF UTILITY. Jeremy Bentham, The Works of Jeremy Bentham, vol. 1 (*Principles of Morals and Legislation, Fragment on Government, Civil Code, Penal Law* [1843] Retrieved from the Online Library of Liberty.

III

By utility is meant that property in any object, whereby it tends to produce benefit, advantage, pleasure, good, or happiness (all this in the present case comes to the same thing), or (what comes again to the same thing) to prevent the happening of mischief, pain, evil, or unhappiness to the party whose interest is considered: if that party be the community in general, then the happiness of the community: if a particular individual, then the happiness of that individual.

[...]

CHAPTER II

OF PRINCIPLES ADVERSE TO THAT OF UTILITY

I

If the principle of utility be a right principle to be governed by, and that in all cases, it follows from what has been just observed, that whatever principle differs from it in any case must necessarily be a wrong one. To prove any other principle, therefore, to be a wrong one, there needs no more than just to show it to be what it is, a principle of which the dictates are in some point or other different from those of the principle of utility: to state it is to confute it.

[...]

XI

Among principles adverse[2] to that of utility, that which at this day seems to have most influence in matters of government, is what may be called the principle of sympathy and antipathy. By the principle of sympathy and antipathy, I mean that principle which approves or disapproves of certain actions, not on account of their tending to augment the happiness, nor yet on account of their tending to diminish the happiness of the party whose interest is in question, but merely because a man finds himself disposed to approve or disapprove of them: holding up that approbation or disapprobation as a sufficient reason for itself, and disclaiming the necessity of looking out for

any extrinsic ground. Thus far in the general department of morals: and in the particular department of politics, measuring out the quantum (as well as determining the ground) of punishment, by the degree of the disapprobation.

XII

It is manifest, that this is rather a principle in name than in reality: it is not a positive principle of itself, so much as a term employed to signify the negation of all principle. What one expects to find in a principle is something that points out some external consideration, as a means of warranting and guiding the internal sentiments of approbation and disapprobation: this expectation is but ill fulfilled by a proposition, which does neither more nor less than hold up each of those sentiments as a ground and standard for itself.

XIII

In looking over the catalogue of human actions (says a partizan of this principle) in order to determine which of them are to be marked with the seal of disapprobation, you need but to take counsel of your own feelings: whatever you find in yourself a propensity to condemn, is wrong for that very reason. For the same reason it is also meet for punishment: in what proportion it is adverse to utility, or whether it be adverse to utility at all, is a matter that makes no difference. In that same *proportion* also is it meet for punishment: if you hate much, punish much: if you hate little, punish little: punish as you hate. If you hate not at all, punish not at all: the fine feelings of the soul are not to be overborne and tyrannized by the harsh and rugged dictates of political utility.

XIV

The various systems that have been formed concerning the standard of right and wrong, may all be reduced to the principle of sympathy and antipathy. One account may serve for all of them. They consist all of them in so many contrivances for avoiding the obligation of appealing to any external standard, and for prevailing upon the reader to accept of the author's sentiment or opinion as a reason, and that a sufficient one, for itself. The phrases different, but the principle the same.[3]

NOTES

1. To this denomination has of late been added, or substituted, the *greatest happiness* or *greatest felicity* principle: this for shortness, instead of saying at length that principle which states the greatest happiness of all those whose interest is in question, as being the right and proper, and only right and proper and universally desirable, end of human action: of human action in every situation, and in particular in that of a functionary or set of functionaries exercising the powers of Government. The word *utility* does not so clearly point to the ideas of *pleasure* and *pain* as the words *happiness* and *felicity* do: nor does it lead us to the consideration of the *number,* of the interests affected; to the *number,* as being the circumstance, which contributes, in the largest proportion, to the formation of the standard here in question; the *standard of right and wrong,* by which alone the propriety of human conduct, in every situation, can with propriety be tried. This want of a sufficiently manifest connexion between the ideas of *happiness* and *pleasure* on the one hand, and the idea of *utility* on the other, I have every now and then found operating, and with but too much efficiency, as a bar to the acceptance, that might otherwise have been given, to this principle.

2. [. . .] In the days of Lord Coke, the light of utility can scarcely be said to have as yet shone upon the face of Common Law. If a faint ray of it, under the name of the *argumentum ab inconvenienti,* is to be found in a list of about twenty topics exhibited by that great lawyer as the co-ordinate leaders of that all-perfect system, the admission, so circumstanced, is as sure a proof of neglect, as, to the statues of Brutus and Cassius, exclusion was a cause of notice. It stands, neither in the front, nor in the rear, nor in any post of honour; but huddled in towards the middle, without the smallest mark of preference. Nor is this Latin *inconvenience* by any means the same thing with the English one. It stands distinguished from *mischief:* and because by the vulgar it is taken for something less bad, it is given by the learned as something worse. *The law prefers a mischief to an inconvenience,* says an admired maxim, and the more admired, because as nothing is expressed by it, the more is supposed to be understood.

Not that there is any avowed, much less a constant opposition, between the prescriptions of utility and the operations of the common law: such constancy we have seen to be too much even for ascetic fervor. From time to time, instinct would unavoidably betray them into the paths of reason: instinct which, however it may be cramped, can never be killed by education. The cobwebs spun out of the materials brought together by "the competition of opposite analogies," can never have ceased being warped by the silent attraction of the rational principle: though it should have been, as the needle is to the magnet, without the privity of conscience.

3. Note: It is curious enough to observe the variety of inventions men have hit upon, and the variety of phrases they have brought forward, in order to conceal from the world, and, if possible, from themselves, this very general and therefore very pardonable self-sufficiency.

   1. One man [Lord Shaftesbury, Hutchinson, Hume, &c.] says, he has a thing made on purpose to tell him what is right and what is wrong; and that it is called a *moral sense:* and then he goes to work at his ease, and says, such a thing is right, and such a thing is wrong—why? "because my moral sense tells me it is."

   2. Another man [Dr. Beattie] comes and alters the phrase: leaving out *moral,* and putting in *common,* in the room of it. He then tells you, that his common sense teaches him what is right and wrong, as surely as the other's moral sense did: meaning by common sense, a sense of some kind or other, which, he says, is possessed by all mankind: the sense of those, whose sense is not the same as the author's, being struck out of the account as not worth taking. This contrivance does better than the other; for a moral sense, being a new thing, a man may feel about him a good while without being able to find it out: but common sense is as old as the creation; and there is no man but would be ashamed to be thought not to have as much of it as his neighbours. It has another great advantage: by appearing to share power, it lessens envy: for when a man gets up upon this ground, in order to anathematize those who differ from him, it is not by a *sic volo sic jubeo* [Ed.: "Thus I wish, thus I command."], but by a *velitis jubeatis* [Ed.: "Is it your will and pleasure?" The form of proposing a law to the people in Ancient Rome.].

3. Another man [Dr. Price] comes, and says, that as to a moral sense indeed, he cannot find that he has any such thing: that however he has an *understanding,* which will do quite as well. This understanding, he says, is the standard of right and wrong: it tells him so and so. All good and wise men understand as he does: if other men's understandings differ in any point from his, so much the worse for them: it is a sure sign they are either defective or corrupt.

4. Another man says, that here is an eternal and immutable Rule of Right: that that rule of right dictates so and so: and then he begins giving you his sentiments upon any thing that comes uppermost: and these sentiments (you are to take for granted) are so many branches of the eternal rule of right.

5. Another man [Dr. Clark], or perhaps the same man (it's no matter) says, that there are certain practices conformable, and others repugnant, to the Fitness of Things; and then he tells you at his leisure, what practices are conformable and what repugnant: just as he happens to like a practice or dislike it.

6. A great multitude of people are continually talking of the Law of Nature; and then they go on giving you their sentiments about what is right and what is wrong: and these sentiments, you are to understand, are so many chapters, and sections of the Law of Nature.

5 The Case of the Speluncean Explorers

LON L. FULLER

The defendants, having been indicted for the crime of murder, were convicted and sentenced to be hanged by the Court of General Instances of the County of Stowfield. They bring a petition of error before this Court. The facts sufficiently appear in the opinion of the Chief Justice.

TRUEPENNY, C. J. The four defendants are members of the Speluncean Society, an organization of amateurs interested in the exploration of caves. Early in May of 4299 they, in the company of Roger Whetmore, then also a member of the Society, penetrated into the interior of a limestone cavern of the type found in the Central Plateau of this Commonwealth. While they were in a position remote from the entrance to the cave, a landslide occurred. Heavy boulders fell in such a manner as to block completely the only known opening to the cave. When the men discovered their predicament they settled themselves near the obstructed entrance to wait until a rescue party should remove the detritus that prevented them from leaving their underground prison. On the failure of Whetmore and the defendants to return to their homes, the Secretary of the Society was notified by their families. It appears that the explorers had left indications at the headquarters of the Society concerning the location of the cave they proposed to visit. A rescue party was promptly dispatched to the spot.

The task of rescue proved one of overwhelming difficulty. It was necessary to supplement the forces of the original party by repeated increments of men and machines, which had to be conveyed at great expense to the remote and isolated region in which the cave was located. A huge temporary camp of workmen, engineers, geologists, and other experts was established. The work of removing the obstruction was frustrated several times by fresh landslides. In one of these, ten of the workmen engaged in clearing the entrance were killed. The treasury of the Speluncean Society was soon exhausted in the rescue effort, and the sum of eight hundred thousand frelars, raised partly by popular subscription and partly by legislative grant, was expended before the imprisoned men were rescued. Success was finally achieved on the thirty-second day after the men entered the cave.

Lon L. Fuller, "The Case of the Speluncean Explorers," *Harvard Law Review*, vol. 62 (1949), pp. 616–45. Reprinted by permission of the *Harvard Law Review* and Mr. John N. Roche.

Since it was known that the explorers had carried with them only scant provisions, and since it was also known that there was no animal or vegetable matter within the cave on which they might subsist, anxiety was early felt that they might meet death by starvation before access to them could be obtained. On the twentieth day of their imprisonment it was learned for the first time that they had taken with them into the cave a portable wireless machine capable of both sending and receiving messages. A similar machine was promptly installed in the rescue camp and oral communication established with the unfortunate men within the mountain. They asked to be informed how long a time would be required to release them. The engineers in charge of the project answered that at least ten days would be required even if no new landslides occurred. The explorers then asked if any physicians were present, and were placed in communication with a committee of medical experts. The imprisoned men described their condition and the rations they had taken with them, and asked for a medical opinion whether they would be likely to live without food for ten days longer. The chairman of the committee of physicians told them that there was little possibility of this. The wireless machine within the cave then remained silent for eight hours. When communication was reestablished the men asked to speak again with the physicians. The chairman of the physicians' committee was placed before the apparatus, and Whetmore, speaking on behalf of himself and the defendants, asked whether they would be able to survive for ten days longer if they consumed the flesh of one of their number. The physicians' chairman reluctantly answered this question in the affirmative. Whetmore asked whether it would be advisable for them to cast lots to determine which of them should be eaten. None of the physicians present was willing to answer the question. Whetmore then asked if there were among the party a judge or other official of the government who would answer this question. None of those attached to the rescue camp was willing to assume the role of adviser in this matter. He then asked if any minister or priest would answer their question, and none was found who would do so. Thereafter no further messages

were received from within the cave, and it was assumed (erroneously, it later appeared) that the electric batteries of the explorers' wireless machine had become exhausted. When the imprisoned men were finally released it was learned that on the twenty-third day after their entrance into the cave Whetmore had been killed and eaten by his companions.

From the testimony of the defendants, which was accepted by the jury, it appears that it was Whetmore who first proposed that they might find the nutriment without which survival was impossible in the flesh of one of their own number. It was also Whetmore who first proposed the use of some method of casting lots, calling the attention of the defendants to a pair of dice he happened to have with him. The defendants were at first reluctant to adopt so desperate a procedure, but after the conversations by wireless related above, they finally agreed on the plan proposed by Whetmore. After much discussion of the mathematical problems involved, agreement was finally reached on a method of determining the issue by the use of the dice.

Before the dice were cast, however, Whetmore declared that he withdrew from the arrangement, as he had decided on reflection to wait for another week before embracing an expedient so frightful and odious. The others charged him with a breach of faith and proceeded to cast the dice. When it came Whetmore's turn, the dice were cast for him by one of the defendants, and he was asked to declare any objections he might have to the fairness of the throw. He stated that he had no such objections. The throw went against him, and he was then put to death and eaten by his companions.

After the rescue of the defendants, and after they had completed a stay in a hospital where they underwent a course of treatment for malnutrition and shock, they were indicted for the murder of Roger Whetmore. At the trial, after the testimony had been concluded, the foreman of the jury (a lawyer by profession) inquired of the court whether the jury might not find a special verdict, leaving it to the court to say whether on the facts as found the defendants were guilty. After some discussion, both the Prosecutor and counsel for the defendants indicated their acceptance of this procedure, and it was adopted by the court. In a lengthy special verdict the jury found the facts as I have related them above, and found further that if on these facts the defendants were guilty of the crime charged against them, then they found the defendants guilty. On the basis of this verdict, the trial judge ruled that the defendants were guilty of murdering Roger Whetmore. The judge then sentenced them to be hanged, the law of our Commonwealth permitting him no discretion with respect to the penalty to be imposed. After the release of the jury, its members joined in a communication to the Chief Executive asking that the sentence be commuted to an imprisonment of six months. The trial judge addressed a similar communication to the Chief Executive. As yet no action with respect to these pleas has been taken, as the Chief Executive is apparently awaiting our disposition of this petition of error.

It seems to me that in dealing with this extraordinary case the jury and the trial judge followed a course that was not only fair and wise, but the only course that was open to them under the law. The language of our statute is well known: "Who ever shall willfully take the life of another shall be punished by death." *N.C.S.A. (N.S.)* § 12-A. This statute permits of no exception applicable to this case; however, our sympathies may incline us to make allowance for the tragic situation in which these men found themselves.

In a case like this the principle of executive clemency seems admirably suited to mitigate the rigors of the law, and I propose to my colleagues that we follow the example of the jury and the trial judge by joining in the communications they have addressed to the Chief Executive. There is every reason to believe that these requests for clemency will be heeded, coming as they do from those who have studied the case and had an opportunity to become thoroughly acquainted with all its circumstances. It is highly improbable that the Chief Executive would deny these requests unless he were himself to hold hearings at least as extensive as those involved in the trial below, which lasted for three months. The holding of such hearings (which would virtually amount to a retrial of the

case) would scarcely be compatible with the function of the Executive as it is usually conceived. I think we may therefore assume that some form of clemency will be extended to these defendants. If this is done, then justice will be accomplished without impairing either the letter or spirit of our statutes and without offering any encouragement for the disregard of law.

FOSTER, J. I am shocked that the Chief Justice, in an effort to escape the embarrassments of this tragic case, should have adopted, and should have proposed to his colleagues, an expedient at once so sordid and so obvious. I believe something more is on trial in this case than the fate of these unfortunate explorers; that is the law of our Commonwealth. If this Court declares that under our law these men have committed a crime, then our law is itself convicted in the tribunal of common sense, no matter what happens to the individuals involved in this petition of error. For us to assert that the law we uphold and expound compels us to a conclusion we are ashamed of, and from which we can only escape by appealing to a dispensation resting within the personal whim of the Executive, seems to me to amount to an admission that the law of this Commonwealth no longer pretends to incorporate justice.

For myself, I do not believe that our law compels the monstrous conclusion that these men are murderers. I believe, on the contrary, that it declares them to be innocent of any crime. I rest this conclusion on two independent grounds, either of which is of itself sufficient to justify the acquittal of these defendants. The first of these grounds rests on a premise that may arouse opposition until it has been examined candidly. I take the view that the enacted or positive law of this Commonwealth, including all of its statutes and precedents, is inapplicable to this case, and that the case is governed instead by what ancient writers in Europe and America called "the law of nature."

This conclusion rests on the proposition that our positive law is predicated on the possibility of men's coexistence in society. When a situation arises in which the coexistence of men becomes impossible, then a condition that underlies all of our precedents and statutes has ceased to exist. When that condition disappears, then it is my opinion that the force of our positive law disappears with it. We are not accustomed to applying the maxim *cessante ratione legis, cessat et ipsa lex* to the whole of our enacted law, but I believe that this is a case where the maxim should be so applied.

The proposition that all positive law is based on the possibility of men's coexistence has a strange sound, not because the truth it contains is strange, but simply because it is a truth so obvious and pervasive that we seldom have occasion to give words to it. Like the air we breathe, it so pervades our environment that we forget that it exists until we are suddenly deprived of it. Whatever particular objects may be sought by the various branches of our law, it is apparent on reflection that all of them are directed toward facilitating and improving men's coexistence and regulating with fairness and equity the relations of their life in common. When the assumption that men may live together loses its truth, as it obviously did in this extraordinary situation where life only became possible by the taking of life, then the basic premises underlying our whole legal order have lost their meaning and force.

Had the tragic events of this case taken place a mile beyond the territorial limits of our Commonwealth, no one would pretend that our law was applicable to them. We recognize that jurisdiction rests on a territorial basis. The grounds of this principle are by no means obvious and are seldom examined. I take it that this principle is supported by an assumption that it is feasible to impose a single legal order upon a group of men only if they live together within the confines of a given area of the earth's surface. The premise that men shall coexist in a group underlies, then, the territorial principle, as it does all of law. Now I contend that a case may be removed morally from the force of a legal order, as well as geographically. If we look to the purposes of law and government, and to the premises underlying our positive law, these men when they made their fateful decision were as remote from our legal order as if they had been a thousand miles beyond our boundaries. Even in a physical sense, their underground prison was separated from our courts and writ-servers by a solid curtain of rock that could be removed only

after the most extraordinary expenditures of time and effort.

I conclude, therefore, that at the time Roger Whetmore's life was ended by these defendants, they were, to use the quaint language of the nineteenth-century writers, not in a "state of civil society" but in a "state of nature." This has the consequence that the law applicable to them is not the enacted and established law of this Commonwealth, but the law derived from those principles that were appropriate to their condition. I have no hesitancy in saying that under those principles they were guiltless of any crime.

What these men did was done in pursuance of an agreement accepted by all of them and first proposed by Whetmore himself. Since it was apparent that their extraordinary predicament made inapplicable the usual principles that regulate men's relations with one another, it was necessary for them to draw, as it were, a new charter of government appropriate to the situation in which they found themselves.

It has from antiquity been recognized that the most basic principle of law or government is to be found in the notion of contract or agreement. Ancient thinkers, especially during the period from 1600 to 1900, used to base government itself on a supposed original social compact. Skeptics pointed out that this theory contradicted the known facts of history, and that there was no scientific evidence to support the notion that any government was ever founded in the manner supposed by the theory. Moralists replied that, if the compact was a fiction from a historical point of view, the notion of compact or agreement furnished the only ethical justification on which the powers of government, which include that of taking life, could be rested. The powers of government can only be justified morally on the ground that these are powers that reasonable men would agree upon and accept if they were faced with the necessity of constructing a new order to make their life in common possible.

Fortunately, our Commonwealth is not bothered by the perplexities that beset the ancients. We know as a matter of historical truth that our government was founded upon a contract or free accord of men. The archaeological proof is conclusive that in the first period following the Great Spiral the survivors of that holocaust voluntarily came together and drew up a charter of government. Sophistical writers have raised questions as to the power of those remote contractors to bind future generations, but the fact remains that our government traces itself back in an unbroken line to that original charter.

If, therefore, our hangmen have the power to end men's lives, if our sheriffs have the power to put delinquent tenants in the street, if our police have the power to incarcerate the inebriated reveler, these powers find their moral justification in that original compact of our forefathers. If we can find no higher source for our legal order, what higher source should we expect these starving unfortunates to find for the order they adopted for themselves?

I believe that the line of argument I have just expounded permits of no rational answer. I realize that it will probably be received with a certain discomfort by many who read this opinion, who will be inclined to suspect that some hidden sophistry must underlie a demonstration that leads to so many unfamiliar conclusions. The source of this discomfort is, however, easy to identify. The usual conditions of human existence incline us to think of human life as an absolute value, not to be sacrificed under any circumstances. There is much that is fictitious about this conception even when it is applied to the ordinary relations of society. We have an illustration of this truth in the very case before us. Ten workmen were killed in the process of removing the rocks from the opening to the cave. Did not the engineers and government officials who directed the rescue effort know that the operations they were undertaking were dangerous and involved a serious risk to the lives of the workmen executing them? If it was proper that these ten lives should be sacrificed to save the lives of five imprisoned explorers, why then are we told it was wrong for these explorers to carry out an arrangement which would save four lives at the cost of one?

Every highway, every tunnel, every building we project involves a risk to human life. Taking these projects in the aggregate, we can calculate with some precision how many deaths the construction of them will require; statisticians can tell you the average cost in human lives of a thousand miles of a four-lane concrete highway. Yet we deliberately and knowingly incur and pay this cost on the assumption that the values obtained for those who survive outweigh the loss. If these things can be said of a society functioning above ground in a normal and ordinary manner, what shall we say of the supposed absolute value of a human life in the desperate situation in which these defendants and their companion Whetmore found themselves?

This concludes the exposition of the first ground of my decision. My second ground proceeds by rejecting hypothetically all the premises on which I have so far proceeded. I concede for purposes of argument that I am wrong in saying that the situation of these men removed them from the effect of our positive law, and I assume that the Consolidated Statutes have the power to penetrate five hundred feet of rock and to impose themselves upon these starving men huddled in their underground prison.

Now it is, of course, perfectly clear that these men did an act that violates the literal wording of the statute which declares that he who "shall willfully take the life of another" is a murderer. But one of the most ancient bits of legal wisdom is the saying that a man may break the letter of the law without breaking the law itself. Every proposition of positive law, whether contained in a statute or a judicial precedent, is to be interpreted reasonably, in the light of its evident purpose. This is a truth so elementary that it is hardly necessary to expatiate on it. Illustrations of its application are numberless and are to be found in every branch of the law. In *Commonwealth v. Staymore* the defendant was convicted under a statute making it a crime to leave one's car parked in certain areas for a period longer than two hours. The defendant had attempted to remove his car, but was prevented from doing so because the streets were obstructed by a political demonstration in which he took no part and which he had no reason to anticipate. His conviction was set aside by this Court, although his case fell squarely within the wording of the statute. Again, in *Fehler v. Neegas* there was before this Court for construction a statute in which the word *not* had plainly been transposed from its intended position in the final and most crucial section of the act. This transposition was contained in all the successive drafts of the act, where it was apparently overlooked by the draftsmen and sponsors of the legislation. No one was able to prove how the error came about, yet it was apparent that, taking account of the contents of the statute as a whole, an error had been made, since a literal reading of the final clause rendered it inconsistent with everything that had gone before and with the object of the enactment as stated in its preamble. This Court refused to accept a literal interpretation of the statute, and in effect rectified its language by reading the word *not* into the place where it was evidently intended to go.

The statute before us for interpretation has never been applied literally. Centuries ago it was established that a killing in self-defense is excused. There is nothing in the wording of the statute that suggests this exception. Various attempts have been made to reconcile the legal treatment of self-defense with the words of the statute, but in my opinion these are all merely ingenious sophistries. The truth is that the exception in favor of self-defense cannot be reconciled with the *words* of the statute, but only with its *purpose*.

The true reconciliation of the excuse of self-defense with the statute making it a crime to kill another is to be found in the following line of reasoning. One of the principal objects underlying any criminal legislation is that of deterring men from crime. Now it is apparent that if it were declared to be the law that a killing in self-defense is murder, such a rule could not operate in a deterrent manner. A man whose life is threatened will repel his aggressor, whatever the law may say. Looking therefore to the broad purposes of criminal legislation, we may safely declare that this statute was not intended to apply to cases of self-defense.

When the rationale of the excuse of self-defense is thus explained, it becomes apparent that precisely the same reasoning is applicable to the case at bar. If in the future any group of men ever find themselves in the tragic predicament of these defendants, we may be sure that their decision whether to live or die will not be controlled by the contents of our criminal code. Accordingly, if we read this statute intelligently it is apparent that it does not apply to this case. The withdrawal of this situation from the effect of the statute is justified by precisely the same considerations that were applied by our predecessors in office centuries ago to the case of self-defense.

There are those who raise the cry of judicial usurpation whenever a court, after analyzing the purpose of a statute, gives to its words a meaning that is not at once apparent to the casual reader who has not studied the statute closely or examined the objectives it seeks to attain. Let me say emphatically that I accept without reservation the proposition that this Court is bound by the statutes of our Commonwealth and that it exercises its powers in subservience to the duly expressed will of the Chamber of Representatives. The line of reasoning I have applied above raises no question of fidelity to enacted law, though it may possibly raise a question of the distinction between intelligent and unintelligent fidelity. No superior wants a servant who lacks the capacity to read between the lines. The stupidest housemaid knows that when she is told "to peel the soup and skim the potatoes" her mistress does not mean what she says. She also knows that when her master tells her to "drop everything and come running" he has overlooked the possibility that she is at the moment in the act of rescuing the baby from the rain barrel. Surely we have a right to expect the same modicum of intelligence from the judiciary. The correction of obvious legislative errors or oversights is not to supplant the legislative will, but to make that will effective.

I therefore conclude that on any aspect under which this case may be viewed these defendants are innocent of the crime of murdering Roger Whetmore, and that the conviction should be set aside.

TATTING, J. In the discharge of my duties as a justice of this Court, I am usually able to dissociate the emotional and intellectual sides of my reactions, and to decide the case before me entirely on the basis of the latter. In passing on this tragic case I find that my usual resources fail me. On the emotional side I find myself torn between sympathy for these men and a feeling of abhorrence and disgust at the monstrous act they committed. I had hoped that I would be able to put these contradictory emotions to one side as irrelevant, and to decide the case on the basis of a convincing and logical demonstration of the result demanded by our law. Unfortunately, this deliverance has not been vouchsafed for me.

As I analyze the opinion just rendered by my brother Foster, I find that it is shot through with contradictions and fallacies. Let us begin with his first proposition: these men were not subject to our law because they were not in a "state of civil society" but in a "state of nature." I am not clear why this is so, whether it is because of the thickness of the rock that imprisoned them, or because they were hungry, or because they had set up a "new charter of government" by which the usual rules of law were to be supplanted by a throw of the dice. Other difficulties intrude themselves. If these men passed from the jurisdiction of our law to that of "the law of nature," at what moment did this occur? Was it when the entrance to the cave was blocked, or when the threat of starvation reached a certain undefined degree of intensity, or when the agreement for the throwing of the dice was made? These uncertainties in the doctrine proposed by my brother are capable of producing real difficulties. Suppose, for example, one of these men had had his twenty-first birthday while he was imprisoned within the mountain. On what date would we have to consider that he had attained his majority—when he reached the age of twenty-one, at which time he was, by hypothesis, removed from the effects of our law, or only when he was released from the cave and became again subject to what my brother calls our "positive law"? These difficulties may seem fanciful, yet they only serve to reveal the fanciful nature of the doctrine that is capable of giving rise to them.

But it is not necessary to explore these niceties further to demonstrate the absurdity of my brother's position. Mr. Justice Foster and I are the appointed judges of a court of the Commonwealth of Newgarth, sworn and empowered to administer the laws of that Commonwealth. By what authority do we resolve ourselves into a Court of Nature? If these men were indeed under the law of nature, whence comes our authority to expound and apply that law. Certainly *we* are not in a state of nature.

Let us look at the contents of this code of nature that my brother proposes we adopt as our own and apply to this case. What a topsy-turvy and odious code it is! It is a code in which the law of contracts is more fundamental than the law of murder. It is a code under which a man may make a valid agreement empowering his fellows to eat his own body. Under the provisions of this code, furthermore, such an agreement once made is irrevocable, and if one of the parties attempts to withdraw, the others may take the law into their own hands and enforce the contract by violence—for though my brother passes over in convenient silence the effect of Whetmore's withdrawal, this is the necessary implication of his argument.

The principles my brother expounds contain other implications that cannot be tolerated. He argues that when the defendants set upon Whetmore and killed him (we know not how, perhaps by pounding him with stones) they were only exercising the rights conferred upon them by their bargain. Suppose, however, that Whetmore had concealed upon his person a revolver, and that when he saw the defendants about to slaughter him he had shot them to death in order to save his own life. My brother's reasoning applied to these facts would make Whetmore out to be a murderer, since the excuse of self-defense would have to be denied to him. If his assailants were acting rightfully in seeking to bring about his death, then of course he could no more plead the excuse that he was defending his own life than could a condemned prisoner who struck down the executioner lawfully attempting to place the noose about his neck.

All of these considerations make it impossible for me to accept the first part of my brother's argument. I can neither accept his notion that these men were under a code of nature which this Court was bound to apply to them, nor can I accept the odious and perverted rules that he would read into that code. I come now to the second part of my brother's opinion, in which he seeks to show that the defendants did not violate the provisions of

N.C.S.A. (N.S.) § 12-A. Here the way, instead of being clear, becomes for me misty and ambiguous, though my brother seems unaware of the difficulties that inhere in his demonstrations.

The gist of my brother's argument may be stated in the following terms: No statute, whatever its language, should be applied in a way that contradicts its purpose. One of the purposes of any criminal statute is to deter. The application of the statute making it a crime to kill another to the peculiar facts of this case would contradict this purpose, for it is impossible to believe that the contents of the criminal code could operate in a deterrent manner on men faced with the alternative of life or death. The reasoning by which this exception is read into the statute is, my brother observes, the same as that which is applied in order to provide the excuse of self-defense.

On the face of things this demonstration seems very convincing indeed. My brother's interpretation of the rationale of the excuse of self-defense is in fact supported by a decision of this Court, *Commonwealth v. Parry,* a precedent I happened to encounter in my research on this case. Though *Commonwealth v. Parry* seems generally to have been overlooked in the texts and subsequent decisions, it supports unambiguously the interpretation my brother has put upon the excuse of self-defense.

Now let me outline briefly, however, the perplexities that assail me when I examine my brother's demonstration more closely. It is true that a statute should be applied in the light of its purpose and that *one* of the purposes of criminal legislation is recognized to be deterrence. The difficulty is that other purposes are also ascribed to the law of crimes. It has been said that one of its objects is to provide an orderly outlet for the instinctive human demand for retribution. *Commonwealth v. Scape.* It has also been said that its object is the rehabilitation of the wrongdoer. *Commonwealth v. Makeover.* Other theories have been propounded. Assuming that we must interpret a statute in the light of its purpose, what are we to do when it has many purposes or when its purposes are disputed?

A similar difficulty is presented by the fact that although there is authority for my brother's interpretation of the excuse of self-defense, there is

other authority which assigns to that excuse a different rationale. Indeed, until I happened on *Commonwealth v. Parry* I had never heard of the explanation given by my brother. The taught doctrine of our law schools, memorized by generations of law students, runs in the following terms: The statute concerning murder requires a "willful" act. The man who acts to repel an aggressive threat to his own life does not act "willfully," but in response to an impulse deeply ingrained in human nature. I suspect that there is hardly a lawyer in this Commonwealth who is not familiar with this line of reasoning, especially since the point is a great favorite of the bar examiners.

Now the familiar explanation for the excuse of self-defense just expounded obviously cannot be applied by analogy to the facts of this case. These men acted not only "willfully" but with great deliberation and after hours of discussing what they should do. Again we encounter a forked path, with one line of reasoning leading us in one direction and another in a direction that is exactly the opposite. This perplexity is in this case compounded, as it were, for we have to set off one explanation, incorporated in a virtually unknown precedent of this Court, against another explanation, which forms a part of the taught legal tradition of our law schools, but which, so far as I know, has never been adopted in any judicial decision.

I recognize the relevance of the precedents cited by my brother concerning the displaced "not" and the defendant who parked overtime. But what are we to do with one of the landmarks of our jurisprudence, which again my brother passes over in silence? This is *Commonwealth v. Valjean.* Though the case is somewhat obscurely reported, it appears that the defendant was indicted for the larceny of a loaf of bread, and offered as a defense that he was in a condition approaching starvation. The court refused to accept this defense. If hunger cannot justify the theft of wholesome and natural food, how can it justify the killing and eating of a man? Again, if we look at the thing in terms of deterrence, is it likely that a man will starve to death to avoid a jail sentence for the theft of a loaf of bread? My brother's demonstrations would compel us to overrule *Commonwealth v. Valjean,* and many other precedents that have been built on that case.

Again, I have difficulty in saying that no deterrent effect whatever could be attributed to a decision that these men were guilty of murder. The stigma of the word *murderer* is such that it is quite likely, I believe, that if these men had known that their act was deemed by the law to be murder they would have waited for a few days at least before carrying out their plan. During that time some unexpected relief might have come. I realize that this observation only reduces the distinction to a matter of degree, and does not destroy it altogether. It is certainly true that the element of deterrence would be less in this case than is normally involved in the application of the criminal law.

There is still a further difficulty in my brother Foster's proposal to read an exception into the statute to favor this case, though again a difficulty not even intimated in his opinion. What shall be the scope of this exception? Here the men cast lots and the victim was himself originally a party to the agreement. What would we have to decide if Whetmore had refused from the beginning to participate in the plan? Would a majority be permitted to overrule him? Or, suppose that no plan were adopted at all and the others simply conspired to bring about Whetmore's death, justifying their act by saying that he was in the weakest condition. Or again, that a plan of selection was followed but one based on a different justification than the one adopted here, as if the others were atheists and insisted that Whetmore should die because he was the only one who believed in an afterlife. These illustrations could be multiplied, but enough have been suggested to reveal what a quagmire of hidden difficulties my brother's reasoning contains.

Of course I realize on reflection that I may be concerning myself with a problem that will never arise, since it is unlikely that any group of men will ever again be brought to commit the dread act that was involved here. Yet, on still further reflection, even if we are certain that no similar case will arise again, do not the illustrations I have given show the lack of any coherent and rational

principle in the rule my brother proposes? Should not the soundness of a principle be tested by the conclusions it entails, without reference to the accidents of later litigational history? Still, if this is so, why is it that we of this Court so often discuss the question whether we are likely to have later occasion to apply a principle urged for the solution of the case before us? Is this a situation where a line of reasoning not originally proper has become sanctioned by precedent, so that we are permitted to apply it and may even be under an obligation to do so?

The more I examine this case and think about it, the more deeply I become involved. My mind becomes entangled in the meshes of the very nets I throw out for my own rescue. I find that almost every consideration that bears on the decision of the case is counterbalanced by an opposing consideration leading in the opposite direction. My brother Foster has not furnished to me, nor can I discover for myself, any formula capable of resolving the equivocations that beset me on all sides.

I have given this case the best thought of which I am capable. I have scarcely slept since it was argued before us. When I feel myself inclined to accept the view of my brother Foster, I am repelled by a feeling that his arguments are intellectually unsound and approach mere rationalization. However, when I incline toward upholding the conviction, I am struck by the absurdity of directing that these men be put to death when their lives have been saved at the cost of the lives of ten heroic workmen. It is to me a matter of regret that the Prosecutor saw fit to ask for an indictment for murder. If we had a provision in our statutes making it a crime to eat human flesh, that would have been a more appropriate charge. If no other charge suited to the facts of this case could be brought against the defendants, it would have been wiser, I think, not to have indicted them at all. Unfortunately, however, the men have been indicted and tried, and we have therefore been drawn into this unfortunate affair.

Since I have been wholly unable to resolve the doubts that beset me about the law of this case, I am with regret announcing a step that is, I believe, unprecedented in the history of this tribunal. I declare my withdrawal from the decision of this case.

KEEN, J. I should like to begin by setting to one side two questions which are not before this Court.

The first of these is whether executive clemency should be extended to these defendants if the conviction is affirmed. Under our system of government, that is a question for the Chief Executive, not for us. I therefore disapprove of that passage in the opinion of the Chief Justice in which he in effect gives instructions to the Chief Executive as to what he should do in this case and suggests that some impropriety will attach if these instructions are not heeded. This is a confusion of governmental functions—a confusion of which the judiciary should be the last to be guilty. I wish to state that if I were the Chief Executive I would go farther in the direction of clemency than the pleas addressed to him propose. I would pardon these men altogether, since I believe that they have already suffered enough to pay for any offense they may have committed. I want it to be understood that this remark is made in my capacity as a private citizen who by the accident of his office happens to have acquired an intimate acquaintance with the facts of this case. In the discharge of my duties as judge, it is neither my function to address directions to the Chief Executive, nor to take into account what he may or may not do, in reaching my own decision, which must be controlled entirely by the law of this Commonwealth.

The second question that I wish to put to one side is that of deciding whether what these men did was "right" or "wrong," "wicked" or "good." That is also a question that is irrelevant to the discharge of my office as a judge sworn to apply, not my conceptions of morality, but the law of the land. In putting this question to one side I think I can also safely dismiss without comment the first and more poetic portion of my brother Foster's opinion. The element of fantasy contained in the arguments developed there has been sufficiently revealed in my brother Tatting's somewhat solemn attempt to take those arguments seriously.

The sole question before us for decision is whether these defendants did, within the meaning of *N.C.S.A.* (N.S.) § 12-A, willfully take the life of Roger Whetmore. The exact language of the statute is as follows: "Who ever shall willfully take the life of another shall be punished by death." Now I should suppose that any candid observer, content to extract from these words their natural meaning, would concede at once that these defendants did "willfully take the life" of Roger Whetmore.

Whence arise all the difficulties of the case, then, and the necessity for so many pages of discussion about what ought to be so obvious? The difficulties, in whatever tortured form they may present themselves, all trace back to a single source, and that is a failure to distinguish the legal from the moral aspects of this case. To put it bluntly, my brothers do not like the fact that the written law requires the conviction of these defendants. Neither do I, but unlike my brothers I respect the obligations of an office that requires me to put my personal predilections out of my mind when I come to interpret and apply the law of this Commonwealth.

Now, of course, my brother Foster does not admit that he is actuated by a personal dislike of the written law. Instead he develops a familiar line of argument according to which the court may disregard the express language of a statute when something not contained in the statute itself, called its "purpose," can be employed to justify the result the court considers proper. Because this is an old issue between myself and my colleague, I should like, before discussing his particular application of the argument to the facts of this case, to say something about the historical background of this issue and its implications for law and government generally.

There was a time in this Commonwealth when judges did in fact legislate very freely, and all of us know that during that period some of our statutes were rather thoroughly made over by the judiciary. That was a time when the accepted principles of political science did not designate with any certainty the rank and function of the various arms of the state. We all know the tragic issue of that uncertainty in the brief civil war that arose out of the conflict between the judiciary, on the one hand, and the executive and the legislature, on the other. There is no need to recount here the factors that contributed to that unseemly struggle for power, though they included the unrepresentative character of the Chamber, resulting from a division of the country into election districts that no longer accorded with the actual distribution of the population, and the forceful personality and wide popular following of the then Chief Justice. It is enough to observe that those days are behind us, and that in place of the uncertainty that then reigned we now have a clear-cut principle, which is the supremacy of the legislative branch of our government. From that principle flows the obligation of the judiciary to enforce faithfully the written law, and to interpret that law in accordance with its plain meaning without reference to our personal desires or our individual conceptions of justice. I am not concerned with the question whether the principle that forbids the judicial revision of statutes is right or wrong, desirable or undesirable; I observe merely that this principle has become a tacit premise underlying the whole of the legal and governmental order I am sworn to administer.

Yet though the principle of the supremacy of the legislature has been accepted in theory for centuries, such is the tenacity of professional tradition and the force of fixed habits of thought that many of the judiciary have still not accommodated themselves to the restricted role which the new order imposes on them. My brother Foster is one of that group; his way of dealing with statutes is exactly that of a judge living in the 3900s.

We are all familiar with the process by which the judicial reform of disfavored legislative enactments is accomplished. Anyone who has followed the written opinions of Mr. Justice Foster will have had an opportunity to see it at work in every branch of the law. I am personally so familiar with the process that in the event of my brother's incapacity I am sure I could write a satisfactory opinion for him without any prompting whatever, beyond being informed whether he liked the effect of the terms of the statute as applied to the case before him.

The process of judicial reform requires three steps. The first of these is to divine some single "purpose" which the statute serves. This is done although not one statute in a hundred has any such single purpose, and although the objectives of nearly every statute are differently interpreted by the different classes of its sponsors. The second step is to discover that a mythical being called "the legislator," in the pursuit of this imagined "purpose," overlooked something or left some gap or imperfection in his work. Then comes the final and most refreshing part of the task, which is, of course, to fill in the blank thus created. . . .

My brother Foster's penchant for finding holes in statutes reminds one of the story told by an ancient author about the man who ate a pair of shoes. Asked how he liked them, he replied that the part he liked best was the holes. That is the way my brother feels about statutes; the more holes they have in them the better he likes them. In short, he doesn't like statutes.

One could not wish for a better case to illustrate the specious nature of this gap-filling process than the one before us. My brother thinks he knows exactly what was sought when men made murder a crime, and that was something he calls "deterrence." My brother Tatting has already shown how much is passed over in that interpretation. But I think the trouble goes deeper. I doubt very much whether our statute making murder a crime really has a "purpose" in any ordinary sense of the term. Primarily, such a statute reflects a deeply felt human conviction that murder is wrong and that something should be done to the man who commits it. If we were forced to be more articulate about the matter, we would probably take refuge in the more sophisticated theories of the criminologists, which, of course, were certainly not in the minds of those who drafted our statute. We might also observe that men will do their own work more effectively and live happier lives if they are protected against the threat of violent assault. Bearing in mind that the victims of murders are often unpleasant people, we might add some suggestion that the matter of disposing of undesirables is not a function suited to private enterprise, but should be a state monopoly. All of which reminds me of the attorney who once argued before us that a statute licensing physicians was a good thing because it would lead to lower life insurance rates by lifting the level of general health. There is such a thing as overexplaining the obvious.

If we do not know the purpose of § 12-A, how can we possibly say there is a "gap" in it? How can we know what its draftsmen thought about the question of killing men in order to eat them? My brother Tatting has revealed an understandable, though perhaps slightly exaggerated revulsion to cannibalism. How do we know that his remote ancestors did not feel the same revulsion to an even higher degree? Anthropologists say that the dread felt for a forbidden act may be increased by the fact that the conditions of a tribe's life create special temptations toward it, as incest is most severely condemned among those whose village relations make it most likely to occur. Certainly the period following the Great Spiral was one that had implicit in it temptations to anthropophagy. Perhaps it was for that very reason that our ancestors expressed their prohibition in so broad and unqualified a form. All of this is conjecture, of course, but it remains abundantly clear that neither I nor my brother Foster knows what the "purpose" of § 12-A is.

Considerations similar to those I have just outlined are also applicable to the exception in favor of self-defense, which plays so large a role in the reasoning of my brothers Foster and Tatting. It is of course true that in *Commonwealth v. Parry* an obiter dictum justified this exception on the assumption that the purpose of criminal legislation is to deter. It may well also be true that generations of law students have been taught that the true explanation of the exception lies in the fact that a man who acts in self-defense does not act "willfully," and that the same students have passed their bar examinations by repeating what their professors told them. These last observations I could dismiss, of course, as irrelevant for the simple reason that professors and bar examiners have not as yet any commission to make our laws for us. But again the real trouble lies deeper. As in dealing with the statute, so in dealing with the exception, the question is not the conjectural *purpose* of the rule, but its *scope*. Now the scope of the exception in favor of self-defense as it has been applied by this Court is plain: it applies to cases of resisting an aggressive threat to the party's own life. It is therefore too clear for argument that this case does not fall within the scope of the exception, since it is plain that Whetmore made no threat against the lives of these defendants.

The essential shabbiness of my brother Foster's attempt to cloak his remaking of the written law with an air of legitimacy comes tragically to the surface in my brother Tatting's opinion. In that opinion Justice Tatting struggles manfully to combine his colleague's loose moralisms with his own sense of fidelity to the written law. The issue of this struggle could only be that which occurred, a complete default in the discharge of the judicial function. You simply cannot apply a statute as it is written and remake it to meet your own wishes at the same time.

Now I know that the line of reasoning I have developed in this opinion will not be acceptable to those who look only to the immediate effects of a decision and ignore the long-run implications of an assumption by the judiciary of a power of dispensation. A hard decision is never a popular decision. Judges have been celebrated in literature for their sly prowess in devising some quibble by which a litigant could be deprived of his rights where the public thought it was wrong for him to assert those rights. But I believe that judicial dispensation does more harm in the long run than hard decisions. Hard cases may even have a certain moral value by bringing home to the people their own responsibilities toward the law that is ultimately their creation, and by reminding them that there is no principle of personal grace that can relieve the mistakes of their representatives.

Indeed, I will go farther and say that not only are the principles I have been expounding those *which are soundest for our present conditions,* but that we would have inherited a better legal system from our forefathers if those principles had been observed from the beginning. For example, with respect to the excuse of self-defense, if our courts had stood steadfast on the language of the statute the result would undoubtedly have been a legislative revision of it. Such a revision would have drawn on the assistance of natural philosophers and psychologists, and the resulting regulation of the matter would have had an understandable and rational basis, instead of the hodgepodge of verbalisms and metaphysical distinctions that have emerged from the judicial and professorial treatment.

These concluding remarks are, of course, beyond any duties that I have to discharge with relation to this case, but I include them here because I feel deeply that my colleagues are insufficiently aware of the dangers implicit in the conceptions of the judicial office advocated by my brother Foster.

I conclude that the conviction should be affirmed.

HANDY, J. I have listened with amazement to the tortured ratiocinations to which this simple case has given rise. I never cease to wonder at my colleagues' ability to throw an obscuring curtain of legalisms about every issue presented to them for decision. We have heard this afternoon learned disquisitions on the distinction between positive law and the law of nature, the language of the statute and the purpose of the statute, judicial functions and executive functions, judicial legislation and legislative legislation. My only disappointment was that someone did not raise the question of the legal nature of the bargain struck in the cave—whether it was unilateral or bilateral, and whether Whetmore could not be considered as having revoked an offer prior to action taken thereunder.

What have all these things to do with the case? The problem before us is what we, as officers of the government, ought to do with these defendants. That is a question of practical wisdom, to be exercised in a context, not of abstract theory, but of human realities. When the case is approached in this light, it becomes, I think, one of the easiest to decide that has ever been argued before this Court.

Before stating my own conclusions about the merits of the case, I should like to discuss briefly some of the more fundamental issues involved—issues on which my colleagues and I have been divided ever since I have been on the bench.

I have never been able to make my brothers see that government is a human affair, and that men are ruled, not by words on paper or by abstract theories, but by other men. They are ruled well when their rulers understand the feelings and conceptions of the masses. They are ruled badly when that understanding is lacking.

Of all branches of the government, the judiciary is the most likely to lose its contact with the common man. The reasons for this are, of course, fairly obvious. Where the masses react to a situation in terms of a few salient features, we pick into little pieces every situation presented to us. Lawyers are hired by both sides to analyze and dissect. Judges and attorneys vie with one another to see who can discover the greatest number of difficulties and distinctions in a single set of facts. Each side tries to find cases, real or imagined, that will embarrass the demonstrations of the other side. To escape this embarrassment, still further distinctions are invented and imported into the situation. When a set of facts has been subjected to this kind of treatment for a sufficient time, all the life and juice have gone out of it and we have left a handful of dust.

Now I realize that wherever you have rules and abstract principles lawyers are going to be able to make distinctions. To some extent the sort of thing I have been describing is a necessary evil attaching to any formal regulation of human affairs. But I think that the area which really stands in need of such regulation is greatly overestimated. There are, of course, a few fundamental rules of the game that must be accepted if the game is to go on at all. I would include among these the rules relating to the conduct of elections, the appointment of public officials, and the term during which an office is held. Here some restraint on discretion and dispensation, some adherence to form, some scruple for what does and what does not fall within the rule, is, I concede, essential. Perhaps the area of basic principle should be expanded to include certain other rules, such as those designed to preserve the free civilmoign system.

But outside of these fields I believe that all government officials, including judges, will do their jobs best if they treat forms and abstract concepts as instruments. We should take as our model, I think, the good administrator, who accommodates procedures and principles to the case at hand, selecting from among the available forms those most suited to reach the proper result.

The most obvious advantage of this method of government is that it permits us to go about our daily tasks with efficiency and common sense.

My adherence to this philosophy has, however, deeper roots. I believe that it is only with the insight this philosophy gives that we can preserve the flexibility essential if we are to keep our actions in reasonable accord with the sentiments of those subject to our rule. More governments have been wrecked, and more human misery caused, by the lack of this accord between ruler and ruled than by any other factor that can be discerned in history. Once we drive a sufficient wedge between the mass of people and those who direct their legal, political, and economic life, our society is ruined. Then neither Foster's law of nature nor Keen's fidelity to written law will avail us anything.

Now when these conceptions are applied to the case before us, its decision becomes, as I have said, perfectly easy. In order to demonstrate this I shall have to introduce certain realities that my brothers in their coy decorum have seen fit to pass over in silence, although they are just as acutely aware of them as I am.

The first of these is that this case has aroused an enormous public interest, both here and abroad. Almost every newspaper and magazine has carried articles about it; columnists have shared with their readers confidential information as to the next governmental move; hundreds of letters-to-the-editor have been printed. One of the great newspaper chains made a poll of public opinion on the question, "What do you think the Supreme Court should do with the Speluncean explorers?" About 90 percent expressed a belief that the defendants should be pardoned or let off with a kind of token punishment. It is perfectly clear, then, how the public feels about the case. We could have known this without the poll, of course, on the basis of common sense, or even by observing that on this Court there are apparently four-and-a-half men, or 90 percent, who share the common opinion.

This makes it obvious, not only what we should do, but what we must do if we are to preserve between ourselves and public opinion a reasonable and decent accord. Declaring these men innocent need not involve us in any undignified quibble or trick. No principle of statutory construction is required that is not consistent with the past practices of this Court. Certainly no layman would think that in letting these men off we

had stretched the statute any more than our ancestors did when they created the excuse of self-defense. If a more detailed demonstration of the method of reconciling our decision with the statute is required, I should be content to rest on the arguments developed in the second and less visionary part of my brother Foster's opinion.

Now I know that my brothers will be horrified by my suggestion that this Court should take account of public opinion. They will tell you that public opinion is emotional and capricious, that it is based on half-truths and listens to witnesses who are not subject to cross-examination. They will tell you that the law surrounds the trial of a case like this with elaborate safeguards, designed to ensure that the truth will be known and that every rational consideration bearing on the issues of the case has been taken into account. They will warn you that all of these safeguards go for naught if a mass opinion formed outside this framework is allowed to have any influence on our decision.

But let us look candidly at some of the realities of the administration of our criminal law. When a man is accused of crime, there are, speaking generally, four ways in which he may escape punishment. One of these is a determination by a judge that under the applicable law he has committed no crime. This is, of course, a determination that takes place in a rather formal and abstract atmosphere. But look at the other three ways in which he may escape punishment. These are: (1) a decision by the Prosecutor not to ask for an indictment; (2) an acquittal by the jury; and (3) a pardon or commutation of sentence by the executive. Can anyone pretend that these decisions are held within a rigid and formal framework of rules that prevents factual error, excludes emotional and personal factors, and guarantees that all the forms of the law will be observed?

In the case of the jury we do, to be sure, attempt to cabin their deliberations within the area of the legally relevant, but there is no need to deceive ourselves into believing that this attempt is really successful. In the normal course of events the case now before us would have gone on all of its issues directly to the jury. Had this occurred we can be confident that there would have been an acquittal or at least a division that would have prevented a conviction. If the jury had been instructed that the men's hunger and their agreement were no defense to the charge of murder, their verdict would in all likelihood have ignored this instruction and would have involved a good deal more twisting of the letter of the law than any that is likely to tempt us. Of course the only reason that didn't occur in this case was the fortuitous circumstance that the foreman of the jury happened to be a lawyer. His learning enabled him to devise a form of words that would allow the jury to dodge its usual responsibilities.

My brother Tatting expresses annoyance that the Prosecutor did not, in effect, decide the case for him by not asking for an indictment. Strict as he is himself in complying with the demands of legal theory, he is quite content to have the fate of these men decided out of court by the Prosecutor on the basis of common sense. The Chief Justice, however, wants the application of common sense postponed to the very end, though like Tatting, he wants no personal part in it.

This brings me to the concluding portion of my remarks, which has to do with executive clemency. Before discussing that topic directly, I want to make a related observation about the poll of public opinion. As I have said, 90 percent of the people wanted the Supreme Court to let the men off entirely or with a more or less nominal punishment. The 10 percent constituted a very oddly assorted group, with the most curious and divergent opinions. One of our university experts has made a study of this group and has found that its members fall into certain patterns. A substantial portion of them are subscribers to "crank" newspapers of limited circulation that gave their readers a distorted version of the facts of the case. Some thought that "Speluncean" means "cannibal" and that anthropophagy is a tenet of the Society. But the point I want to make, however, is this: although almost every conceivable variety and shade of opinion was represented in this group, there was, so far as I know, not one of them, nor a single member of the majority of 90 percent, who said, "I think it would be a fine thing to have the courts sentence these men to be hanged, and then to have another branch of the government come along and pardon them." Yet this is a solution that has more or less

dominated our discussions and which our Chief Justice proposes as a way by which we can avoid doing an injustice and at the same time preserve respect for law. He can be assured that if he is preserving anybody's morale, it is his own, and not the public's, which knows nothing of his distinctions. I mention this matter because I wish to emphasize once more the danger that we may get lost in the patterns of our own thought and forget that these patterns often cast not the slightest shadow on the outside world.

I come now to the most crucial fact in this case, a fact known to all of us on this Court, though one that my brothers have seen fit to keep under the cover of their judicial robes. This is the frightening likelihood that if the issue is left to him, the Chief Executive will refuse to pardon these men or commute their sentence. As we all know, our Chief Executive is a man now well advanced in years, of very stiff notions. Public clamor usually operates on him with the reverse of the effect intended. As I have told my brothers, it happens that my wife's niece is an intimate friend of his secretary. I have learned in this indirect, but, I think, wholly reliable way, that he is firmly determined not to commute the sentence if these men are found to have violated the law.

No one regrets more than I the necessity for relying in so important a matter on information that could be characterized as gossip. If I had my way this would not happen, for I would adopt the sensible course of sitting down with the Executive, going over the case with him, finding out what his views are, and perhaps working out with him a common program for handling the situation. But of course my brothers would never hear of such a thing.

Their scruple about acquiring accurate information directly does not prevent them from being very perturbed about what they have learned indirectly. Their acquaintance with the facts I have just related explains why the Chief Justice, ordinarily a model of decorum, saw fit in his opinion to flap his judicial robes in the face of the Executive and threaten him with excommunication if he failed to commute the sentence. It explains, I suspect, my brother Foster's feat of levitation by which a whole library of law books was lifted from the shoulders of these defendants. It explains also why even my legalistic brother Keen emulated Pooh-Bah in the ancient comedy by stepping to the other side of the stage to address a few remarks to the Executive "in my capacity as a private citizen." (I may remark, incidentally, that the advice of Private Citizen Keen will appear in the reports of this court printed at taxpayer's expense.)

I must confess that as I grow older I become more and more perplexed at men's refusal to apply their common sense to problems of law and government, and this truly tragic case has deepened my sense of discouragement and dismay. I only wish that I could convince my brothers of the wisdom of the principles I have applied to the judicial office since I first assumed it. As a matter of fact, by a kind of sad rounding of the circle, I encountered issues like those involved here in the very first case I tried as Judge of the Court of General Instances in Fanleigh County.

A religious sect had unfrocked a minister who, they said, had gone over to the views and practices of a rival sect. The minister circulated a handbill making charges against the authorities who had expelled him. Certain lay members of the church announced a public meeting at which they proposed to explain the position of the church. The minister attended this meeting. Some said he slipped in unobserved in a disguise; his own testimony was that he had walked in openly as a member of the public. At any rate, when the speeches began he interrupted with certain questions about the affairs of the church and made some statements in defense of his own views. He was set upon by members of the audience and given a pretty thorough pommeling, receiving among other injuries a broken jaw. He brought a suit for damages against the association that sponsored the meeting and against ten named individuals who he alleged were his assailants.

When we came to the trial, the case at first seemed very complicated to me. The attorneys raised a host of legal issues. There were nice questions on the admissibility of evidence, and, in connection with the suit against the association, some difficult problems turning on the question whether the minister was a trespasser or a licensee. As a novice on the bench I was eager to apply my law school learning and I began studying these questions closely, reading all the authorities and preparing well-documented rulings. As I studied the case I became more and more involved in its legal intricacies and I began to get into a state approaching that of my brother Tatting in this case. Suddenly, however, it dawned on me that all these perplexing issues really had nothing to do with the case, and I began examining it in the light of common sense. The case at once gained a new perspective, and I saw that the only thing for me to do was to direct a verdict for the defendants for lack of evidence.

I was led to this conclusion by the following considerations. The melee in which the plaintiff was injured had been a very confused affair, with some people trying to get to the center of the disturbance, while others were trying to get away from it; some striking at the plaintiff, while others were apparently trying to protect him. It would have taken weeks to find out the truth of the matter. I decided that nobody's broken jaw was worth that much to the Commonwealth. (The minister's injuries, incidentally, had meanwhile healed without disfigurement and without any impairment of normal faculties.) Furthermore, I felt very strongly that the plaintiff had to a large extent brought the thing on himself. He knew how inflamed passions were about the affair, and could easily have found another forum for the expression of his views. My decision was widely approved by the press and public opinion, neither of which could tolerate the views and practices that the expelled minister was attempting to defend.

Now, thirty years later, thanks to an ambitious Prosecutor and a legalistic jury foreman, I am faced with a case that raises issues which are at bottom much like those involved in that case. The world does not seem to change much, except that this time it is not a question of a judgment for five or six hundred frelars, but of the life or death of four men who have already suffered more torment and humiliation than most of us would endure in a thousand years. I conclude that the defendants are innocent of the crime charged, and that the conviction and sentence should be set aside.

TATTING, J. I have been asked by the Chief Justice whether, after listening to the two opinions just rendered, I desire to re-examine the position previously taken by me. I wish to state that after hearing these opinions I am greatly strengthened in my conviction that I ought not to participate in the decision of this case.

The Supreme Court being evenly divided, the conviction and sentence of the Court of General Instances is *affirmed*. It is ordered that the execution of the sentence shall occur at 6 A.M., Friday, April 2, 4300, at which time the Public Executioner is directed to proceed with all convenient dispatch to hang each of the defendants by the neck until he is dead.

POSTSCRIPT

Now that the Court has spoken, the reader puzzled by the choice of date may wish to be reminded that the centuries which separate us from the year 4300 are roughly equal to those that have passed since the Age of Pericles. There is probably no need to observe that the *Speluncean Case* itself

is intended neither as a work of satire nor as a prediction in any ordinary sense of the term. As for the judges who make up Chief Justice Truepenny's Court, they are, of course, as mythical as the facts and precedents with which they deal. The reader who refuses to accept this view, and who seeks to trace out contemporary resemblances where none are intended or contemplated, should be warned that he is engaged in a frolic of his own, which may possibly lead him to miss whatever modest truths are contained in the opinions delivered by the Supreme Court of Newgarth. The case was constructed for the sole purpose of bringing into a common focus certain divergent philosophies of law and government. These philosophies presented men with live questions of choice in the days of Plato and Aristotle. Perhaps they will continue to do so when our era has had its say about them. If there is any element of prediction in the case, it does not go beyond a suggestion that the questions involved are among the permanent problems of the human race.

6   Selections From *On Law, Morality, and Politics*

SAINT THOMAS AQUINAS

QUESTION 90: OF THE ESSENCE OF LAW [IN FOUR ARTICLES]

We have now to consider the extrinsic principles of acts. Now the extrinsic principle inclining to evil is the devil, of whose temptations we have spoken in the First Part. But the extrinsic principle moving to good is God, Who both instructs us by means of His law and assists us by His grace, wherefore, in the first place, we must speak of law, in the second place, of grace.

Concerning law, we must consider (1) law itself in general, (2) its parts. Concerning law in general, three points offer themselves for our con-

sideration: (1) its essence, (2) the different kinds of law, (3) the effects of law.

Under the first head, there are four points of inquiry: (1) Whether law is something pertaining to reason? (2) concerning the end of law; (3) its cause; (4) the promulgation of law.

First Article: Is Law Something Pertaining to Reason?

We proceed thus to the First Article:

Objection 1. It would seem that law is not something pertaining to reason. For the Apostle says: "I see another law in my members," etc. But

From Saint Thomas Aquinas, *On Law, Morality, and Politics.* Eds. William P. Baumgarth and Richard J. Regan (Indianapolis: Hackett Publishing Co., 1988), pp. 11–17, 52–55. Copyright © 1988 by Avatar Books of Cambridge. Numbered notes have been omitted.

nothing pertaining to reason is in the members, since the reason does not make use of a bodily organ. Therefore, law is not something pertaining to reason.

Obj. 2. Further, in the reason there is nothing else but power, habit, and act. But law is not the power itself of reason. In like manner, neither is it a habit of reason, because the habits of reason are the intellectual virtues of which we have spoken above. Nor, again, is it an act of reason because then law would cease when the act of reason ceases, for instance, while we are asleep. Therefore, law is nothing pertaining to reason.

Obj. 3. Further, the law moves those who are subject to it to act aright. But it belongs properly to the will to move to act, as is evident from what has been said above. Therefore, law pertains not to the reason but to the will, according to the words of the Jurist: "Whatever pleases the ruler has the force of law".

On the contrary, It belongs to the law to command and to forbid. But it belongs to reason to command, as stated above. Therefore, law is something pertaining to reason.

I answer that Law is a certain rule and measure of acts whereby man is induced to act or is restrained from acting; for *lex* (law) is derived from *ligare* (to bind) because it binds one to act. Now the rule and measure of human acts is reason, which is the first principle of human acts, as is evident from what has been stated above, since it belongs to reason to direct to the end, which is the first principle in all matters of action, according to the Philosopher. Now, that which is the principle in any genus is the rule and measure of that genus, for instance, unity in the genus of numbers, and the first movement in the genus of movements. Consequently, it follows that law is something pertaining to reason.

Reply Obj. 1. Since law is a kind of rule and measure, it may be in something in two ways. First, as in that which measures and rules; and since this is proper to reason, it follows that, in this way, law is in reason alone. Second, as in that which is measured and ruled. In this way, law is in all those things that are inclined to something by reason of some law, so that any inclination arising from a law may be called a law, not

essentially but by participation as it were. And thus the inclination of the members to concupiscence is called "the law of the members."

Reply Obj. 2. Just as, in external action, we may consider the work and the work done—for instance, the work of building and the house built, so in the acts of reason we may consider the act itself of reason, i.e., to understand and to reason, and something produced by this act. With regard to the speculative reason, this is first of all the definition; secondly, the proposition; thirdly, the syllogism or argument. And since also the practical reason makes use of a kind of syllogism in respect to the work to be done, as stated above and as the Philosopher teaches, hence we find in the practical reason something that holds the same position in regard to operations as, in the speculative intellect, the proposition holds in regard to conclusions. Such like universal propositions of the practical intellect that are directed to actions have the nature of law. And these propositions are sometimes under our actual consideration, while sometimes they are retained in the reason by means of a habit.

Reply Obj. 3. Reason has its power of moving from the will, as stated above, for it is due to the fact that one wills the end that the reason issues its commands as regards things ordained to the end. But in order that the volition of what is commanded may have the nature of law, it needs to be in accord with some rule of reason. And in this sense is to be understood the saying that the will of the ruler has the force of law; otherwise, the ruler's will would savor of lawlessness rather than of law.

Second Article: Is the Law Always Directed to the Common Good?

We proceed thus to the Second Article:

Obj. 1. It would seem that the law is not always directed to the common good as to its end. For it belongs to law to command and to forbid. But commands are directed to certain individual goods. Therefore, the end of the law is not always the common good.

Obj. 2. Further, the law directs man in his actions. But human actions are concerned with particular matters. Therefore, the law is directed to some particular good.

Obj. 3. Further, Isidore says, "If the law is based on reason, whatever is based on reason will be a law." But reason is the foundation not only of what is ordained to the common good but also of that which is directed to private good. Therefore, the law is not only directed to the common good but also to the private good of an individual.

On the Contrary, Isidore says that "Laws are enacted for no private profit but for the common benefit of the citizens."

I answer that, As stated above, the law belongs to that which is a principle of human acts because it is their rule and measure. Now, as reason is a principle of human acts, so in reason itself, there is something which is the principle in respect of all the rest; wherefore to this principle chiefly and mainly law must needs be referred. Now the first principle in practical matters, which are the object of the practical reason, is the last end, and the last end of human life is bliss or happiness, as stated above. Consequently, the law must needs regard principally the relationship to happiness. Moreover, since every part is ordained to the whole as imperfect to perfect, and since a single man is a part of the perfect community, the law must needs regard properly the relationship to universal happiness. Wherefore the Philosopher, in the above definition of legal matters, mentions both happiness and the body politic, for he says that we call those legal matters just "which are adapted to produce and preserve happiness and its parts for the body politic" since the political community is a perfect community, as he says in *Politics* I, 1.

Now, in every genus, that which belongs to it most of all is the principle of the others, and the others belong to that genus in subordination to that thing; thus fire, which is chief among hot things, is the cause of heat in mixed bodies, and these are said to be hot insofar as they have a share of fire. Consequently, since the law is chiefly ordained to the common good, any other precept in regard to some individual work must needs be devoid of the nature of a law, save insofar as it is ordered to the common good. Therefore, every law is ordained to the common good.

Reply Obj. 1. A command denotes an application of a law to matters regulated by the law. Now the order to the common good, at which the law aims, is applicable to particular ends. And in this way, commands are given even concerning particular matters.

Reply Obj. 2. Actions are indeed concerned with particular matters, but those particular matters are referable to the common good, not as to a common genus or species, but as to a common final cause, according as the common good is said to be the common end.

Reply Obj. 3. Just as nothing stands firm with regard to the speculative reason except that which is traced back to the first indemonstrable principles, so nothing stands firm with regard to the practical reason unless it be directed to the last end which is the common good, and whatever stands to reason in this sense has the nature of a law.

Third Article: Is the Reason of Any Person Competent To Make Laws?

We proceed thus to the Third Article:

Obj. 1. It would seem that the reason of any person is competent to make laws. For the Apostle says that "when the Gentiles, who have not the law, do by nature those things that are of the law, . . . they are a law to themselves." Now he says this of all in general. Therefore, anyone can make a law for himself.

Obj. 2. Further, as the Philosopher says, "The intention of the lawgiver is to lead men to virtue." But every man can lead another to virtue. Therefore, the reason of any man is competent to make laws.

Obj. 3. Further, just as the ruler of a political community governs the political community, so every father of a family governs his household. But the ruler of a political community can make laws for the political community. Therefore, every father of a family can make laws for his household.

On the contrary, Isidore says, "A law is an ordinance of the people, whereby something is sanctioned by nobles together with commoners." Not everyone, therefore, is competent to make law.

I answer that Law, properly speaking, regards first and chiefly an ordering to the common good. Now to order anything to the common good belongs either to the whole people or to someone who is the vicegerent of the whole people. And, therefore, the making of law belongs either to the whole people or to a public personage who has care of the whole people, since, in all other matters, the directing of anything to the end concerns him to whom the end belongs.

Reply Obj. 1. As stated above, law is in a person not only as in one that rules but also by participation as in one that is ruled. In the latter way, each one is a law to himself, insofar as he shares the direction that he receives from one who rules him. Hence the same text goes on, "who show the work of the law written in their hearts."

Reply Obj. 2. A private person cannot lead another to virtue efficaciously, for he can only advise, and if his advice be not taken, it has no coercive power, such as the law should have in order to prove an efficacious inducement to virtue, as the Philosopher says. But this coercive power is vested in the whole people or in some public personage to whom it belongs to inflict penalties, as we shall state further on. Wherefore, the framing of laws belongs to him alone.

Reply Obj. 3. As one man is a part of the household, so a household is a part of the political community, and the political community is a perfect community, according to *Politics* I, 1. And, therefore, as the good of one man is not the last end but is ordained to the common good, so too the good of one household is ordained to the good of a single political community, which is a perfect community. Consequently, he that governs a family can indeed make certain commands or ordinances but not such as to have properly the nature of law.

Fourth Article: Is Promulgation Essential to a Law?

We proceed thus to the Fourth Article:

Obj. 1. It would seem that promulgation is not essential to a law. For the natural law above all has the nature of law. But the natural law needs no promulgation. Therefore, it is not essential to a law that it be promulgated.

Obj. 2. Further, it belongs properly to a law to bind one to do or not to do something. But the obligation of fulfilling a law touches not only those in whose presence it is promulgated but also others. Therefore, promulgation is not essential to a law.

Obj. 3. Further, the obligation of a law extends even to the future since "laws are binding in matters of the future," as the jurists say. But promulgation is made to those who are present. Therefore, it is not essential to a law.

On the contrary, It is laid down in the *Decretum,* dist. 4, that "Laws are established when they are promulgated."

I answer that, As stated above, a law is imposed on others by way of a rule and measure. Now a rule or measure is imposed by being applied to those who are to be ruled and measured by it. Wherefore, in order that a law obtain the binding force which is proper to a law, it must needs be applied to the men who have to be ruled by it. Such application is made by its being notified to them by promulgation. Wherefore promulgation is necessary for the law to obtain its force.

Thus, from the four preceding articles, the definition of law may be gathered, and it is nothing else than a certain ordinance of reason for the common good, made by him who has care of the community, and promulgated.

Reply Obj. 1. The natural law is promulgated by the very fact that God instilled it into men's minds so as to be known by them naturally.

Reply Obj. 2. Those who are not present when a law is promulgated are bound to observe the law, insofar as it is notified or can be notified to them by others after it has been promulgated.

Reply Obj. 3. The promulgation that takes place now extends to future time by reason of the durability of written characters, by which means it is continually promulgated. Hence Isidore says that "*lex* (law) is derived from *legere* (to read) because it is written."

QUESTION 94: OF THE NATURAL LAW [IN SIX ARTICLES]

Fifth Article: Can the Natural Law Be Changed?

We proceed thus to the Fifth Article:

Obj. 1. It would seem that the natural law can be changed because, on Sir. 17:9, "He gave them instructions, and the law of life," a gloss says: "He wished the law of the letter to be written in order to correct the law of nature." But that which is corrected is changed. Therefore, the natural law can be changed.

Obj. 2. Further, the slaying of the innocent, adultery, and theft are against the natural law. But we find these things changed by God, as when God commanded Abraham to slay his innocent son, and when He ordered the Jews to borrow and purloin the vessels of the Egyptians, and when He commanded Hosea to take to himself "a wife of fornications." Therefore, the natural law can be changed.

Obj. 3. Further, Isidore says that "the possession of all things in common and universal freedom are matters of natural law. But these things are seen to be changed by human laws. Therefore, it seems that the natural law is subject to change.

On the contrary, It is said in the Decretum: "The natural law dates from the creation of the rational creature. It does not vary according to time but remains unchangeable."

I answer that A change in the natural law may be understood in two ways. First, by way of addition. In this sense, nothing hinders the natural law from being changed, since many things, for the benefit of human life, have been added over and above the natural law both by the divine law and by human laws.

Secondly, a change in the natural law may be understood by way of subtraction, so that what previously was according to the natural law ceases to be so. In this sense, the natural law is altogether unchangeable in its first principles, but in its secondary principles, which, as we have said, are like certain proper conclusions closely related to the first principles, the natural law is not changed so that what it prescribes be not right in most cases. But it may be changed in some particular cases of rare occurrence through some special causes hindering the observance of such precepts, as stated above.

Reply Obj. 1. The written law is said to be given for the correction of the natural law, either because it supplies what was wanting to the natural law or because the natural law was perverted in the hearts of some men as to certain matters, so

that they esteemed those things good which are naturally evil, which perversion stood in need of correction.

Reply Obj. 2. All men alike, both guilty and innocent, die the death of nature, which death of nature is inflicted by the power of God on account of original sin, according to 1 Kings: "The Lord kills and makes alive." Consequently, by the command of God, death can be inflicted on any man, guilty or innocent, without any injustice whatever. In like manner, adultery is intercourse with another's wife, who is allotted to him by the law handed down by God. Consequently, intercourse with any woman, by the command of God, is neither adultery nor fornication. The same applies to theft, which is the taking of another's property. For whatever is taken by the command of God, to Whom all things belong, is not taken against the will of its owner, whereas it is in this that theft consists. Nor is it only in human things that whatever is commanded by God is right but also in natural things—whatever is done by God is, in some way, natural, as stated in the First Part.

Reply Obj. 3. A thing is said to belong to the natural law in two ways. First, because nature inclines thereto, e.g., that one should not do harm to another. Secondly, because nature did not bring in the contrary; thus we might say that for man to be naked is of the natural law because nature did not give him clothes, but art invented them. In this sense, "the possession of all things in common and universal freedom" is said to be of the natural law because, to wit, the distinction of possessions and slavery were not brought in by nature but devised by human reason for the benefit of human life. Accordingly, the law of nature was not changed in this respect except by addition.

Sixth Article: Can the Law of Nature Be Abolished from the Heart of Man?

We proceed thus to the Sixth Article:

Obj. 1. It would seem that the natural law can be abolished from the heart of man because, on Rom. 2:14, "When the Gentiles who have not the law," etc., a gloss says that "the law of righteousness, which sin had blotted out, is graven on the heart of man when he is restored by grace." But the law of righteousness is the law of nature. Therefore, the law of nature can be blotted out.

Obj. 2. Further, the law of grace is more efficacious than the law of nature. But the law of grace is blotted out by sin. Much more, therefore, can the law of nature be blotted out.

Obj. 3. Further, that which is established by law is made just. But many things are legally established which are contrary to the law of nature. Therefore, the law of nature can be abolished from the heart of man.

On the contrary, Augustine says, "Thy law is written in the hearts of men, which iniquity itself effaces not." But the law which is written in men's hearts is the natural law. Therefore, the natural law cannot be blotted out.

I answer that, As stated above, there belong to the natural law, first, certain most general precepts that are known to all, and secondly, certain secondary and more detailed precepts which are, as it were, conclusions following closely from first principles. As to those general principles, the natural law, in the abstract, can nowise be blotted out from men's hearts. But it is blotted out in the case of particular action insofar as reason is hindered from applying the general principles to a particular point of practice on account of concupiscence or some other passion, as stated above. But as to the other, i.e., the secondary precepts, the natural law can be blotted out from the human heart either by evil persuasions, just as in speculative matters errors occur in respect of necessary conclusions, or by vicious customs and corrupt habits, as among some men theft and even unnatural vices, as the Apostle states, were not esteemed sinful.

Reply Obj. 1. Sin blots out the law of nature in particular cases, not universally, except perchance in regard to the secondary precepts of the natural law, in the way stated above.

Reply Obj. 2. Although grace is more efficacious than nature, yet nature is more essential to man and therefore more enduring.

Reply Obj. 3. The argument is true of the secondary precepts of the natural law, against which some legislators have framed certain enactments which are unjust.

7 Natural Law and Natural Rights

JOHN FINNIS

LAW AND COERCION

THE central case of law and legal system is the law and legal system of a complete community, purporting to have authority to provide comprehensive and supreme direction for human behaviour in that community, and to grant legal validity to all other normative arrangements affecting the members of that community (see VI.6). Such large claims, advanced by or on behalf of mere men, would have no plausibility unless those said to be subject to legal authority had reason to think that compliance with the law and with the directions of its officers would not leave them subject to the assaults and depredations of their enemies, inside or outside the community. The authority of the law depends, as we shall see at length, on its justice or at least its ability to secure justice. And in this world, as it is, justice may need to be secured by force; failure to attempt to resist by force the depredations of invaders, pirates, and recalcitrants will normally be a failure in justice. If "effectiveness" is to be contrasted (as it need not be) with "justice," the coercive force of law is not merely a matter of effectiveness.

Aristotle gave currency to a regrettable oversimplification of the relationship between law and coercion. He was aware that law typically has two modes of operation, directive and coercive. But he suggested that the need for coercion arises from the recalcitrance of the selfish, the brutish many whose unprincipled egocentricity can be moderated only by a direct threat to their self-interest. But the fact is that recalcitrance—refusal or failure to comply with authoritative stipulations for co-ordination of action for common good—can be rooted not only in obstinate self-centredness, or in careless indifference to common goods and to stipulations made for their sake, but also in high-minded, conscientious opposition to the demands of this or that (or perhaps each and every) stipula-tion. Practical reasonableness from the genuine authority of which conscience, in the modern sense of that term, gets the prestige it deserves (V.9)—demands that conscientious terrorism, for example, be suppressed with as much conscien-tious vigour as other forms of criminality.

Not all lawful coercion is by way of sanction or punishment. Even the most developed legal systems rightly allow a use of force not only in resistance to forcible assaults but also for expelling certain sorts of intruders. All allow the arrest of certain suspected offenders or potential offenders, and of persons and things (e.g. ships) likely other-wise to escape due processes of adjudication. Judgments may be executed, and some other clas-ses of debts satisfied, by seizure, distraint, forced sale. But the context of restrictions with which these measures of coercion are surrounded in a mature legal system is best understood by looking more closely at a threat and use of force employed for a quite distinct purpose: punitive sanctions ("punishment").

The prohibitions of the criminal law have a simple justifying objective: that certain forms of conduct including certain omissions shall occur less frequently than they otherwise would. But the "system" of criminal law is more than that set of prohibitions. The "goal" of the familiar modern systems of criminal law can only be de-scribed as a certain form or quality of communal life, in which the demands of the common good indeed are unambiguously and insistently pre-ferred to selfish indifference or individualistic de-mands for licence but also are recognized as including the good of individual autonomy, so that in this mode of association no one is made to live his life for the benefit or convenience of others, and each is enabled to conduct his own life (to constitute himself over his span of time) with a clear knowledge and foreknowledge of the appropriate common way and of the cost of

deviation from it. Thus the administration, or working-out, of the criminal law's prohibitions is permeated by rules and principles of procedural fairness ("due process of law") and substantive fairness (desert, proportionality), which very sub-stantially modify the pursuit of the goal of elimi-nating or diminishing the undesired forms of conduct: such principles as *nulla poena sine lege* (and rather precise *leges*, at that), and the princi-ples which outlaw retroactive proscription of con-duct (at the known cost of letting some dubious characters slip through the net), and restrain the process of investigation, interrogation, and trial (even at the expense of that *terror* which a Lenin knows is necessary for attaining definite social goals).

One can rightly debate the details of these criminal law systems, and adjust them to changing circumstances. But, in their main features and in-tent, they are justified because the common good of the community is the good of all its members; it is an open-ended good, a participation in all the basic values, and its maintenance is not a simple objective like that of keeping a path free from weeds.

The legal sanction, then, is to be a human response to human needs, not modelled on a cam-paign of "social defence" against a plague of lo-custs, or sparrows. There is the need of almost every member of society to be taught what the requirements of the law—the common path for pursuing the common good—actually are; and taught not by sermons, or pages of fine print, but by the public and (relatively!) vivid drama of the apprehension, trial, and punishment of those who depart from that stipulated common way. There is the need of the actually or potentially recalcitrant (which includes most members of so-ciety, in relation to at least some activity or other) to be given palpable incentive to abide by the law when appeals to the reasonableness of sustaining the common good fail to move. And there is the need to give the law-abiding the encouragement of knowing that they are not being abandoned to the mercies of criminals, that the lawless are not being left to the peaceful enjoyment of ill-gotten gains, and that to comply with the law is not to be a mere sucker: for without this support and assurance the indispensable co-operation of the law-abiding is not likely to be continued.

Quite distinct from the foregoing set of defining purposes or requirements, which derive from the "psychology" of citizens, there is a further defining purpose or requirement, by reason of which legal sanctions constitute *punishment,* rather than merely the "social hygiene" of quarantine stations, asylums for the insane, and preventive detention. Sanctions are punishment because they are required in reason to avoid injustice, to maintain a rational order of proportionate equality, or fairness, as between all members of the society. For when someone, who really could have chosen otherwise, manifests in action a preference (whether by intention, recklessness, or negligence) for his own interests, his own freedom of choice and action, as against the common interests and the legally defined common way-of-action, then in and by that very action he gains a certain sort of advantage over those who have restrained themselves, restricted their pursuit of their own interests, in order to abide by the law. For is not the exercise of freedom of choice in itself a great human good? If the free-willing criminal were to retain this advantage, the situation would be as unequal and unfair as it would be for him to retain the tangible profits of his crime (the loot, the misappropriated funds, the office of profit, the ...). If those in authority allowed the retention of unfairly gained advantages they would not only lose the allegiance of the disadvantaged law-abiding but indeed forfeit their title, in reason, to that allegiance. For the authority of rulers derives from their opportunity to foster the common good, and a fair balance of benefits and burdens within a community is an important aspect of that common good.

Punishment, then, characteristically seeks to restore the distributively just balance of advantages between the criminal and the law-abiding, so that, over the span of time which extends from before the crime until after the punishment, no one should actually have been disadvantaged— in respect of *this* special but very real sort of advantage—by choosing to remain within the confines of the law. This restoration of the order of fairness is accomplished by depriving the criminal

of what he gained in his criminal act (in the presently relevant sense of "gain"): viz. the exercise of self-will or free choice.

What is done cannot be undone. But punishment rectifies the disturbed pattern of distribution of advantages and disadvantages throughout a community by depriving the convicted criminal of his freedom of choice, proportionately to the degree to which he had exercised his freedom, his personality, in the unlawful act. Such deprivation is very commonly by fine; the removal of pecuniary means removes opportunities of choice. But deprivation of freedom may also be accomplished by actual imprisonment, or by the removal of civil liberties. There is no absolute "natural" measure of due punishment: the "law of talion" (life for life, eye for eye, etc.) misses the point, for it concentrates on the material content or consequences of criminal acts rather than on their formal wrongfulness (unfairness) which consists in a will to prefer unrestrained self-interest to common good, or at least in an unwillingness to make the effort to remain within the common way. But some unlawful acts are premeditated, some impulsive, some involve trivia while others are big choices, for high stakes, really pitting the individual's self-will against his fellows; accordingly, there emerges a rough and ready "function" or, more crudely, "scale" of *relatively* appropriate punitive responses.

Finally, sanctions are part of the enterprise of legally ordering society, an enterprise rationally required only by that complex good of individuals which we name the common good. The criminal is an individual whose good is as good as any man's, notwithstanding that he ought in fairness to be deprived of some opportunities of realizing that good. On the supposition (which I have been making, for simplicity, throughout this section) that the legal system and social order in question are substantially just, we are bound by our whole analysis of human good to say that one who defies or contemns the law harms not only others but also himself. He seized the advantage of self-preference, and perhaps of psychological satisfactions and/or of loot, but all at the price of diminishing his personality, his participation in human good; for such participation is only through the *reasonable* pursuit, realization, and enjoyment of basic goods. The punitive sanction ought therefore to be adapted so that, within the framework of its two sets of defining purposes already indicated, it may work to restore reasonable personality in the offender, reforming him for the sake not only of others but of himself: "to lead a *good* and useful life."

UNJUST PUNISHMENT

The foregoing discussion of the role of coercion in the legal ordering of community is a fragmentary illustration of method in jurisprudence. The method is not squeamish about human evil. It is not restricted to the problems of an imaginary "well-ordered" society. Nor does it suppose for a moment that those in authority are exempt from criminality and injustice. But someone pursuing this method will not participate in debates about whether "we would call it punishment" if a judge knowingly sentenced an innocent man, using him as a scapegoat to avert civil commotion. The problem in jurisprudence is not to find or devise definitions which will extend to *all* circumstances in which, regardless of particular points of view, the word being defined could "correctly" be employed. There is place in jurisprudence, of course, for stipulative definitions of words, in order to avert misunderstandings of discourse; and for lexical explorations, in order to assemble reminders of the complexity of human affairs, concerns, and reasonings. But the point of a jurisprudence such as is exemplified in this chapter is to explain certain human institutions by showing how they are responses to the requirements of practical reasonableness.

Authoritative institutions justified by the requirements of practical reasonableness may be, and quite commonly are, deflected to meet the requirements of individual or group bias. In other circumstances (e.g. the international community) these malign influences, or other practical obstacles, work to prevent the full development of such institutions. A sound jurisprudential method will recognize this, but will not water down its explanations of the links between human institutions and the values and requirements of practical

reasonableness. So the explanation of punishment will refer to features which are absent from the punishment of scapegoats. This absence does not require us to amend the explanatory definition of punishment. Nor does that definition require us to forbid the use of the term "punishment" in the scapegoat case. Still less does it require us to banish the study of abuse of authority to some other discipline. It simply requires us to recognize the unjust punishment of scapegoats for what it is: an abusive, corrupt use of a justified human institution or procedure, an abuse aptly referred to by a secondary or nonfocal use of the term "punishment," a term which in its focal use has a proper role in any satisfactory account of what is required for human well-being. The reasons for this role, and the corresponding features of the central case of the institution and the focal use of the term, have been set out in my account.

THE MAIN FEATURES OF LEGAL ORDER

Law needs to be coercive (primarily by way of punitive sanctions, secondarily by way of preventive interventions and restraints). But other main features of legal order will come into view if we pursue the question: Would there be need for legal authority and regulation in a world in which there was no recalcitrance and hence no need for sanctions?

Max Weber decided to define "law" by reference to the problem of recalcitrance and the availability of authorized sanctions. This was explicitly offered as a stipulative definition, and as such is unobjectionable. But it is significant that the complexity and richness of Weber's data, and of the Western language in which he had to discuss those data, overcame his definitional decision. For he felt obliged to distinguish, from among three "pure types" of authoritative coordination (*Herrschaft*), one type that could best be described as *legal*. And the characteristics of this type, as Weber himself described them, had nothing in particular to do with coercion or with a staff of men authorized to impose sanctions. Indeed, he considered legal order to be most purely exemplified in the internal order of a modern bureaucracy, in whose workings coercion, even "psychic" coercion, is characteristically replaced, in large measure, by a sense of duty motivated by a sense of the worth "for its own sake" of compliance with the organization's internal rules. This departure from his own stipulated definition of law is evidence of Weber's sensitivity to data and language—for the many senses or facets of the term "law" (and its equivalents in German, etc.) simply reflect the many concerns, aspirations, and motivations of the societies which use that term for the purposes, and in the course, of the communal life and practices that in turn constitute Weber's sociological data (I.1).

For Weber, then, authoritative coordination is legal in character when it operates by way not of an attitude of obedience to persons but of a disposition to comply with "the law," a legally established order of consistent, abstract rules (normally established intentionally) and principles to be applied to and followed in particular cases—so that those in authority are regarded as "officials" whose office or authority is defined by these rules, and who are to be obeyed only while they act within their legal powers. Here we can leave Weber, observing that the features of law which he thus found, intelligibly clustered in a historically significant constant in many (not all!) phases of human social order, are features enabling us to distinguish law from politics, conventions, manners, etiquette, mores, games, and indeed from every other form or matrix of communal interaction—and to distinguish it with complete adequacy *even in the absence of any problem of recalcitrance* and hence of any need for coercion or sanctions.

The preceding paragraph's description of what is distinctive of legal authority and order does not in fact carry us much further than Aristotle's suggestive but teasing notion of "the rule of law and not of men." Taking for granted the already-mentioned (VI.6) features of comprehensiveness, purported supremacy, and absorptive or ratificatory capacity (features which do not by themselves distinguish legal order from the charismatic personal governance of a sovereign administering "palm-tree justice" by *ad hoc* decrees), we may now briefly list the main features which as a

set (characteristically but not invariably found together) are distinctive of legal order. It will be evident from the list that the ways in which law shapes, supports, and furthers patterns of coordination would be desirable even in a society free from recalcitrance. Just as authority is not required exclusively by the malice or folly of man, so these features of legal order, though adaptable to handling problems of recalcitrance or negligence, are not necessitated exclusively, either individually or as a cluster, by the need to meet or remedy those human deficiencies.

Firstly, then, law brings definition, specificity, clarity, and thus predictability into human interactions, by way of a system of rules and institutions so interrelated that rules define, constitute, and regulate the institutions, while institutions create and administer the rules, and settle questions about their existence, scope, applicability, and operation. There is thus a characteristically legal "circle," a sense in which the system (as the interrelated rules and institutions are significantly but loosely called) "lifts itself by its own bootstraps"— a sense captured by the more scientific but still literally paradoxical axiom that "the law regulates its own creation." My analysis of custom-formation (IX.2) showed, of course, that the circle can be broken and the paradox avoided; but legal thought systematically avoids answering the question which I there answered: how an authoritative rule can be generated without prior authorization.

The primary legal method of showing that a rule is valid is to show (i) that there was at some past time, t_1, an act (of a legislator, court, or other appropriate institution) which according to the rules in force at t_1 amounted to a valid and therefore operative act of rule-creation, and (ii) that since the rule thus created has not determined (ceased to be in force) by virtue either of its own terms or of any act of repeal valid according to the rules of repeal in force at times t_2, t_3 ..., It is a working postulate of legal thought (so fundamental that it is scarcely ever identified and discussed) that whatever legal rule or institution (e.g. contract, settlement, corporation) has been once validly created remains valid, in force or in existence, in contemplation of law, until it terminates according to its own terms or to some valid act or rule of repeal.

Thirdly, then, rules of law regulate not only the creation, administration, and adjudication of such rules, and the constitution, character, and termination of institutions, but also the conditions under which a private individual can modify the incidence or application of the rules (whether in relation to himself or to other individuals). That is to say, individuals may perform juridical acts which, if performed in accordance with rules in force at the time of the performance, count as making a contract or sale or purchase or conveyance or bequest, contracting a marriage, constituting a trust, incorporating a company, issuing a summons, entering judgment. ... All the legal entities thus created have the quality of persistence through time.

Fourthly, we can say that legal thinking (i.e. the law) brings what precision and predictability it can into the order of human interactions by a special technique: the treating of (usually datable) past acts (whether of enactment, adjudication, or any of the multitude of exercises of public and private "powers") as giving, *now,* sufficient and exclusionary reason for acting in a way *then* "provided for." In an important sense the "existence" or "validity" of a legal rule can be explained by saying that it simply is this relationship, this continuing relevance of the "content" of that past juridical act as providing reason to decide and act in the present in the way then specified or provided for. The convenience of this attribution of authoritativeness to past acts is twofold. The past is beyond the reach of persons in the present; it thus provides (subject only to problems of evidence and interpretation) a stable point of reference unaffected by present and shifting interests and disputes. Again, the present will soon be the past; so the technique gives people a way of now determining the framework of their future.

Fifthly, this technique is reinforced by the working postulate ("no gaps") that every present practical question or coordination problem has, in every respect, been so "provided for" by some such past juridical act or acts (if only, in some cases, by provisions stipulating precisely which person or institution is now to exercise a discretion to settle the question, or defining what precise procedure is now to be followed in tackling the question). There is no need to labour the point that this postulate is fictitious and, if taken literally, is descriptively misleading and would restrict unnecessarily the development of the law by nonlegislative means. The postulate is significant simply as a reinforcement of the other four characteristics of law and legal thought already mentioned.

All this, then, stands as a sufficiently distinctive, self-contained, intelligible, and practically significant social arrangement which would have a completely adequate rationale in a world of saints. In the world as it is, these five constellated formal features of legal order are amplified and elaborated in order to meet the problems of fraud and abuse of power, and are supplemented by the law of wrongs and of offences, criminal procedure and punishment (X.1). So it is that legal order has two broad characteristics, two characteristic modes of operation, two poles about which jurisprudence and "definitions of law" tend to cluster. They are exemplified by the contrast between Weber's formal definition of law and his extensive employment of the term "legal"; and they can be summed up in the two slogans: "law is a coercive order" and "the law regulates its own creation."

THE RULE OF LAW

The account just given of five formal features of law's regulation of its own creation and operation was more incomplete than the very brief account of punitive sanctions in section X.1. For it lacked any systematic account of the relation between these formal features and the requirements of justice and the common good. Such an account may best be developed through some consideration of the conditions under which we can reasonably say that the "legal system" is working well.

The name commonly given to the state of affairs in which a legal system is legally in good shape is "the Rule of Law" (capitalized simply to avoid confusion with a particular norm within a legal system). The Rule of Law, the specific virtue of legal systems, has been well analysed by recent writers; so my discussion can be brief. A legal system exemplifies the Rule of Law to the extent (it is a matter of degree in respect of each item of the list) that (i) its rules are prospective, not retroactive, and (ii) are not in any other way impossible to comply with; that (iii) its rules are promulgated, (iv) clear, and (v) coherent one with another; that (vi) its rules are sufficiently stable to allow people to be guided by their knowledge of the content of the rules; that (vii) the making of decrees and orders applicable to relatively limited situations is guided by rules that are promulgated, clear, stable, and relatively general; and that (viii) those people who have authority to make, administer, and apply the rules in an official capacity (*a*) are accountable for their compliance with rules applicable to their performance and (*b*) do actually administer the law consistently and in accordance with its tenor.

The eighth desideratum should remind us that what is loosely called "the legal system" subsists in time, ordering the affairs of subsisting persons; it therefore cannot be understood as merely a set of "rules" as meaning-contents. None of the eight desiderata is merely a characteristic of a meaning-content, or even of the verbal expression of a meaning-content; all involve qualities of institutions and processes. *Promulgation,* for example, is not fully achieved by printing ever so many legible official copies of enactments, decisions, forms, and precedents; it requires also the existence of a professional class of lawyers whose business it is to know their way around the books, and who are available without undue difficulty and expense to advise anybody who wants to know where he stands. Or again, *coherence* requires not merely an alert logic in statutory drafting, but also a judiciary authorized and willing to go beyond the formulae of intersecting or conflicting rules, to establish particular and if need be novel reconciliations, and to abide by those reconciliations when relevantly similar cases arise at different times before different tribunals. Or again, the *prospectivity* of the law can be secured only by a certain restraint in the judicial adoption of new interpretations of the law. At each point we see that the Rule of Law involves certain qualities of process which can be systematically secured only by the

institution of judicial authority and its exercise by persons professionally equipped and motivated to act according to law. Obviously, much more could be said about this institutional aspect of the Rule of Law—of what historical experience has shown to be further desiderata, such as the independence of the judiciary, the openness of court proceedings, the power of the courts to review the proceedings and actions not only of other courts but of most other classes of official, and the accessibility of the courts to all, including the poor.

To complete this review of the content of the Rule of Law, before proceeding to inquire into its point, we need only observe that concern for the Rule of Law does not merely shape or modulate projects which a ruler already has in mind. It also works to suggest new subject matters for authoritative regulation. Consider, for example, the extension of law into a field such as consumer–supplier relations. Just as a rule authorizing a tyrant to do what he wills *is* "a rule of law" (in a thin, rather uninteresting sense) but departs from the Rule of Law, and *is* "a constitution" (in a thin, uninteresting sense) but fails to establish constitutional government, so likewise a rule such as *caveat emptor* is "a rule of law in respect of consumer–supplier relations" but fails to extend legal order into that field. The decision to extend legal order into the field, by way of criminal law, contract and tort law, new institutions for inspection, complaint-investigation, arbitration, etc., is justified not only by the desirability of minimizing tangible forms of harm and economic loss but also by the value of securing, for its own sake, a quality of clarity, certainty, predictability, trustworthiness, in the human interactions of buying and selling, etc.

And here we touch, at last, the reason why the Rule of Law is a virtue of human interaction and community. It is the reason that I touched upon in discussing the law of criminal procedure. Individuals can only be *selves*—i.e. have the "dignity" of being "responsible agents"—if they are not made to live their lives for the convenience of others but are allowed and assisted to create a subsisting identity across a "lifetime." This is the primary value of the predictability which the law seeks to establish through the five formal features discussed above (X.3). But it is also the primary value of that notion of *constitutional* government (*Rechtsstaat*) which, often at the expense of some certainty about the precise location of authority, seeks to guarantee that rulers will not direct the exercise of their authority towards private or partisan objectives. And the motive of constitutional devices such as the so-called "separation of powers" is characteristically expressed not merely by reference to the unjust schemes of arbitrary, partisan, or despotic rulers but also by appeal to the positive good of a certain quality of association and interaction between ruler and ruled: "to the end it may be a government of laws and not of men." Implicitly, a principal component of the idea of constitutional government (which itself is one aspect of the idea of the Rule of Law) is the holding of the rulers to their side of a relationship of reciprocity, in which the claims of authority are respected on condition that authority respects the claims of the common good (of which a fundamental component is respect for the equal right of all to respectful consideration: VII.3).

In short, the five formal features of law (X.3) are the more instantiated the more the eight desiderata listed above are fulfilled. The fundamental point of the desiderata is to secure to the subjects of authority the dignity of self-direction and freedom from certain forms of manipulation. The Rule of Law is thus among the requirements of justice or fairness.

LIMITS OF THE RULE OF LAW

Just as I followed my discussion of punishment (X.1) with a discussion of unjust punishment (X.2), so we should now briefly consider the abuse of the Rule of Law. Lon Fuller and his critics raised the question whether a tyranny devoted to pernicious objectives can pursue those ends through a fully lawful Rule of Law. The debate failed to clarify the relevant sense of "can." It is clear enough that "logical" or "conceptual" possibility is not, and should not be, the focus of discussion here. As we have to stress again and again in an age of conceptual dogmatism, concepts of law and society are legitimately many, and their

employment is subordinated to matters of principle rooted in the basic principles and requirements of practical reasonableness (which themselves generate many concepts and can be expressed in many reasonable forms). Fuller himself seemed to rest with a very different but equally unsatisfying claim that as a matter of historical fact you will not find a tyranny that operated consistently through law. But Fuller's discussion had more underlying sense than his critics were willing to allow, who could see in it no more than either a "logical" or a "historical" claim.

The truly relevant claim, emerging in muted form in Fuller's references to "reciprocity," is this. A tyranny devoted to pernicious ends has no self-sufficient *reason* to submit itself to the discipline of operating consistently through the demanding processes of law, granted that the rational point of such self-discipline is the very value of reciprocity, fairness, and respect for persons which the tyrant, *ex hypothesi*, holds in contempt. The sort of regime we are considering tends to be (i) exploitative, in that the rulers are out simply for their own interests regardless of the interests of the rest of the community; or (ii) ideological, in that the rulers are pursuing a goal they consider good for their community, but pursuing it fanatically (cf.V.6, VII.7), overlooking other basic aspects of human good in community; or (iii) some admixture of exploitative and ideological, such as the Nazi regime. None of these types of tyranny can find in its objectives any rationale for adherence (other than tactical and superficial) to the disciplines of legality. For such regimes are in business for determinate results, not to help persons constitute them *selves* in community (cf. VI.5, VI.8, VII.3, VIII.5-6).

So it is a mistake to say, as some of Fuller's critics have said, that the Rule of Law (his set of eight desiderata) is simply an efficient instrument which, like a sharp knife, may be good and necessary for morally good purposes but is equally serviceable for evil. Adherence to the Rule of Law (especially the eighth requirement, of conformity by officials to pre-announced and stable general rules) is always liable to reduce the efficiency for evil of an evil government, since it systematically restricts the government's freedom of manœuvre.

The idea of the Rule of Law is based on the notion that a certain quality of interaction between ruler and ruled, involving reciprocity and procedural fairness, is very valuable for its own sake; it is not merely a means to other social ends, and may not lightly be sacrificed for such other ends. It is not just a "management technique" in a programme of "social control" or "social engineering."

To this, however, we must add something not sufficiently emphasized in Fuller's account of the virtue of the Rule of Law, but not overlooked in Plato's. In any age in which the ideal of law, legality, and the Rule of Law enjoy an ideological popularity (i.e. a favour not rooted in a steadily reasonable grasp of practical principles), conspirators against the common good will regularly seek to gain and hold power through an adherence to constitutional and legal forms which is not the less "scrupulous" for being tactically motivated, insincere, and temporary. Thus the Rule of Law does not guarantee every aspect of the common good, and sometimes it does not secure even the substance of the common good.

Sometimes, moreover, the values to be secured by the genuine Rule of Law and authentic constitutional government are best served by departing, temporarily but perhaps drastically, from the law and the constitution. Since such occasions call for that awesome responsibility and most measured practical reasonableness which we call statesmanship, one should say nothing that might appear to be a "key" to identifying the occasion or a "guide" to acting in it. Suffice it to make two observations, one practical, the other reflective. The practical corollary is the judicially recognized principle that a written constitution is not a suicide pact, and that its terms must be both restrained and amplified by the "implicit" prohibitions and authorizations necessary to prevent its exploitation by those devoted to its overthrow. (I return to the question of "implied" principles, their source, and their place in legal thought in XI.3 and XII.3, below.) The reflective observation one may add here is that at this point in our analysis we have visibly returned to the basic principle with which we began (IX.4): authority, of which legal rulership is one species, is the responsibility that accrues, as Fortescue said, "by operation of the law of nature"—i.e. for the sake of the standing needs of the good of persons in community—from the sheer fact of power, of opportunity to affect, for good, the common life.

An exploration of the limits of the Rule of Law is an exploration not only of the judicial methodology developed to embody and buttress the Rule of Law, but also of the "general theory of law" which, even when eschewing all concern with "ideologies" and values, faithfully mirrors that methodology and thus, willy-nilly, the concern for values that informs the methodology. A judge unconscious of the limits of a methodology which suffices for normal times will respond inadequately to abnormal problems. In face of a revolution he will say, for example: "A court which derives its existence and jurisdiction from a written constitution cannot give effect to anything which is not law when judged by that constitution." This proposition, like any unqualified statement of constitutionalism (whether judicial or jurisprudential), is self-defeating. For the proposition itself cannot be derived from, and applied in any particular instance simply by reference to, the constitution alone. Usually a constitution will be quite silent on this sort of question. (And why should the matter be affected fundamentally by the written or unwritten character of the constitution?) But even if a written constitution did contain a rule embodying the proposition, there would remain the question whether any given court derives its existence, jurisdiction, or authority from the written constitution alone, whatever that document may assert. Test the matter further. Suppose a constitution specifically provided that no rule or person should have any authority save by virtue of the constitution. There still would remain the question whether acceptance of one part of, or acceptance of authority under, a constitution requires one to accept the whole constitution, including the part which demands that the whole be accepted as exclusive. A constitution may stipulate, so to speak, "All from me or nothing from me." But it cannot thereby prevent anyone from raising the question whether he need accept *that* norm or stipulation. The very raising of the question shows that the answer cannot be determined by any positive rule (written or unwritten) of the "system"—not even a rule stipulating that the question is illegitimate.

A DEFINITION OF LAW

Throughout this chapter, the term "law" has been used with a focal meaning so as to refer primarily to rules made, in accordance with regulative legal rules, by a determinate and effective authority (itself identified and, standardly, constituted as an institution by legal rules) for a "complete" community, and buttressed by sanctions in accordance with the rule-guided stipulations of adjudicative institutions, this ensemble of rules and institutions being directed to reasonably resolving any of the community's coordination problems (and to ratifying, tolerating, regulating, or overriding coordination solutions from any other institutions or sources of norms) for the common good of that community, according to a manner and form itself adapted to that common good by features of specificity, minimization of arbitrariness, and maintenance of a quality of reciprocity between the subjects of the law both amongst themselves and in their relations with the lawful authorities.

This multi-faceted conception of law has been reflectively constructed by tracing the implications of certain requirements of practical reason, given certain basic values and certain empirical features of persons and their communities. The intention has not been lexicographical; but the construction lies well within the boundaries of common use of "law" and its equivalents in other languages. The intention has not been to describe existing social orders; but the construction corresponds closely to many existing social phenomena that typically are regarded as central cases of law, legal system, Rule of Law, etc. Above all, the meaning has been constructed as a *focal* meaning, not as an appropriation of the term "law" in a univocal sense that would exclude from the reference of the term anything that failed to have all the characteristics (and to their full extent) of the central case. And, equally important, it has been fully recognized that each of the terms used to express the elements in the conception (e.g. "making," "determinate,"

"effective," "a community," "sanctioned," "rule-guided," "reasonable," "nondiscriminatory," "reciprocal," etc.) has itself a focal meaning and a primary reference, and therefore extends to analogous and secondary instances which lack something of the central instance. For example, custom is not *made* in the full sense of "made"—for making is something that someone can set himself to do, but no one sets himself (themselves) to make a custom. Yet customs are "made," in a sense that requirements of practical reason are not made but discovered. The way in which each of the other crucial terms is *more or less* instantiated is quite obvious. (If the term "reasonable" arouses misgivings, see VI.1.) Law, in the focal sense of the term, is *fully* instantiated only when each of these component terms is fully instantiated.

If one wishes to stress the empirical/historical importance, or the practical/rational desirability, of sanctions, one may say, dramatically, that an unsanctioned set of laws is "not really law." If one wishes to stress the empirical/historical importance, or the practical/rational desirability of determinate legislative or adjudicative institutions, one may say, dramatically, that a community without such institutions "lacks a real legal system" or "cannot really be said to have 'a legal system'." If one wishes to stress the empirical/historical importance, or the practical/rational desirability, of rules authorizing or regulating private or public change in the rules or their incidence, one may say, dramatically, that a set of rules which includes no such rules "is not a legal system." All these things have often been said, and can reasonably be said provided that one is seeking to draw attention to a feature of the central case of law and not to banish the other non-central cases to some other discipline.

I have by now sufficiently stressed that one would be simply misunderstanding my conception of the nature and purpose of explanatory definitions of theoretical concepts if one supposed that my definition "ruled out as non-laws" laws which failed to meet, or meet fully, one or other of the elements of the definition. But I should add that it would also be a misunderstanding to condemn the definition because "it fails to explain correctly our ordinary concept of law which does allow for the possibility of laws of [an] objectionable kind." For not only does my definition "allow for the possibility"; it also is not advanced with the intention of "explaining correctly our [sc. the ordinary man's] ordinary concept of law." For the truth is that the "ordinary concept of law" (granting, but not admitting, that there is *one* such concept) is quite unfocused. It is a concept which allows "us" to understand lawyers when they talk about sophisticated legal systems, and anthropologists when they talk about elementary legal systems, and tyrants and bandits when they talk about the orders and the customs of their syndicate, and theologians and moralists ... There is no point in trying to explain a common-sense concept which takes its meanings from its very varied contexts and is well understood by everyone in those contexts. My purpose has not been to explain an unfocused "ordinary concept" but to develop a concept for use in a theoretical explanation of a set of human actions, dispositions, interrelationships, and conceptions which (i) hang together as a set by virtue of their adaptation to a specifiable set of human needs considered in the light of empirical features of the human condition, and (ii) are accordingly found in very varying forms and with varying degrees of suitability for, and deliberate or unconscious divergence from, those needs as the fully reasonable person would assess them. To repeat: the intention has been not to explain a concept, but to develop a concept which would explain the various phenomena referred to (in an unfocused way) by "ordinary" talk about law—and explain them by showing how they answer (fully or partially) to the standing requirements of practical reasonableness relevant to this broad area of human concern and interaction.

The lawyer is likely to become impatient when he hears that social arrangements can be *more or less* legal, that legal systems and the rule of law exist as a matter of degree ... and so on. For the lawyer systematically strives to use language in such a way that from its use he can read off a definite solution to definite problems—in the final analysis, judgment for one party rather than the other in a litigable dispute. If cars are to be taxed at such and such a rate, one must be able, as a lawyer, to say (i.e. to rule) of every object that it simply is or is not a car: qualifications, "in this respect ... but in that respect," *secundum quids,* and the like are permissible in argument (and a good lawyer is well aware how open-textured and analogous in structure most terms and concepts are); but just as they do not appear in statutory formulae, so they cannot appear in the final pronouncement of law. And the lawyer, for the same good practical reasons, intrinsic to the enterprise of legal order as I have described it in this chapter, extends his technical use of language to the terms "law," "rule," "legal," "legal system" themselves. To make his point propositionally he will say that a purported law or rule is either valid or invalid. There are no intermediate categories (though there are intermediate states of affairs, e.g. voidable laws, which now are valid, or are treated as valid, or are deemed to be valid, but are liable to be rendered or treated as or deemed invalid). Equipped with this concept of validity, the lawyer aspires to be able to say of every rule that, being valid, it is a legal rule, or, being invalid, is not. The validity of a rule is identified with membership of the legal system (conceived as a set of valid rules), which thus can be considered legally as the set of all valid rules, including those rules which authorized the valid rule-originating acts of enactment and/or adjudication which are (in this conception) the necessary and sufficient conditions for the validity of the valid rules.

There is no need to question here the sufficiency of this set of concepts and postulates for the practical purposes of the lawyer—though questions could certainly be raised about the role of principles (which have no determinate origin and cannot without awkwardness be called valid) in legal argumentation. Rather it must be stressed that the set is a technical device for use within the framework of legal process, and in legal thought directed to arriving at solutions within that process. The device cannot be assumed to be applicable to the quite different problems of describing and explaining the role of legal process within the ordering of human life in society, and the place of legal thought in practical reason's effort to understand and effect real human good. It is a philosophical mistake to declare, in discourse of the latter kinds, that a social order or set of concepts must either be law or not be law, be legal or not legal.

For our purposes, physical, chemical, biological, and psychological laws are only metaphorically laws. To say this is not to question the legitimacy of the discourse of natural scientists, for whose purposes, conversely, what we call "law strictly speaking" is only metaphorically a set of laws. The similarity between our central case and the laws of arts and crafts and applied sciences is greater; in each case we are considering the regulation of a performance by a self-regulating performer whose own notion of what he is up to affects the course of his performance. But the differences still are systematic and significant; as I said before (VII.7, X.l), ordering a society for the greater participation of its members in human values is not very like following a recipe for producing a definite product or a route to a definite goal. "Natural law"—the set of principles of practical reasonableness in ordering human life and human community—is only analogically law, in relation to my present focal use of the term: that is why the term has been avoided in this chapter on Law, save in relation to past thinkers who used the term. These past thinkers, however, could, without loss of meaning, have spoken instead of "natural right," "intrinsic morality," "natural reason, or right reason, in action," etc. But no synonyms are available for "law" in our focal sense.

DERIVATION OF "POSITIVE" FROM "NATURAL" LAW

"In every law positive well made is somewhat of the law of reason ...; and to discern ... the law of reason from the law positive is very hard. And though it be hard, yet it is much necessary in every moral doctrine, and in all laws made for the commonwealth." These words of the sixteenth-century English lawyer Christopher St. German express the fundamental concern of any sound "natural law theory" of law: to understand the relationship(s) between the particular laws of particular societies and the permanently relevant principles of practical reasonableness.

Consider the law of murder. From the layman's point of view this can be regarded as a directive not to intentionally kill (or attempt to kill) any human being, unless in self-defence ... The legal rule, conceived from this viewpoint, corresponds rather closely to the requirement of practical reason, which would be such a requirement whether or not repeated or supported by the law of the land: that one is not to deliberately kill the innocent (in the relevant sense of "innocent"). Now this requirement is derived from the basic principle that human life is a good, in combination with the seventh of the nine basic requirements of practical reason (V.7). Hence Aquinas says that this sort of law is derived from natural law by a process analogous to deduction of demonstrative conclusions from general principles; and that such laws are not positive law only, but also have part of their "force" from the natural law (i.e. from the basic principles of practical reasonableness). Hooker calls such laws "mixedly human," arguing that their matter or normative content is the same as reason necessarily requires, and that they simply ratify the law of reason, adding to it only the additional constraining or binding force of the threat of punishment. Now Aquinas's general idea here is fundamentally correct, but vaguely stated and seriously underdeveloped; and Hooker's clarifications and developments are not in the most interesting direction.

True, some parts of a legal system commonly do, and certainly should, consist of rules and principles closely corresponding to requirements of practical reason which themselves are conclusions directly from the combination of a particular basic value (e.g. life) with one or more of those nine basic "methodological" requirements of practical reasonableness. Discussion in courts and amongst lawyers and legislators will commonly, and reasonably, follow much the same course as a straightforward moral debate such as philosophers or theologians, knowing nothing of that time and place, might carry on. Moreover, the threat of sanctions is indeed, as Hooker remarks, an "expedient" supplementation for the legislator to annex to the moral rule, with an eye to the recalcitrant and wayward in his own society.

But the process of receiving even such straightforward moral precepts into the legal system deserves closer attention. Notice, for example, that legislative draftsmen do *not* ordinarily draft laws in the form imagined by Aquinas: "There is not to be killing"—nor even "Do not kill," or "Killing is forbidden," or "A person shall not [may not] kill." Rather they will say "It shall be [or: is] an offence to ..." or "Any person who kills ... shall be guilty of an offence." Indeed, it is quite possible to draft an entire legal system without using normative vocabulary at all. Now why does the professional draftsman prefer this indicative prepositional form? At the deepest level it is because he has in his mind's eye the pattern of a future social order, or of some aspect of such an order, and is attempting to reproduce that order (on the assumption, which need not be stated or indicated grammatically because it is contextually self-evident, that the participants are to, shall, must, may, etc., act conformably to the pattern). More particularly, a lawyer sees the desired future social order from a professionally structured viewpoint, as a stylized and manageable drama. In this drama, many characters, situations, and actions known to common sense, sociology, and ethics are missing, while many other characters, relationships, and transactions known only or originally only to the lawyer are introduced. In the legally constructed version of social order there are not merely the "reasonable" and "unreasonable" acts which dominate the stage in an individual's practical reasoning; rather, an unreasonable act, for example of killing, may be a crime (and one of several procedurally significant classes of offence), and/or a tort, and/or an act which effects automatic vacation or suspension of office or forfeiture of property, and/or an act which insurers and/or public officials may properly take into account in avoiding a contract or suspending a licence ... etc. So it is the business of the draftsman to specify, precisely, into which of these costumes and relationships an act of killing-under-such-and-such-circumstances fits. That is why *"No one may kill ..."* is legally so defective a formulation.

Nor is all this of relevance only to professional lawyers. The existence of the legal rendering of social order makes a new train of practical reasoning possible, and necessary, for the law-abiding private citizen (see also XI.4). For example, the professionally drafted legislative provision, "It is

an offence to kill," contextually implies a normative direction to citizens. For there is a legal norm, so intrinsic to any legal ordering of community that it need never be enacted: criminal offences are not to be committed. Behind this norm the citizen need not go. Knowing the law of murder (at least in outline), he need not consider the value of life or the requirement of practical reason that basic values be respected in every action. So Hooker is mistaken in suggesting that what the positive law on murder adds to the permanent rule of reason is merely the punitive sanction. As part of the law of the land concerning offences, it adds also, and more interestingly, (i) a precise elaboration of many other legal (and therefore social) consequences of the act and (ii) a distinct new motive for the law-abiding citizen, who acts on the principle of avoiding legal offences as such, to abstain from the stipulated class of action.

Thus, in a well-developed legal system, the integration of even an uncontroversial requirement of practical reasonableness into the law will not be a simple matter. The terms of the requirement *qua* requirement (e.g., in the case we were considering, the term "intentionally") will have to be specified in language coherent with the language of other parts of the law. And then the part which the relevant acts are to play in the legal drama will have to be scripted—their role as, or in relation to, torts, contracts, testamentary dispositions, inheritances, tenures, benefits, matrimonial offences, proofs, immunities, licences, entitlements and forfeitures, offices and disqualifications, etc., etc.

Now very many of these legal implications and definitions will carry the legislator or judge beyond the point where he could regard himself as simply *applying* the intrinsic rule of reason, or even as deducing conclusions from it. Hence the legal project of *applying* a permanent requirement of practical reason will itself carry the legislator into the second of the two categories of human or positive law discerned by Aquinas and Hooker.

For, in Aquinas's view, the law consists in part of rules which are "derived from natural law like conclusions deduced from general principles," and for the rest of rules which are "derived from natural laws like implementations [*determinationes*] of general directives." This notion of *determinatio* he explains on the analogy of architecture (or any other practical art), in which a general idea or "form" (say, "house," "door," "door-knob") has to be made determinate as this particular house, door, doorknob, with specifications which are certainly derived from and shaped by the general idea but which could have been more or less different in many (even in every!) particular dimension and aspect, and which therefore require of the artificer a multitude of choices. The (making of the) artifact is controlled but not fully determined by the basic idea (say, the client's order), and until it is fully determinate the artifact is nonexistent or incomplete. To count as a door in a human habitation, an object must be more than half a metre high and need not be more than 2.5 metres, but no door will be built at all if the artificer cannot *make up his mind* on a particular height. Stressing, as it were, the artificer's virtually complete freedom in reason to choose say 2.2 rather than 2.1 or 2.3 metres, Aquinas says that laws of this second sort have their force "*wholly* from human law," and Hooker names his second category "*merely human laws.*"

These last formulae, so strongly emphasizing the legislator's rational freedom of choice in such cases, can be misleading unless one bears in mind that they enunciate only a subordinate theorem within a general theory. The general theory is that, in Aquinas's words, "*every* law laid down by men has the character of law just in so far as it is derived from the natural law," or in St. German's words, already quoted, "in *every* law positive well made is somewhat of the law of reason." The compatibility between this theory and the subordinate theorem can be best understood by reference to one or two concrete examples.

A first example is hackneyed, but simple and clear. Consider the rule of the road. There is a sense in which (as the subordinate theorem implies) the rule of the road gets "all its force" from the authoritative custom, enactment, or other determination which laid it down. For until the stipulation "drive on the left, and at less than 70 miles per hour" was posited by one of these means, there was no legal rule of the road; moreover, there was no need for the legislator to have a reason for choosing "left" rather than "right" or "70" rather than "65." But there is also a sense in which (as the general theory claims) the rule of the road gets "all its normative force" ultimately from the permanent principles of practical reason (which require us to respect our own and others' physical safety) in combination with nonposited facts such as that traffic is dangerous and can be made safer by orderly traffic flows and limitation of speed, that braking distances and human reaction times are such-and-such, etc.

A second example is richer. If material goods are to be used efficiently for human well-being (cf. V.6), there must normally be a regime of private property: VII.3. This regime will be constituted by rules assigning property rights in such goods, or many of them, to individuals or small groups. But precisely what rules should be laid down in order to constitute such a regime is not settled ("determined") by this general requirement of justice. Reasonable choice of such rules is to some extent guided by the circumstances of a particular society, and to some extent "arbitrary." The rules adopted will thus for the most part be *determinationes* of the general requirement— derived from it but not entailed by it even in conjunction with a description of those particular circumstances: VII.4, 5, 7.

Moreover, in the vast area where the legislator is constructing *determinationes* rather than applying or ratifying determinate principles or rules of reason, there are relatively few points at which his choice can reasonably be regarded as "unfettered" or "arbitrary" (in the sense that it reasonably can be when one confronts two or more feasible alternatives which are in *all* respects equally satisfactory, or equally unsatisfactory, or incommensurably satisfactory/unsatisfactory). The basic legal norms of a law-abiding citizen are "Do not commit offences," "abstain from torts," "perform contracts," "pay debts," "discharge liabilities," "fulfil obligations," etc.; and, taking these norms for granted without stating them, the lawmaker defines offences (from murder to road-traffic offences), torts, the formation, incidents, and discharge of contracts, etc., etc. But this task of definition (and redefinition in the changing conditions of society) has its own principles, which are not the citizen's. The reasonable legislator's principles include the desiderata of the Rule of Law (X.4). But they also include a multitude of other substantive principles related, some very closely, others more remotely, some invariably and others contingently, to the basic principles and methodological requirements of practical reason.

What are these basic norms for the legislator? Normally they are not the subject of direct and systematic enquiry by lawyers. But it should be recalled that "legislator" here, for convenience (and at the expense of some significant differentiations), includes any judiciary that, like the judge at common law, enjoys a creative role. Now the principles that should guide the judge in his interpretation and application of both statutory and common or customary law to particular issues are the subject of scientific discussion by lawyers. *These* principles are almost all "second-order," in that they concern the interpretation and application of other rules or principles whose existence they presuppose. They therefore are not directly the concern of legislators who have authority not merely to interpret and supplement but also to change and abolish existing rules and to introduce novel rules. Nevertheless, the second-order principles are themselves mostly crystallizations or versions (adapted to their second-order role) of "first-order" principles which ought to guide even a "sovereign legislature" in its acts of enactment. Moreover, a legislator who ignores a relevant first-order principle in his legislation is likely to find that his enactments are controlled, in their application by citizens, courts, and officials, by that principle in its second-order form, so that in the upshot the law on the particular subject will tend to turn out to be a *determinatio* of that principle (amongst others).

Many of the second-order principles or maxims employed by lawyers express the desirability of stability and predictability in the relations between one person and another, and between persons and things. Such maxims are obviously connected very closely not only with the formal features of law (X.3) and the desiderata of the Rule of Law (X.4), but also with the willingness of lawyers and indeed of men in society in every age to attribute authoritative force to usage, practice, custom (IX.3). And there is a corresponding first-order principle or set of principles to which any legislator ought to give considerable weight—that those human goods which are the fragile and cumulative achievements of past effort, investment, discipline, etc. are not to be treated lightly in the pursuit of future goods. More prosaically, the tangible expenses and waste of dislocative change are to be taken fully into account—the legislative choice between "drive on the left" and "drive on the right" is a matter of indifference in the abstract, but not in a society where by informal convention people already tend to drive on the left, and have adjusted their habits, their vehicle construction, road design, and street furniture accordingly.

Starting with these second-order maxims favouring continuity in human affairs—i.e. favouring the good of diachronic order, as distinct from the good of a future end-state—we can trace a series of related second-order principles which include the principle of stability but more and more go beyond it to incorporate new principles or values. In each case these are available in first-order form to guide a legislator. Prose-form requires a linear exposition here which oversimplifies and disguises their interrelations: (i) compulsory acquisition of property rights to be compensated, in respect of *damnum emergens* (actual losses) if not of *lucrum cessans* (loss of expected profits), (ii) no liability for unintentional injury, without fault; (iii) no criminal liability without *mens rea;* (iv) estoppel (*nemo contra factum proprium venire potest*); (v) no judicial aid to one who pleads his own wrong (he who seeks equity must do equity); (vi) no aid to abuse of rights; (vii) fraud unravels everything; (viii) profits received without justification and at the expense of another must be restored; (ix) *pacta sunt servanda* (contracts are to be performed); (x) relative freedom to change existing patterns of legal relationships by agreement; (xi) in assessments of the legal effects of purported acts-in-the-law, the weak to be protected against their weaknesses; (xii) disputes not to be resolved without giving both sides an opportunity to be heard; (xiii) no one to be allowed to judge his own cause.

These "general principles of law" are indeed principles. That is to say, they justify, rather than require, particular rules and determinations, and are qualified in their application to particular circumstances by other like principles. Moreover, any of them may on occasion be outweighed and overridden (which is not the same as violated, amended, or repealed) by other important components of the common good, other principles of justice. Nor is it to be forgotten that there are norms of justice that may never be overridden or outweighed, corresponding to the absolute rights of man (VIII.7). Still, the general principles of law which have been recited here do operate, over vast ranges of legislative *determinationes*, to modify the pursuit of particular social goods. And this modification need not be simply a matter of abstaining from certain courses of conduct: the principles which require compensation, or ascertainment of *mens rea*, or "natural justice" ... can be adequately met only by the positive creation of complex administrative and judicial structures.

In sum: the derivation of law from the basic principles of practical reasoning has indeed the two principal modes identified and named by Aquinas; but these are not two streams flowing in separate channels. The central principle of the law of murder, of theft, of marriage, of contract ... may be a straightforward application of universally valid requirements of reasonableness, but the effort to integrate these subject matters into the Rule of Law will require of judge and legislator countless elaborations which in most instances partake of the second mode of derivation. This second mode, the sheer *determinatio* by more or less free authoritative choice, is itself not only linked with the basic principles by intelligible relationship to goals (such as traffic safety ...) which are directly related to basic human goods, but also is controlled by wide-ranging formal and other structuring principles (in both first-and second-order form) which themselves are derived from the basic principles by the first mode of derivation.

In the preceding chapter (IX.1) I said that a principal source of the need for authority is the luxuriant variety of appropriate but competing choices of "means" to "end." Now we can see how this range of choices is both increased *and* controlled by the complex of interacting "principles of law." True, the reasoning of those in authority frequently ends without identifying any uniquely reasonable decision; so the rulers must choose, and their choice (*determinatio*) determines what thereafter is uniquely just for those subject to their authority. But, having stressed that it is thus authority, not simply reasoning, that settles most practical questions in the life of a community, I now must stress the necessary rider. To be, itself, authoritative in the eyes of a reasonable man, a *determinatio* must be consistent with the basic requirements of practical reasonableness, though it need not necessarily or even usually be the *determinatio* he would himself have made had he had the opportunity; it need not even be one he would regard as "sensible." Our jurisprudence therefore needs to be completed by a closer analysis of this authoritativeness or "binding force" of positive law (XI), and by some consideration of the significance of wrongful exercises of authority (XII).

It may, however, be helpful to conclude the present discussion by reverting to the textbook categories, "[positive] law," "sources of law," "morality." The tradition of "natural law" theorizing is not characterized by any particular answer to the questions: "Is every 'settled' legal rule and legal solution settled by appeal exclusively to 'positive' sources such as statute, precedent, and custom? Or is the 'correctness' of some judicial decisions determinable only by appeal to some 'moral' ('extralegal') norm? And are the boundaries between the settled and the unsettled law, or between the correct, the eligible, and the incorrect judicial decision determinable by reference only to positive sources or legal rules?" The tradition of natural law theorizing is not concerned to minimize the range and determinacy of positive law or the general sufficiency of positive sources as solvents of legal problems.

Rather, the concern of the tradition, as of this chapter, has been to show that the act of "positing" law (whether judicially or legislatively or otherwise) is an act which can and should be guided by "moral" principles and rules; that those moral norms are a matter of objective reasonableness, not of whim, convention, or mere "decision"; and that those same moral norms justify (*a*) the very institution of positive law, (*b*) the main institutions, techniques, and modalities within that tradition (e.g. separation of powers), and (c) the main institutions regulated and sustained by law (e.g. government, contract, property, marriage, and criminal liability). What truly characterizes the tradition is that it is not content merely to observe the historical or sociological fact that "morality" thus affects "law," but instead seeks to determine what the requirements of practical reasonableness really are, so as to afford a rational basis for the activities of legislators, judges, and citizens.

CHAPTER THREE

Legal Positivism

8 A Positivist Conception of Law

JOHN AUSTIN

LECTURE I

The matter of jurisprudence is positive law: law, simply and strictly so called: or law set by political superiors to political inferiors. But positive law (or law, simply and strictly so called) is often confounded with objects to which it is related by *resemblance*, and with objects to which it is related in the way of *analogy:* with objects which are *also* signified, *properly* and *improperly,* by the large and vague expression *law.* To obviate the difficulties springing from that confusion, I begin my projected Course with determining the province of jurisprudence, or with distinguishing the matter of jurisprudence from those various related objects: trying to define the subject of which I intend to treat, before I endeavour to analyse its numerous and complicated parts.

A law, in the most general and comprehensive acceptation in which the term, in its literal meaning, is employed, may be said to be a rule laid down for the guidance of an intelligent being by an intelligent being having power over him. Under this definition are concluded, and without

impropriety, several species. It is necessary to define accurately the line of demarcation which separates these species from one another, as much mistiness and intricacy has been infused into the science of jurisprudence by their being confounded or not clearly distinguished. In the comprehensive sense above indicated, or in the largest meaning which it has, without extension by metaphor or analogy, the term *law* embraces the following objects:—Laws set by God to his human creatures, and laws set by men to men.

The whole or a portion of the laws set by God to men is frequently styled the law of nature, or natural law: being, in truth, the only natural law of which it is possible to speak without a metaphor, or without a blending of objects which ought to be distinguished broadly. But, rejecting the appellation law of nature as ambiguous and misleading, I name those laws or rules, as considered collectively or in a mass, the *Divine law,* or the *law of God.*

Laws set by men to men are of two leading or principal classes: classes which are often blended, although they differ extremely; and which, for that

From *The Province of Jurisprudence Determined*, selections from Lectures I and VI. First published in 1832.

reason, should be severed precisely, and opposed distinctly and conspicuously.

Of the laws or rules set by men to men, some are established by *political* superiors, sovereign and subject: by persons exercising supreme and subordinate *government*, in independent nations, or independent political societies. The aggregate of the rules thus established, or some aggregate forming a portion of that aggregate, is the appropriate matter of jurisprudence, general or particular. To the aggregate of the rules thus established, or to some aggregate forming a portion of that aggregate, the term *law,* as used simply and strictly, is exclusively applied. But, as contradistinguished to *natural* law, or to the law of *nature* (meaning, by those expressions, the law of God), the aggregate of the rules, established by political superiors, is frequently styled *positive* law, or law existing *by position*. As contra-distinguished to the rules which I style *positive morality,* and on which I shall touch immediately, the aggregate of the rules, established by political superiors, may also be marked commodiously with the name of *positive law*. For the sake, then, of getting a name brief and distinctive at once, and agreeable to frequent usage, I style that aggregate of rules, or any portion of that aggregate, *positive law:* though rules, which are *not* established by political superiors are also *positive,* or exist *by position,* if they be rules or laws, in the proper signification of the term.

Though *some* of the laws or rules, which are set by men to men, are established by political superiors, *others* are *not* established by political superiors, or are *not* established by political superiors, in that capacity or character.

Closely analogous to human laws of this second class are a set of objects frequently but *improperly* termed *laws,* being rules set and enforced by *mere opinion,* that is, by the opinions or sentiments held or felt by an indeterminate body of men in regard to human conduct. Instances of such a use of the term *law* are the expressions—"The law of honour"; "The law set by fashion"; and rules of this species constitute much of what is usually termed *international law.*

The aggregate of human laws properly so called belonging to the second of the classes above mentioned, with the aggregate of objects *improperly* but by *close analogy* termed laws, I place together in a common class, and denote them by the term *positive morality*. The name *morality* severs them from *positive law,* while the epithet *positive* disjoins them from the *law of God.* And to the end of obviating confusion, it is necessary or expedient that they *should* be disjoined from the latter by that distinguishing epithet. For the name *morality* (or *morals*), when standing unqualified or alone, denotes indifferently either of the following objects: namely, positive morality *as it is,* or without regard to its merits; and positive morality *as it would be,* if it conformed to the law of God, and were, therefore, deserving of *approbation.*

Besides the various sorts of rules which are included in the literal acceptation of the term *law,* and those which are by a close and striking analogy, though improperly, termed laws, there are numerous applications of the term *law,* which rest upon a slender analogy and are merely metaphorical or figurative. Such is the case when we talk of *laws* observed by the lower animals; of *laws* regulating the growth or decay of vegetables; of *laws* determining the movements of inanimate bodies or masses. For where *intelligence* is not, or where it is too bounded to take the name of *reason,* and, therefore, is too bounded to conceive the purpose of a law, there is not the *will* which law can work on, or which duty can incite or restrain. Yet through these misapplications of a *name,* flagrant as the metaphor is, has the field of jurisprudence and morals been deluged with muddy speculation.

Having suggested the *purpose* of my attempt to determine the province of jurisprudence: to distinguish positive law, the appropriate matter of jurisprudence, from the various objects to which it is related by resemblance, and to which it is related, nearly or remotely, by a strong or slender analogy: I shall now state the essentials of a *law* or *rule* (taken with the largest signification which can be given to the term *properly*).

Every *law* or *rule* (taken with the largest signification which can be given to the term *properly*) is a *command*. Or, rather, laws or rules, properly so called, are a *species* of commands.

Now, since the term *command* comprises the term *law,* the first is the simpler as well as the larger of the two. But, simple as it is, it admits of explanation. And, since it is the *key* to the sciences of jurisprudence and morals, its meaning should be analysed with precision.

Accordingly, I shall endeavour, in the first instance, to analyse the meaning of *command:* an analysis which I fear will task the patience of my hearers, but which they will bear with cheerfulness, or, at least, with resignation, if they consider the difficulty of performing it. The elements of a science are precisely the parts of it which are explained least easily. Terms that are the largest, and, therefore, the simplest of a series are without equivalent expressions into which we can resolve them *concisely.* And when we endeavour to *define* them, or to translate them into terms which we suppose are better understood, we are forced upon awkward and tedious circumlocutions.

If you express or intimate a wish that I shall do or forbear from some act, and if you will visit me with an evil in case I comply not with your wish, the *expression* or *intimation* of your wish is a *command.* A command is distinguished from other significations of desire, not by the style in which the desire is signified, but by the power and the purpose of the party commanding to inflict an evil or pain in case the desire be disregarded. If you cannot or will not harm me in case I comply not with your wish, the expression of your wish is not a command, although you utter your wish in imperative phrase. If you are able and willing to harm me in case I comply not with your wish, the expression of your wish amounts to a command, although you are prompted by a spirit of courtesy to utter it in the shape of a request. *Preces erant, sed quibus contradici non posset.* Such is the language of Tacitus, when speaking of a petition by the soldiery to a son and lieutenant of Vespasian.

A command, then, is a signification of desire. But a command is distinguished from other significations of desire by this peculiarity: that the party to whom it is directed is liable to evil from the other, in case he comply not with the desire.

Being liable to evil from you if I comply not with a wish which you signify, I am *bound* or

obliged by your command, or I lie under a *duty* to obey it. If, in spite of that evil in prospect, I comply not with the wish which you signify, I am said to disobey your command, or to violate the duty which it imposes.

Command and duty are, therefore, correlative terms: the meaning denoted by each being implied or supposed by the other. Or (changing the expression) wherever a duty lies, a command has been signified; and whenever a command is signified, a duty is imposed.

Concisely expressed, the meaning of the correlative expressions is this: He who will inflict an evil in case his desire be disregarded utters a command by expressing or intimating his desire. He who is liable to the evil in case he disregard the desire is bound or obliged by the command.

The evil which will probably be incurred in case a command be disobeyed or (to use an equivalent expression) in case a duty be broken is frequently called a *sanction,* or an *enforcement of obedience.* Or (varying the phrase) the command or the duty is said to be *sanctioned* or *enforced* by the chance of incurring the evil.

Considered as thus abstracted from the command and the duty which it enforces, the evil to be incurred by disobedience is frequently styled a *punishment.* But, as punishments, strictly so called, are only a *class* of sanctions, the term is too narrow to express the meaning adequately.

I observe that Dr. Paley, in his analysis of the term *obligation,* lays much stress upon the *violence* of the motive to compliance. In so far as I can gather a meaning from his loose and inconsistent statement, his meaning appears to be this: that unless the motive to compliance be *violent* or *intense,* the expression or intimation of a wish is not a *command,* nor does the party to whom it is directed lie under a *duty* to regard it.

If he means, by a *violent* motive, a motive operating with certainty, his proposition is manifestly false. The greater the evil to be incurred in case the wish be disregarded, and the greater the chance of incurring it on that same event, the greater, no doubt, is the *chance* that the wish will *not* be disregarded. But no conceivable motive will *certainly* determine to compliance, or no conceivable motive will render obedience inevitable.

If Paley's proposition be true, in the sense which I have now ascribed to it, commands and duties are simply impossible. Or, reducing his proposition to absurdity by a consequence as manifestly false, commands and duties are possible, but are never disobeyed or broken.

If he means by a *violent* motive, an evil which inspires fear, his meaning is simply this: that the party bound by a command is bound by the prospect of an evil. For that which is not feared is not apprehended as an evil: or (changing the shape of the expression) is not an evil in prospect.

The truth is that the magnitude of the eventual evil, and the magnitude of the chance of incurring it, are foreign to the matter in question. The greater the eventual evil, and the greater the chance of incurring it, the greater is the efficacy of the command, and the greater is the strength of the obligation: Or (substituting expressions exactly equivalent), the greater is the *chance* that the command will be obeyed, and that the duty will not be broken. But where there is the smallest chance of incurring the smallest evil, the expression of a wish amounts to a command, and, therefore, imposes a duty. The sanction, if you will, is feeble or insufficient; but still there *is* a sanction, and, therefore, a duty and a command.

By some celebrated writers (by Locke, Bentham, and I think, Paley), the term *sanction,* or *enforcement of obedience,* is applied to conditional good as well as to conditional evil: to reward as to punishment. But, with all my habitual veneration for the names of Locke and Bentham, I think that this extension of the term is pregnant with confusion and perplexity.

Rewards are, indisputably, *motives* to comply with the wishes of others. But to talk of commands and duties as *sanctioned* or *enforced* by rewards, or to talk of rewards as *obliging* or *constraining* to obedience, is surely a wide departure from the established meaning of the terms.

If *you* expressed a desire that *I* should render a service, and if you proffered a reward as the motive or inducement to render it, *you* would scarcely be said to *command* the service, nor should I, in ordinary language, be *obliged* to render it. In ordinary language, *you* would *promise* me a reward, on condition of my rendering the service, whilst *I*

might be *incited* or *persuaded* to render it by the hope of obtaining the reward.

Again: If a law holds out a *reward* as an inducement to do some act, an eventual *right* is conferred, and not an *obligation* imposed, upon those who shall act accordingly: The *imperative* part of the law being addressed or directed to the party whom it requires to *render* the reward.

In short, I am determined or inclined to comply with the wish of another, by the fear of disadvantage or evil. I am also determined or inclined to comply with the wish of another, by the hope of advantage or good. But it is only by the chance of incurring *evil* that I am *bound* or *obliged* to compliance. It is only by conditional *evil* that duties are *sanctioned* or *enforced*. It is the power and the purpose of inflicting eventual *evil,* and *not* the power and the purpose of imparting eventual *good,* which gives to the expression of a wish the name of a *command.*

If we put *reward* into the import of the term *sanction,* we must engage in a toilsome struggle with the current of ordinary speech; and shall often slide unconsciously, notwithstanding our efforts to the contrary, into the narrower and customary meaning.

It appears, then, from what has been premised, that the ideas or notions comprehended by the term *command* are the following. (1) A wish or desire conceived by a rational being, that another rational being shall do or forbear. (2) An evil to proceed from the former, and to be incurred by the latter, in case the latter comply not with the wish. (3) An expression or intimation of the wish by words or other signs.

It also appears from what has been premised that *command, duty,* and *sanction* are inseparably connected terms: that each embraces the same ideas as the others, though each denotes those ideas in a peculiar order or series.

"A wish conceived by one, and expressed or intimated to another, with an evil to be inflicted and incurred in case the wish be disregarded," are signified directly and indirectly by each of the three expressions. Each is the name of the same complex notion.

But when I am talking *directly* of the expression or intimation of the wish, I employ the term *command:* The expression or intimation of the wish being presented *prominently* to my hearer; whilst the evil to be incurred, with the chance of incurring it, are kept (if I may so express myself) in the background of my picture.

When I am talking *directly* of the chance of incurring the evil, or (changing the expression) of the liability or obnoxiousness to the evil, I employ the term *duty,* or the term *obligation.* The liability or obnoxiousness to the evil being put foremost, and the rest of the complex notion being signified implicitly.

When I am talking *immediately* of the evil itself, I employ the term *sanction,* or a term of the like import: The evil to be incurred being signified directly; whilst the obnoxiousness to that evil, with the expression or intimation of the wish, are indicated indirectly or obliquely.

To those who are familiar with the language of logicians (language unrivalled for brevity, distinctness, and precision), I can express my meaning accurately in a breath: Each of the three terms *signifies* the same notion, but each *denotes* a different part of that notion, and *connotes* the residue.

Commands are of two species. Some are *laws* or *rules.* The others have not acquired an appropriate name, nor does language afford an expression which will mark them briefly and precisely. I must, therefore, note them as well as I can by the ambiguous and inexpressive name of "*occasional* or *particular* commands."

The term *laws* or *rules* being not unfrequently applied to occasional or particular commands, it is hardly possible to describe a line of separation which shall consist in every respect with established forms of speech. But the distinction between laws and particular commands may, I think, be stated in the following manner.

By every command, the party to whom it is directed is obliged to do or to forbear.

Now where it obliges *generally* to acts or forbearances of a *class,* a command is a law or rule. But where it obliges to a *specific* act or forbearance, or to acts or forbearances which it determines *specifically* or *individually,* a command is occasional or particular. In other words, a class or description of acts is determined by a law or rule, and acts of that class or description are enjoined or forbidden generally. But where a command is occasional or particular, the act or acts, which the command enjoins or forbids, are assigned or determined by their specific or individual natures as well as by the class or description to which they belong.

The statement which I have given in abstract expressions I will now endeavour to illustrate by apt examples.

If you command your servant to go on a given errand, or *not* to leave your house on a given evening, or to rise at such an hour on such a morning, or to rise at that hour during the next week or month, the command is occasional or particular. For the act or acts enjoined or forbidden are specially determined or assigned.

But if you command him *simply* to rise at that hour, or to rise at that hour *always,* or to rise at that hour *till further orders,* it may be said, with propriety, that you lay down a *rule* for the guidance of your servant's conduct. For no specific act is assigned by the command, but the command obliges him generally to acts of a determined class.

If a regiment be ordered to attack or defend a post, or to quell a riot, or to march from their present quarters, the command is occasional or particular. But an order to exercise daily till further orders shall be given would be called a *general* order, and *might* be called a *rule.*

If Parliament prohibited simply the exportation of corn, either for a given period or indefinitely, it would establish a law or rule: a *kind* or *sort* of acts being determined by the command, and acts of that kind or sort being *generally* forbidden. But an order issued by Parliament to meet an impending scarcity, and stopping the exportation of corn *then shipped and in port,* would not be a law or rule, though issued by the sovereign legislature. The order regarding exclusively a specified quantity of corn, the negative acts or forbearances, enjoined by the command, would be determined specifically or individually by the determinate nature of their subject.

As issued by a sovereign legislature, and as wearing the form of a law, the order which I have now imagined would probably be *called* a law. And hence the difficulty of drawing a distinct boundary between laws and occasional commands.

Again: An act which is not an offence, according to the existing law, moves the sovereign to displeasure: and, though the authors of the act are legally innocent or unoffending, the sovereign commands that they shall be punished. As enjoining a specific punishment in that specific case, and as not enjoining generally acts or forbearances of a class, the order uttered by the sovereign is not a law or rule.

Whether such an order would be *called* a law seems to depend upon circumstances which are purely immaterial: immaterial, that is, with reference to the present purpose, though material with reference to others. If made by a sovereign assembly deliberately, and with the forms of legislation, it would probably be called a law. If uttered by an absolute monarch, without deliberation or ceremony, it would scarcely be confounded with acts of legislation, and would be styled an arbitrary command. Yet, on either of these suppositions, its nature would be the same. It would not be a law or rule, but an occasional or particular command of the sovereign One or Number.

To conclude with an example which best illustrates the distinction, and which shows the importance of the distinction most conspicuously, *judicial commands* are commonly occasional or particular, although the commands which they are calculated to enforce are commonly laws or rules.

For instance, the lawgiver commands that thieves shall be hanged. A specific theft and a specified thief being given, the judge commands that the thief shall be hanged, agreeably to the command of the lawgiver.

Now the lawgiver determines a class or description of acts; prohibits acts of the class generally and indefinitely; and commands, with the like generality, that punishment shall follow transgression. The command of the lawgiver is, therefore, a law or rule. But the command of the judge is occasional or particular. For he orders a specific punishment, as the consequence of a specific offence.

According to the line of separation which I have now attempted to describe, a law and a particular command are distinguished thus: Acts of forbearances of a *class* are enjoined *generally* by the former. Acts *determined specifically* are enjoined or forbidden by the latter.

A different line of separation has been drawn by Blackstone and others. According to Blackstone and others, a law and a particular command are distinguished in the following manner: A law obliges *generally* the members of the given community, or a law obliges *generally* persons of a given class. A particular command obliges a *single* person, or persons whom it determines *individually*.

That laws and particular commands are not to be distinguished thus, will appear on a moment's reflection.

For, *first,* commands which oblige generally the members of the given community, or commands which oblige generally persons of given classes, are not always laws or rules.

Thus, in the case already supposed; that in which the sovereign commands that all corn actually shipped for exportation be stopped and detained; the command is obligatory upon the whole community, but as it obliges them only to a set of acts individually assigned, it is not a law. Again, suppose the sovereign to issue an order, enforced by penalties, for a general mourning, on occasion of a public calamity. Now, though it is addressed to the community at large, the order is scarcely a rule, in the usual acceptation of the term. For, though it obliges generally the members of the entire community, it obliges to acts which it assigns specifically, instead of obliging generally to acts or forbearances of a class. If the sovereign commanded that *black* should be the dress of his subjects, his command would amount to a law. But if he commanded them to wear it on a specified occasion, his command would be merely particular.

And, *secondly,* a command which obliges exclusively persons individually determined may amount, notwithstanding, to a law or a rule.

For example, a father may set a *rule* to his child or children: a guardian, to his ward: a master, to his slave or servant. And certain of God's *laws* were as binding on the first man as they are binding at this hour on the millions who have sprung from his loins.

Most, indeed, of the laws which are established by political superiors, or most of the laws which are simply and strictly so called, oblige generally the members of the political community, or oblige generally persons of a class. To frame a system of duties for every individual of the community is simply impossible: and if it is possible, it is utterly useless. Most of the laws established by political superiors are, therefore, *general* in a twofold manner: as enjoining or forbidding generally acts of kinds or sorts; and as binding the whole community, or, at least, whole classes of its members.

But if we suppose that Parliament creates and grants an office, and that Parliament binds the grantee to services of a given description, we suppose a law established by political superiors, and yet exclusively binding a specified or determinate person.

Laws established by political superiors, and exclusively binding specified or determinate persons, are styled, in the language of the Roman jurists, *privilegia*. Though that, indeed, is a name which will hardly denote them distinctly: for, like most of the leading terms in actual systems of law, it is not the name of a definite class of objects, but a heap of heterogeneous objects.[1]

It appears, from what has been premised, that a law, properly so called, may be defined in the following manner.

A law is a command which obliges a person or persons.

But, as contradistinguished or opposed to an occasional or particular command, a law is a command which obliges a person or persons, and obliges *generally* to acts or forbearances of a class.

In language more popular but less distinct and precise, a law is a command which obliges a person or persons to a *course* of conduct.

Laws and other commands are said to proceed from *superiors*, and to bind or oblige *inferiors*. I will, therefore, analyse the meaning of those correlative expressions; and will try to strip them of a certain mystery, by which that simple meaning appears to be obscured.

Superiority is often synonymous with *precedence* or *excellence*. We talk of superiors in rank; of superiors in wealth; of superiors in virtue: comparing certain persons with certain other persons; and meaning that the former precede or excel the latter in rank, in wealth, or in virtue.

But, taken with the meaning wherein I here understand it, the term *superiority* signifies *might:* the power of affecting others with evil or pain, and of forcing them, through fear of that evil, to fashion their conduct to one's wishes.

For example, God is emphatically the *superior* of Man. For his power of affecting us with pain, and of forcing us to comply with his will, is unbounded and resistless.

To a limited extent, the sovereign One or Number is the superior of the subject or citizen: the master of the slave or servant; the father of the child.

In short, whoever can *oblige* another to comply with his wishes is the *superior* of that other, so far as the ability reaches: The party who is obnoxious to the impending evil, being, to that same extent, the *inferior*.

The might or superiority of God is simple or absolute. But in all or most cases of human superiority, the relation of superior and inferior, and the relation of inferior and superior, are reciprocal. Or (changing the expression) the party who is the superior as viewed from one aspect is the inferior as viewed from another.

For example, to an indefinite, though limited extent, the monarch is the superior of the governed: his power being commonly sufficient to enforce compliance with his will. But the governed, collectively or in mass, are also the superior of the monarch: who is checked in the abuse of his might by his fear of exciting their anger; and of

---

[1] Where a *privilegium* merely imposes a duty, it exclusively obliges a determinate person or persons. But where a *privilegium* confers a right, and the right conferred *avails against the world at large*, the law is *privilegium* as viewed from a certain aspect, but is also a general law as viewed from another aspect. In respect of the right conferred, the law exclusively regards a determinate person, and, therefore, is *privilegium*. In respect of the duty imposed, and corresponding to the right conferred, the law regards generally the members of the entire community.

This I shall explain particularly at a subsequent point of my Course, when I consider the peculiar nature of so-called *privilegia*, or of so-called *private laws*.

rousing to active resistance the might which slumbers in the multitude.

A member of a sovereign assembly is the superior of the judge: the judge being bound by the law which proceeds from that sovereign body. But in his character of citizen or subject, he is the inferior of the judge: the judge being the minister of the law, and armed with the power of enforcing it.

It appears, then, that the term *superiority* (like the terms *duty* and *sanction*) is implied by the term *command*. For superiority is the power of enforcing compliance with a wish: and the expression or intimation of a wish, with the power and the purpose of enforcing it, are the constituent elements of a command.

"That *laws* emanate from *superiors*" is, therefore, an identical proposition. For the meaning which it affects to impart is contained in its subject. If I mark the peculiar source of a given law, or if I mark the peculiar source of laws of a given class, it is possible that I am saying something which may instruct the hearer. But to affirm of laws universally "that they flow from *superiors*," or to affirm of laws universally "that *inferiors* are bound to obey them," is the merest tautology and trifling.

Like most of the leading terms in the sciences of jurisprudence and morals, the term *laws* is extremely ambiguous. Taken with the largest signification which can be given to the term properly, *laws* are a species of *commands*. But the term is improperly applied to various objects which have nothing of the imperative character: to objects which are *not* commands; and which, therefore, are *not* laws, properly so called.

Accordingly, the proposition "that laws are commands" must be taken with limitations. Or, rather, we must distinguish the various meanings of the term *laws*, and must restrict the proposition to that class of objects which is embraced by the largest signification that can be given to the term properly.

I have already indicated, and shall hereafter more fully describe, the objects improperly termed laws, which are *not* within the province of jurisprudence (being either rules enforced by opinion and closely analogous to laws properly so called, or being laws so called by a metaphorical application of the term merely). There are other objects improperly termed laws (not being commands) which yet may properly be included within the province of jurisprudence. These I shall endeavour to particularise:

1. Acts on the part of legislatures to explain positive law can scarcely be called laws in the proper signification of the term. Working no change in the actual duties of the governed, but simply declaring what those duties are, they properly are acts of interpretation by legislative authority. Or, to borrow an expression from the writers on the Roman Law, they are acts of authentic interpretation.

But, this notwithstanding, they are frequently styled laws; *declaratory* laws, or declaratory statutes. They must, therefore, be noted as forming an exception to the proposition "that laws are a species of commands."

It often, indeed, happens (as I shall show in the proper place), that laws declaratory in name are imperative in effect: Legislative, like judicial interpretation, being frequently deceptive; and establishing new law, under guise of expounding the old.

2. Laws to repeal laws, and to release from existing duties, must also be excepted from the proposition "that laws are a species of commands." In so far as they release from duties imposed by existing laws, they are not commands, but revocations of commands. They authorise or permit the parties, to whom the repeal extends, to do or to forbear from acts which they were commanded to forbear from or to do. And, considered with regard to this, their immediate or direct purpose, they are often named permissive laws, or, more briefly and more properly, permissions.

Remotely and indirectly, indeed, permissive laws are often or always imperative. For the parties released from duties are restored to liberties or rights, and duties answering those rights are, therefore, created or revived.

But this is a matter which I shall examine with exactness, when I analyse the expressions "legal right," "permission by the sovereign or state," and "civil or political liberty."

3. Imperfect laws, or laws of imperfect obligation, must also be excepted from the proposition "that laws are a species of commands."

An imperfect law (with the sense wherein the term is used by the Roman jurists) is a law which wants a sanction, and which, therefore, is not binding. A law declaring that certain acts are crimes, but annexing no punishment to the commission of acts of the class, is the simplest and most obvious example.

Though the author of an imperfect law signifies a desire, he manifests no purpose of enforcing compliance with the desire. But where there is not a purpose of enforcing compliance with the desire, the expression of a desire is not a command. Consequently, an imperfect law is not so properly a law, as counsel, or exhortation, addressed by a superior to inferiors.

Examples of imperfect laws are cited by the Roman jurists. But with us in England, laws professedly imperative are always (I believe) perfect or obligatory. Where the English legislature affects to command, the English tribunals not unreasonably presume that the legislature exacts obedience. And, if no specific sanction be annexed to a given law, a sanction is supplied by the courts of justice, agreeably to a general maxim which obtains in cases of the kind.

The imperfect laws, of which I am now speaking, are laws which are imperfect, in the sense of *the Roman jurists;* that is to say, laws which speak the desires of political superiors, but which their authors (by oversight or design) have not provided with sanctions. Many of the writers on *morals,* and on the so called *law of nature,* have annexed a different meaning to the term *imperfect.* Speaking of imperfect obligations, they commonly mean duties which are *not legal,* duties imposed by commands of God, or duties imposed by positive morality, as contradistinguished to duties imposed by positive law. An imperfect obligation, in the sense of the Roman jurists, is exactly equivalent to no obligation at all. For the term *imperfect* denotes simply that the law wants the sanction appropriate to laws of the kind. An imperfect obligation, in the other meaning of the expression, is a religious or a moral obligation. The term *imperfect* does not denote that the law

imposing the duty wants the appropriate sanction. It denotes that the law imposing the duty is *not* a law established by a political superior: that it wants that *perfect,* or that surer or more cogent sanction, which is imparted by the sovereign or state.

I believe that I have now reviewed all the classes of objects to which the term *laws* is improperly applied. The laws (improperly so called) which I have here lastly enumerated are (I think) the only laws which are not commands, and which yet may be properly included within the province of jurisprudence. But though these, with the so-called laws set by opinion and the objects metaphorically termed laws, are the only laws which *really* are not commands, there are certain laws (properly so called) which may *seem* not imperative. Accordingly, I will subjoin a few remarks upon laws of this dubious character.

1. There are laws, it may be said, which merely create rights: And, seeing that every command imposes a duty, laws of this nature are not imperative.

But, as I have intimated already, and shall show completely hereafter, there are no laws *merely* creating *rights*. There are laws, it is true, which *merely* create *duties:* duties not correlating with correlating rights, and which, therefore, may be styled *absolute*. But every law, really conferring a right, imposes expressly or tacitly a *relative* duty, or a duty correlating with the right. If it specify the remedy to be given, in case the right shall be infringed, it imposes the relative duty expressly. If the remedy to be given be not specified, it refers tacitly to pre-existing law, and clothes the right which it purports to create with a remedy provided by that law. Every law really conferring a right is, therefore, imperative: as imperative, as if its only purpose were the creation of a duty, or as if the relative duty, which it inevitably imposes, were merely absolute.

The meanings of the term *right* are various and perplexed; taken with its proper meaning, it comprises ideas which are numerous and complicated; and the searching and extensive analysis, which the term, therefore, requires, would occupy more room than could be given to it in the present lecture. It is not, however, necessary that the analysis should be performed here. I purpose, in my earlier lectures, to determine the province of jurisprudence; or to distinguish the laws established by political superiors, from the various laws, proper and improper, with which they are frequently confounded. And this I may accomplish exactly enough, without a nice inquiry into the import of the term *right*.

2. According to an opinion which I must notice incidentally here, though the subject to which it relates will be treated directly hereafter, customary laws must be excepted from the proposition "that laws are a species of command."

By many of the admirers of customary laws (and, especially, of their German admirers), they are thought to oblige legally (independently of the sovereign or state), *because* the citizens or subjects have observed or kept them. Agreeably to this opinion, they are not the *creatures* of the sovereign or state, although the sovereign or state may abolish them at pleasure. Agreeably to this opinion, they are positive law (or law, strictly so called), inasmuch as they are enforced by the courts of justice: But, that notwithstanding, they exist as *positive law* by the spontaneous adoption of the governed, and not by position or establishment on the part of political superiors. Consequently, customary laws, considered as positive law, are not commands. And, consequently, customary laws, considered as positive law, are not laws or rules properly so called.

An opinion less mysterious, but somewhat allied to this, is not uncommonly held by the adverse party: by the party which is strongly opposed to customary law; and to all law made judicially, or in the way of judicial legislation. According to the latter opinion, all judge-made law, or all judge-made law established by *subject* judges, is purely the creature of the judges by whom it is established immediately. To impute it to the sovereign legislature, or to suppose that it speaks the will of the sovereign legislature, is one of the foolish or knavish *fictions* with which lawyers, in every age and nation, have perplexed and darkened the simplest and clearest truths.

I think it will appear, on a moment's reflection, that each of these opinions is groundless: that customary law is *imperative*, in the proper signification of the term; and that all judge-made law is the creature of the sovereign or state.

At its origin, a custom is a rule of conduct which the governed observe spontaneously, or not in pursuance of a law set by a political superior. The custom is transmuted into positive law, when it is adopted as such by the courts of justice, and when the judicial decisions fashioned upon it are enforced by the power of the state. But before it is adopted by the courts, and clothed with the legal sanction, it is merely a rule of positive morality: a rule generally observed by the citizens or subjects; but deriving the only force which it can be said to possess from the general disapprobation falling on those who transgress it.

Now when judges transmute a custom into a legal rule (or make a legal rule not suggested by a custom), the legal rule which they establish is established by the sovereign legislature. A subordinate or subject judge is merely a minister. The portion of the sovereign power which lies at his disposition is merely delegated. The rules which he makes derive their legal force from authority given by the state: an authority which the state may confer expressly, but which it commonly imparts in the way of acquiescence. For, since the state may reverse the rules which he makes, and yet permits him to enforce them by the power of the political community, its sovereign will "that his rules shall obtain as law" is clearly evinced by its conduct, though not by its express declaration.

The admirers of customary law love to trick out their idol with mysterious and imposing attributes. But to those who can see the difference between positive law and morality, there is nothing of mystery about it. Considered as rules of positive morality, customary laws arise from the consent of the governed, and not from the position or establishment of political superiors. But, considered as moral rules turned into positive laws, customary laws are established by the state; established by the state directly, when the customs are promulgated in its statutes; and established by the state circuitously, when the customs are adopted by its tribunals.

The opinion of the party which abhors judge-made laws springs from their inadequate conception of the nature of commands.

Like other significations of desire, a command is express or tacit. If the desire be signified by *words* (written or spoken), the command is express. If the desire be signified by conduct (or by any signs of desire which are *not* words), the command is tacit.

Now when customs are turned into legal rules by decisions of subject judges, the legal rules which emerge from the customs are *tacit* commands of the sovereign legislature. The state, which is able to abolish, permits its ministers to enforce them: and it, therefore, signifies its pleasure, by that its voluntary acquiescence, "that they shall serve as a law to the governed."

My present purpose is merely this: to prove that the positive law styled *customary* (and all positive law made judicially) is established by the state directly or circuitously, and, therefore, is *imperative*. I am far from disputing that law made judicially (or in the way of improper legislation) and law made by statute (or in the properly legislative manner) are distinguished by weighty differences. I shall inquire, in future lectures, what those differences are; and why subject judges, who are properly ministers of the law, have commonly shared with the sovereign in the business of making it.

I assume, then, that the only laws which are not imperative, and which belong to the subject-matter of jurisprudence, are the following:

1. Declaratory laws, or laws explaining the import of existing positive law.
2. Laws abrogating or repealing existing positive law.
3. Imperfect laws, or laws of imperfect obligation (with the sense wherein the expression is used by the Roman jurists).

But the space occupied in the science by these improper laws is comparatively narrow and insignificant. Accordingly, although I shall take them into account so often as I refer to them directly, I shall throw them out of account on other occasions. Or (changing the expression) I shall limit the term *law* to laws which are imperative, unless I extend it expressly to laws which are not.

LECTURE VI

… The superiority which is styled sovereignty, and the independent political society which sovereignty implies, is distinguished from other superiority, and from other society, by the following marks or characters: (1) The *bulk* of the given society are in a *habit* of obedience or submission to a *determinate* and *common* superior: let that common superior be a certain individual person or a certain body or aggregate of individual persons. (2) That certain individual, or that certain body of individuals, is *not* in a habit of obedience to a determinate human superior. Laws (improperly so called) which opinion sets or imposes may permanently affect the conduct of that certain individual or body. To express or tacit commands of other determinate parties, that certain individual or body may yield occasional submission. But there is no determinate person, or determinate aggregate of persons, to whose commands, express or tacit, that certain individual or body renders habitual obedience.

Or the notions of sovereignty and independent political society may be expressed concisely thus. If a *determinate* human superior, *not* in a habit of obedience to a like superior, receives *habitual* obedience from the *bulk* of a given society, that determinate superior is sovereign in that society, and the society (including the superior) is a society political and independent.

To that determinate superior, the other members of the society are *subject;* or on that determinate superior, to other members of the society are *dependent*. The position of its other members toward that determinate superior is *a state of subjection,* or *a state of dependence*. The mutual relation which subsists between that superior and them may be styled *the relation of sovereign and subject, or the relation of sovereignty and subjection*.

Hence it follows that it is only through an ellipsis, or an abridged form of expression, that the *society* is styled *independent*. The party truly independent (independent, that is to say, of a determinate human superior), is not the society, but the sovereign portion of the society: that a certain member of the society, or that certain body of its members, to whose commands, expressed or intimated, the generality or bulk of its members render habitual obedience. Upon that certain person, or certain body of persons, the other members of the society are *dependent,* or to that certain person, or certain body of persons, the other members of the society are *subject.* By "an independent political society," or "an independent and sovereign nation," we mean a political society consisting of a sovereign and subjects, as opposed to a political society which is merely subordinate: that is to say, which is merely a limb or member of another political society, and which therefore consists entirely of persons in a state of subjection.

In order that a given society may form a society political and independent, the two distinguishing marks which I have mentioned above must unite. The *generality* of the given society must be in the *habit* of obedience to a *determinate* and *common* superior; whilst that determinate person, or determinate body of persons, must *not* be habitually obedient to a determinate person or body. It is the union of that positive, with this negative mark, which renders that given society (including that certain superior) a society political and independent.

To show that the union of those marks renders a given society a society political and independent, I call your attention to the following positions and examples.

1. In order that a given society may form a society political, the generality or bulk of its members must be in a habit of obedience to a determinate and common superior.

In case the generality of its members obey a determinate superior, but the obedience be rare or transient and not habitual or permanent, the relation of sovereignty and subjection is not created thereby between that certain superior and the members of that given society. In other words, that determinate superior and the members of that given society do not become thereby an independent political society. Whether that given society be political and independent or not, it is not an independent political society whereof that certain superior is the sovereign portion.

For example: In 1815 the allied armies occupied France; and so long as the allied armies occupied France, the commands of the allied

sovereigns were obeyed by the French government, and, through the French government, by the French people generally. But since the commands and the obedience were comparatively rare and transient, they were not sufficient to constitute the relation of sovereignty and subjection between the allied sovereigns and the members of the invaded nation. In spite of those commands, and in spite of that obedience, the French government was sovereign or independent. Or in spite of those commands, and in spite of that obedience, the French government and its subjects were an independent political society whereof the allied sovereigns were not the sovereign portion.

Now if the French nation, before the obedience to those sovereigns, had been an independent society in a state of nature or anarchy, it would not have been changed by the obedience into a society political. And it would not have been changed by the obedience into a society political, because the obedience was not habitual.

For, inasmuch as the obedience was not habitual, it was not changed by the obedience from a society political and independent, into a society political but subordinate. A given society, therefore, is not a society political, unless the generality of its members be in a *habit* of obedience to a determinate and common superior.

Again: A feeble state holds its independence precariously, or at the will of the powerful states to whose aggressions it is obnoxious. And since it is obnoxious to their aggressions, it and the bulk of its subjects render obedience to commands which they occasionally express or intimate. Such, for instance, is the position of the Saxon government and its subjects in respect of the conspiring sovereigns who form the Holy Alliance. But since the commands and the obedience are comparatively few and rare, they are not sufficient to constitute the relation of sovereignty and subjection between the powerful states and the feeble state with its subjects. In spite of those commands, and in spite of that obedience, the feeble state is sovereign or independent. Or in spite of those commands, and in spite of that obedience, the feeble state and its subjects are an independent political society whereof the powerful states are not the sovereign portion. Although the powerful states are permanently *superior,* and although the feeble state is permanently *inferior,* there is neither a *habit* of command on the part of the former, nor a *habit* of obedience on the part of the latter. Although the latter is unable to defend and maintain its independence, the latter is independent of the former in fact or practice.

From the example now adduced, as from the example adduced before, we may draw the following inference: that a given society is not a society political, unless the generality of its members be in a *habit* of obedience to a determinate and common superior. By the obedience to the powerful states, the feeble state and its subjects are not changed from an independent, into a subordinate political society. And they are not changed by the obedience into a subordinate political society, because the obedience is not habitual. Consequently, if they were a natural society (setting that obedience aside), they would not be changed by that obedience into a society political.

2. In order that a given society may form a society political, habitual obedience must be rendered, by the generality or bulk of its members, to a determinate and common superior. In other words, habitual obedience must be rendered, by the generality or bulk of its members, to one and the same determinate person, or determinate body of persons.

Unless habitual obedience be rendered by the *bulk* of its members, and be rendered by the bulk of its members to *one and the same* superior, the given society is either in a state of nature, or is split into two or more independent political societies.

For example: In case a given society be torn by intestine war, and in case the conflicting parties be nearly balanced, the given society is in one of the two positions which I have now supposed. As there is no common superior to which the bulk of its members render habitual obedience, it is not a political society single or undivided. If the bulk of each of the parties be in a habit of obedience to its head, the given society is broken into two or more societies, which, perhaps, may be styled independent political societies. If the bulk of each of the parties be not in that habit of obedience, the given society is simply or absolutely in a state of nature or anarchy. It is either resolved or broken into its

individual elements, or into numerous societies of an extremely limited size: of a size so extremely limited, that they could hardly be styled societies independent and *political.* For, as I shall show hereafter, a given independent society would hardly be styled *political,* in case it fell short of a *number* which cannot be fixed with precision, but which may be called considerable, or not extremely minute.

3. In order that a given society may form a society political, the generality or bulk of its members must habitually obey a superior determinate as well as common.

On this position I shall not insist here. For I have shown sufficiently in my fifth lecture that no indeterminate party can command expressly or tacitly, or can receive obedience or submission: that no indeterminate body is capable of corporate conduct, or is capable, as a body, of positive or negative deportment.

4. It appears from what has preceded, that, in order that a given society may form a society political, the bulk of its members must be in a habit of obedience to a certain and common superior. But, in order that the given society may form a society political and independent, that certain superior must not be habitually obedient to a determinate human superior.

The given society may form a society political and independent, although that certain superior be habitually affected by laws which opinion sets or imposes. The given society may form a society political and independent, although that certain superior may render occasional submission to commands of determinate parties. But the society is not independent, although it may be political, in case that certain superior may habitually obey the commands of a certain person or body.

Let us suppose, for example, that a viceroy obeys habitually the author of his delegated powers. And, to render the example complete, let us suppose that the viceroy receives habitual obedience from the generality or bulk of the persons who inhabit his province. Now though he commands habitually within the limits of his province, and receives habitual obedience from the generality or bulk of its inhabitants, the viceroy is not sovereign within the limits of his province, nor are he and its inhabitants an independent political society. The viceroy, and (through the viceroy) the generality or bulk of its inhabitants, are habitually obedient or submissive to the sovereign of a larger society. He and the inhabitants of his province are therefore in a state of subjection to the sovereign of that larger society. He and the inhabitants of his province are a society political but subordinate, or form a political society which is merely a limb of another.

9   Law as the Union of Primary and Secondary Rules

H. L. A. HART

A FRESH START

[As I have discussed elsewhere] at various crucial points, the simple model of law as the sovereign's coercive orders failed to reproduce some of the salient features of a legal system. To demonstrate this, we did not find it necessary to invoke (as earlier critics have done) international law or primitive law which some may regard as disputable or borderline examples of law; instead we pointed to certain familiar features of municipal law in a modern state, and showed that these were either distorted or altogether unrepresented in this over-simple theory.

The main ways in which the theory failed are instructive enough to merit a second summary. First, it became clear that though of all the varieties of law, a criminal statute, forbidding or enjoining certain actions under penalty, most resembles orders backed by threats given by one person to others, such a statute nonetheless differs from such orders in the important respect that it commonly applies to those who enact it and not merely to others. Secondly, there are other varieties of law, notably those conferring legal powers to adjudicate or legislate (public powers) or to create or vary legal relations (private powers) which cannot, without absurdity, be construed as orders backed by threats. Thirdly, there are legal rules which differ from orders in their mode of origin, because they are not brought into being by anything analogous to explicit prescription. Finally, the analysis of law in terms of the sovereign, habitually obeyed and necessarily exempt from all legal limitation, failed to account for the continuity of legislative authority characteristic of a modern legal system, and the sovereign, person, or persons could not be identified with either the electorate or the legislature of a modern state.

It will be recalled that in thus criticizing the conception of law as the sovereign's coercive orders we considered also a number of ancillary devices which were brought in at the cost of corrupting the primitive simplicity of the theory to rescue it from its difficulties. But these too failed. One device, the notion of a *tacit* order, seemed to have no application to the complex actualities of a modern legal system, but only to very much simpler situations like that of a general who deliberately refrains from interfering with orders given by his subordinates. Other devices, such as that of treating power-conferring rules as mere fragments of rules imposing duties, or treating all rules as directed only to officials, distort the ways in which these are spoken of, thought of, and actually used in social life. This had no better claim to our assent than the theory that all the rules of a game are "really" directions to the umpire and the scorer. The device, designed to reconcile the self-binding character of legislation with the theory that a statute is an order given to *others*, was to distinguish the legislators acting in their official

Oxford University Press 1961. Reprinted from *The Concept of Law* by H. L. A. Hart (1961) by permission of Oxford University Press.

capacity, as *one* person ordering *others* who include themselves in their private capacities. This device, impeccable in itself, involved supplementing the theory with something it does not contain: this is the notion of a rule defining what must be done to legislate; for it is only in conforming with such a rule that legislators have an official capacity and a separate personality to be contrasted with themselves as private individuals.

[My previous discussions] are therefore the record of a failure and there is plainly need for a fresh start. Yet the failure is an instructive one, worth the detailed consideration we have given it, because at each point where the theory failed to fit the facts it was possible to see at least in outline why it was bound to fail and what is required for a better account. The root cause of failure is that the elements out of which the theory was constructed, viz. the ideas of orders, obedience, habits, and threats, do not include, and cannot by their combination yield, the idea of a rule, without which we cannot hope to elucidate even the most elementary forms of law. It is true that the idea of a rule is by no means a simple one: we have already seen in [a previous discussion] the need, if we are to do justice to the complexity of a legal system, to discriminate between two different though related types. Under rules of the one type, which may well be considered the basic or primary type, human beings are required to do or abstain from certain actions, whether they wish to or not. Rules of the other type are in a sense parasitic upon or secondary to the first; for they provide that human beings may be doing or saying certain things that introduce new rules of the primary type, extinguish or modify old ones, or in various ways determine their incidence or control their operations. Rules of the first type impose duties; rules of the second type confer powers, public or private. Rules of the first type concern actions involving physical movement or changes; rules of the second type provide for operations which lead not merely to physical movement or change, but to the creation or variation of duties or obligations.

We have already given some preliminary analysis of what is involved in the assertion that rules of these two types exist among a given social group, and in this chapter we shall not only carry this analysis a little farther but we shall make the general claim that in the combination of these two types of rule there lies what Austin wrongly claimed to have found in the notion of coercive orders, namely, "the key to the science of jurisprudence." We shall not indeed claim that wherever the word *law* is "properly" used this combination of primary and secondary rules is to be found; for it is clear that the diverse range of cases of which the word *law* is used are not linked by any such simple uniformity, but by less direct relations—often of analogy of either form or content to a central case. What we shall attempt to show, in this and the succeeding chapters, is that most of the features of law which have proved most perplexing and have both provoked and eluded the search for definition can best be rendered clear, if these two types of rule and the interplay between them are understood. We accord this union of elements a central place because of their explanatory power in elucidating the concepts that constitute the framework of legal thought. The justification for the use of the word *law* for a range of apparently heterogeneous cases is a secondary matter which can be undertaken when the central elements have been grasped.

THE IDEA OF OBLIGATION

It will be recalled that the theory of law as coercive orders, notwithstanding its errors, started from the perfectly correct appreciation of the fact that where there is law, there human conduct is made in some sense nonoptional or obligatory. In choosing this starting point the theory was well inspired, and in building up a new account of law in terms of the interplay of primary and secondary rules we too shall start from the same idea. It is, however, here, at this crucial first step, that we have perhaps most to learn from the theory's errors.

Let us recall the gunman situation. A orders B to hand over his money and threatens to shoot him if he does not comply. According to the theory of coercive orders this situation illustrates the notion of obligation or duty in general. Legal obligation is to be found in this situation writ large; A must be the sovereign habitually obeyed and the orders must be general, prescribing courses of conduct, not single actions. The plausibility of the claim that the gunman situation displays the meaning of obligation lies in the fact that it is certainly one in which we would say that B, if he obeyed, was "obliged" to hand over his money. It is, however, equally certain that we should misdescribe the situation if we said, on these facts, that B "had an obligation" or a "duty" to hand over the money. So from the start it is clear that we need something else for an understanding of the idea of obligation. There is a difference, yet to be explained, between the assertion that someone *was obliged* to do something and the assertion that he *had an obligation* to do it. The first is often a statement about the beliefs and motives with which an action is done: B was obliged to hand over his money may simply mean, as it does in the gunman case, that he believed that some harm or other unpleasant consequences would befall him if he did not hand it over and he handed it over to avoid those consequences. In such cases the prospect of what would happen to the agent if he disobeyed has rendered something he would otherwise have preferred to have done (keep the money) less eligible.

Two further elements slightly complicate the elucidation of the notion of being obliged to do something. It seems clear that we should not think of B as obliged to hand over the money if the threatened harm was, according to common judgments, trivial in comparison with the disadvantage or serious consequences, either for B or for others, of complying with the orders, as it would be, for example, if A merely threatened to pinch B. Nor perhaps should we say that B was obliged, if there were no reasonable grounds for thinking that A could or would probably implement his threat of relatively serious harm. Yet, though such references to common judgments of comparative harm and reasonable estimates of likelihood, are implicit in this notion, the statement that a person was obliged to obey someone is, in the main, a psychological one referring to the beliefs and motives with which an action was done. But the statement that someone *had an*

obligation to do something is of a very different type and there are many signs of this difference. Thus not only is it the case that the facts about B's action and his beliefs and motives in the gunman case, though sufficient to warrant the statement that B was obliged to hand over his purse, are *not sufficient* to warrant the statement that he had an obligation to do this; it is also the case that facts of this sort (i.e., facts about beliefs and motives) are *not necessary* for the truth of a statement that a person had an obligation to do something. Thus the statement that a person had an obligation (e.g., to tell the truth or report for military service) remains true even if he believed (reasonably or unreasonably) that he would never be found out and had nothing to fear from disobedience. Moreover, whereas the statement that he had this obligation is quite independent of the question whether or not he in fact reported for service, the statement that someone was obliged to do something, normally carries the implication that he actually did it.

Some theorists, Austin among them, seeing perhaps the general irrelevance of the person's beliefs, fears, and motives to the question whether he had an obligation to do something, have defined this notion not in terms of these subjective facts, but in terms of the *chance* or *likelihood* that the person having the obligation will suffer a punishment or "evil" at the hands of others in the event of disobedience. This, in effect, treats statements of obligation not as psychological statements but as predictions or assessments of chances of incurring punishment or "evil." To many later theorists this has appeared as a revelation, bringing down to earth an elusive notion and restating it in the same clear, hard, empirical terms as are used in science. It has, indeed, been accepted sometimes as the only alternative to metaphysical conceptions of obligation or duty as invisible objects mysteriously existing "above" or "behind" the world of ordinary, observable facts. But there are many reasons for rejecting this interpretation of statements of obligation as predictions, and it is not, in fact, the only alternative to obscure metaphysics.

The fundamental objection is that the predictive interpretation obscures the fact that, where rules exist, deviations from them are not merely grounds for a prediction that hostile reactions will follow or that a court will apply sanctions to those who break them, but are also a reason or justification for such reaction and for applying the sanctions. We have already drawn attention in [a previous discussion] to this neglect of the internal aspect of rules and we shall elaborate on it later in this chapter.

There is, however, a second, simpler objection to the predictive interpretation of obligation. If it were true that the statement that a person had an obligation meant that *he* was likely to suffer in the event of disobedience, it would be a contradiction to say that he had an obligation, (e.g., to report for military service) but that, owing to the fact that he had escaped from the jurisdiction, or had successfully bribed the police or the court, there was not the slightest chance of his being caught or made to suffer. In fact, there is no contradiction in saying this, and such statements are often made and understood.

It is, of course, true that in a normal legal system, where sanctions are exacted for a high proportion of offenses, an offender usually runs a risk of punishment; so, usually the statement that a person has an obligation and the statement that he is likely to suffer for disobedience will both be true together. Indeed, the connexion between these two statements is somewhat stronger than this: at least in a municipal system it may well be true that, unless *in general* sanctions were likely to be exacted from offenders, there would be little or no point in making particular statements about a person's obligations. In this sense, such statements may be said to presuppose belief in the continued normal operation of the system of sanctions much as the statement "he is out" in cricket presupposes, though it does not assert, that players, umpire, and scorer will probably take the usual steps. Nonetheless, it is crucial for the understanding of the idea of obligation to see that in individual cases the statement that a person has an obligation under some rule and the prediction that he is likely to suffer for disobedience may diverge.

It is clear that obligation is not to be found in the gunman situation, though the simpler notion of being obliged to do something may well be defined in the elements present there. To understand the general idea of obligation as a necessary preliminary to understanding it in its legal form, we must turn to a different social situation which, unlike the gunman situation, includes the existence of social rules; for this situation contributes to the meaning of the statement that a person has an obligation in two ways. First, the existence of such rules, making certain types of behaviour a standard, is the normal, though unstated, background or proper context for such a statement; and, secondly, the distinctive function of such statement is to apply such a general rule to a particular person by calling attention to the fact that his case falls under it. We have already seen in [a previous discussion] that there is involved in the existence of any social rules a combination of regular conduct with a distinctive attitude to that conduct as a standard. We have also seen the main ways in which these differ from mere social habits, and how the varied normative vocabulary ("ought," "must," "should") is used to draw attention to the standard and to deviations from it, and to formulate the demands, criticisms, or acknowledgments which may be based on it. Of this class of normative words the words *obligation* and *duty* form an important sub-class, carrying with them certain implications not usually present in the others. Hence, though a grasp of the elements generally differentiating social rules from mere habits is certainly indispensable for understanding the notion of obligation or duty, it is not sufficient by itself.

The statement that someone has or is under an obligation does indeed imply the existence of a rule; yet it is not always the case that where rules exist the standard of behaviour required by them is conceived of in terms of obligation. "He ought to have" and "He had an obligation to" are not always interchangeable expressions, even though they are alike in carrying an implicit reference to existing standards of conduct or are used in drawing conclusions in particular cases from a general rule. Rules of etiquette or correct speech are certainly rules: they are more than convergent habits or regularities of behaviour; they are taught and efforts are made to maintain them; they are used in criticizing our own and other people's behaviour in the characteristic normative vocabulary. "You ought to take your hat off," "It is wrong to say 'you was.' " But to use in connexion with rules of this kind the words *obligation* or *duty* would be misleading and not merely stylistically odd. It would misdescribe a social situation; for though the line separating rules of obligation from others is at points a vague one, yet the main rationale of the distinction is fairly clear.

Rules are conceived and spoken of as imposing obligations when the general demand for conformity is insistent and the social pressure brought to bear upon those who deviate or threaten to deviate is great. Such rules may be wholly customary in origin: there may be no centrally organized system of punishments for breach of the rules; the social pressure may take only the form of a general diffused hostile or critical reaction which may stop short of physical sanctions. It may be limited to verbal manifestations of disapproval or of appeals to the individuals' respect for the rule violated; it may depend heavily on the operation of feelings of shame, remorse, and guilt. When the pressure is of this last-mentioned kind we may be inclined to classify the rules as part of the morality of the social group and the obligation under the rules as moral obligation. Conversely, when physical sanctions are prominent or usual among the forms of pressure, even though these are neither closely defined nor administered by officials but are left to the community at large, we shall be inclined to classify the rules as a primitive or rudimentary form of law. We may, of course, find both these types of serious social pressure behind what is, in an obvious sense, the same rule of conduct; sometimes this may occur with no indication that one of them is peculiarly appropriate as primary and the other secondary, and then the question whether we are confronted with a rule of morality or rudimentary law may not be susceptible of an answer. But for the moment the possibility of drawing the line between law and morals need not detain us. What is important is that the insistence on importance or *seriousness* of social pressure behind the rules is the primary factor determining whether they are thought of as giving rise to obligations.

Two other characteristics of obligation go naturally together with this primary one. The rules supported by this serious pressure are thought important because they are believed to be necessary to the maintenance of social life or some highly prized feature of it. Characteristically, rules so obviously essential as those which restrict the free use of violence are thought of in terms of obligation. So too rules which require honesty or truth or require the keeping of promises, or specify what is to be done by one who performs a distinctive role or function in the social group are thought of in terms of either "obligation" or perhaps more often "duty." Secondly, it is generally recognized that the conduct required by these rules may, while benefitting others, conflict with what the person who owes the duty may wish to do. Hence obligations and duties are thought of as characteristically involving sacrifice or renunciation, and the standing possibility of conflict between obligation or duty and interest is, in all societies, among the truisms of both the lawyer and the moralist.

The figure of a *bond* binding the person obligated, which is buried in the word *obligation,* and the similar notion of a debt latent in the word *duty* are explicable in terms of these three factors, which distinguish rules of obligation or duty from other rules. In this figure, which haunts much legal thought, the social pressure appears as a chain binding those who have obligations so that they are not free to do what they want. The other end of the chain is sometimes held by the group or their official representatives, who insist on performance or exact the penalty: sometimes it is entrusted by the group to a private individual who may choose whether or not to insist on performance or its equivalent in value to him. The first situation typifies the duties or obligations of criminal law and the second those of civil law where we think of private individuals having rights correlative to the obligations.

Natural and perhaps illuminating though these figures or metaphors are, we must not allow them to trap us into a misleading conception of obligation as essentially consisting in some feeling of pressure or compulsion experienced by those who have obligations. The fact that rules of obligation are generally supported by serious social pressure does not entail that to have an obligation under the rules is to experience feelings of compulsion or pressure. Hence there is no contradiction in saying of some hardened swindler, and it may often be true, that he had an obligation to pay the rent but felt no pressure to pay when he made off without doing so. To *feel* obliged and to have an obligation are different though frequently concomitant things. To identify them would be one way of misinterpreting, in terms of psychological feelings, the important internal aspect of rules to which we drew attention in [a previous discussion].

Indeed, the internal aspect of rules is something to which we must again refer before we can dispose finally of the claims of the predictive theory. For an advocate of that theory may well ask why, if social pressure is so important a feature of rules of obligation, we are yet so concerned to stress the inadequacies of the predictive theory; for it gives this very feature a central place by defining obligation in terms of the likelihood that threatened punishment or hostile reaction will follow deviation from certain lines of conduct. The difference may seem slight between the analysis of a statement of obligation as a prediction, or assessment of the chances, of hostile reaction to deviation, and our own contention that though this statement presupposes a background in which deviations from rules are generally met by hostile reactions, yet its characteristic use is not to predict this but to say that a person's case falls under such a rule. In fact, however, this difference is not a slight one. Indeed, until its importance is grasped, we cannot properly understand the whole distinctive style of human thought, speech, and action which is involved in the existence of rules and which constitutes the normative structure of society.

The following contrast again in terms of the "internal" and "external" aspect of rules may serve to mark what gives this distinction its great importance for the understanding not only of law but of the structure of any society. When a social group has certain rules of conduct, this fact affords an opportunity for many closely related yet different kinds of assertion; for it is possible to be concerned with the rules, either merely as an observer who does not himself accept them, or as a member of the group which accepts and uses them as guides to conduct. We may call these respectively the "external" and the "internal points of view." Statements made from the external point of view may themselves be of different kinds. For the observer may, without accepting the rules himself, assert that the group accepts the rules, and thus may from outside refer to the way in which *they* are concerned with them from the internal point of view. But whatever the rules are, whether they are those of games, like chess or cricket, or moral or legal rules, we can if we choose occupy the position of an observer who does not even refer in this way to the internal point of view of the group. Such an observer is content merely to record the regularities of observable behaviour in which conformity with the rules partly consists and those further regularities, in the form of the hostile reaction, reproofs, or punishments, with which deviations from the rules are met. After a time the external observer may, on the basis of the regularities observed, correlate deviation with hostile reaction, and be able to predict with a fair measure of success, and to assess the chances that a deviation from the group's normal behaviour will meet with hostile reaction or punishment. Such knowledge may not only reveal much about the group, but might enable him to live among them without unpleasant consequences which would attend one who attempted to do so without such knowledge.

If, however, the observer really keeps austerely to this extreme external point of view and does not give any account of the manner in which members of the group who accept the rules view their own regular behaviour, his description of their life cannot be in terms of rules at all, and so not in the terms of the rule dependent notions of obligation or duty. Instead, it will be in terms of observable regularities of conduct, predictions, probabilities, and signs. For such an observer, deviations by a member of the group from normal conduct will be a sign that hostile reaction is likely to follow, and nothing more. His view will be like the view of one who, having observed the working of a traffic signal in a busy street for some time, limits himself to saying that when the light turns red there is a high probability that the traffic will stop. He treats the light merely as a natural *sign that* people will behave in certain ways, as clouds are a *sign that* rain will come. In so doing he will miss out on a whole dimension of the social life of those whom he is watching, since for them the red light is not merely a sign that others will stop: they look upon it as a *signal for* them to stop, and so a reason for stopping in conformity to rules which make stopping when the light is red a standard of behaviour and an obligation. To mention this is to bring into account the way in which the group regards its own behaviour. It is to refer to the internal aspect of rules seen from their internal point of view.

The external point of view may very nearly reproduce the way in which the rules function in the lives of certain members of the group, namely those who reject its rules and are only concerned with them when and because they judge that unpleasant consequences are likely to follow violation. Their point of view will need for its expression, "I was obliged to do it," "I am likely to suffer for it if …," "You will probably suffer for it if …," "They will do that to you if…." But they will not need forms of expression like "I had an obligation" or "You have an obligation" for these are required only by those who see their own and other persons' conduct from the internal point of view. What the external point of view, which limits itself to the observable regularities of behaviour, cannot reproduce is the way in which the rules function as rules in the lives of those who normally are the majority of society. These are the officials, lawyers, or private persons who use them, in one situation after another, as guides to the conduct of social life, as the basis for claims, demands, admissions, criticism, or punishment, viz, in all the familiar transactions of life according to rules. For them the violation of a rule is not merely a basis for the prediction that a hostile reaction will follow but a *reason* for hostility.

At any given moment the life of any society which lives by rules, legal or not, is likely to consist in a tension between those who, on the one hand, accept and voluntarily cooperate in maintaining the rules, and so see their own and other persons' behaviour in terms of the rules, and those who, on the other hand, reject the rules and attend to them only from the external point of view as a sign of possible punishment. One of the difficulties facing any legal theory anxious to do justice to the complexity of the facts is to remember the presence of both these points of view and not to define one of them out of existence. Perhaps all our criticisms of the predictive theory of obligation may be best summarized as the accusation that this is what it does to the internal aspect of obligatory rules.

THE ELEMENTS OF LAW

It is, of course, possible to imagine a society without legislature, courts, or officials of any kind. Indeed, there are many studies of primitive communities which not only claim that this possibility is realized but depict in detail the life of a society where the only means of social control is that general attitude of the group toward its own standard modes of behaviour in terms of which we have characterized rules of obligation. A social structure of this kind is often referred to as one of "custom"; but we shall not use this term, because it often implies that the customary rules are very old and supported with less social pressure than other rules. To avoid these implications we shall refer to such a social structure as one of primary rules of obligation. If a society is to live by such primary rules alone, there are certain conditions which, granted a few of the most obvious truisms about human nature and the world we live in, must clearly be satisfied. The first of these conditions is that the rules must contain in some form restrictions on the free use of violence, theft, and deception to which human beings are tempted but which they must, in general, repress if they are to coexist in close proximity to each other. Such rules are in fact always found in the primitive societies of which we have knowledge, together with a variety of others imposing on individuals various positive duties to perform services or make contributions to the common life. Secondly, though such a society may exhibit the tension, already described, between those who accept the rules and those who reject the rules except where fear of social pressure induces them to conform, it is plain that the latter cannot be more than a minority, if so loosely organized a society of persons, approximately equal in physical strength, is to endure: for otherwise those who reject the rules would have too little social pressure to fear. This too is confirmed by what we know of primitive communities where, though there are dissidents and malefactors, the majority live by the rules seen from the internal point of view.

More important for our present purpose is the following consideration. It is plain that only a small community closely knit by ties of kinship, common sentiment, and belief, and placed in a stable environment, could live successfully by such a régime of unofficial rules. In any other conditions such a simple form of social control must prove defective and will require supplementation in different ways. In the first place, the rules by which the group lives will not form a system, but will simply be a set of separate standards, without any identifying or common mark, except of course that they are the rules which a particular group of human beings accepts. They will in this respect resemble our own rules of etiquette. Hence if doubts arise as to what the rules are or as to the precise scope of some given rule, there will be no procedure for settling this doubt, either by reference to an authoritative text or to an official whose declarations on this point are authoritative. For, plainly, such a procedure and the acknowledgement of either authoritative text or persons involve the existence of rules of a type different from the rules of obligation or duty which *ex hypothesi* are all that the group has. This defect in the simple social structure of primary rules we may call its *uncertainty*.

A second defect is the *static* character of the rules. The only mode of change in the rules known to such a society will be the slow process of growth, whereby courses of conduct once thought optional become first habitual or usual, and then obligatory, and the converse process of decay, when deviations, once severely dealt with, are first tolerated and then pass unnoticed. There will be no means, in such a society, of deliberately adapting the rules to changing circumstances, either by eliminating old rules or introducing new

ones: for, again, the possibility of doing this presupposes the existence of rules of a different type from the primary rules of obligation by which alone the society lives. In an extreme case the rules may be static in a more drastic sense. This, though never perhaps fully realized in any actual community, is worth considering because the remedy for it is something very characteristic of law. In this extreme case, not only would there be no way of deliberately changing the general rules, but the obligations which arise under the rules in particular cases could not be varied or modified by the deliberate choice of any individual. Each individual would simply have fixed obligations or duties to do or abstain from doing certain things. It might indeed very often be the case that others would benefit from the performance of these obligations; yet if there are only primary rules of obligation they would have no power to release those bound from performance or to transfer to others the benefits which would accrue from performance. For such operations of release or transfer create changes in the initial positions of individuals under the primary rules of obligation, and for these operations to be possible there must be rules of a sort different from the primary rules.

The third defect of this simple form of social life is the *inefficiency* of the diffuse social pressure by which the rules are maintained. Disputes as to whether an admitted rule has or has not been violated will always occur and will, in any but the smallest societies, continue interminably, if there is no agency specially empowered to ascertain finally, and authoritatively, the fact of violation. Lack of such final and authoritative determinations is to be distinguished from another weakness associated with it. This is the fact that punishments for violations of the rules, and other forms of social pressure involving physical effort or the use of force, are not administered by a special agency but are left to the individuals affected or to the group at large. It is obvious that the waste of time involved in the group's unorganized efforts to catch and punish offenders, and the smouldering vendettas which may result from self help in the absence of an official monopoly of "sanctions," may be serious. The history of law does, however, strongly suggest that the lack of official agencies to determine authoritatively the fact of violation of the rules is a much more serious defect; for many societies have remedies for this defect long before the other.

The remedy for each of these three main defects in this simplest form of social structure consists in supplementing the *primary* rules of obligation with *secondary* rules which are rules of a different kind. The introduction of the remedy for each defect might, in itself, be considered a step from the pre-legal into the legal world, since each remedy brings with it many elements that permeate law. Certainly all three remedies together are enough to convert the régime of primary rules into what is indisputably a legal system. We shall consider in turn each of these remedies and show why law may most illuminatingly be characterized as a union of primary rules of obligation with such secondary rules. Before we do this, however, the following general points should be noted. Though the remedies consist in the introduction of rules which are certainly different from each other, as well as from the primary rules of obligation which they supplement, they have important features in common and are connected in various ways. Thus they may all be said to be on a different level from the primary rules, for they are all *about* such rules; in the sense that while primary rules are concerned with the actions that individuals must or must not do, these secondary rules are all concerned with the primary rules themselves. They specify the ways in which the primary rules may be conclusively ascertained, introduced, eliminated, varied, and the fact of their violation conclusively determined.

The simplest form of remedy for the *uncertainty* of the régime of primary rules is the introduction of what we shall call a "rule of recognition." This will specify some feature or features possession of which by a suggested rule is taken as a conclusive affirmative indication that it is a rule of the group to be supported by the social pressure it exerts. The existence of such a rule of recognition may take any of a huge variety of forms, simple or complex. It may, as in the early law of many societies, be no more than that an authoritative list or text of the rules is to be found in a written document or carved on some public monument. No doubt as a matter of history this step from the pre-legal to the legal may be accomplished in distinguishable stages, of which the first is the mere reduction to writing of hitherto unwritten rules. This is not itself the crucial step, though it is a very important one: what is crucial is the acknowledgement of reference to the writing or inscription as *authoritative* (i.e., as the *proper* way of disposing of doubts as to the existence of the rule). Where there is such an acknowledgement there is a very simple form of secondary rule: a rule for conclusive identification of the primary rules of obligation.

In a developed legal system the rules of recognition are of course more complex; instead of identifying rules exclusively by reference to a text or list they do so by reference to some general characteristic possessed by the primary rules. This may be the fact of their having been enacted by a specific body, or their long customary practice, or their relation to judicial decisions. Moreover, where more than one of such general characteristics are treated as identifying criteria, provision may be made for their possible conflict by their arrangement in an order of superiority, as by the common subordination of custom or precedent to statute, the latter being a "superior source" of law. Such complexity may make the rules of recognition in a modern legal system seem very different from the simple acceptance of an authoritative text: yet even in this simplest form, such a rule brings with it many elements distinctive of law. By providing an authoritative mark it introduces, although in embryonic form, the idea of a legal system: for the rules are now not just a discrete unconnected set but are, in a simple way, unified. Further, in the simple operation of identifying a given rule as possessing the required feature of being an item on an authoritative list of rules we have the germ of the idea of legal validity.

The remedy for the *static* quality of the régime of primary rules consists in the introduction of what we shall call "rules of change." The simplest form of such a rule is that which empowers an individual or body of persons to introduce new primary rules for the conduct of the life of the group, or of some class within it, and to eliminate old rules. As we have already argued in [a previous discussion] it is in terms of such a rule, and not in terms of orders backed by threats, that the ideas of legislative enactment and repeal are to be understood. Such rules of change may be very simple or very complex: the powers conferred may be unrestricted or limited in various ways: and the rules may, besides specifying the persons who are to legislate, define in more or less rigid terms the procedure to be followed in legislation. Plainly, there will be a very close connexion between the rules of change and the rules of recognition: for where the former exists the latter will necessarily incorporate a reference to legislation as an identifying feature of the rules, though it need not refer to all the details of procedure involved in legislation. Usually some official certificate or official copy will, under the rules of recognition, be taken as a sufficient proof of due enactment. Of course if there is a social structure so simple that the only "source of law" is legislation, the rule of recognition will simply specify enactment as the unique identifying mark or criterion of validity of the rules. This will be the case for example in the imaginary kingdom of Rex I depicted in [a previous discussion]: there the rule of recognition would simply be that whatever Rex I enacts is law.

We have already described in some detail the rules which confer on individuals power to vary their initial positions under the primary rules. Without such private power-conferring rules society would lack some of the chief amenities which law confers upon it. For the operations which these rules make possible are the making of wills, contracts, transfers of property, and many other voluntarily created structures of rights and duties which typify life under law, though of course an elementary form of power-conferring rule also underlies the moral institution of a promise. The kinship of these rules with the rules of change involved in the notion of legislation is clear, and as recent theory such as Kelsen's has shown, many of the features which puzzle us in the institutions

of contract or property are clarified by thinking of the operations of making a contract or transferring property as the exercise of limited legislative powers by individuals.

The third supplement to the simple régime of primary rules, intended to remedy the *inefficiency* of its diffused social pressure, consists of secondary rules empowering individuals to make authoritative determinations of the question whether, on a particular occasion, a primary rule has been broken. The minimal form of adjudication consists in such determinations, and we shall call the secondary rules which confer the power to make them "rules of adjudication." Besides identifying the individuals who are to adjudicate, such rules will also define the procedure to be followed. Like the other secondary rules these are on a different level from the primary rules: though they may be reinforced by further rules imposing duties on judges to adjudicate, they do not impose duties but confer judicial powers and a special status on judicial declarations about the breach of obligations. Again these rules, like the other secondary rules, define a group of important legal concepts: in this case the concepts of judge or court, jurisdiction and judgment. Besides these resemblances to the other secondary rules, rules of adjudication have intimate connexions with them. Indeed, a system which has rules of adjudication is necessarily also committed to a rule of recognition of an elementary and imperfect sort. This is so because, if courts are empowered to make authoritative determinations of the fact that a rule has been broken, these cannot avoid being taken as authoritative determinations of what the rules are. So the rule which confers jurisdiction will also be a rule of recognition, identifying the primary rules through the judgments of the courts, and these judgments will become a "source" of law. It is true that this form of rule of recognition, inseparable from the minimum form of jurisdiction, will be very imperfect. Unlike an authoritative text or a statute book, judgments may not be couched in general terms and their use as authoritative guides to the rules depends on a somewhat shaky inference from particular decisions, and the reliability of this must fluctuate both with the skill of the interpreter and the consistency of the judges.

It need hardly be said that in few legal systems are judicial powers confined to authoritative determinations of the fact of violation of the primary rules. Most systems have, after some delay, seen the advantages of further centralization of social pressure; and have partially prohibited the use of physical punishments or violent self help by private individuals. Instead they have supplemented the primary rules of obligation by further secondary rules, specifying or at least limiting the penalties for violation, and have conferred upon judges, where they have ascertained the fact of violation, the exclusive power to direct the application of penalties by other officials. These secondary rules provide the centralized official "sanctions" of the system.

If we stand back and consider the structure which has resulted from the combination of primary rules of obligation with the secondary rules of recognition, change and adjudication, it is plain that we have here not only the heart of a legal system, but a most powerful tool for the analysis of much that has puzzled both the jurist and the political theorist.

Not only are the specifically legal concepts with which the lawyer is professionally concerned, such as those of obligation and rights, validity and source of law, legislation and jurisdiction, and sanction, best elucidated in terms of this combination of elements. The concepts (which bestride both law and political theory) of the state, of authority, and of an official require a similar analysis if the obscurity which still lingers about them is to be dissipated. The reason why an analysis in these terms of primary and secondary rules has this explanatory power is not far to seek. Most of the obscurities and distortions surrounding legal and political concepts arise from the fact that these essentially involve reference to what we have called the internal point of view: the view of those who do not merely record and predict behaviour conforming to rules, but *use* the rules as standards for the appraisal of their own and others' behaviour. This requires more detailed attention in the analysis of legal and political concepts than it has usually received. Under the simple régime of primary rules the internal point of view is manifested in its simplest form, in the use of those rules as the basis of criticism, and as the justification of demands for conformity, social pressure, and punishment. Reference to this most elementary manifestation of the internal point of view is required for the analysis of the basic concepts of obligation and duty. With the addition to the system of secondary rules, the range of what is said and done from the internal point of view is much extended and diversified. With this extension comes a whole set of new concepts and they demand a reference to the internal point of view for their analysis. These include the notions of legislation, jurisdiction, validity, and, generally, of legal powers, private and public. There is a constant pull toward an analysis of these in the terms of ordinary or "scientific" fact-stating or predictive discourse. But this can only reproduce their external aspect: to do justice to their distinctive, internal aspect we need to see the different ways in which the law-making operations of the legislator, the adjudication of a court, the exercise of private or official powers, and other "acts-in-the-law" are related to secondary rules.

In [a subsequent discussion] we shall show how the ideas of the validity of law and sources of law, and the truths latent among the errors the doctrines of sovereignty may be rephrased and clarified in terms of rules of recognition. But we shall conclude this chapter with a warning: though the combination of primary and secondary rules merits, because it explains many aspects of law, the central place assigned to it, this cannot by itself illuminate every problem. The union of primary and secondary rules is at the centre of a legal system; but it is not the whole, and as we move away from the centre we shall have to accommodate, in ways indicated in later chapters, elements of a different character.

The Foundations of a Legal System

RULE OF RECOGNITION AND LEGAL VALIDITY

According to the theory criticized in [a previous discussion] the foundations of a legal system consist of the situation in which the majority of a social group habitually obey the orders backed by threats of the sovereign person or persons, who themselves habitually obey no one. This social situation is, for this theory, both a necessary and a sufficient condition of the existence of law. We have already exhibited in some detail the incapacity of this theory to account for some of the salient features of a modern municipal legal system: yet nonetheless, as its hold over the minds of many thinkers suggests, it does contain, though in a blurred and misleading form, certain truths about certain important aspects of law. These truths can, however, only be clearly presented, and their importance rightly assessed, in terms of the more complex social situation where a secondary rule of recognition is accepted and used for the identification of primary rules of obligation. It is this situation which deserves, if anything does, to be called the foundations of a legal system. In this chapter we shall discuss various elements of this situation which have received only partial or misleading expression in the theory of sovereignty and elsewhere.

Wherever such a rule of recognition is accepted, both private persons and officials are provided with authoritative criteria for identifying primary rules of obligation. The criteria so provided may, as we have seen, take any one or more of a variety of forms: these include reference to an authoritative text; to legislative enactment; to customary practice; to general declarations of specified persons; or to past judicial decisions in particular cases. In a very simple system like the world of Rex I depicted in [a previous discussion], where only what he enacts is law and no legal limitations upon his legislative power are imposed by customary rule or constitutional document, the sole criterion for identifying the law will be a simple reference to fact of enactment by Rex I. The existence of this simple form of rule of recognition will be manifest in the general practice, on the part of officials or private persons, of identifying the rules by this criterion. In a modern legal system where there are a variety of "sources" of law, the rule of recognition is correspondingly more complex: the criteria for identifying the law are multiple and commonly include a written constitution, enactment by a legislature, and judicial precedents. In most cases, provision is made for possible conflict by ranking these criteria in an order of relative subordination and primacy. It is in this way that in our system "common law" is subordinate to "statute."

It is important to distinguish this relative *subordination* of one criterion to another from *derivation,* since some spurious support for the view that all law is essentially or "really" (even if only "tacitly") the product of legislation has been gained from confusion of these two ideas. In our own system, custom and precedent are subordinate to legislation since customary and common law rules may be deprived of their status as law by statute. Yet they owe their status of law, precarious as this may be, not to a "tacit" exercise of legislative power but to the acceptance of a rule of recognition which accords them this independent though subordinate place. Again, as in the simple case, the existence of such a complex rule of recognition with this hierarchical ordering of distinct criteria is manifested in the general practice of identifying the rules by such criteria.

In the day-to-day life of a legal system its rule of recognition is very seldom expressly formulated as a rule; though occasionally, courts in England may announce in general terms the relative place of one criterion of law in relation to another, as when they assert the supremacy of Acts of Parliament over other sources or suggested sources of law. For the most part the rule of recognition is not stated, but its existence is *shown* in the way in which particular rules are identified, either by courts or other officials or private persons or their advisers. There is, of course, a difference in the use made by courts of the criteria provided by the rule and the use of them by others: for when courts reach a particular conclusion on the footing that a particular rule has been correctly identified as law, what they say has a special authoritative status conferred on it by other rules. In this respect, as in many others, the rule of recognition of a legal system is like the scoring rule of a game. In the course of the game the general rule defining the activities which constitute scoring (runs, goals, etc.) is seldom formulated; instead it is *used* by officials and players in identifying the particular phases which count toward winning. Here too, the declarations of officials (umpire or scorer) have a special authoritative status attributed to them by other rules. Further, in both cases there is the possibility of a conflict between these authoritative applications of the rule and the general understanding of what the rule plainly requires according to its terms. This, as we shall see later, is a complication which must be catered for in any account of what it is for a system of rules of this sort to exist.

The use of unstated rules of recognition, by courts and others, in identifying particular rules of the system is characteristic of the internal point of view. Those who use them in this way thereby manifest their own acceptance of them as guiding rules and with this attitude there goes a characteristic vocabulary different from the natural expressions of the external point of view. Perhaps the simplest of these is the expression, "It is the law that ...," which we may find on the lips not only of judges, but of ordinary men living under a legal system, when they identify a given rule of the system. This, like the expression "Out" or "Goal," is the language of one assessing a situation by reference to rules which he in common with others acknowledges appropriate for this purpose. This attitude of shared acceptance of rules is to be contrasted with that of an observer who records *ab extra* the fact that a social group accepts such rules but does not himself accept them. The natural expression of this external point of view is not "It is the law that ..." but "In England they recognize as law ... whatever the Queen in Parliament enacts...." The first of these forms of

expression we shall call an *internal statement* because it manifests the internal point of view and is naturally used by one who, accepting the rule of recognition and without stating the fact that it is accepted, applies the rule in recognizing some particular rule of the system as valid. The second form of expression we shall call an *external statement* because it is the natural language of an external observer of the system who, without himself accepting its rule of recognition, states the fact that others accept it.

If this use of an accepted rule of recognition in making internal statements is understood and carefully distinguished from an external statement of fact that the rule is accepted, many obscurities concerning the notion of legal "validity" disappear. For the word *valid* is most frequently, though not always, used in just such internal statements, applying to a particular rule of a legal system an unstated but accepted rule of recognition. To say that a given rule is valid is to recognize it as passing all the tests provided by the rule of recognition and so as a rule of the system. We can indeed simply say that the statement that a particular rule is valid means that it satisfies all the criteria provided by the rule of recognition. This is incorrect only to the extent that it might obscure the internal character of such statements; for, like the cricketers' "Out," these statements of validity normally apply to a particular case a rule of recognition accepted by the speaker and others, rather than expressly state that the rule is satisfied.

Some of the puzzles connected with the idea of legal validity are said to concern the relation between the validity and the "efficacy" of law. If by "efficacy" is meant that the fact that a rule of law which requires certain behaviour is obeyed more often than not, it is plain that there is no necessary connexion between the validity of any particular rule and *its* efficacy, unless the rule of recognition of the system includes among its criteria, as some do, the provision (sometimes referred to as a rule of obsolescence) that no rule is to count as a rule of the system if it has long ceased to be efficacious.

From the inefficacy of a particular rule, which may or may not count against its validity, we must distinguish a general disregard of the rules of the system. This may be so complete in character and so protracted that we should say, in the case of a new system, that it had never established itself as the legal system of a given group, or, in the case of a once-established system, that it had ceased to be the legal system of the group. In either case, the normal context or background for making any internal statement in terms of the rules of the system is absent. In such cases it would be generally *pointless* either to assess the rights and duties of particular persons by reference to the primary rules of a system or to access the validity of any of its rules by reference to its rules of recognition. To insist on applying a system of rules which had either never actually been effective or had been discarded would, except in special circumstances mentioned below, be as futile as to assess the progress of a game by reference to a scoring rule which had never been accepted or had been discarded.

One who makes an internal statement concerning the validity of a particular rule of a system may be said to *presuppose* the truth of the external statement of fact that the system is generally efficacious, for the normal use of internal statements is in such a context of general efficacy. It would however be wrong to say that statements of validity "mean" that the system is generally efficacious. For though it is normally pointless or idle to talk of the validity of a rule of a system which has never established itself or has been discarded, none the less it is not meaningless nor is it always pointless. One vivid way of teaching Roman Law is to speak *as if* the system were efficacious still and to discuss the validity of particular rules and solve problems in their terms; and one way of nursing hopes for the restoration of an old social order destroyed by revolution, and rejecting the new, is to cling to the criteria of legal validity of the old régime. This is implicitly done by the White Russian who still claims property under some rule of descent which was a valid rule of Tsarist Russia.

A grasp of the normal contextual connexion between the internal statement that a given rule of a system is valid and the external statement of fact that the system is generally efficacious will help us see in its proper perspective the common theory that to assert the validity of a rule is to predict that it will be enforced by courts or some other official action taken. In many ways this theory is similar to the predictive analysis of obligation which we considered and rejected in [a previous discussion]. In both cases alike the motive for advancing this predictive theory is the conviction that only thus can metaphysical interpretations be avoided: that either a statement that a rule is valid must ascribe some mysterious property which cannot be detected by empirical means or it must be a prediction of future behaviour of officials. In both cases also the plausibility of the theory is due to the same important fact: that the truth of the external statement of fact, which an observer might record, that the system is generally efficacious and likely to continue so, is normally presupposed by anyone who accepts the rules and makes an internal statement of obligation or validity. The two are certainly very closely associated. Finally, in both cases alike the mistake of the theory is the same: it consists in neglecting the special character of the internal statement and treating it as an external statement about official action.

This mistake becomes immediately apparent when we consider how the judge's own statement that a particular rule is valid functions in judicial decision; for, though here too, in making such a statement, the judge presupposes but does not state the general efficacy of the system, he plainly is not concerned to predict his own or others' official action. His statement that a rule is valid is an internal statement recognizing that the rule satisfies the tests for identifying what is to count as law in his court, and constitutes not a prophecy of but part of the *reason* for his decision. There is indeed a more plausible case for saying that a statement that a rule is valid is a prediction when such a statement is made by a private person; for in the case of conflict between unofficial statements of validity or invalidity and that of a court in deciding a case, there is often good sense in saying that the former must then be withdrawn. Yet even here, as we shall see when we come … to investigate the significance of such conflicts between official declarations and the plain requirements of the rules, it may be dogmatic to assume that it is withdrawn as a statement now shown to be *wrong*, because it has falsely *predicted* what a court would say. For there are more reasons for withdrawing statements than the fact that they are wrong, and also more ways of being wrong than this allows.

The rule of recognition providing the criteria by which the validity of other rules of the system is assessed is in an important sense, which we shall try to clarify, an *ultimate* rule: and where, as is usual, there are several criteria ranked in order of relative subordination and primacy, one of them is *supreme*. These ideas of the ultimacy of the rule of recognition and the supremacy of one of its criteria merit some attention. It is important to disentangle them from the theory, which we have rejected, that somewhere in every legal system, even though it lurks behind legal forms, there must be a sovereign legislative power which is legally unlimited.

Of these two ideas, supreme criterion and ultimate rule, the first is the easiest to define. We may say that a criterion of legal validity or source of law is supreme if rules identified by reference to it are still recognized as rules of the system, even if they conflict with rules identified by reference to the other criteria, whereas rules identified by reference to the latter are not so recognized if they conflict with the rules identified by reference to the supreme criterion. A similar explanation in comparative terms can be given of the notions of "superior" and "subordinate" criteria which we have already used. It is plain that the notions of a superior and a supreme criterion merely refer to a *relative* place on a scale and do not import any notion of legally *unlimited* legislative power. Yet "supreme" and "unlimited" are easy to confuse— at least in legal theory. One reason for this is that in the simpler forms of legal system the ideas of ultimate rule of recognition, supreme criterion, and legally unlimited legislature seem to converge. For where there is a legislature subject to no constitutional limitations and competent by its enactment to deprive all other rules of law emanating from other sources of their status as law, it is part of the rule of recognition in such a system that enactment by that legislature is the supreme criterion of validity. This is, according to constitutional theory, the position in the United Kingdom. But even systems like that of the United States in

which there is no such legally unlimited legislature may perfectly well contain an ultimate rule of recognition which provides a set of criteria of validity, one of which is supreme. This will be so, where the legislative competence of the ordinary legislature is limited by a constitution which contains no amending power, or places some clauses outside the scope of that power. Here there is no legally unlimited legislature, even in the widest interpretation of "legislature"; but the system of course contains an ultimate rule of recognition and, in the clauses of its constitution, a supreme criterion of validity.

The sense in which the rule of recognition is the *ultimate* rule of a system is best understood if we pursue a very familiar chain of legal reasoning. If the question is raised whether some suggested rule is legally valid, we must, in order to answer the question, use a criterion of validity provided by some other rule. Is this purported bylaw of the Oxfordshire County Council valid? Yes: because it was made in exercise of the powers conferred, and in accordance with the procedure specified, by a statutory order made by the Minister of Health. At this first stage the statutory order provides the criteria in terms of which the validity of the bylaw is assessed. There may be no practical need to go farther; but there is a standing possibility of doing so. We may query the validity of the statutory order and assess its validity in terms of the statute empowering the minister to make such orders. Finally when the validity of the statute has been queried and assessed by reference to the rule that what the Queen in Parliament enacts is law, we are brought to a stop in inquiries concerning validity: for we have reached a rule which, like the intermediate statutory order and statute, provides criteria for the assessment of the validity of other rules; but it is also unlike them in that there is no rule providing criteria for the assessment of its own legal validity.

There are, indeed, many questions which we can raise about this ultimate rule. We can ask whether it is the practice of courts, legislatures, officials, or private citizens in England actually to use this rule as an ultimate rule of recognition. Or has our process of legal reasoning been an idle game with the criteria of validity of a system now discarded? We can ask whether it is a satisfactory form of legal system which has such a rule at its root. Does it produce more good than evil? Are there prudential reasons for supporting it? Is there a moral obligation to do so? These are plainly very important questions; but, equally plainly, when we ask them about the rule of recognition, we are no longer attempting to answer the same kind of question about it as those which we answered about other rules with its aid. When we move from saying that a particular enactment is valid, because it satisfies the rule that what the Queen in Parliament enacts is law, to saying that in England this last rule is used by courts, officials, and private persons as the ultimate rule of recognition, we have moved from an internal statement of law asserting the validity of a rule of the system to an external statement of fact which an observer of the system might make even if he did not accept it. So too when we move from the statement that a particular enactment is valid, to the statement that the rule of recognition of the system is an excellent one and the system based on it is one worthy of support, we have moved from a statement of legal validity to a statement of value.

Some writers, who have emphasized the legal ultimacy of the rule of recognition, have expressed this by saying that, whereas the legal validity of other rules of the system can be demonstrated by reference to it, its own validity cannot be demonstrated but is "assumed" or "postulated" or is a "hypothesis." This may, however, be seriously misleading. Statements of legal validity made about particular rules in the day-to-day life of a legal system whether by judges, lawyers, or ordinary citizens do indeed carry with them certain presuppositions. They are internal statements of law expressing the point of view of those who accept the rule of recognition of the system and, as such, leave unstated much that could be stated in external statements of fact about the system. What is thus left unstated forms the normal background or context of statements of legal validity and is thus said to be "presupposed" by them. But it is important to see precisely what these presupposed matters are, and not to obscure their character. They consist of two things. First, a person who seriously asserts the validity of some given rule of

law, say a particular statute, himself makes use of a rule of recognition which he accepts as appropriate for identifying the law. Secondly, it is the case that this rule of recognition, in terms of which he assesses the validity of a particular statute, is not only accepted by him but is the rule of recognition actually accepted and employed in the general operation of the system. If the truth of this presupposition were doubted, it could be established by reference to actual practice: to the way in which courts identify what is to count as law, and to the general acceptance of or acquiescence in these identifications.

Neither of these two presuppositions are well described as "assumptions" of a "validity" which cannot be demonstrated. We only need the word *validity,* and commonly only use it, to answer questions which arise *within* a system of rules where the status of a rule as a member of the system depends on its satisfying certain criteria provided by the rule of recognition. No such question can arise as to the validity of the very rule of recognition which provides the criteria; it can neither be valid nor invalid but is simply accepted as appropriate for use in this way. To express this simple fact by saying darkly that its validity is "assumed but cannot be demonstrated," is like saying that we assume, but can never demonstrate, that the standard metre bar in Paris which is the ultimate test of the correctness of all measurement in metres, is itself correct.

A more serious objection is that talk of the "assumption" that the ultimate rule of recognition is valid conceals the essentially factual character of the second presupposition which lies behind the lawyers' statements of validity. No doubt the practice of judges, officials, and others, in which the actual existence of a rule of recognition consists, is a complex matter. As we shall see later, there are certainly situations in which questions as to the precise content and scope of this kind of rule, and even as to its existence, may not admit of a clear or determinate answer. Nonetheless it is important to distinguish "assuming the validity" from "presupposing the existence" of such a rule; if only because failure to do this obscures what is meant by the assertion that such a rule *exists.*

In the simple system of primary rules of obligation sketched in the last chapter, the assertion that a given rule existed could only be an external statement of fact such as an observer who did not accept the rules might make and verify by ascertaining whether or not, as a matter of fact, a given mode of behaviour was generally accepted as a standard and was accompanied by those features which, as we have seen, distinguish a social rule from mere convergent habits. It is in this way also that we should now interpret and verify the assertion that in England a rule—though not a legal one—exists that we must bare the head on entering a church. If such rules as these are found to exist in the actual practice of a social group, there is no separate question of their validity to be discussed, though of course their value or desirability is open to question. Once their existence has been established as a fact we should only confuse matters by affirming or denying that they were valid or by saying that "we assumed" but could not show their validity. Where, on the other hand, as in a mature legal system, we have a system of rules which includes a rule of recognition so that the status of a rule as a member of the system now depends on whether it satisfies certain criteria provided by the rule of recognition, this brings with it a new application of the word *exist*. The statement that a rule exists may now no longer be what it was in the simple case of customary rules—an external statement of the *fact* that a certain mode of behaviour was generally accepted as a standard in practice. It may now be an internal statement applying an accepted but unstated rule of recognition and meaning (roughly) no more than "valid given the systems criteria of validity." In this respect, however, as in others a rule of recognition is unlike other rules of the system. The assertion that it exists can only be an external statement of fact. For whereas a subordinate rule of a system may be valid and in that sense "exist" even if it is generally disregarded, the rule of recognition exists only as a complex, but normally concordant, practice of the courts, officials, and private persons in identifying the law by reference to certain criteria. Its existence is a matter of fact.

10   The Model of Rules I

RONALD DWORKIN

1. EMBARRASSING QUESTIONS

Lawyers lean heavily on the connected concepts of legal right and legal obligation. We say that someone has a legal right or duty, and we take that statement as a sound basis for making claims and demands, and for criticizing the acts of public officials. But our understanding of these concepts is remarkably fragile, and we fall into trouble when we try to say what legal rights and obligations are. We say glibly that whether someone has a legal obligation is determined by applying "the law" to the particular facts of his case, but this is not a helpful answer, because we have the same difficulties with the concept of law.

We are used to summing up our troubles in the classic questions of jurisprudence: What is "the law"? When two sides disagree, as often happens, about a proposition "of law," what are they disagreeing about, and how shall we decide which side is right? Why do we call what "the law" says a matter of legal "obligation"? Is "obligation" here just a term of art, meaning only what the law says? Or does legal obligation have something to do with moral obligation? Can we say that we have, in principle at least, the same reasons for meeting our legal obligations that we have for meeting our moral obligations?

These are not puzzles for the cupboard, to be taken down on rainy days for fun. They are sources of continuing embarrassment, and they nag at our attention. They embarrass us in dealing with particular problems that we must solve, one way or another. Suppose a novel right-of-privacy case comes to court, and there is no statute or precedent claimed by the plaintiff. What role in the court's decision should be played by the fact that most people in the community think that private individuals are "morally" entitled to that particular privacy? Supposing the Supreme Court orders some prisoner freed because the police used procedures that the Court now says are constitutionally forbidden, although the Court's earlier decisions upheld these procedures. Must the Court, to be consistent, free all other prisoners previously convicted through these same procedures?[1] Conceptual puzzles about "the law" and "legal obligation" become acute when a court is confronted with a problem like this.

These eruptions signal a chronic disease. Day in and day out we send people to jail, or take money away from them, or make them do things they do not want to do, under coercion of force, and we justify all of this by speaking of such persons as having broken the law or having failed to meet their legal obligations, or having interfered with other people's legal rights. Even in clear cases (a bank robber or a willful breach of contract), when we are confident that someone had a legal obligation and broke it, we are not able to give a satisfactory account of what that means, or why that entitles the state to punish or coerce him. We may feel confident that what we are doing is proper, but until we can identify the principles we are following we cannot be sure that they are sufficient, or whether we are applying them consistently. In less clear cases, when the issue of whether an obligation has been broken is for some reason controversial, the pitch of these nagging questions rises, and our responsibility to find answers deepens.

Certain lawyers (we may call them "nominalists") urge that we solve these problems by ignoring them. In their view the concepts of "legal obligation" and "the law" are myths, invented and sustained by lawyers for a dismal mix of conscious and subconscious motives. The puzzles we find in these concepts are merely symptoms that they are myths. They are unsolvable because unreal, and our concern with them is just one feature

of our enslavement. We would do better to flush away the puzzles and the concepts altogether, and pursue our important social objectives without this excess baggage.

This is a tempting suggestion, but it has fatal drawbacks. Before we can decide that our concepts of law and of legal obligation are myths, we must decide what they are. We must be able to state, at least roughly, what it is we all believe that is wrong. But the nerve of our problem is that we have great difficulty in doing just that. Indeed, when we ask what law is and what legal obligations are, we are asking for a theory of how we use those concepts and of the conceptual commitments our use entails. We cannot conclude, before we have such a general theory, that our practices are stupid or superstitious.

Of course, the nominalists think they know how the rest of us use these concepts. They think that when we speak of "the law" we mean a set of timeless rules stocked in some conceptual warehouse awaiting discovery by judges, and that when we speak of legal obligation we mean the invisible chains these mysterious rules somehow drape around us. The theory that there are such rules and chains they call "mechanical jurisprudence," and they are right in ridiculing its practitioners. Their difficulty, however, lies in finding practitioners to ridicule. So far they have had little luck in caging and exhibiting mechanical jurisprudents (all specimens captured—even Blackstone and Joseph Beale—have had to be released after careful reading of their texts).

In any event, it is clear that most lawyers have nothing like this in mind when they speak of the law and of legal obligation. A superficial examination of our practices is enough to show this for we speak of laws changing and evolving, and of legal obligation sometimes being problematical. In these and other ways we show that we are not addicted to mechanical jurisprudence.

Nevertheless, we do use the concepts of law and legal obligation, and we do suppose that society's warrant to punish and coerce is written in that currency. It may be that when the details of this practice are laid bare, the concepts we do use will be shown to be as silly and as thick with illusion as those the nominalists invented. If so, then

---

[1]See *Linkletter v. Walker*, 381 U.S. 618 (1965).

we shall have to find other ways to describe what we do, and either provide other justifications or change our practices. But until we have discovered this and made these adjustments, we cannot accept the nominalists' premature invitation to turn our backs on the problems our present concepts provide.

Of course the suggestion that we stop talking about "the law" and "legal obligation" is mostly bluff. These concepts are too deeply cemented into the structure of our political practices—they cannot be given up like cigarettes or hats. Some of the nominalists have half-admitted this and said that the myths they condemn should be thought of as Platonic myths and retained to seduce the masses into order. This is perhaps not so cynical a suggestion as it seems; perhaps it is a covert hedging of a dubious bet.

If we boil away the bluff, the nominalist attack reduces to an attack on mechanical jurisprudence. Through the lines of the attack, and in spite of the heroic calls for the death of law, the nominalists themselves have offered an analysis of how the terms "law" and "legal obligation" should be used which is not very different from that of more classical philosophers. Nominalists present their analysis as a model of how legal institutions (particularly courts) "really operate." But their model differs mainly in emphasis from the theory first made popular by the nineteenth century philosopher John Austin, and now accepted in one form or another by most working and academic lawyers who hold views on jurisprudence. I shall call this theory, with some historical looseness, "legal positivism." I want to examine the soundness of legal positivism, particularly in the powerful form that Professor H. L. A. Hart has given to it. I choose to focus on his position, not only because of its clarity and elegance, but because here, as almost everywhere else in legal philosophy, constructive thought must start with a consideration of his views.

2. POSITIVISM

Positivism has a few central and organizing propositions as its skeleton, and though not every philosopher who is called a positivist would subscribe to these in the way I present them, they do define the general position I want to examine. These key tenets may be stated as follows:

a. The law of a community is a set of special rules used by the community directly or indirectly for the purpose of determining which behavior will be punished or coerced by the public power. These special rules can be identified and distinguished by specific criteria, by tests having to do not with their content but with their *pedigree* or the manner in which they were adopted or developed. These tests of pedigree can be used to distinguish valid legal rules from spurious legal rules (rules which lawyers and litigants wrongly argue are rules of law) and also from other sorts of social rules (generally lumped together as "moral rules") that the community follows but does not enforce through public power.

b. The set of these valid legal rules is exhaustive of "the law," so that if someone's case is not clearly covered by such a rule (because there is none that seems appropriate, or those that seem appropriate are vague, or for some other reason) then that case cannot be decided by "applying the law." It must be decided by some official, like a judge, "exercising his discretion," which means reaching beyond the law for some other sort of standard to guide him in manufacturing a fresh legal rule or supplementing an old one.

c. To say that someone has a "legal obligation" is to say that his case falls under a valid legal rule that requires him to do or to forbear from doing something. (To say he has a legal right, or has a legal power of some sort, or a legal privilege or immunity, is to assert, in a shorthand ray, that others have actual or hypothetical legal obligations to act or not to act in certain ways touching him.) In the absence of such a valid legal rule there is no legal obligation; it follows that when the judge decides an issue by exercising his discretion, he is not enforcing a legal right as to that issue.

This is only the skeleton of positivism. The flesh is arranged differently by different positivists, and some even tinker with the bones. Different versions differ chiefly in their description of the fundamental test of pedigree a rule must meet to count as a rule of law.

Austin, for example, framed his version of the fundamental test as a series of interlocking definitions and distinctions.[2] He defined having an obligation as lying under a rule, a rule as a general command, and a command as an expression of desire that others behave in a particular way, backed by the power and will to enforce that expression in the event of disobedience. He distinguished classes of rules (legal, moral or religious) according to which person or group is the author of the general command the rule represents. In each political community, he thought, one will find a sovereign—a person or a determinate group whom the rest obey habitually, but who is not in the habit of obeying anyone else. The legal rules of a community are the general commands its sovereign has deployed. Austin's definition of legal obligation followed from this definition of law. One has a legal obligation, he thought, if one is among the addressees of some general order of the sovereign, and is in danger of suffering a sanction unless he obeys that order.

Of course, the sovereign cannot provide for all contingencies through any scheme of orders, and some of his orders will inevitably be vague or have furry edges. Therefore (according to Austin) the sovereign grants those who enforce the law (judges) discretion to make fresh orders when novel or troublesome cases are presented. The judges then make new rules or adapt old rules, and the sovereign either overturns their creations or tacitly confirms them by failing to do so.

Austin's model is quite beautiful in its simplicity. It asserts the first tenet of positivism, that the law is a set of rules specially selected to govern public order, and offers a simple factual test—what has the sovereign commanded?—as the sole criterion for identifying those special rules. In time, however, those who studied and tried to apply Austin's model found it too simple. Many objections were raised, among which were two

that seemed fundamental. First, Austin's key assumption that in each community a determinate group or institution can be found, which is in ultimate control of all other groups, seemed not to hold in a complex society. Political control in a modern nation is pluralistic and shifting, a matter of more or less, of compromise and cooperation and alliance, so that it is often impossible to say that any person or group has that dramatic control necessary to qualify as an Austinian sovereign. One wants to say, in the United States for example, that the "people" are sovereign. But this means almost nothing, and in itself provides no test for determining what the "people" have commanded, or distinguishing their legal from their social or moral commands.

Second, critics began to realize that Austin's analysis fails entirely to account for, even to recognize, certain striking facts about the attitudes we take toward "the law." We make an important distinction between law and even the general orders of a gangster. We feel that the law's strictures—and its sanctions—are different in that they are obligatory in a way that the outlaw's commands are not. Austin's analysis has no place for any such distinction, because it defines an obligation as subjection to the threat of force, and so founds the authority of law entirely on the sovereign's ability and will to harm those who disobey. Perhaps the distinction we make is illusory—perhaps our feelings of some special authority attaching to the law is based on religious hangover or another sort of mass self-deception. But Austin does not demonstrate this, and we are entitled to insist that an analysis of our concept of law either acknowledge and explain our attitudes, or show why they are mistaken.

H. L. A. Hart's version of positivism is more complex than Austin's, in two ways. First, he recognizes, as Austin did not, that rules are of different logical kinds. (Hart distinguishes two kinds, which he calls "primary" and "secondary" rules.) Second, he rejects Austin's theory that a rule is a kind of command, and substitutes a more elaborate general analysis of what rules are. We must pause over each of these points, and then note how they merge in Hart's concept of law.

---

[2]J. Austin, *The Province of Jurisprudence Determined* (1832).

Hart's distinction between primary and secondary rules is of great importance.[3] Primary rules are those that grant rights or impose obligations upon members of the community. The rules of the criminal law that forbid us to rob, murder or drive too fast are good examples of primary rules. Secondary rules are those that stipulate how, and by whom, such primary rules may be formed, recognized, modified or extinguished. The rules that stipulate how Congress is composed, and how it enacts legislation, are examples of secondary rules. Rules about forming contracts and executing wills are also secondary rules because they stipulate how very particular rules governing particular legal obligations (i.e., the terms of a contract or the provisions of a will) come into existence and are changed.

His general analysis of rules is also of great importance.[4] Austin had said that every rule is a general command, and that a person is obligated under a rule if he is liable to be hurt should he disobey it. Hart points out that this obliterates the distinction between being *obliged* to do something and being *obligated* to do it. If one is bound by a rule he is obligated, not merely obliged, to do what it provides, and therefore being bound by a rule must be different from being subject to an injury if one disobeys an order. A rule differs from an order, among other ways, by being *normative,* by setting a standard of behavior that has a call on its subject beyond the threat that may enforce it. A rule can never be binding just because some person with physical power wants it to be so. He must have *authority* to issue the rule or it is no rule, and such authority can only come from another rule which is already binding on those to whom he speaks. That is the difference between a valid law and the orders of a gunman.

So Hart offers a general theory of rules that does not make their authority depend upon the physical power of their authors. If we examine the way different rules come into being, he tells us, and attend to the distinction between primary and secondary rules, we see that there are two possible sources of a rule's authority:[5]

a. A rule may become binding upon a group of people because that group through its practices *accepts* the rule as a standard for its conduct. It is not enough that the group simply conforms to a pattern of behavior: even though most Englishmen may go to the movies on Saturday evening, they have not accepted a rule requiring that they do so. A practice constitutes the acceptance of a rule only when those who follow the practice regard the rule as binding, and recognize the rule as a reason or justification for their own behavior and as a reason for criticizing the behavior of others who do not obey it.

b. A rule may also become binding in quite a different way, namely by being enacted in conformity with some *secondary* rule that stipulates that rules so enacted shall be binding. If the constitution of a club stipulates, for example, that bylaws may be adopted by a majority of the members, then particular bylaws so voted are binding upon all the members, not because of any practice of acceptance of these particular bylaws, but because the constitution says so. We use the concept of *validity* in this connection: rules binding because they have been created in a manner stipulated by some secondary rule are called "valid" rules.

Thus we can record Hart's fundamental distinction this way: a rule may be binding (a) because it is accepted or (b) because it is valid.

Hart's concept of law is a construction of these various distinctions.[6] Primitive communities have only primary rules, and these are binding entirely because of practices of acceptance. Such communities cannot be said to have "law," because there is no way to distinguish a set of legal rules from amongst other social rules, as the first tenet of positivism requires. But when a particular community has developed a fundamental secondary

---

[3]See H. L. A. Hart, *The Concept of Law*, 89–96 (1961).
[4]*Id*. at 79–88.

[5]*Id*. at 97–107.
[6]*Id. passim*, particularly ch. 6.

rule that stipulates how legal rules are to be identified, the idea of a distinct set of legal rules, and thus of law, is born.

Hart calls such a fundamental secondary rule a "rule of recognition." The rule of recognition of a given community may be relatively simple ("What the king enacts is law") or it may be very complex (the United States Constitution, with all its difficulties of interpretation, may be considered a single rule of recognition). The demonstration that a particular rule is valid may therefore require tracing a complicated chain of validity back from that particular rule ultimately to the fundamental rule. Thus a parking ordinance of the city of New Haven is valid because it is adopted by a city council, pursuant to the procedures and within the competence specified by the municipal law adopted by the state of Connecticut, in conformity with the procedures and within the competence specified by the constitution of the state of Connecticut, which was in turn adopted consistently with the requirements of the United States Constitution.

Of course, a rule of recognition cannot itself be valid, because by hypothesis it is ultimate, and so cannot meet tests stipulated by a more fundamental rule. The rule of recognition is the sole rule in a legal system whose binding force depends upon its acceptance. If we wish to know what rule of recognition a particular community has adopted or follows, we must observe how its citizens, and particularly its officials, behave. We must observe what ultimate arguments they accept as showing the validity of a particular rule, and what ultimate arguments they use to criticize other officials or institutions. We can apply no mechanical test, but there is no danger of our confusing the rule of recognition of a community with its rules of morality. The rule of recognition is identified by the fact that its province is the operation of the governmental apparatus of legislatures, courts, agencies, policemen, and the rest.

In this way Hart rescues the fundamentals of positivism from Austin's mistakes. Hart agrees with Austin that valid rules of law may be created through the acts of officials and public institutions. But Austin thought that the authority of these institutions lay only in their monopoly of power. Hart finds their authority in the background of constitutional standards against which they act, constitutional standards that have been accepted, in the form of a fundamental rule of recognition, by the community which they govern. This background legitimates the decisions of government and gives them the cast and call of obligation that the naked commands of Austin's sovereign lacked. Hart's theory differs from Austin's also, in recognizing that different communities use different ultimate tests of law, and that some allow other means of creating law than the deliberate act of a legislative institution. Hart mentions "long customary practice" and "the relation [of a rule] to judicial decisions" as other criteria that are often used, though generally along with and subordinate to the test of legislation.

So Hart's version of positivism is more complex than Austin's, and his test for valid rules of law is more sophisticated. In one respect, however, the two models are very similar. Hart, like Austin, recognizes that legal rules have furry edges (he speaks of them as having "open texture") and, again like Austin, he accounts for troublesome cases by saying that judges have and exercise discretion to decide these cases by fresh legislation.[7] (I shall later try to show why one who thinks of law as a special set of rules is almost inevitably drawn to account for difficult cases in terms of someone's exercise of discretion.)

3. RULES, PRINCIPLES, AND POLICIES

I want to make a general attack on positivism, and I shall use H. L. A. Hart's version as a target, when a particular target is needed. My strategy will be organized around the fact that when lawyers reason or dispute about legal rights and obligations, particularly in those hard cases when our problems with these concepts seem most acute, they make use of standards that do not function as rules, but operate differently as principles, policies, and other sorts of standards. Positivism, I shall argue, is a model of and for a system of rules,

---

[7] *Id.* ch. 7.

and its central notion of a single fundamental test for law forces us to miss the important roles of these standards that are not rules.

I just spoke of "principles, policies, and other sorts of standards." Most often I shall use the term "principle" generically, to refer to the whole set of these standards other than rules; occasionally, however, I shall be more precise, and distinguish between principles and policies. Although nothing in the present argument will turn on the distinction, I should state how I draw it. I call a "policy" that kind of standard that sets out a goal to be reached, generally an improvement in some economic, political, or social feature of the community (though some goals are negative, in that they stipulate that some present feature is to be protected from adverse change). I call a "principle" a standard that is to be observed, not because it will advance or secure an economic, political, or social situation deemed desirable, but because it is a requirement of justice or fairness or some other dimension of morality. Thus the standard that automobile accidents are to be decreased is a policy, and the standard that no man may profit by his own wrong a principle. The distinction can be collapsed by construing a principle as stating a social goal (i.e., the goal of a society in which no man profits by his own wrong), or by construing a policy as stating a principle (i.e., the principle that the goal the policy embraces is a worthy one) or by adopting the utilitarian thesis that principles of justice are disguised statements of goals (securing the greatest happiness of the greatest number). In some contexts the distinction has uses which are lost if it is thus collapsed.[8]

My immediate purpose, however, is to distinguish principles in the generic sense from rules, and I shall start by collecting some examples of the former. The examples I offer are chosen haphazardly; almost any case in a law school casebook would provide examples that would serve as well. In 1889 a New York court, in the famous case of *Riggs v. Palmer*,[9] had to decide whether an heir named in the will of his grandfather could inherit under that will, even though he had murdered his grandfather to do so. The court began its reasoning with this admission: "It is quite true that statutes regulating the making, proof and effect of wills, and the devolution of property, if literally construed, and if their force and effect can in no way and under no circumstances be controlled or modified, give this property to the murderer."[10] But the court continued to note that "all laws as well as all contracts may be controlled in their operation and effect by general, fundamental maxims of the common law. No one shall be permitted to profit by his own fraud, or to take advantage of his own wrong, or to found any claim upon his own iniquity, or to acquire property by his own crime."[11] The murderer did not receive his inheritance.

In 1960, a New Jersey court was faced, in *Henningsen v. Bloomfield Motors, Inc.*[12] with the important question of whether (or how much) an automobile manufacturer may limit his liability in case the automobile is defective. Henningsen had bought a car, and signed a contract which said that the manufacturer's liability for defects was limited to "making good" defective parts—"this warranty being expressly in lieu of all other warranties, obligations or liabilities." Henningsen argued that, at least in the circumstances of his case, the manufacturer ought not to be protected by this limitation, and ought to be liable for the medical and other expenses of persons injured in a crash. He was not able to point to any statute, or to any established rule of law, that prevented the manufacturer from standing on the contract. The court nevertheless agreed with Henningsen. At various points in the court's argument the following appeals to standards are made: (a) "[W]e must keep in mind the general principle that, in the absence of fraud, one who does not choose to read a contract before signing it cannot later relieve himself of its burdens."[13] (b) "In applying that principle, the basic tenet of freedom of

---

[8]See Chapter 4. See also Dworkin, "Wasserstrom: The Judicial Decision," 75 *Ethics* 47 (1964), reprinted as "Does Law Have a Function?", 74 *Yale Law Journal* 640 (1965).
[9]115 N.Y. 506, 22 N.E. 188 (1889).
[10]*Id.* at 509, 22 N.E. at 189.
[11]*Id.* at 511, 22 N.E. at 190.
[12]32 N.J. 358, 161 A.2d 69 (1960).
[13]*Id.* at 386, 161 A.2d at 84.

competent parties to contract is a factor of importance."[14] (c) "Freedom of contract is not such an immutable doctrine as to admit of no qualification in the area in which we are concerned."[15] (d) "In a society such as ours, where the automobile is a common and necessary adjunct of daily life, and where its use is so fraught with danger to the driver, passengers and the public, the manufacturer is under a special obligation in connection with the construction, promotion and sale of his cars. Consequently, the courts must examine purchase agreements closely to see if consumer and public interests are treated fairly."[16] (e) "[I]s there any principle which is more familiar or more firmly embedded in the history of Anglo-American law than the basic doctrine that the courts will not permit themselves to be used as instruments of inequity and injustice?"[17] (f) "More specifically the courts generally refuse to lend themselves to the enforcement of a 'bargain' in which one party has unjustly taken advantage of the economic necessities of other...."[18]

The standards set out in these quotations are not the sort we think of as legal rules. They seem very different from propositions like "The maximum legal speed on the turnpike is sixty miles an hour" or "A will is invalid unless signed by three witnesses." They are different because they are legal principles rather than legal rules.

The difference between legal principles and legal rules is a logical distinction. Both sets of standards point to particular decisions about legal obligation in particular circumstances, but they differ in the character of the direction they give. Rules are applicable in an all-or-nothing fashion. If the facts a rule stipulates are given, then either the rule is valid, in which case the answer it supplies must be accepted, or it is not, in which case it contributes nothing to the decision.

This all-or-nothing is seen most plainly if we look at the way rules operate, not in law, but in some enterprise they dominate—a game, for example. In baseball a rule provides that if the batter has had three strikes, he is out. An official cannot consistently acknowledge that this is an accurate statement of a baseball rule, and decide that a batter who has had three strikes is not out. Of course, a rule may have exceptions (the batter who has taken three strikes is not out if the catcher drops the third strike). However, an accurate statement of the rule would take this exception into account, and any that did not would be incomplete. If the list of exceptions is very large, it would be too clumsy to repeat them each time the rule is cited; there is, however, no reason in theory why they could not all be added on, and the more that are, the more accurate is the statement of the rule.

If we take baseball rules as a model, we find that rules of law, like the rule that a will is invalid unless signed by three witnesses, fit the model well. If the requirement of three witnesses is a valid legal rule, then it cannot be that a will has been signed by only two witnesses and is valid. The rule might have exceptions, but if it does then it is inaccurate and incomplete to state the rule so simply, without enumerating the exceptions. In theory, at least, the exceptions could all be listed, and the more of them that are, the more complete is the statement of the rule.

But this is not the way the sample principles in the quotations operate. Even those which look most like rules do not set out legal consequences that follow automatically when the conditions provided are met. We say that our law respects the principle that no man may profit from his own wrong, but we do not mean that the law never permits a man to profit from wrongs he commits. In fact, people often profit, perfectly legally, from their legal wrongs. The most notorious case is adverse possession—if I trespass on your land long enough, some day I will gain a right to cross your land whenever I please. There are many less dramatic examples. If a man leaves one job, breaking a contract, to take a much higher paying job, he may have to pay damages to his first employer, but he is usually entitled to keep his new salary. If a man jumps bail and crosses state lines to make a brilliant investment in

---

[14] *Id.*
[15] *Id.* at 388, 161 A.2d at 86.
[16] *Id.* at 387, 161 A.2d at 85.
[17] *Id.* at 389, 161 A.2d at 86 (quoting Frankfurter, J., in *United States v. Bethlehem Steel*, 315 U.S. 289, 326 [1942]).
[18] *Id.*

another state, he may be sent back to jail, but he will keep his profits.

We do not treat these—and countless other counterinstances that can easily be imagined—as showing that the principle about profiting from one's wrongs is not a principle of our legal system, or that it is incomplete and needs qualifying exceptions. We do not treat counterinstances as exceptions (at least not exceptions in the way in which a catcher's dropping the third strike is an exception) because we could not hope to capture these counterinstances simply by a more extended statement of the principle. They are not, even in theory, subject to enumeration, because we would have to include not only these cases (like adverse possession) in which some institution has already provided that profit can be gained through a wrong, but also those numberless imaginary cases in which we know in advance that the principle would not hold. Listing some of these might sharpen our sense of the principle's weight (I shall mention that dimension in a moment), but it would not make for a more accurate or complete statement of the principle.

A principle like "No man may profit from his own wrong" does not even purport to set out conditions that make its application necessary. Rather, it states a reason that argues in one direction, but does not necessitate a particular decision. If a man has or is about to receive something, as a direct result of something illegal he did to get it, then that is a reason which the law will take into account in deciding whether he should keep it. There may be other principles or policies arguing in the other direction—a policy of securing title, for example, or a principle limiting punishment to what the legislature has stipulated. If so, our principle may not prevail, but that does not mean that it is not a principle of our legal system, because in the next case, when these contravening considerations are absent or less weighty, the principle may be decisive. All that is meant, when we say that a particular principle is a principle of our law, is that the principle is one which officials must take into account, if it is relevant, as a consideration inclining in one direction or another.

The logical distinction between rules and principles appears more clearly when we consider

principles that do not even look like rules. Consider the proposition, set out under "(d)" in the excerpts from the *Henningsen* opinion, that "the manufacturer is under a special obligation in connection with the construction, promotion and sale of his cars." This does not even purport to define the specific duties such a special obligation entails, or to tell us what rights automobile consumers acquire as a result. It merely states—and this is an essential link in the *Henningsen* argument—that automobile manufacturers must be held to higher standards than other manufacturers, and are less entitled to rely on the competing principle of freedom of contract. It does not mean that they may never rely on that principle, or that courts may rewrite automobile purchase contracts at will; it means only that if a particular clause seems unfair or burdensome, courts have less reason to enforce the clause than if it were for the purchase of neckties. The "special obligation" counts in favor, but does not in itself necessitate, a decision refusing to enforce the terms of an automobile purchase contract.

This first difference between rules and principles entails another. Principles have a dimension that rules do not—the dimension of weight or importance. When principles intersect (the policy of protecting automobile consumers intersecting with principles of freedom of contract, for example), one who must resolve the conflict has to take into account the relative weight of each. This cannot be, of course, an exact measurement, and the judgment that a particular principle or policy is more important than another will often be a controversial one. Nevertheless, it is an integral part of the concept of a principle that it has this dimension, that it makes sense to ask how important or how weighty it is.

Rules do not have this dimension. We can speak of rules as being *functionally* important or unimportant (the baseball rule that three strikes are out is more important than the rule that runners may advance on a balk, because the game would be much more changed with the first rule altered than the second). In this sense, one legal rule may be more important than another because it has a greater or more important role in regulating behavior. But we cannot say that one rule is more important than another within the system of rules, so that when two rules conflict one supersedes the other by virtue of its greater weight.

If two rules conflict, one of them cannot be a valid rule. The decision as to which is valid, and which must be abandoned or recast, must be made by appealing to considerations beyond the rules themselves. A legal system might regulate such conflicts by other rules, which prefer the rule enacted by the higher authority, or the rule enacted later, or the more specific rule, or something of that sort. A legal system may also prefer the rule supported by the more important principles. (Our own legal system uses both of these techniques.)

It is not always clear from the form of a standard whether it is a rule or a principle. "A will is invalid unless signed by three witnesses" is not very different in form from "A man may not profit from his own wrong," but one who knows something of American law knows that he must take the first as stating a rule and the second as stating a principle. In many cases the distinction is difficult to make—it may not have been settled how the standard should operate, and this issue may itself be a focus of controversy. The first amendment to the United States Constitution contains the provision that Congress shall not abridge freedom of speech. Is this a rule, so that if a particular law does abridge freedom of speech, it follows that it is unconstitutional? Those who claim that the first amendment is "an absolute" say that it must be taken in this way, that is, as a rule. Or does it merely state a principle, so that when an abridgement of speech is discovered, it is unconstitutional unless the context presents some other policy or principle which in the circumstances is weighty enough to permit the abridgement? That is the position of those who argue for what is called the "clear and present danger" test or some other form of "balancing."

Sometimes a rule and a principle can play much the same role, and the difference between them is almost a matter of form alone. The first section of the Sherman Act states that every contract in restraint of trade shall be void. The Supreme Court had to make the decision whether this provision should be treated as a rule in its own terms (striking down every contract "which restrains trade," which almost any contract does) or as a principle, providing a reason for striking down a contract in the absence of effective contrary policies. The Court construed the provision as a rule, but treated that rule as containing the word "unreasonable," and as prohibiting only "unreasonable" restraints of trade.[19] This allowed the provision to function logically as a rule (whenever a court finds that the restraint is "unreasonable" it is bound to hold the contract invalid) and substantially as a principle (a court must take into account a variety of other principles and policies in determining whether a particular restraint in particular economic circumstances is "unreasonable").

Words like "reasonable," "negligent," "unjust," and "significant" often perform just this function. Each of these terms makes the application of the rule which contains it depend to some extent upon principles or policies lying beyond the rule, and in this way makes that rule itself more like a principle. But they do not quite turn the rule into a principle, because even the least confining of these terms restricts the *kind* of other principles and policies on which the rule depends. If we are bound by a rule that says that "unreasonable" contracts are void, or that grossly "unfair" contracts will not be enforced, much more judgment is required than if the quoted terms were omitted. But suppose a case in which some consideration of policy or principle suggests that a contract should be enforced even though its restraint is not reasonable, or even though it is grossly unfair. Enforcing these contracts would be forbidden by our rules, and thus permitted only if these rules were abandoned or modified. If we were dealing, however, not with a rule but with a policy against enforcing unreasonable contracts, or a principle that unfair contracts ought not to be enforced, the contracts could be enforced without alteration of the law.

---

[19] *Standard Oil v. United States,* 221 U.S. 1, 60 (1911); *United States v. American Tobacco Co.,* 221 U.S. 106, 180 (1911).

4. PRINCIPLES AND THE CONCEPT OF LAW

Once we identify legal principles as separate sorts of standards, different from legal rules, we are suddenly aware of them all around us. Law teachers teach them, lawbooks cite them, legal historians celebrate them. But they seem most energetically at work, carrying most weight, in difficult lawsuits like *Riggs* and *Henningsen*. In cases like these, principles play an essential part in arguments supporting judgments about particular legal rights and obligations. After the case is decided, we may say that the case stands for a particular rule (e.g., the rule that one who murders is not eligible to take under the will of his victim). But the rule does not exist before the case is decided; the court cites principles as its justification for adopting and applying a new rule. In *Riggs,* the court cited the principle that no man may profit from his own wrong as a background standard against which to read the statute of wills and in this way justified a new interpretation of that statute. In *Henningsen,* the court cited a variety of intersecting principles and policies as authority for a new rule respecting manufacturers' liability for automobile defects.

An analysis of the concept of legal obligation must therefore account for the important role of principles in reaching particular decisions of law. There are two very different tacks we might take:

a. We might treat legal principles the way we treat legal rules and say that some principles are binding as law and must be taken into account by judges and lawyers who make decisions of legal obligation. If we took this tack, we should say that in the United States, at least, the "law" includes principles as well as rules.

b. We might, on the other hand, deny that principles can be binding the way some rules are. We would say, instead, that in cases like *Riggs* or *Henningsen* the judge reaches beyond the rules that he is bound to apply (reaches, that is, beyond the "law") for extralegal principles he is free to follow if he wishes.

One might think that there is not much difference between these two lines of attack, that it is only a verbal question of how one wants to use the word "law." But that is a mistake, because the choice between these two accounts has the greatest consequences for an analysis of legal obligation. It is a choice between two *concepts* of a legal principle, a choice we can clarify by comparing it to a choice we might make between two concepts of a legal rule. We sometimes say of someone that he "makes it a rule" to do something, when we mean that he has chosen to follow a certain practice. We might say that someone has made it a rule, for example, to run a mile before breakfast because he wants to be healthy and believes in a regimen. We do not mean, when we say this, that he is *bound* by the rule that he must run a mile before breakfast, or even that he regards it as binding upon him. Accepting a rule as binding is something different from making it a rule to do something. If we use Hart's example again, there is a difference between saying that Englishmen make it a rule to see a movie once a week, and saying that the English have a rule that one must see a movie once a week. The second implies that if an Englishman does not follow the rule, he is subject to criticism or censure, but the first does not. The first does not exclude the possibility of a *sort* of criticism—we can say that one who does not see movies is neglecting his education—but we do not suggest that he is doing something wrong *just* in not following the rule.[20]

If we think of the judges of a community as a group, we could describe the rules of law they follow in these two different ways. We could say, for instance, that in a certain state the judges make it a rule not to enforce wills unless there are three witnesses. This would not imply that the rare judge who enforces such a will is doing anything wrong just for that reason. On the other hand we can say that in that state a rule of law requires judges not to enforce such wills; this does imply that a judge who enforces them is doing

---

[20]The distinction is in substance the same as that made by Rawls, "Two Concepts of Rules," 64 *Philosophical Review* 3 (1955).

something wrong. Hart, Austin and other positivists, of course, would insist on this latter account of legal rules; they would not at all be satisfied with the "make it a rule" account. It is not a verbal question of which account is right. It is a question of which describes the social situation more accurately. Other important issues turn on which description we accept. If judges simply "make it a rule" not to enforce certain contracts, for example, then we cannot say, before the decision, that anyone is "entitled" to that result, and that proposition cannot enter into any justification we might offer for the decision.

The two lines of attack on principles parallel these two accounts of rules. The first tack treats principles as binding upon judges, so that they are wrong not to apply the principles when they are pertinent. The second tack treats principles as summaries of what most judges "make it a principle" to do when forced to go beyond the standards that bind them. The choice between these approaches will affect, perhaps even determine, the answer we can give to the question whether the judge in a hard case like *Riggs* or *Henningsen* is attempting to enforce preexisting legal rights and obligations. If we take the first tack, we are still free to argue that because such judges are applying binding legal standards they are enforcing legal rights and obligations. But if we take the second, we are out of court on that issue, and we must acknowledge that the murderer's family in *Riggs* and the manufacturer in *Henningsen* were deprived of their property by an act of judicial discretion applied *ex post facto*. This may not shock many readers—the notion of judicial discretion has percolated through the legal community—but it does illustrate one of the most nettlesome of the puzzles that drive philosophers to worry about legal obligation. If taking property away in cases like these cannot be justified by appealing to an established obligation, another justification must be found, and nothing satisfactory has yet been supplied.

In my skeleton diagram of positivism, previously set out, I listed the doctrine of judicial discretion as the second tenet. Positivists hold that when a case is not covered by a clear rule, a judge must exercise his discretion to decide that case by

what amounts to a fresh piece of legislation. There may be an important connection between this doctrine and the question of which of the two approaches to legal principles we must take. We shall therefore want to ask whether the doctrine is correct, and whether it implies the second approach, as it seems on its face to do. En route to these issues, however, we shall have to polish our understanding of the concept of discretion. I shall try to show how certain confusions about that concept and in particular a failure to discriminate different senses in which it is used, account for the popularity of the doctrine of discretion. I shall argue that in the sense in which the doctrine does have a bearing on our treatment of principles, it is entirely unsupported by the arguments the positivists use to defend it.

5. DISCRETION

The concept of discretion was lifted by the positivists from ordinary language, and to understand it we must put it back in *habitat* for a moment. What does it mean, in ordinary life, to say that someone "has discretion"? The first thing to notice is that the concept is out of place in all but very special contexts. For example, you would not say that I either do or do not have discretion to choose a house for my family. It is not true that I have "no discretion" in making that choice, and yet it would be almost equally misleading to say that I do have discretion. The concept of discretion is at home in only one sort of context; when someone is in general charged with making decisions subject to standards set by a particular authority. It makes sense to speak of the discretion of a sergeant who is subject to orders of superiors, or the discretion of a sports official or contest judge who is governed by a rule book or the terms of the contest. Discretion, like the hole in a doughnut, does not exist except as an area left open by a surrounding belt of restriction. It is therefore a relative concept. It always makes sense to ask, "Discretion under which standards?" or "Discretion as to which authority?" Generally the context will make the answer to this plain, but in some cases the official may have discretion from one standpoint though not from another.

Like almost all terms, the precise meaning of "discretion" is affected by features of the context. The term is always colored by the background of understood information against which it is used. Although the shadings are many, it will be helpful for us to recognize some gross distinctions.

Sometimes we use "discretion" in a weak sense, simply to say that for some reason the standards an official must apply cannot be applied mechanically but demand the use of judgment. We use this weak sense when the context does not already make that clear, when the background our audience assumes does not contain that piece of information. Thus we might say, "The sergeant's orders left him a great deal of discretion," to those who do not know what the sergeant's orders were or who do not know something that made those orders vague or hard to carry out. It would make perfect sense to add, by way of amplification, that the lieutenant had ordered the sergeant to take his five most experienced men on patrol but that it was hard to determine which were the most experienced.

Sometimes we use the term in a different weak sense, to say only that some official has final authority to make a decision and cannot be reviewed and reversed by any other official. We speak this way when the official is part of a hierarchy of officials structured so that some have higher authority but in which the patterns of authority are different for different classes of decision. Thus we might say that in baseball certain decisions, like the decision whether the ball or the runner reached second base first, are left to the discretion of the second base umpire, if we mean that on this issue the head umpire has no power to substitute his own judgment if he disagrees.

I call both of these senses weak to distinguish them from a stronger sense. We use "discretion" sometimes not merely to say that an official must use judgment in applying the standards set him by authority, or that no one will review that exercise of judgment, but to say that on some issues he is simply not bound by standards set by the authority in question. In this sense we say that a sergeant has discretion who has been told to pick any five men for patrol he chooses or that a judge in a dog show has discretion to judge airedales before

boxers if the rules do not stipulate an order of events. We use this sense not to comment on the vagueness or difficulty of the standards, or on who has the final word in applying them, but on their range and the decisions they purport to control. If the sergeant is told to take the five most experienced men, he does not have discretion in this strong sense because that order purports to govern his decision. The boxing referee who must decide which fighter has been the more aggressive does not have discretion, in the strong sense, for the same reason.[21]

If anyone said that the sergeant or the referee had discretion in these cases, we should have to understand him, if the context permitted, as using the term in one of the weak senses. Suppose, for example, the lieutenant ordered the sergeant to select the five men he deemed most experienced, and then added that the sergeant had discretion to choose them. Or the rules provided that the referee should award the round to the more aggressive fighter, with discretion in selecting him. We should have to understand these statements in the second weak sense, as speaking to the question of review of the decision. The first weak sense—that the decisions take judgment—would be otiose, and the third, strong sense is excluded by the statements themselves.

We must avoid one tempting confusion. The strong sense of discretion is not tantamount to license, and does not exclude criticism. Almost any situation in which a person acts (including those in which there is no question of decision under special authority, and so no question of discretion) makes relevant certain standards of rationality, fairness, and effectiveness. We criticize each other's acts in terms of these standards, and there is no reason not to do so when the acts are within the center rather than beyond the perimeter of the doughnut of special authority. So we can say that

---

[21]I have not spoken of that jurisprudential favorite, "limited" discretion, because that concept presents no special difficulties if we remember the relativity of discretion. Suppose the sergeant is told to choose from "amongst" experienced men, or to "take experience into account." We might say either that he has (limited) discretion in picking his patrol, or (full) discretion to either pick amongst experienced men or decide what else to take into account.

the sergeant who was given discretion (in the strong sense) to pick a patrol did so stupidly or maliciously or carelessly, or that the judge who had discretion in the order of viewing dogs made a mistake because he took boxers first although there were only three airedales and many more boxers. An official's discretion means not that he is free to decide without recourse to standards of sense and fairness, but only that his decision is not controlled by a standard furnished by the particular authority we have in mind when we raise the question of discretion. Of course this latter sort of freedom is important; that is why we have the strong sense of discretion. Someone who has discretion in this third sense can be criticized, but not for being disobedient, as in the case of the soldier. He can be said to have made a mistake, but not to have deprived a participant of a decision to which he was entitled, as in the case of a sports official or contest judge.

We may now return, with these observations in hand, to the positivists' doctrine of judicial discretion. That doctrine argues that if a case is not controlled by an established rule, the judge must decide it by exercising discretion. We want to examine this doctrine and to test its bearing on our treatment of principles; but first we must ask in which sense of discretion we are to understand it.

Some nominalists argue that judges always have discretion, even when a clear rule is in point, because judges are ultimately the final arbiters of the law. This doctrine of discretion uses the second weak sense of that term, because it makes the point that no higher authority reviews the decisions of the highest court. It therefore has no bearing on the issue of how we account for principles, any more than it bears on how we account for rules.

The positivists do not mean their doctrine this way, because they say that a judge has no discretion when a clear and established rule is available. If we attend to the positivists' arguments for the doctrine we may suspect that they use discretion in the first weak sense to mean only that judges must sometimes exercise judgment in applying legal standards. Their arguments call attention to the fact that some rules of law are vague (Professor Hart, for example, says that all rules of law

have "open texture"), and that some cases arise (like *Henningsen*) in which no established rule seems to be suitable. They emphasize that judges must sometimes agonize over points of law, and that two equally trained and intelligent judges will often disagree.

These points are easily made; they are commonplace to anyone who has any familiarity with law. Indeed, that is the difficulty with assuming that positivists mean to use "discretion" in this weak sense. The proposition that when no clear rule is available discretion in the sense of judgment must be used is a tautology. It has no bearing, moreover, on the problem of how to account for legal principles. It is perfectly consistent to say that the judge in *Riggs*, for example, had to use judgment, and that he was bound to follow the principle that no man may profit from his own wrong. The positivists speak as if their doctrine of judicial discretion is an insight rather than a tautology, and as if it does have a bearing on the treatment of principles. Hart, for example, says that when the judge's discretion is in play, we can no longer speak of his being bound by standards, but must speak rather of what standards he "characteristically uses."[22] Hart thinks that when judges have discretion, the principles they cite must be treated on our second approach, as what courts "make it a principle" to do.

It therefore seems that positivists, at least sometimes, take their doctrine in the third, strong sense of discretion. In that sense it does bear on the treatment of principles; indeed, in that sense it is nothing less than a restatement of our second approach. It is the same thing to say that when a judge runs out of rules he has discretion, in the sense that he is not bound by any standards from the authority of law, as to say that the legal standards judges cite other than rules are not binding on them.

So we must examine the doctrine of judicial discretion in the strong sense. (I shall henceforth use the term "discretion" in that sense.) Do the principles judges cited in cases like *Riggs* or *Henningsen* control their decisions, as the sergeant's

---

[22] H. L. A. Hart, *The Concept of Law*, 144 (1961).

orders to take the most experienced men or the referee's duty to choose the more aggressive fighter control the decisions of these officials? What arguments could a positivist supply to show that they do not?

1. A positivist might argue that principles cannot be binding or obligatory. That would be a mistake. It is always a question, of course, whether any particular principle is *in fact* binding upon some legal official. But there is nothing in the logical character of a principle that renders it incapable of binding him. Suppose that the judge in *Henningsen* had failed to take any account of the principle that automobile manufacturers have a special obligation to their consumers, or the principle that the courts seek to protect those whose bargaining position is weak, but had simply decided for the defendant by citing the principle of freedom of contract without more. His critics would not have been content to point out that he had not taken account of considerations that other judges have been attending to for some time. Most would have said that it was his duty to take the measure of these principles and that the plaintiff was entitled to have him do so. We mean no more, when we say that a *rule* is binding upon a judge, than that he must follow it if it applies, and that if he does not he will on that account have made a mistake.

   It will not do to say that in a case like *Henningsen* the court is only "morally" obligated to take particular principles into account, or that it is "institutionally" obligated, or obligated as a matter of judicial "craft," or something of that sort. The question will still remain why this type of obligation (whatever we call it) is different from the obligation that rules impose upon judges, and why it entitles us to say that principles and policies are not part of the law but are merely extralegal standards "courts characteristically use."

2. A positivist might argue that even though some principles are binding, in the sense that the judge must take them into account, they cannot determine a particular result. This is a harder argument to assess because it is not clear what it means for a standard to "determine" a result. Perhaps it means that the standard *dictates* the result whenever it applies so that nothing else counts. If so, then it is certainly true that the individual principles do not determine results, but that is only another way of saying that principles are not rules. Only rules dictate results, come what may. When a contrary result has been reached, the rule has been abandoned or changed. Principles do not work that way; they incline a decision one way, though not conclusively, and they survive intact when they do not prevail. This seems no reason for concluding that judges who must reckon with principles have discretion because a set of principles *can* dictate a result. If a judge believes that principles he is bound to recognize point in one direction and that principles pointing in the other direction, if any, are not of equal weight, then he must decide accordingly, just as he must follow what he believes to be a binding rule. He may, of course, be wrong in his assessment of the principles, but he may also be wrong in his judgment that the rule is binding. The sergeant and the referee, we might add, are often in the same boat. No one factor dictates which soldiers are the most experienced or which fighter the more aggressive. These officials must make judgments of the relative weights of these various factors; they do not on that account have discretion.

3. A positivist might argue that principles cannot count as law because their authority, and even more so their weight, are congenitally *controversial*. It is true that generally we cannot *demonstrate* the authority or weight of a particular principle as we can sometimes demonstrate the validity of a rule by locating it in an act of Congress or in the opinion of an authoritative court. Instead, we make a case for a principle, and for its weight, by appealing to an amalgam of practice and other principles in which the implications of legislative and judicial history figure along with appeals to community practices and understandings. There is no litmus paper for testing

the soundness of such a case—it is a matter of judgment, and reasonable men may disagree. But again this does not distinguish the judge from other officials who do not have discretion. The sergeant has no litmus paper for experience, the referee none for aggressiveness. Neither of these has discretion, because he is bound to reach an understanding, controversial or not, of what his orders or the rules require, and to act on that understanding. That is the judge's duty as well.

Of course, if the positivists are right in another of their doctrines—the theory that in each legal system there is an ultimate *test* for binding law like Professor Hart's rule of recognition—it follows that principles are not binding law. But the incompatibility of principles with the positivists' theory can hardly be taken as an argument that principles must be treated any particular way. That begs the question; we are interested in the status of principles because we want to evaluate the positivists' model. The positivist cannot defend his theory of a rule of recognition by fiat; if principles are not amenable to a test he must show some other reason why they cannot count as law. Since principles seem to play a role in arguments about legal obligation (witness, again, *Riggs* and *Henningsen*), a model that provides for that role has some initial advantage over one that excludes it, and the latter cannot properly be inveighed in its own support.

These are the most obvious of the arguments a positivist might use for the doctrine of discretion in the strong sense, and for the second approach to principles. I shall mention one strong counterargument against that doctrine and in favor of the first approach. Unless at least some principles are acknowledged to be binding upon judges, requiring them as a set to reach particular decisions, then no rules, or very few rules, can be said to be binding upon them either.

In most American jurisdictions, and now in England also, the higher courts not infrequently reject established rules. Common law rules—those developed by earlier court decisions—are sometimes overruled directly, and sometimes radically altered by further development. Statutory rules are

subjected to interpretation and reinterpretation, sometimes even when the result is not to carry out what is called the "legislative intent."[23] If courts had discretion to change established rules, then these rules would of course not be binding upon them, and so would not be law on the positivists' model. The positivist must therefore argue that there are standards, themselves binding upon judges, that determine when a judge may overrule or alter an established rule, and when he may not.

When, then, is a judge permitted to change an existing rule of law? Principles figure in the answer in two ways. First, it is necessary, though not sufficient, that the judge find that the change would advance some principle, which principle thus justifies the change. In *Riggs* the change (a new interpretation of the statute of wills) was justified by the principle that no man should profit from his own wrong; in *Henningsen* the previously recognized rules about automobile manufacturers' liability were altered on the basis of the principles I quoted from the opinion of the court.

But not any principle will do to justify a change, or no rule would ever be safe. There must be some principles that count and others that do not, and there must be some principles that count for more than others. It could not depend on the judge's own preferences amongst a sea of respectable extralegal standards, any one in principle eligible, because if that were the case we could not say that any rules were binding. We could always imagine a judge whose preferences amongst extralegal standards were such as would justify a shift or radical reinterpretation of even the most entrenched rule.

Second, any judge who proposes to change existing doctrine must take account of some important standards that argue against departures from established doctrine, and these standards are also for the most part principles. They include the doctrine of "legislative supremacy," a set of principles that require the courts to pay a qualified deference to the acts of the legislature. They also

---

[23]See Wellington and Albert, "Statutory Interpretation and the Political Process: A Comment on Sinclair v. Atkinson," 72 *Yale L. J.* 1547 (1963).

include the doctrine of precedent, another set of principles reflecting the equities and efficiencies of consistency. The doctrines of legislative supremacy and precedent incline toward the *status quo,* each within its sphere, but they do not command it. Judges are not free, however, to pick and choose amongst the principles and policies that make up these doctrines—if they were, again, no rule could be said to be binding.

Consider, therefore, what someone implies who says that a particular rule is binding. He may imply that the rule is affirmatively supported by principles the court is not free to disregard, and which are collectively more weighty than other principles that argue for a change. If not, he implies that any change would be condemned by a combination of conservative principles of legislative supremacy and precedent that the court is not free to ignore. Very often, he will imply both, for the conservative principles, being principles and not rules, are usually not powerful enough to save a common law rule or an aging statute that is entirely unsupported by substantive principles the court is bound to respect. Either of these implications, of course, treats a body of principles and policies as law in the sense that rules are; it treats them as standards binding upon the officials of a community, controlling their decisions of legal right and obligation.

We are left with this issue. If the positivists' theory of judicial discretion is either trivial because it uses "discretion" in a weak sense, or unsupported because the various arguments we can supply in its defense fall short, why have so many careful and intelligent lawyers embraced it? We can have no confidence in our treatment of that theory unless we can deal with that question. It is not enough to note (although perhaps it contributes to the explanation) that "discretion" has different senses that may be confused. We do not confuse these senses when we are not thinking about law.

Part of the explanation, at least, lies in a lawyer's natural tendency to associate laws and rules, and to think of "the law" as a collection or system of rules. Roscoe Pound, who diagnosed this tendency long ago, though that English-speaking lawyers were tricked into it by the fact that

English uses the same word, changing only the article, for "a law" and "the law."[24] (Other languages, on the contrary, use two words: "loi" and "droit," for example, and "Gesetz" and "Recht.") This may have had its effect, with the English-speaking positivists, because the expression "a law" certainly does suggest a rule. But the principal reason for associating law with rules runs deeper, and lies, I think, in the fact that legal education has for a long time consisted of teaching and examining those established rules that form the cutting edge of law.

In any event, if a lawyer thinks of law as a system of rules, and yet recognizes, as he must, that judges change old rules and introduce new ones, he will come naturally to the theory of judicial discretion in the strong sense. In those other systems of rules with which he has experience (like games), the rules are the only special authority that govern official decisions, so that if an umpire could change a rule, he would have discretion as to the subject matter of that rule. Any principles umpires might mention when changing the rules would represent only their "characteristic" preferences. Positivists treat law like baseball revised in this way.

There is another, more subtle consequence of this initial assumption that law is a system of rules. When the positivists do attend to principles and policies, they treat them as rules *manquées.* They assume that *if* they are standards of law they must be rules, and so they read them as standards that are trying to be rules. When a positivist hears someone argue that legal principles are part of the law, he understands this to be an argument for what he calls the "higher law" theory, that these principles are the rules of a law about the law.[25] He refutes this theory by pointing out that these "rules" are sometimes followed and sometimes not, that for every "rule" like "no man shall profit from his own wrong" there is another competing "rule" like "the law favors security of title," and that there is no way to test the

[24]R. Pound, *An Introduction to the Philosophy of Law* 56 (rev. ed. 1954).
[25]See, e.g., Dickinson, "The Law Behind Law" (pts. 1 & 2), 29, *Columbia Law Review* 112, 254 (1929).

validity of "rules" like these. He concludes that these principles and policies are not valid rules of a law above the law, which is true, because they are not rules at all. He also concludes that they are extralegal standards which each judge selects according to his own lights in the exercise of his discretion, which is false. It is as if a zoologist had proved that fish are not mammals, and then concluded that they are really only plants.

6. THE RULE OF RECOGNITION

This discussion was provoked by our two competing accounts of legal principles. We have been exploring the second account, which the positivists seem to adopt through their doctrine of judicial discretion, and we have discovered grave difficulties. It is time to return to the fork in the road. What if we adopt the first approach? What would the consequences of this be for the skeletal structure of positivism? Of course we should have to drop the second tenet, the doctrine of judicial discretion (or, in the alternative, to make plain that the doctrine is to be read merely to say that judges must often exercise judgment). Would we also have to abandon or modify the first tenet, the proposition that law is distinguished by tests of the sort that can be set out in a master rule like Professor Hart's rule of recognition? If principles of the *Riggs* and *Henningsen* sort are to count as law, and we are nevertheless to preserve the notion of a master rule for law, then we must be able to deploy some test that all (and only) the principles that do count as law meet. Let us begin with the test Hart suggests for identifying valid *rules* of law, to see whether these can be made to work for principles as well.

Most rules of law, according to Hart, are valid because some competent institution enacted them. Some were created by a legislature, in the form of statutory enactments. Others were created by judges who formulated them to decide particular cases, and thus established them as precedents for the future. But this test of pedigree will not work for the *Riggs* and *Henningsen* principles. The origin of these as legal principles lies not in a particular decision of some legislature or court, but in a sense of appropriateness developed in the profession and the public over time. Their continued power depends upon this sense of appropriateness being sustained. If it no longer seemed unfair to allow people to profit by their wrongs, or fair to place special burdens upon oligopolies that manufacture potentially dangerous machines, these principles would no longer play much of a role in new cases, even if they had never been overruled or repealed. (Indeed, it hardly makes sense to speak of principles like these as being "overruled" or "repealed." When they decline they are eroded, not torpedoed.)

True, if we were challenged to back up our claim that some principle is a principle of law, we would mention any prior cases in which that principle was cited, or figured in the argument. We would also mention any statute that seemed to exemplify that principle (even better if the principle was cited in the preamble of the statute, or in the committee reports or other legislative documents that accompanied it). Unless we could find some such institutional support, we would probably fail to make out our case, and the more support we found, the more weight we could claim for the principle.

Yet we could not devise any formula for testing how much and what kind of institutional support is necessary to make a principle a legal principle, still less to fix its weight at a particular order of magnitude. We argue for a particular principle by grappling with a whole set of shifting, developing and interacting standards (themselves principles rather than rules) about institutional responsibility, statutory interpretation, the persuasive force of various sorts of precedent, the relation of all these to contemporary moral practices, and hosts of other such standards. We could not bolt all of these together into a single "rule," even a complex one, and if we could the result would bear little relation to Hart's picture of a rule of recognition, which is the picture of a fairly stable master rule specifying "some feature or features possession of which by a suggested rule is taken as a conclusive affirmative indication that it is a rule ..."[26]

---

[26]H. L. A. Hart, *The Concept of Law* 92 (1961).

Moreover, the techniques we apply in arguing for another principle do not stand (as Hart's rule of recognition is designed to) on an entirely different level from the principles they support. Hart's sharp distinction between acceptance and validity does not hold. If we are arguing for the principle that a man should not profit from his own wrong, we could cite the acts of courts and legislatures that exemplify it, but this speaks as much to the principle's acceptance as its validity. (It seems odd to speak of a principle as being valid at all, perhaps because validity is an all-or-nothing concept, appropriate for rules, but inconsistent with a principle's dimension of weight.) If we are asked (as we might well be) to defend the particular doctrine of precedent, or the particular technique of statutory interpretation, that we used in this argument, we should certainly cite the practice of others in using that doctrine or technique. But we should also cite other general principles that we believe support that practice, and this introduces a note of validity into the chord of acceptance. We might argue, for example, that the use we make of earlier cases and statutes is supported by a particular analysis of the point of the practice of legislation or the doctrine of precedent, or by the principles of democratic theory, or by a particular position on the proper division of authority between national and local institutions, or something else of that sort. Nor is this path of support a one-way street leading to some ultimate principle resting on acceptance alone. Our principles of legislation, precedent, democracy, or federalism might be challenged too; and if they were we should argue for them, not only in terms of practice, but in terms of each other and in terms of the implications of trends of judicial and legislative decisions, even though this last would involve appealing to those same doctrines of interpretation we justified through the principles we are now trying to support. At this level of abstraction, in other words, principles rather hang together than link together.

So even though principles draw support from the official acts of legal institutions, they do not have a simple or direct enough connection with these acts to frame that connection in terms of criteria specified by some ultimate master rule of recognition. Is there any other route by which principles might be brought under such a rule?

Hart does say that a master rule might designate as law not only rules enacted by particular legal institutions, but rules established by *custom* as well. He has in mind a problem that bothered other positivists, including Austin. Many of our most ancient legal rules were never explicitly created by a legislature or a court. When they made their first appearance in legal opinions and texts, they were treated as already being part of the law because they represented the customary practice of the community, or some specialized part of it, like the business community. (The examples ordinarily given are rules of mercantile practice, like the rules governing what rights arise under a standard form of commercial paper.)[27] Since Austin thought that all law was the command of a determinate sovereign, he held that these customary practices were not law until the courts (as agents of the sovereign) recognized them, and that the courts were indulging in a fiction in pretending otherwise. But that seemed arbitrary. If everyone thought custom might in itself be law, the fact that Austin's theory said otherwise was not persuasive.

Hart reversed Austin on this point. The master rule, he says, might stipulate that some custom counts as law even before the courts recognize it. But he does not face the difficulty this raises for his general theory because he does not attempt to set out the criteria a master rule might use for this purpose. It cannot use, as its only criterion, the provision that the community regard the practice as *morally* binding, for this would not distinguish legal customary rules from moral customary rules, and of course not all of the community's long-standing customary moral obligations are enforced at law. If, on the other hand, the test is whether the community regards the customary practice as *legally* binding, the whole point of

---

[27]See Note, "Custom and Trade Usage: Its Application to Commercial Dealings and the Common Law," 55 *Columbia Law Review* 1192 (1955), and materials cited therein at 1193 n.l. As that note makes plain, the actual practices of courts in recognizing trade customs follow the pattern of applying a set of general principles and policies rather than a test that could be captured as part of a rule of recognition.

the master rule is undercut, at least for this class of legal rules. The master rule, says Hart, marks the transformation from a primitive society to one with law, because it provides a test for determining social rules of law other than by measuring their acceptance. But if the master rule says merely that whatever other rules the community accepts as legally binding are legally binding, then it provides no such test at all, beyond the test we should use were there no master rule. The master rule becomes (for these cases) a nonrule of recognition; we might as well say that every primitive society has a secondary rule of recognition, namely the rule that whatever is accepted as binding is binding. Hart himself, in discussing international law, ridicules the idea that such a rule could be a rule of recognition, by describing the proposed rule as "an empty repetition of the mere fact that the society concerned … observes certain standards of conduct as obligatory rules."[28]

Hart's treatment of custom amounts, indeed, to a confession that there are at least some rules of law that are not binding because they are valid under standards laid down by a master rule but are binding—like the master rule—because they are accepted as binding by the community. This chips at the neat pyramidal architecture we admired in Hart's theory: we can no longer say that only the master rule is binding because of its acceptance, all other rules being valid under its terms.

This is perhaps only a chip, because the customary rules Hart has in mind are no longer a very significant part of the law. But it does suggest that Hart would be reluctant to widen the damage by

bringing under the head of "custom" all those crucial principles and policies we have been discussing. If he were to call these part of the law and yet admit that the only test of their force lies in the degree to which they are accepted as law by the community or some part thereof, he would very sharply reduce that area of the law over which his master rule held any dominion. It is not just that all the principles and policies would escape its sway, though that would be bad enough. Once these principles and policies are accepted as law, and thus as standards judges must follow in determining legal obligations, it would follow that *rules* like those announced for the first time in *Riggs* and *Henningsen* owe their force at least in part to the authority of principles and policies, and so not entirely to the master rule of recognition.

So we cannot adapt Hart's version of positivism by modifying his rule of recognition to embrace principles. No tests of pedigree, relating principles to acts of legislation, can be formulated, nor can his concept of customary law, itself an exception to the first tenet of positivism, be made to serve without abandoning that tenet altogether. One more possibility must be considered, however. If no rule of recognition can provide a test for identifying principles, why not say that principles are ultimate, and *form* the rule of recognition of our law? The answer to the general question "What is valid law in an American jurisdiction?" would then require us to state all the principles (as well as ultimate constitutional rules) in force in that jurisdiction at the time, together with appropriate assignments of weight. A positivist might then regard the complete set of these standards as the rule of recognition of the jurisdiction. This solution has the attraction of paradox, but of course it is an unconditional surrender. If we simply designate our rule of recognition by the phrase "the complete set of principles in force," we achieve only the tautology that law is law. If, instead, we tried actually to list all the principles in force we would fail. They are controversial, their weight is all important, they are numberless, and they shift and change so fast that the start of our list would be obsolete before we reached the middle. Even if we succeeded, we

---

[28]H. L. Hart, *The Concept of Law* 230 (1961). A master rule might specify some particular feature of a custom that is independent of the community's attitude; it might provide, for example, that all customs of very great age, or all customs having to do with negotiable instruments count as law. I can think of no such features that in fact distinguish the customs that have been recognized as law in England or America, however. Some customs that are not legally enforceable are older than some that are, some practices relating to commercial paper are enforced and others not, and so forth. In any event, even if a distinguishing feature were found that identified all rules of law established by custom, it would remain unlikely that such a feature could be found for principles which vary widely in their subject matter and pedigree and some of which are of very recent origin.

would not have a key for law because there would be nothing left for our key to unlock.

I conclude that if we treat principles as law we must reject the positivists' first tenet, that the law of a community is distinguished from other social standards by some test in the form of a master rule. We have already decided that we must then abandon the second tenet—the doctrine of judicial discretion—or clarify it into triviality. What of the third tenet, the positivists' theory of legal obligation?

This theory holds that a legal obligation exists when (and only when) an established rule of law imposes such an obligation. It follows from this that in a hard case—when no such established rule can be found—there is no legal obligation until the judge creates a new rule for the future. The judge may apply that new rule to the parties in the case, but this is *ex post facto* legislation, not the enforcement of an existing obligation.

The positivists' doctrine of discretion (in the strong sense) required this view of legal obligation, because if a judge has discretion there can be no legal right or obligation—no entitlement—that he must enforce. Once we abandon that doctrine, however, and treat principles as law, we raise the possibility that a legal obligation might be imposed by a constellation of principles as well as by an established rule. We might want to say that a legal obligation exists whenever the case supporting such an obligation, in terms of binding legal principles of different sorts, is stronger than the case against it.

Of course, many questions would have to be answered before we could accept that view of legal obligation. If there is no rule of recognition, no test for law in that sense, how do we decide which principles are to count, and how much, in making such a case? How do we decide whether one case is better than another? If legal obligation rests on an undemonstrable judgment of that sort, how can it provide a justification for a judicial decision that one party had a legal obligation? Does this view of obligation square with the way lawyers, judges and laymen speak, and is it consistent with our attitudes about moral obligation? Does this analysis help us to deal with the classical jurisprudential puzzles about the nature of law?

These questions must be faced, but even the questions promise more than positivism provides. Positivism, on its own thesis, stops short of just those puzzling, hard cases that send us to look for theories of law. When we read these cases, the positivist remits us to a doctrine of discretion that leads nowhere and tells nothing. His picture of law as a system of rules has exercised a tenacious hold on our imagination, perhaps through its very simplicity. If we shake ourselves loose from this model of rules, we may be able to build a model truer to the complexity and sophistication of our own practices.

11   Negative and Positive Positivism

JULES L. COLEMAN

I am indebted to William Wilcox, David Lyons, John Koethe, and especially Ken Kress and an anonymous referee for their thoughtful comments on earlier drafts of this paper. I am also grateful to those who attended presentations of earlier drafts of this paper at Cornell University and the University of Toronto for their helpful remarks.

Every theory about the nature or essence of law purports to provide a standard, usually in the form of a statement of necessary and sufficient conditions, for determining which of a community's norms constitute its law. For example, the naïve version of legal realism maintains that the law of a community is constituted by the official

From *Journal of Legal Studies* 11 (January 1982), pp. 139–64. © 1982 by The University of Chicago. All rights reserved.

pronouncements of judges. For the early positivists like Austin, law consists in the commands of a sovereign, properly so-called. For substantive natural law theory, in every conceivable legal system, being a true principle of morality is a necessary condition of legality for at least some norms. Legal positivism of the sort associated with H. L. A. Hart maintains that, in every community where law exists, there exists a standard that determines which of the community's norms are legal ones. Following Hart, this standard is usually referred to as a rule of recognition. If all that positivism meant by a rule of recognition were "the standard in every community by which a community's legal norms were made determinate," every theory of law would be reducible to one or another version of positivism. Which form of positivism each would take would depend on the particular substantive conditions of legality that each theory set out. Legal positivism would be true analytically, since it would be impossible to conceive of a theory of law that did not satisfy the minimal conditions for a rule of recognition. Unfortunately, the sort of truth legal positivism would then reveal would be an uninteresting one.

In order to distinguish a rule of recognition in the positivist sense from other statements of the conditions of legality, and therefore to distinguish positivism from alternative jurisprudential theses, additional constraints must be placed on the rule of recognition. Candidates for these constraints fall into two categories: restrictions on the conditions of legality set out in a rule of recognition; and constraints on the possible sources of authority (or normativity) of the rule of recognition.

An example of the first sort of constraint is expressed by the requirement that in every community the conditions of legality must be ones of pedigree or form, not substance or content. Accordingly, for a rule specifying the conditions of legality in any society to constitute a rule of recognition in the positivist sense, legal normativity under it must be determined, for example, by a norm's being enacted in the requisite fashion by a proper authority.

The claim that the authority of the rule of recognition is a matter of its acceptance by officials, rather than its truth as a normative principle, and the related claim that judicial duty under a

rule of recognition is one of conventional practice rather than critical morality, express constraints of the second sort.

Ronald Dworkin expresses this second constraint as the claim that a rule of recognition in the positivist sense must be a social, rather than a normative, rule. A social rule is one whose authority is a matter of convention; the nature and scope of the duty it imposes is specified or constituted by an existing, convergent social practice. In contrast, a normative rule may impose an obligation or confer a right in the absence of the relevant practice or in the face of a contrary one. If a normative rule imposes an obligation, it does so because it is a correct principle of morality, not, *ex hypothesi*, because it corresponds to an accepted practice.

Dworkin, for one, conceives of the rule of recognition as subject to constraints of both sorts. His view is that only pedigree standards of legality can constitute rules of recognition, and that a rule of recognition must be a social rule.[1] Is legal positivism committed to either or both of these constraints on the rule of recognition?

I. NEGATIVE POSITIVISM

Candidates for constraints on the rule of recognition are motivated by the need to distinguish legal positivism from other jurisprudential theses: in particular, natural law theory. Positivism denies what natural law theory asserts: namely, a necessary connection between law and morality. I refer to the denial of a necessary or constitutive relationship between law and morality as the separability thesis. One way of asking whether positivism is committed to any particular kind of constraint on the rule of recognition is simply to ask whether any constraints on the rule are required by commitment to the separability thesis.

To answer this question we have to make some preliminary remarks concerning how we

---

[1]Dworkin's claim that positivism is committed to a pedigree standard of legality is too narrow. What he means to argue, I believe, is that positivism is committed to some form of "noncontentful" criterion of legality, of which a pedigree standard would be one. For ease of exposition, I will use "pedigree test" broadly to mean any sort of noncontentful criterion of legality.

are to understand both the rule of recognition and the separability thesis. The notion of a rule of recognition is ambiguous; it has both an epistemic and a semantic sense. In one sense, the rule of recognition is a standard which one can use to identify, validate, or discover a community's law. In another sense, the rule of recognition specifies the conditions a norm must satisfy to constitute part of a community's law. The same rule may or may not be a rule of recognition in both senses, since the rule one employs to determine the law need not be the same rule as the one that makes law determinate. This ambiguity between the epistemic and semantic interpretations of the rule of recognition pervades the literature and is responsible for a good deal of confusion about the essential claims of legal positivism. In my view, legal positivism is committed to the rule of recognition in the semantic sense at least; whether it is committed to the rule of recognition as a standard for identifying law (epistemic sense) is a question to which we shall return later.[2]

In the language that is fashionable in formal semantics, to say that the rule of recognition is a semantic rule is to say that it specifies the truth conditions for singular propositions of law of the form, "it is the law in C that P," where C is a particular community and P a putative statement of law. The question whether the separability thesis imposes substantive constraints on the rule of recognition is just the question whether the separability thesis restricts the conditions of legality for norms or the truth conditions for propositions of law.

The separability thesis is the claim that there exists at least one conceivable rule of recognition (and therefore one possible legal system) that does not specify truth as a moral principle among the truth conditions for any proposition of law.[3]

Consequently, a particular rule of recognition may specify truth as a moral principle as a truth condition for some or all propositions of law without violating the separability thesis, since it does not follow from the fact that, in one community in order to be law a norm must be a principle of morality, being a true principle of morality is a necessary condition of legality in all possible legal systems.

It is tempting to confuse the separability thesis with the very different claim that the law of a community is one thing and its morality another. This last claim is seriously ambiguous. In one sense, the claim that the law of a community is one thing and its morality another may amount to the very strong assertion that there exists no convergence between the norms that constitute a community's law and those that constitute its morality. Put this way, the thesis is an empirical one whose inadequacies are demonstrated by the shared legal and moral prohibitions against murder, theft, battery, and the like.

Instead, the claim may be that one can identify or discover a community's law without having recourse to discovering its morality. This is an epistemic claim about how, in a particular community, one might go about learning the law. It may well be that in some communities—even those in which every legal norm is a moral principle as well—one can learn which norms are law without regard to their status as principles of morality. Whether in every community this is the case depends on the available sources of legal knowledge, not on the existence of a conceptual relationship, if any, between law and morality.

A third interpretation of the thesis that a community's law is one thing and its morality another, the one Dworkin is anxious to ascribe to positivism, is that being a moral principle is not a truth condition for any proposition of law (in any community). Put this way the claim would be false, just in case "it is the law in C that P" (for any community, C, and any proposition of law, P) were true only if P stated a (true) principle of morality. Were the separability thesis understood this way, it would require particular substantive constraints on each rule of recognition, that is, no rule of recognition could specify truth as a moral

---

[2] See pp. 88–90 *infra*.

[3] The phrase "truth as a moral principle as a condition of legality" does seem a bit awkward. However, any other phrase, such as "morality as a condition of legality," or "moral content as a condition of legality" would be ambiguous, since it would be unclear whether the separability thesis were a claim about the relationship between law and critical morality or between law and conventional morality. My understanding of the separability thesis is as a denial of a constitutive relationship between law and critical morality. For another interpretation of the separability thesis see p. 92 *infra*.

principle among its conditions of legality. Were legal positivism committed to both the rule of recognition and to this interpretation of the claim that the law and morality of a community are distinct, Dworkin's arguments in Model of Rules I (MOR-I) would suffice to put it to rest.

However, were the claim that the law of a community is one thing and its morality another understood not as the claim that in every community law and morality are distinct, but as the assertion that they are conceptually distinguishable, it would be reducible to the separability thesis, for it would assert no more than the denial of a constitutive relationship between law and morality.

In sum, "the law of a community is one thing and its morality another," makes either a false factual claim, an epistemic claim about the sources of legal knowledge, or else it is reducible to the separability thesis. In no case does it warrant substantive constraints on particular rules of recognition.

Properly understood and adequately distinguished from the claim that the law and morality of a community are distinct, the separability thesis does not warrant substantive constraints on any particular rule of recognition. It does not follow, however, that the separability thesis imposes no constraints at all on any rule of recognition. The separability thesis commits positivism to the proposition that there exists at least one conceivable legal system in which the rule of recognition does not specify being a principle of morality among the truth conditions for any proposition of law. Positivism is true, then, just in case we can imagine a legal system in which being a principle of morality is not a condition of legality for any norm: that is, just as long as the idea of a legal system in which moral truth is not a necessary condition of legal validity is not self-contradictory.

The form of positivism generated by commitment to the rule of recognition as constrained by the separability thesis I call negative positivism to draw attention both to the character and the weakness of the claim it makes.[4] Because negative positivism is essentially a negative thesis, it cannot be undermined by counterexamples, any one of which will show only that, in some community or other, morality is a condition of legality at least for some norms.

II. POSITIVE POSITIVISM: LAW AS HARD FACTS

In MOR-I, Dworkin persuasively argues that in some communities moral principles have the force of law, though what makes them law is their truth or their acceptance as appropriate to the resolution of controversial disputes rather than their having been enacted in the appropriate way by the relevant authorities. These arguments would suffice to undermine positivism were it committed to the claim that truth as a moral principle could never constitute a truth condition for a proposition of law under any rule of recognition. The arguments are inadequate to undermine the separability thesis, which makes no claim about the truth conditions of any particular proposition of law in any particular community. The arguments in MOR-I, therefore, are inadequate to undermine negative positivism.

However, Dworkin's target in MOR-I is not really negative positivism; it is that version of positivism one would get by conjoining the rule of recognition with the requirement that the truth conditions for any proposition of law could not include reference to the morality of a norm. Moreover, in fairness to Dworkin, one has to evaluate his arguments in a broader context. In MOR-I Dworkin is anxious to demonstrate, not only the inadequacy of the separability thesis, but that of other essential tenets of positivism—or at least what Dworkin takes to be essential features of positivism—as well.

The fact that moral principles have the force of law, because they are appropriate, true, or accepted even though they are not formally enacted, establishes for Dworkin that: (1) the positivist's conception of law as rules must be abandoned; as must (2) the claim that judges exercise discretion—the authority to extend beyond the law to appeal to moral principles—to resolve controversial cases; and (3) the view that the law of every

---

[4]This seems to be in the form of positivism David Lyons advances to meet Dworkin's objections to positivism. Cf. David Lyons, Review: Principles, Positivism, and Legal Theory, 87 Yale L. J. 415 (1977).

community can be identified by use of a noncontroversial or pedigree test of legality.

The first claim of positivism must be abandoned because principles, as well as rules, constitute legal norms; the second because, while positivists conceive of judges as exercising discretion by appealing to moral principles, Dworkin rightly characterizes them as appealing to moral principles, which, though they are not rules, nevertheless may be binding legal standards. The third tenet of positivism must be abandoned because the rule of recognition in Dworkin's view must be one of pedigree, that is, it cannot make reference to the content or truth of a norm as a condition of its legality; and any legal system that includes moral principles among its legal standards cannot have as its standard of authority a pedigree criterion.[5]

The question, of course, is whether positivism is committed to either judical discretion, the model of rules, or to a pedigree or uncontroversial standard of legality. We know at least that it is committed to the separability thesis from which only negative positivism appears to follow. Negative positivism is committed to none of these claims. Is there another form of positivism that is so committed?

Much of the debate between the positivists and Dworkin appears rather foolish, unless there is a version of positivism that makes Dworkin's criticisms, if not compelling, at least relevant. That version of positivism, whatever it is, cannot be motivated by the separability thesis alone. The question then is whether anything other than its denial of the central tenet of natural law theory motivates positivism?

One easy, but ultimately unsatisfying, response is to maintain that Dworkin's objections are to Hart's version of positivism. While this is no doubt true, such a remark gives no indication of what it is in Hart's version of positivism that is essential to positivism generally. Dworkin, after all, takes his criticisms of Hart to be criticisms of

positivism generally, and the question remains whether positivism is committed to the essentials of Hart's version of it.

A more promising line of argument is the following. No doubt positivism is committed to the separability thesis. Still, one can ask whether commitment to the separability thesis is basic or derivative from some other, perhaps programmatic, commitments of legal positivism. That is, one can look at the separability thesis in isolation or as a component, perhaps even a derivative element, of a network of commitments of legal positivism.[6] We are led to negative positivism when we pursue the former route. Perhaps there is a more interesting form of positivism in the cards if we pursue the latter.

Certainly one reason some positivists have insisted upon the distinction between law and morality is the following: While both law and morality provide standards by which the affairs of people are to be regulated, morality is inherently controversial. People disagree about what morality prescribes, and uncertainty exists concerning the limits of permissible conduct and the nature and scope of one's moral obligations to others. In contrast, for these positivists at least, law is apparently concrete and uncontroversial. Moreover, when a dispute arises over whether or not something is law, there exists a decision procedure that, in the bulk of cases, settles the issue. Law is knowable and ascertainable; so that, while a person may not know the range of his moral obligations, he is aware of (or can find out) what the law expects of him. Commitment to the traditional legal values associated with the rule of law requires that law consist in knowable, largely uncontroversial fact; and it is this feature of law that positivism draws attention to and which underlies it.

One can reach the same characterization of law as consisting in uncontroversial, hard facts by ascribing to legal positivism the epistemological

---

[5]But see Rolf Sartorius, Social Policy and Judicial Legislation, 8 Am. Philosophical Q. 151 (1971); Jules Coleman, Review, Taking Rights Seriously, 66 Calif. L. Rev. 885 (1978); and pp. 90–91 *infra*.

[6]The following characterization of positivism in virtue of motivations for the separability thesis was developed after numerous discussions with Professor Dworkin. I am particularly grateful to him for remarks, but it is likely that I have not put the characterizations as well as he would have.

and semantic constraints of logical positivism on legal facts. For the logical positivists, moral judgments were meaningless because they could not be verified by a reliable and essentially uncontroversial test. In order for statements of law to be meaningful, they must be verifiable by such a test (the epistemic conception of the rule of recognition). To be meaningful, therefore, law cannot be essentially controversial.

Once positivism is characterized as the view of law as consisting in hard facts, Dworkin's ascription of certain basic tenets to it is plausible, and his objections to them are compelling. First, law for positivism consists in rules rather than principles, because the legality of a rule depends on its formal characteristics—the manner and form of its enactment—whereas the legality of a moral principle will depend on its content. The legality of rules, therefore, will be essentially uncontroversial; the legal normativity of principles will be essentially controversial. Second, adjudication takes place in both hard and simple cases. Paradigm or simple cases are uncontroversial. The answer to them as a matter of law is clear, and the judge is obligated to provide it. Cases falling within the penumbra of a general rule, however, are uncertain. There is no uncontroversial answer as a matter of law to them, and judges must go beyond the law to exercise their discretion in order to resolve them. Controversy implies the absence of legal duty and, to the extent to which legal rules have controversial instances, positivism is committed to a theory of discretion in the resolution of disputes involving them. Third, positivism must be committed to a rule of recognition in both the epistemic and the semantic senses, for the rule of recognition not only sets out the conditions of legality, it provides the mechanism by which one settles disputes about what, on a particular matter, the law is. The rule of recognition for the positivist is the principle by which particular propositions of law are verified. Relatedly, the conditions of legality set forth in the rule of recognition must be ones of pedigree of form, otherwise the norm will fail to provide a reliable principle for verifying and adjudicating competing claims about the law.

Finally, law and morality are distinct (the separability thesis) because law consists in hard facts, while morality does not.

Unfortunately for positivism, if the distinction between law and morality is motivated by commitment to law as uncontroversial, hard facts, it must be abandoned because, as Dworkin rightly argues, law is controversial, and even where it is, law may involve matters of obligation and right rather than discretion.

There is no more plausible way of understanding Dworkin's conception of positivism and of rendering his arguments against it (at least those in MOR-I) persuasive. The result is a form of positive positivism that makes an interesting claim about the essence of law—that by and large law consists in hard, concrete facts—a claim that Dworkin neatly shows is mistaken. The entire line of argument rests, however, on ascribing to legal positivism either a programmatic or metaphysical thesis about law. It is the thesis of law as hard facts—whether motivated by semantic, epistemic, or normative arguments—that explains not only positivism's commitment to the separability thesis, but its adherence to other claims about law, that is, discretion, the model of rules, and the noncontentful standard of legality.

The argument for law as hard facts that relies on the positivist program of knowable, ascertainable law is straightforwardly problematic. Legal positivism makes a conceptual or analytic claim about law, and that claim should not be confused with programmatic or normative interests certain positivists, especially Bentham, might have had. Ironically, to hold otherwise is to build into the conceptual account of law a particular normative theory of law; it is to infuse morality, or the way law ought to be, into the concept of law (or the account of the way law is). In other words, the argument for ascribing certain tenets to positivism in virtue of the positivist's normative ideal of law is to commit the very mistake positivism is so intent on drawing attention to and rectifying.

The argument for law as hard facts that relies, not on the programmatic interests of some positivists, but on the semantics and epistemology of logical positivism is both more plausible and interesting. Hart's characterization of his inquiry as an analysis both of the concept of law and of how one determines if a norm constitutes valid law as if these were one and the same thing suggests a conflation of semantic and epistemic inquiries of the sort one associates with logical positivism. Recall, in this regard, Hart's discussion of the move from the "prelegal" to the "legal." The move from the prelegal to the legal is accomplished by the addition of secondary rules to the set of primary social rules of obligation: in particular, by the addition of a rule of recognition that solves the problem of uncertainty, that is, the epistemic problem of determining which norms are law. Moreover Hart's discussion of judicial discretion—that is, the absence of legal duty—as arising whenever the application of a general term in a rule of law is controversial further suggests the identification, for Hart at least, of law with fact ascertainable by the use of a reliable method of verification. Still, in order to justify the ascription to positivism of the view that law consists in hard facts, we need an argument to the effect that part of what it means to be a legal positivist is to be committed to some form of verificationism.

The problem with any such argument is that the separability thesis can stand on its own as a fundamental tenet of positivism without further motivation. After all, verificationism may be wrong and the separability thesis right; without fear of contradiction one can assert both a (metaphysical) realist position about legal facts and the separability thesis. (As an aside, this fact alone should suffice to warrant caution in ascribing logical positivism to legal positivism on the grounds that they are both forms of positivism; otherwise one might be tempted to ascribe metaphysical or scientific realism to legal realism on similar grounds, which, to say the least, would be preposterous.)[7] In short, one alleging to be a positivist can abandon the metaphysics of verificationism, hang on to the separability thesis, and

advance the rather plausible position that the motive for the separability thesis—if indeed there is one—is simply that the distinction it insists on between law and morality is a valid one; and, just in case that is not enough, the positivist can point out that there is a school of jurisprudence that denies the existence of the distinction. In effect, the positivist can retreat to negative positivism and justify his doing so by pointing out that the separability thesis needs no further motivation, certainly none that winds up committing the advocate of a sound jurisprudential thesis to a series of dubious metaphysical ones.

While I am sympathetic to this response, it is not going to satisfy Dworkin. There is something unsatisfactory about a theory of law that does not make an affirmative claim about law. Indeed, one might propose as an adequacy condition that any theory of law must have a point about law. Negative positivism fails to satisfy this adequacy condition. Natural law theory satisfies this adequacy condition by asserting that in every conceivable legal system moral truth is a necessary condition of legality—at least for some norms. Since it consists in the denial of this claim, negative positivism makes no assertion about what is true of law in every conceivable legal system. The view Dworkin rightly ascribes to Hart, but wrongly to positivism generally, that the point of positivism is that law consists in hard facts, meets the adequacy condition and makes the kind of claim, mistaken though it may be, that one can sink one's teeth into.

I want to offer an alternative version of positivism, which, like the "law-as-hard-facts" conception, is a form of positive positivism. The form of positive positivism I want to characterize and defend has, as its point, not that law is largely uncontroversial—it need not be—but that law is ultimately conventional: That the authority of law is a matter of its acceptance by officials.

III. POSITIVE POSITIVISM: LAW AS SOCIAL CONVENTION

It is well known that one can meet the objections to positivism Dworkin advances in MOR-I by constructing a rule of recognition (in the semantic

---

[7]That is because legal realism is skeptical about the existence of legal facts. Legal facts are "created" by official action; they are not "out there" to be discovered by judges. Scientific or metaphysical realism maintains exactly the opposite view of facts.

sense) that permits moral principles as well as rules to be binding legal standards.[8] Briefly the argument is this: Even if some moral principles are legally binding, not every moral principle is a legal one. Therefore, a test must exist for distinguishing moral principles that are legally binding from those that are not. The characteristic of legally binding moral principles that distinguishes them from nonbinding moral principles can be captured in a clause in the relevant rule of recognition. In other words, a rule is a legal rule if it possesses characteristic C; and a moral principle is a legal principle if it possesses characteristic $C1$. The rule of recognition then states that a norm is a legal one if and only if it possesses either C or $C1$. Once this rule of recognition is formulated, everything Dworkin ascribes to positivism, other than the model of rules, survives. The (semantic) rule of recognition survives, since whether a norm is a legal one does not depend on whether it is a rule or a principle, but on whether it satisfies the conditions of legality set forth in a rule of recognition. The separability thesis survives just so long as not every conceivable legal system has in its rule of recognition a $C1$ clause; that is, a clause that sets out conditions of legality for some moral principles, or if it has such a clause, there exists at least one conceivable legal system in which no principle satisfies that clause. Finally, one argument for judicial discretion—the one that relies not on controversy but on the exhaustibility of legal standards—survives. That is, only a determinate number of standards possess either C or $C1$, so that a case may arise in which no legal standard under the rule of recognition is suitable or adequate to its resolution. In such cases, judges must appeal to nonlegal standards to resolve disputes.[9]

Given Dworkin's view of positivism as law consisting in hard facts, he might simply object to this line of defense by noting that the "rule of recognition" formed by the conjunction of the conditions of legality for both principles and rules could not be a rule of recognition in the positivist's sense because its reference to morality would make it inherently controversial. Put another way, a controversial rule of recognition could not be a rule of recognition in the epistemic sense; it could not provide a reliable verification principle. For that reason, it could not be a rule of recognition in the positivist sense. Interestingly, that is not quite the argument Dworkin advances. To be sure, he argues that a rule of recognition of this sort could not constitute a rule of recognition in the positivist's sense. Moreover, he argues that such a rule would be inherently controversial. But the argument does not end with the allegation that such a rule would be controversial. The controversial character of the rule is important for Dworkin, not because it is incompatible with law as hard fact or because a controversial rule cannot be a reliable verification principle, but because a controversial rule of recognition cannot be a social rule. A controversial rule of recognition cannot be a conventional one, or one whose authority depends on its acceptance.

At the outset of the essay I distinguished between two kinds of constraints that might be imposed on the rule of recognition: those having to do with substantive conditions of legality and those having to do with the authority of the rule of recognition itself. The difference between Dworkin's arguments against positivism in MOR-I and MOR-II is that, in the former essay, the version of positivism he objects to is constrained in the first way—legality must be determined by a noncontentful (or pedigree) test—whereas the version of positivism he objects to in MOR-II is constrained in the second way—the rule-of-recognition's authority must be a matter of convention.

Against the law-as-convention version of positivism, Dworkin actually advances four related arguments, none of which, I want to argue, is ultimately convincing. These are what I will refer to as: (1) the social rule argument; (2) the

---

[8]See note 5 *supra*.
[9]Often overlooked is the fact that there are two distinct arguments for discretion: One relies on the controversial nature of penumbra cases involving general terms; the other relies on the finiteness of legal standards. The first argument is actually rooted in a theory of language; the second, which would survive a rejection of that theory, relies on gaps in the law. See Coleman, *supra* note 5.

pedigree argument; (3) the controversy argument; and (4) the moral argument.[10]

A. The Social Rule Argument

Legal obligations are imposed by valid legal norms. A rule or principle is a valid one provided it satisfies the conditions of legality set forth in the rule of recognition. The question Dworkin raises in MOR-II concerns the nature of duties under rule of recognition itself. Does the rule of recognition impose duties on judges because they accept it or because the rule is defensible within a more comprehensive moral theory of law? For Dworkin this is the question of whether the rule of recognition is a social or a normative rule.

Dworkin's first argument in MOR-II against law-as-convention positivism is that the social rule theory provides an inadequate general theory of duty. The argument is this: According to the social rule theory an individual has an obligation to act in a particular way only if (1) there is a general practice of acting in that way; and (2) the rule that is constructed or built up from the practice is accepted from an internal point of view. To accept a rule from an internal point of view is to use it normatively as providing reasons both for acting in accordance with it and for criticizing departures from it. But, as Dworkin rightly notes, there may be duties even where no social practice exists, or where a contrary practice prevails. This is just another way of saying that not every duty is one of conventional morality.

If the positivist's thesis is that the social rule theory provides an adequate account of the source of all noninstitutional duties or of the meaning of all claims about such duties, it is surely mistaken. Not all duties imposed by rules are imposed by conventional rules. Fortunately, the law-as-convention version of positivism makes no such claim. The question is not whether the social rule theory is adequate to account for duties generally; it is whether the theory accounts for the duty of judges under a rule of recognition. An

inadequate general theory of obligation may be an adequate theory of judicial duty. Were one to take the social rule argument seriously, it would amount to the odd claim that the rule of recognition cannot be a social rule and, therefore, that obligations under it could not be ones of conventional morality, simply because not every duty-imposing rule is a social rule.

B. The Pedigree Argument

The first serious argument Dworkin makes against the social rule theory of judicial obligation relies, in part, on the arguments in MOR-I. In meeting the objection to MOR-I, I constructed a rule of recognition that set out distinct conditions of legality for both rules (C) and moral principles ($C1$). Let us abbreviate this rule as "C and $C1$." Dworkin's claim is that such a rule cannot be a social rule.

The argument is this: The truth conditions in "$C + C1$" make reference to moral principles as well as to legal rules. Unlike legal rules, moral principles cannot be identified by their pedigree. Because to determine which of a community's moral principles are legal ones will rely on the content of the principles, it will be a matter of some controversy. But if there is substantial controversy, then there cannot be convergence of behavior sufficient to specify a social rule. The social rule theory requires convergence of behavior, that is, a social practice. A nonpedigree standard implies controversy; controversy implies the absence of a social practice; the absence of the requisite social practice means that the rule cannot be a social rule. A rule of recognition that made reference to morality—the kind of rule of recognition we constructed to overcome Dworkin's objections in MOR-I—could not be a social rule and, therefore, could not be a rule of recognition in the positivist's sense.

The argument moves too quickly. Not every reference that a rule of recognition might make to morality would be inherently controversial. It does not follow from the fact that $C + C1$ refers to moral principles that this rule cannot determine legality in virtue of some noncontent characteristic of moral principles. For example, $C1$ could be an

---

[10]Dworkin does not explicitly distinguish among these various arguments, nor does he label any of them. The labels and distinctions are mine.

"entrenchment" requirement of the sort Rolf Sartorius has proposed, so that whether a moral principle is a legal principle will depend on whether it is mentioned in preambles to legislation and in other authoritative documents: The more mentions, the more weight the principle receives.[11] Or *C1* could state that a moral principle is a legal principle only if it is widely shared by members of the community. In short, the legality of a moral principle could be determined by some of its noncontentful characteristics. In such cases, to determine which moral principles are legally binding would be no more troublesome or controversial than to determine which rules are legal ones.

Though not every reference to morality will render a rule of recognition controversial, some ways of identifying which of a community's moral principles are law will. Suppose *C1* makes moral truth a condition of legality, so that a moral principle could not be part of a community's law unless it were true. Whereas its entrenchment is not a controversial characteristic of a moral principle, its truth is. Any rule of recognition that made moral truth a condition of legality would be controversial. A controversial rule of recognition results in divergence of behavior sufficient to undermine its claim to being a social rule. If a rule of recognition is not a social rule, it cannot be a rule of recognition in the positivist's sense.

Not every possible rule of recognition, therefore, would be a social rule. For example, "the law is whatever is morally right" could never be a rule of recognition in the positivist's sense. Because positivism of the sort I want to defend holds that law is everywhere conventional—that (in the language of this discussion) the rule of recognition in every community is a social rule—it must be mistaken.

---

[11]Sartorius, *supra* note 5; Dworkin himself discusses, but wrongly rejects this possibility; see Model of Rules I, in Taking Rights Seriously 977 (1977). See also C. L. Ten's useful discussion, The Soundest Theory of Law, 88 Mind 522 (1979).

C. The Controversy Argument

Dworkin's view is that the rule of recognition in any jurisdiction is either a social rule or a normative rule; it imposes a duty, in other words, either because it is accepted or because it is true. Law-as-convention positivism is the view that, in every community, the rule of recognition is a social rule. At this level, negative positivism is the view that, in at least one conceivable community, the rule of recognition is a social rule. Natural law theory would then be the view that, in every conceivable legal system, the rule of recognition is a normative rule. Dworkin's claim is that the rule of recognition is a normative rule, and therein lies the justification for placing him within the natural law tradition.

The argument in the previous section is compatible with some rules of recognition being normative rules and others being social rules. For example, a rule of recognition that made no reference to morality or, if it did, referred only to noncontentful features of moral principles, might, for all that the previous argument shows, still be a social rule. If it were, Dworkin's arguments, based on the controversial nature of rules of recognition that refer to morality, would be inadequate to establish the normative theory of law.

What Dworkin needs is an argument that no rule of recognition can be a social rule: That regardless of the conditions of legality it sets forth, no rule of recognition can account for certain features of law unless it is a normative rule. Dworkin has such an argument and it appears to be this: Regardless of the specific conditions of legality it sets forth, every rule of recognition will give rise to controversy at some point. For example, a rule that made no reference to morality could still give rise to controversy concerning either the weight to be given to precedent, or the question of whether—and if so, to what extent—the present legislature could bind a future one. Though the rule itself would not be controversial, particular instances of it would be. Were the rule of recognition a social rule, it could not impose duties on judges in such controversial cases. The existence of judicial duties in controversial cases can only be explained by interpreting the rule of recognition as a normative rule.

This argument relies on the fact that even rules of recognition which are by and large uncontroversial will have controversial applications. In those controversial cases, the social rule interpretation of the rule of recognition could not account for the rule's imposing an obligation on judges. That is because, in the social-rule theory, obligations derive from convergent practice; and in both the controversial, as well as the as yet unresolved, cases there exists no convergent practice or opinion from which an obligation might derive.

The rule of recognition is either a social rule or a normative rule. If it imposes obligations in controversial cases, it cannot be a social rule. Therefore, if the rule of recognition imposes a duty upon judges in controversial cases, it must be a normative rule. Because the rule of recognition in every community is a normative rule, the obligations of judges under it are ones of critical rather than conventional morality; and the ultimate authority of law is a matter of morality, not convention.

The argument from controversy presupposes that judges are bound by duty, even in controversial cases, under the rule of recognition. Positivism, it appears, is committed to judicial discretion in such cases and is, therefore, unable to explain either the source or nature of the duty. Because the social rule theory of judicial obligation is unable to explain the fact of judicial obligation in controversial cases, it must be false and, therefore, its alternative, the normative rule theory, true.

One response a positivist might make to Dworkin's argument is to deny that in such cases judges are bound by duty, in which case the failure of the social rule theory to account for judicial duty would not be troublesome. Dworkin quickly dismisses the plausibility of this response with the offhand remark that such a view likens law to a game in which the participants agree in advance that there are no right answers and no duties where sufficient controversy or doubt exists regarding the requirements of a rule. The analogy to a game is supposed to embarrass positivism, but it need not. Anyone even superficially familiar

with Hart's work knows that the bulk of examples he draws upon to illustrate his claims about rules, law, and the nature of adjudication are drawn from games like baseball and chess. So the positivist might welcome, rather than eschew, the analogy to games.

Whether it is advanced to support or to criticize positivism, the alleged analogy to games is unsatisfying. The more interesting tack is to suppose along with Dworkin that judges may be obligated by a rule of recognition, even in its controversial applications, and then ask whether, in spite of Dworkin's arguments to the contrary, the social rule theory can explain this feature of law.

D. The Moral Argument

That Dworkin takes judicial obligations in cases involving controversial applications of the rule of recognition to be ones of critical morality rather than conventional practice is illustrated by the moral argument. Unlike the previous arguments I have outlined, the moral argument is direct and affirmative in the sense that, instead of trying to establish the inadequacies of the social rule theory, its purpose is to provide direct support for the normative interpretation of the rule of recognition. The argument is simply this: In resolving hard or controversial cases that arise under the rule of recognition, judges do not typically cite the practice or opinions of other judges. Because these cases are controversial, there exists no convergent practice among judges to cite. Instead, in order to resolve these disputes, judges typically appeal to principles of political morality. For example, in determining how much weight to give precedent, judges may apply alternative conceptions of fairness. If, as the social rule theory claims, the source of a judge's duty depends on the rule or principle he cites as its basis, the sources of judicial obligation in these controversial cases are the principles of political morality judges cite as essential to the resolution of the dispute. The duty of judges in controversial cases can only be explained if the rule of recognition is a normative one whose authority depends on its moral merits; whose normativity, in other words, depends on moral argument of precisely the sort judges appear to engage in.

E. Summary

Dworkin has three distinct, powerful arguments against law-as-convention positivism. Each argument has a slightly different character and force. The point of the pedigree argument is that a rule of recognition that makes reference to the content of moral principles as a condition of their legality will spur controversy and, because it will, it cannot be a social rule, or, therefore, a rule of recognition in the positivist's sense. The argument is weak in the sense that, even if sound, it would be inadequate to establish the normative account of the rule of recognition. Only controversial rules of recognition fail to be social rules; for all the argument shows, uncontroversial rules of recognition may be social rules.

The more general argument from controversy appears to fill the gap left by the pedigree argument. Here the argument is not that every rule of recognition will be systematically controversial. Instead, the argument relies on the plain fact that even basically uncontroversial rules of recognition will have controversial instances. The social rule theory cannot account for judicial obligation in the face of controversy. If the rule of recognition imposes an obligation on judges in controversial cases, as Dworkin presumes it does, the obligation can be accounted for only if the rule is a normative one whose capacity to impose a duty does not depend on widespread convergence of conduct or opinion. The point of the argument can be put in weaker or stronger terms. One can say simply that obligations in controversial cases exist and positivism cannot account for them; or one can put the point in terms of natural law theory as the claim that the duties that exist are ones of critical morality, rather than conventional practice.

The point of the moral argument is that, in resolving hard cases, judges appear to rely on principles of political morality rather than on convergent social practice. Judges apparently believe that they are bound to resolve these controversies and, more important, that their duty to resolve them in one way rather than another depends on the principles of morality to which they appeal.

IV. CONVENTION AND CONTROVERSY

Each of the objections to the social rule theory can be met.[12] Consider the pedigree argument first, that is, the claim that a rule of recognition which refers to morality—which has a *C1* clause satisfied by some norm—will be controversial and, therefore, cannot be a social rule of recognition. Suppose the clause in the rule of recognition states: The law is whatever is morally correct. The controversy among judges does not arise over the content of the rule of recognition itself. It arises over which norms satisfy the standards set forth in it. The divergence in behavior among officials as exemplified in their identifying different standards as legal ones does not establish their failure to accept the same rule of recognition. On the contrary, judges accept the same truth conditions for propositions of law, that is, that law consists in

---

[12]There are two ways in which we might understand the notion of a social rule. Under one interpretation, not every rule of recognition would be a social rule; under the other, each would be. As both Hart and Dworkin use the term, a social rule is specified by behavior. It cannot be formulated in the absence of a practice, and the nature of the practice determines the scope of the rule and the extent of the duties it imposes. The rule that men must doff their hats upon entering church is a social rule in this sense. Not every rule of recognition, however, is a social rule in this sense for two reasons. First, at least in some jurisdictions, the content of the rule may be specified prior to the existence of an appropriate practice. For example, the formulation of the Constitution of the United States did not require the existence of the relevant judicial practice; it preceded the practice. No doubt ambiguities and other uncertainties in the rule are resolved through judicial practice; nevertheless, the general form and nature of the rule had been specified without regard to practice. Second, whereas Dworkin's contrast between social rule and normative rule theories of law turns on the manner in which legal rules give rise to duties, the rule of recognition is not itself a duty-imposing rule. We might construct a broader notion of a social rule. In this sense a rule will be a social rule if its existence of authority depends, in part, on the existence of a social practice. Here the requirement is not that the rule's proper formulation be specified by practice. Instead, the claim is that the authority of the rule depends on the existence of a practice. The rule itself may be specifiable, at least in general terms and at some points in time, without regard to the practice. However, in the absence of the practice, the rule is empty in that it is incapable of providing justifications for action. In short, its normativity depends on the practice, though its content need not be specified by it. Every rule of recognition for the positivist is a social rule in this sense.

moral truth. They disagree about which propositions satisfy those conditions. While there may be no agreement whatsoever regarding which standards are legal ones—since there is no agreed-upon standard for determining the truth of a moral principle—there is complete agreement among judges concerning the standard of legality. That judges reach different conclusions regarding the law of a community does not mean that they are employing different standards of legality. Since disagreement concerning which principles satisfy the rule of recognition presupposes that judges accept the same rule of recognition, the sort of controversy envisaged by the pedigree argument is compatible with the conventionalist account of the authority of the rule of recognition.

Notice, however, that were we to understand the rule of recognition epistemically, as providing a reliable test for identifying law, rather than as specifying truth conditions for statements of law, the sort of controversy generated by a rule of recognition like the law is whatever is morally right would be problematic, since the proposed rule of recognition would be incapable of providing a reliable test for identifying legal norms. This just draws our attention once again both to the importance of distinguishing between the epistemic and semantic interpretations of the rule of recognition, and to the necessity of insisting upon the semantic interpretation of it.

Even on the semantic interpretation, the phrase "controversy in the rule of recognition" is ambiguous. Controversy may arise, as it does in the previous case, over which norms satisfy the conditions of legality set forth in the rule of recognition; or it can arise over the conditions of legality set out in the rule of recognition. Cases of the first sort are the ones Dworkin envisions arising from a rule of recognition that includes a clause specifying legality conditions for moral principles. These cases are not problematic because controversy presupposes agreement about and acceptance of the rule of recognition. In contrast, the claim that every rule of recognition will be controversial in some of its details is precisely the claim that, in some cases, controversy will arise over the content or proper formulation of the rule of recognition itself. The question that these cases

pose is not whether judges agree about which norms satisfy the same rule of recognition; rather, it is whether judges can be said to be applying the same rule. Since the social rule theory requires of the rule of recognition that its formulation be specified by convergence of behavior or belief, the controversy concerning the proper formulation of the rule means that the rule cannot be a social rule and, therefore, not a rule of recognition in the positivist's sense.

One way of interpreting Dworkin's claim is that, wherever controversy exists in the proper formulation of a rule, the rule cannot be a conventional or social rule. This is counterintuitive, since all rules—those of conventional as well as critical morality—are vague at points and, therefore, their application in some contexts will be controversial. If we take Dworkin to be making the argument that the existence of controversy is straightforwardly incompatible with the idea of a social rule, then no rule could ever be a social rule. Certainly, in spite of the controversial nature of all rules governing behavior, we are able to distinguish (at least in broad terms) the conventional rules from those whose authority depends on their truth.

A more sympathetic and plausible reading of Dworkin is that he does not mean to contest the existence of social rules. Instead his claim is that social rules cannot account for duties beyond the range of convergent practice. Social rules cannot explain duties in controversial cases. With respect to the rule of recognition, the social rule theory cannot account for the obligation of judges to give the correct formulation of the rule of recognition in its controversial instances. On the assumption that judges have such an obligation, the social rule theory fails. Only a normative interpretation of the rule of recognition can explain the duty in cases of divergent opinions or conduct, since the duty, according to the normative theory, does not derive from convergent practice but from sound moral argument.

Schematically, Dworkin's argument is as follows.

1. Every rule of recognition will be controversial with respect to its scope and, therefore, with respect to the nature and scope of the obligations it imposes.

2. Nevertheless, in resolving disputes involving controversial aspects of the rule, judges are under an obligation, as they are in the uncontroversial cases, to give the right answer.

3. The social rule theory which requires convergence of behavior as a condition of an obligation cannot account for the obligation of judges in 2.

4. Therefore, positivism cannot account for judicial obligation in 2.

5. Therefore, only a normative theory of law in which the duty of judges depends on moral argument rather than convergent practice can account for judicial duty in 2.

As I suggested earlier, a positivist might respond by denying the truth of 2, that is, that judges are obligated in controversial cases in which behavior and opinion diverge. Hart, for one, denies 2, and he appears to do so because he accepts 3. That he denies 2 is made evident by his characterizing these kinds of cases as involving "uncertainty in the rule of recognition" in which "all that succeeds is success." If a positivist were to deny 2 to meet Dworkin's objections on the grounds that he (the positivist) accepts 3, it would be fair to accuse him of begging the question. He would be denying the existence of judicial obligation simply because his theory cannot account for it. Moreover, from a strategic point of view, it would be better to leave open the question of whether such duties exist, rather than to preclude the very possibility of their existence as a consequence of the theory; otherwise any argument that made the existence of such duties conceivable would have the effect of completely undermining the theory. Notice, however, that Dworkin is led to an analogous position, since his argument for the normative theory of law (i.e., 5) requires that judges are under obligations in every conceivable controversial case (i.e., 2). The social rule theory logically precludes judicial obligation in such cases; the normative theory requires it. Both theories of law will fail, just in case the existence of judicial duty in controversial cases involving the rule of recognition is a contingent feature of law. In other words, if it turns out that in some legal systems judges have an obligation to

provide a particular formulation of the rule of recognition when controversy arises over its proper formulation, whereas in other legal systems no such duty exists and judges are free to exercise discretion—at least until one or another formulation takes hold—both the theory that logically precludes judicial duties in all controversial cases, and that which logically entails such duties, will fail.

Denying the existence of the duties to which Dworkin draws attention is a strategy that will not serve the positivist well. One alternative would be to admit the existence of the duty in some cases, but to give up the social rule theory according to which the nature and scope of a duty are completely specified by convergent practice in favor of some other theory concerning the way in which conventional or social rules give rise to duties. This is a promising line of argument I am not prepared to discuss here. However, it seems to me that the discussion of conventions in David Lewis's brilliant book, *Convention*,[13] might provide the theoretical foundations for an alternative to the standard social rule theory. Briefly, the idea is that the duties imposed by social rules or conventions are the results of expectations that arise from efforts to coordinate behavior. Vested, warranted expectations may extend beyond the area of convergent practice, in which case the obligations to which a social rule gives rise might cover controversial, as well as uncontroversial, cases.[14]

Another alternative strategy, the one I have been trying to develop, follows the social rule theory in restricting the duty imposed by a conventional rule to the area of convergent practice. In this view, if controversy arises in the rule of recognition itself, it does not follow that the judges are free to exercise discretion in providing a formulation of the rule. What counts is not whether controversy exists, but whether there exists a practice among judges of resolving the controversy in a particular way. And to answer the question of

---

[13]David Lewis, *Convention: A Philosophical Study* (1969).
[14]Gerald Postema has been trying to develop an alternative to the social rule theory that relies heavily on Lewis's theory of conventions. See Gerald J. Postema, Coordination and Convention at the Foundations of Law, 11 J. Legal Stud., this issue.

whether such a practice exists, we do not look to the rule of recognition—whose conditions of legality are presumably in dispute—but to the social rule constituted by the behavior of judges in applying the rule of recognition. Whether a duty exists will depend, in part, on whether the judges have developed an accepted social practice of resolving these controversies in a particular way.

Suppose that, in applying the rule of recognition, judges have developed a practice of resolving controversial instances of it. Suppose further that in some jurisdictions, for example, the United States and England, judges, by and large, resolve such disputes, as Dworkin believes they do, by providing arguments of principle; so that in determining, for example, whether and to what extent the Supreme Court can review the constitutionality of federal legislation, judges argue from principles of political morality, for example, the separation of powers and so on. According to Dworkin, we would have a controversy in the rule of recognition itself that judges would be required to resolve in the appropriate way; and the obligation of judges would derive from principles of morality that constitute the best argument. This is the essence of what I referred to as the "moral argument," and it would show that the rule of recognition is a normative, not a social, rule.

For the traditional positivist, we would have a case in which no obligation existed, where all that succeeded was success: A case in which the judges' recourse to the principles of political morality necessarily involved an exercise of discretion.

Both of these positions are mistaken. If, as Dworkin supposes, judges as a general rule look to moral principles in resolving controversial features of the rule of recognition, then there exists a practice among them of resolving controversial aspects of the rule of recognition in that way; that is, as the moral argument suggests judges in the United States and Britain do. If this is, in fact, the practice of judges in constitutional democracies like ours—as it must be if Dworkin's arguments are to be taken seriously—and if the practice is critically accepted by judges, then there is a legal duty even in controversial cases: A duty that does not derive from the principles judges cite (as in Dworkin) but from their acceptance of the

practice of resolving these disputes by offering substantive moral arguments. All Dworkin's arguments really show is that judges have adopted critically the practice that the best moral argument wins, which explains both their appeal to substantive moral principles and, contrary to the traditional positivist, their duty to do so.

What, in Dworkin's view, is evidence for the normative theory of the rule of recognition—that is, general and widespread appeal to moral principle to resolve controversies in it—is, in my view, evidence of the existence of a social practice among judges of resolving such disputes in a particular way; a practice that specifies part of the social rule regarding judicial behavior. The appeal to substantive moral argument is, then, perfectly compatible with the conventionalist account of law.

To argue that the appeal to moral argument is compatible with the conventionalist account is not to establish that account, since the appeal to moral argument as a vehicle of dispute resolution is also consistent with the normative theory of law. One could argue that, at most, my argument shows only that Dworkin's arguments, which rely on both the controversial nature of law and the appeal to moral principle to resolve controversy, are inadequate to undermine positivism. We need some further reason to choose between the normative and conventional theories of law.

Dworkin has taken the "acid test" for positivism to be whether it can account for judicial behavior in jurisdictions, such as the United States and England, in which both prospective litigants and judges believe that disputes which arise because of controversy in the rule of recognition are to be resolved, not by discretion, but by principled argument. His arguments are all to the effect that positivism cannot account for either the expectations of litigants or the behavior of judges, because positivism is committed to discretion whenever controversy arises. If controversy arises in a rule subordinate to the rule of recognition, positivism is committed to discretion in virtue of the theory of language it adopts that makes so much of the difference between "core" and "penumbra" instances of general terms. If controversy arises in the rule of recognition itself, positivism is committed to discretion because the rule of recognition is a social rule specified by the behavior of judges; and a social rule can impose an obligation only to the extent behavior converges, that is, only in the absence of controversy. I have argued that, contrary to Dworkin, positivism can, in fact, account for the obligations of judges in controversial instances of the rule of recognition, since the existence of controversy does not preclude the existence of conformity of practice in resolving it. If I am correct, neither the existence of controversy nor the appeal to moral argument in certain jurisdictions as necessary to its resolution are incompatible with law-as-convention positivism. What then is the acid test?

For the normative theory of law to be correct, judges must be under a legal obligation to resolve controversies arising in every conceivable rule of recognition by reliance on substantive moral argument. That is because Dworkin's version of the normative theory entails the existence of judicial duty in all cases, and because the resolution of the dispute must involve moral argument. After all, if the rule of recognition is, as Dworkin claims, a normative rule, then its authority rests on sound moral argument and the resolution of disputes concerning its scope must call for moral argument. Were judges to rely on anything else, the authority of the rule of recognition will not be a matter of its moral merits; or if they appeal to nothing at all, then in such jurisdictions we would have reason to believe that judges are under no particular obligation to resolve a controversy in the rule of recognition.

The real acid test seems to be not whether positivism of the sort I am developing can account for judicial obligations in the kinds of cases we are discussing, but whether these obligations constitute a necessary feature of law which, in every jurisdiction, is imposed by moral principle. As long as the existence of such duties is a contingent feature of law, as is the duty to resolve disputes by appealing to moral argument, the normative theory of law is a less plausible account than is the conventionalist theory. Indeed, it seems straightforwardly false, since we can imagine immature legal systems (which are legal systems nonetheless) in which no practice for resolving disputes in the rule of recognition has as yet

developed—where all that succeeds is success. Or we could imagine the development of considerably less attractive practices for resolving such disputes, for example, the flip of a coin: heads, defendant wins; tails, plaintiff does. In the first sort of legal system, it would seem odd to say judges were legally bound to resolve such disputes (though they might always be morally bound to do so), since no practice had as yet developed. Eventually, such a practice is likely to develop, and the range of judicial discretion will narrow as the practice becomes widespread and critically accepted. As the second example shows, the practice that finally develops need not conform to judicial practice in the United States and England. Though judicial discretion narrows as the range of judicial obligation expands, it may do so in a way that is considerably less attractive than the moral argument envisions; in a way that is, in fact, less attractive than a system in which all that succeeded was success.

Unlike traditional positivism, which has trouble explaining judicial behavior in mature legal systems, and the normative theory of law, which has difficulty explaining developing and immature legal systems (for the reasons that the first precludes obligations in controversial cases, while the second requires them), law-as-convention positivism understands such duties to be a contingent feature of law that can be explained as arising from the critical acceptance of a practice of dispute resolution, rather than from the principles of morality which judges under one kind of practice might cite.

V. CONCLUSION

Dworkin makes three correct observations about the controversial nature of some legal standards.

1. A legal system can (and does in the United States and Britain) recognize certain standards as part of the law even though they are "essentially controversial" in the sense that there may be disagreements among judges as to which these are, and there is no decision procedure which, even in principle, can demonstrate what they are, and so settle disagreements.
2. Among such essentially controversial legal standards are moral principles owing their

status as law to their being "true" moral principles, though their "truth" cannot be demonstrated by any agreed-upon test.

3. The availability of such controversial principles fills the "gaps" left by ordinary sources of law, which may be partially indeterminate, vague, or conflicting. So that, at least with respect to the resolution of disputes involving standards subordinate to the rule of recognition, a judge never has to exercise lawmaking power or "discretion" to fill the gaps or remove the indeterminancy if such moral principles are a part of the law.

In this essay, I have drawn distinctions among three versions of positivism and have discussed their relationship to Dworkin's claims: (1) "Negative positivism," the view that the legal system need not recognize as law "controversial" moral standards; (2) "positive, hard-facts positivism," the view that controversial standards cannot be regarded as law and, hence, rejects Dworkin's three points; (3) "positive, social-rule positivism," which insists only on the conventional status of the rule of recognition but accepts Dworkin's three points.

Since the inclusion of controversial moral principles is not a necessary feature of the concept of law, Dworkin's arguments to the effect that such principles figure in judicial practice in the United States and in Britain, are inadequate to undermine the very weak claim of negative positivism. On the other hand, if Dworkin is right—and I am inclined to think that he is—in thinking that controversial moral principles sometimes figure in legal argument, then any form of positivism that is committed to the essentially noncontroversial nature of law is mistaken. Finally, what I have tried to do is to develop a form of positivism which accepts the controversial nature of some legal reasoning, while denying that this is incompatible with the essential, affirmative claim of the theory that law is everywhere conventional in nature. If I am correct, there is a form of positivism

which can do justice to Dworkin's insights while rendering his objections harmless.[15]

---

[15]I have refrained from discussing the arguments against positivism that Dworkin advances in his brilliant essay "Hard Cases" because in that essay Dworkin reveals himself to be much more of a conventionalist than he would have us believe. The main purpose of that essay is to provide a theory of adjudication that makes plain the sense in which right answers and judicial obligations exist in controversial cases. If Dworkin makes his case for right answers, positivism—at least versions of it that deny judicial duty in the face of controversy—must be mistaken. Moreover, Dworkin attempts to show that the theory of adjudication which provides right answers necessarily makes morality part of the concept of law. Some comments regarding at least this latter claim are in order. Dworkin's general theory of adjudication may be explicated as follows. A case, A, comes before an appellate judge. The judge must decide whether to give a decision in favor of the defendant (decision D), or in favor of the plaintiff, ^-D. In making his decision, the judge notes that there exists a large body of settled law, S, that is suitably purged of its "mistakes." (Dworkin has a theory of the way in which judges identify mistaken decisions). Once S has been purged of mistakes, it can be systematized. The judge is required then to construct a theory of law that best explains and justifies S by subsuming S under a set of general principles that constitute the best explanation of S. These principles constitute the soundest theory of the existing law (STL). Dworkin employs the standard philosophic notion of explanation so that if STL explains S, then S follows logically or theoretically from STL. Once STL is constructed, the judge must ask whether either D or ^-D follows from it. If either statement follows logically from STL, the case presents no problem for the positivist. In the event that neither D nor ^-D follows logically from STL, the case is one that, for the positivists at least, calls for discretion, since both conclusions are equally inadequately warranted by the existing law. Dworkin's theory of adjudication here departs from positivism. For while neither D nor ^-D is entailed by STL, either D or ^-D, but not both, "coheres" or "fits" best with it. While neither a decision in favor of the plaintiff nor the defendant is a logical consequence of the soundest theory of law, one, but not the other, is a coherence consequence of it. Whichever is the coherence consequence is the "right" answer, the one the judge is obligated to provide. More important, in determining the right answer the judge is required to invoke considerations of morality, since the soundest theory of law not only explains the settled law but justifies it as well. While I have other systematic objections to the argument for right answers, I doubt that the theory of adjudication Dworkin outlines accurately describes judicial practice everywhere, or that it is a necessary feature of legal practice. More important for our present purposes, the claim that determining right answers necessarily involves a moral theory of law which is incompatible with the conventionalist account of law is simply mistaken. On the contrary, Dworkin's argument is thoroughly conventionalist in

nature. First, Dworkin must be committed to some standard version of a rule of recognition, since he is committed to a judge's being able to identify the existing body of settled law. Like the positivists he criticizes, Dworkin is, therefore, committed to an epistemic rule of recognition—at least for determining settled law. In Dworkin's view, the judge must construct a theory of law that explains the settled law once it is discovered. The theory of law consists in a set of principles which explain and justify S. The argument for the claim that the soundest theory of law is a moral theory rests either on the requirement that the principles justify the law, or on the claim that the principles which constitute the theory are moral principles. In neither case can the argument be sustained. Dworkin's argument for the justification requirement relies on a deeper principle of political responsibility; the judge must be able to give reasons in support of his decisions by showing a consistency between this and previous, similar cases. The notion of justification, however, is ambiguous. There are both weaker and stronger notions of justification. On the other hand, there is the notion of justification that is part of critical morality according to which if a principle or decision is justified it is morally defensible. In this sense, bad law can never be morally justified. But Dworkin (rightly) believes that bad law can be law nonetheless, so he cannot mean that the best theory of law justifies the existing law in the sense that it shows the law to be morally defensible. It is clear, then, that the principle of political responsibility requires the weaker notion of justification. This notion is institutional in nature and is akin to the requirement of consistency or formal justice, the requirement that like cases be treated alike. But then this notion of justification does not establish the link between law and critical morality necessary to undermine positivism. The argument that the best theory of law is a moral theory because it consists in a set of moral principles fails primarily because the principles which constitute the best theory do not do so because they are true, but because they best systemize the existing law.

CHAPTER FOUR

Legal Realism and Skepticism

12   The Path of the Law

O. W. HOLMES, JR.

When we study law we are not studying a mystery but a well-known profession. We are studying what we shall want in order to appear before judges, or to advise people in such a way as to keep them out of court. The reasons why it is a profession, why people will pay lawyers to argue for them or to advise them, is that in societies like ours the command of the public force is entrusted to the judges in certain cases, and the whole power of the state will be put forth, if necessary, to carry out their judgments and decrees. People want to know under what circumstances and how far they will run the risk of coming against what is so much stronger than themselves, and hence it becomes a business to find out when this danger is to be feared. The object of our study, then, is prediction, the prediction of the incidence of the public force through the instrumentality of the courts.

The means of the study are a body of reports, of treatises, and of statutes, in this country and in England, extending back for six hundred years, and now increasing annually by hundreds. In these sibylline leaves are gathered the scattered prophecies of the past upon the cases in which the axe will fall. These are what properly have been called the oracles of the law. Far the most important and pretty nearly the whole meaning of every new effort of legal thought is to make these prophecies more precise, and to generalize them into a thoroughly connected system. The process is one, from a lawyer's statement of a case, eliminating as it does all the dramatic elements with which his client's story has clothed it, and retaining only the facts of legal import, up to the final analyses and abstract universals of theoretic jurisprudence. The reason why a lawyer does not mention that his client wore a white hat when he made a contract, while Mrs. Quickly would be sure to dwell upon it along with the parcel gilt goblet and the sea-coal fire, is that he foresees that the public force will act in the same way whatever his client had upon his head. It is to make the prophecies easier to be remembered and to be understood that the teachings of the decisions of the past are put into general propositions and gathered into textbooks, or that statutes are passed in a general form. The primary rights and duties with which

Oliver Wendell Holmes, Jr., "The Path of the Law," *Harvard Law Review*, vol. 10 (1897), pp. 457–68.

jurisprudence busies itself again are nothing but prophecies. One of the many evil effects of the confusion between legal and moral ideas, about which I shall have something to say in a moment, is that theory is apt to get the cart before the horse, and to consider the right or the duty as something existing apart from and independent of the consequences of its breach, to which certain sanctions are added afterward. But, as I shall try to show, a legal duty so called is nothing but a prediction that if a man does or omits certain things he will be made to suffer in this or that way by judgment of the court—and so of a legal right.

The number of our predictions when generalized and reduced to a system is not unmanageably large. They present themselves as a finite body of dogma which may be mastered within a reasonable time. It is a great mistake to be frightened by the ever increasing number of reports. The reports of a given jurisdiction in the course of a generation take up pretty much the whole body of the law, and restate it from the present point of view. We could reconstruct the corpus from them if all that went before were burned. The use of the earlier reports is mainly historical, a use about which I shall have something to say before I have finished.

I wish, if I can, to lay down some first principles for the study of this body of dogma or systematized prediction which we call the law, for men who want to use it as the instrument of their business to enable them to prophesy in their turn, and, as bearing upon the study, I wish to point out an ideal which as yet our law has not attained.

The first thing for a business-like understanding of the matter is to understand its limits, and therefore I think it desirable at once to point out and dispel a confusion between morality and law, which sometimes rises to the height of conscious theory, and more often and indeed constantly is making trouble in detail without reaching the point of consciousness. You can see very plainly that a bad man has as much reason as a good one for wishing to avoid an encounter with the public force, and therefore you can see the practical importance of the distinction between morality and law. A man who cares nothing for an ethical rule which is believed and practiced by his neighbors is likely nevertheless to care a good deal to avoid being made to pay money, and will want to keep out of jail if he can.

I take it for granted that no hearer of mine will misinterpret what I have to say as the language of cynicism. The law is the witness and external deposit of our moral life. Its history is the history of the moral development of the race. The practice of it, in spite of popular jests, tends to make good citizens and good men. When I emphasize the difference between law and morals I do so with reference to a single end, that of learning and understanding the law. For that purpose you must definitely master its specific marks, and it is for that that I ask you for the moment to imagine yourselves indifferent to other and greater things.

I do not say that there is not a wider point of view from which the distinction between law and morals becomes of secondary or no importance, as all mathematical distinctions vanish in the presence of the infinite. But I do say that that distinction is of the first importance for the object which we are here to consider—a right study and mastery of the law as a business with well-understood limits, a body of dogma enclosed within definite lines. I have just shown the practical reason for saying so. If you want to know the law and nothing else, you must look at it as a bad man, who cares only for the material consequences which such knowledge enables him to predict, not as a good one, who finds his reasons for conduct, whether inside the law or outside of it, in the vaguer sanctions of conscience. The theoretical importance of the distinction is no less, if you would reason on your subject aright. The law is full of phraseology drawn from morals, and by the mere force of language continually invites us to pass from one domain to the other without perceiving it, as we are sure to do unless we have the boundary constantly before our minds. The law talks about rights, and duties, and malice, and intent, and negligence, and so forth, and nothing is easier, or, I may say, more common in legal reasoning, than to take these words in their moral sense, at some stage of the argument, and so to drop into fallacy. For instance, when we speak of the rights of man in a moral sense, we mean to mark the limits of interference with individual freedom which we think are prescribed by conscience, or by our ideal, however reached. Yet it is certain that many laws have been enforced in the past, and it is likely that some are enforced now, which are condemned by the most enlightened opinion of the time, or which at all events pass the limit of interference as many consciences would draw it. Manifestly, therefore, nothing but confusion of thought can result from assuming that the rights of man in a moral sense are equally rights in the sense of the Constitution and the law. No doubt simple and extreme cases can be put of imaginable laws which the statute-making power would not dare to enact, even in the absence of written constitutional prohibitions, because the community would rise in rebellion and fight; and this gives some plausibility to the proposition that the law, if not a part of morality, is limited by it. But this limit of power is not coextensive with any system of morals. For the most part it falls far within the lines of any such system, and in some cases may extend beyond them, for reasons drawn from the habits of a particular people at a particular time. I once heard the late Professor Agassiz say that a German population would rise if you added two cents to the price of a glass of beer. A statute in such a case would be empty words, not because it was wrong, but because it could not be enforced. No one will deny that wrong statutes can be and are enforced, and we should not all agree as to which were the wrong ones.

The confusion with which I am dealing besets confessedly legal conceptions. Take the fundamental question, What constitutes the law? You will find some text writers telling you that it is something different from what is decided by the courts of Massachusetts or England, that it is a system of reason, that it is a deduction from principles of ethics or admitted axioms or what not, which may or may not coincide with the decisions. But if we take the view of our friend the bad man we shall find that he does not care two straws for the axioms or deductions, but that he does want to know what the Massachusetts or English courts are likely to do, in fact. I am much of his mind. The prophecies of what the courts will do in fact,

and nothing more pretentious, are what I mean by the law.

Take again a notion which as popularly understood is the widest conception which the law contains—the notion of legal duty, to which already I have referred. We fill the word with all the content which we draw from morals. But what does it mean to a bad man? Mainly, and in the first place, a prophecy that if he does certain things he will be subjected to disagreeable consequences by way of imprisonment or compulsory payment of money. But from his point of view, what is the difference between being fined and being taxed a certain sum for doing a certain thing? That his point of view is the test of legal principles is shown by the many discussions which have arisen in the courts on the very question whether a given statutory liability is a penalty or a tax. On the answer to this question depends the decision whether conduct is legally wrong or right, and also whether a man is under compulsion or free. Leaving the criminal law on one side, what is the difference between the liability under the mill acts or statutes authorizing a taking by eminent domain and the liability for what we call a wrongful conversion of property where restoration is out of the question? In both cases the party taking another man's property has to pay its fair value as assessed by a jury, and no more. What significance is there in calling one taking right and another wrong from the point of view of the law? It does not matter, so far as the given consequence, the compulsory payment, is concerned, whether the act to which it is attached is described in terms of praise or in terms of blame, or whether the law purports to prohibit it or allow it. If it matters at all, still speaking from the bad man's point of view, it must be because in one case and not in the other some further disadvantages, or at least some further consequences, are attached to the act by the law. The only other disadvantages thus attached to it which I ever have been able to think of are to be found in two somewhat insignificant legal doctrines, both of which might be abolished without much disturbance. One is that a contract to do a prohibited act is unlawful, and the other that if one of two or more joint wrongdoers has to pay all the damages, he cannot recover contribution from his fellows. And that I believe is all. You see how the vague circumference of the notion of duty shrinks and at the same time grows more precise when we wash it with cynical acid and expel everything except the object of our study, the operations of the law.

Nowhere is the confusion between legal and moral ideas more manifest than in the law of contract. Among other things, here again the so-called primary rights and duties are invested with a mystic significance beyond what can be assigned and explained. The duty to keep a contract at common law means a prediction that you must pay damages if you do not keep it—and nothing else. If you commit a tort, you are liable to pay a compensatory sum. If you commit a contract, you are liable to pay a compensatory sum unless the promised event comes to pass, and that is all the difference. But such a mode of looking at the matter stinks in the nostrils of those who think it advantageous to get as much ethics into the law as they can. It was good enough for Lord Coke, however, and here, as in many other cases, I am content to abide with him. In *Bromage v. Genning,*[1] a prohibition was sought in the King's Bench against a suit in the marches of Wales for the specific performance of a covenant to grant a lease, and Coke said that it would subvert the intention of the covenantor, since he intends it to be at his election either to lose the damages or to make the lease. Sergeant Harris for the plaintiff confessed that he moved the matter against his conscience, and a prohibition was granted. This goes further than we should go now, but it shows what I venture to say has been the common law point of view from the beginning, although Mr. Harriman, in his very able little book upon Contracts has been misled, as I humbly think, to a different conclusion.

I have spoken only of the common law, because there are some cases in which a logical justification can be found for speaking of civil liabilities as imposing duties in an intelligible sense. These are the relatively few in which equity will grant an injunction, and will enforce it by putting the defendant in prison or otherwise punishing him unless he complies with the order of the court. But I hardly think it advisable to shape general theory from the exception, and I think it would be better to cease troubling ourselves about primary rights and sanctions altogether, than to describe our prophecies concerning the liabilities commonly imposed by the law in those inappropriate terms.

I mentioned, as other examples of the use by the law of words drawn from morals, malice, intent, and negligence. It is enough to take malice as it is used in the law of civil liability for wrongs—what we lawyers call the law of torts—to show you that it means something different in law from what it means in morals, and also to show how the difference has been obscured by giving to principles which have little or nothing to do with each other the same name. Three hundred years ago a parson preached a sermon and told a story out of *Fox's Book of Martyrs* of a man who had assisted at the torture of one of the saints, and afterward died, suffering compensatory inward torment. It happened that Fox was wrong. The man was alive and chanced to hear the sermon, and thereupon he sued the parson. Chief Justice Wray instructed the jury that the defendant was not liable, because the story was told innocently, without malice. He took malice in the moral sense, as importing a malevolent motive. But nowadays no one doubts that a man may be liable, without any malevolent motive at all, for false statements manifestly calculated to inflict temporal damage. In stating the case in pleading, we still should call the defendant's conduct malicious; but, in my opinion at least, the word means nothing about motives, or even about the defendant's attitude toward the future, but only signifies that the tendency of his conduct under the known circumstances was very plainly to cause the plaintiff temporal harm.[2]

In the law of contract the use of moral phraseology has led to equal confusion, as I have shown in part already, but only in part. Morals deal with the actual internal state of the individual's mind, what he actually intends. From the time of the Romans down to now, this mode of dealing has affected the language of the law as to contract, and the language used has reacted upon the thought. We talk about a contract as a meeting of the minds of the parties, and thence it is inferred in various cases that there is no contract because their minds have not met; that is, because they have intended different things or because one party has not known of the assent of the other. Yet nothing is more certain than that parties may be bound by a contract to things which neither of them intended, and when one does not know of the other's assent. Suppose a contract is executed in due form and in writing to deliver a lecture, mentioning no time. One of the parties thinks that the promise will be construed to mean at once, within a week. The other thinks that it means when he is ready. The court says that it means within a reasonable time. The parties are bound by the contract as it is interpreted by the court, yet neither of them meant what the court declares that they have said. In my opinion no one will understand the true theory of contract or be able even to discuss some fundamental questions intelligently until he has understood that all contracts are formal, that the making of a contract depends not on the agreement of two minds in one intention, but on the agreement of two sets of external signs—not on the parties' having *meant* the same thing but on their having *said* the same thing. Furthermore, as the signs may be addressed to one sense or another—to sight or to hearing—on the nature of the sign will depend the moment when the contract is made. If the sign is tangible, for instance, a letter, the contract is made when the letter of acceptance is delivered. If it is necessary that the minds of the parties meet, there will be no contract until the acceptance can be read—none, for example, if the acceptance be snatched from the hand of the offerer by a third person.

This is not the time to work out a theory in detail, or to answer many obvious doubts and questions which are suggested by these general views. I know of none which are not easy to answer, but what I am trying to do now is only by a series of hints to throw some light on the narrow path of legal doctrine, and upon two pitfalls which, as it seems to me, lie perilously near to it. Of the first of these I have said enough. I hope that my illustrations have shown the danger, both to speculation and to practice, of confounding

morality with law, and the trap which legal language lays for us on that side of our way. For my own part, I often doubt whether it would not be a gain if every word of moral significance could be banished from the law altogether, and other words adopted which should convey legal ideas uncolored by anything outside the law. We should lose the fossil records of a good deal of history and the majesty got from ethical associations, but by ridding ourselves of an unnecessary confusion we should gain very much in the clearness of our thought.

So much for the limits of the law. The next thing which I wish to consider is what are the forces which determine its content and its growth. You may assume, with Hobbes and Bentham and Austin, that all law emanates from the sovereign, even when the first human beings to enunciate it are the judges, or you may think that law is the voice of the Zeitgeist, or what you like. It is all one to my present purpose. Even if every decision required the sanction of an emperor with despotic power and a whimsical turn of mind, we should be interested nonetheless, still with a view to prediction, in discovering some order, some rational explanation, and some principle of growth for the rules which he laid down. In every system there are such explanations and principles to be found. It is with regard to them that a second fallacy comes in, which I think it important to expose.

The fallacy to which I refer is the notion that the only force at work in the development of the law is logic. In the broadest sense, indeed, that notion would be true. The postulate on which we think about the universe is that there is a fixed quantitative relation between every phenomenon and its antecedents and consequents. If there is such a thing as a phenomenon without these fixed quantitative relations, it is a miracle. It is outside the law of cause and effect, and as such transcends our power of thought, or at least is something to or from which we cannot reason. The condition of our thinking about the universe is that it is capable of being thought about rationally, or, in other words, that every part of it is effect and cause in the same sense in which those parts are with which we are most familiar. So in the broadest sense it is true that the law is a logical development, like everything else. The danger of which I speak is not the admission that the principles governing other phenomena also govern the law, but the notion that a given system, ours, for instance, can be worked out like mathematics from some general axioms of conduct. This is the natural error of the schools, but it is not confined to them. I once heard a very eminent judge say that he never let a decision go until he was absolutely sure that it was right. So judicial dissent often is blamed, as if it meant simply that one side or the other were not doing their sums right, and, if they would take more trouble, agreement inevitably would come.

This mode of thinking is entirely natural. The training of lawyers is a training in logic. The processes of analogy, discrimination, and deduction are those in which they are most at home. The language of judicial decision is mainly the language of logic. And the logical method and form flatter that longing for certainty and for repose which is in every human mind. But certainty generally is illusion, and repose is not the destiny of man. Behind the logical form lies a judgment as to the relative worth and importance of competing legislative grounds, often an inarticulate and unconscious judgment, it is true, and yet the very root and nerve of the whole proceeding. You can give any conclusion a logical form. You always can imply a condition in a contract. But why do you imply it? It is because of some belief as to the practice of the community or of a class, or because of some opinion as to policy, or, in short, because of some attitude of yours upon a matter not capable of exact quantitative measurement, and therefore not capable of founding exact logical conclusions. Such matters really are battle grounds where the means do not exist for determinations that shall be good for all time, and where the decision can do no more than embody the preference of a given body in a given time and place. We do not realize how large a part of our law is open to reconsideration upon a slight change in the habit of the public mind. No concrete proposition is self-evident, no matter how ready we may be to accept it, not even Mr. Herbert Spencer's Everyman has a right to do what he wills, provided he interferes not with a like right on the part of his neighbors.

Why is a false and injurious statement privileged, if it is made honestly in giving information about a servant? It is because it has been thought more important that information should be given freely, than that a man should be protected from what under other circumstances would be an actionable wrong. Why is a man at liberty to set up a business which he knows will ruin his neighbor? It is because the public good is supposed to be best subserved by free competition. Obviously such judgments of relative importance may vary in different times and places. Why does a judge instruct a jury that an employer is not liable to an employee for an injury received in the course of his employment unless he is negligent, and why do the jury generally find for the plaintiff if the case is allowed to go to them? It is because the traditional policy of our law is to confine liability to cases where a prudent man might have foreseen the injury, or at least the danger, while the inclination of a very large part of the community is to make certain classes of persons ensure the safety of those with whom they deal. Since the last words were written, I have seen the requirement of such insurance put forth as part of the programme of one of the best known labor organizations. There is a concealed, half-conscious battle on the question of legislative policy, and if any one thinks that it can be settled deductively, or once for all, I only can say that I think he is theoretically wrong, and that I am certain that his conclusion will not be accepted in practice *semper ubique et ab omnibus.*

Indeed, I think that even now our theory upon this matter is open to reconsideration, although I am not prepared to say how I should decide if a reconsideration were proposed. Our law of torts comes from the old days of isolated, ungeneralized wrongs, assaults, slanders, and the like, where the damages might be taken to lie where they fell by legal judgment. But the torts with which our courts are kept busy today are mainly the incidents of certain well-known businesses. They are injuries to person or property by railroads, factories, and the like. The liability for them is estimated, and sooner or later goes into the price paid by the public. The public really pays the damages, and the question of liability, if pressed far enough, is really the question how far it is desirable that the public should ensure the safety of those whose work it uses. It might be said that in such cases the chance of a jury finding for the defendant is merely a chance, once in a while rather arbitrarily interrupting the regular course of recovery, most likely in the case of an unusually conscientious plaintiff, and therefore better done away with. However, the economic value even of a life to the community can be estimated, and no recovery, it may be said, ought to go beyond that amount. It is conceivable that some day in certain cases we may find ourselves imitating, on a higher plane, the tariff for life and limb which we see in the Leges Barbarorum.

I think that the judges themselves have failed adequately to recognize their duty of weighing considerations of social advantage. The duty is inevitable, and the result of the often-proclaimed judicial aversion to deal with such considerations is simply to leave the very ground and foundation of judgments inarticulate, and often unconscious, as I have said. When socialism first began to be talked about, the comfortable classes of the community were a good deal frightened. I suspect that this fear has influenced judicial action both here and in England, yet it is certain that it is not a conscious factor in the decisions to which I refer. I think that something similar has led people who no longer hope to control the legislatures to look to the courts as expounders of the Constitutions, and that in some courts new principles have been discovered outside the bodies of those instruments, which may be generalized into acceptance of the economic doctrines which prevailed about fifty years ago, and a wholesale prohibition of what a tribunal of lawyers does not think about right. I cannot but believe that if the training of lawyers led them habitually to consider more definitely and explicitly the social advantage on which the rule they lay down must be justified, they sometimes would hesitate where now they are confident, and see that really they were taking sides upon debatable and often burning questions.

NOTES
1. I Roll. Rep. 368.
2. See Hanson v. Globe Newspaper Co., 159 Mass. 293, 302.

13 Legal Realism

JEROME FRANK

We have talked much of the law. But what is "the law"? A complete definition would be impossible and even a working definition would exhaust the patience of the reader. But it may not be amiss to inquire what, in a rough sense, the law means to the average man of our times when he consults his lawyer.

The Jones family owned the Blue & Gray Taxi Company, a corporation incorporated in Kentucky. That company made a contract with the A. & B. Railroad Company, also a Kentucky corporation, by which it was agreed that the Blue & Gray Taxi Company was to have the exclusive privilege of soliciting taxicab business on and adjacent to the railroad company's depot.

A rival taxicab company, owned by the Williams family, the Purple Taxi Company, began to ignore this contract; it solicited business and parked its taxicabs in places assigned by the railroad company to the Blue & Gray Company and

Jerome Frank, "Legal Realism," from *Law and the Modern Mind* (New York: Doubleday and Co. Anchor edition 1963), pp. 46–52. Originally published by Brentanos. Inc., in 1930. Copyright © 1930, 1933, 1949 by Coward McCann. Inc. Copyright reviewed in 1958 by Florence K. Frank. Copyright © 1930 by Brentanos, Inc. Reprinted by arrangement with Barbara Kiastern and Peter Smith Publisher, Inc.

sought in other ways to deprive the Blue & Gray Company of the benefits conferred on it by the agreement with the railroad.

The Jones family was angered; their profits derived from the Blue & Gray stock, which they owned, were threatened. They consulted their lawyer, a Louisville practitioner, and this, we may conjecture, is about what he told them: "I'm afraid your contract is not legally valid. I've examined several decisions of the highest court of Kentucky and they pretty clearly indicate that you can't get away with that kind of an agreement in this state. The Kentucky court holds such a contract to be bad as creating an unlawful monopoly. But I'll think the matter over. You come back tomorrow and I'll try meanwhile to find some way out."

So, the next day, the Joneses returned. And this time their lawyer said he thought he had discovered how to get the contract sustained: "You see, it's this way. In most courts, except those of Kentucky and of a few other states, an agreement like this is perfectly good. But, unfortunately, as things now stand, you'll have to go into the Kentucky courts.

"If we can manage to get our case tried in the federal court, there's a fair chance that we'll get a different result, because I think the federal court will follow the majority rule and not the Kentucky rule. I'm not sure of that, but it's worth trying.

"So this is what we'll do. We'll form a new Blue & Gray Company in Tennessee. And your Kentucky Blue & Gray Company will transfer all its assets to the new Tennessee Blue & Gray Company. Then we'll have the railroad company execute a new contract with the new Tennessee Blue & Gray Company, and at the same time cancel the old contract and, soon after, dissolve the old Kentucky Blue & Gray Company."

"But," interrupted one of the Joneses, "what good will all that monkey-business do?"

The lawyer smiled broadly. "Just this," he replied with pride in his cleverness: "The A. & B. Railroad Company is organized in Kentucky. So is the Purple Taxi which we want to get at. The federal court will treat these companies as if they were citizens of Kentucky. Now, a corporation which is a citizen of Kentucky can't bring this

kind of suit in the federal court against other corporations which are also citizens of Kentucky. But if your company becomes a Tennessee corporation, it will be considered as if it were a citizen of Tennessee. Then your new Tennessee company can sue the other two in the federal court, because the suit will be held to be one between citizens of different states. And that kind of suit, based on what we lawyers call 'diversity of citizenship,' can be brought in the federal court by a corporation which organized in Tennessee against corporations which are citizens of another state, Kentucky. And the federal court, as I said, ought to sustain your contract."

"That sounds pretty slick," said one of the Joneses admiringly. "Are you sure it will work?"

"No," answered the lawyer. "You can't ever be absolutely sure about such a plan. I can't find any case completely holding our way on all these facts. But I'm satisfied that's the law and that that's the way the federal court ought to decide. I won't guarantee success. But I recommend trying out my suggestion." His advice was followed. Shortly after the new Tennessee Blue & Gray Company was organized and had entered into the new contract, suit was brought by the Joneses' new Blue & Gray Corporation of Tennessee in the Federal District Court against the competing Purple Company and the railroad company. In this suit, the Blue & Gray Taxi Company of Tennessee asked the court to prevent interference with the carrying out of its railroad contract.

As the Joneses' lawyer had hoped, the federal court held, against the protest of the Purple Company's lawyer, first, that such a suit could be brought in the federal court and, second, that the contract was valid. Accordingly the court enjoined the Purple Company from interfering with the depot business of the Joneses' Blue & Gray Company. The Joneses were elated, for now their profits seemed once more assured.

But not for long. The other side appealed the case to the Federal Circuit Court of Appeals. And the Joneses' lawyer was somewhat worried that that court might reverse the lower federal court. But it didn't, and the Joneses again were happy.

Still the Purple Company persisted. It took the case to the Supreme Court of the United

States. That Court consists of nine judges. And the Joneses' lawyer couldn't be certain just how those judges would line up on all the questions involved. "Some new men on the bench, and you never can tell about Holmes and Brandeis. They're very erratic," was his comment.

When the United States Supreme Court gave its decision, it was found that six of the nine judges agreed with counsel for the Joneses. Three justices (Holmes, Brandeis, and Stone) were of the contrary opinion. But the majority governs in the United States Supreme Court, and the Joneses' prosperity was at last firmly established.

Now, what was "the law" for the Joneses, who owned the Blue & Gray Company, and the Williamses, who owned the Purple Company? The answer will depend on the date of the question. If asked before the new Tennessee Company acquired this contract, it might have been said that it was almost surely "the law" that the Joneses would lose; for any suit involving the validity of that contract could then have been brought only in the Kentucky state court and the prior decisions of that court seemed adverse to such an agreement.

After the suggestion of the Joneses' lawyer was carried out and the new Tennessee corporation owned the contract, "the law" was more doubtful. Many lawyers would have agreed with the Joneses' lawyer that there was a good chance that the Jones family would be victorious if suit were brought in the federal courts. But probably an equal number would have disagreed: they would have said that the formation of the new Tennessee company was a trick used to get out of the Kentucky courts and into the federal court, a trick of which the federal court would not approve. Or that, regardless of that question, the federal court would follow the well-settled Kentucky rule as to the invalidity of such contracts as creating unlawful monopolies (especially because the use of Kentucky real estate was involved) and that therefore the federal court would decide against the Joneses. "The law," at any time before the decision of the United States Supreme Court, was indeed unsettled. (That is, it was unsettled whether the Williamses had the energy, patience, and money to push an appeal. If

not, then the decision of the lower federal court was the actual settled law for the Jones and Williams families.) No one could know what the court would decide. Would it follow the Kentucky cases? If so, the law was that no "rights" were conferred by the contract. Would it refuse to follow the Kentucky cases? If so, rights were conferred by the contract. To speak of settled law governing that controversy, or of the fixed legal rights of those parties, as antedating the decision of the Supreme Court, is mere verbiage. If two more judges on that bench had agreed with Justices Holmes, Brandeis, and Stone, the law and the rights of the parties would have been of a directly opposite kind.

After the decision, "the law" was fixed. There were no other courts to which an appeal could be directed. The judgment of the United States Supreme Court could not be disturbed and the legal "rights" of the Joneses and the Williamses were everlastingly established.

We may now venture a rough definition of law from the point of view of the average man: For any particular lay person, the law, with respect to any particular set of facts, is a decision of a court with respect to those facts so far as that decision affects that particular person. Until a court has passed on those facts no law on that subject is yet in existence. Prior to such a decision, the only law available is the opinion of lawyers as to the law relating to that person and to those facts. Such opinion is not actually law but only a guess as to what a court will decide. (The United States Supreme Court has wittily been called the "court of ultimate conjecture.")

Law, then, as to any given situation is either (*1*) actual law, that is, a specific past decision, as to that situation, or (*2*) probable law, that is, a guess as to a specific future decision.

Usually when a client consults his lawyer about "the law," his purpose is to ascertain not what the courts have actually decided in the past but what the courts will probably decide in the future. He asks, "Have I a right, as a stockholder of the American Taffy Company of Indiana, to look at the corporate books?" Or, "Do I have to pay an inheritance tax to the State of New York on bonds left me by my deceased wife, if our residence was in Ohio, but the bonds, at the time of her death, were in a safety-deposit box in New York?" Or, "Is there a right of 'peaceful' picketing in a strike in the State of California?" Or, "If Jones sells me his Chicago shoe business and agrees not to compete for ten years, will the agreement be binding?" The answers (although they may run "There is such a right," "The law is that the property is not taxable," "Such picketing is unlawful," "The agreement is not legally binding") are in fact prophecies or predictions of judicial action. It is from this point of view that the practice of law has been aptly termed an art of prediction.

14 Ships and Shoes and Sealing Wax

K. N. LLEWELLYN

There is more to the law and to the study of law than the Case System. And now that that most pressing business is over, and you see at least something of what the study of cases is about, we can sit back more at our ease, give fancy freer rein, and loaf a little in such pastures of the law as the old nag will take us to. There is no end of pastures: logic, and legal history, and the Register of Writs; law on the Continent, law among the Cheyenne, juvenile courts; Hohfeldian analysis, the federal Constitution; Bracton and Blackstone, Mansfield, Coke and Bentham; how English law came to America; statutes, the judge in politics, legal research; admission to the bar, the bar itself; use of the library, codes, and the law's delay. Let us pick out a few of these, and stuff our pipes, touch a match, puff, and watch the pictures in the smoke.

I

Perhaps first as to the part that logic plays in law. For if you remember, I have been a little hard on logic. There was a view, and I suppose some hold it still, that law is made up of principles and rules. A master craftsman would be able to arrange them in one great hierarchical scheme. At the apex, ideally, stands a single major premise, the Grand Exalted Ruler of the Order. Under him Kleagles, Klaxons, Klaws, and so on down to the more ordinary rules of law. Under these ordinary rules, in turn, the cases range: the single sets of fact, each in its due appointed place, each one a term in a minor premise of which the major is the rule that holds its class. In less idealized and ambitious form such ordering has repeatedly been attempted for particular fields of law. Indeed, what I have urged upon you as the problem of putting a group of cases together comes in essence to the building of a tiny system of this nature for a tiny field.

Now such a logical system of propositions, however modest in scope, inevitably goes beyond the instances in hand. The essence of inductive construction is the building of a major premise which will include not only the observed phenomena, but all *like* phenomena as well. The most modest, the most purely descriptive logical arrangement of the rules of cases therefore always is broad enough to cover more cases than you start from. As to such further cases, and when viewed still as a system of *description,* your logical set-up now remarks to you as follows: "*If* I am a correct description of the cases, then the future cases *a* and *b* will have the outcome *x*, as have past cases *a* and *b*; and cases *a'* and *b'* will also have that outcome; but the future cases *c* and *d* will like their predecessors have the outcome *y*; so will the cases *c'* and *d'*."

But in law your logical system refuses to remain on the level of description, of arranging existing observation. Backed by the fact and doctrine of precedent, your logical system shifts

From Karl N. Llewellyn, *The Bramble Bush: On Our Law and Its Study* (New York: Oceana Publications, 1951), pp. 70–81.

its content to the level of Ought (this does not affect the logic). Its remarks change in tone and substance. Now they run: "*If I am a correct description of the accepted doctrine,* the future cases *a* and *b are to* have the outcome *x*—they *should* have that outcome, and if the judge is on the job he will see to it that they do." For your logical system has now incorporated into each of its initial data—into each decision from which it is built up—the Ought idea. No longer are these initial data statements *merely* of how courts have held on given facts. They have—thanks to the addition of precedent—become each one a statement simultaneously of how a court *has* held, and in addition of how future courts *ought* to hold. To describe the one is to announce the other, by describing an *authoritative* command to future officials given by the precedents.

The rules that you derive from putting cases together are therefore *rules not merely of description but of Ought,* major premises from which one concludes that if the rule is correct, a particular further case ought to be so decided and not otherwise; to which is added an implication in fact that the judge in the future case will be on his job.

Now on the level of *predicting* what will in fact come to pass, clearly there are three places to attack your rule as you thus set it up. One may attack it by challenging your logic: you have slipped in your reasoning; you have, let us say, indulged in the lawyer's most frequent logical blunder, ambiguous middle, using the same word-symbol in two different senses. Or, and here we recur to the level of observation, you may have so built your alleged rule that it fails to cover some of the cases before you, or covers some of them contrary to their holdings. Then not your logical *de*duction, but the adequacy of your *in*duction is in question. Or, and finally, one may attack you on your implication about future judges; you may have picked a premise perfectly all right as covering your material, you may have deduced soundly the conclusion which follows—and yet your future judge may kick over the traces. To use the language of my last lecture, his *attitude* may not admit acceptance of your reasoning. And, since we have seen that *every single* precedent, *according to what may be the attitude of future judges, is ambiguous,* is wide or narrow at need, it is clear that your original induction must either run in terms of the future judge's attitude in this, or else fail to jibe with what he will do.

Seen in these terms it becomes clear that whereas the deductive aspects of your *application* of a rule once made may be, ideally, perfectly certain, your induction, which precedes, is one which *begins* not with definite, but with indefinite material: one therefore into which elements of judgment, hunches, prediction enter as you freeze it into definite arbitrary form to make possible its logical manipulation; and it is clear that in choosing the definite form you give it, you will be guided by the desire that your conclusion may work out in fact, in life. You will therefore cut the raw material of your single cases according to your *expectation* about how courts will handle each one of them as a precedent. So far, in your role as a non-participant, a business adviser, a man figuring what courts *will* do, in order to arrange his affairs to suit.

But as an advocate, as one about to argue to a court, the matter is somewhat different. There, the rule which you derive by induction is a rule which has one striking characteristic absent in the observer's work. In addition to the cases which are given in the books it must cover the case which you have in hand, and must cover it cogently, and must decide it as you need it decided. Here your job of induction has a predetermined goal. And the inductive reasoning you now put forward is in terms less of what the present court's attitude *is* than of what you desire it to be, and of what you hope you can induce it to be. This does not change the job of making a logically perfect structure—of making what I have called a sound technical ladder to reach the result. But it affects the way in which you deal with the ambiguous raw material of the prior cases. And, since your ladder must be persuasive on the deductive side as well, it affects the way in which you emphasize, arrange, classify the facts of the case in hand, to drive home as significant those aspects of the facts which fit conveniently into the premise you have erected, which nail *this* case down "within the rule."

Indeed, it is time now to challenge what I have thus far assumed: to wit, that on the purely deductive side of these logical structures a *certainty* of conclusion is to be found when you move into the world of fact. Remember again the infinite diversity of fact-situations in life. Remember again, in the court's decision, the level of "interpreting the raw evidence." Remember, finally, that even when the evidence has been interpreted as to what it means—in *fact*—there remains the job of seeing what it means in *law*: of putting the individual facts or groups of facts into those legal abstract categories which are the terms of legal rules: "motorcar" or "vehicle"; "road" or "public highway"—and the rest. What shall we do with a scooter in a private park? There is judgment to be exercised, then, first, in selection of raw evidence; second in interpreting or transforming what has been selected; third, in classifying for legal significance the material after its *fact*-meaning has been assured. And for the advocate there is persuading to be done not only on the side of induction from ambiguous precedents, but also on the side of deduction, of classifying any concrete facts into the abstract fact-categories which are all that rules at law can hope to deal with. Of a truth the logic of law, however indebted it may be to formal logic for method, however nice it may be in its middle reaches, loses all sharp precision, all firm footing, in the two battlegrounds in which the two feet of the ladder stand.

Is this an excuse for sloppiness of logic? It is not. To slip in logic is to curse your case. Even if otherwise good, it then is bad. But to mistake your logic for persuasion is an error as great. Where the material on each end speaks with a forked tongue there rises against you a ladder of logic as impeccable as yours. And there remains to you the problems of *persuasion*—in your initial building of your ladder; and in your argument.

So far we have looked at the relation of logic to the law from the angle of the observer, or adviser, and from the angle of the advocate. We have seen how the counsellor must add to his logic his understanding of the attitude of the judge; and how the advocate must add not only that, but also the wherewithal to persuade the judge to accept a major premise from which the advocate's conclusion flows. *What now of the judge himself?* Is he a machine, merely with a set, an attitude, which goes on mechanically, and which an observer requires only to discover? Is he a weather vane which the advocate can blow this way or that? Is he a despot, free of all control, thanks to the leeway offered by the ambiguities of his material, and able at will, or as a favor, or in caprice, or for a price, to throw the decision this way or that? As to this last question, within limits, yes; but much more truly, no. He *can* throw the decision this way or that. *But not freely.* For to him the logical ladder, or the several logical ladders, are ways of keeping himself in touch with the decisions of the past. This, as a judge, he wishes to do. This, as a judge, he would have to do even if he did not wish. This is the public's check upon his work. This is his own check on his own work. For while it is possible to build a number of divergent logical ladders up out of the same cases and down again to the same dispute, *there are not so many that can be built defensibly.* And of these few there are some, or there is one, toward which the prior cases pretty definitely press. Already you see the walls closing in around the judge. Finally, when all is done, he does remain free to choose—in a sense. But not free in another—for he is a judge. As a human being, his "attitude"—the resultant of his life—conditions him. As a judge—and a potent factor in his attitude—his conscience conditions him. It is his job to decide which ladder leads to the *just* conclusion, or to the *wise* conclusion— when he sees two clear possibilities. He does that job, and in the main he does it well. Often indeed he will not get that far. Often the prior cases push so strongly toward one lineup that he will not even see the chance we here point out to line them up differently. Then, unless the result raises the hair (*his* hair, not yours!), and forces a different outcome so to speak at the muzzle of a gun, the judge will never get as far as inquiring into justice. He will decide "by law" and let it go at that. Particularly, to come back to a point made earlier, will this be true of the weaker, the less skilful judge. Advance upon him with a ladder sound in logic, and he grows uncomfortable: his duty calls for application of the law; his skill does not suffice to find the alternative ladder which a more able or sophisticated mind might find. Again we see wisdom made institutional, caught up and crystallized into a working system: by way of logic the weak judge is penned within the walls his predecessors built; by way of logic the strong judge can scale those walls when in his judgment that is needed. And either phase, and both, promote the common weal.

Now this ad hoc approach to logic, this building of major premises out of a group of cases not so much to find what is in them as to decide a case in hand—this is of the essence of our case-law system. It is not so of every legal system, even of every system built on case law. The classical jurists of Rome seem, though they worked case by case, to have built up a strangely systematic whole; the French and German writers before the Codes had gone a great distance further on that road. *Elegantia juris* is the Latin for it: *form* in the law, in whole and in each part. Our sin is lack of elegance and even taste; our virtue is a sturdy, earthy common sense.

From this angle I think you will understand the attitude of some of your instructors. They show so little interest in the deductive consequences of a proposition. They show no patience in following deductive reasoning through. Put them an inconvenient case within their rule; there is no thrill of battle. The minute they see the inconvenience they will junk the rule, restate it to avoid the bother, and go on. They do not seem depressed. Students who have had rigorous deductive training are amazed—and often are disgusted. I think, with no great reason. Here is a man whose training is ad hoc, who knows our courts to work as he is working. His search is not for a rule which holds, at large, but for a rule which holds good *for the matter in hand*. His interest is in *forming premises* in consonance with the authorities, and premises which decide according to need the case before him. One is as good as another, ad hoc—apart from the question of persuasion. That he is there to teach you. And one thing he can teach you which is worth learning. That is, resilience in *choosing* major premises. This is a pragmatic world. Most major premises

still are dictated by a conclusion needed and already fixed.

Not that I would have your training stop at this. You must have exercise in deduction as well. Fortunately, you have other instructors who lay down major premises and work with them. Though all but one are as weak in logic as the others. They, too, are products of their training ground, our law. And our law has had no love for definitions—except ad hoc. The more careful of our statutes do include some definitions. But for the law at large? Not at all. "In this act," is as far as they purport to go. And even there, they lack (and lack for reason) the touch of Puritan courage of conviction. The definitions follow weasel words: "except when the context or subject matter otherwise requires" *x* shall mean *a* or *b* or *c*. Now deduction without definition of terms is a game of cop and robber: you can have anything you catch. You will find, too, in this academic deductive exercise—as with the legal writers—that what we have seen as a most difficult, ambiguous task is regularly slurred over: to wit the allocation of the raw facts among the generalized "significant" categories of the law.

In short, on the side of logic, the law has much to learn, and we, your instructors, not a little. But, as I hope I have indicated, that does not mean that *you* can get along without it. It means that you have a chance to improve on the techniques now current—if you will season your logic *at each end* with knowledge of the cases, and with common sense.

From this angle, moreover, you will observe another value in the study of the cases. Each opinion is an example of legal reasoning—with and from prior cases. Each opinion is an example of what some court has thought persuasive. Both as to the legal use of logic and as to persuasion there is something here to learn. And please note that there is as much, almost, to learn from the poor reasoning as from the good. A fine opinion is a model piece of work. But an execrable opinion gives an example of a type of mind you have to deal with, too.

In this connection, too, I should like to ask you to observe the difference between logical argument and argumentative statement, between showing a given logical relation between two matters, and *persuading* someone else that it exists by *attributing* the relationship to them in your discussion or description. This appears nowhere more strikingly than in the presentation of the facts with an eye to the rule you are trying to bring them under. Allied in technique, but different logically, is the use of *emotive* words in your argument, which are designed to induce the attitude toward the result your argument requires. The crass case, as you already must have seen, is in old-fashioned pleadings. Watch for these things in the judges' opinions. Not always, but often, they mean that defective logic is being covered up.

II

Now, having raised the question of rules of law as rules of Ought, rules which tell judges and other officials what to do, and having in my first lecture argued that the law really was not so much rules as what the officials did, I fear I must wrestle with the relation between the two. And at the same time with the place in all this scheme of statute law.

Perhaps the best approach to an answer will be to backtrack a little on the assertion in my introduction, and to assert instead (so to speak as a corrected hypothesis) that law must embrace in its very heart and core what the officials do, and that rules take on meaning in life only as they aid one either to predict what officials will do, or to get them to do something. Or, if you prefer to state the dispute aspect of law broadly enough to include the most primitive forms of law within the group, and the still primitive forms of law between the great groups we call states: that a heart and core of living law is how disputes are in fact settled, and that rules take on live meaning only as they bear on that. But whether you go with me in this opinion or not, you will surely agree that rules and results both will need attention. That is one thing. And that the two must never be confused, if you are to see what you are talking about, or where you are going. That is another.

It will pay you to observe here and to sever off one by one what we may call the *levels of discussion* about law, especially in a case class. Cross-level discussion is *never* profitable. One must be conscious, always, of which level he is talking on, and which level the other person is talking on, and see to it that differences in level are corrected. One must, moreover, know and signal his shifting from one level to another. Else false issues, cross-purposes, and general footlessness ensue.

1. a. There is first the question of what the court *actually decided* in a given case: judgment reversed, and new trial ordered. And the question of what express *ratio decidendi* it announced. These are facts of observation. They are the starting point of all discussion. Until you have them there is no use doing any arguing about anything.

   b. There is the question of *what the rule of the case is,* as derived from its comparison with a number of other cases. This is not so simple, but the technical procedures for determining it are clear. Skilled observers should rather regularly be able to agree on two points: (i) the reasonably safe maximum rule the case can be used for; (ii) the reasonably certain minimum rule the case must be admitted to contain.

2. As against both of these, there is the question of the manner, attitude and accuracy of the court's *interpretation* or transformation of the raw evidence. Here judgement factors enter, and you and I may not agree about it. But at least we can keep the level of discussion separate from the levels just above. There we *presuppose* facts as they *result* from this interpretation we are here discussing; and we look to the rule laid down upon the facts already transformed.

3. There is the question of what the *probable* precedent value of the case is, in a given court or in general. Here, too, judgment factors enter very largely, and objective agreement is not to be expected; for we must draw into our thinking the results of our work on the second level, and must draw further things as well. Yet here, too, as to the *level* of discourse

all can agree: it is a question of predicting what some court will in fact do. You can phrase this, if you will, in terms of Ought: what some court will understand this case to tell it to do. I think this latter phrasing slightly misleading, and certainly cumbersome; but defensible it surely is.

4. There is the question of *estimating what consequences the case* (and its consequences in other cases) have to laymen: the relation between the *ways* of the court and the *ways* of those affected by the court. This I take again to be purely on the level of description or prediction, but to be a very complicated matter, and one which involves even more information from outside the cases than does problem 3. The consequences may turn, for instance, on the persons concerned making quite inaccurate prediction of how later cases will eventuate—on their quite misinterpreting the case, on their readjusting their own ways not to their actual environment, but to an *imaginary* environment of court ways.

5. a. There is the question of *evaluating* the court's action in the case—of concluding how desirable it is. And this is of course the most complicated of all, because it includes all the foregoing, and various premises also as to what values are to be taken as the baseline and the goal. What is utterly vital to see at least is that you cannot begin on this *until you have settled* the matters in the first and second problems, and grappled with those in the third and fourth. And, finally, that this matter of evaluation, while it presupposes the others, in no way touches the *level* on which they are discussed.

    b. There is the evaluation of the court's decision or *ratio* from the angle of *doctrine*. Here some premise or concept is *assumed,* as authoritatively given, and the court's action is tested for whether it is or is not dogmatically *correct,* when compared with that premise. Less dogmatically minded thinkers use the same technique, on the same *logical* level, to see not whether the care is "correct," but

whether it *squares* with a given hypothesis (either of doctrine or of prediction)—i.e. to test its consistency with some formulation of a "rule" derived inductively from other cases. It should be clear that this touches neither 3, nor 4, nor (really) even 5a.

Now it would be a case-hardened theorist who proposed to exclude any of these problems from the field of law. Yet I think it equally clear that central to them all is the question of what the courts will do. I think it also clear that after study of a group of cases and estimates of just how far courts do follow what prior courts have done, one can set about constructing generalized statements, generalized predictions of their action. I have no hesitancy in calling these predictions rules; they are, however, thus far only rules *of* the court's action; they are statements of the practices of the court. Thanks to the doctrine of precedent the courts themselves regard them also and simultaneously as rules *for* the court's action, *precepts* for the court. So far, the two phases of prediction and of Ought cover identical territory. Yet the moment that you forsake the relatively solid rock of attempted prediction, you run into difficulty, and for this reason: that when you are told by anyone that a given rule is *the proper rule* (not "an accurate prediction") you are dealing with his value judgment, based on no man knows what. *If* you will keep that fact in mind, and your own feet on the cases, and *if* you will remember especially that the only test of whether and how far a rule *authoritatively prevails as a rule of Ought* is: how far will courts follow it—then you will be safe, whatever language is employed.

How shall I reconcile this position with the fact of statutes? We live under a regime of theoretical separation of powers. So far, at least, that theory holds true in fact, that courts and legislatures agree that when legislatures properly pass statutes, the courts are bound by them. But statutes are rules, they are forms of words on books.

Now the essential differences between statutes and the law of case decisions are these. A judge makes his rule in and around a specific case, and looking backward. The case shapes the rule; the judge's feet are firmly on the particular instance; his rule is commonly good sense, and very narrow. And any innovation is confined regularly within rather narrow limits—partly by the practice of trying hard to square the new decision with old law; it is hard to keep daring innovations even verbally consistent with old rules. And partly innovation is confined through conscious policy: case law rules (though new) are applied *as if* they had always been the law; this derives from our convention that "judges only declare and do not make the law." Knowing that the effect of their ruling will be retroactive, and unable to foresee how many men's calculations a new ruling may upset, the judges move very cautiously into new ground. Then, when a case has been decided, it enters into the sea of common law—available to any court within the Anglo-American world, and peculiarly, within this country. Finally, and important here, case law is flexible around the edges; the rules are commonly somewhat uncertain in their wording, and not too easy to make definite. Else why your study?

But statutes are made relatively in the large, to cover wider sweeps, and looking forward. They apply only to events and transactions occurring *after* they have come into force; that element of caution disappears. They are, moreover, a recognized machinery for readjustment of the law. They represent not single disputes, but whole classes of disputes. They are political, not judicial in their nature, represent readjustments along the lines of balance of power, decide not single cases by a tiny shift of rule, but the rearrangement of a great mass of clashing interests. Statute-making, too, is confined within what in relation to society at large is a straitened margin of free movement; but in comparison to courts the legislature is a horse without a halter. Finally, statutes have a wording fixed and firm. And their effect is local for the single state. You cannot reason from a statute to the common law. The statue of one state affords no ground for urging a like conclusion in another with no similar statute. If anything, the contrary. The presence of a statute argues rather that the common law was otherwise in the state of the statute—and hence everywhere.

Well, say you, these statutory rules with their fixed words take us wholly out of the prediction problem. Here is Ought, naked. That, I fear, I must doubt. For the very basis of this statute is its generality. Made without any particular case in mind—or in some instances, with a single particular case too much in mind, and without the caution drilled by experience into the judges—the language is faced now with a succession of particular cases. And as with the problem of deduction raised above, the question is that of classifying these new ambiguous concrete facts: do they or do they not fit into the statutory boxes? The meaning of the statute in life, like the meaning of case-law rule, turns on the answer. We must turn to prediction, then, of what the courts will do, if we would read the statute. We turn, if we can, to what the judges have already done, to make our prediction sound.

I am not touching here the Constitution, the power of the judges to set constitution above legislation, and to deny that a given statute has validity. I am dealing with the meaning of a statute which by the judges' announcement and practice they hold to bind themselves, and which they set out merely to "apply."

Much of the situation I describe is inherent in the nature of the case. We meet it abroad, where statutes have been drawn with prayer and skill, and judges deemed themselves for years to be almost mechanical interpreters. Even there, we find that it is to decisions we must turn, much of the time, to make out what the statute means, and that the Continentals have awakened to that fact. But in our system there are further reasons. First (to get it out of the way) we have so many statutes which are drawn so poorly that it seems doubtful whether the draftsman himself knew what he wanted, much less what meaning he has put into his words. This evil lessens as the practice of official legislative drafting service grows. But second, we have with us still the relics of a sort of feud between the courts and the legislature, a pride of office, a pride in prestige, a jealousy of skill, technique, of trade. To the courts the common law seemed a coherent system, filling the whole universe of possible disputes with sound solutions. But statutes were single innovations, intrusions upon this system; warts on the body of the common law. Systematic, complete, exclusive codification of the law is strange to us; though the Continentals know it. We see single statutes—warts; we treat them thus. Partly, with reason. Statutes surely require to be fitted in. They cannot stand alone. No language stands alone. It draws life from its background. Technical terms used in a statute, undefined, must draw their meaning from the law which brought them forth. Only the background of the case teaches what the law was which the statute-maker sought to clarify or change. Against that background, then, his meaning must be sought. If you have doubt of this, turn to some clarifying statute, such as the Sales Act, excellent legislation, about a subject, sales of goods, with which you might suppose any businessman familiar. Read over ten or twenty sections, in ignorance of the cases, and see how little they tell you. Finally, the statute must, as I said, be fitted into something. The fitting can be accomplished only by bringing the two together. The necessary accommodation must in part be mutual; the legislature can hardly be deemed, with its single aim in mind, to have willed the wrenching and ruin of all neighboring existing law it did not mention.

But in another aspect this antagonism to the statute has far less point. Statutes are passed precisely to the end of change. Then they should be given scope. Filling a statute out with meaning from the common law is one thing; emasculating it by artificial construction is another. I suspect, as I have indicated, that pride of skill and jealousy had some part in producing that great maxim that statutes in derogation of the common law are to be strictly construed—which means: are to be made to mean as little as they can be made to mean. Some other part is almost surely due to the training of the judges in reading any writing: first, as property lawyers, holding a conveyance down to the closest confine of its terms (what man

would grant away more than he need to?); second, as skilled special pleaders, trained to construe the papers with all cunning against the party who had put them out. It is hardly needful to point out that most of the wordiness of our older statutes reflects this duel of wits against unwilling courts.

On the other hand, we have another maxim of more recent importance: remedial statutes are to be liberally construed. This represents a better insight. But observe here, as in the case of precedents, as throughout the law, the two-faced premise legal technique offers to the judge. At his need, as the case before him urges, he can construe the statute strictly (as "in derogation of the common law") when it would seem to work hardship, or liberally (as "remedial") if that seems indicated.

One more thing I must mention before I leave these statutes: if they are local, territorial in their effect, if they afford no ground for reasoning to the reservoir of law, then when you meet a statute in a case, you can skate over it? It has no *general* bearing? It need not be remembered? *As pure information,* it may be you will not need it, unless like statutes show signs of appearing elsewhere. But as a problem in legal technique, a statute in your case book deserves more intensive study than a common law decision. For whatever the concrete content it may have, it presents to the court a problem: how to interpret—what to do about it? As to that problem, the court's approach and solution are typical of all our courts, typical of a *process* you must know. And of a process which you cannot follow except in its abominable detail. You cannot read a statute like a case. There is no pleasant repetition of the same thought in different forms. Each word stands there. You get it, or you miss the whole. There is nothing that one dares to scant. There is little indeed of dictum in a statute. Eyes out, then, for *each word* of each statute that you meet!

CHAPTER FIVE

Legal Interpretation

15   Integrity in Law

RONALD DWORKIN

THE *McLOUGHLIN* CASE[1]

... Mrs. McLoughlin's husband and four children were injured in an automobile accident in England at about 4 P.M. on October 19, 1973. She heard about the accident at home from a neighbor at about 6 P.M. and went immediately to the hospital, where she learned that her daughter was dead and saw the serious condition of her husband and other children. She suffered nervous shock and later sued the defendant driver, whose negligence had caused the accident, as well as other parties who were in different ways involved, for compensation for her emotional injuries. Her lawyer pointed to several earlier decisions of English courts awarding compensation to people who had suffered emotional injury on seeing serious injury to a close relative. But in all these cases the plaintiff had either been at the scene of the accident or had arrived within minutes. In a 1972 case, for example, a wife recovered—won compensation—for emotional injury; she had come upon the body of her husband immediately after his fatal accident. In 1967 a man who was not related to any of the victims of a train crash worked for hours trying to rescue victims and suffered nervous shock from the experience. He was allowed to recover. Mrs. McLoughlin's lawyer relied on these cases as precedents, decisions which had made it part of the law that people in her position are entitled to compensation....

The judge before whom Mrs. McLoughlin first brought her suit, the trial judge, decided that the precedents her lawyer cited, about others who had recovered compensation for emotional injury suffered when they saw accident victims, were distinguishable because in all those cases the shock had occurred at the scene of the accident, while she was shocked some two hours later and in a different place. Of course not every difference in the facts of two cases makes the earlier one distinguishable: no one could think it mattered if Mrs. McLoughlin was younger than the plaintiffs in the earlier cases.

The trial judge thought that suffering injury away from the scene was an important difference

Reprinted by permission of the publisher from *Law's Empire* by Ronald Dworkin, Cambridge, Mass: Harvard University Press, copyright © 1986 by Ronald Dworkin. Endnotes have been edited and renumbered.

because it meant that Mrs. McLoughlin's injury was not "foreseeable" in the way that the injury to the other plaintiffs had been. Judges in both Britain and America follow the common law principle that people who act carelessly are liable only for reasonably foreseeable injuries to others, injuries a reasonable person would anticipate if he reflected on the matter. The trial judge was bound by the doctrine of precedent to recognize that emotional injury to close relatives at the scene of an accident is reasonably foreseeable, but he said that injury to a mother who saw the results of the accident later is not. So he thought he could distinguish the putative precedents in that way and decided against Mrs. McLoughlin's claim.

She appealed his decision to the next highest court in the British hierarchy, the Court of Appeal. That court affirmed the trial judge's decision—it refused her appeal and let his decision stand—but not on the argument he had used. The Court of Appeal said it *was* reasonably foreseeable that a mother would rush to the hospital to see her injured family and that she would suffer emotional shock from seeing them in the condition Mrs. McLoughlin found. That court distinguished the precedents not on that ground but for the very different reason that what it called "policy" justified a distinction. The precedents had established liability for emotional injury in certain restricted circumstances, but the Court of Appeal said that recognizing a larger area of liability, embracing injuries to relatives not at the scene, would have a variety of adverse consequences for the community as a whole. It would encourage many more lawsuits for emotional injuries, and this would exacerbate the problem of congestion in the courts. It would open new opportunities for fraudulent claims by people who had not really suffered serious emotional damage but could find doctors to testify that they had. It would increase the cost of liability insurance, making it more expensive to drive and perhaps preventing some poor people from driving at all. The claims of those who had suffered genuine emotional injury away from the scene would be harder to prove, and the uncertainties of litigation might complicate their condition and delay their recovery.

Mrs. McLoughlin appealed the decision once more, to the House of Lords, which reversed the Court of Appeal and ordered a new trial. The decision was unanimous, but their lordships disagreed about what they called the true state of the law. Several of them said that policy reasons, of the sort described by the Court of Appeal, might in some circumstances be sufficient to distinguish a line of precedents and so justify a judge's refusal to extend the principle of those cases to a larger area of liability. But they did not think these policy reasons were of sufficient plausibility or merit in Mrs. McLoughlin's case. They did not believe that the risk of a "flood" of litigation was sufficiently grave, and they said the courts should be able to distinguish genuine from fraudulent claims even among those whose putative injury was suffered several hours after the accident. They did not undertake to say when good policy arguments might be available to limit recovery for emotional injury; they left it an open question, for example, whether Mrs. McLoughlin's sister in Australia (if she had one) could recover for the shock she might have in reading about the accident weeks or months later in a letter.

Two of their lordships took a very different view of the law. They said it would be wrong for courts to deny recovery to an otherwise meritorious plaintiff for the *kinds* of reasons the Court of Appeal had mentioned and which the other law lords had said might be sufficient in some circumstances. The precedents should be regarded as distinguishable, they said, only if the moral *principles* assumed in the earlier cases for some reason did not apply to the plaintiff in the same way. And once it is conceded that the damage to a mother in the hospital hours after an accident is reasonably foreseeable to a careless driver, then no difference in moral principle can be found between the two cases. Congestion in the courts or a rise in the price of automobile liability insurance, they said, however inconvenient these might be to the community as a whole, cannot justify refusing to enforce individual rights and duties that have been recognized and enforced before. They said these were the wrong sorts of arguments to make to judges as arguments of law, however cogent they might be if addressed to legislators as arguments for a change in the law.

(Lord Scarman's opinion was particularly clear and strong on this point.) The argument among their lordships revealed an important difference of opinion about the proper role of considerations of policy in deciding what result parties to a lawsuit are entitled to have....

A LARGE VIEW

... Law as integrity denies that statements of law are either the backward-looking factual reports of conventionalism or the forward-looking instrumental programs of legal pragmatism. It insists that legal claims are interpretive judgments and therefore combine backward- and forward-looking elements; they interpret contemporary legal practice seen as an unfolding political narrative. So law as integrity rejects as unhelpful the ancient question whether judges find or invent law; we understand legal reasoning, it suggests, only by seeing the sense in which they do both and neither.

Integrity and Interpretation

The adjudicative principle of integrity instructs judges to identify legal rights and duties, so far as possible, on the assumption that they all were created by a single author—the community personified—expressing a coherent conception of justice and fairness. We form our third conception of law, our third view of what rights and duties flow from past political decisions, by restating this instruction as a thesis about the grounds of law. According to law as integrity, propositions of law are true if they figure in or follow from the principles of justice, fairness, and procedural due process that provide the best constructive interpretation of the community's legal practice. Deciding whether the law grants Mrs. McLoughlin compensation for her injury, for example, means deciding whether legal practice is seen in a better light if we assume the community has accepted the principle that people in her position are entitled to compensation....

Integrity and History

History matters in law as integrity: very much but only in a certain way. Integrity does not require consistency in principle over all historical stages of a community's law; it does not require that judges try to understand the law they enforce as continuous in principle with the abandoned law of a previous century or even a previous generation. It commands a horizontal rather than vertical consistency of principle across the range of the legal standards the community now enforces. It insists that the law—the rights and duties that flow from past collective decisions and for that reason license or require coercion—contains not only the narrow explicit content of these decisions but also, more broadly, the scheme of principles necessary to justify them. History matters because that scheme of principle must justify the standing as well as the content of these past decisions. Our justification for treating the Endangered Species Act as law, unless and until it is repealed, crucially includes the fact that Congress enacted it, and any justification we supply for treating that fact as crucial must itself accommodate the way we treat other events in our political past.

Law as integrity, then, begins in the present and pursues the past only so far as and in the way its contemporary focus dictates. It does not aim to recapture, even for present law, the ideals or practical purposes of the politicians who first created it. It aims rather to justify what they did (sometimes including, as we shall see, what they said) in an overall story worth telling now, a story with a complex claim: that present practice can be organized by and justified in principles sufficiently attractive to provide an honorable future. Law as integrity deplores the mechanism of the older "law is law" view as well as the cynicism of the newer "realism." It sees both views as rooted in the same false dichotomy of finding and inventing law. When a judge declares that a particular principle is instinct in law, he reports not a simple-minded claim about the motives of past statesmen, a claim a wise cynic easily can refute, but an interpretive proposal: that the principle both fits and justifies some complex part of legal practice, that it provides an attractive way to see, in the structure of that practice, the consistency of principle integrity requires. Law's optimism is in that way conceptual; claims of law are endemically constructive, just in virtue of the kind of claims they are. This optimism may be misplaced: legal practice may in the end yield to nothing but a deeply skeptical interpretation. But that is not inevitable just because a community's history is one of great change and conflict. An imaginative interpretation can be constructed on morally complicated, even ambiguous terrain.

THE CHAIN OF LAW

The Chain Novel

… [C]reative interpretation takes its formal structure from the idea of intention, not (at least not necessarily) because it aims to discover the purposes of any particular historical person or group, but because it aims to impose purpose over the text or data or tradition being interpreted. Since all creative interpretation shares this feature, and therefore has a normative aspect or component, we profit from comparing law with other forms or occasions of interpretation. We can usefully compare the judge deciding what the law is on some issue not only with the citizens of courtesy deciding what that tradition requires, but with the literary critic teasing out the various dimensions of value in a complex play or poem.

Judges, however, are authors as well as critics. A judge deciding *McLoughlin* adds to the tradition he interprets; future judges confront a new tradition that includes what he has done. Of course, literary criticism contributes to the traditions of art in which authors work; the character and importance of that contribution are themselves issues in critical theory. But the contribution of judges is more direct, and the distinction between author and interpreter more a matter of different aspects of the same process. We can find an even more fruitful comparison between literature and law, therefore, by constructing an artificial genre of literature that we might call the chain novel.

In this enterprise a group of novelists writes a novel seriatim; each novelist in the chain interprets the chapters he has been given in order to write a new chapter, which then is added to what the next novelist receives, and so on. Each has the job of writing his chapter so as to make the novel being constructed the best it can be, and the complexity of this task models the complexity of deciding a hard case under law as integrity. The imaginary literary enterprise is fantastic but not unrecognizable. Some novels actually have been written in this way, though mainly for a debunking purpose, and certain parlor games for rainy weekends in English country houses have something of the same structure. Television soap operas span decades with the same characters and some minimal continuity of personality and plot, though they are written by different teams of authors even in different weeks. In our example, however, the novelists are expected to take their responsibilities of continuity more seriously; they aim jointly to create, so far as they can, a single unified novel that is the best it can be.[2]

Each novelist aims to make a single novel of the material he has been given, what he adds to it, and (so far as he can control this) what his successors will want or be able to add. He must try to make this the best novel it can be, construed as the work of a single author rather than, as is the fact, the product of many different hands. That calls for an overall judgment on his part, or a series of overall judgments as he writes and rewrites. He must take up some view about the novel in progress, some working theory about its characters, plot, genre, theme, and point, in order to decide what counts as continuing it and not as beginning anew. If he is a good critic, his view of these matters will be complicated and multifaceted, because the value of a decent novel cannot be captured from a single perspective. He will aim to find layers and currents of meaning rather than a single, exhaustive theme. We can, however, in our now familiar way give some structure to any interpretation he adopts, by distinguishing two dimensions on which it must be tested. The first is what we have been calling the dimension of fit. He cannot adopt any interpretation, however complex, if he believes that no single author who set out to write a novel with the various readings of character, plot, theme, and point that interpretation describes could have written substantially the text he has been given. That does not mean his interpretation must fit every bit of the text. It is not disqualified simply because he claims that some lines or tropes are accidental, or even that some events of plot are mistakes because they work against the literary ambitions the interpretation states. But the interpretation he takes up nevertheless must flow throughout the text; it must have general explanatory power, and it is flawed if it leaves unexplained some major structural aspect of the text, a subplot treated as having great dramatic importance or a dominant and repeated metaphor. If no interpretation can be found that is not flawed in that way, then the chain novelist will not be able fully to meet his assignment; he will have to settle for an interpretation that captures most of the text, conceding that it is not wholly successful. Perhaps even that partial success is unavailable; perhaps every interpretation he considers is inconsistent with the bulk of the material supplied to him. In that case he must abandon the enterprise, for the consequence of taking the interpretive attitude toward the text in question is then a piece of internal skepticism: that nothing can count as continuing the novel rather than beginning anew.

He may find, not that no single interpretation fits the bulk of the text, but that more than one does. The second dimension of interpretation then requires him to judge which of these eligible readings makes the work in progress best, all things considered. At this point his more substantive aesthetic judgments, about the importance or insight or realism or beauty of different ideas the novel might be taken to express, come into play. But the formal and structural considerations that dominate on the first dimension figure on the second as well, for even when neither of two interpretations is disqualified out of hand as explaining too little, one may show the text in a better light because it fits more of the text or provides a more interesting integration of style and content. So the distinction between the two dimensions is less crucial or profound than it might seem. It is a useful analytical device that helps us give structure to any interpreter's working theory or style. He will form a sense of when an interpretation fits so poorly that it is unnecessary to consider its substantive appeal, because he knows that this cannot outweigh its embarrassments of fit in deciding whether it makes the novel better, everything taken into account, than its rivals. This sense will define the first dimension for him. But he need not reduce his intuitive sense to any precise

formula; he would rarely need to decide whether some interpretation barely survives or barely fails, because a bare survivor, no matter how ambitious or interesting it claimed the text to be, almost certainly would fail in the overall comparison with other interpretations whose fit was evident. We now can appreciate the range of different kinds of judgments that are blended in this overall comparison. Judgments about textual coherence and integrity, reflecting different formal literary values, are interwoven with more substantive aesthetic judgments that themselves assume different literary aims. Yet these various kinds of judgments, of each general kind, remain distinct enough to check one another in an overall assessment, and it is that possibility of contest, particularly between textual and substantive judgments, that distinguishes a chain novelist's assignment from more independent creative writing. Nor can we draw any flat distinction between the stage at which a chain novelist interprets the text he has been given and the stage at which he adds his own chapter, guided by the interpretation he has settled on. When he begins to write he might discover in what he has written a different, perhaps radically different, interpretation. Or he might find it impossible to write in the tone or theme he first took up, and that will lead him to reconsider other interpretations he first rejected. In either case he returns to the text to reconsider the lines it makes eligible.

Scrooge

We can expand this abstract description of the chain novelist's judgment through an example. Suppose you are a novelist well down the chain. Suppose Dickens never wrote *A Christmas Carol*, and the text you are furnished, though written by several people, happens to be the first part of that short novel. You consider these two interpretations of the central character: Scrooge is inherently and irredeemably evil, an embodiment of the untarnished wickedness of human nature freed from the disguises of convention he rejects; or Scrooge is inherently good but progressively corrupted by the false values and perverse demands of high capitalist society.

Obviously it will make an enormous difference to the way you continue the story which of these interpretations you adopt. If you have been given almost all of *A Christmas Carol* with only the very end to be written—Scrooge already has had his dreams, repented, and sent his turkey— it is too late for you to make him irredeemably wicked, assuming you think, as most interpreters would, that the text will not bear that interpretation without too much strain. I do not mean that no interpreter could possibly think Scrooge inherently evil after his supposed redemption. Someone might take that putative redemption to be a final act of hypocrisy, though only at the cost of taking much else in the text not at face value. This would be a poor interpretation, not because no one could think it a good one, but because it is in fact, on all the criteria so far described, a poor one.

But now suppose you have been given only the first few sections of *A Christmas Carol*. You find that neither of the two interpretations you are considering is decisively ruled out by anything in the text so far; perhaps one would better explain some minor incidents of plot that must be left unconnected on the other, but each interpretation can be seen generally to flow through the abbreviated text as a whole. A competent novelist who set out to write a novel along either of the lines suggested could well have written what you find on the pages. In that case you have a further decision to make. Your assignment is to make of the text the best it can be, and you will therefore choose the interpretation you believe makes the work more significant or otherwise better. That decision probably (though not inevitably) will depend on whether you think that real people somewhat like Scrooge are born bad or are corrupted by capitalism. But it will depend on much else as well, because your aesthetic convictions are not so simple as to make only this aspect of a novel relevant to its overall success. Suppose you think that one interpretation integrates not only plot, but image and setting as well; the social interpretation accounts, for example, for the sharp contrast between the individualistic fittings and partitions of Scrooge's countinghouse and the communitarian formlessness of Bob Cratchit's household. Now your aesthetic judgment—about which reading makes the continuing novel better as a novel—is itself more complex because it must identify and trade off different dimensions of value in a novel. Suppose you believe that the original sin reading is much the more accurate depiction of human nature, but that the sociorealist reading provides a deeper and more interesting formal structure for the novel. You then must ask yourself which interpretation makes the work of art better on the whole. You never may have reflected on that sort of question before—perhaps the tradition of criticism in which you have been trained takes it for granted that one or the other of these dimensions is the more important—but that is no reason why you may not do so now. Once you make up your mind you will believe that the correct interpretation of Scrooge's character is the interpretation that makes the novel better on the whole, so judged.

This contrived example is complex enough to provoke the following apparently important question: Is your judgment about the best way to interpret and continue the sections you have been given of *A Christmas Carol* a free or a constrained judgment? Are you free to give effect to your own assumptions and attitudes about what novels should be like? Or are you bound to ignore these because you are enslaved by a text you cannot alter? The answer is plain enough: neither of these two crude descriptions—of total creative freedom or mechanical textual constraint—captures your situation, because each must in some way be qualified by the other. You will sense creative freedom when you compare your task with some relatively more mechanical one, like direct translation of a text into a foreign language. But you will sense constraint when you compare it with some relatively less guided one, like beginning a new novel of your own.

It is important not only to notice this contrast between elements of artistic freedom and textual constraint, but also not to misunderstand its character. It is *not* a contrast between those aspects of interpretation that are dependent on and those that are independent of the interpreter's aesthetic convictions. And it is not a contrast between those aspects that may be and those that cannot be controversial. For the constraints that you sense as limits to your freedom to read *A Christmas Carol* so as to make Scrooge irredeemably evil are as much matters of judgment and conviction, about which different chain novelists might disagree, as the convictions and attitudes you call on in deciding whether the novel would have been better if he had been irredeemably evil. If the latter convictions are "subjective" (I use the language of external skepticism, reluctantly, because some readers will find it helpful here) then so are the former. Both major types of convictions any interpreter has—about which readings fit the text better or worse and about which of two readings makes the novel substantively better—are internal to his overall scheme of beliefs and attitudes; neither type is independent of that scheme in some way that the other is not....

Our chain-novel example has so far been distorted by the unrealistic assumption that the text you were furnished miraculously had the unity of something written by a single author. Even if each of the previous novelists in the chain took his responsibilities very seriously indeed, the text you were given would show the marks of its history, and you would have to tailor your style of interpretation to that circumstance. You might not find any interpretation that flows through the text, that fits everything the material you have been given treats as important. You must lower your sights (as conscientious writers who join the team of an interminable soap opera might do) by trying to construct an interpretation that fits the bulk of what you take to be artistically most fundamental in the text. More than one interpretation may survive this more relaxed test. To choose among these, you must turn to your background aesthetic convictions, including those you will regard as formal. Possibly no interpretation will survive even the relaxed test. That is the skeptical possibility I mentioned earlier: you will end then by abandoning the project, rejecting your assignment as impossible. But you cannot know in advance that you will reach that skeptical result. You must try first. The chain-novel fantasy will be useful in the later argument in various ways, but that is the most important lesson it teaches. The wise-sounding judgment that no one interpretation could be

best must be earned and defended like any other interpretive claim.

A Misleading Objection

A chain novelist, then, has many difficult decisions to make, and different chain novelists can be expected to make these differently. But his decisions do not include, nor are they properly summarized as, the decision whether and how far he should depart from the novel-in-progress he has been furnished. For he has nothing he *can* depart from or cleave to until he has constructed a novel-in-progress from the text, and the various decisions we have canvassed are all decisions he must make just to do this. Suppose you have decided that a sociorealist interpretation of the opening sections of *A Christmas Carol* makes that text, on balance, the best novel-so-far it can be, and so you continue the novel as an exploration of the uniformly degrading master-servant relation under capitalism rather than as a study of original sin. Now suppose someone accuses you of rewriting the "real" novel to produce a different one that you like better. If he means that the "real" novel can be discovered in some way other than by a process of interpretation of the sort you conducted, then he has misunderstood not only the chain-novel enterprise, but also the nature of literature and criticism. Of course, he may mean only that he disagrees with the particular interpretive and aesthetic convictions on which you relied. In that case your disagreement is not that he thinks you should respect the text, while you think you are free to ignore it. Your disagreement is more interesting: you disagree about what respecting this text means.

LAW: THE QUESTION OF EMOTIONAL DAMAGES

Law as integrity asks a judge deciding a common-law case like *McLoughlin* to think of himself as an author in the chain of common law. He knows that other judges have decided cases that, although not exactly like his case, deal with related problems; he must think of their decisions as part of a long story he must interpret and then continue, according to his own judgment of how to make the developing story as good as it can be. (Of course the best story for him means "best" from the standpoint of political morality, not aesthetics.) We can make a rough distinction once again between two main dimensions of this interpretive judgment. The judge's decision—his postinterpretive conclusions—must be drawn from an interpretation that both fits and justifies what has gone before, so far as that is possible. But in law as in literature the interplay between fit and justification is complex. Just as interpretation within a chain novel is for each interpreter a delicate balance between different types of literary and artistic attitudes, so in law it is a delicate balance between political convictions of different sorts; in law as in literature these must be sufficiently related yet disjoint to allow an overall judgment that trades off an interpretation's success on one type of standard against its failure on another. I must try to exhibit that complex structure of legal interpretation, and I shall use for that purpose an imaginary judge of superhuman intellectual power and patience who accepts law as integrity.

Call him Hercules.[3] In this and the next several chapters [Ed.: not reprinted] we follow his career by noticing the types of judgments he must make and tensions he must resolve in deciding a variety of cases. But I offer this caution in advance. We must not suppose that his answers to the various questions he encounters *define* law as integrity as a general conception of law. They are the answers I now think best. But law as integrity consists in an approach, in questions rather than answers, and other lawyers and judges who accept it would give different answers from his to the questions it asks. You might think other answers would be better. (So might I, after further thought.) You might, for example, reject Hercules's views about how far people's legal rights depend on the reasons past judges offered for their decisions enforcing these rights, or you might not share his respect for what I shall call "local priority" in common-law decisions. If you reject these discrete views because you think them poor constructive interpretations of legal practice, however, you have not rejected law as integrity, but rather have joined its enterprise.

Six Interpretations

Hercules must decide *McLoughlin*. Both sides in that case cited precedents; each argued that a decision in its favor would count as going on as before, as continuing the story begun by the judges who decided those precedent cases. Hercules must form his own view about that issue. Just as a chain novelist must find, if he can, some coherent view of character and theme such that a hypothetical single author with that view could have written at least the bulk of the novel so far, Hercules must find, if he can, some coherent theory about legal rights to compensation for emotional injury such that a single political official with that theory could have reached most of the results the precedents report. He is a careful judge, a judge of method. He begins by setting out various candidates for the best interpretation of the precedent cases even before he reads them. Suppose he makes the following short list:

1. No one has a moral right to compensation except for physical injury.
2. People have a moral right to compensation for emotional injury suffered at the scene of an accident against anyone whose carelessness caused the accident, but have no right to compensation for emotional injury suffered later.
3. People should recover compensation for emotional injury when a practice of requiring compensation in their circumstances would diminish the overall costs of accidents or otherwise make the community richer in the long run.
4. People have a moral right to compensation for any injury, emotional or physical, that is the direct consequence of careless conduct, no matter how unlikely or unforeseeable it is that that conduct would result in that injury.
5. People have a moral right to compensation for emotional or physical injury that is the consequence of careless conduct, but only if that injury was reasonably foreseeable by the person who acted carelessly.
6. People have a moral right to compensation for reasonably foreseeable injury, but not in

circumstances when recognizing such a right would impose massive and destructive financial burdens on people who have been careless out of proportion to their moral fault.

These are all relatively concrete statements about rights and, allowing for a complexity in (3) we explore just below, they contradict one another. No more than one can figure in a single interpretation of the emotional injury cases. (I postpone the more complex case in which Hercules constructs an interpretation from competitive rather than contradictory principles, that is, from principles that can live together in an overall moral or political theory though they sometimes pull in different directions.)[4] Even so, this is only a partial list of the contradictory interpretations someone might wish to consider; Hercules chooses it as his initial short list because he knows that the principles captured in these interpretations actually have been discussed in the legal literature. It obviously will make a great difference which of these principles he believes provides the best interpretation of the precedents and so the nerve of his postinterpretive judgment. If he settles on (1) or (2), he must decide for Mr. O'Brian [the defendant]; if on (4), for Mrs. McLoughlin. Each of the others requires further thought, but the line of reasoning each suggests is different. (3) invites an economic calculation. Would it reduce the cost of accidents to extend liability to emotional injury away from the scene? Or is there some reason to think that the most efficient line is drawn just between emotional injuries at and those away from the scene? (5) requires a judgment about foreseeability of injury, which seems to be very different, and (6) a judgment both about foreseeability and the cumulative risk of financial responsibility if certain injuries away from the scene are included.

Hercules begins testing each interpretation on his short list by asking whether a single political official could have given the verdicts of the precedent cases if that official were enforcing consciously and coherently the principles that form the interpretation. He will therefore dismiss interpretation (1) at once. No one who believed that people never have rights to compensation for emotional injury could have reached the results of those past decisions cited in *McLoughlin* that allowed compensation. Hercules also will dismiss interpretation (2), though for a different reason. Unlike (1), (2) fits the past decisions; someone who accepted (2) as a standard would have reached these decisions, because they all allowed recovery for emotional injury at the scene and none allowed recovery for injury away from it. But (2) fails as an interpretation of the required kind because it does not state a principle of justice at all. It draws a line that it leaves arbitrary and unconnected to any more general moral or political consideration.

What about (3)? It might fit the past decisions, but only in the following way: Hercules might discover through economic analysis that someone who accepted the economic theory expressed by (3) and who wished to reduce the community's accident costs would have made just those decisions. But it is far from obvious that (3) states any principle of justice or fairness....

Law as integrity asks judges to assume, so far as this is possible, that the law is structured by a coherent set of principles about justice and fairness and procedural due process, and it asks them to enforce these in the fresh cases that come before them, so that each person's situation is fair and just according to the same standards. That style of adjudication respects the ambition integrity assumes, the ambition to be a community of principle. But ... integrity does not recommend what would be perverse, that we should all be governed by the same goals and strategies of policy on every occasion. It does not insist that a legislature that enacts one set of rules about compensation today, in order to make the community richer on the whole, is in any way committed to serve that same goal of policy tomorrow. For it might then have other goals to seek, not necessarily in place of wealth but beside it, and integrity does not frown on this diversity. Our account of interpretation, and our consequent elimination of interpretation (3) read as a naked appeal to policy, reflects a discrimination already latent in the ideal of integrity itself.

We reach the same conclusion in the context of *McLoughlin* through a different route, by further reflection on what we have learned about interpretation. An interpretation aims to show what is interpreted in the best light possible, and an interpretation of any part of our law therefore must attend not only to the substance of the decisions made by earlier officials, but also to how—by which officials in which circumstances—these decisions were made. A legislature does not need reasons of principle to justify the rules it enacts about driving, including rules about compensation for accidents, even though these rules will create rights and duties for the future that then will be enforced by coercive threat. A legislature may justify its decision to create new rights for the future by showing how these will contribute, as a matter of sound policy, to the overall good of the community as a whole. There are limits to this kind of justification.... The general good may not be used to justify the death penalty for careless driving. But the legislature need not show that citizens already have a moral right to compensation for injury under particular circumstances in order to justify a statute awarding damages in those circumstances.

Law as integrity assumes, however, that judges are in a very different position from legislators. It does not fit the character of a community of principle that a judge should have authority to hold people liable in damages for acting in a way he concedes they had no legal duty not to act. So when judges construct rules of liability not recognized before, they are not free in the way I just said legislators are. Judges must make their common-law decisions on grounds of principle, not policy: they must deploy arguments why the parties actually had the "novel" legal rights and duties they enforce at the time the parties acted or at some other pertinent time in the past.[5] A legal pragmatist would reject that claim. But Hercules rejects pragmatism. He follows law as integrity and therefore wants an interpretation of what judges did in the earlier emotional damage cases that shows them acting in the way he approves, not in the way he thinks judges must decline to act. It does not follow that he must dismiss interpretation (3) read ... as supposing that past judges acted to protect a general legal right to compensation when this would make the community

richer. For if people actually have such a right, others have a corresponding duty, and judges do not act unjustly in ordering the police to enforce it. The argument disqualifies interpretation (3) only when this is read to deny any such general duty and to rest on grounds of policy alone.

Expanding the Range

Interpretations (4), (5), and (6) do, however, seem to pass these initial tests. The principles of each fit the past emotional injury decisions, at least on first glance, if only because none of these precedents presented facts that would discriminate among them. Hercules must now ask, as the next stage of his investigation, whether any one of the three must be ruled out because it is incompatible with the bulk of legal practice more generally. He must test each interpretation against other past judicial decisions, beyond those involving emotional injury, that might be thought to engage them. Suppose he discovers, for example, that past decisions provide compensation for physical injury caused by careless driving only if the injury was reasonably foreseeable. That would rule out interpretation (4) unless he can find some principled distinction between physical and emotional injury that explains why the conditions for compensation should be more restrictive for the former than the latter, which seems extremely unlikely.

Law as integrity, then, requires a judge to test his interpretation of any part of the great network of political structures and decisions of his community by asking whether it could form part of a coherent theory justifying the network as a whole. No actual judge could compose anything approaching a full interpretation of all of his community's law at once. That is why we are imagining a Herculean judge of superhuman talents and endless time. But an actual judge can imitate Hercules in a limited way. He can allow the scope of his interpretation to fan out from the cases immediately in point to cases in the same general area or department of law, and then still farther, so far as this seems promising. In practice even this limited process will be largely unconscious: an experienced judge will have a sufficient sense of the terrain surrounding his immediate problem to know instinctively which interpretation of a small set of cases would survive if the range it must fit were expanded. But sometimes the expansion will be deliberate and controversial. Lawyers celebrate dozens of decisions of that character, including several on which the modern law of negligence was built.[6] Scholarship offers other important examples.[7]

Suppose a modest expansion of Hercules's range of inquiry does show that plaintiffs are denied compensation if their physical injury was not reasonably foreseeable at the time the careless defendant acted, thus ruling out interpretation (4). But this does not eliminate either (5) or (6). He must expand his survey further. He must look also to cases involving economic rather than physical or emotional injury, where damages are potentially very great: for example, he must look to cases in which professional advisers like surveyors or accountants are sued for losses others suffer through their negligence. Interpretation (5) suggests that such liability might be unlimited in amount, no matter how ruinous in total, provided that the damage is foreseeable, and (6) suggests, on the contrary, that liability is limited just because of the frightening sums it might otherwise reach. If one interpretation is uniformly contradicted by cases of that sort and finds no support in any other area of doctrine Hercules might later inspect, and the other is confirmed by the expansion, he will regard the former as ineligible, and the latter alone will have survived. But suppose he finds, when he expands his study in this way, a mixed pattern. Past decisions permit extended liability for members of some professions but not for those of others, and this mixed pattern holds for other areas of doctrine that Hercules, in the exercise of his imaginative skill, finds pertinent.

The contradiction he has discovered, though genuine, is not in itself so deep or pervasive as to justify a skeptical interpretation of legal practice as a whole, for the problem of unlimited damages, while important, is not so fundamental that contradiction within it destroys the integrity of the larger system. So Hercules turns to the second main dimension, but here, as in the chain-novel example, questions of fit surface again, because

an interpretation is pro tanto more satisfactory if it shows less damage to integrity than its rival. He will therefore consider whether interpretation (5) fits the expanded legal record better than (6). But this cannot be a merely mechanical decision; he cannot simply count the number of past decisions that must be conceded to be "mistakes" on each interpretation. For these numbers may reflect only accidents like the number of cases that happen to have come to court and not been settled before verdict. He must take into account not only the numbers of decisions counting for each interpretation, but whether the decisions expressing one principle seem more important or fundamental or wide-ranging than the decisions expressing the other. Suppose interpretation (6) fits only those past judicial decisions involving charges of negligence against one particular profession—say, lawyers—and interpretation (5) justifies all other cases, involving all other professions, and also fits other kinds of economic damage cases as well. Interpretation (5) then fits the legal record better on the whole, even if the number of cases involving lawyers is for some reason numerically greater, unless the argument shifts again, as it well might, when the field of study expands even more.

Now suppose a different possibility: that though liability has in many and varied cases actually been limited to an amount less than interpretation (5) would allow, the opinions attached to these cases made no mention of the principle of interpretation (6), which has in fact never before been recognized in official judicial rhetoric. Does that show that interpretation (5) fits the legal record much better, or that interpretation (6) is ineligible after all? Judges in fact divide about this issue of fit. Some would not seriously consider interpretation (6) if no past judicial opinion or legislative statement had ever explicitly mentioned its principle. Others reject this constraint and accept that the best interpretation of some line of cases may lie in a principle that has never been recognized explicitly but that nevertheless offers a brilliant account of the actual decisions, showing them in a better light than ever before.[8] Hercules will confront this issue as a special question of political morality. The political history of the community is pro tanto a better history, he thinks, if it shows judges making plain to their public, through their opinions, the path that later judges guided by integrity will follow, and if it shows judges making decisions that give voice as well as effect to convictions about morality that are widespread through the community. Judicial opinions formally announced in law reports, moreover, are themselves acts of the community personified that, particularly if recent, must be taken into the embrace of integrity. These are among his reasons for somewhat preferring an interpretation that is not too novel, not too far divorced from what past judges and other officials said as well as did. But he must set these reasons against his more substantive political convictions about the relative moral value of the two interpretations, and if he believes that interpretation (6) is much superior from that perspective, he will think he makes the legal record better overall by selecting it even at the cost of the more procedural values. Fitting what judges did is more important than fitting what they said.

Now suppose an even more unpatterned record. Hercules finds that unlimited liability has been enforced against a number of professions but has not been enforced against a roughly equal number of others, that no principle can explain the distinction, that judicial rhetoric is as split as the actual decisions, and that this split extends into other kinds of actions for economic damage. He might expand his field of survey still further, and the picture might change if he does. But let us suppose he is satisfied that it will not. He will then decide that the question of fit can play no more useful role in his deliberations even on the second dimension. He must now emphasize the more plainly substantive aspects of that dimension: he must decide which interpretation shows the legal record to be the best it can be from the standpoint of substantive political morality. He will compose and compare two stories. The first supposes that the community personified has adopted and is enforcing the principle of foreseeability as its test of moral responsibility for damage caused by negligence, that the various decisions it has reached are intended to give effect to that principle, though it often has lapsed and reached decisions that

foreseeability would condemn. The second supposes, instead, that the community has adopted and is enforcing the principle of foreseeability limited by some overall ceiling on liability, though it often has lapsed from that principle. Which story shows the community in a better light, all things considered, from the standpoint of political morality?

Hercules's answer will depend on his convictions about the two constituent virtues of political morality we have considered: justice and fairness. It will depend, that is, not only on his beliefs about which of these principles is superior as a matter of abstract justice, but also about which should be followed, as a matter of political fairness, in a community whose members have the moral convictions his fellow citizens have. In some cases the two kinds of judgment—the judgment of justice and that of fairness—will come together. If Hercules and the public at large share the view that people are entitled to be compensated fully whenever they are injured by others' carelessness, without regard to how harsh this requirement might turn out to be, then he will think that interpretation (5) is plainly the better of the two in play. But the two judgments sometimes will pull in different directions. He may think that interpretation (6) is better on the grounds of abstract justice, but know that this is a radical view not shared by any substantial portion of the public and is unknown in the political and moral rhetoric of the times. He might then decide that the story in which the state insists on the view he thinks right, but against the wishes of the people as a whole, is a poorer story, on balance. He would be preferring fairness to justice in these circumstances, and that preference would reflect a higher-order level of his own political convictions, namely his convictions about how a decent government, committed to both fairness and justice, should adjudicate between the two in this sort of case.

Judges will have different ideas of fairness, about the role each citizen's opinion ideally should play in the state's decision about which principles of justice to enforce through its central police power. They will have different higher-level opinions about the best resolution of conflicts between these two political ideals. No judge is likely to hold the simplistic theory that fairness automatically is to be preferred to justice, or vice versa. Most judges will think that the balance between the opinions of the community and the demands of abstract justice must be struck differently in different kinds of cases. Perhaps in ordinary commercial or private law cases, like *McLoughlin*, an interpretation supported in popular morality will be deemed superior to one that is not, provided it is not thought very much inferior as a matter of abstract justice. But many judges will think the interpretive force of popular morality very much weaker in constitutional cases like *Brown vs. Board of Education* [347 U.S. 483 (1954), the landmark Supreme Court decision prohibiting racial segregation in public schools], because they will think the point of the Constitution is in part to protect individuals from what the majority thinks right.

Local Priority

I must call special attention to a feature of Hercules's practice that has not yet emerged clearly. His judgments of fit expand out from the immediate case before him in a series of concentric circles. He asks which interpretations on his initial list fit past emotional injury cases, then which ones fit cases of accidental damage to the person more generally, then which fit damage to economic interests, and so on into areas each further and further from the original *McLoughlin* issue. This procedure gives a kind of local priority to what we might call "departments" of law. If Hercules finds that neither of two principles is flatly contradicted by the accidental damage cases of his jurisdiction, he expands his study into, say, contract cases to see which of these principles, if either, fits contract decisions better. But in Hercules's view, if one principle does *not* fit accident law at all—if it is contradicted by almost every decision in the area that might have confirmed it—this counts dramatically against it as an eligible interpretation of that body of law, even if it fits other areas of the law superbly. He will not treat this doctrine of local priority as absolute, however; he will be ready to

override it, as we shall soon see, in some circumstances.

The compartmentalization of law into separate departments is a prominent feature of legal practice. Law schools divide courses and their libraries divide treatises to distinguish emotional from economic or physical injury, intentional from unintentional torts, tort from crime, contract from other parts of common law, private from public law, and constitutional law from other parts of public law. Legal and judicial arguments respect these traditional divisions. Judicial opinions normally begin by assigning the case in hand to some department of law, and the precedents and statutes considered usually are drawn exclusively from that department. Often the initial classification is both controversial and crucial.

Compartmentalization suits both conventionalism and pragmatism, though for different reasons. Departments of law are based on tradition, which seems to support conventionalism, and they provide a strategy a pragmatist can manipulate in telling his noble lies: he can explain that his new doctrine need not be consistent in principle with past decisions because the latter, properly understood, belong to a different department. Law as integrity has a more complex attitude toward departments of law. Its general spirit condemns them, because the adjudicative principle of integrity asks judges to make the law coherent as a whole, so far as they can, and this might be better done by ignoring academic boundaries and reforming some departments of law radically to make them more consistent in principle with others. But law as integrity is interpretive, and compartmentalization is a feature of legal practice no competent interpretation can ignore.

Hercules responds to these competing impulses by seeking a constructive interpretation of compartmentalization. He tries to find an explanation of the practice of dividing law into departments that shows that practice in its best light. The boundaries between departments usually match popular opinion; many people think that intentional harm is more blameworthy than careless harm, that the state needs a very different kind of justification to declare someone guilty of a crime than it needs to require him to pay compensation for damage he has caused, that promises and other forms of explicit agreement or consent are a special kind of reason for state coercion, and so forth. Dividing departments of law to match that sort of opinion promotes predictability and guards against sudden official reinterpretations that uproot large areas of law, and it does this in a way that promotes a deeper aim of law as integrity. If legal compartments make sense to people at large, they encourage the protestant attitude integrity favors, because they allow ordinary people as well as hard-pressed judges to interpret law within practical boundaries that seem natural and intuitive.

Hercules accepts that account of the point of compartmentalization, and he shapes his doctrine of local priority accordingly. He allows the doctrine most force when the boundaries between traditional departments of law track widely held moral principles distinguishing types of fault or responsibility, and the substance of each department reflects those moral principles. The distinction between criminal and civil law meets that test. Suppose Hercules thinks, contrary to most people's opinion, that being made to pay compensation is just as bad as being made to pay a fine, and therefore that the distinction between criminal and civil law is unsound in principle. He will nevertheless defer to local priority. He will not claim that criminal and civil law should be treated as one department; he will not argue that a criminal defendant's guilt need only be established as probable rather than beyond a reasonable doubt because the probable standard fits the combined department as well as any other.

But Hercules will not be so ready to defer to local priority when his test is not met, when traditional boundaries between departments have become mechanical and arbitrary, either because popular morality has shifted or because the substance of the departments no longer reflects popular opinion.[9] Compartments of law do sometimes grow arbitrary and isolated from popular conviction in that way, particularly when the central rules of the departments were developed in different periods. Suppose the legal tradition of a community has for many decades separated nuisance law, which concerns the discomfort of

interference that activities on one person's land cause to neighbors, from negligence law, which concerns the physical or economic or emotional injuries someone's carelessness inflicts on others. Suppose that the judges who decided the crucial nuisance cases disdained any economic test for nuisance; they said that an activity counts as a nuisance, and must therefore be stopped, when it is not a "natural" or traditional use of the land, so that someone who starts a factory on land traditionally used for farming is guilty of nuisance even though the factory is an economically more efficient use. But suppose that in recent years judges have begun to make economic cost crucial for negligence. They say that someone's failure to take precautions against injuring others is negligent, so that he is liable for the resulting injury if the precaution was "reasonable" in the circumstances, and that the economic cost of the precaution counts in deciding whether it was in fact reasonable.

The distinction between negligence and nuisance law no longer meets Hercules's test, if it ever did. It makes some sense to distinguish nuisance from negligence if we assume that nuisance is intentional, where negligence is unintentional; then the distinction tracks the popular principle that it is worse to injure someone knowingly than unknowingly. But the developments in negligence law I just described are not consistent with that view of the distinction, because failing to guard against an accident is not necessarily unintentional in the required sense. So Hercules would be ready to ignore the traditional boundary between these two departments of law. If he thought that the "natural use" test was silly, and the economic cost test much more just, he would argue that the negligence and nuisance precedents should be seen as one body of law, and that the economic cost test is a superior interpretation of that unified body. His argument probably would be made easier by other legal events that already had occurred. The intellectual climate that produced the later negligence decisions would have begun to erode the assumption of the earlier nuisance cases, that novel enterprises that annoy people are necessarily legal wrongs. Perhaps the legislature would have adopted special statutes rearranging liability for some new forms of inconvenience, like airport noise, that the "natural" theory has decided or would decide in what seems the wrong way, for example. Or perhaps judges would have decided airport cases by straining the historical meaning of "natural" to reach decisions that seemed sensible given developing technology. Hercules would cite these changes as supporting his interpretive argument consolidating nuisance and negligence. If he persuades the profession to his view, nuisance and negligence will no longer be distinct departments of law but joint tenants of a new province that shortly will attract a new name attached to new law school courses and new treatises. This process is in fact under way in Anglo-American law, as is—though less securely—a new unification of private law that blurs even the long-established and once much firmer boundary between contract and tort....

SOME FAMILIAR OBJECTIONS

Hercules Is Playing Politics

Hercules has completed his labors in *McLoughlin*. He declares that the best interpretation of the emotional damage cases, all things considered, is (5): the law allows compensation for all emotional injury directly caused by careless driving and foreseeable by a reasonably thoughtful motorist. But he concedes that in reaching that conclusion he has relied on his own opinion that this principle is better—fairer and more just—than any other that is eligible on what he takes to be the right criteria of fit. He also concedes that this opinion is controversial: it is not shared by all of his fellow judges, some of whom therefore think that some other interpretation, for example (6), is superior. What complaints are his arguments likely to attract? The first in the list I propose to consider accuses Hercules of ignoring the actual law of emotional injury and substituting his own views about what the law should be.

How shall we understand this objection? We might take it in two very different ways. It might mean that Hercules was wrong to seek to justify his interpretation by appealing to justice and fairness, because it does not even survive the proper

threshold test of fit. We cannot assume, without reviewing the cases Hercules consulted, that this argument is mistaken. Perhaps this time Hercules nodded; perhaps if he had expanded the range of his study of precedents further he would have discovered that only one interpretation did survive, and this discovery would then have settled the law, for him, without engaging his opinions about the justice of requiring compensation for accidents. But it is hardly plausible that even the strictest threshold test of fit will always permit only one interpretation, so the objection, understood this way, would not be a general objection to Hercules's methods of adjudication, but only a complaint that he had misapplied his own methods in the particular case at hand.

We therefore should consider the second, more interesting reading of the objection: this claims that a judge must never rely on his personal convictions about fairness or justice the way Hercules did in this instance. Suppose the critic says, "The correct interpretation of a line of past decisions can always be discovered by morally neutral means, because the correct interpretation is just a matter of discovering what principles the judges who made these decisions intended to lay down, and that is just a matter of historical fact." Hercules will point out that this critic needs a political reason for his dictum that interpretations must match the intentions of past judges. That is an extreme form of the position we have already considered, that an interpretation is better if it fits what past judges said as well as did, and even that weaker claim depends on the special arguments of political morality I described. The critic supposes that these special reasons are not only strong but commanding; that they are so powerful that a judge always does wrong even to consider an interpretation that does not meet the standard they set, no matter how well that interpretation ties together, explains, and justifies past decisions.

So Hercules's critic, if his argument is to have any power, is not relying on politically neutral interpretive convictions after all. He, too, has engaged his own background convictions of political morality. He thinks the political values that support his interpretive style are of such fundamental importance as to eliminate any competing commands of justice altogether. That may be a plausible position, but it is hardly uncontroversial and is in no sense neutral. His difference with Hercules is not, as he first suggested, about whether political morality is relevant in deciding what the law is, but about which principles of morality are sound and therefore decisive of that issue. So the first, crude objection, that Hercules has substituted his own political convictions for the politically neutral correct interpretation of the past law, is an album of confusions.

Hercules Is a Fraud

The second objection is more sophisticated. Now the critic says, "It is absurd to suppose that there is any single correct interpretation of the emotional injury cases. Since we have discovered two interpretations of these cases, neither of which can be preferred to the other on 'neutral' grounds of fit, no judge would be forced by the adjudicative principle of integrity to accept either. Hercules has chosen one on frankly political grounds; his choice reflects only his own political morality. He has no choice in the circumstances but to legislate in that way. Nevertheless it is fraudulent for him to claim that he has discovered, through his political choice, what the *law* is. He is only offering his own opinion about what it should be."

This objection will seem powerful to many readers, and we must take care not to weaken it by making it seem to claim more than it does. It does not try to reinstate the idea of conventionalism, that when convention runs out a judge is free to improve the law according to the right legislative standards; still less the idea of pragmatism that he is always free to do this, checked only by considerations of strategy. It acknowledges that judges must choose between interpretations that survive the test of fit. It insists only that there can be no best interpretation when more than one survives that test. It is an objection, as I have framed it, from within the general idea of law as integrity; it tries to protect that idea from corruption by fraud.

Is the objection sound? Why is it fraudulent, or even confusing, for Hercules to offer his judgment as a judgment of law? Once again, two

somewhat different answers—two ways of elaborating the objection—are available, and we cannot do credit to the objection unless we distinguish them and consider each. The first elaboration is this: "Hercules's claim is fraudulent because it suggests that there can be a right answer to the question whether interpretation (5) or (6) is fairer or more just; since political morality is subjective there cannot be a single right answer to that question, but only answers." ... The second elaboration does not rely on skepticism: "Hercules is a fraud even if morality is objective and even if he is right that the principle of foreseeability he settled on is objectively fairer and more just. He is a fraud because he pretends he has discovered what the law is, but he has only discovered what it should be." That is the form of the objection I shall consider here.

We ask of a conception of law that it provide an account of the grounds of law—the circumstances under which claims about what the law is should be accepted as true or sound—that shows why law licenses coercion. Law as integrity replies that the grounds of law lie in integrity, in the best constructive interpretation of past legal decisions, and that law is therefore sensitive to justice in the way Hercules recognizes. So there is no way Hercules *can* report his conclusion about Mrs. McLoughlin's case except to say that the law, as he understands it, is in her favor. If he said what the critic recommends, that she has no legal right to win but has a moral right that he proposes to honor, he would be *misstating* his view of the matter. He would think that a true account of some situations—if he found the law too immoral to enforce, for example—but not of this one. A critic might disagree with Hercules at many levels. He might reject law as integrity in favor of conventionalism or pragmatism or some other conception of law. Or he might accept it but reach different conclusions from Hercules because he holds different ideas about the necessary requirements of fit, or different convictions about fairness or justice or the relation between them. But he can regard Hercules's use of "law" as fraudulent (or grammatically wrong) only if he suffers from the semantic sting, only if he assumes that claims of law are somehow out of order when they are not drawn directly from some set of factual criteria for law every competent lawyer accepts.

One aspect of the present objection, however, might be thought immune from my arguments against the rest. Even if we agree that Hercules's conclusions about Mrs. McLoughlin are presented properly as conclusions of law, it might seem extravagant to claim that these conclusions in any way follow from integrity understood as a distinct political ideal. Would it not be more accurate to say that integrity is at work in Hercules's calculations just up to the point at which he has rejected all interpretations that fail the threshold test of fit, but that integrity plays no part in selecting among those that survive that test? Should we not say that his conception of law is really two conceptions: law as integrity, supplemented—when integrity gives out—by some version of natural law theory? This is not a very important objection; it only suggests a different way of reporting the conclusions it no longer challenges. Nevertheless the observation that prompts it is too crude. For it is a mistake to think that the idea of integrity is irrelevant to Hercules's decision once that decision is no longer a matter of his convictions about fit but draws on his sense of fairness or justice as well.

The spirit of integrity, which we located in fraternity, would be outraged if Hercules were to make his decision in any way other than by choosing the interpretation that he believes best from the standpoint of political morality as a whole. We accept integrity as a political ideal because we want to treat our political community as one of principle, and the citizens of a community of principle aim not simply at common principles, as if uniformity were all they wanted, but the best common principles politics can find. Integrity is distinct from justice and fairness, but it is bound to them in that way: integrity makes no sense except among people who want fairness and justice as well. So Hercules's final choice of the interpretation he believes sounder on the whole—fairer and more just in the right relation—flows from his initial commitment to integrity. He makes that choice at the moment and in the way

integrity both permits and requires, and it is therefore deeply misleading to say that he has abandoned the ideal at just that point....

NOTES

1. *McLoughlin v. O'Brian* [1983] 1 AC 410.
2. Perhaps this is an impossible assignment; perhaps the project is doomed to produce not just an impossibly bad novel but no novel at all, because the best theory of art requires a single creator or, if more than one, that each must have some control over the whole. (But what about legends and jokes? What about the Old Testament, or, on some theories, the *Iliad*?) I need not push that question further, because I am interested only in the fact that the assignment makes sense, that each of the novelists in the chain can have some grasp of what he is asked to do, whatever misgivings he might have about the value or character of what will then be produced.
3. Hercules played an important part in Dworkin, Ronald, *Taking Rights Seriously*. Cambridge, Mass: Harvard University Press, 1978. Chap. 4. Print.
4. See the discussion of critical legal studies later in this article.
5. See Dworkin, *Taking Rights Seriously*, chap. 4.
6. See *Thomas v. Winchester*, 6 N.Y. 397, and *MacPherson v. Buick Motor Co.*, 217 N.Y. 382, 111 N.E. 1050.
7. Haar, Charles M & Daniel W. Fessler, *The Wrong Side of the Tracks*. New York: Simon and Schuster, 1986 (print) is a recent example of integrity working on a large canvas.
8. See, for example, Benjamin Cardozo's decision in *Hynes v. New York Central R.R. Co.*, 231 N.Y. 229.
9. The disagreement between Lords Diplock and Edmund Davies, on the one hand, and Viscount Dilhourne on the other, in the notorious blasphemy case *R. v. Lemon* [1979] I All ER 898, illustrates the importance of not ignoring this connection between changes in popular morality and the boundaries of local priority. The former insisted that the law of blasphemy be interpreted to reflect developments in other parts of criminal law; the latter that blasphemy, for some unexplained reason, be counted an isolated domain of its own.

16   Common-Law Courts in a Civil-Law System

The Role of United States Federal Courts in Interpreting the Constitution and Laws

ANTONIN SCALIA

I am grateful for technical and research assistance by Matthew P. Previn, and for substantive suggestions by Eugene Scalia.

"INTENT OF THE LEGISLATURE"

Statutory interpretation is such a broad subject that the substance of it cannot be discussed comprehensively here. It is worth examining a few aspects, however, if only to demonstrate the great degree of confusion that prevails. We can begin at the most fundamentally possible level. So utterly unformed is the American law of statutory interpretation that not only is its methodology unclear, but even its very *objective* is. Consider the basic question: What are we looking for when we construe a statute?

You will find it frequently said in judicial opinions of my court and others that the judge's objective in interpreting a statute is to give effect to "the intent of the legislature." This principle, in one form or another, goes back at least as far as Blackstone.[1] Unfortunately, it does not square with some of the (few) generally accepted concrete rules of statutory construction. One is the rule that when the text of a statute is clear, that is the end of the matter. Why should that be so, if what the legislature *intended*, rather than what it *said*, is the object of our inquiry? In selecting the words of the statute, the legislature might have misspoken. Why not permit that to be demonstrated from the floor debates? Or indeed, why not accept, as proper material for the court to consider, later explanations by the legislators—a sworn affidavit signed by the majority of each house, for example, as to what they *really* meant?

Another accepted rule of construction is that ambiguities in a newly enacted statute are to be resolved in such fashion as to make the statute, not only internally consistent, but also compatible with previously enacted laws. We simply assume, for purposes of our search for "intent," that the enacting legislature was aware of all those other laws. Well of course that is a fiction, and if we were really looking for the subjective intent of the enacting legislature we would more likely find it by paying attention to the text (and legislative history) of the new statute in isolation.

The evidence suggests that, despite frequent statements to the contrary, we do not really look for subjective legislative intent. We look for a sort of "objectified" intent—the intent that a reasonable person would gather from the text of the law, placed alongside the remainder of the *corpus juris*. As Bishop's old treatise nicely put it, elaborating upon the usual formulation: "[T]he primary object of all rules for interpreting statutes is to ascertain the legislative intent; *or, exactly, the meaning which the subject is authorized to understand the legislature intended*."[2] And the reason we adopt this objectified version is, I think, that it is simply incompatible with democratic government, or indeed, even with fair government, to have the meaning of a law determined by what the lawgiver meant, rather than by what the lawgiver promulgated. That seems to me one step worse than the trick the emperor Nero was said to engage in:

From Antonin Scalia, *A Matter of Interpretation: Federal Courts and the Law: An Essay* (Princeton, N. J.: Princeton University Press, 1997), pp. 3–48, # 1997 Princeton University Press. Reprinted by permission of Princeton University Press.

posting edicts high up on the pillars, so that they could not easily be read. Government by unexpressed intent is similarly tyrannical. It is the *law* that governs, not the intent of the lawgiver. That seems to me the essence of the famous American ideal set forth in the Massachusetts constitution: A government of laws, not of men. Men may intend what they will; but it is only the laws that they enact which bind us.

In reality, however, if one accepts the principle that the object of judicial interpretation is to determine the intent of the legislature, being bound by genuine but unexpressed legislative intent rather than the law is only the *theoretical* threat. The *practical* threat is that, under the guise or even the self-delusion of pursuing unexpressed legislative intents, common-law judges will in fact pursue their own objectives and desires, extending their law-making proclivities from the common law to the statutory field. When you are told to decide, not on the basis of what the legislature said, but on the basis of what it *meant,* and are assured that there is no necessary connection between the two, your best shot at figuring out what the legislature meant is to ask yourself what a wise and intelligent person *should* have meant; and that will surely bring you to the conclusion that the law means what you think it *ought* to mean—which is precisely how judges decide things under the common law. As Dean Landis of Harvard Law School (a believer in the search for legislative intent) put it in a 1930 article:

> [T]he gravest sins are perpetrated in the name of the intent of the legislature. Judges are rarely willing to admit their role as actual lawgivers, and such admissions as are wrung from their unwilling lips lie in the field of common and not statute law. To condone in these instances the practice of talking in terms of the intent of the legislature, as if the legislature had attributed a particular meaning to certain words, when it is apparent that the intent is that of the judge, is to condone atavistic practices too reminiscent of the medicine man.[3]

CHURCH OF THE HOLY TRINITY

To give some concrete form to the danger I warn against, let me describe what I consider to be the prototypical case involving the triumph of supposed "legislative intent" (a handy cover for judicial intent) over the text of the law. It is called *Church of the Holy Trinity v. United* States[4] and was decided by the Supreme Court of the United States in 1892. The Church of the Holy Trinity, located in New York City, contracted with an Englishman to come over to be its rector and pastor. The United States claimed that this agreement violated a federal statute that made it unlawful for any person to "in any way assist or encourage the importation or migration of any alien ... into the United States, ... under contract or agreement ... made previous to the importation or migration of such alien ... , to perform labor or service of any kind in the United States...." The Circuit Court for the Southern District of New York held the church liable for the fine that the statute provided. The Supreme Court reversed. The central portion of its reasoning was as follows:

> It must be conceded that the act of the [church] is within the letter of this section, for the relation of rector to his church is one of service, and implies labor on the one side with compensation on the other. Not only are the general words labor and service both used [in the statute], but also, as it were to guard against any narrow interpretation and emphasize a breadth of meaning, to them is added "of any kind"; and, further, ... the fifth section [of the statute], which makes specific exceptions, among them professional actors, artists, lecturers, singers and domestic servants, strengthens the idea that every other kind of labor and service was intended to be reached by the first section. While there is great force to this reasoning, we cannot think Congress intended to denounce with penalties a transaction like that in the present case. It is a familiar rule, that a thing may be within the letter of the statute and yet not within the statute, because not within its spirit, nor within the intention of its makers.[5]

The Court proceeds to conclude from various extratextual indications, including even a snippet of legislative history (highly unusual in those days), that the statute was intended to apply only to *manual* labor—which renders the exceptions for actors, artists, lecturers, and singers utterly inexplicable. The Court then shifts gears and devotes the last seven pages of its opinion to a lengthy description of how and why we are a religious nation. That being so, it says "[t]he construction invoked cannot be accepted as correct."[6] It concludes:

> It is a case where there was presented a definite evil, in view of which the legislature used general terms with the purpose of reaching all phases of that evil, and thereafter, unexpectedly, it is developed that the general language thus employed is broad enough to reach cases and acts which the whole history and life of the country affirm could not have been intentionally legislated against. It is the duty of the courts, under those circumstances, to say that, however broad the language of the statute may be, the act, although within the letter, is not within the intention of the legislature, and therefore cannot be within the statute.[7]

Well of course I think that the act was within the letter of the statute, and was therefore within the statute: end of case.[8] Congress can enact foolish statutes as well as wise ones, and it is not for the courts to decide which is which and rewrite the former. I acknowledge an interpretative doctrine of what the old writers call *lapsus linguae* (slip of the tongue), and what our modern cases call "scrivener's error," where on the very face of the statute it is clear to the reader that a mistake of expression (rather than of legislative wisdom) has been made. For example, a statute may say "defendant" when only "criminal defendant" (i.e., not "civil defendant") makes sense.[9] The objective import of such a statute is clear enough, and I think it not contrary to sound principles of interpretation, in such extreme cases, to give the totality of context precedence over a single word.[10] But to say that the legislature obviously misspoke is worlds away from saying that the legislature obviously overlegislated. *Church of the Holy Trinity* is cited to us whenever counsel wants us to ignore the narrow, deadening text of the statute, and pay attention to the life-giving legislative intent. It is nothing but an invitation to judicial lawmaking.

There are more sophisticated routes to judicial lawmaking than reliance upon unexpressed legislative intent, but they will not often be found in judicial opinions because they are too obvious a usurpation. Calling the court's desires "unexpressed legislative intent" makes everything seem

all right. You will never, I promise, see in a judicial opinion the rationale for judicial lawmaking described in Guido Calabresi's book, *A Common Law for the Age of Statutes*. It says:

> [B]ecause a statute is hard to revise once it is passed, laws are governing us that would not and could not be enacted today, and ... some of these laws not only could not be reenacted but also do not fit, are in some sense inconsistent with, our whole legal landscape....
> ... There is an alternate way of dealing with [this] problem of legal obsolescence: granting to courts the authority to determine whether a statute is obsolete, whether in one way or another it should be consciously reviewed. At times this doctrine would approach granting to courts the authority to treat statutes as if they were no more and no less than part of the common law.[11]

Indeed, Judge Calabresi says that the courts have already, "in a common law way, ... come to the point of exercising [the law-revising authority he favors] through fictions, subterfuges, and indirection,"[12] and he is uncertain whether they should continue down that road or change course to a more forthright acknowledgment of what they are doing.

Another modern and forthright approach to according courts the power to revise statutes is set forth in Professor Eskridge's recent book, *Dynamic Statutory Interpretation*. The essence of it is acceptance of the proposition that it is proper for the judge who applies a statute to consider "'not only what the statute means abstractly, or even on the basis of legislative history, but also what it ought to mean in terms of the needs and goals of our present day society.'"[13] The law means what it ought to mean.

I agree with Judge Calabresi (and Professor Eskridge makes the same point) that many decisions can be cited which, by subterfuge, accomplish precisely what Calabresi and Eskridge and other honest nontextualists propose. As I have said, "legislative intent" divorced from text is one of those subterfuges; and as I have described, *Church of the Holy Trinity* is one of those cases. What I think is needed, however, is not rationalization of this process but abandonment of it. It is simply not compatible with democratic theory that laws mean whatever they ought to mean, and that unelected judges decide what that is.

It may well be that the statutory interpretation adopted by the Court in *Church of the Holy Trinity* produced a desirable result; and it may even be (though I doubt it) that it produced the unexpressed result actually intended by Congress, rather than merely the one desired by the Court. Regardless, the decision was wrong because it failed to follow the text.

The text is the law, and it is the text that must be observed. I agree with Justice Holmes's remark, quoted approvingly by Justice Frankfurter in his article on the construction of statutes: "Only a day or two ago—when counsel talked of the intention of a legislature, I was indiscreet enough to say I don't care what their intention was. I only want to know what the words mean."[14] And I agree with Holmes's other remark, quoted approvingly by Justice Jackson: "We do not inquire what the legislature meant; we ask only what the statute means."[15]

TEXTUALISM

The philosophy of interpretation I previously have described is known as textualism. In some sophisticated circles, it is considered simpleminded—"wooden," "unimaginative," "pedestrian." It is none of that. To be a textualist in good standing, one need not be too dull to perceive the broader social purposes that a statute is designed, or could be designed, to serve; or too hide-bound to realize that new times require new laws. One need only hold the belief that judges have no authority to pursue those broader purposes or write those new laws.

Textualism should not be confused with so-called strict constructionism, a degraded form of textualism that brings the whole philosophy into disrepute. I am not a strict constructionist, and no one ought to be—though better that, I suppose, than a nontextualist. A text should not be construed strictly, and it should not be construed leniently; it should be construed reasonably, to contain all that it fairly means. The difference between textualism and strict constructionism can be seen in a case my Court decided four terms ago.[16]

The statute at issue provided for an increased jail term if, "during and in relation to ... [a] drug trafficking crime," the defendant "uses ... a firearm." The defendant in this case had sought to purchase a quantity of cocaine; and what he had offered to give in exchange for the cocaine was an unloaded firearm, which he showed to the drug-seller. The Court held, I regret to say, that the defendant was subject to the increased penalty, because he had "used a firearm during and in relation to a drug trafficking crime." The vote was not even close (6–3). I dissented. Now I cannot say whether my colleagues in the majority voted the way they did because they are strict-construction textualists, or because they are not textualists at all. But a proper textualist, which is to say my kind of textualist, would surely have voted to acquit. The phrase "uses a gun" fairly connoted use of a gun for what guns are normally used for, that is, as a weapon. As I put the point in my dissent, when you ask someone, "Do you use a cane?" you are not inquiring whether he has hung his grandfather's antique cane as a decoration in the hallway.

But although the good textualist is not a literalist, neither is he a nihilist. Words do have a limited range of meaning, and no interpretation that goes beyond that range is permissible. My favorite example of a departure from text—and certainly the departure that has enabled judges to do more freewheeling lawmaking than any other—pertains to the Due Process Clause found in the Fifth and Fourteenth Amendments of the United States Constitution, which says that no person shall "be deprived of life, liberty, or property without due process of law." It has been interpreted to prevent the government from taking away certain liberties *beyond* those, such as freedom of speech and of religion, that are specifically named in the Constitution. (The first Supreme Court case to use the Due Process Clause in this fashion was, by the way, *Dred* Scott[17]—not a desirable parentage.) Well, it may or may not be a good thing to guarantee additional liberties, but the Due Process Clause quite obviously does not bear that interpretation. By its inescapable terms, it guarantees only process. Property can be taken by the state; liberty can be taken; even life can be taken; but not without the *process* that our traditions require—notably, a validly enacted law and a fair trial. To say otherwise is to abandon textualism, and to render democratically adopted texts mere springboards for judicial lawmaking.

Of all the criticisms leveled against textualism, the most mindless is that it is "formalistic." The answer to that is, *of course it's formalistic!* The rule of law is *about* form. If, for example, a citizen performs an act—let us say the sale of certain technology to a foreign country—that is prohibited by a widely publicized bill proposed by the administration and passed by both houses of Congress, *but not yet signed by the President,* that sale is lawful. It is of no consequence that everyone knows both houses of Congress and the President wish to prevent that sale. Before the wish becomes a binding law, it must be embodied in a bill that passes both houses and is signed by the President. Is that not formalism? A murderer has been caught with blood on his hands, bending over the body of his victim; a neighbor with a video camera has filmed the crime; and the murderer has confessed in writing and on videotape. We nonetheless insist that before the state can punish this miscreant, it must conduct a full-dress criminal trial that results in a verdict of guilty. Is that not formalism? Long live formalism. It is what makes a government a government of laws and not of men.

INTERPRETING CONSTITUTIONAL TEXTS

Without pretending to have exhausted the vast topic of textual interpretation, I wish to address a final subject: the distinctive problem of constitutional interpretation. The problem is distinctive, not because special principles of interpretation apply, but because the usual principles are being applied to an unusual text. Chief Justice Marshall put the point as well as it can be put in *McCulloch v. Maryland:*

> A constitution, to contain an accurate detail of all the subdivisions of which its great powers will admit, and of all the means by which they may be carried into execution, would partake of the prolixity of a legal

code, and could scarcely be embraced by the human mind. It would probably never be understood by the public. Its nature, therefore, requires, that only its great outlines should be marked, its important objects designated, and the minor ingredients which compose those objects be deduced from the nature of the objects themselves.[18]

In textual interpretation, context is everything, and the context of the Constitution tells us not to expect nit-picking detail, and to give words and phrases an expansive rather than narrow interpretation—though not an interpretation that the language will not bear.

Take, for example, the provision of the First Amendment that forbids abridgment of "the freedom of speech, or of the press." That phrase does not list the full range of communicative expression. Handwritten letters, for example, are neither speech nor press. Yet surely there is no doubt they cannot be censored. In this constitutional context, speech and press, the two most common forms of communication, stand as a sort of synecdoche for the whole. That is not strict construction, but it is reasonable construction.

It is curious that most of those who insist that the drafter's intent gives meaning to a statute reject the drafter's intent as the criterion for interpretation of the Constitution. I reject it for both. I will consult the writings of some men who happened to be delegates to the Constitutional Convention—Hamilton's and Madison's writings in *The Federalist,* for example. I do so, however, not because they were Framers and therefore their intent is authoritative and must be the law; but rather because their writings, like those of other intelligent and informed people of the time, display how the text of the Constitution originally was understood. Thus I give equal weight to Jay's pieces in *The Federalist,* and to Jefferson's writings, even though neither of them was a Framer. What I look for in the Constitution is precisely what I look for in a statute: the original meaning of the text, not what the original draftsmen intended.

But the Great Divide with regard to constitutional interpretation is not that between Framers' intent and objective meaning, but rather that between *original* meaning (whether derived from

Framers' intent or not) and *current* meaning. The ascendant school of constitutional interpretation affirms the existence of what is called The Living Constitution, a body of law that (unlike normal statutes) grows and changes from age to age, in order to meet the needs of a changing society. And it is the judges who determine those needs and "find" that changing law. Seems familiar, doesn't it? Yes, it is the common law returned, but infinitely more powerful than what the old common law ever pretended to be, for now it trumps even the statutes of democratic legislatures. Recall the words from the Fourth-of-July speech of the avid codifier Robert Rantoul: "The judge makes law, by extorting from precedents something which they do not contain. He extends his precedents, which were themselves the extension of others, till, by this accommodating principle, a whole system of law is built up without the authority or interference of the legislator."[19] Substitute the word *people* for *legislator,* and it is a perfect description of what modern American courts have done with the Constitution.

If you go into a constitutional law class, or study a constitutional law casebook, or read a brief filed in a constitutional law case, you rarely will find the discussion addressed to the text of the constitutional provision that is at issue, or to the question of what was the originally understood or even the originally intended meaning of that text. The starting point of the analysis will be Supreme Court cases, and the new issue will presumptively be decided according to the logic that those cases expressed, with no regard for how far that logic, thus extended, has distanced us from the original text and understanding. Worse still, however, it is known and understood that if that logic fails to produce what in the view of the current Supreme Court is the *desirable* result for the case at hand, then, like good common-law judges, the Court will distinguish its precedents, or narrow them, or if all else fails overrule them, in order that the Constitution might mean what it *ought* to mean. Should there be—to take one of the less controversial examples—a constitutional right to die? If so, there is.[20] Should there be a constitutional right to reclaim a biological child put out for adoption by the other parent? Again, if so, there is.[21] If it is good, it is so. Never mind the text that we supposedly are construing; we will smuggle these new rights in, if all else fails, under the Due Process Clause (which, as I have described, is textually incapable of containing them). Moreover, what the Constitution meant yesterday it does not necessarily mean today. As our opinions say in the context of our Eighth Amendment jurisprudence (the Cruel and Unusual Punishments Clause), its meaning changes to reflect "the evolving standards of decency that mark the progress of a maturing society."[22]

This is preeminently a common-law way of making law, and not the way of construing a democratically adopted text. [There is] a famous English treatise on statutory construction called *Dwarris on Statutes.* The fourth of Dwarris's Maxims was as follows: "An act of Parliament cannot alter by reason of time; but the common law may, since *cessante ratione cessat lex* [when the reason for the law ceases, the law itself ceases]."[23] This remains (however much it may sometimes be evaded) the formally enunciated rule for statutory construction: statutes do not change. Proposals for "dynamic statutory construction," such as those of Judge Calabresi and Professor Eskridge, are concededly avant-garde. The Constitution, however, even though a democratically adopted text, we formally treat like the common law. What, it is fair to ask, is the justification for doing so?

One would suppose that the rule that a text does not change would apply a fortiori to a constitution. If courts felt too much bound by the democratic process to tinker with statutes, when their tinkering could be adjusted by the legislature, how much more should they feel bound not to tinker with a constitution, when their tinkering is virtually irreparable. It certainly cannot be said that a constitution naturally suggests changeability; to the contrary, its whole purpose is to prevent change—to embed certain rights in such a manner that future generations cannot readily take them away. A society that adopts a bill of rights is skeptical that "evolving standards of decency" always "mark progress," and that societies always "mature," as opposed to rot.

Neither the text of such a document nor the intent of its framers (whichever you choose) can possibly lead to the conclusion that its only effect is to take the power of changing rights away from the legislature and give it to the courts.

FLEXIBILITY AND LIBERALITY OF THE LIVING CONSTITUTION

The argument most frequently made in favor of The Living Constitution is a pragmatic one: Such an evolutionary approach is necessary in order to provide the "flexibility" that a changing society requires; the Constitution would have snapped if it had not been permitted to bend and grow. This might be a persuasive argument if most of the "growing" that the proponents of this approach have brought upon us in the past, and are determined to bring upon us in the future, were the *elimination* of restrictions upon democratic government. But just the opposite is true. Historically, and particularly in the past 35 years, the "evolving" Constitution has imposed a vast array of new constraints—new inflexibilities—upon administrative, judicial, and legislative action. To mention only a few things that formerly could be done or not done, as the society desired, but now cannot be done:

- Admitting in a state criminal trial evidence of guilt that was obtained by an unlawful search;[24]
- Permitting invocation of God at public-school graduations;[25]
- Electing one of the two houses of a state legislature the way the United States Senate is elected, i.e., on a basis that does not give all voters numerically equal representation;[26]
- Terminating welfare payments as soon as evidence of fraud is received, subject to restoration after hearing if the evidence is satisfactorily refuted;[27]
- Imposing property requirements as a condition of voting;[28]
- Prohibiting anonymous campaign literature;[29]
- Prohibiting pornography.[30]

And the future agenda of constitutional evolutionists is mostly more of the same—the creation of *new* restrictions upon democratic government, rather than the elimination of old ones. *Less* flexibility in government, not *more*. As things now stand, the state and federal governments either may apply capital punishment or abolish it, permit suicide or forbid it—all as the changing times and the changing sentiments of society may demand. But when capital punishment is held to violate the Eighth Amendment, and suicide is held to be protected by the Fourteenth Amendment, all flexibility with regard to those matters will be gone. No, the reality of the matter is that, generally speaking, devotees of The Living Constitution do not seek to facilitate social change, but to prevent it.

There are, I must admit, a few exceptions to that—a few instances in which, historically, greater flexibility has been the result of the process. But those exceptions serve only to refute another argument of the proponents of an evolving Constitution, that evolution always will be in the direction of greater personal liberty. (They consider that a great advantage, for reasons that I do not entirely understand. All government represents a balance between individual freedom and social order, and it is not true that every alteration of that balance in the direction of greater individual freedom is necessarily good.) But in any case, the record of history refutes the proposition that the evolving Constitution will invariably enlarge individual rights. The most obvious refutation is the modern Court's limitation of the constitutional protections afforded to property. The provision prohibiting impairment of the obligation of contracts, for example, has been gutted. I am sure that We the People agree with that development; we value property rights less than the Founders did. So also, we value the right to bear arms less than did the Founders (who thought the right of self-defense to be absolutely fundamental), and there will be few tears shed if and when the Second Amendment is held to guarantee nothing more than the state National Guard. But this just shows that the Founders were right when they feared that some (in their view misguided) future generation might wish to abandon liberties that they considered essential, and so sought to protect those liberties in a Bill of Rights. We may *like* the abridgment of property rights and *like* the elimination of the right to bear arms; but let us not pretend that these are not *reductions of rights*.

Or if property rights are too cold to arouse enthusiasm, and the right to bear arms too dangerous, let me give another example: Several terms ago a case came before the Supreme Court involving a prosecution for sexual abuse of a young child. The trial court found that the child would be too frightened to testify in the presence of the (presumed) abuser, and so, pursuant to state law, she was permitted to testify with only the prosecutor and defense counsel present, with the defendant, the judge, and the jury watching over closed-circuit television. A reasonable enough procedure, and it was held to be constitutional by my Court.[32] I dissented, because the Sixth Amendment provides that "[i]n *all* criminal prosecutions the accused shall enjoy the right … to be confronted with the witnesses against him" (emphasis added). There is no doubt what confrontation meant—or indeed means today. It means face-to-face, not watching from another room. And there is no doubt what one of the major purposes of that provision was: to induce *precisely* that pressure upon the witness that the little girl found it difficult to endure. It is difficult to accuse someone to his face, particularly when you are lying. Now no extrinsic factors have changed since that provision was adopted in 1791. Sexual abuse existed then, as it does now; little children were more easily upset than adults, then as now; a means of placing the defendant out of sight of the witness existed then as now (a screen easily could have been erected that would enable the defendant to see the witness, but not the witness the defendant). But the Sixth Amendment nonetheless gave *all* criminal defendants the right to *confront* the witnesses against them, because that was thought to be an important protection. The only significant things that *have* changed, I think, are the society's sensitivity to so-called psychic trauma (which is what we are told the

child witness in such a situation suffers) and the society's assessment of where the proper balance ought to be struck between the two extremes of a procedure that assures convicting 100 percent of all child abusers, and a procedure that assures acquitting 100 percent of those falsely accused of child abuse. I have no doubt that the society is, as a whole, happy and pleased with what my Court decided. But we should not pretend that the decision did not *eliminate* a liberty that previously existed.

LACK OF A GUIDING PRINCIPLE FOR EVOLUTION

My pointing out that the American people may be satisfied with a reduction of their liberties should not be taken as a suggestion that the proponents of The Living Constitution *follow* the desires of the American people in determining how the Constitution should evolve. They follow nothing so precise; indeed, as a group they follow nothing at all. Perhaps the most glaring defect of Living Constitutionalism, next to its incompatibility with the whole antievolutionary purpose of a constitution, is that there is no agreement, and no chance of agreement, upon what is to be the guiding principle of the evolution. *Panta rhei* [Ed.: from the philosopher Heraclitus, "everything flows"] is not a sufficiently informative principle of constitutional interpretation. What is it that the judge must consult to determine when, and in what direction, evolution has occurred? Is it the will of the majority, discerned from newspapers, radio talk shows, public opinion polls, and chats at the country club? Is it the philosophy of Hume, or of John Rawls, or of John Stuart Mill, or of Aristotle? As soon as the discussion goes beyond the issue of whether the Constitution is static, the evolutionists divide into as many camps as there are individual views of the good, the true, and the beautiful. I think that is inevitably so, which means that evolutionism is simply not a practicable constitutional philosophy.

I do not suggest, mind you, that originalists always agree upon their answer. There is plenty of room for disagreement as to what original meaning was, and even more as to how that original meaning applies to the situation before the court. But the originalist at least knows what he is looking for: the original meaning of the text. Often—indeed, I dare say, usually—that is easy to discern and simple to apply. Sometimes (though not very often) there will be disagreement regarding the original meaning; and sometimes there will be disagreement as to how that original meaning applies to new and unforeseen phenomena. How, for example, does the First Amendment guarantee of "the freedom of speech" apply to new technologies that did not exist when the guarantee was created—to sound trucks, or to government-licensed, over-the-air television? In such new fields the Court must follow the trajectory of the First Amendment, so to speak, to determine what it requires—and assuredly that enterprise is not entirely cut-and-dried, but requires the exercise of judgment.

But the difficulties and uncertainties of determining original meaning and applying it to modern circumstances are negligible compared with the difficulties and uncertainties of the philosophy which says that the Constitution *changes;* that the very act which it once prohibited it now permits, and which it once permitted it now forbids; and that the key to that change is unknown and unknowable. The originalist, if he does not have all the answers, has many of them. The Confrontation Clause, for example, requires confrontation. For the evolutionist, on the other hand, every question is an open question, every day a new day. No fewer than three of the Justices with whom I have served have maintained that the death penalty is unconstitutional,[33] *even though its use is contemplated explicitly in the Constitution.* The Due Process Clause of the Fifth and Fourteenth Amendments says that no person shall be deprived of life without due process of law; and the Grand Jury Clause of the Fifth Amendment says that no person shall be deprived of life without due process of law; and the Grand Jury Clause of the Fifth Amendment says that no person shall be held to answer for a capital crime without grand jury indictment. No matter. Under The Living Constitution the death penalty may have

become unconstitutional. And it is up to each Justice to decide for himself (under no standard I can discern) when that occurs.

In the last analysis, however, it probably does not matter what principle, among the innumerable possibilities, the evolutionist proposes to determine in what direction The Living Constitution will grow. Whatever he might propose, at the end of the day an evolving constitution will evolve the way the majority wishes. The people will be willing to leave interpretation of the Constitution to lawyers and law courts so long as the people believe that it is (like the interpretation of a statute) essentially lawyers' work—requiring a close examination of text, history of the text, traditional understanding of the text, judicial precedent, and so forth. But if the people come to believe that the Constitution is *not* a text like other texts; that it means, not what it says or what it was understood to mean, but what it *should* mean, in light of the "evolving standards of decency that mark the progress of a maturing society"—well, then, they will look for qualifications other than impartiality, judgment, and lawyerly acumen in those whom they select to interpret it. More specifically, they will look for judges who agree with *them* as to what the evolving standards have evolved to; who agree with *them* as to what the Constitution *ought* to be.

It seems to me that that is where we are heading, or perhaps even where we have arrived. Seventy-five years ago, we believed firmly enough in a rock-solid, unchanging Constitution that we felt it necessary to adopt the Nineteenth Amendment to give women the vote. The battle was not fought in the courts, and few thought that it could be, despite the constitutional guarantee of Equal Protection of the Laws; that provision did not, when it was adopted, and hence did not in 1920, guarantee equal access to the ballot but permitted distinctions on the basis not only of age but of property and of sex. Who can doubt that if the issue had been deferred until today, the Constitution would be (formally) unamended, and the courts would be the chosen instrumentality of change? The American people have been converted to belief in The Living Constitution, a "morphing" document that means, from age to age, what it ought to mean. And with that conversion has inevitably come the new phenomenon of selecting and confirming federal judges, at all levels, on the basis of their views regarding a whole series of proposals for constitutional evolution. If the courts are free to write the Constitution anew, they will, by God, write it the way the majority wants; the appointment and confirmation process will see to that. This, of course, is the end of the Bill of Rights, whose meaning will be committed to the very body it was meant to protect against: the majority. By trying to make the Constitution do everything that needs doing from age to age, we shall have caused it to do nothing at all.

NOTES

1. See 1. William Blackstone, Commentaries on the Laws of England, 59–62, 91 (photo. reprint 1979) (1765).
2. Joel Prentiss Bishop, Commentaries on the Written Laws and Their Interpretation, 57–58 (Boston: Little, Brown, & Co. 1882) (emphasis added) (citation omitted).
3. James M. Landis, A Note on "Statutory Interpretation," 43 Harv. L. Rev. 886, 891 (1930).
4. 143 U.S. 457 (1892).
5. Id. at 458–59.
6. Id. at 472.
7. Id.
8. End of case, that is, insofar as our subject of statutory construction is concerned. As Professor Tribe's comments suggest, see post, at 92, it is possible (though I think far from certain) that in its application to ministers the statute was unconstitutional. But holding a provision unconstitutional is quite different from holding that it says what it does not; constitutional doubt may be used validly to affect the interpretation of an ambiguous statute, see United States v. Delaware & Hudson Co., 213 U.S. 366, 407–08 (1909), but not to rewrite a clear one, see Moore Ice Cream Co. v. Rose, 289 U.S. 373, 379 (1933).
9. See Green v. Bock Laundry Mach. Co., 490 U.S. 504 (1989).
10. Id. at 527 (Scalia, J., concurring).
11. Guido Calabresi, A Common Law for the Age of Statutes 2 (1982) (emphasis in original).
12. Id. at 117.
13. William N. Eskridge, Jr., Dynamic Statutory Interpretation 50 (1994) (quoting Arthur Phelps, Factors Influencing Judges in Interpreting Statutes, 3 Vand. L. Rev. 456, 469 (1950).
14. Felix Frankfurter, Some Reflections on the Reading of Statutes, 47 Column. L. Rev. 527, 538 (1947).
15. Oliver Wendell Holmes, Collected Legal Papers 207 (1920), quoted in Schwegmann Bros. v. Calvert Distillers Corp., 341 U.S. 384, 397 (1951) (Jackson, J., concurring).
16. Smith v. United States, 508 U.S. 223 (1993).
17. Dred Scott v. Sandford, 60 U.S. (19 How.) 393, 450 (1857).
18. McCulloch v. Maryland, 17 U.S. (4 Wheat.) 316, 407 (1819).
19. Rantoul, supra note 7, at 318.
20. See Cruzan v. Director, Mo. Dep't of Health, 497 U.S. 261, 279 (1990).
21. See In re Kirchner, 649 N.E.2d 324, 333 (Ill.), cert. denied, 115 S. Ct. 2599 (1995).
22. Rhodes v. Chapman, 452 U.S. 337, 346 (1981), quoting from Trop v. Dulles, 356 U.S. 86, 101 (1958) (plurality opinion).
23. Fortunatus Dwarris, A General Treatise on Statutes, with American Notes and Additions by Platt Potter 122 (Albany, N.Y. 1871).
24. See Mapp v. Ohio, 367 U.S. 643 (1961).
25. See Lee v. Weisman, 505 U.S. 577 (1992).
26. See Reynolds v. Sims, 377 U.S. 533 (1964).
27. See Goldberg v. Kelly, 397 U.S. 254 (1970).
28. See Kramer v. Union Free Sch. Dist., 395 U.S. 621 (1969).
29. See McIntyre v. Ohio Elections Comm'n, 115 S. Ct. 1511 (1995).
30. Under current doctrine, pornography may be banned only if it is "obscene," see Miller v. California, 413 U.S. 15 (1973), a judicially crafted term of art that does not embrace material that excites "normal, healthy sexual desires," Brockett v. Spokane Arcades, Inc., 472 U.S. 491, 498 (1985).
31. See Home Building & Loan Ass'n v. Blaisdell, 290 U.S. 398 (1934).
32. See Maryland v. Craig, 497 U.S. 836 (1990).
33. See Gregg v. Georgia, 428 U.S. 153, 227 (1976) (Brennan, J., dissenting); id. at 231 (Marshall, J., dissenting); Callins v. Colllins, 114 S. Ct. 1127, 1128 (1994) (Blackmun, J., dissenting from denial of certiorari).

17 Comment

RONALD DWORKIN

1

Justice Scalia has managed to give two lectures about meaning with no reference to Derrida or Gadamer or even the hermeneutic circle, and he has set out with laudable clarity a sensible account of statutory interpretation. These are considerable achievements. But I believe he has seriously misunderstood the implications of his general account for constitutional law, and that his lectures therefore have a schizophrenic character. He begins with a general theory that entails a style of constitutional adjudication that he ends by denouncing.

His initial argument rests on a crucial distinction between law and intention. "Men may intend what they will," he says, "but it is only the laws that they enact which bind us," and he is scornful of decisions like *Holy Trinity,* in which the Supreme Court, conceding that the "letter" of a statute forbade what the church had done, speculated that Congress did not intend that result. Indeed, he is skeptical about the very idea of a corporate legislative "intention"; most members of Congress, he says, have never thought about the unforeseen issues of interpretation that courts must face. A careless reader might object, however, that any coherent account of statutory interpretation *must* be based on assumptions about someone's (or some body's) intention, and that Scalia's own account accepts this at several points. Scalia admits that courts should remedy "scrivener's error." He rejects "strict constructionism"—he thinks the Supreme Court's "literalist" decision in the "firearm" case, *Smith v. United States,* was silly. He credits at least some of the "canons" of interpretation as being an "indication" of meaning. And he says that it would be absurd to read the First Amendment's protection of speech and press as not applying to handwritten notes, which are, technically, neither.

Each of these clarifications allows respect for intention to trump literal text, and the careless objection I am imagining therefore claims an inconsistency. Scalia's defenders might say, in reply to the objection, that he is not an *extreme* textualist, and that these adjustments are only concessions to common sense and practicality. But that misunderstands the objection, which is that the concessions undermine Scalia's position altogether, because they recognize not only the intelligibility but the priority of legislative intention, both of which he begins by denying. If judges can appeal to a presumed legislative intent to add to the plain meaning of "speech" and "press," or to subtract from the plain meaning of "uses a firearm," why can they not appeal to the same legislative intent to allow a priest to enter the country? Scalia's answer to this objection must not rely on any self-destructive "practicality" claim. It must rely instead on a distinction between *kinds* of intention, a distinction he does not make explicitly, but that must lie at the heart of his theory if the theory is defensible at all.

This is the crucial distinction between what some officials intended to *say* in enacting the language they used, and what they intended—or expected or hoped—would be the *consequence* of their saying it. Suppose a boss tells his manager (without winking) to hire the most qualified applicant for a new job. The boss might think it obvious that his own son, who is an applicant, is the most qualified; indeed, he might not have given the instruction unless he was confident that the manager would think so too. Nevertheless, what the boss *said,* and *intended* to say, was that the most qualified applicant should be hired, and if the manager thought some other applicant

From Antonin Scalia, *A Matter of Interpretation: Federal Courts and the Law: An Essay* (Princeton, N. J.: Princeton University Press, 1997), pp. 115–28, 144–49. # 1997 Princeton University Press. Reprinted by permission of Princeton University Press.

better qualified, but hired the boss's son to save his own job, he would not be following the standard the boss had intended to lay down.

So what I called the careless objection is wrong. The supposed lapses from Scalia's textualism it cites are not lapses at all, because textualism insists on deference to one kind of intention—semantic intention—and in all his remarks so far cited Scalia is deferring to that. Any reader of anything must attend to semantic intention, because the same sounds or even words can be used with the intention of saying different things. If I tell you (to use Scalia's own example) that I admire bays, you would have to decide whether I intended to say that I admire certain horses or certain bodies of water. Until you had, you would have no idea what I had actually said even though you would know what sounds I had uttered. The phrase "using a firearm" might naturally be used, in some contexts, with the intention of describing only situations in which a gun is used as a threat; the same phrase might be used, in other contexts, to mean using a gun for any purpose including barter. We do not know what Congress actually said, in using a similar phrase, until we have answered the question of what it is reasonable to suppose, in all the circumstances including the rest of the statute, it intended to say in speaking as it did.

When we are trying to decide what someone meant to say, in circumstances like these, we are deciding which clarifying *translation* of his inscriptions is the best. It is a matter of complex and subtle philosophical argument what such translations consist in and how they are possible—how, for example, we weave assumptions about what the speaker believes and wants, and about what it would be rational for him to believe and want, into decisions about what he meant to say. The difficulties are greatly increased when we are translating not the utterances of a real person but those of an institution like a legislature. We rely on personification—we suppose that the institution has semantic intentions of its own—and it is difficult to understand what sense that makes, or what special standards we should use to discover or construct such intentions. Scalia would not agree with my own opinions about these matters.[1] But we do agree on the importance of the distinction I am emphasizing: between the question of what a legislature intended to say in the laws it enacted, which judges applying those laws must answer, and the question of what the various legislators as individuals expected or hoped the consequences of those laws would be, which is a very different matter.

Holy Trinity illustrates the difference and its importance. There can be no serious doubt that Congress meant to say what the words it used would naturally be understood to say. It is conceivable—perhaps even likely—that most members would have voted for an exception for English priests had the issue been raised. But that is a matter of (counterfactual) expectations, not of semantic intention. The law, as Scalia emphasizes, is what Congress has said, which is fixed by the best interpretation of the language it used, not by what some proportion of its members wanted or expected or assumed would happen, or would have wanted or expected or assumed if they had thought of the case.[2] Not everyone agrees with that judgment. Some lawyers think that it accords better with democracy if judges defer to reasonable assumptions about what most legislators wanted or would have wanted, even when the language they used does not embody those actual or hypothetical wishes. After all, these lawyers argue, legislation should reflect what those who have been elected by the people actually think best for the country. Scalia disagrees with that judgment: he thinks it more democratic to give semantic intention priority over expectation intention when the two conflict, as they putatively did in *Holy Trinity*.

2

Now consider the implications of textualism so understood for the most important part of Scalia's judicial duties: interpreting the exceedingly abstract clauses of the Bill of Rights and later rights-bearing amendments. Scalia describes himself as a constitutional "originalist." But the distinction we made allows us a further distinction between two forms of originalism: "semantic" originalism, which insists that the rights-granting clauses be read to say what those who made them intended to say, and "expectation" originalism, which holds that these clauses should be understood to have the consequences that those who made them expected them to have. Consider, to see the difference, the *Brown vs. Board of Education* question: does the Fourteenth Amendment guarantee of "equal protection of the laws" forbid racial segregation in public schools? We know that the majority of the members of Congress who voted for that amendment did not expect or intend it to have that consequence: they themselves sustained racial segregation in the schools of the District of Columbia.[3] So an expectation-originalist would interpret the Fourteenth Amendment to permit segregation and would declare the Court's decision wrong. But there is no plausible interpretation of what these statesmen meant to *say*, in laying down the language "equal protection of the laws," that entitles us to conclude that they *declared* segregation constitutional. On the contrary, as the Supreme Court held, the best understanding of their semantic intentions supposes that they meant to, and did, lay down a general principle of political morality that (it had become clear by 1954) condemns racial segregation. So, on that ground, a semantic-originalist would concur in the Court's decision.

If Scalia were faithful to his textualism, he would be a semantic-originalist. But is he? Notice his brief discussion of whether capital punishment offends the Eighth Amendment's prohibition against "cruel and unusual" punishments. An expectation-originalist certainly would hold that it does not, for the reasons Scalia cites. The "Framers" hardly would have bothered to stipulate that "life" may be taken only after due process if they thought that the Eighth Amendment made capital punishment unconstitutional anyway. But the question is far more complicated for a semantic-originalist. For he must choose between two clarifying translations—two different accounts of what the Framers intended to *say* in the Eighth Amendment. The first reading supposes that the Framers intended to say, by using the words "cruel and unusual," that punishments generally thought cruel at the time they spoke were to be prohibited—that is, that they would have

expressed themselves more clearly if they had used the phrase "punishments widely regarded as cruel and unusual at the date of this enactment" in place of the misleading language they actually used. The second reading supposes that they intended to lay down an abstract principle forbidding whatever punishments are in fact cruel and unusual. Of course, if the correct translation is the first version, then capital punishment does not violate the Eighth Amendment. But if the second, principled translation is a more accurate account of what they intended to say, the question remains open. Just as the manager in my story could only follow his boss's principled instruction by using his own judgment, so judges then could apply the Eighth Amendment only by deciding whether capital punishment is in fact cruel and has now become (as in fact it has become, at least among democracies) unusual.

The textual evidence Scalia cites would be irrelevant for a semantic-originalist who translated the Eighth Amendment in a principled rather than a concrete and dated way. There is no contradiction in the following set of claims. The Framers of the Eighth Amendment laid down a principle forbidding whatever punishments are cruel and unusual. They did not themselves expect or intend that that principle would abolish the death penalty, so they provided that death could be inflicted only after due process. But it does not follow that the abstract principle they stated does not, contrary to their own expectation, forbid capital punishment. Suppose some legislature enacts a law forbidding the hunting of animals that are members of "endangered species" and then, later in its term, imposes special license requirements for hunting, among other animals, minks. We would assume that the members who voted for both provisions did not think that minks were endangered. But we would not be justified in concluding from that fact that, as a matter of law, minks were excluded from the ban even if they plainly *were* endangered. The latter inference would be an example of *Holy Trinity* thinking.

You will now understand my concern about Scalia's consistency, for he cites the view that capital punishment is unconstitutional as so obviously preposterous that it is cause for wonder that three justices who served with him actually held such an opinion.[4] If he were an expectation-originalist, we would not be surprised at that view, or at the evidence he offers to support it. But for a semantic-originalist the question just *cannot* be foreclosed by references to the death penalty in the rest of the Constitution. A semantic-originalist would also have to think that the best interpretation of the Eighth Amendment was the dated rather than the principled translation, and even someone who might be drawn to that dated interpretation could not think the principled one *preposterous*.

On the contrary, it is the dated translation that seems bizarre. It is near inconceivable that sophisticated eighteenth-century statesmen, who were familiar with the transparency of ordinary moral language, would have used "cruel" as shorthand for "what we now think cruel." They knew how to be concrete when they intended to be: the various provisions for criminal and civil process in the Fourth, Fifth, Sixth, and Seventh Amendments do not speak of "fair" or "due" or "usual" procedures, but lay down very concrete provisions. If they had intended a dated provision, they could and would have written an explicit one. Of course, we cannot imagine Madison or any of his contemporaries doing that: they wouldn't think it appropriate to protect what they took to be a fundamental right in such terms. But that surely means that the dated translation would be a plain mistranslation.

So Scalia's impatience with what seems the most natural statement of what the authors of the Eighth Amendment intended to say is puzzling. Part of the explanation may lie in his fear of what he calls a "morphing" theory of the Constitution—that the rights-bearing clauses are chameleons which change their meaning to conform to the needs and spirit of new times. He calls this chameleon theory "dominant," but it is hardly even intelligible, and I know of no prominent contemporary judge or scholar who holds anything like it. True, a metaphorical description of the Constitution as "living" has figured in constitutional rhetoric of the past, but this metaphor is much better understood as endorsing, not the chameleon theory, but the view I just described as the one that Scalia, if he were a semantic-originalist,

might be expected to hold himself—that key constitutional provisions, as a matter of their original meaning, set out abstract principles rather than concrete or dated rules. If so, then the application of these abstract principles to particular cases, which takes fresh judgment, must be reviewed continually, not in an attempt to find substitutes for what the Constitution says, but out of respect for what it says.

I have defended that view in a series of books over the last decade,[5] and some of what I have written might strike Scalia as saying that the Constitution itself changes, though I meant the opposite. I said, for example, that, subject to the constraints of integrity which require judges to keep faith with past decisions, "The Constitution insists that our judges do their best collectively to construct, reinspect, and revise, generation by generation, the skeleton of freedom and equality of concern that its great clauses, in their majestic abstraction, command."[6]

It is that moral and principled reading of the Constitution, not the mythic chameleon claims he describes, that Scalia must produce reasons for rejecting. (Professor Tribe endorses the abstract moral reading of many clauses as well; he proposes that the First Amendment, for example, be read as abstract.[7]) So we may gauge Scalia's arguments against the principled reading by studying his response to Tribe's suggestion. Scalia argues that the First Amendment should be read not as abstract but as dated—that it should be read, that is, as guaranteeing only the rights it generally would have been understood to protect when it was enacted. He makes three points: first, that since many parts of the Bill of Rights are plainly concrete—the Third Amendment's prohibition against quartering troops during peacetime, for example—the "Framers" probably intended to make them all so; second, that the "Framers" presumably would be anxious to ensure that their own views about free speech were respected, even if later generations no longer agreed; and, third, that in any case the "Framers" would not have wanted to leave the development of a constitutionalized moral principle to judges.[8]

These are all arguments for ignoring the natural semantic meaning of a text in favor of speculations about the expectations of its authors, and the Scalia of the preconstitutional part of these lectures would have ridiculed those arguments. First, why shouldn't the "Framers" have thought that a combination of concrete and abstract rights would best secure the (evidently abstract) goals they set out in the preamble? No other national constitution is written at only one level of abstraction, and there is no reason to suppose the authors of the Bill of Rights would have been tempted by that kind of stylistic homogeneity. Second, as I said, Enlightenment statesmen were very unlikely to think that their own views represented the last word in moral progress. If they really were worried that future generations would protect rights less vigorously than they themselves did, they would have made plain that they intended to create a dated provision. Third, we must distinguish the question of what the Constitution means from the question of which institution has final authority to decide what it means. If, as many commentators think, "Framers" expected judges to have that authority, and if they feared the consequences for abstract rights, they would have taken *special* care to write concrete, dated clauses. If, on the contrary, they did not expect judicial review, then Scalia's third argument fails for that reason. The First Amendment turns out to be his *Holy Trinity*.

He ignores, moreover, an apparently decisive argument against a translation of the First Amendment as dated. There *was* no generally accepted understanding of the right of free speech on which the framers could have based a dated clause even if they had wanted to write one. On the contrary, the disagreement about what the right comprises was much more profound when the amendment was enacted than it is now. When the dominant Federalist party enacted the Sedition Act in 1798, its members argued, relying on Blackstone, that "the freedom of speech" meant only freedom from "prior restraint"—in effect, freedom from an advance prohibition—and did not include any protection at all from punishment *after* publication.[9] The opposing Republicans argued for a dramatically different view of the amendment: as Albert Gallatin (Jefferson's future secretary of the treasury) pointed out, it is "preposterous to say,

that to punish a certain act was not an abridgment of the liberty of doing that act." All parties to the debate *assumed* that the First Amendment set out an abstract principle and that fresh judgment would be needed to interpret it. The Federalists relied, not on contemporary practice, which hardly supported their reading,[10] but on the moral authority of Blackstone. The Republicans relied, not on contemporary practice either, but on the logic of freedom. No one supposed that the First Amendment codified some current and settled understanding, and the deep division among them showed that there was no settled understanding to codify.

So Scalia's discussion of the First Amendment is as puzzling as his briefer remarks about the Eighth Amendment. Now consider what he says about the Fourteenth Amendment's guarantee of "equal protection of the laws." He says that that clause "did not, when it was adopted, and hence did not in 1920, guarantee equal access to the ballot but permitted distinctions on the basis not only of age but of property and sex."[11] Why is he so sure that the Equal Protection Clause did not always forbid discrimination on grounds of age, property, or sex (or, for that matter, sexual orientation)? Certainly when the amendment was adopted, few people *thought* that the clause had that consequence, any more than they thought that it had the consequence of making school segregation illegal. But the semantic-originalist would dismiss this as just what the Framers and later generations of lawyers expected, not a matter of what the Framers actually *said*. If we look at the text they wrote, we see no distinction between racial discrimination and any other form of discrimination: the language is perfectly general, abstract, and principled. Scalia now reads into that language limitations that the language not only does not suggest but cannot bear, and he tries to justify this mistranslation by attributing understandings and expectations to statesmen that they may well have had, but that left no mark on the text they wrote. The Equal Protection Clause, we might say, is Scalia's *Holy Trinity* cubed.

What has happened? Why does the resolute text-reader, dictionary-minder, expectation-scorner of the beginning of these lectures change his mind when he comes to the most fundamental American statute of them all? He offers, in his final pages, an intriguing answer. He sees, correctly, that if we read the abstract clauses of the Bill of Rights as they were written—if we read them to say what their authors intended them to say rather than to deliver the consequences they expected them to have—then judges must treat these clauses as enacting abstract moral principles and therefore must exercise moral judgment in deciding what they *really* require. That does not mean ignoring precedent or textual or historical integrity or morphing the Constitution. It means, on the contrary, enforcing it in accordance with its text, in the only way that this can be done. Many conservative judges therefore reject semantic originalism as undemocratic; elected judges, they say, should not have that responsibility. Scalia gives nearly the opposite reason: he says the moral reading gives the people not too little but too much power, because it politicizes the appointment of Supreme Court justices and makes it more likely that justices will be appointed who reflect the changing moods of the majority. He fears that the constitutional rights of individuals will suffer.

History disagrees. Justices whose methods seem closest to the moral reading of the Constitution have been champions, not enemies, of individual rights, and, as the political defeat of Robert Bork's nomination taught us, the people seem content not only with the moral reading but with its individualist implications. Scalia is worried about the decline of what he believes to be

property rights embedded in the Constitution but ignored in recent decades. He reminds liberals that rights of criminal defendants may also be at risk. But even if we were persuaded that the Court has gone too far in neglecting property rights, and also that *Maryland v. Craig* compromised a valid constitutional right, these assumed mistakes would hardly outweigh the advantages to individual freedom that have flowed from judges' treatment of the great clauses as abstract.

It is, however, revealing that this is the scale on which Scalia finally wants his arguments to be weighed, and it may provide a final explanation, if not justification, for the inconsistency of his lectures as a whole. His most basic argument for textualism is drawn from majoritarian theory: he says that it is undemocratic when a statute is interpreted other than in accordance with the public text that was before legislators when they voted and is available to everyone in the community afterwards. His most basic argument for rejecting textualism in constitutional interpretation, on the other hand, reflects his *reservations* about majority rule. As with most of us, Scalia's attitudes about democracy are complex and ambivalent. I disagree with his judgment about which individual rights are genuine and important, and about whether the moral reading is a threat or an encouragement to freedom. But I agree with him that in the end the magnet of political morality is the strongest force in jurisprudence. The power of that magnet is nowhere more evident than in the rise and fall of his own love affair with textual fidelity.

Response to Dworkin

ANTONIN SCALIA

I agree with the distinction that Professor Dworkin draws in part 1 of his Comment, between what he calls "semantic intention" and the concrete expectations of lawgivers. It is indeed the former rather than the latter that I follow. I would prefer the term "import" to "semantic intention"—because that puts the focus where I believe it should be, upon what the text reasonably would

be understood to mean, rather than upon what it was intended to mean. Ultimately, of course, those two concepts chase one another back and forth to some extent, since the import of language depends upon its context, which includes the occasion for, and hence the evident purpose of, its utterance. But so far Professor Dworkin and I are in accord: we both follow "semantic intention."

Professor Dworkin goes on to say, however, that I am not true to this calling, as is demonstrated, he believes, by my conviction that the Eighth Amendment does not forbid capital punishment. I am wrong in this, he says, because "the semantic-originalist ... must choose between two clarifying translations," the first of which "supposes that the Framers intended to say, by using the words 'cruel and unusual,' that punishments generally thought cruel at the time they spoke were to be prohibited—that is, that they would have expressed themselves more clearly if they had used the phrase 'punishments widely regarded as cruel and unusual at the date of this enactment' in place of the misleading language they actually used," and the second of which "supposes that they intended to lay down an abstract principle forbidding whatever punishments are in fact cruel and unusual." This seems to me a false dichotomy, the first part of which caricatures my sort of originalism, much as Professor Tribe did—as a narrow and hidebound methodology that ascribes to the Constitution a listing of rights "in highly particularistic, rule-like terms." In fact, however, I, no less than Professor Dworkin, believe that the Eighth Amendment is no mere "concrete and dated rule," but rather an abstract principle. If I did not hold this belief, I would not be able to apply the Eighth Amendment (as I assuredly do) to all sorts of tortures quite unknown at the time the Eighth Amendment was adopted. What it abstracts, however, is not a moral principle of "cruelty" that philosophers can play with in the future, but rather the existing society's assessment of what is cruel. It means not (as Professor Dworkin would have it) "whatever may be considered cruel from one generation to the next," but "what we consider cruel today"; otherwise, it would be no protection against the moral perceptions of a future, more brutal, generation. It is, in other words, rooted in the moral perceptions *of the time*.

On this analysis, it is entirely clear that capital punishment, which was widely in use in 1791, does not violate the abstract moral principle of the Eighth Amendment. Professor Dworkin is therefore close to correct in saying that the *textual* evidence I cite for the constitutionality of capital punishment (namely, the specific mention of it in several portions of the Bill of Rights) ought to be "irrelevant" to me. To be entirely correct, he should have said "superfluous." Surely the same point *can* be proved by textual evidence, even though (as far as my philosophy is concerned) it need not be. I adduced the textual evidence only to demonstrate that thoroughgoing constitutional evolutionists will be deterred no more by text than by theory.

Professor Dworkin nonetheless takes on my textual point and seeks to prove it wrong. He asserts that making provision for the death penalty in the Constitution does not establish that it was not regarded as "cruel" under the Eighth Amendment, just as making provision for mink-hunting licenses in a statute which forbids the hunting of "endangered species" does not establish that minks can never acquire the protected status of an "endangered species." To begin with, I am not as clear as he is that such a fanciful statute—which simply forbids the hunting of "endangered species" without conferring authority upon some agency to define what species are endangered from time to time—would be interpreted to have a changing content; or, if it were so interpreted, that minks, for which hunting licenses are authorized, can come within that changing content. But if the example does suggest those consequences, it is only because the term "endangered species," unlike the term "cruel punishments," clearly connotes a category that changes from decade to decade. Animal populations, we will all agree, ebb and flow, and hence it is plausible to believe that minks, even though "unendangered" and marked for hunting when the statute was passed, might come under "endangered species" protection in the future. Unlike animal populations, however, "moral principles," most of us think, are permanent. The Americans of 1791 surely thought that what was cruel was cruel, regardless of what a more brutal future generation might think about it. They were embedding in the Bill of Rights *their* moral values, for otherwise all its general and abstract guarantees could be brought to nought. Thus, provision for the death penalty in a Constitution that sets forth the moral principle of "no cruel punishments" is conclusive evidence that the death penalty is not (in the moral view of the Constitution) cruel.

Professor Dworkin asserts that the three arguments I have made against an evolutionary meaning of the Bill of Rights do not comport with my methodology of "semantic intent." I disagree. The first of them, argument from the unquestionably "time-dated" character of the concrete provisions to the conclusion that the more abstract provisions are time-dated as well, is not, as Professor Dworkin asserts, a "speculation[ ] about the expectations of [their] authors," but is rather a quite routine attempt to divine import ("semantic intent") from *context*. In fact, it is nothing more than an application of the canon of construction *noscitur ex sociis* ["words are known by their fellows"], which I discussed in my main essay. The second argument also rests upon context—a context which shows that the purpose of the document in question is to guarantee certain rights, which in turn leads to the conclusion that the passage of time cannot reasonably be thought to alter the content of those rights. And the third, the argument that the repository of ultimate responsibility for determining the content of the rights (the judiciary) is a most unlikely barometer of evolving national morality but a traditional interpreter of "time-dated" laws, rests upon context as well—assuming (as a given) that judicial review is implicit in the structure of the Constitution. Of course if, as both Professor Dworkin and Professor Tribe seem to suggest, it is not a given that the Bill of Rights is to be enforced against the legislature by the courts, then my argument ceases to have force as a justification for my mode of interpretation, but becomes an argument directed to the overall inconsistency of the evolutionists: Why, given what they believe the Bill of Rights is, would they want judges to be its ultimate interpreters?

As for Professor Dworkin's point that the First Amendment cannot possibly be "time-dated" because "[t]here *was* no generally accepted understanding of the right of free speech": On the main points, I think, there was. But even if not, it is infinitely more reasonable to interpret a document as leaving some of the uncertainties of the current state of the law to be worked out in practice and in litigation (statutes do this all the time) than to interpret it as enacting, and making judicially enforceable, an indeterminate moral concept of "freedom of speech." It makes a lot of sense to guarantee to a society that "the freedom of speech you now enjoy (*whatever* that consists of) will never be diminished by the federal government"; it makes very little sense to guarantee that "the federal government will respect the moral principle of freedom of speech, which may entitle you to more, or less, freedom of speech than you now legally enjoy."

Professor Dworkin also criticizes my discussion of the Fourteenth Amendment—in the course of which he confuses, I think, two issues. First, he quotes my statement that the Equal Protection Clause "did not, when it was adopted, and hence did not in 1920, guarantee equal access to the ballot but permitted distinctions on the basis not only of age but of property and sex." He then asks, "Why is he so sure that the Equal Protection Clause did not always forbid discrimination on grounds of age, property, or sex (or, for that matter, sexual orientation)? ... If we look at the text ... , we see no distinction...." In fact, however, as far as access to the ballot goes (which was the subject of my quoted remark), the text of the Fourteenth Amendment is very clear that equal protection does not mean equal access on the basis of (at least) age and sex. Section 2 of the amendment provides for reduction of representation in Congress if a state excludes from the ballot "any of the male inhabitants of such State, being twenty-one years of age." But as for the application of the Equal Protection Clause *generally* (which is what Professor Dworkin proceeds to address), he quite entirely mistakes my position. I certainly do not assert that it permits discrimination on the basis of age, property, sex, "sexual orientation," or for that matter even blue eyes and nose rings. Denial of equal protection on *all* of these grounds is prohibited—but that still leaves open the question of what *constitutes* a denial of equal protection. Is it a denial of equal protection on the basis of sex to have segregated toilets in public buildings, or to exclude women from combat? I have no idea how Professor Dworkin goes about answering such a question. I answer it on the basis of the "time-dated" meaning of equal protection in 1868. Unisex toilets and women assault troops may be ideas whose time has come, and the people certainly are free to require them by legislation; but refusing to do so does not violate the Fourteenth Amendment, because that is not what "equal protection of the laws" ever meant.

Finally, Professor Dworkin dismisses my fears that, in the long run, the "moral reading" of the Constitution will lead to a reduction of the rights of individuals. "History disagrees," he says, since "the people seem content not only with the moral reading but with its individualist implications." Well, there is not really much history to go on. As I have observed, evolutionary constitutional jurisprudence has held sway in the courts for only forty years or so, and recognition by the people that the Constitution means whatever it ought to mean is even more recent. To be sure, there are still notable victories in the Supreme Court for "individual rights," but has Professor Dworkin not observed that, increasingly, the "individual rights" favored by the courts tend to be the same "individual rights" favored by popular majoritarian legislation? Women's rights, for example; racial minority rights; homosexual rights; abortion rights; rights against political favoritism? The glorious days of the Warren Court, when the *judges* knew that the Constitution means whatever it ought to, but the *people* had not yet caught on to the new game (and selected their judges accordingly), are gone forever. Those were the days in which genuinely *unpopular* new minority rights could be created—notably, rights of criminal defendants and prisoners. That era of public naïveté is past, and for individual rights disfavored by the majority I think there are hard times ahead.

NOTES

1. See chapter 9 of my Law's Empire (Harvard University Press, 1986).
2. I am prescinding, as Scalia does, from the question Professor Tribe raises about the constitutionality of the statute considered in Holy Trinity if it is read to say what it was plainly intended to say.
3. For a recent account of the literature, see Michael J. Klarman, *Brown, Originalism and Constitutional Theory: A Response to Professor McConnell*, 81 Virginia Law Review, 1881 (1995).
4. Scalia, "Common-Law Courts in a Civil-Law System," p. 46.
5. See chapter 10 of Law's Empire, supra note 7, chapter 5 of Life's Dominion (Alfred Knopf, 1993), and Freedom's Law: The Moral Reading of the American Constitution (Harvard University Press, 1996).
6. Life's Dominion, supra note 11, 145.
7. I assume that Tribe agrees that some constitutional clauses are semantically principled, though in his lecture he called such clauses "aspirational," a term that is often used to describe ambitions that government should strive to realize as distinct from law it is bound to obey. Many contemporary constitutions, for example, set out "aspirational" declarations of economic and social rights meant to have that function. Scalia may have understood Tribe in that sense in describing Tribe's view of the First Amendment as a beau ideal, based on Justice Scalia's verbal reply to his respondents on the occasion of the Tanner Lectures, March 1995, hereafter referred to as Tanner reply. The abstract principles of the Constitution's text are as much law—as much mandatory and as little aspirational or idealized—as any other clauses. See Freedom's Law, supra note 11.
8. Tanner reply.
9. For a recent description of the arguments over the Sedition Act, see Anthony Lewis, Make No Law (Random House, 1991), chapter 7.
10. See the exchange of views between Professors Leonard Levy and David Anderson, summarized in the former's 1985 edition of his book, Legacy of Suppression.
11. Scalia, "Common-Law Courts in a Civil-Law System," p. 47.

CHAPTER SIX

Critical Approaches to Law

18 Critical Legal Histories

ROBERT W. GORDON

Critical legal writers[1] pay a lot of attention to history. In fact, they have probably devoted more pages to historical description—particularly the intellectual history of legal doctrine—than to anything else, even law and economics. Such a preoccupation within a radical movement is at first glance surprising. After all, lawyers have, by notorious custom, used history conservatively, appealing to continuity and tradition. And in the less common situations in which lawyers have used history to criticize the status quo, they have usually resorted to social and economic history, to show that the original social context of a legal rule reveals it was adopted for wicked or obsolete reasons, rather than to the history of legal doctrine. What could conceivably be radical—or, as some unkindly ask, even interesting—about rewriting the history of doctrine?

I will attempt, in this article, to give a brief account of the impulses that have prompted the Critical scholars to their chosen ways of writing history (or rather histories, since the movement has actually spawned several different historiographical practices). I'll start by trying to describe a vision of law-in-history that has tended, as I'll argue, to dominate liberal legal scholarship. I will then outline some of the Critical insights that have developed—many of them within liberal scholarship itself—to corrode separate components of that dominant vision. Next I'll show how Critical writers have tried to build these insights into a more thorough critique and how this critique has affected the ways in which they go about their work. Finally, I will discuss some common attacks on Critical histories, add a few doubting remarks of my own, and proffer some suggestions and exhortations for future directions. [...]

I. THE DOMINANT VISION: EVOLUTIONARY FUNCTIONALISM

A. Common Threads

Over the last 150 years or so, enlightened American legal opinion has adhered with remarkable fidelity to what, in broad conception, looks like a single set of notions about historical change and the relation of law to such change. Stated baldly, these notions are that the natural and proper evolution of a society (or at least of a "progressive" society, to use Maine's qualification) is towards the type of liberal capitalism seen in the advanced Western nations (especially the United States), and that the natural and proper function of a legal system is to facilitate such an evolution. (The words "natural" and "proper" stress the normative nature of the theory [which I will call "functionalism"]; deviations from the norm are both atypical and bad.) Let me try to break this very general account down into some more manageable pieces, the handful of propositions that compose its core. Readers will, I hope, understand that what I'm constructing is an "ideal type": a list of the propositions that one could expect most legal writers within the dominant tradition to accept most of the time, even if one also could expect that any individual writer would want to qualify or even violently object to one or two of them.

1. "Law" and "society" are separate social categories, each describable independently from the other but related to each other through various mechanisms of causal linkage.

Writers in the dominant tradition make an important, though usually silent, move even before they start saying anything substantive about law-in-history: They divide the world into two spheres, one social and one legal. "Society" is the primary realm of social experience. It is "real life": What's immediately and truly important to people, like desire and its fulfillment, or frustration, goes on there. This realm is the realm of production, commerce, the market, the family. "Law" or "the legal system," on the other hand, is a distinctly secondary body of phenomena. It is a specialized realm of state and professional activity that is called into being by the primary social world in order to serve that world's needs. Law is auxiliary—an excrescence on social life, even if sometimes a useful excrescence.

Though law and society are separate, they are related. And the big theoretical problem for writers who see the world this way is to work out the secret of that relationship. Thus, they ask questions such as, "Is law a dependent or independent

variable?" "Is everything about law—norms, rules, processes, and institutions—determined by society, or does law have 'autonomous' internal structures or logic?" "If it has internal structures, do they enable it to have an independent causal effect—to act as a positive feedback loop—on social life?" Writers in the liberal tradition (like those in the Marxist tradition) have resolved these questions in wildly different ways and reached wildly different conclusions, but they all assume that these *are* the vital questions.

2. Societies have needs.

This proposition is the functionalist heart of the dominant vision. Social needs may be universal—needs such as survival, stability, maintenance of social order, conflict management, organization of production, security against foreign enemies, allocation of scarce resources, or preservation of continuity in the midst of change—or they may be specific to a given stage of social or economic development. One key need is the *need to develop* along the appropriate social evolutionary path.

Needs operate both as pressures and as constraints. They are the motors driving the society to find means for their fulfillment, and they set the limits on the possibilities of social experimentation —limits beyond which lie dysfunction, futility, failure, and chaos.[2]

3. There is an objective, determined, progressive social evolutionary path.

The general idea here is that the causal responsibility for change lies with impersonal forces of historical "becoming." More specifically, the histories of certain advanced Western societies, most notably the United States, describe an evolutionary development that is both natural (in the sense that some version of it will happen in every society unless "artificial" constraints force a deviation) and, on the whole, progressive.

Different generations have described this evolutionary process somewhat differently, but the contemporary United States almost always ends up sitting at the developmental summit. The great eighteenth and nineteenth-century story (the "Scottish Enlightenment" story, whose general outlines still are rooted so firmly in our culture) told of the gradual liberation of the individual from the shackles of feudalism and superstition—from restraints on trade, on free alienation of land, and on free movement of labor; from the oppressions of feudal dues and tithes, and of perpetual subordination to customary hierarchies of ecclesiastical and noble orders; and from established religions. According to this story, the concurrent spread of liberty and commerce yielded a commonwealth of men who were actually or potentially (with some exceptions such as slaves) politically equal property-holders, securely owning and freely exchanging land, labor, and capital.

By the start of our own century, the growth of propertyless classes caused the historians' emphasis to shift away from the concept of progress as the growth of yeoman freeholders and towards the concept of progress as improvement in technology, organization of production, and creation of opportunities for immigrants to rise in society. In our own age of dampened enthusiasms, the labels attached to basic historical changes tend to be more neutral: "industrialization," "modernization," or just "political and economic development." In usage, however, these labels retain a strong normative flavor and occasionally, as in some legal economists' interpretation of the history of societies as one long series of "efficiency" gains, an unabashed Victorian optimism.

What all these histories have in common is their determinist teleologies, whose elemental parts—the "extension of the market," the "breakdown of traditional communities and status hierarchies," the "shift from ascribed to achieved social status," the "triumph of the middle class," the "revolution of production in the factory system," the "rise of the administrative state," and the "development of the multi-divisional form of corporate organization"—are all linked together in a master *process* of social evolution.

Lawyers once played a moderately important role in actually writing these histories. Recent legal writing is more likely just to assume that some objective, generally understood process of development has been working away in the background, and to leave the actual details of the process to vague implication.

4. Legal systems should be described and explained in terms of their functional responsiveness to social needs.

Functionalist sociological legal history has an exceedingly distinguished lineage, beginning with Montesquieu and Adam Smith, continuing through Karl Marx, Max Weber, and Rudolph von Jhering, and virtually all lesser nineteenth-century writers on law, and including among twentieth-century lawyers such figures as Oliver Wendell Holmes, Roscoe Pound, Karl Llewellyn, Franz Neumann, and Willard Hurst. The general functionalist method is to construct (or, as is rather more common, to assume without much discussion) a typology of stages of social development, and then to show how legal forms and institutions have satisfied, or failed to satisfy, the functional requirements of each stage. Obviously, an enormous gap in sophistication and conceptual power separates the best and worst examples of this method. At its best, as in Weber's work, complex bundles of rules are tied through explicit theorizing to elaborate accounts of social development. At its comically vulgar worst, the method produces wholly speculative functional rationales for legal rules in underlying social changes—vacuously described rationales such as "the evolution of the right of privacy was a response to the increasing complexity and interdependence of modern society."

Of all the generalizations produced by this method, one so familiar that it has become a cliché of our common discourse is that capitalist development (or as our forebears preferred to put it, the expansion of commerce) requires legal improvements that increase the certainty and predictability of exchange relationships. I will come back to this assertion, but I should first list the final identifying characteristic of the dominant vision, namely:

5. The legal system adapts to changing social needs.

This concept expresses the confidence that, in the advanced Western nations and especially in the United States, the legal system *has in fact* responded to evolving social needs. Save for egregiously Panglossian writers (Blackstone in some moods is one of these), the proponents of this notion do not feel a need to attribute a social function to every piece of law in the system; most writers will concede that even major legal forms and processes can be dysfunctional for short periods. But a committed functionalist will maintain that, despite undeniable instances of lag and reaction, adaptation is the normal course. The perspective thus tends to produce statements such as the following (presented here for the sake of illustration in their simplest and most unqualified form), which discuss specific changes in legal rules or forms:

— Tort law rules such as the negligence standard and the fellow-servant rule were adopted to meet the needs of early industrial development. (They allowed employers and transportation entrepreneurs to externalize a portion of their costs.) But as technological change increased the risks of accidents stemming from employment and from the use of consumer goods, the law responded with rules of strict liability.

— Warranty rules such as "caveat emptor" reflected a society in which most commercial trading was face-to-face. But with the rise of mass consumer transactions between remote sellers and purchasers and with increasing ignorance about the risks of defects, the law implied warranties of merchantability.

— The corporate form developed in order to fulfill the need for capital accumulation during the period of industrial takeoff.

— Various features of modern corporate organization, including the "business judgment" rule and the rules specifying areas of management "prerogative" exempt from collective bargaining, developed in order to give management broad discretionary decision-making power necessary for efficient maximization of profits in advanced industrial societies.

— Courts and legislatures were competent to handle the problems of regulating the early nineteenth-century economy of competitive individuals. By the late nineteenth century, however, the concentration of corporate enterprise was raising problems of such complexity that administrative agencies were required to handle them.

— Professionalization of the bar—the development of bar associations, law schools, formalized training and entry requirements, the large urban law office, etc.—was necessary to enable lawyers to take on the complex specialized tasks of law in a modern economy.

This perspective also produces some very large claims indeed. The first two examples listed below were commonplace in legal rhetoric through the end of the last century; the third is asserted by some lawyer-economists in our own time:

— The common law over time tends to work itself pure.

— Progressive improvements in legal science have tended to clarify legal doctrine, making it ever more certain and predictable, as well as more adaptable to social needs.

— Common law rules have tended to become more and more efficient.

B. Divisions Within Functionalism

By now it will be evident that my "dominant tradition" is a very broad umbrella, covering legal writers whose views on many issues differ radically, some of whom would be appalled to find themselves sharing even a limited-purpose category with the others. In particular, I mean to group under the common shelter of "evolutionary functionalism" both of the great antagonistic parties of modern American legal thought, labelled here for simplicity's sake "Formalism" and "Realism." Each of these parties has, I think, worked out contrasting visions of what social development consists of and how law has adapted to that development without disturbing the fundamental assumption of progressive adaptation that they hold in common. The parties have clashed instead over such issues as the definition of law and the autonomy of legal decision making.[3]

The Formalist side has a very restrictive notion of law as judge-made law: "The legal system is the domain of the legal specialist; the legislature is in general not part of the legal system but a source of the goals that the legal system is to carry out." Legislation and usually administration as well are thus relegated to the "social" sphere of the great law/society dichotomy. On the Realist side, however, law is "what officials do about disputes," or even more broadly, the work of anyone, including the private bar, whose task is the administration of public policy.

Formalists and Realists also divide over the issue of the "autonomy" of legal decisionmaking processes in relation to political, social, and economic decisionmaking. Formalists think that it is both usual and desirable for legal decisions to follow an internal professional agenda such as "a taught legal tradition" of the common law. The idea is that such decisions will perform their social/functional task of adaptation best if lawyers and judges are not thinking about society at all but only about perfecting their own craft, because a logic of liberty or efficiency is inherent in the practice of that craft. Realists think that this proposition is nonsense, that policymaking can't be socially functional unless it is self-consciously directed towards the satisfaction of social needs. Realists do, however, have their own notion of legal "autonomy": Policymakers ought to be, and sometimes actually are, insulated from the immediate pressures of short-term political or economic interests so they can concentrate on their society's long-run needs.

These differences lead to differing Formalist and Realist approaches to legal history. Formalist legal history focuses exclusively on the development of legal doctrine, where Realist legal history considers doctrine as one component of a general, if not always well-coordinated, policymaking enterprise. Further, formalist legal history considers phenomena outside the legal craft as distorting judicial decision making, or as simply irrelevant to the important story to be told; the Formalist hero is the judge or treatise writer who best clarifies doctrinal categories. Realist history, on the other hand, takes as its main subject the relations of function or dysfunction between law and major trends of social development; the Realist hero is the social engineer who masterfully wields law as an instrument of policy.

Naturally these differences lead to fundamental disagreements about the course of recent history. For many Formalists, the high point of legal development was reached around the end of the nineteenth century, when the ideal of the rule of law as primarily enforced by judges through an autonomous legal order was at its peak of influence. But the Formalists' high is the Realists' low: At that time, abstraction from concrete social forces had put the legal system badly out of synch with the evolving requirements of society, and we only climbed out of this trough of dysfunction through the implementation of the policies of Progressivism and the New Deal.

[...]

III. PARTIAL CRITIQUES: VARIATIONS ON THE DOMINANT THEME

I call the sample of views that follow "partial" critiques because they remain faithful to many elements of the dominant vision while rejecting others. These critiques come from all colors of the political spectrum.

[...]

B. Variation #2—Transpose "Needs" into "Domination"

In other words, every time a mainstream writer says a legal rule or process or institution serves the needs of society, show instead how it serves to maintain the power of a dominant class or group. Opponents of this variation are inclined to call it "Marxist," although the classical Marxist theory of law is just one highly specific subset of this variation.[4] In reality, this general proposition would be adopted as well by many non-Marxists: by elite theorists, including conservatives like Alexander Hamilton, who think the ruling classes *ought* to control the legal system; and by fatalists, who think that for good or ill elites always will be in control and indeed that having control of the legal system is one of the things that helps identify those elites. On the other hand, modern *marxisant* [Marx-inspired] theorists of law and the state, as well as most Critical Legal Studies people, have become so disenchanted with the project of trying to explain law as nothing more than the tool of the ruling class that their ideas can't be adequately treated under this subheading.

The great contribution of this variation has been to put social structure, class, and power—whose very existence much liberal legal writing seems so astonishingly to deny—back into our accounts of law. Histories of legal oppressions—of slavery, Indian Removal laws, Black Codes, labor injunctions—are indispensable reminders that there's often nothing subtle about the way the powerful deploy the legal system to keep themselves organized and their victims disorganized and scared. But the crude versions of the law-as-an-elite-tool theory are as vulnerable as mainstream functionalism to the critique which points out how incredibly difficult it is to relate events in the realm of "law" in any straightforward causal way to those in the realm of "society."

C. Variation #3—Weaken the Instrumental Links Between Law and Society

Instrumentalist theories of law … generally aspire to a positivist style of explanation. The idea is that someday (that Jubilee when all the data have been gathered in) we will be able to generalize convincingly and fairly abstractly about what social conditions will produce what legal responses and what effects upon society those responses will have in their turn. Yet I think it's fair to say that on the whole such statements of regularity in legal-social relations don't stand up very well to historical criticism. These statements keep running up against (a) comparative studies showing that social and economic conditions that are apparently similar in relevant respects actually have produced radically different legal responses, and (b) demonstrations that the social effects of adopting a legal form are *never* predictable from the form itself, because the interpretation of a form, its enforcement by lower-level officials, and the response it's likely to elicit (enthusiasm, indifference,

resistance) may all vary with the minutest particulars of context.

Take, for example, the once familiar proposition that the negligence principle was a functional response to the social needs of industrialization in its earlier phases (because it protected infant industry by externalizing its costs onto farmers, workers, city residents, etc.). The problems with this proposition are that (a) lots of societies industrialized without the negligence principle or after the principle had been around so long that it could hardly be a "response" to industrialization, and (b) the fact that there was a "negligence principle" doesn't by itself imply *any* determinate set of social consequences because the principle can be interpreted (or ignored) by judges, administrators, jurors, or employers so as to produce any imaginable combination of liability and damages (including none of either). These signs of indeterminacy naturally do not daunt the committed functionalist; they only spur him on to more refined hypotheses that will account for most of the variations. But in practice the progressive refinement of general statements about causal relationships between legal and social forms tends rapidly to decompose such statements into the detailed histories of particular societies. One's brave and sweeping original hypothesis of the necessary relation between industrialization and a negligence standard of liability gets boiled down to something like this: "In those places where the negligence principle was recognized and routinely applied in a certain way, it may have helped somewhat to facilitate capital accumulation; in other places, where there seems to have been lots of capital accumulation under different legal conditions, (a) some other form served the same function as the negligence principle, or (b) for various special reasons it wasn't necessary to the accumulation process to have that function served, or (c) perhaps there would have been still more accumulation if there had been a negligence principle." There's nothing wrong with this modest sort of proposition; it's the common stuff of historical writing. But it is an awfully long distance from demonstrating that economic requirements *produced* the form and that it duly performed its functional services to those requirements.

A functionalist thus subdued can continue to argue for a scaled-down determinism: the legal forms that actually emerged in a particular society were necessary to that society's particular requirements. Even if a negligence rule was not necessary for industrialization, perhaps the fellow-servant rule, as administered to workers on the railroads—or just the Pennsylvania Railroad in the 1870s—was critical to that industry's ability to finance its expansion. One can't disprove such an assertion. Because everything that has happened in history is causally connected to everything else, there's no way to be sure that the connections were not forged by a logic of necessity. Even actions that seem chosen or simply accidental just may look that way because we haven't yet discovered the secret logic underlying them.[5] Yet, without for a moment disputing that the forms that industrial capitalism and the negligence principle took in the nineteenth-century United States might be related, is the evolutionary-functionalist hypothesis (law meets the needs of the developing economy) the most *plausible* means of relating these two things? It is here that the comparative data revealing all the myriad paths to capital accumulation and the legal-realist data revealing all the myriad permutations that a legal form undergoes in practice should at least make the functionalist hesitate.

Let me illustrate what I mean through what I mentioned earlier as probably the most frequently asserted functionalist proposition about law: the claim that various regimes of legal rules were necessary or at least very useful to capitalist development because they provided the certainty that facilitated rational calculation. The strongest versions of this claim propose, for example, that the rules of nineteenth-century contract law functionally *responded* to the need for certainty: When commerce summoned loud, "Thou must!," contract whispered low, "I can!" One hears this claim all the time, but it is very difficult to sustain. Such evidence as we have suggests that tracing the common law doctrines and institutions for enforcing contracts to businessmen, those whom one might expect to be society's preferred mouthpiece for voicing her needs, is very difficult. When businessmen say what they want from an enforcement

mechanism, it's usually something along the lines of an arbitration process. To be sure, the legal system may have been wiser than the businessmen about their true needs: Lawyers undeniably thought so, as they liked to promote their products—the common law of contracts, treatises, Restatements, and commercial codifications—for their presumed tendency to "increase the certainty and predictability" of commercial transactions. Yet, in retrospect, the lawyers' goal of certainty appears to have been largely a legal fantasy. Formal rules framed in juristic categories, such as "offer and acceptance" and "consideration," that have no regard for the specific usages of real businesses are not predictable. Nor are rules phrased in terms of general standards of customary fairness, such as "reasonableness" and "good faith," so as to incorporate those usages. And even if such rules were predictable, businessmen don't seem to pay much attention to them until the (rare) prospect of litigation looms.

Further, when one looks at the early nineteenth-century legal system as a whole, rather than just at contract law, and to the system in operation, rather than just its formal doctrinal expressions, can one really say that this system made life more predictable for rational capitalist planning? Sometimes, perhaps. Other times, surely not. The law of that time, for example, rapidly divested a whole slew of previously vested legal rights—rights to monopolize resources, to enjoin nuisances created by new industry, to collect compensation for "indirect" property damage, and so forth. Should one therefore say, "The legal system was a functional response to the capitalist need to destabilize everyone's expectations, to put all property rights at the risk of devastation from competition or from exposure to spillovers from capitalist enterprise?" Early nineteenth-century governments also created commons out of large bundles of previously vested individual entitlements, insisting on the community's power to subject property to takings or regulations for public uses. Should one thus say, "The legal system responds to the need to sacrifice individual expectations to capitalist needs for social overhead capital?" And what if one takes a closer look at what lawyers actually did for their commercial clients?

One would find, it appears, that one of their main jobs in their roles as debt collectors was to mediate in bad times between their creditor clients and the debtors, not pushing collection to the limit but trying to reschedule and scale down debts in order to keep everyone afloat until the upswing of the business cycle—in effect helping to redistribute losses among the whole trading community. Should one then conclude, "The legal system responds functionally to the needs of capitalism not to have legal rules enforced too strictly?" And one still has to account for what looks like a large number of anticapitalist rules, such as those restricting corporate powers, capitalization, and attempts to limit liability. Perhaps here the explanation should be, "The legal system responds to the functional needs of capitalism to make concessions to its anticapitalist opponents." If one should be tempted to dismiss such rules (which I think would be a serious mistake) as aberrant spasms of dysfunctional Luddism, one can hardly do the same with the entire law of slavery or with the crop-lien system—which effectively tied farm labor to the land—that replaced it.

It's worth repeating, since arguments like these are so often misunderstood, that this case for the indeterminacy of legal-economic relations is directed against certain typical propositions of relations of functional necessity, usually expressed in statements that some economic process "required" support from the legal system, which then responded to "meet the needs" of that process. The argument is not that "legal" and "economic" practices bear no or purely random relations to one another (though many Critics [i.e., CLS writers] doubt that these categories are very helpful). Regular, patterned, and moderately predictable (at least in the short-to-medium-term) causal relations are always springing up between specific legal and economic practices—though the lessons of Realism are that one has to get down to very concrete situations before one can describe what they are. These causal relations seem to contemporaries and to historians who study them later to work loosely together into some sort of system. Lawyers make their livings from their experienced insights into the operations of these patterns or systems;

policymakers and investors make informed guesses, which certainly are not always wrong, that the patterns will continue to hold. This argument is that—though contemporaries and historians often believe the contrary—all the pieces of the system are very loosely articulated: Individual pieces, even quite large ones such as the fundamental premises of civil liability, the organization of enterprise in the corporate form, worker's compensation schemes, or even the progressive income tax, could have been even radically different without drastic consequences to the master social-economic processes that the functionalist has supposed to require them....

IV. GENERALIZING AND DEEPENING THE CRITIQUES: CRITICAL LEGAL HISTORIES

Having at last completed the catalogue of variations, let me restate in summary form those that have done the most to inform the varieties of Critical historiography:

1. The conditions of social life and the course of historical development are radically underdetermined, or at least not determined by any uniform evolutionary path.

2. The causal relations between changes in legal and social forms likewise are radically underdetermined: Comparable social conditions (both within the same and across different societies) have generated contrary legal responses, and comparable legal forms have produced contrary social effects.

3. If a society's law can't be understood as an objective response to objective historical processes, neither can it be understood as a neutral technology adapted to the needs of that particular society. Legal forms and practices are political products that arise from the struggles of conflicting social groups that possess very disparate resources of wealth, power, status, knowledge, access to armed force, and organizational capability.

4. Although they are the product of political conflict, legal forms and practices don't shift with every realignment of the balance of

political forces. They tend to become embedded in "relatively autonomous" structures that transcend and, to some extent, help to shape the content of the immediate self-interest of social groups.

5. This relative autonomy means that they can't be explained completely by reference to external political-social-economic factors. To some extent they are independent variables in social experience and therefore they require study elaborating their peculiar internal structures, with the aim of finding out how those structures feed back upon social life. Given what so often appears to be the indeterminacy of instrumental effects, a promising approach for such study may be to treat legal forms as ideologies and rituals whose "effects"—effects that include people's ways of sorting out social experience, giving it meaning, grading it as natural, just, and necessary, or as contrived, unjust, and subject to alteration—are in the realm of consciousness.

6. Our accustomed ways of thinking about law and history are as culturally and historically contingent as "society" and "law" themselves. Though we never can escape completely from the limitations of our environment, we can protect to some extent against the risk of simply projecting our parochial categories onto the past, by a self-conscious effort to relativize our own consciousness, by trying to write the story of its formative context and development, and by trying to reconstruct as faithfully as possible the different mentalities of past societies before translating them into our own.

7. It also will help us to relativize our understanding of the past's relation to the present if we see that our conventional views of that relation are mediated by familiar narrative story lines, which are so deeply entrenched in our consciousness that we are often unaware of their rule over our conception of reality. These story lines, like other mentalities, have a history filled with ideological purposes, and there always exist—and so we always may draw upon—competing stories that impress the same historical experience with radically divergent meanings.

Taken *en bloc* rather than separately, this set of partial critiques adds up to a position that most people who see themselves as doing Critical legal historiography probably would accept. Many, though by no means all, would want to push the critique still further.

A. Blurring the "Law/Society" Distinction

You might think that after the ravages of partial critique there would not be much left of the dominant tradition. But there is. Its skeletal frame, its division of the world into social and legal spheres, tends to endure. Thus, even the more severe of the Partial Critics continue to assume—although conceding that all over the landscape of social life we can see the imprints, some deep and others almost imperceptible, of feedback reactions from the "autonomous" outputs of the legal system—that at bottom the really basic terms of community life are set by conditions and relations we can, and should, describe independently of law: family ties, personal affections, power struggles, technology, consumption preferences, association in interest groups, and the organization of production. These conditions and relations—the realm of "material life" in some formulations; of "basic needs" of all societies or of particular evolutionary stages in evolutionary functionalism; of "the forces of production" in some Marxisms; of the "interests" of individuals or groups in liberal pluralist theory; and finally of the "preferences" of self-constituting individual subjects in the ultimate reduction of classical and neoclassical economics—comprise the "real world" that law may serve or disserve or even partially twist out of shape, but to which law is ancillary. The *fundamental* operations of this world originate before law and go forward independently of it; they fashion in general outline (if not in tiny detail) the agendas and limits of legal systems and are beyond the power of law to alter.

Yet, in practice, it is just about impossible to describe any set of "basic" social practices without describing the legal relations among the people involved—legal relations that don't simply condition how the people relate to each other but to an important extent define the constitutive terms of the relationship, relations such as lord and peasant, master and slave, employer and employee, ratepayer and utility, and taxpayer and municipality. For instance, among the first words one might use to identify the various people in an office likely would be words connoting legal status: "That's the owner over there." "She's a partner; he's a senior associate; that means an associate with tenure." "That's a contractor who's come in to do repairs." "That's a temp they sent over from Manpower." This seems an obvious point, but if it's correct, how can one square it with the standard view of law as peripheral to "real" social relations? Could one, for example, seriously assert that "the law of slavery has tended to play only a marginal role in the administration of slave societies"? Slavery is a legal relationship: It is precisely the slave's bundle of jural rights (or rather lack of them) and duties vis-à-vis others (he can't leave, he can't inherit, he has restricted rights of ownership, he can't insist on his family being together as a unit, etc.) that *makes* him a slave. Change the bundle significantly and you have to call him something else. And how could one say something like "medieval law bolstered (or undermined) the structure of feudal society"? Again, a particular (though concededly in this case very hazily defined) set of legal relations composes what we tend to call feudal society. If those relations change (commutation of in-kind service to money rents, ousting of seignorial jurisdiction to punish offenses, etc.) we speak not simply of changes in "the legal rules regulating feudal institutions," but of the decline of feudalism itself.

I would guess that the notion of the fundamentally constitutive character of legal relations in social life is probably a lot easier to understand when made about slave or feudal societies than about liberal societies. After all, in liberal societies, differences of legal status are not supposed to define social relationships, but merely to channel and facilitate them. In theory, one can, in a liberal society, choose one's legal status to suit one's underlying, material, functional, *real* purposes; with "freedom of contract," one even gets to create that status within the limits set by public law. But a whole generation of Realists taught us to

see that a regime of free contract delegates to those who contract legal powers, subject to a host of important legal exceptions, to coerce performance according to the contract; and the establishment of private property gives the proprietor a set of legal powers, again subject to important legal limitations, to dictate to others the terms of access to his property: and the chartering of a corporation entitles the managerial few to make binding decisions affecting the lives and fortunes of the laboring and shareholding many. These bundles of rights and powers, diminished by exceptions and limitations, with which members of liberal societies are endowed, are critical determinants of the terms of their relations with one another. For instance, it usually matters a lot in an employment relationship whether the employee is employed at will, a major stockholder of the business, an illegal immigrant, married to the employer, protected against being fired for trying to organize other employees, and so forth. In each case, a different complex of background legal entitlements factors into the power relations between the parties. Of course, nobody is going to claim that law explains more than a fraction of the power differences between these people. The employee may be the only person who understands the filing system, or be irresistibly attractive or physically intimidating, or just have been there for ages, or have lots of alternatives in the market (though of course that "market" itself importantly is structured by the legal regulations of what may be owned and traded in it, subject to limitations, and by the property entitlements of all the traders in it).[6] It is, of course, possible to imagine, as for example G. A. Cohen has done in his extremely ingenious attempt to demonstrate that one *can* describe a "material" core of social relations without any "law" in them at all— a Hobbesian power balance of force that is destabilized every time somebody sharpens a stick or lifts a weight. But in actual historical societies, the law governing social relations—even when never invoked, alluded to, or even consciously much thought about—has been such a key element in the constitution of productive relations that it is difficult to see the value (aside from vindicating a wholly abstract commitment to "materialist" world views) of trying to describe those relations apart from law. Power is a function of one's ability to form and coordinate stable alliances with others that will survive setbacks and the temptations of defection to satisfy opportunistic interests. Such organization and coordination are bound to involve something legal. Indeed, one is likely to find the conditions of the Hobbesian state of war precisely in those instances where law has established, explicitly or by silence, a combat zone in which people are endowed with (in Hohfeldian terms[7]) privileges to inflict harm upon one another, and are denied any legal means of restricting that harm (as when the legal regime says a wife can't be raped or that contracts between husband and wife are not enforceable). Clearly (as Cohen for example points out, people can struggle to improve their position vis-à-vis others by *changing* the rules that define their entitlements, but that doesn't alter the fact that the bundle of legal endowments they start out with positions them for the struggle, and may make all the difference as to whether they win, lose, or get a good compromise deal. The new deal, when sufficiently stabilized in practice, simply will be the new legal constitution of their relationship.

More prosaically, the "interests" in the instrumental account that make demands upon the legal system are not self-constituting prelegal entities. They owe important aspects of their identities, traits, organizational forms, and sometimes their very existence to their legal constitution. For example, "taxpayers" are partially families, partnerships, or individuals, because of the legal definition of these units; "New England gas consumers" pressing the Congress for relief from high prices are partially a "regional interest" because of the legal form of territorial representation; "Communists" are not an interest represented as such in labor unions because of legal excommunication; whereas the true identity of the "corporate client" to whom a corporation's lawyer owes her undivided loyalty is an unsolved mystery, because of conflicts in legal theory. For the most part, the legal creation of "interests" and the selection of their representatives proceed too quietly for notice—save on those occasions where formal choice must be made, as in deciding whether the "Sierra Club" may represent people who care about the environment in class actions or administrative proceedings.

Understanding the constitutive role of law in social relationships is often crucial not only in characterizing societies but in accounting for major social change. Robert Brenner's remarkable work on preindustrial Europe for instance, identifies two general patterns of social adjustment to the population declines of the late Middle Ages: a (typically) Western pattern in which the labor shortage resulted in more favorable labor terms for the peasantry, and a (typically) Eastern pattern in which the same shortage brought about an intensification of serfdom, a tightening of the lords' control over their serfs. Brenner's (richly detailed and here much simplified) explanation for this dichotomy is that the landlords' ability to tighten control instead of having to grant concessions depended critically upon the balance of class power that had come to prevail in their particular society. A central component of this power balance was the set of legal relationships that had been established between the classes. Where peasant communities were strongly organized, they had, over the centuries, managed to wring concessions from their lords, which had been institutionalized as law. Thus institutionalized as rights, these concessions could not be withdrawn without provoking massive resistance. Brenner goes on to argue that where (as in France and parts of western Germany) these customary rights of peasant proprietorship persisted through the early modern period, they did so because centralizing states helped to secure these rights against the lords and thus retarded the process of capitalist consolidation of landholdings. In England, by contrast, where such rights had been eroded for a complex of reasons, small proprietors were unable to resist eviction.

Maybe the point that law and society are inextricably mixed seems hard for legal writers to grasp because they sometimes restrict their view of what law is to a bunch of discrete events that occur within certain specialized state agencies (in the most restrictive view, the courts alone) and therefore assume that the only question for a social history of law is the relation between the output of these agencies and social change. But if that output is all there is to law, how on earth are we going to characterize all the innumerable rights, duties, privileges, and immunities that people commonly recognize and enforce, without officials anywhere nearby? Slavery, for instance, may well make its first appearance in the temporary emergency practices of a settlement, harden over the next few planting seasons into invariable custom, and, decades later, when the localities decide they want the help of centralized enforcement authority, become the subject of legislation in slave codes. When should a sociologically minded historian (as opposed, for example, to a legal-positivist jurisprudent) start to speak of the emergence in this society of the legal institutions of slavery? At any point, I should think, when she finds the ordinary practices and discourses of that society assuming or appealing to the collectively shared and maintained notions of right and obligation that support that institution, the moment when power becomes institutionalized as "right." Thus, the social-legal historian who *began* her account of slave law in these settlements with the codifications would rightly be accused of leaving out the most important part of the story. Furthermore, even if the historian refused to recognize custom as law until it was ratified by some official agency, she won't get very far towards understanding the role of law in social change if she looks only for the immediate social effects of marginal changes in discrete enactments and ignores the whole invisible background network of rules (like the basic law of property) that are incorporated silently into people's lives.

Again, since it all seems so incredibly obvious once it's said, what explains the persistent view of law's marginality in social life? Partly, it comes from the view of generations of disillusioned reformers—liberal reformers mostly, I suspect—who have come to doubt whether more than marginal social change can be achieved through deliberate promotion by those in control of the mechanisms of the liberal state. But this proposition is not really about the limits of law; it is about the limits of selective types of attempts to reorient, usually from the top down, selective formal institutions. Most legal change takes place all through

civil society, in thousands of small interactions, usually with no official visibly present at all. It's strange, in a way, that the Realist and Law-and-Society[8] scholars, who taught us to see the law "in action" as well as the law "on the books," so often should be the very same people who revert to restrictive Formalist views of law when they stress, in [Roscoe] Pound's words, "the limits of effective legal action." There is a real disjunction here between their sociological analysis of the law constituting the status quo as dynamic, informal, and political, and their programmatic analysis of the law needed to bring about change as static, formal, and bureaucratic.

The view that law is marginal in social life probably also registers an overreaction to the preceding generation of Formalists, who often behaved as if once you described the legal form of an institution or practice, you had described the *whole* thing. A "corporation" or a "city" appeared as nothing more than a shell of legal rights and powers. The Realist successors to these Formalists yearned to break through the formal shell to (as they often expressed it) the "living" reality beneath it: the "realities" of trade practices, power politics, emotional ties, "behavior," and, of course, social needs. But there is no way to detach essences from their forms: The law (in the catholic sense that I've been using) was all along a part of the reality. If the program of Realists was to lift the veil of legal form to reveal living essences of power and need, the program of the Critics is to lift the veil of power and need to expose the legal elements in their composition.

B. Law as Constitutive of Consciousness

Many Critical writers would, I think, claim not only that law figures as a factor in the power relationships of individuals and social classes, but also that it is omnipresent in the very marrow of society—that lawmaking and law-interpreting institutions have been among the primary sources of the pictures of order and disorder, virtue and vice, reasonableness and craziness, Realism and visionary naiveté, and of some of the most commonplace aspects of social reality that ordinary people carry around with them and use in ordering their lives. To put this another way, the power exerted by a legal regime consists less in the force that it can bring to bear against violators of its rules than in its capacity to persuade people that the world described in its images and categories is the only attainable world in which a sane person would want to live. "Either this world," legal actions are always implicitly asserting, "some slightly amended version of this world, or the Deluge."

A familiar example of the way in which legal categories affect social perceptions would be the carryover into common speech and perceptions of the legal distinction between public and private realms of action, the public being the sphere of collective action for the welfare of all through the medium of government (and thus the only realm of legitimate coercion), and the private being the sphere of individual self-regarding action. Those who have internalized this distinction as part of the natural order of things, as all of us have to some extent, are perfectly capable of deriving from it conclusions such as this: It is an invasion of the privacy and autonomy of a (private) corporation for (public) OSHA [the United States Federal Government's Occupational Safety and Health Administration] inspectors to come upon its premises without a warrant, but the same company's management can post time-study monitors in the workers' washrooms because the workers have (impliedly) consented to this in advance by private contract.

I don't for a moment mean that this particular set of conclusions—in which readers are bound to recognize the classic late nineteenth century mind-set, recently dusted off for revival—flows inexorably from the public/private distinction. One certainly also could conclude, as many people have, that corporations, being organized collectives endowed by law with effective coercive power over people within their jurisdiction (on their property), are like states, and may therefore exercise their power only through politically accountable forms. The crucial point here is that both sets of conclusions are inferred from the same

public/private classification (coercive-collective states vs. freely choosing individuals) that sets fairly severe limits on the ways in which we can imagine the world and how to change it.

Let me try another, perhaps slightly less abstract, example which I hope might illuminate some of the differences between functionalist and Critical styles of historical explanation. A nineteenth-century state that we'll call "Wisconsin" enacts a "lumber-lien" law—that is, a statute giving loggers of wood a priority lien for their wages in the proceeds from the sale of cut timber. How might an historian approach the interpretation of this bit of law? A good straightforward functionalist approach would look for the context of a social "problem" to which the law was an attempted response or solution. Let us suppose that our functionalist historian finds such a problem in the circumstance that logging enterprises were short of liquid capital out of which to pay wages but needed to attract labor into the forests for a long winter's work. The solution to this problem was to give some additional security for wages in the lien, which was somewhat easier to enforce legally and less subject to trumping by other claims than was an ordinary action for breach of contract. There is nothing wrong, it seems, with this explanation as far as it goes. But then one starts to wonder: Why this solution rather than others one could think of—others that were actually adopted in nearby times and places? Here's a quick offhand list of potential solutions that doesn't even begin to exhaust the possibilities: (1) use slave labor in the forests; (2) use conscript labor—either as part of compulsory militia service or as a statutory duty of every able-bodied man in the state; (3) raise the capital fund for wage payments out of taxes; (4) refuse to "intervene in the private contracts" between logger and employer, and let the loggers contract, if they can, for their security interest in the wage bargain; (5) run logging as a state enterprise, paying loggers out of general revenues or out of an excise tax on log sales; (6) make the loggers general partners in the enterprise, entitled to manage company concerns and to share in company profits. In the perspective created by some of these alternatives, the lumber-lien law appears to have been the product of a political consciousness in which, for example, "enterprise" was "private," though the state might be expected to help it out and even "regulate" a bit, and in which labor was "free" but definitely subordinate. The main point I want to make here is that this statute was not only the *product* of such a consciousness but helped to reproduce that consciousness by confirming it. The statute's enactment made some political alternatives that the society had already discarded as bad or unworkable (slavery, conscription, state enterprise) just a tiny bit more unthinkable and made it a tiny bit more difficult to imagine something altogether outside the scope of familiar possibilities (such as the option of laborers as equal partners). In short, the legal forms we use set limits on what we can imagine as practical options: Our desires and plans tend to be shaped out of the limited stock of forms available to us: The forms thus condition not just our power to get what we want but what we want (or think we can get) itself. This perspective completely collapses the distinction that legal writers sometimes make—that indeed I made earlier in this article when discussing the Variations—between "instrumental" and "symbolic" uses of law. One never has more power than when one has so successfully appropriated the symbols of authority that one's actions are not seen as exercises of power at all, but simply as expressions of sound pragmatic common sense.

Another way of looking at what seems to be the key difference of approach between functionalists and their Critical opponents is that the functionalist examines what actually has happened and explains how it all "works," how each development fits into the pattern created by all the others, while the Critic takes each event as situated, not on a single developmental path but on multiple trajectories of possibility, the path actually chosen being chosen not because it had to be but because the people pushing for alternatives were weaker and lost out in their struggle, or because both winners and losers shared a common

consciousness that set the agenda for all of them, highlighting some possibilities and suppressing others completely. How can one identify the counterfactual trajectories, the roads not taken? From the experience of other societies, from the hopes of those who lost the struggle, from routine practices that the same society has tried in other spheres of life without ever dreaming they might be applied to the situation at hand, and from imagination disciplined, as one hopes, by the knowledge of past failures.

C. Indeterminacy Located in Contradiction

The partial critiques attack the twin determinisms of functionalism and evolutionism mostly by means of empirical counterexamples drawn from Legal Realism and the Law-and-Society movement, in the case of functionalism (in practice, the effect of law varies enormously with differences of power politics, cultural predisposition to accept it, strength of local custom, etc.), and from comparative historiography in the case of evolutionism (there are many paths of development and of legal response; indeed variation in developmental paths is partly a function of legal variation). Taken together, these partial critiques add up to the proposition that when you situate law in social context, it varies with variations in that context. Some of the most original and powerful recent Critical writing, however, carries the claim of law's indeterminate relation to social life a significant step further. The same body of law, in the same context, can always lead to contrary results because law is indeterminate at its core, in its inception, not just in its applications. This indeterminacy exists because legal rules derive from structures of thought—the collective constructs of many minds—that are fundamentally contradictory. We are, the theory goes, constantly torn between our need for others and our fear of them, and law is one of the cultural devices we invent in order to establish terms upon which we can fuse with others without their crushing our identities, our freedom, even our lives. One way, therefore, of writing the histories of legal systems is to examine successive attempts to build structures that will facilitate good and prevent bad fusion. Such histories can reliably be expected to exhibit two properties: First, because the structures usually have been built by dominant elites (though with input from those struggling from below), their content will be ideological. That is, their methods of sorting out good from bad interactions will contain a bias in favor of existing orders. Second, and more important because the fundamental contradiction between the needs for fusion and for individuality never has been (perhaps never can be?) overcome, legal structures represent unsuccessful and thus inherently unstable mediations of that contradiction. Over time, therefore, these legal structures will tend to become unglued and to collapse.

According to this vision, modern American legal history is in part the story of how the latest of these great cultural constructs, "liberal legalism," arose and developed its own characteristic set of mediating devices (chief among these being the division of social life into a private sphere of contracting individuals, e.g., "the market," and a strictly limited sphere of constitutional/democratic collective coercion, "the state"); how the construct was purified of its pre-liberal elements and elaborated to its highest pitch in the late nineteenth century; and how, at the moment of its perfection, it started to decay under attacks from without and the pressure of its own internal contradictions—ultimately leaving us where we are now, living in its ruins, no longer believing in its mediating powers, and clinging to it still because we have found nothing to replace it, and being faithless moderns, doubting that we ever can. The general framework of this story has served as the background to a growing number of histories of particular bodies of legal doctrine and theory, each of which locates its special set of rules and principles within the fundamental contradiction and shows how one attempt after another to mediate that contradiction results in failure.

The common thread of these histories is the observation that, for the decision of every case, the contradiction makes available for the decision of every case matched pairs of arguments that are perfectly plausible within the logic of the system,

but that cut in exactly opposite directions. The managers of the legal system preserve their sense that law is actually relatively orderly and predictable, by assembling a bunch of devices to keep these oppositions from becoming too starkly obvious (even to themselves). They classify some of the oppositions as "anomalies and exceptions." They stick others in separate categories (e.g., law/equity). They rule out still others (the capitalist wage-bargain is invalid, at least in times of high unemployment, because concluded under duress; the equal protection clause prohibits rationing scarce social goods by ability to pay) by a separation between law and politics or simply by arbitrary ideological fiat (interpretations of rules that would too much alter the status quo are wrong per se). Nonetheless, these fudging devices are subject to strains that eventually crack them apart. Enemies of the status quo expose obviously ideological contrivances for what they are and develop arguments based on utopian counterpossibilities of the system. ("Freedom of contract" as administered is just the rule of the stronger; contracts can't be really free unless entered into by parties with "equal bargaining power"; hence, "freedom of contract" norms require regulatory schemes equalizing bargaining power.) Ordinary lawyers and judges with no wish whatever to destroy the system lay bare its contradictions in adversary arguments or dissents. And jurists whose main ambition is to *justify* the system by showing how clear and orderly it is at its core end up expounding it so well that its faults appear in plain view.

Anyone who has come to adopt this approach has left functionalism far behind. For if it turns out to be true that law is founded upon contradictions, it cannot also be true that any particular legal form is required by, or a condition of, any particular set of social practices. And, in fact, one of the skills that the fans of this method have developed to an abnormal extent is that of supplying, whenever they hear a claim of functional relation between a legal rule and a social practice, the standard counterclaim, with counterexamples, for an exactly inverse relationship.

[Ed. Argument #1, criticizing the focus on legal doctrine, is omitted]

Argument #2—The Critics who do intellectual-history-of-doctrinal-structures haven't got any theory of the causal relations between legal/doctrinal change and other social change, except their claim that the contradictions within legal structures make such relations completely indeterminate. But this claim of indeterminacy is surely exaggerated—there are lots of regularities in legal/social relations.

This argument has to be broken down a bit to be responded to. I think that, at this stage, the response can be very short because much of it has been answered already. It's true that, for example, the Critics have not produced an analysis—along the lines of the traditionalist-functionalist histories or of instrumental Marxism—that relates changes in the legal system to changes in the economy. The whole point, recall, of the Critics' critique is that the "economy" isn't something separate from the "law," which reacts on law and is in turn reacted upon by it; the idea of their separation is a hallucinatory effect of the liberal reification of "state" and "market" (or "public" and "private") into separate entities. Because the economy is partially composed of legal relations, legal and economic histories are not histories of distinct and interacting entities, but simply are different cross-cutting slices out of the same organic tissue. Again, if the Critics want to make this point convincingly, they will have to start slicing their narratives out of field-level uses of law.

The other argument rests, I think, on a misunderstanding of what the Critics mean by indeterminacy. They don't mean—although sometimes they sound as if they do—that there are never any predictable causal relations between legal forms and anything else. [T]here are plenty of short- and medium-run stable regularities in social life, including regularities in the interpretation and application, in given contexts, of legal rules. Lawyers, in fact, constantly are making predictions for their clients on the basis of these regularities. The Critical claim of indeterminacy is simply that none of these regularities are *necessary* consequences of the adoption of a given regime of rules. The rule system also could have generated a different set of stabilizing conventions leading to exactly the opposite results, and may, upon a shift in the direction of political winds, switch to those opposing conventions at any time.

V. CONCLUSION

As this guided tour comes to an end, what shall we say about the contribution of the Critical historians? Perhaps this: that they have added powerfully to the critique of the functionalist-evolutionary vision that has so long dominated legal studies and that they have produced their own distinctive and exciting brand of doctrinal historiography and successfully taught others how to apply their method. The Critics are still a long way from being able to deliver the brightest promises of their Critical program: thickly described accounts of how law has been imbricated in and has helped to structure the most routine practices of social life. But they are trying; they are getting there.

NOTES

1. Ed: "Critical Legal Studies" (or CLS) is an intellectual movement in law, especially prominent in the 1980s, that argues that law is best understood as a political tool that advances the interest of the powerful, rather than a neutral framework of social cooperation. Professor Gordon's article is reproduced here because it explores many CLS themes.

2. For the purposes of this article, I'm reserving the term "functionalism" for the particular type of explanation outlined here, i.e., one that first posits a set of "primary," more-or-less objective needs or dynamic processes and then explains "secondary" historical phenomena as responses to those needs or processes.

   Some legal writers seem to use "functionalism" in a sense different from mine, to mean any way of explaining legal forms or practices by reference to social "purposes" or "interests"—indeed by reference to anything other than the formal, internal materials of the legal system. This usage seems to me both too broad and too narrow. It's too broad because *any* practice is "functional," and none dysfunctional, if that means it serves somebody's interest or can be seen as part of a system or pattern or process. And it's too narrow because it arbitrarily excludes attempts to show how the "function" of a legal practice might be to meet the formal requirements of (i.e., serve someone's "ideal interest" in) the elegance or completeness of an abstract system. I'd prefer to call this general type of explanation "external" or "contextual" and to label as "instrumental" the particular subset of external explanations that account for legal practices as products of the desires or demands of social classes, groups, or individuals.

3. Incidentally, the fact that Legal Formalism has been politically conservative and Legal Realism more liberal-reformist is only an accident of our recent history. It is easy to imagine a radical formalism, such as the French Revolution's program to remake society in accordance with abstract legal rights, or a conservative Realism, such as German historicism.

4. The classical Marxist theory closely resembles the dominant liberal vision in that it holds legal institutions to be functionally responsive to the needs of the basic modes of production that define successive stages of a macro-historical evolutionary process.

5. Compare, for example, the hypothesis that both the negligence principle and the organizational structures of industry were products of a common political-legal ideology that liked to pretend that everything that happened in corporations was the product of voluntary individual choice.

6. To give another example, assume two people are having an argument in a car. One says, "Get out of my car." The other says, "It's not your car, it's the company's car. I have as much right to be here as you do." The first: "I'm driving today, so as far as you're concerned it's my car: and I want you to get out." This is of course a fairly complex, if utterly commonplace, legal argument—unusual, if at all, only in that the claims and counterclaims are very explicit instead of being just silent background assumptions. Of course, factors other than legal relations may be involved. One of these guys may be a lot bigger than the other or have a long-run stake in the other's amiability or good opinion. But the law of the situation is a potentially critical factor in its resolution.

7. Ed: Wesley Hohfeld, a Yale law professor in the early part of the 20th century, developed an influential analytical framework for understanding legal relations in terms of matched pairs of permissions and obligations.

8. Ed: The Law and Society movement, pioneered by Wisconsin historian Willard Hurst, examines law as a form of social order, and so approaches it from the perspective of history, sociology, and political science, rather than from the perspective of doctrine.

19 From Choice to Reproductive Justice: De-Constitutionalizing Abortion Rights

ROBIN WEST

INTRODUCTION

The preferred moral foundations of the abortion right created in *Roe v. Wade*[1] and its progeny continue to shift, from marital and medical privacy, to women's equality, to individual liberty or dignity, and back, in the minds of both the Supreme Court Justices and the pro-choice advocates and legal scholars that have argued or celebrated these famous cases. What has not shifted is the commitment of the pro-choice community to the right

itself, and to the propriety of its judicial origin. Legal abortion, according to this near-universal pro-choice consensus, is and should be an individual, constitutional right protected against political winds, rather than simply good policy reflected in a state's laws, and it is therefore entirely fitting that we look to the courts, and to the Supreme Court in particular, for its articulation and enforcement. It is the work of the courts and their actors—judges, lawyers, litigants, amici, judicial clerks, and academic commentators—to orate

This article is reprinted with permission of the author. It appeared originally in 118 Yale L.J. 1394 (2009), and is available for download without charge from: Scholarly Commons: http://scholarship.law. georgetown.edu/facpub/23/. Most footnotes, including citations, have been omitted here.

the basis of this important individual right, to develop its contours, and to expand or contract it when appropriate—to subject it in effect to the ordinary and extraordinary processes of constitutional adjudication.

This Essay tabulates some of the costs to feminist ideals that are produced by our reliance on the creation of an individual right as the conceptual vehicle for legal abortion, and our reliance on adjudication as the strategic vehicle for the right's development and justification. I will argue that while the court-focused methods and the various "choice-based" arguments put forward by the pro-choice advocacy community have jointly secured for individuals a fairly robust constitutional right to legal abortion, those same arguments have ill served not only progressive politics broadly conceived, but also have ill served women, both narrowly, in terms of our reproductive lives and needs, and more generally. I ultimately will urge a broader political argument for reproductive justice in women's lives that embraces, but does not center upon, rights-based claims, and for a reorientation of legal resources to secure those claims away from the judicial realm and to state and federal legislative arenas.

The Essay is organized as follows. The first Part asks a (somewhat) rhetorical question: why has there not been more feminist and pro-choice criticism of both *Roe v. Wade* specifically and our reproductive rights jurisprudence more generally? To be clear, there is of course plenty of criticism of *Roe* from those who abhor legal abortion on moral grounds, as well as from legal scholars and Court watchers who object to the Court's perceived freewheeling activism in this field. There is also a fair amount of critique of *Roe* from progressive scholars worried about *Roe*'s demonstrated propensity to create backlash against the Democratic Party and progressivism more generally. What is missing from the massive amounts of critical commentary on *Roe* is an examination by pro-choice scholars of both the abortion right itself and the Court's central role in its creation for the possible harms done to the broader cause of reproductive justice. There is, bluntly, almost none of this scholarship. I will argue that while there are quite understandable reasons for the reluctance of this community to offer constructive critiques, those reasons are not in the end persuasive.

The second Part argues that there are unreckoned moral and political costs of the judicially created, individualist, and negative right to an abortion—costs that ought to be troubling for all, but particularly for feminist legal scholars. Briefly, I look at three such costs of the abortion right, which I refer to as (1) legitimation costs, (2) democratic costs, and (3) aspirational costs. All three of these general types of costs of rights have been well developed in the various "rights critiques" produced by critical legal scholars during the 1970s and 1980s. None, however, has been applied to the particular case of abortion rights. Individual, negative, constitutional rights, according to their critics, keep the state off our backs and out of our lives, but they also run the risk of legitimating the injustices we sustain in the insulated privacy so created; they denigrate the democratic processes that might generate positive law that could better respond to our vulnerabilities and meet our needs; and they truncate our collective visions of law's moral possibilities. All three costs, I will argue, attend to the abortion right created by *Roe v. Wade*. The second and major Part of the Essay specifies how this is so.

1. A MISSING CRITICAL JURISPRUDENCE

Why is there not more pro-choice criticism of *Roe*, and of its varying and various rationales? The lack of such commentary is odder than it might first seem. The liberal adjudicated victories of the Warren and Burger Courts, with the one exception of *Roe*, generated massive amounts of critical commentary from theorists purporting to speak for the interests of the victorious parties in those cases and the communities they roughly represented. *Brown v. Board of Education*,[2] to take the most iconic example, has generated a burgeoning cottage industry of critique, eventually coalescing in the creation of an entire scholarly movement—critical race theory—that was rigorously critical, on leftwing and racial-justice grounds, of that decision's liberal, rights-expansive, and integrationist ideals. Thus, according to its progressive critics, *Brown* hid the massive problems of underfunded public education under the false covering of a legally reformed and racially fair integrationist ideal, and articulated an account of de jure segregation as the evil to be addressed by civil rights law that left an insidious pattern of de facto segregation both intact and legitimated. It birthed an entire ideology of "color blindness" that did little but undercut serious attempts at redistributive racial justice, including affirmative action programs in employment and education both. *Brown* lent a veneer of fairness to purportedly meritocratic hierarchic orderings that result from individual and state decision making and that continue to subordinate poor people. It relied on a cramped and ungenerous vision of "rights" and "integration" that both truncated rather than generated political progress on these and other progressive causes. All of this, again, stems from the champions of racial justice, not antagonists. Other less revered but nevertheless substantial Warren, Burger, and Rehnquist Court progressive victories also have prompted scathing critiques by progressive legal scholars. *Miranda v. Arizona*[3] prompted worry as well as celebration among advocates for the interests of criminal defendants: the right the Court created might constitute a triumph for nothing but a formalistic and legitimating conception of interrogatory justice, setting back, rather than advancing, the cause of respectful and noncoercive treatment of criminal defendants. Likewise, the more recent *Lawrence v. Texas*[4] decision prompted plenty of accolades but also its share of criticism from equality-minded legal scholars. In elevating sex into the realm of those aspects of life and identity so highly regarded as to be worthy of constitutional protection, some argued, it might further burden the work of protecting vulnerable people against sexual harassment and assault.

Whatever the merits of the criticisms of these famously progressive cases, my point here is comparative: unlike *Brown*, *Miranda*, or *Lawrence*, *Roe v. Wade* remains largely insulated from friendly critique. Why is that? I think there are three reasons for the critical reticence. None, however, is a particularly compelling justification.

Part of the story—maybe the major part—is a widespread belief among the pro-choice community in the opinion's relative vulnerability. This alone deters criticism of the decision by those who politically support legal abortion. *Roe*, by contrast to *Brown*, *Miranda*, and even *Lawrence*, seems to be in perpetual and great danger of being overturned. *Roe* is a perennial—permanent?—presidential campaign issue, and has been since it was decided. Its "hanging by a thread" status, furthermore, is perhaps the one sure thing that *will not be* changed by Barack Obama's world-altering victory in 2008. President Obama may replace the retiring liberal Justices with younger liberal Justices, but that will still leave the opinion with only five-to-four support. A Republican presidential victory in 2012 might result in a fifth vote on the Court for overturning *Roe*. Even assuming Democratic administrations far into the future, however, it does not follow that a newly constituted Court dominated by Democratic Party nominees will be committed to *Roe*. The pro-life wing of the Democratic Party will likely grow, not shrink, with Democratic dominance, as will the risk that a Justice appointed by a Democratic president will see his or her way to reverse *Roe*. There is, in short, no end in sight to the compulsive vote counting with respect to *Roe v. Wade*. We are seemingly today, just as we were on November 3, 2008, one judicial appointment away from the decision's reversal.

The second reason has to do with a belief in *Roe*'s efficacy. The gains secured by *Roe* seem more tangible than the gains secured by *Brown* and *Lawrence*, so the potential cost of reckless critique seems higher. *Brown* ended de jure segregation of the schools—but not de facto segregation, and much less real racial subordination: schools as well as neighborhoods remain segregated and unequal in much of the country. *Lawrence* struck from the books criminal statutes that had not been directly enforced anyway, and left untouched the unequal treatment of gay and lesbian citizens on any number of fronts, from marriage to military service, employment, and tenancy rights. There is much to criticize, if one keeps the focus on the paltry consequences of these decisions, compared with what they promised. *Roe*, by contrast, was by no means an empty victory, much less a Trojan horse. Rather, *Roe* sent a clear material and rhetorical signal to women, girls, and the larger society: women's reproductive lives should be, and henceforth would be, governed by a regime of choice—whose choice is not so clear—and not by fate, nature, accident, biology, or men.

The gains of this one decision, in terms of the autonomy and broadened options for women and girls, were felt to be enormous. With the advent of birth control and safe and legal abortion, women can avoid life- and health-threatening pregnancies, can limit the number of children they will mother, and can plan the major sequence of their lives—pregnancies, education, marriage, job, and career—so as to increase hugely their chances of succeeding at all. Without that control, women's and girls' control of these life-changing events is severely compromised. Dangerous, injurious, or simply too many pregnancies in one's teens, twenties, thirties, and forties make completion of high school, college, professional school, graduate school, or vocational training for skilled crafts much harder even to imagine, much less to accomplish. The burdens of unwanted, dangerous, or just too many pregnancies are harder to measure but just as real in private and intimate life. Dangerous pregnancies shorten lives. Too many pregnancies make for difficult and unrewarding mothering. All of it leaves the woman feeling, justifiably, hostage to fate. If she cannot control her reproductivity, she cannot control her life. Without self-sovereignty over her body, all that remains of her life—her work, her sociability, her education, her mothering, and her impact on the world—is miniaturized. She lives a smaller life.

Lastly, there may be no pro-choice criticism of *Roe* because *Roe* got so much exactly right, and it is both understood and appreciated by the pro-choice community for doing so. Criticism, then, might just seem churlish. Thus, it may simply be true that women must have a right to legal abortion if women are to be equal citizens, and it may also be true that equal citizenship is what the Constitution requires. As the political philosopher Eileen McDonagh has argued at length, where

abortion is criminal, women, but not men, are required to donate body parts for a substantial part of their adult lives and at substantial risk to their own health and life, to the cause of nurturing and preserving the life of another, and they are required to do this regardless of whether they consent to this appropriation. Women's ownership of the use of their own bodies is therefore contingent, or conditional, in a way which men's is not: another human life (the fetus) has a primary right to their bodies, and they have no right to ward off what would be a criminal assault were it a *born* child making these demands. This contingent self-sovereignty is not conducive to equal citizenship. If equal citizenship is the goal of the Constitution's declarations of equality and liberty, then women seemingly must have a right to legal abortion in order to achieve it. And equal citizenship does seem to be what our Constitution contemplates, at least as we now understand it. Whatever the problems with *Roe*'s rhetoric or rationale, that conclusion seems both important and right.

None of this, however—*Roe*'s perceived vulnerability, its consequences, or the truth it partially expresses—justifies the relative dearth of critical inquiry by pro-choice scholars into the costs of either *Roe*'s genesis in the Court or its various stated rationales. First, with respect to both the decision's vulnerability and its efficacy, the goal of the pro-choice movement should be women's access to legal and safe abortion, not preservation of a right that may be increasingly hollow. Of course, there is a danger that *Roe* could be overturned (although perhaps smaller than the pro-choice community claims), but there is also a danger with the road we are on: we preserve the right, while growing numbers of women across large swaths of the country lose access to the service. With *Roe* on the books, we are nevertheless witnessing a gradual diminution in the availability of abortion for poor, teenaged, and rural women, as state legislatures pass, and the Court upholds, first funding restrictions, then parental notification requirements, and then waiting periods. The threat to legal, safe, affordable abortion is not so much that the Court may overturn *Roe*, but that abortion will become less and less available, because of the impact of legislative and political decisions made far from the Supreme Court's doors. Either way, the challenge to legal and safe abortion comes primarily from state politics and only secondarily from court action. Fixation on the Court and the narrowing constitutional right it has created as a way to secure legal abortion is just counterproductive.

More important, even if it is true that legal abortion is necessary to women's equal citizenship, it by no means follows that a judicially created individualized constitutional right, rather than political persuasion, is the best way to achieve it, for two reasons. First, it bears emphasizing that what the Court created in *Roe v. Wade* is *not* a right to legal abortion; it is a negative right against the criminalization of abortion in some circumstances. That no more creates a genuine right to a legal abortion than *Brown* created a right to an integrated school. To be a meaningful support for women's equality or liberty, a right to legal abortion must mean much more than a right to be free of moralistic legislation that interferes with a contractual right to purchase one. It must guarantee access to one. And, for a right to legal abortion to guarantee that a woman who needs an abortion will have access to one, whether or not she can pay for it, the state must be required to provide considerable support. But the Court has consistently read the Constitution as not including positive rights to much of anything from the state, and certainly not to abortion procedures. It is so unlikely as to be a certainty that neither this Court nor likely any Court will commence a jurisprudence of positive constitutional rights, by beginning in the contested terrain of mandating public funds for abortions. By comparison, the state legislative arena is not so constrained: it is very much the business of state legislatures to create legislative programs to meet the positive needs of citizens. Whatever obstacles there might be to a legislative initiative to publicly fund abortions, a refusal to see "positive rights" in the Constitution is not among them.

But second, and aside from the growing doctrine that cuts against funding, even a purely negative right, assuming it exists, might be better secured through what is now sometimes called political, popular, or legislative constitutionalism, rather than through the adjudicated Constitution as interpreted by courts. That is, a right to abortion might be better understood to be a part of our constitutional self-understanding that is achieved through political and legislative victories, rather than adjudicative pronouncement. It would not be the first time a right would be better secured politically rather than judicially—think of the "right" to social security, or the "right" to be free of a military draft, or for that matter women's right to equality itself. No Supreme Court decision ever secured any of these in constitutional doctrine, yet they seem at least as secure against political change as the various unenumerated rights the Court has discovered or created. A woman's right to legal abortion likewise might be better inferred from contemporary understandings of equality and citizenship than from any constitutional language or configuration of past cases that a court is likely to recognize as authoritative. This is, at least, a possibility we ought to consider. The academic-feminist attachment not only to *Roe*, but to its origination in the courts, and our resistance to even the suggestion that we have become overly reliant upon courts, precludes our ability to do so.

Neither the vulnerability nor efficacy of *Roe*, nor the partial truth it expresses, is a good reason *not* to engage in critique. There are also, however, costs to the reticence. The lack of such a critique, I will argue, has dulled us to the degree to which the rhetoric of adjudicated abortion rights might have weakened reproductive justice more broadly conceived. But it is also worth noting that even if feminism's or progressivism's or the Democratic Party's sole goal were to strengthen this embattled right, there is a strong pragmatic case for pro-choice feminist critiques of the way that right is now constructed: by its steadfast loyalty to *Roe* the pro-choice community is in danger of losing this war by fighting—even if winning—yesterday's battle. Pro-life movement activists increasingly look to reduce abortions not by reversing *Roe* and criminalizing abortion, but rather through a three-pronged strategy, no part of which is dependent upon *Roe*'s reversal: first, by passing restrictions the Court will uphold even with *Roe* on the books; second, by reducing abortion supply and demand by intimidating clinics and clinicians and shaming the women who use them; and third, by reducing the long-range cost of pregnancy by urging more political and communitarian support for motherhood, particularly for poor women. For pro-life constituencies, the grounds of contestation of legal abortion have shifted to the local, political, and moral, and away from the constitutional-adjudicative. The pro-choice community's fixation on the apparently never-ending project of finding adequate grounds for adjudicated abortion rights blinds it to this development.

The pro-choice community, for purely pragmatic reasons, might be well advised to take up a challenge made a few years ago by Janet Halley and Wendy Brown in a different context—to wit, that we subject liberal constitutional victories to criticism in an unfettered way, as though we were not in fear of the wolf at the door. It is past time to apply this simple-enough prescription to abortion rights. Not only is critique valuable for its own sake, but here, we thereby might push the wolf further back. The *Roe* to *Casey* line of decisions stands in need of progressive, feminist, and pro-choice critique and transformation. The first without the second may well be irresponsibly reckless, but the second without the first is impossible. And both are necessary.

II. CRITIQUE

There are at least three major costs of the right created in *Roe* that seem to be underappreciated by the pro-choice community. All three are suggested by the various critiques of negative rights, of the Left's reliance on courts to create and protect them, and of the liberal-legal political commitments that underlie them, which were pioneered by the critical legal scholarship of the 1970s and 1980s. They are as follows: (1) choice-based arguments for abortion rights legitimate considerable injustice, both in women's reproductive lives and elsewhere; (2) the Court's active role in creating this jurisprudence exacerbates antidemocratic features of U.S. constitutionalism, to women's detriment; and (3) the arguments do not do justice to the aspirational

goals of the women's movement's early arguments for reproductive rights.

A. Legitimation

"Legitimation" has come to mean many things in critical legal scholarship, but two particular meanings are of relevance to the right to abortion; the first concerns the legitimating consequences of legal change, and the second concerns the legitimating consequences of individual choice. In the case of the right to abortion, of course, these are deeply intertwined: the legal change effected by this right is an expansion of individual choice. It is nevertheless helpful to treat them separately.

By the first meaning, apparent gains in justice wrought through legal change are sometimes offset by what might be called the "legitimation costs" of the same legal breakthrough. The idea here is that a concededly just legal change will sometimes legitimate a deeper or broader injustice with the legal institution so improved, thus further insulating the underlying or broader legal institution from critique. This ought to be understood, then, as a cost of the reform—one that, in some circumstances, might be quite high. For example, although *Brown* ended de jure racial segregation of the public schools, it might have thereby legitimated an entire host of evils, including de facto segregation, unequally funded urban schools, private-sphere rather than state-sponsored subordination of African Americans, and the purportedly meritocratic classifications and hierarchies of market economies themselves. All of these are left not just untouched by *Brown*, but legitimated by it. The decision's equation of injustice with state-sponsored racism carries the implicit suggestion that so long as those segregated or underfunded schools, or market-generated hierarchies of class and race privilege, are not polluted by the pernicious impact of state-sponsored racial classifications, then they are not only constitutional, but also morally and politically untroubling. The legitimation cost of *Brown* is the possibly increased insularity against criticism and political reform of these greater injustices. The critics' claim is not that the goal of the legal breakthrough—ending de jure segregation—is undesirable. Rather, the worry is that the goal comes at the cost of legitimating deeper racial injustices. At some point, the critics worry, these legitimation costs might outweigh the benefit of the breakthrough itself.

The second meaning of "legitimation," developed in critical scholarship of the late twentieth century, concerns the nature and role of consent and the specific impact of an individual's consent to the perceived justice of either particular transactions or entire institutions to which consent is given. In liberal market economies and the legal orders that govern them, the act of consent generally insulates the object of consent even from criticism, much less legal challenge. Consent to the terms of a contract, for example, almost always insulates the fairness of the terms of that contract from both public scrutiny and legal attack, regardless of how harmful or injurious that contract turns out to be to any of the parties that consented to it. If the contract was consensual, it cannot possibly be unfair to execute it against a later regretful party, no matter how harmful its terms might appear to be. Widely shared norms against paternalistic legislation,[5] an ideological and seemingly bottomless belief in the ability of individuals to understand and act on their own welfare, skepticism regarding the motivation of regulatory bodies or meddling individuals who would seek to upset consensual individual transactions, and at least for some, a definitional commitment to consent as that which maximizes value, all burden attempts to intervene in or even question contract terms. They may do so through "unconscionability" or "duress" limits in the common law of contract, or through more explicitly regulatory means, such as consumer protection legislation or workers' rights laws. I have argued elsewhere that the same dynamic increasingly limits critique of intimate sexual relations: consensual sex is viewed not only as not rape, but also as not subjected appropriately to moral or political criticism. To subject consensual sex to criticism is puritanical, moralistic, or worse. Lastly, in the public sphere, "consent" operates similarly: the consent of the governed legitimates whatever governance follows. We can generalize from these three examples of the impact of consent in the private, intimate, and public spheres: consent cleans or purifies that to which the consent is given, and thereby insulates it from political critique as well as legal challenge. Questioning the value of that to which consent has been given is politically suspect—because it is unjustifiably paternalist, logically incoherent, or both.

Perhaps the hallmark of late twentieth-century Critical Legal Studies (CLS) writing was the claim that this widely made inference from consent to value is simply unwarranted. People's abilities to ascertain and act on their own self-interest are limited, the critical scholars argued. The capacity of countries, institutions, multinational corporations, social forces, or simply stronger parties to create in individual subjects a willingness to consent to transactions or changes that do not in fact increase their well being is well documented. "Consent" of the weaker can be manufactured to serve the interests of dominant parties, and when it is manufactured, it is not a good measure of the value to the weak of that to which consent was given. Neither skepticism regarding the good motives or knowledge base of the "paternalist," nor faith in the self-regarding preferences of the individual, justify the unexamined inference that a consensual change so extracted is a good one for all affected parties. The degree to which a consensual change is perceived as such is the degree to which it has been unduly legitimated by the consent that preceded it. The legitimation cost of consensual transactions, then, is the sometimes unwarranted belief in the increased value of the change to which consent was proffered.

Are these worries about the legitimating effects of either legal change on the one hand, or individual consent on the other, relevant to *Roe v. Wade*? Does the decision in *Roe*, even assuming the value of the right it created, carry legitimation costs? Placing the question in a historical context, one might recall that Catharine MacKinnon's early critiques of *Roe v. Wade* pointed to two important legitimating effects of that decision—one quite specific and the other more general. First, she argued, constitutionalizing a right to terminate a pregnancy broadly legitimates the sex that produced the pregnancy—sex that might well have been less than fully consensual by both parties. It shifts the focus away from addressing the social and sexual imbalances that result in unwanted pregnancies to the unwanted pregnancy itself, and strongly suggests that the appropriate social and individual response to unwanted sex is to protect the decision to end the pregnancy. This has the effect of minimizing the social costs of sexual inequality for the strong and the weak both, rather than ending the sexual inequality itself. *Roe*, then, legitimates both unwanted sex and the hierarchies of power that generate it. Second, MacKinnon argued, the privacy rationale of *Roe v. Wade* might have the pernicious effect of further insulating the already overly privatized world of intimate relations from either moral critique or political struggle. Men subordinate women, to a large degree, in private: in homes, in bedrooms, in hotel rooms, through pornography, prostitution, marriage, and sex. Extolling the privacy of these relations, and casting a constitutional wall of protection around them for the express purpose of warding off legal intervention or regulation, thus both insulates and valorizes—and hence legitimates—the subordination that occurs within them.

These arguments, I think, were never answered satisfactorily by feminist supporters of *Roe v. Wade*. Completely unaddressed, however, was whether MacKinnon's critique went far enough. The question should have been not only whether MacKinnon was right to complain that *Roe v. Wade* might have the undesirable effect of legitimating, by privatizing, sexual violence, but also whether there are other legitimating costs of this decision, in addition to, and not reducible to, the problem of male sexual coercion.

I think there are such costs. The danger I want to highlight is that the individual right to terminate a pregnancy created by *Roe v. Wade* might have the effect not only of legitimating the coercive sex that might have led to it, but also of legitimating the profoundly inadequate social welfare net and hence the excessive economic burdens placed on poor women and men who decide to parent. As *Roe* and the choice it heralds to opt out of parenting become part of the architecture of our moral and legal lives, we increasingly come to think of the decision to parent, no

less than the decision not to parent, as a chosen consumer good or lifestyle—albeit a very expensive one. As this shift in consciousness occurs, it may come to seem, at least for many, that the only role for a caring or just society, here as elsewhere, is to ensure that that consumer choice to parent or not parent is well informed. Making sure that choices are well informed, after all, exhausts the role of the state in regulating consensual affairs, particularly market-based ones, in a culture that valorizes consensual market transactions.

Consumers of the choice to parent or not to parent, from this "informed consent" model of the role of the just state, should know a few things. They should know that high-quality childcare can only be obtained at a very high cost. They should know that caring for a newborn, nurturing a toddler, and then raising a child, will interfere mightily with the parent's wage-earning potential in a working world that still valorizes the unattached laborer with no commitments to any earthly soul other than his employer. They should know that the quality of public education is spotty—in communities where housing is affordable, the public education is abysmal, and vice versa—and that a purchased private education at elite private schools costs far more than most Americans' paychecks. They should know that publicly funded preventative (as opposed to emergency) healthcare for one's dependents is almost nonexistent. They should know that once the decision is made to become a parent, there is "no exit," or turning back. Parenting is not the sort of at-will employment from which an employee can simply walk away if the terms are not favorable; there are moral, emotional, and legal restraints on one's ability to do so. They should know all of this. All of this increases hugely the price of parenting.

If parenting is a *choice*, however—if it is a status entered freely, as might be a very long and very binding long-term contract—its expense is not a source of injustice or even a cause for worry, so long as the choice is made knowingly. Parenting is indeed expensive. But so are private jets and graduate degrees. If the potential parent—like the potential buyer contemplating whether to buy an airplane paid for in installments and that will require a lot of upkeep—is armed with enough information about her choices, then there is no further need for intervention into the various private markets for the support services—education, healthcare, childcare—from which she might choose when it comes time to employ those services. We now have a "choice" to end a pregnancy—when we parent, no less than when we do not, we have made our choice. And, since *Roe*, many of us *do* now view parenting in this way, and we so view it not just incidentally, but as a part of our fundamental, American, constitutional identity. As Americans, when we choose to parent, we should be well informed; we should make the choice knowing the price. At least here in America, that is no reason to publicly *subsidize* the choice. There is no further reason to help a poor mother pay for it than there is to help a would-be recreational sailor buy a boat that will allow him to sail around the world, or to help the aspiring scholar with the expense of yet another graduate degree. It is one lifestyle choice among several that happens to come with a hefty price tag.

Thus, constitutionalizing this particular right to choose simultaneously legitimates—in both of the senses noted above—the lack of public support given parents in fulfilling their caregiving obligations. By giving pregnant women the choice to opt *out* of parenting by purchasing an abortion, we render parenting a market commodity, and thereby systematically legitimate the various baselines to which she agrees when she opts *in*: an almost entirely privatized system of childcare, a mixed private and public but prohibitively expensive healthcare system, and a publicly provided education system that delivers a product, the quality of which is spotty at best and disastrously inadequate at worst. Narrowly, by giving her the choice, her consent legitimates the parental burden to which *she* has consented. A woman who is poor and chooses to parent will exacerbate her poverty by so choosing, particularly if she "chooses" to parent without a partner. If she "chooses" to parent a special needs child, she will have little assistance for the extraordinary educational, health, and care needs of her child. If she chooses to parent without a partner while she herself lives in poverty, she likewise has so chosen. The choice-based arguments for abortion rights

strengthen the impulse to simply leave her with the consequences of her bargain. She has chosen this route, so it is hers to travel alone. To presume otherwise would be paternalistic. The woman's "choice" mutes any attempt to make her claims for assistance cognizable.

More generally, the choice rhetoric of *Roe* undercuts the arguments for the development of what I have elsewhere called "caregiver rights"— the rights of caregivers, women and men both, to a level of public assistance for their caregiving work. This has consequences for everyone who spends substantial parts of their adult lives caring for the needs of dependents, whether small children or the elderly, and who incurs substantial costs by virtue of so doing. Pregnant women, parents of small children, and the grown children of elderly parents, by virtue of their caregiving obligations, are not capable of the sort of independence that is so highly valued in a culture that prizes rugged individualism above all else. Caregivers are less independent, and therefore less autonomous, than those with no such obligations. Someone tied to the needs of others is that much less free to live the wealth-maximizing, self-regarding, autonomous life presupposed by, and valorized by, a free-market economy in the first place. The right to an abortion gives women a right not to be a caregiver, but at the cost of rhetorically making the difficulties of caregiving all the harder to publicly share, should she opt for it. For privileged women, this is not such a terrible trade off: an economically secure woman gets a right to terminate a pregnancy, and can more or less put up with the bolstered legitimacy of an overly privatized system of health and child care. She can exit the paid labor market for a few years to raise her child, or she can split those obligations with a supportive spouse or partner and continue to work part-time, or she can delegate to others the caregiving work for substantially less than she herself earns so that she need not interrupt her own wage labor. She can, through one of these routes, simply absorb the expense of these choices. The woman only marginally capable of supporting even herself, however, faces a choice between parenting and severe impoverishment, on the one hand, and forgoing children on the other. Are we truly comfortable, morally, with a world that we have created, in which only rich people can parent satisfactorily? Is it a just world, in which poor people are told that perhaps they really should not have children, particularly if they cannot find someone to marry first? The sheer cruelty of this is what the legitimating rhetoric of choice, and of individual rights to privacy, liberty, and dignity, all mask.

B. Democracy

In the last thirty years, a growing body of scholarship from critical legal scholars and progressive political theorists has decried the political Left's heavy reliance on courts, rights, and constitutional law as vehicles for progressive victories, which might better have been secured through ordinary politics. Several themes have emerged from this literature, some of it going back to early critiques of rights penned by the CLS movement, some of it more contemporary and based in understandings of the workings of institutions. Three themes in particular recur in this literature, which, I believe, are of relevance to *Roe*. I will quickly review these concerns, spell out the ways in which *Roe* is exemplary of them, and then suggest in a bit more detail a fourth.

The first concerns the logic of countermajoritarian, constitutional rights. Echoing Marxist critiques, critical scholars have argued for well over a quarter century that while constitutional rights in this country have indeed served the interests of minorities, as their celebrants claim, it has primarily been the interests, privileges, and entitlements of not particularly embattled property owners either to retain their wealth or to buy and sell assets on open markets for profit, against the wishes of those who would challenge them. What they have protected all that privilege against, primarily, is the majoritarian, democratically expressed wish of the less well off—peons, workers, renters, mobs, the poor, or the masses—for a bit of state-sponsored, democratically inspired, redistribution of wealth. With the advent of progressive rights-based movements in the nineteenth and twentieth centuries, this historical alignment of rights and privilege became mixed. Thus, whatever their propertied

pedigree, rights have furthered the causes of abolition, suffrage, labor, and eventually racial justice and reproductive freedom. Nevertheless, purely as a matter of rhetoric and logic, rights are the coin of the realm of the relatively entitled, so to speak, and will likely always remain so. Regardless of content, then, rights and rights rhetoric (or "rights talk," as it used to be called) tend to protect preexisting property entitlements to that which is owned, and contract entitlements to that which can be privately traded, even if just indirectly, by discrediting precisely the democratic, popular, majoritarian, and political deliberation and reform it would take to upend them. Rights generally protect entitlements against political encroachment rather than satisfy even dire need. Any progressive gains achieved by rights must therefore be understood as risking some degree of entrenchment of current distributions of power that favor a wealthy minority against majoritarian redistribution, simply because of the use of rights discourse.

Second, critical scholars argued forcefully that court-generated rights discourse in this country has tended to reinforce pernicious distinctions between the private and the public realms of social life, largely because of its cribbed insistence that injustice almost by definition emanates only from states and from state action rather than from private actors of any sort. What judicially discovered rights mostly give us is a way to ward off overly intrusive or irrational state involvement in our private lives. There are two problems with this. The first has been much belabored: court-generated rights perversely protect rather than stand as a challenge to forms of oppression that are distinctively private, such as unfair employment or contract regimes, patriarchal privilege, or private sphere racism, all of which are accomplished by private actors in some "private" realm. But second, and less noted, the valorization of the "private" realm comes at the expense of degradation of the "public." Consequently, the public-private distinction at the heart of rights discourse feeds a distrust of the machinations of public deliberation—including processes of government, of democracy, and collective action—the use of which is essential to any sort of genuinely progressive political movement against private injustice. For this reason as well, particularly in the economic sphere, the result is an undue, and perhaps unwitting, regressive conservatism.

The third cost of court-created rights identified by rights critics stems from concerns about the methods of reasoning courts employ. Progressive victories secured through adjudication rather than politics must be or at least aim to be consistent with past practice—they must mesh more or less seamlessly with preexisting precedent, policies, decisions, institutional arrangements, and forms. This makes the progressive victory achieved through the courts—including rights-based victories—relatively conservative, compared to what might be achieved politically: the restraint of integrity with the past makes it not even theoretically possible that the victory will be a truly radical one. At the same time, the apparent gain in permanence, depth, certainty, or profundity that seemingly comes from the adjudicative victory being secured through law—the perception that the "right" so discovered is something that has always been deeply embedded in a system of law that has its own roots in antiquity, and is therefore truly there and secured against precipitous change—is an illusion. Rights found by courts can also be abandoned by courts. The right is hostage to the whims of the people on the Supreme Court rather than a working majority of a Senate. It is nevertheless just as much hostage to whimsy. It is a product of power, no less than any traffic ordinance passed by a city council, and just as subject to recall.

These progressive critiques of judicially created rights, pressed in different ways by critical scholars over the past thirty years, all suggest limits to the progressive potential of *Roe v. Wade*. Let me take them in the order outlined above. First, the critics complained that constitutional rights, in spite of their occasional progressive potential, have tended to protect individuals' commodificationist rights to contract and property rather than to serve people's needs, and would likely continue to do so. The right created by *Roe* is no exception. *Roe*'s holding, whether couched in terms of liberty or privacy, did indeed quickly devolve into a bare negative contract right to buy a particular

medical service—an abortion—free of moralistic intrusion by state legislators who would paternalistically intervene into that—or any other—consensual purchase. The right became a stick in a bundle of negative rights to our bodies and labor, that we wield in order to keep the state out of our sex lives: we have a right to birth control, a right to same-sex sex, limited rights to produce and consume pornography, and a right to engage in the commercial and medical consultation necessary to secure an abortion to end the pregnancies in which all that protected sex sometimes result. It has furthered the cause of unfettered sexuality in open markets, for purchase and otherwise, by giving us a property right in the pregnancy and a contract right to purchase the means to end it. It has done nothing, however, to further the satisfaction of the positive needs—whether understood as rights or not—of either pregnant women or parents. By relentlessly celebrating negative rights as the route to women's liberty and equality, and thereby impliedly castigating politically secured legislation as the evil against which negative rights—and hence, liberty and equality both—are constructed, it has undermined the case for the very sorts of positive legislative schemes that might do so.

Second, and as the rights critiques of the "public-private" distinction presaged, the libertarian rhetoric of the opinion has indeed focused attention on pernicious state intermeddling in women's lives, rather than either the private sphere appropriation of women's sexuality caused by male sexual aggression, or the appropriation of women's reproductive and parenting labor in that sphere, as the primary limit on women's equality and liberty. Catharine MacKinnon warned in her early critiques of *Roe* that the pro-choice community ran the risk that it would further obfuscate both the fact and nature of private sphere sexual subordination by aggressively shrouding that sphere, and the subordination that occurs within it, in a constitutionally protected veil of laudatory privacy. The right to abortion, she argued, might further privatize the private by constitutionalizing it, and by so doing thicken the veil of privilege around intimate life, and therefore around the sexual subordinations that occur within it. Events have not proven her wrong to have so worried. The same is true, although she did not so argue, with respect to women's labor, no less than women's sexuality, and with respect to the economic sphere, no less than the sexual. Parenting is economic activity, as well as the consequence of sexual acts that may have been coerced. By insulating the private economic realm of parental choice against public critique and intervention, the economic deprivations occasioned by overly privatized parenting are further shielded against public intervention. The effect is not only the valorization of the "private" activities of sex and parenting, but also the denigration of the public sphere of politics. The public assistance that would be required to alleviate costs borne in private is cast as unwarranted intrusion into an exalted sphere of private economic life, rather than warranted assistance with an almost impossibly privatized burden.

And third, and just as a critical sensibility should have predicted, the right has indeed proven to be both relatively regressive and seemingly unstable. This right's genesis in "law" rather than "politics" has not yielded the permanence or security or respect that law promises. *Roe*, conceived as a "right" so as to withstand the whims of hostile political opinion that would upset it, still seemingly hangs by a legal thread. The Court can broaden it, narrow it, uphold it, or overrule it. Meanwhile, and ironically, the activity it primarily protects—legal and safe abortion in the first trimester of an unwanted pregnancy—enjoys strong majoritarian political support. Rendering legal abortion a constitutional right, rather than an ordinary political one, may not have made it any more secure than it otherwise would have been. We have seemingly gained the regressive features of constitutionalizing this right, without enjoying the gain of security or stability that constitutionalism promises.

There is, though, an additional and less appreciated cost to democracy of conceptualizing legal abortion as a judicially created right that the rights critics never touched on, but is worth addressing more expansively. This cost too has particular poignancy in the domain of abortion rights. When the Court claims privileged and even monopolistic access to the language of moral principle, reasoned discourse, and civil dialogue, it suggests a lesser, distasteful view of the politics it thereby limits. Representative politics is routinely construed by liberal devotees of court-generated rights as the realm of bald power: whimsical, arbitrary, emotive, unprincipled, rent seeking, horse trading, reflective of the "interests" of a basically infantile constituency that does nothing but form arbitrary preferences for unprincipled— unthoughtful—reasons. The public whose interests and preferences are so reflected in politics, in Congress, and in the legislative branches of state governments is portrayed as prone to hysteria, as a body that acts on whims and winds of political sentiment, and as given to unpredictable moments of mob mentality. Politics, as construed by the Court and its liberal devotees, is anything but the highest art of which the species is capable, and anything but deliberative. The Court, by contrast, expresses *law*—and when it does so, it speaks in the language of principle, reason, rationality, integrity, consistency with the past, and dispassionate concern for the future. It speaks with intelligence and wisdom both; it assimilates knowledge from history and judiciously weighs— rather than reacts to—the desires of the interested parties of the present. It takes the long view. It is attentive to enduring principles. It deliberates; it does not react. It engages in civil discourse. The Court, not the Congress, is the institution that permits rational and respectful dissent. It is the Court that keeps the civil conversation going in this country. Therefore, *law*, expressed through courts, is our highest and best form of *politics*. Meanwhile, our *actual* politics—what happens in Washington or Annapolis or Sacramento or downtown Wasilla—is everything this adjudicative conception of our highest politics is not. It is low life.

Roe v. Wade and its progeny are not, of course, responsible for the degradation of politics that has become the natural counterpart of the institution of judicial review, its high-minded justifications, and the reverence we now accord it. It does, though, exemplify it. When the Court speaks of the hallowed right to privacy in which it locates abortion, it speaks of the sanctity of marriage and family, of individual liberty, of equality or dignity, of respect, and of the great and deepest mysteries of life. It speaks of the constituents of individual identity, and of what is most important to a well-led life, of the grand promises of the Fourteenth Amendment, of the importance of precedent to political and social order, of the needs of all of us to be free of a "jurisprudence of doubt," and of the importance of consistency, integrity, and moral principle in decisionmaking and in our law. The contrast between what the Court and commentators say when speaking of this right, and what abortion rights advocates say in the public sphere when defending or addressing the need for legal abortion, could not be starker. When advocates speak of abortion in the public sphere and outside the courts, they do not talk, for the most part, about a "jurisprudence of doubt" or the importance of precedent or of principled judicial decision making, of liberty, dignity, or even equality. Rather, they most often speak of women's bodies. They speak of the dangers to women's health that are posed by many pregnancies. They speak of the lives that have been lost to illegal abortion. They talk a lot about hemorrhaging, and of women and girls bleeding to death in botched back-alley abortions. They speak of fear and terror. They speak of lives shortened, or narrowed, or rendered mean and uncompromising by dangerous pregnancies, or too many unplanned pregnancies, or too many children, or too much mothering. They speak of shattered dreams, or girls with low or no expectations for their own futures. They often speak of abusive stepfamily members, of domestic violence, and child rape. They speak of intentional, deeply wanted pregnancies gone wrong; they talk about diseased fetuses, miscarriages, and tragic choices. They talk about stillbirths and life-threatening complications. They speak of the earthy, present, demanding, felt, fought-over need of women to control their bodies and fate.

The contrast on the other side of this debate, between the rhetoric of the Court and commentators on the one hand, and activists on the other, is if anything even more stark, although it is beginning to narrow somewhat, at least if *Gonzales v. Carhart* is any guide.[6] In the public square,

pro-life advocates speak, argue, petition, canvas, and beseech us to attend to the biological lives of unborn babies. They wield pictures of fetal life and body parts. They deploy sonograms and give voice to silent screams. They push their listeners to identify with the unborn, to open their sympathies and their hearts to the least of these, to pull fetal life into the human community, to recognize us in them and them in us. Conservative legal critics of *Roe v. Wade*, on the other hand, speak rarely if at all of any of this. Rather, they speak of originalism, of constitutional integrity, of the close readings of texts, of plain meaning, and of the lack of the word "privacy" in the text of the Constitution. They worry over the integrity, identity, and future of the Constitution. There is little talk, either on the Court or in the pages of scholarly commentary that is hostile to *Roe*, about fetal life, silent screams, or unborn babies, and even less about the struggles facing women with unwanted or dangerous pregnancies. The discussion is principled, constitutional, and historical. It does not stem from a visceral identification with or sympathy for the plight of murdered babies.

This momentous gulf in the substance of pro-choice and pro-life arguments on the street, versus pro-choice and pro-life arguments on the Court, is understandable: the issue facing the Court, after all, is *not* the morality of abortion, but the power of the states to criminalize it. The contrasting substance of the arguments, however, is in turn reflected in contrasting styles and modes of discourse—and it is that contrast that I wish to problematize. The clerks and Justices of the Court craft arguments for and against legal abortion from the principles, precedent, and constitutional phrases found in the pages of past case law. They then make analogies from those principles and precedents. They reason closely or loosely from original texts—either of the Constitution or of the cases that interpret it. Public advocates of free and legal abortion as well as public advocates for criminalization of abortion speak in a different modulation entirely. They protest, march, yell, organize, canvas, petition, and carry posters depicting coat hangers and fetuses, dead women, and body parts. They make demands rather than arguments: that states either protect the least of us, or stay off our backs. And on both sides, the demands are visceral.

These contrasting modes of discourse around abortion—reasoned, from the bench, and impassioned, on the street—have fueled the perception that the Court, rather than the public square, is the necessary and proper place to decide the legality or criminalization of abortion. The Court epitomizes reason, dispassion, and principled discussion. The debate in the public square epitomizes the hysteria against which the Courts, law, and rights themselves do combat, with the sword of sweet reason. The Court and its product—opinions—jointly constitute and embody the nobility of law. The political branch that represents us, particularly at the local level, is ignoble.

Now, there is much to be said against this picture—most of it already said by the CLS scholars in the 1970s and 1980s. In a nutshell, they argued, the Court's reasoning is neither as rational nor as principled as might first appear. True enough, but this argument missed and itself obfuscated what might be a more consequential point. The now-conventional division of labor spelt out above—that the Court exercises reason in the pursuit of principle, while the legislative branch is an escape valve for the emotive excesses of various publics and an arena for horse trading among their infantile interests and desires—is untrue, not only because it so discounts emotionality, infantilism, and horse trading on the Court, but also because it understates the seriousness, public mindedness, and capacity for reasoned discourse of legislators. Courts are less than fully reasonable, to be sure. And Congress is more than emotive.

But even that friendly amendment understates the damage done by this liberal conception of judicial wisdom and legislative infantilism. The deeper harm is that it misstates the role of passion in politics. Politics at its best, not just its worst, is an admixture of passion and principle. Signs, pictures, and images that evoke empathy may be ingredients of mob un-think, but they are also necessary components of any movement that aims to broaden our moral compass—if we do not think of either women or fetal life as a part of us, we will not legislate, as a people, to protect them. Any politics, but certainly progressive

politics, must seek to expand affective sympathies. The derogation of passionate politics, so deeply embedded in the jurisprudence of an activist, anti-majoritarian, and rights-oriented Court, systematically belittles precisely the sort of politics that is obviously not sufficient, but is likely necessary to any sort of expanded progressive political vision.

Finally, the traditional identification and elevation of reasoned discourse with the Court, which is at the heart of rights-oriented constitutionalism, not only pits the principled decision-making, of which the Court is so proud, against passion, but also pits itself against compromise. Principle cannot abide compromise, but politics cannot proceed without it. The public discussion of abortion has become as raw as it has, in part, because of that fact. When we battle this issue out in court as a clash of principles, we develop those martial arts of the mind that are necessary to that battle. We lose, though, the arts of political compromise. We lose the ability and willingness to craft deals we can live with, the nimbleness of giving a little and getting a little, the commitment to the project of living with and under the roofs that compromise creates. There is much to worry over, of course, in compromise, but there is also much to applaud: it is neighborly, civil, and inclusive.

Adjudicating abortion rights over the last quarter century and more may have dulled our capacities and appreciation for both impassioned, engaged politics and civil compromise. It is not at all clear that the result has been a stronger rather than weaker set of reproductive rights and liberties.

[...]

At least according to contemporary social and legal historians of the time period, advocacy for legal abortion was in effect severed from its trunk largely because of the politics surrounding the Equal Rights Amendment (ERA) movement and then transplanted into the quite different terrain of individual liberty. It then became its own "tree," rooted not so much in women's equality, but in marital, medical, and sexual privacy. Without second-guessing the then-compelling reasons for doing so, it is clear in retrospect that this rerooting strategy carried costs beyond even the legitimation and democratic costs outlined above—it also carried costs for our understanding of what an abortion right is and why we should have one. Understood as one of a series of Supreme Court cases, *Roe v. Wade* and the right it articulates become a chapter in a narrative authored, developed, and controlled by the Court, rather than a part of a narrative of women's rights authored, developed, and controlled by feminists, progressives, or women's rights devotees. Abortion rights are a part of a story consisting of Supreme Court cases, not a part of a story consisting of political victories for women's equality, healthcare, or poor families.

And what is that story? Of course there are several narratives that can be told based on these cases, just as there are any number of patterned ways to assemble beads on a string. One might, for example, think of *Roe* as the first in a possible trajectory of future cases revitalizing a libertarian and antimoralistic strand of *Lochner v. New York*. *Lochner*[7] famously found a right to contract for labor in the Constitution that in turn trumped democratic control of labor markets, and *Roe* likewise found a right to contract for an abortion that trumped democratic control of markets for reproductive services. *Roe*, then, like *Lawrence v. Texas,* might be sensibly viewed as a stepping stone toward a revitalized libertarian understanding of the relation between citizen, state, and contract. The libertarian and antimoralistic language in *Lawrence* also supports such a reading, as commentators have noted.[7,8] Perhaps the extreme administrative and legal intervention into markets that characterized so much of the twentieth century, whether prompted by moralistic impulses or by redistributive impulses, is the anomaly. The norm may be an ecumenical understanding of the individual liberty protected by the substantive prong of the Due Process Clause—a liberty that arguably protects the sale and purchase of labor, contraception, abortions, subprime mortgages, high interest loans, prostitution services, surrogacy services, babies, gambling contracts, guns, or kidneys, and protects all of these contractual transactions against either moralistic or paternalistic intervention. That is one way to string the beads.

Another way to string the beads aligns *Roe* with other cases that establish what I call "lethal rights," or defensive rights to kill. On this

understanding, *Roe* is part of a narrative that also prominently includes *District of Columbia v. Heller.*[8] Thus, the Court in *Heller* created, or discovered, a right to own a handgun, desired not only by gun enthusiasts and hunters, but also by citizens who worry that the state will not defend them against aggressors in their home or elsewhere. The right to own a gun, read in this way, is the complement to the Court's refusal to grant a positive right to a state's protection against private violence;[9] if you do not have a right to the state's protection against violence, but you do have a right to kill in self-defense, then it becomes quite natural that you must have a prior right to the arms necessary to exercise it. Viewed as a bead on *that* string, we might understand *Roe* as granting a right to kill fetal life, made all the more desirable by virtue of the state's refusal to create meaningful systems of health and child care, and the Court's refusal even to consider the possibility of creating a right to such assistance. A right to an abortion looks all the more desirable if one has no right to assistance in dealing with the economic stresses of parenting. It becomes another "defensive" lethal right, necessitated, in part, by an excessively minimalist state.[10] The rights created by the Court in *Heller* and *Roe* have more than a slight family resemblance.

Of course, neither of these radically libertarian understandings of *Roe* are the narratives preferred by *Roe*'s pro-choice celebrants, or by the Court itself. Rather, the dominant narrative puts *Roe* in line with cases protecting sexual expression, not personal liberty, and not self-defense. On the dominant understanding, *Roe* is on a string of beads with *Griswold v. Connecticut,*[11] *Eisenstadt v. Baird,*[12] and *Lawrence,*[13] not with *Lochner*, and certainly not with *Heller*. What *Roe* does, along with *Griswold, Eisenstadt*, and *Lawrence*, is protect an individual's right to have nonreproductive sex. What is stressed, on this story, is the consequence for sexual freedom to be garnered from the right to be free of the risk of pregnancy.

There are undoubtedly other ways to read *Roe*. There are many ways to string a finite number of beads. Nevertheless, the class is not infinite. It is not possible, for example, to read *Roe* as protective of marital, as opposed to individual privacy.[14] That is foreclosed by *Eisenstadt*. It is not possible, I believe, to read *Roe* as a part of an adjudicative, narrative movement toward a robust conception of reproductive justice. That is ruled out by the right's negativity. Reproductive justice requires a state that provides a network of support for the processes of reproduction: protection against rape and access to affordable and effective birth control, healthcare, including but not limited to abortion services, prenatal care, support in childbirth and postpartum, support for breastfeeding mothers, early childcare for infants and toddlers, income support for parents who stay home to care for young babies, and high quality public education for school age children. The Court is not equipped to mandate any of that, and has stated repeatedly that it is not inclined even to suggest that a citizen might have a right to a state that does so. The negative right that it *has* recognized suggests something very different: it suggests at best a right to nonreproductive sex, and at worst, a right to end a pregnancy by killing the fetus so as to free oneself of the burden of impossible parental obligations in an unjust world. Either way, it is not all that clear that women, parents, or children are the beneficiaries.

III. THE OPPORTUNITY COSTS OF CONSTITUTIONALIZED ABORTION RIGHTS

Reproductive justice is a political and moral project. The Court-created abortion right is a judicial and constitutional one. How might the world be different, if the pro-choice community focused on the former a bit more, and the latter a bit less? What opportunities have been foregone, by virtue of the constancy of the gaze on courts? What are *Roe*'s "opportunity costs"? This Part outlines three: political, rhetorical, and moral.

A. Political Costs

First, movement toward a broadened reproductive justice movement could prompt a fresh look at the pro-life movement, which is different than it was thirty years ago, when it coalesced around the overriding goal of reversing *Roe*. Feminist and progressive theorists and advocates routinely characterize the pro-life movement as aimed at reversing *Roe*, and as committed to the project of requiring women to carry pregnancies to term, primarily so as to enforce restrictive and Victorian roles of motherhood, femininity, and sexuality. This depiction, however, is dated. At least parts of that movement, as expressed both by its leadership and by its members, are not single-mindedly focused on overturning *Roe* or on criminalizing abortion, and are not particularly interested in using either pregnancy or motherhood as a way to punish premarital or extramarital sexual activity. Thus, a fair amount of pro-life feminist scholarship is now focused as much on increasing public support for parenting—both for its own sake, and as a means of minimizing the number of abortions—as with minimizing abortions by criminalizing them and incarcerating the doctors that perform them. The change is just as clear outside of the law review pages. Websites such as MomsRising seek to organize mothers—both pro-life and pro-choice, but the focus seems to be on the former—around what have to date been almost exclusively progressive-feminist goals: paid maternity leave, publicly funded childcare, more public assistance for single mothers, more support across the board for working families. These Internet-based movements express more interest in helping women and teens through their pregnancies and with their families, and less or no interest in punishing teenagers for premarital sex.

By putting legal abortion in its place—that is, putting it in the context of a reproductive justice agenda pursued in the legislative arena—pro-choice advocates might find common cause with pro-life movements that responsibly seek greater justice for pregnant women who choose to carry their pregnancies to term, working families, and struggling mothers. I do not mean to suggest that progressive-feminist advocates and scholars have not been actively seeking these goals. Of course they have, and for a good long while. But at the level of theory, the pro-choice movement exists in considerable tension with those goals.[15] And at the level of politics, the antipathy of pro-choice and pro-life advocates has veiled the possibility of coalitions on these issues, where interests are in fact aligned. Pro-life and pro-choice movements have a common interest in reducing the incidence of abortion, both by minimizing the number of unintended pregnancies and lowering the cost of mothering. They should also have a common interest in protecting the ordinary legal rights and interests of pregnant women who complete their pregnancies—rights that also are threatened by a legal regime that generally neglects the demands of reproductive justice.[16] It might be time to give ordinary politics a chance to achieve common goals.

B. Rhetorical Costs

[Second,] turning our attention away from the courts might prompt a profitable return to pragmatism and away from principle in the formulation of arguments for legal abortion. Principled argument on this issue, perhaps like any other, can take us only so far. It does not follow, though, that the alternative is unthinking chaos. There are pragmatic reasons that the power to make this decision should rest with the pregnant woman or girl: she is the one physically burdened for a substantial period of time by the pregnancy, she is the one faced with the decision to raise or relinquish a baby, she is the one to bear the burden of motherhood with little support from the public sphere should she carry the pregnancy to term, and so on. Giving this power over to husbands, fathers, or medical boards when the pregnant woman is the person who will bear the brunt of the decision, and when that "brunt" is as life-altering and as life-shrinking as it currently is, will result in injuries, stunted lives, and some deaths. We should be explaining the pragmatic reasons that women here and now must have control over their own reproductive lives, rather than focus as exclusively as we have on principled constitutional claims that purport to rest on timeless principle. The need to shoehorn arguments for choice into constitutional form has not only forced the "right to an abortion" into its current truncated and negative form, with the costs noted above, it has also muted arguments for reproductive choice that are pragmatic and time-bound. De-constitutionalizing the case for legal abortion, and relocating the

argument so as to appeal to legislative and popular audiences rather than judicial ones might recenter those claims.

C. Moral Costs

Finally, the focus on the abortion right has diverted resources not only from political and legal possibilities for promoting reproductive justice, but also from other forms of social persuasion, including moral argument, that might reduce the number of unwanted pregnancies women experience, whether they result in live births or not. Bluntly, if women and men were encouraged to be more sexually responsible, there would be fewer unintended pregnancies and less need for abortions or abortion rights. There are two moral constraints in particular on individual sexual behavior that seem particularly compelling, the case for which has been neglected, in part, because of an obsessive fixation on rights.

First, it would behoove the pro-choice community to acknowledge—and then insist—that opposite-sex partners who do not intend to conceive have a compelling moral duty to use birth control. The pro-choice community has focused hard on a *right* to use birth control and much less on the duty to do so. For purposes of contrast, look at another historical moment. At the height of the AIDS epidemic, the gay male community embraced a "condom code," the purpose of which was to influence, through moral persuasion, the use of condoms, so as to reduce the incidence of recklessly transmitted HIV. the straight community, there has been nothing even remotely comparable to the condom code with respect to undesired pregnancies. There ought to be. We need a moral code that makes clear that heterosexuals who do not wish to conceive have a duty to use birth control. We currently have none.

Second, a powerful array of societal forces still pushes heterosexual women and girls to have sex that they patently do not desire, some of which leads to unwanted pregnancies. Women who have sex they do not want may regard such sex as a duty, a hassle, a trauma, a bore, a mystery, a pain in the neck, or, perhaps, as something closer to rape—as the cost of staying free of violence.

But whether traumatic or boring, unwanted sex that is not enjoyed is alienating to the woman who experiences it: she gives her body over—willfully, but still she gives it over—for use by a man, as a part of a bargain she has struck that gives her no pleasure. All of this, I have argued at length elsewhere, is a serious but largely unrecognized and deeply alienating harm.[17]

Should she then become pregnant, however, and consent to an unwanted pregnancy, the alienating harm is compounded: she now will have a comparable relation with an unwanted fetus that she initially had with the unwanted sex. Again, her body is being used for the service of another, rather than a part of an integrated self. This can be not just unpleasant but injurious down the road. When a woman who has endured an unwanted pregnancy must later reclaim use of her body, whether for remunerative market-based labor, or for sport, or even for relaxation, she might find it difficult to do. She might find that, having given one's body away against the sovereignty of one's own desire, it is not an easy path back. "Gifts" of one's body to sex and pregnancy are not joyous when they are deeply unwanted. The motion picture *Waitress*—in which unwanted sex leads to an unwanted pregnancy that then morphs into a wanted pregnancy, which eventually produces a loved child—was fiction.

From this, I would argue that a girl or young woman owes a moral duty not just to herself but also to her future self not to engage in sex she does not want, and a boy or man has a duty not to engage in sex undesired by his partner. Our current sex education curricula—whether abstinence only or abstinence plus birth control—says nothing of this. Nor do the pro-marriage urban billboards that are one of the legacies of the Clinton and Bush Administrations' war on welfare mothers: the "Marriage Works" and "Virgin: Teach your kids it's not a dirty word" and "I don't give it up and I'm not giving in" messages that now dot city landscapes, as a quid pro quo for block grants to aid poor families.[18] These abstinence-only curricula and personal responsibility-enhancing billboards all seemingly presuppose that teenagers universally desire vaginally penetrating sex, but that this sex they all want so intensely is bad, and for various unstated reasons they should not engage in it. We do not see billboards instructing the same population that there is no reason at all not to have sex if they want it—that fully desired sex is good—but that they should indeed abstain from sex they do not desire—that they have a duty to each other and to themselves to do so. We do not see billboards conveying the message that while sex is good, uncontracepted or unwanted sex is a moral wrong. Why not? A straightforward public relations campaign, aimed at teenagers and young adults, that sought to convey both norms—that while wanted sex is a human good, one has a duty to use contraception to avoid unwanted pregnancy, and a duty to say no to unwanted sex—could not hurt, and it might do a lot of good. It might also bring down the total number of unwanted pregnancies in the world.

IV. FROM CHOICE TO REPRODUCTIVE JUSTICE

Pro-choice policies, from the outset, should have been generated by ordinary politics, respectful and reflective of a sex-friendly popular morality, and expressed ultimately in ordinary law. The community of advocates and scholars that held those commitments should have looked to the public, legislators, educators, and social structures, rather than to hoary constitutional principles expressed by not particularly trustworthy oracles, for their meaningful articulation, elaboration, and enforcement. The moment for developing such a politics without interference from the Court, however, has long passed. Nevertheless, both sides— pro-life as well as pro-choice—might yet reclaim at least a degree of such a focus, each from where they now stand. There are particularly compelling reasons for the pro-choice community to do so. Political arguments for reproductive justice, made in political fora and divorced from the adjudicative context, might not carry the specific costs of rights discourse theorized by critical writers and highlighted above. First, they need not rest on a commitment to negative rights and libertarian premises. Women need legal abortion not to ward off undue state interference, but in order to live better and more integrated lives in their families and workplaces both. And to live those better and more integrated lives, they require both reproductive choice and better support for their caregiving obligations, as do the men with whom they might partner. Viewed as pragmatic needs for well-led lives, rather than principled demands for rights, better supports for childcare and legal abortion are both components of an as yet unrealized reproductive justice. Only when elevated to the level of constitutional and timeless principle does the argument for one component seem to undercut the case for the other.

Nor should these arguments be put forward in the context of appeals to individual antimajoritarian rights that have the effect, whether intended or unintended, of undercutting the institutional structures of majoritarian democracy. Arguments for legal abortion have strong majoritarian appeal, and are at least as amenable to public deliberation, persuasion, and compromise as the ordinary fodder of political debate. Arguments for legal abortion in legislative and public arenas need not be made in ways that limit the movement for reproductive justice to this most individualistic and self-abdicating "right to an abortion." They need not be "truncated." Repoliticizing reproductive justice arguments, in other words, might not carry the costs of rights-focused constitutional rhetoric.

Finally, a shift in focus away from courts to more democratic fora might open the door to moral and political opportunities to which we have been blinded by the light of the promises of a living Constitution. We might recapture some of those heretofore-slighted opportunities. Most modestly, it might at least break the logjam that now frustrates any sort of coalition between parts of the pro-choice and pro-life communities that undoubtedly share many common interests and goals. Substantial parts of both sides of these movements have an interest in minimizing the demand for abortion through minimizing the cost of mothering, enforcing and strengthening the rights of pregnant women, advocating the responsible use of birth control, insisting upon sensible anti-rape policies, and discouraging unwanted sex. The reproductive justice that might be achieved

through these coalitions—that is, achieved through ordinary modes of political persuasion—might prove more enduring than what we have garnered to date from the Court. It also might prove more deserving.

NOTES
1. 410 U.S. 113 (1973).
2. 347 U.S. 543 (1954), holding unconstitutional racially segregated public schools.
3. 384 U.S. 436 (1966), holding that criminal suspects must be informed of their rights by police before interrogation.
4. 550 U.S. 124, 150–54 (2007) (describing partial-birth abortion, in graphic and morally charged detail).
5. The surrogacy debates of the late 1980s and early 1990s present a stark example of the application of this principle in policy debates.
6. 550 U.S. 124, 150–54 (2007).
7. 198 U.S. 45 (1905).
8. 128 S. Ct. 2783, 2793 (2008) (holding that the right to bear arms is historically a right to self-defense).
9. DeShaney v. Winnebago County Dep't of Soc. Servs., 489 U.S. 189, 195–97 (1989) (holding that due process does not impose any duty on a state to provide members of the general public with adequate protective services).
10. The controversial "right to die" might also be viewed as a right necessitated, in part, by the lack of a right to healthcare, including palliative care. *See generally* THE CASE AGAINST ASSISTED SUICIDE: FOR THE RIGHT TO END-OF-LIFE CARE (Kathleen Foley & Herbert Hendin eds., 2002) (including arguments for a right to assisted suicide as well as arguments for increased palliative care instead of a right to assisted suicide). For a criticism of the argument against assisted suicide, see Ani B. Satz, *The Case Against Assisted Suicide Reexamined*, 100 MICH. L. REV. 1380 (2002).
11. 381 U.S. 479 (1965).
12. 405 U.S. 438 (1972).
13. 539 U.S. 558 (2003).
14. *See Eisenstadt*, 405 U.S. at 453 (making clear that privacy protects individual rather than marital privacy).
15. For an early statement regarding the tension between the negative logic of *Roe* and the struggles of drug-addicted mothers, see Dorothy E. Roberts, *Punishing Drug Addicts Who Have Babies:*

Women of Color, Equality, and the Right of Privacy, 104 HARV. L. REV. 1419, 1477–78 (1991) (arguing that the negative right of privacy created in *Roe* is not helpful to drug-addicted mothers).

16. Both groups, for example, should have a joint interest in protecting the currently embattled rights of pregnant women to make choices regarding their modes of delivery, or of pregnant teenagers to a full education, of pregnant inmates not to be shackled during their deliveries, of new mothers to breastfeed, of mothers of children conceived in rape to be free of coercive pressures by their rapists, and of drug-infected pregnant women to be free of incarceration and have access to healthcare. On shackling female prisoners during pregnancy, see Geraldine Doetzer, *Hard Labor: The Legal Implications of Shackling Female Inmates During Pregnancy and Childbirth*, 14 WM. & MARY J. WOMEN & L. 363, 372–73 (2008) (arguing that shackling inmates during childbirth is unconstitutional). On protecting the rights of mothers to

control their deliveries, see April L. Cherry, *Roe's Legacy: The Nonconsensual Medical Treatment of Pregnant Women and Implications for Female Citizenship*, 6 U. PA. J. CONST. L. 723, 732–36 (2004) (arguing that the structure of *Roe* has led to restrictions on pregnant women's medical choices in the later stages of pregnancy by creating a constitutionally protected state interest in the fetus).

17. *See* Robin West, *Sex, Law and Consent*, in THE ETHICS OF CONSENT: THEORY AND PRACTICE (Alan Wertheimer & William Miller eds., forthcoming 2009).

18. *See* ROBIN WEST, MARRIAGE, SEXUALITY, AND GENDER 134–35, 173 (2007) (discussing the "Marriage Works" campaigns); Heather Harris, *Marriage Works. Or Does It?: A Pro-Marriage Campaign Pops a Lot of Questions but Provides Few Answers*, THE URBANITE MAGAZINE, Sept. 27, 2006, http://www.urbanitebaltimore.com/sub.cfm?ArticleID=461&IssueID=39&SectionID=4.

20   Whiteness as Property

CHERYL I. HARRIS

I. INTRODUCTION

In the 1930s, some years after my mother's family became part of the great river of Black migration that flowed north my Mississippi-born grandmother was confronted with the harsh matter of economic survival for herself and her two daughters. Having separated from my grandfather, who himself was trapped on the fringes of economic marginality, she took one long hard look at her choices and presented herself for employment at a major retail store in Chicago's central business district. This decision would have been unremarkable for a white woman in similar circumstances, but for my grandmother, it was an act of both great daring and self-denial, for in so doing she was presenting herself as a white woman. In the parlance of racist America, she was "passing."

Her fair skin, straight hair, and aquiline features had not spared her from the life of sharecropping into which she had been born in anywhere-nowhere, Mississippi—the outskirts of Yazoo City. But in the burgeoning landscape of urban America, anonymity was possible for a Black person with "white" features. She was transgressing boundaries, crossing borders, spinning on margins, traveling between dualities of Manichean space, rigidly bifurcated into light-dark, good-bad, white-Black. No longer immediately identifiable as "Lula's daughter," she could thus enter the white world, albeit on a false passport, not merely passing, but *tres*passing.

Every day my grandmother rose from her bed in her house in a Black enclave on the south side of Chicago, sent her children off to a Black school, boarded a bus full of Black passengers, and

This article is reprinted, as excerpts, with permission of the author. It appeared originally in 106 Harvard Law Review 1707–1791 (June 1993). Many footnotes, including most citations, have been omitted.

rode to work. No one at her job ever asked if she was Black; the question was unthinkable. By virtue of the employment practices of the "fine establishment" in which she worked, she could not have been. Catering to the upper-middle class, understated tastes required that Blacks not be allowed.

She quietly went about her clerical tasks, not once revealing her true identity. She listened to the women with whom she worked discuss their worries—their children's illnesses, their husbands' disappointments, their boyfriends' infidelities—all of the mundane yet critical things that made up their lives. She came to know them but they did not know her, for my grandmother occupied a completely different place. That place—where white supremacy and economic domination meet—was unknown turf to her white coworkers. They remained oblivious to the worlds within worlds that existed just beyond the edge of their awareness and yet were present in their very midst.

Each evening, my grandmother, tired and worn, retraced her steps home, laid aside her mask, and reentered herself. Day in and day out, she made herself invisible, then visible again, for a price too inconsequential to do more than barely sustain her family and at a cost too precious to conceive. She left the job some years later, finding the strain too much to bear.

From time to time, as I later sat with her, she would recollect that period, and the cloud of some painful memory would pass across her face. Her voice would remain subdued, as if to contain the still-remembered tension. On rare occasions she would wince, recalling some particularly racist comment made in her presence because of her presumed, shared group affiliation. Whatever retort might have been called for had been suppressed long before it reached her lips, for the price of her family's well-being was her silence. Accepting the risk of self-annihilation was the only way to survive.

Although she never would have stated it this way, the clear and ringing denunciations of racism she delivered from her chair when advanced arthritis had rendered her unable to work were informed by those experiences. The fact that self-

denial had been a logical choice and had made her complicit in her own oppression at times fed the fire in her eyes when she confronted some daily outrage inflicted on Black people. Later, these painful memories forged her total identification with the civil rights movement. Learning about the world at her knee as I did, these experiences also came to inform my outlook and my understanding of the world.

My grandmother's story is far from unique. Indeed, there are many who crossed the color line never to return. Passing is well-known among Black people in the United States[1] and is a feature of race subordination in all societies structured on white supremacy. Notwithstanding the purported benefits of Black heritage in an era of affirmative action, passing is not an obsolete phenomenon that has slipped into history.[2]

The persistence of passing is related to the historical and continuing pattern of white racial domination and economic exploitation that has given passing a certain economic logic. It was a given to my grandmother that being white automatically ensured higher economic returns in the short term, as well as greater economic, political, and social security in the long run. Becoming white meant gaining access to a whole set of public and private privileges that materially and permanently guaranteed basic subsistence needs and, therefore, survival. Becoming white increased the possibility of controlling critical aspects of one's life rather than being the object of others' domination.

My grandmother's story illustrates the valorization of whiteness as treasured property in a society structured on racial caste. In ways so embedded that it is rarely apparent, the set of assumptions, privileges, and benefits that accompany the status of being white have become a valuable asset that whites sought to protect and that those who passed sought to attain—by fraud if necessary. Whites have come to expect and rely on these benefits, and over time these expectations have been affirmed, legitimated, and protected by the law. Even though the law is neither uniform nor explicit in all instances, in protecting settled expectations based on white privilege, American law has recognized a property interest in whiteness that, although unacknowledged, now forms the background against which legal disputes are framed, argued, and adjudicated.

My Article investigates the relationships between concepts of race and property and reflects on how rights in property are contingent on, intertwined with, and conflated with race. Through this entangled relationship between race and property, historical forms of domination have evolved to reproduce subordination in the present. In Part II, I examine the emergence of whiteness as property and trace the evolution of whiteness from color to race to status to property as a progression historically rooted in white supremacy[3] and economic hegemony over Black and Native American peoples. The origins of whiteness as property lie in the parallel systems of domination of Black and Native American peoples out of which were created racially contingent forms of property and property rights. I further argue that whiteness shares the critical characteristics of property even as the meaning of property has changed over time. In particular, whiteness and property share a common premise—a conceptual nucleus—of a right to exclude. This conceptual nucleus has proven to be a powerful center around which whiteness as property has taken shape. Following the period of slavery and conquest, white identity became the basis of racialized privilege that was ratified and legitimated in law as a type of status property. After legalized segregation was overturned, whiteness as property evolved into a more modern form through the law's ratification of the settled expectations of relative white privilege as a legitimate and natural baseline.

II. THE CONSTRUCTION OF RACE AND THE EMERGENCE OF WHITENESS AS PROPERTY

The racialization of identity and the racial subordination of Blacks and Native Americans provided the ideological basis for slavery and conquest. Although the systems of oppression of Blacks and Native Americans differed in form—the former involving the seizure and appropriation of labor, the latter entailing the seizure and appropriation of land—undergirding both was a racialized conception of property implemented by force and ratified by law.

The origins of property rights in the United States are rooted in racial domination. Even in the early years of the country, it was not the concept of race alone that operated to oppress Blacks and Indians; rather, it was the *interaction* between conceptions of race and property that played a critical role in establishing and maintaining racial and economic subordination.

The hyperexploitation of Black labor was accomplished by treating Black people themselves as objects of property. Race and property were thus conflated by establishing a form of property contingent on race—only Blacks were subjugated as slaves and treated as property. Similarly, the conquest, removal, and extermination of Native American life and culture were ratified by conferring and acknowledging the property rights of whites in Native American land. Only white possession and occupation of land was validated and therefore privileged as a basis for property rights. These distinct forms of exploitation each contributed in varying ways to the construction of whiteness as property.

A. Forms of Racialized Property: Relationships Between Slavery, Race, and Property

1. The Convergence of Racial and Legal Status.
Although the early colonists were cognizant of race, racial lines were neither consistently nor sharply delineated among or within all social groups. Captured Africans sold in the Americas were distinguished from the population of indentured or bond servants—"unfree" white labor—but it was not an irrebuttable presumption that all Africans were "slaves" or that slavery was the only appropriate status for them.[4] The distinction between African and white indentured labor grew, however, as decreasing terms of service were introduced for white bond servants. Simultaneously, the demand for labor intensified, resulting in a greater reliance on African labor and a rapid

increase in the number of Africans imported into the colonies.

The construction of white identity and the ideology of racial hierarchy also were intimately tied to the evolution and expansion of the system of chattel slavery. The further entrenchment of plantation slavery was in part an answer to a social crisis produced by the eroding capacity of the landed class to control the white labor population. The dominant paradigm of social relations, however, was that, although not all Africans were slaves, virtually all slaves were not white. It was their racial otherness that came to justify the subordinated status of Blacks. The result was a classification system that "key[ed] official rules of descent to national origin" so that "[m]embership in the new social category of 'Negro' became itself sufficient justification for enslaveability." Although the cause of the increasing gap between the status of African and white labor is contested by historians, it is clear that "[t]he economic and political interests defending Black slavery were far more powerful than those defending indentured servitude."

By the 1660s, the especially degraded status of Blacks as chattel slaves was recognized by law." Between 1680 and 1682, the first slave codes appeared, codifying the extreme deprivations of liberty already existing in social practice. Many laws parceled out differential treatment based on racial categories: Blacks were not permitted to travel without permits, to own property, to assemble publicly, or to own weapons; nor were they to be educated. Racial identity was further merged with stratified social and legal status: "Black" racial identity marked who was subject to enslavement; "white" racial identity marked who was "free" or, at minimum, not a slave. The ideological and rhetorical move from "slave" and "free" to "Black" and "white" as polar constructs marked an important step in the social construction of race.

2. Implications for Property.

The social relations that produced racial identity as a justification for slavery also had implications for the conceptualization of property. This result was predictable, as the institution of slavery, lying at the very core of economic relations, was bound up with the idea of property. Through slavery, race and economic domination were fused.

Slavery produced a peculiar, mixed category of property and humanity—a hybrid possessing inherent instabilities that were reflected in its treatment and ratification by the law. The dual and contradictory character of slaves as property and persons was exemplified in the Representation Clause of the Constitution. Representation in the House of Representatives was apportioned on the basis of population computed by counting all persons and "three-fifths of all other persons"—slaves.[5] Gouverneur Morris's remarks before the Constitutional Convention posed the essential question: "Upon what principle is it that slaves shall be computed in the representation? Are they men? Then make them Citizens & let them vote? Are they property? Why then is no other property included?"

The cruel tension between property and humanity was also reflected in the law's legitimation of the use of Blackwomen's bodies as a means of increasing property. In 1662, the Virginia colonial assembly provided that "[c]hildren got by an Englishman upon a Negro woman shall be bond or free according to the condition of the mother ..." In reversing the usual common law presumption that the status of the child was determined by the father, the rule facilitated the reproduction of one's own labor force. Because the children of Blackwomen assumed the status of their mother, slaves were bred through Blackwomen's bodies. The economic significance of this form of exploitation of female slaves should not be underestimated. Despite Thomas Jefferson's belief that slavery should be abolished, like other slaveholders he viewed slaves as economic assets, noting that their value could be realized more efficiently from breeding than from labor. A letter he wrote in 1805 stated: "I consider the labor of a breeding woman as no object, and that a child raised every 2 years is of more profit than the crop of the best laboring man."

Even though there was some unease in slave law, reflective of the mixed status of slaves as humans and property, the critical nature of social relations under slavery was the commodification of human beings. Productive relations in early American society included varying forms of sale of labor capacity, many of which were highly oppressive; but slavery was distinguished from other forms of labor servitude by its permanency and the total commodification attendant to the status of the slave. Slavery as a legal institution treated slaves as property that could be transferred, assigned, inherited, or posted as collateral. For example, in *Johnson v. Butler*,[6] the plaintiff sued the defendant for failing to pay a debt of $496 on a specified date. Because the covenant had called for payment of the debt in "money or negroes," the plaintiff contended that the defendant's tender of one negro only, although valued by the parties at an amount equivalent to the debt, could not discharge the debt. The court agreed with the plaintiff. This use of Africans as a stand-in for actual currency highlights the degree to which slavery "propertized" human life.

Because the "presumption of freedom [arose] from color [white]" and the "black color of the race [raised] the presumption of slavery," whiteness became a shield from slavery, a highly volatile and unstable form of property. In the form adopted in the United States, slavery made human beings market-alienable and in so doing, subjected human life and personhood—that which is most valuable—to the ultimate devaluation. Because whites could not be enslaved or held as slaves, the racial line between white and Black was extremely critical; it became a line of protection and demarcation from the potential threat of commodification, and it determined the allocation of the benefits and burdens of this form of property. White identity and whiteness were sources of privilege and protection; their absence meant being the object of property.

Slavery as a system of property facilitated the merger of white identity and property. Because the system of slavery was contingent on and conflated with racial identity, it became crucial to be "white," to be identified as white, to have the property of being white.[7] Whiteness was the characteristic, the attribute, the property of free human beings.

B. Forms of Racialized Property: Relationships Between Native American Land Seizure, Race, and Property

Slavery linked the privilege of whites to the subordination of Blacks through a legal regime that attempted the conversion of Blacks into objects of property. Similarly, the settlement and seizure of Native American land supported white privilege through a system of property rights in land in which the "race" of the Native Americans rendered their first possession rights invisible and justified conquest. This racist formulation embedded the fact of white privilege into the very definition of property, marking another stage in the evolution of the property interest in whiteness. Possession—the act necessary to lay the basis for rights in property—was defined to include only the cultural practices of whites. This definition laid the foundation for the idea that whiteness—that which whites alone possess—is valuable and is property.

Although the Indians were the first occupants and possessors of the land of the New World, their racial and cultural otherness allowed this fact to be reinterpreted and ultimately erased as a basis for asserting rights in land. Because the land had been left in its natural state, untilled and unmarked by human hands, it was "waste" and therefore the appropriate object of settlement and appropriation.[8] Thus, the possession maintained by the Indians was not "true" possession and could safely be ignored. This interpretation of the rule of first possession effectively rendered the rights of first possessors contingent on the race of the possessor. Only particular forms of possession—those that were characteristic of white settlement—would be recognized and legitimated.[9] Indian forms of possession were perceived to be too ambiguous and unclear.

The conquest and occupation of Indian land was wrapped in the rule of law. The law provided not only a defense of conquest and colonization, but also a naturalized regime of rights and disabilities, power and disadvantage that flowed from it, so that no further justifications or rationalizations were required. A key decision defending the right of conquest was *Johnson and Graham's Lessee v.*

M'Intosh,[10] in which both parties to the action claimed the same land through title descendant from different Indian tribes. The issue specifically presented was not merely whether Indians had the power to convey title, but to whom the conveyance could be made—to individuals or to the government that "discovered" land. In holding that Indians could only convey to the latter, the Court reasoned that Indian title was subordinate to the absolute title of the sovereign that was achieved by conquest because "[c]onquest gives a title which the Courts of the conqueror cannot deny...." If property is understood as a delegation of sovereign power—the product of the power of the state—then a fair reading of history reveals the racial oppression of Indians inherent in the American regime of property.

In *Johnson* and similar cases, courts established whiteness as a prerequisite to the exercise of enforceable property rights. Not all first possession or labor gave rise to property rights; rather, the rules of first possession and labor as a basis for property rights were qualified by race. This fact infused whiteness with significance and value because it was solely through being white that property could be acquired and secured under law. Only whites possessed whiteness, a highly valued and exclusive form of property.

C. Critical Characteristics of Property and Whiteness

The legal legacy of slavery and of the seizure of land from Native American peoples is not merely a regime of property law that is (mis)informed by racist and ethnocentric themes. Rather, the law has established and protected an actual property interest in whiteness itself, which shares the critical characteristics of property and accords with the many and varied theoretical descriptions of property.

Although by popular usage property describes "things" owned by persons, or the rights of persons with respect to a thing, the concept of property prevalent among most theorists, even prior to the twentieth century, is that property may "consist[] of rights in 'things' that are intangible, or whose existence is a matter of legal definition."

Property is thus said to be a right, not a thing, characterized as metaphysical, not physical. The theoretical bases and conceptual descriptions of property rights are varied, ranging from first possessor rules, to creation of value, to Lockean labor theory, to personality theory, to utilitarian theory.[11] However disparate, these formulations of property clearly illustrate the extent to which property rights and interests embrace much more than land and personalty. Thus, the fact that whiteness is not a "physical" entity does not remove it from the realm of property.

Whiteness is not simply and solely a legally recognized property interest. It is simultaneously an aspect of self-identity and of personhood, and its relation to the law of property is complex. Whiteness has functioned as self-identity in the domain of the intrinsic, personal, and psychological; as reputation in the interstices between internal and external identity; and, as property in the extrinsic, public, and legal realms. According whiteness actual legal status converted an aspect of identity into an external object of property, moving whiteness from privileged identity to a vested interest. The law's construction of whiteness defined and affirmed critical aspects of identity (who is white); of privilege (what benefits accrue to that status); and of property (what *legal* entitlements arise from that status). Whiteness at various times signifies and is deployed as identity, status, and property, sometimes singularly, sometimes in tandem.

1. Whiteness as a Traditional Form of Property. Whiteness fits the broad historical concept of property described by classical theorists. In James Madison's view, for example, property "embraces every thing to which a man may attach a value and have a right," referring to all of a person's legal rights.[12] Property as conceived in the founding era:

> included not only external objects and people's relationships to them, but also all of those human rights, liberties, powers, and immunities that are important for human well-being, including: freedom of expression, freedom of conscience, freedom from bodily harm, and free and equal opportunities to use personal faculties.[13]

Whiteness defined the legal status of a person as slave or free. White identity conferred tangible and economically valuable benefits and was jealously guarded as a valued possession, allowed only to those who met a strict standard of proof. Whiteness—the right to white identity as embraced by the law—is property if by property one means all of a person's legal rights.

Other traditional theories of property emphasize that the "natural" character of property is derivative of custom, contrary to the notion that property is the product of a delegation of sovereign power. This "bottom up" theory holds that the law of property merely codifies existing customs and social relations. Under that view, government-created rights such as social welfare payments cannot constitute legitimate property interests because they are positivistic in nature. Other theorists have challenged this conception, and argued that even the most basic of "customary" property rights—the rule of first possession, for example—is dependent on its acceptance or rejection in particular instances by the government. Citing custom as a source of property law begs the central question: whose custom?

Rather than remaining within the bipolar confines of custom or command, it is crucial to recognize the dynamic and multifaceted relationship among custom, command, and law, as well as the extent to which positionality[14] determines how each may be experienced and understood. Indian custom was obliterated by force and replaced with the regimes of common law that embodied the customs of the conquerors. The assumption of American law as it related to Native Americans was that conquest *did* give rise to sovereignty. Indians experienced the property laws of the colonizers and the emergent American nation as acts of violence perpetuated by the exercise of power and ratified through the rule of law. At the same time, these laws were perceived as custom and "common sense" by the colonizers. The Founders, for instance, so thoroughly embraced Lockean labor theory as the basis for a right of acquisition because it affirmed the right of the New World settlers to settle on and acquire the frontier. It confirmed and ratified their experience.

The law's interpretation of those encounters between whites and Native Americans not only inflicted vastly different results on them, but also established a pattern—a *custom*—of valorizing whiteness. As the forms of racialized property were perfected, the value and protection extended to whiteness increased. Regardless of which theory of property one adopts, the concept of whiteness—established by centuries of custom (illegitimate custom, but custom nonetheless) and codified by law—may be understood as a property interest.

2. Modern Views of Property as Defining Social Relations.

Although property in the classical sense refers to everything that is valued and to which a person has a right, the modern concept of property focuses on its function and the social relations reflected therein. In this sense, modern property doctrine emphasizes the more contingent nature of property and has been the basis for the argument that property rights should be expanded.

Modern theories of property reject the assumption that property is "objectively definable or identifiable, apart from social context." Charles Reich's ground-breaking work, *The New Property*, was an early effort to focus on the function of property and note the changing social relations reflected and constructed by new forms of property derived from the government. Property in this broader sense encompassed jobs, entitlements, occupational licenses, contracts, subsidies, and indeed a whole host of intangibles that are the product of labor, time, and creativity, such as intellectual property, business goodwill, and enhanced earning potential from graduate degrees. Notwithstanding the dilution of new property since *Goldberg v. Kelly*[15] and its progeny as well as continued attacks on the concept, the legacy of new property infuses the concept of property with questions of power, selection, and allocation. Reich's argument that property is not a natural right but a construction by society resonates in current theories of property that describe the allocation of property rights as a series of choices. This construction directs attention toward issues of relative power and social relations inherent in any definition of property.

3. Property and Expectations.

"Property is nothing but the basis of expectation," according to Bentham, "consist[ing] in an established expectation, in the persuasion of being able to draw such and such advantage from the thing possessed."[16] The relationship between expectations and property remains highly significant, as the law "has recognized and protected even the expectation of rights as actual legal property." This theory does not suggest that all value or all expectations give rise to property, but those expectations in tangible or intangible things that are valued and protected by the law are property.

In fact, the difficulty lies not in identifying expectations as a part of property, but in distinguishing which expectations are reasonable and therefore merit the protection of the law as property. Although the existence of certain property rights may seem self-evident and the protection of certain expectations may seem essential for social stability, property is a legal construct by which selected private interests are protected and upheld. In creating property "rights," the law draws boundaries and enforces or reorders existing regimes of power. The inequalities that are produced and reproduced are not givens or inevitabilities, but rather are conscious selections regarding the structuring of social relations. In this sense, it is contended that property rights and interests are not "natural," but are "creation[s] of law."

In a society structured on racial subordination, white privilege became an expectation and, to apply Margaret Radin's concept, whiteness became the quintessential property for personhood. The law constructed "whiteness" as an objective fact, although in reality it is an ideological proposition imposed through subordination. This move is the central feature of "reification": "Its basis is that a relation between people takes on the character of a thing and thus acquires a 'phantom objectivity,' an autonomy that seems so strictly rational and all-embracing as to conceal every trace of its fundamental nature: the relation between people." Whiteness was an "object" over which continued control was—and is—expected. The protection of these expectations is central because, as Radin notes: "If an object you now control is bound up in your future plans or in your anticipation of your future self, and it is partly these plans for your own continuity that make you a person, then your personhood depends on the realization of these expectations."

Because the law recognized and protected expectations grounded in white privilege (albeit not explicitly in all instances), these expectations became tantamount to property that could not permissibly be intruded upon without consent. As the law explicitly ratified those expectations in continued privilege or extended ongoing protection to those illegitimate expectations by failing to expose or to radically disturb them, the dominant and subordinate positions within the racial hierarchy were reified in law. When the law recognizes, either implicitly or explicitly, the settled expectations of whites built on the privileges and benefits produced by white supremacy, it acknowledges and reinforces a property interest in whiteness that reproduces Black subordination.

4. The Property Functions of Whiteness.

In addition to the theoretical descriptions of property, whiteness also meets the functional criteria of property. Specifically, the law has accorded "holders" of whiteness the same privileges and benefits accorded holders of other types of property. The liberal view of property is that it includes the exclusive rights of possession, use, and disposition. Its attributes are the right to transfer or alienability, the right to use and enjoyment, and the right to exclude others. Even when examined against this limited view, whiteness conforms to the general contours of property. It may be a "bad" form of property, but it is property nonetheless.

(a) Rights of Disposition. Property rights are traditionally described as fully alienable. Because fundamental personal rights are commonly understood to be inalienable, it is problematic to view them as property interests. However, as Margaret Radin notes, "inalienability" is not a transparent term; it has multiple meanings that refer to interests that are nonsalable, nontransferable, or

nonmarket-alienable. The common core of in-alienability is the negation of the possibility of sep-aration of an entitlement, right, or attribute from its holder.

Classical theories of property identified alien-ability as a requisite aspect of property; thus, that which is inalienable cannot be property. As the major exponent of this view, Mill argued that public offices, monopoly privileges, and human beings—all of which were or should have been inalienable—should not be considered property at all. Under this account, if inalienability inheres in the concept of property, then whiteness, inca-pable of being transferred or alienated either in-side or outside the market, would fail to meet a criterion of property.[17]

As Radin notes, however, even under the clas-sical view, alienability of certain property was lim-ited. Mill also advocated certain restraints on alienation in connection with property rights in land and probably other natural resources. In fact, the law has recognized various kinds of inalienable property. For example, entitlements of the regulatory and welfare states, such as transfer payments and government licenses, are inalienable; yet they have been conceptualized and treated as property by law. Although this "new property" has been criticized as being improper—that is, not appropriately cast as property—the principal objec-tion has been based on its alleged lack of produc-tive capacity, not its inalienability.

The law has also acknowledged forms of in-alienable property derived from nongovernmental sources. In the context of divorce, courts have held that professional degrees or licenses held by one party and financed by the labor of the other is marital property whose value is subject to alloca-tion by the court. A medical or law degree is not alienable either in the market or by voluntary transfer. Nevertheless, it is included as property when dissolving a legal relationship.

Indeed, Radin argues that, as a deterrent to the dehumanization of universal commodification, market-inalienability may be justified to protect property important to the person and to safeguard human flourishing. She suggests that non-commodification or market-inalienability of per-sonal property or those things essential to human

flourishing is necessary to guard against the objec-tification of human beings. To avoid that danger, "we must cease thinking that market alienability is inherent in the concept of property." Following this logic, then, the inalienability of whiteness should not preclude the consideration of white-ness as property. Paradoxically, its inalienability may be more indicative of its perceived enhanced value, rather than its disqualification as property.

(b) Right to Use and Enjoyment. Possession of property includes the rights of use and enjoyment. If these rights are essential aspects of property, it is because "the problem of property in political phi-losophy dissolves into … questions of the will and the way in which we use the things of this world." As whiteness is simultaneously an aspect of iden-tity and a property interest, it is something that can both be experienced and deployed as a re-source. Whiteness can move from being a passive characteristic as an aspect of identity to an active entity that—like other types of property—is used to fulfill the will and to exercise power. The state's official recognition of a racial identity that subor-dinated Blacks and of privileged rights in property based on race elevated whiteness from a passive attribute to an object of law and a resource de-ployable at the social, political, and institutional level to maintain control. Thus, a white person "used and enjoyed" whiteness whenever she took advantage of the privileges accorded white people simply by virtue of their whiteness—when she exercised any number of rights reserved for the holders of whiteness. Whiteness as the em-bodiment of white privilege transcended mere be-lief or preference; it became usable property, the subject of the law's regard and protection. In this respect whiteness, as an active property, has been used and enjoyed.

(c) Reputation and Status Property. In con-structing whiteness as property, the ideological move was to conceptualize white racial identity as an external thing in a constitutive sense—an "object[] or resource[] necessary to be a person." This move was accomplished in large measure by recognizing the reputational interest in being regarded as white as a thing of significant value, which like other reputational interests, was intrinsically bound up with identity and personhood. The reputation of being white was treated as a species of property, or something in which a property interest could be asserted.[18] In this context, whiteness was a form of status property.

The conception of reputation as property found its origins in early concepts of property that encompassed things (such as land and personalty), income (such as revenues from leases, mortgages, and patent monopolies), and one's life, liberty, and labor." Thus, Locke's famous pronouncement, "every man has a 'property' in his own 'person,' " undergirded the assertion that one's physical self was one's property.[19] From this premise, one's labor, "the work of his hands," combined with those things found in the common to form property over which one could exercise ownership, control, and dominion. The idea of self-ownership, then, was particularly fertile ground for the idea that reputation, as an aspect of identity earned through effort, was similarly property. Moreover, the loss of reputation was capable of being valued in the market.

The direct manifestation of the law's legitimation of whiteness as reputation is revealed in the well-established doctrine that to call a white person "Black" is to defame her. Although many of the cases were decided in an era when the social and legal stratification of whites and Blacks was more absolute, as late as 1957 the principle was reaffirmed, notwithstanding significant changes in the legal and political status of Blacks. As one court noted, "there is still to be considered the social distinction existing between the races," and the allegation was likely to cause injury. A Black person, however, could not sue for defamation if she was called "white." Because the law expressed and reinforced the social hierarchy as it existed, it was presumed that no harm could flow from such a reversal.

Private identity based on racial hierarchy was legitimated as public identity in law, even after the end of slavery and the formal end of legal race segregation. Whiteness as interpersonal hierarchy was recognized externally as race reputation. Thus, whiteness as public reputation and personal property was affirmed.

(d) The Absolute Right to Exclude. Many theorists have traditionally conceptualized property to include the exclusive rights of use, disposition, and possession, with possession embracing the absolute right to exclude. The right to exclude was the central principle, too, of whiteness as identity, for mainly whiteness has been characterized, not by an inherent unifying characteristic, but by the exclusion of others deemed to be "not white." The possessors of whiteness were granted the legal right to exclude others from the privileges inhering in whiteness; whiteness became an exclusive club whose membership was closely and grudgingly guarded. The courts played an active role in enforcing this right to exclude—determining who was or was not white enough to enjoy the privileges accompanying whiteness. In that sense, the courts protected whiteness as any other form of property.

Moreover, as it emerged, the concept of whiteness was premised on white supremacy rather than mere difference. "White" was defined and constructed in ways that increased its value by reinforcing its exclusivity. Indeed, just as whiteness as property embraced the right to exclude, whiteness as a theoretical construct evolved for the very purpose of racial exclusion. Thus, the concept of whiteness is built on both exclusion and racial subjugation. This fact was particularly evident during the period of the most rigid racial exclusion, as whiteness signified racial privilege and took the form of status property.

At the individual level, recognizing oneself as "white" necessarily assumes premises based on white supremacy: It assumes that Black ancestry in any degree, extending to generations far removed, automatically disqualifies claims to white identity, thereby privileging "white" as unadulterated, exclusive, and rare. Inherent in the concept of "being white" was the right to own or hold whiteness to the exclusion and subordination of Blacks. Because "[i]dentity is ... continuously being constituted through social interactions," the assigned political, economic, and social inferiority of Blacks necessarily shaped white identity. In the commonly held popular view, the presence of Black "blood"—including the infamous "one-drop" consigned a person to being "Black" and evoked the "metaphor ... of purity and contamination" in which Black blood is a contaminant and white racial identity is pure. Recognizing or identifying oneself as white is thus a claim of racial purity, an assertion that one is free of any taint of Black blood. The law has played a critical role in legitimating this claim.

The law relied on bounded, objective, and scientific definitions of race—what Neil Gotanda has called "historical race"—to construct whiteness as not merely race, but race plus privilege. By making race determinant and the product of rationality and science, dominant and subordinate positions within the racial hierarchy were disguised as the product of natural law and biology rather than as naked preferences. Whiteness as racialized privilege was then legitimated by science and was embraced in legal doctrine as "objective fact."

Case law that attempted to define race frequently struggled over the precise fractional amount of Black "blood"—traceable Black ancestry—that would defeat a claim to whiteness. Although the courts applied varying fractional formulas in different jurisdictions to define "Black" or, in the terms of the day, "Negro" or "colored," the law uniformly accepted the rule of hypodescent[20]—racial identity was governed by blood, and white was preferred.

This legal assumption of race as blood-borne was predicated on the pseudosciences of eugenics and craniology that saw their major development during the eighteenth and nineteenth centuries. The legal definition of race was the "objective" test propounded by racist theorists of the day who described race to be immutable, scientific, biologically determined—an unsullied fact of the blood rather than a volatile and violently imposed regime of racial hierarchy.

In adjudicating who was "white," courts sometimes noted that, by physical characteristics, the individual whose racial identity was at issue appeared to be white and, in fact, had been regarded as white in the community. Yet if an individual's blood was tainted, she could not claim to be "white" as the law understood, regardless of the fact that phenotypically she may have been completely indistinguishable from a white person, may have lived as a white person, and have

descended from a family that lived as whites. Although socially accepted as white, she could not *legally* be white. Blood as "objective fact" dominated over appearance and social acceptance, which were socially fluid and subjective measures.

But, in fact, "blood" was no more objective than that which the law dismissed as subjective and unreliable. The acceptance of the fiction that the racial ancestry could be determined with the degree of precision called for by the relevant standards or definitions rested on false assumptions that racial categories of prior ancestors had been accurately reported, that those reporting in the past shared the definitions currently in use, and that racial purity actually existed in the United States. Ignoring these considerations, the law established rules that extended equal treatment to those of the "same blood," albeit of different complexions, because it was acknowledged that, "[t]here are white men as dark as mulattoes, and there are pure-blooded albino Africans as white as the whitest Saxons."

[...]

It is important to note the effect of this hypervaluation of whiteness. Owning white identity as property affirmed the self-identity and liberty of whites and, conversely, denied the self-identity and liberty of Blacks. The attempts to lay claim to whiteness through "passing" painfully illustrate the effects of the law's recognition of whiteness. The embrace of a lie, undertaken by my grandmother and the thousands like her, could occur only when oppression makes self-denial and the obliteration of identity rational and, in significant measure, beneficial. The economic coercion of white supremacy on self-definition nullifies any suggestion that passing is a logical exercise of liberty or self-identity. The decision to pass as white was not a choice, if by that word one means voluntariness or lack of compulsion. The fact of race subordination was coercive and circumscribed the liberty to self-define. Self-determination of identity was not a right for all people, but a privilege accorded on the basis of race. The effect of protecting whiteness at law was to devalue those who were not white by coercing them to deny their identity in order to survive.

[...]

III. BOUND BY LAW: THE PROPERTY INTEREST IN WHITENESS AS LEGAL DOCTRINE IN *PLESSY* AND *BROWN*

Even after the period of conquest and colonization of the New World and the abolition of slavery, whiteness was the predicate for attaining a host of societal privileges, in both public and private spheres. Whiteness determined whether one could vote, travel freely, attend schools, obtain work, and indeed, defined the structure of social relations along the entire spectrum of interactions between the individual and society. Whiteness then became status, a form of racialized privilege ratified in law. Material privileges attendant to being white inhered in the status of being white. After the dismantling of legalized race segregation, whiteness took on the character of property in the modern sense in that relative white privilege was legitimated as the status quo. In *Plessy v. Ferguson*[21] and the case that overturned it, *Brown v. Board of Education*,[22] the law extended protection to whiteness as property, in the former instance, as traditional status-property, in the latter, as modern property.

[...]

Thus, we are left with *Brown's* mixed legacy: *Brown* held that the Constitution would not countenance legalized racial separation, but *Brown* did not address the government's responsibility to eradicate inequalities in resource allocation either in public education or other public services, let alone to intervene in inequities in the private domain, all of which are, in significant measure, the result of white domination. In attempting to remedy state-mandated racial separation by the simple prescription of desegregation, the *Brown* decisions finessed the question of what to do about the inequality produced by state and private policy and practice. *Brown* modified *Plessy's* interpretation of the Equal Protection Clause and accommodated both Blacks' claims for "equality under law" and the global interests of white ruling elites. What remained consistent was the perpetuation of institutional privilege under a standard of legal equality. In the foreground was the change

of formal societal rules; in the background was the "natural" fact of white privilege that dictated the pace and course of any moderating change. What remained in revised and reconstituted form was whiteness as property.

IV. THE PERSISTENCE OF WHITENESS AS PROPERTY

In the modern period, neither the problems attendant to assigning racial identities nor those accompanying the recognition of whiteness have disappeared. Nor has whiteness as property. Whiteness as property continues to perpetuate racial subordination through the courts' definitions of group identity and through the courts' discourse and doctrine on affirmative action. The exclusion of subordinated "others" was and remains a central part of the property interest in whiteness and, indeed, is part of the protection that the court extends to whites' settled expectations of continued privilege.

The essential character of whiteness as property remains manifest in two critical areas of the law and, as in the past, operates to oppress Native Americans and Blacks in similar ways, although in different arenas. This Part first examines the persistence of whiteness as valued social identity; then exposes whiteness as property in the law's treatment of the question of group identity, as the case of the Mashpee Indians illustrates; and finally, exposes the presence of whiteness as property in affirmative action doctrine.

A. The Persistence of Whiteness as Valued Social Identity

Even as the capacity of whiteness to deliver is arguably diminished by the elimination of rigid racial stratifications, whiteness continues to be perceived as materially significant. Because real power and wealth never have been accessible to more than a narrowly defined ruling elite, for many whites the benefits of whiteness as property, in the absence of legislated privilege, may have been reduced to a claim of relative privilege only in comparison to people of color. Nevertheless, whiteness retains its value as a "consolation prize": it does not mean that all whites will win, but simply that they will not lose, if losing is defined as being on the bottom of the social and economic hierarchy—the position to which Blacks have been consigned.

Andrew Hacker, in his 1992 book *Two Nations*, recounts the results of a recent exercise that probed the value of whiteness according to the perceptions of whites. The study asked a group of white students how much money they would seek if they were changed from white to Black. "Most seemed to feel that it would not be out of place to ask for $50 million, or $1 million for each coming black year." Whether this figure represents an accurate amortization of the societal cost of being Black in the United States, it is clear that whiteness is still perceived to be valuable. The wages of whiteness are available to all whites regardless of class position, even to those whites who are without power, money, or influence. Whiteness, the characteristic that distinguishes them from Blacks, serves as compensation even to those who lack material wealth. It is the relative political advantages extended to whites, rather than actual economic gains, that are crucial to white workers. Thus, as Kimberlé Crenshaw points out, whites have an actual stake in racism. Because Blacks are held to be inferior, although no longer on the basis of science as antecedent determinant, but by virtue of their position at the bottom, it allows whites—all whites—to "include themselves in the dominant circle. [Although most whites] hold no real power, [all can claim] their privileged racial identity."

White workers often identify primarily as white rather than as workers because it is through their whiteness that they are afforded access to a host of public, private, and psychological benefits.. It is through the concept of whiteness that class consciousness among white workers is subordinated and attention is diverted from class oppression.

Although dominant societal norms have embraced the idea of fairness and nondiscrimination, removal of privilege and antisubordination principles are actively rejected or at best ambiguously received because expectations of white privilege are bound up with what is considered essential for self-realization. Among whites, the idea persists that their whiteness is meaningful. Whiteness is an aspect of racial identity surely, but it is much more; it remains a concept based on relations of power, a social construct predicated on white dominance and Black subordination.

B. Subordination Through Denial of Group Identity

Whiteness as property is also constituted through the reification of expectations in the continued right of white-dominated institutions to control the legal meaning of group identity. This reification manifests itself in the law's dialectical misuse of the concept of group identity as it pertains to racially subordinated peoples. The law has recognized and codified racial group identity as an instrumentality of exclusion and exploitation; however, it has refused to recognize group identity when asserted by racially oppressed groups as a basis for affirming or claiming rights. The law's approach to group identity reproduces subordination, in the past through "race-ing" a group—that is, by assigning a racial identity that equated with inferior status, and in the present by erasing racial group identity.

In part, the law's denial of the existence of racial groups is predicated not only on the rejection of the ongoing presence of the past, but is also grounded on a basic tenet of liberalism—that constitutional protections inhere in individuals, not groups. As informed by the Lockean notion of the social contract, the autonomous, free will of the individual is central. Indeed, it is the individual who, in concert with other individuals, elects to enter into political society and to form a state of limited powers. This philosophical view of society is closely aligned with the antidiscrimination principle—the idea being that equality mandates only the equal treatment of individuals under the law. Within this framework, the idea of the social group has no place.

Although the law's determination of any "fact," including that of group identity, is not infinitely flexible, its studied ignorance of the issue of racial group identity insures wrong results by assuming a pseudo-objective posture that does not permit it to hear the complex dialogue concerning the identity question, particularly as it pertains to historically dominated groups.

Instead, the law holds to the basic premise that definition from above can be fair to those below, that beneficiaries of racially conferred privilege have the right to establish norms for those who have historically been oppressed pursuant to those norms, and that race is not historically contingent. Although the substance of race definitions has changed, what persists is the expectation of white-controlled institutions in the continued right to determine meaning—the reified privilege of power—that reconstitutes the property interest in whiteness in contemporary form.

In undertaking any definition of race as group identity, there are implicit and explicit normative underpinnings that must be taken into account. The "riddle of identity" is not answered by a "search for essences" or essential discoverable truth, nor by a search for mere "descriptions and redescriptions." Instead, when handling the complex issue of group identity, we should look to "purposes and effects, consequences and functions." The questions pertaining to definitions of race then are not principally biological or genetic, but social and political: what must be addressed is who is defining, how is the definition constructed, and why is the definition being propounded. Because definition is so often a central part of domination, critical thinking about these issues must precede and adjoin any definition. The law has not attended to these questions. Instead, identity of "the other" is still objectified, the complex, negotiated quality of identity is ignored, and the impact of inequitable power on identity is masked. These problems are illustrated in the land claim suit brought by the Mashpee, a Massachusetts Indian tribe.

[...]

C. Subjugation Through Affirmative Action Doctrine

The assumption that whiteness is a property interest entitled to protection is an idea born of systematic white supremacy and nurtured over the years, not only by the law of slavery and "Jim Crow," but also by the more recent decisions and rationales of the Supreme Court concerning affirmative action. In examining both the nature of the affirmative action debate and the legal analysis applied in three Supreme Court cases involving affirmative action—*Regents of University of California v. Bakke*,[23] *City of Richmond v. J.A. Croson Co.*,[24] and *Wygant v. Jackson Board of Education*,[25] it is evident that the protection of the property interest in whiteness still lies at the core of judicial and popular reasoning.

Affirmative action remains a wellspring of contention. If anything, the tone of the debate has sharpened since affirmative action programs were first introduced. The universal battle cry of the political right is that affirmative action means "quotas" for Blacks, and is an economic threat to whites. This equation, although advanced most stridently by the right, has deep resonance among many whites across the political spectrum. In according "preferences" for Blacks and other oppressed groups, affirmative action is said to be "reverse discrimination" against whites, depriving them of their right to equal protection of the laws. Lawsuits brought by white males claiming constitutional injury allegedly produced by affirmative action programs have proliferated and have garnered support in many quarters. Whites concede that Blacks were oppressed by slavery and by legalized race segregation and its aftermath, but protest that, notwithstanding this legacy of deprivation and subjugation, it is unfair to allocate the burden to innocent whites who were not involved in acts of discrimination.

The Supreme Court's rejection of affirmative action programs on the grounds that race-conscious remedial measures are unconstitutional under the Equal Protection Clause of the Fourteenth Amendment—the very constitutional measure designed to guarantee equality for Blacks—is based on the Court's chronic refusal to dismantle the institutional protection of benefits for whites that have been based on white supremacy and maintained at the expense of Blacks. As a result, the parameters of appropriate remedies are not dictated by the scope of the injury to the subjugated, but by the extent of the infringement on settled expectations of whites. These limits to remediation are grounded in the perception that the existing order based on white privilege is not only just "there," but also is a property interest worthy of protection. Thus, under this assumption, it is not only the interests of individual whites who challenge affirmative action that are protected; the interests of whites as whites are enshrined and institutionalized as a property interest that accords them a higher status than any individual claim to relief.

This protection of the property interest in whiteness is achieved by embracing the norm of colorblindness. Current legal definitions interpret race as a factor disconnected from social identity and compel abandonment of race-consciousness. Thus, at the very historical moment that race is infused with a perspective that reshapes it, through race-conscious remediation, into a potential weapon *against* subordination, official rules articulated in law deny that race matters. Simultaneously, the law upholds race as immutable and biological. The assertion that race is color and color does not matter is, of course, essential to the norm of color blindness. To define race reductively as simply color, and therefore meaningless, however, is as subordinating as defining race to be scientifically determinative of inherent deficiency. The old definition creates a false linkage between race and inferiority; the new definition denies the real linkage between race and oppression under systematic white supremacy. Distorting and denying reality, both definitions support race subordination. As Neil Gotanda has argued, color blindness is a form of race subordination in that it denies the historical context of white domination and Black subordination. This idea of race recasts privileges attendant to whiteness as legitimate race identity under "neutral" color-blind principles.

The use of color blindness as the doctrinal mode of protecting the property interest in whiteness is exemplified in three major affirmative action cases decided by the Supreme Court: *Bakke, Croson,* and *Wygant.* The underlying, although unstated, premise in each of these cases is that the expectation of white privilege is valid, and that the legal protection of that expectation is warranted. This premise legitimates prior

assumptions of the right to ongoing racialized privilege and is another manifestation of whiteness as property.

[...]

Together, these cases establish the Court's major doctrinal view of affirmative action as abnormal and against the norm of nondiscrimination. They speak the formal language of equality, but subordinate equality by vesting the expectations of whites that what is unequal in fact will be regarded as equal in law. Thus, they enshrine whiteness as property.

V. DELEGITIMATING THE PROPERTY INTEREST IN WHITENESS THROUGH AFFIRMATIVE ACTION

Within the worlds of de jure and de facto segregation, whiteness has value, whiteness is valued, and whiteness is expected to be valued in law. The legal affirmation of whiteness and white privilege allowed expectations that originated in injustice to be naturalized and legitimated. The relative economic, political, and social advantages dispensed to whites under systematic white supremacy in the United States were reinforced through patterns of oppression of Blacks and Native Americans. Materially, these advantages became institutionalized privileges, and ideologically, they became part of the settled expectations of whites—a product of the unalterable original bargain. The law masks what is chosen as natural; it obscures the consequences of social selection as inevitable. The result is that the distortions in social relations are immunized from truly effective intervention, because the existing inequities are obscured and rendered nearly invisible. The existing state of affairs is considered neutral and fair, however unequal and unjust it is in substance. Although the existing state of inequitable distribution is the product of institutionalized white supremacy and economic exploitation, it is seen by whites as part of the natural order of things that cannot legitimately be disturbed. Through legal doctrine, expectation of continued privilege based on white domination was reified; whiteness as property was reaffirmed.

The property interest in whiteness has proven to be resilient and adaptive to new conditions. Over time it has changed in form, but it has retained its essential exclusionary character and continued to distort outcomes of legal disputes by favoring and protecting settled expectations of white privilege. The law expresses the dominant conception of "rights," "equality," "property," "neutrality," and "power": rights mean shields from interference; equality means formal equality; property means the settled expectations that are to be protected; neutrality means the existing distribution, which is natural; and, power is the mechanism for guarding all of this.

One reason then for the court's hostility toward affirmative action is that it seeks to delegitimate the assumptions surrounding existing inequality. It exposes the illusion that the original or current distribution of power, property, and resources is the result of "right" and "merit." It places in tension the settled expectations of whites, based on both the ideology of white supremacy and the structure of the U.S. economy, that have operated to subordinate and hyperexploit groups identified as the "other." It opens to critique the idea that individualized and discrete claims to remedy identified discrimination will achieve the promise of equality contained in the Fourteenth Amendment. It conceives of equality in transgenerational terms, and demands a new and different sense of social responsibility in a society that defines individualism as the highest good, and the "market value" of the individual as the just and true assessment. It unmasks the limited character of rights granted by those who dominate. In a word, it is destabilizing.

Affirmative action begins the essential work of rethinking rights, power, equality, race, and property from the perspective of those whose access to each of these has been limited by their oppression. This approach follows Mari Matsuda's suggestion of "looking to the bottom" for a more humane and liberating view. From this perspective, affirmative action is required on both moral and legal grounds to delegitimate the property interest in whiteness—to dismantle the actual and expected privilege that has attended "white" skin since the founding of the country. Like "passing," affirmative action undermines the property interest in whiteness. Unlike passing, which seeks the shelter of an assumed whiteness as a means of extending protection at the margins of racial boundaries, affirmative action deprivileges whiteness and seeks to remove the legal protections of the existing hierarchy spawned by race oppression. What passing attempts to circumvent, affirmative action moves to challenge.

Rereading affirmative action to delegitimate the property interest in whiteness suggests that if, historically, the law has legitimated and protected the settled expectations of whites in white privilege, delegitimation should be accomplished not merely by implementing equal treatment, but by *equalizing* treatment among the groups that have been illegitimately privileged or unfairly subordinated by racial stratification. Obviously, the meaning of equalizing treatment would vary, because the extent of privilege and subordination is not constant with reference to all societal goods. In some instances, the advantage of race privilege to poorer whites may be materially insignificant when compared to their class disadvantage against more privileged whites. But exposing the critical core of whiteness as property as the unconstrained right to exclude directs attention toward questions of redistribution and property that are crucial under both race and class analysis. The conceptions of rights, race, property, and affirmative action as currently understood are unsatisfactory and insufficient to facilitate the self-realization of oppressed people.

Here I consider some of the preliminary issues that arise from thinking about affirmative action as a method of attacking whiteness as property. First, I examine how the property interest in whiteness has skewed the concept of affirmative action by focusing on the sin or innocence of individual white claimants with vested rights as competitors of Blacks whose rights are provisional and contingent, rather than on the broader questions of distribution of benefits and burdens. This focus improperly narrows the affirmative action debate to corrective-compensatory issues, to the exclusion of distributive issues. Asking distributive questions about affirmative action is not only conceptually warranted, but is an effective beginning to disentangling whiteness from property through refocusing on the extent to which the existing, distorted distribution results directly from racial subordination. Second, I consider and reject the argument that affirmative action amounts to the illegitimate establishment of a property interest in Blackness. Affirmative action does not embody a conception of Blackness that is the functional opposite of whiteness, because Black identity, unlike whiteness, is not derived from racial subordination. Affirmative action does not reify expectations of continued race-based privilege, for it does not implement a permanent system of unfair advantage that is then naturalized and held outside the boundaries of continued scrutiny. Finally, I argue that, unlike the property interest in whiteness that rests on the distorted notions of identity and property that afford whites the right to exclude "the other," affirmative action implies broader and more highly developed concepts of identity and property.

A. Corrective Justice, Sin, and Whiteness as Property

The distorting prism of whiteness as property further reinforces an exclusively corrective view of affirmative action claims when, in fact, affirmative action embodies aspects of both corrective and distributive justice. [...] Even when the Court has upheld affirmative action plans, it implicitly has accepted the notion that affirmative action burdens—that is, extracts compensation from—innocent whites. Proponents of affirmative action justify requiring the sons to pay for the sins of the fathers by pointing to the compelling interest in eliminating the disadvantage of the present built on the oppression of the past. Even this argument, however, accepts the notion that harm was being done. Significantly, this argument has great moral suasion in popular discourse and is the source of heated debate. The focus on innocent whites changes the affirmative action inquiry from one of rectifying the harm to Blacks to invoking legal protection for the rights of whites who are

innocent of discriminatory acts, although they have benefited from prior discrimination.

Mischaracterizing affirmative action as a claim of bipolar corrective justice between individual Black and white competitors renders invisible parties essential to the proper adjudication of the claims at issue. In some instances, when the claim is between competing Black and white applicants for limited resources, the role of the employer, state agency, or other distributor of the resources is minimized although, as decisionmakers and holders of power, they are obviously major players. In other scenarios, when a white applicant charges that he has been unfairly passed over, Blacks are at the core of the dispute but are not parties to the litigation. By disavowing the essential jurisprudential nature of affirmative action to be both corrective and distributive, conflict that is both private and public in nature becomes wholly privatized and the parties misaligned.

If affirmative action is viewed through the prism of distributive justice, the claim of white innocence no longer seems so compelling, because a distributive justice framework does not focus primarily on guilt and innocence, but rather on entitlement and fairness. Thus, distributive justice as a matter of equal protection requires that individuals receive that share of the benefits they would have secured in the absence of racism.[26] ...

B. Affirmative Action: A New Form of Status Property?

If whiteness as property is the reification, in law, of expectations of white privilege, then according privilege to Blacks through systems of affirmative action might be challenged as performing the same ideological function, only on the other side of the racial line. As evidence of a property interest in Blackness, some might point out that, recently, some whites have sought to characterize themselves as belonging to a racial minority. Equating affirmative action with whiteness as property, however, is false and can only be maintained if history is ignored or inverted and the premises inherent in the existing racial hierarchy are retained. Whiteness as property is derived from the deep historical roots of systematic white supremacy that has given rise to definitions of group identity predicated on the racial subordination of the "other," and that has reified expectations of continued white privilege. This reification differs in crucial ways from the premises, intent, and objectives of affirmative action.

Fundamentally, affirmative action does not reestablish a property interest in Blackness because Black identity is not the functional opposite of whiteness. Even today, whiteness is still intertwined with the degradation of Blacks and is still valued because "the artifact of 'whiteness' ... sets a floor on how far [whites] can fall." Acknowledging Black identity does not involve the systematic subordination of whites, nor does it even set up a danger of doing so. Affirmative action is based on principles of antisubordination, not principles of Black superiority.

The removal of white privilege pursuant to a program of affirmative action would not be implemented under an ideology of subordination, nor would it be situated in the context of historical or present exploitation of whites. It is thus not a matter of implementing systematic disadvantage to whites or installing mechanisms of group exploitation. Whites are not an oppressed people and are not at risk of becoming so. Those whites that are disadvantaged in society suffer not because of their race, but in spite of it. Refusing to implement affirmative action as a remedy for racial subordination will not alleviate the class oppression of poor whites. Indeed, failing to do so will reinforce the existing regime of race and class domination that leaves lower class whites more vulnerable to class exploitation. Affirmative action does not institute a regime of racialized hierarchy in which all whites, because they are white, are deprived of economic, social, and political benefits. It does not reverse the hierarchy, but levels the racial privilege.

Even if one rejects the notion that, properly constructed, affirmative action policies cause whites no injustice, affirmative action does not implement a set of permanent, never-ending privileges for Blacks. Affirmative action does not distort Black expectations because it does not naturalize these expectations. Because affirmative action can only be implemented through conscious

intervention and requires constant monitoring and reevaluation, it does not function behind a mask of neutrality in the realm beyond scrutiny. Affirmative action for Blacks does not reify existing patterns of privilege, nor does it produce subordination of whites as a group. If anything, it might fairly be said that affirmative action creates a property interest in *true* equal opportunity—opportunity and means that are equalized.

C. What Affirmative Action Has Been; What Affirmative Action Might Become

The truncated application of affirmative action as a policy has obscured affirmative action as a concept. The ferocious and unending debate on affirmative action cannot be understood unless the concept of affirmative action is considered and conceptually disengaged from its application in the United States.

As policy, affirmative action does not have a clearly identifiable pedigree, but was one of the limited concessions offered in official response to demands for justice pressed by Black constituencies. Despite uneven implementation in the areas of public employment, higher education, and government contracts, it translated into the attainment by Blacks of jobs, admissions to universities, and contractual opportunities. Affirmative action programs did not, however, stem the tide of growing structural unemployment and underemployment among Black workers, nor did it prevent the decline in material conditions for Blacks as a whole. Such programs did not change the subordinated status of Blacks, in part because of structural changes in the economy, and in part because the programs were not designed to do so.

However, affirmative action is more than a program: it is a principle, internationally recognized, based on a theory of rights and equality. Formal equality overlooks structural disadvantage and requires mere nondiscrimination or "equal treatment"; by contrast, affirmative action calls for *equalizing treatment* by redistributing power and resources in order to rectify inequities and to achieve real equality. The current polarized debate on affirmative action and the intense political and judicial opposition to the concept is thus grounded in the fact that, in its requirement of equalizing treatment, affirmative action implicitly challenges the sanctity of the original and derivative present distribution of property, resources, and entitlements, and directly confronts the notion that there is a protectable property interest in "whiteness." If affirmative action doctrine were freed from the constraint of protecting the property interest in whiteness, if indeed it were conceptualized from the perspective of those on the bottom, it might assist in moving away from a vision of affirmative action as an uncompensated taking and inspire a new perspective on identity as well. The fundamental precept of whiteness—the core of its value—is its exclusivity. But exclusivity is predicated not on any intrinsic characteristic, but on the existence of the symbolic "other," which functions to "create an illusion of unity" among whites. Affirmative action might challenge the notion of property and identity as the unrestricted right to exclude. In challenging the property interest in whiteness, affirmative action could facilitate the destruction of the false premises of legitimacy and exclusivity inherent in whiteness and break the distorting link between white identity and property.

Affirmative action in the South African context offers a point of comparison. It has emerged as one of the democratic movement's central demands, appearing in both the constitutional guidelines and draft Bill of Rights issued by the African National Congress. These documents simultaneously denounce all forms of discrimination and embrace affirmative action as a mechanism for rectifying the gross inequities in South African society.

The South African conception of affirmative action expands the application of affirmative action to a much broader domain than has typically been envisioned in the United States. That is, South Africans consider affirmative action a strategic measure to address directly the distribution of property and power, with particular regard to the maldistribution of land and the need for housing. This policy has not yet been clearly defined, but what is implied by this conception of affirmative action is that existing distributions of property will be modified by rectifying unjust loss and inequality. Property rights will then be respected, but they will not be absolute and will be considered against a societal requirement of affirmative action. In essence, this conception of affirmative action is moving toward the reallocation of power and the right to have a say. This conception is in fact consistent with the fundamental principle of affirmative action and effectively removes the constraint imposed in the American model that strangulates affirmative action principles by protecting the property interest in whiteness.

VI. CONCLUSION

Whiteness as property has carried and produced a heavy legacy. It is a ghost that has haunted the political and legal domains in which claims for justice have been inadequately addressed for far too long. Only rarely declaring its presence, it has warped efforts to remediate racial exploitation. It has blinded society to the systems of domination that work against so many by retaining an unvarying focus on vestiges of systemic racialized privilege that subordinates those perceived as a particularized few—the "others." It has thwarted not only conceptions of racial justice but also conceptions of property that embrace more equitable possibilities. In protecting the property interest in whiteness, property is assumed to be no more than the right to prohibit infringement on settled expectations, ignoring countervailing equitable claims that are predicated on a right to inclusion. It is long past time to put the property interest in whiteness to rest. Affirmative action can assist in that task. Affirmative action, if properly conceived and implemented, is not only consistent with norms of equality, but is essential to shedding the legacy of oppression.

NOTES

1. When I began to relate the subject matter of my research to Black friends and colleagues, in nearly every instance I was told, "I had an uncle ... I had a great aunt ... My grandfather's brother left Alabama to go North as a white man and we never saw or heard from him again," or other similar stories.

2. *See, e.g.*, Doe v. State of Louisiana, 479 So.2d 369, 371 (La. Ct. App. 1985) (rejecting the attempt by a family whose parents had been classified as "colored" to be reclassified as white).

3. I adopt here the definition of white supremacy utilized by Frances Lee Ansley:

> By "white supremacy" I do not mean to allude only to the self-conscious racism of white supremacist hate groups. I refer instead to a political, economic, and cultural system in which whites overwhelmingly control power and material resources, conscious and unconscious ideas of white superiority and entitlement are widespread, and relations of white dominance and non-white subordination are daily re-enacted across a broad array of institutions and social settings.

Frances L. Ansley, *Stirring the Ashes: Race, Class and the Future of Civil Rights Scholarship*, 74 CORNELL L. REV. 993, 1024 n.129 (1989).

4. According to John Hope Franklin, "there is no doubt that the earliest Negroes in Virginia occupied a position similar to that of the white servants in the colony." JOHN H. FRANKLIN, U.S. COMM'N ON CIVIL RIGHTS, FREEDOM TO THE FREE 71 (1963), *cited in* A. LEON HIGGINBOTHAM, JR., IN THE MATTER OF COLOR: Race and the American Legal Process 21 (1978). The legal disabilities imposed on Blacks were not dissimilar to those imposed on non-English servants of European descent, as the principal line of demarcation was between Christian and non-Christian servants. *See* Raymond T. Diamond & Robert J. Cottrol, *Codifying Caste: Louisiana's Racial Classification Scheme and the Fourteenth Amendment*, 29 Loy. L. Rev. 255, 259 n. 19 (1983). Indeed, "the word *slave* had no meaning in English law." THOMAS F. GOSSETT, RACE: THE HISTORY OF AN IDEA IN AMERICA 29 (1963). Later statutory provisions prohibited Blacks who were slaves from attaining their freedom by converting to Christianity. *See, e.g.*, Higginbotham, *supra*, at 200 (citing a South Carolina statute of 1690 that declared "no slave shall be free by becoming a christian").

5. U.S. CONST. art. 1, § 2, cl. 3.

6. 4 Ky. (1 Bibb) 97 (1815).

7. Kenneth Minogue states that property performs the critical function of identification: "[P]roperty is the concept by which we find order in things. The world is a bundle of things, and things are recognized in terms of their attributes or properties." Kenneth R. Minogue, *The Concept of Property and Its Contemporary Significance, in* NOMOS XXII: PROPERTY 3, 11 (J. Roland Pennock & John W. Chapman eds., 1980). Indeed, he suggests that it is impossible to identify anyone or anything except by reference to their properties. *See id.* at 12.

8. Thus, the Indians' claim as first possessors was said to rest on a "questionable foundation," according to John Quincy Adams, because the right of the hunter could not preempt and provide the basis for an exclusive claim for a "few hundreds" against the needs of "millions." His argument reflected a widely held consensus. GOSSETT, *supra* note 14, at 230 (citations omitted). The land that lay in the common, left "wholly to nature," was the proper subject of appropriation by one's labor because these "great tracts of ground ... [that] lie waste ... are more than the people who dwell on it do, or can make use of." JOHN LOCKE, TWO TREATISES OF GOVERNMENT 137, 139 (photo. reprint 1990) (W.S. Carpenter ed., 1924) (3d ed. 1698). The forms of land use typical of Native American peoples were fluid and communal in nature. The American courts have held that governmental seizures of Indian property held under original Indian title do not offend the Takings Clause of the Fifth Amendment. Courts have reasoned that Indian property rights were not protected by the constitutional prohibition against taking private property without just compensation because the property rights of Native Americans were communal and inhered in the tribe rather than an individual. Secondly, courts have contended that Native American people had not established possession of the lands they claimed for. Although they had hunted and fished on the land, they had never enclosed it and allotted the land to individuals. *See* Joseph W. Singer, *Sovereignty and Property*, 86 NW. U. L. REV. 1, 17–18 (1991).

9. This redefinition of possession and occupancy at the theoretical level was accompanied at the practical level by massive land dispossession that restricted Indians to reservations and designated hunting areas, established lines of demarcation by treaty that were later violated, effected land "sales" through fraud, trickery, or coercion, and led ultimately to campaigns of forced removals. *See* GOSSETT, *supra* note 14, at 228. Jefferson's Indian policy, for example, had the stated goal of

"civilizing" the Indians, which resulted in their land being taken by whites for development. The objective of making the Indians "willing to sell" was achieved by the threat of force and encouraging the exchange of lands for goods pushed on them through trading houses. [...]

10. 21 U.S. (8 Wheat.) 543 (1823).

11. Margaret Radin ascribes these concepts as the principal basis for liberal property theories propounded by John Locke, Georg W. Friedrich Hegel, and Jeremy Bentham respectively. *See* Margaret J. Radin, *Property and Personhood*, 34 STAN. L. REV. 957, 958 n.3 (1982). Munzer describes the multiplicity of definitions of property as inviting the despairing conclusion that "any overarching normative theory of property is impossible." MUNZER, *supra* note 58, at 17; *see* Thomas C. Grey, *The Disintegration of Property*, *in* NOMOS XXII: property, *supra* note 38, at 69, 69–82.

12. According to Macpherson, the common seventeenth century usage was very broad: "[M]en were said to have a property not only in land and goods and in claims on revenue from leases, mortgages, patents, monopolies and so on, but also a property in their lives and persons "Macpherson, *supra* note 52, at 7, *see* LAWRENCE BECKER, PROPERTY RIGHTS-PHILOSOPHIC FOUNDATIONS 120 n 11 (1977) (describing the use of the word "property" by Blackstone, Hobbes, and Locke to be referring to all of a person's legal rights).

13. Laura S Underkuffler, *On Property: An Essay*, 100 YALE L J. 127, 128–29 (1990).

14. I use "positionality" here in the sense employed in feminist legal theory. Positionality is a theory of knowledge, a rejection of objective, neutral truth in favor of a truth "situated and partial[,] ... emerg[ing] from particular involvements and relationships ... [that] define the individual's perspective and provide the location for meaning, identity, and political commitment." Katharine T. Bartlett, *Feminist Legal Methods*, 103 HARV. L. REV. 829, 880 (1990).

15. 397 U.S. 254 (1970).

16. Jeremy Bentham, *Security and Equality in Property, in* PROPERTY, *supra* note 52, at 51–52. Curiously, although Bentham argued strongly for the constructed nature of property, he considered the absence of property—poverty—to be natural: "Poverty is not the work of the laws; it is the primitive condition of the human race ... ." *Id.* at 52–53.

A more modern formulation of the relation between property and expectations is advanced by Macpherson, although from an opposing philosophical view. He argues that property is a right or claim that one anticipates or expects will be enforced. *See* Macpherson, *supra* note 52, at 3 ("What distinguishes property from mere momentary possession is that property is a claim that will be enforced by society or the state, by custom or convention of law."). Munzer also notes that "property, conceived as a legal structure of Hohfeldian normative modalities, makes possible legal expectations with respect to things." MUNZER, *supra* note 52, at 29.

17. There is one historical instance in which arguably whiteness was transferred. In Loving v. Virginia, 388 U.S. 1 (1967), the Supreme Court invalidated Virginia's anti-miscegenation statute that prohibited intermarriage between white persons and "colored persons" as violative of the Equal Protection Clause. *See id.* at 12. Significantly, the statute did allow intermarriage between whites and persons of white and American Indian descent. It further defined white persons as those of exclusively Caucasian origin, but granted persons with less than one-sixteenth American Indian blood the status of being white for the purposes of the statute. *See* VA. CODE ANN. § 20–54 (repealed 1968). In conferring the status of honorary white on persons of such heritage, the statute was reflecting the "desire of all to recognize as an integral and honored part of the white race the descendants of John Rolfe and Pocahontas." Bureau of Vital Statistics, *The New Family and Race Improvement*, 17 VA. HEALTH BULL., Extra No. 12, at 18, 19, 26 (New Families Series No. 5, 1925), *cited in* Walter Wadlington, *The* Loving *Case: Virginia's Anti-Miscegenation Statute in Historical Perspective*, 52 VA. L. REV. 1189, 1202 (1966). In one sense, the statute represented a legal conveyance of the property interest in whiteness to those who were technically not white, possibly to ensure the stability of a social order in which many who considered themselves white were not in fact white as defined by law.

18. There have been longstanding debates on whether one's reputation is more correctly characterized as property or liberty. *Compare* Van Alstyne, *supra* note 75, at 479 n.97 (claiming that interests in reputation, traditionally described as interests in liberty, are at least as well described as property interests) *with* MUNZER, *supra* note 52, at 46 n.9

(noting that reputation in Anglo-American law is more often described as a liberty interest than a property interest). Reputational interests, however, have been treated as interests possessing aspects of both in American law. As Robert Post indicates, the concepts of reputation manifested in the common law of defamation at different points in history include reputation as property, reputation as honor, and reputation as dignity. *See* Robert C. Post, *The Social Foundations of Defamation Law: Reputation and the Constitution,* 74 CAL. L. REV. 691, 693 (1986). Reputation is a "melange" lending itself to different descriptions over time. *Id.* at 740.

19. Radin surmises that Locke's use of person in this passage probably refers to ownership of one's physical body. *See* Radin, *supra* note 57, at 965. To construe the Lockean precept of holding property in one's person as meaning property in one's body depends on a particular theory of the person that equates persons with human bodies. However, solving the riddle of the meaning of person is not an essential predicate to recognizing whiteness as property because whatever the concept of personhood, whiteness was bound up with identity and liberty in both private and public spheres.

20. "Hypodescent" is the term used by anthropologist Marvin Harris to describe the American system of racial classification in which the subordinate classification is assigned to the offspring if there is one "superordinate" and one "subordinate" parent.

Under this system, the child of a Black parent and a white parent is Black. MARVIN HARRIS, PATTERNS OF RACE IN THE AMERICAS 37, 56 (1964).

21. 163 U.S. 537 (1896).
22. 347 U.S. 483 (1954).
23. 438 U.S. 265 (1978).
24. 488 U.S. 469 (1989).
25. 467 U.S. 267 (1986).
26. If one assumes relative equality of abilities among the races at birth, then it is only racial subordination that can explain the fact that Blacks have not secured the proportion of society's benefits that they would be expected to have based on their numbers in society. *But see* Posner, *supra* note 251, at 17 ("Many groups are underrepresented in various occupations for reasons of taste, opportunity, or aptitude unrelated to discrimination. There is no basis for a presumption that but for past discrimination … minorities … would supply [a proportional] percent of the nation's lawyers."). Fiscus argues that, if one accepts relative group equality in ability at birth, then race-correlated differences must be due to societal factors that differentiate along racial lines — racism. *See* Fiscus, *supra* note 254, at 24. He rejects the racial ethnicity argument "because any racially correlated variation in taste, opportunity, or aptitude can *only* be explained by either innate racial differences or pervasive societal recognition of race and differential behavior based on it—*i.e., de facto* discrimination." *Id.* at 27.

CHAPTER SEVEN

Is There an Obligation to Obey the Law?

21 Crito

PLATO

Socrates: Here already, Crito? Surely it is still early?

Crito: Indeed it is.

Socrates: About what time?

Crito: Just before dawn.

Socrates: I wonder that the warder paid any attention to you.

Crito: He is used to me now, Socrates, because I come here so often. Besides, he is under some small obligation to me.

Socrates: Have you only just come, or have you been here for long?

Crito: Fairly long.

Socrates: Then why didn't you wake me at once, instead of sitting by my bed so quietly?

Crito: I wouldn't dream of such a thing, Socrates. I only wish I were not so sleepless and depressed myself. I have been wondering at you, because I saw how comfortably you were sleeping, and I deliberately didn't wake you because I wanted you to go on being as comfortable as you could. I have often felt before in the course of my life how fortunate you are in your disposition, but I feel it more than ever now in your present misfortune when I see how easily and placidly you put up with it.

Socrates: Well, really, Crito, it would be hardly suitable for a man of my age to resent having to die.

Crito: Other people just as old as you are get involved in these misfortunes, Socrates, but their age doesn't keep them from resenting it when they find themselves in your position.

Socrates: Quite true. But tell me, why have you come so early?

Crito: Because I bring bad news, Socrates—not so bad from your point of view, I suppose, but it will be very hard to bear for me and your other friends, and I think that I shall find it hardest of all.

Socrates: Why, what is this news? Has the boat come in from Delos—the boat which ends my reprieve when it arrives?

Crito: It hasn't actually come in yet, but I expect that it will be here today, judging from the report of some people who have just arrived from Sunium and left it there. It's quite clear

Hugh Tredennick, trans. From Edith Hamilton and Huntington Cairnes, eds., *The Collected Dialogues of Plato* (Princeton, N.J.: Princeton University Press, 1961). ©1961 Princeton University Press. Reprinted by permission of Princeton University Press.

from their account that it will be here today, and so by tomorrow, Socrates, you will have to … to end your life.

Socrates: Well, Crito, I hope that it may be for the best. If the gods will it so, so be it. All the same, I don't think it will arrive today.

Crito: What makes you think that?

Socrates: I will try to explain. I think I am right in saying that I have to die on the day after the boat arrives?

Crito: That's what the authorities say, at any rate.

Socrates: Then I don't think it will arrive on this day that is just beginning, but on the day after. I am going by a dream that I had in the night, only a little while ago. It looks as though you were right not to wake me up.

Crito: Why, what was the dream about?

Socrates: I thought I saw a gloriously beautiful woman dressed in white robes, who came up to me and addressed me in these words: Socrates, "To the pleasant land of Phthia on the third day thou shalt come."[1]

Crito: Your dream makes no sense, Socrates.

Socrates: To my mind, Crito, it is perfectly clear.

Crito: Too clear, apparently. But look here, Socrates, it is still not too late to take my advice and escape. Your death means a double calamity for me. I shall not only lose a friend whom I can never possibly replace, but besides, a great many people who don't know you and me very well will be sure to think that I let you down, because I could have saved you if I had been willing to spend the money. And what could be more contemptible than to get a name for thinking more of money than of your friends? Most people will never believe that it was you who refused to leave this place although we tried our hardest to persuade you.

Socrates: But my dear Crito, why should we pay so much attention to what "most people" think? The really reasonable people, who have more claim to be considered, will believe that the facts are exactly as they are.

Crito: You can see for yourself, Socrates, that one has to think of popular opinion as well. Your present position is quite enough to show that the capacity of ordinary people for causing trouble is not confined to petty annoyances,

but has hardly any limits if you once get a bad name with them.

Socrates: I only wish that ordinary people *had* an unlimited capacity for doing harm; then they might have an unlimited power for doing good, which would be a splendid thing, if it were so. Actually they have neither. They cannot make a man wise or stupid; they simply act at random.

Crito: Have it that way if you like, but tell me this, Socrates. I hope that you aren't worrying about the possible effects on me and the rest of your friends, and thinking that if you escape we shall have trouble with informers for having helped you to get away, and have to forfeit all our property or pay an enormous fine, or even incur some further punishment? If any idea like that is troubling you, you can dismiss it altogether. We are quite entitled to run that risk in saving you, and even worse, if necessary. Take my advice, and be reasonable.

Socrates: All that you say is very much in my mind, Crito, and a great deal more besides.

Crito: Very well, then, don't let it distress you. I know some people who are willing to rescue you from here and get you out of the country for quite a moderate sum. And then surely you realize how cheap these informers are to buy off; we shan't need much money to settle them, and I think you've got enough of my money for yourself already. And then even supposing that in your anxiety for my safety you feel that you oughtn't to spend my money, there are these foreign gentlemen staying in Athens who are quite willing to spend theirs. One of them, Simmias of Thebes, has actually brought the money with him for this very purpose, and Cebes and a number of others are quite ready to do the same. So, as I say, you mustn't let any fears on these grounds make you slacken your efforts to escape, and you mustn't feel any misgivings about what you said at your trial—that you wouldn't know what to do with yourself if you left this country. Wherever you go, there are plenty of places where you will find a welcome, and if you choose to go to Thessaly, I have friends there who will make much of you and give you complete protection, so that no one in Thessaly can interfere with you.

Besides, Socrates, I don't even feel that it is right for you to try to do what you are doing, throwing away your life when you might save it. You are doing your best to treat yourself in exactly the same way as your enemies would, or rather did, when they wanted to ruin you. What is more, it seems to me that you are letting your sons down too. You have it in your power to finish their bringing-up and education, and instead of that you are proposing to go off and desert them, and so far as you are concerned they will have to take their chance. And what sort of chance are they likely to get? The sort of thing that usually happens to orphans when they lose their parents. Either one ought not to have children at all, or one ought to see their upbringing and education through to the end. It strikes me that you are taking the line of least resistance, whereas you ought to make the choice of a good man and a brave one, considering that you profess to have made goodness your object all through life. Really, I am ashamed, both on your account and on ours, your friends'. It will look as though we had played something like a coward's part all through this affair of yours. First there was the way you came into court when it was quite unnecessary—that was the first act. Then there was the conduct of the defense—that was the second. And finally, to complete the farce, we get this situation, which makes it appear that we have let you slip out of our hands through some lack of courage and enterprise on our part, because we didn't save you, and you didn't save yourself, when it would have been quite possible and practicable, if we had been any use at all.

There, Socrates, if you aren't careful, besides the suffering there will be all this disgrace for you and us to bear. Come, make up your mind. Really it's too late for that now; you ought to have it made up already. There is no alternative; the whole thing must be carried through during this coming night. If we lose any more time, it can't be done; it will be too late. I appeal to you, Socrates, on every ground; take my advice and please don't be unreasonable!

Socrates: My dear Crito, I appreciate your warm feelings very much—that is, assuming that they have some justification. If not, the stronger they are, the harder they will be to deal with. Very well, then, we must consider whether we ought to follow your advice or not. You know that this is not a new idea of mine; it has always been my nature never to accept advice from any of my friends unless reflection shows that it is the best course that reason offers. I cannot abandon the principles which I used to hold in the past simply because this accident has happened to me; they seem to me to be much as they were, and I respect and regard the same principles now as before. So unless we can find better principles on this occasion, you can be quite sure that I shall not agree with you—not even if the power of the people conjures up fresh hordes of bogies to terrify our childish minds, by subjecting us to chains and executions and confiscations of our property.

Well, then, how can we consider the question most reasonably? Suppose that we begin by reverting to this view which you hold about people's opinions. Was it always right to argue that some opinions should be taken seriously but not others? Or was it always wrong? Perhaps it was right before the question of my death arose, but now we can see clearly that it was a mistaken persistence in a point of view which was really irresponsible nonsense. I should like very much to inquire into this problem, Crito, with your help, and to see whether the argument will appear in any different light to me now that I am in this position, or whether it will remain the same, and whether we shall dismiss it or accept it.

Serious thinkers, I believe, have always held some such view as the one which I mentioned just now, that some of the opinions which people entertain should be respected, and others should not. Now I ask you, Crito, don't you think that this is a sound principle? You are safe from the prospect of dying tomorrow, in all human probability, and you are not likely to have your judgment upset by this impending calamity. Consider, then, don't you think that this is a sound enough principle, that one should not regard all the opinions that people hold, but only some and not others? What do you say? Isn't that a fair statement?

Crito: Yes, it is.

Socrates: In other words, one should regard the good ones and not the bad?

Crito: Yes.

Socrates: The opinions of the wise being good, and the opinions of the foolish bad?

Crito: Naturally.

Socrates: To pass on, then, what do you think of the sort of illustration that I used to employ? When a man is in training, and taking it seriously, does he pay attention to all praise and criticism and opinion indiscriminately, or only when it comes from the one qualified person, the actual doctor or trainer?

Crito: Only when it comes from the one qualified person.

Socrates: Then he should be afraid of the criticism and welcome the praise of the one qualified person, but not those of the general public.

Crito: Obviously.

Socrates: So he ought to regulate his actions and exercises and eating and drinking by the judgment of his instructor, who has expert knowledge, rather than by the opinions of the rest of the public.

Crito: Yes, that is so.

Socrates: Very well. Now if he disobeys the one man and disregards his opinion and commendations, and pays attention to the advice of the many who have no expert knowledge, surely he will suffer some bad effect?

Crito: Certainly.

Socrates: And what is this bad effect? Where is it produced? I mean, in what part of the disobedient person?

Crito: His body, obviously; that is what suffers.

Socrates: Very good. Well now, tell me, Crito—we don't want to go through all the examples one by one—does this apply as a general rule, and above all to the sort of actions which we are trying to decide about, just and unjust, honorable and dishonorable, good and bad? Ought we to be guided and intimidated by the opinion of the many or by that of the one—assuming that there is someone with expert knowledge? Is it true that we ought to respect and fear this person more than all the rest put together, and that if we do not follow his guidance we shall spoil and mutilate that part of us which, as we used to say, is improved by right conduct and destroyed by wrong? Or is this all nonsense?

Crito: No, I think it is true, Socrates.

Socrates: Then consider the next step. There is a part of us which is improved by healthy actions and ruined by unhealthy ones. If we spoil it by taking the advice of nonexperts, will life be worth living when this part is once ruined? The part I mean is the body. Do you accept this?

Crito: Yes.

Socrates: Well, is life worth living with a body which is worn out and ruined in health?

Crito: Certainly not.

Socrates: What about the part of us which is mutilated by wrong actions and benefited by right ones? Is life worth living with this part ruined? Or do we believe that this part of us, whatever it may be, in which right and wrong operate, is of less importance than the body?

Crito: Certainly not.

Socrates: It is really more precious?

Crito: Much more.

Socrates: In that case, my dear fellow, what we ought to consider is not so much what people in general will say about us but how we stand with the expert in right and wrong, the one authority, who represents the actual truth. So in the first place your proposition is not correct when you say that we should consider popular opinion in questions of what is right and honorable and good, or the opposite. Of course one might object: All the same, the people have the power to put us to death.

Crito: No doubt about that! Quite true, Socrates. It is a possible objection.

Socrates: But so far as I can see, my dear fellow, the argument which we have just been through is quite unaffected by it. At the same time I should like you to consider whether we are still satisfied on this point, that the really important thing is not to live; but to live well.

Crito: Why, yes.

Socrates: And that to live well means the same thing as to live honorably or rightly?

Crito: Yes.

Socrates: Then in the light of this agreement we must consider whether or not it is right for me to try to get away without an official discharge. If it turns out to be right, we must make the attempt; if not, we must let it drop. As for the considerations you raise about expense and reputation and bringing up children, I am afraid, Crito, that they represent the reflections of the ordinary public, who put people to death, and would bring them back to life if they could, with equal indifference to reason. Our real duty, I fancy, since the argument leads that way, is to consider one question only, the one which we raised just now. Shall we be acting rightly in paying money and showing gratitude to these people who are going to rescue me, and in escaping or arranging the escape ourselves, or shall we really be acting wrongly in doing all this? If it becomes clear that such conduct is wrong, I cannot help thinking that the question whether we are sure to die, or to suffer any other ill effect for that matter, if we stand our ground and take no action, ought not to weigh with us at all in comparison with the risk of doing what is wrong.

Crito: I agree with what you say, Socrates, but I wish you would consider what we ought to *do*.

Socrates: Let us look at it together, my dear fellow; and if you can challenge any of my arguments, do so and I will listen to you; but if you can't, be a good fellow and stop telling me over and over again that I ought to leave this place without official permission. I am very anxious to obtain your approval before I adopt the course which I have in mind. I don't want to act against your convictions. Now give your attention to the starting point of this inquiry—I hope that you will be satisfied with my way of stating it—and try to answer my questions to the best of your judgment.

Crito: Well, I will try.

Socrates: Do we say that one must never willingly do wrong, or does it depend upon circumstances? Is it true, as we have often agreed before, that there is no sense in which wrongdoing is good or honorable? Or have we jettisoned all our former convictions in these last few days? Can you and I at our age, Crito, have spent all these years in serious discussions without realizing that we were no better than a pair of children? Surely the truth is just what we have always said. Whatever the popular view is, and whether the alternative is pleasanter than the present one or even harder to bear, the fact remains that to do wrong is in every sense bad and dishonorable for the person who does it. Is that our view, or not?

Crito: Yes, it is.

Socrates: Then in no circumstances must one do wrong.

Crito: No.

Socrates: In that case one must not even do wrong when one is wronged, which most people regard as the natural course.

Crito: Apparently not.

Socrates: Tell me another thing, Crito. Ought one to do injuries or not?

Crito: Surely not, Socrates.

Socrates: And tell me, is it right to do an injury in retaliation, as most people believe, or not?

Crito: No, never.

Socrates: Because, I suppose, there is no difference between injuring people and wronging them.

Crito: Exactly.

Socrates: So one ought not to return a wrong or an injury to any person, whatever the provocation is. Now be careful, Crito, that in making these single admissions you do not end by admitting something contrary to your real beliefs. I know that there are and always will be few people who think like this, and consequently between those who do think so and those who do not there can be no agreement on principle; they must always feel contempt when they observe one another's decisions.

I want even you to consider very carefully whether you share my views and agree with me, and whether we can proceed with our discussion from the established hypothesis that it is never right to do a wrong or return a wrong or defend oneself against injury by retaliation, or whether you dissociate yourself from any share in this view as a basis for discussion. I have held it for a long time, and still hold it, but if you have formed any other opinion, say so and tell me what it is. If, on the other hand, you stand by what we have said, listen to my next point.

Crito: Yes, I stand by it and agree with you. Go on.

Socrates: Well, here is my next point, or rather question. Ought one to fulfill all one's agreements, provided that they are right, or break them?

Crito: One ought to fulfill them.

Socrates: Then consider the logical consequence. If we leave this place without first persuading the state to let us go, are we or are we not doing an injury, and doing it in a quarter where it is least justifiable? Are we or are we not abiding by our just agreements?

Crito: I can't answer your question, Socrates. I am not clear in my mind.

Socrates: Look at it in this way. Suppose that while we were preparing to run away from here—or however one should describe it—the laws and constitution of Athens were to come and confront us and ask this question: Now, Socrates, what are you proposing to do? Can you deny that by this act which you are contemplating you intend, so far as you have the power, to destroy us, the laws, and the whole state as well? Do you imagine that a city can continue to exist and not be turned upside down, if the legal judgments which are pronounced in it have no force but are nullified and destroyed by private persons?

How shall we answer this question, Crito, and others of the same kind? There is much that could be said, especially by a professional advocate, to protest against the invalidation of this law which enacts that judgments once pronounced shall be binding. Shall we say: Yes,

I do intend to destroy the laws, because the state wronged me by passing a faulty judgment at my trial? Is this to be our answer, or what?

Crito: What you have just said, by all means, Socrates.

Socrates: Then what supposing the laws say: Was there provision for this in the agreement between you and us, Socrates? Or did you undertake to abide by whatever judgments the state pronounced?

If we expressed surprise at such language, they would probably say: Never mind our language, Socrates, but answer our questions; after all, you are accustomed to the method of question and answer. Come now, what charge do you bring against us and the state, that you are trying to destroy us? Did we not give you life in the first place? Was it not through us that your father married your mother and begot you? Tell us, have you any complaint against those of us laws that deal with marriage?

No, none, I should say.

Well, have you any against the laws which deal with children's upbringing and education, such as you had yourself? Are you not grateful to those of us laws which were instituted for this end, for requiring your father to give you a cultural and physical education?

Yes, I should say.

Very good. Then since you have been born and brought up and educated, can you deny, in the first place, that you were our child and servant, both you and your ancestors? And if this is so, do you imagine that what is right for us is equally right for you, and that whatever we try to do to you, you are justified in retaliating? You did not have equality of rights with your father, or your employer—supposing that you had had one—to enable you to retaliate. You were not allowed to answer back when you were scolded or to hit back when you were beaten, or to do a great many other things of the same kind. Do you expect to have such license against your country and its laws that if we try to put you to death in the belief that it is right to do so, you on your part will try your hardest to destroy your country and us its laws in return? And will you, the true devotee of goodness, claim that you are justified in doing so? Are you so wise as to have forgotten that compared with your mother and father and all the rest of your ancestors your country is something far more precious, more venerable, more sacred, and held in greater honor both among gods and among all reasonable men? Do you not realize that you are even more bound to respect and placate the anger of your country than your father's anger? That if you cannot persuade your country you must do whatever it orders, and patiently submit to any punishment that it imposes, whether it be flogging or imprisonment? And if it leads you out to war, to be wounded or killed, you must comply, and it is right that you should do so. You must not give way or retreat or abandon your position. Both in war and in the lawcourts and everywhere else you must do whatever your city and your country command, or else persuade them in accordance with universal justice, but violence is a sin even against your parents, and it is a far greater sin against your country.

What shall we say to this, Crito—that what the laws say is true, or not?

Crito: Yes, I think so.

Socrates: Consider, then: Socrates, the laws would probably continue, whether it is also true for us to say that what you are now trying to do to us is not right. Although we have brought you into the world and reared you and educated you, and given you and all your fellow citizens a share in all the good things at our disposal, nevertheless by the very fact of granting our permission we openly proclaim this principle, that any Athenian, on attaining to manhood and seeing for himself the political organization of the state and us its laws, is permitted, if he is not satisfied with us, to take his property and go away wherever he likes. If any of you chooses to go to one of our colonies, supposing that he should not be satisfied with us and the state, or to emigrate to any other country, not one of us laws hinders or prevents him from going away wherever he likes, without any loss of property. On the other hand, if any one of you stands his ground when he can see how we administer justice and the rest of our public organization, we hold that by so doing he has in fact undertaken to do anything that we tell him. And we maintain that anyone who disobeys is guilty of doing wrong on three separate counts: first because we are his parents, and secondly because we are his guardians, and thirdly because, after promising obedience, he is neither obeying us nor persuading us to change our decision if we are at fault in any way. And although all our orders are in the form of proposals, not of savage commands, and we give him the choice of either persuading us or doing what we say, he is actually doing neither. These are the charges, Socrates, to which we say that you will be liable if you do what you are contemplating, and you will not be the least culpable of your fellow countrymen, but one of the most guilty.

If I asked why, they would no doubt pounce upon me with perfect justice and point out that there are very few people in Athens who have entered into this agreement with them as explicitly as I have. They would say: Socrates, we have substantial evidence that you are satisfied with us and with the state. You would not have been so exceptionally reluctant to cross the borders of your country if you had not been exceptionally attached to it. You have never left the city to attend a festival or for any other purpose, except on some military expedition. You have never traveled abroad as other people do, and you have never felt the impulse to acquaint yourself with another country or constitution. You have been content with us and with our city. You have definitely chosen us, and undertaken to observe us in all your activities as a citizen, and as the crowning proof that you are satisfied with our city, you have begotten children in it. Furthermore, even at the time of your trial you could have proposed the penalty of banishment, if you had chosen to do so—that is, you could have done then with the sanction of the state what you are now trying to do without it. But whereas at that time you made a noble show of indifference if you had to die, and in fact preferred death, as you said, to banishment, now you show no respect for your earlier professions, and no regard for us, the laws, whom you are trying to destroy. You are behaving like the lowest type of menial, trying to run away in spite of the contracts and undertakings by which you agreed to live as a member of our state. Now first answer this question: Are we or are we not speaking the truth when we say that you have undertaken, in deed if not in word, to live your life as a citizen in obedience to us?

What are we to say to that, Crito? Are we not bound to admit it?

Crito: We cannot help it, Socrates.

Socrates: It is a fact, then, they would say, that you are breaking covenants and undertakings made with us, although you made them under no compulsion or misunderstanding, and were not compelled to decide in a limited time. You had seventy years in which you could have left the country, if you were not satisfied with us or felt that the agreements were unfair. You did not choose Sparta or Crete—your favorite models of good government—or any other Greek or foreign state. You could not have absented yourself from the city less if you had been lame or blind or decrepit in some other way. It is quite obvious that you stand by yourself above all other Athenians in your affection for this city and for us its laws. Who would care for a city without laws? And now, after all this, are you not going to stand by your agreement? Yes, you are, Socrates, if you will take our advice, and then you will at least escape being laughed at for leaving the city.

We invite you to consider what good you will do to yourself or your friends if you commit this breach of faith and stain your conscience. It is fairly obvious that the risk of being banished and either losing their citizenship or having their property confiscated will extend to your friends as well. As for yourself, if you go to one of the neighboring states, such as Thebes or Megara, which are both well governed, you will enter them as an enemy to their constitution, and all good patriots will eye you with suspicion as a destroyer of law and order. Incidentally you will confirm the opinion of the jurors who tried you that they gave a correct verdict; a destroyer of laws might very well be supposed to have a destructive influence upon young and foolish human beings. Do you intend, then, to avoid well-governed states and the higher forms of human society? And if you do, will life be worth living? Or will you approach these people and have the impudence to converse with them? What arguments will you use, Socrates? The same which you used here, that goodness and integrity, institutions and laws, are the most precious possessions of mankind? Do you not think that Socrates and everything about him will appear in a disreputable light? You certainly ought to think so.

But perhaps you will retire from this part of the world and go to Crito's friends in Thessaly? That is the home of indiscipline and laxity, and no doubt they would enjoy hearing the amusing story of how you managed to run away from prison by arraying yourself in some costume or putting on a shepherd's smock or some other conventional runaway's disguise, and altering your personal appearance. And will no one comment on the fact that an old man of your age, probably with only a short time left to live, should dare to cling so greedily to life, at the price of violating the most stringent laws? Perhaps not, if you avoid irritating anyone. Otherwise, Socrates, you will hear a good many humiliating comments. So you will live as the toady and slave of all the populace, literally "roistering in Thessaly," as though you had left this country for Thessaly to attend a banquet there. And where will your discussions about goodness and uprightness be then, we should like to know? But of course you want to live for your children's sake, so that you may be able to bring them up and educate them. Indeed! By first taking them off to Thessaly and making foreigners of them, so that they may have that additional enjoyment? Or if that is not your intention, supposing that they are brought up here with you still alive, will they be better cared for and educated without you, because of course your friends will look after them? Will they look after your children if you go away to Thessaly, and not if you go away to the next world? Surely if those who profess to be your friends are worth anything, you must believe that they would care for them.

No, Socrates, be advised by us your guardians, and do not think more of your children or of your life or of anything else than you think of what is right, so that when you enter the next world you may have all this to plead in your defense before the authorities there. It seems clear that if you do this thing, neither you nor any of your friends will be the better for it or be more upright or have a cleaner conscience here in this world, nor will it be better for you when you reach the next. As it is, you will leave this place, when you do, as the victim of a wrong done not by us, the laws, but by your fellow men. But if you leave in that dishonorable way, returning wrong for wrong and evil for evil, breaking your agreements and covenants with us, and injuring those whom you least ought to injure—yourself, your friends, your country, and us—then you will have to face our anger in your lifetime, and in that place beyond when the laws of the other world know that you have tried, so far as you could, to destroy even us their brothers, they will not receive you with a kindly welcome. Do not take Crito's advice, but follow ours.

That, my dear friend Crito, I do assure you, is what I seem to hear them saying, just as a mystic seems to hear the strains of music, and the sound of their arguments rings so loudly in my head that I cannot hear the other side. I warn you that, as my opinion stands at present, it will be useless to urge a different view. However, if you think that you will do any good by it, say what you like.

Crito: No, Socrates, I have nothing to say.

Socrates: Then give it up, Crito, and let us follow this course, since God points out the way.

NOTES

1. Iliad 9, 363.

22   Letter from Birmingham Jail

MARTIN LUTHER KING, JR.

April 16, 1963 My Dear Fellow Clergymen:

While confined here in the Birmingham city jail, I came across your recent statement calling my present activities "unwise and untimely." Seldom do I pause to answer criticism of my work and ideas. If I sought to answer all the criticisms that cross my desk, my secretaries would have little time for anything other than such correspondence in the course of the day, and I would have no time for constructive work. But since I feel that you are men of genuine good will and that your criticisms are sincerely set forth, I want to try to answer your statement in what I hope will be patient and reasonable terms.

I think I should indicate why I am here in Birmingham, since you have been influenced by the view which argues against "outsiders coming in." I have the honor of serving as president of the Southern Christian Leadership Conference, an organization operating in every southern state, with headquarters in Atlanta, Georgia. We have some eighty-five affiliated organizations across the South, and one of them is the Alabama Christian Movement for Human Rights. Frequently we share staff, educational, and financial resources with our affiliates. Several months ago the affiliate here in Birmingham asked us to be on call to engage in a nonviolent direct-action program if such were deemed necessary. We readily consented, and when the hour came we lived up to our promise. So I, along with several members of my staff, am here because I was invited here. I am here because I have organizational ties here.

But more basically, I am in Birmingham because injustice is here. Just as the prophets of the eighth century B.C. left their villages and carried their "thus saith the Lord" far beyond the boundaries of their home towns, and just as the Apostle Paul left his village of Tarsus and carried the gospel of Jesus Christ to the far corners of the Greco-Roman world, so am I compelled to carry the gospel of freedom beyond my own home town. Like Paul, I must constantly respond to the Macedonian call for aid.

Moreover, I am cognizant of the interrelatedness of all communities and states. I cannot sit idly by in Atlanta and not be concerned about what happens in Birmingham. Injustice anywhere is a threat to justice everywhere. We are caught in an inescapable network of mutuality, tied in a single garment of destiny. Whatever affects one directly, affects all indirectly. Never again can we afford to live with the narrow, provincial "outside agitator" idea. Anyone who lives inside the United States can never be considered an outsider anywhere within its bounds.

You deplore the demonstrations taking place in Birmingham. But your statement, I am sorry to say, fails to express a similar concern for the conditions that brought about the demonstrations. I am sure that none of you would want to rest content with the superficial kind of social analysis that deals merely with effects and does not grapple with underlying causes. It is unfortunate that demonstrations are taking place in Birmingham, but it is even more unfortunate that the city's white power structure left the Negro community with no alternative.

In any nonviolent campaign there are four basic steps: collection of the facts to determine whether injustices exist; negotiation; self-purification; and

direct action. We have gone through all these steps in Birmingham. There can be no gainsaying the fact that racial injustice engulfs this community. Birmingham is probably the most thoroughly segregated city in the United States. Its ugly record of brutality is widely known. Negroes have experienced grossly unjust treatment in the courts. There have been more unsolved bombings of Negro homes and churches in Birmingham than in any other city in the nation. These are the hard, brutal facts of the case. On the basis of these conditions, Negro leaders sought to negotiate with the city fathers. But the latter consistently refused to engage in good-faith negotiation.

Then, last September, came the opportunity to talk with leaders of Birmingham's economic community. In the course of the negotiations, certain promises were made by the merchants—for example, to remove the stores' humiliating racial signs. On the basis of these promises, the Reverend Fred Shuttlesworth and the leaders of the Alabama Christian Movement for Human Rights agreed to a moratorium on all demonstrations. As the weeks and months went by, we realized that we were the victims of a broken promise. A few signs, briefly removed, returned; the others remained.

As in so many past experiences, our hopes had been blasted, and the shadow of deep disappointment settled upon us. We had no alternative except to prepare for direct action, whereby we would present our very bodies as a means of laying our case before the conscience of the local and the national community. Mindful of the difficulties involved, we decided to undertake a process of self-purification. We began a series of workshops on nonviolence, and we repeatedly asked ourselves: "Are you able to accept blows without retaliating?" "Are you able to endure the ordeal of jail?" We decided to schedule our direct-action program for the Easter season, realizing that except for Christmas, this is the main shopping period of the year. Knowing that a strong economic-withdrawal program would be the by-product of direct action, we felt that this would be the best time to bring pressure to bear on the merchants for the needed change.

Then it occurred to us that Birmingham's mayoral election was coming up in March, and we speedily decided to postpone action until after election day. When we discovered that the Commissioner of Public Safety, Eugene "Bull" Connor, had piled up enough votes to be in the run-off, we decided again to postpone action until the day after the run-off so that the demonstrations could not be used to cloud the issues. Like many others, we waited to see Mr. Connor defeated, and to this end we endured postponement after postponement. Having aided in this community need, we felt that our direct-action program could be delayed no longer.

You may well ask: "Why direct action? Why sit-ins, marches and so forth? Isn't negotiation a better path?" You are quite right in calling for negotiation. Indeed, this is the very purpose of direct action. Nonviolent direct action seeks to create such a crisis and foster such a tension that a community which has constantly refused to negotiate is forced to confront the issue. It seeks so to dramatize the issue that it can no longer be ignored. My citing the creation of tension as part of the work of the nonviolent resister may sound rather shocking. But I must confess that I am not afraid of the word *tension*. I have earnestly opposed violent tension, but there is a type of constructive, nonviolent tension which is necessary for growth. Just as Socrates felt that it was necessary to create a tension in the mind so that individuals could rise from the bondage of myths and half-truths to the unfettered realm of creative analysis and objective appraisal, so must we see the need for nonviolent gadflies to create the kind of tension in society that will help men rise from the dark depths of prejudice and racism to the majestic heights of understanding and brotherhood.

The purpose of our direct-action program is to create a situation so crisis-packed that it will inevitably open the door to negotiation. I therefore concur with you in your call for negotiation. Too long has our beloved Southland been bogged down in a tragic effort to live in monologue rather than dialogue.

One of the basic points in your statement is that the action that I and my associates have taken in Birmingham is untimely. Some have asked: "Why didn't you give the new city administration time to act?" The only answer that I can give to this query is that the new Birmingham administration must be prodded about as much as the outgoing one, before it will act. We are sadly mistaken if we feel that the election of Albert Boutwell as mayor will bring the millennium to Birmingham. While Mr. Boutwell is a much more gentle person than Mr. Connor, they are both segregationists, dedicated to maintenance of the status quo. I have hope that Mr. Boutwell will be reasonable enough to see the futility of massive resistance to desegregation. But he will not see this without pressure from devotees of civil rights. My friends, I must say to you that we have not made a single gain in civil rights without determined legal and nonviolent pressure. Lamentably, it is an historical fact that privileged groups seldom give up their privileges voluntarily. Individuals may see the moral light and voluntarily give up their unjust posture; but, as Reinhold Niebuhr has reminded us, groups tend to be more immoral than individuals.

We know through painful experience that freedom is never voluntarily given by the oppressor; it must be demanded by the oppressed. Frankly, I have yet to engage in a direct-action campaign that was "well timed" in the view of those who have not suffered unduly from the disease of segregation. For years now I have heard the word "Wait!" It rings in the ear of every Negro with piercing familiarity. This "Wait" has almost always meant "Never." We must come to see, with one of our distinguished jurists, that "justice too long delayed is justice denied."

We have waited for more than 340 years for our constitutional and God-given rights. The nations of Asia and Africa are moving with jetlike speed toward gaining political independence, but we still creep at horse-and-buggy pace toward gaining a cup of coffee at a lunch counter. Perhaps it is easy for those who have never felt the stinging darts of segregation to say, "Wait." But when you have seen vicious mobs lynch your mothers and fathers at will and drown your sisters and brothers at whim; when you have seen hate-filled policemen curse, kick, and even kill your black brothers and sisters; when you see the vast majority of your twenty million Negro brothers smothering in an airtight cage of poverty in the midst of an affluent society; when you suddenly find your tongue twisted and your speech stammering as you seek to explain to your six-year-old daughter why she can't go to the public amusement park that has just been advertised on television, and see tears welling up in her eyes when she is told that Funtown is closed to colored children, and see ominous clouds of inferiority beginning to form in her little mental sky, and see her beginning to distort her personality by developing an unconscious bitterness toward white people; when you have to concoct an answer for a five-year-old son who is asking: "Daddy, why do white people treat colored people so mean?"; when you take a cross-country drive and find it necessary to sleep night after night in the uncomfortable corners of your automobile because no motel will accept you; when you are humiliated day in and day out by nagging signs reading "white" and "colored"; when your first name becomes "nigger," your middle name becomes "boy" (however old you are), and your last name becomes "John," and your wife and mother are never given the respected title "Mrs."; when you are harried by day and haunted by night by the fact that you are a Negro, living constantly at tiptoe stance, never quite knowing what to expect next, and are plagued with inner fears and outer resentments; when you are forever fighting a degenerating sense of "nobodiness"—then you will understand why we find it difficult to wait. There comes a time when the cup of endurance runs over, and men are no longer willing to be plunged into the abyss of despair. I hope, sirs, you can understand our legitimate and unavoidable impatience.

You express a great deal of anxiety over our willingness to break laws. This is certainly a legitimate concern. Since we so diligently urge people to obey the Supreme Court's decision of 1954 outlawing segregation in the public schools, at first glance it may seem rather paradoxical for us

consciously to break laws. One may well ask: "How can you advocate breaking some laws and obeying others?" The answer lies in the fact that there are two types of laws: just and unjust. I would be the first to advocate obeying just laws. One has not only a legal but a moral responsibility to obey just laws. Conversely, one has a moral responsibility to disobey unjust laws. I would agree with St. Augustine that "an unjust law is no law at all."

Now, what is the difference between the two? How does one determine whether a law is just or unjust? A just law is a man-made code that squares with the moral law or the law of God. An unjust law is a code that is out of harmony with the moral law. To put it in the terms of St. Thomas Aquinas: An unjust law is a human law that is not rooted in eternal and natural law. Any law that uplifts human personality is just. Any law that degrades human personality is unjust. All segregation statutes are unjust because segregation distorts the soul and damages the personality. It gives the segregator a false sense of superiority and the segregated a false sense of inferiority. Segregation, to use the terminology of the Jewish philosopher Martin Buber, substitutes an "I-it" relationship for an "I-thou" relationship and ends up relegating persons to the status of things. Hence segregation is not only politically, economically, and sociologically unsound, it is morally wrong and sinful. Paul Tillich has said that sin is separation. Is not segregation an existential expression of man's tragic separation, his awful estrangement, his terrible sinfulness? Thus it is that I can urge men to obey the 1954 decision of the Supreme Court, for it is morally right; and I can urge them to disobey segregation ordinances, for they are morally wrong.

Let us consider a more concrete example of just and unjust laws. An unjust law is a code that a numerical or power majority group compels a minority group to obey but does not make binding on itself. This is *difference* made legal. By the same token, a just law is a code that a majority compels a minority to follow and that it is willing to follow itself. This is *sameness* made legal.

Let me give another explanation. A law is unjust if it is inflicted on a minority that, as a result of being denied the right to vote, had no part in enacting or devising the law. Who can say that the legislature of Alabama which set up that state's segregation laws was democratically elected? Throughout Alabama all sorts of devious methods are used to prevent Negroes from becoming registered voters, and there are some counties in which, even though Negroes constitute a majority of the population, not a single Negro is registered. Can any law enacted under such circumstances be considered democratically structured?

Sometimes a law is just on its face and unjust in its application. For instance, I have been arrested on a charge of parading without a permit. Now, there is nothing wrong in having an ordinance which requires a permit for a parade. But such an ordinance becomes unjust when it is used to maintain segregation and to deny citizens the First Amendment privilege of peaceful assembly and protest.

I hope you are able to see the distinction I am trying to point out. In no sense do I advocate evading or defying the law, as would the rabid segregationist. That would lead to anarchy. One who breaks an unjust law must do so openly, lovingly, and with a willingness to accept the penalty. I submit that an individual who breaks a law that conscience tells him is unjust, and who willingly accepts the penalty of imprisonment in order to arouse the conscience of the community over its injustice, is in reality expressing the highest respect for law.

Of course, there is nothing new about this kind of civil disobedience. It was evidenced sublimely in the refusal of Shadrach, Meshach, and Abednego to obey the laws of Nebuchadnezzar, on the ground that a higher moral law was at stake. It was practiced superbly by the early Christians, who were willing to face hungry lions and the excruciating pain of chopping blocks rather than submit to certain unjust laws of the Roman Empire. To a degree, academic freedom is a reality today because Socrates practiced civil disobedience. In our own nation, the Boston Tea Party represented a massive act of civil disobedience.

We should never forget that everything Adolf Hitler did in Germany was "legal" and everything the Hungarian freedom fighters did in Hungary was "illegal." It was "illegal" to aid and comfort a Jew in Hitler's Germany. Even so, I am sure that, had I lived in Germany at the time, I would have aided and comforted my Jewish brothers. If today I lived in a Communist country where certain principles dear to the Christian faith are suppressed, I would openly advocate disobeying that country's antireligious laws. I must make two honest confessions to you, my Christian and Jewish brothers. First, I must confess that over the past few years I have been gravely disappointed with the white moderate. I have almost reached the regrettable conclusion that the Negro's great stumbling block in his stride toward freedom is not the White Citizen's Counciler or the Ku Klux Klanner, but the white moderate, who is more devoted to "order" than to justice; who prefers a negative peace which is the absence of tension to a positive peace which is the presence of justice; who constantly says: "I agree with you in the goal you seek, but I cannot agree with your methods of direct action"; who paternalistically believes he can set the timetable for another man's freedom; who lives by a mythical concept of time and who constantly advises the Negro to wait for a "more convenient season." Shallow understanding from people of good will is more frustrating than absolute misunderstanding from people of ill will. Lukewarm acceptance is much more bewildering than outright rejection.

I had hoped that the white moderate would understand that law and order exist for the purpose of establishing justice and that when they fail in this purpose they become the dangerously structured dams that block the flow of social progress. I had hoped that the white moderate would understand that the present tension in the South is a necessary phase of the transition from an obnoxious negative peace, in which the Negro passively accepted his unjust plight, to a substantive and positive peace, in which all men will respect the dignity and worth of human personality. Actually, we who engage in nonviolent direct action are not the creators of tension. We merely bring to the surface the hidden tension that is already alive. We bring it out in the open, where it can be seen and dealt with. Like a boil that can never be cured so long as it is covered up but must be opened with all its ugliness to the natural medicines of air and light, injustice must be exposed, with all the tension its exposure creates, to the light of human conscience and the air of national opinion before it can be cured.

In your statement you assert that our actions, even though peaceful, must be condemned because they precipitate violence. But is this a logical assertion? Isn't this like condemning a robbed man because his possession of money precipitated the evil act of robbery? Isn't this like condemning Socrates because his unswerving commitment to truth and his philosophical inquiries precipitated the act by the misguided populace in which they made him drink hemlock? Isn't this like condemning Jesus because his unique God-consciousness and never-ceasing devotion to God's will precipitated the evil act of crucifixion? We must come to see that, as the federal courts have consistently affirmed, it is wrong to urge an individual to cease his efforts to gain his basic constitutional rights because the quest may precipitate violence. Society must protect the robbed and punish the robber.

I had also hoped that the white moderate would reject the myth concerning time in relation to the struggle for freedom. I have just received a letter from a white brother in Texas. He writes: "All Christians know that the colored people will receive equal rights eventually, but it is possible that you are in too great a religious hurry. It has taken Christianity almost two thousand years to accomplish what it has. The teachings of Christ take time to come to earth." Such an attitude stems from a tragic misconception of time, from the strangely irrational notion that there is something in the very flow of time that will inevitably cure all ills. Actually, time itself is neutral; it can be used either destructively or constructively. More and more I feel that the people of ill will have used time much more effectively than have the people of good will. We will have to repent in this generation not merely for the hateful words and actions of the bad people but for the appalling silence of the good people. Human progress never rolls in on wheels of inevitability; it comes through

the tireless efforts of men willing to be coworkers with God, and without this hard work, time itself becomes an ally of the forces of social stagnation. We must use time creatively, in the knowledge that the time is always ripe to do right. Now is the time to make real the promise of democracy and transform our pending national elegy into a creative psalm of brotherhood. Now is the time to lift our national policy from the quicksand of racial injustice to the solid rock of human dignity.

You speak of our activity in Birmingham as extreme. At first I was rather disappointed that fellow clergymen would see my nonviolent efforts as those of an extremist. I began thinking about the fact that I stand in the middle of two opposing forces in the Negro community. One is a force of complacency, made up in part of Negroes who, as a result of long years of oppression, are so drained of self-respect and a sense of "somebodiness" that they have adjusted to segregation; and in part of a few middle-class Negroes who, because of a degree of academic and economic security and because in some ways they profit by segregation, have become insensitive to the problems of the masses. The other force is one of bitterness and hatred, and it comes perilously close to advocating violence. It is expressed in the various black nationalist groups that are springing up across the nation, the largest and best-known being Elijah Muhammad's Muslim movement. Nourished by the Negro's frustration over the continued existence of racial discrimination, this movement is made up of people who have lost faith in America, who have absolutely repudiated Christianity, and who have concluded that the white man is an incorrigible "devil."

I have tried to stand between these two forces, saying that we need emulate neither the "do-nothingism" of the complacent nor the hatred and despair of the black nationalist. For there is the more excellent way of love and nonviolent protest. I am grateful to God that, through the influence of the Negro church, the way of nonviolence became an integral part of our struggle.

If this philosophy had not emerged, by now many streets of the South would, I am convinced, be flowing with blood. And I am further convinced that if our white brothers dismiss as "rabble-rousers" and "outside agitators" those of us who employ nonviolent direct action, and if they refuse to support our nonviolent efforts, millions of Negroes will, out of frustration and despair, seek solace and security in black-nationalist ideologies—a development that would inevitably lead to a frightening racial nightmare. Oppressed people cannot remain oppressed forever. The yearning for freedom eventually manifests itself, and that is what has happened to the American Negro. Something within has reminded him of his birthright of freedom, and something without has reminded him that it can be gained. Consciously or unconsciously, he has been caught up by the zeitgeist, and with his black brothers of Africa and his brown and yellow brothers of Asia, South America, and the Caribbean, the United States Negro is moving with a sense of great urgency toward the promised land of racial justice. If one recognizes this vital urge that has engulfed the Negro community, one should readily understand why public demonstrations are taking place. The Negro has many pent-up resentments and latent frustrations, and he must release them. So let him march; let him make prayer pilgrimages to the city hall; let him go on freedom rides—and try to understand why he must do so. If his repressed emotions are not released in nonviolent ways, they will seek expression through violence; this is not a threat but a fact of history. So I have not said to my people: "Get rid of your discontent." Rather, I have tried to say that this normal and healthy discontent can be channeled into the creative outlet of nonviolent direct action. And now this approach is being termed extremist.

But though I was initially disappointed at being categorized as an extremist, as I continued to think about the matter I gradually gained a measure of satisfaction from the label. Was not Jesus an extremist for love: "Love your enemies, bless them that curse you, do good to them that hate you, and pray for them which despitefully use you, and persecute you." Was not Amos an extremist

for justice: "Let justice roll down like waters and righteousness like an ever-flowing stream." Was not Paul an extremist for the Christian gospel: "I bear in my body the marks of the Lord Jesus." Was not Martin Luther an extremist: "Here I stand; I cannot do otherwise, so help me God." And John Bunyan: "I will stay in jail to the end of my days before I make a butchery of my conscience." And Abraham Lincoln: "This nation cannot survive half slave and half free." And Thomas Jefferson: "We hold these truths to be self-evident, that all men are created equal...." So the question is not whether we will be extremists, but what kind of extremists we will be. Will we be extremists for hate or for love? Will we be extremists for the preservation of injustice or for the extension of justice? In that dramatic scene on Calvary's hill three men were crucified. We must never forget that all three were crucified for the same crime—the crime of extremism. Two were extremists for immorality, and thus fell below their environment. The other, Jesus Christ, was an extremist for love, truth, and goodness, and thereby rose above his environment. Perhaps the South, the nation, and the world are in dire need of creative extremists.

I had hoped that the white moderate would see this need. Perhaps I was too optimistic; perhaps I expected too much. I suppose I should have realized that few members of the oppressor race can understand the deep groans and passionate yearnings of the oppressed race, and still fewer have the vision to see that injustice must be rooted out by strong, persistent, and determined action. I am thankful, however, that some of our white brothers in the South have grasped the meaning of this social revolution and committed themselves to it. They are still all too few in quantity, but they are big in quality. Some—such as Ralph McGill, Lillian Smith, Harry Golden, James McBride Dabbs, Ann Braden, and Sarah Patton Boyle—have written about our struggle in eloquent and prophetic terms. Others have marched with us down nameless streets of the South. They have languished in filthy, roach-infested jails, suffering the abuse and brutality of policemen who view them as "dirty nigger-lovers." Unlike so many of their moderate brothers and sisters, they have recognized the urgency of the moment and sensed the need for powerful "action" antidotes to combat the disease of segregation.

Let me take note of my other major disappointment. I have been so greatly disappointed with the white church and its leadership. Of course, there are some notable exceptions. I am not unmindful of the fact that each of you has taken some significant stands on this issue. I commend you, Reverend Stallings, for your Christian stand on this past Sunday, in welcoming Negroes to your worship service on a nonsegregated basis. I commend the Catholic leaders of this state for integrating Spring Hill College several years ago.

But despite these notable exceptions, I must honestly reiterate that I have been disappointed with the church. I do not say this as one of those negative critics who can always find something wrong with the church. I say this as a minister of the gospel, who loves the church; who was nurtured in its bosom; who has been sustained by its spiritual blessings, and who will remain true to it as long as the cord of life shall lengthen.

When I was suddenly catapulted into the leadership of the bus protest in Montgomery, Alabama, a few years ago, I felt we would be supported by the white church. I felt that the white ministers, priests, and rabbis of the South would be among our strongest allies. Instead, some have been outright opponents, refusing to understand the freedom movement and misrepresenting its leaders; all too many others have been more cautious than courageous and have remained silent behind the anesthetizing security of stained-glass windows.

In spite of my shattered dreams, I came to Birmingham with the hope that the white religious leadership of this community would see the justice of our cause and, with deep moral concern, would serve as the channel through which our just grievances could reach the power structure. I had hoped that each of you would understand. But again I have been disappointed.

I have heard numerous southern religious leaders admonish their worshippers to comply with a desegregation decision because it is the law, but I have longed to hear white ministers declare: "Follow this decree because integration is morally right and because the Negro is your brother." In the midst of blatant injustices inflicted upon the Negro, I have watched white churchmen stand on the sidelines and mouth pious irrelevancies and sanctimonious trivialities. In the midst of a mighty struggle to rid our nation of racial and economic injustice, I have heard many ministers say: "Those are social issues, with which the gospel has no real concern." And I have watched many churches commit themselves to a completely otherworldly religion which makes a strange, unbiblical distinction between body and soul, between the sacred and the secular.

I have traveled the length and breadth of Alabama, Mississippi, and all the other southern states. On sweltering summer days and crisp autumn mornings I have looked at the South's beautiful churches with their lofty spires pointing heavenward. I have beheld the impressive outlines of her massive religious education buildings. Over and over I have found myself asking: "What kind of people worship here? Who is their God? Where were their voices when the lips of Governor Barnett dripped with words of interposition and nullification? Where were they when Governor Wallace gave a clarion call for defiance and hatred? Where were their voices of support when bruised and weary Negro men and women decided to rise from the dark dungeons of complacency to the bright hills of creative protest?"

Yes, these questions are still in my mind. In deep disappointment I have wept over the laxity of the church. But be assured that my tears have been tears of love. There can be no deep disappointment where there is not deep love. Yes, I love the church. How could I do otherwise? I am in the rather unique position of being the son, the grandson, and the great-grandson of preachers. Yes, I see the church as the body of Christ. But, oh! How we have blemished and scarred that body through social neglect and through fear of being nonconformists.

There was a time when the church was very powerful—in the time when the early Christians rejoiced at being deemed worthy to suffer for what they believed. In those days the church was not merely a thermometer that recorded the ideas and principles of popular opinion; it was a thermostat that transformed the mores of society. Whenever the early Christians entered a town, the people in power became disturbed and immediately sought to convict the Christians for being "disturbers of the peace" and "outside agitators." But the Christians pressed on, in the conviction that they were "a colony of heaven," called to obey God rather than man. Small in number, they were big in commitment. They were too God-intoxicated to be "astronomically intimidated." By their effort and example they brought an end to such ancient evils as infanticide and gladiatorial contests.

Things are different now. So often the contemporary church is a weak, ineffectual voice with an uncertain sound. So often it is an archdefender of the status quo. Far from being disturbed by the presence of the church, the power structure of the average community is consoled by the church's silent—and often even vocal—sanction of things as they are.

But the judgment of God is upon the church as never before. If today's church does not recapture the sacrificial spirit of the early church, it will lose its authenticity, forfeit the loyalty of millions, and be dismissed as an irrelevant social club with no meaning for the twentieth century. Every day I meet young people whose disappointment with the church has turned into outright disgust.

Perhaps I have once again been too optimistic. Is organized religion too inextricably bound to the status quo to save our nation and the world? Perhaps I must turn my faith to the inner spiritual church, the church within the church, as the true *ekklesia* and the hope of the world. But again I am thankful to God that some noble souls from the ranks of organized religion have broken loose from the paralyzing chains of conformity and joined us as active partners in the struggle for freedom. They have left their secure congregations and walked the streets of Albany, Georgia, with us. They have gone down the highways of the South on tortuous rides for freedom. Yes, they have gone to jail with us. Some have been dismissed from their churches, have lost the support of their bishops and fellow ministers. But they have acted in the faith that right defeated is stronger than evil triumphant. Their witness has been the spiritual salt that has preserved the true meaning of the gospel in these troubled times. They have carved a tunnel of hope through the dark mountain of disappointment.

I hope the church as a whole will meet the challenge of this decisive hour. But even if the church does not come to the aid of justice, I have no despair about the future. I have no fear about the outcome of our struggle in Birmingham, even if our motives are at present misunderstood. We will reach the goal of freedom in Birmingham and all over the nation, because the goal of America is freedom. Abused and scorned though we may be, our destiny is tied up with America's destiny. Before the pilgrims landed at Plymouth, we were here. Before the pen of Jefferson etched the majestic words of the Declaration of Independence across the pages of history, we were here. For more than two centuries our forebears labored in this country without wages; they made cotton king; they built the homes of their masters while suffering gross injustice and shameful humiliation—and yet out of a bottomless vitality they continued to thrive and develop. If the inexpressible cruelties of slavery could not stop us, the opposition we now face will surely fail. We will win our freedom because the sacred heritage of our nation and the eternal will of God are embodied in our echoing demands.

Before closing I feel impelled to mention one other point in your statement that has troubled me profoundly. You warmly commended the Birmingham police force for keeping "order" and "preventing violence." I doubt you would have so warmly commended the police force if you had seen its dogs sinking their teeth into unarmed, nonviolent Negroes. I doubt that you would so quickly commend the policemen if you were to observe their ugly and inhumane treatment of Negroes here in the city jail; if you were to watch them push and curse old Negro women and young Negro girls; if you were to see them slap and kick old Negro men and young boys; if you were to observe them, as they did on two occasions, refuse to give us food because we wanted to sing our grace together. I cannot join you in your praise of the Birmingham police department.

It is true that the police have exercised a degree of discipline in handling the demonstrators. In this sense they have conducted themselves rather "nonviolently" in public. But for what purpose? To preserve the evil system of segregation. Over the past few years I have consistently preached that nonviolence demands that the means we use must be as pure as the ends we seek. I have tried to make clear that it is wrong to use immoral means to attain moral ends. But now I must affirm that it is just as wrong, or perhaps even more so, to use moral means to preserve immoral ends. Perhaps Mr. Connor and his policemen have been rather nonviolent in public, as was Chief Pritchett in Albany, Georgia, but they have used the moral means of nonviolence to maintain the immoral end of racial injustice. As T. S. Eliot has said: "The last temptation is the greatest treason: To do the right deed for the wrong reason."

I wish you had commended the Negro sit-inners and demonstrators of Birmingham for their sublime courage, their willingness to suffer, and their amazing discipline in the midst of great provocation. One day the South will recognize its real heroes. They will be the James Merediths, with the noble sense of purpose that enables them to face jeering and hostile mobs, and with the agonizing loneliness that characterizes the life of the pioneer. They will be old, oppressed, battered Negro women, symbolized in a seventy-two-year-old woman in Montgomery, Alabama, who rose up with a sense of dignity and with her people decided not to ride segregated buses, and who responded with ungrammatical profundity

to one who inquired about her weariness: "My feets is tired, but my soul is at rest." They will be the young high school and college students, the young ministers of the gospel, and a host of their elders, courageously and nonviolently sitting in at lunch counters and willingly going to jail for conscience's sake. One day the South will know that when these disinherited children of God sat down at lunch counters, they were in reality standing up for what is best in the American dream and for the most sacred values in our Judaeo-Christian heritage, thereby bringing our nation back to those great wells of democracy which were dug deep by the founding fathers in their formulation of the Constitution and the Declaration of Independence.

Never before have I written so long a letter. I'm afraid it is much too long to take your precious time. I can assure you that it would have been much shorter if I had been writing from a comfortable desk, but what else can one do when he is alone in a narrow jail cell, other than write long letters, think long thoughts, and pray long prayers?

If I have said anything in this letter that overstates the truth and indicates an unreasonable impatience, I beg you to forgive me. If I have said anything that understates the truth and indicates my having a patience that allows me to settle for anything less than brotherhood, I beg God to forgive me.

I hope this letter finds you strong in the faith. I also hope that circumstances will soon make it possible for me to meet each of you, not as an integrationist or a civil-rights leader but as a fellow clergyman and a Christian brother. Let us all hope that the dark clouds of racial prejudice will soon pass away and the deep fog of misunderstanding will be lifted from our fear-drenched communities, and in some not too distant tomorrow the radiant stars of love and brotherhood will shine over our great nation with all their scintillating beauty.

Yours for the cause of Peace and
Brotherhood,
Martin Luther King, Jr.

23　Is There a Prima Facie Obligation to Obey the Law?

M. B. E. SMITH

It isn't a question of whether it was legal or illegal. That isn't enough. The question is, what is morally wrong?
—RICHARD NIXON, *"Checkers Speech,"* 1952

Many political philosophers have thought it obvious that there is a prima facie obligation to obey the law; and so, in discussing this obligation, they have thought their task to be more that of explaining its basis than of arguing for its existence. John Rawls has, for example, written:

> I shall assume, as requiring no argument, that there is, at least in a society such as ours, a moral obligation to obey the law, although it may, of course, be overriden in certain cases by other more stringent obligations.[1]

As against this, I suggest that it is not at all obvious that there is such an obligation, that this is something that must be shown, rather than so blithely assumed. Indeed, were he uninfluenced by conventional wisdom, a reflective man might on first considering the question be inclined to deny any such obligation. As H. A. Prichard once remarked, "the mere receipt of an order backed by force seems, if anything, to give rise to the duty of resisting, rather than obeying."[2]

I shall argue that, although those subject to a government often have a prima facie obligation to obey particular laws (e.g., when disobedience has seriously untoward consequences or involves an act that is *malum in se*), they have no prima facie obligation to obey all its laws. I do not hope to prove this contention beyond a reasonable doubt. My goal is rather the more modest one of showing that it is a reasonable position to maintain by first criticizing arguments that purport to establish the obligation and then presenting some positive argument against it.

First, however, I must explain how I use the phrase "prima facie obligation." I shall say that a person *S* has a prima facie obligation to do an act *X* if, and only if, there is a moral reason for *S* to do *X* which is such that, unless he has a moral reason not to do *X* at least as strong as his reason to do *X, S*'s failure to do *X* is wrong.[3] In this discussion it also will be convenient to distinguish two kinds of prima facie obligation via the difference between the two kinds of statement which ascribe them. A specific statement asserts that some particular person has a prima facie obligation to perform some particular act. In contrast, a generic statement (e.g., "Parents have a prima facie obligation to care for their infant children") asserts that everyone who meets a certain description has a prima facie obligation to perform a certain kind of act whenever he has an opportunity to do so. I shall therefore say that a person *S* has a *specific* prima facie obligation to do *X* if, and only if, the specific statement "*S* has a prima facie obligation to do *X*" is true; and that he has a *generic* prima facie obligation to do *X* if, and only if, *S* meets some description D and the generic statement "Those who are D have a prima facie obligation to do *X*" is true.[4]

Now, the question of whether there is a prima facie obligation to obey the law is clearly about a generic obligation. Everyone, even the anarchist,

Reprinted by permission of the Yale Law Journal Company and William S. Hein Company from The Yale Law Journal, Vol. 82, pages 950–973.

would agree that in many circumstances individuals have specific prima facie obligations to obey specific laws. Since it is clear that there is in most circumstances a specific prima facie obligation to refrain from murder, rape, or breach of contract, it is plain that in these circumstances each of us has a specific prima facie obligation not to violate laws which prohibit these acts. Again, disobeying the law often has seriously untoward consequences; and, when this is so, virtually everyone would agree that there is a specific prima facie obligation to obey. Therefore, the interesting question about our obligation vis-à-vis the law is not "Do individual citizens ever have specific prima facie obligations to obey particular laws?," but rather "Is the moral relation of any government to its citizens such that they have a prima facie obligation to do certain things merely because they are legally required to do so?" This is, of course, equivalent to asking "Is there a generic prima facie obligation to obey the law?" Hereafter, when I use the phrase "the prima facie obligation to obey the law" I shall be referring to a generic obligation.

One final point in clarification: As used here, the phrase "prima facie" bears a different meaning than it does when used in legal writing. In legal materials, the phrase frequently refers to evidence sufficiently persuasive so as to require rebuttal. Hence, were a lawyer to ask "Is there a prima facie obligation to obey the law?" a reasonable interpretation of his question might be "May a reasonable man take mere illegality to be sufficient evidence that an act is morally wrong, so long as there is no specific evidence tending to show it is right?" Let us call this the "lawyer's question." Now, the question of primary concern in this inquiry is "Is there any society in which mere illegality is a moral reason for an act's being wrong?" The difference between these questions is that, were there a prima facie obligation to obey the law in the lawyer's sense, mere illegality would, in the absence of specific evidence to the contrary, be evidence of wrongdoing, but it would not necessarily be relevant to a determination of whether lawbreaking is wrong where there is reason to think such conduct justified or even absolutely obligatory. In contrast, if there is a prima facie obligation to obey the law in the sense in which I am using the phrase, the mere illegality of an act is always relevant to the determination of its moral character, despite whatever other reasons are present.[5] Hence, there may be a prima facie obligation to obey the law in the lawyer's sense and yet be no such obligation in the sense of the phrase used here. Near the end of this article I shall return briefly to the lawyer's question; for the present, I raise it only that it may not be confused with the question I wish to examine.

I.

The arguments I shall examine fall into three groups: First, those which rest on the benefits each individual receives from government; second, those relying on implicit consent or promise; third, those which appeal to utility or the general good. I shall consider each group in turn.

Of those in the first group, I shall begin with the argument from gratitude. Although they differ greatly in the amount of benefits they provide, virtually all governments do confer substantial benefits on their subjects. Now, it is often claimed that, when a person accepts benefits from another, he thereby incurs a debt of gratitude toward his benefactor. Thus, if it be maintained that obedience to the law is the best way of showing gratitude toward one's government, it may with some plausibility be concluded that each person who has received benefits from his government has a prima facie obligation to obey the law.

On reflection, however, this argument is unconvincing. First, it may reasonably be doubted whether most citizens have an obligation to act gratefully toward their government. Ordinarily, if someone confers benefits on me without any consideration of whether I want them, and if he does this in order to advance some purpose other than promotion of my particular welfare, I have no obligation to be grateful toward him. Yet the most important benefits of government are not accepted by its citizens, but rather are enjoyed regardless of whether they are wanted. Moreover, a government typically confers these benefits, not to advance the interests of particular citizens, but rather as a consequence of advancing some purpose of its own. At times, its motives are wholly admirable, as when it seeks to promote the general welfare; at others, they are less so, as when it seeks to stay in power by catering to the demands of some powerful faction. But, such motives are irrelevant: Whenever government forces benefits on me for reasons other than my particular welfare, I clearly am under no obligation to be grateful to it.

Second, even assuming arguendo that each citizen has an obligation to be grateful to his government, the argument still falters. It is perhaps true that cheerful and willing obedience is the best way to show one's gratitude toward government, in that it makes his gratitude unmistakable. But, when a person owes a debt of gratitude toward another, he does not necessarily acquire a prima facie obligation to display his gratitude in the most convincing manner: A person with demanding, domineering parents might best display his gratitude toward them by catering to their every whim, but he surely has no prima facie obligation to do so. Without undertaking a lengthy case-by-case examination, one cannot delimit the prima facie obligation of acting gratefully, for its existence and extent depends on such factors as the nature of the benefits received, the manner in which they are conferred, the motives of the benefactor, and so forth. But, even without such an examination, it is clear that the mere fact that a person has conferred on me even the most momentous benefits does not establish his right to dictate all of my behavior; nor does it establish that I always have an obligation to consider his wishes when I am deciding what I shall do. If, then, we have a prima facie obligation to act gratefully toward government, we undoubtedly have an obligation to promote its interests when this does not involve great sacrifice on our part, and to respect some of its wishes concerning that part of our behavior which does not directly affect its interests. But, our having this obligation to be grateful surely does not establish that we have a prima facie obligation to obey the law.

A more interesting argument from the benefits individuals receive from government is the argument from fair play. It differs from the argument from gratitude in contending that the prima facie obligation to obey the law is owed, not to one's government but rather to one's fellow citizens. Versions of this argument have been offered by H. L. A. Hart and John Rawls.

According to Hart, the mere existence of cooperative enterprise gives rise to a certain prima facie obligation. He argues that:

> [W]hen a number of persons conduct any joint enterprise according to rules and thus restrict their liberty, those who have submitted to these restrictions when required have a right to a similar submission from those who have benefitted by their submission. The rules may provide that officials should have authority to enforce obedience and make further rules, and this will create a structure of legal rights and duties, but the moral obligation to obey the rules in such circumstances is due to the cooperating members of the society, and they have the correlative moral right to obedience.[6]

Rawls's account of this obligation in his essay, *Legal Obligation and the Duty of Fair Play*,[7] is rather more complex. Unlike Hart, he sets certain requirements on the kinds of cooperative enterprise that give rise to the obligation: First, that success of the enterprise depends on near-universal obedience to its rules, but not on universal cooperation; second, that obedience to its rules involves some sacrifice, in that obeying the rules restricts one's liberty; and finally, that the enterprise conform to the principles of justice.[8] Rawls also offers an explanation of the obligation: He argues that, if a person benefits from participating in such an enterprise and if he intends to continue receiving its benefits, he acts unfairly when he refuses to obey its rules. With Hart, however, Rawls claims that this obligation is owed not to the enterprise itself, nor to its officials, but rather to those members whose obedience has made the benefits possible. Hart and Rawls also agree that this obligation of fair play—"fair play" is Rawls's term—is a fundamental obligation, not derived from utility or from mutual promise or consent.[9] Finally, both Hart and Rawls conceive of legal systems, at least those in democratic societies, as complex practices of the kind that give rise to the obligation of fair play; and they conclude that those who benefit from such legal systems have a prima facie obligation to obey their laws.

These arguments deserve great respect. Hart and Rawls appear to have isolated a kind of prima facie obligation overlooked by other philosophers, and thereby have made a significant contribution to moral theory. However, the significance of their discovery to jurisprudence is less clear. Although Hart and Rawls have discovered the obligation of fair play, they do not properly appreciate its limits. Once these limits are understood, it is clear that the prima facie obligation to obey the law cannot be derived from the duty of fair play.

The obligation of fair play seems to arise most clearly within small, voluntary cooperative enterprises. Let us suppose that a number of persons have gone off into the wilderness to carve out a new society; and that they have adopted certain rules to govern their communal life. Their enterprise meets Rawls's requirements on success, sacrifice, and justice. We now can examine the moral situation of the members of that community in a number of circumstances, taking seriously Hart's insistence that cooperating members have a right to the obedience of others, and Rawls's explanation of this right and its correlative obligation on grounds of fairness.

Let us take two members of the community, A and B. B, we may suppose, has never disobeyed the rules and A has benefitted from B's previous submission. Has B a right to A's obedience? It would seem necessary to know the consequences of A's obedience. If, in obeying the rules, A will confer on B a benefit roughly equal to those he has received from B, it would be plainly unfair for A to withhold it from B; and so, in this instance, B's right to A's obedience is clear. Similarly, if, in disobeying the rule, A will harm the community, B's right to A's obedience is again clear. This is because in harming the community A will harm B indirectly, by threatening the existence or efficient functioning of an institution on which B's vital interests depend. Since A has benefitted from B's previous submission to the rules, it is unfair for A to do something that will lessen B's chances of receiving like benefits in the future. However, if A's compliance with some particular rule does not benefit B, and if his disobedience will not harm the community, it is difficult to see how fairness to B could dictate that A must comply. Surely, the fact that A has benefitted from B's submission does not give B the right to insist that A obey when B's interests are unaffected. A may in this situation have an obligation to obey, perhaps because he has promised or because his disobedience would be unfair to some other member; but, if he does disobey, he has surely not been unfair to B.

We may generalize from these examples. Considerations of fairness apparently do show that, when cooperation is perfect and when each member has benefitted from the submission of every other, each member of an enterprise has a prima facie obligation to obey its rules when obedience benefits some other member or when disobedience harms the enterprise. For, if in either circumstance a member disobeys, he is unfair to at least one other member and is perhaps unfair to them all. However, if a member disobeys when his obedience would have benefitted no other member, and when his disobedience does no harm, his moral situation is surely different. If his disobedience is then unfair, it must be unfair to the group but not to any particular member. But this, I take it, is impossible: Although the moral properties of a group are not always a simple function of the moral properties of its members, it is evident that one cannot be unfair to a group without being unfair to any of its members. It would seem, then, that even when cooperation is perfect, considerations of fairness do not establish that members of a cooperative enterprise have a simple obligation to obey all of its rules, but have rather the more complex obligation to obey when obedience benefits some other member, or when disobedience harms the enterprise. This does not, it is worth noting, reduce the obligation of fair play to a kind of utilitarian obligation, for it may well be that fair play will dictate in certain circumstances that a man obey when disobedience would have better consequences. My point is merely that the obligation of fair play governs a man's actions only when some benefit or harm turns on whether he obeys. Surely, this is as should be, for questions of fairness typically arise from situations in which burdens or benefits are distributed or in which some harm is done.

The obligation of fair play is therefore much more complex than Hart or Rawls seem to have imagined. Indeed, the obligation is even more complex than the above discussion suggests, for the assumption of perfect cooperation is obviously unrealistic. When that assumption is abandoned, the effect of previous disobedience considered, and the inevitable disparity among the various members' sacrifice in obeying the rules taken into account, the scope of the obligation is still further limited; we then shall find that it requires different things of different members, depending on their previous pattern of compliance and the amount of sacrifice they have made.[10] These complications need not detain us, however, for they do not affect the fact that fairness requires obedience only in situations where noncompliance would withhold benefits from someone or harm the enterprise. Now it must be conceded that all of this makes little difference when we confine our attention to small, voluntary, cooperative enterprises. Virtually any disobedience may be expected to harm such enterprises to some extent, by diminishing the confidence of other members in its probable success and therefore reducing their incentive to work diligently toward it. Moreover, since they are typically governed by a relatively small number of rules, none of which ordinarily require behavior that is useless to other members, we may expect that when a member disobeys he will probably withhold a benefit from some other member, and that he has in the past benefitted significantly from that member's obedience. We may therefore expect that virtually every time the rules of a small, voluntary enterprise call on a member to obey, he will have a specific prima facie obligation to do so because of his obligation of fair play.

In the case of legal systems, however, the complexity of the obligation makes a great deal of difference. Although their success may depend on the "habit of obedience" of a majority of their subjects, all legal systems are designed to cope with a substantial amount of disobedience.[11] Hence, individual acts of disobedience to the law only rarely have an untoward effect on legal systems. What is more, because laws necessarily must be designed to cover large numbers of cases, obedience to the law often benefits no one. Perhaps the best illustration is obedience of the traffic code: Very often I benefit no one when I stop at

a red light or observe the speed limit. Finally, virtually every legal system contains a number of pointless or even positively harmful laws, obedience to which either benefits no one or, worse still, causes harm. Laws prohibiting homosexual activity or the dissemination of birth control information are surely in this category. Hence, even if legal systems are the kind of cooperative enterprise that gives rise to the obligation of fair play, in a great many instances that obligation will not require that we obey specific laws. If, then, there is a generic prima facie obligation to obey the laws of any legal system, it cannot rest on the obligation of fair play. The plausibility of supposing that it does depends on an unwarranted extrapolation from what is largely true of our obligations within small, cooperative enterprises to what must always be true of our obligations within legal systems.

In his recent book, Rawls has abandoned the argument from fair play as proof that the entire citizenry of even just governments has a prima facie obligation to obey the law. He now distinguishes between obligations (e.g., to be fair or to keep promises) and natural duties (e.g., to avoid injury to others). Obligations, according to Rawls, are incurred only by one's voluntary acts, whereas this is not true of natural duties.[12] In his book, he retains the obligation of fair play (now "fairness"); but he now thinks that this obligation applies only to those citizens of just governments who hold office or who have advanced their interests through the government. He excludes the bulk of the citizenry from having a prima facie obligation to obey the law on the ground that, for most persons, receiving benefits from government is nothing they do voluntarily, but is rather something that merely happens to them.[13] He does not, however, take this to imply that most citizens of a reasonably just government are morally free to disobey the law: He maintains that everyone who is treated by such a government with reasonable justice has a natural duty to obey all laws that are not grossly unjust, on the ground that everyone has a natural duty to uphold and to comply with just institutions.[14]

It is tempting to criticize Rawls's present position in much the same way that I criticized his earlier one. One might argue that, while it is true that officeholders and those who have profited by invoking the rules of a just government must in fairness comply with its laws when disobedience will result in harm to that government or when it withholds a benefit from some person who has a right to it, it is simply false that fairness dictates obedience when disobedience does no harm or withholds no benefit. One might argue further that the utility of a just government is such that one has a prima facie duty to obey when disobedience is harmful to it, but that, so long as disobedience does no harm, the government's character is irrelevant to the question of whether one has a prima facie obligation to obey. These criticisms would, I think, show that if we are to base our normative ethics on an appeal to intuitively reasonable principles of duty and obligation, Rawls's present position is no more satisfying than is his earlier one. However, although certainly relevant to an assessment of Rawls's present position, these arguments cannot be regarded as decisive, for in his book Rawls does not rely on a bare appeal to moral intuition. He does not disregard the evidence of intuition, and he is glad to enlist its aid when he can; but, in putting forward particular principles of duty and obligation, he is more concerned with showing that they follow from his general theory of justice. Hence, to refute Rawls's present position, one would have to set out his elaborate theory and then show either that it is mistaken or that the particular claims he makes on its basis do not follow from it. Such a task is beyond the scope of this article; and I shall therefore be content to observe that Rawls's present position lacks intuitive support and, hence, that it rests solely on a controversial ethical theory and a complicated argument based upon it, neither of which have as yet emerged unscathed from the fire of critical scrutiny. His view deserves great respect and demands extended discussion, but it is not one which we must now accept on pain of being unreasonable.

II.

The second group of arguments are those from implicit consent or promise. Recognizing that among the clearest cases of prima facie obligation are those in which a person voluntarily assumes the obligation, some philosophers have attempted to found the citizen's obligation to obey the law upon his consent or promise to do so. There is, of course, a substantial difficulty in any such attempt, viz., the brute fact that many persons have never so agreed. To accommodate this fact, some philosophers have invoked the concept of implicit promise or consent. In the *Second Treatise*, Locke argued that mere residence in a country, whether for an hour or a lifetime, constitutes implicit consent to its law.[15] Plato[16] and W. D. Ross[17] made the similar argument that residence in a country and appeal to the protection of its laws constitutes an implicit promise to obey.

Nevertheless, it is clear that residence and use of the protection of the law do not constitute any usual kind of consent to a government nor any usual kind of promise to obey its laws. The phrases "implicit consent" and "implicit promise" are somewhat difficult to understand, for they are not commonly used; nor do Locke, Plato, or Ross define them. Still, a natural way of understanding them is to assume that they refer to acts which differ from explicit consent or promise only in that, in the latter cases, the person has said "I consent … " or "I promise … ," whereas in the former, he has not uttered such words but rather has performed some act which counts as giving consent or making a promise. Now, as recent investigation in the philosophy of language has shown, certain speech acts are performed only when someone utters certain words (or performs some other conventional act) with the intention that others will take what he did as being an instance of the particular act in question.[18] And it is certain that, in their ordinary usage, "consenting" and "promising" refer to speech acts of this kind. If I say to someone, "I promise to give you fifty dollars," but it is clear from the context that I do not intend that others will take my utterance as a promise, no one would consider me as having promised. Bringing this observation to bear on the present argument, it is perhaps possible that some people reside in a country and appeal to the protection of its laws with the intention that others will take their residence and appeal as consent to the laws or as a promise to obey; but this is surely true only of a very small number, consisting entirely of those enamoured with social contract theory.[19]

It may be argued, however, that my criticism rests on an unduly narrow reading of the words *consent* and *promise*. Hence, it may be supposed that, if I am to refute the implicit consent or promise arguments, I must show that there is no other sense of the words *consent* or *promise* in which it is true that citizens, merely by living in a state and going about their usual business, thereby consent or promise to obey the law. This objection is difficult to meet, for I know of no way to show that there is no sense of either word that is suitable for contractarian purposes. However, I can show that two recent attempts, by John Plamenatz and Alan Gewirth, to refurbish the implicit consent argument along this line have been unsuccessful.[20] I shall not quarrel with their analyses of *consent,* though I am suspicious of them; rather, I shall argue that given their definitions of *consent* the fact that a man consents to government does not establish that he has a prima facie obligation to obey the law.

Plamenatz claims that there are two kinds of consent. The first, which is common garden-variety consent, he terms *direct*. He concedes that few citizens directly consent to their government.[21] He suggests, however, that there is another kind of consent, which he calls *indirect,* and that, in democratic societies, consent in this sense is widespread and establishes a prima facie obligation to obey the law. Indirect consent occurs whenever a person freely votes or abstains from voting.[22] Voting establishes a prima facie obligation of obedience because:

> Even if you dislike the system and wish to change it, you put yourself by your vote under a [prima facie] obligation to obey whatever government comes legally to power.... For the purpose of an election is to give authority to the people who win it and, if you vote knowing what you are doing and without being compelled to do it, you voluntarily take part in a process which gives authority to these people.[23]

Plamenatz does not explain why abstention results in a prima facie obligation, but perhaps his idea is

that, if a person abstains, he in effect acknowledges the authority of whoever happens to win.

The key premise then in the argument is that "the purpose of an election is to give authority to the people who win it," and it is clear that Plamenatz believes that this implies that elections do give authority to their winners. In assessing the truth of these contentions, it is, of course, vital to know what Plamenatz means by "authority." Unfortunately, he does not enlighten us, and therefore we must speculate as to his meaning. To begin, the word *authority,* when used without qualification, is often held to mean the same as "legitimate authority." Since prima facie obligation is the weakest kind of obligation, part of what we mean when we ascribe authority to some government is that those subject to it have at least a prima facie obligation to obey. However, if this is what Plamenatz means by "authority," his argument simply begs the question: For, in order to be justified in asserting that the purpose of an election is to confer authority and that elections succeed in doing this, he must first show that everyone subject to an elected government has a prima facie obligation to obey its law, both those eligible to vote and those ineligible.

It is possible, however, that Plamenatz is using *authority* in some weaker sense, one that does not entail that everyone subject to it has a prima facie obligation to obey. If this is so, his premises will perhaps pass, but he must then show that those who are eligible to take part in conferring authority have a prima facie obligation to obey it. However, it is difficult to see how this can be done. First, as Plamenatz recognizes, voting is not necessarily consenting in the "direct" or usual sense, and merely being eligible to vote is even more clearly not consenting. Hence, the alleged prima facie obligation of obedience incurred by those eligible to vote is not in consequence of their direct consent. Second, Plamenatz cannot appeal to "common moral sentiment" to bolster his argument: This is because if we really believed that those eligible to vote have a prima facie obligation to obey, an obligation not incurred by the ineligible, we should then believe that the eligible have a stronger obligation than those who are ineligible. But, as far as I can tell, we do not ordinarily think that this is true. Finally, Plamenatz cannot rely on a purely conceptual argument to make his point. It is by no means an analytic truth that those subject to elected governments have a prima facie obligation to obey the law.[24] The radical who says, "The present government of the United States was freely elected, but because it exploits people its citizens have no obligation to obey it," has perhaps said something false, but he has not contradicted himself. Plamenatz's argument is therefore either question-begging or inconclusive, depending on what he means by *authority*. Gewirth's argument is similar to Plamenatz's in that he also holds that a person's vote establishes his prima facie obligation of obedience. He argues that men consent to government when "certain institutional arrangements exist in the community as a whole," including "the maintenance of a method which leaves open to every sane, noncriminal adult the opportunity to discuss, criticize, and vote for or against the government."[25] He holds that the existence of such consent "justifies" government and establishes the subject's prima facie obligation to obey because:

> The method of consent combines and safeguards the joint values of freedom and order as no other method does. It provides a choice in the power of government which protects the rights of the electorate more effectively than does any other method. It does more justice to man's potential rationality than does any other method, for it gives all men the opportunity to participate in a reasoned discussion of the problem of society and to make their discussion effective in terms of political control.[26]

As it stands, Gewirth's argument is incomplete. He makes certain claims about the benefits of government by consent that are open to reasonable doubt. Some communists, for example, would hold that Gewirth's method of consent has led to exploitation, and that human rights and freedom are better protected by the rule of the party. This aside, Gewirth's argument still needs strengthening. The fact that certain benefits are given only by government with a method of consent establishes only that such a government is better than

one that lacks such a method. But, to show that one government is better than another, or even to show that it is the best possible government, does not prove that its subjects have a prima facie obligation to obey its laws: There is a prior question, which remains to be settled, as to whether there can be a prima facie obligation to obey any government. Gewirth does not carry the argument farther in his discussion of "consent," but earlier in his paper he hints as to how he would meet this objection. He argues that "government as such" is justified, or made legitimate, by its being necessary to avoid certain evils.[27] Indeed, although he does not so state explicitly, he seems to think that utilitarian considerations demonstrate that there is a prima facie obligation to obey any government that protects its subjects from these evils, but that there is an additional prima facie obligation to obey a government with a method of consent because of the more extensive benefits it offers. In the next section, I shall discuss whether a direct appeal to utility can establish a prima facie obligation to obey the law.

III.

I shall consider three utilitarian arguments: the first appealing to a weak form of act-utilitarianism, the second and third to rule-utilitarian theories. To my knowledge, the first argument has never been advanced explicitly. It is nevertheless worth considering, both because it possesses a certain plausibility and because it has often been hinted at when philosophers, lawyers, and political theorists have attempted to derive an obligation to obey the law from the premise that government is necessary to protect society from great evil. The argument runs as follows:

> There is obviously a prima facie obligation to perform acts which have good consequences. Now, government is absolutely necessary for securing the general good: The alternative is the state of nature in which everyone is miserable, in which life is "solitary, poor, nasty, brutish and short."
> But, no government can long stand in the face of widespread disobedience, and government therefore can promote the general good only so long as its laws are obeyed. Therefore, obedience

to the law supports the continued existence of government and, hence, always has good consequences. From this it follows that there is a prima facie obligation to obey the law.

On even brief scrutiny, however, this argument quickly disintegrates. The first thing to be noticed is that its principle of prima facie obligation is ambiguous. It may be interpreted as postulating either (a) an obligation to perform those acts that have any good consequences, or (b) an obligation to perform optimific acts (i.e., those whose consequences are better than their alternatives). Now, (a) and (b) are in fact very different principles. The former is obviously absurd. It implies, for example, that I have a prima facie obligation to kill whomever I meet, since this would have the good consequence of helping to reduce overpopulation. Thus, the only weak act-utilitarian principle with any plausibility is (b). But, regardless of whether (b) is acceptable—and some philosophers would not accept it[28]—the conclusion that there is a prima facie obligation to obey the law cannot be derived from it, inasmuch as there are obvious and familiar cases in which breach of a particular law has better consequences than obedience. The only conclusion to be derived from (b) is that there is a specific prima facie obligation to obey the law whenever obedience is optimific. But no generic prima facie obligation to obey can be derived from weak act-utilitarianism.[29]

The second utilitarian argument appeals not to the untoward consequences of individual disobedience, but rather to those of general disobedience. Perhaps the most common challenge to those who defend certain instances of civil disobedience is "What would happen if everyone disobeyed the law?" One of the arguments implicit in this question is the generalization argument, which may be expanded as follows:

No one can have a right to do something unless everyone has a right to do it. Similarly, an act cannot be morally indifferent unless it would be morally indifferent if everyone did it. But, everyone's breaking the law is not a matter of moral indifference; for no government can survive in such a circumstance and, as we have already agreed, government is necessary for securing and maintaining the general good. Hence, since the consequences

of general disobedience would be disastrous, each person subject to law has a prima facie obligation to obey it.

In assessing this argument, we must first recognize that the generalization argument is a moral criterion to be applied with care, as virtually everyone who has discussed it has recognized.[30] If we simply note that, if everyone committed a certain act there would be disastrous consequences, and thereupon conclude that there is a prima facie obligation not to commit acts of that kind, we will be saddled with absurdities. We will have to maintain, for example, that there is a prima facie obligation not to eat dinner at five o'clock, for if everyone did so, certain essential services could not be maintained. And, for similar reasons, we will have to maintain that there is a prima facie obligation not to produce food. Now, those who believe that the generalization argument is valid argue that such absurdities arise when the criterion is applied to acts that either are described too generally or are described in terms of morally irrelevant features. They would argue that the generalization argument appears to go awry when applied to these examples because the description "producing food" is too general to give the argument purchase and because the temporal specification in "eating dinner at five o'clock" is morally irrelevant.[31]

However, such a restriction on the generalization argument is fatal to its use in proving a prima facie obligation to obey the law. This is because a person who denies any such obligation is surely entitled to protest that the description "breaking the law" is overly general, on the ground that it refers to acts of radically different moral import.[32] Breaking the law perhaps always has some bad consequences; but sometimes the good done by it balances the bad or even outweighs it. And, once we take these differences in consequences into account, we find that utilitarian generalization, like weak act-utilitarianism, can establish a specific prima facie obligation to obey the law only when obedience is optimific. Were everyone to break the law when obedience is optimific, the consequences undoubtedly would be disastrous; but it is by no means clear that it would be disastrous if everyone broke the law when obedience is not optimific. Since no one knows, with respect to any society, how often obedience is not optimific, no one can be certain as to the consequences of everyone acting in this way. Indeed, for all we know, if everyone broke the law when obedience was not optimific, the good done by separate acts of lawbreaking might more than compensate for any public disorder that might result. In sum, even if the generalization argument is regarded as an acceptable principle of prima facie obligation, the most it demonstrates is that there is a specific prima facie obligation to obey the law whenever the consequences of obedience are optimific.

Some readers—especially those unfamiliar with the recent literature on utilitarianism[33]—may suspect that this last argument involves sleight of hand. They may object:

> In your discussion of the generalization argument, you argued that we have no way of knowing the consequences if everyone disobeyed when obedience was not optimific. But, your argument rests on the premise that the act-utilitarian formula can be applied perfectly, whereas this is in fact impossible. The consequences of many acts are difficult or impossible to foretell; and so, were we all to attempt to be act-utilitarians, we either would make horrendous mistakes or be paralyzed into inaction. In constructing a rule-utilitarian theory of prima facie obligations, we therefore should concentrate not on the consequences of everyone following certain rules, but rather on the consequences of everyone trying to follow them. And, it seems reasonable to believe that, on such a theory, the rule "Obey the law" would receive utilitarian blessing.

As it stand, this objection is overdrawn. My argument does not presuppose that persons generally can succeed in applying the act-utilitarian formula: I merely speculated on the consequences of everyone behaving in a certain way; and I made no assumption as to what made them act that way. Moreover, the objection severely overestimates the difficulty in being a confirmed act-utilitarian. Still, the objection makes one substantial point that deserves further attention. Rule-utilitarian theories that focus on the consequences of everyone accepting (although not always following) a certain set of rules do differ markedly from the generalization argument; and so the question remains as to whether such a theory could establish a prima facie obligation to obey the law. I shall therefore discuss whether the most carefully developed such theory, that given by R. B. Brandt,[34] does just this.

In Brandt's theory, one's obligations are (within certain limits) relative to his society and are determined by the set of rules whose acceptance in that society would have better consequences than would acceptance of any other set.[35] According to this theory, then, there can be a generic prima facie obligation to obey the law within a given society if, and only if, general acceptance of the rule "Obey the law," as a rule of prima facie obligation, would have better consequences than were no rule accepted with respect to obeying the law, as well as better consequences than were some alternative rule accepted (e.g., "Obey the law when obedience to the law is optimific," or "Obey the law so long as it is just"). Now, to many it may seem obvious that the ideal set of rules for any society will contain the rule "Obey the law," on the ground that, were its members not generally convinced of at least a prima facie obligation to obey, disobedience would be widespread, resulting in a great many crimes against person and property. But, there are two reasons to doubt such a gloomy forecast. First, surely we must suppose that in this hypothetical society the laws are still backed by sanctions, thereby giving its members a strong incentive to obey its laws. Second, we also must assume that the members of that society accept other moral rules (e.g., "Do not harm others," "Keep promises," "Tell the truth") that will give them a moral incentive to obey the law in most circumstances. It is, in short, a mistake to believe that unless people are convinced that they have a generic prima facie obligation to obey the law, they cannot be convinced that in most circumstances they have a specific prima facie obligation to obey particular laws. We therefore may expect that, even though members of our hypothetical society do not accept a moral rule about obedience to the law per se, they will feel a prima facie obligation to act in accordance with the law, save when disobedience does no harm. There is, then, no reason to think that an orgy of lawbreaking would ensue were no rule about obedience to the law generally recognized; nor, I think, is there any good reason to believe that acceptance of the rule "Obey the law" would in any society have better consequences than were no such rule recognized. And, if this is so, there is surely no reason to think that recognition of this rule would have better consequences than recognition of some alternative rule. In sum, Brandt's theory requires that we be able to determine the truth-value of a large number of counterfactual propositions about what would happen were entire societies persuaded of the truth of certain moral rules. But, even if we assume—and it is hardly clear that we should[36]—that we can reliably determine the truth-value of such counterfactuals through "common sense" and our knowledge of human nature, Brandt's form of rule-utilitarianism gives no support for the proof of a prima facie obligation to obey the law.

IV.

In the foregoing discussion, I have played the skeptic, contending that no argument has as yet succeeded in establishing a prima facie obligation to obey the law. I want now to examine this supposed obligation directly. I shall assume arguendo that such an obligation exists in order to inquire as to how it compares in moral weight with other prima facie obligations. As we shall see, this question is relevant to whether we should hold that such an obligation exists.

To discuss this question, I must, of course, first specify some test for determining the weight of a prima facie obligation. It will be recalled that I defined "prima facie obligation" in terms of wrongdoing: To say that a person S has a prima facie obligation to do an act X is to say that S has a moral reason to do X which is such that, unless he has a reason not to do X that is at least as strong, S's failure to do X is wrong. Now, we are accustomed, in our reflective moral practice, to distinguish degrees of wrongdoing. And so, by appealing to this notion, we can formulate two principles that reasonably may be held to govern

the weight of prima facie obligations: First, that a prima facie obligation is a serious one if, and only if, an act that violates that obligation and fulfills no other is seriously wrong; and, second, that a prima facie obligation is a serious one if, and only if, violation of it will make considerably worse an act that on other grounds is already wrong.[37] These principles, which constitute tests for determining an obligation's weight, are closely related, and application of either to a given prima facie obligation is a sufficient measure; but I shall apply both to the presumed prima facie obligation to obey the law in order to make my argument more persuasive.

First, however, we should convince ourselves of the reliability of these tests by applying them to some clear cases. I suppose it will be granted that we all have a prima facie obligation not to kill (except perhaps in self-defense), and that this obligation is most weighty. Our first test corroborates this, for, if a person kills another when he is not defending himself, and if he has no specific prima facie obligation to kill that person, his act is seriously wrong. By contrast, our prima facie obligation to observe rules of etiquette—if indeed there is any such obligation—is clearly trifling. This is borne out by our test, for if I belch audibly in the company of those who think such behavior rude, my wrongdoing is at most trivial. The same results are obtained under our second test. If I attempt to extort money from someone my act is much worse if I kill one of his children and threaten the rest than if I merely threatened them all; and so the obligation not to kill again counts as substantial. Similarly, the prima facie obligation to observe the rules of etiquette is again trivial, for if I am rude during the extortion my act is hardly worse than it would have been had I been polite.

By neither of these tests, however, does the prima facie obligation to obey the law count as substantial. As for the first test, let us assume that while driving home at two o'clock in the morning I run a stop sign. There is no danger, for I can see clearly that there was no one approaching the intersection, nor is there any impressionable youth nearby to be inspired to a life of crime by my flouting of the traffic code. Finally, we may assume that I nevertheless had no specific prima facie obligation to run the stop sign. If, then, my prima facie obligation to obey the law is of substantial moral weight, my action must have been a fairly serious instance of wrongdoing. But clearly it was not. If it was wrong at all—and to me this seems dubious—it was at most a mere peccadillo. As for the second test, we may observe that acts which are otherwise wrong are not made more so—if they are made worse at all—by being illegal.[38] If I defraud someone my act is hardly worse morally by being illegal than it would have been were it protected by some legal loophole. Thus, if there is a prima facie obligation to obey the law, it is at most of trifling weight.

This being so, I suggest that considerations of simplicity indicate that we should ignore the supposed prima facie obligation to obey the law and refuse to count an act wrong merely because it violates some law. There is certainly nothing to be lost by doing this, for we shall not thereby recommend or tolerate any conduct that is seriously wrong, nor shall we fail to recommend any course of action that is seriously obligatory. Yet, there is much to be gained, for in refusing to let trivialities occupy our attention, we shall not be diverted from the important questions to be asked about illegal conduct, viz., "What kind of act was it?," "What were its consequences?," "Did the agent intend its consequences?," and so forth. Morality is, after all, a serious business; and we are surely right not to squander our moral attention and concern on matters of little moral significance.

To illustrate what can be gained, let us consider briefly the issue of civil disobedience. Most philosophers who have written on the subject have argued that, at least in democratic societies, there is always a strong moral reason to obey the law. They have therefore held that civil disobedience is a tactic to be employed only when all legal means of changing an unjust law have failed, and that the person who engages in it must willingly accept punishment as a mark of respect for the law and recognition of the seriousness of law-breaking. However, once we abandon the notion that civil disobedience is morally significant per se, we shall judge it in the same way we judge most other kinds of acts, that is, on the basis of their character and consequences. Indeed, we then can treat civil disobedience just as we regard many other species of illegal conduct. If breaking the law involves an act which is *mala in se*, or if it has untoward consequences, we ordinarily are prepared to condemn it and to think that the malefactor ought to accept punishment. But if lawbreaking does not involve an act that is *mala in se*, and if it has no harmful consequences, we do not ordinarily condemn it, nor do we think that its perpetrator must accept punishment, unless evading punishment itself has untoward consequences. If we adopt this view of civil disobedience, we shall have done much to escape the air of mystery that hovers about most discussions of it.

Of course, this is not to say it will be easy to determine when civil disobedience is justified. Some have maintained that the civil disobedience of the last decade has led to increasing violation of laws that safeguard people and property.[39] If this is true, each instance of disobedience which has contributed to this condition has a share in the evil of the result. Others maintain that such disobedience has had wholly good consequences, that it has helped to remedy existing injustice and to restrain government from fresh injustice.[40]

Still others think its consequences are mixed. Which position is correct is difficult to determine. I myself am inclined to believe that, although the consequences have been mixed, the good far outweigh the bad; but I would be hard pressed to prove it. What is clear, however, is that either abandoning or retaining the supposed prima facie obligation to obey the law will not help settle these questions about consequences. But, if we do abandon it, we shall then at least be able to focus on these questions without having to worry about a prima facie obligation of trivial weight that nevertheless somehow must be taken into account. Finally, if we abandon the prima facie obligation to obey the law, perhaps we shall look more closely at the character of acts performed in the course of civil disobedience, and this may, in turn, lead to fruitful moral speculation. For example, we shall be able to distinguish between acts that cannot conceivably violate the obligation of fair play (e.g., burning one's draft card) and acts that may do so (e.g., tax refusal or evasion of military service). This in turn may provide an incentive to reflect further on the obligation of fair play, to ask, for example, whether Rawls is right in his present contention that a person can incur the obligation of fair play only so long as his acceptance of the benefits of a cooperative enterprise is wholly voluntary.

V.

It is now time to take stock. I initially suggested that it is by no means obvious that there is any prima facie obligation to obey the law. In the foregoing, I have rejected a number of arguments that purport to establish its existence. The only plausible argument I have not rejected is the one of Rawls that purports to prove that there is a natural duty to obey the laws of reasonably just governments. However, I did note that his position lacks intuitive support and rests on a controversial ethical theory which has not yet withstood the test of critical scrutiny. Finally, I have shown that even if such an obligation is assumed, it is of trivial weight and that there are substantial advantages in ignoring it. I suggest that all of this makes it reasonable to maintain that there is in no society a prima facie obligation to obey the law.

Before I conclude my discussion, however, I want to tie up one loose thread. Near the beginning of my argument I distinguished the question to be discussed from that which I called the lawyer's question: "May a reasonable man take mere illegality to be sufficient evidence that an act is morally wrong, so long as he lacks specific evidence that tends to show that it is right?" Since I have raised the question, I believe that, for the sake of completeness, I should consider it, if only briefly. To begin, it seems very doubtful that there is, in the lawyer's sense, a prima facie obligation to obey the law. It is undoubtedly true that most instances of lawbreaking are wrong, but it is also true that many are not: This is because there are, as Lord Devlin once remarked, "many fussy regulations whose breach it would be pedantic to call immoral,"[41] and because some breaches of even nonfussy regulations are justified. Now, unless—as in a court of law—there is some pressing need

to reach a finding, the mere fact that most *A*s are also *B*s does not, in the absence of evidence that a particular *A* is not *B*, warrant an inference that the *A* in question is also a *B*: In order for this inference to be reasonable, one must know that virtually all *A*s are *B*s. Since, then, it rarely happens that there is a pressing need to reach a moral finding, and since to know merely that an act is illegal is not to know very much of moral significance about it, it seems clear that, if his only information about an act was that it was illegal, a reasonable man would withhold judgment until he learned more about it. Indeed, this is not only what the fictitious reasonable man would do, it is what we should expect the ordinary person to do. Suppose we were to ask a large number of people: "Jones has broken a law; but I won't tell you whether what he did is a serious crime or merely violation of a parking regulation, nor whether he had good reason for his actions. Would you, merely on the strength of what I have just told you, be willing to say that what he did was morally wrong?" I have concluded only an informal poll; but, on its basis, I would wager that the great majority would answer "I can't yet say—you must tell me more about what Jones did."

More important, it appears to make little difference what answer we give to the lawyer's question. While an affirmative answer establishes a rule of inference that an illegal act is wrong in the absence of specific information tending to show it to be right, it is a rule that would in fact virtually never be applied in any reasonable determination of whether an illegal act is wrong. If, on the other hand, we have specific information about an illegal act that tends to show it to be right, then the rule is irrelevant to our determination of the act's moral character. Should we be inclined, in this instance, to hold the act wrong, we must have specific information that tends to show this: and it is clear that our conclusions about its moral character must be based on this specific information, and not on the supposed reasonableness of holding illegal conduct wrong in the absence of specific information tending to show it is right. On the other hand, if we have specific information tending to show it is right, the rule is applicable but otiose: Since we have ample specific reason to condemn the act, the rule is superfluous to our judgment. It would seem, then, that the rule is relevant only when we have no specific information about the illegal conduct's rightness or wrongness; and this, I suggest, is something that virtually never occurs. When we are prompted to make a moral judgment about an illegal act, we virtually always know something of its character or at least its consequences; and it is these that we consider important in determining the rightness or wrongness of lawbreaking. In short, it seems to make little difference what answer we give to the lawyer's question; I raise it here only that it may hereafter be ignored.

In conclusion, it is, I think, important to recognize that there is nothing startling in what I am recommending, nothing that in any way outrages common sense. Even the most conscientious men at times violate trivial and pointless laws for some slight gain in convenience and, when they do so, they do not feel shame or remorse. Similarly, when they observe other men behaving in a like fashion, they do not think of passing moral censure. For most people, violation of the law becomes a matter for moral concern only when it involves an act that is believed to be wrong on grounds apart from its illegality. Hence, anyone who believes that the purpose of normative ethics is to organize and clarify our reflective moral practice should be skeptical of any argument purporting to show that there is a prima facie obligation to obey the law. It is necessary to state this point with care: I am not contending that reflective and conscientious citizens would, if asked, deny that there is a prima facie obligation to obey the law. Indeed, I am willing to concede that many more would affirm its existence than deny it. But, this is in no way inconsistent with my present point. We often find that reflective people will accept general statements that are belied by their actual linguistic practice. That they also accept moral generalizations that are belied by their actual reflective moral practice should occasion no surprise.

This last point may, however, be challenged on the ground that it implies that there is in our reflective moral practice no distinction between raw power and legitimate authority. As I noted above, the concept of legitimate authority often is analyzed in terms of the right to command, where "right" is used in the strict sense as implying some correlative obligation of obedience. Given this definition, if it is true that the principle "There is a prima facie obligation to obey the law" is not observed in our reflective moral practice, it follows that we do not really distinguish between governments that possess legitimate authority (e.g., that of the United States) and those which do not (e.g., the Nazi occupation government of France). And this, it may justly be held, is absurd. What I take this argument to show, however, is not that the principle is enshrined in our reflective morality, but rather that what we ordinarily mean when we ascribe legitimate authority to some government is not captured by the usual analysis of "legitimate authority." It is a mistake to believe that, unless we employ the concept of authority as it usually is analyzed, we cannot distinguish satisfactorily between the moral relation of the government of the United States vis-à-vis Americans and the moral relation of the Nazi occupation government vis-à-vis Frenchmen. One way of doing this, for example, is to define "legitimate authority" in terms of "the right to command and to enforce obedience," where "right" is used in the sense of "what is morally permissible." Thus, according to this analysis of the notion, the government of the United States counts as having legitimate authority over its subjects because within certain limits there is nothing wrong in its issuing commands to them and enforcing their obedience, whereas the Nazi occupation government lacked such authority because its issuing commands to Frenchmen was morally impermissible. It is not my intention to proffer this as an adequate analysis of the notion of legitimate authority, or to suggest that it captures what we ordinarily mean when we ascribe such authority to some government. These are difficult matters, and I do not wish to address myself to them here. My point is rather that the questions "What governments enjoy legitimate authority?" and "Have the citizens of any government a prima facie obligation to obey the law?" both can be, and should be, kept separate.

NOTES

I wish to thank Judith Jarvis Thomson, Hugo A. Bedau, Gerald Barnes, Murray Kiteley, Robert Ackermann, and Stanley Rothman, for their criticism of earlier drafts of this article.

1. Rawls, J. "Legal Obligation and the Duty of Fair Play." *Law and Philosophy.* Ed. S. Hook. 1964. 3.
2. Prichard, H. A. "Green's Principles of Political Obligation." *Moral Obligation.* 1949. 54
3. The distinction between prima facie and absolute obligation was first made by W. D. Ross in *The Right and the Good*, ch. 2 (1930). My account of prima facie obligation differs somewhat from Ross's; but I believe it adequately captures current philosophical usage. As for absolute obligation, I shall not often speak of it; but when I do, what I shall mean by "*S* has an absolute obligation to do X " is that "*S*'s failure to do X is wrong."
4. My motive for distinguishing generic and specific prima facie obligations is simply convenience, and not because I think it provides a perspicuous way of classifying prima facie obligations. As a classification it is obviously defective: The two kinds of obligation overlap, since in a trivial sense every specific obligation can be construed as a generic one, and there are some prima facie obligations (e.g., the obligation to keep one's promise) that fit neither definition.
5. An example may help to make the point clear. If I promise that I will meet someone at a certain time, I have a prima facie obligation to keep my promise. Now, were this merely a prima facie obligation in the lawyer's sense, without evidence to the contrary the fact that I had promised would be sufficient to hold that a breach of my promise was wrong, yet it would not be evidence of wrongdoing were there reason to believe the breach was justified or even obligatory. But, in fact, this is not what we think of promising. We think that if someone promises to do a thing there is a strong moral reason for him to do it and that, although this reason sometimes may be opposed by stronger reasons to the contrary, its weight does not disappear. In such cases, my promise is yet relevant to what I am absolutely obligated to do, although it is not always determinative. But, even when this reason is outweighed, it still discloses its existence by imposing fresh prima facie obligations (e.g., to tell the person I promised why I broke it). Hence, there is a prima facie obligation to keep one's promise in the sense in which I here use the phrase.
6. H.L.A. Hart, *Are There Any Natural Rights?* 64 Phil. Rev. 185 (1955). I must note that Hart does not use the phrase "prima facie obligation," maintaining that his argument establishes an obligation sans phrase to comply with the rules of cooperative enterprises. However, since his use of "obligation" seems much the same as my use of "prima facie obligation," I shall ignore his terminological scruples.
7. Rawls, supra note 1. The same argument appears, although in less detail, in John Rawls, *Justice as Fairness*, 67 Phil. Rev. 164 (1958), and Rawls, John *The Justification of Civil Disobedience, in Civil Disobedience: Theory and Practice.* Ed. H. A. Bedau. 1969.
8. Rawls, John. "Legal Obligation and the Duty of Fair Play." *Law and Philosophy.* Ed. S. Hook. 1964. 10. According to Rawls, the principles of justice are that

   > everyone have an equal right to the most extensive liberty compatible with a like liberty for all; ... [and] that inequalities are arbitrary unless it is reasonable to expect that they will work out for everyone's advantage and provided that the positions and offices to which they attached or from which they may be gained are open to all.

   Id. at 11.
9. Id. at 13; Hart, supra note 6, at 185.
10. Those intrigued by the mention of these additional factors may be interested to know that, when imperfect cooperation is taken into account, it can be shown that considerations of fairness establish no more than: (1) that a member *A* of a cooperative enterprise has a prima facie obligation to obey when his obedience will benefit some other member *B* from whose submission *A* has previously benefited, and it is not the case that *B* has withheld from *A* more significant benefits than *A* withholds from *B*; and (2) that *A* has a prima facie obligation to obey when his disobedience harms the enterprise and there is some other member *B* from whose submission *A* has benefitted previously and *B* has by his disobedience harmed the enterprise less than the harm that would be done by *A*'s disobedience.

    As for the effect of disparity in sacrifice, it was only recently suggested to me that this factor must be taken into account, and I have not yet attempted to determine its effects precisely. A moment's reflection discloses, however, that this additional factor would make the obligation still more complex. Were anyone to attempt a precise specification of the citizen's obligations vis-à-vis the laws of his government, he would have to master these complexities; but my task is not so ambitious.

11. Indeed, it seems strange that Rawls should have attempted to base the prima facie obligation to obey the law on fair play, since he maintains that this latter obligation is incurred within cooperative enterprises that depend on near-universal cooperation. Rawls, J. "Legal Obligation and the Duty of Fair Play." *Law and Philosophy*. Ed. S. Hood. 1964. 10.

12. Rawls, J. *A Theory of Justice*. 1971. 108.

13. Id., at 336, 344.

14. Id., at 334–37, 350–62.

15. Locke, J. *Two Treatises of Government*. 1690. Bk. 11, { 119.

16. Plato. *Dialogues* Trans. B. Jowett. 1892). 435.

17. Ross, supra note 3, at 27.

18. Cf. Strawson, *Intention and Convention in Speech Acts*, 73 Phil. Rev. 439, 448–49, 457–59 (1964).

19. A similar argument also could be made utilizing the analysis of promising in Searle, J. *Speech Acts: An Essay in the Philosophy of Language*. 1969. 60.

20. Another recent tacit consent theory is found in Tussman, J. *Obligation and the Body Politic* (1960). I shall not discuss this theory, however, because it has already received adequate criticism in Pitkin, *Obligation and Consent I*, 59 Am. Pol. Sci. Rev. 990 (1964). Nor shall I discuss Pitkin's own "hypothetical consent" theory that obedience is owed to those governments to which one ought to consent, because in her discussion of how political obligation is justified she does not appeal to the concept of hypothetical consent. She takes the problem of justifying political obligation to be the question "Why am I ever obligated to obey even legitimate authority?" She gives the question short shrift, however, replying that it is simply part of the meaning of the phrase "legitimate authority" that those subject to legitimate authority have a prima facie obligation to obey it. See Pitkin, *Obligation and Consent II*, 60 Am. Pol. Sci. Rev. 39, 45–49 (1966).

21. Plamenatz, J. *Man and Society*. 1963). 228, 238–39

22. Id., at 239–40.

23. Id.

24. A defender of Plamenatz, John Jenkins, appears to hold that something like this is an analytic truth, maintaining that:

> if a person supposes that he has no obligation to a successful candidate because that candidate happens not to be the person for whom he cast his vote, then there is an excellent case for saying that the man has failed to understand the nature of the electoral process.

John Jenkins, *Political Consent*, 20 Phil. Q. 61 (1970).

This seems a silly claim. Many who voted for George McGovern believe themselves to be under no obligation to Richard Nixon. Some are highly educated and close observers of the political scene. Were such a person to explain his belief that he is not obligated to Nixon solely on the ground that he did not vote for him, we might think him mistaken or wish that he had chosen a better reason, but we should have no reason at all to think that he fails to understand "the nature of the electoral process."

25. Earlier in his discussion Gewirth distinguishes three senses of "consent": an "occurrence" sense, a "dispositional" sense, and an "opportunity" sense. Id. at 131. It is only the last that will concern us here, since he admits that the prima facie obligation to obey the law cannot be shown by relying on the occurrence or the dispositional senses. Gewirth, "Political Justice." *Social Justice*. Ed. R. Brandt. 1962. 138.

26. Id., at 139.

27. Id., at 135.

28. For example, some philosophers would hold that there is a prima facie obligation to refrain from acts that have undesirable consequences, but not that there is an obligation to perform the one act that has the best consequences. See, e.g., Singer, M. G. *Generalization in Ethics*. 1961. Ch. 7

29. For purposes of clarification, I should emphasize that I am here concerned with act-utilitarianism as a theory of prima facie, not absolute, obligation. There is no incongruity here. The consequences of acts count as having great moral significance on virtually every moral theory; and so, one need not be a strict act-utilitarian in order to maintain the principle that there is a prima facie obligation to act optimifically. Indeed, for a strict act-utilitarian such as Bentham, it is pointless to worry about whether there is a prima facie obligation to obey the law: He would hold that there is an absolute obligation to obey the law when, and only when, obedience is optimific, and would there end the discussion. At most, an act-utilitarian would hold that the rule "Obey the law" is a useful rule of thumb, to be followed only when the consequences of obedience or disobedience are difficult to discern.

30. Singer, supra note 28, at ch. 4.

31. I have borrowed these cases and this strategy for handling them from Singer. Id., at 71–83.

32. According to Singer, a mark of a description's being overly general is that the generalization argument is "invertible" with respect to it (i.e., the consequences of everyone's doing the act (given that description) is disastrous and the consequences of everyone's failing to do it is also disastrous). Id., at 76–77. It is relevant to note that the generalization argument is plainly invertible with respect to the description "breaking the law." Sometimes breaking the law is the only way to avoid a great evil; and so, if everyone were always to obey the law, such evils never could be avoided.

33. That the generalization argument and weak act-utilitarianism offer the same advice on the topic of obedience to the law should surprise no one familiar with D. Lyons, *Forms and Limits of Utilitarianism*. 1965. Lyons there shows that act-utilitarianism and the generalization argument are extensionally equivalent. There is, it should be noted, a substantial difference between Lyons's argument for equivalence and the argument I have here offered. Lyons argues for equivalence on a priori grounds, whereas I have relied on the empirical impossibility of determining the consequences of everyone disobeying the law when obedience is not optimific.

34. Brandt, "Toward a Credible Utilitarianism." *Morality and the Language of Conduct*. (Eds. H. N. Casteñeda & G. Nakhnikian. 1963. 107. In the following I shall not be attacking a position Brandt holds, but only an argument that might be offered on the basis of his theory. In fact, in Brandt, "Utility and the Obligation to Obey the Law." *Law and Philosophy*. Ed. S. Hook. 1964. 43, 47–49, Brandt expresses doubt as to whether there is such an obligation.

35. According to Brandt's theory, there is an absolute obligation to perform an act if it:

> conforms with that learnable set of rules the recognition of which as morally binding— roughly at the time of the act—by everyone in the society of the agent, except for the retention by individuals of already formed and decided moral convictions, would maximize intrinsic value.

Brandt, "Toward a Credible Utilitarianism." *Morality and the Language of Conduct*. (Eds. H. N. Casteñeda & G. Nakhnikian. 1963. 107. He distinguishes three levels of rules, the first stating prima facie obligations and the latter two dealing with cases in which lower-level rules conflict. At every level, however, those in the favored set of rules are those whose recognition would have the best consequences (i.e., consequences better than were any alternative rule accepted, as well as better than were no such rule accepted). Id., at 118–119.

36. As an illustration of the difficulty, Brandt suggests that the first-level rule, "Keep your promises," is neither the one that we accept nor the rule about promising that would maximize utility. Id., at 131–132. I think he is right to say that it is not the rule we accept, but how does he know that some more complex rule maximizes utility?

37. The second principle may be thought objectionable on the ground that it trivializes obviously weighty prima facie obligations. It may perhaps be held that, were a man to kill a thousand persons, his act would not have been much worse had he killed but one more. The principle therefore seems to imply that the prima facie obligation not to kill that one person is trivial. The objection is plausible, but misguided. Surely there is a substantial moral difference between killing a thousand persons and killing a thousand-and-one— exactly the difference between killing one person and killing none. To deny this is to imply that the thousand-and-first person's life has little moral significance. At first glance, however, we may be inclined to take the difference to be trivial, because both acts are so monstrous that we should rarely see any point in distinguishing between them. That this objection might be raised against the principle was pointed out to me by Anne Brown.

38. I have taken this point from I. W. Blackstone, *Commentaries* 54: Neither do divine or natural duties (such as, for instance, the worship of God, the maintenance of children, and the like) receive any stronger sanction from being also declared to be duties by the law of the land. The case is the same as to crimes and misdemeanors, which are forbidden by the superior laws and therefore styled *mala in se*, such as murder, theft, and perjury; which contract no additional turpitude from being declared unlawful by the inferior legislature.

39. Whittaker, C. *First Lecture, in Law, Order and Civil Disobedience*. 1967.

40. See Zinn, H. *Disobedience and Democracy*. 1968.

41. Devlin, P. *The Enforcement of Morals*. 1965. 27.

CHAPTER EIGHT

International Law and Human Rights

24   The Legitimacy of International Law

ALLEN BUCHANAN[1]

I. THE CONCEPT OF LEGITIMACY AS APPLIED TO INTERNATIONAL LAW AND INSTITUTIONS

1. The Primacy of Institutional Legitimacy

Although writers on international law and international relations frequently fail to make the distinction, "legitimate" has both a sociological and a normative meaning.[1] An institution that attempts to rule (govern) is legitimate in the normative sense if and only if it has *the right to rule*. Rival theories of legitimacy differ on what the right to rule is and on what conditions must be satisfied for an institution to have the right to rule. Calling an institution legitimate in the sociological sense is a misleading way of saying that it is widely *believed*

to have the right to rule. Here I will focus on the normative sense of "legitimacy."

Both laws and legal institutions are said to be legitimate or illegitimate, but institutional legitimacy is primary in so far as the legitimacy of particular laws or of a corpus of law depends on the legitimacy of the institutions that make, interpret, and apply the laws (although legitimate institutions sometimes may produce illegitimate laws). Accordingly, international laws are legitimate only if the institutions that make them are legitimate. Let us call international lawmaking institutions "ILIs." By an institution here is meant (roughly) a persisting pattern of organized, rule-governed, coordinated behavior. Using this broad sense of "institution," we can say there are three types of ILIs: the institution of treaty making, the institution of customary international law, and global governance institutions, which includes a diversity of entities such as the World Trade Organization (WTO), the United Nations (UN) Security Council, environmental regimes such as that established by the Kyoto Accords, and various

[1] I am grateful to Haim Ganz, Stephen Ratner, Lukas Meyer, Samantha Besson, and JohnTasioulas for their comments on earlier versions of this paper.

judicial and regulatory "government networks" composed of officials from several states. Global governance institutions, though created and sustained through treaties made by states, are increasingly taking on lawmaking functions.

At present, there is nothing approaching an adequate theory of legitimacy for international law. Before much headway can be made on this task, several questions must be answered. (1) What is the distinctive character and point of legitimacy judgments and how do they differ from other evaluations of institutions? (2) What concept or conceptions of legitimacy are relevant to international law and what standards of legitimacy ought ILIs meet, assuming that a particular concept of legitimacy is relevant? (Is there one concept of legitimacy and one set of standards for legitimacy that applies to all ILIs?). (3) What are the chief challenges to the legitimacy of international law? (What features of ILIs call their legitimacy into question?). (4) What is at stake in assessments of the legitimacy of international law—more specifically, why does the legitimacy of ILIs matter and to whom? (5) What conditions should a theory of legitimacy for international law satisfy? (6) What are the main rival approaches to theorizing the legitimacy of international law and which seem most promising, given an account of the conditions such theories should satisfy? The aim of this chapter is to answer these six questions.

2. The Nature of Legitimacy Assessments

Assertions about the legitimacy or illegitimacy of institutions (as opposed to reports about people's beliefs about their legitimacy) are moral evaluations, not statements of legal fact. The issue is whether ILIs have the *moral* right to rule and what does the right to rule entail.[2]

Just as legitimacy judgments cannot be reduced to statements of legal fact, they also are not reducible to statements to the effect that noncompliance with the institution's rules will elicit coercion or that compliance with the rules is advantageous. An institution can be effective in coercively enforcing rules and yet not be legitimate; indeed, in the case of the state it has been precisely its success in coercing that has most urgently

raised the question of its legitimacy. Similarly, an institution might be advantageous—even advantageous to all whom it attempts to govern—and yet it might still be illegitimate, for example, if it came about through usurpation.

The moral evaluation that institutional legitimacy judgments express is also different from that of justice. Although extreme and persisting injustices can render an institution illegitimate, legitimacy is a less demanding standard than justice in the sense that an institution can be legitimate though not fully just.[3] Different parties' legitimacy assessments of a particular institution can agree, even if they have serious disagreements about what justice requires. Thus, legitimacy judgments can facilitate morally based coordinated support—or criticism—of institutions even where consensus on justice is lacking. The current concern about the legitimacy of international law may be due in part to the widespread belief that present disagreements about justice—especially global distributive justice—are not likely soon to be resolved.

Achieving morally based coordination can be of great practical importance when two conditions are satisfied. The first, which I have already suggested, is that there is serious disagreement about justice but considerable consensus that institutions ought to satisfy some moral requirements—a widespread belief that merely being able to enforce their rules and being advantageous relative to the noninstitutional alternative are not sufficient. The second is that the distinctive benefits that an institution creates are most reliably secured if, in addition to the fear of coercion and the expectation of advantage relative to the noninstitutional alternative, there are moral reasons to support the functioning of the institution. Moral reason-based support can enable an institution to function successfully when there are lapses in its ability to coerce, and during periods when there is reason for some to doubt that it is indeed advantageous for all relative to the noninstitutional alternative. Moral reason-based support can reduce the costs of achieving compliance, which might be prohibitively high if the threat of coercion were the only reason for compliance.

3. Stronger and Weaker Senses of "the Right to Rule"

There are stronger and weaker senses of "the right to rule," although prominent accounts of legitimacy often assume that only one of these senses is of central importance for political philosophy. What might be called the dominant philosophical view (DPV) of *state* legitimacy employs a very strong understanding of the right to rule as including six elements: (a) the institution's agents are morally justified in engaging in governance functions, including issuing rules and attaching costs and benefits to various agents to facilitate compliance with them (the justified governance condition); (b) the institution's agents are morally justified in using coercion to secure compliance with the institution's rules (the justified coercion condition); (c) only the institution's agents are morally justified in engaging in governance functions in the domain of action in question (the exclusive justification condition); (d) the institution's agents are morally justified in using coercion to prevent others from attempting to engage in governance activities in its domain (the coercive exclusion condition); and (e) those whom the institution attempts to govern have a content-independent moral obligation to comply with (all) the rules the institution imposes (the content-independent moral obligation condition).[4] A content-independent obligation to comply with a rule is an obligation that exists independently of any assessment of the rule itself. In all legal systems, those to whom the rules are addressed typically have content-*dependent* moral obligations to comply with some of the rules: for example, if the law prohibits murder, one has a moral obligation to comply with this law because it is simply the legal expression of a valid moral rule. Since (e) presumably implies (f), a similar obligation *not to interfere* with the institution's efforts to secure compliance with its rules, there are in fact six elements of legitimacy on this account. Because the DPV was developed with the case of the state in mind, it emphasizes the right to coerce.

The DPV's conception of the right to rule is extraordinarily strong, both with regard to what

counts as *ruling* (that is, governance) and with regard to what counts as having a *right* to rule. It assumes that legitimacy not only involves justified governance (ruling) of some sort (element (a)), but *also* justified coercive governance (element (b)), *and* the exclusive right to use coercion to secure compliance with rules (element (c)), *and* the right to use coercion to exclude others from engaging in governance activities in its domain (element (d)). However, there is no reason to assume that only institutions that govern (rule) in this very strong sense can be said to be legitimate or illegitimate, that is, can have the right to rule or lack it. Indeed, there are many institutions, including all existing international institutions, which do not rule in this robust way and do not even claim to do so. It is *more* plausible to say that the very strong notion of governance encompassed by the dominant philosophical conception of legitimacy is pertinent if we are focusing only on the legitimacy of one peculiar kind of institution, namely, the state.[5]

A better way of understanding the "being morally justified in governing" element of legitimacy is as follows: being morally justified in issuing rules and seeking to secure compliance with them through attaching costs to noncompliance and benefits to compliance. This characterization covers coercion but is not limited to it and can therefore serve as an element in a concept of legitimacy that is applicable to institutions that do not rule coercively, including most ILIs.

The DPV rightly emphasizes that legitimacy, as the term is often used, includes more than being justified in governing if this means merely having the liberty-right to govern.[6] *A* can have the liberty-right to do *X* and it can nonetheless be true that no one has any duty or even any reason not to interfere with *A* doing *X*. Merely being justified in governing in this sense is arguably insufficient for what might be called the focal sense of "legitimacy," because it fails to encompass the distinctive *relational* aspect of legitimacy.[7] More specifically, the mere liberty-right to govern omits the crucial idea that the rules of a legitimate institution *have a privileged status vis à vis our reasons for acting, and that their having this privileged status is not dependent on their content.* At least in what might be called the focal sense of the term, legitimacy involves not only the liberty-right to govern but also *a content-independent requirement of practical support for (or at least non-interference with) the institution's efforts to govern.*[8]

The DPV's very robust requirement of a content-independent *moral obligation* to comply with rules is not needed to capture the idea of a requirement of content-independent practical support and hence is not necessary for legitimacy in the focal, relational sense. The weaker combination of a content-independent moral obligation or substantial content-independent reason not to interfere, along with substantial content-independent *moral reasons* to comply—where these reasons may fall short of grounding an obligation—does the job. Therefore, it is not the case that a proper recognition of the distinction between merely being justified in governing and being legitimate requires anything as strong as the DPV's conception of legitimacy.[9] One can acknowledge that legitimacy as the right to rule involves more than being justified in ruling, without assuming that it entails something as strong as a content-independent moral obligation to comply.

The DPV's understanding of what counts as *rule* (that is, governance) is as unduly strong as its understanding of the right to rule. Many international legal institutions do not claim an *exclusive* right to rule, yet it makes perfectly good sense to ask whether they are legitimate (in a relational sense). For example, the World Trade Organization (WTO) does not claim that it alone is justified in engaging in multilateral efforts to promote the liberalization of trade; it recognizes the legitimacy of regional trade regimes that promote liberalization. Similarly, the International Criminal Court (ICC) does not claim to be the only tribunal that justifiably may prosecute the international crimes specified in its statute; it allows for both prosecution of individuals by their own states and the exercise of "universal jurisdiction" by states over foreign individuals. Second, even when international legal institutions claim the exclusive right to govern in a certain domain, they do not always, or even typically, also claim the right to use coercion to exclude others from

attempting to engage in governance functions. Third, "rule" in the DPV's understanding of the right to rule means governance in the peculiarly strong sense in which *states* (sometimes) govern: seeking to ensure compliance with rules through *coercion*, understood as a credible threat of the use of physical force against noncompliers. Although most international legal institutions do not govern, or attempt to govern, or even claim the right to govern, in this very strong sense, it nevertheless makes sense to ask whether these institutions are legitimate, where legitimacy is understood as relational, as implying more than being morally justified in governing.

My proposal, then, is to proceed on the assumption that for ILIs, legitimacy as the right to rule includes two main elements: (1) the institution must be morally justified in attempting to govern (must have the moral liberty-right or permission to try to govern) in the sense of issuing rules (that prescribe duties for various actors) and attempting to secure compliance with them by imposing costs for noncompliance and benefits for compliance and (2) those toward whom the rules are directed (chiefly, though not exclusively states) have substantial, content-independent moral reasons for compliance, and others (including citizens of states) have substantial content-independent moral reasons for supporting the institution's efforts to secure compliance with its directives or at least have substantial, content-independent moral reasons not to interfere with those efforts.

This formulation has several advantages. First, it acknowledges the fact that most ILIs, like international institutions generally, do not employ coercion to secure compliance with their rules, and do not claim the right to do so. Thus it avoids the error of simply applying to ILIs the very strong conception of legitimacy that may be appropriate for the state. Second, it allows for the fact that there is variation among ILIs as to whether they attempt to achieve or claim exclusive authority over the domain in which they operate. Third, the second conjunct of (2), it recognizes that the legitimacy of ILIs can reasonably be of concern to actors other than states, some of whom may not be subjects of duties the institution attempts to impose.

This understanding of legitimacy seems superior to the Razian conception of authority that John Tasioulas advances, according to which A has the right to rule over B if and only if B's complying with A's rules enables B to do better than B would do were she to act directly on reasons that independently apply to her. The difficulty with the Razian notion is that the mere fact that others would do better were they to obey one does not justify one's attempting to rule over them. So an entity could have authority in the Razian sense but not be justified in attempting to secure compliance with the norms it promulgates. Yet, whatever else having the right to rule entails, it surely includes being justified in attempting to rule.

4. The Chief Challenges to the Legitimacy of International Law

Challenges fall mainly under the following five headings. First, there is a challenge from the perspective of states: it is frequently said that particular ILIs, like the UN Security Council or the WTO, or even the entire international legal order, are unfairly controlled by a handful of powerful states, thereby unfairly disadvantaging weaker ones. Whether it is supposed to be a claim about injustice or about legitimacy is often unclear. It could be both, of course—the idea being that from the perspective of fairness to states, this or that ILI or the current international legal order as a whole is so unjust as to be illegitimate. Some who advance this charge assume that the remedy is state-majoritarian democracy: ILIs should operate according to procedures that assure an equal voice for all states.

A second, quite different challenge to the legitimacy of ILIs is that they are unfair to individuals and nonstate groups such as indigenous peoples, or that they fail to take the legitimate interests of nonstate individuals or groups seriously enough and often operate so as to threaten their welfare. On this view, the unfairness of ILIs regarding states is of concern only so far as it results in unfairness to nonstate individuals or groups or threats to their welfare. Some versions of this challenge assume that some kind of global democracy is required if ILIs are to be legitimate.[10]

The third legitimacy challenge focuses on whether ILIs credibly do the jobs they are supposed to do, or act in accordance with the goals and procedures to which they publicly commit. For example, some have argued that the failure of the Security Council to authorize armed intervention to stop genocides or other forms of mass murder have been so egregious as to undermine the legitimacy of the Council. An institution also may be deemed illegitimate if it is deeply and persistently corrupt. Some have concluded that the massive corruption of the Iraq "Oil For Food" programme, when considered in the light of a long history of corruption or at least poor management in many other cases, impugns the legitimacy of the UN Secretariat, which was in charge of the programme.

The fourth challenge to the legitimacy of ILIs alleges that all or some of them usurp the proper authority of states or, on one variant of the view, of democracies. There are two different ways of understanding this challenge. On the first, less radical variant, the charge is that *as a matter of fact* some ILIs have so seriously encroached on the proper domain of authority of the state (or democratic states) as to render themselves illegitimate, but there is no claim that international law and sovereignty or the sovereignty of democracies are *in principle* incompatible. On the second, more radical variant, the charge is that the supremacy of international law is incompatible in principle with sovereignty or with democratic constitutional sovereignty. According to the second interpretation, ILIs, so far as they claim supremacy for their norms, are *necessarily* illegitimate, at least *vis à vis* constitutional democracies, because by definition the supreme law in a constitutional democracy is determined by its own constitution.

It appears, however, that there is no problem of incompatibility in principle. If democracies can subject themselves to international laws by following processes that accord with their own constitutional principles, there is no bar to saying both that they are bound by those laws and that the constitution is the supreme law of the land. One way of accomplishing this is to create a new constitution or amend an old one so that it recognizes the supremacy of international law, or of some types of international law, such as human rights law. Moreover, if a democratic state ratifies a treaty and incorporates the relevant laws into its domestic legal system through a process that satisfies constitutional requirements, then presumably it will be true to say that the state has a substantial content-independent moral reason to comply and that the citizens of the democracy have a substantial content-independent reason to support their state's compliance—namely, because the law in question became the law of the land through a constitutionally sanctioned process. If the worry is only that international law is being incorporated in ways that violate the democracy's constitution, and proper constitutional processes for incorporation are available, then the objection is not that constitutional democracy and the supremacy of international law are *in principle* incompatible.

The fifth and final challenge to the legitimacy of international law is that ILIs are not themselves democratic. *If* "democracy" here means what it does in the case of the state, namely, that those who make the law must be accountable through periodic electoral processes in which individuals have an equal vote, most theorists agree that democracy (in this "individual-majoritarian" sense) at the global level is not presently feasible or likely to become so in the foreseeable future. Instead of concluding from this that ILIs cannot be legitimate, some argue that they can be, so long as they exemplify the same basic *democratic values* (or principles) that mandate individual-majoritarian democracy in the case of the state. Whether the current democracy deficit is sufficiently serious to deprive the existing international order of legitimacy is a further question, and one which in my judgment has not been adequately addressed.

5. Why and to Whom the Legitimacy of International Lawmaking Institutions Matters

It is misleading to say that international law is created by states, through treaty and custom, both because this formulation overlooks the growing contribution of global governance institutions to international lawmaking and because various nonstate actors increasingly play a role in international lawmaking. The legitimacy of international law is not just a concern of states, but also of nonstate groups and individual citizens, who sometimes reasonably may question the legitimacy of international institutions even though they know that their own states have consented to them. As I noted earlier, individuals and groups still may question the legitimacy of ILIs even though their state voluntarily has consented to them, not because they believe that these institutions treat weaker *states* unfairly, but rather because they believe that these institutions act unfairly toward *them* or threaten *their* welfare. To a large extent, this concern on the part of citizens reflects the growing penetration of international law into life within states. The further we depart from the picture of international laws as being created solely by states and as dealing solely with the relations of states to one another—and the more seriously we take the idea that human beings, not states, are the ultimate objects of moral concern—the clearer it becomes that a satisfactory account of the legitimacy of international law must include more than an explanation of why *states* ought to regard the international institutions through which law is made as having the right to rule. More precisely, appreciating the new face of international law shows just how inadequate the traditional framing of the question of the legitimacy of international law is. The question is much broader than "why should states consider international law binding?"

6. A Deeper Sense of the Question "Is International Law Legitimate?"

There is a still more basic issue about the legitimacy of international law. This is the question of whether or to what extent democratic state leaders and the citizens of democratic states ought to be morally committed to the project of international law—to the endeavour to build and sustain an international legal order. The query here is not whether this or that international law or this or that type of ILI (for example, treaty law or customary law) is legitimate; rather, it concerns the moral status of the goal of developing the rule of law at the global level. This is an important question, even if one concludes that international law as it now exists has a serious legitimacy deficit. Even if no existing international institutions were legitimate, we still could ask whether the project of international law makes moral sense.

Recently some American legal theorists, like some American political leaders, have answered this question in the negative, advocating what I have elsewhere called a purely instrumental stance toward international law.[11] On this view, the citizens of democratic states should direct their state leaders to support international legal institutions only when it is in the national interest to do so or when those citizens happen to have moral "preferences" (such as the "preference" that human rights not be violated) that are best promoted by doing so. There is no noninstrumental reason for entering into any particular international agreement or for keeping agreements already entered into, nor for contributing to the work of building and improving the international legal order.

7. The Ideal of the Rule of Law

The most obvious reply to the purely instrumentalist view is that there are substantial moral reasons to promote *the rule of law* at the international level. Although there is much controversy as to just what the ideal of the rule of law consists of, there is considerable consensus that the principles that constitute it include the following: the law should be general (and when there are departures from generality they should be controlled by processes that are informed by general principles); the law should be understandable and publicly proclaimed; there is a presumption against retroactive law, especially retroactive criminal law; and the administration of the law should be impartial. In a wider sense, the commitment to the rule of law is the commitment to resolving or managing conflicts by effectively institutionalizing the impartial application of publicly known general rules that are based on the assumption that there is to be an accommodation of interests. The commitment to the rule of law in this wider sense goes beyond

the assertion that *if* there is to be international law it should conform to the principles that constitute the ideal of the rule of law; it is the commitment to subjecting international relations to law, in conformity to this ideal.

The traditional answer to the question "Why should we try to subject international relations to the rule of law?" was that doing so is necessary to achieve peace among states. This answer is compatible with the purely instrumental view, but it is also compatible with its rejection, if the commitment to peace is understood to be a moral duty, not merely a matter of rational prudence. Increasingly, the contemporary answer to the question is that subjecting international relations to the rule of law is necessary not only for the sake of peace among states but also for justice, where justice is understood, first and foremost, though not exclusively, as the realization of human rights.

Those who hold the purely instrumental view of international law may do so because they subscribe to a Realist theory of international relations: Realists deny that there is a noninstrumental moral obligation to promote the rule of international law, because they believe that, given the nature of international relations as they understand it, international law never will be capable of making a significant contribution to justice. (In addition, they may in fact hold that the concept of justice has no application to international affairs.) Given the weaknesses of Realism, which have been exposed increasingly in recent years, this reason for denying that there is a noninstrumental moral obligation to support the project of international law is hardly conclusive.

Resolving the dispute between the purely instrumentalist view and the view that there is a moral obligation to promote the rule of international law is clearly beyond the scope of the present investigation. My purpose is only to distinguish different senses of the question "is international law legitimate?" and to indicate that the deepest of these goes to the heart of our understanding of the relationship between law and justice, and our predictions about the human capacity for creating lawful relationships among different societies.

8. Conditions an Adequate Theory of the Legitimacy of International Law Should Satisfy

The preceding analysis yields criteria of adequacy for a theory of the legitimacy of international law. Such a theory must encompass all three types of ILIs—it must provide an account of the legitimacy (or otherwise) of customary law, treaty law, and law produced by global governance institutions. It also must acknowledge that it is no longer true that states alone make international law, accommodating the fact that global governance institutions engage in rulemaking that is not accurately described as the creation of law through state consent, and that nonstate actors, including agents of transnational, nongovernmental organizations, now sometimes contribute to the making of international law.

II. STANDARDS FOR THE LEGITIMACY OF INTERNATIONAL LAW

1. The Simple State-consent View

Proceeding on the assumption that institutions are the primary subject of legitimacy assessments and that the legitimacy of laws depends on the legitimacy of institutions that make them, it may be initially tempting to say that the question of the legitimacy of international law can be answered in a rather simple and straightforward way: rules are legitimate international laws if and only if they are produced through *the institution of state consent*, that is, if they are created in accordance with the procedures that states have consented to for the making of international laws, which include the requirement that states must consent to laws. The state-consent view of legitimacy has been by far the dominant view among international legal theorists. Let us consider the first half of the biconditional: is state consent sufficient for legitimacy?

On the simplest interpretation of the view that state consent is sufficient—the legitimacy of treaty law is assured by the explicit consent of states—the legitimacy of customary international law is assured by a kind of implicit consent

inferred from the behaviour of states, and the legitimacy of law generated by global governance institutions is assured by their being created and sustained by state consent. The attraction of this view lies in an analogy with individual consent: if you and I consent to a certain arrangement as to how we shall treat each other, then surely that arrangement is legitimate. Similarly, it is said, if states consent to a certain arrangement for how their interactions are to be regulated, then it is legitimate.

The analysis of section I indicates that there are several reasons for rejecting the view that *under current and foreseeable conditions* state consent is sufficient for the legitimacy of international laws. The consent of weaker states may be less than substantially voluntary, because stronger states can make the costs of their not consenting prohibitive. Further, in many cases, states do not represent all of or even most of their people; they are not sufficiently democratic to make it reasonable to say that state consent by itself legitimizes what states consent to.

In addition, even if we focused only on treaty law—setting aside the dubious assumption that customary law reasonably can be understood as enjoying state consent—and even if all states represented all their people, it still would not follow that state consent suffices for legitimacy for two distinct reasons. First, the problem of questionable voluntariness still would remain: the fact that a weak state is democratic does not change the fact that it is weak and therefore may face pressures that undermine the voluntariness of its consent. Second, as I already have noted, international law increasingly is not limited to rules to which states can be said to consent in a normatively substantial sense; instead, some important international law is created by global governance institutions of various sorts. Even though these institutions are created by state consent and cannot function without state support, they engage in *ongoing* governance activities, including the generation of laws and law-like rules, that are not controlled by the "specific consent" of states. Hence, the problem of "bureaucratic distance" looms large, even if the states that create these institutions are democratic; the links between the popular will in democratic states that consent to the creation of global governance institutions and the governing functions these institutions perform seem too anaemic to confer legitimacy. Given the reality of bureaucratic distance, the mere fact that democratic states consented to the creation of global governance institutions and have not withdrawn their consent does not seem sufficient to make such institutions legitimate. Finally, to the extent that nonstate actors play a role in the creation of international law, state consent seems insufficient for legitimacy, unless it can be shown that the legitimacy of the contribution these nonstate actors make to the creation of international law somehow is assured by state consent.

So far I have argued that, under current conditions in which (1) there is great disparity of power among states, in which (2) many states do not represent all of their people, and in which (3) there is a serious problem of "bureaucratic distance," state consent is not sufficient for the legitimacy of international institutions nor, therefore, for the legitimacy of the laws they make (given that the legitimacy of the latter derives from the legitimacy of the former). At this point one might argue that *in different circumstances*—where conditions (1), (2), and (3) do not obtain—state consent would be sufficient for legitimacy. In other words, we might view the claim that state consent is sufficient for legitimacy as a claim in the ideal theory of international legal order, not as a claim about what suffices for the legitimacy of international law as it is or is likely to be in the foreseeable future. Whether state consent would be a sufficient condition for legitimacy in ideal theory cannot be determined, however, until the ideal theory is laid out.

More troubling still, we cannot begin to evaluate claims about ideal theory until we specify just what an ideal theory is a theory of. The answer to the question "Would state consent be sufficient for the legitimacy of international lawmaking institutions in ideal theory?" may differ depending upon whether or not we assume that ideal theory is a theory for a world in which only states (as opposed to other political entities, regional or substate) are the primary agents for the establishment of justice.

2. Is State Consent Necessary for Legitimacy?

So far I have argued that, under current conditions, state consent is not sufficient for legitimacy. This leaves open the question of whether it is necessary. If we assume that state consent is a necessary condition for legitimacy under current conditions, then it appears that we must conclude that much of existing international law, perhaps especially customary international law (CIL), is illegitimate. The view that states tacitly or implicitly consent to CIL does not stand up to scrutiny. CIL norms apply to states that did not exist at the time of their emergence, even if they object to them, yet surely their objecting to them is pretty good evidence that they are not now consenting to them. To say that such states have consented to the *process* by which CIL norms emerge is equally unconvincing, given the inability of weaker states to opt out of the process or to do so without excessive costs. To summarize: if state consent is a necessary condition for legitimacy under current conditions, then a substantial portion of existing international law appears to be illegitimate.

Whether state consent is a plausible necessary condition for the legitimacy of international law in ideal theory cannot be determined unless we first have a specification of the background conditions for ideal theory, including the role of states in the overall system the ideal theory prescribes. In contrast, there is a straightforward nonideal theory argument for a norm according to which state consent is a necessary condition for the legitimacy of international law under current conditions: adherence to this norm would reduce the ability of strong states to hijack the project of international law. In other words, the best reason for saying that state consent is a necessary condition for the legitimacy of international law may be that, under current and foreseeable conditions, it provides an important safeguard against the rule of the strong. Whether strict adherence to the requirement of state consent is the only feasible and adequately effective safeguard is a complex issue that cannot be pursued here. It is worth pointing out, however, that strict adherence to the requirement of state consent is a costly way of protecting against predation: it gives every state, including the most oppressive ones, a veto over any progressive change in international law.

3. The Demand for Democratic Legitimacy

A growing awareness of the insufficiency of state consent for legitimacy under current and foreseeable conditions, along with the widespread belief that democracy is a necessary condition for the legitimacy of the state, may explain why the debate about the legitimacy of the international legal order has shifted from a preoccupation with state consent to a debate about the possibilities of "global democracy." A major focus of this discussion has been global governance institutions, in large part because they appear to be controlled inadequately by state consent, or at least by the will of democratic publics, and yet seem to be growing more consequential, not just for state sovereignty, but also for the well-being of individuals. Let us call the "Global Democracy View" the claim that at least one important type of ILI, global governance institutions, cannot be legitimate unless they are democratic in the individual-majoritarian sense. The Global Democracy View often is criticized for being utopian. The idea is that the conditions for global democracy (in the individual-majoritarian sense)—do not exist and are not likely to exist in the foreseeable future. This seems to me to be right, if, as the Global Democracy View holds, the requirement for legitimacy is that ILIs must be democratic in what I referred to earlier as the individual-electoral sense. Here one either might conclude that the standard of democracy now increasingly applied to states is too demanding to be applied to ILIs, or one might conclude that no ILIs are legitimate because they fail to satisfy that standard. Robert O. Keohane and I opt for the former conclusion. We argue that once the distinctive practical function of legitimacy assessments in achieving moral reason-based coordination is understood, it becomes clear that a requirement of global democracy in the individual-majoritarian sense is an unreasonably strong necessary condition in the case of global governance institutions for the

foreseeable future.[12] In a nutshell, we argue that the demand for global democracy in this sense is unreasonably strong given two conditions: first, the benefits that global governance institutions provide are quite valuable and not likely to be provided reliably without them; second, the key values that underlie the demand for global democracy can be approximated reasonably if these institutions satisfy other more feasible conditions, including what we call "Broad Accountability." By the latter we mean that these institutions must cooperate with external epistemic actors—individuals and groups outside the institution, in particular transnational civil society organizations—to create conditions under which the goals and processes of the institution, as well as the current terms of institutional accountability, can be contested and critically revised over time, and in a manner that helps to ensure an increasingly inclusive consideration of legitimate interests, through largely transparent deliberative processes. Broad Accountability, we argue, would provide a reasonable second-best for global democracy in the individual-majoritarian sense, under current, highly nonideal conditions. Although Broad Accountability may not qualify as democracy on some accounts, it does realize some important democratic values.

Rather than recapitulate that argument in detail here, I simply want to note that, even if one could argue, contrary to what Keohane and I contend, that global democracy in the individual-electoral sense is a necessary condition for the legitimacy of ILIs, *it would not be sufficient*. Even the most enthusiastic advocates of democracy at the domestic level ought to admit that the legitimacy of *any* majoritarian electoral process can be undercut if it results in serious and persistent violations of basic human rights, for example, the rights of a minority ethnic or national group. The same would be true at the global level. So, whether or not democracy (in the individual-electoral sense) is a necessary condition for the legitimacy of global governance institutions, it is not sufficient. Nor would global democracy understood as an arrangement that achieves equal political power for all states (rather than all individuals)—what I referred to in section I as the state-majoritarian view—be sufficient for legitimacy, because that too is compatible with serious violations of human rights. In sum, it is difficult to imagine that any institution of governance, democratic or otherwise, at the global or the domestic level, could be legitimate if it persistently engaged in serious violations of basic human rights norms. Of course, on some understandings of democracy (whether global or domestic) respect for basic human rights already is included, but this conflation is unhelpful. A political order could be democratic, even in the very strong sense that each individual has an "equal say" in lawmaking, and yet the laws could provide insufficient protection for human rights or even violate them. So, assuming that the protection of human rights is generally a necessary condition for the legitimacy of a political order, it appears that state consent, even under much more ideal conditions than those in which it now operates, is not sufficient for legitimacy.

III. HUMAN RIGHTS AND INTERNATIONAL LEGITIMACY

It is something of a commonplace that the international legal order is becoming less exclusively state-centered and more concerned with human rights. The Security Council has authorized military interventions to stop large-scale human rights violations in Bosnia and Somalia. *Ad hoc* tribunals and a permanent international criminal court have been created to prosecute war crimes, genocide, and crimes against humanity. The idea that state sovereignty itself is conditional on the protection of human rights seems to be taking hold.

These changes are rightly viewed as moral progress; yet they raise a fundamental issue of legitimacy that those who greet them with enthusiasm have not squarely faced. In order to be legitimate, an international legal order that takes the protection of human rights to be a fundamental goal must address a familiar challenge to the very idea of human rights: what I have elsewhere labeled *the parochialism objection*, according to which what are called *human* rights are not really universal but instead are simply reflections of one particular cultural point of view (variously said to be "Western" or "liberal" or "liberal individualist").

To meet this objection, it is not enough to point out that most states have ratified the major human rights conventions. The question is not whether states have agreed to treat human rights norms *as if they were* universally valid, but rather whether they *are* universally valid. To elide the latter distinction is to assume that state consent, under current conditions, is sufficient for legitimacy. But that claim, I have argued, is indefensible. Nor will it do to say that the international legal system includes institutions that articulate legal international human rights norms and ensure that these norms conform to the criteria for legality in the international legal system. By itself, the legality of a putative human rights norm does nothing to establish that a human right exists. Further, nothing in the texts of human rights conventions seems to provide an adequate response to the fundamental issue of justification that the parochialism objection raises. Indeed, aside from some vague gestures toward human dignity in the Preambles, the texts scrupulously avoid the task of justification.

One might argue that the parochialism objection is hardly credible when applied to *basic* human rights norms such as the rights against enslavement, the right to physical security, the right against religious persecution, and the right to subsistence. And, indeed, it does seem implausible to say that these rights are of value only to "Westerners" or "liberal individualists." The parochialism objection arises anew, however, once we realize that there can be serious disagreements, in some cases apparently rooted in different cultural, religious, or philosophical views, about the specific content of these rights and about how they ought to be balanced against one another in cases of conflict. For example, there may be near-universal agreement that there is a human right not to be subjected to torture or to cruel and inhumane punishment, but cultural variation as to what counts as torture or cruel and inhumane punishment. In brief, even the most basic human rights norms are not self-specifying, and specifications reasonably may be questioned as to whether they are parochial or not. The more fully an intuitively plausible, highly abstract human rights norm becomes legalized—that is, expressed as an international legal human right—the more vulnerable it can become to the charge of parochialism, because legalization involves, *inter alia*, greater specificity.

It is often said that the Universal Declaration of Human Rights and the various human rights treaties that followed it wisely avoided attempting a justification for the norms they asserted. To paraphrase the philosopher Jacques Maritain, it was possible to agree on a list of human rights only on the condition that almost nothing was said about how they are grounded. As an explanation of the absence of a public moral grounding for international human rights law, Maritain's remark is cogent. It does nothing to rebut the parochialism objection, however. Therefore, it also does nothing to allay the worry that an international legal order that increasingly relies on the idea of human rights in its conception of its own legitimacy, in the legitimacy assessments it makes, and in its efforts to enforce the conditions of legitimacy on other institutions, is of questionable legitimacy if it persists in doing so without being able to provide a credible public justification for the claim that it has properly identified and specified a set of genuinely universal rights.

In the end, whether such a justification becomes available will depend not only upon the further development of the moral foundations of the idea of human rights—a task which until recently most contemporary moral and political philosophers, like most international legal theorists, have avoided—but also upon improvements in the global public deliberative processes that occur within the complex array of institutions within which human rights norms are articulated, contested, and revised over time.[13] What I am suggesting is that grappling with this fundamental legitimacy problem requires an investigation of the moral-epistemic functions of these institutions. This means viewing them, not merely as venues in which antecedently justified moral norms are given legal form, but as institutions for global public deliberation that can contribute to the moral justification of human rights norms,

and thereby to their own legitimacy and to the legitimacy of the international legal order as a whole, so far as that order takes human rights seriously.

NOTES

1. Fernando Tesón has focused squarely on the normative sense of legitimacy, and is among the first (if not the first) contemporary international legal scholars writing in English to advance the idea that the legitimacy of states depends upon their satisfying at least minimal standards with respect to the protection of human rights. Tesón, F. *Humanitarian Intervention, An Inquiry Into Law and Morality*. 3rd ed. New York: Transnational Publishers, 2005; and *A Philosophy of International Law*. Boulder, Colo.: Westview Press, 1998.

2. The rest of this section draws on Buchanan, A. and Keohane, R. O. 'The Legitimacy of Global Governance Institutions.' *Ethics & International Affairs* 20/4 (2006): 405.

3. However, an institution might be operating in a perfectly just way yet be illegitimate, if it came about through serious injustice, for example, by usurping the functions of a preexisting legitimate institution.

4. By the dominant philosophical view I mean that view of the legitimacy of the state that generally is assumed in the extensive contemporary analytic philosophical literature on the question of whether there is "a duty to obey the law." For what may be the most developed and carefully reasoned contribution to this literature, see Simmons, J. A. *Justification and Legitimacy, Essays on Rights and Obligations*. Cambridge: Cambridge University Press, 2001. Item (d) above may not be explicit in Simmons's own understanding of legitimacy, but it is included in the Weberian conception of the state as an entity that claims a monopoly on the use of force within a territory, and it seems clear that Simmons and others in the mainstream debate about the obligation to obey the law assume the Weberian conception. However, nothing in my central argument in this paper depends on the claim that the dominant philosophical view includes (d).

5. It is not even clear, however, that the dominant philosophical conception of legitimacy applies to states as they actually are at present, as opposed to how they have been conceived in recent

analytic political philosophy. The dominant philo-sophical conception appears to assume a unitary and unqualified sovereignty that no longer exists, if it ever did. Sovereignty is now increasingly "un-bundled," and distributed in two ways. First, there is increasing political differentiation within states, with various forms of federalism (symmet-rical and asymmetrical) and other kinds of intra-state autonomy regimes, as well as a separation of powers at both the state and Federal levels. Under these conditions of complex political differentia-tion, there may be no definitive answer to the question "Who has exclusive authority over do-main D?"—or at least no answer prior to the ac-tual resolution of some particular conflict over authority, which may or may not occur. Yet it still makes sense to ask whether the state is legitimate. Second, there are substantial external limitations on sovereignty, including the increasingly effective institutionalization of international criminal law and international (and, in the case of the Euro-pean Union, regional) human rights law. These external limitations on sovereignty diminish the authority of the state even within its own territory. Given the internal dispersal of sovereignty and the external limits on it, the dominant philosophical conception of legitimacy appears to be too strong for application to the contemporary state.

6. "Justified" in the phrase "being justified in gov-erning" is itself ambiguous between (a) having a liberty-right to govern, that is, it being morally permissible to govern; and (b) there being good moral reasons in favour of (the institution's) gov-erning. I will operate with the former, weaker no-tion, but nothing in my argument hinges on this.

7. Simmons, J. A. *Justification and Legitimacy.* Above, n. 4, 128.

8. There are different possible interpretations of the idea that these content-independent obligations are "weighty." In particular, it could be argued that the right to rule implies not only that there are content-independent reasons for compliance with the institution's rules, but also that these content-independent reasons are peremptory in the sense that they rule out certain kinds of rea-sons for not complying *ab initio*, rather than merely being weighty relative to them. On this view, if an institution that addresses a rule to

one is legitimate, then the mere fact that not com-plying with its rule would be to one's advantage does not count as a reason that could be weighed against one's reason for compliance. The points I wish to make about the legitimacy of ILIs in this paper do not depend upon resolving the issue of whether the content-independent reasons for compliance are peremptory, but my assumption is that they are and this is one of the reasons for the qualifier "substantial" in the phrase "substan-tial content-independent reasons."

9. This is true even if "being justified" is understood more robustly than "having a mere liberty-right," for example, if it is taken to signify that there are strong reasons in favour of having the institution in question (for example, for prudential reasons).

10. These first two challenges to the legitimacy of ILIs are all seriously incomplete. Each merely cites an unfairness or injustice of ILIs, but then slides immediately to the conclusion that the institution is illegitimate. Something more must be said, be-cause, as I already have noted, injustice does not entail illegitimacy. The gap here is symptomatic of a more general problem: the characteristics that appear to be relevant to legitimacy (fairness, avoidance of discrepancies between institutional goals and actual behaviour, accountability, trans-parency, etc.) are all scalar (they admit of degree), yet at least in some context, the legitimacy must be regarded as a threshold concept (an institution either has it or doesn't), if legitimacy assessments are to play their practical role of distinguishing institutions that have the right to rule from those that don't. Having the right to rule, on the face of it, is not a matter of degree.

11. See e.g. Goldsmith, J., and Posner, E. *The Limits of International Law.* Oxford: Oxford University Press, 2005.

12. Buchanan, A. and Keohane, R. O. "The Legiti-macy of Global Governance Institutions." Above, n. 2.

13. I develop this idea of a complementary relation-ship between philosophical argumentation about the justification of human rights and global public deliberative processes occurring through interna-tional legal institutions in "Human Rights and the Legitimacy of the International Legal Order." *Legal Theory* 14 (2008): 39–70.

25 Outcasting: Enforcement in Domestic and International Law

OONA HATHAWAY & SCOTT J. SHAPIRO

Is international law *law?* In 2009, the American Society of International Law organized a panel at its annual meeting to discuss the question. Most of the panelists, however, began by expressing indignation that such a panel had even been convened. Andrew Guzman thought the question was a "futile" one; Thomas Franck was "surprised that we have gathered here again at the beginning of a new political era to ask this tired old question"; and José Alvarez was "appalled that we are still discussing this 1960s chestnut of a question." Instead, they agreed, the more interesting question— indeed, the proper organizing question of the field—is, "How well does international law do in its effort to influence state behavior?"

We understand this reaction, but we do not share it. The question of whether international law is law matters a great deal. Most fundamentally, it matters from the moral point of view. Law's moral import follows from a basic truth accepted by all but hardcore anarchists: namely, that legal systems are morally valuable institutions.[1] Thus, whether we ought to respect, support, or obey international law depends in part on whether it possesses those properties that make legal regimes worthy of our esteem and allegiance—that is, on whether it is "really" law (an implication, by the way, not lost on critics who deny its legality). But there is an additional—and, we shall see, deeply illuminating— reason why this jurisprudential question ought to be engaged. As we will show in this Article, responding to the critics who argue that international law is not law allows us to make substantial new progress in answering the very question international law scholars *do* care about: *whether* and *how* international law affects state behavior.

The reason is simple. The principal objection made by critics of international law is that international law cannot be real law because *it cannot matter in the way that real law must matter.* In particular, they argue that international law cannot matter in the way it must to be law because it lacks mechanisms of coercive enforcement. Anthony D'Amato describes this objection as follows:

Many serious students of the law react with a sort of indulgence when they encounter the term "international law," as if to say, "Well, we know it isn't *really* law, but we know that international lawyers and scholars have a vested professional interest in calling it 'law.'" Or they may agree to talk about international law *as if* it were law, a sort of quasi-law or near-law. But it cannot be true law, they maintain, because it cannot be enforced: how do you enforce a rule of law against an entire nation, especially a superpower such as the United States or the Soviet Union?

On this objection, international law cannot be real law because real law must be capable of affecting behavior through the threat and exercise of physical coercion. Since international law lacks mechanisms of physically coercive enforcement, it cannot affect behavior in the right way and hence cannot be a real legal system. It follows that answering the skeptic who doubts that international law is law also answers the skeptic who doubts that international law matters. For in order to respond to the first skeptic, one must show that international law is capable of affecting behavior in the right way to be law. But once one shows that international law matters in the right way, one ipso facto shows that it matters!

From the *Yale Law Journal* 121 (2011), pp. 252–281. Many notes, including most citations, have been omitted from this extract. Reprinted by permission of the Yale Law Journal Company.

No doubt, one could try to answer the question of whether international law matters directly without engaging the central objection to international law as law. But there is a crucial advantage to addressing the former question via the latter. For examining whether international law is law first requires one to figure out *all the ways* in which legal systems must be capable of affecting behavior to be law. This inquiry opens up a fascinating range of new possibilities about how law might matter to its subjects. With the help of the fuller account that results, we will see not only that international law is capable of affecting state behavior in the right way to be law; more significantly, it is capable of affecting state behavior in ways that previously have eluded international law scholars. Though international law does not matter to states in the same way that much modern domestic law does, we will show that it matters to them nonetheless. International law has mechanisms of law enforcement and these mechanisms give states reason not to violate the law.

Jurisprudence, then, can be an invaluable tool for empirical investigations of legal phenomena, for the former aims to uncover logical space often neglected by the latter. Indeed, the temptation to overlook important areas of jurisprudential space when analyzing international law is especially strong. After all, the legal systems with which we are most familiar are domestic. In our culture, modern state regimes are the paradigm instances of law. The inclination to focus exclusively on the state and to understand all legal phenomena through this lens is thus completely understandable. But it is also, we argue, a grave mistake.

In this Article, we show that critics of international law have succumbed to this temptation and have taken modern legal systems as their exclusive model for law. They have adopted what we call the "Modern State Conception" of law. The Modern State Conception maintains that regimes are legal systems only when they possess the distinctive capacities of the modern state; namely, they possess a monopoly over the use of force within a territory and use this monopoly to enforce their rules. In the domestic context, the monopoly is shared by a host of interlocking bureaucratic organizations that employ intimidation and violence as a method of enforcement, such as police, militia, prosecutorial agencies, and correctional institutions. In the Modern State Conception, then, law matters through the threat and exercise of violence by such organizations. Skepticism about international law naturally follows from this conception, given that international law does not possess these bureaucratic institutions. Famously, it does not have its own army or police force. While international prosecutorial agencies and prisons have sprung up in recent years, nothing resembling the modern state's enforcement apparatus exists or is likely to exist for the foreseeable future. If law must matter through the threat and exercise of physical coercion by an interlocking system of bureaucratic institutions, then international law cannot matter in the right way to be law.

We argue that the concept of law that lies behind this critique of international law is seriously flawed because of its limited understanding of how rules must be capable of affecting behavior in order to count as law. Its failure stems not simply from the fact that the Modern State Conception insists that legal rules only affect behavior when they are enforced; more important, it falters by adopting an excessively narrow conception of law enforcement itself. The Modern State Conception errs by insisting that law may be enforced only in the same way that it is enforced in modern states. First, it demands that the law can matter only if it is enforced *internally*, i.e., by the regime itself. Second, it requires that law matter only if it is enforced *violently*, i.e., through the threat and exercise of physical force.

This narrow understanding of law enforcement ignores regimes that outsource enforcement to external parties. We argue that, contrary to the Modern State Conception, as long as some party is tasked with using coercion in order to ensure compliance with the rules, the regime itself need not perform the role. We call this *externalized enforcement*. Moreover, we argue that the coercion used to enforce the law need not involve the threat and exercise of violence. Rather, it may involve the threat of exclusion, or as we call it, *outcasting*. Unlike the distinctive method that modern states use to enforce their law, outcasting is nonviolent: it does not rely on bureaucratic organizations, such as police or militia, that employ physical force to maintain order. Instead, outcasting involves denying the disobedient the benefits of social cooperation and membership. And it is frequently carried out by those outside the regime. We call this *externalized outcasting* and argue that it is a form of law enforcement that is ubiquitous in modern international law.

Seeing externalized outcasting as a form of law enforcement helps us see that the traditional critique of international law—that it is not enforced and is therefore both ineffective and not real law—is based on a limited and inaccurate understanding of law enforcement. Disobedience need not be met with the law's iron fist—enforcement simply may involve denying the disobedient the benefits of social cooperation and membership. Once we broaden our understanding of law enforcement to include externalization and outcasting, rather than limiting it to internalization and violence, we will see that international law matters in the way that legal systems must matter.

Although we hope to rebut the principal source of skepticism about the legality of international law, we do not intend to answer completely the question of whether international law is law in this paper. To do so would require us to set out a complete theory of law, demonstrate that this theory deems international law to be a genuine legal system, and respond to the numerous objections lodged against the legality of international law over the last several centuries. Clearly, such a project is beyond the scope of a single article. Our aim is more limited, though we believe it to be quite substantial. For as we will show, responding to the principal objection to international law not only makes headway towards resolving the age-old question of whether international law is law, it also helps uncover certain truths about how international law affects state behavior that have hitherto been ignored by scholars who directly study such questions.

I. SKEPTICISM ABOUT INTERNATIONAL LAW

The question of whether international law is properly considered law is rarely debated these days. This reluctance, however, represents a significant departure from more than a century of preoccupation with this issue. Indeed, until recently, many considered it *the* organizing question of the field of international law.

In this Part, we will review the main objections made by the original skeptics of international law. While these arguments have proven faulty, we will see that it is possible to reformulate them so as to avoid their surface vulnerabilities. Our aim, then, is to continue the long-running conversation that was abruptly, and we think mistakenly, dropped several decades ago. In the process, we will show that adjudicating an issue that no one seems to care about any more will have profound implications for the questions that many now care about intensely.

A. Austin's Objection

The *locus classicus* for the view that international law is not law is John Austin's *The Province of Jurisprudence Determined*. To understand Austin's skepticism, we must briefly recall the basic elements of Austin's theory of law. According to Austin, all rules are general commands. A command is the expression of a wish by a person or determinate body, backed by a threat to inflict an evil in case the wish is not fulfilled, issued by someone who is willing and able to act on the threat. Austin calls the evil resulting from the violation of a command a "sanction."

Having characterized the genus of rules as general commands, Austin proceeds to delimit the species of law. For Austin, only the rules of positive law are "law simply and strictly so called." Positive law consists of those rules issued by the sovereign. The sovereign is someone who habitually is obeyed by the bulk of the community and habitually obeys no one else. Austin took the King-in-Parliament to be the British sovereign because the bulk of British society habitually obeyed the King-in-Parliament, while the King-in-Parliament habitually obeyed no one else.

According to Austin, then, what makes a law *the law* is that it constitutes a general command issued by the sovereign. Given this jurisprudential conception, it is understandable that Austin would reject the legal status of international law:

> [T]he law obtaining between nations is not positive law: for every positive law is set by a given sovereign to a person or persons in a state of subjection to its author.... [T]he law obtaining between nations is law (improperly so called) set by general opinion. The duties which it imposes are enforced by moral sanctions: by fear on the part of nations, or by fear on the part of sovereigns, of provoking general hostility, and incurring its probable evils, in case they shall violate maxims generally received and respected.

International law appears to suffer from two defects in the Austinian model. First, the elements of international law are not commands, for commands are expressions of wishes of some person or well-defined collective body. The community of nations, however, is an "indeterminate" body, and is thus incapable of expressing wishes. International law can be set only by general opinion, not command. Second, laws properly so-called are commands issued by the sovereign. International law, however, lacks a sovereign—there is no nation or supranational body that habitually is obeyed and obeys no one else.

Austin's attack on international law was highly influential. Sir Thomas Holland, who occupied the Chichele Chair of International Law and Diplomacy at Oxford for thirty-six years and wrote the famous treatise *The Elements of Jurisprudence*, argued that international law was "law only by courtesy." Because international law lacks a "political arbiter by which it can be enforced," its rules are best considered as "the moral code of nations." William Edward Hearn, a passionate devotee of Austinian jurisprudence, declared that "[l]aw cannot be predicated of mere customs which are not even true commands, much less the commands of any competent State."

Even those who objected strongly to Austin's theory of law nevertheless agreed with him on the defects of international law as law. Edward Jenks rejected the idea that all laws must be commands and that all laws must be issued by an omnipotent sovereign; yet he thought that international law was not fully law. "Although, in fact, many important nations have agreed to submit certain classes of disputes between one another to judicial or arbitral treatment by international tribunals,... yet such tribunals have no executive authority, and cannot enforce submission to their decisions...." George Paton departed so far from Austin that he claimed that "[i]t is possible to conceive of law without a sovereign authority or a court without compulsory jurisdiction or even perhaps if there are no organs of enforcement." For Paton, the essential feature was instead the regulation of self-help: "[T]he moment when law emerges is when self-help is regulated by the community." Unfortunately, according to Paton, the regulation of self-help in the international sphere was only beginning to emerge. "So long as all declarations of war are lawful, it is difficult to say that a system of law is in operation."

B. The Internality Objection

In *The Concept of Law*, H.L.A. Hart showed that Austin's theory of law is seriously flawed. As he pointed out, Austin was mistaken to claim that all laws arise from commands. Custom, for example, is a recognized source of law in domestic legal systems. But as Hart noted, domestic customary norms are set by the mere opinion and moral sanctions of indeterminate bodies, not by imperatives. Modern legislation cannot be construed as commands either. One cannot command oneself but, as Hart argued, legislators can and typically do enact legislation that applies to themselves. Austin, therefore, cannot impugn international law for not arising from commands, for most domestic law does not arise from commands either.

Hart also showed that the absence of an Austinian sovereign does not detract from the legality of international law insofar as most domestic systems lack a sovereign as well. An Austinian sovereign is legally omnicompetent, but the sovereign's powers in modern domestic regimes are usually limited. The United States Constitution, for example, limits the sovereign powers of the American people, both by making certain constitutional provisions unalterable[2] and prescribing an extremely onerous procedure that must be followed before an amendment is ratified.[3] The United States has a legal system even though it does not have an Austinian sovereign.

While Hart's critique is certainly correct, the Austinian critique can be reframed in a way that captures the essence of the challenge but dodges the Hartian responses. To see how this might be done, let us begin with the core idea behind Austin's theory of law. We might say that, according to Austin, the distinctiveness of the law as a social institution is constituted by the unique way in which it seeks to affect human behavior.

First and foremost, the law distinguishes itself because it seeks to affect behavior through the *enforcement* of its rules. Subjects are encouraged to obey because consequences they care about follow from their decision to comply. Second, the law is distinctive because its enforcement comes in the form of *sanctions* that attach to noncompliance. In Austin's formulation, "evils" follow disobedience. Third, sanctions are imposed by *powerful members* of the population, otherwise known as "officials."

According to Austin, then, the distinctiveness of the law is constituted by *how* it seeks to affect behavior and *by whom*. To be law, a regime must matter through (1) enforcement, which takes the form of (2) sanctions for disobedience (3) imposed by the officials of an extremely powerful group.

Once we notice that Austin's theory is predicated on a view about the distinctive ways in which law seeks to affect behavior, we see that he did not have to insist that all laws are *commands* issued by a *sovereign*. Instead, Austin could have relaxed his jurisprudential model by merely requiring that laws be enforced by sanctions (even if they were not created by commands) and administered by officials of the normative system in question (even if the regime does not have an Austinian sovereign). A regime that does not enforce its rules through the imposition of sanctions, or has sanctions but delegates enforcement to nonregime members, cannot be a legal system.

Notice that this weaker set of conditions still impugns the legality of international law. With few exceptions, which we will explore in Part II, international law does not seek to affect behavior by sanctioning the violation of its rules "internally," that is, through designated international bureaucracies. It relies primarily on nation-states to ensure that violations of the rules are sanctioned. We call this the "Internality Objection."

As an illustration of the Internality Objection, consider the World Trade Organization. The World Trade Organization (WTO), with 153 member states representing more than ninety-seven percent of world trade, is widely considered one of the strongest and most effective international legal organizations of the modern era. And yet, the WTO itself does not have the authority under international law to enforce the rules that it creates. The Internality Objection therefore holds that those rules are not, in fact, law.

The enforcement of international trade law principles of the WTO occurs through "a compulsory third party adjudication system." Under the WTO agreement, member states agree to resolve disputes *exclusively* through the adjudicative procedure, and states are required to abide by decisions issued by the expert panels and the appellate body to avoid retaliation. If the offending party refuses to comply, decisions of the panel are enforced through authorized economic retaliation imposed by the aggrieved state party.

In the context of international trade, therefore, trade law principles are *not* enforced internally, namely, by the officials of the WTO itself. Rather, sanctions are imposed and administered by the officials of the aggrieved state party. The WTO merely authorizes state parties with legitimate complaints to retaliate against noncompliant states through a limited denial of Most Favored Nation status. This authorization permits a state with a legitimate complaint to impose offsetting tariffs and other protectionist measures on a state that is found to have violated its treaty obligations. The WTO, in other words, delegates the enforcement of its rules to the bureaucratic machinery of its members, typically its legislative or executive branches. Enforcement of trade rules is a form of externalized sanctioning: the retaliation is performed by the member states, not the WTO. The WTO is simply the gatekeeper.

According to the Internality Objection, international law cannot be a genuine legal system because it does not enforce its own rules and hence does not seek to affect behavior in the right way. As the WTO example illustrates, the enforcement of international law is not administered by designated international organizations. Rather, sanctions are delegated to external parties, namely, the governmental bureaucracies of member states, to impose and administer.

C. The Brute Force Objection

Having sketched the Internality Objection, we now note a related challenge to international law. Recall the passage quoted above in which Austin states that international law is backed solely by "moral sanctions," i.e., a diffuse hostility that nations express when the rules of international law are broken. This passage suggests that the objection to international law is that it does not sanction the violation of its rules through the use of brute physical force; it merely contents itself with weak "moral" sanctions. Call this the "Brute Force Objection."

Once again, let us illustrate the Brute Force Objection by considering the WTO. As one commentator put it, when states are found to have violated the trade rules, "there is no prospect of incarceration, injunctive relief, damages for harm inflicted, or police enforcement. The WTO has no jailhouse, no bail bondsmen, no blue helmets, no truncheons or tear gas." The WTO, in other words, does not enforce its rules through the threat or exercise of physical force. Member states may not resort to violence either. As mentioned above, trade law is enforced through retaliatory trade measures taken by the aggrieved parties.

The Brute Force Objection is rooted in a widespread intuition that law and physical coercion are intimately connected. Robert Cover famously expressed this intuition at the beginning of his essay, *Violence and the Word*, when he wrote: "Legal interpretation takes place in a field of pain and death." Indeed, Cover thought the link between violence and law to be "obvious" and to sever the connection would be "something less (or more) than law." Similarly, Hans Kelsen

characterized the law as the "organization of force." Law differs from morality and religion on his account insofar as legal demands are backed by socially organized physical coercion.

The Brute Force Objection is distinct from the Internality Objection insofar as it does not focus on *who* enforces the law but rather *how* it is enforced. It claims that legal systems must matter to us in the same way that modern domestic legal systems do, namely, through threat or exercise of brute physical force.

D. The Modern State Conception

The Internality and Brute Force objections are analytically distinct, but they nonetheless frequently come together as a package. Critics often assume that a regime is law only when it (1) contains bureaucratic enforcement mechanisms, i.e., it enjoys internality, *and* (2) those mechanisms employ intimidation and violence to ensure compliance, i.e., it uses physical force. Thus, international law fails on this view to be a legal regime for two reasons: (1) it lacks its own enforcement mechanisms, and (2) it lacks internal mechanisms that employ brute force.

It is not surprising that these two objections are commonly paired. For these objections are simply expressions of different aspects of the same jurisprudential account, namely, what we called the "Modern State Conception" of law. According to the Modern State Conception, a regime counts as a legal one only if it seeks to affect behavior in the manner that modern states do: it must enjoy a monopoly over the use of physical force and employ this monopoly to enforce its rules. The Modern State Conception, in other words, requires legal systems to (1) possess *internal* enforcement mechanisms (2) that use the threat and exercise of *physical force*. It follows on this view that international law is not a proper legal system because it does not contain these sorts of institutions and hence cannot affect behavior in the right way. For this reason, we call the combination of the Internality and Brute Force objections the "Modern State Objection."

The Modern State Objection takes modern domestic legal systems as the paradigm cases of law and judges all other regimes against this ideal. Because international law does not resemble the modern state in the way in which it seeks to control behavior, this objection denies international law jurisprudential status. Consider, in this regard, John Bolton's critique of international treaty law. "It is a flat misunderstanding of reality," Bolton argues, "to believe that there are enforcement mechanisms 'out there' internationally that conform to the kind of legal system that exists in the United States." When a contract is breached in domestic law, he notes, "there is a defined way to get remedies. There is a process to decide which promises are legitimate and a procedure to enforce a court order that a party has breached a promise." By contrast, no similar procedure exists for redressing the violation of treaty obligations.

A treaty is primarily a compact between independent nations. It depends for the enforcement of its provisions on the interest and the honor of the governments that are parties to it. If these fail, its infraction becomes the subject of international negotiations and reclamations, so far as the injured party chooses to seek redress, which may in the end be enforced by actual war.

This is not domestic law at work. Accordingly, there is no reason to consider treaties as "legally" binding internationally, and certainly not as "law" themselves.

Bolton's argument seems to be that treaties cannot generate real legal obligations because there are no force-based mechanisms "out there" to ensure their compliance. Treaties cannot be a source of law, in other words, because there are no treaty police. While contractual breaches can be redressed through the threat or exercise of physical coercion by the state, violations of treaty obligations can be enforced only by the moral sanctions of the international community or the self-help remedy of war.

II. LAW ENFORCEMENT IN THE MODERN STATE CONCEPTION

In the Parts that follow, we will attempt to evaluate the cogency of the Modern State Objection by examining and critiquing its underlying conception of law. It behooves us, therefore, to say a bit more about the Modern State Conception of law and its constitutive elements. To do so, we first must clarify its notion of law enforcement.

A. Primary and Secondary Enforcement

It is commonplace to say that the law enforces its demands by imposing costs on those who violate its rules. But what exactly does this mean? How does the law impose costs on rule violators? Take a trivial example of law enforcement. Suppose you forget to put money in a parking meter when you park your car. The standard response from the police is a parking ticket. A parking ticket is a demand to pay a fixed sum of money because of a parking violation. In other words, the police do not wait until you return to the car and forcibly take your money. Rather, they impose a duty on you to pay the parking violation bureau. Of course, if you fail to pay, the law likely will become more aggressive. The police may end up booting your tire or seizing your car, or the sheriff may come to your house and confiscate goods equal to the value of the fine or, worse, lead you off to jail.

Let us distinguish, accordingly, among three kinds of legal rules. *Conduct rules* tell people which actions they are obligated, prohibited, or permitted to perform. They require us to put money in meters if we want to park, to pay taxes on our income, and not to engage in arson. A subset of conduct rules are *enforcement rules*. The function of enforcement rules is to ensure that the conduct rules are followed. *Primary enforcement rules* are addressed to the conduct rule violators. These rules either impose duties on violators to perform some costly act or deny them a beneficial right. Primary enforcement rules may obligate the conduct rule violator to pay a fine, report to jail, leave the country, wear a red letter, etc., or deny them the right to drive, serve liquor, exclude others from taking their property, etc.

If primary enforcement rules are the law's Plan B, then *secondary enforcement rules* are its Plan C. Secondary enforcement rules come into play when the conduct rule violator fails to follow the primary enforcement rules.[4] These rules either impose duties on people other than the conduct rule violator to perform some harmful act on (or refrain from performing some beneficial act for) the conduct rule violator, or the rules permit people other than the conduct rule violator to perform some harmful act on (or refrain from performing some beneficial act for) the conduct rule violator. Thus, secondary enforcement rules may require the police to apprehend the conduct rule violators, shame them, seize their property, etc., or permit creditors to seize property from debtors, allow crime victims to retaliate against offenders, authorize property owners to physically exclude trespassers, etc.

Primary enforcement rules frequently are backed by multiple secondary enforcement rules. For example, unpaid parking tickets may be enforced through the garnishment of wages. The rule requiring garnishment is a secondary one insofar as it is directed to someone other than the parking scofflaw, namely, the scofflaw's employer. Suppose that the employer fails to withhold wages. The law likely will require officials to take further steps to ensure that the employer complies (e.g., demanding that the employer pay a fine, revoking his license, etc.). Ultimately, the law may require officials to use physical force against the employer (or others). They may shutter the doors, imprison the CEO for contempt, or enter the business premises and take the money themselves. In such cases, law enforcement bottoms out in physical force employed by legal officials.

We can think of legal rules, therefore, as forming *enforcement chains*. The first link in the chain is the conduct rule being enforced by the subsequent rules. Typically, the second link is a primary enforcement rule that imposes duties on those who violate the initial conduct rule. Later links are normally secondary rules that enforce the prior primary rules (and transitively the initial conduct rule).

Enforcement chains also may be split into *subchains*. A jurisdiction may respond to unpaid parking tickets by requiring employers to garnish wages *and* by requiring police to seize the offenders' cars. These subchains likely will be of differing lengths: the law may have contingency plans for the failure of employers to garnish wages but have no response for the failure of the police to seize the cars.

We can now see how the law enforces its rules: it imposes costs on rule violators either by (1) *imposing duties on them or others or both* or (2) *denying them rights or providing rights to others or both*. Primary enforcement rules require conduct rule violators to act in ways deemed costly or deny them the right to act in ways deemed beneficial. Secondary enforcement rules require or permit others to act in ways deemed costly to the conduct rule violator or not to act in ways deemed beneficial. These primary and secondary rules form chains, with each rule designed to enforce earlier links and, ultimately, to ensure that the initial conduct rule is followed.

Having clarified the notion of enforcement, we can now state more clearly the basic presuppositions of the Modern State Conception of law. Its first tenet holds that most conduct rules must be enforced in order to be law.

Enforcement Thesis: Most legal conduct rules are part of law enforcement chains.

The second tenet defines a "law enforcement chain" as one that authorizes or mandates internalized violence.

Internalized Violence Thesis: A law enforcement chain is an enforcement chain that has at least one secondary link that either requires or permits officials to use physical force on the person who violated the initial link or on his or her property.

The Modern State Conception can be seen, therefore, as a theory composed of a necessary condition and a definition. The Enforcement Thesis demands that most legal conduct rules be part of law enforcement chains, while the Internalized Violence Thesis defines a "law enforcement chain" as one that threatens violence by officials at some point in the sequence.

It should be pointed out that the Modern State Conception does not require the regime in question to include the full panoply of coercive bureaucratic institutions characteristic of contemporary states. It need not have police, militia, large prosecutorial agencies, *and* correctional institutions. But it must at least have some such bodies.

It might have police but not public prosecutors; it might have jails, guards, and wardens but not police; it might have police and prosecutors but no prisons. As long as some institution exists whose role is to use the threat or exercise of physical force in order to enforce conduct rules, the Modern State Conception will recognize the regime as law.

Two final clarifications are in order. First, the Modern State Conception does not demand that the law seek to affect behavior *only* through the threat and exercise of violence. Officials may appeal, for example, to the citizenry's sense of moral obligation to obey the law or to their patriotism. The Modern State Conception insists, however, that these motivations are neither necessary nor sufficient for the existence of law. Regardless of how else a regime seeks to affect behavior, at the very least it must do so through internal threats and the exercise of physical force. Second, the Modern State Conception does not demand that obedience to the law be coercively obtained. The motivation for obeying the conduct rules, in other words, need not be "transmitted" up the enforcement chain from the secondary rules threatening force. Why citizens obey the law is left open by the account. The Modern State Conception insists that the law give citizens a certain kind of reason in order to be law, not that they act for that reason.

B. Does International Law Satisfy the Modern State Conception?

The Modern State Objection claims that international law is not law because most of its rules are not part of law enforcement chains. Without its own police, prosecutors, or jailors, international law cannot be enforced by the right people in the right way.

We can imagine two ways in which to respond to the Modern State Objection. One accepts its underlying theory of law, i.e., the Modern State Conception, but argues that international law does indeed satisfy it. The other accepts that international law does not satisfy the Modern State Conception, but argues that the Modern State Conception is itself flawed. Let us discuss each in turn.

The first response to the Modern State Objection maintains that international law fits the Modern State Conception. The best example for such a claim would likely be mutual defense treaties, which are core instruments of international law. The North Atlantic Treaty, and the organization it creates (the North Atlantic Treaty Organization [NATO]), is one of the most robust mutual defense treaties. The provisions for collective self-defense represent the core of the NATO alliance and emerged as a device to deter the threat of Soviet aggression—and to respond to it, if needed. Under Article V of the North Atlantic Treaty, member states commit to come to the aid of one another:

> The Parties agree that an armed attack against one or more of them ... shall be considered an attack against them all and consequently they agree that, if such an armed attack occurs, each of them, in exercise of the right of individual or collective self-defence recognised by Article 51 of the Charter of the United Nations, will assist the Party or Parties so attacked....

Decisions to use force to repel aggression are made and enforced by internal NATO structures. The principal decisionmaking body of NATO is the North Atlantic Council, which is made up of representatives from each of the 26 member states. The Council can direct a response by the NATO Response Force, which operates as a standing army ready to respond to acts of aggression against a member state. The Force provides NATO with the ability to react quickly to situations of threat and engage in high-intensity combat on a modern battlefield for thirty days on its own, or for a longer period as part of a NATO Combined Joint Task Force.

Even NATO, however, suffers from a flaw in the eyes of the Modern State Conception of law enforcement. Yes, it can deploy physical force. And, yes, it has its own forces capable of engaging in that physical force. But the laws it enforces are not its own. It exists, instead, to enforce the U.N. Charter's Article 2(4) prohibition on the use of force and Article 51 right of self-defense. NATO's enforcement mechanism is thus *external* rather than *internal* to the legal system it exists to enforce.

The United Nations Charter offers yet another instance in which international law nearly meets the Modern State Conception, but falls just short. A central principle of international law—codified in Article 2(4) of the United Nations Charter—is the prohibition on the use of aggressive force by a sovereign state against the sovereign territory or political independence of another state. Under Chapter VII of the U.N. Charter, the Security Council is empowered to "determine the existence of any threat to the peace, breach of the peace, or act of aggression" and to take action to "restore international peace and security."

The founders of the United Nations expected that a significant portion of the enforcement actions under Chapter VII would be carried out by forces assembled from member states who would "make available to the Security Council" armed forces and assistance pursuant to special agreements. A Military Staff Committee (MSC) would be responsible for "the strategic direction of any armed forces placed at the disposal of the Security Council."

Had this vision been realized, it would have satisfied the Modern State Conception of law enforcement by giving the United Nations Security Council the power to deploy internal physical force to enforce its decisions. But this vision was never realized. It fell victim to the Cold War before it could take shape. Instead, it is the member states that carry out the enforcement actions specified in Security Council resolutions through *external physical enforcement*.

Even if there are cases in which international law meets the stringent criteria of the Modern State Conception of law (we, as yet, have not identified any), it is inarguable that most of international law does not. Hence when defenders of international law respond to critiques of international law by pointing to such structures, they effectively fall into a trap. Critics are likely to respond to such examples by noting first that the defenders of international law are picking out, at best, a few good examples for their case. Second, they will likely point out that any international law that actually fits this conception of law is arguably antisovereigntist and antidemocratic, for if international law is enforced against member states in the way that domestic law is enforced against individuals in a modern state (through internal threats of force), then international law lays claim to the right to subjugate nation-states to the will of the international organization in the same way that nation-states lay claim to subjugating individuals to the will of the national government. That position may be particularly difficult for advocates of international law to defend when the sovereign state in question is a democracy. Advocates of international law, unprepared to adequately respond to either critique, tend to let the conversation drop at this point—or they deny the legitimacy of the inquiry at all (witness the quotations with which this Article opened).

C. Is the Modern State Conception Valid?

Instead of arguing that international law satisfies the Modern State Conception, the more promising and, in fact, popular strategy in defense of international law has been to argue against the Modern State Conception itself. Thus, most defenders concede that international law is not enforced through the barrel of a U.N. gun, but they deny that enforcement is necessary for legality. In other words, they seek to undercut the Modern State Conception by attacking the Enforcement Thesis. In their view, most conduct rules need not be part of enforcement chains in order to be legal rules. Indeed, they are willing to accept as a conceptual possibility that a regime can still be a legal system even though it does not enforce any of its rules. The fact that international law does not have the right enforcement mechanism, therefore, is not fatal to its legality, for a regime does not need *any* enforcement mechanism to be law, let alone the right kind.

Those who reject the Enforcement Thesis have presented three sorts of arguments in their support. The first kind employs a philosophical thought experiment. Consider a community of extremely conscientious and well-intentioned individuals who are governed by a democratically elected assembly and a cadre of wise judges. Because the members of this community completely and wholeheartedly accept the legitimacy of the governing regime and consequently always obey the rules, the community has no police, jails, or other mechanisms of enforcement. Joseph Raz, for example, imagines a society of angels governed by legislatures and courts that is so obedient that subjects do not need to be threatened with sanctions for breaking the rules.

Many have the intuition that such sanctionless communities have law. If we take this intuition seriously, then we should reject the Enforcement Thesis. For while enforcement is normally required in the actual world, given human weakness and foibles, the thought experiment shows that beings who can be trusted to do what they think is right and, as a result, do not need coercive enforcement can nevertheless have law. Contrary to the Modern State Conception, most legal conduct rules need not be part of enforcement chains, let alone law enforcement chains; in fact, none of them do.

Though we are personally persuaded by this argument, we are aware that many are not. Some reject it because they do not trust intuitions about bizarre hypotheticals. Since we never encounter anything like angelic legal systems, they complain, we cannot be confident in our reactions to such outlandish scenarios. Others reject the argument because their intuitions pull in precisely the opposite direction: they are convinced that "law" without enforcement would not really be law.

Because the status and outcome of such thought experiments are controversial and have failed to persuade many people, we will eschew them in this Article. We will, therefore, restrict our evidence to actual legal systems. A regime will constitute a counterexample to the Modern State Conception only if it exists or has existed and our intuitions are reasonably firm about its jurisprudential status.

A second strategy for rejecting the Enforcement Thesis relies on empirical observation, not philosophical intuition. It proceeds by noting that people normally obey the law out of a sense of moral obligation. Consider Anthony D'Amato's argument against the idea that "enforcement is the hallmark of law":

> Most of "law" concerns itself with the interpretation and enforcement of private contracts, the redress of intentional and negligent harms, rules regarding sales of goods and sales of securities, rules relating to the family and the rights of members thereof, and other such rules, norms, and cases. The rules are obeyed not out of fear of the state's power, but because the rules by and large are perceived to be right, just, or appropriate.

According to D'Amato, coercive enforcement does not play a major role in ordinary compliance with law. Since legal rules are obeyed rather out of a sense of moral obligation, enforcement cannot be constitutive of legality. D'Amato concludes that skeptics who believe that international law cannot be law because it lacks enforcement mechanisms must, therefore, be mistaken.

Unfortunately, D'Amato's argument misses the mark. The Enforcement Thesis does not claim that a regime is a legal system only if its subjects comply out of fear of enforcement. As we noted earlier, this thesis is agnostic on why citizens obey the law. The Enforcement Thesis merely requires that law enforcement mechanisms exist, not that citizens act because of them. Critics of international law, therefore, can recognize that people normally obey law out of moral considerations but also maintain that a regime would not be law if it did not provide them alternative reasons to comply.

D'Amato's argument fails for an additional reason. One cannot infer from the fact that citizens normally obey out of moral considerations that "enforcement is not a hallmark of law." For it is plausible to suppose that regimes are perceived as legitimate only because enforcement mechanisms exist for those who do not accept the legitimacy of the regime. In other words, people are willing to obey the law out of the sense of moral obligation only because they have assurance that they won't be "suckers" and that those who break the rules will be punished for doing so.

The final attempt to undermine the Enforcement Thesis distinguishes sharply between ordinary domestic law and public law. According to this response, the Enforcement Thesis is a plausible requirement to impose on rules that bind ordinary citizens. The rules of criminal law, torts, contract law, and so on are indeed backed by the physically coercive power of the State. By contrast, public law—the rules that bind state actors—are not enforced in this way. Indeed, the argument proceeds, they are not enforceable at all. And because public law is unenforceable, the Enforcement Thesis is not a plausible requirement to impose on this group of legal rules and hence cannot be a principle valid for all legal rules.

Because this is a provocative argument, we should examine it closely. Consider the institution of judicial review. Jack Goldsmith and Daryl Levinson argue that its power to enforce constitutional law is an illusion. They write:

> Courts are cast as powerful enforcement agents, prevailing upon the political branches of government to comply with their commands. But of course courts cannot play any such role. Courts are merely subdivisions of government, lacking the powers of purse and sword that might be used to coerce the compliance of other government officials and their constituents.[5]

Contrary to the received wisdom, courts cannot enforce constitutional law because they are the "least dangerous branch." Judges merely declare a law or action "unconstitutional" but have no power to back up such declarations with coercion.

Courts are not the only powerless ones. According to Goldsmith and Levinson, *no one* can enforce domestic public law. With "no sovereign above the sovereign," there is no body powerful enough to employ coercion against wayward state actors. "[P]ublic law cannot rely on the enforcement capacity of states for compliance. Lacking the kind of 'external' enforcement mechanism that states provide for ordinary domestic law, public law regimes must be internally self-enforcing through some combination of rationally self-interested and normative, internalized, or role-based motivations."

Goldsmith and Levinson extend their argument to public international law. Just as domestic public law is unenforceable against domestic state actors, public international law cannot be enforced against them either. Since there is "no sovereign above the sovereign," there is no way to coerce wayward state actors to comply with the public law of the international realm.

If we accept Goldsmith and Levinson's argument about the unenforceability of public law, then the Enforcement Thesis loses its appeal. Since domestic public law is law despite being unenforceable, rules can be legal norms even though they are not enforced. And if the Enforcement Thesis is invalid, then the Modern State Conception is invalid as well. International law cannot, therefore, be denied the status of legality simply because it lacks mechanisms of coercive enforcement.

The success of this refutation of the Modern State Conception hinges on the claim that domestic public law is unenforceable. But is that true? Consider *United States v. Nixon*. In that case, Richard Nixon refused to hand over the tapes to the special prosecutor investigating Watergate, claiming executive privilege. The Supreme Court unanimously disagreed and ordered the President to turn over the tapes. Nixon complied with this order. Far from being a feckless institution, then, judicial review was a highly effective mechanism of law enforcement. Public law, it would seem, is enforceable after all.

Goldsmith and Levinson might argue that, contrary to appearances, the Court was not the enforcement body in this case. Nixon did not comply because he respected the authority of the Court; rather, he complied because he would certainly have been impeached and convicted otherwise. Even assuming that this claim about Nixon's motivations is true, it is hard to see how it vindicates Goldsmith and Levinson's ultimate thesis about the unenforceability of public law. For it would simply follow that public law was enforced in this instance by the impeachment mechanism. Even if judicial review did not enforce public law in this case, the threat of congressional impeachment did!

Goldsmith and Levinson would, no doubt, reject this inference. Nixon, they would point out, did not have to listen to Congress. As President, he was the Chief Law Enforcement Officer and Commander-in-Chief of the armed forces. If he refused to vacate the Oval Office following impeachment by the House and conviction by the Senate, no one would have physically forced him to do so. His leaving would have had to be his own decision: public law can only be self-enforced by the President, not enforced against him by the Court, Congress or anyone else.

It is hard to know, of course, whether Nixon would have been physically forced to leave the Oval Office if he were impeached, convicted and refused to budge. But the outcome of the hypothetical is irrelevant to the issue of whether impeachment was an effective method of public law enforcement in *United States v. Nixon*. For refusing to leave the Oval Office following impeachment and conviction would have had terrible consequences for Nixon, far worse than relinquishing the reins of power. The dishonor and public scorn that would have been heaped on him for precipitating a constitutional crisis would have been more than he was willing to bear. The threat of impeachment, therefore, was genuinely coercive: it compelled Nixon to comply with the Court because the costs of playing hardball were simply too great.

Goldsmith and Levinson are wrong, therefore, to claim that public law cannot be enforced. As we have seen, impeachment and judicial review can be effective tools for disciplining state actors. Indeed, they are not the only options available. Public law can be enforced at the ballot box: state actors who violate the law can be voted out of office. Others can be fired, fined, or denounced by their superiors. Funding denials are also powerful enforcement tools. Agencies or governmental subdivisions that refuse to follow the law may see their budgets shrink dramatically.

We can now see that there is a missing premise in Goldsmith and Levinson's argument. Recall the passage cited earlier: "Lacking the kind of 'external' enforcement mechanism that states provide for ordinary domestic law, public law regimes must be internally self-enforcing." Even if public law cannot be enforced in the same way as ordinary domestic law, it does not follow that public law cannot be enforced at all. It would follow *only* if law enforcement had to take the form that it does in ordinary domestic law, namely, internalized physical coercion. In other words, Goldsmith and Levinson can establish the unenforceability of public law only by severely limiting the kinds of coercive actions that count as law enforcement.

The reason they do not countenance judicial review, impeachment, elections, firings, and defunding as mechanisms of law enforcement, despite being coercive, is that they are not *physically* coercive.

There is an irony here. The third attempt to rescue international law relies on Goldsmith and Levinson's argument that domestic public law is unenforceable. Since enforcement is not necessary for domestic public law, it must not be necessary for all other forms of public law, including international law. But this argument follows only if we tacitly accept the Modern State Conception's narrow understanding of law enforcement. This effort to undermine the Enforcement Thesis thus unwittingly relies on the Internalized Violence Thesis.

The third attack on the Enforcement Thesis, therefore, ultimately depends on the validity of the Internalized Violence Thesis. Unfortunately, we do not know whether the latter is true. And if we cannot establish its truth, we cannot use it to falsify the Enforcement Thesis and, with it, the Modern State Objection. Indeed, there are strong reasons to reject the Internalized Violence Thesis. As we will see in the next Part, this understanding of law enforcement is far too narrow. Not only does the Internalized Violence Thesis fail to capture the way in which public law is enforced, it does not even comport with the way in which ordinary domestic law has been enforced in other legal systems. And if the Internalized Violence Thesis is not even true of ordinary domestic law, we have no reason to accept it at all.[…]

VI. INTERNATIONAL LAW ENFORCEMENT REIMAGINED

A. Examining International Law as Law

This Article examines and responds to the central critique made by skeptics of international law—that international law cannot be law because it does not matter in the way law must matter. We show that by engaging this critique directly, we can open up logical space that would otherwise not have been apparent. In doing so, we are able to make new progress on an issue that is of pressing interest to international legal scholars—when and whether international law matters.

Yet our aim in engaging the critique of international law as law is not merely instrumental. We aim, as well, to make progress toward answering the broader question of whether international law is *law*. As we stated in the Introduction, we do not attempt a full answer to the question here. Doing so would require us to first articulate a theory of law, which is far beyond the confines of this Article. We have instead sought to make a step toward that goal by engaging the central critique of international law and demonstrating that it is ill founded. We hope in the process that we have shown that the effort to engage the question whether international law is law is not "futile" or "tired," but is fruitful, fresh, and worthy of continued study.

The stakes of this broader debate are immense. The Modern State Conception derives its appeal not only from the fact that all paradigmatic instances of law in the modern world have well-developed enforcement institutions that employ physical intimidation and coercion. Its appeal is also explainable by the fact that the properties which make law *law* are also those properties that make law morally valuable. On the Modern State Conception, internal physical enforcement is necessary for a regime to be a legal system because what makes regimes worthy of respect—indeed morally indispensable in the modern world—is that they can accomplish certain tasks that no other comparable social institution can. Namely, they can wield and focus an enormous amount of physical force to ensure that people obey their demands. In the words of Hans Kelsen, law is "organized force." Thus, despite the fact that legal officials are almost always a small minority of a population, the bureaucratic organization of enforcement personnel harnesses and magnifies their power, thereby enabling them to compel obedience to the will of the law.

In our view, the moral distinctiveness of the law does not derive from its ability to use internally controlled physical coercion in order to enforce its will. Rather, it stems from the fact that legal systems are extremely sophisticated instruments for effecting social change through the creation and application of rules. The idea might be expressed as follows: when a community faces moral problems that are numerous and serious and that require complex, contentious, or arbitrary solutions, certain modes of governance such as improvisation, spontaneous ordering, private bargaining, or communal consensus will be costly to engage in, sometimes prohibitively so. Unless the community has a way of reducing the costs of governance, resolving these moral problems will be expensive at best, and impossible at worst. On our view, the moral indispensability of the law arises from its ability to meet this demand in an efficient manner. By providing a highly nimble and durable method for creating and applying rules, the law enables communities to solve the numerous and serious problems that would otherwise be too costly or risky to resolve.

To be sure, law would not be morally indispensable if it were purely aspirational in nature. Legal systems not only create and apply rules: they also see to it that their demands are met. But as opposed to the Modern State Conception, we do not require that legal systems ensure that their will be done in any particular fashion. Their methods for motivating compliance are a contingent matter. Whether a particular regime deems it appropriate to employ physical force depends on the costs and benefits of doing so. Much will depend on the material wealth of the society, the current state of technology, the legitimacy enjoyed by the regime, the cultural meaning of violence, the climate and geography of the territory, the degree of social interdependence and cooperation, the availability of external sources of coercion, and so on. Indeed, the ability of the law to solve moral problems may in some cases *depend* on its decision to eschew violence as a means of enforcement. As we saw in the case of Iceland [ED: omitted], the egalitarian ethos of the commonwealth demanded that the law be enforced by private individuals. And the Roman Catholic Church took itself to be spiritually barred from using temporal sanctions. If it was to do God's will, it would have to turn the other cheek. So, too, the nature of state sovereignty demands that international law only apply physical force in rare instances. Like Iceland and classical canon law, international law must—and does—rely on another means of law enforcement. And that means, more often than not, is externalized outcasting.

B. Reimagining Possibilities in International Law

Seeing external enforcement and outcasting as modes of law enforcement allows scholars to reimagine the possibilities for international law. Recognizing that international law often operates through external enforcement—by calling on states to enforce the law—can lead us to see the successes and failures of international law in an entirely new light.

Once we see that international law relies heavily on external enforcement, this shifts our attention to how external enforcement works—and when and why it does not. Law that relies on external actors for enforcement is vulnerable in an obvious way to the independent choices of those external actors. An international legal regime might rely on external actors to enforce, but that does not mean they will always do so. Attention, therefore, must be paid to when, why, and how external actors will act to enforce international legal obligations. Seen in this light, the problem of international legal enforcement is turned upside down—when an international legal regime that relies on external enforcement goes unenforced, it is not a failure of the international institution as such, but a failure of states to act. Viewing the problem through this lens, then, offers a new agenda for scholars seeking to understand how to make international legal regimes more effective.

At the same time, once we see outcasting as a central mode of international law enforcement, we see international law enforcement in an entirely new light. International agreements that lack enforcement through physical force do not necessarily lack enforcement. Enforcement through exclusion from the benefits of social cooperation can be as powerful at motivating states to comply with the law as any physical force—and sometimes even more powerful. And not only is outcasting powerful, but it is multifaceted. Different forms of outcasting are better suited to addressing different

sets of challenges. This opens up a new world of possibilities for international law—and a host of new questions for scholars to answer. Why do some variations exist in some contexts and not in others? Are there further variations that could be used to respond to challenges not already met by existing forms of outcasting? Are there areas of international law where outcasting could be better tailored to effectively enforce the law? What barriers exist to making those changes and how might they be overcome? We have attempted to begin this conversation, but much remains to be done.

C. The Sovereigntist Fallacy

The Modern State Conception insists that regimes are legal systems only when they enforce their commands internally through the threat and exercise of physical force. This vision of law places defenders of international law in an indefensible position: if international law is "really" law, then it is like a modern state—with international police ready to use violence to force states to comply with its commands. To be real law under the Modern State Conception, then, international law must live up to the greatest fears of its critics—trampling state sovereignty and democratic self-determination.

We have attempted in this Article to show that this is a false trap. Law enforcement that fits the Modern State Conception is *one* form of law enforcement, but it is not the *only* form. There are other forms of law enforcement that violate the conditions of the Modern State Conception—enforcing commands through external actors, or relying on outcasting rather than physical force, or, as in the case of most of international law, both.

Once we see that international law most often operates not through the tools of the Modern State Conception but instead through externalized outcasting, we can see that the sovereigntist critique of international law stands on a false foundation. By relying on external actors to enforce the law, international law places responsibility for the success or failure of law back upon the states that created it. It is not the blue-helmeted police of the United Nations that enforce the vast majority of international law, but pressures brought to bear by other states. Those states act, moreover, not by threatening physical force. Rather, they create agreements that produce benefits for all their members—and then threaten to exclude those who violate those rules from some or all of the benefits of the regime.

Indeed, the very nature of the international legal system *requires* that it be so. International law, like Icelandic and classical canon law, *must* rely on some means of enforcement other than physical force. International law's lack of the capacities of a modern state is a feature, not a bug, of international law. Yes, international law is not enforced by an international police force—*and that is exactly as it must be.* Just as the presence of a king with the power to physically force compliance with the law would have been inconsistent with the egalitarianism of medieval Iceland and temporal sanctions administered by the Church of the classical period would have sullied the Church's spiritual character; so too would the existence of international police exerting physical power to force states to comply be inconsistent with the very meaning of international law, which is based on respect for the sovereignty and self-determination of states.

It is impossible to overemphasize the importance of state sovereignty in international law. The international legal system is both created by and creates sovereign states. A treaty, for example, is "an international agreement concluded *between States.*" Similarly, customary international law results from a general and consistent practice *of states* followed by them from a sense of legal obligation. At the same time, the very idea of what it is to be a "state" is, in a very real sense, a legal construction—one based on physical facts, to be sure—but nonetheless constructed through shared understandings. Perhaps the most important of these shared understandings is that the quintessential defining characteristic of a "state" is its monopoly over the legitimate use of force within its geographical boundaries. International law thus creates, protects, and reinforces state sovereignty through various legal rules including the obligation not to use aggressive physical force against another sovereign state except in rare circumstances. International law cannot primarily rely on internal physical force against states as a means of law enforcement, because to do so would threaten to collapse the very idea of what it is to be a "state" and thus eliminate the precondition for the existence of international law in the cause of enforcing it.

The recognition that international law most often relies on outcasting rather than physical force turns the sovereigntist critique on its head. If international legal regimes are best understood as arrangements that generate community benefits for member states and impose discipline through outcasting (excluding lawbreakers from the benefits of membership), then international law does not have the power to rob states of their sovereignty. Instead, it only has the power to take away the very benefits that it has itself generated. If that is true, then states that refuse to join international agreements out of a fear that doing so will undermine their sovereignty are simply voluntary outcasts.

NOTES

1. To say that the law is a valuable institution is to make a claim about its potential. The moral value of the law stems from its distinctive ability to solve problems that no other comparable social institutions are capable of solving. When a particular system does not solve these problems, exacerbates them, or creates new problems, it fails to realize its potential and correspondingly lacks moral value. In this respect, law is like marriage and education. While these social institutions are capable of realizing important moral goods, their failure to do so deprives their instantiations of value and may render them morally pernicious.

2. *See* U.S. CONST. art. I, § 9, cl. 1 (prohibiting abolition of the slave trade before 1808); U.S. CONST. art. V (providing that "no State, without its Consent, shall be deprived of its equal Suffrage in the Senate").

3. *See* U.S. CONST. art. V.

4. Secondary enforcement rules can exist even when there are no primary enforcement rules. They are "secondary" rules because they are directed at individuals other than the conduct rule violators.

5. Jack Goldsmith & Daryl Levinson, *Law for States: International Law, Constitutional Law, Public Law*, 122 HARV. L. REV. 1791, 1831 (2009)

26 Human Rights and the Challenge of Cultural Diversity

JAMES W. NICKEL

When governments do cruel and unjust things to their citizens we are now likely to describe those actions as violations of human rights—instead of simply saying that they are unjust, immoral, tyrannical, or barbaric. Appealing to human rights in order to describe and criticize the actions of repressive governments became common as a popular phenomenon in the second half of the twentieth century. Talk of natural rights and of constitutional rights has long been common among philosophers and lawyers, but since 1948, the idea of human rights has gradually been adopted by journalists, politicians, and the public in many parts of the world. Violations of human rights are now frequently recognized and reported as such by journalists, and many people around the world have adopted "human rights violation" as a category of political thought and appraisal.

THE UNIVERSAL DECLARATION OF HUMAN RIGHTS

The human rights movement in its contemporary form emerged after World War II. The carnage. genocides, and destruction of that war led to a determination to do something to prevent aggressive war, to build an international organization to address severe international problems, and to impose standards of decency on the world's governments. The United Nations organization (UN), created in 1945, has played a key role in the development of the contemporary idea of human rights.

The creators of the UN believed that reducing the likelihood of war required preventing severe and large-scale oppression within countries. Because of this belief, even the earliest conceptions of the UN gave the organization a role in promoting rights and liberties. Some early conceptions of the UN Charter suggested that it contain an international bill of rights to which any member nation would have to subscribe, but the idea did not succeed. Instead, the Charter simply committed the UN to promoting human rights. The Charter expressed "faith in fundamental human rights, in the dignity and worth of the human person, in the equal rights of men and women and of nations large and small." (United Nations, 1945: preamble.)[1] Its signatories pledged themselves to "take joint and separate action in cooperation with the organization" to promote "universal respect for, and observance of, human rights and fundamental freedoms for all without distinction as to race, sex, language or religion." (United Nations, 1945: article 1.3.)[2]

Shortly after the approval of the Charter, a UN committee was charged with writing an international bill of rights. It was to be similar in content to bills of rights already existing in some countries, but applying to all people in all countries. The UN took a familiar genre, a national bill of rights, and adapted it for use at the international level. An international bill of rights emerged in December 1948 as the Universal Declaration of Human Rights. The Universal Declaration was a set of proposed standards, rather than a treaty. It recommended promotion of human rights through "teaching and education" and "measures, national and international, to secure their universal and effective recognition and observance." (United Nations, 1948b; for histories of the Universal Declaration see Glendon, 2001; Lauren, 1998; and Morsink, 1999.)[3]

Human rights comprise seven families, six of which are found in the Universal Declaration. First, there are security rights that protect people

(New York: Wiley-Blackwell, 2nd ed. 2007). Adapted with permission of the publisher.

against crimes such as murder, massacre, torture, and rape. Second, there are due process rights that protect against abuses of the legal system such as imprisonment without trial, secret trials, and excessive punishments. Article 5 of the European Convention, for example, says that people facing criminal charges are "entitled to a fair and public hearing within a reasonable time by an independent and impartial tribunal established by law."

Third, there are liberty rights that protect fundamental freedoms in areas such as belief, expression, association, assembly, and movement. For example, Article 11 of the European Convention says that "Everyone has the right to freedom of peaceful assembly and to freedom of association with others, including the right to form and to join trade unions for the protection of his interests." (European Convention, Article 11.)

Fourth, there are rights of political participation that require a democratic political process in which people can participate through actions such as voting, serving in public office, communicating, assembling, and protesting. The African Charter is typical in setting out that "Every citizen shall have the right to participate freely in the government of his country, either directly or through freely chosen representatives in accordance with the provisions of the law." (African Charter Union, 1981.) [4] The American Convention goes further, saying that every citizen shall have the right to "vote and to be elected in genuine period elections, which shall be by universal and equal suffrage and by secret ballot." (Organization of American States, 1969.)[5]

Fifth, there are equality rights that guarantee equal citizenship, equality before the law, and nondiscrimination. For example, article 24 of the American Convention says that: "All persons are equal before the law. Consequently, they are entitled, without discrimination, to equal protection of the law."

Sixth, there are social rights that require governments to ensure that each person has access to subsistence, health care, and education. For example, the Social Covenant sets out a "right of everyone to an adequate standard of living for himself and his family, including adequate food, clothing, and housing ..." (United Nations, 1966b.)[6]

Finally, there are rights addressing the problems of distinctive groups, including women, children, minorities, and indigenous peoples; minority rights; and group rights. Human rights treaties place great emphasis on the right to freedom from discrimination, but they go beyond it to require specific protections for distinctive groups: women, minorities, and indigenous peoples. The Universal Declaration does not include group rights, but several human rights treaties do, beginning with the Genocide Convention. (United Nations, 1948a.)[7] Group rights include protections of ethnic groups against genocide and the ownership by countries of their national territories and resources.

This classification of human rights into seven families is much more fine-grained than the familiar division of human rights into civil and political rights and social rights. It is also more discriminating than Karel Vasek's classification of human rights in terms of three generations. (The first generation of rights was civil and political rights; the second was social rights; and the third generation was "solidarity rights," which include group rights and rights to peace and development. (Vasek, 1977; see also Wellman, 1999.)[8]

The Universal Declaration has been amazingly successful in establishing a fixed worldwide meaning for the idea of human rights. Broadly speaking, the list of human rights that it proposed still sets the pattern for the numerous human rights treaties that have gone into operation since 1948. Those treaties include the European Convention on Human Rights (Council of Europe, 1950),[9] the International Covenant on Civil and Political Rights (United Nations, 1966a),[10] the International Covenant on Economic, Social, and Cultural Rights (United Nations, 1966b),[11] the American Convention on Human Rights (Organization of American States, 1969),[12] and nearly a dozen others.

DEFINING FEATURES OF HUMAN RIGHTS

Human rights, as conceived in the Universal Declaration and subsequent human rights treaties, have a number of general characteristics. Here are six of them:

Lest we miss the obvious, human rights are *rights*. At a minimum this means that human rights have *rightholders* (the people who have them); *addressees* (parties assigned duties or responsibilities); and *scopes* that focus on a freedom, protection, or benefit. Further, rights are mandatory in the sense that some behaviors of the addressees are required or forbidden.

Human rights are universal in the sense that they extend to every person living today. Characteristics such as race, sex, religion, social position, and nationality are irrelevant to whether one has human rights.

Human rights are high priority norms. They are not absolute but are strong enough to win most of the time when they compete with other considerations. As such, they must have strong justifications that apply all over the world and support the independence and high priority of human rights. The Universal Declaration states that human rights are rooted in the dignity and worth of human beings and in the requirements of domestic and international peace and security.

Human rights are not dependent for their existence on recognition or enactment by particular governments. They exist as legal norms at the national and international levels, and as norms of justified or enlightened political morality. In promulgating the Universal Declaration as a "common standard of achievement," the UN did not purport to describe rights already recognized everywhere. Instead, it attempted to set forth an enlightened international political morality that addresses familiar abuses of contemporary political institutions. Subsequently, however, international treaties were used to make human rights norms part of international law. Their proponents would like to see them embedded in all people's beliefs and actions and effectively recognized and implemented in law, government, and international organizations.

Human rights are international standards of evaluation and criticism unrestricted by political boundaries. They provide standards for criticism by "outsiders" such as international organizations, people and groups in other countries, and foreign governments.

Finally, human rights are numerous and specific rather than few and general. Like other bills of rights, the Universal Declaration is a list of specific rights that addresses severe but familiar problems of governments. Accordingly, the Universal Declaration is not a restatement of Locke's rights to life, liberty, and property (Locke, 1986; originally published 1689),[13] although some abstract values are identified in the preamble. Instead, it is a list of roughly two dozen specific rights.

Rights range from abstract to specific (or from general to precise) according to how fully their parts are specified. Indeterminacy can occur in any of the elements of a right. There may be lack of clarity about the identity of the right holders and addressees. The scope of the right, what it offers its holder(s) and requires of its duty bearers, may be imprecisely defined. And we may lack a clear view of the right's weight in competition with other considerations. One of the confusing things about rights is that they have differing degrees of abstractness. A right under a business contract is likely to be quite specific, where constitutional and human rights are usually abstract (and therefore somewhat vague). Abstract rights are just as important as specific rights, so we should not repudiate them simply to achieve some philosophical ideal of precision.

RELATIVISM AND HUMAN RIGHTS

Planet earth is wonderfully varied in its peoples, cultures, religions, and national traditions. Put all those differences together with the idea of universal human rights and the combination may not seem very plausible. How can a single set of rights be appropriate to such a diverse world? Accordingly, the universality and justifiability of human rights are sometimes challenged by appeal to cultural differences, using some notion that a society's norms inevitably are, or should be, relative to its culture and circumstances. The defender of universal human rights may be accused of insensitivity, arrogance, and cultural imperialism. (Talbott, 2005.)[14] *Insensitivity* may be found in failing to recognize differences in values and traditions. *Arrogance* may be found in considering one's own values to be better without having thought deeply about the matter. *Cultural imperialism* may be seen in being prepared to impose one's own culture's values and norms coercively.

When the Universal Declaration was being formulated in 1947, the Executive Board of the American Anthropological Association warned of the danger that the Declaration would be "a statement of rights conceived only in terms of the values prevalent in Western Europe and America," and condemned an ethnocentrism that translates "the recognition of cultural differences into a summons to action." The main concern of the Board was to condemn intolerant colonialist attitudes and to advocate cultural and political self-determination. The Board allowed that "freedom is understood and sought after by peoples having the most diverse cultures," and suggested that in attempting to influence repressive regimes, "underlying cultural values may be called on to bring the peoples of such states to a realization of the consequences of the acts of their governments, and thus enforce a brake upon discrimination and conquest." (American Anthropological Association, 1947.)[15]

In addition to these sensible suggestions the AAA Board also made some stronger assertions. One was that "standards and values are relative to the culture from which they derive" and thus "what is held to be a human right in one society may be regarded as anti-social by another people." The Board also asserted that "respect for differences between cultures is validated by the scientific fact that no technique of qualitatively evaluating cultures has been discovered." (American Anthropological Association, 1947.)[16] This bizarre argument attempts to justify a norm of tolerance by asserting that there is no way of justifying moral and legal norms. If norms are impossible to justify, so are norms that prescribe diversity and tolerance.

Globalization and its accompanying set of transnational influences create unlikely combinations of beliefs, practices, and commitments. The world's countries and cultures are not isolated, insulated, and homogeneous. Most of them have not been so in recent centuries, but they are even

less isolated and homogeneous today than they once were. The walls separating countries are battered and breached not only by trade and other forms of economic interaction, but also by global media and communications systems, legions of travelers, extensive migration, international organizations, and global governance systems—including, of course, the international human rights system. The world long ago ceased to be comprised of separate "culture gardens" that are homogeneous, coherent, and integrated. (Preis, 1996: 288–9.)[17] Instead, cultures are bombarded by outside influences that lead to internal conflict and debates. Disagreement and conflict are part of culture. (Preis, 1996: 305.)[18] This is not to deny, of course, that there are dominant patterns of culture within most countries which help constitute a country's traditions, practices, and institutions.

I shall argue below that there is much more agreement worldwide about human rights than one might initially expect. But there is no doubt that there exists today significant normative disagreement about various features of human rights. Features of human rights that occasion disagreement in many countries include:

- The importance of, and appropriate qualifications to, fundamental freedoms such as freedom of religion, expression, and association;
- The importance of rights of political participation and regular elections;
- Whether social rights are genuine human rights;
- Whether concern for social and economic equality is an appropriate concern of human rights;
- Whether women's rights to nondiscrimination and social and economic equality are important human rights requiring immediate realization through government action;
- The importance of the rights of groups in thinking about human rights.

There is diversity of opinion about these questions in every country. In particular countries one perspective on these questions may be by far the most popular, however, and it may be influenced by political and religious traditions or by economic circumstances. Countries with authoritarian political traditions may have political elites or popular majorities that are unenthusiastic about individual liberties and democratic institutions. Countries with very hierarchical religious traditions may have elites or popular majorities that are unenthusiastic about women's rights, rights of religious and ethnic minorities, and concern for social and economic equality. Countries whose traditions put great emphasis on the importance of community and belonging, particularly at the national level, may have political elites or popular majorities that are enthusiastic about democratic rights and group rights, but unenthusiastic about the fundamental freedoms (which they may consider excessively individualistic).

What follows are eight arguments directed to the cultural relativist. The first three responses attempt to attract the relativist to a human rights perspective. The second set continues that effort by showing how international human rights norms can accommodate a great deal of cultural and political diversity. The last two suggest that substantial acceptance of human rights now exists around the world, and that this acceptance makes irrelevant many relativist worries.

1. Human rights yield far stronger protections of tolerance and security than relativism can support. Many people are attracted to cultural relativism because they think that it promotes tolerance, rejects imperialism and colonialist practices, and shows respect for other countries and cultures. After all, if people restrict the application of their own norms to their own countries or cultures, then they will not find any justification for imposing their own values and norms upon other cultures. Relativism produces tolerance. There may be some truth in this if we are looking at relativism and tolerance from a psychological perspective. It seems likely that people who are keenly aware of cultural and national differences, and who do not see any basis for extending norms across borders, will be inclined towards more tolerant attitudes than universalistic moral absolutists.

But from a logical perspective, relativism provides no support for tolerance across borders. If the culture of A-land fosters very intolerant

attitudes towards the practices of other peoples, and citizens of A-land act intolerantly towards people from B-land, the A-landers are just following their own traditions and cultural norms. To the relativist, that is normal. Suppose that B-land has cultural and political traditions that are tolerant of other countries and cultures, and that our relativist is a native of B-land. Our relativist will not find it appropriate to criticize the intolerance of citizens of A-land because they are just following their longstanding cultural norms. To criticize the A-landers, people from B-land will have to endorse or presuppose a transnational principle of tolerance. (See Talbott, 2005: 43.)[19] And that transnational principle will go against the cultural traditions of some peoples and countries.

If relativists committed to tolerance recognize that there are likely to be occasions on which they will find it necessary to engage in transnational moral and political criticism, they should find attractive international human rights norms that prohibit genocide, prescribe security and nondiscrimination for minority cultures, endorse the self-determination of peoples, and combat racism.

2. The milder forms of relativism are compatible with thinking that at least some human rights are a good idea. A relativist does not need to be a total moral skeptic. She can believe that humans have some reliable abilities to arrive at useful practical norms. Neither the weak nor the strong forms of moral skepticism are proven true by the existence of important moral, political, and legal differences. The nonskeptic can respond that disagreement only shows that some people hold justified moral beliefs and others unjustified ones or, more plausibly, a mixture of the two. Disagreement does not show that reliable and rational methods of settling moral, political, and legal questions are unavailable or impossible. Some people may not know good methods, or they may be incapable of using them well because of bias, irrationality, or lack of knowledge about relevant facts.

Interestingly, the existence of complete agreement on moral issues worldwide would not disprove moral skepticism. That view could still be correct if agreement derived from irrational grounds and was impossible to justify by appeal to rational ones. Skeptics appeal to disagreement and nonskeptics to agreement as evidence for their views, but neither appeal is conclusive. The issue must be argued on other grounds.

One may hope to settle the matter in favor of skeptical relativism by arguing that if there were a rational method for settling moral disagreements, everyone would know it or, at least, that moral philosophers would be able to specify its steps adequately. This argument does not work. It took millennia for human beings to develop rational methods for deciding disputes in scientific matters, and even now there are very significant disputes about the methods of physical sciences. Further, philosophers have offered numerous accounts of the grounds of practical knowledge and argumentation, one of which may be correct.

Cultural relativists tend to prefer that moral and legal norms be decided at the cultural or national level, but this preference is sure to require exceptions. Otherwise the relativist would have to disapprove of having a general criminal law in a multicultural society, and would have to object not just to international human rights but to international law generally. The superiority of indigenous standards is often exaggerated. We know from our own cultures that indigenous institutions often work badly and become outdated. Social and technological changes often make older norms and practices ill-suited to a group's needs. For example, when education and wide availability of electronic media make people more knowledgeable about politics and less willing to have no influence on important political decisions, the absence of even rudimentary democratic institutions becomes a problem. Further, one cannot assume that the existing norms and practices that violate human rights are in fact indigenous. They may themselves have been imported from other authoritarian or hierarchical countries.

The claim that imported standards generally function poorly or not at all is also an exaggeration. Many transplanted institutions and norms can function successfully, especially if a transition period is planned. The parliamentary institutions created in Japan after World War II are one striking example of successful transplantation. Borrowing between countries occurs constantly and ranges from social movements (for example, environmentalism, feminism), political institutions and law (for example, civil service systems, judicial review, ombudsmen, income tax, environmental law) to technology and economics (for example, assembly line production, computers, air transportation).

3. A strong case for international human rights can be made by appealing to widely recognized problems and widely shared values. Many human rights problems come from the dangers of contemporary political and economic institutions. Human rights are needed in all countries because the institutions of the modern state are now used everywhere, and many human rights are socially learned remedies for the built-in dangers of these institutions. As Jack Donnelly says, "[T]he special threat to personal autonomy and equality presented by the modern state requires a set of legal rights, such as the presumption of innocence and rights to due process, fair and public hearings before an independent tribunal, and protection from arbitrary arrest, detention, or exile." (Donnelly, 2003: 46; see also 92.)[20] Differences in values and social traditions are less important than one might think.

As a humble analogy consider the rotary lawnmower, a motorized device with wheels that spins a blade parallel to the ground in order to cut grass. Rotary lawnmowers sometimes injure the operator's feet. The danger is inherent in the device and is realized everywhere the device is used. And people everywhere find cut-up feet to be a bad thing. So, if people in all countries use rotary lawnmowers, their dangers and remedies need to be taught everywhere. If this social learning first occurred in the countries where rotary mowers were first introduced, it was or would have been appropriate to spread its lessons around the world as soon as use of the device began to spread. This is analogous to the modern state, with its built-in dangers that need to be learned and remedied. Once the dangers and remedies have been learned, the lessons ought to be shared with all the users. Indeed, since the European colonial powers both developed and promoted the spread of the institutions of the modern state, they have responsibilities to address its dangers. A recall of the product is not possible, but sharing the lessons about its dangers and remedies is.

The modern state evolved from earlier systems of government, law, and property, and it is implausible to suggest that none of the dangers of the modern state were present in the earlier versions. The dangers of the reckless and corrupt use of political power, of food scarcity due to systems of private agricultural property, and the dangers of democracy have been known and discussed for more than 2,000 years. Further, it is doubtful that Donnelly's view supports all families of human rights. Not all the problems that human rights address derive from abuses of political institutions. Human rights address slavery, patriarchy, and violence against minorities, but these are as much social issues as political ones. We need a view of human rights that is not focused exclusively on problems mainly caused by the state. Still, it is helpful to follow Donnelly in emphasizing the dangers all humans now face from widely used political institutions.

4. Intervention is not the main means of promoting human rights. This is the first of three responses focusing on the ability of international human rights norms to accommodate cultural and political diversity. This response turns to the issue of imperialism. The ugliness and frequent ineffectiveness of international intervention to protect human rights often leads people to its wholesale rejection. (See Talbott, 2005: 107.)[21] I agree that coercive intervention is often likely to be unsuccessful, and emphasize that its costs are very high. It is because of the costs, dangers, and low success rate of coercive intervention that the international human rights movement has predominantly relied on persuasion and pressure rather than coercion to promote human rights. I cannot, however, endorse a wholesale rejection of international intervention to protect human rights. I believe that some interventions have been necessary and successful. These include sanctions against apartheid in South Africa, the NATO [Ed., North Atlantic Treaty Organization] intervention in Kosovo, and the intervention led by Australia in East Timor. And I believe that some interventions did not occur when they should have, a notable example

being intervention to stop the 1994 genocide in Rwanda.

Still, as human rights function today within international organizations, it is just untrue to say that they are mainly about intervention. A better description of their main role is that they encourage and pressure governments to treat their citizens humanely with respect for their lives, liberties, and equal citizenship. They use social pressure and acculturation to promote acceptance and compliance with human rights norms. (See Goodman and Jinks, 2004.)[22]

Because enforcement efforts are costly, dangerous, and often fail to work, it is reasonable to restrict their use to the most severe human rights crises. These tend to be situations in which large numbers of people are being killed. To avoid narrowing the human rights agenda to such crises, means for promoting human rights have been devised that do not require intervention or the imposition of sanctions. These weaker means include educating governments and publics about international human rights standards, treaties that commit countries to human rights norms and require governments to make reports on their progress in realizing them, and nagging and shaming governments by NGOs [Ed., nongovernmental organizations], other governments, and international officials such as the UN High Commissioner for Human Rights.

5. Human rights are compatible with great cultural and political diversity. Human rights are minimal standards open to interpretation at the national level. At the implementation stage countries can take local conditions into account in formulating their constitutional and legal rights. Formulations of human rights use broad language that allows considerable flexibility to interpretation and implementation at the national level. When human rights are enforced by courts, as they are under the European Convention on Human Rights (Council of Europe, 1950),[23] the scope allowed to local interpretation is constrained. But even there, accommodation is promoted by the "margin of appreciation" doctrine. It allows the court to defer to national authorities in matters that are culturally sensitive. (See Hartman, 1981.)[24]

Human rights standards have a number of features allowing them to accommodate diversity. Perhaps the most obvious and important is limited scope—they provide minimal standards in a limited number of areas. For example, the rights one has as a homeowner, teacher, or union member depend not on human rights but on the morality, laws, and customs of one's country. It is possible, of course, that some of the rights found in the Universal Declaration and other human rights documents are insufficiently basic and that one who wanted to preserve local flexibility against international human rights would set the criterion for a "minimal standard" or "basic right" rather high.

Next, the terms used in formulating human rights are often broad or abstract enough to allow considerable latitude to local interpretation. For example, Article 10 of the International Covenant on Civil and Political Rights requires that people in prison be "treated with humanity and with respect for the inherent dignity of the human person." This permits the operation of varying conceptions of human dignity. What counts as an indignity depends somewhat on how most people live and are treated and on what the local culture finds repulsive. If many people work in the fields pulling plows because there are no tractors or beasts of burden, then a punishment involving such work would be no indignity. But if such work is normally done by tractors, and only prisoners are required to pull plows, this may amount to a substantial indignity by suggesting that prisoners are mere beasts or machines.

Further, the possibility of overriding some human rights in emergency situations is explicitly allowed by major human rights treaties. For example, the European Convention allows countries to suspend some rights during "time of war or other public emergency threatening the life of the nation."

Finally, the human rights movement has supported diversity within a structure of basic principles by endorsing the principle of self-determination and, in the UN Charter, the principle of nonintervention in matters essentially within the domestic jurisdiction of a state. It should be understood, however, that these

principles are subject to some important qualifications. The domestic jurisdiction clause does not relieve a country of obligations undertaken in international law, even if they pertain to domestic matters.

6. Human rights collide with culture and religion much less than one might expect. Two beliefs that can collide, in the sense of one contradicting or excluding belief in the other, may fail to do so, or collide only rarely. Let's call this noncollision. For example, a Muslim immigrant to the United States may believe, as a religious ideal, that the United States Constitution should be replaced by an Islamic constitution that makes Islamic law central to American life. But this ideal is so unlikely to be realized in the foreseeable future that he consigns it to the realm of things that are true in theory but which do not have much relevance to daily practice. Indeed, he may admire the US Constitution as a good, practical second best.

There are a number of sources of noncollision. One, just mentioned, is psychological or practical compartmentalization. People often put potentially conflicting beliefs in different realms. Many religious norms and ideals will be placed in the categories of religion and home and family, but be viewed as having limited relevance to current politics and business. Political and legal matters are often kept in their own realm. For example, a requirement that people receive fair trials when charged with a crime does not generally conflict with cultural values or religious beliefs, since those values are unlikely to be focused on criminal trials.

Another explanation of why noncollision occurs is that people can agree on human rights without agreeing on the grounds of human rights. A libertarian may endorse the fundamental freedoms because they take seriously the separateness of persons, where a communitarian who rejects the separateness of persons may also endorse the basic liberties because he thinks they are as important to groups as they are to individuals. (Buchanan, 1989.)[25] And many people will not have fancy theoretical grounds for believing in human rights; they subscribe to them because their friends do or because they seem to work. Rawls's notion of an "overlapping consensus" is based on this; it allows people to support political principles for reasons that are rooted in their own religions, philosophies, and worldviews. (Rawls, 1993.)[26] But this is too ordinary a matter to require a fancy name. It is a commonplace of politics that people support policies for different reasons. For most people, agreement on human rights is not agreement on a philosophy of human rights or a liberal political ideology. Just as people from different ideologies often accept the same political institutions with varying degrees of enthusiasm, people from different ideologies can accept most of the same human rights norms. Further, the cultural and religious views of many people are loosely organized rather than tightly systematized, held with the understanding that some competing considerations have to be accommodated, and viewed as ideals or duties with lots of exceptions rather than as categorical requirements.

If most human rights exhibit noncollision in relation to cultural and religious views, then the diversity of those views does not present a direct problem for most human rights. It will not be possible to infer rejection of human rights from the presence of widely accepted cultural and religious beliefs and practices that seem contrary to human rights. For example, the Buddhist belief that the self is ultimately illusory can often fail to collide with the view of human rights advocates that governments should respect the personal freedoms of their citizens.

It might be alleged that noncollision only works in liberal societies where politics and religion are separated. I doubt this, while allowing that noncollision is more likely when a significant degree of psychological and institutional separation exists between politics and local religions. Even in religiously ordered countries the limitations that religion places on political practices allow considerable flexibility in constitutional arrangements and in matters such as criminal law, due process, and punishment. Further, it cannot be assumed that people in strongly religious countries have no commitment to tolerance or want the religious leaders to be the political leaders.

7. Human rights treaties have been ratified by most governments. This is the first of two responses focusing on the acceptance of human rights by people and governments in all parts of the world. As of 2006, the Civil and Political Covenant has been ratified by 155 countries (out of a total of about 200), and the Social Covenant by 152. The Convention on the Elimination of All Forms of Discrimination against Women has been ratified by 180(!), and the Convention on the Rights of the Child by 192(!!). Part of the explanation for these ratifications is the desire to look good internationally and the absence—in most cases—of irresistible pressure to comply with United Nations human rights treaties. But governments would not have accepted these treaties if they regarded their content as outlandish or totally alien to their visions of the future. Countries that ratify a treaty consent thereby to scrutiny and discussion of their practices.

Many countries have gone beyond ratifying international treaties to incorporate international human rights norms in their national constitutions, bills of rights, and legislation.

8. Human rights are widely accepted by ordinary people around the world. The best way to find out how much agreement and disagreement there is about international human rights is empirical; it involves, among other things, asking people what they think. I have lost confidence in our ability to project beliefs about human rights from other things we think we know about people's cultures, religions, or national traditions. There are several reasons why such projections are risky. First, it may be that only some part of the population holds those beliefs or adheres to those traditions. It's easy to exaggerate the uniformity of culture or religion. Second, people care about their culture, religion, and traditions, but they are not their only big concerns. Third, as we saw above, religious and cultural norms are often loosely applied; full and exact compliance may be unnecessary or too demanding for most people. Fourth, and also mentioned above, different areas of life are somewhat compartmentalized institutionally and psychologically. Fifth, most people know about the dangers of mixing religion and politics.

Polling and other empirical studies are needed to find out what people feel and think about human rights. Such polling is starting to be done worldwide, and its results are sometimes surprising. For example, in a 2002 opinion poll in eight Arab countries, respondents were asked to rank, in order of importance, ten different political issues. "Civil and personal rights" received the highest score in all eight countries, coming in ahead of health care and Palestine (Zogby International, 2002; see also Pew, 2003, and Torney-Purta, 2001.)[27]

If we wanted to find out empirically whether human rights are accepted worldwide, what exactly would we need to investigate? One large question here is exactly what a person who accepts human rights must accept. This problem is analogous to the problem of determining the percentage of people in a country who accept a particular religion. How many of the religion's theological beliefs does an ordinary person need to endorse in order to accept the religion? Understanding worldwide acceptance requires us to analyze what acceptance is, which people must accept human rights, and what propositions about human rights they must endorse. In order to explain worldwide acceptance it will be necessary to explain *acceptance by a person* and *acceptance by a country.*

To accept a norm is to believe in its validity or to have favorable attitudes towards its adoption and use. Sincere acceptance is compatible with having some worries about the norm, or with limited enthusiasm for it. Opinion polls accommodate this by allowing people to choose between strongly agree and agree. Acceptance of a norm is not the same as always complying with a norm. As those who have struggled against temptation know, people frequently violate norms that they sincerely accept. And accepting a norm does not require that one have any particular reasons for one's acceptance.

How many people need to accept human rights for worldwide acceptance? We could give a simple majoritarian answer requiring that more than fifty percent of the world's competent adults accept human rights. But this answer would allow for the possibility that there is one half of the world where nearly everyone accepts human rights and another half where few people do. To avoid that possibility, let's use a country-by-country approach and require that a majority of people in almost all countries accept human rights. Acceptance in a country exists when the appropriate number of people in the country agree with human rights norms. And acceptance in the world exists when almost all of the world's countries accept human rights.

One could answer the "Which people?" question by giving a special place to the opinions of people, such as political leaders and public intellectuals, who are well-placed to influence government policies on human rights, or to officials, such as soldiers and police officers, who are in a position to violate human rights. I will not take this approach, since acceptance by an elite, however influential or practically important, does not constitute general acceptance. Nevertheless, it will be useful for many purposes to have statistics about which subgroups within society accept and reject human rights.

It is hard to decide which beliefs about human rights a person needs to have, to be counted as believing in human rights. There are limits to what ordinary people can be expected to understand about human rights. Articulate acceptance of a complex conception of human rights by ordinary people is not a plausible expectation. Most people have never have thought about what a right is, how rights relate to duties and powers, who the addressees of human rights are, or about the high priority of rights. If the acceptance of human rights requires that ordinary people have complicated understandings of human rights and their place in morality and international law, we will find that few ordinary people accept human rights.

Suppose that we could ask a person ten questions to determine if she accepted human rights. Which questions should we ask? I propose two sorts of questions. One kind of question pertains to the general idea of human rights. For example, does the person have the idea that there should be minimal international standards that apply to people everywhere? The second kind of question pertains to whether a person accepts the kinds of specific norms that are found in contemporary human rights declarations and treaties.

Let's start with the general idea of human rights. I propose to represent this general idea with questions pertaining to (1) universality; (2) high priority; and (3) associated duties. Universality might be tested by propositions such as:

- All people everywhere ought to enjoy decent treatment by governments and societies.
- Rights to life and security are protections that nobody should be denied.

To these propositions people would be asked to indicate whether they strongly disagree, disagree, agree, strongly agree, or have no opinion.

The idea that human rights are mandatory or duty-generating might be tested by propositions such as:

- It is generally wrong for governments to violate human rights such as the right against torture and the right to a fair trial.
- The responsibilities of governments include respecting and protecting people's human rights.

Belief in the high priority of human rights will be tested by formulating propositions about specific rights, or families of rights, as questions about importance. For example, a question about the right to life would be formulated as: "It is very important that people enjoy protections against being killed by agents of the state without trial."

Next we can turn to testing for beliefs about specific human rights. The requirement I propose is that we test for acceptance of representative examples of rights from all of the six families of human rights. These six families are security rights, due process rights, liberty rights, rights of political participation, equality rights, and welfare rights. To illustrate this, here are five propositions to which people could indicate that they strongly disagree, disagree, are ambivalent, agree, strongly agree, or have no opinion:

- It is very important that governments refrain from and protect all people against arbitrary execution and torture.
- It is very important that governments ensure that all people charged with crimes receive a fair trial.

- It is very important that governments respect and protect everyone's rights of political participation, such as voting and engaging in political movements and campaigns.
- It is very important that governments respect and protect everyone's equality before the law, and freedom from discrimination on grounds such as race, sex, or religion.
- It is imperative that governments take steps to ensure that all people have access to basic material needs such as food and shelter, and that all children have access to education.

My proposal, then, is that our ten questions include some that concern the general idea of human rights, and others that are about the main families of particular human rights.

To accept human rights, a person would need to accept most of the items in each group. Thus, if a person agreed to most of the ten propositions about human rights, including most of the ones about the general conception of human rights and most of the ones about specific rights, I would count that person as accepting human rights.

It is obvious that certain questions are more important than others in determining belief in human rights. Believing in the right to life, for example, is more important than believing in the right to freedom of political participation. But I propose not to make any one question the touchstone of believing in human rights. It is hard to identify such propositions, and it is even harder to formulate questions in such a way that a person who believed in human rights might not nevertheless find things in them to disagree with. For example, a person much preoccupied with crime might disagree with "It is generally wrong for governments to violate human rights such as the right against torture and the right to a fair trial," because it contains no exception permitting the severe punishment of rapists and murderers.

Note that under this sketch of what acceptance means there are lots of things that people do not need to accept in order to accept human rights. They do not have to accept any particular reasons for human rights, much less a liberal political ideology. They do not have to accept any precise conception of what a right is. They do not have to distinguish between moral and legal norms. And they do not need to have views about the international enforcement of human rights. But the formulation of the test does incorporate the universality, mandatory character, and high priority of human rights.

If a person agreed to most of the ten propositions about human rights in the way described above, I would count that person as accepting human rights. If, apart from those with no opinion, a majority of competent adults in a country were like the person just described, then I would count that country as accepting human rights. And if almost all countries accepted human rights, then worldwide acceptance of human rights would exist. Note that this describes a world in which there could—and probably would—still be lots of disagreement about human rights among intellectuals, politicians, and the people generally.

Statistical representations of the results of conducting in all countries an opinion poll similar to the one I described would be much more informative than the simple notion of general acceptance that I have defined. Polling data would tell us which rights, and ideas of rights, were accepted by what percentage of people in each country, and would correlate acceptance of each item with variables such as religion, age, sex, ethnicity, religion, level of education, occupation, and political outlook. The data would also tell us about acceptance of human rights by intellectual and political elites.

One might think that the world has far too many human rights problems for worldwide acceptance, or some near approximation of it, to exist. If almost people in almost all countries accepted human rights in the sense defined, surely we would not have the political and human rights problems that we do. This overlooks the fact that rejection of human rights is not the only obstacle to their realization. Even in countries where a majority now accepts human rights, severe social and political problems can remain. Acceptance of human rights, in the sense defined, can exist in countries in which large and influential minorities of people and leaders do not accept human rights. Because large numbers of people do not

participate in the consensus, they may be sources of rejectionist ideas, political insurgencies, ethnic hatreds, terrorism, and the like. Higher levels of acceptance diminish but may not remove this possibility.

Further, large gaps between accepted norms and actual practices may exist. People and governments frequently fail to live up to their human rights beliefs, just as they often fail to live up to their religious and ethical beliefs. And government leaders often fail to bring political and legal institutions into line with human rights. Beyond this, all sorts of disagreements about matters not fully covered by human rights may exist among those who accept human rights. Big disagreements about territory, historic injustices, terrorism, and various political and economic arrangements may still exist.

Finally, many countries will still be poor and troubled. Perhaps their problems will take more peaceful forms if most people accept human rights, but not necessarily. Thugs who do not believe in human rights may still be able to take over the government, loot its resources, and kill and rape its people.

Even though worldwide acceptance of human rights is unlikely to solve many of the world's problems, there clearly are ways in which worldwide acceptance will improve matters. First, political discourse among governments and peoples will often be guided by shared norms, and democratic support will more often be available for government actions to respect, protect, provide for, or promote human rights. Policies such as genocide and ethnic cleansing will be off the table in most countries, particularly those in which eighty or ninety percent of people accept human rights. Second, efforts to promote and protect human rights by international organizations are less likely to be blocked by deep disagreements (as they were during the Cold War) and more likely to be based on consensus. Third, worries about the legitimacy of international efforts to promote and protect human rights will be reduced. Finally, it will be harder to demonize countries and peoples if we know that large majorities in them accept human rights.

FURTHER READING

Baderin, M. "Human Rights and Islamic Law: The Myth of Discord." *European Human Rights Law Review 2 (2005): 165–85.*

Bauer, J., and D. Bell, D., eds. *The East Asian Challenge for Human Rights. Cambridge: Cambridge University Press, 1999.*

Bell, D. *East Meets West: Human Rights and Democracy in East Asia. Princeton: Princeton University Press, 2000.*

Brackney, W., series editor. *Human Rights and the World's Major Religions. Vol. 1: Hass, P., ed. The Jewish Tradition; Vol. 2: Brackney, W., ed. The Christian Tradition; Vol. 3: 'Abd al-Rahim, M., ed. The Islamic Tradition; Vol. 4: Coward, H., ed. The Hindu Tradition; Volume 5: Florida, R., ed. The Buddhist Tradition. Westport, CT: Praeger, 2004.*

Cowan, J., M. Dembour, and R. Wilson, eds. *Culture and Rights: Anthropological Perspectives. Cambridge: Cambridge University Press, 2001.*

Evans, M. and R. Murray, eds. *The African Charter on Human and People's Rights: The System in Practice, 1986–2000. Cambridge: Cambridge University Press, 2002.*

Preis, A. "Human Rights as Cultural Practice: An Anthropological Critique." *Human Rights Quarterly 18 (1996): 286–315.*

Talbott, W. *Which Rights Should be Universal? Oxford: Oxford University Press, 2005.*

Wilson, R., ed. *Human Rights, Culture and Context: Anthropological Perspectives. London: Pluto Press, 1997.*

NOTES

1. United Nations. 1945. *Charter of the United Nations.* In I. Brownlie and G. Goodwin-Gill (eds.), *Basic Documents on Human Rights.* 5th edn. Oxford: Oxford University Press, 2006.

2. Id.

3. United Nations. 1948b. *Universal Declaration of Human Rights.* In I. Brownlie and G. Goodwin-Gill (eds.), *Basic Documents on Human Rights.* 5th edn. Oxford: Oxford University Press, 2006; Glendon, M. 2001. *A World Made New: Eleanor Roosevelt and the Universal;* Lauren, P. 1998. *The Evolution of International Human Rights.* Philadelphia: University of Pennsylvania Press; Morsink, J. 1999. *Universal Declaration of Human Rights: Origins, Drafting, and Intent.* Philadelphia: University of Pennsylvania Press.

4. African Union. 1981. *African Charter on Human and Peoples' Rights.* In I. Brownlie and G. Goodwin-Gill (eds.), *Basic Documents on Human Rights.* 5th edn. Oxford: Oxford University Press, 2006.

5. Organization of American States. 1948. *American Declaration of the Rights and Duties of Man.* In I. Brownlie and G. Goodwin-Gill (eds.), *Basic Documents on Human Rights.* 5th edn. Oxford: Oxford University Press, 2006.

6. United Nations. 1966b. *International Covenant on Economic, Social, and Cultural Rights.* In I. Brownlie and G. Goodwin-Gill (eds.), *Basic Documents.*

7. United Nations. 1948a. *Convention on the Prevention and Punishment of the Crime of Genocide.* In I. Brownlie and G. Goodwin-Gill (eds.), *Basic Documents on Human Rights.* 5th edn. Oxford: Oxford University Press, 2006.

8. Vasek, K. 1977. "A 30-Year Struggle: The Sustained Efforts to Give Force of Law to the Universal Declaration of Human Rights. " *Unesco Courier* 10: 29–30; Wellman, Carl. 1999. *The Proliferation of Rights: Moral Progress or Empty Rhetoric?* Boulder, Colo.: Westview Press.

9. Council of Europe. 1950. *European Convention for the Protection of Human Rights and Fundamental Freedoms.* In I. Brownlie and G. Goodwin-Gill (eds.), *Basic Documents on Human Rights.* 5th edn. Oxford: Oxford University Press, 2006.

10. United Nations. 1966a. *International Covenant on Civil and Political Rights.* In I. Brownlie and G. Goodwin-Gill (eds.), *Basic Documents on Human Rights.* 5th edn. Oxford: Oxford University Press, 2006.

11. Supra, note 6.

12. Supra, note 5.

13. Locke, J. 1986. *The Second Treatise on Civil Government.* New York: Prometheus Books. Originally published 1689.

14. Talbott, W. 2005. *Which Rights Should be Universal?* Oxford: Oxford University Press.

15. American Anthropological Association. 1947. "Statement on Human Rights." *American Anthropologist.* 49: 539–543.

16. Id.

17. Preis, A. 1996. "Human Rights as Cultural Practice: An Anthropological Critique." *Human Rights Quarterly* 18: 286–315.

18. Id.

19. Supra, note 14.

20. Donnelly, J. 2003. *Universal Human Rights in Theory and Practice.* 2nd edn. Ithaca, NY and London: Cornell University Press.

21. Supra, note 14.

22. Goodman, R., and Jinks, D. 2004. "How to Influence States: Socialization and International Human Rights Law." *Duke Law Journal* 54: 621.

23. Council of Europe. 1950. *European Convention for the Protection of Human Rights and Fundamental Freedoms.* In I. Brownlie and G. Goodwin-Gill (eds.), *Basic Documents on Human Rights.* 5th edn. Oxford: Oxford University Press, 2006.

24. Hartman, J. 1981. " Derogation from Human Rights Treaties in Public Emergencies." *Harvard International Law Journal* 22: 1–52.

25. Buchanan, A. 1989. "Assessing the Communitarian Critique of Liberalism." *Ethics* 99: 852–82.

26. Rawls, J. 1993. *Political Liberalism.* New York: Columbia University Press.

27. Zogby, J. J. 2002. *What Arabs Think: Values, Beliefs, and Concerns.* Utica, NY: Zogby International; Pew Research Center. 2003. *Global Attitudes Project.*

27 Should the Ticking Bomb Terrorist Be Tortured?

A Case Study in How a Democracy Should Make Tragic Choices

ALAN M. DERSHOWITZ

Authorizing torture is a bad and dangerous idea that can easily be made to sound plausible. There is a subtle fallacy embedded in the traditional "ticking bomb" argument for torture to save lives."

—Philip Heymann, former Deputy Attorney General

THE CASE FOR TORTURING THE TICKING BOMB TERRORIST

The arguments in favor of using torture as a last resort to prevent a ticking bomb from exploding and killing many people are both simple and simpleminded. Bentham constructed a compelling hypothetical case to support his utilitarian argument against an absolute prohibition on torture:

> Suppose an occasion were to arise, in which a suspicion is entertained, as strong as that which would be received as a sufficient ground for arrest and commitment as for felony—a suspicion that at this very time a considerable number of individuals are actually suffering, by illegal violence inflictions equal in intensity to those which if inflicted by the hand of justice, would universally be spoken of under the name of torture. For the purpose of rescuing from torture these hundred innocents, should any scruple be made of applying equal or superior torture, to extract the requisite information from the mouth of one criminal, who having it in his power to make known the place where at this time the enormity was practising or about to be practised, should refuse to do so? To say nothing of wisdom, could any pretence be made so much as to the praise of blind and vulgar humanity, by the man who to save one criminal, should determine to abandon 100 innocent persons to the same fate?[1]

If the torture of one guilty person would be justified to prevent the torture of a hundred innocent persons, it would seem to follow—certainly to

Reprinted with permission of the publisher from Alan M. Dershowitz, *Why Terrorism Works: Understanding the Threat, Responding to the Challenge* (New Haven, CT: Yale University Press, 2002), pp. 142–62, 250–54. Endnotes have been renumbered.

Bentham—that it would also be justified to prevent the murder of thousands of innocent civilians in the ticking bomb case. Consider two hypothetical situations that are not, unfortunately, beyond the realm of possibility. In fact, they are both extrapolations on actual situations we have faced.

Several weeks before September 11, 2001, the Unites States Immigration and Naturalization Service detained Zacarias Moussaoui after flight instructors reported suspicious statements he had made while taking flying lessons and paying for them with large amounts of cash.[2] The government decided not to seek a warrant to search his computer. Now imagine that they had, and that they discovered he was part of a plan to destroy large occupied buildings, but without any further details. They interrogated him, gave him immunity from prosecution, and offered him large cash rewards and a new identity. He refused to talk. They then threatened him, tried to trick him, and employed every lawful technique available. He still refused. They even injected him with sodium pentothal and other truth serums, but to no avail. The attack now appeared to be imminent, but the FBI still had no idea what the target was or what means would be used to attack it. We could not simply evacuate all buildings indefinitely. An FBI agent proposes the use of nonlethal torture—say, a sterilized needle inserted under the fingernails to produce unbearable pain without any threat to health or life, or the method used in the film *Marathon Man,* a dental drill through an unanesthetized tooth.

The simple cost-benefit analysis for employing such nonlethal torture seems overwhelming: it is surely better to inflict nonlethal pain on one guilty terrorist who is illegally withholding information needed to prevent an act of terrorism than to permit a large number of innocent victims to die.[3] Pain is a lesser and more remediable harm than death; and the lives of a thousand innocent people should be valued more than the bodily integrity of one guilty person. If the variation on the Moussaoui case is not sufficiently compelling to make this point, we can always raise the stakes. Several weeks after September 11, our government received reports that a ten-kiloton nuclear weapon may have been stolen from Russia and

was on its way to New York City, where it would be detonated and kill hundreds of thousands of people. The reliability of the source, code named Dragonfire, was uncertain, but assume for purposes of this hypothetical extension of the actual case that the source was a captured terrorist—like the one tortured by the Philippine authorities—who knew precisely how and where the weapon was being bought into New York and was to be detonated. Again, everything short of torture is tried, but to no avail. It is not absolutely certain torture will work, but it is our last, best hope for preventing a cataclysmic nuclear devastation in a city too large to evacuate in time. Should nonlethal torture be tried? Bentham would certainly have said yes.

The strongest argument against any resort to torture, even in the ticking bomb case, also derives from Bentham's utilitarian calculus. Experience has shown that if torture, which has been deemed illegitimate by the civilized world for more than a century, were now to be legitimated—even for limited use in one extraordinary type of situation—such legitimation would constitute an important symbolic setback in the worldwide campaign against human rights abuses. Inevitably, the legitimation of torture by the world's leading democracy would provide a welcome justification for its more widespread use in other parts of the world. Two Bentham scholars, W. L. Twining and P.E. Twining, have argued that torture is unacceptable even if it is restricted to an extremely limited category of cases:

> There is at least one good practical reason for drawing a distinction between justifying an isolated act of torture in an extreme emergency of the kind postulated above and justifying the institutionalisation of torture as a regular practice. The circumstances are so extreme in which most of us would be prepared to justify resort to torture, if at all, the conditions we would impose would be so stringent, the practical problems of devising and enforcing adequate safeguards so difficult and the risks of abuse so great that it would be unwise and dangerous to entrust any government, however enlightened, with such a power. Even an out-and-out utilitarian can support an absolute prohibition against institutionalised torture on the

ground that no government in the world can be trusted not to abuse the power and to satisfy in practice the conditions he would impose.[4]

Bentham's own justification was based on *case* or *act* utilitarianism—a demonstration that in a *particular case,* the benefits that would flow from the limited use of torture would outweigh its costs. The argument against any use of torture would derive from *rule* utilitarianism—which considers the implications of establishing a precedent that would inevitably be extended beyond its limited case utilitarian justification to other possible evils of lesser magnitude. Even terrorism itself could be justified by a case utilitarian approach. Surely one could come up with a singular situation in which the targeting of a small number of civilians could be thought necessary to save thousands of other civilians—blowing up a German kindergarten by the relatives of inmates in a Nazi death camp, for example, and threatening to repeat the targeting of German children unless the death camps were shut down.

The reason this kind of single-case utilitarian justification is simpleminded is that it has no inherent limiting principle. If nonlethal torture of one person is justified to prevent the killing of many important people, then what if it were necessary to use lethal torture—or at least torture that posed a substantial risk of death? What if it were necessary to torture the suspect's mother or children to get him to divulge the information? What if it took threatening to kill his family, his friends, his entire village?[5] Under a simpleminded quantitative case utilitarianism, anything goes as long as the number of people tortured or killed does not exceed the number that would be saved. This is morality by numbers, unless there are other constraints on what we can properly do. These other constraints can come from rule utilitarianisms or other principles of morality, such as the prohibition against deliberately punishing the innocent. Unless we are prepared to impose some limits on the use of torture or other barbaric tactics that might be of some use in preventing terrorism, we risk hurtling down a slippery slope into the abyss of amorality and ultimately tyranny. Dostoevsky captured the complexity of this dilemma in *The Brothers Karamazov* when he had Ivan pose the following question to Alyosha:

> Imagine that you are creating a fabric of human destiny with the object of making men happy in the end, giving them peace at last, but that it was essential and inevitable to torture to death only one tiny creature—that baby beating its breast with its fist, for instance—and to found that edifice on its unavenged tears, would you consent to be the architect on those conditions? Tell me the truth.

A willingness to kill an innocent child suggests a willingness to do anything to achieve a necessary result. Hence the slippery slope.

It does not necessarily follow from this understandable fear of the slippery slope that we can never consider the use of nonlethal infliction of pain, if its use were to be limited by acceptable principles of morality. After all, imprisoning a witness who refuses to testify after being given immunity is designed to be punitive—that is painful. Such imprisonment can, on occasion, produce more pain and greater risk of death than nonlethal torture. Yet we continue to threaten and use the pain of imprisonment to loosen the tongues of reluctant witnesses.[6]

It is commonplace for police and prosecutors to threaten recalcitrant suspects with prison rape. As one prosecutor put it: "You're going to be the boyfriend of a very bad man." The slippery slope is an argument of caution, not a debate stopper, since virtually every compromise with an absolutist approach to rights carries the risk of slipping further. An appropriate response to the slippery slope is to build in a principled break. For example, if nonlethal torture were legally limited to convicted terrorists who had knowledge of future massive terrorist acts, were given immunity, and still refused to provide the information, there might still be objections to the use of torture, but they would have to go beyond the slippery slope argument.[7]

The case utilitarian argument for torturing a ticking bomb terrorist is bolstered by an argument from analogy—an a fortiori argument. What moral principle could justify the death penalty for past individual murders and at the same time condemn nonlethal torture to prevent future mass murders? Bentham posed this rhetorical question as support for his argument. The death penalty is, of course, reserved for convicted murderers. But again, what if torture was limited to convicted terrorists who refused to divulge information about future terrorism? Consider as well the analogy to the use of deadly force against suspects fleeing from arrest for dangerous felonies of which they have not yet been convicted. Or military retaliations that produce the predictable and inevitable collateral killing of some innocent civilians. The case against torture, if made by a Quaker who opposes the death penalty, war, self-defense, and the use of lethal force against fleeing felons, is understandable. But for anyone who justifies killing on the basis of a cost-benefit analysis, the case against the use of nonlethal torture to save multiple lives is more difficult to make. In the end, absolute opposition to torture—even nonlethal torture in the ticking bomb case—may rest more on historical and aesthetic considerations than on moral or logical ones.

In debating the issue of torture, the first question I am often asked is, "Do you want to take us back to the Middle Ages?" The association between any form of torture and gruesome death is powerful in the minds of most people knowledgeable of the history of its abuses. This understandable association makes it difficult for many people to think about nonlethal torture as a technique for *saving* lives.

The second question I am asked is, "What kind of torture do you have in mind?" When I respond by describing the sterilized needle being shoved under the fingernails, the reaction is visceral and often visible—a shudder coupled with a facial gesture of disgust. Discussions of the death penalty on the other hand can be conducted without these kinds of reactions, especially now that we literally put the condemned prisoner "to sleep" by laying him out on a gurney and injecting a lethal substance into his body. There is no breaking of the neck, burning of the brain, bursting of internal organs, or gasping for breath that used to accompany hanging, electrocution, shooting, and gassing. The executioner has been replaced by a paramedical technician, as the aesthetics of death have become more acceptable. All this tends to cover up the reality that death is forever while nonlethal pain is temporary. In our modern age death is underrated, while pain is overrated.

I observed a similar phenomenon several years ago during the debate over corporal punishment that was generated by the decision of a court in Singapore to sentence a young American to medically supervised lashing with a cane. Americans who support the death penalty and who express little concern about inner-city prison conditions were outraged by the specter of a few welts on the buttocks of an American. It was an utterly irrational display of hypocrisy and double standards. Given a choice between a medically administrated whipping and one month in a typical state lockup or prison, any rational and knowledgeable person would choose the lash. No one dies of welts or pain, but many inmates are raped, beaten, knifed, and otherwise mutilated and tortured in American prisons. The difference is that we don't see—and we don't want to see—what goes on behind their high walls. Nor do we want to think about it. Raising the issue of torture makes Americans think about a brutalizing and unaesthetic phenomenon that has been out of our consciousness for many years.[8]

THE THREE—OR FOUR—WAYS

The debate over the use of torture goes back many years, with Bentham supporting it in a limited category of cases, Kant opposing it as part of his categorical imperative against improperly using people as means for achieving noble ends, and Voltaire's views on the matter being "hopelessly confused."[9] The modern resort to terrorism has renewed the debate over how a rights-based society should respond to the prospect of using nonlethal torture in the ticking bomb situation. In the late 1980s the Israeli government appointed a commission headed by a retired Supreme Court justice to look into precisely that situation. The commission concluded that there are "three ways for solving this grave dilemma between the vital need to preserve the very existence of the state and its citizens, and maintain its character as a law-abiding state." The first is to allow the security services to continue to fight terrorism in "a twilight zone which is outside the realm of law." The second is "the way of the hypocrites: they declare that they abide by the rule of law, but turn a blind eye to what goes on beneath the surface." And the third, "the truthful road of the rule of law," is that the "law itself must insure a proper framework for the activity" of the security services in seeking to prevent terrorist acts.[10]

There is of course a fourth road: namely to forgo any use of torture and simply allow the preventable terrorist act to occur.[11] After the Supreme Court of Israel outlawed the use of physical pressure, the Israeli security services claimed that, as a result of the Supreme Court's decision, at least one preventable act of terrorism had been allowed to take place, one that killed several people when a bus was bombed.[12] Whether this claim is true, false, or somewhere in between is difficult to assess.[13] But it is clear that if the preventable act of terrorism was of the magnitude of the attacks of September 11, there would be a great outcry in any democracy that had deliberately refused to take available preventive action, even if it required the use of torture. During numerous public appearances since September 11, 2001, I have asked audiences for a show of hands as to how many would support the use of nonlethal torture in a ticking bomb case. Virtually every hand is raised. The few that remain down go up when I ask how many believe that torture would actually be used in such a case.

Law enforcement personnel give similar responses. This can be seen in reports of physical abuse directed against some suspects that have been detained following September 11, reports that have been taken quite seriously by at least one federal judge.[14] It is confirmed by the willingness of U.S. law enforcement officials to facilitate the torture of terrorist suspects by repressive regimes allied with our intelligence agencies. As one former CIA operative with thirty years of experience reported: "A lot of people are saying we need someone at the agency who can pull fingernails out. Others are saying, 'Let others use interrogation methods that we don't use.' The only question then is, do you want to have CIA people in the room?" The real issue, therefore, is not whether some torture would or would not be used in the ticking bomb case—it would. The question is whether it would be done openly, pursuant to a

previously established legal procedure, or whether it would be done secretly, in violation of existing law.[15]

Several important values are pitted against each other in this conflict. The first is the safety and security of a nation's citizens. Under the ticking bomb scenario this value may require the use of torture, if that is the only way to prevent the bomb from exploding and killing large numbers of civilians. The second value is the preservation of civil liberties and human rights. This value requires that we not accept torture as a legitimate part of our legal system. In my debates with two prominent civil libertarians, Floyd Abrams and Harvey Silverglate, both have acknowledged that they would want nonlethal torture to be used if it could prevent thousands of deaths, but they did not want torture to be officially recognized by our legal system. As Abrams put it: "In a democracy sometimes it is necessary to do things off the books and below the radar screen." Former presidential candidate Alan Keyes took the position that although torture might be *necessary* in a given situation it could never be *right*. He suggested that a president *should* authorize the torturing of a ticking bomb terrorist, but that this act should not be legitimated by the courts or incorporated into our legal system. He argued that wrongful and indeed unlawful acts might sometimes be necessary to preserve the nation, but that no aura of legitimacy should be placed on these actions by judicial imprimatur.

This understandable approach is in conflict with the third important value: namely, open accountability and visibility in a democracy. "Off-the-book actions below the radar screen" are antithetical to the theory and practice of democracy. Citizens cannot approve or disapprove of governmental actions of which they are unaware. We have learned the lesson of history that off-the-book actions can produce terrible consequences. Richard Nixon's creation of a group of "plumbers" led to Watergate, and Ronald Reagan's authorization of an off-the-books foreign policy in Central America led to the Iran-Contra scandal. And these are only the ones we know about!

Perhaps the most extreme example of such a hypocritical approach to torture comes—not surprisingly—from the French experience in Algeria. The French army used torture extensively in seeking to prevent terrorism during a brutal colonial war from 1955 to 1957. An officer who supervised this torture, General Paul Aussaresses, wrote a book recounting what he had done and seen, including the torture of dozens of Algerians. "The best way to make a terrorist talk when he refused to say what he knew was to torture him," he boasted. Although the book was published decades after the war was over, the general was prosecuted—but not for what he had done to the Algerians. Instead, he was prosecuted for *revealing* what he had done, and seeking to justify it.[16]

In a democracy governed by the rule of law, we should never want our soldiers or our president to take any action that we deem wrong or illegal. A good test of whether an action should or should not be done is whether we are prepared to have it disclosed—perhaps not immediately, but certainly after some time has passed. No legal system operating under the rule of law should ever tolerate an "off-the-books" approach to necessity. Even the defense of necessity must be justified lawfully. The road to tyranny has always been paved with claims of necessity made by those responsible for the security of a nation. Our system of checks and balances requires that all presidential actions, like all legislative or military actions, be consistent with governing law. If it is necessary to torture in the ticking bomb case, then our governing laws must accommodate this practice. If we refuse to change our law to accommodate any particular action, then our government should not take that action.[17]

Only in a democracy committed to civil liberties would a triangular conflict of this kind exist. Totalitarian and authoritarian regimes experience no such conflict, because they subscribe to neither the civil libertarian nor the democratic values that come in conflict with the value of security. The hard question is: which value is to be preferred when an inevitable clash occurs? One or more of these values must inevitably be compromised in making the tragic choice presented by the ticking bomb case. If we do not torture, we compromise the security and safety of our citizens. If we tolerate torture, but keep it off the books and below the radar screen, we compromise principles of democratic accountability. If we create a legal structure for limiting and controlling torture, we compromise our principled opposition to torture

in all circumstances and create a potentially dangerous and expandable situation.

In 1678, the French writer Francois de La Rochefoucauld said that "hypocrisy is the homage that vice renders to virtue." In this case we have two vices: terrorism and torture. We also have two virtues: civil liberties and democratic accountability. Most civil libertarians I know prefer hypocrisy, precisely because it appears to avoid the conflict between security and civil liberties, but by choosing the way of the hypocrite these civil libertarians compromise the value of democratic accountability. Such is the nature of tragic choices in a complex world. As Bentham put it more than two centuries ago: "Government throughout is but a choice of evils." In a democracy, such choices must be made, whenever possible, with openness and democratic accountability, and subject to the rule of law.[18]

Consider another terrible choice of evils that could easily have been presented on September 11, 2001—and may well be presented in the future: a hijacked passenger jet is on a collision course with a densely occupied office building; the only way to prevent the destruction of the building and the killing of its occupants is to shoot down the jet, thereby killing its innocent passengers. This choice now seems easy, because the passengers are certain to die anyway and their somewhat earlier deaths will save numerous lives. The passenger jet must be shot down. But what if it were only *probable*, not certain, that the jet would crash into the building? Say, for example, we know from cell phone transmissions that passengers are struggling to regain control of the hijacked jet, but it is unlikely they will succeed in time. Or say we have no communication with the jet and all we know is that it is off course and heading toward Washington, D.C., or some other densely populated city. Under these more questionable circumstances, the question becomes *who* should make this life and death choice between evils—a decision that may turn out tragically wrong?

No reasonable person would allocate this decision to a fighter jet pilot who happened to be in the area or to a local airbase commander—unless of course there was no time for the matter to be passed up the chain of command to the president or the secretary of defense. A decision of this kind should be made at the highest level possible, with visibility and accountability.

Why is this not also true of the decision to torture a ticking bomb terrorist? Why should that choice of evils be relegated to a local policeman, FBI agent, or CIA operative, rather than to a judge, the attorney general, or the president?

There are, of course, important differences between the decision to shoot down the plane and the decision to torture the ticking bomb terrorist. Having to shoot down an airplane, though tragic, is not likely to be a recurring issue. There is no slope down which to slip.[19] Moreover, the jet to be shot down is filled with our fellow citizens—people with whom we can identify. The suspected terrorist we may choose to torture is a "they"—an enemy with whom we do not identify but with whose potential victims we do identify. The risk of making the wrong decision, or of overdoing the torture, is far greater, since we do not care as much what happens to "them" as to "us."[20] Finally, there is something different about torture—even nonlethal torture—that sets it apart from a quick death. In addition to the horrible history associated with torture, there is also the aesthetic of torture. The very idea of deliberately subjecting a captive human being to excruciating pain violates our sense of what is acceptable. On a purely rational basis, it is far worse to shoot a fleeing felon in the back and kill him, yet every civilized society authorizes shooting such a suspect who poses dangers of committing violent crimes against the police or others. In the United States we execute convicted murderers, despite compelling evidence of the unfairness and ineffectiveness of capital punishment. Yet many of us recoil at the prospect of shoving a sterilized needle under the finger of a suspect who is refusing to divulge information that might prevent multiple deaths. Despite the irrationality of these distinctions, they are understandable, especially in light of the sordid history of torture.

We associate torture with the Inquisition, the Gestapo, the Stalinist purges, and the Argentine colonels responsible for the "dirty war." We recall it as a prelude to death, an integral part of a regime of gratuitous pain leading to a painful demise. We find it difficult to imagine a benign use of nonlethal torture to save lives.

Yet there was a time in the history of Anglo-Saxon law when torture was used to save life, rather than to take it, and when the limited administration of nonlethal torture was supervised by judges, including some who are well remembered in history.[21] This fascinating story has been recounted by Professor John Langbein of Yale Law School, and it is worth summarizing here because it helps inform the debate over whether, if torture would in fact be used in a ticking bomb case, it would be worse to make it part of the legal system, or worse to have it done off the books and below the radar screen.

In his book on legalized torture during the sixteenth and seventeenth centuries, *Torture and the Law of Proof,* Langbein demonstrates the trade-off between torture and other important values. Torture was employed for several purposes. First, it was used to secure the evidence necessary to obtain a guilty verdict under the rigorous criteria for conviction required at the time—either the testimony of two eyewitnesses or the confession of the accused himself. Circumstantial evidence, no matter how compelling, would not do. As Langbein concludes, "no society will long tolerate a legal system in which there is no prospect in convicting unrepentant persons who commit clandestine crimes. Something had to be done to extend the system to those cases. The two-eyewitness rule was hard to compromise or evade, but the confession invited 'subterfuge.'" The subterfuge that was adopted permitted the use of torture to obtain confessions from suspects against whom there was compelling circumstantial evidence of guilt. The circumstantial evidence, alone, could not be used to convict, but it was used to obtain a torture warrant. That torture warrant was in turn used to obtain a confession, which then had to be independently corroborated—at least in most cases (witchcraft and other such cases were exempted from the requirement of corroboration).[22]

Torture was also used against persons already convicted of capital crimes, such as high treason, who were thought to have information necessary to prevent attacks on the state.

Langbein studied 81 torture warrants, issued between 1540 and 1640, and found that in many of them, especially in "the higher cases of treasons, torture is used for discovery, and not for evidence." Torture was "used to protect the state" and "mostly that meant preventive torture to identify and forestall plots and plotters." It was only when the legal system loosened its requirement of proof (or introduced the "black box" of the jury system) and when perceived threats against the state diminished that torture was no longer deemed necessary to convict guilty defendants against whom there had previously been insufficient evidence, or to secure preventive information.[23]

The ancient Jewish system of jurisprudence came up with yet another solution to the conundrum of convicting the guilty and preventing harms to the community in the face of difficult evidentiary barriers. Jewish law required two witnesses and a specific advance warning before a guilty person could be convicted. Because confessions were disfavored, torture was not an available option. Instead, the defendant who had been seen killing by one reliable witness, or whose guilt was obvious from the circumstantial evidence, was formally acquitted, but he was then taken to a secure location and fed a concoction of barley and water until his stomach burst and he died. Moreover, Jewish law permitted more flexible forms of self-help against those who were believed to endanger the community.[24]

Every society has insisted on the incapacitation of dangerous criminals regardless of strictures in the formal legal rules. Some use torture, others use informal sanctions, while yet others create the black box of a jury, which need not explain its commonsense verdicts. Similarly, every society insists that, if there are steps that can be taken to prevent effective acts of terrorism, these steps should be taken, even if they require some compromise with other important principles.

In deciding whether the ticking bomb terrorist should be tortured, one important question is whether there would be less torture if it were done as part of the legal system, as it was in sixteenth- and seventeenth-century England, or off the books, as it is in many countries today. The Langbein study does not definitively answer this question, but it does provide some suggestive insights. The English system of torture was more visible and thus more subject to public accountability, and it is likely that torture was employed less frequently in England than in France. "During these years when it appears that torture might have become routinized in English criminal procedure, the Privy Council kept the torture power under careful control and never allowed it to fall into the hands of the regular law enforcement officers," as it had in France. In England "no law enforcement officer ... acquired the power to use torture without special warrant." Moreover, when torture warrants were abolished, "the English experiment with torture left no traces." Because it was under centralized control, it was easier to abolish than it was in France, where it persisted for many years.[25]

It is always difficult to extrapolate from history, but it seems logical that a formal, visible, accountable, and centralized system is somewhat easier to control than an ad hoc, off-the-books, and under-the-radar-screen nonsystem. I believe, though I certainly cannot prove, that a formal requirement of a judicial warrant as a prerequisite to nonlethal torture would decrease the amount of physical violence directed against suspects. At the most obvious level, a double check is always more protective than a single check. In every instance in which a warrant is requested, a field officer has already decided that torture is justified and, in the absence of a warrant requirement, would simply proceed with the torture. Requiring that decision to be approved by a judicial officer will result in fewer instances of torture even if the judge rarely turns down a request. Moreover, I believe that most judges would require compelling evidence before they would authorize so extraordinary a departure from our constitutional norms, and law enforcement officials would be reluctant to seek a warrant unless they had compelling evidence that the suspect had information needed to prevent an imminent terrorist attack. A record would be kept of every warrant granted, and although it is certainly possible that some individual agents might torture without a warrant, they would have no excuse, since a warrant procedure would be available. They could not claim "necessity," because the decision as to whether the torture is indeed necessary has been taken out of their hands and placed in the hands of a judge. In addition, even if torture were deemed totally illegal without any exception, it would still occur, though the public would be less aware of its existence.

I also believe that the rights of the suspect would be better protected with a warrant requirement. He would be granted immunity, told that he was now compelled to testify, threatened with imprisonment if he refused to do so, and given the option of providing the requested information. Only if he refused to do what he was legally compelled to do—provide necessary information, which could not incriminate him because of the immunity—would he be threatened with torture. Knowing that such a threat was authorized by the law, he might well provide the information.[26] If he still refused to, he would be subjected to judicially monitored physical measures designed to cause excruciating pain without leaving any lasting damage.

Let me cite two examples to demonstrate why I think there would be less torture with a warrant requirement than without one. Recall the case of the alleged national security wiretap placed on the phones of Martin Luther King by the Kennedy administration in the early 1960s. This was in the days when the attorney general could authorize a national security wiretap without a warrant. Today no judge would issue a warrant in a case as flimsy as that one. When Zacarias Moussaoui was detained after raising suspicions while trying to learn how to fly an airplane, the government did not even seek a national security wiretap because its lawyers believed that a judge would not have granted one. If Moussaoui's computer could have been searched without a warrant, it almost certainly would have been.

It should be recalled that in the context of searches, our Supreme Court opted for a judicial check on the discretion of the police, by requiring a search warrant in most cases. The Court has explained the reason for the warrant requirement as follows: "The informed and deliberate determinations of magistrates ... are to be preferred over the

hurried action of officers."[27] Justice Robert Jackson elaborated:

> The point of the Fourth Amendment, which often is not grasped by zealous officers, is not that it denies law enforcement the support of the usual inferences which reasonable men draw from evidence. Its protection consists in requiring that those inferences be drawn by a neutral and detached magistrate instead of being judged by the officer engaged in the often competitive enterprise of ferreting out crime. Any assumption that evidence sufficient to support a magistrate's disinterested determination to issue a search warrant will justify the officers in making a search without a warrant would reduce the Amendment to nullity and leave the people's homes secure only in the discretion of police officers.[28]

Although torture is very different from a search, the policies underlying the warrant requirement are relevant to the question whether there is likely to be more torture or less if the decision is left entirely to field officers, or if a judicial officer has to approve a request for a torture warrant. As Abraham Maslow once observed, to a man with a hammer, everything looks like a nail. If the man with the hammer must get judicial approval before he can use it, he will probably use it less often and more carefully.

There are other, somewhat more subtle, considerations that should be factored into any decision regarding torture. There are some who see silence as a virtue when it comes to the choice among such horrible evils as torture and terrorism. It is far better, they argue, not to discuss or write about issues of this sort, lest they become legitimated. And legitimation is an appropriate concern. Justice Jackson, in his opinion in one of the cases concerning the detention of Japanese-Americans during World War II, made the following relevant observation:

> Much is said of the danger to liberty from the Army program for deporting and detaining these citizens of Japanese extraction. But a judicial construction of the due process clause that will sustain this order is a far more subtle blow to liberty than the promulgation of the order itself. A military order, however unconstitutional, is not apt to last longer than the military emergency. Even during

that period a succeeding commander may revoke it all. But once a judicial opinion rationalizes such an order to show that it conforms to the Constitution, or rather rationalizes the Constitution to show that the Constitution sanctions such an order, the Court for all time has validated the principle of racial discrimination in criminal procedure and of transplanting American citizens. The principle then lies about like a loaded weapon ready for the hand of any authority that can bring forward a plausible claim of an urgent need. Every repetition imbeds that principle more deeply in our law and thinking and expands it to new purposes. All who observe the work of courts are familiar with what Judge Cardozo described as "the tendency of a principle to expand itself to the limit of its logic." A military commander may overstep the bounds of constitutionality, and it is an incident. But if we review and approve, that passing incident becomes the doctrine of the Constitution. There it has a generative power of its own, and all that it creates will be in its own image.[29]

A similar argument can be made regarding torture: if an agent tortures, that is "an incident," but if the courts authorize it, it becomes a precedent. There is, however, an important difference between the detention of Japanese-American citizens and torture. The detentions were done openly and with presidential accountability; torture would be done secretly, with official deniability. Tolerating an off-the-book system of secret torture can also establish a dangerous precedent.

A variation on this "legitimation" argument would postpone consideration of the choice between authorizing torture and forgoing a possible tactic necessary to prevent an imminent act of terrorism until after the choice—presumably the choice to torture—has been made. In that way, the discussion would not, in itself, encourage the use of torture. If it were employed, then we could decide whether it was justified, excusable, condemnable, or something in between. The problem with that argument is that no FBI agent who tortured a suspect into disclosing information that prevented an act of mass terrorism would be prosecuted—as the policemen who tortured the kidnapper into disclosing the whereabouts of his victim were not prosecuted. In the absence of a prosecution, there would be no occasion to judge the appropriateness of the torture.

I disagree with these more passive approaches and believe that in a democracy it is always preferable to decide controversial issues in advance, rather than in the heat of battle. I would apply this rule to other tragic choices as well, including the possible use of a nuclear first strike, or retaliatory strikes—so long as the discussion was sufficiently general to avoid giving our potential enemies a strategic advantage by their knowledge of our policy.

Even if government officials decline to discuss such issues, academics have a duty to raise them and submit them to the marketplace of ideas. There may be danger in open discussion, but there is far greater danger in actions based on secret discussion, or no discussion at all.

Whatever option our nation eventually adopts—no torture even to prevent massive terrorism, no torture except with a warrant authorizing nonlethal torture, or no "officially" approved torture but its selective use beneath the radar screen—the choice is ours to make in a democracy. We do have a choice, and we should make it—before local FBI agents make it for us on the basis of a false assumption that we do not really "have a choice." ...

NOTES

1. Quoted in Twining, W.L. and Twining, P.E. "Bentham on Torture." *Northern Ireland Legal Quarterly,* Autumn 1973: 347. Bentham's hypothetical question does not distinguish between torture inflicted by private persons and by governments.

2. Johnston, David and Shenon, Philip. "F.B.I. Curbed Scrutiny of Man Now a Suspect in the Attacks." *New York Times* 6 Oct. 2001.

3. It is illegal to withhold relevant information from a grand jury after receiving immunity. *See Kastigar v. U.S.* 406 U.S. 441 (1972).

4. Twining and Twining, "Bentham on Torture," pp. 348–49. The argument for the limited use of torture in the ticking bomb case falls into a category of argument known as "argument from the extreme case," which is a useful heuristic to counter arguments for absolute principles.

5. To demonstrate that this is not just in the realm of the hypothetical:

   The former CIA officer said he also suggested the agency begin targeting close relatives of known terrorists and use them to obtain intelligence. "You get their mothers and their brothers and their sisters under your complete control, and then you make that known to the target," he said. "You imply or you directly threaten [that] his family is going to pay the price if he makes the wrong decision."

Drogin, Bob and Miller, Greg. "Spy Agencies Facing Questions of Tactics." *Los Angeles Times* 28 Oct. 2001.

6. One of my clients, who refused to testify against the mafia, was threatened by the government that if he persisted in his refusal the government would "leak" false information that he was cooperating, thus exposing him to mob retaliation.

7. *USA v. Cobb* 1 S.C.R. 587 (2001).

8. On conditions in American prisons, see Dershowitz, Alan M. "Supreme Court Acknowledges Country's Other Rape Epidemic." *Boston Herald* 12 June 1994. The United States may already be guilty of violating at least the spirit of the prohibition against torture. In a recent case the Canadian Supreme Court refused to extradite an accused person to the United States because of threats made by a judge and a prosecutor regarding the treatment of those who did not voluntarily surrender themselves to the jurisdiction of the U.S. court. First, as he was sentencing a coconspirator in the scheme, the American judge assigned to their trial commented that those fugitives who did not cooperate would get the "absolute maximum jail sentence." Then, the prosecuting attorney hinted during a television interview that uncooperative fugitives would be subject to homosexual rape in prison:

Zubrod [prosecutor]: I have told some of these individuals, "Look, you can come down and you can put this behind you by serving your time in prison and making restitution to the victims, or you can wind up serving a great deal longer sentence under much more stringent conditions," and describe those conditions to them. MacIntyre [reporter]: How would you describe those conditions?

Zubrod: *You're going to be the boyfriend of a very bad man if you wait out your extradition.* MacIntyre: And does that have much of an impact on these people?

Zubrod: Well, out of the 89 people we've indicted so far, approximately 55 of them have said, "We give up."

After reading the transcripts, the Supreme Court of Canada held:

The pressures were not only inappropriate but also, in the case of the statements made by the prosecutor on the eve of the opening of the judicial hearing in Canada,

unequivocally amounted to an abuse of the process of the court. We do not condone the threat of sexual violence as a means for one party before the court to persuade any opponent to abandon his or her right to a hearing. Nor should we expect litigants to overcome well-founded fears of violent reprisals in order to be participants in a judicial process. Aside from such intimidation itself, it is plain that a committal order requiring a fugitive to return to face such an ominous climate—which was created by those who would play a large, if not decisive role in determining the fugitive's ultimate fate—would not be consistent with the principles of fundamental justice.

USA v. Cobb 1 S.C.R. 587 (2001). (Thanks to Craig Jones, a student, for bringing this matter to my attention.)

9. Langbein, John. *Torture and the Law of Proof.* Chicago: University of Chicago Press, 1977. 68. Voltaire generally opposed torture but favored it in some cases.

10. A special edition of the *Israel Law Review* in 1989 presented a written symposium on the report on the Landau Commission, which investigated interrogation practices of Israel's General Security Services from 1987 to 1989.

11. A fifth approach would be simply to never discuss the issue of torture—or to postpone any such discussion until after we actually experience a ticking bomb case—but I have always believed that it is preferable to consider and discuss tragic choices before we confront them, so that the issue can be debated without recriminatory emotions and after-the-fact finger pointing.

12. See Dershowitz, Alan M. *Shouting Fire: Civil Liberties in a Turbulent Age.* Boston: Little, Brown, 2002. 476–77:

The Supreme Court of Israel left the security services a tiny window of opportunity in extreme cases. Citing the traditional common-law defense of necessity, the Supreme Court left open the possibility that a member of the security service who honestly believed that rough interrogation was the only means available to save lives in imminent danger could raise this defense. This leaves each individual member of the security services in the position of having to guess how a court would ultimately resolve his case. That is extremely unfair to such investigators. It would have been far better had the court required any investigator who believed that torture was necessary in order to save lives to apply to a judge. The judge would then be in a position either to authorize or refuse to authorize a "torture warrant." Such a procedure would require judges to dirty their hands by authorizing torture warrants or bear the responsibility for failing to do so. Individual interrogators should not have to place their liberty at risk by guessing how a court might ultimately decide a close case. They should be able to get an advance ruling based on the evidence available at the time.

Perhaps the legislature will create a procedure for advance judicial scrutiny. This would be akin to the warrant requirement in the Fourth Amendment to the United States Constitution. It is a traditional role for judges to play, since it is the job of the judiciary to balance the needs for security against the imperatives of liberty. Interrogators from the security service are not trained to strike such a delicate balance. Their mission is single-minded: to prevent terrorism. Similarly, the mission of civil liberties lawyers who oppose torture is single-minded: to vindicate the individual rights of suspected terrorists. It is the role of the court to strike the appropriate balance. The Supreme Court of Israel took a giant step in the direction of striking that balance. But it—or the legislature—should take the further step of requiring the judiciary to assume responsibility in individual cases. The essence of a democracy is placing responsibility for difficult choices in a visible and neutral institution like the judiciary.

13. Sennott, Charles M. "Israeli High Court Bans Torture in Questioning; 10,000 Palestinians Subjected to Tactics." *Boston Globe* 7 Sept. 1999.

14. Osama Awadallah, a green-card holder living in San Diego, has made various charges of torture, abuse, and denial of access to a lawyer. Shira Scheindlin, a federal district court judge in New York, has confirmed the seriousness and credibility of the charges, saying Awadallah may have been "unlawfully arrested, unlawfully searched, abused by law enforcement officials, denied access to his lawyer and family." Lewis, Anthony. "Taking Our Liberties." *New York Times* 9 March 2002.

15. Drogin, Bob and Miller, Greg. "Spy Agencies Facing Questions of Tactics," *Los Angeles Times* 29 Oct. 2001. Philip Heymann is the only person I have debated thus far who is willing to take the position that no form of torture should ever be permitted—or used—even if thousands of lives could be saved by its use. Heymann, Philip B. "Torture Should Not Be Authorized." *Boston Globe* 16 Feb. 2002. Whether he would act on that principled view if he were the responsible government official who was authorized to make this life and death choice—as distinguished from an academic with the luxury of expressing views without being accountable for their consequences—is a more difficult question. He has told me that he probably would authorize torture in an actual ticking bomb case, but that it would

be wrong and he would expect to be punished for it.

16. Daley, Suzanne. "France Is Seeking a Fine in Trial of Algerian War General." *New York Times* 29 Nov. 2001.

17. The necessity defense is designed to allow interstitial action to be taken in the absence of any governing law and in the absence of time to change the law. It is for the nonrecurring situation that was never anticipated by the law. The use of torture in the ticking bomb case has been debated for decades. It can surely be anticipated. See Dershowitz, *Shouting Fire*, pp. 474–76.

Indeed, there is already one case in our jurisprudence in which this has occurred and the courts have considered it. In the 1984 case of *Leon v. Wainwright*, Jean Leon and an accomplice kidnapped a taxicab driver and held him for ransom. Leon was arrested while trying to collect the ransom but refused to disclose where he was holding the victim. At this point, several police officers threatened him and then twisted his arm behind his back and choked him until he told them the victim's whereabouts. Although the federal appellate court disclaimed any wish to "sanction the use of force and coercion, by police officers" the judges went out of their way to state that this was not the act of "brutal law enforcement agents trying to obtain a confession." "This was instead a group of concerned officers acting in a reasonable manner to obtain information they needed in order to protect another individual from bodily harm or death." Although the court did not find it necessary to invoke the "necessity defense," since no charges were brought against the policemen who tortured the kidnapper, it described the torture as having been "motivated by the immediate *necessity* to find the victim and save his life." *Leon v. Wainwright*, 734 F.2d 770, 772–73 (11th Circuit 1984) (emphasis added). If an appellate court would so regard the use of police brutality—torture—in a case involving one kidnap victim, it is not difficult to extrapolate to a situation in which hundreds or thousands of lives might hang in the balance.

18. Quoted in Twining and Twining, "Bentham on Torture," p. 345.

19. For an elaboration of this view, see Dershowitz, *Shouting Fire*, pp. 97–99.

20. The pilot who would have been responsible for shooting down the hijacked plane heading from Pennsylvania to Washington, D.C., on September

11, 2001, has praised the passengers who apparently struggled with the hijackers, causing the plane to crash. These brave passengers spared him the dreadful task of shooting down a plane full of fellow Americans. The stakes are different when it comes to torturing enemy terrorists.

21. Sir Edward Coke was "designated in commissions to examine particular suspects under torture." Langbein, *Torture and the Law of Proof*, p. 73.

22. Ibid., p. 7.

23. Ibid., p. 90, quoting Bacon.

24. *Din Rodef*, or "Law of the Pursuer," refers to the halachic principle that one may kill a person who is threatening someone else's life. This rule was set forth in the twelfth century by Moses Maimonides, a great Talmudic scholar.

25. Langbein, *Torture and the Law of Proof*, pp. 136–37, 139.

26. When it is known that torture is a possible option, terrorists sometimes provide the information and then claim they have been tortured, in order to be able to justify their complicity to their colleagues.

27. *U.S. v. Lefkowitz*, 285 U.S. 452, 464 (1932).

The Fourth Amendment provides that "The right of the people to be secure in their persons, houses, papers, and effects, against unreasonable searches and seizures, shall not be violated, and no Warrants shall issue, but upon probable cause, supported by Oath or affirmation, and particularly describing the place to be searched, and the persons or things to be seized." There are numerous exceptions to the warrant requirement. When there are exigent circumstances, for example, or when a person with authority consents to the search, the police do not need a warrant. Also, police officers can search someone without a warrant if they have lawfully arrested the person. If the police arrest someone inside a car, they can also search the interior of the car and any containers inside the car.

28. *Johnson v. U.S.* 333 U.S. 10, 13–14 (1948).

29. *Korematsu v. U.S.* 323 U.S. 214, 245–46 (1944) (Jackson, J., dissenting).

28   Torture and Positive Law: Jurisprudence for the White House

JEREMY WALDRON

I. LEGAL DEFINITIONS

A. The Texts and the Prohibitions

The law relating to torture comprises a variety of national, regional, and international norms. The basic provision of human rights law is found in the International Covenant on Civil and Political Rights (which I shall refer to hereinafter as the "Covenant"):

> Article 7. No one shall be subjected to torture or to cruel, inhuman or degrading treatment or punishment[1]

Article 4 of the Covenant provides that "[i]n time of public emergency which threatens the life of the nation and the existence of which is officially proclaimed, the States Parties to the present Covenant may take measures derogating from their obligations under the present Covenant to the extent strictly required by the exigencies of the situa-tion," but article 4 also insists that no derogation from article 7 may be made under that provision. The United States ratified the Covenant in 1994, though with the following reservation:

> [T]he United States considers itself bound by Article 7 to the extent that "cruel, inhuman or degrading treatment or punishment" means the cruel and unusual treatment or punishment prohibited by the Fifth, Eighth, and/or Fourteenth Amendments to the Constitution of the United States.[2]

This is part of a pattern of reservations from human rights conventions in which the United States asserts its right to rely on its own

Reprinted with permission of the *Columbia Law Review* 105, no. 6 (October 2005), pp. 1681, 1688–1717. Notes have been renumbered and many citations have been omitted.

constitutional law in any case of overlap with international human rights law where the international standards might prove more demanding.

Besides the Covenant, we also have to consider a more specific document—the international Convention Against Torture (which I shall refer to hereinafter as the "Convention").[3] This instrument requires states to "take effective legislative, administrative, judicial or other measures to prevent acts of torture in any territory under its jurisdiction," and to "ensure that all acts of torture are offences under its criminal law."[4] Again there is a nonderogation provision (implying in effect that states must establish an absolute rather than a conditional or derogable ban on torture), and again, there is a similar reservation relating to cruel, inhuman, and degrading treatment in the U.S. ratification of the Convention. In addition, the Convention goes beyond the Covenant (not to mention other regional human rights instruments such as the European Convention on Human Rights (ECHR)), in that it attempts to give a definition of torture:

> For the purposes of this Convention, the term "torture" means any act by which severe pain or suffering, whether physical or mental, is intentionally inflicted on a person for such purposes as obtaining from him or a third person information or a confession, punishing him for an act he or a third person has committed or is suspected of having committed, or intimidating or coercing him or a third person, or for any reason based on discrimination of any kind, when such pain or suffering is inflicted by or at the instigation of or with the consent or acquiescence of a public official or other person acting in an official capacity. It does not include pain or suffering arising only from, inherent in or incidental to lawful sanctions.

This definition, particularly in its reference to the *intentional* infliction of *severe* pain, was the starting point of the recent American discussion by Jay Bybee and others.[5]

In pursuance of its obligations under the Convention, the United States has enacted legislation forbidding torture outside the United States by persons subject to U.S. jurisdiction.[6] The anti-torture statute makes it an offense punishable by up to twenty years imprisonment to commit, or conspire or attempt to commit torture. The offense is also punishable by death or life imprisonment if the victim of torture dies as a result. Moreover, the statute defines torture as follows:

> "[T]orture" means an act committed by a person acting under the color of law specifically intended to inflict severe physical or mental pain or suffering (other than pain or suffering incidental to lawful sanctions) upon another person within his custody or physical control.[7]

There is an additional definition of "severe mental pain and suffering" in terms of "prolonged mental harm" caused by or resulting from the threat of death, physical torture, or the administration of mind-altering substances to oneself or others.[8]

Finally, there are the Geneva Conventions, which deal with the treatment of various categories of vulnerable individuals in circumstances of armed conflict.[9] The best-known provision is article 17 of the Third Geneva Convention, which provides that "[n]o physical or mental torture, nor any other form of coercion, may be inflicted on prisoners of war to secure from them information of any kind whatever,"[10] In addition, the four Geneva Conventions share a common article 3, which provides as follows:

> Persons taking no active part in the hostilities, including members of armed forces who have laid down their arms ... shall in all circumstances be treated humanely ...
>
> ... [T]he following acts are and shall remain prohibited at any time and in any place whatsoever with respect to the above-mentioned persons:
> (a) violence to life and person, in particular murder of all kinds, mutilation, cruel treatment and torture; ...
> (c) outrages upon personal dignity, in particular[,] humiliating and degrading treatment....[11]

Common article 3 applies to all the persons the Geneva Conventions protect, which include not just prisoners of war, but wounded soldiers, shipwrecked sailors, detained members of irregular forces, and so on.

These provisions, together with the protections that law routinely provides against serious assault and abuse, add up to an interlocking set of prohibitions on torture. They are what I have in mind when I refer to "the prohibition on torture" (or "the rule against torture"), though sometimes one element in this interlocking set, sometimes another, will be most prominent in the arguments that follow.

B. Rules and Backgrounds

What is the effect of these provisions? How should we approach them as lawyers? Should we use the same strategies of interpretation as we use elsewhere in the law? Or is there something special about the prohibitions on torture that requires us to treat them more carefully or considerately? These are the questions that will occupy us throughout the remainder of this article.

I want to begin this discussion by considering the scope and application of the prohibitions on torture. John Yoo has suggested that the Geneva Conventions, read literally, apply to some captives or detainees but not others, and that they do not apply to Al Qaeda and Taliban detainees in the war on terror.[12] What sort of reading, what sort of interpretative approach is necessary to reach a conclusion like that? To answer this question, it is helpful to invoke the old distinction between malum prohibitum and malum in se—two ways in which a legal prohibition may be regarded.

On the malum prohibitum approach, we may think about the text of a given legal provision as introducing a prohibition into what was previously a realm of liberty. Consider the introduction of parking regulations as an analogy. Previously, we were at liberty to park our cars wherever we liked along the streets of our small town. But one day the town government adopts parking regulations, which restrict how long one can park. So now our freedom is limited. Those limits are defined by the regulations that have been enacted: The text of the regulations determines the extent of the prohibition, and we must consult the text to see exactly what is prohibited and what is left free. Overparking is a malum prohibitum offense: It consists of violating the letter of the regulations. If the regulations had not been enacted, there would be no offense. And the corollary of this is that anything that is not explicitly prohibited by the regulations remains as free as before.

The other approach is a malum in se approach. Some things are just wrong, and would be wrong whether positive law prohibited them or not. What legal texts do is articulate this sense of wrongness and fill in the details to make that sense of wrongness administrable. So, for example, a statute prohibiting murder characteristically does not make unlawful what was previously permissible; it simply expresses more clearly the unlawfulness of something which was impermissible all along. It follows that consulting the statutory provision in a rigidly textualist spirit might be inappropriate; it certainly would be inappropriate if one were assuming that anything not prohibited by the exact terms of the text must be regarded as something that one was entirely free to do.

The distinction between malum prohibitum and malum in se might seem to depend on a natural law theory, in which some of law's functions are related to the administration of natural law prohibitions while other functions are related to positive law's capacity to generate new forms of regulation.[13] But that need not be so. All we need in order to make sense of malum in se and distinguish it from malum prohibitum is to discern some preexisting normative background to the prohibition that is legally recognizable. That normative background may be a shared moral sense or it may be some sort of higher or background law: natural law, perhaps, or international law. We should note, however, that the distinction between malum in se and malum prohibitum is not clear-cut. Even in our parking example, there will have been some background reasons governing the way it was appropriate to park even before the regulations were introduced: Do not park unsafely or inconsiderately, do not block access, and so on. These reasons do not evaporate when the explicit regulations are introduced.

Now let us apply these distinctions to the rule against torture. I think it is obvious that the U.S. antitorture statute cannot plausibly be construed according to the malum prohibitum model. It does not represent the first introduction of a prohibition into an area that was previously unregulated and in which everyone was previously at liberty to do what they liked. On the contrary, the statute fulfilled a treaty obligation that the United States already had under the Convention, and it also applied and extended the spirit of existing criminal law. It gave definition to an existing and legally recognized sense of the inherent wrongness of torture. Something similar is true of the Convention itself and also of the Covenant. They themselves are not to be conceived as new pieces of positive international law encroaching into what was previously an unregulated area of freedom. Like all human rights instruments, they have what Gerald Neuman has called a suprapositive aspect: They were "conceived as reflections of nonlegal principles that have normative force independent of their embodiment in law, or even superior to the positive legal system." Though they are formal treaties based on the actual consent of the states that are party to them, they also represent a consensual acknowledgment of deeper background norms that are binding on nations anyway, treaty or no treaty.

It might be thought that the Geneva Conventions are a special case because they are designed to limit armed conflict, and *there* the background or default position is indeed that anything goes. That is, one might think that armed forces are normally at liberty to do anything they like to enemy soldiers in time of war—bombard, shoot, kill, wound, maim, and terrify them—and that the function of the Geneva Conventions is precisely to introduce a degree of unprecedented regulation into what would otherwise be a horrifying realm of freedom. Under this reasoning, the malum prohibitum approach is appropriate, and therefore we have no choice but to consult the strict letter of the texts of the Conventions to see exactly what is prohibited and what has been left as a matter of military freedom. John Yoo's memorandum approaches the Geneva Conventions in that spirit. He implies that absent the Conventions we would be entitled to do anything we like to enemy detainees; grudgingly, however, we must accept some limits (which we ourselves have negotiated and signed up for). But we have signed up for no more than the actual texts stipulate.[14] When we run out of text, we revert to the default position, which is that we can do anything we like. Now—this line of reasoning continues—it so happens that as a result of military action in Afghanistan and Iraq, certain individuals have fallen into our hands as captives who do not have the precise

attributes that the Geneva Conventions stipulate for persons protected by its prohibitions. So—the conclusion runs—the textual prohibitions on maltreatment do not apply to these detainees, and we are back in the military default position: We can do with them whatever we like.

Yoo's approach is wrong in three ways. First, its narrow textualism embodies a bewildering refusal to infer anything along ejusdem generis lines from the existing array of categories of detainees that *are* covered. The Geneva Conventions reiterate elementary protections (against, for instance, torture) for one category of detainee, the same protections for a second category of detainee, the same protections for a third category of detainee, and so on. And now we have detainees in a fourth category that does not exactly fit the literal terms of the first three. It might be reasonable to think that the earlier categories give us a sense of how to go on—how to apply the underlying rule—in new kinds of cases. That is how lawyers generally proceed. That is how we infer, for example, that the Third Amendment to the U.S. Constitution applies to the quartering of sailors, marines, and airmen as well as soldiers. But Professor Yoo proceeds as though the methods of analogy, inference, and reasoned elaboration—the ordinary tools of our lawyerly trade—are utterly inappropriate in this case.

In any case, it is simply not true that the texts of the Geneva Conventions represent the first introduction of prohibitions into a previously unregulated area. The Geneva Conventions, like the Convention Against Torture and the International Covenant, respond to a strongly felt and well-established sense that certain abuses are beyond the pale, whether one is dealing with criminal suspects, political dissidents, or military detainees, and that they remain beyond the pale even in emergency situations or situations of armed conflict. There are certain things that are not to be done to human beings and these international instruments represent our acknowledgment by treaty of that fact. Professor Yoo asserts that the United States cannot regard itself as bound by norms of customary international law or even *jus cogens* norms of international law; he thinks that we must regard ourselves as having a free hand to deal with detainees except to the extent that the exact letter of our treaty obligations indicates otherwise. But such argument as he provides for this assertion relies on the malum prohibitum approach, which, as we have already seen, is inappropriate in this area.

Third, Yoo's analysis lacks a sense of the historic context in which the conventions governing captives and detainees were negotiated and reformulated in 1949. It has been suggested by Scott Horton that the modern Geneva Conventions are in part a response to experience during the Second World War. The conventions then existing were vulnerable to being treated as a patchwork of rules with piecemeal coverage, encouraging Germany, for example, to argue that it could exclude from the benefit of their coverage various categories of detainee such as commandos, partisans, pilots engaged in acts of terror, and those who fought on behalf of a new kind of political entity (the Soviet Union). The conventions were renegotiated in 1949 precisely to prevent this sort of exploitation of loopholes, and it is quite discouraging now to see American lawyers arguing for the inapplicability of the Conventions on grounds that are strikingly similar—new forms of warfare, new types of non-state entity, etc.—to those invoked by Germany in that period.

C. The Interest in Clear Definitions

Let me turn now to the word "torture" itself in these various provisions of municipal and international law. Some of the provisions—the Covenant, for example—offer no elucidation of the meaning of the term. The Covenant just prohibits torture; it does not tell us what torture is. It seems to proceed on the theory that "we know it when we see it,"[15] or that we can recognize this evil using a sort of visceral "puke" test.[16] In a 1990 Senate hearing, a Department of Justice official observed that "there seems to be some degree of consensus that the concept involves conduct the mere mention of which sends chills down one's spine." Is this sufficient? Well, the trouble is that we seem to puke or chill at different things. The response to the Abu Ghraib scandal indicated the lack of any settled consensus in this matter.

Muslim prisoners were humiliated by being made to simulate sexual activity with one another; they were beaten and their fingers and toes were stomped on; they were put in stress postures, hooded and wired, in fear of death if they so much as moved; they were set upon or put in fear of attack by dogs. Was this torture? Many commentators thought it was, but one or two American newspapers resisted the characterization, preferring the word "abuse."[17] Some conservative commentators suggested that what happened was no worse than hazing.[18] The impetus for this distinction seems to be that if we use the word "torture" to characterize what Americans did in Abu Ghraib prison, we might be depriving ourselves of the language we need to condemn much more vicious activities.[19]

Unlike the Covenant, the Convention Against Torture and the U.S. antitorture statute offer more than just a term and an appeal to our intuitions. Their definitional provisions offer us ways to analyze torture in terms of what lawyers sometimes call "the elements of the offense." Criminal law analyzes rape, for example, in terms of a certain sort of physical action (sexual intercourse), under certain circumstances (compulsion by the use or threat of force, or impairment of the victim's ability to control her conduct). Similarly, these provisions analyze torture as a certain sort of action, performed in a certain capacity, causing a certain sort of effect, done with a certain intent, for a certain purpose, and so on. Some of the elements in the antitorture statute and the Convention are the same: Both, for example, distinguish torture from pain or suffering incidental to lawful sanctions. But debates about definition are likely to result from differences in the respective analyses—the analyses of "mental torture," for example, are slightly.[20]

Now, I shall have some harsh things to say about the quest for definitional precision in the remainder of this Section and the next. But nothing that follows is supposed to preclude or even frown upon the sort of analysis or analytic debate that I have just mentioned.

We might ask: What is the point of this restriction? Why narrow the definition of torture so that it covers only severe pain? After all, some theorists have embraced a broad definition of the word. Jeremy Bentham worried about "the delusive power of words" in discussions of torture. But his own definition was very wide: "Torture ... is where a person is made to suffer any violent pain of body in order to compel him to do something ... which done ... the penal application is immediately made to cease." Though he used the term "violent" to qualify "pain," Bentham meant it to refer to the suddenness of the pain's onset, rather than its severity. So, for example, he applied the word "torture" to the case of "a Mother or Nurse seeing a child playing with a thing which he ought not to meddle with, and having forbidden him in vain pinches him till he lays it down." Evidently he thought the interests of clarity would be served by defining torture to include *all* cases of the sudden infliction of pain for the sake of immediate coercion. It is not surprising that Bentham would take this view. He was, after all, a consequentialist and the currency of his consequentialism was pain as well as pleasure. He favored adjusting the meanings of words to facilitate a substantive debate about which inflictions of pain are justified and which are not, rather than assuming in advance that everything taken in by the term "torture" is necessarily illegitimate and then debating the definitional ramifications of that.[21]

Most modern discussions, however, work from the opposite assumption. They begin with the sense that there is something seriously wrong with torture—even if it is not absolutely forbidden—and they approach the issue of definition on that basis. Marcy Strauss, for example, complains that "Amnesty International and others speak of torture when describing sexual abuse of women prisoners, police abuse of suspects by physical brutality, overcrowded cells, the use of implements such as stun guns, and the application of the death penalty." She worries about the consequences of this causal expansion of the term: "[I]f virtually anything can constitute torture, the concept loses some of its ability to shock and disgust.... [U]niversal condemnation may evaporate when the definition is so all encompassing." She implies that we have a certain normative investment in the term—we use it to mark a serious moral judgment—and we

ought to adjust our definition so as to protect that investment.

What do those who are dissatisfied with the vagueness of the phrase "severe pain or suffering" have in mind? What would be a more determinate definition? Presumably, it would be some *measure* of severity, something to turn the existing vague standard into an operationalized rule. Below we shall consider Jay Bybee's attempt to provide just such a measure. But first I want to discuss the very idea of such precision. What motivates the demand for a precise measure of severity? We know that in almost all cases when we replace a vague standard with an operationalized rule, the cost of diminishing vagueness is an increase in arbitrariness. We specify a number, but cases just below that number might seem to be excluded arbitrarily.[22] That sort of arbitrariness can itself reflect badly on the normative investment we have in the relevant provision. So why is this cost worth risking?

I think the argument in favor of precision goes like this. If the terms of a legal prohibition are indeterminate, the person to whom the prohibition is addressed may not know exactly what is required of him, and he may be left unsure as to how the enforcement powers of the state will be used against him. The effect will be to chill that person's exercise of liberty as he tries to avoid being taken by surprise by enforcement decisions.

Is this a compelling argument? We should begin by recalling that the prohibitions on torture contained in the Geneva Conventions and in the Convention Against Torture apply in the first instance to the state and state policy. Is the state in the same position as the ordinary individual in having a liberty interest in bright lines and an interest in not having its freedom of action chilled? I don't think so: We set up the state to preserve and enlarge *our* liberty; the state itself is not conceived as a beneficiary of our libertarian concern. Even the basic logic of liberty seems inapplicable. In the case of individuals, we say that everything that is not expressly forbidden is permitted. But it is far from clear that this principle should apply to the state. Indeed, constitutional doctrine often works the other way around: In the United States, everything that is not explicitly entrusted to the federal government is forbidden to it; it does not have plenary power.[23]

However, although the prohibition on torture is intended mainly as a constraint on state policy, soldiers and other officials do also have an interest as individuals in anticipating war crimes or other prosecutions. The antitorture statute purports to fulfill the obligations of the United States under the Convention by defining torture as an individual criminal offense. Many would say that inasmuch as that statute threatens serious punishment, there is an obligation to provide a tight definition. If that obligation is not fulfilled, they will say, then lenity requires that the defendant be given the benefit of whatever ambiguity we find in the statute. The doctrine of lenity, then, is the basis of the demand for precision.

Against this, however, we need to remember that the charge of torture is unlikely to be surprising or unanticipated by someone already engaged in the deliberate infliction of pain on prisoners: "I am shocked—*shocked!*—to find that 'waterboarding' or squeezing prisoners' genitals or setting dogs on them is regarded as torture." Remember, we are talking about precision or imprecision in regard to a particular element in the definition of torture—the severity element. The potential defendant is one who already knows that he is inflicting considerable pain; that is his intention. The question he faces is whether the pain is severe enough to constitute torture. It seems to me that the working definition in the antitorture statute already gives him all the warning he needs that he is taking a huge risk in relying upon casuistry about "severity" as a defense against allegations of torture.

One other point in this connection. Even if there is a legitimate interest on the part of potential individual defendants in having a precise definition of torture, there is the further question about whether it is appropriate to exploit this in the interest of the state. It is evident from the Yoo memorandum, for example, that an interpretation guided in part by lenity is being used to determine what U.S. policy should be and what U.S. officials should permit and authorize. Defining the sort of bright line that lenity calls for has the effect of carving out space for an official policy of coercive

interrogation that would be much more problematic if the Administration did not present itself as pandering to the individual interest in clear definitions. As we think about the case that can be made for precision, we need to remember that this is how any argument based on lenity is likely to be exploited.

Let us return now to the general question of precision in law. One way of thinking about the need for precise definition involves asking whether the person constrained by the norm in question—state or individual—has a legitimate interest in pressing up as close as possible to the norm, and thus a legitimate interest in having a bright-line rule stipulating exactly what is permitted and exactly what is forbidden. The idea is that the offense may be understood as a threshold on a continuum of some sort; the subject knows that he is on the continuum and that there is a point at which his conduct might be stigmatized as criminal, and the question is whether he has a legitimate interest in being able to move as close to that point as possible. If he *does* have such an interest, then he has an interest in having the precise location of the crucial point on the continuum settled clearly in advance. If he does not, then the demand for precision may be treated less sympathetically.

An example of someone who has such a legitimate interest might be a taxpayer who says, "I have an interest in arranging my affairs to lower my tax liability as much as possible, so I need to know exactly how much I can deduct for entertainment expenses." Another example is the driver who says, "I have an interest in knowing how fast I can go without breaking the speed limit." For those cases, there does seem to be a legitimate interest in having clear definitions. Compare them, however, to some other cases: the husband who says, "I have an interest in pushing my wife around a bit and I need to know exactly how far I can go before it counts as domestic violence"; or the professor who says, "I have an interest in flirting with my students and I need to know exactly how far I can go without falling foul of the sexual harassment rules." *There are some scales one really should not be on,* and with respect to which one really does not have a legitimate interest in knowing precisely how far along the scale one is permitted to go.

Let us apply this to the prohibition on torture. In regard to torture, is there an interest in being able to press up against clear bright-line rules, analogous to the taxpayer's interest in pushing his entertainment deductions to the limit, or the driver's interest in going at exactly 65 mph? The most common argument goes like this: Interrogators have an interest in being as coercive as possible and in being able to inflict as much pain as possible short of violating the prohibition on torture. After all, the point of interrogation is to get people to do what they do not want to do, and for that reason, pressure of some sort is necessary to elicit information that the subject would rather not reveal. Since interrogation as such is not out of bounds, it may be thought interrogators obviously do have a legitimate interest in being on a continuum of pressure, and it is just a question of how far along that continuum we ought to allow them to go. If we fail to specify that point, we might chill any use of pressure in interrogation, even what might turn out to be legitimate pressure.

What is wrong with this argument? Well, it is true that all interrogation *puts pressure* on people to reveal what they would rather not reveal. But there are ways the law can pressure people while still respecting them as persons and without using any form of brutality. And it is quite wrong to suggest that these forms of respectful pressure are marked on the scale of brutality, just down the line from torture. So for example: A hostile witness under subpoena on the witness stand (in a case where there is no issue of self-incrimination) is pressured to answer questions truthfully and give information that he would rather not give. The examination or cross-examination may be grueling, and there are penalties of contempt for refusing to answer and perjury for answering falsely. These are forms of pressure, but they are not on a continuum of brutality with torture. Certainly the penalties for contempt and perjury are coercive: They impose unwelcome costs on certain options otherwise available to the witness. Even so, there is a difference of quality, not just of degree, between the coercion posed by legally

established penalties for noncompliance and the sort of force that involves using pain to break the will of the person being interrogated. I doubt that Professor Dershowitz would agree with what I have just said. Dershowitz argues that "imprisoning a witness who refuses to testify after being given immunity is designed to be punitive—that is painful. Such imprisonment can, on occasion, produce more pain ... than nonlethal torture. Yet we continue to threaten and use the pain of imprisonment to loosen the tongues of reluctant witnesses." But Dershowitz's argument is fallacious in his equation of "punitive" and "painful." Though pain can be used as punishment, only the crudest utilitarian would suggest that all punishment is necessarily painful. Imprisonment works coercively because it is undesired, not because it is, in any literal sense, painful. And it is the literal sense that is needed if we are to say that torture and imprisonment are on a continuum.

Some have argued that there might be a continuum of discomfort associated with interrogation, and we are entitled to ask how far along *that* continuum we are permitted to be. After all, we are not required to provide comfortable furniture for the subject of interrogation to sit in. So, one might ask, "Are we required to ensure that the back of the chair that the subject sits in does not hurt his back or that the seat is not too hard?" If the answer is "No," then surely that means we *are* on a continuum with some of the techniques of interrogation that are arguably torture, like the Israeli technique of shackling a subject in a stress position in a low tilted chair.

To answer this, it is important to understand that torture is a crime of specific intent: It involves the use of pain deliberately and specifically to *break the will* of the subject. Failing to provide a comfortable armchair for the interrogation room may or may not be permissible, but it is in a different category from specifically choosing or designing furniture in a way calculated to break the will of the subject by the excruciating pain of having to sit in it. That latter choice *is* on a continuum with torture—and I want to question whether that is a continuum an official has a legitimate reason for being on. The former choice—failing to provide an armchair or a cushion—is not.

If I am right about all this, then we should be suspicious about the attempt that the Bush Administration has made to pin down a definition of torture and to try to stipulate precisely the point of severity at which the prohibition on torture is supposed to kick in. Far from being the epitome of good lawyering, we might suspect that this enterprise represents an attempt to weaken or undermine the prohibition, by portraying it as something like a speed limit which we are entitled to push up against as closely as we can and in regard to which there might even be a margin of toleration which a good-hearted enforcement officer, familiar with our situation and its exigencies, might be willing to recognize. These suspicions are confirmed, I think, by the character of the actual attempts that have been made to give the prohibition on torture this sort of spurious precision.

D. The Bybee Memorandum

I now want to focus more specifically on the August 2002 memorandum written for the CIA and the White House by Jay Bybee, chief of the Office of Legal Counsel in the Department of Justice. The fifty pages of the Bybee memorandum give what some have described as the most lenient interpretation conceivable to the Convention and other antitorture provisions. Although the memorandum was subsequently officially repudiated, large sections of the Bybee memorandum were incorporated more or less verbatim into what is now known as the Haynes memorandum[24] produced by a working group set up in the Pentagon in January 2003 to reconsider interrogation methods.

According to Bybee, the relevant legal provisions prohibit as torture "only extreme acts" and penalize as torture "only the most egregious conduct." He notes that the American ratification of the Convention Against Torture was accompanied by an express understanding that "in order to constitute torture, an act must be a deliberate and calculated act of an extremely cruel and inhuman nature, specifically intended to inflict excruciating

and agonizing physical or mental pain or suffering." In discussions at the time, it was suggested that the word "torture" should be reserved for practices like "sustained systematic beatings, application of electric currents to sensitive parts of the body and tying up or hanging in positions that cause extreme pain." Administration officials added that such "rough treatment as generally falls into the category of 'police brutality,' while deplorable, does not amount to 'torture.'" Although he conceded that this sort of brutality might amount to "inhuman treatment," Bybee noted that the United States made a reservation to that part of the Convention Against Torture as well, to the effect that the prohibition on inhuman treatment would not apply to the extent that it purported to prohibit anything permitted by the U.S. Constitution as currently interpreted. From all this, Bybee concluded that "certain acts may be cruel, inhuman, or degrading, but still not produce pain and suffering of the requisite intensity to fall within [the] proscription against torture."

It is clear, then, what sort of continuum Bybee thinks interrogators should be on, in the interest of knowing the precise location of a torture threshold. It is not a continuum of pressure, nor is it is a continuum of unwelcome penalties, nor is it a continuum of discomfort. Interrogators, in Bybee's opinion, are permitted to work somewhere along the continuum of the deliberate infliction of pain, and the question is: Where is the bright line along that continuum where the specific prohibition on torture kicks in? If we cannot answer this, Bybee fears, our interrogators may be chilled from *any* sort of deliberate infliction of pain on detainees.

I leave readers to decide whether this is a legally reputable exercise. Bybee purports to draw some support from the jurisprudence of the European Convention of Human Rights, even though the ECHR does not apply to the United States. The leading case is *Ireland v. United Kingdom*, in which the European Court of Human Rights assessed methods of interrogation used by the British in Northern Ireland in the early 1970s. Five techniques of what was called "interrogation in depth" were at issue: sleep deprivation, hooding, white noise, stress postures, and severe limitation on food and water. In holding that the use of these methods did not constitute torture, the Court observed: "[I]t appears ... that it was the intention that the Convention, with its distinction between 'torture' and 'inhuman or degrading treatment,' should by the first of these terms attach a special stigma to deliberate inhuman treatment causing very serious and cruel suffering." Bybee reads that as reinforcing his view that "torture" and "inhuman or degrading treatment" should be regarded as different zones on the same scale, with the first being an extreme version of the second.

However, Bybee failed to mention two things about this decision. First, in *Ireland v. United Kingdom*, the European Commission (as opposed to the Court) of Human Rights had concluded that the five techniques, in combination, *were* torture and not just inhuman or degrading treatment. Both parties to the suit and a minority of judges on the Court accepted this determination. Second, and more important, Bybee failed to mention that *both* categories of conduct were and are absolutely prohibited under the ECHR. The five techniques may not have been termed torture by the Court, but because the Court determined that their application treated the suspects in an inhuman and degrading manner, they were prohibited nonetheless. The fact that there is a verbal distinction in article 3 of the ECHR between torture and inhuman and degrading treatment does not mark an effective normative distinction in the ECHR scheme, so far as the strength and immovability of these prohibitions are concerned. The article 15 nonderogation provision applies to both, and the Court's comments about "special stigma" do not affect that.[25] One does not have to be a legal realist to reckon that since the normative consequences of the discrimination between torture and inhuman and degrading treatment are different between the ECHR and the American torture statute (with its background in the Convention Against Torture), any extrapolation of support from an approach taken under the former is likely to be suspect.

All of this goes to the general character of Bybee's analysis. Let us turn now to its detail. How, exactly, does Bybee propose to pin down a meaning for "severe pain or suffering"? It is all very well to talk about "requisite intensity," but how are we to determine the appropriate measure of severity? With a dictionary in hand, Bybee essays a proliferation of adjectives—"grievous," "extreme," and the like. But they all seem to defy operationalization in the same way: The intensity, the severity, and the agonizing or excruciating character of pain are all subjective and, to a certain extent, inscrutable phenomena. One thing Bybee said, in an attempt to give the definition of torture a somewhat less phenomenological basis, was that "the adjective 'severe' conveys that the pain or suffering must be of such a high level of intensity that the pain is difficult for the subject to endure." But that is not going to give him the distinction he wants. Presumably that is the whole point of *any* pain imposed deliberately in cruel and inhuman interrogation, not just the extreme cases Bybee wants to isolate.

A more promising approach involves drawing on statutes governing medical administration, where Bybee said that attempts to define the phrase "severe pain" had already been made. He wrote this:

> Congress's use of the phrase "severe pain" elsewhere in the United States Code can shed more light on its meaning. Significantly, the phrase "severe pain" appears in statutes defining an emergency medical condition for the purpose of providing health benefits. See, e.g., 8 U.S.C. § 1369 (2000); 42 U.S.C. § 1395w-22 (2000); id. §1395x (2000); id. § 1395dd (2000); id. §1396b (2000); id. § 1396u-2 (2000). These statutes define an emergency condition as one "manifesting itself by acute symptoms of sufficient severity (including *severe pain*) such that a prudent lay person, who possesses an average knowledge of health and medicine, could reasonably expect the absence of immediate medical attention to result in—[(i)] placing the health of the individual ... in serious jeopardy, (ii) serious impairment to bodily functions, or (iii) serious dysfunction of any bodily organ or part." Id. § 1395w-22(d) (3) (B) (emphasis added). Although these statutes address a substantially different subject from Section 2340, they are nonetheless helpful for understanding what constitutes severe physical pain.

From this, Bybee concluded that severe pain amounting to torture must be equivalent in intensity to the pain accompanying serious physical injury, such as organ failure, impairment of body function, or even death.

It is hard to know where to start in criticizing this analysis. One could comment on the strange assumption that a term like "severe pain" takes no color from its context or from the particular purpose of the provision in which it is found, but that it *unproblematically means the same* in a medical administration statute (with the purposes characteristically associated with statutes of this kind) as it does in an antitorture statute (with the purposes characteristically associated with statutes of that kind). Never mind that the latter provision in intended to fulfill our international obligations under the Convention, while the former addresses the resource problems of our quite peculiar healthcare regime. Bybee argues that the medical administration statute can still cast some light on the definition of torture.

Even that glimmer of light flickers out when we consider a couple of glaring defects of basic logic in the detail of the analysis itself. First, the healthcare provision that Bybee refers to uses certain conditions—(i) to (iii) in the excerpt above—to define the phrase "emergency condition," not to define "severe pain." The medical administration statute says that severe symptoms (including severe pain) add up to an emergency condition if any of the three conditions are satisfied.[26] These conditions provided Bybee with his formulations about organ failure and death, but since the antitorture statute does not use the term "emergency condition," the logic of their use in the healthcare statute makes them utterly irrelevant to the definition of severe pain, there or anywhere else.[27] Second, Bybee's analysis reverses the causality implicit in the medical administration statute: That statute refers to the likelihood that a severe condition will *lead to* organic impairment or dysfunction if left untreated, whereas what Bybee infers from the healthcare statute is that pain counts as severe only if it is associated with (naturally read as "caused by") organic impairment or dysfunction. To sum up: Bybee takes a definition of "emergency condition" (in which severe pain happens to be mentioned), reverses the causal relationship required between the emergency condition and organ failure, and concludes—on a matter as important as the proper definition of torture—that the law does not prohibit anything as torture unless it causes the same sort of pain as organ failure.

The quality of Bybee's legal work here is a disgrace when one considers the service to which this analysis is being put. Bybee is an intelligent man, these are obvious errors, and the Department of Justice—as the executive department charged with special responsibility for the integrity of the legal system—had a duty to take special care with this most important of issues. Bybee's mistakes distort the character of the legal prohibition on torture and create an impression that there is more room for the lawful infliction of pain in interrogation than a casual acquaintance with the antitorture statute might suggest. Fortunately, someone in the Administration felt that he had gone too far: This part of Bybee's memorandum was not incorporated into the Haynes memorandum (although most of the rest of it was), and much of the Bybee approach to the definition of torture appears to have been rejected by the Administration in its most recent deliverances on the subject.

II. LEGAL ABSOLUTES

A. Legal Contingency: Is Nothing Sacred?

I now want to step back from all this and ask: What is it about these definitional shenanigans that seems so disturbing? After all, we know there is an element of contingency and manipulation in the definition of any legal rule. As circumstances change, amendments in the law or changes of interpretation seem appropriate. Legal prohibitions are not set in stone. Changing the definitions of offenses or reinterpreting open-ended phrases is part of the normal life of any body of positive law. Why should the law relating to torture be any different?

Well for one thing, we seem to be dealing in this case with not just fine tuning, but a wholesale attempt to gut our commitment to a certain basic norm. As I mentioned earlier, the Bybee memorandum maintains that none of the legislation enacted pursuant to the Convention Against Torture can be construed as applying to interrogations authorized under the President's Commander-in-Chief powers. It does not matter what the legislative definition of torture is—those who act under presidential authority in time of war cannot be construed as covered by it, and any attempt to extend prohibitions on torture to modes of interrogation authorized by the President would be unconstitutional. This is not just tinkering with the details of positive law: It amounts to a comprehensive assault on our traditional understanding of the whole legal regime relating to torture. Even so, we still have to acknowledge that the life of the law is sometimes to change or reinterpret whole paradigms (particularly in constitutional law, where we suddenly decide that a whole area of lawmaking thought out of bounds is in bounds or vice versa).[28] Why is it so shocking in this instance?

The question can be generalized. Law in all its features and all the detail of its terms and application is contingent on politics and circumstances—that is the lesson of legal positivism. Nothing is beyond revision or repudiation. Why then do we have this sense that something *sacred* is being violated in the Bybee memorandum, in John Yoo's arguments, or in the proposal Alan Dershowitz invites us to consider? Can a provision of positive law be sacred, in anything approaching a literal sense, so that it is wrong to even touch or approach its formulation. Is there a literal meaning of "sacred" in this secular age?

Some among the drafters of the European Convention on Human Rights seemed to think so. I am not usually one for citing legislative history, but in this case, it is instructive. The following motion was proposed in the *travaux préparatoires* for the ECHR in 1949 by a United Kingdom delegate, a Mr. F.S. Cocks:

The Consultative Assembly takes this opportunity of declaring that all forms of physical torture ... are inconsistent with civilized society, are offences against heaven and humanity and must be prohibited.

It declares that this prohibition must be absolute and that torture cannot be permitted for any purpose whatsoever, neither for extracting evidence, for saving life nor even for the safety of the State.

It believes that it would be better even for society to perish than for it to permit this relic of barbarism to remain.

Lamenting the rise of torture in the twentieth century, Mr. Cocks added this in his speech moving this proposal:

I feel that this is the occasion when this Assembly should condemn in the most forthright and absolute fashion this retrogression into barbarism. I say that to take the straight beautiful bodies of men and women and to maim and mutilate them by torture is a crime against high heaven and the holy spirit of man. I say that it is a sin against the Holy Ghost for which there is no forgiveness.

Mr. Cocks's fellow delegates applauded his sentiments—nobody disagreed with his fierce absolutism on this issue—but they thought this was inappropriate to include in their report. And you can see their point. It is all very well to talk about "sin against the Holy Ghost" and "offences against heaven and humanity," but these are not exactly legal ideas, and it is unlikely that they resonate even with my good-hearted readers, let alone the steely-eyed lawyers in the Justice Department.

So, can we make sense—without resorting to religious ideas—of the idea of a noncontingent prohibition, a prohibition so deeply embedded that it cannot be modified or truncated in this way?

There are some fairly well-known ways of conceiving the indispensability of certain legal norms. We have already considered the distinction between mala in se and mala prohibita. There is H. L A. Hart's idea of "the minimum content of natural law"—certain kinds of rules that a legal system could not possibly do without, given humans as they are and the world as it is.[29] Less philosophically, we understand that there are things that in theory lawmakers might do but are in fact very unlikely to do. As Leslie Stephen put it, "If a legislature decided that all blue-eyed babies should be murdered, the preservation of blue-eyed babies would be illegal; but legislators must go mad before they could pass such a law, and subjects be idiotic before they could submit to it."

There are also various legal ways to diminish the vulnerability of a norm to revision, redefinition, or repeal. One possibility is that a rule might be entrenched in a constitution as proof against casual or bare majoritarian alteration. A second is that a provision of international law might acquire the status of *jus cogens*, as proof against the vagaries of consent that dominate treaty-based international law. A third possibility is that a human rights norm might be associated with an explicit nonderogation clause as proof against the thought that it is acceptable to abandon rights-based scruples in times of emergency. In fact, there have been attempts in all three of these ways to insulate the prohibition against torture against the contingency of positive law: The Eighth Amendment to the U.S. Constitution might be taken as an example of the first, the identification of international norms against torture as *jus cogens* is an example of the second, and of course the nonderogation provisions of the European Convention on Human Rights in relation to article 3 of that Convention offer a fine example of the third. But all of these are themselves positive law devices, and they too are subject to manipulation. Constitutions can be reinterpreted: For example, the Eighth Amendment prohibition on cruelty is construed nowadays as limited only to punishment imposed as part of the criminal process. And even usually rights-respecting regimes can limit or weaken their support for apparently compelling international obligations by definitional or other maneuvers: Professor Yoo argues that the U.S. President cannot be bound by customary international law; Judge Bybee says that there can be no legislative constraints on the President's ability to authorize torture; and the English Court of Appeal recently determined that the prohibition in the Convention Against Torture on using information obtained by torture (in this case for the purpose of determining whether an individual's detention as a terrorist suspect was justified) applies only to information that has been extracted by torture conducted by agents of the detaining state. In the end, a legal prohibition is only as strong as the moral and political consensus that supports it. And there is the difficulty. The moral and political consensus is weak and uneasy. In these troubled times, it is not hard to make the idea of an absolute prohibition on torture, or any absolute prohibition, look silly, as a matter of moral philosophy. I do not mean that everyone is a consequentialist. There are good deonotological accounts of the rule against torture, but most of them stop short of absolutism. The principle defended by deontologists almost always turns out to be wobbly when sufficient pressure is applied. Even among those who are not already Bentham-style consequentialists, most are moderates in their deontology: They are willing to abandon even cherished absolutes in the face of what Robert Nozick once called "catastrophic moral horror." For a culture supposedly committed to human rights, we have amazing difficulty in even conceiving—without some sort of squirm—the idea of genuine moral absolutes. Academics in particular are so frightened of being branded "unrealistic" that we will fall over ourselves at the slightest provocation to opine that *of course* moral restraints must be abandoned when the stakes are high enough. Extreme circumstances can make moral absolutes look ridiculous, and those in our position cannot afford to be made to look ridiculous.

B. The Dershowitz Strategy

This tendency is exacerbated by the way we pose the question of torture to ourselves. Law school and moral philosophy classes thrive on hypotheticals that involve grotesque disproportion between the pain that a torturer might inflict on an informant and the pain that might be averted by timely use of the information extracted from him: a little bit of pain from the needles for him versus a hundred thousand people saved from nuclear incineration[30] Of course after September 11, 2001, the hypotheticals are beginning to look a little less fantastic. Professor Dershowitz asks: What if on September 11 law enforcement officials had arrested terrorists boarding one of the planes and learned that other planes, then airborne, were heading towards unknown occupied buildings? Would they not have been justified in torturing the terrorists in their custody—just enough to get the information that would allow the target buildings to be evacuated? How could anyone object to the use of torture if it were dedicated specifically to saving thousands of lives in a case like this? That is the question that Dershowitz and others regard as a useful starting point in our thinking about torture. The answer it is supposed to elicit is that torture can never be entirely out of the question, if the facts are clear and the stakes are high enough.

Should it worry us that once one goes down this road, the justification of torture—indeed, the justification of *anything*—is a matter of simple arithmetic coupled with the professor's ingenuity in concocting the appropriate fact situation? As Seth Kreimer observes, "a sufficiently large fear of catastrophe could conceivably authorize almost any plausibly efficacious government action." The tactics used to discredit absolute prohibitions on torture are tactics that can show in the end, "to borrow the formula of Dostoevsky's Ivan Karamazov, … [that] everything is permitted." Dershowitz concedes the point, acknowledging that there is something disingenuous about his own suggestion that judicial torture warrants would be issued to authorize nothing but *nonlethal* torture. If the number of lives that can be saved is twice the number necessary to justify nonlethal torture, why not justify lethal torture or torture with *unsterilized* needles? Indeed, why just torture? Why not judicial rape warrants? Why not terrorism itself? The same kind of hypotheticals will take care of these inhibitions as well.

Still, this concern alone does not dispose of Dershowitz's question. Might we be willing to allow the authorization of torture at least in a "ticking bomb" case—make it a ticking nuclear bomb in your hometown, if you like—where we are sure that the detainee we are proposing to torture has information that will save thousands of lives and will give it up only if subjected to excruciating pain?

For what it is worth, my own answer to this question is a simple "No." I draw the line at torture. I suspect that almost all of my readers will draw the line *somewhere*, to prohibit *some* actions even under the most extreme circumstances—if it is not torture of the terrorist, they will draw the line at torturing the terrorist's relatives, or raping

the terrorist, or raping the terrorist's relatives, all of which can be posited (with a logic similar to Dershowitz's) to be the necessary means of eliciting the information. Then the boot is simply on the other foot: Why is it so easy to abandon one absolute (against torturing terrorists) while remaining committed to other absolutes (against, for instance, raping terrorists' relatives)? We can all be persuaded to draw the line somewhere, and I say we should draw it where the law requires it, and where the human rights tradition has insisted it should be drawn.

But in any case, one's answer is less important than one's estimation of the question. An affirmative answer is meant to make us feel patriotic and tough-minded. But the question that is supposed to elicit this response is at best silly and at worst deeply corrupt. It is silly because torture is seldom used in the real world to elicit startling facts about particular ticking bombs; it is used by American interrogators and others to accumulate lots of small pieces of relatively insignificant information which may become important only when accumulated with other pieces of similar information elicited by this or other means. And it is corrupt because it attempts to use a farfetched scenario, more at home in a television thriller than in the real world, deliberately to undermine the integrity of certain moral positions.

Some replies to Dershowitz's question—and to my mind, they are quite convincing—say that even if the basic fact situation he posits is no longer so fantastic in light of the bizarre horrors of September 11, nevertheless the framing of the hypothetical *is* still farfetched, inasmuch as it asks us to assume that torture warrants will work exactly as Professor Dershowitz says they should work.[31] The hypothetical asks us to assume that the power to authorize torture will not be abused, that intelligence officials will not lie about what is at stake or about the availability of the information, that the readiness to issue torture warrants in one case (where they may be justified by the sort of circumstances Dershowitz stipulates) will not lead to their extension to other cases (where the circumstances are somewhat less compelling), that a professional corps of torturers will not emerge who stand around looking for work, that the existence of a law allowing torture in some cases will not change the office politics of police and security agencies to undermine and disempower those who argue against torture in other cases, and so on.

Professor Dershowitz has ventured the opinion that if his torture-warrant idea had been taken seriously, it is less likely that the abuses at Abu Ghraib prison in Iraq would have occurred. This takes optimism to the point of irresponsibility. What we know about Abu Ghraib and other recent cases is that against the background of any given regulatory regime in these matters, there will be some enthusiasts who are prepared to "push the envelope," trespassing into territory that goes beyond what is legally permitted. In addition, there will always be some depraved individuals who act in a way that is simply abusive *relative to whatever authorization is given.* There is, as Henry Shue notes, "considerable evidence of all torture's metastatic tendency." In the last hundred years or so it has shown itself not to be the sort of thing that can be kept under rational control. Indeed, it is already expanding. The torture at Abu Ghraib had nothing to do with "ticking bomb" terrorism. It was intended to "soften up" detainees so that U.S. military intelligence could get information from them about likely attacks by Iraqi insurgents against American occupiers.

The important point is that the use of torture is not an area in which human motives are trustworthy. Sadism, sexual sadism, the pleasure of indulging brutality, the love of power, and the enjoyment of the humiliation of others—these all-too-human characteristics need to be kept very tightly under control, especially in the context of war and terror, where many of the usual restraints on human action are already loos-ened.[32] If ever there were a case for Augustinian suspicion of the idea that basic human depravity can be channeled to social advantage, this is it. Remember too that we are not asking whether these motives can be judicially regulated in the abstract. We are asking whether they can be regulated in the kind of circumstances of fear, anger, stress, danger, panic, and terror in which, realistically, the hypothetical case must be posed.

NOTES

1. International Covenant on Civil and Political Rights, adopted Dec. 16, 1966 (hereinafter "ICCPR"). There is also a provision in article 7 prohibiting medical experimentation without consent.
2. S. Exec. Rep. No. 102-23, at 22 (1992).
3. Convention Against Torture and Other Cruel, Inhuman or Degrading Treatment or Punishment, adopted Dec. 10, 1984 (hereinafter "Convention Against Torture.")
4. The Convention also imposes requirements of non-refoulement [Ed.: in international law, the refusal to return a victim of true persecution to their persecutor] of refugees likely to face torture, id. art. 3, requirements to ensure that officials are prohibited from using torture and that the prohibition is included in their training, id. art. 10, requirements to promptly investigate allegations of torture, id. art. 12, to protect complainants against retaliation, id. art. 13, and to secure a right to redress and compensation for victims of torture, id. art. 14. There is also a prohibition on the use in legal proceedings or proceedings before any official tribunal of "any statement which is established to have been made as a result of torture … except against a person accused of torture as evidence that the statement was made."
5. See section I.D. of this article.
6. See 18 U.S.C. § 2340 (2000). It is assumed that ordinary provisions of criminal and constitutional law sufficiently prohibit torture within the United States.
7. Id. § 2340(1).
8. Id. § 2340(2).
9. Geneva Convention for the Amelioration of the Condition of the Wounded and Sick in Armed Forces in the Field, opened for signature Aug. 12, 1949, 6 U.S.T. 3114, 75 U.N.T.S. 31 (hereinafter "Geneva Convention I"); Geneva Convention for the Amelioration of the Condition of Wounded, Sick and Shipwrecked Members of Armed Forces at Sea, opened for signature Aug. 12, 1949, 6 U.S.T. 3217, 75 U.N.T.S. 85 (hereinafter "Geneva Convention II"); Geneva Convention Relative to the Treatment of Prisoners of War, opened for signature Aug. 12, 1949, 6 U.S.T. 3316, 75 U.N.T.S. 135 (hereinafter "Geneva Convention III"); Geneva Convention Relative to the Protection of Civilian Persons in Time of War, opened for signature Aug. 12, 1949, 6 U.S.T.

3516, 75 U.N.T.S. 287 (hereinafter "Geneva Convention IV").

10. Geneva Convention III, supra note 9, art. 17.

11. Geneva Convention I, supra note 9, art. 3; Geneva Convention II, supra note 9, art. 3; Geneva Convention III, supra note 9, art. 3; Geneva Convention IV, supra note 9, art. 3.

12. See Memorandum from John Yoo, Deputy Assistant Att'y Gen., & Robert J. Delahunty, Special Counsel, to William J. Haynes II, Gen. Counsel, Dep't of Def. 1 (Jan. 9, 2002) (hereinafter "Yoo Memorandum") 1–2.

13. Blackstone drew this distinction as follows:

> [C]rimes and misdemeanours, that are forbidden by the superior laws, and therefore stifled mala in se; such as murder, theft, and perjury ... contract no additional turpitude from being declared unlawful by the inferior legislature. For that legislature in all these cases acts only ... in subordination to the great lawgiver, transcribing and publishing his precepts.

> 1 William Blackstone, Commentaries *54 (footnote omitted).

14. This impression is based on Yoo Memorandum, supra note 12, at 11 ("[M]embers of the al Qaeda organization do not receive the protection of the laws of war."); id. at 34 ("[C]ustomary international law of armed conflict in no way binds, as a legal matter, the President or the U.S. Armed Forces concerning the detention or trial of members of al Qaeda and the Taliban.").

15. This was what Justice Potter Stewart said, notoriously, about obscenity in Jacobellis v. Ohio, 378 U.S. 184, 197 (1964).

16. Oliver Wendell Holmes once said that a law was constitutional unless it made him want to "puke."

17. Newsday reported the following characterization:

> "Torture is torture is torture," Secretary of State Colin Powell said this week in an interview....
>
> That depends on what papers you read. The media in France, Italy and Germany have been routinely using the word "torture" in the headings of their stories on the abuses in the Abu Ghraib prison....
>
> But the American press has been more circumspect, sticking with vaguer terms such as "abuse" and "mistreatment."... [T]hey may have been taking a cue from Defense Secretary Donald Rumsfeld. Asked about torture in the prison, he said, "What has been charged so far is abuse, which is different from torture. I'm not going to address the 'torture' word."

> Geoffrey Nunberg, Don't Torture English to Soft-Pedal Abuse, Newsday (Nassau Cty., N.Y.), May 20, 2004, at A50.

18. See Frank Rich, The War's Lost Weekend, N.Y. Times, May 9, 2004, § 2, at 1 ("[A] former Army interrogation instructor, Tony Robinson, showed up on [a] Fox show ... to assert that the prison photos did not show torture. 'Frat hazing is worse than this,' the self-styled expert said."). This characterization was seconded by Rush Limbaugh, who said on his radio program:

> "This is no different than what happens at the Skull and Bones initiation, and we're going to ruin people's lives over it, and we're going to hamper our military effort, and then we are going to really hammer them because they had a good time. You know, these people are being fired at every day ... You ever heard of emotional release?"

> Cathy Young, Cruelty Cuts Across Nationality, Gender Lines, Boston Globe, May 10, 2004, at A15.

19. Similarly, Judge Sir Gerald Fitzmaurice asked in his dissent in *Ireland v. United Kingdom* if the five techniques that the British had used in Northern Ireland in the early 1970s—sleep deprivation, hooding, white noise, stress postures, and severe limitations on food and water—were "to be regarded as involving torture, how does one characterize e.g. having one's finger-nails torn out, being slowly impaled on a stake through the rectum, or roasted over an electric grid?" 25 Eur. Ct. H.R. (ser. A) at 130 (1978) (separate opinion of Fitzmaurice, J.).

20. It is a weakness of this article that I say almost nothing about the definition of mental torture. That silence is not supposed to condone what the various Bush Administration memoranda have said on that topic. One cannot do justice to everything in one article, and this one is already too long.

Instead, I want to consider a kind of complaint about definitional looseness (and an attempt to narrow the definition of "torture") that goes well beyond this business of analyzing the elements of the offense. Both the Convention and the antitorture statute refer to the intentional infliction of "severe" pain or suffering. Since pain can be more or less severe, evidently the word "severe" is going to be a site for contestation between those who think of torture in very broad terms and those who think of it in very narrow terms. The word looks as though it is supposed to restrict the application of the word "torture." But as with a requirement to take "reasonable care" or a constitutional prohibition on "excessive" bail, we are not told what exactly the restriction is—that is, we are not told where exactly severity is on the spectrum of pain, and thus where the prohibition on torture is supposed to kick in.

21. Thus Bentham argued, "There is no approving [torture] in the lump, without militating against reason and humanity: nor condemning it without falling into absurdities and contradictions." W. L. Twining & P. E. Twining, Bentham on Torture, 24 N. I. L. Q. 305, 308 (1973) at 308 (quoting Bentham Manuscripts, University College London Collection, box 46, 337).

22. Duncan Kennedy described this sort of arbitrariness with the following example:

    Suppose that the reason for creating a class of persons who lack capacity is the belief that immature people lack the faculty of free will. Setting the age of majority at 21 years will incapacitate many but not all of those who lack this faculty. And it will incapacitate some who actually possess it. From the point of view of the purpose of the rules, this combined over- and underinclusiveness amounts not just to licensing but to requiring official arbitrariness. If we adopt the rule, it is because of a judgment that this kind of arbitrariness is less serious than the arbitrariness and uncertainty that would result from empowering the official to apply the standard of "free will" directly to the facts of each case.

    Duncan Kennedy, Form and Substance in Private Law Adjudication, 89 Harv. L. Rev. 1685, 1689 (1976).

23. Is the state entitled, as we sometimes think individuals are entitled—see Friedrich A. Hayek, The Constitution of Liberty 139–40, 156–57 (1960)—to a legally predictable environment in which it can exercise whatever liberty it has? I was intrigued by a suggestion to this effect by Justice Scalia in his dissent in *Rasul v. Bush*:

    Normally, we consider the interests of those who have relied on our decisions. Today, the Court springs a trap on the Executive, subjecting Guantanamo Bay to the oversight of the federal courts even though it has never before been thought to be within their jurisdiction—and thus making it a foolish place to have housed alien wartime detainees.

    124 S. Ct. 2686, 2706 (2004) (Scalia, J., dissenting).

24. Memorandum from William J. Haynes, II, Gen. Counsel, Dep't of Def., to Donald Rumsfeld, Sec'y of Def. (Nov. 27, 2002).

25. 25 Eur. Ct. H.R. (ser. A) at 66. Indeed, had the Court been confronted with the situation Bybee thinks he faces—a situation in which there is a weaker prohibition on abuse that is merely inhuman, degrading, and cruel than there is on torture—I think it is unlikely that the Court would have rejected the Commission's characterization of the five techniques as torture.

26. 42 U.S.C. U.S.C. § 1395w-22(d) (3)(B).

27. Using these conditions to define "severe pain" would be like taking the following statement—"A dog (particularly a large dog) is a Dalmatian if it has a white coat with black spots"—to imply that the definition of "large dog" required a white coat and black spots. I am grateful to Bill Dailey for this analogy.

28. See, for example, the discussion in Planned Parenthood of Se. Pa. v. Casey, 505 U.S. 833, 861–64 (1992) (citing W. Coast Hotel Co. v. Parrish, 300 U.S. 379 (1937), and Brown v. Bd. of Educ., 347 U.S. 483 (1954), as examples of cases that overruled whole swathes of existing constitutional doctrine).

29. H. L. A. Hart, The Concept of Law 193–200 (2d ed. 1994). Hart famously illuminated this concept with the following example:

    [S]uppose that men were to become invulnerable to attack by each other, were clad perhaps like giant land crabs with an impenetrable carapace … In such circumstances (the details of which can be left to science fiction) rules forbidding the free use of violence … would not have the necessary nonarbitrary status which they have for us, constituted as we are in a world like ours. At present, and until such radical changes supervene, such rules are so fundamental that if a legal system did not have them there would be no point in having any other rules at all.

    H. L. A. Hart, Positivism and the Separation of Law and Morals, 71 Harv. L. Rev. 593, 623 (1958).

30. See Alan M. Dershowitz, Why Terrorism Works (2002), at 132. It is a tradition reaching back to Jeremy Bentham, who wrote:

    Suppose … a suspicion is entertained … that at this very time a considerable number of individuals are actually suffering, by illegal violence, inflictions equal in intensity to those which if inflicted by the hand of justice, would universally be spoken of under the name of torture. For the purpose of rescuing from torture these hundred innocents, should any scruple be made of applying equal or superior torture, to extract the requisite information from the mouth of one criminal, who having it in his power to make known the place where at this time the enormity was practising or about to be practised, should refuse to do so?

Twining & Twining, supra note 21, at 347 n.3 (quoting Bentham Manuscripts, University College London Collection, box 74b, 429 (May 27, 1804)). Bentham refers to the antitorture sentiment in the face of this sort of example as the "blind and vulgar humanity" of those who "to save one criminal, should determine to abandon 100 innocent persons to the same fate."

31. The best version of this answer comes from Henry Shue, who points out that precious few real-world cases have the clean precision of the philosopher's hypothetical; the philosophers' cases remain fanciful in their closure conditions and in the assurances we are given that the authority to torture will not expand and will not be abused. Henry Shue, Torture, 7 Phil. & Pub. Aff. 124, 141–43 (1978).

32. Incidentally, it is worth noting the role that the pornographic character of modern American culture played in determining the sort of images and tableaux that seemed appealing to the torturers at Abu Ghraib. See, e.g., Scott Higham et al., A Prison on the Brink, Wash. Post, May 9, 2004, at A1 ("The photographs featuring piles of naked Iraqis seem as though they were taken from a pornographic magazine."). Is it asking too much to expect that those who "defend to the death" our right to suffuse society with pornographic imagery might acknowledge this as one of its not-entirely-harmless effects?

PART TWO

The Political Morality of Law

WE CAN DISTINGUISH between the concept of law in general and the laws of a particular political community. Sometimes lawyers and philosophers draw this distinction in terms of what they call *general* and *specific* jurisprudence: between, say, the theory of law as such, and the theory of American, British, or Japanese law. Put this way, the distinction can be more confusing than helpful, because the two categories seem to involve different questions. In general jurisprudence (the subject in most of Part I) we ask about the nature of law; we look to uncover essential truths about law, or what must be true of something in order for it to be law, or the set of regulations, principles, or norms that count as a legal system. According to H. L. A. Hart, law is the union of primary and secondary rules, with the most important secondary rule being the rule of recognition. (See Chapter 3 for more on these concepts.) According to Hart, every legal system must have a rule of recognition, and it is this rule that distinguishes it from other legal systems. If Hart is right about general jurisprudence, then specific jurisprudence would amount to an inquiry into the rule of recognition in the United States, Britain, or Japan. But that may or may not be a philosophical question at all; certainly it is not the same sort of question involved in general jurisprudence.

It is, perhaps, helpful to consider at least two other interpretations of specific jurisprudence. In one interpretation, the jurisprudence of British law, say, might be the set of principles that underlie or make the best sense of the various domains of law—torts, contracts, property, criminal law, and so on—within the territories governed by British law. There is no requirement that the principles that rationalize tort law (tort jurisprudence) be the same ones at play in constitutional law or in criminal law. Specific jurisprudence is hence doubly specific. It is specific to (or indexed to) a particular political community and to particular bodies of law within that jurisdiction. These are the issues to which we shall turn in Part Three, where we will examine which principles appear to be at work in various areas of the law—criminal law, torts, contracts, property, and so on.

Though the principles that are embodied or reflected in distinctive areas of the law need not coincide with one another, it would be odd or even troubling if they were in deep and irresolvable conflict. If the principles at work in determining what one could own (property) were completely inconsistent with those governing damage to property (torts) or those governing the use to which one could put one's property (contract), we might well think something about the law was amiss. Imagine, for example, a system that allows people to buy and sell land, but provides no restriction on the state's right to seize that land without compensation, or on the desire of strangers to ride motorcycles across it at will.

Such a legal system would be confusing and ineffective. It could not serve well its coordinating functions. But that would likely not be our deepest concern. We would worry that something had gone wrong morally. For the law is a way of regulating human affairs by providing those subject to it with reasons for acting—which include the state's authority to coercively enforce the law. A body of law that reflects deeply conflicting and incompatible principles might demand inconsistent or contradictory conduct, and its claim to enforce those demands through the use of force would be morally questionable.

This suggests that at some level of generality, the law of well-ordered political communities is or should be consistent—that is, it expresses or embodies a set of consistent moral or political ideals. This does not mean that in specific cases those ideals cannot come into conflict with one another. Indeed they do, and we recognize the need to resolve such conflicts in the law and in our practical lives more generally. It means, however, that in many legal systems, we should expect to find a set of principles of political morality that are of a piece with one another—that express a particular conception of political association embodied in law. In the legal communities that we are focusing on here, those are principles of, broadly speaking, liberal political democracy.

This is what we have in mind by specific jurisprudence under a second interpretation: not the jurisprudence of Britain or Japan, nor of tort and constitutional law, but the jurisprudence of a liberal democracy. What overarching principles justify and limit the exercise of political coercion in a liberal democracy, and which principles must be expressed in law in order for it to give expression to a distinctive liberal ideal? We might refer to these as the principles that make up the political morality of the law. Those principles are the focal point of this second part of the book.

CONSTITUTIONALISM

One of the defining features of a liberal democratic state is the existence of an effective *constitution*. In its most abstract sense, a constitution is the set of norms, usually but not always collected in a single written document, that define and structure the operations of governance. Thus, constitutions are the foundational legal documents of almost all legal orders, liberal or not, and provide—at least in principle—the standard against which the legitimacy of particular laws or exercises of public power can be assessed. All constitutions determine the procedure by which political authorities are elected or appointed; all determine the procedure by which legislatures may make new laws; all define the crucial relationship between military and political authorities. Many, though not all, constitutions define rights held by individuals against the state, including such rights as the right of political assembly, conscience, and rights to fair and open criminal or civil trials. More generally, in liberal states, the constraint function of constitutions is central to their role in the architecture of government. Constitutions limit the kinds of acts that the state can take vis-à-vis its citizens (for instance, prohibiting the state from limiting religious observances to a single faith), as well as the acts that various agencies of the state can perform with respect to each other (for example, prohibiting the executive from adjudicating challenges to its own authority).

As stated, constitutionalism amounts to a catalog of rules—secondary rules, in Hart's terminology—governing how primary rules of behavior can be (and cannot be) established, changed, adjudicated, and applied. The philosophical problem is explaining the coherence and justification of these secondary rules in a liberal political order—specifically, their justification against a relevant alternative: untrammeled democracy. For if we think of our key normative commitment today as one to democracy, to the right and power of a political community to decide, together, how best to deploy collective resources and forces, then the limits imposed by constitutions present several obvious dilemmas, if they are to be justified at all.

A first dilemma, presupposed by the limiting nature of a constitution, is the conflict between the *entrenched* aspect of constitutional norms, and the general principle of democratic authority. It is in the nature of constitutional provisions to be resistant to change by ordinary legislative processes—or else the limits they could place on the desires of political agencies would be very weak. Thus some constitutions (in, e.g., Germany, Israel) explicitly prohibit any future revision to or rescission of their grants of fundamental individual rights. Many others prohibit any change from a "republican" form of government (e.g., France, Turkey), while virtually all constitutions stipulate that changes to their key provisions be made through a heightened democratic requirement, often consisting of a two-thirds legislative majority or some form of popular referendum. While states differ in how rigid or flexible their constitutions are with respect to formal, legal change, virtually all allow a minority of a political community to trump the will of a democratic majority, by privileging the decisions of an (often long-dead) group that wrote and adopted the constitution in the first place.

How to make sense of such democracy-limiting provisions, in a way that leaves them compatible with the values of a liberal political order, has been called a "tactic of pre-commitment." With pre-commitment, a term coined by political theorist Stephen Holmes, a community restricts its immediate freedom of action in order to protect what it regards as immutable (or longer-term) interests—much as Ulysses, before encountering the seductive call of the sirens, orders his sailors to bind him and to ignore his cries to deviate from the ship's established course. Of course, Ulysses's authority to "pre-commit" himself to these restrictions is relatively unproblematic, since he is responsible for his own long- and short-term desires. Holmes explores how this idea can be extended to the problem of how an earlier generation can bind a later, and so constitute a national people extending over time.

A second dilemma concerns how a constitution can be given effect—how, in James Madison's words, the "parchment barriers" of a written constitution can become something more than mere words, actively shaping and constraining government power. Our readings from the *Federalist Papers*—a series of essays by Alexander Hamilton and Madison explaining the virtues of the proposed American constitution—draw upon the ideas of the Baron de Montestquieu, who argued that separate, and to some extent rivalrous, government agencies could police each other's exercise of power, and so keep each other in check. In the American constitutional tradition, represented most famously by *Marbury vs Madison*, 5 U.S. (1 Cranch) 137 (1803), this principle was established through a doctrine of judicial supremacy in review, according to which the federal judiciary has final authority over the constitutional legality of the other branches' actions.

The American constitution's design, and Marshall's emphasis on judicial superiority, represent a significant but by no means definitive form of constitutionalism. Indeed, today, a Western European model of judicial "advice" and the supremacy of a legislative body (or a semi-judicial constitutional council) appears to be ascendant in new constitutions. Under either structure, however, the problem remains of how the judiciary ought to give meaning to fixed constitutional terms, while adapting them to changing circumstances. That jurisprudential problem, as much philosophical as legal, is the subject of Joseph Raz's contribution to this chapter. Raz's argument is complex and difficult to summarize, as is typical for this philosopher. In examining the legitimacy of constitutionalism and its implications for interpretation, Raz identifies the deep connections (as well as distinctions) between constitutional and moral reasoning. Along the way, he rejects the notions that constitutional jurisprudence is nothing but moral reasoning applied, and that any clear distinction can be drawn between statements of what constitutional law is and statements about how it ought to be developed or changed. While Raz's conclusions represent a distinctively American model of constitutionalism, they illuminate a great range of shared practices, including the universal insistence that constitutional reasoning must be *public*, capable of articulation and argument, as individual moral choice need not be. This final constraint, of publicity in decision-making, is arguably the most important feature of constitutionalism.

RIGHTS AND LIBERTY

Our discussion of constitutionalism has focused thus far on the structure of liberal democratic government, and how to preserve that structure against potentially ill-advised changes. We have not addressed the second signal feature of liberal states, usually embodied in their constitutions: their definition of the *rights* of their citizens against the state, and the broader conceptions they embody of people capable of governing themselves, both collectively and individually. Even in states that do not constitutionalize individual rights, such as Great Britain, talk of rights is pervasive. Indeed, justice is sometimes even thought to be entirely a matter of respecting rights. But what are rights?

It is sometimes suggested that rights and duties are just two sides of a coin: all rights have correlative duties, and all duties have correlative rights. In "The Nature and Value of Rights," Joel Feinberg argues that this is not so. The duty to stop at a red light, for example, is not owed to any particular individual or individuals, even though particular others are protected by and benefit from the duty to stop. Therefore, Feinberg asks, can we imagine a world full of duties but without any rights? What would be missing from such a world? The key to our notion of rights, he argues, is to be found in the activity of claiming. When I have a right, I have a ground for asserting certain claims against others. The right entails a correlative duty of others in relation to me, but—crucially—the right is prior to and more basic than the duty.

In a classic essay on rights, H. L. A. Hart questions whether there are natural rights—rights that human beings have qua human beings, not due to membership in some society or special standing vis-à-vis others. Hart claims that if there is one natural right that all people have, it is the right to be free. Finally, Jeremy Waldron dissects a common misconception about rights: the idea that to have a right to do something is tantamount to its being right to do that thing. The fallacy involved may be obvious: my having a speech right to say nasty things about you does not entail that I should do so, nor even that it is morally permissible, but only that it would be wrong for the state to interfere with my actions. But this distinction is nonetheless often elusive in political discussions. Waldron examines the idea of a "right to do wrong" in order to cast light both on the general nature of rights and rights claims, and to highlight the distinction between moral and political assessments and questions.

The nature of rights having been identified, the more urgent question concerns what rights do people in a liberal political order have? More generally, how broad is their liberty of action in relation to potential interference, and when can the presumption of liberty be overridden? This is not merely an abstract question addressed to and by philosophers. It is an unavoidable practical question faced by every democratic legislator. In effect, it is a question of the limits beyond which restrictive lawmaking is morally illegitimate.

John Stuart Mill gives the classic liberal answer to the question. Restricting the liberty of one citizen, he argues, can be justified only to prevent harm to others. We can refer to Mill's position as the "harm to others principle," or, more succinctly, the *harm principle*. Several things should be noted about this principle at the outset. First, by *harm*, Mill means not only direct personal injury such as broken bones or the loss of money, but also more diffuse social harms such as air pollution or the impairment of public institutions. Second, the principle does not propose a sufficient condition for the restriction of liberty, because some harms to others are too slight to outweigh the very real harm or danger involved in the restriction of liberty. Thus, in close cases, legislators must balance (a) the probable cost to the interests to be restricted by proposed coercive legislation *and* (b) the collateral costs of enforcing that legislation, against (c) the probable cost of harms that will be prevented by the proposed legislation. Only when the harms prevented by the statute are greater than the costs the statute will impose is the legislation justified. Finally, the harm principle can be interpreted as a restrictive claim about *reasons*. According to a libertarian understanding of the principle, only one kind of consideration is ever morally relevant to the justification of coercion, namely, that it is necessary to prevent harm to others. It is *never* a relevant reason that the conduct to be restricted is merely offensive (as opposed to harmful) or even that it is intrinsically immoral, nor is it relevant that coercion is necessary to prevent a person from harming himself or herself (as opposed to others).

Few would disagree that something along the lines of "harm prevention" is always *a* relevant reason for coercion (whether harm is taken on its own or as a factor restricting the legitimate exercise of personal sovereignty), but many disagree with the contention that it is the *only* relevant consideration. Thus, no one will seriously suggest that laws against battery, larceny, and homicide are unjustified, but many maintain that the state is also justified, at least in some circumstances, in prohibiting (1) actions that hurt or endanger the actor (the principle of legal paternalism), (2) "immoralities," even when they harm no one but their perpetrators (the principle of legal moralism), and (3) conduct that is offensive though not harmful to others (the offense principle).

These rival doctrines cannot easily be proved or refuted in the abstract. Rather, they are best judged by how faithfully they reflect, and how systematically they organize, our considered judgments in particular cases; for such principles, after all, purport to be explicit renderings of the axioms to which we are committed by the most confident judgments we make in everyday discourse about problems of liberty. The main areas of controversy in which such problems arise are those concerning unorthodox expressions of opinion, "morals offenses" in the criminal law (especially when committed in private by solitary individuals or among consenting adults), pornography and obscenity (especially when offered or displayed to the public or to nonconsenting individuals), activities that are harmful or dangerous to those who voluntarily engage in them (voluntary suicide and euthanasia), otherwise harmless invasions of others' privacy, and conscientious acts of civil disobedience.

The cautious theorist will therefore begin with Mill's harm principle as an account of at least one set of reasons that are always relevant in such controversies, and then apply it to the various problem areas to determine the extent, if any, to which it must be supplemented to provide solutions that are both plausible and consistent. In particular, we must decide, in each area, whether we need recourse to legal paternalism, legal moralism, or the offense principle.

In an analysis of paternalism, Gerald Dworkin considers, in a comprehensive and systematic way, whether paternalistic statutes (defined roughly as those interfering with a person's liberty "for his own good") are ever justified. He treats Mill's rejection of paternalism with respect but points out how widespread paternalistic restrictions are and how drastic their total elimination would be. Laws requiring hunters to wear red caps, and motorcyclists to wear helmets, or those requiring medical prescriptions for certain therapeutic drugs, for example, seem innocuous to most of us. Even more accepted are laws that protect children and incompetents from their own folly, or that may be seen as a kind of "social insurance" against impulsive, dangerous, or irreversible decisions. Dworkin then attempts to find criteria that can be used to separate unjustified paternalistic restrictions from those he thinks any rational person would welcome.

The subject of legal moralism (or the restriction of "victimless" acts on the basis of their inherent immorality) is the focus of the famous debate between Hart and Lord Patrick Devlin, a conservative British judge, concerning the proposal in 1957 by the Wolfenden Commission for Britain to decriminalize homosexual intercourse (a proposal adopted by the British Parliament in 1967). While the specifics may seem dated, the arguments of both Devlin and Hart recur today in debates about establishment of homosexual marriage, as we will see in our chapter on privacy and sexual intimacy. We focus on them here because of the clarity with which Devlin and Hart discuss the presuppositions of the claim that law ought to be used to enforce a society's conventional morality, simply because it is that society's conventional morality. Hart is generally acknowledged to have won the debate, by characterizing Devlin's position as committed to an unrealistic and undesirable conception of society as socially static. But Devlin provides an important articulation of the nature of a tradition, and of the threat ostensibly neutral liberal institutions pose to traditionalism itself as a political value, and not just to particular traditions.

FREEDOM OF EXPRESSION

An especially important application of these questions and principles involves speech and expression. There is no doubt that expressions of opinion, in speech or writing, can sometimes cause vast amounts of harm. Politicians sometimes advocate policies that would lead to disastrous consequences if adopted, and scientists sometimes defend theories that are false and detrimental to scientific progress. If we apply the harm principle in a straightforward, unqualified way—by prohibiting all particular expressions that seem, on the best evidence, likely to cause more harm than good—we might very well justify widespread infringements on what we should take to be a moral right of free speech. To avoid this embarrassing consequence, the partisan of the harm principle will have to propose subtle refinements and mediating norms for the application of this principle, balancing rival interests and social costs, and estimating probabilities, dangers, and risks.

One candidate is a so-called *offense principle* that treats nuisances and other offensive conduct as potentially subject to criminal sanction. Putatively offensive conduct often takes the form of "speech." But where are the boundaries of the offensive? Joel Feinberg provides thought experiment involving a bus ride gone awry to explore our intuitions in his article, "Offensive Nuisances." Ultimately, Feinberg reminds us of the centrality of our self-determination, and points to the boundaries between public and private as a potential key to the question of offense.

The United States has, of course, a distinctive tradition of protecting even profoundly offensive speech—a tradition seen most recently in the *Snyder v. Phelps* case of 2011 (562 U.S. ___; TK 131 S. Ct. 1207; 179 L. Ed. 2d 172), in which the Supreme Court protected the right of anti-gay protestors to picket dead soldiers' funerals with signs such as "God hates you" and "Fag troops."

A famous predecessor of this case is *Cohen v. California* in 1971.[1] Cohen was convicted of disturbing the peace by lingering in the corridors of a public building wearing a jacket emblazoned with the words "Fuck the Draft." In his appeal to the Supreme Court of California and later to the United States Supreme Court, Cohen claimed that his right to free speech, guaranteed by the First and Fourteenth Amendments, had been violated. The California authorities argued that they had properly applied against him a valid statute forbidding "willfully . . . offensive conduct."

There are two ways in which a written or a spoken statement can be offensive: it can express an opinion that some auditors might find offensive, or it can express an opinion in language that is itself offensive, independent of the substantive message it conveys. Neither the United States Constitution nor the libertarian principles of free expression of opinion espoused by Mill and Feinberg would permit legal interference with free speech in order to prevent the expression of an "offensive" opinion. However, restrictions on obscene, scurrilous, and incendiary words, quite apart from their role in the expression of unpopular opinion, might well be justified by the offense principle, and indeed by the Constitution itself, insofar as it tacitly employs the offense principle to mark out a class of exceptions to the free-speech guarantee.

Justice Harlan, however, rejected this approach in his majority opinion in *Cohen*. He argued that the free expression of opinion, protected by the Constitution, extends not merely to the proposition declared by a statement, but also to the speaker's (or writer's) emotions or the intensity of his or her attitudes—in the case at hand, "the depths of [Cohen's] feelings against the Vietnam War and the draft." Harlan's distinction points to an important function of what are ordinarily called obscene words: unseemly epithets can shock and jolt and, by virtue of their very character as socially unacceptable, give expression to intense feelings more accurately than any other words in the language. Thomas Scanlon's article attempts to give philosophical teeth to the doctrine announced by Harlan, of protecting the interests of the audience—we members of the political community—in deciding for ourselves what claims, political or otherwise, have merit and which should be rejected. Scanlon therefore sees the principles of freedom of expression as constitutive of the individual autonomy celebrated by Mill, an autonomy understood as the power to act on reasons one defines for oneself. Scanlon then wrestles with the limits of such principles, in regard to speech that is harmful in Mill's sense, such as a description of how to manufacture weapons of mass destruction, or the communication of criminal plans. Reconciling the attractiveness of such principles with their evident limitations is one of the main challenges of free speech theory.

Of course, the United States is not the only liberal state to struggle with the limits of offensive expression. With the advent of significant Muslim migration into Western European nations committed to a multicultural politics, and the rise of transnational tribunals such as the European Court of Human Rights, conflicts have arisen between freedom of expression and demands of respect for religious symbols. The most notable of recent conflicts involved the so-called "Danish Cartoons" published by a Danish newspaper, the *Jyllands-Posten*, in 2005. These cartoons, mostly of the Prophet Mohammed, were regarded by some Muslims, in Denmark and around the world, as deeply offensive, either simply by showing Mohammed—in defiance of an asserted Islamic prohibition on depicting the prophet at all—or by associating him with terrorism. Riots followed around the world, leaving at last 130 dead and the editor of the *Posten* shaken. Robert Post's article examines the arguments for and against prohibiting offense to religious believers, including whether, under the European law of human rights, the state could have restricted publication either on grounds of offense or public safety. While the legal answer in the U.S. is clear (the First Amendment would clearly prohibit such a restraint), Post's examination shows that the conception of liberal state legitimacy is more complex than one might assume, and reveals the range of defensible liberalisms.

DISTRIBUTIVE JUSTICE AND MATERIAL EQUALITY

We have so far explored several types of reasons why liberty might be limited by the state: to prevent harm or offense, or to enforce conventional morality. There are a variety of different ways of expressing the liberal commitment to liberty. The Millian tradition argues for a presumption in favor of liberty, limited by the harm principle. The basic idea is that the exercise of liberty is particularly valuable, and that because coercion interferes with liberty it requires justification. The harm principle expresses one kind of good reason for coercion. When the political morality of law is approached in this way, the question becomes whether there are other good reasons for interfering with individual liberty, and how those reasons ought to be balanced against liberty. This section focuses on two reasons for interfering with liberty: in order to reach the ideal of equality and in order to protect various personal rights.

Most versions of liberalism associate liberty with a commitment to equality as well; the problem of political philosophy is to determine the relationship between the two. John Rawls, in his landmark *A Theory of Justice* (1971), argues that a liberal state must be committed to both liberty and equality. Rawls develops his argument using a thought experiment he calls "the Original Position": asking what principles reasonable people would choose as a basis for a common government, if they did not know at the time of their choice how they in particular would benefit or be burdened by those principles. Such people choosing under a "veil of ignorance," Rawls argues, would select principles that would provide security against the worst sorts of deprivations—enslavement, denial of religious or expressive freedom, and material destitution. In particular, he argues, although the protection of civil liberties will take absolute priority over equality, a just society, having secured the liberties, should proceed towards an ambitious egalitarian ideal. This ideal is designed to ensure that social and economic inequalities be tolerated only on the grounds that any greater level of equality would leave the poorest of the community worse off—for example by reducing individual incentives for productive work. Our 1985 reading from Rawls, "Justice as Fairness: Political not Metaphysical," reintroduces *A Theory of Justice*'s argument for egalitarian justice in the distribution of goods, while also exploring what sorts of argument may and may not be offered for justice in a politically and morally diverse democratic community.

Rawls's argument in favor of equality is challenged in our readings in two different ways. Soon after the publication of *A Theory of Justice*, Robert Nozick offered the purported counterexample of Wilt Chamberlain, a popular basketball star of the era. Nozick argued that (the fictive) Chamberlain's great wealth, arising wholly from consensual transactions with individuals, could only be "rectified" by impermissible interference with the desires of the individuals who wish to see Wilt play. Thus, concludes Nozick, a demand for egalitarian distributions of wealth is in fundamental conflict with liberal commitments to free choice and the disposition of goods honestly acquired.

Harry Frankfurt, by contrast, argues against the value of economic equality itself as a moral ideal. In regard to distribution of resources, it is most important that everyone has *sufficient* resources, not that everyone has equal resources. Frankfurt notes that in addition to the problematic tension between equality and liberty, a misguided emphasis on the importance of equality is alienating to the individual. One becomes preoccupied with comparison of one's own situation to that of others, rather than reflecting internally about one's own desires and aspirations. Thus, Frankfurt concludes that an emphasis on economic equality results in "moral disorientation."

Frankfurt's view, along with Nozick's, is firmly challenged by Elizabeth Anderson, who argues that it is a mistake to focus only on the material dimension of equality. (Indeed, she concedes the force Frankfurt's critique would have against a purely material conception of equality). Instead, argues Anderson, the relevant dimension of equality is equality of respect: a liberal state should ensure that individuals (and social groups) enjoy material conditions sufficient to ensure their protection from oppression: "Its proper positive aim is not to ensure that everyone gets what they morally deserve, but to create a community in which people stand in relations of equality to others."

PRIVACY AND SEXUAL EQUALITY

The idea of a right to privacy made a major new entry into American constitutional law through the celebrated case of *Griswold v. Connecticut*, decided by the United States Supreme Court in 1965. The decision overturned a Connecticut statute making the use of contraceptives by any person a criminal offense. That statute was unconstitutional, Justice Douglas wrote, because it violated a right of marital privacy "older than the Bill of Rights" but included in the "penumbra" of the First, Fourth, Fifth, Eight, Ninth, and Fourteenth Amendments. A penumbra of a right is a set of further rights not explicitly guaranteed, but properly inferable from the primary right either as necessary means for its fulfillment or as implied by it in certain factual circumstances not necessarily foreseen by those who formulated it. Thus, the right to read whatever one wishes is in the penumbra of the right of free expression, if only because the latter, which is mentioned in the Constitution, would have little point if it existed without the former, which is not mentioned in the Constitution.

Similarly, the Constitution does not specifically spell out a right of marital privacy. Justice Goldberg, in his concurring opinion in *Griswold*, rested his case for marital privacy on the Ninth Amendment's reference to fundamental rights "retained by the people," and Justices Harlan and White in their concurring opinions derived the unconstitutionality of the anti-contraception statute from its "capriciousness, irrationality, and offensiveness to a sense of fairness and justice." The dissenters in *Griswold* (Justices Stewart and Black) suspected that such techniques could be used to find anything a judge thinks just and reasonable in the "penumbra" of a specific guarantee.

The doctrine of privacy applied by the majority opinions in *Griswold* affirms that there is a domain in which the individual's own choice must reign supreme. *Einstadt v. Baird* (1972) extended the right of marital privacy to individuals, married or single, allowing them to use contraceptives if they so choose and freeing them from governmental intrusion in an area that is their business alone. In *Loving v. Virginia* (1967), privacy was made the basis of a person's right to freely decide to marry a person of another race. In *Stanley v. Georgia* (1969), a right to view pornographic films or tapes in one's own home was also said to be implied by the fundamental right to privacy, and in *Roe v. Wade* (1973), a right to choose an abortion was similarly derived. Throughout this period, there was both controversy and confusion. The latter was caused, according to some critics, by a misnaming of the constitutional right in question. The relevant right, for these critics, is one of *autonomy* (self-government) in some fundamental areas of life, not *privacy*, which is quite another thing.

The most controversial of the "privacy" decisions has been the famous abortion case *Roe v. Wade*, which extended the right of privacy to a woman's autonomous choice of whether to terminate her pregnancy during the first two trimesters. Here a woman's autonomy had to be balanced against the state's growing interest in the potentiality of human life—an interest which, the court decided, can become dominant in the third trimester. Abortion is distinctive, if not unique, among other privacy issues in requiring courts and critics to consider not only moral principles and constitutional precedents, but also conceptual or metaphysical questions, such as "What is a person?" In *Planned Parenthood of Southeastern Pennsylvania v. Casey* (1992) the Court settled twenty years of intense controversy by explicitly upholding *Roe v. Wade*. In so doing, however, it kindled new quarrels by permitting more grounds for state regulation of abortions—even to the point of placing a substantial obstacle in the path of a woman seeking an abortion during the first two trimesters. Thus, another constitutional criterion was born: the "undue burden standard," which permits legislatures to regulate privacy rights only up to a point. Beyond that point, according to the standard, the burden placed on a woman bent on exercising her constitutional privacy right becomes an undue burden.

The discussion over a right of privacy took a different turn in 2003, when the Supreme Court overturned a Texas statute prohibiting deviate sexual conduct, including homosexual sodomy. But it did not do so on grounds of a right to privacy—as had previously been the issue in *Bowers v. Hardwick* (1986), in which a Georgia law prohibiting sodomy was *not* overturned after it was decided that there was no constitutional privacy right to engage in homosexual conduct. Rather, the decision in *Lawrence v. Texas*, as with *Casey*, was based on *liberty*. The central feature in the decision is the importance of the freedom to live one's life as one chooses, to be able—in *Casey's* poetic if vague words—to "to define one's own concept of existence, of meaning, of the universe, and of the mystery of human life."

Since *Lawrence* established consensual sexual intimacy as a zone free from state interference, the issue of gay equality and status has shifted to the question of whether gays have a right to marry, where marriage includes not just incidental rights, privileges, and tax status, but application of the particular ceremonial term of marriage to a union between romantic partners. This is now fully a debate not about privacy (since a public status is at issue), nor about liberty (since civil partnerships conferring equivalent rights are available in some states even where marriage is not), but about equal status. The debate, however, has varied only in its specific application, not in its fundamental terms. For religious and political conservatives, such as Justice Antonin Scalia (dissenting in *Casey* and *Lawrence*) and for Robert George, these sexual privacy–liberty–equality cases were decided in error—for they use a denatured concept of liberty to deny the rights of political majorities to establish fundamental moral precepts for their communities. (George has a different argument against majority-led legislative efforts to permit gay marriage.) George's fundamental target is the conception of political liberalism defined by Rawls in his later work, where (among other things) Rawls argued that a liberal state containing a diversity of individual and collective moral and religious views must not exercise coercive power over certain fundamental matters on the basis of sectarian beliefs—even those of a majority. Public power must be wielded only on the basis of reasons that could be common to all members of the community, regardless of their faith or moral outlook, drawing on such shared threads in a liberal polity as a commitment to equality, reciprocal respect, and liberty of conscience. The effect of this restriction of what Rawls called "public reasons," George argues, is to deny to religious members of a community the opportunity to promote those reasons most resonant to them, and thus to privilege ostensibly neutral but substantively partisan liberal views in the public sphere. George's point in this reading is not to insist on the wrongness of gay marriage or sexual intimacy; it is instead to insist on the legitimacy, in democratic debate, of voices that seek to deny gay equality on the basis of traditional views.

In his contribution to the chapter, Leslie Green tries to move past the old debate about minority status equality versus democratic rights, and asks the question whether marriage (now) need be considered to be about sexual intimacy at all. As he points out, two *heterosexual* persons of the same sex can now marry in the states that permit same-sex marriage, just as two gay individuals of different sexes have always been able to marry in states that prohibit gay marriage. Marriage does not or should not, as a legal matter, entail an obligation to have sexual relations with one's marital partner. By shifting the debate about marriage from sexual equality to sex equality, Green hopes to help us move towards a *demoralization* of marriage, and towards more fertile ground for legal and political argument.

FAIRNESS VS. WELFARE

Our final readings in the morality of liberal democratic communities return to perhaps the most fundamental issue concerning the state's basic purpose: should the state aim to ensure fair treatment of individuals at the expense of overall welfare, or should overall welfare be the goal? For example, our system of accident law tends to protect the actual market value of people's goods, even if those goods are much more valuable than average; it is usually much more expensive to crash into a BMW than a Chevrolet. One can argue that such policies are wasteful, and that it would be more efficient (and would better conserve society's resources) if the owners of expensive cars had to pay extra insurance for accidents that are not their fault—just as they have to pay more to insure against faultless damage to their cars. But such a rule might be seen as *unfair* to the BMW owner whose car is wrecked through someone else's lousy driving. Why should she have to pay more for the consequences of someone else's mistake, just because she chose to purchase a more expensive car? Similarly, if one could show that overtime parking could be discouraged by a rare but extremely severe punishment for it, is there any fundamental objection to such a policy, given that it would make parking easier for many, many people?

The case for focusing on general welfare is powerfully made by two economists, Lewis Kaplow and Steven Shavell, on both economic and philosophical grounds. They argue that aggregate individual welfare—understood in such a way that it can include individual "tastes" for fairness—is the basic coin of political argument. Jules Coleman argues that Kaplow and Shavell's view rests on a mistake: By assimilating the value of fairness into the list of items that make up an individual's welfare, they have, in fact, confused a tautological statement about what it is to be a value with a substantive claim that welfare (understood as getting what one values) is more fundamental than fairness. (Alternatively, Coleman suggests, they may mistakenly think that fairness intuitions can be explained away by evolutionary biology, while welfarist intuitions are simply correct.) Coleman offers an alternative way to understand the values of welfare and fairness, in terms of the basic normative interests of individuals in a liberal political community.

Taken together, the essays in this section aim to sketch the debates that a liberal democratic community, committed to the dignity of its members, must have. As we have seen, the principles of a liberal democratic state constitute a family of related ideas, but a family (like any actual family) whose members can often stand in tense relations with one anther. The commitment of orderly politics can interfere with the self-governance of an existing democratic majority, the protection of the autonomy of some can conflict with the protection from harm of others. The problem of managing these tensions is perhaps *the* problem of legal philosophy for a democratic state.

NOTES

1. See, for an extended discussion, Raz, J. *The Morality of Freedom*. Oxford: Clarendon Press, 1986. pt I; and Raz, J. *Ethics in the Public Domain*. Rev. edn. Oxford: Clarendon Press, 1995. essays 9 and 10.

CHAPTER NINE

Constitutionalism

29   The Federalist Papers

Federalist No. 48

These Departments Should Not Be So Far Separated as to Have No Constitutional Control Over Each Other

JAMES MADISON

To the People of the State of New York:

IT WAS shown in the last paper that the political apothegm there examined does not require that the legislative, executive, and judiciary departments should be wholly unconnected with each other. I shall undertake, in the next place, to show that unless these departments be so far connected and blended as to give to each a constitutional control over the others, the degree of separation which the maxim requires, as essential to a free government, can never in practice be duly maintained. It is agreed on all sides, that the powers properly belonging to one of the departments ought not to be directly and completely administered by either of the other departments. It is equally evident, that none of them ought to possess, directly or indirectly, an overruling influence over the others, in the administration of their respective powers. It will not be denied, that power is of an encroaching nature, and that it ought to be effectually restrained from passing the limits assigned to it.

After discriminating, therefore, in theory, the several classes of power, as they may in their nature be legislative, executive, or judiciary, the next and most difficult task is to provide some practical security for each, against the invasion of the others. What this security ought to be, is the great problem to be solved. Will it be sufficient to mark, with precision, the boundaries of these departments, in the constitution of the government, and to trust to these parchment barriers against the encroaching spirit of power? This is the security which appears to have been principally relied on by the compilers of most of the American constitutions. But experience assures us, that the

From the New York Packet. Friday, February 1, 1788.

efficacy of the provision has been greatly over-rated; and that some more adequate defense is indispensably necessary for the more feeble, against the more powerful, members of the government. The legislative department is everywhere extending the sphere of its activity, and drawing all power into its impetuous vortex. The founders of our republics have so much merit for the wisdom which they have displayed, that no task can be less pleasing than that of pointing out the errors into which they have fallen. A respect for truth, however, obliges us to remark, that they seem never for a moment to have turned their eyes from the danger to liberty from the over-grown and all-grasping prerogative of an hereditary magistrate, supported and fortified by an hereditary branch of the legislative authority. They seem never to have recollected the danger from legislative usurpations, which, by assembling all power in the same hands, must lead to the same tyranny as is threatened by executive usurpations. In a government where numerous and extensive prerogatives are placed in the hands of an hereditary monarch, the executive department is very justly regarded as the source of danger, and watched with all the jealousy which a zeal for liberty ought to inspire. In a democracy, where a multitude of people exercise in person the legislative functions, and are continually exposed, by their incapacity for regular deliberation and concerted measures, to the ambitious intrigues of their executive magistrates, tyranny may well be apprehended, on some favorable emergency, to start up in the same quarter. But in a representative republic, where the executive magistracy is carefully limited; both in the extent and the duration of its power; and where the legislative power is exercised by an assembly, which is inspired, by a supposed influence over the people, with an intrepid confidence in its own strength; which is sufficiently numerous to feel all the passions which actuate a multitude, yet not so numerous as to be incapable of pursuing the objects of its passions, by means which reason prescribes; it is against the enterprising ambition of this department that the people ought to indulge all their jealousy and exhaust all their precautions. The legislative department derives a superiority in our governments

from other circumstances. Its constitutional powers being at once more extensive, and less susceptible of precise limits, it can, with the greater facility, mask, under complicated and indirect measures, the encroachments which it makes on the co-ordinate departments. It is not unfrequently a question of real nicety in legislative bodies, whether the operation of a particular measure will, or will not, extend beyond the legislative sphere. On the other side, the executive power being restrained within a narrower compass, and being more simple in its nature, and the judiciary being described by landmarks still less uncertain, projects of usurpation by either of these departments would immediately betray and defeat themselves. Nor is this all: as the legislative department alone has access to the pockets of the people, and has in some constitutions full discretion, and in all a prevailing influence, over the pecuniary rewards of those who fill the other departments, a dependence is thus created in the latter, which gives still greater facility to encroachments of the former. I have appealed to our own experience for the truth of what I advance on this subject. Were it necessary to verify this experience by particular proofs, they might be multiplied without end. I might find a witness in every citizen who has shared in, or been attentive to, the course of public administrations. I might collect vouchers in abundance from the records and archives of every State in the Union. But as a more concise, and at the same time equally satisfactory, evidence, I will refer to the example of two States, attested by two unexceptionable authorities. The first example is that of Virginia, a State which, as we have seen, has expressly declared in its constitution, that the three great departments ought not to be intermixed. The authority in support of it is Mr. Jefferson, who, besides his other advantages for remarking the operation of the government, was himself the chief magistrate of it. In order to convey fully the ideas with which his experience had impressed him on this subject, it will be necessary to quote a passage of some length from his very interesting "Notes on the State of Virginia," p. 195:

> All the powers of government, legislative, executive, and judiciary, result to the legislative body. The concentrating these in the same hands, is pre-

cisely the definition of despotic government. It will be no alleviation, that these powers will be exercised by a plurality of hands, and not by a single one. One hundred and seventy-three despots would surely be as oppressive as one. Let those who doubt it, turn their eyes on the republic of Venice. As little will it avail us, that they are chosen by ourselves. An ELECTIVE DESPOTISM was not the government we fought for; but one which should not only be founded on free principles, but in which the powers of government should be so divided and balanced among several bodies of magistracy, as that no one could transcend their legal limits, without being effectually checked and restrained by the others.

For this reason, that convention which passed the ordinance of government, laid its foundation on this basis, that the legislative, executive, and judiciary departments should be separate and distinct, so that no person should exercise the powers of more than one of them at the same time. BUT NO BARRIER WAS PROVIDED BETWEEN THESE SEVERAL POWERS. The judiciary and the executive members were left dependent on the legislative for their subsistence in office, and some of them for their continuance in it. If, therefore, the legislature assumes executive and judiciary powers, no opposition is likely to be made; nor, if made, can be effectual; because in that case they may put their proceedings into the form of acts of Assembly, which will render them obligatory on the other branches. They have accordingly, IN MANY instances, DECIDED RIGHTS which should have been left to JUDICIARY CONTROVERSY, and THE DIRECTION OF THE EXECUTIVE, DURING THE WHOLE TIME OF THEIR SESSION, IS BECOMING HABITUAL AND FAMILIAR.

The other State which I shall take for an example is Pennsylvania; and the other authority, the Council of Censors, which assembled in the years 1783 and 1784. A part of the duty of this body, as marked out by the constitution, was "to inquire whether the constitution had been preserved inviolate in every part; and whether the legislative and executive branches of government had performed their duty as guardians of the people, or assumed to themselves, or exercised, other or greater powers than they are entitled to by the constitution." In the execution of this trust, the council were necessarily led to a comparison of both the legislative and executive proceedings, with the constitutional powers of these departments; and from the facts enumerated, and to the truth of most of which both sides in the council subscribed, it appears that the constitution had been flagrantly violated by the legislature in a variety of important instances. A great number of laws had been passed, violating, without any apparent necessity, the rule requiring that all bills of a public nature shall be previously printed for the consideration of the people; although this is one of the precautions chiefly relied on by the constitution against improper acts of legislature. The constitutional trial by jury had been violated, and powers assumed which had not been delegated by the constitution.

Executive powers had been usurped. The salaries of the judges, which the constitution expressly requires to be fixed, had been occasionally varied; and cases belonging to the judiciary department frequently drawn within legislative cognizance and determination. Those who wish to see the several particulars falling under each of these heads, may consult the journals of the council, which are in print. Some of them, it will be found, may be imputable to peculiar circumstances connected with the war; but the greater part of them may be considered as the spontaneous shoots of an ill-constituted government. It appears, also, that the executive department had not been innocent of frequent breaches of the constitution. There are three observations, however, which ought to be made on this head: FIRST, a great proportion of the instances were either immediately produced by the necessities of the war, or recommended by Congress or the commander-in-chief; SECONDLY, in most of the other instances, they conformed either to the declared or the known sentiments of the legislative department; THIRDLY, the executive department of Pennsylvania is distinguished from that of the other States by the number of members composing it. In this respect, it has as much affinity to a legislative assembly as to an executive council. And being at once exempt from the restraint of an individual responsibility for the acts of the body, and deriving confidence from mutual example and joint influence, unauthorized measures would, of course, be more freely hazarded, than where the executive department is administered by a single hand, or by a few hands.

The conclusion which I am warranted in drawing from these observations is, that a mere demarcation on parchment of the constitutional limits of the several departments, is not a sufficient guard against those encroachments which lead to a tyrannical concentration of all the powers of government in the same hands.

PUBLIUS.

30   The Federalist Papers

Federalist No. 51

The Structure of the Government Must Furnish the Proper Checks and Balances Between the Different Departments

---

ALEXANDER HAMILTON OR JAMES MADISON

To the People of the State of New York:

TO WHAT expedient, then, shall we finally resort, for maintaining in practice the necessary partition of power among the several departments, as laid down in the Constitution? The only answer that can be given is, that as all these exterior provisions are found to be inadequate, the defect must be supplied, by so contriving the interior structure of the government as that its several constituent parts may, by their mutual relations, be the means of keeping each other in their proper places. Without presuming to undertake a full development of this important idea, I will hazard a few general observations, which may perhaps place it in a clearer light, and enable us to form a more correct judgment of the principles and structure of the government planned by the convention.

In order to lay a due foundation for that separate and distinct exercise of the different powers of government, which to a certain extent is admitted on all hands to be essential to the preservation of liberty, it is evident that each department should have a will of its own; and consequently should be so constituted that the members of each should have as little agency as possible in the appointment of the members of the others. Were this principle rigorously adhered to, it would require that all the appointments for the supreme executive, legislative, and judiciary magistracies should be drawn from the same fountain of authority, the people, through channels having no communication whatever with one another. Perhaps such a plan of constructing the several departments would be less difficult in practice than it may in contemplation appear. Some difficulties, however, and some additional expense would attend the execution of it. Some deviations, therefore, from the principle must be admitted. In the constitution of the judiciary department in particular, it might be inexpedient to insist rigorously on the principle: first, because peculiar qualifications being essential in the members, the primary consideration ought to be to select that mode of choice which best secures these qualifications; secondly, because the permanent tenure by which the appointments are held in that department, must soon destroy all sense of dependence on the authority conferring them.

It is equally evident, that the members of each department should be as little dependent as possible on those of the others, for the emoluments

From the Independent Journal. Wednesday, February 6, 1788.

annexed to their offices. Were the executive magistrate, or the judges, not independent of the legislature in this particular, their independence in every other would be merely nominal.

But the great security against a gradual concentration of the several powers in the same department, consists in giving to those who administer each department the necessary constitutional means and personal motives to resist encroachments of the others. The provision for defense must in this, as in all other cases, be made commensurate to the danger of attack. Ambition must be made to counteract ambition. The interest of the man must be connected with the constitutional rights of the place. It may be a reflection on human nature, that such devices should be necessary to control the abuses of government. But what is government itself, but the greatest of all reflections on human nature? If men were angels, no government would be necessary. If angels were to govern men, neither external nor internal controls on government would be necessary. In framing a government which is to be administered by men over men, the great difficulty lies in this: you must first enable the government to control the governed; and in the next place oblige it to control itself. A dependence on the people is, no doubt, the primary control on the government; but experience has taught mankind the necessity of auxiliary precautions.

This policy of supplying, by opposite and rival interests, the defect of better motives, might be traced through the whole system of human affairs, private as well as public. We see it particularly displayed in all the subordinate distributions of power, where the constant aim is to divide and arrange the several offices in such a manner as that each may be a check on the other that the private interest of every individual may be a sentinel over the public rights. These inventions of prudence cannot be less requisite in the distribution of the supreme powers of the State.

But it is not possible to give to each department an equal power of self-defense. In republican government, the legislative authority necessarily predominates. The remedy for this inconveniency is to divide the legislature into different branches; and to render them, by different modes of election

and different principles of action, as little connected with each other as the nature of their common functions and their common dependence on the society will admit. It may even be necessary to guard against dangerous encroachments by still further precautions. As the weight of the legislative authority requires that it should be thus divided, the weakness of the executive may require, on the other hand, that it should be fortified. An absolute negative on the legislature appears, at first view, to be the natural defense with which the executive magistrate should be armed. But perhaps it would be neither altogether safe nor alone sufficient. On ordinary occasions it might not be exerted with the requisite firmness, and on extraordinary occasions it might be perfidiously abused. May not this defect of an absolute negative be supplied by some qualified connection between this weaker department and the weaker branch of the stronger department, by which the latter may be led to support the constitutional rights of the former, without being too much detached from the rights of its own department?

If the principles on which these observations are founded be just, as I persuade myself they are, and they be applied as a criterion to the several State constitutions, and to the federal Constitution it will be found that if the latter does not perfectly correspond with them, the former are infinitely less able to bear such a test.

There are, moreover, two considerations particularly applicable to the federal system of America, which place that system in a very interesting point of view.

First. In a single republic, all the power surrendered by the people is submitted to the administration of a single government; and the usurpations are guarded against by a division of the government into distinct and separate departments. In the compound republic of America, the power surrendered by the people is first divided between two distinct governments, and then the portion allotted to each subdivided among distinct and separate departments. Hence a double security arises to the rights of the people. The different governments will control each other, at the same time that each will be controlled by itself.

Second. It is of great importance in a republic not only to guard the society against the oppression of its rulers, but to guard one part of the society against the injustice of the other part. Different interests necessarily exist in different classes of citizens. If a majority be united by a common interest, the rights of the minority will be insecure. There are but two methods of providing against this evil: the one by creating a will in the community independent of the majority that is, of the society itself; the other, by comprehending in the society so many separate descriptions of citizens as will render an unjust combination of a majority of the whole very improbable, if not impracticable. The first method prevails in all governments possessing an hereditary or self-appointed authority. This, at best, is but a precarious security; because a power independent of the society may as well espouse the unjust views of the major, as the rightful interests of the minor party, and may possibly be turned against both parties. The second method will be exemplified in the federal republic of the United States. Whilst all authority in it will be derived from and dependent on the society, the society itself will be broken into so many parts, interests, and classes of citizens, that the rights of individuals, or of the minority, will be in little danger from interested combinations of the majority. In a free government the security for civil rights must be the same as that for religious rights. It consists in the one case in the multiplicity of interests, and in the other in the multiplicity of sects. The degree of security in both cases will depend on the number of interests and sects; and this may be presumed to depend on the extent of country and number of people comprehended under the same government. This view of the subject must particularly recommend a proper federal system to all the sincere and considerate friends of republican government, since it shows that in exact proportion as the territory of the Union may be formed into more circumscribed Confederacies, or States oppressive combinations of a majority will be facilitated: the best security, under the republican forms, for the rights of every class of citizens, will be diminished: and consequently the stability and independence of some member of the government, the only other security, must be proportionately increased. Justice is the end of government. It is the end of civil society. It ever has been and ever will be pursued until it be obtained, or until liberty be lost in the pursuit. In a society under the forms of which the stronger faction can readily unite and oppress the weaker, anarchy may as truly be said to reign as in a state of nature, where the weaker individual is not secured against the violence of the stronger; and as, in the latter state, even the stronger individuals are prompted, by the uncertainty of their condition, to submit to a government which may protect the weak as well as themselves; so, in the former state, will the more powerful factions or parties be gradually induced, by a like motive, to wish for a government which will protect all parties, the weaker as well as the more powerful. It can be little doubted that if the State of Rhode Island was separated from the Confederacy and left to itself, the insecurity of rights under the popular form of government within such narrow limits would be displayed by such reiterated oppressions of factious majorities that some power altogether independent of the people would soon be called for by the voice of the very factions whose misrule had proved the necessity of it. In the extended republic of the United States, and among the great variety of interests, parties, and sects which it embraces, a coalition of a majority of the whole society could seldom take place on any other principles than those of justice and the general good; whilst there being thus less danger to a minor from the will of a major party, there must be less pretext, also, to provide for the security of the former, by introducing into the government a will not dependent on the latter, or, in other words, a will independent of the society itself. It is no less certain than it is important, notwithstanding the contrary opinions which have been entertained, that the larger the society, provided it lie within a practical sphere, the more duly capable it will be of self-government. And happily for the REPUBLICAN CAUSE, the practicable sphere may be carried to a very great extent, by a judicious modification and mixture of the FEDERAL PRINCIPLE.

PUBLIUS.

31   Between Authority and Interpretation

JOSEPH RAZ

I. WHAT KIND OF CONSTITUTION?

The writings on constitutional theory fill libraries. They are often presented as, and almost invariably are, writings on the constitutional practice of one country or another.

Whether they offer an analysis of current practices, doctrines that may justify them or critiques of these practices, or suggestions for their improvement, they are valid, if at all, against the background of the political and constitutional arrangements of one country or another, valid for the interpretation of the constitution of one country or another. Few writings on constitutional interpretation successfully address problems in full generality; that is, few offer useful lessons regarding the nature of constitutional interpretation as such. In part this is explained by the ambition of writers on interpretation. Whether or not they mean their writings to provide an account of current interpretive practices in their countries, they almost invariably aim to provide an account of how constitutional interpretation should be carried out, an account of the correct method of constitutional interpretation. They also aim to present their conclusions in a form that will be usable by lawyers and judges, and therefore in a form that shuns very abstract formulations that presuppose much for their interpretation and application. They aspire to help with the solution to important constitutional problems facing their countries, and these aspirations limit the relevance of their conclusions to one jurisdiction, or a few similar ones.

But possibly it is not their underlying aspirations that limit the validity of most writings on constitutional interpretation. Possibly there is no room for a truly universal theory of the subject. After all, the law, including constitutional law,

can vary from country to country, and from period to period even in one country. Even the most basic understanding of the constitution and its role in the life and law of a country may be different in different countries. How can there be a theory of constitutional interpretation that spans all these differences?

Up to a point these doubts are well founded. A powerful case can be made to the effect that a substantive theory of constitutions and of constitutionalism has limited application. Its application is to some countries and to some constitutions only. One reason is that the notion of "a constitution" is used in legal discourse sometimes in a thin sense and sometimes in a variety of thicker senses. In the thin sense it is tautological that every legal system includes a constitution. For in that sense the constitution is simply the law that establishes and regulates the main organs of government, their constitution and powers, and ipso facto it includes law that establishes the general principles under which the country is governed: democracy, if it establishes democratic organs of government; federalism, if it establishes a federal structure; and so on.

The thick sense of "constitution" is less clear, and probably there are several such senses in use in different legal cultures. For the purposes of the present discussion I will regard constitutions as defined by a combination of seven features.

First, incorporating the thin sense, the constitution defines the constitution and powers of the main organs of the different branches of government. (This feature identifies the constitution as *constitutive* of the legal and political structure that is that legal system.)

Second, it is, and is meant to be, of long duration: It is meant to serve as a stable framework for the political and legal institutions of the

Reprinted from *Between Authority and Interpretation* by Joseph Raz (New York: Oxford University Press, 2009).

country, to be adjusted and amended from time to time, but basically to preserve stability and continuity in the legal and political structure, and the basic principles that guide its institutions. (The constitution is *stable*, at least in aspiration.)

Third, it has a canonical formulation. That usually means that it is enshrined in one or a small number of written documents. It (they) is (are) commonly referred to as the constitution. (The constitution—we say when referring to this feature—is *written*.)

Fourth, it constitutes a superior law. This means that ordinary law that conflicts with the constitution is invalid or inapplicable. (The constitution is *superior law*.)

Fifth, there are judicial procedures to implement the superiority of the constitution, that is judicial processes by which the compatibility of rules of law and of other legal acts with the constitution can be tested, and incompatible rules or legal acts can be declared inapplicable or invalid. (The constitution is *justiciable*.)

Sixth, while there usually are legal procedures for constitutional amendment, constitutional amendments are legally more difficult to secure than ordinary legislation. (The constitution is *entrenched*.)

Seventh, its provisions include principles of government (democracy, federalism, basic civil and political rights, etc) that are generally held to express the common beliefs of the population about the way their society should be governed. It serves, you may say, not only as a lawyers' law, but as the people's law. Its main provisions are generally known, command general consent, and are held to be the (or part of the) common ideology that governs public life in that country. (The constitution expresses a *common ideology*.)

This characterization of a constitution (in the thick sense) yields a vague concept. Each one of the seven criteria is vague in application. To give but one example: Is it a condition of a country having a written constitution (condition 3) that there cannot be an "unwritten" part of the constitution—for example, a part that is "customary law"? And if the written-constitution condition is compatible with part of the constitution being unwritten, does it follow that Britain has a written constitution? Remember that although some of its constitution (in the thin sense) is customary or common law, part of it (e.g. the Bill of Rights of 1689, the Act of Union between England and Scotland of 1706, the European Communities Act of 1971) is written law. We know that in the relevant sense Britain does not have a written constitution. But that does not clearly follow from the characterization given, which is vague on the point.

But then the characterization is not meant to draw borderlines, but to focus discussion. Its purpose is to highlight the central features of constitutions—in (one) thick sense—features that explain why (some) constitutions (i.e. constitutions in this thick sense) give rise to theoretical questions that do not apply, at least not to the same degree, to other law. This chapter will consider some questions relating to constitutions in this sense. Some of the questions, even some of the answers, apply to constitutions that meet only some of the specified conditions, or meet them only to some degree. Indeed, some of them apply to ordinary (i.e. nonconstitutional) law as well. But it is useful to discuss them in the constitutional context, and we will not be concerned with the degree to which the problems or their solutions apply elsewhere.

There would be little point in investigating in general terms thick constitutions wherever they are were it not the case that they play a major role in the life of more and more countries. Clearly, not all countries have a constitution in this sense. Britain today and the Roman Empire of old are but two examples of countries that do or did not. The absence of a constitution (in the strong sense) may be due to a variety of factors. One is that the country enjoys a level of political consensus that makes a constitution unnecessary. Such consensus means that everyone knows and accepts the framework of government, the distribution of powers among its organs, and the general principles guiding or constraining the exercise of governmental powers. These are, if you like, matters of understood conventions, with no mechanisms for their enforcement. A consensus of this kind can exist in a small country with a relatively homogeneous and stable population, enjoying relative equality of status and a stable economy. But it can also exist in a large country with a diverse population marked by considerable social and economic stratification, if it is based on a culture of deference and enjoys stable social, demographic, and economic conditions.

Constitutions in the strong sense tend to exist in societies that enjoy relative stability within diversity and change. Such societies must have stability and a sense of a common identity sufficient to ensure the durability and stability of the constitution itself. But being large-scale societies, with many divisions of, for example, religion, class, and ethnic origin, they need the assurance of publicly accountable government, guided by openly administered principles, to strengthen the stability of the political structures and the authority of their legal institutions. A tempting suggestion is that the way to construct a theory of the authority and the proper interpretation of the (thick) constitution is to explore further the social, cultural, and economic conditions that justify it. Surely they hold the clues to an understanding of the nature and function of the constitution and therefore to its authority and interpretation. But the suggestion is misguided. No doubt such an inquiry will be very valuable. It will not, however, yield the hoped-for results. It assumes that the law, constitutional law at the very least, develops exclusively in response to the relatively stable aspects of the social conditions of the country to which it applies. As we know, this is far too rationalistic a view of the development of the law. Much of it depends on the ambitions of powerful personages, the political convenience of the hour. Fluctuating public moods and even temporary economic turns can lead to changes that remain in force many years after the conditions that led to them are forgotten.

Nor are matters any different with constitutions. The thought that their "higher status" and their propensity for longevity make them responsive only to fundamental and lasting social conditions or social trends is mistaken. In 1995, to give but one example, influential voices in the British Labour Party called on it to put constitutional reform at the centre of its platform, because the economic situation in the country seemed to be

improving and might favour the Conservative government in the forthcoming election. Similarly, it is arguable that the courts in Britain would not have been so active between the late 1980s and the mid-1990s in developing new doctrines in public law, leading to a series of humiliating defeats for the government, but for the fact that the Conservatives had been in power for 17 years, meeting very little effective parliamentary opposition. Constitutional politics may not be the same as parliamentary politics, but they are not altogether separate either. Similar examples can be found in the history of other countries, including those with a constitution in the strong sense. Moreover, in our ever-contracting world the adoption of constitutions, and the way they develop, often owes more to fashion than to principle. Certain ways of understanding the constitution become fashionable, perhaps because of the prestige of the country that initiated them. It becomes politically expedient to follow fashion. More than we often like to admit is owed to this factor.

It may be objected that none of these facts matters to constitutional theory, which is a normative theory and therefore unaffected by mere contingencies. In a sense to be explored, a constitutional theory is normative. But that does not mean that it is or should be blind to the basic realities of life. That the adoption and development of constitutions are affected by a variety of short-term factors is no mere aberration in the life of one country or another. It is a universal feature of the political life of all countries with a constitution. Constitutional theory had better allow for that. A theory that condemns all such influences as aberrations to be avoided is too remote from this world to be much use in it.

We will have to come back to this point and explore it further. While the main exploration will have to await a more detailed discussion of the normativity of constitutional theory, we can begin here by making one relevant observation: A good deal of legal development (and this includes constitutional development) is autonomous. This means that its traditions crystallize into practices that are followed in decisions which develop constitutional law. These traditions may be informed by valid considerations, such as concern for the efficiency of government, or for the dignity of individuals, or for the relative autonomy of different regions. But the crucial point is that these considerations do not determine the outcome of the decisions they influence. These considerations will be respected by a variety of constitutional decisions. The decision actually taken is chosen out of habit, or out of respect for the constitutional practices and traditions of that country.

If that is right, and if the autonomous legal traditions of different countries rightly play a major part in determining their constitutional development, then a theory of the constitution cannot be based on social or economic or cultural factors. It cannot be derived from extraneous circumstances. It must allow a major role to internal legal considerations. Therefore, the reflections on a constitutional theory offered here proceed by examining the abstract central features of a constitution, the seven enumerated earlier and some of their implications. The theory abstracts from the possible impact of social conditions, for I assume that they will differ from country to country. I hope, however, that a theory of the constitution will provide the theoretical framework within which the effect of diverse social conditions can be assessed.

I believe that most of what needs saying about the nature of constitutions has already been said. This does not mean, of course, that matters are relatively clear and settled. The problem is not so much that the truth is elusive or obscure and has not yet been seen by anyone, as that a variety of misleading analogies helped lend plausibility to some misguided ideas. I will spend much of this chapter trying to explain why we should not listen to some false sirens.

We can start, though, by recalling one principle that seems to be common ground to many approaches to constitutional studies: Constitutional theory comprises two major parts, an account of the authority of constitutions and an account of the way constitutions should be interpreted. The first explains under what conditions the constitution of a country is legitimate, thus fixing the condition under which citizens have a duty to obey it. In doing that, it provides an account of the principles of political morality that underpin the constitution, in that they justify and legitimize its enforcement, if it is indeed justified. The theory of constitutional interpretation explains the ways the principles of constitutional interpretation in different countries are determined. A principle of constitutional theory that commands widespread support says that the principles of constitutional interpretation depend in part on the theory of constitutional authority. In determining the conditions for constitutional legitimacy, the theory of the authority of the constitution contributes to the determination of principles of interpretation. Unfortunately, this sound principle is also the source of many false analogies motivated by attempts to assimilate the authority of the constitution to that of other parts of the law.

II. THE AUTHORITY OF CONSTITUTIONS

A. The Authority of the Constitution and the Authority of Its Authors

It is tempting to think that the authority of law, of any law, derives from the authority of its maker. Customary law is allowed to be a puzzling exception. But consider enacted law—that is, law whose validity derives from the fact that it was made by a legitimate legal authority acting with the intention to make law. The paradigm example of this kind of law is statutes. They are valid because they were passed by a body authorized in law to pass them. If, for example, the legal validity of a regulation is impugned on the ground that the body that enacted it had no legal power to do so, the charge cannot be repulsed by a claim, however justified, that the rule the regulation embodies is nevertheless legally binding because it is a good rule, one that would be sensible to follow. This does not mean that the merits of rules are irrelevant to legal reasoning. In appropriate contexts, such considerations can guide the interpretation of a statute or regulation whose legal validity is established on other grounds. In some contexts, the merits of having a rule of a certain kind may also justify the courts in adopting it and basing their decision on it, even if this requires overriding existing legal rules. The merit of a rule may also be grounds for giving it binding force, either through the courts, by turning it into a binding precedent, or by legislation. But the merit of a rule is not the sort of consideration which can establish that it is already legally binding.

I belabour this familiar point to bring out the fact, itself obvious, that the identity of the lawmaker is material to the validity of the law, at least in the case of enacted law. It is plausible to think that only if the identity of the lawmaker is the reason for the validity of the law can one make sense of this feature of enacted law. The fact that the law was made by that person or institution provides, on this view, the justification (at least at one level of justification) for holding the enacted rule to be valid in law. That means that with enacted law the authority of the law derives from the authority of its maker.

This is a powerful argument for the claim that the authority of constitutions derives from the authority of their makers. The argument is not that there is no other way in which law can have authority. Customary law shows that there are other ways of establishing the authority of law. Nor is the argument that anything which was made with the intention to make law must, if it is legally valid at all, derive its authority from the authority of its maker. That is not so either. In Britain, to mention just one example, a regulation laying down a rule may be ultra vires, in that the body which adopted it had no power to make law on that matter, and yet the rule which the regulation embodied may be valid, since it also happens to be a long-established common law rule. The argument lies elsewhere: Unless the authority of the constitution derives from the authority of its makers, there is no explaining the fact that it matters that it was made by one body rather than another. But surely it makes all the difference in the world that the constitution was adopted by those who did adopt it, and not by others. It is, we want to say, valid because it was so adopted. Does it not follow, by the force of the argument above, that its authority derives from the authority of those who made it?

As is so often the case, the short answer is both yes and no. To explain it, a longer answer must be given. But first we must dispose of a false answer waiting in the wings. Its interest lies not so much in itself, but in bringing us face to face with one aspect of the perennial question of the relations between law and morality. It may be claimed that the authority of constitutions cannot derive from that of their makers, for their makers, standing at the birth of their states, cannot have authority themselves. All authority derives from the constitution that they themselves made without prior authority to do so.

1. The nature of the authority of the makers of an originating constitution.

To be taken seriously, this argument has to be confined to the few constitutions that can be called "originating" constitutions. Most constitutions are not like that. They are made by legitimate legal authorities as part of a process of legal reform. Even constitutions that stand at the birth of a new independent country are often made in pursuance of legal authority conferred on their makers by the previous legal order in force in these countries, often a colonial regime. This is the way most of the countries of the British Commonwealth acquired their independence. But is not the argument cogent regarding those constitutions to which it applies? It is not.

The argument assumes that only those on whom authority has been conferred by preexisting law can have legitimate authority. That is not, nor can it be, the case. Legal authority is itself a form of claimed moral authority.[1] The point is sometimes lost to sight, for legal structures transmit the authority to make law from one body to another. We are familiar with the fact that the law is a structure of authority, in which each legal authority derives its power from laws made by another. We rely on the authority of one to justify the authority of another. Only infrequently do we appeal to moral reasons to justify a claim to legal authority. This gives discourse about legal authority an appearance of being autonomous, technical, legal discourse. In a way it is. If the constitution and the other rules that establish legal authorities are morally justified, so are the authorities that they establish, and the laws made by those authorities are morally binding. This means that once the moral justification of those ultimate legal rules (i.e. those whose legal validity does not presuppose that of any other law) is established, or assumed, the moral justification of the rest of the law is—up to a point—established by technical legal argumentation. (This is so up to a point only, because, as was noted, the interpretation of the law may well involve further moral or other non-legal considerations.) Since much of the time legal argument is addressed to legal officials who accept the moral validity of the ultimate laws, and much legal argument explains (to clients or lawyers, or to any individual) what is the position in law—on the supposition that it is morally legitimate—regarding one matter or another, much legal argument is technically legal.

None of this denies the fact that the law claims to be morally binding and that on the whole only people who accept that claim, people who accept at least that it is morally permissible to apply the law (to tax people, to determine their property rights, or their right in and to employment, to imprison them, etc.), serve in the authorities that make and apply the law. A theory of law is, therefore and among other things, a theory of the conditions, if any, under which the law is morally legitimate and of the consequences that follow from the assumption that it is morally legitimate. That is also the nature of our investigation into the authority of the constitution. If the constitution is not an originating constitution, if it has been made by a body on which some other law (perhaps an earlier constitution) bestowed power to enact a constitution, then it may be morally legitimate if the law that authorized it is morally legitimate. But if it is an originating constitution, then the question of its moral legitimacy cannot turn on the legitimacy of any other law. It must turn directly on moral argument.

It follows that the argument that an originating constitution cannot derive its authority from the authority of its makers—for they had no such authority—is invalid. It is true that the makers of the constitution had no authority bestowed on them by other laws. But it does not follow that they had no authority, nor that the authority of

the constitution cannot rest on their authority. They may have had moral authority, and it may be the reason for the authority of the constitution.

One may reply that, true as my observations are, they miss the point of the argument they were meant to refute. That argument, it may be said, is about the *legal* authority of originating constitutions, not about their moral authority. In a sense it is true that their framers did not have legal authority. (It is misleading to put the point in this form, but the technical considerations involved need not detain us here.[2]) The crucial point is that our interest in legal authority lies in how it establishes the moral authority of the law, or of parts of it. We are interested in the authority of law, if any, in order to establish whether we have an obligation to respect and obey it.[3] Moreover, the grounds for the authority of the law help to determine how it ought to be interpreted. Judges, perhaps more than anyone else, follow the law because they believe they are morally required to do so. There can be no other way in which they can justify[4] imprisoning people, interfering with their property, jobs, family relations, and so on, decisions that are the daily fare of judicial life.

It may be worth repeating that none of this implies that there is no room for more narrowly focused legal reasoning about whether any institution meets the purely legal conditions for the possession of authority. My claim is only that such an inquiry is of interest because it is embedded in a wider inquiry into the moral legitimacy of that institution's power. Nor do I claim that in any chain of reasoning about legal authority there will be a stage in which the moral considerations affecting legitimacy will be confronted directly or explicitly. Very often they are taken for granted. Nor is it, of course, my claim that whenever the legal conditions for legitimacy are met so are the moral conditions.

2. The argument from the rule of recognition.
This may be an appropriate place to clear out of the way another misguided argument for the independence of the authority of the constitution from that of its authors. Some theorists who broadly follow H.L.A. Hart's theory of law think that the constitution of a country is its rule of

recognition, as that term is used by Hart.[5] Since the rule of recognition exists as a practice of the legal officials, it is, as it were, a living rule, a rule sustained by *current attitudes and conduct*, and not by what happened at the point it came into being. Hence, since the constitution is the rule of recognition, the constitution's authority derives from the current practice of the officials, and not from the authority of its makers.

This argument is easily refuted. For one thing, its conclusion can be turned around and used as a ground for rejecting its central premise: If the constitution is the rule of recognition, then its authority does not derive from the authority of its authors: since its authority does derive from the authority of its authors, it follows that the constitution is not the rule of recognition. There is no reason to prefer the argument to this reversal of it. This lands us in a tie. Fortunately, there are plenty of independent reasons that establish that constitutions are not the rules of recognition of their countries. No constitution can be, if that term is understood in the thick sense in which it is used here. For example, most constitutions may be amended or even repealed and replaced by others in accordance with procedures that they themselves provide. This means that they can be amended or repealed by enactment. The rule of recognition cannot be repealed or amended by an enactment. It can change only as the practice that it is changes. Customary law can be repealed and replaced by statute. There is nothing in the nature of custom to prevent it from being changed by legislation. But once that happens, the law on the point is no longer customary. It is statutory. The rule of recognition, on the other hand, cannot give way to statutory law. It is and always remains customary.

Not only is it a mistake to identify constitutions with rules of recognition, but rules of recognition do not play the legitimating role that constitutions can play.[6] The rule of recognition is unlike the rest of the law. It is the practice—that is, the fact—that the courts and other legal institutions recognize the validity, the legitimacy, of the law, and that they are willing to follow it and apply it to others. As such it is unlike any other legal rule, including other customary legal rules. It is the point (one such point) at which—metaphorically speaking—the law ends and morality begins. It is the fact that enables us to separate legal from moral facts. If the rule of recognition exists—that is, if the appropriate practice of recognition is followed by the courts—then the law exists. But only if they are right in so conducting themselves is the law actually legitimate and binding, morally speaking.

Put it in different terms: Because we can identify a social fact of the judicial recognition of the law by the courts, we can establish that there is a law in a certain country and establish its content even if it is a morally bad and illegitimate system of law. The rule of recognition, being a social fact, enables us to identify the law without recourse to morality. But that is (by and large) all it does. It cannot be sensibly regarded as a conventional rule—that is, we cannot assume it to be a necessary truth that when a judge follows the practice of, let us say, applying acts passed by the Queen in Parliament as binding, he does so because all the courts do so, or because they all hold themselves duty bound to do so (even though they do). He may do so because Acts of Parliament enjoy democratic legitimacy, or for some other reason. The rule of recognition constitutes a normative practice, but not a conventional practice.

3. The argument from consent.

Some people think that the only way in which some people can have authority over others is through the others' consent.[7] Since the constitution is the source of legal authority in the state, its own authority must arise from the consent of the governed. If consent is the source of all authority, then this consent must be the consent of the living, the consent of those subject to the law as it is from time to time. Those who think that consent is the foundation of authority cannot tolerate the supposition that the current generation is subject to the law because it enjoyed the consent of the population living two hundred years ago. Hence, even if a constitution was adopted by a referendum, it is valid not because of the process by which it was adopted originally but because it commands the consent of the public as it is from time to time.

Some variants of this argument modify it to accommodate two objections: First is the fact that some people may refuse their consent by whim in a totally arbitrary or irrational way. When this happens, those who refuse their consent will not be subject to the law of the state. They can break the law with impunity. It seems implausible that it is that easy to escape the authority of the law, that people can escape its authority at will. Second, many people are never actually called upon to give their consent to the constitution. Many may have failed to consent to it simply because it never occurred to them that they should. Again it seems implausible that they will be exempt from the authority of the law. Both objections can be circumvented if one stipulates that the consent that gives rise to the authority of the constitution is not necessarily the actual consent of the governed. Rather, at least regarding those who did not in fact consent, it is the fact that they would have consented—had they been reasonable and rational people (but not necessarily exemplary moral people)—if they had been invited to do so. These variants regard authority as arising out of the hypothetical consent of the governed.

This is not the place to engage in a comprehensive discussion of the weaknesses of consent accounts of authority.[8] Suffice it to say that although in the respects mentioned accounts based on hypothetical consent are stronger than simple consent-based accounts, in others they are weaker: There is some normative force to the fact that one gives one's free and informed[9] consent to an arrangement affecting oneself, which hypothetical consent does not have. Consent, whether wise or foolish, expresses the will of the agent concerning the conduct of his own life. Whatever mess results from his consent is, in part at least, of his own making. Since his life is his own, it is relevant whether it is under his control or not, and consent shows that it is. So even if real consent is a source of authority, it is far from clear that hypothetical consent is. I know of no argument which shows that it is.[10]

In any case, *this* relevance of consent is not of a kind that can establish the legitimacy of any authority. Not being able to argue the case in full, let me give an analogy: Suppose that I consent to a boxing match with an opponent of far superior strength and skill. I am simply mad at him and lose my head in my desire to fight him. That I consented is relevant to what I can say later, when nursing my wounds. It affects the sort of complaints I can make (I can say to my friends, "Why didn't you stop me?" but I cannot say to my enemy, "Why did you fight me?"). It also affects any reasonable judgment of my character. But it does not necessarily establish that my enemy was right to fight me. He should have known that boxing is immoral and that my consent does not make it otherwise. He should have known that the fight will not be fair, given his superiority (he was not fighting in self-defence; it was an arranged fight). You may disagree with the judgments I am relying on here. Even so, you should agree that if they are true, then my consent did not make my enemy's action right. The case of legitimate government is similar: My consent can bar me from certain complaints and can be material to judging my character. But it cannot endow the government with a right to govern if it did not have it—unless consent is relevant to its right in a way that is different from the one I was commenting on earlier. I will assume in the sequel that that aspect of consent is not relevant to our issue.

It is plausible to suppose that whatever merit there is in hypothetical-consent accounts derives from the fact that the kind of hypothetical consent they involve captures whatever it is that matters in real-consent accounts—for example, that it represents the true will of the agent. To that extent they suffer from some of the limitations of real-consent accounts—that is, those which affect not only the form of consent, but its underlying rationale. An important aspect of consent, as of all human action, is that it is given for a reason—that is, a reason the agent regards as a good reason, in light of all the considerations, moral considerations included, that apply to the case. The reasons agents believe in may not be good reasons, or not adequate to the task, and the agents may even know this and give their consent out of weakness of the will. However, I know of no consent-based account of authority that does not assume that the reasons for the consent are cogent and adequate. Indeed, it would be impossible to base authority on consent that is misguided and ill-founded—again, I am afraid, not a point that can be established here. But if so, then the consent is given in the true belief that there is adequate reason to recognize the authority of the institutions, or principles, in question. The question arises whether these considerations are not enough to establish the authority of those bodies or principles, independently of the consent.

Obviously, in many cases consent is required for one to have an obligation. But typically these are cases in which the wisdom of the consent is not in question (for example, with few exceptions, a promise is binding whether or not one's reasons for making it are good reasons). It is equally clear that not all obligations arise out of consent or undertakings (for example, the obligation to keep one's promises does not depend on consenting to do so). Nor do all our obligations to accede to the will of others arise out of consent (for example, we have an obligation to accede, within bounds, to the will of our parents, which—at least in the conditions prevailing in some societies—extends beyond childhood and applies to the relations between adults and their parents as well). So the question arises: If consent to authority is effective only when based on adequate reasons to recognize the authority, why are these reasons not enough in themselves to establish that authority?

This is a serious question, not a rhetorical one. We can well imagine answers that would show that in certain matters no one can have authority over another except with that person's consent. Such may be the case in matters that relate to what we call "private" areas of life. What is much more difficult to imagine is that no political authority can be legitimate without consent—that is, that there is no area over which an authority may have legitimate power independently of consent. Many areas of governmental action (for example, determining the relative contribution of individuals to the maintenance of essential common services, or securing that those who injure others compensate them for the harm caused, when fairness or justice require that they do so) are matters of setting up schemes to facilitate conformity with precepts of justice and morality, and these are typical of matters where obligations that are not voluntary abound.

Assuming that in many areas authority need not depend on consent makes it more likely that in these matters at least consent is not a way of establishing authority at all.[11] For it seems reasonable to suppose that, regarding such matters, the only reasons which justify consent to authority also justify the authority without consent.

If the sketch of the argument offered here can be fleshed out to make a sound argument, then consent is not at all an important way of establishing legitimate political or legal authority. This puts an end to the consent-based argument to show that the authority of constitutions cannot derive from the authority of their authors.

4. The dead hand of the past.

We should turn to the best known and most powerful argument aiming to sever the authority of constitutions from that of their authors. No one, the argument goes, can have authority over future generations. Therefore, the authority of a constitution cannot rest on the authority of its makers. Let us examine it.

First, a couple of obvious qualifications: The argument does not apply to new constitutions. But constitutions are meant to last for a long time, and it is fair to concentrate on older constitutions, as all constitutions are meant to be one day. Equally obviously, at least prima facie, the argument applies equally to old statutes. There may be differences between constitutions and ordinary law, arising out of the differences in their content, which affect the argument. But these remain to be argued for. Neither of these points substantially affects the force of the argument.

The way the argument works is this: We are looking for the conditions under which constitutions can be justified, can enjoy legitimate (moral) authority. Whatever they are, it cannot be the case that the authority of an old constitution can derive from the authority of its authors. For there is no reasonable way of justifying the authority of any institution that allows it to have authority stretching long into the future. How much into the future can authority stretch? Does the power of an authority die with it? And if so, what is the lifetime of an institutional authority (is it the period between elections, does the United States Congress change every two years or every six years, or is it a continuous body that will die only with a fundamental change in its constitution)? Or should we think of the lifetime of an individual authoritative decree, the lifetime of each individual statute or regulation, or that of every constitutional provision? The second seems the more reasonable approach.

The authority of institutions to issue binding decrees is limited in various ways: Some institutions have authority to lay down binding rules about the way banks should be run; others may have authority to direct the running of schools. Possibly, no institution can have unlimited authority regarding all subject matters. Similarly, the authority of any institution is limited by the range of people subject to it. Some have authority over people in Kansas, others over people in France, and so on. The considerations that limit the authority of others over us are, roughly speaking, of the same order as those that establish the immorality of slavery. They set limits to subjugation, to the subordination of one person to the will of another. Just as they do that by setting limits to the subject matter regarding which different authorities can have power and to the range of people over whom their power extends, so those very same considerations limit the temporal validity of their directives. Just as the range of subject matter and people will vary from case to case, so the temporal duration of an authoritative directive will vary depending on the circumstances. But it is reasonable to think, say, that none will be valid one hundred years after its passing. That is, if it were still valid at that time, that would not be due to the authority of its original author.

It is tedious to spell out the argument to this conclusion in full detail. But it may be helpful to provide some pointers to the sort of considerations involved. They come at two levels: (1) the types of factors that determine whether laws are good or bad, and (2) the factors that determine the competence of political authorities to achieve worthwhile goals, which thereby both establish and limit the scope of their legitimate powers.

Considerations of both levels must be combined to establish the boundaries of political authorities.

I will illustrate the first level by mentioning two categories (simplified for the purpose of the present discussion):

(i) Some law, if it is good law, directly[12] implements unconditional moral imperatives. Here one may mention the basic legal protection of personal safety in the criminal law and (to a certain degree) tort law. Some civil rights, like freedom of religion or of thought, are often thought to belong to this category.

(ii) Much law, if it is good law, reflects a fair distribution of opportunities, resources, and amenities among members of the population, given their actual or likely needs, goals, and aspirations, the existing technological and economic resources, and the existing social organization. Laws whose value is to be judged by these criteria should be subject to continuous review, as the factors that make them satisfactory at any time are subject to frequent and significant changes. These include all welfare law, planning and zoning laws, consumer protection legislation, safety regulations, health provisions, education law, and much else.

It may be thought that laws belonging to the first category do not require frequent adjustment. They incorporate into law immutable moral principles. Therefore, it may be argued, the authority of lawmakers to make these kinds of law is long-lasting. But the argument fails on both counts. First, while arguably the moral precepts that these laws are there to enforce are immutable, it does not follow that so are the laws that protect and enforce them. Take a simple example: The moral wrong committed by rape may involve the violation of a universal moral principle. But the legal regulation of rape may rightly vary from place to place and from time to time. To go no further, it is far from a universal principle that rape should constitute a separate offence rather than be assimilated to serious assault. There is no generally cogent reason for there being a one-to-one correlation between type of moral wrong and type of offence. Whether and when a sexual motive should determine the character of the offence, rather than be relevant to the sentence only, whether or when penetration should single out some sex offences from others, whether or when violence matters or not (it is not a necessary ingredient of rape, according to most jurisdictions)—all these are questions sensitive to social conditions, to perceived social meanings, to the informal consequences of criminal convictions, and to many other factors that are as variable as any. Hence, the first step in the argument for a long-lasting authority regarding laws directly implementing universal moral principles of conduct is unsound.

The second leg of the argument is no more sound. To see that, let us waive the objection I raised in the preceding paragraph. Let us assume that there is a category of laws whose validity is as timeless as that of the universal moral principles from which they derive. Would that show that long after their enactment the authority of these laws rests on the authority of their makers? Far from it. This may be the case should the authority of the laws derive from the authority of their makers. But the very fact that they have, as we suppose, timeless authority militates against that view. The timeless authority of these supposed laws depends on their content. If they are timelessly valid, that is because they express universal moral principles. They are not timelessly valid because they were enacted by a fallible social institution or approved by a referendum. For an authority to be able to pass timelessly valid laws of this kind it must be counted as an expert on morality—that is, as having a significantly superior grasp of abstract moral principles than do the people who are bound by its laws. While there seem to be people who acquire moral expertise in some specialized problems of applied morality (e.g. the knotted issue of consent to medical experimentation), there is no reason to think that anyone or any institution can claim expertise in the very abstract basic principles of morality. Therefore, the authority of laws that express such principles cannot derive from that of their authors at all. As I indicated in my comment on the first step of the argument, in fact the authority of the law can be said to derive from that of its author at least inasmuch as the laws determine the temporary, and

socially sensitive, way in which moral principles are to be enshrined into law. But that does not help show that anyone can have lawmaking authority to make laws that last for very long.

On the whole the case for the temporally limited authority of institutions regarding laws of the second kind—those that allocate resources, burdens, and opportunities fairly among people—is easier to establish. It seems impossible to formulate these laws in ways that do not necessitate frequent revision. Given that lawmakers cannot make laws that remain good for long, their authority cannot be the reason for the authority of old laws that they made.

To see this point more clearly we need to turn to the second level of considerations, to the factors that determine the competence of institutions to function well and, therefore, to be legitimate authorities. These have been touched upon in the preceding few paragraphs but deserve separate consideration, however brief.

Broadly speaking, political authority can be based on one or more of three types of considerations: expertise, coordination, and symbolic value. Considerations of expertise underlie, for example, much consumer-protection law, safety-at-work law, and most other safety regulations. They are also relevant to many laws that implement direct moral imperatives. Medical expertise is relevant to the definition of death, as well as health, illness, injury, and the like. Psychological expertise is relevant to many aspects of family law, and so on. To assume that expertise gives lawmakers timeless authority is to assume that either no advance in knowledge in the relevant area or no advance in its spread is likely, or both. Such advances would negate the expertise of the old lawmakers relative to new experts (new advances in knowledge) or relative to the population at large (the spread of knowledge). Either would denude them of legitimate authority insofar as it is based on expertise.

Much law is a matter of securing social coordination. Securing coordination predominates when the law aims to secure social conditions whose achievement depends on the conduct of a number of people, and when, should enough of them not behave in a way conducive to the achievement of the desired conditions, there is no reason (or no sufficient reason) for others to behave in that way either.[13] The law can help to secure coordination, and in fulfilling these functions it can achieve a variety of goals, including all those that fall into the second category listed earlier. In as much as forms of coordination have to be adjusted or replaced by others in changing circumstances, and in as much as there is a limit to anyone's ability to provide for such changes in advance, there is a limit, a temporal limit, on the laws they have power to make.

The third factor that can endow institutions with authority is the symbolic value of their position as legal authorities. Here we have to distinguish between the value of an office and the value of having a certain person, or group of people, holding the office. Some people qualify for positions of high authority in having become symbols of their nations in periods of transition or struggle. The position of Václav Havel in the years immediately following the democratization of Czechoslovakia (and later in the Czech Republic) is an instance of that, and there are many others. Our concern, however, lies in the less common, or at least less easy to document, case in which an institution has acquired symbolic value. Arguably, the Crown has such a position in the United Kingdom. It expresses and symbolizes the unity of the country (which is not a nation-state). The symbolic meaning of an institution is itself reason to recognize it as enjoying morally legitimate standing. While the symbolic value of giving office to certain people does not affect the theory of authority, the fact that an institution has symbolic value may feature in an argument establishing its legitimate authority. But it is unlikely to affect it in a timeless way. After all, there is prima facie reason for not accepting laws as valid unless they are the sorts of laws one should have. That the institution making them is of value does not show that the laws it has enacted are good. Even if the value of the institution may nevertheless provide an argument for recognizing its authority, it is not likely to extend to endowing it with timeless authority.

I have rehearsed these familiar considerations because they are of the kind that tends to establish that no human institution has authority to make

laws that last forever, or for a very long time. It follows that even if new constitutions may derive their authority from the authority of their makers, old constitutions, if morally valid at all, must derive their authority from other sources. While with new law the authority of the law derives from the authority of its makers, the authority of old law must rest on other grounds.

B. Principle and Practice in Justification

1. Difficulties about facts and norms.

This conclusion is liable to appear paradoxical on a number of grounds. It may be thought to give rise to a paradox of change: The constitution that is valid in the United States today is the one that came into force in 1789 and has been amended a few times since, most importantly between 1865 and 1870. But if my conclusion is right, some may object, then some time after its adoption the constitution lapsed and a new different constitution came into place. But this is a simple misunderstanding. My argument is not that the constitution changed, but that the reasons for its validity did. The same law can be valid for a variety of reasons, and these may change without the law changing.

There may be a deeper worry in the background, which I am groping to identify. One strand in it arises out of the worry that my argument leaves unexplained the full role of the original constitution-makers and their importance in the life of some countries. It is not exhausted by their role in the early life of the constitution. There are countries where respect for the authors of the constitution is very much a living political force long after the validity of the constitution has ceased, according to the argument of the preceding section, to depend on their authority. But that need not be an obstacle to accepting the argument. The authors of a constitution, especially the authors of a country's first constitution, sometimes become political symbols, people's respect for whom unites the country and appeal to whose wisdom becomes the common currency of political argument. Such political facts—justified or otherwise—need have no bearing on the narrower issue of the grounds for the legitimate authority of constitutions, where they have such authority. Nor is the fact that the wisdom of the founding fathers, and so on, is appealed to in interpreting a constitution an objection to the argument, for, as will be seen later, local interpretive practices are to a degree self-legitimating.

But these are not the only worries the argument of the preceding section gives rise to. It also raises new questions about the relations between law and morality. We recognize the dual character of the law. On the one hand it is a social rather than a moral fact that the law of one country or another is so and so, and not different. This aspect of the law derives from several features fundamental to our understanding of its nature: First, it explains how there can be not only good and bad law, but also law and governments lacking all (moral) legitimacy, as well as those that are (morally) legitimate.[14] Second, it explains why we cannot learn what the law in a certain country, or on a certain matter, is, simply by finding out what it ought to be. Third, it explains how two people, one believing the law to be legitimate and the other denying its legitimacy, can nevertheless agree on what it is. What accounts for these and other simple but deep features of the law is that it is a social fact, which means that its existence and content can be established as social facts are established, without reliance on moral arguments.[15] On the other hand, the law has a different, normative aspect. It aims to guide people's conduct and it claims moral authority to do so. And while it may fail to enjoy such authority, it must be in principle capable of making its claim good. That is, the law is a social institution that claims moral authority over its subjects and is in principle, by its nature, capable of enjoying such authority.

A theory of law must explain this dual nature of the law as fact[16] and as norm. The doctrine that the (moral) authority of all law derives from the (moral) authority of its authors provides an easy way of doing so. There are, according to the simple version of this explanation, two steps in establishing the moral validity of the law. First, one has to establish the moral authority of the lawmakers to make law, and then one has to establish as a matter of social fact alone that those lawmakers made this particular law—that is, a law with this

particular content. The two aspects of the law are thus separated into these two stages in establishing the legitimate authority of the law. According to this explanation, the moral authority of the law, if it has any, derives in part from its factuality. That it consists in such and such social facts becomes the core of the moral argument for its authority: When these facts are of such and such a character, moral arguments endow the law with moral legitimacy, but when they have this and that character, there is no moral argument that can legitimate the law. This explains why the content of the law can be established independently of any issues regarding its moral legitimacy. Here morality follows the facts: It applies to independently established facts.

But all this presupposes that legislators, in the form of social institutions, mediate between law and morality. They provide the factual anchor of the law; they are part of its factual aspect, which is then submitted to moral scrutiny. Much in this simple picture is correct, but it unnecessarily focuses on legislation as the one feature that allows for an account combining the two aspects of the law. An adequate account of the dual nature of the law along the suggested lines[17] requires (1) that the content and existence of the law be determined by social sources and (2) that the moral argument for the authority of the law depends on the actual nature of the social sources. It does not require that the social sources take the form of legislation. They can be custom, common law, juristic opinions, and much else.[18]

It may help clarify the picture to reflect on the implications for the relations between law and morality of the dual aspect of law. The two aspects of the law are reconciled by the fact that the application of morality to our conduct is mediated by its application to norm-making social facts. This is a special kind of mediation. It is not surprising that our moral rights and duties depend on how things are with us and with the world in which we live: "I should not take this or that action, for there are people around who may get hurt by it." "I should offer assistance to this person, for he fell down and needs help." "I should give the car to my neighbour next week, for I promised to do so." These are common instances of the way the implications of morality depend on facts. But none of them are norm-creating facts.

Not so in its relations to the law. Here morality applies by sanctioning (or condemning) norms generated by the social facts of legislation, custom, and so on. Why must it be mediated in this special way when it comes to law? Not because all moral considerations have to be mediated by socially generated norms. The reasons for this are, at least in part, well understood. The law can help in securing social coordination and in bringing to people the benefits of information that is not generally available. The ability to benefit from such information and to secure social coordination is often advantageous or even necessary to achieve valuable goals, and even for compliance with moral requirements. But why cannot people coordinate their actions or share information without the mediation of legal norms? If moral norms are enough to justify coordination and sharing of information, why do not people act to achieve these goals simply because they are aware of the moral reasons for doing so? Sometimes they do, and when they do legal mediation is not necessary. But sometimes they do not, and for all-too-familiar reasons. Among the reasons that have attracted much attention in recent writings are: (1) the fact of disagreement about which goals one has good (moral) reasons to pursue; (2) collective action problems; and (3) the indeterminacy of moral reasons. These factors sometimes make it difficult to secure coordination and sharing of information, except through the intervention of social or legal authorities whose legitimacy is acknowledged and who possess enough power to enforce a reasonable degree of compliance from those who doubt their legitimacy or who might otherwise be tempted to free ride and so on.

Perhaps the last factor mentioned is the least familiar.[19] The underlying thought is simple: Barring ignorance and disagreement about moral goals or the best ways of implementing them, and barring backsliding, free riding, and their like, were moral considerations to indicate how things should be arranged in society in a univocal way then people would follow these considerations. But when moral considerations underdetermine the goals to be pursued or the ways to pursue them, there may be additional difficulties in securing coordination, and to overcome them the mediation of the law is sometimes helpful, and in some cases necessary. Think of a hypothetical example: Assume that the theory of democracy yields only a general principle—for example, that a democratic government is one where there are formal legal mechanisms making the content of policies and the identity of those in charge of implementing them sensitive to the wishes of the governed, in a way that as far as possible does not give any individual greater political power than that enjoyed by any other. It follows that there can be in principle many morally legitimate ways of organizing democratic governments: federal republics and unitary constitutional monarchies, single-member constituencies, and proportional-representation systems, parliamentary government and elected-presidential systems, and so on. All these radically different systems would be adequate democratic systems of government. Possibly, the circumstances of one country or another will make one or more of them inadequate for that country. But—that is the assumption underlying the example—such considerations will not reduce the number of acceptable systems to one.

In such circumstances mediation through law serves the role of concretizing moral principles—that is, of giving them the concrete content they must have in order for people to be able to follow them. In our example a country must have one or another system of democratic government. So the law determines which one it has. Of course, to do so the law itself must be a matter of social, not moral, fact. Its point and purpose, as far as this example goes, is to supplement morality. To do that, its content cannot be determined by moral considerations. It must reflect social practices or traditions or some other social facts.

These considerations show how the fact that the content of the law is determined by facts and not by norms not only explains the fundamental truisms about the law that I stated earlier, and others like them, but also contributes to an account of how the law is capable of discharging some of its basic functions (such as tackling disagreements about morality and concretizing moral principles). The very same considerations explain how sometimes it is advantageous, morally speaking, for the mediation to be through legislation, whereas in other circumstances it is better for it to be through other means. Legislation would be the preferred method of mediation when changes in the law become desirable frequently, or suddenly, and when the adjustments to the law that become desirable can be worked out through deliberation or negotiation. But other forms of mediation are preferable when the adjustments to the changes can be slow and gradual, when neither deliberation nor negotiation is of much help, and especially when it is important to secure continuity, to discourage premature or hasty change, to deny interest groups the possibility of blackmailing (or twisting the arms of) the rest of the community into agreeing to change, and so on. In brief, mediation should not be carried out exclusively through legislation when the matter is of constitutional importance, that is, when it should form part of an entrenched constitution.

2. Legitimacy through practice.

The discussion of the relations between norm and fact is instructive. But the conclusion it points to may seem problematic. Let me put it in the most paradoxical form: Constitutions, at least old ones, do not derive their authority from the authority of their authors. But there is no need to worry as to the source of their authority. They are self-validating. They are valid just because they are there, enshrined in the practices of their countries.

Obviously to put it thus is to misrepresent the conclusions that the preceding discussion yields. A most important qualification should be added to them: *As long as they remain within the boundaries set by moral principles*, constitutions are self-validating, in that their validity derives from nothing more than the fact that they are there. It should be added that this conclusion follows *if morality underdetermines* the principles concerning the form of government and the content of individual rights enshrined in constitutions. I have said nothing in support of the

underdetermination thesis, nor will I do so here. However, since I believe this to be the case,[20] I will explore here some implications of this position.

The main implication is that within the broad bounds set by moral principles, practice-based law is self-vindicating. The constitution of a country is a legitimate constitution because it is the constitution it has. This conclusion has to be explained and elaborated before we can accept it.

First, the fact that moral principles underdetermine the content of the constitution does not mean that the people or institutions who adopt constitutions or amend them do not do so for reasons, or that they cannot have adequate reasons for their decisions. It only follows that their reasons are not ones of moral principles (i.e. not the moral principles that determine which constitution is legitimate and which is not). For example, a government may support a change in the constitution that is not required by principled moral grounds, for the reason that it is popular with the electorate, or for the reason that it will offer some advantage to a group that is currently resentful and alienated, and will thus help reconcile it to the state or to the larger society. Alternatively, such a change may recommend itself simply because it is a change, and a change will infuse a new spirit in a society that has grown moribund and stagnant, or because every change leads to some people losing power and others gaining power, and it is good to reduce the power of the people or groups who currently hold power in the country.

Such reasons and many others are in a sense moral reasons, and they can be perfectly adequate reasons for adopting changes in a constitution. The point is that none of them is what I will call a "merit reason"; none derives from the moral desirability of any constitutional provision. I will call reasons that bear on the merit of being subject to a particular constitutional provision "merit reasons," to distinguish them from reasons for adopting a constitutional provision or for amending it that do not derive from the good of being subject to it. On the contrary, they are all examples of how constitutional amendment may be justified by reasons that do not bear on the merit of the constitutional change they justify. In that, they are also examples of how ordinary political concerns, even relatively short-term political concerns, can have a legitimate role in the politics of the constitution.

The self-legitimating aspect of practice is not negated by the fact that action for and against constitutional reform may be taken for good reasons. Because reasons of the kind just illustrated are not merit reasons and do not bear on the merit of the content of the constitution, they do not bear on its legitimacy. That is determined primarily by merit reasons that show the content of the constitution to be morally acceptable, and nothing in the examples undercuts the claim that merit reasons typically greatly underdetermine the content of the constitution, leading to the conclusion that within the boundaries they set, constitutions are legitimated by their existence.[21]

3. Stability and continuity.

I introduced the idea of self-legitimation, of the legitimating effect of practice, through reflection on the fact that moral principles underdetermine the content of constitutions, and practice takes up the slack. But as is well known, the self-legitimating power of practice is not confined to this. Conventions are, perhaps, the most familiar example. Conventions illustrate a larger category in which behaviour is justified if, and normally only if, a general practice exists: One should not cross the lawn if there is a general practice not to do so. That things happen in a certain way makes it right, or good, that they should continue to happen in that way.

An important concern of a similar nature is the concern for stability. The need to secure stability is in itself indifferent to the content of the constitutional practices prevailing in any time or place. Whatever they are, the concern for stability indicates that they should be perpetuated. Stability is not always an advantage. In the preceding subsection I noted that shaking things up can be desirable when it can change a moribund or corrupt power structure, infuse a country with a sense of energy and hope, and so on. However, stability is often desirable, and for many reasons. Remember that here as before the reference to the "self-

legitimating" character of the "constitution" is not to the formal legal existence of the constitution but to the constitution as it exists in the practices and traditions of the country concerned. Constitutions are meant to provide a framework for the public life of a country, giving it direction and shape. For this to be achieved, widespread knowledge of the constitution has to be secured. This requires knowledge not only of the text but of its significance—that is, knowledge of the constitutional practices in the country. Until people absorb and adjust to it, a radical constitutional change upsets these practices. It has ramifications regarding different aspects of public life, and there is bound to be a temporary uncertainty regarding the way the reform or change will affect various aspects of constitutional practice. The uncertainty affects people's ability to function. It is made worse if it generates fear of continuous change, leading to a sense of dislocation and loss of orientation.

These are some of the many, mostly familiar reasons for preferring stability to instability. They do not amount to a rejection of change, but they create a reason to prefer continuity to change, unless there are really good reasons for the change. They add to the main and powerful conservative argument: Although it is possible to predict the direct consequences of small changes in legal and social practices—changes that take place within existing frameworks and do not upset them—it is impossible to predict the effect of radical, large-scale changes. They are liable to affect the legal and social framework, which constitutes the background conditions that make predictions of social events possible. Hence, although radical reform may be inspired by cogent reasons to bring about different social conditions, there is no adequate advance reason to believe that it will bring about the hoped-for consequences. In itself this is no argument against radical reform and change. It does not show that radical change is likely to be for the worse. But it does undercut many reasons that people often advocate in pressing for radical change. Taken together with the advantages of stability, it adds to a certain conservative attitude sometimes expressed by saying that in relatively stable and decent societies there is a presumption in favour of continuity against which all proposals for change should be judged.

Broadly speaking, the argument for stability and the underdetermination of constitutional principles by morality combine to establish the self-legitimating aspect of constitutional practices and traditions.[22] Yet lumping them together like this runs the risk of obscuring the two fundamental differences between them.

In the first place the underdetermination argument means that within broad boundaries set by moral principles the very existence of a constitution establishes that it is a good constitution for the country in question. Others would have done, but given that they were not adopted, not they but the one enshrined in the practices of that country is its legitimate constitution. The desirability of stability does not establish that the constitution is legitimate. It applies even to illegitimate constitutions. The drawbacks of instability apply there too, though they are overcome by other considerations.

Second, although the argument from underdetermination allows that, within bounds, existing constitutions are self-legitimating, it does not constitute a reason for not changing the constitution. The constitution is legitimate, but so would be many alternatives we might have in its place. The arguments for stability, on the other hand, although they do not establish the legitimacy of the existing constitution, establish the existence of reasons for not changing an existing constitution.

Things are different if the constitution is morally legitimate—that is, if it instantiates one of the permissible forms of government, if it lies within the permissible as determined by moral considerations. When this is so, the arguments from underdeterminacy and from stability combine to legitimate the constitution and provide a reason for keeping the constitutional tradition going as it is.

What role, if any, do the authors of the constitution play in providing it with legitimacy? Their role can be of enormous practical importance, though it is a secondary role, from a theoretical point of view. Basically they help launch the constitutional tradition, and sometimes their

reputation helps to keep it going. They may endow it with authority in its early years, and the respect in which they are held may be of great importance in determining the willingness of the population, and its politically active groups, to abide by it. This willingness is crucial both to the survival and to the legitimacy of the constitution. But it is so to the extent that it helps to bring the constitution within the bounds of the morally permissible.

III. INTERPRETING CONSTITUTIONS

A. Interpreting the Constitution: On the Nature of Interpretive Doctrines

We can take constitutional interpretation as an established practice and confine ourselves to studying how it is conducted in different countries. Such a study would not be without interest, but from a theoretical point of view its benefits would be limited. A study based on this kind of survey and classification of interpretive techniques would yield an unwieldy plethora of interpretive styles and techniques, varying within countries as well as between countries, and changing over time. It would also reveal large disagreements among judges about the proper methods and techniques of constitutional interpretation. Finally, it would show that not infrequently what judges say is one thing and what they do is another. The practice of some judges does not accord with their more general statements about the nature of constitutional interpretation.

Perhaps in part for these reasons, many legal philosophers have either shied away from writing about interpretation or offered normative accounts of interpretation generally, and of constitutional interpretation in particular. Does this betray the task of explaining the law as it is, rather than as it ought to be? Not necessarily. First, legal interpretation is much more than a method of establishing what the law is. When used by courts and by lawyers, or commentators and academics who focus on the interpretations that courts should adopt, legal interpretation is also a tool for developing the law, changing and reforming it. Second, while it is generally accepted that there is a point in following established interpretive methods, to the extent that they exist, it is also generally accepted that interpretations are subject to objective assessment, that some are defensible and others are not.[23] Moreover, it is part of the practice of legal interpretation as it is in many countries that courts are not bound to follow past interpretive techniques if they can be shown to be mistaken or less desirable than some alternatives. They can modify them or replace them with better ones. This is the case, for example, in all common-law jurisdictions. In such countries the study of sound interpretation is also part of the study of the law as it is. But it is a study of a very special aspect of the law, one that demarcates some of the lawmaking powers of the courts and the circumstances for their legitimate use.

Therefore, when reflecting on constitutional interpretation, we should start not from the fact that certain methods of interpretation are used, and others not, but from the question: Why is interpretation so central to constitutional adjudication? The answer, as always when there is reason to resort to interpretation, turns on a combination of reasons for respecting the constitution as it exists and reasons for remaining open to the possibility that it is in need of reform, adjustment, or development in order to remove shortcomings it always had or shortcomings that emerged as the government or the society that it governs changed over time.

It may be worth emphasizing that this Janus-like aspect of interpretation (that it faces both backward, aiming to elucidate the law as it is, and forward, aiming to develop and improve it) is not special to legal interpretation. It is the mark of interpretation in general that it aims to be true to an original that is being interpreted and to be open to innovation. In the performing arts such as the theatre, for example, good performances interpret the text and in doing so they often express the views of the performers at the same time. This does not mean that all good interpretations are innovative, merely that interpretations can be innovative and therefore are ever open to this possibility. This is not the place to consider the nature of interpretation in general.[24]

But we should reflect on the reasons why constitutional interpretation should be doublesided.

The reason for the backward-looking aspect of constitutional interpretation takes us back to the principle with which we started. The doctrines of constitutional interpretation, it was our assumption from the beginning, are based, at least in part, on the doctrine of sources of the authority of constitutions. Since the authority of a long-established constitution rests primarily on the desirability of securing continuity, the same desirability should inform constitutional interpretation as well. To secure continuity the interpretation should be backward-looking. It should be faithful to the constitution as it exists at that time. If so, should not this consideration dominate constitutional interpretation to the exclusion of all else? The moral importance of the issues decided upon in constitutional cases would not allow this to happen. Courts whose decisions determine the fortunes of many people must base them on morally sound considerations. Nothing else could justify their actions. If we admit that, does it not follow from the preceding argument that the morally correct decision is the one which is purely backward-looking—that is, which does nothing more than set out the content of (the relevant parts of) the constitution as it is at the time? This may be the right course for them to take, but only when it would be morally required, or at least morally reasonable, to rely on considerations of continuity above all else.

In other words, given the impact that constitutional decisions, like many other legal decisions, have on people's lives, they are justified only if they are morally justified. As we saw, considerations of continuity are of great moral importance, and they are the primary considerations determining the continuous legitimacy of the constitution. But they are hardly ever the only moral considerations affecting an issue. When they are not, courts should try to reach decisions that satisfy as much as possible all the relevant considerations, and when it is impossible to satisfy all completely, they should strive to satisfy them as much as possible, given their relative importance. Hence, while on occasion the desirability of continuity in the matter concerned will prevail over all else, often this will not be the case, though even when continuity does not override all else, it should still be taken into account as much as possible. Hence, in such cases, while the courts should still interpret the constitution, for they are still rightly moved by considerations of continuity, they should also give weight to other moral considerations. That is, their interpretation should also be forward-looking. None of this should be taken to imply that all defects in a constitution can be put right through ingenious interpretation. All I am saying is that sometimes this is possible.

Yet again, an objection that this view is misconceived—for it overlooks the fact that the doctrine of constitutional interpretation is a *legal*, not a moral, doctrine—is bound to occur to some. Whatever the moral merit of my observations, the objection goes, it is irrelevant to an understanding of constitutional interpretation. That doctrine is a legal doctrine and there is nothing judges may do other than follow the doctrines of interpretation that are binding on them according to the law of their own country. Let me concede right away that there is something to the objection. Judges who follow the views on interpretation developed here may find themselves morally obliged to disobey the law of their country. That is the result of the fact that I am developing an approach to constitutional interpretation that, for lack of a better word, we may call a moral approach. The law of any country may be at odds with morality in a variety of ways. One of them is the existence of locally binding rules that prohibit the courts from following any morally acceptable interpretation.

I am not proposing the observations in this chapter as a substitute for an examination of the rules and doctrines of interpretation prevailing in this country or that. That is clearly an important task for those interested in the law of the countries concerned. Nevertheless, it would be false modesty to say no more than that the topic of my discussion is different. I am also making claims for its importance. Let me recapitulate: First, while there is every reason for people interested in this or that legal system to study the rules of interpretation binding in it, there is no universal theory of interpretation that applies to all law,

except as a normative theory—that is, of what interpretation should be like. Second, whether they like it or not, courts face moral problems and should behave in a way sanctioned by morality. This may bring them into conflict with the law. Third, quite often the proper ways of interpreting constitutions are controversial. Fourth, typically courts have power to adopt new ways of interpreting the law and to revise established ones when they have good reason to do so.

The last two points are interconnected, and both stem from a fact not yet mentioned: At the most basic level there are not, nor can there be, specifically legal ways of interpretation. Of course, most legal systems have rules of interpretation laid down in legislation or precedent that are special to them. But most interpretation does not, cannot, depend on them. This is not only, not primarily, because rules of interpretation themselves often require to be interpreted. It is primarily because problems of interpretation are rarely problems of the meaning of one term or phrase. They are more often than not questions of the interpretation of sentences, or of articles in statutes or in constitutions, or of moral and political doctrines. And they can arise in unexpected places. No set of explicitly articulated rules of interpretation can deal with all of them. The same is true of rules of interpretation implied in a legal culture, rather than explicitly articulated in its laws. Such rules cannot settle all possible issues of interpretation. All too often interpretation is just a matter of reasoning to a reasonable view on the basis of a variety of considerations, some reinforcing each other, some clashing. There is no way of reducing such reasoning to the application of rules, or other norms, nor is there any way of eliminating the need and the desirability of interpretation that consists in and results from such reasoning.

This explains why the law of interpretation, meaning the rules and doctrines of interpretation in force in any given country, useful as they may be, cannot contain all that can and need be said in an account of legal or constitutional interpretation. Ultimately an account of constitutional interpretation has more to do with understanding legal or constitutional reasoning than with understanding any legal doctrine specific to this or that country. Reasoning that aims to establish the meaning of a law, a work of art, literature, religion, or anything else and that combines respect for its original expression or its traditional or current meaning with openness to innovation is interpretive. For the reasons already given, constitutional reasoning is to a considerable degree interpretive reasoning. But accounts of reasoning are accounts of rationality in belief, and they are universal normative accounts, specific to any locality or subject matter only in the details of their application.

All this was said to explain the importance of a normative account of constitutional interpretation, an account that goes over and above the study of the rules and doctrines of interpretation established in one country or another. But the drift of these remarks raises a different objection to the thought that there can be a general study of constitutional interpretation. If the study of interpretation is just the study of reasoning that is constrained by the condition specified earlier, and if the study of constitutional interpretation is just the study of such reasoning when applied to constitutions, can anything specific be said about it beyond the unhelpful but sound advice that in interpreting constitutions one should reason well? There may be a general account of reasoning, and perhaps even a general account of interpretive reasoning. But once one has mastered those is there anything more that is special to constitutional interpretation and that is not merely an application of the general account of interpretive reasoning to the content of the constitutions of specific countries?

This revives the doubt about the possibility of a general theory of constitutional law raised at the outset, but this time addressed specifically to issues of interpretation. As I explained there, I believe that there is much truth in the doubt. There is no general theory of constitutional interpretation, if that is meant to be a general recipe for the way such interpretation should be conducted that is set out in some detail in order to guide the interpreter every step of the way with practical advice. There is little more that one can say other than "reason well" or "interpret reasonably." What little there is to say consists mainly of pointing out mistakes that have been made attractive by the popularity they enjoy among judges, lawyers, or academic writers.

B. Fidelity and Innovation

Interpretation, it was suggested, lives in spaces where fidelity to an original and openness to novelty mix. It exists in a dialectical tension, as some might say. The reason we find this tension in reasoning about constitutional law, I claimed, is that constitutional decisions are moral decisions that have to be morally justified, and the moral considerations that apply include both fidelity to the law of the constitution as it is, arising out of concern for continuity, and openness to its shortcomings and to injustices its application may yield in certain cases, which leads to openness to the need to develop and modify it.

Two opposing mistakes are invited by this fact. The first is to think that because a good interpretation may combine both elements, the distinction between the constitution, and more generally the law, as it is and as it ought to be is illusory. Constitutional interpretation, one argument runs, establishes the meaning of the constitution. That is, there is no sense in talking of the content of the constitution except as it is determined by a process of interpretation. Since interpretation mixes fidelity and innovation, it undermines both notions. It breaks down the distinction between them, for fidelity assumes that the content of the constitution, to which one is supposed to be faithful, can be established independently of interpretation and, by the same token, so does innovation, since it is identified as deviation from pure fidelity. Without an interpretation-independent identification of the content of the constitution, we cannot tell fidelity from innovation, and since the content cannot be identified independently of interpretation, it follows that there is no coherent meaning to the notion of fidelity to the constitution and none to constitutional innovation either.

This argument fails. I intimated earlier that not all explanations of meaning are interpretations. But we need not rely on this in refuting the argument. It overlooks the fact that the reason fidelity and innovation are often mixed is that we often have reasons to interpret in ways that mix them. But this is not always the case. Sometimes we have reason to interpret the constitution in ways that simply elucidate its content at the moment, warts and all. Such an interpretation—I call it "a conserving interpretation"—will be successful if it is true to the existing meaning of the constitution. It will include no mixing of conflicting elements. It will display no dialectical tension, and it will establish the benchmark by which we can measure other interpretations to see whether they are more or less innovatory.

The failure of the preceding argument does not mean, of course, that there are no other better ones. But I do not know of any successful argument to the same conclusion. It does not follow that in every case we can establish what the law is. The evidence may be incomplete. Moreover, it is not the case that we can establish the legal answer regarding any legal question, since the law is often indeterminate on various issues. As a result, when the constitution is interpreted with the goal of establishing just what it is at a given moment in time, the interpretation will show it to be vague and indeterminate. Granted all these points, it is still the case that when the evidence is available, it is possible to establish what the law is, and therefore to distinguish between innovatory and conserving interpretations. I suspect that one reason that encourages people to assume that it is impossible to interpret the law, to establish its meaning at any given time without changing it at the same time, is the following sort of argument: (1) Courts can always change the law that is relevant to the case in front of them. (2) Courts can change the law only when it is indeterminate. (3) It follows that the law is indeterminate on all issues. (4) Therefore, no interpretation can simply establish what it is without changing it. The argument is invalid, for from the claim that the law is indeterminate on all issues it does not follow that an interpretation cannot merely describe it without changing it. All that follows is that such an interpretation will describe it as indeterminate. More important, the second premise is simply false. Courts can develop the law even when it is determinate. They can and often do simply change it.

This brings us to the second mistake one should avoid, which in some ways is the opposite of the first. Some may think that if there is a distinction between a conserving interpretation that merely states the law as it is and an innovatory one that develops and changes it, then it must be possible to take any interpretation and point to where it stops merely stating the law as it is and starts developing and changing it. It must, in other words, be possible to separate the descriptive and the innovative elements in every interpretive statement. The thought that this is so is encouraged by the fact that sometimes such a separation is indeed possible. But these occasions are relatively rare, and it certainly does not follow from the previous observations that it is ever, let alone always, possible. In clearing the first mistake, I argued for the possibility of comparing different interpretations by their degree of novelty and of distinguishing innovative interpretations from conserving ones. (There could be several of them, since one can provide interpretations that restate the law as it was at different points in time.) That thought is very different from the suggestion that within each interpretation one can separate the elements that are true to the law as it is from those that are innovative. All that my position implies is that when thinking of the reasons that justify an interpretation one can distinguish those that suggest that the interpretation should be faithful to existing law from those that suggest that it should develop or even change the law.

Having cleared these two theoretical mistakes out of the way, we can face one of the main mistakes to which theories of constitutional interpretation are liable. Having established in the preceding section that constitutional interpretation has to answer to a variety of reasons, some urging fidelity to existing law, others urging its development, change, and adaptation, it is natural to expect that the central task of a theory of constitutional interpretation is to spell out the right proportions of innovation and conservation in constitutional interpretations, or to tell one how to determine how much of each to allow in each case. But this is a misconception, which if not checked is bound to breed many false theories. It overlooks the fact that there is no one reason to develop and change constitutional law. When it is adequate to its tasks and to the situation in the country, there is no need to change or to develop it. Modification of the law is called for either when it is undetermined on the issue the court has to decide or when it is less than adequate. In those cases the court should take notice of the reasons for having the law take one shape or another. But those are enormously varied both in nature and in importance. Any moral reason whatsoever can figure in the considerations of a constitutional court on these occasions. There cannot be a general answer to the question of how much importance reasons for change should have in their conflict with reasons for continuity.

Of course, there are certain generalizations one can safely put forward. For example, it is generally (but not universally) the case that the greater are the defects in the constitutional law concerned, the less important is it to preserve continuity and the more important is it to change it. We can also emphasize that sometimes it is possible to reconcile continuity with change, by introducing changes in the law that deviate little from it, especially in matters where established expectations led people to make plans on the basis of existing law. This is particularly true of cases in which the need to resolve legal indeterminacy on this issue or that is the only reason for deviation from existing law. In such cases, it may be that no expectations have been generated, and resolution of the case need not affect stability. One can continue in this vein to offer more helpful generalizations. But they will not amount to a general answer to the question of what is the right mix of innovation and preservation in constitutional decisions.

C. Considerations of the Moral Merit of the Constitution and of Its Institutional Role

So far I have argued for four main conclusions: First, there is no real theory of constitutional interpretation, in the sense of a set of principles that when applied to an interpretive question yield the correct interpretation of the constitutional provision concerned. All a philosophical discussion of

interpretation can do is explain the nature of the activity and its main parameters, and help one to avoid some mistakes. Second, there is a cogent way of distinguishing between innovative and conserving interpretations, and often between more or less innovative (less or more conserving) interpretations. Third, interpretation is central to legal reasoning because in legal reasoning fidelity to an original competes with, and has to be combined with, reasons for innovation. Constitutional interpretation is central to constitutional adjudication because courts are faced with conflicting moral considerations, some militating for continuity, and therefore for giving effect to the constitution as it is at that moment, and some pointing to the need to develop and improve it. Fourth, it makes no sense to ask in general what is the right mix of conservation and innovation in constitutional interpretation.

To help us make further progress with the argument, we need to retreat and consider an objection to the third conclusion—that whatever the merit of innovative interpretations in literature, history, and elsewhere, judicial interpretations of the constitution should be purely conserving. Earlier I argued against this view on the ground that: (1) courts are faced with moral issues and should make morally justified decisions, and (2) the moral considerations they face often point not only to the advantages of continuity, but also to the desirability of modifying and improving the constitutional provisions concerned. My imaginary objector agrees to both premises but denies that the conclusion follows. It seems to follow, he points out, only because I disregarded altogether the importance of institutional considerations to legal decisions. Over and above the moral considerations I gestured toward stands the doctrine of the role of the courts, which says that their job is exclusively to apply the law as it is.[25] Others have the responsibility to improve it. Therefore, the fact that there are good reasons for dissatisfaction with the law as it stands is no justification at all for judicial "activism." It is not the courts' business. They have a job to do and they should confine themselves to doing it and no more.

The value of this objection is that it reminds us of the importance of institutional considerations in justifying political and legal actions. The objection relies on a doctrine of division of labour among various organs of government. But behind it are additional complex considerations of institutional design, relative advantage in performing one task or another, and others necessary for its justification. Philosophers are sometimes prone to let institutional considerations drop out of their sight. I suspect that contributing to this is the fact that institutional considerations do not mark one outcome as better than others. They merely indicate that the court is or is not an appropriate body to adopt one interpretation or another, not that it is better for the law to be this way or that. In other words, institutional considerations do not contribute to showing which result is best. They do, however, show which decision is justified. They act something like side constraints, though they are not necessarily exceptionless.[26]

The objection is that my argument overlooks the effect of institutional constraints and that once the omission is repaired we can see that the courts may not modify the law. Is this really the sole role of the courts? My earlier argument that since the courts have to take a moral decision they have to reach the best moral result was too simple-minded. It took too simple a view of who the agent is. The courts do not act in their own name. They act as organs of the political society, that is—to simplify—of the state. It is the state that has the responsibility to reach the right result. It does not automatically follow, and that is what the institutional objection points to, that it should do so through its courts. The state has other organs, and possibly the courts should always simply apply existing law, and if that is not the right result, that is, if the law should be modified, then it falls to other state organs to modify it.

How, then, are we to determine the responsibility of different organs of state? In the first instance by examining the structure of state organs and the division of powers enshrined in the constitution. But beyond that, we need to examine the moral soundness of that structure. It is not morally sound if following it is not a good way to make sure, inasmuch as that is possible, that the state reaches the right outcome in each case.

In that case it falls to each state organ to consider whether it would not be morally right for it to deviate from existing law in order to secure the best outcome. It ought, of course, to weigh the reasons, of continuity, separation of powers, and others, against doing so. But it cannot avoid taking the question of the desirability of change seriously. There is no need here to explore the structure of that kind of reasoning. The important lesson is that the issue of the relative role of institutions is itself, like all the other issues we have encountered, a moral issue, and the courts have to act on moral considerations that apply to division-of-labor questions.

The salient fact for our concern is that whether or not in this state or that the role of the courts includes responsibility for improving the constitution is a question of the doctrine of constitutional interpretation in force in it. As I observed earlier, in most countries issues of interpretation at this level of generality tend to be subject to dispute and disagreement. Since in such countries there is no established practice on the issue, there is in them no settled law about it, and there is nothing to stop the courts from giving effect to the view of their own role that is morally compelling.

Is that the view which confines the courts to merely applying existing law?[27] That would be their role if and only if there were other state organs fully able to engage in improving the law when necessary. The more entrenched the constitution is, the less likely is it that there are such alternatives.

But does not the fact that constitutions are entrenched show not that there are inadequate means of amending them but rather that it is undesirable that they be amended in ways other than the procedures provided? It may mean that this is what their authors intended, but it does not follow that their view is sound. This is yet another debate that can only be touched upon here. There is a strong case for separating constitutional development and adjustment from the course of ordinary politics. In most circumstances it is advantageous to secure the stability and durability of the framework of governmental institutions and the fundamental principles of their operation from short-term political pressures. But the case for separation is not a case for making it difficult to change constitutional provisions. It is merely a case for a special process controlling their change. The argument against easy changes is the case for stability and continuity in constitutional law. But that case has complex conclusions. It establishes that radical changes in the structure of the constitution should not be easy to effect. Their adoption should require extensive publicity, wide-ranging public debate, and substantial and durable consensus. There is no objection to regular development of the law within existing frameworks. Such modifications do not undermine continuity. By and large they tend to enhance it. So far I have not distinguished between stability in the law—that is, the absence of change in the law—and stability in the social or economic effects of the law. Since the two often go hand in hand, there was no need to distinguish between them. But they go hand in hand only as long as the underlying social, political, or economic conditions do not change. When they do, the law may have to change if it is to continue to have the same social or economic effects. In such a case innovative interpretations that modify the law prevent it from ossifying and getting progressively less and less adequate to its task and requiring major reform. Of course, the cumulative effect of small-change reform may well amount to a radical change in constitutional law over the years. But stability is consistent with slow change, whatever its cumulative effect. Therefore, entrenching the constitution may be justified in that it secures extensive debate and solid consensus behind radical constitutional changes. But it also means that it falls to the courts to take charge of continuous improvements and adjustments within existing structures. The institutional argument against innovative constitutional interpretations by the courts fails.

D. Moral and Legal Considerations: Where the Law Is Autonomous

In the preceding discussion it was assumed that there are two anchors to constitutional interpretation. On the one hand, reasons for continuity militate in favour of conserving interpretation.[28] On the other hand, imperfections in the law militate in favour of innovative interpretation that will develop and modify the constitution. Conserving interpretations articulate or restate the current meaning of the constitutional provisions in question. That means that they aim to capture the meaning these provisions have in current constitutional practice. In the early days of a constitution this will be the meaning intended by its authors, inasmuch as it was expressed in its text as understood given the conventions of meaning and interpretation of the time.[29] In later years this meaning will be gradually overlaid by layers of interpretive decisions and by the way the relevant provisions have come to be understood in the practices of the legal institutions of that country and by its population. Naturally, quite often the constitution so understood will be vague and indeterminate on many issues. How does moral and legal underdetermination affect interpretation?

Indeterminacy in constitutional provisions will favour innovative interpretations. As long as they merely make determined what was underdetermined, they cannot offend against stability. Whatever moral reasons apply to improve the constitutional provisions involved can be given effect. Sometimes, however, there will be indeterminacy both in law and in morality. Nevertheless, the matter must be decided, and the constitutional position has to be settled. How is the court to proceed then?

A distinction introduced in section II.B is relevant here. I distinguished there between merit reasons, which bear on the merit of a constitution and its provisions, and reasons for amending a constitution, or some of its provisions, which have no bearing on the merit of those provisions. The need for a change to infuse a spirit of optimism in a new future, or in order to win the support or allegiance of some segment of the population, were examples of the second type of reason. When addressing the consequences of the incommensurability of reasons, we need to distinguish between incommensurability of all the reasons bearing on a decision and incommensurability in some class of reasons.

Merit reasons which show that one interpretation, innovative or not, makes the constitution better than its alternatives take pride of place in constitutional interpretation. This is not because the balance of these merit reasons always defeats all other reasons with which they may conflict. This is not so. Other reasons may rightly defeat merit reasons on various occasions. The court may, to mention but one familiar consideration, adopt an interpretation that renders the constitution inferior to what it would be on one or more alternative interpretations, in order to placate a hostile legislature or executive, which may otherwise take action to limit the power of the courts or to compromise their independence. Merit reasons are the primary reasons because they define the task of the courts in constitutional interpretation: Their task is to apply the constitution when it is adequate to its task and to improve it when it is wanting. Their success, and therefore the merit of maintaining the existing system of constitutional courts, depends on their being good at this task. If in the long run the constitutional courts are not good at performing their task (i.e. not as good as some alternative might be), then one should reform them or assign some of their functions to another institution. But, to repeat, the fact that merit reasons are primary does not mean that they are the only reasons constitutional courts can take account of, nor that they are always decisive.

In section II.B it was argued that when we consider the legitimacy of a constitution as a whole, merit reasons often underdetermine the verdict. Often the constitution we have is legitimate not because it is superior to any alternative we may have, but because we have it, and there is nothing fundamentally wrong with it; that is it lies within the bounds of the morally permissible. It would be a mistake, however, to think that it *follows* that if the constitution is legitimate then considerations of merit play no role in constitutional interpretation. Given that a country has a legitimate constitution and that it developed institutions and practices to fit its constitution, many considerations of merit apply that would not have applied otherwise. For example, given that in democracies a major consideration in defining the reach of the doctrine of freedom of expression is the importance of the freedom for democratic

politics, the boundaries of the right to free expression will inevitably depend in part on the powers of government, in all its branches. Roughly speaking, the more wide-ranging are the powers of the government, the more extensive is the right to free expression.

Merit reasons also depend on other aspects of the economic, social, and legal life of a country. Compare two examples, both relating to the proper balance between freedom of expression and the protection of the administration of justice from undue influence by the media. First, this balance depends on the conduct of the media in the country. When good sense prevails in practice, freedom of the press can and should be wider than when the conduct of the media is careless of the need to protect the administration of justice from its influence. Second, the balance also depends on whether trials and other legal proceedings take place before juries or before professional judges sitting without lay jurors. In the second example the doctrine of freedom of expression is affected by merit reasons that depend on another aspect of the constitution; in the first example it is affected by social practices that are not enshrined in law. In both cases merit reasons have considerable weight even though the constitution the provisions of which are litigated is not the only morally good one, but merely a morally permissible constitution legitimated by practice.

Having said that, I should add that although merit reasons are central to constitutional adjudication, they will often be incommensurate. They will fail to determine which constitutional provision is better. As was anticipated earlier, this does not mean that there will be no sound reasons for establishing that the courts should prefer one interpretation over others. For the most part, however, these reasons are particularly time-bound and agent-bound. That is, they may be reasons that apply at a particular point in time but lapse fairly quickly, and they may be reasons for the courts to interpret the constitution one way or another, without being reasons for other agents to do so. My example of the way the scope of freedom of expression depends on how mindful the media are of the need to protect the administration of justice illustrates the familiar point that the temporal relativity of reasons for a constitutional interpretation affects merit reasons as well as others. The way nonmerit reasons may be relative to the interpreting agent is illustrated by the example of a preference for an interpretation that will not trigger action by the legislature against the courts. Suppose an individual relies in her dealings with an agency belonging to the executive branch of government on an interpretation that, were it adopted by the courts, would offend the legislature. The executive and its agencies cannot legitimately refrain from accepting the validity of the interpretation because of these considerations. The supposition is that only the courts are in disfavour with the legislature. Organs of the executive should, therefore, adopt the interpretation supported by merit considerations. Unfortunately, if they refuse, the individual may not find relief in the courts, which may be rightly inhibited from adopting the "best" interpretation.

Much more can be said about the relative role of merit and other considerations. But we have to turn back to the issue of incommensurability. Let me summarize the points made so far: (1) Moral reasons motivate all interpretive decisions, both conserving ones and innovative ones. (2) Merit considerations may justify an innovative interpretation even when a conserving interpretation is possible, that is even when the issue is settled by the constitution as it is. That would be the case when the need to improve the law is greater than the need for continuity on the point, and when there is an interpretation that improves the law. (3) When the constitution is underdetermined on the issue in question, the need for improvement exists and meets no direct opposition from considerations of continuity. (4) The fact that the constitutional scheme as a whole is legitimated by practice, and is merely permissible, does not mean that merit considerations are exhausted. (5) Although merit reasons are the primary reasons for innovative interpretations, they are not the only relevant ones. There are sound interpretive reasons that are not merit reasons and that compete with them. (6) Those other reasons can determine the right interpretation to adopt even when both the constitution as it is at the time and the merit reasons fail to resolve the issue at hand. The question is: How are courts to decide cases in which these reasons also fail to resolve the issue and determine the outcome of the case?

Why is this a problem? Rational action is action for a reason that is reasonably thought to be undefeated. It is not action for a reason that defeats all those which conflict with it.[30] We have no difficulty in choosing which orange to pick from a bowl of oranges just because there is nothing to choose between them. Of course, incommensurable reasons are not reasons of equal strength. But the fact that no one incommensurable reason defeats the others should not present a mystery about how we manage to choose what to do when facing incommensurable reasons.

Incommensurability of reasons is pervasive, and while we are far from having a satisfactory philosophical explanation of all its aspects, it does not pose a difficulty in explaining how we can act without belief that the act we perform is supported by stronger reasons than all its alternatives. Yet there is a problem here. It is a problem specific to law and to other public actions. It arises not from a difficulty of squaring incommensurability of reasons with a theory of rational action or rational choice, but from a principle of political morality, namely the principle of the public accountability of public actions. This principle directs not only that courts should take their decisions for cogent reasons and that they should avoid irrelevant reasons, but also that as far as possible the fact that no irrelevant considerations affected the decision should be publicly visible. This principle makes it inappropriate for the courts to act as people do when confronted by incommensurability of reasons for the options facing them. People's choices are in part not dictated by any reason. They reveal dispositions and tastes they have that may or may not be important in their lives, but are nonrational in nature. It is important for institutions acting for the public not to take decisions the explanations for which are the nonrational dispositions or tastes of the people who hold office in them. Public institutions should develop or adopt distancing devices—devices they can rely on to settle such issues in a way that is independent of the personal tastes of the judges or other officials involved.

The need for this distancing is one of the reasons why many judges persist in arguing that at no point did they rely in their decisions on anything other than a conserving interpretation of the law and that there is only one such true interpretation. But the law can and should provide them with genuine distancing devices. Elsewhere I have suggested that legal doctrine can and does play such a role.[31] Legal doctrine can be, of course, no more than what morality dictates. But notoriously doctrine can take a life of its own, detached from moral considerations. This tendency in legal thought is often decried as formalism, conceptualism, or essentialism, and often it deserves the criticism. But criticism is deserved—in constitutional law—only in cases where relying on formal legal reasoning prevents a court from adopting an innovative interpretation that could improve the constitution. In cases where reasons for the two or more best interpretations are incommensurate, reliance on formal legal reasoning is justified; it serves as a distancing device.

I am not arguing, of course, that such distancing devices are always available in the law. On the contrary, I asserted earlier that often they are unavailable and the law is indeterminate. I am simply pointing out the desirability of having them available. We can now return for the last time to the argument expounded earlier in this part, that it is frequently appropriate for courts to adopt an innovative interpretation even when there is a conserving interpretation they could adopt instead. Some legal doctrines and methods of interpretation fall into my category of formal doctrines—ones that are not justified by moral value or whose application to the case at hand cannot be so justified. Formal legal doctrines, I have been arguing, are valuable. But they should not be used to stop the courts from resorting to moral considerations to develop and improve the law.

They should be brought into play only once moral resources have been exhausted, when the courts need to resort to distancing devices to justify their choice between otherwise incommensurate interpretations.

E. Coda: But Is It the Same Constitution?

Possibly this doubt is not yet laid to rest. If the courts make the constitution, does it not follow that many people who believe that, let us say, they are living under a constitution adopted two hundred years ago are mistaken? Is it not the case that if people like me are right then the constitution has been made and remade many times since, and we are not now living under the constitution then adopted? It has to be admitted that people who do not realize that the law of the constitution lies as much in the interpretive decisions of the courts as in the original document that they interpret, and who deny that courts are entitled to adopt innovative interpretations, are making a mistake. But it is not the mistake of thinking that it is the same constitution. It is still the constitution adopted two hundred years ago, just as a person who lives in an eighteenth-century house lives in a house built two hundred years ago. His house had been repaired, added to, and changed many times since. But it is still the same house and so is the constitution.

A person may, of course, object to redecorating the house or to changing its windows, saying that it would not be the same. In that sense it is true that an old constitution is not the same as a new constitution, just as an old person is not the same as the same person when young. Sameness in that sense is not the sameness of identity (the old person is identical with the young person she once was). It is the sameness of all the intrinsic properties of the object. Sometimes there are good reasons to preserve not only the same object, but the same object with all its intrinsic properties intact. In the case of constitutions, such reasons are moral reasons. When they prevail, only a conserving interpretation is appropriate. Like many others, I have pointed out a range of reasons for thinking that they do not always prevail. The point of my coda is to warn against confusing change with loss of identity and against the spurious arguments it breeds. Dispelling errors is all that a general theory of the constitution can aspire to achieve.

NOTES

1. See, for an extended discussion, Raz, J. *The Morality of Freedom*. Oxford: Clarendon Press, 1986. pt I; and Raz, J. *Ethics in the Public Domain*. Rev. edn. Oxford: Clarendon Press, 1995. essays 9 and 10.

2. I discussed some of them in *The Concept of a Legal System*. 2nd edn. Oxford: OUP, 1980. 29–32.

3. The question of the authority of law does not exhaust the issue of political obligation, but it is a major part of it.

4. Possibly, some hold judicial office for reasons of personal advantage even when they believe that it is morally wrong for them to do so. In some oppressive regimes we can imagine judges and other officials perpetrating immoralities out of fear for their life or the life of their families. In such circumstances it may be morally excusable to act as they do. But these are likely to be the exception, and I will disregard such cases in the present discussion.

5. See Hart, H.L.A. *The Concept of Law*. Oxford: OUP, 1961. Rev. edn., 1994.

6. The views expressed in this paragraph and the next are at variance with Hart's own interpretation of the rule of recognition, as explained in the postscript to the revised edition of *The Concept of Law*.

7. Other variants of the argument relate it to democracy rather than consent. The considerations advanced against the version considered in the text have to be adapted to apply to other variants of the argument.

8. I have discussed them in "Government by Consent." *Ethics in the Public Domain* 355.

9. Meaning not that consenting was rational given the information, but that—judged in light of the information generally available at the time—the information known to the agent presented roughly a true picture of the (non-evaluative) features of the situation, in as much as they were relevant to his decision.

10. This is not to deny that arguments which are not consent-based cannot be presented as relating to hypothetical consent: Suppose you have an obligation deriving from whatever source to recognize the authority of certain governments. It follows trivially that if you know your obligations you would consent that you have an obligation to recognize the authority of such governments.

11. Or that it plays only a secondary role in establishing authority over such areas.

12. The directness is important here. Ultimately all moral principles either are or derive from universal principles. The laws belonging to this category are justified by direct reference to universal principles of conduct, without the mediation of complex arguments regarding the way these apply to social and economic conditions.

13. This notion of coordination captures, I believe, the natural meaning of the term as used in political discourse. I have used it in this sense in writing about the justification of authority. Consequently it varies from the artificial sense given the term in game theory.

14. Bad laws, i.e. laws that should be repealed or amended, can have moral legitimacy; that is, one may have a moral obligation to apply them or to obey them.

15. As is well known, this claim needs careful statement that may include clarifications we need not enter into here. It may, for example, be the case that only creatures having a capacity for moral knowledge, and moral life, can have the ability to identify and understand social facts.

16. For reasons of convenience I follow the convention of contrasting fact with norm, or with morality or value. I do not mean to imply that there are no moral facts.

17. And there are possible alternatives that deviate from the simple way in which fact and norm are neatly separated into two distinct stages, and allow some mixing in certain circumstances.

18. Not every social fact can be a source of law. It must satisfy other conditions that need not concern us here.

19. In recent times its importance has been emphasized by Finnis, J. *Natural Law and Natural Rights*. Oxford: OUP, 1979.

20. The fact that morality underdetermines the content of the constitution seems to follow from the thesis that moral values are extensively and significantly incommensurable. I have explored this view in several publications, especially in *The Morality of Freedom*, chapter 13; and *Engaging Reason*. Oxford: OUP, 1999. Chapter 3.

21. This conclusion can be strengthened. Even when an alternative constitution is somewhat better than the one we have, the fact that this is the one we have makes it legitimate. The considerations that support this conclusion and give it more precise meaning arise out of the cost of change and the conservative presumption.

22. One should always remember, but I will not repeat the point again, that the self-legitimating aspect of

constitutional practices is subject to their falling within what is morally acceptable.

23. As is clear, this does not imply accepting that for any question about the interpretation of the law there is only one acceptable answer.

24. For the reasons for denying that every time we understand something we interpret it see the application of Wittgenstein's position in Marmor, A. *Interpretation and Legal Theory.* Oxford: OUP, 1994. For my own stab at a general account of interpretation see chapter 10 of the present volume. [Ed.: Not included in this reading.]

25. We can imagine a more moderate objector who allows the courts creative functions in special circumstances. I am using the extreme position as a way to explain my argument.

26. A notion introduced by Nozick, Robert. *Anarchy, State and Utopia.* New York: Basic Books, 1974. For his notion is of exceptionless side constraints, except in extremis, see 28ff.

27. I am overlooking here the objection to this position that challenges its intelligibility and claims that whatever the courts' intentions, they cannot but engage in developing and modifying the law, at least on occasion. The argument in the text goes a long way beyond that conclusion and establishes that there are occasions when courts should engage in innovative interpretation even when they can avoid doing so.

28. But remember the distinction between continuity in the law and continuity in its effects introduced earlier. The first is needed typically only when it is necessary for the second.

29. This formula is meant to capture the conclusions of chapter 11, "Intention in Interpretation." [Ed.: Not included in this reading.]

30. I am relying here on my analysis in chapter 3 of *Engaging Reason.*

31. Raz, J. "On the Autonomy of Legal Reasoning." *Ethics in the Public Domain* 326.

CHAPTER TEN

What Are Rights?

32   The Nature and Value of Rights

JOEL FEINBERG

1

I would like to begin by conducting a thought experiment. Try to imagine Nowheresville—a world very much like our own except that no one, or hardly any one (the qualification is not important), has *rights*. If this flaw makes Nowheresville too ugly to hold very long in contemplation, we can make it as pretty as we wish in other moral respects. We can, for example, make the human beings in it as attractive and virtuous as possible without taxing our conceptions of the limits of human nature. In particular, let the virtues of moral sensibility flourish. Fill this imagined world with as much benevolence, compassion, sympathy, and pity as it will conveniently hold without strain. Now we can imagine men helping one another from compassionate motives merely, quite as much or even more than they do in our actual world from a variety of more complicated motives.

This picture, pleasant as it is in some respects, would hardly have satisfied Immanuel Kant. Benevolently motivated actions do good, Kant admitted, and therefore are better, *ceteris paribus* than

malevolently motivated actions; but no action can have supreme kind of worth—what Kant called "moral worth"—unless its whole motivating power derives from the thought that it is *required by duty*. Accordingly, let us try to make Nowheresville more appealing to Kant by introducing the idea of duty into it, and letting the sense of duty be a sufficient motive for many beneficent and honorable actions. But doesn't this bring our original thought experiment to an abortive conclusion? If duties are permitted entry into Nowheresville, are not rights necessarily smuggled in along with them?

The question is well-asked, and requires here a brief digression so that we might consider the so-called "doctrine of the logical correlativity of rights and duties." This is the doctrine that (1) all duties entail other people's rights and (2) all rights entail other people's duties. Only the first part of the doctrine, the alleged entailment from duties to rights, need concern us here. Is this part of the doctrine correct? It should not be surprising that my answer is: "In a sense yes and in a sense no."

Etymologically, the word *duty* is associated with actions that are *due* someone else, the

Journal of Value Inquiry, 4, no. 4 (Dec 1970), 243–60. © 1970 Kluwer Academic Publishers. Reprinted with kind permission of Kluwer Academic Publishers.

payments of debts *to* creditors, the keeping of agreements with promises, the payment of club dues, or legal fees, or tariff levies to appropriate authorities or their representatives. In this original sense of "duty," all duties are correlated with the rights of those *to whom* the duty is owed. However, there seem to be numerous classes of duties, both of a legal and nonlegal kind, that are *not* logically correlated with the rights of other persons. This seems to be a consequence of the fact that the word *duty* has come to be used for *any* action understood to be *required,* whether by the rights of others, or by law, or by higher authority, or by conscience, or whatever. When the notion of requirement is in clear focus it is likely to seem the only element in the idea of duty that is essential, and the other component notion—that a duty is something *due* someone else—drops off. Thus, in this widespread but derivative usage, *duty* tends to be used for any action we feel we *must* (for whatever reason) do. It comes, in short, to be a term of moral modality merely; and it is no wonder that the first thesis of the logical correlativity doctrine often fails.

Let us then introduce duties into Nowheresville, but only in the sense of actions that are, or are believed to be, morally mandatory, not in the older sense of actions that are due others and can be claimed by others as their right. Nowheresville now can have duties of the sort imposed by positive law. A legal duty is not something we are implored or advised to do merely; it is something the law, or an authority under the law, *requires* us to do whether we want to or not, under pain of penalty. When traffic lights turn red, however, there is no determinate person who can plausibly be said to claim our stopping as his due, so that the motorist owes it to *him* to stop, in the way a debtor owes it to his creditor to pay. In our own actual world, of course, we sometimes owe it to our *fellow motorists* to stop; but that kind of right-correlated duty does not exist in Nowheresville. There, motorists "owe" obedience to the Law, but they owe nothing to one another. When they collide, no matter who is at fault, no one is morally accountable to anyone else, and no one has any sound grievance or "right to complain."

When we leave legal contexts to consider moral obligations and other extra-legal duties, a greater variety of duties without correlative rights present themselves. Duties of charity, for example, require us to contribute to one or another of a large number of eligible recipients, no one of whom can claim our contribution from us as his due. Charitable contributions are more like gratuitous services, favors, and gifts than like repayments of debts or reparations; and yet we do have duties to be charitable. Many persons, moreover, in our actual world believe that they are required by their own consciences to do more than that "duty" that *can* be demanded of them by their prospective beneficiaries. I cite to you the phrase, quoted by H. B. Acton, of a character in a Malraux novel who "gave all his supply of poison to his fellow prisoners to enable them by suicide to escape the burning alive which was to be their fate and his." This man, Acton adds, "probably did not think that [the others] had more of a right to the poison than he had, though he thought it his duty to give it to them."[1] I am sure that there are many actual examples, less dramatically heroic than this fictitious one, of persons who believe, rightly or wrongly, that they *must do* something (hence the word *duty*) for another person in excess of what that person can appropriately demand (hence the absence of "right").

Now the digression is over and we can return to Nowheresville and summarize what we have put in it thus far. We now find spontaneous benevolence in somewhat larger degree than in our actual world, and also the acknowledged existence of duties of obedience, duties of charity, and duties imposed by exacting private consciences, and also, let us suppose, a degree of conscientiousness in respect to those duties somewhat in excess of what is to be found in our actual world. I doubt that Kant would be fully satisfied with Nowheresville even now that duty and respect for law and authority have been added to it; but I feel certain that he would regard their addition at least as an improvement. I will now introduce two further moral practices into Nowheresville that will make that world very little more appealing to Kant, but will make it appear more familiar to us. These are the practices connected with the notions of *personal desert* and what I call a *sovereign monopoly of rights.*

When a person is said to deserve something good from us what is meant in part is that there would be a certain propriety in our giving that good thing to him in virtue of the kind of person he is, perhaps, or more likely, in virtue of some specific thing he has done. The propriety involved here is a much weaker kind than that which derives from our having promised him the good thing or from his having qualified for it by satisfying the well-advertised conditions of some public rule. In the latter case he could be said not merely to deserve the good thing but also to have a *right* to it, that is to be in a position to demand it as his due; and of course we will not have that sort of thing in Nowheresville. That weaker kind of propriety which is mere desert is simply a kind of *fittingness* between one party's character or action and another party's favorable response, much like that between human and laughter, or good performance and applause.

The following seems to be the origin of the idea of deserving good or bad treatment from others: A master or lord was under no obligation to reward his servant for especially good service; still a master might naturally feel that there would be a special fittingness in giving a gratuitous reward as a grateful response to the good service (or conversely imposing a penalty for bad service). Such an act, although surely fitting and proper, was entirely supererogatory. The fitting response in turn from the rewarded servant should be gratitude. If the deserved reward had not been given him he should have had no complaint, since he only *deserved* the reward, as opposed to having a *right* to it, or a ground for claiming it as his due.

The idea of desert has evolved a good bit away from its beginnings by now, but nevertheless, it seems clearly to be one of those words J. L. Austin said "never entirely forget their pasts."[2] Today servants qualify for their wages by doing their agreed-upon chores, no more and no less. If their wages are not forthcoming, their contractual rights have been violated and they can make legal claim to the money that is their due. If they do less than they agreed to do, however, their employers may "dock" them, by paying them proportionately less than the agreed-upon fee. This is all a matter of right. But if the servant does a

splendid job, above and beyond his minimal contractual duties, the employer is under no further obligation to reward him, for this was not agreed upon, even tacitly, in advance. The additional service was all the servant's idea and done entirely on his own. Nevertheless, the morally sensitive employer may feel that it would be exceptionally appropriate for him to respond, freely on *his* own, to the servant's meritorious service, with a reward. The employee cannot demand it as his due, but he will happily accept it, with gratitude, as a fitting response to his desert.

In our age of organized labor, even this picture is now archaic; for almost every kind of exchange of service is governed by hard-bargained contracts, so that even bonuses can sometimes be demanded as a matter of right, and nothing is given for nothing on either side of the bargaining table. And perhaps that is a good thing; for consider an anachronistic instance of the earlier kind of practice that survives, at least as a matter of form, in the quaint old practice of "tipping." The tip was originally conceived as a reward that has to be earned by "zealous service." It is not something to be taken for granted as a standard response to *any* service. That is to say that its payment is a *gratuity,* not a discharge of obligation, but something given apart from, or in addition to, anything the recipient can expect as a matter of right. That is what tipping originally meant at any rate, and tips are still referred to as "gratuities" in the tax forms. But try to explain all that to a New York cab driver! If he has *earned* his gratuity, by God, he has it coming, and there had better be sufficient acknowledgment of his desert or he'll give you a piece of his mind! I'm not generally prone to defend New York cab drivers, but they do have a point here. There is the making of a paradox in the queerly unstable concept of an "earned gratuity." One can understand how "desert" in the weak sense of "propriety" or "mere fittingness" tends to generate a stronger sense in which desert is itself the ground for a claim of right.

In Nowheresville, nevertheless, we will have only the original weak kind of desert. Indeed, it will be impossible to keep this idea out if we allow such practices as teachers grading students, judges awarding prizes, and servants serving benevolent but class-conscious masters. Nowheresville is a reasonably good world in many ways, and its teachers, judges, and masters will generally try to give students, contestants, and servants the grades, prizes, and rewards they deserve. For this the recipients will be grateful; but they will never think to complain, or even feel aggrieved, when expected responses to desert fail. The masters, judges, and teachers don't *have* to do good things, after all, for *anyone*. One should be happy that they *ever* treat us well, and not grumble over their occasional lapses. Their hoped-for responses, after all, are *gratuities,* and there is no wrong in the omission of what is merely gratuitous. Such is the response of persons who have no concept of *rights,* even persons who are proud of their own deserts.[3]

Surely, one might ask, rights have to come in somewhere, if we are to have even moderately complex forms of social organization. Without rules that confer rights and impose obligations, how can we have ownership or property, bargains and deals, promises and contracts, appointments and loans, marriages and partnerships? Very well, let us introduce all of these social and economic practices into Nowheresville, but *with one big twist*. With them I should like to introduce the curious notion of a "sovereign right–monopoly." You will recall that the subjects in Hobbes's *The Leviathan* had no rights whatever against their sovereign. He could do as he liked with them, even gratuitously harm them, but this gave them no valid grievance against him. The sovereign, to be sure, had a certain duty to treat his subjects well, but this duty was owed not to the subjects directly, but to God, just as we might have a duty to a person to treat his property well, but of course no duty to the property itself but only to its owner. Thus, while the sovereign was quite capable of *harming* his subjects, he could commit no wrong against them that they could complain about, since they had no prior claims against his conduct. The only party *wronged* by the sovereign's mistreatment of his subjects was God, the supreme lawmaker. Thus, in repenting cruelty to his subjects, the sovereign might say to God, as

David after killing Uriah, "Against Thee, Thee only, have I sinned."[4]

Even in *The Leviathan,* however, ordinary people had ordinary rights *against one another*. They played roles, occupied offices, made agreements, and signed contracts. In a genuine "sovereign right–monopoly," as I shall be using that phrase, they will do all those things too, and thus incur genuine obligations toward one another; but the obligations (here is the twist) will not be owed directly *to* promisees, creditors, parents, and the like, but rather to God alone, or to the members of some elite, or to a single sovereign under God. Hence, the rights correlative to the obligations that derive from these transactions are all owned by some "outside" authority.

As far as I know, no philosopher has ever suggested that even our role and contract obligations (in this, our actual world) are all owed directly to a divine intermediary; but some theologians have approached such extreme moral occasionalism. I have in mind the familiar phrase in certain widely distributed religious tracts that "it takes three to marry," which suggests that marital vows are not made between bride and groom directly but between each spouse and God, so that if one breaks his vow, the other cannot rightly complain of being wronged, since only God could have claimed performance of the marital duties as his *own* due; and hence God alone had a claim–right violated by nonperformance. If John breaks his vow to God, he might then properly repent in the words of David: "Against Thee only have I sinned."

In our actual world, very few spouses conceive of their mutual obligations in this way; but their small children, at a certain stage in their moral upbringing, are likely to feel precisely this way toward *their* mutual obligations. If Billy kicks Bobby and is punished by Daddy, he may come to feel contrition for his naughtiness induced by his painful estrangement from the loved parent. He may then be happy to make amends and sincere apology *to Daddy;* but when Daddy insists that he apologize to his wronged brother, that is another story. A direct apology to Billy would be a tacit recognition of Billy's status as a right holder against him, someone he can wrong as well as harm, and someone to whom he is directly accountable for his wrongs. This is a status Bobby will happily accord Daddy; but it would imply a respect for Billy that he does not presently feel, so he bitterly resents according it to him. On the "three-to-marry" model, the relations between each spouse and God would be like those between Bobby and Daddy; respect for the other spouse as an independent claimant would not even be necessary; and where present, of course, never sufficient.

The advocates of the "three-to-marry" model who conceive it either as a description of our actual institution of marriage or a recommendation of what marriage ought to be may wish to escape this embarrassment by granting rights to spouses in capacities other than as promisees. They may wish to say, for example, that when John promises God that he will be faithful to Mary, a right is thus conferred not only on God as promisee but also on Mary herself as third-party beneficiary, just as when John contracts with an insurance company and names Mary as his intended beneficiary, she has a right to the accumulated funds after John's death, even though the insurance company made no promise to her. But this seems to be an unnecessarily cumbersome complication contributing nothing to our understanding of the marriage bond. The life insurance transaction is necessarily a three party relation, involving occupants of three distinct offices, no two of whom alone could do the whole job. The transaction, after all, is defined as the purchase by the customer (first office) from the vendor (second office) of protection for a beneficiary (third office) against the customer's untimely death. Marriage, however, in this our actual world, appears to be a binary relation between a husband and wife, and even though third parties such as children, neighbors, psychiatrists, and priests may sometimes be helpful and even causally necessary for the survival of the relation, they are not logically necessary to our *conception* of the relation, and indeed many married couples do quite well without them. Still, I am not now purporting to describe our actual world, but rather trying to contrast it with a counterpart world of the imagination. In *that* world, it takes three to make almost *any* moral relation and all rights are owned by God or some sovereign under God.

There will, of course, be delegated authorities in the imaginary world, empowered to give commands to their underlings and to punish them for their disobedience. But the commands are all given in the name of the sovereign right–monopoly, who in turn are the only persons to whom obligations are owed. Hence, even intermediate superiors do not have claim–rights against their subordinates but only legal *powers* to create obligations in the subordinates *to* the monopolistic right-holders, and also the legal *privilege* to impose penalties in the name of that monopoly.

2

So much for the imaginary "world without rights." If some of the moral concepts and practices I have allowed into that world do not sit well with one another, no matter. Imagine Nowheresville with all of these practices if you can, or with any harmonious subset of them, if you prefer. The important thing is not what I've let into it, but what I have kept out. The remainder of this paper will be devoted to an analysis of what precisely a world is missing when it does not contain rights, and why that absence is morally important.

The most conspicuous difference, I think, between the Nowheresvillians and ourselves has something to do with the activity of *claiming*. Nowheresvillians, even when they are discriminated against invidiously, or left without the things they need, or otherwise badly treated, do not think to leap to their feet and make righteous demands against one another, though they may not hesitate to resort to force and trickery to get what they want. They have no notion of rights, so they do not have a notion of what is their due; hence they do not claim before they take. The conceptual linkage between personal rights and claiming has long been noticed by legal writers and is reflected in the standard usage in which "claim–rights" are distinguished from the mere liberties, immunities, and powers, also sometimes called "rights," with which they are easily confused. When a person has a legal claim–right to X, it must be the case (1) that he is at liberty in respect to X (i.e., that he has no duty to refrain from or relinquish X), and also (2) that his liberty is the ground of other people's *duties* to grant him X or not to interfere with him in respect to X. Thus, in the sense of claim–rights, it is true by definition that rights logically entail other people's duties. The paradigmatic examples of such rights are the creditor's right to be paid a debt by his debtor, and the landowner's right not to be interfered with by anyone in the exclusive occupancy of his land. The creditor's right against his debtor, for example, and the debtor's duty to his creditor are precisely the same relation seen from two different vantage points, as inextricably linked as the two sides of the same coin.

And yet, this is not quite an accurate account of the matter, for it fails to do justice to the way claim–rights are somehow prior to, or more basic than, the duties with which they are necessarily correlated. If Nip has a claim–right against Tuck, it is because of this fact that Tuck has a duty to Nip. It is only because something from Tuck is *due* Nip (directional element) that there is something Tuck *must* do (modal element). This is a relation, moreover, in which Tuck is bound and Nip is free. Nip not only *has* a right, but he can choose whether or not to exercise it, whether to claim it, whether to register complaints upon its infringement, even whether to release Tuck from his duty, and forget the whole thing. If the personal claim–right is also backed up by criminal sanctions, however, Tuck may yet have a duty of obedience to the law from which no one, not even Nip, may release him. He would even have such duties if he lived in Nowheresville; but duties subject to acts of claiming, duties derivative from and contingent upon the personal rights of others, are unknown and undreamed of in Nowheresville.

Many philosophical writers have simply identified rights with claims. The dictionaries tend to define *claims*, in turn, as "assertions of right," a dizzying piece of circularity that led one philosopher to complain, "We go in search of rights and are directed to claims, and then back again to rights in bureaucratic futility."[5] What then is the relation between a claim and a right?

As we shall see, a right *is* a kind of claim, and a claim is "an assertion of right," so that a formal definition of either notion in terms of the other will not get us very far. Thus if a "formal definition" of the usual philosophical sort is what we are after, the game is over before it has begun, and we can say that the concept of a right is a "simple, undefinable, unanalysable primitive." Here as elsewhere in philosophy this will have the effect of making the commonplace seem unnecessarily mysterious. We would be better advised, I think, not to attempt a formal definition of either *right* or *claim,* but rather to use the idea of a claim in informal elucidation of the idea of a right. This is made possible by the fact that *claiming* is an elaborate sort of rule-governed *activity.* A claim is that which is claimed, the object of the act of claiming. There is, after all, a verb "to claim," but no verb "to right." If we concentrate on the whole activity of claiming, which is public, familiar, and open to our observation, rather than on its upshot alone, we may learn more about the generic nature of rights than we could ever hope to learn from a formal definition, even if one were possible. Moreover, certain facts about rights more easily, if not solely, expressible in the language of claims and claiming are essential to a full understanding not only of what rights are, but also why they are so vitally important.

Let us begin then by distinguishing between: (1) making claim to..., (2) claiming that..., and (3) having a claim. One sort of thing we may be doing when we claim is to *make claim to something.* This is "to petition or seek by virtue of supposed right; to demand as due." Sometimes this is done by an acknowledged right-holder when he serves notice that he now wants turned over to him that which has already been acknowledged to be his, something borrowed, say, or improperly taken from him. This is often done by turning in a chit, a receipt, an I.O.U., a check, an insurance policy, or a deed, that is, a *title* to something currently in the possession of someone else. On other occasions, making claim is making application for titles or rights themselves, as when a mining prospector stakes a claim to mineral rights, or a householder to a tract of land in the public domain, or an inventor to his patent rights. In the one kind of case, to make claim is to exercise rights one already has by presenting title; in the other kind of case it is to apply for the title itself, by showing that one has satisfied the conditions specified by a rule for the ownership of title and therefore that one can demand it as one's due.

Generally speaking, only the person who has a title or who has qualified for it, or someone speaking in his name, can make claim to something as a matter of right. It is an important fact about rights (or claims), then, that they can be claimed only by those who have them. Anyone can claim, of course, *that* this umbrella is yours, but only you or your representative can actually claim the umbrella. If Smith owes Jones five dollars, only Jones can claim the five dollars as his own, though any bystander can *claim that* it belongs to Jones. One important difference then between *making legal claim to* and *claiming that* is that the former is a legal performance with direct legal consequences whereas the latter is often a mere piece of descriptive commentary with no legal force. Legally speaking, *making claim to* can itself make things happen. This sense of "claiming," then, might well be called "the performative sense." The legal power to claim (performatively) one's right or the things to which one has a right seems to be essential to the very notion of a right. A right to which one could not make claim (i.e., not even for recognition) would be a very "imperfect" right indeed!

Claiming that one has a right (what we can call "propositional claiming" as opposed to "performative claiming") is another sort of thing one can do with language, but it is not the sort of doing that characteristically has legal consequences. To claim that one has rights is to make an assertion that one has them, and to make it in such a manner as to demand or insist that they be recognized. In this sense of "claim" many things in addition to rights can be claimed, that is, many other kinds of proposition can be asserted in the claiming way. I can claim, for example, that you, he, or she has certain rights, or that Julius Caesar once had certain rights; or I can claim that certain statements are true, or that I have certain skills, or accomplishments, or virtually anything at all. I can claim that the earth is flat. What is essential to *claiming that* is the manner of assertion. One can assert without even caring very much whether any one is listening, but part of the point of prepositional claiming is to *make sure* people listen.

When I claim to others that I know something, for example, I am not merely asserting it, but rather "obtruding my putative knowledge upon their attention, demanding that it be recognized, that appropriate notice be taken of it by those concerned...."[6] Not every truth is properly assertable, much less claimable, in every context. To claim that something is the case in circumstances that justify no more than calm assertion is to behave like a boor. (This kind of boorishness, I might add, is probably less common in Nowheresville.) But not to claim in the appropriate circumstances that one has a right is to be spiritless or foolish. A list of "appropriate circumstances" would include occasions when one is challenged, when one's possession is denied, or seems insufficiently acknowledged or appreciated; and of course even in these circumstances, the claiming should be done only with an appropriate degree of vehemence.

Even if there are conceivable circumstances in which one would admit rights diffidently, there is no doubt that their characteristic use and that for which they are distinctively well suited is to be claimed, demanded, affirmed, and insisted upon. They are especially sturdy objects to "stand upon," a most useful sort of moral furniture. Having rights, of course, makes claiming possible; but it is claiming that gives rights their special moral significance. This feature of rights is connected in a way with the customary rhetoric about what it is to be a human being. Having rights enables us to "stand up like men," to look others in the eye, and to feel in some fundamental way the equal of anyone. To think of oneself as the holder of rights is not to be unduly but properly proud, to have that minimal self-respect that is necessary to be worthy of the love and esteem of others. Indeed, respect for persons (this is an intriguing idea) may simply be respect for their rights, so that there cannot be the one without the other; and what is called "human dignity" may simply be the recognizable capacity to assert claims. To respect a person then, or to think of him as possessed of human dignity, simply *is* to think of him as a potential maker of claims. Not all of this can be packed into a definition of "rights"; but these are *facts* about the possession of rights that argue well their supreme moral importance. More than anything else I am going to say, these facts explain what is wrong with Nowheresville.

We come now to the third interesting employment of the claiming vocabulary, that involving not the verb "to claim" but the substantive "a claim." What is it to *have a claim* and how is this related to rights? I would like to suggest that *having a claim consists in being in a position to claim, that is, to make claim to or claim that.* If this suggestion is correct it shows the primacy of the verbal over the nominative forms. It links claims to a kind of activity and obviates the temptation to think of claims as *things,* on the model of coins, pencils, and other material possessions which we can carry in our hip pockets. To be sure, we often make or establish our claims by presenting titles, and these typically have the form of receipts, tickets, certificates, and other pieces of paper or parchment. The title, however, is not the same thing as the claim; rather it is the evidence that establishes the claim as valid. On this analysis, one might have a claim without ever claiming that to which one is entitled, or without even knowing that one has the claim; for one might simply be ignorant of the fact that one is in a position to claim; or one might be unwilling to exploit that position for one reason or another, including fear that the legal machinery is broken down or corrupt and will not enforce one's claim despite its validity.

Nearly all writers maintain that there is some intimate connection between having a claim and having a right. Some identify right and claim without qualification; some define "right" as justified or justifiable claim, others as recognized claim, still others as valid claim. My own preference is for the latter definition. Some writers, however, reject the identification of rights with valid claims on the ground that all claims as such are valid, so that the expression "valid claim" is redundant. These writers, therefore, would identify rights with claims *simpliciter.* But this is a very simple confusion. All claims, to be sure, are *put forward* as justified, whether they are justified in fact or not. A claim conceded even by its maker to have no validity is not a claim at all, but a mere demand. The highwayman, for example, *demands* his

victim's money; but he hardly makes claim to it as rightfully his own.

But it does not follow from this sound point that it is redundant to qualify claims as justified (or as I prefer, valid) in the definition of a right; for it remains true that not all claims put forward as valid really are valid; and only the valid ones can be acknowledged as rights.

If having a valid claim is not redundant (i.e., if it is not redundant to pronounce *another's* claim valid), there must be such a thing as having a claim that is not valid. What would this be like? One might accumulate just enough evidence to argue with relevance and cogency that one has a right (or ought to be granted a right), although one's case might not be overwhelmingly conclusive. In such a case, one might have strong-enough argument to be entitled to a hearing and given fair consideration. When one is in this position, it might be said that one "has a claim" that deserves to be weighed carefully. Nevertheless, the balance of reasons may turn out to militate against recognition of the claim, so that the claim, which one admittedly had, and perhaps still does, is not a valid claim or right. "Having a claim" in this sense is an expression very much like the legal phrase "having a prima facie case." A plaintiff establishes a prima facie case for the defendant's liability when he establishes grounds that will be sufficient for liability unless outweighed by reasons of a different sort that may be offered by the defendant. Similarly, in the criminal law, a grand jury returns an indictment when it thinks that the prosecution has sufficient evidence to be taken seriously and given a fair hearing, whatever countervailing reasons may eventually be offered on the other side. That initial evidence, serious but not conclusive, is also sometimes called a prima facie case. In a parallel "prima facie sense" of "claim," having a claim to X is not (yet) the same as having a right to X, but is rather having a case of at least minimal plausibility that one has a right to X, a case that does establish a right, not to X, but to a fair hearing and consideration. Claims, so conceived, differ in degree: some are stronger than others. Rights, however, do not differ in degree: no one right is more of a right than another.[7]

Another reason for not identifying rights with claims *simply* is that there is a well-established usage in international law that makes a theoretically interesting distinction between claims and rights. Statesmen are sometimes led to speak of "claims" when they are concerned with the natural needs of deprived human beings in conditions of scarcity. Young orphans *need* good upbringings, balanced diets, education, and technical training everywhere in the world; but unfortunately there are many places where these goods are in such short supply that it is impossible to provision all who need them. If we persist, nevertheless, in speaking of these needs as constituting rights and not merely claims, we are committed to the conception of a right that is an entitlement *to* some good, but not a valid claim *against* any particular individual; for in conditions of scarcity there may be no determinate individuals who can plausibly be said to have a duty to provide the missing goods to those in need. J. E. S. Fawcett therefore prefers to keep the distinction between claims and rights firmly in mind. "Claims," he writes, "are needs and demands in movement, and there is a continuous transformation, as a society advances [toward greater abundance] of economic and social claims into civil and political rights...and not all countries or all claims are by any means at the same stage in the process."[8] The manifesto writers on the other side who seem to identify needs, or at least basic needs, with what they call "human rights" are more properly described, I think, as urging upon the world community the moral principle that *all* basic human needs ought to be recognized as *claims* (in the customary prima facie sense) worthy of sympathy and serious consideration right now, even though, in many cases, they cannot yet plausibly be treated as *valid* claims, that is, as grounds of any other people's duties. This way of talking avoids the anomaly of ascribing to all human beings now, even those in preindustrial societies, such "economic and social rights" as "periodic holidays with pay."[9]

Still, for all of that, I have a certain sympathy with the manifesto writers, and I am even willing to speak of a special "manifesto sense" of "right," in which a right need not be correlated with another's duty. Natural needs are real claims if only upon hypothetical future beings not yet in existence. I accept the moral principle that to have an unfulfilled need is to have a kind of claim against the world, even if against no one in particular. A natural need for some good as such, like a natural desert, is always a reason in support of a claim to that good. A person in need, then, is always "in a position" to make a claim, even when there is no one in the corresponding position to do anything about it. Such claims, based on need alone, are "permanent possibilities of rights," the natural seed from which rights grow. When manifesto writers speak of them as if already actual rights, they are easily forgiven, for this is but a powerful way of expressing the conviction that they ought to be recognized by states here and now as potential rights and consequently as determinants of *present* aspirations and guides to *present* policies. That usage, I think, is a valid exercise of rhetorical license.

I prefer to characterize rights as valid claims rather than justified ones, because I suspect that justification is rather too broad a qualification. "Validity," as I understand it, is justification of a peculiar and narrow kind, namely justification within a system of rules. A man has a legal right when the official recognition of his claim (as valid) is called for by the governing rules. This definition, of course, hardly applies to moral rights, but that is not because the genus of which moral rights are a species is something other than *claims*. A man has a moral right when he has a claim, the recognition of which is called for—not (necessarily) by legal rules—but by moral principles, or the principles of an enlightened conscience.

There is one final kind of attack on the generic identification of rights with claims, and it has been launched with great spirit in a recent article by H. J. McCloskey, who holds that rights are not essentially claims at all, but rather entitlements. The springboard of his argument is his insistence that rights in their essential character are always *rights to*, not *rights against*:

> My right to life is not a right against anyone. It is my right and by virtue of it, it is normally permissible for me to sustain my life in the face of obstacles. It does give rise to rights against others *in the sense* that others have or may come to have duties to refrain from killing me, but it is essentially a

right of mine, not an infinite list of claims, hypothetical and actual, against an infinite number of actual, potential, and as yet nonexistent human beings....Similarly, the right of the tennis club member to play on the club courts is a right to play, not a right against some vague group of potential or possible obstructors.[10]

The argument seems to be that since rights are essentially rights *to,* whereas claims are essentially claims *against,* rights cannot be claims, though they can be grounds for claims. The argument is doubly defective though. First of all, contrary to McCloskey, rights (at least legal claim–rights) *are* held *against* others. McCloskey admits this in the case of in personam rights (what he calls "special rights") but denies it in the case of in rem rights (which he calls "general rights"):

> Special rights are sometimes against specific individuals or institutions—e.g., rights created by promises, contracts, etc....but these differ from... characteristic...general rights where the right is simply a right to....[11]

As far as I can tell, the only reason McCloskey gives for denying that in rem rights are against others is that those against whom they would have to hold make up an enormously multitudinous and "vague" group, including hypothetical people not yet even in existence. Many others have found this a paradoxical consequence of the notion of in rem rights, but I see nothing troublesome in it. If a general rule gives me a right of noninterference in a certain respect against everybody, then there are literally hundreds of millions of people who have a duty toward me in that respect; and if the same general rule gives the same right to everyone else, then it imposes on me literally hundreds of millions of duties—or duties toward hundreds of millions of people. I see nothing paradoxical about this, however. The duties, after all, are negative, and I can discharge all of them at a stroke simply by minding my own business. And if all human beings make up one moral community and there are hundreds of millions of human beings, we should expect there to be hundreds of millions of moral relations holding between them.

McCloskey's other premise is even more obviously defective. There is no good reason to think that all *claims* are "essentially" *against,* rather than *to.* Indeed most of the discussion of previous claims has been of claims *to,* and as we have seen, the law finds it useful to recognize claims *to* (or "mere claims") that are not yet qualified to be claims *against,* or rights (except in a "manifesto sense" of "rights").

Whether we are speaking of claims or rights, however, we must notice that they seem to have two dimensions, as indicated by the prepositions *to* and *against,* and it is quite natural to wonder whether either of these dimensions is somehow more fundamental or essential than the other. All rights seem to merge *entitlements to* do, have, omit, or be something with *claims against* others to act or refrain from acting in certain ways. In some statements of rights the entitlement is perfectly determinate (e.g., *to* play tennis) and the claim vague (e.g., *against* "some vague group of potential or possible obstructors"); but in other cases the object of the claim is clear and determinate (e.g., *against* one's parents), and the entitlement general and indeterminate (e.g., to be given a proper upbringing). If we mean by "entitlement" that *to* which one has a right and by "claim" something directed at those *against* whom the right holds (as McCloskey apparently does), then we can say that all claim–rights necessarily involve both, though in individual cases the one element or the other may be in sharper focus.

In brief conclusion: To have a right is to have a claim against someone whose recognition as valid is called for by some set of governing rules or moral principles. To have a *claim,* in turn, is to have a case meriting consideration, that is, to have reasons or grounds that put one in a position to engage in performative and propositional claiming. The activity of claiming, finally, as much as any other thing, makes for self-respect and respect for others, gives a sense to the notion of personal dignity, and distinguishes this otherwise morally flawed world from the even worse world of Nowheresville.

NOTES

1. Acton, H. B. "Symposium on 'Rights'." *Proceedings of the Aristotelian Society.* Supplementary Volume 24 (1950): 107–108.

2. Austin, J. L. "A Plea for Excuses." *Proceedings of the Aristotelian Society.* Vol. 57 (1956–57).

3. For a fuller discussion of the concept of personal desert see my "Justice and Personal Desert." *Nomos VI, Justice.* Eds. C. J. Friedrich and J. Chapman. New York: Atherton Press, 1963. 69–97.

4. Psalm 51:4; II Sam. 11. Cited with approval by Thomas Hobbes in *The Leviathan,* Part II, Chap. 21.

5. Supra, note 1.

6. Warnock, G. J. "Claims to Knowledge." *Proceedings of the Aristotelian Society.* Supplementary Volume 36 (1962): 21.

7. This is the important difference between rights and mere claims. It is analogous to the difference between *evidence* of guilt (subject to degrees of cogency) and *conviction* of guilt (which is all or nothing). One can "have evidence" that is not conclusive, just as one can "have a claim" that is not valid. "Prima-facieness" is built into the sense of "claim," but the notion of a "prima-facie right" makes little sense. On the latter point see Melden, A. I. *Rights and Right Conduct.* Oxford: Basil Blackwell, 1959. 18–20; and Morris, Herbert. "Persons and Punishment." *The Monist.* Vol. 52 (1968). 498–499.

8. Fawcett, J. E. S. "The International Protection of Human Rights." *Political Theory and the Rights of Man.* Ed. D. D. Raphael. Bloomington: Indiana University Press, 1967). 125, 128.

9. As declared in Article 24 of *The Universal Declaration of Human Rights* adopted on December 10, 1948, by the General Assembly of the United Nations.

10. McCloskey, H. J. "Rights." *Philosophical Quarterly.* Vol. 15 (1965): 118.

11. Id.

33 Are There Any Natural Rights?

H. L. A. HART[1]

I shall advance the thesis that if there are any moral rights at all, it follows that there is at least one natural right, the equal right of all men to be free. By saying that there is this right, I mean that in the absence of certain special conditions which are consistent with the right being an equal right, any adult human being capable of choice (1) has the right to forbearance on the part of all others from the use of coercion or restraint against him save to hinder coercion or restraint and (2) is at liberty to do (i.e., is under no obligation to abstain from) any action which is not one coercing or restraining or designed to injure other persons.[2]

I have two reasons for describing the equal right of all men to be free as a *natural* right; both of them were always emphasized by the classical theorists of natural rights. (1) This right is one which all men have if they are capable of choice; they have it *qua* men and not only if they are members of some society or stand in some special relation to each other. (2) This right is not created or conferred by men's voluntary action; other moral rights are.[3] Of course, it is quite obvious that my thesis is not as ambitious as the traditional theories of natural rights; for although on my view all men are *equally* entitled to be free in the sense explained, no man has an absolute or unconditional right to do or not to do any particular thing or to be treated in any particular way; coercion or restraint of any action may be justified in special conditions consistently with the general principle. So my argument will not show that men have any right (save the equal right of all to be free) that is "absolute," "indefeasible," or "imprescriptible." This may for many reduce the importance of my contention, but I think that the principle that all men have an equal right to be free, meager as it may seem, is probably all that the political philosophers of the liberal tradition need have claimed to support any program of

From *The Philosophical Review* 64 (1955): 175–91. Reprinted with permission of the publisher.

action even if they have claimed more. But my contention that there is this one natural right may appear unsatisfying in another respect; it is only the conditional assertion that *if* there are any moral rights then there must be this one natural right. Perhaps few would now deny, as some have, that there are moral rights; for the point of that denial was usually to object to some philosophical claim as to the "ontological status" of rights, and this objection is now expressed not as a denial that there are any moral rights but as a denial of some assumed logical similarity between sentences used to assert the existence of rights and other kinds of sentences. But it is still important to remember that there may be codes of conduct quite properly termed moral codes (though we can of course say they are "imperfect") that do not employ the notion of *a* right, and there is nothing contradictory or otherwise absurd in a code or morality consisting wholly of prescriptions or in a code that prescribed only what should be done for the realization of happiness or some ideal of personal perfection.[4] Human actions in such systems would be evaluated or criticized as compliances with prescriptions or as *good* or *bad*, *right* or *wrong*, *wise* or *foolish*, *fitting* or *unfitting*, but no one in such a system would have, exercise, or claim rights, or violate or infringe them. So those who lived by such systems could not of course be committed to the recognition of the equal right of all to be free; nor, I think (and this is one respect in which the notion of a right differs from other moral notions), could any parallel argument be constructed to show that, from the bare fact that actions were recognized as ones which ought or ought not to be done, as right, wrong, good or bad, it followed that some specific kind of conduct fell under these categories.

I

(A) Lawyers have for their own purposes carried the dissection of the notion of a legal right some distance, and some of their results[5] are of value in the elucidation of statements of the form "X has a right to ..." outside legal contexts. There is of course no simple identification to be made between moral and legal rights, but there is an intimate connection between the two, and this itself is one feature that distinguishes a moral right from other fundamental moral concepts. It is not merely that as a matter of fact men speak of their moral rights mainly when advocating their incorporation in a legal system, but that the concept of a right belongs to that branch of morality that is specifically concerned to determine when one person's freedom may be limited by another's[6] and so to determine what actions may appropriately be made the subject of coercive legal rules. The words *droit, diritto,* and *Recht,* used by continental jurists, have no simple English translation and seem to English jurists to hover uncertainly between law and morals, but they do in fact mark off an area of morality (the morality of law) which has special characteristics. It is occupied by the concepts of justice, fairness, rights, and obligation (if this last is not used as it is by many moral philosophers as an obscuring general label to cover every action that morally we ought to do or forbear from doing). The most important common characteristic of this group of moral concepts is that there is no incongruity, but a special congruity in the use of force or the threat of force to secure that what is just or fair or someone's right to have done shall in fact be done; for it is in just these circumstances that coercion of another human being is legitimate. Kant, in the *Rechtslehre,* discusses the obligations that arise in this branch of morality under the title of *officia juris,* "which do not require that respect for duty shall be of itself the determining principle of the will," and contrasts them with *officia virtutis,* which have no moral worth unless done for the sake of the moral principle. His point is, I think, that we must distinguish from the rest of morality those principles regulating the proper distribution of human freedom that alone make it morally legitimate for one human being to determine by his choice how another should act; and a certain specific moral value is secured (to be distinguished from moral virtue in which the good will is manifested) if human relationships are conducted in accordance with these principles even though coercion has to be used to secure this, for only if these principles are regarded will freedom be distributed among human beings as it should be. And it is, I think, a very important feature of a moral right that the possessor of it is conceived as having a moral justification for limiting the freedom of another and that he has this justification, not because the action he is entitled to require of another has some moral quality, but simply because in the circumstances a certain distribution of human freedom will be maintained if he by his choice is allowed to determine how that other shall act.

(B) I can best exhibit this feature of a moral right by reconsidering the question whether moral rights and "duties"[7] are correlative. The contention that they are means, presumably, that every statement of the form "X has a right to..." entails and is entailed by "Y has a duty (not) to...," and at this stage we must not assume that the values of the name-variables "X" and "Y" must be different persons. Now there is certainly one sense of "a right" (which I have already mentioned) such that it does not follow from X's having a right, that X or someone else has any duty. Jurists have isolated rights in this sense and have referred to them as "liberties" just to distinguish them from rights in the centrally important sense of "right" which has "duty" as a correlative. The former sense of "right" is needed to describe those areas of social life where competition is at least morally unobjectionable. Two people walking along both see a ten-dollar bill in the road twenty yards away, and there is no clue as to the owner. Neither of the two are under a "duty" to allow the other to pick it up; each has in this sense a right to pick it up. Of course there may be many things that each has a "duty" not to do in the course of the race to the spot—neither may kill or wound the other—and corresponding to these "duties" there are rights to forbearances. The moral propriety of all economic competition implies this minimum sense of "a right," in which to say that "X has a right to" means merely that X is under no "duty" not to. Hobbes saw that the expression "a right" could have this sense but he was wrong if he thought that there is no sense in which it does follow from X's having a right that Y has a duty or at any rate an obligation.

(C) More important for our purpose is the question whether for all moral "duties" there are correlative moral rights, because those who have given an affirmative answer to this question have usually assumed without adequate scrutiny that to have a right is simply to be capable of benefiting by the performance of a "duty"; whereas in fact this is not a sufficient condition (and probably not a necessary condition) of having a right. Thus animals and babies who stand to benefit by our performance of our "duty" not to ill-treat them are said *therefore* to have rights to proper treatment. The full consequence of this reasoning is not usually followed out; most have shrunk from saying that we have rights against ourselves because we stand to benefit from our performance of our "duty" to keep ourselves alive or develop our talents. But the moral situation that arises from a promise (where the legal-sounding terminology of rights and obligations is most appropriate) illustrates most clearly that the notion of having a right and that of benefiting by the performance of a "duty" are not identical. X promises Y in return for some favor that he will look after Y's aged mother in his absence. Rights arise out of this transaction, but it is surely Y to whom the promise has been made, and not his mother who *has* or *possesses* these rights. Certainly Y's mother is a person concerning whom X has an obligation and a person who will benefit by its performance, but the person *to whom* he has an obligation to look after her is Y. This is something *due to* or *owed to* Y, so it is Y, not his mother, whose right X will disregard and to whom X will have done *wrong* if he fails to keep his promise, though the mother may be physically injured. And it is Y who has a moral *claim* upon X, is *entitled* to have his mother looked after, and who can *waive* the claim and *release* Y from the obligation. Y is, in other words, morally in a position to determine by his choice how X shall act and in this way to limit X's freedom of choice; and it is this fact, not the fact that he stands to benefit, that makes it appropriate to say that he has *a right*. Of course often the person to whom a promise has been made will be the only person who stands to benefit by its performance, but this does not justify the identification of "having a right" with "benefiting by the performance of a duty." It is important for the whole logic of rights that, while the person who stands to benefit by the performance of a duty is discovered by considering what will happen if the duty is not performed, the person who has a right (to whom performance is *owed* or *due*) is discovered by examining the transaction or antecedent situation or relations of the parties out of which the "duty" arises. These considerations should incline us not to extend to animals and babies whom it is wrong to ill-treat the notion of a right to proper treatment, for the moral situation can be simply and adequately described here by saying that it is wrong or that we ought not to ill-treat them or, in the philosopher's generalized sense of "duty," that we have a duty not to ill-treat them.[8] If common usage sanctions talk of the rights of animals or babies it makes an idle use of the expression "a right," which will confuse the situation with other different moral situations where the expression "a right" has a specific force and cannot be replaced by the other moral expressions I have mentioned. Perhaps some clarity on this matter is to be gained by considering the force of the preposition "to" in the expression "having a duty to Y" or "being under an obligation to Y" (where "Y" is the name of a person); for it is significantly different from the meaning of "to" in "doing something to Y" or "doing harm to Y," where it indicates the person affected by some action. In the first pair of expressions, "to" obviously does not have this force, but indicates the person to whom the person morally bound is bound. This is an intelligible development of the figure of a bond (*vinculum juris: obligare*); the precise figure is not that of two persons bound by a chain, but of *one* person bound, the other end of the chain lying in the hands of another to use if he chooses.[9] So it appears absurd to speak of having duties or owing obligations to ourselves—of course we may have "duties" not to do harm to ourselves, but what could be meant (once the distinction between these different meanings of "to" has been grasped) by insisting that we have duties or obligations *to* ourselves not to do harm to ourselves?

(D) The essential connection between the notion of a right and the justified limitation of one person's freedom by another may be thrown into relief if we consider codes of behavior which do not purport to confer rights but only to prescribe what shall be done. Most natural law thinkers down to Hooker conceived of natural law in this way: there were natural duties, compliance with which would certainly benefit man—things to be done to achieve man's natural end; but not natural rights. And there are of course many types of codes of behavior that only prescribe what is to be done, e.g., those regulating certain ceremonies. It would be absurd to regard these codes as conferring rights, but illuminating to contrast them with rules of games, which often create rights, though not, of course, moral rights. But even a code that is plainly a moral code need not establish rights; the Decalogue is perhaps the most important example. Of course, quite apart from heavenly rewards, human beings stand to benefit by general obedience to the Ten Commandments: disobedience is wrong and will certainly harm individuals. But it would be a surprising interpretation of them that treated them as conferring rights. In such an interpretation obedience to the Ten Commandments would have to be conceived as due to or owed to individuals, not merely to God, and disobedience not merely as wrong but as *a wrong to* (as well as harm to) individuals. The Commandments would cease to read like penal statutes designed only to rule out certain types of behavior, and would have to be thought of as rules placed at the disposal of individuals and regulating the extent to which *they* may demand certain behavior from others. Rights are typically conceived of as *possessed* or *owned by* or *belonging to* individuals, and these expressions reflect the conception of moral rules as not only prescribing conduct but as forming a kind of moral property of individuals to which they are as individuals entitled; only when rules are conceived in this way can we speak of *rights* and *wrongs* as well as right and wrong actions.[10]

II

So far I have sought to establish that to have a right entails having a moral justification for limiting the freedom of another person and for determining how he should act; it is now important to see that the moral justification must be of a special kind if it is to constitute a right, and this will emerge most clearly from an examination of the circumstances in which rights are asserted with the typical expression "I have a right to...." It is I think the case that this form of words is used in two main types of situations: (A) when the claimant has some special justification for interference with another's freedom that other persons do not have ("*I* have a right to be paid what you promised for my services"); (B) when the claimant is concerned to resist or object to some interference by another person as having no justification ("*I* have a right to say what I think").

(A) *Special rights.*

When rights arise out of special transactions between individuals or out of some special relationship in which they stand to each other, both the persons who have the right and those who have the corresponding obligation are limited to the parties to the special transaction or relationship. I call such rights special rights to distinguish them from those moral rights that are thought of as rights against (i.e., as imposing obligations upon)[11] everyone, such as those that are asserted when some unjustified interference is made or threatened, as in (B) above.

(i) The most obvious cases of special rights are those that arise from promises. By promising to do or not to do something, we voluntarily incur obligations and create or confer rights on those to whom we promise; we alter the existing moral independence of the parties' freedom of choice in relation to some action and create a new moral relationship between them, so that it becomes morally legitimate for the person to whom the promise is given to determine how the promisor shall act. The promisee has a temporary authority or sovereignty in relation to some specific matter over the other's will which we express by saying that the promisor is under an obligation *to* the promisee to do what he has promised. To some philosophers the notion that moral phenomena—rights and duties or obligations—can be brought into existence by the voluntary action of individuals has appeared utterly mysterious; but this I think has been so because they have not clearly seen how special the moral notions of a right

and an obligation are, nor how peculiarly they are connected with the distribution of freedom of choice; it would indeed be mysterious if we could make actions morally good or bad by voluntary choice. The simplest case of promising illustrates two points characteristic of all special rights: (1) the right and obligation arise not because the promised action has itself any particular moral quality, but just because of the voluntary transaction between the parties; (2) the identity of the parties concerned is vital—only *this* person (the promisee) has the moral justification for determining how the promisor shall act. It is *his* right; only in relation to him is the promisor's freedom of choice diminished, so that if he chooses to release the promisor no one else can complain.

(ii) But a promise is not the only kind of transaction whereby rights are conferred. They may be *accorded* by a person consenting or authorizing another to interfere in matters that, but for this consent or authorization, he would be free to determine for himself. If I consent to your taking precautions for my health or happiness, or authorize you to look after my interests, then you have a right which others have not, and I cannot complain of your interference if it is within the sphere of your authority. This is what is meant by a person surrendering his rights to another; and again the typical characteristics of a right are present in this situation: the person authorized has the right to interfere, not because of its intrinsic character, but because *these* persons have stood in *this* relationship. No one else (not similarly authorized) has any right[12] to interfere in theory, even if the person authorized does not exercise his right.

(iii) Special rights are not only those created by the deliberate choice of the party on whom the obligation falls, as they are when they are accorded or spring from promises, and not all obligations to other persons are deliberately incurred, though I think it is true of all special rights that they arise from previous voluntary actions. A third very important source of special rights and obligations which we recognize in many spheres of life is what may be termed mutuality of restrictions, and I think political obligation is intelligible only if we see what precisely this is and how it differs from the other right-creating transactions (consent, promising) to which philosophers have assimilated it. In its bare schematic outline it is this: when a number of persons conduct any joint enterprise according to rules, and thus restrict their liberty, those who have submitted to these restrictions when required have a right to a similar submission from those who have benefited by their submission. The rules may provide that officials should have authority to enforce obedience and make further rules, and this will create a structure of legal rights and duties, but the moral obligation to obey the rules in such circumstances is *due to* the cooperating members of the society, and they have the correlative moral right to obedience. In social situations of this sort (of which political society is the most complex example) the obligation to obey the rules is something distinct from whatever other moral reasons there may be for obedience in terms of good consequences (e.g., the prevention of suffering); the obligation is due to the cooperating members of the society as such and not because they are human beings on whom it would be wrong to inflict suffering. The utilitarian explanation of political obligation fails to take account of this feature of the situation, both in its simple version that the obligation exists because and only if the direct consequences of a particular act of disobedience are worse than obedience, and also in its more sophisticated version that the obligation exists even when this is not so, if disobedience increases the probability that the law in question or other laws will be disobeyed on other occasions when the direct consequences of obedience are better than those of disobedience.

Of course to say that there is such a moral obligation upon those who have benefited by the submission of other members of society to restrictive rules to obey these rules in their turn does not entail either that this is the only kind of moral reason for obedience or that there can be no cases where disobedience will be morally justified. There is no contradiction or other impropriety in saying, "I have an obligation to do *X*, someone has a right to ask me to, but I now see I ought not to do it." It will in painful situations sometimes be the lesser of two moral evils to disregard what really are people's rights and not perform our

obligations to them. This seems to me particularly obvious from the case of promises: I may promise to do something and thereby incur an obligation just because that is one way in which obligations (to be distinguished from other forms of moral reasons for acting) are created; reflection may show that it would in the circumstances be wrong to keep this promise because of the suffering it might cause, and we can express this by saying, "*I ought not* to do it though *I have an obligation to him* to do it" just because the italicized expressions are not synonyms but come from different dimensions of morality. The attempt to explain this situation by saying that our real obligation here is to avoid the suffering and that there is only a prima facie obligation to keep the promise seems to me to confuse two quite different kinds of moral reason, and in practice such a terminology obscures the precise character of what is at stake when "for some greater good" we infringe people's rights or do not perform our obligations to them.

The social-contract theorists rightly fastened on the fact that the obligation to obey the law is not merely a special case of benevolence (direct or indirect), but something that arises between members of a particular political society out of their mutual relationship. Their mistake was to identify *this* right-creating situation of mutual restrictions with the paradigm case of promising; there are of course important similarities, and these are just the points that all special rights have in common, viz., that they arise out of special relationships between human beings and not out of the character of the action to be done or its effects.

(iv) There remains a type of situation that may be thought of as creating rights and obligations: where the parties have a special natural relationship, as in the case of parent and child. The parent's moral right to obedience from his child would, I suppose, now be thought to terminate when the child reaches the age "of discretion," but the case is worth mentioning because some political philosophies have had recourse to analogies with this case as an explanation of political obligation, and also because even this case has some of the features we have distinguished in special rights, viz., the right arises out of the special relationship of the parties (though it is in this case a natural relationship) and not out of the character of the actions to the performance of which there is a right.

(v) To be distinguished from special rights, of course, are special liberties, where, exceptionally, one person is *exempted* from obligations to which most are subject, but does not thereby acquire a *right* to which there is a correlative obligation. If you catch me reading your brother's diary, you say, "You have no right to read it." I say, "I have a right to read it—your brother said I might unless he told me not to, and he has not told me not to." Here I have been specially *licensed* by your brother who had a right to require me not to read his diary, so I am exempted from the moral obligation not to read it, but your brother is under no obligation to let me go on reading it. Cases where *rights,* not liberties, are accorded to manage or interfere with another person's affairs are those where the license is not revocable at will by the person according the right.

(B) *General rights.*

In contrast with special rights, which constitute a justification peculiar to the holder of the right for interfering with another's freedom, are general rights, which are asserted defensively, when some unjustified interference is anticipated or threatened, in order to point out that the interference is unjustified. "I have the right to say what I think."[13] "I have the right to worship as I please." Such rights share two important characteristics with special rights. (1) To have them is to have a moral justification for determining how another shall act, viz., that he shall not interfere.[14] (2) The moral justification does not arise from the character of the particular action to the performance of which the claimant has a right; what justifies the claim is simply—there being no special relation between him and those who are threatening to interfere to justify that interference—that this is a particular exemplification of the equal right to be free. But there are of course striking differences between such defensive general rights and special rights. (1) General rights do not arise out of any special relationship or transaction

between men. (2) They are not rights that are peculiar to those who have them, but are rights that all men capable of choice have in the absence of those special conditions that give rise to special rights. (3) General rights have as correlatives obligations not to interfere, to which everyone else is subject and not merely the parties to some special relationship or transaction, though of course they will often be asserted when some particular persons threaten to interfere as a moral objection to that interference. To assert a general right is to claim in relation to some particular action the equal right of all men to be free in the absence of any of those special conditions that constitute a special right to limit another's freedom; to assert a special right is to assert in relation to some particular action a right constituted by such special conditions to limit another's freedom. The assertion of general rights directly invokes the principle that all men equally have the right to be free; the assertion of a special right (as I attempt to show in section III) invokes it indirectly.

III

It is, I hope, clear that unless it is recognized that interference with another's freedom requires a moral justification, the notion of a right could have no place in morals; for to assert a right is to assert that there is such a justification. The characteristic function in moral discourse of those sentences in which the meaning of the expression "a right" is to be found—"I have a right to...," "You have no right to...," "What right have you to...?"—is to bring to bear on interferences with another's freedom, or on claims to interfere, a type of moral evaluation or criticism specially appropriate to interference with freedom and characteristically different from the moral criticism of actions made with the use of expressions like "right," "wrong," "good," and "bad." And this is only one of many different types of moral ground for saying "You ought..." or "You ought not...." The use of the expression "What right have you to...?" shows this more clearly, perhaps, than the others; for we use it, just at the point where interference is actual or threatened, to call for the moral *title* of the person addressed to interfere; and we do this often without any suggestion at all that what he proposes to do is otherwise wrong, and sometimes with the implication that the same interference on the part of another person would be unobjectionable.

But though our use in moral discourse of "a right" does presuppose the recognition that interference with another's freedom requires a moral justification, this would not itself suffice to establish, except in a sense easily trivialized, that in the recognition of moral rights there is implied the recognition that all men have a right to equal freedom; for unless there is some restriction inherent in the meaning of "a right" on the type of moral justification for interference that can constitute a right, the principle could be made wholly vacuous. It would, for example, be possible to adopt the principle and then assert that some characteristic or behavior of some human beings (that they are improvident, or atheists, or Jews, or Negroes) constitutes a moral justification for interfering with their freedom; *any* differences between men could, so far as my argument has yet gone, be treated as a moral justification for interference and so constitute a right, so that the equal right of all men to be free would be compatible with gross inequality. It may well be that the expression "moral" itself imports some restriction on what can constitute a moral justification for interference that would avoid this consequence, but I cannot myself yet show that this is so. It is, on the other hand, clear to me that the moral justification for interference that is to constitute a *right* to interfere (as distinct from merely making it morally good or desirable to interfere) is restricted to certain special conditions, and that this is inherent in the meaning of "a right" (unless this is used so loosely that it could be replaced by the other moral expressions mentioned). Claims to interfere with another's freedom based on the general character of the activities interfered with (e.g., the folly or cruelty of "native" practices) or the general character of the parties ("We are Germans; they are Jews") even when well-founded are not matters of moral right or obligation. Submission in such cases, even where proper, is not *due to* or *owed to* the individuals who interfere; it would be equally proper whoever of the same class of persons interfered. Hence other elements in our moral

vocabulary suffice to describe this case, and it is confusing here to talk of rights. We saw in section II that the types of justification for interference involved in special rights was independent of the character of the action to the performance of which there was a right, but depended upon certain previous transactions and relations between individuals (such as promises, consent, authorization, submission to mutual restrictions). Two questions here suggest themselves: (1) On what intelligible principle could these bare forms of promising, consenting, submission to mutual restrictions, be either necessary or sufficient, irrespective of their content, to justify interference with another's freedom? (2) What characteristics have these types of transaction or relationship in common? The answer to both these questions is I think this: If we justify interference on such grounds as we give when we claim a moral right, we are in fact indirectly invoking as our justification the principle that all men have an equal right to be free. For we are in fact saying in the case of promises and consents or authorizations that this claim to interfere with another's freedom is justified because he has, in exercise of his equal right to be free, freely chosen to create this claim; and in the case of mutual restrictions we are in fact saying that this claim to interfere with another's freedom is justified because it is fair; and it is fair because only so will there be an equal distribution of restrictions and so of freedom among this group of men. So in the case of special rights as well as of general rights recognition of them implies the recognition of the equal right of all men to be free.

NOTES

1. I was first stimulated to think along these lines by Mr. Stuart Hampshire, and I have reached by different routes a conclusion similar to his.
2. Further explanation of the perplexing terminology of freedom is, I fear, necessary. *Coercion* includes, besides preventing a person from doing what he chooses, making his choice less eligible by threats; *restraint* includes any action designed to make the exercise of choice impossible and so includes killing or enslaving a person. But neither coercion nor restraint includes *competition*. In terms of the distinction between "having a right to" and "being at liberty to," used above and further discussed in section I, B, all men may have, consistently with

the obligation to forbear from coercion, the *liberty* to satisfy, if they can, such at least of their desires as are not designed to coerce or injure others, even though in fact, owing to scarcity, one man's satisfaction causes another's frustration. In conditions of extreme scarcity this distinction between competition and coercion will not be worth drawing; natural rights are only of importance "where peace is possible" (Locke). Further, freedom (the absence of coercion) can be *valueless* to those victims of unrestricted competition too poor to make use of it; so it will be pedantic to point out to them that though starving they are free. This is the truth exaggerated by the Marxists, whose *identification* of poverty with lack of freedom confuses two different evils.

3. Save those general rights (cf. section II, B) that are particular exemplifications of the right of all men to be free.

4. Is the notion of *a* right found in either Plato or Aristotle? There seems to be no Greek word for it as distinct from "right" or "just" (δικαίον), though expressions like τὰ ἐμά δικαία are, I believe, fourth-century legal idioms. The natural expressions in Plato are τὸ ἐαύτον (ἔχειν) or τὰ τινὶ ὀφειλόμενα, but these seem confined to property or debts. There is no place for a moral right unless the moral value of individual freedom is recognized.

5. As W. D. Lamont has seen: cf. his *Principles of Moral Judgment*. Oxford, 1946; for the jurists, cf. Hohfeld's *Fundamental Legal Conceptions*. New Haven, 1923.

6. Here and subsequently I use "interfere with another's freedom," "limit another's freedom," "determine how another shall act," to mean either the use of coercion or demanding that a person shall do or not do some action. The connection between these two types of "interference" is too complex for discussion here; I think it is enough for present purposes to point out that having a justification for demanding that a person shall or shall not do some action is a necessary though not a sufficient condition for justifying coercion.

7. I write "duties" here because one factor obscuring the nature of a right is the philosophical use of "duty" and "obligation" for all cases where there are moral reasons for saying an action ought to be done or not done. In fact "duty," "obligation," "right," and "good" come from different segments of morality, concern different types of conduct, and make different types of moral criticism or evaluation. Most important are the points (1) that obligations may be voluntarily incurred or created, (2) that they are *owed to* special persons (who have rights), (3) that they do not arise out of the character of the actions that are obligatory, but out of the relationship of the parties. Language roughly though not consistently confines the use of "having an obligation" to such cases.

8. The use here of the generalized "duty" is apt to prejudice the question whether animals and babies have rights.

9. Cf. Campbell, A. H. *The Structure of Stair's Institutes*. Glasgow, 1954. 31.

10. Continental jurists distinguish between *"subjektives"* and *"objektives Recht,"* which corresponds very well to the distinction between a right, which an individual has, and what it is right to do.

11. Cf. section II. B below.

12. Though it may be *better* (the lesser of two evils) that he should.

13. In speech the difference between general and special rights is often marked by stressing the pronoun where a special right is claimed or where the special right is denied. "You have no right to stop him reading the book" refers to the reader's general right. "*You* have no right to stop him reading that book" denies that the person addressed has a special right to interfere, though others may have.

14. Strictly, in the assertion of a general right, both the *right* to forbearance from coercion and the *liberty* to do the specified action are asserted, the first in the face of actual or threatened coercion, the second as an objection to an actual or anticipated demand that the action should not be done. The first has as its correlative an obligation upon everyone to forbear from coercion; the second the absence in anyone of a justification for such a demand. Here, in Hohfeld's words, the correlative is not an obligation but a "no-right."

34   A Right to Do Wrong[1]

JEREMY WALDRON

I

It seems unavoidable that, if we take the idea of moral rights seriously, then we have to countenance the possibility that an individual may have a moral right to do something that is, from the moral point of view, wrong. Consider, for example, the following actions.

> Someone uses all the money that he has won fairly in a lottery to buy racehorses and champagne and refuses to donate any of it to a desperately deserving charity.
>
> An individual joins or supports an organization that he knows has racist leanings, such as the National Front in the United Kingdom; he canvasses support for it among a credulous electorate, and he exercises his own vote in its favor.
>
> Somebody offers deliberately confusing, though not untrue, information about the policies of a political party to a confused and simpleminded voter in an attempt to influence his vote.
>
> An athlete takes part in sports competition with the representatives of an oppressive or racist state, despite the fact that this profoundly demoralizes those who are struggling for the liberalization of that state.
>
> Antiwar activists organize a rowdy demonstration near a cenotaph service on Remembrance Day.
>
> A man refuses to give a stranger in the street the time of day when he asks for it or coldly and rudely rebuffs attempts at conversation in a railway compartment.
>
> Someone refuses to consider evidence that might call in question his or her fundamental opinions and beliefs about the world; for

instance, a biblical fundamentalist refuses even to look at the evidence of the fossil record.

Now, our opinions as to the morality of these actions may differ, and, in real life, our judgments would turn on details and background elements that have to be left out when one is sketching examples such as these. But in each case we can easily imagine circumstances and backgrounds in which the following is a possible, even perhaps the most plausible, moral response: the action in question is morally wrong, but nevertheless it is an action that the agent in question has a moral right to do. Thus someone might say, "It is surely wrong to canvass support for an organization with racist leanings, but equally surely it is something people have a moral right to do." Or they might say, "Certainly, athletes have the moral right to compete in sports with racially selected teams if they want to, but nevertheless it is something that they should not do." This sort of double-barreled response is not unfamiliar in political discourse. But it *sounds* paradoxical, or it sounds as if the person who is making it is equivocating. So the question that I want to examine in this paper is whether there is any *real* inconsistency underlying the appearance of paradox or equivocation in this sort of response. When somebody says of an action, "Action A is wrong" and adds ". . . but you have a right to do it," is he expressing his own uncertainty or indecision as between two contrary positions such that he cannot in the end hold both? Or does the conjunction of these two judgments actually represent a single coherent position that is open to a logically scrupulous person making judgments from the moral point of view?

Obviously, at least some of our uneasiness about the idea of a right to do wrong can be

Ethics, Vol. 92, No. 1, Special Issue on Rights (Oct., 1981): 21–39. Reprinted by permission of The University of Chicago Press. Available also through the *JSTOR* archive, http://www.jstor.org/stable/2380701.

explained away on purely terminological grounds. The *noun* "right" (as in "You have a *right* to join the National Front") is apt to be confused with the *adjective* "right" (as in "You are *right* to join the National Front"), and the latter term is, of course, an antonym of "wrong." So it is perhaps inevitable that the noun "right" tends to acquire by association some color of this antonymy. In a more lucid language, such a connotation might be avoided by having a word for *rights* (say, "claims" or "entitlements") that is different in sound and appearance from the adjective we use for the property *rightness*.

But this glib move does not do away with very many of our misgivings. The connection between the noun "right" and the adjective "right" is not a matter of accidental homonymy, like "pitch" (as in "cricket pitch") and "pitch" (as in "pitch black"), nor is it even merely a matter of common etymology, like "bank" (as in "bank overdraft") and "bank" (as in "river bank"). The connection between "right" and "right" is generally supposed to be more subtle and substantial than that. It is widely believed that statements about rights can be analyzed ultimately into statements about rightness and wrongness or into "ought"-statements, or that both sets of statements are commonly reducible to statements about the realization of goodness or consequential value. The paradox of a right to do wrong is serious because it threatens to introduce incoherence into all these reductive enterprises. Such a threat cannot be removed simply by substituting a fresh string of letters for one of the delinquent terms.

II

The language of rights is now a familiar part of moral discourse. It should not be necessary to emphasize that the topic here is *moral* rights, not legal rights—no matter how the former are supposed to be related to the latter. Clearly, there is no paradox in the suggestion that someone may have a *legal* right to do an act that is morally wrong. Just as individuals may have legal duties that require them to perform wrong acts (e.g., serve in unjust wars), so too they may have legal rights that entitle them to perform actions that are

wrong from the moral point of view. (This, no doubt, is what antiabortionists think about the legal rights created by permissive abortion legislation.) This seems to be possible, no matter whether "legal right" is construed as standing for a Hohfeldian privilege (indicating merely the absence of a legal duty constraining the right-bearer with respect to the action specified) or whether it stands for the stronger claim-right (indicating that others have certain duties to the right-bearer in respect of the action specified).[2] I may be legally at liberty to perform a certain act even though that act is not permissible from the moral point of view; or, others may have a legal duty to me to refrain from interfering with my performance of a certain act, even though the act is morally wrong and their interference morally permissible. All this seems quite straightforward. But legal rights are not our topic here.

When we come to examine the less straightforward topic of moral rights, we find that some moral philosophers have rejected out of hand the possibility that individuals have rights to do what is morally wrong. In 1798, William Godwin wrote, "There cannot be a more absurd proposition than that which affirms the right of doing wrong."[3] More recently, some philosophers seem to have adopted conceptions of moral rights such that the proposition

1. P has a moral right to do A
simply *entails* the negation of

2. P's doing A is morally wrong.

That is, they have adopted conceptions that make the moral permissibility of an action part of what is asserted when it is claimed that the action is the subject of a moral right. For instance, John Mackie says that a moral right is the conjunction of two elements—a freedom and a claim-right. The contribution made by the former element to the proposition that an individual has a right to do some act is this, that the act in question is one that the individual is not morally required not to do. Since a wrong act is an act we *are* morally required not to do, it follows, on Mackie's account, that one cannot have a moral right to do an action that is morally wrong.[4]

But philosophers are by no means unanimous on this. In recent jurisprudence, both Ronald Dworkin[5] and Joseph Raz[6] have insisted that there is no contradiction in the claim that a morally wrong act may be the exercise of a moral right. But neither Raz nor Dworkin has provided any detailed argument for this position. In what follows, I shall show that the conjunction of propositions 1 and 2 above is not, as Mackie suggests, a logical falsehood, and that the fact that it is not tells us a great deal about the nature of moral rights and their function in moral theory.

It may be thought that the issue between Mackie and myself is simply this: is it the case that the formal analysis of a rights-statement always reveals, among other things, a Hohfeldian privilege? Or, more bluntly: do moral rights contain moral privileges? If they do, then the acts that are the subject matter of moral rights cannot be acts prohibited by the moral duties of the right-bearer, and, in this sense, one cannot have a moral right to do what is morally wrong. But unfortunately matters are not so simple. Hohfeld's account of privileges was designed to cope with the analysis of normative systems in which duties were perfectly correlative with claim-rights, as they are, for the most part, in contract, tort, and property law. In such systems, a privilege (being the absence of a duty with respect to some action) is just someone else's lack of a right with respect to that action. The duties whose absence is indicated by a privilege are always and only duties imposed by the rights of others. There is no conception of normative constraints on action other than duties in this strictly correlative sense and, thus, no conception of normative permissibility apart from the lack of constraints defined in this very narrow way.

Now the trouble with applying this neat analysis to the language of morals is that, in the moral sphere, notions like *duty, wrongness,* and *permissibility* are—though relevant to rights—not confined to the area of rights. Certainly, there are some actions that are impermissible, some actions that we have a duty not to do, because they are infringements of the rights of others. But actions may also be morally impermissible or more generally subject to moral criticism for other and more

subtle reasons. They may be seen as wrong because they are vicious, or because they fall short of the standard required by some ideal or principle that is conceived of as a constraint independent of moral rights. So, since wrongness does not necessarily involve the infringement or violation of rights, there is much more to the question of whether one can have a moral right to do what is morally wrong than the simple question of whether moral rights are capable of coming into conflict.

I suppose we could *define* a sense of "morally wrong" so that it applied only to infringements of moral rights. If we were to adopt this artificial way of talking, *then* the issue would just be the Hohfeldian one outlined above. But resolution of that issue would beg the much more interesting question of the relation between the language of moral rights and the rest of moral language in all its exuberance, including those uses of "wrong" and "impermissible" that are not already tied into an artificial reconstruction of rights-talk.

III

In analyzing a problem of this sort, the professional philosopher is likely to be tempted to see whether W. D. Ross's distinction between prima facie and actual duties can be of any use.[7] The distinction is supposed to operate as follows.

When they are stated in general terms, the intuitively apprehended demands of morality often appear to contradict one another. For example, my duty to tell the truth may conflict in a particular case with my duty not to cause distress. Or my duty to keep a promise to meet someone at a certain time may conflict with my duty to give aid to someone else along the way. Now if one and the same act is the subject of conflicting moral requirements, then we have to insist that the general principles of duty that generate the conflict cannot *both* be regarded as stating the individual's *actual* duty with regard to that act in those circumstances. In other words, they cannot both be regarded as indicating what, all things considered, he ought to do. An individual's actual duty cannot be determined until the requirements of all the general principles applicable to the situation in which he finds himself have been weighed and considered. The application of a *single* general principle to a particular case, in advance of this process of weighing and considering, yields only the conclusion that the act in question is what we call a prima facie duty—something that we might conclude would be our duty *tout court* were it not for the fact that other moral considerations are relevant as well.

Obviously, if there is anything in this distinction between prima facie duty and actual duty, it can be applied equally well to rightness and wrongness. Since the idea of duty leads to the idea of the wrongness of the failure to do one's duty, we can talk about prima facie wrongness and actual wrongness in a similar sort of way. It has been argued that the distinction can also be extended to moral rights; indeed, some theorists have claimed that, without such a distinction between prima facie and actual rights, theories of human rights become manifestly implausible.[8] It is argued that, since a general right like the right to liberty may have to be set aside in some cases in favor, say, of the right to life or the right to a decent standard of living, particular cases where these rights conflict cannot be analyzed without recourse to the distinction between prima facie and actual moral constraints.

Can this distinction be of any use in analyzing our paradox of a right to do wrong? At first sight, maybe. Perhaps what are involved when somebody conjoins

1. P has a moral right to do A

and

2. P's doing A is morally wrong

are not final all-things-considered judgments, but rather tentative prima facie judgments about P's doing A, each of them capable of entering into the balance of considerations to establish what, in the final analysis, ought to be done. We can perhaps rewrite 1, then, as

1A. P has a prima facie moral right to do A,

meaning that, under one description at least, P's doing A is the exercise of a moral right, but withholding our final assessment until the significance

of all the possible descriptions of P's doing A is considered. And similarly, 2 is now

2A. P's doing A is prima facie morally wrong.

Understood in this way, the conjunction of 1A and 2A is, of course, not incoherent: neither of the judgments purports to state a final position, and their juxtaposition indicates only that they are both to be weighed in the balance, along with any other judgments relevant to the moral character of P's doing A, to determine what we are finally to say about the matter.

But there is a bit of an ambiguity here. Consider 2. When we shift from 2 to 2A, we indicate that we are to be understood as expressing only a prima facie rather than a final moral judgment. But in saying this we may mean either of two things: (i) We may mean that it is not to be understood as a final judgment *even so far as the wrongness of P's doing A is concerned*. That is, there may be other considerations to be weighed before we finally conclude that P's doing A is morally wrong, quite apart from whether P has a right to do it. (ii) Or we may mean that it *is* to be understood as *a final judgment so far as the wrongness of P's doing A is concerned,* but that the judgment remains prima facie inasmuch as the issue between it and 1 or 1A is still outstanding. Of these two interpretations of the claim that we are making a prima facie rather than a final moral judgment, the rendering of 2 as 2A seems better suited to (i). Similarly, there are two possible interpretations of 1A: (i) that it is not a final judgment even about moral rights, and (ii) that it is final about rights but not final vis-à-vis 2 or 2A. Again, the rendering of 1 as 1A seems better suited to the former interpretation.

But from our point of view, it is the latter interpretation, (ii), of the prima facie claims that is the more interesting. We are more interested in the case where a judgment that is final, so far as the rightness or wrongness of P's doing A is concerned, confronts a judgment that is final so far as the issue of whether P has a moral right to do A is concerned. For instance, to take one of the examples from the list at the start of the paper: we may have balanced up all the conflicting principles and considerations that bear on the issue of whether voting for the National Front is *wrong* (e.g., on the one hand, British society as we know it is in danger of cultural collapse, and, on the other hand, the National Front is a dangerous racist organization); we may have weighed up all the conflicting principles and considerations that bear on the issue of whether one has a moral *right* to vote for the National Front (e.g., on the one hand, being free to vote for the party of one's choice is a necessary right in a true democracy, and, on the other hand, there is a chance that one's vote is being given to a party that would itself reject the democratic process); and we may have reached verdicts that are final in each of these two areas of morality. The question, then, is this: can the distinction between prima facie and actual moral requirements be of any further use in analyzing the confrontation between these two verdicts?

It is difficult to see how it could be. The distinction between prima facie and actual moral requirements is designed for the analysis of cases in which the agent is pulled in opposite directions by a number of general moral requirements whose applicability to this situation he acknowledges. But, whereas it is clear that the judgment expressed in 2, conceived of as a final judgment about the wrongness of the action, pulls the agent in a certain direction—in the direction of refraining from A—it is not at all clear that the judgment expressed in 1, even conceived as a final judgment so far as P's rights are concerned, pulls him in the opposite direction, or indeed in any direction at all.

This point can be understood more clearly in terms of the idea of reasons for action. Obviously, anyone who acknowledges the truth of 2 or 2A recognizes a reason for not doing A in the sort of circumstances in which P is placed. That, at least in part, is what acknowledging the truth of 2 amounts to. But although 2 provides a reason for *not* doing A, there is no corresponding reason *in favor of* doing A provided by an acknowledgment of 1. To assent to the proposition that I have a right to perform some action is not thereby to acknowledge any reason for performing that action.[9] For instance, I have a moral right to marry the partner of my choice (if she will have me), but that does not provide me with any reason

whatever for getting married, let alone for marrying anyone in particular. If I say, "I have a right to marry anyone I choose but I am determined to remain celibate," there is nothing logically odd, not even slightly logically odd, about that conjunction. Perhaps it will be argued that in remaining a bachelor I am in fact exercising the right in question, since the right to marry may be thought to include the right to refuse to get married. (Similarly, choosing to remain silent may be thought of as an exercise of the right of free speech, and so on.) But this point—important as it is— only reinforces my argument. The moral right in itself gives me no reason for undertaking any one course of action rather than another. Thus the fact that P has a right to do A does not of itself give rise to any reason in favor of A that is capable of competing with and being balanced against the reason for not doing A provided by the acknowledged wrongness of the act. It seems, then, that the distinction between prima facie and actual moral requirements, tailored as it is to the analysis of cases in which moral reasons for acting conflict, is inappropriate for the analysis of the tensions that arise in the case of our paradox of a right to do wrong.

IV

Rights, I have said, do not provide reasons for acting, at least not for the people who have them. The same point can be presented another way. If, in some situation, I ask a friend, "What shall I do?" he has not given me any advice at all, he has not prescribed any action, if he answers, "You have a right to do A." By the same token, if somebody asks me, "Why did you vote for the National Front candidate?" or "Why did you spend all that money on racehorses and champagne?" or "Why did you marry someone you loathed?" the answer, "I was exercising my moral rights," is not any sort of appropriate reply. At best it amounts to a refusal to reply, like the retort, "Because I wanted to." Certainly, the reply, "I had a right to do A," goes no way toward *justifying* the doing of A. To justify an action is to show the standard to which in the circumstances it conformed or the worthiness of the goal that it was intended to advance. But to adduce a right is not to do either of these things.

This point has often been overlooked. For instance, A. I. Melden opens his book *Rights and Persons* with the claim: "Actions which would otherwise be arbitrary and capricious may be quite reasonable when they are in fact cases in which rights are being exercised...."[10] But that is precisely what is *not* the case. If an action appears arbitrary or capricious, if, for example, I stand on my head for a week facing west in a public place, or marry somebody I loathe, or burn my stock certificates in a fit of pique, or vote randomly in a general election, my action when questioned is not made to appear one iota more reasonable or defensible, nor is a spectator the slightest bit more likely to understand why I did it, when I reply, "I had a right to do it; I was exercising my right." The spectator may concede that the reply is *true,* but that concession need not in any way diminish his puzzlement or indignation at my behavior.

In what contexts, then, *is* this reply helpful or appropriate? The cutting edge of the claim that P has a right to do A is the correlative claim that other people are morally required to refrain from interfering with P's performance of A. If P has a right to do A, then it follows that it is wrong for anyone to try to stop P from doing A. Thus the assertion, "I have a moral right to do A," is entirely appropriate when my act is challenged in the sense that somebody threatens to interfere coercively. For example, I may be halfway through my speech in favor of the National Front when a radical member of the audience interrupts me, saying, "Give me one good reason why I shouldn't stop you making such an evil racist speech." In these circumstances, the reply, "I have a moral right to make the speech," is, if true, a perfect and sufficient answer. Although it does not provide *me* with any reason or justification for acting, my right provides the radical with a reason for not interfering.

Now our paradox of a right to do wrong arose out of the conjunction of two propositions:

1. P has a moral right to do A

and

2. P's doing A is morally wrong.

We have seen that 1 entails

3. It is morally wrong for anyone to interfere with P's doing A.

The first step toward an understanding of why our paradox does not involve a contradiction is to realize that 2 and 3 are perfectly compatible. In particular, 2 does not entail

4. It is morally permissible for someone to interfere with P's doing A,

which would obviously contradict 3 and therefore 1.

That the wrongness of an act does not by itself entail the moral permissibility of interfering with it is obvious on a number of grounds. First, in almost every case, the act of interfering with wrongdoing will have a significance over and above the mere stopping of the wrongdoing and the suppression of its consequences. It may put the interferer at risk; it may involve the expenditure of public money or the use of other scarce resources such as police manpower; it may enhance or tarnish the reputation of the police; and so on. It may even, as the Christian ethic argues, distract the interferer from the task of his own self-improvement or be the occasion for a sinful act of moral self-indulgence. Clearly, none of these factors is relevant to the issue of whether P's doing A is right or wrong. But they *are* directly relevant to the permissibility of someone's proposed interference with P's doing A. For these reasons, then, it is necessary to drive a wedge between 2 and 4.

It may be thought that driving a wedge between 2 and 4 diminishes the prescriptivity of 2. After all, I can hardly assert 2 sincerely, with its full prescriptive force, and yet remain completely indifferent to the conduct in question. But there is an important distinction to be drawn between self and other here. If I utter 2 sincerely, I commit myself to avoiding A in the sort of circumstances in which P is placed. But I do not commit myself to interfering with P's action. Tolerating wrongdoing does not make me hypocritical or weak willed; I am weak willed only to the extent that I perform actions myself that I believe to be wrong, and I am hypocritical only if I purport to believe that certain actions are wrong that I myself perform. The difference, then, between self and other is this. To stop *myself* from performing wrong actions, no special act of prevention is required; I need only steel myself to my duty (assuming of course that I am not in the grip of any sort of duress or compulsion). But to stop *others* from performing wrong acts (even when their behavior is as voluntary as my own), other positive acts must be performed by me beyond the mere giving of my sincere assent to the moral judgment in question. And, of course, these other acts will have moral ramifications of their own.

Of course, in practice, these distinctions get a bit blurred. Depending on the circumstances, on the personal relationships involved, and so on, merely *telling* someone that he should not do A may be a highly effective way of *getting* him to stop A-ing. The line at which mere prescription and admonition stop and coercion begins is a fine one. Even the mere expression of disapproval—the raised eyebrow or the icy stare—may be felt as a positive show of force. Also, inasmuch as a morality forms part of a way of life, and inasmuch as a person's way of life is defined in part by the persons with whom he chooses to associate, the prescriptivity of a *personal* moral judgment may lead an agent to impose social sanctions of the most far-reaching kind on those around him. There are, then, considerable difficulties in distinguishing interference from mere condemnation, and it should not be thought that driving a wedge between 2 and 4 in our formal reconstruction of the positions involved does anything to remove them. But it would be a mistake merely to abandon the point in the face of these difficulties. What we can say is this: to the extent that expressing an opinion on a moral matter has any effect on the world (over and above its inherent prescriptive effect on the actions of the person expressing it), the issue of whether one ought to express the opinion is a separate issue—a separate *moral* issue—from the issue of the correctness of the opinion itself. The expression of a moral judgment may have any number of effects in the world: it may disturb the peace in a library; it may reveal one's position to enemy soldiers; it may upset one's mother; or it

may coercively interfere with another's freedom. It is not necessary to be a consequentialist to see that in all such cases there is a clear distinction to be drawn between the issue of the *truth* of a moral judgment and the issue of the rightness or wrongness of expressing it. So long as these distinctions are kept in mind, it will be clear that, since 4 does not follow from 2, then 2 and 3 are logically compatible.

We have seen that 1 and 2, the two sides of our paradox, are compatible at least to the extent that 2 does not contradict one of the most important consequences of 1, namely, 3. But while obviously 1 entails 3, it is not obvious that their relation is one of equivalence. Mackie's position, for example, was based on the inference of a further consequence from 1—an assertion of moral permissibility.[11] So a more general argument is needed to show, against Mackie and others, that there is, as it were, nothing *else* in 1 that 2 could contradict.

The same point can be put another way. The considerations I have given in favor of driving a wedge between 2 and 4 apply to *all* cases of wrongdoing, not just those cases of wrongdoing protected by a moral right. In *every* situation where someone does something that is wrong, it is a further question whether it would be right or permissible to interfere with the wrongdoing. But when we move to the cases where there are moral *rights* involved, there is a feeling that the fact that the agent had a right to do what he did provides a *special* reason for not interfering that is not present in the ordinary cases of wrongdoing. So what we have to do now is to make sure that there is nothing in this special reason for noninterference, provided by rights, which is inconsistent with the claim that the action in question is wrong.

In the following section I shall show that we can capture the special reasons against interference provided by rights in a way that does not commit us to rejecting the possibility of a right to do wrong. To this end, I shall provide an argument showing that the *function* of rights in moral theory precludes the imposition of any general requirement on rights to the effect that actions that one has a right to perform must be actions that it is morally permissible for one to perform.

V

The argument I am going to introduce relies on something I want to call the *generality* of moral rights. The statement that an individual P has a moral right to perform a particular action A never stands on its own. It is usually supported by indicating that A is a member of a certain set of actions any of which P has a right to perform in the circumstances. Characteristically, the claim about P's doing A is seen as a particular instance of a more general claim, that P has the right to perform actions of a certain type. For example, when we say that an individual has a right to join the National Front, this claim is defended and debated, not on its own merits, but on the basis of its connection with the wider claim that the individual has the right to join any political group he likes, or, if he chooses, to refrain from political activity altogether. That is, it is put forward as an instance of the right of free political association. Similarly, when I say that a certain person has the right to paste up a particular wall poster, that claim is not contested or defended on its own merits alone but in terms of the wider claim that he has a right to free expression in public of his views—that is, a right to perform any of a number of activities, ranging from addressing a meeting at his workplace to writing a letter to the local newspaper. The general claim is not inferred, as it were, inductively from the more specific claims ("He has the right to put up the wall poster, and he has the right to address his workmates, and he has the right to send a letter to the newspaper—so therefore he must have the right to free expression in public"). The order of argument is the other way round. We establish the general claim and then derive the more specific propositions from it.

Of course, not all argument about rights takes place at the general level. There may be argument as to whether a particular case is really an instance of the wider claim; for example, does the right of free expression include a right constraining the editor of the local newspaper to actually publish my letter? But even here, argument at the level of particular cases looks up and refers back all the time to the nature of the argument for the more general right.

Notice that generality, in this sense, is not the same as what R. M. Hare has called the "universalisability" of evaluative language.[12] A judgment is universalizable if it either is, or is supported by, a judgment in which there are no terms referring to particulars. But a judgment may eschew all reference to particulars and so be universal in Hare's sense and still fail to be general in the sense that I have outlined. For example (moving for a moment from the language of rights to that of deontological prescriptions), the prescription, "One should never tell lies to one's wife on the morning of her birthday" is *less* general than "Don't ever deceive me," even though the former is universal and the latter is not. The greater generality of "Don't ever deceive me" consists just in its application to a wider range of actions than the former prescription. Generality and universality, then, are two different dimensions in terms of which prescriptions may be described, though it is worth reminding ourselves that generality is a matter of degree, whereas a statement is either universal or it is not.[13]

Hare has insisted throughout his work that universalizability is a *logical* feature of evaluative language. I wish to make no such claim on behalf of generality, even in the limited fragment of evaluative language that comprises the language of rights. (The mind boggles even at the preparatory task of deciding what would count as the establishment of such a claim.) Nevertheless, it is, I think, significant that many rights-claims have this feature: particular rights-claims, as well as being universalizable, are also liable to be argued for in terms of a wider, more general right. In particular, this seems to be true of the very rights that are most likely to feature in the paradox of a right to do wrong; it seems to be true, for instance, of all the rights-claims that could be applied to the situations described at the start of this paper. This, as I shall show, is no coincidence.

Before we go on, it is necessary to add an important qualification. The language of rights is far from being a homogeneous fragment of the language of morals and political theory. It includes not only the traditional liberal claims of the right to free speech, to freedom of worship, and so on, in terms of which my argument has been couched so far, but also the more radical "positive" rights to free medical care, decent housing, and other basic assistance from the state and from one's fellow citizens. It also includes claims of *special* rights—the rights both positive and negative that arise out of interpersonal transactions such as promises and contracts.

In the case of these last two categories, the thesis that rights-statements are not just universalizable but also general in the way outlined above seems rather out of place. There is no question of defending, say, P's right to emergency first aid in an accident on the basis of some more general right of P's to choose among any of a number of alternative goods and services. The link with individual choice that seems so important in the case of the liberal rights, and which is probably the basis of the universality feature, seems lost altogether here. If human choice is important in cases like this, it is so only as a general justifying value lurking in the background; we might say, for instance, that the reason why people have a right to free medical care is that, without such a right, any freedom of choice in other areas of life would be so insecure as to be empty. But the immediate subject matter of the right (the receipt of medical care) itself involves no choice.

This is even more apparent in the case of special rights. If I have a right arising out of a promise to use your cottage for the weekend, then that is all I have a right to. There is no more general right that I have in terms of which my right to use your cottage could be defended and which also indicates other particular rights that are open to me.

I suppose that if one were, in Aristotle's words, out to defend a thesis at all costs, one might insist that the rights described in both these cases each cover at least two choices open to the right-bearer. In the case of the promissory right, I may choose either to use the cottage in accordance with the permission granted to me by its owner, or not to use it. So my promissory right covers a plurality of actions. And even in the case of a straightforward right of receipt, such as the right to first aid in an accident, one might want to draw a distinction between *being given a good,* which is a purely passive condition, and *recieving or accepting a good,* which seems to have a slightly

more active flavor to it. So if the right to first aid is redescribed as the right to *accept* first aid, and not just the right to *be given* first aid, then it too may be seen to cover a plurality of actions open to the right-bearer.[14]

In any case, I do not want to pursue this line of thought here. Anyone who wants to apply my argument for the coherence of the paradox of a right to do wrong to cases of special or positive rights of receipt will be obliged to set up some such line of argument. But I prefer to concentrate on cases where the generality and choice elements are clearly prominent, for these are the cases where the paradox arises most acutely.

Particular rights-statements can be conceived of as clustered together into groups represented by general rights-statements. It was indicated earlier that the main characteristic of this general clustering was its relation to justification: debate and justification normally take place at the level of the general rights-statements, not at the level of the particular ones. What we contest or defend is not just the right to do A, but a general right that is the right to choose to do A or B or C or D, and so on.

Now it is important for understanding the notion of a right to do wrong to see in general terms how justification here usually proceeds. As we have seen, the cutting edge of a rights-claim is the claim it entails about the wrongness of interfering with the action that the right-bearer has chosen. So what is defended or contested when a general right is in dispute is the claim that choice within a certain range is not to be interfered with. This claim in turn is usually defended on the basis of the *importance* of the choices in the range in question for the lives of the individuals who are making them. In the ranges of action to which a theory of rights draws attention, individual choices are seen as crucial to personal integrity. To make a decision in these areas is, in some sense, to decide what person one is to be. Some rights-theorists attribute this importance indiscriminately to *all* the choices that an individual makes in his life, and so his rights to perform particular actions are organized into just one cluster under the auspices of a general right to liberty. But most rights-theorists recognize that some of the choices that individuals make are more important than others.[15] There are certain types of choice, certain key areas of decision making, which have a special importance for individual integrity and self-constitution. Particular theorists may differ, of course, as to what these key areas are, but, over the centuries, a certain liberal consensus has evolved: individuals' political activities, their intimate relations with others, their public expressions of opinion, their choice of associates, their participation in self-governing groups and organizations, particularly political organizations and trade unions, their choice of an occupation— all these have been regarded as particularly important in people's definitions of themselves.

In each of these areas, from time to time, a number of alternative actions are possible. That is why the claim that someone has the right to perform one particular action does not stand alone: the claim is understood in the light of the more general proposition that the range of options in which that action is located represents an important area of choice for that person. Moreover, that is why the fact that an individual has the right to perform some particular action does not in itself provide a *reason* for his performing that action. For the claim that he has the right to perform it refers us to the wider area of decision, in which the action is located and in which alternatives are available, and asserts only that his decision making in this area is to be protected. To protect decision making is not to provide a reason for the making of any particular decision.

In the light of all this, it is easy to see why we cannot exclude the possibility that a person has a right to perform some action that is wrong. Presumably, the actions in each of the clusters covered by a general right will each be either morally required, morally prohibited, or morally indifferent. Or, to phrase it a little less rigidly, each action protected by a right will, in its particular circumstances, be an action that is *called for* from the moral point of view, or an action that is *subject to moral criticism,* or an action on which *morality has nothing of importance to say.* (For simplicity, I am ignoring supererogatory acts; their inclusion would not affect the argument except to make it a bit more complicated.)

Now suppose we were to agree with Mackie, for instance, that only morally permissible actions

can be the subject of moral rights. Then the protected choices would be limited to actions that are called for from the moral point of view and actions that are morally indifferent; wrong actions or actions subject to moral criticism would be excluded. But once this restriction had been imposed it would be bound to escalate further. For, if an action is *called for* from the moral point of view, then any alternative to it that is not called for (i.e., any merely indifferent alternative) immediately becomes impermissible and so would be excluded. Thus, if we applied Mackie's condition and allowed only right and indifferent acts to figure as the subject of rights, then the right actions would soon start to dominate. And to the extent that right actions became the dominant subject matter of rights, then rights would lose what we have regarded up to now as their crucial link with the notions of choice and alternatives. One might have the right to do *the right thing* in given circumstances, but only at the cost of not having the right to do anything else in those circumstances. Rights would become what they are at times for Locke—merely the duties of the right-bearer perceived from a subjective point of view.[16]

It may be argued that this dominance of rights by right action need not be total even on Mackie's proposal for, except under very rigorous moralities (such as Godwin's utilitarianism),[17] there are many choice situations in which a number of permissible alternatives are open to the agent, none of which is actually called for from the moral point of view.

But this possibility reveals even greater danger for the idea of moral rights. Suppose that, in view of the argument just developed, we were to modify Mackie's proposal slightly, so that right actions as well as wrong actions were excluded, leaving only morally indifferent actions as the subject matter for rights. Then we seem to be faced with two possibilities that are equally objectionable.

The first possibility is that, by limiting rights to actions that are morally permissible, we would impoverish the content of our theory of rights. To implement the proposal under consideration, we have to imagine some sort of lexical ordering whereby the morality of rightness and wrongness, duty and obligation, requirement and prohibition, even virtue and vice is allowed first into the field of action to pick out as its domain those actions that are of particular moral concern. The morality of rights is allowed to enter the field only when that process has been completed, to clean up the leftovers, as it were. But *what* will be left over when the morality of rightness and wrongness has had its say? The answer seems to be: the banalities and trivia of human life. The decision to begin shaving on chin rather than cheek, the choice between strawberry and banana ice cream, the actions of dressing for dinner and avoiding the cracks on the sidewalk—these would be the sorts of actions left over for the morality of rights to concern itself with. But these are the actions that—apart from the argument here under consideration—would be the ones *least likely to be regarded as an appropriate subject matter for rights.* The areas of decision that we *normally* associate with rights would, on this account, be miles out of range. Because of the very importance that leads us to regard them as subject matter for rights, those areas of decision are bound to be of concern to the other deontological requirements of morality and thus are bound to be excluded from the area of moral indifference where rights are permitted their limited sway. In other words, if rights were confined to actions that were morally indifferent, actions on which the rest of morality had nothing to say, then rights would lose the link with the *importance* of certain individual decisions that, as we have seen, is crucial in their defense.

The other possibility is to let the morality of rights into the field first and to exclude from the domain of rightness and wrongness, duty and obligation, requirement and criticism any action preempted by the morality of rights. But this is equally unacceptable. The decisions that one makes in exercising one's rights are supposed to be decisions that shape the character and direction of one's life and, in some sense, define the person one is to be. It is completely implausible to suppose that the rest of morality could be silent here, that the ethics of rightness and wrongness, goodness and evil, duty and obligation, and virtue and vice could have nothing to say on matters of this importance. When we say, for example, that individuals have the right to marry whom they will or to speak their minds on

matters of public moment, we cannot mean to claim that actions of these sorts are sealed off from moral criticism and evaluation. Quite apart from anything else, the decisions in question cannot be made in an existentialist vacuum. Those who are making them will ask others for advice and for their opinions and evaluations of the various alternatives under consideration. And replies will come not just from those who have some personal interest at stake in the decision but also from those—like parents, priests, politicians, and philosophers—who are capable of seeing and evaluating the chosen actions as emergent fragments of an overall pattern of life. Since exercising a right involves making an important choice, it is incredible to suppose that the practice of assessing, evaluating, guiding, and criticizing important choices—the practice we call "morality"—should be inapplicable to the exercise. To exclude the rest of morality from the evaluation of these choices, and yet to insist that the choices in question are still somehow important (indeed, to justify the exclusion on the basis of this importance), is to come perilously close to self-contradiction.

To sum up. I have spoken as if the morality of rights and the morality of rightness and wrongness—the morality that gives rise to statements like 1 and the morality that gives rise to statements like 2—were distinct. And so they are, for they have distinct functions: the former has the function of protecting choices and the latter the function of guiding them. But they cannot be distinct in their range of application: it cannot be the case that a choice is so important that it needs to be protected but yet so unimportant that guidance is out of the question. If we attempt to allot a distinct sphere of action to each of these fragments of morality, we will end up by impoverishing at least one of them.

If we take the idea of moral rights seriously, then, and if we draw the connections with the ideas of choice and of the importance of certain areas of decision that I have outlined, it is necessary to insist that wrong actions as well as right actions and indifferent actions can be the subject of moral rights. So the clusters of actions that we find subsumed under our general rights are likely to include, in the circumstances that face us, actions that would be stupid, cowardly, tasteless, inconsiderate, destructive, wasteful, deceitful, and just plain wrong, as well as actions that are wise, courageous, cultured, compassionate, creative, honest, and good. This may seem messy to a certain austere type of analytic mind, but it involves no contradiction, as far as I can see, and it is the only way to reconcile the importance of moral rights, as a distinctive ingredient in ethical theory, with the diversity and the wide range of standards of ethical evaluation.

VI

We have seen that the possibility of a right to do wrong, far from being a contradiction in terms, is actually required by the way in which rights function in moral theory and the basis on which we argue for them. But even after these arguments have been given, the sense of paradox is likely to linger. I will conclude by offering some explanations of this.

The residual sense of paradox in the idea of a right to do wrong has, I think, at least four main sources. The first is the terminological consideration I mentioned at the very start of the paper:[18] the associative link between the noun "right" and the adjective "right" is so strong that some feeling of the latter's antonymy with "wrong" is bound to rub off on the former.

The second source is connected with this. The language of rights is put to many uses, and sometimes a sentence like 1 is used just to say that P's doing A was right or at least morally permissible—and no more.[19] This usage is perhaps more noticeable in the second-person negative: "You had no right to do that" is often used as though it were interchangeable with, "You shouldn't have done that." We are all guilty of this usage at times, and it is an obvious source of misgiving about the conjunction of 1 and 2. (It should perhaps be noted also that this is not the only deviant use to which the language of rights is put. Often rights-statements are used as though "right" were loosely synonymous with authority in such a way that "You had no right to do that" is equivalent to "It was not for you to do that" said, for example, to someone who had purported to act in loco parentis. In this sense of "right," there do not seem to be any problems with the idea of a right to do something that is wrong.)[20]

The third source was also alluded to earlier. It may be thought that it is, in the last resort, impossible both to guide choices and to protect them. If we take a sufficiently brutal (perhaps emotivist) view of moral interaction, we may believe that, when somebody tells me that A is wrong, he cannot claim to be respecting my right to do A. To say that an act is wrong, to condemn its performance, and to urge others not to do it—surely all that comes down, in the end, to the very sort of coercion that is ruled out when we say that the action is one which there is a moral right to perform. But it should be obvious that the whole drift of this paper depends on a rejection of that way of looking at things. As Austin and Hare have stressed, there *is* a distinction to be drawn between telling a person to do something and making him do it;[21] so that even if saying that A is wrong involves telling P not to do A, still we can distinguish between moral guidance and coercive interference. But it has to be admitted that, in real life, this distinction is a perilously fine one, and that its fineness is one of the contributing sources of any residual misgivings about the idea of a right to do wrong.

The fourth and final source is based on the pragmatics of rights-talk. There is, as we have seen, no prescriptive incompatibility between 1 and 2: there is nothing in the assertibility conditions of 1 to rule out its conjunction with 2. But now consider the *pragmatics* of the first-person assertion, "I have a right to do A." In real life, such an assertion is not often offered as a contribution to ethical theory—it is most often uttered by someone who intends to do A and is responding to moves by other people to prevent his carrying out that intention. But there is something odd about having the intention to do A and sincerely believing that A is wrong. There is an extremely important logical link, alluded to already in this paper, whose precise nature has not and will not be explained until we have satisfactory theories both of weakness of will and of the relation between prima facie wrongness and actual wrongness, between intending to do A and *dissenting* from the judgment, "My doing A is wrong." And so the pragmatic link that holds between the assertion, "I have a right to do A," and the intention to do A, coupled with the semantic link between the assertion, "My doing A is wrong," and *not* intending to do A, is likely to remain as another source of residual misgiving about the idea of a right to do wrong.

NOTES

1. I am obliged to Bob Durrant, Ronald Dworkin, Les Green, Bob Hargrave, and Gwen Taylor for helpful criticisms of earlier drafts of this paper, and to the editor and referees of Ethics for their encouragement and suggestions.

2. For the distinction between privileges and claim-rights, see Hohfeld, Wesley. Fundamental Legal Conceptions. New Haven, Conn.: Yale University Press, 1923. See also Feinberg, Joel. Social Philosophy. Englewood Cliffs, N.J.: Prentice-Hall, Inc., 1973. 56–59, for a brief and accessible summary.

3. Godwin, William. Enquiry Concerning Political Justice. Ed. K. Codell Carter. Oxford: Clarendon Press, 1971. 88.

4. Mackie, John. "Can There Be a Right-based Moral Theory?" Midwest Studies in Philosophy 3 (1978): 350–59, esp. 351. A similar account is found in Nickel, James. "Dworkin on the Nature and Consequences of Rights." Georgia Law Review 11 (1977): 1115–42, esp. 1117: "And if P has a right to receive X then P does no wrong (morally, if it is a moral right, legally, if it is a legal right) in receiving X."

5. Dworkin, Ronald. Taking Rights Seriously. London: Gerald Duckworth & Co., 1978. 188: "Someone may have the right to do something that is the wrong thing for him to do...."

6. Raz, Joseph. The Authority of Law: Essays on Law and Morality. Oxford: Clarendon Press, 1979. 274: "To show that one has a right to perform the act is to show that even if it is wrong he is entitled to perform it."

7. The distinction was introduced in Ross, W. D. The Right and the Good. Oxford: Clarendon Press, 1930. Chap. 2, pp. 17–56.

8. See, e.g., Brandt, Richard. Ethical Theory. Englewood Cliffs, N.J.: Prentice-Hall, Inc., 1959. 437–39.

9. See Raz, supra, note 6, pp. 266–67.

10. Melden, A. I. Rights and Persons. Oxford: Basil Blackwell, 1977. 1.

11. See section II, above.

12. See Hare, R. M. The Language of Morals. Oxford: Oxford University Press, 1952; and esp. Freedom and Reason. Oxford: Oxford University Press, 1963. passim.

13. In this paragraph, I have drawn heavily on Hare's discussion of universality and generality in Freedom and Reason, id., chap. 3, pp. 38–40.

14. This approach may be taken, e.g., by somebody committed to H. L. A. Hart's "choice theory" of rights: see Hart, H. L. A. "Are There Any Natural Rights?" Philosophical Review 64 (1955) : 175–91 [also collected in the present anthology as Reading 34]; and also "Bentham on Legal Rights." Oxford Essays in Jurisprudence, 2d ser. Ed. A. W. B. Simpson. Oxford: Clarendon Press, 1973. 171–201. Despite superficial similarities, my emphasis on the role of choice in rights does not commit me to anything like Hart's "choice theory." Clearly, one may say that a certain right is necessarily a right to make a certain choice, and that others have a duty to respect that choice, without saying (as Hart says) that the respondent's duty is actually created or imposed by the right-bearer's choice. It seems perfectly intelligible to say that Q may have a duty not to interfere with certain choices made by P, even before P has exercised any of those choices.

15. Dworkin, supra, note 5, pp. 269–72, presents this contrast nicely.

16. See, e.g., Locke, John. Two Treatises of Government. Critical Edition, Vol. 2. Ed. Peter Laslett. Cambridge: Cambridge University Press, 1960. Sec. 11: (the "right" of self-preservation); see also Ryan, Alan. "Locke and the Dictatorship of the Bourgeoisie." Political Studies 13 (1965): 219–30, esp. 223–24.

17. Godwin, supra, note 3, pp. 84–85; "There is not one of our avocations or amusements, that does not, by its effects, render us more or less fit to contribute our quota to the general utility. If then every one of our actions falls within the province of morals, it follows that we have no rights in relation to the selecting them."

18. See section I, above.

19. See Dworkin, supra, note 5, p. 189 and footnote thereto.

20. Some such theory, linking "right" and "authority," seems to be espoused in Anscombe, G. E. M. "On the Authority of the State." Ratio 20 (1978): 1–28.

21. See Austin, J. L. How to Do Things with Words. 2d ed. Eds. J. O. Urmson and Marian Sbisa. Oxford: Oxford University Press, 1975. 101 ff.; and Hare, The Language of Morals, supra, note 12, pp. 12–16.

CHAPTER ELEVEN

Law and Liberty

35   The Liberal Argument—From *On Liberty*

JOHN STUART MILL

The object of this essay is to assert one very simple principle, as entitled to govern absolutely the dealings of society with the individual in the way of compulsion and control, whether the means used be physical force in the form of legal penalties, or the moral coercion of public opinion. That principle, that the sole end for which mankind is warranted, individually or collectively, in interfering with the liberty of action of any of their number, is self-protection. That the only purpose for which power can be rightfully exercised over any member of a civilized community, against his will, is to prevent harm to others. His own good, either physical or moral, is not a sufficient warrant. He cannot rightfully be compelled to do or forbear because it will be better for him to do so; because it will make him happier; because, in the opinions of others, to do so would be wise, or even right. These are good reasons for remonstrating with him, or reasoning with him, or persuading him, or entreating him, but not for compelling him, or visiting him with any evil, in case he does otherwise. To justify that, the conduct from which it is desired to deter him must be calculated to produce evil to some one else. The only part of the conduct of any one, for which he is amenable to society, is that which concerns others. In the part which merely concerns himself, his independence is, of right, absolute. Over himself, over his own body and mind, the individual is sovereign.

It is, perhaps, hardly necessary to say that this doctrine is meant to apply only to human beings in the maturity of their faculties. We are not speaking of children, or of young persons below the age which the law may fix as that of manhood or womanhood. Those who are still in a state to require being taken care of by others must be protected against their own actions as well as against external injury. For the same reason, we may leave out of consideration those backward states of society in which the race itself may be considered as in its nonage. The early difficulties in the way of spontaneous progress are so great that there is seldom any choice of means for overcoming them; and a ruler full of the spirit of improvement is warranted in the use of any expedients that will attain an end, perhaps otherwise unattainable. Despotism is a legitimate mode of government

---

From *On Liberty*, excerpts from Chapters I and II, and all of Chapter IV. First published in 1859.

in dealing with barbarians, provided the end be their improvement, and the means justified by actually effecting that end. Liberty, as a principle, has no application to any state of things anterior to the time when mankind have become capable of being improved by free and equal discussion. Until then, there is nothing for them but implicit obedience to an Akbar or a Charlemagne, if they are so fortunate as to find one. But as soon as mankind have attained the capacity of being guided to their own improvement by conviction or persuasion (a period long since reached in all nations with whom we need here concern ourselves), compulsion, either in the direct form or in that of pains and penalties for non-compliance, is no longer admissible as a means to their own good, and justifiable only for the security of others.

It is proper to state that I forego any advantage which could be derived to my argument from the idea of abstract right, as a thing independent of utility. I regard utility as the ultimate appeal on all ethical questions; but it must be utility in the largest sense, grounded on the permanent interests of man as a progressive being. Those interests, I contend, authorize the subjection of individual spontaneity to external control, only in respect to those actions of each, which concern the interest of other people. If any one does an act hurtful to others, there is a prima facie case for punishing him, by law, or, where legal penalties are not safely applicable, by general disapprobation. There are also many positive acts for the benefit of others, which he may rightfully be compelled to perform; such as, to give evidence in a court of justice; to bear his fair share in the common defence, or in any other joint work necessary to the interest of the society of which he enjoys the protection; and to perform certain acts of individual beneficence, such as saving a fellow creature's life, or interposing to protect the defenseless against ill-usage, things which whenever it is obviously a man's duty to do, he may rightfully be made responsible to society for not doing. A person may cause evil to others not only by his actions but by his inaction, and in either case he is justly accountable to them for the injury. The latter case, it is true, requires a much more cautious exercise of compulsion than the former. To make any one answerable for doing evil to others is the rule; to make him answerable for not preventing evil is, comparatively speaking, the exception. Yet there are many cases clear enough and grave enough to justify that exception. In all things which regard the external relations of the individual, he is *de jure* amenable to those whose interests are concerned, and if need be, to society as their protector. There are often good reasons for not holding him to the responsibility; but these reasons must arise from the special expediencies of the case: either because it is a kind of case in which he is on the whole likely to act better, when left to his own discretion, than when controlled in any way in which society have it in their power to control him; or because the attempt to exercise control would produce other evils, greater than those which it would prevent. When such reasons as these preclude the enforcement of responsibility, the conscience of the agent himself should step into the vacant judgment-seat, and protect those interests of others which have no external protection; judging himself all the more rigidly, because the case does not admit of his being made accountable to the judgment of his fellow-creatures.

But there is a sphere of action in which society, as distinguished from the individual, has, if any, only an indirect interest; comprehending all that portion of a person's life and conduct which affects only himself, or, if it also affects others, only with their free, voluntary, and undeceived consent and participation. When I say only himself, I mean directly, and in the first instance: for whatever affects himself may affect others *through* himself, and the objection which may be grounded on this contingency will receive consideration in the sequel. This, then, is the appropriate region of human liberty. It comprises, first, the inward domain of consciousness; demanding liberty of conscience, in the most comprehensive sense; liberty of thought and feeling; absolute freedom of opinion and sentiment on all subjects, practical or speculative, scientific, moral, or theological. The liberty of expressing and publishing opinions may seem to fall under a different principle, since it belongs to that part of the conduct of an individual which concerns other people; but, being almost of as much importance as the liberty of thought itself, and resting in great part on the same reasons, is practically inseparable from it. Secondly, the principle requires liberty of tastes and pursuits; of framing the plan of our life to suit our own character; of doing as we like, subject to such consequences as may follow; without impediment from our fellow-creatures, so long as what we do does not harm them, even though they should think our conduct foolish, perverse, or wrong. Thirdly, from this liberty of each individual, follows the liberty, within the same limits, of combination among individuals; freedom to unite, for any purpose not involving harm to others: the persons combining being supposed to be of full age, and not forced or deceived.

No society on which these liberties are not, on the whole, respected, is free, whatever may be its form of government; and none is completely free in which they do not exist absolute and unqualified. The only freedom which deserves the name is that of pursuing our own good in our own way, so long as we do not attempt to deprive others of theirs, or impede their efforts to obtain it. Each is the proper guardian of his own health, whether bodily, or mental and spiritual. Mankind are greater gainers by suffering each other to live as seems good to themselves, than by compelling each to live as seems good to the rest....

We have now recognized the necessity to the mental well-being of mankind (on which all their other well-being depends) of freedom of opinion, and freedom of the expression of opinion, on four distinct grounds; which we will now briefly recapitulate.

First, if any opinion is compelled to silence that opinion may, for aught we can certainly know, be true. To deny this is to assume our own infallibility.

Secondly, though the silenced opinion be an error, it may, and very commonly does, contain a portion of truth; and since the general or prevailing opinion on any subject is rarely or never the whole truth, it is only by the collision of adverse opinions that the remainder of the truth has any chance of being supplied.

Thirdly, even if the received opinion be not only true, but the whole truth; unless it is suffered to be, and actually is vigorously and earnestly contested, it will, by most of those who receive it, be held in the manner of a prejudice, with little comprehension or feeling of its rational grounds. And not only this, but, fourthly, the meaning of the doctrine itself will be in danger of being lost, or enfeebled, and deprived of its vital effect on the character and conduct: the dogma becoming a mere formal profession, inefficacious for good, but cumbering the ground, and preventing the growth of any real and heartfelt conviction from reason or personal experience....

OF THE LIMITS TO THE AUTHORITY OF SOCIETY OVER THE INDIVIDUAL

What, then, is the rightful limit to the sovereignty of the individual over himself? Where does the authority of society begin? How much of human life should be assigned to individuality, and how much to society?

Each will receive its proper share, if each has that which more particularly concerns it. To individuality should belong the part of life in which it is chiefly the individual that is interested; to society, the part which chiefly interests society.

Though society is not founded on a contract, and though no good purpose is answered by inventing a contract in order to deduce social obligations from it, every one who receives the protection of society owes a return for the benefit, and the fact of living in society renders it indispensable that each should be bound to observe a certain line of conduct towards the rest. This conduct consists, first, in not injuring the interests of one another; or rather certain interests, which, either by express legal provision or by tacit understanding, ought to be considered as rights; and secondly, in each person's bearing his share (to be fixed on some equitable principle) of the labors and sacrifices incurred for defending the society or its members from injury and molestation. These conditions society is justified in enforcing, at all costs to those who endeavor to withhold fulfillment. Nor is this all that society may do. The acts of an individual may be hurtful to others, or wanting in due consideration for their welfare, without going the length of violating any of their constituted rights. The offender may then be justly punished by opinion, though not by law. As soon as any part of a person's conduct affects prejudicially the interests of others, society has jurisdiction over it, and the question whether the general welfare will or will not be promoted by interfering with it becomes open to discussion. But there is no room for entertaining any such question when a person's conduct affects the interests of no persons besides himself, or needs not affect them unless they like (all the persons concerned being of full age, and the ordinary amount of understanding). In all such cases there should be perfect freedom, legal and social, to do the action and stand the consequences.

It would be a great misunderstanding of this doctrine to suppose that it is one of selfish indifference, which pretends that human beings have no business with each other's conduct in life, and that they should not concern themselves about the well-doing or well-being of one another, unless their own interest is involved. Instead of any diminution, there is need of a great increase of disinterested exertion to promote the good of others. But disinterested benevolence can find other instruments to persuade people to their good than whips and scourges, either of the literal or the metaphorical sort. I am the last person to undervalue the self-regarding virtues; they are only second in importance, if even second, to the social. It is equally the business of education to cultivate both. But even education works by conviction and persuasion as well as by compulsion, and it is by the former only that, when the period of education is past, the self-regarding virtues should be inculcated. Human beings owe to each other help to distinguish the better from the worse, and encouragement to choose the former and avoid the latter. They should be forever stimulating each other to increased exercise of their higher faculties, and increased direction of their feelings and aims toward wise instead of foolish, elevating instead of degrading, objects and contemplations. But neither one person, nor any

number of persons, is warranted in saying to another human creature of ripe years that he shall not do with his life for his own benefit what he chooses to do with it. He is the person most interested in his own well-being: the interest which any other person, except in cases of strong personal attachment, can have in it is trifling, compared with that which he himself has; the interest which society has in him individually (except as to his conduct to others) is fractional, and altogether indirect: while, with respect to his own feelings and circumstances, the most ordinary man or woman has means of knowledge immeasurably surpassing those that can be possessed by anyone else. The interference of society to overrule his judgment and purposes in what only regards himself must be grounded on general presumptions, which may be altogether wrong, and even if right, are as likely as not to be misapplied to individual cases, by persons no better acquainted with the circumstances of such cases than those are who look at them merely from without. In this department, therefore, of human affairs, individuality has its proper field of action. In the conduct of human beings toward one another, it is necessary that general rules should for the most part be observed, in order that people may know what they have to expect; but in each person's own concerns, his individual spontaneity is entitled to free exercise. Considerations to aid his judgment, exhortations to strengthen his will, may be offered to him, even obtruded on him, by others; but he, himself, is the final judge. All errors which he is likely to commit against advice and warning are far outweighed by the evil of allowing others to constrain him to what they deem his good.

I do not mean that the feelings with which a person is regarded by others ought not to be in any way affected by his self-regarding qualities or deficiencies. This is neither possible nor desirable. If he is eminent in any of the qualities which conduce to his own good, he is, so far, a proper object of admiration. He is so much the nearer to the ideal perfection of human nature. If he is grossly deficient in those qualities, a sentiment the opposite of admiration will follow. There is a degree of folly, and a degree of what may be called (though the phrase is not unobjectionable) lowness or depravation of taste, which, though it cannot justify doing harm to the person who manifests it, renders him necessarily and properly a subject of distaste, or, in extreme cases, even of contempt: a person would not have the opposite qualities in due strength without entertaining these feelings. Though doing no wrong to anyone, a person may so act as to compel us to judge him, and feel to him, as a fool, or as a being of an inferior order: and since this judgment and feeling are a fact which he would prefer to avoid, it is doing him a service to warn him of it beforehand, as of any other disagreeable consequence to which he exposes himself. It would be well, indeed, if this good office were much more freely rendered than the common notions of politeness at present permit, and if one person could honestly point out to another that he thinks him in fault, without being considered unmannerly or presuming. We have a right, also, in various ways, to act upon our unfavorable opinion of any one, not to the oppression of his individuality, but in the exercise of ours. We are not bound, for example, to seek his society; we have a right to avoid it (though not to parade the avoidance), for we have a right to choose the society most acceptable to us. We have a right, and it may be our duty to caution others against him, if we think his example or conversation likely to have a pernicious effect on those with whom he associates. We may give others a preference over him in optional good offices, except those which tend to his improvement. In these various modes a person may suffer very severe penalties at the hands of others, for faults which directly concern only himself; but he suffers these penalties only in so far as they are the natural, and, as it were, the spontaneous consequences of the faults themselves, not because they are purposely inflicted on him for the sake of punishment. A person who shows rashness, obstinacy, self-conceit—who cannot live within moderate means—who cannot restrain himself from hurtful indulgences—who pursues animal pleasures at the expense of those of feelings and intellect—must expect to be lowered in the opinion of others, and to have a less share of their favorable sentiments, but of this he has no right to complain, unless he has merited their favor by special

excellence in his social relations and has thus established a title to their good offices, which is not affected by his demerits toward himself.

What I contend for is that the inconveniences which are strictly inseparable from the unfavorable judgment of others are the only ones to which a person should ever be subjected for that portion of his conduct and character which concerns his own good, but which does not affect the interests of others in their relations with him. Acts injurious to others require a totally different treatment. Encroachment on their rights; infliction on them of any loss or damage not justified by his own rights; falsehood or duplicity in dealing with them; unfair or ungenerous use of advantages over them; even selfish abstinence from defending them against injury—these are fit objects of moral reprobation, and, in grave cases, of moral retribution and punishment. And not only these acts, but the dispositions which lead to them, are properly immoral, and fit subjects of disapprobation which may rise to abhorrence. Cruelty of disposition; malice and ill-nature; that most antisocial and odious of all passions, envy; dissimulation and insincerity; irascibility on insufficient cause, and resentment disproportioned to the provocation; the love of domineering over others; the desire to engross more than one's share of advantages (the *pleonexia* of the Greeks); the pride which derives gratification from the abasement of others; the egotism which thinks self and its concerns more important than everything else, and decides all doubtful questions in his own favor—these are moral vices, and constitute a bad and odious moral character: unlike the self-regarding faults previously mentioned, which are not properly immoralities, and to whatever pitch they may be carried, do not constitute wickedness. They may be proofs of any amount of folly, or want of personal dignity and self-respect; but they are only a subject of moral reprobation when they involve a breach of duty to others, for whose sake the individual is bound to have care for himself. What are called duties to ourselves are not socially obligatory, unless circumstances render them at the same time duties to others. The term *duty to oneself,* when it means anything more than prudence, means self-respect or self-development; and for none of these is any one accountable to his fellow-creatures, because for none of them is it for the good of mankind that he be held accountable to them.

The distinction between the loss of consideration which a person may rightly incur by defect of prudence or of personal dignity, and the reprobation which is due to him for an offense against the rights of others, is not a merely nominal distinction. It makes a vast difference both in our feelings and in our conduct toward him, whether he displeases us in things in which we think we have a right to control him, or in things in which we know that we have not. If he displeases us, we may express our distaste, and we may stand aloof from a person as well as from a thing that displeases us; but we shall not therefore feel called on to make his life uncomfortable. We shall reflect that he already bears, or will bear, the whole penalty of his error; if he spoils his life by mismanagement, we shall not, for that reason, desire to spoil it still further: instead of wishing to punish him, we shall rather endeavor to alleviate his punishment, by showing him how he may avoid or cure the evils his conduct tends to bring upon him. He may be to us an object of pity, perhaps of dislike, but not of anger or resentment; we shall not treat him like an enemy of society: the worst we shall think ourselves justified in doing is leaving him to himself, if we do not interfere benevolently by showing interest or concern for him. It is far otherwise if he has infringed the rules necessary for the protection of his fellow-creatures, individually or collectively. The evil consequences of his acts do not then fall on himself, but on others; and society, as the protector of all its members, must retaliate on him; must inflict pain on him for the express purpose of punishment, and must take care that it be sufficiently severe. In the one case, he is an offender at our bar, and we are called on not only to sit in judgment on him, but, in one shape or another, to execute our own sentence: in the other case, it is not our part to inflict any suffering on him, except what may incidentally follow from our using the same liberty in the regulation of our own affairs, which we allow to him in his.

The distinction here pointed out between the part of a person's life which concerns only himself, and that which concerns others, many persons will refuse to admit. How (it may be asked) can any part of the conduct of a member of society be a matter of indifference to the other members? No person is an entirely isolated being; it is impossible for a person to do anything seriously or permanently hurtful to himself, without mischief reaching at least to his near connections, and often far beyond them. If he injures his property, he does harm to those who directly or indirectly derived support from it, and usually diminishes, by a greater or less amount, the general resources of the community. If he deteriorates his bodily or mental faculties, he not only brings evil upon all who depended on him for any portion of their happiness, but disqualifies himself for rendering the services which he owes to his fellow-creatures generally; perhaps becomes a burden on their affection or benevolence; and if such conduct were very frequent, hardly any offense that is committed would detract more from the general sum of good. Finally, if by his vices or follies a person does no direct harm to others, he is nevertheless (it may be said) injurious by his example; and ought to be compelled to control himself, for the sake of those whom the sight or knowledge of his conduct might corrupt or mislead.

And even (it will be added) if the consequences of misconduct could be confined to the vicious or thoughtless individual, ought society to abandon to their own guidance those who are manifestly unfit for it? If protection against themselves is confessedly due to children and persons under age, is not society equally bound to afford it to persons of mature years who are equally incapable of self-government? If gambling, or drunkenness, or incontinence, or idleness, or uncleanliness, are as injurious to happiness, and as great a hindrance to improvement, as many or most of the acts prohibited by law, why (it may be asked) should not law, so far as is consistent with practicability and social convenience, endeavor to repress these also? And as a supplement to the unavoidable imperfections of law, ought not opinion at least to organize a powerful police against these vices, and visit rigidly with social penalties those who are known to practice them? There is no question here (it may be said) about restricting individuality, or impeding the trial of new and original experiments in living. The only things it is sought to prevent are things which have been tried and condemned from the beginning of the world until now; things which experience has shown not to be useful or suitable to any person's individuality. There must be some length of time and amount of experience, after which a moral or prudential truth may be regarded as established: and it is merely desired to prevent generation after generation from falling over the same precipice which has been fatal to their predecessors.

I fully admit that the mischief which a person does to himself may seriously affect, both through their sympathies and their interests, those nearly connected with him, and in a minor degree, society at large. When, by conduct of this sort, a person is led to violate a distinct and assignable obligation to any other person or persons, the case is taken out of the self-regarding class, and becomes amenable to moral disapproval in the proper sense of the term. If, for example, a man, through intemperance or extravagance, becomes unable to pay his debts, or, having undertaken the moral responsibility of a family, becomes from the same cause incapable of supporting or educating them, he is deservedly reprobated, and might be justly punished; but it is for the breach of duty to his family or creditors, not for the extravagance. If the resources which ought to have been devoted to them had been diverted from them for the most prudent investment, the moral culpability would have been the same. George Barnwell murdered his uncle to get money for his mistress, but if he had done it to set himself up in business, he would equally have been hanged. Again, in the frequent case of a man who causes grief to his family by addiction to bad habits, he deserves reproach for his unkindness or ingratitude; but so he may for cultivating habits not in themselves vicious, if they are painful to those with whom he passes his life, or who from personal ties are dependent on him for their comfort. Whoever fails in the consideration generally due to the interests and feelings of others, not being compelled by some more imperative duty, or justified by allowable self-preference, is a subject of moral disapprobation for that failure, but not for the cause of it, nor for the errors, merely personal to himself,

which may have remotely led to it. In like manner; when a person disables himself, by conduct purely self-regarding, from the performance of some definite duty incumbent on him to the public, he is guilty of a social offense. No person ought to be punished simply for being drunk; but a soldier or a policeman should be punished for being drunk on duty. Whenever, in short, there is a definite damage, or a definite risk of damage, either to an individual or to the public, the case is taken out of the province of liberty, and placed in that of morality or law.

But with regard to the merely contingent, or, as it may be called, constructive injury which a person causes to society, by conduct which neither violates any specific duty to the public, nor occasions perceptible hurt to any assignable individual except himself; the inconvenience is one which society can afford to bear, for the sake of the greater good of human freedom. If grown persons are to be punished for not taking proper care of themselves, I would rather it were for their own sake, than under pretense of preventing them from impairing their capacity of rendering to society benefits which society does not pretend it has a right to exact. But I cannot consent to argue the point as if society had no means of bringing its weaker members up to its ordinary standard of rational conduct, except waiting till they do something irrational, and then punishing them, legally or morally, for it. Society has had absolute power over them during all the early portion of their existence: it has had the whole period of childhood and nonage in which to try whether it could make them capable of rational conduct in life. The existing generation is master both of the training and the entire circumstances of the generation to come; it cannot indeed make them perfectly wise and good, because it is itself so lamentably deficient in goodness and wisdom; and its best efforts are not always, in individual cases, its most successful ones; but it is perfectly well able to make the rising generation, as a whole, as good as, and a little better than, itself. If society lets any considerable number of its members grow up mere children, incapable of being acted on by rational consideration of distant motives, society has itself to blame for the consequences. Armed not only with all the powers of education, but with the ascendency which the authority of a received opinion always exercises over the minds who are least fitted to judge for themselves; and aided by the *natural* penalties which cannot be prevented from falling on those who incur the distaste or the contempt of those who know them; let not society pretend that it needs, besides all this, the power to issue commands and enforce obedience in the personal concerns of individuals, in which, on all principles of justice and policy, the decision ought to rest with those who are to abide the consequences. Nor is there anything which tends more to discredit and frustrate the better means of influencing conduct than a resort to the worse. If there be among those whom it is attempted to coerce into prudence or temperance any of the material of which vigorous and independent characters are made, they will infallibly rebel against the yoke. No such person will ever feel that others have a right to control him in his concerns, such as they have to prevent him from injuring them in theirs; and it easily comes to be considered a mark of spirit and courage to fly in the face of such usurped authority, and do with ostentation the exact opposite of what it enjoins; as in the fashion of grossness which succeeded, in the time of Charles II, to the fanatical moral intolerance of the Puritans. With respect to what is said of the necessity of protecting society from the bad example set to others by the vicious or the self-indulgent; it is true that bad example may have a pernicious effect, especially the example of doing wrong to others with impunity to the wrongdoer. But we are now speaking of conduct which, while it does no wrong to others, is supposed to do great harm to the agent himself; and I do not see how those who believe this can think otherwise than that the example, on the whole, must be more salutary than hurtful, since, if it displays the misconduct, it displays also the painful or degrading consequences which, if the conduct is justly censured, must be supposed to be in all or most cases attendant on it.

But the strongest of all the arguments against the interference of the public with purely personal conduct is that when it does interfere, the odds are that it interferes wrongly, and in the wrong place. On questions of social morality, of duty to others, the opinion of the public, that is, of an overruling majority, though often wrong, is likely to be still oftener right; because on such questions they are only required to judge of their own interests; of the manner in which some mode of conduct, if allowed to be practiced, would affect themselves. But the opinion of a similar majority, imposed as a law on the minority, on questions of self-regarding conduct is quite as likely to be wrong as right; for in these cases public opinion means, at the best, some people's opinion of what is good or bad for other people; while very often it does not even mean that; the public, with the most perfect indifference, passing over the pleasure or convenience of those whose conduct they censure, and considering only their own preference. There are many who consider as an injury to themselves any conduct which they have a distaste for, and resent it as an outrage to their feelings; as a religious bigot, when charged with disregarding the religious feelings of others, has been known to retort that they disregard his feelings, by persisting in their abominable worship or creed. But there is no parity between the feeling of a person for his own opinion, and the feeling of another who is offended at his holding it; no more than between the desire of a thief to take a purse, and the desire of the right owner to keep it. And a person's taste is as much his own peculiar concern as his opinion or his purse. It is easy for any one to imagine an ideal public, which leaves the freedom and choice of individuals in all uncertain matters undisturbed, and only requires them to abstain from modes of conduct which universal experience has condemned. But where has there been seen a public which set any such limit to its censorship? or when does the public trouble itself about universal experience? In its interferences with personal conduct it is seldom thinking of anything but the enormity of acting or feeling differently from itself; and this standard of judgment, thinly disguised, is held up to mankind as the dictate of religion and philosophy, by nine-tenths of all moralists and speculative writers. These teach that things are right because they are right; because we feel them to be so. They tell us to search in our own minds and hearts for laws of conduct binding on ourselves and on all others. What can the poor public do but apply these instructions, and make their own personal feelings of good and evil, if they are tolerably unanimous in them, obligatory on all the world?

The evil here pointed out is not one which exists only in theory; and it may perhaps be expected that I should specify the instances in which the public of this age and country improperly invests its own preferences with the character of moral laws. I am not writing an essay on the aberrations of existing moral feeling. That is too weighty a subject to be discussed parenthetically, and by way of illustration. Yet examples are necessary, to show that the principle I maintain is of serious and practical moment, and that I am not endeavoring to erect a barrier against imaginary evils. And it is not difficult to show, by abundant instances, that to extend the bounds of what may be called moral police, until it encroaches on the most unquestionably legitimate liberty of the individual, is one of the most universal of all human propensities.

As a first instance, consider the antipathies which men cherish on no better grounds than that persons whose religious opinions are different from theirs do not practice their religious observances, especially their religious abstinences. To cite a rather trivial example, nothing in the creed or practice of Christians does more to envenom the hatred of Mahomedans against them, than the fact of their eating pork. There are few acts which Christians and Europeans regard with more unaffected disgust than Mussulmans regard this particular mode of satisfying hunger. It is, in the first place, an offense against their religion; but this circumstance by no means explains either the degree or the kind of their repugnance; for wine also is forbidden by their religion, and to partake of it is by all Mussulmans accounted wrong, but not disgusting. Their aversion to the flesh of the "unclean beast" is, on the contrary, of that peculiar character, resembling an instinctive antipathy, which the idea of uncleanness, when once it thoroughly sinks into the feelings, seems always to excite even in those whose personal habits are anything but scrupulously cleanly, and of which

the sentiment of religious impurity, so intense in the Hindoos, is a remarkable example. Suppose now that in a people, of whom the majority were Mussulmans, that majority should insist upon not permitting pork to be eaten within the limits of the country. This would be nothing new in Mahomedan countries.[1] Would it be a legitimate exercise of the moral authority of public opinion? and if not, why not? The practice is really revolting to such a public. They also sincerely think that it is forbidden and abhorred by the Deity. Neither could the prohibition be censured as religious persecution. It might be religious in its origin, but it would not be persecution for religion, since nobody's religion makes it a duty to eat pork. The only tenable ground of condemnation would be that with the personal tastes and self-regarding concerns of individuals the public has no business to interfere.

To come somewhat nearer home: the majority of Spaniards consider it a gross impiety, offensive in the highest degree to the Supreme Being, to worship him in any other manner than the Roman Catholic; and no other public worship is lawful on Spanish soil. The people of all Southern Europe look upon a married clergy as not only irreligious, but unchaste, indecent, gross, disgusting. What do Protestants think of these perfectly sincere feelings, and of the attempt to enforce them against non-Catholics? Yet, if mankind are justified in interfering with each other's liberty in things which do not concern the interests of others, on what principle is it possible consistently to exclude these cases? or who can blame people for desiring to suppress what they regard as a scandal in the sight of God and man? No stronger case can be shown for prohibiting anything which is regarded as a personal immorality than is made out for suppressing these practices in the eyes of those who regard them as impieties; and unless we are willing to adopt the logic of persecutors, and to say that we may persecute others because we are right, and that they must not persecute us because they are wrong, we must beware of admitting a principle of which we should resent as a gross injustice the application to ourselves.

The preceding instances may be objected to, although unreasonably, as drawn from contingencies impossible among us: opinion, in this country, not being likely to enforce abstinence from meats, or to interfere with people for worshiping, and for either marrying or not marrying, according to their creed or inclination. The next example, however, shall be taken from an interference with liberty which we have by no means passed all danger of. Wherever the Puritans have been sufficiently powerful, as in New England, and in Great Britain at the time of the Commonwealth, they have endeavored, with considerable success, to put down all public, and nearly all private, amusements: especially music, dancing, public games, or other assemblages for purposes of diversion, and the theatre. There are still in this country large bodies of persons by whose notions of morality and religion these recreations are condemned; and those persons belonging chiefly to the middle class, who are the ascendant power in the present social and political condition of the kingdom, it is by no means impossible that persons of these sentiments may at some time or other command a majority in Parliament. How will the remaining portion of the community like to have the amusements that shall be permitted to them regulated by the religious and moral sentiments of the stricter Calvinists and Methodists? Would they not, with considerable peremptoriness, desire these intrusively pious members of society to mind their own business? This is precisely what should be said to every government and every public, who have the pretension that no person shall enjoy any pleasure which they think wrong. But if the principle of the pretension be admitted, no one can reasonably object to its being acted on in the sense of the majority, or other preponderating power in the country; and all persons must be ready to conform to the idea of a Christian commonwealth, as understood by the early settlers in New England, if a religious profession similar to theirs should ever succeed in regaining its lost ground, as religions supposed to be declining have so often been known to do.

To imagine another contingency, perhaps more likely to be realized than the one last mentioned, there is confessedly a strong tendency in the modern world toward a democratic constitution of society, accompanied or not by popular political institutions. It is affirmed that in the country where this tendency is most completely realized—where both society and the government are most democratic—the United States—the feeling of the majority, to whom any appearance of a more showy or costly style of living than they can hope to rival is disagreeable, operates as a tolerably effectual sumptuary law, and that in many parts of the Union it is really difficult for a person possessing a very large income to find any mode of spending it, which will not incur popular disapprobation. Though such statements as these are doubtless much exaggerated as a representation of existing facts, the state of things they describe is not only a conceivable and possible, but a probable result of democratic feeling, combined with the notion that the public has a right to a veto on the manner in which individuals shall spend their incomes. We have only further to suppose a considerable diffusion of Socialist opinions, and it may become infamous in the eyes of the majority to possess more property than some very small amount, or any income not earned by manual labor. Opinions similar in principle to these already prevail widely among the artisan class, and weigh oppressively on those who are amenable to the opinion chiefly of that class, namely, its own members. It is known that the bad workmen who form the majority of the operatives in many branches of industry are decidedly of the opinion that bad workmen ought to receive the same wages as good, and that no one ought to be allowed, through piecework or otherwise, to earn by superior skill or industry more than others can without it. And they employ a moral police, which occasionally becomes a physical one, to deter skillful workmen from receiving, and employers from giving, a larger remuneration for a more useful service. If the public have any jurisdiction over private concerns, I cannot see that these people are in fault, or that any individual's particular public can be blamed for asserting the same authority over his individual conduct, which the general public asserts over people in general.

But, without dwelling upon suppositious cases, there are, in our own day, gross usurpations upon the liberty of private life actually practiced, and still greater ones threatened with some expectation of success, and opinions proposed which assert an unlimited right in the public not only to prohibit by law everything which it thinks wrong, but in order to get at what it thinks wrong, to prohibit any number of things which it admits to be innocent.

Under the name of preventing intemperance, the people of one English colony, and of nearly half the United States, have been interdicted by law from making any use whatever of fermented drinks, except for medical purposes: for prohibition of their sale is in fact, as it is intended to be, prohibition of their use. And though the impracticability of executing the law has caused its repeal in several of the States which had adopted it, including the one from which it derives its name, an attempt has notwithstanding been commenced, and is prosecuted with considerable zeal by many of the professed philanthropists, to agitate for a similar law in this country. The association, or "Alliance" as it terms itself, which has been formed for this purpose has acquired some notoriety through the publicity given to a correspondence between its Secretary and one of the very few English public men who hold that a politician's opinions ought to be founded on principles. Lord Stanley's share in this correspondence is calculated to strengthen the hopes already built on him, by those who know how rare such qualities as are manifested in some of his public appearances unhappily are among those who figure in political life. The organ of the Alliance, who would "deeply deplore the recognition of any principle which could be wrested to justify bigotry and persecution," undertakes to point out the "broad and impassable barrier" which divides such principles from those of the association. "All matters relating to thought, opinion, conscience, appear to me," he says, "to be without the sphere of legislation; all pertaining to social act, habit, relation, subject only to a discretionary power vested in the State itself, and not in the individual, to be within it." No mention is made of a third class, different from either of these, *viz.,* acts and habits which are not social, but individual; although it is to this class, surely, that the act of drinking fermented liquors belongs. Selling fermented liquors, however, is trading, and trading is a social act. But the infringement complained of is not on the liberty of the seller, but on that of the buyer and consumer, since the State might just as well forbid him to drink wine as purposely make it impossible for him to obtain it. The Secretary, however, says, "I claim, as a citizen, a right to legislate whenever my social rights are invaded by the social act of another." And now for the definition of these "social rights." "If anything invades my social rights, certainly the traffic in strong drink does. It destroys my primary right of security, by constantly creating and stimulating social disorder. It invades my right of equality, by deriving a profit from the creation of a misery, I am taxed to support. It impedes my right to free moral and intellectual development, by surrounding my path with dangers, and by weakening and demoralizing society, from which I have a right to claim mutual aid and intercourse." A theory of "social rights," the like of which probably never before found its way into distinct language—being nothing short of this—that it is the absolute social right of every individual, that every other individual shall act in every respect exactly as he ought; that whosoever fails thereof in the smallest particular violates my social right, and entitles me to demand from the legislature the removal of the grievance. So monstrous a principle is far more dangerous than any single interference with liberty; there is no violation of liberty which it would not justify; it acknowledges no right to any freedom whatever, except perhaps to that of holding opinions in secret, without ever disclosing them; for the moment an opinion which I consider noxious passes any one's lips, it invades all the "social rights" attributed to me by the Alliance. The doctrine ascribes to all mankind a vested interest in each other's moral, intellectual, and even physical perfection, to be defined by each claimant according to his own standard.

Another important example of illegitimate interference with the rightful liberty of the individual, not simply threatened, but long since carried into triumphant effect, is Sabbatarian legislation. Without doubt, abstinence on one day in the week, so far as the exigencies of life permit, from the usual daily occupation, though in no respect religiously binding on any except Jews, is a highly beneficial custom. And inasmuch as this custom cannot be observed without a general consent to that effect among the industrious classes, therefore, in so far as some persons by working may impose the same necessity on others, it may be allowable and right that the law should guarantee to each the observance by others of the custom by suspending the greater operations of industry on a particular day. But this justification, grounded on the direct interest which others have in each individual's observance of the practice, does not apply to the self-chosen occupations in which a person may think fit to employ his leisure; nor does it hold good, in the smallest degree, for legal restrictions on amusements. It is true that the amusement of some is the day's work of others; but the pleasure, not to say the useful recreation, of many is worth the labor of a few, provided the occupation is freely chosen, and can be freely resigned. The operatives are perfectly right in thinking that if all worked on Sunday, seven days' work would have to be given for six days' wages: but so long as the great mass of employments are suspended, the small number who for the enjoyment of others must still work obtain a proportional increase of earnings; and they are not obliged to follow those occupations, if they prefer leisure to emolument. If a further remedy is sought, it might be found in the establishment by custom of a holiday on some other day of the week for those particular classes of persons. The only ground, therefore, on which restrictions on Sunday amusements can be defended must be that they are religiously wrong; a motive of legislation which never can be too earnestly protested again. *Deorum injuriae Diis curae.* [Latin: "The gods take care of injuries to the gods."] It remains to be proved that society or any of its officers holds a commission from on high to avenge any supposed offense to Omnipotence, which is not also a wrong to our fellow-creatures. The notion that it is one man's duty that another should be religious was the foundation of all the religious persecutions ever perpetrated, and if admitted, would fully justify them. Though the feeling which breaks out in the repeated attempts to stop railway travelling on Sunday, in the resistance to the opening of Museums, and the like has not the cruelty of the old persecutors, the state of mind indicated by it is fundamentally the same. It is a determination not to tolerate others in doing what is permitted by their religion, because it is not permitted by the persecutor's religion. It is a belief that God not only abominates the act of the misbeliever, but will not hold us guiltless if we leave him unmolested.

I cannot refrain from adding to these examples of the little account commonly made of human liberty the language of downright persecution which breaks out from the press of this country, whenever it feels called on to notice the remarkable phenomenon of Mormonism. Much might be said on the unexpected and instructive fact that an alleged new revelation, and a religion founded on it, the product of palpable imposture, not even supported by the *prestige* of extraordinary qualities in its founder, is believed by hundreds of thousands, and has been made the foundation of a society, in the age of newspapers, railways, and the electric telegraph. What here concerns us is that this religion, like other and better religions, has its martyrs; that its prophet and founder was, for his teaching, put to death by a mob; that others of its adherents lost their lives by the same lawless violence; that they were forcibly expelled, in a body, from the country in which they first grew up; while, now that they have been chased into a solitary recess in the midst of a desert, many of this country openly declare that it would be right (only that it is not convenient) to send an expedition against them, and compel them by force to conform to the opinion of other people. The article of the Mormonite doctrine which is the chief provocative to the antipathy which thus breaks through the ordinary restraints of religious tolerance, is its sanction of polygamy; which, though permitted to Mahomedans, and Hindoos, and Chinese, seems to excite unquenchable animosity when practiced by persons who speak English, and profess to be a kind of Christian. No one has a deeper disapprobation than I have of the Mormon institution; both for other reasons, and because, far from being in any way countenanced by the principle of liberty, it is a direct infraction of that principle, being a mere riveting of the chains of one-half of the community, and an emancipation of the other from reciprocity of obligation toward them. Still, it must be remembered that this relation is as much voluntary on the part of the women concerned in it, and who may be deemed the sufferers by it, as is the case with any other form of the marriage institution; and however surprising this fact may appear, it has its explanation in the common ideas and customs of the world, which teaching women to think marriage the one thing needful, make it intelligible that many a woman should prefer being one of several wives, to not being a wife at all. Other countries are not asked to recognize such unions, or release any portion of their inhabitants from their own laws on the score of Mormonite opinions. But when the dissentients have conceded to the hostile sentiments of others, far more than could justly be demanded; when they have left the countries to which their doctrines were unacceptable, and established themselves in a remote corner of the earth, which they have been the first to render habitable to human beings; it is difficult to see on what principles but those of tyranny they can be prevented from living there under what laws they please, provided they commit no aggression on other nations, and allow perfect freedom of departure to those who are dissatisfied with their ways. A recent writer, in some respects of considerable merit, proposes (to use his own words) not a crusade, but a *civilizade,* against this polygamous community, to put an end to what seems to him a retrograde step in civilization. It also appears so to me, but I am not aware that any community has a right to force another to be civilized. So long as the sufferers by the bad law do not invoke assistance from other communities, I cannot admit that persons entirely unconnected with them ought to step in and require that a condition of things with which all who are directly interested appear to be satisfied, should be put an end to because it is a scandal to persons some thousands of miles distant, who have no part or concern in it. Let them send missionaries, if they please, to preach against it; and let them, by any fair means (of which silencing the teachers is not one), oppose the progress of similar doctrines among their own people. If civilization has got the better of barbarism when barbarism had the world to itself, it is too much to profess to be afraid lest barbarism, after having been fairly got under, should revive and conquer civilization. A civilization that can thus succumb to its vanquished enemy must first have become so degenerate that neither its appointed priests and teachers, nor anybody else, has the capacity, or will take the trouble, to stand up for it. If this be so, the sooner such a civilization receives notice to quit, the better. It can only go on from bad to worse, until destroyed and regenerated (like the Western Empire) by energetic barbarians.

NOTES

1. The case of the Bombay Parsees is a curious instance in point. When this industrious and enterprising tribe, the descendants of the Persian fire-worshippers, flying from their native country before the Caliphs, arrived in Western India, they were admitted to toleration by the Hindoo sovereigns, on condition of not eating beef. When those regions afterwards fell under the dominion of Mahomedan conquerors, the Parsees obtained from them a continuance of indulgence, on condition of refraining from pork. What was at first obedience to authority became a second nature, and the Parsees to this day abstain both from beef and pork. Though not required by their religion, the double abstinence has had time to grow into a custom of their tribe; and custom, in the East, is a religion.

36   Paternalism

GERALD DWORKIN

Neither one person, nor any number of persons, is warranted in saying to another human creature of ripe years, that he shall not do with his life for his own benefit what he chooses to do with it.

—MILL

I do not want to go along with a volunteer basis. I think a fellow should be compelled to become better and not let him use his discretion whether he wants to get smarter, more healthy or more honest.

—GENERAL HERSHEY

I take as my starting point the "one very simple principle" proclaimed by Mill *On Liberty* ...

> That principle is, that the sole end for which mankind are warranted, individually or collectively, in interfering with the liberty of action of any of their number, is self-protection. That the only purpose for which power can be rightfully exercised over any member of a civilized community, against his will, is to prevent harm to others. He cannot rightfully be compelled to do or forbear because it will be better for him to do so, because it will make him happier, because, in the opinion of others, to do so would be wise, or even right.

This principle is neither "one" nor "very simple." It is at least two principles; one asserting that self-protection or the prevention of harm to others is sometimes a sufficient warrant and the other claiming that the individual's own good is *never* a sufficient warrant for the exercise of compulsion either by the society as a whole or by its individual members. I assume that no one, with the possible exception of extreme pacifists or anarchists, questions the correctness of the first half of the principle. This essay is an examination of the negative claim embodied in Mill's principle—the objection to paternalistic interferences with a man's liberty.

I

By paternalism I shall understand roughly the interference with a person's liberty of action justified by reasons referring exclusively to the welfare, good, happiness, needs, interests, or values of the person being coerced. One is always well-advised to illustrate one's definitions by examples, but it is not easy to find "pure" examples of paternalistic interferences. For almost any piece of legislation is justified by several different kinds of reasons and even if historically a piece of legislation can be shown to have been introduced for purely paternalistic motives, it may be that advocates of the legislation with an antipaternalistic outlook can find sufficient reasons justifying the legislation without appealing to the reasons that were originally adduced to support it. Thus, for example, it may be that the original legislation requiring motorcyclists to wear safety helmets was introduced for purely paternalistic reasons. But the Rhode Island Supreme Court recently upheld such legislation on the grounds that it was "not persuaded that the legislature is powerless to prohibit individuals from pursuing a course of conduct that could conceivably result in their

From *Morality and the Law*, ed. R. Wasserstrom (Belmont, CA: Wadsworth Publishing, 1971). Reprinted by permission of the publisher.

becoming public charges," thus clearly introducing reasons of a quite different kind. Now I regard this decision as being based on reasoning of a very dubious nature, but it illustrates the kind of problem one has in finding examples. The following is a list of the kinds of interferences I have in mind as being paternalistic.

II

1. Laws requiring motorcyclists to wear safety helmets when operating their machines.
2. Laws forbidding persons from swimming at a public beach when lifeguards are not on duty.
3. Laws making suicide a criminal offense.
4. Laws making it illegal for women and children to work at certain types of jobs.
5. Laws regulating certain kinds of sexual conduct, for example, homosexuality, among consenting adults in private.
6. Laws regulating the use of certain drugs that may have harmful consequences to the user but do not lead to antisocial conduct.
7. Laws requiring a license to engage in certain professions with those not receiving a license subject to fine or jail sentence if they do engage in the practice.
8. Laws compelling people to spend a specified fraction of their income on the purchase of retirement annuities (Social Security).
9. Laws forbidding various forms of gambling (often justified on the grounds that the poor are more likely to throw away their money on such activities than the rich who can afford to).
10. Laws regulating the maximum rates of interest for loans.
11. Laws against duelling.

In addition to laws that attach criminal or civil penalties to certain kinds of action there are laws, rules, regulations, and decrees that make it either difficult or impossible for people to carry out their plans, and which are also justified on paternalistic grounds. Examples of this are:

1. Laws regulating the types of contracts that will be upheld as valid by the courts, for example (an example of Mill's to which I shall

return), no man may make a valid contract for perpetual involuntary servitude.
2. Not allowing assumption of risk as a defense to an action based on the violation of a safety statute.
3. Not allowing as a defense to a charge of murder or assault the consent of the victim.
4. Requiring members of certain religious sects to have compulsory blood transfusions. This is made possible by not allowing the patient to have recourse to civil suits for assault and battery and by means of injunctions.
5. Civil commitment procedures when these are specifically justified on the basis of preventing the person being committed from harming himself. The District of Columbia Hospitalization of the Mentally Ill Act provides for involuntary hospitalization of a person who "is mentally ill, and because of that illness, is likely to injure himself or others if allowed to remain at liberty." The term *injure* in this context applies to unintentional as well as intentional injuries.

All of my examples are of existing restrictions on the liberty of individuals. Obviously one can think of interferences that have not yet been imposed. Thus one might ban the sale of cigarettes, or require that people wear safety belts in automobiles (as opposed to merely having them installed), enforcing this by not allowing a motorist to sue for injuries even when caused by other drivers, if the motorist was not wearing a seat belt at the time of the accident.

I shall not be concerned with activities which, though defended on paternalistic grounds, are not interferences with the liberty of persons, for example, the giving of subsidies in kind rather than in cash on the grounds that the recipients would not spend the money on the goods which they really need, or not including a $1,000 deductible provision in a basic protection automobile insurance plan on the ground that the people who would elect it could least afford it. Nor shall I be concerned with measures such as "truth-in-advertising" acts and Pure Food and Drug legislation, which are often attacked as paternalistic but which should not be considered so. In these cases all that is provided—it is true by the use of compulsion—is information which it is presumed that rational persons are interested in having in order to make wise decisions. There is no interference with the liberty of the consumer unless one wants to stretch a point beyond good sense and say that his liberty to apply for a loan without knowing the true rate of interest is diminished. It is true that sometimes there is sentiment for going further than providing information, for example when laws against usurious interest are passed preventing those who might wish to contract loans at high rates of interest from doing so, and these measures may correctly be considered paternalistic.

III

Bearing these examples in mind, let me return to a characterization of paternalism. I said earlier that I meant by the term, roughly, interference with a person's liberty for his own good. But, as some of the examples show, the class of persons whose good is involved is not always identical with the class of persons whose freedom is restricted. Thus, in the case of professional licensing it is the practitioner who is directly interfered with, but it is the would-be patient whose interests are presumably being served. Not allowing the consent of the victim to be a defense to certain types of crime primarily affects the would-be aggressor, but it is the interests of the willing victim that we are trying to protect. Sometimes a person may fall into both classes, as would be the case if we banned the manufacture and sale of cigarettes and a given manufacturer happened to be a smoker as well.

Thus we may first divide paternalistic interferences into "pure" and "impure" cases. In "pure" paternalism the class of persons whose freedom is restricted is identical with the class of persons whose benefit is intended to be promoted by such restrictions. Examples: the making of suicide a crime, requiring passengers in automobiles to wear seat belts, requiring a Christian Scientist to receive a blood transfusion. In the case of "impure" paternalism in trying to protect the welfare of a class of persons, we find that the only way to do so will involve restricting the freedom of other persons besides those who are benefitted. Now, it might be thought that there are no cases of "impure" paternalism, since any such case could always be justified on nonpaternalistic grounds, that is, in terms of preventing harm to others. Thus we might ban cigarette manufacturers from continuing to manufacture their product on the grounds that we are preventing them from causing illness to others in the same way that we prevent other manufacturers from releasing pollutants into the atmosphere, thereby causing danger to the members of the community. The difference is, however, that in the former but not the latter case the harm is of such a nature that it could be avoided by those individuals affected if they so chose. The incurring of the harm requires, so to speak, the active cooperation of the victim. It would be mistaken theoretically—and hypocritical in practice—to assert that our interference in such cases is just like our interference in standard cases of protecting others from harm. At the very least someone interfered with in this way can reply that no one is complaining about his activities. It may be that impure paternalism requires arguments or reasons of a stronger kind in order to be justified, since there are persons who are losing a portion of their liberty, and they do not even have the solace of having it be done "in their own interest." Of course in some sense, if paternalistic justifications are ever correct, then we are protecting others, we are preventing some from injuring others, but it is important to see the differences between this and the standard case.

Paternalism then will always involve limitations on the liberty of some individuals in their own interest, but it may also extend to interferences with the liberty of parties whose interests are not in question.

IV

Finally, by way of some more preliminary analysis, I want to distinguish paternalistic interference with liberty from a related type with which it is often confused. Consider, for example, legislation that forbids employees to work more than, say, forty hours per week. It is sometimes argued that such legislation is paternalistic, for if employees desired such a restriction on their hours of work, they could agree among themselves to impose it voluntarily. But because they do not, the society imposes its own conception of their best interests upon them by the use of coercion. Hence this is paternalism.

Now it may be that some legislation of this nature is, in fact, paternalistically motivated. I am not denying that. All I want to point out is that there is another possible way of justifying such measures that is not paternalistic in nature. It is not paternalistic because, as Mill puts it in a similar context, such measures are "required not to over-rule the judgment of individuals respecting their own interest, but to give effect to that judgment: they being unable to give effect to it except by concert, which concert again cannot be effectual unless it receives validity and sanction from the law." *(Principles of Political Economy.)*

The line of reasoning here is a familiar one first found in Hobbes and developed with great sophistication by contemporary economists in the last decade or so. There are restrictions that are in the interests of a class of persons taken collectively, but are such that the immediate interest of each individual is furthered by his violating the rule when others adhere to it. In such cases the individuals involved may need the use of compulsion to give effect to their collective judgment of their own interest, by guaranteeing each individual compliance by the others. In these cases compulsion is not used to achieve some benefit that is not recognized to be a benefit by those concerned, but rather because it is the only feasible means of achieving some benefit that *is* recognized as such by all concerned. This way of viewing matters provides us with another characterization of paternalism in general. Paternalism might be thought of as the use of coercion to achieve a good that is not recognized as such by those persons for whom the good is intended. Again, although this formulation captures the heart of the matter—it is surely what Mill is objecting to in *On Liberty*—the matter is not always quite like that. For example, when we force motorcyclists to wear helmets we are trying to promote a good—the protection of the person from injury—that is surely recognized by most of the individuals concerned. It is not that a cyclist doesn't value his bodily integrity; rather, as a

supporter of such legislation would put it, he either places, perhaps irrationally, another value or good (freedom from wearing a helmet) above that of physical well-being or, perhaps, while recognizing the danger in the abstract, he either does not fully appreciate it or he underestimates the likelihood of its occurring. But now we are approaching the question of possible justifications of paternalistic measures, and the rest of this essay will be devoted to that question.

V

I shall begin for dialectical purposes by discussing Mill's objections to paternalism and then go on to discuss more positive proposals.

An initial feature that strikes one is the absolute nature of Mill's prohibitions against paternalism. It is so unlike the carefully qualified admonitions of Mill and his fellow utilitarians on other moral issues. He speaks of self-protection as the *sole* end warranting coercion, of the individual's own goals as *never* being a sufficient warrant. Contrast this with his discussion of the prohibition against lying in *Utilitarianism*:

> Yet that even this rule, sacred as it is, admits of possible exception, is acknowledged by all moralists, the chief of which is where the withholding of some fact … would save an individual … from great and unmerited evil.

> The same tentativeness is present when he deals with justice:

> It is confessedly unjust to break faith with any one: to violate an engagement, either express or implied, or disappoint expectations raised by our own conduct, at least if we have raised these expectations knowingly and voluntarily. Like all the other obligations of justice already spoken of, this one is not regarded as absolute, but as capable of being overruled by a stronger obligation of justice on the other side.

This anomaly calls for some explanation. The structure of Mill's argument is as follows:

1. Since restraint is an evil the burden of proof is on those who propose such restraint.
2. Since the conduct that is being considered is purely self-regarding, the normal appeal to the protection of the interests of others is not available.

3. Therefore we have to consider whether reasons involving reference to the individual's own good, happiness, welfare, or interests are sufficient to overcome the burden of justification.
4. We either cannot advance the interests of the individual by compulsion, or the attempt to do so involves evils that outweigh the good done.
5. Hence the promotion of the individual's own interests does not provide a sufficient warrant for the use of compulsion.

Clearly the operative premise here is (4), and it is bolstered by claims about the status of the individual as judge and appraiser of his welfare, interests, needs, and so on:

> With respect to his own feelings and circumstances, the most ordinary man or woman has means of knowledge immeasurably surpassing those that can be possessed by any one else.
>
> He is the man most interested in his own well-being: the interest which any other person, except in cases of strong personal attachment, can have in it is trifling, compared to that which he himself has.
>
> These claims are used to support the following generalizations concerning the utility of compulsion for paternalistic purposes.
>
> The interferences of society to overrule his judgment and purposes in what only regards himself must be grounded on general presumptions; which may be altogether wrong, and even if right, are as likely as not to be misapplied to individual cases.
>
> But the strongest of all the arguments against the interference of the public with purely personal conduct is that when it does interfere, the odds are that it interferes wrongly and in the wrong place.
>
> All errors that the individual is likely to commit against advice and warning are far outweighed by the evil of allowing others to constrain him to what they deem his good.

Performing the utilitarian calculations by balancing the advantages and disadvantages, we find that: "Mankind are greater gainers by suffering each other to live as seems good to themselves, than by compelling each other to live as seems good to the rest." Ergo, (4).

This classical case of a utilitarian argument with all the premises spelled out is not the only line of reasoning present in Mill's discussion. There are asides, and more than asides, which look quite different, and I shall deal with them later. But this is clearly the main channel of Mill's thought, and it is one that has been subjected to vigorous attack from the moment it appeared—most often by fellow Utilitarians. The link that they have usually seized on is, as Fitzjames Stephen put it in *Liberty, Equality, Fraternity,* the absence of proof that the "mass of adults are so well acquainted with their own interests and so much disposed to pursue them that no compulsion or restraint put upon them by any others for the purpose of promoting their interest can really promote them." Even so sympathetic a critic as H. L. A. Hart is forced to the conclusion that:

> In Chapter 5 of his essay [*On Liberty*] Mill carried his protests against paternalism to lengths that may now appear to us as fantastic.... No doubt if we no longer sympathise with his criticism this is due, in part, to a general decline in the belief that individuals know their own interest best.
>
> Mill endows the average individual with "too much of the psychology of a middle-aged man whose desires are relatively fixed, not liable to be artificially stimulated by external influences; who knows what he wants and what gives him satisfaction or happiness; and who pursues these things when he can."

Now it is interesting to note that Mill himself was aware of some of the limitations on the doctrine that the individual is the best judge of his own interests. In his discussion of government intervention in general (even where the intervention does not interfere with liberty but provides alternative institutions to those of the market) after making claims that are parallel to those just discussed, for example, "People understand their own business and their own interests better, and care for them more, than the government does, or can be expected to do," he goes on to an intelligent discussion of the "very large and conspicuous exceptions" to the maxim that:

> Most persons take a juster and more intelligent view of their own interest, and of the means of

promoting it than can either be prescribed to them by a general enactment of the legislature, or pointed out in the particular case by a public functionary.

Thus there are things:

of which the utility does not consist in ministering to inclinations, nor in serving the daily uses of life, and the want of which is least felt where the need is greatest. This is peculiarly true of those things which are chiefly useful as tending to raise the character of human beings. The uncultivated cannot be competent judges of cultivation. Those who most need to be made wiser and better, usually desire it least, and, if they desire it, would be incapable of finding the way to it by their own lights.

... A second exception to the doctrine that individuals are the best judges of their own interest, is when an individual attempts to decide irrevocably now what will be best for his interest at some future and distant time. The presumption in favor of individual judgment is only legitimate, where the judgment is grounded on actual, and especially on present, personal experience; not where it is formed antecedently to experience, and not suffered to be reversed even after experience has condemned it.

The upshot of these exceptions is that Mill does not declare that there should never be government interference with the economy but rather that:

... in every instance, the burden of making out a strong case should be thrown not on those who resist but those who recommend government interference. Letting alone, in short, should be the general practice: every departure from it, unless required by some great good, is a certain evil.

In short, we get a presumption, not an absolute prohibition. The question is, why doesn't the argument against paternalism go the same way?

I suggest that the answer lies in seeing that in addition to a purely utilitarian argument, Mill uses another as well. As a utilitarian, Mill has to show, in Fitzjames Stephen's words, that: "Self-protection apart, no good object can be attained by any compulsion which is not in itself a greater evil than the absence of the object which the compulsion obtains." To show this is impossible, one

reason being that it isn't true. Preventing a man from selling himself into slavery (a paternalistic measure that Mill himself accepts as legitimate), or from taking heroin, or from driving a car without wearing seat belts may constitute a lesser evil than allowing him to do any of these things. A consistent utilitarian can only argue against paternalism on the grounds that it (as a matter of fact) does not maximize the good. It is always a contingent question that may be returned by the evidence. But there is also a noncontingent argument that runs through *On Liberty*. When Mill states that "there is a part of the life of every person who has come to years of discretion, within which the individuality of that person ought to reign uncontrolled either by any other person or by the public collectively," he is saying something about what it means to be a person, an autonomous agent. It is because coercing a person for his own good denies this status as an independent entity that Mill objects to it so strongly and in such absolute terms. To be able to choose is a good that is independent of the wisdom of what is chosen. A man's "mode of laying out his existence is the best, not because it is the best in itself, but because it is his own mode." It is the privilege and proper condition of a human being, arrived at the maturity of his faculties, to use and interpret experience in his own way.

As further evidence of this line of reasoning in Mill, consider the one exception to his prohibition against paternalism:

In this and most civilised countries, for example, an engagement by which a person should sell himself, or allow himself to be sold, as a slave, would be null and void; neither enforced by law nor by opinion. The ground for thus limiting his power of voluntarily disposing of his own lot in life, is apparent, and is very clearly seen in this extreme case. The reason for not interfering, unless for the sake of others, with a person's voluntary acts, is consideration for his liberty. His voluntary choice is evidence that what he so chooses is desirable, or at least endurable, to him, and his good is on the whole best provided for by allowing him to take his own means of pursuing it. But by selling himself for a slave, he abdicates his liberty; he foregoes any future use of it beyond that single act. He therefore defeats, in his own case, the very purpose which is the justification of allowing him to dispose of himself. He is no longer free; but is thenceforth in a position which has no longer the presumption in its favour, that would be afforded by his voluntarily remaining in it. The principle of freedom cannot require that he should be free not to be free. It is not freedom to be allowed to alienate his freedom.

Now leaving aside the fudging on the meaning of freedom in the last line, it is clear that part of this argument is incorrect. While it is true that *future* choices of the slave are not reasons for thinking that what he chooses then is desirable for him, what is at issue is limiting his immediate choice; and since this choice is made freely, the individual may be correct in thinking that his interests are best provided for by entering such a contract. But the main consideration for not allowing such a contract is the need to preserve the liberty of the person to make future choices. This gives us a principle—a very narrow one—by which to justify some paternalistic interferences. Paternalism is justified only to preserve a wider range of freedom for the individual in question. How far this principle could be extended, whether it can justify all the cases in which we are inclined upon reflection to think paternalistic measures justified, remains to be discussed. What I have tried to show so far is that there are two strains of argument in Mill—one a straightforward utilitarian mode of reasoning, and one that relies not on the goods that free choice leads to but on the absolute value of the choice itself. The first cannot establish any absolute prohibition but at most a presumption and indeed a fairly weak one given some fairly plausible assumptions about human psychology; the second, while a stronger line of argument, seems to me to allow on its own grounds a wider range of paternalism than might be suspected. I turn now to a consideration of these matters.

VI

We might begin looking for principles governing the acceptable use of paternalistic power in cases where it is generally agreed that it is legitimate.

Even Mill intends his principles to be applicable only to mature individuals, not those in what he calls "nonage." What is it that justifies us in interfering with children? The fact that they lack some of the emotional and cognitive capacities required in order to make fully rational decisions. It is an empirical question to just what extent children have an adequate conception of their own present and future interests, but there is not much doubt that there are many deficiencies. For example, it is very difficult for a child to defer gratification for any considerable period of time. Given these deficiencies, and given the very real and permanent dangers that may befall the child, it becomes not only permissible but even a duty of the parent to restrict the child's freedom in various ways. There is however an important moral limitation on the exercise of such parental power, which is provided by the notion of the child eventually coming to see the correctness of his parent's interventions. Parental paternalism may be thought of as a wager by the parent on the child's subsequent recognition of the wisdom of the restrictions. There is an emphasis on what could be called future-oriented consent—on what the child will come to welcome, rather than on what he does welcome.

The essence of this idea has been incorporated by idealist philosophers into various types of "real-will" theory as applied to fully adult persons. Extensions of paternalism are argued for by claiming that in various respects, chronologically mature individuals share the same deficiencies in knowledge, capacity to think rationally, and the ability to carry out decisions that children possess. Hence in interfering with such people we are in effect doing what they would do if they were fully rational. Hence we are not really opposing their will, hence we are not really interfering with their freedom. The dangers of this move have been sufficiently exposed by Berlin in his *Two Concepts of Liberty*. I see no gain in theoretical clarity nor in practical advantage in trying to pass over the real nature of the interferences with liberty that we impose on others. Still the basic notion of consent is important and seems to me the only acceptable way of trying to delimit an area of justified paternalism.

Let me start by considering a case where the consent is not hypothetical in nature. Under certain conditions it is rational for an individual to agree that others should force him to act in ways that, at the time of action, the individual may not see as desirable. If, for example, a man knows that he is subject to breaking his resolves when temptation is present, he may ask a friend to refuse to entertain his requests at some later stage.

A classical example is given in the *Odyssey*, when Odysseus commands his men to tie him to the mast and refuse all future orders to be set free, because he knows the power of the Sirens to enchant men with their songs. Here we are on relatively sound ground in later refusing Odysseus's request to be set free. He may even claim to have changed his mind but, since it is *just* such changes that he wished to guard against, we are entitled to ignore them.

A process analogous to this may take place on a social rather than individual basis. An electorate may mandate its representatives to pass legislation that, when it comes time to "pay the price," may be unpalatable. I may believe that a tax increase is necessary to halt inflation, though I may resent the lower pay check each month. However in both this case and that of Odysseus, the measure to be enforced is specifically requested by the party involved, and at some point in time there is genuine consent and agreement on the part of those persons whose liberty is infringed. Such is not the case for the paternalistic measures we have been speaking about. What must be involved here is not consent to specific measures, but rather consent to a system of government, run by elected representatives, with an understanding that they may act to safeguard our interests in certain limited ways.

I suggest that since we are all aware of our irrational propensities, deficiencies in cognitive and emotional capacities, and avoidable and unavoidable ignorance, it is rational and prudent for us to, in effect, take out "social insurance policies." We may argue for and against proposed paternalistic measures in terms of what fully rational individuals would accept as forms of protection. Now clearly, since the initial agreement is not about specific measures, we are dealing with a more-or-less blank check, and therefore there have to be carefully defined limits. What I am looking for are certain kinds of conditions that make it plausible to suppose that rational men could reach agreement to limit their liberty even when other men's interests are not affected.

Of course as in any kind of agreement schema there are great difficulties in deciding what rational individuals would or would not accept. Particularly in sensitive areas of personal liberty, there is always a danger of the dispute over agreement and rationality being a disguised version of evaluative and normative disagreement.

Let me suggest types of situations in which it seems plausible to suppose that fully rational individuals would agree to having paternalistic restrictions imposed upon them. It is reasonable to suppose that there are "goods" such as health that any person would want to have in order to pursue his own good—no matter how that good is conceived. This is an argument used in connection with compulsory education for children, but it seems to me that it can be extended to other goods that have this character. Then one could agree that the attainment of such goods should be promoted even when not recognized to be such, at the moment, by the individuals concerned.

An immediate difficulty arises from the fact that men are always faced with competing goods, and that there may be reasons why even a value such as health—or indeed life—may be overridden by competing values. Thus the problem with the Christian Scientist and blood transfusions. It may be more important for him to reject "impure substances" than to go on living. The difficult problem that must be faced is whether one can give sense to the notion of a person irrationally attaching weights to competing values.

Consider a person who knows the statistical data on the probability of being injured when not wearing seat belts in an automobile, and knows the types of gravity of the various injuries. He also insists that the inconvenience attached to fastening the belt every time he gets in and out of the car outweighs for him the possible risks to himself. I am inclined in this case to think that such a weighing is irrational. Given his life plans, which we are assuming are those of the average person, his interests and commitments already undertaken, I think it is safe to predict that we can find inconsistencies in his calculations at some point. I am assuming that this is not a man who for some conscious or unconscious reasons is trying to injure himself, nor is he a man who just likes to "live dangerously." I am assuming that he is like us in all the relevant respects, but just puts an enormously high negative value on inconvenience—one which does not seem comprehensible or reasonable.

It is always possible, of course, to assimilate this person to creatures like myself. I also neglect to fasten my seat belt, and I concede such behavior is not rational, but not because I weigh the inconvenience differently from those who fasten the belts. It is just that having made (roughly) the same calculation as everybody else, I ignore it in my actions. (Note: a much better case of weakness of the will than those usually given in ethics tests.) A plausible explanation for this deplorable habit is that, although I know in some intellectual sense what the probabilities and risks are, I do not fully appreciate them in an emotionally genuine manner.

We have two distinct types of situation in which a man acts in a nonrational fashion. In one case he attaches incorrect weights to some of his values; in the other he neglects to act in accordance with his actual preferences and desires. Clearly there is a stronger and more persuasive argument for paternalism in the latter situation. Here we are really not—by assumption— imposing a good on another person. But why may we not extend our interference to what we might call evaluative delusions? After all, in the case of cognitive delusions we are prepared, often, to act against the expressed will of the person involved. If a man believes that when he jumps out the window he will float upwards—Robert Nozick's example—would not we detain him, forcibly if necessary? The reply will be that this man doesn't wish to be injured and if we could convince him that he is mistaken as to the consequences of his action, he would not wish to perform the action. But part of what is involved in claiming that the man who doesn't fasten his seat belts is attaching an incorrect weight to the inconvenience of fastening them is that if he were to be involved in an accident and severely injured he would look back and admit that the inconvenience wasn't as bad as all that. So there is a sense in which, if I could convince him of the consequences of his action, he also would not wish to continue his present course of action. Now the notion of consequences being used here is covering a lot of ground. In one case it's being used to indicate what will or can happen as a result of a course of action, and in the other it's making a prediction about the future evaluation of the consequences— in the first sense—of a course of action. And whatever the difference between facts and values— whether it be hard and fast or soft and slow—we are genuinely more reluctant to consent to interferences where evaluative differences are the issue. Let me now consider another factor that comes into play in some of these situations, which may make an important difference in our willingness to consent to paternalistic restrictions.

Some of the decisions we make are of such a character that they produce changes that are in one or another way irreversible. Situations are created in which it is difficult or impossible to return to anything like the initial stage at which the decision was made. In particular, some of these changes will make it impossible to continue to make reasoned choices in the future. I am thinking specifically of decisions that involve taking drugs that are physically or psychologically addictive and those that are destructive of one's mental and physical capacities.

I suggest we think of the imposition of paternalistic interferences in situations of this kind as being a kind of insurance policy we take out against making decisions that are far-reaching, potentially dangerous, and irreversible. Each of these factors is important. Clearly there are many decisions we make that are relatively irreversible. In deciding to learn to play chess, I could predict in view of my general interest in games that some portion of my free time was going to be preempted and that it would not be easy to give up the game once I acquired a certain competence. But my whole life style was not going to be jeopardized in an extreme manner. Further it might be argued that even with addictive drugs such as heroin one's normal life plans would not be seriously interfered with if an inexpensive and adequate supply were readily available. So this type of argument might have a much narrower scope than appears to be the case at first.

A second class of cases concerns decisions that are made under extreme psychological and sociological pressures. I am not thinking here of the making of the decision as being something one is pressured into—for example, a good reason for making duelling illegal is that unless this is done many people might have to manifest their courage and integrity in ways in which they would rather not do so—but rather of decisions, such as that to commit suicide, which are usually made at a point where the individual is not thinking clearly and calmly about the nature of his decision. In addition, of course, this comes under the previous heading of all-too-irrevocable decisions. Now, there are practical steps that a society could take if it wanted to decrease the possibility of suicide—for example, not paying social security benefits to the survivors or, as religious institutions do, not allowing persons to be buried with the same status as natural deaths. I think we may count these as interferences with the liberty of persons to attempt suicide, and the question is whether they are justifiable.

Using my argument schema the question is whether rational individuals would consent to such limitations. I see no reason for them to consent to an absolute prohibition, but I do think it is reasonable for them to agree to some kind of enforced waiting period. Since we are all aware of the possibility of temporary states, such as great fear or depression, that are inimical to the making of well-informed and rational decisions, it would be prudent for all of us if there were some kind of institutional arrangement whereby we were restrained from making a decision that is so irreversible. What this would be like in practice is difficult to envisage, and it may be that if no practical

arrangements were feasible we would have to conclude that there should be no restriction at all on this kind of action. But we might have a "cooling off" period, in much the same way that we now require couples who file for divorce to go through a waiting period. Or, more far-fetched, we might imagine a Suicide Board composed of a psychologist and another member picked by the applicant. The Board would be required to meet and talk with the person proposing to take his life, though its approval would not be required.

A third class of decisions—these classes are not supposed to be disjoint—involves dangers that are either not sufficiently understood or appreciated correctly by the persons involved. Let me illustrate, using the example of cigarette smoking, a number of possible cases:

1. A man may not know the facts—for example, smoking between one and two packs a day shortens life expectancy 6.2 years, the costs and pain of the illness caused by smoking, et cetera.
2. A man may know the facts, wish to stop smoking, but not have the requisite willpower.
3. A man may know the facts but not have them play the correct role in his calculation because, say, he discounts the danger psychologically since it is remote in time, or inflates the attractiveness of other consequences of his decision that he regards as beneficial.

In case 1 what is called for is education, the posting of warnings, et cetera. In case 2 there is no theoretical problem. We are not imposing a good on someone who rejects it. We are simply using coercion to enable people to carry out their own goals. (Note: There obviously is a difficulty in that only a subclass of the individuals affected wish to be prevented from doing what they are doing.) In case 3 there is a sense in which we are imposing a good on someone, in that given his current appraisal of the facts he doesn't wish to be restricted. But in another sense we are not imposing a good, since what is being claimed—and what must be shown or at least argued for—is that an accurate accounting on his part would lead him to reject his current course of action. Now, we all know that such cases exist, that we are prone to disregarding dangers that are only possibilities, that immediate pleasures are often magnified and distorted.

If in addition the dangers are severe and far-reaching, we could agree to allow the state a certain degree of power to intervene in such situations. The difficulty is in specifying in advance, even vaguely, the class of cases in which intervention will be legitimate. A related difficulty is that of drawing a line so that it is not the case that all ultra-hazardous activities are ruled out, for example, mountain climbing, bull fighting, sports-car racing, et cetera. There are some risks—even very great ones—that a person is entitled to take with his life.

A good deal depends on the nature of the deprivation—for example, does it prevent the person from engaging in the activity completely, or merely limit his participation—and how important to the nature of the activity is the absence of restriction, when this is weighed against the role that the activity plays in the life of the person. In the case of automobile seat belts, for example, the restriction is trivial in nature, interferes not at all with the use or enjoyment of the activity, and does, I am assuming, considerably reduce a high risk of serious injury. Whereas, for example, making mountain climbing illegal completely prevents a person from engaging in an activity that may play an important role in his life and his conception of the person he is.

In general, the easiest cases to handle are those that can be argued about in the terms that Mill thought to be so important—a concern not just for the happiness or welfare, in some broad sense, of the individual, but rather a concern for the autonomy and freedom of the person. I suggest that we would be most likely to consent to paternalism in those instances in which it preserves and enhances for the individual his ability to rationally consider and carry out his own decisions.

I have suggested in this essay a number of types of situations in which it seems plausible that rational men would agree to granting the legislative powers of a society the right to impose restrictions on what Mill calls "self-regarding" conduct. However, rational men knowing something about the resources of ignorance, ill-will, and stupidity available to the lawmakers of a society—a good case in point is the history of drug legislation in the United States—will be concerned to limit such intervention to a minimum. I suggest in closing two principles designed to achieve this end.

In all cases of paternalistic legislation there must be a heavy and clear burden of proof placed on the authorities to demonstrate the exact nature of the harmful effects (or beneficial consequences) to be avoided (or achieved), and the probability of their occurrence. The burden of proof here is twofold—what lawyers distinguish as the burden of going forward and the burden of persuasion. That the authorities have the burden of going forward means that it is up to them to raise the question and bring forward evidence of the evils to be avoided. Unlike the case of new drugs, where the manufacturer must produce some evidence that the drug has been tested and found not harmful, no citizen has to show with respect to self-regarding conduct that it is not harmful or promotes his best interest. In addition the nature and cogency of the evidence for the harmfulness of the course of action must be set at a high level. To paraphrase a formulation of the burden of proof for criminal proceedings—better two men ruin themselves than one man be unjustly deprived of liberty.

Finally I suggest a principle of the least restrictive alternative. If there is an alternative way of accomplishing the desired end without restricting liberty, although it may involve great expense, inconvenience, et cetera, the society must adopt it.

[handwritten: sin = transgress from morality → moral law / crime]

37 Morals and the Criminal Law

LORD PATRICK DEVLIN

[handwritten: crime = sin ?]

The Report of the Committee on Homosexual Offences and Prostitution, generally known as the Wolfenden Report, is recognized to be an excellent study of two very difficult legal and social problems. But it has also a particular claim to the respect of those interested in jurisprudence; it does what law reformers so rarely do; it sets out clearly and carefully what in relation to its subjects it considers the function of the law to be.[1] Statutory additions to the criminal law are too often made on the simple principle that "there ought to be a law against it." The greater part of the law relating to sexual offences is the creation of statute, and it is difficult to ascertain any logical relationship between it and the moral ideas that most of us uphold. Adultery, fornication, and prostitution are not, as the Report[2] points out, criminal offences: homosexuality between males is a criminal offence, but between females it is not. Incest was not an offence until it was declared so by statute only 50 years ago. Does the legislature select these offences haphazardly, or are there some principles that can be used to determine what part of the moral law should be embodied in the criminal? There is, for example, being now considered a proposal to make A.I.D., that is, the practice of artificial insemination of a woman with the seed of a man who is not her husband, a criminal offence; if, as is usually the case, the woman is married, this is in substance, if not in form, adultery. [handwritten: WTF] Ought it to be made punishable when adultery is not? This sort of question is of practical importance, for a law that appears to be arbitrary and illogical, in the end and after the wave of moral indignation that has put it on the statute book subsides, forfeits respect. As a practical question it arises more frequently in the field of sexual morals than in any other, but there is no special answer to be found in that field. The inquiry must be general and fundamental. What is the connection between crime and sin and to what extent, if at all, should the criminal law of England concern itself with the enforcement of morals and punish sin or immorality as such?

The statements of principle in the Wolfenden Report provide an admirable and modern starting point for such an inquiry. In the course of my examination of them I shall find matter for criticism. If my criticisms are sound, it must not be imagined that they point to any shortcomings in the Report. Its authors were not, as I am trying to do, composing a paper on the jurisprudence of morality; they were evolving a working formula to use for reaching a number of practical conclusions. I do not intend to express any opinion one way or the other about these; that would be outside the scope of a lecture on jurisprudence. I am concerned only with general principles; the statement of these in the Report illuminates the entry into the subject and I hope that its authors will forgive me if I carry the lamp with me into places where it was not intended to go.

Early in the Report[3] the Committee put forward: [handwritten: PROTECTION ?]

> … our own formulation of the function of the criminal law so far as it concerns the subjects of this enquiry. In this field, its function, as we see it, is to preserve public order and decency, to protect the citizen from what is offensive or injurious, and to provide sufficient safeguards against exploitation and corruption of others, particularly those who are specially vulnerable because they are young, weak in body or mind, inexperienced, or in a state of special physical, official or economic dependence.
>
> It is not, in our view, the function of the law to intervene in the private lives of citizens, or to seek to enforce any particular pattern of behaviour, further than is necessary to carry out the purposes we have outlined.

From *The Enforcement of Morals* (Oxford: Oxford University Press, 1965). Reprinted with permission of the publisher.

[handwritten: AID = illegal, but not adultery!]

The Committee preface their most important recommendation[4] that homosexual behaviour between consenting adults in private should no longer be a criminal offence, [by stating the argument[5]] that we believe to be decisive, namely, the importance that society and the law ought to give to individual freedom of choice and action in matters of private morality. Unless a deliberate attempt is to be made by society, acting through the agency of the law, to equate the sphere of crime with that of sin, there must remain a realm of private morality and immorality that is, in brief and crude terms, not the law's business. To say this is not to condone or encourage private immorality.

Similar statements of principle are set out in the chapters of the Report that deal with prostitution. No case can be sustained, the Report says, for attempting to make prostitution itself illegal.[6] The Committee refer to the general reasons already given and add: "We are agreed that private immorality should not be the concern of the criminal law except in the special circumstances therein mentioned." They quote[7] with approval the report of the Street Offences Committee,[8] which says: "As a general proposition it will be universally accepted that the law is not concerned with private morals or with ethical sanctions." It will be observed that the emphasis is on *private* immorality. By this is meant immorality that is not offensive or injurious to the public in the ways defined or described in the first passage that I quoted. In other words, no act of immorality should be made a criminal offence unless it is accompanied by some other feature such as indecency, corruption, or exploitation. This is clearly brought out in relation to prostitution: "It is not the duty of the law to concern itself with immorality as such ... it should confine itself to those activities which offend against public order and decency or expose the ordinary citizen to what is offensive or injurious."[9]

These statements of principle are naturally restricted to the subject matter of the Report. But they are made in general terms and there seems to be no reason why, if they are valid, they should not be applied to the criminal law in general. They separate very decisively crime from sin, the divine law from the secular, and the moral from the criminal. They do not signify any lack of support for the law, moral or criminal, and they do not represent an attitude that can be called either religious or irreligious. There are many schools of thought among those who may think that morals are not the law's business. There is first of all the agnostic or freethinker. He does not of course disbelieve in morals, nor in sin if it be given the wider of the two meanings assigned to it in the *Oxford English Dictionary,* where it is defined as "transgression against divine law or the principles of morality." He cannot accept the divine law; that does not mean that he might not view with suspicion any departure from moral principles that have for generations been accepted by the society in which he lives; but in the end he judges for himself. Then there is the deeply religious person who feels that the criminal law is sometimes more of a hindrance than a help in the sphere of morality, and that the reform of the sinner—at any rate when he injures only himself—should be a spiritual rather than a temporal work. Then there is the man who without any strong feeling cannot see why, where there is freedom in religious belief, there should not logically be freedom in morality as well. All these are powerfully allied against the equating of crime with sin.

I must disclose at the outset that I have as a judge an interest in the result of the inquiry that I am seeking to make as a jurisprudent. As a judge who administers the criminal law and who has often to pass sentence in a criminal court, I should feel handicapped in my task if I thought that I was addressing an audience that had no sense of sin or that thought of crime as something quite different. Ought one, for example, in passing sentence upon a female abortionist to treat her simply as if she were an unlicenced midwife? If not, why not? But if so, is all the panoply of the law erected over a set of social regulations? I must admit that I begin with a feeling that a complete separation of crime from sin (I use the term throughout this lecture in the wider meaning) would not be good for the moral law and might be disastrous for the criminal. But can this sort of feeling be justified as a matter of jurisprudence? And if it be a right feeling, how should the relationship between the

Rules for activities

criminal and the moral law be stated? Is there a good theoretical basis for it, or is it just a practical working alliance, or is it a bit of both? That is the problem I want to examine, and I shall begin by considering the standpoint of the strict logician. It can be supported by cogent arguments, some of which I believe to be unanswerable and which I put as follows.

Morals and religion are inextricably joined— the moral standards generally accepted in Western civilization being those belonging to Christianity. Outside Christendom other standards derive from other religions. None of these moral codes can claim any validity except by virtue of the religion on which they are based. Old Testament morals differ in some respects from New Testament morals. Even within Christianity there are differences. Some hold that contraception is an immoral practice and that a man who has carnal knowledge of another woman while his wife is alive is in all circumstances a fornicator; others, including most of the English-speaking world, deny both these propositions. Between the great religions of the world, of which Christianity is only one, there are much wider differences. It may or may not be right for the state to adopt one of these religions as the truth, to found itself upon its doctrines, and to deny to any of its citizens the liberty to practise any other. If it does, it is logical that it should use the secular law wherever it thinks it necessary to enforce the divine. If it does not, it is illogical that it should concern itself with morals as such. But if it leaves matters of religion to private judgment, it should logically leave matters of morals also. A state that refuses to enforce Christian beliefs has lost the right to enforce Christian morals.) ← USA?

If this view is sound, it means that the criminal law cannot justify any of its provisions by reference to the moral law. It cannot say, for example, that murder and theft are prohibited because they are immoral or sinful.) The state must justify in some other way the punishments it imposes on wrongdoers, and a function for the criminal law independent of morals must be found. This is not difficult to do. The smooth functioning of society and the preservation of order require that a number of activities should be regulated.

EX.

The rules that are made for that purpose and are enforced by the criminal law are often designed simply to achieve uniformity and convenience, and rarely involve any choice between good and evil. Rules that impose a speed limit or prevent obstruction on the highway have nothing to do with morals. Since so much of the criminal law is composed of rules of this sort, why bring morals into it at all? Why not define the function of the criminal law in simple terms as the preservation of order and decency and the protection of the lives and property of citizens, and elaborate those terms in relation to any particular subject in the way in which it is done in the Wolfenden Report? The criminal law in carrying out these objects will undoubtedly overlap the moral law. Crimes of violence are morally wrong and they are also offences against good order; therefore they offend against both laws. But this is simply because the two laws in pursuit of different objectives happen to cover the same area. Such is the argument.

Is the argument consistent or inconsistent with the fundamental principles of English criminal law as it exists today? That is the first way of testing it, though by no means a conclusive one. In the field of jurisprudence one is at liberty to overturn even fundamental conceptions if they are theoretically unsound. But to see how the argument fares under the existing law is a good starting point.

It is true that for many centuries the criminal law was much concerned with keeping the peace, and little, if at all, with sexual morals. But it would be wrong to infer from that that it had no moral content or that it would ever have tolerated the idea of a man being left to judge for himself in matters of morals. The criminal law of England has from the very first concerned itself with moral principles. A simple way of testing this point is to consider the attitude that the criminal law adopts towards consent.

Subject to certain exceptions inherent in the nature of particular crimes, the criminal law has never permitted consent of the victim to be used as a defence. In rape, for example, consent negatives an essential element. But consent of the victim is no defence to a charge of murder. It is not a defence to any form of assault that the victim thought his punishment well-deserved and submitted to it; to make a good defence the accused must prove that the law gave him the right to chastise, and that he exercised it reasonably. Likewise, the victim may not forgive the aggressor and require the prosecution to desist; the right to enter a nolle prosequi belongs to the Attorney-General alone. "CONSENT TO CRIME"

Now, if the law existed for the protection of the individual, there would be no reason why he should avail himself of it if he did not want it. The reason why a man may not consent to the commission of an offence against himself beforehand, or forgive it afterwards, is because it is an offence against society. It is not that society is physically injured; that would be impossible. Nor need any individual be shocked, corrupted, or exploited; everything may be done in private. Nor can it be explained on the practical ground that a violent man is a potential danger to others in the community, who have therefore a direct interest in his apprehension and punishment as being necessary to their own protection. That would be true of a man whom the victim is prepared to forgive, but not of one who gets his consent first; a murderer who acts only upon the consent, and maybe the request, of his victim is no menace to others, but he does threaten one of the great moral principles upon which society is based, that is, the sanctity of human life. There is only one explanation of what has hitherto been accepted as the basis of the criminal law, and that is that there are certain standards of behaviour or moral principles that society requires to be observed; and the breach of them is an offence not merely against the person who is injured but against society as a whole.

Thus, if the criminal law were to be reformed so as to eliminate from it everything that was not designed to preserve order and decency or to protect citizens (including the protection of youth from corruption), it would overturn a fundamental principle. It would also end a number of specific crimes. Euthanasia or the killing of another at his own request, suicide, attempted suicide, and suicide pacts, duelling, abortion, incest between brother and sister, are all acts that can be done in private and without offence to others, and need not involve the corruption or exploitation

of others. Many people think that the law on some of these subjects is in need of reform, but no one hitherto has gone so far as to suggest that they should all be left outside the criminal law as matters of private morality. They can be brought within it only as a matter of moral principle. It must be remembered also that although there is much immorality that is not punished by the law, there is none that is condoned by the law. The law will not allow its processes to be used by those engaged in immorality of any sort. For example, a house may not be let for immoral purposes; the lease is invalid and would not be enforced. But if what goes on inside there is a matter of private morality and not the law's business, why does the law inquire into it at all?

I think it is clear that the criminal law as we know it is based upon moral principle. In a number of crimes its function is simply to enforce a moral principle and nothing else. The law, both criminal and civil, claims to be able to speak about morality and immorality generally. Where does it get its authority to do this and how does it settle the moral principles that it enforces? Undoubtedly, as a matter of history, it derived both from Christian teaching. But I think that the strict logician is right when he says that the law can no longer rely on doctrines in which citizens are entitled to disbelieve. It is necessary therefore to look for some other source.

In jurisprudence, as I have said, everything is thrown open to discussion and, in the belief that they cover the whole field, I have framed three interrogatories addressed to myself to answer:

1. Has society the right to pass judgment at all on matters of morals? Ought there, in other words, to be a public morality, or are morals always a matter for private judgment?
2. If society has the right to pass judgment, has it also the right to use the weapon of the law to enforce it?
3. If so, ought it to use that weapon in all cases or only in some; and if only in some, on what principles should it distinguish?

I shall begin with the first interrogatory and consider what is meant by the right of society to pass a moral judgment, that is, a judgment about what is good and what is evil. The fact that a majority of people may disapprove of a practice does not of itself make it a matter for society as a whole. Nine men out of ten may disapprove of what the tenth man is doing and still say that it is not their business. There is a case for a collective judgment (as distinct from a large number of individual opinions that sensible people may even refrain from pronouncing at all if it is upon somebody else's private affairs) only if society is affected. Without a collective judgment there can be no case at all for intervention. Let me take as an illustration the Englishman's attitude to religion as it is now and as it has been in the past. His attitude now is that a man's religion is his private affair; he may think of another man's religion that it is right or wrong, true or untrue, but not that it is good or bad. In earlier times that was not so; a man was denied the right to practise what was thought of as heresy, and heresy was thought of as destructive of society.

The language used in the passages I have quoted from the Wolfenden Report suggests the view that there ought not to be a collective judgment about immorality per se. Is this what is meant by "private morality" and "individual freedom of choice and action"? Some people sincerely believe that homosexuality is neither immoral nor unnatural. Is the "freedom of choice and action" that is offered to the individual freedom to decide for himself what is moral or immoral, society remaining neutral; or is it freedom to be immoral if he wants to be? The language of the Report may be open to question, but the conclusions at which the Committee arrives answer this question unambiguously. If society is not prepared to say that homosexuality is morally wrong, there would be no basis for a law protecting youth from "corruption" or punishing a man for living on the "immoral" earnings of a homosexual prostitute, as the Report recommends.[10] This attitude the Committee make even clearer when they come to deal with prostitution. In truth, the Report takes it for granted that there is in existence a public morality that condemns homosexuality and prostitution. What the Report seems to mean by private morality might perhaps be better described as private behaviour in matters of morals.

This view—that there is such a thing as public morality—can also be justified by a priori argument. What makes a society of any sort is a community of ideas, not only political ideas but also ideas about the way its members should behave and govern their lives; these latter ideas are its morals. Every society has a moral structure as well as a political one: or rather, since that might suggest two independent systems, I should say that the structure of every society is made up both of politics and morals. Take, for example, the institution of marriage. Whether a man should be allowed to take more than one wife is something about which every society has to make up its mind one way or the other. In England we believe in the Christian idea of marriage and therefore adopt monogamy as a moral principle. Consequently the Christian institution of marriage has become the basis of family life and so part of the structure of our society. It is there not because it is Christian. It has got there because it is Christian, but it remains there because it is built into the house in which we live and could not be removed without bringing it down. The great majority of those who live in this country accept it because it is the Christian idea of marriage and for them the only true one. But a non-Christian is bound by it, not because it is part of Christianity but because, rightly or wrongly, it has been adopted by the society in which he lives. It would be useless for him to stage a debate designed to prove that polygamy was theologically more correct and socially preferable; if he wants to live in the house, he must accept it as built in the way in which it is.

We see this more clearly if we think of ideas or institutions that are purely political. Society cannot tolerate rebellion; it will not allow argument about the rightness of the cause. Historians a century later may say that the rebels were right and the Government was wrong and a percipient and conscientious subject of the state may think so at the time. But it is not a matter that can be left to individual judgment.

The institution of marriage is a good example for my purpose because it bridges the division, if there is one, between politics and morals. Marriage is part of the structure of our society and it is also the basis of a moral code that condemns fornication and adultery. The institution of marriage would be gravely threatened if individual judgments were permitted about the morality of adultery; on these points there must be a public morality. But public morality is not to be confined to those moral principles that support institutions such as marriage. People do not think of monogamy as something that has to be supported because our society has chosen to organize itself upon it; they think of it as something that is good in itself and offering a good way of life, and that it is for that reason that our society has adopted it. I return to the statement that I have already made, that society means a community of ideas; without shared ideas on politics, morals, and ethics no society can exist. Each one of us has ideas about what is good and what is evil; they cannot be kept private from the society in which we live. If men and women try to create a society in which there is no fundamental agreement about good and evil, they will fail; if, having based it on common agreement, the agreement goes, the society will disintegrate. For society is not something that is kept together physically; it is held by the invisible bonds of common thought. If the bonds were too far relaxed the members would drift apart. A common morality is part of the bondage. The bondage is part of the price of society; and mankind, which needs society, must pay its price.

Common lawyers used to say that Christianity was part of the law of the land. That was never more than a piece of rhetoric as Lord Sumner said in *Bowman v. The Secular Society.*[11] What lay behind it was the notion I have been seeking to expound, namely that morals—and until a century or so ago no one thought it worth distinguishing between religion and morals—were necessary to the temporal order. In 1675 Chief Justice Hale said: "To say that religion is a cheat is to dissolve all those obligations whereby civil society is preserved."[12] In 1797 Mr. Justice Ashurst said of blasphemy that it was "not only an offence against God but against all law and government from its tendency to dissolve all the bonds and obligations of civil society."[13] By 1908 Mr. Justice Phillimore was able to say: "A man is free to think, to speak, and to teach what he

pleases as to religious matters, but not as to morals."[14]

You may think that I have taken far too long in contending that there is such a thing as public morality, a proposition that most people would readily accept, and may have left myself too little time to discuss the next question, which to many minds may cause greater difficulty: to what extent should society use the law to enforce its moral judgments? But I believe that the answer to the first question determines the way in which the second should be approached, and may indeed very nearly dictate the answer to the second question. If society has no right to make judgments on morals, the law must find some special justification for entering the field of morality: if homosexuality and prostitution are not in themselves wrong, then the onus is very clearly on the lawgiver who wants to frame a law against certain aspects of them to justify the exceptional treatment. But if society has the right to make a judgment and has it on the basis that a recognized morality is as necessary to society as, say, a recognized government, then society may use the law to preserve morality in the same way as it uses it to safeguard anything else that is essential to its existence. If therefore the first proposition is securely established with all its implications, society has a prima facie right to legislate against immorality as such.

The Wolfenden Report, notwithstanding that it seems to admit the right of society to condemn homosexuality and prostitution as immoral, requires special circumstances to be shown to justify the intervention of the law. I think that this is wrong in principle and that any attempt to approach my second interrogatory on these lines is bound to break down. I think that the attempt by the Committee does break down and that this is shown by the fact that it has to define or describe its special circumstances so widely that they can be supported only if it is accepted that the law *is* concerned with immorality as such.

The widest of the special circumstances are described as the provision of "sufficient safeguards against exploitation and corruption of others, particularly those who are specially vulnerable because they are young, weak in body or mind, inexperienced, or in a state of special physical, official or economic dependence."[15] The corruption of youth is a well-recognized ground for intervention by the state, and for the purpose of any legislation the young can easily be defined. But if similar protection were to be extended to every other citizen, there would be no limit to the reach of the law. The "corruption and exploitation of others" is so wide that it could be used to cover any sort of immorality that involves, as most do, the cooperation of another person. Even if the phrase is taken as limited to the categories that are particularized as "specially vulnerable," it is so elastic as to be practically no restriction. This is not merely a matter of words. For if the words used are stretched almost beyond breaking point, they still are not wide enough to cover the recommendations that the Committee make about prostitution.

Prostitution is not in itself illegal, and the Committee do not think that it ought to be made so.[16] If prostitution is private immorality and not the law's business, what concern has the law with the ponce or the brothel keeper or the householder who permits habitual prostitution? The Report recommends that the laws that make these activities criminal offences should be maintained or strengthened and brings them (so far as it goes into principle; with regard to brothels it says simply that the law rightly frowns on them) under the head of exploitation.[17] There may be cases of exploitation in this trade, as there are or used to be in many others, but in general a ponce exploits a prostitute no more than an impressario exploits an actress. The Report finds that "the great majority of prostitutes are women whose psychological makeup is such that they choose this life because they find in it a style of living that is to them easier, freer and more profitable than would be provided by any other occupation...: In the main the association between prostitute and ponce is voluntary and operates to mutual advantage."[18] The Committee would agree that this could not be called exploitation in the ordinary sense. They say: "It is in our view an over-simplification to think that those who live on the earnings of prostitution are exploiting the prostitute as such. What they are really exploiting is the whole complex of the relationship between prostitute and customer; they are, in effect, exploiting the human weaknesses which cause the customer to seek the prostitute and the prostitute to meet the demand."[19]

All sexual immorality involves the exploitation of human weaknesses. The prostitute exploits the lust of her customers and the customer the moral weakness of the prostitute. If the exploitation of human weaknesses is considered to create a special circumstance, there is virtually no field of morality that can be defined in such a way as to exclude the law.

I think, therefore, that it is not possible to set theoretical limits to the power of the state to legislate against immorality. It is not possible to settle in advance exceptions to the general rule or to define inflexibly areas of morality into which the law is in no circumstances to be allowed to enter. Society is entitled by means of its laws to protect itself from dangers, whether from within or without. Here again I think that the political parallel is legitimate. The law of treason is directed against aiding the king's enemies and against sedition from within. The justification for this is that established government is necessary for the existence of society and therefore its safety against violent overthrow must be secured. But an established morality is as necessary as good government to the welfare of society. Societies disintegrate from within more frequently than they are broken up by external pressures. There is disintegration when no common morality is observed and history shows that the loosening of moral bonds is often the first stage of disintegration, so that society is justified in taking the same steps to preserve its moral code as it does to preserve its government and other essential institutions.[20] The suppression of vice is as much the law's business as the suppression of subversive activities; it is no more possible to define a sphere of private morality than it is to define one of private subversive activity. It is wrong to talk of private morality or of the law not being concerned with immorality as such or to try to set rigid bounds to the part the law may play in the suppression of vice. There are no theoretical limits to the power of the state to legislate against treason and sedition, and likewise I think there can be no theoretical limits to legislation against immorality. You may argue that if a man's sins affect only himself it cannot be the concern of society. If he chooses to get drunk every night in the privacy of his own home, is any one except himself the worse for it? But suppose a quarter or a half of the population got drunk every night, what sort of society would it be? You cannot set a theoretical limit to the number of people who can get drunk before society is entitled to legislate against drunkenness. The same may be said of gambling. The Royal Commission on Betting, Lotteries, and Gaming took as their test the character of the citizen as a member of society. They said: "Our concern with the ethical significance of gambling is confined to the effect which it may have on the character of the gambler as a member of society. If we were convinced that whatever the degree of gambling this effect must be harmful we should be inclined to think that it was the duty of the state to restrict gambling to the greatest extent practicable."[21]

In what circumstances the state should exercise its power is the third of the interrogatories I have framed. But before I get to it I must raise a point that might have been brought up in any one of the three. How are the moral judgments of society to be ascertained? By leaving it until now, I can ask it in the more limited form that is now sufficient for my purpose. How is the lawmaker to ascertain the moral judgments of society? It is surely not enough that they should be reached by the opinion of the majority; it would be too much to require the individual assent of every citizen. English law has evolved and regularly uses a standard that does not depend on the counting of heads. It is that of the reasonable man. He is not to be confused with the rational man. He is not expected to reason about anything and his judgment may be largely a matter of feeling. It is the viewpoint of the man in the street—or to use an archaism familiar to all lawyers—the man in the Clapham omnibus. He might also be called the right-minded man. For my purpose I should like to call him the man in the jury box, for the moral judgment of society must be something about which any twelve men or women drawn at random might after discussion be expected to be unanimous. This was the standard the judges applied in the days before Parliament was as active as it is now and when they laid down rules of public policy. They did not think of themselves as making law but simply as stating principles that every right-minded person would accept as valid. It is what Pollock called "practical morality," which is based not on theological or philosophical foundations but "in the mass of continuous experience half-consciously or unconsciously accumulated and embodied in the morality of common sense." He called it also "a certain way of thinking on questions of morality that we expect to find in a reasonable civilized man or a reasonable Englishman, taken at random."[22]

Immorality then, for the purpose of the law, is what every right-minded person is presumed to consider to be immoral. Any immorality is capable of affecting society injuriously and in effect to a greater or lesser extent it usually does; this is what gives the law its *locus standi* [its legal standing before a court]. It cannot be shut out. But—and this brings me to the third question—the individual has a *locus standi* too; he cannot be expected to surrender to the judgment of society the whole conduct of his life. It is the old and familiar question of striking a balance between the rights and interests of society and those of the individual. This is something that the law is constantly doing in matters large and small. To take a very down-to-earth example, let me consider the right of the individual whose house adjoins the highway to have access to it; that means in these days the right to have vehicles stationary in the highway, sometimes for a considerable time if there is a lot of loading or unloading. There are many cases in which the courts have had to balance the private right of access against the public right to use the highway without obstruction. It cannot be done by carving up the highway into public and private areas. It is done by recognizing that each has rights over the whole; that if each were to exercise their rights to the full, they would come into conflict; and therefore that the rights of each must be curtailed so as to ensure as far as possible that the essential needs of each are safeguarded.

I do not think that one can talk sensibly of a public and private morality any more than one can of a public or private highway. Morality is a sphere in which there is a public interest and a private interest, often in conflict, and the problem is to reconcile the two. This does not mean that it is impossible to put forward any general statements about how in our society the balance ought to be struck. Such statements cannot of their nature be rigid or precise; they would not be designed to circumscribe the operation of the lawmaking power, but to guide those who have to apply it. While every decision a court of law makes when it balances the public against the private interest is an ad hoc decision, the cases contain statements of principle to which the court should have regard when it reaches its decision. In the same way it is possible to make general statements of principle it may be thought the legislature should bear in mind when it is considering the enactment of laws enforcing morals.

I believe that most people would agree upon the chief of these elastic principles. There must be toleration of the maximum individual freedom that is consistent with the integrity of society. It cannot be said that this is a principle that runs all through the criminal law. Much of the criminal law that is regulatory in character—the part of it that deals with *malum prohibitum* [wrong because prohibited] rather than *malum in se* [wrong in itself]—is based upon the opposite principle, that is, that the choice of the individual must give way to the convenience of the many. But in all matters of conscience the principle I have stated is generally held to prevail. It is not confined to thought and speech; it extends to action, as is shown by the recognition of the right to conscientious objection in wartime; this example shows also that conscience will be respected even in times of national danger. The principle appears to me to be peculiarly appropriate to all questions of morals. Nothing should be punished by the law that does not lie beyond the limits of toleration. It is not nearly enough to say that a majority dislike a practice; there must be a real feeling of reprobation. Those who are dissatisfied with the present law on homosexuality often say that the opponents of reform are swayed simply by disgust. If that were so it would be wrong, but I do not think one can ignore disgust if it is deeply felt and not manufactured. Its presence is a good indication that the

bounds of toleration are being reached. Not everything is to be tolerated. No society can do without intolerance, indignation, and disgust; they are the forces behind the moral law, and indeed it can be argued that if they or something like them are not present, the feelings of society cannot be weighty enough to deprive the individual of freedom of choice. I suppose that there is hardly anyone nowadays who would not be disgusted by the thought of deliberate cruelty to animals. No one proposes to relegate that or any other form of sadism to the realm of private morality or to allow it to be practised in public or in private. It would be possible no doubt to point out that until a comparatively short while ago nobody thought very much of cruelty to animals and also that pity and kindliness and the unwillingness to inflict pain are virtues more generally esteemed now than they have ever been in the past. But matters of this sort are not determined by rational argument. Every moral judgment, unless it claims a divine source, is simply a feeling that no rightminded man could behave in any other way without admitting that he was doing wrong. It is the power of a common sense and not the power of reason that is behind the judgments of society. But before a society can put a practice beyond the limits of tolerance there must be a deliberate judgment that the practice is injurious to society. There is, for example, a general abhorrence of homosexuality. We should ask ourselves in the first instance whether, looking at it calmly and dispassionately, we regard it as a vice so abominable that its mere presence is an offence. If that is the genuine feeling of the society in which we live, I do not see how society can be denied the right to eradicate it. Our feeling may not be so intense as that. We may feel about it that, if confined, it is tolerable, but that if it spread it might be gravely injurious; it is in this way that most societies look upon fornication, seeing it as a natural weakness that must be kept within bounds, but which cannot be rooted out. It becomes then a question of balance, the danger to society in one scale and the extent of the restriction in the other. On this sort of point the value of an investigation by such a body as the Wolfenden Committee and of its conclusions is manifest.

The limits of tolerance shift. This is supplementary to what I have been saying, but of sufficient importance in itself to deserve statement as a separate principle that lawmakers have to bear in mind. I suppose that moral standards do not shift; so far as they come from divine revelation they do not, and I am willing to assume that the moral judgments made by a society always remain good for that society. But the extent to which society will tolerate—I mean tolerate, not approve—departures from moral standards varies from generation to generation. It may be that over-all tolerance is always increasing. The pressure of the human mind, always seeking greater freedom of thought, is outwards against the bonds of society forcing their gradual relaxation. It may be that history is a tale of contraction and expansion and that all developed societies are on their way to dissolution. I must not speak of things I do not know; and anyway as a practical matter no society is willing to make provision for its own decay. I return therefore to the simple and observable fact that in matters of morals, the limits of tolerance shift. Laws, especially those that are based on morals, are less easily moved. It follows as another good working principle that in any new matter of morals the law should be slow to act. By the next generation the swell of indignation may have abated and the law be left without the strong backing that it needs. But it is then difficult to alter the law without giving the impression that moral judgment is being weakened. This is now one of the factors that is strongly militating against any alteration to the law on homosexuality.

A third elastic principle must be advanced more tentatively. It is that as far as possible privacy should be respected. This is not an idea that has ever been made explicit in the criminal law. Acts or words done or said in public or in private are all brought within its scope without distinction in principle. But there goes with this a strong reluctance on the part of judges and legislators to sanction invasions of privacy in the detection of crime. The police have no more right to trespass than the ordinary citizen has; there is no general right of search; to this extent an Englishman's home is still his castle. The Government is extremely careful in the exercise even of those powers that it claims to

be undisputed. Telephone tapping and interference with the mails afford a good illustration of this. A Committee of three Privy Councillors who recently inquired[23] into these activities found that the Home Secretary and his predecessors had already formulated strict rules governing the exercise of these powers and the Committee were able to recommend that they should be continued to be exercised substantially on the same terms. But they reported that the power was "regarded with general disfavour."

This indicates a general sentiment that the right to privacy is something to be put in the balance against the enforcement of the law. Ought the same sort of consideration to play any part in the formation of the law? Clearly only in a very limited number of cases. When the help of the law is invoked by an injured citizen, privacy must be irrelevant; the individual cannot ask that his right to privacy should be measured against injury criminally done to another. But when all who are involved in the deed are consenting parties and the injury is done to morals, the public interest in the moral order can be balanced against the claims of privacy. The restriction on police powers of investigation goes further than the affording of a parallel; it means that the detection of crime committed in private and when there is no complaint is bound to be rather haphazard, and this is an additional reason for moderation. These considerations do not justify the exclusion of all private immorality from the scope of the law. I think that, as I have already suggested, the test of "private behaviour" should be substituted for "private morality" and the influence of the factor should be reduced from that of a definite limitation to that of a matter to be taken into account. Since the gravity of the crime is also a proper consideration, a distinction might well be made in the case of homosexuality between the lesser acts of indecency and the full offence, which on the principles of the Wolfenden Report it would be illogical to do.

The last and the biggest thing to be remembered is that the law is concerned with the minimum and not with the maximum; there is much in the Sermon on the Mount that would be out of place in the Ten Commandments. We all recognize the gap between the moral law and the law of the land. No man is worth much who regulates his conduct with the sole object of escaping punishment, and every worthy society sets for its members standards that are above those of the law. We recognize the existence of such higher standards when we use expressions such as "moral obligation" and "morally bound." The distinction was well put in the judgment of African elders in a family dispute: "We have power to make you divide the crops, for this is our law, and we will see this is done. But we have not power to make you behave like an upright man."[24]

NOTES

1. The Committee's "statement of juristic philosophy' (to quote Lord Pakenham) was considered by him in a debate in the House of Lords on 4 December 1957, reported in *Hansard Lords Debates,* vol. ccvi at 738; and also in the same debate by the Archbishop of Canterbury at 753 and Lord Denning at 806. The subject has also been considered by Mr. J. E. Hall Williams in the *Law Quarterly Review,* January 1958, vol. lxxiv, p. 76.
2. *The Wolfenden Report: Report of the Committee on Homosexual Offences and Prostitution.* New York: Stein and Day (1963). ¶ 14.
3. Id., ¶ 13
4. Id., ¶ 62.
5. Id., ¶ 61.
6. Id., ¶ 224.
7. Id., ¶ 227.
8. Cmd. 3231 (1928).
9. *The Wolfenden Report,* supra, note 2, ¶ 257.
10. Id., ¶ 76.
11. (1917), A.C. 406, at 457.
12. *Taylor's Case,* 1 Vent. 293.
13. *R. v. Williams,* 26 St. Tr. 653, at 715.
14. *R. v. Boulter,* 72 J.P. 188.
15. *The Wolfenden Report,* supra, note 2, ¶ 13.
16. Id., ¶¶ 224. 285, and 318.
17. Id., ¶¶ 302 and 320.
18. Id., ¶ 223.
19. Id., ¶ 306.
20. It is somewhere about this point in the argument that Professor Hart, in *Law, Liberty and Morality,* discerns a proposition which he describes as central to my thought. He states the proposition and his objection to it as follows (p. 51):

He appears to move from the acceptable proposition that *some* shared morality is essential to the existence of any society [this I take to be the proposition on p. 75] to the unacceptable proposition that a society is identical with its morality as that is at any given moment of its history so that a change in its morality is tantamount to the destruction of a society. The former proposition might be even accepted as a necessary rather than an empirical truth depending on a quite plausible definition of society as a body of men who hold certain moral views in common. But the latter proposition is absurd. Taken strictly, it would prevent us saying that the morality of a given society had changed, and would compel us instead to say that one society had disappeared and another one taken its place. But it is only on this absurd criterion of what it is for the same society to continue to exist that it could be asserted without evidence that any deviation from a society's shared morality threatens its existence.

In conclusion (p. 82) Professor Hart condemns the whole thesis in the lecture as based on "a confused definition of what a society is."

I do not assert that *any* deviation from a society's shared morality threatens its existence any more than I assert that *any* subversive activity threatens its existence. I assert that they are both activities that are capable in their nature of threatening the existence of society so that neither can be put beyond the law.

For the rest, the objection appears to me to be all a matter of words. I would venture to assert, for example, that you cannot have a game without rules, and that if there were no rules there would be no game. If I am asked whether that means that the game is "identical" with the rules, I would be willing for the question to be answered either way in the belief that the answer would lead to nowhere. If I am asked whether a change in the rules means that one game has disappeared and another has taken its place, I would reply probably not, but that it would depend on the extent of the change.

Likewise I should venture to assert that there cannot be a contract without terms. Does this mean that an "amended" contract is a "new" contract in the eyes of the law? I once listened to an argument by an ingenious counsel that a contract, because of the substitution of one clause for another, had "ceased to have effect" within the meaning of a statutory provision. The judge did not accept the argument; but if most of the fundamental terms had been changed, I daresay he would have done.

The proposition that I make in the text is that if (as I understand Professor Hart to agree, at any rate for the purposes of the argument) you cannot have a society without morality, the law can be used to enforce morality as something that is essential to a society. I cannot see why this proposition (whether it is right or wrong) should mean that morality can never be changed without the destruction of society. If morality is changed, the law can be changed. Professor Hart refers (p. 72) to the proposition as "the use of legal punishment to freeze into immobility the

morality dominant at a particular time in a society's existence." One might as well say that the inclusion of a penal section into a statute prohibiting certain acts freezes the whole statute into immobility and prevents the prohibitions from ever being modified.

21. (1951) Cmd. 8190, ¶ 159.
22. *Essays in Jurisprudence and Ethics.* Macmillan, 1882. 278 and 353.
23. (1957) Cmd. 283.
24. A case in the Saa-Katengo at Lialiu, August 1942, quoted in Gluckman, Max. *The Judicial Process Among the Barotse of Northern Rhodesia.* Manchester University Press, 1955. 172.

38   Immorality and Treason

H. L. A. HART

The most remarkable feature of Sir Patrick's lecture is his view of the nature of morality—the morality that the criminal law may enforce. Most previous thinkers who have repudiated the liberal point of view have done so because they thought that morality consisted either of divine commands or of rational principles of human conduct discoverable by human reason. Since morality for them had this elevated divine or rational status as the law of God or reason, it seemed obvious that the state should enforce it, and that the function of human law should not be merely to provide men with the opportunity for leading a good life, but actually to see that they lead it. Sir Patrick does not rest his repudiation of the liberal point of view on these religious or rationalist conceptions. Indeed much that he writes reads like an abjuration of the notion that reasoning or thinking has much to do with morality. English popular morality has no doubt its historical connection with the Christian religion: "That," says Sir Patrick, "is how it got there." But it does not owe its present status or social significance to religion any more than to reason.

What, then, is it? According to Sir Patrick it is primarily a matter of feeling. "Every moral judgment," he says, "is a feeling that no right-minded man could act in any other way without admitting that he was doing wrong." Who then must feel this way if we are to have what Sir Patrick calls a public morality? He tells us that it is "the man in the street," "the man in the jury box," or (to use the phrase so familiar to English lawyers) "the man on the Clapham omnibus." For the moral judgments of society so far as the law is concerned are to be ascertained by the standards of the reasonable man, and he is not to be confused with the rational man. Indeed, Sir Patrick says "he is not expected to reason about anything and his judgment may be largely a matter of feeling."

INTOLERANCE, INDIGNATION, AND DISGUST

But what precisely are the relevant feelings, the feelings that may justify use of the criminal law? Here the argument becomes a little complex. Widespread dislike of a practice is not enough. There must, says

From *The Listener*, 30 July 1959. pp. 162–3. Reprinted by permission of the author. For a fuller development of the ideas expressed here see Hart, *Law, Liberty, and Morality*, Oxford, 1963.

Sir Patrick, be "a real feeling of reprobation." Disgust is not enough either. What is crucial is a combination of intolerance, indignation, and disgust. These three are the forces behind the moral law, without which it is not "weighty enough to deprive the individual of freedom of choice." Hence there is, in Sir Patrick's outlook, a crucial difference between the mere adverse moral judgment of society and one that is inspired by feeling raised to the concert pitch of intolerance, indignation, and disgust.

This distinction is novel and also very important. For on it depends the weight to be given to the fact that when morality is enforced, individual liberty is necessarily cut down. Though Sir Patrick's abstract formulation of his views on this point is hard to follow, his examples make his position fairly clear. We can see it best in the contrasting things he says about fornication and homosexuality. In regard to fornication, public feeling in most societies is not now of the concert-pitch intensity. We may feel that it is tolerable if confined: only its spread might be gravely injurious. In such cases the question whether individual liberty should be restricted is for Sir Patrick a question of balance between the danger to society in the one scale, and the restriction of the individual in the other. But if, as may be the case with homosexuality, public feeling is up to concert pitch, if it expresses a "deliberate judgment" that a practice as such is injurious to society, if there is "a genuine feeling that it is a vice so abominable that its mere presence is an offence," then it is beyond the limits of tolerance, and society may eradicate it. In this case, it seems, no further balancing of the claims of individual liberty is to be done, though as a matter of prudence the legislator should remember that the popular limits of tolerance may shift: the concert-pitch feeling may subside. This may produce a dilemma for the law; for the law may then be left without the full moral backing that it needs, yet it cannot be altered without giving the impression that the moral judgment is being weakened.

A SHARED MORALITY

If this is what morality is—a compound of indignation, intolerance, and disgust—we may well ask what justification there is for taking it, and turning it as such, into criminal law with all the misery that criminal punishment entails. Here Sir Patrick's answer is very clear and simple. A collection of individuals is not a society; what makes them into a society is among other things a shared or public morality. This is as necessary to its existence as an organized government. So society may use the law to preserve its morality like anything else essential to it. "The suppression of vice is as much the law's business as the suppression of subversive activities." The liberal point of view that denies this is guilty of "an error in jurisprudence": for it is no more possible to define an area of private morality than an area of private subversive activity. There can be no "theoretical limits" to legislation against immorality just as there are no such limits to the power of the state to legislate against treason and sedition.

Surely all this, ingenious as it is, is misleading. Mill's formulation of the liberal point of view may well be too simple. The grounds for interfering with human liberty are more various than the single criterion of "harm to others" suggests: cruelty to animals or organizing prostitution for gain do not, as Mill himself saw, fall easily under the description of harm to others. Conversely, even where there is harm to others in the most literal sense, there may well be other principles limiting the extent to which harmful activities should be repressed by law. So there are multiple criteria, not a single criterion, determining when human liberty may be restricted. Perhaps this is what Sir Patrick means by a curious distinction that he often stresses between theoretical and practical limits. But with all its simplicities, the liberal point of view is a better guide than Sir Patrick to clear thought on the proper relation of morality to the criminal law: for it stresses what he obscures—namely, the points at which thought is needed before we turn popular morality into criminal law.

SOCIETY AND MORAL OPINION

No doubt we would all agree that a consensus of moral opinion on certain matters is essential if society is to be worth living in. Laws against murder, theft, and much else would be of little use if they were not supported by a widely diffused conviction that what these laws forbid is also immoral. So much is obvious. But it does not follow that everything to which the moral vetoes of accepted morality attach is of equal importance to society; nor is there the slightest reason for thinking of morality as a seamless web: one which will fall to pieces carrying society with it, unless all its emphatic vetoes are enforced by law. Surely even in the face of the moral feeling that is up to concert pitch—the trio of intolerance, indignation, and disgust—we must pause to think. We must ask a question at two different levels that Sir Patrick never clearly enough identifies or separates. First, we must ask whether a practice that offends moral feeling is harmful, independently of its repercussion on the general moral code. Secondly, what about repercussion on the moral code? Is it really true that failure to translate this item of general morality into criminal law will jeopardize the whole fabric of morality and so of society?

We cannot escape thinking about these two different questions merely by repeating to ourselves the vague nostrum: "This is part of public morality and public morality must be preserved if society is to exist." Sometimes Sir Patrick seems to admit this, for he says in words that both Mill and the Wolfenden Report might have used that there must be the maximum respect for individual liberty consistent with the integrity of society. Yet this, as his contrasting examples of fornication and homosexuality show, turns out to mean only that the immorality the law may punish must be generally felt to be intolerable. This plainly is no adequate substitute for a reasoned estimate of the damage to the fabric of society likely to ensue if it is not suppressed.

Nothing perhaps shows more clearly the inadequacy of Sir Patrick's approach to this problem than his comparison between the suppression of sexual immorality and the suppression of treason or subversive activity. Private subversive activity is, of course, a contradiction in terms, because "subversion" means overthrowing government, which is a public thing. But it is grotesque, even where moral feeling against homosexuality is up to concert pitch, to think of the homosexual behaviour of two adults in private as in any way like treason or sedition, either in intention or effect. We can

make it *seem* like treason only if we assume that deviation from a general moral code is bound to affect that code, and to lead not merely to its modification but to its destruction. The analogy could begin to be plausible only if it was clear that offending against this item of morality was likely to jeopardize the whole structure. But we have ample evidence for believing that people will not abandon morality, will not think any better of murder, cruelty, and dishonesty, merely because some private sexual practice that they abominate is not punished by the law.

Because this is so the analogy with treason is absurd. Of course "No man is an island": what one man does in private, if it is known, may affect others in many different ways. Indeed it may be that deviation from general sexual morality by those whose lives, like the lives of many homosexuals, are noble ones and in all other ways exemplary will lead to what Sir Patrick calls the shifting of the limits of tolerance. But if this has any analogy in the sphere of government it is not the overthrow of ordered government, but a peaceful change in its form. So we may listen to the promptings of common sense and of logic, and say that though there could not logically be a sphere of private treason, there is a sphere of private morality and immorality.

Sir Patrick's doctrine is also open to a wider, perhaps a deeper, criticism. In his reaction against a rationalist morality and his stress on feeling, he has, I think, thrown out the baby and kept the bath water; and the bath water may turn out to be very dirty indeed. When Sir Patrick's lecture was first delivered, *The Times* greeted it with these words: "There is a moving and welcome humility in the conception that society should not be asked to give its reason for refusing to tolerate what in its heart it feels intolerable." This drew from a correspondent in Cambridge the retort: "I am afraid that we are less humble than we used to be. We once burnt old women because, without giving our reasons, we felt in our hearts that witchcraft was intolerable."

This retort is a bitter one, yet its bitterness is salutary. We are not, I suppose, likely, in England, to take again to the burning of old women for witchcraft, or to punishing people for associating with those of a different race or colour, or to punishing people again for adultery. Yet if these things were viewed with intolerance, indignation, and disgust, as the second of them still is in some countries, it seems that on Sir Patrick's principles no rational criticism could be opposed to the claim that they should be punished by law. We could only pray, in his words, that the limits of tolerance might shift.

CURIOUS LOGIC

It is impossible to see what curious logic has led Sir Patrick to this result. For him a practice is immoral if the thought of it makes the man on the Clapham omnibus sick. So be it. Still, why should we not summon all the resources of our reason, sympathetic understanding, as well as critical intelligence, and insist that before general moral feeling is turned into criminal law it is submitted to scrutiny of a different kind from Sir Patrick's? Surely, the legislator should ask whether the general morality is based on ignorance, superstition, or misunderstanding; whether there is a false conception that those who practise what it condemns are in other ways dangerous or hostile to society; and whether the misery to many parties, the blackmail and the other evil consequences of criminal punishment, especially for sexual offences, are well understood. It is surely extraordinary that among the things that Sir Patrick says are to be considered before we legislate against immorality, these appear nowhere; not even as "practical considerations," let alone "theoretical limits." To any theory that, like this one, asserts that the criminal law may be used on the vague ground that the preservation of morality is essential to society, and yet omits to stress the need for critical scrutiny, our reply should be: "Morality, what crimes may be committed in thy name!"

As Mill saw, and de Tocqueville showed in detail long ago in his critical but sympathetic study of democracy, it is fatally easy to confuse the democratic principle that power should be in the hands of the majority with the utterly different claim that the majority with power in their hands need respect no limits. Certainly there is a special risk in a democracy that the majority may dictate how all should live. This is the risk we run, and should gladly run; for it is the price of all that is so good in democratic rule. But loyalty to democratic principles does not require us to maximize this risk: yet this is what we shall do if we mount the man in the street on the top of the Clapham omnibus and tell him that, if only he feels sick enough about what other people do in private to demand its suppression by law, no theoretical criticism can be made of his demand.

CHAPTER TWELVE

The Limits of Freedom of Expression

39   Offensive Nuisances

JOEL FEINBERG

1. DISCLAIMERS: THE RELATIVE TRIVIALITY OF MERE OFFENSE

Passing annoyance, disappointment, disgust, embarrassment, and various other disliked conditions such as fear, anxiety, and minor ("harmless") aches and pains are not in themselves necessarily harmful. Consequently, no matter how the harm principle is mediated, it will not certify as legitimate those interferences with the liberty of some citizens that are made for the sole purpose of preventing such unpleasant states in others. For convenience I will use the word *offense* to cover the whole miscellany of universally disliked mental states ... and not merely that species of the wider genus that are offensive in a strict and proper sense. If the law is justified, then, in using its coercive methods to protect people from mere offense, it must be by virtue of a separate and distinct legitimizing principle, which we can label "the offense principle" and formulate as follows: *It is always a good reason in support of a proposed criminal prohibition that it would probably be an effective way of preventing serious offense (as opposed to injury or harm) to persons other than the actor, and that it is probably a necessary means to that end (i.e., there is probably no other means that is equally effective at no greater cost to other values).* The principle asserts, in effect, that the prevention of offensive conduct *is* properly the state's business.

Like the word *harm*, the word *offense* has both a general and a specifically normative sense, the former including in its reference any or all of a miscellany of disliked mental states (disgust, shame, hurt, anxiety, etc.), and the latter referring to those states only when caused by the wrongful (right-violating) conduct of others. Only the latter sense—*wrongful offense*—is intended in the offense principle as we shall understand it. In this respect there is a parallel with the harm principle. We can also use the verb "to offend" meaning "to cause another to experience a mental state of a universally disliked kind (e.g., disgust, shame)." The offense principle then cites the need to prevent some people from *wrongfully offending* (offending and wronging) others as a reason for coercive legislation. Finally, the word *offense* in

From *Offense to Others*, vol. 2 of *The Moral Limits of the Criminal Law* (New York: Oxford University Press, 1985). Reprinted with permission of the publisher.

the strict and proper sense it bears in ordinary language is specific in a different way. Whereas *offense* in the sense of the offense principle specifies an objective condition—the unpleasant mental state must be caused by conduct that really is wrongful—"offense" in the strict sense of ordinary language specifies a subjective condition—the offending act must be taken by the offended person to wrong him whether in fact it does or not. In the strict and narrow sense, I am offended (or "take offense") when (1) I suffer a disliked state, and (2) I attribute that state to the wrongful conduct of another, and (3) I *resent* the other for his role in causing me to be in the state. The sense of grievance against the other or resentment of him for wronging me in this way is a phenomenological component of the unpleasant experience itself, an element that actually reinforces and magnifies its unpleasantness. If I am disgusted by the sight of a hospital patient's bloody wounds, the experience is one of that miscellany of disliked states I call "offended states of mind in the broad sense," but I can hardly resent the poor fellow for his innocent role in causing me to suffer that state of mind, and indeed there may be nobody to resent, in which case I do not "take offense," which is to say I am not offended in the strict and narrow sense.

The offense principle requires that the disliked state of mind (offense in the broad sense) be produced wrongfully by another party, but not that it be an offense in the strict sense of ordinary language. The victim may not know, or may not care, that another has wrongfully caused his unease, and therefore his unpleasant state of mind will not contain the element of resentment, and thus will not be offense in the strict sense. The offense principle as we shall interpret it then applies to offended states in either the broad or the strict sense—that is either with or without resentment—when these states are in fact wrongfully produced in violation of the offended party's rights. It is necessary that there *be* a wrong, but not that the victim *feel* wronged. And there will always be a wrong whenever an offended state (in the generic sense) is produced in another without justification or excuse.

Since I shall be defending a highly restricted version of the offense principle in this chapter, I should begin with some important disclaimers. To begin with, *offense is surely a less serious thing than harm.* That comparative value judgment seems to me self-evident, yet not simply true by definition. It is possible to deny it without contradiction if only because offense is not strictly commensurable with harm. It is a misconception to think of offenses as occupying the lower part of the same scale as harms; rather offenses are a different sort of thing altogether, with a scale all their own. Yet most people after reflection will probably acknowledge that a person is not treated as badly, other things being equal, when he is merely offended as when he is harmed. We may (at most) be inclined to rank extreme offenses as greater wrongs to their victims than trifling harms, but perhaps that is because they may become so offensive as to be actually harmful, in a minor sort of way. (At any rate the comparison of extreme offense with minor harm is the only place controversy could reasonably arise over the relative seriousness of offenses and harms.) Continued extreme offense … can *cause* harm to a person who becomes emotionally upset over the offense, to the neglect of his real interests. But the offended mental state in itself is not a condition of harm. From the moral point of view, considered in its own nature (apart from possible causal linkages to harmful consequences), it is a relatively trivial thing.

It follows from this evident but unprovable truth that the law should not treat offenses as if they were as serious, by and large, as harms. It should not, for example, attempt to control offensiveness by the criminal law when other modes of regulation can do the job as efficiently and economically. For the control of uncommon and transitory forms of offensiveness, for example, reliance can be placed on individual suits for injunctions, or by court orders initiated by police to cease and desist on pain of penalty, or by licensing procedures that depend on administrative suspension of license as a sanction. These alternatives would not entirely dispense with the need for punishment (which is almost always a disproportionately greater evil to the offender than offended mental states are to his "victims"), but punishment would be reserved as a back-up threat, not inflicted for offending others so much as for defying authority by persisting in prohibited conduct.... It may well be that the ordinary criminal law need not concern itself at all with defining crimes of offensiveness, even though offensiveness is the sort of evil it could in principle be used legitimately to combat. It is more likely, however, that for various practical reasons, reliance on injunctions, administrative orders, and license withdrawals would be insufficient to control *all* properly prohibitable offensive conduct. In some cases, we can know very well in advance that conduct of a certain kind will offend; that is, we don't have to wait for the particular circumstances to decide the question. Moreover, in some cases there will not be time to get an injunction or administrative hearing. By the time that sort of relief is forthcoming, the annoyance has come and gone, and the offense, such as it is, already committed.

Even if there must be defined crimes with specified penalties for purely offensive conduct, however, the penalties should be light ones: more often fines than imprisonment, but when imprisonment, it should be measured in days rather than months or years. Where crimes are divided into the categories of misdemeanor and felony, purely offensive crimes should always be misdemeanors, never felonies. Where penal codes follow the American Law Institute model[1] in dividing offenses into felonies, misdemeanors, petty misdemeanors, and "violations,"[2] harmlessly offensive conduct at its worst should be a petty misdemeanor, but typically only a violation—a status it would share with traffic and parking violations, various illegal sales, and unintentional violations of health or safety codes. When a given crime is both harmful and offensive the punishment can properly be severe, but legislators and judges should make it clear that the severity of the punishment is primarily a function of the harmfulness (or dangerousness) of the criminal act, not a reaction to its offensiveness. The state should punish a very harmful or dangerous but only routinely offensive crime much more severely than a crime that is greatly offensive but harmful or dangerous only to a minor degree.

These strictures would seem too obvious to mention were it not for the fact that they have been traditionally flouted by legislatures. Indeed, it hardly overstates the case to say that until very recently, at least, legislatures have tended to go haywire and treat offensiveness as *more* serious than harm![3] In 1961, Herbert Wechsler[4] made a survey of state penal codes and reported, among other things, that the New York Penal Law provided a maximum sentence of ten years for first degree assault and twenty years for sodomy; that Pennsylvania's Penal Code specified a maximum of seven years' imprisonment for assault with intent to kill, but ten years for pandering; that California provided a maximum of two years for corporal injury to wife or child but fifteen years for "perversion." Mayhem and assault with intent to commit a serious felony got fourteen and twenty years, respectively, in California, but statutory rape and incest got fifty years each. (Is incest two-and-a-half times as great an evil as mayhem?) From colonial times until 1869 North Carolina, following English precedents, punished "the unmentionable crime against nature," even when perpetrated with a willing partner, by the death penalty,[5] a punishment much more severe than that for aggravated battery or grand larceny. But Zechariah Chafee gives the best example I know of perverse judicial zeal to avenge mere offense: "The white slave traffic was first exposed by W. T. Stead in a magazine article, 'The Maiden Tribute.' The English law did absolutely nothing to the profiteers in vice, but put Stead in prison for a year for writing about an indecent subject."[6][!]

Because of legislators' tendency to overreact to offensiveness we should approach the subject with the greatest caution. Any legislator who votes to punish open lewdness or disrespect to the flag with prison terms *far* greater than those provided for genuinely and deliberately harmful acts of battery or burglary must be simply registering his hatred, revulsion, or personal anxiety rather than rationally applying some legislative principle to the facts. No one in his right mind could claim that lewd indecencies or even privately performed sexual deviations that are shocking merely to think about are some sort of menace to individual or collective interests, a threat from which we all urgently need protection at any cost to the offenders. Offensive behavior as such is no kind of menace, but at its worst only a severely irritating nuisance.

2. THE MODEL OF NUISANCE LAW

There are "mere nuisances," however, with which the law in England and America has long been engaged, a concern which has not hitherto disturbed libertarian reformers. The word *nuisance,* which is derived from the French *nuisance,* was sometimes spelled *"anoysance"* in early legal English,[7] which shows its early connection with the idea of annoyance, irritation, or inconvenience. Extreme nuisances can actually reach the threshold of harm, as when building noises in the house next door prevent a student from studying at all on the evening before an examination, or when an obstructed road causes a person to be late for an important appointment. But we are not very happy with nuisances even when they do not cause harm to our interests, but only irritations to our senses or inconvenient detours from our normal course. The offending conduct produces unpleasant or uncomfortable experiences—affronts to sense or sensibility, disgust, shock, shame, embarrassment, annoyance, boredom, anger, fear, or humiliation—from which one cannot escape without unreasonable inconvenience or even harm. We demand protection from nuisances when we think of ourselves as *trapped* by them, and we think it unfair that we should pay the cost in inconvenience that is required to escape them.

In the Anglo-American Law the term *nuisance* refers to two quite different sorts of wrongs: a miscellany of minor criminal offenses bearing the label "public nuisance" or "common nuisance," and a tort called "private nuisance," which consists in an interference with a landowner's use or enjoyment of his land. Private nuisances inconvenience specific individuals in the possession of their land, whereas public nuisances inconvenience random assortments of people ("the public") in the exercise of rights common to all

citizens. Thus, a landowner can sue his neighbor for private nuisance when the latter keeps a howling dog (irritating others) or a malarial pond (alarming others), whereas an intentional or negligent wrongdoer can be convicted of "public nuisance" in a criminal court for unreasonably obstructing a public highway (inconveniencing others), letting odors from his fertilizer plant escape over half the town (discomfiting others), keeping diseased animals (threatening others), storing explosives (alarming others), holding indecent public exhibitions (shocking others), conducting cock fights or dog fights (offending the sensibilities of others), or causing large noisy crowds to gather (disquieting others). Public and private nuisances, of course, have different kinds of legal remedies. Moreover, they have little in common, according to Prosser, except that "each causes inconveniences to someone."[8] But that common element is sufficient to justify both the law's traditional concern, and our own present theoretical interest.

The most interesting aspect of the law of nuisance is its own version of the unavoidable legal balancing act. Both legislators formulating statutes that define public nuisances and courts adjudicating conflicts between neighboring landowners must weigh opposing considerations.... [I]nterest-balancing is required in cases of those conflicts that make some harms unavoidable. Similar considerations apply in the law of nuisance when private and public interests of diverse sorts must be weighted against one another and against such noninterests as inconveniences, annoyances, and "offended mental states." The law of nuisance, in its full complexity, provides a model for the legislative application of an offense principle to the tangled problems of urban civilization. In the case of private nuisances, things may seem somewhat simpler than in criminal nuisance, since there are only two parties whose convenience and interests are directly involved, namely, the inconvenienced or offended plaintiff and the defendant whose conduct occasioned the suit, but even in this case public interests are indirectly involved, and the balancing tests are no easier to apply than in the criminal analogue. Balancing tests are at the very heart of judicial deliberations in tort cases, as they often are in legislative deliberations over the wording of criminal statutes. One influential legal manual explains why that is so:

> Practically all human activities, unless carried on in a wilderness, interfere to some extent with others or involve some risk of interference, and these interferences range from mere trifling annoyances to serious harms. It is an obvious truth that each individual in a community must put up with a certain amount of risk in order that all may get on together. The very existence of organized society depends upon the principle of give and take, live and let live, and therefore the law of torts does not attempt to impose liability or shift the loss in every case where one person's conduct has some detrimental effect on another. Liability is imposed only in those cases where the harm and risk [or inconvenience or offense] to one is greater than he ought to be required to bear under the circumstances, at least without compensation.[9]

Establishing that one person's conduct is a nuisance to someone else, then, is not yet sufficient to warrant legal interference. We must first compare carefully the magnitude of the nuisance to the one against the reasonableness of the conduct of the other, and the necessity "that all may get on together."

In his philosophically rewarding text on the law of torts,[10] William L. Prosser shows us how complicated the comparison of plaintiff and defendant can be, and how, inevitably, consideration of public interests must enter into the measurements. Describing the various factors that weigh on each side of the scale, Prosser tells us that the magnitude of the nuisance (or "seriousness of the inconvenience") to the plaintiff in a private nuisance action depends upon (1) the extent, duration, and character of the interference, (2) the social value of the use the plaintiff makes of his land, and (3) the extent to which the plaintiff can, without undue burden or hardship, avoid the offense by taking precautions against it.[11] These three factors yield the weight to be assigned to the seriousness of the inconvenience. They must be weighed against the reasonableness of the defendant's conduct, which is determined by (1) "the social value of its ultimate purpose, (2) the motive of the defendant [in particular its character as innocent or

spiteful], and (3) whether the defendant by taking reasonable steps can avoid or reduce the inconvenience to the plaintiff without undue burden or inconvenience to himself."[12] Finally, Prosser would have us throw on to the scale the interests of the "public at large," in particular its interest in "the nature of the locality" where the nuisance occurred—to "what particular use it is already devoted"—and given that background, "the suitability of the use made of the land by both plaintiff and defendant."[13]

On both sides of the comparison then, a variety of factors must be considered.

1) *The seriousness of the inconvenience* depends on:
   a) *The extent, duration, and character of the interference.* "The law does not concern itself with trifles," Prosser writes, "or seek to remedy all the petty annoyances and disturbances of everyday life.... Thus it has been held that there is no nuisance arising from the mere unsightliness of the defendant's premises ... or from the temporary muddying of a well, or from an occasional unpleasant odor or whiff of smoke."[14] Constant and unrelieved stench or smoke, on the other hand, and a residence reeking of offal and overrun with vermin, would be "substantial interferences" with a neighbor's enjoyment of his land, and hence genuine nuisances. The law of nuisance treats special susceptibility to annoyance in the same way that the law in general treats abnormal vulnerability to harm.... Hence, "so long as the interference is substantial and unreasonable, and such as would be offensive or inconvenient to the normal person, virtually any disturbance of the enjoyment of the property may amount to a nuisance."[15]
   b) *The social value of the use the plaintiff makes of his land.* Some balance must be struck by the courts, other things being equal, between the uses to which the plaintiff and the defendant put their property when the uses are incompatible. If the plaintiff's "use" during the night

hours is to sleep, and the defendant's is to enjoy large and raucous parties, then even though both have claims based on their property rights to those uses, the incompatibility of the uses may compel the court to declare the plaintiff's employment of greater "value." The court's judgment might be different, however, if the plaintiff's "use" were to throw raucous parties, and the defendant's to operate a blast furnace, or a hospital frequently subject to emergency nocturnal visits by ambulances with noise sirens.

c) *The extent to which the plaintiff can, without undue burden or hardship, avoid the offense by taking precautions against it.* The plaintiff cannot plausibly complain, for example, that occasional smoke from his neighbor's land has entered his own home, when he has neglected to close the windows through which the smoke enters.

2) *The reasonableness of the defendant's conduct* depends on:

a) *The social value of its ultimate purpose.* "The world must have factories, smelters, oil refineries, noisy machinery, and blasting, even at the expense of some inconvenience to those in the vicinity, and the plaintiff may be required to accept and tolerate some not unreasonable discomfort for the general good.... On the other hand, a foul pond, or a vicious or noisy dog will have little if any social value, and relatively slight annoyance from it may justify relief."[16]

b) *The motive of the defendant,* in particular its character as innocent or spiteful: "... where the defendant acts out of pure malice or spite, as by erecting a fence for the sole purpose of shutting off the plaintiff's view ... or leaving the kitchen door open in order to give the plaintiff the benefit of the aroma of cooking onions,[17] his conduct is indefensible from the social point of view, and he is liable for the nuisance."[18]

c) *Whether the defendant, by taking reasonable steps, can avoid or reduce the inconvenience to the plaintiff without undue burden or inconvenience to himself.* This is the counterpart on the defendant's side of the scales of factor 3 in the plaintiff's list. A socially useful factory may be forgiven for emitting moderate amounts of smoke when emission control equipment would cost the owner hundreds of thousands of dollars, but not when the emissions are substantial and unpleasant to others, and can be prevented by minor inexpensive adjustments.

3) *The interest of the community or the public at large* includes not only the social utility of the defendant's conduct and the interest in supporting the resale of the plaintiff's property, but also, as "a decisive consideration in many cases,"[19] the nature of the neighborhood, and the uses to which it has hitherto been devoted. Both for reasons of their physical characteristics and for accidental reasons, various localities have come to be devoted primarily to one specific sort of activity—commerce, industry, agriculture, or residence. Some of these activities are mutually incompatible so that uses of land come to be more or less segregated to prevent conflicts. Sometimes courts are called upon, in effect, "to determine the paramount use to which a locality is [already] devoted."[20] Thus a householder who takes up residence in a manufacturing district cannot complain, as a plaintiff in a private nuisance suit, of the noise, dust, or vibration. On the other hand, the very same amount of noise, dust, or vibration, caused by a factory located in a primarily residential district, will be declared a nuisance to the landowners in its vicinity.

Social philosophers very rarely argue about the role of law in the control of noise, dust, smoke, barking dogs, obstructed roads, and the like. They prefer instead to enter the ancient controversies about the role of law in the control of shocking or unsettling indecencies, obscene utterances, pornography, blasphemy, nudity, and similar affronts to sensibilities. But the offended and otherwise unpleasant states caused by these more interesting activities are objectionable for roughly the same kind of reason as the evils combatted by nuisance law. Even when they are not harms, they are annoying distractions, unwelcome demands on one's attention, a bother that must be coped with however inconvenient it may be at the time to do so. They are, in short, themselves nuisances in a perfectly ordinary sense. When they inconvenience homeowners (or tenants) in their own residences, they are already covered by tort law, and can be remedied by civil suits for damages or injunctive relief. (In that way a householder can protect himself from regular indecent behavior on his neighbor's lawn or obscene signs or pornographic displays on the external walls of his neighbor's house.) If they are to be the concern of the criminal law at all, it should be only when they occur in open places and thereby inconvenience elements of the general public, in the manner of "public" or "common" nuisances. In neither case will the law be justified in interfering with the offending conduct on the sole ground that it *does* annoy or inconvenience someone or other, for the consequences of such massive interference with liberty would be chaotic and paralyzing. Instead, the offense principle will have to be mediated by balancing tests similar to those already employed in the law of nuisance.

3. A RIDE ON THE BUS

There is a limit to the power of abstract reasoning to settle questions of moral legitimacy. The question raised by this chapter is whether there are any human experiences that are harmless in themselves yet so unpleasant that we can rightly demand legal protection from them even at the cost of other persons' liberties. The best way to deal with that question at the start is to engage our imaginations in the inquiry, consider hypothetically the most offensive experiences we can imagine, and then sort them into groups in an effort to isolate the kernel of the offense in each category. Accordingly, this section will consist of a number of vividly sketched imaginary tales, and the reader is asked to project himself into each story and determine as best he can what his reaction would be. In each story the reader should think of himself as a passenger on a normally crowded public bus on his way to work or to some important appointment in circumstances such that if he is forced to leave the bus prematurely, he will not only have to pay another fare to get where he is going, but he will probably be late, to his own disadvantage. If he is not exactly a captive on the bus, then, he would nevertheless be greatly inconvenienced if he had to leave the bus before it reached his destination. In each story, another passenger, or group of passengers, gets on the bus, and proceeds to cause, by their characteristics or their conduct, great offense to *you*. The stories form six clusters corresponding to the kind of offense caused.

A. Affronts to the Senses

Story 1. A passenger who obviously hasn't bathed in more than a month sits down next to you. He reeks of a barely tolerable stench. There is hardly room to stand elsewhere on the bus and all other seats are occupied.

Story 2. A passenger wearing a shirt of violent clashing orange and crimson sits down directly in your forward line of vision. You must keep your eyes down to avoid looking at him.

Story 3. A passenger sits down next to you, pulls a slate tablet from his briefcase, and proceeds to scratch his fingernails loudly across the slate, sending a chill up your spine and making your teeth clench. You politely ask him to stop, but he refuses.

Story 4. A passenger elsewhere in the bus turns on a portable radio to maximum volume. The sounds it emits are mostly screeches, whistles, and static, but occasionally some electronically amplified rock and roll music blares through.

B. Disgust and Revulsion

Story 5. This is much like story 1 except that the malodorous passenger in the neighboring seat continually scratches, drools, coughs, farts, and belches.

Story 6. A group of passengers enters the bus and shares a seating compartment with you. They spread a table cloth over their laps and proceed to eat a picnic lunch that consists of live insects, fish heads, and pickled sex organs of lamb, veal, and pork, smothered in garlic and onions. Their table manners leave almost everything to be desired.

Story 7. Things get worse and worse. The itinerant picnickers practice gluttony in the ancient Roman manner, gorging until satiation and then vomiting onto their tablecloth. Their practice, however, is a novel departure from the ancient custom in that they eat their own and one another's vomit along with the remaining food.

Story 8. A coprophagic sequel to story 7.

Story 9. At some point during the trip the passenger at one's side quite openly and nonchalantly changes her sanitary napkin and drops the old one into the aisle.

C. Shock to Moral, Religious, or Patriotic Sensibilities

Story 10. A group of mourners carrying a coffin enter the bus and share a seating compartment with you. Although they are all dressed in black their demeanor is by no means funereal. In fact they seem more angry than sorrowful, and refer to the deceased as "the old bastard," and "the bloody corpse." At one point they rip open the coffin with hammers and proceed to smash the corpse's face with a series of hard hammer blows.

Story 11. A strapping youth enters the bus and takes a seat directly in your line of vision. He is wearing a T-shirt with a cartoon across his chest of Christ on the cross. Underneath the picture appear the words "Hang in there, baby!"

Story 12. After taking the seat next to you a passenger produces a bundle wrapped in a large American flag. The bundle contains, among other things, his lunch, which he proceeds to eat. Then he spits into the star-spangled corner of the flag and uses it first to

clean his mouth and then to blow his nose. Then he uses the main striped part of the flag to shine his shoes.

D. Shame, Embarrassment (Including Vicarious Embarrassment), and Anxiety

Story 13. The passenger who takes the seat directly across from you is entirely naked. On one version of the story, he or she is the same sex as you; on the other version of the story, he or she is the opposite sex.

Story 14. The passenger in the previous story proceeds to masturbate quietly in his or her seat.

Story 15. A man and woman, more or less fully clothed to start, take two seats directly in front of you, and then begin to kiss, hug, pet, and fondle one another to the accompaniment of loud sighs and groans of pleasure. They continue these activities throughout the trip.

Story 16. The couple of the previous story, shortly before the bus reaches its destination, engage in acts of mutual masturbation, with quite audible instructions to each other and other sound effects.

Story 17. A variant of the previous story which climaxes in an act of coitus, somewhat acrobatically performed as required by the crowded circumstances.

Story 18. The seat directly in front of you is occupied by a youth (of either sex) wearing a T-shirt with a lurid picture of a copulating couple across his or her chest.

Story 19. A variant of the previous story in which the couple depicted is recognizable (in virtue of conventional representations) as Jesus and Mary.

Story 20. The couple in stories 15–17 perform a variety of sadomasochistic sex acts with appropriate verbal communications ("Oh, that hurts so sweet! Hit me again! Scratch me! Publicly humiliate me!").

Story 21. The two seats in front of you are occupied by male homosexuals. They flirt and tease at first, then kiss and hug, and finally perform mutual fellatio to climax.

Story 22. This time the homosexuals are both female and they perform cunnilingus.

Story 23. A passenger with a dog takes an aisle seat at your side. He or she keeps the dog calm at first by petting it in a familiar and normal way, but then petting gives way to hugging, and gradually goes beyond the merely affectionate to the unmistakably erotic, culminating finally with oral contact with the canine genitals.

E. Annoyance, Boredom, Frustration

Story 24. A neighboring passenger keeps a portable radio at a reasonably low volume, and the sounds it emits are by no means offensive to the senses. Nor is the content of the program offensive to the sensibilities. It is, however, a low quality "talk show" which you find intensely boring, and there is no possible way for you to disengage your attention.

Story 25. The two seats to your left are occupied by two persons who put on a boring "talk show" of their own. There is no way you can avoid hearing every animated word of their inane conversation, no way your mind can roam to its own thoughts, problems, and reveries.

Story 26. The passenger at your side is a friendly bloke, garrulous and officious. You quickly tire of his conversation and beg leave to read your newspaper, but he persists in his chatter despite repeated requests to desist. The bus is crowded and there are no other empty seats.

F. Fear, Resentment, Humiliation, Anger (from Empty Threats, Insults, Mockery, Flaunting, or Taunting)

Story 27. A passenger seated next to you reaches into a military kit and pulls out a "hand grenade" (actually only a realistic toy), and fondles and juggles it throughout the trip to the accompaniment of menacing leers and snorts. Then he pulls out a (rubber) knife and

"stabs" himself and others repeatedly to peals of maniacal laughter. He turns out to be harmless enough. His whole intent was to put others in apprehension of harm.

Story 28. A passenger sits next to you wearing a black armband with a large white swastika on it.

Story 29. A passenger enters the bus straight from a dispersed street rally. He carries a banner with a large and abusive caricature of the Pope and an anti-Catholic slogan. (You are a loyal and pious Catholic.)

Story 30. Variants of the above. The banner displays a picture of a black according to some standard offensive stereotype (Step 'n Fetchit, Uncle Tom, etc.) with an insulting caption, or a picture of a sneering, sniveling, hook-nosed Fagin or Shylock, with a scurrilous anti-Jewish caption, or a similar offensive denunciation or lampooning of groups called "Spicks," "Dagos," "Polacks," and so on.

Story 31. Still another variant. A counter-demonstrator leaves a feminist rally to enter the bus. He carries a banner with an offensive caricature of a female and the message, in large red letters: "Keep the bitches barefoot and pregnant."

4. THE MODES AND MEANING OF "OFFENSE"

I have tried to make a number of different points by telling these bloodcurdling tales: that there are at least six distinguishable classes of offended states that can be caused by the blamable conduct of others; that to suffer such experiences, at least in their extreme forms, is an evil; but that to the normal person (like the reader) such experiences, unpleasant as they are, do not cause or constitute harm. It is very important that the reader put himself on the bus and imagine his own reactions, for no amount of abstract argument can convince him otherwise that the represented experiences are in principle of a kind that the state can legitimately make its business to prevent.

When I imagine myself on the bus in these various stories, I find that one of the least unsettling experiences is that of the otherwise well-behaved nude passenger (story 13). Needless to say, I have never seen a nude person on a public bus, so I cannot be certain what my reaction would be. But I know that the sight of a nude body as such never did a normal person any harm, and as for the "unsettling experience" itself, one might escape it, I suppose, by turning one's eyes elsewhere, or escaping into one's private reveries. For all that, however, I suspect that I would be made at least vaguely ill at ease by the nude body (for reasons that urgently require examination—see below), and perhaps less stable persons in such a situation would be thrown into the kind of inner turmoil to which even the reader and I would be subject in most of the other situations.

The examples of "affronts to the senses" are all cases where the gratingly unpleasant experience derives entirely from its sound, color, or odor, and not at all from any symbolic representation, or recognized object. The shirt in story 2 "offends the eye" not because it is recognized as a shirt or because it symbolically asserts or suggests any proposition about shirts or any other subject. It is the sensuous garb of the experience rather than any cognitively mediated content that directly assails the eye, and that is the very feature that distinguishes affronts to the *senses* from shock to the *sensibilities*. That most of us are more disturbed emotionally by assaults on our sensibilities than by direct affronts to our senses is a contingent fact about our psyches and our common culture that could well have been other than it is without violating any law of nature. Story 3 (fingernails scratching slate) is designed to show, moreover, that affronts to senses can be so intensely unpleasant as to be nearly unbearable, even when they do not involve the cognitive faculties (and hence the sensibilities) in the offense. On the other hand, it is likely that the offense in story 1 (a passenger's odor) is influenced to some extent by one's awareness of its source as an unwashed human being, and the revulsion attendant upon that recognition. Precisely the same odor, if it were recognized as one's own, for example, would not be quite an equal offense, presumably, in one's own nostrils. Indeed, the unpleasantness of smells (perhaps more than that of other senses) is very difficult to separate from associated beliefs and sensibilities. The smell of freshly baked macaroni and cheese smells very different from that of much human vomit, yet the latter but not the former, when mediated by recognition, is offensive. A carton of rotten eggs, however, would smell no worse for being recognized as such, or as some particular person's property, and it may well be a transcultural truth that no one finds sulphurous oxide or the smell of skunk in high concentration very pleasant. These examples suggest that some affronts to the olfactory sense may be less dependent on cognition than others.

Another fact suggested by the stories in group A is that offensive sounds and smells can reach much greater extremes of intensity than directly offensive shapes and colors. Quite apart from the point that visual affronts are more easily avoided (we can shut our eyes more easily than our noses and ears), the visual sense seems less vulnerable to affront than the others, a purely neurological fact that has certain obvious implications for the legislator who employs an offense principle mediated by the kind of balancing tests used in the law of nuisance. Eyesores, so called, are for the most part not as great nuisances as noisome stenches and loud or grating sounds.

Disgust and revulsion, as illustrated by the stories in group B, differ from mere sensuous assaults in two important respects. In the first place, their impact on the offended person, while not *always* more intense, is less localized and more profound. Indeed, the etymology of the word *disgust* (from the Latin for "bad taste") suggests that the condition it designates is more likely to involve the digestive tract than the organs of perception. The first definition of the word in *Webster's New International Dictionary* (Third Edition, 1961) presumably captures something like its original sense: "marked aversion or repugnance toward food or toward a particular dish or kind of food...." In a second, more generalized definition, disgust is an extremely disagreeable emotional reaction "excited by exposure to something [anything] highly distasteful or loathesome," for example, the sight of a patient's festering wounds. Whatever the object of the disgust, the term is distinguished only in degree from its near synonym *sicken* ("a disgust so strong that one is affected physically as by a turning of the stomach") and *nausea* ("stronger still, suggesting a loathesomeness that provokes vomiting"). To be acutely disgusted is to suffer as disagreeable a state of mind and body as is possible below the threshold of actual harm, since to be sickened or nauseated is, in most cases, to cross that threshold.

In the second place, disgust—unlike sensuous affront—is always mediated by recognition or belief. What turns the spectator's stomach when he sees the itinerent picnickers in stories 6–8 consume their unusual "food" is not the color, shape, touch, sound—not even the smell—of the objects of their appetite (although these may be independently offensive to the senses), but rather the recognition of those things as objects of a certain kind—live insects, slugs, sex organs, feces, vomit, and so on. If the spectator mistakenly believed that the picnickers were eating eggplant, macaroni and cheese, and sweetbreads, he might still experience some aversion in the circumstances, but it would not amount to disgust or revulsion of the near-sickening kind. Disgust then is an offense not merely to sense but rather to *sensibility*, that susceptibility to offense from witnessing objects or events which, because of the observer's recognition of them as objects of a certain kind, are painful for him to behold.

The sensibilities offended in the stories of group B might be called "lower order sensibilities," and as such they can be contrasted with the moral, religious, and patriotic sensibilities in group C. We are disgusted at the sight of a person eating a dripping, wriggling, live sea slug, simply because we recognize it to be such, and given the character of our gastronomic sensibility, that recognition is quite sufficient to induce disgust. It is not necessary to the process that we hold a moral principle, or even a specific moral conviction, that eating sea slugs is cruel, sinful, or wicked. It is simply disgusting in some prerational, nondiscursive way, and that is an end to the matter. An additional step is involved in the production of disgust by offense to higher-level sensibilities. When we see a strapping young man arrogantly push aside an aged lady in his haste to occupy the only remaining seat on the bus, we recognize

the items in our experience as *young man, aged lady, push,* and *seat,* and that brings to mind a moral principle prescribing the proper conduct of persons of the type perceived. Then, in virtue of the perceived gross violation of that principle, we are disgusted. Similarly, the sight of a person wantonly desecrating a crucifix offends the religious sensibility not simply because the abused object is recognized as a wooden object in the shape of a cross, but because of the conventional symbolism of such shapes, and a whole complex of religious convictions, commitments, and emotions directed to the objects symbolized.[21]

The examples of indecorous sexual conduct in group D include some extreme deviations from prevailing standards of "normalcy" (stories 20–23), but they also include examples of perfectly ordinary and acceptable ways of deriving sexual pleasure when done in private (stories 14–17) and at least one commonplace state of being in which almost everyone in the world participates daily in private (story 13). Why should examples of the latter kinds be so upsetting? Why should conduct perfectly acceptable in itself become "indecent" when performed in public? These examples are not like the instances of disgusting eating in group B. Rather they would seem analogous to examples of "normal eating" in a public place, for example, munching peanuts or eating sandwiches, alone or with a friend, on a bus, activities that are not generally thought shameful, embarrassing, or indecent, but are at the very most, minor violations of etiquette.

Our culture, of course, is far more uptight about sexual pleasures than about "harmless" pleasures of any other kind, which is easy enough to understand given the danger in, and harmful consequences of, sexual behavior in the past—disease, personal exploitation, unwanted pregnancy, and so forth—and the intricate association of sexual taboos with rules of property transfer, legitimacy, marriage, and the like. Perhaps our abundant anxieties and our susceptibilities to shock will all fade away in the future, as improved contraceptive techniques reduce dangers of disease and unwanted pregnancy, and candid treatments of sexual themes in public forums and private conversations become more common still. But that day, despite recent relaxations of attitudes, still seems far off.

The disquietude caused in captive observers by public nudity and sexual behavior is a complicated psychological phenomenon, difficult to explain not only because of wide individual differences, but also because so many psychic elements are involved, and combine in so many possible ways. To begin with, nude bodies and copulating couples, like all forms of nuisance, have the power of preempting the attention and absorbing the reluctant viewer, whatever his preferences in the matter. The presence of such things in one's field of perception commands one's notice; they are distractions that must be attended to and coped with whatever one might prefer to be doing or thinking. Moreover, the problem of coping, for many persons at least, is a bit of a difficult one, not insurmountable, but something of an unpleasant strain. Part, but only part, of the explanation of that displeasure no doubt rests on the fact that nudity and sex acts have an irresistible power to draw the eye and focus the thoughts on matters that are normally repressed. Indeed, most of us spend an inordinate amount of time and energy, even without provocation, in sexual fantasies and the repression of lust. The unresolved conflict between instinctual desires and cultural taboos leaves many people in a state of unstable equilibrium and a readiness to be wholly fascinated, in an ambivalent sort of way, by any suggestion of sexuality in their perceptual fields. There is a temptation to see and savour all, and to permit oneself to become sexually stimulated, as by a pornographic film, but instantly the temptations of voyeurism trigger the familiar mechanism of inhibition and punishment in the form of feelings of shame. The primary basis of one's "offended state" then is this tension between attracting and repressing forces, against a psychic background of total fascination, a combination which can be at once exciting, upsetting, and anxiety-producing. When the precipitating experience is not mere nudity, but actual sexual activity, even of a "normal" kind, it will create a kind of inner agitation at best, and at worst that experience of exposure to oneself of one's "peculiarly sensitive, intimate, vulnerable aspects" which is called *shame*.[22] When one has not been able to prepare one's defenses,

"one's feeling is involuntarily exposed openly in one's face…. We are caught unawares, made a fool of."[23] For some relatively unenlightened persons the result will be a severe psychic jolt; those of us who are better able to cope with our feelings might well resent the necessity to do so and regard it as an irritating distraction and a bore, much the same as any other nuisance.

Understandable doubt has been expressed by some writers over the contention that the public nudity or sexual behavior of others can produce something called "shameful embarrassment" in oneself. Michael Bayles has effectively entered a challenge to that way of describing matters:

> It is difficult to understand how the public nudity of others invades one's privacy or causes one embarrassment. Surely the privacy involved is the nude's, but one has not invaded it. For one to be ashamed of something, it must have a relation to oneself, be something for which one takes responsibility. One can be ashamed of the conduct of one's friends, for one may take vicarious responsibility for their conduct or consider oneself responsible for who one's friends are…."[24]

Shame, in the relevant sense, is "a painful emotion caused by consciousness of guilt, shortcoming, or impropriety in one's own behavior or position, or in the behavior or position of a closely associated person or group."[25] It is, therefore, difficult to understand how the painful emotion felt by the captive observer of nudity or sex play on the bus could possibly be shame, for *he* is not the one who is behaving improperly or indecorously. If the nude passenger or lewd lovers were his fellow countrymen in a foreign country, his children, friends, or business partners, he might well feel ashamed of *them*, but in our hypothetical story, the offending persons are total strangers and the offended observer is in his own country.

Still, for all of that, it does seem natural to describe the offended reaction of the observer as "shame." After all, the unexpected apprehension of nudity or "indecency" can be expected to bring a blush to the face of the observer, which is a recognized symptom both of intense self-consciousness and "shame, modesty, or confusion."[26] How then could the reaction to another's misconduct be

shameful embarrassment? There are at least two answers to this question. First, the "guilt, shortcoming, or impropriety of one's own" that is the object
of the shame may well be the instantaneous reaction
of one's own to the offending experience, a sudden
loss of control, soon recovered, over impulses normally restrained by the firmest reins. One reacts in a
certain way and then is immediately ashamed of that
reaction. Second, one can feel shame or embarrassment vicariously in a way other than that which
Bayles acknowledges. Bayles accounts for those
cases where one person is ashamed of or *because of*
another person with whom he is closely associated
or for whom he is responsible. In those cases some
of the other's shame "rubs off" on him, so to speak.
But there are other cases in which the improper or
inept actions of a total stranger can induce shame or
embarrassment in an observer. In these cases, the
observer, by a kind of sympathetic identification
with the other party that comes naturally to sensitive
and imaginative people, feels ashamed or embarrassed *for* the other party. In these cases the observer feels the shame he would feel were he in
the other's place. In many cases, an observer's painful emotion is complex and contains elements of
shame of both the personal and vicarious kinds.

And sometimes the offended mental state is
still more complex. When the observer can perceive the whole embarrassing situation not only
from his own vantage point, but also imaginatively
from the point of view of the offenders, he comes
to feel that whatever *they* may think about it, his
own presence is a jarring foreign element in their
privacy. His own witness then seems a part of their
humiliation, and since they neither know nor care
about their own public disgrace, their human dignity is further diminished in his eye, to his further
distress. Still another quite independent element
in the unwilling observer's painful emotion may
be the feeling that he is threatened by what is
happening, that either the unrestrained public performers or his own stirred up feelings may surge
out of control. Thus one becomes anxiously ap-
prehensive, and concerned lest unwilling revelations of one's own feeling discredit or embarrass
one at any moment. Another element may be a
response to the whole spectacle, performance *and*
audience, not merely the performers themselves.

What may seem obscene to the observer is not
simply that the offenders are there nude or tu-
mescent in his eye, but that they stand (or lie)
revealed to many other eyes.... The obscenity
consists not in the object of observation but in
the fact that many people are looking and "collectively" experiencing their own inadmissible
feelings. The observer might thus feel embarrassed to be part of the spectacle perceived by
the other members of the observing audience
and also vicariously embarrassed on *their* behalf.
And so, a final element steals into the complex
mental state of the offended observer: a near total
confusion and disarray of feeling.

The stories of abnormal sexual acts (numbers
20–23) provide examples of public behavior that
would be even more disagreeable to witness. Two
elements are present in the painful feelings induced in these stories that are rarely present to
the same degree in mere nudity and ordinary
sex: (1) The witnessed incidents are taken to be
immediately and powerfully *threatening,* and
(2) "lower-level sensibilities" are shocked so that
a spontaneous *disgust* arises to mingle with the
other painful elements in the experience. The
point about threats is best illustrated by the example of male homosexuality. The general nervous-
ness about this subject is even reflected in the way
it is treated in the most iconoclastic pornographic
films. The celebrated film *Emmanuelle,* for example, included numerous scenes of female homosexuality (not very graphically displayed) presumably
because such scenes are thought to be especially
titillating to the males who constitute the bulk of
the audience for those films. But there was not so
much as a suggestion of male homosexuality, a
practice which many males loathe and execrate,
and hold in considerable terror. Not only do homosexual acts violate powerful taboos in our
culture; they also threaten the "ego ideals" of heterosexual men. Homosexuals are the objects of
near universal contempt and ridicule, and their
peculiar practice is held inconsistent with the ideals
of genuine manhood. Hatred of homosexuality,
therefore, is a part of the psychic fortress many
men build around their self-esteem. The point
about disgust is best illustrated by the story about
bestiality (number 23). Not even the story of the

feces-and-vomit-eating picnickers in group B is more disgusting to most of us than that.

After considering such jolts to sensibility, it may seem altogether anticlimactic to turn to the offenses in group E, for the boredom of radio shows and dull conversation are of such a common type that we suffer from it to some degree almost every day of our lives. At their extremes, however, the mental states they induce can be almost as intensely disliked and difficult to tolerate as fingernails on a slate board or unavoidable witness to homosexual couplings. Boredom is sometimes conceived as mere listless aimlessness or ennui, the state of a solitary person who cannot think of anything to do. That condition is unhappy enough, but there is nothing acute or piercing about it, and it is not necessarily an "offense" directly caused by another person. When one is buttonholed by a "cocktail-party bore," or a "discussion-period bore," on the other hand, the displeasure can be so sharp and penetrating as to suggest the pointed revolving tool that "bores" holes in firmly held objects. The bore is persistent and undivertable; he *will* command your attention; there is no escape. The offended state he produces results from another kind of tense inner conflict: one is trying desperately to escape by thinking up stratagems, excuses, and diversions, but clear thinking is impossible in the face of the bore's peremptory demands on one's attention. Often there is no escape possible without unacceptable rudeness, so one resigns oneself in depressed and weary annoyance. At that point one is "crushed with irksome tediousness." The boring people on the bus are surely not that bad, however, if only because (stories 24 and 25) they do not attempt to exact responses from you, whereas in story 26, the officious talker can in the end be requested, without rudeness, to be quiet. But insofar as the boring passengers commandeer one's attention irresistibly, they are nuisances in the same manner, even if to a lesser degree, as their disgusting, shocking, embarrassing, and threatening counterparts in the other stories.

The group insults issued by passengers in the stories in group F, the contemptuous mockery, the deliberate baiting and taunting through the display of offensive signs and symbols, can be the most disturbing behavior of all in its effects on members of the insulted groups, and even on others to whom such conduct is odious. In these cases, as in the others, disagreeable emotions are aroused that have to be coped with, but it is distinctive of these cases that the emotion is the most difficult of all to handle, namely sudden violent anger, conjoined with anxious fear, and a feeling of humiliation and impugned "honor." Again, as soon as the emotion flares it is likely to be followed by a feeling of shame and worry over its presence and a desperate effort at repression. But the offending symbols are still there in one's visual field, still mocking and threatening, nagging and tugging at one's attention, like another kind of efficient boring tool. And attendant upon one's shame is a new anxiety: fear of making a fool of oneself by losing control. These conflicting elements pull a person in all directions and throw him into confusion. Despite the legal doctrine of "fighting words," which permits states to ban "personally abusive epithets ... that are inherently likely to provoke violent reaction,"[27] it is unlikely that present laws would permit one who is personally insulted to accept what he takes to be a challenge and vent his anger in retaliatory aggression, any more than it would permit the sexually excited witness of nudity or indecency on the bus to force his lust on the provoking person. But again, having to cope with one's rage is as burdensome a bore as having to suffer shame, or disgust, or noisome stenches, something unpleasant to experience and inconvenient to accommodate, even when it causes one no harm....

It should be clear at this point that despite the miscellaneous character of "offended states" they have some important characteristics in common. They are at the very least unpleasant to the one who suffers them, though the mode of displeasure varies from case to case. With the exception of irritations to the senses, and only some of these, they are complex states whose unpleasantness is in part a function of the tension between conflicting elements. And, most important from the legislative point of view, they are nuisances, making it difficult for one to enjoy one's work or leisure in a locality that one cannot reasonably be expected to leave in the circumstances. In extreme cases, the offending conduct commandeers one's attention from the outside, forcing one to relinquish control of one's inner state, and drop what one was doing in order to cope, when it is greatly inconvenient to do so.

5. THE RELATION BETWEEN OFFENSE AND PRIVACY

In what manner, if any, do the offensive people on the bus violate the privacy of their fellow passengers? The word *privacy* may seem clear enough in ordinary discourse, but its ever more frequent use in law courts and legislatures has caused increasing bewilderment and controversy. Privacy as a legal category came into American law less than a century ago. Its first appearance was in the law of torts, where it served to protect persons from misappropriation of their names or pictures for commercial purposes, and then was gradually extended to include protection of persons from embarrassing publicity, from being put in a false light by the public attribution of beliefs they do not hold, and most important, from unwarranted intrusion into their personal affairs by such means as wiretapping, electronic surveillance, shadowing, and peeping. The moral rights to be free of these various evils are certainly genuine ones, and the evils themselves, genuine evils. These rights, moreover, had not been adequately protected by the common law before the "right to privacy" was invented or discovered. But they have an irreducibly heterogeneous character summarizable in a unitary way only by such an imprecise phrase as "the right to be let alone." Soon it became popular to designate still other legal protections under the same flexible rubric. The old privilege of confidentiality protecting certain special relationships is now considered a special case of privacy.[28] In torts, the right to privacy came to encompass not only the right not to be known about in certain ways by others, but also the right to avoid "seeing and hearing what others say,"[29] apparently on the ground that "it may be as distasteful to suffer the intrusions of a garrulous and unwelcome guest as to discover an eavesdropper or peeper."[30] In constitutional law, the Supreme Court has come to discover a miscellany of "penumbral rights" of privacy against governmental action that imposes limits even on otherwise valid legislation, including a right to marital privacy that is violated by a state statute prohibiting the sale of contraceptives even to married couples.[31] … The tendency to apply the one concept "privacy" to such a motley collection of rights has alarmed many commentators who fear that so plastic and expansive a concept will obfuscate legal analysis. "Given this disparity of central issues," wrote Paul Freund, "privacy becomes too greedy a legal concept."[32]

Many or most of the disparate legal uses of the idea of privacy, however, can be grouped in one or the other of two families of sense. Elizabeth Beardsley has put the distinction well: "Alleged violations [of privacy] seem to fall into two major categories: conduct by which one person *A* restricts the power of another person *B* to determine for himself whether or not he will perform an act *X* or undergo an experience *E,* and conduct by which one person *A* acquires or discloses information about *B* which *B* does not wish to have known or disclosed."[33] Beardsley labels the right to privacy violated in the former case, the right to *autonomy,* and that violated in the latter case, the right to *selective disclosure.* Window peeping, secret shadowing or photographing, wiretapping, publishing of intimate conversation, intercepted correspondence, candid photographs, and the like all violate a person's privacy in the sense that they invade his right not to be observed or known about in certain ways without his consent. Nothing like that kind of wrong is committed by the offensive passengers on the bus against their fellow travelers, so we can put that notion of privacy aside. A typical violation of privacy in the sense of autonomy occurs when unwanted noises obtrude upon one's experience, restricting one's power to determine for oneself "whether one will do *X,* or undergo *E,* or not." "Noise removes [one's] power to choose effectively between sound and silence, or between one sound and another, as features of [one's] immediate experience."[34] The offensive passengers clearly *do* violate their neighbor's privacy in this sense (autonomy) not only when they are noisy, but also when they are disgusting, shocking, embarrassing, boring, threatening, and enraging, for in each case, they deprive the unwilling spectators of the power to determine for themselves whether or not to undergo a certain experience. No passenger, moreover, would decide, if the choice were left to him, to undergo experiences of these offensively unpleasant kinds. Each must spend the whole bus trip coping with feelings induced in himself from the outside when he would much prefer, presumably, to be doing something else. In being made to experience and be occupied in certain ways by outsiders, and having had no choice in the matter whatever, the captive passengers suffer a violation of their autonomy (assuming that the "boundaries" of the autonomous realm do not shrink to the vanishing point when they enter the public world.)

We can agree with Beardsley that "selective disclosure" and "autonomy" are two different kinds of things commonly called "privacy," while insisting that they are not without a common element that explains why the word *privacy* is commonly applied to both. They are, in short, two species of the genus "privacy" rather than two distinct senses of the word *privacy*. The root idea in the generic concept of privacy is that of a privileged territory or domain in which an individual person has the exclusive authority of determining whether another may enter, and if so, when and for how long, and under what conditions.... Within this area, the individual person is—pick your metaphor—boss, sovereign, owner. The area includes not only the land and buildings he owns and occupies, but his special relationships with spouse, attorney, or priest, and his own mental states or "inner sanctum." His rightful control over his "inner property" is violated when another learns or reveals its secret contents without his consent, for he should be the one who decides what is to be known of them and by whom. His will alone reigns supreme over them. But his sovereignty or ownership is also violated when others obtrude their own sounds, and shapes, and affairs upon his "territory" without his consent, for within the privileged area, he has the sole right to determine what he is to experience, insofar as these matters are rightfully

subject to his control.[35] When he is forced to experience loud or grating sensations, disgusting or enraging activities while on his privileged ground, something like a property right has been violated,[36] and violated in a manner similar to that of "private nuisance." The legislative problem of determining when offensive conduct is a public or criminal nuisance could with equal accuracy be expressed as a problem about determining the extent of personal privacy or autonomy. The former way of describing the matter (in terms of "nuisance") lends itself naturally to talk of *balancing* (the independent value or reasonableness of the offending conduct against the degree of seriousness of the offense caused) whereas the latter way (in terms of "privacy") lends itself naturally to talk of drawing *boundaries* between the various private domains of persons, and between the private domain of any given person and the public world. The metaphors are different; the actual modes of reasoning are the same.

NOTES

1. *Model Penal Code, Proposed Official Draft.* American Law Institute. Philadelphia (1962): § 1.04.
2. Id., at § 1.04, pt. 5. An offense is said to constitute a violation, as opposed to any kind of crime, if no other sentence than a fine, or fine and forfeiture, or other civil penalty is authorized upon conviction by the law defining the offense, and conviction gives rise to no disability or legal disadvantage based on conviction of criminal offense.
3. In this connection it should be noted that the most common generic synonym for "crimes" is neither "harms" nor "injuries," but "offenses."
4. Wechsler, Herbert. "Sentencing, Correction, and the Model Penal Code." *University of Pennsylvania Law Review* 109 (1961): 473, 474.
5. The North Carolina law copied an English statute of 1533 (enacted during the reign of Henry VIII) that made it a felony punishable by death to commit "the vice of buggery." For "vice of buggery" North Carolina substituted "the abominable and detestable crime against nature not to be named among Christians" whether committed with "mankind or beast." In 1869 the penalty was reduced to imprisonment of "not less than five nor more than sixty years."
6. Chafee, Zechariah. *Free Speech in the United States.* Cambridge, Mass.: Harvard University

Press, 1964. 51. Chafee provides another good example (p. 286)—a Montana sedition law from World War I. Thus Montana imposed a penalty of twenty years in prison for various insults to the Constitution, the uniform, and the flag, which were considered too trivial to be federal crimes, until Congress in 1918 inserted the whole Montana law into the middle of the Espionage Act. Nothing could show better the way state war legislation works than the fate of Starr of Montana, as described by a United States judge:

> He was in the hands of one of those too common mobs, bent upon vindicating its peculiar standard of patriotism and its odd concept of respect for the flag by compelling him to kiss the latter. In the excitement of resisting their efforts, Starr said: "What is this thing anyway? Nothing but a piece of cotton with a little paint on it and some other marks in the corner there. I will not kiss that thing. It might be covered with microbes." The state authorities did nothing to the mob, but they had Starr convicted under the Montana Sedition Act for using language "calculated to bring the flag into contempt and disrepute," and sentenced him to the penitentiary for not less than ten nor more than twenty years at hard labor.

7. Prosser, William L. *Handbook of the Law of Torts.* 2d ed. St. Paul: West Publishing Co., 1955. 390, n. 7.
8. Prosser, William L. *Handbook of the Law of Torts.* 4th ed. St. Paul: West Publishing Co., 197. 573.
9. *Restatement of the Law of Torts.* American Law Institute, 1939. § 822, comment j.
10. Prosser, supra, note 8.
11. Id., at 597.
12. Id., at 597–99.
13. Id., at 599–600.
14. Id., at 577–78.
15. Id., at 593.
16. Id., at 597–98.
17. *Medford v. Levy,* 31 W. Va. 649 (1888).
18. Prosser, supra, note 8. 598–99.
19. Id., at 599.
20. Id., at 600.
21. There is an unfortunate tendency in human nature to elevate lower order sensibilities to the status of moral or religious ones, thus masquerading what is in origin little more than a reflexive aversion as some sort of rational or sacred principle. J. S. Mill cited a standard example of this in *On Liberty*, chap. 4, para. 13:

> To cite a rather trivial example, nothing in the creed or practice of Christians does more to envenom the hatred of Mahomedans against them than the fact of their eating pork. There are few acts which Christians and Europeans regard with more unaffected disgust than Mussulmans regard this particular mode of satisfying hunger. It is, in the first place, an offense against their religion; but this circumstance by no means explains either the degree or the kind of their repugnance; for wine is also forbidden by their religion, and to partake of it is by all Mussulmans accounted wrong, but not disgusting. Their aversion to the flesh of the "unclean beast" is, on the contrary, of that peculiar character, resembling an instinctive antipathy, which the idea of uncleanness, when once it thoroughly sinks into the feelings, seems always to excite even in those whose personal habits are anything but scrupulously cleanly....

22. Lynd, Helen. *On Shame and the Search for Identity.* New York: Science Editions, 1961. 33.
23. Id., at 32.
24. Michael D. Bayles, Michael D. "Comments." *Issues in Law and Morality.* Eds. Norman Care and Thomas Trelogan. Cleveland: Case Western Reserve University Press, 1973. 125, n. 4.
25. *Webster's New International Dictionary,* 3d Edition, 1961.
26. Id.
27. See *Chaplinsky v. New Hampshire,* 315 U.S. 568 (1942)....
28. Freund, Paul A. "Privacy: One Concept or Many?" *Nomos* XIII: *Privacy.* Eds. J. R. Pennock and J. W. Chapman. New York: Atherton Press, 1971. 102.
29. Harper, Fowler V. and James, Fleming, Jr. *The Law of Torts.* Vol. 1. Boston: Little, Brown, and Co., 1956. 681.
30. Id.
31. *Griswold v. Connecticut,* 381 U.S. 479 (1965)....
32. Freund, supra, note 28, 192 (footnote 28). See also id., Gross, Hyman. "Privacy and Autonomy."
33. Beardsley, Elizabeth L. "Privacy, Autonomy and Selective Disclosure." *Nomos* XIII: *Privacy.* Eds. J. R. Pennock and J. W. Chapman. New York:

Atherton Press, 1971. 56. Letter variables revised to accord with the convention of this book.

34. Id., at 58.

35. And they cannot be reasonably expected to be very much subject to his control. As Beardsley notes:

> Of course sounds which (like thunder) are not produced by the intentional acts of human beings, or which (like subway clatter) could reasonably have been predicted by X to be part of an environment into which X has chosen to enter, or which (like the roar of compressed air drills and *perhaps* like some recorded music) have a redeeming social utility, have come to be accepted: questions about "violations of privacy" are often not so much as thought of, as far as most of the din of modern life is concerned.
>
> Beardsley, supra, note 33, at 58).

36. This point is well appreciated by Ernest Van den Haag in his: "Own Privacy." *Nomos* XIII: *Privacy*. Eds. J. R. Pennock and J. W. Chapman. New York: Atherton Press, 1971. 150ff. One should point out that *if* the analogy to landed property rights is perfect, then even an unconsented-to intrusion of delightful and appreciated sounds and activities into the private domain is a technical violation of privacy on the model of trespass.

40 Religion and Freedom of Speech: Portraits of Muhammad

ROBERT POST

On September 30, 2005, the Danish newspaper *Jyllands-Posten* solicited and published twelve cartoons depicting the prophet Muhammad.[1] By American standards, the cartoons are prosaic. One is a child's portrait of Muhammad in the desert; another shows Muhammad's face intertwined with Islamic symbols like the crescent and the star; several poke fun at the *Jyllands-Posten,* calling the cartoons a "PR Stunt" and the journalists a "bunch of reactionary provocateurs." Some contain ordinary, rather anodyne satire.[2] One shows Muhammad with a turban in the shape of a bomb; another confuses Muhammad with St. Peter, portraying the prophet at the entrance to a cloud-filled heaven facing a long line of suicide bombers saying, "Stop, Stop. We ran out of virgins."

The consequence of publishing these cartoons has been truly dreadful. There have been riots throughout the world. According to one estimate, 139 people have died.[3] A fatwa has been issued offering a million-dollar bounty for the death of the cartoonists. Newspaper editors have been fired and imprisoned, newspapers closed, and an Italian minister forced to resign for displaying the cartoons on his T-shirt. The Swedish foreign minister was forced to resign for attempting to close a web site that wished to display the cartoons.

Islam contains a rich history of portraying the prophet Mohammed, but the modern fundamentalist sects who now claim to speak for Islam assert that it is forbidden to publish any representation of Muhammad, or, in some versions, of any prophet recognized by Islam. "Merely publishing the image of Muhammad is regarded as blasphemous by many Muslims."[4] For this reason the violent riots protesting the publication of the cartoons no doubt included numerous persons who were "undeniably outraged by what they perceive as blasphemy."[5] The question I shall address in this paper is how the law ought to respond to this outrage. How should the law mediate between the demands of religious sanctity and freedom of speech?

From *Constellations*, Vol. 14, No 1, 2007. © The Author. Journal compilation © Blackwell Publishing Ltd. Reprinted with permission of the publisher.

This is a very narrow question, which concerns only the coercive power of the state. It is quite distinct from the ethical issue of when and how one should speak. All that is legally permitted is not ethically advisable. Carsten Juste, the editor-in-chief *of Jyllands-Posten,* later said that "If I had known that the lives of Danish soldiers and civilians would be threatened, if I had known that, as my finger hovered one centimeter above the send button for publishing the drawings, would I have hit it? No. No responsible editor in chief would have done."[6] Juste was plainly correct to distinguish legal right from ethical propriety. Even if *Jyllands-Posten* were legally entitled to publish cartoons that were offensive, provocative, and likely to lead to violence, it may have been ethically inappropriate to do so. In this paper, I analyze only the question of legal right.

In the United States this question could be easily and accurately answered by any first year law student. Since 1940 our First Amendment has been held to protect from legal sanction all religious polemic, even expression that aims deliberately and provocatively to assault the religious sensibilities of the pious. "In the realm of religious faith, and in that of political belief," our Supreme Court has held:

> sharp differences arise. In both fields the tenets of one man may seem the rankest error to his neighbor. To persuade others to his own point of view, the pleader, as we know, at times, resorts to exaggeration, to vilification of men who have been, or are, prominent in church or state, and even to false statement. But the people of this nation have ordained in the light of history, that, in spite of the probability of excesses and abuses, these liberties are, in the long view, essential to enlightened opinion and right conduct on the part of the citizens of a democracy.

The essential characteristic of these liberties is that under their shield many types of life, character, opinion, and belief can develop unmolested and unobstructed. Nowhere is this shield more necessary than in our own country for a people composed of many races and of many creeds.[7]

It is recognized that "a first great principle of consensus" in First Amendment doctrine is that *"In America, there is no heresy, no blasphemy."*[8]

The American Constitution protects speech in "public discourse," which is to say speech about public figures or circulating in the national media, that seeks intentionally to violate religious sensibilities by causing emotional pain, distress, and outrage.

The American First Amendment, however, is unique. Alongside our commitment to the death penalty, it stands as an outstanding exemplar of American constitutional exceptionalism. In Europe, where the Danish cartoons were published, there is a long history of regulating blasphemy, and as a consequence the question of subjecting the cartoons to legal sanction is very much alive. It is that question that I shall analyze in this paper, with particular emphasis on decisions of the European Court of Human Rights, which set minimum European requirements for the suppression of religiously provocative speech. There are of course many distinct justifications for protecting freedom of speech,[9] but because all European nations are committed to democratic self-governance, I shall in this paper seek to explore the compatibility of blasphemy regulation with the requirements of democracy.

I. SPEECH AND DEMOCRACY

All agree that states aspiring to democratic legitimacy must extend some protection to freedom of speech. The extent and nature of these protections will depend upon many factors, including, most centrally, the meaning of democracy.

I begin with what I take to be the unobjectionable premise that democracy refers to "the distinction between autonomy and heteronomy: Democratic forms of government are those in which the laws are made by the same people to whom they apply (and for that reason they are autonomous norms), while in autocratic forms of government the law-makers are different from those to whom the laws are addressed (and are therefore heteronomous norms)."[10] When we use this definition, we must immediately distinguish democracy from majoritarianism, in which a majority of the people exercise control over their government. Although it is frequently said "any distinct restraint on majority power, such as a principle of freedom of speech, is by its nature anti-democratic, anti-majoritarian,"[11] it is plain that majorities can implement rules that are inconsistent with democracy, as for example by voting a monarchy into office. Although majoritarianism may be intimately associated with the practice of democracy, democracy is not defined by majoritarianism, which is why it is intelligible to conclude that particular exercises of majoritarianism are antidemocratic.

Democracy is distinct from majoritarianism because democracy is a normative idea that refers to substantive political values,[12] whereas majoritarianism is a descriptive term that refers to a particular decision-making procedure. Essential to democracy are the values that allow us to determine whether in specific circumstances particular decision-making procedures are actually democratic. Governments, for example, do not become democratic merely because they hold elections in which majorities govern. Such elections are currently held in North Korea. To know whether these elections make North Korea democratic requires an inquiry into whether these elections are implemented in a way that serves democratic values. It is a grave mistake to confuse democracy with any particular decision-making procedure, and thereby to fail to identify the core values that democracy as a form of government seeks to instantiate.

Because these values are associated with the practice of self-determination, we must ask what it means for a people to engage in the practice of self-governance. This practice is often interpreted to mean that a people be made ultimately responsible for governmental decisions, either by making such decisions directly or by electing those who do. This is the view, for example, of Alexander Meiklejohn or Owen Fiss.[13] But this is an insufficient account of the practice of self-government. For reasons that I shall explain, I think it preferable to say that the practice of self-government requires that a people have the warranted conviction that they are engaged in the process of governing themselves.[14] The distinction is crucial, for it emphasizes the difference between making particular decisions and recognizing particular decisions as one's own. Self-government is about the

authorship of decisions, not about the making of decisions.

We can test this distinction by imagining a situation in which the people retain their collective capacity to decide issues, but in which individuals within the collectivity feel hopelessly alienated from these decisions. Suppose, for example, that in State X citizens are provided with interactive computer terminals that they are required to use in the morning to register their preferences about various issues. Each morning an agenda for decisions (composed by an elected assembly) is presented on the terminal. The citizens of State X must decide what color clothes should be worn; what menu should be served for lunch and dinner; the boundaries of the attendance zones for the neighborhood school; whether a stop sign should be placed at a local intersection; and so on. Assume that citizens of State X can get from their computer whatever information they believe is relevant for their votes, including information about the likely views of other citizens.

Imagine, further, that State X has no public discourse. There are neither newspapers nor broadcast media. The state bans political parties and associations. It proscribes public demonstrations and prohibits individuals from publishing their views to other citizens. Each citizen must make up his or her mind in isolation. Decisions in State X, however, are made on the basis of the majority vote of the collectivity, and all individuals are henceforth required to comply: to wear blue, or to serve chicken for lunch, or to attend a particular school, or to stop at the local intersection. Individuals in State X feel completely alienated from these decisions. They do not identify with them and instead feel controlled and manipulated by the external force of the collectivity.

Would we deem State X an example of a society that engages in self-determination? Although in State X the people retain their ability, "as a collectivity, to decide their own fate,"[15] which is to say to make decisions by majority rule, I very much doubt that we would characterize State X as a democracy. We are much more likely to condemn it as a dystopian tyranny. Rousseau long ago diagnosed the reason for this condemnation: collective decision-making is merely oppressive unless there is some internal connection between the particular wills of individual citizens and the general will of the collectivity.[16]

It is implausible to claim, as Rousseau might be thought to claim, that there can exist a complete identity between the particular wills of individual citizens and the general will of the democratic state. It is enough that individual citizens can recognize in that general will the potentiality of their own authorship.[17] When this occurs, collective decision-making is democratic because it is experienced as self-determination. But when citizens feel alienated from the general will, or from the process by which the general will is created, voting on issues is merely a decision-making mechanism, a mechanism that can easily turn oppressive and undemocratic.

It follows that the value of democracy can be fulfilled only if there is continual mediation between collective self-determination and the individual self-determination of particular[18] If democracy requires that citizens experience their government as their own, as representing them, they must experience the state as in some way responsive to their own values and ideas. How is this theoretically possible under modern conditions of diversity, when the citizens of a state are heterogeneous and disagree with each other? The focus of analysis must shift from specific state decisions to the process by which these decisions are authorized. Citizens must experience that process as responsive to their own values and ideas.

Modern democracies conceive this process in terms of communication. They seek to make the decisions of the state responsive to public opinion, and to protect freedom of speech so that citizens can participate in the formation of public opinion. They hope that the opportunity freely to participate in forming public opinion will allow citizens to experience their government as their own, even if they must live in common with citizens who hold diverse views and otherwise disagree. That is why in the United States we say that the First Amendment, which is antimajoritarian, is nevertheless "the guardian of our democracy."[19] Hans Kelsen, speaking of democracy, puts the matter this way:

A subject is politically free insofar as his individual will is in harmony with the "collective" (or "general") will expressed in the social order. Such harmony of the "collective" and the individual will is guaranteed only if the social order is created by the individuals whose behavior it regulates. Social order means determination of the will of the individual. Political freedom, that is, freedom under social order, is self-determination of the individual by participating in the creation of the social order....

The will of the community, in a democracy, is always created through a running discussion between majority and minority, through free consideration of arguments for and against a certain regulation of a subject matter. This discussion takes place not only in parliament, but also, and foremost, at political meetings, in newspapers, books, and other vehicles of public opinion. A democracy without public opinion is a contradiction in terms.[20]

A democracy must protect the communicative processes by which its citizens work toward an "agreement" that is "uncoerced, and reached by citizens in ways consistent with their being viewed as free and equal persons."[21] Of course, under conditions of modern heterogeneity, actual agreement is impossible, so the notion of agreement functions merely as a "regulative idea" for the formation of public opinion. If we use the term "public discourse" to refer to the communicative processes by which public opinion is formed, we can say that public discourse continuously but unsuccessfully strives to mediate between individual and collective self-determination to produce "a common will, communicatively shaped and discursively clarified in the political public sphere."[22]

In a modern democracy, therefore, citizens are free to engage in public discourse so as to make the state responsive to their ideas and values, in the hope that even if the state acts in ways inconsistent with those ideas and values, citizens can nevertheless maintain their identification with the state. Freedom of speech is thus a necessary condition of democratic legitimacy, but not a sufficient condition. If the state prevents citizens from participating in public discourse when they would otherwise desire to do so, the state loses democratic legitimacy with respect to those citizens, for it prevents them from attempting to make public opinion responsive to their views.

The Danish cartoons of Muhammad that we are considering are plainly part of public discourse.[23] They concern matters of intense public controversy. When Danish author Kåre Bluitgen complained that he could not find an artist brave enough to illustrate his forthcoming children's book about the life of Muhammad, the culture editor of *Jyllands-Posten* decided to test the "fear of violence from Islamic radicals" by inviting members of the Danish Cartoonist Society to depict their interpretations of the Prophet.[24] As Kurt Westergaard, author of the "incendiary but dignified drawing" of Muhammed with a bomb-shaped turban that "has become the metonym for the whole controversy," subsequently explained in an interview: "The cartoon is not directed against Islam as a whole, but against the part of it that obviously can inspire violence, terrorism, death and destruction."[25] Fear of these aspects of Islam is relevant to matters of important public policy, like immigration. If public policy is to be directed by an intelligently informed public opinion, and if citizens are to feel that public policy is potentially responsive to their views, they must be free to express and discuss their perspectives on the matters satirized in the *Jyllands-Posten* cartoons.

II. THE SUPPRESSION OF BLASPHEMY

It follows that if free speech is to serve the value of democratic legitimation, the Danish cartoons ought to be immune from legal censorship. This conclusion, however, is merely the beginning of analysis. We must ask whether there are state interests that might nevertheless justify suppression of the cartoons. In the context of the cartoons, there are three such interests that have been advanced: the suppression of blasphemy, the protection of religious groups, and the prevention of discrimination. I shall discuss each of these in turn.

The state has an interest in suppressing blasphemy insofar as it has an interest in protecting the respect properly due to God.[26] Samuel

Johnson defined blasphemy as "an offering of some indignity unto God himself."[27] English law made blasphemy a crime based upon "the plain principle that the public importance of the Christian religion is so great that no one is allowed to deny its truth."[28] In 1841 the English Commissioners on Criminal Law reported "that the common law of England punishes as an offence any general denial of the truth of Christianity, without reference to the language or temper in which such denial is conveyed."[29]

About the middle of the nineteenth century, British blasphemy law began to evolve. Instead of protecting the respect due to God, it sought to protect the feelings and sensibility of religious groups. In 1883, for example, Lord Coleridge explained that whatever the "old cases" may have said "the mere denial of the truth of Christianity is not enough to constitute the offence of blasphemy."[30] He defined the crime of blasphemous libel instead as the publication of communications "calculated and intended to insult the feelings and the deepest religious convictions of the great majority of the persons amongst whom we live." The point of blasphemy was altered to prevent "outrages to the general feeling of propriety among the persons amongst whom we live."[31] "If the decencies of controversy are observed, even the fundamentals of religion may be attacked without the writer being guilty of blasphemy."[32]

This is essentially the status of the crime of blasphemous libel in Britain today.[33] The crime prohibits "any contemptuous, reviling, scurrilous or ludicrous matter relating to God, Jesus Christ or the Bible," but provides that opinions hostile to Christianity may be expressed in a "decent and moderate" manner.[34] I trace this development in order to emphasize the distinction between a state interest in protecting the respect due to God, and a state interest in protecting the feelings and religious convictions of religious groups. I shall address the former in section II, and the latter in section III.

Even today there exist blasphemy laws that seek to protect the sacred by enforcing the respect due to God. Pakistan, for example, prescribes the death penalty for anyone who "by any imputation, innuendo, or insinuation, directly or indirectly, defiles the sacred name of the Holy Prophet."[35] One teacher at a medical college was prosecuted for speculating that Muhammad's parents might not have been Muslims. Pakistani Christians are particularly vulnerable to legal sanction.

Some who claim that the Danish cartoons ought to be legally suppressed argue that they are blasphemous because they disrespect God or Muhammad, his Prophet. King Abdullah of Jordan, for example, announced that "With all respect to press freedoms, obviously anything that vilifies the Prophet Muhammad, peace be upon him … needs to be condemned."[36] A communiqué from the Organization of the Islamic Conference (OIC), a group comprised of the world's 57 Muslim nations, denounced the "desecration of the image of the Holy Prophet Muhammad in the media."[37] A Hamas legislator proclaimed that "We are angry—very, very, very angry … No one can say a bad word about our prophet."[38]

The question is how a state interest in safeguarding the respect due to God and his prophets can be reconciled with the freedom of speech necessary to serve the function of democratic legitimation. There is an obvious and immediate contradiction between keeping public discourse open to all opinions and excluding from public discourse those who would deny what a particular religion regards as sacred. With respect to those who do not share the religious beliefs protected by a particular blasphemy law, and who are therefore expelled from public discourse, the state is rendered heteronomous. The state loses democratic legitimacy with respect to those who do not believe in the truths protected by a law of blasphemy.

This loss in democratic legitimacy may be acceptable if a state does not aspire democratically to govern those of differing religious beliefs. But most modern states define their jurisdiction in terms of a geographical territory that includes persons of many different beliefs. To the extent democratic legitimacy is important with respect to persons who do not share the beliefs enshrined in a state's blasphemy law, any such loss of democratic legitimacy should be unacceptable.

III. THE PROTECTION OF RELIGIOUS GROUPS

It is no doubt for something like this reason that British blasphemy law evolved in the middle of the nineteenth century, changing from a law designed to protect the sacred into a law designed to protect religious groups. British law was (and is) anomalous, because it protects the religious feelings of only one religious group, Anglicans.[39] But this justification for suppressing speech, if allowed its natural extension, would justify a non-discriminatory prohibition on all speech that offends the religious feelings of any religious group. Many states currently have laws of this kind. Oriana Fallaci, for example, was charged with the crime of blasphemy in Italy because her attacks on Islam "offend a religion acknowledged by the state, by defaming those who profess it."[40]

This form of blasphemy law was considered in 1993 by the European Court of Human Rights in the case of *Otto Preminger Institute v. Austria*. Austrian law imposed criminal penalties on anyone who, through behavior "likely to arouse justified indignation, disparages or insults a person who, or an object which, is an object of veneration of a church or religious community established within the country, or a dogma, a lawful custom or a lawful institution of such church or religious community."[41] Austrian authorities had invoked the statute to justify the seizure of a film, *Liebeskonzil,* that offensively satirized Christian beliefs, portraying "God the Father … both in image and in text as a senile, impotent idiot, Christ as a cretin, and Mary Mother of God as a wanton lady."[42]

In upholding the seizure, the European Court of Human Rights invoked "the right of citizens not to be insulted in their religious feelings by the public expression of views of other persons." It reasoned that "in extreme cases the effect of particular methods of opposing or denying religious beliefs can be such as to inhibit those who hold such beliefs from exercising their freedom to hold and express them," and it accordingly held that "provocative portrayals of objects of religious veneration … can be regarded as malicious violation of the spirit of tolerance, which must also be a feature of democratic society."[43]

The logic of the court was essentially that persons have a right not to be insulted in their religious beliefs, because offense of this kind inhibits the right to practice a religion. Something like this rationale was evident in the controversy over the Danish cartoons. The OIC denounced the cartoons as offending "hundreds of millions of Muslims around the world" and as "meant to disturb and infuriate Muslims." For this reason, OIC argued, the cartoons "could not be considered as an innocent behavior falling within the scope of freedom of expression in which everyone believes."[44] Ayatollah Ali Khamenei condemned the cartoons for "insulting the beliefs of 1.5 billion Muslims."[45] Doudou Diene, the United Nations Special Rapporteur on Contemporary Forms of Racism, Racial Discrimination, Xenophobia and Related Intolerance, urged that the United Nations "treat cases such as the Danish cartoon situation ... as a debate on the balancing of two rights, freedom of expression and freedom of religion."[46] The Rapporteur is reported as stating that "the cartoons are absolutely insulting" and that "beliefs should not be humiliated under the veil of freedom of expression."[47]

If suppressing speech in order to protect the sacred is flatly inconsistent with freedom of speech insofar as it excludes from public discourse those who would dispute the state's conception of the sacred, so suppressing speech in order to protect the sensibility of religious groups is also inconsistent with freedom of speech, because it excludes from public discourse those whose convictions are offensive to religious groups. The European Court of Human Rights offered several arguments for attempting to ameliorate this contradiction.

The first was to claim that a "spirit of tolerance ... must ... be a feature of democratic society."[48] This strategy strikes me as inadequate. The toleration required by democracy refers to action. Democracy demands that we refrain from acting toward each other in ways that are inconsistent with the social order. We must not riot or murder in defense of our beliefs. We must allow others peacefully to practice their beliefs. But democracy does not require toleration in the sense that persons must abandon their independent evaluation of the beliefs and ideas of others.

Democracies encompass groups that dislike and even detest each other, sometimes on religious grounds.[49] To the extent that democracy suppresses my expressions of disapproval or condemnation for the actions of groups that I dislike, it excludes me from the formation of public opinion.

A second strategy adopted by the European Court of Human Rights for minimizing the antidemocratic consequences of suppressing religiously offensive speech was to assert that speech critical of religious beliefs may be suppressed only if it is "gratuitously offensive to others" and thus does "not contribute to any form of public debate capable of furthering progress in human affairs."[50] This argument turns on the distinction between "gratuitous" offense and other forms of offense. We must thus ask when offense is merely "gratuitous" and hence not necessary for public debate.

Consider the example of Dr. Wafa Sultan, a Syrian-American psychiatrist who was raised a Muslim but who has strongly denounced the violence associated with Muslim fundamentalism. She has characterized recent controversies as "a clash between barbarity and rationality." Sultan has since been denounced by Muslim clerics "as an infidel" who has "done Islam more damage than the Danish cartoons mocking the Prophet Muhammad." An Egyptian professor of religious studies charged that "she had blasphemed against Islam, the Prophet Muhammad and the Koran." Sultan "has received numerous death threats."[51]

Sultan's remarks are clearly offensive. But are they gratuitously offensive? They refer to the same issues of violence and sectarianism as do the Danish cartoons. They equally stereotype Muslim attitudes and actions. Sultan's denunciations are probably more offensive than the cartoons because they are more reasoned, comprehensive, and hard-hitting. But should the law regard them as "gratuitous"? To do so would of course turn the law into an instrument for excising any opinion that a religious group might deem offensive. For the reasons I have already discussed, this is not compatible with the use of freedom of speech to establish democratic legitimation.

There is a hint in the European Court of Human Rights decision that the concept of "gratuitous" offense refers to the style of speech rather than to its substance. Speech like Sultan's can offend religious groups and nevertheless receive protection as contributing to public debate if it is sober and rational. But speech that is expressed in an offensive manner, like *Liebeskonzil* (or perhaps the Danish cartoons), is not deemed to contribute to public debate. This is essentially the position of contemporary British blasphemy law, which permits anything to be said, so long as "the decencies of controversy are observed."[52]

Insofar as this is the position of the European Court of Human Rights, it necessarily follows that the Court was incorrect to invoke "the right of citizens not to be insulted in their religious feelings by the public expression of views of other persons." This position assumes that citizens must tolerate insults from speech that is sober and rational, like Sultan's, but that citizens do not have to tolerate insults that flow from a certain style or manner of speech that is condemned as intrinsically offensive.[53] The question is how the law should distinguish between styles of speech that are intrinsically offensive and styles of speech that are inherently protected.[54] If freedom of speech is to serve its function of democratic legitimation, any such distinction must be drawn in such a way as to minimize damage to public debate.

This suggests that the distinction cannot be drawn simply on the basis of the beliefs of discrete religious groups. What any given religious group finds offensive is a matter of contingent history. Before the European religious wars of the seventeenth century, Catholics found deeply offensive the mere existence of Protestants in their community, and vice versa.[55] It would seem that the law cannot transparently apply the beliefs of religious groups without becoming entangled in endless and insoluble contradictions.

More important, the beliefs of particular religious groups may be more or less compatible with the maintenance of the kind of public sphere required for democratic legitimation. One religious group might experience any negative reference to its founding Prophet as intolerably offensive; another might find outrageous and blasphemous any aspersion on the character of its religion or of its followers. As religious groups regard subjects for public discussion and commentary as admissible or inadmissible, the public sphere could shrink in ways that are incompatible with democracy.[56]

The distinction between speech that is consistent with "the decencies of controversy" and speech that is unacceptably offensive, therefore, must be drawn by reference to social norms of dialogue that are endorsed by a democratic state, in part because they are deemed compatible with the function of democratic legitimation. It follows that if a state's interest in the protection of religious groups is to be rendered compatible with freedom of speech, the state must at a minimum distinguish between "gratuitous" and "nongratuitously" offensive speech on the basis of general secular principles that protect all members of society and reflect universally applicable standards of civility. Speech cannot be suppressed merely because it is inconsistent with the religious principles of particular sects.

It does not follow that a democratic state cannot discipline public discourse by enforcing basic norms of civility. European states typically possess laws that prohibit outrageous, indecent, or offensive forms of speech that violate social norms and thereby convey insult, infringe upon honor, or violate dignity. It is clear, however, that although such laws *purport* to enforce civility norms that are universally shared, they *in fact* express the mores of dominant groups. During debates 76 years ago in the British Parliament about the revision of blasphemy law, for example, it was well recognized that "what it really comes to is that, where opinions are strongly held by an educated man, those opinions will be expressed in a way which the law cannot touch, while those expressed by an uneducated man, simply because he is uneducated, will come under the penalties of the law."[57]

American law differs in this regard. In America, by contrast, the First Amendment is interpreted to create a "marketplace of communities" as well as a marketplace of ideas.[58] The First Amendment thus precludes the state from imposing the norms of any one particular community onto the common space of public discourse, which is the arena in which all communities must compete for the allegiance of public opinion. Respect for the equality of diverse communities underlies the American constitutional conclusion that civility norms, which always reflect the view of some particular community, may not be used to regulate speech within public discourse.[59] As a consequence, the First Amendment regards "one man's vulgarity" as "another's lyric."[60]

European states, by contrast, are more normatively hegemonic than America, and are therefore more comfortable enforcing civility norms that distinguish permissible from impressible speech. Hate speech is commonly regulated in Europe. The suppression of speech that is deeply offensive to religious groups is sociologically and theoretically analogous to the suppression of speech that is deeply offensive to racial groups. But whereas in the latter context it is plain that law must ultimately define the boundaries of permissible speech on the basis of civility norms that a secular state is prepared to endorse as its own, in the context of blasphemy there is the suggestion that these norms might be established simply by religious values. This is untenable, for the reasons I have suggested, and as a consequence the European Court of Human Rights was incorrect to uphold the censorship of *Liebeskonzil* on the ground that the "unwarranted and offensive" nature of the film was to be determined merely by reference to the "religious beliefs" of "the overwhelming majority of Tyroleans," who were Roman Catholic.[61]

This conclusion, of course, rests on the priority of using freedom of speech to maintain democratic legitimacy. The conclusion does not follow if a state does not especially prize such legitimacy, or if it believes that the need "to ensure religious peace"[62] trumps in particular circumstances the necessity of democratic legitimation, or if a state's population overwhelmingly shares religious norms so that the state is indifferent to losing democratic legitimacy among religious minorities.

IV. THE PREVENTION OF DISCRIMINATION

A third theme that emerges from the controversy surrounding the Danish cartoons does not concern the protection of religion or religious sensibilities, but instead focuses on the prevention of discrimi-

nation.[63] This theme is explicit in Doudou Diene's response to the cartoons. The UN Special Rapporteur linked the publication of the cartoons to "the development of Islamophobia" and to racial discrimination. He asserted that the cartoons "illustrated the increasing emergence of the racist and xenophobic currents in everyday life."[64] Those who condemned the cartoons argued that they were "a new sign of Europe's growing 'Islamophobia' " because they reinforced "a dangerous confusion between Islam and Islamist terrorism."[65] Civil rights lawyers in Denmark argued that there ought to be "a balance here between freedom of speech and the right not to be subjected to racial discrimination."[66]

States have a significant interest in prohibiting and preventing discrimination against Muslims. This objective is distinct from the interest in prohibiting and preventing speech that Muslims find offensive. Prohibiting discrimination means, in the first instance, forbidding conduct that discriminates. Preventing discrimination, however, might also mean altering the social conditions that cause discrimination. Among these conditions are a fear and dislike of Muslims, which is now captured by the term "Islamophobia." It is not implausible to conclude that speech that promotes Islamophobia is causally connected to discrimination. The nature and strength of this causal connection is a question of contingent, historical fact.

In America the First Amendment would prevent the state from prohibiting speech for this reason. Content-based restrictions on speech cannot be imposed on the ground that the speech might cause a future harm unless the speech "is directed to inciting or producing imminent lawless action and is likely to incite or produce such action."[67] This severe restriction is deemed necessary because a more lax causal connection would invite the government to use the pretext of a causal connection in order to prohibit speech. Classic historical examples of this abuse were statutes prohibiting the advocacy of Communist doctrine on the ground that such speech might cause a future revolution.

European states have on the whole allowed speech to be prohibited on the basis of far looser causal connections between speech and potential future harms. This may be because the legitimacy of European states is typically far more secure than that of the American state, which is constantly battling a deep libertarian streak in the American character. In America it is uniformly said that the "people" are sovereign; in Europe it is more common to say that the "nation" or the "republic" is sovereign. The consequence is that in the United States, as distinct from Europe, the government is continuously deprecated as at the sufferance of the people. The demand for democratic legitimation in the United States is consequently more persistent and insistent than in Europe, and so restrictions on public discourse are correspondingly more disfavored.

Nevertheless, even in Europe the European Court of Human Rights has held that there are some restrictions on the capacity of member states to prohibit offensive racist remarks,[68] although there might be some connection between such remarks and subsequent racial discrimination. National courts in Europe typically impose a requirement of proportionality on such regulation, which means that states must show that the harm of discrimination cannot be ameliorated by means other than the suppression of protected speech. Such alternative means might include educational initiatives about the nature of Islam, affirmative efforts to insure that Muslims receive adequate access to jobs, housing, health care, and food, the regulation of offensive speech that is *not* public discourse (such as speech in the workplace or in schools), and so on.

Assuming that these conditions are satisfied, there still remains the question of the kind of speech that a state might properly prohibit in the interest of preventing racial discrimination, and whether the Danish cartoons would qualify for proscription. Some of the cartoons do invoke stereotypic criticisms of Islam. They comment on Islamic repression of women; on the use of Islamic fundamentalist doctrines to foster violence; on the fear of violent reprisal for publishing criticisms of Islam.[69] These are ideas that have been and will be used by those who would discriminate against Muslims.

But they are also ideas about real and pressing public issues. The relationship between Islam and gender is a lively and controversial question.

Fundamentalist Islamic violence is a public worry throughout Europe. Fear of reprisal for crossing Islamic taboos is omnipresent, as can be seen in the recent contretemps about a German production of Mozart's opera *Idomeneo*.[70] To cut off all public discussion of real and pressing public issues would be unthinkable. And if such issues are to be discussed, the expression of all relevant views must be protected.

How to draw the line between protected expression and speech that can be suppressed because it is likely to cause discrimination is thus a difficult and complex issue. The most obvious way to make this distinction would be to rely on the traditional difference between hate speech and ordinary expression, a difference that is incorporated into the positive law of many countries, like France and Germany.[71] French author Michel Houellebecq, for example, was recently charged with violating France's Pleven Law, which prohibits words that "provoke discrimination, hatred or violence against a person or group of people" on account of ethnicity, nationality, race, or religion. Houellebecq had called the Koran "mediocre" and had asserted that "The dumbest religion, after all, is Islam." He was acquitted on the ground that his comments "constituted mere criticism of Islamic doctrine."[72]

Measured by this standard, the Danish cartoons seem to me rather far from legally prohibited hate speech. They take a position on issues of obvious public moment, but they do not advocate discrimination or oppression or violence; they do not threaten; they do not use racist epithets or names; they do not attack individuals; they do not perpetuate an obvious untruth; they do not portray Muslims as without human dignity. They may exacerbate stereotypes and exaggerations, but that is not the same as hate speech. That is simply the nature of most ideas.

I am grateful for the unflagging assistance of Abha Khanna. The original version of this paper was first presented at the fourteenth annual conference on "The Individual vs. the State" at the Central European University in 2006, and is intended for publication in a forthcoming volume edited by András Sajó, tentatively *entitled Free Speech and Religion: The Eternal Conflict in the Age of Selective Modernization.*

NOTES

1. The cartoons, along with much useful information about the controversy, can be seen at http://www.zombietime.com/mohammed_image_archive/jyllands-posten_cartoons/.

2. The cartoons are certainly a good deal less vicious and racist than the anti-Semitic cartoons that routinely appear in the Arab press, see, e.g., "Major Anti-Semitic Motifs in Arab Cartoons." *Jerusalem Center for Public Affairs.* Web. 1 June 2004. http://www.jcpa.org/phas/phas-21.htm; "Cartoons From the Arab World." *Tom Gross—Mideast Media Analysis.* Web. http://www.tomgrossmedia.com/ArabCartoons.htm, or the anti-Semitic, anti-Holocaust cartoons recently solicited by Iran. See *Iran Cartoon.* Web. http://www.irancartoon.com/. Not to be outdone, the Israeli-based Dimona Comix has announced its own anti-Semitic cartoon context. See *The Drawn Blog.* Web. http://drawn.ca/2006/02/14/israeli-anti-semitic-cartoon-contest/, proclaiming that "We'll show the world we can do the best, sharpest, most offensive Jew hating cartoons ever published! No Iranian will beat us on our home turf!"

3. See *Cartoonbodycount.com.* Web. http://www.cartoonbodycount.com/.

4. Smith, Craig and Fisher, Ian. "Temperatures Rise over Cartoons Mocking Muhammad." *New York Times* 3 Feb. 2006. A3.

5. "Silenced by Islamist Rage." *New York Times* 25 Feb. 2006. A14. It is clear that the riots have also been fomented in part by secular anti-western Arab governments, like Syria, and by Islamic extremists seeking to discredit moderate Arab governments. In an astute discussion of the cartoons, which includes their only reproduction in the American print media, cartoonist Art Spiegelman observed that "the most baffling aspect of this whole affair is why all the violent demonstrations focused on the dopey cartoons rather than on the truly horrifying torture photos seen regularly on Al Jazeera, on European television, everywhere but in the mainstream media of the United States. Maybe it's because those photos of actual violation don't have the magical aura of things unseen, like the damn cartoons." Spiegelman. "Drawing Blood: Outrageous Cartoons and the Art of Courage." *Harper's* June 2006: 47. Spiegelman noted that "none of the millions of protesters saw any of the images. It was enough to be told

that insult was intended. The *Jyllands-Posten* could have saved the $129 it paid to each of its twelve cartoonists and simply printed a front-page headline in 64-point type that shouted 'Yo' Prophet Wears Army Boots!' " (46).

6. Quoted in Cowell, Alan. "Cartoons Force Danish Muslims to Examine Loyalties." *New York Times,* 4 Feb. 2006. A3.

7. *Cantwell v. Connecticut,* 310 U.S. 296, 310 (1940).

8. Kalven, H. *A Worthy Tradition: Freedom of Speech in America.* New York: Harper & Row, 1988. 7 (emphasis in original).

9. For a good summary of the major positions, see Schauer, Frederick. *Free Speech: A Philosophical Enquiry.* Cambridge: Cambridge University Press, 1982.

10. Bobbio, Norberto. *Democracy and Dictatorship: The Nature and Limits of State Power.* Tran. Peter Kennealy. Cambridge: Polity, 1989. 137.

11. Schauer, *Free Speech,* supra, note 9, at 40–41.

12. On democracy as a substantive value, see Michelman, Frank. *Brennan and Democracy.* Princeton: Princeton University Press, 1999.

13. See, e.g., Meiklejohn, Alexander. *Political Freedom: The Constitutional Powers of the People.* New York: Harper & Bros., 1948.

14. The concept of a "warranted conviction" is meant to signify that a subjective conviction of self-government is not a determinative and preclusive condition for the realization of democratic values. The conviction must withstand scrutiny, which means that it must always be open to third parties to attempt to convince a citizen that his or her experience of self-government is delusory.

15. Fiss, Owen. *Liberalism Divided: Freedom of Speech and the Many Uses of State Power.* Boulder: Westview, 1996. 37–38.

16. Rousseau, Jean-Jacques. *The Social Contract.* Tran. Maurice Cranston. Harmondsworth: Penguin, 1968. 58–62. Ironically, Rousseau seemingly contemplated that the general will would be formed through just such an alienated process as I have sketched. "From the deliberations of a people properly informed, and provided its members do not have any communication among themselves, the great number of small differences will always produce a general will and the decision will always be good." Id., at 73. This suggests that Rousseau may have had a finer grasp of the analytic prerequisites of democracy than of

the sociological dynamics necessary for its realization.

17. For a full explication of this argument, see Post, Robert. "Meiklejohn's Mistake: Individual Autonomy and the Reform of Public Discourse." *University of Colorado Law Review* 64 (1993).

18. I have elsewhere argued that "[t]he essential problematic of democracy ... lies in the reconciliation of individual and collective autonomy." Post. *Constitutional Domains: Democracy, Community, Management.* Cambridge: Harvard University Press, 1995. 7. For a full discussion, see Post. "Between Democracy and Community: The Legal Constitution of Social Form." *Democratic Community: Nomos XXXV.* Eds. John W. Chapman and Ian Shapiro. New York: NYU Press, 1993. 178–79.

19. *Brown v. Hartlage,* 456 U.S. 45, 60 (1982).

20. Kelsen, Hans. *General Theory of Law and State.* Tran. Anders Wedberg. New York: Russell & Russell, 1961. 285–88.

21. Rawls, John. "Justice as Fairness: Political Not Metaphysical." *Philosophy and Public Affairs* 14 (1985): 229–30.

22. Habermas, Jürgen. *The Theory of Communicative Action.* Tran. Thomas McCarthy. Cambridge, MA: MIT Press, 1987. 81.

23. Exactly how to draw the boundaries of public discourse is a complex and complicated matter. For a discussion, see Post, Robert. "The Constitutional Concept of Public Discourse: Outrageous Opinion, Democratic Deliberation, and *Hustler Magazine v. Falwell.*" *Harvard Law Review* 103 (1990): 667–84.

24. Smith, Craig. "Adding Newsprint to the Fire." *New York Times* 5 Feb. 2006. 5. A *New York Times* columnist has characterized the "callous and feeble cartoons" published by *Jyllands-Posten* as "cooked up as a provocation by a conservative newspaper exploiting the general Muslim prohibition on images of the Prophet Muhammad to score cheap points about freedom of expression." Kimmelman, Michael. "A Startling New Lesson in the Power of Imagery." *New York Times* 8 Feb. 2006. E1.

25. Quoted in Spiegelman, "Drawing Blood," supra, note 5, at 48. Spiegelman shrewdly observes of this cartoon that "the irate artist successfully discharged himself of the political cartoonist's duty to bring matters to a head. If the drawing had simply not appeared under the rubric of 'Muhammad's Face,' it would have been more immedi-

ately seen to specifically represent the murderous aspect of fundamentalism, the one that ... made this drawing a self-fulfilling prophecy" (48–49).

26. For a discussion, see Post, Robert. "Cultural Heterogeneity and Law: Pornography, Blasphemy, and the First Amendment." *California Law Review* 76 (1988). In England, blasphemy was a common law crime. It was one of the four branches of criminal libel, the other three being obscenity, sedition, and defamation. See Spencer, J.R. "Criminal Libel – A Skeleton in the Cupboard." *Criminal Law Review* (1977). All four branches of libel sought to ensure that speech did not violate established norms of respect and propriety. The particular province of blasphemy was to prevent disrespect toward God, which according to Blackstone could be manifested "by denying his being or providence; or by contumelious reproaches of our Saviour Christ." Blackstone, William. *Commentaries.* Vol. 4:59. 1769.

27. Johnson, Samuel. *A Dictionary of the English Language.* 1756. Benjamin Norton Defoe defined blasphemy as "vile or opprobrious Language, tending to the Dishonour of God." Defoe, *A Compleat English Dictionary.* 1735.

28. Stephen, James Fitzjames. *A History of the Criminal Law of England.* Vol. 2: 475. 1883. The English law of blasphemy was successfully used to prosecute individuals for publishing such works as Thomas Paine's *Age of Reason* (471–73), *Rex v. Williams, Howell's St. Tr.* 26 (K.B. 1797): 653; *Rex v. Carlile (Richard), St. Tr. N.S.* 1 (1819): 1387; Shelley's poem 'Queen Mab,' *Regina v. Moxon, St. Tr. N.S. 4* (1841): 693; and the popular Discourses of an early Deist, a minister and Fellow of Sydney Sussex College at Cambridge, which urged that the miracles reported in the New Testament be interpreted allegorically, rather than literally. *See Rex v. Woolston, Eng. Rep.* 94: 112, *Barn. K.B.* 1 (1729): 162.

29. Commissioners on Criminal Law, *Sixth Report* (1841), 83.

30. *Regina v. Ramsay and Foote, Cox C.C.* 15 (1883): 231, 236.

31. *Regina v. Bradlaugh, Cox C.C.* 15 (1883): 217, 230, 231.

32. *Ramsay and Foote,* supra, note 30, at 238.

33. *Regina v. Lemon,* 1979 App. Cas. 617.

34. *Wingrove v. United Kingdom,* Eur. Comm'n H. R. Dec. & Rep. 24 (1996): 1, 7.

35. For a discussion, see Arzt, Donna E. "Heroes or Heretics: Religious Dissidents under Islamic

Law." *Wisconsin International Law Journal* 14 (1996).

36. Sanger, David E. "Bush Urges Nations to End Violence; Rice Accuses Syria and Iran." *New York Times* 9 Feb. 2006. A14.

37. Fattah, Hassan M. "At Mecca Meeting, Cartoon Outrage Crystallized." *New York Times* 9 Feb. 2006. A1.

38. Smith, Craig S. and Fisher, Ian. "Temperatures Rise Over Cartoons Mocking Muhammad." *New York Times* 3 Feb. 2006. A3.

39. *R. v. Chief Metropolitan stipendiary Magistrate ex parte Choudhury,* W.L.R. 3 (1990): 986; Chase, Anthony. "Legal Guardians: Islamic Law, International Law, Human Rights Law, and the Salman Rushdie Affair." *American University Journal of International Law and Policy* 11 (1996): 419–20. On February 16, 2006, Britain enacted the Racial and Religious Hatred Act of 2006, which provides that "A person who uses threatening words or behaviour, or displays any written material which is threatening, is guilty of an offence if he intends thereby to stir up religious hatred" (§29B). The Act defines "religious hatred" to mean "hatred against a group of persons defined by reference to religious belief or lack of religious belief (§29A). The Act thus prohibits threats that stir up religious hatred against any religious group, not merely Anglicans.

40. Talbot, Margaret. "The Agitator: Oriana Fallaci Directs Her Fury Against Islam." *The New Yorker* 5 June 2006. 61.

41. *Otto Preminger Institut v. Austria,* Eur. Comm'n H.R. Dec. & Rep. 19 (1994): §25; citing §188 of the Austrian Penal Code.

42. Id., at §16; quoting the judgment of the Austrian Regional Court.

43. Id., at §48, 47, 47. In a subsequent decision, the European Court of Human Rights upheld British censorship of a film showing a Catholic saint in a state of sexual ecstasy. *Wingrove v. United Kingdom,* Eur. Comm'n H.R. Dec. & Rep. 24 (1996): 7. The Court's reasoning, however, was far less substantive than in *Otto Preminger Institut.* The Court turned its decision on the conclusion that "a wider margin of appreciation is generally available to the Contracting States when regulating freedom of expression in relation to matters liable to offend intimate personal convictions within the sphere of morals or, especially, religion" (§58):

Moreover, as in the field of morals, and perhaps to an even greater degree, there is no uniform European conception of the requirements of "the protection of the rights of others" in relation to attacks on their religious convictions. What is likely to cause substantial offence to persons of a particular religious persuasion will vary significantly from time to time and from place to place, especially in an era characterised by an ever-growing array of faiths and denominations. By reason of their direct and continuous contact with the vital forces of their countries, State authorities are in principle in a better position than the international judge to give an opinion on the exact content of these requirements with regard to the rights of others as well as on the "necessity" of a "restriction" intended to protect from such material those whose deepest feelings and convictions would be seriously offended.

But see *Affaire Giniewski c. France,* Judgment of January 31, 2006.

44. Goodenough, Patrick. "Growing Anger over Mohammed Cartoons." *CNS News* 3 Jan. 2006. Web.

45. Quoted in Fathi, Nazila. "Contest for Cartoons Mocking the Holocaust Announced in Tehran." *New York Times* 8 Feb. 2006. A10. Dr. Abdulaziz Othman Altwaijri, Director General of the Islamic Educational, Scientific, and Cultural Organization, called for "enacting an international law incriminating offences to religions and prophets" because of the need "to reinforce tolerance among the followers of the divine religions, the aim being to remove the causes that lead to hatred and discrimination and contribute to stirring up conflicts among civilizations and cultures." "At the Congress of Imams and Rabbis in Seville, ISESCO Director General calls for: Abidance by a pact of honour among the followers of the divine religions." *Saudi Press Agency.* Web. 20 Feb. 2006. http://www.sauress.com/en/spaen/ 347291. Two months previously Altwaijri had called upon the Danish Center for Culture and Development "to protest in the manner you deem appropriate against this newspaper as well as against every other information means in your country that damages the image of Islam and Muslims, following in that the policy of tolerance that rejects the contempt of religions and the

profanation of religious sanctities in which believe a billion and a third people on this earth."

46. Press Release, "Special Rapporteur on Racism tells Committee that Racism and Racial Discrimination Are on the Upswing." *United Nations.* Web. 7 Mar. 2006. http://www.unhchr.ch/huricane/huricane.nsf/view01/5F30A01100D70D67C125 712A006FBE18?opendocument.

47. Quoted in Cucuk, Hasan. "UN: Denmark Acted Irresponsibly in Cartoon Crisis." *Zaman Online.* Web. 19 Mar. 2006. http://www.zaman.com/?bl=international&alt=&trh=20060319&hn=31079. This Turkish paper quotes Diene to the effect that the "defense that freedom of speech is limitless contradicts international rules. There is a great need to establish a balance between freedom of speech and freedom of faith. This publication explicitly shows a lack of understanding and emotion for believers. The newspaper also helped Islam and terror to be likened." See also "The Volokh Conspiracy, Another U.N. Official Demanding Speech restrictions, and faulting Denmark for Protecting Speech Too Much." *The Eugene Volokh Blog.* Web. 21 March 2006. http://volokh.com/posts/1142989233.shtml.

48. *Otto Preminger Institut,* supra, note 41, at §47. Recently the Court attempted to explained this principle of tolerance as requiring the Court in prosecutions for blasphemy to weigh "the conflicting interests of the exercise of two fundamental freedoms, namely the right of the applicant to impart to the public his views on religious doctrine, on the one hand, and the right of others to respect for their freedom of thought, conscience and religion, on the other hand" (§55). Case of *İ.A v. Turkey,* 13 September 2005, §27. In *İ.A.* the Court upheld the blasphemy conviction of a novelist for publishing a novel that contained this paragraph: "Look at the triangle of fear, inequality and inconsistency in the Koran; it reminds me of an earthworm. God says that all the words are those of his messenger. Some of these words, moreover, were inspired in a surge of exultation, in Aisha's arms.... God's messenger broke his fast through sexual intercourse, after dinner and before prayer. Muhammad did not forbid sexual relations with a dead person or a live animal" (§13).

49. The European Court of Human Rights implicitly recognized this principle in *Kokkinakis v. Greece,* Judgment of 19 April 1993, which struck down a Greek law prohibiting proselytism, by which was "meant, in particular, any direct or indirect attempt to intrude on the religious beliefs of a person of a different religious persuasion *(eterodoxos),* with the aim of undermining those beliefs, either by any kind of inducement or promise of an inducement or moral support or material assistance, or by fraudulent means or by taking advantage of his inexperience, trust, need, low intellect or naivety" (§16). The European Court of Human Rights held that "a distinction has to be made between bearing Christian witness and improper proselytism. The former corresponds to true evangelism, which a report drawn up in 1956 under the auspices of the World Council of Churches describes as an essential mission and a responsibility of every Christian and every Church. The latter represents a corruption or deformation of it. It may, according to the same report, take the form of activities offering material or social advantages with a view to gaining new members for a Church or exerting improper pressure on people in distress or in need; it may even entail the use of violence or brainwashing; more generally, it is not compatible with respect for the freedom of thought, conscience and religion of others" (§48).

50. *Otto-Preminger Institut,* supra, note 41, at §49. In *İ.A v. Turkey,* the Court explained that freedom of speech "carries with it duties and responsibilities. Amongst them, in the context of religious beliefs, may legitimately be included a duty to avoid expressions that are gratuitously offensive to others and profane (see, for example, *Otto-Preminger-Institut v. Austria,* judgment of 20 September 1994, Series A no. 295-A, pp. 18–19, § 49, *and Murphy v. Ireland,* no. 44179/98, § 67, ECHR 2003-IX). This being so, as a matter of principle it may be considered necessary to punish improper attacks on objects of religious veneration (ibid.)" (§24). See also *Case of Murphy v. Ireland,* March 12, 2003, ¶65.

51. "We have not seen a single Jew blow himself up in a German restaurant. We have not seen a single Jew destroy a church. We have not seen a single Jew protest by killing people.... Only Muslims defend their beliefs by burning down churches, killing people and destroying embassies. This path will not yield any results." Quoted in Broder, John M. "For Muslim Who Says Violence Destroys Islam, Violent Threats." *New York Times* 11 Mar. 2006. A1. Sultan continued, "The clash we are witnessing around the world is

not a clash of religions or a clash of civilizations. ... It is a clash between a mentality that belongs to the Middle Ages and another mentality that belongs to the 21st century. It is a clash between civilization and backwardness, between the civilized and primitive, between barbarity and rationality."

52. The British distinction between style and substance is meant to maintain the openness of public debate. See, e.g., Jones, "Blasphemy, Offensiveness and Law." *British Journal of Political Science* 10 (1980): 142–43:

> The intention behind the distinction is plain. Granted that it is possible to distinguish manner from matter, a law restricting only forms of expression need not prevent the assertion of any substantive point of view. The usual conflict between freedom of opinion and prevention of offense is therefore largely avoided.... The failing of the matter-manner distinction is that it supposes that statements are capable of more or less offensive formulations which are nevertheless identical in meaning. The manner of an assertion is treated as though it were so much verbal wrapping paper whose features had no bearing upon the content of the parcel. In certain cases this assumption may not be unjustified.... More often, however, manner and matter are so integrally related that it is impossible to distinguish the offensive manner from the offensive matter of a statement.

Even the European Court of Human Rights has recognized the ultimate difficulty in any effort to enforce a hard distinction between the style and substance of speech. See, e.g., *Jersild v. Denmark,* Eur. Comm'n H.R. Dec. & Rep. 19 (1994): §31: "The Court recalls that Article 10 protects not only the substance of the ideas and information expressed, but also the form in which they are conveyed."

53. In *Case of İ.A v. Turkey,* the Court upheld a blasphemy prosecution because "the present case concerns not only comments that offend or shock, or a 'provocative' opinion, but also an abusive attack on the Prophet of Islam. Notwithstanding the fact that there is a certain tolerance of criticism of religious doctrine within Turkish society, which is deeply attached to the principle of secularity, believers may legitimately feel themselves to be the object of unwarranted and offensive attacks through the following passages: 'Some of these

words were, moreover, inspired in a surge of exultation, in Aisha's arms.... God's messenger broke his fast through sexual intercourse, after dinner and before prayer. Muhammad did not forbid sexual intercourse with a dead person or a live animal' " (§29).

54. In England in the nineteenth century, Lord Denman sought to draw this distinction in this way:

> [U]pon the question whether it is blasphemous or not I [make] this general observation ... namely, that the question is not altogether a matter of opinion, but that it must be, in a great degree, a question as to the tone, and style, and spirit, in which such inquiries are conducted. Because, a difference of opinion may subsist, not only between different sects of Christians, but also with regard to the great doctrines of Christianity itself; and ... even discussions upon that subject may be by no means a matter of criminal prosecution, but, if they be carried on in a sober and temperate and decent style, even those discussions may be tolerated, and may take place without criminality attaching to them; but that, if the tone and spirit is that of offence, and insult, and ridicule, which leaves the judgment really not free to act, and, therefore, cannot be truly called an appeal to the judgment, but an appeal to the wild and improper feelings of the human mind, more particularly in the younger part of the community, in that case the jury will hardly feel it possible to say that such opinions, so expressed, do not deserve the character [of blasphemy] affixed to them in this indictment.

Regina v. Hetherington, St. Tr. N.S. 4 (1841): 590–91.

55. Consider, for example, Oliver Cromwell's famous directive regarding religious liberty to the Catholics in Ireland: "As to freedom of conscience, I meddle with no man's conscience; but if you mean by that, liberty to celebrate the Mass, I would have you understand that in no place where the power of the Parliament of England prevails shall that be permitted." Quoted in *McDaniel v. Paty,* 435 U.S. 618, 631 n.2 (1978) (J. Brennan. concurring).

56. As an historical matter, toleration in the Christian West only began "when the advocates of competing religious orthodoxies failed to impose their doctrines and standards on the population at

large," so "that they began to accept, reluctantly at first, an ideology which legitimated the reality created by their own failures." Steve Bruce, *A House Divided: Protestantism, Schism, and Secularization* (London: Routledge, 1990), 99–100. It has thus been said that "Religion, any religion, is the enemy of liberal democracy as long as it has not been defanged and privatized. Religion, any religion, is quite explicitly about election and exclusion." Beit-Hallahmi, Benjamin. "The Return of Martyrdom: Honour, Death and Immortality." *Religious Fundamentalism and Political Extremism.* Eds. Leonard Weinberg and Ami Pedahzur. London: Frank Cass, 2004. 32.

57. *Parl. Deb.,H.C.* (5th Ser.) 234 (1930): 535 (remarks of Mr. Kingsley Griffith); see also 499:

> We have writers today who can commit the offence of blasphemy with impunity, if the offence of blasphemy is an attack on the Christian religion. There are men like Sir Arthur Keith, Mr. H. G. Wells, Mr. Bertrand Russell, Mr. Aldous Huxley and others who are able to attack the Christian religion without any danger whatever of their being prosecuted, while poor men, expressing the same point of view more bluntly and crudely, expose themselves to fine and imprisonment. That is a thoroughly unsatisfactory state of the law. After all, if one concedes the right to attack religion … one has to concede to the people who care to do this thing the right to choose their style of doing it. Different styles are needed for different circumstances and different audiences. I do not suppose the kind of style that would go down in a select circle in the West End would be effective amongst the democracy of the East End.

(Remarks of Mr. Thurtle); see also 558 (remarks of Mr. Lansbury).

58. Post, "The Constitutional Concept of Public Discourse," supra, note 23, at 634–35.

59. See Post, Robert. "Community and the First Amendment." *Arizona State Law Journal* 29 (1997).

60. *Cohen v. California,* 403 U.S. 15, 25 (1971).

61. *Otto-Preminger Institut,* supra, note 41, at §56; see also §52. The conclusion in text must have formed the basic premise of the reasoning of the European Court of Human Rights's own judg-

ment in *Kokkinakis v. Greece,* on the not implausible assumption that the Greek Orthodox Church, which is the "the dominant religion in Greece" (quoting the Greek Constitution of 1975), found the proselytism protected by the Court to be "morally reprehensible." *Kokkinakis,* §17; quoting the judgment of the Supreme Administrative Court of Greece in *Symvoulio tis Epikratias.*

62. Id., at §56.

63. See, e.g., Teitel, Ruti. "No Laughing Matter: The Controversial Danish Cartoons Depicting the Prophet Mohammed, and Their Broader Meaning for Europe's Public Square." *Findlaw.* Web. 15 Feb. 2006. http://writ.news.findlaw.com/commentary/20060215_teitel.html.

64. "Special Rapporteur on Racism tells Committee that Racism and Racial Discrimination Are on the Upswing," supra, note 46.

65. Smith, Craig S. and Fisher, Ian. "Temperatures Rise Over Cartoons Mocking Muhammad." *New York Times.* 3 Feb. 2006. A3.

66. Cowell, Alan. "More European Papers Print Cartoons of Muhammad, Fueling Dispute with Muslims." *New York Times* 2 Feb. 2006. A12.

67. *Brandenburg v. Ohio,* 395 U.S. 444, 447 (1969) (per curiam).

68. *Jersild v. Denmark,* Eur. Comm'n H.R. Dec. & Rep. 19 (1994).

69. One cartoon shows Muhammad with a slit covering his eyes in front of two women who are covered everywhere by a veil except for a slit over their eyes; another shows Muhammad with a turban in the shape of a bomb; a third shows the cartoonist frightened at the thought of drawing a portrait of Muhammad.

70. See Dempsey, Judy and Landler, Mark. "Opera Canceled Over a Depiction of Muhammad." *New York Times* 27 Sept. 2006. A1:

> A leading German opera house has canceled performances of a Mozart opera because of security fears stirred by a scene that depicts the severed head of the Prophet Muhammad, prompting a storm of protest here about what many see as the surrender of artistic freedom. The Deutsche Oper Berlin said Tuesday that it had pulled "Idomeneo" from its fall schedule after the police warned of an "incalculable risk" to the performers and the audience … Political and cultural figures throughout Germany

condemned the cancellation. Some said it re-called the decision of European newspapers not to reprint satirical cartoons about Muhammad, after their publication in Denmark generated a furor among Muslims.

The Deutsche Oper Berlin has since rescheduled the opera.

71. For a discussion, see Rosenfeld, Michel. "Hate Speech in Constitutional Jurisprudence: A Com-

parative Analysis." *Cardozo Law Review* 24 (2003).

72. See Vance, Susannah C. "The Permissibility of Incitement to Religious Hatred Offenses under European Convention Principles." *Transnational Law and Contemporary Problems* 14 (2004): 202–03. Houellebecq quoted in Rimensnyder, Sara. "Sins of the Author: Hate and Free Speech." *Reason Foundation. reason.com.* Web. Dec. 2002. http://reason.com/0212/ci.sr.sins.shtml.

41   Freedom of Expression and Categories of Expression

T.M. SCANLON, JR.

I. INTRODUCTION

Freedom of expression, as a philosophical problem, is an instance of a more general problem about the nature and status of rights. Rights purport to place limits on what individuals or the state may do, and the sacrifices they entail are in some cases significant. Thus, for example, freedom of expression becomes controversial when expression appears to threaten important individual interests in a case like the Skokie affair, or to threaten some important national interest such as the ability to raise an army. The general problem is, if rights place limits on what can be done even for good reasons, what is the justification for these limits?

A second philosophical problem is how we decide what these limits are. Rights appear to be something we can reason about, and this reasoning process does not appear to be merely a calculation of consequences. In many cases, we seem to decide whether a given policy infringes freedom of expression simply by consulting our conception of what this right entails. And although there are areas of controversy, there is a wide range of cases in which we all seem to arrive at the same answer. But I doubt that any of us could write out a brief, noncircular definition of freedom of expression whose mechanical application to these clear cases

would yield the answers on which we all agree. In what, then, does our agreement consist?

My aim in this paper is to present an account of freedom of expression that provides at least a few answers to these general questions. I will also address a more specific question about freedom of expression itself. What importance should a theory of freedom of expression assign to categories of expression such as political speech, commercial speech, libel and pornography? These categories appear to play an important role in informal thought about the subject. It seems central to the controversy about the Skokie case, for example, that the proposed ordinance threatened the ability of unpopular *political* groups to hold demonstrations.[1] I doubt whether the residents of Skokie would have been asked to pay such a high price to let some other kind of expression proceed. To take a different example, laws against false or deceptive advertising and the ban on cigarette advertising on television suggest that we are willing to accept legal regulation of the form and content of commercial advertising that we would not countenance if it were applied to other forms of expression. Why should this be so?

While I do not accept all of these judgments, I find it hard to resist the idea that different categories of expression should to some degree be

---

From the University of Pittsburgh Law Review, Vol. 40 (1978–79): 519–550. Reprinted with permission of the publisher.

treated differently in a theory of freedom of expression. On the other hand some ideas of freedom of expression seem to apply across the board, regardless of category: intervention by government to stop the publication of what it regards as a false or misleading view seems contrary to freedom of expression whether the view concerns politics, religion, sex, health, or the relative desirability of two kinds of automobile. So the question is, to what extent are there general principles of freedom of expression, and to what extent is freedom of expression category-dependent? To the degree that the latter is true, how are the relevant categories defined?

I will begin by considering the individual interests that are the basis of our special concern with expression. In section three I will consider how several theories of freedom of expression have been based on certain of these interests, and I will sketch an answer to the first two questions raised above. Finally, in sections four and five, I will discuss the place of categories of expression within the framework I have proposed and apply this to the particular categories of political speech, commercial speech and pornography.

II. INTERESTS

What are the interests with which freedom of expression is concerned? It will be useful to separate these roughly into those interests we have in being able to speak, those interests we have in being exposed to what others have to say, and those interests we have as bystanders who are affected by expression in other ways. Since, however, I want to make it clear that "expression" as I am using it is not limited to speech, I will refer to these three groups of interests as the interests of participants, the interests of audiences, and the interests of bystanders.

A. Participant Interests

The actions to which freedom of expression applies are actions that aim to bring something to the attention of a wide audience. This intended audience need not be the widest possible audience ("the public at large"), but it must be more than

one or two people. Private conversations are not, in general, a matter of freedom of expression, not because they are unimportant to us, but because their protection is not the aim of this particular doctrine. (It is a matter, instead, of privacy or of personal liberty of some other sort.) But private conversations might be viewed differently if circumstances were different. For example, if telephone trees (or whispering networks) were an important way of spreading the word because we lacked newspapers and there was no way for us to gather to hear speeches, then legal restrictions on personal conversations could infringe freedom of expression as well as being destructive of personal liberty in a more general sense. What this shows, I think, is that freedom of expression is to be understood primarily in terms of the interests it aims to protect and only secondarily in terms of the class of actions whose protection is, under a given set of circumstances, an adequate way to safeguard these interests.

The most general participant interest is, then, an interest in being able to call something to the attention of a wide audience. This ability can serve a wide variety of more specific purposes. A speaker may be interested in increasing his reputation or in decreasing someone else's, in increasing the sales of his product, in promoting a way of life, in urging a change in government, or simply in amusing people or shocking them. From a social point of view, these interests are not all equally important, and the price that a society is required to pay in order to allow acts of expression of a particular kind to flourish will sometimes be a function of the value of expression of that kind.

This is one reason why it would be a mistake to look for a distinction between pure speech (or expression), which is protected by freedom of expression, and expression that is part of some larger course of action, which is not so protected. It is true that some acts of expression seem not to qualify for first amendment protection because of the larger courses of action of which they are a part (assault, incitement). But what distinguishes these from other acts of expression is not just that they are part of larger courses of action (which is true of almost all acts of expression), but rather the character of the particular courses of action of which they form a part. Their exclusion from first amendment protection should be seen as a special case of the more general phenomenon just mentioned: the protection to which an act of expression is entitled is in part a function of the value of the larger purposes it serves.

This cannot mean, of course, that the protection due a given act of expression depends on the actual value of the particular purposes at which it aims. It would be clearly antithetical to freedom of expression, for example, to accord greater protection to exponents of true religious doctrines than to exponents of false and misleading ones. Despite the fact that the objectives at which these two groups aim are of very different value, their acts of expression are (other things being equal) accorded equal status. This is so because the "further interest" that is at stake in the two cases is in fact the same, namely the interest we all have in being able to follow and promote our religious beliefs whatever they may be.

Here, then, is one way in which categories of expression arise. We are unwilling to bear the social costs of granting to just any expressive purpose the opportunities for expression that we would demand for those purposes to which we, personally, attach greatest importance. At the most concrete level, however, there is no agreement about the values to be attached to allowing particular acts of expression to go forward. It is just this lack of consensus, and the consequent unacceptability of allowing governments to regulate acts of expression on the basis of their perceived merits, that makes freedom of expression an important issue. In order to formulate a workable doctrine of freedom of expression, therefore, we look for something approaching a consensus on the relative importance of interests more abstractly conceived—the interest in religious expression, the interest in political expression, etc. Even this more abstract consensus is only approximate,[2] however, and never completely stable. As people's values change, or as a society becomes more diverse, consensus erodes. When this happens, either the ranking of interests must change or the categories of interests must be redefined, generally in a more abstract manner.[3] Recent shifts in attitudes toward religion have provoked

changes of both these kinds. As religion (or, as it is more natural to say here, *one's* religion) has come to be seen more as a matter of private concern on a par with other private interests, it has become harder to justify assigning religious concerns the preeminent value they have traditionally received. In order to make contemporary sense of this traditional assignment of values, on the other hand, there has been a tendency to redefine "religion" more abstractly as "a person's ultimate values and deepest convictions about the nature of life," thereby preserving some plausibility for the claim that we can all agree on the importance of religion in one's life even though we may have different beliefs.

The categories of participant interests I have been discussing are naturally identified with familiar categories of expression: political speech, commercial speech, etc. But we should not be too quick to make this identification. The type of protection that a given kind of expression requires is not determined by participant values alone. It also depends on such factors as the costs and benefits to nonparticipants and the reliability of available forms of regulation. Not surprisingly, these other factors also play a role in how categories of expression are defined. As will later become apparent, the lack of clarity concerning these categories results in part from the difficulty of seeing how these different elements are combined in their definition.[4]

B. Audience Interests

The interests of audiences are no less varied than those of participants: interests in being amused, informed on political topics, made aware of the pros and cons of alternatives available in the market, and so on. These audience interests conflict with those of participants in an important way. While participants sometimes aim only at communicating with people who are already interested in what they have to present, in a wide range of important cases their aims are broader: they want to gain the attention of people who would not otherwise consider their message. What audiences generally want, on the other hand, is to have expression available to them should they want to attend to it. Expression that grabs one's attention whether one likes it or not is generally thought of as a cost. But it should not be thought of only as a cost, even from the audience's point of view. As Mill rightly emphasized,[5] there is significant benefit in being exposed to ideas and attitudes different from one's own, though this exposure may be unwelcome. If we had complete control over the expression we are exposed to, the chances are high that we would use this power to our detriment. The important and difficult question however, is, when unwanted exposure to expression is a good thing from the audience's point of view.

This question is relatively easy to answer if we think of it as a problem of balancing temporary costs of annoyance, shock, or distraction against the more lasting benefits of a broadened outlook or deepened understanding. But it becomes more complicated if we take into account the possibility of more lasting costs such as being misled, having one's sensibilities dulled and cheapened, or acquiring foolish desires. This balancing task is simplified in the way we often think about expression by a further assumption about the audience's control. We are inclined to think that what would be ideal from the audience's point of view would be always to have the choice whether or not to be exposed to expression. Similarly, we have a tendency to assume that, having been exposed, an audience is always free to decide how to react: what belief to form or what attitude to adopt. This freedom to decide enables the audience to protect itself against unwanted long-range effects of expression. If we saw ourselves as helplessly absorbing as a belief every proposition we heard expressed, then our views of freedom of expression would be quite different from what they are. Certainly we are not like that. Nonetheless, the control we exercise over what to believe and what attitudes to adopt is in several respects an incomplete protection against unwarranted effects of expression.

To begin with, our decisions about what to believe are often mistaken, even in the best of circumstances. More generally, the likelihood of our not being mistaken, and hence the reliability of our critical rationality as a defense mechanism, varies widely from case to case depending on our emotional state, the degree of background information we possess, and the amount of time and energy we have to assess what we hear. As these things vary, so too does the value of being exposed to expression and the value of being able to avoid it. Commonly recognized cases of diminished rationality such as childhood, panic, and mental illness are just extreme instances of this common variation.

Quite apart from the danger of mistakenly believing what we hear, there is the further problem that a decision to disbelieve a message does not erase all the effects it may have on us. Even if I dismiss what is said or shown to me as foolish and exaggerated, I am slightly different for having seen or heard it. This difference can be trivial but it can also be significant and have a significant effect on my later decisions. For example, being shown powerful photographs of the horrors of war, no matter what my initial reaction to them may be, can have the effect of heightening (or ultimately of dulling) my sense of the human suffering involved, and this may later affect my opinions about foreign policy in ways I am hardly aware of.

Expression influencing us in this way is a good thing, from the point of view of our interests as audiences, if it affects our future decisions and attitudes by making us aware of good reasons for them, so long as it does not interfere with our ability to weigh these reasons against others. Expression is a bad thing if it influences us in ways that are unrelated to relevant reasons, or in ways that bypass our ability to consider these reasons. "Subliminal advertising" is a good example of this. What is bad about it is not just that it is "subliminal," i.e., that we are influenced by it without being aware of that influence. This, I think, happens all the time and is, in many cases, unobjectionable. What is objectionable about subliminal advertising, if it works, is that it causes us to act—to buy popcorn, say, or to read Dostoevsky—by making us think we have a good reason for so acting, even though we probably have no such reason. Suddenly finding myself with the thought that popcorn would taste good or that *Crime and Punishment* would be just the thing is often good grounds for acting in the relevant way. But such a thought is no reason for action if it is produced in me by messages flickered on the screen rather than by facts about my present state that indeed make this a good moment to go out for popcorn or to lie down with a heavy book.

I have assumed here that subliminal advertising works by leading us to form a false belief: we acquire a positive feeling toward popcorn which we then take, mistakenly, to be a sign that we would particularly enjoy some popcorn. One can easily imagine, however, that the effect is deeper.[6] Suppose that what the advertising does is to change us so that we both have a genuine desire for popcorn and will in fact enjoy it. One can still raise the question whether being affected in this way is a good thing for us, but an answer to it cannot rely on the claim that we are made to think that we have a reason to buy popcorn when in fact we do not. For in this case we will have as good a reason to buy popcorn as we ever do: we want some and will enjoy it if we get it. Advertising of this kind will be a bad thing from the audience's point of view if one is worse off for having acquired such a desire, perhaps because it leads one to eat unhealthily, or because it distracts one from other pursuits, or for some other reason.

It is particularly galling to think of such effects being produced in us by another agent whose aim is to have us benefit him through actions we would not otherwise choose. But the existence of a conscious manipulator is not essential to the objections I have presented. It is a bad thing to acquire certain desires or to be influenced by false reasons, and these things are bad whether or not they are brought about by other agents. But while the existence of a conscious manipulator is not essential to this basic objection, it can be relevant in two further ways. What we should want in general is to have our beliefs and desires produced by processes that are reliable—processes whose effectiveness depends on the grounds for the beliefs and on the goodness of the desires it produces. We prefer to be aware of how we are being affected partly because this critical awareness increases the reliability of the process; although, as I have said, this safeguard is commonly overrated. Particularly where effects on us escape our notice, the existence of an agent controlling these effects

can decrease the reliability of the process: the effects produced will be those serving this agent's purposes, and there may be no reason to think that what serves his purposes will be good from our point of view. (Indeed, the reverse is suggested by the fact that he chooses surreptitious means.) So the existence of a controlling agent can be relevant because of its implications for the reliability of the process. Beyond the question of reliability, however, we may simply prefer to have the choice whether or not to acquire a given desire; we may prefer this even where there is no certainty as to which desire it is better to have. This provides a further reason for objecting to effects produced in us by others (although this reason seems to hold as well against effects produced by inanimate causes).

The central audience interest in expression, then, is the interest in having a good environment for the formation of one's beliefs and desires. From the point of view of this interest, freedom of expression is only one factor among many. It is important to be able to hear what others wish to tell us, but this is not obviously more important than having affirmative rights of access to important information or to basic education. Perhaps freedom of expression is thought to differ in being purely negative: it consists merely in not being denied something and is therefore more easily justified as a right than are freedom of information or the right to education, which require others to provide something for us. But this distinction does not withstand a careful scrutiny. To begin with, freedom of expression adequately understood requires affirmative protection for expression, not just the absence of interference. Moreover, even nonintervention involves costs, such as the annoyance and disruption that expression may cause. On the other side, restrictions on freedom of information include not only failures to provide information but also attempts to conceal what would otherwise become public. When a government makes such an attempt for the purpose of stopping the spread of undesirable political opinions, this contravenes the same audience interests as an attempt to restrict publication, and the two seem to be objectionable on the same grounds. The fact that there is in the one case no "participant" whose right to speak is violated, but only a fact that remains undiscovered, seems not to matter.

C. Bystander Interests

I have mentioned that both participants and audiences can sometimes benefit from restrictions on expression as well as from the lack thereof. But the most familiar arguments for restricting expression appeal to the interests of bystanders. I will mention these only briefly. First are interests in avoiding the undesirable side effects of acts of expression themselves: traffic jams, the noise of crowds, the litter from leafletting. Second, and more important, are interests in the effect expression has on its audience. A bystander's interests may be affected simply by the fact that the audience has acquired new beliefs if, for example, they are beliefs about the moral character of the bystander. More commonly, bystanders are affected when expression promotes changes in the audience's subsequent behavior.

Regulation of expression to protect any of these bystander interests can conflict with the interests of audiences and participants. But regulation aimed at protecting bystanders against harms of the first type frequently strikes us as less threatening than that aimed at protecting bystanders against harmful changes in audience belief and behavior. This is true in part because the types of regulation supported by the two objectives are different. Protecting bystanders against harmful side effects of acts of expression calls for regulation only of the time, place, and manner of expression, and in many cases such regulation merely inconveniences audiences and participants. It *need* not threaten central interests in expression. Regulation to protect interests of the second kind, however, must, if it is successful, prevent effective communication of an idea. It is thus in direct conflict with the interests of participants and, at least potentially, of audiences as well. But this contrast is significant only to the degree that there are some forms of effective expression through which participant and audience interests can be satisfied without occasioning bystander harms of the first type: where there is no surplus of effective means

of expression, regulation of time, place, and manner can be just as dangerous as restrictions on content.

III. THEORIES

Although "freedom of expression" seems to refer to a right of participants not to be prevented from expressing themselves, theoretical defenses of freedom of expression have been concerned chiefly with the interests of audiences and, to a lesser extent, those of bystanders. This is true, for example, of Mill's famous defense in *On Liberty*,[7] which argues that a policy of noninterference with expression is preferable to a policy of censorship on two grounds: first, it is more likely to promote the spread of true beliefs, and second, it contributes to the well-being of society by fostering the development of better (more independent and inquiring) individuals. A similar emphasis on audience values is evident in Alexander Meiklejohn's theory.[8] He argues that first amendment freedom of speech derives from the right of citizens of a democracy to be informed in order that they can discharge their political responsibilities as citizens.

This emphasis can be explained, I think, by the fact that theories of freedom of expression are constructed to respond to what are seen as the most threatening arguments for restricting expression. These arguments have generally proceeded by calling attention to the harms that unrestricted expression may bring to audiences and bystanders: the harm, for example of being misled, or that of being made less secure because one's neighbors have been misled or provoked into disaffection and unrest. The conclusion drawn is that government, which has the right and even the duty to protect its citizens against such harms, may and should do so by preventing the expression in question. Responding to this argument, theories of freedom of expression have tended to argue either that the interests in question are not best protected by restricting expression (Mill) or that "protecting" citizens in this way is illegitimate on other grounds (Meiklejohn).

The dialectical objective of Mill's argument helps to explain why, although he professes to be arguing as a utilitarian, he concentrates on just two goods, true belief and individual growth, and never explicitly considers how these are to be balanced off against other goods that would have to be taken into account in a full utilitarian argument.

The surprising narrowness of Meiklejohn's theory can be similarly explained. Meiklejohn was reacting against the idea that a "clear and present danger" could justify a government in acting to protect its citizens by curbing the expression of threatening political ideas. This seemed to him to violate the rights of those it claimed to protect. Accordingly, he sought to explain the "absolute" character of the first amendment by basing it in a right to be informed and to make up one's own mind. But is there such a right? Meiklejohn saw the basis for one in the deliberative role of citizens in a democratic political order. But a right so founded does not apply to all forms of expression. Debates over artistic merit, the best style of personal life, or the promotion of goods in the marketplace may have their importance, but Meiklejohn saw these forms of expression as pursuits on a par with many others, unable to claim any distinct right to immunity from regulation. He was thus led to concede that these activities, in the main, fall outside the area of fundamental first amendment protection or, rather, that they qualify for it only insofar as their general importance makes them relevant to political decisions.

This narrowness is an unsatisfactory feature of what is in many ways an interesting and appealing theory. Moreover, given this emphasis on political rights as the basis of first amendment protection of speech, it is particularly surprising that Meiklejohn's theory should take audience values—the right of citizens to be informed—as the only fundamental ones. For prominent among the political rights of democratic citizens is the right to participate in the political process—in particular, the right to argue for one's own interests and point of view and to attempt to persuade one's fellow citizens. Such rights of participation do not entirely derive from the need of one's fellow citizens to be informed; the right to press one's case and to try to persuade others of its validity would not evaporate if it could be assumed that others were

already perfectly informed on the questions at issue. Perhaps Meiklejohn would respond by saying that what is at stake is not a matter of being informed in the narrow sense of possessing all the relevant information. Democratic citizens also need to have the arguments for alternative policies forcefully presented in a way that makes their strengths and weaknesses more apparent, stimulates critical deliberation and is conducive to the best decision. Surely, it might be asked, when political participation reaches the point where it becomes irrelevant to or even detracts from the possibility of good political decisions, what is the argument in its favor? I will return to this question of the relation between participant and nonparticipant interests in section five.[9]

Several years ago I put forward a theory of freedom of expression[10] that was very much influenced by Meiklejohn's views. Like him, I wanted to state a principle of freedom of expression that had a kind of absoluteness or at least a partial immunity from balancing against other concerns. But I wanted my theory to be broader than Meiklejohn's. I wanted it to cover more than just political speech, and I thought it should give independent significance to participant and audience interests. The basis of my theory was a single, audience-related principle applying to all categories of expression.

> *The Millian Principle:*
> There are certain harms which, although they would not occur but for certain acts of expression, nonetheless cannot be taken as part of a justification for legal restrictions on these acts. These harms are: (a) harms to certain individuals, which consist in their coming to have false beliefs as a result of those acts of expression; (b) harmful consequences of acts performed as a result of those acts of expression, where the connection between the acts of expression and the subsequent harmful acts consists merely in the fact that the act of expression led the agents to believe (or increased their tendency to believe) these acts to be worth performing.[11]

I undertook to defend this principle by showing it to be a consequence of a particular idea about the limits of legitimate political authority: namely that the legitimate powers of government are limited to those that can be defended on grounds compatible with the autonomy of its citizens—compatible, that is, with the idea that each citizen is sovereign in deciding what to believe and in weighing reasons for action.[12] This can be seen as a generalized version of Meiklejohn's idea of the political responsibility of democratic citizens.

The Millian Principle was intended to rule out the arguments for censorship to which Mill and Meiklejohn were responding. It did this by ruling that the harmful consequences to which these arguments appeal cannot count as potential justifications for legal restriction of expression. But there are other ways to arrive at policies that would strike us as incompatible with freedom of expression. One such way would be to restrict expression excessively, simply on the ground that it is a nuisance or has other undesirable consequences of a kind that the Millian Principle does allow to be weighed. So the second component in a theory of the type I described counters "excessive" restriction of this type by specifying that participant and audience interests in expression are to receive high values when they are balanced against competing goods. (As I have indicated, these values vary from one type of expression to another.) But freedom of expression does not only require that there should be "enough" expression. The two further components of the theory require that the goods of expression (for both participants and audiences) should be distributed in ways that are in accord both with the general requirements of distributive justice and with whatever particular rights there may be, such as rights to political participation, that support claims for access to means of expression.

This theory identifies the Millian Principle as the only principle concerned specifically with *expression* (as opposed to a general principle of justice) that applies with the same force to all categories of expression. If correct, then, it would answer one of the questions with which I began.[13] But is it correct? I now think that it is not.[14]

To begin with, the Millian Principle has what seem to be implausible consequences in some cases. For example, it is hard to see how laws against deceptive advertising or restrictions such as the ban on cigarette advertising on television could be squared with this principle. There are, of course, ways in which these objections might be answered. Perhaps the policies in question are simply violations of freedom of expression. If, on the other hand, they are acceptable this is because they are examples of justified paternalism, and my original theory did allow for the Millian Principle to be set aside in such cases.[15] But the theory provided for this exception only in cases of severely diminished rationality, because it took the view that any policy justified on grounds violating the Millian Principle would constitute paternalism of a particularly strong form.[16] The advertising cases seem to be clear counterexamples to this latter claim. More generally, clause (a) of the Millian Principle, taken as a limitation that can be set aside only in cases where our rational capacities are severely diminished, constitutes a rejection of paternalism that is too strong and too sweeping to be plausible. An acceptable doctrine of justified paternalism must take into account such factors as the value attached to being able to make one's own decisions, as well as the costs of so doing and the risks of empowering the government to make them on one's behalf. As the advertising examples show, these factors vary from case to case even where no general loss of rational capacities has occurred.

But the problems of the Millian Principle are not limited to cases of justified paternalism. The principle is appealing because it protects important audience interests—interests in deciding for one's self what to believe and what reasons to act on. As I have remarked earlier, these interests depend not only on freedom of expression, but also on other forms of access to information, education, and so on. Consideration of these other measures shows that there are in general limits to the sacrifices we are willing to make to enhance our decision-making capacity. Additional information is sometimes not worth the cost of getting it. The Millian Principle allows some of the costs of free expression to be weighed against its benefits, but holds that two important classes of costs must be ignored. Why should we be willing to bear unlimited costs to allow expression to flourish provided that the costs are of these particular kinds? Here it should be borne in mind that the

Millian Principle is a restriction on the authority of legitimate governments. Now it may well be that, as I would argue, there is *some* restriction of this kind on the costs that governments may take as grounds for restricting expression, and that this is so because such a restriction is a safeguard that is more than worth the costs involved. But an argument for this conclusion, if it is to avoid the charge of arbitrariness and provide a convincing account of the exact form that the restriction takes, must itself be based on a full consideration of all the relevant costs.

What these objections mainly point to, then, is a basic flaw in the argument I offered to justify the Millian Principle. There are many ways in which the appealing, but notoriously vague and slippery notion of individual autonomy can be invoked in political argument. One way is to take autonomy, understood as the actual ability to exercise independent rational judgment, as a good to be promoted. Referring to "autonomy" in this sense is a vague, somewhat grandiloquent and perhaps misleading way of referring to some of the most important audience interests described in section two. The intuitive arguments I have offered in the present section appeal to the value of autonomy in this sense. These audience interests were also taken into account in the second component of my earlier theory. My argument for the Millian Principle, on the other hand, employed the idea of autonomy in a different way, namely as a constraint on justifications of authority. Such justifications, it was held, must be compatible with the thesis that citizens are equal, autonomous rational agents.[17]

The idea of such a constraint now seems to me mistaken. Its appeal derives entirely from the value of autonomy in the first sense, that is, from the importance of protecting central audience interests. To build these interests in at the outset as constraints on the process of justification gives theoretical form to the intuition that freedom of expression is based on considerations that cannot simply be outweighed by competing interests in the manner that "clear and present danger" or "pure balancing" theories of the first amendment would allow. But to build these audience interests into the theory in this way has the effect of

assigning them greater and more constant weight than we in fact give them. Moreover, it prevents us from even asking whether these interests might in some cases be better advanced if we could shield ourselves from some influences. In order to meet the objections raised to the Millian Principle, it is necessary to answer such questions, and, in general, to take account of the variations in audience interests under varying circumstances. But this is not possible within the framework of the argument I advanced.

Most of the consequences of the Millian Principle are ones that I would still endorse. In particular, I still think that it is legitimate for the government to promote our personal safety by restricting information about how to make your own nerve gas,[18] but not legitimate for it to promote our safety by stopping political agitation which could, if unchecked, lead to widespread social conflict. I do not think that my judgment in the latter case rests simply on the difficulty of predicting such consequences or on the idea that the bad consequences of allowing political controversy will in each such case be outweighed by the good. But I do not think that the difference between the two cases can be found in the distinction between restricting means and restricting reasons, as my original article suggested. The difference is rather that where political issues are involved governments are notoriously partisan and unreliable. Therefore, giving government the authority to make policy by balancing interests in such cases presents a serious threat to particularly important participant and audience interests. To the degree that the considerations of safety involved in the first case are clear and serious, and the participant and audience interests that might suffer from restriction are not significant, regulation could be acceptable.

In this way of looking at things, political speech stands out as a distinctively important category of expression. Meiklejohn's mistake, I think, was to suppose that the differences in degree between this category and others mark the boundaries of first amendment theory. My mistake, on the other hand, was that in an effort to generalize Meiklejohn's theory beyond the category of political speech, I took what were in effect features peculiar to this category and presented them, under the heading of autonomy, as a priori constraints on justifications of legitimate authority.

In order to avoid such mistakes it is useful to distinguish several different levels of argument. At one extreme is what might be called the "level of policy," at which we might consider the overall desirability or undesirability of a particular action or policy, e.g., an ordinance affecting expression. At the other extreme is what might be called the "foundational level." Argument at this level is concerned with identifying the ultimate sources of justification relevant to the subject at hand. In the case of expression, these are the relevant participant, audience, and bystander interests, and the requirements of distributive justice applicable to their satisfaction. Intermediate between these levels is the "level of rights."[19] The question at this level is what limitations and requirements, if any, must be imposed on policy decisions if we are to avoid results that would be unacceptable with respect to the considerations that are defined at the fundamental level? To claim that something is a right, then, is to claim that some limit or requirement on policy decisions is *necessary* if unacceptable results are to be avoided, and that this particular limit or requirement is a *feasible* one, that is, that its acceptance provides adequate protection against such results and does so at tolerable cost to other interests. Thus, for example, to claim that a particular restriction on searches and seizures is part of a right of privacy would be to claim that it is a feasible form of necessary protection for our important and legitimate interests in being free from unwanted observation and intrusion. What rights there are in a given social setting at a given time depends on which judgments of necessity and feasibility are true at that place and time.[20] This will depend on the nature of the main threats to the interests in question, on the presence or absence of factors tending to promote unequal distribution of the means to their satisfaction, and particularly on the characteristics of the agents (private individuals or governments) who make the relevant policy decisions: what power do they have, and how are they likely to use this power in the absence of constraints?

Most of us believe that freedom of expression is a right. That is, we believe that limits on the power of governments to regulate expression are necessary to protect our central interests as audiences and participants, and we believe that such limits are not incompatible with a healthy society and a stable political order. Hundreds of years of political history support these beliefs. There is less agreement as to exactly how this right is to be understood—what limits and requirements on decision-making authority are necessary and feasible as ways of protecting central participant and audience interests and insuring the required equity in the access to means of expression. This is less than surprising, particularly given the fact that the answer to this question changes, sometimes rapidly, as conditions change. Some threats are constant—for example the tendency of governments to block the expression of critical views—and these correspond to points of general agreement in the definition of the right. But as new threats arise—from, for example, changes in the form or ownership of dominant means of communication—it may be unclear, and a matter subject to reasonable disagreement, how best to refine the right in order to provide the relevant kinds of protection at a tolerable cost. This disagreement is partly empirical—a disagreement about what is likely to happen if certain powers are or are not granted to governments. It is also in part a disagreement at the foundational level over the nature and importance of audience and participant interests and, especially, over what constitutes a sufficiently equal distribution of the means to their satisfaction. The main role of a philosophical theory of freedom of expression, in addition to clarifying what it is we are arguing about, is to attempt to resolve these foundational issues.

What reasons are there for taking this view of rights in general and of freedom of expression in particular? One reason is that it can account for much of what we in fact believe about rights and can explain what we do in the process of defending and interpreting them. A second reason is that its account of the bases of rights appears to exhaust the relevant concerns: if a form of regulation of expression presents no threat to the interests I have enumerated, nor to the equitable distribution of the means to their satisfaction, what further ground might there be to reject it as violating freedom of expression? Beyond these two reasons, all I can do in defense of my view is to ask, what else? If rights are not instrumental in the way I have described, what are they and what are the reasons for taking them seriously?

IV. CATEGORIES

Let me distinguish two ways in which arguments about freedom of expression may involve distinctions between categories of expression. First, not every participant or audience interest is capable of exerting the same upward pressure on the costs freedom of expression requires us to bear. Freedom of expression often requires that a particular form of expression—leafletting or demonstrations near public buildings—be allowed despite high bystander costs, because important participant or audience interests would otherwise be inadequately or unequally served. Such arguments are clearly category-dependent: their force depends on the importance of the particular participant or audience interests in question. But, once it is concluded on the basis of such an argument that a given mode of expression must be permitted, there is the further question whether its use must be permitted for any form of expression or whether it may be restricted to those types of expression whose value was the basis for claiming that this mode of expression must be allowed. If the latter, then not only will categories of interests be assigned different weights in arguments about the content of the right of freedom of expression, but the application of this right to particular cases will also involve determining the category to which the acts in question belong. I will refer to these two forms of categorization as, respectively, categories of interests and categories of acts.

This distinction can be illustrated by considering the ways in which "political speech" can serve as a category. For the purposes of this discussion, I will assume that "political" is to be interpreted narrowly as meaning, roughly, "having to do with the electoral process and the activities of government." We can distinguish a category of interests in expression that are political in this

sense, including both participant interests in taking part in the political process and audience (and bystander) interests in the spread of information and discussion about political topics. As a category of acts, on the other hand, "political speech" might be distinguished[21] either by participant intent—expression with a political purpose—or by content and effect—expression that concerns political issues or contributes to the understanding of political issues. These two definitions correspond, roughly, to the two sets of interests just mentioned. I will assume for the moment that the category of political speech is to be understood to include acts falling under either of these definitions.

Although the political interests in expression are not uniquely important, the fact that they are inadequately or very unequally served constitutes a strong reason for enlarging or improving available modes of expression. Their particular importance as a source of upward pressure is something that rational argument about freedom of expression must recognize. Must "political speech" be recognized as a category of acts as well? That is, can the fact that an act of expression has the relevant political intent or content exempt it from regulation that would otherwise be compatible with freedom of expression?

Special standards for defamation applicable to expression concerning "public officials," "public figures" or "public issues"[22] indicate that something like "political speech" does function as a category of acts in the current legal understanding of freedom of expression. Reflection on the *Skokie* case may also suggest that "political speech" has a special place in our intuitive understanding of this right. It seems unlikely that expression so deeply offensive to bystanders would be deemed to be protected by freedom of expression if it did not have a political character—if, for example, its purpose had been merely to provide entertainment or to promote commerce. But I do not see how this interpretation of freedom of expression can be defended, at least unless "political" is understood in a very broad sense in which any important and controversial question counts as a "political issue." Expression that is political in the narrow sense is both important and in need of protection, but it is not unique in either respect. Furthermore, even if "political" is understood broadly, the idea that access to a mode of expression can be made to depend on official determination of the "political" nature of one's purposes or one's message does not sit comfortably with the basic ideas of freedom of expression.

This suggests a second, more plausible analysis of the *Skokie* case, one which relies more heavily on categories of interests and less on categories of acts. The judgment that the Nazi march is protected may reflect the view that no[23] ordinance giving local authorities the power to ban such a march could give adequate protection to central interests in political expression. This argument avoids any judgment as to whether the content and purposes of this particular march were "genuinely political." It relies instead on the judgment that such a march could not be effectively and reliably distinguished from political expression that it is essential to protect.

The distinction between categories of interests and categories of acts can be used to explain some of the ambivalence about categories noted at the beginning of this article. Reference to categories of interests is both important and unavoidable in arguments about freedom of expression. Categories of acts may also be unavoidable—"expression" is itself such a category, and assault, for example, is distinguished from it on the basis of participant intent—but there are good reasons for being wary of categories of acts and for keeping their use to a minimum. Even where there is agreement on the relative importance of various interests in expression, the purposes and content of a given expressive act can be a matter of controversy and likely misinterpretation, particularly in those situations of intense conflict and mistrust in which freedom of expression is most important. (Well-known difficulties in the application of laws against incitement are a good illustration of this point.) Thus the belief that the fundamental principles of freedom of expression must transcend categories derives in part from the recognition that categories of acts rest on distinctions—of intent and content—that a partisan of freedom of expression will instinctively view with suspicion. Nonetheless, in interpreting freedom of expression, we are constantly drawn toward categories

of acts as we search for ways of protecting central interests in expression while avoiding unacceptable costs. The current struggle to define the scope of special standards of defamation[24] is a good example of this process. Identifying the categories of acts that can actually be relied upon to give the protection we want is a matter of practical and strategic judgment, not of philosophical theory.

I have mentioned the possibility of official misapplication as one reason for avoiding categories of acts, but this is not the only problem. A second difficulty is the fact that it is extremely difficult to regulate one category of speech without restricting others as well. Here the recent campaign financing law is an instructive example.[25] The basic aim of restricting money spent during a campaign in order to increase the fairness of this particular competition is entirely compatible with freedom of expression. The problem is that in order to regulate spending effectively, it was deemed necessary to make campaign funds flow through a single committee for each candidate. In order to do this a low limit was placed on the amount any private person or group could spend on expression to influence the campaign. But since spending on expression to influence a campaign cannot be clearly separated from expression on political topics generally, the limit on private spending constituted an unacceptable restriction on expression. Limits on spending for "campaign speech" are in principle as compatible with freedom of expression as limits on the length of speeches in a town meeting: both are acceptable when they enhance the fairness of the proceedings. Unlike a town meeting, however, "campaign speech" is not easily separated from other expression on political topics, hence not easily regulated in a way that leaves this other expression unaffected.

In addition to the difficulty of regulating one category without affecting others, there is the further problem that the categories within which special regulation is held to be permissible may themselves suffer from dangerous overbreadth. I believe that this is true, for example, of the category of commercial speech. Presumably "commercial speech" is to be defined with reference to participant intent: expression by a participant in the market for the purpose of attracting buyers or sellers. It is not identical with advertising, which can serve a wide variety of expressive purposes, and it cannot be defined by its subject matter: *Consumer Reports* has the same subject matter as much commercial speech, but it is entitled to "full" first amendment protection. Why, then, would anyone take commercial speech to be subject to restrictions that would not be acceptable if applied to other forms of expression? This view is widely held, or has been until recently,[26] and it appears to be supported by the acceptability of laws against false or deceptive advertising, the regulation of cigarette advertising, and restriction on the form of classified advertisements of employment opportunities. One reason for this attitude may be that the participant and audience interests at stake in commercial speech—promoting one's business, learning what is available in the market—are not generally perceived as standing in much danger from overrestriction. There is, we are inclined to think, plenty of opportunity for advertising, and we are in no danger of being deprived of needed information if advertising is restricted. In fact, the relevant audience interests are in much more danger from excessive exposure to advertising, and from false and deceptive advertising. In addition, laws against such advertising seem acceptable in a way that analogous laws against false or deceptive political or religious claims would not be, first because there are reasonably clear and objective criteria of truth in this area, and second, we regard the government as much less partisan in the competition between commercial firms than in the struggle between religious or political views.

Much of this is no doubt true, but it does not support the generalization that commercial speech as a category is subject to less stringent requirements of freedom of expression. The restrictions I have mentioned, where they seem justified, can be supported by arguments that are applicable in principle to other forms of expression (for example, by appeals to qualified paternalism, or to the advantages for audiences of protection against an excessive volume of expression). It is a mistake to think that these arguments are applicable only to

commercial speech or that all commercial speech is especially vulnerable to them. In particular, if, as I believe, the assumption that governments are relatively neutral and trustworthy in this area is one reason for our complacent attitude toward regulation of commercial speech, this assumption should be made explicit and treated with care. There are many cases that clearly count as commercial speech in which our traditional suspicions of governmental regulation of expression are as fully justified as they are elsewhere. One such example might be an advertising battle between established energy companies and antiestablishment commercial enterprises promoting alternative energy sources.[27]

V. PORNOGRAPHY

In this final section I will consider the category of pornography. This example will illustrate both the problems of categories, just discussed, and some of the problems concerning participant and audience interests that were discussed in section two above.

The question to ask about pornography is, why restrict it? I will consider two answers. The first appeals to the interest people have in not being unwillingly exposed to offensive material. By offense, I do not mean a reaction grounded in disapproval but an immediate discomfort analogous to pain, fear of acute embarrassment. I am willing to assume for purposes of argument that many people do have such a reaction to some sexual material, and that we should take seriously their interest in being protected against it. I also agree that what offends most people will differ from place to place depending on experience and custom. Therefore the appropriate standards of protection may also vary. But if this were the only reason for restricting pornography the problem would have an easy solution: restrict what can be displayed on the public streets or otherwise forced on an unwilling audience, but place no restrictions whatever on what can be shown in theaters, printed in books, or sent through the mails in plain brown wrappers. The only further requirement is that the inconvenience occasioned by the need to separate the two groups should be fairly shared between them.

The idea that this solution should be acceptable to all concerned rests on specific assumptions about the interests involved. It is assumed that consumers of pornography desire private enjoyment, that sellers want to profit from selling to those who have this desire, and that other people want to avoid being forced to see or hear what they regard as offensive. Rarely will one find three sets of interests that are so easily made compatible. There are of course certain other interests which are left out of this account. Perhaps some people want to enjoy pornography in public; their pleasure depends on the knowledge that they are disturbing other people. Also, sellers may want to reach a larger audience in order to increase profits, so they would like to use more stimulating advertisements. Finally, those who wish to restrict pornography may be offended not only by the sight of it but even by the knowledge that some people are enjoying it out of their sight; they will be undisturbed only if it is stopped. But none of these interests has significant weight. There is, to be sure, a general problem of explaining what makes some interests important and others, like these, less significant; but this is not a problem peculiar to freedom of expression.

Unfortunately, offense is not the only reason to restrict pornography. The main reason, I think, is the belief that the availability, enjoyment, and even the legality of pornography will contribute to undesirable changes in our attitudes toward sex and in our sexual mores. We all care deeply about the character of the society in which we live and raise our children. This interest cannot be simply dismissed as trivial or illegitimate. Nor can we dismiss as empirically implausible the belief that the evolution of sexual attitudes and mores is strongly influenced by the books and movies that are generally available and widely discussed, in the way that we can dismiss the belief that pornography leads to rape. Of course, expression is not the only thing that can influence society in these ways. This argument against pornography has essentially the same form as well-known arguments in favor of restricting nonstandard sexual conduct.[28] If the interest to which these arguments

appeal is, as I have conceded, a legitimate one, how can the arguments be answered?

I think that transactions "between consenting adults" can sometimes legitimately be restricted on the ground that, were such transactions to take place freely, social expectations would change, people's motives would be altered and valued social practices would as a result become unstable and decline. I think, for example, that some commercial transactions might legitimately be restricted on such grounds. Thus Richard Titmuss,[29] opposing legalization of blood sales in Britain, claims that the availability of blood on a commercial basis weakens people's sense of interdependence and leads to a general decline in altruistic motivation. Assuming for the purposes of argument that this empirical claim is correct, I am inclined to think that there is no objection to admitting this as *a* reason for making the sale of blood illegal. To ban blood sales for this reason seems at first to be objectionable because it represents an attempt by the state to maintain a certain state of mind in the population. What is objectionable about many such attempts, which violate freedom of expression, is that they seek to prevent changes of mind by preventing people from considering and weighing possible reasons for changing their minds. Such interventions run contrary to important audience interests. As far as I can see, however, the presence of a market in blood does not put us in a better position to decide how altruistic we wish to be.

There are of course other objections to outlawing the sale of blood, objections based simply on the value of the opportunity that is foreclosed. Being deprived of the opportunity to sell one's blood does not seem to me much of a loss. In the case of proposed restrictions on deviant sexual conduct, however, the analogous costs to the individuals who would be restricted are severe—too severe to be justified by the considerations advanced on the other side. In fact, the argument for restriction seems virtually self-contradictory on this score. What is the legitimate interest that people have in the way their social mores evolve? It is in large part the legitimate interest they have in not being under pressure to conform to practices they find repugnant under pain of being thought odd and perhaps treated as an outcast. But just this interest is violated in an even more direct way by laws against homosexual conduct.

The case for restricting pornography might be answered in part by a similar argument, but there is also a further issue, more intrinsic to the question of freedom of expression. Once it is conceded that we all have legitimate and conflicting interests in the evolution of social attitudes and mores, the question arises how this conflict can fairly be resolved. In particular, is majority vote a fair solution? Can the majority be empowered to preserve attitudes they like by restricting expression that would promote change? The answer to this question is clearly no. One reason is that, as Meiklejohn would emphasize, the legitimacy of majoritarian political processes themselves depends upon the assumption that the voters have free access to information and are free to attempt to persuade and convince each other. Another reason is that, unlike a decision where to build a road, this is an issue that need not be resolved by a clear decision at any one time. There is hence no justification for allowing a majority to squeeze out and silence a minority. A fair alternative procedure is available: a continuing process of "informal politics" in which the opposing groups attempt to alter or to preserve the social consensus through persuasion and example.

This response to the argument for restricting pornography has several consequences. First, since it rests upon viewing public interaction under conditions of freedom of expression as an informal political process that is preferable to majority voting as a way of deciding certain important questions, the response is convincing only if we can argue that this process is in fact fair. It will not be if, for example, access to the main means of expression, and hence the ability to have an influence on the course of public debate, are very unequally distributed in the society. Thus, equity in the satisfaction of participant interests, discussed above as one goal of freedom of expression, arises here in a new way as part of a defense of freedom of expression against majority control.

A second consequence of the argument is that time, place, and manner restrictions on obscene material, which at first seemed a satisfactory

solution to the problem of offense, are no longer so obviously satisfactory. Their appeal as a solution rested on the supposition that, since the interests of consumers and sellers of pornography were either purely private or simply commercial, unwilling audiences were entitled to virtually complete protection, the only residual problem being the relatively trivial one of how to apportion fairly the inconvenience resulting from the need to shield the two groups from each other. But if what the partisans of pornography are entitled to (and what the restrictors are trying to deny them) is a fair opportunity to influence the sexual mores of the society, then it seems that they, like participants in political speech in the narrow sense,[30] are entitled to at least a certain degree of access even to unwilling audiences. I do not find this conclusion a particularly welcome one, but it seems to me difficult to avoid once the most important arguments against pornography are taken seriously. Let me conclude by considering several possible responses.

The argument I have presented starts from the high value to be assigned to the participant interest in being able to influence the evolution of attitudes and mores in one's society. But although some publishers of "obscene" materials have this kind of crusading intent, undoubtedly many others do not. Perhaps the proper conclusion of my argument is not that any attempt to publish and disseminate offensive sexual material is entitled to full First Amendment protection but, at most, that such protection can be claimed where the participant's intent is of the relevant "political" character. This would construe "pornography" as a category of acts in the sense defined above: sexually offensive expression in the public forum need not be allowed where the intent is merely that of the pornographer—who aims only to appeal to a prurient interest in sex —but must be allowed where the participant has a "serious" interest in changing society. To take "the obscene" as a category of acts subject to extraordinary regulation would involve, on this view, the same kind of overbreadth that is involved when "commercial speech" is seen as such a category. In each case features typical of at most some instances are taken to justify special treatment of the category as a whole.

As I indicated in section four above, distinctions based on participant intent cannot be avoided altogether in the application of the right of freedom of expression, but they are nearly always suspect. This is particularly so in the present case; expression dealing with sex is particularly likely to be characterized, by those who disapprove of it, as frivolous, unserious and of interest only to dirty minds. To allow expression in this area to be regulated on the basis of participant intent would be to set aside a normal caution without, as far as I can see, any ground for doing so.

The conclusion that unwilling audiences cannot be fully protected against offensive expression might be avoided in a second way. Even if the "political interest" in expression on sexual topics is an important interest, and even if it supports a right of access to unwilling audiences, there is a further question whether this interest requires the presentation of "offensive" material. Perhaps it would be enough to be entitled to present material that "deals with" the question of sexual mores in a sober and nonoffensive manner. Perhaps Larry Flynt and Ralph Ginzburg should, on the one hand, be free to sell as much pornography as they wish for private consumption, and they should on the other hand be free to write newspaper editorials and books, make speeches, or go on television as much as they can to crusade for a sexually liberated society. But the latter activity, insofar as it presses itself on people's attention without warning, is subject to the requirement that it not involve offense.

On the other side, it can be claimed that this argument rests on an overly cognitive and rationalistic idea of how people's attitudes change. Earnest treatises on the virtues of a sexually liberated society can be reliably predicted to have no effect on prevailing attitudes towards sex. What is more likely to have such an effect is for people to discover that they find exciting and attractive portrayals of sex which they formerly thought offensive or, vice versa, that they find boring and offensive what they had expected to find exciting and liberating. How can partisans of sexual change be given a fair chance to make this happen except

through a relaxation of restrictions on what can be publicly displayed? I do not assume that the factual claims behind this argument are correct. My question rather is, if they were correct what would follow? From the fact that frequent exposure to material previously thought offensive is a likely way to promote a change in people's attitudes, it does not follow that partisans of change are entitled to use this means. Proponents of a change in attitude are not entitled to use just *any* expressive means to effect their aim, even if the given means is the only one that would actually have the effect they desire: audience interests must also be considered. It must be asked whether exposure to these means leads to changes in one's tastes and preferences through a process that is, like subliminal advertising, both outside of one's rational control and quite independent of the relevant grounds for preference, or whether, on the contrary, the exposure to such influences is in fact part of the best way to discover what one really has reason to prefer. I think that a crucial question regarding the regulation of pornography and other forms of allegedly corrupting activity lies here.

It is often extremely difficult to distinguish influences whose force is related to relevant grounds for the attitudes they produce from influences that are the work of irrelevant factors. Making this distinction requires, in many cases, a clearer understanding than we have both of the psychological processes through which our attitudes are altered and of the relevant grounds for holding the attitudes in question. The nature of these grounds, in particular, is often a matter of too much controversy to be relied upon in defining a right of freedom of expression. The power to restrict the presentation of "irrelevant influences" seems threatening because it is too easily extended to restrict any expression likely to mislead.

Subliminal advertising is in this respect an unusual case, from which it is hard to generalize. A law against subliminal advertising could be acceptable on first amendment grounds because it could be framed as a prohibition simply of certain techniques—the use of hidden words or images—thus avoiding controversial distinctions between relevant and irrelevant influences. Where we are concerned with the apparent—as opposed to the hidden—content of expression, however, things become more controversial (even though it is true that what is clearly seen or heard may influence us, and be designed to do so, in ways that we are quite unaware of).

The case for protecting unwilling audiences against influence varies considerably from one kind of offensive expression to another, even within the class of what is generally called pornography. The separation between the way one's attitudes are affected by unwanted exposure to expression and the relevant grounds for forming such attitudes is clearest in the case of pornography involving violence or torture. The reasons for being opposed to, and revolted by, these forms of behavior are quite independent of the question whether one might, after repeated exposure, come to find them exciting and attractive. This makes it plausible to consider such changes in attitude produced by unchosen exposure to scenes of violence as a kind of harm that an unwilling audience is entitled to protection against.[31] The question is whether this protection can be given without unacceptably restricting other persuasive activity involving scenes of violence, such as protests against war.

The argument for protection of unwilling audiences is much weaker where what is portrayed are mildly unconventional sexual attitudes or practices, not involving violence or domination. Here it is more plausible to say that discovering how one feels about such matters when accustomed to them is the best way of discovering what attitude towards them one has reason to hold. The lack of independent grounds for appraising these attitudes makes it harder to conceive of changes produced by expression as a kind of harm or corruption. Even here there are some independent grounds for appraisal, however.[32] Attitudes towards sex involve attitudes towards other people, and the reasons for or against holding *these* attitudes may be quite independent of one's reactions to portrayals of sex, which are, typically, highly impersonal. I believe that there are such grounds for regarding as undesirable changes in our attitudes towards sex produced by pornography, or for that matter by advertising, and for wanting to be able to avoid them. But, in addition to the problem of separability, just mentioned with regard to portrayals

of violence, these grounds may be too close to the substantive issues in dispute to be an acceptable basis for the regulation of expression.

It seems, then, that an argument based on the need to protect unwilling audiences against being influenced could justify restriction of at most some forms of offensive expression. This leaves us with the residual question how much offense must be tolerated in order for persuasion and debate regarding sexual mores to go forward. Here the clearest arguments are by comparison with other categories of expression. The costs that audiences and bystanders are required to bear in order to provide for free political debate are generally quite high. These include very significant psychological costs, as the *Skokie* case indicates. Why should psychological costs of the particular kind occasioned by obscenity be treated differently (or given a particularly high value)? A low cost threshold would be understandable if the issues at stake were trivial ones, but by the would-be restrictors' own account this is not so. I do not find the prospect of increased exposure to offensive expression attractive, but it is difficult to construct a principled argument for restriction that is consistent with our policy towards other forms of expression and takes the most important arguments against pornography seriously.

Versions of this paper were presented at the University of Minnesota and the University of California at Berkeley as well as at the Pittsburgh symposium. I am grateful to members of all these audiences for helpful comments. I have also benefitted greatly from discussions of this topic with Marshall Cohen, Clark Glymour, and Derek Parfit.

Tim Scanlon is Professor of Philosophy at Princeton University.

NOTES

1. Villiage of Skokie v. National Socialist Party of America, 69 Ill. 2d 605, 373 N.E. 2d 21 (1978).
2. How the existence of an approximate consensus, even though it is only approximate, can contribute to the legitimacy of the agreed-upon values as a basis for justification is a difficult problem, which I cannot here discuss.
3. I have assumed here that categories of interests are disrupted by a decrease in consensus and an increase in diversity of views, since this is the

course of change we are most familiar with. I suppose that the reverse process—in which increasing consensus makes an abstract category seem pointlessly abstract and leads to its being redefined to include what was before only a special case—is at least possible. On the former, more familiar kind of transition, see E. Durkheim, *Individualism and the Intellectuals,* in Emile Durkheim on Morality and Society 43 (R. Bellah ed. 1973). See *also* E. Durkheim, Division of Labor in Society (G. Simpson trans. 1933). Perhaps Marx's view of the transition to a socialist society includes an instance of the latter kind.

4. Here libel provides a good example. One reason for assigning it low status as a category of expressive acts is the low value attached to the participant interest in insulting people and damaging their reputations. This is something we sometimes want to do, but it gets low weight in our social calculus. Another reason is the high value we attach to not having our reputations damaged. These are not unrelated, but they do not motivate concern with the same class of actions. Other relevant considerations include the interest we may have in performing or having others perform acts which incidentally damage reputations. A defensible definition of libel as a category of expressive acts will be some resultant of all these factors, not simply of the first or the second alone.

5. J. Mill, On Liberty ch. 2 (C. Shields ed. 1956).

6. Here I am indebted to the discussion following the presentation of this paper at Berkeley, and to comments by members of my graduate seminar for the Spring Term, 1979.

7. J. Mill, supra, note 5.

8. A. Meiklejohn, Political Freedom (1960).

9. See pp. 32–34, infra.

10. Scanlon, *A Theory of Freedom of Expression,* 1 Philosophy & Pub. Aff. 204 (1972).

11. Id., at 213.

12. Id., at 215.

13. See p. 520, supra.

14. In what follows I am indebted to a number of criticisms, particularly to objections raised by Robert Amdur and by Gerald Dworkin.

15. Scanlon, supra, note 10, at 220.

16. Id., at 221.

17. Id., at 215.

18. Id., at 211–13.

19. For a presentation of this view at greater length, see Scanlon, *Rights, Goals, and Fairness,* in Public and Private Morality (S. Hampshire ed. 1978).

20. Of course there may be multiple solutions to the problem; that is, different ways in which a right might be defined to give adequate protection to the interests in question. In such a case what there is a right to initially is *some* protection of the relevant kind. At this point the right is incompletely defined. Once one adequate form of protection becomes established as a constraint on policy making, the other alternatives are no longer necessary in the relevant sense. In this respect our rights are partly determined by convention.

21. Distinguished, that is, from other forms of protected expression. I am concerned here only with what marks speech as political. A full definition of "political speech" (i.e., permissible political expression) would, in order to exclude such things as bombings, take into account features other than those mentioned here. See note 4, supra.

22. See the line of cases following New York Times Co. v. Sullivan, 376 U.S. 254 (1964). See, e.g., Curtis Publishing Co. v. Butts, 388 U.S. 130 (1967); Gertz v. Robert Welch, Inc., 418 U.S. 323 (1974); Herbert v. Lando, 99 S.Ct. 1635 (1979); Hutchinson v. Proxmire, 99 S.Ct. 2675 (1979).

23. Of course an actual decision need only find a particular ordinance unconstitutional. I take it, however, that an intuitive judgment that an action is protected by freedom of expression is broader than this and implies that *no* acceptable ordinance could restrict that action.

24. See cases cited note 22, supra.

25. Buckley v. Valeo, 424 U.S. 1 (1976). Federal Election Campaign Act of 1971, Pub. L. No. 92-225, 86 Stat. 3 (1972), *as amended by* Federal Election Campaign Act Amendments of 1974, Pub. L. No. 93-443, 88 Stat. 1263 (1974), *as amended by* Federal Election Campaign Act Amendments of 1976, Pub. L. No. 94-283, 90 Stat. 475 (1976).

26. See Bates v. State Bar of Arizona, 433 U.S. 350 (1977) *reh. denied* 434 U.S. 881 (1977); Virginia Pharmacy Bd. v. Virginia Consumer Council, 425 U.S. 748 (1976).

27. It might be claimed that insofar as this example has the character I mention, it is an instance of political, not merely commercial, speech. Certainly it does have a political element. Nonetheless, the intentions of the participants (and the interests of audiences) may be thoroughly

commercial. The political element of the controversy triggers First Amendment reactions because it raises the threat of partisan regulation, not because the interests at stake, on the part of either participants or audience, are political.

28. See DEVLIN, THE ENFORCEMENT OF MORALS (1965).

29. R. TITMUSS, THE GIFT RELATIONSHIP chs. 13–15 (1971). See *also* Singer, *Altruism and Commerce,* 2 PHILOSOPHY & PUB. AFF. 312 (1973).

30. Perhaps Meiklejohn would defend "offensive" discussion of sexual topics in a similar fashion, construing it as a form of political speech. Several differences should be noted, however. First, my argument appeals to participant interests rather than to the audience interests Meiklejohn emphasizes. Second, the politics I am concerned with here is an informal process distinct from the formal democratic institutions he seems to have in mind. Participation in this informal process is not important merely as a preliminary to making decisions in one's official capacity as a citizen. But even if Meiklejohn would not construe the political role of citizens this narrowly, a further difference remains. Having an influence on the evolving mores of one's society is, in my view, only one important participant interest among many, and I would not make the validity of all first amendment claims depend on their importance for our role in politics of either the formal or the informal sort. It is true, however, that those ideas controversial enough to he in greatest need of first amendment protection are likely also to be the subject of politics in one or both of these senses. See note 27, supra.

31. Prohibiting the display of such scenes for willing audiences is a separate question. So is their presentation to children. Here and throughout this article I am concerned only with adults.

32. Here the moral status of attitudes and practices may become relevant. Moral considerations have been surprisingly absent from the main arguments for restricting pornography considered in this section: the notion of offense quite explicitly abstracts from moral appraisal, and the importance of being able to influence the future mores of one's society does not depend on the assumption that one's concern with these mores is based in morality. A person can have a serious and legitimate interest in preserving (or eliminating) certain customs even if these are matters of no *moral* significance. But morality is relevant to the argument for audience protection since, if sexual attitudes are a matter of morality, this indicates that they can be appraised on grounds that are independent of subjective reaction, thus providing a possible basis for claiming that a person who has come to have a certain attitude (and to be content with having it) has been made worse off.

CHAPTER THIRTEEN

Distributive Justice and Material Equality

42   A Theory of Justice (Excerpts)

JOHN RAWLS

SEC. 3. THE MAIN IDEA OF THE THEORY OF JUSTICE

My aim is to present a conception of justice that generalizes and carries to a higher level of abstraction the familiar theory of the social contract as found, say, in Locke, Rousseau, and Kant. In order to do this we are not to think of the original contract as one to enter a particular society or to set up a particular form of government. Rather, the guiding idea is that the principles of justice for the basic structure of society are the object of the original agreement. They are the principles that free and rational persons concerned to further their own interests would accept in an initial position of equality as defining the fundamental terms of their association. These principles are to regulate all further agreements; they specify the kinds of social cooperation that can be entered into and the forms of government that can be established. This way of regarding the principles of justice I shall call justice as fairness.

Thus we are to imagine that those who engage in social cooperation choose together, in one joint act, the principles which are to assign basic rights and duties and to determine the division of social benefits. Men are to decide in advance how they are to regulate their claims against one another and what is to be the foundation charter of their society. Just as each person must decide by rational reflection what constitutes his good, that is, the system of ends which it is rational for him to pursue, so a group of persons must decide once and for all what is to count among them as just and unjust. The choice which rational men would make in this hypothetical situation of equal liberty, assuming for the present that this choice problem has a solution, determines the principles of justice.

In justice as fairness the original position of equality corresponds to the state of nature in the traditional theory of the social contract. This original position is not, of course, thought of as an actual historical state of affairs, much less as a primitive condition of culture. It is understood as a purely hypothetical situation characterized so as to lead to a certain conception of justice.[1] Among the essential features of this situation is

From *A Theory of Justice* (Cambridge, Mass.: Belknap Press, rev. ed. 1999). Reprinted with permission of Harvard University Press.

that no one knows his place in society, his class position or social status, nor does any one know his fortune in the distribution of natural assets and abilities, his intelligence, strength, and the like. I shall even assume that the parties do not know their conceptions of the good or their special psychological propensities. The principles of justice are chosen behind a veil of ignorance. This ensures that no one is advantaged or disadvantaged in the choice of principles by the outcome of natural chance or the contingency of social circumstances. Since all are similarly situated and no one is able to design principles to favor his particular condition, the principles of justice are the result of a fair agreement or bargain. For, given the circumstances of the original position, the symmetry of everyone's relations to each other, this initial situation is fair between individuals as moral persons, that is, as rational beings with their own ends and capable, I shall assume, of a sense of justice. The original position is, one might say, the appropriate initial status quo, and thus the fundamental agreements reached in it are fair. This explains the propriety of the name "justice as fairness": it conveys the idea that the principles of justice are agreed to in an initial situation that is fair. The name does not mean that the concepts of justice and fairness are the same, any more than the phrase "poetry as metaphor" means that the concepts of poetry and metaphor are the same.

Justice as fairness begins, as I have said, with one of the most general of all choices which persons might make together, namely, with the choice of the first principles of a conception of justice which is to regulate all subsequent criticism and reform of institutions. Then, having chosen a conception of justice, we can suppose that they are to choose a constitution and a legislature to enact laws, and so on, all in accordance with the principles of justice initially agreed upon. Our social situation is just if it is such that by this sequence of hypothetical agreements we would have contracted into the general system of rules which defines it. Moreover, assuming that the original position does determine a set of principles (that is, that a particular conception of justice would be chosen), it will then be true that whenever social institutions satisfy these principles those

engaged in them can say to one another that they are cooperating on terms to which they would agree if they were free and equal persons whose relations with respect to one another were fair. They could all view their arrangements as meeting the stipulations which they would acknowledge in an initial situation that embodies widely accepted and reasonable constraints on the choice of principles. The general recognition of this fact would provide the basis for a public acceptance of the corresponding principles of justice. No society can, of course, be a scheme of cooperation which men enter voluntarily in a literal sense; each person finds himself placed at birth in some particular position in some particular society, and the nature of this position materially affects his life prospects. Yet a society satisfying the principles of Justice as fairness comes as close as a society can to being a voluntary scheme, for it meets the principles which free and equal persons would assent to under circumstances that are fair. In this sense its members are autonomous and the obligations they recognize self-imposed.

One feature of justice as fairness is to think of the parties in the initial situation as rational and mutually disinterested. This does not mean that the parties are egoists, that is, individuals with only certain kinds of interests, say in wealth, prestige, and domination. But they are conceived as not taking an interest in one another's interests. They are to presume that even their spiritual aims may be opposed, in the way that the aims of those of different religions may be opposed. Moreover, the concept of rationality must be interpreted as far as possible in the narrow sense, standard in economic theory, of taking the most effective means to given ends. I shall modify this concept to some extent, but one must try to avoid introducing into it any controversial ethical elements. The initial situation must be characterized by stipulations that are widely accepted.

In working out the conception of justice as fairness one main task clearly is to determine which principles of justice would be chosen in the original position. To do this we must describe this situation in some detail and formulate with care the problem of choice which it presents. It may be observed, however, that once the principles of justice are thought of as arising from an original agreement in a situation of equality, it is an open question whether the principle of utility would be acknowledged. Offhand it hardly seems likely that persons who view themselves as equals, entitled to press their claims upon one another, would agree to a principle which may require lesser life prospects for some simply for the sake of a greater sum of advantages enjoyed by others. Since each desires to protect his interests, his capacity to advance his conception of the good, no one has a reason to acquiesce in an enduring loss for himself in order to bring about a greater net balance of satisfaction. In the absence of strong and lasting benevolent impulses, a rational man would not accept a basic structure merely because it maximized the algebraic sum of advantages irrespective of its permanent effects on his own basic rights and interests. Thus it seems that the principle of utility is incompatible with the conception of social cooperation among equals for mutual advantage. It appears to be inconsistent with the idea of reciprocity implicit in the notion of a well-ordered society. Or, at any rate, so I shall argue.

I shall maintain instead that the persons in the initial situation would choose two rather different principles: the first requires equality in the assignment of basic rights and duties, while the second holds that social and economic inequalities, for example inequalities of wealth and authority, are just only if they result in compensating benefits for everyone, and in particular for the least advantaged members of society. These principles rule out justifying institutions on the grounds that the hardships of some are offset by a greater good in the aggregate. It may be expedient but it is not just that some should have less in order that others may prosper. But there is no injustice in the greater benefits earned by a few provided that the situation of persons not so fortunate is thereby improved. The intuitive idea is that since everyone's well-being depends upon a scheme of cooperation without which no one could have a satisfactory life, the division of advantages should be such as to draw forth the willing cooperation of everyone taking part in it, including those less well-situated. The two principles mentioned seem to be a fair basis on which those better endowed, or more fortunate in their social position, neither of which we can be said to deserve, could expect the willing cooperation of others when some workable scheme is a necessary condition of the welfare of all. Once we decide to look for a conception of justice that prevents the use of the accidents of natural endowment and the contingencies of social circumstance as counters in a quest for political and economic advantage, we are led to these principles. They express the result of leaving aside those aspects of the social world that seem arbitrary from a moral point of view.

The problem of the choice of principles, however, is extremely difficult. I do not expect the answer I shall suggest to be convincing to everyone. It is, therefore, worth noting from the outset that justice as fairness, like other contract views, consists of two parts: (1) an interpretation of the initial situation and of the problem of choice posed there, and (2) a set of principles which, it is argued, would be agreed to. One may accept the first part of the theory (or some variant thereof), but not the other, and conversely. The concept of the initial contractual situation may seem reasonable although the particular principles proposed are rejected. To be sure, I want to maintain that the most appropriate conception of this situation does lead to principles of justice contrary to utilitarianism and perfectionism, and therefore that the contract doctrine provides an alternative to these views. Still, one may dispute this contention even though one grants that the contractarian method is a useful way of studying ethical theories and of setting forth their underlying assumptions.

Justice as fairness is an example of what I have called a contract theory. Now, there may be an objection to the term "contract" and related expressions, but I think it will serve reasonably well. Many words have misleading connotations which at first are likely to confuse. The terms "utility" and "utilitarianism" are surely no exception. They too have unfortunate suggestions which hostile critics have been willing to exploit; yet they are clear enough for those prepared to study utilitarian doctrine. The same should be true of the term "contract" applied to moral theories. As I have mentioned, to understand it one has to keep in mind that it implies a certain level of abstraction. In particular, the content of the relevant agreement is not to enter a given society or to adopt a given form of government, but to accept certain moral principles. Moreover, the undertakings referred to are purely hypothetical: a contract view holds that certain principles would be accepted in a well-defined initial situation.

The merit of the contract terminology is that it conveys the idea that principles of justice may be conceived as principles that would be chosen by rational persons, and that in this way conceptions of justice may be explained and justified. The theory of justice is a part, perhaps the most significant part, of the theory of rational choice. Furthermore, principles of justice deal with conflicting claims upon the advantages won by social cooperation; they apply to the relations among several persons or groups. The word "contract" suggests this plurality as well as the condition that the appropriate division of advantages must be in accordance with principles acceptable to all parties. The condition of publicity for principles of justice is also connoted by the contract phraseology. Thus, if these principles are the outcome of an agreement, citizens have a knowledge of the principles that others follow. It is characteristic of contract theories to stress the public nature of political principles. Finally there is the long tradition of the contract doctrine. Expressing the tie with this line of thought helps to define ideas and accords with natural piety. There are then several advantages in the use of the term "contract." With due precautions taken, it should not be misleading.

A final remark. Justice as fairness is not a complete contract theory. For it is clear that the contractarian idea can be extended to the choice of more or less an entire ethical system, that is, to a system including principles for all the virtues and not only for justice. Now for the most part I shall consider only principles of justice and others closely related to them; I make no attempt to discuss the virtues in a systematic way. Obviously if justice as fairness succeeds reasonably well, a next step would be to study the more general view suggested by the name "rightness as fairness." But even this wider theory fails to embrace all moral relationships, since it would seem to include

only our relations with other persons and to leave out of account how we are to conduct ourselves toward animals and the rest of nature. I do not contend that the contract notion offers a way to approach these questions, which are certainly of the first importance; and I shall have to put them aside. We must recognize the limited scope of justice as fairness and of the general type of view that it exemplifies. How far its conclusions must be revised once these other matters are understood cannot be decided in advance.

SEC. 4. THE ORIGINAL POSITION AND JUSTIFICATION

I have said that the original position is the appropriate initial status quo which insures that the fundamental agreements reached in it are fair. This fact yields the name "justice as fairness." It is clear, then, that I want to say that one conception of justice is more reasonable than another, or justifiable with respect to it, if rational persons in the initial situation would choose its principles over those of the other for the role of justice. Conceptions of justice are to be ranked by their acceptability to persons so circumstanced. Understood in this way the question of justification is settled by working out a problem of deliberation: we have to ascertain which principles it would be rational to adopt given the contractual situation. This connects the theory of justice with the theory of rational choice.

If this view of the problem of justification is to succeed, we must, of course, describe in some detail the nature of this choice problem. A problem of rational decision has a definite answer only if we know the beliefs and interests of the parties, their relations with respect to one another, the alternatives between which they are to choose, the procedure whereby they make up their minds, and so on. As the circumstances are presented in different ways, correspondingly different principles are accepted. The concept of the original position, as I shall refer to it, is that of the most philosophically favored interpretation of this initial choice situation for the purposes of a theory of justice.

But how are we to decide what is the most favored interpretation? I assume, for one thing, that there is a broad measure of agreement that principles of justice should be chosen under certain conditions. To justify a particular description of the initial situation one shows that it incorporates these commonly shared presumptions. One argues from widely accepted but weak premises to more specific conclusions. Each of the presumptions should by itself be natural and plausible; some of them may seem innocuous or even trivial. The aim of the contract approach is to establish that taken together they impose significant bounds on acceptable principles of justice. The ideal outcome would be that these conditions determine a unique set of principles; but I shall be satisfied if they suffice to rank the main traditional conceptions of social justice.

One should not be misled, then, by the somewhat unusual conditions which characterize the original position. The idea here is simply to make vivid to ourselves the restrictions that it seems reasonable to impose on arguments for principles of justice, and therefore on these principles themselves. Thus it seems reasonable and generally acceptable that no one should be advantaged or disadvantaged by natural fortune or social circumstances in the choice of principles. It also seems widely agreed that it should be impossible to tailor principles to the circumstances of one's own case. We should insure further that particular inclinations and aspirations, and persons' conceptions of their good do not affect the principles adopted. The aim is to rule out those principles that it would be rational to propose for acceptance, however little the chance of success, only if one knew certain things that are irrelevant from the standpoint of justice. For example, if a man knew that he was wealthy, he might find it rational to advance the principle that various taxes for welfare measures be counted unjust; if he knew that he was poor, he would most likely propose the contrary principle. To represent the desired restrictions one imagines a situation in which everyone is deprived of this sort of information. One excludes the knowledge of those contingencies which sets men at odds and allows them to be guided by their prejudices. In this manner the veil of ignorance is arrived at in a natural way. This concept should cause no difficulty if we keep in mind the constraints on arguments that it is meant to express. At any time we can enter the original position, so to speak, simply by following a certain procedure, namely, by arguing for principles of justice in accordance with these restrictions.

It seems reasonable to suppose that the parties in the original position are equal. That is, all have the same rights in the procedure for choosing principles; each can make proposals, submit reasons for their acceptance, and so on. Obviously the purpose of these conditions is to represent equality between human beings as moral persons, as creatures having a conception of their good and capable of a sense of justice. The basis of equality is taken to be similarity in these two respects. Systems of ends are not ranked in value; and each man is presumed to have the requisite ability to understand and to act upon whatever principles are adopted. Together with the veil of ignorance, these conditions define the principles of justice as those which rational persons concerned to advance their interests would consent to as equals when none are known to be advantaged or disadvantaged by social and natural contingencies.

There is, however, another side to justifying a particular description of the original position. This is to see if the principles which would be chosen match our considered convictions of justice or extend them in an acceptable way. We can note whether applying these principles would lead us to make the same judgments about the basic structure of society which we now make intuitively, and in which we have the greatest confidence; or whether, in cases where our present judgments are in doubt and given with hesitation, these principles offer a resolution which we can affirm on reflection. There are questions which we feel sure must be answered in a certain way. For example, we are confident that religious intolerance and racial discrimination are unjust. We think that we have examined these things with care and have reached what we believe is an impartial judgment not likely to be distorted by an excessive attention to our own interests. These convictions are provisional fixed points which we presume any conception of justice must fit. But we have much less assurance as to what is the correct distribution of wealth and authority. Here we may be looking for a way to remove our doubts. We can check an interpretation of the initial situation, then, by the capacity of its principles to accommodate our firmest convictions and to provide guidance where guidance is needed.

In searching for the most favored description of this situation we work from both ends. We begin by describing it so that it represents generally shared and preferably weak conditions. We then see if these conditions are strong enough to yield a significant set of principles. If not, we look for further premises equally reasonable. But if so, and these principles match our considered convictions of justice, then so far well and good. But presumably there will be discrepancies. In this case we have a choice. We can either modify the account of the initial situation or we can revise our existing judgments, for even the judgments we take provisionally as fixed points are liable to revision. By going back and forth, sometimes altering the conditions of the contractual circumstances, at others withdrawing our judgments and conforming them to principle, I assume that eventually we shall find a description of the initial situation that both expresses reasonable conditions and yields principles which match our considered judgments duly pruned and adjusted. This state of affairs I refer to as reflective equilibrium.[2] It is an equilibrium because at last our principles and judgments coincide; and it is reflective since we know to what principles our judgments conform and the premises of their derivation. At the moment everything is in order. But this equilibrium is not necessarily stable. It is liable to be upset by further examination of the conditions which should be imposed on the contractual situation and by particular cases which may lead us to revise our judgments. Yet for the time being we have done what we can to render coherent and to justify our convictions of social justice. We have reached a conception of the original position.

I shall not, of course, actually work through this process. Still, we may think of the interpretation of the original position that I shall present as the result of such a hypothetical course of reflection. It represents the attempt to accommodate within one scheme both reasonable philosophical conditions on principles as well as our considered judgments of justice. In arriving at the favored interpretation of the initial situation there is no point at which an appeal is made to self-evidence in the traditional sense either of general conceptions or particular convictions. I do not claim for the principles of justice proposed that they are necessary truths or derivable from such truths. A conception of justice cannot be deduced from self-evident premises or conditions on principles; instead, its justification is a matter of the mutual support of many considerations, of everything fitting together into one coherent view.

A final comment. We shall want to say that certain principles of justice are justified because they would be agreed to in an initial situation of equality. I have emphasized that this original position is purely hypothetical. It is natural to ask why, if this agreement is never actually entered into, we should take any interest in these principles, moral or otherwise. The answer is that the conditions embodied in the description of the original position are ones that we do in fact accept. Or if we do not, then perhaps we can be persuaded to do so by philosophical reflection. Each aspect of the contractual situation can be given supporting grounds. Thus what we shall do is to collect together into one conception a number of conditions on principles that we are ready upon due consideration to recognize as reasonable. These constraints express what we are prepared to regard as limits on fair terms of social cooperation. One way to look at the idea of the original position, therefore, is to see it as an expository device which sums up the meaning of these conditions and helps us to extract their consequences. On the other hand, this conception is also an intuitive notion that suggests its own elaboration, so that led on by it we are drawn to define more clearly the standpoint from which we can best interpret moral relationships. We need a conception that enables us to envision our objective from afar: the intuitive notion of the original position is to do this for us.

SEC. 5. CLASSICAL UTILITARIANISM

There are many forms of utilitarianism, and the development of the theory has continued in recent years. I shall not survey these forms here, nor take account of the numerous refinements found in contemporary discussions. My aim is to work out a theory of justice that represents an alternative to utilitarian thought generally, and so to all of these different versions of it. I believe that the contrast between the contract view and utilitarianism remains essentially the same in all these cases. Therefore I shall compare justice as fairness with familiar variants of intuitionism, perfectionism, and utilitarianism in order to bring out the underlying differences in the simplest way. With this end in mind, the kind of utilitarianism I shall describe here is the strict classical doctrine, which receives perhaps its clearest and most accessible formulation in Sidgwick. The main idea is that society is rightly ordered, and therefore just, when its major institutions are arranged so as to achieve the greatest net balance of satisfaction summed over all the individuals belonging to it.[3]

We may note first that there is, indeed, a way of thinking of society which makes it easy to suppose that the most rational conception of justice is utilitarian. For consider: each man in realizing his own interests is certainly free to balance his own losses against his own gains. We may impose a sacrifice on ourselves now for the sake of a greater advantage later. A person quite properly acts, at least when others are not affected, to achieve his own greatest good, to advance his rational ends as far as possible. Now why should not a society act on precisely the same principle applied to the group and therefore regard that which is rational for one man as right for an association of men? Just as the well-being of a person is constructed from the series of satisfactions that are experienced at different moments in the course of his life, so in very much the same way the well-being of society is to be constructed from the fulfillment of the systems of desires of the many individuals who belong to it. Since the principle for an individual is to advance as far as possible his own welfare, his own system of desires, the principle for society is to advance as far as possible the welfare of the group, to realize to the greatest extent the comprehensive system of desire arrived at from the desires of its members. Just as an individual balances present and future gains against present and future losses, so a society may balance satisfactions and dissatisfactions between different individuals. And so by these reflections one reaches the principle of utility in a natural way: a society is properly arranged when its institutions maximize the net balance of satisfaction. The principle of choice for an association of men is interpreted as an extension of the principle of choice for one man. Social justice is the principle of rational prudence applied to an aggregative conception of the welfare of the group (§30).[4]

This idea is made all the more attractive by a further consideration. The two main concepts of ethics are those of the right and the good; the concept of a morally worthy person is, I believe, derived from them. The structure of an ethical theory is, then, largely determined by how it defines and connects these two basic notions. Now it seems that the simplest way of relating them is taken by teleological theories: the good is defined independently from the right, and then the right is defined as that which maximizes the good.[5] More precisely, those institutions and acts are right which of the available alternatives produce the most good, or at least as much good as any of the other institutions and acts open as real possibilities (a rider needed when the maximal class is not a singleton). Teleological theories have a deep intuitive appeal since they seem to embody the idea of rationality. It is natural to think that rationality is maximizing something and that in morals it must be maximizing the good. Indeed, it is tempting to suppose that it is self-evident that things should be arranged so as to lead to the most good.

It is essential to keep in mind that in a teleological theory the good is defined independently from the right. This means two things. First, the theory accounts for our considered judgments as to which things are good (our judgments of value) as a separate class of judgments intuitively distinguishable by common sense, and then proposes the hypothesis that the right is maximizing the good as already specified. Second, the theory enables one to judge the goodness of things without referring to what is right. For example, if pleasure is said to be the sole good, then presumably pleasures can be recognized and ranked in value by criteria that do not presuppose any standards of right, or what we would normally think of as such. Whereas if the distribution of goods is also counted as a good, perhaps a higher order one, and the theory directs us to produce the most good (including the good of distribution among others), we no longer have a teleological view in the classical sense. The problem of distribution falls under the concept of right as one intuitively understands it, and so the theory lacks an independent definition of the good. The clarity and simplicity of classical teleological theories derives largely from the fact that they factor our moral judgments into two classes, the one being characterized separately while the other is then connected with it by a maximizing principle.

Teleological doctrines differ, pretty clearly, according to how the conception of the good is specified. If it is taken as the realization of human excellence in the various forms of culture, we have what may be called perfectionism. This notion is found in Aristotle and Nietzsche, among others. If the good is defined as pleasure, we have hedonism; if as happiness, eudaimonism, and so on. I shall understand the principle of utility in its classical form as defining the good as the satisfaction of desire, or perhaps better, as the satisfaction of rational desire. This accords with the view in all essentials and provides, I believe, a fair interpretation of it. The appropriate terms of social cooperation are settled by whatever in the circumstances will achieve the greatest sum of satisfaction of the rational desires of individuals. It is impossible to deny the initial plausibility and attractiveness of this conception.

The striking feature of the utilitarian view of justice is that it does not matter, except indirectly, how this sum of satisfactions is distributed among individuals any more than it matters, except indirectly, how one man distributes his satisfactions over time. The correct distribution in either case is that which yields the maximum fulfillment. Society must allocate its means of satisfaction whatever these are, rights and duties, opportunities and privileges, and various forms of wealth, so as to achieve this maximum if it can. But in itself no distribution of satisfaction is better than another except that the more equal distribution is to be preferred to break ties.[6] It is true that certain common sense precepts of justice, particularly those that concern the protection of liberties and rights, or that express the claims of desert, seem to contradict this contention. But from a utilitarian standpoint the explanation of these precepts and of their seemingly stringent character is that they are those precepts that experience shows should be strictly respected and departed from only under exceptional circumstances if the sum of advantages is to be maximized.[7] Yet, as with all other precepts, those of justice are derivative from the one end of attaining the greatest balance of satisfaction. Thus there is no reason in principle why the greater gains of some should not compensate for the lesser losses of others; or more important, why the violation of the liberty of a few might not be made right by the greater good shared by many. It simply happens that under most conditions, at least in a reasonably advanced stage of civilization, the greatest sum of advantages is not attained in this way. No doubt the strictness of common sense precepts of justice has a certain usefulness in limiting men's propensities to injustice and to socially injurious actions, but the utilitarian believes that to affirm this strictness as a first principle of morals is a mistake. For just as it is rational for one man to maximize the fulfillment of his system of desires, it is right for a society to maximize the net balance of satisfaction taken over all of its members.

The most natural way, then, of arriving at utilitarianism (although not, of course, the only way of doing so) is to adopt for society as a whole the principle of rational choice for one man. Once this is recognized, the place of the impartial spectator and the emphasis on sympathy in the history of utilitarian thought is readily understood. For it is by the conception of the impartial spectator and the use of sympathetic identification in guiding our imagination that the principle for one man is applied to society. It is this spectator who is conceived as carrying out the required organization of the desires of all persons into one coherent system of desire; it is by this construction that many persons are fused into one. Endowed with ideal powers of sympathy and imagination, the impartial spectator is the perfectly rational individual who identifies with and experiences the desires of others as if these desires were his own. In this way he ascertains the intensity of these desires and assigns them their appropriate weight in the one system of desire, the satisfaction of which the ideal legislator then tries to maximize by adjusting the rules of the social system. On this conception of society separate individuals are thought of as so many different lines along which rights and duties are to be assigned and scarce means of satisfaction allocated in accordance with rules so as to give the greatest fulfillment of wants. The nature of the decision made by the ideal legislator is not, therefore, materially different from that of an entrepreneur deciding how to maximize his profit by producing this or that commodity, or that of a consumer deciding how to maximize his satisfaction by the purchase of this or that collection of goods. In each case there is a single person whose system of desires determines the best allocation of limited means. The correct decision is essentially a question of efficient administration. This view of social cooperation is the consequence of extending to society the principle of choice for one man, and then, to make this extension work, conflating all persons into one through the imaginative acts of the impartial sympathetic spectator. Utilitarianism does not take seriously the distinction between persons.

SEC. 11. TWO PRINCIPLES OF JUSTICE

I shall now state in a provisional form the two principles of justice that I believe would be agreed to in the original position. The first formulation of these principles is tentative. As we go on I shall consider several formulations and approximate step-by-step the final statement to be given much later. I believe that doing this allows the exposition to proceed in a natural way.

> The first statement of the two principles reads as follows.
> First: each person is to have an equal right to the most extensive scheme of equal basic liberties compatible with a similar scheme of liberties for others.
> Second: social and economic inequalities are to be arranged so that they are both (a) reasonably expected to be to everyone's advantage, and (b) attached to positions and offices open to all. There are two ambiguous phrases in the second principle, namely "everyone's advantage" and "open to all."

These principles primarily apply, as I have said, to the basic structure of society, and govern the assignment of rights and duties and regulate the distribution of social and economic advantages. Their formulation presupposes that, for the purposes of a theory of justice, the social structure may be viewed as having two more or less distinct parts, the first principle applying to the one, the second principle to the other. Thus we distinguish between the aspects of the social system that define and secure the equal basic liberties of citizenship and the aspects that specify and establish social and economic inequalities. Now, it is essential to observe that the basic liberties are given by a list of such liberties. Important among these are political liberty (the right to vote and to hold public office) and freedom of speech and assembly; liberty of conscience and freedom of thought; freedom of the person, which includes freedom from psychological oppression and physical assault and dismemberment (integrity of the person); the right to hold personal property; and freedom from arbitrary arrest and seizure as defined by the concept of the rule of law. These liberties are all required to be equal by the first principle.

The second principle applies, in the first approximation, to the distribution of income and wealth and to the design of organizations that make use of differences in authority and responsibility. Although the distribution of wealth and income need not be equal, it must be to everyone's advantage, and at the same time, positions of authority and responsibility must be accessible to all.

One applies the second principle by holding positions open, and then, subject to this constraint, arranges social and economic inequalities so that everyone benefits.

These principles are to be arranged in a serial order, with the first principle prior to the second. This ordering means that infringements of the basic equal liberties protected by the first principle cannot be justified, or compensated for, by greater social and economic advantages. These liberties have a central range of application within which they can be limited and compromised only when they conflict with other basic liberties. Since they may be limited when they clash with one another, none of these liberties is absolute; but however they are adjusted to form one system, this system is to be the same for all. It is difficult, and perhaps impossible, to give a complete specification of these liberties independently from the particular circumstances—social, economic, and technological—of a given society. The hypothesis is that the general form of such a list could be devised with sufficient exactness to sustain this conception of justice. Of course, liberties not on the list, for example, the right to own certain kinds of property (e.g., means of production) and freedom of contract as understood by the doctrine of laissez-faire are not basic; and so they are not protected by the priority of the first principle. Finally, in regard to the second principle, the distribution of wealth and income, and positions of authority and responsibility, are to be consistent with both the basic liberties and equality of opportunity.

These principles are to be arranged in a serial order with the first principle prior to they second. This ordering means that a departure from the institutions of equal liberty required by the first principle cannot be justified by, or compensated for, by greater social and economic advantages. The distribution of wealth and income and the hierarchies of authority, must be consistent with both the? liberties of equal citizenship and equality of opportunity.

It is clear that these two principles are rather specific in their content, and their acceptance rests on certain assumptions that I must eventually try to explain and justify. A theory of justice depends upon a theory of society in ways that will become evident as we proceed. For the present, it should be observed that these principles are a special case of a more general conception of justice that can be expressed as follows.

> All social values—liberty and opportunity, income and wealth, and the social bases of self-respect—are to be distributed equally unless an unequal distribution of any, or all, of these values is to everyone's advantage.

Injustice, then, is simply inequalities that are not to the benefit of all. Of course, this conception is extremely vague and requires interpretation.

As a first step, suppose that the basic structure of society distributes certain primary goods, that is, things that every rational man is presumed to want. These goods normally have a use whatever a person's rational plan of life. For simplicity, assume that the chief primary goods at the disposition of society are rights, liberties, opportunities, income, and wealth. These are the social primary goods. Other primary goods such as health and vigor, intelligence and imagination, are natural goods; although their possession is influenced by the basic structure, they are not so directly under its control. Imagine, then, a hypothetical initial arrangement in which all the social primary goods are equally distributed: everyone has similar rights and duties, and income and wealth are evenly shared. This state of affairs provides a benchmark for judging improvements. If certain inequalities of wealth and differences in authority would make everyone better off than in this hypothetical starting situation, then they accord with the general conception.

Now, it is possible, at least theoretically, that by giving up some of their fundamental liberties men are sufficiently compensated by the resulting social and economic gains. The general conception of justice imposes no restrictions on what sort of inequalities are permissible; it only requires that everyone's position be improved. We need not suppose anything so drastic as consenting to a condition of slavery. Imagine instead that people seem willing to forgo certain political rights when the economic returns are significant and their capacity to influence the course of policy by the exercise of these rights would be marginal in any case. It is this kind of exchange that the two principles rule out; being arranged in serial order they do not permit exchanges between basic liberties and economic and social gains except under extenuating circumstances (§§26, 39). The serial ordering of principles expresses an underlying preference among primary social goods. When this preference is rational so likewise is the choice of these principles in this order.

For the most part I shall leave aside the general conception of justice and examine instead the two principles in serial order. The advantage of this procedure is that from the first the matter of priorities is recognized and an effort made to find principles to deal with it. One is led to attend throughout to the conditions under which the absolute weight of liberty with respect to social and economic advantages, as defined by the lexical order of the two principles, would be reasonable. Offhand, this ranking appears extreme and too special a case to be of much interest; but there is more justification for it than would appear at first sight. Or at any rate, so I shall maintain). Furthermore, the distinction between fundamental rights and liberties and economic and social benefits marks a difference among primary social goods that suggests an important division in the social system. Of course, the distinctions drawn and the ordering proposed are at best only approximations. There are surely circumstances in which they fail. But it is essential to depict clearly the main lines of a reasonable conception of justice; and under many conditions, anyway, the two principles in serial order may serve well enough. When necessary we can fall back on the more general conception.

The fact that the two principles apply to institutions has certain consequences. Several points illustrate this. First of all, the rights and basic liberties referred to by these principles are those which are defined by the public rules of the basic structure. Whether men are free is determined by the rights and duties established by the major institutions of society. Liberty is a certain pattern of social forms. The first principle simply requires that certain sorts of rules, those defining basic liberties, apply to everyone equally and that they allow the most extensive liberty compatible with a like liberty for all. The only reason for circumscribing basic liberties and making them less extensive is that otherwise they would interfere with one another.

Further, when principles mention persons, or require that everyone gain from an inequality, the reference is to representative persons holding the various social positions, or offices established by the basic structure. Thus in applying the second principle I assume that it is possible to assign an expectation of well-being to representative individuals holding these positions. This expectation indicates their life prospects as viewed from their social station. In general, the expectations of representative persons depend upon the distribution of rights and duties throughout the basic structure. Expectations are connected: by raising the prospects of the representative man in one position we presumably increase or decrease the prospects of representative men in other positions. Since it applies to institutional forms, the second principle (or rather the first part of it) refers to the expectations of representative individuals. As I shall discuss below, neither principle applies to distributions of particular goods to particular individuals who may be identified by their proper names. The situation where someone is considering how to allocate certain commodities to needy persons who are known to him is not within the scope of the principles. They are meant to regulate basic institutional arrangements. We must not assume that there is much similarity from the standpoint of justice between an administrative allotment of goods to specific persons and the appropriate design of society. Our common sense intuitions for the former may be a poor guide to the latter.

Now the second principle insists that each person benefit from permissible inequalities in the basic structure. This means that it must be reasonable for each relevant representative man defined by this structure, when he views it as a going concern, to prefer his prospects with the inequality to his prospects without it. One is not allowed to justify differences in income or in positions of authority and responsibility on the ground that the disadvantages of those in one position are outweighed by the greater advantages of those in another. Much less can infringements of liberty be counterbalanced in this way. Applied to the basic structure, the principle of utility would have up maximize the sum of expectations of representative men (weighted by the number of persons they represent, on the classical view); and this would permit us to compensate for the losses of some by the benefit from economic and social inequalities. It is obvious, however, that there are indefinitely many ways in which all may be advantaged when the initial arrangement of equality is taken as a benchmark. How then are we to choose among these possibilities? The principles must be specified so that they yield a determinate conclusion. I now turn to this problem.

SEC. 24. THE VEIL OF IGNORANCE

The idea of the original position is to set up a fair procedure so that any principles agreed to will be just. The aim is to use the notion of pure procedural justice as a basis of theory. Somehow we must nullify the effects of specific contingencies which put men at odds and tempt them to exploit social and natural circumstances to their own advantage. Now, in order to do this I assume that the parties are situated behind a veil of ignorance. They do not know how the various alternatives will affect their own particular case, and they are obliged to evaluate principles solely on the basis of general considerations.

It is assumed, then, that the parties do not know certain kinds of particular facts. First of all, no one knows his place in society, his class position or social status; nor does he know his fortune in the distribution of natural assets and abilities, his intelligence and strength, and the like. Nor, again, does anyone know his conception of the good, the particulars of his rational plan of life, or even the special features of his psychology such as his aversion to risk or liability to optimism or pessimism. More than this, I assume that the parties do not know the particular circumstances of their own society. That is, they do not know its economic or political situation, or the level of civilization and culture it has been able to achieve. The persons in the original position have no information as to which generation they belong. These

broader restrictions on knowledge are appropriate in part because questions of social justice arise between generations as well as within them; for example, the question of the appropriate rate of capital saving and of the conservation of natural resources and the environment of nature. There is also, theoretically anyway, the question of a reasonable genetic policy. In these cases too, in order to carry through the idea of the original position, the parties must not know the contingencies that set them in opposition. They must choose principles the consequences of which they are prepared to live with whatever generation they turn out to belong to.

As far as possible, then, the only particular facts which the parties know are that their society is subject to the circumstances of justice, and whatever this implies. It is taken for granted, however, that they know the general facts about human society. They understand political affairs and the principles of economic theory; they know the basis of social organization and the laws of human psychology. Indeed, the parties are presumed to know whatever general facts affect the choice of the principles of justice. There are no limitations on general information, that is, on general laws and theories, since conceptions of justice must be adjusted to the characteristics of the systems of social cooperation they are to regulate, and there is no reason to rule out these facts. It is, for example, a consideration against a conception of justice that, in view of the laws of moral psychology, men would not acquire a desire to act upon it even when the institutions of their society satisfied it. For in this case there would be difficulty in securing the stability of social cooperation. An important feature of a conception of justice that it should generate its own support. Its principles should be such that when they are embodied in the basic structure of society men tend to acquire the corresponding sense of justice and develop a desire to act in accordance with its principles. In this case a conception of justice is stable. This kind of general information is admissible in the original position.

The notion of the veil of ignorance raises several difficulties. Some may object that the exclusion of nearly all particular information makes it difficult to grasp what is meant by the original position. Thus it may be helpful to observe that one or more persons can at any time enter this position, or perhaps, better, simulate the deliberations of this hypothetical situation, simply by reasoning in accordance with the appropriate restrictions. In arguing for a conception of justice we must be sure that it is among the permitted alternatives and satisfies the stipulated formal constraints. No considerations can be advanced in its favor unless they would be rational ones for us to urge were we to lack the kind of knowledge that is excluded. The evaluation of principles must proceed in terms of the general consequences of their public recognition and universal application, it being assumed that they will be complied with by everyone. To say that a certain conception of justice would be chosen in the original position is equivalent to saying that rational deliberation satisfying certain conditions and restrictions would reach a certain conclusion. If necessary, the argument to this result could be set out more formally. I shall, however, speak throughout in terms of the notion of the original position. It is more economical and suggestive, and brings out certain essential features that otherwise one might easily overlook.

These remarks show that the original position is not to be thought of as a general assembly which includes at one moment everyone who will live at some time; or, much less, as an assembly of everyone who could live at some time. It is not a gathering of all actual or possible persons. If we conceived of the original position in either of these ways, the conception would cease to be a natural guide to intuition and would lack a clear sense. In any case, the original position must be interpreted so that one can at any time adopt its perspective. It must make no difference when one takes up this viewpoint, or who does so: the restrictions must be such that the same principles are always chosen. The veil of ignorance is a key condition in meeting this requirement. It insures not only that the information available is relevant, but that it is at all times the same.

It may be protested that the condition of the veil of ignorance is irrational. Surely, some may object, principles should be chosen in the light of all the knowledge available. There are various replies to this contention. Here I shall sketch those which emphasize the simplifications that need to be made if one is to have any theory at all. To begin with, it is clear that since the differences among the parties are unknown to them, and everyone is equally rational and similarly situated, each is convinced by the same arguments. Therefore, we can view the agreement in the original position from the standpoint of one person selected at random. If anyone after due reflection prefers a conception of justice to another, then they all do, and a unanimous agreement can be reached. We can, to make the circumstances more vivid, imagine that the parties are required to communicate with each other through a referee as intermediary, and that he is to announce which alternatives have been suggested and the reasons offered in their support. He forbids the attempt to form coalitions, and he informs the parties when they have come to an understanding. But such a referee is actually superfluous, assuming that the deliberations of the parties must be similar.

Thus there follows the very important consequence that the parties have no basis for bargaining in the usual sense. No one knows his situation in society nor his natural assets, and therefore no one is in a position to tailor principles to his advantage. We might imagine that one of the contractees threatens to hold out unless the others agree to principles favorable to him. But how does he know which principles are especially in his interests? The same holds for the formation of coalitions: if a group were to decide to band together to the disadvantage of the others, they would not know how to favor themselves in the choice of principles. Even if they could get everyone to agree to their proposal, they would have no assurance that it was to their advantage, since they cannot identify themselves either by name or description. The one case where this conclusion fails is that of saving. Since the persons in the original position know that they are contemporaries (taking the present time of entry interpretation), they can favor their generation by refusing to make any sacrifices at all for their successors; they simply acknowledge the principle that no one has a duty to save for posterity. Previous generations have saved or they have not; there is nothing the parties can now do to affect that. So in this instance the veil of ignorance fails to secure the desired result. Therefore, to handle the question of justice between generations, I modify the motivation assumption and add a further constraint. With these adjustments, no generation is able to formulate principles especially designed to advance its own cause, and some significant limits on savings principles can be derived Whatever a person's temporal position, each is forced to choose for all.[8]

The restrictions on particular information in the original position are, then, of fundamental importance. Without them we would not be able to work out any definite theory of justice at all. We would have to be content with a vague formula stating that justice is what would be agreed to without being able to say much, if anything, about the substance of the agreement itself. The formal constraints of the concept of right, those applying to principles directly, are not sufficient for our purpose, The veil of ignorance makes possible a unanimous choice of a particular conception of justice. Without these limitations on knowledge the bargaining problem of the original position would be hopelessly complicated. Even if theoretically a solution were to exist, we would not, at present anyway, be able to determine it.

The notion of the veil of ignorance is implicit, I think, in Kant's ethics. Nevertheless the problem of defining the knowledge of the parties and of characterizing the alternatives open to them has often been passed over, even by contract theories. Sometimes the situation definitive of moral deliberation is presented in such an indeterminate way that one cannot ascertain how it will turn out. Thus Perry's doctrine is essentially contractarian: he holds that social and personal integration must proceed by entirely different principles, the latter by rational prudence, the former by the concurrence of persons of good will. He would appear to reject utilitarianism on much the same grounds suggested earlier: namely, that it improperly extends the principle of choice for one person to choices facing society. The right course of action is characterized as that which best advances social

aims as these would be formulated by reflective agreement, given that the parties have full knowledge of the circumstances and are moved by a benevolent concern for one another's interests. No effort is made, however, to specify in any precise way the possible outcomes of this sort of agreement. Indeed, without a far more elaborate account, no conclusions can be drawn. I do not wish here to criticize others; rather, I want to explain the necessity for what may seem at times like so many irrelevant details.

Now the reasons for the veil of ignorance go beyond mere simplicity. We want to define the original position so that we get the desired solution. If a knowledge of particulars is allowed, then the outcome is biased by arbitrary contingencies. As already observed, to each according to his threat advantage is not a principle of justice. If the original position is to yield agreements that are just, the parties must be fairly situated and treated equally as moral persons. The arbitrariness of the world must be corrected for by adjusting the circumstances of the initial contractual situation. Moreover, if in choosing principles we required unanimity even when there is full information, only a few rather obvious cases could be decided. A conception of justice based on unanimity in these circumstances would indeed be weak and trivial. But once knowledge is excluded, the requirement of unanimity is not out of place and the fact that it can be satisfied is of great importance. It enables us to say of the preferred conception of justice that it represents a genuine reconciliation of interests.

A final comment. For the most part I shall suppose that the parties possess all general information. No general facts are closed to them. I do this mainly to avoid complications. Nevertheless a conception of justice is to be the public basis of the terms of social cooperation. Since common understanding necessitates certain bounds on the complexity of principles, there may likewise be limits on the use of theoretical knowledge in the original position. Now, clearly it would be very difficult to classify and to grade the complexity of the various sorts of general facts. I shall make no attempt to do this. We do however recognize an intricate theoretical construction when we meet one. Thus it seems reasonable to say that, other things equal, one conception of justice is to be preferred to another when it is founded upon markedly simpler general facts, and its choice does not depend upon elaborate calculations in the light of a vast array of theoretically defined possibilities. It is desirable that the grounds for a public conception of justice should be evident to everyone when circumstances permit. This consideration favors, I believe, the two principles of justice over the criterion of utility.

SEC. 29. SOME MAIN GROUNDS FOR THE TWO PRINCIPLES OF JUSTICE

In this section my aim is to use the conditions of publicity and finality to give some of the main arguments for the two principles of justice. I shall rely upon the fact that for an agreement to be valid, the parties must be able to honor it under all relevant and foreseeable circumstances. There must be a rational assurance that one can carry through. The arguments I shall adduce fit under the heuristic schema suggested by the reasons for following the maximin rule. That is, they help to show that the two principles are an adequate minimum conception of justice in a situation of great uncertainty. Any further advantages that might be won by the principle of utility, or whatever, are highly problematical, whereas the hardship if things turn out badly are intolerable. It is at this point that the concept of a contract has a definite role: it suggests the condition of publicity and sets limits upon what can be agreed to.

The first confirming ground for the two principles can be explained in terms of the strains of commitment. The parties have a capacity for justice in the sense that they can be assured that their undertaking is not in vain. Assuming that they have taken everything into account, including the general facts of moral psychology, they can rely on one another to adhere to the principles adopted. Thus they consider the strains of commitment. They cannot enter into agreements that

may have consequences they cannot accept. They will avoid those that they can adhere to only with great difficulty. Since the original agreement is final and made in perpetuity, there is no second chance. In view of the serious nature of the possible consequences, the question of the burden of commitment is especially acute. A person is choosing once and for all the standards which are to govern his life prospects. Moreover, when we enter an agreement we must be able to honor it even should the worst possibilities prove to be the case. Otherwise we have not acted in good faith. Thus the parties must weigh with care whether they will be able to stick by their commitment in all circumstances. Of course, in answering this question they have only a general knowledge of human psychology to go on. But this information is enough to tell which conception of justice involves the greater stress.

In this respect the two principles of justice have a definite advantage. Not only do the parties protect their basic rights, but they insure themselves against the worst eventualities. They run no chance of having to acquiesce in a loss of freedom over the course of their life for the sake of a greater good enjoyed by others, an undertaking that in actual circumstances they might not be able to keep. Indeed, we might wonder whether such an agreement can be made in good faith at all. Compacts of this sort exceed the capacity of human nature. How can the parties possibly know, or be sufficiently sure, that they can keep such an agreement? Certainly they cannot base their confidence on a general knowledge of moral psychology. To be sure, any principle chosen in the original position may require a large sacrifice for some. The beneficiaries of clearly unjust institutions (those founded on principles that have no claim to acceptance) may find it hard to reconcile themselves to the changes that will have to be made. But in this case they will know that they could not have maintained their position anyway. In any case, the two principles of justice an alternative. If the only possible candidates all involved similar risks, the problem of the strains of commitment would have to be waived. This is not the case and judged in this light the two principles seem distinctly superior.

A second consideration invokes the condition of publicity as well as that of the constraints on agreements. I shall present the argument in terms of the question of psychological stability. Earlier I stated that a strong point in favor of a conception of justice is that it generates its own support. When the basic structure of society is publicly known to satisfy its principles for an extended period of time, those subject to these arrangements tend to develop a desire to act in accordance with these principles and to do their part in institutions which exemplify them. A conception of justice is stable when the public recognition of its realization by the social system tends to bring about the corresponding sense of justice. Now, whether this happens depends, of course, on the laws of moral psychology and the availability of human motives. We may observe that the principle of utility seems to require a greater identification with the interests of others than the two principles of justice. Thus the latter will be a more stable conception to the extent that this identification is difficult to achieve. When the two principles are satisfied, each person's liberties are secured and there is a sense defined by the difference principle in which everyone is benefited by social cooperation. Therefore we can explain the acceptance of the social system and the principles it satisfies by the psychological law that persons tend to love, cherish, and support whatever affirms their own good. Since everyone's good is affirmed, all acquire inclinations to uphold the scheme.

When the principle of utility is satisfied, however, there is no such assurance that everyone benefits. Allegiance to the social system may demand that some should forgo advantages for the sake of the greater good of the whole. Thus the scheme will not be stable unless those who must make sacrifices strongly identify with interests broader than their own. But this is not easy to bring about. The sacrifices in question are not those asked in times of social emergency, when all or some must pitch in for the common good. The principles of justice apply to the basic structure of the social system and to the determination of life prospects.

What the principle of utility asks is precisely a sacrifice of these prospects. Even when we are less fortunate, we are to accept the greater advantages of others as a sufficient reason for lower expectations over the whole course of our life. This is surely an extreme demand. In fact, when society is conceived as a system of cooperation designed to advance the good of its members, it seems quite incredible that some citizens should be expected, on the basis of political principles, to accept still lower prospects of life for the sake of others. It is evident then why utilitarians should stress the role of sympathy in moral learning and the central place of benevolence among the moral virtues. Their conception of justice is threatened with instability unless sympathy and benevolence can be widely and intensely cultivated. Looking at the question from the standpoint of the original position, the parties would reject the principle of utility and adopt the more realistic idea of designing the social order on a principle of reciprocal advantage. We need not suppose, of course, that in everyday life persons never make substantial sacrifices for one another, since moved by affection and ties of sentiment they often do. But such actions are not demanded as a matter of justice by the basic structure of society.

Furthermore, the public recognition of the two principles gives greater support to men's self-respect, and this in turn increases the effectiveness of social cooperation. Both effects are reasons for agreeing to these principles. It is clearly rational for men to secure their self-respect. A sense of their own worth is necessary if they are to pursue their conception of the good with satisfaction and to take pleasure in its fulfillment. Self-respect is not so much a part of any rational plan of life as the sense that one's plan is worth carrying out. Now, our self-respect normally depends upon the respect of others. Unless we feel that our endeavors are respected by them, it is difficult if not impossible for us to maintain the conviction that our ends are worth advancing (§67). Hence, for this reason the parties would accept the natural duty of mutual respect which asks them to treat one another civilly and to be willing to explain the grounds of their actions, especially when the claims of others are overruled (§51). Moreover, one may assume that those who respect themselves are more likely to respect each other. Self-contempt leads to contempt of others and threatens their good as much as envy does. Self-respect is reciprocally self-supporting.

Thus a desirable feature of a conception of justice is that it should publicly express men's respect for one another. In this way they insure a sense of their own value. Now, the two principles achieve this end. For when society follows these principles, everyone's good is included in a scheme of mutual benefit, and this public affirmation in institutions of each man's endeavors supports men's self-esteem. The establishment of equal liberty and the operation of the difference principle are bound to have this effect. The two principles are equivalent, as I have remarked, to an undertaking to regard the distribution of natural abilities in some respects as a collective asset, so that the more fortunate are to benefit only in ways that help those who have lost out. I do not say that the parties are moved by the ethical propriety of this idea. But there are reasons for them to accept this principle. For by arranging inequalities for reciprocal advantage and by abstaining from the exploitation of the contingencies of nature and social circumstance within a framework of equal liberties, persons express their respect for one another in the very constitution of their society. In this way they insure their self-respect, as it is rational for them to do.

Another way of putting this is to say that the principles of justice manifest in the basic structure of society men's desire to treat one another not as means only but as ends in themselves. I cannot examine Kant's view here.[9] Instead I shall freely interpret it in the light of the contract doctrine. The notion of treating men as ends in themselves and never as only a means obviously needs an explanation. How can we always treat everyone as an end and never as a means only? Certainly we cannot say that it comes to treating everyone by the same general principles, since this interpretation makes the concept equivalent to formal justice. On the contract interpretation, treating men as ends in themselves implies at the very least

treating them in accordance with the principles to which they would consent in an original position of equality. For in this situation men have equal representation as moral persons who regard themselves as ends and the principles they accept will be rationally designed to protect the claims of their person. The contract view as such defines a sense in which men are to be treated as ends and not as means only.

But the question arises whether there are substantive principles which convey this idea. If the parties wish to express this notion visibly in the basic structure of their society in order to secure each man's rational interest in his self-respect, which principles should they choose? Now, it seems that the two principles of justice achieve this aim: for all have equal basic liberties and the difference principle interprets the distinction between treating men as a means only and treating them also as ends in themselves. To regard persons as ends in themselves in the basic design of society is to agree to forgo those gains that do not contribute to everyone's expectations. By contrast, to regard persons as means is to be prepared to impose on those already less favored still lower prospects of life for the sake of the higher expectations of others. Thus we see that the difference principle, which at first appears rather extreme, has a reasonable interpretation. If we further suppose that social cooperation among those who respect each other and themselves—as manifest in their institutions—is likely to be more effective and harmonious, [then] the general level of expectations, assuming we could estimate it, may be higher when the two principles of justice are satisfied than one might otherwise have thought. The advantage of the principle of utility in this respect is no longer so clear.

The principle of utility presumably requires some who are less fortunate to accept even lower life prospects for the sake of others. To be sure, it is not necessary that those having to make such sacrifices rationalize this demand by having a lesser appreciation of their own worth. It does not follow from the utilitarian doctrine that it is because their aims are trivial or unimportant that some individuals' expectations are less. But the parties must consider the general facts of moral psychology. Surely it is natural to experience a loss of self-respect, a weakening of our sense of the value of accomplishing our aims, when we are already less favored. This is particularly likely to be so when social cooperation is arranged for the good of individuals. That is, those with greater advantages do not claim that they are necessary to preserve certain religious or cultural values that everyone has a duty to maintain. We are not here considering a doctrine of traditional order, nor the principle of perfectionism, but rather the principle of utility. In this instance, then, men's self-respect hinges on how they regard one another. If the parties accept the utility criterion, they will lack the support to their self-respect provided by the public commitment of others to arrange inequalities to everyone's advantage and to guarantee the basic liberties for all. In a public utilitarian society men, particularly the least advantaged, will find it more difficult to be confident of their own worth.

The utilitarian may answer that in maximizing the average utility these matters are already taken into account. If, for example, the equal liberties are necessary for men's self-respect and the average utility is higher when they are affirmed, then of course they should be established. So far so good. But the point is that we must not lose sight of the publicity condition. This requires that in maximizing the average utility we do so subject to the constraint that the utilitarian principle is publicly accepted and followed as the fundamental charter of society. What we cannot do is to raise the average utility by encouraging men to adopt and apply non-utilitarian principles of justice. If, for whatever reasons, the public recognition of utilitarianism entails some loss of self-esteem, there is no way around this drawback. It is an unavoidable cost of the utilitarian scheme given our stipulations. Thus suppose that the average utility is actually greater should the two principles of justice be publicly affirmed and realized in the basic structure. For the reasons mentioned, this may conceivably be the case. These principles would then represent the most attractive prospect, and on both lines of reasoning just examined, the

two principles would be accepted. The utilitarian cannot reply that one is now really maximizing the average utility. In fact, the parties would have chosen the two principles of justice.

We should note, then, that utilitarianism, as I have defined it, is the view that the principle of utility is the correct principle for society's public conception of justice. And to show this one must argue that this criterion would be chosen in the original position. If we like, we can define a different variation of the initial situation in which the motivation assumption is that the parties want to adopt those principles that maximize average utility. The preceding remarks indicate that the two principles of justice may still be chosen. But if so, it is a mistake to call these principles—and the theory in which they appear—utilitarian. The motivation assumption by itself does not determine the character of the whole theory. In fact, the case for the principles of justice is strengthened if they would be chosen under different motivation assumptions. This indicates that the theory of justice is firmly grounded and not sensitive to slight changes in this condition. What we want to know is which conception of justice characterizes our considered judgments in reflective equilibrium and best serves as the public moral basis of society. Unless one maintains that this conception is given by the principle of utility, one is not a utilitarian.[10]

The strains of commitment and the publicity condition, both of which we have discussed in this section, are also important. The first arises from the fact that, in general, the class of things that can be agreed to is included within, but smaller than, the class of things that can be rationally chosen. We can decide to take a chance and at the same time fully intend that, should things turn out badly, we shall do what we can to retrieve our situation. But if we make an agreement, we have to accept the result; and so to give an undertaking in good faith, we must not only intend to honor it, but with reason believe that we can do so. Thus the contract condition excludes a certain kind of randomizing. One cannot agree to a principle if there is a real possibility that it has any outcome that one will not be able to accept. I shall not comment further on the publicity condition except to note that it ties in with the desirability of embedding ideals in first principles, with simplicity and with stability.

The form of the argument for the two principles is that the balance of reasons favors them over the principle of average utility, and assuming transitivity, over the classical doctrine as well. Thus the agreement of the parties depends on weighing various considerations. The reasoning is informal and not a proof, and there is an appeal to intuition as the basis of the theory of justice. Yet when everything is tallied up, it may be clear where the balance of reasons lies. If so, then to the extent that the original position embodies reasonable conditions used in the justification of principles in everyday life, the claim that one would agree to the principles of justice is perfectly credible. Thus they can serve as a conception of justice in the public acceptance of which persons can recognize one another's good faith.

It may be helpful at this point to list some of the main grounds in favor of the two principles of justice over the principle of average utility. That the conditions of generality of principle, universality of application, and limited information are not sufficient by themselves to require these principles is clear from the reasoning for the utility principle. Further assumptions must, therefore, be incorporated into the original position. Thus, I have assumed that the parties regard themselves as having certain fundamental interests that they must protect if they can; and that, as free persons, they have a highest-order interest in maintaining their liberty to revise and alter these ends. The parties are, so to speak, persons with determinate interests rather than bare potentialities for all possible interests, even though the specific character of these interests is unknown to them. They must try to secure favorable conditions for advancing these finite ends, whatever they are . The hierarchy of interests and its relation to the priority of liberty is taken up later , but the general nature of the argument for the basic liberties is illustrated by the case of liberty of conscience and freedom of thought.

In addition, the veil of ignorance is interpreted to mean not only that the parties have no knowledge of their particular aims and ends (except what is contained in the thin theory of the good), but also that the historical record is closed to them. They do not know, and cannot enumerate, the social circumstances in which they may find themselves, or the array of techniques their society may have at its disposal. They have, therefore, no objective grounds for relying on one probability distribution rather than another, and the principle of insufficient reason cannot be invoked as a way around this limitation. These considerations, together with those derived from regarding the parties as having determinate fundamental interests, imply that the expectation constructed by the argument for the utility principle is unsound and lacks the necessary unity.

NOTES

1. Kant is clear that the original agreement is hypothetical. See *The Metaphysics of Morals*, pt. I *(Rechtslehre)*, especially §§47, 52; and pt. II of the essay "Concerning the Common Saying: This May Be True in Theory but It Does Not Apply in Practice," in *Kant's Political Writings*. Ed. Hans Reiss. Trans. H. B. Nisbet. Cambridge: The University Press, 1970. 73–87. For a further discussion see Vlachos, Georges. *La Pensée politique de Kant*. Paris: Presses Universitaires de France, 1962. 326–335; Murphy, J. G. *Kant: The Philosophy of Right*. London: Macmillan, 1970. 109–112, 133–136.

2. The process of mutual adjustment of principles and considered judgments is not peculiar to moral philosophy. For parallel remarks concerning the justification of the principles of deductive and inductive inference see Goodman, Nelson. *Fact, Fiction, and Forecast*. Cambridge, Mass.: Harvard University Press, 1955. 65–68.

3. I shall take Henty Sidgwick's *The Methods of Ethics*, 7th ed. (London, 1907), as summarizing the development of utilitarian moral theory. Book III of his *Principles of Political Economy* (London, 1883) applies this doctrine to questions of economic and social justice, and is a precursor of Pigou, A. C. *The Economics of Welfare*. London: Macmillan, 1920. Sidgwick's *Outlines of the History of Ethics*, 5th ed. (London, 1902), contains a brief history of

the utilitarian tradition. We may follow him in assuming, somewhat arbitrarily, that it begins with Shaftesbury's *An Inquiry Concerning Virtue and Merit* (1711) and Hutcheson's *An Inquiry Concerning Moral Good and Evil* (1725). Hutcheson seems to have been the first to state clearly the principle of utility. He says in *Inquiry,* sec. 111, §8, that "that action is best, which procures the greatest happiness for the greatest numbers; and that, worst, which, in like manner, occasions misery." Other major eighteenth century works are Hume's *A Treatise of Human Nature* (1739), and *An Enquiry Concerning the Principles of Morals* (1751); Adam Smith's *A Theory of the Moral Sentiments* (1759); and Bentham's *The Principles of Morals and Legislation* (1789). To these we must add the writings of J. S. Mill represented by *Utilitarianism* (1863) and F. Y. Edgeworth's *Mathematical Psychics* (London, 1888).

The discussion of utilitarianism has taken a different turn in recent years by focusing on what we may call the coordination problem and related questions of publicity. This development stems from the essays of: Harrod, R. F. "Utilitarianism Revised." *Mind* vol. 45 (1936); Mabbott, J. D. "Punishment." *Mind* vol. 48 (1939); Harrison, Jonathan. "Utilitarianism, Universalisation, and Our Duty to Be Just." *Proceedings of the Aristotelian Society* vol. 53 (1952–53); and Urmson, J. O. "The Interpretation of the Philosophy of J. S. Mill." *Philosophical Quarterly* vol. 3 (1953). See also Smart, J. J. C. "Extreme and Restricted Utilitarianism." *Philosophical Quarterly* vol. 6 (1956), and his *An Outline of a System of Utilitarian Ethics.* Cambridge: The University Press, 1961. For an account of these matters, see Lyons, David. *Forms and Limits of Utilitarianism.* Oxford: The Clarendon Press, 1965; and Gibbard, Allan. "Utilitarianisms and Coordination." (Dissertation, Harvard University, 1971). The problems raised by these works, as important as they are, I shall leave aside as not bearing directly on the more elementary question of distribution which I wish to discuss.

Finally, we should note here the essays of J. C. Harsanyi, in particular: "Cardinal Utility in Welfare Economics and in the Theory of Risk-Taking." *Journal of Political Economy*

(1953), and "Cardinal Welfare, Individualistic Ethics, and Interpersonal Comparisons of Utility." *Journal of Political Economy* (1955); and Brandt, R. B. "Some Merits of One Form of Rule-Utilitarianism." *University of Colorado Studies.* Boulder, Colorado, 1967.

4. On this point see also Gauthier, D. P. *Practical Reasoning.* Oxford: Clarendon Press, 1963. 126f. The text elaborates the suggestion found in "Constitutional Liberty and the Concept of Justice," *Nomos VI: Justice.* Eds. C. J. Friedrich and J. W. Chapman New York: Atherton Press, 1963. 124f, which in turn is related to the idea of justice as a higher-order administrative decision. See "Justice as Fairness." *Philosophical Review* (1958): 185–187. That the principle of social integration is distinct from the principle of personal integration is stated by Perry, R. B. *General Theory of Value.* New York: Longmans, Green, and Company, 1926. 674–677. He attributes the error of overlooking this fact to Emile Durkheim and others with similar views. Perry's conception of social integration is that brought about by a shared and dominant benevolent purpose.

5. Here I adopt W. K. Frankena's definition of teleological theories in *Ethics.* Englewood Cliffs, N.J.: Prentice Hall. Inc., 1963. 13.

6. On this point see Sidgwick, *The Methods of Ethics* (1874). 416f.

7. See Mill, J. S. *Utilitarianism,* ch. V, last two pars.

8. Rousseau, *The Social Contract,* bk. II, ch. IV, par. 5.

9. Kant, Immanuel. *The Foundations of the Metaphysics of Morals. Gesammelten Schriften.* Vol. IV. Berlin: Preussische Akademie der Wissenschaften, 1913. See pp. 427–430, where the second formulation of the categorical imperative is introduced.

10. Thus while Brandt holds that a society's moral code is to be publicly recognized, and that the best code from a philosophical standpoint is the one that maximizes average utility, he does not maintain that the principle of utility must belong to the code itself. In fact, he denies that within the public morality the final court of appeal need be to utility. Thus by the definition in the text, his view is not utilitarian. See Brandt, Richard B. "Some Merits of One Form of Rule Utilitarianism." *University of Colorado Studies* (1967): 58f.

43   Wilt Chamberlain and Distributive Justice (from *Anarchy, State, and Utopia*)

ROBERT NOZICK

The minimal state is the most extensive state that can be justified. Any state more extensive violates people's rights. Yet many persons have put forth reasons purporting to justify a more extensive state. It is impossible within the compass of this [article] to examine all the reasons that have been put forth. Therefore, I shall focus upon those generally acknowledged to be most weighty and influential, to see precisely wherein they fail. In this chapter we consider the claim that a more extensive state is justified, because necessary (or the best instrument) to achieve distributive justice.

The term "distributive justice" is not a neutral one. Hearing the term "distribution," most people presume that some thing or mechanism uses some principle or criterion to give out a supply of things. Into this process of distributing shares some error may have crept. So it is an open question, at least, whether *re*distribution should take place; whether we should do again what has already been done once, though poorly. However, we are not in the position of children who have been given portions of pie by someone who now makes last minute adjustments to rectify careless cutting. There is no *central* distribution, no person or group entitled to control all the resources, jointly deciding how they are to be doled out. What each person gets, he gets from others who give to him in exchange for something, or as a gift. In a free society, diverse persons control different resources, and new holdings arise out of the voluntary exchanges and actions of persons. There is no more a distributing or distribution of shares than there is a distributing of mates in a society in which persons choose whom they shall marry. The total result is the product of many individual decisions which the different individuals involved are entitled to make. Some uses of the term "distribution," it is true, do not imply a previous distributing appropriately judged by some criterion (for example, "probability distribution"); nevertheless, despite the title of this chapter, it would be best to use a terminology that clearly is neutral. We shall speak of people's holdings; a principle of justice in holdings describes (part of) what justice tells us (requires) about holdings. I shall state first what I take to be the correct view about justice in holdings, and then turn to the discussion of alternate views.

THE ENTITLEMENT THEORY

The subject of justice in holdings consists of three major topics. The first is the *original acquisition of holdings*, the appropriation of unheld things. This includes the issues of how unheld things may come to be held, the process, or processes, by which unheld things may come to be held, the things that may come to be held by these processes, the extent of what comes to be held by a particular process, and so on. We shall refer to the complicated truth about this topic, which we shall not formulate here, as the principle of justice in acquisition. The second topic concerns the *transfer of holdings* from one person to another. By what processes may a person transfer holdings to another? How may a person acquire a holding from another who holds it? Under this topic come general descriptions of voluntary exchange, and gift and (on the other hand) fraud, as well as reference to particular conventional details fixed upon in a given society. The complicated truth about this subject (with placeholders for conventional details) we shall call the principle of justice in transfer. (And we shall suppose it also includes

From *Anarchy, State and Utopia* (New York: Basic Books, 1974). Reprinted with permission of the publisher. Citations have been omitted.

principles governing how a person may divest himself of a holding, passing it into an unheld state.)

If the world were wholly just, the following inductive definition would exhaustively cover the subject of justice in holdings.

1. A person who acquires a holding in accordance with the principle of justice in acquisition is entitled to that holding.
2. A person who acquires a holding in accordance with the principle of justice in transfer, from someone else entitled to the holding, is entitled to the holding.
3. No one is entitled to a holding except by (repeated) applications of 1 and 2.

The complete principle of distributive justice would say simply that a distribution is just if everyone is entitled to the holdings they possess under the distribution.

A distribution is just if it arises from another just distribution by legitimate means. The legitimate means of moving from one distribution to another are specified by the principle of justice in transfer. The legitimate first "moves" are specified by the principle of justice in acquisition.[1] Whatever arises from a just situation by just steps is itself just. The means of change specified by the principle of justice in transfer preserve justice. As correct rules of inference are truth-preserving, and any conclusion deduced via repeated application of such rules from only true premises is itself true, so the means of transition from one situation to another specified by the principle of justice in transfer are justice-preserving, and any situation actually arising from repeated transitions in accordance with the principle from a just situation is itself just. The parallel between justice-preserving transformations and truth-preserving transformations illuminates where it fails as well as where it holds. That a conclusion could have been deduced by truth-preserving means from premises that are true suffices to show its truth. That from a just situation a situation *could* have arisen via justice-preserving means does *not* suffice to show its justice. The fact that a thief's victims voluntarily *could* have presented him with gifts does not entitle the thief to his ill-gotten gains. Justice in

holdings is historical; it depends upon what actually has happened. We shall return to this point later.

Not all actual situations are generated in accordance with the two principles of justice in holdings: the principle of justice in acquisition and the principle of justice in transfer. Some people steal from others, or defraud them, or enslave them, seizing their product and preventing them from living as they choose, or forcibly exclude others from competing in exchanges. None of these are permissible modes of transition from one situation to another. And some persons acquire holdings by means not sanctioned by the principle of justice in acquisition. The existence of past injustice (previous violations of the first two principles of justice in holdings) raises the third major topic under justice in holdings: the rectification of injustice in holdings. If past injustice has shaped present holdings in various ways, some identifiable and some not, what now, if anything, ought to be done to rectify these injustices? What obligations do the performers of injustice have toward those whose position is worse than it would have been had the injustice not been done? Or, than it would have been had compensation been paid promptly? How, if at all, do things change if the beneficiaries and those made worse off are not the direct parties in the act of injustice, but, for example, their descendants? Is an injustice done to someone whose holding was itself based upon an unrectified injustice? How far back must one go in wiping clean the historical slate of injustices? What may victims of injustice permissibly do in order to rectify the injustices being done to them, including the many injustices done by persons acting through their government? I do not know of a thorough or theoretically sophisticated treatment of such issues. Idealizing greatly, let us suppose theoretical investigation will produce a principle of rectification. This principle uses historical information about previous situations and injustices done in them (as defined by the first two principles of justice and rights against interference), and information about the actual course of events that flowed from these injustices, until the present, and it yields a description (or descriptions) of holdings in the society. The principle of rectification presumably will make use of its best estimate of subjunctive information about what would have occurred (or a probability distribution over what might have occurred, using the expected value) if the injustice had not taken place. If the actual description of holdings turns out not to be one of the descriptions yielded by the principle, then one of the descriptions yielded must be realized.[2]

The general outlines of the theory of justice in holdings are that the holdings of a person are just if he is entitled to them by the principles of justice in acquisition and transfer, or by the principle of rectification of injustice (as specified by the first two principles). If each person's holdings are just, then the total set (distribution) of holdings is just. To turn these general outlines into a specific theory we would have to specify the details of each of the three principles of justice in holdings: the principle of acquisition of holdings, the principle of transfer of holdings, and the principle of rectification of violations of the first two principles. I shall not attempt that task here.

HISTORICAL PRINCIPLES AND END-RESULT PRINCIPLES

The general outlines of the entitlement theory illuminate the nature and defects of other conceptions of distributive justice. The entitlement theory of justice in distribution is *historical*; whether a distribution is just depends upon how it came about. In contrast, *current-time-slice principles* of justice hold that the justice of a distribution is determined by how things are distributed (who has what) as judged by some *structural* principle(s) of just distribution. A utilitarian who judges between any two distributions by seeing which has the greater sum of utility and, if the sums tie, applies some fixed equality criterion to choose the more equal distribution, would hold a current-time-slice principle of justice. As would someone who had a fixed schedule of trade-offs between the sum of happiness and equality. According to a current-time-slice principle, all that needs to be looked at, in judging the justice of a distribution, is who ends up with what; in comparing any two distributions one need look only at

the matrix presenting the distributions. No further information need be fed into a principle of justice. It is a consequence of such principles of justice that any two structurally identical distributions are equally just. (Two distributions are structurally identical if they present the same profile, but perhaps have different persons occupying the particular slots. My having ten and your having, five, and my having five and your having ten are structurally identical distributions.) Welfare economics is the theory of current-time-slice principles of justice. The subject is conceived as operating on matrices representing only current information about distribution. This, as well as some of the usual conditions (for example, the choice of distribution is invariant under relabeling of columns), guarantees that welfare economics will be a current time-slice theory, with all of its inadequacies.

Most persons do not accept current-time-slice principles as constituting the whole story about distributive shares. They think it relevant in assessing the justice of a situation to consider not only the distribution it embodies, but also how that distribution came about. If some persons are in prison for murder or war crimes, we do not say that to assess the justice of the distribution in the society we must look only at what this person has, and that person has, and that person has, … at the current time. We think it relevant to ask whether someone did something so that he *deserved* to be punished, deserved to have a lower share. Most will agree to the relevance of further information with regard to punishments and penalties. Consider also desired things. One traditional socialist view is that workers are entitled to the product and full fruits of their labor; they have earned it; a distribution is unjust if it does not give the workers what they are entitled to. Such entitlements are based upon some past history. No socialist holding this view would find it comforting to be told that because the actual distribution *A* happens to coincide structurally with the one he desires *D*, *A* therefore is no less just than *D*; it differs only in that the "parasitic" owners of capital receive under *A* what the owners are entitled to under *D*, and the workers receive under *A* what the owners are entitled to under *D*, namely very little. This socialist rightly, in my view, holds onto the notions of earnings, producing, entitlement, desert, and so forth, and he rejects current-time-slice principles that look only to the structure of the resulting set of holdings. (The set of holdings resulting from what? Isn't it implausible that how holdings are produced and come to exist has no effect at all on who should hold what?) His mistake lies in his view of what entitlements arise out of what sorts of productive processes.

We construe the position we discuss too narrowly by speaking of *current*-time-slice principles. Nothing is changed if structural principles operate upon a time sequence of current-time-slice profiles and, for example, give someone more now to counterbalance the less he has had earlier. A utilitarian or an egalitarian or any mixture of the two over time will inherit the difficulties of his more myopic comrades. He is not helped by the fact that *some* of the information others consider relevant in assessing a distribution is reflected, unrecoverably, in past matrices. Henceforth, we shall refer to such unhistorical principles of distributive justice, including the current-time-slice principles, as *end-result principles* or *end-state principles.*

In contrast to end-result principles of justice, *historical principles* of justice hold that past circumstances or actions of people can create differential entitlements or differential deserts to things. An injustice can be worked by moving from one distribution to another structurally identical one, for the second, in profile the same, may violate people's entitlements or deserts; it may not fit the actual history.

PATTERNING

The entitlement principles of justice in holdings that we have sketched are historical principles of justice. To better understand their precise character, we shall distinguish them from another subclass of the historical principles. Consider, as an example, the principle of distribution according to moral merit. This principle requires that total distributive shares vary directly with moral merit; no person should have a greater share than anyone whose moral merit is greater. (If moral merit could be not merely ordered but measured on an interval or ratio scale, stronger principles could

be formulated.) Or consider the principle that results by substituting "usefulness to society" for "moral merit" in the previous principle. Or instead of "distribute according to moral merit," or "distribute according to usefulness to society," we might consider "distribute according to the weighted sum of moral merit, usefulness to society, and need," with the weights of the different dimensions equal. Let us call a principle of distribution *patterned* if it specifies that a distribution is to vary along with some natural dimension, weighted sum of natural dimensions, or lexicographic ordering of natural dimensions. And let us say a distribution is patterned if it accords with some patterned principle. (I speak of natural dimensions, admittedly without a general criterion for them, because for any set of holdings some artificial dimensions can be gimmicked up to vary along with the distribution of the set.) The principle of distribution in accordance with moral merit is a patterned historical principle, which specifies a patterned distribution. "Distribute according to I.Q." is a patterned principle that looks to information not contained in distributional matrices. It is not historical, however, in that it does not look to any past actions creating differential entitlements to evaluate a distribution; it requires only distributional matrices whose columns are labeled by I.Q. scores. The distribution in a society, however, may be composed of such simple patterned distributions, without itself being simply patterned. Different sectors may operate different patterns, or some combination of patterns may operate in different proportions across a society. A distribution composed in this manner, from a small number of patterned distributions, we also shall term "patterned." And we extend the use of "pattern" to include the overall designs put forth by combinations of end-state principles.

Almost every suggested principle of distributive justice is patterned: to each according to his moral merit, or needs, or marginal product, or how hard he tries, or the weighted sum of the foregoing, and so on. The principle of entitlement we have sketched is *not* patterned.[3] There is no one natural dimension or weighted sum or combination of a small number of natural dimensions that yields the distributions generated in accordance with the principle of entitlement. The set of holdings will not be patterned that results when some persons receive their marginal products, others win at gambling, others receive a share of their mate's income, others receive gifts from foundations, others receive interest on loans, others receive gifts from admirers, others receive returns on investment, others make for themselves much of what they have, others find things, and so on. Heavy strands of patterns will run through it; significant portions of the variance in holdings will be accounted for by pattern-variables. If most people most of the time choose to transfer some of their entitlements to others only in exchange for something from them, then a large part of what many people hold will vary with what they held that others wanted. More details are provided by the theory of marginal productivity. But gifts to relatives, charitable donations, bequests to children, and the like, are not best conceived, in the first instance, in this manner. Ignoring the strands of pattern, let us suppose for the moment that a distribution actually arrived at by the operation of the principle of entitlement is random with respect to any pattern. Though the resulting set of holdings will be unpatterned, it will not be incomprehensible, for it can be seen as arising from the operation of a small number of principles. These principles specify how an initial distribution may arise (the principle of acquisition of holdings) and how distributions may be transformed into others (the principle of transfer of holdings). The process whereby the set of holdings is generated will be intelligible, though the set of holdings itself that results from this process will be unpatterned.

The writings of F. A. Hayek focus less than is usually done upon what patterning distributive justice requires. Hayek argues that we cannot know enough about each person's situation to distribute to each according to his moral merit (but would justice demand we do so if we did have this knowledge?); and he goes on to say, "our objection is against all attempts to impress upon society a deliberately chosen pattern of distribution, whether it be an order of equality or of inequality." However, Hayek concludes that in a free society there will be distribution in accordance with value rather than moral merit; that is, in accordance with the perceived value of a person's actions and services to others. Despite his rejection of a patterned conception of distributive justice, Hayek himself suggests a pattern he thinks justifiable: distribution in accordance with the perceived benefits given to others, leaving room for the complaint that a free society does not realize exactly this pattern. Stating this patterned strand of a free capitalist society more precisely, we get "To each according to how much he benefits others who have the resources for benefiting those who benefit them." This will seem arbitrary unless some acceptable initial set of holdings is specified, or unless it is held that the operation of the system over time washes out any significant effects from the initial set of holdings. As an example of the latter, if almost anyone would have bought a car from Henry Ford, the supposition that it was an arbitrary matter who held the money then (and so bought) would not place Henry Ford's earnings under a cloud. In any event, *his* coming to hold it is not arbitrary. Distribution according to benefits to others *is* a major patterned strand in a free capitalist society, as Hayek correctly points out, but it is only a strand and does not constitute the whole pattern of a system of entitlements (namely, inheritance, gifts for arbitrary reasons, charity, and so on) or a standard that one should insist a society fit. Will people tolerate for long a system yielding distributions that they believe are unpatterned? No doubt people will not long accept a distribution they believe is *unjust*. People want their society to be and to look just. But must the look of justice reside in a resulting pattern rather than in the underlying generating principles? We are in no position to conclude that the inhabitants of a society embodying an entitlement conception of justice in holdings will find it unacceptable. Still, it must be granted that, were people's reasons for transferring some of their holdings to others always irrational or arbitrary, we would find this disturbing. (Suppose people always determined what holdings they would transfer, and to whom, by using a random device.) We feel more comfortable upholding the justice of an entitlement system if most of the transfers under it are done for reasons. This does not mean necessarily that all deserve what holdings they receive. It means only that there is a purpose or point to someone's transferring a holding to one person rather than to another; that usually we can see what the transferor thinks he's gaining, what cause he thinks he's serving, what goals he thinks he's helping to achieve, and so forth. Since in a capitalist society people often transfer holdings to others in accordance with how much they perceive these others benefiting them, the fabric constituted by the individual transactions and transfers is largely reasonable and intelligible.[4] (Gifts to loved ones, bequests to children, charity to the needy also are nonarbitrary components of the fabric.) In stressing the large strand of distribution in accordance with benefit to others, Hayek shows the point of many transfers, and so shows that the system of transfer of entitlements is not just spinning its gears aimlessly. The system of entitlements is defensible when constituted by the individual aims of individual transactions. No overarching aim is needed, no distributional pattern is required.

To think that the task of a theory of distributive justice is to fill in the blank in "to each according to his———" is to be predisposed to search for a pattern; and the separate treatment of "from each according to his———" treats production and distribution as two separate and independent issues. On an entitlement view these are *not* two separate questions. Whoever makes something, having bought or contracted for all other held resources used in the process (transferring some of his holdings for these cooperating factors), is entitled to it. The situation is *not* one of something's getting made, and there being an open question of who is to get it. Things come into the world already attached to people having entitlements over them. From the point of view of the historical entitlement conception of justice in holdings, those who start afresh to complete "to each according to his———" treat objects as if they appeared from nowhere, out of nothing. A complete theory of justice might cover this limit case as well; perhaps here is a use for the usual conceptions of distributive justice.

So entrenched are maxims of the usual form that perhaps we should present the entitlement conception as a competitor. Ignoring acquisition and rectification, we might say:

> From each according to what he chooses to do, to each according to what he makes for himself (perhaps with the contracted aid of others) and what others choose to do for him and choose to give him of what they've been given previously (under this maxim) and haven't yet expended or transferred.

This, the discerning reader will have noticed, has its defects as a slogan. So as a summary and great simplification (and not as a maxim with any independent meaning) we have:

> *From each as they choose, to each as they are chosen.*

HOW LIBERTY UPSETS PATTERNS

It is not clear how those holding alternative conceptions of distributive justice can reject the entitlement conception of justice in holdings. For suppose a distribution favored by one of these nonentitlement conceptions is realized. Let us suppose it is your favorite one and let us call this distribution *D*1; perhaps everyone has an equal share, perhaps shares vary in accordance with some dimension you treasure. Now suppose that Wilt Chamberlain is greatly in demand by basketball teams, being a great gate attraction, (Also suppose contracts run only for a year, with players being free agents.) He signs the following sort of contract with a team: In each home game, twenty-five cents from the price of each ticket of admission goes to him. (We ignore the question of whether he is "gouging" the owners, letting them look out for themselves.) The season starts, and people cheerfully attend his team's games; they buy their tickets, each time dropping a separate 25 cents of their admission price into a special box with Chamberlain's name on it. They are excited about seeing him play; it is worth the total admission price to them. Let us suppose that in one season one million persons attend his home games, and Wilt Chamberlain winds up with $250,000, a much larger sum than the average income and larger even than anyone else has. Is he entitled to this income? Is this new distribution

*D*2, unjust? If so, why? There is *no* question about whether each of the people was entitled to the control over the resources they held in *D*1; because that was the distribution (your favorite) that (for the purposes of argument) we assumed was acceptable. Each of these persons *chose* to give 25 cents of their money to Chamberlain. They could have spent it on going to the movies, or on candy bars, or on copies *of Dissent* magazine, or of *Monthly Review.* But they all, at least one million of them, converged on giving it to Wilt Chamberlain in exchange for watching him play basketball. If *D*1 was a just distribution, and people voluntarily moved from it to *D*2, transferring parts of their shares they were given under *D*1 (what was it for if not to do something with?), isn't *D*2 also just? If the people were entitled to dispose of the resources to which they were entitled (under *D*1), didn't this include their being entitled to give it to, or exchange it with, Wilt Chamberlain? Can anyone else complain on grounds of justice? Each other person already has his legitimate share under *D*1. Under *D*1, there is nothing that anyone has that anyone else has a claim of justice against. After someone transfers something to Wilt Chamberlain, third parties *still* have their legitimate shares; *their* shares are not changed. By what process could such a transfer among two persons give rise to a legitimate claim of distributive justice on a portion of what was transferred, by a third party who had no claim of justice on any holding of the others *before* the transfer?[5] To cut off objections irrelevant here, we might imagine the exchanges occurring in a socialist society, after hours. After playing whatever basketball he does in his daily work, or doing whatever other daily work he does, Wilt Chamberlain decides to put in *overtime* to earn additional money. (First his work quota is set; he works time over that.) Or imagine it is a skilled juggler people like to see, who puts on shows after hours.

Why might someone work overtime in a society in which it is assumed their needs are satisfied? Perhaps because they care about things other than needs. I like to write in books that I read, and to have easy access to books for browsing at odd hours. It would be very pleasant and convenient

to have the resources of Widener Library in my back yard. No society, I assume, will provide such resources close to each person who would like them as part of his regular allotment (under *D*1). Thus, persons either must do without some extra things that they want, or be allowed to do something extra to get some of these things. On what basis could the inequalities that would eventuate be forbidden? Notice also that small factories would spring up in a socialist society, unless forbidden. I melt down some of my personal possessions (under *D*1) and build a machine out of the material. I offer you, and others, a philosophy lecture once a week in exchange for your cranking the handle on my machine, whose products I exchange for yet other things, and so on. (The raw materials used by the machine are given to me by others who possess them under *D*1, in exchange for hearing lectures.) Each person might participate to gain things over and above their allotment under *D*1. Some persons even might want to leave their job in socialist industry and work full time in this private sector. I wish merely to note how private property even in means of production would occur in a socialist society that did not forbid people to use as they wished some of the resources they are given under the socialist distribution *D*1. The socialist society would have to forbid capitalist acts between consenting adults.

The general point illustrated by the Wilt Chamberlain example and the example of the entrepreneur in a socialist society is that no end-state principle or distributional patterned principle of justice can be continuously realized without continuous interference with people's lives. Any favored pattern would be transformed into one unfavored by the principle, by people choosing to act in various ways; for example, by people exchanging goods and services with other people, or giving things to other people, things the transferors are entitled to under the favored distributional pattern. To maintain a pattern one must either continually interfere to stop people from transferring resources as they wish to, or continually (or periodically) interfere to take from some persons resources that others for some reason chose to transfer to them. (But if some time limit is to be set on how long people may keep resources others voluntarily transfer to them, why let them keep these resources for *any* period of time? Why not have immediate confiscation?) It might be objected that all persons voluntarily will choose to refrain from actions that would upset the pattern. This presupposes unrealistically (1) that all will most want to maintain the pattern (are those who don't to be "reeducated" or forced to undergo "self-criticism"?), (2) that each can gather enough information about his own actions and the ongoing activities of others to discover which of his actions will upset the pattern, and (3) that diverse and far-flung persons can coordinate their actions to dovetail into the pattern. Compare the manner in which the market is neutral among persons' desires, as it reflects and transmits widely scattered information via prices, and coordinates persons' activities.

It puts things perhaps a bit too strongly to say that every patterned (or end-state) principle is liable to be thwarted by the voluntary actions of the individual parties transferring some of their shares they receive under the principle. For perhaps some *very* weak patterns are not so thwarted. Any distributional pattern with any egalitarian component is overturnable by the voluntary actions of individual persons over time; as is every patterned condition with sufficient content so as actually to have been proposed as presenting the central core of distributive justice. Still, given the possibility that some weak conditions or patterns may not be unstable in this way, it would be better to formulate an explicit description of the kind of interesting and contentful patterns under discussion, and to prove a theorem about their instability. Since the weaker the patterning, the more likely it is that the entitlement system itself satisfies it, a plausible conjecture is that any patterning either is unstable or is satisfied by the entitlement system.

NOTES

1. Applications of the principle of justice in acquisition may also occur as part of the move from one distribution to another. You may find an unheld thing now and appropriate it. Acquisitions also are to be understood as included when, to simplify, I speak only of transitions by transfers.

2. If the principle of rectification of violations of the first two principles yields more than one description of holdings, then some choice must be made as to which of these is to be realized. Perhaps the sort of considerations about distributive justice and equality that I argue against play a legitimate role in *this* subsidiary choice. Similarly, there may be room for such considerations in deciding which otherwise arbitrary features a statute will embody, when such features are unavoidable because other considerations do not specify a precise line; yet a line must be drawn.

3. One might try to squeeze a patterned conception of distributive justice into the framework of the entitlement conception, by formulating a gimmicky obligatory "principle of transfer" that would lead to the pattern. For example, the principle that if one has more than the mean income one must transfer everything one holds above the mean to persons below the mean so as to bring them up to (but not over) the mean. We can formulate a criterion for a "principle of transfer" to rule out such obligatory transfers, or we can say that no correct principle of transfer, no principle of transfer in a free society, will be like this. The former is probably the better course, though the latter also is true.

Alternatively, one might think to make the entitlement conception instantiate a pattern, by using matrix entries that express the relative strength of a person's entitlements as measured by some real-valued function. But even if the limitation to natural dimensions failed to exclude this function, the resulting edifice would *not* capture our system of entitlements to *particular* things.

4. We certainly benefit because great economic incentives operate to get others to spend much time and energy to figure out how to serve us by providing things we will want to pay for. It is not mere paradox mongering to wonder whether capitalism should be criticized for most rewarding and hence encouraging, not individualists like Thoreau who go about their own lives, but people who are occupied with serving others and winning them as customers. But to defend capitalism one need not think businessmen are the finest human types. (I do not mean to join here the general maligning of businessmen, either.) Those who think the finest should acquire the most can try to convince their fellows to transfer resources in accordance with *that* principle.

5. Might not a transfer have instrumental effects on a third party, changing his feasible options? (But what if the two parties to the transfer independently had used their holdings in this fashion?) ... [N]ote ... that this question concedes the point for distributions of ultimate intrinsic noninstrumental goods (pure utility experiences, so to speak) that are transferrable. It also might be objected that the transfer might make a third party more envious because it worsens his position relative to someone else. I find it incomprehensible how this can be thought to involve a claim of justice....

Here ... a theory that incorporates elements of pure procedural justice might find what I say acceptable, *if* kept in its proper place; that is, if background institutions exist to ensure the satisfaction of certain conditions on distributive shares. But if these institutions are not themselves the sum or invisible-hand result of people's voluntary (nonaggressive) actions, the constraints they impose require justification. At no point does *our* argument assume any background institutions more extensive than those of the minimal nightwatchman state, a state limited to protecting persons against murder, assault, theft, fraud, and so forth.

44   Equality as a Moral Ideal

HARRY FRANKFURT

First man: "How are your children?" Second man: "Compared to what?"

I

Economic egalitarianism is, as I shall construe it, the doctrine that it is desirable for everyone to have the same amounts of income and of wealth (for short, "money").[1] Hardly anyone would deny that there are situations in which it makes sense to tolerate deviations from this standard. It goes without saying, after all, that preventing or correcting such deviations may involve costs which—whether measured in economic terms or in terms of noneconomic considerations—are by any reasonable measure unacceptable. Nonetheless, many people believe that economic equality has considerable moral value in itself. For this reason they often urge that efforts to approach the egalitarian ideal should be accorded—with all due consideration for the possible effects of such efforts in obstructing or in conducing to the achievement of other goods—a significant priority.[2]

In my opinion, this is a mistake. Economic equality is not, as such, of particular moral importance. With respect to the distribution of economic assets, what *is* important from the point of view of morality is not that everyone should have *the same* but that each should have *enough*. If everyone had enough, it would be of no moral consequence whether some had more than others. I shall refer to this alternative to egalitarianism—namely, that what is morally important with respect to money is for everyone to have enough—as "the doctrine of sufficiency."[3]

The fact that economic equality is not in its own right a morally compelling social ideal is in no way, of course, a reason for regarding it as undesirable. My claim that equality in itself lacks moral importance does not entail that equality is to be avoided. Indeed, there may well be good reasons for governments or for individuals to deal with problems of economic distribution in accordance with an egalitarian standard and to be concerned more with attempting to increase the extent to which people are economically equal than with efforts to regulate directly the extent to which the amounts of money people have are enough. Even if equality is not as such morally important, a

---

Ethics 98 (October 1987); pp. 21–43. ©1987 by The University of Chicago. All rights reserved. Reprinted with permission of the publisher.

commitment to an egalitarian social policy may be indispensable to promoting the enjoyment of significant goods besides equality or to avoiding their impairment. Moreover, it might turn out that the most feasible approach to the achievement of sufficiency would be the pursuit of equality.

But despite the fact that an egalitarian distribution would not necessarily be objectionable, the error of believing that there are powerful moral reasons for caring about equality is far from innocuous. In fact, this belief tends to do significant harm. It is often argued as an objection to egalitarianism that there is a dangerous conflict between equality and liberty: if people are left to themselves, inequalities of income and wealth inevitably arise, and therefore an egalitarian distribution of money can be achieved and maintained only at the cost of repression. Whatever may be the merit of this argument concerning the relationship between equality and liberty, economic egalitarianism engenders another conflict that is of even more fundamental moral significance.

To the extent that people are preoccupied with equality for its own sake, their readiness to be satisfied with any particular level of income or wealth is guided not by their own interests and needs but just by the magnitude of the economic benefits that are at the disposal of others. In this way egalitarianism distracts people from measuring the requirements to which their individual natures and their personal circumstances give rise. It encourages them instead to insist upon a level of economic support that is determined by a calculation in which the particular features of their own lives are irrelevant. How sizable the economic assets of others are has nothing much to do, after all, with what kind of person someone is. A concern for economic equality, construed as desirable in itself, tends to divert a person's attention away from endeavoring to discover—within his experience of himself and of his life—what he himself really cares about and what will actually satisfy him, although this is the most basic and the most decisive task upon which an intelligent selection of economic goals depends. Exaggerating the moral importance of economic equality is harmful, in other words, because it is alienating.[4]

To be sure, the circumstances of others may reveal interesting possibilities and provide data for useful judgments concerning what is normal or typical. Someone who is attempting to reach a confident and realistic appreciation of what to seek for himself may well find this helpful. It is not only in suggestive and preliminary ways like these, moreover, that the situations of other people may be pertinent to someone's efforts to decide what economic demands it is reasonable or important for him to make. The amount of money he needs may depend in a more direct way on the amounts others have. Money may bring power or prestige or other competitive advantages. A determination of how much money would be enough cannot intelligently be made by someone who is concerned with such things, except on the basis of an estimate of the resources available to those with whose competition it may be necessary for him to contend. What is important from this point of view, however, is not the comparison of levels of affluence as such. The measurement of inequality is important only as it pertains contingently to other interests.

The mistaken belief that economic equality is important in itself leads people to detach the problem of formulating their economic ambitions from the problem of understanding what is most fundamentally significant to them. It influences them to take too seriously, as though it were a matter of great moral concern, a question that is inherently rather insignificant and not directly to the point, namely, how their economic status compares with the economic status of others. In this way the doctrine of equality contributes to the moral disorientation and shallowness of our time.

The prevalence of egalitarian thought is harmful in another respect as well. It not only tends to divert attention from considerations of greater moral importance than equality. It also diverts attention from the difficult but quite fundamental philosophical problems of understanding just what these considerations are and of elaborating, in appropriately comprehensive and perspicuous detail, a conceptual apparatus that would facilitate their exploration. Calculating the size of an equal share is plainly much easier than determining how much a person needs in order to have enough. In addition, the very concept of having an equal share is itself considerably more patent and accessible than the concept of having enough. It is far from self-evident, needless to say, precisely what the doctrine of sufficiency means and what applying it entails. But this is hardly a good reason for neglecting the doctrine or for adopting an incorrect doctrine in preference to it. Among my primary purposes in this essay is to suggest the importance of systematic inquiry into the analytical and theoretical issues raised by the concept of having enough, the importance of which egalitarianism has masked.[5]

II

There are a number of ways of attempting to establish the thesis that economic equality is important. Sometimes it is urged that the prevalence of fraternal relationships among the members of a society is a desirable goal and that equality is indispensable to it.[6] Or it may be maintained that inequalities in the distribution of economic benefits are to be avoided because they lead invariably to undesirable discrepancies of other kinds—for example, in social status, in political influence, or in the abilities of people to make effective use of their various opportunities and entitlements. In both of these arguments, economic equality is endorsed because of its supposed importance in creating or preserving certain noneconomic conditions. Such considerations may well provide convincing reasons for recommending equality as a desirable social good, or even for preferring egalitarianism as a policy over the alternatives to it. But both arguments construe equality as valuable derivatively, in virtue of its contingent connections to other things. In neither argument is there an attribution to equality of any unequivocally inherent moral value.

A rather different kind of argument for economic equality, which comes closer to construing the value of equality as independent of contingencies, is based upon the principle of diminishing marginal utility. According to this argument, equality is desirable because an egalitarian distribution of economic assets maximizes their aggregate utility.[7] The argument presupposes: *(a)* for each individual the utility of money invariably

diminishes at the margin, and *(b)* with respect to money, or with respect to the things money can buy, the utility functions of all individuals are the same.[8] In other words, the utility provided by or derivable from an *nth* dollar is the same for everyone, and it is less than the utility for anyone of dollar *(n − 1)*. Unless *b* were true, a rich man might obtain greater utility than a poor man from an extra dollar. In that case an egalitarian distribution of economic goods would not maximize aggregate utility even if *a* were true. But given both *a* and *b,* it follows that a marginal dollar always brings less utility to a rich person than to one who is less rich. And this entails that total utility must increase when inequality is reduced by giving a dollar to someone poorer than the person from whom it is taken.

In fact, however, both *a* and *b* are false. Suppose it is conceded, for the sake of the argument, that the maximization of aggregate utility is in its own right a morally important social goal. Even so, it cannot legitimately be inferred that an egalitarian distribution of money must therefore have similar moral importance. For in virtue of the falsity of *a* and *b,* the argument linking economic equality to the maximization of aggregate utility is unsound.

So far as concerns *b,* it is evident that the utility functions for money of different individuals are not even approximately alike. Some people suffer from physical, mental, or emotional weaknesses or incapacities that limit the satisfactions they are able to obtain. Moreover, even apart from the effects of specific disabilities, some people simply enjoy things more than other people do. Everyone knows that there are, at any given level of expenditure, large differences in the quantities of utility that different spenders derive.

So far as concerns *a,* there are good reasons against expecting any consistent diminution in the marginal utility of *money.* The fact that the marginal utilities of certain goods do indeed tend to diminish is not a principle of reason. It is a psychological generalization, which is accounted for by such considerations as that people often tend after a time to become satiated with what they have been consuming and that the senses characteristically lose their freshness after repetitive stimulation.[9] It is common knowledge that experiences of many kinds become increasingly routine and unrewarding as they are repeated.

It is questionable, however, whether this provides any reason at all for expecting a diminution in the marginal utility of *money*—that is, of anything that functions as a generic instrument of exchange. Even if the utility of everything money can buy were inevitably to diminish at the margin, the utility of money itself might nonetheless exhibit a different pattern. It is quite possible that money would be exempt from the phenomenon of unrelenting marginal decline because of its limitlessly protean versatility. As Blum and Kalven explain:

> In ... analysing the question whether money has a declining utility it is ... important to put to one side all analogies to the observation that particular commodities have a declining utility to their users. There is no need here to enter into the debate whether it is useful or necessary, in economic theory, to assume that commodities have a declining utility. Money is infinitely versatile. And even if all the things money can buy are subject to a law of diminishing utility, it does not follow that money itself is.[10]

From the supposition that a person tends to lose more and more interest in what he is consuming as his consumption of it increases, it plainly cannot be inferred that he must also tend to lose interest in consumption itself or in the money that makes consumption possible. For there may always remain for him, no matter how tired he has become of what he has been doing, untried goods to be bought and fresh new pleasures to be enjoyed.

There are in any event many things of which people do not, from the very outset, immediately begin to tire. From certain goods, they actually derive more utility after sustained consumption than they derive at first. This is the situation whenever appreciating or enjoying or otherwise benefiting from something depends upon repeated trials, which serve as a kind of "warming up" process: for instance, when relatively little significant gratification is obtained from the item or experience in question until the individual has acquired a special taste for it, has become addicted to it, or has begun in some other way to relate or respond to it profitably. The capacity for

obtaining gratification is then smaller at earlier points in the sequence of consumption than at later points. In such cases marginal utility does not decline; it increases. Perhaps it is true of everything, without exception, that a person will ultimately lose interest in it. But even if in every utility curve there is a point at which the curve begins a steady and irreversible decline, it cannot be assumed that every segment of the curve has a downward slope.[11]

III

When marginal utility diminishes, it does not do so on account of any deficiency in the marginal unit. It diminishes in virtue of the position of that unit as the latest in a sequence. The same is true when marginal utility increases: the marginal unit provides greater utility than its predecessors in virtue of the effect that the acquisition or consumption of those predecessors has brought about. Now when the sequence consists of units of money, what corresponds to the process of warming up—at least, in one pertinent and important feature—is *saving*. Accumulating money entails, as warming up does, generating a capacity to derive, at some subsequent point in a sequence, gratifications that cannot be derived earlier.

The fact that it may at times be especially worthwhile for a person to save money rather than to spend each dollar as it comes along is due in part to the incidence of what may be thought of as "utility thresholds." Consider an item with the following characteristics: it is non-fungible, it is the source of a fresh and otherwise unobtainable type of satisfaction, and it is too expensive to be acquired except by saving up for it. The utility of the dollar that finally completes a program of saving up for such an item may be greater than the utility of any dollar saved earlier in the program. That will be the case when the utility provided by the item is greater than the sum of the utilities that could be derived if the money saved were either spent as it came in or divided into parts and used to purchase other things. In a situation of this kind, the final dollar saved permits the crossing of a utility threshold.[12]

It is sometimes argued that, for anyone who is rational in the sense that he seeks to maximize the utility generated by his expenditures, the marginal utility of money must necessarily diminish. Abba Lerner presents this argument as follows:

> The principle of diminishing marginal utility of income can be derived from the assumption that consumers spend their income in the way that maximizes the satisfaction they can derive from the good obtained. With a given income, all the things bought give a greater satisfaction for the money spent on them than any of the other things that could have been bought in their place but were not bought for this very reason. From this it follows that if income were greater the additional things that would be bought with the increment of income would be things that are rejected when income is smaller, because they give less satisfaction; and if income were greater still, even less satisfactory things would be bought. The greater the income the less satisfactory are the *additional* things that can be bought with equal increases of income. That is all that is meant by the principle of the diminishing marginal utility of income.[13]

Lerner invokes here a comparison between the utility of $G(n)$—the goods that the rational consumer actually buys with his income of n dollars—and "the other things that could have been bought in their place but were not." Given that he prefers to buy $G(n)$ rather than the other things, which by hypothesis cost no more, the rational consumer must regard $G(n)$ as offering greater satisfaction than the others can provide. From this Lerner infers that with an additional n dollars the consumer would be able to purchase only things with less utility than $G(n)$; and he concludes that, in general, "the greater the income the less satisfactory are the additional things that can be bought with equal increases of income." This conclusion, he maintains, is tantamount to the principle of the diminishing marginal utility of income.

It seems apparent that Lerner's attempt to derive the principle in this way fails. One reason is that the amount of satisfaction a person can derive from a certain good may vary considerably according to whether or not he also possesses certain other goods. The satisfaction obtainable from a certain expenditure may therefore be greater if some other expenditure has already been made. Suppose that the cost of a serving of popcorn is the same as the cost of enough butter to make it delectable, and suppose that some rational consumer who adores buttered popcorn gets very little satisfaction from unbuttered popcorn, but that he nonetheless prefers it to butter alone. He will buy the popcorn in preference to the butter, accordingly, if he must buy one and cannot buy both. Suppose now that this person's income increases so that he can buy the butter too. Then he can have something he enjoys enormously: his incremental income makes it possible for him not merely to buy butter in addition to popcorn but also to enjoy buttered popcorn. The satisfaction he will derive by combining the popcorn and the butter may well be considerably greater than the sum of the satisfactions he can derive from the two goods taken separately. Here, again, is a threshold effect.

In a case of this sort, what the rational consumer buys with his incremental income is a good—$G(i)$—which, when his income was smaller, he had rejected in favor of $G(n)$ because having it alone would have been less satisfying than having only $G(n)$. Despite this, however, it is not true that the utility of the income he uses to buy $G(i)$ is less than the utility of the income he used to buy $G(n)$. When there is an opportunity to create a combination that is (like buttered popcorn) synergistic in the sense that adding one good to another increases the utility of each, the marginal utility of income may not decline even though the sequence of marginal items—taking each of these items by itself—does exhibit a pattern of declining utilities.

Lerner's argument is flawed in virtue of another consideration as well. Since he speaks of "the *additional* things that can be bought with equal increases of income," he evidently presumes that a rational consumer uses his first n dollars to purchase a certain good and that he uses any incremental income beyond that to buy something else. This leads Lerner to suppose that what the consumer buys when his income is increased by i dollars (where i is equal to or less than n) must be something that he could have bought and which he chose not to buy when his income was only n dollars. But this supposition is unwarranted. With an income of $(n + i)$ dollars, the consumer need not use his money to purchase both $G(n)$ and $G(i)$. He might use it to buy something that costs more than either of these goods—something that was too expensive to be available to him at all before his income increased. The point is that if a rational consumer with an income of n dollars defers purchasing a certain good until his income increases, this does not necessarily mean that he "rejected" purchasing it when his income was smaller. The good in question may have been out of his reach at that time because it cost more than n dollars. His reason for postponing the purchase may have had nothing to do with comparative expectations of satisfaction or with preferences or priorities at all.

There are two possibilities to consider. Suppose on the one hand that, instead of purchasing $G(n)$ when his income is n dollars, the rational consumer saves that money until he can add an additional i dollars to it and then purchases $G(n + i)$. In this case it is quite evident that his deferral of the purchase of $G(n + i)$ does not mean that he values it less than $G(n)$. On the other hand, suppose that the rational consumer declines to save up for $G(n + i)$ and that he spends all the money he has on $G(n)$. In this case too it would be a mistake to construe his behavior as indicating a preference for $G(n)$ over $G(n + i)$. For the explanation of his refusal to save for $G(n + i)$ may be merely that he regards doing so as pointless because he believes that he cannot reasonably expect to save enough to make a timely purchase of it.

The utility of $G(n + i)$ may not only be greater than the utility either of $G(n)$ or of $G(i)$. It may also be greater than the sum of their utilities. That is, in acquiring $G(n + i)$ the consumer may cross a utility threshold. The utility of the increment i to his income is then actually greater than the utility of the n dollars to which it is added, even though i equals or is less than n. In such a case, the income of the rational consumer does not exhibit diminishing marginal utility.

IV

The preceding discussion has established that an egalitarian distribution may fail to maximize aggregate utility. It can also easily be shown that, in virtue of the incidence of utility thresholds, there are conditions under which an egalitarian distribution actually minimizes aggregate utility.[14]

Thus, suppose that there is enough of a certain resource (e.g., food or medicine) to enable some but not all members of a population to survive. Let us say that the size of the population is ten people, that a person needs at least five units of the resource in question to live, and that forty units are available. If any members of this population are to survive, some must have more than others. An equal distribution, which gives each person four units, leads to the worst possible outcome, namely, everyone dies. Surely in this case it would be morally grotesque to insist upon equality! Nor would it be reasonable to maintain that, under the conditions specified, it is justifiable for some to be better off only when this is in the interests of the worst off. If the available resources are used to save eight people, the justification for doing this is manifestly not that it somehow benefits the two members of the population who are left to die.

An egalitarian distribution will almost certainly produce a net loss of aggregate utility whenever it entails that fewer individuals than otherwise will have, with respect to some necessity, enough to sustain life—in other words, whenever it requires a larger number of individuals to be below the threshold of survival. Of course, a loss of utility may also occur even when the circumstances involve a threshold that does not separate life and death. Allocating resources equally will reduce aggregate utility whenever it requires a number of individuals to be kept below *any* utility threshold without ensuring a compensating move above some threshold by a suitable number of others.

Under conditions of scarcity, then, an egalitarian distribution may be morally unacceptable. Another response to scarcity is to distribute the available resources in such a way that as many people as possible have enough or, in other words, to maximize the incidence of sufficiency. This alternative is especially compelling when the amount of a scarce resource that constitutes enough coincides with the amount that is indispensable for avoiding some catastrophic harm— as in the example just considered, where falling below the threshold of enough food or enough medicine means death. But now suppose that there are available, in this example, not just forty units of the vital resource, but forty-one. Then maximizing the incidence of sufficiency by providing enough for each of eight people leaves one unit unallocated. What should be done with this extra unit?

It has been shown above that it is a mistake to maintain that *where some people have less than enough, no one should have more than anyone else.* When resources are scarce, so that it is impossible for everyone to have enough, an egalitarian distribution may lead to disaster. Now, there is another claim that might be made here, which may appear to be quite plausible but which is also mistaken: *where some people have less than enough, no one should have more than enough.* If this claim were correct, then—in the example at hand—the extra unit should go to one of the two people who have nothing. But one additional unit of the resource in question will not improve the condition of a person who has none. By hypothesis, that person will die even with the additional unit. What he needs is not one unit but five.[15] It cannot be taken for granted that a person who has a certain amount of a vital resource is necessarily better off than a person who has a lesser amount, for the larger amount may still be too small to serve any useful purpose. Having the larger amount may even make a person worse off. Thus it is conceivable that while a dose of five units of some medication is therapeutic, a dose of one unit is not better than none but actually toxic. And while a person with one unit of food may live a bit longer than someone with no food whatever, perhaps it is worse to prolong the process of starvation for a short time than to terminate quickly the agony of starving to death.

The claim that no one should have more than enough while anyone has less than enough derives its plausibility, in part, from a presumption that is itself plausible but that is nonetheless false: to wit,

giving resources to people who have less of them than enough necessarily means giving resources to people who need them and, therefore, making those people better off. It is indeed reasonable to assign a higher priority to improving the condition of those who are in need than to improving the condition of those who are not in need. But giving additional resources to people who have less than enough of those resources, and who are accordingly in need, may not actually improve the condition of these people at all. Those below a utility threshold are not necessarily benefited by additional resources that move them closer to the threshold. What is crucial for them is to attain the threshold. Merely moving closer to it either may fail to help them or may be disadvantageous.

By no means do I wish to suggest, of course, that it is never or only rarely beneficial for those below a utility threshold to move closer to it. Certainly it may be beneficial, either because it increases the likelihood that the threshold ultimately will be attained or because, quite apart from the significance of the threshold, additional resources provide important increments of utility. After all, a collector may enjoy expanding his collection even if he knows that he has no chance of ever completing it. My point is only that additional resources do not necessarily benefit those who have less than enough. The additions may be too little to make any difference. It may be morally quite acceptable, accordingly, for some to have more than enough of a certain resource even while others have less than enough of it.

V

Quite often, advocacy of egalitarianism is based less upon an argument than upon a purported moral intuition: economic inequality, considered as such, just seems wrong. It strikes many people as unmistakably apparent that, taken simply in itself, the enjoyment by some of greater economic benefits than are enjoyed by others is morally offensive. I suspect, however, that in many cases those who profess to have this intuition concerning manifestations of inequality are actually responding not to the inequality but to another feature of the situations they are confronting. What I believe they find intuitively to be morally objectionable, in the types of situations characteristically cited as instances of economic inequality, is not the fact that some of the individuals in those situations have *less* money than others but the fact that those with less have *too little*.

When we consider people who are substantially worse off than ourselves, we do very commonly find that we are morally disturbed by their circumstances. What directly touches us in cases of this kind, however, is not a quantitative discrepancy but a qualitative condition—not the fact that the economic resources of those who are worse off are *smaller in magnitude* than ours but the different fact that these people are so *poor*. Mere differences in the amounts of money people have are not in themselves distressing. We tend to be quite unmoved, after all, by inequalities between the well-to-do and the rich; our awareness that the former are substantially worse off than the latter does not disturb us morally at all. And if we believe of some person that his life is richly fulfilling, that he himself is genuinely content with his economic situation, and that he suffers no resentments or sorrows that more money could assuage, we are not ordinarily much interested—from a moral point of view—in the question of how the amount of money he has compares with the amounts possessed by others. Economic discrepancies in cases of these sorts do not impress us in the least as matters of significant moral concern. The fact that some people have much less than others is morally undisturbing when it is clear that they have plenty.

It seems clear that egalitarianism and the doctrine of sufficiency are logically independent: considerations that support the one cannot be presumed to provide support also for the other. Yet proponents of egalitarianism frequently suppose that they have offered grounds for their position when in fact what they have offered is pertinent as support only for the doctrine of sufficiency. Thus they often, in attempting to gain acceptance for egalitarianism, call attention to disparities between the conditions of life characteristic of the rich and those characteristic of the poor. Now, it is undeniable that contemplating

such disparities does often elicit a conviction that it would be morally desirable to redistribute the available resources so as to improve the circumstances of the poor. And, of course, that would bring about a greater degree of economic equality. But the indisputability of the moral appeal of improving the condition of the poor by allocating to them resources taken from those who are well off does not even tend to show that egalitarianism is, as a moral ideal, similarly indisputable. To show of poverty that it is compellingly undesirable does nothing whatsoever to show the same of inequality. For what makes someone poor in the morally relevant sense—in which poverty is understood as a condition from which we naturally recoil—is not that his economic assets are simply of lesser magnitude than those of others.

A typical example of this confusion is provided by Ronald Dworkin. Dworkin characterizes the ideal of economic equality as requiring that "no citizen has less than an equal share of the community's resources just in order that others may have more of what he lacks."[16] But in support of his claim that the United States now falls short of this ideal, he refers to circumstances that are not primarily evidence of inequality but of poverty: "It is, I think, apparent that the United States falls far short now [of the ideal of equality]. A substantial minority of Americans are chronically unemployed or earn wages below any realistic 'poverty line' or are handicapped in various ways or burdened with special needs; and most of these people would do the work necessary to earn a decent living if they had the opportunity and capacity" (Dworkin, p. 208). What mainly concerns Dworkin—what he actually considers to be morally important—is manifestly not that our society permits a situation in which a substantial minority of Americans have *smaller shares* than others of the resources that he apparently presumes should be available for all. His concern is, rather, that the members of this minority *do not earn decent livings*.

The force of Dworkin's complaint does not derive from the allegation that our society fails to provide some individuals with as much as others but from a quite different allegation, namely, our society fails to provide each individual with "the opportunity to develop and lead a life he can regard as valuable both to himself and to [the community]" (p. 211). Dworkin is dismayed most fundamentally not by evidence that the United States permits economic inequality, but by evidence that it fails to ensure that everyone has enough to lead "a life of choice and value" (p. 212) —in other words, that it fails to fulfill for all the ideal of sufficiency. What bothers him most immediately is not that certain quantitative relationships are widespread but that certain qualitative conditions prevail. He cares principally about the value of people's lives, but he mistakenly represents himself as caring principally about the relative magnitudes of their economic assets.

My suggestion that situations involving inequality are morally disturbing only to the extent that they violate the ideal of sufficiency is confirmed, it seems to me, by familiar discrepancies between the principles egalitarians profess and the way in which they commonly conduct their own lives. My point here is not that some egalitarians hypocritically accept high incomes and special opportunities for which, according to the moral theories they profess, there is no justification. It is that many egalitarians (including many academic proponents of the doctrine) are not truly concerned whether they are as well off economically as other people are. They believe that they themselves have roughly enough money for what is important to them, and they are therefore not terribly preoccupied with the fact that some people are considerably richer than they. Indeed, many egalitarians would consider it rather shabby or even reprehensible to care, with respect to their own lives, about economic comparisons of that sort. And, notwithstanding the implications of the doctrines to which they urge adherence, they would be appalled if their children grew up with such preoccupations.

VI

The fundamental error of egalitarianism lies in supposing that it is morally important whether one person has less than another regardless of how much either of them has. This error is due in part to the false assumption that someone who is economically worse off has more important unsatisfied needs than someone who is better off. In fact the morally significant needs of both individuals may be fully satisfied or equally unsatisfied. Whether one person has more money than another is a wholly extrinsic matter. It has to do with a relationship between the respective economic assets of the two people, which is not only independent of the amounts of their assets and of the amounts of satisfaction they can derive from them but also independent of the attitudes of these people toward those levels of assets and of satisfaction. The economic comparison implies nothing concerning whether either of the people compared has any morally important unsatisfied needs at all, nor concerning whether either is content with what he has.

This defect in egalitarianism appears plainly in Thomas Nagel's development of the doctrine. According to Nagel: "The essential feature of an egalitarian priority system is that it counts improvements to the welfare of the worse off as more urgent than improvements to the welfare of the better off.... What makes a system egalitarian is the priority it gives to the claims of those at the bottom.... Each individual with a more urgent claim has priority ... over each individual with a less urgent claim."[17] And in discussing Rawls's Difference Principle, which he endorses, Nagel says the Difference Principle: "establishes an order of priority among needs and gives preference to the most urgent."[18] But the preference actually assigned by the Difference Principle is not in favor of those whose needs are most urgent; it is in favor of those who are identified as worst off. It is a mere assumption, which Nagel makes without providing any grounds for it whatever, that the worst off individuals have urgent needs. In most societies the people who are economically at the bottom are indeed extremely poor, and they do, as a matter of fact, have urgent needs. But this relationship between low economic status and urgent need is wholly contingent. It can be established only on the basis of empirical data. There is no necessary conceptual connection between a person's relative economic position and whether he has needs of any degree of urgency.[19]

It is possible for those who are worse off not to have more urgent needs or claims than those who are better off, because it is possible for them to have no urgent needs or claims at all. The notion of "urgency" has to do with what is *important*. Trivial needs or interests, which have no significant bearing upon the quality of a person's life or upon his readiness to be content with it, cannot properly be construed as being urgent to any degree whatever or as supporting the sort of morally demanding claims to which genuine urgency gives rise. From the fact that a person is at the bottom of some economic order, moreover, it cannot even be inferred that he has *any* unsatisfied needs or claims. After all, it is possible for conditions at the bottom to be quite good; the fact that they are the worst does not in itself entail that they are bad or that they are in any way incompatible with richly fulfilling and enjoyable lives.

Nagel maintains that what underlies the appeal of equality is an "ideal of acceptability to each individual."[20] On his account, this ideal entails that a reasonable person should consider deviations from equality to be acceptable only if they are in his interest in the sense that he would be worse off without them. But a reasonable person might well regard an unequal distribution as entirely acceptable even though he did not presume that any other distribution would benefit him less. For he might believe that the unequal distribution provided him with quite enough, and he might reasonably be unequivocally content with that, with no concern for the possibility that some other arrangement would provide him with more. It is gratuitous to assume that every reasonable person must be seeking to maximize the benefits he can obtain, in a sense requiring that he be endlessly interested in or open to improving his life. A certain deviation from equality might not be *in* someone's interest because it might be that he would in fact be better off without it. But as long as it does not *conflict* with his interest, by obstructing his opportunity to lead the sort of life that it is important for him to lead, the deviation from equality may be quite acceptable. To be wholly satisfied with a certain state of affairs, a reasonable person need not suppose that there is

no other available state of affairs in which he would be better off.[21]

Nagel illustrates his thesis concerning the moral appeal of equality by considering a family with two children, one of whom is "normal and quite happy" while the other "suffers from a painful handicap."[22] If this family were to move to the city the handicapped child would benefit from medical and educational opportunities that are unavailable in the suburbs, but the healthy child would have less fun. If the family were to move to the suburbs, on the other hand, the handicapped child would be deprived but the healthy child would enjoy himself more. Nagel stipulates that the gain to the healthy child in moving to the suburbs would be greater than the gain to the handicapped child in moving to the city: in the city the healthy child would find life positively disagreeable, while the handicapped child would not become happy "but only less miserable."

Given these conditions, the egalitarian decision is to move to the city; for "it is more urgent to benefit the [handicapped] child even though the benefit we can give him is less than the benefit we can give the [healthy] child." Nagel explains that this judgment concerning the greater urgency of benefiting the handicapped child "depends on the worse off position of the [handicapped] child. An improvement in his situation is more important than an equal or somewhat greater improvement in the situation of the [normal] child." But it seems to me that Nagel's analysis of this matter is flawed by an error similar to the one that I attributed above to Dworkin. The fact that it is preferable to help the handicapped child is not due, as Nagel asserts, to the fact that this child is worse off than the other. It is due to the fact that this child, and not the other, suffers from a painful handicap. The handicapped child's claim is important because his condition is *bad*—significantly undesirable—and not merely because he is *less well off* than his sibling.

This does not imply, of course, that Nagel's evaluation of what the family should do is wrong. Rejecting egalitarianism certainly does not mean maintaining that it is always mandatory simply to maximize benefits and that therefore the family should move to the suburbs because the normal child would gain more from that than the handicapped child would gain from a move to the city. However, the most cogent basis for Nagel's judgment in favor of the handicapped child has nothing to do with the alleged urgency of providing people with as much as others. It pertains rather to the urgency of the needs of people who do not have enough.[23]

VII

What does it mean, in the present context, for a person to have enough? One thing it might mean is that any more would be too much: a larger amount would make the person's life unpleasant, or it would be harmful or in some other way unwelcome. This is often what people have in mind when they say such things as "I've had enough!" or "Enough of that!" The idea conveyed by statements like these is that *a limit has been reached,* beyond which it is not desirable to proceed. On the other hand, the assertion that a person has enough may entail only that *a certain requirement or standard has been met,* with no implication that a larger quantity would be bad. This is often what a person intends when he says something like "That should be enough." Statements such as this one characterize the indicated amount as sufficient while leaving open the possibility that a larger amount might also be acceptable.

In the doctrine of sufficiency the use of the notion of "enough" pertains to *meeting a standard* rather than to *reaching a limit.* To say that a person has enough money means that he is content, or that it is reasonable for him to be content, with having no more money than he has. And to say this is, in turn, to say something like the following: the person does not (or cannot reasonably) regard whatever (if anything) is unsatisfying or distressing about his life as due to his having too little money. In other words, if a person is (or ought reasonably to be) content with the amount of money he has, then insofar as he is or has reason to be unhappy with the way his life is going, he does not (or cannot reasonably) suppose that money would—either as a sufficient or as a necessary condition—enable him to become (or to have reason to be) significantly less unhappy with it.[24]

It is essential to understand that having enough money differs from merely having enough to get along or enough to make life marginally tolerable. People are not generally content with living on the brink. The point of the doctrine of sufficiency is not that the only morally important distributional consideration with respect to money is whether people have enough to avoid economic misery. A person who might naturally and appropriately be said to have just barely enough does not, by the standard invoked in the doctrine of sufficiency, have enough at all.

There are two distinct kinds of circumstances in which the amount of money a person has is enough—that is, in which more money will not enable him to become significantly less unhappy. On the one hand, it may be that the person is suffering no substantial distress or dissatisfaction with his life. On the other hand, it may be that although the person is unhappy about how his life is going, the difficulties that account for his unhappiness would not be alleviated by more money. Circumstances of this second kind obtain when what is wrong with the person's life has to do with noneconomic goods such as love, a sense that life is meaningful, satisfaction with one's own character, and so on. These are goods that money cannot buy; moreover, they are goods for which none of the things money can buy are even approximately adequate substitutes. Sometimes, to be sure, noneconomic goods are obtainable or enjoyable only (or more easily) by someone who has a certain amount of money. But the person who is distressed with his life while content with his economic situation may already have that much money.

It is possible that someone who is content with the amount of money he has might also be content with an even larger amount of money. Since having enough money does not mean being at a limit beyond which more money would necessarily be undesirable, it would be a mistake to assume that for a person who already has enough the marginal utility of money must be either negative or zero. Although this person is by hypothesis not distressed about his life in virtue of any lack of things that more money would enable him to obtain, nonetheless it remains possible that he would enjoy having some of those things. They would not make him less unhappy, nor would they in any way alter his attitude toward his life or the degree of his contentment with it, but they might bring him pleasure. If that is so, then his life would in this respect be better with more money than without it. The marginal utility for him of money would accordingly remain positive.

To say that a person is content with the amount of money he has does not entail, then, that there would be no point whatever in his having more. Thus someone with enough money might be quite *willing* to accept incremental economic benefits. He might in fact be *pleased* to receive them. Indeed, from the supposition that a person is content with the amount of money he has it cannot even be inferred that he would not *prefer* to have more. And it is even possible that he would actually be prepared to *sacrifice* certain things that he values (e.g., a certain amount of leisure) for the sake of more money.

But how can all this be compatible with saying that the person is content with what he has? What *does* contentment with a given amount of money preclude, if it does not preclude being willing or being pleased or preferring to have more money or even being ready to make sacrifices for more? It precludes his having an *active interest* in getting more. A contented person regards having more money as *inessential* to his being satisfied with his life. The fact that he is content is quite consistent with his recognizing that his economic circumstances could be improved and that his life might as a consequence become better than it is. But this possibility is not important to him. He is simply not much interested in being better off, so far as money goes, than he is. His attention and interest are not vividly engaged by the benefits that would be available to him if he had more money. He is just not very responsive to their appeal. They do not arouse in him any particularly eager or restless concern, although he acknowledges that he would enjoy additional benefits if they were provided to him.

In any event, let us suppose that the level of satisfaction that his present economic circumstances enable him to attain is high enough to meet his expectations of life. This is not fundamentally a matter of how much utility or satisfaction his various activities and experiences provide. Rather, it is most decisively a matter of his attitude toward being provided with that much. The satisfying experiences a person has are one thing. Whether he is satisfied that his life includes just those satisfactions is another. Although it is possible that other feasible circumstances would provide him with greater amounts of satisfaction, it may be that he is wholly satisfied with the amounts of satisfaction that he now enjoys. Even if he knows that he could obtain a greater quantity of satisfaction overall, he does not experience the uneasiness or the ambition that would incline him to seek it. Some people feel that their lives are good enough, and it is not important to them whether their lives are as good as possible.

The fact that a person lacks an active interest in getting something does not mean, of course, that he prefers not to have it. This is why the contented person may without any incoherence accept or welcome improvements in his situation and why he may even be prepared to incur minor costs in order to improve it. The fact that he is contented means only that the possibility of improving his situation is not *important* to him. It only implies, in other words, that he does not resent his circumstances, that he is not anxious or determined to improve them, and that he does not go out of his way or take any significant initiatives to make them better.

It may seem that there can be no reasonable basis for accepting less satisfaction when one could have more, that therefore rationality itself entails maximizing, and, hence, that a person who refuses to maximize the quantity of satisfaction in his life is not being rational. Such a person cannot, of course, offer it as his reason for declining to pursue greater satisfaction that the costs of this pursuit are too high; for if that were his reason then, clearly, he would be attempting to maximize satisfaction after all. But what other good reason could he possibly have for passing up an opportunity for more satisfaction? In fact, he may have a very good reason for this: namely, *that he is satisfied with the amount of satisfaction he already has.* Being satisfied with the way things are is unmistakably an excellent reason for having no great interest in changing them. A person who is indeed satisfied with his life as it is can hardly be criticized, accordingly, on the grounds that he has no good reason for declining to make it better.

He might still be open to criticism on the grounds that he *should not* be satisfied—that it is somehow unreasonable, or unseemly, or in some other mode wrong for him to be satisfied with less satisfaction than he could have. On what basis, however, could *this* criticism be justified? Is there some decisive reason for insisting that a person ought to be so hard to satisfy? Suppose that a man deeply and happily loves a woman who is altogether worthy. We do not ordinarily criticize the man in such a case just because we think he might have done even better. Moreover, our sense that it would be inappropriate to criticize him for that reason need not be due simply to a belief that holding out for a more desirable or worthier woman might end up costing him more than it would be worth. Rather, it may reflect our recognition that the desire to be happy or content or satisfied with life is a desire for a satisfactory amount of satisfaction and is not inherently tantamount to a desire that the quantity of satisfaction be maximized.

Being satisfied with a certain state of affairs is not equivalent to preferring it to all others. If a person is faced with a choice between less and more of something desirable, then no doubt it would be irrational for him to prefer less to more. But a person may be satisfied without having made any such comparisons at all. Nor is it necessarily irrational or unreasonable for a person to omit or to decline to make comparisons between his own state of affairs and possible alternatives. This is not only because making comparisons may be too costly. It is also because if someone is satisfied with the way things are, he may have no motive to consider how else they might be.[25]

Contentment may be a function of excessive dullness or diffidence. The fact that a person is free both of resentment and of ambition may be due to his having a slavish character or to his vitality being muffled by a kind of negligent lassitude. It is possible for someone to be content merely, as it were, by default. But a person who is content with resources providing less utility than he could have may not be irresponsible or indolent or deficient in imagination. On the contrary, his decision to be content with those resources—in other words, to adopt an attitude of willing acceptance toward the fact that he has just that much—may be based upon a conscientiously intelligent and penetrating evaluation of the circumstances of his life.

It is not essential for such an evaluation to include an *extrinsic* comparison of the person's circumstances with alternatives to which he might plausibly aspire, as it would have to do if contentment were reasonable only when based upon a judgment that the enjoyment of possible benefits has been maximized. If someone is less interested in whether his circumstances enable him to live as well as possible than in whether they enable him to live satisfyingly, he may appropriately devote his evaluation entirely to an *intrinsic* appraisal of his life. Then he may recognize that his circumstances do not lead him to be resentful or regretful or drawn to change and that, on the basis of his understanding of himself and of what is important to him, he accedes approvingly to his actual readiness to be content with the way things are. The situation in that case is not so much that he rejects the possibility of improving his circumstances because he thinks there is nothing genuinely to be gained by attempting to improve them. It is rather that this possibility, however feasible it may be, fails as a matter of fact to excite his active attention or to command from him any lively interest.[26]

APPENDIX

Economic egalitarianism is a drily formalistic doctrine. The amounts of money its adherents want for themselves and for others are calculated without regard to anyone's personal characteristics or circumstances. In this formality, egalitarians resemble people who desire to be as rich as possible but who have no idea what they would do with their riches. In neither case are the individual's ambitions, so far as money is concerned, limited or measured according to an understanding of the goals that he intends his money to serve or of the importance of these goals to him.

The desire for unlimited wealth is fetishistic, insofar as it reflects with respect to a *means* an attitude—namely, desiring something for its own sake—that is appropriate only with respect to an *end*. It seems to me that the attitude taken by John Rawls toward what he refers to as "primary goods" ("rights and liberties, opportunities and powers, income and wealth")[27] tends toward fetishism in this sense. The primary goods are "all purpose means," Rawls explains, which people need no matter what other things they want: "Plans differ, since individual abilities, circumstances, and wants differ … ; but whatever one's system of ends, primary goods are a necessary means" (Rawls, p. 93). Despite the fact that he identifies the primary goods not as ends but as means, Rawls considers it rational for a person to want as much of them as possible. Thus, he says: "Regardless of what an individual's rational plans are in detail, it is assumed that there are various things which he would prefer more of rather than less. While the persons in the original position do not know their conception of the good, they do know, I assume, that they prefer more rather than less primary goods" (Rawls, pp. 92–93). The assumption that it must always be better to have more of the primary goods rather than less implies that the marginal utility of an additional quantity of a primary good is invariably greater than its cost. It implies, in other words, that the incremental advantage to an individual of possessing a larger quantity of primary goods is never outweighed by corresponding incremental liabilities, incapacities, or burdens.

But this seems quite implausible. Apart from any other consideration, possessing more of a primary good may well require of a responsible individual that he spend more time and effort in managing it and in making decisions concerning its use. These activities are for many people intrinsically unappealing; and they also characteristically involve both a certain amount of anxiety and a degree of distraction from other pursuits. Surely it must not be taken simply for granted that incremental costs of these kinds can never be greater than whatever increased benefits a corresponding additional amount of some primary good would provide.

Individuals in the original position are behind a veil of ignorance. They do not know their own conceptions of the good or their own life plans. Thus it may seem rational for them to choose to possess primary goods in unlimited quantities: since they do not know what to prepare for, perhaps it would be best for them to be prepared for anything. Even in the original position, however, it is possible for people to appreciate that at some point the cost of additional primary goods might exceed the benefits those goods provide. It is true that an individual behind the veil of ignorance cannot know at just what point he would find that an addition to his supply of primary goods costs more than it is worth. But his ignorance of the exact location of that point hardly warrants his acting as though no such point exists at all. Yet that is precisely how he does act if he chooses that the quantity of primary goods he possesses be unlimited.

Rawls acknowledges that additional quantities of primary goods may be, for some individuals, more expensive than they are worth. In his view, however, this does not invalidate the supposition that it is rational for everyone in the original position to want as much of these goods as they can get. Here is how he explains the matter:

> I postulate that they [i.e., the persons in the original position] assume that they would prefer more primary social goods rather than less. Of course, it may turn out, once the veil of ignorance is removed, that some of them for religious or other reasons may not, in fact, want more of these goods. But from the standpoint of the original position, it is rational for the parties to suppose that they do want a larger share, since in any case they are not compelled to accept more if they do not wish to, nor does a person suffer from a greater liberty. (Rawls, pp. 142–43.)

I do not find this argument convincing. It neglects the fact that dispensing with or refusing to accept primary goods that have been made available is itself an action that may entail significant costs. Burdensome calculations and deliberations may be required in order for a person to determine whether an increment of some primary good is worth having, and making decisions of this sort may involve responsibilities and risks in virtue of which the person experiences considerable anxiety. What is the basis, moreover, for the claim that no one suffers from a greater liberty? Under a variety of circumstances, it would seem, people may reasonably prefer to have fewer alternatives from which to choose rather than more. Surely liberty, like all other things, has its costs. It is an error to suppose that a person's life is invariably improved, or that it cannot be made worse, when his options are increased.[28]

NOTES

1. This version of economic egalitarianism (for short, simply "egalitarianism") might also be formulated as the doctrine that there should be no inequalities in the distribution of money. The two formulations are not unambiguously equivalent because the term "distribution" is equivocal. It may refer either to a pattern of possession or to an activity of allocation, and there are significant differences in the criteria for evaluating distributions in the two senses. Thus it is quite possible to maintain consistently both that it is acceptable for people to have unequal amounts of money and that it is objectionable to allocate money unequally.

2. Thus, Thomas Nagel writes: "The defense of economic equality on the ground that it is needed to protect political, legal and social equality … [is not] a defense of equality per se—equality in the possession of benefits in general. Yet the latter is a further moral idea of great importance. Its validity would provide an independent reason to favor economic equality as a good in its own right" "Equality." *Mortal Questions.* Cambridge: Cambridge University Press, 1979. 107.

3. I focus attention here on the standard of equality in the distribution of money chiefly in order to facilitate my discussion of the standard of sufficiency. Many egalitarians, of course, consider economic equality to be morally less important than equality in certain other matters: e.g., welfare, opportunity, respect, satisfaction of needs. In fact, some of what I have to say about economic egalitarianism and sufficiency applies as well to these other benefits. But I shall not attempt in this essay to define the scope of its applicability, nor shall I attempt to relate my views to other recent criticism of egalitarianism (e.g., Temkin, Larry S. "Inequality." *Philosophy and Public Affairs* 15 [1986]: 99–121; Goodin, Robert E. "Epiphenomenal Egalitarianism." *Social Research* 52 [1985]: 99–117).

4. It might be argued (as some of the editors of *Ethics* have suggested to me) that pursuing equality as an important social ideal would not be so alienating as pursuing it as a personal goal. It is indeed possible that individuals devoted to the former pursuit would be less immediately or less intensely preoccupied with their own economic circumstances than those devoted to the latter. But they would hardly regard the achievement of economic equality as important for the society unless they had the false and alienating conviction that it was important for individuals to enjoy economic equality.

5. I shall address some of these issues in section VII.

6. In the Sterling Memorial Library at Yale University (which houses 8.5 million volumes), there are 1,159 entries in the card catalog under the subject heading "liberty" and 326 under "equality." Under "fraternity," there are none. This is because the catalog refers to the social ideal in question as "brotherliness." Under that heading there are four entries! Why does fraternity (or brotherliness) have so much less salience than liberty and equality? Perhaps the explanation is that, in virtue of our fundamental commitment to individualism, the political ideals to which we are most deeply and actively attracted have to do with what we suppose to be the rights of individuals, and no one claims a right to fraternity. It is also possible that liberty and equality get more attention in certain quarters because, unlike fraternity, they are considered to be susceptible to more or less formal treatment. In any event, the fact is that there has been very little serious investigation into just what fraternity is, what it entails, or why it should be regarded as especially desirable.

7. Nagel endorses this argument as establishing the moral importance of economic equality. Other formulations and discussions of the argument may be found in: Arrow, Kenneth. "A Utilitarian Approach to the Concept of Equality in Public Expenditures." *Quarterly Journal of Economics* 85 (1971): 409–410; Blum, Walter and Kalven, Harry. *The Uneasy Case for Progressive Taxation.* Chicago: University of Chicago Press, 1966; Lerner, Abba. *The Economics of Control.* New York: Macmillan Publishing Co., 1944; Samuelson, Paul. *Economics.* New York: McGraw-Hill Book Co., 1973, and "A. P. Lerner at Sixty." *Collected Scientific Papers of Paul A. Samuelson.* Vol. 3. Ed. Robert C. Merton. Cambridge, Mass.: MIT Press, 1972. 643–52.

8. Thus, Arrow says: "In the utilitarian discussion of income distribution, equality of income is derived

from the maximization conditions if it is further assumed that individuals have the same utility functions, each with diminishing marginal utility." Supra, note 7, at 409. And Samuelson offers the following formulation: "If each extra dollar brings less and less satisfaction to a man, and if the rich and poor are alike in their capacity to enjoy satisfaction, a dollar taxed away from a millionaire and given to a median-income person is supposed to add more to total utility than it subtracts." *Economics*, supra, note 7, at 164, n. 1.

9. "With successive new units of [a] good, your total utility will grow at a slower and slower rate because of a fundamental tendency for your psychological ability to appreciate more of the good to become less keen. This fact, that the increments in total utility fall off, economists describe as follows: as the amount consumed of a good increases, the marginal utility of the good (or the extra utility added by its last unit) tends to decrease." Samuelson, *Economics*, supra, note 7, at 431.

10. Blum and Kalven, supra, note 7, at 57–58.

11. People tend to think that it is generally more important to avoid a certain degree of harm than to acquire a benefit of comparable magnitude. It may be that this is in part because they assume that utility diminishes at the margin, for in that case the additional benefit would have less utility than the corresponding loss. However, it should be noted that the tendency to place a lower value on acquiring benefits than on avoiding harms is sometimes reversed: when people are so miserable that they regard themselves as "having nothing to lose," they may well place a higher value on improving things than on preventing them from becoming (to a comparable extent) even worse. In that case, what is diminishing at the margin is not the utility of benefits but the disutility of harms.

12. In virtue of these thresholds, a marginal or incremental dollar may have conspicuously greater utility than dollars that do not enable a threshold to be crossed. Thus, a person who uses his spare money during a certain period for some inconsequential improvement in his routine pattern of consumption—perhaps a slightly better quality of meat for dinner every night—may derive much less additional utility in this way than by saving up the extra money for a few weeks and going to see some marvelous play or opera. The threshold effect is particularly integral to the experience of collectors, who characteristically derive greater satisfaction from obtaining the item that finally completes a collection—whichever item it happens to be—than from obtaining any of the other items in the collection. Obtaining the final item entails crossing a utility threshold: a complete collection of twenty different items, each of which when considered individually has the same utility, is likely to have greater utility for a collector than an incomplete collection that is of the same size but that includes duplicates. The completeness of the collection itself possesses utility, in addition to the utility provided individually by the items of which the collection is constituted.

13. Lerner, supra, note 7, at 26–27.

14. Conditions of these kinds are discussed in Rescher, Nicholas. *Distributive Justice*. Indianapolis: Bobbs-Merrill Co., 1966. 28–30.

15. It might be correct to say that he does need one unit if there is a chance that he will get four more, since in that case the one unit can be regarded as potentially an integral constituent of the total of five that puts him across the threshold of survival. But if there is no possibility that he will acquire five, then acquiring the one does not contribute to the satisfaction of any need.

16. Dworkin, Ronald. "Why Liberals Should Care about Equality." *A Matter of Principle*. Cambridge, Mass.: Harvard University Press, 1985. 206. Page numbers in parentheses in the text that follows refer to this work.

17. Nagel, supra, note 2, at 118.

18. Id., at 117.

19. What I oppose is the claim that when it comes to justifying attempts to improve the circumstances of those who are economically worst off, a good reason for making the attempt is that it is morally important for people to be as equal as possible with respect to money. The only morally compelling reason for trying to make the worse off better off is, in my judgment, that their lives are in some degree bad lives. The fact that some people have more than enough money suggests a way in which it might be arranged for those who have less than enough to get more, but it is not in itself a good reason for redistribution.

20. Nagel, supra, note 2, at 123.

21. For further discussion, see section VII.

22. Quotations from his discussion of this illustration are from Nagel, supra, note 2, at 123–24.

23. The issue of equality or sufficiency that Nagel's illustration raises does not, of course, concern the distribution of money.

24. Within the limits of my discussion it makes no difference which view is taken concerning the very important question of whether what counts is the attitude a person actually has or the attitude it would be reasonable for him to have. For the sake of brevity, I shall henceforth omit referring to the latter alternative.
25. Compare the sensible adage: "If it's not broken, don't fix it."
26. People often adjust their desires to their circumstances. There is a danger that sheer discouragement, or an interest in avoiding frustration and conflict, may lead them to settle for too little. It surely cannot be presumed that someone's life is genuinely fulfilling, or that it is reasonable for the person to be satisfied with it, simply because he does not complain. On the other hand, it also cannot be presumed that when a person has accommodated his desires to his circumstances, this is itself evidence that something has gone wrong.
27. Rawls, John. *A Theory of Justice*. Cambridge, Mass.: Harvard University Press, 1971. 92. Additional references to this book appear in parentheses in the following text.
28. For pertinent discussion of this issue, see Dworkin, Gerald. "Is More Choice Better than Less?" *Midwest Studies in Philosophy*. Vol. 7. Eds. P. French, T. Uehling, and H. Wettstein. Minneapolis: University of Minnesota Press, 1982. 47–61.

45   What Is the Point of Equality?

ELIZABETH S. ANDERSON*

If much recent academic work defending equality had been secretly penned by conservatives, could the results be any more embarrassing for egalitarians? Consider how much of this work leaves itself open to classic and devastating conservative criticisms. Ronald Dworkin defines equality as an "envy-free" distribution of resources.[1] This feeds the suspicion that the motive behind egalitarian policies is mere envy. Philippe Van Parijs argues that equality in conjunction with liberal neutrality among conceptions of the good requires the state to support lazy, able-bodied surfers who are unwilling to work.[2] This invites the charge that egalitarians support irresponsibility and encourage the slothful to be parasitic on the productive. Richard Arneson claims that equality requires that, under certain conditions, the state subsidize extremely costly religious ceremonies that its citizens feel bound to perform.[3] G. A. Cohen tells us that equality requires that we compensate people for being temperamentally gloomy, or for being so incurably bored by inexpensive hobbies that they can only get fulfilling recreation from expensive diversions.[4] These proposals bolster the objection that egalitarians are oblivious to the proper limits of state power and permit coercion of others for merely private ends. Van Parijs suggests that to fairly implement the equal right to get married, when male partners are scarce, every woman should be given an equal tradable share in the pool of eligible bachelors and have to bid for whole partnership rights, thus implementing a transfer of wealth from successful brides to compensate the losers in love.[5] This supports the objection that egalitarianism, in its determination to correct perceived unfairness everywhere, invades our privacy and burdens the personal ties of love and affection that lie at the core of family life.

*I thank Louise Antony, Stephen Everson, Allan Gibbard, Mark Hansen, Don Herzog, David Hills, Louis Loeb, Martha Nussbaum, David Velleman, and audience participants at the University of North Carolina and the University of Chicago, where I delivered earlier versions of this article. Special thanks go to Amy Gutmann, for her penetrating comments at the thirty-first annual Philosophy Colloquium at Chapel Hill, N.C.

From *Ethics*. Vol. 109, No. 2 (January 1999): 287–337. © 1999 by The University of Chicago. All rights reserved. Reprinted with permission of the publisher. Also available online from JSTOR: http://www.jstor.org/stable/10.1086/233897

Those on the left have no less reason than conservatives and libertarians to be disturbed by recent trends in academic egalitarian thought. First, consider those whom recent academic egalitarians have singled out for special attention: beach bums, the lazy and irresponsible, people who can't manage to entertain themselves with simple pleasures, religious fanatics. Thomas Nagel[6] and Gerald Cohen give us somewhat more sympathetic but also pitiable characters in taking stupid, talentless, and bitter people to be exemplary beneficiaries of egalitarian concern. What has happened to the concerns of the politically oppressed? What about inequalities of race, gender, class, and caste? Where are the victims of nationalist genocide, slavery, and ethnic subordination?

Second, the agendas defined by much recent egalitarian theorizing are too narrowly focused on the distribution of divisible, privately appropriated goods, such as income and resources, or privately enjoyed goods, such as welfare. This neglects the much broader agendas of actual egalitarian political movements. For example, gay and lesbian people seek the freedom to appear in public as who they are, without shame or fear of violence, the right to get married and enjoy benefits of marriage, to adopt and retain custody of children. The disabled have drawn attention to the ways the configuration of public spaces has excluded and marginalized them, and campaigned against demeaning stereotypes that cast them as stupid, incompetent, and pathetic. Thus, with respect to both the targets of egalitarian concern and their agendas, recent egalitarian writing seems strangely detached from existing egalitarian political movements.

What has gone wrong here? I shall argue that these problems stem from a flawed understanding of the point of equality. Recent egalitarian writing has come to be dominated by the view that the fundamental aim of equality is to compensate people for undeserved bad luck—being born with poor native endowments, bad parents, and disagreeable personalities, suffering from accidents and illness, and so forth. I shall argue that in focusing on correcting a supposed cosmic injustice, recent egalitarian writing has lost sight of the distinctively political aims of egalitarianism. The proper negative aim of egalitarian justice is not to eliminate the impact of brute luck from human affairs, but to end oppression, which by definition is socially imposed. Its proper positive aim is not to ensure that everyone gets what they morally deserve, but to create a community in which people stand in relations of equality to others.

In this article, I will compare the implications of these two conceptions of the point of equality. The first conception, which takes the fundamental injustice to be the natural inequality in the distribution of luck, can be called "luck egalitarianism" or "equality of fortune." I shall argue that equality of fortune fails the most fundamental test any egalitarian theory must meet: that its principles express equal respect and concern for all citizens. It fails this test in three ways. First, it excludes some citizens from enjoying the social conditions of freedom on the spurious ground that it's their fault for losing them. It escapes this problem only at the cost of paternalism. Second, equality of fortune makes the basis for citizens' claims on one another the fact that some are inferior to others in the worth of their lives, talents, and personal qualities. Thus, its principles express contemptuous pity for those the state stamps as sadly inferior and uphold envy as a basis for distributing goods from the lucky to the unfortunate. Such principles stigmatize the unfortunate and disrespect the fortunate by failing to show how envy can obligate them. Third, equality of fortune, in attempting to ensure that people take responsibility for their choices, makes demeaning and intrusive judgments about people's capacities to exercise responsibility and effectively dictates to them the appropriate uses of their freedom.

The theory I shall defend can be called "democratic equality." In seeking the construction of a community of equals, democratic equality integrates principles of distribution with the expressive demands of equal respect. Democratic equality guarantees all law-abiding citizens effective access to the social conditions of their freedom at all times. It justifies the distributions required to secure this guarantee by appealing to the obligations of citizens in a democratic state. In such a state, citizens make claims on one another by virtue of their equality, not their inferiority, to others. Because the fundamental aim of citizens in constructing a state is to secure everyone's freedom, democratic equality's principles of distribution neither presume to tell people how to use their opportunities nor attempt to judge how responsible people are for choices that lead to unfortunate outcomes. Instead, it avoids bankruptcy at the hands of the imprudent by limiting the range of goods provided collectively and expecting individuals to take personal responsibility for the other goods in their possession.

JUSTICE AS EQUALITY OF FORTUNE

The following passage by Richard Arneson aptly describes the conception of justice I aim to criticize:

> The concern of distributive justice is to compensate individuals for misfortune. Some people are blessed with good luck, some are cursed with bad luck, and it is the responsibility of society—all of us regarded collectively—to alter the distribution of goods and evils that arises from the jumble of lotteries that constitutes human life as we know it ... Distributive justice stipulates that the lucky should transfer some or all of their gains due to luck to the unlucky.[7]

This conception of justice can be traced to the work of John Rawls,[8] and has been (I believe mistakenly) attributed to him. Equality of fortune is now one of the dominant theoretical positions among egalitarians, as evidenced by the roster of theorists who endorse it, including Richard Arneson, Gerald Cohen, Ronald Dworkin, Thomas Nagel, Eric Rakowski, and John Roemer.[9] Philippe Van Parijs also incorporates this principle into his theory of equality of resources or assets. Luck egalitarianism relies on two moral premises: that people should be compensated for undeserved misfortunes and that the compensation should come only from that part of others' good fortune that is undeserved.

Part of the appeal of equality of fortune comes from its apparently humanitarian impulse. When decent people see others suffer for no good reason—say, children dying from starvation—they tend to regard it as a matter of obligation that the more fortunate come to their aid. Part of its appeal comes from the force of the obviously correct claim that no one deserves their genetic endowments or other accidents of birth, such as who their parents are or where they were born. This seems to weaken claims of those blessed by their genes or social circumstances to retain all of the advantages that typically flow from such good fortune. Besides these intrinsic sources of appeal, proponents of equality of fortune have tried to build support for egalitarianism by responding to many of the formidable objections that conservatives and libertarians have made against egalitarians of the past.

Consider the following litany of objections to equality. Some critics argue that the pursuit of equality is futile. For no two people are really equal: the diversity of individuals in their talents, aims, social identities, and circumstances ensures that in achieving equality in some domain, one will inevitably create inequalities in others.[10] Give people the same amount of money and the prudent will get more happiness from it than the imprudent. Recent egalitarians have effectively responded to these charges by paying close attention to the problem of defining the proper space in which equality is desirable. Equality is a viable goal once the space of egalitarian concern is defined and the resulting inequalities in other domains are shown to be acceptable. Other critics charge that the quest for equality is wasteful because it would rather throw away goods that can't be evenly divided than let some have more than others.[11] What's worse, it may call for leveling down people's talents when all cannot be lifted to the same high standards.[12] Recent egalitarians adopt a "leximin" criterion of equality, permitting inequalities as long as they benefit, or, more permissively, don't harm the worst off.[13] So they don't care much about income disparities among the very prosperous. Many proponents of equality of fortune also accept a strong principle of self-ownership, and so deplore interference with people's choices to develop their talents or forced appropriation of those talents.[14]

Luck egalitarians have been most responsive to criticisms of equality based on ideals of desert, responsibility, and markets. Critics of equality object that egalitarians take goods away from the deserving.[15] Proponents of equality of fortune reply that they take from the fortunate only that portion of their advantages that everyone acknowledges is undeserved. On the receiving side, the critics protest that egalitarianism undermines personal responsibility by guaranteeing outcomes independent of people's personal choices.[16] In response, luck egalitarians have moved from an equality of outcome to an equality of opportunity conception of justice: they ask only that people start off with equal opportunities to achieve welfare or access to advantage, or that they start off with an equal share of resources.[17] But they accept the justice of whatever inequalities result from adults' voluntary choices. All place great stress on the distinction between the outcomes for which an individual is responsible—that is, those that result from her voluntary choices—and the outcomes for which she is not responsible— good or bad outcomes that occur independent of her choice or of what she could have reasonably foreseen. Luck egalitarians dub this the distinction between "option luck" and "brute luck."[18]

The resulting theories of equality of fortune thus share a common core: a hybrid of capitalism and the welfare state. For the outcomes for which individuals are held responsible, luck egalitarians prescribe rugged individualism: let the distribution of goods be governed by capitalist markets and other voluntary agreements.[19] This reliance on markets responds to the objection that egalitarianism does not appreciate the virtues of markets as efficient allocative mechanisms and as spaces for the exercise of freedom.[20] For the outcomes determined by brute luck, equality of fortune prescribes that all good fortune be equally shared and that all risks be pooled. "Good fortune" means, primarily, unproduced assets such as unimproved land, natural resources, and the income attributable to native endowments of talent. Some theorists would also include the welfare opportunities attributable to possession of unchosen favorable mental and physical traits. "Risks" mean any prospects that reduce one's welfare or resources. Luck egalitarians thus view the welfare state as a giant insurance company that insures its citizens against all forms of bad brute luck. Taxes for redistributive purposes are the moral equivalent of insurance premiums against bad luck. Welfare payments compensate people against losses traceable to bad brute luck, just like insurance policies do.

Ronald Dworkin has articulated this insurance analogy most elaborately.[21] He argues that justice demands that the state compensate each individual for whatever brute risks they would have insured themselves against, on the assumption that all were equally likely to suffer from the risk. The state steps in to provide social insurance when private insurance for a risk is not available to all on equal and affordable terms. Where such private insurance is available, brute luck is automatically converted into option luck, for society can hold individuals responsible for purchasing insurance on their own behalf.[22] In its pure form, luck egalitarianism would insist that if individuals imprudently fail to do so, no demand of justice requires society to bail them out. Most luck egalitarians recoil from this thought, however, and thus justify mandatory insurance, or other restrictions on individuals' liberty to squander their share of good fortune, on paternalistic grounds.[23]

Luck egalitarians disagree with one another primarily over the space in which they advocate equality. Should egalitarians seek equality of resources or assets (Dworkin, Rakowski, Roemer), real freedom—that is, legal rights plus the means to achieve one's ends (Van Parijs), equal opportunity for welfare (Arneson), or equal access to advantage—a mixed bag of internal capabilities, opportunities for welfare, and resources (Cohen, Nagel)? This looks like a wide diversity of views, but the central disagreement among them separates luck egalitarians into two camps: one which accepts equality of welfare as a legitimate (if not the only) object of egalitarian concern (Arneson, Cohen, Roemer, probably Nagel), and one which only equalizes resources (Dworkin, Rakowski, Van Parijs). All parties accept an analysis of an individual's welfare in terms of the satisfaction of her informed preferences. The role of individual preferences in equality of fortune shall be a central object of my critique, so it pays to consider these differences.

Should egalitarians care whether people have equal opportunities for welfare, or only that their share of resources be equal? Resource egalitarians object to taking welfare as an equalisandum because of the problem of expensive tastes.[24] Some people—spoiled brats, snobs, sybarites—have preferences that are expensive to satisfy. It takes a lot more resources to satisfy them to the same degree that a modest, self-controlled person can be satisfied. If equalizing welfare or opportunities for welfare were the object of equality, then the satisfaction of self-controlled people would be held hostage to the self-indulgent. This seems unfair. Resource egalitarians argue, therefore, that people should be entitled to equal resources, but be held responsible for developing their tastes so that they can live satisfactorily within their means.

Against this view, those who believe welfare is a legitimate space of egalitarian concern offer three arguments. One is that people value resources for the welfare they bring. Shouldn't egalitarians care about what ultimately matters to people, rather than focusing on merely instrumental goods?[25] Second, they argue that resource egalitarians unfairly hold people responsible for all of their preferences and for the costs of satisfying them. Although some preferences are voluntarily cultivated by individuals, many others are shaped by genetic and environmental influences beyond their control and are highly resistant to deliberate change. Moreover, an individual may not be responsible for the fact that satisfying them is so expensive. For example, an unforeseeable event may cause a dramatic shortage of a once abundant means of satisfying some taste, and thereby escalate its price. Welfarists argue that it is unfair, and inconsistent with the basic premise of luck egalitarianism, to hold people responsible for their involuntary, or involuntarily expensive, tastes.[26] Third, they argue that people with handicaps are entitled to more resources (medical treatment, guide dogs, etc.) than others, on account of their handicap, and that resource egalitarians can't accommodate this intuition. This is because being handicapped is analytically equivalent to having preferences that are involuntarily expensive to

satisfy. The preference for mobility may be the same between an ambulatory and a paraplegic person, but the cost of satisfying the latter's preference is much higher, although not by the choice of the paraplegic person. The paraplegic has an involuntarily expensive taste for mobility. If resource egalitarians accept the liberal requirement that theories of justice must be neutral among competing conceptions of the good, they cannot discriminate between involuntarily expensive tastes for mobility on the part of the handicapped and involuntarily expensive tastes for rare champagne on the part of gourmets.[27]

I shall consider the first and third defenses of welfarism later in this article. The second defense is open to the following reply by resource egalitarians. Justice demands that the claims that people are entitled to make on others should be sensitive not only to the benefits expected on the part of the claimants but to the burdens these claims place on others. These burdens are measured by the opportunity costs of the resources devoted to meeting them, which are a function of the preferences of others for the same resources. For egalitarian purposes, the value of a bundle of external resources should thus be determined not by how much welfare the owner can get from it, but by the price it would fetch in a perfectly competitive market if everyone could bid for it and all enjoyed the same monetary assets.[28]

The importance of this reply is that it shows how even resource egalitarians give subjective preferences a central role to play in the measurement of equality. For the value of resources is measured by the market prices they would command in a hypothetical auction, and these prices are a function of everyone's subjective preferences for those resources. Everyone is said to have an equal bundle of resources when the distribution of resources is envy-free: no one prefers someone else's bundle of resources to their own. Resource egalitarians agree that unproduced external resources should be distributed equally in this envy-free sense, and that such a distribution is identical to what would be achieved in a perfectly competitive auction open to everyone, if everyone had equal information, talents, bidding skills, and cash available for bidding.[29] The difference between resource egalitarians and welfare egalitarians thus does not consist in whether the measure of equality is based on subjective preferences. They differ only in that for welfare egalitarians, the claims a person makes are dependent on her tastes, whereas for resource egalitarians, they are a function of everyone's tastes.

The different conceptions of equality of fortune differ in many details, which I cannot cover here. I have sketched what I take to be the crucial differences among them. My aim, however, has been to identify the features these conceptions of justice share, for I want to show that these features reflect a fundamentally flawed conception of justice. In the next two sections, I shall present a series of cases in which luck egalitarianism generates injustice. Not every version of equality of fortune is vulnerable to each counterexample; but each version is vulnerable to one or more counterexamples in each section.

THE VICTIMS OF BAD OPTION LUCK

The state, says Ronald Dworkin, should treat each of its citizens with equal respect and concern.[30] Virtually all egalitarians accept this formula, but rarely have they analyzed it. Instead, they invoke the formula, then propose their favored principle of egalitarian distribution as an interpretation of it, without providing an argument proving that their principle really does express equal respect and concern for all citizens. In this section, I will argue that the reasons luck egalitarians offer for refusing to come to the aid of the victims of bad option luck express a failure to treat these unfortunates with equal respect and concern. In the next section, I will argue that the reasons luck egalitarians offer for coming to the aid of the victims of bad brute luck express disrespect for them.

Luck egalitarians say that, assuming everyone had equal opportunity to run a particular risk, any outcomes due to voluntary choices whose consequences could reasonably be foreseen by the agent should be born or enjoyed by the agent. The inequalities they generate neither give rise to redistributive claims on others if the outcome is bad, nor are subject to redistributive taxation if the outcome is good.[31] This, at least, is the doctrine in its hard-line form. Let us start with Rakowski's version of equality of fortune, since his sticks most closely to the hard line.

Consider an uninsured driver who negligently makes an illegal turn that causes an accident with another car. Witnesses call the police, reporting who is at fault; the police transmit this information to emergency medical technicians. When they arrive at the scene and find that the driver at fault is uninsured, they leave him to die by the side of the road. According to Rakowski's doctrine, this action is just, for they have no obligation to give him emergency care. No doubt, there are sound policy reasons for not making snap judgments of personal responsibility at the scene of an emergency. The best policy is to rescue everyone and sort questions of fault out later. But this is of no help to the luck egalitarian. There is the uninsured driver, hooked up to a respirator, fighting for his life. A judicial hearing has found him at fault for the accident. According to Rakowski, the faulty driver has no claim of justice to continued medical care. Call this the problem of *abandonment of negligent victims.*

If the faulty driver survives, but is disabled as a result, society has no obligation to accommodate his disability. Arneson joins Rakowski on this point.[32] It follows that the post office must let the guide dogs of the congenitally blind guide their owners through the building, but it can with justice turn away the guide dogs of faulty drivers who lost their sight in a car accident. No doubt it would be too costly for the state to administer such a discriminatory system. But this administrative consideration is irrelevant to the question of whether luck egalitarianism identifies the right standard of what *justice* requires. Call this the problem of *discrimination among the disabled.*

Luck egalitarians abandon even prudent people to their fates when the risks they run turn sour. "If a citizen of a large and geographically diverse nation like the United States builds his house in a flood plain, or near the San Andreas fault, or in the heart of tornado country, then the risk of flood, earthquake, or crushing winds is one he chooses to bear, since those risks could be all but eliminated by living elsewhere."[33] We must not forget the threat of hurricanes devastating the Gulf and East Coasts. Shall all Americans be expected to crowd into Utah, say, to be entitled to federal disaster relief?[34] Rakowski's view effectively limits disaster relief to only those citizens who reside in certain portions of the country. Call this the problem of *geographical discrimination among citizens.*

Consider next the case of workers in dangerous occupations. Police officers, firefighters, members of the armed forces, farmers, fishers, and miners suffer from significantly higher than average risks of injury and death at work. But these are "exemplary instances of option luck" and hence can generate no claims to publicly subsidized medical care or aid to dependents if an accident occurs.[35] Rakowski would have to allow that people *drafted* into the armed forces would be entitled to veterans' disability payments. However, his doctrine implies that patriotic volunteers, having run the risks of battle by choice, could justly be required to pay for their rehabilitation themselves. Call this the problem of *occupational discrimination.*

Dependent caretakers and their children face special problems under equality of fortune. Many people who care for dependents—children, the ill and infirm—command no market wage for discharging their obligations to those who cannot take care of themselves, and lack the time and flexibility to earn a decent wage. For this reason, dependent caretakers, who are almost all women, tend to be either financially dependent on a wage earner, dependent on welfare payments, or extremely poor. Women's financial dependence on a male wage earner results in their systematic vulnerability to exploitation, violence, and domination.[36] But Rakowski's doctrine implies that this poverty and resulting subordination is by choice and therefore generates no claims of justice on others. It is a "lifestyle," perhaps taken up from deep conviction but precisely for that reason not something that can be pursued at the expense of those who don't share their "zeal" or "belief" that one owes duties of care to family members.[37] If women don't want to be subject to such poverty

and vulnerability, they shouldn't choose to have children.

Nor do children have any claim to assistance from anyone but their parents. From the point of view of everyone else, they are an unwelcome intrusion, who would reduce the fair shares of natural resources to which the first comers are entitled were they allowed to lay a claim to such shares independently of their claim to their parents' shares. "It is ... unjust to declare ... that because two people decide to have a child ... *everyone* is required to share their resources with the new arrival, and to the same extent as its parents. With what right can two people force all the rest, through deliberate behavior rather than bad brute luck, to settle for less than their fair shares after resources have been divided justly?"[38] The desire to procreate is just another expensive taste, which resource egalitarians need not subsidize.

Rakowski's view is, certainly, on the harsh end among luck egalitarians. Most luck egalitarians would consider the time at which a person enters society as irrelevant to their claim to their fair share of the bounties of nature. Children are not responsible either for their parents' lack of wealth or for their parents' decision to reproduce. Thus it is a matter of bad brute luck, requiring compensation, if their parents lack the means to give them their fair share. But the women who devote themselves to caring for children are another story. Since women are not on average less talented than men, but choose to develop and exercise talents that command little or no market wage, it is not clear whether luck egalitarians have any basis for remedying the injustices that attend their dependence on male wage earners. Call this the problem of *vulnerability of dependent caretakers.*

On Rakowski's hard-line version of equality of fortune, once people risk and lose their fair share of natural wealth, they have no claims against others to stop their free fall into misery and destitution. Equality of fortune imposes no constraints on the structure of opportunities generated by free markets. Nothing would prevent people, even those whose gambles were prudent but who suffered from bad option luck, from subjection to debt peonage, sweatshops, or other forms of exploitation. The inequalities and suffering permitted by this view are unlimited. Call these the problems of *exploitation* and the *lack of a safety net.*

Rakowski could insist that private or public insurance be made available to all to prevent such conditions. Then it would be the fault of individuals who failed to purchase such insurance that they were so destitute and vulnerable to exploitation. But justice does not permit the exploitation or abandonment of anyone, even the imprudent. Moreover, a person's failure to keep up with all of the insurance payments needed to protect herself against innumerable catastrophes need not reflect imprudence. If her option luck is particularly bad, she may not be able to pay for all that insurance and still provide for her family's basic needs. Under these conditions, it is perfectly rational, and indeed morally obligatory, to serve the family's urgent needs over its speculative needs—for example, to drop some insurance in order to pay for food. Call this the problem of the *abandonment of the prudent.*

Rakowski's version of equality of fortune treats the victims of bad option luck most harshly. His distributive rules are considerably more harsh than even those found in the United States, which does not ration health care on the basis of fault, protects all the disabled from discrimination, provides federal disaster relief to all residents of the country, requires employers to provide worker disability plans, provides veterans' benefits and at least temporary welfare for impoverished families with dependent children, requires minimum wages, and forbids slavery, debt peonage, and at least some kinds of sweatshop exploitation. Do other luck egalitarians do a better job than Rakowski in shielding the victims of bad option luck from the worst fates? Dworkin's theory offers no better protection than Rakowski's against predatory practices in the free market, once people have lost their fair share of resources through bad option luck. Nor would it help dependent caretakers, or people who are disabled as a result of choices they made.

Van Parijs would guarantee everyone the maximum unconditional basic income that could be sustained in a society. If this income were significant, it would certainly help dependent caretakers, the disabled and involuntarily unemployed, and anyone else down on their luck.[39] However, Van Parijs concedes that the size of this income might be very low, even zero.[40] The chief difficulty with his proposal is that his basic income would be awarded to all unconditionally, regardless of whether they were able or performing socially useful work. Lazy, able-bodied surfers would be just as entitled to that income as dependent caretakers or the disabled. In order to offer an incentive for people to work and thereby provide the tax revenue to fund a basic income, there would have to be a substantial gap between the basic income and the wage provided by the lowest paid unskilled job. Such a low basic income might be satisfactory to footloose beach bums, who might be happy camping on the beach. But it would hardly be enough for struggling parents, the involuntarily unemployed, or the disabled, who have special expenses. Were the guaranteed basic income tied to a requirement that able-bodied people engage in socially useful work, it could be raised to a much higher level. Van Parijs's proposal effectively indulges the tastes of the lazy and irresponsible at the expense of others who need assistance.[41]

Arneson proposes that everyone be guaranteed equal opportunity for welfare. Upon reaching adulthood, everyone should face a range of choices such that the sum of expected utilities for each equally accessible life history is equal to the sum of utilities that any other person faces in their possible life histories. Once these opportunities are guaranteed, people's fates are determined by their choices and option luck.[42] Like Dworkin's and Rakowski's theories, Arneson's theory guarantees equality, indeed even a minimally decent life, only *ex ante,* before one has made any adult choices. This is small comfort to the person who led a cautious and prudent life, but still fell victim to extremely bad option luck.[43] Arneson might reply by incorporating into people's prospective decision-trees their preferences for facing (or not having to face) certain options at each moment in time. However, this could undermine personal responsibility altogether by allowing people to rule out even minor losses consequent upon whatever choices they may make.[44] In addition, we have seen that Arneson would not require accommodation of people who are disabled by their own fault. Dependent caretakers also would not get much help from Arneson. As Roemer says, explaining Arneson's and Cohen's position, "Society should not compensate people for their choice of [a more altruistic, self-sacrificing] path because it owes people no compensation on account of their moral views."[45] People who want to avoid the vulnerabilities that attend dependent caretaking must therefore decide to care only for themselves. This is egalitarianism for egoists alone. One wonders how children and the infirm are to be cared for, with a system that offers so little protection to their caretakers against poverty and domination.

Cohen's and Roemer's theories are the only ones to question the structure of opportunities generated by markets in response to people's choices. Cohen argues that equality demands equality of access to advantage, and defines advantage to include not just welfare but freedom from exploitation or subjection to unfair bargains.[46] Roemer's version of market socialism, in which households would share equally in the returns to capital through a universal grant, would also prevent the worst outcomes generated by laissez faire capitalism, such as debt peonage and sweatshop labor. However, as theorists from the Marxist tradition, they focus on the exploitation of wage laborers to the exclusion of non-wage-earning dependent caretakers.[47]

What do luck egalitarians say in response to these problems? None recognize the sexist implications of assimilating the performance of moral obligations to care for dependents to the class of voluntarily expensive tastes. Most are sensitive to the fact that an egalitarian view that guarantees equality only *ex ante*, before adults start making choices for themselves, and makes no provision for people after that, will in fact generate substantial inequalities in people's fates as they lead their lives, to the point where the worst off will often be extremely badly off. They assume that the prudent will prevent such fates by taking advantage of the availability of private (or, where needed, public) insurance. All agree, then, that the chief

difficulty for luck egalitarians is how to insure against the wretchedness of the imprudent.

Arneson has considered this problem most deeply within the terms of luck egalitarianism. He argues that it is sometimes unfair to hold people responsible for the degree to which they are responsible agents. The capacities needed for responsible choice—foresight, perseverance, calculative ability, strength of will, self-confidence—are partly a function of genetic endowments and partly of the good fortune of having decent parents. Thus, the imprudent are entitled to special paternalistic protection by society against their poor choices. This might involve, for example, mandatory contributions to a pension plan to provide for old age.[48] The other luck egalitarians agree that pure equality of fortune might have to be modified by a significant dose of paternalistic intervention, to save the imprudent from the worst consequences of their choices. However, in their view, *only* paternalistic reasons can justify making mandatory the various universal social insurance programs characteristic of modern welfare states: social security, health and disability insurance, disaster relief, and so forth. *Only* paternalistic reasons justify meting out individuals' basic income grant on a monthly basis, rather than in a lump sum upon coming of age.[49] Call this the problem of *paternalism*.

Let us pause to consider whether these policies express respect for citizens. Luck egalitarians tell the victims of very bad option luck that, having chosen to run their risks, they deserve their misfortune, so society need not secure them against destitution and exploitation. Yet a society that permits its members to sink to such depths, due to entirely reasonable (and, for dependent caretakers, even obligatory) choices, hardly treats them with respect. Even the imprudent don't deserve such fates. Luck egalitarians do entertain modifications of their harsh system, but only on paternalistic grounds. In adopting mandatory social insurance schemes for the reasons they offer, luck egalitarians are effectively telling citizens that they are too stupid to run their lives, so Big Brother will have to tell them what to do. It is hard to see how citizens could be expected to accept such reasoning and still retain their self-respect.

Against these objections, one might argue as follows.[50] First, given their concern that no one suffer undeserved misfortune, luck egalitarians ought to be able to argue that some outcomes are so awful that no one deserves to suffer them, not even the imprudent. Negligent drivers don't deserve to die from a denial of health care. Second, paternalism can be an honest and compelling rationale for legislation. For example, it is no great insult for a state to pass laws requiring the use of seat belts, so long as the law is democratically passed. Self-respecting people can endorse some paternalistic laws as simply protecting themselves from their own thoughtlessness.

I accept the spirit of these arguments. But they suggest desiderata for egalitarian theory that move us away from equality of fortune. The first argument points to the need to distinguish between goods that society guarantees to all citizens and goods that may be entirely lost without generating any claims to compensation. This is not simply a matter of defining minimum guaranteed aggregate levels of welfare or property endowments. A negligent driver might suffer far more from the death of her son in a car accident she caused than from denial of rehabilitative surgery to her injured leg. Society owes her no compensation for the worse suffering, even if it brings her below some threshold of welfare, but ought not to deprive her of health care, even if she would not drop below that level without it. Egalitarians must try to secure certain *kinds* of goods for people. This thought goes against the spirit of equality of fortune, which aims for comprehensive indemnification of people against undeserved losses of all kinds within the general space of equality they specify (welfare or resources). Arneson's argument for the indistinguish-ability of the needs of the handicapped from the desires of anyone with involuntarily expensive tastes illustrates this.

The second argument raises the question of how to justify liberty-limiting laws that aim to provide benefits to those whose liberty is limited. Seat belt laws are fine, but represent an insignificant case, because the liberty they limit is trifling. When the liberty being limited is significant, as in the case of mandatory participation in a social insurance scheme, citizens are owed a more dignified explanation than that Big Brother knows better than they do where their interests lie. It is a desideratum of egalitarian theory that it be capable of supplying such an explanation.

THE VICTIMS OF BAD BRUTE LUCK

Consider now the victims of bad brute luck: those born with serious genetic or congenital handicaps, or who become significantly disabled due to childhood neglect, illness, or accidents for which they cannot be held responsible. Luck egalitarians assimilate to this category those who have little native talent and those whose talents do not command much market value. Van Parijs would also include in this group anyone who is dissatisfied with their other native endowments, whether of nonpecuniary talents, beauty and other physical features, or of agreeable personality traits.[51] Cohen and Arneson would add, also, those people who have involuntarily expensive tastes or chronically depressed psychic states.[52] Equality of fortune says that such victims of bad brute luck are entitled to compensation for their defective internal assets and internal states.

Where luck egalitarians tend to be either harsh or paternalistic toward the victims of bad option luck, they seem compassionate toward the victims of bad brute luck. The chief appeal of equality of fortune to those of an egalitarian bent lies in this appearance of humanitarianism. Equality of fortune says that no one should have to suffer from undeserved misfortune and that priority in distribution should be given to those who are blamelessly worst off. I shall argue here that the appearance of humanitarianism is belied by the doctrine of equality of fortune in two ways. First, its rules for determining who shall be included among the blamelessly worst off fail to express concern for everyone who is worst off. Second, the reasons it offers for granting aid to the worst off are deeply disrespectful of those to whom the aid is directed.

When is a deficit in internal assets so bad as to require compensation? One doesn't want anyone with any trivial personal dissatisfaction, such as having bad hair, to be entitled to compensation. Dworkin argues that the people who should be compensated for defects in internal assets are those who would have purchased insurance against their having the defect if they were behind a veil of ignorance and did not know whether they would have that defect. It follows, uncharitably, that people who have an extremely rare but severe disability could be ineligible for special aid just because the chances of anyone suffering from it were so minute that it was *ex ante* rational for people not to purchase insurance against it. The proposal discriminates between people with rare and common disabilities.[53] In addition, Dworkin's proposal would treat two people with the same disability differently, depending on their tastes.[54] A risk-averse blind person could be entitled to aid denied to a risk-loving blind person, on the grounds that the latter probably would not have insured against being blind, given the probabilities. These are further cases of discrimination among the disabled.

Dworkin's criterion of compensable disability, since it depends on people's individualized preferences for insurance, also falls prey to the problem of *expensive tastes*.[55] Suppose a vain person would get hysterical over the prospect of being genetically determined to have a hooked nose. A person's anxiety over this prospect might be enough to make it rational for her to take out insurance for plastic surgery before knowing how her nose would turn out. It is hard to see how such a preference could create an obligation on the part of society to pay for her plastic surgery. Moreover, many people don't see hooked noses as such a bad thing, and many of these people have hooked noses: they would rightly feel insulted if society treated having a hooked nose as such a grievous defect that it was entitled to compensation.

To avoid being held hostage to expensive, idiosyncratic, and frivolous tastes, Van Parijs, following Ackerman,[56] has proposed that the class of people whose internal asset deficiencies are entitled to compensation be determined by the principle of *undominated diversity*. The idea is to arrive at an objective criterion of disability to which everyone would assent, given the great

heterogeneity in internal assets and in tastes for them. Consider the total internal assets of person A. If there exists a person B such that *everyone* would prefer having B's total set of internal assets to having A's, then A's diversity of assets is *dominated* by B's. A is then considered so wretched that no one thinks any of his internal assets is valuable enough to make up for his internal defects to the extent of making his assets at least equal to B's. This condition seems bad enough to warrant compensation, from anyone's point of view. The amount of compensation is set to the point at which for any B, at least one person prefers A's set of internal and external assets to B's.

Against the criterion of undominated diversity, one could complain that if an odd religious sect considered the severely disabled blessed because closer to God on account of their disabilities, then none of the disabled would be entitled to special aid, even those who rejected the religion. Van Parijs finds this example far-fetched: only those who have a real appreciation of the disadvantages of having the disability, and whose preferences are intelligible to the wider public, should have their preferences count in the test. But a real case is ready to hand: most people who identify as members of the Deaf community do not believe that being Deaf is such a grievous defect that there is any hearing person whose abilities are preferable to theirs. Van Parijs bites the bullet at this point, and says that if this is so, then the deaf are not entitled to any special aid, whether they identify as part of the Deaf community or not. In their own judgment, they find their abilities to be satisfactory without the aid, so why provide it to them?[57]

A similar problem afflicts welfarist egalitarian theories such as Arneson's. Cohen objects that in Arneson's view, if Tiny Tim would still be happy without his wheelchair and sullen Scrooge would be consoled by having the money it costs, then Tim should have to give up his wheelchair to Scrooge.[58] The trouble is that these theories, in relying on subjective evaluations, and in aggregating over different dimensions of well-being, allow private satisfactions to count as making up for publicly imposed disadvantages. If people find happiness in their lives despite being oppressed by others, this hardly justifies continuing the oppression. Similarly, would it be all right to compensate for natural inequalities, such as being born ugly, by means of social advantages, such as getting preferential hiring over the beautiful?[59] Call this the problem of *using private (dis)satisfaction to justify public oppression*. It suggests a further desideratum of egalitarian theory, that the form of remedy it supplies match the type of injustice it addresses.

So far I have stressed the injustices equality of fortune inflicts upon those excluded from aid. Consider now those whom equality of fortune singles out as the exemplary beneficiaries of aid. Consider Thomas Nagel's view: "When racial and sexual injustice have been reduced, we shall still be left with the great injustice of the smart and the dumb, who are so differently rewarded for comparable effort.... Perhaps someone will discover a way to reduce the socially produced inequalities (especially the economic ones) between the intelligent and the unintelligent, the talented and the untalented, or even the beautiful and the ugly."[60] What do luck egalitarians have to say to those cursed by such defects in their internal assets? Suppose their compensation checks arrived in the mail along with a letter signed by the State Equality Board explaining the reasons for their compensation. Imagine what these letters would say.

> To the disabled: Your defective native endowments or current disabilities, alas, make your life less worth living than the lives of normal people. To compensate for this misfortune, we, the able ones, will give you extra resources, enough to make the worth of living your life good enough that at least *one* person out there thinks it is comparable to someone else's life.
>
> To the stupid and untalented: Unfortunately, other people don't value what little you have to offer in the system of production. Your talents are too meager to command much market value. Because of the misfortune that you were born so poorly endowed with talents, we productive ones will make it up to you: we'll let you share in the bounty of what we have produced with our vastly superior and highly valued abilities.
>
> To the ugly and socially awkward: How sad that you are so repulsive to people around you

that no one wants to be your friend or lifetime companion. We won't make it up to you by being your friend or your marriage partner—we have our own freedom of association to exercise—but you can console yourself in your miserable loneliness by consuming these material goods that we, the beautiful and charming ones, will provide. And who knows? Maybe you won't be such a loser in love once potential dates see how rich you are.

Could a self-respecting citizen fail to be insulted by such messages? How dare the state pass judgment on its citizens' worth as workers and lovers! Furthermore, to require citizens to display evidence of personal inferiority in order to get aid from the state is to reduce them to groveling for support. Nor is it the state's business to pass judgment on the worth of the qualities of citizens that they exercise or display in their private affairs. Even if everyone thought that A was so ugly or socially unappealing that they preferred socially attractive B's personal qualities, it is none of the state's business to attach an official stamp of recognition on such private judgments. If it is humiliating to be widely regarded by one's associates as a social clod, think how much more degrading it would be for the state to raise such private judgments to the status of publicly recognized opinions, accepted as true for purposes of administering justice. Equality of fortune *disparages the internally disadvantaged* and *raises private disdain to the status of officially recognized truth.*

Let us not think that the problem here lies only in the consequences of sending the insulting notes along with the compensatory checks. Of course, actually sending such notes would only add insult to injury. Even if such notes were not sent, general knowledge of the grounds upon which citizens laid claim to special aid would be stigmatizing. A conesquentialist might therefore recommend that the State Equality Board conduct its investigations in secrecy and shroud its reasonings in euphemism and dissimulation. It is hard to see how the board could gather the information it needed to implement luck egalitarian principles without branding some of its citizens as inferior. How could one tell whether someone's state were so pitiable that everyone preferred someone else's internal assets to hers without taking a poll? Yet such objections to government house utilitarianism, however formidable, do not get to the core of the problem with equality of fortune.

Whether it communicates its reasons for aid or not, equality of fortune bases its distributive principles on considerations that can only express *pity* for its supposed beneficiaries. Look back at the reasons offered for distributing extra resources to the handicapped and those low in talent or personal appeal: in each case, it is some relative deficiency or defect in their persons or their lives. People lay claim to the resources of egalitarian redistribution in virtue of their inferiority to others, not in virtue of their equality to others. Pity is incompatible with respecting the dignity of others. To base rewards on considerations of pity is to fail to follow principles of distributive justice that express equal respect for all citizens. Luck egalitarianism therefore violates the fundamental expressive requirement of any sound egalitarian theory.[61]

One might argue that the concern expressed by equality of fortune is simple humanitarian compassion, not contemptuous pity. We must be clear about the difference. Compassion is based on an awareness of suffering, an intrinsic condition of a person. Pity, by contrast, is aroused by a comparison of the observer's condition with the condition of the object of pity. Its characteristic judgment is not "she is badly off" but "she is worse off than me." When the conditions being compared are internal states in which people take pride, pity's thought is "she is sadly inferior to me." Compassion and pity can both move a person to act benevolently, but only pity is condescending.

In virtue of their distinct cognitive bases, humanitarian compassion and pity motivate action on different principles. Compassion does not yield egalitarian principles of distribution: it aims to relieve suffering, not to equalize it. Once people have been relieved of suffering and neediness, compassion generates no further impetus toward equality of condition.[62] Furthermore, compassion seeks to relieve suffering wherever it exists, without passing moral judgment on those who suffer. International humanitarian organizations such as

the Red Cross offer aid to all the victims of war, including even the aggressors. By contrast, equality of fortune seeks to equalize assets even when people are not actually suffering from internal deficits, but merely get fewer advantages from them than others get from theirs. And it restricts its sympathy to those who are blamelessly disadvantaged. Equality of fortune therefore does not express compassion. It focuses not on the absolute misery of a person's condition but on the gap between least and most fortunate. Thus, among the more fortunate who are moved by equality of fortune, it evokes the pathos of distance, a consciousness of the benefactors' own superiority to the objects of their compassion. This is pity.

If pity is the attitude the more fortunate express toward the less fortunate when they adopt luck egalitarianism as their principle of action, what is the attitude the less fortunate express toward the more fortunate when they make claims in accordance with the theory? The resourcist luck egalitarians are explicit on this point: it is envy. Their criterion of an equal distribution of resources is an envy-free distribution: one which is such that no one wants anyone else's bundle of resources.[63] The two attitudes are well-suited to each other: the most generous attitude the envied could appropriately have toward the envious is pity. While this makes equality of fortune emotionally consistent, it hardly justifies the theory. Envy's thought is "I want what you have." It is hard to see how such wants can generate *obligations* on the part of the envied. To even offer one's own envy as a reason to the envied to satisfy one's desire is profoundly disrespectful.

Luck egalitarianism thus fails to express concern for those excluded from aid, and fails to express respect for those included among its beneficiaries as well as for those expected to pay for its benefits. It fails the most fundamental tests any egalitarian theory must meet.

THE ILLS OF LUCK EGALITARIANISM: A DIAGNOSIS

We have seen that equality of fortune underwrites a hybrid institutional scheme: free markets, to govern the distribution of goods attributable to factors for which individuals are responsible, and the welfare state, to govern the distribution of goods attributable to factors beyond the individual's control. Equality of fortune can thus be seen as an attempt to combine the best of capitalism and socialism. Its free market aspects promote efficiency, freedom of choice, "consumers' sovereignty," and individual responsibility. Its socialist aspects give everyone a fair start in life and protect the innocent against bad brute luck. Equality of fortune could be seen as a doctrine to which socialists might naturally gravitate, after learning the lessons of the follies of comprehensive centralized state economic planning and the considerable virtues of market allocations. By incorporating a very large role for market decisions within their institutional arrangements, luck egalitarians might appear to have disarmed the traditional conservative and libertarian critiques of egalitarianism.

But the counterintuitive judgments that luck egalitarians pass on the cases discussed above suggest a more dismal judgment: equality of fortune appears to give us some of the worst aspects of capitalism and socialism. Egalitarianism ought to reflect a generous, humane, cosmopolitan vision of a society that recognizes individuals as equals in all their diversity. It should promote institutional arrangements that enable the diversity of people's talents, aspirations, roles, and cultures to benefit everyone and to be recognized as mutually beneficial. Instead, the hybrid of capitalism and socialism envisioned by luck egalitarians reflects the mean-spirited, contemptuous, parochial vision of a society that represents human diversity hierarchically, moralistically contrasting the responsible and irresponsible, the innately superior and the innately inferior, the independent and the dependent. It offers no aid to those it labels irresponsible, and humiliating aid to those it labels innately inferior. It gives us the cramped vision of the Poor Laws, where unfortunates breathe words of supplication and submit to the humiliating moral judgments of the state.

How could luck egalitarians go so wrong? Consider first the ways equality of fortune invites problems in the ways it relies on market decisions. It offers a very inadequate safety net for the

victims of bad option luck. This reflects the fact that equality of fortune is essentially a "starting-gate theory": as long as people enjoy fair shares at the start of life, it does not much concern itself with the suffering and subjection generated by people's voluntary agreements in free markets.[64] The fact that these evils are the product of voluntary choices hardly justifies them: free choice within a set of options does not justify the set of options itself. In focusing on correcting the supposed injustices of nature, luck egalitarians have forgotten that the primary subject of justice is the institutional arrangements that generate people's opportunities over time.

Some luck egalitarians, most notably Dworkin, also use market decisions to provide guidance on appropriate state allocations at the start of life. The guiding idea here is that individual autonomy is protected by "consumers' sovereignty." Thus, Dworkin suggests that the market prices people actually pay for insurance against bodily injury might be used as a guide for the state's awards of compensation for people who are blamelessly injured in the same ways.[65] But actual market prices for insurance reflect two factors irrelevant to determining the compensation the state might owe to the involuntarily injured: the need to keep compensation extremely low to reduce the moral hazard for nonfatal injuries (high compensation might tempt people to risk greater injuries), and the fact that people insure only against the costs of injury that the state does not already indemnify them against (e.g., workplace disability, public accommodations for the disabled).

Dworkin's resort to the hypothetical insurance purchases of people who don't know their abilities suffers from a larger problem: he never explains why such hypothetical market choices have any relevance at all to determining what citizens owe one another. Since these choices were not, in fact, made, the failure to reflect them in state allocations violates no one's actual autonomous choices. Individuals' market choices vary according to their tastes. But what one is obligated to do for others is not, in general, determined either by one's own or even by the beneficiaries' tastes. We have seen that such taste relativity licenses discrimination against citizens with rare disabilities and against risk-loving citizens. But even if certain people are willing to take risks with themselves, it doesn't follow that they give up their claim on fellow citizens to provide them with the same social insurance benefits against *involuntarily* caused disabilities to which their risk-averse fellows are entitled. Moreover, even if everyone would rationally purchase some insurance for themselves—say, for plastic surgery to correct minor defects in appearance—this fact is hardly sufficient to generate an *obligation* for society to pay for it. If everyone wants it, they could of course vote to include plastic surgery in a national health-care plan. But if they voted not to include it and leave everyone to purchase such insurance from their private resources, it is hard to see how any citizen could have a complaint of justice against the decision of the voters. It is one thing for everyone to decide that something is worth purchasing for their private consumption, quite another to decide that citizens acting collectively are obligated to socialize the costs of providing it to everyone. I conclude that *people's real or hypothetical market choices offer no guidance whatsoever to what citizens are obligated to provide to one another on a collective basis.* This suggests another desideratum for egalitarian theory: it must supply principles for collective willing—that is, for what citizens should will together, not just for what each can will individually.

Now, consider the ways luck egalitarianism invites problems in the ways it relies on socialist principles. Equality of fortune tells us that no one should suffer from undeserved misfortune. To implement its principles, the state must make judgments of moral desert or responsibility in assigning outcomes to brute or option luck. To determine whether a smoker who picked up the habit while a soldier should get state-funded medical treatment for lung cancer, other people must judge whether he should have shown stronger resolve against smoking, given the social pressures he faced from peers and advertisers while serving in the army, the anxiety-reducing benefits of smoking in the highly stressful situation of combat, the opportunities he was offered to overcome his habit after the war, and so forth.[66]

F. A. Hayek has identified the central problem with such merit-based systems of reward: in order to lay a claim to some important benefit, people are forced to obey other people's judgments of what uses they should have made of their opportunities, rather than following their own judgments.[67] Such a system requires the state to make grossly intrusive, moralizing judgments of individual's choices. Equality of fortune thus *interferes with citizens' privacy and liberty.* Furthermore, as Arneson and Roemer make clear, such judgments require the state to determine how much responsibility each citizen was capable of exercising in each case. But it is disrespectful for the state to pass judgment on how much people are responsible for their expensive tastes or their imprudent choices.[68]

Furthermore, equality of fortune would not really promote personal responsibility in the way that it claims. To be sure, it denies compensatory rewards to people who are judged responsible for their bad fortune. But this gives individuals an *incentive to deny personal responsibility for their problems,* and to represent their situation as one in which they were helpless before uncontrollable forces. Better social conditions for fostering the spread of a passive, whining victim's mentality could hardly be constructed. They allow citizens to lay claim to such goods as basic medical benefits only at the cost of making an undignified spectacle of themselves. Moreover, it is easier to construct a sob story recounting one's undeserved misfortunes than it is to engage in productive work that is valued by others. In giving people an incentive to channel their self-seeking energies in the former rather than the latter direction, equality of fortune generates a huge *deadweight loss* to society.

In promoting such an unhappy combination of capitalist and socialist institutions, equality of fortune succeeds not in establishing a society of equals, but only in reproducing the stigmatizing regime of the Poor Laws, in which citizens lay claim to aid from the state only on condition that they accept inferior status. Poor Law thinking pervades the reasoning of luck egalitarians. This is most evident in their distinction between the deserving and the undeserving disadvantaged—between those who are not responsible for their misfortune and those who are. Like the Poor Law regime, it abandons those disadvantaged through their own choices to their miserable fates, and defines the deserving disadvantaged in terms of their innate inferiority of talent, intelligence, ability, or social appeal.

Moreover, in classifying those who devote the bulk of their energies to caring for dependents with those who have a voluntarily expensive taste for charity, equality of fortune *assumes atomistic egoism and self-sufficiency as the norm for human beings.* It promises equality only to those who tend only to their own self-interest, who avoid entering into relationships with others that might generate obligations to engage in dependent care-taking, and who therefore can manage to take care of themselves through their own wage earning, without having to depend on market-generated income provided by anyone else. But such a norm for human beings cannot be universalized. Long periods of dependency on others' caretaking are a normal and inevitable part of everyone's life cycle. It is therefore an indispensable condition of the continuation of human society that many adults devote a great deal of their time to such caretaking, however poorly such work may be remunerated in the market. And this, in turn, entails some dependency of caretakers on income generated by others. Equality of fortune, in representing the dependency of caretakers as voluntary deviance from a falsely universalized androcentric norm, ends up justifying the subordination of women to male wage earners and the stigmatization of dependent caretaking relative to self-sufficient wage earning. A more perfect reproduction of Poor Law thinking, including its sexism and its conflation of responsible work with market wage-earning, could hardly be imagined.[69]

WHAT IS THE POINT OF EQUALITY?

There must be a better way to conceive of the point of equality. To do so, it is helpful to recall how egalitarian political movements have historically conceived of their aims. What have been the inegalitarian systems that they have opposed? In-

egalitarianism asserted the justice or necessity of basing social order on a hierarchy of human beings, ranked according to intrinsic worth. Inequality referred not so much to distributions of goods as to relations between superior and inferior persons. Those of superior rank were thought entitled to inflict violence on inferiors, to exclude or segregate them from social life, to treat them with contempt, to force them to obey, work without reciprocation, and abandon their own cultures. These are what Iris Young has identified as the faces of oppression: marginalization, status hierarchy, domination, exploitation, and cultural imperialism.[70] Such unequal social relations generate, and were thought to justify, inequalities in the distribution of freedoms, resources, and welfare. This is the core of inegalitarian ideologies of racism, sexism, nationalism, caste, class, and eugenics.

Egalitarian political movements oppose such hierarchies. They assert the equal moral worth of persons. This assertion does not mean that all have equal virtue or talent. Negatively, the claim repudiates distinctions of moral worth based on birth or social identity—on family membership, inherited social status, race, ethnicity, gender, or genes. There are no natural slaves, plebeians, or aristocrats. Positively, the claim asserts that all competent adults are equally moral agents: everyone equally has the power to develop and exercise moral responsibility, to cooperate with others according to principles of justice, to shape and fulfill a conception of their good.[71]

Egalitarians base claims to social and political equality on the fact of universal moral equality. These claims also have a negative and a positive aspect. Negatively, egalitarians seek to abolish oppression—that is, forms of social relationship by which some people dominate, exploit, marginalize, demean, and inflict violence upon others. Diversities in socially ascribed identities, distinct roles in the division of labor, or differences in personal traits, whether these be neutral biological and psychological differences, valuable talents and virtues, or unfortunate disabilities and infirmities, never justify the unequal social relations listed above. Nothing can justify treating people in these ways, except just punishment for crimes and defense against violence. Positively, egalitarians seek a social order in which persons stand in relations of equality. They seek to live together in a democratic community, as opposed to a hierarchical one. Democracy is here understood as collective self-determination by means of open discussion among equals, in accordance with rules acceptable to all. To stand as an equal before others in discussion means that one is entitled to participate, that others recognize an obligation to listen respectfully and respond to one's arguments, that no one need bow and scrape before others or represent themselves as inferior to others as a condition of having their claim heard.[72]

Contrast this democratic conception of equality with equality of fortune. First, democratic equality aims to abolish socially created oppression. Equality of fortune aims to correct what it takes to be injustices generated by the natural order. Second, democratic equality is what I shall call a relational theory of equality: it views equality as a social relationship. Equality of fortune is a distributive theory of equality: it conceives of equality as a pattern of distribution. Thus, equality of fortune regards two people as equal so long as they enjoy equal amounts of some distributable good—income, resources, opportunities for welfare, and so forth. Social relationships are largely seen as instrumental to generating such patterns of distribution. By contrast, democratic equality regards two people as equal when each accepts the obligation to justify their actions by principles acceptable to the other, and in which they take mutual consultation, reciprocation, and recognition for granted. Certain patterns in the distribution of goods may be instrumental to securing such relationships, follow from them, or even be constitutive of them. But democratic egalitarians are fundamentally concerned with the relationships within which goods are distributed, not only with the distribution of goods themselves. This implies, third, that democratic equality is sensitive to the need to integrate the demands of equal recognition with those of equal distribution.[73] Goods must be distributed according to principles and processes that express respect for all. People must not be required to grovel or demean themselves before others as a condition of laying claim

to their share of goods. The basis for people's claims to distributed goods is that they are equals, not inferiors, to others.

This gives us a rough conception of equality. How do we derive principles of justice from it? Our investigation of equality of fortune has not been completely fruitless: from its failures, we have gleaned some desiderata for egalitarian principles. First, such principles must identify certain goods to which all citizens must have effective access over the course of their whole lives. Some goods are more important from an egalitarian point of view than others, within whatever space of equality is identified as of particular concern for egalitarians. And starting-gate theories, or any other principles that allow law-abiding citizens to lose access to adequate levels of these goods, are unacceptable. Second, egalitarians should be able to justify such guarantees of lifetime accessibility without resorting to paternalism. Third, egalitarian principles should offer remedies that match the type of injustice being corrected. Private satisfactions cannot make up for public oppression. Fourth, egalitarian principles should uphold the responsibility of individuals for their own lives without passing demeaning and intrusive judgments on their capacities for exercising responsibility or on how well they have used their freedoms. Finally, such principles should be possible objects of collective willing. They should be capable of supplying sufficient reasons for citizens acting together to collectively guarantee the particular goods of concern to egalitarians.

Let us take up the last desideratum first. The determination of what can or must be collectively willed has been the traditional task of social contract theory. In liberal democratic versions of social contract theory, the fundamental aim of the state is to secure the liberty of its members. Since the democratic state is nothing more than citizens acting collectively, it follows that the fundamental obligation of citizens to one another is to secure the social conditions of everyone's freedom.[74] Because libertarians also embrace this formula, it might be thought to lead to inegalitarian implications. Instead of repudiating this formula, democratic equality interprets it. It claims that the social condition of living a free life is that one stand in relations of equality with others.

This claim might seem paradoxical, given the prevailing view that represents equality and freedom as conflicting ideals. We can see how it is true by considering the oppressive relationships that social equality negates. Equals are not subject to arbitrary violence or physical coercion by others. Choice unconstrained by arbitrary physical coercion is one of the fundamental conditions of freedom. Equals are not marginalized by others. They are therefore free to participate in politics and the major institutions of civil society. Equals are not dominated by others; they do not live at the mercy of others' wills. This means that they govern their lives by their own wills, which is freedom. Equals are not exploited by others. This means they are free to secure the fair value of their labor. Equals are not subject to cultural imperialism: they are free to practice their own culture, subject to the constraint of respecting everyone else. To live in an egalitarian community, then, is to be free from oppression to participate in and enjoy the goods of society, and to participate in democratic self-government.

Egalitarians thus differ from libertarians in advocating a more expansive understanding of the social conditions of freedom. Importantly, they view private relations of domination, even those entered into by consent or contract, as violations of individual freedom. Libertarians tend to identify freedom with formal, negative freedom: enjoying the legal right to do what one wants without having to ask anyone else's permission and without interference from others. This definition of freedom neglects the importance of having the means to do what one wants. In addition, the definition implicitly assumes that, given the material means and internal capacity to do what one wants, the absence of interference from others is all one needs to do what one wants. This ignores the fact that most of the things people want to do require participation in social activities, and hence communication and interaction with others. One cannot do these things if others make one an outcast. A libertarian might argue that freedom of association entails the right of people to refuse to associate with others on any grounds. Yet, a

society embodying such an unconditional right hardly needs physical coercion to force others to obey the wishes of those with the power to exclude others from participation in social life. The same point applies to a society in which property is so unequally distributed that some adults live in abject dependence on others, and so live at the mercy of others. Societies that permit the creation of outcasts and subordinate classes can be as repressive as any despotic regime.

EQUALITY IN THE SPACE OF FREEDOM: A CAPABILITIES APPROACH

Amartya Sen has proposed a better way to understand freedom. Consider the states of being and doing that constitute a person's well-being: a person can be healthy, well-nourished, physically fit, literate, an active participant in community life, mobile, happy, respected, confident, and so forth. A person may also care about other states of being and doing that reflect her autonomous ends: she may want to be outgoing, to raise children, practice medicine, play soccer, make love, and so forth. Call such states *functionings*. A person's *capabilities* consist of the sets of functionings she can achieve, given the personal, material, and social resources available to her. Capabilities measure not actually achieved functionings, but a person's freedom to achieve valued functionings. A person enjoys more freedom the greater the range of effectively accessible, significantly different opportunities she has for functioning or leading her life in ways she values most.[75] We can understand the egalitarian aim to secure for everyone the social conditions of their freedom in terms of capabilities. Following Sen, I say that egalitarians should seek equality for all in the space of capabilities.

Sen's capability egalitarianism leaves open a large question, however. *Which* capabilities does society have an obligation to equalize? Some people care about playing cards well, others about enjoying luxury vacations in Tahiti. Must egalitarians, in the name of equal freedom, offer free card-playing lessons and state subsidized vacations in exotic lands? Surely there are limits to which capabilities citizens are obligated to provide one another. We should heed our first desideratum, to identify particular goods within the space of equality that are of special egalitarian concern.

Reflection on the negative and positive aims of egalitarianism helps us meet this requirement. Negatively, people are entitled to whatever capabilities are necessary to enable them to avoid or escape entanglement in oppressive social relationships. Positively, they are entitled to the capabilities necessary for functioning as an equal citizen in a democratic state. While the negative and positive aims of egalitarianism overlap to a large extent, they are not identical. If functioning as an equal citizen were all that egalitarians cared about, they could not object to forced clitoridectomy, by which men control women's sexuality in private relations. But egalitarians also aim at abolishing private relations of domination, and therefore support the functionings needed for individual sexual autonomy. If having the capabilities needed to avoid oppression were all that mattered, then egalitarians would not oppose discrimination among the relatively privileged—for example, the glass ceiling for female executives. But egalitarians also aim at enabling all citizens to stand as equals to one another in civil society, and this requires that careers be open to talents.

Democratic equality thus aims for equality across a wide range of capabilities. But it does not support comprehensive equality in the space of capabilities. Being a poor card player does not make one oppressed. More precisely, the social order can and should be arranged so that one's skill at cards does not determine one's status in civil society. Nor is being a good card player necessary for functioning as a citizen. Society therefore has no obligation to provide free card lessons to citizens. Democratic equality satisfies the first desideratum of egalitarian theory.

Consider further the capabilities that democratic equality does guarantee to citizens. Let us focus on the capabilities necessary for functioning as an equal citizen. Citizenship involves functioning not only as a political agent—voting, engaging in political speech, petitioning government, and so forth—but participating as an equal in civil society. Civil society is the sphere of social life that is

open to the general public and is not part of the state bureaucracy, in charge of the administration of laws. Its institutions include public streets and parks, public accommodations such as restaurants, shops, theaters, buses and airlines, communications systems such as broadcasting, telephones, and the Internet, public libraries, hospitals, schools, and so forth. Enterprises engaged in production for the market are also part of civil society, because they sell their products to any customer and draw their employees from the general public. One of the important achievements of the civil rights movement was to vindicate an understanding of citizenship that includes the right to participate as an equal in civil society as well as in government affairs. A group that is excluded from or segregated within the institutions of civil society, or subject to discrimination on the basis of ascribed social identities by institutions in civil society, has been relegated to second-class citizenship, even if its members enjoy all of their political rights.

So, to be capable of functioning as an equal citizen involves not just the ability to effectively exercise specifically political rights, but also to participate in the various activities of civil society more broadly, including participation in the economy. And functioning in these ways presupposes functioning as a human being. Consider, then, three aspects of individual functioning: as a human being, as a participant in a system of cooperative production, and as a citizen of a democratic state. To be capable of functioning as a human being requires effective access to the means of sustaining one's biological existence—food, shelter, clothing, medical care—and access to the basic conditions of human agency—knowledge of one's circumstances and options, the ability to deliberate about means and ends, the psychological conditions of autonomy, including the self-confidence to think and judge for oneself, freedom of thought and movement. To be capable of functioning as an equal participant in a system of cooperative production requires effective access to the means of production, access to the education needed to develop one's talents, freedom of occupational choice, the right to make contracts and enter into cooperative agreements with others, the right to receive fair value for one's labor, and recognition by others of one's productive contributions. To be capable of functioning as a citizen requires rights to political participation, such as freedom of speech and the franchise, and also effective access to the goods and relationships of civil society. This entails freedom of association, access to public spaces such as roads, parks, and public accommodations including public transportation, the postal service, and telecommunications. This also entails the social conditions of being accepted by others, such as the ability to appear in public without shame, and not being ascribed outcast status. The freedom to form relationships in civil society also requires effective access to private spaces, since many such relationships can only function when protected from the scrutiny and intrusions of others. Homelessness—that is, having only public dwelling—is a condition of profound unfreedom.

Three points should be made about the structure of egalitarian guarantees in the space of freedom or capabilities. First, democratic equality guarantees not actual levels of functioning, but effective access to those levels. Individuals are free to choose to function at a lower level than they are guaranteed. For example, they might choose to join a religious group that discourages political participation. Moreover, democratic equality can make access to certain functionings —those requiring an income—conditional upon working for them, provided that citizens have effective access to those conditions—they are physically capable of performing the work, doing so is consistent with their other duties, they can find a job, and so forth. Effective access to a level of functioning means that people can achieve that functioning by deploying means already at their disposal, not that the functioning is unconditionally guaranteed without any effort on their own part. Thus, democratic equality is consistent with constructing the incentive systems needed for a modern economy to support the production needed to support egalitarian guarantees in the first place.

Second, democratic equality guarantees not effective access to equal levels of functioning but effective access to levels of functioning sufficient to stand as an equal in society. For some functionings, equal citizenship requires equal levels. For example, each citizen is entitled to the same number of votes in an election as everyone else. But for other functionings, standing as an equal does not require equal levels of functioning. To be capable of standing as an equal in civil society requires literacy. But in the U.S. context, it does not require literacy in any language other than English, nor the ability to interpret obscure works of literary theory. Democratic equality does not object if not everyone knows a foreign language, and only a few have a Ph.D.-level training in literature. In other countries, multilingual literacy might be required for equal standing.

Third, democratic equality guarantees effective access to a package of capabilities sufficient for standing as an equal over the course of an entire life. It is not a starting-gate theory, in which people could lose their access to equal standing through bad option luck. Access to the egalitarian capabilities is also market-inalienable: contracts whereby individuals irrevocably transfer their fundamental freedoms to others are null and void.[76] The rationale for establishing such inalienable rights might seem difficult to grasp from the point of view of the rights holder. Why shouldn't she be free to trade some of her egalitarian-guaranteed freedoms for other goods that she prefers? Isn't it paternalistic to deny her the freedom to trade?

We can avoid this thought by considering the point of view of the obligation holder. The counterpart to an individual's inalienable right to the social conditions of her freedom is the unconditional obligation of others to respect her dignity or moral equality. Kant would put the point as follows: every individual has a worth or dignity that is not conditional upon anyone's desires or preferences, not even the individual's own desires. This implies that there are some things one may never do to other people, such as to enslave them, even if one has their permission or consent. Contracts into slavery or servitude are therefore invalid. In basing inalienable rights on what others are obligated to do rather than on the rights bearer's own subjective interests, democratic equality satisfies the second desideratum of egalitarian theory: to justify lifetime guarantees without resorting to paternalism.

One advantage of the capabilities approach to equality is that it allows us to analyze injustices in regard to other matters besides the distribution of resources and other divisible goods. One's capabilities are a function not just of one's fixed personal traits and divisible resources, but of one's mutable traits, social relations and norms, and the structure of opportunities, public goods, and public spaces. Egalitarian political movements have never lost sight of the whole range of targets of egalitarian assessment. For example, feminists work to overcome the internal obstacles to choice—self-abnegation, lack of confidence, and low self-esteem—that women often face from internalizing norms of femininity. Gays and lesbians seek the ability to publicly reveal their identities without shame or fear, which requires significant changes in social relations of contempt and hostility, and changes in norms of gender and sexuality. The disabled aim to reconfigure public spaces to make them accessible and adapt work situations to their needs, so that they can participate in productive activity. No mere redistribution of divisible resources can secure the freedoms these groups seek.

Of course, democratic equality is also concerned with the distribution of divisible resources. It requires that everyone have effective access to enough resources to avoid being oppressed by others and to function as an equal in civil society. What counts as "enough" varies with cultural norms, the natural environment, and individual circumstance. For example, cultural norms and climate influence what kind of clothing one needs to be able to appear in public without shame and with adequate protection from the elements. Individual circumstances, such as disabilities, influence how much resources one needs to function as an equal. People without use of their legs may need more resources—wheelchairs, specially adapted vans—to achieve mobility comparable to that of ambulatory persons. Equality in the space of capabilities may therefore demand an unequal division of resources to accommodate the disabled.[77] What citizens ultimately owe one another is the social conditions of the freedoms people need to function as equal citizens. Because of differences in their internal capacities and social situations, people are not equally able to convert resources into capabilities for functioning. They are therefore entitled to different amounts of resources so they can enjoy freedom as equals.

Suppose we abstract from the fact that people have different internal physical and mental capabilities. Would democratic equality demand that external resources be divided equally from the start, as equality of fortune holds? There is no reason to think so. The capabilities relevant to functioning as a human being, as a participant in the system of social cooperation, and as an equal citizen do not include all functionings or all levels of functioning. To function as a human being, one needs adequate nutrition. To eat without being relegated to a sub-human status, one needs access to sources of nutrition besides pet food or the dumpster. But to be able to function as a dignified human being, one does not need the quantity or quality of food intake of a gourmet. Democratic equality therefore requires that everyone have effective access to adequate nutrition, as well as sources of nutrition that one's society considers dignified—fit for consumption in social gatherings. It does not require that everyone have the resources needed for an equal opportunity to function as a gourmet. It therefore does not require criteria for equality of resources that depend on the morally dubious idea that the distribution of resources should be sensitive to considerations of envy.

PARTICIPATION AS AN EQUAL IN A SYSTEM OF COOPERATIVE PRODUCTION

So far we have considered what citizens are obligated to provide one another. But how are such things to be produced, and by what means and principles shall they be distributed? In stressing the concept of obligation, democratic equality heads off the thought that in an egalitarian society everyone somehow could have a right to receive goods without anyone having an obligation to produce them. Democratic equality seeks equality in the capability or effective freedom to achieve functionings that are part of citizenship, broadly construed. For those capable of working and with access to jobs, the actual achievement of these functionings is, in the normal case, conditional on participating in the productive system. Contrary to Van Parijs's view, citizens do not owe one another the real freedom to function as beach bums. Most able-bodied citizens, then, will get access to the divisible resources they need to function by earning a wage or some equivalent compensation due to them on account of their filling some role in the division of labor.

In deciding principles for a just division of labor and a just division of the fruits of that labor, workers are to regard the economy as a system of cooperative, joint production.[78] I want to contrast this image of joint production with the more familiar image that invites us to regard the economy as if it were a system of self-sufficient Robinson Crusoes, producing everything all by themselves until the point of trade. By "joint production," I mean that people regard every product of the economy as jointly produced by everyone working together. From the point of view of justice, the attempt, independent of moral principles, to credit specific bits of output to specific bits of input by specific individuals represents an arbitrary cut in the causal web that in fact makes everyone's productive contribution dependent on what everyone else is doing. Each worker's capacity to labor depends on a vast array of inputs produced by other people—food, schooling, parenting, and the like. It even depends on workers in the recreation and entertainment industries, since enjoyment of leisure activities helps restore energy and enthusiasm for work. In addition, the productivity of a worker in a specific role depends not only on her own efforts, but on other people performing their roles in the division of labor. Michael Jordan could not make so many baskets if no one kept the basketball court swept clean. Millions of people could not even get to work if public transportation workers went on strike. The comprehensiveness of the division of labor in a modern economy implies that no one produces everything, or indeed anything, they consume by their own efforts alone. In regarding the division of labor as a comprehensive system of joint production, workers and consumers regard themselves as collectively

commissioning everyone else to perform their chosen role in the economy. In performing their role in an efficient division of labor, each worker is regarded as an agent for the people who consume their products and for the other workers who, in being thereby relieved from performing that role, become free to devote their talents to more productive activities.

In regarding the economy as a cooperative venture, workers accept the demand of what G. A. Cohen has defined as the principle of interpersonal justification:[79] any consideration offered as a reason for a policy must serve to justify that policy when uttered by anyone to anyone else who participates in the economy as a worker or a consumer. The principles that govern the division of labor and the assignment of particular benefits to the performance of roles in the division of labor must be acceptable to everyone in this sense. To see how interpersonal justification works within the context of the economy considered as a system of cooperative, joint production, consider three of the cases equality of fortune gets wrong: disability compensation for workers in dangerous occupations, federal disaster relief, and dependent caretakers with their children.

Rakowski argues that workers who choose particularly dangerous occupations, such as farming, fishing, mining, forestry, firefighting, and policing, have no claims to medical care, rehabilitation, or compensation if they are injured on the job.[80] Since they engage in these occupations by choice, any bad fortune they suffer on the job is a form of option luck, the consequences of which must be born by the worker alone. Cohen's test invites us to consider how persuasive this argument is, when uttered to the disabled workers by the consumers who eat the food, use the metal and wood, and enjoy the protection from fire and crime that these workers provide. These consumers are not free to disclaim all responsibility for the bad luck that befalls workers in dangerous occupations. For they commissioned these workers to perform those dangerous tasks on their own behalf. The workers were acting as agents for the consumers of their labor. It cannot be just to designate a work role in the division of labor that entails such risks and then assign a package of benefits to performance in the role that fails, given the risks, to secure the social conditions of freedom to those who occupy the role. The principle "let us be served by occupations so inadequately compensated that those in them shall lack the means necessary to secure their freedom, given the risks and conditions of their work" cannot survive the test of interpersonal justification.

Similar reflections apply to those who choose to live and work in areas prone to particularly severe natural disasters, such as residents near the San Andreas fault. Rakowski argues that such residents should be excluded from federal disaster relief because they live there by choice.[81] But they live there because other citizens have, through their demand for California products, commissioned them to exploit the natural resources in California. To deny them federal disaster relief is to invoke the rejected principle above. Economists may object that, on balance, it may not be efficient to continue production in a particular region, and that disaster relief, in subsidizing the costs of living in disaster-prone regions, perpetuates a costly error. However, if, on balance, citizens decide that a region should be designated uninhabitable, because the costs of relief are too high, the proper response is not to leave its residents in the lurch but to designate their relief toward helping them relocate. Citizens are not to be deprived of basic capabilities on account of where they live.[82]

The case of nonwage-earning dependent caretakers and children might seem to fall outside the purview of society as system of cooperation. But this is to confuse the economy with the market sector.[83] Nonwage-earning dependent caretakers contribute to production in at least three ways. First, most engage in household production—cleaning, cooking, and so forth—which services, if not performed, would have to be hired out. Second, they raise the future workers of the economy and help rehabilitate the sick and injured ones so they can return to work. Third, in discharging the obligations everyone has to dependents, considered as human beings, and the obligations all family members have toward their dependent kin, they relieve others of such responsibility and thereby free them to participate in the market

economy. Fathers would not be so productive in the market if the nonwage-earning or part-time working mothers of their children did not relieve them of so much of their responsibility to engage in direct caretaking.[84] The principle "let us assign others to discharge our caretaking obligations to dependents, and attach such meager benefits to performance in this role that these caretakers live at our mercy" cannot survive interpersonal justification, either. Dependent caretakers are entitled to enough of a share of their partner's income that they are not vulnerable to domination and exploitation within the relationship. This principle supports Okin's proposal that paychecks be split between husband and wife.[85] If this is not sufficient to eliminate caretakers' vulnerability in domestic partnership, a case can be made for socializing some of the costs of dependent care through a child-care (or elder-care) subsidy, as is common in western Europe. Ultimately, full equality may not be achievable simply through the redistribution of material resources. Equality may require a change in social norms, by which men as well as women would be expected to share in caretaking responsibilities.[86]

Against the proposal to socialize the costs of dependent care, Rakowski insists that children are entitled only to resources from their parents, not from others. Even if they will provide benefits to others when they grow up and participate in the economy, it is unjust to make people pay for benefits they never asked for, and in any event most of those benefits will accrue to other family members.[87] If the economy consisted of isolated, economically self-sufficient family groups, as in a primitive hunter-gatherer society, one could see Rakowski's point. But in a society with an extensive division of labor, his assumptions make no sense. As long as one doesn't plan to commit suicide once the next generation enters the workforce, one can't help but demand the labor services of future generations. Moreover, most of what people produce in a market economy is consumed by nonfamily members. In regarding the whole society as a system of cooperation that jointly produces the economy's entire output, democratic equality acknowledges everyone's profound mutual dependency in modern society.

It rejects the atomistic norm of individual self-sufficiency as based on a failure to recognize the dependency of wage earners on the work of those whose labor is not for sale. In adjusting entitlements to account for the fact that adults have moral responsibilities to take care of dependents, democratic equality also rejects equality of fortune's reduction of moral obligations to expensive tastes and its consequent guarantee of equality only to egoists. Democratic equality says that no one should be reduced to an inferior status because they fulfill obligations to care for others.

The conception of society as a system of cooperation provides a safety net through which even the imprudent are never forced to fall. It provides that no role in the productive system shall be assigned such inadequate benefits that, given the risks and requirements of the job, people could be deprived of the social conditions of their freedom because they have fulfilled its requirements. Society may not define work roles that amount to peonage or servitude, nor, if it can avoid it, pay them so little that an able-bodied person working full time would still lack basic capabilities.[88] One mechanism for achieving a decent minimum would be a minimum wage. A minimum wage need not raise unemployment if low-wage workers are given sufficient training to make them more productive or if the higher wage induces employers to supply their workers with productivity-enhancing tools. Benefits could also be attached to work by other means, such as socially provided disability and old-age pension schemes, and tax credits for earned income. Democratic equality also favors a qualified entitlement to work on the part of willing, able-bodied adults. Unemployment insurance is a poor substitute for work, given the central importance of participation in productive activity to living life as an equal in civil society. So is "workfare," if, as is typically the case in the United States, it means forcing people to engage in make-work for aid while depriving them of the dignity of a real job with a real wage.

It is instructive to consider what democratic equality says to those with low talents. Equality of fortune would offer compensation to those with low talents, precisely because their innate inferiority makes their labor so relatively worthless to others, as judged by the market. Democratic equality calls into question the very idea that inferior native endowments have much to do with observed income inequalities in capitalist economies. The biggest fortunes are made not by those who work but by those who own the means of production. Even among wage workers, most of the differences are due to the fact that society has invested far more in developing some people's talents than others, and that it puts very unequal amounts of capital at the disposal of each worker. Productivity attaches mainly to work roles, not to individuals. Democratic equality deals with these facts by stressing the importance of educating the less advantaged and by offering firms incentives to increase the productivity of low-wage jobs through capital investment.

Moreover, in regarding society as a system of cooperation, democratic equality has a less demeaning rationale than equality of fortune for state interventions designed to raise the wages of low-wage workers. Society need not try to make the impossible and insulting judgment of whether low-wage workers are there by choice or by the fact that their meagre native endowments prevent them from getting better work. Instead, it focuses on appreciation for the roles that low-wage workers fill. In performing routine, low-skill tasks, these workers free other people to make more productive uses of their talents. Those occupying more productive roles owe much of their productivity to the fact that those occupying less productive roles have freed them from the need to spend their time on low-skill tasks. Fancy corporate executives could not cut so many lucrative deals if they had to answer their own telephone calls. Such reflections express appreciation for the ways that everyone benefits from the diversity of talents and roles in society. They also undermine the thought that workers at the top make a lopsided contribution to the social product and thereby help motivate a conception of reciprocity that would squeeze the gap between the highest- and lowest-paid workers.

Would democratic equality support a wage-squeezing policy as demanding as Rawls's difference principle? This would forbid all income inequalities that do not improve the incomes of the worst off.[89] In giving absolute priority to the worst off, the difference principle might require considerable sacrifices in the lower middle ranks for trifling gains at the lowest levels. Democratic equality would urge a less demanding form of reciprocity. Once all citizens enjoy a decent set of freedoms, sufficient for functioning as an equal in society, income inequalities beyond that point do not seem so troubling in themselves. The degree of acceptable income inequality would depend in part on how easy it was to convert income into status inequality—differences in the social bases of self-respect, influence over elections, and the like. The stronger the barriers against commodifying social status, political influence, and the like, the more acceptable are significant income inequalities.[90] The moral status of free market allocations is strengthened the more carefully defined is the domain in which these allocations have free rein.

DEMOCRATIC EQUALITY, PERSONAL RESPONSIBILITY, AND PATERNALISM

Democratic equality guarantees effective access to the social conditions of freedom to all citizens, regardless of how imprudently they conduct their lives. It does not deprive negligent or self-destructive citizens of necessary medical care. It does not discriminate among the disabled depending on how much they can be held responsible for their disability. Under democratic equality, citizens refrain from making intrusive, moralizing judgments about how people ought to have used the opportunities open to them or about how capable they were of exercising personal responsibility. It need not make such judgments, because it does not condition citizens' enjoyment of their capabilities on whether they use them responsibly. The sole exception to this principle concerns criminal conduct. Only the commission of a crime can justify taking away a person's basic liberties and status as an equal in civil society. Even convicted criminals, however, retain their status as equal human beings, and so are still entitled to basic

human functionings such as adequate nutrition, shelter, and medical care.

One might object to democratic equality on the grounds that all these guarantees invite personal irresponsibility, just as critics of equality have long suspected. If people are going to be bailed out of the situations they get into because of their own imprudence, then why act prudently? Egalitarians must face up to the need to uphold personal responsibility, if only to avoid bankrupting the state. There are two general strategies for doing so. One is to insure only against certain causes of loss: to distinguish between the losses for which people are responsible and those for which they are not, and to indemnify individuals only against the latter. This is the approach of luck egalitarianism, which leads to Poor Law thinking, and intrusive and disrespectful judgments of individuals. The second strategy is to insure only against the losses of certain types of goods: to distinguish between guaranteed and unguaranteed types of goods within the space of egalitarian concern, and to insure individuals only against the loss of the former. This is the approach of democratic equality.

Democratic equality does not indemnify individuals against all losses due to their imprudent conduct. It only guarantees a set of capabilities necessary to functioning as a free and equal citizen and avoiding oppression. Individuals must bear many other losses on their own. For example, a person who smokes would be entitled to treatment for resulting lung cancer, regardless of their degree of responsibility for smoking. But she would not be entitled to compensation for the loss of enjoyment of life brought about by her confinement in the hospital and reduced lung capacity, for the dread she feels upon contemplating her mortality, or for the reproach of her relatives who disapprove of her lifestyle. Individuals thus have plenty to lose from their irresponsible conduct, and therefore have an incentive to behave prudently. Luck egalitarianism can't take advantage of this incentive structure, because it indemnifies individuals against the loss of all kinds of goods (kinds of resources or sources of welfare) within its space of egalitarian concern. It therefore must resort to moral judgments about the cause of loss in order to promote individual responsibility.

Democratic equality has two further strategies for promoting individual responsibility. First, it offers equality in the space of capabilities, which is to say opportunities or freedoms. Individuals still have to exercise responsible agency to achieve most of the functionings effective access to which society guarantees. In the typical case of an able-bodied adult, for instance, access to a decent income would be conditioned on responsible performance of one's duties in one's job, assuming a job was available.

Second, most of the freedoms that democratic equality guarantees are prerequisites to exercising responsible agency. Responsible agency requires real options, awareness of these options, deliberative skills, and the self-respect needed to trust one's own judgment. Democratic equality guarantees the education needed to know and deliberate about one's options, and the social bases of self-respect. Moreover, people will do almost anything to secure what they need to survive. In ensuring effective access to the means of subsistence through legitimate routes, democratic equality prevents the criminal behavior that would be spurred by a society that let people fall below subsistence or that deprived people of dignified legitimate means of subsistence. It also avoids the powerful incentives to deny personal responsibility that are built into equality of fortune, because it ensures that people will always have legitimate means at their disposal to get access to their basic capabilities, without having to resort to deception about their role in getting into their predicament.

It might be objected that democratic equality, in guaranteeing such goods as medical care to all, still requires an objectionable subsidy of irresponsible behavior. Why should prudent nonsmokers have to pay more for universal health insurance, because so many fools choose to smoke? If the costs of some particularly dangerous activity are high, and if the activity is not performed in one's capacity as a participant in the productive system, then justice permits a tax on that activity to cover the extra costs of medical care for those injured by engaging in it. A tax on each pack of cigarettes, adjusted to cover the medical costs of treating smokers, would force smokers to absorb the extra costs of their behavior.

If it is just to force smokers to absorb these costs *ex ante*, why isn't it equally just to force them to absorb these costs *ex post*, as some luck egalitarians hold? Roemer's plan does this, by discounting the medical subsidy people are entitled to according to their degree of personal responsibility.[91] Besides entangling the state in intrusive moralizing judgments of personal responsibility, Roemer's plan leaves people vulnerable to such a deprivation of their capabilities that they cannot function as an equal. This is unjust. By making smokers pay for the costs of their behavior *ex ante*, democratic equality preserves their freedom and equality over the course of their whole lives.

It might be objected that democratic equality, in guaranteeing a specific set of capabilities to citizens, paternalistically violates the freedom of citizens and violates the requirement of liberal neutrality among conceptions of the good. Suppose a smoker would prefer to have cheaper cigarettes than to be provided medical care? Shouldn't citizens be free to choose what goods they prefer to have? Thus, citizens should be entitled to the welfare equivalent of medical care and not be forced to consume medical care at the cost of other things they might prefer. This line of thought supports equality in the space of opportunities for welfare, rather than in capabilities for equal citizenship.

These objections fail to appreciate the distinction between what people want and what other people are obligated to give them. The basic duty of citizens, acting through the state, is not to make everyone happy but to secure the conditions of everyone's freedom. In securing for citizens only the capabilities they need to function as equal citizens, the state is not declaring that these capabilities are more important for individual happiness than some others that they might prefer. It leaves individuals free to decide for themselves how useful or important are the goods that the state guarantees to them. It guarantees certain capabilities to citizens, not because these are the most important ones as judged from the standpoint of the best conception of the good, but because these are the ones citizens are obligated to provide one another in common.

But why can't any given citizen waive his right to guaranteed health care, in return for its welfare equivalent? Citizens can, with justice, refuse to provide what any individual regards as the welfare equivalent of health care. As Thomas Scanlon has stressed, the fact that someone would rather have help in building a temple to his god than to be decently fed does not generate a greater claim on others to subsidize his temple than to ensure his access to adequate nutrition.[92] Furthermore, the obligation to provide health care is unconditional and can't be rescinded, even with the permission of the person to whom the obligation is owed. We are not permitted to abandon people dying by the side of the road, just because they gave us permission to deny them emergency medical care.[93]

One might object that democratic equality fails to respect neutrality among competing conceptions of the good. Some citizens will find the capability sets guaranteed them far more useful than others. For example, those whose conception of the good involves widespread participation in civil society will find their good more fully secured by democratic equality than those who prefer to lead their lives in insular religious cults. Democratic equality is therefore biased in favor of certain conceptions of the good.

This objection misunderstands the point of neutrality. As Rawls has stressed, given the fact the people hold conflicting conceptions of the good, liberal states need some basis for judging claims of justice that does not rest on partisan views of the good. The point of view of citizens acting collectively—the political point of view—does not claim authority in virtue of promoting the objectively best or most important goods but in virtue of being a possible object of collective willing. Neutral goods are the goods we can reasonably agree to collectively provide, given the fact of pluralism.[94] Thus, the capabilities citizens need to function as equals in civil society count as neutral goods for purposes of justice, not because everyone finds these capabilities equally valuable, but because reasonable people can recognize that these form a legitimate basis for making moral claims on one another.[95] By contrast, reasonable persons need not recognize the desire to build a temple to their god as a legitimate basis for a claim to public subsidy. A person who does not worship that god could reasonably object to the state taxing her to subsidize someone else's involuntarily expensive religious desires.

Consider now what equality of fortune and democratic equality have to say to the person who decides, prudently or imprudently, not to purchase health insurance for himself. According to equality of fortune, there are two options. One is to allow the person to decline health insurance and abandon him if he needs emergency care. The other is to tell him, "You are too stupid to run your own life. Therefore, we will force you to purchase health insurance, because we know better than you what is for your own good." Democratic equality passes no judgment on whether it would be prudent or imprudent for any given individual to purchase health insurance. It tells the person who would not purchase insurance for himself: "You have a moral worth that no one can disregard. We recognize this worth in your inalienable right to our aid in an emergency. You are free to refuse this aid once we offer it. But this freedom does not absolve you of the obligation to come to the aid of others when their health needs are urgent. Since this is an obligation we all owe to our fellow citizens, everyone shall be taxed for this good, which we shall provide to everyone. This is part of your rightful claim as an equal citizen." Which rationale for providing health insurance better expresses respect for its recipients?

THE DISABLED, THE UGLY, AND OTHER VICTIMS OF BAD LUCK

According to democratic equality, the distribution of nature's good or bad fortune is neither just nor unjust. Considered in itself, nothing in this distribution calls for any correction by society. No claims to compensation can be generated by nature's effects alone. This may seem an unduly harsh doctrine. Does it not leave the congenitally disabled, ugly, and stupid out in the cold, even though they do not deserve their sorry fates?

Democratic equality says no. Although the distribution of natural assets is not a matter of justice, what people do in response to this distribution is.[96] People may not make the possession of a disability, repugnant appearance, or low intelligence the occasion for excluding people from civil society, dominating them, beating them up, or otherwise oppressing them. In a liberal democratic state, all citizens are entitled to the social conditions of their freedom and standing as equals in civil society, regardless of handicap, physical appearance, or intelligence.[97] Moreover, these conditions are sensitive to variations in people's circumstances, including their disabilities. People who can't walk are entitled to accommodation in civil society: to wheelchairs, ramps on public buildings, and so forth. However, these conditions are not sensitive to variations in people's tastes. Everyone has an entitlement to the same package of capabilities, whatever else they may have, and regardless of what they would prefer to have. Thus, if a person who needs a wheelchair to get around has an involuntarily expensive taste for engaging in particular religious rituals, and would prefer having this taste satisfied to having a wheelchair, democratic equality does not substitute a subsidy for her rituals for the wheelchair. For individuals need to be able to move around civil society to have equal standing as citizens, but they do not need to be able to worship in particularly expensive ways in order to function as equals.

Richard Arneson objects to this distinction between disabled people and people with involuntarily expensive tastes. For disabilities are just another kind of involuntarily expensive taste. It's not the disabled individual's fault that it costs more for her to get around in a wheelchair than it takes ambulatory people to make the same journey. Once we see that it is the involuntariness of the costs of her tastes that entitles her to special subsidy, one must allow people with other involuntarily expensive tastes to make equal claims on behalf of their preferences. Arneson claims that only an illegitimate perfectionist doctrine—the claim that mobility is intrinsically more important than worship—can support discrimination between the disabled and those with other involuntarily expensive tastes.[98]

Democratic equality takes no stand on what goods individuals should value more, when they are thinking only of their own interests. It provides the social conditions for equal citizenship, and not the conditions for equal ability to fulfill the demands of one's gods, because citizens are obligated to provide the first and are not obligated to provide the second. Arneson argues that capabilities are diverse, and the resources available to provide them scarce. Some trade-offs among capabilities must therefore be accepted. Some index is therefore needed to rank the importance of different capabilities. If one rejects perfectionist doctrines, the only basis for constructing an index of capabilities is subjective, based on the importance to the individual of having that capability.[99]

Against Arneson, democratic equality follows Scanlon in insisting that the weight that a citizen's claim has on others depends solely on the content of her interest and not on the importance she places on it in her own conception of the good.[100] In some cases, the weight of an interest can be determined by considering its impact on a person's standing as an equal in society. Some deprivations of capabilities express greater disrespect than others, in ways any reasonable person can recognize. From a public point of view, it is more disrespectful to deny a person in a wheelchair access to the public schools than it is to deny her access to an amusement park ride that only accommodates the walking. This is true even if she'd rather go through the Fun House than learn how to read. In other cases, where the concepts of equal standing and respect don't yield a determinate answer to how capabilities should be ranked, the ranking may legitimately be left up to democratic legislation. Even here, voters are not to ask themselves what priorities they give to different capabilities for citizenship in their private choices, but what priorities they want the state to assign to these different capabilities, given that these goods shall be provided in common. The answers to the questions are likely to diverge, if only because many capabilities are more valuable to others than to their possessors. Most people gain much more from other people's freedom of speech than from their own.[101]

It might be argued that democratic equality is still too harsh to those who are disabled through bad brute luck. It would not compensate them for all of the miseries they face. For example, democratic equality would ensure that the deaf have equal access to civil society, but not that they be compensated for the loss of the pleasures of hearing itself. Yet the lives of the deaf are less happy for lacking these pleasures, and should be compensated on that account.

It is useful to ask what the deaf demand on their own account, in the name of justice. Do they bemoan the misery of not being able to hear, and demand compensation for this lack? On the contrary: like the disabled more generally, they resent being cast as poster children for the abled to pity, because they do not want to have to cast their claims as appeals to the condescending benevolence of kindly patrons. Many deaf people identify as part of a separate Deaf community that repudiates the intrinsic choiceworthiness of hearing itself. They insist that sign language is just as valuable a form of communication as is speech and that the other goods obtainable through hearing, such as appreciation of music, are dispensable parts of any conception of good. One needn't pass judgment on the intrinsic choiceworthiness of hearing to appreciate the rhetorical uses of denying it: the Deaf want to cut the hearing down to size, to purge the arrogant assumption of the hearing that the lives of the Deaf are somehow less worth living. They want to make claims on the hearing in a manner that expresses the dignity they see in their lives and community, rather than in a manner that appeals to pity for their condition.[102] They do this by denying that their condition, considered in itself, is anything to be pitied.

Equality of fortune, despite the fact that it considers the treatment of the disabled as a core case, has difficulty with such ideas. This is due to the fact that it relies on subjective measures of welfare or of the worth of personal assets. Subjective measures invite all the wrong thoughts on the part of the abled. Van Parijs's criterion of undominated diversity allows the disabled to make claims of justice regarding their disability only if everyone regards their condition as so wretched that everyone would prefer being someone else.

This test asks the abled to take the horror they feel upon imagining that they had a disability as their reason for compensating the disabled. To regard the condition of the disabled as intrinsically horrible is insulting to the disabled people who lead their lives with dignity. Arneson's criterion of equal opportunity for welfare implies that as long as the disabled have equal chances for happiness, they have no claims to special accommodation. Survey research shows that the disabled experience the same range of happiness as the abled.[103] Thus, by Arneson's criterion, it is all right to exclude the disabled from public life because they are happy enough without being included.

Subjective measures of people's condition generate either pity for the disabled or reluctance to consider their claims of justice. The way to escape this dilemma is to take seriously what the disabled are actually complaining about. They do not ask that they be compensated for the disability itself. Rather, they ask that the social disadvantages others impose on them for having the disability be removed. "The inequality of people mobilizing in wheelchairs ... manifests itself not in the inability to walk but in exclusion from bathrooms, theaters, transportation, places of work, [and] life-saving medical treatment."[104] Democratic equality can handle this distinction. It demands, for instance, that the disabled have good enough access to public accommodations that they can function as equals in civil society. To be capable of functioning as an equal does not require that one's access be equally fast, comfortable, or convenient, or that one get equal subjective utility from using public accommodations. There may be no way to achieve this. But the fact that, with current technology, it takes an extra minute to get into city hall does not compromise one's standing as an equal citizen.

Democratic equality thus supports the use of objective tests of unjust disadvantage. Such tests fit the claims of justice that the disabled make on their own behalf. For example, what the Deaf find objectionable is not that they can't hear, but that everyone else has rigged the means of communication in ways that leave them out of the conversation. One can detect this injustice without investigating anyone's preferences or subjective states. The test for a satisfactory remedy is equally objective. The Americans with Disabilities Act, for example, embodies an objective standard of accommodation. "Rather than speculating on how the *subjective personal response* of unimpaired agents would be transfigured by the onset of physical or mental impairment, this standard calls for projecting how *objective social practice* would be transformed were unimpaired functioning so *atypical* as to be of merely marginal importance for social policy."[105] The act asks us to imagine how communications in civil society would be arranged if nearly everyone were deaf, and then try to offer to the Deaf arrangements approximating this.

The objective standards of injustice and remedy proposed by democratic equality have several advantages over those proposed by equality of fortune. They match the remedy to the injustice: if the injustice is exclusion, the remedy is inclusion. Democratic equality does not attempt to use private satisfactions to justify public oppression. Objective standards do not insultingly represent the disabled as deserving aid because of their pitiful internal condition. They locate the unjust disadvantage of disability in the way others treat the disabled. Democratic equality also does not assimilate the disabled to the situation of those suffering from involuntarily expensive tastes. Having a disability is not like being so spoiled that one can't help wanting expensive toys.

Should other victims of bad brute luck be treated like the handicapped? Equality of fortune thinks so—it extends its concern to the ugly, the stupid, and the untalented as well. Democratic equality does not pass judgment on the worth of people's native endowments, and so has nothing special to say to the stupid and the untalented. Instead, it focuses on the productive roles that people occupy, in recognition of the fact that society attaches economic benefits to performance in a role rather than to the possession of talent in itself. Democratic equality requires that sufficient benefits be attached to performance in every role that all workers can function as equals in society. Talent brings noneconomic advantages as well, such as the admiration of others. Democratic equality finds no injustice in this advantage,

because one doesn't need to be admired to be able to function as an equal citizen. As justice requires, most residents of modern democracies live in a state of civilization where the attainment of honor is not a condition of enjoying basic freedoms. In places where this is not so, such as certain tough inner-city neighborhoods, it is clear that the injustice lies not in the fact that some individuals are unfortunately born with lower native endowments of courage, but that the social order is arranged so that only those willing to display uncommonly high degrees of ruthlessness can enjoy personal security.

What about the ugly? Are they not entitled to compensation for their repugnant appearance, which makes them so unwelcome in social settings? Some luck egalitarians would view this bad luck as calling for a remedy, perhaps in the form of publicly subsidized plastic surgery. Democratic equality refuses to publicly endorse the demeaning private judgments of appearance which are the basis of such claims to compensation. Instead, it asks whether the norms based on such judgments are oppressive. Consider a birth defect, affecting only a person's appearance, that is considered so abhorrent by current social norms that people tend to shun those who have it. Since the capability to participate in civil society as an equal citizen is a fundamental freedom, egalitarians demand that some remedy be provided for this. But the remedy need not consist in plastic surgery that corrects the defect. An alternative would be to persuade everyone to adopt new norms of acceptable physical appearance, so that people with the birth "defect" were no longer treated as pariahs. This is not to call for the abolition of norms of beauty altogether. The norms need only be flexible enough to deem the person an acceptable presence in civil society. They need not entitle such a person to claim equal beauty to others, since successful functioning as a contestant in a beauty pageant, or as a hot prospect for a Saturday night date, are not among the capabilities one needs to function as an equal citizen.

By directing attention to oppressive social norms of beauty, democratic equality avoids the disparaging scrutiny of the ugly through the lens of the oppressive norms themselves. This lets us see that the injustice lies not in the natural misfortune of the ugly but in the social fact that people shun others on account of their appearance. To change the person rather than the norm insultingly suggests that the defect lies in the person rather than in society. Other things equal, then, democratic equality prefers altering social norms to redistributing material resources in response to the disadvantages faced by the unsightly. Of course, other things are often not equal. It may be very difficult and costly to change prevailing norms of beauty that cruelly dictate who cannot appear in public without provoking shock and rejection. The liberal state can't do too much in this regard without overstepping its proper bounds; thus, this task must be delegated mainly to egalitarian social movements, which vary in their abilities to transform social norms. Under these conditions the better option may well be to supply the plastic surgery. Democratic equality, in focusing on equality as a social relationship, rather than simply as a pattern of distribution, at least enables us to see that we have a choice between redistributing material resources and changing other aspects of society to meet the demands of equality.

DEMOCRATIC EQUALITY AND THE OBLIGATIONS OF CITIZENS

Democratic equality refocuses egalitarian theorizing in several ways. It conceives of justice as a matter of obligations that are not defined by the satisfaction of subjective preferences. This ensures that people's rights do not depend on arbitrary variations in individual tastes and that people may not claim rights without accepting corresponding obligations to others. Democratic equality applies judgments of justice to human arrangements, not to the natural order. This helps us see that people, not nature, are responsible for turning the natural diversity of human beings into oppressive hierarchies. It locates unjust deficiencies in the social order rather than in people's innate endowments. Instead of lamenting the human diversity of talents and trying to make up for what is represented as innate deficiencies in talent, democratic equality offers a way of conceiving and harnessing human diversity so that it ben-

efits everyone and is recognized as doing so. Democratic equality conceives of equality as a relationship among people rather than merely as a pattern in the distribution of divisible goods. This helps us see how egalitarians can take other features of society besides the distribution of goods, such as social norms, as subject to critical scrutiny. It lets us see how injustices may be better remedied by changing social norms and the structure of public goods than by redistributing resources. And it allows us to integrate the demands of equal distribution and equal respect, ensuring that the principles by which we distribute goods, however equal resulting patterns may be, do not in fact express contemptuous pity for the beneficiaries of egalitarian concern. Democratic equality thus offers a superior way to understand the expressive demands of justice—the demand to act only on principles that express respect for everyone. Finally, in refocusing academic egalitarian theorizing, democratic equality holds out the promise of reestablishing connections with actually existing egalitarian movements. It is not a moral accident that beach bums and people who find themselves slaves to their expensive hobbies are not organizing to make claims of justice on behalf of their lifestyles. Nor is it irrelevant that the disabled are repudiating forms of charity that appeal to pity for their condition and are struggling for respect from others, not just handouts. Democratic equality helps articulate the demands of genuine egalitarian movements in a framework that offers some hope of broader appeal.

NOTES

1. Dworkin, Ronald. "What Is Equality? II. Equality of Resources." *Philosophy and Public Affairs* 10 (1981): 285.
2. Van Parijs, Philippe. "Why Surfers Should Be Fed: The Liberal Case for an Unconditional Basic Income." *Philosophy and Public Affairs* 20 (1991): 101–31.
3. Arneson, Richard. "Equality and Equality of Opportunity for Welfare." in *Equality: Selected Readings.* Eds. Louis Pojman and Robert Westmoreland. New York: Oxford University Press, 1997. 231.
4. Cohen, G. A. "On the Currency of Egalitarian Justice." *Ethics* 99 (1989): 922–23, 930–31.

5. Van Parijs, Phillipe. *Real Freedom for All.* Oxford: Clarendon, 1995. 127.

6. Nagel, Thomas. "The Policy of Preference." *Mortal Questions.* Cambridge: Cambridge University Press, 1979. 91–105.

7. Arneson, Richard. "Rawls, Responsibility, and Distributive Justice." *Justice, Political Liberalism, and Utilitarianism: Themes from Harsanyi.* Eds. Maurice Salles and John A. Weymark. Cambridge: Cambridge University Press (in press).

8. Rawls, John. *A Theory of Justice.* Cambridge, Mass.: Harvard University Press, 1971. 100–104.

9. Nagel, Thomas. *Equality and Partiality.* New York: Oxford University Press, 1991. 71; Rakowski, Eric. *Equal Justice.* New York: Oxford University Press, 1991; Roemer, John. "A Pragmatic Theory of Responsibility for the Egalitarian Planner." *Egalitarian Perspectives.* Cambridge: Cambridge University Press, 1994. 179–80.

10. von Hayek, Friedrich August. *The Constitution of Liberty.* Chicago: University of Chicago Press, 1960. 87.

11. Raz, Joseph. *The Morality of Freedom.* Oxford: Clarendon, 1986. 227.

12. Nozick, Robert. *Anarchy, State, and Utopia.* New York: Basic, 1974. 229.

13. Cohen, G. A. "Incentives, Inequality, and Community." *Equal Freedom.* Ed. Stephen Darwall. Ann Arbor: University of Michigan Press, 1995. 335; Van Parijs, *Real Freedom for All*, supra, note 5, at 5.

14. Arneson, "Equality and Equality of Opportunity for Welfare," supra, note 3, at 230; Dworkin, "Equality of Resources," supra, note 1, at 311–12; Rakowski, supra, note 9, at 2; Van Parijs, *Real Freedom for All*, supra, note 5, at 25.

15. Bauer, P. T. *Equality, the Third World, and Economic Delusion.* Cambridge, Mass.: Harvard University Press, 1981.

16. Mead, Lawrence. *Beyond Entitlement: The Social Obligations of Citizenship.* New York: Free Press, 1986.

17. Arneson, "Equality and Equality of Opportunity for Welfare," supra, note 3, at 235.

18. Dworkin, "Equality of Resources," supra, note 1, at 293.

19. Cohen is the only prominent luck egalitarian to regard society's reliance on capitalist markets as an unfortunate if—in the foreseeable future—necessary compromise with justice, rather than as a vital instrument of just allocation. See Cohen, "Incentives, Inequality, and Community," supra, note 13, at 395. Roemer, John. *Egalitarian Perspectives.* Cambridge: Cambridge University Press, 1994, supports a complex version of market socialism on distributive grounds, but these grounds do not appear sufficient to demonstrate the superiority of market socialism to, say, Van Parijs's version of capitalism.

20. See Hayek, supra, note 10.

21. Dworkin, "Equality of Resources," supra, note 1.

22. Rakowski, supra, note 9, at 80–81.

23. Arneson, "Equality and Equality of Opportunity for Welfare," supra, note 3, at 239; Dworkin, "Equality of Resources," supra, note 1, at 295; Rakowski, supra, note 9, at 76.

24. Dworkin, Ronald. "What Is Equality? I. Equality of Welfare." *Philosophy and Public Affairs* 10 (1981): 228–40.

25. Arneson, "Equality and Equality of Opportunity for Welfare," supra, note 3, at 237.

26. Id., at 230–31; Cohen, "On the Currency of Egalitarian Justice." pp. 522–23.

27. Arneson, Richard. "Liberalism, Distributive Subjectivism, and Equal Opportunity for Welfare." *Philosophy and Public Affairs* 19 (1990): 185–87, 190–91.

28. Dworkin, "Equality of Resources," supra, note 1, at 285–89.

29. Id., at 285–89; Rakowski, supra, note 9, at 69; Van Parijs, *Real Freedom for All*, supra, note 5, at 51.

30. Dworkin, Ronald. *Taking Rights Seriously.* Cambridge, Mass.: Harvard University Press, 1977. 272–73.

31. Rakowski, supra, note 9, at 74–75.

32. Arneson, "Liberalism, Distributive Subjectivism, and Equal Opportunity for Welfare," supra, note 27, at 187.

33. Rakowski, supra, note 9, at 79.

34. Id., at 80. Rakowski allows that, in areas that suffer from no more than average risk of natural disaster, "any losses resulting from whatever risk were a necessary concomitant to the ownership of property essential to live a moderately satisfying life" and would be fully compensable, "as instances of bad brute luck." But once private insurance becomes available, brute luck converts to option luck and uninsured parties are on their own again.

35. Id., at 79.

36. Okin, Susan Moller. *Justice, Gender, and the Family.* New York: Basic, 1989. 134–69.

37. Rakowski, supra, note 9, at 109.

38. Id., at 153.

39. Van Parijs, "Why Surfers Should Be Fed," supra, note 2, at 131.

40. Van Parijs, *Real Freedom for All*, supra, note 5, at 76.

41. Barry, Brian M. "Equality, Yes, Basic Income, No." *Arguing for Basic Income.* Ed. Philippe Van Parijs. New York: Verso, 1992. 138.

42. Arneson, "Equality and Equality of Opportunity for Welfare," supra, note 3.

43. Roemer, John. *Theories of Distributive Justice.* Cambridge, Mass.: Harvard University Press, 1996. 270.

44. Rakowski, supra, note 9, at 47.

45. Roemer, *Theories of Distributive Justice*, supra, note 43, at 270.

46. Cohen, "On the Currency of Egalitarian Justice," supra, note 4, at 908.

47. Roemer, John. "The Morality and Efficiency of Market Socialism." *Ethics* 102 (1992): 448–64.

48. Arneson, "Equality and Equality of Opportunity for Welfare," supra, note 3, at 239.

49. Van Parijs, *Real Freedom for All*, supra, note 5, at 47; Arneson, Richard. "Is Socialism Dead? A Comment on Market Socialism and Basic Income Capitalism." *Ethics* 102 (1992): 485–511, p. 510.

50. Amy Gutmann made these points in her public comments on an earlier version of this article, delivered at the thirty-first annual Philosophy Colloquium at Chapel Hill, N.C.

51. Van Parijs, *Real Freedom for All*, supra, note 5, at 68.

52. Arneson, "Liberalism, Distributive Subjectivism, and Equal Opportunity for Welfare," supra, note 27; Cohen, "On the Currency of Egalitarian Justice," supra, note 4, at 930–31.

53. Rakowski, supra, note 9, at 99.

54. Van Parijs, *Real Freedom for All*, supra, note 5, at 70.

55. Id.

56. Ackerman, Bruce. *Social Justice in the Liberal State.* New Haven, Conn.: Yale University Press, 1980. 115–21.

57. Van Parijs, *Real Freedom for All*, supra, note 5, at 77.

58. Cohen, "On the Currency of Egalitarian Justice," supra, note 4, at 917–18.

59. Pogge, Thomas. "Three Problems with Contractarian-Consequentialist Ways of Assessing Social Institutions." *The Just Society.* Eds. Ellen Frankel Paul, Fred Miller, Jr., and Jeffrey Paul. Cambridge: Cambridge University Press, 1995. 247–48.

60. Nagel, "The Policy of Preference," supra, note 6, at 105.

61. This is a concern with what attitudes the theory expresses, not with the consequences of expressing those attitudes. Self-respecting citizens would reject a society based on principles that treat them as inferiors, even if the principles are kept secret. Government house utilitarianism is thus no solution. Nor is it a satisfactory defense of equality of fortune to recommend that society adopt more generous distributive policies than the theory requires so as to avoid insulting people. The question is not whether to deviate from what justice requires so as to avoid bad consequences. It is whether a theory of justice based on contemptuous pity for its supposed beneficiaries satisfies the egalitarian requirement that justice must be founded on equal respect for persons.

62. Raz, *The Morality of Freedom*, supra, note 11, at 242.

63. Dworkin, "Equality of Resources," supra, note 1, at 285; Rakowski, supra, note 9, at 65–66; Van Parijs, *Real Freedom for All*, supra, note 5, at 51.

64. Dworkin denies that his is a "starting-gate theory," but only because he would allocate compensation for unequal talents over the course of a lifetime. "Equality of Resources," supra, note 1, at 309–11.

65. Id., at 299.

66. What if someone runs a health risk that only increases her already significant chance of illness? Let scientific studies apportion the risks of illness due to involuntary causes (e.g., faulty genes) and voluntary causes (e.g. eating a fatty diet), and discount the resources contributed to care for the ill by the proportion to which their risk was one they ran voluntarily. Rakowski, supra, note 9, at 75. Roemer accepts this logic, but insists that people's responsibility for their conditions should be discounted by unchosen sociological as well as genetic influences. Thus, if two people with lung cancer smoke the median number of years for their sociological type (determined by sex, race, class, occupation, parents' smoking habits, etc.), then they are entitled, other things equal, to equal indemnification against the costs of their cancer, even if one smoked for eight years and the other for twenty-five years. Roemer, "A Pragmatic Theory of Responsibility for the Egalitarian

Planner," supra, note 9, at 183. His intuition is that people who exercise comparable degrees of responsibility, adjusted to make up for the different social influences on their behavior, should be entitled to equal degrees of compensation against the costs of their behavior. Roemer does not consider the expressive implications of the state, assuming that different classes of citizens should be held to different standards of responsible behavior.

67. Hayek, supra, note 10, at 95–97.

68. Korsgaard, Christine. "Commentary on G. A. Cohen and Amartya Sen." *The Quality of Life*. Eds. Martha Nussbaum and Amartya Sen. Oxford: Clarendon, 1993. 61.

69. Young, Iris Marion. "Mothers, Citizenship, and Independence: A Critique of Pure Family Values." *Ethics* 105 (1995): 535–56, makes a similar critique, unconnected to luck egalitarianism, of contemporary welfare reform movements. Van Parijs's version of luck egalitarianism might seem to escape from Poor Law thinking because it promises an unconditional income to everyone, regardless of whether they work for a wage. However, as noted above, even his view implicitly takes the tastes of the egoistic adult without caretaking responsibilities as the norm. For the gap between the minimum wage and the unconditional income will be set by the incentives needed to bring the marginal footloose egoist into the labor market. The fate of nonwage-earning dependent caretakers will thus depend on the labor–leisure trade-offs of beach bums, rather than on their own needs. The more attached to leisure the beach bum is, the lower must the unconditional income be.

70. Young, Iris Marion. *Justice and the Politics of Difference*. Princeton, N.J.: Princeton University Press, 1990.

71. Rawls, John. "Kantian Constructivism in Moral Theory." *Journal of Philosophy* 77 (1980): 525. The use of "equally" to modify "moral agents" might seem otiose: why not just say that all competent adults are moral agents? Egalitarians deny a hierarchy of types of moral agency—e.g., any theory that says there is a lower type of human only able to follow moral commands issued by others and a higher type able to issue or discover moral commands for themselves.

72. Anderson, Elizabeth. "The Democratic University: The Role of Justice in the Production of Knowledge." *Social Philosophy and Policy* 12 (1995): 186–219. Does this requirement mean that we must always listen patiently to those who have proven themselves to be stupid, cranky, or dishonest? No. It means: 1) that everyone must be granted the initial benefit of the doubt, 2) a person can be ignored or excluded from discussion only on demonstrated grounds of communicative incompetence or unwillingness to engage in fair discussion, and 3) reasonable opportunities must be available to the excluded to demonstrate their communicative competence and thereby win back a place in the conversation.

73. Fraser, Nancy. "From Redistribution to Recognition? Dilemmas of Justice in a 'Postsocialist' Age." *Justice Interruptus*. New York: Routledge, 1997. 11–39; Honneth, Axel. *The Struggle for Recognition*. Trans. Joel Anderson. Cambridge: Polity Press, 1995.

74. Korsgaard, supra, note 68.

75. Sen, Amartya. *Inequality Reexamined*. Cambridge, Mass.: Harvard University Press, 1992. 39–42, 49.

76. Radin, Margaret. "Market Inalienability." *Harvard Law Review* 100 (1987): 1849–1937. A person might have to forfeit some of her market inalienable freedoms, however, if she is convicted of a serious crime.

77. Sen, *Inequality Reexamined*, supra, note 75, at 79–84.

78. I shift from talk of "citizens" to talk of "workers" in part because the moral implications of regarding the economy as a system of cooperative production cross international boundaries. As the economy becomes global, we are all implicated in an international division of labor subject to assessment from an egalitarian point of view. We have obligations not only to the citizens of our country but to our fellow workers, who are now found in virtually every part of the globe. We also have global humanitarian obligations to everyone, considered simply as human beings—to relieve famine and disease, avoid fomenting or facilitating aggressive warfare, and the like. Alas, I do not have the space to consider the international implications of democratic equality.

79. Cohen, "Incentives, Inequality, and Community," supra, note 13, at 348.

80. Rakowski, supra, note 9, at 79.

81. Id.

82. What about rich people who build their vacation homes in disaster-prone areas? They haven't been commissioned by others to live there, nor does it seem fair to force taxpayers to insure their luxurious estates. Democratic equality cannot allow even unproductive citizens to lose everything, but it does not indemnify them against all their losses either. It only guarantees sufficient relief to get them back on their feet, not to shod them in luxurious footwear. If even this relief seems too expensive, an egalitarian state can forbid people from inhabiting disaster-prone areas, or tax people who do to cover the excess costs of disaster relief. What it may not do is let them live there at their own risk and then abandon them in their hour of need. Such action treats even the imprudent with impermissible contempt.

83. Waring, Marilyn. *If Women Counted*. San Francisco: HarperCollins, 1990.

84. Williams, Joan. "Is Coverture Dead?" *Georgetown Law Journal* 82 (1994): 2227.

85. Okin, supra, note 36, at 180–82

86. Fraser, Nancy. "After the Family Wage: A Postindustrial Thought Experiment," *Justice Interruptus,* supra, note 73, at 41–66.

87. Rakowski, supra, note 9, at 153.

88. It might be thought that poor societies cannot afford even basic capabilities for all workers. However, Sen's studies of the standard of living in India and China show that even extremely poor societies can supply an impressive set of basic capabilities—decent nutrition, health, literacy, and the like—to all of their members, if they apply themselves to the task. See, e.g., Sen, Amartya. *Commodities and Capabilities*. Amsterdam: North-Holland, 1985.

89. Rawls, *A Theory of Justice,* supra, note 8, at 75–78.

90. Walzer, Michael. *Spheres of Justice*. New York: Basic, 1983; Kaus, Mickey. *The End of Equality*. New York: Basic, 1992.

91. Roemer, "A Pragmatic Theory of Responsibility for the Egalitarian Planner," supra, note 9, at 179–96.

92. Scanlon, Thomas. "Preference and Urgency." *Journal of Philosophy* 72 (1975): 659–60.

93. This point is entirely distinct from the right to refuse medical care. It is one thing for an individual to exercise the right to refuse medical care when offered, quite another for others to refuse to offer medical care when needed.

94. Rawls, John. *Political Liberalism*. New York: Columbia University Press, 1993.

95. De Marneffe, Peter. "Liberalism, Liberty, and Neutrality." *Philosophy and Public Affairs* 19 (1990): 255–58.

96. Rawls, *A Theory of Justice,* supra, note 8, at 102.

97. Some exceptions would have to be made for those so severely mentally disabled or insane that they cannot function as agents. In addition, children are entitled not immediately to all of the freedoms of adults, but to the social conditions for the development of their capacities to function as free and equal citizens.

98. Arneson, "Liberalism, Distributive Subjectivism, and Equal Opportunity for Welfare," supra, note 27, at 159, 187, 190–94.

99. Arneson, "Equality and Equality of Opportunity for Welfare," supra, note 3, at 236–37.

100. Scanlon, "Preference and Urgency," supra, note 92, at 659.

101. Raz, Joseph. "Rights and Individual Well-Being." *Ethics in the Public Domain*. Oxford: Clarendon, 1994. 52–55.

102. Wrigley, Owen. *The Politics of Deafness*. Washington, D.C.: Gallaudet University Press, 1996, discusses the potentials and problems of reconceiving disability (being *deaf*) as community (being *Deaf*) after the manner of identity politics.

103. Silvers, Anita. "Reconciling Equality to Difference: Caring (f)or Justice for People with Disabilities." *Hypatia* 10 (1995): 54, n. 9.

104. Id., at 48.

105. Id., at 49.

CHAPTER FOURTEEN

Privacy and Sexual Equality

46   Public Reason and Political Conflict: Abortion and Homosexuality

ROBERT P. GEORGE

Is it possible for people who sharply disagree about important questions of morality, including those pertaining to abortion and homosexuality, to constitute a stable political society whose basic constitutional principles can be affirmed as just by all reasonable parties? This question is not about the possibility of political compromise; rather, it concerns the possibility of a certain type of moral agreement. This type of moral agreement is not agreement about whether abortion or homosexual conduct, for example, are right or wrong. Instead, it is agreement about basic principles of justice for a society composed of people who disagree about such issues.

One possibility is for people who disagree about the morality of particular acts or practices to agree upon fair procedures for the political resolution of moral disagreements. For example, people who disagree about the morality of abortion might, as a constitutional matter, agree upon democratic procedures for setting public policy on abortion. However, people of strong and settled conviction on either side of the debate over abortion cannot reasonably be satisfied of the justice of the fundamental law of their country simply because the procedures used to arrive at a resolution were democratic. From the pro-life point of view, any regime of law (including one whose pedigree is impeccably democratic) that deprives unborn human beings of their right to legal protection against homicide is gravely unjust. Similarly, from the pro-choice viewpoint, restrictions on a woman's right to abortion are seriously unjust even if they were put in place by democratic procedures. From either perspective, the question of abortion is viewed as a matter of fundamental justice whose proper resolution is essential to the full moral legitimacy of the constitutional order. In this respect, the social conflict over abortion closely resembles the conflict over slavery. Of course, pro-life and pro-choice advocates may, for their own partisan reasons, or as part of a

From *The Yale Law Journal*, Vol. 106, No. 8, Symposium: Group Conflict and the Constitution: Race, Sexuality, and Religion (Jun., 1997): pp. 2475–2504 Reprinted with permission of The Yale Law Journal Company, Inc. Footnotes omitted.

modus vivendi, agree to a constitutional requirement that public policy on abortion be settled by democratic procedures. But agreement of this sort is not agreement on basic principles of justice.

A number of leading liberal political theorists have proposed a different, and more radical, possibility. They contend that people who disagree about abortion, homosexuality, and other matters of allegedly "private" or "personal" morality can and should agree as a matter of fundamental justice to a constitutional principle that forbids government from substantially restricting or burdening people's liberty, or denying them equality of treatment, on the basis of controversial moral judgments about such matters. This principle is one version of what is sometimes referred to as "antiperfectionism." Its proponents seek to provide the ground of a moral right, for example, to legal abortion and the legal recognition of same-sex unions, a ground that can rationally be affirmed as a principle of political justice even by people who believe that abortion and homosexual conduct are seriously immoral.

Why should people agree to the antiperfectionist principle? After all, the question of whether abortion and homosexuality are purely "private" or "personal" matters—matters that implicate no significant *public* interests—is as much in dispute as the question of whether these acts are immoral. From the pro-life point of view, abortion is no more "private" than infanticide and other forms of homicide. From the perspective of those who object to the public recognition or promotion of same-sex sexual relationships, the issue is no more a matter of merely "personal" morality than was (and is) the issue of polygamy. Understandably, critics of antiperfectionism suspect that it represents a kind of philosophical sleight of hand designed to induce dissenters from substantive liberal moral beliefs to accede to liberal hegemony in matters of public policy pertaining to issues such as abortion and homosexuality.

Are antiperfectionism's critics correct? Or can a sound argument in defense of antiperfectionism be developed? In this essay, I shall consider the recent effort of John Rawls and some of his followers to defend antiperfectionist liberalism in the form of a doctrine of "political justice." Their

criteria of legitimate political advocacy and action in societies marked by group conflict over issues such as abortion and homosexuality centers around the idea of "public reason." I shall try to show that their arguments fail to provide compelling grounds for embracing antiperfectionism, and I shall illustrate this point by criticizing: (1) the sketch of a defense of a right to abortion proposed by Rawls in *Political Liberalism* and developed in greater detail by Judith Jarvis Thomson; and (2) Stephen Macedo's Rawlsian argument for the legal recognition of same-sex "marriages." I will then provide suggestions as to how people with such disagreements can discuss and debate their beliefs in a peaceful and civil manner.

I. POLITICAL LIBERALISM AND THE RATIONALIST BELIEVERS

A. The Rawlsian Conception

In his profoundly influential book, *A Theory of Justice*, Rawls defended a strict antiperfectionism. This defense was embedded in a general theory of justice ("justice as fairness") that Rawls now says relied on a premise which the theory itself rules out, namely, the idea that "in the well-ordered society of justice as fairness, citizens hold the same comprehensive doctrine, and this includes aspects of Kant's comprehensive liberalism, to which the principles of justice as fairness might belong." The problem with this idea is that neither liberalism, considered as a "comprehensive doctrine," nor any other comprehensive view is held by citizens generally in pluralistic societies such as ours. Nor is it reasonable under the circumstances of political freedom that characterize modern constitutional democratic regimes to expect that "comprehensive liberalism," or any competing comprehensive view, ever would be adopted by citizens generally. Rawls refers to this state of affairs as "the fact of reasonable pluralism," and it is the starting point of his revised argument for an antiperfectionist resolution of the problem of moral disagreement.

Rawls labels his revised proposal "political liberalism." His idea (or ideal) is that, for constitutional democratic societies such as ours, citizens are to conduct their public political discussions of constitutional essentials and matters of basic justice within the framework of what each sincerely regards as a reasonable political conception of justice, a conception that expresses political values that others as free and equal also might reasonably be expected reasonably to endorse.

In this framework, "deeply opposed though reasonable comprehensive doctrines may live together and all affirm the political conception of a constitutional regime." Debates over constitutional essentials and matters of basic justice are, for moral reasons (and not as a mere modus vivendi), to be conducted in terms of a "strictly political conception of justice," such as "justice as fairness" as revised by Rawls in *Political Liberalism*. These debates are not to be conducted in terms of moral doctrines of justice, whether secular (e.g., Kantian or Millian liberalism) or religious (e.g., Catholic or Jewish), which are "general in scope" and in dispute among reasonable citizens. In sharing a common "political" conception of justice, the partisans of competing reasonable comprehensive doctrines participate in an "overlapping consensus" on basic principles of justice, thus making social stability (despite the fact of pervasive moral disagreement about personal and social life) not only possible, but also possible "for the right reasons."

The alternative to a common commitment to a "political" conception of justice is for citizens in pluralistic societies to debate issues of constitutional essentials and matters of basic justice by appealing to general moral doctrines of justice connected to their various reasonable comprehensive views. In that case, liberalism—representing one comprehensive view with its own reasonable, but controversial, moral and metaphysical doctrines—would compete for ascendancy in the public square with a range of alternative religious and secular comprehensive views, some reasonable, some not, but all characterized by controversial moral and metaphysical doctrines of their own. Rawls argues against this alternative, not on pragmatic grounds (such as fear that the conflict of comprehensive views at this level could lead to civil strife), but on moral grounds. A strictly "political" conception of justice is, he maintains, the fairest and most reasonable way of settling

constitutional essentials and matters of basic justice. "Political," as opposed to "comprehensive" or "metaphysical," liberalism consists precisely in the adoption of such a conception.

What this means concretely is that, whenever constitutional essentials and matters of basic justice are at stake, political actors—including citizens as voters and public political advocates—are forbidden to act on the basis of principles drawn from their comprehensive doctrines, except to the extent that "public reasons, given by a reasonable political conception, are presented sufficient to support whatever the comprehensive doctrines are introduced to support." In this way, political liberalism constrains—sometimes quite radically—appeals to, and actions based upon, comprehensive doctrines including comprehensive liberalism. It does so on grounds entirely separate from the putative falsity, unsoundness, or unreasonableness of those doctrines or the specific principles drawn from them. Appeals to comprehensive doctrines are never legitimate in legislative assemblies or in the public acts and pronouncements of executive officers. Nor, above all, may judges in a constitutional democracy with judicial review justify their decisions by appealing to principles drawn from comprehensive doctrines.

Undoubtedly having in mind criticisms of *A Theory of Justice* advanced by Alasdair MacIntyre, Michael Sandel, Charles Taylor, and others, Rawls insists that "[p]olitical liberalism is not a form of Enlightenment liberalism, that is, a comprehensive liberal and often secular doctrine founded on reason and viewed as suitable for the modern age now that the religious authority of Christian ages is said to be no longer dominant." It is, rather,

> a political conception of political justice for a constitutional democratic regime that a plurality of reasonable doctrines, both religious and nonreligious, liberal and nonliberal, may freely endorse, and so freely live by and come to understand its virtues. Emphatically, it does not aim to replace comprehensive doctrines, religious or nonreligious, but intends to be equally distinct from both and, it hopes, acceptable to both.

"Political liberalism" claims to be "impartial" between the viewpoints represented by the range of competing reasonable comprehensive doctrines, be they liberal or nonliberal, secular or religious. Indeed, according to Rawls, "political liberalism does not attack or criticize any reasonable view." He says that "rather than confronting religious and nonliberal doctrines with a comprehensive liberal philosophical doctrine, the thought is to formulate a liberal political conception that those nonliberal doctrines might be able to endorse."

If Rawls is correct, not only people who subscribe to one or another comprehensive form of liberalism, but also traditional Catholics, evangelical Protestants, and orthodox Jews—assuming their viewpoints are reasonable (something Rawls seems to suggest he is willing to assume)—ought to be able reasonably to embrace a purely "political" liberalism while in no way compromising their fundamental moral and religious beliefs and commitments. Precisely to the extent that they are reasonable, various comprehensive views, including religious ones, can be part of the overlapping consensus of political liberalism that ensures social stability.

Although he observes that a de facto modus vivendi might, in particular circumstances, develop into an overlapping consensus, Rawls emphatically denies that the overlapping consensus constitutes, or necessarily results from, a mere modus vivendi. The key is that the overlapping consensus is characterized by a certain type of reasonable moral agreement about what, at a basic level defined by principles and ideals, constitute fair terms of social cooperation among people who, being reasonable, view each other as free and equal citizens. Thus, "political liberalism," though representing a "freestanding" conception of justice, is a moral conception, containing "its own intrinsic normative and moral ideal."

Terms of cooperation offered by citizens to their fellow citizens are fair, according to Rawls, only to the extent that "citizens offering them … reasonably think that those citizens to whom such terms are offered might also reasonably accept them." Rawls refers to this requirement as "the criterion of reciprocity." It is the core of what Rawls calls "the liberal principle of legitimacy," namely, that "our exercise of political power is fully proper only when it is exercised in

accordance with a constitution the essentials of which all citizens as free and equal may reasonably be expected to endorse in the light of principles and ideals acceptable to their common human reason." Only when political power is thus exercised do political actors (including voters) act consistently with the ideal of "public reason."

B. The "Rationalist Believers"

A central point and effect of the liberal principle of legitimacy and the ideal of public reason is to exclude as illegitimate, in the framing of a constitution and in legislative and judicial deliberations touching upon constitutional essentials or basic matters of justice, certain principles and other propositions even though they are, or may well be, true. It is easy enough to see how such an exclusion might, in certain circumstances, be reasonable, prudent, and thus warranted as part of a modus vivendi. It is far from obvious, however, that people are obligated morally, in circumstances in which they are not obliged as a matter of political prudence, to refrain from acting on principles that they reasonably believe to be true and that are not ruled out as reasons for political action by their reasonable comprehensive doctrines of justice and political morality.

Of course, a particular comprehensive view might identify reasons, even reasons of principle and not mere prudence, for declining to enforce by law or otherwise to take political action based on certain types of moral obligations. Certain comprehensive liberalisms, such as the liberalisms of John Stuart Mill and Joseph Raz, purport to identify such principles. It is, of course, crucial to Rawls's project to avoid an appeal to any such comprehensive liberalism. His claim is that the rational moral force of the liberal principle of legitimacy and of the ideal of public reason depends in no way on the truth of comprehensive liberalism in any form.

When citizens disagree with one another about certain basic moral, political, and religious questions, what does it mean for them to propose terms of social cooperation that they reasonably think their fellow citizens can reasonably accept? If the criterion of reciprocity and the principle of legitimacy are interpreted narrowly, it simply requires that those citizens proposing terms of social cooperation must reasonably think that they are giving their fellow citizens who disagree with them about particular fundamental matters sound reasons, accessible to them as rational persons, for changing their minds. Under such a narrow interpretation, the scope of public reason would be correspondingly wide. Although it would exclude appeals to sheer authority, or "secret knowledge," or to putative truths revealed only to an elect few and not accessible to reasonable persons as such, it would not rule out in advance of argument on the merits any principle or proposition, however controversial, which is (or can be) defended by rational argument.

Of course, this interpretation (and the very wide view of public reason it would authorize) is not one Rawls can accept, for it does not limit the field of acceptable doctrines of political morality to political liberalism. It will not serve to exclude ideals and principles drawn from comprehensive forms of liberalism, for example. More to the point, it will not rule out certain notable nonliberal comprehensive views that similarly appeal to our "common human reason." The broad tradition of natural law thinking, for example, proposes what amounts to its own principle of public reason when it asserts that questions of fundamental law and basic matters of justice ought to be decided in accordance with natural law, natural right, natural rights, or natural justice. If Rawls is to sustain his bold claim that "[o]nly a political conception of justice that all citizens might reasonably be expected to endorse can serve as a basis of public reason and justification," he must defend a broad version of the legitimacy principle, one that restricts the scope of public reason sufficiently to exclude not only comprehensive doctrines that appeal to secret knowledge or private revelation, but also comprehensive doctrines that appeal to publicly accessible reasons. Relatedly, he must show that the putatively strictly "political" conception of justice can guarantee the liberal conclusions he favors on questions that from the liberal point of view touch upon constitutional essentials and matters of basic justice, without smuggling into the justification for these conclusions disputed principles or propositions drawn from a comprehensive liberalism.

In *Political Liberalism*, Rawls considers the case of "rationalist believers who contend that [their] beliefs are open to and can be fully established by reason." Oddly, he says that this contention is "uncommon," when it is, in fact, the claim of what Sir Isaiah Berlin, whose own sympathies are plainly liberal, has called "a central strand in the whole tradition of western thought." In any event, Rawls's remarkably brief argument against the so-called rationalist believers is based entirely on the claim that they unreasonably deny "the fact of reasonable pluralism." If I understand accurately what Rawls means by "rationalist believers," then I am something of one myself. I certainly do not deny that people in our culture, including reasonable people, disagree about fundamental moral questions, such as the morality of abortion and homosexual acts. Nor need people like me deny that some measure of moral disagreement is in some sense inevitable under circumstances of political and religious freedom. In precisely what sense, then, do we, according to Rawls, deny the fact of reasonable pluralism?

To be faithful to his own methodological scruples, Rawls must avoid denying the truth of the reasonable, albeit controversial, moral, metaphysical, and religious claims that he wishes to exclude as reasons for political action under the principle of legitimacy. He must, therefore, adduce grounds other than their falsity for their exclusion. If he is reduced to arguing on the merits for the falsity of these claims, the case for "political liberalism" has been fatally compromised. Rawls's strategy is not to deny the truth of the claims of rationalist believers, but merely to deny that their claims "can be publicly and fully established by reason." This denial can be sustained, however, only by addressing the merits of the actual arguments that the rationalist believers publicly advance in support of their beliefs, arguments that the liberal principle of legitimacy and the Rawlsian ideal of public reason are meant to rule out in advance, irrespective of their soundness, on grounds independent of the truth or falsity of the principles the arguments are meant to vindicate.

Rawls's insistence that he is not denying the truth of rationalist believers' beliefs, but only their assertion that these beliefs can be publicly and fully established by reason, is therefore unavailing. Rationalist believers do not claim on the basis of secret knowledge or special revelation that their beliefs are publicly justifiable by rational argument; on the contrary, they defend their views precisely by offering public justification, that is, rational arguments in support of the principles and propositions on the basis of which they propose political action. These arguments are either sound or unsound. If sound, there is no reason to exclude the principles and propositions they vindicate as "illegitimate" reasons for political action. If unsound, they should be rejected—on rationalist believers' own terms—precisely for that reason.

Consider the matter from the viewpoint of people to whom the arguments of rationalist believers are addressed. Those who, upon reflection, are persuaded by arguments that appeal to their "common human reason" obviously have no ground for excluding as in principle "illegitimate" or "contrary to public reason" these principles and propositions as reasons for political action. People who are not persuaded will consider that the arguments advanced for these principles and policies are unsound or, in any event, insufficient to warrant belief in, and action based on, the principles and propositions in support of which they are advanced. They will, of course, consider those who are persuaded to be in error (and vice versa), but they have no grounds for supposing them to be acting in violation of a principle of legitimacy by preparing to exercise public power, or to support the exercise of such power, for "nonpublic" reasons.

Do rationalist believers deny the possibility of reasonable disagreement? Rawls says that, "[i]t is unrealistic—or worse, it arouses mutual suspicion and hostility—to suppose that all our differences are rooted in ignorance and perversity, or else in the rivalries for power, status, or economic gain." True, but rationalist believers recognize that many differences, including certain political differences, arise from considerations that are underdetermined by reason such as matters of taste or sentiment, or from reasonably guided, albeit still rationally underdetermined, prior commitments and the distinctive perspectives and responsibilities flowing from them, or from the diversity of reasonable beliefs about the likely consequences of alternative possible courses of action. There may be in such cases a variety of unreasonable opinions; but there need not be a uniquely reasonable or correct one.

In other matters, however, including fundamental political matters such as questions of human rights, there are uniquely morally correct beliefs that are, in principle, available to every rational person, or so rationalist believers hold. Differences with regard to such matters may be "reasonable," in the sense that reasonable persons can err about such matters (which may be complicated and difficult), and, indeed, can sometimes err without subjective moral fault. Still, some error of reason must be responsible for anyone's failure to arrive at a correct opinion with regard to such matters. Errors may be rooted in inattention to or ignorance of certain facts or values, subrational influences that block insight but may be subjectively nonculpable, logical failure, or other mistakes in judgment that can be induced or at least facilitated by particular cultures.

Is this view unreasonable? Rawls speaks of competing comprehensive views that are "perfectly reasonable" and of persons subscribing to different views who are nonetheless "fully reasonable." Unless he is to violate his own methodological scruples by appealing to some form of moral relativism, Rawls cannot declare the view of rationalist believers to be unreasonable because they hold that conflicting views on moral questions, including some questions of human rights, on which "reasonable people disagree" cannot be equally reasonable. There is nothing unreasonable in holding that the view of those in error is less than fully or perfectly reasonable, and that they, to the extent that their view deviates from the correct one, are (perhaps nonculpably) being less reasonable than their opponents who have managed to get to the truth of the matter at issue.

Indeed, it is difficult to see how Rawls himself could defend a contrary position. After all, there are reasonable people who reject "political liberalism." Rawls must suppose that they are in error. Persons who consider other people to be in error can, of course, do so compatibly with a recognition of their own fallibility. Nevertheless, to the extent that their view deviates from the correct one—perhaps because they misunderstand or fail to appreciate the force of one or more of Rawls's central arguments—Rawls must suppose that they are being less reasonable than those who grasp his arguments, appreciate their force, and therefore affirm the superiority of "political liberalism" to its alternatives.

Must rationalist believers reject Rawls's account of the sources of reasonable disagreement in connection with what he calls "the burdens of judgment"? That account is not without its ambiguities. If, however, it is read in such a way as to avoid its collapse into relativism, then Rawls's idea of "fully reasonable," or even "perfectly reasonable," though erroneous, views refers to false beliefs that are formed by people without subjective fault. This is what people generally have in mind when, although themselves persuaded of the truth of a certain view, they nevertheless allow that the relevant subject matter is one about which "reasonable people can disagree." The possibility of reasonable disagreement in this sense is, however, no reason to exclude public argument as to the truth of the matters in question. John Finnis's remark on this point strikes me as entirely apt: "Public reasoning should be directed to overcoming the relevant mistakes, not preemptively surrendering to them."

In *A Theory of Justice*, Rawls defended his substantive principles of justice by way of a "political constructivism" that asked what principles reasonable parties in an original position, behind a "thick" veil of ignorance, and thus possessed of merely a "thin" theory of the good, would choose for a society in which they would eventually occupy a place. In *Political Liberalism*, he indicates that the principle of legitimacy and the limits or guidelines of public reason "have the same basis as the substantive principles of justice." This is shaky, for neither Rawls nor his followers have ever provided any reason to believe that perfectionist principles that would not be chosen under conditions of artificial ignorance by the unnaturally risk-averse parties in the original position are unjust,

or are not valid principles of justice. The key point is this: From the proposition that principles that would be chosen by such parties under such conditions are just (and are principles of justice), it simply does not follow that perfectionist principles that might very well be chosen by reasonable and reasonably well-informed persons outside the Rawlsian original position are unjust (or are not principles of justice).

II. ABORTION AND PUBLIC REASON

Although his desire to defend "political liberalism" requires Rawls to resist the very wide view of public reason that could be endorsed by natural law theorists or other so-called rationalist believers, he is nevertheless eager to show that the scope of his doctrine of public reason is not excessively narrow. For example, his "political liberalism" allows people to resort to beliefs drawn from their comprehensive doctrines in a variety of areas that do not touch upon "constitutional essentials" and matters of "basic justice." Even in areas that do touch upon such matters, Rawls's theory allows appeals to comprehensive doctrines subject to the proviso that citizens making such appeals "in due course" show that their position can be justified in terms of public reason.

In *Political Liberalism*, Rawls offers the following explanation of the demands of public reason:

> What public reason asks is that citizens be able to explain their vote to one another in terms of a reasonable balance of public political values, it being understood by everyone that of course the plurality of reasonable comprehensive doctrines held by citizens is thought by them to provide further and often transcendent backing for those values. In each case, which doctrine is affirmed is a matter of conscience for the individual citizen. It is true that the balance of political values a citizens holds must be reasonable, and one that can be seen to be reasonable by other citizens; but not all reasonable balances are the same. The only comprehensive doctrines that run afoul of public reason are those that cannot support a reasonable balance of political values.

Precisely at this point, Rawls inserts a footnote, which, "[a]s an illustration," takes up what he describes as "the troubled question of abortion." After stipulating "that we are dealing with the normal case of mature adult women," he asks the reader to "consider the question in terms of these three important political values: the due respect for human life, the ordered reproduction of political society over time, including the family in some form, and finally the equality of women as equal citizens." After acknowledging, parenthetically, that these are not the only important political values, he declares that "any reasonable balance of these three values will give a woman a duly qualified right to decide whether or not to end her pregnancy during the first trimester."

How, one may ask, could this bold conclusion be justified without appeal to moral or metaphysical views widely in dispute about the status of embryonic and fetal human beings, or the justice or injustice of choices either to bring about their deaths or to perform acts with the foreseeable side effect of bringing about their deaths? Here is Rawls's entire justification: "[A]t this early stage of pregnancy the political value of the equality of women is overriding, and this right is required to give it substance and force." Why does the value of women's equality override the value of fetal life? Rawls does not say. The absence of argument for this claim is especially remarkable in view of the fact that opponents of abortion contend that the right to life (which, in their view, the unborn share with all other human beings) is fundamental and inviolable and, as such, cannot be "balanced" against other considerations. Rawls goes on to comment that he does not think that the introduction of other political values into the calculation would alter his conclusion, and, indeed, that a reasonable balance of political values might allow a right to abortion even beyond the first trimester, "at least in certain circumstances." He explicitly declines to argue the point further, however, stating that his purpose in raising the question of a right to abortion at all is simply "to illustrate the point of the text by saying that any comprehensive doctrine that leads to a balance of political values excluding that duly qualified right in the first trimester is to that extent unreasonable."

Needless to say, Rawls's footnote has elicited vigorous criticism. As an argument for a right to abortion, it does worse than beg centrally important questions—it ignores them altogether. Moreover, it seems plainly, if silently, to import into the analysis of the question a range of undefended beliefs of precisely the sort that "political liberalism" is supposed to exclude. This smuggling in of controversial moral and metaphysical beliefs is especially egregious in view of the fact that abortion is often put forward as a question that simply cannot be resolved, one way or the other, without introducing such beliefs into the deliberations. As such, it presents a particular challenge to Rawls's central argument that constitutional essentials and matters of basic justice ought to be resolved by appeal to a purely "political" conception of justice, rather than to general doctrines of justice as parts of reasonable comprehensive views.

In a footnote to the introduction of the new paperback edition of *Political Liberalism*, Rawls acknowledges the force of some of these criticisms and offers a brief reply:

> Some have quite naturally read the [original] footnote ... as an argument for the right to abortion in the first trimester. I do not intend it to be one. (It does express my opinion, but an opinion is not an argument.) I was in error in leaving it in doubt that the aim of the footnote was only to illustrate and confirm the following statement in the text to which the footnote is attached: "The only comprehensive doctrines that run afoul of public reason are those that cannot support a reasonable balance [or ordering] of political values [on the issue]." To try to explain what I meant, I used three political values (of course, there are more) for the troubled issue of the right to abortion, to which it might seem improbable that political values could apply at all. I believe a more detailed interpretation of those values may, when properly developed in public reason, yield a reasonable argument. I don't say the most reasonable or decisive argument; I don't know what that would be, or even if it exists.

At this point, Rawls cites with approval, noting only that he would add several (unspecified) "addenda" to it, Judith Jarvis Thomson's argument for a right to abortion in her then-recent article,

Abortion: Whose Right? Here is Thomson's summation of her argument:

> First, restrictive regulation [of abortion] severely constrains women's liberty. Second, severe constraints on liberty may not be imposed in the name of considerations that the constrained are not unreasonable in rejecting. And third, the many women who reject the claim that the fetus has a right to life from the moment of conception are not unreasonable in doing so.

The affinities of Thomson's approach with Rawlsian political liberalism are obvious. The central pro-life claims are: (1) Human beings in the embryonic and fetal stages, like innocent human beings at all other stages of life, have a right not to be directly (or otherwise unjustly) killed; and (2) like all other human beings, they are entitled to the (equal) protection of the laws against homicide. Thomson defends the right to abortion, not by claiming that the central pro-life claims are false, but by arguing that their truth or falsity is irrelevant to the political resolution of the question of abortion. What matters is that people are "not unreasonable" in judging the central pro-life claims to be false. Therefore, even those who judge them to be true should refrain from taking political action that would restrict women's freedom based on their judgment. They should join those who consider the central pro-life claims to be false in a sort of Rawlsian overlapping consensus that recognizes a woman's right to abortion.

Here, I submit, we have fully on display all the equivocations, ambiguities, and weaknesses of the Rawlsian criterion of reciprocity, liberal principle of legitimacy, and doctrine of public reason. Immediately after offering the summary of her argument I quoted a moment ago, Thomson, evidently struggling to be generous, says that, "[t]here is of course room for those who accept Catholic doctrine on abortion to declare it in the public forum"; but, she adds, "those who accept the doctrine ought not say that reason requires us to accept it, for that assertion is false." What is Thomson claiming here? Is it that the central pro-life claims should be rejected because they are untrue or, even if true, somehow unreasonable? To establish that, she would have to engage

pro-life arguments on the merits and refute them. She makes no serious effort to do so. To have done so would, in any event, have shifted the ground of the argument for a right to abortion from the sphere of Rawlsian "public reason" to an unrestricted debate of a sort that would engage, in violation of Rawlsian scruples, principles connected with competing comprehensive doctrines.

What Thomson seems to mean is that not all "reasonable people" accept pro-life claims, or that the rejection of pro-life claims does not mark a person as "unreasonable." There are, as I suggested earlier, important ways in which assertions like these are true. Contrary to what Thomson supposes, however, nothing follows from the ways in which they are true for the questions whether women have a right to abortion or the unborn have a right not to be aborted. If, in truth, the latter right obtains, and thus the pro-life position is more reasonable than its alternative, then the fact that reasonable people, perhaps without culpability, hold the contrary view in no way vitiates the human right of the unborn not to be killed, or confers upon women a moral right to the more or less unrestricted legal freedom to bring about their deaths. What matters, from the moral point of view, is that basic human rights be identified where they obtain and, to the extent possible, protected.

In the end, Thomson's argument that people are "not unreasonable" in rejecting the pro-life position boils down to an assertion that the argument over the moral status of the human conceptus and early embryo ends in a sort of stalemate: "While I know of no conclusive reason for denying that fertilized eggs have a right to life, I also know of no conclusive reason for asserting that they do have a right to life." Yet one is entitled to this conclusion about the moral status of newly conceived human beings (Thomson's "fertilized eggs") only if one can make an argument sufficient to support it. Such an argument also would have to rebut the arguments put forward to show that the unborn have a right to life even in the earliest stages of their existence. Apart from a few references to *Evangelium Vitae* [papal encyclical of Pope John Paul II, 25 March 1995],

Thomson cites no such arguments at all. There is all the difference in the world between rebutting these arguments and ruling them out in advance on the ground that they implicate deep moral and metaphysical questions in dispute among reasonable people subscribing to competing comprehensive doctrines.

What are the arguments to be rebutted if Thomson is to show that there is nothing unreasonable in rejecting the central pro-life claims? Perhaps these arguments are so tendentious, obscure, or otherwise lacking in rational force that she is justified in ruling them out in advance as legitimate grounds for political action on pro-life principles. In considering the claim that "a human being's life begins at conception," Thomson observes parenthetically, and without further comment or citation, that "[w]e are invited to accept that premise on the ground that the conceptus—a fertilized human egg—contains a biological code that will govern its entire future physical development, and therefore is already a human being." Her suggestion, it seems, is not that the ground adduced for accepting the premise is false, but rather that it is inadequate. It is worth pausing here to consider the implications of the genetic coding and completeness of the human conceptus and early embryo. A human being is conceived when a human sperm containing twenty-three chromosomes fuses with a human egg also containing twenty-three chromosomes (albeit of a different kind) producing a single-cell human zygote containing, in the normal case, forty-six chromosomes that are mixed differently from the forty-six chromosomes as found in the mother or father. Unlike the gametes (that is, the sperm and egg), the zygote is genetically unique and distinct from its parents. Biologically, it is a separate organism. It produces, as the gametes do not, specifically human enzymes and proteins. It possesses, as they do not, the active capacity or potency to develop itself into a human embryo, fetus, infant, child, adolescent, and adult.

Assuming that it is not conceived in vitro, the zygote is, of course, in a state of dependence on its mother. But independence should not be confused with distinctness. From the beginning, the newly conceived human being directs its own

integral organic functioning. It takes in nourishment and converts it to energy. Given an hospitable environment, it will "develop continuously without any biological interruptions, or gaps, throughout the embryonic, fetal, neo-natal, childhood and adulthood stages—until the death of the organism." Thus, according to Dianne Nutwell Irving:

> [T]he biological facts demonstrate that at syngamy we have a truly *human* nature. It is not that he or she will become a human being—he or she already *is* a human being.... [A] human zygote or embryo is not a *possible* human being; nor is he or she *potentially* a human being; he or she *is* a human being.

Jed Rubenfeld, in his influential article, *On the Legal Status of the Proposition that "Life Begins at Conception,"* asserts the contrary. He claims that arguments that life begins at conception are "virtually unintelligible."[2] If this were true, then Thomson would seem to be justified in effectively ruling such arguments out in advance as reasons for legal restrictions on abortion. The trouble with Rubenfeld's assertion is that he engages no serious scholarly argument in favor of the proposition he claims to be not merely false or inadequate but "virtually unintelligible." Although he cites serious scholarly work in his analyses of claims that "life begins" at various biological marker events in prenatal development such as the point in brain development at which interneural connections within the cerebral cortex make possible higher mental functioning, he fails to engage a single serious scholarly defense of the proposition whose legal status the title of his article promises to explore. The sole citation he gives for "these arguments" before declaring them to be "virtually unintelligible" is a "well-known antiabortion pamphlet written by Dr. John Willke of the National Right to Life Committee." To make matters worse, it is unclear whether Rubenfeld has even read this source, since he refers to it only parenthetically as having been discussed by Frances Olsen (a pro-choice scholar) in a 1989 *Harvard Law Review* article.

Had Rubenfeld examined the scholarly literature, he could not have imagined, as Thomson did, that the ground of the belief that the lives of new human individuals begin at conception is the bare proposition that "[f]ertilization may be said to represent the moment of genetic completion." This is what Thomson seems to have in mind in referring to the "biological code that will govern its entire future physical development." In response to the argument that life begins at conception, as he imagines it, Rubenfeld says that "[e]very cell in our bodies is genetically complete," yet nobody supposes that every human cell is a distinct human being with a right to life. This misses the point of the argument that there comes into being at conception, not a mere clump of human cells, but a distinct, unified self-integrating organism, which develops itself, truly himself or herself, in accord with its own genetic blueprint. The significance of genetic completeness for the status of newly conceived human beings is that no outside genetic material is required to enable the zygote to mature into an embryo, the embryo into a fetus, the fetus into an infant, the infant into a child, the child into an adolescent, the adolescent into an adult. What the zygote needs to function as a distinct self-integrating human organism, a human being, it already possesses.

At no point in embryogenesis does the distinct organism that came into being when it was conceived undergo substantial change or a change of natures. It is human and will remain human. This was the point of Justice Byron White's remark in his dissenting opinion in *Thornburgh v. American College of Obstetricians & Gynecologists* that "there is no nonarbitrary line separating a fetus from a child." Rubenfeld quotes White's observation and then purports to demolish what he takes to be "[t]he argument based on the gradualness of gestation," by pointing out that, "[n]o nonarbitrary line separates the hues of green and red. Shall we conclude that green is red? That night is day?"

The point of the argument is not that development is "gradual," but rather that it is continuous and is the development of a single lasting being. The human zygote that actively develops itself is, as I have pointed out, a genetically complete organism directing its own integral organic functioning. As it matures, in utero and ex utero,

it does not "become" a human being, for it is a human being already, albeit an immature human being, the way a newborn infant is an immature human being who will undergo quite dramatic growth and development over time.

These considerations undermine the familiar argument, recited by Rubenfeld, that "[a]n unfertilized ovum also has the potential to develop into a whole human being, but that does not make it a person." The ovum is not a whole human being. It is, rather, a part of another human being (the woman whose ovum it is) with merely the potential to give rise to, in interaction with a part of yet another human being (a man's sperm cell), a new and whole human being. Unlike the zygote, it lacks both genetic distinctness and completeness, as well as the active capacity to develop itself into an adult member of the human species. It is living human cellular material, but, left to itself, however hospitable its environment, it will never become a human being. It will "die" as a human ovum, just as countless skin cells "die" daily as nothing more than skin cells. If successfully fertilized by a human sperm, which, like the ovum (but dramatically unlike the zygote), lacks the active potential to develop into an adult member of the human species, then substantial change—a change of natures—will occur. There will no longer be merely an egg, which was part of the mother, sharing her genetic composition, and a sperm, which was part of the father, sharing his genetic composition; there will be a genetically complete, distinct, unified, self-integrating human organism whose nature differs from that of the gametes—not mere human material, but a human being.

These considerations also make clear that Michael Lockwood, who takes a line on these issues similar to Rubenfeld's, is quite incorrect to say that "we were never week-old embryos, any more than we were sperm or ova." It truly makes no sense to say that "I" was once a sperm (or an unfertilized egg) that matured into an adult. Conception was the occasion of substantial change (that is, change from one complete individual entity to another) that brought into being a distinct self-integrating organism with a specifically human nature. By contrast, it makes every bit as much sense to say that I was once a week-old embryo as to say that I was once a week-old infant or a ten-year-old child. It was the new organism created at conception that, without itself undergoing any change of substance, matured into a week-old embryo, a fetus, an infant, a child, an adolescent, and, finally, an adult.

Rubenfeld has another argument: Cloning processes give to nonzygotic cells the potential for development into distinct, self-integrating human beings; thus to recognize the zygote as a human being is to recognize all human cells as human beings, which is absurd. It is true that a distinct, self-integrating human organism that came into being by a process of cloning would be, like a human organism that comes into being as a monozygotic twin, a human being. That being, no less than human beings conceived by the union of sperm and egg, would possess a human nature and the active potential to mature as a human being. However, even assuming the possibility of cloning human beings from nonzygotic human cells, the nonzygotic cell must be activated by a process that effects substantial change and not mere development or maturation. Left to itself, apart from an activation process capable of effecting a change of substance or natures, the cell will mature and die as a human cell, not as a human being. When speaking of the conceptus, Thomson refers to the biological code that will govern "*its* entire future physical development"; her syntax points to the relevant entity and reveals the truth that each of us is the human being—that is, the distinct, self-integrating organism—we were as an adolescent, a child, an infant, a fetus, an embryo, and a zygote. Each of us is the "it" who has now experienced the physical development that was in its future when, at conception, it was coded for that development.

I have set forth in some detail the argument that the life of a human being begins at conception, and considered some (though by no means all) of the counterarguments, not to show that the unborn have a right to life (though I believe that they do) or that there is no general right to abortion (though I believe there is not), but to show that the case for the right to life cannot be easily rebutted, nor can the case for a right to abortion—even a "duly qualified" right to abortion "in the first trimester"—be established without engaging the deep moral and metaphysical questions on the basis of which people divide over the question of abortion. If I am correct, Rawlsian "political liberalism" does not offer a way of resolving the social and political conflict surrounding the issue on the basis of principles of justice that can be identified and applied independently of any particular view on these questions. Neither the considerations suggested by Rawls himself nor those advanced by Thomson give those on the pro-life side anything approaching a sufficient reason to surrender in their political struggle for legal protection of the unborn against abortion. They, like their opponents on the pro-choice side, may have good reasons to seek political compromises with their opponents on legislative proposals for the restriction or regulation of abortion, or even to seek a modus vivendi at the constitutional level on the best terms they can obtain. But nothing in the idea of "public reason" gives them grounds to suppose that justice itself requires them to shift from being "politically pro-life" to being merely "personally opposed to abortion, but politically pro-choice."

III. HOMOSEXUAL ACTS, MARRIAGE, AND PUBLIC REASON

If abortion is the most explosive issue in our "culture war," questions pertaining to the legal treatment of homosexual acts and relationships are emerging as the second most incendiary. Assuming that public policy issues regarding sex and marriage go to matters of constitutional essentials and basic justice, Rawlsian political liberalism offers itself as the morally best, or most reasonable, way to resolve political issues concerning homosexual acts and other questions of public policy pertaining to sex and marriage. This way avoids, indeed rules out, appeal to underlying moral and metaphysical questions in dispute among people who give their allegiance to competing comprehensive views. If Rawls is right, reasonable people who reject comprehensive liberalism in favor of views that include more conservative positions on homosexual acts and other questions of sexual morality ought reasonably to be able to join comprehensive liberals in an overlapping consensus on the proper political resolution of these questions.

Disagreements over public policies regarding homosexual conduct and relationships certainly reflect different, incompatible understandings of sexual morality connected to different "comprehensive views." Underlying and informing these different understandings are, once again, profound differences about the nature of human persons and values. Is pleasure intrinsically good and, as such, a noninstrumental reason for action? Or can pleasure, in itself, provide nothing more than subrational motivation? Is the body an aspect of the personal reality of the human being whose body it is? Or is the body a subpersonal part of the human being whose personal reality is the conscious and desiring self that uses the body as an instrument? Is the idea of a true bodily union of persons an illusion? Or are marital acts realizations of precisely such a union? Do nonmarital sexual acts instrumentalize the bodies of those performing them in such a way as to damage their personal integrity? Or are mutually agreeable sexual acts of whatever type morally innocent and even valuable means of sharing pleasure and intimacy and expressing feelings of tenderness and affection?

People's judgments and understandings regarding these and related issues, judgments and understandings that are rarely formal and are usually merely implicit, determine their places on the spectrum ranging from various forms of sexual liberationism to strict forms of conservative sexual morality. Some proponents of moderate liberalism on questions of sexual morality oppose promiscuity and adultery but maintain that the judgment of traditional natural law theorists and others that fornication and sodomy are intrinsically nonmarital and immoral is misguided. They believe that nonadulterous and nonpromiscuous sexual acts and relationships between loving and devoted partners, whether of opposite sexes or the same sex, can be morally good even outside of marriage. Moreover, they argue that the state should, to be fair to people who are homosexually oriented, make marriage licenses, or at least benefits

equivalent to those conferred by legal marriage, available to otherwise eligible same-sex couples.

Together with a coauthor, Gerard V. Bradley, I recently debated issues of marriage and sexual morality, including the question of homosexual acts and relationships, with Stephen Macedo in the pages of the *Georgetown Law Journal*. Professor Macedo argues that government has an obligation in justice to its homosexually oriented citizens to issue marriage licenses on a nondiscriminatory basis to same-sex couples. If I understand Macedo's argument correctly, he defends a conception of marriage as essentially an emotional and, possibly, spiritual union of two loving and devoted persons who may be of opposite sexes or the same sex. The intimacy and overall value of their union is, or may be, enhanced by the partners' cooperation in the performance of mutually agreeable sexual acts. Professor Bradley and I defend an alternative conception of marriage—one that we believe to be reflected in traditional American and British marriage law, especially in the law governing consummation of marriage. We argue that marriage is a one-flesh (i.e., *bodily*, as well as emotional, dispositional, and spiritual) union of a male and a female spouse consummated and actualized by sexual acts that are reproductive in type. Such acts consummate and, we maintain, actualize the intrinsic good of marriage whether or not reproduction is desired by the spouses in any particular marital act, or is even possible for them in a particular act or at all.

Macedo is no sexual liberationist. He evidently opposes promiscuity and believes that even consensual sex acts can, in some cases, violate personal integrity or some other moral value. Nor does he maintain that marriage is a mere social or legal convention that lacks a nature of its own and can therefore legitimately be manipulated to serve the subjective ends of individuals or the state, whatever they happen to be. He shares with people such as Bradley and me the view that not all forms of consensual sexual association ought to be recognized as marriages by the state. He disagrees with us, however, on questions of the nature of marriage and the role and value of sex within it.

Bradley and I summarize our argument as follows:

(1) Marriage, considered not as a mere legal convention, but, rather, as a two-in-one-flesh communion of persons that is consummated and actualized by sexual acts of the reproductive type, is an intrinsic ... human good; as such, marriage provides a noninstrumental reason for spouses, whether or not they are capable of conceiving children in their acts of genital union, to perform such acts. (2) In choosing to perform nonmarital orgasmic acts, including sodomitical acts—irrespective of whether the persons performing such acts are of the same or opposite sexes (and even if those persons are validly married to each other)—persons necessarily treat their bodies and those of their sexual partners (if any) as *means* or *instruments* in ways that damage their personal (and interpersonal) integrity; thus, regard for the basic human good of integrity provides a conclusive moral reason not to engage in sodomitical and other nonmarital sex acts.

Macedo denies these claims. He argues that the organic bodily union of persons we believe to be possible in marital intercourse, whether or not procreation is possible, is illusory. Thus the reproductive-type acts of spouses cannot possibly have the unitive value and significance we ascribe to them. Marital intercourse cannot be what we claim it is, namely, the biological matrix of the multilevel reality of marriage. The most sex can do for people, beyond making it possible for them to become parents, is to enable them to share pleasure, thus enhancing and enabling them to express in a special way the caring, affectionate, and intimate emotional bond between them.

Macedo also argues that, by confining humanly valuable and morally upright sex to marital intercourse, natural law theorists such as Bradley and I unreasonably exclude sex acts which, though nonmarital (at least in our sense), are nevertheless humanly valuable in their capacity to express and enhance the emotional bonds between lovers. Moreover, he maintains that we are wrong to deny, as we do, that pleasure is an intrinsic good, or that the instrumentalizing of the body to the end of gaining or sharing pleasurable sensations is intrinsically bad. Thus he denies that nonmarital sex inevitably damages personal or interpersonal integrity. Bradley and I respond to Macedo's critique of our views by arguing that his understanding of sex and marriage implicates him in a philosophically untenable person-body dualism. This is most apparent in his denial that human males and females unite biologically when they mate, and in his related understanding of sexual organs as "equipment" that serves the goods of pleasure and procreation but cannot make possible a truly personal union of spouses as the biological matrix of the multi-level (bodily, emotional, dispositional, spiritual) reality of their marriage. Implicit in these denials, we believe, is the idea that the body is a subpersonal aspect of the human being that serves the conscious and desiring aspect—the true "self"—which inhabits and uses the body. Were Macedo to acknowledge what we believe to be the case, namely, "that the biological reality of human beings is 'part of, not merely an instrument of, their *personal* reality,'" then it is difficult to see how he could resist our claim that "the biological union of spouses in marital acts constitutes a truly *interpersonal* communion," whose value is intrinsic, and not merely instrumental to pleasure or the sharing of pleasure, the expression of tender and affectionate feelings, or any other extrinsic goal.

My point in introducing the debate between Macedo and Bradley and myself is not to try to settle the issues but merely to illustrate that the arguments advanced on both sides plainly implicate a body of assumptions reflective of our respective commitments to very different "comprehensive views." As a result, I suspect, people whose comprehensive view is essentially liberal will find Macedo's argument much more persuasive than ours; those with nonliberal comprehensive views—including traditional-minded Christians, Jews, and other believers—are likely to find our argument more compelling. Still, neither side makes any appeal to principles or propositions that are not publicly available to rational persons. Neither side invokes any form of secret knowledge or revelation. Each side offers people on the other side reasons, which such people may or may not find persuasive, for changing their minds.

My concern for now is not with the truth or falsity of the claims made on either side, or the validity of the arguments advanced on either side to support its claims, but with the relevance of the truth or falsity of these claims to the resolution of questions of public policy pertaining to sex and marriage and particularly to questions of homosexual acts and relationships. My claim is that political liberalism does not provide a workable alternative to the conflict of comprehensive views on such questions. On the contrary, law and policy in this area should be shaped in accordance with the truth and will inevitably be shaped by people's ideas about the truth of the moral and metaphysical claims at stake in the debate among advocates of competing comprehensive views.

The case for resolving policy questions in this area on the basis of "political liberalism" is articulated by Macedo himself. Although he contends that the view of marriage and sexual morality that Bradley and I put forward as a ground for public policymaking ought to be rejected as unreasonably narrowing the range of morally valuable sexual conduct and relationships, he argues, in the alternative, that our view constitutes an illegitimate ground for public policy even if it is true and the competing moral view he defends is false. The upshot of his position for questions of public policy pertaining to homosexual acts and relationships is that justice requires the state to grant marriage licenses to same-sex partners and to recognize their relationship as marital even if, in truth, their sex acts cannot be marital (or morally upright) and their relationship cannot, morally speaking, be a marriage. That is the proposition I am interested in here.

Noting that "[i]t may be, indeed, that Bradley and George and I disagree … deeply in our understandings of what it is to have reasons for action, about the nature of goods, and perhaps even about the relationship between mind and body," Macedo argues that, "[i]f our disagreements indeed lie in these difficult philosophical quarrels, about which reasonable people have long disagreed, then our differences lie precisely in the territory that John Rawls rightly … marks off as

inappropriate to the fashioning of our basic rights and liberties." He continues:

> It is inappropriate to carve up basic rights and principles of justice on the basis of reasons and arguments whose force depends on accepting particular religious convictions. So too it is inappropriate to deny people fundamental aspects of equality based on reasons and arguments whose force can only be appreciated by those who accept difficult-to-assess claims about the nature and incommensurability of basic goods, the relationship between intrinsic and instrumental value, and the dispute over whether pleasure is a reason for action.

Macedo's Rawlsian argument is certainly appealing on its face. The deep moral and metaphysical questions to which he refers are indeed difficult ones about which reasonable people have long disagreed. Claims on either side of these questions are, as he says, difficult to assess. How could it be right, then, to "deny people fundamental aspects of equality" on the basis of such claims? I certainly do not think it is ever right to deny people fundamental aspects of equality. The question is whether we can identify fundamental aspects of equality pertaining to marriage while prescinding from questions of the nature and value of marriage that, inevitably, implicate deeper moral and metaphysical questions of the sort that Rawls and Macedo wish to rule out of bounds as grounds for public policymaking. Macedo implicitly supposes that we can; I think we cannot.

Macedo's claim about "denying fundamental aspects of equality" can be sustained only if we presuppose the truth of his own comprehensive liberalism. If the nature and value of marriage are, in truth, what Macedo's comprehensive view supposes them to be, then it is indeed a violation of equality to deny marriage licenses and the full legal benefits of marriage to same-sex partners. This violation occurs, however, only because homosexual partners can in fact realize in their sexual acts and relationships the same constitutive value or values (pleasure, intimacy, the expression of tender feelings) that can be realized by heterosexual spouses. No principle of equality is violated, however, if, in truth, homosexual sexual acts and relationships *cannot* realize the constitutive value or values of marriage—if marriage truly is, as Bradley and I contend, a bodily communion of persons consummated and actualized by sexual acts that are reproductive in type.

On Macedo's view and on mine, marriage is an important value that society and government have an obligation to help make available to people and which the government should not deny to people who are capable of fulfilling its requirements. What follows from this, in my view, is society's obligation to "get it right," that is, to embody in its law and policy a morally sound conception of marriage. This obligation seems to me especially stringent in view of the fact that whatever understanding of marriage is embodied in law and public policy will profoundly shape the public's understanding of the nature and value of marriage, and, thus, affect people's capacities to live out true marriages and participate in their value. This is an area in which moral neutrality strikes me as not only undesirable, but unattainable. The conflict of comprehensive views is unavoidable.

IV. CIVILITY, RECIPROCITY, AND THE CONFLICT OF "COMPREHENSIVE VIEWS"

The morally charged political disputes of our day, particularly the dispute over abortion, are often compared with the conflict over slavery in the United States in the middle of the nineteenth century. By that point in time, some supporters of slavery were no longer content to defend the "peculiar institution" as a "necessary evil," the toleration of which was required where abolition would allegedly produce disastrous, and therefore morally unacceptable, social and economic consequences. Instead, they contended that slavery was morally good and right, and that the position of their abolitionist opponents constituted, not a noble—albeit practically unattainable—moral ideal, but a form of moral and religious fanaticism that threatened the rights of slaveholders. The conflict of comprehensive views over slavery ultimately defied political compromise and proved to be incompatible with peace and social stability. The matter was finally resolved, but only after a

civil war and at a price of nearly three-quarters of a million lives.

Anyone who reflects on the carnage of the American Civil War will applaud Rawls and others for their efforts to come to terms with "the fact of moral pluralism." For those of us who judge, however, that "political liberalism" cannot provide a rational alternative to the conflict of comprehensive views, at least when it comes to morally charged issues such as abortion and homosexuality, the question arises whether it is possible to identify rational standards or ideals of political discourse and action to regulate the conflict. How should people treat those of their fellow citizens with whom they sharply disagree about profoundly important questions of morality, justice, and human rights? What, if anything, do citizens who find themselves in such disagreement owe to each other as a matter of justice in the sphere of political advocacy?

The question of one's obligations toward fellow citizens with whom one disagrees is itself a moral question, indeed, a moral question that implicates, or may implicate, constitutional essentials and matters of basic justice such as questions of freedom of speech and the press, and the right to vote. Deliberation about one's obligations to those who advocate policies that one believes to be seriously unjust will be informed by one's general or "comprehensive" views about justice. There is, I believe, no reason to suppose that people can or should attempt to prescind from their "comprehensive views" in determining their obligations to those with whom they find themselves in morally charged political conflict.

However, a certain substantial "overlapping consensus" in fact exists between a great many thoughtful people on both sides of contemporary debates over issues such as abortion and homosexuality regarding people's obligations to their political opponents. Most fundamentally, perhaps, there is a significant level of moral as well as pragmatic agreement about the need to respect basic freedoms of speech, press, and religion, and the right to vote. Of course, there is a measure of disagreement at the margins about the scope of some of these rights. Differences break out, for example, over the free speech rights of advertisers of abortion services, on the one hand, and of protesters and sidewalk counselors at abortion clinics, on the other. Nevertheless, most pro-life and pro-choice advocates respect the rights of their opponents to express and publicize their views and arguments.

Furthermore, it seems at least possible for citizens who differ fundamentally over certain basic moral questions to share a "deliberative" conception of democracy that includes the mutually recognized obligations of citizens to treat those with whom they disagree with civility and respect. In a valuable new book on the subject of moral conflict in the context of democratic politics, Amy Gutmann and Dennis Thompson have remarked that the "core idea" of "deliberative democracy" is that "when citizens or their representatives disagree morally, they should continue to reason together to reach mutually acceptable decisions." Gutmann and Thompson do not suppose that these efforts will always be successful, or that, somehow, by reasoning together, differences of "comprehensive views" can be made to melt away. Nor do they imagine that regulative principles of debate and discussion—such as the principles of "reciprocity," "publicity," and "accountability" that figure centrally in what they call "the constitution" of deliberative democracy—will dictate substantive policies, liberal or otherwise, on issues such as abortion. Their claim, rather, is that "reciprocity," which they consider to be deliberative democracy's "first principle," demands that people recognize that others who come down on what they judge to be the wrong side of a disputed moral question may nevertheless be reasonable and honest people who deserve, therefore, to be reasoned with and treated with respect. Yet reasoning with people and treating them with respect does not entail tolerating what one judges to be grave injustices so as not to offend those who judge otherwise. Nor does it mean that one ought not to oppose injustices resolutely and forcefully in one's advocacy and action. Nor does it mean that one may not protest against injustices or even practice civil disobedience to prevent them. It does mean, however, that one has certain obligations to one's opponents, obligations that are not mere matters of politeness.

Deliberative democracy is more than a matter of competing to assemble majorities for positions that one believes to be in one's interest or even morally right. In a deliberative democracy, citizens understand and accept the duty to justify their positions to their fellow citizens who disagree with them. In this respect, it includes something like an ideal of "public reason," but not one so narrow as to exclude, as Rawls's ideal of public reason purports to do, reasonable alternatives to liberal positions on such issues as abortion and homosexuality. In other words, it does not "load the dice" in favor of substantive liberal policies.

A sound principle of public reason for a deliberative democracy would indeed require citizens and policymakers to justify their political advocacy and action by appeal to principles of justice and other moral principles accessible to their fellow citizens by virtue of their "common human reason." It would, however, exclude no reasonable view in advance of its dialectical consideration "on the merits" in public debate. Nor would it exclude religious views as such. What it would exclude, rather, as grounds of public policymaking generally, are appeals to sheer authority (religious or otherwise) or to "secret knowledge," or the putative truths revealed only to an elite (or the elect) and not available, in principle, to rational persons as such. A sound principle of public reason would, in short, be very wide. Its goal would be the "perfectionist" one of settling law and public policy in accordance with what is true as a matter of justice, human rights, and political morality generally.

I have indicated elsewhere my own broad agreement with the conception of deliberative democracy advanced by Gutmann and Thompson, albeit indicating certain areas in which I would be inclined to amend, and, more important, extend their conception of "reciprocity." Inasmuch as Gutmann and Thompson plainly are committed to a broadly liberal comprehensive view, and I am not, this agreement of moral principle about regulative ideals that should govern morally charged political conflict reflects an "overlapping consensus" that goes beyond the mutual recognition of basic political rights. A consensus of this sort holds out the promise that reasonable people of good-will who have arrived at sharply different conclusions about basic questions of morality, justice, and human rights may nevertheless recognize

moral reasons to conduct their political disputes with civility and enjoy the common goods of peace and social stability that are the fruit of such civility.

47   Sex-Neutral Marriage

LESLIE GREEN[1]

I

First, my title. Why not "gay marriage"? That will not do, because civil marriage is the name of a legal relation, and legal relations cannot themselves have sexual orientations and, a fortiori, cannot have the orientation we label "gay." Then how about "same-sex marriage"? That is much better, provided we remember it is the married and not the marriage that has the same sex as something else. Marriage laws can, however, be *neutral* with respect to sex, and so they are in places like Argentina, Belgium, Canada, Iceland, the Netherlands, Norway, Portugal, South Africa, Spain, and Sweden. "But," you complain, "this is pedantry, and it shows why legal philosophers should not be allowed near lawyers. Everyone knows what 'gay marriage' means: it means a marriage contracted between a couple of gay men or a couple of lesbians. And everyone knows what 'same-sex' marriage means: it means a marriage contracted between two people of the same sex." Maybe so. But everyone also knows that these terms are now used interchangeably, and it

therefore follows that everyone has made a glaring mistake, for "gay marriage" and "same-sex marriage," on the definitions proposed, have meanings that are certainly not interchangeable. If you doubt it, consider the following observation in the case of *Baehr v. Lewin*, in which Hawaii's Supreme Court declared that, absent some very powerful justification, sex-restricted marriage laws will be found discriminatory.[1] In a footnote, the court offered this piece of pedantry or, as I see it, especially careful analysis:

"Homosexual" and "same-sex" marriages are not synonymous; by the same token, a "heterosexual" same-sex marriage is not, in theory, oxymoronic.... Parties to a "union between a man and a woman" may or may not be homosexuals. Parties to a same-sex marriage could theoretically be either homosexuals or heterosexuals.[2]

The Hawaiian court made no use of this nice point, but one of the dissenters did in *Goodridge et al. v. Department of Public Health*—though not for a benign purpose. In 2003, the Supreme Judicial Court of Massachusetts was the first in the United States to find sex-restricted marriage invalid under a state constitution and to order as a remedy that marriage licences be provided.[3] The majority declared the power to marry a fundamental right, and found that the state provided no rational basis, let alone a compelling one, for restricting it to couples of different sexes. The decision was not overtly based on considerations of equality, but a concurring judgment offered that more direct route to the result. Justice F.X. Spina, in a dissent, disagreed. He wrote;

---

[1]Leslie Green, Professor of the Philosophy of Law, University of Oxford. Email: leslie.green@law.ox.ac.uk. This article was first delivered as the Leon Green 16 Memorial Lecture at the School of Law, University of Texas at Austin. I am grateful for that invitation, and especially to Larry Sager and Brian Leiter for their hospitality and criticisms. I have also profited from comments by Cécile Fabre, Andy Koppelman, Jeffrie Murphy and Denise Réaume.

From *Current Legal Problems*, Volume 64 (2011), pp. 1–21. © The Author 2011. Reprinted with permission of Oxford University Press. All rights reserved.

[T]he marriage statutes do not discriminate on the basis of sexual orientation. As the court correctly recognizes, constitutional protections are extended to individuals, not couples. The marriage statutes do not disqualify individuals on the basis of sexual orientation from entering into marriage. All individuals, with certain exceptions not relevant here, are free to marry. Whether an individual chooses not to marry because of sexual orientation or any other reason should be of no concern to the court.[4]

There is an error in this analysis (which I shall explain below); but there is also an important truth, and it is the one noticed in *Baehr*. Neither the common law of marriage nor the impugned statute disqualified anyone on the basis of his or her sexual orientation from entering into marriage as the law defines it. The power to marry has never been conditional on the sexualities of the parties, not in any of the states and not in any other common-law jurisdiction. A marriage between a lesbian and a gay man is everywhere perfectly valid.

Now that I draw your attention to it, you may say this is true but irrelevant. If you think that sex-restricted marriage offends liberty and dignity, or even if you are just willing to tolerate sex-neutral marriage, you will not be reassured. If you think sex-neutral marriage outrages the nation's values or God's plans, you will not be worried. Both views are mistaken. The fact that the capacity to marry is already and everywhere neutral with respect to sexual orientation shows how little interest the law takes in sex within marriage. This is as it should be and, as I shall argue, the law should now go further still.

II

To see why the *Baehr* footnote is correct, we need to attend to some preliminaries about the concepts of sex, sexual orientation, and gender, and the way these categories interact with marriage.

Sex classifies people as male or female. It does not do so along a bright line. The distinction rests on a cluster of biological indicia (including chromosomal, anatomical, and endocrinal factors) that do not themselves draw bright lines, that are in some cases continuous variables, and that do not always co-vary in lockstep. So while it is true the vast majority of people are unambiguously female or male, there are also some whose sex is indeterminate.

Sexual orientation classifies people according to the relation between their own sex and the sex of the people with whom they would, or could, enjoy sexual activities (at least under ideal conditions). Sexual orientation is even less determinate than sex, the indeterminacies of which it inherits. It compounds them with the further indeterminacy about what it is to *enjoy* sexual activities, and even with the indeterminacy of what it is to *engage in sexual activity* with someone. None of this is news. It is common knowledge that there are people—in fact, lots of people—who are neither clearly straight, gay, nor clearly bisexual, because human sexual appetites shade into each other in boundaryless ways, and only some of the shades and hues achieve social salience. These homely truths do not, I hasten to add, sustain any of the extravagant claims about the radical indeterminacy or constructedness of sex or sexuality once popular in some corners of literary and cultural theory. There are clear cases of both females and heterosexuals, and although these categories are *our* categories and have an interesting genealogy—they are not arbitrary, they have explanatory power, and they will probably play a role in any morally adequate view of human nature.[5]

Last of all, there is *gender*, the behaviours, attitudes and social roles that, in a particular society, are conventionally considered appropriate to a given sex. Gender is as socially constructed as it gets, and in this way it differs from sex. Like many other animals, human beings are sexed, and our remote ancestors included sexed species long before they got around to socially constructing anything. We do sometimes hear radical-sounding claims to the effect that sex runs no deeper than gender and is constructed by similar processes.[6] Way out on the fringes, we sometimes catch wind of slogans like this: "sex is gender, all the way down." But these ill-considered thoughts prove incoherent, for they leave us without a way of identifying the gender-norms that we supposedly project onto our formless anatomies in order to produce sex. To know whether it is a violation of any gender-norm for Robin to wear a dress, drive a truck, or have sex with a man, one first has to know Robin's (presumed) *sex*.[7] If one cannot identify norm-violation and norm-conformity, one cannot identify the norms, and shapeless norms cannot be projected onto something else to give it shape. (Related problems beset the Victorian tendency to equate sexual orientation with a kind of "gender inversion," which is oddly revived in Monique Wittig's rhetorically powerful, but literally false, claim that lesbians are not women.[8])

I stress these abstract points for three reasons. First, they help us see why the *Baehr* footnote states a plain truth. Although there is a conceptual connection between sexual orientation and sex, law may restrict the power to marry by sex without thereby restricting it by sexual orientation. The common law prevented gay men from marrying each other, but it also prevented heterosexual men from marrying each other, and it permitted lesbians to marry gay men. The common law cared about sex-difference in marriage, and about little else.

Second, the existence of a conceptual connection between sexual orientation and sex provides a toe-hold for advocates in jurisdictions that permit discrimination on grounds of sexual orientation.[9] In *Baehr v. Lewin*, lawyers tried to persuade the court that sex-restricted marriage discriminates on grounds of sex, notwithstanding that the rule neither favoured one sex over the other, nor constituted any indignity to the status of women or men. But the restriction did, quite obviously, discriminate on grounds of sexual orientation and in many jurisdictions that is how such cases would be tried. Nina Baehr was, after all, disadvantaged not as a woman, but as a lesbian. But neither the Hawaiian constitution nor the US constitution has been construed to prohibit discrimination against lesbians and, outside certain enclaves of tolerant opinion, there is in fact doubt among Americans whether "sexual orientation discrimination" even picks out a moral wrong. (Which helps explain why, among the mature democracies, only in the United States did the idea that gay rights are "special rights" get real political traction.)

In such unpromising territory, it would be understandable if a liberal advocate tried to shoehorn Baehr's complaint into a protected ground of discrimination. Moreover, the choice of sex, however morally or theoretically unsatisfactory, is not exactly arbitrary. It is because we individuate sexualities by the relation between the sex of the subject and the sex of the eroticized object that we take lesbians and straight men to have different sexualities, notwithstanding their shared sexual interest in women. Even overt and intentional discrimination on grounds of sexual orientation makes necessary, if implicit, reference to sex: it has to target people whom it supposes to be attracted to people of the same *sex*. If you add to that the idea that such target-practice helps police gender roles (by reinforcing the rule that no one should stray from the sexual activities conventionally approved for someone of that sex) you can see how it might help the Nina Baehrs of the world get what they need, notwithstanding the fact that their law is indifferent to, or even supports, discrimination on grounds of sexual orientation. (It also shows how excellent advocacy can make for bad theory.)

The third reason for exploring the relations among these concepts is that it helps us understand the possibility and significance of gaps between people's sexual orientations and their sexual identities as partly constituted by social norms. Although laws and legal relations help shape the identities we call "straight" and "gay," attaching these identities to people is fallible. Some straight-identified men have stable and significant erotic interests in other men. Some homosexually inclined women neither identify nor are identified as lesbian or bisexual. It is an open question whether a homosexually inclined boy or girl will ever grow into an adult gay male or a lesbian. For one thing, where they live such identities may not be available or may have little social salience. Or countervailing factors may dominate: the fact that a woman marries a man may lead friends and family, or in some cases even herself, wrongly to suppose that she is heterosexual. The fallibility of identity-ascriptions is of considerable importance. Only if people can make mistakes about their own sexualities can we make adequate sense of the wonderful, and sometimes terrible, discovery that one's own sexual capacities are other than what one supposed, or give content to the familiar thought that gay people may "come out" or remain closeted, or understand what it is to lead an authentic life given one's erotic constitution.[10] The existence of identity-independent facts about sexual desire proves crucial to any satisfactory account of sexual liberty, which is of value not only in choosing how we are to conduct our lives, or in choosing which identities to adopt or elaborate, but also in discovering who we already are. That is why to restrict a marriage-oriented lesbian to a set of (gay, bisexual, or straight) men from which to seek a spouse, is to strike so closely at her personhood.

III

The *Baehr* court buried the observation with which I began in a footnote, qualifying it as something that might "theoretically" be true. You can see the point. At the same time, the fact that parties to a valid marriage may have any sexual orientation whatever is not *a theory*. For one thing, it is a sociological reality: think of the marriages—happy, average, or miserable—of Maynard Keynes, Harold Nicholson, Vita Sackville-West, Virginia Woolf, Stephen Spender, John Cheever, Leonard Bernstein, or Bruce Chatwin. We have no idea at all what proportion of people married to someone of another sex are not straight, or not entirely straight, but there is no doubt that it is a lot higher than anyone lets on. Second, and more important here, the "theoretical" truth is a matter of trite law. In every American state and throughout the common-law world a gay man may marry a lesbian or a straight woman, and in jurisdictions with sex-neutral marriage laws two straight women or two straight men may lawfully marry.

Let us examine more closely the relationship that includes such pairings. Civil marriage is a legal status constituted by a cluster of powers, rights, immunities, and duties. Its precise shape varies from place to place, but it typically includes powers of decision, rights of public recognition and recipience of benefits, immunity from certain kinds of intrusions on the relationship, and duties

of mutual support and fidelity. One of the primary purposes of that complex legal institution is to support the practice of social marriage, i.e. to affirm and secure valuable extra-legal relationships. Marriage has a life outside the law—indeed, it began its life outside the law. Were social or religious marriages not important in their own right civil marriage would not have the significance for us that it does. This is not to deny the existence of interaction and feedback between social practices and legal institutions. Unmarried couples living conjugally often take something like civil marriage as the model for their informal relationships, and marriage adapts (often slowly) to the changing character of the lives that its subjects live, as seen in the liberalization of divorce after women entered the workforce in massive numbers and thus became somewhat less dependent on their husbands.

The priority of the social relationship is evident in the structure of current debates. While people contest whether the law should *recognize* a marriage between people of the same sex (or among groups larger than two or, in an earlier era, between people of different races), no one denies that such marriages already exist as a matter of social or religious practice. In the United States, there are at least half a million same-sex couples living together, some of whom have had church weddings, and about a fifth of the total, including a third of the women, are raising children together.[11] In Canada, the world's first modern civil[12] marriage between couples of the same sex came into being when an Ontario court ordered that two such preexisting religious marriages be retroactively registered as legally valid.[13] However you look at it, many same-sex couples are already married. What is in issue is only whether the law owes them the kind of support, respect, and recognition that it already gives mixed-sex couples. While the laws of marriage do therefore constitute civil marriage, they do so in order to recognize and support social marriage. Attempts to justify sex-restrictions on civil marriage by reference to bald assertions about the very definition of "marriage" are thus misguided. Polygamous marriages, same-sex marriages, arranged marriages, interracial marriages, and foreign marriages are all marriages and, none of them falls anywhere near the borderline cases of what we are willing to recognize as a kind of "marriage." The live question is which of these, if any, also merit legal support.

Moral assessment of civil marriage involves a two-stage inquiry. If the underlying social relationships are vicious, for instance if they are irredeemably sexist or oppressive, then they ought not to be supported at all. Some argue that the sexist past of social marriage calls into question how far we should encourage an institution that has done so much ill. But even if the underlying relations are reparable, benign, or desirable, we still need to decide whether civil marriage is the right *way* to support them. Law may cramp, deform, or distort intimacies, as suggested by Robert Louis Stevenson's quip that marriage is "a sort of friendship recognized by the police." Legal marriage may also have distributive consequences that adversely affect those who cannot afford to marry, or cannot afford not to. Finally, there is room for concern about the package deal that marriage always is. Marriage may be a contract; but if so it is a take-it-or-leave-it contract of adhesion, subject to limited antenuptial powers to vary property arrangements and, in some jurisdictions, the grounds on which it may be terminated. Generally speaking, civil marriage is one-size-fits-all. It is supple enough to allow many couples to elaborate lives tailored to their own needs and temperaments; but they do so within the frame it permits, including not only its rights but also its duties, some of which can survive termination of the marriage.

Coming to an overall assessment of an institution that complex is no simple matter. There are arguments in favour of the integrated package: common forms allow for generic social interactions that form the basis of much of our common life, especially amongst strangers. Questions of whom to invite to dinner, who counts as next-of-kin, to whom condolences should be sent—even things as trivial as how to interpret photographs on a colleague's desk—these are all made simpler when people organize their primary relationships through marriage. Apart from such social consequences, marriage may also foster an environment that secures important individual

goods, such as stable love, intimacy, psychological security, and perhaps even personal autonomy.[14] On the other hand, marriage can also be limiting, and the artificial security and centrality that law provides it may weaken other morally valuable bonds so that, for example, deep friendships become fewer and less durable among those who marry.[15] In any case, it may well be that we can provide all the support that personal relationships deserve in some more articulated, piecemeal way, without the downside risks of marriage.

These issues are all well known, and I will not attempt an assessment here, save to note that it is clearly a vast exaggeration to suggest that civil marriage is a necessary institution or fundamental building-block of human society. (Civil marriage may be fundamental to the way the modern state counts and controls people; but that is not an argument in its favour.) I shall nonetheless suppose that a reformed but recognizable version of marriage, if not "actually existing" marriage, is a morally permissible institution and one that helps secure genuine goods for many people, even if "many" does not amount to all or even a majority.

In view of this ambivalent assessment, one of the features of marriage as we have it takes on a special significance. Throughout modern common law and civilian systems, marriage is a voluntary scheme. It contrasts with social arrangements in which girls could be married off, usually for a price, without their consent (something not to be confused with so-called "arranged" marriages, in which the arrangement is a causal, but not normative, precondition of the union). It also contrasts with the nonvoluntary duties of support and rights to property that legal systems typically impose on couples who have lived together in conjugal relations of sufficient duration or with morally serious consequences (e.g. having had children together).

Civil marriage is a status entered by exercise of a legal power, that is, a capacity to create or vary legal relations. It is one of our voluntary powers, along with the powers to make a will, settle a trust, or enter a contract. By calling this power voluntary I mean only: (i) no one has any legal duty to get married (or at least no duty that they did not themselves assume), and (ii) marriage requires the consent of both parties. This is consistent with the following: Some people (usually women) are pressured into marriage. However, unless such pressure is inconsistent with what the law regards as a voluntary exercise of their normative powers, they are legally married. Of course, there is no reason for us to be uncritical about that pressure, nor about other sorts of social inducement to marry. A woman who cannot get health insurance unless she marries a man whose job provides it marries him voluntarily in the eyes of the law. If we deplore that state of affairs, then we will need to think about what sort of healthcare system is consistent with the aspiration that marriage should never be a desperate grasp for a life raft. Nor does the centrality of consent commit us to some sort of contractualism as an adequate theory of the moral dimensions of marriage —Hegel was right to say that if marriage is established by contract, it is nonetheless a contract to transcend contractual relations. But I shall nonetheless suppose that where the institution marriage does exist, its voluntary aspect is of great value in any society as complex and fluid as our own. It has instrumental value in allowing people to create and reinforce valuable relationships with immediate effect; it also provides them with an orderly way of bringing those relationships to an end when they have failed. The voluntary aspect of marriage also has noninstrumental value, for the exchange of consents is a solemn and fitting expression of the sort of relationship that the couple initiates or confirms, a relationship of commitment, albeit with an element of give-and-take.

IV

The voluntary character of marriage is clearly expressed in the law's requirements for the capacity to marry. Age and the general capacity to enter into voluntary agreements are normally the only limits on who may marry. People must be old enough, and they must be capable of understanding and agreeing to the nature and character of the commitment—though with respect to the latter the law gives them a very wide berth. Generally speaking, anyone who can contract can also marry. There are, notoriously, also other conditions on

the validity of marriage—restrictions as to the quantity and identity of people with whom one may exercise one's marital powers (for example: no one already married, no close kin, and in some jurisdictions no one of the same sex). These regulate the shape and scope of marriage and, unlike the capacity conditions they do so in a way that is not obviously supportive of individual autonomy. So there is tension between the voluntary, contractual, aspect of marriage, and the restrictions on its shape and scope.

In light of this, consider again Justice Spina's dissent in *Goodridge*. He is correct in saying that the power to marry is not conditioned by the sexualities of the parties. This is the point I have insisted on. Not only is it true, it is important, for things might have been otherwise. The law might have required tests of sexual orientation as a condition of a marriage licence, or it might have otherwise restricted marriage to those whom it considers to be straight, or at least straight enough. Moreover, before *Goodridge*, marriage in Massachusetts was sex-restricted, so it would be hard to deny that there could be *some* rational basis for preventing people who are not straight enough from entering into a (potentially) unhappy different-sex marriage—at any rate, courts accepted much less plausible reasons as rational bases for barring gay people from openly serving in the military, or teaching in public schools, or adopting children. Those rights really are restricted by sexual orientation and they exhibit a vice of which sex-restricted marriage laws are free.

In 2006, New York's Court of Appeals considered whether there might be any rational basis for a procreationist marriage law that took no interest in whether a couple could possibly have children, unless it was for the reason that they were a same-sex couple. Justice R. S. Smith thought the answer obvious:

> While same-sex couples and opposite-sex couples are easily distinguished, limiting marriage to opposite-sex couples likely to have children would require grossly intrusive inquiries, and arbitrary and unreliable line-drawing. A legislature that regarded marriage primarily or solely as an institution for the benefit of children could rationally

find that an attempt to exclude childless opposite-sex couples from the institution would be a very bad idea.[16]

Now, the idea that same-sex and opposite-sex couples are "easily distinguished" shows a surprising lack of interest in the leading cases on the definition of "sex" for the purposes of marriage, including *Corbett v. Corbett*[17] and *Littleton v. Prange*.[18] (One of the side-benefits of a sex-neutral marriage regime is that judicial energy wasted in trying to draw lines in such cases of transsexuals' marriage can be redirected to more useful projects.) But Judge Smith's explanation fails not only for its lack of inquisitiveness, but because it misses the glaringly obvious point that *age* is a fairly reliable, nonarbitrary and nonintrusive indicator of a woman's capacity to reproduce. We have workable age floors for driving, drinking, and voting; we insist on an age floor for marrying. There is no reason that an age ceiling for marrying would be more intrusive than these, and no reason that such a rough attempt to identify women with procreative capacities would be more arbitrary than the floor's attempt to identify women with contractual capacities.

Of course, the answer lies elsewhere, and it is not far to seek. There would be something morally, and probably constitutionally, repugnant in a regime that invalidated the marriages of post-menopausal women. A legislature that so restricted marriage would be invading a particularly intimate decision, and failing to support a relationship that can bring great good to the lives of the elderly. After all, people sometimes wish to marry even on their deathbeds.

Now sexual orientation is, I acknowledged in section II, vaguer than sex. But it is not so vague that legislators and judges found themselves unable to define homosexuality in order to *stop* lesbians and gay men from serving in the military, teaching in schools, adopting children, or becoming Scout masters. Nor has its vagueness prevented more tolerant jurisdictions from being able to prohibit discrimination on grounds of sexual orientation. The reason the law does not contemplate tests of sexual orientation—or reproductive capacity—for the marriageable is

not a matter of the difficulty in designing or applying such tests; it is that such tests would be widely regarded as improper, and rightly so. Moreover, sexual orientation is generally invisible, so a marriage between a lesbian and a gay man, unlike a marriage between two straight men, need not offend conventional forms, so the usual pressures in the direction of moralistic conformism are here attenuated.

V

Let us now return to the issue of discrimination. The conceded fact that sex-restricted marriage powers have value *even* for lesbians and gay men does not show that Justice Spina was correct in denying that sex-restrictive marriage statutes discriminate on the basis of sexual orientation. The fact that a legal power is not granted on the basis of X does not show that the power does not discriminate on the grounds of X. To know that, we need to know not only who gets the power, but what the power enables them to do. Consider some examples. Suppose library cards are available to people of any religion or none, provided that they are used to borrow a Bible once a week. Suppose drivers' licences are available indifferently to men and to women, but that women are by their terms prohibited from driving alone. We would have no trouble here identifying the relevant discrimination, notwithstanding that the powers were granted on neutral grounds. Likewise, the fact that anyone in Massachusetts could, without regard to sexual orientation, use their marital powers to marry someone of a *different* sex does not begin to show that the marriage law was non-discriminatory.

Discrimination can be wrong for two different kinds of reason. First, it may deny people their entitlements owing to the bigotry, prejudice, and superstition of others. I assume the soundness of the standard modern position according to which same-sex relationships can be not only unobjectionable, but also good in ways that merit social support. (I do not pause to prove this; none of the old arguments to the contrary have any plausibility, and they flourish only among sectarian religions.) For the state irrationally to deny these relationships support is to fail in its (non-comparative) duty to protect the interests of people in those relationships. In view of the importance and character of the interests involved, this amounts to an insult to their dignity. Think of this as the vertical axis of non-discrimination. It requires acknowledging that the interests of people in same-sex relationships matter because these people and their lives matter. At a minimum, it requires preventing the prejudices and superstitions of others from affecting their life chances (and also the life chances of their children). Note, this argument does not require showing that same-sex and different-sex conjugal relationships are the *same*, or *equally* good, or even *comparable*—it requires only showing that each is *good enough*, perhaps in its own unique way, to merit the kinds of support that marriage laws can provide, and that to refuse this support on irrational grounds amounts to discrimination.

But there is also a second, horizontal axis of dimension to which comparison is more central. Here, the nerve of the argument is that what different-sex couples *already* have, same-couples should *also* have. I said above that civil marriage is, morally speaking, a close call: it is a permissible, but not morally necessary, institution. Perhaps it would be better if no one had these powers—perhaps, as critics from the right and left have often suggested, the state should get out of the marriage business entirely and protect the secular interests in other ways, leaving religions and other voluntary associations free to define their marriages however they please. But until this happens, everyone similarly situated should not only have some power to marry, they should, as far as this turns on public policy, get the same value from that power. I am not here endorsing the general principle that no one should get a benefit unless everyone else also gets it. When we are dealing with goods that are scarce or indivisible, that policy can be wasteful. But those considerations plainly do not apply in this case. (Or if they do, they do not favour rationing by sexual orientation.) Moreover, in our actual circumstances, the horizontal inequality constitutes a dignitary wrong, for the comparative disadvantage treats homosexual relationships and,

derivatively, those who have best reason to enter them, as second class.

The presence of such discrimination is not inconsistent with gay people getting *some* value from sex-restricted powers of marriage. For one thing, it is worth quite a lot to bisexual people. For another, some gay people might want to enter a different-sex marriage for many of the reasons straight people do: money, immigration, insurance, family, companionship, and, no doubt in some cases, love.[19] Neither of these points negates the burden of discrimination in other cases.

VI

I have been stressing the voluntary character of the power to marry as relevant to the justification for the law's indifference to sexuality when it comes to capacity. Some think there is an objection to this argument. Robert George, for example, asserts:

> Professor Bradley and I defend [a] conception of marriage ... which we believe to be reflected in traditional American and British marriage law, especially in the law governing consummation of marriage. We argue that marriage is a one-flesh (i.e., bodily, as well as emotional, dispositional, and spiritual) union of a male and a female spouse consummated and actualized by sexual acts that are reproductive in type.[20]

On George's account, particular sexual capacities are a necessary component of marriage, for it is only a certain kind of sex act that can actualize a "one-flesh" union, and that union is what marriage *essentially* is. This is not the obvious point that the law of marriage was shaped by an interest in children and child rearing. It is a metaphysical conjecture wholly unrelated to the civil law of marriage.

Actually, it is doubtful that any intelligible secular principle can be wrought from the "one-flesh" dogma—unless it is the beautiful idea that Plato's Aristophanes provides as a metaphor for the unifying power of love. Of course, Aristophanes would have laughed at the suggestion that a longing for one's other half is limited to a half of the opposite sex. His speech in the *Symposium* praises the universality of such love. The "one-flesh" dogma is a familiar enough piece of sectarian ideology—an ideology ostentatiously unconcerned with basic truths about human psychology and biology—but it is foreign to our legal systems. The common law never required that marriage be consummated by a sexual act that is "reproductive in type." That is a tenet of the Roman Church, which holds that a marriage between baptised Catholics becomes indissoluble only after they "have in a human manner engaged together in a conjugal act in itself apt for the generation of offspring."[21] That requirement is, at least in theory, stringent about what it is to engage in sex in a "human manner": it wants a heterosexual penetrative sex act in which a penis ejaculates into a vagina, preferably uninhibited by "unnatural" barriers.[22]

The common law always took a more parsimonious view. Although it delicately describes the act, in the words of great nineteenth century jurist Dr Lushington, as "ordinary and complete intercourse,"[23] its idea of what that amounts to may be surprising. Consummation at common law was nothing less, but emphatically nothing more, than the penetration of a vagina by a penis to a sufficient depth and duration to please the trier of fact. Since it was a test of capacity, one such act was enough. The act did not need to be enjoyable for either party—what we would now regard as marital rape was, as an instance of consummation, just fine. Since it had nothing to do with procreation, so far from being "reproductive in type," it could be an act whose very nature was incompatible with orgasm on the husband's part. It could be deliberately undertaken at a time or in a manner when it was biologically certain that it would not be reproductive in type. What's more, before the law would take any interest in it, a failure to consummate a marriage had to have a particular causal history: preferably, a physical or psychological incapacity and, if on the part of the petitioner, a permanent incapacity unknown to himself at the time of the marriage. Willful refusal to have sex would generally not support nullity[24] (presumably on the theory that those who willfully refuse might change their minds), though some courts were satisfied if the requisite act felt "invincibly repugnant" to the petitioner.[25]

Notice that the capacity to consummate a sex-restricted marriage is very undemanding. In all likelihood almost all lesbians and gay men possess it. A lesbian, after all, is not in the standard case a woman who *cannot* have sex with men, she is a woman who does not much *enjoy* having sex with men. (In this respect, lesbians have something in common with some of their straight sisters, but with the compensating advantage of enjoying sex with women.) One might suppose that, in light of the act prescribed for consummation, not enjoying heterosexual activity would have an asymmetric consequence for men. The evidence refutes it. The incapacity to sustain arousal sufficient for one performance of the specified act is untypical of homosexuals of either sex: many gay men have had sex with women, and gave it up only because they found it unenjoyable, or at any rate less enjoyable than sex with men.

A typical lesbian and gay man could successfully consummate a mixed-sex marriage, if they wished. And if they did not? Would those unconsummated marriages be invalid, and does that not show that sex is, after all, central to the creation of a valid marriage? It does not, and this principle long antedates the common law. From the time of the Roman lawyers, marriage was validated not by sex but by consent. We read in the Digest, "*Nuptias non concubitus sed consensus facit.*"[26] Common lawyers ultimately adopted the same view. Blackstone's *Commentaries* would summarize matters this way:

> Our law considers marriage in no other light than as a civil contract.... And, taking it in this civil light, the law treats it as it does all other contracts; allowing it to be good and valid in all cases, where the parties at the time of making it were, in the first place, willing to contract; secondly, able to contract; and, lastly, actually did contract, in the proper forms and solemnities required by law.[27]

This did coexist with the doctrine of nullity. But that is consistent with the ancient rule that the formation and validity of a marriage depends on consent alone. Failure to consummate a marriage may leave it voidable, that is, open to being annulled by a court—but only under very stringent conditions and only at the request of one of the parties. Matters are different when a putative marriage fails to satisfy one of its constitutive conditions. A "marriage" of someone who is underage, who lacks the capacity to consent, who did not in fact consent, or, at common law, who is of the same sex, creates no legal relations in the first place.[28] Such marriages are void as a consequence of their failure to satisfy constitutive conditions of marriage. An unconsummated marriage is a different matter. Unless and until some court is requested to act, and acts, it is valid, gives rise to all the rights and duties of marriage, and is entitled to be recognized as such for all legal purposes. Moreover, the courts would not intervene to void an unconsummated marriage except at the initiative of one of the parties, and then only in the lifetime of the couple. In effect, the law of consummation gave the spouses another voluntary power: the power to apply to have their marriage annulled, if they wished, on certain narrowly defined grounds. It did not establish a validity condition for marriage; it did not constitute a marriage; it did not define the concept of marriage.

This limited power to apply for nullification, restricted in the ways that it is, was another means by which the law promoted individual autonomy and privacy. It gave people a way to re-shape their lives after a significant relationship failed them. Remember that, in the formative era of this doctrine, fornication was not only a sin but a crime, and that divorce was impossible or difficult, so there was in theory (and sometimes in practice) no reliable way for people to satisfy themselves beforehand that their betrothed would turn out to have the sexual capacities they were hoping for.

The law did presume that people contracting a marriage envisioned a sexual relationship as one of its features, which relationship would be frustrated if either of the parties lacked the requisite capacity. In that context, and in solicitude for the privacy of marriage, a second-best solution was to give them a special power of exit if things did not turn out as the law presumed them to want. That this was a rebuttable presumption is shown by the fact that if they did not care to have sex the courts would themselves take no interest in that fact and

their marriage would remain forever valid. Nor would the courts permit anyone *else* to apply to have their marriage annulled on the suspicion that they were not having sex. So far from making a certain sex act part of the essence of marriage, the common law of nullity reflects and supports the idea that all that is a matter reserved to the couple. Indeed, in spite of its other differences even canon law presumes that spouses who have lived together after the celebration of their marriage have consummated it, unless the contrary is proven,[29] which, in the nature of things, leaves it pretty much in the hands of the couple.

So the law of consummation neither contradicts nor even qualifies the central truth that in the traditional law of marriage, the essence of the relationship is not coitus but consensus. Unsurprisingly, then, that law was indifferent to the sexual orientation of the parties to *any* marriage and, as I said, different-sex marriages between homosexuals are everywhere valid. Justice Spina wrote: "Whether an individual chooses not to marry because of sexual orientation or any other reason should be of no concern to the court." We can revise that mistaken dictum in a way that more accurately represents matters: "Whether a person chooses *not* to have sex with another, because of his sexual orientation or any other reason, inside marriage or out, should be of no concern to a court." And who would deny that? The traditional law of marriage did not.

If sex matters so little to marriage, then procreation matters even less, since potentially reproductive sex is only a (very small) proper subset of all human sex acts. In fact, the religious ideology according to which the essence of marriage is connected to reproductive capacity is something that intrudes in the case law only *after* lesbians and gay men began litigating for marriage rights. In 1948, when such cases were unimaginable, the House of Lords denied a man an annulment whose suspicious wife refused to have sex with him unless he used a condom, stating that procreation "does not appear to be a principle end of marriage as understood in Christendom."[30] That may have been contrary to the *Book of Common Prayer*, but it was, and remains, a fair statement about civil marriage.

VII

I have been exploring some issues in the law of marriage as it stands; I conclude with a reformist proposal. The nullity of same-sex marriages never had anything to do with consummation. Quite the contrary: the penis–vagina definition of consummation was a *consequence* of the sex-restricted definition of marriage, and the parties' sexual capacities got such legal relevance as they had only after a marriage had been established by their own consent. The problem for same-sex couples was that the law would not let them get to square one. That is why the House of Lords, struggling in 1970 with the question of the validity of a transsexual's marriage, said "sex is clearly an essential determinant of the relationship called marriage, because it is and always has been recognised as the union of man and woman. It is the institution on which the family is built, and in which the capacity for natural heterosexual intercourse is an essential element."[31] There are many troubling things in this decision but the Lords are on firm ground in saying that the rationale runs *from* the declared necessity for different sexes in a marriage *to* the criteria for consummation, here interpreted as involving the "capacity for natural heterosexual intercourse." But for the Lords' worry that the Corbetts' was a putative marriage between two people who were, in their opinion, people of the same sex, there would have been no independent worry about consummation. It is a nice question, then, what should become of the doctrine of nullity in jurisdictions whose sex-neutral marriage laws have resolved the Lords' initial worry.

One Canadian judge, writing before Parliament removed the sex restriction on the power to marry, thought this constituted an independent objection to the validity of same-sex marriage. "A change of the nature proposed would create new issues of social and community concern," he wrote. "For example, a marriage not consummated by intercourse is voidable. There is no evidence before me as to what would constitute consummation in a gay or lesbian relationship if it should be a factor in the formation of the relationship at all."[32] Now, the idea that there would

be "community concern" about how same-sex couples might consummate their marriages is bizarre. Moreover, as I argued above, consummation was never a factor in the formation of marriage in the first place. But we can reformulate the question: If an unconsummated marriage is voidable, what sex acts should be taken to consummate the marriage of a same-sex couple? Not the penis–vagina transaction that does the trick for different-sex couples. As I said, most lesbians and gay men can perform that act, but the doctrine of consummation requires, not a free-floating sexual capacity, but a capacity actualized with one's spouse. There is no need here to fuss about counterfactual conditionals: if the spouses in a marriage cannot come up with at least one penis and one vagina between them there is no question of applying to them the common law rule. But what is the alternative? Should we require some analogical act? This would be both legally and morally unsatisfactory. How are we to determine which acts are adequately analogical—which aspects of the penis–vagina transaction must be preserved under the transformation, and why? And should the analogical act—or disjunctive list of acts—be the same for male couples as for female ones? Or should we say that same-sex marriages are consummated by whatever sex acts the couples choose, at least when they can come to an agreement?

It is difficult to warm to any of these proposals, not least because in a sex-neutral marriage regime they seem unfair to *different*-sex couples. Consider this: as things stand, an incapacity for, or invincible repugnance to, oral, manual, or anal sex will not give grounds for annulling a different-sex marriage—not even if that has been someone's highest erotic hope for the marriage. No annulment for them—they will either have to get therapy or a divorce. Why then should the expectations of same-sex couples be treated more favourably? The better answer is that the power to nullify a marriage on grounds of any sort of sexual incapacity should now be terminated by the courts or, where they lack that power, by legislation. Divorce laws should permit people to leave marriages they find sexually unsatisfying; and if they are so opposed to divorce that they cannot bring themselves to do that, they had better satisfy themselves before entering the marriage that they will be able to find some kind of sexual satisfaction thereafter.

The fixation on a sex act that guaranteed littlebeyond an erectable penis and penetrable vagina—a standard that took no notice of procreation or of pleasure, and one that could be brutally satisfied by an act that was in all but name rape—is not a fixation of which the law should remain proud, and certainly not one that it should extend by some contorted analogy into the realm of sex-neutral marriage. Sex, and sexuality, never mattered that much to the law of marriage in the first place; we should clear the remaining residue of a world well lost.

NOTES

1. *Baehr v. Lewin*, 74 Haw 530, 580, 852 P 2d 44, 67 (1993).
2. Id., at 544 n 11, 852 P 2d 52, n 11.
3. Nina Baehr won her case in Hawaii, but lost her marriage when the voters amended the state constitution in order to prevent her marrying.
4. *Goodridge et al v. Department of Public Health et al*, 440 Mass. 309, 351, 798 N.E.2d 941, 975 (2004).
5. On the moral significance of sex, see Haslanger, Sally "Gender, Race: (What) Are They? (What) Do We Want Them To Be?" *Noûs* 34 (2000): 31–55.
6. Butler, Judith. *Bodies that Matter: On the Discursive Limits of "Sex."* London: Routledge, 1993. 2–3. One who flirts with the idea that sex is gender, but cannot quite bring himself to argue for it, is Thomas Laqueur in his *Making Sex: Body and Gender from the Greeks to Freud*. Cambridge, Mass.: Harvard University Press, 1985.
7. "Presumed," because people are generally held to the gender norms of the sex they *present*; only when they fail to pass are they held to the gender norms of the sex they actually *are*. (This does not suppose that a person's actual sex is his or her sex at birth; it supposes only there can be a distinction between what someone is and how he is regarded.) One's presumed sex may be determined by gender presentation, but that does not show that sex is gender.
8. Wittig, Monique. "The Straight Mind." *The Straight Mind and Other Essays*. Boston: Beacon Press 1992. 32.
9. Andrew Koppelman has been a tireless advocate of this strategy in the United States. See Koppelman, Andrew. "Why Discrimination Against Lesbians and Gay Men is Sex Discrimination." 69 *NYUL Rev* 197 (1994). For criticism see Stein, Edward. "Evaluating the Sex Discrimination Argument for Lesbian and Gay Rights." 49 *UCLA L Rev* 471 (2001), and in reply see Koppelman. "Defending The Sex Discrimination Argument for Lesbian and Gay Rights: A Reply to Edward Stein." 49 *UCLA L Rev* 539 (2001).
10. See Green, Leslie. "Sexuality, Authenticity, and Modernity." *Philosophy of Law*. 5th Ed. Eds. Joel Feinberg and Jules Coleman. Boston: Wadsworth, 1999. 538–48.
11. Simmons, Tavia and O'Connell, Martin. "Married-Couple and Unmarried-Partner Households: 2000." *Census 2000 Special Reports*. US Census Bureau, February 2003.
12. On the reason for the qualification, see Boswell, John. *Same Sex Unions in Premodern Europe*. New York: Villard Books, 1994.
13. *Halpern v. Canada (Attorney General)* (2003) 65 OR (3d) 161; (2003), 225 DLR (4th) 529.
14. For an (ambitious) argument that marriage helps spouses achieve individual autonomy, see Bennett, Christopher. "Liberalism, Autonomy, and Conjugal Love" 9 *Res Publica* 285 (2003).
15. Americans' networks of people with whom they can discuss important matters seem to be shrinking to the married couple: Macpherson, Miller, Smith-Lovin, Lynne, and Brashears, Matthew. "Social Isolation in America." 71 *Am Soc Rev* 353 (2006). The authors suppose that the intensification of marital ties is a *consequence* of the weakening of other relationships; it would be interesting to test the opposite causal hypothesis, that the valorization of marriage in the United States *produces* social isolation.
16. *Hernandez v. Robles*, 855 NE 2d 1 20, 7 NY 3d 388, 365 (2006).
17. *Corbett v. Corbett* (otherwise Ashley) 2 All ER 33 (PDA 1970).
18. *Littleton v. Prange* 9 SW 3d 223 (Tex App 1999), *cert denied*, 531 US 872 (2000).
19. See Whitney, Catherine and Henny, Christine. *Uncommon Lives: Gay Men and Straight Women*. New York: New American Library, 1991.
20. George, Robert P. "Public Reason and Political Conflict: Abortion and Homosexuality." 106 *Yale L J* 2475 (1997): 2497.

21. Canon 1061.1. *The Canon Law: Letter and Spirit.* Canon Law Society of Great Britain and Ireland. Collegeville, Minn: Liturgical Press, 1995.

22. For commentary, see id., at 2073.

23. *D-E v. A-G (falsely calling herself D-E)* (1845) 1 Rob Eccl 279, 298.

24. *Heil v. Heil*, (1942) SCR 160. England introduced willful refusal to consummate a marriage as a statutory ground for nullity in 1937, and it is still present: *Matrimonial Causes Act* 1973, s 12(b). The Church of England opposed the introduction of "wilful refusal" as a ground of nullity, see Church of England, *The Church and the Law of Nullity of Marriage* (SPCK 1955) 31–32.

25. *Gajamugan v. Gajamugan* (1979), 10 RFL (2d) 280 (Ont H Ct).

26. 30, Ulp 1 36 ad Sabinum.

27. Blackstone, William. *Commentaries on the Laws of England*. Book 1 ch 15. Philadelphia: J.B. Lippincott Co., 1893. He goes on to cite the Digest on the primacy of *consensus* over *concubitus*.

28. Though courts have on equitable grounds ordered property settlements and even support of a former "spouse" notwithstanding a nullity.

29. Canon 1061.2.

30. *Baxter v. Baxter* [1948] 2 All ER 886.

31. *Corbett v. Corbett* (otherwise Ashley) [1970] 2 All ER 33.

32. *EGALE Canada Inc v. Canada (Attorney General of)*, [2001] BCLR (3d) 122, Reversed on appeal: Barbeau *v British Columbia (Attorney General)*, [2003] 13 BCLR (4th) 1.

CHAPTER FIFTEEN

Law and Economics

48   Welfare Economics and Notions of Fairness

LOUIS KAPLOW AND STEVEN SHAVELL

In section A, we discuss the basic nature of welfare economics, and, in section B, we describe the fundamental difference between normative evaluation that employs notions of fairness and evaluation that is based on welfare economics. In section C, we provide an overview of our critique of the use of notions of fairness in the assessment of legal policy. Finally, in section D, we comment on the correspondence between notions of fairness and social norms of everyday life, and we consider how this correspondence helps to explain the appeal that notions of fairness possess. As we explain in this section, the reasons that notions of fairness have some attraction do not justify the use of the notions as independent principles in evaluating legal rules.

A. WELFARE ECONOMICS

In economic analysis that is designed to evaluate social policy, two steps are necessarily involved. The first is to determine the effects of the policy, that is, to undertake positive analysis, for the effects of the policy will enter into its assessment. To evaluate a legal rule concerning driving behavior, for example, one must ascertain the rule's influence on accident frequency.

The second step is to evaluate the effects of the policy in order to determine its social desirability, that is, to engage in normative analysis. This step involves the framework of welfare economics and is our focus in the present section and throughout the book. The hallmark of welfare economics is that policies are assessed exclusively in terms of their effects on the well-being of individuals. Accordingly, whatever is relevant to individuals' well-being is relevant under welfare economics, and whatever is unrelated to individuals' well-being is excluded from consideration under welfare economics. Because of the central importance of the concept of well-being to welfare economics and to understanding how analysis under that approach differs from analysis based on notions of fairness, we devote subsection 1 to an elaboration of the idea of well-being. There we emphasize that well-being is to be understood expansively, to include everything that is of concern to an individual.

From *Fairness versus Welfare*. Cambridge, Mass.: Harvard University Press, 2002. Reprinted with permission of the publisher.

To complete the assessment of a policy under welfare economics, it is necessary to aggregate the information about each individual's well-being to form an overall social judgment. We discuss this aspect of welfare economics in subsection 2. Because under welfare economics the evaluation of a policy depends on how it influences individuals' well-being and on nothing else, the ultimate judgment about a policy under welfare economics is clear in cases in which all individuals are made better off or all are made worse off by the policy. When, however, some individuals gain and others lose under a policy—that is, when the policy affects the distribution of income and well-being—the welfare-economic approach requires one to make a distributive judgment, a point that we elaborate in subsection 3. But the assessment under welfare economics is still based exclusively on how the policy affects individuals' well-being.

Before proceeding with our discussion of the nature of welfare economics, let us consider how welfare economic analysis of legal policy is conducted. Suppose that an analyst wishes to compare a regime of negligence-based liability for automobile accidents with a pure no-fault insurance regime. Initially, the analyst would engage in positive analysis, which involves identifying differences in the effects of the regimes; under welfare economics, the relevant differences are those that pertain to individuals' well-being. Thus, the analyst would examine the influence of liability on driving behavior, taking into account that liability creates incentives to drive safely, that these incentives are mitigated by drivers' ownership of liability insurance, and other factors. Also, the analyst would consider that important incentives to drive safely exist even under a no-fault regime, namely, drivers' concerns about injury to themselves and about traffic laws. In addition, the analyst would identify the effects of the two regimes on the financial risks that individuals bear. Under the negligence regime, victims of automobile accidents would receive compensation through the legal system when they suffered harm due to negligence, and the extent of compensation would depend on injuring drivers' assets and liability insurance coverage; of course, victims might also possess their own first-party insurance coverage.

Under a no-fault regime, all victims would be compensated through first-party insurance coverage. Furthermore, the analyst would compare the aggregate administrative costs under the two regimes, that is, litigation costs plus private insurance costs under the negligence regime versus insurance costs under the no-fault regime.

After identifying the various effects of the two regimes on individuals' well-being, the analyst employing welfare economics would combine them to make an overall evaluation of the regimes. For example, if individuals tend to be alike—to drive for similar amounts of time, to pose and be subject to essentially equal accident risks—the analyst would simply determine the net of all of the costs and benefits of each system and choose the one producing the greatest net benefit per person. If, however, individuals differ in relevant respects, the analyst would have to consider distributive issues as well. Suppose, for example, that adopting a no-fault regime would produce large gains for the middle class and the wealthy and result in small losses to the poor, and that the analyst viewed this distributive effect negatively. Then the analyst would favor the no-fault regime only if the adverse effect on distribution were modest relative to its other benefits, or if there were some other way (notably through income taxes and transfer programs) to compensate the poor. Under welfare economics, the analyst would consider these and other factors relevant to individuals' well-being, but the analyst would not take into account factors that do not bear on individuals' well-being, notably, whether liability under the negligence rule is required by corrective justice or other notions of fairness that some would accord independent significance.

1. Individuals' Well-Being

Under welfare economics, normative evaluations are based on the well-being of individuals. Economists often use the term "utility" to refer to the well-being of an individual, and, when there is uncertainty about future events, economists use an ex-ante measurement of well-being, "expected utility."[1]

The notion of well-being used in welfare economics is comprehensive in nature. It incorporates in a positive way everything that an individual might value—goods and services that the individual can consume, social and environmental amenities, personally held notions of fulfillment, sympathetic feelings for others, and so forth. Similarly, an individual's well-being reflects in a negative way harms to his or her person and property, costs and inconveniences, and anything else that the individual might find distasteful. Well-being is not restricted to hedonistic and materialistic enjoyment or to any other named class of pleasures and pains.[2] The only limit on what is included in well-being is to be found in the minds of individuals themselves, not in the minds of analysts.[3]

We note that the concept of well-being, which covers situations involving uncertainty, incorporates the value of protection against risk. Accordingly, well-being is generally increased by the availability of insurance and other means of compensation, including legal redress for injury. In the language of economics, individuals generally are risk averse and thus are made better off by insurance, or implicit insurance, against financial risk.[4]

We further note a particular source of well-being that has special relevance to our book, namely, the possibility that individuals have a taste for a notion of fairness, just as they may have a taste for art, nature, or fine wine. For example, an individual might derive pleasure from knowing that vicious criminals receive their just deserts (independent of the anticipated effects of punishment on the incidence of crime) or that legal rules reflect a favored conception of fairness.[5] In such cases, satisfying the principle of fairness enhances the individual's well-being, just as would satisfying his preference for wine. (Our discussion of social norms in section D will help to explain why individuals may in fact have tastes regarding notions of fairness.)[6]

One should sharply distinguish the preceding observation—about how tastes for notions of fairness, when they exist, are a component of individuals' well-being and thus are relevant under welfare economics—from the views about notions of fairness that we criticize in this book. Under those views, notions of fairness are held to be direct bases for legal policy assessment and to possess importance independent of whether individuals have tastes for the notions (in the sense that satisfaction of such tastes affects their well-being). Under welfare economics, by contrast, the relevance to policy analysis of a notion of fairness depends solely on how much, if at all, individuals' well-being is affected by their tastes for fairness. As a consequence, the welfare economic importance of fairness depends on what individuals' tastes happen to be and thus involves a question that is entirely empirical in character; philosophers' or policy analysts' views of which notions of fairness should be endorsed by members of an enlightened society are irrelevant. It is our understanding, however, that legal academics, policy analysts, philosophers, and others who invoke notions of fairness when assessing legal policy do not view their arguments and concerns as involving individuals' actual tastes (although they may well believe in some instances that many people are in agreement with them, or they may wish to convince others to adopt their beliefs).[7] Rather, they believe that notions of fairness should serve as independent principles to be used in assessing legal policy. Hence, the role of notions of fairness under welfare economics—solely as a taste that individuals might have—is quite different from the role of notions of fairness that we will be criticizing.

Before continuing, we observe that we will usually assume that individuals comprehend fully how various situations affect their well-being and that there is no basis for anyone to question their conception of what is good for them. Therefore, when we say that an individual is better off, there will be no doubt about what we mean. We focus on instances in which well-being is unambiguous because our purpose is to address whether legal policy analysis should consider solely effects on individuals' well-being—however that notion is best understood or measured—or also (or instead) should consider factors that are independent of individuals' well-being. We note, however, that our assumption that well-being is unambiguous is one of convenience; if individuals do not understand how situations affect their well-being, our argument may be applied to individuals' actual well-being—what they would prefer if they correctly understood how they would be affected—rather than to individuals' well-being as reflected in their mistaken preferences.[8] In any event, questions about which legal policies actually promote individuals' well-being are logically distinct from whether and to what extent well-being should be the focus of policy assessment in the first place.

2. Social Welfare and Individuals' Well-Being

Under the rubric of welfare economics, the conception of social welfare is based on individuals' well-being. Specifically, social welfare is postulated to be an increasing function of individuals' well-being and to depend on no other factors. It is also generally supposed that each individual's well-being affects social welfare in a symmetric manner, which is to say that the idea of social welfare incorporates a basic notion of equal concern for all individuals.

In several different respects, the approach of welfare economics involves value judgments. First, value judgments underlie the assumptions that social welfare depends on individuals' well-being, that this dependence is positive, and that factors unrelated to individuals' well-being are irrelevant. In other words, to adopt welfare economics is to adopt the moral position that one should be concerned, positively and exclusively, with individuals' well-being. Moreover, because analysts generally assume that each individual's well-being affects social welfare in a symmetric manner, welfare economics is understood to include, as we said, a requirement that individuals count equally in an important sense.

Second, a method of aggregation is of necessity an element of welfare economics, and value judgments are involved in aggregating different individuals' well-being into a single measure of social welfare. The choice of a method of aggregation involves the adoption of a view concerning matters of distribution (as we explore further in subsection 3). Various methods of aggregation are possible. For example, under the utilitarian approach, social welfare is taken to be the sum of

individuals' utilities. Alternatively, the well-being of worse-off individuals might be given additional weight, as under the approach associated with John Rawls, wherein social welfare corresponds to the utility of the worst-off individuals. In this book, we do not defend any specific way of aggregating individuals' well-being; that is, we do not endorse any particular view about the proper distribution of well-being or income. Rather, we argue, in essence, that legal policy analysis should be guided by reference to *some* coherent way of aggregating individuals' well-being, in contrast to the view that policy analysis should be guided by notions of fairness and thus, at least in part, without regard to individuals' well-being.

To some readers, there may appear to be a tension between our accepting the legitimacy of distributive judgments within welfare economics and our criticizing notions of fairness, particularly since many views about distribution are expressed using the language of fairness. In fact, however, there is no tension, because of the manner in which we define notions of fairness for purposes of this inquiry and because of the substance of our criticism. As we elaborate in section B and throughout the book, our definition of notions of fairness includes all principles—but only those principles—that give weight to factors that are independent of individuals' well-being. And, as we elaborate in the next subsection, distribution can play an important role even under a system of evaluation that is concerned exclusively with individuals' well-being. Moreover, the criticisms of notions of fairness that we offer are not criticisms of the language that analysts use or of the need to make value judgments in assessing legal policy; rather, they are specific criticisms of giving weight to factors that are independent of individuals' well-being. Hence, our analysis does not affect distributive judgments that are confined to individuals' well-being.

3. Comments on Social Welfare and the Distribution of Income

In this subsection, we elaborate on how questions about the distribution of income[9] fit within the framework of welfare economics, especially because the relevance of income distribution under welfare economics contrasts sharply with the popular view that income distribution is unimportant under normative economic analysis of law.

Our main point is that many basic concerns about the overall distribution of income are encompassed by the welfare economic approach.[10] This can be seen by reflecting on the implications of the fact that social welfare depends on individuals' well-being. First, the distribution of income will matter to social welfare because a dollar of income often will raise the utility of some individuals more than that of others. Notably, redistributing income from the rich to the poor will tend to raise social welfare, assuming that the marginal utility of income is greater for the poor than for the rich.[11] Second, the distribution of income may matter to social welfare because it affects the distribution of well-being, and, under the welfare-economic approach, social welfare may depend directly on how equally well-being is distributed among individuals. For example, as previously noted, more weight might be placed on the well-being of less-well-off individuals, in which case social welfare would tend to be higher if income were redistributed from the better off to the worse off (independently of whether the marginal utility of income for the worse off were greater than that for the better off).[12] Third, the distribution of income may matter to social welfare because some individuals' well-being may depend directly on the distribution of income, as when individuals feel sympathy toward those who are less fortunate.[13] We also note that, in accord with the foregoing, there is a substantial body of work by economists on matters concerning income distribution.[14]

The significance of the distribution of income under welfare economics raises the question of why much normative economic analysis of social policy and, in particular, of law does not address distributive concerns directly. To a degree, this omission may reflect some analysts' lack of concern about the distribution of income.[15] However, we now wish to explain why ignoring distributive effects in legal policy analysis is often the most sensible course even though the distribution of income is generally viewed to be important, as it is under welfare economics.

First, when undertaking any kind of analysis, it is often useful to focus on certain factors in order best to understand their effects, leaving other considerations aside. Thus, as a matter of analytical convenience, economists may choose to study stylized models in which individuals' well-being and social welfare are determined in a simple manner, and, in particular, one in which the distribution of income does not affect social welfare.[16] For example, in a model of accidents, we might consider a hypothetical world where individuals' well-being and social welfare depend only on a simple aggregate, such as total accident losses plus prevention costs plus legal administrative costs.[17] Such a model and social goal would be useful to examine if the purpose were to understand accident prevention and incentives. Use of the model would hardly mean that the analyst actually considered the distribution of income (or other factors, such as risk-bearing costs) to be irrelevant to the determination of true social welfare.

Second, many legal rules probably have little effect on the distribution of income. For example, in contractual settings, price adjustments will often negate the distributive effects of rules (if a seller is adversely affected by a rule, he will raise his price). In important tort domains, such as automobile accidents, injurers and victims will, on average, tend to have similar incomes; hence, the distributive effects of the choice of legal rules will be small. Likewise, in many areas of corporate law, most investors will be on each side of a type of transaction (approximately) equally often, so any distributive effects of rules that are favorable to one type of party will tend to cancel out in the balance. If legal rules are likely to have little distributive effect, it will do little harm to ignore this effect in the analysis.

Third, when legal rules do have distributive effects, the effects usually should not be counted as favoring or disfavoring the rules because distributional objectives can often be best accomplished directly, using the income tax and transfer (welfare) programs. One reason economists have tended to favor these direct means of redistribution is that they reach all individuals and are based explicitly on income. In contrast, particular legal rules affect only relatively small fractions of the population and ordinarily constitute relatively crude means of redistribution. For example, a pro-plaintiff tort rule will affect only people involved in accidents, and the resulting redistribution will be haphazard because whether and to what extent plaintiffs are poorer than defendants will vary greatly from context to context. In addition, the income tax and transfer programs tend to involve less distortion and inefficiency than does redistribution through legal rules. The reason is that redistribution through legal rules entails both the inefficiency of redistribution generally (due to adverse effects on work incentives) and the additional cost involved in adopting less efficient legal rules.

It therefore appears that there are sound reasons for much normative economic analysis of law not to take explicit account of the distribution of income.[18] As we have stressed, these reasons derive from judgments about the best ways to organize analysis and to accomplish distributive objectives, not from a belief that distributive concerns lack normative importance. If these reasons are inapplicable in a particular setting, a proper welfare economic analysis will take distributional concerns into account.

The foregoing analysis helps to illuminate the view that the appropriate social goal is "wealth maximization"; maximizing the total dollar value of, or willingness to pay for, social resources. Many legal academics seem to be under the impression that wealth maximization is *the* economic measure of social welfare. This belief is perhaps not surprising, both because wealth maximization possesses some intuitive appeal and because it is the goal that Richard Posner advanced two decades ago in the most sustained attempt by a legal scholar to defend a normative law and economics approach. However, wealth—and thus wealth maximization—is not a well-defined concept; to compute wealth, one must know the prices of different goods and services, yet there is no natural set of prices to use.[19] More important, and more obvious, even if we possessed an unambiguous way of computing wealth, wealth still would not constitute a measure of social welfare under

welfare economics, because wealth is not defined in terms of individuals' well-being. As we have explained, a measure of social welfare under welfare economics must be a function of individuals' well-being. (This observation also reconciles the fact that total wealth is independent of its distribution, with the point that distributive concerns may be an important determinant of social welfare under welfare economics.)

As a practical matter, though, the defects in the conceptual and normative foundations of wealth maximization do not imply that analysis based on wealth maximization will usually be misguided. As we have mentioned, it may be analytically useful to study models in which social welfare equals some simple wealth-like aggregate.[20] In addition, maximization of wealth (defined, perhaps, with respect to current prices) may in fact reasonably approximate maximization of social welfare in many contexts. Thus, under welfare economics, although wealth is not in itself deemed to be valuable, analysis that assesses policies based on their aggregate impact on wealth will often prove useful. (We observe that the preceding point about wealth applies as well to "efficiency." Efficiency is also a concept that captures aggregate effects of policies on individuals' well-being, and invocations of efficiency should thus be understood to entail a concern for individuals' well-being rather than obeisance to some technical or accounting notion.[21] Moreover, that efficiency does not reflect a concern for the distribution of income indicates that efficiency, like wealth, is only a proxy measure of social welfare, and one that is incomplete in an important respect.)

Finally, to avoid possible confusion, we offer a comment on the meaning of the term "distribution." Here, we use the term to refer to concerns about the overall allocation of income or wealth—that is, about economic equality and inequality—of the sort we outline at the beginning of this subsection. However, concerns about who should prevail in a particular legal dispute are also often described as distributive. In such contexts, the word "distributive" refers to the allocation of a particular loss between the disputing parties (rather than to the degree of inequality in the distribution of income in the society), and the appropriate allocation is understood to be determined by notions of fairness such as corrective justice (rather than by a conception of the appropriate distribution of income in society as a whole).[22] Welfare economics is not concerned with distribution in this situational sense per se, although the division of losses between parties to disputes may often affect individuals' well-being in a number of respects.[23]

4. Concluding Remark

Our portrayal of welfare economics probably differs from the understanding that many legal academics (and others) have of the normative basis of law and economics, particularly with regard to the conception of individuals' well-being and the relevance of the distribution of income. In part, this divergence in views may exist because the welfare economic framework developed by economists has not been adequately presented in legal academic discourse.[24] In any event, we hope that our providing a fuller description of welfare economics will lead to a better appreciation of its appeal. We also hope that the foregoing discussion will clarify the contrast between welfare economics and policy assessment based on notions of fairness.

B. NOTIONS OF FAIRNESS

1. The Basic Nature of Notions of Fairness

Notions of fairness—which we take in this book to include ideas of justice, rights, and related concepts—provide justification and language for legal policy decisions.[25] For example, under corrective justice, an individual who wrongfully injures another must compensate him, a requirement that has implications for the design of tort law. Under the promise-keeping principle, individuals must keep promises, and by extension they must perform their contracts. Under retributive justice, punishment should be in proportion to the gravity of wrongful acts, and thus criminal sanctions should fit the crimes committed.[26]

Although it does not seem possible to adduce a general definition of notions of fairness because they are so many and varied, we can identify a feature that is common to all notions of fairness that concern us in this book and that is central to our argument. *Notions of fairness have the property that evaluations relying on them are not based exclusively—and sometimes are not dependent at all—on how legal policies affect individuals' well-being.*[27] Indeed, some analysis based on notions of fairness is entirely nonconsequentialist, in that it does not depend on any effects of legal rules. In such cases, it follows automatically that fairness-based analysis is independent of the effects of legal rules on individuals' well-being.[28] More commonly, analysts who accord weight to certain notions of fairness also take into account the consequences of legal rules; nevertheless, such analysts do not base their assessment of legal rules exclusively on the effects of the rules on individuals' well-being.

To illustrate this basic feature of notions of fairness, let us elaborate on the classical principle of corrective justice, which requires a person who wrongfully harms another to compensate the victim. (For convenience, we will consider a pure version of the principle, under which the evaluation of a legal rule depends entirely on the extent to which it satisfies the principle and not on anything else, notably, the effects of a legal rule on individuals' well-being.) Application of this principle of fairness relies on a description of the circumstances of an adverse event: A person's conduct is examined to see if it was wrongful and caused harm—and, if so, the principle requires that person to pay compensation to the victim. By definition, then, the fair treatment of individuals depends on the situational character of an event. The determination of whether treatment is fair does not depend—as it would under welfare economics—on how that treatment will influence individuals' behavior and, in turn, on how such behavior will affect individuals' well-being.

Of course, requiring fair treatment will, in reality, have consequences. If wrongful, harmful conduct is penalized, we would expect there to be less of it, with attendant effects on individuals' well-being. (For example, holding negligent drivers liable will tend to reduce accidents, increase resources devoted to precautions, result in expenditures on litigation, and provide compensation to some risk-averse victims.) But assessing such effects is not part of an analysis based on the notion of fairness that we have posited, because such normative analysis is avowedly independent of how the pursuit of fairness will influence the well-being of individuals. (Thus, the negligence rule may be favored even if there is little reduction in accidents, litigation costs are large, and compensated victims are already insured and thus bear no risk.) It follows from this characterization of fairness-based normative analysis and our prior description of welfare economics that the two approaches are potentially in conflict: Welfare economics is concerned exclusively with effects on individuals' well-being, whereas notions of fairness like the principle of corrective justice that we have been discussing are not at all concerned with such effects.

Our example involved a pure principle of fairness, under which legal rules are evaluated with no regard for individuals' well-being. Although analysis based on such notions of fairness is embraced by some legal academics and by strictly deontological philosophers (notably, Kant[29]), a different stance is typical, as we said. In particular, it is our impression that most analysts of legal policy who attach importance to notions of fairness hold mixed normative views. That is, not only do they give weight to notions of fairness, but they also place weight, and perhaps significant weight, on how legal policies affect individuals' well-being—either because they understand individuals' well-being to be encompassed by some notions of fairness, or because they consider both fairness and individuals' well-being in reaching a final judgment. For example, a fairness-minded analyst might believe the negligence rule to be more fair than strict liability, if all else is equal, but might ultimately favor strict liability if the negligence rule turns out to be too expensive to administer.[30]

We emphasize, however, that we take notions of fairness to be principles used in normative analysis such that at least some weight is given to factors that are independent of individuals' well-being. One could certainly define notions of fairness more broadly, to include as well principles

that are equivalent to those of welfare economics. (And certain notions of fairness familiar to some readers may well have this feature, which is to say that these notions give exclusive weight to how legal rules affect individuals' well-being.) Moreover, as we discuss at many points below, notions of fairness are sometimes invoked not as evaluative principles in their own right, but rather as rules of thumb or proxy principles that may help identify legal rules that increase individuals' well-being. (For example, if wrongful acts are usually harmful acts, a practice of penalizing those who commit wrongful acts will tend to deter harmful activity.) But many notions of fairness are not ordinarily understood in this way, and our criticism of the use of notions of fairness obviously does not extend either to welfare economics or to the possibility that notions of fairness may serve as proxy principles for enhancing welfare rather than as independent evaluative criteria.[31]

Thus, to reiterate what we state at the outset of this subsection, *we employ the terminology of "notions of fairness" to refer only to principles that accord weight to factors that are independent of individuals' well-being.* Relatedly, we direct our criticism of fairness-based analysis precisely at those circumstances in which the legal rules that are chosen when weight is given to notions of fairness differ from the legal rules that would be selected under welfare economics.[32] That is, we define notions of fairness as we do—to include all principles that give weight to factors independent of individuals' well-being, but only such principles—because the substance of our argument depends precisely on this characteristic.[33] Moreover, the leading notions of fairness that are used in legal policy analysis in a wide range of fields of law indeed have just this feature: Analysis based on such notions does give weight to factors independent of individuals' well-being and, as a consequence, does result in different prescriptions from those of welfare economics.

2. Further Comments on Notions of Fairness

We now describe some problematic aspects of the meaning, nonconsequentialist nature, and ex-post character of many notions of fairness. These difficulties, however, are independent of our main criticisms of the use of notions of fairness and accordingly are set aside in much of the book.

(a) Meaning

It is frequently difficult to ascertain what analysts mean when they discuss the fairness of legal rules. Analysts often use words like "fairness" without defining them. (For example, when discussing tort law, analysts may simply remark that a rule or result is "fair" or "unfair," leaving the reader to guess what that signifies.[34]) Moreover, when analysts do provide some elaboration of their concepts, their explanations are often incomplete in important respects. (They might, for instance, refer to corrective justice but fail to articulate what constitutes a wrong, even though wrongdoing is a main condition for requiring compensation under corrective justice.) Additionally, many analysts do not supply a basis for determining the scope of application of notions of fairness. (Corrective justice on its face is applicable to many areas of law but is invoked mainly in tort. Should we view corrective justice as applicable to contract law too, or is there an unstated limitation on its domain?) Relatedly, analysts rarely explain how they resolve the conflicts that arise among the different notions of fairness that may apply in a situation. (If one principle of justice requires the use of strict liability in order to compensate the innocent victim and another requires use of the negligence rule to avoid punishing nonculpable actors, what meta-principle determines which rule should govern?[35])

Although in principle these deficiencies concerning meaning and scope might be remedied, they generally have not been, and we are left with considerable uncertainty about what fairness-based analysis actually entails, even in very basic settings.[36] In each instance, we examine pertinent notions of fairness that are identified in the academic literature on the legal subject under consideration or that seem to be applicable even if not articulated in scholarly writing. When we are uncertain about which legal rule should be understood as most fair under a given notion of fairness, we simply consider each of the relevant possibilities.

(b) Nonconsequentialist Character

Adherence to nonconsequentialist notions of fairness seems to raise a basic tension with what one would imagine to be analysts' underlying motivation for caring about fairness. Namely, if consequences are ignored, the amount of fairness or unfairness is also ignored. To illustrate, a principle of fairness may favor a legal rule that prevents sellers from disadvantaging buyers in some way, even though the rule will result in buyers being hurt even more, taking into account that they will pay for the protection through higher prices. One would then have to ask whether such a result is really fairer to buyers. Or consider the notion of retributive justice that calls for punishment that fits the wrongful act. It is possible that a higher level of punishment would reduce or eliminate the occurrence of wrongs. Presuming that the theory's demand for punishment is motivated by the evil associated with wrongdoing (that is, wrongful acts are themselves unfair), it should be troubling that insistence on fair punishment may result in avoidable wrongdoing.[37] (Also, any unfairness associated with imposing a higher punishment is arguably mitigated by the fact mat the higher punishment might rarely if ever have to be imposed.) We suspect that such conflicts have not been recognized because analysts focus on particular notions of fairness that, on their own terms, have a nonconsequentialist character. As a result, analysts are not inclined to pay attention to the effects of legal rules even when such effects concern the incidence of unfairness itself. (The following subsection offers a related reason that this difficulty with many notions of fairness has largely been ignored.)

(c) Ex-Post Character

We find that most notions of fairness reflect an ex-post perspective on the situations under examination, in contrast to the inclusive approach of welfare economics. In this subsection, we briefly explain this point and suggest that it both lends support to our main arguments, which we sketch in section C, and helps reconcile the widespread appeal of notions of fairness with their shortcomings as independent evaluative principles.

As we discuss in subsection B.1, above, notions of fairness typically are used to reach conclusions based upon situational characteristics of events. Furthermore, it is often true—particularly in legal contexts—that an important, indeed central aspect of the events under examination, is what in fact has happened.[38] That is, the assessments are usually made from an ex-post perspective. Thus, when asking what rule is just as between an injurer and a victim in the accident context, it is generally assumed that an accident has in fact happened. In examining remedies for breach of contract, the focus is on those cases in which there is actually a breach. When determining what punishment is just for a convicted criminal, the discussion takes for granted that the criminal has been captured. In this respect, fairness-oriented analysts tend to focus on particular outcomes. Moreover, these outcomes are often relatively unlikely ones, given the acts in question. (Most instances of negligence do not cause accidents; for many types of crime, most criminals are not caught.[39])

In addition to directing attention to particular, and often unlikely, outcomes, analysis based on notions of fairness frequently ignores important aspects of ex-ante behavior that may well be responsible for the ultimate results. Individuals select what level of care to take, which affects the likelihood of accidents; they decide whether to enter into contracts (and at what price) and whether to breach; and they choose whether to commit criminal acts. Each of these decisions, moreover, may plausibly be influenced by what legal rule actors anticipate will be applied ex post, and it is these legal rules that notions of fairness are being used to select.[40]

Thus, in important respects, many notions of fairness focus on particular consequences and thereby ignore or undervalue other plausibly relevant aspects of the situation under examination. In this sense, the judgments reached under such notions of fairness are based on incomplete characterizations of situations. (There is, of course, no error in logic to the extent that the excluded considerations are deemed irrelevant; we argue later, however, that upon analysis it is difficult to sustain the view that such basic features of individuals'

behavior and possible outcomes are morally irrelevant.) In contrast, welfare economics takes into account any effect of a legal rule that is pertinent to anyone's well-being. Accordingly, ex-ante behavior, all of its possible outcomes, and the potential effects of legal rules thereon are central features that are examined under welfare-economic analysis.

A priori, a welfare economic approach to policy assessment would seem superior to one based on notions of fairness to the extent that the former reflects a complete consideration of factors that plausibly seem relevant and the latter does not. Moreover, in our subsequent analysis of particular notions of fairness in specific legal contexts, we find that the two approaches often lead to different policy prescriptions precisely in those cases in which the ex-post perspective implicit in fairness-based analysis omits an important consideration that welfare-economic analysis captures. For example, notions of fairness pertaining to remedies for breach of contract seem to lead us astray in part because they do not take into account that remedies that seem fair ex post will tend to lead parties to adjust other contract terms (such as the contract price) ex ante in a manner that nullifies or even reverses the apparent effect of the seemingly fair legal rule, or to change parties' decisions whether to enter contracts or to commit breaches in the first place. When fair levels of punishment are set, standard application of the proportionality principle under theories of retributive justice tends to be problematic precisely in those cases in which the probability of apprehension is low. In such cases, penalties that seem unfairly high ex post (that is, applied to those few criminals who are captured) may actually be moderate or low in an expected sense, which is relevant to whether potential criminals will in fact choose to commit crimes and, arguably, to whether sanctions should be viewed as unfairly high.

Thus, when notions of fairness and welfare economics favor different legal policies, we argue in many contexts that the prescriptions of welfare economics are more compelling because they reflect a more complete and accurate assessment of what legal rules actually do. Of course, a form of analysis that accounts for a broader range of effects of legal rules and that determines their effects more accurately is superior only if the actual effects of legal rules are deemed relevant in the first instance. And as we have discussed, many— or all—effects of legal rules are considered to be irrelevant under many notions of fairness, especially those notions advanced by deontological moral philosophers. Our analysis, however, raises questions about whether this view can plausibly be defended once its implications are fully understood.

Finally, we observe that the ex-post perspective of many notions of fairness helps explain their broad appeal. When policy analysts or members of the public at large consider what rule seems fair in a given situation, we tend to focus (as just described) on what has actually happened, for that is what we see in the case before us. We do not tend to focus on what did *not* happen (even when that may have been, ex ante, a much more likely outcome), and we do not directly observe the ex-ante-choice situation and how behavior may differ in the future as a consequence of the legal rule that we choose to apply to the situation at hand.

This tendency to focus on what is salient—and in particular, on what has actually happened—is related to familiar and prevalent cognitive biases.[41] Because the application of many notions of fairness seems to fit the pattern of certain types of errors in mental processing, cognitive psychology would seem to offer a partial explanation for the apparent attractiveness of fairness-based analysis.[42] As a normative matter, however, if the appeal of notions of fairness, when they conflict with welfare economics, derives from what amount to mistakes in judgment, there is no basis for giving the notions weight as independent evaluative principles, to be pursued at the expense of individuals' well-being.

(d) Concluding Remark

We will later examine the foregoing problems but we do not make them the focus of our critique because they are not inherent in the idea of giving weight to notions of fairness. Leading notions of fairness, as articulated over the centuries and today, may have uncertain meaning and application, but perhaps more elaborate or rather different versions of the notions could be developed and a

system for resolving conflicts among them could be created. Moreover, if they accounted for the consequences of legal rules and reflected a perspective that incorporated all plausibly relevant factors, such modified notions of fairness might not be subject to the difficulties that we have identified.[43] Nevertheless, the apparent existence of serious yet largely unrecognized internal deficiencies in many prominent notions of fairness suggests that, despite their distinguished lineage, these notions have not received sufficiently rigorous scrutiny. Furthermore, these sorts of problems in themselves raise questions about the plausibility of justifications for the notions (which, as we note in subsection C.2, are not generally supplied).

More important, even if the problems discussed in this subsection were overcome, there would remain the central point that we identify in subsection B.1: Under notions of fairness, legal rules would still be evaluated based on factors that are independent of individuals' well-being. This property of notions of fairness is the focus of our critique, to which we now turn.

C. OVERVIEW OF OUR ARGUMENT

1. The Argument for Welfare Economics and against Notions of Fairness

Our argument for basing the evaluation of legal rules entirely on welfare economics, giving no weight to notions of fairness, derives from the fundamental characteristic of fairness-based assessment: Such assessment does not depend exclusively on the effects of legal rules on individuals' well-being. As a consequence, satisfying notions of fairness can make individuals worse off; that is, reduce social welfare. Furthermore, individuals will be made worse off overall whenever consideration of fairness leads to the choice of a regime different from that which would be adopted under welfare economics because, by definition, the two approaches conflict when a regime with greater overall well-being is rejected on grounds of fairness.[44]

This point takes on special force when, as we show in important situations, fairness-based analysis leads to the choice of legal rules that reduce the well-being of *every* individual. In particular, in symmetric contexts—those in which all individuals are identically situated (for example, an accident setting in which all are equally likely to be injurers or victims)—it is *always* the case that everyone will be worse off when a notion of fairness leads to the choice of a different legal rule from that chosen under welfare economics. The explanation for this result is straightforward. Because everyone is identically situated, whenever welfare economics leads to the choice of one rule over another, it must be that everyone is better off under the preferred rule. Hence, whenever a notion of fairness leads one to choose a different rule from that favored under welfare economics, everyone is necessarily worse off as a result.

Indeed, the possibility that pursuing a notion of fairness may make everyone worse off is always present (whether or not the notion applies in symmetric contexts): It can be demonstrated that consistently adhering to any notion of fairness will sometimes entail favoring regimes under which every person is made worse off.[45] And it is not possible to circumvent this problem by modifying notions of fairness in any plausible manner.[46] That any notion of fairness will sometimes make everyone worse off raises a sharp question: To whom is one being fair?

We observe that the foregoing conclusion is important in assessing the soundness of a notion of fairness regardless of whether pursuing the notion will in fact make everyone worse off in the particular setting under consideration or how often that would be so. We emphasize this observation because of the common belief among policy analysts that the Pareto principle—which holds that one should always favor a policy under which everyone is better off—has little relevance in making policy decisions because it will rarely be true that one legal rule will literally make everyone better off than does another rule. Our argument is that, although adherence to the Pareto principle may not directly determine policy *choices* in most real situations, it nevertheless has powerful implications for what *criteria* for making policy choices one can plausibly employ. That is, if one adheres to the view that it cannot be normatively good to make everyone worse off, then logical consistency

requires that one can give no weight in normative analysis to notions of fairness because doing so entails the contrary proposition that sometimes it is normatively desirable to adopt a policy that makes everyone worse off. To restate the point, demonstrating that a theory, in some part of its intended domain of application, contradicts a principle to which one subscribes, shows the theory to be unacceptable.[47]

We also wish to observe that the previously discussed symmetric case—in which notions of fairness make everyone worse off whenever their prescriptions differ from those of welfare economics—arguably has special significance under a number of broadly endorsed principles of normative analysis. In particular, we suggest that, upon examination, the Golden Rule, Kant's categorical imperative, and the construct of a veil of ignorance can each be seen to imply the requirement that all normative principles be tested in a symmetric setting. The reason is that normative analysis is understood to proceed from a disinterested perspective, which can be made explicit by imagining that one is equally likely to be in any possible role, that one will occupy each and every role, or some equivalent assumption—and it is precisely symmetric settings that have this property.[48] Thus, our argument that following notions of fairness always makes everyone worse off in symmetric settings (whenever there is a conflict with the prescriptions of welfare economics) poses an unrecognized but real challenge to those who find compelling the types of moral theories just described and (as many do) also advance notions of fairness. It would seem either that such analysts must systematically favor notions that always make everyone worse off in the type of setting that they believe should be used to test moral concepts, or that they must abandon their notions of fairness in favor of welfare economics.

The conclusion that in some circumstances all individuals will be made worse off as a consequence of pursuing any notion of fairness reveals that fairness-based analysis stands in opposition to human welfare at the most basic level. Now, as we state in the introduction, it is true that it is virtually a tautology to assert that fairness-based evaluation entails some sort of reduction in individuals' well-being, for notions of fairness are principles of evaluation that give weight to factors unrelated to individuals' well-being. Nevertheless, we do not believe that the full import of fairness-based analysis for human welfare is appreciated. Indeed, policy-oriented legal academic literature that uses notions of fairness as criteria for assessing legal rules rarely confronts or even acknowledges the existence of the conflict between giving weight to notions of fairness and advancing individuals' well-being. In order for the conflict to be better appreciated, we examine a range of important legal settings and discuss in specific terms how prominent notions of fairness lead to outcomes under which individuals are worse off.

2. On the Rationale for Notions of Fairness

The second aspect of our critique of fairness-based analysis concerns the rationale for notions of fairness. We have just stated that furthering notions of fairness, whenever they favor policies different from those endorsed under welfare economics, leads to reductions in individuals' well-being. Moreover, we presume that legal policy analysts and policymakers care about individuals' well-being. Hence, it is especially important to explore what the rationale for notions of fairness might be.

Thus, we ask what society might be thought to gain—in what sense a better state of affairs might be said to exist—by pursuing commonly advanced notions of fairness at the expense of individuals' well-being. In this inquiry, we consider the legal academic and philosophical literature endorsing the particular notions of fairness that are put forward in each setting and attempt to identify the motivation for advancing notions of fairness at the cost of individuals' well-being. We also reflect on the essential features of the paradigmatic legal situations that we analyze and endeavor to determine why what is viewed as the fairer outcome might seem attractive.

We find that little explicit justification for notions of fairness—even those developed by prominent writers over the years—has in fact been offered. Relatedly, many theorists seem to rely heavily on conclusory metaphors, such as the

idea espoused by some retributivists that punishment is justified in order to restore a sort of moral balance in the world. This shortcoming, we believe, helps to explain the previously identified problems of determining the meaning of notions of fairness and of resolving internal tensions: When a principle's underlying rationale is unknown, we should not be surprised that it will be difficult to ascertain whether and how various factors affect its proper application.

Moreover, the motivations that we are able to identify (from the literature or from reflection on relevant situations) do not really provide good reasons for viewing notions of fairness as independent evaluative principles, even from the apparent perspective of those who favor giving weight to these concepts. In some instances, there seems to be little relationship between the purposes offered (or those that might be imagined) to support the notions of fairness and the actual implications of the notions for the choice of legal rules. For example, in some basic settings, the only effect of choosing punishment in accordance with retributive justice (aside from raising the costs of the legal system and increasing the number of innocent victims of crime) is to preserve the profitability of crime to some potential criminals—who themselves are viewed as wrongdoers according to retributive theory. Or, pursuing the principle of corrective justice, under which wrongdoers must compensate victims for harm done independently of whether requiring such payments reduces individuals' well-being, has as its only other feature that in certain settings it favors some types of individuals over others based solely on characteristics determined by chance elements that seem morally arbitrary from any plausible perspective.

An additional problem with the defenses offered for notions of fairness concerns the source of the underlying arguments. Sometimes, proponents of principles of fairness support the principles by reference to their consistency with existing legal doctrine. Such a claim, however, relies on positive analysis that by its very nature cannot provide a normative justification for the use of the principles for purposes of evaluation, including assessment of the very legal rules that were examined when identifying the principles of fairness.

Also, fairness proponents often appeal to intuitions or instincts. Yet, as we discuss at length (in section D), this source of insight is an unreliable grounding in the context we are examining; the intuitions and instincts themselves usually have a basis in promoting individuals' well-being (rather than in some independent, conflicting purpose); and reliance on these sources is self-defeating because an important purpose of explicit normative analysis of legal policy is to identify when our intuitions or instincts may lead us astray. Finally, some fairness arguments seem implicitly to be motivated by the circumstances of a specific group of people (such as victims of wrongful acts). But as we state above, pursuing a notion of fairness can make literally everyone worse off, necessarily including anyone whose plight might have motivated the notion of fairness in the first place. In this respect, it may not be surprising that, upon reflection, it is difficult to identify rationales for notions of fairness: Most moral theories seem concerned in some way with individuals, whereas, by definition, notions of fairness are concerned with factors that are unrelated to and thus (when they differ from welfare economics) opposed to individuals' well-being.

Our contention that the rationales that seem to underlie notions of fairness do not justify treating these notions as independent evaluative principles is not, of course, one that can be established through logical deduction, for logic alone cannot tell us what our first principles of evaluation should be. Nevertheless, we believe that the deficiencies just described are indeed present and that, upon reflection, notions of fairness are difficult to defend. We also suggest that the problems identified in subsection B.2 concerning the meaning and internal coherence of notions of fairness raise serious questions about the possible bases for most notions of fairness, which should make it less surprising that careful scrutiny reveals the notions to be untenable.

Our two conclusions, about how the pursuit of notions of fairness makes individuals worse off and about the lack of affirmative warrant for using notions of fairness as evaluative principles, raise the question of why legal policy analysts (including ourselves), policymakers, and philosophers,

among others, find these notions so appealing. We devote significant attention to this question throughout this book and offer a number of related answers (including one, concerning the ex-post character of notions of fairness, that we already discussed in subsection B.2(c)). An important part of the explanation, we believe, is suggested by the analysis in the next section.

D. NOTIONS OF FAIRNESS AND SOCIAL NORMS

We submit that there is often a correspondence—indeed, sometimes an identity—between notions of fairness that are used as independent principles for the evaluation of legal rules and various social norms that guide ordinary individuals in their everyday lives. Moreover, we suggest that this relationship between notions of fairness and social norms helps to reconcile the attraction that notions of fairness possess with our argument that such notions should not be given independent weight in the assessment of legal rules. Our discussion draws on a long tradition of work in the social sciences, evolutionary biology, and philosophy, including early contributions of Hume, Mill, Sidgwick, and Darwin, and many of our conclusions concerning implications for understanding fairness arguments relate to themes developed in the more recent work of Baron and Hare. In subsection D.1 we examine the functions that social norms serve.

1. The Nature of Social Norms

Ordinary individuals routinely draw on social norms in determining how they should behave in their daily lives—in interactions with friends, relatives, business associates, and the like—and social norms serve as principles in educating and governing children. These norms include such principles as telling the truth, keeping promises, not harming others, and being held accountable when one does cause harm.

Many notions of fairness employed to assess legal rules correspond to these social norms. For example, the promise-keeping theory of contract law may be identified with the social norm that individuals should keep their promises. The notions of corrective justice in tort and retributive justice in criminal law seem to be closely related to social norms about not harming others and being held responsible when one does so. Moreover, these notions of fairness contain limits on what sanctions are appropriate (the punishment should fit the crime rather than be excessive) that are similar to limits embodied in social norms (adverse reactions to wrongs should be proportionate, to avoid becoming wrongs themselves). Each notion of fairness employed by legal analysts that we consider indeed corresponds to an identifiable social norm.

Having stated that there seems to be a relationship between notions of fairness and social norms, we now sketch what appears to be the role of social norms in regulating individuals' behavior in the informal situations that they confront in everyday life. Once we describe this function of social norms, we will be able to discuss how it bears on our understanding of notions of fairness used in legal policy analysis.

Social norms tend to be valuable regulators of everyday conduct for two reasons. First, the presence of internalized social norms—against lying, larceny, or littering, for example—reduces the incidence of selfish, undesirable behavior. Individuals will have a motive to follow social norms if those who violate them experience feelings of guilt and encounter social disapproval, whereas those who comply with the norms feel virtuous and receive praise from others. That is, when a principle is embodied in an internalized social norm, there exists a system of internal rewards and punishments and related external (yet extralegal) rewards and punishments—in the form of social approval and disapproval—that serves to induce individuals to behave in accord with the principle. If, instead, individuals were unconstrained by social norms, their selfish tendencies would more often lead them to act opportunistically, such as by lying when they might gain thereby, stealing when they are stronger than their victim, or littering at their convenience. Thus, social norms can play an important role in channeling individuals' behavior in a socially desirable manner.

If social norms are to be effective in countering opportunistic inclinations in the way just described, it seems that, given the nature of human psychology, they must operate as rather broad, superior principles that are generally not subject to case-by-case analysis and exception. Feelings of guilt or outrage, for example, seem likely to be more powerful if they are spontaneous reactions rather than products of dispassionate consideration and calculation. Moreover, if social norms called on individuals to make complex, situation-specific judgments, individuals' ability to rationalize and their tendency to misperceive events in a manner that aligns with their self-interest might dilute the norms' effectiveness. The type of "man who can say to himself without questioning or hesitation, 'Thou shalt not commit adultery' or 'Never, never tell a. lie' is more likely, in the course of his life, to do what is optimific than one who is prepared to question these principles, in the sense of 'contemplate breaking them', on any but rather extraordinary occasions." Finally, to the extent that the social norms to which we adhere are instilled in us when we are very young, it is particularly important that the application of the norms not allow the individuals subject to them substantial discretion and room for judgment in determining when they apply.

A second reason that social norms can be valuable is that they may serve as useful proxy principles, heuristics, or rules of thumb that promote individuals' welfare. Such use of norms is valuable because most decisions that individuals make are of such small consequence that refined consideration of possible actions would be a waste of effort. In addition, it would be very costly, if not infeasible, for many individuals to acquire the analytical skills and knowledge necessary to behave otherwise. Relatedly, if decisions were made on a case-by-case basis, individuals would inevitably make some errors, particularly in certain settings, such as when a decision would produce immediate, tangible benefits or costs. Adhering to rules—such as always saving a given portion of one's paycheck or never having more than two drinks—may well reduce the rate of errors even though the rules themselves do not always prescribe the behavior that is truly best under the circumstances. (We note that these sorts of benefits from following norms may complement the preceding function of curbing opportunistic behavior toward others: For example, never telling a lie may usually be ideal even from a selfish perspective because possible retaliation, loss of reputation, and so forth may make lying unlikely to be profitable in the long run.) Like the first function of social norms, curbing opportunistic behavior toward others, this benefit from following norms is obtained only if individuals are inclined to follow the norms rather automatically; reflective analysis of whether norms should be followed in each particular case would be self-defeating in light of the norms' purposes. It is also necessary that the norms be simple and general in application.

NOTES

1. More precisely, the primitive element for analysis of an individual's well-being is that individual's ordering of possible outcomes. The analyst assigns numerical tags—utility indexes—to the outcomes to reflect the ordering: That is, if one outcome is preferred to another, the preferred outcome is assigned a higher utility. Thus, if outcome A is preferred to B, which in turn is preferred to C, A might be assigned utility of 10, B assigned utility of 8, and C assigned utility of 5; equivalently, A might be assigned utility of 100, B utility of 18, and C utility of 16. Any assignment of utility numbers such that the utility of A is highest and that of C lowest would represent the individual's preference ordering equally well. The point is that utility numbers need not be interpreted as objective, measurable quantities, but rather should be understood as constructed, auxiliary numbers selected by the analyst to represent the underlying rank ordering of the individual. When uncertainty is involved, the theory of how utility represents preferences is more refined. But the underlying idea that utility numbers are chosen by the analyst remains the same. See Raiffa (1968, 86–89) and Savage (1972, chapter 5). We note that the utility index needs to be specified further when one aggregates individuals' well-being to compute social welfare.

2. See, for example, Becker (1993, 386); and Little (1985, 1187 n.2), who refers to the "oft-refuted accusation that economists ignore the psyche" in objecting to the use of the term "material welfare"

as an apt description of Pigou's early twentieth-century economic writings.

We observe that the early utilitarians, many of whom espoused hedonism and its variants, did not in fact hold narrow views of well-being, despite conventional wisdom to the contrary. See, for example, Bentham ([1781] 1988, 33), listing, at the outset of a chapter on the kinds of pains and pleasures, some "simple pleasures," which include, in addition to pleasures of the senses and wealth, the pleasures of skill, amity, a good name, piety, benevolence, imagination, and association. Mill criticized the view that utilitarianism is limited to certain categories of pleasure. See Mill ([1861] 1998, 54–57). (Interestingly, he pointed out that the Greek philosopher Epicurus, who addressed such issues, was mischaracterized as having a narrow view of pleasure. Id. (56).) In fact, Mill appears to have endorsed higher intellectual pleasures as superior to more basic pleasures of the senses (although there is some dispute among modern scholars as to whether Mill held this position as a matter of principle, in seeming conflict with his other arguments, or purely as an empirical matter). Compare Sidgwick (1907, 402): "The term Pleasure is not commonly used so as to include clearly *all* kinds of consciousness which we desire to retain or reproduce: in ordinary usage it suggests too prominently the coarser and commoner kinds of such feelings; and it is difficult even for those who are trying to use it scientifically to free their minds altogether from the associations of ordinary usage …"

3. Some philosophers, such as Scanlon, have expressed skepticism about the concept of well-being. See, for example, Scanlon (1998). Many such arguments, however, do not seem pertinent to the concept as we have defined it in the text. For example, some doubts reflect the view that well-being is not understood in a sufficiently expansive manner, whereas we impose no restrictions on what may be included. Other doubts involve resistance to the idea of interpreting well-being as an objective concept specified by an analyst, rather than according to what the individuals under consideration really care about, but the former is not how we define well-being. We consider some common objections concerning the make-up of individuals' preferences in section VIII.B. (Different reservations reflect the view that individuals' well-being as they experience it should not be the basis for normative analysis; these reservations

do relate to the substantive argument of our book.)

Let us also comment briefly on the relationship between our conception of individuals' well-being and the views of modern political theorists and legal academics advancing what are referred to as "communitarian" or "republican" theories of individuals and the role of the state. See, for example, Arendt (1963); MacIntyre (1984); Pocock (1975); Sandel (1982); Taylor (1989); Walzer (1983); Fallon (1989), expressing skepticism about republican theories in a survey that focuses on constitutional law scholarship; and Gardbaum (1992), emphasizing, in a survey of political theorists and legal scholars, the lack of a necessary connection between their descriptive claims about the nature of individuals and their normative claims. The literature advances a descriptive claim, which is that individuals' desires are importantly influenced by the communities in which they live. This view does not bear on our definition of well-being or on our analysis, both of which are independent of the origins of well-being. Thus, we might imagine that individuals' desires are in part inherited; in part influenced by family; in part determined by interactions with others, including the community at large; in part shaped by legal rules and institutions (see subsection VIII.B.2); and so forth. Some such theorists also advance normative claims that do conflict with our argument. Notably, some insist that community participation should be encouraged for its own sake (rather than for instrumental reasons ultimately related to the promotion of individuals' well-being, such as that individuals would find participation rewarding, that it would lead them to behave better toward each other, or that it would improve the quality of laws or the functioning of government) or that particular conceptions of the good (independent of individuals' actual well-being) should be promoted. A theme of our analysis is that it is difficult to defend such notions, because they imply that members of society should pursue a course of action that, when it conflicts with a welfare-based approach, can only be detrimental to their well-being. See also subsection VIII.B.4, addressing the idea that an analyst's notion of the good should be substituted for individuals' actual well-being.

4. The assumption that an individual is risk averse is equivalent to the assumption that an individual's utility increases with income, but at a decreasing rate—that is, the marginal utility of income decreases with the level of income. The assumption means that an additional dollar produces less of an increase in utility the more income one already has, which will tend to be true because individuals are inclined to allocate scarce dollars first to those goods and services that they value most highly.

Risk-averse individuals will, for example, refuse an even-odds bet for $1,000 because the utility gain if they win $1,000 is less than the utility loss if they lose $1,000. By similar reasoning, subjecting individuals to the risk of an uncompensated, uninsured loss (say, a 10% chance of losing $10,000) will reduce their utility more than would subjecting them to a certain loss with the same expected value ($1,000). This trait implies that individuals will tend to find the purchase of insurance attractive. In essence, insurance involves the transfer of income from situations in which income is relatively high (and thus the marginal utility from income is relatively low) to situations in which income is low (and thus the marginal utility from income is relatively high); such a transfer increases expected utility.

To elaborate on the reason that risk-averse individuals are made better off by insurance, suppose that I have an income of $50,000 but am subject to a 50% risk of losing $20,000 tomorrow. Assume further that my marginal utility per dollar is higher when my income is low—say, it is 4 per dollar when my income is $30,000 (that is, $50,000–$20,000) and only 2 per dollar when my income is $50,000. To keep the analysis simple, let us now consider my decision to enter into the following simple contract with an insurance company: I pay them $1 today and they agree to pay me $2 tomorrow if I indeed lose $20,000. This contract will increase my expected utility. To see that this is true, consider the two possibilities: If I do lose the $20,000, I have paid my $1 insurance premium but receive a $2 payment from the insurance company, so my net income is $30,001, $1 higher than without the insurance. If I do not lose the $20,000, I have paid my premium of $1, so my income is $49,999. In sum, I have a 50% chance of gaining $1 when I am relatively poor—which increases my utility by 4—and a 50% chance of losing $1 when I am relatively rich—which decreases my utility by only 2. The resulting effect on my expected utility is a gain of 1: $(50\% \times 4) + (50\% \times -2) = 1$. This gain indicates how insurance increases expected utility. (The logic of the example suggests that I would prefer to purchase complete insurance, paying a premium of $10,000 for a payment of $20,000 in the event of loss, giving me a certain income of $40,000. As Long as my coverage is not yet complete, the utility gain from additional coverage, when I am relatively worse off, will exceed the utility loss from paying the premium in the event that no loss occurs, when I am better off.)

5. The latter possibility is related to the idea that individuals might be displeased if the law failed to "express" their beliefs. See, for example, Sunstein (1996a). See also Adler (2000, 1364–74), surveying writings on expressive theories.

6. In particular, our discussion suggests that individuals are inculcated with fairness norms such that they feel virtuous when they act fairly and remorseful when they act unfairly, and that they are motivated to take actions in response to the unfair behavior of others. Such feelings and motivations tend to constitute, or be associated with, tastes for notions of fairness, which in turn may be satisfied to a greater or lesser degree by a particular legal rule. Mill states that:

> [V]irtue [is something that was] originally a means, and which if it were not a means to anything else, would be and remain indifferent, but which by association with what it is a means to, comes to be desired for itself, and that too with the utmost intensity…. What was once desired as an instrument for the attainment of happiness, has come to be desired for its own sake. In being desired for its own sake it is, however, desired as *part* of happiness. (Mill [1861] 1998, 83)

Certain eighteenth-century moral philosophers address the relationship between notions of fairness and individuals' moral sense, which is understood as akin to tastes in some respects. See Hutcheson ([1725–1755] 1994) and Hume ([1751] 1998).

7. For example, in the literature on retributive justice, commentators insist that their conception of fairness is distinct from individuals' tastes. See subsection VI.D.2. Usually, however, the philosophical and legal academic literature on notions of fairness does not explicitly address the relationship, if any, between such notions and individuals' tastes. Yet it is clear from the arguments given in the literature that the writers' endorsement of notions of fairness is not based on the notions' importance as tastes. In addition, this writing essentially lacks empirical content, whereas it would necessarily be substantially empirical if it were concerned with fairness as a taste. Moreover, the literature sometimes

advances notions of fairness that are opposed to the popular will, as, for instance, when the popular will supports less protection of criminal defendants. See, for example, Husak (1995, 154): "[C]ritical morality is distinct from the conventional mores of communities. Public opinion polls consistently reveal that many citizens are prepared to sacrifice rights in order to help reduce crime. Only the application of a critical morality can justify the protection of rights against the apparent willingness of many citizens to relinquish them." Also, even those who invoke public opinion to support their views do not suggest that the weight given to notions of fairness should be determined entirely by the strength of individuals' desire for more fairness in preference, say, to more fine wine. Finally, we note that some positions of philosophers are clearly distinguished from popular views:

> But it is quite absurd to want to comply with popularity in the first investigation, on which all correctness of basic principles depends. Not only can this procedure never lay claim to the very rare merit of a true philosophic popularity, since there is no art in being commonly understandable if one thereby renounces any well-grounded insight; it also produces a disgusting hodge-podge of patchwork observations and half-rationalized principles, in which shallow pates revel because it is something useful for everyday chitchat, but the insightful … avert their eyes. … (Kant [1785] 1997, 21–22)

The suggestion that what are presented as moral views really involve individuals' tastes tends to be put forward by critics, not by fairness proponents describing their own views. See, for example, R. Posner (1998, 1644), giving an example, and id. (1645), suggesting that "many moral claims are just the gift wrapping of theoretically ungrounded (and ungroundable) preferences or aversions."

8. For elaboration, see section VIII.B. We also note that much of our more formal argument has an even broader application. Namely, if an analyst thought that a concept of well-being that was qualitatively different from the welfare economic one (say, an objective view of the good life) was normatively compelling, important parts of our analysis would still hold. In particular, there would be no change in the logic of our argument that giving any weight to a notion of fairness that is independent of well-being always raises the

possibility that everyone would be made worse off; everyone being made worse off would be interpreted by reference to the analyst's own conception of individuals' well-being. Of course, the foregoing observation could easily be taken too far—for example, by defining each individual's well-being as equivalent to the degree to which a policy satisfies some notion of fairness that is not conventionally understood to have anything to do with individuals' well-being. Such language usage would obscure important differences in normative positions.

In addition, although many who adhere to conceptions of well-being that differ from the welfare economic one should find much of our analysis convincing, other aspects of our argument favor the welfare economic conception because it is rooted in the actual well-being of individuals. To be sure, many analysts seem to define individuals' well-being not as something that has any relationship to individuals' actual preferences or feelings, however well-informed, but rather as some conception that the analyst holds dear. We find such usage (like the aforementioned usage that would collapse all notions of fairness into well-being) confusing and misleading, both because well-being seems to refer to an actual rather than an external and conceptual state of existence and because referring to well-being as that of an individual suggests that the actual individual in question, rather than an analyst, is the direct object of concern. See subsection VIII.B.4. On different conceptions of well-being, see generally Griffin (1986), Ng (2000, chapter 4), Nussbaum and Sen (1993), and Sumner (1996).

9. We discuss the distribution of income rather than the distribution of well-being because much analysis of distributive issues refers to the distribution of income and because many redistributive policies operate through individuals' incomes. As should be apparent from our discussion, however, welfare economics also incorporates distributive issues involving well-being that may arise independently of income differences (such as when individuals have different physical capacities). For convenience, however, we do not generally refer as well to the distribution of well-being, even when such language might be more accurate.

10. However, not all criteria for assessing the proper distribution of income are admissible under welfare economics. In particular, arguments favoring equality, not by reference to individuals' well-being, but based upon some standard independent of

well-being, are outside the scope of welfare economics and therefore are among the notions of fairness that are subject to our critique. For example, John Rawls is concerned with the distribution of primary goods rather than the distribution of well-being. See Rawls (1980, 526–27), stating that primary goods "are *not* to be understood as general means essential for achieving whatever final ends a comprehensive empirical or historical survey might show people usually or normally to have in common" (emphasis added), and explaining that his position revises suggestions in *A Theory of Justice*, in which the list of primary goods might have seemed to depend purely on psychological, statistical, or historical facts about people, rather than on a conception of the person that is fixed prior to examining general social facts. In similar spirit, Amartya Sen considers individuals' "capabilities" rather than their actual well-being as conventionally understood. See, for example, Sen (1985).

These alternative formulations often have implications similar to those of a social welfare function based upon individuals' well-being. When they do not, however, we find them unpersuasive for reasons analogous to the criticisms of notions of fairness that we offer in this book. Specifically, when the analyst decides which goods are primary or which capabilities are to count, and what importance each is to have, and then weights them differently from how the actual individuals in society weight them—which is precisely when this formulation has different implications from those of welfare economics—individuals will be made worse off. The reason is that they will be given less of those things that they value more than the analyst does and more of those things that they value less than the analyst does. Indeed, such alternative approaches sometimes would favor regimes under which everyone is worse off. This claim is easiest to see in the case in which all individuals have the same preferences and the analyst's formulation does not correspond to individuals' preferences, which is to say, whenever the analyst's approach differs from welfare economics. (The claim is a direct implication of the proof in Kaplow and Shavell (2001).) This analysis suggests that these alternative formulations can be viewed as a species of paternalism, see subsection VIII.B.1, but a sort that is not ultimately based on raising individuals' actual well-being. See, for example, Baron (1993, 152–54), suggesting that the importance of particular goods and capabilities can be explained with regard to their effects on individuals' well-being and noting that proponents may find such explanations inadequate, but asking: "[W]hat alternative kind of justification can be provided [?] ... What reason would anyone have to endorse a norm for satisfying desires that people do not have ... at the expense of desires that people have in fact?"; and Sumner (1996, 42–80), criticizing "objective" theories of welfare, including Rawls's and Sen's formulations, because they are detached from what actually matters to individuals.

11. In the case of a utilitarian social welfare function, for example, redistributing a dollar from an individual with lower marginal utility of income to one with higher marginal utility of income will, all else being equal, raise social welfare: Because the utility of the former individual will fall less than the utility of the latter individual will rise, total utility will be greater. (With regard to many other social welfare functions, individuals' marginal utility will similarly tend to be relevant but may not be decisive because of the next factor identified in the text.) A familiar implication of the diminishing marginal utility of income is that, under a utilitarian social welfare function, complete equality will be optimal if all individuals' utility functions are the same and there are no incentive effects associated with redistribution. And as Lerner has shown, if utility functions differ but the state cannot determine who has which utility function, it still follows that an equal distribution is optimal. See Lerner (1944, 28–34). See also Sen (1973, 83–87), showing that an equal distribution also maximizes any standard social welfare function in these circumstances.

12. That is, under such a social welfare function, it is possible for social welfare to be higher when two individuals' levels of well-being are more nearly equal, even if the sum total of their well-being is the same. In contrast, under the utilitarian social welfare function, only the total utility matters, not the distribution of utility (although recall that the distribution of *income* does matter, see note 28). There is a debate about whether and to what extent social welfare should be taken to depend on the distribution of individuals' well-being, but this is a debate within the framework of welfare economics. That is, the debate is about how social welfare depends on individuals' well-being, not whether it should. However the debate is resolved, note that social welfare depends only on

individuals' well-being; information on aspects of a situation other than their effects on well-being is irrelevant in assessing social welfare.

13. To illustrate, suppose that parents care about the welfare of their children and that many children turn out to be poor. Then a government program that helps poor children contributes to social welfare in two ways: directly, by increasing the well-being of the poor children, and indirectly, by increasing the well-being of the parents of poor children, who have higher utility because their children are better off. Similar logic applies to the case in which the well-being of the wealthy depends on the plight of the poor or that in which the poor envy the rich. See, for example, Duesenberry (1949, 101), Hochman and Rodgers (1969), and Boskin and Sheshinski (1978).

14. That is, some of those who undertake research in normative law and economics do not understand their efforts to be grounded in welfare economics, as we describe it. On this point, see our discussion of wealth maximization later in this subsection.

15. Economists are often criticized for using stylized models and for making restrictive assumptions, but such criticism reflects a misunderstanding of scientific method. Stylized models are helpful for understanding problems, and the statement of assumptions makes explicit the domain of one's analysis. Economists' use of assumptions actually is similar to legal academics' and philosophers' use of "hypotheticals," the stipulated facts of which constrain one to analyze the implications of given assumptions in an orderly fashion.

16. In the stylized model, losses and costs might be expressed in terms of only one good, and the well-being of each individual might be taken to equal the quantity of that good that he has. Relatedly, a common aspect of the economic approach is to express all costs and benefits in terms of a common denominator. In law and economics writing, this denominator is usually money. However, as the text to follow indicates, this approach does not entail embracing "wealth maximization" as the ultimate principle. See also subsection VIII. D.1, on valuing life, pain and suffering, and other nonpecuniary factors. We note that any logically consistent and complete system for evaluating legal rules is, in fact, equivalent to expressing everything, including factors sometimes viewed as incommensurable, in terms of a common denominator. See infra, note 29, presenting a formal statement of assessment based on fairness, and

note 114 in chapter VIII, further discussing the issue of incommensurability.

17. For example, in our own work, we sometimes analyze models in which only incentives are at issue, while at other times we undertake analysis in which income distribution is important. Other analysts may choose to specialize completely; for example, some public finance economists and legal academics who study the tax system focus primarily on matters pertaining to the distribution of income. Academic writing is properly viewed as a large, cooperative enterprise, within which each work seeks to make a contribution without necessarily being concerned with all aspects of the enterprise. In this context, specialization makes sense. See also subsection VII.B.2, discussing the proper approach to policy research by legal academics.

    We recognize that some economic analysts of law, like other analysts, too readily make policy recommendations based upon incomplete analysis. This is a problem to be avoided, but it does not bear on the value of making explicit simplifying assumptions for the purpose of advancing the understanding of complex problems.

18. A separate argument concerns differences among legal institutions; in particular, some would favor judges choosing legal rules on distributive grounds because legislatures may not engage in the optimal degree of redistribution, due to the balance of political forces. We do not address here matters of accountability and other questions involving the proper division of labor in this regard, but we do offer two observations that are usually overlooked by those who advocate that courts actively engage in redistribution. First, on average and in the long run, it is not clear that judges, who are elected or are appointed by elected officials, have significantly different distributive preferences from legislators. Hence, judicial redistribution that deviates from the legislative plan, if successful, would not over the long run produce a different distributive outcome, but it would result in inefficiencies both in periods in which judges redistributed more than the legislature would on its own and in periods in which they redistributed less. Second, legislatures can directly overturn court decisions (outside the constitutional context, which does not substantially regulate the extent of redistribution), and, in any event, legislatures set income taxes and transfer programs freely. Furthermore, many legal rules fall partially or wholly within the legislative domain to begin with. Hence, it seems unlikely that judges could succeed in implementing a regime that was significantly more or less redistributive than the one favored by the legislature.

19. One reason that there is no single, natural set of prices is that prevailing prices depend upon the distribution of wealth. (For example, if there is more inequality of wealth, there may be more demand for luxury goods, resulting in higher prices for such goods, and less demand for goods favored by the poor, lowering their prices.) In addition, prices are influenced by legal rules. (For example, products subject to stricter safety requirements will tend to sell at higher prices.) Moreover, the absence of a natural set of prices is not a problem that can be resolved by a simple price index adjustment, similar to adjustments for pure inflation, because relative prices differ. See generally Arrow (1958), discussing conceptual issues in measuring price, and id., at 77, stating that "[t]here seems no recourse but to recognize frankly that a standard of living [the cost of which a consumer price index is designed to measure] is not any fixed basket of goods, but a subjective level of satisfaction"—which, we note, is a notion that wealth maximization eschews by focusing on wealth rather than well-being. For a sketch of the development of Posner's views on wealth maximization and how they relate to the problem of defining wealth, see Kornhauser (1998).

20. Although there is no natural set of prices to use in measuring wealth, this problem may be overcome when undertaking such partial analysis by taking prices as given, or, as in some models, by implicitly stipulating that there is a single good (which thus becomes the common denominator for measuring, say, accident, prevention, and administrative costs). See supra, note 17.

21. Schelling offers a similar observation:

    Unfortunately, economists use the term "efficiency[,]" [which] sounds more like engineering than human satisfaction, and if I tell you that it is not "efficient" to put the best runway lights at the poorer airport you are likely to think you know exactly what I mean and not like it, perhaps also not liking me. If I tell you that "not efficient" merely means that I can think of something better—something potentially better from the points of view of all parties concerned—you can at least be excused for wondering why I use "efficient" in such an unaccustomed way. The only explanation I can think of is that economists talk mainly to each other. (Schelling 1981, 52)

Regrettably, legal academics often understand efficiency as a technical concept, divorced from its roots in individuals' well-being, so that they see pursuing the economic goal of efficiency as unrelated to concerns for human welfare. See, for example, Schwartz (1997, 1802): "[W]hile deterrence can be seen as a way of achieving the somewhat austere goal of economic efficiency, deterrence *also* has deep roots in a humane and compassionate view of the law's functions." (emphasis added); and id., at 1831: "But if accident prevention is an economic goal, it is *also* a generous, warm-hearted, compassionate, and humane goal. As such, it is a goal that can be and is in fact supported by a broad range of scholars." (Emphasis added.)

22. For further discussion of this issue and the related literature in the accident context, including comments on the difficulty many corrective justice proponents have had in distinguishing these notions of distribution, see section III.B.

23. For example, the prospect of payment or compensation may affect incentives, individuals' well-being when they are risk averse, and the overall distribution of income. But, setting aside these and any other ways that lawsuits may affect individuals' well-being, the bare fact that money may change hands in a lawsuit in certain circumstances, thereby changing how a loss is divided between the two parties, is of no consequence under welfare economics.

24. Some have suggested that much existing policy-oriented law and economics work does not follow the welfare economic approach as we describe it. We think that there is less truth to this point than meets the eye (see, for example, our comments in subsection 3, about the role of income distribution in the analysis of legal rules under welfare economics), but we do not seek to evaluate the existing body of work here.

25. Most arguments that invoke one of these terms can be expressed using other related terms. For example, the notion that it is "unfair" for one who is injured to be denied compensation from the wrongdoer may also be described as a form of "injustice" or as a violation of a "right" to compensation. Although some writers distinguish among these terms, we find it convenient to use a single term—we have chosen "fairness"—to refer

to any principle that does not depend solely on the well-being of individuals, as this section explains. Hence, our arguments concerning fairness-based analysis are broadly applicable to analyses based on justice or rights. Compare Hare (1981, chapter 9), stating that arguments drawing on "justice" and "rights" have the same character as those generally invoking our intuitive moral principles, on which see note 108, and thus have no real independent role in critical moral thinking. ... Indeed, defenders of rights often support them in ways that suggest an instrumental concern with promoting individuals' well-being. ... Of course, the idea that rights may be important on consequentialist grounds, relating to the promotion of individuals' well-being, has long been familiar. See, for example, Mill (1859).

26. Id.

27. What we mean by a notion of fairness can be expressed using the apparatus of welfare economics. We define social welfare, $W(x)$, as a function that depends exclusively on individuals' utility functions, denoted $Ui(x)$, and thus welfare does not depend directly on the situation x itself (that is, independently of how x might affect individuals' utilities). In contrast, a method of policy assessment that gives weight to a notion of fairness corresponds to a function $Z(x)$ that differs from (that is, cannot be expressed in the form of) the $W(x)$ function previously defined. Consider:

$$Z(x) = F(U1(x), U2(x), ..., Un(x), x).$$

Here, $Z(x)$ may depend not only on each individual's utility, but also directly on x, which includes all characteristics of the situation that will prevail under a legal regime. Thus, it is possible that a characteristic of the situation that affects no one's utility nevertheless affects $Z(x)$. Moreover, it may be that a characteristic that affects individuals' utilities influences $Z(x)$, but in a different manner. For example, a principle that says punishment should be proportional to the harm caused by an act depends on factors that do matter to people: Punishment matters to those punished and, because of deterrence, to others; and harm matters to victims. But under the principle in question, punishment is not assessed solely with regard to how it affects individuals' well-being—the $Ui(x)$— as was the case with the $W(x)$ function.

Some readers may be skeptical about whether a notion of fairness can be expressed in such formal terms. It should be understood, however, that this formulation simply involves a manner of communication. As we explained with regard to the social welfare function used in welfare economics, the only essential point is that, whatever the principle of evaluation, it provides an ordering of all potentially relevant situations (legal regimes), denoted here for convenience by the variable *x*. Now, any numerical value can be assigned to any situation (regime), as long as the analyst assigns a higher number to regimes viewed more favorably than others, so that $Z(x) > Z(X')$ may then be interpreted to mean that situation *x* is socially preferred to situation *X'*. Thus, the main assumptions entailed in expressing a notion of fairness as a function, $Z(x)$, are that the notion indicates a preference among various regimes and that the notion is followed in a consistent manner.

28. Sidgwick describes "intuitional" ethics—in his taxonomy, the alternative to egoism and utilitarianism—as:

> the view of ethics which regards as the practically ultimate end of moral actions their conformity to certain rules or dictates of Duty unconditionally prescribed.... Writers who maintain that we have "intuitive knowledge" of the rightness of actions usually mean that this rightness is ascertained by simply "looking at" the actions themselves, without considering their ulterior consequences. (Sidgwick 1907, 96)

See, for example, id., at 98; Davis (1991), surveying and criticizing deontological, that is, nonconsequentialist, theories of contemporary philosophers; and Fletcher (1972, 540–41): "Whether the victim is [entitled to recover under the proposed theory] depends exclusively on the nature of the victim's activity when he was injured and on the risk created by the defendant. The social costs and utility of the risk are irrelevant, as is the impact of the judgment on socially desirable forms of behavior." We will not usually distinguish between notions of fairness that do not depend on any consequences and those that do depend on consequences but not on individuals' well-being. (It is, of course, logically possible to have consequentialist principles that are independent of welfare. For example, one could seek to reduce the number of wrongful acts—without regard for the cost of doing so or for how much individuals would benefit—because one deems wrongful acts to be evil per se.) Because our claim is that

consequences for individuals' well-being are what should count in evaluation, not consequences unrelated to their well-being, we do not see a consequentialist fairness principle that is unrelated to well-being as better than a nonconsequentialist principle. In any event, as we discuss in chapters III–VI, most non-welfarist notions of fairness seem to be nonconsequentialist.

We also observe that, although many advance notions of fairness are avowedly nonconsequentialist, their stance is in some respects hard to interpret because of the difficulty in defining which acts are to be considered morally relevant without reference to their actual or expected consequences, particularly given the focus under many moral theories on what individuals "will" to occur, that is, what they voluntarily choose to cause. (For example, to define which acts constitute murder, one would have to refer to acts having expected consequences that include the death of another person.)

It must be observed, too, that it is difficult to draw the line between an act and its consequences: as the effects consequent on each of our volitions form a continuous series of indefinite extension, and we seem to be conscious of causing all these effects, so far as at the moment of volition we foresee them to be probable. However, we find that in the common notions of different kinds of actions, a line is actually drawn between the results included in the notion and regarded as forming part of the act, and those considered as its consequences. (Sidgwick 1907, 96–97)

29. Kant states that morality is a quality of the will, and he asserts:

> A good will is not good because of what it effects or accomplishes, because of its fitness to attain some proposed end, but only because of its volition, that is, it is good in itself and, regarded for itself, is to be valued incomparably higher than all that could merely be brought about by it. (Kant [1785] 1997, 8)

See id., at 10: "[T]he true vocation of reason must be to produce a will that is good, not perhaps *as a means* to other purposes, but *good in itself*...."

We note that, despite Kant's clear statements in his *Groundwork of the Metaphysics of Morals* ([1785] 1997) and the conventional understanding of his body of work, which is that he is a purely deontological philosopher who entirely rejects alternatives such as utilitarianism, Kant scholars have identified important inconsistencies in Kant's writing that raise some questions about the conventional interpretation:

> As Kant himself points out in reply to criticisms by Christian Garve … , he never asserted, and nothing he says implies, that happiness is not of the utmost importance [citing a 1793 Kant essay]. The unconditional character of morality means that the desire for your own happiness must not stop you from doing what is right; it does not mean that morality is the only good and important thing. Happiness is conditionally valuable, but when its condition is met, it is a genuine good. The moral law commits us to the realization of the good things that rational beings place value on. A world in which good people are miserable is morally defective. (Korsgaard 1996, 28)

Jeffrie Murphy (1987) has found similar inconsistencies in Kant's treatment of the purposes of punishment, as we discuss in note 17 in chapter VI.

Another aspect of Kant's writing that makes it hard to understand him as a consistent deontologist is his belief that duties to others should be assessed in a way that resembles the method of welfare economics. See, for example, Korsgaard (1996, 349), observing that "Kant agrees that we have a duty to promote the happiness of others," and that, in examining this duty, Kant believed that " '[w]hat they count as belonging to their happiness is left up to them to decide'" (quoting Kant ([1797] 1983)); and Sidgwick (1907, 386): "And we find that when [Kant] comes to consider the ends at which virtuous action is aimed, the only really ultimate end which he lays down is the object of Rational Benevolence as commonly conceived—the happiness of other men." See also O'Neill (1989, 6), noting that Kant added to the second edition of his *Critique of Pure Reason* a motto, taken from Bacon, that included the statement that "they should be confident that I seek to support not some sect or doctrine but the basis of human greatness and well-being."

In addition to such statements, which seem to take a positive view of a consequentialist, welfare-based approach, Kant also makes consequentialist arguments to illustrate or support his seemingly deontological maxims. Thus, when he attempts to deduce requirements of morality from the categorical imperative:

> he fails, almost grotesquely, to show that there would be any contradiction, any logical (not to say physical) impossibility, in the adoption by all rational beings of the most outrageously immoral rules of conduct. All he shows is that the *consequences* of their universal adoption would be such as no one would choose to incur. (Mill [1861] 1998, 51–52)

See id., at 97, observing that Kant's insistence that a principle be capable of adoption as a law by all rational beings cannot possibly rule out utter selfishness, so that giving meaning to Kant's principle requires that we understand rational beings as having a purpose of providing benefit to their collective interest. See generally Hare (1997, chapter 8, entitled "Could Kant Have Been a Utilitarian?").

30. As the preceding text suggests, such an outcome might be rationalized in one of two ways. First, the applicable notion of fairness may itself be understood as including a concern for individuals' well-being, in which case the fairness of making injurers compensate victims may be deemed to depend upon the cost of administering such compensation—perhaps because administrative costs must be borne by innocent victims, innocent taxpayers, or injurers who, although culpable, may be viewed as excessively punished if they bear a total cost larger than the harm they caused. Second, the notion of fairness may be independent of well-being but still not be decisive when well-being is affected. Thus, one might posit that the negligence rule is more fair but nevertheless favor strict liability because its cost savings exceed the extent of any unfairness associated with using it. Fairness-minded analysts are usually unclear about how they might incorporate consequences, particularly for individuals' well-being, into their analysis, but how a mixed view might be formulated is not relevant for our purposes.

31. However, our discussion in subsection VII.B.2 and elsewhere suggests that there is value in policy analysts' being clear and explicit about their objectives; in this respect, the language or fairness can be problematic even if it is used to express a welfare-economic-equivalent notion because fairness has many different meanings, some of which stand apart from, and are opposed to, individuals' well-being.

32. The reader should recall from subsection A.3 that many notions of fairness that are concerned with the distribution of income are principles that are concerned exclusively with individuals' well-being

and thus can be seen as encompassed by welfare economics.

33. We remind the reader of our discussion in subsection A.2, which explains how our critique of notions of fairness is easily reconciled with our view that considerations of income distribution are admissible under welfare economics.

34. Compare Sidgwick (1907, 264): "[T]here is no case where the difficulty is greater, or the result more disputed, than when we try to define Justice."; id., at 342–43, observing that moral notions are often left as "vague generalities," that we cannot make them definite without losing their broad acceptance, and that there may be alternative interpretations or no way to make them definite; id., at 375, stating that a view of justice holds that "we ought to give every man his own," but that we cannot define "his own" except as equal to "that which it is right he should have," rendering the formulation tautological; and id., at 392, explaining that the notion that morality depends on the "General Good," which consists in virtue, which depends on common morality, the prescriptions of which depend on a notion of the "General Good," is a further example of the circularity of moral theories. Bentham, commenting on the state of contemporary jurisprudence, expresses similar concerns:

> Had the science of architecture no fixed nomenclature belonging to it—were there no settled names for distinguishing the different sorts of buildings, nor the different parts of the same building from each other—what would it be? It would be what the science of legislation, considered with respect to its *form*, remains at present.
>
> Were there no architects who could distinguish a dwelling-house from a barn, or a side-wall from a ceiling, what would architects be? They would be what all legislators are at present. (Bentham [1781] 1988, 335)

This failure to provide definitions is not confined to analysts. It appears that judges, although they frequently invoke notions of fairness, often do not move beyond vague generalities:

> The most striking characteristic of fairness–rightness reasoning is the extent to which generalized, bottom-line assertions of fairness dominated [in the products liability opinions surveyed]. Nearly three-quarters of the decisions containing opinions relying upon fairness included general assertions—specific fairness reasons appeared in less than half of the fairness-based decisions. ... This recurring pattern of reliance upon vague assertions suggests that the judges grasped the concept of fairness intuitively, but found it somewhat difficult to explain analytically. (Henderson 1991, 1590–92).

35. As Mill observes:

> Not only have different nations and individuals different notions of justice, but, in the mind of one and the same individual, justice is not some one rule, principle, or maxim, but many, which do not always coincide in their dictates, and in choosing between which, he is guided either by some extraneous standard or by his own personal predilections. (Mill [1861] 1998, 99)

See, for example, id., at 100: "Each [principle] is triumphant so long as he is not compelled to take into consideration any other maxims of justice than the one he has selected, but as soon as their several maxims are brought face to face, each disputant seems to have exactly as much to say for himself as the others"; Sidgwick (1907, 271), observing that one "cannot get any new principle for settling any conflict that may present itself among such duties, by asking 'what Justice requires of us' "; and id., at 350, stating that we have not been furnished "with a single definite principle, but with a whole swarm of principles, which are unfortunately liable to come into conflict with each other; and of which even those that when singly contemplated have the air of being self-evident truths, do not certainly carry with them any intuitively ascertainable definition of their mutual boundaries and relations." See also Hardin (1986, 67): "[C]onflicts between rights are fundamentally problematic for a rights theory that begins with rights and that therefore has no prior principle from which to resolve the conflict." Most of the particular examples offered in this paragraph in the text will be discussed in section III.B, especially in the footnotes, where we address the views of corrective justice proponents in some detail.

36. Compare Hare (1997, 31), discussing the impossibility of identifying which cases are covered by a moral principle without first identifying what it is about certain acts or consequences that makes them "wrong" in the first place.

37. We observe that these points constitute a criticism of notions of fairness on the assumption that fairness-minded analysts would deem more of the injustice with which their notions of fairness are

concerned to be a bad thing. But in strict logic, an analyst could say, for example, that the injury to buyers through market-price adjustments is the fault of the market rather than of the legal rule that set the market forces in motion. Or one could say that punishment and evil acts go hand in hand, but the extent of evil is of no concern to society—in other words, evil is something that, in itself, is a matter of indifference, even though it is a thing that, for some reason, provides a justification for punishing those who bring it about. Because the actual rationale for most notions of fairness is not well articulated in the literature, it is difficult to know whether the consequentialist internal critique sketched in the text would in fact be viewed as troubling by scholars who promote notions of fairness, particularly deontological philosophers. Nevertheless, we suspect that many others would view our observations as relevant.

38. There is an irony here: On one hand, as discussed in subsections B.1 and B.2(b), most notions of fairness are understood to be nonconsequentialist, whereas on the other hand, their application is very much dependent upon the consequences—often fortuitous ones—of individuals' acts. Some proponents of fairness-based analysis would, however, take issue with principles that depend on the consequences of acts rather than on the acts themselves, as understood from the point of view of the actor at the moment he decides to commit the act; accordingly, some of the analysis in the text would be inapplicable. See, for example, note 3 in chapter III, discussing an argument about the relevance of "moral luck" to the principle of corrective justice. In any event, most notions of fairness are nonconsequentialist (as the term is conventionally understood) in that, when choosing a legal rule to govern particular outcomes, fairness-oriented analysts do not consider relevant how the rules under consideration would affect what outcomes are likely to occur.

39. Even many intentional acts, such as certain breaches of contract, are probabilistic in nature—and often quite unlikely—when viewed ex ante. Thus, it may be that virtually everyone would breach a contract if a particular contingency arose, but, at the time a contract is originally made, that contingency is remote, whereas contingencies under which promisors will in fact perform are overwhelmingly more likely.

40. That many notions of fairness implicitly ignore how the rules in question affect whether wrongs

occur in the first instance is noted in subsection B.2(b).

41. See generally Nisbett and Ross (1980) (survey); Baron and Hershey (1988), explaining how the particular outcomes of initial decisions influence assessments of the quality of those decisions; Fischhoff (1975), presenting experimental evidence of hindsight bias; and Tversky and Kahneman (1973), identifying the tendency of subjects to evaluate the probability of events based on the information that is most available or salient.

42. Baron has recently pursued this line of argument. See, for example, Baron (1993, 1998).

43. Fairness proponents have not, however, attempted to put forth notions of fairness that meet the sorts of objections that we have just noted. Indeed, the thrust of many arguments (especially those of philosophers) advancing notions of fairness has been anticonsequentialist and ex post in character, so substituting theories that are consequentialist and that adopt a more inclusive ex-ante perspective would conflict with the spirit of the proponents' enterprise. Moreover, if one made the necessary modifications, one would then have notions of fairness that are much closer to the objectives of welfare economics: To apply them, one would have to trace the effects of legal rules and, in the end, trade off competing effects. The primary remaining possible distinction would be that fairness-based analysis would give different weight to the effects than would welfare economics. For example, under welfare economics, the value of deterring a wrong depends on the amount of harm thereby avoided, where harm is measured by the negative effects of the wrong on individuals' well-being. For a notion of fairness not to collapse into welfare economics, it would need to specify a different methodology for assigning weights to wrongful acts—that is, the weights would have to be independent of how the acts affect individuals' well-being.

44. The thrust of our argument is similar to that of consequentialist philosophers (often, it turns out, utilitarians) who criticize nonconsequentialists (deontologists):

> [A]ny system of deontological ethics ... is open to a persuasive type of objection which may well be found convincing by some of those people who have the welfare of humanity at heart.... [T]here must be some possible cases in which the dictates of the system clash with those of

human welfare, indeed in which the deontological principles prescribe actions which lead to avoidable human misery. (Smart 1973, 5)

45. For a formal proof of our claim (which does not make use of symmetric settings), see Kaplow and Shavell (2001). Rather than sketch the proof here, we present a heuristic explanation, applicable to asymmetric cases, that we think better conveys the relevant intuition.

(1) Consider rules X and Y, and suppose that rule X is deemed better under welfare economics but rule Y is deemed better under a notion of fairness. The welfare-economic assessment means that, under the analyst's choice of the social welfare function, which embodies a distributive judgment, the overall situation under X is superior. See subsections A.2 and A.3.

(2) Now, construct a regime X' with the following characteristics: The overall level of social welfare and the extent of fairness are each the same as under rule X, but the distribution of well-being is the same as under rule Y—that is, the ratio of any two individuals' well-being is the same. (How do we identify such a regime? Consider all conceivable regimes with the same distribution of well-being as under rule Y and the same degree of fairness as under rule X. Now, in some such regimes, everyone will be better off than under rule X, so social welfare will be higher in such regimes than under rule X; and, in others, everyone will be worse off than under rule X. Since we can imagine all regimes in between, we can consider one in particular, which we are calling X', in which social welfare is the same as under rule X.)

(3) Next, compare situations X and X'. Even though the distributions are different, by construction (step 2) the overall level of social welfare is the same under the two regimes (and also, by construction, the extent of fairness is the same). If, for example, equality is greater under X' than under X, we would suppose that average incomes are lower under X'. The point is that, *whatever distributive judgment the analyst thinks appropriate,* it will be true by definition that, if one undertakes the above construction, the proper evaluation will rate X and X' equally, for social welfare (as defined under welfare economics) and the level of fairness are each the same in both situations.

(4) Finally, compare situations X' and Y. We know that the level of social welfare is higher under X' than under Y. (This is because we began, in step 1, with a case in which social welfare was higher under X than under Y, and, in step 2, we constructed X' such that it has the same level of social welfare as X; hence, social welfare under X' must be greater than under Y.) But because, in step 2, we constructed X' to have the same distribution as Y, it must necessarily be the case that everyone is better off under X' than under Y. (If total social welfare is greater under X' than under Y and the distribution of well-being is the same under both, it must be that every individual has a higher level of well-being under X'.)

This demonstration establishes that, if one insists on giving weight to a notion of fairness in an asymmetric case, then, whenever one chooses a rule different from one chosen under welfare economics, one expressly rejects a regime (here, X) that is equivalent—taking into account the combination of efficiency and distribution, and also holding fairness constant— to another regime (here, X') under which everyone would be better off than under the regime (here, Y) favored by the notion of fairness. In sum, even though in the asymmetric case the fairness-preferred rule may not itself make everyone worse off than under the alternative favored by welfare economics, choosing such a rule entails—if one is logically consistent— expressing a normative preference in another (constructed) situation for a rule under which everyone would be worse off. (We observe that the heuristic argument presented in this footnote differs from our formal proof and makes stronger implicit assumptions. The only substantial assumption required for our proof is that notions of fairness are, in mathematical parlance, continuous m a particular sense: The fairness assessment cannot change infinitely at the margin in response to a small, finite change in the level of some consumption good. For example, it cannot be that the notion of fairness under consideration gives more weight to, say, the population having one more peanut than it gives to an arbitrarily large degree of unfairness.)

We observe that, in the economics literature on social choice theory, a result exists that is a special case of the one that appears in the above-cited reference. Sen shows that following a particular notion of fairness—under which a stated domain of individuals' activity may not be regulated, even if that activity may affect the well-being of others—can lead to violation of the Pareto principle (that is, the principle that social choices should never make everyone worse off). See Sen (1970).

The logic of his proof, in essence, is that allowing individuals to create externalities may make everyone worse off. Our argument, by contrast, applies to all notions of fairness, most of which do not have the feature that generated Sen's result.

We also note that Sen interprets the conflict he adduces as raising questions about the underlying appeal of the Pareto principle. We do not, however, find his interpretation plausible. Sen's condition (which he calls "liberalism" and which he and others have subsequently described as an implication of a form of libertarianism) might seem merely to protect a sphere of individuals' activity. Yet in fact, his condition is tantamount to a prohibition on individuals' voluntary waiver of their "rights" in the specified sphere (in exchange for some concession from others), and this implicit prohibition is the source of the conflict with the Pareto principle that Sen identifies. Thus, this conflict actually has its roots in a limitation on individuals rights. Moreover, protecting a sphere of individuals' activity—commonly implemented by granting certain rights against government action—is familiarly justified on grounds of promoting individuals' well-being, because this sort of restriction on the government, while making some welfare-improving policies unavailable, produces an even greater expected gain by reducing the potential for the government's abuse of power. See, for example, Hardin (1986, 69–73) and subsection VIII.A.2. Sen's subsequent responses to these and other reactions to his argument seem to us to shift ground in a manner that eliminates the conflict he originally identified. In a later article, for example, Sen suggests that a contract by which parties mutually waive their rights may not work for a number of reasons: It may not be enforceable; enforcement may involve other adverse costs; and individuals may not in fact wish to enter into such a contract, because they prefer minding their own business. See Sen (1992, 144–46). In each instance, however, Sen no longer rejects in principle the state in which each party's rights are overridden and both parties are better off. Instead, such a state is deemed to be infeasible or for various reasons is not understood to make the parties better off after all. See also subsection VIII.B.3, addressing whether other-regarding preferences should be ignored in determining what is socially desirable.

46. This conclusion follows immediately from our proof that any notion of fairness conflicts with the Pareto principle, see Kaplow and Shavell (2001), because any modified notion of fairness—if it has not been altered so as to require an exclusively welfare-economic assessment—is still, formally, a notion of fairness; hence, our proof remains applicable to any modified notion....

We also note that, even if one could somehow modify some principle of fairness to avoid the objection that it may lead to choices under which the well-being of all individuals is reduced, one would have to ask whether the original motivation for the notion of fairness (whatever it might be) applies to the modified principle with sufficient force to justify its adoption. For example, if we view some act as intrinsically evil under a notion of fairness, but the notion becomes modified so that we give this evil no weight when such acts make everyone better off (but not when, say, they make almost everyone better off but a single person is ever-so-slightly worse off), a serious question arises whether we can still maintain the view that the act is intrinsically evil.... Compare Sidgwick (1907, 341–43), raising the question, in the context of discussing the need to modify moral principles to avoid conflicts, whether "the correctly qualified proposition will present itself with the same self-evidence as the simpler but inadequate one; and whether we have not mistaken for an ultimate and independent axiom one that is really derivative and subordinate."

Focusing on the symmetric case and on how it differs from asymmetric cases sheds further light on the inevitability of the conflict with the Pareto principle. First, as already explained in the text, any notion of fairness—however modified—will *always* make everyone worse off in the symmetric case whenever it favors a different regime from that favored under welfare economics. Second, as we elaborate in the tort context, the only important difference between symmetric and asymmetric cases is that the choice of legal rules may affect the distribution of income in the latter case. But, as explained in subsections A.2 and A.3, welfare economics already encompasses concerns about the distribution of income (or, more broadly, the distribution of well-being). That is, our definition of notions of fairness, which refers to all evaluative principles that differ from welfare economics, refers to notions based on matters other than concerns about income distribution, Hence, the only pertinent difference between the symmetric and asymmetric cases seems to be a factor (income distribution) that is separate from the concern of all notions of fairness that we consider. To sum up the argument, if notions of fairness are deemed to be flawed in the symmetric case because they can only make everyone worse off, and if asymmetric cases (that is to say, all other cases) do not differ from the symmetric case in a manner that is normatively relevant to the notions, then it follows that the notions are flawed in all cases. (This claim is related to the preceding point in this footnote because, in essence, the present argument is that, whatever the underlying basis for the notion of fairness is, it does not vary between symmetric cases, in which conflicts with the Pareto principle always arise, and asymmetric cases, in which such conflicts often do not arise.)

47. The importance of logical consistency in moral theory is often emphasized by philosophers. See, for example, Hare (1963, 93); id., at 100–02, criticizing those who attempt to escape from the demands of consistency by refusing to make moral judgments in certain cases that prove problematic for their theory; Hare (1997, 22): "Logic does not forbid the adoption of different moral standards by different people; it simply prohibits a single person from adopting inconsistent standards at the same time ..."; Sidgwick (1907, 6): "[A] fundamental postulate of Ethics [is] that so far as two methods conflict, one or (the] other of them must be modified or rejected"; and id., at 341, emphasizing the need for consistency and noting that "we frequently find ethical writers treating this point very lightly." See also Rawls (1980, 546), offering the following prescription when examining basic matters of justice: "[I]t is sensible to lay aside certain difficult complications. If we can work out a theory that covers the fundamental case, we can try to extend it to other cases later. Plainly a theory that fails for the fundamental case is of no use at all."

To many, the need for consistency will be evident, yet it is worth elaborating briefly. The application of a theory in a particular context can depend on any number of factors that are recognized under the theory. Thus, under welfare economics, if the amount of harm caused under a given regime or its administrative costs were to differ, the assessment might well change because, under the terms of the theory, assessments depend on individuals' well-being and these factors affect well-being. It does not follow, however, that it would be acceptable tor an adherent or welfare economics to offer a different assessment after a change in a factor that did not influence well-being, for to do so would, essentially by definition,

entail a rejection of welfare economics (which itself rules out the relevance of any such factor). Similarly, if one believed that a principle of fairness was absolute, and if that principle were nonconsequentialist (and thus necessarily independent of the effects of regimes on individuals' well-being), one could not favor a different regime from that dictated by the principle in order to avoid the problem that in some cases following the principle would lead to everyone being worse off. To do so would be to adopt a different principle. Compare note 55 in chapter III, discussing the issue in the tort context.

Nor can one avoid the problem that we describe in the text by adopting less absolute views of fairness, including commonly held mixed views that give weight to effects on individuals' well-being as well as to notions of fairness. On one hand, such mixed views can surely be consistent. On the other hand, we show at many points that such mixed views may in fact favor regimes under which everyone is worse off (and that this proposition is true whenever any weight, however little, is given to notions of fairness). Indeed, the discussion in the text of the symmetric case, indicating how any notion of fairness makes everyone worse off whenever it differs from welfare economics in that setting, is fully applicable to mixed views that give *any* weight to a notion of fairness. See also note 50 in chapter III, illustrating how, in the reciprocal case in the tort context, giving any weight to any notion of fairness will sometimes lead one to favor a legal rule under which everyone is worse off. And, as explained in note 49, supra, our proof that all notions of fairness sometimes make everyone worse off applies to any modification of the notions (as long as any weight to fairness remains), and hence to any mixed view.

48. To understand why principles like the categorical imperative essentially require an assumption of symmetry, let us consider an example. Suppose that there are strong people and weak people. A strong person would be happy to live by the principle that "might makes right" because such a rule would be to his advantage. Furthermore, in the absence of a symmetry assumption, the categorical imperative does not interfere with his adopting this principle because, if it were adopted as a general rule for society, he would still benefit from it, because he is strong. In order for the categorical imperative to rule out principles like "might makes right," which are little more than

statements of self-interest, it is necessary to imagine either that everyone is identical (neither strong nor weak) or that each of us is in each position (strong and weak) for a commonly specified period of time. This is precisely what is assumed to be true when one examines symmetric settings. See, for example, Hare (1963, 93–95); Hare (1997, 130–35), discussing Kant's categorical imperative; Korsgaard (1996, 100–01), stating that Kant's model of immoral conduct is built on the sort of case in which the problem is the temptation to make oneself an exception; and Sidgwick (1907, 389), criticizing Kant by observing: "[S]till a strong man, after balancing the chances of life, may easily think that he and such as he have

more to gain, on the whole, by the general adoption of the egoistic maxim ..." See also Sidgwick (1907, 380), noting that formulas like the Golden Rule are incomplete because "there may be differences in the circumstances—and even in the natures—of two individuals, A and B, which would make it wrong for A to treat B in the way in which it is right for B to treat A"; and Rawls (1980, 529): "[T]he background setup of the original position ... situates [the parties] symmetrically [so that persons are not] advantaged or disadvantaged by the contingencies of their social position, the distribution of natural abilities, or by luck and historical accident over the course of their lives."

49   The Grounds of Welfare (Review of Kaplan & Shavell, *Fairness versus Welfare*)

JULES L. COLEMAN

Louis Kaplow and Steven Shavell are talented and distinguished legal academics who for the past several years have been working jointly on a massive project in normative law and economics. The project's goal is to answer the question: What are the criteria by which legal policies (rules, standards, decisions, and other authoritative acts) ought to be assessed and proposals calling for their reform to be evaluated? In answering this question, they consider two normative frameworks—one defined by a concern for the impact of policies on human welfare, the other defined by a concern for various principles of fairness. Thus, the title of the book: *Fairness Versus Welfare*.[1] There is no surprise ending, as from the outset Kaplow and Shavell are clear that they judge welfare the unambiguous winner of the competition.

Previous iterations of the book have been in circulation for some time and available on the

Internet.[2] In addition, Kaplow and Shavell have made the rounds of law and economics workshops for several years,[3] taking the opportunity such occasions provide to set out and defend the book's central claims. Beyond that, the book has been the subject of numerous conferences and panels at professional meetings. It is unlikely, therefore, that many intended readers are not already familiar with its claims and the arguments marshaled on their behalf.

Even so, it is useful to distinguish among three groups of potential readers. The first two groups are the representatives of protagonists. On the one side are the deontologists—philosophers and legal theorists committed to the idea that some or other deontic considerations must play an independent role in assessing legal practice as well as calls for its reform. Along with everyone from Plato and Aristotle to Kant, Rawls, and Dworkin, Kaplow and Shavell are kind enough explicitly to include me in this group. This group is their target. As Kaplow and Shavell see it, no argument they could muster might convince the

Jules Coleman is a professor of law at Harvard Law School.

From *Yale Law Journal* 112 (2003): 1511–1543. Reprinted with permission of the publisher.

deontologists of the error of their ways, so hopelessly are the deontologists in the grip of a mistaken view. On the other side stand the fellow travelers along the law-and-economics highway. This group represents Kaplow and Shavell's natural allies. Although the argument of the book might firm their resolve, and harden them in battles with the deontologists, it is not necessary to persuade them. The argument of the book will be lost on the first group and otiose for the second. This leaves the uncommitted law professor searching for an analytical and normative framework within which to organize her thinking and through which to sharpen her critical lens. The book is self-consciously aimed at capturing the hearts and minds of this segment of the legal academy.[4]

It should come as something of a surprise, then, that among the most vehement critics of Kaplow and Shavell's project are other advocates of an economic approach to the law.[5] Whereas most deontologists are likely merely to dismiss Kaplow and Shavell as unsophisticated and their arguments as inadequately nuanced, the majority of law-and-economics scholars are anxious to dissociate themselves from a thesis they are convinced is dangerous to the cause. Why? The answer is that the book openly endorses precisely the imperialistic claims with which others have saddled the law-and-economics movement, often in an effort to discredit it as inadequately catholic or, in the extreme, uncivilized.[6] Whereas the vast majority of law-and-economics scholars have been trying to make the case for including efficiency among the factors suitable to assessing legal reform proposals, the entire point of the Kaplow and Shavell argument is that the *only* considerations that can figure in a rational reform policy are those of human welfare—or efficiency properly construed.

One might suppose that any book that triggers so much fear and loathing—that sends its natural allies scampering for shelter and engenders apoplexy among its targets—has to be either really dreadful or of fundamental importance. *Fairness Versus Welfare* is neither. The book is divided into two parts of very unequal length. In the first part, the authors distinguish the two competing normative frameworks of fairness and welfare from one another and set forth the general framework by which they shall adjudicate between the two.[7] In the second, and by far the longer, section of the book, they set out to make good on the strategy of evaluation by comparing fairness and welfare in a wide range of areas of the law—both private and public.[8] The argument of the book requires for its success treating the two parts of the book as connected. That is because the objection to fairness is that the price of fairness is too high in terms of its likely impact on welfare, and so it is the burden of the second part to establish just how extensive those detrimental effects are likely to be.[9] In this sense, the second part forms the evidentiary base for the thesis of the first part.

In fact, however, the second part of the book can stand on its own and constitutes a significant contribution to discussions of the impact on human welfare of various regimes of rules, standards, and policies in a wide range of areas of the law. The source of consternation for "friend" and foe alike is the first part of the book. Whereas the second part is nearly invaluable to anyone interested in policy analysis and legal reform, the first part's argument is entirely unsuccessful. Unfortunately, the overall argument of the book depends crucially on it.

Fairness Versus Welfare claims that welfare, and not fairness, is the standard appropriate to assessing the law and calls for its reform. This is a normative claim and, as such, requires normative argument on its behalf. Any suitable argument for the authors' claim then will consist in a set of reasons or grounds for the claim that welfare, and not fairness, is the appropriate basis for assessing law and its reform. The burden of providing an account of what is to count as grounds or reasons for that claim is the task of the first part of the book: the evaluative framework. Sadly, instead of discharging that obligation, *Fairness Versus Welfare* serves up empty tautological claims and underdeveloped putative causal explanations—explanations, moreover, that were they in fact adequate, would be so strong as to undermine, rather than support, the book's overall thesis. *Fairness Versus Welfare* makes a bold normative claim, but it offers no argument adequate to support it.

In part I of this Review, I summarize the debate on the normative foundation of efficiency prior to the publication of the Kaplow and Shavell book. In part II, I criticize Kaplow and Shavell's argument that welfare is the uniquely appropriate standard for the assessment of the law and proposals for its reform. In part III of this Review, I sketch an alternative account of the value of welfare. On that view, however, whatever it is about welfare that explains its value and aptness for assessing the law also explains why fairness is valuable and appropriate to assessing the law. In short, Kaplow and Shavell's account of welfare fails to explain its value and its role in evaluating the law. On the other hand, any plausible account of welfare that is capable of explaining its value explains as well the value of fairness and its appropriateness to evaluating the law and proposals for its reform. The central claim of the book is not just inadequately defended, but, at the end of the day, unsupportable.

I. WHY EFFICIENCY? THE DEBATE PRIOR TO *FAIRNESS VERSUS WELFARE*

Law and economics has attained such a dominant position within the modern legal academy that we can be excused for forgetting how relatively young a field it is. Richard Posner's *Economic Analysis of Law*[10] is the work most responsible for thrusting an economic approach to law onto the broader academic landscape. The distinctive feature of that book was the claims it made on behalf of the explanatory prowess of economic efficiency. In the face of the familiar Critical Legal Studies objection that the law lacks coherence and objective, rational content,[11] proponents of the economic analysis of law, led by Posner, argued that the law is a rational, coherent, and relatively determinate body of standards, the coherence and determinate content of which are explained by the principle of efficiency. As Posner and those who followed him argued, vast areas of the law—especially the private law—could be rationally reconstructed as if they were designed to produce an efficient allocation of resources.[12] The claim was

not that the law should promote efficiency—only that it did.

This desire to shy away from efficiency as a normative ideal could not be sustained, however. For law is the sort of institution that claims a legitimate authority for itself.[13] By its nature, law is coercive. Coercion is, by definition, an interference with human autonomy and personal prerogatives. To the extent that personal autonomy and human prerogatives are presumptively good, coercion is presumptively bad. It requires a defense. Law claims just such justification for itself. The claim may turn out to be false—sometimes or often. Still, the claim is not incoherent or necessarily false. This means that law must be the sort of thing of which the claim could be true. Those who claim that the law is efficient also claim that this fact about it contributes to its legitimacy. If that is so, it is natural to ask what principles of justified political or legal authority efficiency embodies or expresses. Posner understood the importance and appropriateness of this line of inquiry and saw it as his burden to answer the question: What justifies efficiency?

The burden of economic analysis is to identify a political or moral value beyond efficiency itself that would be adequate to justify the state's employing its coercive machinery in order to achieve it. How could the best interpretation of legal practice identify it as efficient if there were nothing to be said from the moral point of view on behalf of efficiency? Law's efficiency might merely undermine, rather than support, its claim to legitimacy. Nor would it be enough to associate some or other moral value with efficiency. After all, not everything of value is justly pursued through the law. The problem is not merely to identify some or other moral value achieved by efficiency, but to find one that would justify promoting efficiency through the coercive machinery of the law.

In setting out to meet this challenge, one might have expected Posner to avail himself of the strategy of identifying economic analysis with classical forms of utilitarianism. In promoting efficiency, the law promotes utility. To the extent it is appropriate for law to promote utility, it is similarly appropriate for it to seek to achieve an efficient allocation of resources. Since Bentham at least, the claim that the law appropriately pursues utility has an illustrious pedigree. The alliance between efficiency and utility would have seemed natural in part because law and economics relies on the Pareto criteria of efficiency. The Pareto criteria are themselves understood in terms of the role they have played in solving problems within utilitarian moral and political theory.

We can distinguish between Pareto optimality and Pareto superiority. We begin by defining Pareto superiority and then define Pareto optimality in terms of it. A state of affairs S is Pareto superior to another, A, if and only if no one prefers A to S and at least one person prefers S to A. The notion of Pareto optimality is then defined with respect to Pareto superiority. A state of affairs S is Pareto optimal provided there is no state of affairs Sn that is Pareto superior to it.

The Pareto rankings were introduced into the utilitarian literature in the early part of the last century in order to solve the so-called interpersonal comparability problem. They allow one to compare social states without making interpersonal comparisons of utility. If S is Pareto superior to A, then because at least one person's welfare or utility is improved and no one's is reduced, a move from A to S increases overall utility. There is no need to make any interpersonal utility comparisons, as there would be if a move from A to S created both winners and losers. Thus, social scientists generally (Pareto himself was a sociologist, not an economist) took the Pareto rankings as a way of rendering claims about overall utility verifiable and thus meaningful.[14] Given its role within both economic analysis and utilitarian moral theory, it is only natural to think, therefore, that the foundation for the economic approach to law is utilitarianism as mediated by Paretianism. The political or moral value captured by efficiency is utility, and economic analysis is part of the grand utilitarian tradition tracing itself back to Sidgwick and Bentham and beyond.

Natural as the alliance would appear, Posner would have none of it, and for the simple reason that he had been convinced by the classic objections to utilitarianism.[15] Maximizing utility can often lead to injustice, sacrificing the one for the good of the many. Utilitarianism is a defective moral theory, an inappropriate standard on which to justify state coercion—or so Posner himself thought. If efficiency is, as he thought it was, an appropriate standard of state action, then one would have to look elsewhere to explain its normative attractiveness. To find a moral foundation suitable to efficiency, Posner looked to a particular conception of Kantian moral theory—one that emphasized the importance of individual autonomy as expressed in the capacity to consent.

The argument he devised went as follows.[16] States of affairs that are Pareto superior make no one worse off and at least one person better off. For that reason no one could object to them. In other words, everyone would agree or consent to them. States of affairs that are Pareto optimal have no states Pareto superior to them. Any movement from a Pareto-optimal state will make someone worse off, and so not everyone will consent to it. People will consent to Pareto-superior states and will never unanimously consent to departures from Pareto-optimal states. Thus, the Pareto rankings reflect a commitment to consent and autonomy, not to utility. We need to distinguish the history of the Pareto rankings from the principles of morality to which they actually give expression. The history is utilitarian; the justification is Kantian. Or so Posner argued.

Welcome though it was, Posner's argument generated a bevy of critical responses, including mine. In the first place, very little efficiency analysis in the law actually invokes the Pareto criteria. Most efficiency analysis relies instead on the Kaldor–Hicks criterion.[17] One state of affairs, S, is Kaldor–Hicks efficient to another, A, if and only if the winners under S could compensate the losers such that, after compensation, no one would prefer A to S and at least one person would prefer S to A. For this reason, some advocates of law and economics, like Guido Calabresi, came to refer to the Kaldor–Hicks criterion as the "potential Pareto" principle.[18] States of affairs are Kaldor–Hicks efficient to others if and only if they could (were compensation actually paid) be Pareto superior. Of course, compensation is not paid, and so they are not in fact Pareto superior. That they are potentially Pareto superior has as much bearing on how they should be treated as the fact that I am potentially President of the United States has on how I should be treated now. The fact is that unlike the Pareto criteria, Kaldor–Hicks allows for both winners and losers. If the worries about interpersonal comparability are legitimate, Kaldor–Hicks reintroduces them; it does not solve them.

Those concerns are exacerbated by the fact that the Kaldor–Hicks criterion is subject to the Scitovsky Paradox. Scitovsky showed that two states of affairs can be Kaldor–Hicks efficient to one another.[19] This means that Kaldor–Hicks is not even a weakly transitive ordering relationship. Because Kaldor–Hicks does not observe transitivity, one cannot infer from the fact that S is Kaldor–Hicks efficient to A that S has more utility than A. But if Kaldor–Hicks cannot be defended on the grounds that it embodies utility, it certainly cannot be defended on Kantian grounds. For there are losers under Kaldor-Hicks-efficient states of affairs, and one cannot infer their consent to being made a loser.[20] My first set of objections to Posner's argument, then, had three elements. First, efficiency analysis in the law invokes Kaldor–Hicks and not Pareto. Second, because Kaldor–Hicks is intransitive, it cannot reliably track utility and cannot be defended on utilitarian grounds. Third, if we assume that losers do not consent to their losses, Kaldor–Hicks cannot be defended on Posner's conception of Kantian grounds either.

It would be a mistake to think that these problems are reserved only for Kaldor–Hicks, for even were economic analysis restricted to the Pareto criteria, there is no Kantian, autonomy, or consent argument in the offing. Consider first the criterion of Pareto optimality. A Pareto-optimal state is one that has no states Pareto superior to it. Any movement from a Pareto-optimal state will produce losers. So it may be reasonable to assume that movement *from* a Pareto-optimal state would not be unanimously agreed to. But it does not mean that movement *to* a Pareto-optimal state from a prior state would be consented to, nor does it mean that everyone would consent to the Pareto-optimal state in which they find themselves. A Pareto-optimal state can itself be the result of a Pareto-noncomparable change, one that produces winners as well as losers. If we presume that the

losers in going to a Pareto-optimal state would not consent to the move, then the move to a Pareto-optimal state would not have been consented to.

A simple example illustrates the general point. At time t, everyone has nine units of X each except Jones, who has one unit of X. At $t+1$, Jones has one hundred units of X and everyone else has only one unit of X each. Any move from $t+1$ will make Jones worse off and thus the allocation at $t+1$ is Pareto optimal. By the same token, the move to the situation at $t+1$ would not have been consented to by anyone other than Jones. That does not mean that $t+1$ is not Pareto optimal. It is. It's just that the Pareto optimality of the world at $t+1$ tells us nothing about whether or not it is or would be consented to.

If we move on to consider Pareto superiority, we locate the real problem with Posner's defense of efficiency. Posner's thought is that because no one is made worse off under a Pareto improvement and at least one person is made better off, it follows that no one would object to—or, more strongly, that everyone would consent to—Pareto improvements. But this is either false or a logical consequence of the definition of the notion of preference. In neither case can the fact that parties would prefer this or that be a *reason* or *ground* for their consent. The argument after all is simply this: People prefer S to A; therefore, people would consent to S (over A). The first clause is supposed to represent the idea of Pareto superiority, the second that of consent. The second is thus the grounds of the first. In fact, people sometimes choose to do what they do not prefer to do, and do not do what they would otherwise prefer to do, often because they think it wrong to act as they would otherwise prefer. So we cannot infer choice from preference. We could of course infer choice (or consent) from preference, but only if we build the notion of choice into the definition of what it is to have a preference. Often that is in fact what we do. To say that S prefers A is just to say that S has a disposition to choose A when the option is available. But when we do that, we cannot employ the notion of choice as an independent moral basis for the Pareto ranking. Quite the contrary, in fact. We are merely defining the Pareto rankings in terms of hypothetical choices. In other words, the consent argument for Pareto superiority either fails or is best understood as a definition of rational self-interest.

To sum up: (1) Kaldor–Hicks, and not the Pareto criteria, is the basic standard of efficiency in law and economics. The Kaldor–Hicks criterion is intransitive. Two states of affairs can be Kaldor–Hicks efficient to one another. Utility observes transitivity, but Kaldor–Hicks efficiency does not. This suggests that Kaldor–Hicks does not embody or express the utilitarian ideal. (2) States of affairs that satisfy the Kaldor–Hicks standard may produce losers as well as winners. The losers cannot be expected to consent to their losses, or at least we cannot infer that they will. Therefore, there is no Kantian or consent defense for Kaldor–Hicks efficiency. (3) Nor is there a consent-based defense of Pareto optimality in the offing. On the assumption that losers will not consent to their losses, all we can say is that once at a Pareto-optimal point, individuals will not unanimously consent to departures from it. (4) Nor can one infer that Pareto-superior states are consented to. One can infer that Pareto-superior states are preferred to those states Pareto inferior to them. But the fact that they are preferred does not entail that they are consented to, unless preference is defined in terms of consent. In that case, the claim that Pareto-superior states are consented to expresses a definition, and thus consent cannot ground or justify Pareto superiority, being completely constitutive of it. Or so I have argued.

II. FAIRNESS VERSUS WELFARE: ASSESSING THE KAPLOW–SHAVELL ARGUMENT

This is the backdrop against which we approach our discussion of the Kaplow–Shavell book—a book that explicitly limits itself to addressing only these and other issues in normative law and economics. This is *not* a book that extols the explanatory virtues of efficiency or the importance of modeling legal problems as ones about the efficient allocation of resources.[21] It is a book whose central claim is that considerations of welfare are the only defensible grounds on which to assess

legal policy and proposals calling for legal reform.[22] This is a claim that presupposes the value of efficiency, that invites us to reconsider the very same questions that Posner and his critics took up 20 years ago. At the end of the day, after all, the book's claim is interesting only if both fairness and welfare are at least prima facie plausible candidates for assessing legal practice. Were fairness not even a plausible candidate for assessing legal practice, the claim that welfare is more appropriate to the evaluation of the law than is fairness would be both unimportant and uninteresting. Were welfare an implausible candidate for assessing legal practice, the claim that it is more appropriate than fairness in evaluating law would be no more than a bad joke.

This means that several burdens fall to Kaplow and Shavell. In the first place, because the aim of the book is to compare welfare and fairness with regard to their value as standards for evaluating the law, they owe us accounts of welfare and fairness.[23]

We need to know what it is we are comparing. It would be demanding too much to require that Kaplow and Shavell defend one or another conception of fairness and welfare as uniquely correct or better than a range of plausible alternatives. Whereas Kaplow and Shavell need not defend accounts of welfare and fairness as correct, they do need to offer accounts of each that answer to several adequacy conditions. One crucial adequacy condition is the requirement that any account offered *must* have the resources sufficient to explain why welfare and fairness are valuable. More than that, really. The accounts offered must have resources adequate to explain why both are apt for the assessment of law. Not every value, after all, is one suitably pursued through the coercive machinery of the law. An account of welfare that left it mysterious why a rational policymaker might think that legal policies ought to be assessed according to their impact on welfare would fail as an account of welfare. Similarly, an account of the nature of fairness that left it mysterious why a rational policymaker might argue that the law ought to conform to the demands of fairness would fail as an account of fairness. Even if it is too strong an adequacy condition to impose on an account of either welfare or fairness that it be capable of explaining the aptness of either *for assessing law*, the condition is minimally necessary to make the Kaplow–Shavell book interesting. After all, their explicit aim is to show that welfare is a more appropriate criterion for assessing legal policy than is fairness, and that project is interesting only insofar as fairness and welfare are both plausible criteria for assessing legal policy in the first place.

Beyond that, Kaplow and Shavell must provide a standard for deciding between the two. They need to defend that standard as appropriate and argue that applying it to the relevant facts leads to the conclusion that welfare is uniquely apt to the assessment of legal policy. Focusing on the standard itself for a moment, it is important to note that it might take a broader or a narrower scope. Someone might defend the unique appropriateness of welfare (or fairness) as a tool for assessing legal practice by showing first that welfare (or fairness) is the correct standard for assessing *all* human action. Or one might argue that welfare (or fairness) is uniquely appropriate to assessing the law while setting to one side concerns about which norms are appropriate to the assessment of human or political actions more broadly.

Most, but not necessarily all, deontologists adopt the view that the standards appropriate to assessing political or legal action need not apply to human conduct more generally. This means that the aptness, say, of corrective or retributive justice for assessing tort and criminal law respectively is not in general thought to depend on whether compensatory or punitive practices within the family are similarly regulated by principles of corrective and retributive justice. In contrast, utilitarians incline to the view that the principle of utility is appropriate for the assessment of legal or political action just because all action is appropriately assessed by its impact on utility. The principle plays out differently in different contexts, but it remains the appropriate ultimate standard of assessment in all.

Because of this difference in scope of application, the standard for assessing the appropriateness of fairness and welfare as normative frameworks for the law has to be tailored to law. A welfarist

or utilitarian is free to believe and contend that welfare or utility is uniquely suitable to assessing human conduct broadly, but she cannot count it against her deontologist rivals that retributive or corrective justice is not.[24] She cannot, that is, unless she is also prepared to offer an additional argument to the effect that a norm is appropriate to assessing legal practice only if it is appropriate to assessing human conduct more generally—only, in other words, if she is prepared to argue that the political must be derivable from the ethical. Kaplow and Shavell offer no such argument, nor do I have reason to think that they would be inclined to do so. Thus, they must take on the deontologist on the narrower ground that welfare is superior to fairness as a criterion for assessing legal practice, setting to one side the relative merits of both in assessing human conduct more generally.

To sum up to this point: To support the claim the book makes, Kaplow and Shavell must first provide accounts of welfare and fairness that explain why both are apt for the assessment of legal policy. Then they need both to identify a standard for choosing between the two and to defend its appropriateness. Finally, they need to argue—on the basis of relevant facts about law, fairness, and welfare, together with the relevant evaluative standard—that welfare is uniquely appropriate to the assessment of law. This is the kind of argument the central claim of the book demands. The most striking feature of the book is that there are no such arguments in it. There are no explicit substantive accounts of either welfare or fairness offered, no argument presented that explains why either is valuable or apt for assessing the law. Nor is a standard for choosing between the two articulated, let alone defended as correct, and so there is no argument from such a standard to the book's central conclusion. What then is there?

There is instead the following—what I will refer to as the "main argument":

1. A person's welfare is a function of what he or she values.[25]
2. To say that a person values something is to say that it can be represented as an argument in his utility function, or that it is the logical object of one of his preferences.[26]

3. Fairness is thought to be valuable.[27]
4. To say that fairness is valuable is ambiguous between the claim that (a) fairness is something that persons (some or all) prefer, and the claim that (b) fairness is valuable apart from whether or not persons prefer it.[28]
5. If fairness is valuable insofar as it is the object of a preference, then fairness is a constituent of a person's welfare.[29]
6. If fairness is a constituent of welfare, then pursuing fairness improves welfare or is in any event compatible with welfare.[30]
7. If, however, the value of fairness is independent of its being preferred or valued by someone, then pursuing fairness is incompatible with welfare maximization.[31]
8. Therefore, whether pursuing fairness is compatible with welfare depends on whether it is an independent value. Fairness as an independent value is incompatible with welfare because it diminishes welfare.[32]
9. Therefore, understood as an independent value—that is, something whose value is independent of whether it is the object of anyone's desire or preference—fairness is inappropriate as a standard of assessment.[33]
10. Because fairness so conceived is an inappropriate standard for assessing conduct of any sort, it is inappropriate to assessing the law.

This has the form of an argument, but it may be a mere tautology. Insofar as fairness is valuable as the object of desire, pursuing it is compatible with welfare. To the extent it is valuable apart from anyone's preference for it, pursuing it is counter to preference satisfaction, and to the extent that preference satisfaction is constitutive of welfare, it is incompatible with welfare. This is no more than a tautology, and, remarkably, Kaplow and Shavell admit as much.[34] Nor is it an informative tautology. It is not, in other words, a truth whose existence or import is revealed only upon seeing the connections brought to light by the argument. It simply follows from the view of welfare as constituted by the objects of one's preferences and of fairness as the remainder, that is, as logically independent of one's preferences, that if we pursue the latter we do so at the expense of

the former. No elaborate argument is needed to support that claim or to have its insights revealed tous.

Because the argument does no more than reveal the analytic relationship between conceptions of fairness and welfare, whatever claims it makes about how fairness decreases welfare can be recast as claims about how welfare diminishes fairness.[35] Thus, any conclusion about the relative appropriateness of welfare as against fairness for assessing the law can be recast as a conclusion about how fairness is more appropriate than welfare. In fact, neither conclusion would be warranted by the argument. The argument merely elaborates a tautology, and no normative conclusion follows from a tautology. One could conclude from this argument that welfare is preferable to fairness as a standard for assessing law only if one could also conclude that fairness is preferable to welfare—such is the nature of the tautology. Either conclusion is simply a non sequitur; a fortiori, so is the conclusion Kaplow and Shavell draw. So much for the main argument.

Unfortunately, this is the only relatively explicit argument Kaplow and Shavell offer. There are, however, a variety of considerations that appear to play a significant role in their overall assessment of the case for welfare as against fairness, and if we identify and attend to them we may be able to construct another argument on behalf of their central claim. Kaplow and Shavell strongly believe that moral, political, and legal philosophers drawn to deontic considerations grossly underestimate and otherwise fail fully to appreciate the extent to which pursuing fairness can diminish welfare.[36] So even if it is analytic that fairness decreases welfare, it is important to note just how much it does, or, more accurately, how much in principle it could. No one would endorse the pursuit of fairness were there reason to think that doing so could make everyone worse off. Yet that is precisely the sort of disaster pursuing fairness could occasion, or so they argue.[37]

Kaplow and Shavell draw two implications from the strongly adverse effects of fairness on welfare. The first is that those who support deontic standards for assessing law incur an argumentative burden. Given that (1) welfare is appropriate to assessing legal practices and that (2) fairness can impose tremendous costs on welfare, the burden is to explain why the law ought nevertheless to conform to the demands of fairness. That is a burden that falls on the deontologist, and there is no comparable burden on the welfarist. Assuming next that (1) and (2) above are true, it is then puzzling that actual policymakers and ordinary folk, as well as political philosophers, urge that legal policy should conform to the demands of fairness. In other words, in spite of the easily demonstrated adverse effects of fairness on welfare, there remain deeply rooted deontic intuitions, whose existence calls out for explanation. It is central to Kaplow and Shavell's thinking that they believe that they have identified just such an explanation. It is, broadly speaking, an evolutionary argument.[38] Possessing strong deontic beliefs is evolutionarily selected for. Such beliefs contribute to human survival and thus to human welfare. Evidence, moreover, of this fact is the extent to which such intuitions are reflected in the informal norms that guide relations among us.

If we put these considerations together, we can construct what I will refer to as the "subsidiary argument":

1. It is indeed a tautology that pursuing fairness diminishes welfare.[39] This is no more interesting than is the equally true claim that pursuing welfare diminishes fairness.

2. Though (1) is a tautology, the important point is that deontologists underestimate the extent to which pursuing fairness can in fact diminish welfare. In the extreme case, pursuing fairness can make everyone worse off as judged by each person's conception of her welfare.[40]

3. This means that fairness can be very detrimental indeed to welfare.[41]

4. Still, in spite of the detrimental impact of fairness on welfare, many people believe that we ought to assess policies in terms of their fairness, and not in terms of their impact on welfare.[42]

5. Given what we know about the value of welfare and the detrimental impact of fairness on it, the existence and persistence of such a belief is puzzling. This puzzle begs for an explanation. The explanation can be located in the mechanisms of evolutionary biology. Having strong deontic intuitions reflected in practices has evolutionary value. It contributes to survival and to human welfare accordingly.[43]

6. Thus, we can offer a *reasoned* explanation for the value of welfare and a *causal* explanation for the belief in the value of fairness. Reasoned explanations rationalize and, in doing so, justify or explain the value of welfare. In contrast, causal explanations deflate the justificatory claims made on behalf of fairness.[44]

7. Therefore, because welfare is rationalizable as a standard, it is appropriate to evaluating the law. In contrast, it is the belief in the value of fairness that is explained—not by reasons, but by causes. So we must assess the law by considerations of welfare, even as we recognize the forces of nature that pull us to fairness: a pull our rational selves must resist if we are to do what is right.[45]

The main argument is an elaborated tautology offered in support of a non sequitur. The subsidiary argument is not a tautology, but it is no less problematic and unpersuasive. Let's begin with the thought that philosophers drawn to assessing legal practices and policies along broadly speaking deontic lines (fairness or justice) underestimate the extent to which pursuing the latter can diminish welfare. Presumably this is an empirical claim about deontologists, and, if so, it is false. Each of the traditional and widely known objections to utilitarianism put forth by deontologists presupposes that pursuing fairness or justice comes at a very high price to utility (or welfare). All the old war-horse examples—including the case of punishing the innocent—are constructed around the conflict between fairness and welfare (broadly construed). In the usual case, considerations of security and welfare make an overwhelming argument for punishing an innocent man. The question is whether we ought to. The deontologist argues we cannot. There is simply no way of understanding the deontologist's argument other than by attributing to him an implicit acknowledgment of the high cost to welfare of acting in conformity with the demands of justice. Indeed, there is no way of understanding any of the standard deontological objections to utilitarianism of this form other than as acknowledgments of the claim that conformity to justice demands much in the way of costs to welfare. So much is taken for granted. It is a further question whether the deontological arguments are always convincing—that, in other words, the costs to welfare are worth the price of justice. And it is a further question still whether deontologists must be committed to the view that no price to welfare is too high when incurring it is necessary to conform to the demands of justice. But there is simply no question that deontologists are more than adequately aware of the extent to which conforming to the demands of justice can come at a very high cost indeed to welfare.

Kaplow and Shavell similarly fail to appreciate that if what they offer up is a good argument, it is as telling against the welfarist as it is against the deontologist. For if conforming to justice can greatly diminish welfare, it is equally true that pursuing welfare can greatly diminish justice. The very same counterexamples to utilitarianism that presuppose the extent to which one must forgo welfare to conform to the demands of fairness can be read as indicating the extent to which pursuing welfare imposes costs on fairness. Isn't that just the point of the punishing-the-innocent kind of example? That is, if all we have in mind is pursuing welfare, then we run the risk of imposing the greatest sorts of injustices—including punishing those we know to be innocent of wrongdoing. Similar remarks are in order for all such counterexamples to utilitarianism. In just the same way that they require the deontologist to confront the cost to welfare of conformity with justice, they force the welfarist to confront the cost to fairness of a single-minded pursuit of welfare. That is why so much ink has been spilt on these examples. They vividly raise the conflicts between two different conceptions of right action, and the costs of a single-minded devotion to either. Not only is it simply false that deontologists fail to appreciate the costs to welfare of commitment to conformity with fairness, but also, if true, the

charge applies equally to the economist. We have uncovered no truth about deontology or about its relationship to welfare. All Kaplow and Shavell have provided are vivid examples of how the conflict between welfare and fairness—a conflict that is inevitable, given the way they conceptualize the two—might play out in actual practice.

The most puzzling feature of the Kaplow–Shavell argument is the apparent sense that there is something perplexing about strong deontic intuitions that calls for a causal explanation.[46] Every component of this part of their argument is problematic—from the claim that deontic intuitions, but not welfarist ones, need explanation, to the explanation itself, to the implication that to offer a causal explanation of such intuitions is somehow to deflate their justificatory force. Beyond that, again there is the problem that they fail to see that if the arguments they marshal forward are adequate against the deontologist, they are equally compelling against the welfarist. Let's take up these problems in turn, beginning with the suggestion that there is reason to think that strong deontic intuitions somehow call for explanation.

Given the value of welfare and the detrimental impact of pursuing fairness on it, Kaplow and Shavell wonder why it is that otherwise intelligent people would insist that the law should conform to the demands of fairness. The view that the law should cannot be defended by reason. The best one can hope to do is to explain why philosophers and others nevertheless insist on it. Where Kaplow and Shavell fail to see the possibility of justification, they offer an explanation instead. The belief in the value of fairness cannot be justified, but it can be explained. Indeed, the fact that it can be explained is part of what counts against the claim itself. This is a difficult idea, and some care must be taken to understand it and its significance within their overall argument.

To this end, it is helpful to distinguish between two (of many possible) views about the relationship between explanatory and normative projects. The first of these is represented by a particular form of philosophical naturalism, what we may call "replacement naturalism."[47] Replacement naturalism is the view that normative projects—whether in epistemology, jurisprudence, or the philosophy of mind—are hopeless. Because normative projects cannot succeed, the only projects left worth pursuing are explanatory ones.

A familiar example from epistemology illustrates the general strategy of argument. We can think of the central projects in epistemology in the following way. Begin by thinking of sensory experience as epistemic inputs and beliefs; theories, or worldviews as epistemic outputs. The project of epistemology is to determine which outputs are warranted by a given set of inputs. This is the project of identifying the criteria of warranted or justified belief. Beliefs are warranted if they are appropriately supported by the inputs. What constitutes appropriate support or justification? In this sense, traditional epistemology is "justification-centered." Famously, Quine argued that there are no a priori discoverable rules that uniquely pick out some beliefs as warranted and others as not, given a set of epistemic inputs. Philosophy has nothing to contribute to helping us identify the norms of sound or good reasoning—the norms that, if followed, would uniquely warrant some beliefs and not others.[48] Instead of trying to determine the norms governing good reasoning—those which, if followed, would warrant beliefs—we should study how people in fact reason. Traditional epistemology would be reduced to a chapter buried somewhere in a psychology textbook as its justificatory projects gave way to explanatory projects of cognitive psychology; thus the phrase "replacement naturalism."

From the view that explanatory inquiries substitute for normative ones, we can distinguish a family of views around the claim that causal explanations have normative consequences. There are of course many senses in which explanations are normative, and many ways in which explanations can play a role in normative arguments, none of which need be controversial. Not all the views one might have about the relationship of explanation to justification are so innocent, and in a moment I want to focus on one particularly controversial claim. According to the claim on which I want to focus, a causal explanation of why someone asserts the claim she does bears on our assessment of the merits of the claim itself. In particular, in the

form of the claim upon which Kaplow and Shavell rely, causal explanations of the beliefs we have and the claims we make can deflate those beliefs and claims.

Before focusing on this claim and its centrality to their argument, it is important to contrast it a bit further with some more familiar law-and-economics attitudes regarding the place of explanatory and normative projects. Some advocates of law and economics are skeptical of the value of normative projects and are inclined instead to restrict themselves to explanatory endeavors. This makes them naturalists of a sort, self-aware or not. Others are not skeptical of normative judgments as such, but feel that the special role of economic analysis is not to advance normative judgments but to contribute to the rationality of the judgments we reach by uncovering important causal connections, for example between liability rules and accident rates. Most law and economics contributes to the wisdom of our judgments and the defensibility of our social policies in precisely this way.

Kaplow and Shavell eschew these more modest understandings of the way in which causal explanations can figure in normative arguments in favor of the much stronger claim that a causal explanation of the beliefs individuals have deflates the merits of the beliefs themselves.[49] As they see it, the fact that there is a persuasive causal explanation for why many people—including philosophers, policymakers, and ordinary folk—believe that the law ought to promote fairness should figure in our assessment of the claim itself. Why else would they introduce, in the course of defending welfare against fairness, the fact that such an explanation exists?

There are two connected claims here: first, that there is a persuasive causal explanation of why individuals insist on the view that the law ought to be assessed by its conformity to the demands of fairness; and second, that the fact that there is such an explanation counts in our assessment of the underlying merits of the claims of fairness. This latter claim is the interesting one for our purposes. There is no denying that it is bold and distinctive and, as we shall see in a moment, essential to their overall argument. Bold, distinctive, and essential to the argument it may be, but plausible and adequately defended it is not. Worse, were the claim sound, it would likely undermine rather than support their overall thesis.

Without qualification, the view that the existence of a causal explanation of the fact that someone holds or asserts a particular claim undermines the truth of the claim asserted simply cannot be sustained. Often, the best causal explanation of why someone might assert that P is the truth of P. So it cannot be that causal explanations as such undermine the truth of the claim the assertion of which is being explained. The thesis must be narrowed or weakened. Even if most causal explanations have no bearing on the truth of the claims asserted, some explanations might. Which causal explanations of the beliefs we have go to our assessment of the merits of our beliefs, and why? Kaplow and Shavell obviously believe that evolutionary explanations of our beliefs have a bearing on the merits of the beliefs themselves. For they argue both that there is an evolutionary explanation for the fact that individuals believe in the value of fairness as appropriate to assessing the law, and that this fact cuts against the claim of fairness and indirectly supports the claim of welfare.

As they see it, evolution shows that it is to our collective advantage to believe that our affairs should be regulated by fairness, and so it should come as no surprise that individuals insist that our affairs be regulated by fairness. On their view, we insist on fairness because it is to our advantage to do so, not because our affairs really ought to be regulated by fairness. Once we are suitably attuned to the evolutionary advantages of our strong deontic intuitions—advantages evidenced, they claim, by the extent to which our informal norms and practices embody fairness[50]—the grip of those principles on us is correspondingly weakened. Learning the source weakens the grip, and in this way evolutionary explanations figure in our justifiably discounting the content of the claims of fairness.

It is easy to confuse this view with a familiar and more plausible one that is common in everyday discourse. In a heated debate on tort reform, one participant advances the view that a cap should be imposed on damage awards for medical malpractice, and another replies by noting that the advocate of capped damage awards is a surgeon who has been sued successfully for medical malpractice. In so replying, she means to deflate the surgeon's claim. Another person advances the view that rents in New York City should remain stabilized, and others dismiss her view on the grounds that she lives in a rent-stabilized apartment. In these cases, reflecting on the source of the claims, we are not surprised by the opinions both advocate, and we are properly skeptical of their motives. Even so, while we may be skeptical of the motives in each case and wary of the arguments adduced, the fact remains that both the surgeon and the apartment dweller may be right. They are interested advocates, and this may increase their burden to make a compelling case, but such a case can be made. And for the obvious reason that the causal story goes to the reliability (one way or another) of the witness, not to the truth of what is asserted.

Kaplow and Shavell are making a stronger claim. For it is not their view that once we learn the evolutionary origins of the belief in fairness that we should adopt a skeptical posture to those who advocate fairness—a posture that would incline us to demand more in the way of normative argument before we are persuaded by the truth of the underlying claim. Their view is that the evolutionary argument for fairness, by itself, is part of the argument against it and for welfare.

I have attributed this claim to Kaplow and Shavell, but they nowhere explicitly make the claim or defend it. My claim is not that Kaplow and Shavell explicitly advance this view. Rather, my claim is that we must attribute such a view to them to make their argument work. To appreciate the centrality of this claim to their overall argument, we need to retrace the argument up to the point at which the evolutionary argument for the belief in fairness is introduced.

The basic argument rests on just a few ideas. As I have reconstructed it, the basic thought is that welfare is valuable and that pursuing fairness is detrimental to it. This cannot suffice to defeat fairness for the simple reason that we can run the argument in reverse. Fairness is valuable, and pursuing welfare is detrimental to it. The charge against fairness is then strengthened with the observation that pursuing fairness can *greatly* diminish welfare. This is no help either, since the same is true of fairness: Pursuing welfare can greatly limit our ability to act in accordance with the demands of fairness. This is basically the argument of the book, but for two ancillary discussions—one on the evolutionary origins of the belief in fairness and another on, loosely speaking, the plasticity of our deontic intuitions.[51]

This means that in the absence of the evolutionary argument, Kaplow and Shavell have adduced no considerations against fairness and for welfare that could not be recast to cut the other way. Without the evolutionary argument, nothing they say cuts one way or the other. The evolutionary argument thus carries a very heavy burden. It is all that stands between their having made the case for welfare and their having made no case at all. The evolutionary argument is supposed to introduce considerations that cut against fairness and for welfare. And how can that be unless the existence of an evolutionary explanation for fairness counts against the claims of fairness and for welfare? There is no way to read the evolutionary argument in the context of the book other than as an effort to deflate the claims of fairness and thus indirectly to make the case for welfare.

With so much riding on the evolutionary argument, we should pause for a moment to identify what Kaplow and Shavell would have to demonstrate in order to make good on it. Evolutionary arguments are a species of causal explanations. Causal explanations of why someone believes or asserts what he does typically do not bear on the merits of those beliefs or assertions. So one thing Kaplow and Shavell need to do is to explain why evolutionary explanations do. More than that, of course; they would need to explain why evolutionary arguments deflate rather than bolster the merits of the beliefs whose existence they are said to explain. At the most basic level, of course, they would need to show that evolution (or something like it) actually selects for beliefs. In addition, they would have to show that evolution has selected for the belief in fairness. Even this would not be enough, for they would have to

show that even though evolution selects for the belief in fairness, it does not select for the belief in welfare. For if evolution selects for the belief in welfare, the entire project would collapse.

Kaplow and Shavell meet none of these adequacy conditions. They offer no basis on which to distinguish evolutionary arguments from other causal or functional explanations—that is, no grounds for thinking that evolutionary explanations go to the underlying merits of the beliefs we have in a way in which other causal explanations do not. They offer no grounds for thinking that evolutionary arguments deflate rather than bolster the merits of our beliefs that have evolutionary origins. They provide no reason for thinking that evolutionary factors select for beliefs. If evolution selects for beliefs, they provide no reason for thinking it would select for the belief in fairness and not for the belief in welfare.

We can set aside many of these worries for now because, even on its own terms, the argument fails. It is something of an exaggeration to say that Kaplow and Shavell offer an evolutionary explanation for the belief in fairness, or for strong deontic intuitions more generally. They do little more than gesture at an evolutionary-style argument.[52] Roughly, the argument is that there are evolutionary advantages to believing that human affairs ought to be regulated by considerations of fairness. Once we understand the evolutionary benefits of maintaining strong deontic intuitions, the puzzle is solved. Those who insist on evaluating the law by its conformity with the demands of fairness are advancing a view that cannot be sustained by appeal to reason or to value, but which can be explained evolutionarily—as a false but valuable one.

If Kaplow and Shavell are correct, the belief in the value of fairness (as valuable independent of its connection to welfare) is mistaken. Not just a harmless false belief either, but one that, to the extent that it has affected our legal practices, has been the source of waste, misery, and misfortune. The correct belief is in the value of welfare. The claim that evolution selects for fairness implies that evolution would select for a false belief. Other things being equal, we should want an accurate road map of the world as we try to negotiate our way through it. After all, an inaccurate road map will likely lead us astray. If we think of our beliefs as constituting a map of the world, why shouldn't we expect evolution to select for true beliefs, rather than for false ones? Some of the beliefs on which we rely in making our way through life are normative ones—beliefs about how we ought to behave, what we owe one another, and how governments should regulate affairs among us. Shouldn't we expect evolution to select for true normative beliefs, not for false ones?

We don't have to claim that evolution must select for true beliefs in order to undermine Kaplow and Shavell's argument. It is enough to note that they provide no reason for thinking that evolution would select for this particular false belief in the value of fairness as opposed to the true belief in the value of welfare. If anything, there is at least as much reason for thinking that evolution selects for welfare as for fairness. If evolution selects for beliefs, it is likely to select for beliefs that contribute to our capacity to negotiate the world successfully. In general, true rather than false beliefs are more likely to contribute to our capacity to negotiate the world. There is probably a better evolutionary argument for the economist's insistence on welfare than there is for the philosopher's insistence on fairness. Given their view that an evolutionary explanation of the beliefs deflates the content of the beliefs, this would not be a good outcome for them. On the one hand, evolutionary pressures explain the belief in welfare. On the other hand, they are committed to the view that evolutionary arguments deflate. The deflation claim seemed helpful when there was reason to think that evolutionary considerations would cut against fairness. The argument looks less helpful when it is likely to cut against welfare.

These evolutionary considerations are even more troubling than we have suggested so far. If true beliefs are the ones that are in fact evolutionarily selected for and if the evolutionary argument cuts against them, then the only claims that are not undercut by evolution are the ones evolution does not select for: namely, false, unhelpful ones. Could anything be more implausible than this? In fact, all this is best taken as a *reductio* of the entire form of argument.

This line of objection seems so devastating to the evolutionary argument that I wonder whether I have misunderstood the role that evolutionary considerations are to play in their thinking. Perhaps the evolutionary argument is offered to make a different point, namely that everything, even the belief in fairness, survives only because it contributes to welfare. That argument might run as follows. We have three categories of beliefs on which we might act: the belief in the value of welfare; the belief in the value of fairness, where fairness is reducible to an argument in this or that person's utility function; and the belief in fairness, where fairness is thought to be something valuable whether or not anyone has a taste for it.[53] Acting on the belief in the value of welfare (other things being equal) promotes welfare. Acting on the belief in the value of fairness as something valuable insofar as individuals have a taste for it also promotes welfare (other things being equal). There is an apparent tension when philosophers and others argue that we should act on a belief in the value of fairness as something valuable whether or not anyone has a taste for it. Such action would appear to be inconsistent with welfare. But the evolutionary argument shows us that this inconsistency is more apparent than real. For the belief in fairness as an independent value itself survives only because it is welfare enhancing. Evolution shows us that everything converges on welfare, even fairness; everything that survives contributes to welfare.

If this is the argument Kaplow and Shavell have in mind, then rather than supporting the central thesis of the book, it overwhelms it. If everything survives because it contributes to welfare, then that's all there is to it. It does not matter how we assess the law. If we think it appropriate to assess the law by its impact on welfare, that's good because doing so contributes to welfare. If, on the other hand, we come to the view that we ought to assess the law by the extent to which it conforms to the demands of fairness, no problem. For we have come to that belief evolutionarily. And if we have come to that view evolutionarily, acting on such a view contributes to welfare. The problem with interpreting the evolutionary argument this way is that it makes a joke of the book's project; there is no meaningful sense in which there is a competition between fairness and welfare. The only competition is between direct and less direct methods of attaining welfare. Indeed, promoting welfare is hardly something that we attain, for at the end of the day, evolution makes it impossible for us to do anything else. Hardly the stuff of a classic work.

Kaplow and Shavell's reliance on evolutionary theory is a methodological nightmare. In the first place, the appeal to evolutionary considerations cannot be taken literally since evolution does not select for particular beliefs. They claim that because there are advantages to a belief in fairness, there must be an evolutionary-type argument for it. But they also believe that the belief in the value of fairness is false, and moreover that such a belief has many disadvantages as well. This is hardly adequate material to support an evolutionary hypothesis that would explain the persistence of a false belief.[54] There is better reason to suppose that there is an evolutionary argument for the belief in the value of welfare—a belief Kaplow and Shavell insist is both true and beneficial. They provide no reason for thinking that evolutionary arguments go to the merits of the beliefs we have when other causal-functional explanations do not, and no reason for thinking that such explanations deflate rather than inflate the underlying claims. Worse, if evolutionary explanations do go to the underlying merits, that would put Kaplow and Shavell in a bind. There is an evolutionary argument for welfare, and, on their view, such an argument should undermine the claims of welfare. If, however, the evolutionary argument is introduced to show that everything reduces to welfare at the end of the day, then it proves too much.

Forgetting the methodological confusions that ravage the argument itself, and focusing only on what inferences we can draw from it, several options are available. If there is an evolutionary argument for fairness, then there is one for welfare. If evolutionary arguments deflate the normative beliefs they explain, the claim to the value of welfare as well as claims to the value of fairness are equally deflated. If evolutionary arguments are irrelevant to the content of the claims the belief in which they explain, then the evolutionary argument is a non sequitur. If the evolutionary argument shows that everything is reducible to welfare, then it makes a mockery of the book. At the end of the day, the evolutionary argument is either a non sequitur, proves nothing, or proves too much. In no case can it shoulder the burdens Kaplow and Shavell have placed on it.

It might be helpful if we synthesize all the arguments of the first part of the book.

1. From the main argument we can derive the conclusion that pursuing fairness reduces welfare.
2. From the subsidiary argument, we get illustrations of the extent to which it might.
3. From the subsidiary argument, we also get a causal explanation of the belief that pursuing fairness is appropriate.
4. From the subsidiary argument, therefore, we derive a deflationism about the normative claims for fairness.
5. When all of these considerations are put together, we have an argument for the conclusion that pursuing welfare (as against the alternative of pursuing fairness) is uniquely appropriate to the legal domain.

The problems with the argument can be put as follows:

1. Given how they define the terms, the claim that fairness diminishes welfare is a tautology and can be recast as the claim that welfare diminishes fairness.
2. The subsidiary argument illustrates not just that fairness can greatly diminish welfare, but that welfare can in fact greatly diminish fairness as well.
3. To the extent that the subsidiary argument offers an adequate causal explanation of strong deontic intuitions, the same argument applies to strong welfarist intuitions.
4. To the extent to which evolutionary or causal explanations more generally deflate normative claims on behalf of deontic beliefs, they deflate analogous claims made on behalf of welfare.
5. On the other hand, there is no reason to suppose that causal explanations deflate justificatory claims in either case.

The problem with *Fairness Versus Welfare* is that it makes a normative claim but offers no normative arguments to support it. Instead, Kaplow and Shavell present a mixture of tautological claims about the relationship between fairness and welfare, and putative causal explanations of the fact that individuals have strong deontic intuitions. The former are empty and cannot support a normative claim. In truth, the latter fail to rise above the level of mere speculations. Even as adequate causal explanations, such factors are irrelevant to the truth of the underlying claims on behalf of fairness. And, as I have demonstrated over and over, if the evolutionary argument is a problem for the deontologist, it is a problem for the welfarist as well. At the end of the day, of course, the existence of a possible causal-functional explanation of why we believe what we do has no bearing on the truth of what we believe.

III. WELFARE AND FAIRNESS REDUX: OUTLINING AN ALTERNATIVE VIEW

The central claim of the book is that the law should be assessed by its impact on welfare and not by its conformity to the demands of fairness. This claim is interesting only if both welfare and fairness are plausible frameworks within which to evaluate the law. An argument appropriate to sustaining the book's claim, therefore, would begin with substantive accounts of both welfare and fairness. Such accounts would be adequate insofar as each possessed resources sufficient to explain the value of welfare (and fairness) as well as the aptness of each for evaluating the law. Once adequate accounts of welfare and fairness were in place, an appropriate argument would then set forth and defend a criterion for choosing between welfare and fairness so conceived.

Kaplow and Shavell provide no criterion for choosing between fairness and welfare—which is puzzling in a book entitled *Fairness Versus Welfare*. They provide evidence that requiring the law to conform to the demands of fairness limits the extent to which it can promote welfare. Many

of these very same examples, however, also illustrate the extent to which promoting welfare restricts the extent to which the law might satisfy the demands of fairness. And so the evidence they offer, while interesting in its own right, has, in the absence of a criterion for choosing between welfare and fairness, no bearing on the book's fundamental claim.

The reader should recall that it is Kaplow and Shavell, and not their deontologist target, who make the radical claim. They claim that the law should be assessed *only* by its impact on welfare, and never by its conformity with the demands of fairness. The deontologist need make no comparable claim. The deontologist need not, and likely does not, claim that the law ought not to be assessed by its impact on welfare. He claims only that in addition to being assessed by its impact on welfare, the law ought to be assessed as well by the extent to which it conforms to the demands of justice. Kaplow and Shavell reject even that modest claim. One would think, with the stakes so high and the claims so strong, that Kaplow and Shavell would offer and defend a criterion for making the choice—but they do not.

Nor, should it be said, do they offer an account of fairness or of its value. Indeed, they explicitly reject the need to provide an account of what fairness is.[55] Therefore, they offer no criterion for distinguishing corrective from retributive justice, and both from distributive justice. All are lumped together under the general rubric, fairness, whose value or aptness as a standard for assessing the law remains completely obscure. On their view, it is not necessary to explain what fairness is or why pursuing fairness is valuable, because their argument is that whatever fairness is and whatever is valuable about it, pursuing it is detrimental to welfare.

If truth be told, the only serious claim they make is that fairness is detrimental to welfare, and we have gone to great lengths to establish the limited interest of this claim in making out the book's fundamental conclusion. Even so, one would think that with so much riding on the claim, Kaplow and Shavell would go to similar lengths to spell out the nature of welfare and to explain its value and appropriateness to assessing the law. If it is decisive against fairness that it is detrimental to welfare, then welfare must be pretty damn important. It may be, but whether it is depends in part on what we take welfare to be. So we need an account of what welfare is and an explanation of its extraordinary value.

In fact, Kaplow and Shavell offer precious little by the way of an account of the nature of welfare. They have even less to say about the value of welfare—apparently content to observe that no one denies that welfare is valuable.[56] Although Kaplow and Shavell do not offer what anyone would regard as an account of welfare, they do offer a general picture of its constitutive elements.[57] There is enough in that picture for us to differentiate it from other possible conceptions of human welfare, and to ask whether welfare, so conceived, is something of such value that it could provide the only standard suitable for assessing the law.

In what follows, I argue for two points. First, on any interpretation of welfare plausibly attributed to Kaplow and Shavell, it is unclear what the value of welfare is. It is even less clear why one would insist that welfare, so conceived, is uniquely appropriate to assessing the law. If I am right, the central claim of the book is entirely unsupported by their arguments. Beyond that, I argue that any conception of welfare adequate to explain its value would also explain the moral significance of deontic considerations and their aptness for assessing the law. Whatever it is about human welfare that makes it appropriate to assessing the law explains why assessing the law in terms of its justice and fairness is similarly appropriate. Any argument offered in defense of their central claim merely defeats it. Thus, I suggest that not only is the central claim of the book unsupported, it is unsupportable.

Let's begin with their partial conception of welfare. In their framework, the constitutive elements of a person's welfare are her preferences.[58] A person can have welfare only insofar as she has preferences that obey a set of rationality constraints. If a person has a set of preferences over all possible social states, and these preferences obey familiar rationality constraints, then a person can have welfare; and her welfare is determined by the satisfaction of her preferences. The more her preferences are satisfied, the greater her welfare. Maximizing preference satisfaction maximizes welfare (for an agent).

The basic elements of welfare are preferences and their satisfaction. This leads to the natural identification of welfare with preference satisfaction. This identification is too quick, however, for the notion of preference satisfaction is ambiguous between a logical and a psychological sense. In the logical sense, to satisfy a preference is to realize it. To satisfy Jones's preference that P is to bring P about. Whether a person's preferences are satisfied in the logical sense is one thing; whether he is satisfied in the sense of experiencing pleasure, joy, happiness, or gratification as a result is another thing altogether.[59]

We might flesh out Kaplow and Shavell's account of welfare in two distinct ways corresponding to these two notions of satisfaction. In the logical sense, a person's welfare is maximally satisfied when his desires are maximally realized. If this is what welfare is, why is welfare in this sense something of value? The value of welfare in this sense cannot be the value we associate with gratification, joy, or pleasure. Rather, the value of welfare is the value of seeing to it that people get what they want. And their getting what they want—having their desires or preferences realized—is valuable independent of what individuals want and whether getting what they want is met with pleasure, joy, or gratification, on the one hand, or consternation and regret on the other. Often we regret what we have chosen to do and what we have done, what we desire to do and the actions that flow from those desires. What is so valuable about seeing to it that individuals get what they want—if what they prefer brings them no happiness or joy, or if what they want is bad for them and for others—that the law should promote welfare in this sense?

In contrast, if welfare is understood in terms of psychological satisfaction, then it is not obvious what the value is of satisfying preferences in the logical sense. After all, the psychological state that we desire to bring about by acting on the basis of our preferences may sometimes be achieved only by frustrating rather than by realizing our desires.

By the same token, because individuals may secure gratification or satisfaction from all sorts of activities that are bad for them and for others as well, why would anyone think that maximizing satisfaction in the psychological sense should be the goal of law?

Although Kaplow and Shavell offer no general account of welfare, they do understand welfare in terms of preference satisfaction. But preference satisfaction is an ambiguous notion. There is an important difference between satisfaction in the logical and the psychological sense, and the relationship between the two notions is anything but unproblematic. Satisfying preferences in the logical sense is no guarantor of satisfying them in the psychological sense. On the other hand, satisfaction in the psychological sense can require frustrating rather than satisfying preferences in the logical sense. On neither account is the value of welfare obvious. And its unique or distinctive appropriateness for assessing the law remains mysterious.

I don't mean to suggest that gratification or psychological satisfaction is undesirable or valueless. Nor am I suggesting that realizing one's desires is similarly without appeal or value. Still, whatever the value of either may be, it cannot carry the normative burden with which Kaplow and Shavell saddle it. For their view is that welfare conceived in either sense is uniquely appropriate to legal policy in a way in which fairness is not.[60]

This brings us to my second, and ultimately more important, point. Any plausible account of welfare that explains its value and aptness for assessing the law also explains the value of fairness and its aptness for assessing the law. We do better in understanding the nature of welfare and its value if we think of an individual's welfare not in terms of his preferences, but in terms of what is in his interests—not in terms of what he desires, but in terms of what is good for him. Among the distinguishing features of persons is that in addition to having preferences, they are planning agents. They can formulate projects and plans, invest in and execute them. They can form views about what it is they want from life, and guide their behavior by the plans they make, the agreements they reach, and the norms that regulate their

affairs with others. This is part of what it is to live a life of one's own—what it is for a life to be something one does rather than something that happens to one.

Persons have interests not only in what they desire and in realizing those desires, but also in autonomy and security. They are interested not only in having their desires realized and in securing gratification and pleasure. They also have an interest in organizing a life in a way that makes sense of the desires they have. They have an interest in contributing to the way their life unfolds. The capacity to live a life, and not merely to have a life happen to one, depends on being able to express one's autonomy and on being protected against persons who are unprepared to mitigate their action in the light of the interests of others. Of course, any plausible theory of what is valuable to a person would include the ability to act on the basis of one's preferences and desires. But that is because autonomous action is valuable to persons understood as planning agents who bear a special relationship of ownership and responsibility to how their life goes, and not because people have a taste for autonomy.

In the context of this brief review, I cannot develop this line of argument in detail. I have said a bit more about it elsewhere, and views of this sort are familiar in the literature more broadly.[61] The idea here is that once we acknowledge that human welfare matters because of something about what it is to be a person—that is, to be an agent capable of living a life of one's own, where how one's life goes is in part a matter of what one does and not just a function of what happens to one—it is obvious that the very same kinds of considerations that explain the value of welfare explain our strong deontic intuitions as well. Principles that restrict the extent to which we can pursue our own interests without regard for the impact of our actions on the interests and rights of others express a commitment to this ideal of the person. We can think of distributive justice in roughly the same way. It is a precondition of one's life being something one does, rather than something that happens to one, that one have resources at one's disposal adequate to that end. One who is completely the victim of misfortune and bad luck is robbed of the capacity to realize oneself or one's personality in the world. Welfare matters because the self-respect and dignity of persons matter. The conditions of self-respect and human dignity require us to mitigate our actions in ways that take into account the interests of others, and to regulate our conduct by norms that fairly and justly adjudicate among those competing interests.

Once we realize that welfare is connected to a person's interests—what is good for him, and not merely to what he desires or to his gratification or joy—it should be clear that whatever it is in that account that explains the value of welfare explains as well the importance of the law's regulating human affairs according to various principles of justice and fairness. It is something about people, and not something about realizing desires or gratifying psychological states, that makes human welfare valuable. But whatever it is about persons that ultimately warrants concern for human welfare warrants the view that justice must regulate affairs between persons. It is not that justice is a constituent of welfare or welfare a constituent of justice. Rather, both are important and distinct reflections of the dignity and importance of persons. Any theory of the law that would direct us to evaluate our practices by considering only welfare or justice and not the other could do so only by impoverishing the idea of the person. In doing so, it would indict itself more than any critic, sympathetic or otherwise, could.

NOTES

1. LOUIS KAPLOW & STEVEN SHAVELL, FAIRNESS VERSUS WELFARE (2002).
2. See Louis Kaplow & Steven Shavell, *Fairness Versus Welfare*, 114 HARV. L. REV. 961 (2001); Louis Kaplow & Steven Shavell, Principles of Fairness Versus Human Welfare: On the Evaluation of Legal Policy (Nov. 2000), *at* http://www.law.harvard.edu/programs/olin_center.
3. See KAPLOW & SHAVELL, supra, note 1, at xxi-xxii (listing workshops at which the authors have presented portions of the book).
4. See id., at 79–81, 389–94.
5. See, e.g., Howard F. Chang, *A Liberal Theory of Social Welfare: Fairness, Utility, and the Pareto Principle*, 110 YALE L.J. 173 (2000); Howard F. Chang, *The Possibility of a Fair Paretian*, 110 YALE L.J. 251 (2000).
6. Cf. Joseph William Singer, *Something Important in Humanity*, 37 HARV. C.R.-C.L. L. REV. 103, 124–30 (2002) (accusing Kaplow and Shavell of imperialistically insisting upon an overly cramped conception of the human good).
7. KAPLOW & SHAVELL, supra, note 1, at 3–81. The book concludes with a few chapters that elaborate upon the framework presented in the first part of the book. For purposes of my bipartite division, these chapters can be treated as addenda to the first part.
8. Id., at 85–378.
9. See id., at 58 (noting that later chapters will document the extent to which fairness-based policies and rules diminish human welfare).
10. RICHARD A. POSNER, ECONOMIC ANALYSIS OF LAW (1972). The book is currently in its sixth edition.
11. E.g., Joseph William Singer, *The Player and the Cards: Nihilism and Legal Theory*, 94 YALE L.J. 1 (1984).
12. POSNER, supra, note 10, at 98–100.
13. This claim is often associated with Raz. See JOSEPH RAZ, THE AUTHORITY OF LAW 29–30 (1979).
14. It is worth pointing out that the so-called "interpersonal comparison" problem arose during the heyday of logical positivism, and that the problem may well be no more than an artifact of a mistaken semantic and metaphysical thesis, and not a real problem at all. At least, that is my view.
15. See Richard A. Posner, *Utilitarianism, Economics, and Legal Theory*, 8 J. LEGAL STUD. 103, 111–19 (1979).
16. See Richard A. Posner, *The Ethical and Political Basis of the Efficiency Norm in Common Law Adjudication*, 8 HOFSTRA L. REV. 487, 488–97 (1980).
17. See Jules L. Coleman, *Efficiency, Exchange, and Auction: Philosophic Aspects of the Economic Approach to Law*, 68 CAL. L. REV. 221, 237–47 (1980); Jules L. Coleman, *Efficiency, Utility, and Wealth Maximization*, 8 HOFSTRA L. REV. 509, 525 (1980) [hereinafter Coleman, *Efficiency, Utility, and Wealth Maximization*].
18. GUIDO CALABRESI & PHILIP BOBBITT, TRAGIC CHOICES 85–86 (1978).
19. See T. de Scitovszky, *A Note on Welfare Propositions in Economics*, 9 REV. ECON. STUD. 77 (1941); see also Coleman, *Efficiency, Utility, and Wealth Maximization*, supra, note 17, at 519 n.14 (providing a brief demonstration of the paradox).

20. Coleman, *Efficiency, Utility, and Wealth Maximization*, supra, note 17, at 533-39. On the other hand, if we ask whether individuals would choose to have policy made according to Kaldor–Hicks, then the answer might be "Yes" under well-defined circumstances, but these are the same conditions that Harsanyi showed would lead individuals to adopt average utilitarianism with interpersonal utility comparisons. See John C. Harsanyi, *Cardinal Utility in Welfare Economics and the Theory of Risk-Bearing*, 61 J. POL. ECON. 434 (1953). In that case, efficiency analysis is just a (perhaps) mathematically more sophisticated way of representing a commitment to average utilitarianism. But the defense of utilitarianism or efficiency (understood as Kaldor–Hicks) is not in terms of any particular moral value. Rather, it is simply a logical consequence of the notion of rationality defined in a particular way. Average utility falls out of our notion of rational choice and risk neutrality. Rational, risk-neutral parties will prefer or choose (the same thing on this theory, since to prefer is to be disposed to choose under appropriate circumstances) a principle of average utility as a way of distributing resources among themselves. This is what Harsanyi proves, and as David Gauthier once remarked, one does not argue against theorems. What one does is show that this is not a defense of the moral attractiveness of utilitarianism, but a consequence of a certain conception of rationality (in conjunction with the formulation of a particular choice problem). One would then have to show what moral value, if any, is embodied in this particular conception of rationality, and so on.

21. See KAPLOW & SHAVELL, supra, note 1, at 4 n.3.

22. See id., at 3 ("Our central claim is that the welfare-based normative approach should be exclusively employed in evaluating legal rules.") See also id., at 5 ("[T]he design of the legal system should depend solely on concerns for human welfare.")

23. In a book of this length, a reviewer is likely to find much with which to take issue. Indeed, I found no shortage of such disagreements, but I want to limit my discussion to this, the central argument of the book. I cannot resist, however, pointing out that the authors often show themselves incapable of taking on the issues they tackle on the philosophical grounds they have chosen. One place where their lack of philosophical understanding is especially noteworthy is right at the core of the book—otherwise I would be inclined just to let the issue pass.

One of their persistent criticisms of deontologists is that we do not seem capable of settling on a shared definition of various of the notions of fairness at play. See, e.g., id., at 45–47, 86–99. We do not, for example, agree about what corrective justice is or about the nature of retributivism or distributive justice. This criticism is doubly mistaken. Most important, philosophers of law are not in the business of defining "fairness" or cognate terms like "corrective justice" and "retributivism." We are not providing a semantic or metasemantic account of terms, but a theoretical account of the nature of the thing to which the term arguably refers. We disagree with one another about what fairness is, what corrective and distributive justice are, and, indeed, what welfare is. Ours is not a disagreement in the first instance as to the semantic content of "fairness" or "corrective justice," for example. In claiming that fairness is appropriate to the assessment of law, we cannot be understood as making the claim that the content of "fairness" is appropriate to assessing law. Our disagreements are theoretical, not semantic or metasemantic (although as philosophers of language, we may—and do—have such disagreements as well). And once we realize that our disagreements are theoretical, not semantic, it is hardly surprising that we disagree. After all, the content of political principles—and the demands they impose—are nothing if not controversial.

24. It is worth noting, as Rawls has, that the classical utilitarians were concerned primarily with questions of institutional design and not with human conduct more broadly or with specific details of legal practice. See JOHN RAWLS, A THEORY OF JUSTICE 22 (1971). Concern for the role the principle of utility plays in answering every minute detail of legal practice is very much a modern phenomenon, and not a particularly attractive one either.

25. KAPLOW & SHAVELL, supra, note 1, at 18. The reader should note that what I refer to as the "main argument" synthesizes claims that the authors make at various points in the first part of the book; Kaplow and Shavell themselves do not lay out their contentions in so systematic a form.

26. See id., at 18 n.6.

27. See, e.g., id., at 10 (recognizing that "notions of fairness are … widely employed and respected").

28. See id., at 11–12, 21–23.

29. See id., at 21 (noting that individuals can have a taste for fairness, just as they can have a taste for fine wine).

30. See id., ("[When an individual has a taste for fairness], satisfying the principle of fairness enhances the individual's well-being ... .")
31. See id., at 52, 58.
32. See id.,
33. See id., at 56.
34. Id., at 7, 58.
35. Perhaps the point is better put by claiming that welfare precludes pursuing certain demands of fairness, rather than by claiming that welfare diminishes or decreases fairness. The latter way of casting the claim suggests that fairness, like welfare, is something that can be added up and maximized. It need not be, and probably is not.
36. KAPLOW & SHAVELL, supra, note 1, at 58 ("[W]e do not believe that the full import of fairness-based analysis for human welfare is appreciated.")
37. Id., at 52–58.
38. See id., at 62–70.
39. Id., at 7, 58.
40. Id., at 58.
41. Id. Elaborating upon this claim is, of course, the main purpose of the book's large second part.
42. Id., at 62.
43. See id., at 62–70.
44. See id., at 62–63, 69–72, 77. For instance, Kaplow and Shavell argue as follows:

    > [The] source of the appeal of notions of fairness—that they are associated with social norms to which we have an attachment—does not carry any implication that they should receive weight as evaluative principles when choosing legal rules. Quite the contrary is the case. ... If we were self-conscious about the role of social norms and the origins of our instincts and intuitions about them, we would not be led to attach independent weight to notions of fairness for the purpose of assessing legal policy.

    Id., at 71–72.
45. See id., at 69–72, 77, 80–81. Kaplow and Shavell perhaps put the point most starkly in the following passage:

    > [L]egal policy analysts—being members of society and thus under the influence of internalized social norms—naturally find appealing those legal rules and institutions that seem fair, without appreciating the extent to which those feelings may be independent of whether particular legal regimes actually enhance the well-being of members of society. It is this tendency that we argue

should be resisted. ... After all, the very purpose of academic discourse—and a central obligation of those designing and reforming the legal system—is to go beyond the relatively reflexive responses of ordinary individuals, so that we can identify when our instincts and intuitions about what is the best policy lead us astray.

    Id., at 80–81.
46. For example, Kaplow and Shavell note:

    > Our two conclusions, about how the pursuit of notions of fairness makes individuals worse off and about the lack of affirmative warrant for using notions of fairness as evaluative principles, raise the question of why legal policy analysts (including ourselves), policymakers, and philosophers, among others, find these notions so appealing.

    Id., at 62.
47. See Brian Leiter, *Naturalism and Naturalized Jurisprudence*, in ANALYZING LAW: NEW ESSAYS IN LEGAL THEORY 79 (Brian Bix ed., 1998) (distinguishing among types of naturalism); see also JULES L. COLEMAN, THE PRACTICE OF PRINCIPLE 210–17 (2001) (assessing the prospects of a naturalized jurisprudence).
48. See W.V. QUINE, *Epistemology Naturalized*, in ONTOLOGICAL RELATIVITY AND OTHER ESSAYS 69 (1969) (arguing from confirmation holism and the underdetermination thesis against a priori, justification-centered epistemology).
49. I do not mean to suggest that Kaplow and Shavell, jointly or severally, do not pursue these more modest projects elsewhere, including elsewhere in this book. Rather, the point is that the central argument they make against fairness depends on this stronger thesis.
50. See KAPLOW & SHAVELL, supra, note 1, at 63–69.
51. These latter considerations are introduced partly to bolster the evolutionary argument and partly as an independent argument against fairness.
52. In doing so, they do not indicate that they understand the limits within which evolutionary arguments are appropriate. Evolution does not select for particular beliefs held by particular persons. If anything, it selects for human capacities, for example the capacity to have beliefs, or to reason, etc. Too often, evolutionary arguments are really no more than metaphors for a "style" of argument. This is not the place to explore the extent to which social scientists have misunderstood and

misapplied evolutionary arguments. For a recent conference on the use of evolutionary arguments in the law, see Symposium, *ASU-Gruter Conference on Law, Behavioral Biology, and Economics*, 41 JURIMETRICS J. 287 (2001).

53. The difference between the two conceptions of fairness is this: In one sense, fairness is valuable because someone values it (as judged by the fact that he or she has a taste for it). In the other sense, fairness is valuable, and therefore individuals ought to value it—that is, they ought to prefer it or have a taste for it. It is a reason on which they ought to act.

54. My claim is not that evolution selects for true beliefs. My view is that evolution does not select for beliefs in general. If it did select for beliefs, I would not claim that it selects only for true beliefs. There are of course persistent false beliefs, and it is an interesting question as to why they survive as long as they do given powerful countervailing evidence. That is an issue for those more versed in evolutionary epistemology than I. My point is the very modest one that other things being equal there is a better armchair case—and that, after all, is all that Kaplow and Shavell offer—to be made on behalf of the evolutionary advantages of the belief in welfare than there is for the belief in fairness.

55. KAPLOW & SHAVELL, supra, note 1, at 5 n.7, 38–39 & n.48.

56. This is no place for casual empiricism. Similar casual empiricism would ground the value of fairness, for there are few among us, I suspect, who would deny that fairness is valuable.

57. See KAPLOW & SHAVELL, supra, note 1, at 18–24, 409–36.

58. Id.

59. A person can have his preferences satisfied—that is, realized—after he is dead. His preference is therefore satisfied in the logical sense, but he secures no satisfaction in the psychological sense. The dead may be raised but that does not mean they can get a rise out of having their preferences satisfied in the logical sense. That, after all, is one of the unhappy consequences of being dead.

60. I have heard proponents of law and economics argue more than once and always with a straight face for a version of preference utilitarianism or preference welfarism based on a general normative skepticism. On such views, there are no objective values; nothing is good or bad objectively. All we have are people's preferences or desires. The problem here is the obvious one that one cannot have it both ways. One cannot defend the normative value of satisfying preferences while at the same time rejecting the objectivity of value. What is the value, one might ask, of satisfying preferences when nothing has objective value? One cannot defend normative claims on a foundation of normative skepticism. Sometimes this claim is weakened and recast as the view that individual preferences are normatively less controversial than are the claims of justice, of what we owe one another. But this is anything but obvious. I would argue that quite the opposite is true. What is not mysterious to us is that we have no right to disregard the interests and rights of others. What is mysterious is why, in spite of this, we give such a special standing to our own interests. There may be a psychological explanation for why we accord our own interests pride of place, but what calls out for justification is the normative priority we accord our own desires. That position is—if anything is—mysterious and, in any case, quite controversial morally speaking.

61. See, *e.g.*, COLEMAN, supra, note 47, at 59–63; ARTHUR RIPSTEIN, EQUALITY, RESPONSIBILITY, AND THE LAW (1999); Ronald Dworkin, *What Is Equality? Part 1: Equality of Welfare*, 10 PHIL. & PUB. AFF. 185 (1981), reprinted in RONALD DWORKIN, SOVEREIGN VIRTUE 11 (2000); Ronald Dworkin, *What Is Equality? Part 2: Equality of Resources*, 10 PHIL. & PUB. AFF. 283 (1981), reprinted in DWORKIN, supra,, at 65.

PART THREE

Philosophy and the Law

IN PART ONE WE EXPLORED various views about the nature of law and its authority. Whatever the differences among them, all jurisprudential accounts treat law as a system of governance—that is, a set of institutions and practices that are designed to regulate our affairs with one another. Some theories emphasize the distinctive nature of laws as commands or authoritative directives; others draw our attention to the characteristic ways in which legal rules are enforced by sanctions. Still others emphasize the role that law plays in securing morally valuable goods. In the legal system typical of liberal democracies, legal rules enable collective self-governance, embody such values as liberty and equality, are criticizable if not enforced fairly, and contribute to the safety and security of those to whom the law is addressed. The relationship in liberal democracies between law and the principles of political morality, which constrain law's scope and animate its content, is the focus of much of the discussion in part 2.

In this part, we change and sharpen our focus, from the law as such, and the broad outlines of democratic governance through law, to some of the specific bodies of law that aim to regulate our individual behavior. In particular, we will look at the principles undergirding the law of serious wrongdoing (criminal law), the law of noncriminal harms and accidents (tort law), the law of agreements (contract law), and the law of possession (property law).

With the exception of criminal law, these bodies of law are collectively known as "private law," in that they generally regulate the relations among individuals—their rights and duties to one another. Even criminal law, nominally a matter of the individual's relation to the state, has an important private dimension, since much of criminal law concerns the outer limits of how we can treat each other.[1]

Unsurprisingly, philosophers have long thought most about both constitutional and criminal law. Constitutional law is naturally thought of as embodying our most fundamental liberal ideals—justice, fairness, liberty, and equality. Similarly, criminal law helps determine the legal limits of human freedom. Its complement (what it does not prohibit) is, then, the state's conception of what freedom is and should be. The person who commits a crime has done something he or she has no liberty or freedom to do and in doing so renders him- or herself vulnerable to being punished. Normally, a criminal act requires both physical conduct contrary to a criminal prohibition and a certain state of mind, which the law refers to with the Latin expression *mens rea.* Murder, for example, involves the conduct of causing the death of another person, with either the intention of causing that death, or a willful indifference to whether death might be caused (for instance, an arsonist who burns down a house not caring whether it is inhabited). Merely causing a death unintentionally—a pure accident—is not murder, though it may be the lesser crime of manslaughter, if proper care would have avoided the death. It is this combination of physical and mental facts that makes punishing the criminal appropriate; the punishment is fitting because it is deserved, in terms of what the criminal did and caused, and the attitude or will expressed in that doing.

Our legal practices of criminal punishment mirror in important ways our moral practice of blaming agents for their mischievous conduct. Someone who is morally culpable for what she has done deserves blame, and (other things being equal) everyone in the moral community is authorized to blame her for it. Someone who has committed a crime has acted in a punishment-worthy manner and is liable to the state (acting in everyone's name) punishing her for having done so. These links—between our moral and legal standards of culpability on the one hand, and blaming and punishing on the other—explain in part the centrality of criminal law to the philosophy of law.

Though philosophers since Cesare Beccaria and Immanuel Kant have emphasized important issues in criminal law—notably the justification of punishment and the conditions that must be satisfied in order for an agent to be subject to it—there has lately been a flourishing of philosophical interest in several areas of private law: primarily in torts, contracts, and property. The law of property identifies what sorts of things can count as property under the law and what it means to "own" property. The law of contract sets the terms under which individuals can dispose of their property as they see fit. Tort law sets out the rights to redress that individuals have in the event that others fail to respect their property.

The essays in this part of the text focus on philosophical issues in criminal law and other issues that arise in the private law of torts, contracts, and property. As a preliminary matter, it is important to distinguish between two notions of individual or personal responsibility that are central to criminal and private law: *responsibility for acts* and *responsibility for outcomes.* Often these go together: a murderer is responsible for the act of killing as well as the death he caused. By contrast, a person who willfully attempts to kill another is responsible for her action and arguably deserves to be punished for attempted murder. But if she fails in her attempt, she is not responsible for anyone's death, and there is no outcome that she also must answer for. In contrast, a ship's captain decides to dock his ship in order to prevent damage from a storm, but the storm slams the boat into the pier, damaging the boat. Even if the captain has done nothing wrong—no action for which he is responsible or to blame in a sense that would warrant his being criminally punished—the damage to the bulkhead may be an outcome for which he is responsible and therefore a loss for which he must compensate the boat's owner.

Arguably, the concept of responsibility for acts is especially important to criminal liability, whereas the concept of responsibility for outcomes is at the center of liability in private law. The first series of essays in this part of the book—those by Joel Feinberg, Christopher Kutz, and Thomas Nagel—sort out these distinctions, examining the different bases of responsibility. Nagel's essay expands on a theme touched upon by Feinberg: the tension between our ideal of responsibility and the way chance events undermine that ideal. The tension between responsibility and chance runs throughout the law, both criminal and civil. This is reflected, for instance, in both our practices of tort liability for accidents, and in the difficulties justifying our practice of punishing successful crimes more severely than attempted ones, even if the success is only a matter of luck (a topic we return to below).

PUNISHMENT AND RESPONSIBILITY

The essays in this section consider a wide range of issues pertaining to our legal practices of punishment. The concept of legal punishment, in its own right, is of central theoretical importance to a philosopher of law. In addition, solutions to the puzzles it poses for the philosopher are also presupposed by problems, both theoretical and practical, throughout the substantive criminal law. Questions about the necessary conditions of criminal liability, for example, are often answered in different ways by philosophers with differing conceptions of the nature and moral grounding of punishment. That these two types of disagreement should appear together is no mere coincidence. Differing views about the conditions of criminal responsibility can derive specifically from prior disagreements over the nature of punishment. Even in the practical contexts in which law cases are adjudicated, decisions often hinge upon which definition of punishment a judge's argument endorses.

The philosophy of punishment has, since at least the eighteenth century, largely been characterized by an impasse between utilitarian views, represented in our readings by Cesare Beccaria (1738–1794), an Italian philosopher and jurist who became an important influence on the English philosopher Jeremy Bentham; and retributivist, or desert-based views, represented in our readings by the German moral philosopher and epistemologist, Immanuel Kant (1724–1804). Utilitarian approaches treat punishment as a tool, and ask of it, when is this tool *useful?* That is, when will punishing someone do more good than harm? Since punishment, by its nature, harms the criminal being punished (by inflicting suffering) and his or her family (by depriving them of the criminal's support), and costs society (who must pay for jails or executions), a rational punishment must produce sufficient offsetting good—for instance by scaring (deterring) the criminal or others enough that they will abide by the law in the future.

Retributivists, by contrast, do not ask what punishment is good for, or whether it brings happiness or not to society. They ask, rather, whether punishment is *deserved*, in virtue of the wrong done by the criminal. Someone who has done wrong, say the retributivists, merits punishment, just as someone who has done well merits reward. Punishment is a fitting public response to the criminal's violation of the law. Retributivists point out that, on the utilitarian's instrumentalist view, there is no reason to restrict punishment to guilty criminals: it might, for example, be worthwhile in utilitarian terms for a society to make a show of punishing some people whether or not they were guilty, because of the deterrent effect on others. (In World War II France, the Nazis engaged in exactly this behavior, executing 50 innocent hostages in reprisal for the killing of one German officer by the French Resistance.) Similarly, if it could be shown that punishing a wicked criminal would not serve any social purpose that could not be achieved simply by *pretending* he had been punished—because the criminal would certainly not reoffend, for example—then a utilitarian society would be wrong to punish him. Such indifference to innocence and guilt, says the retributivist, shows that utilitarianism is not a moral philosophy of punishment at all.

The utilitarians have a response, to be sure. First, they point out, a punishment system that did not restrict itself carefully to lines of innocence and guilt (but deploying clemency as appropriate) would sow confusion and social unrest—indeed, the Nazi tactics largely hardened the Resistance. Whether or not utilitarians could, in principle, countenance punishment of the innocent, no such institutional system would make utilitarian sense. Second, retributivists have the burden of showing why, rationally, one person's wrongdoing justifies another person (or society) to inflict serious suffering, which ordinarily is forbidden by morality. Simply insisting that the suffering is *deserved* renames the problem rather than solving it. So retributivism seems to have as much of a problem with morality as utilitarianism.

The two theories rested more or less at this impasse for nearly two centuries. But in the 1950s there seemed for a time to be promise of a resolution of the traditional impasse in the philosophy of punishment. The promising new developments were primarily due to more careful definitions of the term *legal punishment*. Largely through the examples of Anthony Flew, Stanley Benn, Herbert Hart, and John Rawls, philosophers began to distinguish between *defining* and *justifying* punishment, between particular instances of punishment and punishment as a general practice within an institutional structure, and between moral and legal guilt, among other things. The hope was that the new distinctions and more accurate definitions would permit reformulations of ancient unitary questions now seen to be separable. No one view carried the day, but people were especially excited by the idea that the general practice of punishment is something retributive in its defining operations and utilitarian in its justifying aims. The influential definition from Flew had five conditions. To paraphrase, one party's treatment of another can properly be called legal punishment only if (1) it is hard treatment (2) inflicted for a violation of legal rules (3) on the actual or supposed violator (4) imposed and administered by human beings other than the supposed violator himself (5) who have the authority to do so under the rules of the governing legal system. If the sense of punishment captured by Flew's definition is the "general practice" sense, then the practice it analyzes seems clearly justifiable by its likely deterrence of would-be violators. But, unlike other utilitarian theories, it does not define a practice whose internal or constitutive rules could ever permit the knowing punishment of the innocent. That kind of barbarism, in fact, is explicitly ruled out by condition (3) of the definition.

Joel Feinberg, in his 1964 article, "The Expressive Function of Punishment," had no quarrel with the basic Flew strategy. Feinberg argued, however, that Flew's definition was inadequate—though not in a way directly relating to Flew's main purpose. Feinberg argued that the five-pronged Flew definition was too broad. Although all the legal practices we would normally call punishment are indeed punishment according to Flew's definition, some of the practices we would not call punishment ("in the strict and narrow sense of special interest to the moralist") also fall within the scope of the definition. Feinberg had in mind as properly excludable the sanctions he called "mere penalties," such as parking tickets, taxes, and football penalties. To exclude them from the class of dealings properly called punishments, he proposed that a sixth condition be added to Flew's definition: namely, that proper punishments, unlike mere penalties, express (often through their conventional symbolism) resentment, disapproval, condemnation, or reprobation. Now the definition seemed neither too broad nor too narrow.

Once this expressive function of punishment is recognized, however, new questions arise. To what extent, and by what methods, should criminal punishment express to the community and to the offender messages about what is heinous or shameful? If official expression of condemnation is an aim of punishment, does this justify public shaming of offenders?

We also must mention another possible resolution of the impasse: a *hybrid* theory of punishment. According to that theory, since moral guilt is said to be a necessary condition for an act of legal punishment to be justified, then social utility cannot, by itself, be sufficient; and since social utility is deemed necessary, it follows that moral guilt, all by itself, cannot be sufficient. Since the retributivist holds that moral guilt is sufficient to justify punishment, even in the absence of expected good consequences for *anybody,* then that theory is false. And since the utilitarian holds that social utility is sufficient, even without moral guilt, to justify legal punishment, then this theory is false too. Thus, both pure theories would have to give up their claims that their favorite justifying factors (moral guilt in the one case, social utility in the other) are sufficient for successful justification of punishment. The mixed theory would then hold that (1) moral guilt is necessary, but not alone sufficient; (2) social utility is necessary, but not alone sufficient; (3) moral guilt and social utility are severally necessary and jointly sufficient.

The adherent of the mixed theory is then relieved of the burden of defending two of the most embarrassing claims customarily made by philosophers of punishment. The first embarrassing claims is Kant's, that even if a desert island community were to disband and scatter throughout the world, they have a *duty* to execute all the convicted murderers in their custody, their moral guilt being sufficient justification for punishment, even stipulating that the murderers would never reoffend. The hybrid theory says that if no net social utility will be produced, then there is no rational reason to punish. On this mixed theory, the utilitarian is also relieved, categorically, of having to defend the possibility of punishing the innocent. But the mixed theory of punishment has had more difficulty dealing with a third question distinguished by Feinberg in his "Classic Debate" article: "How should we determine how much punishment is the correct amount?" Or put differently, "How should we interpret the requirement that 'the punishment must fit the crime?' "Insofar as the mixed theory is committed *both* to retributive and to utilitarian considerations, it must find a way to blend those normally irreconcilable factors in deciding how much punishment to mete out. And that is not easy to do.

Retributive punishments have been associated with some of the most unsavory of human emotions. Not only do these emotions produce the attitudes and judgments that are then embodied in retributivist punishments, they are themselves strengthened by the retributive practices and made even more disreputable. Nietzsche is a marvelously insightful philosopher and literary psychologist who can be quite convincing as he explains and exposes the typical mechanism by which people acquire the emotional dispositions that he lumps under the French term *ressentiment:* "resentment, fear, anger, cowardice, hostility, aggression, cruelty, sadism, envy, jealousy, guilt, self-loathing, hypocrisy, and [especially] self-deception."

The idea of punishment as vengeance has never been popular with philosophers because it gives a major role in the justification of legal punishment to a response that most philosophers regard as primitive, superstitious, and irrational. Retributivists especially have taken great pains to distance themselves from any theory that even tolerates vengeance, much less to one that enshrines it near the top of the hierarchy of justificatory aims for punishment. Retributivists have been constantly challenged to answer the utilitarian accusation that retribution is merely self-gratifying vengeance in disguise. In recent years, perhaps under the growing influence of the victims' rights movement, there has been something of a change in this scenario. Formerly, retributivists unanimously abhorred vengeance; now some of them, instead of denying the connection between retribution and vengeance, suggest that vengeance need not be as disreputable as philosophers have long believed. In particular, they suggest that *victims* of crimes are in a position to demand vengeance, since nonvictims—though they can demand that there be a return of the criminal's wrongdoing back on him "out of principle," or for some similarly impersonal moral reason—cannot themselves be the ones to enjoy retaliating or getting even. Also, if vengeance is thought to be a way of coping with such barely tolerable intense emotions as wrath and hatred, it can be claimed uniquely by a victim, if it can be claimed by anyone.

The law prohibits bank robberies, but being forced to rob a bank with a gun to one's head may constitute extreme duress and excuse someone who has participated in this crime from punishment. In offering the excuse of extreme duress, the bank robber in this example should be understood not as claiming that his robbing the bank is justified or permitted but that he does not deserve to be punished for having done so. Speeding is also against the law. Yet someone who speeds in order to rush an extremely ill passenger to the hospital may be justified in doing so. Whereas the bank robber allows that robbing the bank is wrong even in his case, the speeding driver denies that she has done anything wrong. Both may escape liability to punishment, but for different reasons.

Excused wrongs are wrongs nonetheless; justified departures from rules are not wrongs at all. Someone acting with either an excuse or a justification is innocent of any wrong and for that reason ought not be punished—or so the argument goes. That's the prevailing view. But is it correct?

To punish someone who acts with an excuse or a justification is to punish someone who is innocent, and to punish innocents is to harm them. But is it always wrong to harm the innocent? Do we wrong innocents every time we harm them? Aren't we sometimes justified in harming the innocent? Here is an example: in March 1987, the ferry *The Herald of Free Enterprise* began to sink in the North Sea, off the shore of Belgium. Passengers attempting to escape from the sinking vessel along an outside ladder found themselves prevented by a man who had begun to climb down but became paralyzed by fear and froze in place, blocking the ladder. According to witnesses, one of the other passengers then pushed the frightened passenger off the ladder, killing him but enabling a much larger number to escape to safety.

Imagine that you are the passenger who can push the frightened man off the ladder. You have already tried to reason with him and to urge him to descend on his own. You push him off and climb into a lifeboat. Could it be the case that morality prevents you from taking these steps to protect yourself at the cost of his life? You kill, him to be sure, but it is hard to see how you *wrong* him in doing so. Wronging him would mean that he has a *right* that you not push him off—and that (assuming you have no other options) you let yourself die. Imagine now that if you do not push him off, he will survive the wreck, while you (and perhaps others) will die. It seems that even here, when it is you (and others) or him, you do not wrong him by pushing him out of the way. True, it might be praiseworthy to sacrifice yourself so that he might live, and perhaps even a duty if you have some special professional responsibility to protect him. But assume you have no such duty. It seems you would be justified in killing an innocent threat to save your own life and the lives of your fellow passengers. And note that your being at liberty to take his life to protect your own life and the lives of others is not because the man has done something wrong; we have been assuming that his fear reaction is entirely involuntary and beyond his control.

It is natural to think of punishment as harm imposed on a wrongdoer for wrong done, and to justify it accordingly. In other views, punishment is justified as a form of deterrence: wrongdoers are punished to reduce future wrongdoing. Deterrence views, however, are really self-defense views. Punishment is a kind of self-defense in which we harm some to protect ourselves against the threats that others (or the punished person) might pose. We have just seen that it is permissible sometimes to harm an innocent who poses a threat—indeed, we have seen that it is sometimes permissible even to kill an innocent who threatens us—to protect ourselves. If that is so, and it is, why wouldn't we be justified—at least on some occasions—in punishing the innocent? At the very least, examples like this one invite us to explore the differences (if any) between what we are entitled to do to someone to ward off or counter a threat prior to its being realized and what we would be entitled to do to the very same person once he or she has wronged us.

We can all agree that the frightened man has suffered a stroke of very bad luck—lots of bad luck in fact. He walked innocently onto a dangerous boat whose risks he could not have foreseen. That would have been bad enough, for he surely would have suffered while clinging to the ladder before being rescued. But his luck is much worse because you also need to escape behind him and he is paralyzed by fear. If he ends up blocking you and others, he'll have to live with your deaths for the remainder of his life. But he's even more unlucky, perhaps, because you are prepared to push him off and so relieve him both of his guilt and his life.

Luck is everywhere. When we evaluate the law, we do so in part by how it responds to luck—by its relative sensitivity to luck. The areas of the law we are discussing here are concerned with two different kinds of luck: causal and constitutive. *Causal luck* is central to the distinction between responsibility for acts and responsibility for outcomes. Imagine that Jones and Smith both shoot at Brown with the intention of mortally wounding him. Suppose that Jones succeeds but Smith does not. In fact, the reason Smith fails is that Jones's bullet hits Brown and forces his head back so that Smith's bullet misses the target. That Smith misses is a matter of luck, nothing else. Should the fact that Jones succeeds while Smith fails count toward how much each should be punished? Should Jones suffer a greater punishment than Smith? From the moral point of view aren't they both equally culpable and equally dangerous? What role, if any, should causal luck play in the doling out of punishments or, as we shall see, in legal liabilities more generally?

Now consider *constitutive luck*. We do not choose our birth. The same is true, arguably, of many of our moral and cognitive capacities. These attributes are differentially distributed among us, and in that sense it is a matter of luck whether we are morally sensitive and fully competent to comply with the rules that apply to us. In this sense, our capacity to comply with what the law requires of us is itself partially a matter of luck. Arguably, some excuses in criminal law—in particular those that relieve the mentally handicapped or ill from liability to punishment—accommodate or are sensitive to forms of constitutive luck. What is so special about constitutive luck? Why accommodate constitutive luck but not causal luck? Do the differences in the way criminal law alternatively punishes and excuses the effects of luck reflect superficial if widespread customs rooted in emotional reactions? Or deep philosophical conceptions of individual moral responsibility and agency? Or a utilitarian concern for maximizing overall welfare? Or systematic consideration of how society should fairly allocate the burdens of life's misfortunes and favors? Or basic concerns of administrability (what can be charged and proven in courts)? Clearly different criminal law doctrines and different jurisdictions will reflect these possible aims and concerns variously, as will different writers. But the basic concerns of individual desert, social fairness, welfare, and efficiency are the bedrock values for the evaluation of criminal law, as well as the bodies of the private law that we will now consider.

PROPERTY AND OWNERSHIP

Property is perhaps the most basic subject of the private law. We can ask a variety of questions about property and ownership. We can ask what sorts of things can be owned, who can own them, what ownership amounts to, and what justifies the institutions of property and the particular rights in property that people have.

When most people think about property, they associate it with tangible property: houses, cars, televisions, stereo systems, and land. On the other hand, almost everyone agrees that people cannot be property. Some ideas can be property, but not all abstract entities can be. After all, the number 10 is not the sort of thing that can belong to anyone, though this or that material instance of the numeral "10" could be. I don't own the number 57, but I do own the brass numerals 57 that appear on the front door of my home. When we use the term *property* in these contexts, we have in mind the idea of ownership. Property is something one can own.

Some theorists, notable among them John Locke, argue that the right to property is inalienable. To say that a right is inalienable is to say that it cannot be traded or sold. (It cannot be alienated.) This may seem puzzling, since selling property is commonplace. To understand what Locke meant, we must distinguish between two claims. The first is that the right to property is inalienable. The second is that the right to a particular piece of property is inalienable. When Locke and others claim that the right to property is inalienable, they do not mean that individuals are not free to trade or sell particular parcels of property they own. Rather, the claim is that the right to have property of any sort is inalienable. No person can decide to give up the right to have property at all, or trade or sell that right to someone else. Of course, even a person who has the right to property may choose never to exercise it and thus never to own anything at all.

What is property? The prevailing view is that property is itself a bundle of rights in things. Among the most basic rights associated with property are the right to exclude others and to alienate. If I own my house, then I can exclude others from moving into it. They cannot do so without my consent. It does not follow that I can take any steps I like to exclude them, nor does it mean that I can exclude everyone who needs to enter my property. So I cannot usually shoot trespassers who mean me no harm, and I must allow the police and fire department access to my property when there is an emergency.

In some views, what distinguishes communist or socialist forms of political society from liberal ones is their respective approaches to the question of property. Even a socialist or communist political order can allow private property (no one wants to share a toothbrush!), recognizing its importance to persons; but they are likely to hold that most property is and should be owned collectively, especially productive property such as farmland or factories. By contrast, although in liberal societies there are public parks and government facilities, such societies (like our own) tend to hold that productive property is best owned privately. But what is so special about private property that individuals can be said to have an inalienable right to it? This is one of the fundamental questions of political philosophy.

Some philosophical arguments for private property, such as those made by Immanuel Kant and G. W. F. Hegel, tie property to personality, action, and choice. Each of us has a conception of what would be valuable for us in our lives and worthy of our pursuit. We form projects, plans, and goals, and we have aspirations and seek ways of fulfilling ourselves over the course of a life. This requires that we have some property that we can mold to our uses. The way we mold property to our uses reflects our goals, ambitions, and plans. Self-respect and human autonomy are intimately connected to the ownership and control of property. Such views therefore share ground with the view of Locke, mentioned above, according to which one cannot alienate one's right to property, since the right to own property partly constitutes one's status as a moral agent in a political community.

Another important set of philosophical debates addresses the question of whether one can own another person. Of course, the horror of involuntary slavery has long existed. But philosophers have asked whether the idea that we own ourselves permits us morally to choose to sell ourselves to others, as with other forms of property. (For instance, a Chinese immigrant might commit himself to years of service in a New York restaurant, in order to send money back home.) Is our ownership of ourselves alienable? If we believe that having property means that one has exclusive control over its use, then it is easy to see why I can't own you and you can't own me. For, understanding us as separate, individually responsible persons means, among other things, that what we do must at least in part be under our own control, not the control of others. To give ourselves to slavery is to relinquish our standing as morally responsible beings; so it would be a kind of contradiction to say that we have the moral right to give up the status that gives us moral rights in the first place.

But if we cannot own one another, what is left of the idea that we own ourselves? Locke, for one, thought that self-ownership was the basis of his claim that we each own our labor, as the product of ourselves. Locke argued that individuals obtain a moral claim on property by mixing their labor with it, for instance by tilling a patch of soil. But this ability to take possession of unclaimed resources, Locke also thought, is limited by the requirement that one take only so much as one can use without spoilage, and that there be "enough and as good" left over for others—the so-called "Lockean proviso." In his essay in chapter 19, Jeremy Waldron challenges the Lockean argument. These issues of fairness in acquisition are also addressed in Tony Honoré's classic piece on the nature of ownership.

CONTRACTING AND PROMISING

As we saw in our readings on the concept of law, H. L. A. Hart draws an important distinction between primary and secondary legal rules. On one interpretation of the distinction, primary rules impose legal obligations, whereas secondary rules confer legal powers. Primary rules limit the scope of individual liberty, whereas secondary rules expand the scope of individual freedom. Hart also distinguishes between public and private power-conferring rules. Good examples of public power-conferring rules are the laws that create the legislature and judiciary, and set out the respective powers they have to make and interpret law. Examples of private power-conferring rules include the laws granting private persons the right to wed and to pass on their property to their heirs through the institution of wills. Private power-conferring rules enable individuals to create legally enforceable normative relationships with one another.

It is helpful to think about the law of contract in terms of Hart's notion of power-conferring rules. The law confers a power on individuals to bind themselves to one another and to have the scheme of rights and duties they create thereby be enforceable by law. The domain within which parties can determine their legal relations with one another is surprisingly broad. And from a legal point of view, the range of activities that are "contracts" is surprisingly large. Every time we shop, whether for groceries or clothing, in person or online, we are entering into contracts of one sort or another.

I have many first-order duties under the law that are not of my choosing, but part of what is distinctive about contract law is that the majority of the duties I have in contract are self-imposed. I voluntarily undertake to impose burdens upon myself. Though not all of the duties imposed on me by contract are self-imposed, the vast majority of the most important ones are. In a nutshell, it's up to me to bind myself by contract. Indeed if someone else forces me to sign a contract against my will, the terms of the contract will not be imposed upon me. The fact that contracts are self-imposed obligations has led many philosophers and legal theorists to identify contracts with promises. In Anglo-American law, contract is a set of mutual promises backed by something of value—what the law calls *consideration*. You must get something of value from me in return for your promise to me, and vice versa, for our contract to count.

One reason for identifying contracts with promises is that doing so might explain why the terms of a contract into which you have freely entered can legitimately be imposed upon you. Since you have a moral obligation in general to keep the promises you make, you have an obligation to measure up to your end of a contract. And since the person to whom you have made a promise is in the distinct position of being able to demand that you keep your promise to him, he is in the unique position of being able to demand your performance. So in thinking of contracts as promises, one is able to answer two basic questions in the theory of contract law: what grounds the obligation to comply with a contract, and who has the power to enforce contracts?

Perhaps the most famous proponent of the view that contracts are promises is Charles Fried. The selection in chapter 19 drawn from Fried's seminal work on the relation of contract to promise makes the case for thinking of contracts as promises.

It is natural to see contracts as promises, but this view is nevertheless quite controversial. In fact, most contemporary legal theorists reject it. One of the reasons for rejecting the view that contracts are promises has to do with the damage award for breach of contract. Suppose I promise to take you to lunch on Tuesday, but when Tuesday rolls around I fail to show up. I have broken my promise to you, and you have a right to complain—unless of course I had a very good reason for breaking my promise and could not alert you in advance that I would be unable to follow through on my commitment. What can you reasonably demand of me for the wrong I have done you? Assuming you still want to have lunch with me and that both of us are available tomorrow, it is perfectly permissible for you to demand that I take you to lunch tomorrow. Similarly, if I promised to paint your house on Thursday but fail to show up, you are well within your rights to demand that I paint your house as promised some other day—sooner rather than later. In both cases, having broken my promise, it is logically impossible for me to fulfill it. But it is still possible for me to do what I promised, i.e. take you to lunch or paint your house. In legal jargon, we say that I am still capable of providing you with *specific performance*. I can still perform the act I promised even if I can't fulfill the promise itself.

Now switch for a second to *your* perspective on my failures. It seems that in the ordinary case of a broken promise, you have every right to demand specific performance from me. Or to put it another way, you certainly don't have to offer a special explanation for demanding of me that I do what it was I promised to do. In other words, it doesn't fall to you to explain why, now that I have failed to take you to lunch or paint your house, that I still should do so. Were I to apologize to you and offer you money instead, you might well be offended. Imagine I said the following to you: "Did you rely on having lunch with me? Did you forgo having lunch with someone else instead? How much would you have enjoyed that lunch? How valuable would it have been to you? What, in other words, did it cost you to rely on having lunch with me? Let's forget about having lunch together and let me just pay you your 'reliance costs.'" "Or suppose I said something like this: "How excited were you about having lunch with me? What were you expecting from the experience? Let's forget about having lunch together and let me pay you your 'expectation costs' instead."

This would be bizarre coming from a friend, to be sure. Perhaps you'll take me up on either offer, but you needn't. You can quite rightly demand specific performance and not have to justify your doing so. One way of expressing this thought is to say that specific performance is the natural response to a breach of promise.

The problem is that specific performance is not the typical or natural response to a breach of contract. Expectation damages are. This is an important divergence between contract and promise that has led many to doubt the plausibility of the view that contracts are promises—that they are binding in the way that promises are and for the same reasons. These issues are addressed in Anthony Kronman's piece on why contract law, unlike promising, makes specific performance a very unusual response to breach.

There are other ways in which contracts diverge from promises. If I promise to paint your house for $10,000 next week, then unless something comes up that makes my performance impossible, I am under an obligation to do so. If, in the interim, your neighbor offers me $21,000 to paint his house next week, I should tell him I cannot do it; and I should give him as a reason the fact that I am already committed to painting your house then. The fact that your neighbor has offered me a better deal is not the sort of consideration that makes my meeting my obligation to you "impossible." It just makes it less financially attractive.

Contract law is different. Suppose I had contracted with you to paint your house for $10,000 and your neighbor came along offering me $21,,000 to paint his house during the time I had committed to painting yours. In contract, I would simply breach my contract with you, paint your neighbor's house instead and collect $21,000, pay you $10,000 (more or less) to cover your damages (i.e., your cost to get your house painted by someone else), and keep the difference—a net gain of $1,000 (more or less) to me over what I would have earned ($10,000) if I had kept my contract with you. This practice even has a name among contracts scholars: *efficient breach*. The idea is that you are rendered harmless by my paying you $10,000, while both your neighbor and I are made better off. With so much good to go around, why would anyone complain? (It is a good question to ask, even were it permissible for me to breach the contract, pay you $10,000, and move on to paint the other house for more than $10,000 net, whether your complaint would be equally good against my neighbor who made the offer of $21,000 to me?) Why should it matter whether you collect from me who breached or the other offeree who induced my breach? It does matter and the fact that it does is important.

It is one thing to ask whether any of the three of us would or should complain, and another to ask whether there is something in this arrangement worth complaining about. If there is, what might it be? In a sense, this is the question that Seana Shiffrin takes up in her essay on the divergence between contract and promise. If most people believe that the practices of contracting and promising are closely connected, then this divergence between them raises moral and psychological problems. I am supposed to keep my promises except when my promises are contracts, in which case I don't have to keep them if the conditions for an efficient breach exist. But surely I should keep my promises if I can, and not just if it is profitable to do so. This divergence between the requirements of law and morality is particularly troubling when the legal practice is so closely tied in our consciousness to the moral one.

TORTS AND COMPENSATION

In the previous section we explored one of the powers associated with the ownership of property, namely alienation: the power to trade or sell what you own. We turn our attention here to another legal institution that grows up around property, an institution that protects property (but not just property): the institution of tort law. Tort law protects persons and their property by imposing duties not to harm individuals or their property and by providing repair for harm that results from breach of those duties. Normally this repair takes the form of compensation, and, infrequently, punitive damages as well.

Recall our discussion of causal luck and punishment. Imagine that you and I each drive recklessly down two different streets. Your street is populated by Olympic-quality athletes, and as they see you approaching, each employs his or her extraordinary reflexes to avoid the danger your recklessness poses. I am not nearly so lucky. I have made a wrong turn and find myself driving down the sun-baked streets of Sun City, Arizona, where most residents are in the latter stages of their lives and find even games of shuffleboard demanding. There is no chance that any of them can escape my oncoming car, and I smash into one electric golf cart after another.

Let us suppose for the sake of the argument that the only difference between us is that I injure, while you do not, those people each of us has recklessly put at risk. We are equally careless in regard to the welfare of others and equally to blame for the risks we have imposed. The difference between us is entirely a matter of luck. If the criminal law punishes us commensurate with our culpability, it is reasonable to suppose that it will do what it can to minimize the differences in punishment we are subject to for our recklessness. In contrast, the causal upshots of our actions make all the difference to the law of torts. Because you injured no one, you will escape tort liability, whereas the very same conduct will render me liable to the unfortunate victims of my recklessness.

However bad your behavior, you have, in fact, caused no harm. Though no worse, my conduct has wreaked much havoc, for which I may well have to answer. Can the significant differences in the legal consequences for what we have done be rationalized by the simple idea that the law must treat us fairly—not just with regard to those whom we put at risk, but with regard to one another as well?

One thought is that the difference in the way the law treats us can be explained by the simple fact that I have done something that you have not done. For while we have both driven badly, I have caused suffering and harm that you have not. But we assumed from the outset that this fact is simply a matter of causal luck. And how can I be responsible for the consequences that are not matters under my control but are instead matters of luck? One might think that luck is the antithesis of responsibility, not an essential ingredient of it. If that is the case, then if our liability is to track our responsibility, and if fairness requires that our respective liabilities reflect our responsibility, then how can this difference in the way the law treats us be justified?

Suppose a referee in a football game makes a terrible call, putting one team in position to win the game with a field goal at the last second. The team does so and wins the game, even though they were outplayed from start to finish. The losing team may have deserved to win, but they did not. Their record now shows an additional loss. On the other side of the coin, the winning team is entitled to a victory, and it will show up on their record as such. Even if it is one we might agree that they did not deserve, it is nevertheless one they are entitled to. In saying they are entitled to the victory, we are not saying they deserve it; and so we are not making any claims about whether their performance was praiseworthy or otherwise noteworthy. On the other hand, we are saying that no one can take the victory away from them; and we are saying that if the victory is enough to catapult them into the playoffs, then no one can keep them out of the playoffs. Good luck, yes. But the outcomes of the luck they can legitimately claim as their own.

If we were to take an accounting of our lives, we might ask the following question: was I a good or a bad person? What does my "moral balance sheet" look like? To answer that question, we would likely try to identify the praiseworthy and blameworthy things that we have done over the course of our lives and assess ourselves accordingly. For those of us who believe in God and Heaven, we might even imagine that this is precisely the sort of accounting that will determine whether we make our way into Heaven or are relegated to a less attractive afterlife.

But this is not the only question we might ask ourselves in taking an accounting of our lives. For we may well ask the following questions as well: What difference did I make? How is the world different as a result of my being in it? What events happened in the world that were my doing (fully or partially)? What can I take credit for? What must I answer for? In asking these questions, we are not primarily concerned with the nature of the character we have displayed in our actions and undertakings, so much as the events and states of affairs that are connected to us in ways that make them "ours": ours to answer for or take credit for.

The underlying idea is that while various notions of luck may be inimical to the notion of responsibility that figures in moral accounting of the first sort, whether I am a good or bad person, it is unavoidable—indeed it is essential—to the notion of responsibility that is at work in moral accounting of the second sort.

It is one thing to show that there is a notion of responsibility that includes luck and that is essential to our senses of ourselves as good or bad people. It is another thing altogether to show that various practices relying on that notion are justified. Moreover, although we might think that we cannot do without various practices of moral crediting and debiting, we would certainly deem such practices wrong or unfair in some situations. Football games and records are one thing. It is another thing to hold people to account under the law, with its coercive authority and power, for the consequences of actions that are merely a matter of luck.

To be sure, liability based on outcome responsibility puts one at the mercy of bad luck. But it is not always unfair to impose costs or losses on the basis of luck. Go back to our original example, in which you and I drive recklessly down different streets. I suffer bad luck and you benefit from good luck. In effect, by driving recklessly, both of us have purchased tickets in a lottery. The "prize" is potential liability. We have both taken a chance. Luck will now come into play to see if either of us "wins." Winning or (better in this case) losing is a matter of luck, but that doesn't make it unfair; nor does it make it unfair if one of us loses and other does not. What matters is whether the lottery is fair. The fairness of the lottery is not undermined by luck, but the fairness of liability based on luck depends on the fairness of the lottery. Negligent and reckless actors are purchasing tickets in the lottery, and if the lottery is fair, they can have no complaints when their tickets are cashed.

We do not have to rely on the idea of a lottery in order to understand the centrality and legitimacy of outcome responsibility in tort law. Instead, we can focus on the idea of a duty not to harm. At the core of tort law is the principle that each of us is under a range of duties not to harm others. These duties are not voluntarily undertaken as they are in contracts. Instead, they result from the fact that our undertakings often impose risks on others. In exercising my liberty by driving my car on the streets of New York, I put the security of other motorists and pedestrians at risk. I have a duty not to harm other pedestrians or motorists by driving carelessly.

This is a duty not merely to be careful or to drive carefully. I have a duty not to harm those whom I endanger by my driving. This is important because while I can control the levels of care with which I drive, I cannot fully control what happens beyond that. Luck and outcome responsibility are presupposed by the very idea of the duties we owe one another in torts.

The fact that tort law relies on the notion of a duty not to harm explains the importance of outcome responsibility, but it also invites some very deep questions. It is reasonable to suppose that one aim of the law of torts is to protect the important interests each of us has in the security of our persons and property. But if that is so, then the law should be primarily concerned with whether or not I am careless or reckless in my undertakings and not whether, on a particular occasion, my mischief leads to harm. To be sure, if I carelessly risk injuring people, then sooner or later my carelessness will lead to harm; and that is why we want to keep me from driving carelessly. The way to do that is to hold me liable for creating unreasonable risks—quite apart from additional material harm resulting as a consequence of my doing so. But if we go that route, we eliminate the centrality of outcome responsibility, and we will have to rethink the grounds for distinguishing between criminal culpability and tort liability. These are among the questions that Jules Coleman takes up in two essays reprinted in chapter 19. In "Corrective Justice and Wrongful Gain," Coleman explores the various rationales in current tort law for linking injurers and victims; in

"In Doing Away With Tort Law," Coleman explains what would be lost if we decided to abandon tort law in favor of another set of institutions for penalizing wrongdoers and compensating victims of wrongdoing.

NOTES

1. Dividing bodies of law involves complications. For example, murder is both a crime and the tort of wrongful death. Someone who commits murder is subject to criminal punishment—for example, life imprisonment—and also may have a duty to compensate the family and estate of the murdered person. The deliberate breach of a contractual promise also can be considered an intentional tort. And the rights described by property law have force in virtue of the backstop provided by the criminal law, for example the crimes of trespass or larceny.

CHAPTER SIXTEEN

General Principles of Responsibility

50   Action and Responsibility

JOEL FEINBERG

What is the difference between a full-fledged human action and a mere bodily movement? Discussion of this ancient question, long at an impasse, was revitalized a decade and a half ago by H. L. A. Hart in a classic article on the subject[1] in which he argued that the primary function of action sentences is to ascribe responsibility, and that even in nonlegal discourse such sentences are "defeasible" in the manner of certain legal claims and judgments. It is now widely agreed, I think, that Professor Hart's analysis, although it contains insights of permanent importance, still falls considerably short of the claims its author originally made for it. Yet, characteristically, there appears to be very little agreement over which features of the analysis are "insights" and which "mistakes." I shall, accordingly, attempt to isolate and give some nourishment to what I take to be the kernel of truth in Hart's analysis, while avoiding, as best I can, his errors. I shall begin with that class of action sentences for which Hart's analysis has the greatest prima facie plausibility—those attributing to their subjects various kinds of substandard and performance.

I[2]

If I throw down my cards at the end of a hand of poker and, with anger in my voice, say to another player "You kept an ace up your sleeve!" or, more simply, "You cheated," then surely I am doing more than "describing his bodily movements"; I am *charging* him with an offense, *accusing* him of a wrong. It is at least plausible to interpret utterances of that sort as claims that a person is deserving of censure or punishment for what he did. Charges of deceit, cruelty, and the like no doubt are the most dramatic examples of pronouncements ascribing subpar performance. It would probably be a mistake, however, to consider them to the exclusion of other, no less typical ascriptions of defective behavior. "Condemnatory verbs,"[3] such as "cheat" and "murder," are of course used to impute faulty actions, but they are not the only verbs that serve this function. Such words as "miscalculate" and "stammer" also have faultiness built into their meaning; miscalculating is a faulty way of calculating, and stammering is a defective way of speaking. Yet

From *Doing and Deserving: Essays in the Theory of Responsibility* (Princeton, NJ: Princeton University Press, 1970), pp. 119–51. Reprinted with permission of the publisher.

miscalculators and stammerers are not (necessarily) deserving of censure or punishment. Similarly, we speak of failing tests and muffing lines, of bumbling, botching, breaking, and spoiling—all defective ways of acting, but none necessarily morally defective.

Of the many distinctions that can be drawn between various kinds of faulty-action sentences, perhaps the most interesting philosophically is the distinction between the "defeasible" and "nondefeasible" species. Hart borrowed the term "defeasible" from the law of property, where it is used to refer to an estate or legal interest in land which is "subject to termination or 'defeat' in a number of different contingencies but remains intact if no such contingencies mature."[4] He then extended its meaning to cover all legal claims that are regarded as provisionally established at a certain stage of the litigation process but still vulnerable to defeat, annulment, or revocation at some later stage of the proceedings. Defeasibility, then, if I understand Hart's intentions, is closely associated with the legal notion of a prima facie case: "A litigating party is said to have a prima facie case when the evidence in his favor is sufficiently strong for his opponent to be called upon to answer it. A prima facie case, then, is one which is established by sufficient evidence, and can be overthrown only by rebutting evidence adduced on the other side."[5] If a plaintiff in a civil action fails to state a claim that, if established, would amount to a prima facie case, then there is nothing against which the defendant need defend himself and he wins a directed verdict. If the plaintiff does state a claim that, if established, would amount to a prima facie case, then there are a variety of defensive postures open to a defendant. He might deny some of the plaintiff's factual allegations, he might argue that the court lacks jurisdiction, or he might make an "affirmative defense," that is, in effect provisionally grant the plaintiff's prima facie case but put forward some one or more of a variety of justifications, excuses, or claimed immunities. The burden of proof switches at this point from plaintiff to defendant. And this is just one of several procedural consequences of the distinction between prima facie case and affirmative defense. In a criminal grand jury trial the *only* question

before the court is whether or not there is evidence tending to establish a prima facie case against the accused; hence the jury need not even hear the evidence for the defense.

The notion of defeasibility, then, is inextricably tied up with an adversary system of litigation and its complex rules governing the sufficiency and insufficiency of legal claims, presumptive and conclusive evidence, the roles of contending parties, and the burden of proof. Of course, there are no rules of comparable complexity and precision governing our everyday nontechnical use of "faulty-action sentences." At most, therefore, the assertion that these everyday ascriptions are defeasible suggests only that there are revealing analogies between them and legal claims in respect to their presumptiveness and vulnerability. In particular, I think, Hart would emphasize the vulnerability of both to defeat by excuses (such as accident or mistake) and justifications (such as forced choice of the lesser evil, special privilege, or consent) but not by such other affirmative defenses as diplomatic immunity, expiration of the statute of limitations, and so on. The point is that, given certain rules of courtroom procedure, various types of excuse and justification are among those defenses that can defeat legal claims and charges even when all the other conditions necessary and normally sufficient for their success (the "prima facie case") are satisfied. But in everyday life outside of courtrooms there is rarely a conception of "prima facie case" at all comparable in definiteness to the legal model (after all, in the law what is to be included in a prima facie case is largely determined by administrative convenience and other considerations having no counterparts in private life); hence outside of the law the notion of "necessary and normally sufficient conditions" will be necessarily vague, though not necessarily obscure.

Some ascriptions of "faulty action" are subject to "defeat" or withdrawal, then, if it should turn out that the subject had an excuse or justification for what he did. The very word by which the act is ascribed has, in some instances, this vulnerability to defeat built into its meaning. Consider the verb "cheat," for example. If we find a poker player with an ace up his sleeve, we have established a powerful presumption that he has cheated. Unless he can satisfactorily explain himself, the ascription to him of cheating will be fully warranted by the evidence. But note that part of the evidence is "positive" in nature, consisting of public facts described in positive affirmations, while another part of the evidence consists of "negative" facts about the accused's intentions, beliefs, or abilities (for example, he was not forced or coerced, nor did he slip or fall by accident, nor did he make an honest mistake about the facts or about what was permitted by the rules, and so on) and is therefore usually considered his burden to rebut in an "affirmative defense." The word "cheat" affords an especially clear illustration, for its character as defeasible by excuses seems part of its very meaning, as is shown by the obvious absurdity of such phrases as "unintentional cheating" and "accidental cheating." (Compare "accidental murder" and "unintentional lie.") If the "defeating" excuse is accepted, the fault imputation *must* be withdrawn; this is what it means for a fault imputation to be defeasible, and it allows us to show that "cheat," "murder," and "lie" refer to defeasibly faulty actions.

Even when the actor has an excuse that completely defeats the ascription to him of one kind of faulty action (such as murdering or lying), there may nevertheless be another ascription of faulty behavior (such as killing or speaking falsely) that applies to him, excuses notwithstanding. Non-defeasibly faulty actions fall below some standard or other and thus may be regrettable, defective, or untoward, even though the actor cannot rightly be blamed (in a stronger sense) for them.

There are many clear examples of both defeasible and non-defeasible imputations of faulty action. "He broke the window" and "He broke down and cried" are both non-defeasible, whereas their distant relative "He broke faith with his friend" is defeasible. A man who accidentally breaks a window nevertheless breaks the window. We may forgive him because his faulty performance was accidental, but, for all that, we do not withdraw the fault-imputing verb or "defeat" its imputation. He broke down and cried *understandably* perhaps, but the explanation does not

cancel the fact of the breakdown. Breaking faith, however, is a fish from another kettle. One cannot break faith unintentionally; for if what one did was done by mistake or accident, it cannot properly be called "breaking faith." We should have to withdraw the charge of faith breaking altogether once we acknowledged the excuse. Faith breaking, in short, is defeasible. Other examples of *nondefeasible* charges of faulty performance are: "He drove dangerously," "He dropped the ball" (in a baseball game), "He spoke falsely." But "He drove recklessly," "He fumbled the ball" (in baseball), and "He lied" are all *defeasible*. All of these statements alike are ascriptions of performances that are in some way faulty or defective; but some we would withdraw if the subject had a proper excuse, whereas the others we cannot withdraw so long as we admit that conditions "normally sufficient" for their truth are satisfied.

What is the basis of the distinction between defeasible and nondefeasible ascriptions of faulty performance? Both kinds of ascriptions express blame, at least in the very general sense that they attribute to an agent a performance somehow defective or subpar. The distinctive feature of the defeasible ascriptions is that they express a blame *above and beyond* the mere defectiveness of the ascribed action. Still, as we have seen, it would be much *too* strong to say that all the verbs in the defeasible ascriptions, unlike their more "neutral" counterparts, always express moral condemnation (although it is sometimes plausible to say this of some of them). In what way, then, is their blame "stronger" and "beyond" mere ascription of fault?

There is, I should like to suggest, something quasi-judicial or quasi-official about the defeasible ascriptions, even when uttered outside of institutional contexts, which helps distinguish them from the nondefeasible ones. To lie or cheat, to fail to show due care, to fumble the ball or flub one's lines, is not merely to do something untoward or defective; it is also to be "to blame" for doing it. This in turn means that the doing of the untoward act can be *charged* to one, or *registered* for further notice, or "placed as an entry on one's *record*." Outside of institutional contexts, of course, there are no formal records, but only reputations.

Perhaps that is what the notion of a "moral record" comes to. The concept of a record, however, is primarily and originally an institutional concept. Our formal records are found in offices of employment, schools, banks, and police dossiers, and they are full of grades and averages, marks and points, merits, demerits, debits, charges, credits, and registered instances of "fault." These records have a hundred different uses, from determining the value of a baseball player to his team to dictating decisions about whether to trust, hire, fire, reward, or punish someone. Without all these records and their informal analogue (reputation), there would be no point to talk of being "to blame" and no need for the defeasible ascriptions of fault.

To defeat the charge of being to blame by presenting a relevant strong excuse is to demonstrate that an action's faultiness is not properly "registrable" on one of the agent's records, not chargeable to "his account." The reason why a faulty action is sometimes not chargeable to an agent's record even though the action was, under another description, his is that it was performed under such circumstances that to enter it on the relevant record would make it misleading and thus defeat its point or purpose. In a baseball game, for example, a fielder is normally said to have fumbled a ball when he is able to get his glove on it without having to run very far and yet is unable to hold on to the ball once he touches it. If the ball, however, strikes a pebble and takes a bad hop before reaching the fielder's glove, the fielder is not then properly chargeable either with an "error" on his official record or with having "fumbled the ball" on his "unofficial record" or reputation. And the reason for the acceptability of this "strong defense" is found in the very purpose of keeping fielders' records, namely, to allow interested parties to make as accurate as possible an appraisal of the contribution of each player to the success or failure of the team.[6] If we charge fielders with the consequences of fortuitous events, the records will lose their accuracy and fail, accordingly, to achieve their purpose. A similar account, I think, could be given of the rationale of entries on other professional, legal, and even "moral" records.

It might be argued against this sketchy account that *any* kind of fault can be put on some sort of record or other, hence "registrability" cannot very well be the characteristic which distinguishes defeasible from nondefeasible faults. But the point I am endeavoring to make is not one about logical conceivability; it is one about practical plausibility. On what sort of record might we register that Jones drove dangerously, if it should turn out that the risk he created by driving ten miles an hour over the speed limit was amply justified by his purpose in getting a critically ill passenger to the hospital? Should we put this down as a fault on his *driving record*? Surely not, if the point of keeping a driving record is to reveal what kind of driver a man is—safe and capable or careless and dangerous. Jones drove dangerously on this occasion, to be sure, but the circumstances were so special that his behavior did nothing to reveal his *predominant tendencies;* hence to register it as a fault would not promote the purpose of the record itself. Smith speaks falsely on a given occasion. On what imaginable record might this have a point as an entry? On his *moral record*? Surely not, unless he spoke with intent to deceive, in which case he *lied*—and that is registrable. In general, I should think, a person's faulty act is registrable only if it reveals what sort of person he is in some respect about which others have a practical interest in being informed.

There are at least three different types of "registrable" (defeasible) faults, each exhibiting its own peculiarities. Depending on their purposes, record keepers might register (1) instances of defective skill or ability (for example, "fumbles"), (2) instances of defective or improper care or effort (negligence, laziness), and (3) instances of improper intention (cheating, breaking faith). There are similarities in the uses to which these three distinct types of entries might be put—and also differences. In all three types of cases, to be forewarned is to be forearmed. If there are numerous instances of cheating on a man's record, then we had better not play cards with him, or if we play, we should watch him closely. Similarly, if a man's record shows him to be careless and absentminded, then we should not hire him to be a night watchman; and if Butterfingers's fielding average is substantially lower than Orthodigits's, we had better install the latter at third base in the ninth inning with our team ahead in a close game.

On the other hand, corresponding to the three types of faults, there are important differences in the modes of treatment we might inflict on their possessors. We should not punish or censure the fumbler, for example, even if we were in a position to do so, except of course to make him try harder; but then the censure is for defective effort, not defective skill. However else we are to analyze punishment and censure, we must include an element of expressed disapproval, perhaps even hostility and resentment; and these attitudes and judgments, while they might intensify desire and even change intention, could have little effect (except perhaps inhibiting) on skill. Censure apparently works best in fortifying the motivation of otherwise careless, distractible, and lazy people, that is, those with faulty records of the second type. There is now some reason to think that manifest hostility, warnings, and threats work less well in correcting faults of improper intention and, in respect at least to the most severe defects of this sort, are useless or self-defeating. To *express* disapproval, for example, to the man with a powerful grudge against society may simply intensify his hatred and promote, rather than hinder, further hateful and destructive behavior.

If we mean by "blame" any sort of outwardly manifested disapproval of a person for his defective performance, then the relations between blaming and "being to blame" are diverse and complex indeed. The defeasible fault imputations charge only that a man is *to blame* for his defective performance (and not merely that the performance *was* defective), but not that he is properly subject to any kind of overt blame for it. Whether to blame him or not depends on what use we wish to make of his "record," and this in turn depends upon our prior purposes, the nature of the fault, and the prospects of "utility."

In summary: I have distinguished three different stages in our responses to faulty performance. We can simply note that a given act is Jones's and that it was in some way faulty or defective. At this

stage we need not use the language of defeasible fault ascriptions at all. We might simply say, for instance, that he dropped the ball, departed from the blueprints, spoke falsely, or whatever. At a second stage we might resort to the language of defeasible ascriptions and charge him, for example, with fumbling the ball, botching the job, or lying. Here we not only ascribe to him an action that is somehow defective, we also hold him *to blame* for it. This involves registering the defective performance on the actor's relevant record or, in the absence of a formal record and an institutional context, making it part of his reputation. At a third stage we may put the record or reputation, with the fault duly registered therein, to any one of a great variety of *uses*, including, among other things, overt blame. If we think, on the basis of the record, that overt blame is what the actor deserves, we might say that he is properly subject— or liable—to blame, and then that judgment could be characterized as an *ascription of liability*. But being "to blame" and being subject to further blaming performances are two quite distinct things: the former is usually necessary but not always sufficient for the latter.

We shall stop at the first stage (nondefeasible fault ascription) if an appropriate defense defeats the charge that the defect is registrable. Or we may stop at the second stage (register that the actor is "to blame" for the fault) where there are no persons granted the right or authority by relevant rules to respond overtly and unfavorably to the actor for his registered fault. Finally, where there are such rules, we may proceed to the third stage and properly judge the actor liable to such responses as censure, demotion, or punishment. In respect to the normal non-faulty action, however, we do not even get to the first stage.

Utilitarian considerations clearly have no relevance as reasons at the first two stages. It is less clear, but equally true, that they have no relevance at the third stage either—that is, no relevance to the question of whether liability judgments may be made. A person can properly be said to be liable to blame, censure, or punishment even when in fact no likely good, or much likely harm, would come from responding to him in these ways. To say that he is liable—or properly subject—to these responses is to say that another *may* so respond *if* he wishes; that is, the rules *permit* a response. What is "proper," in other words, is that others should have a certain discretion, not that they should exercise it in a certain way. Whether those with discretion *should* do what they *may* do depends on utilitarian considerations, for surely there is no rational point in acting in a manner that will do more harm than good, if rules grant us the liberty to do otherwise. The actual responsive behavior, then, when it follows a judgment of liability,[7] constitutes still a fourth stage, and it is only at this stage that the principle of utility has relevant application.

II

Can we conclude by accepting this complicated version of Hart's analysis as holding good for faulty-action sentences only? Was Hart simply misled, as some critics[8] have charged, by his own unrepresentative selection of examples, oddly failing to notice the difference between such accusations as "He murdered her" (and "He fumbled the ball"), on the one hand, and such normal, non-accusing sentences as "He closed the door," on the other? This is a tidy way of disposing of Hart's view, but I suspect that it does less than full justice to his insight. Hart must surely have intended, and perhaps with good reason, that the notions of ascriptiveness and defeasibility throw some light on the normal cases of action as well as on defective performance. This is the critical possibility that will be explored in the remainder of this essay.

Is there any sense in which normal-action sentences ascribe responsibility? If we consider the matter closely, we shall discover at least five closely related but distinguishable things that might be meant by the phrase "ascription of responsibility."

Straightforward Ascriptions of Causality

A meteorologist might ascribe today's weather in New England to yesterday's pressure system over the Great Lakes, meaning simply that the latter is the cause of the former. In similar ways we fre-

quently ascribe causality not only to the presence or absence of impersonal events, states, and properties, but also to the actions, omissions, properties, and dispositions of human beings. Ascriptions of causality, whether to impersonal or to personal sources, often use the language of responsibility. A low-pressure system over the Great Lakes, we might naturally say, was *responsible* for the storms in New England; and in precisely the same (causal) sense we might say that a man's action was responsible for some subsequent event or state of affairs, imputing no more blame or credit or guilt or liability to the man than we do to the low-pressure system when we ascribe causality to it. When we assert, then, that Smith is responsible for *X,* we can mean simply that *X* is the result of what Smith did or, in equivalent terms, that Smith did something (say, turned the knob) and thereby caused *X* (the door's opening) to happen.

Gilbert Ryle has argued that we do not speak of persons being responsible for states of affairs unless we are charging them with some sort of offense.[9] There is a point overstated in this claim, but not one that militates against a purely causal sense of "responsible." The point is this: we do not ordinarily raise the question of responsibility for something unless that something has somehow excited our interest; and, as a matter of fact, the states of affairs that excite our interest are very often unhappy ones. But sometimes, unexpectedly, happy circumstances need accounting for too, and sometimes the interest aroused is the desire to understand, not the desire to give credit or blame.

"It makes sense," Ryle argues, "to ask whether a boy was responsible for breaking a window, but not whether he was responsible for finishing his homework in good time."[10] It must be admitted that the latter question *usually* does not "make sense," but it is not difficult to imagine circumstances in which it would be a perfectly natural query. A parent comes home at any early hour and, to his great surprise, discovers Johnny's difficult new math lesson correctly completed and prominently displayed on the dining room table. The parent's interest *may* be purely intellectual: How on earth, he may wonder, did this astonishing event come about? Could Johnny, of all people, be responsible for it? More likely, the parent's interest, at least in part, will be a consequence of his concern to give credit to Johnny, to improve his estimate of him, to have grounds for praising and encouraging him, and so on. But, in this case, he must satisfy himself first that it was indeed Johnny who did (was responsible for) the work and not someone else; and, as we shall see, the language of responsibility is peculiarly well qualified for the raising and settling of such questions.

There are also easily imaginable circumstances in which we might ask of a perfectly whole and unbroken pane of glass who was responsible for it, that is, who caused it to be that way. Obviously, this query would be natural and intelligible if the window in question had been broken for many years and its owner had throughout that time been indifferent or even hostile to the suggestion that he repair it. The point that emerges is that it is *departures from norms* that excite interest in the ways that entitle us to use the language of responsibility. Where there is no departure from a norm, a necessary contextual condition for the intelligible use of such language is violated, and queries about responsibility may seem otiose or melodramatic.

Quite the same point can be made about some purely causal inquiries, even when the word "responsible" is not used. When we ask a question of the form "What caused *X* to happen?" we expect a simple answer, mentioning a single factor (or small number of factors) that explains why some departure from the normal course of events has occurred. We expect to receive an answer, in such cases, of the form "The cause of *X* was so-and-so" or else, perfectly equivalently, "So-and-so was *responsible* for *X*." But if *X* itself was no departure from the usual, then to ask what caused it, or what was responsible for it, would be as otiose as to ask of the president of the Women's Christian Temperance Union what caused her to be sober today.

Ascriptions of Causal Agency

In order to characterize the second class of responsibility ascriptions properly, it is necessary to introduce a rough distinction between complex and simple acts. There are, of course, a great number of ways in which actions can be complex, but only one of these concerns us here—that which can be called "causal complexity." An action is "causally complex" if it produces results, intentionally or not, by means of other, relatively simple, constitutive acts. The clearest examples are achievements of certain tasks and goals. To accomplish such a task as moving one's furniture to a warehouse or rescuing a drowning swimmer, one must first take a number of other steps, such as lifting chairs or diving into the water. The complex task in these examples is performed by means of a series of purposively connected "subacts," just as one closes a door *by* pushing and latching it.

A causally simple case of doing, on the other hand, requires no earlier doing as a means. Smiling and frowning are simple actions, and so are raising one's arm and shutting one's eyes. To do any of these things, it is not first necessary to do something else. Nor is it necessary to do something in one's mind as a kind of triggering—to set off a volition or "flex an occult nonmuscle."[11] In very special circumstances, of course, these normally simple acts can be complex. I may have to make myself smile, for social purposes, by a kind of interior girding of my tired facial muscles[12]; but normally one smiles spontaneously without having to cause oneself to do so.

Any distinction in terms of simplicity and complexity is, naturally, a matter of degree. Winking and smiling are usually perfectly simple actions; grasping, clutching, throwing, only slightly more complex; baking a cake or building a house, more complex still. Some relatively complex actions, such as walking, rising, and sitting down, do not involve in their bare descriptions any reference to an external object transformed or manipulated. These can be distinguished from those complex actions—usually referred to by transitive verbs, such as "open," "close," "rescue," and "kill"—with their objects. I refer here only to the latter by the phrase "causally complex actions." Whereas verbs expressing simple action, then, can be either transitive (raising an arm) or intransitive (smiling), the causally complex action verbs are typically transitive.

Now, with respect to causally connected sequences of acts and consequences, our language provides us with numerous alternative ways of talking. J. L. Austin describes one of these options: "a single term descriptive of what he did may be made to cover either a smaller or a larger stretch of events, those excluded by the narrower description being then called 'consequences,' or 'results,' or 'effects,' or the like of his act."[13] Thus we can say that Peter opened the door and thereby caused Paul (who was inside) to be startled, in this way treating Peter's act as the cause of a subsequent effect; or we can say (simply) "Peter startled Paul" (by opening the door) and in that way incorporate the consequence into the complex action. If Paul suffered a heart attack and died, we can say that Peter's opening the door caused his death, or that Peter's startling him caused his death, or simply that Peter killed him (by doing those things).

This well-known feature of our language, whereby a man's action can be described almost as narrowly or as broadly as we please, might fittingly be called the "accordion effect," because an action, like the folding musical instrument, can be squeezed down to a minimum or else stretched way out. He turned the key, he opened the door, he startled Paul, he killed Paul—all of these things we might say that Peter *did* with one identical set of bodily movements. Because of the accordion effect, we can usually replace any ascription of causal responsibility to a person by an ascription of agency or authorship. We can, if we wish, inflate our conception of an action to include one of its effects, and more often than not our language obliges us by providing a relatively complex action word for the purpose. Instead of saying that Peter did *A* (a relatively simple act) and thereby caused *X* in *Y*, we might say something of the form "Peter *X*-ed *Y* "; instead of "Peter opened the door causing Paul to be startled," "Peter startled Paul."

Ascriptions of causal responsibility, then, are often precisely equivalent to ascriptions of the second type, which I have called ascriptions of causal agency. When this is the case, whatever difference exists between the two forms of expression is merely a matter of rhetorical emphasis or grammatical convenience.[14] Both say something about causation, the one quite explicitly, the other in the language of agency or authorship.

There are, however, at least two kinds of exceptions to the rule that causal ascriptions to human agency can be translated into ascriptions of causal agency. The first class of exceptions is relatively uninteresting. It may happen, as a purely contingent matter of fact, that there is no single action word in the language that is precisely equivalent to a given causal phrase. In the second, more interesting class of exceptions, transitive verbs of action are available to tempt us, but they cannot be substituted for straightforward causal idioms without distortion of sense. Substitutivity commonly fails in cases of interpersonal causation—where one person, whether by accident or design, causes another person to act. Dr. Ortho, by making certain learned remarks about the musculature of the forearm, may cause Humphrey thoughtfully to wiggle his finger. Even though it would be correct to say that Dr. Ortho's remark caused Humphrey to move his finger, we cannot say that Dr. Ortho *moved* the finger himself. Here is an instance, then, where "causing to move" is not the same as "moving." Hart and Honoré in their impressive work *Causation in the Law*[15] have argued that a fully voluntary act "negatives" causal connection between an earlier causal factor and some upshot. Their theory does not seem to fit the present example, though, for Humphrey's action might well have been unconstrained, undeceived, and very deliberate—that is, "fully voluntary"—and yet, for all that, it would remain true that it was caused by Dr. Ortho's remark. What the example shows, apparently, is not that a voluntary act "negatives" causal connection, but rather that it precludes the extension of causal agency.

Ascriptions of Simple Agency

Simple actions (or "basic actions," as they are often called) are those that have no causal component. In order to open a door, we must first do something else that will *cause* the door to open; but to move one's finger in the normal way, one simply moves it—no prior causal activity is required. Hence ascriptions of simple agency are ascriptions of agency through and through. One cannot play the accordion with them.

That there are such things as simple acts should be beyond controversy, partly because each person has direct experience of them in his own case and partly because a denial of their existence leads to an infinite regress and attendant conceptual chaos. If, before we could *do* anything, we had to do something else first as a means, then clearly we could never get started. As one writer puts it, "If there are any actions at all, there are basic actions."[16]

Imputations of Fault

This motley group, discussed in part I, have, amidst their many dissimilarities, several important features in common. All of them ascribe agency, simple or (more commonly) causal, for a somehow defective or faulty action. Many of them, but not all, are defeasible. Rather than be qualified in certain ways, these will be withdrawn altogether and replaced with nondefeasible faulty-act ascriptions. If they cannot be so "defeated," however, they are properly entered on a relevant record of the agent's; that is, they are *registrable*. As registered faults, they are *nontransferable*. In the relevant sense of "being to blame," no one is to blame but the agent; hence no one else can "take the blame" (or "shoulder the responsibility") for him.

Ascriptions of Liability

These are different in kind from the fault imputations, even though they are often intertwined or confused with them. The one kind imputes a faulty act, simple or complex, to an agent as its author; the other ascribes, either to the agent or to someone else, liability under a set of rules or customs to some further response for it. Unlike imputations of fault, ascriptions of liability can be transferable, vicarious, or "strict," that is, independent of actual fault. In some situations under some rules, a faultless spectator may effectively say, "I'll take the responsibility for that" or "Charge that to my account," and the liability really does transfer as a result.

There are several morals to be drawn immediately from this fivefold classification. In the first place, all five types of ascription can be made in the language of responsibility. Sometimes "responsibility" *means* causal assignability, sometimes authorship, causal or simple, sometimes fault imputability or creditability, sometimes liability. Often ascriptions of responsibility blend authorship and liability, these being intimately related in that the most usual (though not the only) reason for holding a person liable for an action (or event) is that he performed (or caused) it. Another thing to notice about the classification is that the first three uses of "responsible," in ascriptions of straightforward causality, causal agency, and simple agency, apply to the "normal case" of action, where questions of fault, desert of punishment, and the like do not arise. Quite clearly, action sentences *do* ascribe responsibility in these senses.

The classification also suggests what it means to say that a sentence *ascribes* responsibility, in any of the senses of "responsibility." It was very important to Hart in his original article to argue that action sentences are typically "ascriptive" rather than "descriptive." But this is a confusion. Any kind of action sentence can be *used* either descriptively or ascriptively. We describe a person's actions when we have been considering that person and wondering what he did—when the question before our minds is not "Who did it?" but rather "What did *he* do?" When we have occasion to ascribe an action to a person, we have the action, so to speak, in our hands, and we want to know what to do with it, whom to pin it on.

If we wish to know who killed Cock Robin, this must be because we know that *someone* killed Cock Robin, but we do not know *who*. Where complex actions are involved, this sort of curiosity is common, for we can often examine the effects of an action in separation from the action itself and then wonder to whom to ascribe the consequences. A perfectly simple action, however, has no detachable part to examine in leisurely abstraction from the rest. Except for the simple act itself, there is no further "ascriptum" to ascribe. The statement "Jones smiled," when it appears routinely in a novelist's narrative or a newspaper article, simply describes or reports what Jones did at a certain moment. The novelist or journalist has not *assigned* a smile to Jones, as if he had the smile first and then selected Jones to put it on.

Still, rare as they might be, there are occasions for ascribing simple acts. A simple-action sentence is used ascriptively only when a question of personal identity has, for one reason or another, arisen. "Who was that man who smiled?" one might ask, and another might chime in "Oh, did someone smile? Who was it?" Now the stage is set for an ascription. An ascription of simple action is but an identification of the doer of an already-known doing.[17]

Some philosophers have argued that it is an "improper way of talking" to speak, after the fact, of a person's being responsible *for his own actions,* that strictly speaking what a person can be held responsible for are the "consequences, results, or upshots of the things he does."[18] This is quite true if we mean by "responsible" *causally* responsible; for, with rare exceptions, we do not cause our actions, we simply do them. It would be extraordinary, however, if such a widespread idiom as "responsibility for one's actions" always embodied such a crude mistake, and our classification reveals several "proper" uses to which it might be put. First of all, to be responsible for one's own complex actions (for example, closing a door) is properly to have one's simpler actions identified as the cause of an upshot. The knife cuts both ways: if "being responsible for the door's being shut" (by having caused it to close) is a permissible way of speaking, then so is talk of being responsible *for closing* the door, which, in virtue of the accordion effect, is strictly equivalent to it. Secondly, to be responsible for one's simple actions is only to be properly identifiable as their doer. "It was Mary who smiled" ascribes the responsibility for *smiling* to Mary and says nothing whatever about causal upshots. This is especially clear when the simple action is faulty, as, for example, a socially inappropriate smirk or leer. The report that someone had smiled in church, if it were to have received currency in colonial Massachusetts where such simple activity was a crime, would have set the stage for a noncausal responsibility ascription. To say then that it was Mary who did it would be to ascribe responsibility to Mary *for smiling,* not in the sense of doing some thing to cause the smile to appear, but rather in the sense of being properly identifiable as the doer of the deed.

III

The fivefold classification of responsibility ascriptions thus does tend to support Hart's view that action sentences are ascriptive. It suggests at least that, for all kinds of action sentences, there is some context in which they can be used ascriptively, that is, to identify the "author." On the other hand, it does nothing to support his view that all action sentences ascribe *liability* to formal responses from others, or that they are all defeasible in the manner of legal charges and accusations. In this section the classification will be used to restore still more of Hart's view, though perhaps not in the way he intended it to be understood.

We have already noticed one way in which the puzzling term "ascription" can be understood. Ascriptions in this sense have a necessary subjective condition or contextual presupposition. What is not an ascription in one context may well be so in another, depending on the concerns of the speaker. If the question is "What did Jones do?" then the sentence "Jones did A" *describes* what Jones did; but if the question is "Who did *A*?" then "Jones did *A*" *ascribes A* to Jones. This simple distinction may seem to have very little importance, since ascriptions and descriptions, so understood, may say the same thing about a man with only different emphases provided by our interest. The distinction between ascriptions and descriptions, however, sometimes reverberates with deeper overtones. Instead of a mere matter of emphasis, the distinction is taken to be one of type. P. T. Geach,[19] for example, in criticizing Hart, compares the distinction between descriptive and ascriptive with the better known contrast between descriptive and *pre*scriptive as if they were distinctions of the same order; and K. W. Rankin contrasts "matters of ascription" with "matters of fact."[20] Now whether the sentence "Jones did, *A*" is used to *ascribe A* to Jones or to *describe* what Jones did, as we have understood those terms, it surely registers, in either case, a matter of fact. The indicative mood is well suited to express what the sentence does in either use; and ascriptions as well as descriptions can be true or false and are "about" what happened. If ascriptions are to be contrasted, then, with "matters of fact," some new conception of ascriptiveness is involved. The question to be considered now is whether, in this new sense of ascription, there is any reason for treating action sentences as ascriptive.

The stronger notion of ascriptiveness can be explained, I think, in the following way. There is a familiar commonsense distinction between questions calling for *decisions* and those requiring *discoveries*. I must decide at which restaurant to dine tomorrow, but first I must discover the solution of an equation or the population of a town. In the first case, even when all the facts are in, I have a certain amount of discretion; in the latter case, I am bound or committed totally by the facts—I cannot escape the conclusions they dictate. This distinction has been expressed in a great variety of ways: questions of policy versus questions of fact, practical versus theoretical, regulative versus constitutive, and so on. Some philosophers have denied either the existence or the importance of the distinction: Platonists tend to reduce questions of decision to questions of discovery, and pragmatists assimilate the theoretical to the practical. Common sense, however, holds firm to the distinction, even when puzzled about how to explain it or where to draw the line. Philosophers who contrast "ascriptive" with "factual," I suggest, have this distinction in mind. By "ascriptive sentences" they mean (among other things) sentences not *wholly* theoretical or factual, having an irreducibly discretionary aspect.

A second characteristic of ascriptions, closely connected with the first, is what may be called their "contextual relativity." We may have an option of ascribing X to either A, B, or C. To which of these X is properly ascribable may depend on numerous factors other than the relevant characteristics of A, B, and C. Our decision may turn on our own degree of knowledge or ignorance, on our practical purposes, on the type of ascription or the nature of the "context," on our long-range policies, on institutional rules and practices, on "values," and so on. Some of these

considerations may conflict and thus call for careful weighing—which is to say that they require not merely decision, but *judgment*. Finally, our well-considered ascriptive judgments may exhibit something like what Hart calls "defeasibility," although outside of legal and quasi-legal contexts talk of "cases" and "claims" and "defenses" may not seem quite at home.

Let us return to the fivefold classification to see what it can tell us now about ascriptiveness construed as irreducibly discretionary, contextually relative, and "something-like-defeasible." The first thing it reveals is that ascriptions of causality, even when they do not involve persons and their actions, commonly exhibit ascriptiveness construed in this fuller way. This is not to suggest that many "causal laws" are decided upon rather than discovered, or that scientists have any discretion at all in discovering and formulating laws of nature. Where scientists and others have some discretion is in a rather different sort of inquiry—when some unexplained happening has occurred, or some interesting or important state of affairs has been discovered, and we must decide to what cause to attribute it. Here, often, even after all of the facts are known, we have some choice, if what we wish to do is to *select* from the welter of causal factors that made some contribution to the event in question one to be denominated *the* cause.[21]

Frequently the selection from among many causal candidates of "the cause" seems so obvious that we may lose sight altogether of the fact that we are selecting, singling out, deciding. But that causal ascriptions are selective becomes clear to anyone who tries to give a *complete* causal explanation of some event in terms of all the conditions severally necessary and jointly sufficient for its occurrence. *All* of these conditions are equally important to the event, a naïve person might argue, in that all were equally necessary to its occurrence. Equally important to the event perhaps, but not equally important to the investigator. The investigator talks of "the cause" in the first place only because he suspects that there is some single event or condition among the many causal contributors to the outcome which it will be of special interest or importance to him or others to identify.

Which "contributor"[22] to an event is to be labeled the cause of that event, then, is always a matter of selection, often an occasion for decision, even for difficult judgment, and is generally "relative" to a variety of contextual considerations. Cataloguing the many forms of causal relativity is a large task, but three might be mentioned here. First, selecting the cause of an event is relative to what is usual or normal in a given context. I. M. Copi bids us ponder the fate of the insurance investigator who reports back to his company that the cause of a mysterious fire in the house of a policyholder was "the presence of oxygen in the air." What the company clearly wanted him to discover was not just any necessary condition, but rather "the incident or action which in the presence of those conditions normally present, made the difference this time."[23] Leaving the insurance investigator to be dealt with by his employers, we can without difficulty think of contexts where his ascription would not have raised an eyebrow. "... it is easy to imagine cases," write Hart and Honoré, "where the exclusion of oxygen would be normal, e.g., when some laboratory experiment or delicate manufacturing process depended on its exclusion for safety from fire and hence for success, and in such cases it would be correct to identify the abnormal presence of oxygen as the cause of the fire."[24] What is "the cause," then, depends on what is normal, and what is normal varies with the context.

Another form of causal relativity is relativity to ignorance. Consider how we might explain to a group of workers in a welding shop how an explosion occurred in a nearby warehouse. We might say that the explosion was the result of a spark which, let us suppose, was the last conspicuous event preceding the eruption. But in a welding shop sparks are flying all the time. They are perfectly routine, and hence they cannot explain anything as extraordinary as an explosion. Given the context naturally assumed by the welding shop workers, one must cite as the cause much earlier events, such as the storing of TNT or leaky gasoline drums. The analogy with history, and its own brand of causal relativity, is plain. Historiographers ascribe the causes of wars, revolutions, and other such explosions, and as a rule they write for

their own contemporaries. Historiographers of later ages then write of the same events but for a later group of contemporaries with a later set of conceptions of what is routine. As a result, the earlier writer ascribes "the cause" to some political or economic equivalent of the spark, and the later opts for TNT or a leaky gasoline can. One of the functions of an explanation of particular occurrences is to render them intelligible, to induce understanding of them. Intelligibility, however, is always intelligibility *to* someone, and understanding is always *someone's* understanding, and these are in part functions of what is already known or assumed to be normal or routine.

A third sort of causal relativity is relativity of practical interest. "It is a well-known fact," wrote R. B. Perry, "that we describe as the cause of an event that particular condition by which we hope to control it."[25] Accordingly, we tend to select as "the cause" of an event that causal condition which—in Collingwood's felicitous metaphor—has a handle on it that we can grasp and manipulate; and thus even causal generalizations tend to function directively or, as Douglas Gasking puts it, as "recipes" for cooking up desired effects.

The very meaning we assign the word "cause" is likely to vary with our purposes. Those who are concerned to produce something beneficial seek "the cause" of what they wish to produce in some new condition that, when conjoined with the conditions usually present, will be *sufficient* for the desired thing to come into existence. On the other hand, those whose primary aim is to eliminate something harmful are for the most part looking for causes in the sense of *necessary* condition. That is because, in order to succeed in such a task, one must find some condition in whose absence the undesirable phenomenon would not occur and then must somehow eliminate *that* condition. Not just any necessary condition, however, will do as "the cause"; it must be a necessary condition that technicians can get at, manipulate, modify, or destroy. Our purposes here determine what we will accept as "the cause," and when it is the cause of an illness or a crime wave we are after, accessibility and manipulability are as important to our purposes as the "necessity" of the condition. Indeed, we will accept as the cause of some unhappy state even some necessary condition that, from the point of view of theory, is obvious or trivial, provided only that it *is* necessary and that it is something we can get at.

It would be an oversimplification, however, to identify "the cause" of an infelicitous condition with *any* manipulable necessary condition, no matter how trivial—an oversimplification not of the processes of nature, but of human purposes themselves. However much we wish to get rid of defects and infelicities in our bodies, machines, and societies, we never wish to eliminate them at *any price*. What we want when we look for "the cause" of unfortunate happenings is an *economical* means of eliminating them, the right price being determined by our many implicit underlying purposes.

A boozy pedestrian on a dark and rainy night steps into the path of a careless speeding motorist and is killed. What caused this regrettable accident? Since liabilities are at stake, we can expect the rival attorneys to give conflicting answers. But more than civil liability is involved. A reformer argues that the liquor laws are the cause, claiming that as long as liquor is sold in that region we can count on so many deaths a year. From traffic engineers, city planners, and educators we can expect still different answers; and in a sense they might all be right, if they named genuine "causal factors." But that is not what their discussion is all about. Should we prevent such accidents by spending a million dollars as the traffic engineer recommends? Or fifty million as the city planner urges? Each would uproot a necessary condition, but at what expense! Perhaps the moralist is on the right track, but do we really wish to penalize thousands of innocent responsible whisky drinkers in order to prevent the deaths of a careless few? In such ways as these are interests and purposes drawn into the context of ascribing causes. They form an implicit part of every causal field determining in part the direction in which we point when we pick "the cause" of an event.

In virtue of their discretionary character and their contextual relativity, causal ascriptions characteristically exhibit a kind of vulnerability logically analogous to the defeasibility of some legal claims and accusations. When a humanly interesting event occurs, it is always possible to mention dozens of factors that have made important causal contributions to its occurrence. Even events that occurred years earlier may so qualify. (Sometimes the straw that breaks the camel's back is in the middle, or even at the bottom, of the pile.) To cite any one of these as "the cause" is always to invite a "rebuttal" from a partisan of one of the other "causal candidates," just as to make an accusation is always to invite a defense; and to show in a proper way that a certain condition did make a contribution or was an indispensable condition is only to make out a presumption of causal importance that holds unless rebutted in one of the many diverse allowable ways.

In general, properly rebuttable causal ascriptions commit the error not of misdescribing, but of representing the less important as the more important. When it is said that the presence of oxygen in the air caused the fire, or that the cause of the stomach ache was the drink of whisky (rather than an unsuspected ulcer), or that the riot was caused by the unprecedented presence of a Negro student in the dormitory, it is less to the point to call these statements false than to call them unwise, misleading, or unfair, in the manner of otherwise accurate accounts that put their emphases in the wrong places. To be sure, but for the oxygen, the drink, the presence of the Negro,[26] there would have been no fire, ache, or riot. However, for the purposes of our more comprehensive understanding and control of such events, other equally necessary causal factors are far more important and deserve to be mentioned first.

Given that causal ascriptions, both those that assign "the cause" to impersonal factors and those that select out human actions, are "ascriptive" in the stronger sense, it follows immediately, in virtue of the accordion effect, that ascriptions of causal agency are so too. If "Jones caused the door to close" is ascriptive, then "Jones closed the door" must be so equally. If "causing a war by an act of assassination" is ascriptive, then the still more complex act of "starting a war" must be so as well. We have found a sense, then, in which one large class of action sentences—those attributing causal agency—are ascriptive and "something-like-defeasible" *even when the activity in question is in no way faulty.*

Ascriptions of simple agency, however, cannot be analyzed in this way, for a simple doing is not the upshot of a prior doing to which it may be ascribed, and a fortiori we have no discretion to *decide* whether to *select* a prior doing as "the cause" of the simple doing in question. Whether or not a man smiled is entirely a question of fact whose answer is to be discovered, not "decided" or "selected" presumptively.

Insofar as the word "smile" is *vague*, of course, there is room for discretion in its application to a borderline case; but the discretion here, which is hardly peculiar to simple-action words, is of a different sort. Whether we call a borderline-colored object blue or green, we are likely to say, is a matter of indifference or "a mere question of words." But when we deny that a question of causation is wholly factual, we are not contrasting "question of fact" with "question of language"; nor are we implying that its resolution by a decision is indifferent or arbitrary. We are implying instead that a decision cannot be made without a reference to our own practical purposes and values, which is quite another thing.

Simple-action sentences, then, such as "Jones moved his finger," can be used ascriptively to identify an agent, but they are not ascriptive in the further strong sense that we are left with discretion to accept or reject them even after all the facts are in. Thus, in summary, Hart's critics are right in charging him with overburdening the notion of ascriptiveness, for we have found at least one class of action sentences, the action-simples, which are not ascriptive in the sense that is opposed to "wholly factual." But we have restored a good part of Hart's original theory (considerably reinterpreted) that is often rejected, inasmuch as we have shown that one substantial class of action sentences that do not necessarily impute faults are nevertheless very often ascriptive in a strong sense, and that these sentences, as is revealed by the characteristic ways in which they might be rebutted, are "something-like-defeasible" as well.

IV

How important is this restoration of a part of Hart's original thesis? The answer to that depends in large measure on one's philosophical interests and strategies. For problems of jurisprudence and moral psychology, I should think, the ascriptive and defeasible character of the action sentences of most interest to those disciplines is a matter of great importance indeed. But for "the problem of action" (or of "voluntary action"), construed as a problem of metaphysics, where the concern is to distinguish activity from passivity as very general conceptual categories, the notions of ascriptiveness and defeasibility appear to be of no help whatever. It is no accident that writers in ethics and jurisprudence, when troubled by "the problem of action," typically select as their examples more or less complex, teleologically connected sequences of behavior that cause harm or happiness, success or failure, to self or others. They are likely to ask, for example, what distinguishes a voluntary killing from a mere accidental homicide, or a voluntary from an involuntary signing of a contract, or in general an act freely and deliberately performed from one done in circumstances that gave the agent "no choice." The best answer to *this* question about voluntary action, it seems to me, is the one Hart and Honoré gave in *Causation in the Law*: "In common speech, and in much legal usage, a human action is said not to be voluntary or not fully voluntary if some one or more of a quite varied range of circumstances are present...."[27]

These circumstances make a lengthy enumeration. They include, Hart and Honoré inform us,[28] physical compulsion, concussion, shock, dizziness, hypnosis; the motives of self-preservation, preservation of property, safeguarding of other rights, privileges, or interests of self or others; legal or moral obligation; unreflective, instinctive, or automatic movement; mistake, accident, or even negligence. Voluntariness ("actness"?) in this sense is a matter of degree. An action done under a threat of physical violence, for example, comes closer to being fully voluntary than an act done under the threat of death. Further, voluntariness in this sense has no direct and invariant connection with liability. An agent may be held strictly accountable for an action that is considerably "less than fully voluntary" if the act is sufficiently harmful; and where the harm is enormously great (for example, giving military secrets to the enemy), no degree short of complete involuntariness may relieve the agent of liability.[29]

Writers concerned with the metaphysical problem of action typically select as *their* examples such simple movements as raising one's arm or moving one's finger. When they ask what distinguishes a voluntary from an involuntary act, they are inquiring about the difference between an *action* (said with emphasis) and a mere bodily movement—for example, between a wink and a mere eye-twitch. Involuntariness in this sense (lack of muscular control) is only one of the circumstances that can render an act less than fully voluntary in the other sense. That is, some actions which *are* actions through and through, and not automatic twitches or "mere bodily movements," are nevertheless not fully voluntary in the sense discussed earlier because they may be done in response to threats or under moral obligation, and so on. Now whether an action in the sense opposed to mere bodily motion is properly to be ascribed to a person whose arm has moved is not a question that has anything to do with excuses, presumptions, and practical purposes. It has every appearance of being strictly about "the facts," although just what kind of facts it is about is part of the metaphysical perplexity that the question naturally engenders.

On the other hand, whether or not a causally complex act is to be ascribed to a person whose relatively simple act was a causal factor in the production of some upshot depends, as we have seen, on how important a causal contribution it made, as determined by our prior assumptions and practical purposes. It is misleading to attribute "*X*-ing *Y*" to a man as his doing when other factors made more important contributions. When the action in question is "faulty," then sometimes the "other conditions" are mitigating *excuses* (the agent's sickness or fatigue), sometimes not—as when between the agent's act and the upshot a dozen unanticipated causal factors intervened. "Burning down a forest" cannot be ascribed to a camper whose campfire is suddenly scattered by unprecedented hurricane winds, even though, but for his relatively simple act of making a fire, the forest would never have burned; and to cite the abnormal winds as causally more important factors is not to cite an excuse. Nor does one offer an excuse in pointing out that Jones did not "burn down the forest" because twelve other campfires also burned out of control and any one of them would have been sufficient to consume the whole forest. This consideration does not necessarily relieve Jones of *fault*. What it does is override the presumption that Jones's action is the crucial causal factor in the production of the outcome. But "overriding presumptions of causal importance" and "defeating imputations of personal fault," while of course not one and the same thing, are still sufficiently similar for their comparison to be mutually illuminating; and the discretionary character, contextual relativity, and presumptiveness of the causal ascription, though surely not identical with Hart's "ascriptiveness" and "defeasibility," are strongly analogous to them.

Simple noncausal doings, however, resist these comparisons; and to Wittgenstein's puzzling question "What is left over if I subtract the fact that my arm goes up from the fact that I raise my arm?"[30] the notions of ascriptiveness and defeasibility can provide no answer. Here, as elsewhere in philosophy, analytic techniques help answer the penultimate questions, while the ultimate ones, being incapable of *answer*, must be settled in some other way.

NOTES

1. Hart, H. L. A. "The Ascription of Responsibility and Rights." *Proceedings of the Aristotelian Society* 49 (1948/49): 171–194.
2. I am grateful to George Pitcher for pointing out some serious errors in an earlier version of this section. I fear there may still be much in it that he disagrees with.
3. The term is Pitcher's. See his penetrating article "Hart on Action and Responsibility." *The Philosophical Review* 69 (1960): 226–235.
4. Hart, supra, note 1, at 175.
5. *Black's Law Dictionary.* 4th ed. St. Paul: West Publishing Co., 1951. 1353.

6. This is very close to the function of "records" in history. Cf. H. L. A. Hart and A. M. Honoré: "History is written not only to satisfy the need for explanation, but also the desire to identify and assess contributions made by historical figures to changes of importance; to triumphs and disasters, and to human happiness or suffering." *Causation in the Law*. Oxford: Clarendon Press, 1959. 59.

7. More commonly "the record" is used as a ground for direct responsive behavior, and judgments of liability are expressed, if at all, only in justification (showing that one had the right to do what one did) of the responsive action after the fact. A special kind of case is provided by those judgments to the effect that a person is liable to be called upon "to answer" or "to give an accounting" of his conduct. These can occur as early as the second stage, when it remains to be established whether prima facie faulty behavior is registrably faulty.

8. E.g., Pitcher, supra, note 3, and Geach, P. T. "Ascriptiveness." *The Philosophical Review* 69 (1960): 221.

9. Ryle, Gilbert. *The Concept of Mind*. New York: Barnes & Noble, 1949. 69.

10. Id.

11. Id., at 74: "To frown intentionally is not to bring about a frown-causing exertion of some occult nonmuscle."

12. Cf. Ralph Waldo Emerson: "There is a mortifying experience ... I mean 'the foolish face of praise,' the forced smile we put on in company where we do not feel at ease, in answer to conversation which does not interest us. The muscles, not spontaneously moved but moved by a low usurping wilfulness, grow tight about the outline of the face, with the most disagreeable sensation." *Essays, First Series*. Boston: 1847. 56–57. Available online from *Ralph Waldo Emerson Texts*. http://www.emersoncentral.com/essays1.htm

13. Austin, J. L. "A Plea for Excuses." *Philosophical Papers*. Oxford: Clarendon Press, 1961. 149.

14. Cf. John Salmond: "The distinction between an act and its consequences, between doing a thing and causing a thing, is a merely verbal one." *Jurisprudence*. 11th ed. London: Sweet & Maxwell, 1957. 402.

15. Hart and Honoré, *Causation and the Law*, supra, note 6, chs. 2–6. Hart and Honoré's "voluntary intervention thesis" is discussed critically in Feinberg, Joel. "Causing Voluntary Actions." *Doing and Deserving*. Princeton: Princeton University Press, 1970. 152–86.

16. Danto, Arthur C. "Basic Actions." *American Philosophical Quarterly* 2 (1965): 142.

17. It is only when statements of nonfaulty simple agency are used ascriptively (in the sense explained in the text) that they are ever called "judgments of responsibility." When they are naturally characterized as responsibility judgments, "responsibility" always bears the sense of "proper identifiability." When a simple action has taken place that for some reason interests us in itself, and yet we do not know the author's identity, we may ask "Who did it?" The statement, in those circumstances, that "Mary did it" ascribes responsibility for the interesting act only in the sense that it identifies the doer of an already known doing. We may, however, have no interest whatever in the simple act in question except that it was done by the person who (we later learn) is Mary. Thus, having looked right at Mary as she moves her hand to her head, we may turn to a friend and ask "Who is that girl who just raised her hand?" When our friend says that it is Mary who raised her hand, his reply can hardly be described as an ascription of responsibility to Mary for raising a hand. That is because focal interest in these circumstances is on the actor, not the act. We are concerned in this example to learn Mary's identity not because she did an interesting deed; on the contrary, her deed is interesting to us only because it is hers. Hence no question of responsibility for it arises.

18. Pitcher, supra, note 3, at 227.

19. Geach, supra, note 8, at 221.

20. Rankin, K. W. *Choice and Chance*. Oxford: Basil Blackwell, 1961. 29 and passim.

21. A great deal has been written in recent years about causal ascriptions. I am probably most indebted to Dray, William H. *Laws and Explanation in History*. London: Oxford University Press, 1957; Gasking, Douglas. "Causation and Recipes." *Mind* 64 (1955); Hanson, N. R. "Causal Chains." *Mind* 64 (1955); Hart and Honoré, *Causation and the Law*, supra, note 6; and Mackie, J. L. "Responsibility and Language." *Australasian Journal of Philosophy* 33 (1955).

22. There are circumstances in which "the cause" need not even be a necessary condition. See Hart and Honoré, *Causation and the Law*, supra, note 6, at 116–121. Moreover, we do not have complete discretion in selecting, according to our purposes and policies, the cause from the causal conditions,

as Hart and Honoré have effectively and thoroughly demonstrated.

23. Copi, I. M. *Introduction to Logic.* 1st ed. New York: Macmillan, 1952. 327.

24. Hart H. L. A. and Honoré, A. M. "Causation in the Law." *Law Quarterly Review* 72 (1956): part 1, 75.

25. Perry, Ralph Barton. *General Theory of Value.* Cambridge: Harvard University Press, 1926. 394.

26. For an account of the difficult integration of the University of Georgia, see Trillin, Calvin. "An Education in Georgia." *New Yorker* 13 July 1963:

> On the ... night of the riot, their [the white girls'] behaviour changed drastically. After the first brick and the first coke bottle had crashed into her room, Charlayne [Hunter] went to a

partly partitioned office ... and stayed there during most of what followed. A group of [white] coeds soon formed a circle in front of the office and marched around, each screaming an insult as she got to the door. They kept yelling "Does she realize she's causing all this trouble?"

27. Hart and Honoré, *Causation in the Law,* supra, note 6, at 38.

28. Id., at 134 ff.

29. Cf. Aristotle, *Nichomachean Ethics,* 1110a 20–1110b, and Hart and Honoré, *Causation in the Law,* supra, note 6, at 147.

30. *Philosophical Investigations.* Tran. G. E. M. Anscombe. Oxford: Basil Blackwell, 1953. Part 1, §621.

51   Responsibility

CHRISTOPHER KUTZ

1 INTRODUCTION

Claims of responsibility are notoriously multifarious. H. L. A. Hart's tale of the drunken captain, here adapted slightly, still shows this best:

> (1) As captain of the ship, Smith was responsible for the safety of his passengers and crew. (2) But he drank himself into a stupor on his last voyage and was responsible for the loss of the ship and many of its passengers. (3) The doctors initially thought his drinking might have been the product of a paralytic depression, but later concluded that he had, in fact, been fully responsible at the time he became drunk. Smith initially maintained that the exceptional winter storms were responsible for the loss of the ship, but at trial, (4) after he was found criminally responsible for his negligent conduct and sentenced to ten years imprison-

ment, (5) he declared that no legal penalty could alleviate his guilt, for which he sought to atone. (6) Some of the survivors of the wreck, however, declared that they wished to put their nightmare behind them, and forgave Smith. (7, 8) Meanwhile, the president of the cruise line issued the following statement: "Although the company must accept its legal responsibility for the loss of life and property, we bear no culpability for the disaster, since Smith fraudulently concealed from us his earlier employment problems, and our alcohol screens turned up no evidence of his drinking."[1]

The story rehearses different uses of "responsibility" in our everyday social, moral, and legal discourse; the numbers distinguish either different senses of responsibility, or different exemplary contexts in which someone takes responsibility or is held responsible. Here is Hart's catalogue: First is a claim of *role* responsibility: Smith, in virtue of his position as captain, had specific obligations to safeguard his ship and his passengers. A claim of role responsibility states the

I am grateful to Cambridge University Press for permission to reuse passages also appearing in my *Complicity: Ethics and Law for a Collective Age* (New York: Cambridge University Press, 2000).

From the *Oxford Handbook of Jurisprudence and Philosophy of Law.* Eds. J. Coleman, S. Shapiro, & K.E. Himma. New York: Oxford University Press, 2004. 548–587. Reprinted with permission of the publisher.

expectations of an agent's conduct towards some charge. Second is a claim of *causal* responsibility: the captain's insobriety is cited as the cause of the vessel's loss. Causal responsibility might be better thought of as a species of explanatory responsibility, causation being typically the best explanation of an event.[2] Third is a claim of *capacity* responsibility: the captain's decision to drink was not the product of a pathology, or some other nondeliberative causal process, but rather reflected his exercise of a power of rational self-determination. Being responsible, in this sense, simply is a matter of having the competency of self-government. Four, five, six, and seven relate to claims of different kinds of individual *liability* responsibility, respectively accountability to the demands of the criminal law, tort law, and morality. Finally, eight involves a claim of *collective* responsibility, a claim whose distinguishing feature is that the responsible subject involves a plurality of individuals.

Much of the modern literature involves attempts to refine, reduce, and compare elements of Hart's taxonomy—to show, for example, why moral and criminal liability share a common foundation, why role responsibility is the foundation for liability responsibility, or why collective responsibility cannot be reconciled with individual responsibility. R. A. Duff, for example, distinguishes causal, prospective, and retrospective responsibility, making claims of causal responsibility factual and the other two normative. Prospective responsibility (what I have called role responsibility) is defined by norms governing conduct, and retrospective responsibility is accountability for failure to meet those norms. Capacity responsibility is then defined derivatively, in terms of whether an individual is an appropriate candidate for prospective or retrospective responsibility; only responsible agents can be held responsible.[3] T. M. Scanlon similarly distinguishes between judgments of substantive and attributive responsibility. Judgments of substantive responsibility involve claims about what people are required to do for one another, and judgments of attributive responsibility are judgments that some act or event is a proper basis of moral appraisal.[4] Finally, Stephen Perry, following Tony Honoré, makes a

distinction within the field of attributive responsibility, between act and outcome responsibility.[5]

However we slice the idea of responsibility, it is apparent that we need considerable information to deploy the term. First, we need to know the *object* of the agent's putative responsibility. Is it a task, a status, someone's well-being, conduct, or an event? Secondly, we need the *ground* for demanding this responsibility—that he performed some act, caused the event, was invested with duties of a specific sort. His having or lacking a capacity for responsibility enters as a precondition of his responsibility, but being responsible includes the nature of his relation to the act, state, or outcome, whether he did it, caused it, manifested it, and so on.

In other words, we need to know whether the agent accepted the role, performed the act, caused the harm; and whether the agent did so consensually or involuntarily, intentionally or accidentally, sanely or madly. The idea that attributions of responsibility rest solely on facts about agents and their relations to certain harmful (or favorable) events or states is familiar and attractive. To give this idea a name, let us call it *retributivism*. The fundamental idea of retributivism is that responsibility is a moral property of agents that consists in or supervenes upon underlying facts of agency and upon agents' connections to the world. Such facts uniquely determine the moral desert of the agent; it is then a primary job of our moral and legal institutions to mete out to agents the response they deserve. On the simple retributivist picture, responsibility is a moral fact, pertaining to a relation between an agent and an object of assessment.

The retributive conception of responsibility is not wrong. It is radically incomplete. For claims of responsibility are more elliptical than I have so far indicated, in two ways. First, beyond the facts of agency, capacity, and causation, we need to know the *response* demanded of and to the agent, and conditions of *warrant* for that response: is it (among the range of possibilities) contrition, or civil liability, or criminal punishment, and what are the criteria for appropriate application of each? The truth of a claim of responsibility depends on the mode of demanded response. Smith, for example, may be justly liable in tort but not in criminal law. If his fault is minimal or nonexistent, then resentment by his victims may be unwarranted, even though he himself must properly regard the accident with great regret.

Attributions of responsibility occur not in a juridical vacuum, but in specific interpersonal and circumstantial contexts. Such attributions are fundamentally *relational:* they depend upon the character of moral, legal, and social relations among the actor, the victim, and the evaluator. Consequently, we need to know what I will call the *position,* or identity, of the respondent to the agent, as well as the relation between them. The justification for demanding a given response depends on the position and the relation of the respondent to the agent. Is the respondent a victim, a court, the agent himself or herself, a bystander? Smith, arguably, owes his victims but not the state an apology; and the state, but not his victims, has a right to punishment after a fair trial. At that, Smith may only be justly punished by the state with the appropriate jurisdictional relationship to him—even a scrupulous adjudication of the merits of his conduct by an alien court would be irrelevant to the justice of his punishment.

Relational and positional dependence reflect a number of deep facts about responsibility claims. First, the complex set of practices involved in taking responsibility, projecting responsibilities, and finding and holding persons and collectives responsible can only be made sense of against the background set of social, political, and legal relationships and their constitutive norms. Secondly, the contextual and relation-dependent nature of responsibility claims means that, fundamentally, responsibility is a social practice and not the neutral registration of independent moral facts. Claims of responsibility are things *we do,* revelations of our agency. Thus, thirdly, making responsibility claims, of ourselves or others both constitutes and transforms our agency and our relations to one another. Consequently, judgments of responsibility must be understood in terms of the ideals of agency and community that they reflect and effect.

The fundamentally relational character of responsibility is reflected in a recent efflorescence of philosophical work on moral and legal responsibility, including the works mentioned above. This literature has demonstrated, sometimes merely implicitly and sometimes despite itself, that the traditional chestnuts of the topic—such as the problem of psychological determinism, the legitimacy of strict liability, or the distinction between tort and criminal responsibility—will be cracked not with a priori arguments but instead with examinations of the relationships and expectations that give point and structure to our responsibility practices. Indeed, shifts and divisions within recent philosophical literature make sense only with the realization that different theories reflect different conceptions of the background relations. The shift in contemporary moral and legal thinking, away from the systemic view of consequentialism and towards a deontology focusing on individual responsibility, manifests the central social and political dilemma of late modernity: reconciling individual meaning and autonomy within the increasingly consolidated social world.

The subject of responsibility could clearly consume much of the subject matter of law, including many matters treated elsewhere in this volume. This article will not pretend to be a complete treatment of the idea, but rather is a sketch of some important subthemes within the topic. Section 2 discusses moral responsibility. Moral responsibility serves as a template for more institutionalized forms of responsibility, thus the capacities it presupposes and its criteria of liability can illuminate other forms. Section 3 takes up criminal responsibility, notably the problems of finding an adequate theory of criminal legislation, appropriate response, and criteria of responsibility. I will try to show that the periodic oscillations between managerial and retributive approaches to punishment reflect a deeper debate about the nature of state–social relations. In Section 4 I treat the exemplary case of tort liability, focusing on the debate in tort theory between instrumentalist and corrective justice views. Again, my aim is to show how a relational understanding of responsibility clarifies the debates within tort theory.

Thus, I leave several topics for further exploration. In particular, I do not discuss the question of what Ronald Dworkin has called "political responsibility," that is, the responsibility on the part of the state generally or state officials particularly to justify their conduct—a responsibility particularly at issue in jurisprudence and administrative law.[6] Although political responsibility might be thought of as a version of role responsibility (at least in many instances), I have omitted its discussion because it belongs properly to jurisprudence, discussed extensively in this volume, and to political theory more broadly. Engaging those questions would force too great a digression from the central focus of this chapter on individual responsibility. For similar reasons I will not treat, except in passing, the subject of "social responsibility," as it relates to the social welfare obligations of individuals or other entities. Finally, my discussion of legal responsibility in private law is limited to tort law, although the subject of responsibility in contract law also raises interesting philosophical questions, for example, about the relation between promise and contract, and the justification of promissory estoppel and unconscionability principles.[7] For the most part, however, the relevant issues of agency and repair, and the social ideals they presuppose, are aired in the tort law discussion.

2 MORAL RESPONSIBILITY

Moral responsibility names a set of practices, and our conduct, consequences, and character are the objects of those practices. We hold ourselves and each other morally responsible for how we act, what we bring about, and who we are. This is an entirely unremarkable claim, and would seem a natural starting point for discussions of moral responsibility. But philosophical discussions of moral responsibility have instead often been waylaid by the challenge of reconciling a conception of responsibility with a naturalistic understanding of human deliberation and action. The philosophical problem of responsibility arises from two powerful ideas. On the one hand, it seems that we do not morally praise or blame others for acts not somehow the products of their choices; and even

when the acts are the products of their choices, we will withdraw blame if we discover that, for some reason, the person could not have chosen other than as he or she did. Had the ship been sunk by an unnoticeable iceberg, Captain Smith would have been off the hook.[8] This observation is then transformed into the metaphysically more ambitious claim that moral responsibility for an act (or the consequences of an act) requires both that the agent could have done otherwise, and that the agent is responsible because his or her choice was the cause of the act. On the other hand, any plausible conception of humanity's place in nature must make room for the idea that our choices and actions are as subsumed under natural laws as all other phenomena.

The conjunction of a naturalistic understanding of human action, thus subsumed, and the conception of responsibility in terms of a capacity to choose freely among a range of options generates the metaphysical free will problem. For a naturalistic understanding of human action suggests either that choices are the determinate products of antecedent events, or that they are the products of pure indeterminacy. Either way, the conception of responsibility as capacity to do otherwise is undermined.[9] Moral responsibility, extrapolated from this argument, is a fundamental aspect of our social lives, and yet it seems to require a kind of freedom unavailable in the world we inhabit.

There are two things to notice about the genesis of this problem, both related to the concept of responsibility from which it arises. First, the problem arises from an underspecified understanding of responsibility: the putative requirement of free choice is taken roughly as an intuitive axiom. The result has been to interpret the notion of free choice in terms of counterfactual possibilities, and then to compare that interpretation against claims about physical necessity. Secondly, the understanding of responsibility is basically *solipsistic,* in that only facts about the agent, his choice, and his acts, are relevant to the ascription of responsibility; relations to other agents are irrelevant. The result is that the metaphysical notion of being responsible is taken as primary, and the notions of holding or taking responsibility are derivative. One is morally responsible in general if one possesses the relevant capacity for free choice, and morally responsible for a particular act or event if that act or event resulted from such a choice.

The metaphysical problem of free will has inspired much difficult and interesting work.[10] But the mere capacity conception of responsibility, coupled with the disregard for the social relations in which ascriptions of responsibility are embedded, has meant that the metaphysical debates tended to reveal little about the underlying notion. The social and psychological meaning of responsibility was neglected. This all changed with Peter Strawson's seminal "Freedom and Resentment," an article that aimed to reverse the traditional direction of explanation. Rather than explain the notion of holding someone responsible in terms of a capacity for responsibility, Strawson suggested taking the idea of holding responsible as primary, and then understanding the capacity sense of responsibility in terms of the liability sense of responsibility. The result is to ground the abstract notion of moral responsibility in a set of social practices of holding ourselves and one another responsible, not in a metaphysical conception of free choice. Obversely, Strawson extracts the incapacity for responsibility from our social practices of excuse. The hope, then, is that the metaphysical free will problem can be disarmed by showing that the social practices of excuse do not generalize under the threat of causal determinism but are, rather, context-specific.[11]

What Strawson noticed was that ascriptions of responsibility have a crucial affective dimension. Our practices of accountability are made up of natural patterns of emotional reaction, or "reactive attitudes," to the welcome and unwelcome attitudes of others manifested in their conduct towards us.[12] When I blame you for slapping me on the back of the neck, I am venting my resentment at the hostility implicit in your act; and when I am grateful to you for courteously holding the door for me, I am expressing my delight at the goodwill you demonstrate. My responses to your actions flow principally from my assumptions about the sentiments expressed by your conduct, not the consequences produced by it. Thus, when I discover that the attitude to which I am reacting is absent or different than I had supposed, my reaction naturally transforms. If I discover that you slapped my neck in order to swat away a bee, then I will no longer resent the action as an attack upon me. Or, if I discover that you have been merely careless in swinging your hand around, I may revise my resentment to focus upon your disregard rather than your hostility. My reactions similarly shift when the attitude is present, but has a suspect aetiology—perhaps an effect of your paranoid delusions. Now I do not resent your hostility, but try to understand it, because it no longer expresses your considered sentiments, but only the state of your mental health.

There are two points to notice here. First is that the capacities and incapacities presupposed by our reactive attitudes are straightforwardly psychological, not metaphysical. *Will* thus names an item accessible to naturalistic investigation. Since there is no evident reason to think that the truth or falsehood of determinism bears on the nature or exercise of these capacities, the psychological concept of responsibility can be unyoked from the metaphysical concept. Once the two are unyoked, it is difficult to see the motivation for the metaphysical problem our ordinary responses, as distinct from the intrinsic philosophical interest in whether our behaviour has ultimate external causes. The test for this claim is whether, if we really believed determinism was true, our ordinary responses would erode. But that test is pragmatic, not logical, and cannot be resolved by theoretical discussion. Strawson's view thus opens up conceptual space for an independent investigation of the norms internal to the practices of responsibility, norms whose content can be divorced—in great part even if not entirely—from metaphysics.

Secondly, and relatedly, our disinclination to express reactive attitudes to partly or wholly non-responsible agents is explained not merely by the quality of their wills, but by the nature of our relations with them. Thus, the norms governing our practices of responsibility are in part *social* norms, deriving from and governing our relations with others. Though children and the insane do indeed manifest attitudes of hostility and goodwill, we tend to take what Strawson calls an "objective" rather than a "participant's" view of their attitudes. Instead of attempting to define the quality that responsible agents' wills have and nonresponsible agents' wills lack, Strawson emphasizes the way that our awareness of cognitive and affective limitations in nonresponsible agents naturally precludes them from participating in the relationships characteristic of adult society.[13] We see them not as accountable subjects but as the objects of understanding, treatment, or education—that is, as quasi-participants in therapeutic relationships.

It should be clear from this brief description that a Strawsonian view does not insist that we must have these reactive attitudes in every case in which they might be warranted. To borrow an example from Jay Wallace, a rogue might act in a way that would warrant recrimination, but be so charming that we cannot work up the indignation.[14] Moral responsibility is, in any event, a normative rather than descriptive concept: someone's being responsible is a matter of being warranted by the relevant social norms in having certain attitudes towards them. Just as I may form unwarranted attitudes towards someone whom I mistakenly take to be responsible, so I may fail to form warranted attitudes. Studies of the moral emotions by such writers as Patricia Greenspan, Jean Hampton, Michael Moore, Herbert Morris, Jeffrie Murphy, Samuel Scheffler, Gabriele Taylor, Bernard Williams, and Richard Wollheim, also have contributed to a normative understanding of our emotional responses.[15] We also may extend the notion of a warranted response from affect alone to acts of contrition, punishment, gratitude, and reward. In its most general sense, to be responsible is for certain responses to be warranted, in virtue of what one has done and why one has done it.

The claim that responses are warranted by governing social norms necessarily implies some social relativism. Relativity to social norms can arise in at least two innocuous ways: social norms define the nature of the act in question and they regulate the appropriate response. A remark that is a mild tease in one society (or social subgroup) can be a grave insult in another; and an insult that demands redress in one place may permit cheek-turning in another. But anchoring responsibility in local norms may seem to imply as well a

less palatable, more thoroughgoing relativism, leaving no room to criticize quaint local traditions such as scapegoating or ritual sacrifice. Moreover, social norms conflict and are frequently indeterminate in their demands even when they do not conflict. Thus, the Strawsonian approach may well lead to questions of responsibility that can receive only partial and limited answers.

There are, however, a couple of responses to these worries. First, social norms are rooted in a collection of human needs, wants, and dispositions that are only semiplastic—influenced but not fully determined by physical and social environments. The Strawsonian account recognizes local variation, to its considerable advantage; but the degree of that variation should not be overestimated. In every culture where accidents and injuries happen—which is to say in every culture—the responsibility practices that arise will persist only if they cohere with other normative and explanatory concepts. Practices bearing too little relation to such basic considerations as causality and proportionality, for example, are unlikely to flourish over time, for they will fail to cohere with other basic cultural and scientific institutions. Although pockets of magical thinking will surely persist in any culture, they are unlikely to remain the bedrock of responsibility practices. There thus will be room in any culture with a notion of causality (which is to say every practically feasible culture) for criticism of pure scapegoating. Moreover, nothing in the Strawsonian account precludes grounding (or criticizing) some set of responsibility practices in terms of some nonrelative ethical standards (for example, standards of fairness or equal treatment). Warrant can emerge from local context, or from absolute ethical standards (if they exist), or both; no deep relativism is implied.

The second point concerns indeterminacy. It is a consequence of the Strawsonian view that when responsibility norms conflict (either local or absolute norms), there will be no clear answer what response is warranted, despite disagreement among the participants in the debate. But "underdeterminacy" is the better term for this state of affairs, not "indeterminacy," for it is not the case that no response is warranted, but rather that the set of applicable norms is insufficient to warrant any unique response. And it seems a virtue of the Strawsonian account to imply such underdeterminacy, for underdeterminacy is surely also a feature of the moral (and legal) lives the account aims to reflect. Moreover, underdeterminacy, unlike indeterminacy, makes room for argument, as participants contest the relative weight or priority of different potential norms, for example when the spirit of a rule is best honoured by an exception, or when mercy's place must be subordinated to collective security.

So Strawson's suggestion is helpful, not just for the way in which it allows us to avoid metaphysical thickets, but by making room for the relational and positional character of responsibility. It should now be clear that the attitudes and expressions of agents only warrant response given a certain understanding of the nature of the relationship between agent and respondent. In Strawson's very rough division, the relationship must be either participatory or potentially participatory: the agent to whom we respond must be someone with whom we will or could cooperate in social life. Our attitudes and expressions both indicate and constitute the nature of a participatory relationship. In general, we care about our relationships with others in virtue of the ways they can make our lives good (or bad), both in themselves, and as vehicles for promoting our interests. So the responses characteristic of accountability are warranted by the point and demands of the relationship. What we take responsibility and hold each other responsible for are deviations between our actual conduct and the norms constitutive of the relevant relationship.

Acknowledging relationality entails, as Strawson point out, a necessary variability in warranted responses depending upon the nature of the relationship in question: what might constitute callous indifference between friends or lovers is simply good manners between commercial transactors.[16] For example, if I carelessly break a neighbour's vase at a party while dancing on his grand piano, my neighbour is warranted in resenting my carelessness and asking for an apology, though not in, say, smashing my glasses. Reciprocally, an apology or restitution is warranted on my part (and perhaps even obligatory). But my responsibility does not end with a simple interaction between my neighbour and myself. There are countless other positions from which other agents may respond to my act. For example, other guests at the party may also feel indignant at having their pleasant evening disrupted by my loutish behaviour, and they may expect a public display of contrition for their sake, though they could not appropriately feel personally aggrieved in the same way as my neighbour. Perhaps some of the guests are relatives of my neighbour, however, and they may take the event more personally than friends and acquaintances present. I may also be accountable to my own family for the harm, since they will now be embarrassed before the neighbour, and I may owe them a promise to take more care in the future. Finally, to and from the public at large only very constrained responses are warranted. Although anyone who heard about my accident could consider me a fool, and say so, a more direct response to me personally would be thought self-righteous and nosy; and it would be self-abasing of me to confess my shame to a random person met in the street.

This essential and obvious fact of responsibility, its relational and positional dependence, is unexplained on the retributive, desert-based model. The retributivists' exclusive focus upon an agent's intentional state and actions dictates that all warranted responses flow from a single constant value: what the agent deserves. The response warranted by desert is thus univocal, dependent upon facts about the agent rather than the agent's relations to others. One could object that the variability of warranted responses can be made consistent with the retributive model: an agent "deserves" multiple and varied responses from different people. On this interpretation, "desert" just means that some response (or set of responses) is warranted on some ground. Although there is nothing objectionable about this use, it falls well short of the traditional ambitions of the desert model, namely itself to provide a justification for hard treatment and prescribe the upper and lower limits of that treatment.

Strawson's own account works best where the form of background participatory relationship that grounds and warrants response is most conspicuous, that is, in the domain that I have called social accountability. His account is less helpful in explaining the special character of our moral responses to agents with whom we share no particular set of relationships—for example, my reaction upon reading in the paper that an employer has exploited its workers. Here I am outraged, towards the employer and on behalf of the workers, though I cannot in any deep sense identify myself with either of their positions. Strawson says that the relationship among moral respondents in such cases is simply a "generalized" form of the claim to goodwill made by members of participatory social relationships. He does so in order to explain what he calls the "vicarious" nature of moral reactions: responses like moral indignation are "essentially capable" of being directed at others' attitudes towards third parties as well as at attitudes directed towards ourselves.[17] Strawson says these vicarious reactions are "humanly connected" with participant reactions, though he does not explain the nature of this connection.[18] Strawson is surely right to suggest that it is a deeply rooted fact that humans—or at least members of minimally cohesive societies—have a propensity to pass judgment generally on others' compliance with social norms.[19] Indeed, it is hard to imagine how a society could maintain its normative structure if its members were not disposed to monitor and censure each other for noncompliance. It is in this propensity, layered and modified through cultural forms, that the institutions of judgment, punishment, and repair find their ground.

Sometimes responses to agents are not motivated by the attitudes those agents manifest, nor by their failure to conform their conduct to appropriate norms. Sometimes an agent's mere causal linkage with a harm may warrant a response from others. The responses characteristic of accountability for consequences also can only be understood in terms of the moral and social relationships among the parties, and their different positions with respect to the harm. The striking asymmetry in accountability for consequences between the responses of agents themselves, on the one hand, and victims and onlookers, on the other, has not been fully appreciated. In particular, agents can reproach themselves for faultless conduct that causes a harm, even when their victims, and onlookers, do not reproach them. This asymmetry of responses to consequences reflects the deep role that causal relations have for agents in structuring their understanding of (or relationship to) themselves. Those affected by the agent, in contrast, care less about causal relations in the absence of faulty conduct.

Although conduct-based responses are warranted by the way that agents' behaviour manifests attitudes of respect, contempt, or indifference regardless of whether that conduct causes harm, consequence-based responses are warranted by the fact of a harm regardless of whether the conduct was faulty. Causality, in isolation from conduct, indicates nothing about how agents have previously viewed their relations with others. The ready-to-hand example of the significance of causality is Oedipus. Despite their initial strangeness, the characters' reactions in *Oedipus Rex* can be intelligible to modern readers once the magical elements of fatalism and pollution are stripped away. Reasons of consequence explain these reactions: "incest," after all, describes a situation, not a content of will, or an attitude. Oedipus has, by his own actions, brought on (and engaged in) this situation, and this contingent, causal connection grounds his horror and self-reproach.[20]

Oedipus's response to the fact of his causal role is what Bernard Williams calls "agent-regret": regret that a state of affairs obtains whose occurrence involved one's own agency.[21] Agent-regret rests on no sense of wrongdoing, and is compatible with impeccable conduct, even conduct so recognized by the agent.[22] However, it seems a mistake to distinguish agent-regret fully from guilt, for although an awareness of wrongful acting is a typical part of guilt, awareness of having done something awful, even if unwittingly, can suffice.[23] Oedipus's response was partly shame at his incestuous disgrace. But his horrible self-mutilation can only be explained by something else, something that we can recognize as a form of guilt: a gesture at repaying a wrong he has done. The causal relation itself need not be entirely direct to trigger guilt. If, while tending a friend's cat, it slips outdoors despite my protections and gets hit by a car, I will feel not merely sorry for my friend but guilty towards her. Although the death is not my fault, I have provided for its occasion, and so my relations to her differ from those of any other sympathetic friend. Indeed, because of the friend's trust in me, I am likely to feel even worse than the driver who, also let us assume faultlessly, actually killed the cat.[24]

These examples bring out a striking feature of consequential accountability: where conduct is not at issue, there is an especially radical asymmetry in response among the various positions that the harm itself creates. My friend is unlikely to resent me, even though I feel guilty. More precisely, if the accident is not my fault, then my friend would be unwarranted in resenting my role, since I will not have acted badly, although my feelings will be warranted by my causal role and our prior relationship, as well as by the protective role I assumed towards his cat.[25] Likewise, Oedipus's compatriots more pity than despise him for his crime. The principal reason for this asymmetry is that agents' causal relations necessarily inform their conceptions of themselves, of who they are. For victims, by contrast, the significance of the harm consists largely in the mere fact of its occurrence, and not its causal link to a particular agent.

The relation between agents and their effects is one of identity, in a certain sense. What an agent has caused is an important part of that agent's history and life, as important as what that agent has intentionally done, believed, and hoped for. The regret signals the fundamental unluckiness of the causal connection between this agent and those consequences. Because regret for faultless accidents maps the agent's actual (as opposed to idealized) course through the world, the general absence of such regret is found primarily among children and extreme Kantians, for whom the fantasy or ideal world is more salient than the real. As H. L. A. Hart and Tony Honoré have suggested, it is through claims of causal authorship that "[i]ndividuals come to understand themselves as distinct persons, to whatever extent they do, and to acquire a sense of self-respect ...."[26] It is important to note, however, that "what I have

done" does not name a naturally limited universe of events: agents are causally related to infinitely many events, under infinitely many descriptions, and only some of those events, under some descriptions, will be salient. The concept of what an agent has done is given itself by our practices of accountability and conception of causation. Beyond bodily movements themselves, the extension of an agent's field of causal influence is given by a complex and deeply rooted normative conception.[27]

The shape of that conception—what causal relations are picked out as warranting a response—isthe subject of an enormous literature. Although some writers have attempted to locate normative considerations in a metaphysical conception of causation, most have instead adopted a nonnormative, context-neutral conception, then relied on pragmatics to explain ordinary usage.[28] According to generic conceptions, a person's act is typically one item among enormously many causally relevant events and conditions that are jointly sufficient for an event's occurrence. As many philosophers have argued, whether that act is highlighted as noteworthy ("*the* cause"), by the agent or another, depends in part upon its relation to stable background conditions, its role in durable structures of events, its susceptibility to intervention or control, and so on.[29] The relevance of the agent's intervention in the cat and Oedipal cases is obvious. But I want to suggest that, in more difficult cases, agents' social and moral relations to others are especially important to agents' seeing their acts as causally connected to harms. This is particularly true of omissions, as when my failure to bring a sick child promptly to the doctor results in suffering: the nature of my accountability will depend upon my relation to the child. But my seeing myself as the positive cause of another's misery also depends upon my understanding of the structure of our mutual relations. If we are competitors in business and my low prices unintentionally drive you into bankruptcy, I may see your failure to meet my prices, rather than my own act, as the cause of your demise.[30] In contrast, if we are friends and my unintentional act results in your suffering, I am likely to reproach myself for my causal role and do what I can to make amends.

My gesture of repair as an agent is, in these cases, more complicated than just the reaffirming or re-establishing of the character of a relationship between agent and victim. When I see myself as accountable for a harm I merely cause, and when repair of that harm is at least possible in part, my gesture of repair is directed at myself as well as at my victim. It is directed at the victim in so far as it is an attempt to compensate for a burden I have imposed. And it is directed at myself in so far as it provides a way for me to transform my trajectory through the world, eliminating what is unfortunate about what I have done. Here we see a further asymmetry in the responsive positions of agent and victim, particularly in cases of faultless wrongdoing: although my victim may be indifferent to the source of compensation, I may feel that it must, in symbolic part at least, come from me.[31] And even if neither I nor my victim feels it necessary that I provide the compensation, an apology or other gesture of repair may also be called for, and that can come only from me.

This account of causation as a source of reasons warranting response may seem circular, for if merely singling out a causally relevant factor as the cause depends upon a prior conception of appropriate relations between the parties, then the relevant notion of causation is doing no independent normative work.[32] The notion of cause and warranted response are indeed interdependent and so, in a sense, functionally circular, but the circularity is not vicious. We make our causal contributions in social as well as physical space; the norms and interests that define that social space inevitably play a role in helping to delineate the causal relations we perceive. Once we have identified a given act as the cause of some harm, on the basis of background expectations of appropriate behaviour, then we are led to modify our conception of that background, and so alter our future perceptions of what is a cause and what a mere condition. My friend forgives me this time for letting the cat out; either the driver or the cat itself may be regarded as the cause of its death. But if several more cats die while in my care, my friend's

perceptions of my causal role in the harms, and so her responses to me, will undoubtedly change.

As I have said, the position of victims, and the responses warranted by their relations to the harm, differ dramatically from the agents' own responses, particularly in cases of faultless causation; and these responses also depend upon the way victims view their relations to agents and onlookers. For agents, their causal relation to a harm warrants feelings of self-reproach. But because the agents manifested no ill conduct or will, victims' resentment on that basis is unwarranted. No prior moral or social relationship has been devalued by the harm, but only a distribution of goods distorted. As a result, the victim's response is more likely to be a demand for compensation unaccompanied by reproach. Whether this claim for compensation is seen as having normative force, by victim or agent, is itself a product of the relationships among the parties and society at large. "It wasn't my fault," when true, is a perfect excuse from accountability for conduct, but it bears no direct relationship to the moral question of compensation. Given a certain understanding of social and moral relationships, "that you caused it" can sufficiently warrant a claim for compensation. (The embedding of compensatory demand in the relationships constituted by a legal system, in the form of tort law, is the subject of section 4.)

So far my discussion has concerned the event paradigm of greatest traditional interest to moral philosophers, when one person injures another directly. But it is worth noting that many of the harms and miseries of modern life fall outside the paradigm of direct action. Think of buying a table made of tropical wood that comes from a defoliated rain forest, or using a CFC-based air-conditioner, along with 10,000,000 others, and so jointly putting a hole in the ozone layer; being a citizen of a nation that bombs another country's factories in a reckless attack on terrorists; or inhabiting a region seized long ago from its aboriginal occupants; helping to design an automobile that the manufacturer knowingly sells with a dangerously defective fuel system, or working in a healthcare bureaucracy that carelessly allows the distribution of HIV-contaminated blood. All of these examples are instances of a mediated relation to harm, where injury is brought about through the actions of others. And many of them are cases where what any one individual does makes no difference; only together do individuals cause harm.

These mediated relations to harm are the domain of *complicity*. Just as purely consequential responsibility tests will-oriented models of responsibility, so complicitous accountability puts pressure on consequence-oriented models. For it is a familiar fact of our moral and legal practices that we blame, punish, and demand compensation from complicitous agents even though what they did made no difference. The bank would have been robbed regardless, the ozone hole formed, the battle fought. The puzzle arises because, if causal contribution is necessary to responsibility, then no one is responsible, for no one makes a difference. And even when an individual difference is made, say when one person acts as lookout during a robbery, our practices of blame and rules of punishment go far beyond the causal contribution. What complicitous responsibility centrally challenges is an appealing, intuitive principle of responsibility, that someone can only be responsible for events over which he had control. Call this the "control principle."[33] An account of responsibility that aims to reveal rather than replace these pervasive practices of responsibility will have to show how responsibility can outrun both causation and control, without becoming simply a free-form virtual guilt shared by all.

In other work I have tried to do this.[34] Briefly, I argue that once we have in hand an analytical understanding of cooperation, a normative account of complicity follows suit. Individuals who cooperate share what I call *participatory intentions*, that is, intentions to do their parts of some collective act. Participatory intentions ground our basic practice of action- and outcome-ascription in cooperative contexts, so that, for example, when two of us together write an opera, you writing the music and I the book, each of us can truly say, "We wrote the opera." Each of us should be regarded as an author of the opera, albeit an inclusive author, in virtue of our individual collective participation in its creation. Responsibility for it—praise or blame—then tracks

the ascription of authorship. This is because the will of each can be deemed manifest in the collective product.

Now, differences in particular causal contributions change the responses warranted to particular individuals; it is reasonable to celebrate Mozart more than his librettist, Da Ponte. And there is a truth in the control principle: individuals who cannot control *whether* they participate at all (hostages or dupes, for example) cannot be held responsible for the collective harm.[35] But in cases of full overdetermination, when no individual really does make a causal difference, blame (or praise) may still fairly lie. Derek Parfit's famous "harmless torturers," each of whom gives a torture victim an individually imperceptible but aggregatively awful electrical jolt, provides a stark example of the problem.[36] Parfit himself struggles to accommodate consequentialist ethics to a form of responsibility that seems, on its face, precisely independent of individual consequence. Others have attempted to develop a theory of causation that makes sense of such cases.[37] I am sceptical, myself, whether these approaches work, even on their own terms. Whatever the ultimate account of complicitous responsibility, however, it will have to go at least partly by way of the participatory intentions of the agents—their will, independent of its effects, to join in a collective act that does injury. For in the absence of any salient individual causal contribution, surely it is the cooperation itself that explains responsibility. Implication follows participation.

3 CRIMINAL RESPONSIBILITY

A working theory of criminal responsibility presupposes an answer to one question, and must answer two more questions. It presupposes an answer to the question of what norms should define the domain of criminal law. And it must provide answers to the following questions: first, what counts as a violation of those norms; and second, what responses are warranted by their violation? Clearly, these questions must be answered together if they are to be answered intelligibly. If the criminal norms aim primarily at conduct as opposed to consequence, then the criteria of responsibility will emphasize causation over quality of will. If the norms protect very great or vulnerable interests, then more serious responses are likely to be deemed warranted. And if the responses deemed warranted for violation are very severe, then the criteria of responsibility ought to be narrow—assuming some background political principles against the infliction of suffering or favouring the retention of individual liberty. This is not to say that a theory of one of these subjects determines answers to the other two, but only the more modest point that the criminal norms, criteria of responsibility, and responsive practices must hang together in reflective equilibrium.

Criminal norms have traditionally protected the most important interests in life, security of body, and security of possession. By protecting these interests from malicious incursion, criminal law makes social life possible by making social trust possible. Relying on state power to quell each other's urges to act selfishly or viciously, we can forge the cooperative relations that make our lives good.[38] It is true that the reach of criminal norms in modern times has extended beyond these core interests into many regulatory domains. These regulatory domains often use only weak criteria of responsibility, forgoing requirements of knowledge and intent. The extended reach of criminal norms provokes worry even when the actual sanctions are not severe, because the expressive, condemnatory aspect of criminal norms carries over from the core concerns.[39] But what determines whether a given interest will be expressed and protected through criminal law is only in part a function of its intrinsic importance. It is also a function of the special responsive position of the state as the expressive and enforcement agency, as well as of the state's relations to other social institutions. Demands for a moralized criminal law—a law punishing private, consensual behaviour on grounds of its immorality—reflect in their proponents not just a concern to maintain a (probably illusory) normative status quo, but also a deep insecurity about the capacity of non-coercive social institutions to govern behaviour. "There oughtta be a law!" is spoken not by the discoverer of a new norm, but by someone unhappy about an old norm's current efficacy. A similar point holds for the criminalization of regulatory matters: the choice to rely upon sanctions, as opposed to tax- or market-based approaches, often reflects both an articulated judgment about the efficacy of different means to the same result, as well as more inchoate beliefs about the need for state authority to supplement private forms of social ordering.

Just as contested ideals of state–civil society relations explain debates about the allocation of authority between criminal and other norms, so they also explain debates about the proper response to violations of those norms and criteria of responsibility. Discussions of warranted response have typically come in the form of different theories of punishment. Theories of punishment divide into two groups. On the one hand, there are true theories of punishment, which attempt to offer a justification for the intentional and condemnatory hard treatment of violators of criminal norms. In this group there is some discussion of the proper sort of hard treatment, whether it includes physical pain, execution, incarceration, or shaming penalties. But discussion primarily focuses on how to justify a treatment whose unpleasantness is assumed—whether it is to be justified in retributivist or expressive terms.[40] The second group consists not in theories of punishment per se, but in theories of the proper treatment of offenders, where the proper treatment may not involve state-inflicted suffering at all. All such theories are, self-evidently, instrumentalist, and utilitarian theories are the most obvious examples. Hard treatment will be justified, if it is, through its role in deterring other crime or in subordinating the offender to social authority. Gentler rehabilitative and educative theories also fall into this group, as do reparative theories—that is, approaches to offence that attempt to mend the social ties severed by the criminal offence.[41] Finally come theories that represent a hybrid of instrumental and intrinsic concerns. Hart's theory of punishment, further developed by Mackie and Scanlon, takes this form: a system of punishment whose infliction is sensitive to offenders' wills is justified both as a means of maintaining civil order against a background of general liberty, and as a system peculiarly appropriate to beings who value the ability to determine by choice whether they will come into conflict with the state.[42]

Contrast criminal responsibility with moral responsibility. Within morality's broad limits, variety reigns. Friends and family members can reproach each other for minor defects of character as social acquaintances cannot. The fury and rage expressed by lovers at betrayal, well-warranted though it may be, would be wholly out of place even between friends. Likewise, the poignant guilt properly felt at the betrayal of a friend might well be considered self-lacerating if it were directed at all moral transgressions. Social morality is effective precisely because there is room for play in its joints. Though the norms governing warranted response have shifted enormously through time and across cultures, and depended crucially upon the state's eagerness and capacity to keep the civil peace, there have always been limits to appropriate response, even if those responses have greatly transgressed the generally pacific borders of contemporary Western elite social morality. I will stipulate here, however, that absent circumstances of self-defence, the limits of moral response are the limits of language and feeling. Physically violent or coercive responses to individuals are only morally permitted to the state.

Legal systems protect the interests that morality protects, centrally the means and liberties necessary to live well as a rational and reflective, project-centred agent. To the extent that legal systems do anything more than simply express (vehemently) these norms, then it is necessary to conceive law instrumentally to some extent, judging systems better or worse in their capacity to secure these interests. But this need not be a crassly functionalist conception of law any more than of morality, which also performs a function of protecting the interests and relationships that make our lives good. Law is good because the interests it protects are valuable; and legal responses are warranted by the importance of those interests. If liberties and well-being are values within the law, then legal responses that compromise those values are suspect. Although the restrictions upon moral wrongdoing and free riding that legal institutions dictate are not themselves objectionable compromises to agents'

interests, the use of threats and application of sanctions to guarantee those restrictions do compromise autonomy.

It follows that if coercive measures by the state are warranted at all, they are warranted because no noncoercive measures are adequate to protect social interests once moral and legal forms of accountability have failed. Unlike social and moral responses, whose verbal or emotional nature is only of concern to those for whom the relationships they protect have value, coercive responses are of concern to any self-interested agent. Although legal systems may depend primarily, as Mackie suggests, upon the efficacy of an adverse legal characterization of certain acts, coercive threats play an essentially ancillary role in motivating those unswayed by a desire to maintain morally appropriate relations.[43]

The interests justifying legal responses themselves limit those responses. If, as under liberal regimes, legal systems aim to protect meaningful forms of individual autonomy and social cooperation in general, then individuals' autonomy interests will be of concern as well in the administration of legal sanctions. As Hart (and Scanlon following him) have argued, this concern for autonomy, rather than a concern for rectifying moral wrongs, can best explain the general restriction of penal sanctions to cases of voluntary conduct.[44] By making the infliction of those legal sanctions that severely infringe individual autonomy depend upon the choices individuals make, the state has done what it can to ensure the autonomy of each citizen. Due process considerations also serve to protect individual autonomy from undue state interference. The concern for autonomy also helps to explain the criminal law's "act requirement," that only voluntary attempts and commissions are punishable, and not inchoate plans or involuntary movements.[45] Because who an agent is and what an agent causes are far less sensitive to choice, criminal punishment on these bases is far more restricted.[46]

The debates among theories of punishment have famously tended to stress an ideal of the person, enhanced or compromised by the relevant punitive practice. Immanuel Kant famously denounced the "serpent windings of utilitarianism" on the grounds that it uses the offender simply as a means of general social control, thus failing to respect him as a rational agent meriting concern for his own ends.[47] By contrast, critics of the retributivist ideal preferred by Kant, according to which it is intrinsically good or right to ensure that wrongdoers suffer, have worried that talk of the rightfulness of punishment served mainly to mask the punisher's desire to humiliate, a desire coming from a sense of resentment, not justice. As Nietzsche put it (with characteristic exaggeration), Kant's "categorical imperative reeks of cruelty."[48]

Disputed ideals of the person do drive the debate over punishment, but to focus only on the person punished involves a kind of ethical solipsism. Equally important is an ideal, not of the individual, but of social and political relations. Different theories of punishment implicate, and are implied by, different conceptions of the proper relation of the individual to the community. What must strike anyone working in the area of punishment theory is the way in which different theories have come to dominate or recede, it seems, as a matter of shifts in broader political views. When Hart began writing on punishment, for example, the philosophical status quo was reformist and rehabilitative, not retributive. Along with other writers, he rejected rehabilitative theories out of a concern about the reduction of the offender to a psychological system to be manipulated by the state.[49] Hart rejected retributivist theories of punishment as well, partly on the familiar conceptual ground that they depended upon a "mysterious piece of moral alchemy" that made two ordinarily impermissible acts amount to justice.[50] But his conceptual argument (or observation—he hardly took retributivist theories seriously enough to argue against them) can be fairly seen as a product of a general sentiment that retributivism in punishment was faintly barbaric, as compared with enlightened utilitarian social policy. By the 1980s, however, retributivist theories had come to flourish, propelled in significant part by the work of Michael Moore and Andrew von Hirsch.[51] It seems hardly coincidental that fashion in philosophical theories of punishment has tracked fashion in political practice (or

vice versa), as particularly United States penal policy has shifted from rehabilitative to fiercely punitive practice and increasing emphasis on individual rather than social responsibility.[52]

This sociology of recent theorizing is meant to do more than point out the obvious fact that philosophers too are creatures and creators of the Zeitgeist. It also demonstrates the analytical point that theories of warranted response must be interpreted in terms of the background conception of social relations they presume. I have already mentioned how rejection of rehabilitative theories was early driven by worries about the therapeutic politics they presumed.[53] The rejection of utilitarian theories has as much to do with their treatment of individuals as means, as with the more general, managerial conception they hold of the state. In utilitarian political theory of a crude but familiar kind, the state is conceived as an expert at social engineering, attempting to maximize net social satisfaction.[54] Doubts about utilitarian political theory, related both to its implicit dependence on expertise and to its failure to see individual members of society as cooperating agents, not just joint consumers, have led to its displacement in the field of distributive justice.[55] A theory of punishment resting on a conception of the state as social manager is equally undermined by these doubts. Retributivist theories, with their emphasis on individual dignity, point up the defects of utilitarian views. But retributivists have thus far failed to come up with a conception of the state that makes the infliction of just punitive deserts a legitimate objective of the state.[56] It certainly is possible to conceive of the state as the people's agent in delivering deserts, both retributive and distributive; but this conception is hardly uncontroversial, resting as it does on a metaphysically robust and preinstitutional understanding of desert.[57] The reparative justice theories now emerging reflect a more communitarian ideal of social relations in their focus on reconciling individuals with their societies. Unless there is reason to think that some particular political conception will come to hold sway—and I see no such reason—the relationality of responsibility means that debates among punishment theories will go unresolved.

The concomitant of the relationality of criminal responsibility is its positionality. It is not merely a legal conceit that, although the prosecutor represents "the people," the court represents impartial justice. For the position of justice taken by the law is very special and circumscribed. When legal institutions assume the partisan position of the victim and the posture of resentment, the rights and liberties of defendants are severely compromised, situations for which the sedition trials of the twentieth century are the best exemplars.[58] The warranted response of victims to hostile behaviour is resentment; but resentment is wholly inappropriate from the institutions of justice. The position the criminal law represents is not simply an integration over all social and moral positions, and legal responses do not represent whole, overall responses to wrongs. Instead, legal responses are ideally made from a particular position, that of the state, and represent one form of response among many. Regardless of what individuals deserve, the state's responses flow from the relations that tie each individual to one another, agent and victim alike, and are limited by the claims internal to those relationships.

Reminding ourselves of the special position of the state is particularly helpful in getting a handle on the old chestnut of theories of punishment, why unsuccessful attempts should be punished less severely than successfully completed crimes. On one side is the view that the proper basis of punitive, as opposed to compensatory, responsibility is either the social danger of the defendant's conduct, the contempt for legal norms evinced by that conduct, or both, and that these bases are the same for unsuccessful and successful attempters alike.[59] Since the basis of responsibility is the same, there is no reason to punish differently. Adjusting punishment to actual harm, on this view, simply confuses punitive and compensatory responses. Proponents of differentiated punishment, by contrast, observe that our moral responses as a matter of fact track the harm we do. We blame ourselves more when misjudgment results in real harm; and we resent more the malevolent acts of others, simply because those acts cause us harm.[60] The connection between this bit of moral phenomenology and state punishment is a retributive theory of punishment, according to which the state's role is to administer a (univocal) moral desert.

The relation between luck and responsibility is deeply vexed, and it is unclear, to say the least, whether our practices of responsibility can be fully regimented or rationalized in terms of specific bases of response.[61] Reconciling responsibility with luck is a deep problem, perhaps an insoluble one, for moral theory. But it must only be solved for the theory of punishment if state punishment ought genuinely to mimic interpersonal moral response and resentment—whether it really is to be Sidgwickian "resentment universalized."[62] If the argument for distinguishing successful from unsuccessful attempts can be given no firmer basis than coherence with interpersonal moral practice, then there is no good case to adding actual harm as a factor in calculating punishment, independent of social danger and antisocial will. To do otherwise is to confuse the particular purposes of the criminal responsibility system with the more general expressive and constitutive functions played by our practices of moral responsibility.

The second main point of intersection between criminal law and philosophical interest concerns the criteria of responsibility. In Anglo-American law, the criteria of criminal responsibility converge with the criteria of moral responsibility: where moral claims are warranted, so generally is legal sanction; and where there is moral excuse or justification, so too there is legal excuse or justification. Although the expressive function of criminal law makes overlap between moral blame and criminal guilt likely, the very high degree of convergence in modern doctrine and statute is the product of the concerted effort by a number of criminal scholars, notably Hart, Sanford Kadish, Herbert Wechsler, and Glanville Williams, to limit the encroachment of strict liability doctrines.[63] That said, any specifically legal conception of culpability must recognize that legal authority is always exercised in doubt. Criminal law presents the most serious epistemic problems, given its focus upon individual intentions. Intentions are inferred from scatterings of circumstance, causal explanations are shaped by the interests of the contesting parties. Unfortunately, just resolution of cases requires good information; and good information is generally expensive and difficult to obtain. No individual accused of a crime can be expected, practically or normatively, to divulge a culpable state of mind. The distinction between premeditated and spontaneous homicide, for example, can be the difference between execution and incarceration. Premeditated homicide can be proven by evidence of advance planning. However, the most subjectively inclined courts have held that killing can count as premeditated in the absence of planning, so long as the accused has the opportunity to reflect on the decision to kill.[64] Since obviously no killer will admit to premeditation, and since there is rarely a surviving witness to the crime, the judge or jury's decision often teeters upon a scaffolding of circumstantial evidence and psychological inference.

Despite pervasive doubt and uncertainty, decisions must be made and distinctions drawn, whether in the name of retributive justice or credible deterrence. It is therefore no wonder that evidentiary matters play a central role in the criminal process. Some of the restrictions upon the evidence that can be procured by the state and brought to bear in the courtroom, such as the requirement of a duly authorized warrant for a comprehensive search, stem from a generalized concern about the limits of police intrusion. But other restrictions reflect fundamentally epistemic concerns, such as the exclusion of evidence of a defendant's prior criminal history, or of hearsay reports of the defendant's statements. Although prior criminal history is clearly relevant to proof of the crime in question, such evidence is rightly excluded in many cases on the grounds that its effect upon juries is more prejudicial than probative.[65] Without these protective evidentiary rules, a system of criminal responsibility could not possibly be applied in justice.

Contrast the circumstances of criminal justice with those of moral theory. Although moral philosophers since Kant have warned of the inscrutability of individual intention in the first- as well as third-person cases, most moral theories ignore these epistemic problems, including Kant's own moral theory.[66] Deontologists focus on agents' underlying intentions and self-conceptions; and

utilitarians resort to the idealized fiction of fully informed, "ethical" preferences in order to justify their criterion of right action.[67] Whether agents have acted wrongly and are accountable for so acting thus depends upon deep facts about their deliberative and motivational capacities, fine-grained attributions of intentional content, unequivocal motivation, and empirically adequate predictions of future consequences.

In general, the moral judgments we make and the responses we offer may be wildly out of line with the evidence necessary to support their application. The jerk who cuts me off on the highway may be distracted by great personal loss. But this possibility is unlikely to stop me from thinking him a jerk. Moral theory and practice can live by idealized epistemic standards because the stakes in the moral game are low in any particular case. The relationships that social morality plays the dominant role in protecting can usually be repaired through apology and understanding. I may unfairly resent your failure to meet me, not realizing that you had a sick child to take care of. When you have a chance to explain, or when I otherwise discover the reason for your absence, all is again put right between us.

By contrast, the belated acquittal of someone unjustly convicted puts little right, for nothing can repair the violence done to one's sense of autonomy and worth by unjust punishment. To be imprisoned, publicly despised, and stripped of elementary civil rights is to have one's political, social, and moral identity undermined or lost: it is to become an object of the state's authority, rather than a subject who authorizes the state's exercise of that power.[68] Freedom and compensation may be valid claims stemming from unjust process or sentence, but they are not a full means of repair. Given the moral and human costs of wrongful conviction, it surely follows that a necessary condition of a just penal institution is that it make very few mistakes. Legal judgments have little point unless actually applied and enforced; they are worthless merely as indicators of moral norms. But in order to be legitimate, legal judgments must be well-rooted in both fact and political morality. Legal theorists and moral philosophers who distinguish sharply between normative and evidentiary issues run the risk of ignoring the social space, with its costs and limitations, in which legal rules are necessarily embedded.[69] The problem is that an awareness of the law's epistemic constraints can quickly become licence for a cavalier cynicism about alibi and excuse. To the extent that exculpatory considerations are narrowed because of difficulties of proof, so broadens the scope of legal intrusion.

Within these epistemic constraints, two different kinds of criteria are generally relevant to criminal responsibility: criteria of capacity, and criteria of intentionality. The capacity demanded for criminal liability is, roughly, that demanded for moral responsibility: a capacity to govern oneself by practical reason, responsive to the moral and factual considerations that obtain. The requisite capacity for practical rationality evidently incorporates a number of different components: a perceptual component, for establishing the nature of one's environment; a conative component, through which one finds some possibilities of action desirable as goals and others undesirable; an evaluative-cognitive component, for weighing the reasons for and against the potential goals; an instrumental-cognitive component, for determining how to realize those goals; and a volitional component, through which one actually acts on the desired goals.[70] Note that there is nothing about the having or exercise of this capacity that is incompatible with causal determinism[71] This is not meant to beg the free will problem, but only to point out that the metaphysical capacity to act otherwise demanded by incompatibilists is a further requirement, going beyond the core practical capacity.[72] And even if compatibilist understandings of moral responsibility are not, finally, acceptable, it is plausible to argue that here is one point where legal and moral criteria of responsibility may reliably diverge. For the moral notion may well be thought to import a theologically or metaphysically ambitious conception of responsibility, related to divine judgment or existential meaningfulness. The sublunary ambitions of law, meanwhile, might be satisfied with a conception of fair attributability, for which the practical reason capacity suffices.[73]

Metaphysical debates notwithstanding, those persons without the capacity to reason practically are manifestly to be treated or incapacitated, not punished. It remains a vexed question in law and philosophy what sort of rational incapacities fatally undermine culpability.[74] The traditional M'Naghten requirement is that the defendant will only be excused from responsibility if he does not "know the nature or the quality of the act he was doing; or if he did know it, that he did not know what he was doing was wrong."[75] This is obviously an extremely restrictive definition, according to which a defendant who understood the wrongness of his act, but was compelled to do so by satanic voices in his head, would not be excused. The purely cognitive definition was therefore expanded by the American Legal Institute into the requirement that the defendant be able to "appreciate the criminality of his conduct" and "to conform his conduct to the requirements of law."[76] Other definitions have been put forward as well, notably the short-lived but famous definition offered by the federal court of appeals for the D.C. Circuit, that a defendant be deemed nonresponsible if his unlawful act was "the product of mental disease or mental defect."[77]

None of these definitions fully captures the idea of incapacity that juries almost certainly operate with, but all indicate the general scope of the questions surrounding criteria of responsibility.[78] The genuinely difficult questions come at the margins of capacity, for example with agents who suffer delusions but who know that they do so (as with many schizophrenics), or with agents who recognize the wrongness of their acts but who seem completely to lack ordinary concern for wrongness.[79] Given the general lack of knowledge about the nature of mental illness and the inhospitability of legal proceedings to nuanced discussion, epistemic constraints are tightest in this domain. This is mainly a problem for retributivists, who may find that any operationalizable criteria of mental capacity will err, either by demanding treatment for those who ought be punished, or by demanding punishment for those demanding treatment. For instrumentalists, the choice between incapacitating and punitive responses is less significant.[80]

Moral responsibility hinges on conduct—in the sense of intentional activity—and causation. The most serious moral responses, such as blame and recrimination, fall where conduct and causation run together: when the agent causes harm with a will that evinces lack of respect for another's interests. Criminal responsibility follows suit. Liability for most crimes is based upon a combination of criteria regarding the defendant's bodily acts and their consequences, and the intentions, knowledge, or awareness with which those acts were done and their consequences produced. The terms *subjective* and *objective* are used, respectively, for the intentional and the conduct, circumstance, and consequence criteria, often also called the *mens rea* and *actus reus* elements of a crime.

Unfortunately, "subjective" and "objective" are also used for a wholly different contrast in criminal law, to distinguish between individualized and normalized standards. In this sense, subjective criteria predicate liability upon the actual capacities and beliefs of the agent, where objective criteria predicate liability upon the capacities and beliefs that could reasonably be expected of a generally competent rational agent.[81] At the risk of departing somewhat from standard legal usage, I will use the terms *individualized* and *normalized* for this sense of "subjective" and "objective" criteria. Philosophical questions arise about both sorts of criteria.

Standardly, criminal liability requires that a single agent perform the specified acts or cause the specified harms, with or because of a specified mental state or states. First-degree murder, for example, requires the subjective element of a premeditated intention to kill, as well, of course, as the "objective" result that the agent has caused another's death in acting upon that very intention. Second-degree, or "depraved-heart" homicide, does not require killing as an aim, but does require that the defendant believe killing a likely consequence of his actions. For some crimes, the defendant's mental state must be highly determinate: larceny requires not only the objective taking of another's property, but a subjective intent to deprive the other permanently of that property. And there are many crimes that can be committed with a still culpable but not intentional mental state, such as recklessness or gross negligence. The defendant must be engaged in some activity intentionally (e.g. driving), but need not be driving with an intent to kill to be found guilty of vehicular homicide. It suffices if the defendant's objective conduct consists of driving, that conduct causes a death, and, for recklessness, that he is aware of the risks his driving presents. Crimes committed negligently must be handled differently, for the question is not whether the defendant had any particular mental state, but whether he lacked a state he should have had, namely attention to the relevant risks.[82] Clearly, subjective and objective criteria interpenetrate, for the objective conduct component is itself intentional—for example, the taking of property, or the killing of another—and may merely be accompanied rather than caused by the relevant subjective state. The subjective component is not, therefore, generally an explanation of the conduct, but rather a mental state relevant to the assessment of the defendant's moral culpability.[83]

The subjective and objective criteria of responsibility invoke the traditional analytical philosophical problems of giving an account of intentional action, including the problems of relating intention to bodily movement, individuating acts, and intentional omissions; and writers in criminal legal theory have pursued these philosophical problems.[84] But it is unclear that a legal theory needs a deep philosophical account of these problems. Take the problem of act individuation: a defendant throws down a match, thus setting fire to a house and killing the inhabitants. There is a philosophical dispute between so-called fine-grained individuators, such as Alvin Goldman, who argue that the defendant performs many different acts (throwing down the match, burning down the house, and killing the inhabitants), and coarse-grained individuators, such as Donald Davidson, who argue that the defendant performs but one act, the bodily movement of throwing down the match, which act can be described in many different ways, as a house burning, inhabitant killing, and so on.[85] The relevant questions of criminal responsibility are, however, neutral between these issues in action theory.

These questions include whether, for example, the burning or the killing can be traced causally to the match throwing; whether the defendant intended the burning or the killing, or was reckless towards those consequences; and whether the burning and the killing merit independent, cumulative punishments. They are not purely metaphysical questions or problems of action theory. They are, rather, normative, and will be answered instead by reference to a theory of punishment. The terms of these theories are the folk or commonsensical notions of deliberation, foresight, intention, and action; the normative challenge lies in relating these terms to a scale of culpability.[86] Even the difficult questions raised by automatism and mind control must be answered in terms of a normative theory of responsibility and the criteria of self-governance, theories that need only presuppose and not analyse the basic idea of doing something for a reason.

More difficult philosophical questions about responsibility arise regarding the question whether the punishment system should deploy individualized or normalized criteria of responsibility. Claims of specific (not general-incapacity) excuse from responsibility or justification are the main place issues of individualized and normalized criteria, and arise typically when the defendant unreasonably believes that justifying or excusing circumstances obtain. A defendant who commits a crime under the unreasonable belief that his life is being threatened might plead duress or self-defence. But these issues also arise with crimes defined partly in terms of results, such as homicide. Return to the arsonist, and suppose that anyone reasonably intelligent would have realized there was a substantial chance people might be sleeping in this house.[87] But this defendant was in fact so addled or unintelligent that she was not in fact aware of the risk. Should she be punished for reckless homicide nonetheless—that is, causing death not intentionally but with a conscious disregard of the relevant risks—on the grounds that any reasonable person would have been aware of those risks, even if she was not? The case for an individualized standard, which would acquit in this instance, is that however indefensible her conduct, she must evince the particular culpable mental state which the law targets. If the justification for punishing someone with that mental state depends on the wickedness of agents with that state, then punishment is morally unjustified; and if the punishment's justification is deterring agents from acting recklessly, then it also misses its target, since she was not, by her own lights, acting recklessly. Similarly in the excuse and justification contexts, there is a strong moral case for individualized standards: the defendant simply did not have the ill will targeted by the criminal norm. Nor is the failure of deterrence in these cases worrisome since, in the excuse case, the norm is not expected to deter in such circumstances, and in the justification case, the norm should not deter.[88]

Now, these considerations only reach so far. First, even if she was not specially deterred by the punishment, others might generally be, and might also be dissuaded from acting recklessly with the hope of being acquitted on erroneous individualized grounds. Secondly, at most these considerations show that punishing her for reckless killing is unwarranted; punishment for negligent killing might still be warranted; and there is no obvious reason to distinguish sharply between the punishment schedules for each. Thirdly, the epistemic limitations of the criminal process may suggest that a fairer process will be one that deploys normalized standards rather than one that is likely to fail if it attempts to discern individual beliefs. These are largely pragmatic considerations. But some, most recently Arthur Ripstein, have tried to make a positive, principled case for normalized standards.[89] Criminal norms are devices for allocating autonomy, where "autonomy" means control over person and property—as I put it before, they define a minimum normative content for social and moral relations. In a liberal state, a legitimate system of criminal norms allocates autonomy equally, giving each citizen the same measure of protection and control. The defendant here failed to take the interests of others into account, not by acting badly in the face of awareness of the relevant risks to potential victims, but by failing to consider the risks at all. If she is acquitted, the victims will, in effect, have been deprived of the measure of autonomy to which state norms entitle them. One need not think of punishment as compensation to the victims to think they have a claim on state punishment here. Given the necessarily expressive dimension of punishment, an acquittal may be thought to signal that the state condones the way in which the defendant failed to give due regard to the victims' interests. As Ripstein puts it, the state would otherwise condone the defendant's substitution of private rationality for public reasonableness. Nor does there appear to be unfairness towards the defendant. Assuming she had the capacity to advert to the risks, the norm under which she is punished is a reasonable constraint on her behaviour, and so she has not received less protection to her own autonomy than to which she is entitled.[90] After all, she could have avoided punishment altogether simply by not torching the house.

Of course, this argument, like the argument for subjectivism, might be taken instead to support the more limited point, that there be some state response to the particular flaw in the defendant's conduct, namely, that she caused harm through unreasonably failing to advert to the relevant risks. What the argument shows is that there should be a criminal norm prohibiting negligence. Punishment for negligence still incorporates normalized standards of conduct into the criminal law, but by establishing a separate criminal norm. Declining to integrate normalized standards into particular offences, however, may well serve purposes of analytical clarity, as well as focusing attention on the normative question of what response is appropriate for the particular kind of conduct engaged in by the defendant. The same point holds true for claims of excuse or justification founded in unreasonable beliefs: there is clearly a justifiable (and often taken) middle path of treating these as cases of "imperfect defences," and mitigating but not eliminating punishment.

What the dispute between individualized and normalized standards ultimately reveals is, again, how important it is to see criminal law's criteria of responsibility as constitutive of interpersonal normative relations. The debate cannot be settled without an account of the conduct citizens owe one another, the specific meaning and response demanded by failure to meet that standard of conduct, and the role of the state in creating, expressing, and defending that standard. The impulse towards individualized standards comes from a view of the state as principally responsible for denouncing or punishing failures to meet that standard; the impulse towards normalized standards from a view of the state as principally responsible for ensuring a fair allocation of autonomy among citizens. Hart famously argued that the law of excuse should be understood not to conceal a particular moral conception of responsible agency, but rather as a way of maximizing citizens' liberty against the background of a deterrence system, by maximizing citizens' ability to control the incidence of coercive force.[91] Hart's view offers a healthy reminder of the importance of understanding the distinctive relation between the state and citizens in a liberal order, by relating it to the political value of autonomy instead of moral values implicated by retribution. But it is too narrow a view, for we also expect the state to express the moral force of the conduct norms we set for ourselves. We must not complicate our understanding of the state's functions, and so complicate our understanding of the criteria of criminal responsibility, when we realize that these criteria define both our relations to one another as well as our relations to the state.

4 LEGAL RESPONSIBILITY FOR ACCIDENTS

In contemporary legal theory, criminal law concerns responsibility for acts and tort law, responsibility for outcomes. As we have seen, this theoretical contrast can mislead, since one can be criminally responsible for the consequences of one's conduct (e.g., murder), and one can be responsible in tort on the basis of one's conduct (e.g., an intentional injury). What chiefly distinguishes tort from criminal law is the nature of the warranted response: tort law governs the state creation of a compensatory response from the agent towards the victim, where criminal law, at least conventionally, solely involves a response from the state towards the agent.[92] Tort and criminal law should thus be understood as complements, not necessarily treating different objects of responsibility, but as involving different responses. The complementary nature of criminal and tort liability is worth bearing in mind even in those instances where only one form could lie, as when someone violates a criminal norm without causing any harm (e.g. a failed attempt), or causes harm without transgressing a criminal norm. The latter is the domain of accident, when ordinarily permissible activities go awry and cause harm.

If tort law is defined as the legal norms governing compensatory responses from injurers to victims, then it is apparent that tort law is only one of many possible systems treating responsibility for accidents. Rather than dictate or enforce responses between injurers and victims, the state could, for example, simply ensure victim compensation through a mandatory insurance fund, as in New Zealand.[93] Or the state could make injury an occasion for punishment, leaving victims with only the moral compensation of seeing justice done. But the system on which most of the world has converged takes as a central feature the linking of injurers and victims through the enforcement of private compensatory response. Accordingly, the task modern legal theorists have set for themselves is a defence of the legal practice of accountability for accidents.

The range and depth of modern theories of tort is great. What I will do is indicate some of the general patterns of theorizing and to show how the choice among them mainly turns on the ideal of interpersonal and political relations they presuppose. One major division runs through modern theorizing, between what can be called *allocative* and *attributive* theories of responsibility, each side of the division reflecting a different conception of the relation among individuals and between them and the state.[94] Allocative theories of responsibility treat accidental harm as an incident of communal life, to be handled collectively in the first instance, with individuals bearing liability only if that serves the collective interest. Attributive theories, by contrast, treat harms as problems for individuals; the task of a legal system is to recognize and enforce the reparative obligations individuals have towards one another.

Consequentialist theories, of which the economic models are the most thoroughly worked out, typify the allocative approach. A normative goal is posited, for example, utility or wealth maximization, and then various principles are defended on the grounds that when accident costs are so allocated, utility will indeed be maximized, through readjustment of incentives, spreading effects, and so forth.[95] It becomes an empirical question whether, say, a fault principle best achieves the normative goal. Moreover, pursuit of the consequentialist goal may dictate principles that depart very far from ordinary tort practice, such as simply allocating the costs of the accident among the wealthiest. It will thus be purely contingent whether the legal principles of tort reflect anything like the common-sense moral paradigm of injurer repair. But nonconsequentialist approaches may also have an allocative structure, such as Jules Coleman's earlier "annulment theory" of tort. According to the annulment theory, the purpose of tort law is to ensure the rectification of wrongful losses and wrongful gains, where "wrongful" is determined by reference to the norms governing legitimate transfer of holdings and liberties.[96] On this view, the function of tort law is to maintain the allocation of holdings provided by the prevailing scheme of distributive justice. Still other allocative approaches are suggested by egalitarian theories, for example, following the principle that accident costs ought to be distributed in such a way that both preserves an equal initial distribution of resources and demands a display of equal concern by individuals.[97]

Alternatively, the costs of accidents might be allocated so as to maximize individual autonomy, with autonomy conceived broadly in terms of individuals' capacity to engage in effective planning.[98] All these allocative principles might generate the same set of operational principles—fault-based injurer liability, no-fault social insurance, strict liability—but the emergence of those principles would be in each instance grounded in a collective responsibility for the costs of accidents. Allocations of responsibility to individuals are derivative.

Attributive theories of tort law, by contrast, make individual ascriptions of responsibility primary. The theory of individual responsibility may be moral, in the sense of being prior to political institutions, or it may be political; but the task of a system of legal responsibility is to give effect to the underlying claims and duties of individual responsibility. So-called libertarian theories of tort law exemplify the attributive approach.[99] On a libertarian view generally, agents are regarded as entitled, as a matter of prepolitical, natural right, to the profits of their causal interventions. Costs would then be treated symmetrically, as also the entitlement, albeit unwanted, of productive agency. It is a further consideration on the libertarian view that injury diminishes the legitimate entitlements of the victim, depriving him of (some of) the value of his holdings in a way inconsistent with the norms of legitimate transfer.[100] But the central concept is one of responsibility for one's accidents, where responsibility is understood in terms of causation.

Now, theories grounding responsibility on causation suffer from a crippling defect, familiar already from my discussion of moral responsibility: in a metaphysical sense, a broad variety of conditions and events count equally as causes of a given harm; only pragmatic, normative criteria can distinguish them. As Ronald Coase pointed out, most accidental injuries arise from an interaction between plaintiffs and defendants—one walking while the other is driving, one using a product while the other is producing it, and so forth.[101] Indeed, in the modern world of mass torts and mass production, causal criteria hardly exclude anyone from liability. Take the Bhopal disaster of 1984, when a pesticide plant leaked poisonous gas, killing thousands of nearby residents. The disaster seems to have been the product of lax supervisory and maintenance standards at the plant, under-trained employees, understating as a result of low profits, the absence of effective regulatory authority within the relevant Indian ministries, inadequate monitoring by US headquarters, much less by Union Carbide shareholders; coupled with the decision by residents to move to or remain near an industrial facility whose central product was highly toxic.[102] Clearly, different causally implicated parties bear very different levels of responsibility for the tragedy. So causal criteria at best determine a range of liability candidates. Only by reference to further, normative criteria can one

party be designated "the cause," or one "injurer" and the other "victim," terms that load a direction of causation and not merely a description of harm.

Others have offered attributive theories of legal responsibility grounded in a richer notion of moral responsibility than mere causation. Ernest Weinreb, for example, treats tort liability as simply the reflection of individuals' moral responsibilities to remedy the rights they infringe. Moral compensatory responsibility rests, in turn, on a basically Kantian understanding of the requirements of practical reason. A rational agent who wills an act must perforce accept responsibility for the consequences of that act; to impose the costs of one's act on others willy-nilly is to fail to respect the demand that one act only in accordance with principles that all might follow.[103] Compensatory responsibility is self-attributed, in the sense that it follows from the exercise of practical reason.[104] Jules Coleman's intermediate work, *Risks and Wrongs,* similarly ties legal reparative obligations to moral claims of compensation, claims grounded in a normative conception of individual agency.[105] Unlike his earlier, purely allocative "annulment theory" of tort, which focused on the general claim of victims that their wrongful losses be remedied, Coleman's newer agency-centred theory aims to show the special moral obligations agents have "to repair the wrongful losses for which they are responsible."[106] This principle of corrective justice, Coleman suggests, is simply immanent in our particular and contingent social practices.[107] However, the extension of this moral principle to legal responsibility is indirect. A legal system *may* implement the corrective-justice principle directly, through the sort of enforceable, individualized reparative obligations characteristic of the tort system. Or it may not implement corrective justice, and instead implement some sort of purely allocative scheme in which individual reparative obligations do not directly figure.[108]

Finally, there are theories combining both allocative and attributive aspects. Stephen Perry, building on Tony Honoré's notion of "outcome responsibility," offers a theory of tort liability grounded independently in agents' moral responsibility for the outcomes they produce and over which they have control.[109] This claim of responsibility, not yet rising to a compensatory duty, flows from the phenomenology of agency, as I discussed above in reference to moral responsibility: our self-understanding as persisting, embedded agents depends, in part, upon our seeing ourselves as marking the world.[110] As Perry realizes, the interactive contexts that dogged libertarian theories pose a challenge for him as well, for injuries arising from intersecting activities will typically reflect the agency and control of all parties. (Though you hit me with your car, I might have chosen not to go for a walk, and so I equally controlled the outcome.) Thus Perry supplements the notion of outcome responsibility, which limits prima-facie candidacy for liability, with an allocative principle according to which accident costs ought to lie with those at fault, or who otherwise impose unusual risks on others. Similarly, Coleman, with Arthur Ripstein, has recently put forth a conception fusing allocative and attributive considerations.[111] On their view, corrective justice is still a matter of instantiating the attributive principle that individuals must bear the costs of their own conduct. This principle is immanent in a contingent set of social practices and not, as with Perry, derived from a moral theory of agency. But the question of which costs individuals "own" should not be understood simply as a matter of social convention. The question of cost ownership must, rather, be answered by reference to a political theory concerning the proper allocation of risk and responsibility.[112] In short, Coleman and Ripstein make a political, allocative principle primary and then attribute specific reparative duties on the basis of the liability criteria it specifies, while Perry makes a moral, attributive principle primary, and then deploys a political, allocative one.[113]

The debate among tort theorists partly reflects different descriptive concerns: some theorists, such as Epstein and Calabresi, meant their contributions to be largely revisionary, while others, such as Perry, Coleman, and Posner, have claimed to be providing accounts sensitive to the actual content of doctrine, albeit accounts that aim to justify that doctrine. But, as with debates about criminal responsibility, what is really at stake are the distinctive ideals of social relations

the views manifest. Further attention to this point by theorists might obviate the pressure to find a basically a priori argument for a moral or political principle justifying reparative obligations.[114] I argued in section 2 that some notion of responsibility is clearly rooted in the experience of agency itself, as well as demanded by the facts of communal, conflicting life. But the responses specific to that notion, in other words the *content* of responsibility, will inevitably be a product of specific institutional arrangements and social life. It is, of course, a task for historians to document the emergence and transformation of the principles structuring tort law—as has been done, for instance, for the fault principle in Anglo-American law, showing its subsequent limitation in workplace and product contexts as a response to economic, social, and intellectual pressures.[115] The philosophical point is not to reject tort theory in favour of history, but rather to recognize the central place that contingent social norms must play in even a philosophical account.

Return to the central debate between purely allocative, economic theories and purely attributive, corrective justice theories. Even assuming that a purely attributive theory can deal with the problem of interaction, the choice between theories depends primarily on a normative conception of the social arrangements to be regulated under the appropriate regime. With highly regularized domains of activity, such as automobile driving, industrial employment, and perhaps mass production and consumption, the systemic, managerial model of social relations presupposed by an economic approach seems both appropriate and attractive.[116] These are, in other words, the domains in which a public regulatory response seems correct: they present a collective problem of managing, spreading, and reducing costs, arising out of a generally valued and common activity, and in which the state can legitimately and effectively exercise authority. Within such a specified domain, the anti-individualism and cross-individual trade-offs that characterize the economic approach can be cabined, unthreatening to more general political ideals of individualism. By contrast, an untrammelled extension of an allocative approach to the general run of activity may indeed threaten those social and moral ideals. But much depends on the degree to which legal forms of responsibility are understood to reflect moral forms; and this too will surely vary with the relevant domain of activity, and with the particular social understanding of the relation between law and social morality. In the absence of a conception of such relations, the idea that an agent has a duty to pay compensation is empty. In some social conditions, ideals of personal responsibility and individual autonomy may indeed be threatened by tort doctrine.[117] In other conditions, the subsumption under allocative principles of even quite a broad range of activities may simply reflect an underlying collectivist ethos.

Again, my point is not that philosophical reflection on legal responsibility is beholden to particular cultural practice. An especially valuable form of philosophical activity is to point to alternative, more desirable social and political ideals, whether or not these are actually instantiated in legal practice, or are otherwise internal to the culture. I do not, above all, mean to endorse a blanket relativism towards social and legal practice; they are, of course, open to any manner of rational, critical treatment that one's metaethics provide. Another task is to engage in philosophy's traditional task of conceptual clarification, attempting to render perspicuous the principles and ideals animating a given legal culture, as well as showing what those ideals logically entail. What I mean to point out is simply that a relational understanding of tort law brings out the relevant dependence on social and moral ideals, and properly focuses attention on the normative crux of theoretical debates.[118]

5 CONCLUSION

I began with a catalogue of the many uses of responsibility, but this article has generally sought a unity within the subject. I have emphasized the way claims of responsibility can only be understood as specific social practices, responsive to a background set of social, moral, and political relations and ideals. This basically Strawsonian path through the thickets of responsibility seems to me independently correct, as a way of illuminating

important features of claims and responses of responsibility. But it also casts a useful light on a set of debates within legal theory, between retributivists and utilitarians in criminal law, for example, and between allocationists and attributivists in tort. These debates seem currently at a philosophical standstill, though they shift from one decade to the next. But the general turn in moral and legal theorizing about responsibility, towards a relational conception, gives reason to hope that these debates may begin to move ahead, as their adherents confront and attempt to justify the ideals their accounts presuppose. And reconstructing responsibility has importance beyond what it shows about philosophical debate. For it is in understanding responsibility that we see ourselves as actors, creators, empathizers, and sufferers. It is in understanding responsibility, in short, that we know ourselves as persons.

NOTES

1. Hart, H. L. A. "Postscript: Responsibility and Retribution." *Punishment and Responsibility.* New York: Oxford University Press, 1968. 211.

2. I ignore the question whether omissions can be, strictly speaking, causes.

3. Duff, R. A. "Responsibility." *Routledge Encyclopedia of Philosophy.* Ed. E. J. Craig. New York: Routledge, 1998. R: 290–4.

4. Scanlon, T. M. *What We Owe to Each Other.* Cambridge, Mass.: Harvard University Press, 1998. 248.

5. Perry, Stephen. "Responsibility for Outcomes, Risk, and the Law of Torts." *Philosophy and the Law of Torts.* Ed. Gerald Postema. Cambridge: Cambridge University Press, 2001. 72–130.

6. Dworkin, Ronald "Hard Cases." *Taking Rights Seriously.* Cambridge, Mass.: Harvard University Press, 1975. 88. See also Nagel, Thomas. "Ruthlessness in Public Life." *Mortal Questions.* Cambridge: Cambridge University Press, 1979. 75–90.

7. See Kutz, C. *Complicity: Ethics and Law for a Collective Age.* New York: Cambridge University Press, 2000. Ch. 21. See also the essays collected in *The Theory of Contract Law: New Essays.* Ed. Peter Benson. New York: Cambridge University Press, 2001).

8. The obvious possibility that Captain Smith is an alcoholic raises difficult questions about the fairness of holding him responsible. Current medical

wisdom regards alcoholism as an organic disease, and so not something for which alcoholics can be held responsible. Presumably, if Smith's drinking is a product of his alcoholism, then the consequences of that drinking would be attributable to his disease, not to him. But neither law nor conventional social practice fully exonerates alcoholics from the consequences of their drinking. Whether or not they should is an important subject for debate.

9. This discussion is obviously greatly simplified and abbreviated. See Fischer, John Martin. "Introduction." *Moral Responsibility.* Ed. John Martin Fischer. Ithaca: Cornell University Press, 1986; Fischer, John Martin and Ravizza, Mark. *Responsibility and Control.* Cambridge: Cambridge University Press, 1998; Fischer, John Martin. "Recent Work on Moral Responsibility." *Ethics* 110 (1999): 93–139; Williams, Bernard. "How Free Does the Will Need to Be?" *Making Sense of Humanity.* Cambridge: Cambridge University Press, 1995. 3–21; Watson, Gary. "Free Action and Free Will." *Mind* 96 (1987): 145–72. Fischer and Watson include extensive bibliographies.

10. For some especially valuable work, see van Inwagen, Peter. *An Essay on Free Will.* New York: Oxford University Press; the work by Fischer mentioned in note 8; Bok, Hilary. *Freedom and Responsibility.* Princeton: Princeton University Press, 1999; and Wolf, Susan. *Freedom within Reason.* New York: Oxford University Press, 1990).

11. See Wallace, R. Jay. *Responsibility and the Moral Sentiments.* Cambridge, Mass.: Harvard University Press, 1994 for a deep exploration of Strawson's argument.

12. Strawson, Peter. "Freedom and Resentment." *Free Will.* Ed. Gary Watson. New York: Oxford University Press, 1982. 62.

13. Id., at 66.

14. Wallace, *Moral Sentiments,* supra, note 11, at 76.

15. See Greenspan, P. S. *Practical Guilt: Moral Dilemmas, Emotions and Social Norms.* New York: Oxford University Press, 1995; Moore, Michael S. *Placing Blame.* New York: Oxford University Press, 1997 (esp. "The Moral Worth of Retribution"); Morris, Herbert. *On Guilt and Innocence.* Los Angeles: University of California Press, 1976; Murphy, Jeffrie G. and Hampton, Jean. *Forgiveness and Mercy.* Cambridge: Cambridge University Press, 1988; Scheffler, Samuel. *Human Morality.* New York: Oxford University Press, 1993; Taylor, Gabriele. *Pride, Shame, and Guilt.* New York: Oxford University Press, 1985; Williams, Bernard. *Shame and Necessity.* Berkeley: University of California Press, 1993; and Wollheim, Richard. *The Sheep and the Ceremony.* Cambridge: Cambridge University Press, 1979.

16. Strawson, "Resentment," supra, note 12, at 71.

17. Id., at 71.

18. Id., at 72.

19. David Hume makes such a claim in his *Enquiry,* though he grounds the disposition in a notion of self-interest generously expanded by our capacities of sympathetic identification. Hume, David. *An Enquiry Concerning the Principles of Morals.* Ed. J. B. Schneewind. Indianapolis: Hackett Publishing, 1983. §5, pt. I.

20. See Bernard Williams's discussion of the Oedipus example in his *Shame and Necessity.* Berkeley: University of California Press, 1993. 56–60.

21. Williams, Bernard. "Moral Luck." *Moral Luck.* Cambridge: Cambridge University Press, 1981. 20–39.

22. Id., at 28. As Williams notes, one of the roles played by other moral agents may be to insist upon the rightness of conduct in order to erase the significance of an agent's connection to the harm.

23. Taylor, *Pride,* supra, note 15, at 91.

24. Of course, the driver also now stands in a special normative relation to my friend, the cat's owner, owing her at least the courtesy of informing her that the cat is dead.

25. This is not to say that I would be morally wrong not to feel at all guilty, but only lacking a full grasp of the relevant moral norms. And self-laceration is clearly out of place.

26. Hart, H. L. A. and Honoré, Tony. *Causation in the Law.* 2nd edn. New York: Oxford University Press, 1985. p. lxxx. See also Honoré's discussion of "outcome responsibility" and its relationship to identity in Honoré, Tony, "The Morality of Tort Law—Questions and Answers." *Philosophical Foundations of Tort Law.* Ed. David G. Owen. New York: Oxford University Press, 1995. 81–3.

27. This is consistent with a certain understanding of Donald Davidson's claim that "We never do more than move our bodies; the rest is up to nature." Davidson, Donald. "Agency." *Essays on Actions and Events.* New York: Oxford University Press, 1981. 59. The "accordion effect" that licences further ascriptions of events to my agency relies on causal relations external to me, but the

particular relations singled out are, as Davidson would acknowledge, deeply dependent upon our normative concerns. See also Feinberg, Joel. "Action and Responsibility." *Doing and Deserving.* Princeton: Princeton University Press, 1970. 119–51.

28. Hart and Honoré's *Causation in the Law,* supra, note 26, is still the leading work on the morally relevant notion of causation. But see also Feinberg, Joel. *Harm to Others.* New York: Oxford University Press, 1984; and Wright, Richard. "Causation in Tort Law." *California Law Review* 73 (1985): 1775–98. For other important accounts of a generic conception of causation, see also Mackie, J. L. *The Cement of the Universe.* New York: Oxford University Press, 1974; and Lewis, David. "Causation & Postscript." *Philosophical Papers.* New York: Oxford University Press, 1984. 159–213. Michael Moore began a project of demonstrating that the ordinary language of degrees of causation and intervening causation reflects the actual metaphysics of causation. See Moore, Michael. "Causation and Responsibility." *Social Philosophy & Policy* 16 (1999: 1–51; and cf. "The Metaphysics of Causal Intervention." *California Law Review,* 88 (2000): 827–77, 876–7.

29. Lewis, "Causation," supra, note 28.

30. That I will see it this way says much about my view of what constitutes appropriate relations among competitors.

31. Williams makes a similar point, in "Moral Luck," supra, note 21, at 28–9. I do not mean to claim that agents usually will feel this way, except in the most tragic of circumstances.

32. This charge of circularity is the standard criticism of tort lawyers' use of the notion of "proximate cause": to say of a party's conduct that it was the proximate cause of the harm is virtually to foreclose the question of liability. Much of *Causation in the Law* can be seen as an attempt to give independent content to the notion of proximate cause. Section 4 takes up the issue of causation in tort law.

33. The "control principle" is endorsed, in varying forms, by Husak, Douglas. *Philosophy of Criminal Law.* Totowa, NJ: Rowman & Littlefield, 1987. 98; and by Stephen Perry, "Responsibility for Outcomes," supra, note 5, at 82.

34. I treat this subject at length in Kutz, Christopher. *Complicity: Ethics and Law for a Collective Age.* Cambridge: Cambridge University Press, 2000.

35. More difficult questions arise concerning those who control their initial participation, but not its ultimate extent—those who get taken on a ride, so to speak. Presumably they are accountable by reference for the risk they run in participating in a potentially injurious enterprise.

36. Parfit, Derek. *Reasons and Persons.* New York: Oxford University Press, 1984. 80. If the example is too surreal, consider the huge bombing fleet that burned Dresden in World War II. No one plane made a difference, but each contributed to a collective horror. I discuss the Dresden case extensively in *Complicity,* supra, note 34, ch. 4.

37. See Goldman, Alvin I. "Why Citizens Should Vote: A Causal Responsibility Approach." *Social Philosophy and Policy* 16 (1999): 201–17.

38. Tort and contract law have similar functions, also stabilizing cooperation. Richard Posner's economic analysis of criminal law, according to which the purpose of criminal norms is to prevent intentional bypass of market transactions, can be expressed less crassly in terms of making consensual, cooperative relations possible.

39. See, famously, *United States v. Dotterweich,* 320 US 277 (1943) (president of pharmaceutical company convicted of interstate shipping of misbranded and adulterated drugs, despite lack of knowledge or intent).

40. See Moore, "Moral Worth of Retribution," supra, note 15; Morris, "Persons and Punishment." *On Guilt and Innocence,* supra, note 15; Feinberg, Joel. "The Expressive Theory of Punishment." *Doing and Deserving.* Princeton: Princeton University Press, 1970.

41. See e.g. Wootton, Barbara. *Social Science and Social Pathology.* London: Allen & Unwin, 1959; Hampton, Jean. "The Moral Education Theory of Punishment." *Philosophy and Public Affairs* 13 (1984): 208–38; Sayre-McCord, Geoffrey. "Criminal Justice and Legal Reparations as an Alternative to Punishment." *Noûs* 35 (2001): 502-529; Garvey, Steven. "Punishment as Atonement." *University of California Law Review* 46 (1999): 1801–58.

42. See Hart, H. L. A. "Legal Responsibility and the Excuses." *Punishment and Responsibility,* supra, note 1, at 28–53; Mackie, J. L. "The Grounds of Responsibility." *Law, Morality, and Society.* Eds. P. M. S. Hacker and Joseph Raz. Oxford: Oxford University Press, 1977; Scanlon, T. M. "The Significance of Choice." *Equal Freedom.* Ann Arbor: University of Michigan Press, 1995.

39–104. See also Brudner, Alan. "Agency and Welfare in the Penal Law." *Action and Value in Criminal Law*. Eds. Stephen Shute, John Gardner, and Jeremy Horder. New York: Oxford University Press, 1993. 21–53.

43. Mackie,"Grounds of Responsibility," supra, note 42, at 187–8.

44. Hart, "Legal Responsibility and the Excuses," supra, note 9; Scanlon, "Significance of Choice," supra, note 42.

45. With the important and largely deplorable exception of Anglo-American conspiracy law, according to which liability can be incurred at a very early stage of planning.

46. It is worth noting that criminal sentencing is heavily characterological, especially in death penalty proceedings. Punishment is aggravated or mitigated in proportion to the moral worth of the convicted.

47. Kant, Immanuel. "Doctrine of Right." *The Metaphysics of Moral.*, Ed. and trans. Mary Gregor. Cambridge: Cambridge University Press, 1991. 331–3.

48. Nietzsche, Friedrich. *On the Genealogy of Morals.* Ed. and trans. Walter Kaufmann. New York: Vintage, 1967. book II, §6. Nietzsche's own preferred alternative to punishment, at least in the moral realm, was a kind of confident forgetting exemplified by Mirabeau. *Genealogy*, book I, ¶10, p. 39.

49. The most famous statement rejecting the rehabilitative ideal is in Lewis, C. S. "The Humanitarian Theory of Punishment." *Res Judicatae* 6 (1953): 224–30; see also the essays collected in Kadish, Sanford. *Blame and Punishment*. New York: MacMillan, 1987. Isaiah Berlin's objections to a politics grounded in a notion of "positive liberty" also echo concerns about the manipulative state. Berlin, Isaiah. "Two Concepts of Liberty." *Four Essays on Liberty*. New York: Oxford University Press, 1970. 118–72.

50. Hart, "Postscript," supra, note 1, at 234.

51. See Moore, *Placing Blame*, supra, note 15; and von Hirsch, Andrew. *Doing Justice*. New York: Hill and Wang, 1976.

52. The public shift is easily seen in California's politics, usually a harbinger of national trends, a politics that resulted in such successful ballot initiatives as, in 1994, a "three strikes" law that incarcerates a wide range of recidivists for life (codified as Cal. Penal Code §1170.12); and, in February 2000, Proposition 21, a ballot measure

that greatly expanded the reach of prosecutorial authority over the young. It passed overwhelmingly. For a general discussion of changes in criminological practice, see Garland, David. *Punishment and Modern Society: A Study in Social Theory*. Chicago: University of Chicago Press, 1993.

53. Doubts—possibly mistaken—about the effectiveness of rehabilitative measures probably contributed more to their loss of public support.

54. This is, roughly, Henry Sidgwick's view, see Sidgwick, Henry. *Methods of Ethics*. Indianapolis: Hackett Publishing, 1981. It is this view of utilitarianism that John Rawls criticizes in *A Theory of Justice*. Rev. edn. Cambridge, Mass.: Harvard University Press, 1999. §5.

55. Although cooperative models of utilitarianism are available; see Regan, Donald. *Utilitarianism and Cooperation*. New York: Oxford University Press, 1980.

56. This criticism is made by Jeffrie Murphy in "Retributivism, Moral Education, and the Liberal State." *Criminal Justice Ethics* 4 (1985): 3–11.

57. For response, see Moore, "Moral Worth of Retribution," supra, note 15, at 150–1; for the controversy, see Scanlon, "Significance of Choice," supra, note 42; and Scheffler, Samuel. "Liberalism, Desert, and Reactive Attitudes." *Philosophy and Public Affairs* 21 (1992): 299–323.

58. Even when the state is apparently the victim, as in tax fraud or treason, we must keep in mind that it has no tax or security interests of its own, but only those of its citizens. This derivative status renders its position, normatively at least, wholly unlike the positions of unmediated victimhood.

59. For representative statements of this view, see Kadish, Sanford. "Luck of the Draw." *Blame and Punishment*, supra, note 49; Feinberg, Joel. "Equal Punishment for Failed Attempts." *Arizona Law Review* 37 (1995): 117–34; Schulhofer, Stephen. "Harm and Punishment: A Critique of the Emphasis on the Results of Conduct in the Criminal Law." *University of Pennsylvania Law Review*, 122 (1974): 1497.

60. See Moore, Michael S. "The Independent Moral Significance of Wrongdoing." *Placing Blame*, supra, note 15, at 191–248; Katz, Leo. "Why the Successful Assassin is More Wicked than the Unsuccessful One." *California Law Review* 88 (2000): 791–812.

61. For the deeper philosophical discussion of moral luck, see Nagel, Thomas. "Moral Luck." in

Mortal Questions. New York: Cambridge University Press, 1979. 24–38; and Williams, "Moral Luck," supra, note 21.

62. See Sidgwick, *Methods of Ethics,* supra, note 54, at 280–1.

63. The American Legal Institute's Model Penal Code is Wechsler's lasting legacy; for Williams see his *Criminal law: The General Part.* London: Stevens and Sons. 2nd edn. 1961. Where strict liability still obtains, in the regulatory domain mentioned above, or in specific doctrines of, for example, publicans' vicarious liability, the penalties are generally comparatively mild, and liability can often be tied, through the exercise of prosecutorial discretion, to some failure of role responsibility.

64. See *Sandoval v People,* 117 Colo. 558, 192 P. 2d 423 (1948) ("[I]t matters not how short the interval between the determination to kill and infliction of the mortal wound, if the time was sufficient for one thought to follow another").

65. See e.g. *Brinegar v United States,* 338 US 160 (1949) ("[M]uch evidence of real and substantial probative value goes out on considerations irrelevant to its probative weight but relevant to possible misunderstanding or misuse by the jury"). Note that evidence of a defendant's criminal history is often brought in after conviction, at the sentencing stage, as an aggravating factor.

66. See Kant, Immanuel *Groundwork of the Metaphysics of Morals.* Trans. Mary Gregor. Cambridge: Cambridge University Press, 1998. Ch. 2, 407: "We are pleased to flatter ourselves with the false claim to a nobler motive, but in fact we can never, even by the most strenuous self-examination, get to the bottom of our secret impulses; for when moral value is in question, we are concerned, not with the actions which we see, but with their inner principles, which we cannot see." That said, Kant's mechanism of evaluating potential maxims does seem to presuppose a large amount of self-knowledge.

67. See e.g. Herman, Barbara. "Moral Deliberation and the Derivation of Duties." *The Practice of Moral Judgment.* Cambridge, Mass.: Harvard University Press, 1993. 132–58; Brandt, Richard. *A Theory of the Good and the Right.* New York: Oxford University Press, 1979; and Harsanyi, John. "Rule Utilitarianism and Decision Theory." *Erkenntnis* 11 (1977): 25–53.

68. One can, of course, take on a new identity as a result of imprisonment, just or unjust. My point is that one cannot return naïvely to the normal positions of an equal citizen. One becomes either an antisocial rebel, or a sentimental citizen.

69. Douglas Husak is an example of a legal theorist who may distinguish too sharply between the two. He argues that questions of the difficulty of proving mens rea do not bear upon the justice of a mens rea requirement. Husak, *Philosophy of Criminal Law,* supra, note 33, at 59–60. Although I agree with Husak that intentionality requirements should not easily be compromised for the sake of easing the burden of proof, I do not think the position generalizes to the autonomy of liability rules from epistemic questions.

70. For a more thorough examination of the relevant self-governing capacity, see Fischer and Ravizza, *Responsibility and Control,* supra, note 9; and Moore, Michael S. "The Legal View of Persons." *Law and Psychiatry.* Cambridge: Cambridge University Press, 1984. 44–112.

71. Since it demands that one's actions flow from a process of reasoned action, it does seem incompatible with any notion of physical indeterminacy that would make action or decision essentially random.

72. For discussion see Fischer and Ravizza, *Responsibility and Control,* supra, note 9, at 44–51; Morse, Stephen J. "Diminished Capacity." Shute, *Action and Value,* supra, note 42, at 239–78; Scanlon, "Significance of Choice," supra, note 42, at 61–64.

73. This is again to emphasize the special responsive position of the state, and to deny, contra Moore, that it should take the role played by God in a godless world.

74. Another small philosophical literature has emerged concerning the "actual" blameworthiness of corporate actors, where this question is usually approached through the metaphysical question whether corporations are moral persons. See, e.g., French, Peter. *Collective and Corporate Responsibility.* New York: Columbia University Press, 1984; and May, Larry. *The Morality of Groups.* Notre Dame, Indiana: Notre Dame University Press, 1987. The metaphysical discussion seems to me largely to miss the genuinely central question. Given that all groups are groups of people, what are individuals' responsibilities for what their groups do? Examining complicity seems to me the better way to approach the problem, than to inquire in what sense General Motors can be properly blamed. Of course, there are important

questions about the *effectiveness* of different measures directed at corporate groups. For an excellent discussion, see Fisse, Brent and Braithwaite, John. *Corporations, Crime, and Accountability.* Cambridge: Cambridge University Press, 1993.

75. *Regina v M'Naghten*, 8 Eng. Rep 718 (1843).

76. Model Penal Code §4.01.

77. *Durham v United States*, 214 F.2d 845, 862 (D. C. Cir. 1954).

78. See Moore, "The Legal Concept of Insanity," supra, note 15, at 245, for this surely correct observation.

79. See Deigh, John. "Empathy and Universalizability." *Ethics* 105 (1995): 743–63; see also Fischer and Ravizza, *Responsibility and Control*, supra, note 9, at 76–81.

80. There would be a problem for instrumentalists if defendants could easily demonstrate insanity, then simulate a quick recovery, thus avoiding both punishment and lengthy incapacitation; the deterrence system would clearly be undermined. For better or worse, this does not seem an actual problem, as confinement of the criminally insane is notoriously lengthy.

81. See e.g. Hart, "Legal Responsibility," supra, note 9.

82. Both recklessness and negligence raise questions of individualized versus normalized standards, questions I treat shortly.

83. This description, in fact, only works for the individual-actor paradigm. In cases of complicity, the accomplice has a culpable mens rea, namely an intention to further the principal's criminal objective, but his actions fall well short of the actus reus component of the offence. For a superb discussion, see Kadish, Sanford H. "Complicity, Cause, and Blame: A Study in Doctrine." *California Law Review* 73 (1985): 323–410. As with the harmless torturers mentioned above, the justification in liability has to be grounded almost entirely in the accomplice's participatory intention, not in his causal contribution. See my *Complicity*, supra, note 7, at 220–36.

84. See, e.g., Moore, Michael, *Act and Crime.* New York: Oxford University Press, 1993; and Duff, Antony. *Intention, Agency, and Criminal Liability.* New York: Oxford University Press, 1990.

85. Goldman, Alvin I. "Action and Crime: A Fine-Grained Approach." *University of Pennsylvania Law Review* 142 (1994): 1563–86; Davidson, Donald. "Agency." *Essays on Actions and Events.*

New York: Oxford University Press, 1980. 43–61.

86. For discussion of this point, see Ripstein, Arthur. *Equality, Responsibility, and the Law.* New York: Cambridge University Press, 1999. 14; and Hornsby, Jennifer. "On What's Intentionally Done." *Action and Value*, supra, note 42, at 55–74.

87. These facts are loosely taken from *R. v Hyam* [1973] Q.B. 99 (C.A) (defendant set fire to house hoping to frighten romantic rival, killing the rival's two daughters). Similar issues are raised by crimes that make specific beliefs part of the definition, notably rape, which in some formulations makes the defendant's belief that the victim does not consent an element of the crime. In the notorious English *Morgan* case, it was held that a defendant's unreasonable but sincere belief that a woman had consented to intercourse could be a complete defence to the rape charge; now, it is often held that the defendant's belief about consent must be reasonable. *R. v Morgan* [1976] A. C. 182. (The defendants in question were supposedly persuaded by Morgan that his wife enjoyed intercourse under duress.)

88. The relation between deterrence and the excuses raises the important distinction between conduct rules, addressed to citizens, and decision rules, addressed to adjudicators. Excuse rules are arguably decision rules alone, and should not play a role in citizens' deliberations. See Dan-Cohen, Meir. "Conduct Rules and Decision Rules: On Acoustic Separation in Criminal Law." *Harvard Law Review* 97 (1984): 625–77.

89. See Ripstein, *Equality*, supra, note 86, at 163–70. Ripstein's argument is much subtler and more complex than I show here.

90. Compare Scanlon, "Significance of Choice," supra, note 42, at 89–96.

91. Hart, "Legal Responsibility," supra, note 9.

92. As I mentioned above, the practice of criminal law might come to include a reparative or restitutionary element, through which the state oversees a response from agent to victim. See Barnett, Randy. *The Architecture of Freedom.* New York: Oxford University Press, 1998. The pure restitutionary, such as that by Barnett, simply replaces criminal with tort law; it ignores the reasons to repair other relations sundered by criminal acts, including relations to the state.

93. For a recent reassessment of New Zealand's alternative to a tort system, see Wilkinson, Bryce.

"New Zealand's Failed Experiment with State Monopoly Accident Insurance." *Green Bag* 2d 2 (1998): 45–55.

94. I borrow these terms, along with much else in my discussion, from Jules Coleman; see Coleman, Jules. "Second Thoughts and Other First Impressions." *Analyzing Law.* Ed. Brian Bix. New York: Oxford University Press, 1998. 301–306. But borrowing so much from Coleman is merely to keep company with much of the rest of tort theory in the last two decades.

95. See e.g. Calabresi, Guido. *The Costs of Accidents.* New Haven: Yale University Press, 1970; Landes William N. and Posner, Richard A. *The Economic Structure of Tort Law.* Cambridge, Mass.: Harvard University Press, 1987; and Shavell, Steven. *Economic Analysis of Accident Law.* Cambridge, Mass.: Harvard University Press, 1987.

96. See Coleman, Jules. "Tort Law and the Demands of Corrective Justice." *Indiana Law Journal* 67 (1992): 349–79.

97. Such an approach is suggested by Dworkin, Ronald. *Law's Empire.* Cambridge, Mass: Harvard University Press, 1986. 276–312. In his "What is Equality? Part 2: Equality of Resources." *Philosophy and Public Affairs* 10 (1981): 283–345, Dworkin lays the ground for an alternative approach, according to which accident costs should allocated to individuals when those costs reflect, in a specified sense, choices of those individuals; and otherwise should be allocated so as to preserve an egalitarian distribution of resources. This approach is further developed in Rakowski, Eric. *Equal Justice.* New York: Oxford University Press, 1991. 227–43.

98. This approach is suggested by Hart's theory of criminal liability, discussed above.

99. Richard Epstein's early view, in "A Theory of Strict Liability." *Journal of Legal Studies* 2 (1973): 151–204, is still taken as exemplary of libertarian theories of tort. While Epstein still considers himself a libertarian, his more recent work, in *Simple Rules for a Complex World.* Cambridge, Mass.: Harvard University Press, 1995, seeks a utilitarian foundation for tort law. Whether or not Epstein can reconcile libertarianism with utilitarianism, his newer view is clearly allocative—which may reduce actually held, genuinely libertarian theories of tort to a null set.

100. As a corollary, if no agent is responsible for the victim's loss, finding compensation in a manda-tory insurance pool would be an illegitimate taking.

101. Coase, Ronald. "The Problem of Social Cost." *Journal of Law & Economics* 3 (1960). For a rich development of this point, see Perry, Stephen "The Impossibility of General Strict Liability." *Canadian Journal of Law & Jurisprudence* 1 (1988): 147–71.

102. See the comprehensive *New York Times* series of reports on the disaster, "The Bhopal Disaster: How it Happened." in the 28, 29, and 31 Jan. 1994 issues, all p. A1. The Bhopal plant was operated by Union Carbide India, whose shares were 50.9% owned by Union Carbide Co. (US), 22% directly by the Government of India, and the remainder among 23,000 Indian citizens.

103. Weinreb, Ernest. *A Theory of Private Law.* Cambridge, Mass.: Harvard University Press, 1995.

104. For a suggestive development of a Kantian view of tort liability, see Herman, Barbara "What Happens to the Consequences?" in *Practice of Moral Judgment,* supra, note 67, at 94–112.

105. Coleman, Jules. *Risks and Wrongs.* Cambridge: Cambridge University Press, 1992. 314–18.

106. Id., at 324.

107. Coleman, Jules. "The Practice of Corrective Justice." *Philosophical Foundations,* supra, note 26, at 63. To say that the principle of corrective justice is contingent, however, is not to say that it is merely contingent, in any sense of "merely" beyond the metaphysical. For the principle that agents have special reason to repair their wrongs resonates throughout a set of ideals of agency, concern for others, and personhood. The principle, in other words, depends on a broad set of relational practices. Echoes of Strawson are strong.

108. Coleman, *Risks,* supra, note 105, at 386–406. The state may not justifiably do nothing, at least if it has a defensible ideal of distributive justice.

109. See Perry, "Responsibility for Outcomes," supra, note 5; Perry, Stephen. "The Moral Foundations of Tort Law." *Iowa Law Review* 77 (1992): 449–513; Honoré, Tony. "Responsibility and Luck." *The Law Quarterly Review* (1988): 530–53.

110. Perry, "Moral Foundations," supra, note 109, at 498. Perry suggests that outcome-responsibility is grounded only in one's responses to one's own outcomes. But, being the social beings we are, surely our reactions to what others do, and theirs to us, contribute to the phenomenological importance of causation and control.

111. See Coleman, Jules and Ripstein, Arthur. "Mischief and Misfortune." *McGill Law Journal* 41 (1995): 91–130; see also Ripstein's independent exploration in Ripstein, *Equality, Responsibility,* supra, note 86.

112. In the version of liberal political theory Coleman and Ripstein defend, the proper allocation is one that ensures an equal allocation of security, thus deploying normalized standards of liability, and reflects a deliberate ranking of the relative value of different activities. Coleman and Ripstein, "Mischief," supra, note 111, at 126–29.

113. Since Coleman and Ripstein make attribution subsidiary to allocation, their argument may seem to threaten to collapse corrective justice into distributive justice, as Perry argues. Perry, "Mischief." 154. But if corrective justice is distinguished from distributive justice by its generation of agent-specific obligations, then Coleman and Ripstein have indeed put forth a corrective justice view, albeit one rooted in distributive justice. Alternatively, they could be read as showing that distributive justice must be understood in terms of both agent-general and agent-specific reasons. See Coleman, "Second Thoughts," supra, note 94, at 312–16.

114. It would be equally a mistake to rely on a Strawsonian invocation of "natural" patterns of response, the "natural" being clearly a product of the social.

115. The English case *Holmes v Mather* [1875] 10 Ex. 21 contains the first prominent claim that negligent or willful misconduct is a necessary element in a legal claim for compensation. Morton Horwitz argues that the move to negligence in American law expressed a deliberate social policy of subsidizing emerging industries. He notes also, however, that jurists focused on fault as a useful tool for determining liability in cases of joint collision, of which there were suddenly many. Horwitz, Morton. *The Transformation of American Law. 1780–1860.* Cambridge: Mass., Harvard University Press, 1977. 85–99. See also Friedman, Lawrence M. *A History of American Law.* 2nd edn.. New York: Simon & Schuster, 1985.

116. See e.g. Justice Roger Traynor's famous concurrence in the products liability case *Escola v Coca Cola Bottling Co.*, 24 Cal. 2d 453,461,150 P.2d 436, 440 (1944), in which he defends enterprise liability in terms of insurance and incentive effects.

117. The social transformation may come to be viewed generally positively, as is arguably the case in the domain of industrial accidents, with the shift from no employer liability without fault to nofault workers' compensation.

118. Coleman and Ripstein are, as I have noted, particularly conscious of this dimension of tort theory.

52   Moral Luck

THOMAS NAGEL

Kant believed that good or bad luck should influence neither our moral judgment of a person and his actions, nor his moral assessment of himself.

> The good will is not good because of what it effects or accomplishes or because of its adequacy to achieve some proposed end; it is good only because of its willing, i.e., it is good of itself. And, regarded for itself, it is to be esteemed incomparably higher than anything which could be brought about by it in favor of any inclination or even of the sum total of all inclinations. Even if it should happen that, by a particularly unfortunate fate or by the niggardly provision of a stepmotherly nature, this will should be wholly lacking in power to accomplish its purpose, and if even the greatest effort should not avail it to achieve anything of its end, and if there remained only the good will (not as a mere wish but as the summoning of all the means in our power), it would sparkle like a jewel in its own right, as something that had its full worth in itself. Usefulness or fruitlessness can neither diminish nor augment this worth.[1]

From *Moral Luck*. New York: Cambridge University Press, 1991. 24–38. Reprinted with permission of the publisher.

He would presumably have said the same about a bad will: whether it accomplishes its evil purposes is morally irrelevant. And a course of action that would be condemned if it had a bad outcome cannot be vindicated if by luck it turns out well. There cannot be moral risk. This view seems to be wrong, but it arises in response to a fundamental problem about moral responsibility to which we possess no satisfactory solution.

The problem develops out of the ordinary conditions of moral judgment. Prior to reflection it is intuitively plausible that people cannot be morally assessed for what is not their fault, or for what is due to factors beyond their control. Such judgment is different from the evaluation of something as a good or bad thing, or state of affairs. The latter may be present in addition to moral judgment, but when we blame someone for his actions we are not merely saying it is bad that they happened, or bad that he exists: we are judging him, saying he is bad, which is different from his being a bad thing. This kind of judgment takes only a certain kind of object. Without being able to explain exactly why, we feel that the appropriateness of moral assessment is easily undermined by the discovery that the act or attribute, no matter how good or bad, is not under the person's control. While other evaluations remain, this one seems to lose its footing. So a clear absence of control, produced by involuntary movement, physical force, or ignorance of the circumstances, excuses what is done from moral judgment. But what we do depends in many more ways than these on what is not under our control—what is not produced by a good or a bad will, in Kant's phrase. And external influences in this broader range are not usually thought to excuse what is done from moral judgment, positive or negative.

Let me give a few examples, beginning with the type of case Kant has in mind. Whether we succeed or fail in what we try to do nearly always depends to some extent on factors beyond our control. This is true of murder, altruism, revolution, the sacrifice of certain interests for the sake of others—almost any morally important act. What has been done, and what is morally judged, is partly determined by external factors. However jewel-like the good will may be in its own right,

there is a morally significant difference between rescuing someone from a burning building and dropping him from a twelfth-story window while trying to rescue him. Similarly, there is a morally significant difference between reckless driving and manslaughter. But whether a reckless driver hits a pedestrian depends on the presence of the pedestrian at the point where he recklessly passes a red light. What we do is also limited by the opportunities and choices with which we are faced, and these are largely determined by factors beyond our control. Someone who was an officer in a concentration camp might have led a quiet and harmless life if the Nazis had never come to power in Germany. And someone who led a quiet and harmless life in Argentina might have become an officer in a concentration camp if he had not left Germany for business reasons in 1930.

I shall say more later about these and other examples. I introduce them here to illustrate a general point. Where a significant aspect of what someone does depends on factors beyond his control, yet we continue to treat him in that respect as an object of moral judgment, it can be called moral luck. Such luck can be good or bad. And the problem posed by this phenomenon, which led Kant to deny its possibility, is that the broad range of external influences here identified seems on close examination to undermine moral assessment as surely as does the narrower range of familiar excusing conditions. If the condition of control is consistently applied, it threatens to erode most of the moral assessments we find it natural to make. The things for which people are morally judged are determined, in more ways than we at first realize, by what is beyond their control. And when the seemingly natural requirement of fault or responsibility is applied in light of these facts, it leaves few prereflective moral judgments intact. Ultimately, nothing or almost nothing about what a person does seems to be under his control.

Why not conclude, then, that the condition of control is false—that it is an initially plausible hypothesis refuted by clear counter-examples? One could in that case look instead for a more refined condition that picked out the kinds of lack of control that really undermine certain moral judgments, without yielding the unacceptable conclusion, derived from the broader condition, that most or all ordinary moral judgments are illegitimate.

What rules out this escape is that we are dealing not with a theoretical conjecture but with a philosophical problem. The condition of control does not suggest itself merely as a generalization from certain clear cases. It seems correct in the further cases to which it is extended beyond the original set. When we undermine moral assessment by considering new ways in which control is absent, we are not just discovering what *would* follow given the general hypothesis, but are actually being persuaded that in itself the absence of control is relevant in these cases too. The erosion of moral judgment emerges not as the absurd consequence of an over-simple theory, but as a natural consequence of the ordinary idea of moral assessment, when it is applied in view of a more complete and precise account of the facts. It would therefore be a mistake to argue from the unacceptability of the conclusions to the need for a different account of the conditions of moral responsibility. The view that moral luck is paradoxical is not a *mistake,* ethical or logical, but a perception of one of the ways in which the intuitively acceptable conditions of moral judgment threaten to undermine it all.

It resembles the situation in another area of philosophy, the theory of knowledge. There too conditions that seem perfectly natural, and which grow out of the ordinary procedures for challenging and defending claims to knowledge, threaten to undermine all such claims if consistently applied. Most skeptical arguments have this quality: they do not depend on the imposition of arbitrarily stringent standards of knowledge, arrived at by misunderstanding, but appear to grow inevitably from the consistent application of ordinary standards.[2] There is a substantive parallel as well, for epistemological skepticism arises from consideration of the respects in which our beliefs and their relation to reality depend on factors beyond our control. External and internal causes produce our beliefs. We may subject these processes to scrutiny in an effort to avoid error, but our conclusions at this next level also result, in part, from

influences that we do not control directly. The same will be true no matter how far we carry the investigation. Our beliefs are always, ultimately, due to factors outside our control, and the impossibility of encompassing those factors without being at the mercy of others leads us to doubt whether we know anything. It looks as though, if any of our beliefs are true, it is pure biological luck rather than knowledge.

Moral luck is like this because, although there are various respects in which the natural objects of moral assessment are out of our control or influenced by what is out of our control, we cannot reflect on these facts without losing our grip on the judgments.

There are roughly four ways in which the natural objects of moral assessment are disturbingly subject to luck. One is the phenomenon of constitutive luck—the kind of person you are, where this is not just a question of what you deliberately do, but of your inclinations, capacities, and temperament. Another category is luck in one's circumstances—the kind of problems and situations one faces. The other two have to do with the causes and effects of action: luck in how one is determined by antecedent circumstances, and luck in the way one's actions and projects turn out. All of them present a common problem. They are all opposed by the idea that one cannot be more culpable or estimable for anything than one is for that fraction of it that is under one's control. It seems irrational to take or dispense credit or blame for matters over which a person has no control, or for their influence on results over which he has partial control. Such things may create the conditions for action, but action can be judged only to the extent that it goes beyond these conditions and does not just result from them.

Let us first consider luck, good and bad, in the way things turn out. Kant, in the above-quoted passage, has one example of this in mind, but the category covers a wide range. It includes the truck driver who accidentally runs over a child, the artist who abandons his wife and five children to devote himself to painting,[3] and other cases in which the possibilities of success and failure are even greater. The driver, if he is entirely without fault, will feel terrible about his role in the event, but will not have to reproach himself. Therefore this example of agent regret[4] is not yet a case of *moral* bad luck. However, if the driver was guilty of even a minor degree of negligence —failing to have his brakes checked recently, for example— then if that negligence contributes to the death of the child, he will not merely feel terrible. He will blame himself for the death. And what makes this an example of moral luck is that he would have to blame himself only slightly for the negligence itself if no situation arose that required him to brake suddenly and violently to avoid hitting a child. Yet the negligence is the same in both cases, and the driver has no control over whether a child will run into his path.

The same is true at higher levels of negligence. If someone has had too much to drink and his car swerves onto the sidewalk, he can count himself morally lucky if there are no pedestrians in its path. If there were, he would be to blame for their deaths, and would probably be prosecuted for manslaughter. But if he hurts no one, although his recklessness is exactly the same, he is guilty of a far less serious legal offence and will certainly reproach himself and be reproached by others much less severely. To take another legal example, the penalty for attempted murder is less than that for successful murder— however similar the intentions and motives of the assailant may be in the two cases. His degree of culpability can depend, it would seem, on whether the victim happened to be wearing a bulletproof vest, or whether a bird flew into the path of the bullet—matters beyond his control.

Finally, there are cases of decision under uncertainty—common in public and in private life. Anna Karenina goes off with Vronsky, Gauguin leaves his family, Chamberlain signs the Munich agreement, the Decembrists persuade the troops under their command to revolt against the czar, the American colonies declare their independence from Britain, you introduce two people in an attempt at matchmaking. It is tempting in all such cases to feel that some decision must be possible, in the light of what is known at the time, that will make reproach unsuitable no matter how things turn out. But this is not true; when someone acts in such ways he takes his life, or his moral position, into his hands, because how things turn out determines what he has done. It is possible *also* to assess the decision from the point of view of what could be known at the time, but this is not the end of the story. If the Decembrists had succeeded in overthrowing Nicholas I in 1825 and establishing a constitutional regime, they would be heroes. As it is, not only did they fail and pay for it, but they bore some responsibility for the terrible punishments meted out to the troops who had been persuaded to follow them. If the American Revolution had been a bloody failure resulting in greater repression, then Jefferson, Franklin, and Washington would still have made a noble attempt, and might not even have regretted it on their way to the scaffold, but they would also have had to blame themselves for what they had helped to bring on their compatriots. (Perhaps peaceful efforts at reform would eventually have succeeded.) If Hitler had not overrun Europe and exterminated millions, but instead had died of a heart attack after occupying the Sudetenland, Chamberlain's action at Munich would still have utterly betrayed the Czechs, but it would not be the great moral disaster that has made his name a household word.[5]

In many cases of difficult choice the outcome cannot be foreseen with certainty. One kind of assessment of the choice is possible in advance, but another kind must await the outcome, because the outcome determines what has been done. The same degree of culpability or estimability in intention, motive, or concern is compatible with a wide range of judgments, positive or negative, depending on what happened beyond the point of decision. The mens rea that could have existed in the absence of any consequences does not exhaust the grounds of moral judgment. Actual results influence culpability or esteem in a large class of unquestionably ethical cases ranging from negligence through political choice.

That these are genuine moral judgments rather than expressions of temporary attitude is evident from the fact that one can say in advance how the moral verdict will depend on the results. If one negligently leaves the bath running with the baby in it, one will realize, as one bounds up the stairs toward the bathroom, that if the baby has drowned one has done something awful, whereas if it has not one has merely been careless. Someone who launches a violent revolution against an authoritarian regime knows that if he fails he will be responsible for much suffering that is in vain, but if he succeeds he will be justified by the outcome. I do not mean that any action can be retroactively justified by history. Certain things are so bad in themselves, or so risky, that no results can make them all right. Nevertheless, when moral judgment does depend on the outcome, it is objective and timeless and not dependent on a change of standpoint produced by success or failure. The judgment after the fact follows from a hypothetical judgment that can be made beforehand, and it can be made as easily by someone else as by the agent.

From the point of view that makes responsibility dependent on control, all this seems absurd. How is it possible to be more or less culpable depending on whether a child gets into the path of one's car, or a bird into the path of one's bullet? Perhaps it is true that what is done depends on more than the agent's state of mind or intention. The problem then is, why is it not irrational to base moral assessment on what people do, in this broad sense? It amounts to holding them responsible for the contributions of fate as well as for their own—provided they have made some contribution to begin with. If we look at cases of negligence or attempt, the pattern seems to be that overall culpability corresponds to the product of mental or intentional fault and the seriousness of the outcome. Cases of decision under uncertainty are less easily explained in this way, for it seems that the overall judgment can even shift from positive to negative depending on the outcome. But here too it seems rational to subtract the effects of occurrences subsequent to the choice, that were merely possible at the time, and concentrate moral assessment on the actual decision in light of the probabilities. If the object of moral judgment is the person, then to hold him accountable for what he has done in the broader sense is akin to strict liability, which may have its legal uses but seems irrational as a moral position.

The result of such a line of thought is to pare down each act to its morally essential core, an inner act of pure will assessed by motive and intention. Adam Smith advocates such a position in *The Theory of Moral Sentiments*, but notes that it runs contrary to our actual judgments.

> But how well soever we may seem to be persuaded of the truth of this equitable maxim, when we consider it after this manner, in abstract, yet when we come to particular cases, the actual consequences that happen to proceed from any action have a very great effect upon our sentiments concerning its merit or demerit, and almost always either enhance or diminish our sense of both. Scarce, in any one instance perhaps, will our sentiments be found, after examination, to be entirely regulated by this rule, which we all acknowledge ought entirely to regulate them.[6]

Joel Feinberg points out further that restricting the domain of moral responsibility to the inner world will not immunize it to luck. Factors beyond the agent's control, like a coughing fit, can interfere with his decisions as surely as they can with the path of a bullet from his gun.[7] Nevertheless the tendency to cut down the scope of moral assessment is pervasive, and does not limit itself to the influence of effects. It attempts to isolate the will from the other direction, so to speak, by separating out constitutive luck. Let us consider that next.

Kant was particularly insistent on the moral irrelevance of qualities of temperament and personality that are not under the control of the will. Such qualities as sympathy or coldness might provide the background against which obedience to moral requirements is more or less difficult, but they could not be objects of moral assessment themselves, and might well interfere with confident assessment of its proper object—the determination of the will by the motive of duty. This rules out moral judgment of many of the virtues and vices, which are states of character that influence choice but are certainly not exhausted by dispositions to act deliberately in certain ways. A person may be greedy, envious, cowardly, cold, ungenerous, unkind, vain, or conceited, but behave perfectly by a monumental effort of will. To possess these vices is to be unable to help having certain feelings under certain circumstances, and to have strong spontaneous impulses to act badly. Even if one controls the impulses, one still has the vice. An envious person hates the greater success of others. He can be morally condemned as envious even if he congratulates them cordially and does nothing to denigrate or spoil their success. Conceit, likewise, need not be displayed. It is fully present in someone who cannot help dwelling with secret satisfaction on the superiority of his own achievements, talents, beauty, intelligence, or virtue. To some extent such a quality may be the product of earlier choices; to some extent it may be amenable to change by current actions. But it is largely a matter of constitutive bad fortune. Yet people are morally condemned for such qualities, and esteemed for others equally beyond control of the will: they are assessed for what they are *like*.

To Kant this seems incoherent because virtue is enjoined on everyone and therefore must in principle be possible for everyone. It may be easier for some than for others, but it must be possible to achieve it by making the right choices, against whatever temperamental background.[8] One may want to have a generous spirit, or regret not having one, but it makes no sense to condemn oneself or anyone else for a quality that is not within the control of the will. Condemnation implies that you should not be like that, not that it is unfortunate that you are.

Nevertheless, Kant's conclusion remains intuitively unacceptable. We may be persuaded that these moral judgments are rational, but they reappear involuntarily as soon as the argument is over. This is the pattern throughout the subject.

The third category to consider is luck in one's circumstances. I shall mention it briefly. The things we are called upon to do, the moral tests we face, are importantly determined by factors beyond our control. It may be true of someone that in a dangerous situation he would behave in a cowardly or heroic fashion, but if the situation never arises, he will never have the chance to distinguish or disgrace himself in this way, and his moral record will be different.

A conspicuous example of this is political. Ordinary citizens of Nazi Germany had an opportunity to behave heroically by opposing the regime. They also had an opportunity to behave badly, and most of them are culpable for having failed this test. But it is a test to which the citizens of other countries were not subjected, with the result that even if they, or some of them, would have behaved as badly as the Germans in like circumstances, they simply did not and therefore are not similarly culpable. Here again one is morally at the mercy of fate, and it may seem irrational upon reflection, but our ordinary moral attitudes would be unrecognizable without it. We judge people for what they actually do or fail to do, not just for what they would have done if circumstances had been different.[9]

This form of moral determination by the actual is also paradoxical, but we can begin to see how deep in the concept of responsibility the paradox is embedded. A person can be morally responsible only for what he does; but what he does results from a great deal that he does not do; therefore he is not morally responsible for what he is and is not responsible for. (This is not a contradiction, but it is a paradox.)

It should be obvious that there is a connection between these problems about responsibility and control and an even more familiar problem, that of freedom of the will. That is the last type of moral luck I want to take up, though I can do no more within the scope of this essay than indicate its connection with the other types. If one cannot be responsible for consequences of one's acts due to factors beyond one's control, or for antecedents of one's acts that are properties of temperament not subject to one's will, or for the circumstances that pose one's moral choices, then how can one be responsible even for the stripped-down acts of the will itself, if *they* are the product of antecedent circumstances outside of the will's control?

The area of genuine agency, and therefore of legitimate moral judgment, seems to shrink under this scrutiny to an extensionless point. Everything seems to result from the combined influence of factors, antecedent and posterior to action, that are not within the agent's control. Since he cannot be responsible for them, he cannot be responsible for their results—though it may remain possible to take up the aesthetic or other evaluative analogues of the moral attitudes that are thus displaced.

It is also possible, of course, to brazen it out and refuse to accept the results, which indeed seem unacceptable as soon as we stop thinking about the arguments. Admittedly, if certain surrounding circumstances had been different, then no unfortunate consequences would have followed from a wicked intention, and no seriously culpable act would have been performed; but since the circumstances were not different, and the agent in fact succeeded in perpetrating a particularly cruel murder, that is what he did, and that is what he is responsible for. Similarly, we may admit that if certain antecedent circumstances had been different, the agent would never have developed into the sort of person who would do such a thing; but since he *did* develop (as the inevitable result of those antecedent circumstances) into the sort of swine he is, and into the person who committed such a murder, that is what he is blameable for. In both cases one is responsible for what one actually does—even if what one actually does depends in important ways on what is not within one's control. This compatibilist account of our moral judgments would leave room for the ordinary conditions of responsibility—the absence of coercion, ignorance, or involuntary movement—as part of the determination of what someone has done—but it is understood not to exclude the influence of a great deal that he has not done.[10]

The only thing wrong with this solution is its failure to explain how skeptical problems arise. For they arise not from the imposition of an arbitrary external requirement, but from the nature of moral judgment itself. Something in the ordinary idea of what someone does must explain how it can seem necessary to subtract from it anything that merely happens - even though the ultimate consequence of such subtraction is that nothing remains. And something in the ordinary idea of knowledge must explain why it seems to be undermined by any influences on belief not within the control of the subject—so that knowledge seems impossible without an impossible foundation in autonomous reason. But let us leave

epistemology aside and concentrate on action, character, and moral assessment.

The problem arises, I believe, because the self that acts and is the object of moral judgment is threatened with dissolution by the absorption of its acts and impulses into the class of events. Moral judgment of a person is judgment not of what happens to him, but of *him*. It does not say merely that a certain event or state of affairs is fortunate or unfortunate or even terrible. It is not an evaluation of a state of the world, or of an individual as part of the world. We are not thinking just that it would be better if he were different, or did not exist, or had not done some of the things he has done. We are judging *him*, rather than his existence or characteristics. The effect of concentrating on the influence of what is not under his control is to make this responsible self seem to disappear, swallowed up by the order of mere events.

What, however, do we have in mind that a person must *be* to be the object of these moral attitudes? While the concept of agency is easily undermined, it is very difficult to give it a positive characterization. This is familiar from the literature on free will.

I believe that in a sense the problem has no solution, because something in the idea of agency is incompatible with actions being events, or people being things. But as the external determinants of what someone has done are gradually exposed, in their effect on consequences, character, and choice itself, it becomes gradually clear that actions are events and people things. Eventually nothing remains that can be ascribed to the responsible self, and we are left with nothing but a portion of the larger sequence of events, which can be deplored or celebrated, but not blamed or praised.

Though I cannot define the idea of the active self that is thus undermined, it is possible to say something about its sources. There is a close connection between our feelings about ourselves and our feelings about others. Guilt and indignation, shame and contempt, pride and admiration are internal and external sides of the same moral attitudes. We are unable to view ourselves simply as portions of the world, and from inside we have a rough idea of the boundary between what is us and what is not, what we do and what happens to us, what is our personality and what is an accidental handicap. We apply the same essentially internal conception of the self to others. About ourselves we feel pride, shame, guilt, remorse—and agent regret. We do not regard our actions and our characters merely as fortunate or unfortunate episodes—though they may also be that. We cannot simply take an external evaluative view of ourselves—of what we most essentially are and what we do. And this remains true even when we have seen that we are not responsible for our own existence, or our nature, or the choices we have to make, or the circumstances that give our acts the consequences they have. Those acts remain ours and we remain ourselves, despite the persuasiveness of the reasons that seem to argue us out of existence.

It is this internal view that we extend to others in moral judgment—when we judge *them* rather than their desirability or utility. We extend to others the refusal to limit ourselves to external evaluation, and we accord to them selves like our own. But in both cases this comes up against the brutal inclusion of humans and everything about them in a world from which they cannot be separated and of which they are nothing but contents. The external view forces itself on us at the same time that we resist it. One way this occurs is through the gradual erosion of what we do by the subtraction of what happens.[11]

The inclusion of consequences in the conception of what we have done is an acknowledgment that we are parts of the world, but the paradoxical character of moral luck that emerges from this acknowledgment shows that we are unable to operate with such a view, for it leaves us with no one to be. The same thing is revealed in the appearance that determinism obliterates responsibility. Once we see an aspect of what we or someone else does as something that happens, we lose our grip on the idea that it has been done and that we can judge the doer and not just the happening. This explains why the absence of determinism is no more hospitable to the concept of agency than is its presence—a point that has been noticed often. Either way the act is viewed externally, as part of the course of events.

The problem of moral luck cannot be understood without an account of the internal conception of agency and its special connection with the moral attitudes as opposed to other types of value. I do not have such an account. The degree to which the problem has a solution can be determined only by seeing whether in some degree the incompatibility between this conception and the various ways in which we do not control what we do is only apparent. I have nothing to offer on that topic either. But it is not enough to say merely that our basic moral attitudes toward ourselves and others are determined by what is actual; for they are also threatened by the sources of that actuality, and by the external view of action that forces itself on us when we see how everything we do belongs to a world that we have not created.

NOTES

1. Kant, Immanuel. *Foundations of the Metaphysics of Morals.* [Also known as *Groundwork for the Metaphysics of Morals.* Trans. Thomas Kingsmill Abbot. Ed. Lara Denis. Orchard Park, NY: Broadview Press (2005).] First section, third paragraph.

2. See Clarke, Thompson. "The Legacy of Skepticism." *The Journal of Philosophy* LXIX, no. 20 (November 9, 1972): 754–69.

3. Such a case, modelled on the life of Gauguin, is discussed by Bernard Williams in "Moral Luck" *Proceedings of the Aristotelian Society* supplementary vol. L (1976):115–35 (to which the original version of this essay was a reply). He points out that, though success or failure cannot be predicted in advance, Gauguin's most basic retrospective feelings about the decision will be determined by the development of his talent. My disagreement with Williams is that his account fails to explain why such retrospective attitudes can be called moral. If success does not permit Gauguin to justify himself to others, but still determines his most basic feelings, that shows only that his most basic feelings need not be moral. It does not show that morality is subject to luck. If the retrospective judgment were moral, it would imply the truth of a hypothetical judgment made in advance, of the form "If I leave my family and become a great

painter, I will be justified by success; if I don't become a great painter, the act will be unforgivable."

4. Williams' term, supra, note 3.

5. For a fascinating but morally repellent discussion of the topic of justification by history, see Merleau-Ponty, Maurice. *Humanisme et Terreur.* Paris: Gallimard, 1947. Translated as *Humanism and Terror.* Boston: Beacon Press, 1969.

6. Smith, Adam. *The Theory of Moral Sentiments.* Pt. II, sect. 3, Introduction, para. 5 (1759).

7. Feinberg, Joel. "Problematic Responsibility in Law and Morals." *Doing and Deserving.* Princeton: Princeton University Press, 1970.

8. See Kant, *Foundations of the Metaphysics of Morals,* supra, note 1, at first section, eleventh paragraph"

> If nature has put little sympathy in the heart of a man, and if he, though an honest man, is by temperament cold and indifferent to the sufferings of others, perhaps because he is provided with special gifts of patience and fortitude and expects or even requires that others should have the same—and such a man would certainly not be the meanest product of nature—would not he find in himself a source from which to give himself a far higher worth than he could have got by having a good-natured temperament?

[FN 9 deleted. Ed.]

9. Circumstantial luck can extend to aspects of the situation other than individual behavior. For example, during the Vietnam War even U.S. citizens who had opposed their country's actions vigorously from the start often felt compromised by its crimes. Here they were not even responsible; there was probably nothing they could do to stop what was happening, so the feeling of being implicated may seem unintelligible. But it is nearly impossible to view the crimes of one's own country in the same way that one views the crimes of another country, no matter how equal one's lack of power to stop them in the two cases. One is a citizen of one of them, and has a connection with its actions (even if only through taxes that cannot be withheld) that one does not have with the other's. This makes it possible to be ashamed of one's country, and to feel a victim of moral bad luck that one was an American in the 1960s.

10. The corresponding position in epistemology would be that knowledge consists of true beliefs formed in certain ways, and that it does not require all aspects of the process to be under the knower's control, actually or potentially. Both the correctness of these beliefs and the process by which they are arrived at would therefore be importantly subject to luck. The Nobel Prize is not awarded to people who turn out to be wrong, no matter how brilliant their reasoning.

11. See P. F. Strawson's discussion of the conflict between the objective attitude and personal reactive attitudes in "Freedom and Resentment," *Proceedings of the British Academy* 1962. Reprinted in *Studies in the Philosophy of Thought and Action.* Ed. P. F. Strawson. London: Oxford University Press, 1968; and in Strawson, P. F. *Freedom and Resentment and Other Essays.* London: Methuen, 1974.

CHAPTER SEVENTEEN

The Function and Limits of Punishment

53 Of Crimes and Punishments

CESARE BECCARIA

CH. 2: OF THE RIGHT TO PUNISH

Every punishment that does not arise from absolute necessity, says the great Montesquieu, is tyrannical. A proposition that may be made more general thus: every act of authority of one man over another, for which there is not an absolute necessity, is tyrannical. It is upon this then that the sovereign's right to punish crimes is founded; that is, upon the necessity of defending the public liberty, entrusted to his care, from the usurpation of individuals; and punishments are just in proportion, as the liberty, preserved by the sovereign, is sacred and valuable.

Let us consult the human heart, and there we shall find the foundation of the sovereign's right to punish; for no advantage in moral policy can be lasting that is not founded on the indelible sentiments of the heart of man. Whatever law deviates from this principle will always meet with a resistance that will destroy it in the end; for the smallest force continually applied will overcome the most violent motion communicated to bodies.

No man ever gave up his liberty merely for the good of the public. Such a chimera exists only in romances. Every individual wishes, if possible, to be exempt from the compacts that bind the rest of mankind.

The multiplication of mankind, though slow—being too great for the means which the earth, in its natural state, offered to satisfy necessities that every day became more numerous—obliged men to separate again, and form new societies. These naturally opposed the first, and a state of war was transferred from individuals to nations.

Thus it was necessity that forced men to give up a part of their liberty. It is certain, then, that every individual would choose to put into the public stock the smallest portion possible, as much only as was sufficient to engage others to defend it. The aggregate of these, the smallest portions possible, forms the right of punishing; all that extends beyond this is abuse, not justice.

Observe that by *justice* I understand nothing more than that bond that is necessary to keep the interest of individuals united, without which men

Excerpted from Cesare Beccaria (1738–1794), *On Crimes and Punishments*. Originally published in Italian in 1764. Translated from the French by Edward D. Ingraham, 1819. Available online at http://www.constitution.org/cb/crim_pun.htm constitution.org would return to their original state of barbarity. All punishments that exceed the necessity of preserving this bond are in their nature unjust. We should be cautious how we associate with the word *justice* an idea of anything real, such as a physical power, or a being that actually exists. I do not, by any means, speak of the justice of God, which is of another kind, and refers immediately to rewards and punishments in a life to come.

CH. 3: CONSEQUENCES OF THE FOREGOING PRINCIPLES

The laws only can determine the punishment of crimes; and the authority of making penal laws can only reside with the legislator, who represents the whole society united by the social compact. No magistrate then (as he is one of the society) can with justice inflict on any other member of the same society punishment that is not ordained by the laws. But as a punishment, increased beyond the degree fixed by the law, is the just punishment with the addition of another, it follows that no magistrate, even under a pretence of zeal, or the public good, should increase the punishment already determined by the laws.

If every individual be bound to society, society is equally bound to him, by a contract that from its nature equally binds both parties. This obligation, which descends from the throne to the cottage, and equally binds the highest and lowest of mankind, signifies nothing more than that it is the interest of all, that conventions, which are useful to the greatest number, should be punctually observed. The violation of this compact by any individual is an introduction to anarchy.

The sovereign, who represents the society itself, can only make general laws to bind the members; but it belongs not to him to judge whether any individual has violated the social compact or incurred the punishment in consequence. For in this case there are two parties, one represented by the sovereign, who insists upon the violation of the contract, and the other is the person accused, who denies it. It is necessary then that there should be a third person to decide this contest; that is to say, a judge, or magistrate, from whose

determination there should be no appeal; and this determination should consist of a simple affirmation or negation of fact.

If it can only be proved that the severity of punishments, though not immediately contrary to the public good, or to the end for which they were intended—viz., to prevent crimes—be useless, then such severity would be contrary to those beneficent virtues that are the consequence of enlightened reason, which instructs the sovereign to wish rather to govern men in a state of freedom and happiness than of slavery. It would also be contrary to justice and the social compact.

CH. 27: OF THE MILDNESS OF PUNISHMENTS

The course of my ideas has carried me away from my subject, to the elucidation of which I now return. Crimes are more effectually prevented by the *certainty* than the *severity* of punishment. Hence in a magistrate the necessity of vigilance, and in a judge of implacability, which, that it may become an useful virtue, should be joined to a mild legislation. The certainty of a small punishment will make a stronger impression than the fear of one more severe, if attended with the hopes of escaping; for it is the nature of mankind to be terrified at the approach of the smallest inevitable evil, whilst hope, the best gift of Heaven, hath the power of dispelling the apprehension of a greater, especially if supported by examples of impunity, which weakness or avarice too frequently afford.

If punishments be very severe, men are naturally led to the perpetration of other crimes, to avoid the punishment due to the first. The countries and times most notorious for severity of punishments were always those in which the most bloody and inhuman actions and the most atrocious crimes were committed; for the hand of the legislator and the assassin were directed by the same spirit of ferocity, which on the throne dictated laws of iron to slaves and savages, and in private instigated the subject to sacrifice one tyrant to make room for another.

In proportion as punishments become more cruel, the minds of men, as a fluid rises to the same height with that which surrounds it, grow hardened and insensible; and the force of the passions still continuing, in the space of an hundred years the *wheel* terrifies no more than formerly the *prison*. That a punishment may produce the effect required, it is sufficient that the *evil* it occasions should exceed the *good* expected from the crime, including in the calculation the certainty of the punishment, and the privation of the expected advantage. All severity beyond this is superfluous, and therefore tyrannical.

Men regulate their conduct by the repeated impression of evils they know, and not by those with which they are unacquainted. Let us, for example, suppose two nations, in one of which the greatest punishment is *perpetual slavery*, and in the other *the wheel*: I say, that both will inspire the same degree of terror, and that there can be no reasons for increasing the punishments of the first that are not equally valid for augmenting those of the second to more lasting and more ingenious modes of tormenting, and so on to the most exquisite refinements of a science too well known to tyrants.

There are yet two other consequences of cruel punishments, which counteract the purpose of their institution, which was, to prevent crimes. The *first* arises from the impossibility of establishing an exact proportion between the crime and punishment; for though ingenious cruelty hath greatly multiplied the variety of torments, yet the human frame can suffer only to a certain degree, beyond which it is impossible to proceed, be the enormity of the crime ever so great. The *second* consequence is impunity. Human nature is limited no less in evil than in good. Excessive barbarity can never be more than temporary, it being impossible that it should be supported by a permanent system of legislation; for if the laws be too cruel, they must be altered, or anarchy and impunity will succeed.

Is it possible without shuddering with horror to read in history of the barbarous and useless torments that were coolly invented and executed by men who were called sages? Who does not tremble at the thoughts of thousands of wretches, whom their misery—either caused or tolerated by the laws, which favoured the few and outraged the many—had forced in despair to return to a state of nature; or accused of impossible crimes, the fabric of ignorance and superstition; or guilty only of having been faithful to their own principles; who, I say, can, without horror, think of their being torn to pieces, with slow and studied barbarity, by men endowed with the same passions and the same feelings? A delightful spectacle to a fanatic multitude!

CH. 47: OF THE MEANS OF PREVENTING CRIMES

It is better to prevent crimes than to punish them. This is the fundamental principle of good legislation, which is the art of conducting men to the maximum of happiness, and to the minimum of misery, if we may apply this mathematical expression to the good and evil of life. But the means hitherto employed for that purpose are generally inadequate, or contrary to the end proposed. It is impossible to reduce the tumultuous activity of mankind to absolute regularity; for, amidst the various and opposite attractions of pleasure and pain, human laws are not sufficient entirely to prevent disorders in society. Such, however is the chimera of weak men, when invested with authority. To prohibit a number of indifferent actions is not to prevent the crimes that they may produce, but to create new ones, it is to change at will the ideas of virtue and vice, which, at other times we are told, are eternal and immutable. To what a situation should we be reduced if everything were to be forbidden that might possibly lead to a crime? We must be deprived of the use of our senses: for one motive that induces a man to commit a real crime there are a thousand that excite him to those indifferent actions that are called crimes by bad laws. If then the probability that a crime will be committed is in proportion to the number of motives, to extend the sphere of crimes will be to increase that probability. The generality of laws are only exclusive privileges, the tribute of all to the advantages of a few.

Would you prevent crimes? Let the laws be clear and simple, let the entire force of the nation be united in their defence, let them be intended rather to favour every individual than any particular classes of men, let the laws be feared, and the laws only. The fear of the laws is salutary, but the fear of men is a fruitful and fatal source of crimes. Men enslaved are more voluptuous, more debauched, and more cruel than those who are in a state of freedom. These study the sciences, the interest of nations, have great objects before their eyes, and imitate them; but those, whose views are confined to the present moment, endeavour, amidst the distraction of riot and debauchery, to forget their situation; accustomed to the uncertainty of all events, for the laws determine none, the consequences of their crimes become problematical, which gives an additional force to the strength of their passions.

In a nation indolent from the nature of the climate, the uncertainty of the laws confirms and increases men's indolence and stupidity. In a voluptuous but active nation, this uncertainty occasions a multiplicity of cabals and intrigues, which spread distrust and diffidence through the hearts of all, and dissimulation and treachery are the foundation of their prudence. In a brave and powerful nation, this uncertainty of the laws is at last destroyed, after many oscillations from liberty to slavery, and from slavery to liberty again.

CH. 61: CONCLUSION

I conclude with this reflection, that the severity of punishments ought to be in proportion to the state of the nation. Among a people hardly yet emerged from barbarity, they should be most severe, as strong impressions are required; but, in proportion as the minds of men become softened by their intercourse in society, the severity of punishments should be diminished, if it be intended that the necessary relation between the object and the sensation should be maintained.

From what I have written results the following general theorem, of considerable utility, though not conformable to custom, the common legislator of nations:

> *That a punishment may not be an act of violence, of one, or of many, against a private member of society, it should be public, immediate, and necessary, the least possible in the case given, proportioned to the crime, and determined by the laws.*

54   The Right to Punish

IMMANUEL KANT

The Right of administering Punishment, is the Right of the Sovereign as the Supreme Power to inflict pain upon a Subject on account of a Crime committed by him. The Head of the State cannot therefore be punished; but his supremacy may be withdrawn from him. Any Transgression of the public law which makes him who commits it incapable of being a Citizen, constitutes a Crime, either simply as a private Crime (*crimen*), or also as a public Crime (*crimen publicum*). Private crimes are dealt with by a Civil Court; Public Crimes by a Criminal Court.—Embezzlement or peculation of money or goods entrusted in trade, Fraud in purchase or sale, if done before the eyes of the party who suffers, are Private Crimes. On the other hand, Coining false money or forging Bills of Exchange, Theft, Robbery, etc., are Public Crimes, because the Commonwealth, and not merely some particular individual, is endangered thereby. Such Crimes may be divided into those of a base character (*indolis abjectæ*) and those of a violent character (*indolis violentiæ*). Judicial or Juridical Punishment (*pœna forensis*) is to be distinguished from Natural Punishment (*pœna naturalis*), in which Crime as Vice punishes itself, and does not as such come within the cognizance

From "The right of punishing and of pardoning." *The Philosophy of Law: An Exposition of the Fundamental Principles of Jurisprudence as the Science of Right.* Trans. W. Hastie. Edinburgh: Clark, 1887. [1798], Pt II E.

of the Legislator. Juridical Punishment can never be administered merely as a means for promoting another Good either with regard to the Criminal himself or to Civil Society, but must in all cases be imposed only because the individual on whom it is inflicted has committed a Crime. For one man ought never to be dealt with merely as a means subservient to the purpose of another, nor be mixed up with the subjects of Real Right. Against such treatment his Inborn Personality has a Right to protect him, even although he may be condemned to lose his Civil Personality. He must first be found guilty and punishable, before there can be any thought of drawing from his Punishment any benefit for himself or his fellow citizens. The Penal Law is a Categorical Imperative; and woe to him who creeps through the serpent windings of Utilitarianism to discover some advantage that may discharge him from the Justice of Punishment, or even from the due measure of it, according to the Pharisaic maxim: "It is better that one man should die than that the whole people should perish." For if Justice and Righteousness perish, human life would no longer have any value in the world.—What, then, is to be said of such a proposal as to keep a Criminal alive who has been condemned to death, on his being given to understand that if he agreed to certain dangerous experiments being performed upon him, he would be allowed to survive if he came happily through them? It is argued that Physicians might thus obtain new information that would be of value to the Commonweal. But a Court of Justice would repudiate with scorn any proposal of this kind if made to it by the Medical Faculty; for Justice would cease to be Justice, if it were bartered away for any consideration whatever.

But what is the mode and measure of Punishment which Public Justice takes as its Principle and Standard? It is just the Principle of Equality, by which the pointer of the Scale of Justice is made to incline no more to the one side than the other. It may be rendered by saying that the undeserved evil which anyone commits on another is to be regarded as perpetrated on himself. Hence it may be said: "If you slander another, you slander yourself; if you steal from another, you steal from yourself; if you strike another,

you strike yourself; if you kill another, you kill yourself." This is the Right of RETALIATION (*jus talionis*); and properly understood, it is the only Principle which in regulating a Public Court, as distinguished from mere private judgment, can definitely assign both the quality and the quantity of a just penalty. All other standards are wavering and uncertain; and on account of other considerations involved in them, they contain no principle conformable to the sentence of pure and strict Justice. It may appear, however, that difference of social status would not admit the application of the Principle of Retaliation, which is that of "Like with Like." But although the application may not in all cases be possible according to the letter, yet as regards the effect it may always be attained in practice, by due regard being given to the disposition and sentiment of the parties in the higher social sphere. Thus a pecuniary penalty on account of a verbal injury may have no direct proportion to the injustice of slander; for one who is wealthy may be able to indulge himself in this offence for his own gratification. Yet the attack committed on the honour of the party aggrieved may have its equivalent in the pain inflicted upon the pride of the aggressor, especially if he is condemned by the judgment of the Court, not only to retract and apologize, but to submit to some meaner ordeal, as kissing the hand of the injured person. In like manner, if a man of the highest rank has violently assaulted an innocent citizen of the lower orders, he may be condemned not only to apologize but to undergo a solitary and painful imprisonment, whereby, in addition to the discomfort endured, the vanity of the offender would be painfully affected, and the very shame of his position would constitute an adequate Retaliation after the principle of "Like with Like." But how then would we render the statement: "If you steal from another, you steal from yourself"? In this way, that whoever steals anything makes the property of all insecure; he therefore robs himself of all security in property, according to the Right of Retaliation. Such a one has nothing, and can acquire nothing, but he has the Will to live; and this is only possible by others supporting him. But as the State should not do this gratuitously, he must for this purpose yield his powers to the State to be used in penal labour; and thus he falls for a time, or it may be for life, into a condition of slavery.—But whoever has committed Murder, must die. There is, in this case, no juridical substitute or surrogate that can be given or taken for the satisfaction of Justice. There is no Likeness or proportion between Life, however painful, and Death; and therefore there is no Equality between the crime of Murder and the retaliation of it but what is judicially accomplished by the execution of the Criminal. His death, however, must be kept free from all maltreatment that would make the humanity suffering in his Person loathsome or abominable. Even if a Civil Society resolved to dissolve itself with the consent of all its members—as might be supposed in the case of a People inhabiting an island resolving to separate and scatter themselves throughout the whole world—the last Murderer lying in the prison ought to be executed before the resolution was carried out. This ought to be done in order that every one may realize the desert of his deeds, and that bloodguiltiness may not remain upon the people; for otherwise they might all be regarded as participators in the murder as a public violation of Justice.

The Equalization of Punishment with Crime is therefore only possible by the cognition of the Judge extending even to the penalty of Death, according to the Right of Retaliation. This is manifest from the fact that it is only thus that a Sentence can be pronounced over all criminals proportionate to their internal wickedness; as may be seen by considering the case when the punishment of Death has to be inflicted, not on account of a murder, but on account of a political crime that can only be punished capitally. A hypothetical case, founded on history, will illustrate this. In the last Scottish Rebellion there were various participators in it—such as Balmerino and others—who believed that in taking part in the Rebellion they were only discharging their duty to the House of Stuart; but there were also others who were animated only by private motives and interests. Now, suppose that the Judgment of the Supreme Court regarding them had been this: that every one should have liberty to choose between the punishment of Death or Penal Servitude for life. In view of such an alternative, I say

that the Man of Honour would choose Death, and the Knave would choose servitude. This would be the effect of their human nature as it is; for the honourable man values his Honour more highly than even Life itself, whereas a Knave regards a Life, although covered with shame, as better in his eyes than not to be. The former is, without gainsaying, less guilty than the other; and they can only be proportionately punished by death being inflicted equally upon them both; yet to the one it is a mild punishment when his nobler temperament is taken into account, whereas it is a hard punishment to the other in view of his baser temperament. But, on the other hand, were they all equally condemned to Penal Servitude for life, the honourable man would be too severely punished, while the other, on account of his baseness of nature, would be too mildly punished. In the judgment to be pronounced over a number of criminals united in such a conspiracy, the best Equalizer of Punishment and Crime in the form of public Justice is Death. And besides all this, it has never been heard of, that a Criminal condemned to death on account of a murder has complained that the Sentence inflicted on him more than was right and just; and any one would treat him with scorn if he expressed himself to this effect against it. Otherwise it would be necessary to admit that, although wrong and injustice are not done to the Criminal by the Law, yet the Legislative Power is not entitled to administer this mode of Punishment; and if it did so, it would be in contradiction with itself.

However many they may be who have committed a murder, or have even commanded it, or acted as art and part in it, they ought all to suffer death; for so Justice wills it, in accordance with the Idea of the juridical Power as founded on the universal Laws of Reason. But the number of the Accomplices (*correi*) in such a deed might happen to be so great that the State, in resolving to be without such criminals, would be in danger of soon also being deprived of subjects. But it will not thus dissolve itself, neither must it return to the much worse condition of Nature, in which there would be no external Justice. Nor, above all, should it deaden the sensibilities of the People by the spectacle of Justice being exhibited in the mere carnage of a slaughtering bench. In such circumstances the Sovereign must always be allowed to have it in his power to take the part of the Judge upon himself as a case of Necessity,—and to deliver a Judgment which, instead of the penalty of death, shall assign some other punishment to the Criminals, and thereby preserve a multitude of the People. The penalty of Deportation is relevant in this connection. Such a form of Judgment cannot be carried out according to a public law, but only by an authoritative act of the royal Prerogative, and it may only be applied as an act of grace in individual cases.

Against these doctrines, the Marquis BECCARIA has given forth a different view. Moved by the compassionate sentimentality of a humane feeling, he has asserted that all Capital Punishment is wrong in itself and unjust. He has put forward this view on the ground that the penalty of death could not be contained in the original Civil Contract; for, in that case, every one of the People would have had to consent to lose his life if he murdered any of his fellow citizens. But, it is argued, such a consent is impossible, because no one can thus dispose of his own life.—All this is mere sophistry and perversion of Right. No one undergoes Punishment because he has willed to be punished, but because he has willed a punishable Action; for it is in fact no Punishment when any one experiences what he wills, and it is impossible for any one to will to be punished. To say, "I will to be punished, if I murder anyone," can mean nothing more than, "I submit myself along with all the other citizens to the Laws" ; and if there are any Criminals among the People, these Laws will include Penal Laws. The individual who, as a Co-legislator, enacts Penal Law, cannot possibly be the same Person who, as a Subject, is punished according to the Law; for, *quâ* Criminal, he cannot possibly be regarded as having a voice in the Legislation, the Legislator being rationally viewed as just and holy. If any one, then, enact a Penal Law against himself as a Criminal, it must be the pure juridically law-giving Reason (*homo noumenon*), which subjects him as one capable of crime, and consequently as another Person (*homo phenomenon*), along with all the others in the Civil Union, to this Penal Law. In other words, it is not the People taken distributively, but the Tribunal of public Justice, as distinct from the Criminal, that prescribes Capital Punishment; and it is not to be viewed as if the Social Contract contained the Promise of all the individuals to allow themselves to be punished, thus disposing of themselves and their lives. For if the Right to punish must be grounded upon a promise of the wrongdoer, whereby he is to be regarded as being willing to be punished, it ought also to be left to him to find himself deserving of the Punishment; and the Criminal would thus be his own Judge. The chief error (πρωτονψενδοζ) of this sophistry consists in regarding the judgment of the Criminal himself, necessarily determined by his Reason, that he is under obligation to undergo the loss of his life, as a judgment that must be grounded on a resolution of his Will to take it away himself; and thus the execution of the Right in question is represented as united in one and the same person with the adjudication of the Right.

There are, however, two crimes worthy of death, in respect of which it still remains doubtful whether the Legislature have the Right to deal with them capitally. It is the sentiment of Honour that induces their perpetration. The one originates in a regard for womanly Honour, the other in a regard for military Honour; and in both cases there is a genuine feeling of honour incumbent on the individuals as a Duty. The former is the Crime of MATERNAL INFANTICIDE (*infanticidium maternale*); the latter is the Crime of KILLING A FELLOW-SOLDIER in a Duel (*Commilitonicidium*). Now Legislation cannot take away the shame of an illegitimate birth, nor wipe off the stain attaching from a suspicion of cowardice, to an officer who does not resist an act that would bring him into contempt, by an effort of his own that is superior to the fear of death. Hence it appears that in such circumstances, the individuals concerned are remitted to the State of Nature; and their acts in both cases must be called Homicide, and not Murder, which involves evil intent (*homicidium dolosum*). In all instances the acts are undoubtedly punishable; but they cannot be punished by the Supreme Power with death. An illegitimate child comes into the world outside of the Law which properly regulates Marriage, and it is thus born beyond the pale or constitutional protection of the Law. Such a child is introduced, as it were, like prohibited goods, into the Commonwealth, and as it has no legal right to existence in this way, its destruction might also be ignored; nor can the shame of the mother when her unmarried confinement is known, be removed by any legal ordinance. A subordinate Officer, again, on whom an insult is inflicted, sees himself compelled by the public opinion of his associates to obtain satisfaction; and, as in the state of Nature, the punishment of the offender can only be effected by a Duel, in which his own life is exposed to danger, and not by means of the Law in a Court of Justice. The Duel is therefore adopted as the means of demonstrating his courage as that characteristic upon which the Honour of his profession essentially rests; and this is done even if it should issue in the killing of his adversary. But as such a result takes place publicly and under consent of both parties, although it may be done unwillingly, it

cannot properly be called Murder (*homicidium dolosum*).—What then is the Right in both cases as relating to Criminal Justice? Penal Justice is here in fact brought into great straits, having apparently either to declare the notion of Honour, which is certainly no mere fancy here, to be nothing in the eye of the Law, or to exempt the crime from its due punishment; and thus it would become either remiss or cruel. The knot thus tied is to be resolved in the following way. The Categorical Imperative of Penal Justice, that the killing of any person contrary to the Law must be punished with death, remains in force; but the Legislation itself and the Civil Constitution generally, so long as they are still barbarous and incomplete, are at fault. And this is the reason why the subjective motive–principles of Honour among the People, do not coincide with the standards which are objectively conformable to another purpose; so that the public Justice issuing from the State becomes Injustice relatively to that which is upheld among the People themselves.

55 The Classic Debate

JOEL FEINBERG

The traditional debate among philosophers over the justification of legal punishment has been between partisans of the "retributive" and "utilitarian" theories. Neither the term *retributive* nor the term *utilitarian* has been used with perfect uniformity and precision, but, by and large, those who have been called utilitarians have insisted that punishment of the guilty is at best a necessary evil justified only as a means to the prevention of evils even greater than itself. *Retributivism*, on the other hand, has labeled a large miscellany of theories united only in their opposition to the utilitarian theory. It may best serve clarity, therefore, to define the utilitarian theory with relative precision (as above) and then define retributivism as its logical contradictory, so that the two theories are not only mutually exclusive but also jointly exhaustive.

Discussion of the various varieties of retributivism can then proceed. Perhaps the leading form of the retributive theory includes major elements identifiable in the following formulations:

> It is an end in itself that the guilty should suffer pain.... The primary justification of punishment is always to be found in the fact that an offense has been committed which deserves the punishment, not in any future advantage to be gained by its infliction.[1]
>
> * * *
>
> Punishment is justified only on the ground that wrongdoing merits punishment. It is morally fitting that a person who does wrong should suffer in proportion to his wrongdoing. That a criminal should be punished follows from his guilt, and the severity of the appropriate punishment depends on

Published in previous editions as part of the introduction to this section.

LAWBREAKING= WRONGDOING

the depravity of the act. The state of affairs where a wrongdoer suffers punishment is morally better than one where he does not, and is so irrespective of consequences.[2]

RETRIBUTIVISM

Justification, according to these accounts, must look backward in time to guilt rather than forward to "advantages"; the formulations are rich in moral terminology ("merits," "morally fitting," "wrongdoing," "morally better"); there is great emphasis on *desert.* For those reasons, we might well refer to this as a "moralistic" version of the retributive theory. As such it can be contrasted with a "legalistic" version, according to which punishment is for lawbreaking, not (necessarily) for wrongdoing. Legalistic retributivism holds that the justification of punishment is always to be found in the fact that a rule has been broken for the violation of which a certain penalty is specified, whether or not the offender incurs any moral guilt. The offender, properly apprised in advance of the penalty, voluntarily assumes the risk of punishment, and when he or she receives comeuppance, he or she can have no complaint. As one recent legalistic retributivist put it:

> Punishment is a corollary not of law but of lawbreaking. Legislators do not choose to punish. They hope no punishment will be needed. Their laws would succeed even if no punishment occurred. The criminal makes the essential choice: he "brings it on himself."[3]

Both moralistic and legalistic retributivism have "pure" and "impure" variants. In their pure formulations, they are totally free of utilitarian admixture. Moral or legal guilt (as the case may be) is not only a necessary condition for justified punishment, it is quite sufficient "irrespective of consequences." In the impure formulation, both guilt (moral or legal) and conducibility to good consequences are necessary for justified punishment, but neither is sufficient without the other. This mixed theory could with some propriety be called "impure utilitarianism" as well as "impure retributivism." Since we have stipulated, however, that a retributive theory is one that is not wholly utilitarian, we are committed to the latter usage.

A complete theory of punishment will not only specify the conditions under which punishment should and should not be administered, it will also provide a general criterion for determining the amount or degree of punishment. It is not only unjust to be punished undeservedly and to be let off although meriting punishment, it is also unfair to be punished severely for a minor offense or lightly for a heinous one. What is the right amount of punishment? There is one kind of answer especially distinctive of retributivism in all of its forms: an answer in terms of fittingness or proportion. The punishment must *fit* the crime; its degree must be *proportionate* to the seriousness or moral gravity of the offense. Retributivists are often understandably vague about the practical interpretations of the key notions of fittingness, proportion, and moral gravity. Sometimes aesthetic analogies are employed (such as matching and clashing colors, or harmonious and dissonant chords). Some retributivists, including Immanuel Kant, attempt to apply the ancient principle of *lex talionis* (the law of retaliation): The punishment should match the crime not only in the degree of harm inflicted on its victim, but also in the mode and manner of the infliction: fines for larceny, physical beatings for battery, capital punishment for murder. Other retributivists, however, explicitly reject the doctrine of retaliation in kind; hence, that doctrine is better treated as a logically independent thesis commonly associated with retributivism rather than as an essential component of the theory.

Defined as the exhaustive class of alternatives to the utilitarian theory, retributivism of course is subject to no simple summary. It will be useful to subsequent discussions, however, to summarize that popular variant of the theory which can be called *pure moralistic retributivism* as consisting (at least) of the following propositions:

1. Moral guilt is a necessary condition for justified punishment.
2. Moral guilt is a sufficient condition ("irrespective of consequences") for justified punishment.
3. The proper amount of punishment to be inflicted upon the morally guilty offender is that amount which fits, matches, or is proportionate to the moral gravity of the offense.

That it is never justified to punish a morally blameless person for his or her "offense" (thesis 1) may not be quite self-evident, but it does find strong support in moral common sense. Thesis 2, however, is likely to prove an embarrassment for the pure retributivist, for it would have him or her approve the infliction of suffering on a person (albeit a *guilty* person) even when no good to the offender, the victim, or society at large is likely to result. "How can two wrongs make a right, or two evils a good?" he or she will be asked by the utilitarian, and in this case it is the utilitarian who will claim to speak for "moral common sense." In reply, the pure retributivist is likely to concede that inflicting suffering on an offender is not "good in itself," but will also point out that single acts cannot be judged simply "in themselves" with no concern for the context in which they fit and the events preceding them which are their occasion. Personal sadness is not a "good in itself" either, and yet when it is a response to the perceived sufferings of another it has a unique appropriateness. Glee, considered "in itself," looks much more like an intrinsically good mental state, but glee does not morally fit the perception of another's pain any more than an orange shirt aesthetically fits shocking pink trousers. Similarly, it may be true (the analogy is admittedly imperfect) that "while the moral evil in the offender and the pain of the punishment are each considered separately evils, it is intrinsically good that a certain relation exist or be established between them."[4] In this way the pure retributivist, relying on moral intuitions, can deny that a deliberate imposition of suffering on a human being is either good in itself or good as a means, and yet find it justified, nevertheless, as an essential component of an intrinsically good relation. Perhaps that is to put the point too strongly. All the retributivist needs to establish is that the complex situation preceding the infliction of punishment can be made better than it otherwise would be by the addition to it of the offender's suffering.

The utilitarian is not only unconvinced by arguments of this kind, he or she is also likely to find a "suspicious connection" between philosophical retributivism and the primitive lust for vengeance. The moralistic retributivist protests that he or she eschews anger or any other passion and seeks not revenge, but justice and the satisfaction of desert. Punishment, after all, is not the only kind of treatment we bestow upon persons simply because we think they deserve it. Teachers give students the grades they have earned with no thought of "future advantage," and with eyes firmly fixed on past performance. There is no necessary jubilation at good performance or vindictive pleasure in assigning low grades. And much the same is true of the assignments of rewards, prizes, grants, compensation, civil liability, and so on. Justice requires assignment on the basis of desert alone. To be sure, there is:

> a great danger of revengeful and sadistic tendencies finding vent under the unconscious disguise of a righteous indignation calling for just punishment, since the evil desire for revenge, if not identical with the latter, bears a resemblance to it sufficiently close to deceive those who want an excuse.[5]

Indeed, it is commonly thought that our modern notions of retributive justice have grown out of earlier practices, like the vendetta and the law of deodand, that were through and through expressions of the urge to vengeance.[6] Still, the retributivist replies, it is unfair to *identify* a belief with one of its corruptions, or a modern practice with its historical antecedents. The latter mistake is an instance of the "genetic fallacy" that is committed whenever one confuses an account of how something came to be the way it is with an analysis of what it has become.

The third thesis of the pure moralistic retributivist has also been subject to heavy attack. Can it really be the business of the state to ensure that happiness and unhappiness are distributed among citizens in proportion to their moral deserts? Think of the practical difficulties involved in the attempt simply to apportion pain to moral guilt in a given case, with no help from utilitarian considerations. First of all, it is usually impossible to punish an offender without inflicting suffering on those who love or depend upon him and may themselves be entirely innocent, morally speaking. In that way, punishing the guilty is self-defeating from the moralistic retributive point of view. It will do more to increase than to diminish the

CONTRADICTION

disproportion between unhappiness and desert throughout society. Secondly, the aim of apportioning pain to guilt would in some cases require punishing "trivial" moral offenses, like rudeness, as heavily as more socially harmful crimes, since there can be as much genuine wickedness in the former as the latter. Thirdly, there is the problem of accumulation. Deciding the right amount of suffering to inflict in a given case would entail an assessment of the character of the offender as manifested throughout his or her whole life (and not simply at one weak moment) and also an assessment of his or her total lifelong balance of pleasure and pain. Moreover, there are inevitably inequalities of moral guilt in the commission of the same crime by different offenders, as well as inequalities of suffering from the same punishment. Application of the pure retributive theory then would require the abandonment of fixed penalties for various crimes and the substitution of individuated penalties selected in each case by an authority to fit the offender's uniquely personal guilt and vulnerability.

The utilitarian theory of punishment holds that punishment is never good in itself, but is (like bad-tasting medicine) justified when, and only when, it is a means to such future goods as correction (reform) of the offender, *protection* of society against other offenses from the same offender, and *deterrence* of other would-be offenders. (The list is not exhaustive.) Giving the offender the pain he deserves because of his wickedness is either not a coherent notion, on this theory, or else not a morally respectable independent reason for punishing. In fact, the utilitarian theory arose in the eighteenth century as part of a conscious reaction to cruel and uneconomical social institutions (including prisons) that were normally defended, if at all, in righteously moralistic terms.

For purposes of clarity, the utilitarian theory of punishment should be distinguished from utilitarianism as a general moral theory. The standard of right conduct generally, according to the latter, is conducibility to good consequences. Any act at all, whether that of a private citizen, a legislator, or a judge, is morally right if and only if it is likely, on the best evidence, to do more good or less harm all around than any alternative conduct open to the actor. (The standard for judging the goodness of consequences, in turn, for Jeremy Bentham and the early utilitarians was the amount of human happiness they contained, but many later utilitarians had more complicated conceptions of intrinsic value.) All proponents of general utilitarianism, of course, are also supporters of the utilitarian theory of punishment, but there is no logical necessity that in respect to punishment a utilitarian be a general utilitarian across the board.

The utilitarian theory of punishment can be summarized in three propositions parallel to those used above to summarize pure moralistic retributivism. According to this theory:

1. Social utility (correction, prevention, deterrence, etc.) is a necessary condition for justified punishment.
2. Social utility is a sufficient condition for justified punishment.
3. The proper amount of punishment to be inflicted upon the offender is that amount which will do the most good or the least harm to all those who will be affected by it.

The first thesis enjoys the strongest support from common sense, though not so strong as to preclude controversy. For the retributivist, as has been seen, punishing the guilty is an end in itself quite apart from any gain in social utility. The utilitarian is apt to reply that if reform of the criminal could be secured with no loss of deterrence by simply giving him or her a pill that would have the same effect, then nothing would be lost by not punishing him or her, and the substitute treatment would be "sheer gain."

Thesis 2, however, is the utilitarian's greatest embarrassment. The retributivist opponent argues forcefully against it that in certain easily imaginable circumstances it would justify punishment of the (legally) innocent, a consequence that all would regard as a moral abomination. Some utilitarians deny that punishment of the innocent could *ever* be the alternative that has the best consequences in social utility, but this reply seems arbitrary and dogmatic. Other utilitarians claim that "punishment of the innocent" is a self-contradiction. The concept of punishment, they argue,[7] itself implies hard treatment imposed upon the guilty as a conscious and deliberate response to their guilt. That guilt is part of the very definition of punishment, these writers claim, is shown by the absurdity of saying "I am punishing you for something you have not done," which sounds very much like "I am curing you even though you are not sick." Since all punishment is understood to be for guilt, they conclude, they can hardly be interpreted as advocating punishing without guilt. H. L. A. Hart[8] calls this move a "definitional stop," and charges that it is an "abuse of definition," and indeed it is, if put forward by a proponent of the general utilitarian theory. If the right act in all contexts is the one that is likely to have the best consequences, then conceivably the act of framing an innocent man could sometimes be right; and the question of whether such mistreatment of the innocent party could properly be called "punishment" is a mere question of words having no bearing on the utilitarian's embarrassment. If, on the other hand, the definitional stop is employed by a defender of the utilitarian theory of the justification of punishment who is not a utilitarian across the board, then it seems to be a legitimate argumentative move. Such a utilitarian is defending official infliction of hard treatment (deprivation of liberty, suffering, etc.) on *those who are legally guilty,* a practice to which he or she refers by using the word *punishment,* as justified when and only when there is probably social utility in it.

No kind of utilitarian, however, will have plausible recourse to the definitional stop in defending thesis 3 from the retributivist charge that it would, in certain easily imaginable circumstances, justify excessive or insufficient penalties. The appeal again is to moral common sense: It would be manifestly unfair to inflict a mere two-dollar fine on a convicted murderer, or life imprisonment, under a balance of terror policy, for parking offenses. In either case, the punishment imposed would violate the retributivist's thesis 3, that the punishment be proportional to the moral gravity of the offense. And yet, if these were the penalties likely to have the best effects generally, the utilitarian in the theory of punishment would be committed to their support. He or she could

not argue that excessive or deficient penalties are not "really" punishments. Instead he would have to argue, as does Jeremy Bentham, that the proper employment of the utilitarian method simply could not lead to penalties so far out of line with our moral intuitions as the retributivist charges.

So far vengeance has not been mentioned except in the context of charge and countercharge between theorists who have no use for it. There are writers, however, who have kind words for vengeance and give it a central role in their theories of the justification of punishment. We can call these approaches the Vindictive Theory of Punishment (to distinguish them from legalistic and moralistic forms of retributivism) and then subsume its leading varieties under either the utilitarian or the retributive rubrics. Vindictive theories are of three different kinds: (1) The *escape-valve version,* commonly associated with the names of James Fitzjames Stephen and Oliver Wendell Holmes, Jr., and currently in favor with some psychoanalytic writers, holds that legal punishment is an orderly outlet for aggressive feelings, which would otherwise demand satisfaction in socially disruptive ways. The prevention of private vendettas through a state monopoly on vengeance is one of the chief ways in which legal punishment has social utility. The escape-valve theory is thus easily assimilated by the utilitarian theory of punishment. (2) The *hedonistic version* of the vindictive theory finds the justification of punishment in the pleasure it gives people (particularly the victim of the crime and his or her loved ones) to see the criminal suffer for the crime. For most utilitarians, and certainly for Bentham, any kind of pleasure— even spiteful, sadistic, or vindictive pleasure, just insofar as it *is* pleasure—counts as a good in the computation of social utility, just as pain—any kind of pain—counts as an evil. (This is sufficient to discredit hedonistic utilitarianism thoroughly, according to its retributivist critics.) The hedonistic version of the vindictive theory, then, is also subsumable under the utilitarian rubric. Finally, (3) the *romantic version* of the vindictive theory, very popular among the uneducated, holds that the justification of punishment is to be found in the emotions of hate and anger it expresses, these emotions being those allegedly felt by all normal or right-thinking people. I call this theory "romantic," despite certain misleading associations of that word, because, like any philosophical theory so labeled, it holds that certain emotions and the actions they inspire are self-certifying, needing no further justification. It is therefore not a kind of utilitarian theory and must be classified as a variety of retributivism, although in its emphasis on feeling it is in marked contrast to more typical retributive theories that eschew emotion and emphasize proportion and desert.

Some anthropologists have traced vindictive feelings and judgments to an origin in the "tribal morality" that universally prevails in primitive cultures, and which presumably governed the tribal life of our own prehistoric ancestors. If an anthropologist turned his attention to our modern criminal codes, he would discover evidence that tribalism has never entirely vacated its position in the criminal law. There are some provisions for which the vindictive theory (in any of its forms) would provide a ready rationale, but for which the utilitarian and moralistic retributivist theories are hard put to discover a plausible defense. Completed crimes, for example, are punished more severely than attempted crimes that fail for accidental reasons. This should not be surprising since the more harm caused the victim, his or her

loved ones, and those of the public who can identify imaginatively with them, the more anger there will be at the criminal. If the purpose of punishment is to satisfy that anger, then we should expect that those who succeed in harming will be punished more than the bunglers who fail, even if the motives and intentions of the bunglers were every bit as wicked.

NOTES

1. Ewing, A. C. *The Morality of Punishment*. London: Kegan Paul, 1929. 13.
2. Rawls, John. "Concepts of Rules." *The Philosophical Review* 54 (1955): 4–5.
3. Mabbott, J. D. "Punishment." *Mind* 58 (1939): 161.
4. Ewing, A. C. *Ethics*. New York: Macmillan, 1953. 169–70.
5. Ewing, *Morality of Punishment*, supra, note 1, at 27.
6. See Holmes, O. W. Jr. *The Common Law*. Boston: Little, Brown, 1881; and Maine, Henry. *Ancient Law*. Boston: Beacon Press, 1963.
7. See, for example, Quinton, Anthony. "On Punishment." *Analysis* 14 (1954): 1933–42.
8. Hart, H. L. A. *Punishment and Responsibility*. New York and Oxford: Oxford University Press, 1968. 5–6.

56   Responsibility, Restoration, and Retribution

R. A. DUFF

Retributivism, the idea that what justifies criminal punishment is that it is deserved for past criminal wrongdoing, famously (or notoriously) underwent a revival in the 1970s—a revival whose influence is still evident both in penal philosophy and in penal policy. With the benefit of hindsight, we can now more clearly identify a number of problems with that revival: what we must then ask is whether those problems are fatal. Can a robust version of retributivism (I comment later on

what makes for a robust version) be rendered plausible in our contemporary penal and philosophical climate, or is it time to move on beyond retributivism to some quite different kind of penal philosophy?

I will argue that penal philosophy and policy should retain a central place for a suitably understood idea of retribution. This argument involves paying closer attention than penal theorists often pay to the criminal process that precedes

From *Restorative Justice and Criminal Justice: Competing or Reconciliable Paradigms?* Ed. A. von Hirsch. Oxford: Hart Publishing, 2003. 43–59. Reprinted with permission of the publisher.

punishment and to the conception of responsible citizenship that should structure such a process. It will also involve showing how a practice of appropriately retributive punishments can meet some of the main concerns of advocates of "restorative justice" by providing a better account than they often provide of what needs to be restored in the aftermath of crime, and how it can be restored. These tasks will occupy sections III and IV, preceded (in section II) by a discussion of the idea of crime as that to which punishment is a response. First, however, we should attend briefly to the problems that impaired the retributivist revival.

I. PROBLEMS FOR RETRIBUTIVISM

We should not underplay the importance of the retributivist revival of the 1970s, but we must also recognize its weaknesses. One weakness was that it was more forceful as a negative critique of the consequentialist attitudes that had dominated penal thinking in the preceding decades than as advocacy for a robust or "positive" retributivism that takes the aim of punishment to be the imposition of an offender's penal deserts. That negative critique could trade, in part, on the perceived failure of consequentialist policies of crime prevention to achieve their overambitious aims, but that failure was relative rather than total. The cry that "Nothing works"[1] proved to be as much an exaggeration as the extravagant claims about what would work to which it was responding: a more modest attention to specific kinds of program focused on specific kinds of offense or offender, guided by a more realistic conception of what should count as working, showed that some kinds of penal provision can be modestly effective in reducing some kinds of crime by some kinds of offender. But the retributivist critique did not really depend on the efficiency or otherwise of consequentialist programs, since its real target was the moral inadequacy of a purely consequentialist perspective. The most salient inadequacy was the failure of any such perspective to do justice to the rights of the (relatively) innocent: the right of those who have committed no crime not to be subjected to the coercive attentions of the penal system; the right of those who have committed

crimes not to be punished unduly harshly. But even if strict consequentialism is open to such objections, this does not force us to abandon primarily consequentialist penal thinking: all it requires is the adoption of the kind of "side-constrained" model that became popular in subsequent years. We are to pursue the consequential ends that give punishment its "general justifying aim," but we may not do so by means that violate the nonconsequentialist demands of justice or fairness. Nor indeed does this require us to accept even a negative form of retributivism, which tells us that we may not punish the innocent, or punish the guilty more harshly than they deserve: at least the first of these constraints may be explained, as Hart explained it, by appeal not to retributive desert, but to the importance of choice. Citizens should, as far as possible, be subject to the coercive penal attention of the law only when they have chosen to act in a way that they were warned would make them liable to such attention.[2]

Some retributivist revivalists also, and more pertinently, raised objections to the ways in which consequentialist approaches portrayed and treated not the innocent, but the guilty. If, for instance, the aim of penal treatment was supposed to reform offenders so that they would become law-abiding citizens, the objection was that this would (or might) treat them not as responsible agents, but as objects to be manipulated or reconditioned.[3] If the aim was to deter potential offenders, the objection was that this would treat offenders as means to some social end, in breach of the Kantian injunction to respect each other as ends. If such objections as these are sound, they undermine not only purely consequentialist accounts of punishment, but also side-constrained accounts that preserve a consequentialist-justifying aim, since it is the very pursuit of that aim that is argued to violate the demands of respect for responsible agency. However, this kind of objection was not developed in enough plausible detail to persuade those who were not yet anticonsequentialist. Reformative or rehabilitative programs were admittedly often advocated (even if they were not operated) in ways that did not portray those subjected to them as responsible agents—and some of their advocates would argue that this was wholly appropriate, either because the idea of responsible agency was a myth that we should now abandon, or because, even if responsible agency was still a reality, offenders were not responsible agents.[4] But not every kind of reformative program had this character; and if to be a responsible agent is to be one whose conduct can be guided by a grasp of reasons for action, deterrent punishment can be said to treat those against whom it is threatened as responsible agents, since it offers reasons for refraining from crime. It is, of course, still true that those who are punished are used as means to deter others (assuming that any plausible deterrent theory must appeal to general and not merely to special deterrence). But apart from the obscurity of just what the Kantian proscription means, what it formally proscribes is treating others *merely* as means; to which deterrent theorists can respond that, if punishment is conditional on the voluntary commission of a crime, it does not treat the person punished *merely* as a means.[5]

However, even if critics of consequentialism can render normatively implausible not only a pure, but even a side-constrained consequentialism, this does not yet deliver retributivism. It could appear to do so only if, first, we assume that these two types of account exhaust the possible justifications of criminal punishment—that if it is to be justified, its justification must be either consequentialist or retributivist; and, second, we beg the institution by assuming that punishment must be justified—that the task for normative penal theory is to ask not whether, but precisely how, punishment is justified. The first assumption is at best arguable, though if we use "retributivism" (unhelpfully) to cover any and every nonconsequentialist justification of punishment it becomes a truism. The second assumption is clearly wrong, though the lack of proper attention to abolitionist ideas among penal theorists for so many years suggests that it was often implicitly made.[6] A full-scale retributivist revival required not merely a critique (however powerful) of consequentialism, but a normatively plausible account of punishment as retribution; which brings us to the second major weakness in the retributive revival of the 1970s.

The intuition that the guilty deserve to suffer may be widely and deeply felt, as becomes evident, at least in Britain and the United States, in the aftermath of any horrific crime. But intuitions, however deeply felt and widely shared, cannot simply be accepted: they must be critically analyzed and appraised. In particular, in the context of punishment, we need to ask precisely *what* criminal wrongdoers deserve to suffer; *why* they deserve to suffer it (how it is that crime makes such suffering appropriate); and why it should be the business of the state to create and maintain an institution whose purpose is to impose that deserved suffering.

Retributive revivalists did try to answer these questions, but their answers were not, on the whole, persuasive, which meant that positive retributivism still looked too much like an intuition in search of a theory. One popular answer, for instance, which did at least address the questions noted above, was that in committing a crime, the criminal took unfair advantage of the law-abiding self-restraint of those who refrained from crime, thus gaining for himself an unjust benefit. Punishment, as the imposition of a burden that matched that benefit, served to remove his unfair advantage and restore the balance of benefits and burdens that the crime disturbed; this was a proper task for the state, since it was a matter of doing justice to and between citizens. Such a view still has its supporters, who have worked hard to render it more plausible—with some success;[7] but it still seems to its critics to fail to capture either the reasons why we should criminalize such wrongs as murder and rape, or the point or focus of convicting and punishing those who perpetrate them. I cannot discuss other retributivist answers here, but simply note that this challenge, to make plausible normative sense of the idea that punishment is justified as retribution for past wrongdoing, is one that retributivist revivalists struggled to meet.

Their task was made harder by two limitations on their approach. First, punishment was too often portrayed simply as some (unspecified) kind of burden or suffering to be imposed by the state on a passive recipient—which makes all too tempting the abolitionist's portrayal of punishment as a matter of "delivering pain,"[8] and all too reasonable the consequent thought that delivering pain cannot be a proper task or ambition for a liberal state, or for a polity that aspires to be humane. If we are to make plausible sense of the idea of retribution, we need to attend more carefully to the character and meaning of the suffering that punishment is meant to involve, and to the kind of response that it must aim to evoke in those who are punished. It is indeed a defining feature of punishment that it is intended to be burdensome, or in some sense painful, but that is not to say that the immediate aim of punishment must be understood simply as the imposition of a burden or the delivery of pain. Retributivists would do better to begin by offering a richer characterization of an appropriate formal response to wrongdoing, and then show how that response must be burdensome or in some appropriate sense painful if it is to have the meaning it requires. I will return to this point in section IV.

The second limitation on many retributivist accounts (indeed, on many accounts, whether retributivist or nonretributivist) of criminal punishment is that they tend to treat punishment in isolation from its institutional context, and in particular from the criminal process by which it is preceded. This reflects a general failure by philosophical theorists to take the criminal process, and in particular the criminal trial, seriously enough, as if that process serves simply to connect crime to punishment by identifying those who are eligible for punishment and by determining the punishment for which they are eligible. We will understand punishment better if we see it as part of a larger process through which we respond, as a polity, to criminal wrongdoing—and if we pay more attention to the role that defendants play in that larger process.

Retributivist theorizing about punishment has moved on since the 1970s; more recent theorists have tried to meet the challenges faced by the earlier revivalists. This is not the place for a survey of recent retributivist thinking.[9] Instead, I will briefly note some new challenges that retributivist thought faces, before going on to show how both the old and the new challenges can be met. One striking point is that retributivism is now challenged in both its positive and negative guises. For a long time it seemed that even if ambitiously positive forms of retributivism could not be made normatively plausible, a negative retributivism (or, at least, the constraints that it implies) was an important part of any acceptable penal theory or practice: that is, whatever aims punishment should be used to serve, we should not punish those whom we know to be innocent, or punish the guilty more harshly than they deserve.[10] It might not be clear whether such principles are best explained by appeals to retributive desert, or to a nonretributive idea of fairness,[11] or to a sophisticated form of consequentialism (Braithwaite and Pettit 1990),[12] but it was very widely agreed that a justifiable system of criminal punishment must respect them. Hence the attractions of "mixed" theory, including "limiting retributivism,"[13] which seemed to do justice both to the retributivist thought that punishment must be warranted by past criminal wrongdoing and to the consequentialist concern that any such practice can be justified only if it secures consequential goods sufficient to outweigh its manifest costs. However, even such a modest retributivism faces at least three new (or renewed) kinds of challenge.

The first comes most vividly from proponents of "therapeutic justice," discussed by Doug Husak,[14] and reflects a renewed confidence that some things do work—that, for instance, specialist courts advised by sensible experts, with access to adequate resources, and with appropriately modest ambitions, can impose sentences that will achieve real successes in crime reduction and the rehabilitation of offenders. This movement challenges retributivist ideas not merely because it is consequentialist in spirit, since the same is true of the familiar kinds of side-constrained consequentialism, but because, like many therapeutic movements, it is impatient with the insistence on a backward-looking proportionality (at least one that does relative justice as between different offenders) that characterizes any retributivism. What must matter, from this perspective, is what is needed to achieve the desired results (results that will, of course, benefit the offender as much as others); although the costs and burdens must be proportionate to that benefit, it would be absurd, for instance, to scale back the program that an offender is required to undertake simply on the grounds that it is disproportionately burdensome relative to the offense that brought him before the court, and to the sentences that others who committed similar offenses have received.

A second challenge comes from "preventive" justice—from the increasing tendency for governments concerned with "security," and the efficient prevention of crime and other kinds of harm, to adopt measures that aim to preempt criminal conduct rather than just to respond to it. Some such measures are imposed on convicted offenders by way of extra or indefinite terms of detention for reasons of public safety or protection; others involve what are formally civil rather than criminal orders that impose restrictions on people who have not as yet been convicted of any offense in order to prevent the crimes that, it is feared, they or others might commit.[15] Such provisions are familiar in the context of offenses related to terrorism, and might be seen as posing a threat not so much to retributive conceptions of punishment as to the very idea of punishment as a response to past wrongdoing. That threat appears most dramatically when it is suggested, explicitly or implicitly, that those who commit terrorist attacks should be treated not as defendants or offenders within the framework, and so under the protection, of the criminal law, but as enemies, outlaws, or "unlawful combatants";[16] but it is not far from the surface whenever politicians and policy makers are swept up by the idea of a "war" against crime—or against certain kinds of crime.

A third challenge comes from the by-now-multifarious forms of "restorative justice," itself the offspring of older abolitionist ideas. This challenge, too, is not merely to retributivism as a particular penal philosophy (although the contrast is often drawn between "restorative" and "retributive" justice), but to the very practice of punishment—and indeed to the very idea of criminal law. More precisely, that is the challenge that comes from some radical advocates of "restorative justice." Some programs or practices that are called "restorative" figure as part of or complements to the traditional criminal justice processes of trial, conviction, and punishment. They might,

for instance, take place during (though not formally as part of) the offender's sentence,[17] or they might take place between conviction and sentencing, and affect the sentencing decision, while the sentence might itself include participation in a restorative program.[18] It is important to think about what the aims of such processes should be and how those aims relate to the traditional aims of punishment. The following discussion bears on these questions. However, my main focus will be on restorative justice processes that are seen not as aspects of or complements to the criminal justice process, but as alternatives to it, since they raise more sharply the questions I want to consider about the proper role of retribution in penal theory. Rather than being prosecuted, convicted, and sentenced, the offender agrees to enter a restorative process, which typically involves a meeting with the victim and other interested parties, and (it is hoped) an agreement on some kind of reparative action.[19] Even here there are, of course, more and less radical approaches. The less radical approach portrays restorative justice programs as modes of diversion from the criminal process—a kind of diversion that is, it is claimed, appropriate for certain kinds of offense or offender (notably for relatively minor victimizing offenses and for young offenders), but that would not, it is implicitly admitted, be appropriate for all kinds of offense and offender. The more radical approach portrays restorative justice not merely as an alternative to, but as a replacement for, criminal justice: we should (as far and as soon as is practicable) abandon the entire apparatus of criminal law, criminal process, and criminal punishment in favor of more "civil," informal practices that aim to repair harm and restore relationships rather than to condemn wrongs and punish their perpetrators. It is this conception of restorative justice that carries forward the ambitions of abolitionist theorists who similarly sought to abolish not merely this or that kind of especially oppressive or destructive punishment, nor indeed (though this is ambitious enough) criminal punishment as such, but all of criminal law, in favor of processes very like those now urged by radical advocates of restorative justice.[20]

According to such radical critics of criminal law, we should talk and think not of crimes that must be condemned and punished, but of "conflicts" or "troubles" that need to be resolved or repaired. We should focus not on wrongs whose perpetrators must be prosecuted by the formal force of the law and subjected to the pains of criminal punishment, but on harms that need to be repaired and relationships that need to be restored. In response to such conflicts or troubles we should not focus on "the offender" as the person whom we must condemn and punish, but on all those with an interest in the matter. Instead of criminal courts that subject lone defendants to the accusing, condemnatory attention of the criminal law, "steal" conflicts from those to whom they properly belong, and inhibit any productive engagement with those conflicts by their abstractions and their professionalism, we need informal fora in which those involved in the affair, either directly or as concerned fellow members of the local community, can come together to work out what to do. Instead of imposing punishments that aim simply to deliver pain, we need to help the interested parties come to agree on reparative measures that will mend the harm and restore the relationships that have been damaged.

I do not suggest that this kind of radical abolitionism is common among advocates of restorative justice, or that they typically share all its concerns and attitudes. However, I do think that we can make progress toward a better understanding of the need for punishment as retribution, and of the role that ideas of repair and restoration can properly play in a system of criminal law and punishment, by starting with radical abolitionism and seeing where and why it goes wrong. We will then also be able to appraise less radical types of restorative justice—and, I will argue, to see that the kind of restoration that crime makes necessary is, properly understood, compatible with retributive punishment (once *that* idea is properly understood).

It is this abolitionist challenge that provides the focus for this essay. Part of what motivates the challenge, and gives it its moral force, is the manifest destructiveness and inhumanity of so much of what now passes for punishment in our existing institutions of criminal justice; another part lies in the rather crude brutalism of some retributivist thought, with its emphasis on making offenders suffer—on imposing a kind of pain that is purely backward-looking and that lacks any redemptive or constructive character. It must, of course, remain a defining feature of any penal theory that is to be recognizably retributive that what it justifies is precisely the imposition of something burdensome or unwelcome, and of any theory that is to count as robustly retributivist that what it justifies is precisely the intention or attempt to impose such burdens; but we will see in what follows that such intentions and attempts may not be best described simply as the intention or attempt "to make the guilty suffer."

There is another kind of abolitionism that I cannot discuss here—one that does not reject the very idea of the criminal law, but does reject or seek to undermine the idea of responsible agency on which criminal punishment depends, arguing that we should be looking instead for efficient kinds of treatment that will prevent further criminal conduct (though one question is whether the idea of crime can survive the removal of that conception of responsible criminal agency). A simple version of this kind of abolitionism is found in psychiatrists who portray crime as a (symptom of) mental disorder;[21] another is found in Wootton's argument that we should cease to attend to *mens rea* as a condition of guilt, or to try to distinguish the culpably responsible from the excusably disordered.[22] This species of abolitionism offers a salutary reminder that criminal punishment can be less oppressively coercive, and can be subject to more stringent principled constraints, than some of the alternatives to it;[23] but what matters for present purposes is that it denies or sidesteps the idea of personal responsibility, whereas advocates both of restorative justice and of retributive punishment insist on the importance of personal responsibility—although they differ sharply in their understandings of what such responsibility brings with it.

II. CRIMES, WRONGS, AND HARMS

Before we can talk usefully about criminal punishment, we must talk about crime itself: although it might not be a necessary truth that crime entails punishment, since we could retain a kind of criminal law while doing away with punishment, criminal punishment presupposes crime as that for which it is imposed. Furthermore, as I noted above, the most radical kind of penal abolitionism argues not that we should respond to crime in nonpunitive ways, but that we should cease to use the concept of crime at all—that we should see our social world through a different conceptual lens.

The criminal law deals in wrongdoing: in its substantive mode, it defines certain kinds of conduct as (criminally) wrongful; in its adjudicative mode, it provides the procedures through which accusations of the commission of such wrongs can be dealt with; in its punitive mode, it provides for the punishments (or other disposals) that are to be imposed on the perpetrators of such wrongs. To understand its punitive mode, we must understand its substantive mode (the topic of this section) and its adjudicative mode (the topic of section III).

To say that the criminal law deals in wrongdoing is, of course, not yet to say that it deals in *moral* wrongdoing: a system of law could define as "legal wrongs" conduct that violates its rules without implying that such conduct is morally wrong. Indeed, to insist that the criminal law does and should deal in moral wrongdoing might be understood to imply a type of legal moralism, according to which the proper aim of criminal law is to condemn and punish moral wickedness, that many contemporary liberals reject. Now, I do think that legal moralism rests on an important truth about the nature of criminal law as a distinctive type of legal regulation: what is defined as criminal must be so defined because it is believed to be morally wrong.[24] The point is not just that, as even staunch opponents of legal moralism might agree,[25] moral wrongfulness should be a necessary condition of criminalization: it is, more ambitiously, that the criminal law's focus should be on the moral wrongfulness of the criminalized

conduct—that that is the proper object of criminalization.[26] I do not mean by this that we have reason to criminalize every kind of moral wrongdoing (Moore 1997):[27] a sensible legal moralism will incorporate the familiar liberal view that some kinds of moral wrongdoing are, "in brief and crude terms, not the law's business"—not even in principle the criminal law's business.[28] Crimes are "public" wrongs, which is to say that they are wrongs that properly concern "the public"—all citizens, simply by virtue of their shared membership of the polity. We must look to political theory—a theory of the proper aims and functions of the state, and an accompanying account of the nature of the civic enterprise of living together as a polity—if we are to work out what kinds of wrongs are in that sense public.[29]

The key claim for present purposes concerns not the precise contours of such a theory (of the state, of political community, of the role of criminal law in a political community, and thus ultimately of criminalization), but that it will have a place for criminal law as a practice focused on wrongdoing. I take it that it does not need arguing that our extralegal, social lives have an essential moral dimension. Though there are various conceptual lenses through which we see our own and others' actions (whether we are in deliberative or evaluative mode), and though that of morality might not be omnipresent or even always the most important, it is nonetheless one essential lens. The moral character of what we and others do is significant, and both our deliberation and our judgment should sometimes focus on it. Nor indeed need abolitionists deny (although some seem inclined to) that this is true of our extralegal lives. What concerns them is the question of whether and how the law should view us through that lens. To see why it should, and why we therefore need a criminal law that takes wrongdoing seriously, we can begin simply, with a limited, shallow description of a kind of occurrence to which advocates and critics of criminal law might respond rather differently. It is established, let us suppose, that A deliberately broke a window of B's house (knowing that it was not his own house) in order to get in and take whatever items of salable value he could find; that he took B's laptop and some money (without B's consent), intending to sell the laptop to make some money; and that he caused various kinds of damage in his search for valuables.

That is a description on whose truth we should be able to agree, whatever our view of the criminal law and of punishment—partly, of course, because it is a very limited description. It is limited in the "thickness" of the concepts it applies: it does not talk of theft, or dishonesty, or of a violation of B's home.[30] It is limited in its scope: it tells us nothing about either A's or B's background, condition, or social or financial status; nothing about the social and political conditions under which they live; nothing about any past dealings or acquaintanceship between A and B. It is limited in its depth: it tells us nothing about A's motives, beyond his concern to obtain money, or about the life and character from which this action emerged, and nothing about the psychological impact on B. Nor indeed does it tell us who "we" are in relation to the affair: whether we are neighbors of A or B, or both; or friends or family; or residents of the same village, city, or country; or observers who just read about it from afar.

On the face of it, this occurrence involves both harm and wrong. B suffers material harm to his house, he loses some of his possessions, and a fuller description might show that he has also suffered psychological distress and longer-term harm (anxiety, fear, insecurity). As so far described, the occurrence involves no harm to A, but a fuller description might reveal that he too has suffered various kinds of harm—the poverty or drug use that led him to see this as the best or only way to obtain money; the fear of detection; perhaps the remorse at what he did to B. Now, the harms that B suffers, as so far described (at least if we leave out the details of what he felt or feels), can be identified and understood as harms without reference to the actions that caused them:[31] they could, in principle, have resulted from natural causes. At first glance, however, we should also say that A has wronged B: only at first glance, since it could turn out, on closer inquiry, that no wrong was done (one can imagine various accounts that would have this implication); but at

least at first glance, since as so far described, it looks as if A has wrongfully invaded B's house, stolen his possessions, and damaged his property; and perhaps also presumptively, since the facts as so far stated seem to warrant an inference of wrongdoing absent some countervailing explanation.

One question that I cannot pursue here concerns the relationship between the harm that B has undoubtedly suffered and the wrong that A has presumptively done to B. It is at the least arguable that if A has wronged B, this does not merely add a wrong to that harm, but changes the character of the harm itself. We cannot separate what B has suffered into a set of harms plus a set of wrongs, but should rather see being burgled, suffering theft, and willful damage to one's property as a harmful wrong or a wrongful harm that cannot be analyzed into two distinct constituents.[32] If that is right, it poses a serious problem for abolitionists who urge us to focus on harms rather than on wrongs,[33] since an adequate understanding of the harms—one that does justice to what those who suffer them have suffered—will need to include reference to the wrongfulness of those harms. Even apart from that possibility, however, we must ask whether the polity's public conception of this affair between A and B, as determined by its formal, legal institutions, should focus solely on the harm that was caused (and on who is to pay for it, and on how that question should be determined), or should also take formal notice of the wrong that B has presumptively suffered. Surely the obvious answer is that it should—and we collectively should—take such formal notice. We owe this, we might say, to victims of such wrongs: as fellow citizens, we owe it to them to notice and to care about what they have suffered—and what they have suffered includes the wrong. We owe it, we might also say, to ourselves collectively, as members of a polity that defines itself by a shared commitment to certain values, including those at stake in this affair: for to be committed to a value is to be committed to taking note of its violation. But we also owe it, we might add, to A (to all those who commit such wrongs). To take each other seriously as citizens is, in part, to take proper notice of our "public" conduct, including our commissions of public wrongs.

More generally, an essential part of what makes a society a political community (rather than a mere collection of unassociated strangers) is some shared understanding of the values that define their civic life. Central to those values is a conception of how people should behave toward each other, of the (perhaps fairly minimal) constraints they should observe in their dealings with each other. The more significant of those values and constraints require some public, formal expression, and this is the first function of criminal law as a distinctive type of law: it constitutes a public declaration and definition of those wrongs of which, as violations of its core defining values, the polity should take formal note. There is, of course, much more to be said about how those values and the correlative wrongs are to be identified, and about the proper scope of such a criminal law;[34] nor have I yet said anything about how we should collectively and formally respond to the commission of such wrongs. All I have suggested so far is that we do, as a polity, need a formal institution with this central feature of the criminal law: an institution that defines, and by implication condemns, a range of public wrongs. The question then is this: How should a polity respond to the (actual or suspected) commission of such wrongs?

III. RESPONSIBILITY AND CALLING TO ACCOUNT

A polity that takes its self-defining values seriously, and that takes its members seriously (a polity, that is, whose members take each other seriously) as citizens who are both bound and protected by those values, cannot ignore violations of those values or the wrongs that citizens do to each other.[35] One way in which it takes note of such wrongs is by publicly defining and declaring them as wrongs: this is, I suggested in the previous section, an initial function of criminal law. But what should it do after the event?

Part of what it should do, part of what we should do as citizens, concerns the victims of such wrongs: we owe them a recognition of what they have suffered, and help in coping with it (though it will not always be clear what kind of "coping" is possible). In part, of course, that recognition and help will focus on whatever harms they have suffered, as sympathy for that suffering and assistance in trying to repair the harm (in so far as it is reparable). However, they have suffered not just harm, but wrong, and our collective response must address that dimension as well. Now, for two reasons, we can most appropriately address that dimension by tackling, or trying to tackle, the person(s) who wronged them.

First, it is plausible to think that part of what we owe to the victims is to seek to call those who wronged them to account for those wrongs—and that this is also something we owe to ourselves collectively in so far as we share those wrongs as their victims' fellow citizens.[36] This is a common complaint by victims when the police do not investigate "their" crime with what they take to be sufficient commitment, or when prosecutors do not bring charges against "their" offender: that "their" crimes have not been taken seriously enough. It is also a common motivation for civil suits in cases of allegedly negligent killing: those who lost loved ones in a train crash, or in a workplace accident, or in a hospital, and who suspect that this was due to negligence by the rail company or the employer, or doctors, might bring a case whose formal aim must be compensation, but whose real aim (they argue) is to call to account those whose negligence caused their loss. What they properly seek is not (just) compensation for whatever independently identifiable harm they have suffered, but an accounting for the wrong.

Second, once we see what is properly involved in "tackling" the wrongdoer, we can also see that this is something that we collectively owe to those who commit as well as to those who suffer such wrongs. Granted, on one familiar but crude kind of retributive view, what victims properly demand is that those who wronged them be made to suffer: this goes with the idea that what wrongdoers deserve is to suffer, and that the polity's first or primary responsibility is to make sure that they suffer. Such a demand for suffering is admittedly one aspect both of public opinion and of many victims' responses to their crimes, and if we focus on that demand, it is indeed hard to see its satisfaction as something that we owe to those who are to be made to suffer: if that is what punishment is, the idea of a right to be punished is as absurd as its critics claim. However, this is not the only salient demand, nor, I think, is it the demand on which we should initially focus.[37] We should instead focus on the demand that the wrongdoer be called or held to account for what he has done—that he answer for it. This is, I suspect, as powerfully felt a demand as the demand that he be made to suffer, as is perhaps evidenced most clearly in the case of international criminal trials: what matters, to many people, is not so much that those who have perpetrated "crimes against humanity" be punished (what punishment, we might ask, could fit such wrongs?), but that they be called to public account for what they have done. But to call someone to account is to treat and address him as a responsible agent, and as a fellow member of a relevant normative community. I can be called to account only if I am a responsible agent who can be expected to answer for what he has done, and only by fellows who are themselves committed to the values for an alleged violation of which I am now called to account, and who participate in the particular form of life within which I am thus called. To call someone to account for an alleged wrong, however condemnatory that calling is, is therefore also to show him a certain kind of respect, or even concern, as a fellow who is, along with us, both bound and protected by the values to which that calling appeals.

Advocates of restorative justice often also make the idea of responsibility salient in their accounts of how we should collectively respond to (what we now see as) crime. What is important, they argue, is to develop structures and procedures through which responsibility can be discussed, negotiated, accepted, and discharged—through which people can come to take responsibility for what they have done, and work out how to discharge that responsibility through reparative actions. They differ, however, over just what those structures and procedures should be, and sometimes fail to appreciate the significance of the distinctive kind of calling to account that (I will argue) the criminal law can provide.

One important point that should have emerged from the previous section is that we must attend not just to harms, but to wrongs. It is not just a matter of determining (or negotiating) responsibility for a harm that was caused, but of determining responsibility for wrongdoing. The former kind of responsibility would be standardly discharged by repairing or paying for the harm. We need to ask how the latter can be discharged, and what goes with accepting it, but the point to note here is that a process that is to do justice to victims and to what they have suffered must aim not merely to call a harm causer to account, or bring him to recognize his responsibility for that harm, but to call a wrongdoer to account for the wrong he has done.

Further important issues are raised by the emphasis that advocates of restorative justice often place on informal negotiation between the parties most directly involved in the affair, rather than a formal determination by a court. What matters, they argue, is that people should be able to discuss their concerns, explain their actions and reactions, freely and openly. They should be able to come to accept their own responsibilities, and to recognize that the responsibility for a harm might well not be properly allocated to just one person—that often it may be shared in complex and nuanced ways that cannot be captured in the formal process of a criminal trial, which is focused on just one person, the defendant. These are certainly valuable features of the ways in which we can conduct our social lives, and it might well be that, even when a "conflict" in which we find ourselves involves criminal conduct, we would do better to try to resolve our problems through such an informal process rather than by appealing to the formal (and coercive) apparatus of the criminal law. But such informal processes will not always be adequate.

First, they privatize the conflict: but some kinds of wrong should be treated as public matters that concern us all as citizens. That is why, as argued in the previous section, we need a criminal law, which defines a category of public wrongs that are our collective business; and a public wrong requires a public response.

Second, the wrongs that we should treat as public are typically wrongs that require categorical recognition and condemnation rather than (or at least before) the kind of nuanced negotiation (and compromise) that a "conflict"-oriented process is likely to involve. No doubt we should sometimes (perhaps more often than we are inclined to) ask versions of Christie's question, "How wrong was the thief, how right was the victim?"[38] No doubt we will sometimes come to see that, having initially portrayed ourselves as innocent victims, we should accept some responsibility for what happened in a way that thereby reduces the responsibility of the person we portrayed as the perpetrator. Sometimes, however, that is inappropriate. One reason for this is that sometimes it is simply not plausible to argue that the victim was in any immediate way even partly responsible for the crime. And although it is true that, if we delved more deeply into the conditions from which the crime emerged, we might see reason to share a deeper kind of responsibility more broadly,[39] it is also important to our conception of ourselves and each other as agents that we take full responsibility for our actions. But another reason is that—although, when what is at stake is who should pay to repair some harm that has been caused, a victim who is partly responsible for the harm should bear part of the cost so that responsibility that is shared is thereby reduced for each person—this is not how responsibility is properly allocated for wrongs. It might be true, for instance, that the victim of a rape behaved negligently in exposing herself to a risk of being attacked; it might be appropriate for her to criticize herself or for a friend to criticize her for her imprudence. But while "contributory negligence" plays a proper role in civil cases, since it warrants the conclusion that responsibility, and thus the cost of the harm, should be shared between plaintiff and defendant, no such conclusion is warranted in a criminal case. It would be insulting for a criminal court to ask, "How wrong was the rapist, how right was the victim?" in such a case. The defendant cannot be allowed to argue, by way of mitigation, that the victim's negligence was a contributory factor in the crime; her negligence does nothing to reduce the attacker's culpable responsibility. In this context, unlike that of liability to pay for harm, responsibility that is shared is not thereby reduced for each of those who share it, and it would be misleading to talk of the rapist and his victim sharing responsibility: his attack constitutes, in moral terms, an utterly *novus actus interveniens* ("new intervening act" breaking the causal chain), for which he alone is criminally responsible. The attacks that constitute paradigmatically criminal *mala in se* are wrongs from which every citizen should be able to expect to be, as it were, categorically safe, and which are therefore to be categorically condemned rather than negotiated.[40] That is why, for instance, it is right to prosecute domestic violence as a criminal offense rather than simply seeing it as a private matter to be negotiated between the people directly involved. Such violence must be marked, categorically, as wrong, and it is a kind of wrong in which we should, collectively, take an active interest as fellow citizens of both victim and perpetrator.[41]

One further aspect of informal procedures is worth noting: that it is harder to set limits on what is raised for critical discussion. What begins as a conflict between neighbors over a precise, limited issue can easily spread out, once discussion begins, to bring in other aspects of their lives. If the aim is to restore their relationship, anything about the relationship that is problematic can be brought up. This is, of course, sometimes just what is needed, especially in a close-knit community, but it is worrying for those who are committed to an idea of liberal political community that respects the boundaries of our personal lives. In such a polity we are related to, and deal with, the majority of fellow citizens not, admittedly, as complete strangers (we recognize them as fellows), but as people with whom our bonds are limited and relatively shallow. We share a civic life with them, but that life is only one dimension of our lives, and we should be able to keep much about the other dimensions of our lives private—shared only with members of those smaller groups with whom we choose to share or with whom we find ourselves living in greater intimacy. When we commit wrongs that count as "public," we must be willing to answer for them publicly, but even then the realm of private life and thought should be protected. The fact that I committed a wrong against a fellow citizen should not give my fellows the right to discuss every aspect of my life that bothers them. But that is just what can happen in an informal, unconstrained discussion of our "conflict."

I have suggested so far that a polity that takes wrongdoing as seriously as it should (i.e., as something neither reducible to nor unimportant as compared to harm), and whose members aspire to treat each other with appropriate respect and concern as responsible citizens, should make provision for those who commit public wrongs to be called to account for them (and, as well, for those accused of committing such wrongs to be called to answer those accusations), but it should also protect alleged and actual wrongdoers against responses that intrude into what should still be the private realms of their lives. I have also suggested that the kinds of processes favored by advocates of restorative justice might not be of this proper kind. But we do have an institution that, in the aspiration that its forms and rhetoric imply, even if sadly all too infrequently in its actual operations, is of that kind: the criminal trial.

Philosophers who write about criminal law have tended to focus on substantive criminal law, and on the punishments that those who commit crimes may incur. But the process that connects crime to punishment is also important to a normative understanding of criminal law; indeed, the formal and public aspects of that process are central to the criminal law's purpose. That process includes the investigation of crime and the treatment of suspected offenders,[42] but we can focus here on the criminal trial as the formal culmination of the criminal process.

It might be tempting to see the criminal trial in purely instrumental terms, as a method of establishing who is to be subjected to the punishments (or other kinds of coercive measures) that give the trial its point; but this does not do justice to important aspects of criminal trials or their role in a democratic system of law. Rather, we should see the criminal trial as a formal process through which an alleged wrongdoer is called to answer to his fellow citizens by the court that speaks in their name. He is called, initially, to answer to the

charge of wrongdoing—either by pleading "guilty," thus admitting his culpable commission of the wrong, or by pleading "not guilty," thus challenging the prosecution to prove his guilt. If the prosecution does prove that he committed the offense, he must then answer for that commission, either by offering a defense—a justification or excuse showing that he should not be condemned for committing the offense—or by submitting himself to the court's formal condemnation and to the sentence it imposes. The criminal trial is thus a formal analogue of the informal moral processes through which we call each other to account for wrongs that we have committed. It addresses the defendant not simply as someone who is the subject of a formal inquiry, but as a citizen who is to participate in the process, and who is expected to answer to his fellows for his alleged violation of the values that define their polity.[43]

The criminal trial, as thus understood, provides an appropriate response to what the law defines as crimes. It constitutes the kind of calling to account that, I have suggested, criminal wrongdoing requires—a calling that takes the wrongdoing seriously and addresses its agent as a responsible citizen. It is precisely focused on the wrongdoing, not just on the harm that might also have been caused, and focuses on that wrongdoing as a public rather than a private matter: the polity as a whole calls the alleged perpetrator to account for a wrong that concerns all citizens. However, that calling to account respects the boundaries of private life. What is at issue is whether the defendant is guilty of the particular wrong specified in the indictment, and only matters bearing directly on that issue are to figure in the trial.

If the prosecution proves that the defendant committed the crime charged, and disproves any exculpatory defense that he offers, he is convicted of the crime. A conviction is not just a formal finding that he did commit the crime, and is therefore eligible for punishment: it also condemns his criminal action, and censures him as its agent.[44] That, we can say, is one thing that a criminal wrongdoer deserves, and one thing that we owe to his victim: a formal, public condemnation of his crime. That is also a kind of punishment, since condemnation by one's fellow citizens is intended to be painfully burdensome as a justified response to one's wrongdoing. It could indeed be seen as a particularly pure kind of punishment, since (leaving aside for the moment the further consequences that may attend a conviction) it is burdensome or painful only in virtue of its meaning as a condemnation, whereas the "hard treatment" that postconviction punishments typically involve is burdensome independently of any meaning that it might have.[45]

However, conviction is not typically the end of the matter for the offender; nor indeed is it typically thought to constitute an adequate response to his crime. It is time to turn, finally, to the material punishments that normally follow a conviction.

IV. THE MEANING AND PURPOSE OF PUNISHMENT

Although I promised at the start of this essay to defend a robust retributivism, I have not yet said anything, retributivist or otherwise, about the role of punishment in the kind of criminal law sketched in the previous two sections. By a "robust" retributivism, I mean one that takes the past wrongdoing for which a person is punished to be not merely a necessary condition of punishment, or a source of limits on the severity of punishment, but the (or a) primary focus of punishment: punishment is to be justified as an appropriate response to that wrongdoing. It might now seem, however, that I have made it harder rather than easier to justify punishment at all, let alone retributive punishment. For I have been emphasizing the respect and concern that citizens owe each other as fellow members of the polity, a respect and concern that is due to offenders as well as to victims. But how can the deliberate infliction of penal hardship be consistent with, let alone expressive of, that concern and respect? Should we not follow an abolitionist route and look for nonpunitive provisions and procedures that could restore and repair the civic relationships that crime has damaged?

It is certainly true that the kind of criminal law and criminal process I have sketched does not make punishment necessary. We could, in principle, do nothing more to or with offenders after their convictions: the polity formally censures them, and that is all. If we find this quite unacceptable, we need to ask why. Is it, for instance, because a criminal process that did not culminate in punishment would be unacceptably ineffective in preventing crime; or because it would not inflict the suffering that wrongdoers deserve; or because such a process would not take crime seriously enough? But even if we must do something more than convict, and thus censure, criminal wrongdoers, it is not yet clear that—or, why that—"more" must be punishment. We could, for instance, subject the convicted offender to whatever "measures" might seem to be necessary and potentially effective in preventing future offending.[46] But this would hardly be to treat or respect them as responsible citizens. Or we could require them to make some appropriate kind of reparation or restitution, or to pay compensation for what they have done. This brings us closer to the territory of restorative justice,[47] but we have to ask what could count as reparation or compensation not just for whatever harm was caused, but for the wrong that was done.

Both the reform of future conduct and reparation for past wrongdoing are important purposes for the criminal process. My suggestion is, however, that if we are to pursue those aims in a way that is consistent with the respect that we owe each other as citizens, and in a way that does justice to the wrongs that crimes involve (and to those who suffer and those who perpetrate such wrongs), we should do so through a system of retributive punishment—a system that will also serve the reconciliatory aims urged by advocates of restorative justice in a manner appropriate to a liberal polity. What follows is a necessarily bare sketch of this suggestion.[48]

We can begin with the by-now-familiar idea that punishment serves a communicative purpose: it communicates (directly to the offender, but also to all citizens) the censure that the crime deserves.[49] It is in that sense retributive: it is justified as a response to the wrong for which it is imposed and must be appropriate in its character and severity to that wrong. But such communication is not purely backward-looking: for to censure someone for their past conduct is also to say both that they should take care to reform their future conduct to avoid such wrongdoing, and that they should make some suitable reparation to those whom they wronged. The question then is, how can penal "hard treatment," the imposition of something that is burdensome independently of its censorial meaning, serve such aims of a communicative process? One familiar, and by itself not wholly persuasive, answer is that the hard treatment makes the communication more effective by making it harder to ignore.[50] But we can say something more than that by looking more carefully at each dimension of the two-way communicative process that punishment should ideally be.

First, punishment communicates censure from the polity to the offender. The aim should be not just to ensure that he hears the censure, but to persuade him to attend to it, in the hope that he will be persuaded by it to repent his crime (and thus also to see the need to reform his future conduct). But merely verbal censure, as conveyed by a conviction, or purely symbolic punishments are likely to be inadequate, since they are all too easily ignored or forgotten. It is all too easy, and too tempting, for us to distract ourselves from giving our wrongdoing the remorseful attention it deserves. One function of burdensome punishment, then, is to make it harder for the offender to ignore the message that punishment communicates. It is a way of helping to keep his attention focused on his wrongdoing and its implications, with a view to inducing and strengthening a properly repentant understanding of what he has done.[51] Such an understanding will include a recognition of the need to reform his future conduct (unless the crime was a genuine aberration), and although such reform must ultimately be something that he achieves for himself as a responsible agent, punishment can help in that endeavor. This is one of the central aims of probation, and of the kinds of program that may be offered to offenders to help them confront and deal with the sources of their crimes. If the program is so focused on the crime itself and its immediate causes that we can say that an offender who refused to undertake the program would be refusing to take his crime

seriously, undertaking the program could be required as part of the punishment.[52]

Second, something must also be communicated from the offender to the polity, and to the victim (when there is a victim). He has committed a wrong against the victim, and against the polity's values, and he must "make up" for that wrong by making some reparation to them. The criminal law is, as we have seen, focused on wrongs rather than on harms. What matters, therefore, is not (just) reparation for whatever harm was caused, but moral reparation for the wrong that was done. It is this aspect of the reparation that crime makes necessary that is missing from accounts of restorative justice that urge us to focus on repairing or making good the harm that was caused. But what could constitute reparation for a wrong? Central to such moral reparation is apology. If I recognize that I have wronged you, I must recognize that I owe you an apology. Apology expresses my repentant recognition of the wrong I did. It owns the wrong as mine, but disowns it as something that I now repudiate. It implies a sincere commitment to avoid doing wrong in future, and it expresses my desire to seek forgiveness from and reconciliation with the person I wronged.

A verbal apology is often sufficient reparation: nothing more is, or should be, expected. Sometimes, however, when the wrong is more serious, or when the victim and the wrongdoer do not stand in the kind of relationship in which words can carry sufficient moral weight, words are not enough, since words can be too cheap and too easy. If the apology is to address the wrong adequately, if it is to show the victim that the wrong is taken seriously, and if it is to focus the wrongdoer's attention on the wrong as it should be focused, it must take a more than merely verbal form. That "more than merely verbal form" will involve something burdensome that the wrongdoer undertakes—some task that he undertakes for the benefit of the victim or the wider community, some penitential suffering that he undergoes, perhaps some burdensome program aimed at dealing with the root of his wrongdoing. The key point to notice here is that it must be burdensome to him if it is to serve its apologetic purpose.

Something that was not burdensome, something that cost no more than mere words, would be no more adequate an apology than mere words; if I am to give material form to my repentant recognition of the burden of guilt that I now carry, that form must itself be something burdensome.

The second communicative aspect of punishment, then, is the communication of apology from the offender to those whom he wronged—the direct victim, and the wider community. The burdensome punishment gives material form, and so greater moral force, to that apology. Of course, we know that many offenders who undergo punishment are not truly apologetic; in undergoing their punishment they are not expressing a genuinely repentant recognition of the wrong they have done. Criminal punishment is, on this account, a species of required apology: the offender is required to go through the motions of apology, even if he does not mean it.

It might now be objected that such required apologies lack real value, and that to require people to apologize is inconsistent with a due respect for them as responsible moral agents.[53] But we can still see value even in required apologies whose sincerity is unknown or doubtful: they make clear to the offender what he ought to do (apologize sincerely) and to the victim that the community recognizes and takes seriously the wrong he has suffered. As to respect, what punishment requires of the offender is not actual repentance, but that he undergo the ritual of apology and moral reparation. It is still up to him to make, or refuse to make, that apology a genuine one.[54] By requiring him to undergo the burdensome sanction that would constitute appropriate reparation for his wrong, we hope that he will come to recognize the need for that reparation himself, and to make it his own, but that is up to him.

To say that punishment has these two communicative dimensions is not to suggest that it should be divided into two parts. The burdensome punishment that is imposed on or required of an offender in order to bring him to confront and recognize his crime should also be a burden that would constitute moral reparation for his crime. It is precisely by requiring him to undertake or undergo such a burden as reparation for

his crime that we hope to bring him to a clearer, repentant understanding of that crime. Punishment is, on this view, a kind of secular penance.

This communicative enterprise—the communication of censure to the offender and the ritual of apology that he is required to undertake or undergo—also serves a reconciliatory aim. It is not, admittedly, well-suited to restore the kinds of personal relationship on which those who advocate restorative justice sometimes focus: it is not apt to reconcile spouses, family members, partners, friends, or neighbors, if reconciliation is understood as the restoration of those bonds of affection and close mutual concern by which such relationships are structured. But that kind of reconciliation of those kinds of relationship is not the criminal law's business, or indeed the business of the liberal state, beyond perhaps offering mediation services that citizens can use if they so wish. The criminal law's proper concern is with our relationship as fellow citizens, a relationship that is, as far as the law is concerned, somewhat distant and formal. It is that relationship that crime, as a breach of our civic values, damages. It is that relationship that can be repaired by the punishment that the offender undertakes or undergoes, *if* his fellow citizens play their proper part in the ritual. They will play that part if they accept the completion of the ritual as adequate moral reparation for the wrong without inquiring into the sincerity of the apology that is thus offered. For while, in our more intimate relationships, apologies, and the rituals through which they may be expressed, are only of value if they are sincere, in the civic life of a liberal polity that takes privacy seriously, what matters is that the ritual is undertaken.[55]

On this account, criminal punishment is robustly retributive, since it is focused on and justified by the crime for which it is imposed. It is justified as an appropriate response to that crime, a response that marks the character and seriousness of the crime and constitutes an appropriate, public, and formal reparation for it. It is not, however, merely retributive, since it also looks to the future: to the offender's (self-) reform, and to the restoration of the bonds of citizenship that the crime damaged. Nor is it opposed, as advocates of restorative justice often take it to be opposed, to ideas of restoration and reparation. It is something that citizens can properly impose on each other, and accept for themselves, as the appropriate way in which the distinctive damage wrought by crime can be repaired and civic relationships restored.

I have offered only the barest sketch of this conception of punishment. Much more needs to be said (but not here) about the details of this conception, about its implications for the operations of a criminal justice system (in particular, for sentencing), and about how we should respond to the gaping chasm between this ideal of what criminal punishment ought to be and our existing penal practices.[56] I hope, however, that I have said enough to show how we can hope to meet the challenges faced by retributivism and remedy the weaknesses that, I have argued, undermined the retributivist revival of the 1970s—in part by getting a clearer view of just what kind of burden punishment should be intended to impose (what it is that offenders can be said to deserve), and by setting punishment in the context of criminal law as a whole. That was why I spent so long, in sections II and III, on the idea of criminal law and on the criminal trial. We can best make sense of criminal punishment by seeing it as an aspect of the way in which a polity can properly deal with public wrongdoing—wrongdoing that is defined as public by the criminal law, and whose perpetrators are called to account in the criminal trial.

ACKNOWLEDGMENT

Thanks to participants in two workshops in Leiden at which earlier sketches of this essay were presented, and especially to Peter Ramsay for his detailed comments, and to Erik Luna and Michael O'Hear for advice on American restorative justice programs.

NOTES

1. Martinson, R. "What works? Questions and Answers about Prison Reform" *Public Interest* 10 (1974): 22–54.
2. Hart, H. L. A. *Punishment and Responsibility.* Oxford: Oxford University Press, 1968. Chap 1–2. It is less clear whether the second constraint, on the excessive punishment of the guilty, could be explained without recourse to retributive ideas of desert. See Feinberg, Joel. *Harmless Wrongdoing.* New York: Oxford University Press, 1988.
3. Lewis, C. S. "The Humanitarian Theory of Punishment." *Res Judicatae* 6 (1953): 231–37. Reprinted in, *Readings in Ethical Theory*, 2nd ed., ed. W. Sellars and J. Hospers. New York: Appleton-Century-Crofts, 1970; Morris, H. "Persons and Punishment." *The Monist* 52 (1968): 475–79.
4. Menninger, K. *The Crime of Punishment.* New York: Viking Press, 1968; Skinner, B. F. *Beyond Freedom and Dignity.* New York: Bantam, 1972.
5. Kant, I. *Groundwork of the Metaphysic of Morals.* (1785). Trans. H. Paton. *The Moral Law.* London: Hutchinson, 1948.
6. Philosophers of punishment have recently begun to take more seriously the idea that we should seek to abolish punishment rather than justify it. See, e.g., Golash, D. *The Case Against Punishment.* New York: New York University Press, 2005; Boonin, D. *The Problem of Punishment.* Cambridge: Cambridge University Press, 2008. There is still, however, a striking lack of engagement with the rich literature of abolitionism.
7. Dagger, R. "Playing Fair with Punishment." *Ethics* 103 (1993): 473–88.
8. Christie, R. *Limits to Pain.* London: Martin Robertson, 1981.
9. Duff, R. A. "Penal Communications: Recent Work in the Philosophy of Punishment." *Crime and Justice: A Review of Research.* Vol. 20. Ed. Michael Tonry. Chicago: University of Chicago Press, 1996.
10. However, there has been persistent controversy over whether "upward departures" from desert constraints could be justified for offenders reliably identified as "dangerous." See, recently, von Hirsch, A. and Ashworth, A. J. *Proportionate Sentencing: Exploring the Principles.* Oxford: Oxford University Press, 2005. chap. 4; Robinson, P. H. *Distributive Principles of Criminal Law: Who Should be Punished How Much?* New York: Oxford University Press, 2008. chap. 6.
11. See supra, note 2, and accompanying text.
12. Braithwaite, J., and Pettit, P. *Not Just Deserts: A Republican Theory of Criminal Justice.* Oxford: Oxford University Press, 1990.
13. Morris, N. *The Future of Imprisonment.* Chicago: University of Chicago Press, 1974; Morris, N. and Tonry, M. *Between Prison and Probation:*

Intermediate Punishments in a Rational Sentencing System. New York: Oxford University Press, 1990.

14. Husak, D. "Retributivism, Proportionality, and the Challenge of the Drug Court Movement." *Retributivism Has a Past. Has It a Future?* Ed. Michael Tonry. New York: Oxford University Press, 2011.

15. Zedner, L. "Preventive Justice or Pre-punishment? The Case of Control Orders." *Current Legal Problems* 60 (2007): 174–203; Zedner, L. and Ashworth, A. J. "Defending the Criminal Law: Reflections on the Changing Character of Crime, Procedure, and Sanctions." *Criminal Law and Philosophy* 2 (2008): 21–51; Ashworth, A. J. and Zedner, L. "Preventive Orders: A Problem of Under-Criminalization?" In *The Boundaries of the Criminal Law*. Eds. R. A. Duff, L. Farmer, S. E. Marshall, M. Renzo, and V. Tadros. Oxford: Oxford University Press, 2011.

16. Compare Jakobs's notorious distinction between "*Bürgerstrafrecht*," and "*Feindstrafrecht*." See Gomez-Jara Díez, C. "Enemy Combatants Versus Enemy Criminal Law." *New Criminal Law Review* 11 (2008): 529–62.

17. See, e.g., the Wisconsin prison program of meetings between offenders and victims organized by Janine Geske, a former Wisconsin Supreme Court justice. Umbreit, M., Vos, B., Coates, R. B., and Lightfoot, E. "Restorative Justice in the Twenty-First Century: A Social Movement Full of Opportunities and Pitfalls." *Marquette Law Review* 89 (2005): 251–304.

18. Gabbay, Z. "Holding Restorative Justice Accountable." *Cardozo Journal of Conflict Resolution* 8 (2006): 85–141; Luna, E., and Poulson, B. "Restorative Justice in Federal Sentencing: An Unexpected Benefit of Booker?" *McGeorge Law Review* 37 (2006): 787–818; O'Hear, M. "Rethinking Drug Courts: Restorative Justice as a Response to Racial Injustice." *Stanford Law and Policy Review* 20 (2009): 463–500.

19. Braithwaite, J. "Restorative Justice: Assessing Optimistic and Pessimistic Accounts." *Crime and Justice: A Review of Research*. Vol. 25. Ed. Michael Tonry. Chicago: University of Chicago Press, 1999; Johnstone, G. *Restorative Justice: Ideas, Values, Debates*. Cullompton, Devon, UK: Willan, 2002; von Hirsch, A., Roberts, J., Bottoms, A. E., Roach, K., and Schiff, M., eds. *Restorative Justice and Criminal Justice*. Oxford: Hart, 2003; Johnstone, G., and D. van Ness, eds. *Handbook of Restorative Justice Reader*. Cullompton, Devon, UK: Willan, 2006.

20. For some central examples of this kind of abolitionism, see Christie, N. "Conflicts as Property." *British Journal of Criminology* 17 (1977): 1–15; Christie, N. *Limits to Pain*, supra, note 8; Hulsman, L. "Critical Criminology and the Concept of Crime." *Crime, Law, and Social Change* 10 (1986): 63–80; Hulsman, L. "The Abolitionist Case: Alternative Crime Policies." *Israel Law Review* 25 (1991): 681–709; Bianchi, H. *Justice as Sanctuary: Toward a New System of Crime Control*. Bloomington: Indiana University Press, 1994.

21. Menninger, *The Crime of Punishment*, supra, note 4.

22. Wootton, B. *Crime and the Criminal Law*. London: Stevens & Sons, 1963. Discussed in Matravers, M. "Is Twenty-first Century Punishment Post-desert?" *Retributivism Has a Past. Has It a Future?* Ed. Michael Tonry. New York: Oxford University Press, 2011. Also compare the use of supposedly nonpunitive "measures," discussed by de Keijser, J. "Never Mind the Pain; It's a Measure! Justifying Measures as Part of the Dutch Bifurcated System of Sanctions." In *Retributivism Has a Past. Has It a Future?* Ed. Michael Tonry. New York: Oxford University Press, 2011.

23. Compare also Bianchi's support for compulsory "sanctuary," supra, note 7.

24. Only "because it is believed," since legislators can of course criminalize what they mistakenly believe to be morally wrong. Tadros, V., and Tierney, S. "The Presumption of Innocence and the Human Rights Act." *Modern Law Review* 67 (2004): 402–34.

25. Feinberg, Joel. *Harm to Others*. New York: Oxford University Press, 1984.

26. Duff, R. A. *Answering for Crime*. Oxford: Hart, 2007.

27. Moore, M. S. *Placing Blame: A General Theory of the Criminal Law*. Oxford: Oxford University Press, 1997.

28. Wolfenden, J. *Report of the Committee on Homosexual Offences and Prostitution* (The Wolfenden Report). London: HM Stationery Office, 1957.

29. Marshall, S. E., and Duff, R. A. "Criminalization and Sharing Wrongs." *Canadian Journal of Law and Jurisprudence* 11 (1998); Marshall, S. E., and Duff, R. A. "Public and Private Wrongs." *Essays in Criminal Law in Honour of Sir Gerald Gordon*. Eds. J. Chalmers, F. Leverick, and L. Farmer. Edinburgh: Edinburgh University Press, 2010.

30. On "thick" concepts, see Williams, B. *Ethics and the Limits of Philosophy*. London: Fontana, 1985. chap. 8; Duff, R. A. "Law, Language and Community." *Oxford Journal of Legal Studies* 18 (1998):189–206.

31. Something that Feinberg makes central to his account of harm. Feinberg, *Harm to Others*, supra, note 25.

32. Duff, *Answering for Crime*, supra, note 26.

33. Walgrave, L. "Imposing Restoration Instead of Inflicting Pain." *Restorative Justice and Criminal Justice: Competing or Reconcilable Paradigms?*, Eds. A. von Hirsch, J. Roberts, A. E. Bottoms, K. Roach, and M. Schiff. Oxford: Hart, 2003.

34. It might seem that such a criminal law could deal with *mala in se*, wrongs that can be identified as wrongs independently of law, but not with *mala prohibita*, whose wrongness cannot be identified independently of the law. For a response to this objection, see Duff, *Answering for Crime*, supra, note 26, at chap. 4, sect. 4, and chap. 7, sect. 3.

35. I focus here on the domestic criminal law of a national polity and on wrongs committed against each other by its citizens. Further accounts must be given of international criminal law and of how domestic criminal law also binds and protects noncitizens, but these will be further accounts. Domestic criminal law is still the familiar paradigm of criminal law, and the law's primary addressees are the polity's citizens.

36. On sharing wrongs, see Marshall and Duff, "Criminalization and Sharing Wrongs," supra, note 29, at 7–22. The point is not that the harm or wrong is done to us collectively rather than (just) to the victim, it is that we share in his wrong as his fellows.

37. On sharing wrongs, see id., Marshall and Duff.

38. Compare Kleinig's comments on the meaning and proper role of the question "what does wrongdoing deserve?" Kleinig, J. "What Does Wrongdoing Deserve?" In *Retributivism Has a Past. Has It a Future?* Ed. Michael Tonry. New York: Oxford University Press, 2011.

39. On a "relational theory of blame," according to which responsibility "lies with individuals and with societies of which they are a part, so that, neither individualized nor denied, it is shared," compare Norrie, A. W. *Punishment, Responsibility, and Justice*. Oxford: Oxford University Press, 2000. 220–21

40. Contrast Bergelson, V. *Victims' Rights and Victims' Wrongs; Comparative Liability In Criminal Law.* Stanford, CA: Stanford University Press, 2009. Bergelson argues that in criminal law a defendant's responsibility can be reduced by the victim's own share of responsibility for the crime. But her argument is undermined by a failure to take seriously enough the fact that while, in a civil case, responsibility shared is responsibility reduced, in a criminal case that is not (always or necessarily) so.

41. Compare Dobash, R. E. and Dobash, R. P. *Women, Violence and Social Change*. London: Routledge, 1992. chap. 7; and Dempsey, M. M. *Prosecuting Domestic Violence*. Oxford: Oxford University Press, 2009.

42. Ashworth, A. J., and Redmayne, M. *The Criminal Process*. 3rd ed. Oxford: Oxford University Press, 2005; Sanders, A. and Young, R. *Criminal Justice*. 3rd ed. Oxford: Oxford University Press, 2006; Kleinig, J. *Ethics and Criminal Justice: An Introduction*. Cambridge: Cambridge University Press, 2008.

43. For further explanation and defense of this conception of the criminal trial, see Duff, R. A., Farmer, L. Marshall, S. E. and Tadros, V. *The Trial on Trial (3): Towards a Normative Theory of the Criminal Trial*. Oxford: Hart, 2007. It should be clear that this is an account of what trials should be, not of what they actually are in our existing courts.

44. That is why jury nullification plays an important role in a democratic polity: it marks a citizens' judgment that the defendant does not deserve condemnation. Abramson, J. *We, the Jury: The Jury System and the Ideal of Democracy*. Cambridge, MA: Harvard University Press, 2000. chap. 2.

45. On "hard treatment," see Feinberg, J. *Doing and Deserving*. Princeton, NJ: Princeton University Press, 1970; Duff, R. A. "Penal Communications: Recent Work in the Philosophy of Punishment," supra, note 9.

46. Wootton, *Crime and the Criminal Law*; de Keijser, "Never Mind the Pain"; and Matravers, "Is Twenty-first Century Punishment Post-desert?" supra, note 22.

47. Golash, *The Case Against Punishment*; and Boonin, *The Problem of Punishment*, supra, note 6.

48. It is also in part a response to the final parts of Kleinig, J. "What Does Wrongdoing Deserve?" supra, note 38.

49. On punishment as expressive see Feinberg, supra, note 23; von Hirsch, A. *Censure and Sanctions*. Oxford: Oxford University Press, 1993; Duff, R.

A. *Punishment, Communication, and Community.* New York: Oxford University Press, 2001; Markel, D. "State, Be Not Proud: A Retributivist Defense of the Commutation of Death Row and the Abolition of the Death Penalty." *Harvard Civil Rights-Civil Liberties Law Review* 40 (2005): 407–80; Markel, D. "Executing Retributivism: Panetti and the Future of the Eighth Amendment." *Northwestern Law Review* 103 (2009): 1163–222.

50. Kleinig, J. "Punishment and Moral Seriousness." *Israel Law Review* 25 (1991): 401–21.

51. I talk of "burdensome punishment" rather than of "hard treatment" to avoid suggesting that the main aim is to hurt. Community service orders and probation are paradigm examples of communicative punishments: they are intended to be burdensome, but it might be misleading to describe them as "hard treatment."

52. See, e.g., the CHANGE program for domestically violent men, Dobash and Dobash, supra, note 41. One worry about "therapeutic" justice is that it ignores this requirement that what we require an offender to undertake must be something focused on and justifiable as a response to his crime.

53. See, e.g., von Hirsch and Ashworth, supra, note 10, for this and other criticisms.

54. Garvey, S. "Punishment as Atonement." *UCLA Law Review* 47 (1999): 1801–58; Tudor, S. K. "Accepting One's Punishment as Meaningful Suffering." *Law and Philosophy* 20 (2001): 581–604; Bennett, C. *The Apology Ritual: A Philosophical Theory of Punishment.* Cambridge: Cambridge University Press, 2008. For some insightful criticism, see Tasioulas, J. "Punishment and Repentance." *Philosophy* 81 (2006): 279–322.

55. We should recognize, however, that "*if* his fellow citizens play their proper part in the ritual" marks a vital condition on the legitimacy of criminal punishment—a condition that, like so many other of the conditions that a just system of punishment must satisfy, is all too often and obviously not satisfied at the moment.

56. But see Duff, *Punishment, Communication, and Community*, supra, note 49.

57   The Expressive Function of Punishment

JOEL FEINBERG

It might well appear to a moral philosopher absorbed in the classical literature of his discipline, or to a moralist sensitive to injustice and suffering, that recent philosophical discussions of the problem of punishment have somehow missed the point of his interest. Recent influential articles[1] have quite sensibly distinguished between questions of definition and justification, between justifying general rules and particular decisions, between moral and legal guilt. So much is all to the good. When these articles go on to *define* "punishment," however, it seems to many that they leave out of their ken altogether the very element that makes punishment theoretically puzzling and morally disquieting. Punishment is defined, in effect, as the infliction of hard treatment by an authority on a person for his prior failing in some respect (usually an infraction of a rule or command).[2] There may be a very general sense of the word *punishment* which is well expressed by this definition; but even if that is so, we can distinguish a narrower, more emphatic sense that slips through its meshes. Imprisonment at hard labor for committing a felony is a clear case of punishment in the emphatic sense; but I think we would be less willing to apply that term to parking tickets, offside penalties, sackings, flunkings, and disqualifications. Examples of the latter sort that I propose to call *penalties* (merely), so that I may inquire further what distinguishes punishment, in the strict and narrow sense that interests the moralist, from other kinds of penalties.[3]

One method of answering this question is to focus one's attention on the class of nonpunitive penalties in an effort to discover some clearly identifiable characteristic common to them all, and

From *Doing and Deserving: Essays in the Theory of Responsibility* (Princeton, N.J.: Princeton University Press, 1970), pp. 95–118. Reprinted by permission of the author.

absent from all punishments, on which the distinction between the two might be grounded. The hypotheses yielded by this approach, however, are not likely to survive close scrutiny. One might conclude, for example, that mere penalties are less severe than punishments, but although this is generally true, it is not necessarily and universally so. Again we might be tempted to interpret penalties as mere "price-tags" attached to certain types of behavior that are generally undesirable, so that only those with especially strong motivation will be willing to pay the price.[4] So, for example, deliberate efforts on the part of some western states to keep roads from urban centers to wilderness areas few in number and poor in quality are essentially no different from various parking fines and football penalties. In each case a certain kind of conduct is discouraged without being absolutely prohibited: Anyone who desires strongly enough to get to the wilderness (or park overtime, or interfere with a pass) may do so provided he is willing to pay the penalty (price). On this view penalties are, in effect, licensing fees, different from other purchased permits in that the price is often paid afterward rather than in advance. Since a similar interpretation of punishments seems implausible, it might be alleged that this is the basis of the distinction between penalties and punishments. However, while a great number of penalties can, no doubt, plausibly be treated as retroactive license fees, this is hardly true of all of them. It is certainly not true, for example, of most demotions, firings, and flunkings, that they are "prices" paid for some already consumed benefit; and even parking fines are sanctions for rules "meant to be taken seriously as ... standard[s] of behavior,"[5] and thus are more than mere public parking fees.

Rather than look for a characteristic common and peculiar to the penalties on which to ground the distinction between penalties and punishments, we would be better advised, I think, to cast our attention to the examples of punishments. Both penalties and punishments are authoritative deprivations for failures; but apart from these common features, penalties have a miscellaneous character, whereas punishments have an important additional characteristic in common. That

characteristic, or specific difference, I shall argue, is a certain expressive function: Punishment is a conventional device for the expression of attitudes of resentment and indignation, and of judgments of disapproval and reprobation, either on the part of the punishing authority himself or of those "in whose name" the punishment is inflicted. Punishment, in short, has a *symbolic significance* largely missing from other kinds of penalties.

The reprobative symbolism of punishment and its character as "hard treatment," while never separate in reality, must be carefully distinguished for purposes of analysis. Reprobation is itself painful, whether or not it is accompanied by further "hard treatment"; and hard treatment, such as fine or imprisonment, because of its conventional symbolism, can itself be reprobatory; but still we can conceive of ritualistic condemnation unaccompanied by any *further* hard treatment, and of inflictions and deprivations which, because of different symbolic conventions, have no reprobative force. It will be my thesis in this essay that (1) both the hard treatment aspect of punishment and its reprobative function must be part of the *definition* of legal punishment; and (2) each of these aspects raises its own kind of question about the *justification* of legal punishment as a general practice. I shall argue that some of the jobs punishment does, and some of the conceptual problems it raises, cannot be intelligibly described unless (1) is true; and (2) that the incoherence of a familiar form of the retributive theory results from failure to appreciate the force of (2).

I. PUNISHMENT AS CONDEMNATION

That the expression of the community's condemnation is an essential ingredient in legal punishment is widely acknowledged by legal writers. Henry M. Hart, for example, gives eloquent emphasis to the point:

> What distinguishes a criminal from a civil sanction and all that distinguishes it, it is ventured, is the judgment of community condemnation which accompanies ... its imposition. As Professor Gardner wrote not long ago, in a distinct but cognate connection:

The essence of punishment for moral delinquency lies in the criminal conviction itself. One may lose more money on the stock market than in a courtroom; a prisoner of war camp may well provide a harsher environment than a state prison; death on the field of battle has the same physical characteristics as death by sentence of law. It is the expression of the community's hatred, fear, or contempt for the convict which alone characterizes physical hardship as punishment.

If this is what a "criminal" penalty is, then we can say readily enough what a "crime" is.... It is conduct which, if duly shown to have taken place, will incur a formal and solemn pronouncement of the moral condemnation of the community.... Indeed the condemnation plus the added [unpleasant physical] consequences may well be considered, compendiously, as constituting the punishment.[6]

Professor Hart's compendious definition needs qualification in one respect. The moral condemnation and the "unpleasant consequences" that he rightly identifies as essential elements of punishment are not as distinct and separate as he suggests. It is not always the case that the convicted prisoner is first solemnly condemned and then subjected to unpleasant physical treatment. It would be more accurate in many cases to say that the unpleasant treatment itself expresses the condemnation, and that this expressive aspect of his incarceration is precisely the element by reason of which it is properly characterized as punishment and not mere penalty. The administrator who regretfully suspends the license of a conscientious but accident-prone driver can inflict a deprivation without any scolding, express or implied; but the reckless motorist who is sent to prison for six months is thereby inevitably subject to shame and ignominy—the very walls of his cell condemn him and his record becomes a stigma.

To say that the very physical treatment itself expresses condemnation is to say simply that certain forms of hard treatment have become the conventional symbols of public reprobation. This is neither more nor less paradoxical than to say that certain words have become conventional vehicles in our language for the expression of certain attitudes, or that champagne is the alcoholic beverage traditionally used in celebration of great events, or that black is the color of mourning. Moreover, particular kinds of punishment are often used to express quite specific attitudes (loosely speaking, this is part of their "meaning"); note the differences, for example, between beheading a nobleman and hanging a yeoman, burning a heretic and hanging a traitor, hanging an enemy soldier and executing him by firing squad.

It is much easier to show that punishment has a symbolic significance than to say exactly what it is that punishment expresses. At its best, in civilized and democratic countries, punishment surely expresses the community's strong *disapproval* of what the criminal did. Indeed it can be said that punishment expresses the *judgment* (as distinct from any emotion) of the community that what the criminal did was wrong. I think it is fair to say of our community, however, that punishment generally expresses more than judgments of disapproval; it is also a symbolic way of getting back at the criminal, of expressing a kind of vindictive resentment. To any reader who has in fact spent time in a prison, I venture to say, even Professor Gardner's strong terms—"hatred, fear, or contempt for the convict"—will not seem too strong an account of what imprisonment is universally taken to express. Not only does the criminal feel the naked hostility of his guards and the outside world—that would be fierce enough—but that hostility is self-righteous as well. His punishment bears the aspect of legitimized vengefulness; hence there is much truth in J. F. Stephen's celebrated remark that "The criminal law stands to the passion of revenge in much the same relation as marriage to the sexual appetite."[7]

If we reserve the less dramatic term *resentment* for the various vengeful attitudes, and the term *reprobation* for the stern judgment of disapproval, then perhaps we can characterize *condemnation* (or denunciation) as a kind of fusing of resentment and reprobation. That these two elements are generally to be found in legal punishment was well understood by the authors of the Report of the Royal Commission on Capital Punishment:

Discussion of the principle of retribution is apt to be confused because the word is not always used in the same sense. Sometimes it is intended to mean vengeance, sometimes reprobation. In the first sense the idea is that of satisfaction by the State of a wronged individual's desire to be avenged; in the second it is that of the State's marking its disapproval of the breaking of its laws by a punishment proportionate to the gravity of the offense [my italics].[8]

II. SOME DERIVATIVE SYMBOLIC FUNCTIONS OF PUNISHMENT

The relation of the expressive function of punishment to its various central purposes is not always easy to trace. Symbolic public condemnation added to deprivation may help or hinder deterrence, reform, and rehabilitation—the evidence is not clear. On the other hand, there are other functions of punishment, often lost sight of in the preoccupation with deterrence and reform, that presuppose the expressive function and would be impossible without it.

1. Authoritative Disavowal

Consider the standard international practice of demanding that a nation whose agent has unlawfully violated the complaining nation's rights should punish the offending agent. For example, suppose that an airplane of nation *A* fires on an airplane of nation *B* while the latter is flying over international waters. Very likely high authorities in nation *B* will send a note of protest to their counterparts in nation *A* demanding, among other things, that the transgressive pilot be punished. Punishing the pilot is an emphatic, dramatic, and well-understood way of *condemning* and thereby *disavowing* his act. It tells the world that the pilot had no right to do what he did, that he was on his own in doing it, that his government does not condone that sort of thing. It testifies thereby to government *A*'s recognition of the violated rights of government *B* in the affected area, and therefore to the wrongfulness of the pilot's act. Failure to punish the pilot tells the world that government *A* does not consider him to have been personally at fault. That in turn is to claim responsibility for the act, which in effect labels

that act as an "instrument of deliberate national policy," and therefore an act of war. In that case either formal hostilities or humiliating loss of face by one side or the other almost certainly follows. None of this makes any sense without the well-understood reprobative symbolism of punishment. In quite parallel ways punishment enables employers to disavow the acts of their employees (though not civil liability for those acts), and fathers the destructive acts of their sons.

2. Symbolic Nonacquiescence: "Speaking in the Name of the People"

The symbolic function of punishment also explains why even those sophisticated persons who abjure resentment of criminals and look with small favor generally on the penal law are likely to demand that certain kinds of conduct be punished when or if the law lets them go by. In the state of Texas, so-called "paramour killings" are regarded by the law as not merely mitigated, but completely justifiable.[9] Many humanitarians, I believe, will feel quite spontaneously that a great injustice is done when such killings are left unpunished. The sense of violated justice, moreover, might be distinct and unaccompanied by any frustrated schadenfreude toward the killer, lust for blood or vengeance, or metaphysical concern lest the universe stay "out of joint." The demand for punishment in cases of this sort may instead represent the feeling that paramour killings deserve to be *condemned*, that the law in condoning, even approving of them, speaks for all citizens in expressing a wholly inappropriate attitude toward them. For, in effect, the law expresses the judgment of the "people of Texas," in whose name it speaks, that the vindictive satisfaction in the mind of the cuckolded husband is a thing of greater value than the very life of his wife's lover. The demand that paramour killings be punished may simply be the demand that this lopsided value judgment be withdrawn and that the state *go on record* against paramour killings, and the law *testify to the recognition* that such killings are wrongful. Punishment no doubt would also help deter killers. This too is a desideratum and a closely related one, but it is not to be identified with reprobation; for deterrence might be achieved by a dozen other techniques, from simple penalties and forfeitures to exhortation and propaganda; but effective public denunciation and, through it, symbolic nonacquiescence in the crime, seem virtually to require punishment.

This symbolic function of punishment was given great emphasis by Kant, who, characteristically, proceeded to exaggerate its importance. Even if a desert island community were to disband, Kant argued, its members should first execute the last murderer left in its jails, "for otherwise they might all be regarded as participators in the [unpunished] murder...."[10] This Kantian idea that in failing to punish wicked acts society endorses them and thus becomes *particeps criminis* ("one who has a share in the crime") does seem to reflect, however dimly, something embedded in common sense. A similar notion underlies whatever is intelligible in the widespread notion that all citizens share the responsibility for political atrocities. Insofar as there is a coherent argument behind the extravagant distributions of guilt made by existentialists and other literary figures, it can be reconstructed in some such way as this: To whatever extent a political act is done "in one's name," to that extent one is responsible for it. A citizen can avoid responsibility in advance by explicitly disowning the government as his spokesman, or after the fact through open protest, resistance, and so on. Otherwise, by "acquiescing" in what is done in one's name, one incurs the responsibility for it. The root notion here is a kind of "power of attorney" a government has for its citizens.

3. Vindication of the Law

Sometimes the state goes on record through its statutes, in a way that might well please a conscientious citizen in whose name it speaks, but then through official evasion and unreliable enforcement, gives rise to doubts that the law really means what it says. It is murder in Mississippi, as elsewhere, for a white man intentionally to kill a Negro; but if grand juries refuse to issue indictments or if trial juries refuse to convict, and this is well understood by most citizens, then it is in a purely formal and empty sense indeed that killings of Negroes by whites are illegal in Mississippi. Yet the law stays on the books, to give ever-less-convincing lip service to a noble moral judgment. A statute honored mainly in the breach begins to lose its character as law, unless, as we say, it is *vindicated* (emphatically reaffirmed); and clearly the way to do this (indeed the only way) is to punish those who violate it.

Similarly, *punitive damages,* so called, are sometimes awarded the plaintiff in a civil action, as a supplement to compensation for his injuries. What more dramatic way of vindicating his violated right can be imagined than to have a court thus forcibly condemn its violation through the symbolic machinery of punishment?

4. Absolution of Others

When something scandalous has occurred and it is clear that the wrongdoer must be one of a small number of suspects, then the state, by punishing one of these parties, thereby relieves the others of suspicion, and informally absolves them of blame. Moreover, quite often the absolution of an accuser hangs as much in the balance at a criminal trial as the inculpation of the accused. A good example of this can be found in James Gould Cozzen's novel, *By Love Possessed*. A young girl, after an evening of illicit sexual activity with her boyfriend, is found out by her bullying mother, who then insists that she clear her name by bringing criminal charges against the boy. He used physical force, the girl charges; she freely consented, he replies. If the jury finds him guilty of rape, it will by the same token absolve her from (moral) guilt; and her reputation as well as his rides on the outcome. Could not the state do this job without punishment? Perhaps, but when it speaks by punishing, its message is loud, and sure of getting across.

III. THE CONSTITUTIONAL PROBLEM OF DEFINING LEGAL PUNISHMENT

A philosophical theory of punishment that, through inadequate definition, leaves out the condemnatory function, not only will disappoint the moralist and the traditional moral philosopher; it will seem offensively irrelevant as well to the constitutional lawyer, whose vital concern with punishment is both conceptual, and therefore genuinely philosophical, and practically urgent. The distinction between punishment and mere penalties is a familiar one in the criminal law, where theorists have long engaged in what Jerome Hall calls "dubious dogmatics distinguishing 'civil penalties' from punitive sanctions, and 'public wrongs' from crimes."[11] Our courts now regard it as true (by definition) that all criminal statutes are punitive (merely labeling an act a crime does not make it one unless sanctions are specified); but to the converse question whether all statutes specifying sanctions are *criminal* statutes, the courts are reluctant to give an affirmative reply. There are now a great number of statutes that permit "unpleasant consequences" to be inflicted on persons and yet are surely not criminal statutes—tax bills, for example, are aimed at regulating, not forbidding, certain types of activity. How to classify borderline cases as either "regulative" or "punitive" is not merely an idle conceptual riddle; it very quickly draws the courts into questions of great constitutional import. There are elaborate constitutional safeguards for persons faced with the prospect of punishment; but these do not, or need not, apply when the threatened hard treatment merely "regulates an activity."

The 1960 Supreme Court case of *Flemming v. Nestor*[12] is a dramatic (and shocking) example of how a man's fate can depend on whether a government-inflicted deprivation is interpreted as a "regulative" or "punitive" sanction. Nestor had immigrated to the United States from Bulgaria in 1913, and in 1955 became eligible for old-age benefits under the Social Security Act. In 1956, however, he was deported in accordance with the Immigration and Nationality Act, for having been a member of the Communist Party from 1933 to 1939. This was a hard fate for a man who had been in America for forty-three years and who was no longer a Communist; but at least he would have his social security benefits to support him in his exiled old age. Or so he

thought. Section 202 of the amended Social Security Act, however,

> provides for the termination of old-age, survivor, and disability insurance benefits payable to … an alien individual who, after September 1, 1954 (the date of enactment of the section) is deported under the Immigration and Nationality Act on any one of certain specified grounds, including past membership in the Communist Party.[13]

Accordingly, Nestor was informed that his benefits would cease.

Nestor then brought suit in a federal district court for a reversal of the administrative decision. The court found in his favor and held § 202 of the Social Security Act unconstitutional, on the grounds that:

> termination of [Nestor's] benefits amounts to punishing him without a judicial trial, that [it] constitutes the imposition of punishment by legislative act rendering § 202 a bill of attainder; and that the punishment exacted is imposed for past conduct not unlawful when engaged in, thereby violating the constitutional prohibition on ex post facto laws.[14]

The Secretary of Health, Education, and Welfare, Mr. Flemming, then appealed this decision to the Supreme Court.

It was essential to the argument of the district court that the termination of old-age benefits under § 202 was in fact punishment, for if it were properly classified as nonpunitive deprivation, then none of the cited constitutional guarantees was relevant. The constitution, for example, does not forbid all retroactive laws, but only those providing punishment. (Retroactive tax laws may also be hard and unfair, but they are not unconstitutional.) The question before the Supreme Court then was whether the hardship imposed by § 202 was punishment. Did this not bring the Court face to face with the properly philosophical question "What is punishment?" and is it not clear that under the usual definition that fails to distinguish punishment from mere penalties, this particular judicial problem could not even arise?

The fate of the appellee Nestor can be recounted briefly. The five man majority of the court held that he had not been punished—this despite Mr. Justice Brennan's eloquent characterization of him in a dissenting opinion as "an aging man deprived of the means with which to live after being separated from his family and exiled to live among strangers in a land he quit forty-seven years ago."[15] Mr. Justice Harlan, writing for the majority, argued that the termination of benefits, like the deportation itself, was the exercise of the plenary power of Congress incident to the regulation of an activity.

> Similarly, the setting by a State of qualifications for the practice of medicine, and their modification from time to time, is an incident of the State's power to protect the health and safety of its citizens, and its decision to bar from practice persons who commit or have committed a felony is taken as evidencing an intent to exercise that regulatory power, and not a purpose to add to the punishment of ex-felons.[16]

Mr. Justice Brennan, on the other hand, argued that it is impossible to think of any purpose the provision in question could possibly serve except to "strike" at "aliens deported for conduct displeasing to the lawmakers."[17]

Surely Justice Brennan seems right in finding in the sanction the expression of congressional reprobation, and therefore "punitive intent"; but the sanction itself (in Justice Harlan's words, "the mere denial of a noncontractual governmental benefit"[18]) was not a conventional vehicle for the expression of censure, being wholly outside the apparatus of the criminal law. It therefore lacked the reprobative symbolism essential to punishment generally, and was thus, in its hybrid character, able to generate confusion and judicial disagreement. It was as if Congress had "condemned" a certain class of persons privately in stage whispers, rather than by pinning the infamous label of criminal on them and letting that symbol do the condemning in an open and public way. Congress without question "intended" to punish a certain class of aliens and did indeed select sanctions of appropriate severity for that use; but the deprivation they selected was not of an appropriate kind to perform the function of public condemnation. A father who "punishes" his son

for a displeasing act the father had not thought to forbid in advance, by sneaking up on him from behind and then throwing him bodily across the room against the wall, would be in much the same position as the legislators of the amended Social Security Act, especially if he then denied to the son that his physical assault on him had had any "punitive intent," asserting that it was a mere exercise of his parental prerogative to rearrange the household furnishings and other objects in his own living room. This would be to tarnish the paternal authority and infect all later genuine punishments with hollow hypocrisy. This also happens when legislators go outside the criminal law to do the criminal law's job.

In 1961 the New York State Legislature passed the so-called "Subversive Drivers Act" requiring "suspension and revocation of the driver's license of anyone who has been convicted, under the Smith Act, of advocating the overthrow of the Federal government." *The Reporter* magazine[19] quoted the sponsor of the bill as admitting that it was aimed primarily at one person, Communist Benjamin Davis, who had only recently won a court fight to regain his driver's license after his five-year term in prison. *The Reporter* estimated that at most a "few dozen" people would be kept from driving by the new legislation. Was this punishment? Not at all, said the bill's sponsor, Assemblyman Paul Taylor. The legislature was simply exercising its right to regulate automobile traffic in the interest of public safety:

> Driving licenses, Assemblyman Taylor explained... are not a "right" but a "valuable privilege." The Smith Act Communists, after all, were convicted of advocating the overthrow of the government by force, violence, or assassination. ("They always leave out the assassination," he remarked. "I like to put it in.") Anyone who was convicted under such an act had to be "a person pretty well dedicated to a certain point of view," the assemblyman continued, and anyone with that particular point of view "can't be concerned about the rights of others." Being concerned about the rights of others, he concluded, "is a prerequisite of being a good driver."[20]

This shows how transparent can be the effort to mask punitive intent. The Smith Act ex-convicts were treated with such severity and in such circumstances that no nonpunitive legislative purpose could *plausibly* be maintained; yet that *kind* of treatment (quite apart from its severity) lacks the reprobative symbolism essential to clear public denunciation. After all, aged, crippled, and blind persons are also deprived of their licenses, so it is not *necessarily* the case that reprobation attaches to that kind of sanction. And so victims of a cruel law understandably claim that they have been punished, and retroactively at that. Yet strictly speaking they have not been *punished;* they have been treated much worse.

IV. THE PROBLEM OF STRICT CRIMINAL LIABILITY

The distinction between punishments and mere penalties, and the essentially reprobative function of the former, can also help clarify the controversy among writers on the criminal law about the propriety of so-called "strict liability offenses"— offenses for the conviction of which there need be no showing of "fault" or "culpability" on the part of the accused. If it can be shown that he committed an act proscribed by statute then he is guilty irrespective of whether he had justification or excuse for what he did. Perhaps the most familiar examples come from the traffic laws: Leaving a car parked beyond the permitted time in a restricted zone is automatically to violate the law, and penalties will be imposed however good the excuse. Many strict liability statutes do not even require an overt act; these proscribe not certain conduct but certain *results.* Some make mere unconscious possession of contraband, firearms, or narcotics a crime, others the sale of misbranded articles or impure foods. The liability for so-called "public welfare offenses" may seem especially severe:

> [W]ith rare exceptions, it became definitely established that *mens rea* is not essential in the public welfare offenses, indeed that even a very high degree of care is irrelevant. Thus a seller of cattle feed was convicted of violating a statute forbidding misrepresentation of the percentage of oil in the product, despite the fact that he had employed a reputable chemist to make the analysis and had even understated the chemist's findings.[21]

The rationale of strict liability in public welfare statutes is that violation of the public interest is more likely to be prevented by unconditional liability than by liability that can be defeated by some kind of excuse; that even though liability without "fault" is severe, it is one of the known risks incurred by businessmen; and that besides, the sanctions are *only fines,* hence not really "punitive" in character. On the other hand, strict liability to *imprisonment* (or "punishment proper") "has been held by many to be incompatible with the basic requirements of our Anglo-American, and indeed, any civilized jurisprudence."[22] Why should this be? In both kinds of case, defendants may have sanctions inflicted upon them even though they are acknowledged to be without fault; and the difference cannot be simply that imprisonment is always and necessarily a greater hurt than fine, for this is not always so. Rather, the reason why strict liability to imprisonment (punishment) is so much more repugnant to our sense of justice than is strict liability to fine (penalty) is simply that imprisonment in modern times has taken on the symbolism of public reprobation. In the words of Justice Brandeis, "It is … imprisonment in a penitentiary, which now renders a crime infamous."[23] We are familiar with the practice of penalizing persons for "offenses" they could not help. It happens every day in football games, business firms, traffic courts, and the like. But there is something very odd and offensive in *punishing* people for admittedly faultless conduct; for not only is it arbitrary and cruel to *condemn* someone for something he did (admittedly) without fault, it is also self-defeating and irrational.

Though their abundant proliferation[24] is a relatively recent phenomenon, statutory offenses with nonpunitive sanctions have long been familiar to legal commentators, and long a source of uneasiness to them. This is "indicated by the persistent search for an appropriate label, such as 'public torts,' 'public welfare offenses,' 'prohibitory laws,' 'prohibited acts,' 'regulatory offenses,' 'police regulations,' 'administrative misdemeanors,' 'quasi-crimes,' or 'civil offenses.'"[25] These represent alternatives to the unacceptable categorization of traffic infractions, inadvertent violations of commercial regulations, and the like, as *crimes*, their perpetrators as *criminals*, and their penalties as *punishments*. The drafters of the new Model Penal Code have defined a class of infractions of penal law forming no part of the substantive criminal law. These they call "violations," and their sanctions "civil penalties."

Section 1.04. Classes of Crimes: Violations

(1) An offense defined by this Code or by any other statute of this State, for which a sentence of [death or of] imprisonment is authorized, constitutes a crime. Crimes are classified as felonies, misdemeanors, or petty misdemeanors.

[(2), (3), (4) define felonies, misdemeanors, and petty misdemeanors.]

(5) An offense defined by this Code or by any other statute of this State constitutes a violation if it is so designated in this Code or in the law defining the offense or if no other sentence than a fine, or fine and forfeiture or other civil penalty is authorized upon conviction or if it is defined by a statute other than this Code which now provides that the offense shall not constitute a crime. A violation does not constitute a crime and conviction of a violation shall not give rise to any disability or legal disadvantage based on conviction of a criminal offense.[26]

Since violations, unlike crimes, carry no social stigma, it is often argued that there is no serious injustice if, in the interest of quick and effective law enforcement, violators are held unconditionally liable. This line of argument is persuasive when we consider only parking and minor traffic violations, illegal sales of various kinds, and violations of health and safety codes, where the penalties serve as warnings and the fines are light. But the argument loses all cogency when the "civil penalties" are severe—heavy fines, forfeitures of property, removal from office, suspension of a license, withholding of an important "benefit," and the like. The condemnation of the faultless may be the most flagrant injustice, but the good-natured, noncondemnatory infliction of severe hardship on the innocent is little better. It is useful to distinguish violations and civil penalties from crimes and punishments; but it does not follow that the safeguards of culpability requirements and due process that justice demands for the latter are always irrelevant encumbrances to the former. Two things

are morally wrong: (1) to condemn a faultless man while inflicting pain or deprivation on him however slight (unjust punishment); and (2) to inflict unnecessary and severe suffering on a faultless man even in the absence of condemnation (unjust civil penalty). To exact a two-dollar fine [Feinberg wrote in a simpler time, before Denver boots and $100 parking fines!] from a hapless violator for overtime parking, however, even though he could not possibly have helped it, is to do neither of these things.

V. JUSTIFYING LEGAL PUNISHMENT; LETTING THE PUNISHMENT FIT THE CRIME

Public condemnation, whether avowed through the stigmatizing symbolism of punishment or unavowed but clearly discernible (mere "punitive intent"), can greatly magnify the suffering caused by its attendant mode of hard treatment. Samuel Butler keenly appreciated the difference between reprobative hard treatment (punishment) and the same treatment sans reprobation:

[W]e should hate a single flogging given in the way of mere punishment more than the amputation of a limb, if it were kindly and courteously performed from a wish to help us out of our difficulty, and with the full consciousness on the part of the doctor that it was only by an accident of constitution that he was not in the like plight himself. So the Erewhonians take a flogging once a week, and a diet of bread and water for two or three months together, whenever their straightener recommends it.[27]

Even floggings and imposed fastings do not constitute punishments, then, where social conventions are such that they do not express public censure (what Butler called "scouting"); and as therapeutic treatments simply, rather than punishments, they are easier to take.

Yet floggings and fastings do hurt, and far more than is justified by their Erewhonian (therapeutic) objectives. The same is true of our own state mental hospitals, where criminal psychopaths are often sent for "rehabilitation": Solitary confinement may not hurt *quite* so much when called "the quiet room," or the forced support of heavy fire extinguishers when called "hydrotherapy";[28]

but their infliction on patients can be so cruel (whether or not their quasi-medical names mask punitive intent) as to demand justification.

Hard treatment and symbolic condemnation, then, are not only both necessary to an adequate definition of *punishment;* each also poses a special problem for the justification of punishment. The reprobative symbolism of punishment is subject to attack not only as an independent source of suffering but as the vehicle of undeserved responsive attitudes and unfair judgments of blame. One kind of skeptic, granting that penalties are needed if legal rules are to be enforced, and also that society would be impossible without general and predictable obedience to such rules, might nevertheless question the need to add condemnation to the penalizing of violators. Hard treatment of violators, he might grant, is an unhappy necessity, but reprobation of the offender is offensively self-righteous and cruel; adding gratuitous insult to necessary injury can serve no useful purpose. A partial answer to this kind of skeptic has already been given. The condemnatory aspect of punishment does serve a socially useful purpose: It is precisely the element in punishment that makes possible the performance of such symbolic functions as disavowal, nonacquiescence, vindication, and absolution.

Another kind of skeptic might readily grant that the reprobative symbolism of punishment is necessary to and justified by these various derivative functions. Indeed, he may even add deterrence to the list, for condemnation is likely to make it clear where it would not otherwise be so that a penalty is not a mere price tag. Granting that point, however, this kind of skeptic would have us consider whether the ends that justify public condemnation of criminal conduct might not be achieved equally well by means of less painful symbolic machinery. There was a time, after all, when the gallows and the rack were the leading clear symbols of shame and ignominy. Now we condemn felons to penal servitude as the way of rendering their crimes infamous. Could not the job be done still more economically? Isn't there a way to stigmatize without inflicting any further (pointless) pain to the body, to family, to creative capacity?

One can imagine an elaborate public ritual, exploiting the trustiest devices of religion and mystery, music and drama, to express in the most solemn way the community's condemnation of a criminal for his dastardly deed. Such a ritual might condemn so very emphatically that there could be no doubt of its genuineness, thus rendering symbolically superfluous any further hard physical treatment. Such a device would preserve the condemnatory function of punishment while dispensing with its usual physical forms—incarceration and corporal mistreatment. Perhaps this is only idle fantasy; perhaps there is more to it. The question is surely open. The only point I wish to make here is one about the nature of the question. The problem of justifying punishment, when it takes this form, may really be that of justifying our particular symbols of infamy.

Whatever the form of skeptical challenge to the institution of punishment, however, there is one traditional answer to it that seems to me to be incoherent. I refer to that form of the Retributive Theory that mentions neither condemnation nor vengeance, but insists instead that the ultimate justifying purpose of punishment is to match off moral gravity and pain, to give each offender exactly that amount of pain the evil of his offense calls for, on the alleged principle of justice that the wicked should suffer pain in exact proportion to their turpitude.

I will only mention in passing the familiar and potent objections to this view.[29] The innocent presumably deserve not to suffer just as the guilty are supposed to deserve to suffer; yet it is impossible to hurt an evil man without imposing suffering on those who love or depend on him. Deciding the right amount of suffering to inflict in a given case would require an assessment of the character of the offender as manifested through his whole life, and also his total lifelong balance of pleasure and pain, an obvious impossibility. Moreover, justice would probably demand the abandonment of general rules in the interests of individuation of punishment since there will inevitably be inequalities of moral guilt in the commission of the same crime, and inequalities of suffering from the same punishment. If not dispensed with, however, general rules must list all crimes in the order of their moral gravity, all punishments in the order of their severity, and the matchings between the two scales. But the moral gravity scale would have to list motives and purposes, not simply types of overt acts, for a given crime can be committed from any kind of "mental state," and its "moral gravity" in a given case surely must depend in part on its accompanying motive. Condign punishment then would have to match suffering to motive (desire, belief, etc.), not to dangerousness or to amount of harm done. Hence some petty larcenies would be punished more severely than some murders. It is not likely we should wish to give power to judges and juries to make such difficult moral judgments. Worse than this, the judgments required are not merely "difficult," they are in principle impossible. It may seem "self-evident" to some moralists that the passionate impulsive killer, for example, deserves less suffering for his wickedness than the scheming deliberate killer; but if the question of comparative *dangerousness* is left out of mind, reasonable men not only can but will disagree in their appraisals of comparative blameworthiness, and there appears no rational way of resolving the issue.[30] Certainly, there is no rational way of demonstrating that one deserves exactly twice or three-eighths or twelve-ninths as much suffering as the other; yet on some forms, at least, of this theory, the amount of suffering inflicted for any two crimes should stand in exact proportion to the "amounts" of wickedness in the criminals.

For all that, however, the pain-fitting-wickedness version of the retributive theory does erect its edifice of moral superstition on a foundation in moral common sense, for justice *does* require that in some (other) sense "the punishment fit the crime." What justice requires is that the *condemnatory aspect* of the punishment suit the crime, that the crime be of a kind that is truly worthy of reprobation. Further, the degree of disapproval expressed by the punishment should "fit" the crime only in the unproblematic sense that the more serious crimes should receive stronger disapproval than the less serious ones, the seriousness of the crime being determined by the amount of harm it generally causes and the degree

to which people are disposed to commit it. That is quite another thing than requiring that the hard treatment component, considered apart from its symbolic function, should "fit" the moral quality of a specific criminal act, assessed quite independently of its relation to social harm. Given our conventions, of course, condemnation is expressed by hard treatment, and the degree of harshness of the latter expresses the degree of reprobation of the former; still this should not blind us to the fact that it is social disapproval and its appropriate expression that should fit the crime, and not hard treatment (pain) as such. Pain should match guilt only insofar as its infliction is the symbolic vehicle of public condemnation.

NOTES

1. See especially the following: Flew, A. "The Justification of Punishment." *Philosophy* 29 (1954): 291–307; Benn, S. I. "An Approach to the Problems of Punishment." *Philosophy*. 33 (1958): 325–341; and Hart, H. L. A. "Prolegomenon to the Principles of Punishment." *Proceedings of the Aristotelian Society* 60 (1959–60): 1–26.

2. Hart and Benn both borrow Flew's definition. In Hart's paraphrase (Hart, "Prolegomenon," supra, note 1, at 4), punishment:

   (i) … must involve pain or other consequences normally considered unpleasant. (ii) It must be for an offense against legal rules. (iii) It must be of an actual or supposed offender for his offense. (iv) It must be intentionally administered by human beings other than the offender. (v) It must be imposed and administered by an authority constituted by a legal system against which the offense is committed.

3. The distinction between punishments and penalties was first called to my attention by Dr. Anita Fritz of the University of Connecticut. Similar distinctions in different terminologies have been made by many. Pollock and Maitland speak of "true afflictive punishments" as opposed to outlawry, private vengeance, fine, and emendation. (*History of English Law.* 2d ed. Vol. II, 451 ff.) The phrase "afflictive punishment" was invented by Bentham (*Rationale of Punishment*, London, 1830): "These [corporal] punishments are almost always attended with a portion of ignominy, and this does not always increase with the organic

pain, but principally depends upon the condition [social class] of the offender" Id., at 83.

James Stephen says of legal punishment that it "should always connote ... moral infamy." *History of the Criminal Law*. Vol. II, 171. Lasswell and Donnelly distinguish "condemnation sanctions" and "other deprivations." "The Continuing Debate over Responsibility: An Introduction to Isolating the Condemnation Sanction." Yale Law Journal 68 (1959). The traditional common law distinction is between "infamous" and "noninfamous" crimes and punishments. Conviction of an "infamous crime" rendered a person liable to such postpunitive civil disabilities as incompetence to be a witness.

4. That even punishments proper are to be interpreted as taxes on certain kinds of conduct is a view often associated with Oliver Wendall Holmes, Jr. For an excellent discussion of Holmes's fluctuations on this question see Howe, Mark De Wolfe. *Justice Holmes, The Proving Years*. Cambridge, Mass., 1963. 74–80. For illuminating comparisons and contrasts of punishment and taxation, see also Fuller, Lon. *The Morality of Law*. New Haven, 1964. chap. II, part 7, and Hart, H. L. A. *The Concept of Law*. Oxford: Oxford University Press, 1961. 39.

5. H. L. A. Hart, supra, note 4.

6. Hart, Henry M. "The Aims of the Criminal Law." *Law and Contemporary Problems* 23 (1958): II, A, 4.

7. *General View of the Criminal Law of England*. 1st ed. London, 1863. 99.

8. *Report of the Royal Commission on Capital Punishment*. London, 1953. 17–18.

9. The Texas Penal Code (Art. 1220) states: "Homicide is justifiable when committed by the husband upon one taken in the act of adultery with the wife, provided the killing takes place before the parties to the act have separated. Such circumstances cannot justify a homicide when it appears that there has been, on the part of the husband, any connivance in or assent to the adulterous connection." New Mexico and Utah have similar statutes. For some striking descriptions of perfectly legal paramour killings in Texas, see Bainbridge, John. *The Super-Americans*. New York: Garden City Publishing, 1961. 238 ff.

10. Kant, Immanuel. *The Philosophy of Law* Trans. W. Hastie. Edinburgh, 1887. 198.

11. Hall, Jerome. *General Principles of Criminal Law*. 2d ed. Indianapolis, 1960. 328, hereafter cited as *GPCL*.

12. *Flemming v. Nestor* 363 U.S. 603, 80 S. Ct. 1367 (1960).

13. Id., at 1370.

14. Id., at 1374 (interspersed citations omitted).

15. Id., at 1385.

16. Id., at 1375–76.

17. Id., at 1387.

18. Id., at 1376.

19. *The Reporter* 11 May 1961, 14.

20. Id.

21. Hall, *GPCL*, supra, note 11, at 329.

22. Wasserstrom, Richard A. "Strict Liability in the Criminal Law." *Stanford Law Review* 12 (1960): 730.

23. *United States v. Moreland*, 258 U.S. 433, 447–48. Quoted in Hall, *GPCL*, supra, note 11, at 327.

24. Howard, Colin. "Not Proven." *Adelaide Law Review* 1 (1962): 274:

> A depth study of Wisconsin statutes in 1956 revealed that of 1,113 statutes creating criminal offenses [punishable by fine, imprisonment, or both] that were in force in 1953, no less than 660 used language in the definitions of the offenses that omitted all reference to a mental element, and which therefore, under the canons of construction that have come to govern these matters, left it open to the courts to impose strict liability if they saw fit.

The study cited is: Remington, Robinson, and Zick. "Liability Without Fault Criminal Statutes." *Wisconsin Law Review* (1956): 625–636.

25. Perkins, Rollin M. *Criminal Law*. Brooklyn, 1957. 701–2.

26. American Law Institute, *Model Penal Code, Proposed Official Draft*. Philadelphia, 1962.

27. Butler, Samuel. *Erewhon*. London, 1901. chapter 10.

28. These two examples are cited in Allen, Francis A. "Criminal Justice, Legal Values and the Rehabilitative Ideal." *Journal of Criminal Law, Criminology and Police Science* 50 (1959): 229.

29. For more convincing statements of these arguments, see *inter alia*: Ross, W. D. *The Right and the Good*. Oxford, 1930. 56–65; Mabbott, J. D. "Punishment." *Mind* 49 (1939); Ewing, A. C. *The Morality of Punishment*. London, 1929. chap. 1; and Dostoevsky, F. *The House of the Dead*.

30. Cf. Michael, Jerome and Wechsler, Herbert. "Note on Deliberation and Character." *Criminal Law and Its Administration*. Chicago, 1940. 170–72.

58   Persons and Punishment

HERBERT MORRIS

They acted and looked ... at us, and around in our house, in a way that had about it the feeling—at least for me—that we were not people. In their eyesight we were just things, that was all.

—MALCOLM X

We have no right to treat a man like a dog.

—Governor Lester Maddox of Georgia

Alfredo Traps in Friedrich Dürrenmatt's tale ["Traps"] discovers that he has brought off, all by himself, a murder involving considerable ingenuity. The mock prosecutor in the tale demands the death penalty "as reward for a crime that merits admiration, astonishment, and respect." Traps is deeply moved; indeed, he is exhilarated, and the whole of his life becomes more heroic, and, ironically, more precious. His defense attorney proceeds to argue that Traps was not only innocent, but incapable of guilt, "a victim of the age." This defense Traps disavows with indignation and anger. He makes claim to the murder as his and demands the prescribed punishment—death.

The themes to be found in this macabre tale do not often find their way into philosophical discussions of punishment. These discussions deal with large and significant questions of whether or not we ever have the right to punish, and if we do, under what conditions, to what degree, and in what manner. There is a tradition, of course, not notable for its present vitality, that is closely linked with motifs in Dürrenmatt's tale of crime and punishment. Its adherents have urged that justice requires a person be punished if he is guilty. Sometimes—though rarely—these philosophers have expressed themselves in terms of the criminal's *right to be punished.* Reaction to the

claim that there is such a right has been astonishment combined, perhaps, with a touch of contempt for the perversity of the suggestion. A strange right that no one would ever wish to claim! With that flourish the subject is buried and the right disposed of. In this paper the subject is resurrected.

My aim is to argue for four propositions concerning rights that will certainly strike some as not only false but preposterous: first, that we have a right to punishment; second, that this right derives from a fundamental human right to be treated as a person; third, that this fundamental right is a natural, inalienable, and absolute right; and, fourth, that the denial of this right implies the denial of all moral rights and duties. Showing the truth of one, let alone all, of these large and questionable claims is a tall order. The attempt or, more properly speaking, the first steps in an attempt follow.

1.

When someone claims that there is a right to be free, we can easily imagine situations in which the right to be free is infringed and easily imagine situations in which there is a point to asserting or claiming the right. With the right to be punished, matters are otherwise. The immediate reaction to the claim that there is such a right is puzzlement. And the reasons for this are apparent. People do not normally value pain and suffering. Punishment is associated with pain and suffering. When we think about punishment we naturally think of the strong desire most persons have to avoid it, to accept, for example, acquittal of a criminal charge with relief and eagerly, if convicted, to hope for pardon or probation. Adding, of course, to the paradoxical character of the claim of such a right is difficulty in imagining circumstances in which it would be denied one. When would one rightly demand punishment and meet with any threat of the claim being denied?

So our first task is to see when the claim of such a right would have a point. I want to approach this task by setting out two complex types of institutions, both of which are designed to maintain some degree of social control. In the one a central concept is punishment for wrongdoing and in the other the central concepts are control of dangerous individuals and treatment of disease.

Let us first turn attention to the institutions in which punishment is involved. The institution I describe will resemble those we ordinarily think of as institutions of punishment; they will have, however, additional features we associate with a system of just punishment.

Let us suppose that men are constituted roughly as they now are, with a rough equivalence in strength and abilities, a capacity to be injured by each other and to make judgments that such injury is undesirable, a limited strength of will, and a capacity to reason and to conform conduct to rules. Applying to the conduct of these men are a group of rules, ones I shall label *primary*, which closely resemble the core rules of our criminal law, rules that prohibit violence and deception and compliance with which provides benefits for all persons. These benefits consist in noninterference by others with what each person values, such matters as continuance of life and bodily security. The rules define a sphere for each person, then, which is immune from interference by others. Making possible this mutual benefit is the assumption by individuals of a burden. The burden consists in the exercise of self-restraint by individuals over inclinations that would, if satisfied, directly interfere or create a substantial risk of interference with others in proscribed ways. If a person fails to exercise self-restraint even though he might have, and gives in to such inclinations, he renounces a burden that others have voluntarily assumed and thus gains an advantage that others, who have restrained themselves, do not possess. This system, then, is one in which the rules establish a mutuality of benefit and burden and in which the benefits of

noninterference are conditional upon the assumption of burdens.

Connecting punishment with the violation of these primary rules, and making public the provision for punishment, is both reasonable and just. First, it is only reasonable that those who voluntarily comply with the rules be provided some assurance that they will not be assuming burdens that others are unprepared to assume. Their disposition to comply voluntarily will diminish as they learn that others are with impunity renouncing burdens they are assuming. Second, fairness dictates that a system in which benefits and burdens are equally distributed have a mechanism designed to prevent a maldistribution in the benefits and burdens. Thus, sanctions are attached to noncompliance with the primary rules so as to induce compliance with the primary rules among those who may be disinclined to obey. In this way the likelihood of an unfair distribution is diminished.

Third, it is just to punish those who have violated the rules and caused the unfair distribution of benefits and burdens. A person who violates the rules has something others have—the benefits of the system—but by renouncing what others have assumed, the burdens of self-restraint, he has acquired an unfair advantage. Matters are not even until this advantage is in some way erased. Another way of putting it is that he owes something to others, for he has something that does not rightfully belong to him. Justice—that is, punishing such individuals—restores the equilibrium of benefits and burdens by taking from the individual what he owes, that is, exacting the debt. It is important to see that the equilibrium may be restored in another way. Forgiveness—with its legal analogue of a pardon—while not the righting of an unfair distribution by making one pay his debt is, nevertheless, a restoring of the equilibrium by forgiving the debt. Forgiveness may be viewed, at least in some types of cases, as a gift after the fact, erasing a debt, which, had the gift been given before the fact, would not have created a debt. But the practice of pardoning has to proceed sensitively, for it may endanger, in a way the practice of justice does not, the maintenance of an equilibrium of benefits and burdens. If all are indiscriminately pardoned less incentive is provided individuals to restrain their inclinations, thus increasing the incidence of persons taking what they do not deserve.

There are also in this system we are considering a variety of operative principles, compliance with which provides some guarantee that the system of punishment does not itself promote an unfair distribution of benefits and burdens. For one thing, provision is made for a variety of defenses, each one of which can be said to have as its object diminishing the chances of forcibly depriving a person of benefits others have if that person has not derived an unfair advantage. A person has not derived an unfair advantage if he could not have restrained himself or if it is unreasonable to expect him to behave otherwise than he did. Sometimes the rules preclude punishment of classes of persons such as children. Sometimes they provide a defense if on a particular occasion a person lacked the capacity to conform his conduct to the rules. Thus, someone who in an epileptic seizure strikes another is excused. Punishment in these cases would be punishment of the innocent, punishment of those who do not voluntarily renounce a burden others have assumed. Punishment in such cases, then, would not equalize but rather cause an unfair distribution in benefits and burdens.

Along with principles providing defenses there are requirements that the rules be prospective and relatively clear so that persons have a fair opportunity to comply with the rules. There are, also, rules governing, among other matters, the burden of proof, who shall bear it and what it shall be; the prohibition on double jeopardy; and the privilege against self-incrimination. Justice requires conviction of the guilty, and requires their punishment, but in setting out to fulfill the demands of justice we may, of course, because we are not omniscient, cause injustice by convicting and punishing the innocent. The resolution arrived at in the system I am describing consists in weighing as the greater evil the punishment of the innocent. The primary function of the system of rules was to provide individuals with a sphere of interest immune from interference. Given this goal, it is determined to be a greater evil for society to interfere unjustifiably with an individual by depriving him of good than for the society to fail to punish those that have unjustifiably interfered.

Finally, because the primary rules are designed to benefit all and because the punishments prescribed for their violation are publicized and the defenses respected, there is some plausibility in the exaggerated claim that in choosing to do an act violative of the rules an individual has chosen to be punished. This way of putting matters brings to our attention the extent to which, when the system is as I have described it, the criminal "has brought the punishment upon himself" in contrast to those cases where it would be misleading to say "he has brought it upon himself," cases, for example, where one does not know the rules or is punished in the absence of fault.

To summarize, then: first, there is a group of rules guiding the behavior of individuals in the community that establish spheres of interest immune from interference by others; second, provision is made for what is generally regarded as a deprivation of some thing of value if the rules are violated; third, the deprivations visited upon any person are justified by that person's having violated the rules; fourth, the deprivation, in this just system of punishment, is linked to rules that fairly distribute benefits and burdens and to procedures that strike some balance between not punishing the guilty and punishing the innocent, a class defined as those who have not voluntarily done acts violative of the law, in which it is evident that the evil of punishing the innocent is regarded as greater than the nonpunishment of the guilty.

At the core of many actual legal systems one finds, of course, rules and procedures of the kind I have sketched. It is obvious, though, that any ongoing legal system differs in significant respects from what I have presented here, containing "pockets of injustice."

I want now to sketch an extreme version of a set of institutions of a fundamentally different kind, institutions proceeding on a conception of man that appears to be basically at odds with that operative within a system of punishment.

Rules are promulgated in this system that prohibit certain types of injuries and harms.

In this world we are now to imagine when an individual harms another his conduct is to be regarded as a symptom of some pathological condition in the way a running nose is a symptom of a cold. Actions diverging from some conception of the normal are viewed as manifestations of a disease in the way in which we might today regard the arm and leg movements of an epileptic during a seizure. Actions conforming to what is normal are assimilated to the normal and healthy functioning of bodily organs. What a person does, then, is assimilated, on this conception. to what we believe today, or at least most of us believe today, a person undergoes. We draw a distinction between the operation of the kidney and raising an arm on request. This distinction between mere events or happenings and human actions is erased in our imagined system.[1]

There is, however, bound to be something strange in this erasing of a recognized distinction, for, as with metaphysical suggestions generally, and I take this to be one, the distinction may be reintroduced but given a different description, for example, "happenings with X type of causes" and "happenings with Y type of causes." Responses of different kinds, today legitimated by our distinction between happenings and actions, may be legitimated by this new manner of description. And so there may be isomorphism between a system recognizing the distinction and one erasing it. Still, when this distinction is erased certain tendencies of thought and responses might naturally arise that would tend to affect unfavorably values respected by a system of punishment.

Let us elaborate on this assimilation of conduct of a certain kind to symptoms of a disease. First, there is something abnormal in both the case of conduct, such as killing another, and a symptom of a disease such as an irregular heartbeat. Second, there are causes for this abnormality in action such that once we know of them we can explain the abnormality as we now can explain the symptoms of many physical diseases. The abnormality is looked upon as a happening with a causal explanation rather than an action for which there were reasons. Third, the causes that account for the abnormality interfere with the normal functioning of the body, or, in the case of killing,

with what is regarded as a normal functioning of an individual. Fourth, the abnormality is in some way a part of the individual, necessarily involving his body. A well going dry might satisfy our three foregoing conditions of disease symptoms, but it is hardly a disease or the symptom of one. Finally, and most obscure, the abnormality arises in some way from within the individual. If Jones is hit with a mallet by Smith, Jones may reel about and fall on James who may be injured. But this abnormal conduct of Jones is not regarded as a symptom of disease. Smith, not Jones, is suffering from some pathological condition.

With this view of man the institutions of social control respond, not with punishment, but with either preventive detention, in case of "carriers," or therapy in the case of those manifesting pathological symptoms. The logic of sickness implies the logic of therapy. And therapy and punishment differ widely in their implications. In bringing out some of these differences I want again to draw attention to the important fact that, although the distinctions we now draw are erased in the therapy world, they may, in fact, be reintroduced but under different descriptions. To the extent they are, we really have a punishment system combined with a therapy system. I am concerned now, however, with what the implications would be were the world indeed one of therapy and not a disguised world of punishment and therapy, for I want to suggest tendencies of thought that arise when one is immersed in the ideology of disease and therapy.

First, punishment is the imposition, upon a person who is believed to be at fault, of something commonly believed to be a deprivation, where that deprivation is justified by the person's guilty behavior. It is associated with resentment, for the guilty are those who have done what they had no right to do by failing to exercise restraint when they might have and where others have. Therapy is not a response to a person who is at fault. We respond to an individual, not because of what he has done, but because of some condition from which he is suffering. If he is no longer suffering from the condition, treatment no longer has a point. Punishment, then, focuses on the past; therapy on the present. Therapy is normally associated with compassion for what one undergoes, not resentment for what one has illegitimately done.

Second, with therapy, unlike punishment, we do not seek to deprive the person of something acknowledged as a good, but seek rather to help and to benefit the individual who is suffering by ministering to his illness in the hope that the person can be cured. The good we attempt to do is not a reward for desert. The individual suffering has not merited by his disease the good we seek to bestow upon him but has, because he is a creature that has the capacity to feel pain, a claim upon our sympathies and help.

Third, we saw with punishment that its justification was related to maintaining and restoring a fair distribution of benefits and burdens. Infliction of the prescribed punishment carries the implication, then, that one has "paid one's debt" to society, for the punishment is the taking from the person of something commonly recognized as valuable. It is this conception of "a debt owed" that may permit, as I suggested earlier, under certain conditions, the nonpunishment of the guilty, for operative within a system of punishment may be a concept analogous to forgiveness, namely pardoning. Who it is that we may pardon and under what conditions—contrition with its elements of self-punishment no doubt plays a role—I shall not go into, though it is clearly a matter of the greatest practical and theoretical interest. What is clear is that the conceptions of "paying a debt" or "having a debt forgiven" or pardoning have no place in a system of therapy.

Fourth, with punishment there is an attempt at some equivalence between the advantage gained by the wrongdoer—partly based upon the seriousness of the interest invaded, partly on the state of mind with which the wrongful act was performed—and the punishment meted out. Thus, we can understand a prohibition on "cruel and unusual punishments" so that disproportionate pain and suffering are avoided. With therapy, attempts at proportionality make no sense. It is perfectly plausible giving someone who kills a pill and treating for a lifetime within an institution one who has broken a dish and manifested accident proneness. We have the concept of "painful treatment." We do not have the concept of "cruel treatment." Because treatment is regarded as a benefit, though it may involve pain, it is natural that less restraint is exercised in bestowing it than in inflicting punishment. Further, protests with respect to treatment are likely to be assimilated to the complaints of one whose leg must be amputated in order for him to live, and, thus, largely disregarded. To be sure, there is operative in the therapy world some conception of the "cure being worse than the disease," but if the disease is manifested in conduct harmful to others, and if being a normal operating human being is valued highly, there will naturally be considerable pressure to find the cure acceptable.

Fifth, the rules in our system of punishment governing conduct of individuals were rules violation of which involved either direct interference with others or the creation of a substantial risk of such interference. One could imagine adding to this system of primary rules other rules proscribing preparation to do acts violative of the primary rules, and even rules proscribing thoughts. Objection to such suggestions would have many sources, but a principal one would consist in its involving the infliction of punishment on too great a number of persons who would not, because of a change of mind, have violated the primary rules. Though we are interested in diminishing violations of the primary rules, we are not prepared to punish too many individuals who would never have violated the rules in order to achieve this aim. In a system motivated solely by a preventive and curative ideology there would be less reason to wait until symptoms manifest themselves in socially harmful conduct. It is understandable that we should wish at the earliest possible stage to arrest the development of the disease. In the punishment system, because we are dealing with deprivations, it is understandable that we should forbear from imposing them until we are quite sure of guilt. In the therapy system, dealing as it does with benefits, there is less reason for forbearance from treatment at an early stage.

Sixth, a variety of procedural safeguards we associate with punishment have less significance in a therapy system. To the degree objections to double jeopardy and self-incrimination are based on a wish to decrease the chances of the innocent being convicted and punished, a therapy system, unconcerned with this problem, would disregard such safeguards. When one is out to help people there is also little sense in urging that the burden of proof be on those providing the help. And there is less point to imposing the burden of proving that the conduct was pathological beyond a reasonable doubt. Further, a jury system that, within a system of justice, serves to make accommodations to the individual situation and to introduce a human element would play no role or a minor one in a world where expertise is required in making determinations of disease and treatment.

In our system of punishment an attempt was made to maximize each individual's freedom of choice by first of all delimiting by rules certain spheres of conduct immune from interference by others. The punishment associated with these primary rules paid deference to an individual's free choice by connecting punishment to a freely chosen act violative of the rules, thus giving some plausibility to the claim, as we saw, that what a person received by way of punishment he himself had chosen. With the world of disease and therapy all this changes and the individual's free choice ceases to be a determinative factor in how others respond to him. All those principles of our own legal system that minimize the chances of punishment of those who have not chosen to do acts violative of the rules tend to lose their point in the therapy system, for how we respond in a therapy system to a person is not conditioned upon what he has chosen but rather on what symptoms he has manifested or may manifest, and what the best therapy for the disease is that is suggested by the symptoms.

Now, it is clear I think that were we confronted with the alternatives I have sketched, between a system of just punishment and a thoroughgoing system of treatment, a system, that is, that did not reintroduce concepts appropriate to punishment, we could see the point in claiming that a person has a right to be punished, meaning by this that a person has a right to all those institutions and practices linked to punishment. For these would provide him with, among other things, a far greater ability to predict what would happen to him on the occurrence of certain events than the therapy system. There is the inestimable value to each of us of having the responses of others to us determined over a wide range of our lives by what we choose rather than what they choose. A person has a right to institutions that respect his choices. Our punishment system does; our therapy system does not.

Apart from those aspects of our therapy model that would relate to serious limitations on personal liberty, there are clearly objections of a more profound kind to the mode of thinking I have associated with the therapy model.

First, human beings pride themselves in having capacities that animals do not. A common way, for example, of arousing shame in a child is to compare the child's conduct to that of an animal. In a system where all actions are assimilated to happenings we are assimilated to creatures—indeed, it is more extreme than this—whom we have always thought possessed of less than we. Fundamental to our practice of praise and order of attainment is that one who can do more—one who is capable of more and one who does more is more worthy of respect and admiration. And we have thought of ourselves as capable where animals are not of making, of creating, among other things, ourselves. The conception of man I have outlined would provide us with a status that today, when our conduct is assimilated to it in moral criticism, we consider properly evocative of shame.

Second, if all human conduct is viewed as something men undergo, thrown into question would be the appropriateness of that extensive range of peculiarly human satisfactions that derive from a sense of achievement. For these satisfactions we shall have to substitute those mild satisfactions attendant upon a healthy, well-functioning body. Contentment is our lot if we are fortunate; intense satisfaction at achievement is entirely inappropriate.

Third, in the therapy world nothing is earned and what we receive comes to us through compassion, or through a desire to control us. Resentment is out of place. We can take credit for nothing but must always regard ourselves—if there are selves left to regard once actions disappear—as fortunate recipients of benefits or unfortunate carriers of disease who must be controlled. We know that within our own world human beings who have been so regarded and who come to accept this view of themselves come to look upon themselves as worthless. When what we do is met with resentment, we are indirectly paid something of a compliment.

Fourth, attention should also be drawn to peculiar evil that may be attendant upon regarding a man's actions as symptoms of disease. The logic of cure will push us toward forms of therapy that inevitably involve changes in the person made against his will. The evil in this would be most apparent in those cases where the agent, whose action is determined to be a manifestation of some disease, does not regard his action in this way. He believes that what he has done is, in fact, "right" but his conception of "normality" is not the therapeutically accepted one. When we treat an illness we normally treat a condition that the person is not responsible for. He is "suffering" from some disease and we treat the condition, relieving the person of something preventing his normal functioning. When we begin treating persons for actions that have been chosen, we do not lift from the person something that is interfering with his normal functioning, but we change the person so that he functions in a way regarded as normal by the current therapeutic community. We have to change him and his judgments of value. In doing this we display a lack of respect for the moral status of individuals, that is, a lack of respect for the reasoning and choices of individuals. They are but animals who must be conditioned. I think we can understand and, indeed, sympathize with a man's preferring death to being forcibly turned into what he is not.

Finally, perhaps most frightening of all would be the derogation in status of all protests to treatment. If someone believes that he has done something right, and if he protests being treated and changed, the protest will itself be regarded as a sign of some pathological condition, for who would not wish to be cured of an affliction? What this leads to are questions of an important kind about the effect of this conception of man upon what we now understand by reasoning.

Here what a person takes to be a reasoned defense of an act is treated, as the action was, on the model of a happening of a pathological kind. Not just a person's acts are taken from him but also his attempt at a reasoned justification for the acts. In a system of punishment a person who has committed a crime may argue that what he did was right. We make him pay the price and we respect his right to retain the judgment he has made. A conception of pathology precludes this form of respect.

It might be objected to the foregoing that all I have shown—if that—is that if the only alternatives open to us are a *just* system of punishment or the mad world of being treated like sick or healthy animals, we do in fact have a right to a system of punishment of this kind. But this hardly shows that we have a right *simpliciter* to punishment as we do, say, to be free. Indeed, it does not even show a right to a just system of punishment, for surely we can, without too much difficulty, imagine situations in which the alternatives to punishment are not this mad world but a world in which we are still treated as persons and there is, for example, not the pain and suffering attendant upon punishment. One such world is one in which there are rules, but responses to their violation is not the deprivation of some good, but forgiveness. Still another type of world would be one in which violation of the rules were responded to by merely comparing the conduct of the person to something commonly regarded as low or filthy, and thus, producing by this mode of moral criticism, feelings of shame rather than feelings of guilt.

I am prepared to allow that these objections have a point. While granting force to the above objections I want to offer a few additional comments with respect to each of them. First, any existent legal system permits the punishment of individuals under circumstances where the conditions I have set forth for a just system have not been satisfied. A glaring example of this would be criminal strict liability that is to be found in our own legal system. Nevertheless, I think it would be difficult to present any system we should regard as a system of punishment that would not still have a great advantage over our imagined therapy *jail = shame?*

system. The system of punishment we imagine may more and more approximate a system of sheer terror in which human beings are treated as animals to be intimidated and prodded. To the degree that the system is of this character it is, in my judgment, not simply an unjust system but one that diverges from what we normally understand by a system of punishment. At least some deference to the choice of individuals is built into the idea of punishment. So there would be some truth in saying we have a right to any system of punishment if the only alternative to it was therapy.

Second, people may imagine systems in which there are rules and in which the response to their violation is not punishment but pardoning, the legal analogue of forgiveness. Surely this is a system to which we would claim a right as against one in which we are made to suffer for violating the rules. There are several comments that need to be made about this. It may be, of course, that a high incidence of pardoning would increase the incidence of rule violations. Further, the difficulty with suggesting pardoning as a general response is that pardoning presupposes the very responses that it is suggested it supplant. A system of deprivations, or a practice of deprivations on the happening of certain actions, underlies the practice of pardoning and forgiving, for it is only where we possess the idea of a wrong to be made up or of a debt owed to others, ideas we acquire within a world in which there have been deprivations for wrong acts, that we have the idea of pardoning for the wrong or forgiving the debt.

Finally, if we look at the responses I suggested would give rise to feelings of shame, we may rightly be troubled with the appropriateness of these responses in any community in which each person assumes burdens so that each may derive benefits. In such situations might it not be that individuals have a right to a system of punishment so that each person could be assured that inequities in the distribution of benefits and burdens are unlikely to occur, and if they do, procedures exist for correcting them? Further, it may well be that, everything considered, we should prefer the pain and suffering of a system of punishment to a world in which we only experience shame on the doing

of wrong acts, for with guilt there are relatively simple ways of ridding ourselves of the feeling we have, that is, gaining forgiveness or taking the punishment, but with shame we have to bear it until we no longer are the person who has behaved in the shameful way. Thus, I suggest that we have, wherever there is a distribution of benefits and burdens of the kind I have described, a right to a system of punishment.

I want also to make clear in concluding this section that I have argued, though very indirectly, not just for a right to a system of punishment, but for a right to be punished once there is in existence such a system. Thus, a man has the right to be punished rather than treated if he is guilty of some offense. And, indeed, one can imagine a case in which, even in the face of an offer of a pardon, a man claims and ought to have acknowledged his right to be punished.

2.

The primary reason for preferring the system of punishment as against the system of therapy might have been expressed in terms of the one system treating one as a person and the other not. In invoking the right to be punished, one justifies one's claim by reference to a more fundamental right. I want now to turn attention to this fundamental right and attempt to shed light—it will have to be little, for the topic is immense—on what is meant by "treating an individual as a person."

When we talk of not treating a human being as a person or "showing no respect for one as a person" what we imply by our words is a contrast between the manner in which one acceptably responds to human beings and the manner in which one acceptably responds to animals and inanimate objects. When we treat a human being merely as an animal or some inanimate object our responses to the human being are determined, not by his choices, but ours, in disregard of or with indifference to his. And when we "look upon" a person as less than a person or not a person, we consider the person as incapable of rational choice. In cases of not treating a human being as a person we interfere with a person in such a way that what is done, even if the person is involved in the doing, is done not by the person, but by the user of the person. In extreme cases there may even be an elision of a causal chain so that we might say that X killed Z even though Y's hand was the hand that held the weapon, for Y's hand may have been entirely in X's control. The one agent is in some way treating the other as a mere link in a causal chain. There is, of course, a wide range of cases in which a person is used to accomplish the aim of another and in which the person used is less than fully free. A person may be grabbed against his will and used as a shield. A person may be drugged or hypnotized and then employed for certain ends. A person may be deceived into doing other than he intends doing. A person may be ordered to do something and threatened with harm if he does not and coerced into doing what he does not want to do. There is still another range of cases in which individuals are not used, but in which decisions by others are made that affect them in circumstances where they have the capacity for choice and where they are not being treated as persons.

But it is particularly important to look at coercion, for I have claimed that a just system of punishment treats human beings as persons; and it is not immediately apparent how ordering someone to do something and threatening harm differs essentially from having rules supported by threats of harm in case of noncompliance.

There are affinities between coercion and other cases of not treating someone as a person, for it is not the coerced person's choices but the coercer's that are responsible for what is done. But unlike other indisputable cases of not treating one as a person, for example using someone as a shield, there is some choice involved in coercion. And if this is so, why does the coercer stand in any different relation to the coerced person than the criminal law stands to individuals in society?

Suppose the person who is threatened disregards the order and gets the threatened harm. Now suppose he is told, "Well, you did after all bring it upon yourself." There is clearly something strange in this. It is the person doing the threatening and not the person threatened who is responsible. But our reaction to punishment, at

least in a system that resembles the one I have described, is precisely that the person violating the rules brought it upon himself. What lies behind these different reactions?

There exist situations in the law, of course, which resemble coercion situations. There are occasions when in the law a person might justifiably say, "I am not being treated as a person but being used," and where he might properly react to the punishment as something "he was hardly responsible for." But it is possible to have a system in which it would be misleading to say, over a wide range of cases of punishment for non-compliance, that we are using persons. The clearest case in which it would be inappropriate to so regard punishment would be one in which there were explicit agreement in advance that punishment should follow on the voluntary doing of certain acts. Even if one does not have such conditions satisfied—and obviously such explicit agreements are not characteristic—one can see significant differences between our system of just punishment and a coercion situation.

First, unlike the case with one person coercing another "to do his will," the rules in our system apply to all, with the benefits and burdens equally distributed. About such a system it cannot be said that some are being subordinated to others or are being used by others or gotten to do things by others. To the extent that the rules are thought to be to the advantage of only some, or to the extent there is a maldistribution of benefits and burdens, the difference between coercion and law disappears.

Second, it might be argued that at least any person inclined to act in a manner violative of the rules stands to all others as the person coerced stands to his coercer, and that he, at least, is a person disadvantaged as others are not. It is important here, I think, that he is part of a system in which it is commonly agreed that forbearance from the acts proscribed by the rules provides advantages for all. This system is the accepted setting; it is the norm. Thus, in any coercive situation, it is the coercer who deviates from the norm, with the responsibility of the person he is attempting to coerce defeated. In a just punishment situation, it is the person deviating from the norm—indeed he might be a coercer—who is responsible, for it is the norm to restrain oneself from acts of that kind. A voluntary agent diverging in his conduct from what is expected or what is the norm is regarded, on general causal principles, as the cause of what results from his conduct.

There is, then, some plausibility in the claim that, in a system of punishment of the kind I have sketched, a person chooses the punishment that is meted out to him. If, then, we can say in such a system that the rules provide none with advantages that others do not have, and further, that what happens to a person is conditioned by that person's choice and not that of others, then we can say that it is a system responding to one as a person.

We treat a human being as a person provided: first, when we permit the person to make the choices that will determine what happens to him; and second, when our responses to the person are responses respecting the person's choices. When we respond to a person's illness by treating the illness, it is neither a case of treating nor of not treating the individual as a person. When we give a person a gift we are neither treating nor are we not treating him as a person, unless, of course, he does not wish it, chooses not to have it, yet we compel him to accept it.

3.

This right to be treated as a person is a fundamental human right belonging to all human beings by virtue of their being human. It is also a natural, inalienable, and absolute right. I want now to defend these claims, so reminiscent of an era of philosophical thinking about rights that many consider to have been seriously confused.

If the right is one that we possess by virtue of being human beings, we are immediately confronted with an apparent dilemma. If to treat another as a person requires that we provide him with reasons for acting, and avoid force or deception, how can we justify the force and deception we exercise with respect to children and the mentally ill? If they, too, have a right to be treated as persons are we not constantly infringing their rights? One way out of this is simply to restrict

the right to those who satisfy the conditions of being a person. Infants and the insane, it might be argued, do not meet these conditions, and they would not then have the right. Another approach would be to describe the right they possess as a prima facie right to be treated as a person. This right might then be outweighed by other considerations. This approach generally seems to me, as I shall later argue, inadequate.

I prefer this tack: Children possess the right to be treated as persons, but they possess this right as an individual might be said in the law of property to possess a future interest. There are advantages in talking of individuals as having a right, though complete enjoyment of it is postponed. Brought to our attention, if we ascribe to them the right, is the legitimacy of their complaint if they are not provided with opportunities and conditions assuring their full enjoyment of the right when they acquire the characteristics of persons. More than this, all persons are charged with the sensitive task of not denying them the right to be a person and to be treated as a person by failing to provide the conditions for their becoming individuals who are able freely and in an informed way to choose, and who are prepared themselves to assume responsibility for their choices. There is an obligation imposed upon us all, unlike that we have with respect to animals, to respond to children in such a way as to maximize the chances of their becoming persons. This may well impose upon us the obligation to treat them as persons from a very early age, that is, to respect their choices and to place upon them the responsibility for the choices to be made. There is no need to say that there is a close connection between how we respond to them and what they become. It also imposes upon us all the duty to display constantly the qualities of a person, for what they become they will largely become because of what they learn from us is acceptable behavior.

In claiming that the right is a right that human beings have by virtue of being human, there are several other features of the right, that should be noted, perhaps better conveyed by labelling them *natural*. First, it is a right we have apart from any voluntary agreement into which we have entered. Second, it is not a right that derives from some defined position or status. Third, it is equally apparent that one has the right regardless of the society or community of which one is a member. Finally, it is a right linked to certain features of a class of beings. Were we fundamentally different than we now are, we would not have it. But it is more than that, for the right is linked to a feature of human beings that, were that feature absent—the capacity to reason and to choose on the basis of reasons—profound conceptual changes would be involved in the thought about human beings. It is a right, then, connected with a feature of men that sets men apart from natural phenomena.

The right to be treated as a person is inalienable. To say of a right that it is inalienable draws attention, not to limitations placed on what others may do with respect to the possessor of the right, but rather to limitations placed on the dispositive capacities of the possessor of the right. Something is to be gained in keeping the issues of alienability and absoluteness separate.

There are a variety of locutions qualifying what possessors of rights may and may not do. For example, on this issue of alienability, it would be worthwhile to look at, among other things, what is involved in abandoning, abdicating, transferring, and waiving one's rights. And with respect to each of these concepts we should also have to be sensitive to the variety of uses of the term *rights*. What it is, for example, to waive a Hohfeldian "right" in his strict sense will differ from what it is to waive a right in his "privilege" sense.

Let us look at only two concepts very briefly, those of transferring and waiving rights. The clearest case of transferring rights is that of transferring rights with respect to specific objects. I own a watch and owning it I have a complicated relationship, captured in this area rather well I think by Hohfeld's four basic legal relationships, to all persons in the world with respect to the watch. We crudely capture these complex relationships by talking of my "property rights" in or with respect to the watch. If I sell the watch, thus exercising a capacity provided by the rules of property, I have transferred rights in or with respect to the watch to someone else, the buyer, and the buyer now stands, as I formerly did, to all persons in the world in a series of complex relationships with respect to the watch.

While still the owner, I may have given to another permission to use it for several days. Had there not been the permission and had the person taken the watch, we should have spoken of interfering with or violating or, possibly, infringing my property rights. Or, to take a situation in which transferring rights is inappropriate, I may say to another "go ahead and slap me—you have my permission." In these types of situations philosophers and others have spoken of "surrendering" rights or, alternatively and, I believe, less strangely, of "waiving one's rights." And recently, of course, the whole topic of "waiving one's right to remain silent" in the context of police interrogation of suspects has been a subject of extensive litigation and discussion.

I confess to feeling that matters are not entirely perspicuous with respect to what is involved in "waiving" or "surrendering" rights. In conveying to another permission to take a watch or slap one, one makes legally permissible what otherwise would not have been. But in saying those words that constitute permission to take one's watch one is, of course, exercising precisely one of those capacities that leads us to say he has, while others have not, property rights with respect to the watch. Has one then waived his right in Hohfeld's strict sense, in which the correlative is a duty to forebear on the part of others?

We may wish to distinguish here waiving the right to have others forbear to which there is a corresponding duty on their part to forbear, from placing oneself in a position where one has no legitimate right to complain. If I say the magic words "take the watch for a couple of days" or "go ahead and slap me," have I waived my right not to have my property taken or a right not to be struck or have I, rather, in saying what I have, simply stepped into a relation in which the rights no longer apply with respect to a specified other person? These observations find support in the following considerations. The right is that which gives rise, when infringed, to a legitimate claim against another person. What this suggests is that the right is that sphere of interference that entitles us to complain or gives us a right to complain.

From this it seems to follow that a right to bodily security should be more precisely described as "a right that others not interfere without permission." And there is the corresponding duty not to interfere unless provided permission. Thus when we talk of waiving our rights or "giving up our rights" in such cases, we are not waiving or giving up our right to property nor our right to bodily security, for we still, of course, possess the right not to have our watch taken without permission. We have rather placed ourselves in a position where we do not possess the capacity, sometimes called a right, to complain if the person takes the watch or slaps us.

There is another type of situation in which we may speak of waiving our rights. If someone without permission slaps me, there is an infringement of my right to bodily security. If I now acquiesce or go further and say, "Forget it," or, "You are forgiven," we might say that I had waived my right to complain. But here, too, I feel uncomfortable about what is involved. For I do have the right to complain (a right without a corresponding duty) in the event I am slapped, and I have that right whether I wish it or not. If I say to another after the slap, "You are forgiven," what I do is not waive the right to complain but rather make illegitimate my subsequent exercise of that right.

Now, if we turn to the right to be treated as a person, the claim that I made was that it was inalienable, and what I meant to convey by that word of respectable age is that (1) it is a right that cannot be transferred to another in the way one's right with respect to objects can be transferred, and (2) that it cannot be waived in the ways in which people talk of waiving rights to property or waiving, within certain limitations, one's right to bodily security.

While the rules of the law of property are such that persons may, satisfying certain procedures, transfer rights, the right to be treated as a person logically cannot be transferred anymore than one person can transfer to another his right to life or privacy. What, indeed, would it be like for another to have our right to be treated as a person? We can understand transferring a right with respect to certain objects. The new owner stands where the old owner stood. But with a right to be treated as a person what could this mean? My having the right meant that my choices were respected. Now if I transfer it to another this will mean that he will possess the right that my choices be respected? This is nonsense. It is only each person himself that can have his choices respected. It is no more possible to transfer this right than it is to transfer one's right to life.

Nor can the right be waived. It cannot be waived because any agreement to being treated as an animal or an instrument does not provide others with the moral permission to so treat us. One can volunteer to be a shield, but then it is one's choice on a particular occasion to be a shield. If, without our permission, without our choosing it, someone used us as a shield, we may, I should suppose, forgive the person for treating us as an object. But we do not thereby waive our right to be treated as a person, for that is a right that has been infringed and what we have at most done is put ourselves in a position where it is inappropriate any longer to exercise the right to complain.

This is the sort of rights, then, such that the moral rules defining relationships among persons preclude anyone from morally giving others legitimate permissions or rights with respect to one by doing or saying certain things. One stands, then, with respect to one's person, as the nonowner of goods stands to those goods. The nonowner cannot, given the rule-defined relationships, convey to others rights and privileges that only the owner possesses. Just as there are agreements nonenforceable because void as contrary to public policy, so there are permissions our moral outlook regards as without moral force. With respect to being treated as a person, one is "disabled" from modifying relations of others to one.

The right is absolute. This claim is bound to raise eyebrows. I have an innocuous point in mind in making this claim.

In discussing alienability we focused on incapacities with respect to disposing of rights. Here what I want to bring out is a sense in which a right exists despite considerations for refusing to accord the person his rights. As with the topic of alienability there are a host of concepts that deserve a close look in this area. Among them are according, acknowledging, annulling, asserting, claiming, denying, destroying, exercising, infringing, insisting upon, interfering with, possessing, recognizing, and violating.

The claim that rights are absolute has been construed to mean that "assertions of rights cannot, for any reason under any circumstances, be denied." When there are considerations that warrant refusing to accord persons their rights, there are two prevalent views as to how this should be described: there is, first, the view that the person does not have the right, and second, the view that he has rights, but of a prima facie kind, and that these have been outweighed or overcome by the other considerations. "We can conceive times when such rights must give way, and, therefore, they are only prima facie and not absolute rights." (Brandt)

Perhaps there are cases in which a person claims a right to do a certain thing, say with his property, and argues that his property rights are absolute, meaning by this he has a right to do whatever he wishes with his property. Here, no doubt, it has to be explained to the person that the right he claims he has, he does not in fact possess. In such a case the person does not have and never did have, given a certain description of the right, a right that was prima facie or otherwise, to do what he claimed he had the right to do. If the assertion that a right is absolute implies that we have a right to do whatever we wish to do, it is an absurd claim and as such should not really ever have been attributed to political theorists arguing for absolute rights. But, of course, the claim that we have a prima facie right to do whatever we wish to do is equally absurd. The right is not prima facie either, for who would claim, thinking of the right to be free, that one has a prima facie right to kill others, if one wishes, unless there are moral considerations weighing against it?

There are, however, other situations in which it is accepted by all that a person possesses rights of a certain kind, and the difficulty we face is that of according the person the right he is claiming

when this will promote more evil than good. The just act is to give the man his due and giving a man what it is his right to have is giving him his due. But it is a mistake to suppose that justice is the only dimension of morality. It may be justifiable not to accord to a man his rights. But it is no less a wrong to him, no less an infringement. It is seriously misleading to turn all justifiable infringements into noninfringements by saying that the right is only prima facie, as if we have, in concluding that we should not accord a man his rights, made out a case that he had none. To use the language of "prima facie rights" misleads, for it suggests that a presumption of the existence of a right has been overcome in these cases, where all that can be said is that the presumption in favor of according a man his rights has been overcome. If we begin to think the right itself is prima facie, we shall, in cases in which we are justified in not according it, fail sufficiently to bring out that we have interfered where justice says we should not. Our moral framework is unnecessarily and undesirably impoverished by the theory that there are such rights.

When I claim, then, that the right to be treated as a person is absolute, what I claim is that, given that one is a person, one always has the right so to be treated, and that, although there may possibly be occasions morally requiring not according a person this right, this fact makes it no less true that the right exists and would be infringed if the person were not accorded it.

4.

Having said something about the nature of this fundamental right, I want now, in conclusion, to suggest that the denial of this right entails the denial of all moral rights and duties. This requires bringing out what is surely intuitively clear, that any framework of rights and duties presupposes individuals that have the capacity to choose on the basis of reasons presented to them, and that what makes legitimate actions within such a system are the free choices of individuals. There is, in other words, a distribution of benefits and burdens in accord with a respect for the freedom of choice and freedom of action of all. I think that the best way to make this point may be to sketch some of the features of a world in which rights and duties are possessed.

First, rights exist only when there is some conception of some things valued and others not. Secondly, and implied in the first point, is the fact that there are dispositions to defend the valued commodities. Third, the valued commodities may be interfered with by others in this world. A group of animals might be said to satisfy these first three conditions. Fourth, rights exist when there are recognized rules establishing the legitimacy of some acts and ruling out others. Mistakes in the claim of right are possible. Rights imply the concepts of interference and infringement, concepts the elucidation of which requires the concept of a rule applying to the conduct of persons. Fifth, to possess a right is to possess something that constitutes a legitimate restraint on the freedom of action of others. It is clear, for example, that if individuals were incapable of controlling their actions, we would have no notion of a legitimate claim that they do so. If, for example, we were all disposed to object when his territory is invaded, then the objection would operate in a causal way, or approximating a causal way, in getting the behavior of noninterference. In a system of rights, on the other hand, there is a point to appealing to the rules in legitimating one's complaint. Implied, then, in any conception of rights are the existence of individuals capable of choosing, and capable of choosing on the basis of considerations with respect to rules. The distribution of freedom throughout such a system is determined by the free choice of individuals. Thus, any denial of the right to be treated as a person would be a denial undercutting the whole system, for the system rests on the assumption that spheres of legitimate and illegitimate conduct are to be delimited with regard to the choices made by persons.

This conclusion stimulates one final reflection on the therapy world we imagined.

The denial of this fundamental right will also carry with it, ironically, the denial of the right to treatment to those who are ill. In the world as we now understand it, there are those who do wrong and who have a right to be responded to as persons who have done wrong. And there are those who have not done wrong but who are suffering from illnesses that in a variety of ways interfere with their capacity to live their lives as complete persons. These persons who are ill have a claim upon our compassion. But more than this they have, as animals do not, a right to be treated as persons. When any individual is ill he is entitled to that assistance which will make it possible for him to resume his functioning as a person. If it is an injustice to punish an innocent person, it is no less an injustice, and a far more significant one in our day, to fail to promote as best we can through adequate facilities and medical care the treatment of those who are ill. Those human beings who fill our mental institutions are entitled to more than they do in fact receive; they should be viewed as possessing the right to be treated as a person, so that our responses to them may increase the likelihood that they will enjoy fully the right to be so treated. Like the child, the mentally ill person has a future interest we cannot rightly deny him. Society is today sensitive to the infringement of justice in punishing the innocent; elaborate rules exist to avoid this evil. Society should be no less sensitive to the injustice of failing to bring back to the community of persons those whom it is possible to bring back.

NOTES

1. Russell, Bertrand. *Roads to Freedom*. London: George Allen and Unwin Ltd., 1918. 135:

   When a man is suffering from an infectious disease, he is a danger to the community, and it is necessary to restrict his liberty of movement. But no one associates any idea of guilt with such a situation. On the contrary, he is an object of commiseration to his friends. Such steps as science recommends are taken to cure him of his disease, and he submits as a rule without reluctance to the curtailment of liberty involved meanwhile. The same method in spirit ought to be shown in the treatment of what is called "crime."

Skinner, B. F. *Science and Human Behavior*. B. F. Skinner Foundation, 1953, 2005. Web. http://www.bfskinner.org/BFSkinner/Society_files/Science_and_Human_Behavior.pdf. 115–6:

> We do not hold people responsible for their reflexes—for example, for coughing in church. We hold them responsible for their operant behavior—for example, for whispering in church or remaining in church while coughing. But there are variables that are responsible for whispering as well as coughing, and these may be just as inexorable. When we recognize this, we are likely to drop the notion of responsibility altogether and with it the doctrine of free will as an inner causal agent.

Karpman, Benjamin. "Criminal Psychodynamics." *Journal of Criminal Law and Criminology* 47 (1956): 9:

> Basically, criminality is but a symptom of insanity, using the term in its widest generic sense to express unacceptable social behavior based on unconscious motivation flowing from a disturbed instinctive and emotional life, whether this appears in frank psychoses, or in less obvious form in neuroses and unrecognized psychoses ... If criminals are products of early environmental influences in the same sense that psychotics and neurotics are, then it should be possible to reach them psychotherapeutically.

Menninger, Karl. "Therapy, Not Punishment." *Harper's Magazine* August 1959. 63–64:

> We, the agents of society, must move to end the game of tit-for-tat and blow-for-blow in which the offender has foolishly and futilely engaged himself and us. We are not driven, as he is, to wild and impulsive actions. With knowledge comes power, and with power there is no need for the frightened vengeance of the old penology. In its place should go a quiet, dignified, therapeutic program for the rehabilitation of the disorganized one, if possible, the protection of society during the treatment period, and his guided return to useful citizenship, as soon as this can be effected.

59   Forgiveness and Resentment

JEFFRIE MURPHY

Understand, and forgive, my mother said, and the effort has quite exhausted me. I could do with some anger to energize me, and bring me back to life again. But where can I find that anger? Who is to help me? My friends? I have been understanding and forgiving my friends, my female friends, for as long as I can remember.... Understand and forgive.... Understand husbands, wives, fathers, mothers. Understand dogfights above and the charity box below, understand fur-coated women and children without shoes. Understand school—Jonah, Job, and the nature of the Deity; understand Hitler and the bank of England and the behavior of Cinderella's sisters. Preach acceptance to wives and tolerance to husbands; patience to parents and compromise to the young. Nothing in this world is perfect; to protest takes the strength needed for survival. Grit your teeth, endure. Understand, forgive, accept, in the light of your own death, your own inevitable corruption....

Oh mother, what you taught me! And what a miserable, crawling, snivelling way to go, the worn-out slippers neatly placed beneath the bed, careful not to give offense.

—FAY WELDON, *Female Friends*

To err is human; to forgive, supine.

—S. J. PERELMAN

From Jeffrie G. Murphy and Jean Hampton. *Forgiveness and Mercy* (New York: Cambridge University Press, 1988), pp. 14–34. Reprinted with permission of the publisher.

I. INTRODUCTION

Forgiveness, Bishop Butler teaches, is the forswearing of resentment—the resolute overcoming of the anger and hatred that are naturally directed toward a person who has done one an unjustified and nonexcused moral injury.[1] By his emphasis on the forswearing of resentment, Butler indicates that he quite properly wants to draw a distinction between forgiveness (which may be a virtue and morally commanded) and forgetting (which may just happen). Forgiveness is the sort of thing that one does for a reason, and where there are reasons there is a distinction between good ones and bad ones.

What, then, are the good reasons for forgiveness? Butler has useful things to say in response to this question, but his response is limited by a perspective that strikes me as too consequentialist. Resentment, he argues, can provoke bad consequences—especially such antisocial actions as personal revenge. Forgiveness is thus justified primarily as a way of avoiding such undesirable consequences. Resentment does indeed perform a useful social job—the job of reinforcing the rules of morality and provoking defenses of those rules—but when it is allowed to range beyond this useful function, as human weakness and vanity typically allow it to, it becomes counterproductive and even seriously harmful to the social fabric. Tendencies to forgive thus are to be supported to the degree that they help individuals to overcome or avoid such excesses.

This is surely part of the story, but—as Butler himself sometimes sees—there is considerably more to be told. Butler stresses that the passion of resentment functions in a defensive role—defensive of the rules of morality and of the social fabric those rules define. But he never fleshes out this insight in sufficient detail adequately to highlight central features of the context wherein resentment and forgiveness have their life.

In my view, resentment (in its range from righteous anger to righteous hatred) functions primarily in defense, not of *all* moral values and norms, but rather of certain *values of the self*. Resentment is a response not to general wrongs but to wrongs against oneself; and these resented wrongs can be of two sorts: resentment of direct violations of one's rights (as in assault) *or* resentment that another has taken unfair advantage of one's sacrifices by free riding on a mutually beneficial scheme of reciprocal cooperation. Only the immediate victim of crime is in a position to resent a criminal in the first way; all the law-abiding citizens, however, may be in a position to resent the criminal (and thus be secondary victims) in the second way—at least on Herbert Morris's well-known theory of such matters.[2]

I am, in short, suggesting that the primary value defended by the passion of resentment is *self-respect,* that proper self-respect is essentially tied to the passion of resentment, and that a person who does not resent moral injuries done to him (of either of the above sorts) is almost necessarily a person lacking in self-respect. Thus some of the primary reasons justifying forgiveness will be found, not in general social utility, but in reasons directly tied to an individual's self-respect or self-esteem, his perception of his own worth, of what he is owed. In some limited sense, then, I side with Stephen: Resentment (perhaps even some hatred) is a good thing, for it is essentially tied to a noncontroversially good thing—self-respect. Let me elaborate on this a bit.

As noted by thinkers as otherwise diverse as Butler and Nietzsche, resentment has a very unattractive—even dangerous and unhealthy—dimension. This is something I would not want to deny. In addition to many of its other disadvantages, resentment can stand as a fatal obstacle to the restoration of equal moral relations among persons, and thus it cannot always be the final "bottom line" as the response we take to those who have wronged us. Forgiveness heals and restores; and, without it, resentment would remain as an obstacle to many human relationships we value. This can be seen most clearly in such intimate relationships as love and friendship. The people with whom we are most intimate are those who can harm us the most, for they are the persons to whom we have let down our guard and exposed our vulnerabilities. Because of the nature of intimacy, moral injuries here tend to be not just ordinary injustices but also *betrayals*. Thus resentment here can be deep and nearly intractable—as revealed in the quip of Cosmus, Duke of Florence: "You shall read that we are commanded to forgive our enemies; but you never read that we are commanded to forgive our friends."[3] Deep as these hurts of intimacy may be, however, what would be the consequence of never forgiving any of them? Surely it would be this: the impossibility of ever having the kind of intimate relationships that are one of the crowning delights of human existence. The person who cannot forgive is the person who cannot have friends or lovers.

For this reason, it is easy to see why forgiveness is typically regarded as a virtue. Forgiveness is not always a virtue, however. Indeed, if I am correct in linking resentment to self-respect, a too-ready tendency to forgive may properly be regarded as a *vice* because it may be a sign that one lacks respect for oneself. Not to have what Peter Strawson calls the "reactive attitude" of resentment when our rights are violated is to convey—emotionally—either that we do not think we have rights or that we do not take our rights very seriously.[4] Forgiveness may indeed restore relationships, but to seek restoration at all cost—even at the cost of one's very human dignity—can hardly be a virtue. And, in intimate relationships, it can hardly be true love or friendship either—the kind of love and friendship that Aristotle claimed is an essential part of the virtuous life. When we are willing to be doormats for others, we have, not love, but rather what the psychiatrist Karen Horney calls "morbid dependency."[5] If I count morally as much as anyone else (as surely I do), a failure to resent moral injuries done to me is a failure to care about the moral value incarnate in my own person (that I am, in Kantian language, an end in myself) and thus a failure to care about the very rules of morality.[6] To put the point in yet another way: If it is proper to feel *indignation* when I see third parties morally wronged, must it not be equally proper to feel *resentment* when I experience the moral wrong done to myself? Morality is not simply something to be believed in; it is something to be *cared* about. This caring includes concern about those persons (including oneself) who are the proper objects of moral attention.

Interestingly enough, a hasty readiness to forgive—or even a refusal to display resentment initially—may reveal a lack of respect, not just for oneself, but for others as well. The Nietzschean view, for example, is sometimes portrayed (perhaps unfairly) as this: There is no need for forgiveness, because a truly strong person will never feel resentment in the first place. Why? Because he is not so weak as to think that other people—even those who harm him—matter enough to have any impact on his self-respect. We do not resent the insect that stings us (we simply *deal* with it), and neither should we resent the human who wrongs us.[7]

According to Paul Lauritzen, a similar indifference to injury by others (a refusal to view it as genuine injury) can be found in some strands of Christianity. If one believes that the Kingdom of God is imminent, interests and well-being become radically redefined; and, since earthly injury is no longer counted as harm, there is no occasion for resentment.[8]

Socrates also poses an interesting case here. On his stated view (in *Apology*, for example) a good person cannot be harmed or injured. Thus, if one regards oneself as a good person, then one—though positively brimming over with self-respect—will presumably never have occasion to resent, because one will never regard oneself as having been injured in any morally relevant way. Given the degree to which Socrates dealt with his enemies with ridicule and sarcasm, it is by no means clear that he actually practiced what he preached in this regard. Neither is it clear that the view he advocated is unambiguously desirable—even as an ideal. Could this level of insulation from others be compatible with true love or friendship or meaningful membership in any human relationship or community, for example?[9] Although there is something attractive and worth discussing about this view, most of us would probably want to reject it as too demeaning of other human beings and our moral relations with them. I shall thus for the present assume the following: Forgiveness is acceptable only in cases where it is consistent with self-respect, respect for others as responsible moral agents, and allegiance to the rules of morality (i.e., forgiveness must not involve complicity or acquiescence in wrongdoing).[10]

II. THE NATURE AND JUSTIFICATION OF FORGIVENESS

Enough by way of introduction. Having presented an overview of the problem of forgiveness, let me now move to a more detailed consideration of the two basic questions concerning forgiveness: (1) What is forgiveness; that is, how is the concept to be analyzed and distinguished from other concepts with which it may be confused? and (2) when, if at all, is forgiveness justified? (If it is never justified, then a tendency to bestow it can surely not be a virtue.)

First the question of meaning. I have already indicated, following Butler, that forgiveness essentially involves an attempt to overcome resentment. This feature allows us to distinguish forgiveness from three other concepts with which it is often confused: *excuse, justification,* and *mercy.* To excuse is to say this: What was done was morally wrong; but, because of certain factors about the agent (e.g., insanity), it would be unfair to hold the wrongdoer responsible or blame him for the wrong action. To justify is to say this: What was done was prima facie wrong; but because of other morally relevant factors, the action was—*all* morally relevant factors considered—the right thing to do. And why is neither of these forgiveness? Because we may forgive only what it is initially proper to resent; and, if a person has done nothing wrong or was not responsible for what he did, there is *nothing to resent* (though perhaps much to be sad about). Resentment—and thus forgiveness—is directed toward *responsible wrongdoing*; and therefore, if forgiveness and resentment are to have an arena, it must be where such wrongdoing remains intact—i.e., neither excused nor justified. ("Father forgive them for they know not what they do" would go better as "Father *excuse* them for they know not what they do.")

Forgiveness is also not mercy. To be merciful is to treat a person less harshly than, given certain rules, one has a right to treat that person. For example, the rules of chivalry give me the right to kill you under certain circumstances of combat. If you beg for mercy, you are begging that I do something less severe than kill you. When Portia advises Shylock to show mercy, she is asking that he accept a payment less harsh than the one that, given the terms of his bargain, he has a right to demand. Three things are present in such cases: some notion of just or rightful authority, some notion of the supplicant's having fallen afoul of certain public rules, and the consideration of a certain external action (a killing, a payment of a "pound of flesh"). None of these is necessarily involved in forgiveness. Forgiveness is primarily a matter of how I *feel* about you (not how I treat you), and thus I may forgive you in my heart of hearts or even after you are dead. (I cannot show you mercy in my heart of hearts or after you are dead, however.) I may think I have forgiven you; but, when old resentments rise up again, I may say, "I was wrong—I really have not forgiven you after all." But if I have shown you mercy, this has been done—once and for all. Also, with respect to mercy, it is not necessary that I—in showing it—must be the one wronged or injured by your wrongful conduct. (It is not even necessary that anyone be wronged.) All that is required is that you stand under certain rules and that I have authority to treat you in a certain harsh way because of those rules. But the matter is different with forgiveness. To use a legal term, I do not have *standing* to resent or forgive you unless I have myself been the victim of your wrongdoing. I may forgive you for embezzling my funds; but it would be ludicrous for me, for example, to claim that I had decided to forgive Hitler for what he did to the Jews. I lack the proper standing for this. Thus, I may legitimately resent (and hence consider forgiving) only wrong done to *me*.[11] If I forgive, this will primarily be a matter of my forswearing my resentment toward the person who has wronged me—a change of attitude quite compatible with my still demanding certain harsh public consequences for the wrongdoer. My forgiving you for embezzling my funds is not, for example, incompatible with a demand that you return my funds or even with a demand that you suffer just legal punishment for what you have done. Neither does my forgiveness entail that I must trust you with my money in the future. Forgiveness restores moral equality but not necessarily equality in every respect—for example, equality of trust. Some harsh treatment would, of course, be incompatible with forgiveness—namely, harsh treatment the very point of which would be to show you how much I hate and resent you. But when the harsh treatment is based on other factors (e.g., a concern with legal justice), forgiveness need pose no obstacle to such treatment.

Having become clearer on what forgiveness is not, let us return to Butler's account of what it is: the forswearing of resentment. Butler's puzzle was this: How could a loving God who commanded that we love our neighbor implant in us so unloving a passion as resentment? Is not this attitude unambiguously bad and any actions or practices based on it (retributive punishment perhaps) also bad? In answering *no* to this question, Butler suggests that resentment understandably arouses suspicion because it is often inappropriate (e.g., directed toward trivial affronts instead of real injuries) and sometimes provokes excessive behavior (e.g., vigilante activity). As Butler sees, however, it would be a mistake to condemn a passion simply because it admits of pathological or irrational extensions. (What passion does not?) Resentment expresses respect for the demands of morality (particularly, as I have argued, for the demands for *self-respect*) and is thus—when so described—consistent, in Butler's view, with any reasonable interpretation of a gospel of love. (Butler has no patience with attempts to view the Christian ethic as irrational sentimentality.) What is not consistent with a gospel of love is being dominated by the passion of resentment or acting unjustly on the basis of that passion; and thus Butler sees forgiveness as a virtue that functions to check resentment and keep it within proper bounds.

Is forgiveness then nothing but the overcoming (or attempt at overcoming) of resentment? Is every instance where resentment is overcome a case of the virtue of forgiveness? I (agreeing, I believe, with Butler) think not; and two sorts of cases will aid in establishing this negative answer. First, consider the case of *forgetting*. Sometimes we lose a vivid memory of old wrongs, become bored with our resentments, and simply forget. But this just *happens* to us; that is, it is totally nonvoluntary. As such, it seems too removed from agency to count as a moral virtue—though it still might be a desirable disposition of character to possess. Thus, to the extent that forgiveness is properly regarded as a moral virtue, it strikes me as a mistake to identify forgiving with forgetting. We tend to use the phrase "forgive and forget," and I do not believe the phrase is redundant.[12]

Or consider this second case: You have wronged me deeply, and I deeply resent you for it. The resentment eats away at my peace of mind—I lose sleep, snap at my friends, become less effective at my work, and so on. In short, my resentment so dominates my mental life that I am being made miserable. In order to regain my peace of mind, I go to a behavior-modification therapist to have my resentment extinguished. (Let us suppose there are such techniques.) Have I forgiven you? Surely not—at least not in any sense where forgiveness is supposed to be a moral virtue. For my motivation here was not moral at all; it was purely *selfish:* the desire to promote my own mental health.

What is starting to emerge from this discussion is this: The question "What is forgiveness?" cannot after all be sharply distinguished from the question "How is forgiveness justified?" As the foregoing cases show, not all instances of ceasing to resent will be ones of forgiveness—for example, forgetting is not. We cannot define forgiveness and *then* ask what moral reasons make it appropriate; because, I suggest, my ceasing to resent will not constitute forgiveness unless it is *done for a moral reason*. Forgiveness is not the overcoming of resentment *simpliciter*; it is rather this: forswearing resentment on moral grounds.

What, then, are the moral grounds; that is, what sorts of reasons justify or at least render appropriate an act of forgiveness? Let me start to answer this question simply by listing five reasons that are, in ordinary life and discourse, those most often given as grounds for forgiveness. We will then consider if this is just a laundry list or if some rational principle unites them or some set of them. The reasons are these:

I will forgive the person who has willfully wronged me, because:

1. He repented or had a change of heart, *or*
2. He meant well (his motives were good),[13] *or*
3. He has suffered enough, *or*
4. He has undergone humiliation (perhaps some ritual humiliation, e.g., the apology ritual of "I beg forgiveness"), *or*
5. Of [for] old times' sake (e.g., "He has been a good and loyal friend to me in the past").

Let me say something about what these reasons tend to have in common and then say something in detail about each one. But first recall the background here: Acceptable grounds for forgiveness must be compatible with self-respect, respect for others as moral agents, and respect for the rules of morality or the moral order. Can forgiveness ever be consistent with such constraints? I think that it can be for cases where we can draw a distinction between the immoral *act* and the immoral *agent;* for then we can follow Saint Augustine's counsel and "hate the sin but not the sinner." It is, of course, impossible to hate the sin and not the sinner if the sinner is intimately identified with his sin—if the wrongdoer is intimately identified with his wrongdoing. But to the extent that the agent is separated from his evil act, forgiveness *of him* is possible without a tacit approval of his evil act. A similar divorce of act from agent will also help to square forgiveness with self-respect. One reason we so deeply resent moral injuries done to us is not simply that they hurt us in some tangible or sensible way; it is because such injuries are also *messages*—symbolic communications. They are ways a wrongdoer has of saying to us, "I count but you do not," "I can use you for my purposes," or "I am here up high and you are there down below." Intentional wrongdoing *insults* us and attempts (sometimes successfully) to *degrade* us—and thus it involves a kind of injury that is not merely tangible and sensible. It is moral injury, and we care about such injuries. (As Justice Holmes observed, even a dog notices and cares about the difference between being tripped over accidentally and being kicked intentionally.) Most

of us tend to care about what others (at least *some* others, some significant group whose good opinion we value) think about us—how much they think we matter. Our self-respect is *social* in at least this sense, and it is simply part of the human condition that we are weak and vulnerable in these ways. And thus when we are treated with contempt by others it attacks us in profound and deeply threatening ways. We resent (or worse) those who so attack us, and want to separate ourselves from them—to harm them in turn or at least to banish them from the realm of those whose well-being should be our concern.

But what if they come to separate or divorce themselves from their own evil act? (True repentance is a clear way of doing this.) Then the insulting message is no longer present—no longer endorsed by the wrongdoer. We can then join the wrongdoer in condemning the very act from which he now stands emotionally separated. Thus to the degree that the items on the preceding list represent ways in which an agent can be divorced from his evil act, they represent grounds for forgiveness that are compatible with self-respect and respect for the rules of the moral order. To explore this idea of "divorce of act from agent," let us now look a bit more closely at each of the five listed reasons.

1. Repentance

This is surely the clearest way in which a wrongdoer can sever himself from his past wrong. In having a sincere change of heart, he is withdrawing his endorsement from his own immoral past behavior; he is saying, "I no longer stand behind the wrongdoing, and I want to be separated from it. I stand with you in condemning it." Of such a person it cannot be said that he is *now* conveying the message that he holds me in contempt. Thus I can relate to him now, through forgiveness, without fearing my own acquiescence in immorality or in judgments that I lack worth. I forgive him for what he now is.

2. Good motives

Sometimes people wrong us without meaning to convey that they hold us in contempt or think we are of less worth than they are. Paternalism is a good example to illustrate this point. A person who interferes with my liberty for what he thinks is my own good is, in my judgment, acting wrongly; that is, he is interfering in my "moral space" in a way he has no right to. His grounds for interfering, however, are well meaning (i.e., he seeks to do me good) even if his actions are misguided and morally insensitive. (Perhaps he is overattentive to utilitarian considerations at the expense of considerations of rights and justice.) It is hard to view the friend who locks my liquor cabinet because he knows I drink too much as on exactly the same moral level as the person who embezzles my funds for his own benefit—even though both are violating my rights. Thus the case for forgiving the former (at least the first time) strikes me as having some merit.

3. Enough suffering

The claim "He has suffered enough" as grounds for forgiveness may understandably be viewed with suspicion; for example, we may think it was involved in such controversial events as President Gerald Ford's pardon of Richard Nixon on the grounds that Nixon, disgraced and forced to resign as president, had suffered enough. But two cautions are relevant here. First, Nixon was not simply forgiven (if he was forgiven at all); he was treated with *mercy*. To pardon someone is not to change the way one feels about him, but is to let him avoid what may well be his just deserts. Second, just because *some* suffering may be relevant to forgiveness, it does not follow that *any* suffering is. The suffering occasioned by falling from a position that (as one's wrongful actions demonstrate) one had no right to occupy in the first place hardly seems relevant from the moral point of view.[14]

But what would relevant suffering be? I am not sure, actually, and some part of me wants to throw this consideration out entirely as simply confusion or even superstition. And yet some other part of me cannot quite do this. There is the thought, widespread in our culture, that *suffering is redemptive*. (One thinks, for example, of the old Oedipus in *Oedipus at Colonus*.) This connection between suffering and redemption could,

of course, simply be a kind of empirical claim—e.g., the claim that suffering tends to provoke repentance. If so, then the intelligible content of "He has suffered enough" is redundant, collapsing into point 1 above. So too if the suffering is simply guilt or other pangs of conscience. Perhaps there is something in this thought: Wrongdoers attempt to *degrade* us, to bring us low—lower than themselves. We will find it difficult to forgive and restore relations with them in this posture without acquiescing in our own lowered status—something that any self-respecting person is loath to do. But suffering tends to bring people low, to reduce them, to humble them. If so, then enough equality may be restored in order to forgive them consistent with self-respect. They may not have severed themselves from their own evil acts, but there is perhaps a sense in which they have been severed. Given the hurt and sadness that may come to be present in a person's life, it may be difficult and improper to retain, as one's *primary* view of that person, the sense that he is essentially "the one who has wronged me." Perhaps he does and should become in one's mind simply "that poor bastard."

4. Humiliation

What I want to say about humiliation continues the preceding thought about suffering and involves the role of *ritual* in our moral life. We tend to think that rituals are practices that primitive savages have, and that we civilized folks have outgrown this sort of thing. But we are deeply mistaken when we think this. Philosophers have not, I think, paid sufficient attention to the role of ritual in moral relations—a role that illuminates certain aspects of forgiveness.[15] As I mentioned before, wrongdoers attempt (sometimes successfully) to degrade or insult us; to bring us low; to say, "I am on high while you are down there below." As a result, we in a real sense *lose face* when done a moral injury—one reason why easy forgiveness tends to compromise self-esteem. But our moral relations provide for a ritual whereby the wrongdoer can symbolically bring himself low (or raise us up—I am not sure which metaphor best captures the point)—in other words, the humbling ritual of *apology*, the language of which is often that of *begging* for forgiveness. The posture of begging is not very exalted, of course, and thus some symbolic equality—necessary if forgiveness is to proceed consistently with self-respect—is now present. Sometimes, of course, the apology is more than mere ritual; indeed, in the best of cases it is likely to be a way of manifesting repentance. Here it will collapse into point 1. At other times we will settle simply for the ritual—so long as it is not transparently insincere.[16]

5. Old times' sake

As with repentance, we have here a clear case of divorce of act from agent. When you are repentant. I forgive you for what you *now* are. When I forgive you for old times' sake, I forgive you for what you *once were*. Much of our forgiveness of old friends and parents, for example, is of this sort.

The upshot of what I have argued thus far is this: Forgiveness of a wrongdoer on the basis of any of the preceding grounds (grounds that in various ways divorce act from agent) may be consistent with self-respect, respect for others, and respect for the rules of the moral order. All this shows, of course, is that forgiveness—when directed (for example) toward a truly repentant wrongdoer—is permissible, not wrong because not inconsistent with self-respect. But if forgiveness is a virtue, then it must be that sometimes it is not merely permissible that I forgive, but that I *ought* to forgive and can be properly criticized if I do not. Perhaps nobody has a *right* to be forgiven (imposing on others a perfect duty to forgive him), but surely forgiveness—if a virtue—must be like charity in at least this way: Just as charity requires that I sometimes ought to assist those having no right to my assistance, so does forgiveness require that I sometimes ought to forgive those having no right to my forgiveness.

How might one argue for this stronger view? One argument has been latent in what I have said thus far. Although repentance does not give one a right to be forgiven, there is a sense in which it may make resentment *inappropriate*—for why should I resent you now for holding me in contempt when your sincere repentance makes it clear that you do not now hold me in contempt? There is a clear sense in which it is simply not *rational* to

continue holding attitudes when I have come to see their inappropriateness and thus—as a rational being—I ought to forswear those attitudes. Just as rational beings value true beliefs, so they should, I think, value appropriate attitudes—attitudes fitting to their objects. This is why rational beings will seek to root out such things as phobias and other neurotic emotions from their psychologies; and so too, I should think, for inappropriate attitudes of resentment. This then is one argument for why we sometimes *ought* to forgive others— why forgiveness is sometimes more than merely permissible, why forgiveness is—in short—sometimes a virtue.

But there are other arguments as well. Two of them I associate particularly with the Christian tradition; and, since neither relies on the divorce between act and agent that I have made central, it will be worth exploring them briefly to see if they add a significant new dimension to the understanding of forgiveness. The arguments are these:

1. We should forgive in order to reform the wrongdoer; i.e., we should forgive, not because the wrongdoer has repented, but as a step toward bringing his repentance about, making it at least easier for him.
2. We should forgive because we ourselves need to be forgiven. (This, I take it, is the point of the parable of the unforgiving servant in Matt. 18:21–35.)

These grounds for forgiveness may be what prompted Feuerbach and others to suggest that forgiveness cannot be accounted for in ordinary moral and secular terms—that it takes us beyond morality and into a religious dimension that transcends or suspends the ordinarily ethical.[17] I know that some people value obscurity and mystery for their own sake, but I am myself inclined to resist these leaps into special realms. Sometimes we can mine these religious traditions for nuggets of secular value—i.e., values we can recognize even if we do not accept the theological views in which they were originally embedded. Thus we can sometimes avoid leaps into the mysterious and edifying if we will simply think about the matter a bit more. Point 1 above, for example, could be a kind of empirical prediction—almost therapeutic in nature—about what is likely to produce repentance and reform; and, as such, this ground for forgiveness is surely compatible with one's own self-respect. Less clear, however, is the degree to which it is compatible with respect for the wrongdoer. Suppose you had wronged someone. How would you like it if that person assumed that you could not come to repentance on your own but required the aid of his ministry of forgiveness? Might you not feel patronized—condescended to? Forgiveness can be an act of weakness, but it can also be an act of arrogance. Seeing it this way, the wrongdoer might well resent the forgiveness. "Who do you think you are to forgive me?" he might respond to such well-meaning meddling.

But what about point 2—the need we all have for being forgiven? Recall the parable of the unforgiving servant: A lord had decided to punish and generally ruin his servant's life because that servant had not paid a debt that he owed to the lord. The servant prostrated himself and begged piteously, however, and the lord was moved by compassion and forgave him his debt. Shortly after this, that very servant called in a debt owed to him by one of his underlings. He was unmoved by the pleas of his debtor, however. He refused to forgive the debt and consigned his debtor to prison. The lord, learning of this, called the servant in. Telling the servant that he should have showed compassion comparable to the compassion he received, the lord withdrew his forgiveness of the servant and "delivered him to the tormentors." Jesus concludes the parable by saying: "So likewise shall my heavenly Father do also unto you, if ye from your hearts forgive not every one his brother their trespasses."

What exactly is the argument in favor of forgiveness that is being given here? On one interpretation, the whole appeal looks pretty dreadful—of the kind that Nietzsche liked to note when arguing that Christianity is simply sublimated *ressentiment.* For on the surface the parable looks like nothing but an appeal to our baser instincts of *fear:* If you do not forgive others, then God will not forgive you and then you are in for it. One might reject this appeal either because one does not believe in God or because one will try to

resist, on grounds of moral integrity, being bullied by appeals to one's lesser nature. How, in short, can an act of forgiveness exemplify a moral virtue if it is motivated simply by a fear of what some supernatural sorehead will do if one fails to forgive?[18]

But such a rejection would, I think, be too quick. As is often the case with religious parables, there is deep moral insight waiting to be discovered if one will simply explore them with some patience. And the insight in the present parable (which can surely be granted by the most secular or even atheistic reader) is to be seen in its character as a parable on *moral humility.* Each of us, if honest, will admit two things about ourselves: (1) We will within the course of our lives wrong others—even others about whom we care deeply; and (2) because we care so deeply about these others and our relationships with them, we will want to be forgiven by them for our wrongdoings. In this sense we do all need and desire forgiveness and would not want to live in a world where the disposition to forgive was not present and regarded as a healing and restoring virtue. Given that this is the sort of world we all need and want, is it not then incumbent upon each of us to cultivate the disposition to forgive—not the flabby sentimentality of forgiving every wrong, no matter how deep or unrepented, but at least the willingness to be open to the possibility of forgiveness with hope and some trust? Only a person so arrogant as to believe that he will never wrong others or need to be forgiven by them could (in Kantian language) consistently will membership in a world without forgiveness. To see that none of us is such a person is a lesson in moral humility and is, at least in part, the message of the parable.

Suppose one accepts all of this. To what degree can the virtue of forgiveness, so conceived, be relevant to the law? It surely has at least this relevance: To the degree that Stephen is correct in his view that the law institutionalizes resentment, then to that same degree the law has a reason to go easy on those persons who have been forgiven or for whom forgiveness is appropriate. To the degree that the law does more than institutionalize resentment, however, forgiveness is without relevance to legal response. And surely the law does more—considerably more—than merely institutionalize resentment. As Hobbes taught us, for example, law functions to maintain obedience to rules without which civilized life would be impossible; and if one believed that the punishment of an individual was required to maintain these rules, one could consistently advocate such punishment even if one had forgiven the individual to be punished. To forgive a wrongdoer involves a change of heart toward that person (the overcoming of resentment toward him), but this is not necessarily a change in one's view on how that wrongdoer is to be treated. Because I have ceased to hate the person who has wronged me it does not follow that I act inconsistently if I still advocate his being forced to pay compensation for the harm he has done or his being forced to undergo punishment for his wrongdoing—that he, in short, get his just deserts.[19]

The arena of resentment and forgiveness is individual and personal in a way that legal guilt and responsibility are not. I have the proper standing to forgive injuries done to me, but I do not have the proper standing to let people off the hook for all of their legal accountability. To do the latter is to show *mercy* and is necessarily to *act* (and not just to feel) in a certain way. Forgiveness and mercy are often confused, but they should not be. (Some of Butler's remarks about the social and legal dimensions of forgiveness, for example, might more clearly apply to the topic of mercy.) There is a sense, however, in which mercy may be the legal analogue of forgiveness with this difference: Forgiveness involves the *overcoming* of certain passions (resentment, hatred) when they are inappropriate, whereas mercy involves acting in a certain way *because* of certain passions (love, compassion). Both may be virtues, but they are different virtues and operate in different sorts of context....

NOTES

1. Butler, Joseph. Sermon VIII, "Upon Resentment," and Sermon IX, "Upon Forgiveness of Injuries." *Fifteen Sermons*. London, 1726.
2. Morris, Herbert. "Persons and Punishment." *The Monist* 52 (October 1968); reprinted in his collec-

tion of essays *Guilt and Innocence*. Berkeley: University of California Press, 1976.
3. Quoted in Francis Bacon's essay "Of Revenge" (1597).
4. Strawson, Peter. "Freedom and Resentment." *Proceedings of the British Academy*. 1962.
5. Horney, Karen. *Neurosis and Human Growth*. New York: Norton, 1950.
6. See Hill, Thomas E. Jr. "Servility and Self-Respect." *The Monist* 57 (January 1973): 87–104.
7. "To be incapable of taking one's enemies, one's accidents, even one's misdeeds seriously for very long—that is the sign of strong, full natures in whom there is an excess of the power to form, to mold, to recuperate and to forget.... Such a man shakes off with a single shrug many vermin that eat deep into others." Nietzsche, Friedrich. *On the Genealogy of Morals*. Trans. Walter Kaufmann. New York: Random House, 1967. Essay I, Section 10, p. 39.
8. See Lauritzen, Paul. "Forgiveness: Moral Prerogative or Religious Duty?" *Journal of Religious Ethics* 15 (Fall 1987): 141–54.
9. For an exploration of some of these issues, see my "Violence and the Socratic Theory of Legal Fidelity." *Retribution, Justice, and Therapy: Essays in the Philosophy of Law* (Dordrecht: Reidel, 1979. 40–57.
10. For a discussion of the ways in which forgiveness may involve complicity in wrongdoing, see "Forgiveness." *Proceedings of the Aristotelian Society*. (1973–4); reprinted in Kolnai, Aurel. *Ethics, Value, and Reality*. Indianapolis: Hackett, 1978.
11. In "Rebellion" (Dostoevsky, *The Brothers Karamazov*), Ivan considers the suffering of innocents—especially children—and is outraged at the thought that anyone except the children (or perhaps their mothers) could forgive the injuries suffered:

> Sometimes, of course, I will psychologically identify with some persons and will see injuries to them as in some sense injuries to me. I may feel this way, for example, about my children. Here resentment does have a life. There is enormous individual variation, of course, in the degree to which people are psychologically identified with others—even strangers.

12. Although I am not here able to pursue the matter in any depth, I should at least note that forgetting is in fact more complex than this account suggests. As both Nietzsche and Freud have taught us, some cases that appear to involve mere nonvoluntary forgetting might, when analyzed in depth, prove

to be complex (though unconscious) rational strategies—strategies for which an individual might legitimately be held accountable. Here cases that initially look like mere forgetting might merit reclassification as forgetting of a more complex sort or even as forgiving.

13. This point is stressed in Beardsley, Elizabeth. "Understanding and Forgiveness." *The Philosophy of Brand Blanshard*. Ed. Paul Arthur Schilpp. La Salle, Ill.: Open Court, 1981.

14. See *U.S. v. Bergman,* 416 F. Supp. 496 (S.D.N.Y., 1976). Rabbi Bergman was convicted of criminal fraud in connection with the operation of some of his nursing homes. He tried to avoid a prison sentence by arguing that he had been disgraced and had thus suffered enough. Judge Frankel was underwhelmed by this argument and suggested that, as Bergman's crimes demonstrated, he was "suffering from loss of public esteem ... that had been, at least in some measure, wrongly bestowed and enjoyed."

15. One philosopher who has appreciated the role of ritual in our moral life is Gareth Matthews. See his "Ritual and the Religious Feelings." *Explaining Emotions*. Ed. Amelie Oksenberg Rorty. Berkeley: University of California Press, 1980. 339–53.

16. On the role of humiliation ("humbling of the will"), see Fingarette, Herbert. "Presidential Address." *Proceedings of the American Philosophical Association* (1977).

17. For a discussion of Feuerbach and others on this matter, see Wood, Allen. *Kant's Moral Religion*. Ithaca, N.Y.: Cornell University Press, 1970. Chap. 6.

18. For an argument that this characterization of the response to divine commands may be superficial, see my "Kantian Autonomy and Divine Commands." *Faith and Philosophy* 4 (July 1987): 276–81. See also Geach, Peter. "The Moral Law and the Law of God." *God and the Soul*. London: Routledge & Kegan Paul, 1969.

19. Why, then, should the beneficiary of forgiveness care that he is forgiven if he must still face harsh consequences? Surely he will care for the same reason that the victim of his original injustice cared about the intangible harm he received. Normal human beings, in normal human relations, simply care deeply about the attitudes that (some) other people have toward them—about the messages of respect or lack of respect that are conveyed. Thus most of us can easily imagine a case where, although repentant, we are justly punished yet forgiven (even loved) and another case where we are justly punished and not forgiven (even hated). The punishment will hurt the same in both cases, and yet who would not prefer the former to the latter? Recall Melville's *Billy Budd* and how deeply both Billy and Captain Vere cared—independently of the legal consequences that each knew were inevitable—about how each *felt* about the other. Is there anything at all puzzling about this?

60   Should We Execute Those Who Deserve to Die?

STEPHEN NATHANSON

Many people believe that murderers deserve to die and therefore that the state ought to execute them. I will call this reasoning the "argument from desert."

The argument from desert has very broad appeal, and death penalty opponents need to show that it is mistaken if their position is to be taken seriously. In order to show this, death penalty opponents must make a convincing case for the truth of at least one of the following statements:

1. People who commit murder do not deserve to die.

2. Even if people who commit murder deserve to die, it is wrong for the state to execute them.

From *An Eye for an Eye: The Morality of Punishing by Death* (Lanham, MD: Rowman & Littlefield, 1987), pp. 42–59. Reprinted with permission of the publisher.

If either one of these statements can be established, then the argument from desert fails.

I will try to show that both of these statements are true and therefore that the argument from desert does not provide a morally sound justification for the death penalty.

GIVING PEOPLE WHAT THEY DESERVE

In beginning our consideration of the argument from desert, let us assume that death penalty advocates are correct in asserting that murderers deserve to die. Although it may appear that if we assume this, then the argument for the death penalty is unstoppable, this impression is mistaken. There is no inconsistency in conceding that murderers deserve to die and still opposing the death penalty. These two beliefs are consistent because there may be quite good reasons in particular cases why people should not get what they deserve. This is especially true when the body that is to give someone his just deserts is the government.

One reason for not giving a person what he deserves is that doing so conflicts with other obligations that one has. [According to] the brutalization hypothesis, ... executions actually cause homicides. If this hypothesis is true, it provides the government with a powerful reason not to execute convicted murderers, even if they deserve to die. The reason is that the government's policy of giving murderers their just deserts would be carried out at the cost of having innocent people lose their lives. Faced with a choice between giving murderers what they deserve and protecting innocent lives, the government ought to choose protection of the innocent over execution of the guilty. It is more important to save innocent lives than to terminate guilty ones, and it is a more central function of government that it protect people's well-being than that it carry out the distribution of just deserts.

This example is somewhat hypothetical because the brutalization effect remains controversial and has not yet influenced governmental policy. In any case, there are many ways in which our legal system currently departs from a policy of giving people what they deserve. One such case is the prohibition of double jeopardy. Our system does not permit a person to be tried more than once for a particular crime. If he is tried and acquitted, that is the end of it.

Now imagine a case of a person who has been accused of murder. He is tried and acquitted, and as he leaves the courthouse, he tells reporters, "I did it, and I got away with it." If this person did commit the murder and if murderers deserve to die, then he deserves to die. Nonetheless, the government may not prosecute him again for this charge and may not punish him, even though, from a moral point of view, he deserves to die. In this case, the prohibition on double jeopardy outweighs whatever obligation there might be to give this person what he deserves.

Considering this situation, one could claim, of course, that it shows that the legal system is defective and that we ought to abolish the double jeopardy rule. There are good reasons, however, for retaining the prohibition of double jeopardy. It protects all citizens from continued threats and harassment by government officials. If we could always be brought back for retrial even though we had been acquitted of the crime in question, then we would be continually exposed to threats by unscrupulous officials. The double jeopardy rule provides a significant protection for all citizens, and it is wise to keep the rule, even if this means sometimes failing to give the guilty what they deserve.

If giving people what they deserve were the only function of the legal system, these problems would not arise. The design of our legal system incorporates other aims, however. We have already seen this in discussing the costs of capital punishment and the necessity for procedural safeguards surrounding its use. The effect of these multiple aims is that we must sometimes sacrifice the goal of giving people what they deserve in order to satisfy other goals of greater importance. So, even if one concedes that murderers deserve to die, one need not grant that the government ought to execute them. This is because executing them may conflict with other important goals or ideals.

Death penalty supporters might concede this point in principle but deny that any such conflicts arise with respect to the death penalty. The question we must answer, then, is whether there are significant legal or moral goals and ideals that conflict with the imposition of the death penalty.

FURMAN V. GEORGIA

The Eighth Amendment to the United States Constitution prohibits the use of cruel and unusual punishments, and in 1972, the Supreme Court decided that the death penalty, *as it was then administered,* was cruel and unusual.[1]

Although each justice wrote a separate opinion in *Furman v. Georgia,* the most significant argument that emerged against the death penalty was based on the view that the death penalty was imposed in an arbitrary manner. In a widely accepted analysis of the Court's action, Charles Black has written:

> The decisive ground of the 1972 *Furman* case anti-capital punishment ruling—the ground persuasive to the marginal justices needed for a majority—was that, out of a large number of persons "eligible" in law for the punishment, a few were selected as if at random, by no stated (or perhaps statable) criteria, while all the rest suffered the lesser penalty of imprisonment.[2]

In focusing, then, on how the death penalty was administered, the Court was not concerned with whether the actual executions were performed in a cruel and unusual manner. Rather, the justices were concerned with the procedures under which death penalty sentences were being determined, and they judged the punishment to be unacceptable because life and death decisions were being made in an arbitrary way.

In understanding the Court's reasoning, it is important to recall that current laws do not embody the judgment that all people guilty of homicide deserve to die. Some killings are not even called "murder," but are classified as manslaughter, usually because there was no intention to kill. Even among murders, the laws of many states distinguish between first and second degrees of murder. Only those guilty of first-degree murder are eligible for the death penalty, and even among these, judges or juries may decide that their crimes were not sufficiently terrible to merit death. The aim of this system of classifications is to select those killings that are the very worst and to impose the death penalty only in these cases. Underlying this system, then, is the judgment that only those guilty of the worst murders deserve to die. Some people who murder deserve a lesser punishment.

The Court's complaint with the administration of the death penalty was that this system of grading punishments according to the crime was not working. Decisions concerning executions were being made arbitrarily and not on the basis of facts about the crime. This was happening because the law contained no clear criteria that juries could apply when deciding which murderers ought to be executed and which ought to be imprisoned. In the absence of clear criteria, these judgments were determined by legally irrelevant factors.

In explaining their positions, different justices on the Court emphasized different forms of arbitrariness. Justice Stewart objected to the random aspects of the sentencing process, explaining his objection as follows:

> These death sentences are cruel and unusual in the same way that being struck by lightning is cruel and unusual. For, of all the people convicted of rapes and murders in 1967 and 1968, *many just as reprehensible as these*, the petitioners are among *a capriciously selected random handful* upon whom the sentence has in fact been imposed.[3]

In other words, there was no reasonable basis for the execution of these people and the imprisonment of others. Many were equally reprehensible, and so it was "cruel and unusual" to single out only a few for the severest punishment.

Other justices stressed a fact that had long been emphasized by death penalty opponents, its discriminatory application. According to them, the application of the death penalty was arbitrary but not entirely random. Rather, racial bias created a situation in which blacks were more likely to be executed than whites. In fact, prejudice had a significant double effect on sentencing, since blacks who killed whites were among those most likely to be executed, while whites who killed blacks were the least likely to be sentenced to die.[4] Similarly, economic and social status influenced these judgments in illegitimate ways. These were the arbitrary features stressed by Justice Douglas. As he wrote:

> In a Nation committed to equal protection of the laws there is no permissible "caste" aspect of law enforcement. Yet we know that the discretion of judges and juries in imposing the death penalty enables the penalty to be selectively applied, feeding prejudices against the accused if he is poor and despised and lacking political clout, or if he is a member of a suspect or unpopular minority, and saving those who by social position may be in a more protected position.[5]

Douglas argued, then, that the death penalty was cruel and unusual because it was applied to people (or not applied to them) for reasons that were legally irrelevant and impermissible. It would violate the Constitution to have a law that permitted the execution only of poor people or members of racial minorities. Since this was how the death penalty was operating in fact, its use under those conditions was unconstitutional.

THE MORAL BASIS OF THE *FURMAN* DECISION

In considering these issues, the Supreme Court was treating them as matters of constitutional law. The question facing the Court was whether the arbitrary imposition of the death penalty made it unconstitutional. Nonetheless, the issues involved in the *Furman* case are not solely matters of constitutional law. For opponents of the death penalty, the pattern of arbitrary and discriminatory sentencing is itself a deplorable moral injustice. Even if these practices were permissible under the Constitution, they would still be morally unjust.

I believe that this moral condemnation is appropriate and that the Court's reasoning has moral as well as legal force. The *Furman* argument illuminates the true but paradoxical judgment that it can be morally unjust to punish someone for a crime even if he morally deserves to be punished.

In order to see that it can actually be unjust to give someone what he deserves, imagine a group of 50 people, all of whom have committed dreadful murders. Suppose that each one's act is so horrible that we would have no trouble concluding that each one deserved to die. In spite of this, however, only those with red hair are sentenced to die, while all others are given lesser sentences. In this situation, the red-headed murderers would certainly feel that they were being treated unjustly, and I think that they would be correct.

Even if a person deserves to die, that is not enough to make his execution just. In addition, it is necessary that he be executed *because* he deserves to die. In the case I have described, we cannot explain why the red-headed murderers were sentenced to die by saying that they deserved it. This explanation is insufficient because others who were equally deserving were not sentenced to die. So, if we try to explain the decision to execute some but not others, the explanation would be that they were people with red hair who had committed heinous murders. Yet, it is surely unjust to execute someone *because* he is a red-headed murderer rather than a blond- or black-haired murderer. This would be cruel and unusual in the sense stressed by Douglas, since it would involve basing the degree of punishment on features of a person that are irrelevant. It is especially unjust if the punishment is determined by features of a person over which he has little or no control.

Even if we grant, then, that only those who deserve to die are ever sentenced to die, we would be forced to see the death penalty as unjust if its actual imposition depended on such factors as race, economic status, ability to acquire adequate legal representation, or other facts that have nothing to do with a person's culpability. That is the underlying moral argument of the *Furman* decision, and it is a powerful, important moral argument, even apart from its constitutional significance.

ELIMINATING ARBITRARINESS

The problem of arbitrariness has been addressed by death penalty supporters in two ways. After the *Furman* decision, state legislatures passed new laws that were designed to eliminate the influence of arbitrary features from death penalty impositions. Two strategies were pursued. In some states, the death penalty was made mandatory for certain types of crimes. Anyone convicted of them would be executed so that both randomness and discrimination could play no role. This strategy was rejected by the Supreme Court. In *Woodson v. North Carolina*, it ruled that mandatory death sentences were unconstitutional, since they failed to permit consideration of individual differences among defendants.[6]

The second legislative strategy was to leave room for judgment but to eliminate arbitrariness by providing specific guidelines for juries to follow in deciding on the appropriate sentence. This is the strategy of "guided discretion," under which the law leaves the final judgment to juries but specifies what kinds of reasons may be used in determining whether a particular murderer ought to be executed or imprisoned. Typically, these guidelines consist of lists of aggravating and mitigating circumstances, features of the crimes or persons that may make the crime worse or less bad. The new laws also included other procedural safeguards, such as automatic appeals or reviews of death sentences and separate sentencing hearings, which allow defendants to present additional factors on their behalf.

In its 1976 decision in *Gregg v. Georgia*,[7] the Supreme Court ruled that statutes incorporating "guided discretion" and other safeguards were constitutional because they made arbitrariness sufficiently unlikely. In making this ruling, the Court did not reject the *Furman* argument that arbitrarily imposed executions are cruel and unusual. Rather, it claimed that arbitrariness had been sufficiently eliminated so as to guarantee fair proceedings and controlled, unbiased sentencing.

The *Gregg* decision has prompted death penalty opponents to argue that "guided discretion" is an illusion and that even under the new laws, sentences in capital cases continue to be arbitrary and discriminatory. I do not at this point want to consider the evidence for these claims. Instead, I simply want to point out that if these claims are correct, then the Court would be bound to return to its earlier judgment that the death penalty was unconstitutional. This is because the Court did not reject the argument that *if* the death penalty is arbitrarily administered, then it violates the

Constitution. Instead, it decided that under the new laws, the death penalty would no longer be administered arbitrarily.

AGAINST THE ARGUMENT FROM ARBITRARINESS

Although death penalty supporters have tried to make death sentencing less arbitrary, some of them explicitly reject the use of the argument from arbitrariness as a criticism of the death penalty. While favoring fairer sentencing, they think that the Court was wrong to accept the argument from arbitrariness in the first place. They think that the death penalty can be just even if it is administered in an arbitrary and discriminatory way. For those who hold this position, evidence showing the continued influence of arbitrary and discriminatory factors would have no force because, in their view, it never was legally or morally relevant to the question of whether death is a just punishment.

This rejection of the argument from arbitrariness has been stated forcefully by Ernest van den Haag, a longtime defender of the death penalty. According to van den Haag:

> [T]he abolitionist argument from capriciousness, or discretion, or discrimination, would be more persuasive if it were alleged that those selectively executed are not guilty. But the argument merely maintains that some other guilty but more favored persons, or groups, escape the death penalty. This is hardly sufficient for letting anyone else found guilty escape the penalty. On the contrary, that some guilty persons or groups elude it argues for extending the death penalty to them.[8]

For van den Haag, the only injustice that occurs here is that some people who deserve death are not executed. In his opinion, however, the failure to execute these fortunate people does not show that it is unjust to execute others who are no more deserving of death but are simply less fortunate.

From van den Haag's point of view, the justice of punishments is entirely a matter of individual desert. As he writes:

> Justice requires punishing the guilty—as many of the guilty as possible, even if only some can be

punished, and sparing the innocent—as many of the innocent as possible, even if not all are spared. It would surely be wrong to treat everybody with equal injustice in preference to meting out justice at least to some.... [If] the death penalty is morally just, however discriminatorily applied to only some of the guilty, it does remain just in each case in which it is applied.[9]

According to van den Haag, then, the justice of individual punishments depends on individual guilt alone and not on whether punishments are equally distributed among the class of guilty people.

Van den Haag's argument is important because it threatens to undermine the moral basis of the *Furman* decision. It dismisses as irrelevant the abolitionist argument that the death penalty is unjust because its use in the United States has been inextricably bound up with patterns of racial discrimination. Even if we find this history abhorrent, we may yet think that van den Haag's argument is plausible. Its plausibility derives from the fact that we believe that it is often legitimate to punish or reward people, even though we know that others who are equally deserving will not be punished or rewarded. Here are two cases where common sense appears to support van den Haag's view about the requirements of justice:

A. A driver is caught speeding, ticketed, and required to pay a fine. Although we know that the percentage of speeders who are actually punished is extremely small, we would probably regard it as a joke if the driver protested that he was being treated unjustly or if someone argued that no one should be fined for speeding unless all speeders were fined.

B. A person performs a heroic act and receives a substantial reward, in addition to the respect and admiration of his fellow citizens. Because he deserves the reward, we think it just that he receive it, even though many equally heroic persons are not treated similarly. That most heroes are unsung is no reason to avoid rewarding this particular heroic individual.

Both of these cases appear to support van den Haag's view that we should do justice in individual cases whenever we can, and that our failure to

treat people as they deserve in all cases provides no reason to withhold deserved punishment or reward from particular individuals. If this is correct, then we must give up the argument from arbitrariness and accept van den Haag's view that "unequal justice is justice still."

ARBITRARY DECISIONS ABOUT WHO DESERVES WHAT

In order to evaluate this objection to the argument from arbitrariness, we need to look at the original argument more closely. What a closer look reveals is that there is in fact more than one problem of arbitrariness. Van den Haag fails to take note of this, and for this reason, his discussion leaves untouched many of the central issues raised by the argument.

We need to distinguish two different arguments, which I will call the *argument from arbitrary judgment* and the *argument from arbitrary imposition*. In making this distinction, I do not mean to contrast two stages in the actual legal process. Rather, the contrast is meant to help us focus on two different grounds for the claim that the death penalty is unjust because it is arbitrary.

Van den Haag assumes that judges and juries can and do make nonarbitrary judgments about what people deserve, and that the problem of arbitrariness arises only in the imposition of punishments. For him, the arbitrariness arises when we try to determine who among those who deserve to die will actually be executed. This is what I want to call the *argument from arbitrary imposition*. It assumes that we know who deserves to die, and it objects to the fact that only some of those who deserve to die are executed. This version of the argument is expressed by Justice Stewart in the passage I quoted earlier, and it is this argument that van den Haag addresses.

In doing so, however, he completely neglects the *argument from arbitrary judgment*. According to this argument, the determination of *who* deserves to die is itself arbitrary. It is not simply that arbitrary factors determine who among the deserving will be condemned to die. Rather, the problem is that the judgment concerning who deserves to die is itself a product of arbitrary factors.

In other words, van den Haag assumes that we know who the deserving are, but this is just the assumption that the second form of the argument challenges.

Charles Black is clearly drawing our attention to the problem of arbitrary judgment when he writes that:

> [T]he official choices—by prosecutors, judges, juries, and governors—that divide those who are to die from those who are to live are on the whole not made, and cannot be made, under standards that are consistently meaningful and clear, but ... they are often made, and in the foreseeable future will continue to be made, under no standards at all or under pseudostandards without discoverable meaning.[10]

If Black is correct, judgments about who deserves a particular punishment are arbitrary because the law does not contain meaningful standards for distinguishing those who deserve death from those who deserve imprisonment. Given this lack of standards, factors that should have no influence will in fact be the primary bases of decision.

This important argument is completely neglected by van den Haag. In order to defend the death penalty against this criticism, he would have to show that our laws contain adequate criteria for deciding whether people deserve death or imprisonment, and that judges and juries have made judgments of desert in a nonarbitrary way. Van den Haag makes no effort to do this. He simply assumes that the legal system does a good job of distinguishing those who deserve to die from those who do not. This, however, is just what the argument from arbitrary judgment challenges.

Van den Haag's assumption may gain plausibility from his tendency to oversimplify the kinds of judgments that need to be made. In contrast with Black, who stresses the complexity of the law of homicide and the many steps in the legal process leading toward punishment, van den Haag is content with the abstract maxim that "justice requires punishing the guilty ... and sparing the innocent." This maxim makes it look as if officials and jurors are faced with the simple choice of dividing people into two neat categories, the guilty and the innocent. And if we think of these as *factual* rather than *legal* categories, it makes it look as if the only judgment that they must make is whether one person did or did not kill another.

In fact, of course, the judgments that must be made are much more complicated than this. To be guilty of a murder that merits the death penalty is not the same as having killed another person. Although the basic factual judgment that one person has caused the death of another is itself not always easy to make, the legal judgments involved are more complex still. Of those who kill, some may have committed no crime at all if their action is judged to be justifiable homicide. For those guilty of some form of homicide, we need to decide how to classify their act within the degrees of homicide. What did the killer intend to do? Was he under duress? Was he provoked by the victim? Did he act with malice? Had the act been planned or was it spontaneous? These are among the factual issues that arise when juries try to determine the legal status of the action. Beyond these are legal questions. Was the act murder or manslaughter? And if it was murder, was it first or second degree murder? And if it was first degree murder, did any of the mitigating or aggravating circumstances characterize the act? These are the sorts of issues that actually confront prosecutors, juries, and judges, and they go well beyond the more familiar "whodunit" types of questions.[11]

If prosecutors, juries, and judges do not have clear criteria by which to sort out these issues, or if the criteria can be neglected in practice, then judgments about who deserves to face death rather than imprisonment will be arbitrary. This would undermine van den Haag's optimistic assumption that it is only those who genuinely deserve execution who are sentenced to die.

In stressing the complexities of the judgments involved, I have tried to show why it is plausible to believe that the resulting judgments could well be influenced by arbitrary factors. Further, I assume that, if we are not confident that the death penalty is imposed on those who truly deserve it, then we would reject the punishment as unjust. This is the moral force of the argument from arbitrary judgment. Even if those who deserve to die ought to be executed, we ought not to allow the state to execute them if the procedures adopted by the state are unlikely to separate the deserving from the undeserving in a rational and just manner. History supports the view that the death penalty has been imposed on those who are less favored for reasons that have nothing to do with their crimes. The judgment that they deserved to die has often been the result of prejudice, and their executions were unjust for this reason.[12]

IS THE SYSTEM STILL ARBITRARY?

One may wonder, however, whether this sort of arbitrary judgment is still occurring in the administration of the death penalty. Is there any evidence for the continued presence of this form of arbitrariness? Didn't the Supreme Court's *Gregg* decision show that this sort of arbitrariness is no longer a problem?

To decide whether the problem of arbitrariness remains, one could either examine the new laws themselves to see whether the criteria for selecting those who deserve death are clear and adequate, or one could study the actual legal process and its results to see what factors play a role in leading to actual sentences. Both types of investigations have been carried out, and the case for continuing arbitrariness and discrimination is quite strong. Since my primary purpose here is to show that the existence of arbitrariness is morally relevant to our assessment of the death penalty, I will mention only a few points that indicate that the system remains flawed by arbitrariness. Others have made the case for the persistence of arbitrariness with force and in great detail.[13]

In his book *Capital Punishment: The Inevitability of Caprice and Mistake*,[14] Charles Black shows how unclear are the lists of mitigating and aggravating circumstances that are supposed to guide juries in their sentencing decisions. His purely legal analysis is strongly supported by evidence about the actual workings of the system. In a study of sentencing under the new post-*Furman* laws, William Bowers and Glen Pierce found strong evidence of continued and systematic racial discrimination in the process leading to a sentence of death. I will mention just a few items from their study.

Under the new laws, as they were applied between 1972 and 1977, the highest probability of a death sentence was found to occur in those cases where the killer was black and the victim white. The lowest probability of execution was found where the victim was black and the killer white. This same pattern emerged in a study by William Bowers and Glen Pierce of sentencing in Florida, Georgia, Texas, and Ohio. In Ohio and Florida during this period, there were 127 cases of whites killing blacks, and not one of these murderers was sentenced to death. At the same time, blacks who killed whites in these states had about a 25 percent chance of receiving a death sentence.

The following chart, taken from the Bowers and Pierce study, shows the relationship between the races of victims and killers and the probability of a death sentence as this was exhibited in Ohio between 1974 and 1977.[15]

Racial Grouping	Total	Death Sentences	Death Sentence Probability
Black kills white	173	44	.254
White kills white	803	37	.046
Black kills black	1,170	20	.017
White kills black	47	0	.000

These findings strongly suggest that judgments about the seriousness of crimes and the amount of blameworthiness attaching to criminals are strongly influenced by deep-seated racial prejudices. It appears that judges and juries regard the killing of a white by a black as a more serious crime than the killing of a black by a white. Thus, they judge that blacks killing whites deserve more severe punishments than whites killing blacks. Given the bluntness of our ordinary moral judgments and the deep roots of racial prejudice in our society, it is perhaps not surprising that these results occur. But it is clear that no law that embodied these criteria, grading crimes by the race of victims and offenders, would be constitutional. Yet the administration of our laws reveals the de facto operation of just these discriminatory criteria.

Whatever role the criteria for assessing murders play, they do not effectively prevent the operation of discriminatory influences, and so they fail to eliminate the arbitrariness that the *Furman* ruling condemned. Rather than genuinely guiding judgments, the lists of mitigating and aggravating circumstances seem only to provide the language by which juries can justify judgments made on other grounds. This view is further supported by other data in the Bowers and Pierce study. If one compares the Florida and Georgia death penalty statutes, the following difference emerges. In Georgia, the law lists ten aggravating circumstances. If a jury finds one of these circumstances characterizing a particular murder, it can recommend death, and the judge *must* accept their recommendation. In Florida, eight aggravating circumstances are listed, and the jury must determine that aggravating circumstances outweigh mitigating ones. On this basis, they can recommend death, but the judge need not accept their judgment.

As a result of these differences, Florida juries must find more aggravating circumstances to support a recommendation of death than do Georgia juries. It is plausible to suppose that murders in Florida and Georgia do not themselves differ in systematic ways. If jury judgments about aggravating circumstances differ systematically, that would suggest that judgments about whether the defendant ought to be executed are made independently of the criteria and then fitted to the criteria in order to provide a legal rationalization for the decision. In particular, although it is implausible to suppose that murders committed in Florida are objectively worse than those committed in Georgia, we might expect to find that juries discover more aggravating circumstances in Florida so as to justify their independent conviction that a particular individual deserves to die.

This is just what Bowers and Pierce found. Although juries in Georgia found 46 percent of the murders they considered to be especially vile or heinous, Florida juries found these features in 89 percent of the murders they judged. Likewise, although Georgia juries found the factor of "risk to others" in only 1 percent of the cases facing them, Florida juries found that 28 percent of their murders involved a risk to the lives of others beyond the victim. Similar results are found in all but

one of the categories compared, further confirming the judgment that "guided discretion" remains a rather unguided and arbitrary process. The criteria function more as rationalizations of sentencing decisions than as determinants of them.

Finally, although there are many stages in the legal process leading to an execution, the Supreme Court's decision in *Gregg* focused only on the question of whether juries were provided with adequate guidelines in capital cases. It is important to recall, however, that important decisions are made by prosecutors, judges, governors, and clemency boards as well. The case of prosecutors is especially important and instructive. Prosecutors must decide what charges to file, whether to try to convict a person of manslaughter or murder, and whether to press for the death penalty. In making these decisions, they often consider how good a chance they have of winning a case. This does not seem unreasonable, but it is easy to see how this could perpetuate and play upon racial and other prejudices. The black defendant or killer of a white victim may be more likely to be charged with first degree murder in the first place because the prosecutor expects to find a jury that is less sympathetic to these defendants.[16] In many cases, those who are already disadvantaged in society have a greater chance of being charged with more serious crimes, while others more fortunate never face a life or death judgment from a jury because their killing has been classified as manslaughter by the prosecutor. The process is unjustly discriminatory and is arbitrary as well because the judgment is not based on a notion of what the defendant deserves. It is based on a calculation of success or failure in court, which is itself influenced by factors that ought to play no role in the legal process.

CONCLUSIONS

We have seen that the system of capital punishment does not operate so as to execute people only on the basis of what they deserve. Other arbitrary factors play a significant role in determining who is to die for killing another human being. In *Furman v. Georgia,* the Supreme Court recognized that an injustice could occur even in cases where a person who is condemned to die actually deserves that punishment. I have tried to explain the moral basis for considering this an injustice.

I have also considered the objection that arbitrariness is irrelevant because justice requires only that those who are punished deserve it. How others are treated is irrelevant. In replying to this objection, I noted the importance of distinguishing two forms of the argument from arbitrariness— the argument from arbitrary judgment and the argument from arbitrary imposition. What I have tried to show is that van den Haag neglects the argument from arbitrary judgment and assumes that all those who are sentenced to die deserve this treatment. This optimistic assumption is unfounded, however, and I have cited some of the evidence that death sentences remain arbitrary and discriminatory in spite of the guided discretion system that the Supreme Court approved in *Gregg v. Georgia* and has upheld in subsequent decisions.

I should note that, although much of the arbitrariness I have discussed arises from patterns of racial prejudice in the United States, this argument is not only relevant to the death penalty in our society. There is nothing unique about the situation in which societies contain both favored and unfavored groups. The groups may be identified by race, religion, class, political orientation, or other features. Wherever these divisions exist, arbitrariness and discrimination will be obstacles to the just administration of the law.

NOTES

1. *Furman v. Georgia*, 408 U.S. 238 (1972).
2. Black, Charles. *Capital Punishment: The Inevitability of Caprice and Mistake*. 2nd ed. New York: Norton, 1981. 20.
3. From *Furman v. Georgia*, 408 U.S. 238, 239 (1972); reprinted in Bedau, H. *The Death Penalty in America*. 3rd ed. New York: Oxford University Press, 1982. 263–64, emphasis added.
4. For extensive evidence of racial discrimination in the imposition of the death penalty, see Bowers, W. *Legal Homicide*. Boston: Northeastern University Press, 1984. Chs. 3 and 7.
5. Reprinted in Bedau, supra, note 3, at 255.
6. 428 U.S. 280–324 (1976); excerpted in Bedau, supra, note 3, at 288–293.
7. *Gregg v. Georgia*, 428 U.S. 153 (1976).
8. "The Collapse of the Case Against Capital Punishment," *National Review* 31 March 1978, 397. A briefer version of this paper appeared in the *Criminal Law Bulletin* 14 (1978): 51–68 and is reprinted in Bedau, supra, note 3, at 323–33.
9. Id., emphasis added.
10. Black, supra, note 2, at 29.
11. For an interesting account of a case in which classification problems emerge quite vividly, see Phillips, Steven. *No Heroes, No Villains*. New York: Random House, 1977.
12. For historical material about the United States, see Bowers, *Legal Homicide*, supra, note 4, part I.
13. For this evidence, see Black, *Capital Punishment*, supra, note 2, passim; Bowers, William and Pierce, Glen. "Racial Discrimination and Criminal Homicide under Post-Furman Statutes." In Bowers, *Legal Homicide*, supra, note 4, ch. 7, and reprinted in Bedau, supra, note 3, at 206–23; Bentele, Ursula. "The Death Penalty in Georgia: Still Arbitrary." *Washington University Law Quarterly* 62 (1985): 573–646; and Gross, Samuel and Mauro, Robert. "Patterns of Death: An Analysis of Racial Disparities in Capital Sentencing and Homicide Victimization." *Stanford Law Review* 37 (1984): 27–153.
14. See supra, note 2.
15. For a chart showing these figures in full, see Bowers, supra, note 4, at 225; reprinted in Bedau, supra, note 3, at 213.
16. On this point, see Bentele, supra, note 13, at 615.

CHAPTER EIGHTEEN

Principles of Criminal Liability

61   THE M'NAGHTEN RULES

HOUSE OF LORDS, 1843

(Question I.) "What is the law respecting alleged crimes committed by persons afflicted with insane delusion in respect of one or more particular subjects or persons: as for instance, where, at the time of the commission of the alleged crime, the accused knew he was acting contrary to law, but did the act complained of with a view, under the influence of insane delusion, of redressing or revenging some supposed grievance or injury, or of producing some supposed public benefit?"

(Answer I.) "Assuming that your lordships' inquiries are confined to those persons who labor under such partial delusions only, and are not in other respects insane, we are of opinion that notwithstanding the accused did the act complained of with a view, under the influence of insane delusion, of redressing or avenging some supposed grievance or injury, or of producing some public benefit, he is nevertheless punishable, according to the nature of the crime committed, if he knew at the time of committing such crime that he was acting contrary to law, by which expression we understand your lordships to mean the law of the land."

(Q.II.) "What are the proper questions to be submitted to the jury where a person alleged to be afflicted with insane delusion respecting one or more particular subjects or persons is charged with the commission of a crime (murder, for example), and insanity is set up as a defence?"

(Q.III.) "In what terms ought the question to be left to the jury as to the prisoner's state of mind at the time when the act was committed?"

(A.II and A.III.) "As these two questions appear to us to be more conveniently answered together, we submit our opinion to be that the jury ought to be told in all cases that every man is presumed to be sane, and to possess a sufficient degree of reason to be responsible for his crimes, until the contrary be proved to their satisfaction; and that to establish a defence on the ground of insanity it must be clearly proved that, at the time of committing the act, the accused was labouring under such a defect of reason, from disease of the mind, as not to know the nature and quality of the

10 *Cl. 2nd F.* 200 at p. 209. See: "Daniel M'Naghten's Case." *United Kingdom House of Lord's Decisions.* British and Irish Legal Information Institute (BAILII). Web. http://www.bailii.org/uk/cases/UKHL/1843/J16.html

act he was doing, or, if he did know it, that he did not know he was doing what was wrong. The mode of putting the latter part of the question to the jury on these occasions has generally been whether the accused at the time of doing the act knew the difference between right and wrong: which mode, though rarely, if ever, leading to any mistake with the jury, is not, as we conceive, so accurate when put generally and in the abstract as when put with reference to the party's knowledge of right and wrong, in respect to the very act with which he is charged. If the question were to be put as to the knowledge of the accused solely and exclusively with reference to the law of the land, it might tend to confound the jury, by inducing them to believe that an actual knowledge of the law of the land was essential in order to lead to conviction: whereas, the law is administered upon the principle that everyone must be taken conclusively to know it, without proof that he does know it. If the accused was conscious that the act was one that he ought not to do, and if that act was at the same time contrary to the law of the land, he is punishable; and the usual course, therefore, has been to leave the question to the jury, whether the accused had a sufficient degree of reason to know that he was doing an act that was wrong; and this course we think is correct, accompanied with such observations and explanations as the circumstances of each particular case may require."

(Q.IV.) "If a person under an insane delusion as to existing facts commits an offence in consequence thereof, is he thereby excused?"

(A.IV.) "The answer must, of course, depend on the nature of the delusion; but making the same assumption as we did before, namely, that he labors under such partial delusion only, and is not in other respects insane, we think he must be considered in the same situation as to responsibility as if the facts with respect to which the delusion exists were real. For example, if under the influence of his delusion he supposes another man to be in the act of attempting to take away his life, and he kills that man, as he supposes in self-defence, he would be exempt from punishment. If his delusion was that the deceased had inflicted a serious injury to his character and fortune, and he killed him in revenge for such supposed injury, he would be liable to punishment."

62   The Insanity Defense

AMERICAN LAW INSTITUTE

ARTICLE 4. RESPONSIBILITY

Section 4.01. Mental Disease or Defect Excluding Responsibility

1. A person is not responsible for criminal conduct if at the time of such conduct as a result of mental disease or defect he lacks substantial capacity either to appreciate the criminality of his conduct or to conform his conduct to the requirements of law.

2. The terms "mental disease or defect" do not include an abnormality manifested only by repeated criminal or otherwise antisocial conduct.

Alternative formulations of paragraph (1).

a. A person is not responsible for criminal conduct if at the time of such conduct as a result of mental disease or defect his capacity either to appreciate the criminality of his conduct or to conform his conduct to the requirements of law is so substantially impaired that he cannot justly be held responsible.

b. A person is not responsible for criminal conduct if at the time of such conduct as a result of mental disease or defect he lacks substantial capacity to appreciate the criminality of his conduct or is in such state that the prospect of conviction and punishment cannot constitute a significant restraining influence upon him.

COMMENTS §4.01. ARTICLE 4. RESPONSIBILITY

Section 4.01. Mental Disease or Defect Excluding Responsibility

The Problem of Defining the Criteria of Irresponsibility

1. No problem in the drafting of a penal code presents larger intrinsic difficulty than that of determining when individuals whose conduct would otherwise be criminal ought to be exculpated on the ground that they were suffering from mental disease or defect when they acted as they did. What is involved specifically is the drawing of a line between the use of public agencies and public force to condemn the offender by conviction, with resultant sanctions in which there is inescapably a punitive ingredient (however constructive we may attempt to make the process of correction) and modes of disposition in which that ingredient is absent, even though restraint may be involved. To put the matter differently, the problem is to discriminate between the cases where a punitive-correctional disposition is appropriate and those in which a medical-custodial disposition is the only kind the law should allow.

2. The traditional M'Naghten rule resolves the problem solely in regard to the capacity of the individual to know what he was doing and to know that it was wrong. Absent these minimal elements of rationality, condemnation and punishment are obviously both unjust and futile. They are unjust because the individual could not, by hypothesis, have employed reason to restrain the act; he did not and he could not know the facts essential to bring reason into play. On the same ground, they are futile. A madman who believes that he is squeezing lemons when he chokes his wife or thinks that homicide is the command of God is plainly beyond reach of the restraining influence of law; he needs restraint but condemnation is entirely meaningless and ineffective. Thus the attacks on the M'Naghten rule as an inept definition of insanity or as an arbitrary definition in terms of special symptoms are entirely misconceived. The *rationale* of the position is that these are cases in which reason cannot operate and in which it is totally impossible for individuals to be deterred. Moreover, the category defined by the rule is so extreme that to the ordinary man the exculpation of the persons it encompasses bespeaks no weakness in the law. He does not identify such persons and himself; they are a world apart.

Jurisdictions in which the M'Naghten test has been expanded to include the case where mental disease produces an "irresistible impulse" proceed on the same *rationale*. They recognize, however, that cognitive factors are not the only ones that preclude inhibition; that even though cognition still obtains, mental disorder may produce a total incapacity for self-control. The same result is sometimes reached under M'Naghten proper, in the view, strongly put forth by Stephen, that "knowledge" requires more than the capacity to verbalize right answers to a question, it implies capacity to function in the light of knowledge. Stephen, *History of English Criminal Law*, Vol. 2, p. 171.... In modern psychiatric terms, the "fundamental difference between verbal or purely intellectual knowledge and the mysterious other kind of knowledge is familiar to every clinical psychiatrist; it is the difference between knowledge divorced from affect and knowledge so fused with affect that it becomes a human reality." Zilboorg, "Misconceptions of Legal Insanity," 9 *Am. J. Orthopsychiatry*, pp. 540, 552....

3. The draft accepts the view that any effort to exclude the nondeterrables from strictly penal sanctions must take account of the impairment of volitional capacity no less than of impairment of cognition; and that this result should be achieved directly in the formulation of the test, rather than left to mitigation in the application of M'Naghten.

It also accepts the criticism of the "irresistible impulse" formulation as inept in so far as it may be impliedly restricted to sudden, spontaneous acts as distinguished from insane propulsions that are accompanied by brooding or reflection....

Both the main formulation recommended and alternative (a) deem the proper question on this branch of the inquiry to be whether the defendant is without capacity to conform his conduct to the requirements of law....

Alternative (b) states the issue differently. Instead of asking whether the defendant had capacity to conform his conduct to the requirements of law, it asks whether, in consequence of mental disease or defect, the threat of punishment could not exercise a significant restraining influence upon him. To some extent, of course, these are the same inquiries. To the extent that they diverge, the latter asks a narrower and harder question, involving the assessment of capacity to respond to a single influence, the threat of punishment. Both Dr. Guttmacher and Dr. Overholser considered the assessment of responsiveness to this one influence too difficult for psychiatric judgment. Hence, though the issue framed by the alternative may well be thought to state the question that is most precisely relevant for legal purposes, the Reporter and the Council deemed the inquiry impolitic upon this ground. In so far as nondeterrability is the determination that is sought, it must be reached by probing general capacity to conform to the requirements of law. The validity of this conclusion is submitted, however, to the judgment of the Institute.

4. One further problem must be faced. In addressing itself to impairment of the cognitive capacity, M'Naghten demands that impairment be complete: the actor must *not* know. So, too, the irresistible impulse criterion presupposes a complete impairment of capacity for self-control. The extremity of these conceptions is, we think, the point that poses largest difficulty to psychiatrists when called upon to aid in their administration. The schizophrenic, for example, is disoriented from reality; the disorientation is extreme; but it is rarely total. Most psychotics will respond to a command of someone in authority within the mental hospital; they thus have some capacity to conform to a norm. But this is very different from the question whether they have the capacity to conform to requirements that are not thus immediately symbolized by an attendant or policeman at the elbow. Nothing makes the inquiry into responsibility more unreal for the psychiatrist than limitation of the issue to some ultimate extreme of total incapacity, when clinical experience reveals only a graded scale with marks along the way....

We think this difficulty can and must be met. The law must recognize that when there is no black and white it must content itself with different shades of gray. The draft, accordingly, does not demand *complete* impairment of capacity. It asks instead for *substantial* impairment. This is all, we think, that candid witnesses, called on to infer the nature of the situation at a time that they did not observe, can ever confidently say, even when they know that a disorder was extreme.

If substantial impairment of capacity is to suffice, there remains the question whether this alone should be the test or whether the criterion should state the principle that measures how substantial it must be. To identify the degree of impairment with precision is, of course, impossible both verbally and logically. The recommended formulation is content to rest upon the term *substantial* to support the weight of judgment; if capacity is greatly impaired, that presumably should be sufficient. Alternative (a) proposes to submit the issue squarely to the jury's sense of justice, asking expressly whether the capacity of the defendant "was so substantially impaired that he cannot justly be held responsible." Some members of the Council deemed it unwise to present questions of justice to the jury, preferring a submission that in form, at least, confines the inquiry to fact. The proponents of the alternative contend that since the jury normally will feel that it is only just to exculpate if the disorder was extreme, that otherwise conviction is demanded, it is safer to invoke the jury's sense of justice than to rest entirely on the single word *substantial,* imputing no specific measure of degree. The issue is an important one and it is submitted for consideration by the Institute.

5. The draft rejects the formulation warmly supported by psychiatrists and recently adopted

by the Court of Appeals for the District of Columbia in *Durham v. United States,* 214, F. 2d 862 (1954), namely, "that an accused is not criminally responsible if his unlawful act was the product of mental disease or defect." ...

The difficulty with this formulation inheres in the ambiguity of "product." If interpreted to lead to irresponsibility unless the defendant would have engaged in the criminal conduct even if he had not suffered from the disease or defect, it is too broad: an answer that he would have done so can be given very rarely; this is intrinsic to the concept of the singleness of personality and unity of mental processes that psychiatry regards as fundamental. If interpreted to call for a standard of causality less relaxed than but-for cause, there are but two alternatives to be considered: (1) a mode of causality involving total incapacity or (2) a mode of causality which involves substantial incapacity. See Wechsler, "The Criteria of Criminal Responsibility," 22 *U. of Chi. L. Rev.* (1955), p. 367. But if either of these causal concepts is intended, the formulation ought to set it forth.

The draft also rejects the proposal of the majority of the recent Royal Commission on Capital Punishment, namely, "to leave to the jury to determine whether at the time of the act the accused was suffering from disease of the mind (or mental deficiency) to such a degree that he ought not to be held responsible." *Report* (1953), par. 333, p. 116.

While we agree, as we have indicated, that mental disease or defect involves gradations of degree that should be recognized, we think the legal standard ought to focus on the *consequences* of disease or defect that have a bearing on the justice of conviction and of punishment. The Royal Commission proposal fails in this respect.

6. Paragraph (2) of section 4.01 is designed to exclude from the concept of "mental disease or defect" the case of so-called "psychopathic personality." The reason for the exclusion is that, as the Royal Commission put it, psychopathy "is a statistical abnormality; that is to say, the psychopath differs from a normal person only quantitatively or in degree, not qualitatively; and the diagnosis of psychopathic personality does not carry with it any explanation of the causes of the abnormality." While it may not be feasible to formulate a definition of "disease," there is much to be said for excluding a condition that is manifested only by the behavior phenomena that must, by hypothesis, be the result of disease for irresponsibility to be established. Although British psychiatrists have agreed, on the whole, that psychopathy should not be called "disease," there is considerable difference of opinion on the point in the United States. Yet it does not seem useful to contemplate the litigation of what is essentially a matter of terminology; nor is it right to have the legal result rest upon the resolution of a dispute of this kind.

63 Scientific Challenges to Criminal Responsibility

STEPHEN J. MORSE

Free will and human agency are considered foundational for ascriptions of criminal responsibility in Anglo-American jurisprudence. As United States Supreme Court Justice Oliver Wendell Holmes famously observed, "even a dog distinguishes between being stumbled over and being kicked."[1] And, as Supreme Court Justice Jackson wrote in

Morissette v. U.S., concisely noting both conditions:

> The contention that an injury can amount to a crime only when inflicted by intention is no provincial or transient notion. It is as universal and persistent in mature systems of law as belief

---

Written for this volume.

in freedom of the human will and a consequent ability and duty of the normal individual to choose between good and evil. A relation between some mental element and punishment for a harmful act is almost as instinctive as the child's familiar exculpatory "But I didn't mean to"....[2]

Now, however, the emerging discoveries of genetics and neuroscience challenge both foundations for responsibility.[3] In a 2002 editorial published in *The Economist*, the following warning was given: "Genetics may yet threaten privacy, kill autonomy, make society homogeneous and gut the concept of human nature. But neuroscience could do all of these things first."[4]

Despite the rapid advances in both sciences in the last decade—including the sequencing of the human genome and the increasing use of functional magnetic resonance imaging [fMRI] to measure brain physiology—there have been no revolutionary breakthroughs in morality and law. The same has been true of various other sciences that were predicted to revolutionize the law, including behavioral psychology, sociology, and psychodynamic psychology, to name but a few. This will also be true of neuroscience and genetics, which are simply the newest sciences on the block. Neither is going to do the terrible things *The Economist* fears, at least not in the foreseeable future. Despite the impressive advances in neuroscience and genetics, at present neither has much to contribute to criminal law. At most, in the near to intermediate term these sciences may make modest contributions to legal policy and case adjudication. Nonetheless, there has been irrational exuberance about their potential contribution of neuroscience, an issue I have addressed previously and referred to as "Brain Overclaim Syndrome."[5]

Genetics and the new neuroscience seem poised to demonstrate that our behavior is determined by physical events in the brain and that we therefore cannot be morally or legally responsible. The crude way of putting it is that blame and punishment are not justified if your genes and brain "made you do it." Neuroscientific discoveries also are alleged to demonstrate that mental states do not causally explain our behavior. If this is true, it provides another, independent ground for the claim that no one can ever be genuinely responsible.

Neither challenge succeeds at present. The challenge to free will—the ability to act uncaused by anything but yourself—from neurophysical and genetic determinism is the same as similar challenges in the past, but it fails for three reasons. First, free will is not a criterion for the application of any legal rule. Second, free will is not foundational for criminal responsibility. Third, there is a philosophically plausible response to those who claim that determinism—whether based on the theories and findings of neuroscience, genetics, or any other discipline—and responsibility are incompatible. Thus, I conclude that, for the moment, the positive doctrines of legal and moral responsibility are safe from the newest scientific assaults.

The neuroscientific attack on agency—on our apparent ability to guide our behavior according to our beliefs, desires, and intentions—is more troubling because it claims that the presumptions of morality and the law about human agency are inconsistent with our new understanding of the link between our genes, the brain, and behavior. Roughly speaking, the law implicitly adopts the folk-psychological model of the person, which explains behavior in terms of desires, beliefs, and intentions. If practical reason plays no role in explaining our behavior, as some neuroscientists and geneticists claim, current responsibility doctrines and practices would have to be radically altered or jettisoned altogether. I suggest, however, that the conceptual and scientific support for this argument is thin at present and that there is good ground to believe that our conception of persons as agents is unlikely to disappear. Consequently, legal and moral doctrines that depend on agentic personhood are secure—at least for now.

There is no necessary connection between the findings of neuroscience and genetics and legal or moral policies or decisions. In their current state, the new sciences may have fewer implications for law and society than popular imagination and even many scientists believe. The law's concept of the person and the nature of law itself are both so fundamental to our understanding of ourselves and of society that even the most sophisticated and detailed scientific understanding of brain function and genetics is unlikely at present to redefine or to replace them.

THE LAW'S CONCEPT OF THE PERSON

The legal concept of the *person* is an agent who is capable of acting intentionally and for reasons. We are social creatures whose interactions are not governed primarily by innate repertoires. We are able to guide our behavior in light of reasons we may have for acting, and do not solely and blindly follow instinct. Therefore, rules will inevitably be necessary to help order our interactions in any minimally complex social group. Human beings have developed extraordinarily diverse ways of living together, but all societies are governed by rules addressed to beings capable of following those rules.

Law is a practical system of rules and institutions that evaluates, guides, and governs human action. Law gives people reasons to behave one way or another by making the consequences of noncompliance clear, or through peoples' understanding of the reasons that support a particular rule. As an action-guiding system of rules, law shares many characteristics with other sources of guidance, such as morality and custom, but law is different because its rules and institutions are created and enforced by the state.

The nature of law as a guidance system entails that it is addressed to potentially intentional agents that can be guided by reasons. The law's concept of the person as a potentially intentional agent is inseparable from the nature of law itself. Actions—that is, intentional bodily movements—unlike other phenomena, can be explained by physical causes and by reasons. Although physical causes explain the structure and mechanisms of genes and of the brain and nervous system (and all the other moving parts of the physical universe), only human action and other intentionally-produced states can also be explained by reasons. Genes and neural networks have no mental states, no sense of past, present, and future, no aspirations. Only persons do. Law views human action as reason-governed and treats people as intentional agents, not simply as part of

the biophysical flotsam and jetsam of the causal universe. It could not be otherwise. It makes no sense to ask a bull that gores a matador, "Why did you do that?" But this question makes sense and is vitally important when addressed to a person who sticks a knife into the chest of another human being. It makes a great difference to us if the knife wielder is a surgeon who is cutting with knowledge of the patient's consent or a person who is enraged at the victim and intends to kill him. Only human beings are fully intentional creatures. To ask why a person acted a certain way is to ask for reasons for action, not for reductionist biophysical, psychological, or sociological explanations. I am not positing the existence of nonnatural or mysterious properties, such as a soul. Nor do I assume that our nonmaterial minds are somehow independent of our physical bodies but yet are in causal connection with our bodies. The brain enables the mind and the mind is intimately connected to our bodies, but we have no idea how it does so at present. I assume that a perfectly naturalistic set of causes from many levels of explanation, from many fields, can explain intentionality and consciousness. But only persons can deliberate about what action to perform and can determine their conduct by practical reason.

Causal explanations that depend on desires and beliefs, which philosophers and some psychologists refer to as "folk psychology," are the type of explanation we all use every day to understand ourselves, other people, and our interactions with others in the world. Folk psychologists disagree about what mental entities exist and about other issues, but all insist that mental states play a partially explanatory role in human action. Folk psychology fully recognizes that biological, sociological, and other psychological variables also play a causal role, but that mental states are crucial for explaining human action. Indeed, many philosophers claim, the task of neuroscience is to explain folk psychology, to understand how the brain enables conscious intentionality.

As noted, we have no idea how the brain enables the mind (and scant information about precisely how abnormal psychology is caused by the brain), but when we solve this problem—if we ever do—the solution will revolutionize our understanding of biological processes. Our view of ourselves and our moral, legal, and political arrangements are likely to be as profoundly altered as our understanding of biological processes. For now, however, despite the impressive gains in neuroscience and genetics and related disciplines, we still do not know mechanistically how action happens, even if we are convinced, as I am, that at some level a physicalist account of some sort must be correct.

People use legal and moral rules as potential *reasons for action*. Unless people were capable of understanding and using legal rules as premises in deliberation, law would be powerless to affect human behavior. Only by its influence on practical reason can law directly and indirectly affect the world we inhabit. For the law, then, a person is a practical reasoner. It assumes simply that people are capable of acting for reasons and are generally capable of minimal rationality according to mostly conventional, socially-constructed standards of rationality.

RESPONSIBILITY MEANS THE CAPACITY FOR RATIONALITY

Law can guide action only if human beings can understand and conform to legal requirements. Legally responsible agents—most adult people—therefore have the capacity to grasp and be guided by good reason in particular legal contexts. Responsibility has nothing to do with "free will" understood as some independent criterion for responsibility. Legal cases and commentary concerning responsibility are replete with talk about "free will." Nevertheless, the truth of a fully physically caused universe, which is sometimes referred to as "determinism," is not part of the criteria for any legal doctrine that holds some people nonresponsible. Although all behavior may have physical causes in a physical, material universe, it does not follow that all behavior is excused, because causation per se has nothing to do with responsibility. For example, many variables have caused you to be reading this chapter now, but you are perfectly responsible for intentionally reading it. Being caused to read it (because it was assigned to you) is not evidence of an incapacity for rationality, and presumably no one is literally forcing you to read it. If causation negated responsibility, no one would be morally responsible, and holding people legally responsible would be extremely problematic. An assertion about "free will" is simply a conclusory statement about responsibility that must have been reached based on other criteria such as the presence or absence in this situation of rationality or coercion.

The criminal law is thus most consistent with the philosophical position termed "compatibilism," which holds, roughly, that even if determinism is true, agents can still be responsible if they can direct their conduct by their reasons. According to this view, responsibility is possible even if persons do not have the godlike power to act uncaused by anything but themselves.[6] This position is probably the dominant view held by professional philosophers. In the modern world that takes science seriously, it is perhaps the only view that is consistent both with what we know about the physical world (because it does not require a mysterious contra-causal power) and with the deontological and consequentialist moral and legal theories and practices we have adopted.

Rationality is the touchstone of responsibility. What rationality demands will differ across contexts. For example, a person is competent to contract if he or she is capable of understanding the nature of the bargain; a person is criminally responsible if the agent was capable of knowing the nature of his or her conduct or the applicable law. The usual legal presumptions are that adults are capable of minimal rationality and responsibility and that the same rules may be applied to all.

There is no uncontroversial definition of rationality in the relevant disciplines that study it, such as philosophy, economics, and psychology. Moreover, how much and what type of rationality is required for responsibility in various legal contexts is a social, moral, and political issue that divides people. For example, the United States Supreme Court was asked to decide whether the criteria for competence to stand trial should be different from the criteria for competence to plead guilty. In a closely divided decision, the Court decided that the same criteria should apply, but science could not answer this question because it is not a scientific issue. Whatever the outcome might be about such a controversy within a legal system, the debate is about human action. But the rationality criterion for responsibility is perfectly consistent with the facts—most adults are capable of minimal rationality virtually all the time—and with moral theories concerning fairness and justice, such as just deserts for action, that we have good reason to accept.

The law also contains coercion or compulsion criteria for nonresponsibility, but these criteria are demanding and much less frequently provide an excusing condition. Properly understood, coercion obtains when the agent is placed through no fault of her own in a threatening "hard choice" situation from which she cannot readily escape and in which she yields to the threat. The classic example in criminal law is the excuse of duress, which requires that the criminal must be threatened with death or serious bodily harm unless she commits the crime, and that a person of "reasonable firmness" would have yielded to the threat. The agent has acted intentionally and rationally to avoid death or grievous bodily harm. The genuine justification for excusing is that requiring human beings not to yield to such serious threats is simply too much to ask of creatures like ourselves. How hard the choice has to be can vary across contexts. A compulsion excuse for crime might require a greater threat than a compulsion excuse for a contract. But in no case does compulsion have anything to do with whether the behavior was caused—all behavior is caused—or with free will as a general philosophical concept.

A persistent, vexed question is how to assess the responsibility of people who seem to be acting in response to some inner compulsion, or, in more ordinary language, seem to have trouble controlling themselves. But what does it mean to say that an agent who is acting cannot control himself? I have explored this puzzle elsewhere,[7] and have arrived at the conclusion that rationality defects best explain these cases. Here, in short form, is what I think:

People who act in response to such inner states are intentional agents. Simply because an abnormal biological condition played a causal role—and neuroscientific evidence sometimes confirms this—does not per se mean the person could not control himself or had great difficulty doing so.

Compulsion understood as extremely hard choice, and not causation or free will, is the issue. The law's assessment of human action in terms of rationality or common sense criteria such as "self-control" is the question. Lack of control can only be finally demonstrated behaviorally, by evaluating action. Although neuroscientific and genetic evidence may provide assistance in performing this evaluation, science could never tell us how much control ability is required for responsibility. That question is social, moral, political, and, ultimately, legal.

In principle, no amount of increased understanding of behavioral causes, from any form of science, threatens the law's notion of responsibility unless it shows definitively that we humans (or some subset of us) are not intentional, minimally rational creatures. And no information about biological or social causes shows this directly. It will have to be demonstrated behaviorally by showing that the person, or people in general, do not act intentionally or are incapable of rationality. Even if a person has undoubted brain abnormalities or suffered various forms of severe environmental deprivation, if the person behaves minimally rationally, the person will be responsible.

For example, the question in the Hinckley case—the case of the young man who attempted to assassinate President Reagan and others—was whether he was out of touch with reality, and, if so, how much. That must be evaluated behaviorally by examining his beliefs and thoughts, such as his obsession with the actress Jody Foster, whom he was trying to impress. The issue in deciding whether teen murderers should be sentenced to life without the possibility of parole—a case being decided by the United States Supreme Court as this chapter is being written—is whether they suffer from sufficiently less rationality than adults; and, that too, must be evaluated by examining the reasoning and judgment of adolescents.[8] Brains do not have defective judgment; conscious, intentional agents—*persons*—do. I am an opponent of life imprisonment without the possibility of parole for adolescent murderers. Nevertheless, if our society decides morally and legally that the capacity for rationality that normal late adolescents exhibit *is* sufficient for this draconian sentence, even if their brains are less developed than those of adults, then brain science alone cannot demonstrate that the sentence is unjustified.

Many people continue mistakenly to believe that causation, especially abnormal causation, is per se an excusing condition, an analytic error that I have called "the fundamental psycho-legal error." It leads people to try to create a new excuse every time an allegedly valid new "syndrome" or other cause is discovered that plays a role in behavior. But syndromes and other causes do not have excusing force unless they sufficiently diminish rationality in the context in question. In that case, it is diminished rationality that is the excusing condition, not the presence of any particular type of cause, whether neural, genetic, or a combination of the two. Finally, causation is not the equivalent of compulsion. If it were, all behavior would be compelled, but most human action does not take place as a result of threats or as a result of an allegedly irresistible internal urge.

In short, although our behavior is caused, most of the time we are sufficiently rational and uncompelled to be held morally responsible. That is why free will is not even foundational for responsibility. It is simply a brute true fact about the world that most agents are rational and uncompelled, and these facts are consistent with track deontological and consequentialist theories of justice we have reason to endorse. Again, compatibilism is the philosophical position about responsibility that best explains our legal rules and practices and that is most in accord with our scientific account of ourselves. Metaphysical libertarianism— the belief that we have contracausal freedom— would also be consistent with our theories, rules, and practices, but it is simply a panicky, implausible metaphysics of action. In the philosophy of responsibility, the view that people can be responsible even if determinism (or something like it) is true and even if we do not have the god-like power of being able to act uncaused by anything but ourselves is known as "compatibilism."

Neuroscience and genetics will surely discover much more about the conditions that can compromise rationality or produce internal compulsion, and thus they may potentially lead to a broadening of current legal excusing doctrines or to a widening of the class of people who can raise a plausible claim under current law. Neuroscience may help to adjudicate excusing and mitigating claims more accurately. But unless neuroscience or genetics demonstrate that no one is capable of minimal rationality, or that everyone is compelled—both of which are implausible claims—our fundamental criteria for responsibility will be intact.

THE SCIENTIFIC CHALLENGE TO PERSONHOOD AND RESPONSIBILITY

Advances in neuroscience and genetics have revealed hitherto unimagined biological causes of behavior, including abnormal neurotransmitters, that may increase the risk of antisocial or otherwise problematic behavior,[9] but we have no convincing conceptual or empirical reason to abandon our view of ourselves as creatures whose desires, beliefs, and intentions play a causal role in explaining our behavior. Empirical discoveries might indicate that mental causation does not exist as we think it does, but discovering a brain correlate or cause of an action does not mean that it is not an action. If actions exist, they have causes, including causes arising in the brain. The real question is whether scientific, empirical studies have shown that intentional behavior is rare or nonexistent. Despite our strong intuition and first person experience that mental states are ubiquitous and genuinely explanatory, increasing numbers of scientists and philosophers claim that this is an illusion. Some go so far as to claim that we are "mere victims of neuronal circumstances." According to this view, which I will abbreviate as "VNC," our mental states play no causal role in explaining our behavior. The person disappears, and with it moral and legal responsibility.

The claim advanced by many that mental states do no explanatory work presents a challenge to the coherence of all law, and not just to responsibility practices. If the concept of mental causation that underlies folk psychology and current conceptions of responsibility is false, our responsibility practices, and many others, would appear unjustifiable. Such extreme claims are not straw persons. Here is a lengthy quote from a widely noticed article by neuroscientists Joshua Greene (also a philosopher) and Jonathan Cohen that expresses the mechanistic conception.[10]

> [A]s more and more scientific facts come in, providing increasingly vivid illustrations of what the human mind is really like, more and more people will develop moral intuitions that are at odds with our current social practices.... Neuroscience has a special role to play in this process for the following reason. As long as the mind remains a black box, there will always be a donkey on which to pin dualist and libertarian positions.... What neuroscience does, and will continue to do at an accelerated pace, is elucidate the "when," "where" and "how" of the mechanical processes that cause behavior. It is one thing to deny that human behavior is purely mechanical when your opponent offers only a general philosophical argument. It is quite another to hold your ground when your opponent can make detailed predictions about how these mechanical processes work, complete with images of the brain structures involved and equations that describe their function.... At some further point ... [p]eople may grow up completely used to the idea that every decision is a thoroughly mechanical process, the outcome of which is completely determined by the results of prior mechanical processes. What will such people think as they sit in their jury boxes? Will jurors of the future wonder whether the defendant ... *could have done otherwise*? Whether he really *deserves* to be punished...? We submit that these questions, which seem so important today, will lose their grip in an age when the mechanical nature of human decision making is fully appreciated. The law will continue to punish misdeeds, as it must for practical reasons, but the idea of distinguishing the truly, deeply guilty from those who are merely victims of neuronal circumstances will, we submit, seem pointless.

Alternatively, to use another of Greene and Cohen's arguments, suppose that "neuroscience holds the promise of turning the black box of the mind into a *transparent bottleneck.*"[11] They mean that the brain is the final mechanistic pathway through which all types of explanations of behavior must ultimately operate, and that neuroscience will be able to demonstrate that brain mechanisms, not mental states, are doing all the work.[12] They speculate that we may someday possess "extremely high-resolution scanners that can simultaneously

track the neural activity and connectivity of every neuron in the human brain ..." and, that with the help of computers and software, can help people see the neural events that are alone causally responsible for their behavior.[13] If such mechanistic understanding and knowledge were available and widespread, Greene and Cohen are probably correct that notions of responsibility would wither away because most would believe that it was the brain that "did it," not the agent, and we don't hold brains morally responsible.

This picture of human activity exerts a strong pull on the popular, educated imagination as well as on the theorizing of scientists. Indeed, what if all these thinkers who claim that we are just victims of neuronal circumstances are correct? Suppose neuroscience convinces us that agency and folk psychology are an illusion, that intentional bodily movements and reflexes are morally indistinguishable because both are simply the outcomes of mechanistic biophysical processes? What if all the contending conceptions about responsibility depend on a mistake about human activity? What if, for example, conscious mental states such as intentions and decisions do not in fact explain actions, but are simply post-hoc rationalizations the brain creates to "make sense of" the bodily motions or nonmotions that our brains produce? We are just mechanisms and not really agents at all. Will the agentic person disappear and be replaced by the biological victim of neuronal circumstances? This is truly a radical challenge to moral and legal responsibility.

If Cohen and Greene are right, we are all allegedly "merely victims of neuronal circumstances." But are we? And will the criminal justice system as we know it, which includes robust notions of personhood and desert, wither away as an outmoded relic of a pre-scientific and cruel age? Not only criminal law is in peril. What will be the fate of contracts, for example, when a biological machine that was formerly called a person claims that it should not be bound because it did not make a contract? The contract was simply the outcome of various "neuronal circumstances." Although I predict that we will see far more numerous attempts to introduce neuroevidence in the future, the dystopia that Greene and Cohen predict is not likely to come to pass.

It is important to note from the outset, however, that compatibilism or other responses to the determinist challenges will not save the disappearing person. Determinism is consistent with either of two inconsistent views of human behavior. The truth of determinism is consistent with the existence of agency, but it is also consistent with the nonexistence of agency. In other words the truth of determinism is consistent with both the causal role and noncausal role of mental states in partially explaining behavior. Compatibilism presupposes that a folk psychological account of action is accurate and that distinctions based on it, such as the difference between actions and nonactions, or between agents who are and are not capable of minimal rationality, should make a moral and legal difference. Compatibilism denies that something more than rational, intentional action is necessary to ground responsibility. The new VNC claims deny precisely this. The person and responsibility can only be saved if VNC is false or, if it is true, we learn to live with the illusion that it is false. Otherwise, all agency-based conceptions of responsibility must be abandoned.

At present, no such radical, external challenge from neuroscience even remotely approaches plausibility. It is true that the law's fundamental presuppositions about personhood and action are open to profound objection. Most fundamentally, action and consciousness are scientific and conceptual mysteries.[14] We do not know how the brain enables the mind,[15] although we do know that it does, and we do not know how action is possible. At most we have hypotheses or a priori arguments. Dualism—the view that our "nonmaterial" minds and physical brains are separate, independent entities and that the former has a causal connection with the latter—is now largely discredited, but a satisfying physicalist account of the brain–mind–action connection eludes us.[16] How can such tenuously understood concepts be justifiable premises for legal practices such as blaming and punishing? If our picture of ourselves that includes the causal efficacy of mental states is wrong, as many neuroscientists claim, then our responsibility practices are unjustified according to any moral theory we currently embrace. On the other hand, given how little we know about the brain–mind and brain–action connection, to claim based on neuroscience or genetics that we should radically change our picture of ourselves and our practices is scientific overclaim.

To see in more specific detail why we need not abandon our robust conception of agency despite such VNC claims, let us turn to the indirect and allegedly direct evidence for them. The real question is whether scientific and clinical investigations have shown that intentional agency is rare or nonexistent; that conscious will is largely or entirely an illusion. Four kinds of indirect evidence are often adduced: first, demonstrations that a very large part of our activity is undeniably caused by variables we are not in the slightest aware of; second, studies indicating that more activity than we think takes place when our consciousness is divided or diminished; third, laboratory studies that show that people can be experimentally misled about their causal contribution to their apparent behavior; and, fourth, evidence that particular types of psychological processes seem to have their biological substrate in specific regions of the brain. None of these types of evidence offers logical support to VNC, however.

Just because a person may not be aware of all the causes that produced the formation of an intention does not mean that he did not form an intention, that he was not a fully conscious agent when he did so, and that his intention played no causal role in explaining the person's behavior. Even if human beings were never aware of the causes of their intentions to act, and of their actions, it would not necessarily follow that they were not acting consciously, intentionally, and for reasons that make eminent sense to anyone under the circumstances.

Human consciousness can undeniably be divided or diminished by a wide variety of normal and abnormal causes.[17] We have known this long before contemporary scientific discoveries of what causes such states and how they correlate with genetic abnormalities or with brain structure and processes. Law and morality agree that if an agent's capacity for consciousness is nonculpably diminished, responsibility is likewise diminished. Let us assume that divided or diminished consciousness is more common than it appears to be. Nevertheless, neither of these assumptions supports the more radical, general VNC thesis, and the arguments for automatistic imperialism—the claim that most human behavior is automatic and not the product of intentions—have been termed the "automaticity juggernaut."[18]

Demonstrating that divided or partial consciousness is more common than it appears certainly extends the range of cases in which people are not responsible or have diminished responsibility. Such studies do not demonstrate, however, that most human bodily movements that appear intentional and rational (apparently rational actions) occur when the person has altered consciousness. One cannot generalize to all human behavior from genuinely deviant cases or cases in which a known abnormality is present. A model of action (or, we should say, nonaction) built on spasms and sleepwalking, for example, is hardly a threat to orthodox notions of individual responsibility.

There is substantial empirical evidence to suggest that laboratory manipulations of unsuspecting subjects can cause the subjects to believe that their intentions were producing action when this was not the case.[19] That subjects can be cleverly misled by experimental manipulations hardly indicates that intentions generally play no role in explaining our behavior. Self-deception under laboratory conditions of deceit does not entail that intentions generally do not causally explain action. Evolution's explanatory default is surely not that we are virtually always self-deceived about whether our intentions are causally linked to our actions. Successful human existence would be impossible if this were true.

Finally, there is accumulating evidence that various psychological processes have their biological substrates in localized regions of the brain. We have long known from studies of patients with brain lesions that many behavioral activities are biologically based in highly specific regions. For example, there is substantial evidence that ability to recognize faces is localized in a region of the temporal lobe of the right hemisphere referred to as the "fusiform face area." Should this area become lesioned, the subject loses the ability to recognize faces, a condition called *prosopagnosia*.[20] Now, however, functional neuroimaging techniques permit the exploration of brain activity during more complicated psychological processes, and can identify biological substrates for the processes. For example, a recent study demonstrated that investigators could determine from the subject's pattern of brain activity which mental process—adding or subtracting—a subject had covertly intended to, but had not yet, performed.[21]

The localization evidence is immensely interesting and suggestive, but it does not indicate that mental states play no role in causally explaining behavior. There must be a biological substrate in the brain for all human behavior. If your brain is dead, you are dead and not behaving at all. Nor is it surprising that particular regions of the brain are associated with particular psychological processes. For example, a leading, albeit controversial, theory of how the mind works suggests that it is composed of different systems that perform different functions.[22] Although we do not know how the brain enables the mind, it makes sense to assume that specific psychological processes would have one or many brain substrates that are specific for discrete psychological processes. Based on what we already know about localization, and on the reasonable assumption that it would be inefficient if all regions of the brain needed equal activation to support all psychological processes, significant localization is most likely to be true. Even if all this is correct, however, it does not follow that mental states do no causal explanatory work. It demonstrates at most that the neural network substrates for specific mental functions may be located in specific regions of the brain.

What is needed to support VNC is a general, direct demonstration that causal intentionality is an illusion, but no such general demonstration has yet been produced by scientific study. The most interesting evidence has arisen from studies done by neuroscientist Benjamin Libet[23] and those who have followed him, which have generated an immense amount of comment.[24] Indeed, many claim that Libet's work is the first direct neurophysiological evidence of VNC.[25] Libet's exceptionally creative and careful studies demonstrate that measurable electrical brain activity associated with intentional actions occurs in the relevant motor area of the brain about 550 milliseconds before the subject actually acts and for about 350–400 milliseconds before the subject is consciously aware of the intention to act. Some have claimed that such findings demonstrate that the causes of our actions are independent of our conscious thoughts and actions and that the latter play no genuine role in explaining behavior.

Let us assume then, with cautious reservations,[26] the basic scientific methodological validity of these studies.[27] The crucial question then becomes whether the interpretation of these findings as supporting VNC is valid. Michael Moore has usefully shown that the Libetian conception of the role of brain events in causing behavior is confused.[28] Indeed, it is not clear precisely what the claim is, but the most profound challenge would be that mental states are epiphenomenal, meaning that they exist but are causally inert. If this is true, the folk psychological basis for all law is incoherent. Alfred Mele has shown that Libet's work does not establish VNC, has exposed numerous confusions about the relation of the brain to mental states and action, and has usefully described the type of experiment that might achieve this result.[29] Rather than repeat their analyses, which bear close reading, this section will instead offer a more empirical and commonsense critique.

It does not follow from Libet's discovery of the temporal ordering that conscious intentionality does no causal work. It simply demonstrates that nonconscious brain events precede conscious experience. Once again, although we have no idea how the brain enables the mind, but this seems precisely what one would expect of the mind–brain. Electrical impulses move quickly among neurons, but some lag between brain activity and conscious experience seems unsurprising. Prior electrical activity does not mean that intentionality played no causal role. Electrical activity in the brain is precisely that: electrical activity in the brain, and not a mental state such as a decision or an intention. A perfectly plausible reading of Libet's work is that various nonconscious causal variables, including nonconscious urges, precede action—who would have thought

otherwise?—but intentionality is nonetheless necessary for action.

Libet also suggests that people can "veto" the act during the delay between becoming aware of the intention and performing the intended action, which he surprisingly conceives of as an undetermined act. This has been termed "free won't." Surprisingly, then, Libet himself appears to be a closet libertarian. Other researchers appear to have localized the part of the brain that is the substrate for this activity of vetoing.[30] But, in addition to the implausibility of the veto being undetermined according to the underlying logic of Libet's position that brain events are the causes of action,[31] the conceptual foundations of the interpretation that the subjects were exercising a genuine veto are shaky at best.[32] This suggestion undermines the claim that the brain rather than the mind is doing all the work because it is an agent's mental state, a newly formed intention to veto, that causes the agent not to perform the act. In short, Libet's work presupposes conscious agency at every step in the process: if there is reason to believe vetoes resulting in inaction are intentional, then there is no reason to believe actions are simply the product of brain events. Acting and vetoing action are indistinguishable on Libet's own account, properly understood.

Libet's task involved "random" finger movements that involved no deliberation whatsoever and no rational motivation for the specific movements involved.[33] This is a far cry from the behavioral concerns of the criminal law or morality, which address intentional conduct in contexts when there is always good reason to refrain from harming another or to act beneficently. In fact, it is at present an open question whether Libet's paradigm is representative of intentional actions in general, because Libet's experimental task was such trivial behavior.[34]

In addition to direct problems with the alleged implications of Libet's work, there are also good reasons to reject it. Answers to the possibility of VNC are rooted in common sense, a plausible theory of mind, our evolutionary history, and practical necessity. Virtually every neurologically intact person consistently has the experience of first person agency, the experience that one's intentions flow from one's desires and beliefs and result in action. Our folk psychology seems so well-rooted in experience, so central to human life, and so apparently explanatory that the likelihood of replacing it with some purely reductionistic biophysical account of our behavior seems implausible and even mysterious. As the philosopher of mind Jerry Fodor has written:

> [I]f commonsense intentional psychology were really to collapse, that would be, beyond comparison, the greatest intellectual catastrophe in the history of our species; if we're that wrong about the mind, then that's the wrongest we've ever been about anything. The collapse of the supernatural, for example, didn't compare.... Nothing except, perhaps, our commonsense physics ... comes as near our cognitive core as intentional explanation does. We'll be in deep, deep trouble if we have to give it up....
>
> ... But be of good cheer; everything is going to be all right.[35]

Folk psychology has much explanatory power and is capable of scientific investigation.[36] There is compelling psychological evidence that intentions play a causal role in explaining behavior. For example, subjects who form an intention to implement a means to achieve a goal are much more likely to succeed at achieving that goal.[37] For another example, a review of neuroimaging studies found strong support that the subjective nature and the intentional content of mental processes (e.g., thoughts, feelings, beliefs, volition) significantly influence the various levels of brain functioning and brain plasticity. Furthermore, these findings indicate that mentalistic variables have to be seriously taken into account to reach a correct understanding of the neural bases of behavior in humans. In short, to use the review's title, "mind matters."[38] Finally, despite Mele's attempt, it is hard to imagine the nature of a scientific study that would prove conclusively that mental states do no work to creatures that have created that study and will assess it with mental states.

The plausible theory of mind that might support mental-state explanations is thoroughly material, but nonreductive and nondualist. It hypothesizes that all mental and behavioral activity is the causal product of lawful physical events in the brain, that mental states are real, that they are caused by lower-level biological processes in the brain, that they are realized in the brain—the mind–brain—but not at the level of neurons, and that mental states can be causally efficacious.[39] It accepts that a fully causal story about behavior will be multifield and multilevel.

There is a perfectly plausible evolutionary story about why folk psychology is causally explanatory and why human beings need rules such as those provided by law. We have evolved to be self-conscious creatures that act for reasons and are reasons-responsive. Acting for reasons is inescapable for creatures like ourselves who inevitably care about the ends they pursue and about what reasons they have to act in one way rather than another.[40] Because we are social creatures whose interactions are not governed primarily by innate repertoires, it is inevitable that rules will be necessary to help order our interactions in any minimally complex social group.[41] As a profoundly social species, it seems apparent that our ancestors would have been much less successful, and therefore much less likely to be our ancestors, if they were unable to understand the intentions of others, not sure they could convert their intentions into action, and were not also equipped with powerful assumptions that that stranger coming over the hill is equipped with the same capacity for harmful intentions as they are.[42]

One of the qualities that makes us most human is the ability to infer that others have independent mental states, and then to use that information to understand and predict the behavior of others. Psychologists call this having a "theory of mind."[43] Human beings who do not develop an adequate "theory of mind," such as those with autism, experience profound difficulties in their interpersonal lives. The lengthy conservation of mental states and their ubiquity and centrality suggest that they do play an important causal role and that they are very evolutionarily expensive if they do not. This is of course not an incontrovertible analytic argument against VNC, but surely the burden of persuasion is on those who argue the contrary. At the very least, we remain entitled to presume that conscious intentions are causal until the burden is met.

I conclude that Libet's influential work, which allegedly directly demonstrates the truth of VNC, is fascinating, but does not prove that humans are generally not conscious, intentional agents, or capable of employing their conscious intentionality when they have good reason to do so.[44] Even if the work is methodologically valid, various conceptual and interpretive arguments undermine the claim that Libet has demonstrated that VNC is true, and there are good reasons to reject it.

In short, despite the often astonishing findings and impressive advances in neuroscience and genetics, there is no compelling evidence yet that VNC is true. We are nowhere close to demonstrating epiphenomenalism experimentally (indeed, it would be hard to imagine what that study would look like), the best theories about reduction suggest that it is probably false, and evolution and common sense suggest that it is false. Future discoveries may undermine this conclusion, however, so I now turn to the implications of VNC.

VNC, alas, can provide no guidance about what people should do next and, in any event, degenerates into self-referential incoherence. Suppose that you were convinced by the mechanistic view that you were not an intentional, rational agent after all. (Of course, the notion of being "convinced" would be an illusion, too.[45] Being convinced means that you were persuaded by evidence or argument, but a mechanism is not persuaded by anything. It is simply neurophysically transformed.) What should you do now? You know that it is an illusion to think that your deliberations and intentions have any causal efficacy in the world. (Again, what does it mean according to the purely mechanistic view to "know" something? But enough.) You also know, however, that you experience sensations such as pleasure and pain and that you care about what happens to you and to the world. You cannot just sit quietly and wait for your neurotransmitters to fire or for your genes to operate as they will. You cannot wait for determinism to happen. You must, and will of course, deliberate and act.

If one still thought that VNC was correct and that standard notions of genuine moral responsibility and desert are therefore impossible,

one might nevertheless continue to believe that the law would not necessarily have to give up the concept of incentives. Indeed, Greene and Cohen concede that we would have to keep punishing people for practical purposes.[46] Through poorly understood automatic processes, it is possible that various potential rewards and punishments would shape behavior even if they did not do so as premises in practical reasoning. Such an account would be consistent with "black box" accounts of economic incentives. For those who believe that a thoroughly naturalized account of human behavior entails an ethical view of complete consequentialism, such a conclusion might not be unwelcome.

On the other hand, this view seems to entail the same internal contradiction just explored. What is the nature of the "agent" that is discovering the laws governing how incentives shape behavior? Could understanding and providing incentives via social norms and legal rules simply be epiphenomenal interpretations of what the brain has already done? How do "we" "decide" which behaviors to reward or punish? What role does "reason"—a property of thought and agents, not a property of brains—play in this "decision"? Once again, the VNC account seems to swallow itself. Moreover, VNC proponents of consequentialism could hardly complain about those who refuse to "accept" what the proponents think rationality requires. The allegedly misguided people who resist are simply the victims of their automatic brain states. They cannot be expected intentionally to use their capacity for reason to accept what the VNC consequentialists believe reason demands. Indeed, the consequentialist's belief is also either an illusory or causally ineffective mental state.

Even if our mental states play no genuinely causal role (about which, once again, we will never be certain until we solve the mind–body problem) human beings will find it almost impossible not to treat themselves as rational, intentional agents unless there are major changes in the way our brains work. Moreover, if one uses the truth of pure mechanism as a premise in deciding what to do, this premise yields no particular moral, legal, or political conclusions. VNC cannot tell us which goals we should pursue and it cannot explain or justify our present practices. It will provide no guide to how one should live or how one should respond to the truth of VNC. Normativity depends on reason and thus VNC is normatively inert.

LEGAL REFORM

Under what conditions will the new neuroscience and genetics suggest reform of existing legal doctrines (rules)? The law is in many respects a conservative enterprise and will always resist the supposed reforms other disciplines suggest. For example, despite the extraordinary advances in the understanding of mental disorder in the last half century, and consistent calls for reform, the dominant version of the insanity defense—which excuses if the disordered defendant did not know what he was doing or did not know that it was wrong—is scarcely changed from the form adopted in 1843 by English law in the *M'Naghten* case. This is unsurprising. Advances in mental health science can teach us much about why some people lack rationality, and can help identify and treat those people, but it cannot tell society which rationality defects are sufficient to excuse a wrongdoer. As we have seen, deciding who is blameworthy and deserves to be punished is a social, moral, political, and ultimately legal question about which science must fall silent.

Legal rules do of course change in response to shifting political, moral, and empirical discoveries. Racial discrimination was banned by civil rights legislation simply because it was wrong; it is now unlawful to dump toxic waste in large part because science demonstrated the health hazards. But before legislators and judges will be rationally justified in changing existing legal rules in response to the discoveries of any scientific discipline, at the least they should be convinced, first, that the data are valid; second, that the data are genuinely relevant to a particular rule; third, that the data convincingly imply that specific changes to those rules would have desirable effects; and, fourth, that those changes will not infringe other values that may be more important. This is a tall order.

Although I am not an expert in all areas of law, I am unaware of any major proposed or implemented doctrinal changes in any area of law

based on the new neuroscience or genetics. Again, this is not surprising. Nonetheless, when a discipline's theory and data are reasonably developed, the doctrinal implications are potentially clear, and consensually valid goals are not being undermined, doctrine will change in response to discoveries from other disciplines.

Assuming future consensus about findings, which may well be a counterfactual assumption, I predict that neuroscience will not have widespread, profound influence on doctrine in most areas unless, as I have suggested before, its discoveries radically alter our conception of ourselves. On the other hand, one can imagine substantial changes in discrete doctrines.

NEW NEUROSCIENCE, NEW GENETICS, OLD PROBLEMS

The new neuroscience and genetics pose familiar moral, social, political, and legal challenges that can be addressed using equally familiar conceptual and theoretical tools. Discoveries that increase our understanding and control of human behavior may raise the stakes, but they don't change the game. Future discoveries may so radically alter the way we think about ourselves as persons and about the nature of human existence that massive shifts in moral, social, political, and legal concepts, practices, and institutions may ensue. For now, however, neuroscience and genetics pose no threat to the ordinary notions of personhood and responsibility that undergird our morals, politics, and law.

NOTES

1. Holmes, Oliver Wendell Jr. *The Common Law* 7 (Transaction ed. 2005) (1963).
2. *Morissette v. United States*, 342 U.S. 246, 250–51 (1952).
3. I recognize that legal and moral responsibility need not coincide. Because Anglo-American punishment theory holds that desert is a necessary condition for punishment—at least at the core of criminal law—I shall assume that moral and legal responsibility do coincide in the core.
4. "The Ethics of Brain Sciences: Open Your Mind." *The Economist* 23 May 2002, 77, www.economist.com/node/1143317/print.

5. Morse, Stephen J. "Brain Overclaim Syndrome and Criminal Responsibility: A Diagnostic Note." *Ohio State Journal of Criminal Law* 3 (2006): 397.

6. *Oxford Handbook of Free Will*. Ed. Robert Kane. New York: Oxford University Press, 2005. See part IV for a survey of the many possible forms of compatibilism on offer today. See generally Kane, Robert. *A Contemporary Introduction to Free Will* (2005) (providing balanced consideration of compatibilism and other theories concerning free will and responsibility).

7. Morse, Stephen J. "Uncontrollable Urges and Irrational People." *Virginia Law Review* 88 (2002): 1025.

8. The U.S. Supreme Court decided, in June 2012, that life imprisonment without parole for juvenile murderers is unconstitutional. *Miller v. Alabama*, No. 10-9646 (June 25, 2012).

9. See, e.g., Caspi, Avshalom, et al. "Role of Genotype in the Cycle of Violence in Maltreated Children." *Science* 297 (2002): 851; Goldstein, Rita Z. and Volkow, Nora D. "Drug Addiction and Its Underlying Neurobiological Basis: Neuroimaging Evidence for the Involvement of the Frontal Cortex." *Am. J. Psychiatry* 159 (2002): 1542; Potenza, Marc N. et al. "Gambling Urges in Pathological Gambling: A Functional Magnetic Resonance Imaging Study." *Archives of General Psychiatry* 60 (2003): 828; Stein Murray B., et al. "Genetic and Environmental Influences on Trauma Exposure and Posttraumatic Stress Disorder Symptoms: A Twin Study." *Am. J. Psychiatry* 159 (2002): 1675.

10. Greene, Joshua and Cohen, Jonathan. "For the law, neuroscience changes nothing and everything." *Law and the Brain*. Eds. S. Zeki and O. Goodenough. (2006) 207, 217–218.

11. Id., at 217–218, emphasis added.

12. Id.

13. I will assume that the scanning and computing abilities that the argument employs are possible, although the brain has 10^{11} cells and at least 10^{15} connections. Is it really likely, however, that the computer would predict what precise sentences we would speak? At present, of course, the speculation is pure science fiction and, in my opinion, is likely to remain so. The real problem with the argument is not that it assumes a (barely) plausible computational ability, but that it assumes that mental states can be reduced simply to brain states, an assumption that the next subsection addresses.

14. See Audi. *Action, Intention and Reason*. (1993) 1–4 (describing the "basic philosophical divisions" in each of the four major problem areas in action theory); McGinn, Colin. *The Mysterious Flame: Conscious Minds in a Material World* (1999) (describing the immense difficulty of explaining consciousness and doubting the ability of human beings to do so).

15. McHugh Paul R. and Slavney, Philip R. *The Perspectives of Psychiatry*. 2d ed. 1998. 11–12.

16. It is almost impossible not to talk "dualistically" in ordinary speech and writing. Every time a monist neuroscientist uses a personal pronoun in speaking or writing, for example, he seems to imply that there is a genuine "him" or "her" that is somehow distinguishable from his brain activity. This does not mean, however, that the neuroscientist (or anyone else) is really a crypto-dualist. It is simply an inevitable feature of current language, and perhaps it always will be.

17. See Cummings, Jeffrey L. and Mega, Michael S. *Neuropsychiatry and Behavioral Neuroscience*. (2003). 333–43 (description of dissociative and related states and their causes and treatments). Vaitl, D., Birbaumer, N., et al. "Psychobiology of Altered States of Consciousness." *Psychol. Bull.* 131 (2005): 98.

18. Kihlstrom, John F. "The Automaticity Juggernaut—or, Are We Automatons After All?" *Are We Free? Psychology and Free Will*. Eds. John Baer, James C. Kaufman, and Roy F. Baumeister. (2008). 155–173.

19. See Bargh, John A. "Bypassing the Will: Toward Demystifying the Nonconscious Control of Social Behavior." *The New Unconscious*. (2005), 37, 51–54 (reviewing the evidence and concluding that the "will" is not primarily responsible for action).

20. Tanaka, James W. "Object Categorization, Expertise, and Neural Plasticity." *The Cognitive Neurosciences*. 3d ed. Vol. III. Ed. Michael S. Gazzaniga. (2004). 877, 883.

21. Haynes, John-Dylan et al. "Reading Hidden Intentions in the Human Brain." *Current Biology* 17 (2007): 323, 323–28. It is important to recognize that the brain activity accurately predicted only which *type* of process the subject had covertly formed the intention to perform. It did not identify the specific content of the intention, such as which two numbers the subject intended

to add or subtract. Despite the enormous advances in cognitive neuroscience, we do not know how to read minds using neuroimaging or any other technique. Cf. Farah, Martha J. "Bioethical Issues in the Cognitive Neurosciences/" *The Cognitive Neurosciences*, supra, note 20, at 1309, 1309–10 (referring to the ability to identify traits and states as "a crude form of mindreading").

22. See, e.g., Fodor, Jerry A. *The Modularity of Mind* (1983) (providing a strict modular theory).

23. Libet, Benjamin. "Do We Have Free Will." *The Volitional Brain: Towards a Neuroscience of Free Will*. Eds. Benjamin Libet, et al. (1999). 47 (summarizing the findings and speculating about their implications). For a more recent, powerful demonstration of a similar finding, see Soon, C. S., et al. "Unconscious Determinants of Free Decisions in the Human Brain." Nature *Neuroscience* 11 (2008): 543.

24. Wegner, Daniel. *The Illusion of Conscious Will*. (2002). 54–55 (characterizing the recounting of Libet's results as a "cottage industry" and noting the large and contentious body of commentary).

25. Banks, William P. and Pocket, Susan. "Benjamin Libet's Work on the Neuroscience of Free Will." *The Blackwell Companion to Consciousness*. Eds. Max Velmans and Susan Schneider (2007) 658.

26. See, e.g., Walter, Henrik. *Neurophilosophy of Free Will: From Libertarian Illusions to a Concept of Natural Autonomy*. Trans. Cynthia Klor. (2001) 250–252; Zhu, Jing. "Reclaiming Volition: An Alternative Interpretation of Libet's Experiment." *J. Consciousness Stud.* Nov. 2003: 61, 61–77.

27. Banks and Pocket, supra, note 25, at 659–662 (concluding after a careful review of possible artifacts that "readiness potentials do start before the subject consciously 'decides' to move").

28. Moore, Michael S. "Libet's Challenges to Responsible Human Agency."*Conscious Will and Responsibility: A Tribute to Benjamin Libet*. Eds. Walter Sinnott-Armstrong and Lynn Nadel. New York: Oxford University Press, 2010.

29. Mele, Alfred R. *Effective Intentions: The Power of the Conscious Will* (2009). See also, Bennett, M.R. and Hacker, P.M.S. *Philosophical Foundations of Neuroscience*. (2003). 228–231 (criticizing Libet's account of action).

30. See Brass, Maurice and Haggard, Patrick. "To Do or Not to Do: The Neural Signature of Self-Control." *J. Neurosci.* 27 (2007): 9141 (identifying the part of the brain that is activated when the "veto" is exercised).

31. Banks and Pockett, supra, note 33, at 667.

32. Mele, supra, note 29, at 34–35.

33. Participating in the study and cooperating with the investigator can be rationally motivated, of course. But the experimental task was to move one's finger randomly, for no good reason.

34. Banks and Pockett, supra, note 25, at 662–663.

35. Fodor, Jerry A. *Psychosemantics: The Problem of Meaning in the Philosophy of Mind* xii (1987).

36. See, e.g., Malle, Bertram F. *How The Mind Explains Behavior: Folk Explanations, Meaning and Social Interaction* (2004) (providing a full theoretical account and empirical support). There is also growing recognition within psychology that "mental-state inference is one of the most fundamental tools of social cognition." Malle, Bertram F. "Folk Theory of Mind: Conceptual Foundations of Human Social Cognition." *The New Unconscious*. (2005) 225, 229.

37. See, Holton, Richard. *Willing, Wanting, Waiting*. (2009) 5–9 (reviewing psychologist Peter Gollwitzer's work and explaining how it supports the role of a distinct psychological kind, intention, as playing a causal role in behavior); Mele, supra, note 29, at 134–36

38. Beauregard, Mario. "Mind Does Really Matter: Evidence from Neuroimaging Studies of Emotional Self-Regulation, Psychotherapy, And Placebo Effect." *Progress in Neurobiology* 81 (2007): 218.

39. See, e.g., Searle, John R., *Mind: A Brief Introduction*. New York, Oxford University Press, 2004. 113–14 (terming his position "biological naturalism" about consciousness).

40. Bok, Hilary. *Freedom and Responsibility*. Princeton: Princeton University Press, 1998. 75–91, 129–31, 146–51.

41. Alexander Larry, *The Rule of Rules: Morality, Rules and the Dilemmas of Law*. (2001) 11–25 (explaining why rules are necessary in a complex society and contrasting their account with H.L.A. Hart's theory).

42. See Wood Justin N., et al., "The Perception of Rational, Goal-Directed Action in Nonhuman Primates." *Science* 317 (2007): 1402, 1405 (demonstrating that the ability to understand the intentions of other creatures evolved in primates 40 million years ago); see also Herrmann, Esther, et al. "Humans Have Developed Specialized Skills of Social Cognition: The Cultural Intelligence

Hypothesis." *Science* 317 (2007): 1360 (comparing chimpanzees and orangutans to two-and-a-half-year-old humans and discovering that they have approximately equal cognitive skills concerning the physical world, but that humans have superior cognitive skills for understanding social interaction).

43. Dawon, Geraldine and Toth, Karen. "Autism Spectrum Disorders." *Developmental Psychopathology* 2d. ed. Vol. 3. Eds. Dante Cicchetti and Donald J. Cohen. (2006) 327.

44. See Fodor, Jerry. "Making the Connection." *Times Literary Supplement* 17 May 2002. 4 (arguing that the new neuroscience rarely has much to contribute when the phenomenon in question is complex social behavior).

45. See Dennett, Daniel C. "Calling in the Cartesian Loans." *Behav. Brain Scis.* 27 (2004): 661 (wondering, in response to Professor Wegner, who is this "we" that inhabits the brain).

46. Greene and Cohen, "For the law," supra, note 10, at 218.

64   Attempts

GIDEON YAFFE

INTRODUCTION

Criminal attempts—failed efforts to complete crimes—are sometimes, despite the fact of their failure, spectacles. Think of John Hinckley's failed effort to kill President Ronald Reagan, or the September 11th terrorists' failed effort to fly United Flight 93 into the White House. Attempts are also very commonly prosecuted and just as commonly punished, even when they are far from spectacular. There is no shortage of prisoners who never managed to finish the crimes that they were trying to commit. In our present, modern frame of mind, nothing can seem more natural or appropriate than to criminalize and punish not just successful efforts to commit crimes, but failed efforts also. The failures are sometimes as bad or worse than the successes.

The simple intuitive appeal of the idea that attempts are to be punished belies the complexity and confusion that surrounds their adjudication. Some cases are black and white, to be sure, but a startling percentage are not. We have a much less clear idea than we need of what, exactly, we have criminalized in criminalizing attempt. And so it is often very difficult to tell if a particular defendant has committed a criminal attempt; the courts do not know exactly what they are looking for.[1] This confusion manifests itself, for instance, in the many and various descriptions of the conditions that must be met for the defendant's conduct to constitute more than "mere preparation," many of which are overtly metaphorical ("direct movement towards" completion, for instance[2]). But it comes up in many other places, also, often in contexts in which the problems seem, at first glance, to be more tractable than courts have actually found them to be.

Consider, for instance, the problem of so-called "impossibility": The defendant in *United States v. Crow*[3] had multiple conversations in an Internet chatroom with someone going by the name of "StephieFL." During the course of their conversations, StephieFL claimed to be a 13-year-old girl. In fact, the messages were written by an undercover (adult) police officer. Crow

The material in this paper developed out of my book, *Attempts: In the Philosophy of Action and the Criminal Law* (Oxford, 2010). Thanks are owed to the many people who helped me in the writing of that book. Drafts of this paper were presented at Yale Law School and the University of Pennsylvania Law School. Thanks to audiences on both occasions. Thanks also to Bruce Ackerman, Larry Alexander, Fecundo Alonso, Mitch Berman, Michael Bratman, Jules Coleman, Antony Duff, Kim Ferzan, Claire Finkelstein, Heather Gerken, Heidi Hurd, Dan Kahan, Paul Kahn, Leo Katz, Chris Kutz, Tracey Meares, Michael Moore, Stephen Morse, Jed Rubenfeld, Scott Shapiro, and Ken Simon.

Written for this volume.

tried to convince StephieFL to send him sexually explicit photographs of herself, and was charged with attempting sexual exploitation of a minor. The completed offense requires a showing to the effect that the person exploited is indeed a minor. Did Crow attempt sexual exploitation of a minor, or does the fact that it was an adult he was actually in contact with show that he did not? After all, given that Crow was chatting with an adult there was no chance at all that his conduct would succeed in sexually exploiting a minor.

On appeal, Crow questioned the validity of the indictment against him on the grounds that it failed to state an essential element of the crime with which it charged him, namely that the person he was attempting to sexually exploit was in fact a minor. In raising this objection, whatever its merits in this particular case, Crow was raising a general issue about which an answer is required: Do circumstantial elements of completed crimes need to be in place for attempts of those crimes (and, if not, why not)? But the court, having no idea what the answer is to this question, upholds the indictment on the grounds, essentially, that even flawed indictments can be valid, so that whether or not the crime requires that the target is a child, the indictment stands. This bit of reasoning gives the court cover in its desire to avoid addressing the important issue, but, still, the issue remains unaddressed. The court's problem is that the judges are quite certain that Crow was *trying* to sexually exploit *a child* in the sense of relevance to criminal responsibility. What they are ill-equipped to explain is how that's consistent with the fact that the only candidate for the person he was trying to sexually exploit, namely the one he was chatting with, *was an adult*.[4] The result is that they lack the tools they need to explain why they decide the case as they decide it.

While this is just one example, judges in this domain appear to be behaving in the way that legal realists have for years taken to be endemic to judicial behavior: they seem to decide first, and rationalize later through appeal to technical legal concepts, or, as in *Crow*, by bypassing issues of importance on procedural grounds even when proper procedure permits engagement with them.

There is little uniformity across jurisdictions, or even within them, in how courts deal with attempt cases. And even courts that handle such cases in a consistent manner have no idea what principles, if any, support their approach. Struck by the difficulty of discovering, and darkness surrounding, principled solutions to adjudicatory problems about attempts, Jerome Hall wrote in 1940:

> Whoever has speculated on criminal attempt will agree that the problem is as fascinating as it is intricate. At every least step it intrigues and cajoles; like *la belle dame sans merci*, when solution seems just within reach, it eludes the zealous pursuer, leaving him to despair ever of enjoying the sweet fruit of discovery.[5]

Despair no longer. This paper offers a framework for thinking about attempts that solves the "impossibility" problem, and can be used to develop solutions to several other problems about attempts. We need not bow, in this domain, to the powerful impulse to describe what is happening in the law of attempt in the terms of the legal realist. There are valid principles on the basis of which to decide attempt cases; they have just been overlooked until now. And quite often judges are cottoning on to those principles, even if they are incapable of articulating them. In fact, as will be suggested here, it is no surprise that they are, for the relevant principles are entrenched in ordinary moral thought of the sort that informs many commonplace interactions between people outside of the legal domain. Those principles are incorporated into the law, it will be suggested, whenever we proscribe completed conduct.

Section 1 identifies the simple and intuitive grounds for criminalizing attempts in the first place. The section also argues that neither of two ordinary notions of what it is to try to act can be the sense of relevance to criminal law, given the grounds for the criminalization of attempt. Sections 2 and 3 offer an alternative account of the nature of attempt of relevance to criminal law, an account that is motivated by the observations offered in section 1. Section 2 offers an account of the nature of intention, which is the central component of attempt. The account of intention

TRYING = ATTEMPT

builds on and develops recent work in the philosophy of action. Section 3 uses section 2's account of intention to explain what it is *to try* in the sense of relevance to the criminal law. Section 4 uses the view of attempt developed in sections 2 and 3 to solve the problem of "impossibility." So, the paper provides a conceptual framework for thinking about attempt and explains how it helps in one corner of attempt law.

1. THE SOURCE OF AN ATTEMPT'S CRIMINALITY: THE CRIMINALITY OF COMPLETION

1.1 The Transfer Principle

The confusion in the courts can potentially be remedied by an account of what, exactly, the crime of attempt is. If we knew exactly what it is to attempt, we could check to see whether someone like Crow did, indeed, attempt the crimes he is charged with attempting. Theorists of attempt, who have tried to give such accounts, are typically divided into the "subjectivists" and the "objectivists." Struck by the fact that attempts are often harmless—the bullet misses, the child is not abducted, no drugs cross the border—subjectivists conclude that it must be that attempts are properly punished thanks to their *mens rea* elements. From this point of view, attempts are thought crimes. The fundamental challenge for subjectivists, then, is to explain why it is not monstrous for a liberal society to punish attempts. The task of meeting this challenge is typically undertaken by offering an explanation for how the mental states involved in attempt differ from other thoughts that it would be monstrous to punish (e.g. they involve *resolute* intention of a sort that is manifested in action, and not merely idle thoughts). Objectivists, by contrast, start with the thought that if attempts were thought crimes, it would be monstrous to punish them, and so it must be that they are properly punished thanks to the conduct that they involve; the emphasis is on *actus reus* rather than *mens rea*. The challenge for objectivists, then, is to explain what it is about the conduct involved in attempt thanks to which it is punishable despite being harmless (e.g. it risks

harm, is "proximate" to harm, or would result in harm if not prevented).[6]

Neither subjectivists nor objectivists have taken seriously the idea that to attempt is *to try*. Trying, like all the forms of action that statutes criminalize, consists of mental states and conduct. So the fact that it involves these two parts does not distinguish trying from any other form of action. Neither subjectivists nor objectivists have tried to explain the criminalization of attempt through appeal to what distinguishes trying from other forms of conduct. This simple fact suggests a middle way worthy of exploration. Perhaps attempts are crimes because of the peculiar thing they are, namely tryings, and not because they involve something else (bad thoughts, bad conduct) that there are independent grounds for criminalizing.

As a first step towards developing this admittedly abstract thought, consider something important that we find in ordinary morality. The father tells the child not to jump on the sofa; no ice cream if she does. Moments later, the child starts to climb onto the sofa with the intention of jumping on it. He stops her and says, "That's just what I told you not to do!" Imagine that the precocious child replies, "No, you told me not to *jump on the sofa*, you didn't tell me not to *try to* jump on the sofa. But all I managed to do was *try.*" She speaks the simple truth. But, still, she would deserve to lose out on ice cream. In promising to penalize completion we also, just like that, also promise to penalize attempt. And so it is in the law: criminalization of attempts is accomplished, usually, *automatically* through the criminalization of completion.[7] There is an ordinary notion of trying that we take to be worthy of censure by the state whenever completion is worthy of such censure. It can seem as though we need not *say* what it is to attempt for all that needs to be said *is said already* in describing completion. In this respect, the logic of the law mirrors the logic of everyday morality.

The point can be made in a different way. Imagine that you are asked why it is a crime to *attempt* murder. In answer you will cite those features of *murder* that make *it* worthy of criminalization. Chances are, you won't say a word about

Action / conduct

attempt at all. What this implies is that we take the features of a form of completed action in virtue of which *it* is properly considered a crime to somehow *transfer* to the attempt. We criminalize attempts under the following principle, which I will call the "Transfer Principle": *If a form of conduct is legitimately criminalized, then so are attempts to engage in that form of conduct.*

Under the Transfer Principle, the criminality of the completed crime spreads only to attempts to perform *that crime.* The criminality of attempted battery derives from the criminality *of battery*, and not from the criminality of, say, theft. The Transfer Principle supports criminalizing an attempt, then, only if *a description* that applies to the attempt—words that correctly describe what is attempted—is also an apt *description* of a kind of conduct that is legitimately criminalized thanks to the fact that it meets that description.

So the Transfer Principle has an important implication, an implication that tells us where we *should start* in thinking about attempt. Determining what is properly criminalized *as* an attempt requires determining what ordinary notion of trying is implicated in the Transfer Principle. In what sense of the term "try" is trying to jump on the couch implicated in the proscription against jumping on it? Or, to put the question in the legal context, in what sense of the term "try" is trying to commit a crime implicated in the proscription against committing it? In short, we need to know the necessary and sufficient conditions for trying in the way that inherits criminality from that which one is trying to do.

1.2 The Wide and Narrow Senses of "Try"

We might think this problem is easy to solve: just appeal to our ordinary notion of trying. We could then assess whether or not particular legal doctrines concerning attempt sort defendants as they ought by seeing whether or not our ordinary notion of trying sorts them in the same way. However, things are not so simple. There are several "ordinary" notions of trying. In fact, a quick glance at ordinary usage of the term "try" suggests that there are at least two senses of the

ordinary term that are *different* from the sense of relevance to the law. And this leaves us wondering in what ordinary sense trying is implicitly prohibited whenever we prohibit completion. We can see that these two ordinary senses of trying are inadequate to our task by seeing that trying, in those senses, sits uneasily with the Transfer Principle.

Under one ordinary usage of the term "try," what might be called the "wide" sense of the term, anything that would be true of the person's act were he to succeed in doing as he intends can be appealed to in a description of what he is trying to do.[8] We particularly find this usage in cases of mistake. So, for instance, consider someone who is paid a sum to carry a pound of white powder into the United States from abroad. He is quite certain that the powder is cocaine, but couldn't care less. Provided he gets paid, the stuff could be heroin or talcum; he's indifferent. Is this person trying to smuggle cocaine? Or to put the same question another way, does the phrase "to smuggle cocaine" correctly describe what this person is trying to do? In the wide sense of "try" this is an *attempted cocaine smuggling* because if the intended smuggling had come to pass, it would have been a smuggling *of cocaine.* In this respect, the wide sense of trying yields a result that is appropriate to the criminal law. Conduct like this hypothetical person's is of the sort that is implicitly prohibited as an attempt to smuggle cocaine when cocaine smuggling is prohibited; the Transfer Principle applies, and the wide sense of trying supports that result. So far so good.

But the wide sense of "try" does not capture what we are after, as we can see from considering other kinds of cases. In the wide sense, a person who tries to take a suitcase that he reasonably but falsely believes to be his own has attempted *theft.* Imagine, for instance, that the suitcase looks exactly like his and happens to have his luggage tag, with his name on it, attached to it. He reaches for the suitcase, acting on an intention to take it, and is stopped by the suitcase's true owner who explains that the luggage tags were switched by mistake by the airline employees. It's a simple mistake. Is it an attempted theft in the sense of relevance to criminal law? Of course not. But it counts as such under the wide sense of "try," since

UNLIKE SMUGGLING

were this person to have succeeded in taking the suitcase, he would have taken something that was not his own.

The problem here is not only conflict with intuition about what should be criminal. We can see this in part by noticing that had the person in the example just given been charged with the crime of attempted theft he would have been able to cite the fact that he did not know the suitcase was his in his defense, and such a defense would have succeeded. Such a person would never, for this reason, be convicted of attempted theft. The problem is that under the wide sense of trying, such a person would be speaking falsely were he to say, in his defense, "I wasn't trying to steal anything." A person can respond to an accusation either by showing that he did not do what he is accused of having done, or by showing that, although he did it, he is not rightly punished for it (because it is justified, for instance, or because he was insane when he did it). In the example just described, the first sort of response is appropriate, but it is denied to the defendant under the wide sense of trying; under the wide sense of trying, the defendant *was* trying to take someone else's property. The problem is that such a person ought not to be understood as needing to account for his behavior in light of the fact that completed theft is a crime; he did not attempt theft in the sense in which the criminality of completed theft transfers, and so he can admit that those who attempt theft need to account for their behavior and simply deny that he is among them. Theft is criminal for reasons that do not transfer to all wide attempts, and so the wide sense of attempt is not the one that informs the Transfer Principle, or the ordinary practice that shows the Transfer Principle to be implicit in everyday thought.

Under an alternative "narrow" conception of trying to act, also found in ordinary language, what a person is trying to do is determined entirely by the set of conditions that he is committed, by his intention, to promoting. The narrow conception has its appeal. Under it, the person who thinks the bag he tries to take is his is *not attempting theft*, since he is in no sense committed by his intention to making it more likely that the

"NARROW" = INTENT /COMMITMENT

bag that he takes is not his; in fact, he would have held back from trying to take the bag had he known it belonged to someone else. But the narrow conception implies that the smuggler of white powder who believes the stuff is cocaine, but does not care, is *not* attempting to bring cocaine into the United States. After all, he is not committed to making it more likely that *cocaine* should be smuggled. Were someone to convince him that the stuff is talcum he would still smuggle it because he is being paid to smuggle it, no matter what it is. Something has gone wrong. The narrow conception of trying to act cannot be the sense that informs criminal law; it provides too stringent a standard for attempt. Put in the language of the Transfer Principle, the criminality of the completed acts in cases of this sort does not transfer to attempts to commit the corresponding crimes *under the narrow conception of trying*, despite the fact that, intuitively, the conduct in question was criminalized when we criminalized completion. There is *some* ordinary sense of trying under which criminality *does* transfer in these cases. What follows is that the narrow conception is not the sense of "trying" under which attempt is criminalized.

So, if it is neither the "wide" nor the "narrow" sense, what sense of trying *is* of relevance to the criminal law? The answer will be offered in section 3 of this paper. Not surprisingly, progress on the problem of specifying the kind of trying that inherits its criminality from success starts with reflection on the nature of intention. Trying, after all, necessarily involves, although it is not exhausted by, intending.[9] As we will see, it is through an appreciation of the nature of intending that we will be able to develop an account of the kind of trying that is implicitly prohibited whenever completion is prohibited.

2. INTENTION

2.1 The Rationally-Constituted Nature of Intention

Intention is a distinctive state of mind. Intending an event is different from believing it will occur, for instance. Most who believe that the sun will

Belief vs. Intention

GIDEON YAFFE • Attempts 859

rise tomorrow, do not intend it. Intending an event also differs from wanting it to occur. Someone who wants to eat the chocolate cake for dessert may, nonetheless, intend to have no dessert at all. Intending differs also from wishing, hoping and anticipating. This is not to say that intending bears no relationship to these other attitudes. Typically, for instance, those who intend particular events also believe that those events might occur. There is at least this close connection between intention and belief, and there will be similar connections of many different sorts between intention and desire, intention and wish, and so on. But, still, intentions are different from these other mental states.

It is a project in philosophy of mind to determine how intention differs from these other mental states. The project is to specify the necessary and sufficient conditions that must be met for a person to be intending a particular event or condition, including the event of performing a particular action. It is a closely related project in the philosophy of law to identify the necessary and sufficient conditions that must be met for a person to be intending a particular event or condition *in the sense of relevance to intentional torts*, or *in the sense of relevance to formation in contract*, or *in the sense of relevance to intentional discrimination*, or *in the sense of relevance to criminal responsibility*. However, it is an hypothesis worth exploring that all of the various senses of the legal term "intention" circle around a core notion that has its natural home in ordinary discourse. It is that core notion that has been investigated by philosophers of mind and action. If indeed such a core notion informs the law, then it is important for those interested in criminal responsibility to understand what philosophers of mind have discovered about the nature of intention.

As a first step, consider the following example. A shopper goes to the store, equipped with a list of things to buy. He walks around filling his cart. Meanwhile, a spy follows him and writes down everything that the shopper puts in the cart. At the end of the trip, both the shopper and the spy have a list that matches the world: both of their lists correspond to the contents of the cart. But these two lists had very different

functions. The shopper's list functioned to make the world match it; the spy's list functioned to match the world as it came to be. Were a third party to surreptitiously remove eggs from the cart, the fact that the shopper's list includes eggs ought to lead him to fix the situation by putting more eggs in his cart; he should change the world to match his list. By contrast, the fact that the spy's list includes eggs (he wrote that down before the third party removed them) ought to lead him to cross it off his list; he ought to change the list to match the world. The shopper's list is like an intention, the spy's like a belief.[10] Intrinsically, both consist in nothing but a representation of the world. But they have different functions.

With those functions come rational pressures. The shopper's list will not function as it ought if the shopper has another, conflicting list that he is also taking steps to fulfill. He is thus under rational pressure not to be working from two conflicting lists. The shopper's list will also not function as it ought if it does not prompt the shopper to place the things that are on it in his cart. The shopper, that is, is under rational pressure to engage in conduct that he believes will cause it to be the case that the list matches the world. By contrast, the spy's list is not functioning as it ought if it causes him to place things on the list in the cart. The spy is under rational pressure *not* to cause the world to match his list, but, instead, to change his list to match the world when there is mismatch. The spy's list, that is, does not function as it ought if it does not cause him to cross things off his list when the shopper removes them from the cart. And so the spy is under rational pressure to do just that.

What this example suggests is that the right way to inquire about how intention differs from other mental states is to reflect on the distinctive *functional role* of intention. What are intentions *for*? What do they help us to do that other mental states, such as beliefs, desires, hopes, wishes, etc., do not help us to do? We should expect that together with an account of the functional role of intention will come an account of principles of rationality governing those who have intentions. If we know what intentions are for, we will also have some idea of what kinds of things a rational agent who has an intention will do, or what kinds of other attitudes, including beliefs and other intentions, he will have.

Michael Bratman's important work on intention, which he began publishing in the 1980s, provides a great deal of insight about the functional role of intention and the associated norms of rationality that govern those who intend. Under what Bratman calls "the planning theory of intention," intention's function is *to make the world as intended and to make that happen in a way that allows agents to efficiently achieve long-term goals.* So, for instance, it is part of an intention's role to provide for coordination between one's self at one time and one's self at another. The person who intends in the morning to cook spaghetti for dinner will not succeed in doing as he intends unless his midday self helps by stopping at the store for spaghetti. His intention prompts such help by leading the midday self to do just that. In this example, the intention plays its role by prompting the formation of intentions to undertake necessary means, but often an intention plays its role by instead preventing the agent from acting in a particular way. Deliberation, for instance, is a costly activity. When deciding this morning what to have for dinner, the agent has to focus his energies on thinking that through instead of doing a variety of other things; and he might have to collect information, such as information about who will be joining him for dinner, or information about what time he will be free to start cooking. This expensive deliberative process culminates in the formation of the intention to have spaghetti. The intention, in turn, functions to cut off later deliberation about what to have for dinner in the absence of new information. It is because the intention *settles the question* of what to have for dinner that at midday the agent heads straight for the spaghetti aisle rather than rethinking what to buy at the store.

Reflection on the various roles that plans play in making temporally extended behavior possible and effective leads to the articulation of several norms of rationality that govern those with intentions. A fully rational agent who intends to do something, for instance, will not intend to do acts incompatible with completing necessary means to doing as intended. A fully rational agent who intends to do something will not at the same time believe with certainty that he will fail to do as intended. We can argue over the details of how to formulate the relevant norms of rationality governing those who intend. But our purposes here will not require settling such arguments. Intrinsically, an intention is just like any other mental state that represents a future state of the world, such as a future state of one's body. But what distinguishes intentions from other such representations are the norms of rationality under which a person labors thanks to what the intention is for. The intention's primary function is to make the world as it represents the world as being so as to further the agent's goals, and if it is to play that role successfully, the agent must not defeat it by constructing conflicting plans, or by failing to undertake means to its fulfillment. There are many ways to fail to live up to one's intentions. The insight of this view of intention is that many such failures are *normative* failures. They are failures to conform to norms of rationality that apply to the agent only thanks to the fact that he has an intention to act in a particular way.

2.2 Intention-Based Commitments and Responsibility

There are two interrelated and important points, points of importance to understanding criminal law, about the insight that intention is characterized and distinguished from other mental states by the norms of rationality that govern those who have intentions. First, the position sits comfortably with a particular sense in which to intend something is to be *committed* to it. In what is, perhaps, the paradigm case, to be committed to something is not just to have a reason to promote it, but it is also for that reason to be special to oneself and, in many cases, to derive from one's own will. We all have a reason to promote world peace, but only some of us are committed to it. Those who are have a reason to promote it that derives from the fact that they have chosen to, or devoted themselves to, its promotion. The having of such a reason involves, undoubtably among other things, rational pressure to deliberate in certain distinctive ways. A rational person, committed to world peace, is under pressure to at least *consider* the fact that a particular company provides support to an ongoing war when deciding whether to buy that company's products. And such a person is under pressure to at least *grant some weight* to that consideration when deliberating about what to do. In fact, these are two forms of rational pressure that we are under when we intend to act. A cashier who intends to steal from his employer is under distinctive rational pressure both about what facts he considers, and what weight to give them, in his deliberations about what to do. In considering whether to underreport the day's sales, he ought, rationally, to consider the fact that by doing so he increases his chances of stealing from his employer. He may decide not to do it—maybe he has another, better plan for stealing—but, still, he is not fully rational if he does not grant that consideration some weight in his deliberations (provided that it occurs to him that it will help him to commit the intended theft, and provided that he does not give up his intention). In short, intentions constitute commitments to particular, intended conditions *precisely because* what it is to intend is, in part, to be under rational pressures with respect to that which is intended. To intend is to structure one's own rationality. It is to generate reasons for oneself, reasons that do not apply to others.

The second point of importance that follows from the conception of intentions as constituted in part by the norms of rationality governing those who have them is intertwined with the first. The rationally constituted nature of intention provides us with an explanation for why intention is of such paramount importance to culpability and criminal responsibility. What a person intends tells us a great deal about what kinds of considerations he recognizes as giving him reason, and about how he weighs those considerations in his deliberations about what to do.[11] In fact, it is in part constitutive of those facts. Someone who intends to steal from his employer takes the fact that the contents of the cash drawer *belong to his employer* as either providing him with no reason not to take those contents, or as providing a reason of insufficient

significance to outweigh considerations in favor of stealing. These facts about the person's modes of recognition and response to reasons are of crucial importance to assessing his responsibility. They are part of what explains why he deserves censure for the act of stealing. He deserves that censure not merely because his employer suffers at his hand—although that is, of course, significant—but also because he has misused, misdirected, his capacities for the recognition and response to reasons, capacities that are distinctive of moral agents.[12]

Intention, norms of rationality, commitment, and modes of recognition and response to reasons constitute a family of intertwined notions bearing deep and important relations to culpability and criminal responsibility. They are at the heart of what is distinctive about human agency. They are at the heart of what we respond to in others when we judge them to be blameworthy for wrongdoing, both in and out of criminal law contexts. Our resentment and outrage when confronted with another's wrongdoing, not to mention our guilt and remorse when confronted with our own, is a response to corruption in the way the actor recognized and responded to reasons and thereby guided his conduct. Part of what we are outraged *about* is that the actor could not care less that the property he took was not his, or cared insufficiently about the fact that another would be harmed by his act, or cared too much about lining his own pockets. The actor's intentions and commitments are of particular importance because they are inextricably connected with modes of recognition and response to reasons, but also because there is a meaningful sense in which modes of recognition and response to reasons that have their source in intention and commitment are self-inflicted; they have their source in the agent's will.

2.3 Broadening Our Perspective on Intention-Based Commitments

But this is not all that needs to be said about the nature of intention, if we are to develop an adequate account of what it is to try to act, an account that ought to, and sometimes does,

INTENTION ≠ PROMOTION

COMMITMENT (3)

inform the law governing criminal attempt. We cannot just take what philosophers of action have discovered and apply it; we need to go beyond what has been discovered about the nature of intention by Bratman; we need to make further philosophical progress.[13] In particular, more needs to be said about the range of commitments that are constituted by our intentions. Reflection on the issue demonstrates that there are at least three different kinds of commitment that one can have to a condition thanks to the fact that one has a particular intention. As we will see, all three kinds of commitment turn out to be important to the proper adjudication of criminal attempts.

In the typical case—so typical, in fact, as to blind us to the existence of untypical cases—someone who intends a particular condition is thereby committed to increasing the likelihood that the world should be in that condition. The effort to live up to this commitment often manifests itself in "tracking" behavior—behavior in response to the encounter of obstacles to the realization of the intended conditions that dampens their effect. So, for instance, a person who intends to prevent another from leaving a room will not just lock the door, but will also respond, if he can, when the prisoner picks the lock; perhaps he will then throw the deadbolt, or push the prisoner back into the room, or call in reinforcements, or take some other action that will correct for the facts that are defeating, or threatening to defeat, the world from matching his intention. In fact, he is under *rational pressure* to "track" the condition in this way. The sense in which he is committed to the condition is constituted by such rational pressures. Since the pressures in questions are pressures to take steps to improve the chances of the condition's coming to be, call this a commitment of *promotion*.

It is very tempting to say that *all* intention-based commitments to conditions are commitments of promotion. In fact, virtually everyone who has written about intention has assumed this, usually implicitly.[14] Bratman, for instance, insists that among the distinctive norms governing those who intend are norms of "means–end coherence" which place intending agents under normative pressure to intend acts that they believe to

be necessary to fulfilling their intentions. And, to be sure, there are such pressures wherever there are intention-based commitments *of promotion*; rationality requires us to intend necessary means to a condition's occurrence whenever we are committed to increasing the likelihood of that condition's obtaining. In assuming that norms of means–end coherence apply to intending agents *no matter what they intend*, Bratman is assuming that every time a person intends a condition he thereby incurs a commitment of promotion with respect to that condition.

But the assumption is false. Say that I intend to go running at 9:00 AM. As I'm about to start running, I notice a clock that says it's 8:00 AM; I had forgotten that the time changed as a result of daylight savings time. I go running anyway and I'm done by 8:30. Did I do what I intended to do? Well, I went running, as intended. But I didn't go running *at 9:00 AM*, which was part of what I intended. So, I did all that I was committed by my intention *to promoting*. But there is still a meaningful sense in which the world did not match my intention; to fully match my intention I would have had to run at 9:00 AM, not at 8:00. The result: Included in the content of my intention was the condition that I run at 9:00 AM. But despite its inclusion in the content of my intention, that condition is not one that I incurred any commitment to promote.

Who cares? As will be demonstrated below, *we* should care; that is, *we* who care about criminal responsibility and the mental states required for it should care about this. But a first step to seeing why this matters is to see that our intentions *commit* us, in a sense now to be described, to intended conditions even when we lack commitments to promote those conditions.

Say that when I am getting ready to run I see that it is, indeed, 9:00 AM. But I change my mind and decide not to run. When asked why I changed my mind, I say, "Well, it's 9:00 AM." Something has gone wrong. I can reconsider my intention for many good reasons—I remember a pressing 9:15 appointment, the hills are steeper than expected, it starts to rain, there are too many dogs around, etc. If I did not intend to run *at 9:00 AM*, I could even reconsider in light of the fact that *it is*

9:00 AM—maybe I think it is too late in the morning to run. What I cannot do in full rationality is reconsider *for that reason* given that *that* was part of what I intended in the first place. The fact that the condition is included in the content of my intention, then, places me under a very particular form of rational pressure: it places me under pressure *not to reconsider* the intention in light of the fact that the condition is met. Call this a commitment of *non-reconsideration*. As the example illustrates, it is possible to have an intention-based commitment of nonreconsideration with respect to a particular condition without having a commitment to promote the condition.

And there is yet another kind of intention-based commitment that one can have to a condition in the absence of a commitment of promotion with respect to the condition. Imagine that, acting on my intention to go running at 9:00 AM, I go running and so I fail to call a friend whom I promised to call at 9:00 AM. The friend complains. I respond, "Although I did intend to go running at 9:00 AM, it didn't really matter to me what time it was; I would have been happy to run at 8:00." My friend will see this, and quite rightly, as utterly irrelevant. Given that I intended to run *at 9:00 AM*, I can't complain that that's what happened, or shield myself from responsibility for the fact that it was 9:00 AM when I ran, by pointing out that I was not committed to *promoting* that fact. At least, I cannot do so without irrationality. Thanks to my intention, that is, I have incurred a particular commitment towards the condition that it is 9:00 AM when I run. Call this a commitment of *noncomplaint*. A person cannot rationally complain that the world turns out the way he intended it to be, or, more carefully, a very particular kind of complaint is silenced, namely, the complaint that might be expressed by saying, "*That's* not what I intended." Even if it was not something that he was committed to promoting it was still something that he intended and so something that he was committed to not complaining about when it came to pass. Commitments of noncomplaint are commitments to acquiesce to the world's turning out a certain way, a form of acquiescence that precludes us from pointing to the absence of a commitment to promote that condition in justifying our behavior.

Again, why should we care? Why should we think that subtleties about the differences between the kinds of commitments engendered by our intentions matter to criminal responsibility? Read on.

3. THE LEGALLY RELEVANT SENSE OF "TRY"

3.1 The Guiding Commitment View

At the end of section 1 it was argued that neither of two ordinary senses of "trying" are the sense in which trying to do something is implicitly prohibited by our prohibitions of it. The "wide" sense, under which anything that would be true of your act were you to do as you intend contributes to what you are trying to do, is too wide; too much is criminalized as attempt under that conception. The "narrow" sense, under which only that which you are committed by your intention *to promoting* contributes to what you are trying to do, is too narrow; much that ought to be criminalized as attempt under that conception is not so criminalized. It was then promised that further reflection on the nature of intention would allow us to articulate the necessary and sufficient conditions of trying in the sense that is consistent with, and supports, the Transfer Principle. Now that we have a view of the nature of intention in hand, we are in position to fulfill that promise.

Despite its problem the narrow sense of trying gets something right: what a person tries to do, in the sense of relevance to criminal law, is a function of what he is committed to by the intention on which he is acting. But to limit the range of relevant conditions to those that we have an intention-based commitment *to promoting* is to overlook the other ways, discussed in section 2, in which our intentions can commit us to particular conditions. And this is the key to understanding the sense of trying that is relevant to the criminal law. *To try to act, in the sense of relevance to the criminal law, is to have an intention that commits one (in one of the three senses of intention-based commitment) to each of the conditions involved in completion, and for one's behavior to be guided by that intention.* I call this the "Guiding Commitment View" of attempt.

Under the Guiding Commitment View, to use an example from section 1, a defendant who attempts to take a bag that he falsely but reasonably believes to be his own has not attempted theft under the Guiding Commitment View. His intention does not commit him, in any sense, to the bag belonging to someone else. This condition is not represented by his intention and so he incurs no intention-based commitment to it. As we will see in section 4, the Guiding Commitment View, in contrast to the narrow view of trying, also implies that the person who believes the white powder is cocaine, and tries to transport it across the border, has attempted to smuggle cocaine. So, in contrast to the wide and the narrow senses of trying, the Guiding Commitment View provides us with a way of conceptualizing these examples that is consistent with the Transfer Principle. As we will see in section 4, the Guiding Commitment View also provides us with a defensible and independently plausible resolution of a difficult problem of adjudication.

3.2 Guidance and "Mere Preparation"

It is important to emphasize that there are two parts to trying under the Guiding Commitment View: intention-based commitment, and behavior guided by intention. Much has been said already here about intention-based commitment, but more needs to be said about guidance. To be guided by an intention is to be moved, or motivated, by it to do that which is intended. Specifying, however, how motivation differs from other causal influences of intention is no easy matter. A person intends to climb the stairs. This intention causes two things: it causes him to announce "I will ascend the staircase!" and it causes him to take the first step. The intention motivates the taking of the first step, but does not *motivate* the pronouncement. In making the pronouncement he is motivated, instead, by an intention to tell the world of his plans. But how do we distinguish the two causal influences of the intention to climb the staircase? The intention to climb the staircase

does *cause* the pronouncement; he certainly wouldn't make the pronouncement if he did not have that intention. So why is the intention's influence on the one form of behavior (the first step) motivational, but not on the other (the pronouncement)? The best we can do in answer is to note that were the causal sequence leading to the first step to continue without obstacles and without change of mind, the agent would climb the stairs. The same is not true of the causal sequence leading to the pronouncement. *That* causal sequence will culminate instead in his informing the world of his plans. So, the right way to determine whether the influence of a person's intention on his behavior is motivational, and so is an instance of *guidance*, is to ask the following question: Had he ability and opportunity to act, and did not change his mind, would the causal sequence in question have culminated in action?

Efforts on the parts of courts and legislators to concoct "tests" for the act element of attempt can be construed as efforts to provide independent descriptions of those acts that give us sufficient evidence for thinking that the defendant's intention was having a causal influence on his behavior of a sort that would culminate in commission of the crime, given ability, opportunity and no change of mind. For instance, reflection on the notion of "proximity" animating Oliver Wendell Holmes's influential "dangerous proximity test" leads to this conclusion.[15] According to Holmes the defendant's act suffices for the act element of attempt just in case it brought him into dangerous proximity of completion of the crime. But the only coherent and normatively defensible conception of "proximity" in this domain is counterfactual: the defendant's act is in "dangerous proximity" of completion just in case all that needs to be added to get completion is ability, opportunity, and absence of change of mind. Demonstrating that all the various tests for the act element of attempt are either indefensible, or amount to efforts to capture this idea, requires looking at the details of all of the various tests that have been offered, and not just one; I have undertaken that task elsewhere and will not do so here.[16] For our purposes here, however, it suffices to note that the frustrating imprecision that is necessarily involved in this approach—under what conditions, *exactly*, is the relevant counterfactual true?—cannot be overcome *for principled reasons*. Since to try, in the sense of relevance to criminal law, is to be guided by an intention that commits one to success, the best characterization of the act element of attempt will be an account of what it is to be guided by an intention. And it is highly unlikely that we can do better in distinguishing guidance from other influences of intention on behavior than to appeal to what would happen in the absence of obstacles or change of mind. Like it or not, *that's* the question we have to answer in order to determine if the defendant's conduct suffices for attempt.

3.3 Neither "Subjectivism" Nor "Objectivism"

The Guiding Commitment View preserves exactly what we find in ordinary moral thought, and which is expressed in the Transfer Principle. We justify criminalizing an attempt to commit a crime by citing the features of the very crime attempted. We do not justify criminalizing an attempt to do one thing by citing the features of *something other than what was attempted* in explanation. So, we need an account of trying to act that preserves this tight connection. We need an account that allows us to identify the attempt in the way that exhibits congruity between it and completion. The Guiding Commitment View serves the turn. It identifies the sense of trying that is relevant to criminal law.

The truth about attempts has eluded theorists of criminal law precisely because they start in the wrong places; they do not start with the question of what kind of failure, what kind of trying, we have implicitly prohibited in our prohibitions of success. As indicated earlier, subjectivists start with the idea that attempts are thought crimes involving some special species of thoughts that it is acceptable to criminalize (such as *resolute* intentions). Objectivists start with the idea that attempts are crimes involving actions that approximate, or bear some close relation to, harmful conduct of the sort that we typically criminalize (such

as conduct that is "proximate" to completion, or imposes a serious risk of completion).

What subjectivist and objectivist approaches share is the belief that the first and most natural description of the conduct involved in a criminal attempt is a description under which it is not in any sense wrongful. "All he *did*," we say, "was light a match. What could be criminal about *that*?" The subjectivist embraces the claim that the act is not in itself wrongful and concludes that the criminality of the attempt must derive from the accompanying mental state. The objectivist, by contrast, seeks an alternative description of the act under which it is wrongful in explanation of the attempt's criminality. The problem with both approaches is that the first and most natural description of the act is a description under which it *is* wrongful. The act is the act of *trying* to burn down another's house, or *trying* to have sex with a minor, or *trying* to bring drugs across the border. These are wrongful, prohibited, behaviors; they were prohibited when we prohibited burning down another's house, having sex with a minor and bringing drugs across the border. Trying was prohibited when success was prohibited. The place to start in thinking about attempts is with an effort to identify this kind of trying. And, as we have seen, this leads to the Guiding Commitment View.

In fact, it is something in the nature of the conceptualization of criminal behavior endemic to criminal law and its practice that gives rise to the error shared by subjectivists and objectivists alike. It is because criminal law practitioners and theorists insist on dividing crimes into *actus reus* and *mens rea* components that they have overlooked the right way to start thinking about attempts. Implicit in the divide is the thought that the *actus reus* and *mens rea* components of crimes make independent contributions to the criminality of the conduct. And often this is indeed the case. Burning another's property is morally salient; it is something one needs to answer for. *Intending* to burn another's property is also morally salient. When we put these two things together, there is crime. In this case, the act has features that make it morally salient independently of the mental states that gave rise to it; someone's property, after all, was burned; someone's legally protected interests were invaded. If we assume that this is true of all crimes, then we quickly find ourselves on the road to either subjectivism or objectivism, for the truth is that many an attempted crime is not wrongful under any description that applies to it independently of the mental states that gave rise to it. The conduct in question is wrongful alright, but only under descriptions that are not *mens rea*-independent, namely descriptions that specifically identify the fact that the conduct is *a trying*. To describe the act as *trying to burn another's property* is to describe it in a way that implicates and refers to the mental state that gave rise to it, namely an intention that committed the actor to each of the features of completed arson. Students of criminal law are taught to characterize the *actus reus* in a way that is independent of the *mens rea*. Given this, it is no wonder that those who follow such a method take the central puzzle about attempt to derive from the thought that it involves conduct that is not on its face wrongful; they have been taught to attach a description to the act that leaves out exactly that in virtue of which it *is* wrongful, namely that it is an instance of *trying* to do something wrongful.

When we avoid this error we find ourselves on the middle way. We find ourselves with the Guiding Commitment View. And down that road, as we will see by considering one example in the next section, lie solutions to many difficult problems encountered by those tasked with adjudicating attempted crimes.

4. CIRCUMSTANCES AND "IMPOSSIBILITY"

4.1 Clearing Ground and Setting Aside Legal and Factual Impossibility

There is perhaps no area of criminal law in which there is more confusion, both on the parts of courts and commentators, than in the adjudication of so called "impossible" attempts. Consider an appealing line of thought that leads to a disastrous set of doctrines, namely the doctrines employing the distinction between "legal" and "factual" impossibility. Start with cases sometimes

dubbed as "pure legal impossibility" cases: A married man tries to commit adultery and fails. The object of his affections is not interested. Ashamed and falsely believing that adultery is illegal he runs to his local police station to turn himself in for attempted adultery. The police laugh in his face and send him home. Why? Because: *it is not a crime to attempt to do something that would not be criminal were you to have done as intended.* Had the attempted adulterer succeeded, he would have committed no crime, and so his attempt was no crime. So far so good. Or so it seems.

But now let's extend that principle. Consider a case which has occupied the imagination of many a criminal law theorist, namely *People v. Jaffe*.[17] The defendant, a suspected "fence," was charged with an attempt to receive stolen property after he purchased some fabric that he believed to be stolen but which was in fact falsely represented to him as stolen as part of a sting operation. At least part of what Jaffe intended was to receive property. But in doing as intended, Jaffe did not commit a crime, since the property he intended to receive was not stolen. Apply the principle appealed to in the case of the attempted adulterer and it appears to follow that Jaffe has not attempted receipt of stolen property. To keep the sky from falling—if Jaffe did not attempt receipt of stolen property, attempt liability radically shrinks as do the tools available to law enforcement—judges sought a distinction between a case like the attempted adulterer and a case like *Jaffe*. It is not implausible to think that what distinguishes the cases is that the attempted adulterer made a mistake of law, while Jaffe made a mistake of fact. And hence a bit of doctrine is born: if the obstacle to completion is factual, the attempt is criminal (the case is one of "factual impossibility"), while if the obstacle is legal, the attempt is not criminal (the case is one of "legal impossibility").

But the doctrine is a disaster, and, thankfully, has almost disappeared in the United States. The problems are many, and need not be rehearsed here.[18] What is of importance to us is a subtle error that leads to the doctrine, an error that we must not make in thinking about cases like *Jaffe*. The reason that the attempted adulterer has committed no crime is that he is not committed by his intention to all of the components of any crime. He is committed, instead, to the components of a noncriminal form of conduct, namely adultery. The mistake is in thinking that the right question to ask is "Would the attempted adulterer have committed a crime had he done as intended?" This is the wrong question since it invites an answer in which we appeal to facts about the world to which the defendant is not committed by his intention—namely any facts that would be in place were he to do as intended. (Essentially, it involves tacitly assuming that the sense of "try" of relevance to the criminal law is the wide sense discussed in section 1.) The right question to ask about Jaffe is not, "Would he have committed a crime had he done as intended?"—a question to which the answer is "no." The right question is "Was he committed by his intention to all of the components of the crime of receipt of stolen property?"—a question to which the answer may be "yes" (for reasons to be explained below). We need to attend not to what would be the case were the defendant to do as intended, but, instead, to that to which he is committed by his intention.

This change in orientation radically changes the problem. The important issue not only has nothing to do with the fact–law distinction, it also has nothing to do with impossibility. Sometimes we are committed by our intentions to things that can't come to pass, sometimes to things that can. What is crucial is *what we are committed to*, not whether it can come to pass.

The next step is to remember that, as emphasized in section 2, a person can be committed by his intention to a condition without being committed *to promoting* that condition. We can also be committed to not reconsidering our intention in light of the presence of the condition, and, thanks to an intention, we can be committed to not complaining that the world is in a certain condition. When we have these forms of commitment we are under no pressure to adopt necessary means to realizing the condition to which we are committed. Under the Guiding Commitment View, when a person who is not committed to promoting a condition, but is committed to it in

one of these other two ways, the condition can be appealed to in a characterization of what he is trying to do. So, if Jaffe was committed in one of these ways by his intention to the property being stolen, then he attempted receipt *of stolen property,* in the sense that is criminalized under the Transfer Principle. Was he?

4.2 Belief and the Rebuttable Presumption

It is obvious that in a case like *Jaffe* a crucial fact about the defendant that informs our belief that he attempted a crime is that he *believed* that the property he received was stolen. Similarly, Crow, recall, *believed* that the person he tried to sexually exploit, "StephieFL," was a minor. And there are many other cases with the same structure, not all of which have led to conviction for attempt.[19] In *United States v. Berrigan*,[20] for instance, the defendant thought that he was smuggling letters out of the prison in which he was housed *without the warden's knowledge.* In fact, the warden knew all about it and was allowing the letters to leave so as to help the police to track the activity outside the prison that Berrigan was directing through the letters. The court acquitted Berrigan of the attempt to smuggle letters out without the warden's knowledge on the grounds that belief in the presence of the condition (namely that the warden did not know) was insufficient for the attempt.[21] How should we think about the relevance of belief in these cases?

One might think that any view, such as the Guiding Commitment View, that requires for attempt an *intention-based* commitment to each of the conditions involved in the completed crime must say that belief is insufficient in cases like *Jaffe, Crow,* and *Berrigan.* After all, it is common to believe a condition to be in place without it being something to which one is committed by one's intention. The runner believes that he lives in Los Angeles, but we cannot infer from this fact, together with the fact that he intends to go running, the further claim that he intends to go running *in Los Angeles.* That is something that he takes for granted, not something that he directs his will towards in the form of an intention. (We would not expect the neural correlate of his intention to carry information about Los Angeles, but only information about running.) Perhaps it is like that with Jaffe, or Crow, or Berrigan. Perhaps they believe that the relevant conditions are in place, without those conditions being things to which they are committed by their intentions.

And, indeed, this is possible. It is just extremely unlikely. There are quite complicated principles that govern the flow of information from one mental state to another; sometimes content bleeds from one mental state to another and sometimes it does not. Often, people who believe that Obama is Hawaiian and believe that Obama is President also believe that a Hawaiian is President. But a particular person might not have this further belief. He might not "put two and two together." If asked if a Hawaiian has ever been President he might have to think about it, or he might even answer "no" before realizing that it is an implication of other things that he believes. Failures to put two and two together have two related sources of importance. Sometimes we fail to put two and two together because one belief or the other is buried, or dispositional; it is not "before the mind" in the way that it would need to be to serve as a premise in reasoning through which its content would bleed into the other. This might be the case for someone who knows that Obama is Hawaiian but has not given that any thought in some time. Alternatively, a person can fail to put two and two together because one of the facts is extremely unimportant to him; it is insalient. Someone who doesn't care about such things will not have the thought that the President is a dog owner, even if he has the thought that Obama is a dog owner, and the thought that he is President.

These examples involve beliefs, but we find the same limitations on content moving from a belief to an intention. Someone who intends to vote for Obama might not intend to vote for a dog owner, even though he knows that Obama is a dog owner. That fact just does not matter to him. Or even if it does matter to him, it might not be before his mind at the time that he intends to vote for Obama. But notice how rare it is in criminal cases like *Jaffe, Crow,* and *Berrigan* for either

the relevant beliefs to be buried, or for the conditions to be insalient to the defendant. This is *possible* but it is incredibly rare in the criminal law context. It is rare enough, in fact, for the fact of belief in the relevant condition to provide a rebuttable presumption that the condition is included in the content of the defendant's intention. Given that he believes that the property is stolen and intends to receive property, we can be virtually certain that Jaffe intends to receive *stolen* property; given that he believes that StephieFL is thirteen and intends to sexually exploit her, we can be virtually certain that Crow intends to sexually exploit *a minor*; given that he believes the warden is ignorant of his activities and intends to send letters, we can be virtually certain that Berrigan intends to send letters *without the warden's knowledge.* Can we be *certain* that the relevant conditions bleed from the defendants' beliefs to their intentions? It is not a conceptual truth, but in the absence of evidence that defeats the claim, there is every reason to think the intention includes a representation of the believed condition.

So, if we ask, "What is the appropriate *mens rea* standard in attempt with respect to the circumstantial elements of the completed crime?," the answer is "intent." That is an implication of the Guiding Commitment View that we should embrace. But mental states "lower" on the *mens rea* hierarchy can provide extremely good evidence, *sufficient* evidence in the absence of rebuttal, for the needed intention. If there are remaining intuitions that intent is too high a standard in this domain, they arise from a failure to appreciate the fact that one can intend a condition, and thereby be committed to it, without having any commitment to promote it. To say that Crow intends to sexually exploit *a minor* is not to say that he would have dropped his pursuit of her photographs had he discovered she was not a minor. Maybe he would have been happy to receive sexually explicit pictures of either a minor or an adult. Who knows? But still, given that he intended to sexually exploit a minor, he was committed to her being a minor in both the senses of nonreconsideration and noncomplaint. He could not without irrationality have changed his mind on encountering further evidence of her minor

1) PROMOTION 2) NONRECONSIDERATION 3) NONCOMPLAINT

status; nor could he complain that the world came out differently from the way he intended if, in the end, he sexually exploited a minor. These are commitments that he incurs compatible with the absence of any commitment on his part to see to it, or promote, the object of his sexual exploitation being a minor. And it is thanks to the fact that he has these intention-based commitments that he is properly said to have attempted *to sexually exploit a minor* in the sense of relevance to criminal law.

4.3 Recklessness and the Relevance of the Facts

Cases in which the defendant believes the relevant circumstantial element of the completed crime to be present are not, by any means, the only sort. A defendant who tries to take something that he lacks permission to take might fall short of belief that he lacks permission; perhaps he is merely reckless in this respect—his wife was supposed to ask permission for him to take his neighbor's car, but he's not sure if she remembered. His belief is aptly characterized as probabilistic, rather than "flat out." He does not flat out believe that he lacks permission; he believes, instead, that there's a decent chance he lacks permission. Did such a defendant attempt theft? A defendant who tries to buy a stereo off the back of a truck falls short of belief that the stereo is stolen, maybe it's just a roaming garage sale, but is aware of a good chance that it is. Did such a defendant attempt to receive stolen property?

Notice that these recklessness cases are importantly different from those involving defendants who are negligent, or even blamelessly oblivious to the presence of certain conditions. In negligent attempts, there is no mental state the content of which can bleed into the content of the intention. And hence there is no intention-based commitment to the relevant condition. This is why it is just false to say that someone who tries to have sex with someone underage, but whom he unreasonably believes to be an adult, has *attempted rape*. This is false even if negligence, or less, will suffice for the completed crime. When it comes to the attempt, we need intention-based commitment.

And when there is no mental representation of the relevant condition, there is no such commitment.

Under the Guiding Commitment View, the question in recklessness cases, by contrast to negligence cases, is parallel to the question involved in the flat out belief cases: Is the defendant committed to the condition (that he lacks permission, that the property is stolen) by his intention? If so, then we can appeal to the condition in describing what he is trying to do (*steal* rather than merely take; receive *stolen* property); and if not, then we cannot. And, to a point, although *only* to a point, the solution is the same as well: the content of the probabilistic belief can be presumed to bleed into the content of the intention in the absence of a failure on the defendant's part to put two and two together. However, there is an important difference. When the content of the probabilistic belief bleeds into the content of the intention, the defendant does not intend to receive *stolen* property, but intends, instead, to receive *possibly stolen* property. And so we have a new question: Does an intention-based commitment to the property's *possibly* being stolen suffice for the kind of commitment to its *being* stolen that is needed for attempt to receive stolen property?

The answer is, for reasons to be explained, that it suffices *only if the property is actually stolen*. In short, whether or not the intention to receive possibly stolen property constitutes a commitment to the property's being stolen depends on whether it is, in fact, stolen. To see this, start by noticing that an intention to receive possibly stolen property does not generate a commitment of nonreconsideration with respect to the property's being stolen. A person with that intention whose doubt is removed—the guy on the back of the truck, for instance, says, "By the way, this stuff is hot."—could without irrationality reconsider his intention in light of the newly formed belief that the property *is* stolen. A rational agent might be willing to go through with the purchase when he's not certain and be unwilling to go through with it when he is. So, if the intention to receive possibly stolen property commits one to its being stolen it cannot be because it generates a commitment of *nonreconsideration*.

What about a commitment to not complaining? Here there are conditions in which the intention in question generates such a commitment. Say, for instance, that the stereo is purchased and the purchaser is arrested, and it is demonstrated that the stereo is stolen. Can the purchaser rationally deflect criticism from himself by noting that at least the world is not in a condition he *intended* it to be in? No, for the world *is in exactly the condition that he intended it to be in* in intending to receive *possibly* stolen property. This is to say that the defendant has a commitment of noncomplaint with respect to the property's being stolen. But notice: *he only has that commitment if the property is actually stolen*. If the property turns out not to be stolen, then *that* is something that he is committed to not complaining about. What he is committed to not complaining *about* is a function of how things are. What follows is that when the defendant is merely reckless with respect to the relevant condition, he has attempted the crime *only if the condition is actually in place*. So, whether or not the prosecution bears a burden to show that the condition is in place depends on what the defendant's mental state is. If the defendant believes the condition to be in place, then the prosecution bears no such burden. But if the defendant is merely reckless with respect to the condition, then the prosecution must establish that the condition is in place in order to establish that the defendant attempted the crime. Put conversely: *when the prosecution is able to prove only that the defendant was reckless with respect to a particular circumstance, then they must also prove that the circumstance was in place in order to show that the defendant attempted the crime.*

One of the things that is uncovered here is the root of a particular source of confusion in the conceptualization of attempt. We recognize, and without difficulty, that when it comes to a completed crime like receipt of stolen property, there are two different and separable questions to ask in this domain: First: was the property stolen? Second: did the defendant *believe* that the property was stolen? There are two questions because there are two different morally salient facts—one about the property's status, and another about the mental state of the defendant with respect to that fact.

But when theorists have tackled cases of "impossible" attempt—cases like *Jaffe, Crow,* or *Berrigan,* or equivalent cases involving recklessness rather than knowledge—the question of whether the circumstances need to be in place has seemed to be inextricably intertwined with the question of what the defendant's mental attitude needs to be towards the circumstance. But there's a reason that these two things seem entwined in attempt: *they are entwined in attempt.* When what the defendant intends is, for instance, to sexually exploit someone who *might be a minor,* he's attempting to sexually exploit *a minor* only if *the victim is in fact a minor.* The facts are relevant to what his mental state commits him to. And what his mental state commits him to is relevant to what he is trying to do in the sense of relevance to the criminal law. And what he is trying to do in that sense is relevant to whether he has committed a criminal attempt, because we criminalize attempts under the Transfer Principle. The abstract bit of progress made here in philosophy of mind and action— noting the range of commitments to conditions other than conditions to promote them that are constituted by our intentions—is not merely that; it is, instead, identifying something about which those who care about crime and culpability *ought* to care.

CONCLUSION

The philosopher P. F. Strawson, writing about free will, insisted that in thinking about that topic we remind ourselves of some "commonplaces":

> We should think of the many different kinds of relationship which we can have with other people— as sharers of a common interest; as members of the same family; as colleagues; as friends; as lovers; as chance parties to an enormous range of transactions and encounters. Then we should think, in each of these connections in turn, and in others, of the kind of importance we attach to the attitudes and intentions towards us of those who stand in these relationships to us, and of the kinds of reactive attitudes and feelings to which we ourselves are prone.…
>
> The object of these commonplaces is to try to keep before our minds something it is easy to forget when we are engaged in philosophy, especially

in our cool, contemporary style, viz. what it is actually like to be involved in ordinary interpersonal relationships, ranging from the most intimate to the most casual.[22]

As Strawson saw it, the necessary conditions of moral responsibility are those that we find to be implicit in indispensable social practices of interaction and engagement with others. He urged us—in thinking about what human beings must be like such that we can be held morally responsible for our behavior, and hold others responsible—to focus on the varied and complex facts about others and ourselves to which we respond as part of social life, and to which certain responses and not others are particularly appropriate. It is because of its role *there* that, for instance, intention is so important to responsibility. It is one of the things to which we respond with, among other things, resentment and gratitude; it is one of the things to which some responses, including moral emotional responses, though not others, are appropriate.

It is not just this that "our cool contemporary style" can lead us to forget. It can lead us to forget, also, the degree to which the assignment of criminal responsibility *ought to be*, even if it is too rarely, itself an entrenched and integral part of the web of social interactions to which we are necessarily subject thanks to living together in a state. We need an account of what is and should be involved in the assignment of criminal responsibility that demonstrates and exhibits this entrenchment. We must recover the sense in which the assignment of criminal responsibility is an essential part of participation in the many and varied relationships we have with each other as citizens.

The study of criminal responsibility for attempt is not special in this regard. But it is one place in which the theorist is likely to despair, as Jerome Hall did, of the possibility of providing an account of what we are, or should be doing, that bears deep links to the simple interactions of everyday life. We are prone to conceive of the activity as nothing more, for instance, than the *post hoc* rationalization of the zealous desire to intervene earlier and earlier in the lives of those who, for independent reasons if for any at all, we have

classified as inhabiting the wrong side of the law. But this is just pessimism. The law of attempt is the simple interaction between father and daughter writ large. It bears more than an analogical relation to the prohibition of that form of trying which we prohibit implicitly when we prohibit conduct. In fact, it *is* that prohibition. Or, at least, so it has been argued here.

NOTES

1. Although many codes have specific sections criminalizing attempts, it is common for codes to say no more than that it is a crime to attempt a crime without specifying what conditions need to be met for a person's behavior to constitute an attempt. Cf. Cal. Pen. Code §664 (2012), ALM GL ch. 274 §6 (2011), MCLS §750.92, Tenn. Code. Ann. §39-12-101 (2011).
2. Cf. *People v Collins*, 234 N.Y. 355 (1922), *Gregg v. United States*, 113 F.2d 687 (8th Cir. 1940)(requiring "direct movement towards"completion) crime).
3. *United States v. Crow*, 164 F.3d 229 (5th Cir. 1999).
4. Impressed by this point, some courts have embraced the result the *Crow* court endeavors to avoid and acquitted defendants of attempt. On facts very similar to those in *Crow*, for instance, the court in *Aplin v. State*, 898 NE 2d 1240 (2008), acquitted the defendant on the grounds that his conduct "did not constitute the offense of attempted Sexual Misconduct with a Minor, because Detective Claasen [who was posing as a 14 year old girl in his Internet conversations with the defendant] is an adult." (at 884).
5. Hall, J. "Criminal Attempt—A Study of Foundations of Criminal Liability." *Yale Law Journal* 49 (1940): 789.
6. Too many thinkers have taken positions on attempt to allow for anything close to an exhaustive classification here of each as subjectivist or objectivist. The distinction is made in Fletcher, George. *Rethinking Criminal Law.* Oxford: Oxford University Press, 2000. 166–197. Fletcher defends a form of objectivism, as does Duff, R. A. *Criminal Attempts.* Oxford: Oxford University Press, 1996. Objectivist leanings, at least, can be detected in, for instance, Holmes, Oliver Wendell Jr. *The Common Law*, 1881. 69–70; Sayre, Francis. "Criminal Attempts." *Harvard Law Review* 41 (1928): 821–859; Westen, Peter. "Impossible Attempts: A

Speculative Thesis." *Ohio State Criminal Law Journal* 5 (2008): 523–565. Subjectivism's proponents include Ashworth, Andrew. "Criminal Attempts and the Role of Resulting Harm under the Code and in the Common Law." *Rutgers Law Journal* 19 (1988): 725–72; Alexander, Larry and Ferzan, Kimberly. *Crime and Culpability: A Theory of Criminal Law.* Cambridge: Cambridge University Press, 2009; Smith, J. C. "Two Problems in Criminal Attempts." *Harvard Law Review* 70 (1957): 422–48.

7. Of course, some statutes explicitly prohibit attempt as well as completion. E.g., D.C. Code Ann. §22–303 (2006) says that "Whoever maliciously injures or breaks or destroys, *or attempts to injure or break or destroy* … any public or private property" shall be punished. But this does not undermine the point. In such cases, there are two sources of the criminalization of the attempt: the statute prohibiting the attempt, and the statute prohibiting the completion.

8. In his classic 1957 article, "Two Problems of Criminal Attempts," supra, note 6, J.C. Smith claims that what I am calling the wide sense of trying is the sense of relevance to the criminal law of attempts. For the reasons explained below, Smith is mistaken.

9. This claim is actually disputed by philosophers of action. I argue against the consensus view among philosophers in my "Trying, Intending and Attempted Crimes." *Philosophical Topics* 32: 505–532; and *Attempts.* New York: Oxford University Press, 2010. Ch. 2.

10. The example is Elizabeth Anscombe's. See Anscombe, G.E.M *Intention.* Cambridge: Harvard University Press, 1957. 56.

11. For discussion of the impact on this point on a difficult *mens rea* problem, see my "Conditional Intention and Mens Rea." *Legal Theory* 10: 273–310.

12. For views of the nature of responsibility that are supportive of this point, see, for instance, Fischer, John and Ravizza, Mark. *Responsibility and Control: A Theory of Moral Responsibility.* Cambridge: Cambridge University Press, 1998; Scanlon, T.M. "The Significance of Choice." *The Tanner Lectures on Human Values,* 1986. 151–216; Wolf, Susan. *Freedom Within Reason.* Oxford: Oxford University Press, 1990.

13. We also need to reconceptualize some of the rationality conditions on intention that he proposed. For discussion, see my "Trying, Intending and Attempted Crimes." *Philosophical Topics,* 32: 505–532.

14. An exception, arguably, is Hector Neri-Castaneda, whose work in the philosophy of action deserves to receive much more attention than it is currently receiving. For a start, see "Intentions and the Structure of Intending." *Journal of Philosophy* 68 (1971): 453–466.

15. Oliver Wendell Holmes, *The Common Law,* supra, note 6, at 68–9.

16. See my *Attempts,* supra, note 9, ch. 10.

17. *People v. Jaffe,* 185 N.Y. 497, 78 N.E. 169 (1906).

18. One obvious problem is that many obstacles that courts hope to classify as "factual" are legally constituted. The property that Jaffe received had been stolen and then recovered. That recovered property is not properly classified as "stolen" is a legal fact, but such a case would ordinarily be classified as one of factual impossibility. It is difficult to see why.

19. Cf. *Laughner v. State,* 769 N.E.2d 1147 (Ind. Ct. App. 2002) (soliciting sex from an undercover agent defendant thought was a minor was attempt); *U.S. v. Butters,* 267 Fed. Appx. 773 (10th Cir. 2008) (deeming the lack of an actual minor "irrelevant"). But compare to *Gibbs v. State,* 898 N.E.2d 1240 (Ind. Ct. App. 2008) (holding a case could not be proved because it did not actually involve a minor), *overruled by King v. State,* 921 N.E.2d 1288 (Ind. 2010), and *People v. Thousand,* 241 Mich. App. 102 (2000) (dismissing charge of attempt because defendant's "object of desire" was actually an adult and not a minor), *rev'd,* 465 Mich. 149 (2001).

20. *United States v. Berrigan,* 482 F.2d 171 (3d Cir. 1973).

21. One recent case reaches the same kind of conclusion through very different reasoning from that employed in *Berrigan.* In *Moore v. State,* 388 Md 623 (2005), the defendant made arrangements with an undercover detective whom he believed to be 14 years old to meet to have sex. The appellate court notes that the completed crime is strict liability with respect to age, and so can be committed by someone in the absence of an intention to have sex with a minor; even someone who intends to have sex with an adult can be guilty of the completed offense provided that the person he has sex with is actually a minor. The court then analogizes strict liability crimes to crimes of negligence, like involuntary manslaughter, that cannot be committed with intent. Someone who intends to kill is guilty of a purposive homicide rather than involuntary manslaughter and this gives rise to the rule that there is no crime of attempted involuntary

manslaughter, or of any other crime that cannot be completed with intent. (I argue that this rule is based on mistaken logic in *Attempts*, supra, note 9, ch. 6; even crimes that cannot be completed with intent can be attempted.) Extending this well-known rule, the court concludes that it is not possible to attempt a strict liability crime such as that at issue in the case, and acquits. After all, reasons the court, completed strict liability crimes do not involve intent any more than crimes of negligence do. The problem with the court's reasoning is that strict liability crimes, unlike involuntary manslaughter and other crimes of negligence, *can* be committed by someone with

the intention that an attempter has; they just don't *require* such an intention. So even those who think that there are no attempts of crimes like involuntary manslaughter can consistently hold that there are attempts of strict liability crimes. In fact, some courts have taken it to be *easier* to attempt crimes of strict liability; they have thought that in such cases not even belief that the relevant circumstantial element is in place is required for the attempt. Cf. *Commonwealth v. Dunne*, 474 N.E. 2d 538 (1985).

22. Strawson, P.F. "Freedom and Resentment." *Free Will.* Ed. G. Watson. Oxford: Oxford University Press, 1982. 63–4.

65   Beneficence, Law, and Liberty: The Case of Required Rescue

LIAM MURPHY

INTRODUCTION

English-speaking lawyers continue to be resistant to the idea of positive legal obligation, whether civil or criminal, and in this they differ from lawyers in Continental Europe and Latin America. This is in one way surprising, because English is the language not only of the common law but also of utilitarianism, a normative theory that explains all of morality and political justice in terms of positive obligation—the single positive obligation to benefit people as much as possible. But perhaps it is precisely this greater exposure to utilitarian thought that has made English-speaking lawyers more sensitive to the uncomfortable implications of the legal enforcement of positive duties. The main normative ground offered for the rejection of positive legal duties has been that they constitute excessive interference with individual liberty, and perhaps only those who take seriously the idea of truly extreme positive moral or political duties, such as are implied by utilitarianism, would make this rather dramatic objection. After all, the specific legal duty that has been at the heart of this

debate is a duty to rescue a person in distress when this can be done at little cost or danger, something that most of these same lawyers assume that almost all people would in any case do. If this were the most intrusive duty that came to mind when thinking about positive duties it seems unlikely that great revulsion at the infringement of individual liberty would naturally arise in one's breast. But if much more extensive positive duties come to mind, such as Lord Macaulay's imagined duty to travel across India to provide medical services, then a concern with liberty is easier to understand. It is noteworthy, indeed, that in explaining his rejection of a criminal duty to render assistance for the Indian Penal Code of 1837, Macaulay paid special attention to the fact that Edward Livingston had included such a duty in his 1833 draft penal code for Louisiana. In including such a provision, Livingston was following Bentham.

This negative connection with utilitarianism is partly speculative, and there are of course other aspects of the history and structure of the

From *Georgetown Law Journal* 89 (2000–2001): 605. Reprinted with permission of the publisher. All footnotes have been omitted.

common law that would figure in an explanation of its traditional antagonism to positive duties. But my focus in this article is normative; I concentrate on what has been offered by way of normative defense of the traditional view by judges and legal theorists, and in this connection the influence of utilitarian normative thought is not unlikely to have been important.

The main argument in defense of the traditional view, as I have said, has been that positive legal duties threaten the common law's traditional deference to individual liberty. I will argue that this avowed concern with individual liberty is disingenuous, or at any rate mistaken. Positive duties as such do not raise a significant concern about liberty in particular. What they do raise, for some of us at least, is the potential for serious material cost—serious diminution of our welfare or well-being. This was Macaulay's main objection to a legal duty to rescue, and none of the many defenses of such duties that have followed Macaulay have adequately addressed it.

This is not to say that the common law's aversion to positive legal obligations is justified, but rather to say that the possibility of very costly legal duties presents the most compelling ground for such aversion. As there are no easy solutions to the problem of cost, it is not surprising that we have not managed to improve on Macaulay's discussion.

Insofar as legal theory is concerned with the normative justification of the imposition of civil or criminal liability, it can neither ignore the underlying problem of cost, nor avoid it in an unprincipled way by drawing arbitrary lines. Moreover, it will not be sufficient for legal theory to offer purely practical explanations of why costly positive legal duties would not make sense. A full defense of positive legal duties must ultimately appeal to a fundamental normative principle that is itself plausible; and plausible in general, not just as a criterion for torts and the criminal law, but for all areas of government policy and indeed personal conduct apart from the law as well. For example, it will not do to defend minimal positive criminal duties by way of utilitarian argument, noting that there are good practical utilitarian reasons for keeping the costs of such duties low, without

addressing the problem of the apparently unacceptable levels of sacrifice utilitarianism requires in the realm of personal conduct.

Though legal theory must address the problem of the costs of positive duties as it arises generally in moral and political theory, this does not mean that it must embrace a particular solution to that problem. I will argue that all plausible views on the underlying normative problem converge in supporting the legitimacy of the kind of minimal criminal duty to rescue that is typical in Continental Europe, and is becoming quite popular in the United States. This "overlapping consensus" among plausible normative views is, I argue, sufficient to justify legal duties to rescue.

It may seem that, despite the attention it has received from legal theorists, the issue of legal duties to rescue is in practical terms rather trivial. Most opponents of legal duties to rescue are quick to insist that the person who fails to perform an easy rescue is a "moral monster," but they also note, as I have said, that such monsters are rare. This low level of *need* for a legal duty to rescue is sometimes said to strengthen the case against introducing it. But it could also be thought to show that the whole debate is somewhat pointless, because so little turns on it in practice.

It is a mistake to assume that only those legal questions that promise significant immediate practical payoff are important. A good reason for the traditional common law aversion to legal duties to rescue may also be a good reason to resist positive legal duties of all kinds. The implications of such a conclusion are potentially of enormous practical significance, especially when we move from the issue of the positive duties of individuals to the positive (constitutional) duties of government. One writer has even taken the extreme step of claiming that the general absence of personal liability for failure to rescue is a ground for rejecting the constitutional *legitimacy* of transfer payments and "welfare obligations."

So it is the broader significance of antagonism to positive legal duties that largely justifies our interest in the special case of duties to rescue. Here we have a simple example of a highly contested positive legal duty where the case in favor is clear. We can learn a lot about the idea that positive legal duties are in principle undesirable by focusing on this example. More generally, legal duties to rescue provide an excellent case study for thinking about the appropriate methodology for moral and political argument about what the substantive content of the law should be.

In any case, it is simply not true that the issue of the legal duty to rescue is unimportant in practice. It is thought to be so because people "don't need the law" to incline them to provide emergency assistance where it can be done at low risk. But even if it is right to assume that it is a rare person who lacks the minimal level of benevolence needed to move her to perform an easy rescue, this line of thought ignores the fact that strong contrary inclinations will often be present in such situations. For example, in the well-known Kitty Genovese case, it is asserted that a fear of "getting involved" kept people from calling the police. The point is clearest in the internationally most famous instance of alleged failure to rescue—that of the Princess of Wales and the paparazzi. One does not have to believe that if the photographers had, as it was initially alleged (the charges were later dropped), failed to call for the emergency services when the Princess of Wales was dying in front of them, they would have shown themselves to have been totally devoid of any benevolent impulses. These photographers had an enormous incentive not to waste any time calling for assistance: As they knew very well indeed, photographs of the Princess were worth extraordinary amounts of money.

With the possibility of strong self-interested reasons pushing in the opposite direction, it is clear that an assumption of widespread minimal benevolence does not establish the practical irrelevance of a duty to rescue. Now, of course, it is true that not even France's very stringent criminal duty—which, as all the world must now know, provides for a sanction of up to five years in prison and a fine of around $66,000 (500,000 FF)—can eradicate failures to rescue from French soil. But so too, of course, are legal duties not to murder ineffective in very many cases. The point is not that no one in a jurisdiction imposing a legal duty to rescue will ever fail to perform an easy rescue, but rather that the case for such a duty

does not turn on the prevalence of imaginary moral monsters who are entirely indifferent to human life or who like to see people die just for the fun of it. All too familiar human motivations can rather easily overcome whatever degree of concern for human life we would like to think is distributed among people generally.

I begin my argument by introducing the traditional debate about the duty to rescue and canvassing the structural and doctrinal issues that such duties raise for criminal law in section I.A. and tort law in section I.B. I argue that in the criminal context there is no serious structural problem raised by the enactment of a duty to rescue. Matters are less straightforward in tort law, but the structure of tort doctrine may also be sufficiently flexible to accommodate such a duty. The real problems in this area are therefore normative. I discuss a variety of normative objections to the duty in section II, and argue that the traditional focus on individual liberty is misplaced and misleading. This leaves the problem of setting principled limits to the interference with individual well-being by way of legal institutions. section III explains the scope of this problem for legal theory; section IV argues that any plausible view on the matter will justify the kinds of minimally sanctioned criminal duties that have been enacted in a small number of U.S. states. The desirability of civil liability for failures to rescue, it turns out, is less clear.

I. THE DUTY TO RESCUE AND THE COMMON LAW

In common-law countries, liability for failing to assist a person in immediate peril, even though one could do so at little danger or cost, is exceptional both at tort and at criminal law. Indeed, liability for any kind of omission or failure to act is exceptional. As an initial question, we must examine whether this legal preference for commission over omission—misfeasance over nonfeasance—is made necessary by central structural features of legal doctrine. This section begins by noting the exceptions to the general rule of no liability for omissions in criminal law.

A. Criminal law

1. Commission by Omission

In the celebrated case of *People v. Beardsley*, a man had left for dead a woman, not his wife, whom he had observed taking morphine and camphor tablets before she fell into a coma. The Supreme Court of Michigan overturned his conviction for manslaughter, observing: "The fact that this woman was in his house created no such duty as exists in law and is due from a husband towards his wife…. Such an inference would be very repugnant to our moral sense." After quoting these same sentences, Graham Hughes has this to say:

> To be temperate about such a decision is difficult. In its savage proclamation that the wages of sin is death, it ignores any impulse of charity and compassion. It proclaims a morality which is smug, ignorant, and vindictive. In a civilized society, a man who finds himself with a helplessly ill person who has no other source of aid should be under a duty to summon help, whether the person is his wife, his mistress, a prostitute, or a Chief Justice. The *Beardsley* decision deserves emphatic repudiation by the jurisdiction which was responsible.

The State of Michigan has found it possible to resist Professor Hughes's eloquence these past forty years—*Beardsley* has not been repudiated.

The facts of *Beardsley* raise the issue of crimes of commission by omission. The contrast here is with genuine crimes of omission, discussed in the next section, in which a statute directly imposes a positive duty to act—such as the duty to stop to render assistance when involved in an automobile accident. In a crime of commission by omission, the charge is not that the accused violated an explicit duty to act in a particular way, but that an omission attracts liability for a crime of commission. The doctrinal link that renders an omission sufficient for liability for a crime of commission is the existence of some independent duty to perform the omitted act. The trial court in *Beardsley* erred, however, in holding that the defendant's commonsense moral duty to render assistance was sufficient for these purposes; as the Michigan Supreme Court noted, the independent duty in question must be a legal duty.

This remains the standard account of the doctrine, but as Professor Hall long ago pointed out, it is not terribly informative. Not just any independent legal duty will be sufficient to attract liability for any given offense. Instead, a series of particular legal duties has been recognized by courts as sufficient to trigger liability for a failure to act. Such duties may be found in statute or contract, or they may be entirely creatures of the courts. Thus, one basis for liability for commission by omission is failure to perform some statutory (not necessarily criminal) duty to act. If a person breaches a statutory duty to render assistance at the scene of an accident and the victim dies, this failure to perform the legal duty to assist may be the basis of a prosecution for manslaughter by way of the doctrine of commission by omission. An example of commission by way of failure to perform a contractual duty is a railroad gateman omitting to lower the gate to warn motorists of an approaching train. The range of duties to act that have been judicially recognized—without the involvement of legislatures or any explicit undertaking by the defendant—is wide, but most of them are based on the existence of some special relationship between the defendant and the victim, such as the relationship of husband and wife, parent and child, and others.

The emptiness of the slogan that commission by omission requires an independent legal duty and not just a moral duty should be evident. The duty of husbands to render assistance to wives became an independent legal duty sufficient to ground prosecution for homicide when the courts began to treat it as such sometime in the nineteenth century. As Hughes explains, the slogan:

> is a relic of the principle worked out in the nineteenth-century manslaughter cases that the common-law duty to care for children could be used as a base on which to found a homicide conviction if death ensued through neglect, but that this duty could not be extended into a more general duty to aid those in distress where the status relationship of paternal support was absent.

In its current usage, the slogan simply means that a duty will be deemed merely "moral" when a court finds insufficient grounds for commission by omission liability to attach. This aspect of the jurisprudence of criminal omissions has provided courts with what Hughes calls "a facade behind which to hide the progress of the law." This is unfortunate from Hughes's perspective because, "as often happens with such protective devices, the refusal to acknowledge the reality of the progress has impeded the advance."

Though I share Hughes's perspective, I find more troubling the rather neglected fact that the control of judges over the expansion of liability for commission by omission raises serious problems of legality. Even when the independent positive duty is imposed by statute, its sufficiency for liability for commission by omission is typically a decision for the courts. As Professor Fletcher notes, most discussions of liability for omissions are either, in the pro-liability camp, "concerned about condemning the injustice of not punishing immoral omission," or, in the anti-liability camp, concerned about protecting individual liberty; hardly anyone is concerned about "the issue of legality in letting courts roam freely about our moral sentiments."

I will not dwell on the issue of legality in this article. I raise it here because it is one reason why criminal liability for omissions would be better based on explicit provisions to that effect, rather than by piggybacking on crimes of commission. Repudiation of *Beardsley* should take the form of an explicit statutory provision requiring the positive act of rendering assistance, rather than further extension of liability for commission by omission.

2. Omission

Though provisions criminalizing failure to assist are the norm in Continental Europe and Latin America, in the common-law world they are currently found in only a few U.S. states and Australia's Northern Territory. Rhode Island's provision is exemplary:

> Any person at the scene of an emergency who knows that another person is exposed to, or has suffered, grave physical harm shall, to the extent that he or she can do so without danger or peril to himself or herself or to others, give reasonable assistance to the exposed person. Any person violating the provisions of this section shall be guilty

of a petty misdemeanor and shall be subject to imprisonment for a term not exceeding six (6) months or by a fine of not more than five hundred dollars ($500), or both.

Similar provisions are found in Minnesota and Vermont. Though the Rhode Island "duty to assist" provision appears innocuous enough, it is this kind of minimal duty to render aid that has been at the center of the debate about positive legal duties. Some of the reasons offered for opposition to such duties have been based in features of the structure of Anglo-American criminal law doctrine. I consider those objections here, leaving the normative objections to section II.

That there should be structural–doctrinal objections to duties to rescue is prima facie somewhat puzzling, as such duties are hardly unique in providing for liability for omissions. I have mentioned the ubiquitous duty imposed on motorists that they stop when involved in an accident; equally ubiquitous are duties imposed on parents to provide for the minimal needs of their children and on income earners to file tax returns. In one enlightened common-law country, Australia, all resident citizens have the duty to enroll with the electoral office and to vote in federal, state, and local elections. But despite the familiarity of these types of positive criminal duty, it is undeniable that their existence sits somewhat uncomfortably with some general doctrinal principles of criminal law. As criminal liability for omissions came to the common law slowly and rather recently, this appearance of conflict is perhaps not so surprising after all.

We have already considered the legality problems raised by crimes of commission by omission. Statutory provisions imposing liability for omissions directly obviously raise no such problems. But these provisions do raise concerns, among scholars at least, with respect to at least three other general requirements of the criminal law: the act requirement, causation, and *mens rea*. Furthermore, potential structural concerns arise in situations of multiple victims and multiple potential rescuers.

Criminal liability is said to require a (voluntary) act. What then do we say about omissions? It is not helpful to defend the conceptual propriety of regarding omissions as kinds of acts. It is true that the word "omission" seems out of place in the context of some failures to act, such as my current failure to do some act that has not even crossed my mind; there is thus some plausibility to the view that omissions are a distinct subcategory of nonactions. Nevertheless, the concept of omission is clearly not robust enough in our legal and moral practice to carry much normative weight on its own. Even if we were comfortable thinking of omissions as kinds of acts, they would clearly be very special kinds of acts, and the substantive question would immediately arise whether these special kinds of acts were appropriately criminalized. Conceptual intuitions about what counts as an omission will not be sufficiently reliable to help us. We will need to *define* omissions as nonactions with certain characteristics, and then we will have to evaluate the significance of those characteristics.

The most sensible approach is to interpret the act requirement as aiming not so much at the distinction between doing and not doing, but at the distinction between thought and action. Thus it is the criminalization of thought alone that the act requirement rules out. A crime must consist in either an act or a failure to act. This is the approach of the *Model Penal Code*. Michael Moore takes a slightly different approach, defending a strict interpretation of the act requirement—what is required is indeed an act, in the usual sense of a willed bodily movement. He then treats omissions as exceptions to the act requirement. This reflects Moore's view that punishment for action is the standard case, while punishment for omission is non-standard and requires special justification. Because the difference between Professor Moore's approach and that of the *Model Penal Code* turns on a particular normative view about the proper purpose of criminal law, I postpone further discussion of Moore's view until the next section.

The best way to think about the causation requirement mirrors the best way to think about the act requirement. Thus it is pointless to attempt to defend a philosophical account of causation such that we can say that, for example, my

omitting to save a drowning person caused his death. Causation is an ancient and fascinating philosophical topic, but it is unlikely to be relevant to substantive criminal law. This is fortunate, as the issue is so puzzling, and disagreement about it so persistent, that we would be in poor shape if the substantive question of liability for omissions required prior conclusions on the correct philosophical theory of causation. Luckily, there is no need for lawyers to settle on one particular philosophical understanding of causation; this is evident enough from the vague and avowedly nonmetaphysical notion of proximate causation that is at the heart of the legal causation requirement. At the doctrinal level, indeed, there is no problem with saying that omissions are causes: They are "actual" or but-for causes, and whether they pass the proximate causation test is a question not so much of the theory of causation but of the proper limits of criminal liability—the very substantive question that we are investigating for the case of omissions. If a legal theorist proposes that the limits of criminal liability should be set in part by asking whether the defendant caused the harm according to the correct philosophical—as opposed to legal—theory of causation, then the appropriate response is to examine that philosophical theory of causation and see whether its claimed normative significance is plausible. It should be remembered, however, that if omissions turn out not to be causes, the upshot will not be conservative—the well-established crimes of commission by omission will turn out to be outside the scope of legitimate criminalization.

The only genuine doctrinal puzzle raised by criminal liability for omissions lies with the requirement of *mens rea*. Professor Hughes argues that satisfaction of the *mens rea* requirement for crimes of omission puts pressure on the traditional maxim that "ignorance of the law is no excuse." The maxim, Hughes writes, "ought to have no application in the field of criminal omissions, for the mind of the offender has no relationship to the prescribed conduct if he has no knowledge of the relevant regulation. The strictest liability that makes any sense is a liability for culpable ignorance." Though this seems to overstate the problem, Hughes has identified an important distinction between crimes of commission and crimes of omission with respect to *mens rea*.

Professor Hughes criticizes Glanville Williams for offering this test of the intentionality of an omission: "If the defendant had been asked at any time, while the omission was continuing, 'Are you doing so-and-so?' (which the statute makes it his duty to do), would the true answer based on the facts … be: 'I am not'? If so, the omission is intentional." Hughes points out that although he will say that he is not climbing Mount Everest if asked while at home eating an orange, it does not follow that he is, at the moment asked, intentionally not so climbing. But the problem here raised seems not to be unique to omissions.

I would prefer to cast Hughes's point as follows. To conclude that an action or its omission was intentional we require that the agent was aware that the description made relevant by the criminal provision applied to her action or omission; for a conclusion that the action or its omission was reckless or negligent, we require that the agent knew or ought to have known that it was likely that the relevant description applied to her act or omission. Where the agent performed an action, we can typically apply these tests without inquiring into the state of mind of the agent with respect to the existence of a legal duty. Where the agent omitted to do something, by contrast, we may often be unable to apply these tests without such an inquiry. When I break the window of the house and crawl through the resulting hole, I am aware that the description "breaking and entering" applies to my act even if that phrase isn't literally before my conscious mind. I don't need to know that I have a duty not to break and enter before I know that is what I am doing—as opposed to, say, removing immediate obstacles to my progress in a northerly direction. And if, upon leaving the restaurant, I pick an umbrella from the basket at random, I can be said to consciously disregard a substantial and unjustifiable risk that I am taking someone else's umbrella, and thus said to be reckless with respect to the relevant description, even if I have no knowledge of the prohibition on theft.

With omissions, on the other hand, it is often the case that the only thing that could connect the mind of the agent to the relevant description is her state of mind with regard to the legal duty to perform the omitted act. Hughes gives the example of the pharmacist who does not know about the legal duty to register the sale of poisons. In such a case, Hughes says, "liability should depend upon the culpability of his ignorance." The point here is that whether the pharmacist's failure to register the sale of a poison was reckless or negligent depends entirely on whether the pharmacist knew or ought to have known that there was a good chance that there was a *duty* to register sales. There is simply no other way that the description, "failing to register the sale of a poison," could become linked in the appropriate way to the agent's state of mind. No doubt the pharmacist also failed to dance a jig in celebration of the sale; for "failing to dance a jig" or "failing to register" to be relevant descriptions, something is required to pick them out from the crowd of possibilities. Thus also, if a convicted felon fails to register as required by a city ordinance, while having no inkling of any such regulation or of the likelihood of its existence, it is implausible to say that the failure was intentional or reckless— though it might be arguable that it was negligent on the ground that felons ought to consider the possibility of special regulations governing their movements.

The asymmetry between actions and omissions here is clear, and it is due to the simple fact that at any one time there are so many potentially legally relevant things that I am not doing. But the asymmetry is not as stark as Hughes suggests. Clearly, some omitted actions are sufficiently salient to justify saying that the omission was intentional without any knowledge of the duty to act: If I fail to rescue a child I know to be drowning in front of me, for no reason other than that I cannot be bothered to get out of my chair, it is not at all unnatural to say that I intentionally failed to prevent the drowning. Furthermore, some prohibited *actions* are not of sufficient salience, under the relevant description, to count as intentional absent knowledge of the prohibition. If a city were to pass an ordinance (without debate or advertisement) prohibiting people strolling in the city park from intentionally coming within fifteen feet of the river (for some reason, perhaps having to do with hatching birds, not apparent to the lay person), and a person were to stroll within the proscribed area, the only way that we could resolve whether the person did so with the required *mens rea* would be to inquire whether she was aware of the ordinance—and this remains the case even if, had the person been asked whether she was within fifteen feet of the river, the stroller would have replied that, as it happened, she was.

An inquiry into the agent's state of mind with respect to the existence of the legal duty is typically not necessary to establish *mens rea* when a person has acted in some way, because the descriptions of that act that are likely to be legally relevant will be familiar enough in ordinary life— the issue of knowledge, recklessness, or negligence with respect to the description can be solved without such an inquiry. With certain highly unusual descriptions, however, the inquiry may be necessary. So the problem Hughes discusses, though much more significant in cases of omission, is not unique to them. The moral to draw from his insight is that mistakes of law, in the sense of ignorance of the existence of the legal duty, will negate the required mental state much more commonly in the case of offenses of omission. But we do not need to go further and say that the entire requirement of *mens rea* is inapplicable in the case of omissions.

A final pair of possible structural objections to duty to rescue provisions are more practical than doctrinal; they concern the possibility of situations of multiple victims or multiple potential rescuers. But in fact neither situation is problematic. In the case of multiple victims, a rescuer complying with our exemplary Rhode Island provision would continue to render assistance to as many people as she could, so long as this involved no peril to her and so long as the cost sustained remained reasonable; beyond that, she is acting above and beyond the call of legal duty. Where there are multiple potential rescuers, it is not absurd to think that if none of them does anything to help the victim, each of them could be held criminally liable. It may not be

practical to prosecute all such people, but selective apprehension and prosecution, so long as the selection criterion is legitimate, should raise no greater problem than does selective apprehension and prosecution of speeding motorists. And if one person out of the crowd does act, there is no problem with the liability of the others—the victim no longer needs any help, and so they are no longer under any legal duty. It may be thought that there is a puzzle about who should make the first move in this kind of case, but there is not. Utilitarian wisdom, but also simple common sense, tells us that the person best placed to help (in terms of effectiveness and cost) should be the one. Of course, if the best-placed person does not act, the legal duty does not exonerate the others. What is required is that, taking into account everything that is going on around you (including the behavior of others) you render reasonable assistance if you can. Needless to say, in many cases people lack information about exactly who is best placed to help, who next best, and other factors that would help them decide whether to act. What reasonable people do in such circumstances is react to events as they unfold; one takes the first steps to render assistance, ready to back off if it becomes apparent that there is a superior rescuer at hand.

It could be said that this response to what is essentially a practical objection is speculative. To the contrary, the objection itself ignores a rather long history of experience with legal duties to rescue. The population and the courts of France, to take just one example, have managed to cope with criminal and civil duties to rescue for some fifty years. If the problem of multiple potential rescuers were serious enough to warrant rejection of the duty to rescue, one would expect some supporting evidence to have emerged by now. It is somewhat astonishing to read practical objections such as these that take no account of the existence of a world in which the impossible has come to pass. In any case, such objections also apply to current common-law doctrine. If twenty school teachers all failed to throw a rope to a drowning elementary school pupil at the school rowing regatta, would our courts be unable to find a way to impose liability?

II. LAW AND LIBERTY

A. Millians

Though all agree that the person who fails to effect an easy rescue is a moral monster, there is a good deal of disagreement about why. At the level of moral theory, there should be no room for disagreement: The duty to rescue is a duty of beneficence, a positive duty requiring people to benefit others, even total strangers. Most defenders of legal duties to rescue are anxious to avoid this natural characterization, however. The reason for this will emerge as we begin to consider the normative objections that have been raised against a legal duty to rescue.

All normative objections to a legal duty to rescue depend upon at least one, but sometimes two, kinds of normative premises. One premise of any argument that there is a general reason of political morality to resist legal duties to rescue must be some view about the appropriate aims of the law. More specifically, whether explicitly stated or not, there will be a premise about the positive aims of the particular branch of the law under discussion. The second kind of premise, which may or may not be present in any given argument, is a claim about the negative constraints that apply to the pursuit of the specified aim. Thus, for example, one might hold that the aim of the criminal law is to promote the social good and also accept, as a constraint on legitimate pursuit of that aim by government, a certain set of individual rights.

My aim in this Part is not to critique the various premises of the arguments discussed—that would be too great a task—but rather to show that these premises do not lead to the conclusion that legal duties to rescue are illegitimate or obviously unwise. I will begin with the criminal law, and with a theorist who is gratifyingly explicit about the premises of his arguments.

In *Harm to Others,* the first volume of his four-volume work, *The Moral Limits of the Criminal Law,* Joel Feinberg presents an elaboration and defense of what he sees as the central thrust of John Stuart Mill's essay, *On Liberty.* As a utilitarian, Mill held that the aim of the law was to promote happiness, or well-being. As a constraint on all attempts to promote general well-being by means of coercion—either by the state or by informal social pressure—Mill presented his harm principle, stating that "the only purpose for which power can be rightfully exercised over any member of a civilized community, against his will, is to prevent harm to others." The harm principle was not, for Mill, a departure from utilitarianism, but rather a specification of what utilitarianism, properly understood, implied about interferences with people's liberty.

As H.L.A. Hart emphasizes in his discussion and defense of Mill's position, there are two strands to the harm principle: the rejection of paternalism and the rejection of what Hart calls "legal moralism," which is the view that a legitimate aim of the law is the enforcement of morality for its own sake. Both strands are evident in Mill's sentences immediately following the one just quoted:

> His own good, either physical or moral, is not a sufficient warrant. He cannot rightfully be compelled to do or forbear because it will be better for him to do so, because it will make him happier, because, in the opinions of others, to do so would be wise, or even right.

As Hart points out, the two strands of Mill's position do not stand or fall together; Hart is himself less concerned about resisting paternalism than legal moralism. For us, however, the crucial point is that these are the main two strands of Mill's position and that the use of the word "harm" is not meant to mark out an important distinction between harm and *benefit.* This seems clear enough from the fact that Mill, like Bentham before him, explicitly endorses a legal duty to rescue. Mill states that "in all things which regard the external relations of the individual, he is *de jure* amenable to those whose interests are concerned, and if need be, to society as their protector." He goes on to say that the decision whether to enforce a person's positive responsibility to other persons depends largely on "expediences," and his discussion makes clear his view that the enforcement of duties of beneficence is in general less expedient than the enforcement of negative duties not to cause harm.

It is therefore rather surprising that Feinberg, who is an enthusiastic supporter of a criminal duty of easy rescue, should find it so important to cast the duty to rescue as a duty to prevent harm—*as opposed to* a duty to confer a benefit. The key contrast for Feinberg here is not that between a positive and a negative duty, for he is willing to construe the harm principle as allowing for the enforcement of positive duties to prevent harm rather than just negative duties not to cause harm. Instead, he thinks it important for the legitimacy of a duty to rescue that it be understood as the positive duty to prevent harm rather than the positive duty to confer a benefit.

One of Feinberg's concerns is that if the moral duty to rescue is understood as a duty of beneficence, then rescuees are merely beneficiaries and they cannot be said to have a *right* that the rescuer take action. In this connection he discusses Mill's version of the traditional distinction between perfect and imperfect duties. For Mill, a perfect duty is one that correlates with some particular person's claim, or right. Thus my duty not to kill correlates with each person's right not to be killed. A duty of beneficence, by contrast, is open-ended—on any plausible account, I can fulfill my duty while many people remain unbenefited. These unbenefited people are not wronged by me—I do not violate their rights—for it is in the nature of imperfect duties that I must make some choices between equally worthy beneficiaries. Furthermore, if I fail entirely in my duty and assist no one, I violate no one's rights even though I have acted wrongly. This feature of duties of beneficence does cause some difficulties in the tort context, as we saw. But Feinberg is concerned about it because on his account of the harm principle, harms are violations of rights. On Feinberg's relaxed view of rights, just about any setback to a person's interest can count as a violation of a right, so his insistence that criminal prohibitions are legitimate only when they protect individual rights is clearly not motivated by some sense that rights protect especially important interests. His concern is rather that for each crime there must be an identifiable victim, lest we countenance illiberal "victimless crimes." But this is strange; as Feinberg himself acknowledges, there are many crimes for which there may be no identifiable victim—violation of a criminal pollution prohibition is one obvious example. The phrase "victimless crime" is most naturally understood to refer to crimes condemned as paternalistic, such as sexual conduct between consenting adults or the use of narcotics, but this is not the problem with the duty to rescue.

The more important source of Feinberg's desire to understand a duty to rescue as a duty to prevent harm rather than as a duty to benefit is his apparent concern that the latter understanding opens the door to legitimate legal duties of beneficence beyond the rescue context. This too could seem a strange concern, because it could seem that rescue situations are distinctive enough that commitment to the duty to rescue need imply nothing about what other legal duties of beneficence may be legitimate. However, it is extremely difficult to find a plausible normative basis for distinguishing rescue contexts from other contexts in which one person can benefit another. We can seek to define a rescue situation, or at least offer paradigm examples, but it is very hard to justify treating these situations as distinctive in any normatively relevant way. This issue is discussed in some detail in the next section; I mention it here to show that one apparently easy way out is not available to Feinberg.

If Feinberg is right, then the significance of the issue of legal duties to rescue is much less than many of us, especially opponents of the duty, have supposed. Feinberg wants to present the moral duty to rescue as sui generis. This would mean that we can support its legal enforcement without signing on to the idea that it is in general legitimate to coerce one citizen to benefit another. But opponents of the legal duty to rescue are right on this issue—one cannot support the enforcement of the duty to rescue without admitting the prima facie legitimacy of legally-enforced beneficence generally. As I said in the introduction, it is this wider implication of the legitimacy of legal duties to rescue that largely explains the importance of the topic.

On an ordinary understanding, *A* fails to benefit *B* when *A* could, but does not, perform an action that would make *B* better off. On this ordinary understanding, a failure to rescue is a failure to benefit. Feinberg insists, however, that our ordinary understanding of the verb "to benefit" is ambiguous in an important way. If *A* fails to halt some deterioration in *B*'s well-being and bring *B* back up to *B*'s "normal baseline," then, Feinberg says, this is not really a case of failing to benefit, but rather a case of harming, or at least failing to prevent harm. Genuine—that is, *mere*— benefits are those that "advance another's interest to a point beyond his normal baseline." If someone fails to render a genuine benefit, that person has not harmed or failed to prevent harm, she has merely failed to benefit. The point of all this is to give an account of "mere benefit" that marks off rescue contexts as involving something morally more serious than the mere opportunity for *A* to benefit *B*. The idea is that if *B*'s life was proceeding just fine prior to some sudden turn for the worse, then *A*'s failure to help *B* back to normal life is not a mere failure to benefit, but rather a failure to prevent harm (which is morally much more serious). By contrast, we must assume, where *B* has suffered a slow and steady decline, but is about to die (perhaps of starvation), any benefit from *A* would count as a genuine—that is, mere—benefit; for in that case *B* has no normal baseline to be returned to. The discontinuity that appears in the classic rescue case, and that Feinberg appeals to in his account of failing to prevent harm, is lacking.

Feinberg is of course free to define terms as he likes, but his idea that the failure to aid is morally much less serious in the latter case than in the former strikes me as very implausible. Why are the transient and unexpected crises of the moderately well-off more worthy of our attention than the chronic and predictable dangers faced by a badly-off person—even a badly-off person I may confront with my own eyes? I doubt that Feinberg would be happy to have the point put this way, but this is the position to which his attempt to take the duty to rescue out of the realm of controversy leads.

We can conclude that a duty to rescue is what it appears to be: a duty of beneficence. We can further conclude that this fact should cause a Millian liberal no concern. Legal enforcement of

a duty to rescue is clearly not paternalistic. Nor need it be motivated by a concern to enforce morality for its own sake—the case for a criminal duty to rescue does not rest on legal moralism. To be clear about this point, we must not confuse the fact that a legal duty to rescue would be the enforcement of a moral duty with the legal-moralist claim that the aim of the enforcement of the duty to rescue is to enforce morality. It is obvious enough that most of the criminal law enforces moral duties; the Millian liberal insists that the purpose of this enforcement is to benefit society, not to enforce morality for its own sake.

One might wonder at this point where liberty enters into Mill's liberalism as I (following Hart) have described it. The answer is that for Mill, the value of liberty, or more precisely of "negative liberty" (the absence of coercive interference) lies in its contribution to a person's well-being. Human beings who make their own decisions about how to live, who (as Joseph Raz puts it) make their own lives, can be said to be autonomous. Mill values negative liberty as a contribution to autonomy, which he believes to be a central aspect of people's well-being.

Negative liberty contributes to autonomy just because coercive interference reduces autonomy. The most obvious way in which coercion reduces autonomy is by restricting those basic requirements of an autonomous life which we may refer to collectively as a person's positive freedom—the availability of a full range of options and the ability to make reasonable choices among them. Thus we can say that interference with my negative freedom matters because it reduces my positive freedom, which in turn impairs my autonomy and thus reduces my well-being.

To bring these points to bear on Mill's harm principle, we can see that paternalistic coercion may be said both to reduce my positive freedom and to undermine my autonomy more directly by expressing contempt for my ability to create my own life. As Mill puts it, "He who lets the world, or his own portion of it, choose his plan of life for him, has no need of any other faculty than the ape-like one of imitation." Mill's opposition to legal moralism is also connected to the value of autonomy insofar as autonomy is valued as an aspect of human well-being. As we have said, on Mill's account the purpose of the law is to promote human well-being. Human well-being is not promoted by the enforcement of morality for its own sake, unless acting morally is intrinsically valuable for a person. Mill obviously rejects this view. Most straightforwardly, we can see that coercion contrary to the harm principle is bad because it reduces a person's negative liberty (and thus potentially reduces her autonomy) *while doing nothing to promote the interests of anyone else.* But a duty to rescue can legitimately be enforced precisely for the reason that, though it does diminish the negative liberty of the person coerced, it promotes the interests of others. Of course, if the promotion of the interests of others actually achieved by such a provision were outweighed by the loss in autonomy caused by the interference with negative liberty, such a provision would make no sense for a Millian liberal. But as a legal duty of easy rescue would interfere with liberty only minimally, it is not surprising that Mill felt it unnecessary to defend his support for it.

Given that there is no reason whatsoever for a Millian liberal to question the legitimacy of the legal enforcement of a duty of easy rescue, what is surprising is that so many people, in a Mill-dominated tradition, have thought that such a duty would indeed involve an unacceptable interference with liberty. One plausible explanation, mentioned at the start of this article, is that the utilitarianism of our tradition has alerted many people to the possibility that legal duties of beneficence a good deal more stringent than a duty of easy rescue will also survive the balancing test of liberty lost versus interests of others served. Given that there are many people in any given country who are capable of being benefited to a significant degree, it may turn out that this balancing test is satisfied even when the losses to the people coerced—if not of liberty, then at least of money—are very great. I return to this issue in the next section.

Another important explanation is that our tradition is not just Millian; it is also, to a significant degree, libertarian or "Lockean." And the libertarian understanding of the right to liberty raises entirely different problems for the duty to rescue.

Before turning to that other strand of liberalism, however, we need to discuss the views of a prominent opponent of criminal duties to rescue who, though he disagrees with Mill on the proper aims of the criminal law, is broadly Millian in his understanding of the value of liberty. This will also allow us to investigate a third explanation for the otherwise surprising opposition to legal duties to rescue—many people believe, contrary to what I have asserted, that positive duties in their very nature pose rather significant threats to individual liberty understood in Millian terms.

In his recent book, *Placing Blame*, Michael Moore defends the legal moralist view of the criminal law: The purpose of the criminal law is to enforce morality. He reaches this position by way of his defense of a retributivist theory of punishment. He thus departs radically from Mill's utilitarian account of the proper aim of the criminal law as well as from the broader textbook account of that aim as the prevention of social harm—or, as I would rather put it, the promotion of the social good. But Moore does believe that there are countervailing considerations that should temper the aim of enforcing morality. One important consideration of this kind is the general value of negative liberty.

Moore's idea is not that individuals have a *right* to be free of legal coercion. Moore accepts Ronald Dworkin's argument that any such right, so often overridden by legitimate law as it obviously is, is too weak to be worthy of the name. In so doing, Moore also embraces Dworkin's understanding of the term "right," an understanding that is very different from that of Feinberg mentioned above. Dworkin uses "right" in the stronger and more standard sense of a constraint on what may be done to a person even for the sake of promoting general welfare. Rights in this strong sense thus correlate with negative duties whose moral importance cannot be reduced to a concern with the promotion of human well-being, or indeed even with the minimization of rights violations. As Robert Nozick illustrates, if you have the right not to be assaulted, I am duty bound not to assault you even for the sake of preventing several other assaults to other people. In discussions of rights that follow, I too will have in mind this strong sense of the term.

So Moore accepts that there is no moral right to negative liberty. The conflict between liberty and the aim of the criminal law is rather a conflict between two values; the value of enforcing morality and the value of negative liberty. Moore is thus content to employ the traditional idea of a "presumption of liberty" in this context, which is simply that infringement of negative liberty is always regrettable just because freedom from coercion is always valuable, and so any criminal duty must have enough to be said in favor of it to outweigh the loss of liberty it brings. Freedom from coercion is valuable, according to Moore, because positive liberty—by which he means strictly the range of options available to a person—has intrinsic value. Moore does not go on to defend the value of positive liberty in terms of its contribution to autonomy, but in holding that the value of negative liberty lies in its instrumental contribution to positive liberty, he remains squarely in the Millian tradition.

Moore believes that negative criminal duties will generally have a better chance of overcoming the presumption of liberty than positive duties. This, for Moore, explains and justifies the traditional position on the duty to rescue in common-law countries and the reluctance to embrace positive criminal duties of any kind. There are two mutually enhancing aspects to the argument. First, Moore claims that negative moral duties are generally more important, or weighty, than positive moral duties, and thus the legal moralist case in favor of their criminalization is stronger. Second, he claims that positive duties generally interfere with liberty more than do negative duties.

Neither of these claims seems at all plausible to me. It is a well-known assumption of common-sense morality that it is worse to cause some harm rather than allow it to happen; thus it is worse to drown a baby than to allow it to die. But it does not follow that all negative duties are morally more stringent than all positive duties. The duty not to lie is obviously less stringent than the duty to save a drowning child at low cost, or, indeed, to take care of one's own children, even at high cost.

Responding to this point—mindful especially of the strong positive duties people are commonly taken to have toward their children—Moore suggests that the relevant distinction may be that between agent-relative and agent-neutral duties, the former being more stringent than the latter. This widely-used distinction, originally formulated by Thomas Nagel, can be drawn in various ways. I find the following account congenial: agent-neutral duties give all of us the same aim; agent-relative (or "deontological") duties give different agents different aims. The paradigm agent-neutral duty would be a (positive) duty of beneficence; paradigm agent-relative duties would be the (negative) duties not to violate rights. But some positive duties, such as the duty of a parent to take care of his own children, are also agent-relative. Moore's suggestion is that while the negative–positive distinction roughly marks out the more stringent from the less stringent duties, the distinction between agent-relative and agent-neutral duties does so more accurately.

There are several problems with Moore's shift to the distinction between agent-neutral and agent-relative duties. In the first place, the moral duty to rescue (which, as a duty of beneficence, is an agent-neutral duty) is widely thought by the critics of legal duties to rescue to be very stringent indeed (recall the moral monsters). Second, the shift of focus to the contrast between agent-relative and agent-neutral duties makes it quite clear that the negative–positive distinction in itself carries no weight on the question of the stringency of moral duties. This is an uncomfortable result for a theorist who has put so much weight on the importance of the act requirement in criminal law. Indeed, because the distinction between agent-relative and agent-neutral duties does not track action and inaction, we are left with no account of *why* we should believe the former to be more weighty than the latter—Moore simply asserts that this is the case. Without some account of why we should take this view, legal moralists must rely on case-by-case commonsense intuitions about which particular moral duties are, in fact, more important.

Moore is actually prepared to grant that the positive (and agent-neutral) moral duty to perform an easy rescue is more weighty than some negative (and agent-relative) duties which are nevertheless criminalized. This is not fatal to his position, he believes, because there is always the other aspect to his argument—that concerning the impact on liberty. In discussing Samuel Freeman's claim that there is much greater reason for the legal moralist to criminalize failing to rescue a child than stealing her purse, Moore grants that the moral duty to save may be more important than the moral duty not to steal, yet insists that the "liberty differential is still there." But the claim that "it diminishes liberty less to prohibit theft than it does to require life-saving activities" is preposterous. Recall that for Moore the importance of negative liberty lies in its contribution to positive liberty, or the range of available options for choice. As the opportunity to effect an easy rescue never arises in the vast majority of people's lives, the thought that there is a serious interference with people's opportunities for choice here is so evidently bizarre that it calls for some explanation. One possibility, once again, is that Moore and others who make this claim must have other, more demanding, duties of beneficence in mind—the utilitarian duty always to perform that act which will maximize expected aggregate well-being does indeed appear to be very invasive of positive liberty. Be that as it may, the fact remains that it is not credible to say that the Rhode Island provision constitutes more than a de minimis interference with the liberty of Rhode Islanders.

The claim that a duty not to steal is in general *not* very invasive of liberty is also clearly false. Only well-off people who rarely seriously contemplate the option of theft would ever be tempted to think as much. There is, indeed, an obvious and simple political point to be made about the claim that negative duties as a class interfere with liberty less than positive duties as a class: The richer one is, the more plausible this will seem; the poorer one is, the less plausible it will seem. If we focus our minds on the options of a destitute and uneducated person in the United States, and think of the entire range of negative criminal duties lined up against her, the suggestion that she remains free of significant interference with her liberty,

because, thank goodness, she has no positive duties imposed on her, should strike us as absurd.

It is important to remember that I make these responses to the second aspect of Moore's argument without challenging his view that negative liberty is always valuable because its infringement leaves us with a smaller range of options for choice. Thus, as against two of his critics, I agree with Moore that the value of liberty is not dependent on my desiring the options in question, and agree also that there is value in being able to choose to do things that may be wrong or worthless. Furthermore, though I am inclined to think that positive liberty is nevertheless in some sense *more* valuable the more the relevant options matter (either subjectively or objectively), we can for the sake of argument grant Moore that this is not so. The rejection of the idea that positive duties generally interfere with liberty less than negative duties does not at all depend on disagreement with Moore's conception of liberty; it depends rather on two simple points about the way that different duties impact on a person's opportunities for choice.

To repeat and expand on these points, the first is that the extent to which a positive duty will interfere with liberty—diminish the number of options for choice—depends crucially on the pervasiveness of the duty's application to a person's life. The popular claim that positive duties are terribly detrimental to liberty, and much more so than negative duties, seems to be based on the thought that while a negative duty merely cuts off one option, a positive duty cuts off all options *but* one. But this abstract way of putting the point is very misleading precisely because it focuses on the single moment when the duty must be performed, rather than a person's life as a whole. Life is full of positive duties that hardly interfere at all with our total range of options for choice. A positive duty to take out the garbage once a week is very different from the positive duty to become a garbage collector. Likewise, a duty to perform an easy rescue would reduce most people's opportunity sets not at all; a duty to spend every day standing by the river watching for trouble would of course be very detrimental to liberty, but we shouldn't confuse the two duties.

The second point is the more important of the two, as it reveals in stark form the ideological nature of the traditional aversion to positive duties *as opposed to* negative duties. One of the things that most determines a person's set of possible options is the amount of resources at her disposal. The familiar negative duties prohibiting attacks on person and property are extremely detrimental to the positive liberty of those who lack resources; indeed, the coercive prohibitions of theft and violence are far more restrictive of the liberty of the destitute than any positive legal duty anyone has ever seriously proposed.

The rejection of the claim that negative duties are less detrimental to liberty than positive duties obviously has force beyond the context of Moore's legal moralist theory of the criminal law. It applies to any account of the criminal law that includes, as a constraint on whatever aim the criminal law is taken to have, a concern for the value of negative liberty conceived of as a means to positive liberty.

B. Libertarians

To find some general reason of political morality to oppose positive legal duties, we therefore need to turn from Millian liberalism to the libertarian version of rights-based liberalism that in the English-speaking world derives primarily from standard interpretations of Locke. The central claim of libertarian political theory that touches on our topic is that all persons have a right to negative liberty. Here, freedom from coercion is not understood as a value, much less an instrumental value in the service of positive liberty, but rather, simply, as a natural right. Indeed, many writers in this tradition emphasize that in their view the commitment to negative liberty implies no commitment at all to any form of positive liberty. What makes freedom from interference at the hands of other human beings so important? Why is it prima facie so much worse if I am prohibited from proceeding along a road by rocks that you put there rather than by ones that fell? The idea is simply that a special wrong is done when people coerce other people. Freedom is a right, and rights, in the strong sense of the term

that we are using, are all about constraints on what people can do to one another.

Thus the heart of the libertarian account of law's legitimate content is the constraint that individuals' rights must not be violated by the legal regime—especially not individuals' rights to be free of coercion. Of course, it is obvious to everyone that coercion is, as Hayek says, "unavoidable," for the very reason that coercion or its threat is necessary to prevent coercion. This leads straight to the idea that it is no violation of my right not to be coerced for me to be coerced into not violating someone else's right not to be coerced. But libertarians usually go much further and allow that coercion is legitimate for the sake of protecting the whole range of rights that are generally taken for granted in a market economy—notably a right against all forms of aggression, a right to private property (as somehow identified via principles of acquisition and transfer), contractual rights, and the right to be free of fraud. Thus libertarians believe that coercion, and rights infringement generally, is justified for (and only for) the sake of protecting a certain familiar list of individual rights. When it is recalled that on the account of rights we have been employing, and which is employed by contemporary libertarians, there is no such thing as a positive right to aid, it is not hard to see how libertarians reach the conclusion that "the state may not use its coercive apparatus for the purpose of getting some citizens to aid others."

The most prominent opponent of a tort duty of easy rescue among contemporary legal theorists has been Richard Epstein. In his early writings on the topic, the main thrust of his opposition was that affirmative legal obligations constituted an illegitimate interference with individual liberty—understood along libertarian lines. As such, the rejection of duties of easy rescue came with radical implications. Because one of the rights on the libertarians' standard list is the right to private property, redistributive taxation turns out to be illegitimate because it infringes on the right to private property while protecting no other right. In his book *Takings*, Epstein does not shrink from this conclusion. Nevertheless, Epstein has long believed that there are areas of the law that cannot be made compatible with libertarianism and must instead be subjected to a kind of supplementary utilitarian analysis. Furthermore, in *Takings,* Epstein explicitly rejects Nozick's thoroughgoing libertarianism on the ground that he cannot see how the state can be justified if all forced exchanges are ruled out. Once rights can be infringed for the sake of the general good, however, the cat is out of the bag, and it is not surprising that shortly after the publication of *Takings* Epstein announced that the traditional natural rights view he had been espousing was defensible on utilitarian grounds.

Even though Epstein no longer holds to libertarianism at the foundational level, an inchoate form of the libertarian view would appear to be widespread among opponents of legal duties to rescue and thus it is important to discuss it a little further. One point has already been alluded to: If one argues against legal duties to rescue on libertarian grounds, one had better be prepared to reject as illegitimate whole swathes of familiar legal regulation. A possible way of containing these radical implications would be to tamper with the libertarian's typical list of rights. Many of the most radical implications of the doctrine flow from the supposed absolute moral right to property; if this right were removed from the list, redistributive taxation would come out as legitimate while forced labor and legal duties to rescue would remain illegitimate, for violating the right to negative liberty. Given the difficulties facing accounts of an absolute moral right to private property, and given the overwhelming normative implausibility of the libertarian's traditional opposition to any form of redistribution away from market outcomes, this would seem a promising way to save the core idea of this form of liberalism. However, it is not so easy to deradicalize libertarianism. Under this view, noncontractual positive duties to act will remain illegitimate; the duty to file a tax return will be rejected even if automatic withholding for the sake of redistribution will not. And there are of course all the other noncontractual positive duties we have mentioned along the way—to register for the draft, to "rescue" one's aged parent, among others; all these legal duties will fall along with the duty to rescue. Libertarianism remains

radical so long as it insists that the only permissible ground for coercion is to prevent the coercee from infringing the negative rights of another.

The fact that libertarianism is a radical view does not disprove it, of course; it merely makes clear the high stakes of any libertarian argument against the duty to rescue. Whether libertarianism is a plausible political theory is obviously not an issue we can settle here. What is important to note, however, is that such a discussion would focus on, first, the plausibility of the libertarians' list of rights, and, second, the claim that these rights can justifiably be infringed only in order to prevent the coercee from infringing the rights of others. This description makes it clear that despite libertarian rhetoric, the evaluation of libertarianism has little to do with the question of whether one is in favor of more or less liberty; it has rather to do with a very particular focus on the moral force of certain rights. Whether it is therefore appropriate to call libertarians "rights-fetishists" depends upon your point of view, but it does seem right to say that libertarianism is a misleading label.

To see this more clearly, consider the libertarian slogan that liberty may be limited only for the sake of liberty; this suggests that the whole of political morality can be understood in terms of negative liberty. As Sidgwick characterized the view one hundred years ago (commenting optimistically that it was "now perhaps somewhat antiquated"), "all natural Rights, on this view, may be summed up in the Right to Freedom; so that the complete and universal establishment of this Right would be the complete realization of Justice—the Equality at which Justice is thought to aim being interpreted as Equality of Freedom." The trouble is simply that so much of what the libertarian list of rights protects has nothing to do with freedom—especially not on the negative conception of freedom that libertarians insist is the only conception they mean to employ. The most obvious, and politically most important, illustration of this once again concerns the right to private property. In what sense is the prohibition of theft a case of coercion for the sake of protecting liberty? But the point holds even for the right against aggression, which cannot be equated with the right to be free from coercion. For example, it is not in the least clear why prohibiting *A* from poisoning *B*'s water so as to cause *B* occasional headaches is a case of coercing *A* for the sake of protecting *B*'s liberty; it is not, indeed, even clear why prohibiting *A* from killing *B* is a case of limiting liberty for the sake of liberty. If there is a single conception of freedom animating libertarian political morality at all, it is obviously a strongly moralized conception. The idea must either be that any violation of *B*'s rights is by definition a restriction of *B*'s liberty, or that whenever *A* is prohibited from violating *B*'s rights *A*'s liberty is by definition not thereby restricted. But such definitions are clearly ideological because the resulting notion of freedom bears almost no relation to either negative freedom or any version of positive freedom.

This concludes our survey of the various versions of the claim that duties of easy rescue constitute an excessive degree of interference with liberty. We have found no version of the claim to be plausible. It is true that libertarian political morality, unlike Millian liberalism, does provide *a* reason to reject legal duties to rescue (along with all noncontractual positive duties)—such duties are said to violate our rights. But evaluation of libertarian theories of political morality is, as I have said, beyond our scope. As such theories have implications far beyond the issue of the duty to rescue and yet are also—to my mind at least—deeply implausible, this is not such a great loss to our evaluation of the case against legal duties to rescue. Nevertheless, it must be acknowledged that the discussion that follows will be beside the point for committed and consistent libertarians. What even they must admit, however, is that their opposition to legal duties to rescue is not grounded in a concern with individual liberty.

III. THE (UNAVOIDABLE) PROBLEM OF DEMANDS

In a few pages in his notes to the Indian Penal Code, Macaulay presents in lucid form the most serious problem raised by duties to rescue. The problem has two parts. The first is that it is very difficult to find defensible normative grounds on which to distinguish rescue situations from nonrescue situations. As a descriptive matter, rescue situations are sudden, unexpected emergencies involving severe suffering or threat to life. But Macaulay rightly wondered how, once duties to render aid in such situations are accepted, it could be consistently maintained that the rich have no duty to save beggars in Calcutta from slow but certain death by starvation. The second problem is that in rescue and nonrescue situations alike, there is the potential for enormous loss to the benefactor. This second problem is sometimes referred to, following Macaulay's own words, as the "line-drawing problem." I call it the *problem of demands*. A duty to render aid is, as I have said, a duty of beneficence. The duty of beneficence embraced by utilitarians imposes demands with no limit: We must go on benefiting others until the point where further benefits will burden the donor as much as they will benefit the donee. For even moderately well-off people, compliance with this duty would make for a *radical* change of lifestyle. But if this optimizing duty of beneficence is to be rejected as obviously absurd in virtue of the demands it makes, what more reasonable duty of beneficence should we embrace?

Before expanding on these problems, we need to answer a crucial question. As presented, Macaulay's problems are problems of moral–political theory. What is their relevance to the issue of the legitimacy or desirability of legal duties to rescue? Why do we need to be able to have a complete account of the morality of beneficence before we can conclude that there is no objection to at least the kind of minimal legal duty of beneficence found in Rhode Island?

The first point to make is that even if these two problems of moral theory were irrelevant to legal theory, strictly analogous problems would be relevant. Suppose a legal theorist were to hold that the criminal law aims to promote the social good and that criminal duties such as the Rhode Island provision do this and therefore should be enacted. Such a theorist must still answer this question: Why stop with minimal duties to rescue? Why not enact more demanding legal duties of beneficence as well? It will not do to reply that more demanding duties may or may not be called for, but because they seem to be controversial, we can ignore them. Despite what some defenders of legal duties to rescue say, this problem is not one that can be solved by careful drafting. In the absence of any principled basis for drawing the line of legally required beneficence at a particular point, the legitimacy of any actual rescue provision, no matter how minimal, will remain in doubt, and concerns about later extensions of the legal duty of beneficence will remain.

So at the very least problems analogous to Macaulay's must be dealt with in any principled legal-theoretic defense of legal duties to rescue. But I want to make a stronger claim than that. Legal theory itself must confront Macaulay's two problems *as problems of moral theory*. This claim is significant, because it renders inadequate one possible principled basis for a strict limit on the extent of legally required beneficence. As we will see in section IV, there are very important *practical* reasons why it would most likely not make sense, even for a utilitarian, to support general (that is, not limited to rescue) contexts and highly demanding legal duties of beneficence. Thus, a utilitarian defender of Rhode Island-style duties to rescue could claim to have the very best kind of reason to support the enactment of only minimally demanding and rescue-specific legal duties of beneficence. Minimal duties, focused in particular on emergencies, would do more good than harm, but general and more demanding legal duties of beneficence would do more harm than good. A practical explanation for limiting duties to rescue, however, will not be adequate if a legal theorist must *also* be able to explain why, on her view, people do not face extremely demanding moral duties of beneficence. The practical reasons that recommend only limited legal duties of beneficence do not apply in the moral sphere.

Why does a defense of legal duties of beneficence require a plausible account of moral duties of beneficence as well? First, suppose we take the legal moralist view of the criminal law (for the remainder of this section it will not be necessary to distinguish between the criminal law question and the tort question). On that view, the purpose of the law is to enforce morality, so it is abundantly clear that the question of moral theory is a question for lawmakers as well. I think it fair to assume that Macaulay operated with a legal moralist view of the criminal law. And it was his lack of comfort with the idea of enforcing one particular duty of beneficence while not being able to say why other more stringent duties of beneficence should not, on pain of inconsistency, also be enforced, that led him to exclude the duty to rescue from the code. So any legal moralist who wishes to be able to give a principled defense of legal duties to rescue needs to take Macaulay's problems seriously.

The more important and interesting point, however, is that the theorist who holds that the purpose of the law is to promote the social good must also take Macaulay's problems seriously. Legal theorists working in a normative vein provide, naturally enough, normative arguments about what the content of the law should be. But in reaching their conclusions about the preferred content of certain specific legal rules, they often do not ask whether the fundamental principles to which their arguments appeal are plausible *in general*. In particular, they do not ask whether those fundamental principles, used in some specific context of institutional design, are plausible in other areas of institutional design; nor do they ask whether those principles are plausible as principles for personal conduct. The most obvious example of this phenomenon is found in the frequent avowal of utilitarianism as the correct account of the aim of promoting the social good, and thus the correct principle to guide institutional design, by legal academics who would certainly reject the idea that they must live their lives by the extremely demanding utilitarian criterion of personal conduct.

There is, I believe, no justification for the assumption that principles that govern specific questions of institutional design need not be plausible generally, including at the level of personal conduct. The issue of the connection between norms for institutional design and norms for personal conduct is important and controversial, and I can do no more than briefly set out my own view.

Traditionally, moral and political philosophers believed that the very same fundamental normative principles governed both institutional design and personal conduct. Thus, for example, though classical utilitarians such as Bentham were primarily interested in institutional design, this focus was due more to a belief in this issue's practical importance and to a skepticism about human motivation than to some sense that the principle of utility did not also apply directly to people. The idea that different principles govern on the one hand institutional design (the subject of justice) and on the other hand personal conduct (the subject of morality) is due to Rawls. This dualist view of political morality, as I call it, is a central theme of both *A Theory of Justice* and *Political Liberalism*. But I see no good reason to follow Rawls here, and one very good reason not to. The main problem with dualism emerges when we ask what connects just institutions to actual people. There must be such a connection: Even if different normative principles govern institutional design and personal conduct, some normative principle must nevertheless connect institutions to people—institutions do not get to be just all of their own accord. Rawls posits a "natural duty of justice"—people have a duty to sustain and promote just institutions. This provides the necessary normative link between people and institutions, but it also brings out what I believe to be the deep implausibility of the dualist approach. On this view, the obligations people have with respect to matters of justice are always and only to perfect institutions, even when the *aims* of such institutions could be better promoted in some other way. But I believe we have little interest in institutions for their own sake; we are interested in them primarily for what they can do. If, in a given situation, trying to make institutions more closely correspond to some criterion of justice will achieve less than some direct attempt by people to, say, promote well-being (if that is the criterion for institutional design), then people should pass institutions by. The overwhelming practical importance of institutions in achieving the aims of justice in the typical case should not blind us to the fact that what matters to us, ultimately, is not whether our institutions are just, in the sense that they achieve our aims, but rather simply the extent to which those aims are achieved, however that might be done.

Thus, whatever fundamental normative principles we use to evaluate institutions must also be used to evaluate ourselves. We cannot breezily evaluate legal institutions such as tort law or the criminal law with the utilitarian criterion without thinking about the implications of that criterion in the realm of personal conduct. If the utilitarian criterion is correct, it is correct generally; we do not have some fetishistic attachment to utilitarian institutions and no direct concern with the promotion of human well-being independently of institutional design. Therefore, though there are, as I have said, good utilitarian reasons to limit any legal duty of beneficence to the kind of minimal duty found in Rhode Island, that does not mean that a utilitarian supporter of such provisions can ignore Macaulay's problems. If the only way to justify a legal duty to rescue is by appeal to a fundamental principle that we reject as unacceptably demanding as a principle of personal conduct, the case for the legal duty must fail.

This first reason illustrates why a legal theorist who holds that the aim of the law is the promotion of the social good cannot ignore Macaulay's two problems. It is rather fundamental, and does not turn on any particular commitments of political morality. A second reason why the problems may be unavoidable is more specific and substantive. A theorist who holds that the aim of the law is the promotion of the social good might hold that there is nevertheless an important constraint on the pursuit of that aim: The law cannot promote the social good by requiring people to sustain sacrifice beyond what they are morally required to sacrifice voluntarily. This would be a genuine constraint on the law, so that, if it is accepted, legal duties of beneficence that are more demanding than the duties of beneficence found in the best view of morality would be illegitimate.

Having shown the importance of Macaulay's problems for the issue of legally required beneficence, I return now to setting out those problems in greater detail. The first problem is that of explaining why beneficence should be required in rescue situations but not for the sake of meeting desperate needs that are mundane and chronic.

None of the criteria that one might suggest to mark out rescue cases as generating special and especially stringent obligations of beneficence seems on reflection to carry any weight. In his recent book *Living High and Letting Die*, Peter Unger devotes considerable attention to this issue. He considers nine possible factors that might mark out rescue cases as having special normative significance, and rejects all of them. The force of Unger's discussion comes not just from direct reflection on the plausibility of the various possible criteria, but also from his ability to construct, for each factor, a case that seems to prompt the wrong intuitive response. For example, to those who suppose that physical proximity is what underlies the stronger obligation to help in a rescue case, Unger offers the case of a motorist who, rather than confronting a bleeding victim on the side of the road, hears over his CB radio that a twenty-mile detour will take him to a bleeding victim. Unger notes that people he has asked tend to feel that it would be just as wrong to fail to rescue in both cases. But if a rescue situation is marked out by the factor of proximity, this is the wrong answer.

Unger's eventual conclusion is that in most of the cases where we readily accept a stringent obligation to meet the needs of others, those needs are very conspicuous to the person in question. He further claims that while "our basic moral values" support a stringent duty of beneficence for rescue and nonrescue cases alike, our "futility thinking"—roughly the thought that anything we can do to help will be a mere drop in the ocean—blinds us to this obligation in most cases. In cases like the typical rescue case, however, the needs of the victim are sufficiently conspicuous to us to break the hold of the futility thinking. The upshot of this is that there is nothing morally special about rescue cases; the widespread assumption to the contrary is due entirely to the psychological effect that a dramatic confrontation with a particular person's needs has on our futility thinking.

I find Unger's exhaustive argument against the existence of a distinct normative category comprising rescue cases convincing. At least, we can be confident that there is no simple or obvious

way to mark out a distinct principle of beneficence that concerns rescue situations only.

In any case, even if we could explain the special moral significance of rescue cases (thus disposing of Macaulay's first problem), Macaulay's second problem, the problem of demands, would remain. This problem is most obvious for a general requirement of beneficence (that is, one not limited to rescue contexts), but an open-ended duty to rescue could also generate extreme demands. We can ignore any duty to rescue that requires an agent to sustain expected burdens greater than the expected benefit of her act. But even a duty that requires a person to act so long as the expected benefit is substantially greater than the expected burden to her can yield extreme demands. Thus a boat owner who would not normally take a fifty-fifty risk on her life by going out into the storm would nonetheless be required to do so by such a duty if there is the same chance of rescuing all of the ten people from the capsized yacht.

Rescue situations can also generate extreme demands of other kinds, not just threats to the rescuer's life. Suppose that a group of astronomers plan an observation that must take place at sea at a particular date and time, and spend many hundreds of thousands of dollars in preparation. Just as the astronomers are about to take their readings, they receive a Mayday signal; if they rescue the sailors in distress, the project will come to nothing.

Clearly, an unlimited duty to rescue can generate extreme demands. Nevertheless, even more dramatic demands of beneficence emerge with principles of beneficence that are not restricted to rescue contexts. The utilitarian's optimizing principle of beneficence requires of ordinarily well-off people such enormous sacrifice that it is widely regarded as absurd. There is no need to dwell on the details of the sacrifices that the world's moderately well-off must sustain before further beneficial efforts would do no more good than harm. But one point must be emphasized. It is not plausible to say that the losses that would flow from compliance with the optimizing principle of beneficence are all, or even most importantly, losses in liberty. The problem of demands is simple: Compliance with the optimizing principle of beneficence would have a terrible impact on the agent's resources (including time) and thus on her well-being. It is true that if one were required to give all one's money away, this would greatly reduce one's positive freedom; but we must remember that if positive freedom matters, it matters just because it is an aspect of human well-being. The demands of utilitarianism fall heavily on all aspects of well-being, including the more mundane, but nevertheless central, goods of leisure and pleasure. Thus a claim that utilitarianism must be rejected because it interferes so heavily with freedom in particular must depend on the idea that the most important element of human well-being is the extent of the range of choices for action—either as an intrinsic good, or as a means to autonomy. Because this idea is so controversial, it is misleading to describe the costs to complying agents solely in the lofty language of liberty. The degree to which one makes one's own life surely does matter; but it is not the only thing that matters.

What, then, is to be done? If commitment to a duty to rescue brings with it a commitment to a general moral requirement of beneficence, and if the most straightforward general moral requirement of beneficence is the optimizing requirement of the utilitarians, it would seem that commitment to legal duties to rescue comes at the price of embracing the allegedly absurd demands of that requirement. What is needed, obviously, is an account of a general principle of beneficence that does not impose absurd demands. This, it turns out, is an extremely complicated matter. All I will do here is lay out some possibilities. If one of these approaches to the morality of beneficence is plausible, it may be possible to defend legal duties of beneficence without committing oneself to an implausible personal morality.

The first possibility is to hold tight with the utilitarians' optimizing principle of beneficence, extreme demands and all; with this approach we simply deny that a moral principle making such extreme demands is absurd and must be rejected. This extremist view is not unrepresented among philosophers. A second (and more popular) view

responds to the extreme demands of the *optimizing* principle of beneficence by embracing a *non-optimizing* principle—one that gives out at a certain point when the demands get too great (we can call this a "limited principle of beneficence"). Though natural, this response faces severe problems. In the first place, Macaulay's worry about the basis on which the line is drawn remains. It is hard to come up with criteria for the limit to required beneficence that do not seem simply to track our natural tendency to think that the way we live now cannot be too bad. More fundamentally, it is very hard to know how we are to assess the demands of a moral requirement. What baseline should be used? In particular, how are we take into account the fact that, though I might be worse off if I take some beneficent action than if I do not, I am still very much better off, overall, because of the beneficence of my community that is expressed in the form of social and legal institutions that do me so much good? Once we take into account how much good comes to us from the compliance of other people it is hard to see any moral principle as demanding, in an overall sense, at all.

In the face of these problems, it is worth exploring a third possibility: The problem with the demands of the optimizing principle of beneficence is not that they are extreme, but that they are, in a special way, unfair. For it is characteristic of the optimizing principle that in situations of partial compliance, where not everyone is acting as a good optimizer, those who *are* complying must take up the slack left by the others. Thus, a complying person may have to do more than she otherwise would not just because of natural disasters, for example, but also because others are not doing what they ought to do. This requirement that one shoulder not only one's own share of what should be a collective effort but also the shares of others can be regarded as unfair. If this is right, what we can call a "collective principle of beneficence," according to which people must sustain only that amount of sacrifice they would be required to sustain if everyone were doing their part, becomes attractive.

The collective principle of beneficence faces its own problems, of course. Most simply but also most fundamentally, not everyone agrees that the reason why the demands of the optimizing principle of beneficence are absurd is that they are unfair in situations of partial compliance. Even under full compliance, the optimizing principle can make very high demands, and this can still seem objectionable. At the same time, in some contexts doing one's fair share may not seem to be enough.

I have introduced the three responses to the problem of demands—the hold-tight utilitarian response, the response of the limited principle of beneficence, and the response of the collective principle of beneficence—not to defend one of them over the others, but to lay out our options. Fortunately, when we turn back to the question of the desirability of legal duties to rescue, each of the three moral views yields the same verdict: Rhode Island-style duties to rescue may be desirable but more extensive legal duties of beneficence are very unlikely to be.

IV. AN OVERLAPPING LEGAL CONSENSUS AMONG PLAUSIBLE MORAL VIEWS

A. A Criminal Duty

I favor the solution to Macaulay's problem of demands that is offered by the collective principle of beneficence. But this difficult issue of moral theory does not need to be finally resolved before we can justify some legal duties to rescue. As I have argued, legal theory must address the problem of demands as it emerges in moral theory because the fundamental principles we use to guide institutional design must also be plausible in the realm of personal conduct. Thus if there were no plausible alternative to the utilitarian's optimizing principle of beneficence, defense of Rhode Island's criminal duty to rescue would require the acceptance of that principle's truly radical implications in the personal realm. But there are alternatives to the optimizing principle, and at least one of them, the collective principle, seems to me to be plausible. And both of the two alternatives agree with the utilitarian verdict that legally required beneficence should be restricted to criminal duties to

rescue with strictly limited demands. As luck would have it then, legal theory can to a certain extent side-step Macaulay's problems after all.

It is not hard to see that a general criminal duty of beneficence (one not limited to rescue contexts) would make no sense, even for utilitarians. A general duty of beneficence requires the promotion of overall well-being. It is obvious enough that if the state has this aim, the best way to discharge it is by setting up institutional structures that transfer resources, provide education and health care, and other social services—not by criminally enforcing "a thousand points of light." Of course if the state does *not* promote general well-being, a moral principle of beneficence will require (better-off) *people* to do so. But our question is now not what people should do, morally speaking; our question is whether there should be a legal requirement of general beneficence. On the view that the aim of the criminal law is to promote the social good, the state must obviously take a holistic view of its responsibilities—it should not try to achieve through the criminal law what can be better achieved in other ways. And on the legal moralist view too, if the state can in effect discharge people's responsibilities of beneficence for them via the tax and transfer system or other mechanisms, and indeed do a better job of it than people could themselves, then there is no call for enforcing individuals' duties of beneficence. The general point is that overall well-being is best promoted through the organized and coordinated efforts of well-trained people. This holds true for most emergency situations as well—that is why we have police forces and fire departments. The only kind of situation in which the involvement of the ordinary civilian is indispensable, even under an ideal set of institutions, is one calling for immediate attention by whoever happens to be both aware of the problem and able to act. Often, all that is required in such cases is that the bystander summon trained experts, but because we cannot and do not want to have policemen on every corner, this summoning function is very important indeed.

These considerations suggest that criminal duties of beneficence should, like the Rhode Island provision, be limited to emergency scenes—to situations where action by a particular private citizen will make all the difference. But though emergencies are the only *general type* of case where the involvement of private individuals is indispensable, it is surely true that individuals can do a lot of good in other contexts too, even under ideal institutions. Should not a utilitarian therefore favor a mopping-up legal duty of beneficence—with the defense available that no liability attaches where a given beneficent course of action would not have been necessary if the state had been doing its beneficent job as well as is possible? Such a legal duty does not require people to do what could better be done by the state, but it is objectionable nevertheless for the way in which it would operate in practice. A mopping-up duty would put an inordinate informational burden on individuals, who would constantly need to be assessing whether there is good to be done that could not, ideally, be better done by the state. Restricting the application of the duty to cases in which a person has actual knowledge that some cost-justified benefit can be conveyed would reduce these burdens, but the determination of whether the benefit could, ideally, have been better handled by the state would still be extremely burdensome. And a rule that is costly for each individual to comply with is also costly for the state to administer. These costs of deliberation and investigation, not to mention the costs of people's apprehension about possible failure to fulfill such an obtuse duty, must be taken into account by a utilitarian. In addition, insofar as positive freedom contributes to a person's well-being, we must remember the presumption of liberty: All criminal duties come at the basic cost of curtailing people's range of choices. If these costs are outweighed by the benefits achieved, there is no utilitarian objection to the mopping-up duty. It seems very doubtful, however, that the aggregate costs would be less than the aggregate good such a criminal duty might achieve.

We thus have two considerations that govern the shape of desirable criminal duties of beneficence. Such a duty should apply only to situations where the involvement of individuals is indispensable; and it should specify such situations in advance, rather than requiring people to determine the matter for themselves. The duty to rescue is a criminal duty of beneficence that fits this bill. But is it the only such duty? Granting the need to limit the duty to emergency situations, what is the reason for further limiting it to situations that involve grave suffering or the threat of death? From a utilitarian perspective, there is no magic in the magnitude of the benefit conveyed on each occasion. Whether the legal duty of beneficence should be extended to cover emergency cases involving moderate need, or even to situations where the destruction of valuable property can be prevented, depends only on whether the extra benefits of such an extension outweigh any additional burdens it would bring. It seems to me that this test would not be met because the extension would yield a great benefit only if it applied to a large number of cases. But even if it did apply to a large number of cases, the additional administrative costs and costs to positive liberty would likewise be large. Thus, the net benefits of extending the duty seem likely to be small at best. Any assessment of the benefits and burdens of a particular legal rule is in large part speculative; a sensible rule of thumb would be that the costs of legal regulation should be incurred only where the expected net benefit is substantial. The reason for moderate confidence in the overall net benefits of the duty to rescue is that it has the potential to bring out a very great net improvement in overall well-being in each situation to which it applies.

So far we have seen that practical considerations support limiting legal duties of beneficence to rescue contexts even if we accept the optimizing principle of beneficence. These considerations apply *mutatis mutandis* to our two alternative principles of beneficence. Matters are less straightforward when it comes to the issue of demands. As we saw, rescue cases can give rise to extreme demands even where the expected benefit of the rescue is very great. Should the criminal law require a person to take a fifty-percent chance of losing her life for the sake of a fifty-percent chance of saving twenty? To address this question, we need to take each of our three principles of beneficence in turn. If we take a legal moralist approach to the criminal law or accept the constraint against legally required sacrifice beyond what a person is in any case morally required to sustain, then the upper bound of the legitimate demands of legally required beneficence will lie wherever the relevant moral principle of beneficence puts it.

Let us again start, then, with the implications of the optimizing principle of beneficence. Like most other actual legal duties to render aid, the Rhode Island provision requires only "reasonable" assistance, and specifies that this will never involve danger or peril to the rescuer. As a matter of statutory interpretation, it is not plausible to read this latter limitation such that a rescue attempt is required only if it would involve no risk whatever of physical harm. Even walking to the edge of the dock to toss the life preserver entails *some* risk to my life (I could slip and fall off, hitting my head on the rocks). In any event, a sensible legal duty to rescue will require rescue attempts so long as only a minimal risk of serious harm is involved. This means that the risk that a good swimmer will get a cramp and drown if she swims out into the calm lake to rescue a floundering child would not be sufficient to justify inaction. But an average swimmer (as opposed to an off-duty, professional surf lifeguard) should not be required to head off into rough surf to attempt to rescue someone caught in a rip tide.

From a utilitarian perspective, it is clear enough that people who have no special training, and thus cannot count on any substantial probability of succeeding in a rescue attempt, should not be encouraged, let alone required by the criminal law, to take substantial risks with their own lives. Of course, it may be that a particular boat owner can count on roughly a fifty-percent chance of success, and so, if there are twenty people to be saved, the optimizing principle of beneficence would, as a moral matter, require her to take the chance. The utilitarian legislator's first–best result would be a provision that requires such a person to act without encouraging dangerous rescue attempts by the rest of us. It is not clear, however, that this can be done. A provision could specify that rescue attempts are required so long as "the effort, risk, or cost of acting is disproportionately less than the harm or damage avoided." Whether a particular person is liable for nonrescue would then turn on an investigation of her actual chances of success and (perhaps) her awareness of those

chances. But though courts in tort cases deal routinely with the idea that more can be expected of some people than of others, such an approach seems very unwise in the current context. As noted, it is not for the best to encourage people with no particular skills to take unknown (to them) levels of risk with their own lives; yet, the suggested language would do just that. It would be possible to require particular classes of rescuers to sustain a higher level of risk, but this also seems unnecessary because the relevant classes of people are likely already to be on the job when the opportunity to attempt a rescue arises.

So much for the risk of physical harm. Equally difficult is the issue of all other kinds of loss. The drafters of the Rhode Island provision take the standard approach of not specifying what "reasonable" nonphysical cost might amount to. Is this what utilitarianism recommends? A utilitarian rescuer must weigh the value of the chance of saving a life or preventing or alleviating severe suffering against some very different kind of value, such as a simple loss of money. A utilitarian lawmaker understands that this kind of cost-benefit analysis cannot reliably be done on the spot. Because the criminal law should not encourage wasteful rescue expenditures, the utilitarian lawmaker aims to encourage potential rescuers to attempt a rescue only in those cases where the expected benefit clearly outweighs the expected loss. Because it is doubtful that any useful specific criteria could be extracted from the range of possible cases and written into the law, this aim could not be better served than by asking the trier of fact to determine whether "reasonable" efforts were used. Even if further criteria were available, making the duty more complicated would greatly weaken its educative–expressive role, which may be more important than its role as a deterrent. The presence of such a duty in the criminal law reminds us of our responsibilities toward other people, even total strangers, and the more qualified the duty, the less powerful this message.

Triers of fact can get things badly wrong, and potential rescuers can know this. The loose reasonableness standard, coupled with ex-ante mistrust of triers of fact, could thus seem to encourage rescue efforts that are not cost justified.

This potential problem provides a further reason to limit the duty to rescue to cases of severe suffering or threat to life, because in these cases it is hard for an individual to expend too much in the way of material resources. Moreover, in the criminal context the prosecution's high burden of proof should allow people to be less mistrustful of triers of fact than may be warranted in the civil context.

It is clear that even an ideal trier of fact might decide that a person ought reasonably to permit the ruin of his million dollar yacht in order to rescue some drowning people, and utilitarians would have no grounds for regret. Thus, even if I am right that utilitarianism would recommend a legal duty to make only reasonable efforts, this may still leave us with a legal duty of beneficence that some will find too demanding.

As it happens, there is a utilitarian answer to this problem. Saul Levmore has plausibly argued that the most efficient incentive package for legal duties to rescue combines a (small) sanction for failure to rescue with a small reward for rescuing as required. By a small reward, Levmore means one that does no more than compensate the rescuer for her expenses. Such is the arrangement in France and Germany. The upshot of this result is that even in those cases where reasonable rescue is very costly for the rescuer, an optimal legal regime would reimburse those costs. Most states' crime victims' compensation statutes already provide for compensation for rescuers in the context of violent crimes. And in the noncrime context, existing principles of restitution may already provide for such compensation where the rescue is carried out pursuant to a legal duty such as the Rhode Island provision. If so, providing for compensation would require no further legal innovation—unless it was thought, as seems plausible, that the compensation should flow not from the person rescued, but from the community at large by way of a statutory compensation scheme.

I will not rehearse the details of Levmore's argument about the optimal size of the rescue "carrot"; but we should briefly address the issue of the rescue "stick"—the penalty for violation. On a legal moralist approach, the penalty for violation should depend on our judgment of the severity of the moral wrong done by the person who fails to assist. One of the problems with the commission by omission approach to failure to save a life is that it makes it impossible for the law to be sensitive to the difference between the moral wrongness of killing versus letting die—a commonsense distinction that many moral philosophers take very seriously. A statutory duty to rescue, however, can treat letting die as far less serious than homicide, and existing provisions do just that. The maximum penalty for failure to assist in Vermont is a fine of $100, Rhode Island's maximum of $500 and six months imprisonment is at the high end in the common-law world, and the norm in Europe and Latin America is for a penalty of either a fine or no more than a year's imprisonment.

But we do not have to be retributivists to have a reason to distinguish between the sanctions appropriate for positive harming as opposed to failure to aid. Though the incentives for failing to aid *can* be great, as in the case of the Princess of Wales, it is generally true that the payoff available from doing positive harm will be much greater—simply because one can do harm all on one's own and thus choose to harm where it is most profitable. Similarly, a person motivated by great hatred and anger will rarely be able to satisfy his desire by merely letting harm befall someone. Thus, in a deterrence analysis, the sanction for failing to harm should generally not be as severe as the sanction for harming. Indeed rather minimal sanctions would seem to be adequate, and this is what we observe.

It appears then that if we accept the optimizing principle of beneficence as part of our account of the aim of the criminal law, we will nevertheless restrict criminal duties of beneficence to duties to rescue with minimal demands and minimal sanctions for violation. I have argued, however, that such a principle of beneficence is very implausible in the realm of personal conduct. Thus we must examine whether our two alternative principles of beneficence, the limited principle and the collective principle, also support this kind of minimal legal duty to rescue. Of course neither principle will support a legal duty to rescue that is *more* demanding than the utilitarian duty. What needs to be shown, to satisfy legal moralists and those who embrace a constraint against imposing sacrifice beyond what a person is morally required to make independently of law, is that this minimal legal duty to rescue is not more demanding than is compatible with the collective and limited principles of beneficence.

As a matter of personal morality, the operation of the limited principle and the collective principle in rescue contexts turns out to be a very complicated matter. But the main point is simple: Because rescue contexts are not normatively special, and because under both principles the sacrifice required for the sake of benefiting others is not unlimited, there will be some situations in which these principles will not require a person to perform even a very easy and cheap rescue that is certain to succeed. This may seem to ruin the case for legal duties to rescue; the only principles of beneficence that seem to have a hope of being plausible generally do not in the end support a blanket legal requirement to rescue, no matter how minimal.

Here again the option of compensation makes all the difference. Remembering that more-than-minimal risks of physical harm would not be required, even by a legal duty based on the optimizing principle of beneficence, the provision for compensation of material expenses means that those who comply with the legal duty to rescue sustain no significant net sacrifice at all; the problem of demands is, in the end, sidestepped at the level of institutional design.

Thus plausible principles of beneficence do appear to converge in recommending legal duties to rescue that require minimal risk-taking and that provide for both compensation and a moderate sanction for violation. Needless to say, this conclusion is not irresistible. For one thing, I have not considered the possibility that there are ancillary bad effects of criminal duties to rescue that, together with the costs already discussed, outweigh the good these duties would do. This does not seem to me to be likely, but I will not investigate the issue here. As already noted, I do not pretend to have conclusively established that the benefits of a legal duty to rescue substantially outweigh even the costs so far considered. All these arguments involve speculation; their conclusions can only be regarded as more or less plausible. My main aim has been to uncover the structure of the legal, moral–political, and practical issues that underlie the debate about the duty to rescue and to outline some plausible options available to us. And what I do claim to have shown is that if there is a reason to oppose all criminal duties to rescue, it will not be because such duties are offensive to plausible considerations of political morality. So long as compensation is provided, all plausible principles of beneficence support such duties and no plausible arguments grounded in individual liberty count against them. Rather, it will be because an exhaustive evaluation of the benefits and burdens of criminal duties to rescue leaves us insufficiently confident that such duties yield a clear net benefit. That almost all the countries of Continental Europe and Latin America should be wrong about this practical issue, and the handful of common-law countries right, seems to me prima facie dubious. But it could be so.

CONCLUSION: LAW, MORALITY, AND STATE

Criminal duties to render aid of the kind that are now increasingly popular in the United States face no objection on the ground of their interference with liberty, and moreover may be desirable, all things considered. The problem of finding a plausible moral principle of beneficence must be addressed by defenders of legally required beneficence but it need not be finally solved, because it turns out that all the plausible options would support appropriately limited criminal duties to rescue. The reasons why more extensive legal duties of beneficence are not appropriate on any of the plausible views about the morality of beneficence are practical: State institutions can do a better job of promoting well-being than can individuals in all but emergency contexts, and even in those contexts there are good reasons not to legally require people to sustain a substantial risk of death or injury attempting to aid others.

In conclusion, I would like to make two observations that turn on the fact that the reasons why only strictly constrained legal duties of beneficence are defensible and are, indeed, essentially practical. First, we may have here one of those areas of normative thought where the law misleads us about political morality. The fact that it would be absurd to enact a criminal duty to promote social welfare generally may lead us to conclude, wrongly, that the duties people have in respect of beneficence are minimal or optional, especially outside rescue contexts. This would be a serious mistake. It is true that when we think about what kind of criminal duty of beneficence would make sense we must consider how the state might better promote welfare via some other institutional means: In an ideal society, very little may end up being the responsibility of individuals, especially not on pain of criminal sanction. But it is also true that if the state *fails* to set up the appropriate institutions, then moral requirements of beneficence apply directly to people, regardless of the law. The fact that an ideal state would make it unnecessary for people to be that much concerned, in their daily lives, about social welfare does not mean that we need not be concerned about social well-being in our actual, nonideal situation. And so, as I have said, the fundamental normative principles to which we appeal when trying to describe ideal legal institutions had better be ones we can live with in our actual, nonideal world.

The second observation returns us to the issue of the positive responsibilities of government. If I am right, there is no fundamental objection of political morality to the very idea of positive legal obligations. But notice the difference between the case of people and that of government. In the case of people, we saw that the problem of finding a reasonable moral principle of beneficence did not have to be finally resolved by legal theory because all the candidate principles yielded the same recommendation on the issue of legally required beneficence. When we turn to states, however, the practical reasons for accepting only strictly constrained legal requirements of beneficence disappear. At least, the nature of the practical arguments changes dramatically, and the practical potential for the state to do good is obviously vastly greater than is the case for individuals. Thus, when we are addressing the responsibilities of states, the question of which principle of beneficence we accept as a matter of political morality cannot be avoided. Whether the state's duties of beneficence to its members should be constitutionalized is another matter. But it must not be pretended that the fundamental question of what a decent community must do to promote the well-being of its members need not be reached— either because there is some intrinsic incompatibility between the idea of positive state obligation and the basic values of our legal culture, or because, practically speaking, putting beneficence into the law would never make any sense.

And so we see that acceptance of legal duties to rescue, and thus of *some* requirement of beneficence, does indeed open the can of worms that some commentators have been so keen to keep closed.

CHAPTER NINETEEN

Philosophy and Private Law

66 Of Property from *The Second Treatise of Government*

JOHN LOCKE

§25

Whether we consider natural reason, which tells us, that men, being once born, have a right to their preservation, and consequently to meat and drink, and such other things as nature affords for their subsistence; or revelation, which gives us an account of those grants God made of the world to Adam, and to Noah, and his sons; it is very clear, that God, as king David says, Psal. cvx. 16, "has given the earth to the children of men;" given it to mankind in common. But this being supposed, it seems to some a very great difficulty how any one should ever come to have a property in any thing: I will not content myself to answer, that if it be difficult to make out property, upon a supposition that God gave the world to Adam and his posterity in common, it is impossible that any man, but one universal monarch, should have any property, upon a supposition that God gave the world to Adam, and his heirs in succession, exclusive of all the rest of his posterity. But I shall endeavour to show how men might come to have a property in several parts of that which God gave to mankind in common, and that without any express compact of all the commoners.

§26

God, who hath given the world to men in common, hath also given them reason to make use of it to the best advantage of life and convenience. The earth, and all that is therein, is given to men for the support and comfort of their being. And though all the fruits it naturally produces, and beasts it feeds, belong to mankind in common, as they are produced by the spontaneous hand of nature; and nobody has originally a private dominion, exclusive of the rest of mankind, in any of them, as they are thus in their natural state: yet being given for the use of men, there must of necessity be a means to appropriate them some way or other before they can be of any use, or at all beneficial to any particular man. The fruit, or venison, which nourishes the wild Indian, who knows no enclosure, and is still a tenant in

From The Second Treatise of Civil Government (1690), ch, 5. Available at http://www.constitution.org/jl/2ndtreat.htm.

common, must be his, or so his, *i.e.* a part of him, that another can no longer have any right to it, before it can do him any good for the support of his life.

§27

Though the earth, and all inferior creatures, be common to all men, yet every man has a property in his own person: this nobody has any right to but himself. The labour of his body, and the work of his hands, we may say, are properly his. Whatsoever then he removes out of the state that nature hath provided, and left it in, he hath mixed his labour with, and joined to it something that is his own, and thereby makes it his property. It being by him removed from the common state nature hath placed it in, it hath by this labour something annexed to it that excludes the common right of other men. For this labour being the unquestionable property of the labourer, no man but he can have a right to what that is once joined to, at least where there is enough, and as good, left in common for others.

§28

He that is nourished by the acorns he picked up under an oak, or the apples he gathered from the trees in the wood, has certainly appropriated them to himself. Nobody can deny but the nourishment is his. I ask then, when did they begin to be his? When he digested? or when he ate? or when he boiled? or when he brought them home? or when he picked them up? and it is plain, if the first gathering made them not his, nothing else could. That labour put a distinction between them and common: that added something to them more than nature, the common mother of all, had done; and so they became his private right. And will any one say, he had no right to those acorns or apples he thus appropriated, because he had not the consent of all mankind to make them his? Was it a robbery thus to assume to himself what belonged to all in common? If such a consent as that was necessary, man had starved, notwithstanding the plenty God had given him. We see in commons, which remain so by compact, that it is the taking any part of what is common, and removing it out of

the state nature leaves it in, which begins the property; without which the common is of no use. And the taking of this or that part does not depend on the express consent of all the commoners. Thus the grass my horse has bit; the turfs my servant has cut; and the ore I have digged in any place, where I have a right to them in common with others; become my property, without the assignation of consent of any body. The labour that was mine, removing them out of that common state they were in, hath fixed my property in them.

§29

By making an explicit consent of every commoner necessary to any one's appropriating to himself any part of what is given in common, children or servants could not cut the meat, which their father or master had provided for them in common, without assigning to every one his peculiar part. Though the water running in the fountain be every one's, yet who can doubt but that in the pitcher is his only who drew it out? His labour hath taken it out of the hands of nature, where it was common, and belonged equally to all her children, and hath thereby appropriated it to himself.

§30

Thus this law of reason makes the deer that Indian's who hath killed it; it is allowed to be his goods who hath bestowed his labour upon it, though before it was the common right of every one. And amongst those who are counted the civilized part of mankind, who have made and multiplied positive laws to determine property, this original law of nature, for the beginning of property, in what was before common, still takes place; and by virtue thereof, what fish any one catches in the ocean, that great and still remaining common of mankind; or what ambergris any one takes up here, is by the labour that removes it out of that common state nature left it in made his property who takes that pains about it. And even amongst us, the hare that any one is hunting is thought his who pursues her during the chase: for being a beast that is still looked upon as common, and no man's private possession; whoever has employed so much labour about any of that kind, as to find and pursue her, has thereby removed her from the state of nature, wherein she was common, and hath begun a property.

§31

It will perhaps be objected to this, that "if gathering the acorns, or other fruits of the earth, &c. makes a right to them, then any one may engross as much as he will." To which I answer, Not so. The same law of nature, that does by this means give us property, does also bound that property too. "God has given us all things richly," 1 Tim. vi. 17, is the voice of reason confirmed by inspiration. But how far has he given it us? To enjoy. As much as any one can make use of to any advantage of life before it spoils, so much he may by his labour fix a property in: whatever is beyond this, is more than his share, and belongs to others. Nothing was made by God for man to spoil or destroy. And thus, considering the plenty of natural provisions there was a long time in the world, and the few spenders; and to how small a part of that provision the industry of one man could extend itself, and engross it to the prejudice of others; especially keeping within the bounds, set by reason, of what might serve for his use; there could be then little room for quarrels or contentions about property so established.

§32

But the chief matter of property being now not the fruits of the earth, and the beasts that subsist on it, but the earth itself; as that which takes in, and carries with it all the rest; I think it is plain, that property in that too is acquired as the former. As much land as a man tills, plants, improves, cultivates, and can use the product of, so much is his property. He by his labour does, as it were, enclose it from the common. Nor will it invalidate his right, to say every body else has an equal title to it, and therefore he cannot appropriate, he cannot enclose, without the consent of all his fellow commoners, all mankind. God, when he gave the world in common to all mankind, commanded man also to labour, and the penury of his condition required it of him. God and his reason commanded him to subdue the earth, i.e., improve it

for the benefit of life, and therein lay out something upon it that was his own, his labour. He that, in obedience to this command of God, subdued, tilled, and sowed any part of it, thereby annexed to it something that was his property, which another had no title to, nor could without injury take from him.

§33

Nor was this appropriation of any parcel of land, by improving it, any prejudice to any other man, since there was still enough, and as good left; and more than the yet unprovided could use. So that, in effect, there was never the less left for others because of his enclosure for himself: for he that leaves as much as another can make use of, does as good as take nothing at all. Nobody could think himself injured by the drinking of another man, though he took a good draught, who had a whole river of the same water left him to quench his thirst; and the case of land and water, where there is enough of both, is perfectly the same.

§34

God gave the world to men in common; but since he gave it them for their benefit, and the greatest conveniencies of life they were capable to draw from it, it cannot be supposed he meant it should always remain common and uncultivated. He gave it to the use of the industrious and rational (and labour was to be his title to it), not to the fancy or covetousness of the quarrelsome and contentious. He that had as good left for his improvement as was already taken up, needed not complain, ought not to meddle with what was already improved by another's labour: if he did, it is plain he desired the benefit of another's pains, which he had no right to, and not the ground which God had given him in common with others to labour on, and whereof there was as good left as that already possessed, and more than he knew what to do with, or his industry could reach to.

§35

It is true, in land that is common in England, or any other country, where there is plenty of people under government, who have money and commerce, no one can enclose or appropriate any part without the consent of all his fellow-commoners; because this is left common by compact, i.e., by the law of the land, which is not to be violated. And though it be common, in respect of some men, it is not so to all mankind, but is the joint property of this county, or this parish. Besides, the remainder, after such enclosure, would not be as good to the rest of the commoners as the whole was when they could all make use of the whole; whereas in the beginning and first peopling of the great common of the world it was quite otherwise. The law man was under was rather for appropriating. God commanded, and his wants forced him to labour. That was his property, which could not be taken from him wherever he had fixed it. And hence subduing or cultivating the earth, and having dominion, we see are joined together. The one gave title to the other. So that God, by commanding to subdue, gave authority so far to appropriate: and the condition of human life, which requires labour and materials to work on, necessarily introduces private possessions.

§36

The measure of property nature has well set by the extent of men's labour and the conveniencies of life: no man's labour could subdue, or appropriate all; nor could his enjoyment consume more than a small part; so that it was impossible for any man, this way, to intrench upon the right of another, or acquire to himself a property, to the prejudice of his neighbour, who would still have room for as good and as large a possession (after the other had taken out his) as before it was appropriated. This measure did confine every man's possession to a very moderate proportion, and such as he might appropriate to himself, without injury to any body, in the first ages of the world, when men were more in danger to be lost, by wandering from their company, in the then vast wilderness of the earth, than to be straitened for want of room to plant in. And the same measure may be allowed still without prejudice to any body, as full as the world seems; for supposing a man, or family, in the state they were at first peopling of the world by the children of Adam, or Noah; let him plant in some inland, vacant places of America, we

shall find that the possessions he could make himself, upon the measures we have given, would not be very large, nor, even to this day, prejudice the rest of mankind, or give them reason to complain, or think themselves injured by this man's encroachment; though the race of men have now spread themselves to all the corners of the world, and do infinitely exceed the small number was at the beginning. Nay, the extent of ground is of so little value, without labour, that I have heard it affirmed, that in Spain itself a man may be permitted to plough, sow, and reap, without being disturbed, upon land he has no other title to, but only his making use of it. But, on the contrary, the inhabitants think themselves beholden to him, who, by his industry on neglected, and consequently waste land, has increased the stock of corn, which they wanted. But be this as it will, which I lay no stress on; this I dare boldly affirm, that the same rule of propriety, viz. that every man should have as much as he could make use of, would hold still in the world, without straitening any body; since there is land enough in the world to suffice double the inhabitants, had not the invention of money, and the tacit agreement of men to put a value on it, introduced (by consent) larger possessions, and a right to them; which, how it has done, I shall by and by show more at large.

§37

This is certain, that in the beginning, before the desire of having more than man needed had altered the intrinsic value of things, which depends only on their usefulness to the life of man; or had agreed, that a little piece of yellow metal, which would keep without wasting or decay, should be worth a great piece of flesh, or a whole heap of corn; though men had a right to appropriate, by their labour, each one to himself, as much of the things of nature as he could use: yet this could not be much, nor to the prejudice of others, where the same plenty was still left to those who would use the same industry. To which let me add, that he who appropriates land to himself by his labour, does not lessen, but increase the common stock of mankind: for the provisions serving to the support of human life, produced by one acre of enclosed and cultivated land, are (to speak much within compass) ten times more than those which are yielded by an acre of land of an equal richness lying waste in common. And therefore he that encloses land, and has a greater plenty of the conveniencies of life from ten acres, than he could have from an hundred left to nature, may truly be said to give ninety acres to mankind: for his labour now supplies him with provisions out of ten acres, which were by the product of an hundred lying in common. I have here rated the improved land very low, in making its product but as ten to one, when it is much nearer an hundred to one: for I ask, whether in the wild woods and uncultivated waste of America, left to nature, without any improvement, tillage, or husbandry, a thousand acres yield the needy and wretched inhabitants as many conveniencies of life as ten acres equally fertile land do in Devonshire, where they are well cultivated?

Before the appropriation of land, he who gathered as much of the wild fruit, killed, caught, or tamed as many of the beasts, as he could; he that so employed his pains about any of the spontaneous products of nature, as any way to alter them from the state which nature put them in, by placing any of his labour on them, did thereby acquire a propriety in them: but if they perished, in his possession, without their due use; if the fruits rotted, or the venison putrefied, before he could spend it; he offended against the common law of nature, and was liable to be punished; he invaded his neighbour's share, for he had no right, farther than his use called for any of them, and they might serve to afford him conveniencies of life.

§38

The same measures governed the possession of land too: whatsoever he tilled and reaped, laid up and made use of, before it spoiled, that was his peculiar right; whatsoever he enclosed, and could feed, and make use of, the cattle and product was also his. But if either the grass of his enclosure rotted on the ground, or the fruit of his planting perished without gathering and laying up; this part of the earth, notwithstanding his enclosure, was still to be looked on as waste, and

might be the possession of any other. Thus, at the beginning, Cain might take as much ground as he could till, and make it his own land, and yet leave enough to Abel's sheep to feed on; a few acres would serve for both their possessions. But as families increased, and industry enlarged their stocks, their possessions enlarged with the need of them; but yet it was commonly without any fixed property in the ground they made use of, till they incorporated, settled themselves together, and built cities; and then, by consent, they came in time to set out the bounds of their distinct territories, and agree on limits between them and their neighbours; and by laws within themselves settled the properties of those of the same society: for we see that in that part of the world which was first inhabited, and therefore like to be best peopled, even as low down as Abraham's time, they wandered with their flocks, and their herds, which was their substance, freely up and down; and this Abraham did, in a country where he was a stranger. Whence it is plain, that at least a great part of the land lay in common; that the inhabitants valued it not, nor claimed property in any more than they made use of. But when there was not room enough in the same place for their herds to feed together, they by consent, as Abraham and Lot did, Gen. xiii. 5, separated and enlarged their pasture, where it best liked them. And for the same reason Esau went from his father, and his brother, and planted in Mount Seir, Gen. xxxvi. 6.

§39

And thus, without supposing any private dominion and property in Adam, over all the world, exclusive of all other men, which can no way be proved, nor any one's property be made out from it; but supposing the world given, as it was, to the children of men in common, we see how labour could make men distinct titles to several parcels of it, for their private uses; wherein there could be no doubt of right, no room for quarrel.

§40

Nor is it so strange, as perhaps before consideration it may appear, that the property of labour should be able to overbalance the community of land: for it is labour indeed that put the difference of value on every thing; and let any one consider what the difference is between an acre of land planted with tobacco or sugar, sown with wheat or barley, and an acre of the same land lying in common, without any husbandry upon it, and he will find, that the improvement of labour makes the far greater part of the value. I think it will be but a very modest computation to say, that of the products of the earth useful to the life of man, nine-tenths are the effects of labour: nay, if we will rightly estimate things as they come to our use, and cast up the several expenses about them, what in them is purely owing to nature, and what to labour, we shall find, that in most of them ninety-nine hundredths are wholly to be put on the account of labour.

§41

There cannot be a clearer demonstration of any thing, than several nations of the Americans are of this, who are rich in land, and poor in all the comforts of life; whom nature having furnished as liberally as any other people with the materials of plenty, *i.e.* a fruitful soil, apt to produce in abundance what might serve for food, raiment, and delight; yet, for want of improving it by labour, have not one-hundredth part of the conveniencies we enjoy: and a king of a large and fruitful territory there feeds, lodges, and is clad worse than a day labourer in England.

§42

To make this a little clear, let us but trace some of the ordinary provisions of life, through their several progresses, before they come to our use, and see how much of their value they receive from human industry. Bread, wine, and cloth, are things of daily use, and great plenty; yet notwithstanding, acorns, water, and leaves, or skins, must be our bread, drink, and clothing, did not labour furnish us with these more useful commodities: for whatever bread is more worth than acorns, wine than water, and cloth or silk than leaves, skins, or moss, that is wholly owing to labour and industry; the one of these being the food and raiment which unassisted nature furnishes us with; the other, provisions which our industry and

pains prepare for us; which, how much they exceed the other in value, when any one hath computed, he will then see how much labour makes the far greatest part of the value of things we enjoy in this world: and the ground which produces the materials is scarce to be reckoned in as any, or, at most, but a very small part of it; so little, that even amongst us, land that is left wholly to nature, that hath no improvement of pasturage, tillage, or planting, is called, as indeed it is, waste; and we shall find the benefit of it amount to little more than nothing.

This shows how much numbers of men are to be preferred to largeness of dominions; and that the increase of lands, and the right of employing of them, is the great art of government: and that prince, who shall be so wise and godlike, as by established laws of liberty to secure protection and encouragement to the honest industry of mankind, against the oppression of power and narrowness of party, will quickly be too hard for his neighbours: but this by the by. To return to the argument in hand.

§43

An acre of land, that bears here twenty bushels of wheat, and another in America, which, with the same husbandry, would do the like, are, without doubt, of the same natural intrinsic value: but yet the benefit mankind receives from the one in a year is worth £5. and from the other possibly not worth a penny, if all the profit an Indian received from it were to be valued, and sold here; at least, I may truly say, not one thousandth. It is labour, then, which puts the greatest part of the value upon land, without which it would scarcely be worth any thing: it is to that we owe the greatest part of all its useful products; for all that the straw, bran, bread, of that acre of wheat, is more worth than the product of an acre of as good land, which lies waste, is all the effect of labour: for it is not barely the ploughman's pains, the reaper's and thresher's toil, and the baker's sweat, is to be counted into the bread we eat; the labour of those who broke the oxen, who digged and wrought the iron and stones, who felled and framed the timber employed about the plough, mill, oven, or any other utensils, which are a vast number, requisite to this corn, from its being seed to be sown to its being made bread, must all be charged on the account of labour, and received as an effect of that: nature and the earth furnished only the almost worthless materials, as in themselves. It would be a strange "catalogue of things, that industry provided and made use of, about every loaf of bread," before it came to our use, if we could trace them; iron, wood, leather, bark, timber, stone, bricks, coals, lime, cloth, dyeing, drugs, pitch, tar, masts, ropes, and all the materials, made use of in the ship, that brought any of the commodities used by any of the workmen, to any part of the work: all which it would be almost impossible, at least too long, to reckon up.

§44

From all which it is evident, that though the things of nature are given in common, yet man, by being master of himself, and "proprietor of his own person, and the actions or labour of it, had still in himself the great foundation of property"; and that which made up the greater part of what he applied to the support or comfort of his being, when invention and arts had improved the conveniencies of life, was perfectly his own, and did not belong in common to others.

§45

Thus, labour, in the beginning, gave a right of property wherever any one was pleased to employ it upon what was common, which remained a long while the far greater part, and is yet more than mankind makes use of. Men, at first, for the most part, contented themselves with what unassisted nature offered to their necessities: and though afterwards, in some parts of the world, (where the increase of people and stock, with the use of money, had made land scarce, and so of some value) the several communities settled the bounds of their distinct territories, and by laws within themselves regulated the properties of the private men of their society, and so, by compact and agreement, settled the property which labour and industry began: and the leagues that have been made between several states and kingdoms, either expressly or tacitly disowning all claim and right to the land in the others' possession, have,

by common consent, given up their pretences to their natural common right, which originally they had to those countries, and so have, by positive agreement, settled a property amongst themselves, in distinct parts and parcels of the earth; yet there are still great tracts of ground to be found, which (the inhabitants thereof not having joined with the rest of mankind in the consent of the use of their common money) lie waste, and are more than the people who dwell on it do or can make use of, and so still lie in common; though this can scarce happen amongst that part of mankind that have consented to the use of money.

§46

The greatest part of things really useful to the life of man, and such as the necessity of subsisting made the first commoners of the world look after, as it doth the Americans now, are generally things of short duration; such as, if they are not consumed by use, will decay and perish of themselves: gold, silver, and diamonds, are things that fancy or agreement hath put the value on, more than real use, and the necessary support of life. Now of those good things which nature hath provided in common, every one had a right (as hath been said) to as much as he could use, and property in all that he could effect with his labour; all that his industry could extend to, to alter from the state nature had put it in, was his. He that gathered a hundred bushels of acorns or apples, had thereby a property in them; they were his goods as soon as gathered. He was only to look that he used them before they spoiled, else he took more than his share, and robbed others. And indeed it was a foolish thing, as well as dishonest, to hoard up more than he could make use of. If he gave away a part to any body else, so that it perished not uselessly in his possession, these he also made use of. And if he also bartered away plums, that would have rotted in a week, for nuts that would last good for his eating a whole year, he did no injury; he wasted not the common stock; destroyed no part of the portion of the goods that belonged to others, so long as nothing perished uselessly in his hands. Again, if he would give his nuts for a piece of metal, pleased with its colour; or exchange his sheep for shells, or wool for a sparkling pebble or a diamond, and keep those by him all his life, he invaded not the right of others; he might heap as much of these durable things as he pleased; the exceeding of the bounds of his just property not lying in the largeness of his possession, but the perishing of any thing uselessly in it.

§47

And thus came in the use of money, some lasting thing that men might keep without spoiling, and that by mutual consent men would take in exchange for the truly useful, but perishable supports of life.

§48

And as different degrees of industry were apt to give men possessions in different proportions, so this invention of money gave them the opportunity to continue and enlarge them: for supposing an island, separate from all possible commerce with the rest of the world, wherein there were but an hundred families, but there were sheep, horses, and cows, with other useful animals, wholesome fruits, and land enough for corn for a hundred thousand times as many, but nothing in the island, either because of its commonness, or perishableness, fit to supply the place of money; what reason could any one have there to enlarge his possessions beyond the use of his family and a plentiful supply to its consumption, either in what their own industry produced, or they could barter for like perishable, useful commodities with others? Where there is not something, both lasting and scarce, and so valuable, to be hoarded up, there men will not be apt to enlarge their possessions of land, were it ever so rich, ever so free for them to take: for I ask, what would a man value ten thousand, or an hundred thousand acres of excellent land, ready cultivated, and well stocked too with cattle, in the middle of the inland parts of America, where he had no hopes of commerce with other parts of the world, to draw money to him by the sale of the product? It would not be worth the enclosing, and we should see him give up again to the wild common of nature, whatever was more than would supply the conveniencies of life to be had there for him and his family.

§49

Thus in the beginning all the world was America, and more so than that is now; for no such thing as money was any where known. Find out something that hath the use and value of money amongst his neighbours, you shall see the same man will begin presently to enlarge his possessions.

§50

But since gold and silver, being little useful to the life of man in proportion to food, raiment, and carriage, has its value only from the consent of men, whereof labour yet makes, in great part, the measure; it is plain, that men have agreed to a disproportionate and unequal possession of the earth; they having, by a tacit and voluntary consent, found out a way how a man may fairly possess more land than he himself can use the product of, by receiving, in exchange for the overplus, gold and silver, which may be hoarded up without injury to any one; these metals not spoiling or decaying in the hands of the possessor. This partage of things in an inequality of private possessions, men have made practicable out of the bounds of society, and without compact; only by putting a value on gold and silver, and tacitly agreeing in the use of money: for in governments, the laws regulate the right of property, and the possession of land is determined by positive constitutions.

§51

And thus, I think, it is very easy to conceive, "how labour could at first begin a title of property" in the common things of nature, and how the spending it upon our uses bounded it. So that there could then be no reason of quarrelling about title, nor any doubt about the largeness of possession it gave. Right and conveniency went together; for as a man had a right to all he could employ his labour upon, so he had no temptation to labour for more than he could make use of. This left no room for controversy about the title, nor for encroachment on the right of others; what portion a man carved to himself was easily seen: and it was useless, as well as dishonest, to carve himself too much, or take more than he needed.

67 Of the Origin of Justice and Property from *A Treatise of Human Nature*

DAVID HUME

We now proceed to examine two questions, viz. *concerning the manner, in which the rules of justice are establish'd by the artifice of men; and concerning the reasons, which determine us to attribute to the observance or neglect of these rules a moral beauty and deformity.* These questions will appear afterwards to be distinct. We shall begin with the former.

Of all the animals with which this globe is peopled, there is none towards whom nature seems, at first sight, to have exercis'd more cruelty than towards man, in the numberless wants and necessities with which she has loaded him, and in the slender means which she affords to the relieving these necessities. In other creatures these two particulars generally compensate each other. If we consider the lion as a voracious and carnivorous animal, we shall easily discover him to be very necessitous; but if we turn our eye to his make and temper, his agility, his courage, his arms, and his force, we shall find that his advantages hold proportion with his wants. The sheep and ox are depriv'd of all these advantages; but their appetites are moderate, and their food is of easy purchase. In man alone, this unnatural conjunction of infirmity, and of necessity, may be observ'd in its greatest perfection. Not only the food, which is requir'd for his sustenance, flies his search and approach, or at least requires his labour to be produc'd, but he must be possess'd of cloaths and lodging, to defend him against the injuries of the weather; tho' to consider him only in himself, he is provided neither with arms, nor force, nor other natural abilities, which are in any degree answerable to so many necessities.

'Tis by society alone he is able to supply his defects, and raise himself up to an equality with his fellow-creatures, and even acquire a superiority above them. By society all his infirmities are compensated; and tho' in that situation his wants multiply every moment upon him, yet his abilities are still more augmented, and leave him in every respect more satisfied and happy, than 'tis possible for him, in his savage and solitary condition, ever to become. When every individual person labours apart, and only for himself, his force is too small to execute any considerable work; his labour being employ'd in supplying all his different necessities, he never attains a perfection in any particular art; and as his force and success are not at all times equal, the least failure in either of these particulars must be attended with inevitable ruin and misery. Society provides a remedy for these *three* inconveniencies. By the conjunction of forces, our power is augmented: By the partition of employments, our ability encreases: And by mutual succour we are less expos'd to fortune and accidents. 'Tis by this additional *force, ability,* and *security,* that society becomes advantageous.

But in order to form society, 'tis requisite not only that it be advantageous, but also that men be sensible of its advantages; and 'tis impossible, in their wild uncultivated state, that by study and reflexion alone, they should ever be able to attain this knowledge. Most fortunately, therefore, there is conjoin'd to those necessities, whose remedies are remote and obscure, another necessity, which having a present and more obvious remedy, may justly be regarded as the first and original principle of human society. This necessity is no other than that natural appetite betwixt the sexes, which unites them together, and preserves their union, till a new tye takes place in their concern for their common offspring. This new concern becomes also a principle of union betwixt the parents and offspring, and forms a more numerous society; where

From *A Treatise of Human Nature* [1739], Bk. III, Pt. ii, sec. 2. 2nd ed., ed. L. A. Selby-Bigge. Available at http://oll.libertyfund.org/title/342. Footnotes have been omitted.

the parents govern by the advantage of their superior strength and wisdom, and at the same time are restrain'd in the exercise of their authority by that natural affection, which they bear their children. In a little time, custom and habit operating on the tender minds of the children, makes them sensible of the advantages, which they may reap from society, as well as fashions them by degrees for it, by rubbing off those rough corners and untoward affections, which prevent their coalition.

For it must be confest, that however the circumstances of human nature may render an union necessary, and however those passions of lust and natural affection may seem to render it unavoidable; yet there are other particulars in our *natural temper,* and in our *outward circumstances,* which are very incommodious, and are even contrary to the requisite conjunction. Among the former, we may justly esteem our *selfishness* to be the most considerable. I am sensible, that, generally speaking, the representations of this quality have been carried much too far; and that the descriptions, which certain philosophers delight so much to form of mankind in this particular, are as wide of nature as any accounts of monsters, which we meet with in fables and romances. So far from thinking, that men have no affection for any thing beyond themselves, I am of opinion, that tho' it be rare to meet with one, who loves any single person better than himself; yet 'tis as rare to meet with one, in whom all the kind affections, taken together, do not over-balance all the selfish. Consult common experience: Do you not see, that tho' the whole expence of the family be generally under the direction of the master of it, yet there are few that do not bestow the largest part of their fortunes on the pleasures of their wives, and the education of their children, reserving the smallest portion for their own proper use and entertainment. This is what we may observe concerning such as have those endearing ties; and may presume, that the case would be the same with others, were they plac'd in a like situation.

But tho' this generosity must be acknowledg'd to the honour of human nature, we may at the same time remark, that so noble an affection, instead of fitting men for large societies, is almost as contrary to them, as the most narrow selfishness. For while each person loves himself better than any other single person, and in his love to others bears the greatest affection to his relations and acquaintance, this must necessarily produce an opposition of passions, and a consequent opposition of actions; which cannot but be dangerous to the new-establish'd union.

'Tis however worth while to remark, that this contrariety of passions wou'd be attended with but small danger, did it not concur with a peculiarity in our *outward circumstances,* which affords it an opportunity of exerting itself. There are three different species of goods, which we are possess'd of; the internal satisfaction of our mind, the external advantages of our body, and the enjoyment of such possessions as we have acquir'd by our industry and good fortune. We are perfectly secure in the enjoyment of the first. The second may be ravish'd from us, but can be of no advantage to him who deprives us of them. The last only are both expos'd to the violence of others, and may be transferr'd without suffering any loss or alteration; while at the same time, there is not a sufficient quantity of them to supply every one's desires and necessities. As the improvement, therefore, of these goods is the chief advantage of society, so the *instability* of their possession, along with their *scarcity,* is the chief impediment.

In vain shou'd we expect to find, in *uncultivated nature,* a remedy to this inconvenience; or hope for any inartificial principle of the human mind, which might controul those partial affections, and make us overcome the temptations arising from our circumstances. The idea of justice can never serve to this purpose, or be taken for a natural principle, capable of inspiring men with an equitable conduct towards each other. That virtue, as it is now understood, wou'd never have been dream'd of among rude and savage men. For the notion of injury or injustice implies an immorality or vice committed against some other person: And as every immorality is deriv'd from some defect or unsoundness of the passions, and as this defect must be judg'd of, in a great measure, from the ordinary course of nature in the constitution of the mind; 'twill be easy to know, whether we be guilty of any immorality, with regard to others, by considering the natural, and usual force of those several affections, which are directed towards them. Now it appears, that in the original frame of our mind, our strongest attention is confin'd to ourselves; our next is extended to our relations and acquaintance; and 'tis only the weakest which reaches to strangers and indifferent persons. This partiality, then, and unequal affection, must not only have an influence on our behaviour and conduct in society, but even on our ideas of vice and virtue; so as to make us regard any remarkable transgression of such a degree of partiality, either by too great an enlargement, or contraction of the affections, as vicious and immoral. This we may observe in our common judgments concerning actions, where we blame a person, who either centers all his affections in his family, or is so regardless of them, as, in any opposition of interest, to give the preference to a stranger, or mere chance acquaintance. From all which it follows, that our natural uncultivated ideas of morality, instead of providing a remedy for the partiality of our affections, do rather conform themselves to that partiality, and give it an additional force and influence.

The remedy, then, is not deriv'd from nature, but from *artifice;* or more properly speaking, nature provides a remedy in the judgment and understanding, for what is irregular and incommodious in the affections. For when men, from their early education in society, have become sensible of the infinite advantages that result from it, and have besides acquir'd a new affection to company and conversation; and when they have observ'd, that the principal disturbance in society arises from those goods, which we call external, and from their looseness and easy transition from one person to another; they must seek for a remedy, by putting these goods, as far as possible, on the same footing with the fix'd and constant advantages of the mind and body. This can be done after no other manner, than by a convention enter'd into by all the members of the society to bestow stability on the possession of those external goods, and leave every one in the peaceable enjoyment of what he may acquire by his fortune and industry. By this means, every one knows what he may safely possess; and the passions are

restrain'd in their partial and contradictory motions. Nor is such a restraint contrary to these passions; for if so, it cou'd never be enter'd into, nor maintain'd; but it is only contrary to their heedless and impetuous movement. Instead of departing from our own interest, or from that of our nearest friends, by abstaining from the possessions of others, we cannot better consult both these interests, than by such a convention; because it is by that means we maintain society, which is so necessary to their well-being and subsistence, as well as to our own.

This convention is not of the nature of a *promise:* For even promises themselves, as we shall see afterwards, arise from human conventions. It is only a general sense of common interest; which sense all the members of the society express to one another, and which induces them to regulate their conduct by certain rules. I observe, that it will be for my interest to leave another in the possession of his goods, *provided* he will act in the same manner with regard to me. He is sensible of a like interest in the regulation of his conduct. When this common sense of interest is mutually express'd, and is known to both, it produces a suitable resolution and behaviour. And this may properly enough be call'd a convention or agreement betwixt us, tho' without the interposition of a promise; since the actions of each of us have a reference to those of the other, and are perform'd upon the supposition, that something is to be perform'd on the other part. Two men, who pull the oars of a boat, do it by an agreement or convention, tho' they have never given promises to each other. Nor is the rule concerning the stability of possession the less deriv'd from human conventions, that it arises gradually, and acquires force by a slow progression, and by our repeated experience of the inconveniences of transgressing it. On the contrary, this experience assures us still more, that the sense of interest has become common to all our fellows, and gives us a confidence of the future regularity of their conduct: And tis only on the expectation of this, that our moderation and abstinence are founded. In like manner are languages gradually establish'd by human conventions without any promise. In like manner do gold and silver become the common measures of exchange, and are esteem'd sufficient payment for what is of a hundred times their value.

After this convention, concerning abstinence from the possessions of others, is enter'd into, and every one has acquir'd a stability in his possessions, there immediately arise the ideas of justice and injustice; as also those of *property, right,* and *obligation.* The latter are altogether unintelligible without first understanding the former. Our property is nothing but those goods, whose constant possession is establish'd by the laws of society; that is, by the laws of justice. Those, therefore, who make use of the word *property,* or *right,* or *obligation,* before they have explain'd the origin of justice, or even make use of it in that explication, are guilty of a very gross fallacy, and can never reason upon any solid foundation. A man's property is some object related to him: This relation is not natural, but moral, and founded on justice. 'Tis very preposterous, therefore, to imagine, that we can have any idea of property, without fully comprehending the nature of justice, and shewing its origin in the artifice and contrivance of men. The origin of justice explains that of property. The same artifice gives rise to both. As our first and most natural sentiment of morals is founded on the nature of our passions, and gives the preference to ourselves and friends, above strangers; 'tis impossible there can be naturally any such thing as a fix'd right or property, while the opposite passions of men impel them in contrary directions, and are not restrain'd by any convention or agreement.

No one can doubt, that the convention for the distinction of property, and for the stability of possession, is of all circumstances the most necessary to the establishment of human society, and that after the agreement for the fixing and observing of this rule, there remains little or nothing to be done towards settling a perfect harmony and concord. All the other passions, beside this of interest, are either easily restrain'd, or are not of such pernicious consequence, when indulg'd. *Vanity* is rather to be esteem'd a social passion, and a bond of union among men. *Pity* and *love* are to be consider'd in the same light. And so too *envy* and *revenge,* tho' pernicious, they operate only by intervals, and are directed against

particular persons, whom we consider as our superiors or enemies. This avidity alone, of acquiring goods and possessions for ourselves and our nearest friends, is insatiable, perpetual, universal, and directly destructive of society. There scarce is any one, who is not actuated by it; and there is no one, who has not reason to fear from it, when it acts without any restraint, and gives way to its first and most natural movements. So that upon the whole, we are to esteem the difficulties in the establishment of society, to be greater or less, according to those we encounter in regulating and restraining this passion.

'Tis certain, that no affection of the human mind has both a sufficient force, and a proper direction to counter-balance the love of gain, and render men fit members of society, by making them abstain from the possessions of others. Benevolence to strangers is too weak for this purpose; and as to the other passions, they rather inflame this avidity, when we observe, that the larger our possessions are, the more ability we have of gratifying all our appetites. There is no passion, therefore, capable of controlling the interested affection, but the very affection itself, by an alteration of its direction. Now this alteration must necessarily take place upon the least reflection; since 'tis evident, that the passion is much better satisfy'd by its restraint, than by its liberty, and that by preserving society, we make much greater advances in the acquiring possessions, than by running into the solitary and forlorn condition, which must follow upon violence and an universal licence. The question, therefore, concerning the wickedness or goodness of human nature, enters not in the least into that other question concerning the origin of society; nor is there any thing to be consider'd but the degrees of men's sagacity or folly. For whether the passion of self-interest be esteemed vicious or virtuous, 'tis all a case; since itself alone restrains it: So that if it be virtuous, men become social by their virtue; if vicious, their vice has the same effect.

Now as 'tis by establishing the rule for the stability of possession, that this passion restrains itself; if that rule be very abstruse, and of difficult invention; society must be esteem'd, in a manner, accidental, and the effect of many ages. But if it be found, that nothing can be more simple and obvious than that rule; that every parent, in order to preserve peace among his children, must establish it; and that these first rudiments of justice must every day be improv'd, as the society enlarges: If all this appear evident, as it certainly must, we may conclude, that 'tis utterly impossible for men to remain any considerable time, in that savage condition, which precedes society; but that his very first state and situation may justly be esteem'd social. This, however, hinders not, but that philosophers may, if they please, extend their reasoning to the suppos'd *state of nature;* provided they allow it to be a mere philosophical fiction, which never had, and never cou'd have any reality. Human nature being compos'd of two principal parts, which are requisite in all its actions, the affections and understanding; 'tis certain, that the blind motions of the former, without the direction of the latter, incapacitate men for society: And it may be allow'd us to consider separately the effects, that result from the separate operations of these two component parts of the mind. The same liberty may be permitted to moral, which is allow'd to natural philosophers; and 'tis very usual with the latter to consider any motion as compounded and consisting of two parts separate from each other, tho' at the same time they acknowledge it to be in itself uncompounded and inseparable.

This *state of nature,* therefore, is to be regarded as a mere fiction, not unlike that of the *golden age,* which poets have invented; only with this difference, that the former is describ'd as full of war, violence and injustice; whereas the latter is painted out to us, as the most charming and most peaceable condition, that can possibly be imagin'd. The seasons, in that first age of nature, were so temperate, if we may believe the poets, that there was no necessity for men to provide themselves with cloaths and houses as a security against the violence of heat and cold. The rivers flow'd with wine and milk: The oaks yielded honey; and nature spontaneously produc'd her greatest delicacies. Nor were these the chief advantages of that happy age. The storms and tempests were not alone remov'd from nature; but those more furious tempests were unknown to human breasts, which now cause such uproar,

and engender such confusion. Avarice, ambition, cruelty, selfishness, were never heard of: Cordial affection, compassion, sympathy, were the only movements, with which the human mind was yet acquainted. Even the distinction of *mine* and *thine* was banish'd from that happy race of mortals, and carry'd with them the very notions of property and obligation, justice and injustice.

This, no doubt, is to be regarded as an idle fiction; but yet deserves our attention, because nothing can more evidently shew the origin of those virtues, which are the subjects of our present enquiry. I have already observ'd, that justice takes its rise from human conventions; and that these are intended as a remedy to some inconveniences, which proceed from the concurrence of certain *qualities* of the human mind with the *situation* of external objects. The qualities of the mind are *selfishness* and *limited generosity:* And the situation of external objects is their *easy change,* join'd to their *scarcity* in comparison of the wants and desires of men. But however philosophers may have been bewilder'd in those speculations, poets have been guided more infallibly, by a certain taste or common instinct, which in most kinds of reasoning goes farther than any of that art and philosophy, with which we have been yet acquainted. They easily perceiv'd, if every man had a tender regard for another, or if nature supplied abundantly all our wants and desires, that the jealousy of interest, which justice supposes, could no longer have place; nor would there be any occasion for those distinctions and limits of property and possession, which at present are in use among mankind. Encrease to a sufficient degree the benevolence of men, or the bounty of nature, and you render justice useless, by supplying its place with much nobler virtues, and more valuable blessings. The selfishness of men is animated by the few possessions we have, in proportion to our wants; and 'tis to restrain this selfishness, that men have been oblig'd to separate themselves from the community, and to distinguish betwixt their own goods and those of others.

Nor need we have recourse to the fictions of poets to learn this; but beside the reason of the thing, may discover the same truth by common experience and observation. 'Tis easy to remark, that a cordial affection renders all things common among friends; and that married people in particular mutually lose their property, and are unacquainted with the *mine* and *thine,* which are so necessary, and yet cause such disturbance in human society. The same effect arises from any alteration in the circumstances of mankind; as when there is such a plenty of any thing as satisfies all the desires of men: In which case the distinction of property is entirely lost, and every thing remains in common. This we may observe with regard to air and water, tho' the most valuable of all external objects; and may easily conclude, that if men were supplied with every thing in the same abundance, or if *every one* had the same affection and tender regard for *every one* as for himself; justice and injustice would be equally unknown among mankind.

Here then is a proposition, which, I think, may be regarded as certain, *that 'tis only from the selfishness and confin'd generosity of men, along with the scanty provision nature has made for his wants, that justice derives its origin.* If we look backward we shall find, that this proposition bestows an additional force on some of those observations, which we have already made on this subject.

First, we may conclude from it, that a regard to public interest, or a strong extensive benevolence, is not our first and original motive for the observation of the rules of justice; since 'tis allow'd, that if men were endow'd with such a benevolence, these rules would never have been dreamt of.

Secondly, we may conclude from the same principle, that the sense of justice is not founded on reason, or on the discovery of certain connexions and relations of ideas, which are eternal, immutable, and universally obligatory. For since it is confest, that such an alteration as that above-mention'd, in the temper and circumstances of mankind, wou'd entirely alter our duties and obligations, 'tis necessary upon the common system, *that the sense of virtue is deriv'd from reason,* to shew the change which this must produce in the relations and ideas. But 'tis evident, that the only cause, why the extensive generosity of man, and the perfect abundance of every thing, wou'd

destroy the very idea of justice, is because they render it useless; and that, on the other hand, his confin'd benevolence, and his necessitous condition, give rise to that virtue, only by making it requisite to the publick interest, and to that of every individual. 'Twas therefore a concern for our own, and the publick interest, which made us establish the laws of justice; and nothing can be more certain, than that it is not any relation of ideas, which gives us this concern, but our impressions and sentiments, without which every thing in nature is perfectly indifferent to us, and can never in the least affect us. The sense of justice, therefore, is not founded on our ideas, but on our impressions.

Thirdly, we may farther confirm the foregoing proposition, *that those impressions, which give rise to this sense of justice, are not natural to the mind of man, but arise from artifice and human conventions.* For since any considerable alteration of temper and circumstances destroys equally justice and injustice; and since such an alteration has an effect only by changing our own and the publick interest; it follows, that the first establishment of the rules of justice depends on these different interests. But if men pursu'd the publick interest naturally, and with a hearty affection, they wou'd never have dream'd of restraining each other by these rules; and if they pursu'd their own interest, without any precaution, they wou'd run headlong into every kind of injustice and violence. These rules, therefore, are artificial, and seek their end in an oblique and indirect manner; nor is the interest, which gives rise to them, of a kind that cou'd be pursu'd by the natural and inartificial passions of men.

To make this more evident, consider, that tho' the rules of justice are establish'd merely by interest, their connexion with interest is somewhat singular, and is different from what may be observ'd on other occasions. A single act of justice is frequently contrary to *public interest;* and were it to stand alone, without being follow'd by other acts, may, in itself, be very prejudicial to society. When a man of merit, of a beneficent disposition, restores a great fortune to a miser, or a seditious bigot, he has acted justly and laudably, but the public is a real sufferer. Nor is every single act of justice, consider'd apart, more conducive to private interest, than to public; and 'tis easily conceiv'd how a man may impoverish himself by a signal instance of integrity, and have reason to wish, that with regard to that single act, the laws of justice were for a moment suspended in the universe. But however single acts of justice may be contrary, either to public or private interest, 'tis certain, that the whole plan or scheme is highly conducive, or indeed absolutely requisite, both to the support of society, and the well-being of every individual. 'Tis impossible to separate the good from the ill. Property must be stable, and must be fix'd by general rules. Tho' in one instance the public be a sufferer, this momentary ill is amply compensated by the steady prosecution of the rule, and by the peace and order, which it establishes in society. And even every individual person must find himself a gainer, on ballancing the account; since, without justice, society must immediately dissolve, and every one must fall into that savage and solitary condition, which is infinitely worse than the worst situation that can possibly be suppos'd in society. When therefore men have had experience enough to observe, that whatever may be the consequence of any single act of justice, perform'd by a single person, yet the whole system of actions, concurr'd in by the whole society, is infinitely advantageous to the whole, and to every part; it is not long before justice and property take place. Every member of society is sensible of this interest: Every one expresses this sense to his fellows, along with the resolution he has taken of squaring his actions by it, on condition that others will do the same. No more is requisite to induce any one of them to perform an act of justice, who has the first opportunity. This becomes an example to others. And thus justice establishes itself by a kind of convention or agreement; that is, by a sense of interest, suppos'd to be common to all, and where every single act is perform'd in expectation that others are to perform the like. Without such a convention, no one wou'd ever have dream'd, that there was such a virtue as justice, or have been induc'd to conform his actions to it. Taking any single act, my justice may be pernicious in every respect; and 'tis only upon the supposition, that others are to imitate my example, that I can be induc'd to embrace that virtue; since nothing but this combination can render justice advantageous, or afford me any motives to conform my self to its rules.

We come now to the *second* question we propos'd, *viz. Why we annex the idea of virtue to justice, and of vice to injustice.* This question will not detain us long after the principles, which we have already establish'd. All we can say of it at present will be dispatch'd in a few words: And for farther satisfaction, the reader must wait till we come to the *third* part of this book. The *natural* obligation to justice, *viz.* interest, has been fully explain'd; but as to the *moral* obligation, or the sentiment of right and wrong, 'twill first be requisite to examine the natural virtues, before we can give a full and satisfactory account of it.

After men have found by experience, that their selfishness and confin'd generosity, acting at their liberty, totally incapacitate them for society; and at the same time have observ'd, that society is necessary to the satisfaction of those very passions, they are naturally induc'd to lay themselves under the restraint of such rules, as may render their commerce more safe and commodious. To the imposition then, and observance of these rules, both in general, and in every particular instance, they are at first mov'd only by a regard to interest; and this motive, on the first formation of society, is sufficiently strong and forcible. But when society has become numerous, and has encreas'd to a tribe or nation, this interest is more remote; nor do men so readily perceive, that disorder and confusion follow upon every breach of these rules, as in a more narrow and contracted society. But tho' in our own actions we may frequently lose sight of that interest, which we have in maintaining order, and may follow a lesser and more present interest, we never fail to observe the prejudice we receive, either mediately or immediately, from the injustice of others; as not being in that case either blinded by passion, or byass'd by any contrary temptation. Nay when the injustice is so distant from us, as no way to affect our interest, it still displeases us; because we consider it as prejudicial to human society, and pernicious to every one that approaches the person guilty of it. We partake of their uneasiness by *sympathy;* and as every thing, which gives uneasiness in human actions, upon the general survey, is call'd Vice, and whatever produces satisfaction, in the same manner, is denominated Virtue; this is the reason why the sense of moral good and evil follows upon justice and injustice. And tho' this sense, in the present case, be deriv'd only from contemplating the actions of others, yet we fail not to extend it even to our own actions. The *general rule* reaches beyond those instances, from which it arose; while at the same time we naturally *sympathize* with others in the sentiments they entertain of us. *Thus self-interest is the original motive to the* establishment *of justice: but a* sympathy *with public interest is the source of the* moral approbation, *which attends that virtue.*

Tho' this progress of the sentiments be *natural,* and even necessary, 'tis certain, that it is here forwarded by the artifice of politicians, who, in order to govern men more easily, and preserve peace in human society, have endeavour'd to produce an esteem for justice, and an abhorrence of injustice. This, no doubt, must have its effect; but nothing can be more evident, than that the matter has been carry'd too far by certain writers on morals, who seem to have employ'd their utmost efforts to extirpate all sense of virtue from among mankind. Any artifice of politicians may assist nature in the producing of those sentiments, which she suggests to us, and may even on some occasions, produce alone an approbation or esteem for any particular action; but 'tis impossible it should be the sole cause of the distinction we make betwixt vice and virtue. For if nature did not aid us in this particular, 'twou'd be in vain for politicians to talk of *honourable* or *dishonourable, praiseworthy* or *blameable.* These words wou'd be perfectly unintelligible, and wou'd no more have any idea annex'd to them, than if they were of a tongue perfectly unknown to us. The utmost politicians can perform, is, to extend the natural sentiments beyond their original bounds; but still nature must furnish the materials, and give us some notion of moral distinctions.

As publick praise and blame encrease our esteem for justice; so private education and instruction contribute to the same effect. For as parents easily observe, that a man is the more useful, both to himself and others, the greater degree of probity and honour he is endow'd with; and that those principles have greater force, when custom and education assist interest and reflexion: For these reasons they are induc'd to inculcate on their children, from their earliest infancy, the principles of probity, and teach them to regard the observance of those rules, by which society is maintain'd, as worthy and honourable, and their violation as base and infamous. By this means the sentiments of honour may take root in their tender minds, and acquire such firmness and solidity, that they may fall little short of those principles, which are the most essential to our natures, and the most deeply radicated in our internal constitution.

What farther contributes to encrease their solidity, is the interest of our reputation, after the opinion, *that a merit or demerit attends justice or injustice,* is once firmly establish'd among mankind. There is nothing, which touches us more nearly than our reputation, and nothing on which our reputation more depends than our conduct, with relation to the property of others. For this reason, every one, who has any regard to his character, or who intends to live on good terms with mankind, must fix an inviolable law to himself, never, by any temptation, to be induc'd to violate those principles, which are essential to a man of probity and honour.

I shall make only one observation before I leave this subject, *viz.* that tho' I assert, that in the *state of nature,* or that imaginary state, which preceded society, there be neither justice nor injustice, yet I assert not, that it was allowable, in such a state, to violate the property of others. I only maintain, that there was no such thing as property; and consequently cou'd be no such thing as justice or injustice. I shall have occasion to make a similar reflexion with regard to *promises,* when I come to treat of them; and I hope this reflexion, when duly weigh'd, will suffice to remove all odium from the foregoing opinions, with regard to justice and injustice.

OF THE RULES, WHICH DETERMINE PROPERTY

Tho' the establishment of the rule, concerning the stability of possession, be not only useful, but even absolutely necessary to human society, it can never serve to any purpose, while it remains in such general terms. Some method must be shown, by which we may distinguish what particular goods are to be assign'd to each particular person, while the rest of mankind are excluded from their possession and enjoyment. Our next business, then, must be to discover the reasons which modify this general rule, and fit it to the common use and practice of the world.

 'Tis obvious, that those reasons are not deriv'd from any utility or advantage, which either the *particular* person or the public may reap from his enjoyment of any *particular* goods, beyond what wou'd result from the possession of them by any other person. 'Twere better, no doubt, that every one were possess'd of what is most suitable to him, and proper for his use: But besides, that this relation of fitness may be common to several at once, 'tis liable to so many controversies, and men are so partial and passionate in judging of these controversies, that such a loose and uncertain rule wou'd be absolutely incompatible with the peace of human society. The convention concerning the stability of possession is enter'd into, in order to cut off all occasions of discord and contention; and this end wou'd never be attain'd, were we allow'd to apply this rule differently in every particular case, according to every particular utility, which might be discover'd in such an application. Justice, in her decisions, never regards the fitness or unfitness of objects to particular persons, but conducts herself by more extensive views. Whether a man be generous, or a miser, he is equally well receiv'd by her, and obtains with the same facility a decision in his favours, even for what is entirely useless to him.

It follows, therefore, that the general rule, *that possession must be stable,* is not apply'd by particular judgments, but by other general rules, which must extend to the whole society, and be inflexible either by spite or favour. To illustrate this, I propose the following instance. I first consider men in their savage and solitary condition; and suppose, that being sensible of the misery of that state, and foreseeing the advantages that wou'd result from society, they seek each other's company, and make an offer of mutual protection

and assistance. I also suppose, that they are endow'd with such sagacity as immediately to perceive, that the chief impediment to this project of society and partnership lies in the avidity and selfishness of their natural temper; to remedy which, they enter into a convention for the stability of possession, and for mutual restraint and forbearance. I am sensible, that this method of proceeding is not altogether natural; but besides that I here only suppose those reflexions to be form'd at once, which in fact arise insensibly and by degrees; besides this, I say, 'tis very possible, that several persons, being by different accidents separated from the societies, to which they formerly belong'd, may be oblig'd to form a new society among themselves; in which case they are entirely in the situation above mention'd.

 'Tis evident, then, that their first difficulty, in this situation, after the general convention for the establishment of society, and for the constancy of possession, is, how to separate their possessions, and assign to each his particular portion, which he must for the future inalterably enjoy. This difficulty will not detain them long; but it must immediately occur, as the most natural expedient, that every one continue to enjoy what he is at present master of, and that property or constant possession be conjoin'd to the immediate possession. Such is the effect of custom, that it not only reconciles us to any thing we have long enjoy'd, but even gives us an affection for it, and makes us prefer it to other objects, which may be more valuable, but are less known to us. What has long lain under our eye, and has often been employ'd to our advantage, *that* we are always the most unwilling to part with; but can easily live without possessions, which we never have enjoy'd, and are not accustom'd to. 'Tis evident, therefore, that men wou'd easily acquiesce in this expedient, *that every one continue to enjoy what he is at present possess'd of;* and this is the reason, why they wou'd so naturally agree in preferring it.

But we may observe, that tho' the rule of the assignment of property to the present possessor be natural, and by that means useful, yet its utility extends not beyond the first formation of society; nor wou'd any thing be more pernicious, than the constant observance of it; by which restitution wou'd be excluded, and every injustice wou'd be authoriz'd and rewarded. We must, therefore, seek for some other circumstance, that may give rise to property after society is once establish'd; and of this kind, I find four most considerable, *viz.* Occupation, Prescription, Accession, and Succession. We shall briefly examine each of these, beginning with *Occupation*.

The possession of all external goods is changeable and uncertain; which is one of the most considerable impediments to the establishment of society, and is the reason why, by universal agreement, express or tacit, men restrain themselves by what we now call the rules of justice and equity. The misery of the condition, which precedes this restraint, is the cause why we submit to that remedy as quickly as possible; and this affords an easy reason, why we annex the idea of property to the first possession, or to *occupation*. Men are unwilling to leave property in suspence, even for the shortest time, or open the least door to violence and disorder. To which we may add, that the first possession always engages the attention most; and did we neglect it, there wou'd be no colour of reason for assigning property to any succeeding possession.

There remains nothing, but to determine exactly, what is meant by possession; and this is not so easy as may at first sight be imagin'd. We are said to be in possession of anything, not only when we immediately touch it, but also when we are so situated with respect to it, as to have it in our power to use it; and may move, alter, or destroy it, according to our present pleasure or advantage. This relation, then, is a species of cause and effect; and as property is nothing but a stable possession, deriv'd from the rules of justice, or the conventions of men, 'tis to be consider'd as the same species of relation. But here we may observe, that as the power of using any object becomes more or less certain, according as the interruptions we may meet with are more or less probable; and as this probability may increase by insensible degrees; 'tis in many cases impossible to determine when possession begins or ends; nor is there any certain standard, by which we can decide such controversies. A wild boar, that falls into our snares, is deem'd to be in our possession, if it be impossible for him to escape. But what do we

mean by impossible? How do we separate this impossibility from an improbability? And how distinguish that exactly from a probability? Mark the precise limits of the one and the other, and shew the standard, by which we may decide all disputes that may arise, and, as we find by experience, frequently do arise upon this subject.

But such disputes may not only arise concerning the real existence of property and possession, but also concerning their extent; and these disputes are often susceptible of no decision, or can be decided by no other faculty than the imagination. A person who lands on the shore of a small island, that is desert and uncultivated, is deem'd its possessor from the very first moment, and acquires the property of the whole; because the object is there bounded and circumscrib'd in the fancy, and at the same time is proportion'd to the new possessor. The same person landing on a desert island, as large as *Great Britain*, extends his property no farther than his immediate possession; tho' a numerous colony are esteem'd the proprietors of the whole from the instant of their debarkment.

But it often happens, that the title of first possession becomes obscure thro' time; and that 'tis impossible to determine many controversies, which may arise concerning it. In that case long possession or *prescription* naturally takes place, and gives a person a sufficient property in any thing he enjoys. The nature of human society admits not of any great accuracy; nor can we always remount to the first origin of things, in order to determine their present condition. Any considerable space of time sets objects at such a distance, that they seem, in a manner, to lose their reality, and have as little influence on the mind, as if they never had been in being. A man's title, that is clear and certain at present, will seem obscure and doubtful fifty years hence, even tho' the facts, on which it is founded, shou'd be prov'd with the greatest evidence and certainty. The same facts have not the same influence after so long an interval of time. And this may be receiv'd as a convincing argument for our preceding doctrine with regard to property and justice. Possession during a long tract of time conveys a title to any object. But as 'tis certain, that, however every thing be produc'd in time, there is nothing real, that is produc'd by time; it follows, that property being produc'd by time, is not any thing real in the objects, but is the offspring of the sentiments, on which alone time is found to have any influence.

We acquire the property of objects by *accession*, when they are connected in an intimate manner with objects that are already our property, and at the same time are inferior to them. Thus the fruits of our garden, the offspring of our cattle, and the work of our slaves, are all of them esteem'd our property, even before possession. Where objects are connected together in the imagination, they are apt to be put on the same footing, and are commonly suppos'd to be endow'd with the same qualities. We readily pass from one to the other, and make no difference in our judgments concerning them; especially if the latter be inferior to the former.

The right of *succession* is a very natural one, from the presum'd consent of the parent or near relation, and from the general interest of mankind, which requires, that men's possessions shou'd pass to those, who are dearest to them, in order to render them more industrious and frugal. Perhaps these causes are seconded by the influence of *relation,* or the association of ideas, by which we are naturally directed to consider the son after the parent's decease, and ascribe to him a title to his father's possessions. Those goods must become the property of some body: But *of whom* is the question. Here 'tis evident the persons children naturally present themselves to the mind; and being already connected to those possessions by means of their deceas'd parent, we are apt to connect them still farther by the relation of property. Of this there are many parallel instances.

68   Two Worries About Mixing One's Labour

JEREMY WALDRON

I

Does the idea of *mixing one's labour* provide the basis for a plausible account of the genesis of property rights in Locke's state of nature?[1] Or is it merely a dramatic and rhetorical way of expressing the force of other arguments based ultimately on, say, utility or desert? In this paper I will argue that the idea of the mixing of labour is fundamentally incoherent and that therefore it can add nothing at all, apart from an oddly worded metaphor, to whatever other arguments Locke wants to put forward for the proposition that individuals working on goods owned in common in the state of nature are entitled to the products of their labour.

The considerations that Locke puts forward for this proposition fall into at least four main groups. First, dominating the whole account in the *Two Treatises,* there is an argument based on a principle of *need*. Unilateral acquisition of

entitlements by individual labour is presented as the only sensible way of allocating material resources to human needs in the state of nature. The idea is that, if unilateral appropriation were not permissible, people would be obliged to perish in the meantime while more consensual arrangements were being set up.[2] Secondly, and complementing this, there are considerations of *efficiency*. In a society where private property can be acquired by labour, everyone is better off, even the non-proprietors. As Locke puts it: "a King of a large fruitful Territory" where original communism still prevails "feeds, lodges, and is clad worse than a day Labourer in England."[3] Thirdly, there is an argument based on something like a *labour theory of value*. Locke suggests that, in the case of many important resources, the labour that has been expended on them is the source of so much of the value they possess that the labourer is entitled to the resource in roughly the same way

From *The Philosophical Quarterly,* 33, no. 130 (January 1983), pp. 37–44 Reprinted with permission of the publisher.

that a creator is entitled to his creation.[4] Fourthly, we seem at times to catch sight of a strand of argument based on a principle of *desert*. God has commanded men to labour; so "the Industrious and the Rational" are entitled to the products of their labour inasmuch as they have shown by their initiative that they are people of more merit than "the quarrelsome and Contentious" who complain about private appropriation.[5]

In addition to these four considerations, we have what appears to be an independent line of argument based on the idea that a labourer mixes his labour with the object on which he works. This is presented in a very well-known passage which I shall quote in full:

> Though the Earth and all inferior Creatures be common to all Men, yet every Man has a Property in his own Person. This no Body has any Right to but himself. The Labour of his Body, and the Work of his Hands, we may say, are properly his. Whatsoever then he removes out of the State that Nature hath provided, and left it in, he hath mixed his Labour with, and joyned to it something that is his own, and thereby makes it his Property. It being by him removed from the common state Nature placed it in, hath by this labour something annexed to it, that excludes the common right of other Men. For this Labour being the unquestionable Property of the Labourer, no man but he can have a right to what that is once joyned to, at least where there is enough, and as good left in common for others.[6]

There is no mention here—at least, no explicit mention—of any considerations of need, efficiency, value or desert. The argument looks as though it is meant to stand up on its own. In what follows I am going to consider it as such, and I shall leave aside the (interesting) exegetical question of whether Locke really intended this as an independent line of argument. It is sufficient, I think, that many interpreters have taken it as such.

There are good reasons for adopting this approach. It is well known that none of the four arguments I mentioned provides a watertight case for private property. Two of them at least— the argument based on the labour theory of value and the argument based on desert—appear equally capable of being adapted to socialist

conclusions: anything said about the desert of, or the value added by, an independent Lockean appropriator seems equally applicable to the case of an employee working industriously on resources already appropriated by someone else.[7] But, although each of the arguments is incomplete, perhaps they complement each other and together make up a convincing case for private property. If this is how we want to interpret them, then at some stage each strand of argument has to be examined on its own, to see how valid it is in itself, and what support it is capable of lending to the others. One of my conclusions in this paper will be that the argument involving the mixing of labour is, by itself, incapable of establishing anything at all, and so cannot help any of the others. Its appearance as part of the complex Lockean case for property is a distraction: it makes that case look more substantial than it really is.

An additional reason for examining the argument about the mixing of labour is that it has become important once again in political philosophy. In *Anarchy, State, and Utopia*, Robert Nozick insists that any adequate conception of economic justice must have a place for a principle of justice in acquisition—a principle that specifies the ways in which individuals may appropriate previously unowned resources. Nozick did not think it necessary to spell out the details of such a principle himself, but he alluded to the Lockean principle of mixing one's labour, and offered a number of criticisms of it.[8] Those criticisms have provided the inspiration for the present paper. But I think they indicate, not merely that the argument based on mixing labour is incomplete or that it needs to be spelled out in more detail, but rather that it is defective to the point of incoherence, and cannot operate as a principle of justice in acquisition.

II

If there *is* a line of argument in the passage I quoted above, it must go something like this:

1. A person who labours on an object mixes his labour with that object.
2. But that person owns the labour which he mixes with the object.

3. So the object which has been laboured on contains something which the labourer owns.
4. To take the object out of the labourer's control without his consent would violate the entitlement mentioned in (2) and (3).
5. Therefore, no one may take the object out of the labourer's control without his consent.
6. But this amounts to an entitlement in the labourer over the object.
7. Thus, a person who has laboured on an object is entitled to that object.

In this way, an entitlement to an object is seen to be generated out of the prior entitlement to one's labour, on the basis that recognizing the former is the only way to uphold and maintain respect for the latter once the labour has become mixed with the object.

So the idea that labour is literally *mixed with* an object is clearly crucial. Without it there would be no way of transferring the force of the entitlement to labour to the object which has been laboured on. Let us consider the idea of mixing one's labour, then, in a literal way, to see whether it makes sense. On the face of it, the proposition:

(P) Individual A mixes his labour with object O

seems to involve some sort of category mistake. Surely the only things that can be *mixed* with objects are other objects. But labour consists of *actions* not objects. How can a series of actions be mixed with a physical object? Admittedly, from time to time, for various reasons, philosophers have purported to quantify over actions and events, treating them, in some contexts at least, as entities in their own right.[9] But I do not think that disposes of the difficulty in the present case.

We can see this if we compare (P) with a more straightforward proposition about mixing:

(Q) The cook mixes the egg with the batter.

In (Q), there seem to be three objects referred to—the cook, the egg, and the batter. There is also, if you like, the action of mixing the egg into the batter. Now we may treat this action as an entity or we may not. What matters for my criticism is that, entity or not, the action is certainly not identical with any of the other entities involved. It is distinct from the egg and the batter and the cook. That seems quite straightforward.

Let us try a similar analysis of (P). Again, we may say that there are at least three entities referred to:

(P1) the labourer, A, who is the analogue of the cook;

(P2) the labour of A, which, like the egg, is (supposedly) the subject-matter of the mixing; and

(P3) the object, O, the analogue of the batter, into which the labour is being mixed.

So far so good. But where is the fourth element, the analogue of the action of mixing? Perhaps it is the labour of *A;* after all, the Lockean claim is that *by labouring* the producer mixes his labour with the product. But A's labour features *already* in the account we have given, as the ingredient, (P2), which is being mixed in. So instead of the four distinct elements which we had in the straightforward case of (Q), we have now at most only three. There is the mixer, the thing being mixed in, and the thing into which it is being mixed; *but there is no distinct action of mixing.* Or, if you like, we can put it the other way round. There is the mixer, the action of mixing, and the object into which something is being mixed; *but there is nothing which is being mixed in.* We have ingredient and mixture but no mixing, or mixing and mixture but no ingredient. Either way, the ordinary notion of mixing seems quite inappropriate to the case that Locke is describing. The situation lacks the requisite plurality.[10]

Our original hunch about a category mistake has led us to discover a much deeper flaw. It is not just that the idea of mixing one's labour treats labour as a *thing* which can be mixed with other things. It is rather that the phrase "mixing one's labour" is shown to have the logical form of "mixing one's mixing." And that just seems defective.

Is there any way in which Locke's argument can be rescued from this apparently devastating criticism? An attempt may be made along the following lines. Perhaps (P) is being used by Locke in the first premise of the argument in a way which distinguishes it, in terms of its logical form, from

(Q). If this is the case, then the fact that (P) does not conform to the logic of (Q) no more makes (P) ill-formed than the difference between, say, "*A* has a pain in his foot" and "*A* has a growth in his foot" makes the first of these ill-formed. In other words, it may be objected, on behalf of the Lockean argument, that we are interpreting the idea of mixing one's labour too literally. There may be some other perfectly legitimate sense for (P) which does not require the plurality of elements which (Q) requires.

There are two things to say about this objection. First, it is not at all clear that one *can* come up with an interpretation of (P) which will *both* avoid my attack *and* do the work in the argument which Locke seems to want the notion of mixing one's labour to do. Remember that the mixing of labour with an object is supposed to *explain and justify* the principle of labourers' entitlements. It is no good suggesting, for instance, that (P) is just a fancy or rhetorical way of saying "*A* labours on *Q*." For that leaves premise (1) of the Lockean argument saying redundantly that a person who labours on an object labours on an object. The notion implicit in (3)—that the object thereby comes to *contain* the person's labour—is left completely mysterious. The question would still remain open: why does labouring on an object generate an entitlement for the labourer over the object in question? If the argument we are considering has any independent force at all, then Locke is using (P) to *answer*, not to beg, this question. Any reinterpretation of (P), then has to be able to fill that role.

Secondly, the criticism I have made is not only of the expression "mixing one's labour" but also of some of the other expressions used by Locke in the section quoted: labour is said to be "joyned" and "annexed" to objects by the labourer. These expressions, in their ordinary sense, all share the logical form of (Q): that is, they all involve the idea of someone's bringing one thing into relation with another. So they are equally open to the criticism that, in the case of labouring on an object, there are *not* two things to be brought into relation with one another but only one thing and an action that is performed on it. Just as we do not ordinarily talk of *mixing* actions

with objects, so we do not ordinarily talk of *joining* or *annexing* them to objects, and my criticism explains why.

III

Even if this difficulty did not exist, there would be another grave problem in Locke's idea of mixing one's labour which prevents it doing the job in argument that he wants it to do.

The argument, as we saw, depends on the claim that if something to which I am entitled (e.g., my labour) becomes mixed with some other object, then the only way to safeguard and maintain my entitlement to the former is to entitle me to the latter object in which it has become embedded. In the literature, this claim has been attacked on a number of grounds. Robert Nozick raises the question whether deliberately mixing something one owns with something one does not own should not be regarded as a way of losing the former rather than as a way of gaining the latter.[11] Other critics have suggested that, even if labour does become irretrievably embedded in an object so that it cannot afterwards be disentangled from what was not the producer's property in the first place, nevertheless we need not concede that the producer is entitled to the product in full. Our available devices of ownership are subtle enough to allow us to confer on him a more modest entitlement, more in keeping with the proportion between his contribution and the naturally given raw material. So he may be allowed, for instance, a limited degree of control over and benefit from the product, or he may be entitled to *other* goods which have exactly the value of the improvements he made to the objects he worked on.[12] Even if this is not possible in Locke's state of nature, it is certainly possible now in civil society. So it is difficult to see how property entitlements generated initially by Lockean entitlements to the *whole* product of labour (value added plus raw materials) can operate today as moral side constraints on the pursuit of the economic and distributive goals of civil society.

But the second objection that I want to develop is more fundamental than this. I dispute whether entitling the producer to the whole product of his labour can even be regarded as *a way* of protecting his entitlement to the labour, let alone as the only way of doing so. Even if we assume, for the moment, that the idea of mixing labour makes sense, still, once the mixing takes place, the labour is to all intents and purposes lost in the object. There is no longer a question of protecting anyone's entitlement to *it*, since the labour, qua labour, no longer exists.

Once again, a straightforward analogy can assist us. Suppose there is a vat of wet cement lying about which belongs to nobody in particular, and I drop my ham sandwich into it. Before I can retrieve the sandwich, the cement hardens into a concrete block. (Or, better still: as in Locke's case, the cement is lying about and I *intend* to drop my sandwich into it, not wanting to retrieve it.) Can I now claim the concrete block in order to protect my entitlement to the sandwich? Can I object, when someone takes the block out of my control, that he is violating my entitlement to the sandwich? Surely that would be regarded as some sort of joke. My ham sandwich has gone; whatever the justice of my claim to the concrete block, it has nothing to do with my claim still to be the owner of the sandwich. An entitlement to an object consists in the right to use, control, and dispose of the object. But even if I am allowed to use, control, or dispose of the concrete block, I can do none of these things with regard to the sandwich.

Of course, things would be different if there were any possibility of recovering the sandwich from the block, but sandwiches do not usually survive such experiences. And, anyway, to put the case on all fours with the one Locke is describing, we have to conceive of the mixture of concrete and sandwich as irreversible. (Otherwise Locke has no answer to the point that the producer is entitled, at most, to be given back his labour.) So the sandwich as such is as good as lost, despite the fact that we know where it is. As something which can be the subject matter of an ongoing entitlement, generating other entitlements by its attachment to other things, it no longer exists for us.

No doubt the concrete block is different from what it would have been if the sandwich had not been dropped into the cement; presumably it is a little larger and its internal structure is slightly different. But the question raised by the alteration is just this: "Who is to have the concrete block, altered in this way by the insertion of the sandwich?" That may be an important question. But what has transpired makes the question "Who is to have the sandwich?" irrelevant to that.

Similarly, in the case of an object with which labour has been "mixed." The fact that the object has been laboured on certainly makes a difference to it. But the question is now: "Who is to have the object, given that labour has made this difference to it?" In finding the answer to this question, or, more important, in finding a justification for the obvious answer, the further question, "Who is to have the labour which made the difference?" is no use at all.

This becomes even clearer when we approach the troubled question of what it is to own, or be entitled to, one's labour. The notion that labour is, in any plausible sense, the *property* of the labourer has been severely criticized in the literature.[13] If it means anything at all, it means, presumably, that the labourer has a right to liberty. Nobody else has any such right over the labourer's actions as would entitle him to dispose of those actions without the labourer's consent. But ownership in this sense has no relevance *now* to labour that has freely been expended in the past. There is no intelligible question of my liberty *now* in respect of actions I performed freely *yesterday*. The idea of the ownership of labour, understood in this libertarian sense, cannot do any work once the actions which constitute the labour have taken place.

In *A Discourse on Property*, James Tully suggests that by "owning one's labour," Locke simply means being the conscious agent (initiator, creator) of the actions concerned.[14] If so, then Locke can make *some* sense of the idea that one continues to own one's labour after it has been "mixed" with an object: it continues to be the case that one was the agent of those actions. But he can do this only at the expense of severing the link between *ownership of* labour and *entitlement or right to* labour. Any right-related notion of ownership is going to be inapplicable to labour once it has been irretrievably mixed with or annexed to an object.

It has to be emphasized that these considerations are not intended to show that producers are *not* entitled to the products of their labour. Surely the fact that a labourer has made such a difference to an object is of considerable importance in determining the just way to dispose of the product. The problem for political philosophers is to explain *why* this is so. Here what I have shown is that one strand of argument in the famous explanation tendered by John Locke is defective to the point of incoherence. But nothing has been said against the other components of the Lockean case.[15]

NOTES

1. Locke, John. *Two Treatises of Government.* Ed. Peter Laslett. Cambridge, 1960. Part II, chapter 5.
2. Id., at I, §86, II, §28.
3. Id., at II, §41.
4. Id., at II, §§40–44.
5. Id., at II, §§32 and 34.
6. Id., at II, §27.
7. I owe this point to David Miller's paper, "Justice and Property." *Ratio* 22 (1980): 7.
8. Nozick, Robert. *Anarchy, State, and Utopia.* Oxford, 1974. 150, 160, 174–5, and 202–3.
9. Cf. Davidson, Donald. "The Logical Form of Action Sentences." *Actions and Events.* Oxford, 1980.
10. This view seems to be shared by Olivecrona, Karl. "Locke's Theory of Appropriation." *Philosophical Quarterly* 24 (1974): 226, where he remarks: "It would be absurd to contend that the 'labour' of killing a deer or picking an acorn from the ground is, in the exact sense of the expression, 'mixed' with the deer or the acorn respectively. Locke cannot have meant it so." But that is what Locke writes. Olivecrona does not indicate why he thinks the contention absurd.
11. Nozick, supra, note 8, at 174–5.
12. This objection is particularly important in the case of land: see Becker, Lawrence. *Property Rights: Philosophic Foundations.* London: 1977. 34; and Tully, James. *A Discourse on Property: Locke and His Adversaries.* Cambridge, 1980. 117–9.
13. See, especially, Day, J. P. "Locke on Property." *Philosophical Quarterly* 16 (1966): 207.
14. Tully, supra, note 12, at 106–10.
15. The idea that human labour comes to be "contained" in a product as a result of the process of production is, of course, heavily relied on by Marx, in *Capital* and elsewhere. It is worth considering whether similar criticisms apply to his account. I am inclined to think that they do not, inasmuch as Marx is not relying on the labour-mixing idea as a basis for entitlement, but rather for his theories of value and alienation. But that would be a subject for a separate paper.

69   Ownership

A. M. HONORÉ

Ownership is one of the characteristic institutions of human society. A people to whom ownership was unknown, or who accorded it a minor place in their arrangements, who meant by *meum* and *tuum* no more than "what I (or you) presently hold" would live in a world that is not our world. Yet to see why their world would be different, and to assess the plausibility of vaguely conceived schemes to replace "ownership" by "public administration," or of vaguely stated claims that the importance of ownership has declined or its character changed in the twentieth century, we need first to have a clear idea of what ownership is.

I propose, therefore, to begin by giving an account of the standard incidents of ownership: i.e., those legal rights, duties and other incidents which apply, in the ordinary case, to the person who has the greatest interest in a thing admitted by a mature legal system. To do so will be to analyse the concept of ownership, by which I mean the "liberal" concept of "full" individual

From *Oxford Essays in Jurisprudence: A Collaborative Work.* Ed. A. G. Guest. (Oxford: Oxford University Press, 1961), pp. 107–47. Notes have been renumbered.

ownership, rather than any more restricted notion to which the same label may be attached in certain contexts.

Secondly, I propose to say something about the notion of title, about the types of rule which legal systems adopt in order to decide who is to own a thing and, if two or more persons have claims to a thing, how priority between them is to be settled. Thirdly, I touch briefly on some instances of split ownership, in which the standard incidents are divided between two or more persons. Last comes the topic of the restriction of ownership in the social interest and the relation between ownership and public administration. This order of treatment should have the following advantage: once the standard case of full ownership has been depicted the variants and possible alternatives stand out more clearly in contrast, and are easier to understand and assess. On the other hand, this treatment is not meant to prejudge the issue, how far private ownership should stretch and to what extent it should be modified in the public interest. That issue, though it lies outside the scope of this essay, can be understood only with the help of an adequate analysis of the concept of ownership.

I. THE LIBERAL CONCEPT OF OWNERSHIP

If ownership is provisionally defined as the *greatest possible interest in a thing which a mature system of law recognizes,* then it follows that, since all mature systems admit the existence of "interests" in "things," all mature systems have, in a sense, a concept of ownership. Indeed, even primitive systems, like that of the Trobriand islanders, have rules by which certain persons, such as the "owners" of canoes, have greater interests in certain things than anyone else.[1]

For mature legal systems it is possible to make a larger claim. In them certain important legal incidents are found, which are common to different systems. If it were not so, "He owns that umbrella," said in a purely English context, would mean something different from "He owns that umbrella," proferred as a translation of *Cette parapluie est à lui.* Yet, as we know, they mean the

same. There is indeed, a substantial similarity in the position of one who "owns" an umbrella in England, France, Russia, China, and any other modern country one may care to mention. Everywhere the "owner" can, in the simple uncomplicated case, in which no other person has an interest in the thing, use it, stop others using it, lend it, sell it or leave it by will. Nowhere may he use it to poke his neighbour in the ribs or to knock over his vase. Ownership, *dominium, propriété, Eigentum,* and similar words stand not merely for the greatest interest in things in particular systems but for a type of interest with common features transcending particular systems. It must surely be important to know what these common features are.

In stressing the importance of such common features, I do not wish to go beyond the claim that these resemblances exist *de facto* and can be explained by the common needs of mankind and the common conditions of human life. It would be rash to assert that the features discussed are *necessarily* common to different mature systems, or that their range and ubiquity proves that what is called "general jurisprudence" is a reputable pursuit. These assertions may indeed be true, but for my purposes it is enough to show that the standard incidents of ownership do not vary from system to system in the erratic, unpredictable way implied by some writers but, on the contrary, have a tendency to remain constant from place to place and age to age.

Nor must the present thesis be confused with the claim that all systems attach an equal importance to ownership (in the full, liberal sense) or regard the same things as capable of being owned. The latter claim would be patently false. In the Soviet Union, for instance, important assets such as land, businesses and collective farms are in general withdrawn from "personal ownership" (viz., the liberal type of ownership) and subjected to "government" or "collective" ownership, which is a different, though related institution.[2] The notion of things "outside commerce," not subject to private ownership but to special regulation by the state or public authorities is an ancient one and has retained its importance in modern continental law.[3] Again, there is a case for saying that, in the early Middle Ages, land in England could not plausibly be said to be "owned" because the standard incidents of which I shall speak were so divided between lord and tenant that the position of neither presented a sufficient analogy with the paradigm case of owning a thing.[4]

Indeed, in nearly all systems there will be some things to which not all the standard incidents apply, some things which cannot be sold or left by will, some interests which cannot endure beyond a lifetime, some things (flick knives, Colorado beetles) which it is forbidden to use or to use in certain ways. If the differences between these cases and the paradigm case are striking enough, we shall be tempted to say that the things in question are not or cannot be owned, but it would be a mistake to conclude that the legal systems in which these cases occur do not recognize ownership. Whether a system recognizes ownership, and to what extent it permits ownership (who may own, what may be owned), are widely differing questions. No doubt liberal societies are more inclined than socialist societies to extend the list of items that can be owned, but it does not follow that, when a socialist system permits ownership, or "personal ownership," it is permitting something different from what is permitted in the corresponding case in a liberal society. It may well be—and all the evidence indeed supports the view—that socialist societies recognize the "liberal" notion of "full" ownership, but limit the range of things that can be owned. Perhaps definitions of ownership contained in codes are not a safe guide. Still, it is striking that the French civil code, enacted in an atmosphere of liberal individualism, defines ownership as "the right of enjoying and disposing of things in the most absolute manner, provided that one abstains from any use forbidden by statute or subordinate legislation";[5] while the Soviet civil code, framed in a socialist context, provides, in very similar language, that "within the limits laid down by law, the owner has the right to possess, to use and to dispose of his property."[6] Obviously much here depends on what limits are laid down by law in each system; in fact, so far as articles subject to "personal ownership" are concerned, the limits in the two systems hardly differ.

One further caveat. I set out to describe the incidents of ownership in the simple cases in which one would not hesitate to say "X owns that thing; that is X's book or house," even though Y may have borrowed it, or Y may be X's tenant. In doing this I do not lose sight of the existence of more complicated cases in which layman and lawyer alike may be puzzled to know which, of two or more persons interested in a thing, to call owner, or whether to say, on the other hand, that neither or none is owner. Just as the rules of a system may so restrict the permissible ways of dealing with certain types of thing that we are inclined to say that such things are not capable of being owned in that system, or can be owned only [in] a sense different from the full, liberal sense we are to investigate, so the rules of a system may provide for the splitting of interests in a type of thing which, in general, is admittedly capable of being owned. Houses can be owned, and there is no conceptual difficulty in locating the ownership of a house let on a short lease. But if A lets B a house on a lease for 2,000 years it may be very unclear, at least to the layman, whether A or B or neither should be called owner. (In this case, legal usage designates A owner despite the tenuous character of his reversionary right.) Again, can a mortgagor be said to "own" a house which is mortgaged? (Legal usage here refuses to designate the mortgagee owner despite the potentially indeterminate character of his interest.) No obvious linguistic convention governs the answer to such problems, and, if the rules of a legal system demand an answer, it must be sought in positive law, in the comparative strength of competing analogies with the paradigm case and in the light shed on the problem by the social context. The fact that there are such cases of split ownership and that they present baffling problems to one who is compelled to fix on one interested person as *the* owner of the thing, does not make it worthless to try to delineate the incidents present in the ordinary, uncomplicated case. On the contrary, such a delineation is essential in order that it may be possible to assess the strength of the analogies in the peripheral cases. What must, however, be recognized at the outset, is that the actual use of "owner" and "ownership" extends beyond the standard case now to be described and that to delineate the standard case is here, as with most legal notions, not to provide a code for the use of the word. For instance, the sixteen or so pages of Burrows's *Words and Phrases Judicially Defined*,[7] concerned with the interpretation of the word "owner" in various statutes, amply reveal how the courts have wrestled with provisions extending the legal meaning of "owner" beyond the standard cases. But it is important to see that the very existence of such problems of statutory interpretation presupposes that there are paradigm cases in which the interpretation of "owner" is clear.

Thus where a statute provided[8] that " 'owner' in relation to land, includes every person who jointly or severally whether at law or in equity, is entitled" to the profits of the land, etc., Griffith C.J. pointed out that the term "owner" "Prima facie connotes entire dominion. Section 3 [the definition section] extends the meaning so as to take in certain persons who possess some, but not all, of the rights of absolute owners. Although, therefore, the language of the definition is in form inclusive, and not exhaustive, it must be read as if the words 'besides the absolute owner' were inserted after 'includes.'"[9] This presupposes that we know, without the help of an interpretation clause, what is meant by "absolute owner," Again, when Jessel M.R. said in a case on the interpretation of the Highways Act, 1835, "I am clearly of the opinion that the term 'owner' means the man in occupation, who may be either the actual owner or else only the occupying tenant,"[10] he could not meaningfully have said this unless there were available criteria for the identification of the interest called "ownership" and so of the "actual owner" in the majority of cases.

The Standard Incidents

I now list what appear to be the standard incidents of ownership. They may be regarded as necessary ingredients in the notion of ownership, in the sense that, if a system did not admit them, and did not provide for them to be united in a single person, we would conclude that it did not know the liberal concept of ownership, though it might still have a modified version of ownership, either of a primitive or sophisticated sort. But the listed incidents are not individually necessary—though they may be together sufficient—conditions for the person of inherence to be designated "owner" of a particular thing in a given system. As we have seen, the use of "owner" will extend to cases in which not all the listed incidents are present.

Ownership comprises the right to posses, the right to use, the right to manage, the right to the income of the thing, the right to the capital, the right to security, the rights or incidents of transmissibility and absence of term, the prohibition of harmful use, liability to execution, and the incident of residuarity: this makes eleven leading incidents. Obviously, there are alternative ways of classifying the incidents; moreover, it is fashionable to speak of ownership as if it were just a bundle of rights, in which case at least two items in the list would have to be omitted.

No doubt the concentration in the same person of the right (liberty)[11] of using as one wishes, the right to exclude others, the power of alienating and an immunity from expropriation is a cardinal feature of the institution. Yet it would be a distortion—and one of which the eighteenth century, with its overemphasis on subjective rights, was patently guilty—to speak as if this concentration of patiently garnered rights was the only legally or socially important characteristic of the owner's position. The present analysis, by emphasizing that the owner is subject to characteristic prohibitions and limitations, and that ownership comprises at least one important incident independent of the owner's choice, is an attempt to redress the balance.

(1) The right to possess
The right to possess, viz., to have exclusive physical control of a thing, or to have such control as the nature of the thing admits, is the foundation on which the whole superstructure of ownership rests. It may be divided into two aspects, the right (claim) to be put in exclusive control of a thing and the right to remain in control, viz., the claim that others should, not without permission, interfere. Unless a legal system provides some rules and

procedures for attaining these ends it cannot be said to protect ownership.

It is of the essence of the right to possess that it is *in rem* in the sense of availing against persons generally. This does not, of course, mean that an owner is necessarily entitled to exclude everyone from his property. We happily speak of the ownership of land, yet a largish number of officials have the right of entering on private land without the owner's consent, for some limited period and purpose. On the other hand, a general licence so to enter on the "property" of others would put an end to the institution of landowning as we now know it.

The protection of the right to possess (still using "possess" in the convenient, though over-simple, sense of "to have exclusive physical control") should be sharply marked off from the protection of mere present possession. To exclude others from what one presently holds is an instinct found in babies and even, as Holmes points out,[12] in animals, of which the seal gives a striking example. To sustain this instinct by legal rules is to protect possession but not, as such, to protect the right to possess and so not to protect ownership. If dispossession without the possessor's consent is, in general, forbidden, the possessor is given a right in rem, valid against persons generally, to remain undisturbed, but he has no *right to possess in rem* unless he is entitled to recover from persons generally what he has lost or had taken from him, and to obtain from them what is due to him but not yet handed over. Admittedly there may be borderline cases in which the right to possess is partially recognized, e.g., where a thief is entitled to recover from those who oust him and all claiming under them, but not from others.

The protection of the right to possess, and so of one essential element in ownership, is achieved only when there are rules allotting exclusive physical control to one person rather than another, and that not merely on the basis that the person who has such control at the moment is entitled to continue in control. When children understand that Christmas presents go not to the finder but to the child whose name is written on the outside of the parcel, when a primitive tribe has a rule that a dead man's things go not to the first taker but to his son or his sister's son, we know that they have at least an embryonic idea of ownership.

To have worked out the notion of "having a right to" as distinct from merely "having," or, if that is too subjective a way of putting it, of rules allocating things to people as opposed to rules merely forbidding forcible taking, was a major intellectual achievement. Without it society would have been impossible. Yet the distinction is apt to be overlooked by English lawyers, who are accustomed to the rule that every adverse possession is a root of title, i.e., gives rise to a right to possess,[13] or at least that "de facto possession is prima facie evidence of seisin in fee and right to possession."[14]

The owner, then, has characteristically a battery of remedies in order to obtain, keep and, if necessary, get back the thing owned. Remedies such as the actions for ejectment and wrongful detention and the *vindicatio* are designed to enable the plaintiff either to obtain or to get back a thing, or at least to put some pressure on the defendant to hand it over. Others, such as the actions for trespass to land and goods, the Roman possessory interdicts and their modern counterparts are primarily directed towards enabling a present possessor to keep possession. Few of the remedies mentioned are confined to the owner; most of them are available also to persons with a right to possess falling short of ownership, and some to mere possessors. Conversely, there will be cases in which they are not available to the owner, for instance because he has voluntarily parted with possession for a temporary purpose, as by hiring the thing out. The availability of such remedies is clearly not a necessary and sufficient condition of owning a thing; what is necessary, in order that there may be ownership of things at all, is that such remedies shall be available to the owner in the usual case in which no other person has a right to exclude him from the thing.

(2) *The right to use*

The present incident and the next two overlap. On a wide interpretation of "use," management and income fall within use. On a narrow interpretation, "use" refers to the owner's personal use and enjoyment of the thing owned. On this interpretation it excludes management and income.

The right (liberty) to use at one's discretion has rightly been recognized as a cardinal feature of ownership, and the fact that, as we shall see, certain limitations on use also fall within the standard incidents of ownership does not detract from its importance, since the standard limitations are, in general, rather precisely defined, while the permissible types of use constitute an open list.

(3) The right to manage

The right to manage is the right to decide how and by whom the thing owned shall be used. This right depends, legally, on a cluster of powers, chiefly powers of licensing acts which would otherwise be unlawful, and powers of contracting: the power to admit others to one's land, to permit others to use one's things, to define the limits of such permission, and to contract effectively in regard to the use (in the literal sense) and exploitation of the thing owned. An owner may not merely sit in his own deck chair but may validly license others to sit in it, lend it, impose conditions on the borrower, direct how it is to be painted or cleaned, contract for it to be mended in a particular way. This is the sphere of management in relation to a simple object like a deck chair. When we consider more complex cases, like the ownership of a business, the complex of powers which make up the right to manage seems still more prominent. The power to direct how resources are to be used and exploited is one of the cardinal types of economic and political power; the owner's legal powers of management are one, but only one possible basis for it. Many observers have drawn attention to the growth of managerial power divorced from legal ownership; in such cases it may be that we should speak of split ownership or redefine our notion of the thing owned. This does not affect the fact that the right to manage is an important element in the notion of ownership; indeed, the fact that we feel doubts in these cases whether the "legal owner" *really* owns is a testimony to its importance.

Management often takes the form of making contracts relating to the thing owned, whether with servants or agents or independent contractors.

This fact, and the growing relative importance of management in comparison with personal use, at least in regard to some types of thing such as businesses, has led some observers to the neat conclusion that, over a wide sphere, *obligatio* has swallowed up res.[15] Even if the contrast were an apt one (and, after all, an obligatio is a res, a chose in action a chose) the sentiment would be exaggerated because many powers of management are exercised otherwise than by way of contract, not to mention powers of alienation. The point would be better made by saying that, in the owner's battery of rights, powers have increased in calibre while liberties have declined.

(4) The right to the income

To use or occupy a thing may be regarded as the simplest way of deriving an income from it, of enjoying it. It is, for instance, expressly contemplated by the English income tax legislation that the rent-free use or occupation of a house is a form of income, and only the inconvenience of assessing and collecting the tax presumably prevents the extension of this principle to movables. Income in the more ordinary sense (fruits, rents, profits) may be thought of as a surrogate of use, a benefit derived from forgoing personal use of a thing and allowing others to use it for reward; as a reward for work done in exploiting the thing; or as the brute product of a thing, made by nature or by other persons. Obviously the line to be drawn between the earned and unearned income from a thing cannot be firmly drawn.

The owner's right to the income, which has always, under one name or another, bulked large in an analysis of his rights, has assumed still greater significance with the increased importance of income relative to capital. Legally it takes the form of a claim sometimes in rem, sometimes in personam to the income. When the latter is in the form of money, the claim before receipt of the money is in personam; and since the income from many forms of property, such as shares and trust funds, is in this form, there is another opportunity for introducing the apophthegm that obligatio has swallowed up res.

(5) *The right to the capital*

The right to the capital consists in the power to alienate the thing and the liberty to consume, waste, or destroy the whole or part of it: clearly it has an important economic aspect. The latter liberty need not be regarded as unrestricted; but a general provision requiring things to be conserved in the public interest, so far as not consumed by use in the ordinary way, would perhaps be inconsistent with the liberal idea of ownership.

Most people do not wilfully destroy permanent assets; hence the power of alienation is the more important aspect of the owner's right to the capital of the thing owned. This comprises the power to alienate during life or on death, by way of sale, mortgage, gift or other mode, to alienate a part of the thing and partially to alienate it. The power to alienate may be subdivided into the power to make a valid disposition of the thing and the power to transfer the holder's title (or occasionally a better title) to it. The two usually concur but may be separated, as when *A* has a power of appointment over property held by *B* in trust.[16] Again, in some systems, a sale, mortgage, bequest, etc, may be regarded as valid though the seller or mortgagor cannot give a good title. By giving a good title is meant transferring to the transferee the rights of the owner including his power of alienation.

An owner normally has both the power of disposition and the power of transferring title. Disposition on death is not permitted in many primitive societies but seems to form an essential element in the mature notion of ownership. The tenacity of the right of testation once it has been recognized is shown by the Soviet experience. The earliest writers were hostile to inheritance, but gradually Soviet law has come to admit that citizens may dispose freely of their "personal property" on death, subject to limits not unlike those known elsewhere.[17]

(6) *The right to security*

An important aspect of the owner's position is that he should be able to look forward to remaining owner indefinitely if he so chooses and he remains solvent. His right to do so may be called the right to security. Legally, this is in effect an immunity from expropriation, based on rules which provide that, apart from bankruptcy and execution for debt, the transmission of ownership is consensual.

However, a general right to security, availing against others, is consistent with the existence of a power to expropriate or divest in the state or public authorities. From the point of view of security of property, it is important that when expropriation takes place, adequate compensation should be paid; but a general power to expropriate subject to paying compensation would be fatal to the institution of ownership as we know it. Holmes's paradox, that where specific restitution of goods is not a normal remedy,[18] expropriation and wrongful conversion are equivalent, obscures the vital distinction between acts which a legal system permits as rightful and those which it reprobates as wrongful: but if wrongful conversion were general and went unchecked, ownership as we know it would disappear, though damages were regularly paid.

In some systems, as in English law, a private individual may destroy another's property without compensation when this is necessary in order to protect his own person or property from a greater danger.[19] Such a rule is consistent with security of property only because of its exceptional character. Again, the state's (or local authority's) power of expropriation is usually limited to certain classes of thing and certain limited purposes. A general power to expropriate any property for any purpose would be inconsistent with the institution of ownership. If, under such a system, compensation were regularly paid, we might say either that ownership was not recognized in that system, or that money alone could be owned, "money" here meaning a strictly fungible claim on the resources on the community. As we shall see, "ownership" of such claims is not identical with the ownership of material objects and simple claims.

(7) *The incident of transmissibility*

It is often said that one of the main characteristics of the owner's interest is its "duration." In England, at least, the doctrine of estates made lawyers familiar with the notion of the "duration" of an interest, and Maitland, in a luminous metaphor, spoke of estates as "projected upon the plane of time."[20]

Yet this notion is by no means as simple as it seems. What is called "unlimited" duration (*perpetuite*)[21] comprises at least two elements (i) that the interest can be transmitted to the holder's successors and so on ad infinitum (The fact that in medieval land law all interests were considered "temporary"[22] is one reason why the terminology of ownership failed to take root, with consequences which have endured long after the cause has disappeared); (ii) that it is not certain to determine at a future date. These two elements may be called "transmissibility" and "absence of term" respectively. We are here concerned with the former.

No one, as Austin points out,[23] can enjoy a thing after he is dead (except vicariously) so that, in a sense, no interest can outlast death. But an interest which is transmissible to the holder's successors (persons designated by or closely related to the holder who obtain the property after him) is more valuable than one which stops with his death. This is so both because on alienation the alienee or, if transmissibility is generally recognized, the alienee's successors, are thereby enabled to enjoy the thing after the alienor's death so that a better price can be obtained for the thing, and because, even if alienation were not recognized, the present holder would by the very fact of transmissibility be dispensed pro tanto from making provision for his intestate heirs. Hence, for example, the moment when the tenant in fee acquired a heritable (though not yet fully alienable) right was a crucial moment in the evolution of the fee simple. Heritability by the state would not, of course, amount to transmissibility in the present sense: it is assumed that the transmission is in some sense *advantageous* to the transmitter.

Transmissibility can, of course, be admitted, yet stop short at the first, second, or third generation of transmittees. The owner's interest is characterized by *indefinite* transmissibility, no limit being placed on the possible number of transmissions, though the nature of the thing may well limit the actual number.

In deference to the conventional view that the exercise of a right must depend on the choice of the holder,[24] I have refrained from calling transmissibility a right. It is, however, clearly something in which the holder has an economic interest, and it may be that the notion of a right requires revision in order to take account of incidents not depending on the holder's choice which are nevertheless of value to him.

(8) *The incident of absence of term*

This is the second part of what is vaguely called "duration." The rules of a legal system usually seem to provide for determinate, indeterminate, and determinable interests. The first are certain to determine at a future date or on the occurrence of a future event which is certain to occur. In this class come leases for however long a term, copyrights, etc. Indeterminate interests are those, such as ownership and easements, to which no term is set. Should the holder live forever, he would, in the ordinary way, be able to continue in the enjoyment of them forever. Since human beings are mortal, he will in practice only be able to enjoy them for a limited period, after which the fate of his interest depends on its transmissibility. Again, since human beings are mortal, interests for life, whether of the holder or of another, must be regarded as determinate. The notion of an indeterminate interest, in the full sense, therefore requires the notion of transmissibility, but, if the latter were not recognized, there would still be value to the holder in the fact that his interest was not due to determine on a fixed date or on the occurrence of some contingency, like a general election, which is certain to occur sooner or later.

On inspection it will be found that what I have called indeterminate interests are really determinable. The rules of legal systems always provide some contingencies such as bankruptcy, sale in execution, or state expropriation on which the holder of an interest may lose it. It is true that in most of these cases the interest is technically said to be transmitted to a successor (e.g.,, a trustee in bankruptcy) whereas in the case of determinable interests the interest is not so transmitted. Yet the substance of the matter is that the present holder may lose his interest in certain events. It is never, therefore, certain that, if the present holder and his successors so choose, the interest will never determine as long as the thing remains in existence. The notion of indeterminate interests can only be saved by regarding the purchaser in insolvency or execution, or the state, as succeeding to the same interest as that had by the previous holder. This is an implausible way of looking at the matter, because the expropriability and executability of a thing is not an incident of value to the owner, but a restriction on the owner's rights imposed in the social interest. It seems better, therefore, to deny the existence of indeterminate interests and to classify those which are not determinate according to the number and character of the contingencies on which they will determine. This affords a justification for speaking of a "determinable fee," of "fiduciary ownership," etc., for these do not differ essentially from "full ownership," determinable on bankruptcy or expropriation.

(9) *The prohibition of harmful use*

An owner's liberty to use and manage the thing owned as he chooses is in mature systems of law, as in primitive systems, subject to the condition that uses harmful to other members of society are forbidden. There may, indeed, be much dispute over what is to count as "harm," and to what extent give-and-take demands that minor inconvenience between neighbours shall be tolerated. Nevertheless, at least for material objects, one can always point to abuses which a legal system will not allow.

I may use my car freely but not in order to run my neighbour down, or to demolish his gate, or even to go on his land if he protests; nor may I drive uninsured. I may build on my land as I choose, but not in such a way that my building collapses on my neighbour's land. I may let off fireworks on Guy Fawkes night, but not in such a way as to set fire to my neighbour's house. These and similar limitations on the use of things are so familiar and so obviously essential to the existence of an orderly community that they are not often thought of as incidents of ownership; yet, without them "ownership" would be a destructive force.

(10) *Liability to execution*

Of a somewhat similar character is the liability of the owner's interest to be taken away from him for debt, either by execution of a judgment debt or on insolvency. Without such a general liability the growth of credit would be impeded and ownership would, again, be an instrument by which the owner could defraud his creditors. This incident, therefore, which may be called *executability*, seems to constitute one of the standard ingredients of the liberal idea of ownership.

It is a question whether any other limitations on ownership imposed in the social interest should be regarded as among its standard incidents. A good case can certainly be made for listing *liability to tax* and *expropriability by the state* as such. Although it is often convenient to contrast taxes on property with taxes on persons, all tax must ultimately be taken from something owned, whether a material object, or a fund, or a chose in action. A general rule exempting the owners of things from paying tax from those things would therefore make taxation impracticable. But it may be thought that to state the matter in this way is to obliterate the useful contrast between taxes on what is owned and taxes on what is earned. Although therefore, a society could not continue to exist without taxation, and although the amount of tax is commonly dependent on what the taxpayer owns or earns, and must be paid from his assets, I should not wish to press the case for the inclusion of liability to tax as a standard incident of ownership. Much the same will hold good of expropriability; for though some state or public expropriation takes place in every society, and though it is not easy to see how administration could continue without it, it tends to be restricted to special classes of property. We are left with the thought that it is, perhaps, a characteristic of ownership that the owner's claims are ultimately postponed to the claims of the public authority, even if only indirectly, in that the thing owned may, within defined limits, be taken from the owner in order to pay the expenses of running the state or to provide it with essential facilities.

Ownership and Lesser Interests

The interest of which the standard incidents have been depicted is usually described as the *greatest* interest in a thing recognized by the law and is contrasted with lesser interests (easements, short leases, licences, special property, mere detention). It is worthwhile looking a little more closely at this distinction, for it partly depends on a point that the foregoing analysis has not brought to light.

I must emphasize that we are not now concerned with the topic of split ownership—cases where the standard incidents are so divided as to raise a doubt which of two or more persons interested should be called owner. We are dealing with those simpler cases in which the existence of *B*'s interest in a thing, though it restricts *A*'s rights, does not call in question *A*'s ownership of the thing.

The first point that strikes us is that each of the standard incidents of ownership can apply to the holder of a lesser interest in property. The bailee has possession of, and often the right to possess, the goods bailed. The managing director of a company has the right of managing it. The life tenant or usufructuary of a house is entitled to the income from it. The donee of a power of appointment is entitled to dispose of the capital subject to the power. The holder of an easement has a transmissible and nondeterminate right in the land subject to the easement. Yet, without more, we feel no temptation to say that the bailee owns the thing, the managing director the company, the life tenant the house, the donee the capital, or the easement holder the land. What criteria do we use in designating these as "lesser interests"?

One suggested view is that the rights of the holder of a lesser interest can be enumerated while the "owner's" cannot.[25] This rests on a fallacy about enumeration. The privileges, for instance, exercisable over a thing do not together constitute a finite number of permissible actions. The "owner" and the lessee alike may do an indefinite number and variety of actions, viz., any action not forbidden by a rule of the legal system.

A second view is that the criterion used is the fact that, at least as regards *some* incidents, the holder of the lesser interest has more restricted rights than the owner. The lessee's interest is determinate, the "owner's" merely determinable. But, conversely, the lessee has the right to possess and manage the property and take its income; in these respects the "owner's" interest is, for the time being, more restricted than his own. Nor will it help to say that the "owner's" rights are more extensive than those of the holder of a lesser interest as regards *most* of the incidents listed, for, in such cases as lease, this would lead to the conclusion that the lessee has as much claim to be called owner as the reversioner.

A third suggestion is that some one incident is taken as the criterion. It is possible, however, for all the listed rights, to put examples which would lead to the opposite result from that sanctioned by usage. If *A* lets *B* a car on hire, *B* possesses it but *A* "owns" it. The holder of a life interest or usufruct manages and takes the income of the thing, but the *dominus* or reversioner "owns" it. When trust property is subject to a power of appointment, the donee of the power can dispose of it but the trustee "owns" it. When property is subject to a *fideicommissum*, the fiduciary has no transmissible right (unless the fideicommissum fails), yet he is "owner" while the fideicommissary may, exceptionally, have such a right. A person who holds an interest *in diem* may "own," while one who has a potentially indeterminate interest *ex die* does not as yet do so.

Besides these examples, where any of the suggested criteria would give a result at variance with actual lay and legal usage, there are many others where the rights in question apply to both or neither of the persons holding an interest in the thing. For instance, some writers appear to treat "duration"[26] as the criterion for distinguishing between ownership and lesser interests. Yet the holder of an easement, like the "owner" of land, has a transmissible and indeterminate right over it, while, *per contra*, neither the "owner" nor the licensee of a copyright has an indeterminate right.

It would be easy but tedious to list examples for the other rights; clearly, if a criterion is to be found, it must be sought elsewhere. A hopeful avenue of inquiry seems to be the following: what happens on the determination of the various interests in the thing under consideration? This brings us to a further standard incident of ownership, viz., its residuary character.

(11) Residuary character

A legal system might recognize interests in things less than ownership and might have a rule that, on the determination of such interests, the rights in question lapsed and could be exercised by no one, or by the first person to exercise them after their lapse. There might be leases and easements; yet, on their extinction, no one would be entitled to exercise rights similar to those of the former lessee or of the holder of the easement. This would be unlike any system known to us and I think we should be driven to say that in such a system the institution of ownership did not extend to anything in which limited interests existed. In such things there would, paradoxically, be interests less than ownership but no ownership.

This fantasy is intended to bring out the point that it is characteristic of ownership that an owner has a residuary right in the thing owned. In practice, legal systems have rules providing that, on the lapse of an interest, rights, including liberties, analogous to the rights formerly vested in the holder of the interest, vest in or are exercisable by someone else, who may be said to acquire the "corresponding rights." Of course, the "corresponding rights" are not the same rights as were formerly vested in the holder of the interest. The easement holder had a right to exclude the owner; now the owner has a right to exclude the easement holder. The latter right is not identical with, but corresponds to, the former.

It is true that corresponding rights do not always arise when an interest is determined. Sometimes, when ownership is abandoned, no corresponding right vests in another; the thing is simply *res derelicta*. Sometimes, on the other hand, when ownership is abandoned, a new ownership vests in the state, as is the case in South Africa when land has been abandoned.

It seems, however, a safe generalization that, whenever an interest less than ownership terminates, legal systems always provide for corresponding rights to vest in another. When easements terminate, the "owner" can exercise the corresponding rights, and when bailments terminate, the same is true. It looks as if we have found a simple explanation of the usage we are investigating, but this turns out to be but another deceptive short cut. For it is not a sufficient condition of *A*'s being the owner of a thing that, on the determination of *B*'s interest in it, corresponding rights vest in or are exercis-able by *A*. On the determination of a sublease, the rights in question become exercisable by the lessee, not by the "owner" of the property.

Can we then say that the "owner" is the ultimate residuary: When the sublessee's interest determines the lessee acquires the corresponding rights; but when the lessee's right determines the "owner" acquires these rights. Hence the "owner" appears to be identified as the ultimate residuary. The difficulty is that the series may be continued, for on the determination of the "owner's" interest the state may acquire the corresponding rights; is the state's interest ownership or a mere expectancy?

A warning is here necessary. We are approaching the troubled waters of split ownership. Puzzles about the location of ownership are often generated by the fact that an ultimate residuary right is not coupled with present alienability or with the other standard incidents we have listed. Was the feudal lord's right of escheat ownership or merely an expectancy? When land was given in *emphyteusis*, was the *emphyteuta* or the reversioner owner? Other puzzles are created by cases of cross-residuarity. When property is held subject to a fideicommissum in the modern law, the fideicommissary benefits from the lapse of the fiduciary's rights and vice versa; so which is really residuary?

We are of course here concerned not with the puzzles of split ownership but with simple cases in which the existence of *B*'s lesser interest in a thing is clearly consistent with *A*'s owning it. To explain the usage in such cases it is helpful to point out that it is a necessary but not sufficient condition of *A*'s being owner that, either immediately or ultimately, the extinction of other interests would ensure for his benefit. In the end, it turns out that residuarity is merely one of the standard incidents of ownership, important no doubt, but not entitled to any special status.

The Thing Owned

"To own" is transitive; the object of ownership is always spoken of as a "thing" in the legal sense, a *res*. There is, clearly, a close connexion between the idea of ownership and the idea of things owned, as is shown by the use of words such as "property" to designate both. We ought, apparently, to be able to throw some light on ownership by investigating "things."

Outside the law, external material objects are thought of as the prime examples of things and, in this sense, things are contrasted with persons. But, in a wide sense, any object of discourse may be called a thing—events, states, emotions, actions, processes are all things. The extra-legal use of "thing" is therefore not likely to help us in finding out what can be owned.

In the law we find the following position. As regards external material objects, it is natural to speak of ownership. A person "owns" a book, house, or car. The terminology of ownership is also extended to some things other than material objects. A person may "own" a copyright, leasehold property, goodwill, a business, patent rights. In these cases the analogy with the incidents of the ownership of external material objects is a close one.

In other cases the holder of a right is said to "have" rather than own the interest in question. Thus, one "has" an easement, or a chose in action, or a reputation. Here the analogy with the ownership of material objects is less strong or, as in the case of easements, the alternative expression is adopted to avoid confusion with the ownership of the material object to which the right relates.

In other cases again, we speak not of "having" a thing but of "having a right" to or in something. Thus, a person does not either "own" or "have" his body or liberty. He has a right to bodily security or liberty. Here the analogy with the ownership of a thing is tenuous; thus, these rights are inalienable. Finally, there are interests which the law refuses to recognize: one does not own, have, or have a right to them. An example in English law is privacy.

In any viable society we shall expect certain interests (having a house, clothes, food, preserving one's body from harm) to be protected, but, as regards many other interests, (copyright, reputation, privacy, shares) there will be nothing absurd in a system which does not protect them, though it may be an inconvenient system. There will be no way of telling, apart from knowing the details of a system, whether such interests are protected and, *a fortiori*, no way of telling whether they are conceived as consisting in the ownership of things. Apart from the basic interests mentioned, protection of an interest is not merely the recognition of a social necessity. The meaning of the words "right" or "thing" will not help one to guess what the decision has been or is likely to be.

Much the same may be said of the difference between simple rights and interests conceived in terms of ownership. A person is not, in most systems, regarded as owning his body, reputation, skill, honour or dignity. At most he has a simple right to these things, which are therefore not legally "things." By a "simple right," I mean one which is protected by law but is not alienable or transmissible. Now, it may be that the doctrine that one does not own one's body, etc. is influenced by the linguistic fact that such aspects of one's person do not fall within the prime class of things, external material objects. But a more likely explanation is simply that it has been thought undesirable that a person should alienate his body, skill or reputation, as this would be to interfere with human freedom. When human beings were regarded as alienable and ownable they were, of course, also regarded as being legally things: and it is quite easy to conceive arrangements under which one could, for instance, lease one's reputation or one's skill for a term of years, so that the lessee could sue for infringements of the lessor's good name or for the fruits of his work. It may, indeed, be argued that contracts for the assignment of goodwill and contracts of service are examples of at least partial alienations of these interests.

However that may be, it is clear that to stare at the meaning of the word "thing" will not tell us which protected interests are conceived in terms of ownership. When the legislature or courts think that an interest should be alienable and transmissible they will reify it and say that it can be owned, that it is property. They will not say that it can be owned and is a res because of a prior conviction that it falls within the appropriate definition of "thing." The investigation of "things" seems to peter out in a false trail.

A more promising approach is to try to classify the things that can be owned. An obvious classification is into material objects and things that are not material objects (incorporeals). According to one school of thought, this division is so important that only corporeals can really be owned; according to another, it is so unimportant that we ought always to speak of owning rights over material objects, never of owning the objects themselves; in this way we shall keep in mind the parallel with the ownership of incorporeal rights.

Both schools propose a departure from lay and legal usage that stands in need of justification. The former has little to commend it. Consider the difference between "owning" land and "owning" (having) an easement over land. The first counts as the ownership of a material object, the second of an incorporeal. Yet their incidents are in every way similar and, in both cases, include the right to exclude others from interfering with or obstructing a particular physical thing, a right which at first sight might seem to differentiate the ownership of material objects from the ownership of incorporeals. It is true that, when we come to consider claims, we find cases in which either there is no right to exclude others or no right to exclude them from a particular physical thing.

Copyright is an example of one type of claim. It involves the right to prevent others from publishing, etc. one's written work without consent, and hence a sort of right to exclude others; but this right does not relate to a particular physical thing, a particular book. It relates to all material objects which have certain characteristics, viz., that they are copies of the work in question. Again, it is not clear that the incident of prohibition of harmful use applies in a straightforward way to copyrights: on the other hand convincing analogues of the other standard incidents are to be found. Thus it may be said that the notion of ownership applies to copyrights in an extended and somewhat weaker sense than that in which it applies to material objects and interests in them.

Debts due and other choses in action present an example of another type of claim. Here the claim is to the performance of some positive act. No right to exclude others is involved, and, as in the case of copyrights, no question of harmful use arises. On the other hand, incidents such as alienability (nowadays) and transmissibility do apply to choses in action. Hence the ownership of choses in action is to be understood in a still weaker sense than that of copyrights.

It seems, therefore, as if a more useful classification of things owned than that into corporeals and incorporeals would be into material objects and rights in them, claims, and collections of objects and claims. Slightly expanding this, we get the following list:

a. Material objects and interests in material objects;
b. Claims, and interests in claims;
c. Fixed collections of material objects, claims, or both;
d. Variable collections of material objects, claims, or both;
e. Funds.

The list is self-explanatory, "claims" being understood to exclude such claims as amount to interests in material objects. The introduction of fixed and variable collections is necessary in order to accommodate the ownership of estates, businesses, etc., either frozen at a point of time (fixed collection), such as the date of a person's death, or varying from time to time, as in the case of the spouses' "ownership" of a joint estate when they are married in community of property. A "fund" is the monetary equivalent of a collection of things, or claims, or both.

It is a commonplace that the ownership of funds has become of great importance in the twentieth century. With this development a new twist has been given to the notion of ownership, and one which is inherent in the notion of owning a variable collection of things.

A variable collection of things may be owned and managed like a particular thing but, as a matter of convenience, lesser interests in and claims to the collection are not construed as giving the holder powers of management or security against the alienation of particular items in the collection. Such claims are in effect claims to the income or capital of a fund which may vary in value and will in any case be composed of varying items. They are claims on the fund, not claims on the items, and they may well be divorced from what in any case is notionally separable, the management of the individual items.

The modern world presents us with many examples where the ownership of property consists in claims on a variable collection or fund. Of the former the interest of a wife married in community of property is a striking instance. She has no power of managing the community assets and her claim is restricted to whatever items may be found in the collection of community assets on the dissolution of the marriage. Another example is the ownership by members of an unincorporated association of the association's assets. Prominent instances of the latter are the ownership of shares, the ownership of interests in trust funds and floating charges: all the instances of *Gesamthandseigentum* [communal ownership] in German law fall into one of these classes.[27]

Such claims on collections and funds present a still remoter analogy with the ownership of interests in material objects than the simple claims previously considered. The incidents of possession, management, and the prohibition of harmful use apply, if at all, in a sketchy form. Alienability, transmissibility, income and (sometimes) capital rights remain. Since, among forms of property holding, claims on collections and funds are now of outstanding importance economically, we might either say that, over a wide field, the character of things owned has altered, or that the character of ownership has altered. I see no reason for preferring one form of expression to the other; our investigation has revealed, what we began by suspecting, that the notions of ownership and of the thing owned are interdependent. We are left, not with an inclination to adopt a terminology which confines ownership to material objects, but with an understanding of a certain shift in meaning as ownership is applied to different classes of things owned.

It remains to consider the view that the thing owned should always be spoken of as a right. This

is certainly an odd-looking proposal, since "owning" in ordinary use involves "having certain rights to" a thing. If, therefore, we are to substitute for "owning a pen" "owning certain rights in a pen," it would seem to follow that the owner should correctly be said to have certain rights in certain rights in a pen; but why stop at the second order of rights?

Of course, the force of the proposal is a protest against the habit of thinking of the ownership of a thing, particularly a material object, as if it consisted only in a relation between a person and a thing, and not at all in relations between the owner and other persons. Yet to speak always of owning rights rather than things would be doubly misleading. Ownership, as we have seen, is not just a bundle of rights, as it is no help towards understanding our society to speak as if it were. Secondly, the idiom which directly couples the owner with the thing owned is far from pointless; where the right to exclude others exists, there is indeed (legally) a very special relation between the holder of the right and the thing, and this is a rational way of marking it.[28]

II. TITLE

It is not enough for a legal system to recognize the possibility of people owning things. There must be rules laying down how ownership is acquired and lost and how claims to a thing are to rank *inter se*. This brings us to the notion of title, a word which is used in two main senses. First, it refers to the conditions of fact which must be fulfilled in order that a person may acquire a claim to a thing. In this sense, delivery, registration, seizure and succession on death may be titles to the ownership of property. "Mode of acquisition" or "mode of loss" will do as well for this meaning as "title"; so I use "title" in the second sense.

This is the sense in which a title to a thing is a claim—valid against persons generally, though not necessarily against everyone—to the possession of the thing. It is true that in ordinary legal usage "title" involves a great deal more than this; it implies, for instance, a power of alienating the holder's interest and the transmissibility of that interest. The restricted sense I have given to "title" is, however, adequate for the present discussion.

Clearly every owner has a title to the thing owned, provided that the thing admits of being possessed; even if it does not admit of this, there will be prior and posterior claims to the thing, as in the case of choses in action, and the owner will have such a claim. It is also clear that several persons may have titles to the same thing; thus, a mere possessor has, under some systems of law, a better right to possess than any later possessor of the thing not deriving title from an earlier possessor. Taking possession is regarded under such systems as a mode of acquiring a right to possess, valid against persons generally, not merely against a trespasser or disseisor. Hence there may be problems of priority of title. What is not, at first sight, clear is whether the name "owner" should be confined to the person with the best title to a thing out of all possible claimants (*the* title, a *good* title) or whether we should in such cases speak of two or more "owners" of the thing ranking in a certain order.

Modes of Acquisition

These obviously vary from system to system. It is often thought that light can be thrown on the concept of possession by a study of the conditions for acquiring possession; ought not the same procedure to be fruitful in the study of ownership? Holmes, following a general theory about the analysis of legal concepts, approaches the matter in this way,[29] but without yielding more than a catalogue of modes of acquisition. On the other hand, some writers who wish to justify the institution of ownership as a fair one, in spite of the apparent injustice involved in excluding all save the owner from the thing owned, argue that, though there are various modes of derivative acquisition, there is only one mode of original acquisition, namely taking possession.[30] They go on to say that the labour involved in taking or making the thing justifies the taker in retaining it against subsequent claimants and transmitting it to others.

The argument is certainly not, apart from its other defects, consistent with positive law. Thus, in South Africa, land cannot be acquired by *occupatio* but only (apart from irrelevant exceptions) by Government grant, statute or thirty years' prescription. The truth is that modes of acquisition, original and derivative, are many and various; one of the functions of expressions such as "he is owner" is precisely to draw similar legal conclusions from varying states of fact.[31]

If, therefore, we are to seek moral reasons why particular persons ought to own particular things we shall need different reasons for different modes of acquisition; and derivative modes of acquisition stand in need of justification as much as original. There are in fact good reasons why the commonest modes of original acquisition (making and taking) and of derivative acquisition (consent and debt) should be recognized. If these are thought morally satisfactory, we have arrived at a justification for the adoption by a legal system of certain modes of acquisition; what we have not found is a justification for the institution of ownership. I do not, of course, wish to imply that none can be found.

Modes of Loss

Once derivative modes of acquisition are recognized, modes of loss or extinction must also be recognized. These give little difficulty when the loss is with the consent of the previous owner or through his debt, but a good deal when the system admits, as many systems do, the possibility of acquiring title or barring a prior title by lapse of time or, as in English Land Law, of acquiring a "title" in the sense defined above, albeit imperfect, by the simple act of squatting or dispossessing the present holder.

In such cases the later acquisition may have the effect either of divesting the earlier or of creating a second, concurrent title: in the latter event, the two titles may continue indefinitely to run concurrently, or the earlier may lapse or become unenforceable after a period of time.

One or Many Titles

This is a convenient point at which to try to classify legal systems according to the number of independent titles which they permit. By "independent" I mean "not derived from a common source."

In the simplest type of system only a single independent title is possible. Such a system may be called *unititular*. Under it, if the title to a thing is in *A,* no title to it can be acquired (independently) by *B,* except by a process which divests *A.* There is only one "root of title" for each thing, and the present title can ultimately be traced back to that root.

In some ways a unititular system is simple, but it may seem to leave unprotected persons whose interests are deserving of protection. It does not provide for the grading of claims to a thing; it proceeds on the view that only one claim is worthy of protection against persons generally, and that other claims need not be recognized, save, perhaps, that a person in possession may be protected against a trespasser or disseisor, a fact which, as we have seen, does not by itself give the possessor a title. A unititular system may be conservative in its working, if acquisition without the consent of the previous owner is made difficult, or may be "active" and may favour enterprise, or even banditry, if acquisition without the consent of the previous owner is easy.

Classical Roman law at first sight approximates to the "active" unititular system, Justinian's law to the "conservative" version, since the period for acquiring by usucapion or prescription and so divesting the previous owner was increased in the latter case. But on a closer examination the Roman system looks conservative at all periods; the mere thief or trespasser and their successors are never favoured, because nothing stolen or taken by force can be acquired in this way, and the owner of such things can never be divested against his will.[32]

It may be thought that the statement that Roman law was substantially unititular is inconsistent with the distinction between Quiritary and "bonitary" ownership. This is true only so far as "defeasible" bonitary owners are concerned. The Quiritary and bonitary "owners" did not hold by independent titles where the "bonitary" ownership was indefeasible. The praetorian, "bonitary" owner derived title from the Quiritary owner. The

division between the two is a case of split ownership, not of independent titles. The *bona fide possessor in via usucapiendi* also had a title, a type of "bonitary" ownership, defeasible only by the true owner; this is, perhaps, the only exception in Roman law to the rule that there was only one title. When the periods of usucapion were short, it was not an exception of much importance; after a year or two there was, once again, only a single title. As the periods were increased the exception grew in importance. Roman law held to the theory that, in such cases, there was only one *dominus.*

Under a unititular system, one way of ascertaining the true owner is by tracing title to the original acquirer. With land, especially, this is seldom practicable. The remedy may lie in rules either of substance or procedure. A substantive rule creating a mode of acquisition which has a divesting effect may meet the need, especially if the period is fairly short. A ruthless form of divesting is found in French law, where the maxim that possession of movables is equivalent to title is interpreted to mean that, if a bailee of goods delivers them by way of sale, gift, etc. to another, he thereby divests the title of the bailor, leaving him to his action for damages against the bailee.

In Roman law, given the rule that theft or violent dispossession was a bar to acquisition running with the thing, it was theoretically necessary to trace title to the original source in order to see whether a "vice" affected the property. If therefore the difficulty of proof of title is, as Hargreaves asserts,[33] a reason against adopting the terminology of ownership, his argument would apply with as much force to Roman and modern civil law as to English law.

In practice, in modern systems based on Roman law, rules of evidence help to overcome the practical difficulties. Possession, unless otherwise explained, is regarded as evidence of ownership and an earlier possession is regarded as better evidence of ownership than a later, independent possession. Registration of title is really an evidentiary device of the same order. In most systems registration does not have a divesting effect;[34] the register may be rectified at the instance of the true owner (or, in a multititular system, someone with a better title than the registered owner).

The register merely makes it possible to discover without difficulty who is presumptively owner.

With *unititular* systems we may contrast *multititular* systems. As we have seen, these turn on the possibility of acquiring title without the consent of the present owner of a thing by a process which does not have a divesting effect. Such systems may take either a "conservative" or an "active" form. In the former the earlier titles continue to be valid indefinitely or for a very long time. In the latter either the right or the remedy is barred after a relatively short period. Again, if the title of a thief or trespasser is recognized, the system is thereby rendered more "active."

The English system as regards both land and chattels falls into the multititular category. As regards land, a title could and can be acquired without the consent of the previous owner by mere disseisin or dispossession.[35] It was a principle of the medieval law that a disseisor ipso facto acquired an estate in fee, albeit a tortious estate. "Every fee simple is not *legitimum,* for a disseisor, abator, intruder, usurper, etc. have a fee simple, but it is not a lawful fee."[36] In the modern law it seems that a dispossession adverse to the present holder gives the trespasser or squatter an estate in fee simple;[37] despite Holdsworth,[38] every adverse possession is a root of title,[39] though the title may lapse on abandonment.[40]

Such ease of acquisition is consistent with a unititular system. Thus in the early land law disseisin had a divesting effect; the disseisee had a mere right of entry, which might be tolled, and was inalienable. Since the nineteenth-century reforms the disseisee or his modern equivalent can alienate his interest *inter vivos* or on death and it descends to his personal representatives.[41] Hence, as Megarry and Wade say, when S dispossesses O, "S's possession gives all the rights and powers of ownership: S has, in fact, a legal estate, a fee simple absolute in possession. But so also has O, until such time as his title is extinguished by limitation. There is no absurdity of speaking of two or more adverse estates in the land, for their validity is relative."[42]

If, then, S and O both have fees simple, shall we say that both are owners of the land? Or shall we call S, the present possessor, alone owner, but

say that his ownership may be divested; or, again, that O, since his claim is ultimately entitled to prevail, is alone owner? One cannot expect clear criteria for answering such questions. S, however, has every incident of ownership except security against divesting, while O has every such incident except present enjoyment. There is much to be said, therefore, for treating them as independent owners rather than as persons sharing a single, split ownership.

On the other hand, it may be argued that, in view of such puzzles, it would be better not to speak of the ownership of land in English law at all. This argument ignores the many straightforward cases in which there is a single tenant in fee simple and no competing title.

Hargreaves, who argues against speaking of "ownership" in English land law, relies on the fact that in actions for the recovery of land the plaintiff need only prove a better title than the defendant, not that his title is the best of all possible titles.[43] Now, a multititular system must have rules for enabling the holders of titles to recover possession and for regulating priorities between the holders of competing titles. There will not, therefore, be any prodecural need in such a system to provide a special remedy (e.g., a *vindicatio*) for the person with the best title. The holder of the best title can make use of the remedies (e.g., ejectment) available to those with *a title.* The point of such a system is that proof of any title will suffice except against a person who can show a better. But, of course, if priorities are regulated someone must have top priority; *maius ius* implies *maximum ius.* Surely the holder of *maximum ius,* at least, cannot be denied the title of owner? It will, however, be never necessary, though always sufficient, when he claims the possession of land, for him to prove that he has *maximum ius.*

English land law exhibits a highly "active" system of regulating title, owing to the relatively short period of limitation coupled with the recognition of the disseisor's title. Sociological writers may detect in this the mores of the Germanic tribes who invaded Britain; but as the twelve-year period of limitation is a modern innovation, the system has not always been as "active" as it now is.

The English law of title to chattels is also mul-tititular. It is not clear, however, that a thief ac-quires title except against a later wrongdoer;[44] hence the rules for chattels are in some ways less "active" than for land. Divesting, may however, take place either by limitation or by certain con-sensual dispositions (sale in market overt, sale by factors). The Sale of Goods Act makes a sharp distinction between the holder of *the title,* who can give a "good title" to the goods and the holders of lesser titles.[45] Only the former can make a valid disposition of the thing by way of sale. Hence there is no temptation to speak of goods as having more than one independent owner.

From what has been said, it emerges that mul-tititular systems are more flexible than unititular systems, though they are not necessarily more "active." The difference between these two ways of regulating title has often been construed as a difference between two conceptions of ownership. This, I suggest, is a mistake. The only difference of importance between the place of ownership in the two schemes is procedural: what has to be proved in an action. But whether a plaintiff must prove that he is owner, and what is to be understood by ownership, are entirely distinct questions.

III. SPLIT OWNERSHIP

Space does not permit more than a few brief re-marks on the subject of split ownership and the fragments (*Eigentumssplitter*) created by splitting. Historically, there have been many reasons for separating the standard incidents into two or more parcels; indeed, historically speaking, the metaphor of "splitting" may mislead, for in some cases full ownership has been built up from the fragments, not vice versa. Thus, the alienable, her-itable and indefeasible fee simple was evolved from the inalienable and intransmissible tenancy in fee, subject to onerous incidents of tenure.

But looked at from the point of view of their social function, the various cases of splitting fall into two main classes. Many of them are directed towards maintaining intact a physical thing or col-lection or, in more modern times, a fund, in order that this asset may serve a family or a business[46] or an association over a substantial period. In this class fall such examples of splitting as concurrent interests in property (joint tenancy, tenancy in common, co-ownership, the interest of spouses in a community estate, the interest of members of an unincorporated association in the property of the association); and the ownership of property by juristic persons (corporations sole, *Stiftungen,* the state, joint stock companies). Secondly, split-ting may serve the purpose of specialization, by separating management from the enjoyment of income or disposition of the capital; the benefi-ciary obtains the advantage of expert management of the property but also runs some risk. In this second class fall such devices as trusts, the Dutch *bewind* (administration), and incorporated companies.

Most of these institutions have been carefully analysed by specialist writers. Some of them pres-ent problems to a lawyer who has to work with a rule that every thing must have one and only one independent "owner." Ought we, for instance, to speak of "equitable ownership" or only of "equi-table interests"? In answer to such questions gen-eralities are unhelpful. If the context is one in which stress is laid on income rights we may be tempted to speak of "equitable ownership" but, if powers of alienation are in question, the holder of the legal estate will alone qualify (if anyone) to be called owner.

There is, however, one device, formerly used mainly to keep a thing or fund in a family over a period, which has not been analysed as carefully as it deserves. This is the device of the *estate.* Its originality has been exaggerated by some, mini-mized by others. Considering it in its mature form, it provides for the present alienability of an indefinite number of successive interests in a thing, of which, however, not more than one may be a fee simple. Only one of these, obviously, can be presently vested in possession. It further provides for the creation of limited interests which may extend beyond a lifetime, such as estates tail. Finally, it provides for certain rules of descent to regulate the devolution of the thing in the cases where the interest is regarded as extending beyond a lifetime, e.g., again in the case of an entail. These are interesting devices, though not in every way successful. For instance, the freedom thereby given to property owners to impose fetters on future generations turned out to be excessive, and counteracting devices such as the barring of entails were found desirable to redress the balance.

It is important, however, to see that to speak of the ownership of estates, of "many things each with its owner,"[47] rather than the ownership of land or funds does not of itself constitute an original contribution to our legal resources. It would be quite possible, indeed, to reproduce *all* the important features of the doctrine of estates in the terminology of Roman and civilian systems. We have only to think of a set of rules whereby (i) all usufructs and other *iura in re aliena* are freely alienable, (ii) an indefinite number of successive vested usufructs may coexist (As regards all but one, *dies cedit sed nondum venit*), (iii) multiple usufructs extending beyond a lifetime may be created and (iv) these are of various types, to which names are given, and for each a particular mode of devolution and termination is prescribed. Such a scheme would incorporate all the innovations introduced by the doctrine of estates. Would there, however, be any point, if it were introduced, in continuing to distinguish between *dominium* and *iura in re aliena*?

Clearly there would. The distinction would still neatly fit a vast mass of cases, in which the complexities of successive and multiple usufructs were absent, and also most cases in which they were present. But when multiple usufructs were introduced which might extend to an indefinite succession of usufructuaries (corresponding to entails) it would come to seem rather pointless to continue to call the ultimate reversioner *dominus,* because of the uncertainty that he would ever come into possession. There would, indeed, be an inclination to call the "usufructuary-in-tail" *dominus.* But, obviously, at this limit, it would be clearer to abandon the terminology of ownership and speak simply of *A* as having a "usufruct-in-tail," and of *B* as having a "reversion." Only at this limit, however, would the contrast between

dominum and *iura in re aliena* fade and its utility disappear.

There does not, then, seem any good reason why the introduction of the doctrine of estates should lead us to abandon the terminology of ownership; the puzzles it presents in peripheral cases are like those presented by other forms of split ownership in such cases, and may, of course, lead a lawyer, very reasonably, not to use the contrast of ownership with lesser interests *in those cases.*

IV. SOCIAL CONTROL

"Absolute" is perhaps the most ambiguous word met in discussions of ownership. Sometimes it is used to deny the "temporary" (intransmissible or determinate) character of an interest,[48] sometimes to deny its defeasible character (liable to be divested by another, liable to escheat or forfeiture),[49] sometimes to emphasize its exemption from social control.

In the last sense, ownership has never been absolute. Even in the most individualistic ages of Rome and the United States, it has had a social aspect. This has usually been expressed in such incidents of ownership as the prohibition of harmful use, liability to execution for debt, to taxation and to expropriation by the public authority.

Emphasis on the social aspect of ownership has, however, varied from age to age. Those "sacred and inviolable" rights, which, according to the *Declaration of the Rights of Man,* no one could be forced to cede except for *public necessity*[50] have become, in French law, liable to expropriation on grounds of *public utility*[51] and subject to a general doctrine forbidding "abuse." According to the liberal conception of ownership, there is a sharp distinction between government and ownership, *imperium* and *dominium.* Though, in a loose sense, the state may be said to have an "eminent domain" over at least the land comprising its territory, this does not carry with it rights to possess, enjoy, or alienate it, so that the sense in which the state is owner is very loose indeed. The interest of the state, according to this conception, is confined to powers of expropriation and a minimum of restrictive regulation, together with the expectancy of acquiring property as *bona vacantia* or by escheat in a few rather remote contingencies.

Socialism has led to a revised view of the relation between government and ownership, at least as regards some important types of property,[52] such as land and businesses. This means, in practice, that the owner's privileges of using and powers of managing a thing as he wishes have been curtailed and that the social interest in the productive use of things has been affirmed by legislation. Negatively, this process has meant that, in the interests of health and comfort, many substances cannot be used at all or can only be used in certain ways. The sale of drugs is minutely controlled, only smokeless fuel may be used in certain areas, garden hoses may not be used at certain periods. Such instances, multiplied a thousand fold, have come to seem so natural that we hardly realize that the social interest in the use of things, the conservation of resources and in the details of manufacturing processes is a modern, though it is also a primitive, conception.

Positive control by the state shades into prohibition. The positive duty to exploit one's property in a socially beneficial way, as opposed to the prohibition of a harmful exploitation, has not been generally imposed or its implications fully worked out. The British Agriculture Act imposed an obligation on farmers to observe the rules of good husbandry;[53] the owners of patents can in certain cases be compelled to allow their exploitation.[54] According to the Russian civil law book of 1944, the state has a general right to order forfeiture of property in case of mismanagement; there is also a general prohibition on the use of property to exploit others.[55]

A different form of state control is exercised by drawing a distinction between different types of ownership. In Russia the ownership of collective farmers, of handicraftsmen and of the Government are all treated as differing from "personal ownership" and from one another.[56]

The difference lies, of course, in the right of officials to interfere in the management of the former categories and in state regulation of income

rights deriving from the property; also in differing rules about alienation. In this way the sphere of operation of ownership in the liberal sense is narrowed and a form of state participation in management substituted in the remaining sphere.

A third form of social control consists in the exercise by officials of the management of things in the "private" ownership of the state. Such arrangements present the form but not the substance of ownership in the liberal sense. Management and enjoyment are split, and political control, directly or indirectly, is exercised over the allocation of resources and the uses to which the thing owned is put. The nationalized industries in the United Kingdom follow this pattern of control.

Fourthly, social control may be exercised by a restriction on the type of thing that is subject to ownership by persons other than the state, as in the Russian building lease, where the building is owned by a private individual, the land remaining in state ownership.[57] In effect, this restricts the privileges of the building owner in the general interest.

It remains to be seen which combination of these techniques will prove most effective and most acceptable to the people who have to operate them. So far, they have not, singly or together, reached the point in any country at which they could be said to have displaced the liberal conception of ownership and replaced it by a social conception. In practice the two overlap, and operate side by side, together with various types of split ownership and ownership of funds which diverge, to a greater or less extent, from the standard instances depicted in the first Section. The final picture is that of a set of related institutions of great complexity which are best studied against the background of the basic model—a single human being owning, in the full liberal sense, a single material thing.

NOTES

1. Malinowsky, *Crime and Custom in Savage Society*, p. 18.
2. Gsovski, *Soviet Civil Law*, p. 56g.
3. Vegting, *Domaine public et res extra commercium*.

4. Pollock and Maitland, *History of English Law to 1290.*, Vol. 11, p. 4
5. *Code civil*, art. 544.
6. Soviet civil code, art. 58.
7. (1934), Vol. IV, pp. 130–146.
8. Land Tax Assessment Act, 1910, s. 3.
9. *Union Trustee Co. of Australia, Ltd. v. Land Tax Federal Commission* (1915), 20 C.L.R. 526, at p. 531.
10. *Woodard v. Billericay Harbour Board* (1879), 11 Ch. D. 214, at p. 217.
11. In this article I identify rights with claims, liberties etc. For a criticism of this identification see (1960), 34 Tulane L.R. 453.
12. *The Common Law*, p. 213.
13. Pollock & Wright, *Possession in the Common Law* (1888), pp. 91, 95; Wade and Megarry, *The Law of Real Property* (2nd ed.), p. 955.
14. *N.R.M.A. Insurance, Ltd. v. B. & B. Shipping and Marine Salvage Co. (Pty), Ltd.* (1947), 47 S.G.R. (N.S.W.) 273.
15. J. W. Jones. "Forms of Ownership." *Tulane L.R.* 22 (1947): 83, 93.
16. Hanbury, *Modern Equity* (1952), p. 114.
17. Constitution of the U.S.S.R., 1936, s. 10; Gsovski, supra, note 2, at 620.
18. Holmes (1897), 10 Harv. L.R. 457, 461.
19. *Cape v. Sharpe*, [1912] 1 K.B. 496; *Cresswell v. Sirl*, [1948] 1 K.B. 241.
20. Pollock & Maitland, supra, note 4, Vol. II, p. 10.
21. Planiol-Ripert-Esmein, *Traite pratique de droit civil franc̦ais* (1952), Vol. II, p. 220.
22. Hargreaves, *Introduction to the Principles of Land Law* (1952), p. 47.
23. Austin, *Jurisprudence*, 4th ed., (1873), p. 817.
24. Hart, *Definition and Theory in Jurisprudence* (1953), p. 16: (1951), 79, L.Q.R. 49.
25. J. von Gierke, *Sachenrecht* (1948), p. 67. *Cf.,* Markby, *Elements of Law considered with reference to Principles of General Jurisprudence* (6th ed.), pp. 157–158.
26. *Cf.,* Turner, *Some Reflections on Ownership in English Law* (1941), 19 Can. B. R. 342.
27. Palandt, *Burgeliches Gesetzbuch* (1956), p. 806.
28. *Cf.,* Wilson, G. P. "Jurisprudence and the Discussion of Ownership." *Camb. L.J.* (1957): 216.
29. *The Common Law*, p. 245.
30. Locke, *Second Treatise on Civil Government*, ch. 5, s. 26.
31. This is overlooked by A. Ross. "Tu-Tu." *Harv. L. R.* 70 (1956-7): 812.
32. To this Cod. 7.39.8 makes a small exception.
33. Hargreaves, "Terminology and Title in Ejectment." *L.Q.R.* 56 (1940): 376, 377.
34. Wade and Megarry, *The Law of Real Property* (2nd ed.), p. 960 n. 33.
35. Littleton, *Tenures*, ss. 473, 519, 520; *Asher v. Whitlock* (1865), L.R. 1 Q.B. 1; *Allen v. Roughley* (1955), 94. C.L.R. 98.
36. Coke on *Littleton*, 2a; see also *ibid.*, 297a.
37. *The Time Limit of Actions*, p. 125.
38. *History of English Law*, Vol. VII, p. 64.
39. Some authorities go no further than to say that possession is prima facie evidence of seisin in fee and so of a title: *Allen v. Roughley* (supra, note 35), *per* Dixon J., at p. 109.
40. *Allen v. Roughley* (supra, note 35), per Williams J., at p. 118.
41. Cheshire, *Modern Law of Real Property* (8th ed.), p. 30.
42. Wade and Megarry. *The Law of Real Property* (2nd ed.), p. 958.
43. *Terminology and Title in Ejectment* (1949), 56 L. Q.R. 376, 377.
44. *Buckley v. Gross* (1863), 3 B. & S. 566.
45. Sale of Goods Act, 1893, ss. 21–23.
46. Gower, *Principles of Modern Company Law* (1954), p. 10.
47. Pollock and Maitland, supra, note 4, at 4.
48. Hargreaves, *Introduction to the Principles of Land Law* (1952), p. 44.
49. Id., at 46.
50. *Declaration of the Rights of Man*, art, 17.
51. Code civil, art. 545.
52. Friedmann, *Law and Social Change in Contemporary Britain* (1951), ch. 2.
53. Agriculture Act, 1947, ss. 9–11. The Agriculture Act, 1958, Second Schedule, repealed s. 9.
54. Patents and Designs Act, 1949, s. 16.
55. Gsovski, supra, note 2, at 557.
56. Gsovski, supra, note 2, at 569.
57. Gsovski, supra, note 2, at 580.

70   *Contract as Promise*

CHARLES FRIED

CONTRACT AS PROMISE

It is a first principle of liberal political morality that we be secure in what is ours—so that our persons and property not be open to exploitation by others, and that from a sure foundation we may express our will and expend our powers in the world. By these powers we may create good things or low, useful articles or luxuries, things extraordinary or banal, and we will be judged accordingly—as saintly or mean, skillful or ordinary, industrious and fortunate or debased, friendly and kind or cold and inhuman. But whatever we accomplish and however that accomplishment is judged, morality requires that we respect the person and property of others, leaving them free to make their lives as we are left free to make ours. This is the liberal ideal. This is the ideal that distinguishes between the good, which is the domain of aspiration, and the right, which sets the terms and limits according to which we strive. This ideal makes what we achieve our own and our failures our responsibility too—however much or little we may choose to share our good fortune and however we may hope for help when we fail.[1]

Everything must be available to us, for who can deny the human will the title to expand even into the remotest corner of the universe? And when we forbear to bend some external object to our use because of its natural preciousness we use it still, for it is to our judgment of its value that we respond, our own conception of the good that we pursue. Only other persons are not available to us in this way—they alone share our self-consciousness, our power of self-determination; thus to use them as if they were merely part of external nature is to poison the source of the moral power we enjoy. But others *are* part of the external world, and by denying ourselves access to their persons and powers, we drastically shrink the scope of our efficacy. So it was a crucial moral discovery that free men may yet freely serve each others' purposes: the discovery that beyond the fear of reprisal or the hope of reciprocal favor, morality itself be enlisted to assure not only that you respect me and mine but that you actively serve my purposes.[2] When my confidence in your assistance derives from my conviction that you will do what is right (not just what is prudent), then I trust you, and trust becomes a powerful tool for our working our mutual wills in the world. So remarkable a tool is trust that in the end we pursue it for its own sake; we prefer doing things cooperatively when we might have relied on fear or interest or worked alone.[3]

The device that gives trust its sharpest, most palpable form is promise. By promising we put in another man's hands a new power to accomplish his will, though only a moral power: What he sought to do alone he may now expect to do with our promised help, and to give him this new facility was our very purpose in promising. By promising we transform a choice that was morally neutral into one that is morally compelled. Morality, which must be permanent and beyond our particular will if the grounds for our willing are to be secure, is itself invoked, molded to allow us better to work that particular will. Morality then serves modest, humdrum ends: We make appointments, buy and sell, harnessing this loftiest of all forces.

What is a promise, that by my words I should make wrong what before was morally indifferent? A promise is a communication—usually verbal; it says something. But how can my saying something put a moral charge on a choice that before was morally neutral? Well, by my misleading you, or by lying.[4] Is lying not the very paradigm of doing wrong by speaking? But this won't do, for

From *Contract as Promise: A Theory of Contractual Obligation* (Cambridge, MA: Harvard University Press, 1981), pp. 7–39. Notes have been renumbered. Reprinted with permission of the publisher.

a promise puts the moral charge on a *potential* act—the wrong is done later, when the promise is not kept—while a lie is a wrong committed at the time of its utterance. Both wrongs abuse trust, but in different ways. When I speak I commit myself to the truth of my utterance, but when I promise I commit myself to *act,* later. Though these two wrongs are thus quite distinct there has been a persistent tendency to run them together by treating a promise as a lie after all, but a particular kind of lie: a lie about one's intentions. Consider this case:

> I. I sell you a house, retaining an adjacent vacant lot. At the time of our negotiations, I state that I intend to build a home for myself on that lot. What if several years later I sell the lot to a person who builds a gas station on it? What if I sell it only one month later? What if I am already negotiating for its sale as a gas station at the time I sell the house to you?[5]

If I was already negotiating to sell the lot for a gas station at the time of my statement to you, I have wronged you. I have lied to you about the state of my intentions, and this is as much a lie as a lie about the state of the plumbing.[6] If, however, I sell the lot many years later, I do you no wrong. There are no grounds for saying I lied about my intentions; I have just changed my mind. Now if I had *promised* to use the lot only as a residence, the situation would be different. Promising is more than just truthfully reporting my present intentions, for I may be free to change my mind, as I am not free to break my promise.

Let us take it as given here that lying is wrong and so that it is wrong to obtain benefits or cause harm by lying (including lying about one's intentions). It does not at all follow that to obtain a benefit or cause harm by breaking a promise is also wrong. That my act procures me a benefit or causes harm all by itself proves nothing. If I open a restaurant near your hotel and prosper as I draw your guests away from the standard hotel fare you offer, this benefit I draw from you places me under no obligation to you. I should make restitution only if I benefit *unjustly,* which I do if I deceive you—as when I lie to you about my intentions in example I.[7] But where is the injustice

if I honestly intend to keep my promise at the time of making it, and later change my mind? If we feel I owe you recompense in that case too, it cannot be because of the benefit I have obtained through my promise: We have seen that benefit even at another's expense is not alone sufficient to require compensation. If I owe you a duty to return that benefit it must be because of the promise. It is the promise that makes my enrichment at your expense unjust, and not the enrichment that makes the promise binding. And thus neither the statement of intention nor the benefit explains why, if at all, a promise does any moral work.

A more common attempt to reduce the force of a promise to some other moral category invokes the harm you suffer in relying on my promise. My statement is like a pit I have dug in the road, into which you fall. I have harmed you and should make you whole. Thus the tort principle might be urged to bridge the gap in the argument between a statement of intention and a promise: I have a duty just because I could have foreseen (indeed it was my intention) that you would rely on my promise and that you would suffer harm when I broke it. And this wrong then not only sets the stage for compensation of the harm caused by the misplaced reliance, but also supplies the moral predicate for restitution of any benefits I may have extracted from you on the strength of my promise.[8] But we still beg the question. If the promise is no more than a truthful statement of my intention, why am *I* responsible for harm that befalls you as a result of my change of heart? To be sure, it is not like a change in the weather—I might have kept to my original intention—but how does this distinguish the broken promise from any other statement of intention (or habit or prediction of future conduct) of mine of which you know and on which you choose to rely? Should your expectations of me limit my freedom of choice? If you rent the apartment next to mine because I play chamber music there, do I owe you more than an expression of regret when my friends and I decide to meet instead at the cellist's home? And in general, why should my liberty be constrained by the harm you would suffer from the disappointment of the expectations you choose to entertain about my choices?

Does it make a difference that when I promise you do not just happen to rely on me, that I communicate my intention to you and therefore can be taken to know that changing my mind may put you at risk? But then I might be aware that you would count on my keeping to my intentions even if I myself had not communicated those intentions to you. (*You* might have told me you were relying on me, or you might have overheard me telling some third person of my intentions.) It might be said that I become the agent of your reliance by telling you, and that this makes my responsibility clearer: After all, I can scarcely control all the ways in which you might learn of my intentions, but I *can* control whether or not I tell you of them. But we are still begging the question. If promising is no more than my telling you of my intentions, why do we both not know that I may yet change my mind? Perhaps, then, promising is like telling you of my intention and telling you that I don't intend to change my mind. But why can't I change my mind about the latter intention?

Perhaps the statement of intention in promising is binding because we not only foresee reliance, we invite it: We intend the promisee to rely on the promise. Yet even this will not do. If I invite reliance on my stated intention, then that is all I invite. Certainly I may hope and intend, in example I, that you buy my house on the basis of what I have told you, but why does that hope bind me to do more than state my intention honestly? And that intention and invitation are quite compatible with my later changing my mind. In every case, of course, I should weigh the harm I will do if I do change my mind. If I am a doctor and I know you will rely on me to be part of an outing on which someone may fall ill, I should certainly weigh the harm that may come about if that reliance is disappointed. Indeed I should weigh that harm even if you do not rely on me, but are foolish enough not to have made a provision for a doctor. Yet in none of these instances am I bound as I would be had I promised.[9]

A promise invokes trust in my future actions, not merely in my present sincerity. We need to isolate an additional element, over and above benefit, reliance, and the communication of intention. That additional element must *commit* me, and commit me to more than the truth of some statement. That additional element has so far eluded our analysis.

It has eluded us, I believe, because there is a real puzzle about how we can commit ourselves to a course of conduct that absent our commitment is morally neutral. The invocation of benefit and reliance are attempts to explain the force of a promise in terms of two of its most usual effects, but the attempts fail because these effects depend on the prior assumption of the force of the commitment. The way out of the puzzle is to recognize the bootstrap quality of the argument: To have force in *a particular case* promises must be assumed to have force generally. Once that general assumption is made, the effects we intentionally produce by a particular promise may be morally attributed to us. This recognition is not as paradoxical as its abstract statement here may make it seem. It lies, after all, behind every conventional structure: games,[10] institutions and practices, and most important, language.

Let us put to one side the question of how a convention comes into being, or of when and why we are morally bound to comply with its terms, while we look briefly at what a convention is and how it does its work. Take the classical example of a game. What the players do is defined by a system of rules—sometimes quite vague and informal, sometimes elaborate and codified. These rules apply only to the players—that is, to persons who invoke them. These rules are a human invention, and their consequences (castling, striking out, winning, losing) can be understood only in terms of the rules. The players may have a variety of motives for playing (profit, fun, maybe even duty to fellow players who need participants). A variety of judgments are applicable to the players—they may be deemed skillful, imaginative, bold, honest, or dishonest—but these judgments and motives too can be understood only in the context of the game. For instance, you can cheat only by breaking rules to which you pretend to conform.

This almost canonical invocation of the game example has often been misunderstood as somehow applying only to unserious matters, to play, so that it is said to trivialize the solemn objects (like law or promises) that it is used to explain. But this is a mistake, confusing the interests involved, the reasons for creating and invoking a particular convention, with the logical structure of conventions in general. Games are (often) played for fun, but other conventions—for instance religious rituals or legal procedures—may have most earnest ends, while still other conventions are quite general. To the last category belongs language. The conventional nature of language is too obvious to belabor. It is worth pointing out, however, that the various things we do with language—informing, reporting, promising, insulting, cheating, lying—all depend on the conventional structure's being firmly in place. You could not lie if there were not both understanding of the language you lied in and a general convention of using that language truthfully. This point holds irrespective of whether the institution of language has advanced the situation of mankind and of whether lying is sometimes, always, or never wrong.

Promising too is a very general convention—though less general than language, of course, since promising is itself a use of language.[11] The convention of promising (like that of language) has a very general purpose under which we may bring an infinite set of particular purposes. In order that I be as free as possible, that my will have the greatest possible range consistent with the similar will of others, it is necessary that there be a way in which I may commit myself. It is necessary that I be able to make nonoptional a course of conduct that would otherwise be optional for me. By doing this I can facilitate the projects of others, because I can make it possible for those others to count on my future conduct, and thus those others can pursue more intricate, more far-reaching projects. If it is my purpose, my will that others be able to count on me in the pursuit of their endeavor, it is essential that I be able to deliver myself into their hands more firmly than where they simply predict my future course. Thus the possibility of commitment permits an act of generosity on my part, permits me to pursue a project whose content is that *you* be permitted to pursue *your* project. But of course this purely altruistic motive is not the only motive worth facilitating. More central to our concern is the situation where we facilitate each other's projects, where the gain is reciprocal. Schematically the situation looks like this:

You want to accomplish purpose A and I want to accomplish purpose B. Neither of us can succeed without the cooperation of the other. Thus I want to be able to commit myself to help you achieve A so that you will commit yourself to help me achieve B.

Now if A and B are objects or actions that can be transferred simultaneously there is no need for commitment. As I hand over A you hand over B, and we are both satisfied. But very few things are like that. We need a device to permit a trade over time: to allow me to do A for you when you need it, in the confident belief that you will do B for me when I need it. Your commitment puts your future performance into my hands in the present just as my commitment puts my future performance into your hands. A future exchange is transformed into a present exchange. And in order to accomplish this all we need is a conventional device which we both invoke, which you know I am invoking when I invoke it, which I know that you know I am invoking, and so on.

The only mystery about this is the mystery that surrounds increasing autonomy by providing means for restricting it. But really this is a pseudo-mystery. The restrictions involved in promising are restrictions undertaken just in order to increase one's options in the long run, and thus are perfectly consistent with the principle of autonomy—consistent with a respect for one's own autonomy and the autonomy of others. To be sure, in getting something for myself now by promising to do something for you in the future, I am mortgaging the interest of my future self in favor of my present self. How can I be sure my future self will approve?[12] This is a deep and difficult problem about which I say more later. Suffice it to say here that unless one assumes the continuity of the self and the possibility of maintaining complex projects over time, not only the morality of promising but also any coherent picture of the person becomes impossible.

The Moral Obligation of Promise

Once I have invoked the institution of promising, why exactly is it wrong for me then to break my promise?

My argument so far does not answer that question. The institution of promising is a way for me to bind myself to another so that the other may expect a future performance, and binding myself in this way is something that I may want to be able to do. But this by itself does not show that I am morally obligated to perform my promise at a later time if to do so proves inconvenient or costly. That there should be a system of currency also increases my options and is useful to me, but this does not show why I should not use counterfeit money if I can get away with it. In just the same way the usefulness of promising in general does not show why I should not take advantage of it in a particular case and yet fail to keep my promise. That the convention would cease to function in the long run, would cease to provide benefits if everyone felt free to violate it, is hardly an answer to the question of why I should keep a particular promise on a particular occasion.

David Lewis has shown[13] that a convention that it would be in each person's interest to observe if everyone else observed it will be established and maintained without any special mechanisms of commitment or enforcement. Starting with simple conventions (for example that if a telephone conversation is disconnected, the person who initiated the call is the one who calls back) Lewis extends his argument to the case of language. Now promising is different, since (unlike language, where it is overwhelmingly in the interest of all that everyone comply with linguistic conventions, even when language is used to deceive) it will often be in the interest of the promisor *not* to conform to the convention when it comes time to render his performance. Therefore individual self-interest is not enough to sustain the convention, and some additional ground is needed to keep it from unraveling. There are two principal candidates: external sanctions and moral obligation.

David Hume sought to combine these two by proposing that the external sanction of public opprobrium, of loss of reputation for honesty, which society attaches to promise-breaking, is internalized, becomes instinctual, and accounts for the sense of the moral obligation of promise.[14] Though Hume offers a possible anthropological or psychological account of how people feel about promises, his is not a satisfactory *moral* argument. Assume that I can get away with breaking my promise (the promisee is dead), and I am now asking why I should keep it anyway in the face of some personal inconvenience. Hume's account of obligation is more like an argument *against* my keeping the promise, for it tells me how any feelings of obligation that I may harbor have come to lodge in my psyche and thus is the first step toward ridding me of such inconvenient prejudices.

Considerations of self-interest cannot supply the moral basis of my obligation to keep a promise. By an analogous argument neither can considerations of utility. For however sincerely and impartially I may apply the utilitarian injunction to consider at each step how I might increase the sum of happiness or utility in the world, it will allow me to break my promise whenever the balance of advantage (including, of course, my own advantage) tips in that direction. The possible damage to the institution of promising is only one factor in the calculation. Other factors are the alternative good I might do by breaking my promise, whether and by how many people the breach might be discovered, what the actual effect on confidence of such a breach would be. There is no a priori reason for believing that an individual's calculations will come out in favor of keeping the promise always, sometimes, or most of the time.

Rule-utilitarianism seeks to offer a way out of this conundrum. The individual's moral obligation is determined not by what the best action at a particular moment would be, but by the rule it would be best for him to follow. It has, I believe, been demonstrated that this position is incoherent: Either rule-utilitarianism requires that rules be followed in a particular case even where the result would not be best all things considered, and so the utilitarian aspect of rule-utilitarianism is abandoned; or the obligation to follow the rule is so qualified as to collapse into act-utilitarianism after all.[15] There is, however, a version of rule-utilitarianism that makes a great deal of sense. In this version the utilitarian does not instruct us what our individual moral obligations are but rather instructs legislators what the best rules are.[16] If legislation is our focus, then the contradictions of rule-utilitarianism do not arise, since we are instructing those whose decisions can *only* take the form of issuing rules. From that perspective there is obvious utility to rules establishing and enforcing promissory obligations. Since I am concerned now with the question of individual obligation, that is, moral obligation, this legislative perspective on the argument is not available to me.

The obligation to keep a promise is grounded not in arguments of utility but in respect for individual autonomy and in trust. Autonomy and trust are grounds for the institution of promising as well, but the argument for *individual* obligation is not the same. Individual obligation is only a step away, but that step must be taken.[17] An individual is morally bound to keep his promises because he has intentionally invoked a convention whose function it is to give grounds—moral grounds—for another to expect the promised performance.[18] To renege is to abuse a confidence he was free to invite or not, and which he intentionally did invite. To abuse that confidence now is like (but only *like*) lying: the abuse of a shared social institution that is intended to invoke the bonds of trust. A liar and a promise-breaker each *use* another person. In both speech and promising there is an invitation to the other to trust, to make himself vulnerable; the liar and the promise-breaker then abuse that trust. The obligation to keep a promise is thus similar to but more constraining than the obligation to tell the truth. To avoid lying you need only believe in the truth of what you say when you say it, but a promise binds into the future, well past the moment when the promise is made. There will, of course, be great social utility to a general regime of trust and confidence in promises and truthfulness. But this just shows that a regime of mutual respect allows men and women to accomplish what in a jungle of unrestrained self-interest could not be accomplished. If this advantage is to be firmly established, there must exist a ground for mutual confidence deeper

than and independent of the social utility it permits.

The utilitarian counting the advantages affirms the general importance of enforcing *contracts*. The moralist of duty, however, sees *promising* as a device that free, moral individuals have fashioned on the premise of mutual trust, and which gathers its moral force from that premise. The moralist of duty thus posits a general obligation to keep promises, of which the obligation of contract will be only a special case—that special case in which certain promises have attained legal as well as moral force. But since a contract is first of all a promise, the contract must be kept because a promise must be kept.

To summarize: There exists a convention that defines the practice of promising and its entailments. This convention provides a way that a person may create expectations in others. By virtue of the basic Kantian principles of trust and respect, it is wrong to invoke that convention in order to make a promise, and then to break it.

What a Promise Is Worth

If I make a promise to you, I should do as I promise; and if I fail to keep my promise, it is fair that I should be made to hand over the equivalent of the promised performance. In contract doctrine this proposition appears as the expectation measure of damages for breach. The expectation standard gives the victim of a breach no more or less than he would have had had there been no breach—in other words, he gets the benefit of his bargain.[19] Two alternative measures of damage, reliance and restitution, express the different notions that if a person has relied on a promise and been hurt, that hurt must be made good; and that if a contract-breaker has obtained goods or services, he must be made to pay a fair (just?) price for them.[20] Consider three cases:

> II-A. I enter your antique shop on a quiet afternoon and agree in writing to buy an expensive chest I see there, the price being about three times what you paid for it a short time ago. When I get home I repent of my decision, and within half an hour of my visit—before any other customer has come to

your store—I telephone to say I no longer want the chest.

II-B. Same as above, except in the meantime you have waxed and polished the chest and had your delivery van bring it to my door.

II-C. Same as above, except I have the use of the chest for six months, while your shop is closed for renovations.

To require me to pay for the chest in case II-A (or, if you resell it, to pay any profit you lost, including lost business volume) is to give you your expectation, the benefit of your bargain. In II-B if all I must compensate is your effort I am reimbursing your reliance, and in II-C to force me to pay a fair price for the use I have had of the chest is to focus on making me pay for, restore, an actual benefit I have received.

The assault on the classical conception of contract, the concept I call contract as promise, has centered on the connection—taken as canonical for some hundred years—between contract law and expectation damages. To focus the attack on this connection is indeed strategic. As the critics recognize and as I have just stated, to the extent that contract is grounded in promise, it seems natural to measure relief by the expectation, that is, by the promise itself. If that link can be threatened, then contract itself may be grounded elsewhere than in promise, elsewhere than in the will of the parties. In his recent comprehensive treatise, *The Rise and Fall of Freedom of Contract*, Patrick Atiyah makes the connection between the recourse to expectation damages and the emerging enforceability of executory contracts—that is, contracts enforced, though no detriment has been suffered in reliance and no benefit has been conferred. (Case II-A is an example of an executory contract.) Before the nineteenth century, he argues, a contractual relation referred generally to one of a number of particular, community-sanctioned relations between persons who in the course of their dealings (as carriers, innkeepers, surgeons, merchants) relied on each other to their detriment or conferred benefits on each other. It was these detriments and benefits that had to be reimbursed, and an explicit promise—if there happened to be one— was important primarily to establish the reliance or to show that the benefit had been conferred in expectation of payment, not officiously or as a gift. All this, Atiyah writes, turned inside out when the promise itself came to be seen as the basis of obligation, so that neither benefit nor reliance any longer seemed necessary and the proper measure of the obligation was the promise itself, that is, the expectation. The promise principle was embraced as an expression of the principle of liberty—the will binding itself, to use Kantian language, rather than being bound by the norms of the collectivity—and the award of expectation damages followed as a natural concomitant of the promise principle.

The insistence on reliance or benefit is related to disputes about the nature of promising. As I have argued, reliance on a promise cannot alone explain its force: There is reliance because a promise is binding, and not the other way around. But if a person is bound by his promise and not by the harm the promisee may have suffered in reliance on it, then what he is bound to is just its performance. Put simply, I am bound to do what I promised you I would do—or I am bound to put you in as good a position as if I had done so. To bind me to do no more than to reimburse your reliance is to excuse me to that extent from the obligation I undertook. If your reliance is less than your expectation (in case II-A there is no reliance), then to that extent a reliance standard excuses me from the very obligation I undertook and so weakens the force of an obligation I chose to assume. Since by hypothesis I chose to assume the obligation in its stronger form (that is, to render the performance promised), the reliance rule indeed precludes me from incurring the very obligation I chose to undertake at the time of promising. The most compelling of the arguments for resisting this conclusion and for urging that we settle for reliance is the sense that it is sometimes harsh and ungenerous to insist on the full measure of expectancy. (This is part of Atiyah's thrust when he designates the expectation standard as an aspect of the rigid Victorian promissory morality.) The harshness comes about because in the event the promisor finds the obligation he assumed too burdensome.

This distress may be analyzed into three forms: (1) The promisor regrets having to pay for what he has bought (which may only have been the satisfaction of promising a gift or the thrill of buying a lottery ticket or stock option), though he would readily do the same thing again. I take it that this kind of regret merits no sympathy at all. Indeed if we gave in to it we would frustrate the promisor's ability to engage in his own continuing projects and so the promisor's plea is, strictly speaking, self-contradictory. (2) The promisor regrets his promise because he was mistaken about the nature of the burdens he was assuming—the purchaser in case II-A thought he would find the money for the antique but in fact his savings are depleted, or perhaps the chest is not as old nor as valuable as he had imagined, or his house has burned down and he no longer needs it. All of these regrets are based on mistaken assumptions about the facts as they are or as they turn out to be…. [T]he doctrines of mistake, frustration, and impossibility provide grounds for mitigating the effect of the promise principle without at all undermining it.

Finally there is the most troublesome ground of regret: (3) The promisor made no mistake about the facts or probabilities at all, but now that it has come time to perform he no longer values the promise as highly as when he made it. He regrets the promise because he regrets the value judgment that led him to make it. He concludes that the purchase of an expensive antique is an extravagance. Compassion may lead a promisee to release an obligation in such a case, but he releases as an act of generosity, not as a duty, and certainly not because the promisor's repentance destroys the force of the original obligation. The intuitive reason for holding fast is that such repentance should be the promisor's own responsibility, not one he can shift onto others. It seems too easy a way of getting out of one's obligations. Yet our intuition does not depend on suspicions of insincerity alone. Rather we feel that holding people to their obligations is a way of taking them seriously and thus of giving the concept of sincerity itself serious content. Taking this intuition to a more abstract level, I would say that respect for others as free and rational requires taking seriously their capacity to determine their own values. I invoke again the distinction between the right and the good. The right defines the concept of the self as choosing its own conception of the good. Others must respect our capacity as free and rational persons to choose our own good, and that respect means allowing persons to take responsibility for the good they choose. And, of course, that choosing self is not an instantaneous self but one extended in time, so that to respect those determinations of the self is to respect their persistence over time. If we decline to take seriously the assumption of an obligation because we do not take seriously the promisor's prior conception of the good that led him to assume it, to that extent we do not take him seriously as a person. We infantilize him, as we do quite properly when we release the very young from the consequences of their choices.[21]

Since contracts invoke and are invoked by promises, it is not surprising that the law came to impose on the promises it recognized the same incidents as morality demands. The connection between contract and the expectation principle is so palpable that there is reason to doubt that its legal recognition is a relatively recent invention. It is true that over the last two centuries citizens in the liberal democracies have become increasingly free to dispose of their talents, labor, and property as seems best to them. The freedom to bind oneself contractually to a future disposition is an important and striking example of this freedom (the freedom to make testamentary dispositions or to make whatever present use of one's effort or goods one desires are other examples), because in a promise one is taking responsibility not only for one's present self but for one's future self. But this does not argue that the promise principle itself is a novelty—surely Cicero's, Pufendorf's and Grotius's discussions of it[22] show that it is not—but only that its use has expanded greatly over the years.

Remedies in and around the Promise

Those who have an interest in assimilating contract to the more communitarian standards of tort law have been able to obscure the link between contract and promise because in certain cases the natural thing to do *is* to give damages for the harm that has been suffered, rather than to give the money value of the promised expectation. But it does not follow from these cases that expectation is not a normal and natural measure for contract damages. First, these are situations in which the harm suffered is the measure of damages because it is hard to find the monetary value of the expectation. A leading case, *Security Stove & Mfg. Co. v. American Railway Express Co.*,[23] illustrates the type. The plaintiff stove manufacturer had arranged to have a new kind of stove shipped by the defendant express company to a trade convention, at which the plaintiff hoped to interest prospective buyers in his improved product. The president and his workmen went to the convention, but the defendant failed to deliver a crucial part of the exhibit in time, and they had nothing to show. Plaintiff brought suit to recover the cost of renting the booth, the freight charges, and the time and expenses lost as a result of the fruitless trip to the convention. The recovery of these items of damages, which (with the possible exception of the prepaid booth rental) seem typical examples of reliance losses, is generally agreed to have been appropriate. There was no way of knowing what results the plaintiff would have obtained had he succeeded in exhibiting his product at the convention. There was no way of knowing what his expectancy was, and so the court gave him his loss through reliance. But this illustrates only that where expectancy cannot be calculated, reliance may be a reasonable surrogate. It is reasonable to suppose that the plaintiff's expectation in *Security Stove* was at least as great as the monies he put out to exhibit his goods—after all, he was a businessman and is assumed to have been exhibiting his goods to make an eventual profit. If it could somehow be shown that the exhibit would have been a failure and the plaintiff would have suffered a net loss, the case for recovery would be undermined, and most authorities would then deny recovery.[24,25]

Second are the cases in which the amount needed to undo the harm caused by reliance is itself the fairest measure of expectation:

> III-A. Buyer approaches manufacturer with the specifications of a small, inexpensive part—say a bolt—for a machine buyer is building.
> Manufacturer selects the part and sells it to buyer. The bolt is badly made, shears, and damages the machine.

The value of the thing promised, a well-made bolt, is negligible, but to give buyer his money back and no more would be a grave injustice. Here it does seem more natural to say that the manufacturer induced buyer's reasonable reliance and should compensate the resulting harm. But it is equally the case that it is a fair implication of the simple-seeming original transaction that manufacturer not only delivered and promised to transfer good title to the bolt, but promised at the same time that the bolt would do the job it was meant to do.[26,27]

It is for the (perhaps wholly innocent) breach of this implied promise that we hold manufacturers liable. The soundness of this analysis is brought home if we vary the facts slightly:

> III-B. Same as above, except buyer purchases the bolt over the counter in a local hardware store, saying nothing about its use.

To make the owner of the hardware store or the manufacturer of the bolt responsible for large damages in this case seems unfair. One can say that this is because they could not *foresee* harm of this magnitude arising out of their conduct.

(A tort locution: The man who negligently jostles a package containing a bomb could not *foresee* and is not responsible for harm of the ensuing magnitude when the package explodes.) But one can as well cast the matter again in contractual terms, saying that they did not undertake this measure of responsibility. After all, if in the first version of this example the buyer and manufacturer had agreed that manufacturer would be responsible only up to a certain amount, say ten times the cost of the bolt, such a limitation would generally be respected. So in certain cases tort and contract ideas converge on the same result.[28] In III-A we may say that buyer justifiably relied on manufacturer. He relied in part because of the (implied) promise or warranty, and of course it is a primary function of promises to induce reliance. Consider finally this variation:

> III-C. Manufacturer makes not bolts but tinned goods. Buyer buys a can of peas at a

grocer's and serves them to a guest who chips a tooth on a stone negligently included in the can.

Manufacturer promised the guest nothing. (In legal terminology there is between them no privity of contract.) Yet manufacturer should be responsible for the guest's injuries, just as the driver of a car should be responsible for the injuries of a pedestrian whom he negligently hits, though there too privity of contract is lacking.[29] One may say that the guest reasonably relied on the purity of the peas he ate, just as a pedestrian must rely on the due care of motorists. But I never argued that promise is the *only* basis of reliance or that contract is the only basis of responsibility for harms to others.

Third, there are cases in which wrongs are committed and loss is suffered in and around the attempt to make an agreement. In these cases too reliance is the best measure of compensation. A striking example is *Hoffman v. Red Owl Stores*:[30] A prospective Red Owl supermarket franchisee sold his previously owned business and made other expenditures on the assumption that his negotiations to obtain a Red Owl franchise would shortly be concluded. The award of reliance damages was not a case of enforcement of a promise at all, since the parties had not reached the stage where clearly determined promises had been made. Reliance damages were awarded because Red Owl had not dealt fairly with Hoffman. It had allowed him to incur expenses based on hopes that Red Owl knew or should have known were imprudent and that Red Owl was not prepared to permit him to realize. Red Owl was held liable not in order to force it to perform a promise, which it had never made, but rather to compensate Hoffman for losses he had suffered through Red Owl's inconsiderate and temporizing assurances.[31]

There is nothing at all in my conception of contract as promise that precludes persons who behave badly and cause unnecessary harm from being forced to make fair compensation. Promissory obligation is not the only basis for liability; principles of tort are sufficient to provide that people who give vague assurances that cause foreseeable harm to others should make compensation.

Cases like *Hoffman* are seen to undermine the conception of contract as promise: If contract is really discrete and if it is really based in promise, then whenever there has been a promise in the picture (even only a potential promise) contractual principles must govern the whole relation. To state the argument is to reveal it as a non sequitur. It is a logical fallacy of which the classical exponents of contract as promise were themselves supremely guilty in their reluctance to grant relief for fraud or for mistakes that prevented a real agreement from coming into being. Modern critics of contractual freedom have taken the classics at their word. Justice often requires relief and adjustment in cases of accidents in and around the contracting process, and the critics have seen in this a refutation of the classics' major premise.... Here it is sufficient to introduce the notion that contract as promise has a distinct but neither exclusive nor necessarily dominant place among legal and moral principles. A major concern of this book is the articulation of the boundaries and connection between the promissory and other principles of justice.[32]

The tendency to merge promise into its adjacent concepts applies also to the relation between it and the principle of restitution, which holds that a person who has received a benefit at another's expense should compensate his benefactor, unless a gift was intended. This principle does indeed appeal to a primitive intuition of fairness. Even where a gift was intended, the appropriateness at least of gratitude if not of a vague duty to reciprocate is recognized in many cultures. Aristotle refers the principle to the imperative that some balance be retained among members of a society, but this seems to restate the proposition rather than to explain it.[33] Since restitution, like reliance, is a principle of fairness that operates independently of the will of the parties, the attempt to refer promissory obligation to this principle is another attempt to explain away the self-imposed character of promissory obligation. I have already argued that this cannot be done without begging the question. Certainly the restitution principle cannot explain the force of a promise for which no benefit has yet been or ever will be given in return. (The legal recognition of such gift promises is tangled in the confusions of the doctrine of consideration, which is the subject of [the next section].) The reduction of promise to restitution (or to restitution plus reliance) must fail. There are nevertheless breaches of promise for which restitution is the correct principle of relief:[34]

> IV. In a case like *Security Stove,* where the freight charges have been prepaid but the goods never picked up or delivered as agreed, let us suppose the express company could show that the contemplated exhibit would have been a disaster and that the stove company was much better off never having shown at the fair. Perhaps in such a case there should be no award of reliance damages, but should the express company be allowed to keep the prepayment? Should it be able to argue that the stove company is lucky there was a breach?

In terms of both expectation and harm the stove company should get nothing. Its expectation is shown to be negative, and it suffered no harm. And yet it is entirely clear that Railway Express should make restitution. They did nothing for the money and should not keep it. But is this enforcing the promise? Not at all:

> V. I owe my plumber ten dollars, so I place a ten-dollar bill in an envelope, which I mistakenly address and send to you.

On what theory can I get my ten dollars back from you? You made no promise to me. You have *done* me no wrong, and so that is not the ground of my demand that you return the money—though you wrong me now if you do not accede to my demand. The principle is a general one: It is wrong to retain an advantage obtained without justification at another's expense. And what justification can you offer for keeping the ten dollars?[35,36] What justification can Railway Express offer for keeping the freight charges in case IV? That it has done the stove company a favor by spoiling the exhibit? But this is no favor the stove company asked for and not one that Railway Express had a right to thrust on it. And surely Railway Express cannot say it received the money properly under a contract, since it has utterly repudiated that contract. The contract drops out leaving Railway Express without a justification. In this state of affairs the stove company wins.

Promise and restitution are distinct principles. Neither derives from the other, and so the attempt to dig beneath promise in order to ground contract in restitution (or reliance, for that matter) is misconceived. Contract is based on promise, but when something goes wrong in the contract process—when people fail to reach agreement, or break their promises—there will usually be gains and losses to sort out. The *Red Owl* case is one illustration. Here is another:

> VI. Britton signs on to work for Turner for a period of one year at an agreed wage of $120 to be paid at the end of his service. After nine months of faithful service he quits without justification, and Turner without difficulty finds a replacement for him.

On one hand Britton has not kept his promise; on the other Turner has had a substantial benefit at his expense.[37] The promise and restitution principles appear to point in opposite directions in this situation.... For the present it is sufficient to note that it is the very distinctness of the principles that causes such questions to arise. Certainly nothing about the promise principle, the conception of contract as promise, entails that all disputes between people who have tried but failed to make a contract or who have broken a contract must be decided solely according to that principle.

CONSIDERATION

It is a standard textbook proposition that in Anglo-American law a promise is not binding without consideration. Consideration is defined as something either given or promised in exchange for a promise.[38] As it stands this proposition is too unqualified to be quite accurate. Into the nineteenth century a promise contained in a document bearing a seal was binding without consideration in most common law jurisdictions. In the last hundred years there has been a gradual movement to abolish the effect of the seal by legislation,[39] while statutes in different jurisdictions have made a wide variety of particular promises binding without consideration: promises to keep an offer open,[40] to release a debt,[41] to modify an obligation,[42] to pay for past favors.[43] Nevertheless, the trend away from the seal as an anachronistic relic and the narrow, episodic nature of the statutory exceptions leaves the doctrine of consideration as very much the norm.

It is the doctrine of consideration that leads some to see contract as distinct from promise; it is consideration that leads people to say that promise may be all well and good as a ground of moral obligation, but the law is concerned with different and more serious business.[44] What is this more serious business? One intuitive idea is that exchanges are enforced because one who welches on an exchange is a kind of cheat or thief: He has obtained a benefit and now refuses to pay for it. But this intuitive sense does not fit the facts—at least in the many cases of executory contracts where the "cheat" has not yet received anything in exchange for his promise except the "victim's" own promise. Where you have given in exchange for my promise nothing more than your own return promise, it is a bootstrap argument to reason that you must be allowed to recover because I by my breach appropriate to myself a value without rendering the agreed-upon exchange. The only value I have received or you given is just your promise, and so I benefit at your expense only on the premise that your promise is enforceable. But that premise is inadmissible in an argument designed to show that promises are enforceable only so far as necessary to prevent one party from deriving a one-sided benefit. This is not to say that exchanges of promises are not truly exchanges, only that the prevention of unjust enrichment cannot be the basis for enforcing such promissory exchanges. An analogous argument obtains to block the suggestion that the doctrine of consideration shows that the law of contracts is concerned not to enforce promises but to compensate harm suffered through reliance.

Exactly what kind of challenge does the doctrine of consideration pose to my thesis of contract as promise? If consideration implies a basis other than promise for contractual obligation, what exactly is that basis? To answer these questions and thus take the measure of the challenge, we must examine the present doctrine in some detail. The doctrine comprises two propositions: (A) The consideration that in law promotes a mere promise into a contractual obligation is something, or the promise of something, given in exchange for the promise. (B) The law is not at all interested in the adequacy of the consideration. The goodness of the exchange is for the parties alone to judge—the law is concerned only that there *be* an exchange.[45] Thus the classic conception seeks to affirm both exchange and freedom of contract. These two ideas turn out to be contradictory.

Consider first the leading case of *Hamer v. Sidway*:[46]

> I. An uncle promises his nephew that he will pay him $5,000 if the nephew will neither smoke nor drink until his twenty-first birthday. The nephew complies, but the uncle's executor refuses to pay, claiming the promise was made without consideration.

The court held that the nephew's forbearance was sufficient consideration, even if the nephew had benefited from this forbearance and indeed even if the nephew had had no desire to smoke or drink in that period. It was enough that he had the right to do so and did not exercise it. The law will not inquire into actual motives. This seems reasonable. Imagine a concert manager refusing to pay a pianist an agreed fee on the ground that the pianist would have been glad to perform for nothing. Such subjective inquiries are obviously objectionable. How then should we deal with this case:

> II. A father, wanting to assure his son of a gift but not having the funds in hand, promises to pay $5,000 in return for a peppercorn or some other worthless object.[47]

Such a promise, we are told, is unenforceable because the peppercorn is "a mere pretense."[48] When the law says that there must be an exchange, it means just that and not a charade pretending to be an exchange. This too seems reasonable, but how can we decide that the exchange in this case is a charade without looking either at motive—which *Hamer* forbids us to do—or at the substance of the exchange, which the second of the two premises (B) stated at the outset of this section forbids?

The concept of exchange is highly abstract. Perhaps the inquiry would be advanced if we used the more evocative term "bargain,"[49] which is in fact traditionally used to explain consideration. To this we may add Holmes's suggestion that consideration does not necessarily require an actual bargain, but "reciprocal *conventional* inducement."[50] This means either a real bargain *or* the kind of exchange that in general constitutes an actual bargain, though in a particular case the usual motive might be missing. People do not usually exchange large sums of money for peppercorns, but they regularly bargain about the terms of compensation for a musical performance. How else, after all, are pianists supposed to make a living? Thus the suggestion is that a transaction counts as a bargain either if it was so intended or if it belongs to a type of transactions that people generally bargain about. It looks as if the law can then go about its business of enforcing promissory exchanges without having to look at their substance—that is, allowing people the freedom to make whatever bargains seem best to them. If the doctrine of consideration did at least this, the only question left to answer would be what there is about bargains that makes them among promises the privileged objects of legal recognition.

An examination of some cases shows, however, that this simple notion depending on the intuitive idea of bargain cannot account for all of the epicycles of the doctrine of consideration:

> III. An author promises his agent that the agent will have the exclusive right to deal with his manuscript during six months, in return for the agent's adding the manuscript to his list. The agent does not promise to make any effort at all to place the manuscript, but he does insist that without the exclusive right he will do nothing.

The common law holds that a promisor in the author's position is not bound, because the agent has given no consideration—he has promised nothing in return for the author's promise, nor paid for the exclusive privilege of considering the manuscript.[51] Yet there is a bargain in the sense that the author has obtained something he wants—namely, the *chance* that this agent might peddle his manuscript—something he could not have obtained other than in return for his promise. And in general the common law has refused to admit the enforceability of options, unless the beneficiary has given or promised something of value for the option. Such arrangements are said to lack mutuality.[52]

Lack of mutuality is only one ground for denying enforcement to arrangements that are bargains in fact. Here is another:

> IV. A widow promises to repay a debt owed by her deceased husband in return for the creditor bank's canceling the estate's debt. The husband's estate is without assets, and no part of the canceled debt could ever have been collected.

Is there not consideration for the widow's promise? Let us assume the widow knows that the released claim is worthless. Nevertheless she considers the prospect of clearing her husband's name worth exchanging for a promise to pay the debt. Is this not a bargain? We can even imagine the bank and the widow actually haggling about the details of the promise. Yet the court said that since the bank gave nothing of value, the widow's promise was unenforceable.[53], [54] The widow believed she was "buying" something of value to her, so this is not even a case of a pretended bargain. Perhaps the court found the transaction too far from the central paradigm of a bargain, too remote from the model of some standard commercial transaction; but if so, case III is hard to explain. Perhaps, then, the court had a sense that the widow was being put upon in a difficult situation; but such transactions have been held to lack consideration even where no widows are involved, while plenty of hard bargains made by distressed widows are enforced. Consider this case:

> V. A small contractor borrows money from one of his craftsmen and becomes bankrupt without repaying it. Many years later, he makes an explicit written promise to pay this debt, even though it has long ago become unenforceable.

In this case courts typically do enforce the subsequent promise, using the puzzling rationale that the prior obligation is somehow sufficient to support a later promise—the passage of time and the bar of bankruptcy being held to be only formal defects which the subsequent promise removes.[55] Whatever the substantive merit of allowing recovery in such cases, the stated explanation is obviously gibberish. To be consistent the courts would have to find that in such cases there was no bargain, any more than in the case of the widow, since one does not bargain for what one already has: the repentant contractor has already got clear of all obligation the money that he subsequently promises to repay. This notion that you cannot bargain for what you already have is illustrated in these so-called moral consideration cases:

VI. A workman throws himself in the way of a falling object, saving his employer's life but suffering disabling injuries. The grateful employer promises a pension, which the employer's executors refuse to continue after the employer's death, on the grounds that it was promised without consideration.

VII. A family nurses to health over a considerable period the adult son of a distant father. When the father learns of this kindness, he promises recompense but does not keep his promise.

In the second of these cases the court accepted the consequences of the bargain theory and refused enforcement.[56] In the first that result was apparently too repellent to accept and the court granted enforcement—by a process of reasoning too strained to repeat.[57] But the problem of promises about prior obligations may arise as well in contexts where not gratitude but calculation is the motive:

VIII. Architect threatens to abandon supervision of an industrial construction project at a crucial stage unless the desperate owner promises to pay an additional fee.[58]

IX. Builder discovers that the land on which he has contracted to build consists of a shallow crust of hard earth with swamp underneath. Completing the project would be far more costly than he had expected. Although the builder clearly accepted the risk of such a surprise, the owner promises to pay an additional sum on successful completion of the work.[59]

X. Debtor is hard pressed and promises to pay creditor an already-overdue debt in three monthly installments in return for creditor's promise to forgive the promised interest on the debt.[60]

In each of these cases, the promisor later reneges. Owners in cases VIII and IX claim that they received nothing for their promises and so refuse the extra payment. In the first of these the defense succeeded and the architect did not recover; in the second the defense failed and builder recovered. The creditor in X later claims the interest on the debt on the ground that debtor paid nothing for creditor's promise to forgive the interest. The common law has regularly enforced the original debt in full against the debtor in spite of the creditor's promise of partial forgiveness.[61]

The bargain theory of consideration not only fails to explain why this pattern of decisions is just; it does not offer *any* consistent set of principles from which all of these decisions would flow. These cases particularly cannot be accounted for by the two guiding premises of the doctrine of consideration: (A) that only promises given as part of a bargain are enforceable; (B) that whether there is a bargain or not is a formal question only. As in the cases of the author and the widow (III and IV), so in each of these cases there has been a bargain in fact: The owners and creditor have promised something in return for an assurance or performance. The difference is that in cases VIII–X there is a unilateral modification of earlier bargains so that the promisors (the two owners and the creditor) make new promises, but get no more (creditor gets *less*) than they were entitled to under their old bargains. Nevertheless, new bargains have been made, and propositions A and B are satisfied.[62]

The intuitive appeal of the decisions, at least in the two building cases, VIII and IX, may be easily explained. Architect has owner over a barrel: Their original bargain made owner depend on him, and the second bargain exploits the vulnerability created by the owner's trust in that original promise. The builder in IX, by contrast, has had a nasty surprise, though by the terms of the original deal the risk of such a surprise was his. Finally, case X may be one where debtor, like the builder, falls on unexpected difficulties, or it may be more like IX: exploitation of the creditor's unwillingness to suffer the expense and hazards of suing for his money.[63]

The formal device to deal with these modification cases is the doctrine that consideration not only must be bargained for but must be "fresh"—that the promisor cannot, as it were, sell the same thing twice.[63] So perhaps we might just add to A and B a new premise, A': that what is given or promised in return for a promise must not be something that is already owed to the promisor. Never mind for a moment why we are adding this premise, ask only if now the courts can proceed formally—that is, in compliance with premise B—to decide which promises are to be enforced. This new theory of consideration (consisting now of three propositions) would certainly block the blackmailing architect in VIII, but only at the cost of blocking the quite reasonable accommodation between the builder and the owner in IX. And it offers no way to distinguish reasonable from extortionate compositions between debtors and creditors. (The common law does indeed fail to make that distinction, applying it indiscriminately to all debtor compositions.)

The rigors of this expanded theory might be mitigated if we treated a contract modification as if builder and owner in IX had cancelled their old contract and entered into a new one containing the desired additional compensation for builder. At the time of the modification each still owed the other some duty under the old contract (builder to build; owner to pay). Without looking at motives and content (premise B), we can treat the putative mutual release of these outstanding obligations as a bargain, and having done so the way is clear to the making of a new bargain on whatever terms the parties choose.[64] Neat? Alas, it is not to be. For if the trick works in case IX where we want it to, it will work in VIII too, where we do not. If we exclude the trick in both, A bars too much; if we allow it in both, whatever we hoped to accomplish by A' is circumvented. And if we allow it only where the purpose is "reasonable" or the new arrangement fair on its merits, we violate B. Indeed the situation is worse still: The trick will not work at all for any case like

X, reasonable or not. At the time debtor and creditor contemplate a modification, the only outstanding obligation is the debtor's, so there can be no *mutual* release of obligations, no mutual bargain to tear up the old contract. (In a case like X the debtor would have to offer some actual fresh consideration.) But some cases like X will be as appealing as IX or as unappealing as VIII, yet none can be accommodated.

I conclude that the standard doctrine of consideration, which is illustrated by the preceding ten quite typical common law cases, does not pose a challenge to my conception of contract law as rooted in promise, for the simple reason that that doctrine is too internally inconsistent to offer an alternative at all. The matrix of the inconsistency is just the conjunction of propositions A and B. Proposition B affirms the liberal principle that the free arrangements of rational persons should be respected. Proposition A, by limiting the class of arrangements to bargains, holds that individual self-determination is not a sufficient ground of legal obligation, and so implies that collective policies may after all override individual judgments, frustrating the projects of promisees after the fact and the potential projects of promisors. Proposition A is put forward as if it were neutral after all, leaving the parties their "freedom of contract." But there is a sense in which any promisor gets something for his promise, if only the satisfaction of being able to realize his purpose through the promise. Freedom of contract is freedom of promise, and, as my illustrations show, the intrusions of the standard doctrines of consideration can impose substantial if random restrictions on perfectly rational projects.

The anomalous character of the doctrine of consideration has been widely recognized. A variety of statutes abrogate some of its more annoying manifestations, such as the unenforceability of gratuitous options or of contract modifications. There have also been proposals for its virtual abolition.[65] Before commenting on these proposals briefly at the end of this [section], I must turn to a perspective on the doctrine that rescues it from its gravest anomalies and does indeed pose a challenge to my view.

In a recent work, John Dawson compares the common law to French and German law and concludes that an impulse shared by all of these systems distinguishes gratuitous promises, that is, promises to make a gift, from true bargains.[66] Another comparativist, Arthur von Mehren, writing in *The International Encyclopedia of Comparative Law*,[67] also contrasts bargains to promises to make a gift, dubbing the latter economically sterile.[68] Dawson faults the common law not for making this distinction, but for assuming "a doctrinal overload" in using the doctrine of consideration to regulate or exclude promises that hold an offer open (options) and promises that modify or discharge existing arrangements. Dawson emphasizes what he believes is the basic idea of the doctrine of consideration, the substantive, intuitive idea of bargain. Options and modifications fall under that notion because they are part of a "deal"; they are related to bargains. An option is the first step along the way to a bargain. Cases like VIII—X also occur as part of the bargaining process; modifications and discharges should be facilitated to keep that process flexible and serviceable. Substantive unfairness should be controlled not by the manipulation of formalities but by substantive inquiry under the aegis of the doctrines of duress and unconscionability.[69]

This conception challenges my thesis that the basis of contract is promise by locating that basis now in a distinct collective policy, the furtherance of economic exchange. A promise may be necessary, on this view, but it is the largely commercial needs of the market that ground contract. As an explanation this is certainly more satisfying than the incoherent formalities of the common law doctrine, but it too fails on inspection. Neither Dawson's proposal nor French and German law limit contract to commercial transactions: Deals between private individuals selling or exchanging property in no recognized or customary market and family settlements of many sorts are everywhere recognized as binding. It could hardly be otherwise, for to deny a private individual the facility for, say, selling his car or his house to a friend, would lessen the free transferability of property and thus its value, while creating a wholly unjustifiable monopoly in some vaguely defined merchant class. So apparently at least these transactions are not economically "sterile." Rather it is agreed all around that the gift, the donative promise, is the villain of the piece, because of its "sterility." But why is my enforceable promise to sell my brother-in-law my automobile less sterile than my promise to give it to my nephew? The law recognizes the *completed* transaction (after I actually hand over or sign over the automobile), presumably in recognition of my right to do with my property as I choose. In a sense the completed transaction in both cases is quite fertile enough: It is an expression of my will, it increases my satisfaction in some broad sense, and it does so by increasing the satisfaction of my nephew or brother-in-law. Both actual transfers are useful just in the sense that any freely chosen, significant act of mine is useful to me, and therefore is of net utility to society unless it harms someone else. Allowing people to *make* gifts (let us assume freely, deliberately, reasonably) serves social utility by serving individual liberty.[70], [71] Given the preceding [section's] analysis of promise, there simply are no grounds for not extending that conclusion to *promises* to make gifts. I make a gift because it pleases me to do so. I promise to make a gift because I cannot or will not make a present transfer, but still wish to give you a (morally and legally) secure expectation.

I conclude that the life of contract is indeed promise, but this conclusion is not exactly a statement of positive law. There are too many gaps in the common law enforcement of promises to permit so bold a statement. My conclusion is rather that the doctrine of consideration offers no coherent alternative basis for the force of contracts, while still treating promise as necessary to it. Along the way to this conclusion I have made or implied a number of qualifications to my thesis. The promise must be freely made and not unfair.... It must also have been made rationally, deliberately. The promisor must have been serious enough that subsequent legal enforcement was an aspect of what he should have contemplated at the time he promised.[72] Finally, certain promises, particularly those affecting the situation and expectations of various family members, may require substantive regulation because of the legitimate interests of third parties. In a classic article, "Consideration as Form,"[73] Lon Fuller argued that the doctrine of consideration serves several, often convergent policies. The law hesitates to enforce casual promises where promisor or promisee or both would be surprised to find the heavy machinery of the law imposed on what seemed an informal encounter. Requiring an exchange increases the chance that the parties had in contemplation serious business with serious consequences. Moreover, by requiring an exchange, the law allows contracts to be channeled into a number of predetermined types of arrangements, and the existence of these types itself alerts the parties to a conventional set of problems to be considered and a conventional set of answers to those problems. Finally, the requirement of an exchange might exclude the more dubious and meretricious kinds of gift in which strangers are promised the moon, to the prejudice of a spouse or children.

This last qualification is captured in the law by the term "intention to create legal relations." The term as it stands is misleading. No one supposes that two merchants who make a deal must entertain some additional intention to create legal relations in order for that deal to be binding in law. On the other hand, given the consensual basis of contract as promise, the parties should in principle be free to exclude legal enforcement so long as this is not a fraudulent device to trap the unwary. See, e.g., *Spooner v. Reserve Life Insurance*.[74] In a particular case it may be a difficult problem of interpretation whether such a purpose is fairly to be implied. In a particular case it will be a task for interpretation to determine whether legal enforcement would not do violence to the intention of the parties—as with so-called social promises. According to Fuller these are convergent reasons for requiring consideration, because none is either necessary or sufficient. There is the important category of family settlements, and surely these should not be denied enforceability indiscriminately. Furthermore, by using the correct forms it is possible to cast wholly novel transactions—transactions unsupported by the gloss of custom and experience—in an enforceable mold. Finally, the doctrine of consideration makes it possible to lend enforceability to arrangements that are trivial

if not frivolous, so long as the forms are observed. And indeed, so long as the forms are observed, it is possible that a person who makes a promise will be legally bound even if he did not intend to be legally bound—if he intended only to promise and to take some value in exchange for his promise. Consideration in Fuller's view is like a rather awkward tool, which has the virtue of being able to pound nails, drive screws, pry open cans, although it does none of these things well and although each of them might be done much better by a specialized tool. (The archaic institution of the promise under seal might be compared for its ability to serve these useful ends with more or less convenience.)

The movement in the law rather suggests that we may have in the not-too-distant future a more candid set of principles to determine which promises should be enforceable in terms of the fairness of each type. We are moving in that direction as a result of decisions and statutes lending validity to types of promises whose legitimacy had been in doubt under the doctrine of consideration: option contracts, firm offers, compromises of debts, modification of contracts, and the whole domain of promissory estoppel. Secondly, we are moving in that direction as a result of a more open willingness to stigmatize certain promises as unfair or unconscionable and to deny enforcement on that ground rather than on the ground of insufficient consideration.[75]

NOTES

1. On the right and the good the critical discussion is Rawls, John. *Theory of Justice*. Cambridge, 1971. §§68, 83–85, which harks back to Kant, Immanuel. *Groundwork of the Metaphysics of Morals*. Trans. Paton. New York: Harper Torchbooks, 1964, where the contrast is made between the right and happiness. See also Ross, W. D. *The Right and the Good*. Oxford, 1930; Dworkin, Ronald. "Liberalism." *Public and Private Morality*. Ed. S. Hampshire. Cambridge, England, 1978. On the relation between liberalism and responsibility, see Hayek, Friedrich. *The Constitution of Liberty*. Chicago, 1960. Ch. 5; Fried, Charles. *Right and Wrong*. Cambridge, 1978. 124–126; Rawls, supra at 519. For a different view see

Macpherson, C. B. *The Political Theory of Possessive Individualism—Hobbes to Locke.* Oxford, 1962.

2. Kant, Immanuel. *The Metaphysical Elements of Justice.* Trans. Ladd. Indianapolis, 1965. 54–55.

3. See Fried, Charles. *An Anatomy of Values.* Cambridge, 1970. 81–86; Sidgwick, Henry. *Elements of Politics,* quoted in Kessler, Friedrich and Gilmore, Grant. *Contracts* 4. 2d ed. Boston, 1970.

4. Bok, Sissela. *Lying: Moral Choice in Public Life.* New York, 1978; Fried, *Right and Wrong,* supra, note 1, ch. 3.

5. This example is based on *Adams v. Gillig,* 199 N. Y. 314, 92 N.E. 670 (1930).

6. See generally Keeton, Page. "Fraud: Statements of Intention." *Texas L. Rev.* 15 (1937): 185.

7. See generally Goff, Robert and Jones, Gareth. *The Law of Restitution.* 2d. ed. London, 1978. Ch. 1.

8. For a strong statement of the tort and benefit principles as foundations of contract law, see Atiyah, Patrick. *The Rise and Fall of Freedom of Contract.* Oxford, 1979. 1–7. A remarkable article stating the several moral principles implicit in contract law is Gardner, George. "An Inquiry into the Principles of the Law of Contracts." *Harv. L. Rev.* 46 (1932): 1.

9. For a review of Anglo-American writing on promise from Hobbes to modern times, see Atiyah, supra, note 8, at 41–60, 649–659. There has been a lively debate on the bases for the moral obligation of promises in recent philosophical literature. Some philosophers have taken a line similar to that of Atiyah and Gilmore, deriving the obligation of promise from the element of reliance. The strongest statement is MacCormick, Neil. "Voluntary Obligations and Normative Powers." *Proceedings of the Aristotelian Society* supp. vol. 46 (1972): 59. See also Ardal, Pall. "And That's a Promise." *Phil. Q.* 18 (1968): 225; McNeilly, F. S. "Promises Demoralized." *Phil. Rev.* 81 (1972): 63. Warnock, G. J. *The Object of Morality.* London, 1971. Ch. 7 offers an effective refutation along the lines in the text, but his affirmative case proposes that the obligation of a promise rests on the duty of veracity, the duty to make the facts correspond to the promise. For an excellent discussion of this last suggestion and a proposal that accords with my own, see Locke, Don. "The Object of Morality and the Obligation to Keep a Promise." *Canadian J. of Philosophy* 2 (1972): 135. Locke's emphasis on trust seems a clearer and sounder version of H. A. Prichard's proposal that the obligation of a Promise rests on a more general "agreement to keep agreements." Prichard, H. A. *Moral Obligation.* Oxford, 1957. Ch. 7.

10. A number of the philosophers who disagree with the Atiyah–MacCormick argument emphasize the conventional aspect of the invocation of the promissory form, as well as the self-imposed nature of the obligation. E.g. Raz, Joseph. "Voluntary Obligations." *Proceedings of the Aristotelian Society* supp. vol. 46 (1972): 79; Raz, "Promises and Obligations." *Law, Morality and Society.* Eds. Hacker, Raz. Oxford, 1977; Searle, John. *Speech Acts.* Cambridge, 1969. 33–42, 175–188; Searle, "What Is a Speech Act?" *The Philosophy of Language.* Ed. John Searle. Oxford, 1971. The locus classicus of this view of promising is Rawls, John. "Two Concepts of Rules." *Phil. Rev.* 64 (1955): 3. The general idea goes back, of course, to Ludwig Wittgenstein, *Philosophical Investigations* §23. For Hume's account of the conventional nature of promissory obligation, see *A Treatise of Human Nature.* Ed. Selby-Bigge. Oxford, 1888. 516–525.

11. The contention of Cavell, Stanley. *The Claim of Reason.* Oxford, 1979. 293–303 that promising is not a practice or an institution, because unlike the case of a game one cannot imagine setting it up or reforming it and because promising is not an office, seems to me beside the point. Kant's discussion, supra, note 2, shows that morality can mandate that there be a convention with certain general features, as does Hume's discussion, supra, note 10, though Hume's morality is a more utilitarian one.

12. Note that this problem does not arise where I make a present sacrifice for a future benefit, since by hypothesis I am presently willing to make that sacrifice and in the future I only stand to gain.

13. Lewis, David. *Convention.* Cambridge, 1969.

14. Supra, note 10.

15. Here I side with Lyons, David. *The Forms and Limits of Utilitarianism.* Oxford, 1965 in a continuing debate. For the most recent statement of the contrary position, see Brandt, Richard. *A Theory of the Good and Right.* Oxford, 1979. For an excellent introduction, see Smart, J. J. C. and Williams, Bernard. *Utilitarianism: For and Against.* Cambridge, England, 1973. I argue that it is a mistake to treat Rawls's discussion of promising in "Two Concepts of Rules." Supra, note 10, as an instance of rule utilitarianism in my review of Atiyah, *Harv. L. Rev.* 93 (1980): 1863n 18. See also Landesman, Charles. "Promises and Practices." *Mind* 75 (1966): (n.s.) 239.

16. This was in fact Bentham's general perspective. See also Brandt, supra, note 15.

17. Compare Rawls, supra, note 1, ch. 6, where it is argued that (a) the deduction of the principles of justice for institutions, and (b) a showing that a particular institution is just are not sufficient to generate an obligation to comply with that institution. Further principles of natural duty and obligation must be established.

18. See Locke, supra, note 9; Prichard, supra, note 9; Raz, supra, note 10.

19. American Law Institute, *Restatement (1st) of the Law of Contracts* [hereafter cited as *Restatement* (1st) or (2d)], §329, Comment a: "In awarding compensatory damages, the effort is made to put the injured party in as good a position as that in which he would have been put by full performance of the contract...."; Farnsworth, E. Allan. "Legal Remedies for Breach of Contract." *Colum. L. Rev.* 70 (1970): 1145; Gardner, supra, note 8; Goetz, Charles and Scott, Robert. "Enforcing Promises: An Examination of the Basis of Contract." *Yale L. J.* 80 (1980): 1261.

20. See Fuller and Perdue. "The Reliance Interest in Contract Damages." *Yale L. J.* 46 (1936, 1937): 52, 373; Gardner, supra, note 8.

21. For discussions of these issues see Fried, supra, note 3, at 169–177; Rawls, supra, note 1, §85; and the essays in *The Identities of Persons.* Ed. Amelie Rorty. Berkeley, 1976, and *Personal Identity.* Ed. John Perry. Berkeley, 1975.

22. See Atiyah, supra, note 8, at 140–141 for a discussion of these early sources. See my review of Atiyah, *Harv. L. Rev.* 93 (1980): 1858, 1864–1865 for a further discussion of these and other early sources.

23. 227 Mo. App. 175, 51 S.W.2d 572 (1932).

24. A case like this may be seen as involving no more than the allocation of the burden of proof as to the expectation. The plaintiff shows his reliance costs and says that prima facie his expectation was at least that great. The burden then shifts to the defendant to show that indeed this was a losing proposition and the expectation was less than the reliance. It seems only fair that since the defendant's breach prevented the exhibition from taking place and thus prevented the drama on which the expectation depended from being played out, the defendant should at least bear the risk of showing that the venture would have been a failure.

25. *Restatement* (1st) §333(d).

26. In law the latter promise is called a warranty—a promise not merely that the promisor will do something in the future, but a taking of responsibility over and above the responsibility of well-meaning honesty that something is the case. For instance, a dealer may warrant that a violin is a Stradivarius. This means more than that he in good faith believes it to be one: he is promising that if it is not, he will be responsible. Uniform Commercial Code (hereafter cited as UCC) §2-714, Cf. *Smith v. Zimbalist*, 2 Cal. App. 2d 324, 38 P.2d 170 (1934), hearing denied 17 Jan. 1935.

27. Gardner, supra, note 8, at 15, 22–23.

28. This is the problem that is standardly dealt with in contract texts under the rubric of consequential damages, or the principle in *Hadley v. Baxendale*, 9 Exch. 341 (1854). See Gardner, supra, note 8, at 28–30. Holmes, in *Globe Refining Co. v. Landa Cotton Oil Co.*, 190 U.S. 540 (1903) explained the limitation of liability for consequential damages in terms of the agreement itself: The defendant is liable only for those risks he explicitly or tacitly agreed to assume. This conception has been generally rejected in favor of a vaguer standard by which defendant is liable for any risks of which he had "reason to know" at the time of the agreement. UCC §2-715, comment 2. Holmes's test seems more consonant with the thesis of this work. See Pothier, *The Law of Obligations*, quoted in Fuller, Lon and Eisenberg, Melvin. *Basic Contract Law*. 3rd ed. St. Paul, 1972. 27. The difference between the two positions is not great: first, because it is always within the power of the parties to limit or expand liability for consequential damages by the agreement itself, UCC §2-719(3); second, because the "reason to know" standard means that the defendant at least has a fair opportunity to make such an explicit provision.

29. UCC §2-318; Prosser, William. *Torts*. 4th ed. St. Paul, 1971. Ch. 17.

30. 133 N. W.2d 267, 26 Wis.2d 683 (1965).

31. See Henderson, Stanley. "Promissory Estoppel and Traditional Contract Doctrine." *Yale L. J.* 78 (1969): 343, 357–360; see generally Kessler, Friedrich and Fine, Edith. "Culpa in Contrahendo, Bargaining in Good Faith, and Freedom of Contract: A Comparative Study." *Harv. L. Rev.* 77 (1964): 401.

32. There is a category of cases that has become famous in the law under the rubric of promissory estoppel or detrimental reliance. In these cases there has indeed generally been a promise, but

the basis for legal redress is said to be the plaintiff's detrimental reliance on the promise. Courts now tend to limit the amount of the redress in such cases to the detriment suffered through reliance. But these cases also do not show that reliance and harm are the general basis for contractual recovery. Rather these cases should be seen for what they are: a belated attempt to plug a gap in the general regime of enforcement of promises, a gap left by the artificial and unfortunate doctrine of consideration....

33. *Nicomachean Ethics,* bk. V, iv-v.

34. See Dawson, John "Restitution or Damages?" *Ohio St. L. J.* 20 (1959): 175; Gardner, supra, note 8, at 18–27.

35. That you thought it was a present, spent it, and would now have to dip into the grocery budget to pay me back? Well, that might be a justification if it were true.

36. Goff and Jones, supra, note 7, at 69; the problem raised in the footnote is treated at 88–89.

37. *Britton v. Turner,* 6 N.H. 281 (1834).

38. *Restatement* (1st) §19. The definition of consideration is as follows: (1) something of value must have been given in exchange for the promise to be enforced [see *Restatement* (1st) §75(1), *Restatement (2d)* §17(1)]; (2) with manifestation of mutual assent of the parties to make such an exchange (the "bargaining for" requirement) [*Restatement* (1st) §75(1), *Restatement (2d)* §71(1–2)].

39. The common law rule is that consideration is not required for enforcement of a promise under seal. See *Restatement* (1st) §110; *Restatement* (2d) §95 (1); Williston, Samuel. *Contracts.* Vol. 1. 3rd ed. Mt. Kisco: Walter Jaeger, 1957 (hereafter cited as Williston with volume number) §217; Corbin, Arthur. *Contracts.* Vol. 1. (St. Paul, 1963. §252 (hereafter cited as Corbin with volume number). This is, however, a matter that has been the subject of extensive legislative action. See 1 Williston §219A, 1 Corbin §254, and *Restatement (2d)* §95, tent. draft no. 1–7, ch. 4, at 189 for a summary of the state of the law. Roughly half the states still recognize the seal, though many in a weakened form; the effect of a seal may range from a complete substitute for consideration to a substantive though rebuttable presumption of consideration, to an allocation of pleading requirements and burdens of proof on the issue, to mere allocation of the issue to judge or jury. The other

half of the states and UCC §2–203 have explicitly abolished the effect of the seal altogether.

40. UCC §2-205 removes the requirement of consideration for a promise to hold open an offer to buy or sell goods, but limits the period of irrevocability to three months and requires a writing separately signed by the promisor. See N.Y. Gen. Oblig. Law §5–1109 for a similar but more general provision.

41. 1 Williston §120, notes 7–9, for a summary.

42. E.g. UCC §2–209; N.Y. Gen. Oblig. Law §5–1103.

43. E.g. Cal. Civ. Code §1606; Ga. Code Ann. §20–303.

44. See Eisenberg, Melvin. "Donative Promises." *U. Chi. L. Rev.* 47 (1980): 1, 2–7, for an excellent discussion and review of the authorities; see also Goetz, Charles and Scott, Robert. "Enforcing Promises: An Examination of the Basis of Contract." *Yale L.J.* 89 (1980): 1261–1262. The neglect of donative promises is noted with regret by Pound, Roscoe. "Promise or Bargain?" *Tulane L. Rev.* 33 (1959): 455.

45. "It is an elementary principle that the law will not enter into an inquiry as to the adequacy of the consideration." 1 Williston §115, at 454, citing *Westlake v. Adams,* 5 C.B. (n.s.) 248. See 1 Williston §115 and 1 Corbin §127 for numerous examples of consideration considered inadequate but held sufficient. See also *Restatement* (1st) §81 and (2d) §79. The commentators as well as the cases agree in deriving the law's decision not to engage in such "objective" valuation from the freedom of the parties to set their own values and draw their own contract. See also Professor Atiyah's account of the historical origins of the adequacy doctrine, which traces it directly to the complex of notions that underlie the freedom of contract. Atiyah. *The Rise and Fall of Freedom of Contract.* Oxford, 1979. 448–451.

46. 124 N.Y. 538, 27 N.E. 256 (1891).

47. Based on ill. 5, *Restatement* (2d) §71.

48. Id., at comment b. See also *Fischer v. Union Trust Co.,* 138 Mich. 612, 101 N.W. 852 (1904); 1 Corbin §118; 1 Williston §111.

49. See Dawson, John. *Gifts and Promises.* New Haven, 1980. 199–207, and particularly at 203 where Dawson disposes of Gilmore's "surprising ... suggestion" that the bargain theory was invented by Holmes.

50. *The Common Law.* Boston, 1881. 292–293.

51. Case III is based on *Wood v. Lucy, Lady Duff-Gordon,* 222 N.Y. 88, 118 N.E. (1917) (Cardozo,

J.), although Cardozo implied a promise by the agent to make reasonable efforts. The general problem of which the option-to-agent cases are an instance is generally known as the problem of mutuality of obligation. See *Restatement* (2d) §79 (c) and comment f.

52. See Corbin, Arthur. "The Effect of Options on Consideration." *Yale L. J.* 34 (1925): 571; Corbin, "Nonbinding Promises as Consideration." *Colum. L. Rev.* 26 (1926): 550.

53. Cases where a person exacts a promise by threat to bring baseless litigation can be dealt with under the doctrine of duress.... by reason of both the bankruptcy and the passage of time.

54. Case IV is based on *Newman & Snell's State Bank v. Hunter*, 243 Mich. 331, 220 N.W. 665 (1928). Williston regards this celebrated case as an anomalous violation of the doctrine of adequacy. Corbin straightforwardly attacks the result in his most magisterial phrase: "This is believed to be erroneous." 1 Corbin §127, note 83. The "market value" of the note is of no relevance, if the widow bargained for it, and the bank did not have to turn it over.

55. Case V is based on *Zabella v. Pakel*, 242 F.2d 452 (7th Cir. 1958). See *Restatement* (2d) §82, 83.

56. *Mills v. Wyman*, 3 Pick. 207 (Mass. 1825).

57. *Webb v. McGowin*, 27 Ala. App. 82, 168 So. 196 (1935).

58. *Lingenfelder v. Wainwright Brewery Co.*, 103 Mo. 578, 15 S.W. 844 (1891).

59. *Linz v. Schuck*, 106 Md. 220, 67 A.A. 286 (1907).

60. Based on *Foakes v. Beer*, 9 A.C. 605 (House of Lords 1884).

61. The rule in *Foakes v. Beer*, while generally adhered to, has given rise to much criticism and opposition. See note 6, supra, for statutory incursions upon it. Williston accepts this case wholeheartedly (1 Williston §120) and considers it merely a particularly clear instance of the pre-existing duty rule (see 1 Williston §120, §130A, at 542). It has been argued persuasively that this now-standard interpretation is in fact a misinterpretation of the leading cases. See Ames, James Barr. "Two Theories of Consideration." *Harv. L. R.* 12 (1899): 515, and Ferson, Merton. "The Rule in *Foakes v. Beer*." *Yale L. J.* 31 (1926): 15.

62. See Dawson, supra, 15 note 13, at 220-221; Ames, supra, note 25, at 528; Fuller, Lon. "Consideration and Form." *Colum. L. Rev.*: 799, 818; and Beale, Joseph. "Notes on Consideration." *Harv. L. Rev.* 17: 71, 71–72. Perhaps the clearest

and most elegant exposition of this point, however, is Corbin's discussion at 1A Corbin §172.

63. See Williston, Samuel. "Successive Promises of the Same Performance." *Harv. L. Rev.* 5 (1894): 27.

64. See *Schwartzreich v. Baumanbasch, Inc.*, 231 N.Y. 196, 131 N.E. 887 (1921); 1 Williston §130A, at 540: "If for a single moment the parties were free from the original contract so that each of them could refuse to enter into any bargain whatever relating to the same subject matter, a subsequent agreement on any terms would be good."

65. The most striking of these are Samuel Williston's Model Written Obligations Act (in force only in Pennsylvania) and Lord Wright's call, as yet unanswered, in "Ought the Doctrine of Consideration to Be Abolished from the Common Law?" *Harv. L. Rev.* 49 (1936): 1225. Though he disapproves, Professor Atiyah quite correctly observes that these calls are the logical entailments of freedom of contract and the promise principle. Atiyah, [*The Rise and Fall of Freedom of Contract* (1979)], supra, note 8, at 134–40, 440, 452–54, 687–90; and see Fried, review of Atiyah, *Harv. L. Rev.* 93 (1980): 1858, 1865–67.

66. Dawson, supra, note 13.

67. Vol. VII (forthcoming), and see von Mehren, "Civil Law Analogues to Consideration." *Harv. L. Rev.* 72 (1959): 1009.

68. The sterility notion receives its classical statement in Claude Bufnoir, *Propriete et Contract*. Paris, 1990. 487.

69. See generally Goetz and Scott, supra, note 7, at 1265–1266; Eisenberg, supra, note 7, at 4.

70. The objection might be raised that in the case of the promise to make a gift my account of the moral basis for promissory obligation does not hold: It is not obvious that a disappointed promisee, who has suffered no losses in reliance on the promise, is "used" or his confidence "abused" when he is not given a promised gift. And yet abuse there is. The promisor for reasons of his own has chosen to create in the promisee what is, by hypothesis, a firm expectation fixed in moral obligation. The promisee thinks he has something—a moral entitlement—which is what the promisor wants him to think he has. And now, having created this expectation, the promisor chooses to disappoint it. Consider an analogous case drawn from the morality of lying: I tell you that I have just heard you have been awarded the Nobel Prize in philosophy. One hour later, before you have had a chance to spend the prospective

prize money or even to announce this fact, I tell you that the whole thing was a joke. I have lied to you. I have abused your confidence and used you. Now in both this case and the gift-promise case the harm may have been trivial and perhaps the wrong done rather marginal, but that is beside the point. In both instances for analogous reasons I have indeed wronged you.

71. See Kant, *The Metaphysical Elements of Justice,* supra, note 2. In economic terms both gifts and promises are Pareto-efficient transactions. See Hochman, Harold and Rogers, James. "Pareto Optimal Redistribution." *Am. Econ. Rev.* 59 (1969): 542.

72. See Hart, Henry and Sacks, Albert. "The Invitation to Dinner Case." *The Legal Process* Tentative ed. Cambridge, 1958. And legal enforcement may violate the understanding of one but not the other party. Compare *Armstrong v. M'Ghee and Addison,* (Westmoreland County Ct. Pa. 1795) 261....

73. *Colum. L. Rev.* 41 (1941): 799. See also Patterson, Edwin. "An Apology for Consideration." *Colum. L. Rev.* 58 (1958): 929; Atiyah, supra, note 8.

74. *Spooner v. Reserve Life Insurance,* 47 Wash. 2d 454, 287, P.2d 735 (1955).

75. For a less sanguine view, see Pound, supra, note 7 at 455:

> While the progress of the law had been more and more toward what had been taken to be the moral position that promises, as such, ought to be kept, and while until recently the law throughout the world had seemed to come almost (one might all but say substantially) to that position, there has begun a noticeable relaxation of the strict moral doctrine as to the obligation of intentional and advised promise. From antiquity the moral obligation to keep a promise had been a cardinal tenet of ethical philosophers, publicists, and philosophical jurists …
>
> Today, what we were taking to be the last step in bringing the law of contracts into complete accord with the precept of morals has been, at least for the time being, arrested, and we are told that the supposed moral foundation is illusory. Men are not to be bound by promises. They are only to be held to bargains. The Marxian economic interpretation, the rise of the service state, and the humanitarian theory of liability, in different ways and in varying degrees, have seemed to be leading to a radically different view of the significance of a promise …

71 Specific Performance

ANTHONY T. KRONMAN

In an important article,[1] Calabresi and Melamed distinguish two different techniques for protecting legal entitlements. One they call a "property" rule and the other a "liability" rule. According to Calabresi and Melamed, a right or entitlement is protected by a property rule when it can be appropriated by a nonowner only if he first purchases permission to do so from the owner of the right.[2] When a right is protected by a rule of this sort, one who appropriates it without the owner's permission will always be subject to a special sanction—typically, a fine or imprisonment.[3] If a right is protected by a liability rule, in contrast, a nonowner who unilaterally appropriates it need only compensate the owner, after the taking, for any loss the owner suffers.[4] The compensatory amount which a nonowner must pay for taking a right protected by a liability rule is set by a representative of the state rather than by the owner of

I would like to thank Gerhard Casper, Walter Hellerstein, Edmund Kitch, Thomas Jackson, William Landes, Richard Posner, George Priest, Antonin Scalia, and Franklin Zimring for their helpful comments on an earlier draft of this article. I would also like to thank Ms. Brigitte Bell, a second-year student at the University of Chicago Law School, for her valuable research assistance.

From "Specifc Performance," *University of Chicago Law Review* vol. 45 (1978), p. 351. Available through Yale Law School Faculty Scholarship Repository, http://digitalcommons.law.yale.edu/fss_papers/1072.

the right in a voluntary transaction between owner and taker.

Calabresi and Melamed attempt to explain why some legal entitlements are protected by a property rule and others by a liability rule. They suggest that in certain cases the cost of negotiating the voluntary transfer of a right may be sufficiently high to frustrate the transfer. Where this is so, a property rule, which is intended to encourage transfers of this sort, is likely to promote an inefficient allocation of resources. This point is illustrated by automobile accidents and pollution torts.[5] In both cases, a voluntary transfer of entitlements is almost certain to be prohibitively expensive: in the case of an automobile accident because of the cost of identifying the victim beforehand, and in the case of pollution torts because of free-rider and hold-out complications which are likely to make any negotiated settlement enormously difficult and time-consuming.

Where the costs of voluntarily transferring a particular entitlement are low, Calabresi and Melamed argue, economic considerations strongly support the use of a property rule to protect that entitlement.[6] This argument is illustrated by the use of property rules in the criminal law: "[T]he thief or rapist ... could have negotiated [a voluntary transfer of what he takes] without undue expense (at least if the good was one which we allowed to be sold at all) because we assume he knew what he was going to do and to whom he would do it."[7] In such cases, liability rules are inappropriate because they "represent only an approximation of the value of the object to its original owner and willingness to pay such an approximate value is no indication that it is worth more to the thief than the owner."[8]

In their discussion of property and liability rules, Calabresi and Melamed do not consider one very important species of legal right: the kind of right that is created by contractual agreement, the right to the performance of a promise. All of the examples in their article are drawn from the law of torts, crimes, or real property. Since contract rights have special features that distinguish them from the various entitlements created and protected by these other branches of the law, it is appropriate to ask whether contract rights should be protected by a property rule or a liability rule.

In contract law, a liability rule permits a promisor to breach his promise provided he compensates the other party by payment of money damages. The fundamental alternative to money damages, in the law of contracts, is specific performance. A promise may be said to be specifically enforceable when the law gives its owner, the promisee, a right to require the actual (or "specific") performance of the promise. The right to positively enjoin a promise, like the right to negatively enjoin a nuisance, may be viewed as an entitlement protected by a property rule. In both cases, the owner of the right is in a position to force the would-be taker to negotiate a voluntary transfer of the particular entitlement. If the taker acts unilaterally (by simply refusing to perform, or by continuing to pollute), he can be compelled by an injunctive order to honor the owner's entitlement; and if he then refuses to honor the injunction itself, he may be forced to make a payment (not necessarily pecuniary) to the state or the promisee greater than that required to compensate the promisee for his loss.[9] Moreover, if performance is still possible, a supplemental injunction mandating performance will likely issue, again backed up by civil and criminal contempt sanctions.

If one approaches the question from the theoretical perspective developed by Calabresi and Melamed, there are two considerations suggesting that all (or most) contract rights should be protected with a property rule. First, a contract typically involves only two parties.[10] Where only two parties are involved, the special hold-out and free-rider difficulties that plague multiparty negotiations do not arise.[11] Second, and more important, the parties to a contract already know one another and so need not worry about the special problems of identification arising, for example, in the case of automobile accidents. These considerations suggest that the costs of negotiating a voluntary transfer of contract rights are likely to be low. Following Calabresi and Melamed, this should be regarded as a reason for protecting rights of this sort with a property rule.[12]

This view, however, appears to have had little influence in shaping our law of contract remedies.[13] The normal remedy for breach of contract is, of course, money damages.[14] Specific performance is exceptional.[15] The Anglo-American law of contracts protects most contract rights with a liability rule, only a few with a property rule.

It is natural to wonder whether the peculiar mix of property and liability rules in the law of contracts can be explained on economic grounds. Although a great deal has been written about the efficiency of our law of contract damages, this more basic question has been largely ignored.[16] The first two parts of this article argue that, in general, the combination of property and liability rules employed in the law of contracts makes economic sense. In part III conventional explanations for the courts' refusal to enforce private contractual provisions purporting to grant the promisee a right to compel specific performance are skeptically examined. In the final part of the paper, I criticize judicial willingness to permit a promisor to defeat his promisee's property rule protection by transferring the promised goods or services to a good faith purchaser. It is suggested that economic considerations support the constructive trust approach to this problem adopted by some courts.

I. THE "UNIQUENESS" TEST

Specific performance is an equitable remedy[17] which a court, in its sound discretion,[18] may grant a promisee whose money damages remedy is inadequate.[19] The situations in which courts are prepared to order specific performance are heterogeneous. Typical situations include contracts for the sale of land;[20] contracts for the sale of heirlooms, antiques,[21] and certain licenses[22] and patent rights[23] that can only be obtained from the promisor; contracts for the sale of a majority of shares in a particular corporation;[24] and long-term output and requirements contracts.[25] Occasionally, an employment[26] or construction[27] contract will also be specifically enforced.

The most important common feature of these diverse cases is the central role played by the idea of "uniqueness."[28] If the "subject matter of [a] contract is unique in character and cannot be duplicated" or if obtaining "a substantial equivalent involves difficulty, delay, and inconvenience,"[29] a court will be more apt to compel specific performance. "The fact that such a duplicate or equivalent cannot be so obtained does not necessarily show that money damages are not an adequate remedy, but is a fact that tends strongly in that direction."[30] Conversely, if the subject matter of a contract is such that "its substantial equivalent for all practical purposes is readily obtainable from others than the defendant in exchange for a money payment, this fact will usually in the absence of other factors be sufficient to show that money damages are an adequate remedy for breach."[31]

As the cases illustrate, the subject matter of a particular contract may be thought unique for a variety of reasons.[32] Nevertheless, courts often use the concept of uniqueness in a way which suggests that it has some relatively fixed and well-recognized meaning. An economic analysis of the law of specific performance must begin with a workable conception of uniqueness.

In common discourse "unique" means without a substitute or equivalent.[33] In the framework of conventional economic analysis, however, the concept of uniqueness is troublesome. Although it might seem reasonable to define the economic uniqueness of a good in terms of its attributes or properties, this is not the definition economists employ. Economists recognize this sort of uniqueness—they call it "technological" uniqueness—but they do not define the substitutability of goods in these terms.[34] For the purposes of economic theory, the substitutability of a particular good is determined by observing consumer behavior, not by cataloguing the various properties of the good. If an alteration in the relative price of one good affects the demand for another, then these two goods are said to be economic substitutes. The degree of their substitutability is called the "cross-elasticity of demand."[35]

On this view, every good has substitutes, even if only very poor ones. Because all goods compete for consumer attention, a substantial change in the relative price of any good always affects the consumption of other goods. Economists are interested in determining how great a change in the price of one good is required to effect a change of given magnitude in the consumption of certain other goods. But these are really questions of degree, resting on the underlying assumption—fundamental to economic theory—that all goods are ultimately commensurable.[36] If this assumption is accepted, the idea of a unique good loses meaning.

This point can be illustrated by a case that under present law would almost certainly be held to involve a unique good.[37] Suppose that *A* contracts with Sotheby's to purchase the handwritten manuscript of Hobbes's *Leviathan*. If Sotheby's refuses to perform—perhaps because it has a more attractive offer from someone else—*A* will undoubtedly be disappointed. Yet no matter how strong his affection for Hobbes, it is likely there are other things that would make *A* just as happy as getting the manuscript for the contract price. For example, *A* may be indifferent between purchasing the manuscript at the specified price and having 25 hours of violin lessons for the same amount.[38] If so, then *A* will be fully compensated for the loss he suffers by Sotheby's breach[39] upon receiving the difference between the cost of 25 hours worth of violin lessons and the contract price. However, despite the fact that the manuscript has an economic substitute, a court would be likely to order specific performance of the contract (assuming Sotheby's still had the manuscript in its possession)[40] on the ground that the subject matter of the contract is unique.

Pursuing the matter further, it is not difficult to see why *A*'s money damages remedy is likely to be inadequate, and on the basis of this insight to develop an economic justification for the uniqueness test. Under a money damages rule, a court must calculate the amount Sotheby's is required to pay *A* to give *A* the benefit of his bargain. The amount necessary to fully compensate *A* is equal to the amount he requires to obtain an appropriate substitute. So in fixing the amount Sotheby's must pay *A*, the court must first determine what things *A* would regard as substitutes and then how much of any particular substitute would be required to compensate him for his loss.[41]

In the hypothetical case, however, it would be very difficult and expensive for a court to acquire the information necessary to make these determinations. Perhaps some information of this sort would be produced by the parties. For example, *A* could introduce evidence to establish a past pattern of consumption from which the court might draw an inference as to what would be a satisfactory substitute for the manuscript. Sotheby's could then attempt to rebut the evidence and establish some alternative theory of preferences and substitutes. But of course it would be time-consuming to produce information this way, and any inference a court might draw on the basis of such information would be most uncertain.

Moreover, this uncertainty cannot be avoided by simply looking to the selling price of other manuscripts or even the expected resale price of the Hobbes manuscript itself (unless, of course, *A* is a professional dealer).[42] It would be risky to infer the value *A* places on the Hobbes manuscript from the value placed on it by others,[43] and riskier still to infer it from the value others place on the manuscripts of, for example, Harrington's *Oceana* or Locke's *Second Treatise*. If a court attempts to calculate *A*'s money damages on the basis of such information, there is a substantial probability that the award will miss the mark and be either under- or overcompensatory.

Of course, if a court could accurately identify a substitute for the manuscript, it could disregard the fact that *A* may value the manuscript in excess of the price that he, or anyone else, has agreed to pay for it. But where it is difficult to identify a satisfactory substitute (as I assume it is here), the goal of compensation requires that an effort be made to determine the value the promisee places on the promisor's performance, as distinct from what the promisee, or anyone else, has offered to pay for it.

Although it is true in a certain sense that all goods compete in the market—that every good has substitutes[44]—this is an empty truth. What matters, in measuring money damages, is the volume, refinement, and reliability of the available information about substitutes for the subject matter of the breached contract. When the relevant information is thin and unreliable, there is a substantial risk that an award of money damages will either exceed or fall short of the promisee's actual loss. Of course this risk can always be reduced—but only at great cost when reliable information is difficult to obtain. Conversely, when there is a great deal of consumer behavior generating abundant and highly dependable information about substitutes, the risk of error in measuring the promisee's loss may be reduced at much smaller cost. In asserting that the subject matter of a particular contract is unique and has no established market value, a court is really saying that it cannot obtain, at reasonable cost, enough information about substitutes to permit it to calculate an award of money damages without imposing an unacceptably high risk of undercompensation on the injured promisee. Conceived in this way, the uniqueness test seems economically sound.[45]

The following case will illustrate this point. A contracts with B for the purchase of 100 ball bearings. B breaches his promise to deliver, and A sues. If there are two or more sellers of ball bearings, and if there is substantial empirical evidence indicating that the cross-elasticity of demand is very high for ball bearings offered by different sellers, a court is warranted in assuming that most purchasers of ball bearings regard those sold by one seller as a satisfactory substitute for those sold by any other. For this reason, a court may also justifiably assume that a compensatory damages payment to A which enables him to purchase ball bearings from someone other than B (without incurring costs in excess of those he had originally anticipated), is likely to put A in precisely the position he would have been in had B performed his promise. The better the evidence that most buyers regard one brand of ball bearings as a substitute for another, the more confident a court can be that it has correctly calculated the magnitude of the promisee's loss.

It is of course true that even with very complete information about substitutes, a court may err in calculating money damages. It might be that A prefers B's ball bearings to those of any other seller because he believes they will last longer. Normally this preference would be reflected in the market price for B's ball bearings; if one brand

of ball bearings lasts longer than others, it should command a premium of some sort. But this may not be the case. It may be that A's knowledge and experience with B's ball bearings are not shared by other purchasers. If A attaches some special value to B's ball bearings not reflected in their price, he will be undercompensated if his damages are calculated on the assumption that the cost of a substitute is the cost of obtaining ball bearings from another seller. To prevent undercompensation, A must prove that he will suffer a special loss as a result of B's breach, but this may be difficult and costly to establish.

The conclusion to be drawn from this analysis is a simple one. Whenever a court calculates money damages, there is some risk that it will undercompensate the injured party.[46] But the magnitude of this risk is inversely related to the completeness and reliability of the information on which the court bases its award. At one extreme, where there is a well-developed market generating evidence of substitutability, this risk is minimal. At the other extreme, where there is no market or at most a few isolated transactions, this risk is substantial. There is a point between these two extremes at which the risk becomes unacceptably large (or, what amounts to the same thing, at which the risk can only be reduced by incurring unacceptable costs). This is the point separating those contracts that are specifically enforceable from those that are not—the point to which the uniqueness test obliquely refers.

There is an additional, perhaps less obvious, reason why money damages are most likely to be undercompensatory when the subject matter of a contract is unique. In searching for a particular good, a consumer will almost always incur certain costs—the costs of locating the good, obtaining information about it, and so on.[47] When these costs are incurred before formation of a contract, they are generally not compensable under a money damages rule.[48] Under a money damages rule, a disappointed promisee is usually unable to recover precontractual search costs, and is limited, instead, to compensation for the increased cost of obtaining a substitute after the promisor breaches.

Where a good is not unique, information acquired in searching for the good is likely to have some independent usefulness, which will survive a breach by the promisor. For example, if *A* wishes to purchase ball bearings, he will first obtain information about the ball-bearing market. If he then makes a contract with *B*, which *B* breaches, *A* will of course have to obtain some additional information before he can arrange for a substitute purchase.[49] But much of the information acquired prior to his contract with *B* will still have value for *A*—it will still be economically useful. On the other hand, where *A* contracts for the purchase of a unique good, say, a one-of-a-kind stamp, this is less likely to be the case. *A* may have expended a substantial sum in locating the stamp, and although it is possible that some of the information acquired in the course of his search will be generally useful, it is more likely that much of the information is valuable to *A* only because it aided the discovery of the stamp in question.

Under a money damages rule, *A* will not be compensated for these search costs if his seller breaches. But of course he will be compensated (that is, he will obtain the desired return) if he can compel specific performance of the contract. That precontractual search costs are not compensable under a money damages rule is less worrisome when the information generated by the search represents a capital stock that can be exploited in subsequent transactions.[50] But when it does not, the likelihood is increased that money damages will be undercompensatory.[51]

The uniqueness test reflects the unwillingness of courts to impose a risk of undercompensation on promisees when that risk is substantial. What justifies this reluctance? One plausible answer is that a promisor should not be permitted to benefit from his own misconduct by placing that risk on someone who is, after all, an innocent victim of his breach.

This justification is attractive because it appeals to a powerful moral sentiment. Unfortunately, when stated in its most abstract form, it proves too much. If the fact of breach is an adequate reason for protecting the promisee from a risk of undercompensation, it is unclear why a promisor should ever be permitted to substitute money damages for the actual performance of his obligation. The moral justification is not

wrong; it is merely unhelpful since it fails to explain why some contracts are specifically enforceable and others are not. Before a court concludes that it would be wrong to impose a particular risk on the promisee, it should first determine that the promisee has not agreed to bear the risk, nor been compensated for doing so. The moral justification for specific enforcement presupposes a solution to this initial problem of risk allocation.

A second, essentially economic, justification for the uniqueness test consists in showing that the test draws the line between specific performance and money damages in the way that most contracting parties would draw it were they free to make their own rules concerning remedies for breach and had they deliberated about the matter at the time of contracting. If this is true, the uniqueness test promotes efficiency by reducing the costs of negotiating contracts.[52] In general, this way of thinking about the rules of contract law requires consideration of the ex-ante interests of parties engaged in a hypothetical bargaining process, struggling with a problem of rational choice under conditions of uncertainty. As I shall attempt to show in the next section, an analysis based upon ex ante considerations does suggest, if only somewhat tentatively, that contracting parties would be more likely to provide for specific performance where the subject matter of their contract is unique, and for money damages where it is not.

II. SPECIFIC PERFORMANCE AND THE EX ANTE INTERESTS OF PROMISOR AND PROMISEE

When would the parties to a contract freely agree to a judicially enforceable[53] provision giving the promisee an option[54] to specifically enforce the other party's promise? Other things equal, a promisee will always prefer to have such a provision included in the contract, for it gives him an additional right which he would not otherwise possess. Other things equal, a promisor will always prefer a contract without such a provision—a contract, in other words, which he may unilaterally breach on the condition that he make a subsequent compensatory payment to the promisee.

Consequently, a promisee intent upon writing a specific performance provision—a property rule —into the contract will have to pay to secure the promisor's consent. Similarly, a promisor must make a payment of some sort[55] in order to exclude a provision for specific enforcement from the contract. If and only if the benefit which the promisee realizes from a specific performance provision exceeds the cost of the provision to the promisor will the provision be included in the final contract.

When the subject matter of a contract is unique, the risk is greater that the promisee's money damage remedy will be undercompensatory.[56] Since a right to compel specific performance reduces this risk, promisees—as a class—should be willing to pay more for a provision giving them a right of this sort when there is no developed market generating information about the value of the subject matter of their contract.

However, if a specific performance provision is likely to be more beneficial to a promisee when the subject matter of his contract is unique, it is also likely to be more costly to his promisor under the same circumstances. In the first place, a right in the promisee to compel specific performance increases the probability of costly negotiations for transfer of the promisee's contract rights.[57] This of course always reinforces the promisor's preference for a money damages rule. However, a promisor is likely to regard this reason as especially compelling where the subject matter of his contract is unique, since the lack of information about substitutes will almost certainly make the parties' negotiations longer and more complicated and thus more costly.

Second, if the promisee is entitled to specifically enforce the promisor's obligation, the promisor who wishes to breach will have to make a release payment to the promisee and buy his way out of the contract. The amount of the release payment demanded by the promisee will be greater than what the promisor would have to pay the promisee under a money damages rule.[58] This is so whether or not the subject matter of the contract is unique. But the difference between what the promisee would accept in exchange for a release and what he may be expected to receive under a court-administered money damages rule is

likely to be larger where the subject matter of his contract is unique, because the risk that court-awarded damages will be undercompensatory is greater. For these two reasons, a specific performance provision will be more expensive to the promisor when the subject matter of his contract is unique.

Thus far, it would appear that the benefits to the promisee and the costs to the promisor of a specific performance provision are proportional; both are greater when the subject matter of the contract is unique. There is, however, an additional consideration influencing their ex ante deliberations that provides some basis for thinking that the parties to a contract will be more likely to provide for specific performance when the subject matter of their agreement is unique.

The cost of a specific performance provision to the promisor will be determined, in part, by his own estimate of the likelihood that he will want to breach the contract. If he fully intends to perform, and thinks breach unlikely, a promisor will be less hostile to a contract with a specific performance provision than he would otherwise be. One important factor influencing the promisor's thinking in this regard is the probability that he will receive a better offer for his goods or services in the interim between formation of the contract and performance. The higher the probability, the greater the likelihood he will want to breach. The probability of receiving an attractive alternative offer may be especially low where the subject matter of the contract is unique.[59] In this case there is by definition no developed market, transactions are spotty at best, and therefore a promisor will often justifiably think it highly unlikely that he will receive any alternative offer (let alone a better one) for the promised goods or services. Indeed, where the subject matter of his contract is genuinely unique, a promisor may estimate the likelihood of a preferable alternative offer as close to zero, and thus be nearly indifferent as to what remedies the promisee will enjoy in the highly unlikely event of breach.

Although the promisor thinks breach highly improbable, the promisee may not. Despite the promisor's insistence that he intends to perform, the promisee may be skeptical. As long as he is anxious about the promisor's performance, the promisee will be concerned about the adequacy of his own remedies, and where the subject matter of his contract is unique he will likely have a decided preference for a contract that gives him the right to specifically enforce the other party's promise. Consequently, in the case of a contract for a unique good or service, the benefits the promisee derives from a specific performance provision are apt to outweigh its costs to the promisor, who, free of doubts about his own reliability, may regard the inclusion of such a provision as a relatively costless way of enticing the promisee to enter the contract on advantageous terms.

In the case of a contract for nonunique goods or services, by contrast, the existence of a developed market increases the likelihood that the promisor will receive alternative offers before he has performed the contract. The promisor will therefore be anxious to retain the freedom and flexibility enjoyed under a money damages rule.

Moreover, the promisor will be especially anxious in this case to avoid the additional transaction costs that would be incurred if he had to negotiate a voluntary transfer of the promisee's contract rights. Although these costs will tend to be smaller where the subject matter of the contract is not unique, they can never be less than some fixed minimum (the cost of contacting the promisee, notifying him of an intention to breach, obtaining a release statement of some sort, and so on). Where there is an established market in the goods or services involved, prices will ordinarily be grouped rather closely around a single point. The probability is therefore greater that any alternative offer the promisor does receive will not be sufficiently high to cover the cost of negotiating a release plus the amount he must pay the promisee for the release. Thus the likelihood increases that a promisor who has agreed to a specific performance provision will find himself in the undesirable position of having to decline an alternative offer that he would accept under a money damages rule. In some cases the alternative offer will cover the release payment but will be refused solely because the transaction costs of negotiating a transfer of the promisee's contract rights are prohibitively high. The promisor should therefore be

willing to make a small payment to the promisee, perhaps in the form of a slightly reduced contract price, in order to exclude a specific performance provision and thus avoid these potential transaction costs. Because the transaction costs avoided by the promisor would not have benefited the promisee, the latter will be better off with the reduced contract price if he regards the risk of undercompensation under a money damages rule as minimal. The promisee will generally regard this risk as slight where there is a developed market generating information about suitable substitutes.

In sum, promisors and promisees will typically favor a money damages rule if the subject matter of their contract is not unique. When the contract is for unique goods or services, on the other hand, the benefit to the promisee of a specific performance provision is likely to be substantial and the promisor may well regard his own breach as only a remote possibility, so the opposite conclusion seems more plausible. There is thus some basis for believing the uniqueness test reflects the typical solution that contracting parties would arrange for themselves in light of their ex ante interests.

III. SPECIFIC PERFORMANCE AND FREEDOM OF CONTRACT

I have argued that ex ante considerations provide some basis for thinking the uniqueness test is economically rational.[60] The argument attempted to show that if contracting parties were entirely free to select their own remedies, their choice would generally correspond to the mix of property and liability rules adopted by the law of contracts. But ex ante arguments for the efficiency of a particular legal rule assume that individuals remain free to contract around that rule, and a legal system that denies private parties the right to vary rules in this way will tend to be less efficient than a system that adopts the same rules but permits contractual variation.[61]

This raises an important question. If, under the uniqueness standard, a promisee does not have the right to specifically enforce a particular promise, can he create a right of this sort by private agreement?[62] It is easy to imagine situations in which a promisee might wish to do this. For example, A may wish to enter a specifically enforceable contract for the purchase of ball bearings because he believes that special considerations, which will be difficult to establish in a lawsuit, are likely to make his normal money damages remedy undercompensatory. Similarly, some sellers of ball bearings may be willing to agree to a specific performance provision in order to secure a better contract price or a new customer. For example, a new entrant in an industry, lacking an established reputation, may conclude that agreeing to a specific performance provision is the least costly way to communicate to prospective clients his confidence in his ability to perform.

In the well-known case of *Stokes v. Moore*,[63] the plaintiffs, partners operating a small loan business, hired and later dismissed defendant Stokes. They then sued to enforce a covenant not to compete, which had been incorporated in the contract of employment. The contract contained a clause stating that if Stokes breached his promise not to compete, "a restraining order or injunction [might] be issued and entered against [him] in any court of equity jurisdiction."[64] Although it affirmed the trial judge's decision to issue a temporary injunction, the Supreme Court of Alabama viewed unfavorably the parties' attempt to create a right to injunctive relief by private agreement:

> We do not wish to express the view that an agreement for the issuance of an injunction, if and when a stipulated state of facts arises in the future, is binding on the court to that extent. Such an agreement would serve to oust the inherent jurisdiction of the court to determine whether an injunction is appropriate when applied for and to require its issuance even though to do so would be contrary to the opinion of the court.[65]

The court added, however, that "the provision for an injunction is important in its influence upon an exercise of the discretionary power of the court to grant a temporary injunction."[66]

The few cases directly addressing this question reach a similar result.[67] A private agreement that purports to give one party the right to specifically enforce the promise of another will be given some weight by courts in deciding whether to grant injunctive relief. But no court will consider itself foreclosed by the parties' contract from refusing

specific relief. A contractual provision accompanied by a lengthy description of those aspects of the transaction that make specific performance desirable is likely to carry more weight than a provision unadorned by supporting explanation.[68] But in no event will the contract provision prevent a court from independently determining the appropriateness of injunctive relief.[69]

Perhaps judicial unwillingness to honor provisions such as the one in *Stokes* reflects a desire to avoid private abuse of a powerful and intrusive remedy. This is a legitimate concern. But if the purpose in scrutinizing a private agreement of the *Stokes* variety is to prevent abuse by an overreaching promisee, this end could be served as adequately and more directly by other legal tools—for example, by traditional common law doctrines of fraud, duress, and good faith.[70] If the concern is abuse of the contracting process, courts should focus on the voluntariness of the parties' agreement.

It may be, however, that courts prohibit the private creation of injunctive remedies not because specific performance provisions evidence some procedural unfairness in the parties' dealings, but rather because they are perceived to be substantively unacceptable limitations on personal freedom. A provision of the kind involved in *Stokes* might be viewed as a modified contract of self-enslavement, an attempt to transfer an entitlement whose transfer is prohibited by law (an "inalienable" right or entitlement in the scheme proposed by Calabresi and Melamed).[71] This idea is echoed in some of the older specific performance cases involving construction and employment contracts.[72]

Such an argument carries little weight in a case like *Stokes,* where the promise to be enforced is a negative one—a promise to refrain from doing something. More important, the argument is overdrawn. It is true that certain forms of domination (for example, slavery and peonage) are regarded as inherently bad. Our legal system prohibits these forms of domination, whether they are created by consensual act or by force. On the other hand, there are many relations of domination recognized and protected by law so long as they are voluntarily established and maintained. The relation created by a contract of employment is an important example of legally protected domination.

The nature, completeness, and duration of self-imposed limitations on personal freedom determine their legal and moral acceptability. Slavery is objectionable largely because it involves near-total control. By contrast the domination an employer exercises is partial and limited—the employer only controls certain aspects of his employee's life. Nevertheless, employees are not generally required by judicial order to submit to employer control. The judicial order, it may be argued, makes a crucial difference: if the employment relation is created or maintained by the threat of judicial sanctions, it is almost certain to be plagued by acrimony and ill-will. But although the unpleasantness of a forced employment relation should certainly be taken into account by an employer contemplating a suit for specific performance, it should not be a basis for refusing to impose such a relation upon parties who have agreed to an injunctive provision in their contract. Moreover, if the party in breach anticipates that the relation will be unbearable, he can buy his release from the contract.

Judicial insistence that the specific enforcement of certain contracts would create an objectionable form of personal servitude is made yet more puzzling by the numerous cases in which courts have been perfectly willing to negatively enjoin the party in breach from employing his time or talents save in performance of the contract.[73] This sort of decree will often have the same effect as a positive injunction to perform.

There is another common explanation for the reluctance of courts to enforce private injunctive agreements: the specific enforcement of contracts (especially employment and construction contracts) entails special administrative costs which normally can be avoided under a money damages rule, and private individuals should not be allowed to shift the special costs associated with this form of relief to the taxpayers who subsidize the legal system.[74] The assumption on which this argument rests, however, may be mistaken. It is ancient dogma that specific performance necessarily means increased judicial involvement in the enforcement and supervision of contractual duties. This might be true, but so might the opposite

conclusion: if all promises were specifically enforceable, or if private parties were permitted to contract into a specific performance rule at their discretion, a resulting increase in the voluntary transfer of contract rights might lower the number of breaches—and perhaps even of lawsuits—and in this way reduce the actual involvement of courts in contractual relationships.

In comparing the administrative costs, broadly defined, of a property rule mandating specific performance with a liability rule directing an award of money damages, the following factors must be taken into account: (1) the frequency of litigation under both rules; (2) the administrative cost of resolving litigated disputes under both rules; (3) the portion of the administrative costs involved in dispute resolution borne by the parties and the portion borne by society under both rules; (4) the likelihood and cost, under each rule, of pretrial settlement; and (5) special institutional costs, such as the potential loss in court prestige that results from noncompliance with a direct order to perform, and the cost of invoking the court's contempt powers.

To say the least, it is unclear how these administrative costs add up under the two rules. Until these questions have been explored, it is unwise to assume that the legal invalidity of private agreements purporting to create a right of specific enforcement is justified on the ground that specific relief is a more costly remedy than money damages and that a greater portion of the costs of specific performance is borne by third parties.

A promisee could attempt to achieve indirectly the special protection associated with a property rule by insisting, as a condition of entering the contract, that the other party promise to pay a penalty upon breach—a penalty in excess of any damages payment necessary to compensate the promisee. A provision of this sort, if enforceable, would have the same effect as the sanctions that back up both injunctive orders and criminal prohibitions: it would encourage the prospective taker of an entitlement to purchase the entitlement from its owner in a voluntary market transaction. However, a contractual provision that is *deliberately designed* to be penal will not be enforced.[75] The legal prohibition of penal clauses is an important obstacle facing parties who wish to contract into a property rule.[76]

In sum, although the parties to a contract may have legitimate reasons for wishing to contract into a property rule, the courts will generally not enforce a specific performance provision unless the contract would be specifically enforceable without it. The reluctance of courts to enforce such provisions reflects concern that recognition of a private power of injunction would sanction a morally offensive form of involuntary servitude and increase judicial involvement in the enforcement and supervision of contractual obligations. I have suggested that the former rationale is overdrawn and without much force in most cases in which parties to a contract knowingly and voluntarily agree to a specific performance provision, and I have argued that the latter justification is neither intuitively compelling nor empirically established. On the other hand, economic considerations suggest that the parties to a contract should be allowed to contract into a property rule: they are in the best position to determine which remedial devices will serve their respective interests most satisfactorily.

IV. THIRD PARTIES, PENALTIES, AND THE CONVERSION PROBLEM

So far, I have treated property rules and liability rules as though they were sharply distinguishable, and have implicitly assumed that a particular entitlement will always fall cleanly under one rule or the other. Following Calabresi and Melamed,[77] I have distinguished property rules from liability rules by their penal character. It is not sufficient to define a property rule as a rule forbidding the appropriation of an entitlement without the owner's consent. A rule that forbids such a taking but merely requires a taker to compensate the owner of the right is a liability rule. An owner's right is protected by a property rule only if the taking triggers the application of some special sanction whose cost to the taker is likely to exceed the payment he would have to make to compensate the owner for his loss.[78] In the simplest contract cases, specific performance vindicates an entitlement protected by a property rule in just this way. Suppose that Smith promises to sell a unique parcel of land

to Jones.[79] If Smith refuses to deliver the land because he has received a more attractive offer from Miller, Jones can obtain an injunction ordering Smith to perform his promise. And if Smith still refuses to transfer the property to Jones, he may be cited for contempt and fined or imprisoned.

Suppose, however, that instead of merely refusing to sell the land to Jones, Smith actually sells it to Miller, a good faith purchaser, before Jones learns of the second sale and is able to enjoin Smith from disposing of the property. The varying judicial responses to this elementary problem suggest three things: first, that the distinction between property rules and liability rules, while analytically useful, does not capture the full range of entitlement-protecting devices employed in the law of contracts; second, that the choice of a rule for protecting contractual entitlements may be affected by considerations other than those already discussed—in particular, by the interests of third parties; and finally, that in some cases the law appears to irrationally tolerate the deliberate conversion of property rules to liability rules.

There are three ways in which the courts have treated promisees in Jones's position. Not infrequently, they simply limit the promisee to his damages remedy, on the ground that specific performance is no longer possible since the property has been conveyed to an innocent third party.[80] Sometimes, however, a court will impose a constructive trust for the promisee's benefit on the profit realized by the resale (that is, the difference between the resale price and the original contract price), even though this may exceed the damages the promisee has suffered.[81] And finally, on rare occasions, a court will require the good faith purchaser to retender the property and then compel specific performance of the original contract.[82]

The first approach sanctions the conversion of property rules to liability rules. If a promisee in Jones's position receives only court-awarded money damages,[83] he may be undercompensated. Since the justification for protecting the promisee's original entitlement with a property rule was to avoid placing this risk on the promisee, it is puzzling that the promisor should be permitted to impose this risk by simply breaching his contract and putting himself in a position where he is unable to perform. These cases would be less disturbing if there were ground for confidence that courts in measuring the promisee's money damages treat the resale price of the property as strong (or conclusive) evidence of its market value.[84] But it is often difficult to tell from the reported versions of the cases what weight, if any, has been given to the resale price in calculating damages. More important, several cases suggest the resale price is just one factor, among many, that a court may either consider or ignore in determining the amount of the promisee's damage award.[85]

A recent illustrative case is *Grummel v. Hollenstein*.[86] Grummel contracted with Hollenstein to make certain improvements on the latter's property, in return for which Hollenstein promised to convey to Grummel a portion of the property in question. Grummel made the improvements, but Hollenstein refused to convey all of the property to which Grummel was entitled. Part of the property promised Grummel was conveyed to a third party before the initiation of the lawsuit.

Grummel sued to compel specific performance of Hollenstein's promise to convey. The trial court refused to grant specific performance, on the ground that it was "impossible to enforce the agreement of the parties"[87] since the property had been sold. Instead, the trial court awarded Grummel money damages of $40,000. Although it is unclear how the award was calculated, it appears that the trial court considered the "value of the land" and the value of the improvements made by Grummel. After trial but before the entry of judgment against Hollenstein, Grummel discovered the price at which the property had been sold: $156,000. Grummel petitioned the trial court to reopen its judgment to consider the newly discovered evidence. The trial court declined to do so.

On appeal, it was held: (1) the trial court had correctly refused to grant specific performance; (2) having done so, it was justified in then awarding money damages; and (3) the trial court was also justified in refusing to reopen its judgment in order to consider Grummel's new evidence. In so holding, the Supreme Court of Arizona said:

> The measure of damages in lieu of specific performance is generally determined by the same rules obtaining in regard to damages for breach of contract in an action at law....
>
> Although we cannot determine the precise formula applied by the court in arriving at the amount of damages sustained by the plaintiff, we cannot thereby conclude that the court was not justified in the figure it reached. Exact damages in a case of this nature are difficult, if not impossible, to calculate mathematically....
>
> [The trial court's refusal to consider Grummel's evidence of the property's resale price] is a matter lying within the sound discretion of the trial court.[88]

Under the relaxed approach endorsed by the Arizona court, the difference between resale price and original contract price will often exceed the damages awarded the promisee. By encouraging the promisor to believe that he is likely to gain more by selling to a third party than he will be required to pay in damages to his original promisee, the approach adopted by the Arizona court increases the probability that the promisor will breach without having first negotiated a transfer of the promisee's contract rights. To the extent this is true, the promisee's initial right to compel specific performance loses its value and degenerates to a liability claim. There is no justification—certainly no economic one[89]—for permitting this deliberate conversion of property rules to liability rules.

Under a constructive trust approach, the conversion problem is less serious. Since it eliminates any profit the promisor might make by selling the property to someone other than his original promisee, imposition of a constructive trust should greatly weaken the promisor's incentive to breach the original contract without having first negotiated a release. But a constructive trust is not inherently penal: it does not always require a taker to pay more than is necessary to compensate the owner of an entitlement for his loss. On the other hand, the cost imposed on a breaching party by a constructive trust is not measured by the estimated harm suffered by the promisee (as is the case with an award of money damages).[90] In this latter respect, a constructive trust resembles the injunctive remedies that are commonly used to prevent the conversion of property rules to liability rules.

There is, however, one obvious way in which a constructive trust gives the promisee something less than full property rule protection. If a thief steals a car, and then sells it to a good faith purchaser, the original owner can retrieve the automobile.[91] He does not lose his right to the car because it happens to find its way into the hands of an innocent third party. By contrast, under a constructive trust approach, a promisee receives only what is sometimes called "substitutionary" relief[92]— something other than the thing contracted for. If a promisee's entitlement were protected against conversion to the same extent as a property owner's entitlement to be free from theft, he would be able to retrieve the promised goods from a good faith purchaser. There are, in fact, a few cases reaching this result, albeit in two steps:[93] first, the good faith purchaser is compelled to return the property to the promisor and then the original contract is specifically enforced.

An important economic consideration helps to explain why a good faith purchaser usually prevails over the prior promisee and why this rule makes more sense in the law of contracts than an analogous principle would in the law of theft. In general, it is desirable to avoid a conflict between equally innocent claimants. And it makes economic sense to put the risk of conflict of this sort on the party able to prevent it at the lowest cost. Often this will be the original promisee, who is frequently in the best position to publicize his interest in the property and thereby put third parties on notice. The law gives the promisee adequate incentive to publicize his interest by denying him the right to recover the promised property from a purchaser in good faith.[94] This argument applies with less force to the theft situation. Although it may be expensive for a good faith purchaser to determine whether his vendor has title to the goods he is selling, it may well be less expensive for him to do so than for owners to publicly record their interest in all their property[95]—especially property in their possession, for possession is usually adequate notice of a property claim. In short, the constructive trust approach to the conversion problem in contract law is generally the economically soundest.

Perhaps the most interesting feature of the constructive trust is its hybrid character. The use of such a trust remedy seems more consistent than an ordinary damages remedy with the initial decision to protect the entitlement in question with a property rule. On the other hand, a constructive trust does not accord the promisee a right to recover his property from a good faith purchaser—a right typically enjoyed by the victim of theft. The right to insist that a trust be imposed on the money realized from the sale of the promised property is more than a right to money damages and less than a right to pursue the property itself into the hands of a good faith purchaser. It is hard to categorize the trust remedy as either a liability rule or a property rule. Although the distinction between liability rules and property rules (and the underlying distinction between compensation and punishment) provides a useful beginning point for analysis, a rigid insistence on the distinction obscures the fact that certain remedies exhibit features characteristic of both sorts of rules, and straddle the line between them.[96]

NOTES

1. Calabresi & Melamed, *Property Rules, Liability Rules and Inalienability: One View of the Cathedral*, 85 Harv. L. Rev. 1089 (1972). They also discuss a third technique for protecting entitlements—inalienability. The law restricts or forbids the sale of inalienable rights. Id., at 1111–15. For a treatment of property and liability rules from a philosophical perspective, see R. Nozick, Anarchy, State and Utopia 54–87 (1974).
2. Calabresi & Melamed, supra, note 1, at 1092
3. Id., at 1126. See also R. Nozick, supra, note 1, at 57.
4. Calabresi & Melamed, supra, note 1, at 1092.
5. Id., at 1108–09, 1115–24.
6. Id., at 1126–27.
7. Id., at 1127.
8. Id., at 1125.
9. Instructive cases are collected in O. Fiss, Injunctions 714–814 (1972).
10. This is, of course, not true in every case. Perhaps the most important exception is the third-party beneficiary contract. In this article, I ignore the complications posed by these more elaborate contractual arrangements.

11. This distinguishes a contract negotiation from the pollution case discussed in Calabresi & Melamed, supra, note 1, at 1106–08, and from at least some eminent domain proceedings. For a discussion of the conflicting philosophical ideals that have informed judicial interpretation of the compensation clause, see B. Ackerman, Private Property and the Constitution (1977).

12. There is an additional consideration strengthening the case for protecting contractual entitlements with a property rule. According to Calabresi & Melamed, supra, note 1, at 1108–09, 1119, the use of a property rule in both automobile accidents and pollution torts is likely to inhibit an efficient allocation of the resources involved. It is not obvious that specifically enforcing all contractual entitlements would have similar misallocative consequences.

    Suppose that A contracts with B to buy B's piano. Suppose, in addition, that A has the right to specifically enforce B's promise. If C values the piano more than A, he will offer to pay B a premium for breaking his contract with A, and if the premium is large enough, B will be able to buy his way out of the contract, and the piano will go directly to C. Of course, the premium may be too small to cover both the release payment A demands and the costs of negotiating a settlement. If so, the piano will go to A, who will in turn sell it to C. Once again, the piano ends up in the hands of C, the higher-valuing user, but this time after two transfers rather than one. The allocative outcome is the same in both cases; the only difference is a distributional one.

    The result, under a money damages rule, should be identical. If the difference between C's offer and the original contract price exceeds what B must pay A in damages, B will breach and the piano will go to C. However, the piano will remain in C's hands only if he values it more than A. If A's actual loss—the amount he would have demanded for relinquishing his right to B's performance in the first place—exceeds the value C places on the piano, A will now contract to buy the piano from C. Of course, this will only happen if A's money damages are undercompensatory (if they do not reflect his actual loss). But there is always a risk that the representative of the state who determines the amount of the payment will underestimate the extent of the harm suffered by the injured party. The important point is that the piano will go to the higher-valuing user, whether or not the damages awarded the original promisee are compensatory.

One might argue that under a money damages rule the cost of moving resources to their ultimate consumers will be less than what it would be if all contract rights were specifically enforceable. It is true that a promisor who must perform or pay a penalty will be more likely to attempt to buy his way out of a contract before breaching than a promisor who is only required to pay damages if he fails to perform. In some cases, this will mean an additional transaction, which could be avoided under a money damages rule. In other cases, however, a property rule may prevent the transfer of a particular resource to a lower-valuing user and thus eliminate the necessity of an additional exchange shifting the resource back to the original promisee. Furthermore, the onus of a property rule might give promisors an increased incentive to carefully identify their various opportunities before committing themselves contractually—with the result that resources would be more likely to flow directly to higher-valuing users. On balance, it is certainly not obvious that a decision to protect contractual entitlements with a property rule would increase the total cost of moving resources to their most efficient uses.

13. See generally Barbour, *The History of Contract in Early English Equity,* in Oxford Studies in Social and Legal History (1914); Washington, *Damages in Contract at Common Law* (pts. 1–2), 47 & 48 Law Q. Rev. 345, 90 (1931–1932).

14. 11 S. Williston, Contracts §1338 (3d ed. W. Jaeger 1968); 5 A. Corbin, Contracts §993 (1960); Farnsworth, *Legal Remedies for Breach of Contract,* 70 Colum. L. Rev. 1145–47(1970).

15. The limited use of specific performance is a fairly recent historical development. See G. Treitel, The Law of Contract 834–41 (3d ed. 1970); Dawson, *Specific Performance in France and Germany,* 57 Mich. L. Rev. 495, 532, 537–38 (1959). This development has been criticized as inconsistent with natural justice. Union Pacific Ry. Co. v. Chicago Ry. Co., 163 U.S. 564, 600 (1896) (Fuller, C.J.). Not all legal systems draw the line between specific performance and money damages in the same way. See R. Pound, An Introduction to the Philosophy of Law 240 (1922); Beardsley, *Compelling Contract Performance in France,* 1 Hastings Int'l & Comp. L. Rev. 93 (1977); Dawson, supra,; Grossfeld, *Money Sanctions for Breach of Contract in a Communist Economy,* 72 Yale L.J. 1326, 1333 (1963); Treitel, *Remedies for Breach of Contract,* in VII International Encyclopedia of Comparative Law (ch. 16) 2 (1976).

16. See, e.g., Barton, *The Economic Basis of Damages for Breach of Contract*, 1 J. LEG. STUD. 277 (1972); Birmingham, *Damage Measures and Economic Rationality: The Geometry of Contract Law*, 1969 DUKE L.J. 49; Birmingham, *Breach of Contract, Damage Measures, and Economic Efficiency*, 24 RUTGERS L. REV. 273 (1970); Posner & Rosenfield, *Impossibility and Related Doctrines in Contract Law: An Economic Analysis*, 6 J. LEG. STUD. 83 (1977); Schwartz, *Sales Law and Inflations*, 50 S. CAL. L. REV. 1 (1976). Professor Posner briefly discusses the more fundamental issue—whether there are economic consideratons that explain why the law of contracts provides for specific performance in some cases and money damages in others. R. POSNER, ECONOMIC ANALYSIS OF LAW §§4.2, 4.12 (2d ed. 1977).

17. E. FRY, A TREATISE ON THE SPECIFIC PERFORMANCE OF CONTRACTS §3 (6th ed. 1921); J. POMEROY, A TREATISE ON THE SPECIFIC PERFORMANCE OF CONTRACTS §§1–3 (3d ed. with J. Mann 1926); 11 S. WILLISTON, CONTRACTS §1418 (3d ed. W. Jaeger 1968). See, e.g., Klein v. Shell Oil Co., 386 F.2d 659 (8th Cir. 1967).

18. E.g., Lee v. Crane, 270 Ala. 651, 653,120 So. 2d 702, 703 (1960). Although certain kinds of contracts (such as contracts for the sale of land) are, as a general rule, specifically enforced, courts do not feel bound by traditional categories and will sometimes exercise their discretion to deny specific performance of an agreement that would normally be specifically enforceable. See, e.g., Paddock v. Davenport, 107 N.C. 710, 12 S.E. 464 (1890) (specific performance of a contract for the sale of an interest in land denied on the ground that money damages would adequately compensate the vendee). See also cases cited at note 20, infra

19. "[W]e do not give specific relief ordinarily but only exceptionally where pecuniary relief is considered inadequate." R. POUND, supra, note 15, at 240. Money damages are generally regarded as inadequate when they are too difficult to assess. See City Stores Co. v. Ammerman, 266 F. Supp. 766 (D.D.C. 1967), *aff'd per curiam*, 394 F.2d 950 (D.C. Cir. 1968) (contract for a lease in a shopping center). The difficulties of assessing money damages are likely to be especially acute in cases involving long-term output and requirements contracts. See, e.g., American Smelting & Ref. Co. v. Bunker Hill & Sullivan Mining & Concentrating Co., 248 F. 172 (D. Ore. 1918). See generally E. FRY, supra, note 17, at §§49–90; J. POMEROY, supra, note 17, at §§28–34, 47–50; RESTATEMENT OF CONTRACTS §358 (1932); 11 S. WILLSTON, supra, note 14, at §1418.

20. Contracts for the transfer of real property have traditionally been specifically enforced. "Where land, or any estate therein, is the subject matter of the agreement, the equitable jurisdiction is firmly established." J. POMEROY, supra, note 17, at §10. Not only are contracts for the sale of land specifically enforced, covenants running with the land and options to purchase land are specifically enforceable as well. See Mobil Oil Corp. v. Brennan, 385 F.2d 951 (5th Cir. 1967) (covenant running with the land); Abdallah v. Abdallah, 359 F.2d 170 (3d Cir. 1966) (option to purchase real property); McCullough v. Newton, 348 S.W.2d 138 (Mo. 1961) (sale of land).

More recently, however, courts have exhibited greater willingness to deny specific performance of contracts for the transfer of real property, on the ground that the plaintiff has an adequate remedy at law. See Watkins v. Paul, 95 Idaho 499, 511 P.2d 781 (1973); Suchan v. Rutherford, 90 Idaho 288, 295–96, 410 P.2d 434, 443 (1966); Duckworth v. Michel, 172 Wash. 234, 19 P.2d 914 (1933). In the two Idaho cases, the court asserted that the vendee's purpose in entering the contract was not to obtain the land and put it to a specific use, but rather pecuniary profit. For a general discussion of the problem, see J. DAWSON & W. HARVEY, CASES ON CONTRACTS 180 (3d ed. 1977); Bird & Fanning, *Specific Performance of Contracts to Convey Real Estate*, 23 KY. L.J. 380 (1935) (approves the tendency of modern courts to assess more carefully the adequacy of money damages in land cases).

21. Contracts involving heirlooms and antiques are specifically enforceable on the theory that the article involved typically has sentimental significance and value over and above its pecuniary worth. The classic case is Pusey v. Pusey, 23 Eng. Rep. 465 (1684), in which specific performance was granted for the transfer of an ancient horn given the Pusey family by the Danish King Canute. The horn had more than sentimental value, however. It signified conveyance of certain realty. See also Burr v. Bloomsburg, 101 N.J. Eq. 615, 33 A. 962 (1927) (sale of a diamond ring); Falcke v. Gray, 62 Eng. Rep. 250 (1859) (sale of two china jars). The court in *Falcke*, while denying specific performance on other grounds, said: "In the present case the contract is for the purchase of articles of unusual beauty, rarity and distinction, so that damages

would not be an adequate compensation for non-performance...." 62 Eng. Rep. at 252–53.

22. Cf. Nelson v. Richia, 232 F.2d 827 (1st Cir. 1956) (sale of a business with a licensed trade name, buyer required to perform).

23. Cf. Patent & Licensing Corp. v. Olsen, 188 F.2d 522 (2d Cir. 1951) (employee ordered to assign patents on process developed in course of employment to employer); McFarland v. Stanton Mfg. Co., 53 N.J. Eq. 649, 33 A. 962 (1895) (patented improvements on a process ordered handed over to transferee of original patent); Whitcomb v. Whitcomb, 85 Vt. 76, 81 A. 97 (1912) (partner ordered to assign patent to partnership that had equitable ownership of the patent). See generally J. POMEROY, supra, note 17, at §20.

24. [I]t is clear that specific performance is a particularly appropriate remedy for enforcement of "buy-sell" agreements of shares of stock of closely-held corporations. Money damages would not be adequate. It is extremely difficult to determine the value of stock in a closely-held corporation and money damages would not accomplish the primary purpose of such ... agreements—to prevent outsiders from entering the business. *In re* Brown's Estate, 446 Pa. 401, 409, 289 A.2d 77, 81 (1972) (footnotes omitted). Cf. King v. Stevenson, 445 F.2d 565, 572 (7th Cir. 1971) (specific performance of an agreement to allow the president of a corporation to purchase sufficient stock to retain control of the business); Bumgardner v. Leavitt, 35 W. Va. 194, 203, 13 S.E. 67, 71 (1891) (specific performance would be granted to defendant to prevent a takeover by antagonistic interests, therefore plaintiff is entitled to specific performance on ground of mutuality of remedy). See generally E. FRY, supra, note 17, at §§1496–1529; J. POMEROY, supra, note 17, at §§17–19.

25. See, e.g., Laclede Gas. Co. v. Amoco Oil Co., 522 F.2d 33 (8th Cir. 1975) (supply of gas to residential subdivisions); Campbell Soup Co. v. Wentz, 172 F.2d 80 (3d Cir. 1948) (sale of carrots, specific performance denied on other grounds); Hunt Foods v. D'Odisbo, 98 F.Supp. 267 (N.D. Cal. 1951) (peaches); American Smelting & Ref. Co. v. Bunker Hill &Sullivan Mining & Concentrating Co., 248 F. 172, 182–83 (D. Ore. 1918) (lead-silver ore); Eastern Rolling Mill Co. v. Michlovitz, 157 Md. 51, 65–69, 145 A. 378, 383–85 (1929) (scrapiron); Michigan Sugar Co. v. Falkenhagen, 243 Mich. 698, 220 N.W. 760 (1928) (sugar beets); St. Regis Paper Co. v. Santa Clara Lumber Co., 173 N.Y. 149, 65 N.E. 967 (1903). In many cases, the grant of specific performance is coupled with an injunction forbidding transfer of the goods to third parties. See generally 11 S. WILLISTON, supra, note 14, at §1419B.

26. Specific performance of employment contracts has traditionally been denied on three grounds: (1) the presumed adequacy of the plaintiff's legal remedy; (2) the difficulty of supervision; and (3) the aura of involuntary servitude associated with the compulsion of services. 11 S. WILLISTON, supra, note 14, at §1423. See, e.g., Tucker v. Warfield, 119 F.2d 12 (D.C. Cir. 1941) (contract to take care of plaintiff and provide her with all the necessities of life). Nevertheless, employment contracts are sometimes indirectly enforced through injunctions forbidding the defendant to perform similar work for anyone else. Lumley v. Wagner, 42 Eng. Rep. 687 (Ch. 1852). In one interesting case, the reason given for considering specific enforcement of an employment contract was that the interest of the employee—who was to be paid in stocks—was inextricably bound up with that of his employer. McCutcheon v. National Acceptance Corp., 143 Fla. 663, 197 So. 475 (1940). Cf. *In re* Staklinski & Pyramid Elec. Co., 6 N.Y.2d 159, 160 N.E.2d 78,188 N.Y.S.2d 541 (1959) (arbitration award granting specific enforcement of employment contract against employer upheld as not contrary to public policy). See generally E. FRY, supra, note 17, at §§110–15, 852–54; J. POMEROY, supra, note 17, at §24; RESTATEMENT, supra, note 19, at §379; 11 S. WILLISTON, supra, note 14, at §1423.

27. E.g., City Stores Co. v. Ammerman, 266 F. Supp. 766, 776–80 (D.D.C. 1967), *aff'd per curiam*, 394 F.2d 950 (D.C. Cir. 1968). Construction contracts have generally been thought to create special problems of judicial supervision. Nevertheless, construction contracts have been specifically enforced when the construction materials were of a special type and could be obtained only through the builder, Rector of St. David's v. Wood, 24 Ore. 396, 34 P. 18 (1893), or when it was held to be in the public interest to compel completion of the construction, Gas Securities Co. v. Antero & L.P. Reservoir Co., 259 F. 423 (8th Cir.), *cert, denied*, 250 U.S. 667 (1919) (a reservoir construction project secured through public bonds and partially completed at the time of breach). See generally J. POMEROY, supra, note 17, at §23; 11 S. WILLISTON, supra, note 14, at §1422A.

28. The uniqueness test is explicitly incorporated in the Uniform Commercial Code, §2–716(1). According to the Official Comment, this section introduces a "new concept of what are 'unique' goods." Under the rule stated in §2–716(1):

> Specific performance is no longer limited to goods that are already specific or ascertained at the time of contracting.... Output and requirements contracts involving a particular or peculiarly available source or market present today the typical commercial specific performance situation, as contrasted with contracts for the sale of heirlooms or priceless works of art that were usually involved in the older cases.

U.C.C. §2–716, Comment 2. If the Comment ended there, it could be concluded that the Code has merely adopted a well-established principle, and given it a broader and economically more sophisticated interpretation. But the Comment continues: "However, uniqueness is not the sole basis of the remedy under this section, for the relief [specific performance] may also be granted 'in other proper circumstances' and inability to cover is strong evidence of 'other proper circumstances.'" Id., This suggests that the draftsmen contemplated a second, independent basis for awarding specific performance in particular cases. It is unclear, however, what this independent basis might be. The problem of construing "other proper circumstances" may be avoided by reading it as nothing more than a restatement of the proposition that (according to the Comment) is implicit in the Code's notion of uniqueness—that uniqueness can only be determined by looking at "the total situation that characterizes the contract." Id. Read in this way, §2–716(1) states only one test, not two. Although this reading treats "other proper circumstances" as nothing but a clarification of the uniqueness test, it is fairly consistent with the developing caselaw. See Laclede Gas Co. v. Amoco Oil Co., 522 F.2d 33, 40 (8th Cir. 1975); Kaiser Trading Co. v. Associated Metals & Minerals Corp., 321 F. Supp. 923, 932–33 (N.D. Cal. 1970).

29. 5 A. CORBIN, supra, note 14, at §1142.

30. Id.

31. Id., (emphasis added).

32. See, e.g., Camphell Soup Co. v. Wentz, 172 F.2d 80 (3d Cir. 1948) (seeds for special variety of carrots had been supplied by buyer); Huddleston v. Williams, 267 Ala. 447, 103 So. 2d 809 (1958) (papers necessary for poodle registration); Elliott v. Hones, 11 Del. Ch. 343, 101 A. 872 (1917) (horse had particular qualities giving it promise of development into a valuable race horse); Thompson v. Commonwealth, 197 Va. 208, 89 S.E.2d 64 (1955) (contract to build and deliver legislative electronic voting machines not readily available on the open market).

Under the Uniform Commercial Code, "the test of uniqueness ... must be made in terms of the total situation that characterizes the contract." U.C.C. §2–716, Comment 2. Thus, in De Moss v. Conart Motor Sales, Inc., 34 Ohio Op. 535, 72 N. E.2d 158 (Ct. C.P. 1947), *aff'd on other grounds,* 149 Ohio St. 299, 78 N.E.2d 675 (1948), the court granted specific performance for the sale of a car because a manufacturing shortage had caused extensive delays. Specific performance was also held appropriate where the plaintiff sought to purchase a fiberglass boat manufactured only by the defendant, Gay v. Seafarer Fiberglass Yachts, Inc., 14 U.C.C. Rep. 1335 (N.Y. Sup. Ct. 1974); where the parties to the contract had stipulated that the cotton in question was unique, R.L. Kimsey Cotton Co., Inc., v. Ferguson, 233 Ga. 962, 214 S.E.2d 360 (1975); where the competitor's toner and developer for a copying machine were "distinctly inferior," Copylease Corp. v. Memorex Corp., 408 F. Supp. 758 (S.D.N.Y. 1976); and where it was unlikely that the plaintiff could locate a "substantially identical piece of used equipment [transformer] ... in order to perform its contract with [a] third party," Ace Equipment Co., Inc. v. Aqua Chem., Inc., 73 Pa. D. & C. 300, 302 (Ct. C.P. 1975). However, a substantial change in the price of substitutes is not itself ground for awarding specific performance. Duval Co. v. Malcolm, 233 Ga. 784,214 S.E.2d 356 (1975); Hilmor Sales Co. v. Helen Neuschaefer Div. of Supronico, Inc., 6 U.C.C. Rep. 325 (N.Y. Sup. Ct. 1969).

33. See, e.g., 11 OXFORD ENGLISH DICTIONARY 235 (1961) (defining "unique" as "unequalled").

34. G. STIGLER, THE THEORY OF PRICE 25–26 (3d ed. 1966).

35. Id., at 31–33.

36. This proposition has most often been explained and defended in utilitarian terms. See, e.g., J. HICKS, VALUE AND CAPITAL 42–52 (2d ed. 1946); P. SAMUELSON, FOUNDATIONS OF ECONOMIC ANALYSIS 90–117 (1947). Recently, however, one economist has attempted to demonstrate that the law of the negatively sloped demand curve (on which the notion of universal substitutability depends)

may be "derived fundamentally from scarcity alone rather than from an assumption [of the sort made in all utility theories] that behavior is 'rational,'" G. BECKER, ECONOMIC THEORY 11 (1971). See id., at 11–23. See also Becker, *Irrational Behavior and Economic Theory,* 70 J. POL. ECON. 1 (1962).

37. Cf. Lowther v. Lord Lowther, 33 Eng. Rep. 230 (1806) (terms of sale of a painting by Titian held proper issue for equity).

38. The aim of compensation is to put the injured party in the position he would have been in if the invasion of his legally protected interest had not occurred. So stated, the principle of compensation determines the damages for a tortious injury as well as for breach of a contractual obligation. The principle of compensation may be stated in economic terms: "Something compensates X for Y's act if receiving it leaves X on at least as high an indifference curve as he would have been on, without it, had Y not so acted." R. NOZICK, supra, note 1, at 57.

39. Of course, not every imaginable loss is compensable by a payment of money. How can the loss of one's spouse or child be compensated in this way?

40. Specific performance is typically not granted when the seller is no longer in possession of the promised property. Denton v. Stewart, 29 Eng. Rep. 1156 (Ch. 1786) (house had been sold to a third party for valuable consideration). "Even though the impossibility of performing his contract is due to the defendant's own fault, equity will not decree that he shall do what is clearly beyond his power." 11 S. WILLISTON, supra, note 14, at §1422. But when possible, courts will sometimes grant partial specific performance coupled with an abatement in the price. See Skelly Oil Co. v. Ashmore, 365 S. W.2d 582 (Mo. 1963). If the seller has resold the property, a court will occasionally cancel the second sale in order to grant specific performance to the first purchaser. In Groves v. Prickett, 420 F.2d 1119 (9th Cir. 1970), the court, in order to enforce plaintiff shareholders' right of first refusal, cancelled a sale of stock to non-shareholders. See also Abdallah v. Abdallah, 359 F.2d 170, 173 (3d Cir. 1966).

41. If there are several substitutes, the court must also identify the least costly one, for the party in breach should not be required to pay more than the smallest amount necessary to fully compensate the disappointed promisee.

42. If A is a professional dealer, interested in reselling the manuscript, it is perhaps reasonable to treat his loss as equal to the difference between the contract price and the price at which he could have sold it to someone else at the time of *B*'s breach (or the time of performance). Even in this case, however, money damages may be undercompensatory. This would be so, for example, if *A* did not anticipate an immediate resale but planned, instead, to hold the manuscript as an investment property.

43. Suppose that *A* promises to pay $10 for the manuscript, but would only be willing to sell it, if he already owned it, for $15. Suppose, in addition, that *B* receives an offer to sell the manuscript to *C* for $18, and that *C* values it at $20. To fully compensate *A*, *B* should be required to pay him $5. But it may be very difficult to estimate the value *A* places on the manuscript. It will be tempting to give *A* the difference between the contract price and the resale price, $8, but this will be overcompensatory. On the other hand, if *C* offers to pay $12 for the manuscript (still valuing the manuscript at $20), the same measure of damages will be undercompensatory for *A*. *A* will receive just $2 in damages, will be unable to persuade *B* to sell the manuscript for $15 or less, since *C* will bid the price up, and will be unable to convince *C*—if *C* has obtained possession of the manuscript—to sell it for a similar amount. In neither case will *A* get the manuscript.

Of course, if the manuscript has already been sold to a third party, a new set of considerations (involving the protection of good faith purchasers) must be taken into account. See text and notes at notes 77–96, infra.

44. See Dr. Miles Medical Co. v. John D. Park & Sons Co., 220 U.S. 373, 412 (1911) (Holmes, J., dissenting).

45. See generally G. STIGLER, supra, note 34, at 85–89. In a perfectly competitive market, the goods offered by different sellers are assumed to be homogeneous. Even where two or more goods are not homogeneous, however, there will be many circumstances in which they may usefully be characterized as belonging to the same market or, if the term "market" is reserved for the limiting case of perfect competition, as members of a "product group." See C. FERGUSON & J. GOULD, MICROECONOMIC THEORY 315 (1975). In defining different product groups, one important factor is likely to be the volume and refinement of our information about the cross-elasticity of demand for particular goods.

46. Calabresi and Melamed make this point in the context of criminal sanctions. See Calabresi & Melamed, supra, note 1, at 1125.

47. G. STIGLER, THE ORGANIZATION OF INDUSTRY 171–90 (1968).

48. See Chicago Coliseum Club v. Dempsey, 265 Ill. App. 542, 553 (1932); 5 A. CORBIN, supra, note 14, at §§992, 1034.

49. For example, *A* may need to locate another seller. If he already knows several sellers of ball bearings, *A* may have to acquire only a small amount of new information before arranging a substitute transaction (looking up the telephone number of one of *B*'s competitors, confirming price and delivery terms, and so forth). Before contracting with *B*, however, *A* is likely to have obtained a great deal of general information about the properties and relative advantages of different sorts of ball bearings, and this information will continue to be of use after *B*'s breach.

50. If the information represents a capital stock of this sort, its value must be amortized over a number of individual transactions.

51. As part of a money damages award, a court could include compensation for the estimated cost of finding a substitute even where the subject matter of the particular contract is unique. But when the promised performance is unique, the cost of locating a substitute will be difficult to estimate, and the likelihood is rather high that any court-determined award will be undercompensatory. Of course a court could simply give the promisee carte blanche to locate a satisfactory substitute on his own and then recover his search costs from the promisor. This is an untenable alternative, however, for it would encourage an overinvestment in searching and invite fraud by the promisee. See also note 41, supra.

52. See generally R. POSNER, supra, note 16, at 69.

53. This is a counterfactual assumption. See text and notes at notes 62–69, infra.

54. The provision should be thought of as an option because a promisee who is entitled to specific performance may always forego this right and pursue a money damages remedy instead.

55. Although the payment will probably assume the form of a straightforward reduction in the contract price, it may be made in other ways as well (for example, by the inclusion of warranty or delivery terms more favorable to the promisee).

56. See text and notes at notes 41–51 supra.

57. Of course, the inclusion of a specific performance provision will not make a voluntary transfer of the promisee's contract rights inevitable. The promisor can always breach without having first negotiated his release. On the whole, however, it is more likely that the promisor will attempt to buy his way out of the contract before breaching under a specific performance rule than under a money damages rule. See text and notes at notes 1–9 supra.

    One complication not discussed in this article concerns post-breach negotiations. Under either a money damages rule or a specific performance rule, negotiations of this sort are likely to occur if both parties think it in their best interest to avoid litigation. However, the parties may be more likely to conduct post-breach negotiations (rather than litigate or do nothing) under one rule than under the other. This will depend upon the predicted costs of negotiating a settlement and the anticipated benefits of litigation in each case. These problems are sufficiently complicated to warrant separate treatment, but I do not believe they affect the basic soundness of my argument.

58. The amount of the release payment will also be greater than the benefits the promisee expects from performance. There will, of course, always be a ceiling on what the promisor will agree to pay the promisee. This ceiling will be determined by two things: the penalty the promisor will incur if he breaches without having purchased a release from the promisee, and the amount he stands to lose if he performs the contract. The promisor will never pay the promisee more than the lesser of these two amounts for a release.

    The amount that the promisor *actually* pays the promisee will fall somewhere between the maximum payment he is prepared to make, and the minimum payment the promisee is prepared to accept (assuming, of course, that the former exceeds the latter—if it does not, there can be no negotiated release). This price will be determined primarily by the bargaining skills and relative informational advantages of the parties.

59. This conclusion does not ineluctably follow from the definition of uniqueness. There may be great demand for a good in short supply. For example, there may be several collectors willing to pay more than the contract price for a manuscript of Hobbes's *Leviathan*. In the case of currently produceable goods, however, widespread demand for a good should lead to increased production of the good. So in the typical commercial context, the assertion seems plausible.

60. See text and notes at notes 52–59, supra.

61. Posner & Rosenfield, *Impossibility and Related Doctrines in Contract Law: An Economic Analysis.*,

6 J. Leg. Stud. 83, 89 (1977); R. Posner, Economic Analysis of Law §4.1 (2d ed. 1977).

62. Clearly a promisee of a contract that would be specifically enforceable can agree to give up his right to compel performance.

63. 262 Ala. 59, 77 So. 2d 331 (1955).

64. Id., at 61, 77 So. 2d at 334.

65. Id., at 64, 77 So. 2d at 335.

66. Id.

67. See generally McNeil, *Power of Contract and Agreed Remedies,* 47 Cornell L.Q. 495, 520–23 (1962). Professor McNeil collects the principal cases in notes 88–92 of his article. See also Denkin v. Sterner, 10 Pa. D. & C. 2d 203 (Ct. C.P. 1956) (refusing to enforce a contractual provision purporting to give the seller of refrigeration equipment the right on buyer's default to confess judgment against the buyer for the full amount of the unpaid contract price).

68. See Peters, *Remedies for Breach of Contracts Relating to the Sale of Goods Under the Uniform Commercial Code: A Roadmap for Article Two,* 73 Yale L. J. 199, 252 (1963).

69. This is more frequently expressed by saying that specific performance is a discretionary remedy, and that "the right to specific performance is not absolute, like the right to recover the legal judgment." Pomeroy, supra, note 17, at §35. See also id., at §46. It is well established that "[n]either party to a contract can insist, as a matter of right, upon a decree for its specific performance." Snell v. Mitchell, 65 Me. 48, 50 (1876). Only if a promise would be specifically enforced in the absence of a contractual provision purporting to give the promisee the power to enjoin its performance, will a court compel the promisor to do what he initially agreed to do and not permit him to substitute money damages: "If one who contracts to render personal service agrees that in case of breach the remedies of specific performance and imprisonment shall be available to the employer, the agreement would not be effective." 5 A. Corbin, supra, note 14, at §1432.

70. See Epstein, *Unconscionability: A Critical Reappraisal,* 18 J. Law & Econ. 293 (1976).

71. See Calabresi & Melamed, supra, note 1, at 1111–15.

72. See 11 S. Williston, supra, note 14, at §1423.

73. See, e.g., Philadelphia Ball Club v. LaJoie, 202 Pa. 210, 51 A. 973 (1902).

74. See, e.g., Marble Co. v. Ripley, 77 U.S. 339, 358–59 (1870); Northern Delaware Indus. Dev. Corp. v. E.W. Bliss Co., 245 A.2d 431 (Del. Ch.

1968); Edelen v. Samuels, 126 Ky. 295, 306–07, 103 S.W. 360, 363 (1907). *Northern Delaware,* which denied specific performance of a "massive, complex, and unfinished construction contract," has been vigorously criticized. Comment, *Specific Performance of Construction Contracts—Archaic Principles Preclude Necessary Reform,* 47 Notre Dame Law. 1025, 1029–33 (1972).

In recent years, courts have exhibited greater willingness to grant specific performance in situations in which the remedy has traditionally been disfavored on the grounds that it is either too intrusive or too difficult to administer. See *In re* Grayson-Robinson Stores, Inc. & Iris Constr. Corp., 8 N.Y.2d 133, 168 N.E.2d 377, 202 N.Y.S.2d 303 (1960) (enforcement of an arbitration award ordering specific performance of a contract to construct a portion of a shopping center); *In re* Staklinski & Pyramid Elec. Co., 6 N.Y.2d 159, 160 N.E.2d 78, 188 N.Y.S.2d 541 (1959) (enforcement of arbitration award ordering employer to reinstate a discharged employee).

75. The enforcement of penal provisions has been carefully discussed, from an economic point of view, in a recent, and excellent, article. See Goetz & Scott, *Liquidated Damages, Penalties, and the Just Compensation Principle: Some Notes on an Enforcement Model and a Theory of Efficient Breach,* 77 Colum. L. Rev. 554 (1977). Goetz and Scott argue that the "penalty rule" (the rule that a liquidated damages provision will not be enforced if it is penal in nature) is economically unsound since "its uncritical application frequently induces a costly reexamination of the [parties'] initial allocation of risks and may also deny the non-breaching party either adequate compensation for the harm caused by the breach or the opportunity to insure optimally against such harm." Id., at 556. They suggest that "the modern development of unconscionability" offers "a less costly alternative to the sweeping invalidation powers exercised under the penalty rule." Id., at 594.

In their attack on the penalty rule, Goetz and Scott emphasize the importance of what they call "noncompensable idiosyncratic value." I have described the same phenomenon in this article as the "risk of undercompensation." See text and notes at notes 41–46, supra. The analysis of penalty clauses Goetz and Scott advance in their article complements, in many ways, my treatment of specific performance, and I find myself in general agreement with both their theoretical conclusions and proposals for change.

76. Hostility to the use of penal clauses might be based in part upon the conviction that breaking a promise and committing a crime are qualitatively different wrongs and that the legal system ought to prevent private individuals from obliterating the line between them. This conviction is more puzzling than it first appears. Crimes and breaches of contract are both invasions of legally protected interests. In both cases the taker typically knows in advance whose right he is invading and has the time to negotiate a voluntary transfer of that right. Given this important similarity, one might conclude that the right to the performance of a promise and the right to be free from criminal attack should be protected in the same manner.

I have argued that a mix of property and liability rules appears to be the best way of protecting contract rights. See text and notes at notes 37–59, supra. The criminal law could adopt a similar mix: crimes involving the appropriation of a unique good (for example, rape or murder) would be punished by imprisonment or fine while crimes involving the taking of a non-unique good (for example purse-snatching) would give rise only to a claim for compensation. Of course, the criminal law does not employ this approach—nearly all rights to be free from crime are protected by a property rule.

Focusing on the similarity between breaking a promise and committing a crime conceals differences of a more important kind, differences that explain why property rules are used more sparingly in contract law than in criminal law. To explore these differences fully is beyond the scope of this article, but a few suggestive comments can be made. The widespread use of property rules in the criminal law might be explained on the ground that criminal takings not only harm the victim, but inspire fear in the community. Cf. Michelman, *Property, Utility and Fairness: Comments on the Ethical Foundations of "Just Compensation" Law,* 80 HARV. L. REV. 1165, 1214 (1967) (discusses "demoralization" resulting from injury inflicted by "deliberate social action"). To some extent, however, general confidence among promisees is undermined whenever a contract is broken. See Llewellyn, *What Price Contract?—An Essay in Perspective,* 40 YALE L.J. 704, 725 n.47 (1931). Of course the costs to the community of a crime may be much greater than the costs of a breach of contract because a crime is usually thought to be a more alarming invasion of rights than breach of a contractual obligation.

Many crimes exhibit three features that help explain this perception. First, a criminal may well avoid detection, but a promisor will rarely be able to conceal his breach from the promisee. For this reason, the punishment for a crime must be increased to reflect the risk of nonapprehension, but damages for breach of contract need not be likewise inflated. See generally Becker, *Crime and Punishment: An Economic Approach,* 76 J. POL. ECON. 169 (1968). Moreover, even if apprehended, a criminal may have disposed of the property acquired in the crime and is likely to be insolvent, Calabresi & Melamed, supra, note 1, at 1125, n. 69; thus compensation from the criminal is often impossible.

In the second place, breach of contract rarely entails a risk of physical violence; a criminal taking often does. Most people are likely to view their own life and physical well-being as paradigmatic examples of unique goods. Potential victims of crime are thus justifiably concerned that they may suffer a noncompensable loss.

Third, the relation between promisor and promisee is almost always voluntarily established. In contrast, most crimes can be committed by strangers. A taking that occurs in the context of a voluntarily created relationship often seems less offensive than one that does not. Perhaps this is because we believe an individual has greater control over the risks to which he is exposed in the former situation than he does in the latter; perhaps because a taking by a stranger is thought to involve some additional harm to the special set of interests defined by the elusive concept of privacy.

These three features distinguish most serious criminal takings from breaches of contracts. They also help explain and justify the widespread use of property rules in the criminal law. But the dramatic differences between crime and breach of contract do not suggest that contract rights should not be protected by property rules, and so they do not justify judicial reluctance to enforce private contractual attempts to create property rule protection.

77. Although they do not make this point explicitly, it is, I believe, implied by their discussion of criminal sanctions. See Calabresi & Melamed, supra, note 1, at 1124–27.

78. The penal nature of the sanction backing up an injunctive order is clearest where noncompliance constitutes a criminal contempt.

[I]f the defendant does that which he has been commanded not to do, the disobedience is a thing accomplished. Imprisonment cannot undo or remedy what has been done nor afford any compensation for the pecuniary injury caused by the disobedience. If the sentence is limited to imprisonment for a definite period, the defendant is furnished no key, and he cannot shorten the term by promising not to repeat the offense. Such imprisonment operates, not as a remedy coercive in its nature, but solely as punishment for the completed act of disobedience.

Gompers v. Bucks Stove & Range Co., 221 U.S. 418, 442–43 (1911).

But even if the contempt is civil in nature, and the sanction imposed by the court designed merely to coerce compliance with its order, the severity of the sanction (its "cost" to the defendant) is determined not by what will compensate the injured party but by what is required to compel the defendant's obedience. See United States v. United Mine Workers, 330 U.S. 258, 304 (1947); Sunbeam Corp. v. Golden Rule Appliance Co., 252 F.2d 467, 469 (1958); Pekelis, *Legal Techniques and Political Ideologies: A Comparative Study*, 41 MICH. L. REV. 665, 673–74 (1943).

79. See note 20, supra.
80. E.g., Harris v. Nelson, 331 Ill. 225, 229–30, 162 N. E. 833, 835 (1928). See also Cushing v. Levi, 117 Cal. App. 94, 3 P.2d 958 (1951) (original purchaser granted money damages when the property was sold to a good faith purchaser, the vendor's wife having refused, in bad faith, to join in the conveyance to the original vendee); Holden v. Efficient Craftsman Corp., 234 N.Y. 437, 138 N.E. 85 (1923).
81. "The general principle, upon which this doctrine proceeds, is that, from the time of the contract for the sale of land, the vendor, as to the land, becomes a trustee for the vendee, and the vendee, as to the purchase money, a trustee for the vendor, who has a lien upon the land therefor." J. STORY, 1 EQUITY JURISPRUDENCE §789 (12th ed. 1877). See Krabbenhaft v. Gossau, 337 Ill. 396, 411, 169 N. E. 258, 264 (1929); Forthman v. Deters, 206 Ill. 159, 173, 69 N.E. 97, 102 (1903); Timko v. Useful Homes Corp., 114 N.J. Eq. 433, 168 A. 824 (1933); Barrett v. McAllister, 33 W. Va. 738, 759, 11 S.E. 220, 228 (1890). See also POMEROY, supra, note 17, at §465.
82. E.g., Groves v. Prickett, 420 F.2d 1119,1122–25 (9th Cir. 1970) (right of first refusal in sale of stock); cf. Abdallah v. Abdallah, 359 F.2d 170, 174 (3d Cir. 1966) (option to purchase land).
83. See Milkman v. Ordway, 106 Mass. 232, 253 (1870).
84. If damages were measured in this way, the results of a money damages rule and a constructive trust approach would coincide in practice, though not in theory.
85. Cushing v. Levi, 117 Cal. App. 94, 3 P.2d 958 (1933), is illustrative. In *Cushing*, the plaintiff agreed to pay $80,000 for some real property. The property was subsequently sold to a good faith purchaser for $112,500. At trial, the market value of the property at the time of breach was determined to be $90,000, and the plaintiff was awarded $11,000 in damages—despite the uncontroverted evidence of a higher resale price. This result was affirmed on appeal.
86. 90 Ariz. 356, 367 P.2d 960 (1962).
87. Id., at 359, 367 P.2d at 962.
88. Id., at 360–61, 367 P.2d at 963.
89. See note 12, supra.
90. The award, under a constructive trust approach, is measured by the promisor's benefit rather than the promisee's loss. Of course, these two amounts may coincide.

[In some cases, however,] a benefit has been received by the defendant but the plaintiff has not suffered a corresponding loss, or, in some cases, any loss, but nevertheless the enrichment of the defendant would be unjust. In such cases, the defendant may be under a duty to give to the plaintiff the amount by which he has been enriched. Thus where a person with knowledge of the facts wrongfully disposes of the property of another and makes a profit thereby, he is accountable for the profit and not merely for the value of the property of the other with which he wrongfully dealt.

RESTATEMENT OF RESTITUTION §1, Comment e (1937). See also id., at §§160, 202.

91. See generally 5 A. CORBIN, supra, note 14, at §§601, 602. A thief does have the power to invest his purchaser with good title to certain types of property and thereby insulate the latter from attack by the original owner. Money, instruments in bearer form, and, in certain situations, goods entrusted to the thief are three notable examples. See U.C.C. §§3–202, 3–302, 2–403. For a general discussion of the good faith purchase idea in different branches of commercial law, see Gilmore, *The Commercial Doctrine of Good Faith Purchase*, 63 YALE L.J. 1057 (1954).

92. Farnsworth, *Legal Remedies for Breach of Contract*, 70 Colum. L. Rev. 1145, 1151 (1970); Treitel, *Remedies for Breach of Contract*, in VII International Encyclopedia of Comparative Law (ch. 16) 2 (1976).

93. See cases cited at note 82, supra.

94. This is perfectly compatible with the use of a constructive trust. In order to give the promisee an incentive to notify prospective purchasers of the promised property, it is not necessary to limit his claim against the promisor to money damages. So long as the promisee cannot recover the property from a good faith purchaser, he will still have an incentive to put third parties on notice. This incentive will be large if the promisee's remedy against the promisor is worthless, as when the latter is insolvent or unavailable.

95. A full treatment of the economics of good-faith purchase is beyond the scope of this article. An analysis of this sort would have to consider three things: (1) the cost to the initial claimant of preventing the illicit appropriation of his entitlement (for example, by monitoring the behavior of the would-be taker or taking precautionary steps to secure his property); (2) the cost to the initial claimant of publicizing his entitlement; and (3) the cost to the second purchaser of verifying his transferor's right to dispose of the property in question. These are obvious considerations, and have no doubt shaped the development of good-faith purchase provisions in many areas of the law (for example, in the law of negotiable instruments). See U.C.C. §§3–301—3–305.

96. Calabresi and Melamed point out that property and liability rules may be employed in varying combinations to protect the entitlements of parties with conflicting interests. Calabresi & Melamed, supra, note 1, at 1122 n.62. They also recognize that different institutions (for example, the courts or political bodies) may be used to achieve the desired combination of rules in any particular case. Id. What they overlook is the complexity and variety of the legal techniques that have been developed, in different settings, to force the voluntary market transfer of entitlements. The most striking evidence of this is their failure to discriminate between injunctive relief and criminal sanctions. Compare id. at 1116 (injunctions) with id. at 1126 (criminal sanctions).

72   The Divergence of Contract and Promise

SEANA VALENTINE SHIFFRIN

In U.S. law, a contract is described as a legally enforceable promise. So to make a contract, one must make a promise. The legal norms regulating these promises diverge in substance from the moral norms that apply to them. This divergence raises questions about how the moral agent is to navigate both the legal and moral systems. This article provides a new framework to evaluate the divergence between legal norms and moral norms generally, and applies it to the case of contracts and promises. It introduces and defends an approach to the relationship between morality and law that adopts the perspective of moral agents subject to both sets of norms, and argues that the law should accommodate the needs of moral agency. Although the law should not aim to

I am grateful for help and critical comments from Iman Anabtawi, Sarah Coolidge, Richard Craswell, Meir Dan-Cohen, Ronald Dworkin, Melvin Eisenberg, Barbara Fried, James Gordley, Mark Greenberg, Tom Grey, Jeffrey Helmreich, Barbara Herman, Doug Kysar, Stephen Munzer, Liam Murphy, Thomas Nagel, Melanie Phillips, Todd Rakoff, Jennifer Roche, William Rubenstein, Steven Shiffrin, and audience members at the Analytical Legal Philosophy Conference, Boalt Hall, the Harvard Law School Faculty Colloquium, the NYU Law and Philosophy Colloquium, the September Group, and the Stanford Legal Studies Colloquium. This article began as the Kadish Lecture at Boalt Hall and I am especially grateful to Sandy Kadish for its instigation.

From "The Divergence of Contract and Promise," *Harvard Law Review* vol. 120 (2007), pp. 708–753. Reprinted with permission of the publisher.

enforce interpersonal morality as such, the law's content should be compatible with the conditions necessary for moral agency to flourish. Some aspects of contract not only fail to support the morally decent person, but also contribute to a legal and social culture that is difficult for the morally decent person to accept. Indeed, U.S. contract law may sometimes make it harder for the morally decent person to behave decently.

INTRODUCTION

In U.S. law, a contract is described as a legally enforceable promise. So to make a contract, one must make a promise. One is thereby simultaneously subject to two sets of norms—legal and moral. As I argue, the legal norms regulating these promises diverge in substance from the moral norms that apply to them. This divergence raises questions about how the moral agent is to navigate both the legal and moral systems. In this article I provide a new framework to evaluate the divergence between legal norms and moral norms generally and apply it to the case of contracts and promises.

By claiming that contract diverges from promise, I mean that although the legal doctrines of contract associate legal obligations with morally binding promises, the contents of the legal obligations and the legal significance of their breach do not correspond to the moral obligations and the moral significance of their breach.[1] For instance, the moral rules of promise typically require that one keep a unilateral promise, even if nothing is received in exchange. By contrast, contract law only regards as enforceable promises that are exchanged for something or on which the promisee has reasonably relied to her detriment. When breach occurs, the legal doctrine of mitigation, unlike morality, places the burden on the promisee to make positive efforts to find alternative providers instead of presumptively locating that burden fully on the breaching promisor. Morality classifies intentional promissory breach as a wrong that, in addition to requiring compensation, may merit punitive reactions, albeit sometimes minor ones; these may include proportionate expressions of reprobation, distrust, and self-inflicted reproofs,

such as guilt. Contract law's stance on the wrongfulness of promissory breach is equivocal at best, manifested most clearly by its general prohibition of punitive damages.

To analyze this substantive divergence between legal and moral norms, I introduce and defend an approach to the relationship between morality and law that adopts the perspective of moral agents subject to both sets of norms and argue that the law should accommodate the needs of moral agency. Although the law should not aim to enforce interpersonal morality as such, the law's content should be compatible with the conditions necessary for moral agency to flourish. Some aspects of U.S. contract law not only fail to support the morally decent person, but also contribute to a legal and social culture that is difficult for the morally decent person to accept. Indeed, U.S. contract law may sometimes make it harder for the morally decent person to behave decently.

For some, the divergence between contract and morality calls for a direct condemnation of contract law's content. If contract law's business is to enforce promises, its structure, as a whole, should reflect the moral structure of promises.[2] Others regard the divergence between contract norms and moral norms as not significant per se, whether because the law, especially private law, should not directly enforce morality as such, or because promise and contract occupy different realms with independent purposes: promise establishes rules for formalizing trust in interpersonal interactions; contract establishes rules that help to enable a flourishing system of economic cooperation for mutual advantage.[3]

My own view does not fit neatly into either of these camps, which I see as marking two poles of a broader, but artificial, dichotomy. This dichotomy seems to be the product of a set of familiar but overly general, overly blunt questions, such as whether law should reflect interpersonal morality and, in particular, whether contract should mirror the moral rules of promising. These questions frame the issues in ways that obscure an important position about the relation between legal and moral norms that maintains that the law should accommodate moral agency, but neither directly reflect nor entirely ignore interpersonal morality.

The law must be attentive to the full range of normative positions because law represents a special form of normative cooperative activity. Yet, because law is a cooperative activity of mutual governance that takes institutional form, its normative values and principles may well be distinct from, though informed by, those comprising interpersonal morality.[4]

This article approaches these topics by exploring the demands and tensions to which contract law, in particular, subjects moral agents. It starts from the more general premise that law must be made compatible with the conditions for moral agency to flourish—both because of the intrinsic importance of moral agency to the person and because a just political and legal culture depends upon a social culture in which moral agency thrives. The content and normative justifications of a legal practice—at least one that is pervasive and involves simultaneous participation in a moral relationship or practice—should be capable of being known and accepted by a self-consciously moral agent.[5] Legal rules must be constructed and justified in ways that take into account the fact that law embodies a system of rules and practices that moral agents inhabit, enforce, and are subject to alongside other aspects of their lives, especially their moral agency. Although I provide some motivation for these premises from a liberal perspective, for the most part I take them as starting points.

Part I expands briefly on these premises and on the distinctive liberal approach they offer to problems concerning the intersection of law and morality. The remainder of the article applies this approach to the specific problems raised by the divergence between contract and promise. The overarching aim is to explore how an accommodationist approach would frame some issues in contract and to identify some new questions it would raise. This article does not champion particular positions about the proper content of contract law, although toward the end it gestures at an alternative theoretical conception of contract informed by an accommodationist approach.

Part II argues that contract and promise do indeed diverge. Part III argues that the divergence is problematic. Although the divergence may not yield contradictory requirements, some prominent justifications for the divergent aspects of contract could not be known and accepted by moral agents. Further, the divergence raises the concern that the culture created by contract law and its justifications might make it more difficult to nurture and sustain moral agency, in particular the virtues associated with fidelity. Part IV rejects the suggestion that these difficulties could be bypassed, by disentangling promise and contract through an explicit reconception of contract law as a normative system utterly distinct from promises. Contract law must at least be constrained by some of the needs and rationales of the system of promising. Part V closes with preliminary thoughts about how contract theory could be continuous with (rather than merely cabined by) these constraints.

I. MAKING ROOM FOR MORAL AGENCY

Two standard strains of argument address the relationship between contract and promise. Reflective approaches take interpersonal morality as a template for legal rules, sometimes implicitly. Such approaches operate as though the law should reflect everyday moral judgments whenever possible, whether because this is the nature of law or because, as a matter of political philosophy, it is what law should aim to do. A reflective approach may be particularly tempting in contract law because contracts and promises are so closely intertwined.

By contrast, separatist approaches treat law and morality generally, or contract and promise in particular, as independent domains. Some separatists regard reflective approaches as illiberal. For normative, political reasons, they regard it as inappropriate for the law to incorporate or enforce the rules of interpersonal morality as such. Other separatists have different, positive reasons for treating the domains as distinct. They believe that law, or perhaps specifically contract, has its own goals and purposes, such as establishing the foundation for a maximally efficient system of exchange. Their pursuit does not require engagement with other moral concerns. So, it is not the business of contract law per se to reflect or respond to the norms of interpersonal morality. Separatists acknowledge that individuals may be subject to moral demands that regulate their behavior, but separatists nonetheless maintain that compliance with these demands is each individual's responsibility. Since contract law's purpose is not to enforce interpersonal morality or promises as such, there is no special worry associated with contract law's divergence from promise. Participants in contract, as in other legal domains, may have to constrain their pursuit of its goals to accommodate other personal and social values, but that represents a flaw neither in the separatist conception of contract nor in its divergence from promise.

Both approaches harbor some elements of truth and so neither seems correct. I subscribe to an intermediate position that advocates accommodating moral agency but not enforcing morality as such. I agree with separatists that there is no direct and reliable route from the content of interpersonal morality to the appropriate content of the corresponding area of law. Legal domains may pursue normative purposes and principles of their own that are not straightforwardly derived from interpersonal morality. Furthermore, the standard liberal concerns about direct enforcement of morality have some traction.

It does not follow, however, that legal principles in these domains should be entirely insensitive to or divorced from the demands of interpersonal morality. Such insensitivity is not dictated by a commitment to liberal principles. Liberalism does not require that the theory of justice and the law must be predicated on a model that works equally well for amoral and moral agents. Quite the contrary. John Rawls's theory, for example, explicitly and plausibly presupposes that agents have developed moral capacities that underlie their capacity for a sense of justice.[6] These moral capacities are not so fine-tuned that they consist of only those abilities necessary to understand and comply with the terms of justice narrowly understood. Rather, they depend on a broader, fuller moral personality.

Indeed, mastery and appreciation of promissory norms must figure among these requisite

moral capacities, however broadly or narrowly construed.[7] Absent a culture of general mastery and appreciation of promissory norms and the moral habits and sensitivities that accompany them, I doubt that a large-scale, just social system could thrive and that its legal system could elicit general patterns of voluntary obedience. Further, I doubt that, absent a strong promissory culture, the individual relationships that give rise to and sustain moral agency and relationships of equality could flourish. Whether or not all norms and virtues of moral agency must be accommodated by the legal system, those associated with promissory norms seem quite central to the possibility of a flourishing system of justice.[8]

When the directives of law and morality regulate the same phenomena, moral agents have to negotiate two distinct sets of norms. The rules of contract and promise present a salient instance of this navigation problem. Especially because there are moral duties to obey the law, legal rules should be sensitive to the demands placed on moral agents so that law-abiding moral agents do not, as a regular matter, face substantial burdens on the development and expression of moral agency.[9]

Respecting this constraint yields an intermediate stance between the position that law should promote moral behavior for its own sake and the position that interpersonal morality should be irrelevant to the form and justification of law. To wit, even if enforcing interpersonal morality is not the proper direct aim of law, the requirements of interpersonal morality may appropriately influence legal content and legal justifications to make adequate room for the development and expression of moral agency. The influence that is exerted, however, need not result in efforts to mirror interpersonal morality closely.

A. Liberalism and the Accommodation of Moral Agents

These reasons to reject separatist views do not commit us either to a version of reflectivism or to some other illiberal approach. We can be sensitive to the conditions for supporting moral agency and, for that reason, fashion law to be responsive to the content of interpersonal morality without running afoul of liberal strictures that counsel against enforcement of morality or that declare the priority of the right over the good.[10] Two main commitments underlie these strictures. First, the theory of justice must be articulated and defended without relying on any particular comprehensive theory of the good. Its contours are not subject to objection on the mere grounds that they fail to promote or reflect the commitments of any such theory. Second, agents have a primary commitment to abide by the requirements of justice, a commitment that overrides conflicts presented by agents' specific conceptions of the good.

These commitments do not preclude efforts to ensure law's compatibility with the conditions for moral agency. The idea that the right is prior to the good does not entail that the law's content should never be sensitive to the norms of interpersonal morality. The requirements of justice do not fully determine all aspects of law. Contract provides a salient example. The principles of right may require a system of distributive justice, which may in turn require a system of contract. Any adequate contract law may need to have certain features, but all of its particulars may not be fully determined by the principles of justice narrowly construed. For example, considerations of justice may not decisively settle whether to adopt the mailbox rule. Settling the specifics of contract law may depend, in part, on other features of the culture and the society, including components of interpersonal morality. For instance, *if* contract law's aim were to protect against harm suffered from breach of promise, measured in terms of reasonable reliance, what counts as a reasonable form of reliance might depend on the cultural context and the degree to which easy trust is encouraged; the degree to which trust is encouraged might, in turn, be a matter settled partly by the norms of morality and not merely by cultural customs.

To be sure, in many circumstances, liberal principles of justice may preclude the direct implementation of moral commitments for their own sake, or direct appeal to them as a rationale for legal decisions. Such principles prohibit both direct and indirect state pressure to engage in activities whose value depends on authentic and voluntary participation, such as which private relationships to pursue or which ideas to express. Think of the speech and religion protections. Further, to invoke a familiar Rawlsian theme, liberal principles prohibit state endorsement of positions or values, social disagreement about which creates the very need for a theory and system of justice, but reliance on which is not necessary for the system to fulfill its purposes.

Not all components of moral agency or principles of morality fall into these special categories. In particular, the rules of promissory commitment generally do not demand authentic endorsement or performance for their value, nor are they controversial in the ways that create the very need for a system of justice.[11]

I advocate an intermediate position—that law's contents must be structured to make room for moral agents. It calls for the accommodation of moral agents, although the envisioned accommodation differs from some other common forms and connotations of accommodation.[12] Often, "accommodation" refers to adjustments or exceptions to otherwise valid laws that are made for unusual agents or outliers. The sort of accommodation defended here, by contrast, is more foundational. It would inform the guidelines for the shape of the general law and would extend to all moral agents. It would not merely and weakly exempt some agents from legal requirements to permit them to engage in certain behaviors or ways of life. This version of accommodation contains the stronger, positive requirement that the legal system's rules and justifications should be acceptable to moral agents without disrupting their moral agency.

B. What Accommodating Moral Agency Requires

I have been arguing that the legal system should be fashioned, justified, and interpreted to accommodate the opportunity for the governed to lead a full and coherently structured moral life. What does this commitment entail in the case of contract? I start from the following premise: when a legal practice is pervasive and involves simultaneous participation in a moral relationship or practice, the content and normative justification for the legal practice must be acceptable to a reasonable moral agent with a coherent, stable, and unified personality. Law's justification should not depend upon its being opaque or obscure or upon the ignorance, amorality, or split personality of the citizens it governs.[13] From this basic premise follow three more specific principles that regulate the interrelation between moral norms and legal norms, at least in those pervasive, regular contexts that involve the simultaneous participation of moral agents in parallel legal and moral relationships or practices.

First, what legal rules directly require agents to do or to refrain from doing should not, as a general matter, be inconsistent with leading a life of at least minimal moral virtue. "Minimal moral virtue" should be understood in a way that does not presuppose any particular comprehensive conception of the good or ideal of virtue.

Second, the law and its rationale should be transparent and accessible to the moral agent. Moreover, their acceptance by the agent should be compatible with her developing and maintaining moral virtue. Although knowledge of the justifications of law is not required or expected of every citizen, understanding the law's rationale should not present a conflict for the interested citizen qua moral agent. This is not merely because the agent is subject to the law and that to which she is subject should be justifiable to her. Within a democratic society, the law should be understood as ours—as authored by us and as the expression of our joint social voice.

This second principle governs both the reasons that actually motivate government agents to impose and enforce divergent rules, as well as the strongest available justifications for the divergence. Examination of the latter reveals whether the divergence is intrinsically problematic. This task is the focus of this article. Nonetheless, it is possible for there to be an adequate theoretical justification for a divergent rule that is not actually the basis of a court's or a legislature's adoption of that rule. A court or legislature might be guided by poor reasons even when better reasons could be provided for the position. In such a case, we might say that the particular instance of

imposition was impermissible because its rationale was not acceptable to a moral agent, even if the rule itself is not intrinsically problematic.[14] In addition, adoption of an intrinsically permissible rule for an impermissible reason may be problematic because even the implicit endorsement of unacceptable reasons[15] may have a corrosive effect on the moral culture and thereby implicate the next principle.

Third, the culture and practices facilitated by law should be compatible with a culture that supports morally virtuous character. Even supposing that law is not responsible for and should not aim to enforce virtuous character and interpersonal moral norms, the legal system should not be incompatible with or present serious obstacles to leading a decent moral life. A principled requirement that the law facilitate a culture that is compatible with moral virtue need not go so far as to enforce moral virtue. In some circumstances, this goal may better be realized by doing quite the opposite. One may facilitate moral virtue by affording opportunities to be virtuous and by refraining from offering strong incentives or encouragements to misbehave; direct enforcement of virtue for its own sake, in some contexts, can be counterproductive—particularly when it is a necessary aspect of the virtuous conduct that it be voluntary and that it be evident to others that it is voluntarily performed.[16]

The remainder of my discussion investigates whether the divergence of contract from promise can satisfy these principles. The next two parts argue that although contract law does not violate the first principle by issuing directives that contradict moral requirements, it may violate the second and third principles. Defenses of the rules of contract law often invoke rationales the acceptance of which is incompatible with maintaining one's moral convictions. Further, the rules themselves may contribute to a culture that challenges moral agency.

II. THE DIVERGENCE OF PROMISE AND CONTRACT

I now turn to the particulars of the divergence between contract and promise. I focus specifically on the ways in which contract law expects less of the promisor and more of the promisee than morality does.[17] Chiefly, I examine the treatment of remedies in contract and promise, although I occasionally draw on other helpful examples.

In this part and the two parts following, the argument proceeds in three steps that correspond to the three principles for accommodating moral agency just articulated. First, contract and promise diverge in some significant ways, although not by directly generating inconsistent directives. Second, some of the standard arguments for the doctrines' divergence are exactly the sort of justifications that a virtuous agent could not accept. Third, even though some reasons for the divergence may be acceptable to a virtuous agent, the divergence itself may risk another difficulty by contributing to a culture that may be in tension with the conditions for the maintenance of moral character.

Before launching this argument, a few further assumptions about contract and promise should be made explicit. With respect to promising, I will assume, but not defend, that there are definite norms of promising that all moral agents are required to respect.[18] Generally, however, all that is required to raise the sorts of questions contemplated in this article is the weaker assumption that there are *some* definite promissory norms—whether or not they are exactly as I describe—that bind moral agents within an aspirationally democratic, large-scale society such as ours.[19]

Of course, the moral contours of the promissory terrain are not always evident on the ground. In addition, there is a range of commitments that agents may form—some of which are promises, some of which are not, some of which have many but not all of the features of promises, and some whose nature is unclear. There are live philosophical and linguistic puzzles about promising, as well as gray areas and cases along a spectrum, just as with many other moral activities. Often, subtle, contextual distinctions must be deployed within the practice and along its boundaries—to do such things as differentiate promises from mere declarations of intention in context, given that we do not always require invocation of the phrase "I promise" to make a promise. This article works with clear cases of promises and puts aside these genuine unclarities, however, because they do not bear on the issues with which the article is concerned. For the same reason, this article also brackets much of the complexity, nuance, and qualification within contract law in favor of a simpler, perhaps overly blunt, treatment of its central doctrines.

Finally, the main argument does not presuppose a particular theory about the purposes of contract law. Hence, it begins without a detailed account of contract law's purposes. Rather, it starts from contract law's explicit self-representation of its relationship to promising to explore how well this self-representation sits alongside the moral agent's commitments.

U.S. contract law represents that a contract is an enforceable promise. Contracts do not merely resemble promises in that both involve voluntary agreements, usually concerning future activity, and often use identical language. (Later, I return to the significance of the close resemblance itself.) In U.S. law, promises are embedded within contracts and form their basis. The *Restatement of Contracts* defines a contract as "a *promise* ... for the breach of which the law gives a remedy, or the performance of which the law in some way recognizes as a duty."[20] The *Restatement*'s definition of a promise is not technical. It invokes the familiar notion of the communication of an intention, the content and context of which justify the recipient in believing that a commitment has been made through its communication.[21] The language of *promises, promisees,* and *promisors* saturates contract law—in decisions, statutes, and the *Restatement*. It also permeates the academic literature through its common characterization of contracts as the law of enforceable promises, and by its formulation of the foundational questions of contract as which promises to enforce, why, and how.[22] Notably, in U.S. law, promises of the right sort may form the basis for a contract without an additional intention to enter into a legally binding arrangement.[23] Suppose we start by taking the law's self-description seriously and conceive of contracts as resting upon promises per se. As I argue below, a virtuous agent could not accept this self-description as accurate while also accepting the justification and structure of some of the divergence of contract from morality.

A. The Divergence between Promise and Contract

As I have already observed, U.S. contract law diverges from the morality of promises. Contract law would run parallel to morality if contract law rendered the same assessments of permissibility and impermissibility as the moral perspective, except that it would replace moral permissibility with legal permissibility[24] and it would use its distinctive tools and techniques to express and reflect those judgments. For example, typically a promisor is morally expected to keep her promise through performance.[25] Absent the consent of the promisee, the moral requirement would not be satisfied if the promisor merely supplied the financial equivalent of what was promised. Financial substitutes might be appropriate if, for good reason, what was promised became impossible or very difficult to perform. Otherwise, intentional, and often even negligent, failure to perform appropriately elicits moral disapprobation. If contract law ran parallel to morality, then contract law would—as the norms of promises do—require that promisors keep their promises as opposed merely to paying off their promisees. The only difference is that it would require this as a legal, and not merely a moral, matter.

1. Specific performance and damages

Contract law, however, diverges from morality in this respect. Contract law's dominant remedy is not specific performance but expectation damages. Usually, the financial value of the performance is demanded from the promisor, but actual performance is not required (even when it is possible), except in special circumstances.[26] Further, intentional promissory breach is not subject to punitive damages,[27] that is, to those legal damages that express the judgment that the behavior represents a wrong.[28] Notably, U.S. law typically makes damages for emotional distress and attorney's fees unavailable upon breach.[29]

There are two further examples of the divergence over the significance of performance. First, one cannot obtain an order of specific performance even when one successfully alleges anticipatory repudiation. Even prior to the directed time of performance, a court is unlikely to direct specifically that the promised performance should occur. On the contrary, moral observers would direct that the performance should occur as promised, unless the promisee waives. The difference between the moral and legal reaction to breach does not appear only after the specified time for performance elapses.

Second, under the *Hadley* rule,[30] promisors are liable only for those consequential damages that could reasonably have been foreseen at the time of the contract's formation.[31] From a moral perspective, this is quite strange. If one is bound to perform, but without excuse voluntarily elects to breach one's duty, a case could be made that the promisor should be liable for all consequential damages. If foreseeability should limit this liability at all, what would matter morally is what was foreseeable at the time of breach, rather than at the time of formation. Whereas the former reflects the idea that breach is a wrong for which the promisor must take responsibility, the latter fits better with the idea that the contract merely sets a price for potential promissory breach.

The law thereby fails to use its distinctive powers and modes of expression to mark the judgment that breach is impermissible as opposed to merely subject to a price. For this reason, I find unpersuasive the possible rejoinder that contract and promise deliver the same primary judgments—namely, that breach of promise is wrong—but that they diverge only with respect to legal and moral remedies. There are standard legal remedies (as well as legal terms) that signify that a wrong has been done. In other areas of private law, remedies such as punitive damages and specific performance are more commonly invoked.[32] Contract has a distinctive remedial regime that not only diverges from its moral counterpart, but also reflects an underlying view that promissory breach is not a wrong, or at least not a serious one.

2. Mitigation

The mitigation doctrine provides another example of divergence. Contract law requires the promisee to mitigate her damages. It fails to supply relief for those damages she could have avoided through self-help, including seeking another buyer or seller, advertising for a substitute, or finding a replacement. As a general rule, morality does not impose such requirements on disappointed promisees. True, morality does not look sympathetically upon promisees who stay idle while easily avoidable damages accumulate. But this is a far cry from what contract expects of the promisee and what it fails to demand of the breaching promisor. Following the norms of promising, promisors would not readily expect the promisee to accept a substitute for the promised performance, at least not without a strong excuse or justification for nonperformance. Were a substitute unavoidable or justified, promissory norms would ordinarily place the burden on the promisor, rather than the promisee, to locate and provide it. It may sometimes be permissible for the promisor to *ask* the promisee to shoulder this burden when the substitute is *much* easier for the promisee to obtain or when the promisor is ill-suited to select a replacement (as when the promisee's judgment is necessary for the replacement to serve the promisee adequately). Still, even in such cases, it would usually be unacceptable for the promisor to insist were the promisee to refuse.

The difficulties in measuring and fully compensating for the costs incurred in mitigation provide another rationale for the moral stance and the trouble some scholars have with respect to the current legal rule.[33] But concerns about whether compensation can be full and adequate do not exhaust the moral reasons for declining to impose a strong responsibility to mitigate on the promisee. It is morally distasteful to expect the promisee to do work that could be done by the promisor when the occasion for the work is the promisor's own wrongdoing. That expectation is especially distasteful when its rationale is that it makes the promisor's wrongdoing easier, simpler, more convenient, or less costly.

Might it be objected that the promisee, while within her rights to refuse, should not, morally, refuse a promisor's request that she mitigate? It might be thought to be stingy and overly punitive to refuse such a request.[34] If so, it might be maintained that the mitigation doctrine does in fact run parallel to morality.

Sometimes it can be morally wrong for the promisee to refuse to mitigate, especially when the costs of refusal are very steep and disproportionate to the seriousness of what is promised. But whether it is morally wrong for the promisee to refuse may depend on a number of factors to which the law is insensitive, including the closeness of the relationship, the history of the relationship, the reason for breach, the reason the promisor wants to shift the burden, and how cumbersome mitigation activities would be.

It might be suggested that the law's insensitivity to these factors is the byproduct of the need to formulate a clear rule. This is not an entirely satisfying diagnosis. The law is capable of fashioning clear, but more sensitive, rules in other equally complex contexts. Furthermore, it is unclear why, if a blunt rule is necessary, it should be fashioned to favor systematically the breaching promisor and not the promisee. Not only is the promisor the party responsible for the breach, but the wrong committed by the unreasonably reluctant mitigator-promisee is not the sort that is typically the appropriate object of legal enforcement. This wrong may fall within the category of wrongs the law should allow because interference in this particular domain might preclude recognizable realization of the virtuous thing to do—namely, to be gracious and forgiving in the face of another's wrong.[35]

3. Punitive and liquidated damages

Not only are punitive damages unavailable as a response to garden-variety, intentional breach, but willing parties are not permitted to elect them in advance through legally enforceable agreements.[36] It is a delicate question whether this bar exhibits true divergence. On the one hand, agents typically cannot specify the moral seriousness of their conduct and, in particular, their misconduct: the moral status of conduct that is truly misconduct is usually independent of agents' attitudes or will. This feature of morality might lend support to the view that the rule in contracts runs parallel to morality.

On the other hand, promises occupy an interesting part of moral territory because, through them, agents themselves can alter the moral valence of some future conduct. A promise may render an action mandatory and important, when it otherwise would have been optional and, perhaps, unimportant. This created status can then be undone yet again through the consent and waiver of the promisee. Further, although I have been speaking of promises in a rather univocal way, a number of different sorts of commitments are available to agents. Parties can have tacit understandings that have many of the features of formal, strict promises. Certain sorts of affirmations or agreements constitute commitments that can be promise-like without using the most formal terms of promising. Within our moral practices of promising, agents can signify an understanding that there is a commitment but that it is fairly loose and flexible; it is not illusory, but it is subject to change for lesser reasons than would normally be acceptable for standard promises. Consider the following commitment: "I promise to be there if I can, but life is complicated right now and I can't commit for sure." The issuer is surely bound to appear if her schedule is free and her car and legs function; she is bound to turn down new, unanticipated, and conflicting requests for commitment or attendance; but she is not duty-bound to attend if it turns out that working late is necessary to meet a preexisting deadline. We are also able to signal when such looseness and flexibility is out of order, such as when one makes a solemn commitment to be there *no matter what*. One might regard the ability to specify punitive damages as a very rough legal counterpart to the poorly defined mechanisms through which parties mark a particular promissory relation as especially serious or not. If so, then the law does show divergence by disallowing enforceable specifications of liquidated damages that exceed rough approximations of market value.[37] As I say, though, this would be a rather rough method of capturing this aspect of promising—both because it might better be captured through more clearly specified content within the contract, for example through conditions of performance, and because it marks a departure from the more general inability of moral agents to specify for themselves the significance of their own moral failures and the appropriate remedies.

B. An Objection to the Claim of Divergence

Given the plasticity of our promising practices, might the claims about divergence be challenged by arguing that contract law does not treat promises differently than does the moral system, but rather that it produces different promises with particular contents? One might attempt to recharacterize the divergent contract rules that I identify instead as rules that inform the content of what is promised between contractors. Justice Holmes famously declared that a contract to perform should be understood not as a promise to perform, full stop, but as a promise either to perform or to pay damages: "The duty to keep a contract at common law means a prediction that you must pay damages if you do not keep it—and nothing else."[38] Moreover, we might generally regard the promises that contractors enter into as implicitly incorporating the background contract law and, in turn, producing complementary terms. On this rendering, contract does not diverge from the rules of promising, but rather provides a complex background structure for certain promises, a structure that then infuses their content.[39]

This rejoinder is unpersuasive for several reasons. The first, which I mention only to put aside, is that it does not pertain to the claim that the doctrine of consideration diverges from morality. This strategy can only work, if it does at all, to recharacterize gap filling, the specific conceptions of the duties in a promise, and the responses to breaches of binding promises as specifications of the particular content of a binding promise. But it cannot address the divergence between the different *sorts* of promises that contracts and morality treat as binding, for instance their divergence over whether unilateral promises bind.

Even when the reconceptualization strategy is pertinent, it seems unpersuasive. If the promise to perform were plausibly interpreted as really a promise either to perform or to pay compensatory damages, it still would not eliminate the divergence over punitive damages. If the breaching party fails to perform *and* fails to pay damages voluntarily, there is a breach *even on the reinterpretation* of the meaning of the relevant promise.

The law will respond only by providing expectation damages. It will not respond to this recharacterized promise and its breach with measures reflecting disapprobation.[40]

Should we go further and reinterpret the content of the promise as a promise only to perform *or* to pay compensatory damages, whether voluntarily or through compulsion upon legal complaint? This further recharacterization provokes another worry, namely about the assumption that the contents of promises are indefinitely plastic and utterly up to their makers. I have my doubts about this assumption. It is out of bounds to say: "I solemnly promise to do *X*, but I may fail to do so if something better comes along; moreover, if it does, you can only expect *X*'s market value from me, although you may need to enlist the help of others to pry it out of my clenched fist. Further, let us now declare that should I fail, it will not be the sort of thing deserving of moral reprobation so long as eventually you are made whole monetarily. Moreover, it is not the sort of thing you may be upset with me over or view as showing my bad character." This is not a full-fledged promise. Its elaboratory remarks defy the language of its opening gambit. They clarify that it is not a promise at all, while attempting to elicit the interlocutor's acknowledgment of that fact. Rather, it seems to be the statement of an intention to act, along with an acknowledgment that the statement will, in this context, render the utterer susceptible to one sort of liability at the hands of another. But there is no commitment by the utterer to *do* anything at all. Although one can declare within a promise some of the conditions under which the promised performance may not occur, those conditions cannot coherently extend so far as to include any situation in which the promisor has a change of heart or entertains a better offer.

Further, I doubt that one may alter by declaration or by agreement the moral significance of a broken promise (even within its terms and even if the promise itself already has a weight of its own that is partly settled by the parties). A promise may make a nonobligatory action obligatory, but only because the object of the obligation is within the promisor's power in the first place (at least for standard sorts of promises). By contrast, the power to alter the significance and appropriateness of *others'* reactions to a broken obligation is not within the power of the promisor. It does not seem to be the sort of thing that could be altered by consent or made *part* of the content of the promise. In response to another's wrong, we have the elective power to forgive, but forgiveness involves, among other things, recognition of a past wrong, not a power to make it the case that the wrong was never a wrong. Because contract's divergences involve features that are not in the power of moral agents to elect, these divergences should not be understood as components of a framework that infuses the content of certain promises.

III. IS THE DIVERGENCE PROBLEMATIC?

Although many aspects of the promissory and contractual regimes diverge from one another, the two are not flatly inconsistent. Contract law does not require promisors to breach or to respond inappropriately to breach.[41] It will not place pressure on the promisor to behave morally, but neither will it directly proscribe moral behavior by promisors. Nonetheless, despite their prescriptive consistency, the justifications for the divergence may violate the tenet that the virtuous agent should be able to accept the justification for the divergence.

A. Efficient Breach

A common justification for the remedies scheme in contract is that of the so-called "efficient breach." The justification may be stated in two ways. The stronger version contends that, morally, we should facilitate efficient breach because it promotes overall economic welfare and therefore overall social welfare. Take, for example, Professor David Slawson's claim: "People ought not to be liable for punitive damages merely for breaching a contract. They have done nothing wrong if they pay full compensation. Indeed, society loses if people do not breach contracts that would cost them more to perform than to pay compensation for breaching."[42] The weaker version concedes that breach of promise may indeed be morally wrong but maintains that it also can promote greater net economic gain, at least between the parties; that is to say, the economic gains to the promisor from breach may exceed the economic losses to the promisee.[43] Because facilitating efficient economic transactions is the main point of contract law and because orders of specific performance and punitive damages would deter efficient breach, contract law disallows them.[44] On this characterization, contract law is thought to have distinctive purposes that punitive damages would obstruct. Although breach may be immoral, that fact falls outside the domain of concern of contracts per se.[45]

Although it is disputed whether orders of specific performance and punitive damages are in fact economically inefficient in the specified respect,[46] for the purposes of this article I will assume that the premise of efficient breach theory is correct. That is, I will assume that punitive damages and specific performance orders would deter some efficient breaches or would increase transaction costs in such a way that a contract law with punitive damages and more permissive specific performance rules would be less economically efficient in the specified sense than one without them.

Could the virtuous agent accept some version of efficient breach theory as a justification for these remedial rules? The stronger version of the theory would seem to be precluded by her moral commitments. A virtuous agent cannot believe both that a promise can be binding even if a better opportunity comes along that competes with fulfilling the promise *and* that breach of contract, involving breach of promise, is, all things considered, morally justified merely because it leads to (even only marginally) greater economic welfare.

The weaker version of the efficient breach theory does not, by contrast with the stronger version, hold that a party's breach of promise is morally justified, but rather that contract is indifferent to the moral status of the actions it recommends, promotes, or allows; it has distinct purposes that, on occasion, are furthered by breach of contract and so should be facilitated in those circumstances. Perhaps a moral agent

should not breach promises, but this is not the concern of contract law.

Could the virtuous agent accept this argument as a justification for contract law's divergence from promise? She might have difficulty. This line of argument does not merely reject moral norms as a source of guidance for law, but harbors a strong conception of the independence of the domains—namely that a legal domain may pursue purposes that are not constrained by moral norms. It is not clear that a moral agent can accept a rule the justification of which is based on the rule's promoting the full-blown pursuit of a putatively valuable end when this full-blown pursuit would conflict with the moral agent's fundamental moral commitments.

That is, under efficient breach theory, what propels the lack of punitive damages is an affirmative normative position: agents *should* breach when it would yield net economic gain. So punitive damages must be foregone in order to make breach, and thereby a more efficient system of exchange, more likely. A virtuous agent can surely accept that there may be good aspects to wrongful breach on certain occasions. Yet, if such breach is indeed, all things considered, wrong, a virtuous agent cannot accept the economic benefits of breach as constituting a sufficient, or even a partial, contributory justification for the law's content. The challenge would be all the greater if the primary, positive justification for the law's content were the desirability of *encouraging* (and not merely making more likely) the wrongful conduct per se. In that case, the law (or its justification) would be suggesting a prescriptive recommendation to act wrongfully. It is hard to see how a virtuous agent could embrace that recommendation, whether explicit or implicit.

To be clear, the argument currently on the surgical table is not that it is none of contract law's business whether breach is immoral, so that we must therefore reject punitive damages because the only possible argument for them would be breach's immorality. That sort of argument (to which I will return) does not contain any implicit recommendation to breach. It does not, on its face, suffer the difficulty of asking a moral agent to accept the idea that it would be a good thing if people broke their promises and that we should create incentives for them to do so. How could a moral agent think both that breach of promise is, all things considered, wrong, and also that it makes sense for us, as a community of moral agents, to create a system in which we attempt to encourage, however mildly, breach of promise (all the while holding out the possibility of deploying our moral condemnation of breach)?[47]

B. Distinctively Legal Normative Arguments

The root of the problem is that the efficient breach theory is driven by an underlying general *normative* position that directly conflicts with promissory norms, and not by a distinctively *legal* normative argument, by which I mean a moral argument whose range is specifically tailored to the special, normatively salient properties of law and its appropriate content and shape. An example of distinctively legal grounds of justification will illuminate the contrast between legal grounds and more general moral grounds. The reluctance to order specific performance could be justified on familiar, distinctively law-regarding grounds, such as the difficulty and expense of ordering and supervising performance by a reluctant party and, in some cases, the unseemly and disproportionately domineering nature of such state-enforced orders on individuals.[48] These are often persuasive grounds, though less so when performance merely involves the transfer or receipt of nonunique manufactured goods or the provision of services by representatives of a firm rather than by any particular individuals or employees. Whether or not these grounds are persuasive, they are distinctively legal. They do not question the general proposition that specific performance is the appropriate moral response to breach or anticipatory repudiation; rather, they resist the idea that specific performance should be implemented through legal means because of distinctive features associated with law and legal mechanisms.

Are there further distinctively legal grounds that would justify the divergences I identified earlier?

1. *Liquidated damages and punitive damage agreements*

One might support the rule against punitive damage agreements on the distinctively legal grounds that they circumvent the state's monopoly on punishment. The law asserts a monopoly on punishment to prevent vigilantism and to ensure that punishment is meted out fairly and manifests horizontal equity. Legally administered punishment is also supposed to express the voice of the community. Punitive damage agreements allow parties privately to determine appropriate levels of punishment and then to commandeer the legal system to administer the punishment; this may threaten the interest in horizontal equity and in the community's authority to determine appropriate, proportionate responses to wrongs. Perhaps, then, the ban on punitive damage agreements might be justified on the grounds that contract law should not provide the means for private parties to circumvent the limits on private self-help established by tort and criminal law.

By relying on distinctively legal reasons, this theory avoids being in direct tension with commitments presupposed by promissory norms. It may not be entirely successful, however, in providing a complete explanation for the ban on punitive damage agreements. Whether this argument succeeds depends on an issue I will identify here but not attempt to resolve; namely, whether the social interest is in a monopoly on punishment, narrowly understood, or in exclusively determining the wider range of all remedial reactions to legal wrongs and breaches. If the social interest is in preventing the circumvention of the monopoly on punishment, a more limited means than a complete ban on contractual punitive damages would suffice. For instance, one could forbid those agreements that specify alternative damages, whether stronger or weaker than what the law otherwise provides, for independently tortious or criminal activity, but still allow other sorts of punitive damage agreements concerning mere intentional breach. If the social interest is in exercising authoritative and exclusive judgment over the significance of and reactions to breaches of law, however, then the wider ban on all punitive damages agreements makes more sense.[49]

As for the argument about horizontal equity, it would seem strange sometimes to require punitive damages to be administered in horizontally equitable ways[50] but then to permit great variation by the election of the parties. This argument faces obstacles, however. First, concerns about horizontal equity may have less traction when the parties agree specifically to the penalty. Second, variable punitive damages may make more sense in contract because the seriousness of the promise can vary between parties; variable punitive damages may represent a rough means by which to mark this difference, although in ways that blur the line between the substance of the promise and the remedy for breach.[51] By contrast, one might think that the significance of torts and crimes are less subject to manipulation or alteration by the parties involved. This is not a straightforward matter by any means. Consent may transform some actions that would be torts or crimes into legal activities. Still, if nonconsensual activity that comprises a tort or crime occurs, the parties cannot transform the moral seriousness of such nonconsensual, wrongful activity by agreement (whether ex post or ex ante). Agreement can play some role in establishing how serious a promise is, but it cannot, as I argued earlier, alter whether breach is a wrong.

Finally, to succeed, this defense of the ban on punitive damage agreements would have to distinguish between liquidated damages and consideration. The ban on punitive damages, put roughly, disallows liquidated damages that exceed approximated expectation damages; the doctrines of adequacy of consideration and unconscionability are far more permissive about inequitable exchanges, however, and allow consideration that may patently exceed the value of what is received in return. This creates a difficulty for any defense of the ban on punitive damage agreements, because many punitive damage agreements can be recast as forms of consideration. Graduated payment schedules that appear in the body of a contract may present alternative courses of performance and thereby appear to be complex articulations of enforceable contractual duties, even though they achieve the same result as liquidated damage clauses that overreach and are invalidated as

penalties.[52] Some theory of what makes a voluntarily elected penalty a penalty would have to be provided to vindicate a defense of the ban. Perhaps that can be done.[53] If these challenges could indeed be met, the defense would be permissible from an accommodationist perspective because its appeal to distinctively legal normative considerations makes it perfectly compatible with acceptance by a morally virtuous agent.[54]

2. Gift promises and consideration

A different sort of distinctively legal argument appeals to the special hazards associated with legal rules. Professor Melvin Eisenberg and others make arguments of this sort about gift promises. Professor Eisenberg argues that legal enforceability of unilateral promises would cast doubt upon whether their performance was motivated by altruism and care, or by concern about legal liability.[55] This argument has the right structure because it specifically concerns the *legal* status of gift promises. Nonetheless, it seems only partly to justify the consideration rule.

First, many unilateral promises are not tendered as gifts, at least not in the sense presupposed by the argument. They are not always proferred as purely altruistic measures, designed in part to begin, reinforce, or symbolize a particular sort of intimate or special relationship. Second, the argument assumes that *performance* of the promise must be motivated by altruism and care in order for the value of the gift to be realized. Why doesn't the voluntary nature of the offer or promise of the gift sufficiently realize the purely voluntary component of gift promises? Why must its delivery also remain voluntary to achieve the values associated with gifts?

Professor Eisenberg's argument seems motivated, in part, by an effort to preserve the meaning of the gift for the recipient. But it is unclear that the existence of a legal enforcement mechanism would undo or cast significant doubt upon the motivations for compliance with gift promises between intimates. Often, in these circumstances, the motivations for compliance are fairly transparent, especially between parties who already share a special relationship. Further, the existence of legal remedies is unlikely to introduce muddiness.

Typical transaction costs and risks make it rather unlikely that promisees will sue for breach for most sorts of gift promises. This is known to both parties, rendering it implausible that the promisor's motivation for fulfilling the promise is fear of legal enforcement activities and implausible for the promisee to worry that this is the promisor's motivation. Even putting aside standard transaction costs, legal enforcement is still unlikely because its initiation by the promisee would often do further damage to the underlying relationship—damage that may be disproportionate to the contemplated breach. These hazards are also likely to be known by both parties, again often affecting what motivations are in play and what motivations are surmised.[56] Although Professor Eisenberg's defense provides another good example of a distinctively legal argument, I remain unconvinced of its details and application.

C. Is the Divergence Objectionable?

The presupposition that divergent contract rules are suspect and in need of distinctively legal justification might be challenged in two ways. First, one might claim that the line between moral reaction and legal reaction captures exactly the appropriate level of concern about breach of promise.[57] Promissory breach merits personal disapprobation but not necessarily the community's concern. Second, one might press the view that law and morality occupy separate spheres. Perhaps there is a presumption against the law issuing prescriptives that directly contradict moral requirements, but there is no further presumption that the law should exhibit parallelism with moral norms.

A direct, comprehensive answer to these objections might take another article. But a taste of that answer might be gleaned by asking a more internal question about the relationship between different doctrinal areas—namely, what explains why tort and criminal law levy penalties but contract law does not? It cannot be sufficient to argue that tort and criminal law offer penalties in response to legal wrongs, not moral wrongs, or at least not moral wrongs as such. This just raises the question why breach is not a legal wrong. That

question is essentially a variation on the initial question and does not move us further along.

One might claim that tort and criminal law concentrate on a special set of cases involving especially bad behavior, often involving the infliction of physical harm. Tort and criminal law address a distinct range of moral wrongs, deserving of greater punishment than the decentralized, unofficial moral system can safely deliver. It might further be argued that the prevention and condemnation of physical harms serve special moral ends: they are ends that form some of the impetus for a legal system and that must be served for the system to function; further, they are relatively uncontroversial ends endorsed by a wide range of moral views.

Let me take these points in turn. Tort and criminal law do not specialize in physical harms only—think of white-collar crimes, fraud, and defamation. Why are these wrongs palpably worse, necessarily, than intentional breach of trust? The answer is not obvious. Nor can it be plausibly maintained that physical security uniquely serves what is needed for social or legal functioning. Confidence that one can, by and large, trust others' word and their professed commitments is also essential to harmonized and civilized systems of social functioning. On the direct question of whether the mainstay of tort and criminal law—physical security—is more important morally than breach of trust, I do not know how to begin to evaluate the claim. Lapses in physical security can certainly cause more dramatic, immediate trauma; lapses in fidelity and confidence in others may cause more subtle forms of social and psychological corrosion.[58]

Maybe different legal reasons explain the distinctions. Perhaps threats to physical security are more tempting and so require greater deterrence, or perhaps self-enforcement is both more tempting and more dangerous if people orient themselves toward in-kind responses. Then the prospect of strong and decisive enforcement that includes state-administered punishment could be necessary to deter destructive retaliation for physical harms but not for promissory breach. With respect to the latter, unorganized social responses backstopped by a legal compensatory regime might be both safe and optimally deterrent.

This explanation differs from those just discussed because it does not point to a moral distinction between the wrongs but to a distinction between the habits and tendencies associated with responses to those wrongs, habits, and tendencies that themselves call for different sorts of legal responses. It therefore has a distinctively legal structure, but I doubt it will succeed on the merits. It depends not only on questionable empirical claims about moral practice, but also on how we conceive the point of contracts. On the empirical front, I worry that the culture of trust and promising is fragile in subtle ways that are difficult to track; it may require greater and more explicit forms of support, such as legal recognition, because threats to it are less salient than the threats to social order posed by acts of violence.[59] But I put this aside to pursue a different point about the significance of such empirical claims.

If the purpose of contract were purely to facilitate economic exchange, say by analogy to electronic banking, or to serve that and other goals such as deterring dangerous private vigilantism, the argument just rehearsed would have some force if empirically true. But if contract has a more robust normative function, the issue is harder. That is, if contract serves a positive normative purpose and not merely an instrumental and deterrent backstopping role, then empirical facts about the minimal remedies necessary to achieve instrumental and deterrent purposes would not be sufficient to establish that minimal remedies are appropriate. The moral purposes served by contract might require remedies that reflect the wrong of breach, independent of whether such remedies serve deterrent purposes or do so in a maximally efficient way.[60]

I will return to the sort of moral conception I have in mind in part V. Before doing so, I want to address a final concern about the divergence between promise and contract to which I have adverted but have not explained. It provides an independent reason to investigate the justifications and effects of divergence.

IV. CULTURE AND THE MAINTENANCE OF MORAL CHARACTER

Thus far, I have claimed that there may be problems for a system of contract that invokes and is activated by promises as such, but whose rules diverge significantly from those of promise for reasons that are not distinctively legal. I have been focusing on how moral agents should regard a justification for a legal rule that celebrates the breach of a moral commitment, even though the rule merely permits it. I stand by the idea that the justification for a legal rule should be acceptable to the moral agent without compromising her virtue, but it may seem strange to place so much weight upon the content of a justification that may in fact be known to few.

Putting aside the merits of a transparency requirement, the rule and its justification may play a role in creating a wider culture in which pressure develops not to comply with the moral commitment, whether just because it is not legally required or because the legal permission spawns cultural habits that render moral compliance precious or alien. This possibility raises a further worry about a legal regime that introduces divergent norms that apply to agents simultaneously alongside moral norms—namely, whether moral individuals can participate in both cultures without running the risk that their participation will corrode the habits and expectations associated with moral practice.[61]

I will begin with an example to help elucidate what I have in mind, although I do not think it is wise to hang too much on any particular case. I do not know whether disapproval often follows a corporate officer's conscientious objection to taking advantage of an efficient breach. But I have witnessed several conversations in which one party regarded another with incredulity for thinking that she was morally bound not to break her lease against her landlord's will for convenience, suggesting that it made her a "chump," a moral fetishist for feeling bound given that the landlord could readily (though unwillingly) find a substitute renter.[62] Related exchanges occur with respect to contractors. A promisee fumes that the contractor did not come on time or, more realistically, did not come at all, despite repeated, firm promises. Her interlocutor regards her outrage as strange, observing that no more should have been expected; contractors regularly fail to show up on time when something better comes along, so it isn't a big deal—"it's business."

To be clear, I am not advancing the empirical assertion that a weakening of promissory honor is or will be the effect of the divergence of contract and promise, if only because of the almost comic difficulties in adducing persuasive evidence and examples. You may respond to my case by saying: "What do you mean? Breaking the lease is perfectly reasonable. In fact, it's what the landlord should expect." I respond: "Aha! That only shows how deep the corrosion goes. You've been infected too!" You demur and so on.[63]

To avoid such exchanges, it may be more fruitful to retreat to a more abstract level, to ponder how human moral agents nurture and maintain their habits and dispositions of moral agency. The basic concern begins with a background supposition about good behavior and forms of habituation in thought, emotion, and behavior. Namely, a great deal of morally virtuous behavior depends upon cultivating sound instincts and habits and allowing these to guide one's behavior. Morally good agents do not and cannot consciously redeliberate about all the relevant considerations bearing on a decision on every occasion. For everyday matters, agents must often depend on past deliberations that have become encoded into their general cognitive, emotional, and behavioral reactions to moral choices. Much of this deliberation and encoding is supported directly by social institutions and influenced more indirectly by the behaviors they encourage and render salient or standard.[64] This may be especially true when the law plays (or is meant to play) a leadership role in shaping social practice. If this abbreviated account is plausible, then we should be concerned about law's assigning significantly different normative valences and expectations to practices that bear strong similarity to moral practices, especially if we expect both practices to occur frequently and often alongside each other.

That is, we should be concerned that the one will influence the other, making it more difficult to maintain those habits and reactions that are essential to the moral behavior. To expect otherwise, one would need to rely heavily on a clear delineation of the different behaviors and their proper contexts, as well as on our abilities to compartmentalize tightly.[65]

Suppose the law of legally binding agreements, through its structure or justifications, encouraged individuals to associate the conditions of binding agreements with quid-pro-quo exchange or to engage freely in promissory breach when breach yields only marginal economic net gains. The worry would be that these associations and behaviors would influence how the moral agent approached promises—that the divergent treatment of agreements in contract would exert a subtle influence over time on how seriously the moral agent regarded unilateral promises and how casually she regarded promissory breach. This problem may be particularly acute for those who regard the moral practice of promising as resting on a social convention, since the boundaries of that convention are not sharply defined and could well be influenced or partly constituted by the social conventions within law.[66]

Contract and promise have features that strongly trigger this general concern. Contractual agreements are entered into frequently and are a part of daily life. They bear a strong resemblance (if, ex hypothesi, not identity) to promises. Even if contracts are not defined in terms of promises, both contracts and promises involve voluntary agreements, can be written or oral, and may range over the same subject matter. Further, their boundaries are not especially clear, rendering it tempting to move back and forth from one set of norms to the other.

Of course, we could identify the onset of contractual relations in a clearer way to put parties on greater notice that these agreements are subject to special rules and may be treated differently than promises. Suppose that could be done and it would be worth the associated education and transaction costs to make people aware of the distinction and special rules associated with contracts. Even so, I am not sure such clarity would eliminate the difficulty, in part because, even if the distinction is underlined, the same agreement may be both promise and contract. Defining a contract as distinct from a promise does not make the contract cease to be a promise as well. Further, once the distinction is transparent, parties may explicitly ask each other for both contractual and promissory assurances. If the very same agreement is subject to both contractual and promissory norms and these norms diverge, then the difficulties re-emerge. Additionally, the norms themselves, or their justifications, may point in different directions. This may either place the agent directly in a state of conflict, or more weakly, in a position in which it is tempting to treat and regard the two as alike. If contract is more forgiving of transgressions, as I have suggested, this may exert a subtle influence to treat promises less seriously.

These factors give us some reason to be cautious about endorsing the suggestion that the problems discussed in the prior part could be avoided merely by explicitly construing contract and promise as separate domains and by recasting contracts as entities distinct from promises. They may also give us reason to be cautious about even those divergences that can be grounded in distinctive legal normative justifications.

A. Poker and Corporate Etiquette

Of course, there are many occasions on which it is permissible to act in ways that in other contexts would be wrong. In a poker game, for instance, it is permissible to try to mislead the other players about the content of one's cards for personal gain. Not only is misleading behavior in this context permissible and consistent with the general prohibition on deception, but we do not much worry that our behavior in poker games will corrode the relevant aspects of our moral character—our resolve not to lie and to take truth-telling and candor seriously. Games provide many examples in which sharp dealing and an effort to obstruct others or to cause them to suffer loss is encouraged, whereas such conduct would be morally disallowed in other contexts. Or, to consider another context to which Professor Meir Dan-Cohen has called our attention, we do not expect sincerity

from the clerk of a large corporation who thanks us for our business.[67] Why, then, shouldn't we regard the norms of contract as analogous to the norms of games or the norms in business contexts similar to Dan-Cohen's example? In these contexts, different norms of conduct govern and are not perceived to constitute a threat to our moral agency.

Games like poker and the special behaviors permitted and encouraged within them are relatively unusual activities that are fairly rigidly defined and separated from the normal course of events in life and in relationships. One may mislead only about a narrow range of topics. Within poker, these topics are limited to what cards one has and one's confidence in one's hand. Available moves in the game are not defined in terms of moral activities outside of the game. The boundaries are rigid enough that it would be inappropriate, to say the least, to ask one's fellow player, "Yes, but what cards do you really have?" Further, the game of poker and other game-like activities often require particular behaviors to achieve their aims. Trying to cause another to lose (by winning) is necessary for the aims of competition to be realized. This also explains, in part, why different standards of candor are applied to lawyers and those giving testimony in adversarial settings.[68]

By contrast, contracts pervade our lives. We cannot easily opt out of them or treat them as merely an occasional leisure activity. No clear boundaries delineate the realm of activities in which contracts and contractual norms may be encountered from the realm of activities in which promises and compliance with promissory norms is expected. The lack of clarity would persist even if promise and contract were explicitly declared to be separate domains. Unlike in poker and in Professor Dan-Cohen's case of the clerk, it is not inappropriate or a clunky category mistake in the case of a contractual commitment to ask for further reassurance—to ask "Do you really mean it? … You're really *promising*?" Contract is not taken to be a category of behavior incompatible with promising. It is hard to see how it could be, given the prevalence of and pervasive need for contractual and promissory commitments. Finally, it is not clear, especially in light of contract law's explicit invocation of the language of promising, that the aims of contract do intrinsically rely on relaxing or abandoning moral behavior. Indeed, that is partly what is at stake in this article.[69]

The contrast between poker and contractual promises is not stark, but rather falls on a continuum. For instance, we may have reason to be wary of the professional poker player, for whom the game is not occasional but a way of life, unless she is awfully attentive to her character and to maintaining the boundaries between the game and her other relationships. Many lawyers lose their moral bearings. But professionals are not the only ones at risk. Professor Tom Grey reported to me that a group of couples he knew used to get together in the 1970s for evenings of Diplomacy, an especially long and intense war game. By contrast with poker, it involves the forging of alliances followed by their ultimate rupture. "[C]alculated lying and backstabbing" are "crucial parts of the game play."[70] After a period of time, the group had to stop meeting because the breaches of trust involved in the game were threatening their interpersonal relationships of trust outside the game.

Nor is it clear that we should be altogether casual or sanguine about the situation of Professor Dan-Cohen's clerk. It helps tremendously when the clerk truthfully represents the position or sentiments of management or the company as a whole, the represented party is sincere, and it is understood that the clerk represents another party.[71] This already distinguishes the case from the divergence between contract and promise. In the latter, the typically disallowed behavior is not directly in the service of representing someone who is acting in a standardly moral way.

It is more disturbing if the clerk lies on behalf of management. Professor Dan-Cohen objects that someone in the corporate office may have decided that thanking customers was politic but that no person at the corporation may have any real feelings of gratitude, so that the clerk is not representing anyone's gratitude at all.[72] However, although the corporation itself may not have a mental state of gratitude or any individual employee who cares, corporations do have practices, commitments, principles, and cultures. There is a

difference between a corporation that behaves in an appreciative, respectful manner toward its customers and one that treats them purely as means. Representing the former as grateful can be appropriate, even if the particular agents who design and recite the script are not themselves grateful, whereas representing the latter as grateful is deceptive. In the latter case, the fact that the clerk plays a defined role does not exempt him from fault, though the clerk may bear less fault than the script's authors higher up in management.

In both cases, it helps that the clerk's role has defined boundaries—that the clerk says these sorts of things only while at work, while being paid to represent another. The clerk's personal insincerity may be partly distinguished from the case of contract and promise. But, given the dominance of work in our lives and its spillover effects on other facets of our lives and personalities, it may be regrettable that we ask workers to display personal insincerity routinely and that we have come to expect to treat and to be treated by others with personal insincerity. These expectations are exactly the sort of phenomena that may provoke concern about moral drift in the culture.[73]

B. Individual versus Corporate Agents

It may be objected that I am writing as though contracting usually takes place between individual persons—especially individuals who have preexisting bonds or who are even emotionally vulnerable to one another. But many contracts are formed between businesses or other sorts of organizations. Do I really mean to suggest that the failures of businesses to adhere to promissory norms when transacting with each other have special moral significance per se, and further, that these failures may inflict damage on the external promissory culture?

My answer is, yes—at least sometimes. To some extent, I share the intuition that promissory breach between businesses is of significantly less moment, although I worry that in part my intuition is the product of an overly blunt anticorporatism. It may represent a general stance that sweeps too broadly to include small businesses as well as megacorporations and uses an indiscriminate brush not well tailored to the underlying concerns about inequality and homogeneity. There may, however, be something worthy at its root, namely a reaction to the fact that a person intrinsically matters in a way that an economic construct, even one affecting and composed of people, does not. The insult of promissory breach against a business may not sting as harshly as when it is suffered by a person. Some of my reaction also reflects attention to a different frame of reference than the one I have been discussing. That is, the more permissive intuition with respect to breach between organizations may not be a response to the general rule or practice but rather may encapsulate more particularized ethical assessments of singular cases of business-to-business breach within closely competitive contexts. It may be understandable for a party to breach when its competitors have no compunctions against doing so when it is to their advantage, when refraining from doing so would place it at a severe competitive disadvantage, and when it would be very difficult to alter the terms of interaction on a reciprocal basis through unilateral action. Even if these intuitions are appropriate to singular instances given the rules that govern the context, the overall structure of these contexts themselves may be challenged as I have been suggesting.

Further useful distinctions can be drawn between individual and organizational promisors and promisees, and in particular between contracts involving individuals and those involving only experienced organizational actors.[74] It may also matter whether the contractors have repeated interactions, whether they are members of the same linguistic or geographical community, and whether the contractual formation involves communication between people or merely filling out forms on the Internet. The distinctions between different types of contractual agents and different types of contractual content may bear mightily on the relevant analysis and the overall conclusions we reach. We should therefore be wary of overly general diagnoses and conclusions.

Nonetheless, contract norms that authorize or encourage intentional breach of promise for gain among organizational actors should still

give us some pause. True, an organizational actor as such cannot have disappointed feelings or expectations, at least if expectations are taken to be mental states. But for reasons I explore elsewhere,[75] I am disinclined to think that the presence of such mental states is at all essential to the binding nature of a promise (although the consequences, including the parties' potential disappointment, may sometimes bear on a promise's strength and seriousness). Furthermore, although the organizations that make commitments are not persons, persons compose them. Within business transactions, individuals often make and receive promises. An individual representing the seller company may aver to another individual representing the buyer: "Bob, I promise you, a thousand cases will be delivered tomorrow." Individuals make decisions whether to honor or breach these promises. The promises are not thereby made personal, but the involvement of individuals in the acts of commitment, receipt, and intentional breach matters. Individuals solicit one another's trust in the process of forging promissory relations between their organizations.[76] Even if these promises are not addressed to individuals as such and the individuals delivering them are not the formal promisors,[77] there is something troubling about a legal system that encourages persons, whether representing themselves or others, to fail to take these solicitations seriously and to take different attitudes depending upon whether they represent themselves, others, or other entities.

Consider assertion, by analogy. Although promising differs from assertion in some respects,[78] they bear a close relationship to one another.[79] At least with respect to moderately serious matters,[80] one's moral obligations not to lie or mislead do not change when one represents or addresses a business or another sort of enterprise. (Perhaps the duty of forthcomingness and the degree of wrongfulness vary, but the fact that one is speaking to the representative of an organization in itself does not alter in fundamental ways the obligation to speak truthfully.) Why should the moral norms of promising be different? Both involve the solicitation of trust. True, in a large organizational structure, the party that initiates or authorizes the breach may be a different person from the one who makes the promise, whereas the liar is often the same person who makes the representation that attempts to draw upon another's trust. But this may not matter since the party who breaches is bound, via the relation of representation, by the invitation made by the promise giver.

Of course, one can respond that the offeror should not regard her solicitation on behalf of an organization as her own, and that the recipient of this promise should not invest her trust in the offeror as she might were the promise offered to her qua individual, in a more personal context. Perhaps. However, I do not fully grasp what motivates the "should" other than perhaps a counsel of prudence. If this prescription would not be justified as an organizing principle with respect to the sincerity of assertions, even if a more relaxed attitude toward assertion would lead to financial gain, why would it be justified with respect to promising? In any case, it is unclear whether this should be a telling point for those of us who do not believe that the moral force of a promise (or the duties following assertion) depends on whether the promisee relies or expects performance to occur.[81]

More troubling is the implicit suggestion that legal norms should encourage and expect recipients to respond this charily to one another's entreaties. This, of course, returns us to territory we have already visited, involving the degree of alienation the legal system should expect and encourage from its citizens in their everyday activities, including those involving work and economic exchange. A system that leans heavily on such alienation and compartmentalization is dispiriting to defend, to put it mildly.

V. TOWARD AN ALTERNATIVE CONCEPTION

My primary aim has been to develop and advance an accommodationist approach that renders the norms of interpersonal morality relevant to the shape of law, but in a distinctive way that draws on the perspective of moral agents as subjects of law. My secondary aim has been to deploy this approach to sound some alarms about the divergence of promise and contract, particularly with respect to contract's remedial doctrines. What I have argued so far may be summarized as follows: Moral agency must be accommodated either out of respect for agents' basic, reasonable interests in leading moral lives, or because a robust culture of promissory commitment is necessary for a flourishing political society. In either case, we have a political interest in ensuring that we, as a community, do not invoke and recognize promises within our political institutions while treating them in ways inconsistent with their value, through the stance we take toward them in our rationales for various rules. To be sure, our purpose in invoking promises may not be directly to support or encourage the culture of promising as such. Indeed, we may invoke promises, in part, because such invocation is convenient. The concept of a promise operates as shorthand that is readily accessible and familiar to most citizens, even those who are not legal initiates. The use of a moral concept as shorthand is one way to make legal outcomes more accessible and to facilitate transparency. Still, if we invoke promises, directly or indirectly, we have a duty, taking something of the form of a side constraint, not to act or reason in ways that are in tension with the maintenance of a moral culture of promising.

Along the way, I have also made gestures in the direction of a more positive theory of contract that would treat the conditions of moral agency and the culture of promising in a more complementary way—a conception of contract that would incorporate sensitivity to the moral culture of promising, rather than merely regarding these concerns as a constraint on the pursuit of our other purposes, such as collective wealth enhancement. I will end with tentative remarks about a distinctively legal normative conception of contract that would sit more comfortably with our moral agency.

Promises and fidelity to them do not, of course, require law in the way systems of real property require law, or at least socially recognized boundaries.[82] So what is the purpose of a legal regime dedicated to the enforcement of some subset of promises? Suppose one did not start from a purely instrumental point of view. Would generally morally compliant and highly proficient agents who are not shy about making and keeping promises have reasons to establish a system of contract?

I believe they would. In related work, I have defended the claim that in addition to the work they may do in facilitating cooperation or the pursuit of parties' ends or projects, promises play a significant moral function in interpersonal relationships.[83] Promises and their availability provide a concrete (and I believe indispensable) way for parties to reaffirm their equal moral status and respect for each other under conditions in which possibly divergent present or future interests create vulnerability. The promissory commitment represents an effort to disable and manage some of the hazardous mechanisms and effects of power, hierarchy, and vulnerability. These reasons may be extended to illuminate the function of promises between nonintimates as well. For the purposes of this article, I assume these claims are true.[84]

One might then understand contract as the public complement to the private promissory relationship. In creating a contract, the parties render public their efforts to manage morally their disparate interests, as well as the associated latent or emergent vulnerabilities this disparity may create or feed. Creation of a contract invites this relationship to be witnessed, recognized, and scrutinized by the public.[85] The purpose of rendering the relationship public might vary according to circumstance and content. In some cases, contracts provide assurance—going public is meant to assuage concerns that one or more parties have about the security of the arrangement. Motivations like these are familiar in both business contexts and familial contexts, including the public promises involved in marriage. But the emphasis on contract as primarily a mode of assurance, a response to the worry that things may go wrong, is exaggerated.[86] Contract law may play an important function even outside nonideal moral circumstances. Parties may well seek to create contracts for reasons that are not predominantly grounded in fear, lingering distrust of their promissory partners, or even more innocuous concerns about inadvertent breach.

For other parties, by contrast, going public may be a demonstration of feelings of strong security in the relationship and in the reliability of the commitment; one or both parties may be so confident of the commitment that they are happy to render it public and regard their willingness to do so as a symbol of their good intentions. Again, motivations like these are familiar in both business contexts and familial contexts, including the public promises involved in marriage. In other cases, contract serves a positive gap-filling function; parties may come to the essence of an agreement but rely on public rules designed to provide reasonable accommodations of the parties' interests and any relevant public interest to resolve open questions.[87] In still other cases, given what is at issue in the agreement—for example, the use of important resources—going public may be mandatory because public oversight of such resources is necessary to protect broader interests.[88]

Except in cases of the latter type, why should the public attend to these commitments and expend effort to enforce them, as well as establish norms that fill in the gaps that promissory parties fail to anticipate or resolve? A partial answer refers to reasons quite familiar from our discourse about contract. First, although promises solve and manage certain dynamics of vulnerability, they also generate new vulnerabilities. The public has an interest in protecting parties from the consequences and harm caused by breaches that result from these vulnerabilities. Second, and more broadly, the reinforcement of equal status facilitated by promises takes on a political value when made public. In addition to the political interest in a culture of taking commitment seriously, there are reasons to affirm and support such public declarations of equal status and such good faith efforts to manage diversity and vulnerability morally. That such a system also tends to create efficient systems of economic exchange is an important side benefit that may affect many of our decisions about how to structure the institution, but only in ways complementary to our other moral purposes.

This quick articulation is admittedly vague, but it provides a flavor of a set of rationales that could supply normative, moral reasons for an institution of contract without relying upon any direct aim to enforce interpersonal morality or to encourage virtuous behavior. Contract, on this view, is not an effort to get people to act virtuously, to prompt people to keep their promises for the right reasons, to ensure that private relationships go as well as possible, or to get people to make promises when morally appropriate to do so. It is not an effort to legalize as much as possible the interpersonal moral regime of promising, but rather to provide support for the political and public values associated with promising.

Understood in this way, a variety of the divergent aspects of contract law make sense, especially those associated with evidentiary concerns. Requirements of writing—for example, the parol evidence rule or the statute of frauds—may be understood more generally in terms of the conditions of making something verifiable to outside assessors and the public. The unconscionability and public policy doctrines manifest the limits on what commitments the public can support, given the underlying purpose of supporting equality as well as our other social aims.[89] The doctrines of mistake and impracticability presuppose notions of reasonable risk that represent our sense of which endeavors and which assumptions of risk are worth our affirmation and efforts. These characterizations refer back to public, legally normative values, but they are not in implicit or explicit tension with the view that the underlying moral promises are binding.

Although this normative conception of the purposes of contract law can readily support some divergences between promise and contract, it *may* be inconsistent with some others discussed in the body of this article,[90] such as the general unavailability of punitive damages in contract. At the least, some standard arguments for these doctrines are in tension with the maintenance of the conditions of moral agency. Given the overriding nature of our moral commitments, as well as the dependence of a well-functioning democracy on a flourishing moral culture, there may be reason to reexamine these doctrines and their justifications, and to strive for greater convergence between promise and contract.

Many legal theorists have been particularly troubled by the idea of separating criminal law, tort, or constitutional law from moral concerns. Some have been more sanguine about conceiving of contract law as an amoral domain driven by aims entirely insensitive or indifferent to the concerns of interpersonal morality.[91] I suspect that quite the opposite is true. Contract law cannot properly be regarded as an amoral domain in the least. From an accommodationist perspective, the nesting of promise into the self-conception of contract, the ubiquity of promises and contracts, and the elemental role of commitment in social life require a legal approach to contract that is deliberately sensitive to the demands of interpersonal morality.

NOTES

1. Although this article discusses those aspects of contract that diverge from promissory norms, other parts of contract law depend fairly explicitly upon a variety of moral judgments and concepts, not to mention the concept of a promise itself. For instance, the past consideration doctrine contains an exception for cases in which there is an independent moral obligation to do what one has promised. See E. ALLAN FARNSWORTH, CONTRACTS §§2.7–2.8, at 56–63 (4th ed. 2004). Some cases and doctrines involve appeal to moral concepts of fairness or reasonableness. Not all of these cases and doctrines can be recast more narrowly as judgments about what *justice* requires. Aspects of the immorality doctrine, for instance, may not be reducible to efforts to enforce the spirit or the letter of other aspects of public policy. This partial convergence between morality and contract would call for justification if one took the position that contract and promise are entirely separate domains.

2. See, e.g., Peter Linzer, *On the Amorality of Contract Remedies—Efficacy, Equity, and the Second Restatement*, 81 COLUM. L. REV. 111 (1981); Frank Menetrez, *Consequentialism, Promissory Obligation, and the Theory of Efficient Breach*, 47 UCLA L. REV. 859, 879–80 (2000). Professor Charles Fried seems to take this position in *Contract As Promise*. See CHARLES FRIED, CONTRACT AS PROMISE 1–3, 17–21 (1981); see also id., at 17 ("The moralist of duty thus posits a general obligation to keep promises, of which the obligation of contract will be only a special case—that special

case in which certain promises have attained legal as well as moral force."). At points, though, Professor Fried's position is more qualified and ambiguous. It may well be compatible with the ideas I develop below.

Professor Fried's substantive criticisms of contract's moral content, however, are limited to the consideration doctrine. Interestingly, Professor Fried does not discuss punitive damages. He endorses the mitigation doctrine, characterizing it as an altruistic duty toward the promisor that is without cost to the promisee. See id., at 131. Oddly, given his methodology, he does not consider whether the norms of promising in fact include this duty. See LOUIS KAPLOW & STEVEN SHAVELL, FAIRNESS VERSUS WELFARE 161 n.18 (2002) (mentioning Professor Fried's puzzling endorsement of expectation damages rather than specific performance); DORI KIMEL, FROM PROMISE TO CONTRACT 110–11 (2003) (discussing Professor Fried's treatment of mitigation).

3. See FRIED, supra, note 2, at 2–3 (citing PATRICK ATIYAH, THE RISE AND FALL OF FREEDOM OF CONTRACT (1979); LAWRENCE FRIEDMAN, CONTRACT LAW IN AMERICA (1965); GRANT GILMORE, THE DEATH OF CONTRACT (1974); MORTON J. HORWITZ, THE TRANSFORMATION OF AMERICAN LAW, 1780–1860, at 160–210 (1977); Duncan Kennedy, *Form and Substance in Private Law Adjudication*, 89 HARV. L. REV. 1685 (1976); Duncan Kennedy, *The Structure of Blackstone's Commentaries*, 28 BUFF. L. REV. 205, 356 (1979); Anthony T. Kronman, *Contract Law and Distributive Justice*, 89 YALE L.J. 472 (1980); Ian R. Macneil, *The Many Futures of Contracts*, 47 S. CAL. L. REV. 691 (1974)); see also KAPLOW & SHAVELL, supra, note 2, at 162–65, 182–85, 190–97 (arguing that promise-keeping notions conflict with a welfare-maximizing view of contract and advocating the latter); Richard Craswell, *Contract Law, Default Rules, and the Philosophy of Promising*, 88 MICH. L. REV. 489 (1989) [hereinafter Craswell, *Contract Law*] (arguing that theories of promise have little relevance for the "background rules" of contract); Richard Craswell, *Two Economic Theories of Enforcing Promises, in* THE THEORY OF CONTRACT LAW 19 (Peter Benson ed., 2001) [hereinafter Craswell, *Two Economic Theories*]; Anne de Moor, *Are Contracts Promises?, in* OXFORD ESSAYS IN JURISPRUDENCE 103 (John Eekelaar & John Bell eds., 3d series 1987) (casting doubt on the equation of contract with promise).

4. See Barbara Herman, *Reasoning to Obligation*, 49 INQUIRY 44, 60 (2006) (observing that coercion may be morally permissible and even required within a legal institutional context even though it would not be justified in interpersonal contexts); Seana Valentine Shiffrin, *Speech, Death, and Double Effect*, 78 N.Y.U. L. REV. 1135, 1181–84 (2003) (discussing the general point in the context of the First Amendment and rules that govern intentions).

5. In a prior work, I used the perspective of our collective role as moral agents engaged in enforcement to justify the unconscionability doctrine. See Seana Valentine Shiffrin, *Paternalism, Unconscionability Doctrine, and Accommodation*, 29 PHIL. & PUB. AFF. 205 (2000). Such arguments might extend to some applications of the immorality doctrine as well. In this article, I consider our role as subjects of contractual rules, albeit subjects who have a role in the authorship of the rules to which we are subject.

6. See JOHN RAWLS, A THEORY OF JUSTICE 395–587 (1971).

7. See Seana Valentine Shiffrin, Promising, Intimate Relationships, and Conventionalism 42–52 (Dec. 1, 2006) (unpublished manuscript, on file with the Harvard Law School Library) (arguing that promisors must have the ability to bind themselves with a promise "if they are to have the ability to conduct relationships of adequate moral character"); see also H.L.A. HART, THE CONCEPT OF LAW 197 (2d ed. 1994) (recognizing the social necessity of rules respecting promises); RAWLS , supra, note 6, at 346–48 (noting the obligation, derived from the "principle of fairness," to comply with promises). This is not to endorse the view that the duty to obey rests on a promise or a contract.

8. Some reports about Tongan and Iranian culture may complicate claims about the universality of promising, but it is difficult to determine exactly what they show. See Fred Korn & Shulamit R. Decktor Korn, *Where People Don't Promise*, 93 ETHICS 445 (1983) (discussing the absence of promising in Tonga Island culture); Michael Slackman, *The Fine Art of Hiding What You Mean To Say*, N.Y. TIMES, Aug. 6, 2006, §4 (Week in Review), at 5 (discussing the prevalence of what appear to be insincere promises in Iranian culture). Some of this evidence could be interpreted to show that in some cultures, it is hard to tell when sincere commitments are expressed, but not that promises as such have little or no significance.

Further, the purported departures from the culture of promising take place in contexts of hierarchical, unequal structures; thus, they may not serve as counterevidence of the importance of promising in maintaining social relations of equality amid local conditions of vulnerability. Tongan society is so pervasively hierarchical that much of its social interaction and dialogue is colored by status differences. See, *e.g.*, Kerry E. James, *Tonga's Pro-Democracy Movement*, 67 PAC. AFF. 242, 243 (1994) (noting the Tongan "traditions of rank and hierarchy"); Adrienne L. Kaeppler, *Poetics and Politics of Tongan Laments and Eulogies*, 20 AM. ETHNOLOGIST 474, 476 (1993) (drawing on Tongan rituals and pronouncements to show that "hierarchical principles of status and rank pervade life and death"); Adrienne L. Kaeppler, *Rank in Tonga*, 10 ETHNOLOGY 174, 174, 177, 188, 191 (1971) (arguing that the inequality inherent in Tongan society remains in force and has withstood the small movement for democratic reform); Kerry E. James, *Pacific Islands Stakeholder Participation in Development: Tonga* 17 (World Bank, Pac. Islands Discussion Paper Series No. 4, 1998) (describing Tongan society as traditional and hierarchical).

9. I assume that the rules of morality have much substantive content independent of and prior to the law. That is, their content is not fully determined by law's contents and those moral principles requiring obedience to law.

10. See, e.g., JOHN RAWLS, POLITICAL LIBERALISM 173–211 (1993); JOHN RAWLS, *The Priority of the Right and Ideas of the Good, in* COLLECTED PAPERS 449 (Samuel Freeman ed., 1999).

11. Performance of some intrafamilial promises may be an exception, and this may in part (though only in part) explain the resistance to enforcing intrafamilial promises. See, e.g., KIMEL, supra, note 2, at 72–87 (discussing the inadequacy of the contract framework for pursuing the value of personal relationships); see also infra section II.A.2 (discussing mitigation); infra, section III.B.2 (discussing gift promises).

12. I discuss some more familiar forms of accommodation and their role within liberalism in Seana Valentine Shiffrin, *Egalitarianism, Choice-Sensitivity, and Accommodation, in* REASON AND VALUE: THEMES FROM THE MORAL PHILOSOPHY OF JOSEPH RAZ 270 (R. Jay Wallace et al. eds., 2004), and Shiffrin, supra, note 5.

13. I use "citizens" as a shorthand for those regularly subject to a legal regime's requirements.

14. I note, but do not address here, the further question of whether a regime that showed *convergence* between legal and moral rules, but whose legal justifications were unacceptable to moral agents, would also be suspect. I believe it would be, but that position requires greater argument than there is room for in this article.

15. As is well known, there are concerns about how we can coherently refer to the reasons that motivated a legislature, given that it may pass legislation without discussion of, much less consensus on, reasons for that legislation. I put these issues aside here, although a fuller account of legislative rationale must face them, as some have attempted to do. See, e.g., Elizabeth S. Anderson & Richard H. Pildes, *Expressive Theories of Law: A General Restatement*, 148 U. PA. L. REV. 1503, 1520–27 (2000) (asserting that the expressive meaning of collective action is not only a matter of legislative intent, but also a function of public understanding); Elena Kagan, *Private Speech, Public Purpose: The Role of Governmental Motive in First Amendment Doctrine*, 63 U. CHI. L. REV. 413, 438–42 (1996) (arguing that governmental motive could be determined by looking at the legislation produced).

16. For a discussion of the claim that factors of this sort support the consideration rule, see infra, section III.B.

17. In some contexts, however, contract may be more demanding of the promisor than morality. This is certainly the popular notion of contract among laypeople. In close interpersonal relationships, there may be more room for interpretative flexibility than in contract. The law must come to a definitive conclusion about what a clause means; sometimes this serves the promisee's interests, as when the promisor is deemed to bear the risk of ambiguity—perhaps because he is the drafter or because he knows more about the industry. See RESTATEMENT (SECOND) OF CONTRACTS §201(2) (1979). By contrast, moral partners may be obliged to acknowledge directly the ambiguity of the meaning of a promise and strike a compromise given two competing reasonable understandings. Further, as Professor Bernard Williams notes, in many informal contexts promissory parties should adjust their understandings of one another when compliance becomes more difficult than anticipated, especially when unforeseen circumstances

arise. BERNARD WILLIAMS, TRUTH AND TRUTHFULNESS 112 (2002). By contrast, contract law adopts stricter rules, placing the burden on the party who reasonably bears the risk of unforeseen circumstances. See, e.g., RESTATEMENT (SECOND) OF CONTRACTS §154. Sometimes this will place a higher burden on the promisor than morality might.

    I put these examples of divergence aside. The divergence they exhibit is less stark than the examples I consider in the body of this article. Contracting promisors often bear the burden of interpretative ambiguity, but not always. The promisee bears the burden when there is mutual misunderstanding, causing the contract to be dissolved. See id., §152. Moreover, promisors will be bailed out in those cases of impracticability that threaten the survival of their operations. See id., §261. These forms of divergence, unlike the ones on which I focus in the body of the article, seem to be the product of the distinctive function of a large legal system to provide clear, predictable rules for conflict resolution and definitive adjudication when informal, more contextual mechanisms fail. Their content is explained by the effort to place the burdens of such stark rules, when necessary, on the parties who are more able to protect themselves ex ante against those burdens. The divergences I discuss in the body of the article do not share these features.

18. I discuss the central significance of promising to the moral agent in Shiffrin, supra, note 7. My own approach does not take promises and their main moral force as resting on or deriving from a social convention, though many aspects of how we signal, understand, and fill in promissory gaps are, of course, based on local conventions. Most of this article's points, however, do not depend on the rejection of conventionalism but only on the moral rules of promising being understood in the broad terms I describe.

19. See also supra, notes 7–9 and accompanying text.

20. RESTATEMENT (SECOND) OF CONTRACTS §1 (emphasis added).

21. See id.

22. See, e.g., P.S. ATIYAH, PROMISES, MORALS, AND LAW (1981); FRIED, supra, note 2, at 7–14; ROSCOE POUND, AN INTRODUCTION TO THE PHILOSOPHY OF LAW 133–68 (rev. ed.1954); W. DAVID SLAWSON, BINDING PROMISES 173 (1996); Morris R. Cohen, *The Basis of Contract*, 46 HARV. L. REV. 553, 571–92 (1933); Craswell, *Two Economic Theories*, supra, note 3, at 19–44; Melvin Aron Eisenberg,

Donative Promises, 47 U. CHI. L. REV. 1, 1 (1979); Melvin A. Eisenberg, *The Theory of Contracts, in* THE THEORY OF CONTRACT LAW, supra, note 3, at 206, 240–64; Charles J. Goetz & Robert E. Scott, *Enforcing Promises: An Examination of the Basis of Contract*, 89 YALE L.J. 1261 (1980); James Gordley, *Contract Law in the Aristotelian Tradition, in* THE THEORY OF CONTRACT LAW, supra, note 3, at 265, 268–97.

23. See RESTATEMENT (SECOND) OF CONTRACTS §21 ("Neither real nor apparent intention that a promise be legally binding is essential to the formation of a contract, but a manifestation of intention that a promise shall not affect legal relations may prevent the formation of a contract.").In other countries, the presumption sometimes runs the other way. For instance, in British law, the intention to enter into legal relations is presumed for promises between commercial entities but must be positively proved for social and familial promises to become contracts. See THE ENFORCEABILITY OF PROMISES IN EUROPEAN CONTRACT LAW 113 (James Gordley ed., 2001). American law also evinces reluctance to enforce certain sorts of familial promises, though this resistance is not articulated through a doctrine that there must be additional intent to enter into legal relations.

24. Legal impermissibility would substitute for moral impermissibility, legal requirement for moral requirement, and so on.

25. See FRIED, supra, note 2, at 17.

26. See, e.g., U.C.C. §2–716 (2005) (explaining that specific performance may be available when goods are unique, the buyer cannot find cover, and under other "proper circumstances"); RESTATEMENT (SECOND) OF CONTRACTS §359(1) (explaining that specific performance is not available when damages adequately protect the expectation interest); 5A ARTHUR L. CORBIN, CORBIN ON CONTRACTS §1139 (1964) (discussing specific performance as only a supplemental remedy).

27. See, e.g., RESTATEMENT (SECOND) OF CONTRACTS §355. Punitive damages are available in cases of fraud or other violations of contract law that are also torts. For a brief period, California awarded punitive damages for "bad faith" contractual breach. But this doctrine covered only the very narrow class of cases in which the breaching party not only breached, but also contested liability without a good faith belief in the defense. Seaman's Direct Buying Serv., Inc. v. Standard Oil Co., 686 P.2d 1158, 1167 (Cal. 1984); see also

Nicholson v. United Pac. Ins. Co.,710 P.2d 1342, 1348 (Mont. 1985). *Freeman & Mills, Inc. v. Belcher Oil Co.*, 900 P.2d 669 (Cal.1995), sharply limited the doctrine to the insurance context a decade later. Even under *Seaman's*, intentional breach with a ready payment of compensatory damages would still have been perfectly acceptable. Nonetheless, the quite modest application of punitive damages in *Seaman's* was still met with consternation. It was severely constricted after three of its authors, Rose Bird, Joseph Grodin, and Cruz Reynoso, were all unseated from the California Supreme Court in the 1986 election. Although the retention election focused on their positions on the death penalty, Professor David Slawson obliquely suggests some connection between the election and those who blamed the court's decision for higher liability insurance costs. See SLAWSON, supra, note 22, at 110–11.Some states still recognize some form of bad faith breach and subject it to punitive damages. See id., at 112–32.

28. See, e.g., Robert D. Cooter, *Punitive Damages, Social Norms, and Economic Analysis*, 60 LAW & CONTEMP. PROBS. 73, 73–74 (1997) (stating that punitive damages represent legal recognition of a serious wrong).

29. See RESTATEMENT (SECOND) OF CONTRACTS §353 (allowing damages for emotional distress only when breach causes bodily harm or when serious emotional distress is "a particularly likely result" of breach); 24 RICHARD A. LORD, WILLISTON ON CONTRACTS §66:67 (4th ed.2002) (reporting that attorney's fees are generally not recoverable in contracts cases because they are viewed as penal, that the Uniform Commercial Code does not provide for punitive damages, and that the common law rule regarding attorney's fees was not purposefully abrogated by the Uniform Commercial Code provision for consequential damages).

30. Hadley v. Baxendale, 156 Eng. Rep. 145 (Ex. 1854).

31. See id.; RESTATEMENT (SECOND) OF CONTRACTS §351(1).

32. Despite the official distaste for punitive damages in contract, Professor Marc Galanter reports a greater rate of punitive damage awards for successful plaintiffs in contracts cases than in torts cases. Marc Galanter, *Contract in Court; or Almost Everything You May or May Not Want To Know About Contract Litigation*, 2001 WIS. L. REV. 577, 604–06. It is difficult to know what to make of his data without further details of the cases and the nature of the successful claims. As his data show, most of the punitive damage awards are provided in employment cases or in cases in which the behavior at issue was also tortious, though it was classified as a contracts cause of action. Id., at 605 tbl.7.

33. See Richard Craswell & Alan Schwartz, *Notes on Mitigation and Reliance by the Promise*e, *in* FOUNDATIONS OF CONTRACT LAW 64, 64–67 (Richard Craswell & Alan Schwartz eds., 1994).

34. See FRIED, supra, note 2, at 131; Melvin A. Eisenberg, *The Duty To Rescue in Contract Law*, 71 FORDHAM L. REV. 647, 654–55 (2002).

35. Interestingly, French law does not impose a similar duty of mitigation on the promisee, and some acts of mitigation in the United States would be seen as breach by the promisee in France. See de Moor, supra, note 3, at 106–07.

36. See U.C.C. §2-718(1) (2005); RESTATEMENT (SECOND) OF CONTRACTS §356(1).

37. Id.

38. Oliver Wendell Holmes, Jr., *The Path of the Law*, 10 HARV. L. REV. 457, 462 (1897); see also OLIVER WENDELL HOLMES, JR., THE COMMON LAW 235–36 (Transaction Publishers 2005) (1881) (discussing the exceptionality of specific performance and noting that "[t]he only universal consequence of a legally binding promise is, that the law makes the promisor pay damages if the promised event does not come to pass").

39. See, e.g., KAPLOW & SHAVELL, supra, note 2, at 191–92. Richard Craswell may also be read as taking this position. See Craswell, *Contract Law*, supra, note 3, at 490 ("[T]he fidelity principle is consistent with any set of background rules because those rules merely fill out the details of what it is a person has to remain faithful to, or what a person's prior commitment is deemed to be.").

40. But cf. supra, note 27 (discussing a limited exception to the general lack of disapprobation).

41. Does corporate law require those with a fiduciary duty of care or of loyalty to shareholders to pursue an efficient breach if it would clearly enhance share value? The question is probably academic. The duty holder who wishes to comply in the face of an opportunity for efficient breach could probably successfully invoke the business judgment rule by claiming that breach was not clearly in the company's or the shareholders' long-term interest, whether because of standard uncertainties in markets or reputational costs associated with

intentional breach and the consequent financial repercussions, or because intentional breach conflicts with the company's mission statement. See STEPHEN M. BAINBRIDGE, CORPORATION LAW AND ECONOMICS 414 (2002). But suppose the duty holder forswore these defenses or they were overcome. Could a duty holder defend against a charge of breach of fiduciary duty for failure to pursue an efficient breach of contract on the ground that intentional breach of promise is immoral? It might depend on the jurisdiction. The general rule is that corporate directors are to maximize shareholder wealth. See, e.g., Dodge v. Ford Motor Co., 170 N.W. 668, 683–84 (Mich. 1919). Many, but not all, states allow or require those with fiduciary duties to take into account third-party interests, including the interests of contracting parties and the community. See BAINBRIDGE, supra, at 414; see also 1 AM. LAW INST., PRINCIPLES OF CORPORATE GOVERNANCE: ANALYSIS AND RECOMMENDATIONS §2.01(b)(2) (1992) (recommending that governance statutes permit corporations to take into account appropriate ethical considerations). The issue also arises in other contexts in which there are fiduciary duties, such as those of an executor. Professor Liam Murphy brought my attention to *Ahmed Angullia Bin Hadjee Mohamed Salleh Angullia v. Estate & Trust Agencies (1927), Ltd.*, [1938] A.C. 624 (P.C.) (appeal taken from Sing.), which held that an executor never has a duty to break an enforceable contract because breach is an unlawful act. Id., at 635.

42. SLAWSON, supra, note 22, at 122 (emphasis omitted); see also Robert L. Birmingham, *Breach of Contract, Damage Measures, and Economic Efficiency*, 24 RUTGERS L. REV. 273, 284–85 (1969) (arguing that it would be socially desirable to encourage "[r]epudiation of obligations … where the promisor is able to profit from his default" after paying expectation damages); Linzer, supra, note 2, at 115–16, 138–39 (criticizing efficient breach generally but defending, in the limited commercial domain in which people enter contracts for economic reasons, the argument that "law, economics, and arguably common sense all condone the deliberate and willful breach"); A. Mitchell Polinsky & Steven Shavell, *Punitive Damages: An Economic Analysis*, 111 HARV. L. REV. 869, 939 (1998) (noting that punitive damage awards for breach of contract often result in "excessive and expensive performance … thereby lowering the welfare of the contracting parties").

43. I aim merely to describe the argument, not to endorse its notion of efficiency, which is yet another aspect of the justification that may be challenged.

44. Some discussions frame efficiency arguments in contract in these weaker terms, although not always explicitly so. See, e.g., Richard Craswell, *Contract Remedies, Renegotiation, and the Theory of Efficient Breach*, 61 S. CAL. L. REV. 629, 636–38 (1988) (discussing efficient breach in light of the goal of contract damages—to give compensation); Craswell, *Two Economic Theories*, supra, note 3, at 27 (arguing that efficiency-based liability may not be compatible with promises, strictly construed, but that we should recognize another intermediate form of commitment that is compatible with efficiency-based liability); E. Allan Farnsworth, *Legal Remedies for Breach of Contract*, 70 COLUM. L. REV. 1145, 1216 (1970) (describing the system of contractual remedies as "heavily influenced by the economic philosophy of free enterprise" and showing "a marked solicitude for men who do not keep their promises"); Lewis A. Kornhauser, *An Introduction to the Economic Analysis of Contract Remedies*, 57 U. COLO. L. REV. 683, 686, 692 (1986) (stating that economic analyses view the purpose of contract law as the promotion of efficiency and that "the purpose of contract remedies is to induce the parties to act efficiently").

Neither characterization fits the defense of efficient breach that holds that it does not involve a breach of promise at all because breach in such circumstances is what the parties would have wanted if they had formed a complete contract. See, e.g., Steven Shavell, *Contracts, in* THE NEW PALGRAVE DICTIONARY OF ECONOMICS AND THE LAW 436, 439 (Peter Newman ed., 1998). I put this third characterization aside because it deserves a longer treatment than there is room for in this article. In brief, the argument assumes that people would always have made the best bargain for themselves from an economic point of view had they made a complete contract and that what they did promise is determined by what rational economic actors would have promised had they focused on the relevant contingency. Both of these premises, among others, seem contestable.

45. This description of the doctrine of efficient breach does not depend upon a comprehensive consequentialist view. For instance, an adherent might reject consequentialism as a moral position for individuals or even as the general foundation for legal doctrines, but merely posit that the purpose of

the domain of contract law in particular is to create an economically efficient system for transfers and exchanges. Thus, its doctrines should be fashioned to pursue that aim, and in this limited domain consequentialist reasoning is appropriate. This more moderate description of the doctrine of efficient breach and its underlying justification thereby differs from that offered and criticized by Frank Menetrez, supra, note 2. For a more comprehensive consequentialist view, see Craswell, *Two Economic Theories,* supra, note 3, at 19–20, 26–34. Professor Craswell argues that economic analysis of contract has a broad scope and evaluates the effects of legal rules on a variety of parties' incentives and behaviors beyond performance, including incentives to rely, to insure, and to prepare to perform. See id.

46. See, e.g., Craswell, supra, note 44, at 635; Richard Craswell, *Instrumental Theories of Compensation: A Survey,* 40 SAN DIEGO L. REV. 1135, 1145 & nn.10–11 (2003); Daniel Friedmann, *The Efficient Breach Fallacy,* 18 J. LEGAL STUD. 1, 6–7 (1989); Linzer, supra, note 2, at 131; Ian R. Macneil, *Efficient Breach of Contract: Circles in the Sky,* 68 VA. L. REV. 947, 951–53 (1982).

47. Why not condemn the efficient breach recommendation simply on the grounds that it is morally wrong? Why make the more complicated appeal to what justification the moral agent could accept? First, appeal to the moral agent involves a narrower and differently contoured sensitivity to the role of moral judgments in legal justification. Direct appeals to moral judgments might authorize eliminating certain options merely on the grounds that such options were morally bad ones. An accommodationist perspective need not accept that argument. A moral agent could not accept a rule that generated such morally bad options by direct appeal to their moral qualities but *could* accept as a reason that autonomous agents should have the opportunity to decide for themselves what to do. Second, the appeal to the moral agent reflects the correct order of explanation. The efficient breach justification is not rejected because it is morally wrong but because it cannot be endorsed by a moral agent and is therefore inconsistent with the imperative to accommodate. Arguments for accommodation do not appeal directly to the correctness of the position of moral agents but rather to the essential importance of morality to moral agents and the significance of their character traits for the flourishing of just institutions and cultures. As with religious accommodation, these

grounds are compatible with greater neutrality toward the correctness of substantive moral views than is an approach that engages in more direct moral evaluation.

48. See, e.g., STEPHEN A. SMITH, CONTRACT THEORY 400–01 (2004) (discussing the liberty objection to specific performance).

49. See above for a discussion of the parallel moral phenomenon that agents cannot alter by declaration the moral significance or seriousness of immoral behavior.

50. See, e.g., State Farm Mut. Auto. Ins. Co. v. Campbell, 538 U.S. 408, 428 (2003).

51. See supra, section II.A.3.

52. See FARNSWORTH, supra, note 1, at 817–18.

53. I sketch some criteria in Seana Valentine Shiffrin, *Are Credit Card Late Fees Unconstitutional?,* 15 WM. & MARY BILL RTS. J. (Dec. 2006), and suggest that determining whether a term is a penalty requires analysis of the form of the contract, its wording, and its primary function. For example, late charges should be understood as penalties if these charges do not represent the point of the exchange and are framed as responses to a failure to perform another duty that is the point of the contractual relationship.

54. This defense would extend only to the ban on punitive damage agreements; it would not explain the general ban on punitive damages as a remedy in contract.

55. See Eisenberg, *The Theory of Contracts,* supra, note 22, at 230; Melvin Aron Eisenberg, *The World of Contract and the World of Gift,* 85 CAL. L. REV. 821, 846–52 (1997); see also KIMEL, supra, note 2, at 46–49, 72–74; Gordley, supra, note 22, at 330.

56. Cf. Anthony J. Bellia, Jr., *Promises, Trust, and Contract Law,* 47 AM. J. JURIS. 25, 34 (2002) (arguing that legal enforcement is not a perfect substitute for voluntary performance). Professor Bellia also observes that legally enforceable promises may help to form the basis for a relationship that then becomes dependent on other sources of trust. Further, even in solid interpersonal relationships, an offer to make a legally binding promise may help to reinforce the relationship of trust. Id., at 36.

57. See SMITH, supra, note 48, at 419–20 (endorsing in part and criticizing in part this suggestion).

58. One might suggest that although there is a moral consensus that promises matter and that remedial reactions to breach are appropriate, the moral remedial rules are opaque. Reasonable people may

differ about the seriousness of breach or how stringent the appropriate moral remedies should be. Further, the moral significance of any promise varies substantially according to context, the situation of the parties, and their mutual understandings. Given the controverted and highly contextual nature of the moral specifics, there is reason for the legal system to adopt a conservative posture within its rules of contractual enforcement. In response: It is unclear that the moral status of many torts and their appropriate remedies is clearer and less controverted than that of breach. In any case, even if a blunt, conservative rule is called for, it is not clear why these epistemic worries support our current promisor-favoring approach rather than a promisee-favoring approach. At least in cases of intentional breach, the latter seems the more conservative approach since the promisor can avoid being subject to the burdens associated with the rule by fulfilling the promise.

59. To be sure, it is not a simple matter whether fragile cultures gain strength from the blunt and sometimes intrusive methods of the law. Concerns that legal recognition and involvement may harm organized religion more than they help make up one of the traditional strands of argument behind the Establishment Clause. See, e.g., Daniel O. Conkle, *Toward a General Theory of the Establishment Clause*, 82 Nw. U. L. Rev. 1113, 1181–82 (1988); Steven H. Shiffrin, *The Pluralistic Foundations of the Religion Clauses*, 90 Cornell L. Rev. 9, 42–47 (2004); William W. Van Alstyne , *What Is "An Establishment of Religion"?*, 65 N.C. L. Rev. 909, 914 (1987).

60. Some moral conceptions recognize moral ends other than economic efficiency in contract. See, e. g., Atiyah, supra, note 22, at 68–69, 138–46; Fried, supra, note 2; Kimel, supra, note 2, at 22–27, 100–07; Randy E. Barnett, *A Consent Theory of Contract*, 86 Colum. L. Rev. 269, 296–305 (1986); Peter Benson, *The Idea of a Public Basis of Justification for Contract*, 33 Osgoode Hall L. J. 273, 314–19 (1995); Curtis Bridgeman, *Corrective Justice in Contract Law: Is There a Case for Punitive Damages?*, 56 Vand. L. Rev. 237, 260–68 (2003); Gordley, supra, note 22, at 307–08, 327–30; Jody Kraus, *Reconciling Autonomy and Efficiency in Contract Law: The Vertical Integration Strategy*, 11 Phil. Issues 420 (2001) (critiquing economic efficiency as a normative grounding for contract while arguing for an autonomy-based theory whose implementation is sensitive to effi-

ciency considerations); Daniel Markovits, *Contract and Collaboration*, 113 Yale L.J.1417, 1419–21 (2004); T.M. Scanlon, *Promises and Contracts, in* The Theory of Contract Law 86, 86–93 (Peter Benson ed., 2001); Liam Murphy, Theories of Contract (Sept. 2004) (unpublished manuscript, on file with the Harvard Law School Library); Peter Benson, *The Expectation and Reliance Interests in Contract Theory: A Reply to Fuller and Perdue*, 1 Issues in Legal Scholarship, June 2001, art. 5, at 26–31, http://www.bepress.com/cgi/viewcontent.cgi?article=1004&context=ils. Some of these conceptions advance distinctively legal and normative arguments about contract. Others do not.

61. Professors Kaplow and Shavell also briefly raise this possibility, but they do not pursue it because they regard it as a factor only relevant within a welfare economics analysis, one they believe would not entail a significant change in contract rules. See Kaplow & Shavell, supra, note 2, at 211–13.

62. The ethical context in this situation may be complex, I grant, especially when month-to-month leases are unavailable and parties must make year-long commitments to gain access to a requisite good, thereby depriving them of needed flexibility.

63. I am not alone in worrying, however, about the decline of the culture of promising and its interrelation to legal norms and the expectations a legally shaped culture will induce. Roscoe Pound voiced similar anxieties. See Pound, supra, note 22, at 159–68.

64. See Thomas Nagel, Equality and Partiality 169–79 (1991); Samuel Scheffler, Human Morality 133–45 (1992); Barbara Herman, *Morality and Everyday Life*, 74 Proc. & Addresses of the Am. Phil. Ass'n 29, 34, 36 (2000).

65. This argument is developed and applied to the cases of compelled speech and compelled association in Seana Valentine Shiffrin, *What Is Really Wrong with Compelled Association?*, 99 Nw. U. L. Rev. 839, 839–55 (2005), and in Vincent Blasi & Seana V. Shiffrin, *The Story of* West Virginia State Board of Education v. Barnette*: The Pledge of Allegiance and the Freedom of Thought, in* Constitutional Law Stories 433, 454–75 (Michael C. Dorf ed., 2004).

66. See Kaplow & Shavell, supra, note 2, at 163 (arguing that conventionalists have failed to specify the full content of the social convention and that "legal rules themselves are part of the social institution of promising"). I will not lean on this point both because I am not a conventionalist and

because the problem holds for nonconventionalists as well.

67. MEIR DAN-COHEN, HARMFUL THOUGHTS 247–49 (2002).

68. Witnesses and lawyers need not volunteer some facts that they would otherwise be required to volunteer by conventions of cooperative conversation; lawyers may withhold elements of their strategies and advocate positions they do not personally hold. The moral permissibility of these behaviors depends in part on the well-defined boundaries of the practice as well as the underlying justifications for the practice.

69. The majority of the aims of contract law are surely compatible with moral constraints. In part V, I sketch one more positive and unified account of the aim of contract law that dovetails with the moral norms of promising.

70. Wikipedia, Diplomacy, http://en.wikipedia.org/wiki/Diplomacy_(board_game) (last visited Dec. 10, 2006). "A stab can be crucial to victory, but may have negative repercussions in interpersonal relations.... In some circles cheating is not only allowed, but also actively encouraged. Players are allowed and expected to move pieces between turns, add extra armies … , listen in to private conversations, change other players' written move orders and just about anything else they can get away with. In tournament play, however, these forms of cheating are generally prohibited, leaving only the lying and backstabbing which is prevalent wherever *Diplomacy* is played." *Id.*

71. In such cases, it may even be questioned whether this is a real case of insincerity. His "Thanks for shopping here!" may be an abbreviated form of "The company thanks you for shopping here!" See DAN-COHEN, supra, note 67, at 247–48.

72. See id., at 248–49.

73. Cf. Roy Kreitner, *Fear of Contract*, 2004 WIS. L. REV. 429, 469 (arguing that contract law should "make room" for the predispositions of managers, employees, and judges for fairness and cooperative behavior).

74. See, e.g., David Charny, *Nonlegal Sanctions in Commercial Relationships*, 104 HARV. L. REV. 373, 457–60 (1990); Alan Schwartz & Robert E. Scott, *Contract Theory and the Limits of Contract Law*, 113 YALE L.J. 541, 544–46, 550, 618 (2003) (distinguishing between intercorporate transactions and transactions involving individuals and less sophisticated organizations); see also Kreitner, supra, note 73, at 466–74 (agreeing

that efficiency concerns should be more dominant in interbusiness transactions but questioning whether those concerns should be exclusive).

75. See generally Shiffrin, supra, note 7 (discussing the solicitation of trust as a critical component of forging promises).

76. See ERIC A. POSNER, LAW AND SOCIAL NORMS 150 (2000) (observing that "what appears to be an arm's-length contract between two anonymous firms is often the result of negotiations between two friends who belong to the same social club or sit on the board of the same charitable organization"); Lisa Bernstein, *Opting Out of the Legal System: Extralegal Contractual Relations in the Diamond Industry*, 21 J. LEGAL STUD. 115, 119–25 (1992) (describing the relationship between trading clubs and transactions in the diamond industry) [hereinafter Bernstein, *Opting Out of the Legal System*]; Lisa Bernstein, *Private Commercial Law in the Cotton Industry: Creating Cooperation Through Rules, Norms, and Institutions*, 99 MICH. L. REV. 1724, 1745–54 (2001) (stressing the importance of personal relations and one-on-one encounters in commercial cotton agreements).

77. Daniel Markovits suggests, by contrast, that these considerations may be dispositive. See Markovits, supra, note 60, at 1465–68.

78. See Gary Watson, *Asserting and Promising*, 117 PHIL. STUD. 57 (2004) (discussing some of the differences between promises and assertions).

79. See JUDITH JARVIS THOMSON, THE REALM OF RIGHTS 294–321 (1990).

80. Here I mean only to bracket games, jokes, and cases such as Professor Dan-Cohen's, which regard the sincerity of pleasantries by representatives.

81. I reject the view that the promisee must rely on, or develop an expectation of, performance for a promise to be binding. See Shiffrin, supra, note 7.

82. The counterclaim, insofar as it encompasses the claim that socially recognized boundaries are essential to promising, engages the debate about conventionalism and promising. See, e.g., Shiffrin, supra, note 7 (defending a nonconventionalist view of promising). But see supra, note 66.

83. Shiffrin, supra, note 7.

84. For a more complete treatment of this issue, see id.

85. Why would the interest in rendering the relationship public require law? Could other forms of social disclosure perform this function? I will only gloss these important questions. In brief, some alternative forms can work, albeit in discrete, insular, and small-scale contexts. See, e.g., Bernstein, *Opting*

Out of the Legal System, supra, note 76, at 115, 119–30, 132–35; see also Charny, supra, note 74, at 392–97, 412, 417–19 (discussing nonlegal sanctions for breach and the limited contexts of their effectiveness). Our culture, interestingly, lacks a clear public forum other than law in which the socially cooperative community has an official voice. The need for law to serve as our collective voice may not be an essential feature of all cooperative life, although it may be an essential feature of large-scale democratic societies. In more homogeneous cultures, religious bodies may serve as an authoritative social voice, the pronouncements of which nonetheless do not have the status of (civil) law. Given our religious and other sorts of heterogeneity (as well as the economic and civil liberty structure that nurtures such heterogeneity), it may be no accident that we lack a unifying intermediate and independent institution other than law that serves as an official public forum and voice.

86. For instance, Professor Scanlon's claim that the institution of contracts is "centrally concerned with what is to be done when contracts have not been fulfilled" and his stress on contracts as furthering the "value of assurance" reflect an overly narrow conception of the function of contract. Scanlon, supra, note 60, at 93, 99.

87. See, e.g., Craswell, *Contract Law*, supra, note 3.

88. See Gordley, supra, note 22, at 280.

89. See Shiffrin, supra, note 5.

90. Of course, some legal-normative grounds may be given for the doctrine of consideration. Exchange or its promise signals to the parties (or may serve as evidence to third parties) that a promise is legally relevant. These are permissible sorts of reasons, but they do not provide convincing support for the proposition that consideration is a necessary condition of achieving such ends, especially given the risks of creating cultural confusion about the moral significance of quid pro quo requirements. See above; see also Scanlon, supra, note 60, at 306–07.

91. See, e.g., JULES L. COLEMAN, RISKS AND WRONGS 73–74, 192–93, 197 (1992). See *generally* Daniel A. Farber, *Economic Efficiency and the Ex Ante Perspective*, in THE JURISPRUDENTIAL FOUNDATIONS OF CORPORATE AND COMMERCIAL LAW 54, 66–69, 79–80 (Jody S. Kraus & Steven D. Walt eds., 2000) (discussing the intellectual history of law and economics).

73 Doing Away with Tort Law

JULES L. COLEMAN

I. INTRODUCTION

Guido Calabresi famously argues that tort law occupies the normative space between contract law on the one hand and criminal law on the other. It shares attributes of both but provides us with a practical and normative avenue of exchange that neither alone is capable of.

Both contract and tort regulate the transfer of resources. Contract law, however, regulates free exchange, whereas tort law regulates forced exchanges. The criminal law imposes mandatory norms that it enforces by punishments. The norms of tort law are not mandatory. They are optional in the sense that tort law provides agents with a menu of prices one has to pay for noncompliance with the relevant norms.[1] Contract law facilitates the exercise of liberty, and criminal law restricts the scope of individual liberty. Tort law, in contrast, neither prohibits nor encourages the exercise of liberty; instead, it prices its exercise.

A legal order without tort law would lack a mechanism for giving legal effect to forced, but nevertheless desirable, transfers of resources. Just as long as there are good reasons for such transfers in a liberal society, there will be an essential role for tort law to play.

The picture of tort law that Calabresi paints is even more prominent in what is perhaps his most important essay, *Property Rules, Liability Rules, and Inalienability: One View of the Cathedral.* There, Calabresi and his coauthor, Douglas

From *Loyola Los Angeles Law Review* 41 (2008): 1149.

Melamed, draw a distinction between the grounds for allocating rights and the grounds and means for protecting them. Once allocated, rights or entitlements can be secured by property, liability, or inalienability rules. Liability rules are distinctive to torts, and they protect entitlements, not by providing right holders with the legal power to block transfers against their will, but instead by providing them with compensation for the loss in value they experience when others others "take the right" without consent.[2]

For all the influence it has had, the Calabresi-Melamed framework is fundamentally confused. The central idea is that property, liability, and inalienability rules are mechanisms for protecting rights, but liability rules, for example, may be no such thing.[3] A liability rule does not confer any primary or basic normative powers on those who have entitlements. Quite the contrary in fact: a liability rule in the Calabresi-Melamed sense confers a normative power on those without rights to infringe, invade or take what others have a right to on the condition that in doing so they pay compensation for the losses, if any, the right holder experiences. In a phrase, then, a liability rule confers a "conditional power" on those without rights and grants no normative powers to those with rights.[4]

To be sure, the interests of right holders are partially secured by liability rules, but a right is a way of protecting those interests by conferring powers on the right holder, not by conferring powers on others. So we might say in the famous case of *Vincent v. Lake Erie Transportation Co.*, for example, that in the normal course of events the dock owner has a right to exclude the boat from mooring itself to the dock in the absence of the dock holder's consenting to his doing so. The power to exclude, then, is one of the ways in which the right protects the relevant interest. And this power allows us to understand the role of necessity—as created by the impending storm—in altering the structure of the normative relationship between dock and boat. For what necessity does is preempt one aspect of the normative powers associated with owning the dock; namely, the normative power to exclude.

Necessity, in other words, limits or constrains the normative powers that are part of the right. So, built into the right is the normative power;

and we recognize circumstances under which the exercise of those powers would be unjustified, or circumstances under which the powers are extinguished—whether in part or whole, temporarily or permanently. Necessity is one such special circumstance. The problem in the notion of a liability rule, as Calabresi-Melamed understand it, is that every circumstance is one in which the non-right-holder has the normative powers that we would normally associate with the right holder. If one takes rights seriously, it simply cannot be the case that rules protecting rights do so by conferring powers to compel transfers against the will of right holders.

In both of these important papers, Calabresi means to identify an irreducible or ineliminable role for tort law and for the notion of a liability rule that he takes to be central to it. But he can do so only by misunderstanding the relationship between liability and rights—or so I have argued. This misunderstanding suggests, perhaps, that Calabresi's heart is elsewhere, that liability in torts is more tenuous and less central to our legal practices than the arguments in these essays imply.

It should not be surprising, therefore, that Calabresi has also produced the most compelling work suggesting that tort law is anything but essential to liberal legal regime: *The Costs of Accidents*. Calabresi's book is best known for the thought that tort law has three independent, if related, goals: primary, secondary and tertiary cost reduction. Optimal deterrence (primary cost reduction) is accomplished by preventing those accidents worth preventing (i.e., those in which the costs of prevention are less than the costs of the accident discounted by the probability of its occurrence). Risk spreading (secondary cost reduction) is achieved by optimally reducing the impact of the costs of accidents that ought not be prevented by spreading the costs maximally over persons and time. Finally, tertiary cost reduction is produced by optimizing primary and secondary cost reduction at the lowest possible administrative cost. As the famous expression goes: the goal of accident law is to minimize the sum of the costs of accidents and the costs of avoiding them.

To be sure, Calabresi notes that there are compensatory aims of tort law and that the system itself must conform to the demands of fairness. His *One View* essay countenances that both entitlement allocation and protection decisions must be responsive to "fairness" and "other justice considerations." That said, there is no denying that *The Costs of Accidents* is best known for the distinctions Calabresi draws among various forms of cost avoidance and the relationship of tort law to the optimal reduction in accident costs.

Nevertheless, I want to focus on three parts of the Calabresi framework that are at once more basic and less obvious. The first is the emphasis on the "accident" as the paradigmatic tort. The second is the shift from a private action in which a court asks whose responsibility the accident is to the social context in which the question is: what is to be done about accidents—taken as a whole? Third, the normatively important feature of accidents is their costs.

It is nearly impossible to overstate the significance of each of these three building blocks of *The Costs of Accidents*. In effect, what Calabresi does is turn tort law into the law of *accidents*: accidents are a *social problem*, and the goal of tort law is to minimize and fairly or justly distribute their *costs*. Tort law is then a technology: a way of solving a social problem—the problem of accidents and their costs.

If tort law is the law of accidents and if accidents and their costs present a social problem, then we should want to know how good a job tort law does at solving the problem—especially when compared with a range of plausible alternatives. If tort law is an effective technology, we should be happy to keep it around; if not, we should consider abandoning it in favor of a better alternative. Indeed, in many ways, that is precisely the question Calabresi takes himself to be asking.

It should be obvious that this way of thinking about tort law is very much at odds with the argument in the *Mixed Society* and *One View* essays. In those essays, tort law is presented as an ineliminable component of a liberal legal regime. In *The Costs of Accidents*, however, tort law is a mere technology whose value rests on its ability to help solve a social problem, and not on how it adds shape to the normative structure of our relationships with one another.

This conflict in Calabresi's thinking about tort law has gone largely, if not entirely, unnoticed. That is surprising, because at least on the surface, the views are incompatible. According to the *One View* and *Mixed Society* essays, tort law is normatively and practically ineliminable; according to *The Costs of Accidents*, it is anything but. However, once one appreciates the notion of liability rule with which Calabresi has been operating, taking much of tort theory along with him in so doing, much of the surface contrast disappears. The Calabresian framework has little to do with rights as constraints on conduct, it is reformist to the core and sees tort law as a technology—whether to authorize forced transfers or to reduce costs by doing so.

II. TORTS, CRIMES AND CONTRACTS

Should we do away with tort law? This strikes me as the wrong question. There are three better questions we might ask instead. First, is it easier to imagine doing away with tort law than it is (or would be) to imagine doing away with the criminal law or contracts, for example? Second, if so, why would that be? Third, what would be lost, if anything, were we to do away with tort law?

Here is a plausible argument that suggests it would be very difficult to do without a criminal law. There is some conduct that is wrong, and those who engage in it (under certain conditions) deserve to be punished. There is some conduct, one might say, for which the responses of indignation and resentment are altogether fitting. Those responses are given expression publicly through punishment, and were we to do without a criminal law we would lack, one could argue, the appropriate way in which to express collectively the moral sentiments such conduct evokes.

To be sure, there was a time when it was fashionable to conceive of criminals as "sick" and deserving not of punishment but of treatment. Herbert Morris may not have been the first, but he may well have been the most eloquent critic of this view, noting that punishment, not treatment, is implicated in the very idea of responsible human agency. To treat someone as responsible for what he has done is to recognize that (under certain conditions) what he has done grounds an appropriate response in him (guilt, shame, remorse) and in others (indignation, disappropriation, resentment), and that these responses are misrepresented, if they are expressed at all, in our treating wrongdoers as sick and in need of health care. Punishment, whose content varies with prevailing practices—historically and culturally—nevertheless has remained a particularly apt way of giving expression to the ways in which the concepts of wrong, responsible agency and the reactive attitudes are interwoven in our self-understanding and in our normative lives.

Arguably, the capacity for human agency entails the ability both to act for reasons and to be a source of reasons for action as well. Practices in which we join efforts with others for mutual advantage are paradigmatic, if not essential, ways of expressing our capacity for agency and our ability to be sources of reasons for our own actions. Promising and contracting, for example, are basic forms of social organization. To contract with another is in some sense not merely to bind oneself to the will of another, but to bind oneself moreover to a joint plan. As Michael Bratman and others have pointed out, our status as planning agents is more central to our self-understanding than is our understanding of ourselves as social agents. And so, too, it is difficult to imagine doing away with contract law as we know it.

On the other hand, not only can we imagine doing away with tort law, serious theorists have proposed doing precisely that. And if that were not enough, an entire country has been engaged in doing away with large parts of it in favor of a social insurance scheme. It may be difficult if not altogether impossible to imagine doing away with contract or the criminal law; doing away with tort law, in contrast, is apparently anything but unthinkable.

One reason we are so comfortable imagining doing away with tort law is that we are operating with a conception of tort law we have inherited from Calabresi, one in which tort law is a mere technology—a potential solution to a social problem and not a body of law rooted either in fundamental features of our agency or one that otherwise maps onto our moral lives or which reflects the normative structure of our relationships

with one another. It is this, the conventional wisdom, however, and not the law of torts, that leads us astray.

III. WRONGS AND LIABILITY

In *Risks and Wrongs*, I draw distinctions among three ways in which wrongs, wrongdoing and compensation are related: (1) *X wrongs Y* and *Y* is *harmed as* a result of the wrong. *X* incurs a *duty of repair* to *Y*. The *ground* of the duty is the fact that *X* wrongfully breached his duty to *Y* and his doing so is responsible for the harm that *Y* suffers. (2) *X harms Y* but does *Y no wrong* provided he compensates him. The ground of the *duty to compensate* is that it is necessary to right, justify, or make permissible what would *otherwise* be a wrong to *Y*. (3) *X wrongs Y* but he is *justified* in doing so. If compensation is owed, it is not because *X* has acted wrongfully, nor does compensation right what would otherwise be a wrong. *X*'s conduct is permissible whether or not he compensates *Y*; yet he owes *Y* compensation.

The paradigm tort is represented by (1), which is to say that the paradigm tort is an unjustified and unexcused wrong. Liability in such a case protects the underlying right but does not legitimate a forced transfer.

The problem with the Calabresian view of liability rules is that it does not distinguish among these three cases. If anything, it treats them all as instances of (2), whereas (2), in fact, represents a small subset of the cases in which liability is imposed on torts.

We need an alternative conception of tort law, one that will better illuminate the relationships among the concepts central to it—especially that between wrong and liability—and which will explain what values and ideals are expressed by and embodied in it. I propose that we replace the three building blocks of the conventional view—accidents, costs and liability rules—with three others: wrongs, responsibility, and repair.

A. Wrongs and Relations

To be sure, accidents constitute the greatest number of torts. But "accident" covers a broad range of cases, and its use obscures rather than reveals what is essentially tortious about them. The accidents that are torts are, like other torts, by and large wrongs. It is the fact that they are wrongs, not the fact that they are accidents, that brings them within the ambit of the law.

I have elsewhere emphasized the distinction between *wrongdoing* and *wrong*, both of which imply the notion of a norm. Wrongdoing is a failure to comply with a norm of good behavior. "Be careful, prudent and thoughtful," and "attend adequately to the interests of others." These express norms of good behavior. We might admire those who comply with them, and be disappointed in or even fear those who do not. But unless there is a norm that imposes a duty on others to be careful, prudent and thoughtful, one wrongs no one for one's failures of care, prudence or thoughtfulness. One can be careless with the interests of those to whom one owes a duty of care, and one can be careless with regard to those one owes no such duty. A thoughtful person would be attentive to the interests of all those whom one's conduct may impact, but only those who have a right to one's attention and care can be wronged by the thoughtlessness. Parents owe duties to their children, for example, that they do not owe to others' children. Though it may mark a shortcoming in one's parents that they show too little regard for the well-being of children everywhere, the failure to do so may be a wrong to no one. If, however, they were to demonstrate a similar lack of concern for their children's well-being, it would constitute a breach of duty and a wrong to them. This scenario illustrates the important point that even though any failure to be adequately concerned with the interests of others may mark a shortcoming in someone, it does not constitute a wrong to another in the absence one's owing a duty of concern and care to the aggrieved party.

We can capture the distinction by saying that wrongs are *relational*: they are breaches of duty one owes to another. Wrongdoing, in contrast, is not relational in the same way. It consists of a failure to comply with a norm of good behavior.

We can point to another difference between the two norms. Not only can one act badly without wronging another, one can wrong another without acting badly. If I owe you a duty not to trespass on your property, then I wrong you if I do, even if I do so for very good reasons. If I promise to meet you for lunch, I owe you a duty to do so. I may have good reasons for breaking the promise, acting on which would display the goodness of my character; yet if I fail to show up then—provided that you have not released me from my obligation—I have wronged you. And so on.

The domain of tort law is *wrongs*, not *wrongdoing*. And wrongs are relational. Though one may have a specific duty in torts to a particular agent—as servants to masters or innkeepers to patrons—most of the relational duties in torts are more broadly characterized. In negligence, for example, the duty is to take adequately into account the security of those who fall within the ambit of foreseeable risk associated with one's conduct.

Both Cardozo and Andrews agree in *Palsgraf* that the question is whether the Long Island Railroad ("LIRR") breached a duty that it owed the plaintiff, Mrs. Palsgraf. In Andrews's view, the duty to Mrs. Palsgraf derives from the norm requiring that we exercise due care. In contrast, Cardozo's view is that the general norm of due care is not enough to establish the existence of a specific duty to Mrs. Palsgraf. There must be a relation between the railroad and Mrs. Palsgraf sufficient to impose on the railroad a duty of care to her in particular. Cardozo's claim is that we cannot derive such a duty from a general norm exhorting us to behave carefully.

There is a way of reading Andrews, however, that narrows the difference between Cardozo and him. On this reading, it is not just that there is a norm of a general sort endorsing or commanding due care. The norm should be understood instead as imposing a requirement or duty of due care—a duty we owe one another, through which each of us can hold the rest accountable to comply. Failure to exercise care to *anyone* is a breach of the duty of care that each and every one of us can be upset, even indignant, about. Understood in this way, Andrews and Cardozo agree that a tort requires a wrong and that a wrong consists in the breach of a specific duty of care. They differ with respect to the *scope* of the duty of care one has to others; more specifically, they disagree about the scope of the duty that is necessary to support a claim in torts.

This reading of Andrews supports the view that a defendant who breaches the duty of care to one person but who in doing so injures or harms another has committed a wrong, a breach which may ground the injured party's claim in torts, provided the victim can establish the right kind of "responsibility relationship" between the wrong and the harm she suffers. Cardozo's point is that unless the wrong is a *wrong to her* (and not just a duty to someone)—which must rely on a preexisting duty to her—tort law offers her no mode of recourse. And so for Cardozo, it does no good to treat the norm requiring care as a duty-imposing norm, for without a specific duty to Mrs. Palsgraf, there is no basis of liability to her because there is no wrong to her.[5]

Whatever their differences, both Cardozo and Andrews share the view that the core of a tort is a wrong—a breach of duty. They differ not just about the scope of the duty, but also about what wrongs can support a claim to repair or the standing to seek recourse in torts.

Though central both to torts and to my account of it, the notion of duty is in fact problematic in the economic analysis, for the duty requirement is a limitation on the scope of liability and (at least on the surface of things) means that some of the costs of one's mischievous conduct will be externalized. Efficiency requires internalizing externalities, and the duty requirement allows some of the costs of mischief to be externalized inefficiently.

In addition, whereas the notion of a duty and its breach reminds us that tort law has an essential relational dimension, the conventional view emphasizes an entirely different relationship: that between *each* litigant and the goal of optimal deterrence. Instead of asking whether the injurer has breached a duty to the victim, the fundamental question is whether the injurer or the victim is in a better position to reduce accidents and at what cost. So there is the relationship of the injurer to the goals of deterrence and the relationship of the victim to the goals of deterrence, and there is some interest perhaps in the relationship between the two insofar as coordination between their accident prevention measures may be

necessary to achieve optimal deterrence. But the picture of tort law we have inherited from Calabresi attaches no normative significance to the relationship between injurer and victim as such. It has no place for the duty requirement and no conception of a relational wrong. Without either, it cannot hope to capture the distinctiveness of tort law.

B. Persons as Constraints

Surely a defender of the conventional view will object that it has a concept of wrong. A wrong is a failure to take cost-justified precautions. But the Learned Hand formula is not a concept of a *wrong*. It is merely an account of adequate care: a person acts badly when he fails to exercise adequate care, and the care that is adequate is that which is economically efficient. A person who fails to take cost-justified precautions behaves badly. The notion of a wrong relies on the concept of a duty, and the question is not what is required of us to discharge the duties we have, but to whom do we have duties and why do we have the duties we have? The Learned Hand formula does not address those questions; it presupposes that they have already been answered.

My worries about the conventional view go deeper in two ways. First, even if a defender of the conventional view could introduce the concepts of wrong and duty, my concern is that these concepts do no independent work in the analysis or explanation of torts. The concepts are treated as "empty vessels" lacking content. That content is filled in by the concept of efficiency, thereby reducing "wrong" to "inefficiency." The concepts are introduced merely to be eliminated by reduction. All the explanatory and normative work is being done by efficiency.

My second worry is more substantive than methodological. In the conventional view, the normative significance of persons is captured in the idea that we are all locations or sites of welfare. This idea is what makes the Learned Hand formula even remotely plausible; what counts are the relative costs of harm and precaution—not where they reside. To the extent there are other concerns that bear on what the state can do to us in the name of minimizing costs or maximizing welfare, they are matters of equity or redistribution. The notions of breach, duty, right, and wrong derive the content that they have within the conventional view, in part because the conventional view identifies the normatively significant property of persons as their being sites and potential producers (or destroyers) of welfare.

In the alternative view, we are each committed to recognizing the normative significance of one another, and what is normatively significant about each of us is that we are independent constraints on the behavior of the rest of us. In my actions, I must treat you as a constraint on what I am able to do if I am to act in a way that is respectful of you.

Each of us has a capacity for agency, which is an ability not merely to wish but to act, and to act to further our ends as we conceive them. If we recognize this fact about us and we recognize as well that each of us is constrained by the rest of us, then we are committed to living by norms that make each of us accountable to the rest of us. This idea can itself be spelled out in a number of ways. Some have thought that the norms that guide us must be ones that no one to whom they apply could reasonably reject.

In a previous essay, *Mischief and Misfortune*, I argued that the view that each of us is a constraint on the rest of us implies a principle of fairness such that no one of us can unilaterally determine the terms of interactions between us. In torts this means, for example, that you cannot decide for both of us what the distribution of risk between us shall be. Such a norm would rule out a wide range of potential liability rules. Suppose, for example, that the injurer would be liable to the victim only for the harms that he *intends* to inflict. In effect, such a rule allows the injurer to determine the distribution of the risks between injurer and victim because a fact about the injurer alone—the content of his intentions—controls the distribution of risk between the parties (in violation of fairness).

C. Causation and Responsibility

The second key building block of a tort is the notion of responsibility. It is not enough that the injurer breach a duty of care to the plaintiff and that the plaintiff suffer harm: the harm must be attributable to the injurer as his doing; that is, his responsibility. Without that, there is wrong and harm but no grounds for attributing the harm to the injurer as something for which he must answer.

The defendant–injurer is held to answer for the plaintiff–victim's misfortune only if he is responsible for it. In torts, the notion of responsibility is expressed in causal concepts—the conjunction of "cause-in-fact" and "proximate cause." The conventional view, influenced as it is by its economic roots, is quite ambivalent about the concept of causation. On one hand, causation is inescapable since the fundamental claim of the traditional view is that efficiency requires that agents internalize the social costs of their activities. Externalities are the causal upshot of one's doings. So causation as a transitive, robust, and coherent notion is an inescapable commitment of the conventional view. The entire view makes no sense at all if expressions like "*A* causes *B*" make no sense. Without that, we have no concept of an externality.

On the other hand, the classic text, Ronald Coase's *The Problem of Social Cost*, argues for what seems to be the contradictory position, that causal relations are reciprocal and not transitive. For when cows trample corn, Coase's view is that we can no more claim that the cows cause the damage to the corn than we can say that the corn caused the damage by being there.

As I read the conventional view, then, it does not offer a concept of *responsibility* beyond that which is presumably implicated in the notion of causation. The problem is that the conventional view is itself of two minds when it comes to causation. Worse, the two views are incompatible with each other. Worse still, neither view is plausible on its own terms.

As Arthur Ripstein and I have argued in *Mischief and Misfortune*, the basic mistake is treating externalities as a naturalistic, rather than a normative, concept. The naturalistic notion of an externality is that of a *causal upshot*. And it is this notion of causation that economists appear to rely on. The problem is that the concept of an externality is a *normative*, not a naturalistic, notion. Whether certain costs are costs of my activity (and thus externalities) or yours (and thus *not*) is not a matter of causation, but depends instead on what we owe one another in regard to the distribution of risk between us. Externalities are derivative of the concept of a duty of care, and the duties we have to one another are themselves regulated by the principle of fairness, which I articulated in the previous section. This is what is meant by claiming that the notion of an externality is normative, not naturalistic; it relies on fairness in the distribution of risk, as expressed in the duties of care we owe to one another and not on the causal upshots of what we do to one another.

Ironically, this is not only the correct view, but it is one implicit in Coase's own argument—at least important aspects of it are. The correct interpretation of Coase is that we cannot determine whether the damage caused to corn by trampling cows is a cost of ranching or farming until we know whether the rancher owes a duty of care to the farmer or vice versa.

Coase makes a mess of this insight when he expresses the causal relationship as reciprocal, a very different point. The causal relationship is not reciprocal. Cows trample the corn and cause damage in doing so. But it does not follow that the cows should pay. Whether they should pay depends on what "cows" owe "corn," which is a normative matter—one regulated by fairness—not a naturalistic one.

Where did Coase go wrong? The answer is really quite revealing. He begins with the idea that if *A* damages *B*—that is, if the costs *B* suffers are *A*'s doing—then *A* should be liable to *B*. But he notes that there are many reasons why on some occasions if *A* damages *B*, it is *B*, not *A*, who should bear the costs.[6] How can he block the inference that seems so natural, namely, if *A* causes *B* damage, *A* should pay? He has two options. One is to say that the inference is invalid. The second is to say that the inference is valid, but we cannot really make sense of the idea that *A* damages *B* because the causal relationship is reciprocal. If causation is reciprocal, we have as much reason for thinking that *B* should pay as we do for thinking that *A* should.

I do not have enough time in this article or in whatever remains of my academic life to detail all the mistakes and confusions in this view.

Fortunately, there is no need to do so. My aim is ultimately to help Coase, not hang him out to dry. What he really should say is what he really meant to say: the fact that cows trample corn does not settle the question of who should pay for the damage. The problem is not that causation is reciprocal, rather it is that the inference from causation to liability is not valid. Once we adopt this strategy, however, we cannot analyze the notion of responsibility in terms of causation: not because causation is reciprocal, but because responsibility is a normative notion in a way in which causation, as Coase and others understand it, is not.

Once we understand Coase in this way, we get a deeper understanding of the Coase Theorem.[7] If the standard for determining the correct distribution of risk between the parties is efficiency, then it is irrelevant what the initial duties of care between the parties are. The idea is that as long as the parties are able to negotiate and the barriers to their doing so are sufficiently low, all that any liability rule can do is determine who has to pay whom (or to use Calabresi's phrase, "who has to bribe whom"). The optimal level of costs will be achieved through negotiation regardless of the legal or other imposition of liability. But to say that causation is irrelevant to efficiency is a far cry from saying that causation is reciprocal.

The traditional view is doubly problematic. First, it reduces responsibility to causation, and then it eliminates causation as central to torts. But responsibility is at the heart of a tort, and the view we have inherited from the economists has virtually no place for it. So once again, we have to start afresh.

There are two notions of responsibility in the law: responsibility for acts and responsibility for outcomes. Suppose that two individuals, Smith and Jones, act in precisely the same way and that in doing so their actions reveal the very same defect of will or character, thus rendering them both equally to blame for their actions. Imagine that they are both driving recklessly. It happens, however, that Smith is driving down a street populated entirely by Olympic athletes, each of whom is able to escape the risks that Smith's recklessness imposes upon them. Jones is not nearly so lucky. None of those he puts at risk, each the resident of an assisted-living community out on a day trip, is able to avoid the risks he imposes on them. As a result, each of them is injured by Jones's mischief.

A familiar line of argument claims that from a moral responsibility point of view there is no difference between Smith and Jones; all that distinguishes them from one another is luck—good luck in Smith's case, bad luck in Jones's. Luck and not responsibility is the difference between the two of them. There is only one notion of responsibility, and that is responsibility for actions, not outcomes. The causal upshots of what one does—unlike what one should do—are beyond one's control.

There is, however, a genuine and distinct notion of responsibility, that of responsibility for outcomes. This notion figures in the full range of our practices of debiting and crediting. It is also central to our self-understanding—our capacity to pick out our achievements and failures, as well as the marks we make in the world: the differences our lives have made in and to the world. There is, after all, a difference between the question of whether our hearts and character are pure and the question of whether we have made any difference in the world: how the world is different, if at all, for what we have contributed to it.

There are two questions we need to ask about this conception of responsibility: one analytic, the other normative. First, what are the conditions of outcome responsibility? Specifically, what must be true of a person, an outcome (event or state of affairs) and the relationship between them for the agent to be outcome responsible for the state of affairs? The second question is whether the notion of outcome responsibility provides a morally sound basis for imposing liability or, as I prefer, whether it grounds liability to a duty of repair.

We do not have to settle on the correct account of the conditions of outcome responsibility to recognize that some such notion is necessary to connect the injurer's breach with the victim's harm if we are to hold the injurer accountable for it.[8] When it comes to the normative question of whether imposing liability in torts on the basis of outcome responsibility is morally appropriate, however, we cannot content ourselves quite so easily.[9]

Take the case in which Smith and Jones both drive recklessly; Smith escapes damaging anyone,

whereas Jones is less fortunate and injures those he puts at risk. There may be no difference between the two of them with regard to their culpability or blameworthiness. That does not imply that there are no moral differences between them at all. Those who are the victims of Jones's recklessness have perfectly sound moral claims to repair against Jones, which no one, not even they, have against Smith. After all, there is nothing that Smith has done to them, nothing he need apologize to them for and no outcome that he must answer for. The same is not true of Jones. The victim's misfortune is connected to Jones's mischief in ways that ground their claim to repair against him and that give him something he has to answer for. Their claim against him is not merely a convenience but something that has a sound moral basis, and part of that basis is the fact that Jones is "outcome responsible" for the mess in which they now find themselves.

D. The Duty of Repair

The final building block of my account—at least the last I will discuss in this article—is that of a duty of repair. If an injurer is outcome responsible to the victim for a harm that he ought to have foreseen and which he should have avoided (which is to say that he was under a duty to avoid), then the harm is his doing, and he has to answer for it. The key feature of tort law is that it makes injurers accountable by imposing upon them a *duty of repair* that they owe to those they have wronged. Some, like John Goldberg and Ben Zipursky, offer a somewhat different account of this key feature of tort law, and it is worth noting the difference between their account and mine. Goldberg and Zipursky urge that what is distinctive about tort law is not just that the injurer incurs a duty of repair for the damage his wrong has occasioned. Rather, it is that tort law confers a right or option on the victim to impose the duty of repair on the injurer.

Neither Goldberg and Zipursky nor I deny that the injurer has incurred a duty of repair in torts. Their point is that the feature an account of tort law must explain is not the duty of repair but the grounds of the right to impose that duty—which is available to the victim (or those with the legal authority to act on his behalf) and not others.

The duty of repair is the conclusion of a practical inference whose premises include the duty of care, its breach, a compensable harm and the relationship of outcome responsibility between the breach and the harm. When those conditions are satisfied, a practical conclusion is warranted: namely, that the injurer owes the victim repair. The duty of repair is central to torts.

Liability in torts is not, as the conventional view would have it, a distribution of costs. The liability question in torts is not who should bear the costs of this accident or of accidents more generally. Rather, it is *liability to a duty of repair*; or if Goldberg and Zipursky are right, and they may well be, the defendant found liable is liable to the plaintiffs having the option of imposing the duty of repair upon him.[10]

IV. TWO OBJECTIONS

In the Calabresian picture, tort law has goals: primarily those of accident-cost avoidance and fairness in the distribution of accident costs. Tort law is a technology for achieving those goals. The key concepts within this picture of tort law are accidents, costs, and liability as a distributional notion. If tort law is not an effective tool for achieving its goals, we should consider the possibility that we would do well to jettison it in favor of some other scheme that would better reduce accident costs or more fairly distribute them.

My account is very different. We may study, teach, and write about tort cases from the standpoint of the law's failures. That makes perfect sense in many ways, but we have to avoid the temptation to let this distort our understanding of tort law. Like other areas of the law, the aim is to govern behavior and regulate affairs by specifying norms. The norms of tort law are not expressions of what is to count as good or bad behavior with regard to care. Nor are they prohibitions or proscriptions as in the criminal law. The norms of tort law specify relational duties: their grounds and content.

A tort is a wrong in two ways. It is a failure to comply with one of these norms and is a wrong in

that sense. It is also the breach of a particular duty to the person to whom one owes a specific duty of care under the general norm. The failure to comply with the general norm gives everyone a reason to be indignant; but it is the breach of the duty to the victim that gives her and her alone a reason to resent (if there is such a reason in the particular case).

A wrong—even two wrongs—does not a tort make. There must be harm and the right sort of "responsibility relationship"—what I have, employing the common parlance, referred to as "outcome responsibility"—between the breach and the harm. With that comes the duty to repair and the option conferred on the victim to impose it (and to call upon the state to enforce it). Instead of the concepts of accidents, costs and liability, we have the concepts of wrongs, responsibility and repair. If we want to do away with tort law, we need to appreciate what values will be lost, not what technology will be abandoned. We will get a handle on those values only if we come to understand the significance of ordering our affairs with one another in the ways that are expressed by the central notions of a tort: wrongs, responsibility and repair.

Before I say something about that, I want to ward off two related objections to the approach I am taking. Some take me to be suggesting that tort law serves no goals or that it cannot be assessed by how well it achieves its goals. The second objection is that the tort law I am describing exists only in my mind.

After all, there is no denying that modern negligence law is focused on accidents or that it emerges during a period when social reformers are quite open to the possibility that alternative institutional mechanisms might also address accidents. Any account of the normative foundations of tort law must be an account of accident law that is consistent with a decision to have dealt with accidents in some way other than tort law.

Neither of these objections is persuasive. Those who advance the first objection are obviously confusing me with somebody else. It would surely count against tort law if it resulted in far more wrongs being committed or if the costs of administering it were too high. We can surely evaluate our social institutions by their consequences. We can attribute goals to our institutions and assess them accordingly, but analyzing the concepts that figure prominently in the practice in terms of those goals is something else altogether.

I have made this point elsewhere by reporting on an experience I had with my former colleague, Burke Marshall. I had received an invitation to a dinner that was a tribute in his honor, and when I ran into Burke soon after receiving the invitation, I congratulated him on receiving the honor of the tribute. Burke responded sardonically that it was a mere fundraiser. It may well be that the goal—even the function—of the tribute was to raise money. But the event in question was a *tribute*, and if we analyze what tributes are in terms of the goals we sometimes (often or even always) have in feting one another, we will surely miss something about what tributes are.

I do not deny that tort law serves a range of human interests and goals, but it does so in a particular way; and if we want to understand what tort law is, we need to know something about the distinctive way in which tort law functions to serve the ends and goals we associate with it. The account I offer is an explanation of the central organizing concepts of tort law and their relationships to one another.

With this in mind, it is easy to see why I find the second objection equally unpersuasive. Of course I am aware that modern tort law focuses primarily on accidents and that we could have dealt with accidents in any number of ways. But why would it follow that all of those ways must be normatively continuous with one another? I would have thought that quite the contrary is true. In dealing with a class of accidents through tort law, we are suggesting that what is important about at least some of them is *not* their costs, but the fact that they are wrongs. Even the accidents that do not result from wrongs impose costs, and were costs all we cared about, we might well deal with all accidents very differently than we do. Regarding the view under consideration, we are to suppose that all accidents are alike and the reasons we have for reducing them are roughly the same; we just choose different instruments for doing so for practical or technological reasons. But that is

just what I am denying. I am arguing that what is different among the instrumentalities for reducing accidents is precisely the norms that are expressed or embodied in the institutions that seem apt for some categories of accidents and not for others.

V. CONCLUSION

Now what? Nothing I have said implies that we ought not do away with tort law. Indeed, nothing I have said implies that we should not make this decision on the basis of tort law's relative capacity to reduce accident costs effectively. My point is that we would not know what we are losing in the event we do away with tort law until we understand what tort law really is. If we are to understand the values at risk, we cannot allow ourselves the conceit that the conventional view gives us a plausible account of what tort law is.

NOTES

1. In addition, the burden of "prosecuting" failures to comply with tort law falls to particular victims.
2. The loss in value is determined by third parties—usually, but not necessarily, juries.
3. I am *not* claiming that liability rules cannot protect rights. I *am* claiming that liability rules as Calabresi and Melamed conceive of them do not and cannot protect *rights*. They can secure the *interests* protected by rights, but not by protecting them through recognition of rights.
4. This is not quite right. A liability rule in the Calabresi-Melamed sense confers a power on rights-invaders to invade rights on the condition that they are prepared to compensate those whose rights they invade; and confers an *option* on those whose rights are invaded to demand the payment due them.
5. Cardozo offers us a formulation of one such norm: roughly, each of us owes a duty of care to everyone who falls within the ambit of foreseeable risk. That norm specifies the content of the duty and the conditions under which it arises. It is not a norm requiring us to behave carefully; it is a norm specifying conditions under which certain duties arise and to whom we have them.
6. For example, even if *A* damages *B*, *B* may be the cheaper cost avoider, and therefore should bear the loss, which would invert her proper incentive to reduce the risk.

7. Roughly defined, the Coase Theorem contends that in the absence of transaction costs, parties will bargain to an efficient result, regardless of the underlying legal rule.

8. Though the idea of outcome responsibility as a basic moral notion is linked to the groundbreaking work of Tony Honoré, the best account of the conditions of outcome responsibility is given by Stephen Perry. In Perry's account, an agent is outcome responsible for a state of affairs provided he has the capacity both to have foreseen and avoided it.

9. I am allowing myself some liberties here. It is clearly true that whether imposing liability to repair in torts based on a notion of outcome responsibility is fair or morally appropriate must depend to some extent on the analysis of outcome responsibility. Still, I am assuming that some analysis in the neighborhood of Perry's is correct, and will work with that assumption in hand.

10. The notion of a liability rule invites the view of torts as a distributive or allocative institution: what is being allocated are the costs created by certain kinds of mischievous conduct. The question is, who is liable for those costs? But this is an entirely mistaken picture—though one I was under the grip of for a very long time.

74   Corrective Justice and Wrongful Gain

JULES COLEMAN

Richard Posner's essay "The Concept of Corrective Justice in Recent Theories of Tort Law"[1] falls into three distinct but related sections. In the first part of the paper Posner attempts to characterize the principle(s) of corrective justice. In the second part, he criticizes the efforts of a number of other tort theorists, including George Fletcher, Richard Epstein, and myself, who have attempted to ground the law of torts on a foundation of corrective justice. Having himself previously advanced an efficiency-based conception of the law of torts, Posner goes on to argue in the third part of the essay that the principle of corrective justice is itself required by the principle of efficiency. By laying an economic foundation for the principle of corrective justice, Posner argues not only for the compatibility of the most promising line of moral defense of tort law with the dominant economic one, but for the primacy of the latter as well.

Posner has graciously provided me with the opportunity to respond to his paper. In a series of essays, some of which have appeared in philosophy journals, others of which have surfaced in law reviews, and one of which has appeared as a chapter in a very overpriced book, I have explored the moral foundations of tort law. It would not be unfair—indeed, it may be too generous—to say that in these essays I have advanced a theory of torts based on the principle of corrective justice. In what follows I first summarize (in a very compressed fashion) my view of the role of corrective justice in tort theory, then briefly contrast it with those of Epstein and Fletcher, and finally consider Posner's objections to it.

I. LIABILITY, RECOVERY, AND A CONCEPTION OF CORRECTIVE JUSTICE

Central to my account of torts is the distinction between the grounds of liability and recovery—in other words, between the two questions: (1) What are the grounds necessary and sufficient to justify a victim's claim to recompense? and (2) Under what conditions ought an injurer be obligated to provide compensation to his victims? That the grounds of recovery and liability are at least analytically distinguishable is illustrated by the fact that a society could establish an insurance scheme to compensate all accident victims, while only those injurers who are at fault in causing an accident would be required to contribute to the

From *The Journal of Legal Studies* vol. 11 (June 1982): pp. 421–440. Reprinted with permission of the publisher. Most citations have been omitted.

insurance pool. Were we to separate liability and recovery in this way, being at fault in causing harm would be a necessary condition of liability, but not of the victim's case for recovery. Whether a system that separated liability from recovery in this particular way would be just or efficient remains to be worked out. For now the point is simply that the considerations that ground a claim to recompense need not coincide with those that ground the obligation to repair.

Once the distinction between the foundations of recovery and liability is drawn, the next question concerns the role of corrective justice in each. This in turn requires a conception of corrective justice. In my view, corrective or compensatory justice is concerned with the category of wrongful gains and losses. Rectification, in this view, is a matter of justice when it is necessary to protect a distribution of holdings (or entitlements) from distortions that arise from unjust enrichments and wrongful losses. The principle of corrective justice requires the annulments of both wrongful gains and losses.

This conception of corrective justice puts a great burden on the concepts of wrongful gain and wrongful loss. Without offering a set of conditions necessary and sufficient for a loss or gain to count as wrongful, I have tried in my previous work to characterize the basic idea by examples. Within the category of wrongful losses are those one suffers through the fault or wrongful conduct of another; within the class of unjust enrichments are those one secures through one's wrongdoing, as in many instances of fraud and theft. A compensable or undeserved loss need not, however, be the result of another's wrongdoing. Sometimes the justifiable (i.e., nonwrongful) taking of what another has a well-established right to justifies a claim to rectification. An instance of a justifiable taking that creates a compensable loss is given by the following example of Joel Feinberg's:

Suppose that you are on a back-packing trip in the mountain country when an unanticipated blizzard strikes the area with such ferocity that your life is imperiled. Fortunately, you stumble onto an unoccupied cabin, locked and boarded up for the winter, clearly somebody else's private property. You smash in a window, enter, and

huddle in a corner for three days until the storm abates. During this period you help yourself to your unknown benefactor's food supply and burn his wooden furniture in the fireplace to keep warm. Surely you are justified in doing all these things, and yet you have infringed the clear rights of another person.

Feinberg argues, and I concur, that in spite of the justifiability of what you have done, you owe the owner of the cabin compensation for breaking his window and consuming his food and furniture.

Though these examples do not define in any strict sense the operative notion of wrongfulness, they help to characterize it sufficiently to make the notion a useful one.

Given this general conception of corrective justice, the above examples of wrongful gain and loss, as well as the central distinction between the grounds of recovery and liability, we can begin to spell out my account of the role of corrective justice in tort theory.

In torts a distinction is drawn between the rules of fault (or conditional) and strict (or unconditional) liability. In fault liability, a victim is not entitled to recover his loss unless it is the result of another's fault, and an injurer is liable only for those harms that are his fault. In strict liability, neither the victim's claim to recompense nor the injurer's responsibility to make repair require that the injurer's conduct be at fault.

A. Corrective Justice and the Fault Principle

Consider first the role of corrective justice in grounding recovery and liability under the fault principle. Under the fault principle a victim is entitled to repair only if his loss results from another's fault. A loss that is the consequence of another's fault is, in the sense just characterized, a wrongful one. Since the principle of corrective justice requires annulling wrongful losses, it supports the victim's claim to recompense in fault liability.

The relationship between corrective justice and the principle that an individual ought to be liable for the untoward consequences of his fault is somewhat more complex. There are two kinds of cases in which the principle of corrective justice gives direct support to the principle of fault liability: (1) those cases in which an individual's fault results not only in another's loss, but in his gain as well; and (2) those cases in which an individual secures a wrongful gain through his fault, though his gain is not the result of another's loss. Unjust enrichment through fraud is an example of a wrongful gain secured at another's expense; non-harm-causing but nevertheless negligent motoring is often an example of conduct that creates wrongful gain in the absence of a corresponding wrongful loss.

Consider the case of negligent motoring more carefully. Negligent motoring may or may not result in an accident. Whether or not it does, individuals who drive negligently often secure a wrongful gain in doing so, namely, the "savings" from not taking adequate safety precautions—those required of the reasonable man of ordinary prudence. This form of wrongful gain is not, ex hypothesi, the result of anyone else's wrongful loss. On the other hand, if a negligent motorist causes another harm, he normally secures no *additional* wrongful gain in virtue of his doing so. In this respect faulty motoring differs from the usual case of fraud or theft. Because harmful, negligent motoring does not generally result in any wrongful gain (apart from that which is the result of negligence itself), the obligation to repair the victim's wrongful loss cannot be entirely grounded on a foundation of corrective justice. There is, in other words, no wrongful gain correlative of the wrongful loss the faulty injurer imposes upon his victim, and no reason, therefore, as a matter of corrective justice alone, for imposing the victim's loss upon his injurer. The wrongful gain negligent motorists secure is logically distinct from any loss they may cause others, and so the occasion of another's loss cannot be the moral basis for annulling these gains as a matter of justice.

This is bound to appear controversial; some additional distinctions might make it appear less so. A full theory of justice in tort liability and recovery would distinguish among four issues: (1) the foundation of a claim that a person has suffered a compensable loss, or that he has secured an unjust gain; (2) the mode of rectification—that is, the manner in which unjust gains and losses are to

be eliminated; (3) the character of rectification—that is, whether a particular form of compensation (e.g., money) is always, sometimes, or rarely appropriate; and (4) the extent of rectification—that is, just how much of a person's loss (or gain) ought to be eliminated.

The central claim of my thesis is the rather straightforward one (I believe) that determining whether a gain or loss is wrongful determines the answer only to the first of these issues. If there is a wrongful loss, it ought to be annulled; the same goes for wrongful or unwarranted gains. Nevertheless, the principle of corrective justice that enables us to identify compensable losses and unjust enrichments does not commit us to adopting any particular mode of rectification. The principle that determines which gains and losses are to be eliminated does not by itself specify a means for doing so. Presumably there is more than one way of rectifying undeserved gains and losses. So when I claim that if an injurer who through his fault imposes a wrongful loss on another—but who does not thereby gain—has an obligation to repair, his obligation cannot derive directly from the principle of corrective justice; I mean only to be emphasizing the obvious fact that he has secured no gain which would be the concern of corrective justice to rectify. His victim's claim to recompense is, on the other hand, a matter of corrective justice. And if we feel that the injurer should rectify his victim's loss, it must be for reasons other than the fact that doing so is required by justice in order to annul his gain.

Once we have adopted a system of tort liability we have committed ourselves to a particular mode of rectifying wrongful gains and losses—a method that imposes victims' losses on their injurers whether or not the loss occasions a wrongful gain. That particular mode of rectification is in no sense required by the principle of corrective justice. There may be reasons other than those that derive from a theory of corrective justice for imposing an innocent victim's loss on his injurer. Consider three such arguments: First, one might argue from the principle of retributive justice for the imposition of liability of faulty injurers. Such an argument would hold that wrongdoing, whether or not secures personal gain, is sinful and ought to be punished or sanctioned. Imposing liability in torts is a way of sanctioning mischief. Therefore liability is imposed on the faulty injurer not to rectify his gain—of which there may be none—but to penalize his moral wrong. Or one could argue from the principle that claim rights impose correlative duties to the conclusion that the victim's right, which is grounded in corrective justice, imposes a correlative duty to repair on his injurer.[2] Or one might take yet another tack and seek to ground the injurer's obligation to repair in considerations of deterrence or accident cost avoidance. This argument might take the following form. To be at fault is to act in an inefficient manner; it is to fail to take appropriate accident-avoidance measures when the cost of doing so is less than the cost of the harm to the victim discounted by the probability of its occurrence. An injurer who is at fault in harming another is obligated to make restitution because his doing so provides him with an incentive to take such precautions as are reasonable and necessary in the future, and because doing so in general has the long-term effect of reducing the sum of accident and accident-avoidance costs.[3] Were one to take an "economic approach" to the liability of the faulty injurer and a "corrective-justice" approach to the right of his victim to secure recompense, the net result would be a merger of economic and moral theories of fault liability, albeit a more narrowly defined one than Posner contemplates.

B. Corrective Justice and Strict Liability

Consider now the relationship between the principle of corrective justice and liability and recovery under the rule of unconditional or strict liability. The conception of unwarranted or wrongful gain and loss central to the principle of corrective justice includes losses and gains that result from justified "takings." Unlike the wrongful losses in fault liability, the unwarranted losses in these cases are not the result of wrongdoing in the ordinary sense. The "taking" itself may be reasonable or justified, as it is in Feinberg's example, and as it is in cases like *Vincent v. Lake Erie Transp. Co.*[4] Consequently, there is no wrong in the doing; were there any wrong at all it would consist in taking what another has a legitimate right to (un-

der specifiable circumstances) and not rendering adequate compensation for having done so.

Understood in this way, corrective justice may explain those strict liability cases that can adequately be modeled on the idea of a taking. Corrective justice might therefore explain *Vincent v. Lake Erie*, but probably not strict liability for either ultrahazardous activities or defective products. Just how much of strict liability the principle of corrective justice explains will depend on the proper analysis of what constitutes a taking—and that is no easy matter.

Again, one has to be careful to avoid misunderstanding the claim. It does not follow from what I have said that those areas of strict liability, like ultrahazardous or products liability, which do not involve takings in the ordinary sense, cannot be justified or rationally explained. My point is simply that appealing to the principle of corrective justice—properly understood—will not help to explain them. There may be other considerations, both of morality and economics, that neatly rationalize existing strict liability law. My purpose is simply to determine which, if any, of the existing law of torts might be defensible within a certain conception of corrective justice. If it turns out, as I think it does, that only certain well-defined areas of tort law principle can be comprehended by a single principle, so much the better for my view, for it demonstrates theoretically what we knew pretheoretically—that the law of torts is extremely complex and that it resists simple analysis.

II. EPSTEIN AND FLETCHER ON CORRECTIVE JUSTICE

Considerations of corrective justice ground four claims related to liability and recovery in torts: (1) the claim to recompense of a victim of another's fault, (2) the liability of a faulty injurer who gains through his mischief, (3) the claim of a victim in strict liability for a takings-like loss, and (4) the injurer's liability for a taking. In contrast, both Epstein and Fletcher appear to believe that all, or nearly all, of torts can be explained by subsumption under a theory of corrective justice. The interesting question concerns how it is that the three of us, each of whom believes that corrective justice is central to an adequate analysis of torts, reach such different conclusions.

There really is not much of a mystery, however. The key difference is that both Epstein and Fletcher share a strategy which is first to identify an element common to both strict and fault liability, then to argue that this common element is central to liability and recovery, then finally to confer normativity upon this feature of both fault and strict liability by subsuming it under a particular conception of corrective justice.[5] Fletcher and Epstein disagree about which element is the operative shared component in strict and fault liability. For Epstein it is the fact that in both fault and strict liability the injurer causes the victim's loss; for Fletcher it is the fact that the injurer harmed the victim through his nonreciprocal risk taking.

Epstein's arguments are motivated in part by a desire to deemphasize the role of fault in determing both liability and recovery. The desire to eliminate the centrality of fault to torts must be understood against the background of a failed moral theory of fault liability and an increasingly accepted economic account of it. Let me explain. At one time the prevailing moral theory of torts seized upon the introduction of the fault requirement in the mid-nineteenth century as a shift away from the immoral criterion of strict liability to a moral foundation for liability. Instead of imposing liability without regard to the culpability or blameworthiness of the injurer—as was the case in strict liability—fault liability injected a concern for the moral character of the injurer's conduct into the formula that was to determine the appropriateness of imposing another's loss upon him.

The concern of torts for the moral character of the injurer's conduct has always been rather minimal, however. It is the lesson of *Vaughan* v. *Menlove* that an individual may be at fault in torts even if he is not morally at fault for his conduct, his fault being determined by his failure to comply with a standard of reasonable care, whether or not he is capable of compliance. Because moral culpability is not a condition of fault in torts, previous efforts to provide a moral account of fault liability have stalled. Moreover, by the early 1970s, the prevailing view had become that the only plausible, coherent account of fault in torts was an

economic one: to be at fault is simply to fail to take the precautions necessary to avoid an inefficient (in cost–benefit terms) harm. In short, the standard of fault liability which moralists had hoped would anchor a moral theory of torts appeared not only to escape moral analysis, but to be firmly rooted in economic theory. Theorists intent on defending a moral account of torts were faced with a choice: either they could provide an alternative moral account of the fault principle, or they could reexamine, even eliminate, the role of fault in a moral theory of torts. (I have pursued the former route; Epstein and Fletcher have taken the latter.)

In reducing the role of fault liability Epstein focuses his attention on the fact that wherever liability is appropriate, someone has caused another harm. The moral freight that, in the traditional view, had been carried by the fault requirement is borne, in Epstein's view, by the causal condition. Unlike a theory of torts that relies on fault, the theory that relies on the causal condition can theoretically (at least) ground all of tort law under a comprehensive moral principle, since the causal condition, unlike the fault condition, is a necessary element in both fault and strict liability.

Though Epstein has always emphasized the causal condition as central to a moral account of tort liability, his view about the principle that confers moral significance on the causal condition has undergone subtle but significant changes.

In his early essay, "A Theory of Strict Liability," Epstein appears to have held the view that the best way to understand and (where possible) justify tort liability is by rooting it in a more comprehensive theory of personal responsibility. Tort liability is justly imposed provided the conditions of tort liability conform to the requirements of an agent's being responsible for his conduct. Epstein's view is that a satisfactory account of personal responsibility must be developed in terms of an analysis of causation and volition.

Running alongside the responsibility thesis in Epstein's early work is a very undeveloped argument, which relies on corrective justice as the basis of tort liability. Prior to the incidence of harm, individuals are in a state of "equilibrium" or "balance." Liability in torts provides the mechanism for redressing imbalances caused by harmful conduct: liability and recovery in torts reestablish the previously existing equilibria. The causal condition remains central to a just theory of liability since the principle of corrective justice requires annulling gains and losses caused by harmful conduct.

Both the responsibility thesis and the simple corrective-justice accounts of tort liability are seriously flawed. I have argued that although considerations of personal responsibility are relevant to a full theory of torts, Epstein is mistaken in thinking that the analysis of responsibility (which would be a normative theory) could be adequately developed in terms of an analysis of causation (which would involve a natural or scientific theory). One can be responsible not only for what one does, but for what one fails to do as well. If an individual wrongly fails to act, he may be culpable for his failure to prevent harm. Though it would be philosophically confused to say that his failure to act caused the harm, there might be sufficient reasons for ascribing the resulting harm to him as his responsibility.

The problem with the theory of corrective justice that relies on the fact that A caused B harm as sufficient both for (prima facie) liability and recovery (respectively) is simply that not every way in which A harms B is wrongful. Not every loss B suffers at A's hands is a wrongful one; not every gain A secures at B's expense is an unjust one.

Epstein's most recent view emerges from these lines of criticism. In answering the charge that A may have a duty to prevent harm to B so that his failure to do so may be both wrongful and the resulting harm to B his responsibility, Epstein denies that B has any *right* to rescue against A. And in answering the objection to the corrective-justice theory that not every harm creates a wrongful loss, Epstein's response is that only those harms that involve invasions of property *rights* are compensable. In short, the emerging Epstein view is that corrective justice requires annulling only gains and losses owing to the invasion of an individual's rights.

This account of corrective justice maintains a commitment to the causal requirement as central to a just theory of liability not because causing harm is sufficient to trigger the principle's application, but because the concept of a "right invasion" is to be spelled out in causal terms. Causation,

then, is necessary to liability, but no longer sufficient to justify even the prima facie case. For it is also necessary that the injurer's conduct invade one or more of the victim's rights.

I take up Epstein's latest view elsewhere, so I will confine these remarks to a few observations. One way of understanding this view is as follows: Epstein has simply adopted my general conception of corrective justice—that wrongful gains and losses are to be annulled. He has then chosen to analyze the difficult and troublesome notion of wrongfulness in terms of the more basic idea of a property-right violation. Wrongful losses are those that result from the invasion of a property right. So what a judge in a tort case is deciding upon is whether B has a property right against A which A has failed adequately to respect. If the claim "A invaded B's right" is true, then it follows on this view that B has a further right against A to recompense for whatever loss A's invasion occasioned.

My view, which I will not defend here, is that the latest Epstein account is both too strong and too weak. It is too strong because it makes the fact that the victim's loss resulted from a right invasion a necessary condition of liability, whereas in fact not every compensable loss requires that the harm for which one seeks recovery results from the invasion of a right. It is too weak because it maintains that if a person's property rights are violated it follows that he is entitled to recompense, whereas it does not follow either as a matter of logic or moral argument that every right violation triggers a right to repair.

For Fletcher, the guiding principle in determining liability and recovery is the principle of nonreciprocity of risk. A person is entitled to recover whenever he is the victim of harm caused by another's nonreciprocal risk taking; an individual is liable in torts whenever he has no excuse for having caused another harm through his nonreciprocal risk taking. An individual imposes a nonreciprocal risk on others whenever it is different in degree or kind from those risks others impose on him. Examples of nonreciprocal risk taking include engaging in ultrahazardous activities and keeping wild animals on one's property (while one's neighbors confine their affections to traditional domestic pets). The principle of nonreciprocity of risk therefore explains strict liability for harms that result from such activities. Strict liability is appropriate in those cases in which one risk taker imposes risks different from those others in general impose upon him.

There are other activities, however, in which individuals generally impose a certain level of risk on one another. Motoring is one. Liability is not imposed whenever an individual motorist harms another. In Fletcher's view that is because activities like motoring involve a level of reciprocal risk taking. For such activities liability is not strict. In order for liability to be imposed a motorist must negligently harm another. In other words, liability is appropriate only for risks that exceed the general level of shared risk. These nonreciprocal risks are all that is meant, in Fletcher's view, by negligence.

In fault as well as in strict liability, the key to recovery is nonreciprocity of risk. The difference between fault and strict liability is to be understood in terms of the level of risk that constitutes the "background" against which the criterion of nonreciprocity is to be applied. The fault criterion is appropriate to activities of mutual involvement, like motoring, in which there exists a shared level of background or reciprocal risk taking. A faulty or negligent risk is one that exceeds the level of common or background risk. In activities that do not by nature involve participants imposing similar risks on one another, activities like blasting, strict liability is the appropriate criterion.

Fletcher is considerably less clear about what it is that confers moral significance on nonreciprocity of risk. He cites Aristotle on corrective justice as the source of nonreciprocity of risk's claim to moral significance, but the actual argument he advances on its behalf relies on Rawls. The difference is important. Whereas Aristotle is concerned with corrective justice, Rawls is concerned with principles of distributive justice.

Citing Rawls, Fletcher argues for nonreciprocity of risk by constructing a principle of distributive justice that he takes to be an analogue of Rawls's first principle of justice. Fletcher contends that each individual is entitled to the maximum degree of security compatible with a like level of security for all. (The "analogy" is to Rawls's principle that each individual is entitled to the most extensive liberty compatible with a like liberty for all.) Fletcher goes on to define security as freedom from harm without compensation. So defined, everyone has a right not to be harmed without being compensated. If we take Fletcher at his word, it is the fact that one has suffered harm that entitles one to recompense, not the fact that one's harm results from another's nonreciprocal risk taking. The principle that is supposed to impart moral significance on the criterion of nonreciprocity of risk actually has the effect of eliminating it. With nonreciprocity as a condition of liability out of the way, Fletcher's view collapses into Epstein's—in fact, into a less defensible version of Epstein's, since Epstein is committed to the weaker proposition that causing harm is sufficient to establish the prima facie case for liability only.

To maintain the centrality of nonreciprocity of risk in Fletcher's theory one must reformulate the principle that is to confer moral significance on it. This can be accomplished in a number of ways, each of which is problematic. First, one might redefine the notion of security more narrowly as freedom from exposure to nonreciprocal risk taking. An individual's right to security is then the freedom from having nonreciprocal risks imposed on him. If the right one has is to freedom from nonreciprocal risks, then the right to recover that is based upon it does not require that one actually suffer a harm. Exposure to nonreciprocal risk, whether or not it results in harm, triggers the right to recompense. The effect is to eliminate as central to liability what is currently necessary in both strict and fault liability: the requirement that one who seeks relief must establish a loss, not just the threat or risk of loss.

It will not do to redefine security even more narrowly as freedom from harm due to nonreciprocal risk, for that would trivialize the enterprise by restating the criterion of recovery as the principle that supposed to justify it: people are entitled to recover for harms caused by nonreciprocal risk taking because there is a principle that people have such a right.

I want to develop a more sympathetic reading of Fletcher that involves ignoring his efforts to ground the principle of nonreciprocity of risk in a Rawlsian conception of distributive justice.

I prefer to read Fletcher as follows: First, assume that he has adopted a conception of corrective justice like mine or Aristotle's. Then understand the criterion of nonreciprocity of risk as his way of characterizing wrongful gains and losses. In other words, ascribe to Fletcher the position that justice requires annulling wrongful gains and losses; then interpret his account of nonreciprocity of risk as a characterization of what it is that makes a gain or loss wrongful. Our views would then be much closer than they otherwise appear to be. The advantage of this would be that by identifying wrongful loss with losses that result from nonreciprocal risk taking, he can provide a criterion of wrongfulness that is applicable to all of tort law—both strict and fault liability. My conception of wrongfulness is considerably more narrow and explains only a small area of strict liability law. The problem with his view might then be that the notion of nonreciprocity of risk is too broad a characterization of wrongfulness to function within the principle of corrective justice.

To sum up: Epstein, Fletcher, and myself reach different conclusions regarding the extent to which the principle of corrective justice could figure in an adequate theory of liability and recovery in torts for the following reasons. Epstein advances both a simple and a more complex theory of corrective justice. According to the simple theory, corrective justice requires annulling losses caused by harmful conduct. This conception of corrective justice is broad enough to make the fact that A caused B harm sufficient to trigger its application. Since causing harm is (presumably) a necessary element in both strict and fault liability, Epstein's conception of corrective justice turns out to be sufficient to ground all of liability and recovery in torts.

According to the more complex theory of corrective justice, the facts that A harmed B and that in doing so A invaded a right of B's are both separately necessary and jointly sufficient to justify rectification. The best way to read this amendment to the simple view is as resulting from Epstein's sensitivity to the objection that not every harm one suffers at the hands of another creates a compensable loss. To meet that objection to the simple view Epstein restricts compensable losses to those occasioned by the invasion of a property

right. Because Epstein must also believe that as a matter of fact all recoverable losses in torts involve property-right invasions, he can maintain the view that the principle of corrective justice grounds most, if not all, of tort law.

Fletcher does not explicitly put forward a conception of corrective justice, but it would be fair to ascribe to him a much narrower conception of it than the one Epstein first put forth, for example, one like mine or Aristotle's, which requires that a loss or gain be wrongful in order to trigger its application. Fletcher and I differ because we have different conceptions of what makes a gain or loss a wrongful one. Because Fletcher believes that nonreciprocity of risk is central to both strict and fault liability, and because nonreciprocity of risk is one way of fleshing out the notion of wrongfulness in the principle of corrective justice, Fletcher, like Epstein (but for different reasons), is led to the conclusion that corrective justice explains most of torts.

When the emerging Epstein view and the principle of reciprocity are understood in the way in which I have been suggesting, it would be fair to ascribe to both Epstein and Fletcher the same conception of the principle of corrective justice I have advanced. The differences between us could be pinpointed as involving the ways which each of us analyzes the notion of wrongfulness. Whereas Fletcher and I may be said to adopt the same principle of corrective justice, the principle of nonreciprocity of risk constitutes a much broader conception of what makes a gain or loss compensable or wrongful than does the account I have been developing. Epstein's theory of wrongful losses as involving invasions of property rights is both broader and narrower than my own. It is narrower in the sense that my view allows compensation for losses even where the invasion of a property right is not established; it is broader in the sense that he believes that as a matter of fact every compensable loss in torts involves the invasion of a property right.

Let me close this section by saying something about the difference between my view and Aristotle's. In my view, the principle of corrective justice explains a good deal more of tort law than it would for Aristotle. Although Aristotle's conception of corrective justice is very similar to mine, he appears to have held that a wrongful gain or loss requires that a wrong has been done. In that case, the principle of corrective justice could not explain any of strict liability. In contrast, my view is that a loss or gain may sometimes be wrongful, as in a justified taking, even if the conduct that creates it is not wrongful. Moreover, Aristotle appears to have further limited the notion of a wrong to deliberate or intentional wrongdoing. In that case the principle of corrective justice would be unable to account for much of fault liability in which liability is imposed for what one unintentionally but negligently does.

III. POSNER'S OBJECTIONS

I come finally to Posner's objections. Though Posner appears to find much to recommend the position he ascribes to me, he finds fault with three related components of my argument. Two of his objections concern the limitations I place on the argument for liability from the principle of corrective justice; the third concerns the question of whether requiring potential victims to purchase first-party insurance coverage actually enables them to secure full compensation in the event of injury.

One of the central points of my thesis is that, whereas the victim of another's fault has a claim as a matter of corrective justice to recompense, the obligation to make him whole may or may not be as a matter of corrective justice the injurer's responsibility. Objecting to this claim Posner asks rhetorically, "[I]f the injurer is not the source of the compensation, someone else, who is innocent, must be, and why is not that innocent party a victim of the wrongdoer's injurious conduct?" Again, after ascribing to me the view that "the victim of an accident in which the injurer was at fault is entitled to compensation ... the injurer is not required as a matter of justice to be the source of compensation because he does not gain by his wrongful act, as he would if we were speaking of a theft rather than an accident," Posner argues that because faulty injurers avoid the costs of taking adequate safety precautions, they in fact gain by their injurious conduct. Because they gain by their wrongdoing, liability is appropriately imposed upon them.

In sum, Posner's objections are: (1) if a faulty injurer is not the source of compensation, some "innocent" third party must be, and this constitutes an injustice; and (2) each faulty injurer gains from his wrongdoing in a sense sufficient to warrant imposing the victim's loss upon him as a matter of corrective justice.

Taken together these points constitute a serious challenge to central features of my argument. Consider the second objection first. Surely Posner is right in thinking that by and large faulty injurers gain by their failing to satisfy the standard of reasonable care. In fact, their gain, the savings from failing to exercise the care required of others, is a wrongful one, since it is the consequence of their fault. Nevertheless, as I have already pointed out to Posner, and earlier in this paper, this gain in savings is secured by negligent individuals whether or not their negligence results in another's loss. The gain in savings is not triggered by the harm a particular individual's negligence causes another. In contrast to a theft, it is not a gain that results from another's loss. Posner acknowledges the distinction, but goes on to say that he fails to understand the importance of distinguishing between wrongful gains that result from another's loss and those which do not in determining whether an individual's conduct is wrongful.

Posner's response misses the point, however. The distinction is not relevant to determining if an individual's gain from his actions is wrongful; I did not suggest that it was. The distinction may play an important role, however, in determining whether the victim's loss should be imposed upon his particular injurer. In making *that* determination it is relevant to inquire whether the injurer's gain is correlative of the victim's loss, for if the injurer's gain exists independently of the victim's loss, then it is not the victim's loss that provides the moral basis for annulling the injurer's gain.

Furthermore, there are ways other than imposing the victim's loss on him of annulling the gain faulty injurers secure by avoiding the costs of adequate precautions: for example, by imposing fines for negligence. Indeed, because the gains owing to taking inadequate precautions accrue to all negligent individuals, it is in fact more appropriate to annul the gain in savings by fines imposed on each. In this way we can treat this category of wrongful gains similarly by not imposing any additional burden on those particular faulty injurers who, though they do not gain further by their mischief, are unfortunate enough to cause another harm. In short, Posner is right to insist upon the fact that wrongful gain is sufficient to impose as a matter of corrective justice a victim's loss on his negligent injurer.

Posner's other objection is that if the faulty injurer is not required to compensate his victim, an innocent individual—either the victim or some third party—will be forced to do so, and that imposing the loss on an innocent individual constitutes an injustice. (Indeed, Posner goes so far as to refer to these innocent individuals as "victims" of the faulty party's conduct.) This objection goes astray from the start. It simply does not follow in a system in which faulty injurers were not made liable to victims of their mischief that innocent individuals would be coerced into doing so in their stead. Surely, it is at least logically possible that everyone would agree ex ante to distribute accident costs without regard to fault—for example, in accordance with a deep-pocket or risk-spreading principle. In such a system individuals other than those at fault in causing particular accidents would help to pay for the costs of accidents, though no injustice of the sort Posner imagines would exist. Alternatively, the costs of accidents as they accumulate over time could be allocated among faulty individuals—whether or not the fault of each results in harm—without any individual being liable to any particular victim of his fault. Instead, each negligent motorist, for example, would pay according to the degree of his fault rather than according to the extent of the damage his fault causes. (After all, minor faults often occasion major damage, and serious wrong-doing may result in little, if any, damage at all.) In both counterexamples to Posner's objection, the negligent motorist is not obligated to his victim, yet the result is not that some innocent third party is unjustly held liable instead.

Both of these counterexamples imagine modes of rectifying wrongful losses other than the tort system. Perhaps Posner's objection is more telling if we limit ourselves to the tort system. Then his objection appears to be the following: In torts, the victim of another's wrongdoing has a right to recompense. This right constitutes a valid claim against someone. If the obligation to repair is not imposed upon the faulty injurer, the victim's loss will fall on some innocent party or other. According to Posner, my view is that if the faulty injurer does not gain from his conduct, he has no obligation as a matter of corrective justice to render compensation. Absent such an obligation, the victim's loss must indeed fall on someone else (i.e., an innocent person). Therefore (given the tort system as the appropriate mode of rectification), my position generates injustice.

Though more promising, this line of argument fails as well. The argument begins by assuming a particular mode of rectification, namely, that the desired way of annulling undeserved gains and losses is by conferring on victims a right to redress and by imposing on their injurers the corresponding obligation to repair. There is nothing in my view that is incompatible with establishing a tort system to annul wrongful losses. Given the tort system, it would be my view that the obligation to repair the victim's loss falls upon his faulty injurer. It is also my view, however, that it cannot logically be any part of the reason for imposing the duty to repair on the faulty injurer in such cases that in doing so we rectify or annul his wrongful gain. He simply enjoys no gain that needs to be rectified. The duty to repair his victim's loss, in other words, may be rightly his responsibility in a tort system, though it is not a duty of corrective justice.

These objections to my view rest on an ambiguity concerning whether the tort system as a particular mode of rectification is to be assumed, or whether instead it needs some sort of justification. I take the latter approach; and because I do, I emphasize the fact that in the absence of wrongful gain the tort system will not be required by corrective justice. Some other principles must therefore ground our choice of this particular mode of rectification. Posner's last objection takes the tort system as given, then chides me for not being able to explain the faulty injurer's liability as rooted in corrective justice and accuses me of imposing the obligation to repair on an innocent third party. But if we take the tort system as given, my view does in fact impose the obligation to repair upon the faulty injurer; and though it imposes the obligation to repair upon the faulty injurer, it does not explain that obligation as required by the principle of corrective justice itself. Instead, whatever principle it is that leads us to adopt the tort system as the desired means of rectification (and I am not sure we should be driven in that direction) will be the principle that explains why we impose the victim's loss on his injurer. But to deny that the relevant principle is one of corrective justice is not tantamount to asserting that I cannot provide an explanation of the injurer's liability.

Given the tort system, one might object that I am making far too much of these subtle distinctions among the various ways of grounding the injurer's liability. After all, or so the argument might go, I am not denying that (under these circumstances) the faulty injurer has an obligation to make his victim whole. Provided the injurer is obligated to repair, why should it matter whether the duty derives from corrective justice, deterrence, or from a principle like Posner's? It does matter, however, for two very different reasons.

First, the concern of my work has been in part to explore the limits of the corrective-justice theory of torts. The limits on the role of corrective justice in imposing liability are therefore important. Second, it is important, I think, to distinguish between the question of whether a particular individual has a duty and the question of whether justice requires that the encumbered individual, rather than someone else, discharge the duty. If the faulty injurer's duty to repair is a matter of corrective justice, that means, in my view, that he has secured a wrongful gain. If someone else discharges the duty on his behalf, that is, compensates his victim, an injustice remains since the injurer's gain is left unrectified. In contrast, if the faulty injurer's duty does not derive from the principle of corrective justice, that means that his victim's loss does not translate into his wrongful gain. If someone other than the faulty injurer fully compensates the victim, no

corrective injustice is done, since there exists no wrongful gain that is left unrectified.

The distinction I insist on among the various sources of one's obligation to repay is relevant in determining whether principles of justice permit or prohibit various means for compensating victims. Certain debts of repayment, like the criminal's debt to society, cannot, consistent with principles of justice, be discharged by others, for example, through an insurance scheme for criminal liability. The debt of repayment one has in virtue of the wrongful gain one secures at another's expense is another debt that must as a matter of justice be discharged by the encumbered party. Failure to do so leaves a wrongful gain unrectified. On the other hand, if I am right, the debt of repayment a faulty injurer who does not gain by his mischief owes his victim is one that can, consistent with the principle of corrective justice, be discharged by another. This feature of the debt of repayment in torts is, I have argued, central to any defense of no-fault insurance schemes.

NOTES

1. Richard Posner, The Concept of Corrective Justice, 10 J. Legal Stud. 187 (1981).
2. One obvious problem with this line of defense is that it assumes a particular mode of rectifying the innocent victim's wrongful loss, namely, by conferring upon him a claim right to recompense. Such a claim right logically imposes a duty on someone—usually the injurer. Assuming a system of correlative rights and duties, that is, a tort system, begs the justificatory question, namely, Why choose this rather than some other mode of rectification?
3. This line of argument is intended to be a "catch-all" for the wide variety of economic analyses of fault liability. Whatever their differences, these accounts all believe that fault is a criterion of economic efficiency and that liability is imposed on the basis of fault to reduce inefficient costs.
4. 10 Minn. 456, 124 NW 221 (1910).
5. Richard Epstein, "A Theory of Strict Liability," 2 J. Legal Stud. 151 (1973); George Fletcher, Fairness and Utility in Tort Theory, 85 Harv. L. Rev. 537 (1972).